10,000 ILLUSTRATIONS FROM THE BIBLE

FOR PASTORS, TEACHERS, STUDENTS, SPEAKERS, AND WRITERS

7,891 SCRIPTURE TEXTS, 10,000 ILLUSTRATIONS, 30,000 CROSS REFERENCES
ALPHABETICALLY ARRANGED UNDER 1,800 TOPICAL HEADINGS

BY

CHARLES E. LITTLE

BAKER BOOK HOUSE
Grand Rapids, Michigan

Previously published under the titles:

Biblical Lights and Side-Lights
10,000 Biblical Illustrations

Six printings in hard cover

Paperback edition issued September 1981

Sixth printing, September 1992

ISBN: 0-8010-5606-3

Printed in the United States of America

PREFACE.

THE frequent use of illustrations by the Great Teacher, and by nearly all effective speakers, strongly commends the illustrative method to all who teach or speak in public.

Illustrations render special service in popular discourse. They condense a chain of logic in a striking simile, or crystallize a moral lesson in an impressive incident.

Biblical illustrations possess marked peculiarities. They not only interest the mind of the hearer, but their sacred associations secure his respect. The Bible dignifies the address in which it is reverently quoted. Besides this, it may be observed that while the repetition of other illustrations weary the hearer, those from the Bible are fresh forever. Familiarity often increases their effectiveness, as when a lawyer illustrates the insufficiency of circumstantial evidence by reference to Joseph's bloody coat, and Jacob's deep distress when he exclaimed, "An evil beast hath devoured him." Joseph's garment in the hands of Potiphar's wicked wife, and the unjust disgrace and imprisonment which followed, would not only furnish an incident deeply impressive to the ordinary juryman, but familiarity would lend force to the illustration.

In this volume are collected and alphabetically arranged under suitable topics, ten thousand quotations of Biblical facts, incidents, and striking statements. These selections cover a wide field of thought, and relate to almost every variety of character and to the varied experiences of human life. They may be applied not only to the truths of religion, but also in presenting those pertaining to science, philosophy, art, and political society.

In the preparation of this work reference has been had to the wants of speakers and writers in every profession ; but the needs of religious instructors have been especially considered. Here the minister may find valuable assistance in the preparation of his discourses, and also in selecting pulpit lessons and Bible readings.

The Sunday-school teacher may use these illustrations as side-lights to illuminate the lessons. Bible students generally are here supplied with a vast amount of illustrative material, which without such a compilation could only be obtained at the cost of much valuable time and laborious research.

The plan of the book assumes a general knowledge of Biblical history on the part of the reader ; hence the abbreviation of quotations by ellipses of unessential words, and thereby a condensation of the volume. To lessen the time employed in seeking illustrations from these pages, a catch-word printed in italics follows the title of each article. By this means the quotation will usually be suggested without reading it. Sometimes the catch-word supplies an explanatory term.

In place of a general index, a system of cross-references is adopted, which will enable the reader to find without index-turning, where in this work topics of like import are illustrated, and a line of catch-words gives a key to each quotation referred to. This feature greatly increases the amount of illustrative materials, and at the same time facilitates their speedy selection. The textual index will show where any particular verse is used in this volume.

If this compilation shall be of practical service, in the hands of those for whom it has been prepared, the author will be satisfied with his humble endeavor.

CHARLES E. LITTLE.

BIBLICAL ILLUSTRATIONS.

1. ABANDONMENT in Anger. *Divine.* ⁸ They have turned aside quickly out of the way which I commanded them : they have made them a molten calf, and have worshipped it. ¹⁰ Now therefore let me alone, that my wrath may wax hot against them, and that I may consume them.—Ex., ch. 32.

2. —— **of Blasphemers.** *By Apostles.* ²⁰ Hymeneus and Alexander ; whom I have delivered unto Satan, that they may learn not to blaspheme.—1 Tim., ch. 1.

3. —— **for Christ.** *Disciples.* ²⁹ Jesus said, There is no man that hath left house, or brethren, or sisters, or father, or mother, or wife, or children, or lands, for my sake, and the gospel's, ³⁰ But he shall receive a hundredfold now in this time, houses, and brethren, and sisters, and mothers, and children, and lands, with persecutions ; and in the world to come eternal life.—Mark, ch. 10.

4. —— **to Destruction.** *Flood.* ⁷ I will destroy man whom I have created from the face of the earth ; both man, and beast, and the creeping thing, and the fowls of the air ; for it repenteth me that I have made them.—Gen., ch. 6.

5. —— **of Home.** *Abram.* ¹ The Lord had said unto Abram, Get thee out of thy country, and from thy kindred, and from thy father's house, unto a land that I will shew thee.—Gen., ch. 12.

6. —— **Just.** *Israelites.* ¹³ Yet ye have forsaken me, and served other gods : wherefore I will deliver you no more. ¹⁴ Go and cry unto the gods which ye have chosen ; let them deliver you in the time of your tribulation.—Judges, ch. 10.

7. —— **of Jesus.** *Gethsemane.* ⁵⁶ Then all the disciples forsook him, and fled.—Matt., ch. 26.

8. —— **Merited.** *Sinners.* ²⁸ Then shall they call upon me, but I will not answer ; they shall seek me early, but they shall not find me : ²⁹ For that they hated knowledge, and did not choose the fear of the Lord : ³⁰ They would none of my counsel : they despised all my reproof.—Prov., ch. 1.

9. —— **of Sanctuary.** *Divine.* ⁷ The Lord hath cast off his altar, he hath abhorred his sanctuary, he hath given up into the hand of the enemy the walls of her palaces.—Lam., ch. 2.

10. —— **A Surprising.** *Ark.* ⁵ When the ark of the covenant of the Lord came into camp, all Israel shouted with a great shout, so that the earth rang again.—1 Sam., ch. 4. [The Philistines captured the ark.]

11. —— **of Transgressors.** *Israelites.* ¹ But the children of Israel committed a trespass in the accursed thing. ⁴ So there went up thither of the people about three thousand men ; and they fled before the men of Ai.—Josh., ch. 7.

12. —— **of Work.** *Mark.* ³⁷ And Barnabas determined to take with them John, whose surname was Mark. ³⁸ But Paul thought not good to take him with them, who departed from them from Pamphylia, and went not with them to the work.—Acts, ch. 15.

13. —— **Unconscious.** *Samson.* ²⁰ And she said, The Philistines *be* upon thee, Samson. And he awoke out of his sleep, and said, I will go out as at other times before, and shake myself. And he wist not that the Lord was departed from him.—Judges, ch. 16.

See other illustrations under :

DEPARTURE.

FUGITIVE.

Criminal. Jacob..flee thou to Laban, my   3487
Infant. Take the young child..flee into Egypt   3488
Noble. Pharaoh sought to slay Moses..fled   3489
Protected. Not deliver unto his master the   3490
Return. [Onesimus] departed for a season   3491

SECESSION.

Political. If this city be builded..no portion on   7642
"   I will chastise you with scorpions   7643

SEPARATION.

Drunkards. Not to keep company..not to eat   7758
Godly. Separated from I. all the mixed   7759
Impossible. Neither death nor life..able to   7764
Reason of. For they will turn away thy son   7778
Sorrowful. They kissed one another and wept   7780
Spiritual. Fan is in his hand..wheat..chaff   7781
Sinners. Blessed..when they shall separate   7883
By Sin. As a shepherd divideth his sheep..goats   7789
"   Your iniquities have separated..your   7784
Unavoidable. Ye cannot drink the cup of the L.   7787

14. ABDUCTION, A justifiable. *Jehosheba.* [2]Jehosheba, the daughter of king Joram, sister of
Ahaziah, took Joash the son of Ahaziah. and
stole him from among the king's sons *which were*
slain ; and they hid him, and his nurse, in the
bed-chamber from Athaliah, so that he was not
slain.—2 KINGS, ch. 11.

See other illustrations under :

KIDNAPPING.

Crime. If a man..stealing brethren..thief shall   4805
Wives. Children of Benjamin..took wives   4806
Child. [Mothers before Solomon] Not my son   8767

—— ABHORRENCE. —— ——

See illustrations under :

Covetous. .Wicked blesseth the covetous..L.   1786
Outrage. [Concubine] Twelve pieces and sent   2729
Resentment. Why weepeth..is thy servant a   1526
Social. Abhor me..spare not to spit in my face   1097
Worship. I will take it up by force..men   1281
"   Ye brought the lame..sick..offering   1630

15. ABILITY of God. *Jerusalem.* [27]Behold,
I *am* the Lord, the God of all flesh : Is there any
thing too hard for me ?.. [28]Behold, I will give
this city into the hand of the Chaldeans, and of
Nebuchadrezzar king of Babylon.—JER., ch. 32.

16. —— —— *To save.* [25]He is able also to
save them to the uttermost that come unto God
by him, seeing he ever liveth to make intercession for them.—HEB., ch. 7.

17. —— —— *To deliver.* [When the three
Hebrews came from the fiery furnace, Nebuchadnezzar said,] [29]I make a decree, That every
people, nation, and language, which speak any
thing amiss against the God of Shadrach,
Meshach, and Abed-nego, shall be cut in
pieces, and their houses shall be made a dunghill ; because there is no other God that can
deliver after this sort.—DAN., ch. 3.

See other illustrations under :

ART.

Architect. [Bezaleel] Filled with the spirit..to   510
Music. [David] Cunning in playing..man of war   71
War. [Uzziah] Made engines..invented by   509

BUSINESS.

Capacity. [Pharaoh to Joseph] None so discreet   985
Diligence. Man diligent in business..stand before   986
Frauds. Take thy bill, quickly..write fifty   988
Spiritual. [Stewards] Men..honest..full of H. S.   991
Success. Joseph gathered up all the money   993
Talent. [Cattle] The feebler were Laban's   994

DEXTERITY.

Slingers. 700 left-handed..sling stones at a hair   2283
Soldiers. Could use both the right hand and the   3784

GIFTS.

Diversity. To one is given..spirit..wisdom [Paul]   3537
"   To one..five talents..according to   3538
Lesser. I give you power to tread on serpents   3541

INVENTORS.

Family. [Jubal] Handle harp and organ.   4645
Weapon. I can slay a man for my hurt..[Lamech]   4658

POWER.

Delegated. Why could we not cast him out   6312
Endowment. Filled..began to speak with other   6313
God gives. [Samson] L. blessed..Spirit began   6314
God only. [Peter] By our own power made   6315
Loss. [Samson] Shake myself..wist not L. was   6316
Might. Not by might, nor by power..great   6317
Promised. [Joshua] Not any able to stand   6318
Prayer. [Hezekiah] prayed Sennacherib..85,000   6319
Preaching. My speech..demonstration of the S.   6320
Ruling. Rebuked the wind, the raging water   6321
Spiritual. [Stephen] Not able to resist the   6322
Spirit. [Samson] Cords..upon his arms..as flax   6323
Sudden. [Joseph] No man lift up his hand or   6324
Tears. [Moses] Babe wept..had compassion on   6327
Temptation. All these will I [Satan] give thee   6325
Waiting. Wait for the promise..receive power   6329
Weakness. I am weak, though anointed [David]   6328

Differ. They fell before Jonathan..slew after   1784
Doubted. I am not able to bear all this people   453
Presumed. James and John..can ye drink of the   447

18. ABSENCE, Detrimental. *Thomas.* [24]On
Easter evening, Thomas, one of the twelve,
called Didymus, was not with them when Jesus
came.—JOHN, ch. 20. [He remained in painful
doubt for one week. Was relieved when present.]

19. —— Falsely excused. *Jonathan.* [28]Answered Saul, David earnestly asked *leave* of me
to go to Bethlehem : [29]And he said, Let me
go, I pray thee ; for our family hath a sacrifice in the city, and my brother, he hath commanded me *to be there.*—1 SAM., ch. 20. [He
was hidden near by in a field.]

See other illustrations under :

Loss. Sojourned seven years..house and land   1536
Unaccountable. Wot not what has become of   2129
        See ABANDONMENT and references.

20. ABSTINENCE, Extreme. *Nazarite.* [3]He
shall separate *himself* from wine and strong
dŕink, and shall drink no vinegar of wine, or
vinegar of strong drink, neither shall he drink
any liquor of grapes, nor eat moist grapes, or
dried.. [4]Eat nothing that is made of the vine
tree, from the kernels even to the husk.—
NUM., ch. 6.

21. —— in Excitement. *Saul.* [9]He was three
days without sight, and neither did eat nor
drink.—ACTS, ch. 9.

22. —— Famishing from. *Slave.* [David pursued the Amalekites,] [11]And they found an
Egyptian in the field..and gave him bread..
and they made him drink water ; [12]And they
gave him a piece of a cake of figs, and two
clusters of raisins : and when he had eaten, his
spirit came again to him : for he had eaten no
bread, nor drunk *any* water, three days and
three nights.—1 SAM., ch. 30.

23. —— in Mourning. *David.* [Joab assassi

nated Abner.] ³⁵ All the people came to cause David to eat meat while it was yet day, David sware, saying, So do God to me, and more also, if I taste bread, or aught else, till the sun be down.—2 SAM., ch. 3.

24. —— **Necessitated.** *Jesus said,* ³¹ Come ye yourselves apart into a desert place, and rest a while : for they were many coming and going, and they had no leisure so much as to eat.— MARK, ch. 6.

25. —— **Passionate.** *Jonathan.* ³³ Saul cast a javelin at him to smite him: whereby Jonathan knew that it was determined of his father to slay David. ³⁴ So Jonathan arose from the table in fierce anger, and did eat no meat the second day of the month : for he was grieved for David because his father had done him shame.—1 SAM., ch. 20.

26. —— **A priestly.** *Law.* ⁸ The Lord spake unto Aaron, saying, ⁹ Do not drink wine nor strong drink, thou, nor thy sons..when ye go into the tabernacle of the congregation, lest ye die : *it shall be* a statute for ever.—LEV., ch. 10.

27. —— **in Time of Peril.** *Paul.* [They had anchored near to land,] ³³ And while the day was coming on, Paul besought *them* all to take meat, saying, This day is the fourteenth day that ye have tarried and continued fasting, having taken nothing.—ACTS, ch. 27.

28. —— **Protracted.** *Moses.* ²⁸ Moses was there [in the mount] with the LORD forty days and forty nights ; he did neither eat bread, nor drink water.—EX., ch. 34.

29. —— —— *Wilderness.* ¹ Then was Jesus led up of the Spirit into the wilderness to be tempted of the devil. ² And when he had fasted forty days and forty nights, he was afterward a hungered.—MAT., ch. 4.

30. —— **Self-denying.** *David.* [David longed for it,] ¹⁶ And the three mighty men brake through the host of the Philistines, and drew water out of the well of Beth-lehem, that *was* by the gate..and brought *it* to David : Nevertheless he would not drink thereof, but poured it out unto the Lord. ¹⁷ And he said, Be it far from me, O Lord, that I should do this : *is not this* the blood of the men that went in jeopardy of their lives ?—2 SAM., ch. 23.

31. —— **Sorrowful.** *David's Child.* ¹⁵ It was very sick. ¹⁶ David therefore besought God for the child ; and David fasted, and went in, and lay all night upon the earth. ¹⁷ And the elders of his house..went..to raise him up from the earth : but he would not, neither did he eat bread with them.—2 SAM., ch. 12.

32. —— **Total.** *Rechabites.* ⁵ I set before the sons..of the Rechabites pots full of wine, and cups ; and I said..Drink ye wine. ⁶ But they said, We will drink no wine..our father commanded us, saying, Ye shall drink no wine, *neither* ye, nor your sons for ever.—JER., ch. 35.

See other illustrations under :

APPETITE.

FAMINE.

HUNGER.

TEMPERANCE.

— ABSTRACTION. —— ——

See illustrations under :

— ABSURDITY. —— ——

See illustrations under :

33. ABUNDANCE, Countless. *Egypt.* ⁴⁹ Joseph gathered corn as the sand of the sea, very much, until he left numbering ; for it *was* without number.—GEN., ch. 41.

34. —— **Gifts from.** *Wisdom.* ⁴³ Jesus called his disciples, and saith..This poor widow hath cast more in, than all they which have cast into the treasury : ⁴⁴ For all *they* did cast in of their abundance ; but she of her want did cast in all that she had, *even* all her living.—MARK, ch. 12.

35. —— **from Little.** *Elisha.* ⁴² A man brought the man of God bread of the first-fruits, twenty loaves of barley, and full ears of corn in the husk thereof. And he said, Give unto the people, that they may eat. ⁴³ And his servitor said, What, should I set this before a hundred men ?..and they did eat, and left.—2 KINGS, ch. 4.

36. —— **A miraculous.** *Loaves and Fishes.* ⁴³ They took up twelve baskets full of the fragments, and of the fishes. ⁴⁴ And they that did eat of the loaves were about five thousand men.—MARK, ch. 6.

37. —— **Sudden.** *Four Lepers.* [At Samaria,] ³ Said one to another, Why sit we here until we die ? ⁸..Came to the uttermost part of the camp, they went into one tent, and did eat and drink and carried thence silver, and gold, and raiment, and went and hid *it ;* and came again, and entered into another tent, and carried thence *also*, and went and hid *it*.—2 Kings, ch. 7.

38. —— **A surprising.** *Quails.* [18] Ye have wept in the ears of the Lord, saying, Who shall give us flesh to eat? for *it was* well with us in Egypt. [31] And there went forth a wind from the Lord, and brought quails from the sea, and let *them* fall by the camp..a day's journey on this side..and on the other side, round about the camp, and as it were two cubits *high*..[32] And the people..all day, and..night, and all the next day..gathered the quails.—Num., ch. 11.

See other illustrations under:

Excessive. [Building tabernacle,] The people   3512
Gold. The weight of gold that came to Solomon   3635
Improvement. Take the talent..him that hath   4365
Plenty. [Canaan] Land of wheat, barley, vines   6224
Poverty. There was a..rich man..fared   6225
Secret. He which soweth sparingly shall reap   3811
Sacrifices. Solomon sacrificed sheep..not to be   8760
Valuables. Hezekiah had exceeding much riches   4187
See **RICHES** and references.

39. ABUSE of Mercy. *Pharaoh.* [34] When Pharaoh saw that the rain and the hail and the thunders were ceased, he sinned yet more, and hardened his heart, he and his servants.—Ex., ch. 9.

40. —— **of Privileges.** *Corinthians.* [17]..Ye come together not for the better, but for the worse. [18] For first of all..in the church, I hear that there be divisions among you.. [20] When ye come together therefore into one place, *this* is not to eat the Lord's supper. [21] For in eating every one taketh before *other* his own supper: and one is hungry and another is drunken.—1 Cor., ch. 11.

41. —— **Religious.** *Serpent.* [4] Hezekiah brake in pieces the brazen serpent that Moses had made: for unto those days the children of Israel did burn incense to it.—2 Kings, ch. 18.

See other illustrations under:

CRUELTY.

Ambition. [Athaliah] saw her son was dead   1857
Brutal. 10,000 men..Did Judah..cast from the   1858
Failure. Egyptians set taskmasters to afflict   1859
Insulting. Herod's soldiers smote him..spit on   1860
Pride. Mordecai bowed not..Haman sought to   1861
Reward. He that is cruel troubleth his own flesh   1862
Savage. Slew..the sons of Hezekiah before his   1863
War. [Joab] put them under saws..harrows of   1864

INSOLENCE.

Added. [Danite robbers] said unto Micah, What   4530
Fraternal. With whom hast thou left those few   4531
Injustice. There is no straw..ye are idle   4532
Resented. Whatsoever is pleasant in thine eyes   4333

Avarice. Buy the poor for silver..for a pair of   5917
Friends. Hanun cut off their garments in the   3431
Insulting. Samson's wife..given to his friend   4496
Merciless. Took him by the throat saying, Pay   5347
Power. The rich man..took the poor man's lamb   4499

42. ACCESS, Bold. *Compassion.* [15] We have not a high priest which cannot be touched with the feeling of our infirmities; but was in all points tempted like as *we are, yet* without sin. [16] Let us therefore come boldly unto the throne of grace.—Heb., ch. 4.

43. —— **Conditioned.** *Benjamin.* [Joseph said to his brethren,] [23] Except your youngest brother come down with you, ye shall see my face no more.—Gen., ch. 44.

44. —— **Denied.** *Absalom.* [Having caused the murder of his brother Amnon, Absalom fled into exile for three years. Joab then brought him to Jerusalem. David] [24] The king said, Let him turn to his own house, and let him not see my face. So Absalom returned to his own house, and saw not the king's face.—2 Sam., ch. 14.

45. —— **Improved.** *Blood.* [18] Ye are not come unto the mount that might be touched, and that burned with fire, nor unto blackness, and darkness, and tempest. [22] But ye are come unto mount Sion, and unto the city of the living God. [24] And to Jesus the mediator of the new covenant, and to the blood of sprinkling, that speaketh better things than *that of* Abel.—Heb., chap. 12.

46. —— **Prohibited.** *Royal.* [Mordecai desired Queen Esther to intercede with King Ahasuerus in behalf of the Jews. She replied,] [11] Whosoever, whether man or woman, shall come unto the king into the inner court, who is not called, *there is* one law of his to put *him* to death, except such to whom the king shall hold out the golden sceptre, that he may live.—Esther, ch. 4.

47. —— **Provision for.** *Door.* [7] I am the door of the sheep. [9] I am the door: by me if any man enter in, he shall be saved, and shall go in and out, and find pasture.—John, ch. 10.

48. —— **Restricted.** *On Mount Sinai.* [21] Go down, charge the people, lest they break through unto the Lord to gaze, and many of them perish. [23] And Moses said..unto the Lord, The people cannot come up to mount Sinai: For thou chargedst us, saying, Set bounds about the mount, and sanctify it.—Ex., ch. 19.

49. —— **Preparation for.** *Sprinkling.* [19] When Moses had spoken every precept to all the people according to the law, he took the blood of calves and of goats, with water, and scarlet wool, and hyssop, and sprinkled both the book and all the people, [20] Saying, This *is* the blood of the testament which God hath enjoined unto you.—Heb., ch. 9. [Soon God appeared on Sinai.]

50. —— **after Preparation.** *Sinai.* [After the priests, people, and altar were sprinkled with blood,] [9] Then went up Moses, and Aaron, Nadab, and Abihu, and seventy of the elders.. [10] And they saw the God of Israel: and *there was* under his feet as it were a paved work of a sapphire stone, and as it were the body of heaven in *his* clearness.—Ex., ch. 24.

See other illustrations under:

PRAYER.

Closet. When thou prayest, enter..closet..shut   6353
Earnestness. Bartimeus..hold his peace..cried   6364
Humiliation. Manasseh besought the L...humbled   6377
Preparation. Wash ye..cease to do evil; do well   6393
Penitence. Publican..afar off..smote on his   6403
Useless. Elijah mocked them..pervadventure he   6449

Denied. Then shall they seek me..not find   8

51. ACCEPTANCE, Ambition for. *Paul.* [9] We labour, that, whether present or absent, we may be accepted of him.—2 Cor., ch. 5.

52. —— **Authenticated.** *Voice.* [At Jesus' baptism,] [16]..lo, the heavens were opened unto him, and he saw the Spirit of God descending like a dove, and lighting upon him: [17] And lo a voice from heaven, saying, This is my beloved Son, in whom I am well pleased.—MAT., ch. 3.

53. —— **Assurance of.** *Manoah.* ²² Manoah said unto his wife, We shall surely die, because we have seen God. ²³ But his wife said.. If the Lord were pleased to kill us, he would not have received a burnt offering and a meat offering at our hands, neither would he have shewed us all these *things,* nor..have told us *such things* as these.—JUDGES, ch. 13.

54. —— **in Dedication.** *Tabernacle.* [At the dedication of the tabernacle,] ²³ Moses and Aaron came out, and blessed the people : and the glory of the Lord appeared unto all the people. ²⁴ And there came a fire out from before the Lord, and consumed upon the altar the burnt offering and the fat : *which* when all the people saw, they shouted, and fell on their faces.—LEV., ch. 9.

55. —— **Denied.** *Jewish Offerings.* ¹³..ye brought *that which was* torn, and the lame, and the sick ; thus ye brought an offering : should I accept this of your hand? saith the Lord.—MAL., ch. 1.

56. —— **Evidence of.** *Gideon.* [He made an offering for his angel guest.] ²¹ The angel of the Lord put forth the end of the staff that *was* in his hand, and touched the flesh and the unleavened cakes ; and there rose up fire out of the rock, and consumed the flesh and the unleavened cakes. Then the angel..departed.—JUDGES, ch. 6.

57. —— **Manifested.** *Abram.* [Abram divided the sacrifices, and waited.] ¹⁷ When the sun went down, and it was dark, behold a smoking furnace, and a burning lamp..passed between those pieces. ¹⁸ In that same day the Lord made a covenant with Abram.—GEN., ch. 15.

58. —— **of Piety.** *Peter.* [After the vision of the sheet let down from heaven, Peter witnessed the conversion of Cornelius the Gentile, and said,] ³⁴..Of a truth I perceive that God is no respecter of persons : ³⁵ But in every nation he that feareth him, and worketh righteousness, is accepted with him.—ACTS, ch. 10.

59. —— **by Sacrifice.** *Abel.* ⁴ Abel..brought of the firstlings of his flock and of the fat thereof. And the Lord had respect unto Abel and to his offering : ⁵ But unto Cain and his offering he had not respect.—GEN., ch. 4.

60. —— **according to Sacrifice.** *Widow.* ⁴¹ Jesus sat over against the treasury, and beheld how the people cast money into the treasury : and many that were rich cast in much.. ⁴³..This poor widow hath cast more in, than all they which have cast into the treasury.—MARK, ch. 12.

61. —— **Terms of.** *Sacrifice.* ⁷ Will the Lord be pleased with thousands of rams, *or* with ten thousands of rivers of oil? Shall I give my firstborn *for* my transgression, the fruit of my body *for* the sin of my soul? ⁸..What doth the Lord require of thee, but to do justly, and to love mercy, and to walk humbly with thy God?—MICAH, ch. 6.

62. ACCIDENT, A destructive. *Wall.* [In the city of Aphek,] ³⁰..a wall fell upon twenty and seven thousand of the men *that were* left. [After a destructive battle.]—1 KINGS, ch. 20.

63. —— **Fatal.** *Mother.* [One woman said to Solomon,] ¹⁹ This woman's child died in the night ; because she overlaid it.—1 KINGS, ch. 3.

64. —— **Impossible.** *Kine.* ¹⁰..the Philistines took two milch kine, and tied them to the cart, and shut up their calves at home : ¹¹ And they laid the ark of the Lord upon the cart.. ¹² And the kine took the straight way to the way of Beth-shemesh, *and* went along the highway, lowing as they went, and turned not aside *to* the right hand or *to* the left.—1 SAM., ch. 6.

65. —— **Lameness from.** *Jonathan's Son.* ⁴..Mephibosheth was five years old when the tidings came of Saul and Jonathan out of Jezreel, and his nurse took him up, and fled : and.. as she made haste to flee, he fell, and became lame.—2 SAM., ch. 4.

66. —— **Loss by.** *Axe.* ⁵ As one was felling a beam, the axe head fell into the water : and he cried, Alas, master ! for it was borrowed.—2 KINGS, ch. 6.

67. —— **Misjudged.** *Tower.* ⁴ Or those eighteen, upon whom the tower in Siloam fell, and slew them, think ye that they were sinners above all men that dwelt in Jerusalem? ⁵ I tell you, Nay : but, except ye repent, ye shall all likewise perish.—LUKE, ch. 13.

68. ——**A pardonable.** *Chance.* ²² If he thrust him suddenly without enmity, or have cast upon him any thing without laying of wait, ²³ Or with any stone..seeing *him* not..that he die, and *was* not his enemy, neither sought his harm.—NUM., ch. 35.

69. —— **Unpunished.** *Axe.* ⁴..Whoso killeth his neighbour ignorantly, whom he hated not in time past ; ⁵ As when a man goeth into the wood.. to hew wood, and his hand fetcheth a stroke with the axe to cut down the tree, and the head slippeth from the helve, and lighteth upon his neighbour, that he die ; he shall flee unto one of those cities, and live.—DEUT., ch. 19.

70. ACCIDENTS, Fatal. *Refuge.* ¹¹ Ye shall appoint you cities to be cities of refuge..that the slayer may flee thither, which killeth any person at unawares.—NUM., ch. 35.

71. ACCOMPLISHMENTS, Numerous. *David.*
[18] *Is* cunning in playing, and a mighty valiant man, and a man of war, and prudent in matters, and a comely person, and the Lord *is* with him. —1 Sam., ch. 16.

See other illustrations under :

DEXTERITY.

Slingers. 700 left handed..sling stones at a hair	2283
Soldiers. Could use both the right hand and the	3784

Art. [Bezaleel] Wisdom..devise curious works	3519
Music. [Jubal] Handled the harp or the organ	4645
Naturalist. [Solomon] Spake of all trees..cedar	583
Philosopher. [Solomon] Spake 3,000 proverbs	583
" [Animals] Brought them unto	10028

See **MUSIC** and references.

72. ACCOUNTABILITY, Future. *Debtor.*
[23] Therefore is the kingdom of heaven likened unto a certain king, which would take account of his servants. [24] And when he had begun to reckon, one was brought unto him, which owed him ten thousand talents.—Mat., ch. 18.

73. —— for Gifts. *Pounds.* [12].. A certain nobleman went into a far country to receive for himself a kingdom, and to return. [13] And he called his ten servants, and delivered them ten pounds, and said..Occupy till I come.—Luke, ch. 19. [One hid his pound in a napkin.]

74. —— Minute. *Judgment.* [35] A good man out of the good treasure of the heart bringeth forth good things : and an evil man out of the evil treasure bringeth forth evil things. [36]..Every idle word that men shall speak, they shall give account thereof in the day of judgment. [37]..By thy words thou shalt be justified, and by thy words thou shalt be condemned.—Mat., ch. 12.

75. —— Personal. *Steward.* [1]..There was a certain rich man, which had a steward..was accused..that he had wasted his goods. [2]..Said unto him, How is it that I hear this of thee? give an account of thy stewardship ; for thou mayest be no longer steward.—Luke, ch. 16.

See other illustrations under :

JUDGMENT.

Awards. As ye did not..these..not to me	4761
Effect. [David] Was afraid..how shall the ark	4767
Humiliating. [Herod] Smote him..eaten of	4768
Heedless. [Uzzah] Put..hand to the ark..smote	4769
Individual. Not on a wedding garment	4770
Preparation. Commandeth to repent..appointed	4774
Repeated. [Sapphira] Have buried thy husband	4775
Swift. [Only by Moses]..Miriam..leper	4776
Sorrow. Cast..unprofitable servant into outer	8224
Servant. [Paul] Reasoned of righteousness	4779

See **RESPONSIBILITY** and references.

76. ACCUSATION, An astounding. *Jesus.*
[Jesus healed and pardoned the paralytic.] [6] But there were certain of the scribes sitting there, and reasoning in their hearts, [7] Why doth this *man* thus speak blasphemies? who can forgive sins but God only ?—Mark, ch. 2.

77. —— A fraudulent. *Potiphar's Wife.* [10] She spake to Joseph day by day, he hearkened not unto her, to lie by her, *or* to be with her. [When Potiphar returned, his wife said,] [17]..The Hebrew servant..came in unto me to mock me : [18] And..as I lifted up my voice and cried, he left his garment with me, and fled out.—Gen., ch. 39.

78. —— A false. *King Saul.* [7] Saul said unto his servants..Will the son of Jesse give every one of you fields and vineyards, *and* make you all captains of thousands, and captains of hundreds ; [8] That all of you have conspired against me.—1 Sam., ch. 22. [David did not intrigue.]

79. —— —— Of Treachery. [12] Jeremiah went forth..to separate himself thence in the midst of the people. [13] And when he was in the gate of Benjamin, a captain of the ward *was* there, whose name *was* Irijah..and he took Jeremiah..saying, Thou fallest away to the Chaldeans. [15] Wherefore the princes were wroth.. and smote him, and put him in prison in the house of Jonathan the scribe.—Jer., ch. 37.

80. —— Investigated. *Traitor.* [18] As they sat and did eat, Jesus said, Verily I say unto you, One of you which eateth with me shall betray me. [19] And they began to be sorrowful, and to say unto him one by one, *Is* it I? and another said, *Is* it I?—Mark, ch. 14.

81. —— Meekness under. *Jesus.* [9] Herod questioned with him in many words ; but he answered him nothing. [10] And the chief priests and scribes stood and vehemently accused him. —Luke, ch. 23.

82. —— Misapplied. *Ahab.* [There was a long drouth in the land.] [17] When Ahab saw Elijah ..Ahab said..Art thou he that troubleth Israel? [18] And he answered, I have not troubled Israel ; but thou, and thy father's house, in that ye have forsaken the commandments of the Lord, and thou hast followed Baalim.—1 Kings, ch. 18.

83. —— Malicious. *Samaritans.* [Being denied a part in the rebuilding of the temple, they sought to hinder it,] [6] And in the reign of Ahasuerus..wrote they *unto him* an accusation against the inhabitants of Judah and Jerusalem.—Ezra, ch. 4.

84. —— Resented. *Disgraceful.* [6] Saul had a concubine, whose name *was* Rizpah..and *Ishbosheth* said to Abner, Wherefore hast thou gone in unto my father's concubine? [8] Then was Abner very wroth..and said, Am I a dog's head, which against Judah do shew kindness this day unto the house of Saul thy father..and have not delivered thee into the hand of David, that thou chargest me to day with a fault concerning this woman ?—2 Sam., ch. 3.

85. —— Falsely Sustained. *Stephen.* [The Jews arrested Stephen,] [13] And set up false witnesses, which said, This man ceaseth not to speak blasphemous words against this holy place, and the law.—Acts, ch. 6.

86. —— Suppressed. *Adulteress.* [3] The scribes and Pharisees brought unto him a woman taken in adultery ; [5] Now Moses in the law commanded us, that such should be stoned : but what sayest thou ? [7]..He that is without sin among you, let him first cast a stone at her. [9] And they..being convicted by *their own* conscience, went out one by one, beginning at the eldest, *even* unto the last.—John, ch. 8.

87. —— Unsustained. *Jesus.* [13] Pilate, when he had called together the chief priests..rulers and the people, [14] Said..Ye have brought this man unto me, as one that perverteth the people ; and behold, I, having examined *him* before you, have found no fault in this man touching those things whereof ye accuse him : [15] No, nor yet Herod.—Luke, ch. 23.

88. —— Withheld. *Michael.* [9] Michael the

archangel, when contending with the devil he disputed about the body of Moses, durst not bring against him a railing accusation, but said, The Lord rebuke thee.—JUDE.

See other illustrations under:

Astounding. [Concubine] No such deed done 2729
Bigotry. Withered hand..they watched..might 780
Confessed. Is not the hand of Joab..in this 2732
Evasion. Wherefore dealt ye so ill as to tell 2727
Fanaticism. His friends..said, He is beside 3036
Hypocritical. Why was not this sold..given 3088
Idleness. Make brick..ye are idle, ye are idle 4270
Malicious. Behold a gluttonous man, a wine 3089
"   Feigning themselves just men 1111
Reaction. Cast them [accusers] into the den of 439
Self. For my sake this great tempest [Jonah] 7205
Sinners. The woman..she gave me of the tree 4221
Unexplainable. The cup was found in Benjamin's 2749
Unsuppressed. What meaneth this bleating 2750

See **BLAME** and references.

89. ACQUAINTANCE, Influence of. *Herod.*
²⁰ Herod feared John, knowing that he was a just man and a holy, and observed him ; and when he heard him, he did many things, and heard him gladly.—MARK, ch. 6.

See **ASSOCIATES** and references.

90. ACQUITTAL, Punishment after. *Pilate.*
¹⁴ Ye have brought this man unto me, as one that perverteth the people ; and, behold, I, having examined *him* before you, have found no fault in this man touching those things whereof ye accuse him : ¹⁵ No, nor yet Herod. —LUKE, ch. 23.

See other illustrations under:

Confident. I am pure from the blood of all 7223
Manslaughter. Thief smitten..die..no blood shed 7268
Necessity. Lord, let us not perish for this man's 7205
Restitution. Borrow..if the owner be with it 7273
Warning. Turn thee..wherefore should I smite 7252

See **JUSTICE** and references.

91. ACTION instead of Eloquence. *Moses.*
¹⁰ O my Lord, I *am* not eloquent, neither heretofore, nor since thou hast spoken unto thy servant ; but I *am* slow of speech, and of a slow tongue.. ¹⁷ And thou shalt take this rod in thine hand, wherewith thou shalt do signs.— Ex., ch. 4.

92. ACTIVITY, Astonishing. *Jesus.* ²⁰ The multitude cometh together again, so that they could not so much as eat bread. ²¹ And when his friends heard *of it,* they went out to lay hold on him : for they said, He is beside himself.— MARK, ch. 3.

93. —— Benevolent. *Jesus.* ³⁵ Jesus went about all the cities and villages, teaching in their synagogues, and preaching the gospel of the kingdom, and healing every sickness and every disease among the people.—MAT., ch. 9.

94. —— —SPIRITUALITY. *Martha—Mary.*
³⁹ Mary sat at Jesus' feet, and heard his word. ⁴⁰ But Martha was cumbered about much serving.. ⁴² Mary hath chosen that good part, which shall not be taken away from her.—LUKE, ch. 10.

See other illustrations under:

DEEDS.

Authenticated. If I do not the works..believe not 2094
Evince. World began..not heard..opened eyes 2095
Test. Which of these three was neighbor 2096
Words. Said..Lord he is God..slew prophets 2097

EFFORT.

Concentrated. Fight neither small nor great 2605
Deliverance. Why sit we here till we die? 2606
Fruitless. The king labored to deliver Daniel 2607
Humble. Jesus said..loose him and let him go 2608
Ill-considered. This man began to build 2609
Personal. Have mercy on me..my daughter is 2610
Sphere. Witnesses..uttermost part of the earth 2611
Single. With the spear..I will not smite the 2612
Singleness. I determined not to know anything 2613
Union. They strengthened their hands with gold 2614
"   Men and women brought bracelets and 2615
Unavailing. Earneth wages to put in a bag with 2616
Victory without. Stand still and see the salvation 2617

EARNESTNESS.

Angelic. [Lot] While he lingered..laid hold 2568
Bold. Second time..Joab's field..set it on fire 2569
Checked. Running and kneeled..master what 2570
Chosen. Every one that lappeth of the water 2571
Hospitality. [Lot] Pressed upon them greatly 2572
Important. Aaron ran..plague begun..incense 2573
Influence. Because of his importunity he will 2574
Lack. [Joash] Should have smitten 5 or 6 times 2575
Rewarded. Whoso first after the troubling 2576
Safety. Look not behind..escape to the mount 2577
"   [Bartimeus] Cried the more a great 2578
Seeking. Uncovered the roof..broke it..down 2579

ZEAL.

Age. [Caleb, 85 years] Give me this..Anakim 9974
Affecting. Many..afoot out of all cities..out went 9975
Acknowledged. [Epaphras] laboring fervently 9976
Affectionate. Brought spices very early in the 9977
Desirable. Good to be zealously affected always 9981
Excelling. Priests were too few..Levites did 9983
Energetic. [Nehemiah] contend..cursed 9984
Holy. Behold the men ye put in prison..teaching 9989
Hurtful. Say nothing..he began to blaze abroad 9991
Ministerial. Three years..I warned every one 10000
Misunderstood. [Jesus] Friends said, He is 9997
Prosperous. [Hezekiah] In every work..with 10005
Rewarded. Give my covenant..he was zealous 10013
Reformers. I chased him from me [Nehemiah] 10009
Reformation. Made a scourge..drove them out 10012
Sudden. Service..set in order..done suddenly 10016
Seeker's. [Zaccheus] Ran before, climbed..tree 10020
"   Made haste, came down, received 10014
Testify. Left her waterpot. come see a man 10022
Unwavering. None of these things move me 10025
Working. From the rising..morning..till the stars 10026

Earnest. The kingdom of heaven..violent take it 9784
Evince. If..a great people..land of the giants 9811
Faith. Go show..as they went they were 2886
Gentleness. Youth drew not his sword, for he 9966
Industrious. She hasted..ran..drew for..camels 4442
Rewarded. Let not your hands be weak 9804

See **BUSINESS** and references.
See **WORK** and references.

95. ACUTENESS of Perception. *David.* [Joab suborned a widow of Tekoah to disguise herself, and by a parable incline David's heart toward Absalom the fratricide.] ¹⁹ *Is not* the hand of Joab with thee in all this? And the woman answered.. *As* thy soul liveth, my lord the king, none can turn to the right hand or to the left from aught that my lord the king hath spoken : for thy servant Joab, he bade me, and he put all these words in the mouth of thine handmaid.—2 SAM., ch. 14.

Also see

Weatherwise. When ye see a cloud rise..shower 2341

96. ADDRESS, An irresistible. *Stephen.*
⁹ There arose certain of the synagogue of the Libertines, and Cyrenians, and Alexandrians, and of them of Cilicia and of Asia, disputing with Stephen. ¹⁰ And they were not able to resist the wisdom and the spirit by which he spake.—ACTS, ch. 6.

See SPEECH and references.

— **ADMIRATION.** — —

See illustrations under:

PRAISE.

Self. Let another praise thee..not thine own	6330
Praise. Loved the praise of men more than..of G.	6331
Dangerous. In all Israel..none so much to be	6332
Hypocrites. Love to pray..corners of the streets	6337

VANITY.

Forbidden. Be not called Rabbi..are brethren	9160
Humbled. Haman arrayed Mordecai..proclaimed	9162
Punished. Hezekiah showed them all..silver	9161
Religious. To be seen ..garments..love greetings	9163

Applause. Pinnacle..devil..cast thyself down	486
" How can ye believe which receive	485
Beauty for. Lord planted a garden..there he put	656
Jesus. His fame spread abroad..about Galilee	3000
Military. [Uzziah] made engines..name spread	3001
Troublesome. Could no more enter the city	3002
Unexpected. Whole world..be told..woman	3003
Wisdom. All the earth sought to Solomon to	3304

97. ADJURATION, A foolish. *Saul.* [The Israelites were victorious after long subjugation. The Philistines were panic-stricken,] ²⁴ And the men of Israel were distressed that day : for Saul had adjured the people, saying, Cursed *be* the man that eateth *any* food until evening, that I may be avenged on mine ene- mies. So none of the people tasted *any* food. —1 SAM., ch. 14. [Jonathan, his brave son, ate in ignorance of the adjuration. The fam- ished people afterward ate flesh with the blood, thus breaking the law.]

98. —— Sacred. *Trial of Jesus.* ⁶³ Jesus held his peace. And the high priest..said..I adjure thee by the living God, that thou tell us whether thou be the Christ, the Son of God. ⁶⁴ Jesus saith..Thou hast said : nevertheless I say unto you, Hereafter shall ye see the Son of man sit- ting on the right hand of power, and coming in the clouds of heaven.—MAT., ch. 26.

See OATH and references.

99. ADMINISTRATION, Change of. *Egypt.*
⁸ There arose up a new king over Egypt, which knew not Joseph.—EX., ch. 1.

100. —— Rejected. *Samuel's Sons.* ³ Walked not in his ways, but turned aside after lucre, and took bribes, and perverted judgment. ⁴ Then all the elders of Israel came to Samuel, ⁵ And said, Now make us a king to judge us like all the na- tions.—1 SAM., ch. 7.

101. —— Change of. *Moses.* [The ten spies returned to Moses with their evil report of the land of Canaan, which alarmed the people.] ⁴ And they said .Let us make a captain, and let us return into Egypt.—NUM., ch. 14.

See GOVERNMENT and references.

102. ADMONITION disregarded. *Mordecai.*
³ The king's servants..said unto Mordecai, Why transgressest thou the king's commandment? ⁴ ..When they spake daily unto him, and he

hearkened not unto them..they told Haman, to see whether Mordecai's matters would stand : for he had told them that he *was* a Jew.— ESTHER, ch. 3.

103. —— A fraternal. *Paul.* ¹⁴ If any man obey not our word by this epistle, note that man, and have no company with him, that he may be ashamed. ¹⁵ Yet count *him* not as an enemy, but admonish *him* as a brother.—2 THESS., ch. 3.

104. —— An incredible. *Passover.* ¹⁸ As they sat and did eat, Jesus said, Verily I say unto you, One of you which eateth with me shall betray me.—MARK, ch. 14.

See other illustrations under:

ADVICE.

Foolish. Said his wife..curse God and die	152
Good. Naaman's servants said, If the prophet had	153
Unfortunate. Let a gallows be made fifty cubits	154

CAUTION.

Believers. Moses sent them to spy out the land	1548
Building. Lest not be able to finish	676
Eating. Put a knife to thy throat..given to	1068
Forgetfulness. Take heed lest thou forget..seen	3347
Fear. Howbeit no man spake openly..for fear	3432
" Did not confess him lest..put out	3433
Hearing. Increased..30..60..100 fold..he that	1069
Hypocrisy. Beware of the scribes..love greetings	321
Lack. Let about 3000..smite Ai..fled	1532
" I made as if they were beaten..and fled	1522
Strife. Consulteth whether he be able to meet	677
Necessary. The simple believe every word	1070
Prudent. [Micah] saw they were too strong	1071
Wise. Fool uttereth all his mind..wise	1072

WARNING.

Additional. Lazarus..send him..I have five	9340
Destruction. [Scorners] I also will laugh at your	9317
Dream. Have nothing to do with that just man	9318
Dangers. Beware thou pass not such a place	9319
Despised. Get you out of this place..mocked	9320
Disobedience. If thine heart turn away..surely	9321
Doubted. Before the cock crow thou shalt deny	9322
Example. Sodom and G. are set for an example	9323
" Remember Lot's wife [Jesus]	9324
Experience. Alexander..did me much harm	9325
Faithful. Three years I ceased not to warn every	9326
Heedless. Sword come..blood on his own head	9327
Heeded. Noah being warned of God..prepared	9328
Historical. These things were our examples	9329
" Did not Solomon..sin by these things	9330
Ignored. Abner said, Turn thee aside from	9331
Punishment. [Leprosy] Remember what the	9332
Preserved. Angel..Joseph..Herod will seek the	9333
Personal. Before the cock crow..deny me thrice	9334
Repeated. Moses..go down and charge the	9335
Saved. He that taketh warning shall deliver	9336
Solemn. All ye shall be offended..me this night	9337
Sorrowful. One of you shall betray me	9338
Wicked. Korah..fire devoured 250 men	

WATCHING.

Failure. Watch..know not what. hour L. cometh	9345
Hinderances. Take heed..lest..overcharged	9346
Necessary. Be vigilant..the devil as a roaring lion	9356
Vigilance. Watch..lest coming suddenly..you	9352

Farewell. Take heed..lest thou forget [Moses]	4542
Ignorance. Word..understandeth it not..cometh	4545
Improvement. That observe..but do not after	4546

See BLAME and references.

105. ADOPTION by Attraction. *Esther.* [7] Mordecai brought up..Esther, his uncle's daughter : for she had neither father nor mother, and the maid *was* fair and beautiful ; whom Mordecai ..took for his own daughter.—ESTHER, ch. 2.

106. —— **Grateful.** *Mephibosheth.* [1]..David said, Is there yet any that is left of the house of Saul, that I may shew him kindness for Jonathan's sake ? [11]..Mephibosheth shall eat at my table, as one of the king's sons.—2 SAM., ch. 9.

107. —— **through Sympathy.** *Moses.* [Pharaoh's daughter opened the ark where Moses lay, and] [6]..the babe wept. And she had compassion on him, and said, This *is one* of the Hebrew's children. [10] And the child grew, and she brought him unto Pharaoh's daughter, and he became her son.—EX., ch. 2.

108. ADORNMENT, Christian. *Paul.* [9] That women adorn themselves in modest apparel, with shamefacedness and sobriety ; not with braided hair, or gold, or pearls, or costly array ; [10] But..with good works.—1 TIM., ch. 2.

See BEAUTY and references.

109. ADULTERY, Accusation of. *Potiphar's Wife.* [19] When his master heard the words of his wife, saying, After this manner did thy servant to me ; that his wrath was kindled. [20] And Joseph's master took him, and put him into the prison, a place where the king's prisoners *were* bound.—GEN., ch. 39.

110. —— *Resentment.* [7] *Ish-bosheth* said to Abner, Wherefore hast thou gone in unto my father's concubine ? [8] Then was Abner very wroth..and said, Am I a dog's head, which against Judah do shew kindness this day unto the house of Saul.—2 SAM., ch. 3.

111. —— **Concealment of.** *Darkness.* [15] The eye also of the adulterer waiteth for the twilight, saying, No eye shall see me : and disguiseth *his* face. [16] In the dark they dig through houses, *which* they had marked for themselves in the daytime : they know not the light. [17] For the morning *is* to them even as the shadow of death : if *one* know *them*, *they are in* the terrors of the shadow of death.—JOB, ch. 24.

112. —— **Divorce for.** *Jesus.* [9]..Whosoever shall put away his wife, except *it be* for fornication, and shall marry another, committeth adultery : and whoso marrieth her which is put away doth commit adultery.—MAT., ch. 19.

113. —— **Destructive.** *Solomon.* [27] Can a man take fire in his bosom, and his clothes not be burned ? [28] Can one go upon hot coals, and his feet not be burned ? [32] Whoso committeth adultery with a woman lacketh understanding : he *that* doeth it destroyeth his own soul.—PROV., ch. 6.

114. —— **Incipient.** *Jesus.* [28]..Whosoever looketh on a woman to lust after her hath committed adultery with her already in his heart.—MAT., ch. 5.

Also see
Incestuous. Thou shall be as one of the fools in I. 4379

115. ADULTERESS, Arts of the. *Harlot.* [9] In the twilight, in the evening, in the black and dark night : [10]..Behold, there met him a woman *with* the attire of a harlot, and subtile of heart. [13] So she caught him, and kissed him, *and* with an impudent face said : [14] *I have* peace

offerings with me ; this day have I paid my vows.—PROV., ch. 7.

116. —— **Destructive.** *Influence.* [18] Her house inclineth unto death, and her paths unto the dead. [19] None that go unto her return again, neither take they hold of the paths of life.—PROV., ch. 2.

117. —— **Deception of the.** *The End.* [3] The lips of a strange woman drop *as* a honeycomb, and her mouth *is* smoother than oil. [4] But her end is bitter as wormwood, sharp as a two-edged sword. [5] Her feet go down to death ; her steps take hold on hell.—PROV., ch. 5.

118. —— **Pardoned.** *Jesus.* [10]..Woman, where are those thine accusers ? hath no man condemned thee ? [11] She said, No man, Lord. And Jesus said unto her, Neither do I condemn thee : go, and sin no more.—JOHN, ch. 8.

See other illustrations under :
Harlot. Is loud and stubborn, her feet abide not   3801
"   Strong men slain by her..way to hell   3802
Peril. Her house is the way to hell..death   3803
Sodomite. Daughters of Lot..child by their own   4381

119. ADVANCE by Faith. *Red Sea.* [15] The Lord said unto Moses, Wherefore criest thou unto me ? speak unto the children of Israel, that they go forward : [16] But lift thou up thy rod, and stretch out thine hand over the sea, and divide it : and the children of Israel shall go on dry *ground* through the midst of the sea.—EX., ch. 14.

120. —— **Signal for.** *Trees.* [The Philistines were in the valley of Rephaim,] [23] And when David inquired of the Lord, he said, Thou shalt not go up ; *but* fetch a compass behind them, and come upon them over against the mulberry trees. [24]..When thou hearest the sound of a going in the tops of the mulberry trees..then thou shalt bestir thyself : for then shall the Lord go out before thee, to smite the host.— 2 SAM., ch. 5.

121. —— —— *Challenge.* [The Philistines were in their strong hold. To his armor bearer] [8]..said Jonathan, Behold, we will pass over unto *these* men.. [9] If they say..Tarry until we come to you ; then we will stand still in our place, and will not go up unto them. [10] But if they say thus, Come up unto us ; then we will go up : for the Lord hath delivered them into our hand ; and this *shall be* a sign unto us.— 1 SAM., ch. 14.

See other illustrations under :
Christian. Path of the just, shineth more and   6631
Fig-Tree. Cut it down, why cumbereth the   4366
Spiritual. I see men as trees, walking   6634
Hindered. L. took off their chariot wheels..let us   6632
Improvement. Whosoever hath, to him shall be   4365
See IMPROVEMENT and references.

122. ADVENT, The first. *Bethlehem.* [7] Mary brought forth her firstborn son, and wrapped him in swaddling clothes, and laid him in a manger ; because there was no room for them in the inn.—LUKE, ch. 2.

123. —— **The second.** *Heavens.* [30] Then shall appear the sign of the Son of man in heaven : and then shall all the tribes of the earth mourn, and they shall see the Son of man coming in the clouds of heaven with power and great glory. [31] And he shall send his angels with a great sound of a trumpet, and they shall gather together his elect from the four winds, from one end of heaven to the other.—MAT., ch. 24.

124. —— —— *Resurrection.* [16] The Lord himself shall descend from heaven with a shout, with the voice of the archangel, and with the trump of God ; and the dead in Christ shall rise first. [17] Then we which are alive *and* remain shall be caught up together, with them in the clouds, to meet the Lord in the air : and so shall we ever be with the Lord.—1 THESS., ch. 4.

125. ADVENTURERS, Organization of. *Adullamites.* [Saul threatened his life, so] [1] David.. escaped the cave Adullam : and when..all his father's house heard *it*, they went down thither to him. [2] And every one *that was* in distress, and..in debt, and..discontented, gathered themselves unto him ; and he became a captain over them..about four hundred men. —1 SAM., ch. 22.

Also see
Adulteress. Caught..kissed him..impudent face   115

126. ADVERSITY bewailed. *Change.* [Naomi returned to Bethlehem and said,] [20]..the Almighty hath dealt very bitterly with me. [21] I went out full, and the Lord hath brought me home again empty : why *then* call ye me Naomi, seeing the Lord hath testified against me, and the Almighty hath afflicted me?—RUTH, ch. 1.

127. —— **Comfort in.** *Job.* [12] I delivered the poor that cried, and the fatherless, and *him that had* none to help him. [13] The blessing of him that was ready to perish came upon me : and I caused the widow's heart to sing for joy. [15] I was eyes to the blind, and feet *was* I to the lame. [16] I *was* a father to the poor.—JOB, ch. 29.

128. —— **Distrust in.** *Israelites.* [8] I will bring you in unto the land..which I did swear to give it to Abraham, to Isaac, and to Jacob ; and I will give it you for a heritage : I *am* the Lord. [9] And Moses spake so unto the children of Israel : but they hearkened not unto Moses for anguish of spirit, and for cruel bondage.—Ex., ch. 6.

129. —— **Enemy in.** *Shimei.* [David fled out of Jerusalem from Absalom.] [6] Shimei cast stones at David, and..the servants..and all the mighty men *were* on his right hand and on his left. [7] And thus said..Come out, come out, thou bloody man, and thou man of Belial : [8] The Lord hath returned upon thee all the blood of the house of Saul.—2 SAM., ch. 16.

130. —— **Fainting under.** *Proverb.* [10] *If* thou faint in the day of adversity, thy strength *is* small.—PROV., ch. 24.

131. —— **Friends in.** *Provisions.* [David fled from Absalom. See No. 129.] [27]..When David was come to Mahanaim..Shobi..and Machir, and Barzillai.. [28] Brought beds, and basins, and earthen vessels, and wheat, and barley, and flour, and parched *corn*, and beans, and lentiles, and parched *pulse*, [29] And honey, and butter, and sheep, and cheese of kine, for David, and for the people that *were* with him, to eat..in the wilderness.—2 SAM., ch. 17.

132. —— **Grief in.** *Mephibosheth.* [After Absalom drove David out of Jerusalem,] [24]..Mephibosheth the son of Saul had neither dressed his feet, nor trimmed his beard, nor washed his clothes, from the day the king departed until the day he came *again* in peace.—2 SAM., ch. 19.

133. —— **Hope in.** *Jeremiah.* [31] The Lord will not cast off for ever : [32] But though he cause grief, yet will he have compassion according to the multitude of his mercies. [33] For he doth not afflict willingly, nor grieve the children of men.—LAM., ch. 3.

134. —— **Helpless in.** *Obdurate.* [24] Because I have called, and ye refused.. [27] When your fear cometh as desolation, and your destruction cometh as a whirlwind ; when distress and anguish cometh upon you. [28] Then shall they call upon me, but I will not answer ; they shall seek me early, but they shall not find me.— PROV., ch. 1.

135. —— **Misunderstood.** *Jacob.* [His brothers demanded Benjamin to go with them and buy corn in Egypt.] [38] Jacob said, My son shall not go down with you ; for his brother is dead, and he is left alone : if mischief befall him by the way in which ye go, then shall ye bring down my gray hairs with sorrow to the grave.—GEN., ch. 42. [The discovery of Joseph followed.]

136. —— **Misconstrued.** *Idolaters.* [The apostate Jews in Egypt said,] [17]..then had we plenty of victuals, and were well, and saw no evil. [18] But since we left off to burn incense to the queen of heaven, and to pour out drink offerings unto her, we have wanted all *things*, and have been consumed by the sword and by the famine.—JER., ch. 44.

137. —— **Misinterpreted.** *Galileans.* [1]..some told him of the Galileans, whose blood Pilate had mingled with their sacrifices. [2] Jesus..said ..Suppose ye that these Galileans were sinners above all the Galileans, because they suffered such things ? [3] I tell you, Nay : but, except ye repent, ye shall all likewise perish.—LUKE, ch. 13.

138. —— **National.** *Jews.* [16] They mocked the messengers of God, and despised his words. and misused his prophets, until the wrath of the Lord arose against his people, till *there was* no remedy. [17] Therefore he brought upon them the king of the Chaldees, who slew their young men..and had no compassion upon young man or maiden, old man, or him that stooped for age : he gave *them* all into his hand.—2 CHRON., ch. 36.

139. —— **Obduracy in.** *Jews.* [16] *As for* the word that thou hast spoken..in the name of the Lord, we will not hearken unto thee. [17] But we will certainly do whatsoever thing goeth forth out of our own mouth, to burn incense unto the queen of heaven.—JER., ch. 44. [The Jews in Egypt were in great adversity.]

140. —— —— *Ahaz.* [22] In the time of his distress did he trespass yet more against the Lord.. [23] For he sacrificed unto the gods of Damascus, which smote him : and he said, Because the gods of the kings of Syria help them, *therefore* will I sacrifice to them, that they may help me. But they were the ruin of him, and of all Israel.—2 CHRON., ch. 28.

141. —— **Punishment by.** *Idolaters.* [8] They rebelled against me, and would not hearken.. they did not every man cast away the abominations of their eyes, neither did they forsake the idols of Egypt : then I said, I will pour out my fury upon them, to accomplish my anger against them in..the land of Egypt.—Ezek., ch. 20.

142. —— Rejoicing in. *Habakkuk.* [17]Although the fig tree shall not blossom, neither *shall* fruit *be* in the vines ; the labor of the olive shall fail, and the fields shall yield no meat ; the flock shall be cut off from the fold, and *there shall be* no herd in the stalls : [18]Yet I will rejoice in the Lord, I will joy in the God of my salvation.—Hab., ch. 3.

143. —— Rejected in. *Israelites.* [13]Ye have forsaken me, and served other gods : wherefore I will deliver you no more. [14]Go and cry unto the gods which ye have chosen ; let them deliver you in the time of your tribulation.—Judges, ch. 10.

144. —— Times of. *King Asa.* [5]In those times *there was* no peace to him that went out, nor to him that came in, but great vexations *were* upon all the inhabitants of the countries. [6]And nation was destroyed of nation, and city of city : for God did vex them with all adversity.—2 Chron., ch. 15.

145. —— Weakness in. *Job.* [Eliphaz said,] [4]Thy words have upholden him that was falling, and thou hast strengthened the feeble knees. [5]But now it is come upon thee, and thou faintest ; it toucheth thee, and thou art troubled.—Job, ch. 4.

146. ADVERSITIES, Changes by. *Job.* [1]But now *they that are* younger than I have me in derision, whose fathers I would have disdained to have set with the dogs of my flock.—Job, ch. 30.

147. —— Improvement by. *Ezra.* [13]After all that is come upon us for our evil deeds..seeing that thou our God hast punished us less than our iniquities *deserve*. [14]Should we again break thy commandments..wouldest not thou be angry with us till thou hadst consumed *us*, so that *there should be* no remnant nor escaping ?—Ezra, ch. 9.

148. —— Many. *Job's.* [Messengers came to Job in quick succession, saying,] [14]..The oxen were ploughing, and the asses feeding.. [15]And the Sabeans fell *upon them*, and took them.. [16]..The fire of God is fallen from heaven, and hath burned up the sheep. [17]..The Chaldeans..fell upon the camels, and have carried them away. [18]..Thy sons and thy daughters *were* eating and drinking wine in their eldest brother's house. [19]And..there came a great wind..and smote the four corners of the house, and it fell upon the young men, and they are dead.—Job, ch. 1.

149. —— Overwhelming. *Eli.* [A messenger came to Eli and said,] [17]..Israel is fled before the Philistines, and there hath been also a great slaughter..and thy two sons also, Hophni and Phinehas, are dead, and the ark of God is taken. [18]..When he made mention of the ark..he fell from off the seat backward by the side of the gate, and his neck brake..he was an old man, and heavy.—1 Sam., ch. 4.

150. —— Restoration from. *Job.* [12]The Lord blessed the latter end of Job more than his beginning : for he had fourteen thousand sheep, and six thousand camels, and a thousand yoke of oxen, and a thousand she asses. [13]He had also seven sons and three daughters.—Job, ch. 42.

151. —— Unendurable. *Job.* [12]I was at ease, but he hath broken me asunder : he hath also taken *me* by my neck, and shaken me to pieces, and set me up for his mark.—Job, ch. 16.

See other illustrations under:

CALAMITY.

Destructive. Wall fell upon 27,000 men that were	995
Feared. His strength shall be hunger bitten	1000
of God. Earth opened her mouth and swallowed	996
Hardened. I have smitten you with blasting	1001
Indiscriminating. The L. maketh the earth	1002
Misjudged. Tower in Siloam fell think..they	1003
Predicted. Shall not be left one stone upon	997
Reflection. O that I were..days of my youth	1004
Sin. Taken the accursed thing..therefore could	998
Waiting. Jonah sat..see what would become	999

DESPONDENCY.

Bereavement. Joseph is, without doubt, rent in	2226
Complaint. Since I came to Pharaoh..done evil	2227
Constitutional. Let us go..die with him	2230
Continued. My heart is smitten and withered like	2228
Cure. David was greatly distressed..spake of	2229
Difficulties. People was much discouraged	2231
Hope. Why art thou cast down, O my soul	2232
Hasty. Sun beat..Jonah fainted..wished to die	2233
Ill-timed. Handful of meal..little oil..die	2234
Loneliness. I only am left, and they seek my life	2235
Memories. By the rivers of Babylon we wept	2236
Over-care. If thou deal thus with me, kill me	2237
Prayer. How long wilt thou forget me, O L.	2239
Public. Moses heard the people weeping..door	2238
Peril. Esau cometh..400 men..Jacob afraid	2240
Singular. Lord take away my life..not better	2242
Vows. L. made a reproach unto me..derision	2243
Without. Troubled on every side..not in despair	2244

DESTRUCTION.

Flood. They ate..drank..married..destroyed	2254
" Every living..man..cattle..fowl	2256
Grave. Hope of a tree if it be cut down	2258
Israelites. The affliction of I. was very bitter	2253
Losses. Riches certainly make themselves wings	9080
Red Sea. Waters returned..covered the chariots	2257
Sodom. They bought..sold..planted..builded	2255

LAMENTATION.

Adversity. Let the day perish wherein I was	4883
Fathers. O my son Absalom ! my son, my son	4884
General. Thrust out right eyes..people..voices	4885
Ill-timed. Would to G. we had been content.	4886
Jesus. O Jerusalem, Jerusalem..would I have	4887
for Jesus. Weep not for me, but weep for	4888
National. In every province. Jews..weeping and	4889
Tearful. Oh that my head were waters..fountain	4890

MOURNING.

Abstinence. [Abner assassinated] If I taste	5603
Bereavement. I am distressed for thee, my	5604
Beneficial. Better to go to the house of mourning	5605
Comfort. Asleep..sorrow not as others which	5598
Feigned. Be as a woman..long time mourned	5606
Good. Mary..told them..as they mourned and	5600
Genuine. Widows..weeping and showing	5601
Intense. David went up..wept..barefoot	5607
Joy. Jesus came and touched the bier	5608
Last. Thou mourn at the last..body consumed	5609
Time. Great and very sore lamentation	5610
Wicked. King wept at the grave of Abner	5611

SICKNESS.

Destructive. Elisha was sick..my father !..the	7852
Despondency. He will cut me off with pining	7853
Jesus in. Nobleman saith, Sir, come down ere my	7854

Overwork. Nigh unto death, not regarding his	7856
Punished. L. will make plagues..sore sickness	7857
Pretended. Saul sent..to take David, she said	7858
Reflections. I shall behold man no more	7859
Relieved. Simon's wife's mother..fever	7860
Sinners. Take a present..inquire..shall I recover	7861
Unimproved. [Hezekiah healed.] Rendered not	7855
Wasting. My leanness..witness against me [Job]	7862

SUFFERING.

Apostolic. [Paul] Five times..stripes..thrice	8452
For Christ. [Paul and Silas] Laid many stripes	8449
Chosen. Moses..choosing rather to suffer..than	8453
Faithful. Were stoned..sawn asunder, were	8448
Frevented. Keeper of the prison drew out his	8458
Recompensed. Moses..had respect unto the	8454
Sacred. Remove this cup..not my will [Jesus]	8455
Subdued. Bit the people..died, therefore..we	8451
Support. Sufferings of this present time not	8450

SUICIDE.

Imitated. Armor bearer saw that Saul was dead	8456
Mortification. Counsel was not followed..hanged	8457
Soldier's. Archers hit him..sore wounded..sword	8459
Traitor's. Cast down..silver..hanged himself	8460

TRIALS.

Business. Day the drought consumed me..frost	8923
Blessing. Blessed are ye when men shall revile	8925
" I am exceeding joyful in all our	8948
Character. Saw the Egyptians dead..feared the L.	8914
Darkness. I cry out of wrong, but I am not heard	8930
Despair. There was a great earthquake..sun	8946
Faith. Trial of your faith..more precious than	8916
Follow. Three days in the wilderness..no water	8929
Impenitence. Thy sons..as a wild bull in a net	8917
Joyful. Took joyfully the spoiling of your goods	8935
Life. God commanded..Thou shalt not eat	8918
Multiplied. All my inward friends abhorred me	8936
" In labors more abundant..stripes	8940
Proportioned. Led them not..was near..lest	8921
Recompensed. These..came out of great	8949
Severe. Take now thy son..Isaac..burnt	8922
" We hunger and thirst and are naked	8939
" In perils of waters..robbers..heathen	8941
Use. Nations which the L. left to prove I.	8943
" Branch that beareth not fruit..purgeth it	8944
Winnow. When affliction or persecution ariseth	8928

Confession. Pharaoh..L. is righteous, I and	1489
Fasting. David fasted..lay all night upon the	3057
Impenitence. Ahaziah fell through a lattice..was	4347
Preparation. Before your feet stumble on the	4178
Union. Every one that was in distress..gathered	3446

See **AFFLICTIONS** and references.
See **BEREAVEMENT** and references.
See **SORROW** and references.
See **TROUBLE** and references.

152. ADVICE, Foolish. *Curse God.* [9] Said Job's wife unto him, Dost thou still retain thine integrity? curse God, and die.—JOB, ch. 2.

153. —— Good. *Naaman's* [13] ..Servants.. said, My father, *if* the prophet had bid thee *do some* great thing, wouldest thou not have done *it?* how much rather then, when he saith to thee, Wash, and be clean?—2 KINGS, ch. 5.

154. —— Unfortunate. *Gallows.* [14] Said Zeresh his wife and all his friends..Let a gallows be made of fifty cubits high..that Mordecai may be hanged thereon : then go thou in merrily with the king unto the banquet. And the thing pleased Haman.—ESTHER, ch. 5.

See other illustrations under :

COUNSEL.

Dying. I go..show thyself a man [David]	1746
Evil. Rehoboam consulted with the young men	1748
Friends. Let a gallows be made 50 cubits high	1740
Good. Rehoboam consulted with the old men	1749
Influential. David..the lords favor thee not	1750
Malicious. Come let us take counsel together	1751
Neglected. Took not counsel of the L.	1741
Oracular. Counsel of Ahithophel..as..oracle of	1742
Opposing. Ahithophel said to Absalom..Hushai	1747
Payment. Saul to servant..what shall we bring	1744
Peace. Joab, hear the words..handmaid	1743
Rejection. Ahithophel saw..not followed	1745
Safety. In the multitude of counsellors..safety	1739
Unfortunate. Why sit we here until we die?	1738

WITCHCRAFT.

Abolished. Workers with familiar spirits..Josiah	9649
Doubters. Go into Judea, that thy disciples also	4338
Famous. Seek me a woman..a familiar spirit	9647
Influential. They all gave heed..least..greatest	9650

Appreciated. D. said to Abigail, Blessed be thy	2368
Commendation. [Hurtful] These men are the	6896
Consoling. Thy words have upholden him that	145

See **ADMONITION** and references.

155. ADVOCATE, A friendly. *Blastus.* [20] Herod was highly displeased with them of Tyre and Sidon : but they came with one accord to him, and, having made Blastus the king's chamberlain their friend, desired peace ; because their country was nourished by the king's *country.*—ACTS, ch. 12.

156. —— The Sinner's. *Jesus.* [1]..If any man sin, we have an advocate with the Father, Jesus Christ the righteous : [2] And he is the propitiation for our sins.—1 JOHN, ch. 2.

See other illustrations under :

Fraternal. Jonathan answered, Wherefore shall   2107
See **INTERCESSION** and references.

157. AFFECTION, Compassionate. *The Prodigal Son.* [20] He arose, and came to his father. But when he was yet a great way off, his father saw him, and had compassion, and ran, and fell on his neck, and kissed him.—LUKE, ch. 15.

158. —— Condescending. *Centurion.* [2] A certain centurion's servant, who was dear unto him, was sick, and ready to die. [3] And when he heard of Jesus, he sent..beseeching him that he would come and heal his servant.—LUKE, ch. 7.

159. —— Divided. For *Saul* and *David.* [17] Jonathan caused David to swear again..for he loved him as he loved his own soul. [30] Then Saul's anger was kindled against Jonathan..Thou son of the perverse rebellious *woman*, do not I know that thou hast chosen the son of Jesse to thine own confusion?—1 SAM., ch. 20.

160. —— in Death. *Crucifixion.* [26] When Jesus therefore saw his mother, and the disciple standing by, whom he loved, he saith..Woman, behold thy son ! [27] Then saith he to the disciple, Behold thy mother !..That disciple took her unto his own *home.*—JOHN, ch. 19.

161. —— A Demagogue's. *Absalom.* [4]..Oh that I were made judge in the land.. [5]..When any man came nigh *to him* to do him obeisance, he put forth his hand, and took him, and kissed him.. [6]..So Absalom stole the hearts of the men of Israel. —2 SAM., ch. 15.

162. —— Energizes. *Ark of Bulrushes.* [The

mother of Moses] ³..took for him an ark of bulrushes, and daubed it with slime and with pitch, and put the child therein ; and she laid *it* in the flags by the river's brink. ⁴ And his sister stood afar off, to wit what would be done to him.--Ex., ch. 2.

163. —— **Extraordinary.** *David.* ³³ The king was much moved, and went up to the chamber over the gate, and wept : and as he went, thus he said, O my son Absalom ! my son, my son Absalom ! would God I had died for thee, O Absalom, my son, my son !--2 Sam., ch. 18.

164. —— **Fraternal.** *Joseph.* ³⁰ Joseph made haste ; for his bowels did yearn upon his brother : and he sought *where* to weep ; and he entered into *his* chamber, and wept there. ³¹ And he washed his face, and went out, and refrained himself, and said, Set on bread.--Gen., ch. 43.

165. —— **Filial.** *Joseph.* ²⁹ Joseph made ready his chariot, and went up to meet Israel his father, to Goshen..and he fell on his neck, and wept on his neck a good while.--Gen., ch. 46.

166. —— **Family.** *Jewish.* ¹¹ Naomi said, Turn again, my daughters [in law]. ¹⁴ And they lifted up their voice, and wept again : and Orpah kissed her mother in law ; but Ruth clave unto her.--Ruth, ch. 1.

167. —— **of Friendship.** *Jesus.* ⁵ Jesus loved Martha, and her sister, and Lazarus. ³ Therefore his sisters sent unto him, saying, Lord, behold, he whom thou lovest is sick.--John, ch. 11.

168. —— **in the Future Life.** *Dives.* ²⁷..Send him, Lazarus, to my father's house : ²⁸ For I have five brethren ; that he may testify unto them, lest they also come into this place of torment.--Luke, ch. 16.

169. —— **A fictitious.** *Judas.* ⁴⁸ He that betrayed him gave them a sign, saying, Whomsoever I shall kiss, that same is he ; hold him fast. --Mat., ch. 26.

170. —— **Grateful.** *Sinner.* ³⁷..A woman.. which was a sinner, when she knew that *Jesus* sat at meat in the Pharisee's house, brought an alabaster box of ointment, ³⁸ And stood at his feet behind *him* weeping, and began to wash his feet with tears, and did wipe *them* with the hairs of her head, and kissed his feet, and anointed *them* with the ointment.--Luke, ch. 7.

171. —— **A second Husband's.** *Weeping.* ¹⁵ Ish-bosheth sent, and took Michal [David's former wife] from *her* husband, *even* from Phaltiel.. ¹⁶..went with her along weeping behind her to Bahurim. Then said Abner unto him, Go, return.--2 Sam., ch. 3.

172. —— **Maternal.** *Hannah.* ¹⁸ Samuel ministered before the Lord, *being* a child, girded with a linen ephod. ¹⁹ Moreover his mother made him a little coat, and brought *it* to him from year to year.--1 Sam., ch. 2.

173. —— **Manifested.** *Ointment.* ³ Then took Mary a pound of ointment of spikenard, very costly, and anointed the feet of Jesus, and wiped his feet with her hair : and the house was filled with the odor.--John, ch. 12.

174. —— **Nourished.** *Isaac.* ²⁸ Isaac loved Esau, because he did eat of *his* venison.--Gen., ch. 25.

175. —— **Natural.** *David.* [After murdering his brother,] ³⁸ Absalom fled..to Geshur, and was there three years. ³⁹ And *the soul of* King David longed to go forth unto Absalom : for he was comforted concerning Amnon, seeing he was dead.--2 Sam., ch. 13.

176. —— **an Obstacle.** *Kiss.* ¹⁹..Elijah passed by Elisha, and cast his mantle upon him. ²⁰ And he left the oxen, and ran after Elijah, and said, Let me, I pray thee, kiss my father and my mother, and *then* I will follow thee. And he said, Go back again : for what have I done to thee ?--1 Kings, ch. 19.

177. —— **Partiality in.** *Jacob.* ³ Israel loved Joseph more than all his children, because he *was* the son of his old age : and he made him a coat of *many* colours. ⁴ And when his brethren saw that their father loved him more than all his brethren, they hated him, and could not speak peaceably unto him.--Gen., ch. 37.

178. —— **Paternal.** *Father's.* ²⁴..The father of the child cried out, and said with tears, Lord, I believe ; help thou mine unbelief. ²⁵ When Jesus saw that the people came running together, he rebuked the foul spirit.--Mark, ch. 9.

179. —— **Special.** *Passover.* ²³ Now there was leaning on Jesus' bosom one of his disciples, whom Jesus loved. ²⁴ Simon Peter therefore beckoned to him, that he should ask who it should be of whom he spake.--John, ch. 13.

180. —— **A questioned.** *Peter.* ¹⁷..Simon, *son* of Jonas, lovest thou me ? Peter was grieved because he said unto him the third time, Lovest thou me ? And he said unto him, Lord, thou knowest all things ; thou knowest that I love thee.--John, ch. 21.

181. —— **Supreme, Spiritual.** *Jesus.* ²⁵ There went great multitudes..Jesus turned, and said.. ²⁶ If any *man* come to me, and hate not his father, and mother, and wife, and children, and brethren, and sisters, yea, and his own life also, he cannot be my disciple.--Luke, ch. 14.

182. —— **Tender.** *Paul.* ⁴ Out of much affliction and anguish of heart I wrote unto you with many tears ; not that ye should be grieved, but that ye might know the love which I have more abundantly unto you. ⁷ So that contrariwise ye *ought* rather to forgive *him*, and comfort *him*, lest perhaps such a one should be swallowed up with overmuch sorrow.--2 Cor., ch. 2.

183. —— **Tested.** *Sacrifice.* ⁷ Isaac spake unto Abraham..My father : and he said, Here *am* I, my son. And he said, Behold the fire and the wood ; but where *is* the lamb for a burnt offering ?--Gen., ch. 22.

184. —— **Verified.** *Solomon.* ²⁵ The king said, Divide the living child in two, and give half to the one, and half to the other. ²⁶ Then spake the woman..for her bowels yearned upon her son..O my lord, give her the living child, and in no wise slay it. But the other said, Let it be neither mine nor thine, *but* divide it.--1 Kings, ch. 3.

185. —— **Zealous.** *Mary.* ¹..Cometh Mary Magdalene early, when it was yet dark..and seeth the stone taken away from the sepulchre. ² Then she runneth, and cometh to Simon Peter, and to the other disciple.--John, ch. 20.

186. AFFLICTION bewailed. *Naomi.* [21] I went out full, and the Lord hath brought me home again empty : why *then* call ye me Naomi, seeing the Lord hath testified against me, and the Almighty hath afflicted me ?—RUTH, ch. 1.

187. —— Blessed. *Eliphaz said,* [17] Behold, happy *is* the man whom God correcteth : therefore despise not thou the chastening of the Almighty : [18] For he maketh sore, and bindeth up : he woundeth, and his hands make whole. —JOB, ch. 5.

188. —— Bodily. *Job.* [4] Satan answered the Lord. Skin for skin, yea, all that a man hath will he give for his life. [5] But put forth thine hand now, and touch his bone and his flesh, and he will curse thee to thy face.—JOB, ch. 2.

189. —— Conversion in. *Nobleman.* [46]..there was a certain nobleman, whose son was sick at Capernaum.. [53] So the father knew that *it was* at the same hour, in the which Jesus said unto him, Thy son liveth : and himself believed, and his whole house.—JOHN, ch. 4.

190. —— Compensated. *Manasseh.* [12] When he was in affliction, he besought the Lord his God, and humbled himself greatly before the God of his fathers. [13]..And he was entreated of him..and brought him again to Jerusalem into his kingdom. Then Manasseh knew that the Lord he *was* God.—2 CHRON., ch. 33.

191. —— Corrective. *David.* [67] Before I was afflicted I went astray : but now have I kept thy word. [71] *It is* good for me that I have been afflicted ; that I might learn thy statutes. — Ps. 119.

192. —— Compassionated. *Naomi.* [Attended by Ruth, she returned to her native place a poor widow,] [19]..And..when they were come to Bethlehem..all the city was moved about them, and they said, *Is* this Naomi ?—RUTH, ch. 1.

193. —— Comfort in. *Jeremiah.* [31] The Lord will not cast off for ever. [32] But though he cause grief, yet will he have compassion according to the multitude of his mercies. [33] For he doth not afflict willingly, nor grieve the children of men.—LAM., ch. 3.

194. —— —— *Eliphaz.* [3] Behold, thou hast instructed many, and thou hast strengthened the weak hands. [4] Thy words have upholden him that was falling, and thou hast strengthened the feeble knees.—JOB, ch. 4.

195. —— Chosen. *Moses.* [24] By faith Moses, when he was come to years, refused to be called the son of Pharaoh's daughter ; [25] Choosing rather to suffer affliction with the people of God, than to enjoy the pleasures of sin for a season ; [26] Esteeming the reproach of Christ greater riches than the treasures in Egypt.— HEB., ch. 11.

196. —— Encouragement in. *Paul.* [18] I reckon that the sufferings of this present time *are* not worthy *to be compared* with the glory which shall be revealed in us.—ROM., ch. 8.

197. —— Inefficacious. *Ahaz.* [22] In the time of his distress did he trespass yet more against the Lord.. [23] For he sacrificed unto the gods of Damascus, which smote him.—2 CHRON., ch. 23.

198. —— Impatience under. *Job's Wife.* [9]..Dost thou still retain thine integrity ? curse God, and die. [10] But he said unto her, Thou speakest as one of the foolish women speaketh. What ? shall we receive good at the hand of God, and shall we not receive evil ?—JOB, ch. 2.

199. —— Jesus wanted in. *Sisters of Lazarus.* [2] Lazarus was sick. [3] Therefore his sisters sent unto him, saying, Lord, behold, he whom thou lovest is sick.—JOHN, ch. 11.

200. —— Manifested. *Job.* [20] Job arose, rent his mantle, shaved his head, fell down upon the ground, and worshipped. [21] And said..the Lord gave, and the Lord hath taken away ; blessed be the name of the Lord.—JOB, ch. 1.

201. —— Punishment by. *Israelites.* [8] But they rebelled against me, and would not hearken unto me : they did not every man cast away the abominations of their eyes, neither did they forsake the idols of Egypt : then I said, I will pour out my fury upon them, to accomplish my anger against them in the midst of the land of Egypt.—EZEK., ch. 20.

202. —— —— *Eliphaz said,* [7] Remember, I pray thee, who *ever* perished, being innocent ? or where were the righteous cut off ? [8] Even as I have seen, they that plough iniquity, and sow wickedness, reap the same.—JOB, ch. 4.

203. —— not a Punishment. *Blindness.* [2] His disciples asked..Master who did sin, this man, or his parents, that he was born blind ? [3] Jesus answered, Neither hath this man sinned, nor his parents.—JOHN, ch. 9.

204. —— Prosperity in. *Israelites.* [11] Therefore they did set over them taskmasters to afflict them with their burdens. [12] But the more they afflicted them, the more they multiplied and grew.—EX., ch. 1.

205. —— Prolonged. *Eighteen years.* [11]..there was a woman which had a spirit of infirmity eighteen years, and was bowed together, and could in no wise lift up *herself.* [12] And when Jesus saw her, he..said..Woman, thou art loosed from thine infirmity.—LUKE, ch. 13.

206. —— —— *Thirty-eight years.* [4] An angel went down at a certain season into the pool, and troubled the water : whosoever then first after.. stepped in was made whole of whatsoever disease he had. ⁵ And a certain man was there, which had an infirmity thirty and eight years.—JOHN, ch. 5.

207. —— —— *Forty years.* ² A certain man lame from his mother's womb was..laid daily at the gate of the temple which is called Beautiful, to ask alms.. ²² For the man was above forty years old, on whom this miracle of healing was shewed.—ACTS, chs. 3 and 4.

208. —— **Repentance in.** *Pharaoh.* [The firstborn were all dead.] ³¹ Pharaoh called for Moses and Aaron by night, and said, Rise up, and get you forth from among my people, both ye and the children of Israel ; and go, serve the Lord..³²Also take your flocks and your herds, as ye have said, and be gone ; and bless me also.—Ex., ch. 12.

209. —— —— *Manasseh.* ¹¹..the king of Assyria..took Manasseh among the thorns, and bound him with fetters, and carried him to Babylon. ¹² And when he was in affliction, he besought the Lord his God, and humbled himself greatly before the God of his fathers.—2 CHRON., ch. 33.

210. —— **Regarded.** *Israelites* ²³..sighed by reason of the bondage, and they cried, and their cry came up unto God by reason of the bondage. ²⁴ And God heard their groaning, and God remembered his covenant.—Ex., ch. 2.

211. —— **Refinement by.** *Furnace.* ¹⁰ Behold, I have refined thee, but not with silver ; I have chosen thee in the furnace of affliction.—ISA., ch. 48.

212. —— **Temptations in.** *Job.* ⁹..Doth Job fear God for naught? ¹² And the Lord said unto Satan, Behold all that he hath *is* in thy power ; only upon himself put not forth thine hand.—JOB, ch. 1.

213. —— **Weariness in.** *Job.* ³ So am I made to possess months of vanity, and wearisome nights are appointed to me. ⁴ When I lie down, I say, When shall I arise, and the night be gone? and I am full of tossings to and fro unto the dawning of the day.—JOB, ch. 7.

214. —— **Useful.** *Paul.* ¹⁷ Our light affliction, which is but for a moment, worketh for us a far more exceeding *and* eternal weight of glory ; ¹⁸ While we look not at the things which are seen, but at the things which are not seen.—2 COR., ch. 4.

See other illustrations under :

BEREAVEMENT.

Consolation. Now he is dead..wherefore should I	736
Despondency. Jacob rent..put sackcloth	737
Genuine. Widows stood by weeping and show	738
Mourning. [Jacob] Egyptians mourned for him	739
" [Joseph] Beyond Jordan..very sore	740
Repeated. Dead man..only son of his mother	741
Sudden. Job's children..great wind..house fell	742
Submission. Take Benjamin..If I am bereaved	743
Universal. L. smote all the firstborn in the land	744

See ADVERSITY and references.
See DEATH.

215. AGE, Apostasy in old. *Solomon.* ⁴..When Solomon was old..his wives turned away his heart after other gods.. ⁵ For Solomon went after Ashtoreth the goddess of the Zidonians, and after Milcom the abomination of the Ammonites.—1 KINGS, ch. 11.

216. —— **Blessings of old.** *Jacob.* ⁷ Joseph

brought in Jacob his father, and set him before Pharaoh ; and Jacob blessed Pharaoh.—GEN., ch. 47.

217. —— **Beauty of old.** *Gray Hair.* ²⁹ The glory of young men *is* their strength : and the beauty of old men *is* the gray head.—PROV., ch. 20.

218. —— **Crown of old.** *Hoary Head.* ³¹ The hoary head *is* a crown of glory, *if* it be found in the way of righteousness.—PROV., ch. 16.

219. —— **Courage in old.** *Caleb.* ¹²..Give me this mountain, whereof the Lord spake in that day..the Anakim *were* there, and *that* the cities *were* great *and* fenced : if so be the Lord *will be* with me, then I shall be able to drive them out, as the Lord said. ¹⁴ And Caleb drove thence the three sons of Anak.—JOSH., chs. 14 and 15.

220. —— **Old, and Children.** *Joseph.* ²² Joseph lived a hundred and ten years. ²³ And..the children also of Machir the son of Manasseh were brought up upon Joseph's knees.—GEN., ch. 50.

221. —— **Contentment in old.** *Barzillai.* ³⁴ Barzillai said unto the king, How long have I to live, that I should go up with the king unto Jerusalem? ³⁵ I *am* this day four score years old : ³⁷ Let thy servant, I pray thee, turn back again, that I may die in mine own city, *and be buried* by the grave of my father and of my mother.—2 SAM., ch. 19.

222. —— **Counsels of old.** *Rehoboam.* ⁸ He forsook the counsel of the old men..and consulted with the young men that were grown up with him.—1 KINGS, ch. 12.

223. —— **Duties of pious old.** *Paul.* ¹..speak thou.. ² That the aged men be sober, grave, temperate, sound in faith, in charity, in patience. ³ The aged women likewise, that *they* be in behaviour as becometh holiness.—TITUS, ch. 2.

224. —— —— *Anna.* ³⁶ There was one Anna, a prophetess.. ³⁷ She *was* a widow of about four score and four years, which departed not from the temple, but served *God* with fastings and prayers night and day.—LUKE, ch. 2.

225. —— **Enfeebled by old.** *David.* ¹..King David was old ; and they covered him with clothes, but he gat no heat. ²..servants said, Let there be sought a young virgin : and let her stand before the king, and let her cherish him, and let her lie in thy bosom, that my lord the king may get heat.—1 KINGS, ch. 1.

226. —— **Fruitful old.** *David.* ⁵..Solomon my son *is* young and tender, and the house *that is* to be builded for the Lord *must be* exceeding magnifical, of fame and of glory throughout all countries : I will *therefore* now make preparation for it. So David prepared abundantly before his death.—1 CHRON., ch. 22.

227. —— **Glory of old.** *Children's Children.* ⁶ Children's children *are* the crown of old men ; and the glory of children *are* their fathers.—PROV., ch. 17.

228. —— **A good old.** *David.* ²⁷ The time that he reigned over Israel *was* forty years.. ²⁸ And he died in a good old age, full of days, riches, and honour.—1 CHRON., ch. 29.

229. —— **Grief in old.** *Samuel.* ¹..When Samuel was old..he made his sons judges over Israel. ³ And his sons walked not in his ways, but turned aside after lucre, and took bribes and perverted judgment.—1 SAM., ch. 8.

230. —— **Honorable old.** *Job.* [Eliphaz said,] [26] Thou shalt come to *thy* grave in a full age, like as a shock of corn cometh in in his season. JOB, ch. 5.

231. —— **A happy old.** *Job.* [15] . . were no women found *so* fair as the daughters of Job : and their father gave them inheritance among their brethren. [16] After this lived Job a hundred and forty years, and saw his sons, and his son's sons, *even* four generations.—JOB, ch. 42.

232. —— **Infirmities of old.** *Description.* [3] In the day when the keepers of the house shall tremble, and the strong men shall bow themselves, and the grinders cease because they are few, and those that look out of the windows be darkened. [4] And the doors shall be shut in the streets, when the sound of the grinding is low, and he shall rise up at the voice of the bird, and all the daughters of music shall be brought low : [5] Also *when* they shall be afraid of *that which is* high, and fears *shall be* in the way, and the almond tree shall flourish, and the grasshopper shall be a burden, and desire shall fail.—ECCL., ch. 12.

233. —— **Perfection in old.** *Abram.* [1]. . when Abram was ninety years old and nine, the Lord appeared to Abram, and said unto him, I *am* the Almighty God ; walk before me, and be thou perfect.—GEN., ch. 17.

234. —— **Respect for old.** *Elihu.* [6] Elihu . . said, I *am* young, and ye *are* very old ; wherefore I was afraid, and durst not show you mine opinion. [7] I said, Days should speak, and multitude of years should teach wisdom.—JOB, ch. 32.

235. —— **Sorrowful old.** *Eli.* [17] The messenger . . said, Israel is fled before the Philistines . . a great slaughter . . thy two sons also, Hophni and Phinehas, are dead, and the ark of God is taken. [18] . . When he made mention of the ark of God . he fell from off the seat backward . . and his neck brake . . for he was an old man, and heavy. —1 SAM., ch. 4.

236. —— **Sinning in old.** *Noah after the Flood.* [20] Noah began *to be* a husbandman, and he planted a vineyard : [21] And he drank of the wine, and was drunken. [He was six hundred years old.] —GEN., ch. 6.

237. —— **Senses in old.** *Barzillai.* [34] Barzillai said unto the king . . [35] I *am* this day fourscore years old : *and* can I discern between good and evil ? can thy servant taste what I eat or what I drink ? can I hear any more the voice of singing men and singing women ? wherefore then should thy servant be yet a burden unto my lord the king ?—2 SAM., ch. 19.

238. —— **Training for pious old.** *Solomon.* [6] Train up a child in the way he should go : and when he is old he will not depart from it.—PROV., ch. 22.

239. —— **Testimony of pious old.** *Joshua.* [2] Joshua called for all Israel, their elders . . heads . . judges, and for their officers, and said . . I am old . . [14] . this day I *am* going the way of all the earth : and ye know in all your hearts and in all your souls, that not one thing hath failed of all the good things which the Lord your God spake concerning you.—JOSH., ch. 23.

240. —— **Walking with God in old.** *Enoch.*

[23] All the days of Enoch were three hundred sixty and five years : [24] And Enoch walked with God : and he *was* not ; for God took him.— GEN., ch. 5.

241. —— **Unhappy old.** *Jacob.* [38] . . My son shall not go down with you ; for his brother is dead, and he is left alone ; if mischief befall him by the way . . then shall ye bring down my gray hairs with sorrow to the grave.—GEN., ch. 42.

242. —— **Vigorous old.** *Moses.* [7] Moses *was* a hundred and twenty years old when he died : his eye was not dim, nor his natural force abated.—DEUT., ch. 34.

243. —— —— *Caleb.* [10] . . I *am* this day four score and five years old. [11] . . I *am as* strong this day as *I was* in the day that Moses sent me : as my strength *was* then, even so *is* my strength now, for war, both to go out, and to come in.— JOSH., ch. 14.

244. —— **Responsibility of.** *Manhood.* [20] We know that this is our son, and that he was born blind : [21] But by what means he now seeth, we know not ; or who hath opened his eyes, we know not : he is of age ; ask him : he shall speak for himself.—JOHN, ch. 9.

245. AGED, Duty of the. *Teachers.* [2] Hear this, ye old men . . Hath this been in your days, or even in the days of your fathers ? [3] Tell ye your children of it, and *let* your children tell their children, and their children another generation.—JOEL, ch. 1.

246. —— **Respected the.** *Job.* [7] When I went out to the gate through the city, *when* I prepared my seat in the street ! [8] The young men saw me, and hid themselves : and the aged arose, *and* stood up.—JOB, ch. 29.

247. —— **Righteousness of the.** *Zacharias and Elisabeth.* [6] They were both righteous before God, walking in all the commandments and ordinances of the Lord blameless. [7] . . And they both were well stricken in years.—LUKE, ch. 1.

248. AGES, Extraordinary. *Patriarchs.* [Adam, 930 years ; Seth, 912 years ; Enos, 905 years ; Cainan, 910 years ; Mahalaleel, 895 years ; Jared, 962 years ; Enoch, 365 years ; Methuselah, 969 years ; Lamech, 777 years ; Noah, 950 years ; Abraham, 175 years : Isaac, 180 years.]

See other illustrations under :

Blessed. L. blessed the latter end of Job more	150
Blindness in. Isaac was old . . eyes were dim	834
" Ahijah . . his eyes were set by . . age	840
Cruelty to. Chaldeans . . no compassion for age	1440
Children of. Israel loved Joseph more . . son of old.	177
Counsels of. I set before you a blessing . . curse	1236
Disregarded. They that are younger than I	146
Emotions. Ancient men . . shouted, wept	2626
Fears. My son shall not go down . . mischief	241
Pleasures of. Wherefore . . a burden . . the king	237
Paternity in. Z. and E. . well stricken in years . . son	1153
" Abram was 100 years old . . Isaac born	1193
Respected. Elihu waited till Job had spoken	4061
Revealed. Sat according to his birthright	5661
Reflections. Ancient men had seen the first house	957

249. AGENT, Necessary. *Moses.* [15] Wherefore criest thou unto me ? speak unto the children of Israel, that they go forward : [16] But lift thou up thy rod, and stretch out thine hand over the sea, and divide it : and the children of

Israel shall go on dry *ground* through the midst of the sea.—Ex., ch. 14.

250. —— **A simple.** *Naaman.* ¹⁰ Elisha sent, saying, Go and wash in Jordan seven times.. and thou shalt be clean. ¹¹ But Naaman was wroth, and went away, and said, Behold, I thought, He will surely come out to me, and stand, and call on the name of the Lord his God, and strike his hand over the place, and recover the leper.—2 Kings, ch. 5.

See other illustrations under:

AMBASSADORS.

Dangerous. Hezekiah showed them all..his	309
Disregarded. Forbear..that he destroy thee not	310
Maltreated. Hanun took David's servants and	311
Rejected. Beat one..killed another..and stoned	312
Spiritual. We are ambassadors for C..as though G.	313

251. AGENCY, Boastful. *Axe—Saw.* ¹⁵ Shall the axe boast itself against him that heweth therewith? or shall the saw magnify itself against him that shaketh it? as if the rod should shake *itself* against them that lift it up, *or* as if the staff should lift up *itself, as if it were* no wood.—Isa., ch. 10.

252. —— **Responsibility for indirect.** *David.* ²²..said unto Abiathar, I knew *it* that day, when Doeg the Edomite *was* there, that he would surely tell Saul: I have occasioned *the death* of all the persons of thy father's house. ²³ Abide thou with me, fear not..with me thou *shalt be* in safeguard.—1 Sam., ch. 22.

253. —— **Only a seeming.** *Waters of Marah.* ²⁴ The people murmured..What shall we drink? ²⁵ And he cried unto the Lord; and the Lord shewed him a tree, *which* when he had cast into the waters, the waters were made sweet.—Ex., ch. 15.

254. —— **A strange.** *Clay.* ⁶..He spat on the ground, and made clay of the spittle, and he anointed the eyes of the blind man with the clay, ⁷ And said, Go, wash in the pool of Siloam.—John, ch. 9.

255. AGENCIES, Natural and providential. *Moses' Mother.* ³..She took for him an ark of bulrushes, and daubed it with slime and with pitch, and put the child therein; and she laid *it* in the flags by the river's brink. ⁴ And his sister stood afar off, to wit what would be done to him. ⁵ And the daughter of Pharaoh came down to wash *herself* at the river.—Ex., ch. 2.

See other illustrations under:

INFLUENCE.

Bequeathed. Elisha took the mantle..waters	4468
Care. Neither to eat flesh..drink wine..further	4469
Example. L. teach us to pray..as John also	4470
Felt. Herod feared John..knowing that	4471
Leaders. Have any of the rulers believed	4472
Personal. Elisha lay upon the child..mouth upon	4477
Parental. Will drink no wine..our father	4473
Posthumous. G. testifying..gifts..yet speaketh	4474
" Touched the bones of Elisha	4475
Pernicious. Pharisees neither go in..nor suffer	4476
Regarded. Fearful and faint-hearted?..return	4479
Responsibility. Offend..little ones. better	4478
Rank. Ladies have heard..deed of the queen	4480
Supernatural. Ark on the cart..two cows	4481
Sorrowful. Showing the coats..garments which	4482

INSTRUMENT.

Disdained. Eliab..anger was kindled..left the	4552
Destroying. Waters returned..covered the host	4553
Feeble. Syrians to hear the noise of chariots	4560
Gods. Angel said..call for Peter..he shall tell	4561
Insignificant. Sampson..jaw bone of an ass	4555
" David prevailed over the Philistines	4662
Only. Why marvel..as though by our own power	4563
Quality. Philistines..fell before Jonathan	4564
Simple. When he beheld the serpent of brass he	4556
Saving. Red sea..waters were a wall unto them	4557
Sinful. We believe, not because of thy saying	4558
Strange. L. prepared a great fish to swallow Jonah	4559
Weak. [Plagues] frogs..flies..lice..hail	4565
Waiting. Then fled Moses..land of Madian	4566

MEANS.

Defense. Hezekiah..built up the walls..made	5255
Escape. They let him down the wall in a basket	5256
Heroic. Soldiers cut off the ropes of the boat	5257
Ingenious. Ark of bulrushes..pitch..stood	5258
Insignificant. Touched their eyes..eyes were	5259
Not neglected. Take a lump of figs..laid it on the	5260
Prayer. We made our prayer..set a watch..day	5261
Prudential. Jesus..would not walk in Jewry	5262
Strange. Moses..rod of God..held up his hand	5263
" Sound of the trumpet..people shouted	5264
Use of. Think on me when it shall be well with thee	5265
Unworthy. If I make not thy life..went for his	5266

256. AGITATION from Deception. *Isaac.* ³²..Who *art* thou? And he said I *am* thy son, thy firstborn, Esau. ³³ And Isaac trembled very exceedingly, and said, Who? where *is* he that hath taken venison, and brought *it* me, and I have eaten of all before thou camest, and have blessed him?—Gen., ch. 27.

257. —— **Diffuses the Truth.** *Paul.* ¹⁶..saw the city wholly given to idolatry. ¹⁷ Therefore disputed he in the synagogue with the Jews, and with the devout persons, and in the market daily.—Acts, ch. 17.

258. —— **Deplored.** *Israelites.* ²¹..ye have made our savour to be abhorred in the eyes of Pharaoh, and..to put a sword in their hand to slay us. ²² And Moses..said, Lord, wherefore hast thou so evil entreated this people? why *is it* that thou hast sent me?—Ex., ch. 5.

259. —— **A general.** *Of Philistines.* ¹⁴..that first slaughter, which Jonathan and his armourbearer made, was about twenty men, within as it were a half acre of land.. ¹⁵ And there was trembling in the host, in the field, and among all the people: the garrison, and the spoilers, they also trembled, and the earth quaked: so it was a very great trembling.—1 Sam., ch. 14.

260. —— **A Mountain's.** *Sinai.* ¹⁸..Mount Sinai was altogether on a smoke, because the Lord descended upon it in fire: and the smoke thereof ascended as the smoke of a furnace, and the whole mount quaked greatly.—Ex., ch. 19.

261. —— **Overcome by.** *Guard.* ²..the angel ..came and rolled back the stone from the door, and sat upon it. ³ His countenance was like lightning, and his raiment white as snow: ⁴ And for fear of him the keepers did shake, and became as dead *men*.—Mat., ch. 28.

262. —— **Physical and mental.** *Belshazzar.* ⁵..the king saw part of the hand that wrote. ⁶..countenance was changed, and his thoughts troubled him, so that the joints of his loins were loosed, and his knees smote one against another. ⁷ The king cried aloud to bring in the astrologers.—Dan., ch. 5.

263. —— **from Terror.** *Eliphaz.* [13] In thoughts from the visions of the night, when deep sleep falleth on men. [14] Fear came upon me, and trembling, which made all my bones to shake. [15] Then a spirit passed before my face ; the hair of my flesh stood up.—Job, ch. 4.

See other illustrations under :

ALARM.

Conscience. Pray for thy servants..we die not	273
Death. Egyptians were urgent..we be all dead	274
Failure. Priests..doubted..whereunto this would	275
Manifestation. Belshazzar..countenance was	276
Preaching. Paul reasoned..Felix trembled	277
Reasonable. Esau cometh..400 men..Jacob	278
Superstitious. Jesus walking on the sea..troubled	279
Sinners. Adam and his wife hid themselves	280
" Let not God speak with us..die	281
Sudden. Seeing the prison doors open..sword	282
Spiritual. Sirs, what must I do to be saved	283
Tempest. Entreat..be no more mighty thunderings	284
Unnecessary. My money is restored..heart failed	285

EMOTION.

Changed. Jesus showed them his hands..disciples	2625
Exhibited. Shaphan read it..the king rent his	2622
Irrepressible. Joseph made haste..sought where	2623
Mixed. Ancient men..seen the first..wept	2626
" From the sepulchre with fear and great	2627
Opposite. If these should hold their peace	2628
Worship. Mourn not..they heard..law	2624

Cause. Eli sat..watching..his heart trembled for	444
Restless. Would God it were even !..would	7266
Spiritual. It shall bruise thy head..bruise his	451
Sleepless. Darius..sleep went from him..early to	458
Sickness. Nobleman besought him..come..ere	459
Strong. Jesus..groaned in the spirit and was	3198
Suppressed. Haman was full of indignation	3199
Truth. Not come to send peace, but a sword	450
Vexatious. Delilah..pressed him daily..urged	9187

264. AGONY, The Saviour's. *Garden.* [38] ..My soul is exceeding sorrowful, even unto death. —Mat., ch. 26. [44] And being in an agony he prayed more earnestly : and his sweat was as it were great drops of blood falling down to the ground.—Luke, ch. 22.

See SORROW *and references.*

265. AGRARIANS, Hebrew. *God said,* [53] ..the land shall be divided for an inheritance according to number of names. [54] To many thou shalt give the more inheritance, and to few thou shalt give the less.—Num., ch. 26.

266. AGREEMENT, A fraudulent. *Gibeonites.* [4] They did work wilily, and..made as if they had been ambassadors, and took old sacks..and wine bottles, old, and rent, and bound up ; [5] And old shoes and clouted..and old garments..and all the bread..was dry *and* mouldy.—Josh., ch. 9.

267. —— **Ignored.** *Laborers.* [10] ..They likewise received every man a penny. [11] And..they murmured against the good man.. [12] Saying, These last have wrought *but* one hour, and thou hast made them equal unto us, which have borne the burden and heat of the day.—Mat., ch. 20.

268. —— **Refused.** *King of Edom.* [Near to Canaan Israel asked,] [17] Let us pass..through thy country : we will not pass through the fields, or..vineyards, neither will we drink *of*..the wells : we will go by the king's *high* way, we will not turn to the right hand nor to the left.. [18] And Edom said..Thou shalt not pass by me,

lest I come out against thee with the sword.— Num., ch. 20.

See other illustrations under :

CONDITIONS.

Acceptance. What doth the L. require?..do	1470
Access. Except your youngest brother come	1471
Blessing. If thou shalt see me..taken..it shall	1472
Severe. This condition..I may thrust out..right	1473

COVENANT.

Broken. Moses saw the calf..cast the tables	1807
Blood. Moses took the blood and sprinkled	1808
Evil. What will ye give me?..30 pieces of silver	1809
Friendship. Jonathan caused David to sware	1810
People's. All the people stood to the covenant	1811
Perpetuated. Walk before me..thy seed after thee	1812
Ratified. Burning lamp passed between the pieces	1813
Reformation. Made a covenant..be the Lord's	1814
Renewed. Clave to their brethren..curse	1815
Self-denial. Get thee out of thy country..be	1816
Sign. Set my bow in the clouds..token	1817

VOW.

Despondency. I will not speak any more in his	9246
Inconsistent. Cursed be the man that eateth any	9247
Obedience. People entered into a curse and into	9248
Observance. Better..shouldest not vow than..not	9249
Rash. Jepthah..whatsoever cometh..burnt	9250
Sailors. Took up Jonah and cast him..made vows	9251
Trouble. Hannah vowed..I will give him..L.	9252
" Jephthah came..his daughter came	9253
Teetotaller. Neither shall he drink any liquor of	9254

UNITY.

by Creation. Made of one blood all nations of	9121
Delightful. How pleasant it is..brethren in unity	9122
Dangerous. All people is one..nothing	9123
Diversity. Many members, yet but one body	9124
Dependence. Eye can not say..hand..no need	9125
Impracticable. Image..feet were of iron and	9126
Occupation. Because..of the same craft abode	9127
Prayer for. All may be one as thou, Father, art in	9128
Remarkable. Were of one heart..all things	9129
Spirit. By one Spirit we are all baptized into one	9130
Suffering in. Whether one member suffer, all	9131

Falsehood. Ye have agreed together to tempt	2985
Forced. Great cry in Egypt..go and serve the L.	1554

See UNION.

269. AGRICULTURE, Employment in. *Adam.* [15] The Lord God took the man, and put him into the garden of Eden to dress it and to keep it.—Gen., ch. 2.

270. —— —— *Cain.* [2] ..Cain was a tiller of the ground. [3] Cain brought of the fruit of the ground an offering unto the Lord.—Gen., ch. 4.

271. —— **Forbidden.** *Rechabites.* Rechab commanded, [7] Neither shall ye build house, nor sow seed. nor plant vineyard, nor have *any.*—Jer., ch. 35.

272. —— **Independence in.** *Proverb.* [19] He that tilleth his land shall have plenty of bread : but he that followeth after vain *persons* shall have poverty enough.—Prov., ch. 28.

See other illustrations under :

FRUIT.

Commends. The man's rod that I shall choose	3469
Expected. Sent his servants..might receive	3470
God Gives. Tabernacle..rod of Aaron..yielded	3471
Lack. Saw a fig tree..nothing but leaves	3473
Object. If it bear fruit well..if not..cut	3476
Sign. Figs ; the good figs very good..bad, very	3478
Repentance. Bringeth not..good fruit..cast..fire	3479
Preserved. In making war..not destroy the trees	3481

GARDEN.

Agony. In an agony he prayed..blood falling   3502
Coveted. Naboth had a vineyard..Ahab said   3503
Familiar. Garden..Jews ofttimes resorted   3504
Lord's. The L. G. planted a garden..in Eden   3506
Sacred. In the garden a sepulchre..they laid   3507

HARVEST.

Abundant. Joseph gathered corn..without   3803
First Fruits. Bring a sheaf of the first fruits of   3804
Great. The field is the world..reapers the angels   3805
Gleaning. [Boaz to Ruth,] Glean not in another   3806
Prayer. That he will send forth laborers   3807
Promise. While earth remaineth, seed-time and   3808
Poor Man's. Not make clean the corners..the   3809
Sowing. Plowman..open and break the clods   3810
Secret. He which soweth sparingly shall reap   3811

Choice. King Uzziah..had much..loved   3046
Deliverer. Gideon threshed wheat by the wine   3047
Discouragements. Although the fig tree shall not   1379
Danger. Noah began to be a husbandman   236
Dangers. Samson..300 foxes..burnt shocks of   438
Enterprising. Elisha was plowing with 12 yoke of   3045
Growth. Blade..ear..full corn in the ear   3750
Indolence. I went by the field of the slothful   4436
Indispensable. Every branch..beareth not..sway   3483
Misplaced. No place for seed..figs..vines   5639
Plenty. Land of wheat..barley..vines..fig trees   6224
Poor. Nebuzaradan left the poor to be   6304
Prosperous. What shall I do?..no room..fruits   3272
Skill in. Fig tree..let it alone this year, I will dig   642
Type. Flourish like the palm..fruit..age   3340
   "   Like a tree planted by the rivers   3745
   "   Becometh greater than all herbs   3748
   "   Soul shall be as a well-watered garden   3739
Vanity. I planted me gardens and orchards   7396
Varied. Bring forth fruit, some 30..60..100 fold   3486

273. ALARM of Conscience. *Israelites.* ¹⁸ The Lord sent thunder and rain that day : and all the people greatly feared the Lord and Samuel. ¹⁹ And..said unto Samuel, Pray for thy servants.. that we die not : for we have added unto all our sins *this* evil, to ask us a king.—1 SAM., ch. 12.

274. —— Death creates. *Egyptians.* ³⁰..there was a great cry in Egypt : for *there was* not a house where *there was* not one dead. ³³ And the Egyptians were urgent..that they might send them out of the land in haste ; for they said, We *be* all dead men.—Ex., ch. 12.

275. —— from Failure. *Priests.* ²³ The prison truly found we shut with all safety, and the keepers standing without before the doors : but when we had opened, we found no man within. ²⁴ Now when the high priest and the captain of the temple and the chief priests heard these things, they doubted of them whereunto this would grow.—ACTS, ch. 5.

276. —— Manifestations of. *Belshazzar* ⁵..saw the hand that wrote. ⁶ Then the king's countenance was changed, and his thoughts troubled him, so that the joints of his loins were loosed, and his knees smote one against another. ⁷ The king cried aloud to bring in the astrologers.— DAN., ch. 5.

277. —— from Preaching. *Felix.* ²⁴ When Felix came..he sent for Paul, and heard him concerning the faith in Christ. ²⁵ And as he reasoned of righteousness, temperance, and judgment to come, Felix trembled.—ACTS, ch. 24.

278. —— A reasonable. *Jacob.* ⁶..Esau..

cometh to meet thee, and four hundred men with him. ⁷ Then Jacob was greatly afraid and distressed.—GEN., ch. 32.

279. —— Superstitious. *Disciples.* ²⁵ In the fourth watch of the night Jesus went unto them, walking on the sea. ²⁶ And..they were troubled, saying, It is a spirit ; and they cried out for fear. —MAT., ch. 14.

280. —— of Sinners. *Adam and Eve.* ⁸ They heard the voice of the Lord God walking in the garden in the cool of the day : and..hid themselves from the presence of the Lord God amongst the trees.—GEN., ch. 3.

281. —— *Israelites.* ¹⁸ All the people saw the thunderings, and the lightnings, and the noise of the trumpet, and the mountain smoking : and..they removed, and stood afar off. ¹⁹ And they said unto Moses, Speak thou with us, and we will hear : but let not God speak with us, lest we die.—Ex., ch. 20.

282. —— A sudden. *Jailer.* ²⁷ The keeper of the prison awaking..and seeing the prison doors open, he drew out his sword, and would have killed himself, supposing that the prisoners had been fled.—ACTS, ch. 16.

283. —— Spiritual. *Jailer.* ²⁹ He called for a light, and sprang in, and came trembling, and fell down before Paul and Silas, ³⁰ And brought them out, and said, Sirs, what must I do to be saved ?—ACTS, ch. 16.

284. —— at a Tempest. *Pharaoh.* ²⁷ Pharaoh said..I have sinned this time : the Lord *is* righteous, and I and my people *are* wicked. ²⁸ Entreat the Lord (for *it is* enough) that there be no *more* mighty thunderings and hail ; and I will let you go.—Ex., ch. 9.

285. —— Unnecessary. *Sons of Jacob.* ²⁷ As one of them opened his sack.. ²⁸ And he said unto his brethren, My money is restored ; and, lo, *it is* even in my sack : and their heart failed *them*, and they were afraid, saying one to another, What *is* this *that* God hath done unto us? —GEN., ch. 42.

See **FEAR** and references.

286. ALIENATION, Family. *Betrayment.* Jesus said, ¹² The brother shall betray the brother to death, and the father the son ; and children shall rise up against *their* parents, and shall cause them to be put to death.—MARK, ch. 13.

287. —— Heedless. *Lost Sheep.* ⁴ What man of you, having a hundred sheep, if he lose one of them, doth not leave the ninety and nine in the wilderness, and go after that which is lost, until he find it ?—LUKE, ch. 15.

288. —— Unconscious. *Lost Coin.* ⁸ What woman, having ten pieces of silver, if she lose one piece, doth not light a candle, and sweep the house, and seek diligently till she find it ?— LUKE, ch. 15.

289. —— Wilful. *Lost Son.* ¹² The younger of them said..Father, give me the portion of goods that falleth *to* me. ¹³ And not many days after..gathered all together, and took his journey into a far country, and there wasted his substance with riotous living.—LUKE, ch. 15.

See other illustrations under :

INSANITY.

Exhibited. Hairs were grown like eagle's   4514
Feigned. David..feigned himself mad..spittle   4515

Moral. Pharaoh said..see my face no more   4516
Occasional. Evil spirit from God came upon Saul   4517
Sinners. When he came to himself..bread   4518
So-called. His friends said..he is beside himself   4519
     Paul, thou art beside thyself..mad   4520

LUNACY.

Diabolic. In the tombs crying and cutting himself   5154
Moral. [Gadarenes] Began to pray him to depart   5155

Paternal. Let [Absalom]..not see my face   3070

290. ALLIANCE, A contaminating. *Ahaz.*
[7] Ahaz sent..to Tiglath-pileser king of Assyria, saying..come up, and save me out of the hand of the king of Syria, and..of the king of Israel. [10] Ahaz went to Damascus to meet Tiglath-pileser..and saw an altar..and king Ahaz sent to Urijah the priest, the fashion of the altar.—2 KINGS, ch. 16.

291. —— A dangerous. *David.* [3] Said the princes of the Philistines, What *do* these Hebrews *here?* [4]..Make this fellow return..and let him not go..lest in the battle he be an adversary to us : for wherewith should he reconcile himself unto his master? *should it* not *be* with the heads of these men?—1 SAM., ch. 29.

292. —— Forbidden. *Egyptian.* [1] Woe to them that go down to Egypt for help ; and stay on horses, and trust in chariots, because *they are* many ; and in horsemen, because they are very strong ; but they look not unto the Holy One of Israel, neither seek the Lord !—ISA., ch. 31.

293. —— Failure of. *Egyptian.* [3] The Egyptians *are* men, and not God ; and their horses flesh, and not spirit. When the Lord shall stretch out his hand, both he that helpeth shall fall, and he that is holpen shall fall down, and they all shall fail together.—ISA., ch. 31.

294. —— A treacherous. *Gibeonites.* [4] They did work wilily..and made as if..ambassadors, and took old sacks..and wine bottles, old, and rent, and bound up ; [5] And old shoes and clouted ..and old garments..and all the bread of their provision was dry *and* mouldy. [15] And Joshua ..made a league with them.—JOSH., ch. 9.

295. ALLIES, The Lord's. *Women.* [1]..he went throughout every city and village, preaching..and the twelve *were* with him. [2] And certain women, which had been healed of evil spirits and infirmities, Mary called Magdalene, out of whom went seven devils,[3] And Joanna the wife of Chuza Herod's steward, and Susanna, and many others, which ministered unto him of their substance.—LUKE, ch. 8.

See HELP and references.

296. ALTAR in every Place. *Abram.* [He came to Sichem,] [7]..and there builded he an altar unto the Lord, who appeared unto him. [8] And he removed from thence unto a mountain on the east of Beth-el, and pitched his tent.. and there he builded an altar.—GEN., ch. 12.

297. —— Discarded, the old. *Ahaz.* [10]..king Ahaz..saw an altar that *was* at Damascus : and.. sent to Urijah the priest..the pattern of it.. [11] And Urijah..built an altar.—2 KINGS, ch. 16.

298. —— A despised. *Offerings.* [7] Ye offer polluted bread upon mine altar ; and ye say, Wherein have we polluted thee? In that ye say, The table of the Lord *is* contemptible. [8] And if ye offer the blind for sacrifice, *is it* not evil? and if ye offer the lame and sick, *is it* not evil? offer it now unto thy governor ; will he be pleased with thee..?—MAL., ch. 1.

299. —— A plain. *Earth.* [24] An altar of earth thou shalt make unto me, and shalt sacrifice thereon thy burnt offerings, and thy peace offerings, thy sheep, and thine oxen.—EX., ch. 20.

300. —— A protected. *Sword.* [29]..the altar of the burnt offering..at Gibeon. [30] But David could not go before it to inquire of God : for he was afraid because of the sword of the angel of the Lord.—1 CHRON., ch. 21.

301. —— Repaired before Worship. *At Carmel.* [30]..Elijah said..Come near unto me. And all the people came near unto him. And he repaired the altar of the Lord *that was* broken down.— 1 KINGS, ch. 18.

302. —— of Refuge. *Adonijah.* [5]..Adonijah ..exalted himself, saying, I will be king : and he prepared him chariots and horsemen, and fifty men to run before him. [50]..Adonijah feared because of Solomon, and arose, and went, and caught hold on the horns of the altar.—1 KINGS, ch. 1.

303. —— A rent. *Jeroboam's.* [1]..there came a man of God out of Judah..unto Beth-el : and Jeroboam stood by the altar to burn incense.. [5] The altar also was rent, and the ashes poured out..according to the sign which the man of God had given by the word of the Lord.--1 KINGS, ch. 13.

304. —— of Witness. *Trans-Jordan Tribes.* [26]..Let us..build us an altar, not for burnt offerings, nor for sacrifice : [27] But *that* it *may be* a witness between us, and you, and our generations after us, that we might do the service of the Lord..with our burnt offerings, and with our sacrifices..that your children may not say to our children in time to come, Ye have no part in the Lord.—JOSH., ch. 22.

305. ALTARS, Idolatrous. *Manasseh.* [4]..he built altars in the house of the Lord.. [5] And he built altars for all the host of heaven in the two courts of the house of the Lord.—2 KINGS, ch. 21.

Also see
Rejected. L. hath cast off his altar..abhorred.

306. ALTERNATIVE, Only. *Four Lepers.* [4] If we say, We will enter into the city, then the famine *is* in the city, and we shall die there : and if we sit still here, we die also. Now therefore come, and let us fall unto the host of the Syrians : if they save us alive, we shall live ; and if they kill us, we shall but die.—2 KINGS, ch. 7.

See DECISION and references.

307. AMAZEMENT, A great. *Christ on the Sea.* [50]..they all saw him, and were troubled..Be of good cheer : it is I ; be not afraid. [51] And he went..into the ship ; and the wind ceased : and they were sore amazed in themselves beyond measure, and wondered.—MARK, ch. 6.

308. —— Natural. *Stilling the Storm.* [24]..he arose, and rebuked the wind and the raging of the water : and they ceased, and there was a calm. [25]..And they being afraid wondered, saying..What manner of man is this ! for he commandeth even the winds and water, and they obey him.—LUKE, ch. 8.

See other illustrations under :

AGITATION.

309. AMBASSADORS, Dangerous. *Babylonians.*
[13]..Hezekiah shewed them all the house of his
precious things, the silver, and the gold, and
the spices, and the precious ointment, and *all*
the house of his armour, and all that was found
in his treasures.—2 KINGS, ch. 20. [He entertained them, and lost all.]

310. —— Disregarded. *Josiah.* [The king of
Egypt] [21]..sent ambassadors to him, saying..
I come not against thee this day, but against the
house wherewith I have war : for God commanded me to make haste : forbear thee from
meddling with God, who *is* with me, that he destroy thee not.—2 CHRON., ch. 35. [Josiah was
slain.]

311. —— Maltreated. *Half-shaved.* [4]..Ha-
nun took David's servants, and shaved off the
one half of their beards, and cut off their garments in the middle, *even* to their buttocks, and
sent them away.—2 SAM., ch. 10.

312. —— Rejected. *Parable.* [35]..the husbandmen took his servants, and beat one, and killed
another, and stoned another. [36]Again, he sent
other servants more than the first : and they did
unto them likewise.—MAT., ch. 21.

313. —— Spiritual. *Paul.* [20]..we are ambassadors for Christ, as though God did beseech
you by us : we pray *you* in Christ's stead, be ye
reconciled to God.—2 COR., ch. 10.

See MINISTERS and references.

314. AMBITION lost in Age. *Eighty years old.*
[33]..the king said unto Barzillai, Come thou..
with me in Jerusalem. [34]And Barzillai said unto the king, How long have I to live, that I should
go up with the king unto Jerusalem?—2 SAM.,
ch. 19.

315. —— Cruelty of. *Athaliah.* [1]..when Athaliah the mother of Ahaziah saw that her son

was dead, she..destroyed all the seed royal..
[3]..And Athaliah did reign over the land.—2
KINGS, ch. 11.

316. —— A Christian's. *Paul.* [9]..we labour,
that, whether present or absent, we may be accepted of him.—2 COR., ch. 5.

317. —— Evil. *Diotrephes.* [9]..Diotrephes,
who loveth to have the preeminence among them,
receiveth us not. [10]..prating against us with
malicious words : and not content therewith,
neither doth he himself receive the brethren,
and forbiddeth them that would, and casteth
them out of the church.—3 JOHN.

318. —— A fatal. *Asahel.* [22]..Abner said
again to Asahel, Turn thee aside from following
me : wherefore should I smite thee to the ground ?
..[23] Howbeit he refused to turn aside : wherefore
Abner with the hinder end of the spear smote
him under the fifth *rib.*—2 SAM., ch. 2. [He
sought the honour of killing the general and
taking his arms as trophies.]

319. —— Prevents Faith. *Honour.* [Jesus
said,] [44]How can ye believe, which receive honour one of another, and seek not the honour
that *cometh* from God only ?—JOHN, ch. 5.

320. —— for Greatness. *Apostles.* [Jesus
said,] [33]..What was it that ye disputed among
yourselves by the way? [34]But they held their
peace : for..they had disputed..who *should* be
the greatest.—MARK, ch. 9.

321. —— of Hypocrites. *Scribes.* [46]Beware of
the scribes, which desire to walk in long robes,
and love greetings in the markets, and the
highest seats in the synagogues, and the chief
rooms at feasts.—LUKE, ch. 20.

322. —— for Honours. *James and John.*
[35]..James and John, the sons of Zebedee, come
..saying, Master, we would that thou shouldest
do for us whatsoever we shall desire.. [37]..Grant
unto us that we may sit, one on thy right hand,
and the other on thy left hand, in thy glory.—
MARK, ch. 10.

323. —— Instructed. *Child.* [2]..Jesus called
a little child unto him, and set him in the midst
of them.. [4]Whosoever therefore shall humble
himself as this little child, the same is greatest
in the kingdom of heaven.—MAT., ch. 18.

324. —— A laudable. *Paul.* [19]..from Jerusalem, and round about unto Illyricum, I have fully
preached the gospel of Christ. [20]Yea..not
where Christ was named, lest I should build
upon another man's foundation.—ROM., ch. 15.

325. —— A Mother's. *Chief Seats.* [20]Then
came..the mother of Zebedee's children..desir-
ing a certain thing.. [21]And he said..What wilt
thou? She said..Grant that these my two
sons may sit, the one on thy right hand, and the
other on the left, in thy kingdom.—MAT., ch.
20.

326. —— Promotion fires. *Korah.* [8]..Moses
said unto Korah.. [9] *Seemeth it but* a small thing
unto you, that the God of Israel hath separated
you from the congregation. [10]And he hath
brought thee near *to him.*.and seek ye the
priesthood also.—NUM., ch. 16.

327. —— Promotion without. *David.* [11]..Are
here all *thy* children ? And he said, There remaineth yet the youngest, and, behold, he
keepeth the sheep. And Samuel said unto Jesse,

Send and fetch him.—1 Sam., ch. 16. [He was anointed king.]

328. —— **A presumptuous.** *Thistle.* ⁹..The thistle that *was* in Lebanon sent to the cedar that *was* in Lebanon, saying, Give thy daughter to my son to wife : and there passed by a wild beast..and trod down the thistle.—2 Kings, ch. 14.

329. —— **Temptation from.** *Eve.* ⁵..in the day ye eat thereof, then your eyes shall be opened, and ye shall be as gods, knowing good and evil. ⁶And when the woman saw that the tree *was* good for food, and that it *was* pleasant to the eyes, and a tree to be desired to make *one* wise, she took of the fruit.—Gen., ch. 3.

330. —— **Unholy.** *Korah's Company.* ³..they gathered..against Moses and against Aaron, and said.. *Ye take* too much upon you, ⁵seeing all the congregation *are* holy, every one of them, and the Lord *is* among them : wherefore then lift ye up yourselves above the congregation.— Num., ch. 16.

331. —— **An unspiritual.** *Simon.* ¹⁸..Simon saw that through laying on of the apostles' hands the Holy Ghost was given, he offered them money, ¹⁹Saying, Give me also this power, that on whomsoever I lay hands, he may receive the Holy Ghost.—Acts, ch. 8.

332. —— **Unsatisfied.** *Haman.* ¹²..Esther the queen did let no man come in with the king unto the banquet..but myself ; and to morrow am I invited..also with the king. ¹³Yet all this availeth me nothing, so long as I see Mordecai the Jew sitting at the king's gate.—Esther, ch. 5.

333. —— **Without.** *Saul.* ²¹..Saul..was taken : and when they sought him, he could not be found. ²²..And the Lord answered, Behold, he hath hid himself among the stuff. ²³And they ran and fetched him thence.—1 Sam., ch. 10. [They crowned him.]

See other illustrations under :

CROWN.

FAME.

HONOR.

OFFICE.

334. AMBUSCADE, An ineffective. *Syrians.* ⁸..the king of Syria..and took counsel with his servants, saying, In such and such a place *shall be* my camp. ⁹And [Elisha] sent unto the king of Israel, saying, Beware that thou pass not such a place ; for thither the Syrians are come down.—2 Kings, ch. 6.

335. —— **A successful.** *Abimelech.* ⁴³..he took the people, and divided them into three companies, and laid wait in the field..the people *were* come forth out of the city ; and he rose up against them, and smote them. ⁴⁴And..rushed forward, and stood in the entering of the gate of the city.—Judges, ch. 9.

336. AMUSEMENT of Curiosity. *Athenians.* ²¹For all the Athenians, and strangers which were there, spent their time in nothing else, but either to tell or to hear some new thing.—Acts, ch. 18.

337. —— **Dangerous.** *Dancing.* [The elders] ²⁰..commanded the children of Benjamin, saying, Go and lie in wait in the vineyards ; ²¹..if the daughters of Shiloh come out to dance in dances, then come ye..and catch you every man his wife of the daughters of Shiloh.—Judges, ch. 21.

338. —— **an End.** *Rich Fool.* ¹⁹..I will say to my soul, Soul, thou hast much goods laid up for many years ; take thine ease, eat, drink, *and* be merry. ²⁰But God said unto him, *Thou* fool, this night thy soul shall be required.—Luke, ch. 12.

339. —— **A fatal.** *Philistines.* ²⁵..when their hearts were merry..they called for Samson out of the prison house ; and he made them sport : and they set him between the pillars. ³⁰..And he bowed himself with *all his* might ; and the house fell upon the lords, and upon all the people.—Judges, ch. 16.

340. —— **Idolatry an.** *Israelites.* ¹⁶..the people sat down to eat and to drink, and rose up to play. ¹⁹..as he came nigh unto the camp ..he saw the calf, and the dancing : and Moses' anger waxed hot.—Ex., ch. 32.

341. —— **Perilous.** *Amalekites.* ¹⁶..*they were* spread abroad upon all the earth, eating and drinking, and dancing, because of all the great spoil that they had taken..of the Philistines, and..of Judah. ¹⁷And David smote them from the twilight even unto the evening of the next day : and there escaped not a man.—1 Sam., ch. 30.

342. —— **Royal.** *Herodias' Daughter.* ¹¹..Herod on his birthday made a supper to his lords, high captains, and chief *estates* of Galilee ; ²²And ..the daughter of..Herodias came in, and danced, and pleased Herod.—Mark, ch. 6.

343. —— **Sorrow after.** *Herod.* ²⁵And she.. asked, saying, I will that thou give me by and by in a charger the head of John the Baptist. ²⁶And the king was exceeding sorry.—Mark, ch. 6.

See **PLEASURE** and references.

— ANARCHY. ——

344. ANCESTRY respected. *Samaritan Woman.* ¹²Art thou greater than our father Jacob, which gave us the well, and drank thereof himself, and his children, and his cattle ?—John, ch. 4.

See other illustrations under :

Gigantic. Man of great stature..born to the giant 3516
Good. Faith..grandmother Lois..mother Eunice 1282
Imitated. Abijam walked in the sins of his father 1187
"   Children gather wood, the fathers 1188
Resemblance. [Murderers of Jesus] Children of 1204

345. ANGEL of the Annunciation. *Gabriel.*
[30]..the angel said..Fear not, Mary : for thou
hast found favor with God. [31] And, behold, thou
shalt conceive..and bring forth a son, and
shalt call his name Jesus.—LUKE, ch. 1.

346. —— A destroying. *Against Assyrians.*
[35]..that night..the angel of the Lord..smote in
the camp of the Assyrians a hundred fourscore
and five thousand : and when they arose early in
the morning, behold, they *were* all dead corpses.
—2 KINGS, ch. 19.

347. —— Hiding from an. *Ornan.* [18]..the
angel of the Lord commanded Gad to say to
David, that David should..set up an altar..in
the threshingfloor of Ornan.. [20] And Ornan
turned back, and saw the angel ; and his four
sons with him hid themselves.—1 CHRON., ch. 21.

348. —— A manlike. *Manoah's.* [6]..the woman came and told her husband, saying, A man
of God came..like the countenance of an angel
of God, very terrible: but I asked him not whence
he *was.*—JUDGES, ch. 13.

349. —— A mysterious. *Manoah's.* [20]..when
the flame went up toward heaven..the angel of
the Lord ascended in the flame of the altar : and
Manoah and his wife looked on *it,* and fell on
their faces to the ground.—JUDGES, ch. 13.

350. —— Messenger. *To Zacharias.* [19]..I am
Gabriel, that stand in the presence of God ; and
am sent to speak unto thee, and to shew thee
these glad tidings.—LUKE, ch. 1.

351. —— A shining. *By Cornelius.* [30]..Cor-
nelius said, Four days ago I was fasting until this
hour ; and at the ninth hour I prayed in my
house, and, behold, a man stood before me in
bright clothing.—ACTS, ch. 10.

352. —— Sent by an. *Philip.* [26]..the angel of
the Lord spake unto Philip, saying, Arise, and
go toward the south..desert. [27] And he..went :
and, behold..a eunuch of great authority under
Candace, queen of the Ethiopians, who had the
charge of all her treasure, and had come to Jerusalem for to worship.—ACTS, ch. 8.

353. —— A sustaining. *Garden.* [42]..Father,
if thou be willing, remove this cup from me :
nevertheless, not my will, but thine, be done.
[43] And there appeared an angel unto him from
heaven, strengthening him.—LUKE, ch. 22.

354. —— A swift. *Gabriel.* [21]..while I *was*
speaking in prayer, even the man Gabriel..be-
ing caused to fly swiftly, touched me about the
time of the evening oblation.—DAN., ch. 9.

355. —— Terrifying. *Sepulchre Guard.* [3] His
countenance was like lightning, and his raiment
white as snow : [4] And for fear of him the keepers
did shake, and became as dead *men.*—MAT., ch.
28.

356. —— —— Women. [5]..entering into the
sepulchre, they saw a young man sitting on the
right side, clothed in a long white garment ; and
they were affrighted.—MARK, ch. 16.

357. —— —— Gideon. [22]..when Gideon perceived that he *was* an angel of the Lord, Gideon

said, Alas, O Lord God ! for because I have seen
an angel of the Lord face to face.—JUDGES, ch. 6.

358. —— —— At the Altar. [29]..the tabernacle..which Moses made..and the altar of the
burnt offering, *were*..at Gibeon. [30] But David
could not go before it to inquire of God : for he
was afraid because of the sword of the angel of
the Lord.—1 CHRON., ch. 21.

359. —— Deliverance by. *Peter and John.*
[19]..the angel of the Lord by night opened the
prison doors, and brought them forth. [23]..The
prison truly found we shut with all safety, and
the keepers standing without..but we found no
man within.—ACTS, ch. 5.

360. ANGELS, Encouragement from. *Mahanaim.* [1]..Jacob went on his way, and the angels
of God met him. [2] And..he said, This *is* God's
host : and he called the name of that place Mahanaim.—GEN., ch. 32.

361. —— guard the Faithful. *In Dothan.*
[17]..Elisha..said, Lord, I pray thee, open his
eyes..And the Lord opened the eyes of the
young man ; and he saw: and, behold, the
mountain *was* full of horses and chariots of fire
round about Elisha.—2 KINGS, ch. 6.

362. —— Humility of. *Seraphim.* [1]..I saw
also the Lord sitting upon a throne, high and
lifted up.. [2] Above it stood the seraphim : each
one had six wings ; with twain he covered his
face, and with twain he covered his feet, and
with twain he did fly.—ISA., ch. 6.

363. —— Hosts of. *John saw.* [11] I beheld,
and I heard the voice of many angels round
about the throne..and the number of them was
ten thousand times ten thousand, and thousands
of thousands.—REV., ch. 5.

364. —— In human Form. *Ascension.* [10] While
they looked steadfastly toward heaven as he went
up, behold, two men stood by them in white apparel.—ACTS, ch. 1.

365. —— —— Abraham. [1] The Lord appeared unto him in the plains of Mamre : and
he sat in the tent door in the heat of the day :
[2] And he..looked and, lo, three men stood by
him.—GEN., ch. 18.

366. —— Reserved Helpers. *In Gethsemane.*
[51] One of them..drew his sword, and struck a
servant..and smote off his ear.. [53] Thinkest
thou that I cannot now pray to my Father, and
he shall presently give me more than twelve legions of angels ?—MAT., ch. 26.

367. —— Ministry of. *To Shepherds.* [10]..fear
not : for, behold, I bring you good tidings of
great joy, which shall be to all people. [13] And
suddenly there was with the angel a multitude
of the heavenly host praising God.—LUKE, ch. 2.

368. —— —— To Peter. [6]..Peter was sleeping between two soldiers, bound with two
chains : and the keepers before the door.. [7] And,
behold, the angel..came upon *him,* and a light
shined..and he smote Peter on the side, and
raised him up, saying, Arise up quickly. And
his chains fell off from *his* hands.—ACTS, ch. 12.

369. —— Secondary Ministry of. *To Cornelius.*
[The angel said,] [5]..send men to Joppa, and call
for..Peter : [6] He lodgeth with one Simon a tanner, whose house is by the sea side : he shall tell
thee what thou oughtest to do.—ACTS, ch. 10.

370. —— **Honor God's Poor.** *Lazarus.* ²²..the beggar died, and was carried by the angels into Abraham's bosom : the rich man also died, and was buried.—LUKE, ch. 16.

371. —— **Provision by.** *Elijah.* ⁵..as he.. slept under a juniper tree..an angel touched him, and said..Arise *and* eat. ⁶..*There was a* cake baken on the coals, and a cruse of water at his head.—1 KINGS, ch. 19.

372. —— **Succor the Tempted.** *Jesus.* ¹⁰..Get thee hence, Satan : for it is written, Thou shalt worship the Lord thy God, and him only shalt thou serve. ¹¹ Then the devil leaveth him, and, behold, angels came and ministered unto him. —MAT., ch. 4.

See other illustrations under :
Office. To gather together the elect from the four　123
　" 　Mountain was full of horses and chariots　2974

373. ANGER, Consuming. *Murmurers.* ⁴⁹..they that died in the plague were fourteen thousand and seven hundred, besides them that died about the matter of Korah.—NUM., ch. 16.

374. —— **Composure amid.** *Stephen.* ⁵⁹..they stoned Stephen, calling upon *God,* and saying, Lord Jesus, receive my spirit. ⁶⁰ And he kneeled down, and cried with a loud voice, Lord, lay not this sin to their charge. And when he had said this, he fell asleep.—ACTS, ch. 7.

375. —— **A childish.** *Jonah.* ⁹..God said to Jonah, Doest thou well to be angry for the gourd ? And he said, I do well to be angry, *even* unto death.—JONAH, ch. 4.

376. —— **Control of.** *Proverb.* ³² *He that* is slow to anger *is* better than the mighty ; and he that ruleth his spirit than he that taketh a city. —PROV., ch. 16.

377. —— **Destroying.** *Korah.* ²⁰..the Lord spake unto Moses and unto Aaron, saying, ²¹ Separate yourselves from among this congregation, that I may consume them in a moment.—NUM., ch. 16.

378. —— **Great Day of.** *Judgment.* ¹⁵..the kings..the great..the rich..the chief captains ..mighty men..hid themselves in the dens and in the rocks of the mountains ; ¹⁶ And said to the mountains and rocks, Fall on us, and hide us from the face of him that sitteth on the throne, and from the wrath of the Lamb : ¹⁷ For the great day of his wrath is come : and who shall be able to stand ?—REV., ch. 6.

379. —— **from Disparagement.** *Cain.* ⁴..the Lord had respect unto Abel and to his offering : ⁵ But unto Cain and to his offering he had not respect. And Cain was very wroth, and his countenance fell.—GEN., ch. 4.

380. —— **from Defeat.** *Elihu.* ² Then was kindled the wrath of Elihu..against Job..because he justified himself rather than God. ³ Also against his three friends..because they had found no answer, and *yet* had condemned Job.—JOB, ch. 32.

381. —— **Envious.** *Elder Son.* ²⁷..Thy brother is come ; and thy father hath killed the fatted calf, because he hath received him safe and sound..thou never gavest me a kid, that I might make merry with my friends : ²⁸ And he was angry, and would not go in..his father.. intreated him.—LUKE, ch. 15.

382. —— **Folly of.** *Naaman.* ¹¹..Naaman was wroth, and went away, and said, Behold, I thought, He will surely come out to me, and stand, and call on the name of the Lord..and strike his hand over the place.. ¹² Are not Abana and Pharpar, rivers of Damascus, better ?—2 KINGS, ch. 5.

383. —— **Fratricidal.** *Esau.* ⁴¹..Esau hated Jacob because..his father blessed him: and Esau said in his heart, The days of mourning for my father are at hand ; then will I slay my brother Jacob.—GEN., ch. 27.

384. —— **Great.** *Idolaters.* ⁶..the children of Israel did evil again..and served Baalim, and Ashtaroth, and the gods. ⁷ And the anger of the Lord was hot..and he sold them into the hands of the Philistines, and..the children of Ammon. —JUDGES, ch. 10.

385. —— **at Half-heartedness.** *Solomon.* ⁹..the Lord was angry with Solomon, because his heart was turned from the Lord..which had appeared unto him twice.—1 KINGS, ch. 11.

386. —— **of Indignation.** *Moses.* ¹⁹..he saw the calf, and the dancing : and Moses' anger waxed hot, and he cast the tables out of his hands, and brake them.. ²⁰ And he took the calf..and burnt *it*..and ground *it* to powder, and strewed *it* upon the water, and made the children of Israel drink *of it.*—Ex., ch. 32.

387. —— —— *Jonathan.* ³³..Jonathan knew that it was determined of his father to slay David. ³⁴ So Jonathan arose from the table in fierce anger, and did eat no meat the second day of the month : for he was grieved for David.—1 SAM., ch. 20.

388. —— —— *Nehemiah.* [In their distress the poor Jews sold their children to their wealthy brethren.] ⁶ And I was very angry when I heard their cry and these words. ⁷. and I rebuked the nobles, and the rulers, and said unto them, Ye exact usury, every one of his brother.—NEH., ch. 5.

389. —— **Intensified.** *Three Worthies.* ¹⁸..we will not serve thy gods, nor worship the golden image.. ¹⁹ Then was Nebuchadnezzar full of fury, ..*therefore* he..commanded..they should heat the furnace one seven times more than it was wont to be heated.—DAN., ch. 3.

390. —— **Jesus in.** *At Capernaum.* ⁵..when he had looked round about on them with anger, being grieved for the hardness of their hearts, he saith unto the man, Stretch forth thine hand ..and his hand was restored.—MARK, ch. 3.

391. —— **at Murmuring.** *Israelites.* ¹..*when* the people complained..the Lord heard *it ;* and his anger was kindled ; and the fire of the Lord burnt among them, and consumed *them that were* in the uttermost parts of the camp.—NUM., ch. 11.

392. —— **Malicious.** *Pharisees.* [Jesus] ¹⁰..said unto the man, Stretch forth thy hand. And he did so : and his hand was restored whole as the other. ¹¹ And they were filled with madness ; and communed..what they might do to Jesus.—LUKE, ch. 6.

393. —— **Overruled.** *Nebuchadnezzar.* ²⁸..Nebuchadnezzar..said, Blessed *be* the God of Shadrach, Meshach, and Abed-nego, who hath sent his angel, and delivered his servants that trusted in him.. ²⁹ Therefore I make a decree,

That every people, nation, and language, which speak any thing amiss against the God..shall be cut in pieces.—DAN., ch. 3.

394. —— **God provoked to.** *Ahab.* [31]..as if it had been a light thing for him to walk in the sins of Jeroboam..he took to wife Jezebel..and went and served Baal.. [33]..made a grove ; and Ahab did more to provoke the Lord..to anger than all the kings of Israel that were before him. 1 KINGS, ch. 16.

395. —— **Provoked to.** *Moses.* [22] They angered *him* also at the waters of strife, so that it went ill with Moses for their sakes : [33] Because they provoked his spirit, so that he spake unadvisedly with his lips.—Ps. 106.

396. —— —— *Paul.* [4]..ye fathers, provoke not your children to wrath : but bring them up in the nurture and admonition of the Lord.— EPH., ch. 6.

397. —— **Pacification of.** *Jacob* [13]..took of that which came to his hand a present for Esau his brother.—GEN., ch. 32.

398. —— —— *David's.* [18]..Abigail made haste, and took two hundred loaves, and two bottles of wine, and five sheep ready dressed, and five measures of parched *corn*, and a hundred clusters of raisins, and two hundred cakes of figs, and laid *them* on asses.—1 SAM., ch. 25.

399. —— **Petulant.** *Nabal.* [They asked for food.] [10]..Nabal answered David's servants.. Who is David? and who *is* the son of Jesse ? there be many servants nowadays that break away..from his master.—1 SAM., ch. 25.

400. —— **from wounded Pride.** *Haman.* [5]..when Haman saw that Mordecai bowed not, nor did him reverence, then was Haman full of wrath. [6] And he thought scorn to lay hands on Mordecai alone ; for they had shewed him the people of Mordecai.—ESTH., ch. 3.

401. —— **Parental.** *Saul.* [28]..Jonathan answered Saul, David earnestly asked *leave* of me *to go* to Bethlehem : [29]..Therefore he cometh not unto the king's table. [30] Then Saul's anger was kindled against Jonathan.—1 SAM., ch. 20.

402. —— **at Rebellion.** *Calf.* [8]..they have made them a molten calf..worshipped it..sacrificed thereunto, and said, These *be* thy gods, O Israel, which have brought thee up out of the land of Egypt. [10] Now therefore let me alone, that my wrath may wax hot against them, and that I may consume them.—Ex., ch. 32.

403. —— **Righteous.** *Saul.* [2]..Nahash the Ammonite answered them, On this *condition* will I make *a covenant* with you, that I may thrust out all your right eyes, and lay it *for* a reproach upon all Israel.. [6] And the Spirit of God came upon Saul..and his anger was kindled greatly.— 1 SAM., ch. 11.

404. —— **of Resentment.** *Herod,* [16]..when he saw that he was mocked of the wise men, was exceeding wroth..and slew all the children that were in Bethlehem, and in all the coasts thereof, from two years old and under.--MAT., ch. 2.

405. —— —— *Elder Son* [25]..drew nigh to the house, he heard music and dancing.. [28] And he was angry, and would not go in.—LUKE, ch. 15.

406. —— **Relentless.** *Herodias.* [18]..John had said unto Herod, It is not lawful for thee to have thy brother's wife. [19] Therefore Herodias had a quarrel against him, and would have killed him. —MARK, ch. 6.

407. —— **at Sedition.** *Miriam and Aaron.* [9]..Hath the Lord indeed spoken only by Moses ? hath he not spoken also by us ? And the Lord heard *it*.. [9] And the anger of the Lord was kindled against them.—NUM., ch. 12.

408. —— **Surrender of.** *Jesus.* [23]..if thou bring thy gift to the altar, and there rememberest that thy brother hath aught against thee ; [24] Leave there thy gift before the altar, and go thy way ; first be reconciled to thy brother, and then come and offer thy gift.—MAT., ch. 5.

409. —— **Slowness to.** *Proverb.* [17] *He that is* soon angry dealeth foolishly. [29] *He that is* slow to wrath *is* of great understanding : but *he that is* hasty of spirit exalteth folly.—PROV., ch. 14.

410. —— **A strange.** *Ninevites.* [10]..God saw ..that they turned from their evil way ; and God repented of the evil, that he had said that he would do unto them.. [1] But it displeased Jonah exceedingly, and he was very angry.—JONAH, chs. 3 and 4.

411. —— **Sectarian.** *Saul.* [11]..I punished them oft in every synagogue, and compelled *them* to blaspheme ; and being exceedingly mad against them, I persecuted *them* even unto strange cities.—ACTS, ch. 26.

412. —— **Tyrannical.** *Pharaoh.* [4]..Wherefore do ye, Moses and Aaron, let the people from their works ? get you unto your burdens.. [9] Let there be more work laid upon the men.—Ex., ch. 5.

413. —— **Undeserved.** *Caleb and Joshua.* [7]..The land, which we passed through to search it, *is* an exceeding good land. [10] But all the congregation bade stone them with stones.— NUM., ch. 14.

414. —— **Unreasonable.** *Nebuchadnezzar.* [12]..the king was angry and very furious, and commanded to destroy all the wise *men* of Babylon. [13]..and they sought Daniel and his fellows to be slain.—DAN., ch. 2.

415. —— **Victims of.** *Potiphar's.* [19]..his wrath was kindled. [20] And Joseph's master took him, and put him into the prison.—GEN., ch. 39.

See other illustrations under:

Forgotten. Is thy servant a dog..do this? 4419
God Gives. S. of G. came upon Saul..anger 4420
Hot. Saw the calf..Moses' anger waxed hot 4421
at Hypocrisy. Jesus looked on them with anger 4422
at Injustice. Elihu..wrath kindled..yet had con 4423
Improper. Indignation..Why..waste of the 4424
Judgment. Remaineth..a certain fearful 4425
Murderous. When they heard..filled with wrath 4426
National. People arose as one man..to do to 4427
Natural. Ten heard it..moved with indignation 4428
Partisan. Sadducees..were filled with indignation 4429
Pride. Haman was full of indignation against M. 4430
Righteous. I may thrust out all your right eyes 4431
Religious. Against Job..because he justified 4432
at Sinners. David's anger was kindled..restore 4433
Severity. L. was wroth and..to tormentors 4434

INSOLENCE.

Added. [Danite robbers] said unto Micah, What 4530
Fraternal. With whom hast thou left those few 4531
Injustice. There is no straw..ye are idle 4532
Resented. Whatsoever is pleasant in thine eyes 4533
Friends. Hanun cut off their garments in the 3431

RESENTMENT.

Cruel. Herod slew all the children..Bethlehem 7183
Indignant. Woman was fallen..hands on the 7184
of Self-Seeking. Much displeased with James and 7185

RETALIATION.

Cowardly. Joab took Abner aside..smote him 7289
Disallowed. Been said, An eye for an eye 7290
Jewish. Life shall go for life, eye for eye 7291

REVENGE.

Avoided. Flee thou to Laban..brother's fury turn 7304
Brother's. When I say, Smite Amnon, then kill 7305
"   Joab smote Abner..for the blood of 7306
Best. If thine enemy be hungry, give him bread 7307
Frustrated. Haman was come..Hang Mordecai 7308
Ignored. Spake against Moses..M. cried unto the 7309
"   Shall not Shimei be put to death? 7310
Justifiable. Philistines burnt her..S. smote them 7311
Nursed. Absalom spake neither good nor bad 7312
Proposed. Then will I slay my brother Jacob 7313
Price. That they may be destroyed..I will pay 7314
Prayer. O L. G. strengthen me..avenged of the P. 7315

VENGEANCE.

Averted. Let not my lord regard..Nabal 9169
"   Kept me..from coming to shed blood 9170
Blood. Cain said..every one that findeth me..stay 9171
Call. Stoned [Zachariah]..in house of the L. 9172
Divine. To me belongeth vengeance and 9173
"   If I whet my glittering sword 9174
Declined. Not a man be put to death [Saul] 9175
Fear. Joseph will peradventure hate us 9176
with God. My G., think thou upon Tobiah 9177
Inappropriate. I forgave thee..shouldst thou not 9178
Mistaken. Command fire..to consume them 9179
Monstrous. Haman thought scorn..Mordecai 9180
Prohibited. If ye from your hearts forgive not 9182
Undesired. Behold the head of Ishbosheth 9183
for Vengeance. David commanded..slew them 9184

Displeasure. Brought young children..disciples 2414
"   I hate your feast days..let judgment 2411
Enmity. Citizens hated him..will not have..reign 2676
Estrangement. Younger son..journey into a far 2725
Jealousy. Ten heard it..much displeased with 7185

416. ANGUISH of Bereavement. *Shunammite.*
[27]..when she came to [Elisha]..she caught him
by the feet : but Gehazi came near to thrust her
away. And the man of God said, Let her alone ;
for her soul *is* vexed within her.—2 KINGS, ch. 4.

417. —— Bitter. *Esau.* [34]..Esau..cried with
a great and exceeding bitter cry, and said unto
his father, Bless me, *even* me also, O my father.
—GEN., ch. 27.
See other illustrations under :

DESPAIR.

Affliction. Let me not see the death of the child 2213
Anguish. Slay me, for anguish is come upon me 2214
Awaking. Wine was gone out..heart died within 2215
Deliverance. Been better for us to serve the Egyp 2216
Needless. Widow..meal..oil..me and my son eat 2217

DISTRESS.

Cry of. Great cry..none like it, nor shall be 2437
Derided. They that see me, shoot out the lip 2438
Described. I was a derision to all my people 2439
Exasperation. What shall I do..people ready to 3440
Famine. Delicate women..shall eat..children 3441
Friend. Gedaliah..took Jeremiah out of prison 3443
Great. Thrust..right eyes..people wept 3444
Little Faith. Why are ye fearful..little faith..calm 3442
Needless. Saul had adjured..food 3445
Refuge. Ahaz sacrificed unto the gods that smote 3446

LAMENTATION.

Adversity. Let the day perish wherein I was 4883
Fathers. O my son Absalom ! my son, my son 4884
General. Thrust out right eyes..people..voices 4885
Ill-timed. Would to G. we had been content. 4886
Jesus. O Jerusalem, Jerusalem..would I have 4887
for Jesus. Weep not for me, but weep for 4888
National. In every province..Jews..weeping and 4889
Tearful. Oh that my head were waters..fountain 4890

MOURNING.

Abstinence. [Abner assassinated] If I taste 5603
Bereavement. I am distressed for thee, my 5604
Beneficial. Better to go to the house of mourning 5605
Comfort. Asleep..sorrow not as others which 5598
Feigned. Be as a woman..long time mourned 5606
Good. Mary..told them..as they mourned and 5600
Genuine. Widows..weeping and showing 5601
Intense. David went up..wept..barefoot 5607
Joy. Jesus came and touched the bier 5608
Last. Thou mourn at the last..body consumed 5609
Time. Great and very sore lamentation 5610
Wicked. King wept at the grave of Abner 5611

REMORSE.

Needful. People that came..smote their breasts 7067
Prevented. Lest swallowed up with overmuch sor 7068
Treachery. Judas..went and hanged himself 7069

Agony. My soul is exceeding sorrowful..unto death 264
Boldness. I will go into the king..if I perish 2218
Disappointment. Saw his counsel was not follow 2325
Sacrifices. Took his eldest son..for burnt offering 2221
See SORROW and References.

418. ANIMALS, Authority over. *Man.* [6]Thou
madest him to have dominion over the works of
thy hands ; thou hast put all *things* under his
feet : [7]All sheep and oxen, yea, and the beasts
of the field ; [8]The fowl of the air, and the fish
of the sea.—Ps. 8.

419. —— Accursed. *Serpent.* [14]..Because
thou hast done this, thou *art* cursed above all
cattle, and above every beast of the field ; upon
thy belly shalt thou go, and dust shalt thou eat
all the days of thy life : [15]And I will put enmity between thee and the woman.—GEN., ch. 3.

420. —— Contrasted. *Beasts.* [20]Thou makest
darkness, and it is night : wherein all the beasts
of the forest do creep *forth.* [21]The young lions
roar after their prey, and seek their meat from

God. ²² The sun ariseth, they gather themselves together, and lay them down in their dens.—Ps. 104.

421. —— **Dominion over.** *Adam.* ²⁸..God said unto them..Replenish the earth and subdue it : and have dominion over the fish of the sea, and over the fowl of the air, and over every living thing that moveth upon the earth.—GEN., ch. 1.

422. —— **Destructive.** *Bears.* ²³..There came forth little children out of the city, and mocked him..Go up, thou bald head ; ²⁴ And he..cursed them in the name of the Lord. And there came forth two she bears out of the wood, and tare forty and two children of them.—2 KINGS, ch. 2.

423. —— **Dangerous.** *Wild.* ⁶..A lion out of the forest shall slay them, *and* a wolf of the evenings shall spoil them, a leopard shall watch over their cities : every one that goeth out thence shall be torn in pieces : because their transgressions are many.—JER., ch. 5.

424. —— **End of the.** *Solomon.* ²⁰ All go unto one place ; all are of the dust, and all turn to dust again. ²¹ Who knoweth the spirit of man that goeth upward, and the spirit of the beast that goeth downward to the earth?—ECCL., ch. 3.

425. —— **for Food.** *Vegetarians.* ¹..the Spirit speaketh expressly, that in the latter times some shall depart from the faith. ³..*commanding* to abstain from meats, which God hath created to be received with thanksgiving.—1 TIM., ch. 4.

426. —— **Instincts of.** *God.* ⁵ Who hath sent out the wild ass free ? or who hath loosed the bands of the wild ass ? ⁶ Whose house I have made the wilderness, and the barren land his dwellings.—JOB, ch. 39.

427. —— —— *Overruled.* ⁶..the ravens brought him bread and flesh in the morning, and bread and flesh in the evening.—1 KINGS, ch. 17.

428. —— **Divinely guided.** *Kine.* ⁷..take two milch kine, on which there hath come no yoke, and tie the kine to the cart, and bring their calves home from them.. ¹² And the kine took the straight way to the way of Beth-shemesh, *and* went along the highway, lowing as they went, and turned not aside *to* the right hand or *to* the left.—1 SAM., ch. 6. [They returned the ark of God to Israel.]

429. —— **Kindness to.** *Rebekah.* ¹⁹..she said, I will draw *water* for thy camels also, until they have done drinking. ²⁰ And she hasted, and emptied her pitcher into the trough, and ran again unto the well..and drew for all his camels.—GEN., ch. 24.

430. —— **Instruction from.** *Ant.* ⁶ Go to the ant, thou sluggard ; consider her ways, and be wise.. ⁸ Provideth her meat in the summer, *and* gathereth her food in the harvest.—PROV., ch. 6.

431. —— **Kindness of.** *Dogs.* ²⁰..There was a certain beggar named Lazarus, which was laid at his gate, full of sores, ²¹ And desiring..the crumbs which fell from the rich man's table : moreover the dogs came and licked his sores.—LUKE, ch. 16.

432. —— **King of.** *Leviathan.* ¹ Canst thou draw out leviathan with a hook? or his tongue with a cord *which* thou lettest down? ² Canst

thou put a hook into his nose? or bore his jaw through with a thorn?.. ³⁴ He beholdeth all high *things:* he *is* a king over all the children of pride.—JOB, ch. 41.

433. —— **Forbidden mixing.** *Jews.* ¹⁰ Thou shalt not plough with an ox and an ass together.—DEUT. ch. 22.

434. —— —— **Profitable.** *Fish.* ²⁷..Go thou to the sea, and cast an hook, and take up the fish that first cometh up ; and when thou hast opened his mouth, thou shalt find a piece of money.—MAT., ch. 17.

435. —— **Punishment by.** *Israelites.* ²¹..if ye..will not hearken unto me.. ²² I will..send wild beasts amongst you, which shall rob you of your children, and destroy your cattle, and make you few in number ; and your *high* ways shall be desolate.—LEV., ch. 26.

436. —— **Providence feeds.** *Birds.* ²⁶ Behold the fowls of the air : for they sow not, neither do they reap, nor gather into barns ; yet your heavenly Father feedeth them.—MAT., ch. 6.

437. —— **Restrained.** *Lions.* ²¹..said Daniel unto the king.. ²² My God hath sent his angel, and hath shut the lions' mouths, that they have not hurt me.—DAN., ch. 6.

438. —— **Revenge by.** *Foxes.* ⁴..Samson.. caught three hundred foxes..and turned tail to tail, and put a firebrand in the midst between two tails. ⁵..he let *them* go into the standing corn of the Philistines, and burnt up both the shocks, and also the standing corn, with the vineyards *and* olives.—JUDGES, ch. 15.

439. —— **Unrestrained.** *Lions.* ²⁴..they brought those men which had accused Daniel, and they cast *them* into the den of lions, them, their children, and their wives ; and the lions.. brake all their bones in pieces or ever they came at the bottom of the den.—DAN., ch. 6.

See other illustrations under :

BIRDS.

Care. Bird's nest. not take dam with the young	785
" Two sparrows sold for a farthing..not fall	1040
Emblematic. Eagle stirreth up her nest..fluttereth	782
Food. All day..night..next day..gathered quails	786
Service. Ravens brought him bread and flesh	787
Symbolic. Jesus, when he was baptized..dove	783
Welcome. Dove came to Noah..in her mouth an	784

HORSES.

Fast. Jehu rode in a chariot..driveth furiously	2517
Forbidden. Shall not multiply horses..return to	4093
Fire. Appeared horses and chariot of fire..Elijah	4094
Many. Solomon had 40,000 stalls of horses	4095
Sacred. Horses that the kings of Judah..given to	4096
Terrible. Out of his nostrils goeth smoke..flame	4833
White. Armies..in heaven, followed on white hor	4097

Artificial. What shall the trespass..two gold mice	6028
" The golden earrings..molten calf	4281
" Moses made a serpent of brass	7793
Conciliation. Jacob..to Esau..goats..sheep..cam	1462
Captured. 675,000 sheep and 72,000 beeves	911
Dominion. Fear of you shall be upon every beast	3286
Weak. Frogs..flies..lice..locusts..caterpillars..in	4565
Zoologist. Solomon spake of beasts and fowl and	10029

440. ANNUNCIATION, The. *Mary.* ²⁶..the angel Gabriel was sent from God unto..Nazareth, ²⁷ To a virgin espoused to a man whose name was Joseph..and the virgin's name *was* Mary.—LUKE, ch. 1.

441. —— to Zacharias. *Gabriel.* [11]..there appeared unto him an angel of the Lord standing on the right side of the altar of incense.. [13] But the angel said..Fear not, Zacharias : for thy prayer is heard ; and thy wife Elisabeth shall bear thee a son, and thou shalt call his name John.—LUKE, ch. 1.

442. ANNOUNCEMENT, A painful. *Betrayal.* [21]..as they did eat, he said..one of you shall betray me. [22] And they were exceeding sorrowful, and began every one of them to say unto him, Lord, is it I?—MAT., ch. 26.

See MESSENGERS *and references.*

443. ANNOYANCE, A wearisome. *Delilah.* [26]..when she pressed him daily with her words, and urged him, so that his soul was vexed unto death ; [17] That he told her all his heart.—JUDGES, ch. 16.

See TROUBLE *and references.*

444. ANOINTING for Service. *Saul.* [9]..when he had turned his back to go from Samuel, God gave him another heart.. [10] And..a company of prophets met him ; and the Spirit of God came upon him, and he prophesied among them.— 1 SAM., ch. 10. [Samuel had anointed him king of Israel.]

See other illustrations under :

BAPTISM.
Administration. Jesus himself baptized not 631
Christ's. Went up out of the water..dove..voice 632
Imperfect. Apollos..knowing only the b. of John 633
Promised. Ye shall be baptized with the H. S. 634
Prerequisite. If thou believest, with all thine heart 635
Reformation. Washed their stripes and was baptiz 636
Received. Tongues like as of fire, and sat on each 637
Type. Baptized unto Moses in the cloud..sea 638
Many. Jerusalem and all Judea..all the region 639

BLOOD.
Acceptance. Moses took the blood sprinkled. peo 852
Behold. Side posts..upper door post of the house 854
Cleansing. If the blood of bulls blood of Christ 856
Consecration. Put it on the tip of Aaron's right ear 857

445. ANSWER, A hasty. *Proverb.* [13] He that answereth a matter before he heareth it, it is folly and shame unto him.—PROV., ch. 18.

446. —— An insincere. *Chief Priests.* [25] The baptism of John, whence was it? from heaven, or of men? And they reasoned with themselves, saying, If we shall say, From heaven ; he will say unto us, Why did ye not then believe him? [26] But if we shall say, Of men ; we fear the people.. [27] And they answered Jesus..We cannot tell.—MAT., ch. 21.

447. —— An ill-considered. *James and John.* [38]..Ye know not what ye ask : can ye drink of the cup that I drink of? and be baptized with the baptism that I am baptized with? [39]..they said..We can.—MARK, ch. 10.

448. —— An unwise. *Rehoboam.* [13]..the king answered the people roughly, and forsook the old men's counsel.. [14] And spake to them after the counsel of the young men, saying, My father made your yoke heavy, and I will add to your yoke.—1 KINGS, ch. 12. [Ten tribes seceded.]

449. —— A wise. *Pharisees.* [17]..What thinkest thou? Is it lawful to give tribute unto Cesar, or not? [20] And he saith..Whose is this image and superscription? [21] They say..Cesar's. Then saith he, Render therefore unto Cesar the things which are Cesar's ; and unto God the things that are God's.—MAT., ch. 22.

See other illustrations under :
Responsive. The people answered amen, amen. 7209
" One cried unto another, holy, holy 7210

450. ANTAGONISM, Spiritual. *Serpent.* [14]..Because thou hast done this. [15]..I will put enmity between thee and the woman, and between thy seed and her seed ; it shall bruise thy head, and thou shalt bruise his heel.—GEN., ch. 3.

451. —— of Truth. *Sword.* [34] Think not that I am come to send peace on earth : I came not to send peace, but a sword. [35] For I am come to set a man at variance against his father, and the daughter against her mother, and the daughter in law against her mother in law.—MAT., ch. 10.

See ENMITY *and references.*

452. ANTIDOTE, An effectual. *Poison.* [40]..as they were eating of the pottage..they cried out..O thou man of God, there is death in the pot. [41] But he said, Then bring meal. And he cast it into the pot ; and he said, Pour out for the people..And there was no harm in the pot.—2 KINGS, ch. 4.

See other illustrations under :
CURE.
All Persons. Laid his hands on every one and heal 1867
All Diseases. Stepped in, was made whole of what 1868
Faith. When..beheld the serpent of brass he lived 1869
Gratitude. She arose and ministered unto them 1870
Means. Made clay of the spittle..anointed eyes 1871
Progressive. See men as trees walking..clearly 1872
Threefold. Possessed with a devil, blind and dumb 1873
Wonderful. Stretch forth thy hand..as the other 1874

REMEDY.
Improbable. Anointed the eyes of the blind man 7058
Look. As Moses lifted up the serpent..S. of man 7059

453. ANXIETY, Burdensome. *Moses.* [13]..they weep unto me, saying, Give us flesh, that we may eat. [14] I am not able to bear all this people alone, because it is too heavy for me. [15] And if thou deal thus with me, kill me, I pray thee.—NUM., ch. 11.

454. —— for God's Cause. *Eli.* [12]..there ran a man of Benjamin out of the army, and came to Shiloh..with his clothes rent, and with earth upon his head. [13] And..lo, Eli sat upon a seat by the way side watching : for his heart trembled for the ark of God.—1 SAM., ch. 4.

455. —— forbidden. *Future.* [22]..Take no thought for your life, what ye shall eat ; neither for the body, what ye shall put on.. [24] Consider the ravens : for they neither sow nor reap ; which neither have storehouse nor barn ; and God feedeth them : how much more are ye better than the fowls?—LUKE, ch. 12.

456. —— Parental. *Joseph and Mary.* [48]..his mother said..Son, why hast thou thus dealt with us? behold, thy father and I have sought thee sorrowing.—LUKE, ch. 2.

457. —— Relief of. *Spirit.* [19]..when they deliver you up, take no thought how or what ye shall speak : for it shall be given you in that same hour what ye shall speak.—MAT., ch. 10.

458. —— Sleepless. *Darius.* [18]..the king went to his palace, and passed the night fasting : neither were instruments of music brought

..and his sleep went from him. .¹⁹..very early in the morning..went in haste unto the den of lions.—DAN., ch. 6.

459. —— **because of Sickness.** *Nobleman.* ⁴⁷..besought him that he would come down, and heal his son : for he was at the point of death. ⁴⁹ The nobleman saith unto him, Sir, come down ere my child die.—JOHN, ch. 4.

460. —— **Worldly.** *Martha.* ⁴¹..Jesus..said ..Martha, Martha, thou art careful and troubled about many things. ⁴² But one thing is needful.— LUKE, ch. 10.

See other illustrations under :

AGITATION.

Deception. Who art thou ?..Esau..Isaac trembled   256
Diffuses. Disputed he in the synagogue..market   257
Deplored. [Israelites] Made..abhorred..slay us   258
General. [Philistines] Trembling in the host..field   259
Mount. Sinai..quaked greatly   260
Overcome. [At sepulchre] keepers did shake   261
Physical. Belshazzar's thoughts troubled..knees   262
Terror. [Job's vision.] Trembling. my bones   263

ALARM.

Conscience. Pray for thy servants..we die not   273
Death. Egyptians were urgent..we be all dead   274
Failure. Priests..doubted..whereunto this would   275
Manifestation. Belshazzar..countenance was   276
Preaching. Paul reasoned..Felix trembled   277
Reasonable. Esau cometh..400 men..Jacob   278
Superstitious. Jesus walking on the sea..troubled   279
Sinners. Adam and his wife hid themselves   280
"   Let not God speak with us..die   281
Sudden. Seeing the prison doors open..sword   282
Spiritual. Sirs, what must I do to be saved?   283
Tempest. Entreat..be no more mighty thunderings   284
Unnecessary. My money is restored..heart failed   285

CARE.

Beginning. Counteth the cost..sufficient to finish   1032
Others. Samaritan..had compassion..took care   1033

CARE OF GOD.

Animals. Behold the fowls..Father feedeth them   1035
Acknowledged. God, which fed me all my life   1036
Birds. Bird's nest..not take the dam with the   1034
Delicate. He that toucheth you, toucheth..his eye   1037
Defending. Hast thou not made a hedge about   1038
Illustrated. Two sparrows..a farthing..Father   1039
Perfect. He shall feed his flock like a Shepherd   1040
Protecting. Mountain was full..chariots of fire   1041
Shepherd's. L. is my shepherd ; I shall not want   1042
Sheltering. As an eagle..young..on her wings..so   1043
Sustaining. L. shall guide thee..be like..garden   1044
Sleepless. He that keepeth thee will not slumber   1045
Tender. As a hen gathereth her chickens..wings   1046

CARES.

Burdensome. Martha was cumbered about much   1047
Disturbing. Abundance of the rich will not suffer   1048
Ministerial. Besides..the care of all the churches   1049
Wealth. What shall I do..I have no room   1050

DANGER.

Appalled. Jesus went before them..amazed   1906
Escape. Disciples let him down by night in a   1909
Haste. Let them in Judea..flee to the mountains   1911
Intimidates. Peter saw..afraid and beginning to   1912
Jesus. Storm..on the lake..Master, we perish   1913

RESTLESSNESS.

Care. He thought..Thou fool, this night thy soul   7265
Fear. Would God it were morning   7266

See FEAR and references.

461. APOSTASY, Angelic. *Devil.* ⁶..the angels which kept not their first estate, but left their own habitation, he hath reserved in everlasting chains under darkness unto the judgment of the great day.—JUDE.

462. —— **in old Age.** *Solomon.* ⁴..when Solomon was old..his wives turned away his heart after other gods. ⁵ For Solomon went after Ashtoreth the goddess of the Zidonians, and after Milcom the abomination of the Ammonites.—1 KINGS, ch. 11.

463. —— **Deception in.** *Paul.* ¹..the Spirit speaketh expressly, that in the latter times some shall depart from the faith, giving heed to seducing spirits, and doctrines of devils ; ² Speaking lies in hypocrisy ; having their conscience seared with a hot iron.—1 TIM., ch. 4.

464. APOSTATE, Enmity of. *Alexander.* ¹⁴ Alexander the coppersmith did me much evil.. ¹⁵ Of whom be thou ware also ; for he hath greatly withstood our words.—2 TIM., ch. 4.

465. —— **Hopeless.** *Presumption.* ¹⁶..if we sin wilfully after that we have received the knowledge of the truth, there remaineth no more sacrifice for sins. ¹⁷ But a certain fearful looking for of judgment and fiery indignation, which shall devour the adversaries.—HEB., ch. 10.

466. —— **Inconsiderate.** *Esau.* ³³..he sold his birthright unto Jacob. ³⁴ Then Jacob gave Esau bread and pottage of lentiles ; and he did eat and drink, and rose up, and went his way. Thus Esau despised *his* birthright.—GEN., ch. 25.

467. —— **to Idolatry.** *Ahab* ³¹..took to wife Jezebel the daughter of Ethbaal king of the Zidonians, and went and served Baal, and worshipped him.—1 KINGS, ch. 16.

468. —— **in Prosperity.** *Jeshurun.* ¹⁵..Jeshurun waxed fat, and kicked : thou art waxen fat, thou art grown thick, thou art covered *with fatness ;* then he forsook God *which* made him, and lightly esteemed the Rock of his salvation. —DEUT., ch. 32.

469. —— **Responsibility for.** *Drowned.* ⁶..whoso shall offend one of these little ones which believe in me, it were better for him that a mill-stone were hanged about his neck, and *that* he were drowned in the depth of the sea. —MAT., ch. 18.

470. —— **a Shipwreck.** *Hymeneus—Alexander.* ¹⁹ Holding faith, and a good conscience ; which some having put away, concerning faith have made shipwreck : ²⁰ Of whom is Hymeneus and Alexander ; whom I have delivered unto Satan, that they may learn not to blaspheme.—1 TIM., ch. 1.

See BACKSLIDING and references.

471. APPAREL, Angelic. *Ascension.* ¹⁰..while they looked steadfastly toward heaven as he went up, behold, two men stood by them in white apparel.—ACTS, ch. 1.

472. —— **Separate.** *Law.* ⁵ The woman shall not wear that which pertaineth unto a man, neither shall a man put on a woman's garment : for all that do so *are* abomination unto the Lord.— DEUT., ch. 22.

See CLOTHES and references.

473. APPEAL for Sympathy. *Saul.* ⁸..*there is none that sheweth me that my son hath made a* league with the son of Jesse, and *there is* none of you that is sorry for me, or sheweth unto me that my son hath stirred up my servant against me, to lie in wait, as at this day?—1 SAM., ch. 22.

See other illustrations under:

Tender. Not to go..weep and break mine heart   2686
Urgent. Sir, come down ere my child die   2685
   See **PRAYER** and references.

474. APPEARANCES conceal. *Joseph.* ⁷..Joseph saw his brethren, and he knew them, but made himself strange..and spake roughly..and he said..Whence come ye?—GEN., ch. 42.

475. —— Evil. *Tribute.* ²⁷..lest we should offend them, go thou to the sea, and cast a hook, and take up the fish that first cometh up ; and when thou hast opened his mouth, thou shalt find a piece of money : that take, and give unto them.—MAT., ch. 17.

476. —— False. *Scribes.* ⁴⁶Beware of the scribes, which desire to walk in long robes, and love greetings in the markets, and the highest seats in the synagogues, and the chief rooms at feasts. ⁴⁷Which devour widows' houses, and for a shew make long prayers.—LUKE, ch. 20.

477. —— Hurtful. *Example.* ¹⁰..if any man see thee which hast knowledge sit at meat in the idol's temple, shall not the conscience of him which is weak be emboldened to eat those things which are offered to idols ; ¹¹And through thy knowledge shall the weak brother perish, for whom Christ died?—1 COR., ch. 8.

478. —— uncertain. *Eliab.* ⁶..he looked on Eliab, and said, Surely the Lord's anointed is before him. ⁷..the Lord said unto Samuel, Look not on his countenance, or on the height of his stature ; because I have refused him : for *the Lord seeth* not as man seeth ; for man looketh on the outward appearance, but the Lord looketh on the heart.—1 SAM., ch. 16.

See other illustrations under:

DISGUISE.

Battle. Ahab said, I will disguise myself   2382
Failure. Ahijah said, Come in, wife of Jeroboam   2383
Insufficient. Saul disguised himself [visited a witch]2384
Penetrated. Is not the hand of Joab in this?   2385

Display. Ahasuerus..court..white, green and blue 2409
Deception. Israel made as if beaten..Ai   6544
Fashion. Ahaz went to Damascus..fashion..altar   290
Hypocrites. Ye devour widows' houses, and for a 6548
Lip-service. This people draweth nigh..with   5049
Public. If any man see thee at meat in the idol's 1558
   See **DECEPTION** and references.

479. APPETITE, Control of. *Solomon.* ¹When thou sittest to eat with a ruler, consider diligently what *is* before thee. ²And put a knife to thy throat, if thou *be* a man given to appetite. ³Be not desirous of his dainties : for they *are* deceitful meat.—PROV., ch. 23.

480. —— Dangers of. *Israelites.* ⁴..wept again, and said, Who shall give us flesh to eat? ⁵We remember the fish, which we did eat in Egypt freely ; the cucumbers, and the melons, and the leeks, and the onions, and the garlic.—NUM., ch. 11.

481. —— Heedless. *Israelites.* ³¹..they smote the Philistines..and the people were very faint. ³²..flew upon the spoil, and took sheep, and oxen, and calves, and slew *them* on the ground :

and the people did eat *them* with the blood.—1 SAM., ch. 14.

482. —— Sin from. *Israelites.* ¹⁹..ye have wept in the ears of the Lord, saying, Who shall give us flesh to eat? for *it was* well with us in Egypt : therefore the Lord will give you flesh.. ²⁰..even a whole month, until it come out at your nostrils, and it be loathsome unto you.—NUM., ch. 11.

483. —— Temptation by. *Jesus.* ²..when he had fasted forty days and forty nights, he was afterward a hungered. ³..the tempter..said, If thou be the Son of God, command that these stones be made bread.—MAT., ch. 4.

484. —— Unrestrained. *Esau.* ³²..Esau said, Behold, I *am* at the point to die : and what profit shall this birthright do to me? ³⁴Then Jacob gave Esau bread and pottage of lentiles ; and he did eat and drink, and rose up, and went his way. Thus Esau despised *his* birthright.—GEN., ch. 25.

   See **FOOD** and references.

485. APPLAUSE, Love of. *Pharisees.* ⁴⁴How can ye believe, which receive honour one of another, and seek not the honour that *cometh* from God only?—JOHN, ch. 5.

486. —— Temptation to seek. *Jesus.* ⁵..the devil taketh him up into the holy city, and setteth him on a pinnacle of the temple. ⁶And saith..If thou be the Son of God, cast thyself down.—MAT., ch. 4.

See other illustrations under:

FAME.

Increasing. His fame spread abroad..about   3000
Military. Uzziah made..engines..to shoot   3001
Troublesome. Blaze abroad the matter..desert   3002
Unexpected. In the whole world..woman hath   3003
Wisdom. All the earth sought to Solomon   3004

Flattery. [Herod] People gave a shout..voice of   3254
Victory. Women came singing..dancing to meet   1902
Withheld. No prophet is without honor save..own 4073

487. APPLICATION, Direct. *Traitor.* ²¹..Verily, I say unto you, that one of you shall betray me. ²²And they were exceeding sorrowful. ²⁵Then Judas, which betrayed him, answered and said, Master, is it I? He said unto him, Thou hast said.—MAT., ch. 26.

488. —— Personal. *Parable.* ⁴..There came a traveller unto the rich man, and he spared to take of his own flock and of his own herd..but took the poor man's lamb.. ⁷And Nathan said to David, Thou *art* the man.—2 SAM., ch. 12.

489. —— Unmistakable. *Peter.* ¹⁰..by the name of Jesus Christ of Nazareth, whom ye crucified, whom God raised from the dead, *even* by him doth this man stand here before you whole. ¹²Neither is there salvation in any other.—ACTS, ch. 4.

   See **MINISTRY** and references.

490. ARBITRATOR, A wise. *Solomon.* ²⁵..Divide the living child in two, and give half to the one, and half to the other. ²⁶Then spake the woman whose the living child *was*..for her bowels yearned upon her son, and she said, O my lord, give her the living child.—1 KINGS, ch. 3.

See other illustrations under:

Declined. Master speak..that he divide the inher 2724
   See **STRIFE** and references.

491. ARCHITECT, An inspired. *Bezaleel.* [2]..I have called by name Bezaleel..[3] And I have filled him with the spirit of God, in wisdom, and in understanding, and in knowledge, and in all manner of workmanship.—Ex., ch. 31. [He built the tabernacle.]

492. ARCHITECTURE, Ornamental. *Temple.* [32]..he carved upon them carvings of cherubim and palm trees and open flowers, and overlaid *them* with gold, and spread gold upon the cherubim, and upon the palm trees.—1 KINGS, ch. 6.

See other illustrations under :

BUILDER.

Jotham. Built cities in the mountains..castles and   953
Unsuccessful. Laid the foundation..not able   954
Visionary. I will pull down my barns and build   955

BUILDERS.

Joyful. Walls completed..wives and children rejoi   956
"   [Temple] Ancient men..wept..many   957
Stupendous. [Babel] Tower whose top may reach   959
Volunteer. [Temple] Who is there..let him go up   958

BUILDING.

Glorious. [Temple] Solomon built..cedar..gold   960
Hindered. People of the land..weakened the hands   961
Necessitated. Jerusalem..waste..gates burned   962
Outgrown. Elisha..the place..dwell..too strait   963
Prevented. Confound their language..left off to   964
Prohibited. [Rechabites] Neither..build house   965
Revival after. Ezra had prayed..people wept..very   966
Spiritual. Built upon the foundation..corner-stone   967

FOUNDATION.

Only. Other foundation can no man lay   3399
Second Temple. People shouted..because..was   3401
Various Uses. Build on..gold..wood..stubble   3402

FOUNDER.

Celebrated. Hiram..worker in brass..came to S.   3403

HOUSE.

Gifts. [Tabernacle] Brought bracelets, earrings   4131
Ill-founded. Built his house upon the sand..fell   4122
Ivory. Ahab..ivory house..and the cities..built   4121
Mansion. In my Father's house are many mansion   4123
Polluted. Manasseh built altars..graven image   4135
Refuge. Adonijah feared..caught hold..horns of   4136
Residence. Anna..departed not from the temple   4137
Temporary. Jonah made him a booth..see   4125

HOUSE OF GOD.

Abandoned. L. hath cast off his altar..abhorred   4126
Closed. Ahaz shut up..doors..made high places   4127
Despoiled. Chaldees..carried the pots, shovels   4128
Destroyed. Break down the carved work..cast   4129
Expensive. Costing £939,907,687 [Jamieson]
Given for Bribery. Ahaz took away a portion   4132
Grandeur. David said..must be exceeding m.   4133
Neglected. Dwell in your ceiled houses, and this   4134
Robbed. Shishak took..treasures..shields of gold   4138
"   Ahaz..cut in pieces the vessels   4139
Repairing. Jehoida took a chest and bored a hole   4140

MECHANIC.

Apostle. [Paul and Aquila] were tent-makers   5268
Christ. Is not this the carpenter?..offended   5269
Expert. Hiram..worker in brass..came to S.   5270
Independence. Not be chargeable..wrought with   5272
Original. Tubal Cain an instructor of every artific   5271
Opposition. Alexander the coppersmith did..harm   5273
"   Called workmen of like occupation   5274
Renown. Not any..hew timber..like Sidonians   5276
Without. No smith..lest Hebrews make swords   5277

Ark. Dimensions 300 x 50 x 30 cubits   493
Caution. When thou buildest a new h.—Deut. 22 : 8

Folly. Foolish man built his house on the—Mat. 7 : 26
Needed. It is time that the Lord's house—Hag. 1 : 2
Pride. Is not this great Babylon that I—Dan. 4 : 30
Presented. Centurion..hath built us a syn—Luke 7 : 5
Silence. No tool of iron was heard—1 Kings 6 : 7
Slow. Solomon was building his own h.—1 Kings 7 : 1
Splendor. Wall was of Jasper..city—Rev. 21 : 18
Season. Jotham built in the forests—2 Chron. 27 : 4
Unrighteous. Woe to him that buildeth by—Jer. 22 : 13
Ultimate. He that built all things is God—Heb. 3 : 4
Wisdom. Wise man built his house on the—Mat. 7 : 24

493. ARK, Noah's. *Description.* [15]..The length of the ark *shall be* three hundred cubits, the breadth of it fifty cubits, and the height of it thirty cubits. [16] A window shalt thou make to the ark..and the door..in the side..*with* lower, second, and third *stories.*—GEN., ch. 6.

Also see

Mother of Moses. Ark of bulrushes..pitch   4484

494. ARMOR, A defenceless. *Goliath.* [5]..he had a helmet of brass..and..a coat of mail : and the weight of the coat *was* five thousand shekels of brass. [6] And *he had* greaves of brass upon his legs, and a target of brass between his shoulders. —1 SAM., ch. 17. [A pebble killed him.]

495. —— A rejected. *David.* [39]..David girded his sword upon his armor, and he essayed to go ; for he had not proved *it.* And David said unto Saul, I cannot go with these.—1 SAM., ch. 17.

496. ARMS, Destitution of. *Israelites.* [19]..there was no smith found throughout all the land of Israel : for the Philistines said, Lest the Hebrews make *them* swords or spears. [22]..in the day of battle..there was neither sword nor spear found in the hand of any..that *were* with Saul and Jonathan.—1 SAM., ch. 13.

497. ARMY, A great. *Uzziah.* [12] The whole number of the chief..of the mighty men of valour *were* two thousand and six hundred. [13] And under their hand *was* an army, three hundred thousand and seven thousand and five hundred.—2 CHRON., ch. 26.

498. —— impressed. *Saul.* [52]..there was sore war against the Philistines all the days of Saul : and when Saul saw any strong man, or any valiant man, he took him unto him.—1 SAM., ch. 14.

499. —— A strange. *David's.* [2]..every one that *was* in distress..that *was* in debt, and..*that was* discontented, gathered themselves unto him ; and he became a captain over them.. about four hundred men.—1 SAM., ch. 22.

500. —— A standing. *Saul.* [2] Saul chose him three thousand *men* of Israel..and the rest of the people he sent every man to his tent. —1 SAM., ch. 13.

501. —— A scattered. *Zedekiah.* [4]..the city was broken up, and all the men of war *fled* by night.. [5]..The Chaldees pursued after the king, and overtook him in the plains of Jericho : and all his army were scattered from him.— 2 KINGS, ch. 25.

See WAR and references.

502. ARROGANCE, Contemptible. *Bramble.* [15]..the bramble said unto the trees, If in truth ye anoint me king over you, *then* come *and* put your trust in my shadow ; and if not, let fire come out of the bramble, and devour the cedars of Lebanon.—JUDGES, ch. 9.

503. ARSON, Revenge by. *Ephraimites.* [1]..went northward, and said unto Jephthah, Wherefore passedst thou over to fight against the children of Ammon, and didst not call us to go with thee? we will burn thine house upon thee with fire.—JUDGES, ch. 12.

504. ART, An acquired. *Benjamites.* [16]..there were seven hundred chosen men lefthanded ; every one could sling stones at a hair *breadth,* and not miss.—JUDGES, ch. 20.

505. —— Beginning of. *Eden.* [8]..the Lord God planted a garden eastward in Eden ; and there he put the man whom he had formed.—GEN., ch. 2.

506. —— Defence by. *Chariots.* [19]..The Lord was with Judah ; and he drave out *the inhabitants of* the mountain ; but could not drive out the inhabitants of the valley, because they had chariots of iron.—JUDGES, ch. 1.

507. —— Destruction of corrupted. *Canaanites.* [52]..Ye shall drive out all the inhabitants.. and destroy all their images, and destroy all their molten images.—NUM., ch. 33.

508. —— in Deception. *Rebekah.* [15]..upon Jacob her younger son : [16]..she put the skins of the kids of the goats upon his hands, and upon the smooth of his neck.—GEN., ch. 27.

509. —— Helped by. *Uzziah.* [15]..he made in Jerusalem engines, invented by cunning men, to be on the towers and upon the bulwarks, to shoot arrows and great stones withal. And his name spread far abroad.—2 CHRON., ch. 26.

510. —— Inspiration for. *Bezaleel.* [31]..he hath filled him with the spirit of God, in wisdom, in understanding, and in knowledge, and in all manner of workmanship ; [32] And to de-

vise curious works, to work in gold, and in silver, and in brass, [33] And in the cutting of stones. —Ex., ch. 35.

511. —— Prostituted. *Calf.* [3]..all the people brake off the golden earrings which *were* in their ears, and brought *them* unto Aaron. [4] And he..fashioned it with a graving tool, after he had made it a molten calf.—Ex., ch. 32.

512. —— Restricted. *Altar.* [25]..if thou wilt make me an altar of stone, thou shalt not build it of hewn stone : for if thou lift up thy tool upon it, thou hast polluted it.—Ex., ch. 20.

513. —— shadowed. *Athens.* [16]..while Paul waited..at Athens, his spirit was stirred in him, when he saw the city wholly given to idolatry. —ACTS, ch. 17.

514. —— Woman's. *Ark.* [3]..when she could no longer hide him, she took for him an ark of bulrushes, and daubed it with slime and with pitch, and put the child therein ; and she laid *it* in the flags by the river's brink.—Ex., ch. 2.

515. ARTS, Deceptive. *Ephesians.* [19] Many of them also which used curious arts brought their books together, and burned them before all *men :* and they counted the price..fifty thousand *pieces* of silver.—ACTS, ch. 19.

516. —— of Wickedness. *Adulteress.* [16] I have decked my bed with coverings of tapestry, with carved *works,* with fine linen of Egypt. [17] I have perfumed my bed with myrrh, aloes, and cinnamon.—PROV., ch. 7.

517. ARTIFICE, Discovered. *David.* [19]..the king said, *Is not* the hand of Joab with thee in all this? And the woman answered..*As* thy soul liveth, my lord the king, none can turn to the right hand or to the left from aught that my lord the king hath spoken.—2 SAM., ch. 14.

518. ASCENSION, An Angel's. *Flame.* [20]..when the flame went up toward heaven from off the altar..the angel of the Lord ascended in the flame..and Manoah and his wife ..fell on their faces to the ground.—JUDGES, ch. 13.

519. —— of Enoch. *Translation.* [5] By faith Enoch was translated that he should not see death ; and was not found, because God had translated him : for..he had this testimony, that he pleased God.—Heb., ch. 11.

520. —— **of Elijah.** *Whirlwind.* [11]..as they still went on, and talked..*there appeared* a chariot of fire, and horses of fire, and parted them both asunder ; and Elijah went up by a whirlwind into heaven.—2 Kings, ch. 2.

521. —— **of Jesus.** *Blessing.* [50]..he led them out as far as to Bethany, and he lifted up his hands and blessed them. [51] And..while he blessed them, he was parted from them, and carried up into heaven.—Luke, ch. 24.

Also see
Comforting. Jacob dreamed..angels ascending   2503

522. ASPIRANT, A contemptible. *Bramble.* [15]..The bramble said unto the trees, If in truth ye anoint me king over you, *then* come *and* put your trust in my shadow ; and if not, let fire come out of the bramble, and devour the cedars of Lebanon.—Judges, ch. 9.

See other illustrations under :

AMBITION.

Fatal. Asahel refused to turn aside..Abner smote   318
Hypocrites. Scribes..love greetings..highest seats   321
Impious. Diotrephes..loveth the pre-eminence   317
Promotion. Brought you near him..Seek..priest   326
Reproved. [Disciples] had disputed which..great   320
Unsatisfied. [Haman] No man come in with the   332

523. ASSASSINATION, A foul. *Kissed Amasa.* [10]..Amasa took no heed to the sword that *was* in Joab's hand : so he smote him therewith in the fifth *rib*, and shed out his bowels to the ground, and struck him not again ; and he died. —2 Sam., ch. 20.

524. —— **Hired.** *Amnon.* [28]..Absalom had commanded his servants, saying, Mark ye now when Amnon's heart is merry with wine, and when I say unto you, Smite Amnon ; then kill him, fear not.—2 Sam., ch. 13.

525. —— **Patriotic.** *King of Moab.* [17]..he brought the present unto Eglon king of Moab.. [21] And Ehud put forth his left hand, and took the dagger from his right thigh, and thrust it into his belly.—Judges, ch. 3.

526. —— **Revenged by.** *Abner.* [27] When Abner was returned to Hebron, Joab took him aside in the gate to speak with him quietly, and smote him there under the fifth *rib*, that he died, for the blood of Asahel his brother.— 2 Sam., ch. 3.

See other illustrations under :

ASSASSINATION.

Attempted. Saul..to smite David..slipped away   5615
Atrocious. Ish-bosheth lay on a bed at noon..as   5619
Escape. Saul sent unto David's house..watch   5624
Prevented. Bound ourselves..curse..kill Paul   5752
Patriotic. Jael..smote the nail into his temples   3962
Suffocation. Hazael took a thick cloth..face   5634

527. ASSEMBLY, An eager. *Jesus.* [20]..the multitude cometh together again, so that they could not so much as eat bread. [21] And when his friends heard *of it*, they went out to lay hold on him : for they said, He is beside himself.— Mark, ch. 3.

528. —— **An evil.** *Murderers.* [3] Then assembled together the chief priests, and the scribes, and the elders of the people, unto the palace of the high priest, who was called Caiaphas. [4] And

consulted that they might take Jesus by subtilty, and kill *him*.—Mat., ch. 26.

529. —— **A great.** *Josiah.* [2]..the king went up into the house of the Lord..and the priests, and the prophets, and all the people, both small and great : and he read in their ears all the words of the book.—2 Kings, ch. 23.

530. —— **An important.** *Mount Carmel.* [19]..Gather to me all Israel..and the prophets of Baal four hundred and fifty, and the prophets of the groves four hundred.. [Fire fell upon Elijah's altar.] [39] And when all the people saw *it*, they fell on their faces : and they said, The Lord, he *is* the God.—1 Kings, ch. 18.

531. —— **of Nobility.** *Nebuchadnezzar.* [3]..the princes, the governors, and captains, the judges, the treasurers, the counsellors, the sheriffs, and all the rulers of the provinces, were gathered together unto the dedication of the image.— Dan., ch. 3.

532. —— **of Nations.** *Judgment.* [31] When the Son of man shall come in his glory, and all the holy angels with him, then shall he sit upon the throne of his glory ; [32] And before him shall be gathered all nations.—Mat., ch. 25.

533. —— **A persistent.** *Five Thousand.* [31].. Come ye yourselves apart into a desert place, and rest a while : for there were many coming and going, and they had no leisure so much as to eat. [33]..and many..ran afoot thither out of all cities, and outwent them, and came together unto him.—Mark, ch. 6.

534. —— **A pious.** *Ezra.* [1]..all the people gathered themselves together as one man into the street that *was* before the water gate ; and they spake unto Ezra the scribe to bring the book of the law of Moses.. [3]..and the ears of all the people *were attentive* unto the book.— Neh., ch. 8.

See other illustrations under :

ARMY.

Great. [Uzziah's army,] 37,500 men   497
Impressed. Saul saw any strong man he took   498
Strange. Every one..in distress, debt, discontented   499
Standing. Saul chose 3000..the rest..his tent   500
Scattered. [Zedekiah's,] Chaldees pursued..army   501

MOB.

Bigots. Two hours cried out, Great is Diana   5487
Disturbance. Lewd fellows of the baser sort..up   5488
Murderous. City was moved..people ran..took   5489
Trial by. Cried..loud voice..ran upon Stephen   5491
Tumultuous. Left beating Paul..some cried one   5490
Workmen. By this craft we have our wealth   5492

Immense. [Israelites] About 600,000 footmen be   2631
Overflowing. [At Capernaum] No room, not..   1850
Slaughter. Jehu said, Proclaim an assembly for   5251
  See REVIVAL.

535. ASSESSMENT for Tribute. *Menahem.* [19] Pul the king of Assyria came against the land : and Menahem gave Pul a thousand talents of silver..to confirm the kingdom in his hand. [About $1,811,000.] [20] And Menahem exacted the money of Israel, *even* of all the mighty men of wealth, of each man fifty shekels of silver. [About $27 each.]—2 Kings, ch. 15.

See other illustrations under :

TAX.

Burdensome. That which thou puttest on me I   8595
Collector. Levi sitting at the receipt of custom   8596

TAXATION.

Exempted. Ministers..not be lawful to impose.. 8597
    "   King will make his house free in Israel 8598
Endangered. Then will they not pay tribute..the 8599
Eminence by. He shall stand up a raiser of taxes 8600
Foreign. Jehoiakim..according to his taxation 8601
Lawful. Render unto Cesar the things..are C. 8602
Oppressive. We have borrowed money for the 8603
Secession. Make..this heavy yoke lighter..will 8604
Universal. Joseph also went up..to be taxed with 8605

TRIBUTE.

Sheep. King of Moab rendered..100,000 lambs 8952
Useless. Ahaz took a portion..but he helped him 8954

536. ASSIMILATION, Gospel. *Leaven.* 33..the kingdom of heaven is like unto leaven which a woman took, and hid in three measures of meal, till the whole was leavened.—MAT., ch. 13.

537. ASSISTANCE, Independent of. *Paul.* 33 I have coveted no man's silver, or gold, or apparel. 34..these hands have ministered unto my necessities, and to them that were with me.—ACTS, ch. 20. [To Ephesian elders.]

See other illustrations under:

HELP.

Appeal. Come over into Macedonia and help 3925
    "   Help my lord, O King..hid her son 3926

HELPER.

Angelic. [Gethsemane] An angel..from..strength 3937
Builders. Whosoever remaineth..help him with 3942
Dependence. Aaron and Hur stayed up his hands 3943
Divine. I will be with thy mouth and teach 3928
    "   Let us flee from..Israel, the L. fighteth 3929
    "   Wherewith shall I save Israel? Gideon 3930
    "   King of Syria..more with us..him 3931
    "   Samuel..stone..called it Ebenezer 3938
Excused. Mary hath chosen that good part..not 7812
Forbidden. Woe to them that ..to Egypt for help 292
Fraternal. Ye shall pass over before your brethren 3927
Hurtful. Ahaz took a portion..he helped him not 3932
Injurious. Uzziah when he was strong..heart lift 3933
Needed. If there be no man to save us..will 3934
Pay. Who is there that would shut the doors for 7818
Petition. Come..save me..of the king of Syria 290
Provided. L. saw..saved them by..Jeroboam 3939
Reserved. Father..will give me twelve legions 3935
Rewarded. Give you a cup of water..not lose his 7819
Sought. [Canaanite woman] Send her away..L. 3936
Woman. I will make him a help meet 3941
Wanted. I have no man..to put me in 3940

538. ASSOCIATES, Apostasy from. *Solomon.* 1..king Solomon loved many strange women, together with the daughter of Pharaoh, women of the Moabites, Ammonites, Edomites, Zidonians, *and* Hittites. 5..and his wives turned away his heart.—1 KINGS, ch. 11.

539. —— Burdensome. *David.* 39..I am this day weak, though anointed king ; and these men the sons of Zeruiah be too hard for me.— 2 SAM., ch. 3.

540. —— Beneficial. *Sons and Wives.* 1..Come thou and all thy house into the ark ; for thee have I seen righteous before me in this generation. 7 And Noah went in, and his sons, and his wife, and his sons' wives with him, into the ark.—GEN., ch. 7.

541. —— Corrupt. *Israelites.* 34 They did not destroy the nations, concerning whom the Lord commanded them : 35 But were mingled among the heathen, and learned their works. 36 And

they served their idols : which were a snare unto them.—Ps. 106.

542. —— Dangerous. *Sodomites.* 11..Lot chose him all the plain of Jordan ; and Lot journeyed east.. 12..Lot dwelt in the cities of the plain, and pitched *his* tent toward Sodom. 13 But the men of Sodom *were* wicked and sinners before the Lord exceedingly.—GEN., ch. 13.

543. —— Forbidden. *Paul.* 11..I have written unto you not to keep company, if any man that is called a brother be a fornicator, or covetous, or an idolater, or a railer, or a drunkard, or an extortioner ; with such a one no not to eat.— 1 COR., ch. 5.

544. —— —— Disobedient. 14..if any man obey not our word by this epistle, note that man, and have no company with him, that he may be ashamed. 15 Yet count *him* not as an enemy, but admonish *him* as a brother.—2 THESS., ch. 3.

545. —— Hurtful. *Canaanites.* 55..if ye will not drive out the inhabitants of the land..then ..those which ye let remain of them *shall be* pricks in your eyes, and thorns in your sides, and shall vex you in the land wherein ye dwell.— NUM., ch. 33. [See No. 541.]

546. —— Intolerable. *Sodomites.* [God] 7..delivered just Lot, vexed with the filthy conversation of the wicked : 8 For that righteous man dwelling among them, in seeing and hearing, vexed *his* righteous soul from day to day with *their* unlawful deeds.—2 PET., ch. 2.

547. —— Ill-chosen. *Peter.* 54..Peter followed him afar off, even into the palace of the high priest : and he sat with the servants, and warmed himself at the fire.—MARK, ch. 14.

548. —— Influence of. *Solomon.* 24 Make no friendship with an angry man ; and with a furious man thou shalt not go. 25 Lest thou learn his ways, and get a snare to thy soul.—PROV., ch. 22.

549. —— Likeness to. *Antediluvians.* 2..the sons of God saw the daughters of men that they *were* fair ; and they took them wives of all which they chose.—GEN., ch. 6. [See No. 552.]

550. —— Saved by. *Paul.* 13..the woman which hath a husband that believeth not, and if he be pleased to dwell with her, let her not leave him. 14 For the unbelieving husband is sanctified by the wife, and the unbelieving wife is sanctified by the husband.—1 COR., ch. 7.

551. —— —— Brothers. 14 Simon..and Andrew his brother, James and John [his brother], Philip and Bartholomew, 15 Matthew and Thomas, James the *son* of Alpheus, and Simon called Zelotes, 16 And Judas *the brother* of James, and Judas Iscariot, which also was the traitor.— LUKE, ch. 6. [Three pairs of brothers.]

552. —— Uncorrupted by. *Antediluvians.* 5 God saw that the wickedness of man *was* great in the earth, and *that* every imagination of the thoughts of his heart *was* only evil continually. 8 But Noah found grace in the eyes of the Lord.— GEN., ch. 6.

553. —— Worthy. *Hebrew Children.* 16 Melzar took away the portion of their meat, and the wine that they should drink ; and gave them pulse. 17..God gave them knowledge and skill in all learning and wisdom : and Daniel had understanding in all visions and dreams.—DAN., ch. 1.

554. ASSOCIATIONS, Happy. *Queen of Sheba to Solomon.* [8] Happy *are* thy men, happy *are* these thy servants, which stand continually before thee, *and* that hear thy wisdom.—1 KINGS, ch. 10.

555. —— **Helpful.** *Jehoram.* [14] Elisha said, As the Lord of hosts liveth, before whom I stand, surely, were it not that I regard the presence of Jehoshaphat the king of Judah, I would not look toward thee, nor see thee.—2 KINGS, ch. 3.

See other illustrations under:

ALLIANCE.

Contaminating. Ahaz went to Damascus..fashion 290
Dangerous. Make [David] return..in the battle.. 291
Failure. Egyptians are men, and not God 293
Forbidden. Woe..go down to Egypt for help 292
Treacherous. Gibeonites..Joshua..league with the 294

SOCIETY.

Changed. Now they that are younger..in derision 8150
Conservator. Ye are the salt of the earth 8151
Influence. He that walketh with wise men shall 8152
Miserable. Every one that was in distress 8153
Needful. It is not good for man to be alone 8154
Respect of. Young men..hid themselves, and the 8155

Condemned. This man receiveth sinners and eateth 778
Influence. Herod feared John, knowing..heard 89
Ruinous. Taketh seven other..more wicked than 1112
  See FRIEND and FRIENDSHIP.
  See UNION and UNITY.

556. ASSUMPTION rebuked. *Highest Seat.* [8] When thou art bidden..to a wedding, sit not down in the highest room; lest a more honourable man than thou be bidden of him; [9]..Give this man place; and thou begin with shame to take the lowest room.—LUKE, ch. 14.

Also see

Contemptible. The bramble..trees..anoint me king 561
  See ARROGANCE and references.

557. ASSURANCE, Believer's. *Job.* [25] I know *that* my Redeemer liveth, and *that* he shall stand at the latter *day* upon the earth.—JOB, ch. 19.

558. —— **A full.** *Paul.* [38] I am persuaded, that neither death, nor life, nor angels, nor principalities, nor powers, nor things present, nor things to come, [39] Nor height, nor depth, nor any other creature, shall be able to separate us from the love of God.—ROM., ch. 8.

559. —— **A heavenly.** *Paul.* [1]..we know that, if our earthly house of *this* tabernacle were dissolved, we have a building of God, a house not made with hands, eternal in the heavens.—2 COR., ch. 5.

560. —— **Inferential.** *Manoah.* [23]..his wife said unto him, If the Lord were pleased to kill us, he would not have received a burnt offering and a meat offering at our hands, neither would he have shewed us all these *things*.—JUDGES, ch. 13.

561. —— **Impudent.** *Bramble.* [15] The bramble said unto the trees, If in truth ye anoint me king over you, *then* come *and* put your trust in my shadow; and if not, let fire come out of the bramble, and devour the cedars of Lebanon.—JUDGES, ch. 9.

562. —— **A personal.** *Paul.* [20]..I am not ashamed; for I know whom I have believed, and am persuaded that he is able to keep that which

I have committed unto him against that day.—1 TIM., ch. 1.

563. —— **The Victor's.** *Paul.* [35] Who shall separate us from the love of Christ? *shall* tribulation, or distress, or persecution, or famine, or nakedness, or peril, or sword? [37] Nay, in all these things we are more than conquerors through him that loved us.—ROM., ch. 8.

See other illustrations under:

CONFIDENCE.

Believers. Though I walk through the valley 1518
Blind. Know I that the L..I have a priest 1519
Caution. They are smitten down..as at the first 1520
Disappointed. Ark came..I. shouted..ark taken 1521
False. King [of Ai] wist not..ambush 1522
Future. Doth deliver..trust he will deliver 1523
Intelligent. I know whom I have believed 1524
Joyful. How great is thy goodness..trust thee 1525
Over. Is thy servant a dog..do this? [Hazael] 1526
Peril. Have the sentence of death..we trust 1527
Piety begets. L. was with Joseph..into his hand 1528
Strong. L. delight in us..fear them not 1529
Self. Peter said..I will lay down my life 1530
Triumphant. Although the fig tree shall not b. 1531
Unwarranted. Let two or three three thousand go 1532
Unfortunate. Confidence..like a broken tooth and 1533
Undermining. Neither let Hez. make you trust..L. 1534
Warranted. L. is my rock, fortress, deliverer 1535

TRUST.

Active. Hezekiah clave to the L..rebelled against 9008
Courageous. Thou comest..I come..in the name 9009
Experience. L. who delivered me..the paw of the 9010
Egotists. Pharisee..I..I..I..I..I 9011
Fearless. Our G..is able to deliver us..furnace 9012
  " Though I walk through the valley 9013
  " The Lord is on my side, I will not fear 9014
Fixed. Though he slay me, yet will I trust 9015
Foolish. Bramble said..Put your trust in my 9016
Honoured. Cried to G. in the battle..trust in him 9017
  " Angel smote..Assyrians 185,000 9018
Ill-timed. Let us fetch the ark..it may save us 9020
Providence. May boldly say, The L. is my helper 9021
Self. Philistine..saw David..disdained him 9022

Faith's. Enoch..had this testimony..pleased God 519
  See FAITH and references.

564. ASTONISHMENT, Great. *Disciples.* [24]..he arose, and rebuked the wind and the raging of the water: and they ceased, and there was a calm. [25]..And they being afraid wondered, saying..What manner of man is this? for he commandeth even the winds and water, and they obey him.—LUKE, ch. 8.

565. —— **at a Mystery.** *Nebuchadnezzar.* [24]..Nebuchadnezzar the king was astonied, and rose up in haste..and said..Did not we cast three men bound into the midst of the fire? [25]..Lo, I see four men loose, walking.—DAN., ch. 3.

566. —— **Sacred.** *Manoah.* [20]..the angel of the Lord ascended in the flame of the altar: and Manoah and his wife looked on *it*, and fell on their faces to the ground. [22] And Manoah said, We shall surely die, because we have seen God.—JUDGES, ch. 13.

567. —— **at Speech.** *Tongues.* [7]..they were all amazed and marvelled, saying..Behold, are not all these which speak Galileans? [8] And how hear we every man in our own tongue, wherein we were born?—ACTS, ch. 2.

568. —— **Overwhelming.** *Disciples.* [48]..he cometh unto them, walking upon the sea. [50]..Be of good cheer : it is I ; be not afraid. [51] And he went..into the ship ; and the wind ceased : and they were sore amazed in themselves beyond measure, and wondered.—MARK, ch. 6.

See other illustrations under :

Resurrection. Mary..I know not..turned and saw 6518

See AMAZEMENT and references.

569. ASTROLOGERS puzzled. *Babylonians.* [8] Then came in all the king's wise *men :* but they could not read the writing, nor make known to the king the interpretation thereof.—DAN., ch. 5.

See other illustrations under :

SORCERY.

Captivating. Simon bewitched the people..all 8202
Renounced. Simon himself believed..was bapt'd 8203
    "   [Ephesians] used curious arts 8204

WITCHCRAFT.

Abolished. Workers with familiar spirits..put 9649
Work of. The woman saw Samuel, she cried..loud 9648

Curious Arts. [Ephesians] used curious arts..burn 908
Imposition. Magicians..cast down..rod..serpent 5162

570. ATHEISM, Folly of. *David.* [1]..The fool hath said in his heart, *There is* no God.—Ps. 14.

571. ATONEMENT accepted. *Abel.* [4] Abel, he also brought of the firstlings of his flock and of the fat thereof. And the Lord had respect unto Abel and to his offering.—GEN., ch. 4.

572. —— **Blood of.** *Law.* [11] The life of the flesh *is* in the blood ; and I have given it to you upon the altar to make an atonement for your souls : for it *is* the blood *that* maketh an atonement for the soul.—LEV., ch. 17.

573. —— **Death stayed by.** *Plague.* [47] Aaron ..ran into the midst of the congregation..and he put on incense, and made an atonement for the people. [4b] And he stood between the dead and the living ; and the plague was stayed.—NUM., ch. 16.

574. —— **of Justice.** *Sheba.* [21]..Sheba..hath lifted up his hand against..David : deliver him only, and I will depart from the city. And the woman said unto Joab, Behold, his head shall be thrown to thee over the wall.—2 SAM., ch. 20.

575. —— **omitted.** *Cain.* [3]..Cain brought of the fruit of the ground an offering unto the Lord.. [5] But unto Cain and to his offering he had not respect. And Cain was very wroth.—GEN., ch. 4.

576. —— **Sorrow of.** *Gethsemane.* [38]..My soul is exceeding sorrowful, even unto death.. [39]..O my Father, if it be possible, let this cup pass from me.—MAT., ch. 26.

577. —— **Sufferings of.** *Cross.* [46]..Jesus cried with a loud voice, saying, Eli, Eli, lama sabachthani ? that is to say, My God, my God, why hast thou forsaken me ?—MAT., ch. 27.

See other illustrations under :

BLOOD.

Access. Boldness to enter the holiest by the blood 851
Acceptance. Moses took the blood..sprinkled 852
Behold. Strike it on..door posts..houses 854
Blood for. Slain [Ish-bosheth]..blood at your hand 855
Cleansing. If the blood of bulls .more the blood of 856
Consecration. Aaron's right ear..thumb..great toe 857
Changed to. Rod smote..river..turned to blood 858

Defilement. [David] Not build..shed much blood 859
Protection. When I see the blood I will pass over 860
Prohibition. Eateth any manner of blood..cut him 861
Redemption. Not..silver and gold..precious..of C. 862
Responsibility. Intend..this man's blood upon us 863
Speaking. Blood of sprinkling speaketh better 864
Sprinkling. Moses sprinkled..people..Behold 865
Sweat. [Gethsemane] His sweat was as it were 866
Truth. Moses sprinkled both the book and..people 867
Testament. This cup is the N. T. in my blood 868

REDEMPTION.

Blood. Not..silver and gold..blood of Christ 6910
Power. Horse and his rider..cast into the sea 6911

578. ATROCITY, Impious. *Pilate.* [1]..some ..that told him of the Galileans, whose blood Pilate had mingled with their sacrifices.—LUKE, ch. 13.

See CRUELTY and references.

579. ATTACHMENT, Affectionate. *Jesus.* [On the night of his betrayal,] [6]..cometh he to Simon Peter ; and Peter saith unto him, Lord, dost thou wash my feet ?—JOHN, ch. 13.

580. —— **claimed.** *Jesus.* [37] He that loveth father or mother..son or daughter more than me is not worthy of me. [38] And he that taketh not his cross, and followeth after me, is not worthy of me.—MAT., ch. 10.

581. —— **An inseparable.** *Ruth.* [16]..whither thou goest, I will go ; and where thou lodgest, I will lodge : thy people *shall be* my people, and thy God my God : [17] Where thou diest, will I die, and there will I be buried : the Lord do so to me, and more also, *if aught* but death part thee and me.—RUTH, ch. 1.

See FRIENDSHIP and references.

582. ATTENDANCE, A divine. *Joshua.* [The Lord said,] [9]..Be strong and of a good courage ; be not afraid, neither be thou dismayed : for the Lord thy God *is* with thee whithersoever thou goest. —JOSH., ch. 1.

See other illustrations under :

GUIDE.

Blind. Woe unto you, ye blind guides 3760
Divine. By day in a pillar of cloud..night..fire 3757
Human. Leave us not..be to us instead of eyes 3758
Necessary. How can I, except some..guide me 3759

GUIDANCE.

Divine. The kine took the straight way..to B. 3761
Explained. Lest peradventure..see war and they 3762
Gentle. I will guide thee with mine eye 3763
Promised. Acknowledge him..direct thy paths 3764
Waiting. If the cloud were not taken up 3765

PRESENCE.

Acknowledged. I have seen..the L. is with him 6512
Conditioned. Neither will I be with you except 6513
Effect. No man shall be able to stand before thee 6514
Indicated. Priests could not..minister..cloud 6515
Indispensable. If thy presence go not with me 6516
Jesus. Into the ship, the wind ceased..amazed 6517
    "   I know not..turned and saw Jesus 6518
    "   [Disciples'] eyes were holden [at Emmaus] 6519
    "   Did not our heart burn within us 6520
Misjudged. After..after..a still small voice 6521
Manifested. Cloud covered the tabernacle..fire 6522
Questioned. Meribah..saying is the L..among us 6523
Sign. Hearest the sound..mulberry trees..bestir 6524
Undiscovered. Here am I, thou didst call me [Sam] 6525
Withdrawn. Ye have turned..the L. will not be 6526

583. AUTHOR, A voluminous. *Solomon.* [32] He spake three thousand proverbs : and his songs were a thousand and five. [33] And he spake of trees, from the cedar tree that *is* in Lebanon even unto the hyssop that springeth out of the wall : he spake also of beasts, and of fowl, and of creeping things, and of fishes.—1 Kings, ch. 4.

See other illustrations under :

BOOK.

Blood. Moses..sprinkled both the book..people 901
Completed. If any add..God shall add the plagues 902
Christian. Ye are our epistle..read of all men 903
Discovered. I have found the book of the law 904
of God. Forgive..and if not blot me out..thy book 905
Life. Written in the Lamb's book of life 906
Remembrance. Book of remembrance was written 907

BOOKS.

Burned Books. [Ephesians] used curious arts..b. 908
Increase. Of making.many. there is no end 909
Lost Books. Books of Arnon..book of Jasher 910

584. AUTHORITY, A Brother's. *David* [29]..said, Let me go, I pray thee ; for our family hath a sacrifice in the city ; and my brother, he hath commanded me *to be there.*—1 Sam., ch. 20.

585. —— Comparison of. *Adulteress.* [4]..Master, this woman was taken in adultery, in the very act. [5] Now Moses in the law commanded us, that such should be stoned : but what sayest thou ?—John, ch. 8.

586. —— False. *Bethel Prophet.* [11]..there dwelt an old prophet in Beth-el ; [18] He said..I *am* a prophet also as thou *art;* and an angel spake unto me by the word of the Lord, saying, Bring him back with thee into thine house, that he may eat bread and drink water. *But* he lied unto him.—1 Kings, ch. 13.

587. —— Obedience to. *Israelites.* [16]..they answered Joshua, saying, All that thou commandest us we will do, and withersoever thou sendest us, we will go.—Josh., ch. 1.

588. —— Power of. *Military.* [The centurion said to Jesus,] [8]..having under me soldiers..I say unto one, Go, and he goeth ; and to another, Come, and he cometh ; and to my servant, Do this, and he doeth *it.*—Luke, ch. 7.

589. —— questioned. *Jesus.* [23] When he was come into the temple, the chief priests and the elders..said, By what authority doest thou these things ? and who gave thee this authority ?—Mat., ch. 21.

590. —— recognized. *Jesus.* [15]..made a scourge of small cords, he drove them all out of the temple, and the sheep, and the oxen ; and poured out the changers' money, and overthrew the tables ; [16] And said unto them that sold doves, Take these things hence ; make not my Father's house a house of merchandise.—John, ch. 2.

591. —— Supreme. *Jesus.* [24] They..awoke him, saying, Master, Master, we perish. Then he arose, and rebuked the wind and the raging of the water : and they ceased, and there was a calm. [25]..What manner of man is this ! for he commandeth even the winds and water, and they obey him.—Luke, ch. 8.

See other illustrations under :

INFLUENCE.

Felt. Herod feared John..did many things 4471
Leaders. Have any of the rulers..believed on him 4472

Parental. Rechabites..father commanded..drink 4473
Posthumous. He being dead, yet speaketh 4474
Pernicious. Pharisees..neither go in yourselves 4476
Refused. Ahasuerus commanded Vashti..came not 4480
Supernatural. Cart..ark..kine took the straight 4481

POWER.

Delegated. Faith as a..of mustard seed..remove 6312
Endowment. All filled with the H. G. and began 6313
God given. [Samson,] S. of the L. began to move 6314
God only. Why marvel..we had made..to walk 6315
Lost. Samson wist not that the L. was departed 6316
Might or. Not.by might nor by power..O great 6317
Promised. Not any man be able to stand..thee 6318
Prayer. Prayed against Sennacherib..185,000 slain 6319
Preaching. Demonstration of the S. and..power 6320
Ruling. Rebuked the wind.. raging..they ceased 6321
Spiritual. Not able to resist the..Stephen spake 6322
by Spirit. Spirit..came mightily upon Samson 6323
Sudden. Pharaoh said unto Joseph, And without 6324
Temptation. All the kingdoms..if..worship me 6325
Testimony. After the H. G. is come..be witnesses 6326
Tears. The babe [Moses] wept..she had compas'n 6327
Weakness. I am..weak though..king [David] 6328
Waiting. Jerusalem..wait for the promise of the 6329

Credentials. Art thou he..? Tell John..blind see 1824
"   Rod of Aaron was budded..almonds 1825
Dominion. Fear of you..upon every beast of the 2490
See GOVERNMENT.

592. AVARICE begets Falsehood. *Ananias.* [1]..a certain man named Ananias, with Sapphira his wife, sold a possession, [2] And kept back *part* of the price..and brought a certain part, and laid *it* at the apostles' feet.—Acts, ch. 5.

593. —— Oppression from. *Jews.* [4] Hear this, O ye that swallow up the needy, even to make the poor of the land to fail, [5]..making the ephah small and the shekel great, and falsifying the balances by deceit ? [6] That we may buy the poor for silver, and the needy for a pair of shoes ; *yea,* and sell the refuse of the wheat ? —Amos, ch. 8.

594. —— Victim of. *Judas.* [4]..he went his way, and communed with the chief priests and captains, how he might betray him unto them. [5] And they were glad, and covenanted to give him money.—Luke, ch. 22.

See COVETOUSNESS and references.

595. AWAKENING of Conscience. *Herod* [his murderer] [14]..said, That John the Baptist was risen from the dead, and therefore mighty works do shew forth themselves in him.—Mark, ch. 6.

596. —— through Fear. *Crucifixion.* [54] When the centurion, and they that were with him, watching Jesus, saw the earthquake, and those things that were done, they feared greatly, saying, Truly this was the Son of God.—Mat., ch. 27.

597. —— A great. *Reign of Josiah.* [2] The king went up into the house of the Lord..and the priests, and the prophets, and all the people, both small and great : and he read in their ears all the words of the book.—2 Kings, ch. 23.

598. —— A general. *John.* [5] There went out unto him all the land of Judea, and they of Jerusalem, and were all baptized of him in the river of Jordan, confessing their sins.—Mark, ch. 1.

599. —— **A sudden.** *Jailer.* [29] He called for a light, and sprang in, and came trembling, and fell down before Paul and Silas, [30] And brought them out, and said, Sirs, what must I do to be saved?—ACTS, ch. 16.

600. —— **in Trouble.** *Egyptians.* [24]..in the morning watch the Lord looked unto the.. Egyptians through the pillar of fire and of the cloud, and troubled the..Egyptians, [25] And took off their chariot wheels, that they drave them heavily : so that the Egyptians said, Let us flee from the face of Israel.—Ex., ch. 14.

601. —— **by the Truth.** *Felix.* [25] As [Paul] reasoned of righteousness, temperance, and judgment to come, Felix trembled, and answered, Go thy way for this time ; when I have a convenient season, I will call for thee.—ACTS, ch. 24.

602. —— **Unexpected.** *Sons of Jacob.* [21] They said one to another, We *are* verily guilty concerning our brother, in that we saw the anguish of his soul, when he besought us, and we would not hear ; therefore is this distress come upon us.—GEN., ch. 42.

See other illustrations under :

CONVICTION.

Awakening. Made manifest by the light..Awake   1682
Deeds. By this I know thou art..man of God   1684
Examination. Searched the Scriptures..many b'd   1685
Heaven sent. Suddenly there shined a light   1686
Heartfelt. Pricked in their heart..[Pentecost]   1687
Irresistible. Fire fell..consumed..stones..dust   1694
Necessary. Sprung up..no deepness of earth   1688
Prayer. Make me to know my transgression   1689
Resisted. Miracles before them..believed not   1690
Rational. When he came to himself..I will arise   1691
Sensitive. David's heart smote him..Saul's skirt   1692
Smiting. David's heart smote him..numbered   1693
Sudden. People saw it..fell..L. he is God   1694
Speechless. Beholding the man..healed..say n.   1695
Truth. Josiah..heard..the book of the..he rent   1696
Thorough. Digged deep..the foundation on a rock   1697
Transient. Centurion..earthquake..was the S. of   1698
Willing. Nathanael..Thou art the Son of God   1699

CONTRITION.

Accepted. Because..heart was tender..heard thee   1664
Annual. In the seventh month..afflict your souls   1665
Bitter. [Passover] Eat the flesh with bitter herbs   1666

Reading. Baruch read the book..they were afraid   749
    "   Shaphan read it..king rent his clothes   752
    "   All the people wept when they heard   763
    See REVIVAL and references.

603. AWE, Alarming. *Manoah.* [22] Manoah said unto his wife, We shall surely die, because we have seen God.—JUDGES, ch. 13.

604. —— **Painful.** *Gideon.* [22] When Gideon perceived that he *was* an angel of the Lord, Gideon said, Alas, O Lord God ! because I have seen an angel of the Lord face to face.—JUDGES, ch. 6.

See other illustrations under :

REVERENCE.

Attitude. Ezra opened the book..people stood up   7316
Affectionate. Mary stood at his feet, behind him   7317
Age. Joseph brought in Jacob..blessed Pharaoh   7318
Careful. Put off thy shoes from thy feet..holy   7319
Commanded. No man..be seen..all the mount   7320
Commended. Peter fell down at Jesus'..fisher   7321
Esteem. Mephibosheth..fell on his face and did   7322
Joyous. There came a fire..people shouted and   7323

Manifested. [Joshua] Loose thy shoe from off   7324
Necessary. To this man will I look..contrite spirit   7325
    "   Men of Bethshemesh..looked into the   7326
Preserved by. Third captain..fell on his knees   7327
Unworthy of. All the king's servants..reverenced   7328
The Word. Ezra opened the book..people stood   7329
Worthy. Sent his son..they will reverence my son   7330
Youthful. [Young ruler] came running and kneel   7331

PROSTRATION.

Involuntary. I am he..they fell to the ground   6705
Sinners. Saul fell to the earth..Saul, Saul   6706
    "   [King] Saul fell on the earth   6707
of God. Moses hid his face..look upon God   3580

605. BABES, Spiritual. *Paul.* [1]..I, brethren, could not speak unto..you as unto spiritual, but as unto carnal, *even* as unto babes in Christ. [2] I have fed you with milk, and not with meat : for hitherto ye were not able *to bear it*, neither yet now are ye able.—1 COR., ch. 3.

See other illustrations under :

INFANTS.

Accident. Woman's child died..she overlaid it   4450
Heaven. Suffer little children..Such..heaven   4451
Murder. Every son..cast into the river. [Pharaoh]   4452
Massacre. Herod..slew all..in Bethlehem two yrs.   4453
Regarded. Brought infants..Jesus called them   4454
Sympathy. [Moses] Babe wept..She had comp'n   107
    See CHILD.

606. BACHELOR, Justification of the. *Paul.* [26] This is good for the present distress, *I say*, that it *is* good for a man so to be. [27] Art thou bound unto a wife? seek not to be loosed. Art thou loosed from a wife? seek not a wife.—1 COR., ch. 7.

607. —— **The unfortunate.** *Adam.* [18] The Lord God said, *It is* not good that the man should be alone ; I will make him a help meet for him.—GEN., ch. 2.

See other illustrations under :

Relief. Daughters of Shiloh come out to dance   5243
Seducing Spirits. In the latter times..forbidding   5919
    See MARRIAGE.

— BACKBITING. —— ——

See illustrations under :

SLANDER.

Antidote. They may by your good works..glorify   8101
Base. This fellow doth cast out devils by Beelzebub   8102
Disgraceful. We found this man a pestilent fellow   8103
Folly. He that uttereth a slander is a fool   8104
Hurtful. Then will they not pay tribute   8105
Impious. He saved others ; himself he cannot save   8106
Joyful. Blessed..men revile you..rejoice   8107
Loyalty. Ziba said..he abideth at Jerusalem   8108
Malicious. Diotrephes..prating against us   8109
Opposed. It is reported..be their king   8110
Refuted. If Satan cast out Satan..divided   8111
Rebels. The people is greater than we   8112
Sinners. Thou art an austere man   8113
Satan's. Touch all that he hath..will curse   8114
Secret. A whisperer separateth friends   8115
Unbelief. Would to G. we had died..by flesh pots   8116

Satan's. God doth know..ye shall be as gods   8117

608. BACKSLIDERS, Compassion for. *Paul.* [6] Sufficient to such a man *is* this punishment, which *was inflicted* of many. [7] So that contrariwise ye *ought* rather to forgive *him*, and comfort *him*, lest perhaps such a one should be swallowed up with overmuch sorrow.—2 COR., ch. 2.

609. —— **Deterioration of.** *Seven Spirits.* [45] Then goeth he, and taketh with himself seven other spirits more wicked than himself, and they enter in and dwell there ; and the last *state* of that man is worse than the first.—Mat., ch. 12.

610. —— —— *Worse.* [20] If after they have escaped the pollutions of the world. .they are again entangled therein, and overcome, the latter end is worse with them than the beginning.— 2 Peter, ch. 2.

611. —— **entreated.** *Jeremiah.* [12] Go and proclaim these words. .and say, Return, thou backsliding Israel, saith the Lord ; *and* I will not cause mine anger to fall upon you : for I *am* merciful, saith the Lord, *and* I will not keep *anger* for ever. [13] Only acknowledge thine iniquity.—Jer., ch. 3.

612. —— **Folly of.** *David.* [176] I have gone astray like a lost sheep : seek thy servant.—Ps. 119.

613. —— **Image of.** *Dog—Sow.* [22] It is happened unto them according to the true proverb, The dog *is* turned to his own vomit again ; and, The sow that was washed to her wallowing in the mire.—2 Peter, ch. 2.

614. —— **Penitence of.** *Jews.* [21] A voice was heard upon the high places, weeping *and* supplications of the children of Israel ; for they have perverted their way, *and* they have forgotten the Lord their God. [22] Return, ye backsliding children, *and* I will heal your backslidings. Behold, we come unto thee ; for thou *art* the Lord our God.—Jer., ch. 3.

615. —— **Unhappiness of.** *Saul.* [14] The Spirit of the Lord departed from Saul, and an evil spirit from the Lord troubled him. . [17] And Saul said. .Provide me now a man that can play well, and bring *him* to me.—1 Sam., ch. 16.

616. BACKSLIDING angers God. *Solomon.* [9] The Lord was angry with Solomon because his heart was turned from the Lord. .which had appeared unto him twice.—1 Kings, ch. 11.

617. —— **in old Age.** *Noah.* [20] Noah. . planted a vineyard : [21] And he drank of the wine, and was drunken ; and he was uncovered within his tent.—Gen., ch. 9. [More than six hundred years old.]

618. —— **Beginning of.** *Peter.* [58] Peter followed him afar off unto the high priest's palace, and went in, and sat with the servants, to see the end.—Mat., ch. 26.

619. —— **Cause of.** *Stony Ground.* [16] When they have heard the word, immediately receive it with gladness ; [17] And have no root in themselves, and so endure but for a time ; afterward, when affliction or persecution ariseth for the word's sake, immediately they are offended.— —Mark, ch. 4.

620. —— **detected.** *Proverb.* [14] The backslider in heart shall be filled with his own ways. —Prov., ch. 14.

621. —— **Folly of.** *Broken Cistern.* [13] My people have committed two evils ; they have forsaken me the fountain of living waters, *and* hewed them out cisterns, broken cisterns, that can hold no water.—Jer., ch. 2.

622. —— **Origin of.** *Loss of Love.* [4] . .I have *somewhat* against thee, because thou hast left thy first love. [5] Remember therefore from whence thou art fallen, and repent, and do the first works ; or else I. .will remove thy candlestick out of his place.—Rev., ch. 2.

623. —— **Profitless.** *Amaziah.* [15] The anger of the Lord was kindled against Amaziah, and he sent unto him a prophet, which said. .Why hast thou sought after the gods of the people, which could not deliver their own people out of thine hand ?—2 Chron., ch. 25.

624. —— **Perilous.** *"Die."* [24] When the righteous turneth away from his righteousness, and committeth iniquity. .shall he live ? All his righteousness that he hath done shall not be mentioned : in his trespass. .and in his sin. .in them shall he die.—Ezek., ch. 18.

625. —— **repeated.** *Abram.* [18] Pharaoh called Abram, and said, What *is* this *that* thou hast done unto me ? why didst thou not tell me that she *was* thy wife ?—Gen., ch. 12. [2] Abraham said of Sarah his wife, She *is* my sister : and Abimelech king of Gerar. .took Sarah.—Gen., ch. 20.

626. —— **by Wandering.** *Sheep.* [6] All we like sheep have gone astray ; we have turned every one to his own way.—Isa., ch. 53.

See other illustrations under :

—— **BADGE.** —— ——

See illustrations under :

—— **BALANCE.** —— ——

See illustrations under :

627. BALDNESS no Deformity. *Law.* [40] The man whose hair is fallen off his head, he *is* bald ; *yet is* he clean.—Lev., ch. 13.

628. —— **ridiculed.** *Bethel Children.* [23] As he was going up by the way, there came forth little children out of the city, and mocked him, and said unto him, Go up, thou bald head. . [24] . .there came forth two she bears. .and tare forty and two children of them.—2 Kings, ch. 2.

See other illustrations under:

Hair pulled. I contended..plucked off their hair   3780
Humiliating. Instead of well set hair, baldness   3845

629. BANISHMENT from Paradise. *Adam.*
24 He drove out the man : and he placed at the
east of the garden of Eden cherubim, and a
flaming sword which turned every way, to keep
the way of the tree of life.—GEN., ch. 3.

630. —— Punishment by. *Rebels.* [Wrote
Artaxerxes,] 26 Whosoever will not do the law
of thy God, and the law of the king, let judgment be executed speedily upon him, whether
it be unto death, or to banishment, or to confiscation of goods, or to imprisonment.—EZRA,
ch. 7.

See other illustrations under:

EXILE.

Command. [Abram] Get thee out of thy country   2802
Criminal. David mourned for [Amnon]..Absalom   2803
Infant. Take the young child..mother..Egypt   2804
Necessary. Flee..to Laban my brother, to Haran   2805
Painful. Sold Joseph to the Ishmaelites..into   2806

Mourning. By the rivers of Babylon..we wept   1029
Noble. Pharaoh sought to slay Moses..fled   3489
Return. Return to Zion with songs   1028
Spiritual. Fan is in his hand..wheat..chaff   7781
Sinners. Blessed..when they shall separate   7883
by Sin. As a shepherd divided his sheep..goats   7789
    "   Your iniquities have separated..your   7784

—— BANQUET. ——

See illustrations under:

FEAST.

Ancient. Sarah..made cakes..Abraham..calf   3172
Birthday. Herod on his birthday made a supper   3173
Charitable. Call the poor, the lame..blind   3174
Complimentary. At Bethany..they made Jesus a   3175
    "   Levi made Jesus a great feast   3176
Death. Job's sons and daughters..brother's house 3177
Ended sadly. Merry with wine..smite Amnon   3178
Farewell. Elisha..oxen, and slew them..people   3179
Great. Solomon offered 22,000 oxen and 120,000 s. 3180
Idolatrous. [Calf] People..eat..drink..rose up to 3181
Impious. Belshazzar made a feast to a thousand   3182
Joyous. [Tabernacles] Seven days shall dwell in 3183
Marriage. Jesus and his disciples were called   3184
National. Three times..keep a feast unto me..year 3186
Royal. Ahasuerus made a feast at Sushan   3185

631. BAPTISM, Administration of. *Jesus.* 2 Jesus himself baptized not, but his disciples.—
JOHN, ch. 4.

632. —— of Christ. *Jordan.* 16 Jesus, when
he was baptized, went..out of the water : and,
lo, the heavens were opened unto him, and he
saw the Spirit of God descending like a dove,
and lighting upon him : 17 and lo a voice from
heaven, saying, This is my beloved Son, in whom
I am well pleased.—MAT., ch. 3.

633. —— Imperfect. *Apollos.* 24..Apollos..
an eloquent man, *and* mighty in the Scriptures,
came to Ephesus. 25..being fervent in the
spirit, he spake and taught diligently the things
of the Lord, knowing only the baptism of John.
—ACTS, ch. 18.

634. —— promised, Spirit. *Jesus.* 5 John truly
baptized with water ; but ye shall be baptized
with the Holy Ghost not many days hence. 8 Ye
shall receive power, after that the Holy Ghost is
come upon you.—ACTS, ch. 1.

635. —— Prerequisite for. *Eunuch.* 36..See,
here is water ; what doth hinder me to be baptized ? 37 And Philip said, If thou believest
with all thine heart, thou mayest. And he answered..I believe that Jesus Christ is the Son of
God.—ACTS, ch. 8.

636. —— Reformation before. *Jailer.* 33 He
took them the same hour of the night, and
washed *their* stripes ; and was baptized, he and
all his, straightway.—ACTS, ch. 16.

637. —— received, Spirit. *Pentecost.* 2 Suddenly there came a sound from heaven as of a
rushing mighty wind, and it filled all the house..
3 And there appeared unto them cloven tongues
like as of fire, and it sat upon each of them.—
ACTS, ch. 2.

638. —— Type of. *Sea.* 22 The children of
Israel went into the midst of the sea upon the
dry *ground :* and the waters *were* a wall unto
them on their right hand, and on their left.—
EX., ch. 14. 2 And were all baptized unto MOSES
in the cloud and in the sea.—1 COR., ch. 10.

639. —— Numerous. *Baptist.* 5 Then went
out to him Jerusalem, and all Judea, and all the
region round about Jordan. 6 And were baptized of him in Jordan, confessing their sins.—
MAT., ch. 3.

See other illustrations under:

Anointing. Spirit of the L. came..[Saul] prophesied 444
    "   Samuel anointed him..S. of the L.   8276

640. BARGAIN, A bad. *Esau.* 30 Esau said to
Jacob, Feed me, I pray thee, with that same red
pottage : for I *am* faint.. 33 And Jacob said, Swear
to me this day ; and he sware unto him : and he
sold his birthright unto Jacob.—GEN., ch. 25.

641. —— Tricks in. *Jews.* 14 *It is* naught, *it
is* naught, saith the buyer : but when he is gone
his way, then he boasteth.—PROV., ch. 20.

Also see:

Ignored. Received every man a penny..murmured   267
    See BUSINESS and references.

642. BARRENNESS, Condemnation of. *Fig
Tree.* 8 Let it alone this year also, till I shall
dig about it, and dung *it :* 9 And if it bear fruit,
well : and if not, *then* after that thou shalt cut it
down.—LUKE, ch. 13.

See other illustrations under:

Cause. He that soweth sparingly, shall reap also 3811
Indolence. I went by the field of the slothful   3436
Natural. No place for seed..figs..vines [Desert] 5639
Prevented. Add to your faith..neither be barren 3484
    "   He that abideth in me..I in him..much   3485
Rejected. Man's rod that I shall choose..bear   3469
    "   Saw a fig tree..nothing but leaves   3473
    "   Branch that bringeth not forth good   3479
Trustful. Although the fig tree shall not blossom 1379
    "   Tree planted by the rivers..fruit in his 3745

643. BATTLE, Disarmed for. *Israelites.* 19 There
was no smith found throughout all the land of
Israel : for the Philistines said, Lest the Hebrews make *them* swords or spears : 22 So in the
day of battle..there was neither sword nor spear
found in the hand of any of the people.—1 SAM.,
ch. 12.

644. —— without Fighting. *Judah.* [Jaha-
ziel] 15 said, Hearken ye, all Judah, and..Jerusa-
lem, and thou king Jehoshaphat, Thus saith the
Lord..Be not afraid nor dismayed by reason of
this great multitude : for the battle *is* not yours,

but God's.. [17] Ye shall not *need* to fight in this *battle:* set yourselves, stand ye *still,* and see the salvation of the Lord.—2 CHRON., ch. 20. [The allies killed each other.]

645. —— **Hailstones in.** *Amorites.* [11] As they fled from before Israel..the Lord cast down great stones from heaven upon them..and they died ..more..died with hailstones than *they..*slew with the sword.—JOSH., ch. 10.

646. —— **The Lord's.** *Moses.* [1] When thou goest out to battle against thine enemies, and seest horses, and chariots,*and* a people more than thou, be not afraid of them : for the Lord thy God *is* with thee.—DEUT., ch. 20.

647. —— —— *David.* [47] All this assembly shall know that the Lord saveth not with sword and spear : for the battle is the Lord's, and he will give you into our hands. [48] And..the Philistine arose, and came and drew nigh to meet David.—1 SAM., ch. 17.

648. —— **Prayer in.** *Reuben, Gad, Manasseh.* [20]..the Hagarites were delivered into their hand, and all that *were* with them : for they cried to God in the battle, and he was entreated of them. —1 CHRON., ch. 5.

649. —— **A sanguinary.** *Syrians.* [29] The battle was joined : and the children of Israel slew of the Syrians a hundred thousand footmen in one day.—1 KINGS, ch. 20.

650. —— **Spirits of.** *Enemies.* [25] When Jehoshaphat and his people came to take away the spoil..they found among them an abundance both riches with the dead bodies, and precious jewels, which they stripped off for themselves, more than they could carry away : and they were three days in gathering of the spoil, it was so much.—2 CHRON., ch. 20.

651. —— —— *Hagarites.* [Reuben, Gad, and Manasseh] [21]..took away their cattle ; of their camels fifty thousand, and of sheep two hundred and fifty thousand, and of asses two thousand, and of men a hundred thousand. [22] For there fell down many slain, because the war *was* of God.—1 CHRON., ch. 5.

652. —— **Skill in.** *David.* [40] He took his staff ..and chose him five smooth stones out of the brook..and his sling *was* in his hand : and he drew near to the Philistine.—1 SAM., ch. 17.

653. —— **Unfit for.** *David.* [38] Saul armed David with his armour, and he put a helmet of brass upon his head ; also..a coat of mail. [39] And David girded his sword upon his armour, and he assayed to go ; for he had not proved *it.* And David said..I cannot go with these.—1 SAM., ch. 17.

Also see :

Intemperance. Benhadad was drinking himself d. 2528
   See WAR and references.

654. BEARD, Indignity to the. *Half shaved.* [4]..Hanun took David's servants, and shaved off the one half of their beards, and cut off their garments in the middle, *even* to their buttocks, and sent them away.—2 SAM., ch. 10.

655. —— **shaven in Affliction.** *Penitents.* [5] There came certain from Shechem, from Shiloh, and from Samaria, *even* fourscore men, having their beards shaven, and their clothes rent. —JER., ch. 41.

See other illustrations under :
Distinction. If I be shaven then..become like   8375
Neglected. Mephibosheth..nor trimmed his beard 3731

656. BEAUTY for Admiration. *Eden.* [8] The Lord God planted a garden eastward in Eden ; and there he put the man.. [9] And out of the ground made the Lord God to grow every tree that is pleasant to the sight.—GEN., ch. 2.

657. —— **A Babe's.** *Moses.* [20]..Moses was born, and was exceeding fair, and nourished up in his father's house three months.—ACTS, ch. 7.

658. —— **A chosen.** *Rebekah.* [16] The damsel *was* very fair to look upon, a virgin.—GEN., ch. 24.

659. —— **commends.** *Esther.* [7]..Esther..had neither father nor mother, and the maid *was* fair and beautiful ; whom Mordecai, when her father and mother were dead, took for his own daughter.—ESTHER, ch. 2.

660. —— **Dangers of.** *Sarai—Abram.* [11]..said unto Sarai his wife..thou *art* a fair woman to look upon : [12] Therefore..when the Egyptians shall see thee..they shall say, This *is* his wife : and they will kill me.—GEN., ch. 12.

661. —— —— *Sons of God.* [2] That the sons of God saw the daughters of men that they *were* fair ; and they took them wives of all which they chose. [3] And the Lord said, My Spirit shall not always strive with man.—GEN., ch. 6.

662. —— **with Discretion.** *Abigail.* [3]..*was* a woman of good understanding, and of a beautiful countenance.. [32] And David said to Abigail.. [33]..thy advice..has kept me this day from coming to *shed* blood.—1 SAM., ch. 25.

663. —— **Exhibition of.** *Ahasuerus.* [10] On the seventh day, when the heart of the king was merry with wine, he commanded.. [11] To bring Vashti the queen..with the crown royal, to shew the people and the princes her beauty : for she *was* fair.—ESTHER, ch. 1.

664. —— **Favorite.** *Rachel.* [16]..the younger *was* Rachel. [17] Leah *was* tender eyed ; but Rachel was beautiful and well favoured. [18] And Jacob loved Rachel.—GEN., ch. 29. [Leah is supposed to have had soft blue eyes.]

665. —— **Floral.** *Lilies.* [28]..Consider the lilies of the field, how they grow ; they toil not, neither do they spin : [29] And yet..even Solomon in all his glory was not arrayed like one of these. —MAT., ch. 6.

666. —— **Masculine.** *Saul.* [2]..Saul, a choice young man, and a goodly : and *there was* not among the children of Israel a goodlier person than he : from his shoulders and upward *he was* higher than any of the people.—SAM., ch. 9.

667. —— —— *David* [12]..*was* ruddy, *and* withal of a beautiful countenance, and goodly to look to. And the Lord said, Arise, anoint him.—1 SAM., ch. 16.

668. —— **Personal.** *Absalom.* [25]..there was none to be so much praised as Absalom for his beauty : from the sole of his foot even to the crown of his head there was no blemish in him. —2 SAM., ch. 14.

669. —— **Surpassing.** *Job's Daughters.* [15] In all the land were no women found *so* fair as the daughters of Job.—JOB, ch. 42.

See other illustrations under :

CLOTHES.

Influence. Sit thou here in a good place 1353
Mutilated. Hanun cut off their garments in the 1354
Rending. Reuben returned unto the pit..rent his 1355
" David took hold on his clothes..rent 1356
Unwashed. Mephibosheth.. nor washed his clothes 1357

CLOTHING.

Beautiful. [High priest's.] A robe and a broidered 1358
Deception. Old shoes and clouted..old garments 1359
Disguised. False prophets..in sheep's clothing 1360
First. Sewed fig leaves together..coats of skins 1361
Gift. Jonathan stripped himself..gave..David 1362
" His mother made Samuel a little coat 1363
Indestructible. 40 years..raiment waxed not old 1364
Ornamental. Chains and bracelets and mufflers 1365
Plain. Raiment of camel's hair and a leathern 1366
Preserved. Let us not rend it, but cast lots for it 1367
Showy. Women adorn themselves in modest 1368
Sins. [Dives] was clothed in purple and fine linen 1369
Separate. Neither shall a man put on a woman's 1370
Tasteful. [Model woman] clothing is silk and 1371

FLOWERS.

Beauty. Consider the lilies..glory 3261
Desirable. Put him into the garden of Eden 3505
Faith. If then G. so clothe the grass..you 3262

JEWELRY.

Adornment. Women adorn..not with braided hair 108
Abundance. Weight of the golden earrings 1700 4724
Given. Men and women..brought bracelets and 4725
Lord's Jewels. Be mine..when I make up my 4726
Inspired. Bezaleel..to work in gold..stones 4536

ORNAMENT.

Female. Adorning..not wearing of gold or 5928
Inspiration. Filled Bezaleel..to work in gold 5929
Sacrifice. People brake off golden earrings..calf 5930
Stripped. L. will take away..their tinkling 5931

Age. Beauty of old men is their gray hair 216
" Hoary head is a crown of glory..way of 218
Architecture. Carved..cherubim..palm trees 492
" Must be exceeding magnifical of 4133
Palace. Ahab..ivory house 4121
Spiritual. Their soul shall be as a watered garden 3739

— BED. —

See illustrations under:

Adulteress'. I have decked my bed with tapestry 515
Death. Ahaziah..thou shalt not come down 6961
Great. Bedstead of iron..9 cubits was the length 3493
Luxurious. Lie upon beds of ivory..their couches 5159
Murdered in. Ish-bosheth lay on a bed at noon 1117
Prophet's. Let us make a little chamber..for him 4109
Sickness. Thou wilt make all his bed in his sickness 695
Uncomfortable. Bed is shorter than that a man 7258

670. BEGGAR, A blind. *Bartimeus.* [46] Blind Bartimeus.. sat by the highway side begging. [47] And when he heard that it was Jesus of Nazareth, he began to cry out..Jesus, *thou* Son of David, have mercy on me.—MARK, ch. 10.

671. — A changed. *Lazarus.* [22] The beggar died, and was carried by the angels into Abraham's bosom.—LUKE, ch. 16.

672. — A fraudulent. *Gehazi.* [20] The servant of Elisha..said, Behold, my master hath spared Naaman this Syrian, in not receiving at his hands..I will run after him, and take somewhat of him.. [22]..And he said..My master hath sent me, saying..there be come to me..two young men..of the prophets: give them..a talent of silver, and two changes of garments.—2 KINGS, ch. 5.

673. — A devout. *Joseph.* [52] Went unto

Pilate, and begged the body of Jesus. [53] And he took it down, and wrapped it in linen, and laid it in a sepulchre.—LUKE, ch. 23.

674. — An undeserving. *Sluggard.* [4] The sluggard will not plough by reason of the cold ; *therefore* shall he beg in harvest, and *have* nothing.—PROV., ch. 20.

See other illustrations under :
Daily. Lame man..laid daily..gate..Beautiful 205
Misery. Lazarus..full of sores..fed with the crumbs 431
See POVERTY.

675. BEGINNING of all, The. *Creation.* [1] In the beginning God created the heaven and the earth. [2] And the earth was without form, and void ; and darkness *was* upon the face of the deep.—GEN., ch. 1.

676. —— Cautious. *Tower.* [28] Which of you, intending to building a tower, sitteth down first, and counteth the cost, whether he have *sufficient* to finish *it ?* [29] Lest haply, after he hath laid the foundation, and is not able to finish *it*, all that behold *it* begin to mock him.—LUKE, ch. 14.

**677. —— —— ** *War.* [31] What king, going to make war..sitteth not down first, and consulteth whether he be able with ten thousand to meet him that cometh against him with twenty thousand?—LUKE, ch. 14.

678. — A dangerous. *Peter.* [58] Peter followed him afar off unto the high priest's palace, and went in, and sat with the servants, to see the end.—MAT., ch. 26.

— BEHAVIOR. —

See illustrations under :

CONDUCT.

Disposition. Samaritan had compassion 1467
Observed. David behaved himself..much set by 1468
Strange. Turned aside quickly..calf and worship 1469

DISCRETION.

Necessary. King consulteth..war..or..peace 2366
Part of. Let not thy voice be heard..lose thy life 2367
Success. David said to Abigail..Blessed be thy 2368
Safety. Paul perceived that one part were Saddu's 2369
Want of. As a jewel of gold in a swine's snout 2370
" Nabal said, Who is David?..his master 2371

POLITENESS.

Cultivated. May we know what this new doctrine 6232
Inculcated. Sit down in the lowest room 6233
Tender. Is your father well, the old man of whom 6234
Treacherous. Jacob took Amasa..to kiss him 6235

679. BELIEF from Conviction. *Bereans.* [11] Were more noble than those in Thessalonica, in that they received the word with all readiness of mind, and searched the Scriptures daily, whether these things were so.—ACTS, ch. 17.

680. —— from Signs. *Nobleman* [47] Besought him that he would come down, and heal his son ..at the point of death. [48] Then said Jesus.. Except ye see signs and wonders, ye will not believe.—JOHN, ch. 4.

See other illustrations under :

ASSURANCE.

Believers. I know that my Redeemer liveth 557
Full. Neither death nor life. separate us 558
Heavenly. If our earthly house be dissolved 559
Inferential. If to kill us..would not receive 560
Impudent. Bramble said..put your trust in 561
Personal. I know..he is able to keep 562
Victor's. Who shall separate us from..C. 563

CONFIDENCE.

Believers. Though I walk through the valley 1518
Blind. Know I that the L..I have a priest 1519
Caution. They are smitten down..as at the first 1520
Disappointed. Ark came..I. shouted..ark taken 1521
False. King [of Ai] wist not..ambush 1522
Future. Doth deliver..trust he will deliver 1523
Intelligent. I know whom I have believed 1524
Joyful. How great is thy goodness..trust thee 1525
Over. Is thy servant a dog..do this? [Hazael] 1526
Peril. Have the sentence of death..we trust 1527
Piety begets. L. was with Joseph..into his hand 1528
Strong. L. delight in us..fear them not 1529
Self. Peter said..I will lay down my life 1530
Triumphant. Although the fig tree shall not b. 1531
Unwarranted. Let two or three three thousand go 1532
Unfortunate. Confidence..like a broken tooth and 1533
Undermining. Neither let Hez. make you trust..L. 1534
Warranted. L. is my rock, fortress, deliverer 1535

EVIDENCE.

Astounding. Divided her..12 pieces..sent 2729
Circumstantial. Potiphar's wife..left his garment 2730
Confirmatory. Thou art one..thy speech agreeth 2731
Confirmed. Is not the hand of Joab in this? 2732
Convincing. Man..healed standing..say nothing 2733
Deeds. If I do not the works..believe me not 2734
Divine. Tell John..blind see the lame walk 2735
Fraudulent. Gibeonites..old shoes..old garments 2736
False. Sought false witness..two false witnesses 2737
Innocence. So do God..if I taste bread..sun be 2738
Lord's. Kine took the straight way..lowing 2739
Misconstrued. Tower..fell..sinners above all 2740
Mistaken. Keep my saying..never see death 2741
Manufactured. Took Joseph's coat..dipped in 2742
Practical. Reach hither thy hand, and thrust it 2743
Rejected. We would seek a sign..Jonas was three 2744
Satisfying. Now we believe..heard him ourselves 2745
Suggestive. Dagon was fallen..before the ark of 2746
Sincerity. Used curious arts..their books..burned 2747
Trial. Ten days..give us pulse to eat..looked upon 2748
Unexplainable. Cup was found in Benjamin's sack 2749
Unsuppressed. What meaneth then this fleeting 2750
Understood. Saw the boldness..with Jesus 2751

TRUST.

Active. Hezekiah clave to the L..rebelled against 9008
Courageous. Thou comest..I come..in the name 9009
Experience. L. who delivered me..the paw of the 9010
Egotists. Pharisee..I..I..I..I..I 9011
Fearless. Our G..is able to deliver us..furnace 9012
   " Though I walk through the valley 9013
   " The Lord is on my side, I will not fear 9014
Fixed. Though he slay me, yet will I trust 9015
Foolish. Bramble said..Put your trust in my 9016
Honoured. Cried to G. in the battle..trust in him 9017
   " Angel smote..Assyrians 185,000 9018
Ill-timed. Let us fetch the ark..it may save us 9020
Providence. May boldly say, The L. is my helper 9021
Self. Philistine..saw David..disdained him 9022
   See **FAITH** and references.

681. BELIEVERS, Joy of. *Unspeakable.*
[8] Whom having not seen, ye love ; in whom, though now ye see *him* not, yet believing, ye rejoice with joy unspeakable and full of glory.— 1 PETER, ch. 1.

682. —— Possibilities of. *All Things.* [22] Ofttimes it hath cast him into the fire, and into the waters, to destroy him : but if thou canst do anything, have compassion on us, and help us. [23] Jesus said..If thou canst believe, all things *are* possible to him that believeth.—MARK, ch. 9.

683. —— Weak. *Corinthians.* [1] I, brethren, could not speak unto you as unto spiritual, but as unto carnal, *even* as unto babes in Christ. [2] I have fed you with milk, and not with meat.— 1 COR., ch. 3.

684. BENEFITS, Return from. *Fig Tree.* [7]..Behold, these three years I come seeking fruit on this fig tree, and find none : cut it down ; why cumbereth it the ground ?—LUKE, ch. 13.

See other illustrations under :

ACCOUNTABILITY.

Future. King which would take account of..servants 72
Gifts. Delivered them ten pounds..till I come 73
Minute. Every idle word..give account thereof 74
Personal. Wasted his goods..give account 75

GIFT.

Art. Bezaleel..filled him..gold..silver..brass 3519
Better. Silver and gold..none, but such as I have 3521
Children. Children are a heritage of the L. 3523
Declined. Daniel answered, Let thy gifts be to 3535
   " Esau said, I have enough, my brother 3536
Farewell. Do for thee..double portion of thy 3524
Ghastly. Give me in a charger the head of John B. 3525
Hypocrisy. Saul said, I will give her..snare 3526
Influence. Gift maketh room for him 3527
Impossible. Sit..not mine to give..for whom 3528
Jesus. Wise men..gold, frankincense, and myrrh 3543
Thanksgiving. Purim..sending portions..gifts to 3546
Unspeakable. God so loved the world..gave..Son 3529
Unaccepted. David said to Ornan..nay..will buy 3530
Valuable. Only handful of meal..little oil 3531
Value of. Two mites..widow hath cast in more 3548

GIFTS.

no Cleansing. Shall I give the fruit of my body for 3532
Children. Abraham gave all that he had to Isaac 3533
Contemptible. Not bring the price of a dog..L. thy 3534
Diversity. To one is given by the Spirit 3537
Differ. Unto one he gave five talents..another two 3538
Disappointment. Cities which Solomon..pleased 3539
Festival. Every one a cake..piece of flesh..wine 3540
Grace. I give you power..in this rejoice not 3541
Gratitude. Lacketh not one man of us..jewels of 3542
Rule. [Rebuilding] Gave after their ability 3544
Supported by. Aaron shall have no inheritance 3545
Trouble. Opened his sack..espied his money 3547
Various. For tabernacle—Ex. 35 : 23-28

Forgotten. Hezekiah rendered not again according 7855
Remembered. Bless the L. O my soul, and forget 6333

685. BENEFACTORS censured. *Moses.* [20] They met Moses and Aaron, who stood in the way, as they came forth from Pharaoh : [21] And they said ..ye have made our savour to be abhorred in the eyes of Pharaoh.—Ex., ch. 5.

**686. —— —— ** *Moses.* [11] They said unto Moses, Because *there were* no graves in Egypt, hast thou taken us away to die in the wilderness ?.. [12] *Is* not this the word that we did tell thee in Egypt, saying, Let us alone, that we may serve the Egyptians ?—Ex., ch. 14.

687. —— honoured. *Bartimeus.* [51] Lord, that I might receive my sight. [52] And Jesus said.. Go thy way ; thy faith hath made thee whole. And immediately he received his sight, and followed Jesus in the way.—MARK, ch. 10.

688. —— remembered. *Centurion.* [4] When they came to Jesus, they besought him instantly, saying, That he was worthy for whom he should do this : [5] For he loveth our nation, and he hath built us a synagogue.—LUKE, ch. 7.

689. —— **slandered.** *Moses—Aaron.* ³² The earth opened her mouth, and swallowed them up, and their houses, and all the men that *appertained* unto Korah, and all *their* goods.. ⁴¹..all ..murmured against Moses and against Aaron, saying, Ye have killed the people of the Lord.— Num., ch. 16.

See other illustrations under :

COMPASSION.

Appeal. Son..spirit teareth him..have compassion	1423
Active. Jesus went about all the cities..healing	1424
Brother's. Joseph said, Fear not..comforted them	1425
Commended. [Good Samaritan] Go thou and do	1426
Debtors. To be sold and his wife..had compassion	1427
Denied. Took him by the throat..Pay me	1428
Lowly. Israel sighed..G. heard the groaning	1429
Moved. We have sinned..grieve for the misery of	1430
Penitent. While..a great way off..compassion	1431
Public. City was moved..Is this Naomi ?	1432
Patriotic. O Jerusalem..how often..ye would not	1433
Practical. Leper..Jesus..with compassion	1434
Reproof. Forgive him and comfort him	1435
Required. Shouldest thou not have..on thy fellow	1436
Sensitive. Not a high priest which cannot be	1437
Unmoved. [Joseph] We saw the anguish..would	1438
Womanly. Daughter of Pharaoh..babe wept..had	1439
Without. Chaldees..had no compassion..old	1440

GIVERS.

Disposition. Whose heart stirred him up..willing	3551
Grateful. Certain women which had been healed	3552
Happy. People rejoiced, for they offered willingly	3553
Lovely. Not grudgingly..loveth a cheerful giver	3554
Royal. Did Araunah as a king, give unto the king	3555

HELP.

Appeal. Come over into Macedonia and help	3925
" Help my lord, O King..hid her son	3926

Remembered. Thou..shalt remember..L. led thee 5370

See **BENEVOLENCE.**

See **FRIENDS.**

690. BENEVOLENCE according to Ability. *Antiochians.* ²⁹ The disciples, every man according to his ability, determined to send relief unto the brethren..in Judea.—Acts, ch. 11.

691. —— **Active.** *Jesus.* ³⁵ Jesus went about all the cities and villages, teaching in their synagogues, and preaching the gospel..and healing ..every disease among the people.—Mat., ch. 9.

692. —— **to Brethren.** *Law.* ³⁵ If thy brother be waxen poor..then thou shalt relieve him : *yea, though he be* a stranger, or a sojourner.. ³⁷ Thou shalt not give him thy money upon usury, nor lend him thy victuals for increase.— Lev., ch. 25.

693. —— **blesses the Giver.** *Isaiah.* ¹⁰ *If* thou draw out thy soul to the hungry, and satisfy the afflicted soul ; then shall thy light rise in obscurity, and thy darkness *be* as the noonday : ¹¹ And the Lord shall guide thee continually, and satisfy thy soul in drought, and make fat thy bones : and thou shalt be like a water garden, and like a spring of water, whose waters fail not.—Isa., ch. 58.

694. —— **benefits Children.** *David.* ²⁵ I have been young, and *now* am old ; yet have I not seen the righteous forsaken, nor his seed begging bread. ²⁶ *He is* ever merciful, and lendeth ; and his seed *is* blessed.—Ps. 37.

695. —— **Consolations of.** *David.* ¹ Blessed *is* he that considereth the poor : the Lord will deliver him in time of trouble. ³ The Lord will strengthen him upon the bed of languishing : thou wilt make all his bed in his sickness. —Ps. 41.

696. —— **Cheerful.** *Paul.* ⁷ Every man according as he purposeth in his heart, *so let him give ;* not grudgingly, or of necessity : for God loveth a cheerful giver.—2 Cor., ch. 9.

697. —— **Compensated.** *Resurrection.* ¹³ When thou makest a feast, call the poor, the maimed, the lame, the blind : ¹⁴ And thou shalt be blessed ; for they cannot recompense thee : for thou shalt be recompensed at the resurrection of the just.—Luke, ch. 14.

698. —— **Delicacy in.** *Boaz.* ¹⁵ Boaz commanded his young men, saying, Let her glean even among the sheaves. ¹⁶..And let fall also *some* of the handfuls of purpose for her, and leave *them,* that she may glean *them.*—Ruth, ch. 2.

699. —— **Essential.** *Law.* ²⁵ A certain lawyer..tempted him, saying, Master, what shall I do to inherit eternal life ? ²⁶ He said..What is written in the law ?.. ²⁷ And he answering said, Thou shalt love the Lord..and thy neighbour as thyself. ²⁸ And he said..Thou hast answered right : this do, and thou shalt live.— Luke, ch. 10.

700. —— **Female.** *Women.* ¹ He went throughout every city and village, preaching.. and the twelve *were* with him, ² And certain women, which had been healed of evil spirits and infirmities.. ³..ministered unto him of their substance.—Luke, ch. 8.

701. —— **better than Fasting.** *To Poor.* ⁶ *Is* not this the fast that I have chosen ? to loose the bands of wickedness, to undo the heavy burdens, and' to let the oppressed go free, and that ye break every yoke ? ⁷..deal thy bread to the hungry..bring the poor that are cast out to thy house ? when thou seest the naked, that thou cover him.—Isa., ch. 58.

702. —— **Great.** *Zaccheus.* ⁸ Zaccheus..said ..Behold, Lord, the half of my goods I give to the poor.—Luke, ch. 19.

703. —— **Hospitable.** *Nehemiah.* ¹⁷ There *were* at my table a hundred and fifty of the Jews and rulers, besides those that came unto us from among the heathen that *are* about us.— Neh., ch. 5.

704. —— **an Investment.** *Paul.* ³⁵ I have shewed you..how..ye ought to support the weak, and to remember the words of the Lord Jesus..It is more blessed to give than to receive.—Acts, ch. 20.

705. —— **ignoring.** *Proverb.* ¹³ Whoso stoppeth his ears at the cry of the poor, he also shall cry himself, but shall not be heard.—Prov., ch. 21.

706. —— **Imposition on.** *Gehazi.* ²² My master hath sent me, saying..there be come to me..two young men of the sons of the prophets : give them, I pray thee, a talent of silver, and two changes of garments.—2 Kings, ch. 5. [Elisha had declined the gifts of Naaman.]

707. —— **Increase by.** *Elisha.* ⁴² Brought the man of God bread of the first fruits, twenty loaves of barley, and full ears of corn in the husk thereof. And he said, Give unto the people.. ⁴³ And his servitor said, What, should I set this before a hundred men?.. ⁴⁴ So he set *it* before them, and they did eat, and left *thereof.*—2 Kings, ch. 4.

708. —— **Joys of.** *Job.* ¹¹ When the ear heard *me*, then it blessed me ; and when the eye saw *me*, it gave witness to me : ¹² Because I delivered the poor that cried, and the fatherless, and *him that had* none to help him.—Job, ch. 29.

709. —— **Law of.** *Commandment.* ²⁸ One of the scribes..asked him, Which is the first commandment of all? ²⁹ And Jesus answered.. ³⁰..Thou shalt love the Lord thy God with all thy heart.. ³¹ And the second *is* like, *namely* this, Thou shalt love thy neighbour as thyself. There is none other commandment greater than these.—Mark, ch. 12.

710. —— **A Memorial.** *Cornelius.* ³ An angel of God coming in.. ⁴..he was afraid, and said, What is it, Lord? And he said..Thy prayers and thine alms are come up for a memorial before God.—Acts, ch. 10.

711. —— **Divine Measure of.** *Widow.* ⁴³ This poor widow hath cast more in, than all they which have cast into the treasury : ⁴⁴ For all *they* did cast in of their abundance ; but she of her want did cast in all that she had, *even* all her living.—Mark, ch. 12.

712. —— **Office of.** *Job.* ¹⁵ I was eyes to the blind, and feet *was* I to the lame. ¹⁶ I *was* a father to the poor : and the cause *which* I knew not I searched out. ¹⁷ And I brake the jaws of the wicked, and plucked the spoil out of his teeth.—Job, ch. 29.

713. —— **High Office of.** *Judgment.* ³⁷..Lord, when saw we thee a hungered, and fed *thee ?* or thirsty, and gave *thee* drink? ⁴⁰ And the King shall answer..Inasmuch as ye have done *it* unto one of these least of these my brethren, ye have done *it* unto me.—Mat., ch. 25.

714. —— **Pious.** *Cornelius.* ¹ There was.. Cornelius, a centurion of the..Italian *band*, ² *A* devout *man*, and one that feared God with all his house, which gave much alms to the people, and prayed to God always.—Acts, ch. 10.

715. —— **Primitive.** *Communistic.* ⁴⁴ All that believed were together, and had all things common ; ⁴⁵ And sold their possessions and goods, and parted them to all *men*, as every man had need.—Acts, ch. 2.

716. —— **Practical.** *D o r c a s.* ³⁹ All the widows stood by him weeping, and shewing the coats and garments which Dorcas made.—Acts, ch. 9.

717. —— **of the Poor.** *Widow.* ¹² She said.. I have not a cake, but a handful of meal in a barrel, and a little oil in a cruse.. ¹³ And Elijah said..Fear not..but make me thereof a little cake first.—1 Kings, ch. 17.

718. —— **Procrastinated.** *Proverb.* ²⁷ Withhold not good from them to whom it is due, when it is in the power of thine hand to do *it.* ²⁸ Say not unto thy neighbour, Go, and come again, and to-morrow I will give ; when thou hast it by thee.—Prov., ch. 3.

719. —— **Religious.** *Jacob.* ²⁰ Jacob vowed ..If God will be with me, and will keep me in this way that I go.. ²¹..then shall the Lord be my God.. ²²..and of all that thou shalt give me I will surely give the tenth unto thee.—Gen., ch. 28.

720. —— **by Rule.** *Zaccheus.* ⁸ Zaccheus.. said..Behold, Lord, the half of my goods I give to the poor ; and if I have taken any thing from any man by false accusation, I restore *him* fourfold.—Luke, ch. 19.

721. —— **Riches for.** *Paul.* ¹⁷ Charge them that are rich in this world.. ¹⁸ That they do good, that they be rich in good works, ready to distribute, willing to communicate.—1 Tim., ch. 6.

722. —— **refused.** *Priest.* ³⁰ A certain *man* ..fell among thieves, which stripped him of his raiment, and wounded *him*, and departed, leaving *him* half dead. ³¹..There came down a certain priest that way ; and when he saw him, he passed by on the other side.—Luke, ch. 10.

723. —— **Real.** *Samaritan.* ³³ A certain Samaritan..came where he was ; and..he had compassion *on him*, ³⁴ And went to *him*, and bound up his wounds, pouring in oil and wine, and set him on his own beast, and brought him to an inn, and took care of him.—Luke, ch. 10. [See No. 731.]

724. —— **repaid.** *Measure.* ³⁸ Give, and it shall be given unto you ; good measure, pressed down, and shaken together, and running over, shall men give into your bosom. For with the same measure that ye mete withal it shall be measured to you again.—Luke, ch. 6.

725. —— **rewarded, The least.** *Water.* ⁴¹ Whosoever shall give you a cup of water to drink in my name, because ye belong to Christ, verily I say unto you, he shall not lose his reward.—Luke, ch. 9.

726. —— **Systematic.** *Paul.* ² Upon the first *day* of the week let every one of you lay by him in store, as *God* hath prospered him, that there be no gatherings when I come.—1 Cor., ch. 16.

727. —— **with Sacrifice.** *Macedonians.* ² In a great trial of affliction, the abundance of their joy and their deep poverty abounded unto the riches of their liberality. ³ For to *their* power, ..yea, and beyond *their* power *they were* willing of themselves ; ⁴ Praying us with much entreaty that we would receive the gift.—2 Cor., ch. 8.

728. —— **Sufficient.** *Socialistic.* ³⁴ Neither was there any among them that lacked : for as many as were possessors of lands or houses sold them, and brought the prices.. ³⁵ And laid *them* down at the apostles' feet : and distribution was made unto every man according as he had need. —Acts, ch. 4.

729. —— **to the Sick.** *Jesus.* ⁴⁰ When the sun was setting, all they that had any sick with divers diseases brought them unto him ; and he laid his hands on every one of them, and healed them.—Luke, ch. 4.

730. —— **Spirit of.** *Apostles.* ⁸ Heal the sick, cleanse the lepers, raise the dead, cast out devils : freely ye have received, freely give.—Mat., ch. 10.

731. —— **Sentimental.** *Levite.* ³² A Levite.. came and looked *on him*, and passed by on the other side.—Luke, ch. 10. [See Nos. 722, 723.]

732. —— **a Test.** *Young Ruler.* ²¹ Jesus beholding him loved him, and said..One thing thou lackest : go thy way, sell whatsoever thou hast, and give to the poor, and thou shalt have treasure in heaven.—Mark, ch. 10.

733. —— **Unselfish.** *Feast.* [12]..When thou makest a dinner..call not thy friends, nor thy brethren, neither thy kinsmen, or *thy* rich neighbours ; lest they also bid thee again, and a recompense be made thee. [13] But..call the poor, the maimed, the lame, the blind.—LUKE, ch. 14.

734. —— **Willing.** *Tabernacle.* [21] Every one whose heart stirred him up, and..his spirit made willing..brought the Lord's offering to the work of the tabernacle.. [22]..both men and women.. *and* brought bracelets, and earrings, and rings, and tablets, all jewels of gold.—Ex., ch. 35.

735. —— **according to Willingness.** *Paul.* [12] If there be first a willing mind, *it is* accepted according to that a man hath, *and* not accordin to that he hath not.—2 COR., ch. 8.

See other illustrations under :

KINDNESS.

Appreciated. Barzillai..I will feed thee in	4808
Animals. Rebekah : I will draw for thy camels	4809
Bereavement. In the choice of our sepulchres, bury	4810
Brethren. Waken poor ; thou shalt relieve him	4811
Conquerors. Saul..Is this thy voice..David..wept	4812
Christians. Disciples..relief unto brethren..Judea	4814
Captives. Clothed naked..shod them..eat and	4815
Father. If ye..know how to give..much more..F.	4816
Gratitude. Mephibosheth..kindness for Jonathan's	4817
Insulted. David sent to comfort him..cut	4819
Inopportune. Ahab..because thou hast let go	4820
Loan. Hath pity..lendeth to the Lord	4821
Providential. Boaz unto Ruth..abide here	4822
Prosperity. I delivered the poor that cried [Job]	4823
Prisoner. Jeremiah put these..rags under..arms	4824
Remembered. Lest I destroy you, for ye showed	4825
Rewarded. Rahab..hid them with the flax. Saved	4826
Substitutional. I was eyes to the blind..feet [Job]	4827
Servant. Centurion's servant who was dear to him	4828
Strangers. Drink my lord..wasted..gave him	4829
Timely. Barzillai brought beds..flour..butter..to	4830
Unexpected. Shall I smite them?..Let bread	4831
Widow. Harvest..forgot a sheaf..be for the	4832

SYMPATHY.

Abundant. What mean ye to weep and break mine	8545
Bereavement. Much people..with her..he had	8546
" Many of the Jews came to Martha	8547
Distrusted. Thinkest thou that David..hath sent	8549
Eyes. Mine eye affected mine heart because of	8550
by Experience. Touched with the feeling	8551
Erring. Forgive..lest swallowed up with overmuch	8552
" Count him not as an enemy, but..a brother	8553
Forbidden. If any man lie in wait..eye shall not	8554
in Heaven. Not a high-priest, which cannot be	8555
Ill-rewarded. Hanun shaved off one half of their	8556
for Jesus. Great company of people and women	8557
Manifested. [See Nos. 8547, 8557.]	
Offices. I was eyes to the blind, and feet..lame	8559
Power. Behold the babe wept. She had compassion	8560
Public. All the city was moved..Is this Naomi?	8561
Practical. Samaritan..went to him and bound up	8563
Power. What mean ye to weep and break mine	8564
Return. Weep not for me, but weep for yourselves	8565
Sentimental. Levite..looked on him and passed by	8566
Silent. Sat down upon the ground 7 days..none	8567
Tender. O that mine head were waters, and mine	8568
" Mine eye runneth down with rivers of	8569
" Saw her weeping..Jews also..Jesus wept	8570
Unshaken. I am ready not to be bound only, but	8571

Enemies. Love your enemies, bless them that	6121
Liberal. As we have opportunity..do good..all	6125

Philanthropic. Jeremiah..is like to die for hunger   6118
"   Jesus..went about doing good   6120

See **BENEFITS** and **BENEFACTORS.**
See **MERCY.**

736. BEREAVEMENT, Consolation in. *David.* [18]..the servants of David feared to tell him that the child was dead.. [23] But now he is dead, wherefore should I fast ? can I bring him back again ? I shall go to him, but he shall not return to me.—2 SAM., ch. 12.

737. —— **Despondency in.** *Joseph.* [34] Jacob rent his clothes, and put sackcloth upon his loins, and mourned for his son many days. [35] And all his sons and all his daughters rose up to comfort him ; but he refused to be comforted ; and he said, For I will go down into the grave unto my son mourning.—GEN., ch. 37.

738. —— **A genuine.** *Dorcas.* [29] All the widows stood by him weeping, and shewing the coats and garments which Dorcas made.—ACTS, ch. 9.

739. —— **Official Mourning in.** *Jacob.* [3] The Egyptians mourned for him threescore and ten days.—GEN., ch. 50.

740. —— *Joseph.* [9] There went up.. chariots and horsemen : and it was a very great company. [10] And they came..beyond Jordan ; and there they mourned with a great and very sore lamentation..seven days.—GEN., ch. 50.

741. —— **Repeated.** *Nain.* [12] When he came nigh to the gate of the city, behold, there was a dead man carried out, the only son of his mother, and she was a widow : and much people of the city was with her.—LUKE, ch. 7.

742. —— **Sudden.** *Job.* [18] Thy sons and thy daughters *were* eating and drinking wine in their eldest brother's house : [19] And..a great wind from the wilderness..smote the four corners of the house, and it fell upon the young men, and they are dead.—JOB, ch. 1.

743. —— **Submission in.** *Israel.* [13] Take also your brother, and arise, go again.. [14] And God Almighty give you mercy before the man, that he may send away your other brother, and Benjamin. If I be bereaved *of my children*, I am bereaved.—GEN., ch. 42.

744. —— **Universal.** *Egypt.* [29] At midnight the Lord smote all the firstborn in the land of Egypt, from the firstborn of Pharaoh that sat on his throne unto the firstborn of the captive that *was* in the dungeon.—Ex., ch. 12.

See other illustrations under :

WIDOW.

Dilemma. Creditor is come to take my two sons	9542
Gifts. Poor widow cast in more than all	9543
Impoverished. I went out full..home again empty	9544
Importunate. I will avenge her, lest..continual	9545
Pious. [84 yrs.] Departed not from the temple	9546
Remembered. Barrel of meal shall not waste	9547
" Elijah said, See, thy child liveth	9548
Relieved. Go sell the oil and pay the debt	9549
Son of. Hiram..cunning to work in. brass	9550
Seven times. Whose wife shall she be of the seven ?	9551

WIDOWS.

Care for. Widows were neglected in the daily	9552
Home. Naomi's husband died. Also Ruth's and	9553
Provision. Seven men of honest report..this	9554
Resurrection. Neither marry nor are given in	9555
Wronging. Pharisees..devour widows' houses	9556

See **DEATH.**

745. BETRAYAL, Dastardly. *Joab.* ⁹ Joab said to Amasa, *Art* thou in health, my brother? And Joab took Amasa by the beard with the right hand to kiss him. ¹⁰ But Amasa took no heed to the sword that *was* in Joab's hand : so he smote him therewith in the fifth *rib.*—2 SAM., ch. 20.

746. —— —— *Judas* ⁴⁸ Gave them a sign, saying, Whomsoever I shall kiss, that same is he ; hold him fast. ⁴⁹ And forthwith he came to Jesus, and said, Hail, Master ; and kissed him. —MAT., ch. 26.

747. —— A Lover's. *Samson.* ¹⁸ When Delilah saw that he had told her all his heart, she sent .. for the lords of the Philistines, saying, Come up this once, for he hath shewed me all his heart. ²¹ The Philistines took him, and put out his eyes.—JUDGES, ch. 16.

748. —— Woe of. *Jesus.* ²⁴ Woe unto that man by whom the Son of man is betrayed ! it had been good for that man if he had not been born. —MAT., ch. 26.

See other illustrations under :

TRAITOR.

Conspiring. Ahithophel is among the conspirators 8871
Defeated. Ahithophel saw his counsel not followed 8872
Repenting. Judas brought..30 pieces of silver 8873
Remorse. Judas..cast down the 30 pieces..hanged 8874
Suspected. Which..is for the king of Israel? 8875

749. BETROTHAL, Privilege of. *Israelite.* ⁷ What man *is there* that hath betrothed a wife, and hath not taken her ? let him go and return unto his house, lest he die in the battle, and another man take her.—DEUT., ch. 20.

See MARRIAGE.

750. BIBLE, Alarm from the. *Jews.* ¹⁵ Baruch read the book in the ears of the people. ¹⁶ Now.. when they had heard all the words, they were afraid both one and other.—JER., ch. 36.

751. —— studied in Childhood. *Timothy.* ¹⁴ Continue thou in the things which thou hast learned..knowing of whom thou hast learned *them ;* ¹⁵ And that from a child thou hast known the holy Scriptures.—2 TIM., ch. 3.

752. —— Edification from the. *Paul.* ³² Brethren, I commend you to God, and to the word of his grace, which is able to build you up, and to give you an inheritance among all them which are sanctified.—ACTS, ch. 20.

753. —— awakens Emotion, The. *Josiah.* ¹⁰.. Shaphan read it before the king. ¹¹ And.. when the king had heard the words of the book of the law..he rent his clothes.—2 KINGS, ch. 22.

754. —— in the Home. *Teaching.* ⁶ These words, which I command thee.. ⁷ And thou shalt teach them diligently unto thy children, and shalt talk of them when thou sittest in thine house, and when thou walkest by the way, and when thou liest down, and when thou risest up. —DEUT., ch. 6.

755. —— warms the Heart, The. *Disciples.* [See No. 758.]

756. —— in the Heart. *David.* ³⁰ The mouth of the righteous speaketh wisdom, and his tongue talketh of judgment. ³¹ The law of his God *is* in his heart; none of his steps shall slide.—Ps. 24.

757. —— Ignorance of. *Sadducees.* ²⁸ In the resurrection, whose wife shall she be of the

seven ? for they all had her. ²⁹ Jesus answered.. Ye do err, not knowing the Scriptures, nor the power of God.—MAT., ch. 22.

758. —— reveals Jesus, The. *Emmaus.* ³¹ Their eyes were opened, and they knew him ; and he vanished out of their sight. ³² And they said to one another, Did not our heart burn within us, while he talked with us by the way, and while he opened to us the Scriptures ?—LUKE, ch. 24.

759. —— Kept by the. *David.* ⁴ Concerning the works of men, by the word of thy lips I have kept *me from* the paths of the destroyer.—Ps. 17.

760. —— Light of the. *Lamp.* ¹⁰⁵ Thy word *is* a lamp unto my feet, and a light unto my path.—Ps. 119.

761. —— Mighty in the. *Apollos.* ²⁴ A certain Jew named Apollos.. an eloquent man, *and* mighty in the Scriptures, came to Ephesus.— ACTS, ch. 18.

762. —— misquoted. *Satan.* ⁶ For it is written, He shall give his angels charge concerning thee [to keep thee in all thy ways] : and in *their* hands they shall bear thee up, lest at any time thou dash thy foot against a stone.—MAT., ch. 4.

763. —— brings Prosperity, The. *God.* ⁸ This book of the law shall not depart out of thy mouth ; but thou shalt meditate therein day and night, that thou mayest observe to do according to all that is written therein : for then thou shalt make thy way prosperous, and then thou shalt have good success.—JOSH., ch. 1.

764. —— awakens Penitence, The. *Jews.* ⁹ Nehemiah.. and Ezra.. and the Levites.. said unto all the people, This day *is* holy unto the Lord your God ; mourn not, nor weep. For all the people wept, when they heard the words of the law.—NEH., ch. 8.

765. —— The People's. *Joshua.* ² When ye shall pass over Jordan unto the land..thou shalt set thee up great stones, and plaster them with plaster : ³ And.. write upon them all the words of this law.—DEUT., ch. 27.

766. —— Perpetuity of the. *For ever.* ²⁴ All flesh *is* as grass, and all the glory of man as the flower of grass. The grass withereth, and the flower thereof falleth away : ²⁵ But the word of the Lord endureth for ever.—1 PETER, ch. 1.

767. —— -Reading appointed. *Moses to Joshua.* ¹⁰.. At the end of *every* seven years, ¹¹ When all Israel is come.. before the Lord.. thou shalt read this law.. in their hearing. ¹² Gather the people together, men, and women, and children, and thy stranger that *is* within thy gates.—DEUT.,.ch. 31.

768. —— -Reading, An effective. *Josiah.* ² The king went up into the house of the Lord.. and the priests, and the prophets, and all the people, both small and great : and he read in their ears all the words of the book of the covenant which was found in the house of the Lord.. ³.. And all the people stood to the covenant.—2 KINGS, ch. 23.

769. —— -Reading, A faithful. *Joshua.* ³⁴ He read all the words of the law, the blessings and cursings.. ³⁵ There was not a word of all that Moses commanded, which Joshua read not before all the congregation of Israel, with the women, and the little ones, and the strangers.— JOSHUA, ch. 8.

770. —— -Reading, An earnest. *Ezra.* ³ He read therein..from the morning until midday, before the men and the women, and those that could understand ; and the ears of all the people *were attentive* unto the book of the law. —NEH., ch. 8.

771. —— -Reading, Explanatory. *Levites.* ⁸ They read in the book in the law of God distinctly, and gave the sense, and caused *them* to understand the reading.—NEH., ch. 8:

772. —— for Rulers. *The King.* ¹⁸ When he sitteth upon the throne of his kingdom..he shall write him a copy of this law in a book.. ¹⁹ And it shall be with him, and he shall read therein all the days of his life.—DEUT., ch. 17.

773. —— Reverence for the. *Jews.* ⁵ Ezra opened the book in the sight of all the people.. and when he opened it, all the people stood up : ⁶ And Ezra blessed the Lord, the great God. And all the people answered, Amen, Amen, with lifting up their hands : and they bowed their heads, and worshipped.—NEH., ch. 8.

774. —— Study of the. *Eunuch.* ²⁹ The Spirit said. .join thyself to this chariot. ³⁰And Philip ran thither¹ to *him*, and heard him read the prophet Esaias.—ACTS, ch. 8.

775. —— Students of the. *Bereans.* ¹¹ These were more noble than those in Thessalonica, in that they received the word with all readiness of mind, and searched the Scriptures daily, whether those things were so.—ACTS, ch. 17.

776. —— understood, The. *Jesus* [journeying to Emmaus]. ⁴⁵ Then opened he their understanding, that they might understand the Scriptures, ⁴⁶ And said. .Thus it is written, and thus it behooved Christ to suffer, and to rise from the dead the third day.—LUKE, ch. 24.

See other Illustrations under:
SCRIPTURE.
Addition. If any man shall add unto these things   7623
Diminution. If..take away from the words of the   7624
Efficacy. As the rain cometh..so shall my word   7625
Regarded. Because it was the preparation   7627

Discovered. I have found the book of the law   904
Sprinkled. Moses..sprinkled both the book and   901
World's. Ye are our epistle..read of all men   903

777. BIGOTRY, Blindness of. *Jews.* ⁴⁸ Then answered the Jews, and said. .Say we not well that thou art a Samaritan, and hast a devil ?— JOHN, ch. 8.

778. —— Fastidious. *Pharisees.* ² The Pharisees and scribes murmured, saying, This man receiveth sinners, and eateth with them.—LUKE, ch. 15.

779. —— Love kills. *Gentile.* ²⁹ Moses said unto Hobab. .Moses' father-in-law, We are journeying unto the place of which the Lord said, I will give it you : come thou with us, and we will do thee good : for the Lord hath spoken good concerning Israel.—NUM., ch. 10.

780. —— Religious. *Jews.* ¹. .he entered.. the synagogue ; and there was a man there which had a withered hand. ² And they watched him, whether he would heal him on the sabbath day ; that they might accuse him.—MARK, ch. 3.

781. —— Unhappiness of. *Priests.* ¹⁴ The blind and the lame came to him in the temple ; and he healed them. ¹⁵ And when the chief

priests and scribes saw the wonderful things that he did, and the children crying. .Hosanna to the Son of David ; they were sore displeased. —MAT., ch. 21.

See other illustrations under :
PREJUDICE.
Alarmed. Deal wisely..any war..fight against us   6466
Blinded. When Moses is read the vail..their heart   6467
Children. Disciples rebuked them..Jesus called   6468
Custom. Disciples marvelled..talked with the   6469
Communion. Can any good..? Thou art the S. of   6470
Concession to. Paul circumcised him because   6471
Destructive. Rejected the counsel of God against   6472
National. How is it..being a Jew..Samaria ?   6473
"   This fellow came..sojourn..needs be a   6474
Obstacle. We have found him..any good   6475
Obstinate. Stretch forth thine hand..might   6476
Offended. Is not this the carpenter..? were   6477
Piety. Since we left off to burn incense..consumed   6478
Race. Spake against Moses..married an Ethiop'n   6479
Removed. God hath showed..not call any   6480
Sectarian. Saw one casting out devils..forbade   6481
Super-religious. If a prophet..known..she is a s.   6482
Sinners. Murmured..guest with a man..a sinner   6483

Conscientious. It is not lawful for thee to carry   1556
Knowledge. Born in sins, and dost thou teach us   2788

782. BIRD, An emblematic. *Eagle.* ¹¹ As an eagle stirreth up her nest, fluttereth over her young, spreadeth abroad her wings, taketh them, beareth them on her wings : ¹² So the Lord alone did lead him.—DEUT., ch. 32.

783. —— A symbolical. *Dove.* ¹⁶ Jesus, when he was baptized, went up straightway out of the water : and, lo, the heavens were opened unto him, and he saw the Spirit of God descending like a dove, and lighting upon him.— MAT., ch. 3.

784. —— A welcome. *Dove.* ¹¹ The dove came in to him in the evening, and, lo, in her mouth *was* an olive leaf plucked off : so Noah knew that the waters were abated from off the earth.—GEN., ch. 8.

785. BIRDS, God's Care of. *Nest.* ⁶ If a bird's nest chance to be. .in any tree, or on the ground, *whether they be* young ones or eggs. .thou shalt not take the dam with the young : ⁷. .let the dam go, and take the young to thee ; that it may be well with thee, and *that* thou mayest prolong *thy* days.—DEUT., ch. 22.

786. BIRDS for Food. *Quails.* ³¹ A wind from the Lord. .brought quails from the sea, and let *them* fall by the camp, as it were a day's journey on this side, and as. .on the other side . .and as it were two cubits *high*. . ³² And the people stood up all that day, and all *that* night, and all the next day, and they gathered the quails.—NUM., ch. 11.

787. —— Service by. *Ravens.* ⁵ Elijah went and dwelt by the brook Cherith. . ⁶ And the ravens brought him bread and flesh in the morning, and. .in the evening ; and he drank of the brook.—1 KINGS, ch. 17.

See other illustrations under :
Care. Two sparrows sold for a farthing..not fall   1040
Heedless. As a bird wandereth from her nest   7261
Invisible. Riches..fly away as an eagle toward   7417

788. BIRTH, Humble. *Jesus.* ⁷ She brought forth her firstborn son, and wrapped him in swaddling clothes, and laid him in a manger ;

because there was no room for them in the inn. —LUKE, ch. 2.

789. —— a Misfortune. *Traitor.* [24]..woe unto that man by whom the Son of man is betrayed ! it had been good for that man if he had not been born.—MAT., ch. 26.

See other illustrations under :

CHILD.

Holy. John..filled with the H. G. from..womb   1146
Joy. Elisabeth's full time came..her cousins   1150

790. BIRTHDAY Celebration. *Herod.* [21]..Herod on his birthday made a supper to his lords, high captains, and chief *estates* of Galilee ; [22] And..the daughter of..Herodias came in, and danced, and pleased Herod.—MARK, ch. 6.

791. —— Lamented. *Job.* [3] Let the day perish wherein I was born, and the night *in which* it was said, There is a man child conceived. [4] Let that day be darkness ; let not God regard it from above, neither let the light shine upon it.—JOB, ch. 3.

Also see :

Celebration. Sons and daughters were eating and 3177

792. BIRTHRIGHT despised. *Esau.* [33]..he sold his birthright unto Jacob. [34] Then Jacob gave Esau bread and pottage of lentiles ; and he did eat and drink, and rose up, and went his way. Thus Esau despised *his* birthright.—GEN., ch. 25.

793. —— of the Firstborn. *Inheritance.* [17] He shall acknowledge the son of the hated *for the* firstborn, by giving him a double portion of all that he hath : for he *is* the beginning of his strength ; the right of the firstborn *is* his.— DEUT., ch. 21.

794. —— Priesthood by. *Law.* [2] Sanctify unto me all the firstborn..among the children of Israel, *both* of man and of beast : it *is* mine.— Ex., ch. 13.

See other illustrations under :

Privileges. Abraham had two sons, the one by a   3415
Spiritual. If children then heirs..joint heirs with   1202

795. BISHOPS, Qualifications of. *Paul.* [7] A bishop must be blameless, as the steward of God ; not selfwilled, not soon angry, not given to wine, no striker ; not given to filthy lucre ; [8] But a lover of hospitality, a lover of good men, sober, just, holy, temperate ; [9] Holding fast the faithful word.—TITUS, ch. 1.

— BLACKSMITH. —— ——

See illustrations under :

First. Tubal-Cain..artificer in brass and iron   4658
Needed. Was no smith..all the land of Israel   5277

796. BLAME assumed. *Judah.* [9] I will be surety for [Benjamin] ; of my hand shalt thou require him : if I bring him not unto thee..then let me bear the blame for ever.—GEN., ch. 43.

797. —— given Benefactors. *Moses and Aaron.* [21] And they said unto them, The Lord look upon you, and judge ; because ye have made our savour to be abhorred in the eyes of Pharaoh, and in the eyes of his servants, to put a sword in their hand to slay us.—Ex., ch. 5.

798. —— Misapplied. *Israelites.* [The Lord destroyed Korah and his company.] [41] All the congregation of the children of Israel murmured against Moses and against Aaron, saying, Ye have killed the people of the Lord.—NUM., ch. 16.

799. —— for Others. *Egyptians.* [7] Pharaoh's servants said..How long shall this man be a snare unto us? let the men go, that they may serve the Lord their God : knowest thou not yet that Egypt is destroyed ?—Ex., ch. 10.

See other illustrations under :

ACCUSATION.

Astounding. Why doth this man speak blasphemies? 76
Fraudulent. The Hebrew..came in..to mock me   77
False. Saul said..all..have conspired against me   78
"   Thou fallest away to the Chaldeans..in prison 79
Investigated. One of you..betray me..Is it I?   80
Meekness. Herod..questioned..Jesus answered him 81
Misapplied. I have not troubled I. but thou   82
Malicious. Samaritans wrote [Ahasuerus] an a.   83
Resented. Abner said, Am I a dog's head..chargest 84
Sustained. [Stephen.] Set up two false witnesses 85
Suppressed. Convicted..own conscience went out 86
Unsustained. I have examined him..no fault   87
Withheld. Michael durst not bring..railing a.   88

CENSURE.

Preparation. First cast out the beam out of thine 1077
Severe. Did tell thee in Egypt..Let us alone   1078

CENSORIOUSNESS.

Reproved. Why beholdest thou the mote in thy   1080
Unbrotherly. Speak not evil one of another   1081

COMPLAINERS.

Punished. Our soul loatheth..bread..sent fiery 1445
Unreasonable. The first supposed..received more 1446
Unprincipled. These are..walking in their own 1447
Wicked. Did bring up an evil report..the plague 1448

CONDEMNATION.

Cause of. If ye were blind, ye should have no sin 1475
Future. How..not having a wedding garment?   1476
Innocent. Pilate saith, Crucify him..no fault   1477
Others. First cast out the beam..own eye   1478
Reason of. Because..not believed in the..Son of 1479
Reversed. I know thee..hard man..cast ye   1480
Unjust. Wrath of Elihu against Job..justified   1481
Unconscious. David said..shall surely die..Thou 1482

CRITICISM.

Contemptuous. Mical said..How glorious was the 1837
Disparaging. What do these feeble Jews?   1838
Enemies. Not good..because..reproach of the   1839

FAULTS.

Faultfinder. Why..not sold for 300 pence..poor 3087
"   J. B..hath a devil..Son..gluttonous 3088
Fastidious. Why do ye eat..with sinners?   3089
Official. Enemies could find none..fault..in Daniel 3086
One. When my master..house of Rimmon..lean 3083
Overlooked. Sins of Jehu..golden calves..done 4350
Unchurched. Neglect to hear the church..heathen 3084

FAULTFINDERS.

Fastidious. Why do ye eat..with sinners   3087
Hypocritical. Why was not this..sold for 300 pence 3088
Malicious. John B..he hath a devil..Son of man 3089

REPROACH.

Affliction. I was a reproach..especially among my 7128
Christ's. Away with such a fellow..not fit to live 7129
Cowardice. Should such a man as I flee?   7130
Fear. Many believed..not confess him..put out 7131
Intended. Thrust out right eyes..for a reproach 7132
Idolaters. Therefore I made thee a reproach and a 7133
Joy. Blessed are ye when men shall separate   7134
Neglect. Jerusalem lieth waste..be no more a.   7135
Proverb. Thou shalt become a proverb and a   7136
Shame. For thy sake..shame hath covered my   7137
Unconscious. What have we spoken..vain to serve 7138
Welcomed. Esteeming the reproach of Christ   7139

REPROOF.

Accepted. Separate yourselves..congregation said 7141
Appreciated. Entereth..wise..more than 100   7140
Christian. Tell him his fault between thee and him 7145
Good. Let the righteous smite me..an excellent   7147
Prudence. As an ear-ring of gold..a wise reprover 7152
Sarcastic. [Abner] Wherefore..not kept my lord 7155
Sensible. [David] Arise..speak comfortably unto 7156
Sharp. Be it far from the L..Get behind me S.   7154
Simony. [Simon Magus] Thy heart is not right   7153
Unwelcome. Reprove not a scorner..hate thee   7157
Welcomed. He that reproveth..find more favor   7159

MURMURING.

Disappointment. This evil place?..no place of figs 5639
Discouragement. People was much discouraged   5640
Distrust. Would G. that we had died in Egypt   5641
Fear. Did tell thee..been better serve the E.   5642
God. Hath not the potter power over the clay   5643
Mercenaries. These last have wrought but one   5644
Neglect. Murmuring of the Greeks against the   5645
Punished. Fire of the L. burnt them..uttermost   5646
Severity. What shall I do?..almost ready to stone 5647
Thirst. Three days..no water..bitter..what shall 5648

Accepted. Become surety for the lad..bear the   8422
Popular. Peter separated..fearing..the circum.   2709
Sympathy, Disobedient. Not as an enemy but..as 2711

800. BLAMELESS Conduct. *Christians.* ¹⁴ Do all things without murmurings and disputings : ¹⁵ That ye may be blameless and harmless, the sons of God, without rebuke, in the midst of a crooked and perverse nation, among whom ye shine as lights in the world.—PHIL., ch. 2.

See INNOCENCE.

801. BLASPHEMY, Accused of. *Jesus.* ³² For which of those works do ye stone me ? ³³ The Jews answered him..For a good work we stone thee not ; but for blasphemy ; and because that thou, being a man, makest thyself God.—JOHN, ch. 10.

802. —— Evidence of. *Trial of Jesus.* ⁶⁴..Hereafter shall ye see the Son of man sitting on the right hand of power, and coming in the clouds of heaven. ⁶⁵ Then the high priest rent his clothes, saying, He hath spoken blasphemy ; what further need have we of witnesses ?—MAT., ch. 26.

803. —— forbidden. *Commandment.* ⁷ Thou shalt not take the name of the Lord thy God in vain : for the Lord will not hold him guiltless that taketh his name in vain.—EX., ch. 20.

804. —— The greatest. *Holy Spirit.* ³² Whosoever speaketh a word against the Son of man, it shall be forgiven him : but whosoever speaketh against the Holy Ghost, it shall not be forgiven him, neither in this world, neither in the *world* to come.—MAT., ch. 12.

805. —— Heedless. *Gehazi.* ²⁰ Gehazi, the servant of Elisha..said, Behold, my master hath spared Naaman this Syrian, in not receiving at his hands..but, *as* the Lord liveth, I will run after him, and take somewhat of him.—2 KINGS, ch. 5.

806. —— Habit of. *Stephen.* ¹² The elders, and the scribes..brought *him* to the council, ¹³ And set up false witnesses, which said, This man ceaseth not to speak blasphemous words against this holy place, and the law.—ACTS, ch. 6.

807. —— Murdered for. *Jesus.* ⁶ Pilate saith..Take ye him, and crucify *him* : for I find no fault in him. ⁷ The Jews answered him.. by our law he ought to die, because he made himself the Son of God.—JOHN, ch. 19.

808. —— No. *Jesus.* [He healed and forgave the palsied,] ⁶ But there were certain of the scribes sitting there, and reasoning in their hearts, ⁷ Why doth this *man* thus speak blasphemies? who can forgive sins but God only ?—MARK, ch. 2.

809. —— Punishment of. *Stones.* ¹⁰ The son of the Israelitish *woman* and a man of Israel strove together in the camp ; ¹¹ And the Israelitish woman's son blasphemed the name *of the Lord,* and cursed.. ¹⁴ Bring forth him that hath cursed without the camp ; and let all that heard *him* lay their hands upon his head, and let all the congregation stone him.—LEV., ch. 24.

810. —— A strange. *Peter.* ⁷⁰ Peter, Surely thou art *one* of them : for thou art a Galilean, and thy speech agreeth *thereto.* ⁷¹ But he began to curse and to swear, *saying,* I know not this man of whom ye speak.—MARK, ch. 14.

811. —— Unpardonable. *Spirit.* [Jesus said,] ³¹..All manner of sin and blasphemy shall be forgiven unto men : but the blasphemy *against* the *Holy* Ghost shall not be forgiven unto men. —MAT., ch. 12.

See other illustrations under

OATH.

Covenant. Ezra made chief priests..sware   5751
Casuistry. Swear by the temple it is nothing   1063
Conspirators'. Bound ourselves with..slain Paul 6752
Friendship. Jonathan caused D..because he   1810
Obedience. Nobles entered into an oath, to walk in 9248
Strange. Peter began to curse and to swear   4631
Wicked. Herod..Whatsoever thou shalt ask   5754

Compelled. I compelled to blaspheme [Saul]   1574
Change. Before a blasphemer..obtained mercy   5354
Counselled. His wife said..Curse God and die   52
Contemptuous. Philistine cursed David by his gods 920
Intimidation. Peter began to curse and to swear 4631

812. BLASPHEMERS, Abandoned. *Disciples.* ¹⁹ concerning faith have made shipwreck : ²⁰ Of whom is Hymeneus and Alexander ; whom I have delivered unto Satan, that they may learn not to blaspheme.—1 TIM., ch. 1.

813. BLEMISH disqualifies. *Priesthood.* ¹⁷ Whosoever *he be* of thy seed..that hath *any* blemish, let him not approach to offer the bread of his God. ¹⁸..a blind man, or a lame, or he that hath a flat nose, or any thing superfluous, ¹⁹ Or a man that is brokenfooted, or brokenhanded, ²⁰ Or crookbacked, or a dwarf, or that hath a blemish in his eye.—LEV., ch. 21.

814. —— Without. *Absalom.* ²⁵ There was none to be so much praised as Absalom for his beauty : from the sole of his foot even to the crown of his head there was no blemish in him. —2 SAM., ch. 14.

See other illustrations under :

FAULTS.

Fastidious. Why do ye eat..with sinners ?   3089
Faultfinder. Why..not sold for 300 pence..poor 3087
   "   J. B..hath a devil..Son..gluttonous 3088
Official. Enemies could find none..fault..in Daniel 3086
One. When my master..house of Rimmon..lean 3083
Overlooked. Sins of Jehu..golden calves..done 4350
Unchurched. Neglect to hear the church..heathen 3084

INFIRMITY.

Age. Can I discern what I eat or drink..hear 4464
" David was old..clothes..gat no heat 4465
" Keepers of the house shall tremble..bow 4466
" Moses 120 years..eye was not dim 4467
Overlooked. Temptation..in my flesh ye despised 4463

Baldness. He is bald, yet he is clean 627
Drunkards. Tables are full of vomit and filthiness 2376
Humiliating. Hanun..shaved off half their beards 2377
Ridiculed. Go up, thou bald head 628
Soldier's. That men say not a woman slew him 2386
Young Ruler. All..observed..one thing thou 4876

815. BLESSING, An after. *Job.* ¹² The
Lord blessed the latter end of Job more than
his beginning : for he had fourteen thousand
sheep, and six thousand camels, and a thousand
yoke of oxen, and a thousand she asses. ¹³ He
had also seven sons and three daughters.—Job,
ch. 42.

816. —— Disguised. *Jacob.* ¹³ Take also
your brother..go again.. ¹⁴ And God Almighty
give you mercy before the ·man, that he may
send away your other brother, and Benjamin.
If I be bereaved *of my children*, I am bereaved.—
Gen., ch. 43. [Joseph was thereby discovered.]

817. —— A double. *Water.* [The allied
kings were famishing for water, during the war
with Moab. God gave water,] ²². .the sun shone
upon the water, and the Moabites saw the water
on the other side *as* red as blood : ²³ And they
said, This *is* blood : the kings are surely slain,
and they have smitten one another : now therefore, Moab, to the spoil.—2 Kings, ch. 3. [They
were easily defeated.]

818. —— in Fruitage. *Rod.* ⁷ Moses laid
up the rods before the Lord in the tabernacle..
⁸..on the morrow..the rod of Aaron..was budded, and brought forth buds, and bloomed blossoms, and yielded almonds.—Num., ch. 17.

819. —— A farewell. *Christ.* ⁵⁰ He led them
..to Bethany, and he lifted up his hands, and
blessed them. ⁵¹ And..while he blessed them,
he was parted from them, and carried up into
heaven.—Luke, ch. 24.

820. —— Greatness by God's. *Abram.*
⁵ Neither shall thy name any more be called
Abram, but..Abraham ; for a father of many
nations have I made thee. ⁶ And I will make
thee exceeding fruitful, and I will make nations
of thee, and kings shall come out of thee.—
Gen., ch. 17.

821. —— An irrevocable. *Jacob.* ³³ Isaac
trembled very exceedingly, and said, Who?
where *is* he that hath taken venison, and brought
it me, and I have eaten..and have blessed him?
yea, *and* he shall be blessed.—Gen., ch. 27.

822. —— Increase of. *Israelites.* ¹² The
more they afflicted them, the more they multiplied and grew. And they were grieved because
of the children of Israel.—Ex., ch. 1.

823. —— Misused, A. *Strange Fire.* ¹ Nadab
and Abihu, the sons of Aaron, took either of
them his censer..and put incense thereon, and
offered strange fire before the Lord, which he
commanded them not. ² And there went out
fire from the Lord, and devoured them.—Lev.,
ch. 10.

824. —— more than asked. *Paralytic.*
⁴ They let down the bed wherein the sick of
the palsy lay. ⁵ When Jesus saw their faith, he
said..Son, thy sins be forgiven thee. ¹¹..Arise,
and take up thy bed, and go thy way.—Mark,
ch. 2.

825. —— of Obedience. *Temporalities.*
³ Blessed *shalt* thou *be* in the city, and..in the
field. ⁴ Blessed *shall be* the fruit of thy body,
and..of thy ground, and..of thy cattle, the increase of thy kine, and the flocks of thy sheep.
⁵ Blessed *shall be* thy basket and thy store.—
Deut., ch. 28.

826. —— Qualification for. *Conquest.*
² Moses my servant is dead..go over this Jordan, thou, and all this people. ³ Every place
that the sole of your foot shall tread upon, that
have I given unto you.—Joshua, ch. 1.

See other illustrations under :
ACCEPTANCE.

Ambition for. We labor that..we may be accepted 51
Authenticated. Voice from heaven, This is my..Son 52
Assurance. If..to kill us..not have received 53
Dedication. Then came a fire..upon the altar 54
Denied. Brought that which was torn, lame 55
Fire. Fire out of the rock consumed the flesh 56
Manifested. Burning lamp passed between..pieces 57
Piety. In every nation he that feareth..worketh 58
Sacrifice. L. had respect unto Abel..offering 59
" Widow hath cast more in than all 60
Terms. Do justly, love mercy..walk humbly 61

Farewell. While he blessed them he was parted 3040
in Chastisement. Happy is the man whom the L. 187

See PROSPERITY.

827. BLIND believe and see, The. *Two Blind
Men.* ²⁸ Jesus saith unto them, Believe ye that
I am able to do this? They said unto him, Yea,
Lord. ²⁹ Then touched he their eyes, saying,
According to your faith, be it unto you.—Mat.,
ch. 9.

828. —— delivered, The. *Clay.* ⁶ He spat
on the ground, and made clay of the spittle, and
he anointed the eyes of the blind man with the
clay, ⁷ And said..Go, wash in the pool of Siloam.—John, ch. 9.

829. —— easily led, The. *Syrians.* ¹⁸..Elisha
prayed..Smite this people..with blindness.
And he smote them with blindness.. ¹⁹ And
Elisha said unto them..follow me, and I will
bring you to the man whom ye seek. But he
led them to Samaria.—2 Kings, ch. 6.

830. —— restored, The. *Spittle.* ²³ He took
the blind man by the hand, and led him out of
the town ; and when he had spit on his eyes,
and put his hands upon him.. ²⁵..he was restored.—Mark, ch. 8.

831. BLINDNESS of Age. *Isaac.* ¹ When
Isaac was old, his eyes were dim, so that he
could not see.—Gen., ch. 27.

832. —— An affecting. *Zedekiah.* [The last
Jewish king was conquered,] ⁷ And they slew
the sons of Zedekiah before his eyes, and put
out the eyes of Zedekiah, and bound him with
fetters of brass, and carried him to Babylon.—
2 Kings, ch. 25.

833. —— by Brightness. *Paul.* ¹¹ When I
could not see for the glory of that light, being
led by the hand..I came into Damascus.—Acts,
ch. 22.

834. —— and Bondage. *Samson.* ²¹ The
Philistines..put out his eyes, and brought him

down to Gaza, and bound him with fetters of brass ; and he did grind in the prison house.—Judges, ch. 16.

835. —— of Bigots. *Pharisees.* [52] Then said the Jews..Now we know that thou hast a devil. Abraham is dead, and the prophets ; and thou sayest, If a man keep my saying, he shall never taste of death.—John, ch. 8.

836. —— Disqualified by. *Priesthood.* [17] Let him not approach to offer the bread of his God. [18] For whatsoever man *he be* that hath a blemish, he shall not approach : a blind man.—Lev., ch. 21.

837. —— inflicted. *Sodomites.* [Angels] [11]..smote the men that *were* at the door of the house with blindness, both small and great : so that they wearied themselves to find the door.—Gen., ch. 19.

838. —— Infirmity of. *Ahijah.* [2] Jeroboam said to his wife..disguise thyself..[3]..he shall tell thee what shall become of the child. [4] And Jeroboam's wife did so..and went to Shiloh.. But Ahijah could not see ; for his eyes were set by reason of his age.—1 Kings, ch. 14.

839. —— Judicial. *Jews.* [Two days before his death, Jesus said,] [39]..Esaias said, [40] He hath blinded their eyes, and hardened their heart ; that they should not see with *their* eyes, nor understand with *their* heart, and be converted.—John, ch. 12.

840. —— in Leadership. *Guides.* [16] Woe unto you, *ye* blind guides, which say, Whosoever shall swear by the temple, it is nothing ; but whosoever shall swear by the gold of the temple, he is a debtor ! [17] *Ye* fools and blind : for whether is greater, the gold, or the temple that sanctifieth the gold.—Mat., ch. 23.

841. —— Protected in. *Stumblingblock.* [14] Thou shalt not curse the deaf, nor put a stumblingblock before the blind, but shalt fear thy God : I *am* the Lord.—Lev., ch. 19.

842. —— of Prejudice. *Jews.* [13]..Moses, *which* put a vail over his face, that the children of Israel could not steadfastly look to the end of that which is abolished : [14] But their minds were blinded : for until this day remaineth the same vail untaken away in the reading of the old testament.—2 Cor., ch. 3.

843. —— Relief from. *Bartimeus.* [On his last journey to Jerusalem,] [51] Jesus..said..What wilt thou that I should do unto thee ? The blind man said..Lord, that I might receive my sight. [52] Jesus said..Go thy way ; thy faith hath made thee whole. And immediately he received his sight.—Mark, ch. 10.

844. —— Ruin from. *Jews.* [41] He beheld the city, and **w**ept over it, [42] Saying, If thou hadst known..the things *which belong* unto thy peace ! but now they are hid from thine eyes. [43] For the days shall come..that thine enemies shall cast a trench.—Luke, ch. 19.

845. —— removed. *Syrians.* [20] When they were come into Samaria..Elisha said, Lord, open the eyes of these *men*.. And the Lord opened their eyes..and, behold, *they were* in the midst of Samaria.—2 Kings, ch. 6.

846. —— by Satan. *Pharaoh.* [After the eighth plague of locusts,] [7] Pharaoh's servants said..How long shall this man be a snare unto

us? let the men go, that they may serve the Lord their God : knowest thou not yet that Egypt is destroyed?—Ex., ch. 10.

847. —— Spiritual. *Description.* [18] Having the understanding darkened, being alienated from the life of God through the ignorance that is in them, because of the blindness of their heart : [19] Who being past feeling have given themselves over unto lasciviousness, to work all uncleanness with greediness.—Eph., ch. 4.

848. —— Unconscious. *Pharisees.* [39] Jesus said, For judgment I am come into this world, that they which see not might see ; and that they which see might be made blind. [40] And *some* of the Pharisees..said unto him, Are we blind also?—John, ch. 9.

849. —— Visitation of. *Elymas.* [Paul said,] [11]..thou shalt be blind, not seeing the sun for a season. And immediately there fell on him a mist and a darkness ; and he went about seeking some to lead him by the hand.—Acts, ch. 13.

Also see:
Temporary. Saul..three days without sight   21

850. BLOOD, Atonement by. *Abel.* [3] Cain brought of the fruit of the ground.. [4] And Abel ..firstlings of his flock and of the fat thereof. And the Lord had respect unto Abel and to his offering : [5] But unto Cain and to his offering he had not respect.—Gen., ch. 4.

851. —— Access by. *Paul.* [19] Having therefore, brethren, boldness to enter into the holiest by the blood of Jesus, [20] By a new and living way, which he hath consecrated for us, through the vail, that is to say, his flesh.—Heb., ch. 10.

852. —— Acceptance by. *Sinai.* [19] When Moses had spoken every precept..he took the blood of calves and of goats, with water, and scarlet wool, and hyssop, and sprinkled both the book and all the people.. [22]..and without shedding of blood is no remission.—Heb., ch. 9.

853. —— Appearance of. *Moabites.* [22] Early in the morning..the sun shone upon the water, and the Moabites saw the water on the other side *as* red as blood : [23] And they said, This *is* blood : the kings..have smitten one another : now therefore, Moab, to the spoil.—2 Kings, ch. 3.

854. —— Behold the. *Israelites.* [Slaying of the paschal lamb in Egypt.] [7] They shall take of the blood, and strike *it* on the two side posts and on the upper doorpost of the houses, wherein they shall eat it.—Ex., ch. 12.

855. —— for Blood. *Rechab and Baanah.* [They had slain Ish-bosheth.] [11] How much more, when wicked men have slain a righteous person in his own house upon his bed ? shall I not therefore now require his blood of your hand?.. [12] And David commanded his young men, and they slew them.—2 Sam., ch. 4.

856. —— Cleansing. *Jesus.* [13] If the blood of bulls and of goats, and the ashes of a heifer sprinkling the unclean, sanctifieth to the purifying of the flesh ; [14] How much more shall the blood of Christ..purge your conscience from dead works to serve the living God?—Heb., ch. 9.

857. —— of Consecration. *Priests.* [Moses] [22] brought..the ram of consecration : and Aaron and his sons laid their hands upon the head of the ram. ²³ And he slew *it;* and Moses took of the blood of it, and put *it* upon the tip of Aaron's right ear, and upon the thumb of his right hand, and upon the great toe of his right foot.—LEV., ch. 8. [Also on Aaron's sons.]

858. —— **Changed to.** *River.* ²⁰ He lifted up the rod, and smote the waters that *were* in the river. . and all the waters. . were turned to blood. —EX., ch. 7.

859. —— **Defilement of.** *David.* ⁸. . hast made great wars : thou shalt not build a house unto my name, because thou hast shed much blood upon the earth.—1 CHRON., ch. 22.

860. —— **Protection by.** *Israelites.* ¹² I will pass through the land of Egypt this night, and will smite all the firstborn. . ¹³ And the blood shall be to you for a token upon the houses where ye *are:* and when I see the blood, I will pass over you.—EX., ch. 12.

861. —— **Prohibition of.** *Food.* ¹⁰ Whatsoever man *there be* of the house of Israel, or of the strangers. . that eateth any manner of blood ; I will even set my face against that soul. . and will cut him off from among his people.—LEV., ch. 17.

862. —— **Redeemed by.** *Christ.* ¹⁸ Ye know that ye were not redeemed with corruptible things, *as* silver and gold. . ¹⁹ But with the precious blood of Christ, as of a lamb without blemish.—1 PETER, ch. 1.

863. —— **Responsibility for.** *Peter and John.* ²⁷ They set *them* before the council : and the high priest asked them, ²⁸. . Did we not straitly command you that ye should not teach in this name ? and. behold, ye have filled Jerusalem with your doctrine, and intend to bring this man's blood upon us.—ACTS, ch. 5.

864. —— **The Speaking.** *Better Things.* ²² Ye are come unto mount Zion. . ²⁴ And to Jesus the mediator of the new covenant, and to the blood of sprinkling, that speaketh better things than *that of* Abel.—HEB., ch. 12.

865. —— **The Sprinkling.** *Israelites.* ⁸ Moses took the blood, and sprinkled *it* on the people, and said, Behold, the blood of the covenant, which the Lord hath made with you.—EX., ch. 24.

866. —— **Sweat of.** *Gethsemane.* ⁴³ There appeared an angel. . strengthening him. ⁴⁴ And being in an agony he prayed more earnestly : and his sweat was as it were great drops of blood falling down to the ground.—LUKE, ch. 22.

867. —— **with the Truth.** *Sinai.* [See No. 852.]

868. —— **Testament in the.** *Jesus.* ¹⁹ He took bread, and gave thanks, and brake *it,* and gave unto them, saying, This is my body which is given for you : this do in remembrance of me. ²⁰ Likewise also the cup. . saying, This cup *is* the new testament in my blood, which is shed for you.—LUKE, ch. 22.

See other illustrations under :

Aversion. Drink his blood. . disciples went back 2486
Cry. The voice of thy brother's blood crieth unto 7245
Disgrace. Come out, come out, thou bloody man 6752
Monster. Whose blood Pilate mingled with their 7511
Scruples. Not lawful to put them into the treasury 5552

869. BOASTING, A glorious. *Paul.* ²² Are they Hebrews ? so *am* I. Are they Israelites ?

so *am* I. Are they the seed of Abraham ? so *am* I. ²³ Are they ministers of Christ ?. . I *am* more ; in labours more abundant, in stripes above measure, in prisons more frequent, in deaths oft.—2 COR., ch. 11.

870. —— **Inoffensive.** *Paul.* ¹⁴ If I have boasted any thing to him of you, I am not ashamed ; but as we spake all things to you in truth, even so our boasting, which *I made* before Titus, is found a truth.—2 COR., ch. 7.

871. —— **in Prayer.** *Pharisee.* ¹¹ The Pharisee stood and prayed thus with himself, God, I thank thee, that I am not as other men *are,* extortioners, unjust, adulterers, or even as this publican. ¹² I fast twice in the week, I give tithes of all that I possess.—LUKE, ch. 18.

872. —— **prevented.** *Gideon.* ² The Lord said unto Gideon, The people that *are* with thee *are* too many for me to give the Midianites into their hands, lest Israel vaunt themselves against me, saying, Mine own hand hath saved me. ³. . proclaim. . Whosoever *is* fearful and afraid, let him return.—JUDGES, ch. 13.

873. —— **rebuked.** *Peter.* ³⁷. . Lord, why cannot I follow thee now ? I will lay down my life for thy sake. ³⁸ Jesus answered him, Wilt thou lay down thy life for my sake ? Verily, verily, I say unto thee, The cock shall not crow, till thou hast denied me thrice.—JOHN, ch. 13.

See illustrations under :

VANITY.

Forbidden. Be not called Rabbi. . are brethren 9160
Humbled. Haman arrayed Mordecai. . proclaimed 9162
Punished. Hezekiah showed them all. . silver 9161
Religious. To be seen. . garments. . love greetings 9163

Brief. Haman told them. . king had promoted him 6561
Contemptuous. I will give thy flesh to the fowls 920
Disdainful. I know not the L.. let I. go 6559
Folly. Man wise in his own conceits. . more hope 7698
Glorious. L. be for a crown of glory. . diadem of 3561
Humbled. Is not this great Babylon that I have 6583
Profane. Prince of T.. I am a god. . a man not God 6558
Pride. Are not Abana and Pharpar. . better than 6553
Shameful. It is naught. . buyer. . then he boasteth 641
Success. The might of mine hand. . me this 6582
Untimely. Boast not thy self of to-morrow for 3498

— BOAT. ——

See illustrations under :
Immense. Length of the ark 300 cubits, the breadth 493
Ingenious. Mother made an ark of bulrushes 162

874. BODY AND MIND, Care of. *Hebrew Children.* [Nebuchadnezzar commanded the selection of] ⁴ Children in whom *was* no blemish, but well favoured, and skilful in all wisdom, and cunning in knowledge, and understanding science, and such as *had* ability in them to stand in the king's palace. ⁵ And the king appointed them a daily provision. . three years.—DAN., ch. 1.

875. BODY, Surrender of the. *Three Worthies.* ²⁸ Nebuchadnezzar. . said, Blessed *be* the God. . who hath sent his angel, and delivered his servants that trusted in him. . and yielded their bodies, that they might not serve nor worship any god, except their own God.—DAN., ch. 3.

See other illustrations under :

BEAUTY.

Babe. Moses was born. . exceeding fair 657
Chosen. Rebekah. . the damsel was very fair 658

Commended. Esther..the maid was fair and 659
Dangers. Sarah..thou art a fair woman 660
Discretion. Abigail was a woman of beautiful 662
Exhibition. Vashti the queen..show her beauty 663
Favorite. Rachel was beautiful..well favored 664
Masculine. Saul..not a goodlier person..than he 666
  " David..beautiful countenance..good 667
Personal. Absalom..praised for his beauty 668
Surpassing. No woman so fair..daughters of Job 669
  " The daughters of men were fair 661

FLESH.

Gethsemane. Findeth them asleep..flesh is weak 3257
Evil. Works of the flesh..are these 3258

Begged. Joseph went to Pilate and begged the 9409
Contention. Michael..with the devil..about the 6890
Diversity. Body is not one member, but many 2469
Deformed. 18 years was bowed together, and could 205
Emblem. Bread..This is my body, which is given 861
Future. Sown a natural body, it is raised a 7279
Light. Light of the body is the eye..full of light 1928
Resurrected. Many bodies of the saints which 8304
Subjected. I keep my body under..lest I myself 7702

876. BOILS, Plague of. *Egypt.* ¹⁰ They took ashes of the furnace..and Moses sprinkled it up toward heaven ; and it became a boil breaking forth *with* blains upon man, and upon beast. ¹¹ And the magicians could not stand before Moses because of the boils.—Ex., ch. 9.

877. —— Smitten with. *Job.* ⁷ So went Satan forth..and smote Job with sore boils from the sole of his foot unto his crown.—Job, ch. 2.

Also see :
Cured. Lump of figs..laid it on the boil 5260

878. BOLDNESS, Angels urge to. *Peter and John.* ¹⁹ The angel of the Lord by night opened the prison doors, and brought them forth, and said, ²⁰ Go, stand and speak in the temple to the people all the words of this life.—Acts, ch. 5.

879. —— Apostolic. *Council.* ²⁵ Then came one..saying, Behold, the men whom ye put in prison are standing in the temple, and teaching the people.—Acts, ch. 5.

880. —— of Believers. *Three Worthies.* ¹⁶ Shadrach, Meshach, and Abed-nego, answered ..O Nebuchadnezzar, we *are* not careful to answer thee in this matter. ¹⁷ If it be *so*, our God whom we serve is able to deliver us from the burning fiery furnace, and he will deliver *us*.—Dan., ch. 3.

881. —— Brazen. *Ahab.* ¹⁷ When Ahab saw Elijah..Ahab said..Art thou he that troubleth Israel ? ¹⁸ And he answered, I have not troubled Israel ; but thou, and thy father's house, in that ye have forsaken the commandments of the Lord, and thou hast followed Baalim.—1 Kings, ch. 18.

882. —— of Innocence. *Sons of Jacob.* ⁸ The money, which we found in our sacks' mouths, we brought again unto thee out of the land of Canaan : how then should we steal out of thy lord's house silver or gold ? ⁹ With whomsoever of thy servants it [the cup] be found, both let him die, and we also will be my lord's bondmen. —Gen., ch. 44.

883. —— Influence of. *Council.* ¹³ When they saw the boldness of Peter and John, and perceived that they were unlearned and ignorant men, they marvelled ; and they took knowledge

of them, that they had been with Jesus.—Acts, ch. 4.

884. —— for the Right. *Command.* ¹ When thou goest out to battle against thine enemies, and seest horses, and chariots, *and* a people more than thou, be not afraid of them : for the Lord thy God *is* with thee.—Deut., ch. 20. .

885. —— in Sin. *Ahab.* ³¹ As if it had been a light thing for him to walk in the sins of Jeroboam..he took to wife Jezebel..of the Zidonians, and went and served Baal.. ³² And he reared up an altar for Baal.—1 Kings, ch. 16.

886. —— in Shame. *Absalom.* ²² They spread Absalom a tent upon the top of the house ; and Absalom went in unto his father's concubines in the sight of all Israel.—2 Sam., ch. 16.

887. —— in Prayer. *Paul.* ¹⁵ We have not a high priest which cannot be touched with the feeling of our infirmities.. ¹⁶ Let us therefore come boldly unto the throne of grace, that we may obtain mercy, and find grace to help in time of need.—Heb., ch. 4.

888. —— A venturesome. *Walking on the Sea.* ²⁸ Peter..said, Lord, if it be thou, bid me come unto thee on the water. ²⁹ And he said, Come. And..Peter..walked on the water, to go to Jesus. ³⁰ But when he saw the wind boisterous, he was afraid ; and beginning to sink, he cried.. Lord, save me.—Mat., ch. 14.

See COURAGE and references.

889. BONDS broken. *Samson.* ¹² Delilah ..took new ropes, and bound him therewith, and said..The Philistines *be* upon thee, Samson.. And he brake them from off his arms like a thread.—Judges, ch. 16.

890. —— Innocence in. *Arrested.* ¹² The band and the captain and officers of the Jews took Jesus, and bound him, ¹³ And led him away to Annas first.—John, ch. 18.

891. —— Imprisonment with. *Paul.* ³²..when they saw the chief captain and the soldiers, they left beating of Paul. ³³ Then the chief captain ..took him, and commanded *him* to be bound with two chains.—Acts, ch. 21.

892. —— Resting in. *Peter.* ⁶ When Herod would have brought him forth, the same night Peter was sleeping between two soldiers bound with two chains.—Acts, ch. 12.

893. —— A strong Man in. *Samson.* ²¹ The Philistines..put out his eyes..and bound him with fetters of brass ; and he did grind in the prison house.—Judges, ch. 16.

See other illustrations under :
Bravery. Bonds..abide me ; but none of these 2261
Christians. The unity of the Spirit in the bond—Eph. 4 : 3
Sinner's. Simon..thou art in the bond of iniquity 6417

894. BONDAGE, Degrading. *Gibeonites.* ²² Joshua..spake..saying, Wherefore have ye beguiled us.. ²³ Now therefore ye *are* cursed, and there shall none of you be freed from being bondsmen, and hewers of wood and drawers of water for the house of my God.—Josh., ch. 9.

895. —— Rigorous. *Egyptian.* ¹⁰ The taskmasters of the people..spake..Thus saith Pharaoh, I will not give you straw. ¹¹ Go ye, get you straw where ye can find it : yet not aught of your work shall be diminished.—Ex., ch. 5.

896. —— Unendurable. *Israelites.* ¹⁸ Another king arose, which knew not Joseph. ¹⁹ The same dealt subtilely..and evil entreated our fathers, so that they cast out their young children, to the end they might not live.—ACTS, ch. 7.

897. —— to Wealth. *Young Ruler.* ²¹ Jesus beholding him loved him, and said..go thy way, sell whatsoever thou hast, and give to the poor, and come, take up the cross, and follow me. ²² And he was sad..and went away grieved : for he had great possessions.—MARK, ch. 10.

898. BONES, Life-giving. *Elisha.* ²¹ As they were burying a man..they spied a band *of men* [Moabites] ; and they cast the man into the sepulchre of Elisha : and when the man..touched the bones of Elisha, he revived, and stood up.—2 KINGS, ch. 13.

899. —— Made of. *Eve.* ²¹ The Lord God caused a deep sleep to fall upon Adam..and he took one of his ribs, and closed up the flesh.. ²² And the rib..made he a woman.—GEN., ch. 2.

900. —— Removal of. *Joseph's.* ¹⁹ Moses took the bones of Joseph with him : for he had straitly sworn the children of Israel, saying, God will surely visit you ; and ye shall carry up my bones away hence with you.—Ex., ch. 13.

901. BOOK, A blood-sprinkled. *Law.* ¹⁹ When Moses had spoken every precept..he took the blood of calves and of goats, with water, and scarlet wool, and hyssop, and sprinkled both the book and all the people.—HEB., ch. 9.

902. —— A completed. *Bible.* ¹⁸ If any man shall add unto these things, God shall add unto him the plagues that are written in this book : ¹⁹ And if any man shall take away from the words of the book of this prophecy, God shall take away his part out of the book of life.—REV., ch. 22.

903. —— The Christian a. *Heart.* ² Ye are our epistle written in our hearts, known and read of all men : ³ *Forasmuch as ye are* manifestly declared to be the epistle of Christ ministered by us, written not with ink, but with the Spirit of the living God ; not in tables of stone, but in fleshly tables of the heart.—2 COR., ch. 3.

904. —— The discovered. *Law.* ⁸ Hilkiah the high priest said unto Shaphan the scribe, I have found the book of the law in the house of the Lord. And Hilkiah gave the book to Shaphan, and he read it.—2 KINGS, ch. 22.

905. —— of God. *Record.* ³¹ Oh, this people have sinned a great sin, and have made them gods of gold. ³² Yet now, if thou wilt forgive their sin— ; and if not, blot me, I pray thee, out of thy book which thou hast written. ³³ And the Lord said unto Moses, Whosoever hath sinned against me, him will I blot out of my book.—Ex., ch. 32.

906. —— of Life, The. *Record.* ²⁷ There shall in no wise enter into it anything that defileth, neither *whatsoever* worketh abomination, or *maketh* a lie : but they which are written in the Lamb's book of life.—REV., ch. 21.

907. —— of Remembrance. *History.* ¹⁶ They that feared the Lord spake often one to another : and the Lord hearkened, and heard *it*, and a book of remembrance was written before him for them that feared the Lord, and that thought upon his name.—MAL., ch. 3.

908. —— Burned, Bad. *Ephesians.* ¹⁹ Many of them also which used curious arts brought their books together, and burned them before all *men :* and they counted the price..and found it fifty thousand *pieces* of silver.—ACTS, ch. 19.

909. —— Increase of. *Solomon.* ¹² Of making many books *there is* no end ; and much study *is* a weariness of the flesh.—ECCL., ch. 12.

910. —— Lost. *Lost.* ¹⁴ It is said in the book of the wars of the Lord, What he did in the Red sea, and in the brooks of Arnon.— NUM., ch. 21. ¹³ The sun stood still, and the moon stayed, until the people had avenged themselves.. *Is* not this written in the book of Jasher?—JOSHUA, ch. 10. [29] The acts of David ..they *are* written in the book of Samuel the seer, and in the book of Nathan the prophet, and in the book of Gad the seer.—1 CHRON., ch. 29.

See other illustrations under:

Proverbs. Solomon spake 3000 proverbs   583
See BIBLE.

911. BOOTY, A great. *Israelites.* [From the Midianites,] [32]..the booty..which the men of war had caught, was six hundred thousand and seventy thousand and five thousand sheep.. [33] And threescore and twelve thousand beeves... [34] And threescore and one thousand asses.—NUM., ch. 31.

See other illustrations under:

PILLAGE.

Jerusalem. Shishak took away the treasure   6180
Temple. Chaldeans carried to Babylon..gold   6179

SPOILS.

Battle. Jehoshaphat found riches with the dead   8314
"   [From Hagarites] they took camels 50,000   8315
Coveted. I saw..Babylonish garment..200 shekels 8316
Declined. I will not take anything [Abram]   8317
Expected. To Sisera a prey of divers colours of 8318
Forbidden. Keep yourselves from the accursed   8319

912. BORROWER a Servant, The. *Proverb.* [7] The rich ruleth over the poor, and the borrower *is* servant to the lender.—PROV., ch. 22.

913. —— Trouble of a. *Axe.* [4] When they came to Jordan, they cut down wood. [5] But as one was felling a beam, the axe head fell into the water : and he cried, and said, Alas, master ! for it was borrowed.—2 KINGS, ch. 6.

914. BORROWERS, Distress of. *Jews.* [3] Some ..said, We have mortgaged our lands, vineyards, and houses, that we might buy corn, because of the dearth. [5]..and, lo, we bring into bondage our sons and our daughters to be servants.—NEH., ch. 5.

915. —— Ruined by. *Egyptians.* [35] They borrowed of the Egyptians jewels of silver, and jewels of gold, and raiment : [36] And the Lord gave the people favour..so that they lent unto them *such things as they required :* and they spoiled the Egyptians.—EX., ch. 12.

916. BORROWING forbidden. *Paul.* [8] Owe no man anything, but to love one another.—ROM., ch. 13.

See other illustrations under:

DEBTS.

Compromised. Take thy bill..quickly and write   2006
Forgiven. Every seven years..creditor shall   2007
Miracle. Go sell the oil and pay the debt   2009
Severity. Fellow servants took him by the throat 2008

DEBTORS.

Army. Every one that was in debt..gathered   2010
Destructive. Same servant [debtor] took him by   2011
Gratitude. To whom little is forgiven..loveth little 2012
Insolvent. Have mortgaged our lands, vineyards   2013
Protected. When thou dost lend..not go into his 2014

Law. If a man borrow..make it good   7275

917. BOTANY, Knowledge of. *Solomon.* [33] He spake of trees, from the cedar tree that *is* in Lebanon even unto the hyssop that springeth out of the wall.—1 KINGS, ch. 4.

See other illustrations under:

Apostates. Latter times some..abstain from meat 9167
Beginning. Let the earth bring forth grass   9164
Development. First the blade, then the ear..full 9165
Mystery. Seed..spring and grow..knoweth not   9166
Vegetarians. I have given you every herb..fruit 9168

918. BRAVERY, Useless. *Peter.* [10] Simon Peter having a sword drew it, and smote the high priest's servant, and cut off his right ear. —JOHN, ch. 18.

919. —— Youthful. *David.* [32] Let no man's heart fail because of him : thy servant will go and fight with this Philistine. [33] And Saul said ..Thou art not able to go against this Philistine ..for thou *art but* a youth, and he a man of war from his youth.—1 SAM., ch. 17.

See COURAGE and references.

920. BRAVADO, Impious. *Goliath.* [43] The Philistine cursed David by his gods. [44] And ..said to David, Come to me, and I will give thy flesh unto the fowls of the air, and to the beasts of the field.—1 SAM., ch. 17.

See BOASTING.

921. BRETHREN, Compassion toward. *Debtors.* [28] The same servant went out, and found one of his fellow servants, which owed him a hundred pence : and he..took *him* by the throat, saying, Pay me that thou owest. [33] Shouldest not thou also have had compassion on thy fellow servant, even as I had pity on thee?—MAT., ch. 18.

922. —— Dangerous. *Paul.* [25] I have been in the deep ; [26] *In* journeyings often, *in* perils of waters, *in* perils of robbers, *in* perils by *mine own* countrymen, *in* perils by the heathen, *in* perils in the city, *in* perils in the wilderness, *in* perils in the sea, *in* perils among false brethren.—2 COR., ch. 11.

923. —— Encouragement from. *Romans.* [15] When the brethren heard of us, they came to meet us as far as Appii Forum, and the Three Taverns, whom when Paul saw, he thanked God, and took courage.—ACTS, ch. 28.

924. —— Forgiveness of. 490 *Times.* [21] Peter ..said, Lord, how shalt my brother sin against me, and I forgive him ? till seven times ? [22] Jesus saith..I say not unto thee, Until seven times : but, Until seventy times seven.—MAT., ch. 18.

925. —— False. *Paul.* [4] False brethren unawares brought in..came in privily to spy out our liberty which we have in Christ Jesus, that they might bring us into bondage.—GAL., ch. 2.

926. —— Love of. *Christian.* [7] Beloved, let us love one another : for love is of God ; and every one that loveth is born of God, and knoweth God. [8] He that loveth not, knoweth not God ; for God is love.—1 JOHN, ch. 4.

927. —— Practical. [16] He laid down his life for us : and we ought to lay down *our* lives for the brethren. [17] But whoso hath this world's good, and seeth his brother have need, and shutteth up his bowels *of* compassion from him, how dwelleth the love of God in him?—1 JOHN, ch. 3.

928. —— Spurious. *Tares.* [28] The servants said..Wilt thou then that we go and gather them up ? [29] But he said, Nay ; lest while ye gather up the tares, ye root up also the wheat with them. [30] Let both grow together until the harvest.—Mat., ch. 13.

929. —— Unity of. *Refreshing.* [1] Behold, how good and how pleasant *it is* for brethren to dwell together in unity ! [2] *It is* like the precious ointment upon the head, that ran down upon the beard, *even* Aaron's beard. . [3] As the dew of Hermon, *and as the dew* that descended upon the mountains of Zion.—Ps. 133.

See other illustrations under :

FRATRICIDE.

First. In the field, Cain. against Abel slew him	3406
Terrible. Ahimelech . slew his [70] brethren	3407

UNION.

Building. Whosoever remaineth . help with silver	9099
Charity. Disciples . to send relief . in Judea	9103
Communistic. All that believed. all things	9104
Communion. If the household be too small	9105
Diversity. Many members, yet but one body	9124
Dependence. Eye can not say to the hand. no	9125
Important. Shall your brethren go to war. sit	9112
Prayer. Aaron and Hur stayed up [Moses'] hands	9113
Remarkable. Neither said. things he possessed	9129
Strength. If the Syrians be too strong. help me	9117
Spiritual. By one S. we are all baptized into one	9130
Suffering. One member suffer all. with it	9131

Discord. Doth the L. hate. he that soweth discord	2467
Peace. Let there be no strife. we be brethren	9080
Unworthy. If any that is called a brother be drunk	543

See **BROTHER.**

See **COMMUNION** and references.

930. BRIBERY for Concealment. *Soldiers.* [12] They gave large money unto the soldiers, [13] Saying, Say ye, His disciples came by night, and stole him *away* while we slept.—Mat., ch. 28.

931. —— Desecrated for. *Ahaz.* [20] Tilgath-pilneser king of Assyria came. and distressed him. . [21] For Ahaz took away a portion *out* of the house of the Lord. and gave *it* unto the king of Assyria : but he helped him not.—2 Chron., ch. 28.

932. —— of Friendship. *Delilah.* [5] The lords of the Philistines . said unto her, Entice him, and see wherein his great strength *lieth*, and by what *means* we may prevail against him, that we may bind him to afflict him : and we will give thee every one of us eleven hundred *pieces* of silver.—Judges, ch. 16.

933. —— Horrible. *Judas.* [14] Then one of the twelve, called Judas Iscariot, went unto the chief priests, [15] And said. . What will ye give me, and I will deliver him unto you ? And they covenanted with him for thirty pieces of silver.—Mat., ch. 26.

934. —— Official. *Felix.* [26] He hoped also that money should have been given him of Paul, that he might loose him : wherefore he sent·for him the oftener, and communed with him.—Acts, ch. 24.

935. —— —— Rulers. [23] Thy princes *are* rebellious, and companions of thieves : every one loveth gifts, and followeth after rewards : they judge not the fatherless, neither doth the cause of the widow come unto them.—Isa., ch. 1.

See other illustrations under .

Judgment. Samuel's sons. took bribes and	100
Scorned. Shaketh his hand from holding of bribes	4051

936. BROKERS, Expulsion of. *Jesus.* [Near the beginning of his ministry, and also near its close,] [15] When he had made a scourge of small cords, he drove them all out of the temple, and the sheep and the oxen ; and poured out the changers' money, and overthrew the tables ; [16] And said unto them that sold doves, Take these things hence ; make not my Father's house a house of merchandise.—John, ch. 2; also Mat., ch. 21.

937. BROTHER, Authority of a. *Young David.* [29] He said, Let me go, I pray thee ; for our family hath a sacrifice in the city ; and my brother, he hath commanded me *to be there.*—1 Sam., ch. 20.

938. —— A bloody. *Abimelech.* [5] He went unto his father's house at Ophrah, and slew his brethren the sons of Jerubbaal, *being* threescore and ten persons, upon one stone. yet Jotham the youngest son. hid himself.—Judges, ch. 9.

939. —— A Christian. *Andrew.* [41] He first findeth his own brother Simon, and saith. . We have found the Messias, which is, being interpreted, the Christ. [42] And he brought him to Jesus.—John, ch. 1.

940. —— Contempt for a. *Eliab.* [28] Eliab's anger was kindled against David, and he said, Why camest thou down hither ? and with whom hast thou left those few sheep in the wilderness ? I know thy pride, and the naughtiness of thine heart ; for thou art come down that thou mightest see the battle.—1 Sam., ch. 17. [Eliab was his oldest brother.]

941. —— Deed of a. *Samaritan.* [34] Went to him, and bound up his wounds, pouring in oil and wine, and set him on his own beast, and brought him to an inn, and took care of him. [35] And on the morrow when he departed, he took out two pence, and gave *them* to the host, and said. . Take care of him : and whatsoever thou spendest more, when I come again, I will repay thee.—Luke, ch. 10.

942. —— A disdainful. *Elder Son.* [28] He was angry, and would not go in : therefore came his father out, and entreated them. . [30] But as soon as this thy son was come, which hath devoured thy living with harlots, thou hast killed for him the fatted calf.—Luke, ch. 15.

943. —— The erring. *Paul.* [14] If any man obey not our word by this epistle, note that man, and have no company with him, that he may be ashamed. [15] Yet count *him* not as an enemy, but admonish *him* as a brother.—2 Thess., ch. 3.

944. —— A favorite. *Benjamin.* [34] He. *sent* messes unto them from before him : but Benjamin's mess was five times so much as any of theirs. And they drank, and were merry with him.—Gen., ch. 43.

945. —— The Lord's. *Christian.* [49] He stretched forth his hand toward his disciples, and said, Behold my mother and my brethren ! [50] For whosoever shall do the will of my Father which is in heaven, the same is my brother, and sister, and mother.—Mat., ch. 12.

946. —— A loving. *Joseph.* [30] Joseph made haste ; for his bowels did yearn upon his brother : and he sought *where* to weep ; and he entered into *his* chamber, and wept there.—Gen., ch. 43.

947. —— A revengeful. *Esau.* [41] Esau hated

Jacob because..his father blessed him..said in his heart, The days of mourning for my father are at hand : then will I slay my brother Jacob. —GEN., ch. 27.

948. —— —— *Absalom.* [28] When Amnon's heart is merry with wine, and when I say unto you, Smite Amnon ; then kill him, fear not : have not I commanded you? be courageous, and be valiant. [29] And the servants of Absalom did. —2 SAM., ch. 13. [Amnon had dishonoured Absalom's sister.]

949. —— **Regard for a.** *Weak.* [9] Take heed lest..become a stumblingblock to them that are weak. [10] For if any man see thee which hast knowledge sit at meat in the idol's temple, shall not the conscience of him..be emboldened to eat those things which are offered to idols ; [11] And through thy knowledge shall the weak brother perish, for whom Christ died ?—1 COR., ch. 8.

950. —— **A rejected.** *Obstinate.* [15] If thy brother shall trespass against thee.. [17] If he shall neglect to hear them, tell *it* unto the church : but if he neglect to hear the church, let him be unto thee as a heathen man and a publican.— MAT., ch. 18.

951. —— **A poor.** *No Usury.* [35] If thy brother be waxen poor, and fallen in decay with thee ; then thou shalt relieve him : *yea, though he be* a stranger, or a sojourner.. [37] Thou shalt not give him thy money upon usury, nor lend him thy victuals for increase.—LEV., ch. 25.

952. —— **Christian.** *Apostles.* [13] He chose twelve, whom also he named apostles ; [14]..Peter, and Andrew his brother, James and John [his brother].. [15]..James the *son* of Alpheus.. [16] And Judas *the brother* of James.—LUKE, ch. 6.

See **BRETHREN** *and references.*

953. BUILDER, A royal. *Jotham.* [3] He built the high gate of the house of the Lord, and on the wall of Ophel he built much. [4] Moreover he built cities in the mountains of Judah, and in the forests he built castles and towers.—2 CHRON., ch. 27.

954. —— **An unsuccessful.** *Tower.* [28] Which of you, intending to build a tower, sitteth not down first, and counteth the cost, whether he have *sufficient* to finish it ? [29] Lest haply, after he hath laid the foundation, and is not able to finish *it*, all that behold *it* begin to mock him, [30] Saying, this man began to build, and was not able to finish.—LUKE, ch. 14.

955. —— **A visionary.** *Rich Fool.* [17] He thought within himself, saying, What shall I do, because I have no room where to bestow my fruits ? [18]..This will I do : I will pull down my barns, and build greater ; and there will I bestow all my fruits and my goods.—LUKE, ch. 12.

956. BUILDERS, Joyful. *Walls.* [42] And the singers sang loud, with Jezrahiah *their* overseer. [43] Also that day they offered great sacrifices, and rejoiced..the wives also and the children rejoiced : so that the joy of Jerusalem was heard even afar off.—NEH., ch. 12.

957. —— **Shouts of.** *Temple.* [12] But many of the priests and Levites and chief of the fathers, *who were* ancient men, that had seen the first house, when the foundation of this house was laid before their eyes, wept with a loud voice ; and many shouted aloud for joy.—EZRA, ch. 3.

958. —— **Volunteer.** *Exiles.* [Cyrus proclaimed,] [3] Who *is there* among you of all his people? his God be with him, and let him go up to Jerusalem, which *is* in Judah, and build the house of the Lord.—EZRA, ch. 1.

959. BUILDING, A great. *Babel.* [3] They had brick for stone, and slime..for mortar. [4] And they said, Go to, let us build us a city, and a tower whose top *may reach* unto heaven ; and let us make us a name, lest we be scattered abroad upon the face of the whole earth.— GEN., ch. 11.

960. —— **A glorious.** *Temple.* [14] Solomon.. [15]..built the walls..within with boards of cedar, both the floor..and the..ceiling : [22] And the whole house he overlaid with gold..also the whole altar that *was* by the oracle he overlaid with gold. [29] And he carved all the walls..with carved figures of cherubim and palm trees and open flowers, within and without.—1 KINGS, ch. 6.

961. —— **hindered.** *Adversaries.* [4] The people of the land weakened the hands of the people of Judah, and troubled them in building, [5] And hired counsellors against them, to frustrate their purpose.. [17] *Then* sent the king.. [21]..commandment to cause these men to cease, and that this city be not builded.—EZRA, ch. 4.

962. —— **necessitated.** *Walls.* [Nehemiah said,] [17] Ye see the distress that we *are* in, how Jerusalem *lieth* waste, and the gates thereof are burned with fire : come, and let us build up the wall of Jerusalem, that we be no more a reproach.—NEH., ch. 2.

963. —— **An outgrown.** *School.* [1] The sons of the prophets said unto Elisha, Behold now, the place where we dwell with thee is too strait for us. [2] Let us go..unto Jordan..and let us make us a place there, where we may dwell.. Go ye.—2 KINGS, ch. 6.

964. —— **prevented.** *Babel.* [6] This they begin to do : and now nothing will be restrained from them, which they have imagined to do. [7] Go to, let us go down, and there confound their language.. [8] So the Lord scattered them ..upon the face of all the earth : and they left off to build the city.—GEN., ch. 11.

965. —— **prohibited.** *Rechabites.* [6] Jonadab the son of Rechab our father commanded us, saying..ye, nor your sons for ever : [7] Neither shall ye build house..but all your days ye shall dwell in tents.—JER., ch. 35.

966. —— **Revival after.** *Jews.* [After the temple was rebuilt,] [1] When Ezra had prayed, and when he had confessed, weeping and casting himself down before the house of God, there assembled unto him out of Israel a very great congregation of men and women and children : for the people wept very sore.—EZRA, ch. 10.

967. —— **A spiritual.** *Christians.* [20] Are built upon the foundation of the apostles and prophets, Jesus Christ being himself the chief corner *stone*; [21] In whom all the building fitly framed together groweth unto a holy temple in the Lord : [22] In whom ye also are builded together for a habitation of God through the Spirit.— EPH., ch. 2.

See **ARCHITECTURE** *and references.*

968. BURDEN of Cares. *Martha.* 40 Martha was cumbered about much serving, and came to him [to complain of Mary]. 41 And Jesus answered.. Martha, Martha, thou art careful and troubled about many things : 42 But one thing is needful.—LUKE, ch. 10.

969. —— divided, The. *In Babylon.* 4 Whosoever remaineth.. let the men of his place help him with silver, and with gold, and with goods, and with beasts, besides the freewill offering for the house of God that *is* in Jerusalem.—EZRA, ch. 1. [Volunteers went up to rebuild the temple.]

970. —— divested. *Race.* 1 Wherefore, seeing we also are compassed about with so great a cloud of witnesses, let us lay aside every weight, and the sin which doth sin easily beset *us*, and let us run with patience the race that is set before us.—HEB., ch. 12.

971. —— Equality in bearing. *Reuben and Gad.* 5 Let this land be given unto thy servants for a possession, *and* bring us not over Jordan. 6 And Moses said.. Shall your brethren go to war, and shall ye sit here?—NUM., ch. 32.

972. —— according to Strength. *War.* 17 God led them *through* the way of the land of the Philistines, although that *was* near.. Lest peradventure the people repent when they see war, and they return to Egypt : 18 But God led the people about, *through* the way of the wilderness.—EX., ch. 13.

See CARE *and references.*

973. BURGLAR, Killing a. *Night.* 2 If a thief be found breaking up, and be smitten that he die, *there shall* no blood *be shed* for him. 3 If the sun be risen upon him, *there shall be* blood *shed* for him.—EX., ch. 22.

See CRIME *and references.*

974. BURIAL denied. *Idolaters.* 1 Saith the Lord, they shall bring out the bones of the kings of Judah.. his princes.. priests.. prophets, and.. of the inhabitants of Jerusalem, out of their graves : 2 And they shall spread them before the sun, and the moon, and all the host of heaven, whom they have loved, and whom they have served.—JER., ch. 8.

975. —— Life from. *Revived.* 21 As they were burying a man.. behold, they spied a band *of men* [Moabites] ; and they cast the man into the sepulchre of Elisha : and when the man.. touched the bones of Elisha, he revived, and stood up on his feet.—2 KINGS, ch. 13.

976. —— A living. *Korah.* 32 The earth opened her mouth, and swallowed them up, and their houses, and all the men that *appertained* unto Korah, and all *their* goods.—NUM., ch. 16.

977. —— A mournful. *Abner.* 31 King David *himself* followed the bier. 32 And they buried Abner in Hebron : and the king lifted up his voice, and wept at the grave of Abner ; and all the people wept.—2 SAM., ch. 3.

978. —— A mysterious. *Moses.* 5 Moses.. died.. according to the word of the Lord. 6 And he buried him in a valley in the land of Moab.. but no man knoweth of his sepulchre unto this day.—DEUT., ch. 34.

979. —— A Patriarch's. *Jacob.* 7 Joseph went up to bury his father : and with him went up all the servants of Pharaoh, the elders of his house, and all the elders of the land of Egypt, 8 And all the house of Joseph, and his brethren, and his father's house.—GEN., ch. 50.

980. —— A perfumed. *Asa.* 14 They buried him in his own sepulchres.. and laid him in the bed which was filled with sweet odours and divers kinds *of spices* prepared by the apothecaries' art : and they made a very great burning for him.—2 CHRON., ch. 16.

981. BURIAL-PLACE, A chosen. *Barzillai* [to David]. 37 Let thy servant.. turn back again, that I may die in mine own city, *and be buried* by the grave of my father and of my mother.—2 SAM., ch. 19.

982. —— First. *Cave.* 17 The field of Ephron.. in Machpelah.. and the cave which *was* therein, and all the trees that *were* in the field, that *were* in all the borders round about, were made sure 18 Unto Abraham.—GEN., ch. 23.

983. —— A Family. *Machpelah.* [Expiring, Jacob said,] 30 Bury me with my fathers in the cave that *is* in the field of Ephron the Hittite. 31 There they buried Abraham and Sarah.. Isaac and Rebekah.. and there I buried Leah.—GEN., ch. 49.

See other illustrations under :

GRAVE.

Chosen. Bury me with my fathers in the cave	3703
First Bargain. Care of Machpelah.. money as it is	3704
Longed for. O that thou wouldest hide me in the	3705
Crematory. Valiant men.. body of Saul.. sons	1828
Funeral, Joyous. I say unto thee, Arise.. dead sat	3492

984. BUSINESS abandoned. *Levi.* [Jesus] 27.. saw a publican, named Levi, sitting at the receipt of custom : and he said unto him, Follow me. 28 And he left all, rose up, and followed him.—LUKE, ch. 5.

985. —— Capacity for. *Joseph.* 39 Pharaoh said unto Joseph, Forasmuch as God hath shewed thee all this, *there is* none so discreet and wise as thou *art :* 40 Thou shalt be over my house, and according unto thy word shall all my people be ruled.—GEN., ch. 41.

986. —— Diligence in. *Proverb.* 29 Seest thou a man diligent in his business ? he shall stand before kings ; he shall not stand before mean men.—PROV., ch. 22.

987. —— Excuses. *Great Supper.* 5 They made light of *it*, and went their ways, one to his farm, another to his merchandise.—MAT., ch. 22.

988. —— Frauds in. *Unjust Steward.* 5 How much owest thou unto my lord ? 6 And he said, A hundred measures of oil. And he said.. Take thy bill, and sit down quickly, and write fifty. 7.. another.. said, A hundred measures of wheat. And he said unto him, Take thy bill, and write fourscore.—LUKE, ch. 16.

989. —— Hindrances of. *Invited Guests.* 18 They all with one *consent* began to make excuse. The first said.. I have bought a piece of ground, and I must needs go and see it : 19 And another said, I have bought five yoke of oxen, and I go to prove them.—LUKE, ch. 14.

990. —— before Pleasure. *Abraham's Servant.* 32 The man came into the house : and he ungirded.. and gave straw and provender for the camels, and water to wash his feet.. 33.. set *meat* before him to eat : but he said, I will not eat, until I have told mine errand.—GEN., ch. 24.

991. —— **Spiritual Men for.** *Stewards.* ² It is not reason that we should leave the word of God, and serve tables. ³ Wherefore, brethren, look ye out among you seven men of honest report, full of the Holy Ghost and wisdom, whom we may appoint over this business.— ACTS, ch. 6.

992. —— **Secrecy in.** *Fugitive.* ² David said unto Ahimelech the priest, The king hath commanded me a business, and hath said..Let no man know any thing of the business whereabout I send thee.—1 SAM., ch. 21. [He asked for bread and a sword.]

993. —— **Success in.** *Joseph.* ¹⁴ Joseph gathered up all the money that was found in the land of Egypt, and..of Canaan, for the corn which they bought..brought the money into Pharaoh's house.—GEN., ch. 47.

994. —— **Talent for.** *Jacob.* ⁴² The feebler were Laban's, and the stronger Jacob's. ⁴³ And the man increased exceedingly, and had much cattle, and maidservants, and menservants, and camels, and asses.—GEN., ch. 30.

See other illustrations under :

BORROWING.

Distress. Have mortgaged our lands..buy corn　914
Forbidden. Owe no man any thing, but to love　916
Ruin. Borrowed..spoiled the Egyptians　915
Servant. Borrower is servant of the lender　912
Trouble. Axe head fell into the water..borrowed　913

DEBTS.

Compromised. Take thy bill..quickly and write　2006
Forgiven. Every seven years..creditor shall　2007
Miracle. Go sell the oil and pay the debt　2009
Severity. Fellow servants took him by the throat　2008

DEBTORS.

Army. Every one that was in debt..gathered　2010
Destructive. Same servant [debtor] took him by　2011
Gratitude. To whom little is forgiven..loveth little　2012
Insolvent. have mortgaged our lands, vineyards　2913
Protected. When thou dost lend..not go into his　2014

FRAUD.

Appearances Gibeonites..took old sacks..old　3468
Commerce. Take thy bill..quickly..write fifty　3409
Demagogue. O that I were a judge..do justice　2171
Pious. Sons of the prophets, give..silver [Gehazi]　3410
Religious. His enemy..sowed tares among the　3411
Spiritual. Simon offered money..Holy Ghost　3412
Traitors. Whomsoever I shall kiss..is he　3413
Wages. Hire of the labourers kept..crieth　3414

MERCHANTS.

Babylon. Merchants..weep and mourn for her　5371
Intruders. Drove them all out of the temple　5372

TRADE.

Benefits of. Let them trade..their substance..be　8858
Beating down. It is naught..giveth away　8859
Dishonesty. Making the ephah small..shekel great 8860
"　　　False balance is abomination to the L.　8861
"　　　Given to covetousness..dealeth　8862
Lawful. Servants called..how much gained by　8863
Luxuries. Gold and silver..pearls..odors..chariots 8864
Protection. Our craft is in danger to be set at　8865
Sabbath. Bought fish and..ware..sold on the S.　8866
"　　　I testified against..lay hands on you　8867
Tricks. Not have divers weights. divers measures 8868
Union. Called together workmen of like　8869

Bargain. Feed me red pottage..sold his birthright 640

Costs. Counteth the cost..not able to finish　1736
Extortion. We have borrowed money..I shook my 2829
"　　Not to keep company with..extor.　2831
Law. If a man borrow..make it good　7275
Tricks. It is naught, saith the buyer..boasteth　641
Unprofitable. If he gain the whole world and lose 5051
　　See MONEY and references.

995. CALAMITY, A destructive. *Wall.* ²⁹ The children of Israel slew of the Syrians a hundred thousand footmen in one day. ³⁰ But the rest fled to Aphek, into the city ; and there a wall fell upon twenty and seven thousand of the men *that were* left.—1 KINGS, ch. 20.

996. —— **God sent.** *Korah.* ³¹ As he had made an end of speaking.. ³² The earth opened her mouth, and swallowed them up, and their houses, and all the men that *appertained* unto Korah.—NUM., ch. 16.

997. —— **Predicted, A.** *Temple.* ² Jesus said ..See ye not all these things ? verily I say unto you, There shall not be left here one stone upon another, that shall not be thrown down.—MAT., ch. 24.

998. —— **from Sin.** *Achan.* [The Lord said to defeated Joshua,] ¹¹ They have even taken of the accursed thing, and have also stolen, and dissembled also, and they have put *it* even among their own stuff. ¹² Therefore the children of Israel could not stand before their enemies.—JOSH., ch. 7.

999. —— **Waiting for a.** *Nineveh.* ⁵ Jonah went..and sat on the east side of the city, and there made him a booth, and sat under it in the shadow, till he might see what would become of the city.—JONAH, ch. 4.

1000. CALAMITIES, Fear of. *The Wicked.* ¹⁰ The snare *is* laid for him in the ground, and a trap for him in the way. ¹¹ Terrors shall make him afraid on every side, and shall drive him to his feet. ¹² His strength shall be hungerbitten, and destruction *shall be* ready at his side.—JOB, ch. 18.

1001. —— **Hardened by.** *Israelites.* ⁹ I have smitten you with blasting and mildew : when your gardens..vineyards..fig trees and..olive trees increased, the palmerworm devoured *them :* yet have ye not returned unto me, saith the Lord.—AMOS, ch. 4.

1002. —— **Indiscriminate.** *Judgments.* ¹ The Lord maketh the earth empty..waste, and turneth it upside down.. ² And it shall be, as with the people, so with the priest ; as with the servant, so with his master ; as with the maid, so with her mistress ; as with the buyer, so with the seller ; as with the lender, so with the borrower.—ISA., ch. 24.

1003. —— **Misjudged.** *Jesus.* ⁴ Those eighteen, upon whom the tower in Siloam fell, and slew them, think ye that they were sinners above all men that dwelt in Jerusalem ? ⁵ I tell you, Nay : but, except ye repent, ye shall all likewise perish.—LUKE, ch. 13.

1004. —— **Overwhelming.** *Eli.* ¹⁷ The messenger..said, Israel is fled before the Philistines..a great slaughter..thy two sons also, Hophni and Phinehas, are dead, and the ark of God is taken. ¹⁸..he fell from off the seat backward..and his neck brake !—1 SAM., ch. 4.

1005. —— **Reflection in.** *Job.* ² Oh that I

were as *in* months past, as *in* the days *when* God preserved me ; ³ When his candle shined upon my head, *and when* by his light I walked *through* darkness ; ⁴ As I was in the days of my youth. —JOB, ch. 29.

1006. —— Sudden. *Job.* ¹⁵ The oxen..the Sabeans took them.. ¹⁶ While he *was* yet speaking, there came also another, and said, The fire of God..hath burned up the sheep. ¹⁷ While he *was* yet speaking, there came also another, and said, The Chaldeans..fell upon the camels. ¹⁸ While he *was* yet speaking, there came also another, and said, Thy sons and thy daughters. —JOB, ch. 1. [All were dead.]

See other illustrations under :

DESTRUCTION.

Complete. The waters returned..remained not o.	2249
Fire. Burnt all the houses in Jerusalem and	2250
General. Every living substance was destroyed	2251
Grave. Man dieth and wasteth..where is he ?	2252
Preserved. Not blot out the name of I..saved	2253
Sudden. Did eat..married wives..until the day	2254
Unexpected. They sold, they planted, they builded	2255
Vandals. Man was famous..break down the	2256

SHIPWRECK.

Perils by. Thrice I suffered shipwreck [Paul]	7839
Saved in. Some on boards and some on broken	7840

Anguish. Slay me, for anguish is come upon me	2213
Awakening. Wine was gone out..heart died	2215
Changes. L. maketh the earth empty..upside d.	4435
Cry. Great cry..none like it, nor shall be	2437
Derided. They that see me, shoot out the lip	2438
Discouragement. It had been better..serve the	2216
" What shall I do..ready to stone	3440
Famine. Delicate woman..shall eat..children	3441
Great. May thrust out the right eyes..people	3444
Interpretation. Their gods are gods of the hills	5455
" L. hath forsaken us..Midianites	5457
Neglect. House upon the sand..floods came	3267
Refuge. Ahaz sacrificed..unto the gods that	3446
Sixth Seal. Earthquake and the sun became black	8947

1007. CALL to Apostleship. *Matthew.* [In Galilee, Jesus] ²⁷ Saw a publican, named Levi, sitting at the receipt of custom : and he said unto him, Follow me. ²⁸ And he left all, rose up, and followed him.—LUKE, ch. 5.

1008. —— of Children. *Samuel.* ³ Ere the lamp of God went out in the temple..and Samuel was laid down *to sleep ;* ⁴ The Lord called Samuel : and he answered, Here *am* I. ⁵ And he ran unto Eli, and said..thou calledst me.— 1 SAM., ch. 3.

1009. —— Dishonoured, A. *At Capernaum.* ⁵⁹ He said..Follow me. But he said, Lord, suffer me first to go and bury my father. ⁶⁰ Jesus said..Let the dead bury their dead : but go thou and preach the kingdom of God.—LUKE, ch. 9.

1010. —— to Earnestness. *Looking Back.* ⁶¹ Lord, I will follow thee ; but let me first go bid them farewell, which are at home.. ⁶² And Jesus said..No man, having put his hand to the plough, and looking back, is fit for the kingdom of God.—LUKE, ch. 9.

1011. —— An instrumental. *Moses.* ¹⁸ Take thee Joshua..a man in whom *is* the spirit, and lay thine hand upon him : ¹⁹ And set him before Eleazar the priest, and before all the congregation ; and give him a charge in their sight.— NUM., ch. 27.

1012. —— A ministerial. *Levite.* ⁹ I am a Levite..and I go to sojourn where I may find *a place.* ¹⁰ And Micah said..Dwell with me, and be unto me a father and a priest, and I will give thee ten *shekels* of silver by the year, and a suit of apparel, and thy victuals. So the Levite went in.—JUDGES, ch. 17.

1013. —— Obedience to Christ's. *Peter— Andrew.* ¹⁶ He saw Simon and Andrew his brother casting a net into the sea : for they were fishers. ¹⁷ And Jesus said..Come ye after me, and I will make you to become fishers of men. ¹⁸ And straightway they forsook their nets, and followed him.—MARK, ch. 1.

1014. —— to Preach. *Paul.* ¹⁶ Necessity is laid upon me ; yea, woe is unto me, if I preach not the gospel ! ¹⁷ For if I do this thing willingly, I have a reward : but if against my will, a dispensation *of the gospel* is committed unto me.—1 COR., ch. 9.

1015. —— Response to God's. *Isaiah.* ⁶ Then flew one of the seraphim..having a live coal in his hand..from off the altar : ⁷ And he laid *it* upon my mouth, and said, Lo, this hath touched thy lips ; and thine iniquity is taken away.. ⁸ Also I heard the voice of the Lord, saying, Whom shall I send, and who will go for us ? Then said I, Here *am* I ; send me.—ISA., ch. 6.

1016. —— of the Spirit. *Isaiah.* ²⁰ Thine eyes shall see thy teachers : ²¹ And thine ears shall hear a word behind thee, saying, This *is* the way, walk ye in it, when ye turn to the right hand, and when ye turn to the left.—ISA., ch. 30.

1017. —— Sacrifice at Christ's. *James—John.* ¹⁹ He saw James..and John his brother..mending their nets. ²⁰ ..He called them : and they left their father Zebedee in the ship with the hired servants, and went after him.—MARK, ch. 1.

1018. —— in a Vision. A. *Paul.* ⁹ There stood a man of Macedonia..saying, Come over into Macedonia, and help us. ¹⁰ And..immediately we endeavoured to go into Macedonia, assuredly gathering that the Lord had called us for to preach the gospel unto them.—ACTS, ch. 16.

See other illustrations under :

COMMANDMENT.

First. Love the L. with all thine heart..neighbour	1391
Ignored. N. and A..offered strange fire..devoured	1392
Nature. Let there be light..was light.	1393
New. Love one another	1394
Smallest. Bird's nest chance to be..dam..young	1395

INVITATION.

Bountiful. Come unto me..eat the fat of the land	4649
Benevolence. Whosoever is of a willing heart	4650
Christian. Can any good come out of Nazareth	4651
Divine. Ho, every one that thirsteth, come	4652
Gospel. Sent..servants to call..to the wedding	4653
Grace. Spirit and the bride say, Come	4654
Heavenward. Come..we will do thee good..L.	4655
Pressing. I stand at the door and knock..voice	4656
Solicited. Bid me come unto thee upon the water	4657

Unexpected. Elisha was plowing with 12 yoke	3045
Special. Gideon. Go in this thy might..I sent thee	1422

1019. CALM commanded. *Sea.* ²³ They were filled *with water,* and were in jeopardy. ²⁴ And they..awoke him, saying, Master, Master, we perish. Then he arose, and rebuked the wind and the raging of the water : and they ceased, and there was a calm.—LUKE, ch. 8.

1020. —— **A holy.** *Stephen.* [59] They stoned Stephen, calling upon *God*, and saying, Lord Jesus, receive my spirit. [60] And he kneeled down, and cried with a loud voice, Lord, lay not this sin to their charge. -And when he had said this, he fell asleep.—ACTS, ch. 7.

Also see :

Sleep. Peter was sleeping between two soldiers 1441

— CANDOR. —— ——

See illustrations under SINCERITY.

— CALUMNY. —— ——

See illustrations under SLANDER.

— CAPRICE. —— ——

See illustrations under :

Opinions. Barbarians saw..murderer..a god 1096
Social. Now they..have me in derision 1097

1021. CAPTAIN, A divine. *Angel.* [13] When Joshua was by Jericho..he..behold, there stood a man over against him with his sword drawn in his hand : and Joshua..said..*Art* thou for us, or for our adversaries? [14] And he said, Nay ; but *as* captain of the host of the Lord am I now come.—JOSH., ch. 5.

See WAR and references.

1022. CAPTIVE, Compassion for the. *Divine.* [God said to Moses,] [5] I have also heard the groaning of the children of Israel, whom the Egyptians keep in bondage ; and I have remembered my covenant.—EX., ch. 6.

1023. —— **A victorious.** *Samson.* [14] Philistines shouted against him : and the Spirit of the Lord came mightily upon him, and the cords that *were* upon his arms became as flax that was burnt with fire, and his bands loosed from off his hands. [15] And he found a new jawbone of an ass..and slew a thousand men therewith.—JUDGES, ch. 15.

1024. —— **Kindness to.** *Judah.* [15] The men ∴took the captives, and with the spoil clothed all that were naked..and gave them to eat and to drink, and anointed them, and carried all the feeble of them upon asses..to Jericho, the city of palm trees, to their brethren.—2 CHRON., ch. 28.

1025. —— **Mercy to.** *Syrians.* [21] The king of Israel said unto Elisha..shall I smite *them?*.. [22]..Thou shalt not smite *them :* wouldest thou smite those whom thou hast taken captive..set bread and water before them, that they may eat and drink, and go to their master.—2 KINGS, ch. 6.

1026. —— **Mourning of.** *Jews.* [1] By the rivers of Babylon, there we sat down, yea, we wept, when we remembered Zion. [2] We hanged our harps upon the willows in the midst thereof. —Ps. 137.

1027. CAPTIVES, Songless. *Jews.* [3] There they that carried us away captive required of us a song ; and they that wasted us *required of us* mirth, *saying*, Sing us *one* of the songs of Zion. [4] How shall we sing the Lord's song in a strange land ?—Ps. 137.

1028. —— **Return from.** *Joyful.* [10] The ransomed of the Lord shall return, and come to Zion with songs and everlasting joy upon their heads : they shall obtain joy and gladness, and sorrow and sighing shall flee away.—ISA., ch. 35.

1029. —— **Sin brings.** *Jews.* [22] The children of Israel walked in all the sins of Jeroboam ..[23] Until the Lord removed Israel out of his sight.. So was Israel carried away out of their own land to Assyria.—2 KINGS, ch. 17.

1030. —— *Israelites.* [12] The Lord strengthened Eglon the king of Moab against Israel, because they had done evil.. [14] So the children of Israel served Eglon..eighteen years. —JUDGES, ch. 3.

1031. —— **An unexpected.** *At Ziklag.* [3] David and his men came to the city, and, behold, *it was* burned with fire ; and their wives..sons, and..daughters, were taken captives. [4] Then David and the people..lifted up their voice and wept, until they had no more power to weep.— 1 SAM., ch. 30.

See BONDAGE and references.

1032. CARE at the Beginning. *Builder.* [28] Which of you, intending to build a tower, sitteth not down first, and counteth the cost, whether he have *sufficient* to finish *it ?* [29] Lest haply, after he hath laid the foundation, and is not able to finish *it*, all that behold *it* begin to mock him.—LUKE, ch. 14.

1033. —— **for Others, Christian.** *Samaritan.* [33] When he saw him, he had compassion.. [34]..and bound up his wounds, pouring in oil and wine, and set him on his own beast, and brought him to an inn, and took care of him.— LUKE, ch. 10.

1034. —— **for Birds.** *Birds.* [6] If a bird's nest chance, to be .. in any tree, or on the ground, *whether they be* young ones, or eggs, and the dam sitting upon the young, or upon the eggs, thou shalt not take the dam with the young : [7]..that it may be well with thee..mayest prolong *thy* days.—DEUT., ch. 22.

1035. —— **of God for Animals.** *Fowls.* [Jesus said,] [26] Behold the fowls of the air : for they sow not, neither do they reap, nor gather into barns ; yet your heavenly Father feedeth them. Are ye not much better than they ?—MAT., ch. 6.

1036. —— **of God acknowledged.** *Jacob.* [15] He blessed Joseph, and said, God, before whom my fathers Abraham and Isaac did walk, the God which fed me all my life long unto this day, [16] The Angel which redeemed me from all evil, bless the lads.—GEN., ch. 48.

1037. —— **of God, Delicate.** *Eye.* [8] Thus saith the Lord of hosts..he that toucheth you, toucheth the apple of his eye. [9] For, behold, I will shake mine hand upon them.—ZECH., ch. 2.

1038. —— **of God, Defending.** *Hedge.* [9] Satan ..said, Doth Job fear God for nought ? [10] Hast not thou made a hedge about him, and about his house, and about all that he hath on every side ?—JOB, ch. 1.

1039. —— **of God illustrated.** *Sparrows.* [Jesus said,] [29] Are not two sparrows sold for a farthing ? and one of them shall not fall on the ground without your Father.—MAT., ch. 10.

1040. —— **of God, Perfect.** *Promise.* [11] He shall feed his flock like a shepherd : he shall gather the lambs with his arm, and carry *them* in his bosom, *and* shall gently lead those that are with young.—ISA., ch. 40.

1041. —— **God's protecting.** *Horses of Fire.* [15] Alas, my master ! how shall we do ? [16] And he answered, Fear not : for they that *be* with us *are* more than they that *be* with them. [17] And Elisha prayed..And the Lord opened the eyes of the young man ; and he saw : and, behold, the mountain *was* full of horses and chariots of fire round about Elisha.—2 KINGS, ch. 6.

1042. —— **The Good Shepherd's.** *David.* [1] The Lord *is* my shepherd ; I shall not want. [2] He maketh me to lie down in green pastures : he leadeth me beside the still waters.—Ps. 23.

1043. —— **of God, Sheltering.** *Eagle.* [11] As an eagle stirreth up her nest, fluttereth over her young, spreadeth abroad her wings, taketh them, beareth them on her wings : [12] *So* the Lord alone did lead him.—DEUT., ch. 32.

1044. —— **of God, Sustaining.** *Drought.* [11] The Lord shall guide thee continually, and satisfy thy soul in drought, and make fat thy bones : and thou shalt be like a watered garden, and like a spring of water, whose waters fail not.— ISA., ch. 58.

1045. —— **of God, Sleepless.** *In Night.* [3] He will not suffer thy foot to be moved : he that keepeth thee will not slumber.—Ps. 121.

1046. —— **of God, Tender.** *Wings.* [Jesus said,] [34] O Jerusalem, Jerusalem, *thou* that killest the prophets, and stonest them .. how often would I have gathered thy children together, even as a hen gathereth her chickens under *her* wings, and ye would not !—MAT., ch. 23.

See other illustrations under :
DELIVERANCE.

PRESERVATION.

1047. CARES, Burdensome. *Martha.* [40] Martha was cumbered about much serving..and said, Lord, dost thou not care that my sister hath left me to serve alone ? bid her therefore that she help me. [41] And Jesus answered..Martha, Martha, thou art careful and troubled about many things.—LUKE, ch. 10.

1048. —— **Disturbing.** *The Rich.* [12] The sleep of a labouring man *is* sweet, whether he eat little or much : but the abundance of the rich will not suffer him to sleep.—ECCL., ch. 5.

1049. —— **Ministerial.** *Paul.* [27] In weari-

ness and painfulness, in watchings often, in hunger and thirst, in fastings often, in cold and nakedness. [28] Beside those things that are without, that which cometh upon me daily, the care of all the churches.—2 COR., ch. 11.

1050. —— **of Wealth.** *Dives.* [16] The ground of a certain rich man brought forth plentifully : [17] And he thought within himself, saying, What shall I do, because I have no room where to bestow my fruits ? [18]..I will pull down my barns, and build greater.—LUKE, ch. 12.

See other illustrations under :
ADMONITION.

ALARM.

ANXIETY.

CAUTION.

DISCRETION.

PRUDENCE.

WATCHING.

Dead. Rizpah.. from the beginning of harvest till 9344
Failure. Disciples, and findeth them asleep 9345
Hinderances. Overcharged with surfeiting..cares 9346
Malicious. Watched him whether he would heal 9347
Prayer. When the fowls came..Abram drove them 9348
   " We made our prayer..and set a watch 9349
   " Anna..fastings and prayers night and day 9350
   " Jesus..continued all night in prayer to G. 9351
Vigilant. Watch..lest coming suddenly he find 9352
Watched. Compassed about..cloud of witnesses 9353
World's. Herod feared John..observed him 9354

WATCHFULNESS.
Lack. Foolish virgins..said give us of your oil 9855
Necessary. Be vigilant..the devil as a roaring lion 9856
Personal. Appointed watches..every one..against 9857
Rewarded. Blessed are those servants..shall find 9858

Discipline. Nay; lest while ye gather up the tares 2338
Famine. Eat bread by weight..water by measure 3024
Influence. Nor to drink wine..whereby thy 4469
Useless. Which..by taking thought can add one 3333

1051. CARELESSNESS with Fire. *Law.* [6] If fire break out, and catch in thorns, so that the stacks of corn, or the standing corn, or the field, be consumed *therewith*; he that kindled the fire shall surely make restitution.—Ex., ch. 22.

1052. —— Presumptuous. *Ox.* [35] If one man's ox hurt another's, that he die, then they shall sell the live ox, and divide the money of it; and the dead *ox* also they shall divide. [36] Or if it be known that the ox hath used to push in time past, and his owner hath not kept him in, he shall surely pay ox for ox; and the dead shall be his own.—Ex., ch. 21.

1053. —— Responsibility for. *Pit.* [33] If a man shall open a pit..and not cover it, and an ox, or an ass fall therein; [34] The owner of the pit shall make *it* good..and the dead *beast* shall be his.—Ex., ch. 21.

See other illustrations under:
FORGETFULNESS.
Adversity. Whom I loved have turned against me 3346
Caution. Take heed..lest thou forget..thine eyes 3347
of God. Have eaten..full, beware..forget the L. 3342
   " Jeshurun..lightly esteemed the rock 3343
   " When silver and gold is multiplied..forget 3344
Religious. I will not go..He went back with him 3348
Sanctuary. If I forget thee, O Jerusalem..tongue 3345
Spiritual. Face in a glass..straightway forgetteth 3349

INDIFFERENCE.
Hearing. Foolish man who built..upon the sand 4405
Inconsiderate. Here is thy pound which I have 4406
Provoking. Wrath because..have not hearkened 4407
Pitiless. Saw him and passed by..other side 4408
Sin. I have sinned..What is that to us? 4409
Sinners. Made light of it and went their ways 4410
Unbelievers. They did eat..until the day Noe 4411

INDIFFERENT.
Curse. Curse ye Meroz..came not..help of the L. 4412
Woe. Woe unto thém that are at ease in Zion 4413

Neglect. What honour hath been done to Mordecai 5696
Poor. When saw we thee a hungered..in prison 5709
Ungrateful. Yet did not the chief butler remember 3096

—— CARICATURE. —— ——
See
Profane. Clothed Jesus with purple..crown 6600

1054. CARNAGE permitted. *All the Jews by Haman.* [9] Let it be written that they may be destroyed: and I will pay ten thousand talents of silver.—Esth., ch. 3.

See other illustrations under:
CRUELTY.
Captives. Joab put them under saws..harrows 1864
   " Judah cast [10,000 men of Sier] from the 1858
Maternal. Athaliah. destroyed all the seed royal 1857

MASSACRE.
Intended. Letters were sent by post..to destroy 5249
Infants. Herod.. slew all the children..in Bethlehem 5250
Treacherous. Jehu said, Proclaim an assembly for 5251

1055. CASTE abolished. *Peter.* [At Cornelius's house,] [28] Ye know how that it is an unlawful thing for a man that is a Jew to..come unto one of another nation; but God hath shewed me that I should not call any man common or unclean.—Acts, ch. 10.

1056. —— Egyptian. *Joseph.* [32] They set on for him by himself, and for them by themselves, and for the Egyptians..by themselves: because the Egyptians might not eat bread with the Hebrews; for that *is* an abomination unto the Egyptians.—Gen., ch. 43.

1057. —— ignored. *"The Canaanite."* [14] And he ordained twelve..Thomas, and James..and Thaddeus, and Simon the Canaanite.—Mark, ch. 3.

1058. —— Jewish. *Samaritans.* [9] Saith the woman of Samaria unto him, How is it that thou, being a Jew, askest drink of me, which am a woman of Samaria? for the Jews have no dealings with the Samaritans.—John, ch. 4.

1059. —— No more. *Vision.* [11] A great sheet knit at the four corners, and let down to the earth: [12] Wherein were all manner of four-footed beasts..wild beasts, and creeping things, and fowls.. [13] And there came a voice to him, Rise, Peter; kill, and eat.. [34] Then Peter..said, Of a truth I perceive that God is no respecter of persons: [35] But in every nation he that feareth him, and worketh righteousness, is accepted with him.—Acts, ch. 10.

1060. —— No Respect for. *Death.* [29] At midnight the Lord smote all the firstborn in the land of Egypt, from the firstborn of Pharaoh that sat on his throne unto the firstborn of the captive that *was* in the dungeon.—Ex., ch. 12.

1061. —— Religious. *John.* [38] Master, we saw one casting out devils in thy name..and we forbade him, because he followeth not us. [39] But Jesus said, Forbid him not.—Mark, ch. 9.

1062. —— Super-religious. *Pharisee.* [38] Began to wash his feet with tears, and did wipe *them* with the hairs of her head, and kissed his feet, and anointed *them* with the ointment. [39] The Pharisee..spake within himself..if he were a prophet, would have known who and what manner of woman *this is*..for she is a sinner.—Luke, ch. 7.

See other illustrations under:
Race. Haman..scorned to lay hands..showed him 400
   " Miriam..spake against Moses..married 1378
Wealth. If there come in your assembly a man 1353

1063. CASUISTRY, False. *Pharisees.* [16] Woe unto you, *ye* blind guides, which say, Whosoever shall swear by the temple, it is nothing; but whosoever shall swear by the gold of the temple, he is a debtor!—Mat., ch. 23.

1064. —— Hypocritical. *Pharisees.* [23] Woe unto you, scribes and Pharisees, hypocrites! for ye pay tithe of mint and anise and cummin, and have omitted the weightier *matters* of the law, judgment, mercy, and faith.—MAT., ch. 23.

See CONSCIENCE and references.

1065. CATHOLICITY, Example of. *John.* [See No. 1061.]

1066. —— Reward of. *Jesus.* [41] Whosoever shall give you a cup of water to drink in my name, because ye belong to Christ..he shall not lose his reward.—MARK, ch. 9.

See other illustrations under :
LIBERALITY OF OPINION.
Christian. Let not him that eateth despise 4951
Sabbath. The sabbath was made for man, not 4953
Unselfish. Eldad..Medad prophesy..enviest thou 4959

1067. CAUTION, Confidence without. *Benjamites* [32] Said, They *are* smitten down before us, as at the first. But the children of Israel said, Let us flee, and draw them from the city unto the highways.. [44] And there fell of Benjamin eighteen thousand men.—JUDGES, ch. 20.

1068. —— in Eating. *Proverb.* [1] When thou sittest to eat with a ruler, consider diligently what *is* before thee : [2] And put a knife to thy throat, if thou *be* a man given to appetite. [3] Be not desirous of his dainties : for they are deceitful meat.—PROV., ch. 23.

1069. —— in Hearing. *Sower.* [8] Other fell on good ground, and..increased, and brought forth, some thirty, and some sixty, and some a hundred. [9] And he said..He that hath ears to hear, let him hear.—MARK, ch. 4.

1070. —— Necessary. *Proverb.* [15] The simple believeth every word : but the prudent *man* looketh well to his going. [16] A wise *man* feareth, and departeth from evil : but the fool rageth, and is confident.—PROV., ch. 14.

1071. —— A prudent. *Retreat.* [25] The children of Dan said unto him, Let not thy voice be heard among us, lest angry fellows run upon thee, and thou lose thy life, with the lives of thy household. [26] ..And when Micah saw that they *were* too strong for him, he turned and went back unto his house.—JUDGES, ch. 18.

1072. —— of the Wise. *Proverb.* [11] A fool uttereth all his mind : but a wise *man* keepeth it in till afterwards.—PROV., ch. 29.

See CARE and references.

1073. CAVE, Home in a. *David.* [1] David.. escaped to the cave Adullam..and all his father's house..went down thither to him.—1 SAM., ch. 22.

1074. —— Refuge in a. *Elijah.* [He went] [8] Unto Horeb the mount of God. [9] And he came thither unto a cave, and lodged there.—1 KINGS, ch. 19.

See other illustrations under :
Burial. Machpelah..the cave and all the trees 4893
" Grave it was a cave..stone lay—John 11 : 38
Hidden. Five kings were found hid in a cave 9508
" Because of the Midianites—Judges 6 : 2
" I. were in a strait..hide..caves 3278
" Obadiah took 100 prophets and hid 3417
Home. Lot dwelt in a cave..two daughters 4042

1075. CELEBRATION, A worthy. *Jerusalem.* [35] They cast their garments upon the colt, and they set Jesus thereon. [36] ..they spread their clothes in the way. The whole multitude of the disciples began to rejoice and praise God with a loud voice.. [38] Saying, Blessed *be* the King that cometh in the name of the Lord : peace in heaven, and glory in the highest.—LUKE, ch. 19.

See other illustrations under :
FEAST.
Ancient. Sarah..made cakes..Abraham..calf 3172
Birthday. Herod on his birthday made a supper 3173
Charitable. Call the poor, the lame..blind 3174
Complimentary. At Bethany..they made Jesus a 3175
" Levi made Jesus a great feast 3176
Death. Job's sons and daughters..brother's house 3177
Ended sadly. Merry with wine..smite Amnon 3178
Farewell. Elisha..oxen, and slew them..people 3179
Great. Solomon offered 22,000 oxen and 120,000 s. 3180
Idolatrous. [Calf] People..eat..drink..rose up to 3181
Impious. Belshazzar made a feast to a thousand 3182
Joyous. [Tabernacles] Seven days shall dwell in 3183
Marriage. Jesus and his disciples were called 3184
National. Three times..keep a feast unto me..year 3186
Royal. Ahasuerus made a feast at Sushan 3185

Angelic. One cried unto another, Holy, holy, holy 3999
Ark of God. David danced..Sound of the trumpet 1903
Deliverance. Miriam and women..timbrels, dances 1899
Enemies conquered. Saul and all..rejoiced 4078
Philistines slaughtered. Women came singing 1902
Purim. Make them days of feasting and joy 3536
Sacrament. This is my body..do in remembrance 7062
Victory. Amalekites..were eating and drinking 9983

1076. CEMETERY, The first mentioned. *Jacob.* [29] Bury me with my fathers.. [30] In the cave that *is* in the field of Machpelah..which Abraham bought..for a..burying place.—GEN., ch. 49.

See other illustrations under :
BURIAL.
Denied. Bring out the bones of the kings..spread 974
Life from. Touched the bones of Elisha, he revived 975
Living. Earth opened her mouth and swallowed 976
Mournful. David..lifted up his voice..grave of 977
Mysterious. Moses died..no man knoweth his 978
Patriarchs. All the servants of Pharaoh..elders 979
Perfumed. Asa's grave..filled with sweet odours 980

GRAVE.
Chosen. Bury me with my fathers in the cave 3703
First Bargain. Cave of Machpelah..money..worth 3074
Longed for. O that thou wouldest hide me in the g. 3705

Crematory. Valiant men..body of Saul..sons..burnt 1828
Funeral, Joyous. I say unto thee Arise..dead sat up 3492

1077. CENSURE, Preparation for. *Jesus.* [5] Thou hypocrite, first cast out the beam out of thine own eye ; and then shalt thou see clearly to cast out the mote out of thy brother's eye.— MAT., ch. 7. [See No. 1080.]

1078. —— Severe. *Israelites.* [12] *Is* not this the word that we did tell thee in Egypt, saying, Let us alone, that we may serve the Egyptians? For *it had been* better for us..than that we should die in the wilderness.—Ex., ch. 14.

1079. —— Undeserved. *Israelites.* [20] They met Moses and Aaron..as they came forth from Pharaoh : [21] And..said..ye have made our savour to be abhorred in the eyes of Pharaoh, and..his servants, to put a sword in their hand to slay us.—Ex., ch. 5.

1080. CENSORIOUSNESS reproved. *Jesus.*
[3] Why beholdest thou the mote that is in thy
brother's eye, but considerest not the beam that
is in thine own eye? [4] Or how wilt thou say..
Let me pull out the mote out of thine eye ; and,
behold, a beam *is* in thine own eye.—MAT., ch.
7. [See No. 1077.]

1081. —— Unbrotherly. *James.* [11] Speak
not evil one of another, brethren. He that
speaketh evil of *his* brother, and judgeth his
brother, speaketh evil of the law, and judgeth
the law.—JAMES, ch. 4.

See BLAME and references.

1082. CEREMONY, A powerless. *Gehazi.*
[31] Gehazi..laid the staff upon the face of the
child ; but *there was* neither voice, nor hearing.
Wherefore he went..saying, The child is not
awaked.—2 KINGS, ch. 4.

See other illustrations under :

POLITENESS.

Cultivated. May we know what this new doctrine 6232
Inculcated. Sit down in the lowest room..go up 6233
Treacherous. Art thou in health,my brother?..smote 6234
Tender. Is your father well, the old man of whom 6235

Formal. Honoureth me with their lips.'.heart is far 3375
Failure. Gehazi laid the staff upon the face 3373
Heartless. Ye said, What a weariness is it 3374
Prayer. I thank..I fast..I give 3376
Royal. Ahasuerus..made a feast..vessels..drinking 2409

1083. CHALLENGE to Battle. *Goliath.* [16] The
Philistine said, I defy the armies of Israel this
day ; give me a man, that we may fight together.
[11] Saul and all Israel..were dismayed, and greatly
afraid.—1 SAM., ch. 17.

1084. —— of Champions. *Duels.* [14] Abner
said to Joab, Let the young men..play before us
..[15] Then..twelve of Benjamin, which *pertained*
to Ish-bosheth the son of Saul, and twelve of
the servants of David. [16] And they caught every
one his fellow by the head, and *thrust* his sword
in his fellow's side ; so they fell down together.
—2 SAM., ch. 2.

1085. —— a Prayer. *Elijah.* [22] Said Elijah
..I, *even* I only, remain a prophet of the Lord ;
but Baal's prophets *are* four hundred and fifty
men.. [24] And call ye on the name of your gods,
and I will call on the name of the Lord : and
the God that answereth by fire, let him be God
..the people..said, It is well spoken.—1 KINGS,
ch. 18.

1086. —— for War. *Jehu.* [1] Jehu wrote
letters..to them that brought up Ahab's *children,*
saying.. [3] Look even out the best and meetest of
your master's sons, and set *him* on his father's
throne, and fight for your master's house.—2
KINGS, ch. 10.

See other illustrations under :

Awaiting. If they say thus, Come up..will go up 121
Defiant. Pharaoh..Who is the L..I should obey 2117
Impious. Belshazzar commanded to bring..vessels 2116

1087. CHAMPION, A Boastful. *Goliath.*
[10] The Philistine said, I defy the armies of Israel
this day.. [44] And..said to David, Come to me,
and I will give thy flesh unto the fowls of the
air, and to the beasts of the field.—1 SAM., ch. 17.

See other illustrations under :

HEROISM.

Christian. Bonds..abide me..none of these things 3959
Needless. Three mighty men brake through..well 3961

Numbers. Shamgar slew 600 with an ox-goad   3962
Patriotic. Jael..smote the nail into his [Sisera's]   3957
   "   Woman cast a stone upon Abimelech   3958

MIGHTY MEN.

Adino. Mighty men whom David had..chief among 5332
Abishai. Chief among the three..against 300..slew 5336
Benaiah. Slew the lion-like men of Moab   5337
Eleazer. Smote the Philistines..hand clave to his 5333
Shammah. Stood in the midst..slew the Philistines 5334
Three. Brake through the host of the Philistines 5335

Benaiah. Plucked the spear out of the Egyptian's 1543
Captains. See Abner, Abishai, and Joab—1 and 2 Sam.
Faith. He took his staff..five smooth stones   9443
Lords. They cried, The sword of the L. and Gideon 8532
Ominous. David saw the angel having a drawn   8534
   "   Joshua was by Jericho..stood a man   1021
Outfit. Take the sword of the S. which is the sword 8539

1088. CHANCE disproved. *Kine.* [11] They
laid the ark of the Lord upon the cart.. [12] And
the kine took the straight way to..Beth-shemesh
..lowing as they went, and turned not aside *to*
the right hand or *to* the left.—1 SAM., ch. 6.
[They left their calves behind.]

See other illustrations under :

EXPERIMENT.

Dietetic. Ten days, let them give us pulse to eat 2817
Faith's. Peter walked on the water to go to Jesus 2818

FUTURE.

God's Will. If the L. will, we shall live and do this 3494
Ignorance. If thou hadst known..hid from thine 3495
Piety. Let me first go and bid them farewell 3496
Presuming. I will pull down my barns..ease, eat 3497
Uncertainty. Boast not..of to-morrow..knowest 3498
Unseen. God said, Thou fool, this night thy soul 3499

LOT.

Condemnation. Brought his household..Achan 5087
   "   Let us cast lots that we may 5088
Called. Custom of the priests, his lot was to burn 5089
Division. Divide the land by lot for an inheritance 5090
Gambling. Soldiers..took his coat..cast lots for it 5091
Prayer. They prayed..gave forth their lots 5092

VENTURE.

Believers. Went into the midst of the sea..waters 9185
Shot. Drew a bow at a venture and smote the 9186

Manslaughter. Axe..head slippeth upon his 5214
   "   [Jewish law, Num. 35 : 9-29.]

1089. CHANGE by Conversion. *Saul.* [19] Then
was Saul certain days with the disciples which
were at Damascus.. [20] And straightway he
preached Christ in the synagogues, that he is
the Son of God.—ACTS, ch. 9.

1090. —— deplored. *Job.* [2] Oh that I were
as *in* months past, as *in* the days *when* God preserved me.. [3] When his candle shined upon my
head, *and when* by his light I walked *through*
darkness.—JOB, ch. 29.

1091. —— of Disposition. *King Saul.* [14] The
Spirit of the Lord departed from Saul, and an
evil spirit from the Lord troubled him.—1 SAM.,
ch. 16.

1092. —— A delivering. *From Haman.*
[1] When the king's..decree drew near to be put
in execution, in the day that the enemies of the
Jews hoped to have power over them..it was
turned to the contrary, that the Jews had rule
over them that hated them.—ESTHER, ch. 9.

1093. —— A happy. *Four Lepers.* [8] Came
to the uttermost part of the camp, they went in-

to one tent, and did eat and drink, and carried thence silver and gold.. ⁹ Then they said.. We do not well : this day *is* a day of good tidings, and we hold our peace.—2 KINGS, ch. 7.

1094. —— **Impossible.** *Blessing.* ³³ Isaac trembled very exceedingly, and said, Who? where *is* he that hath taken venison, and brought *it* me, and I have.. blessed him? yea, *and* he shall be blessed.—GEN., ch. 27.

1095. —— **An official.** *Administration.* ²² Moses.. took Joshua, and set him before Eleazar the priest, and before all the congregation : ²³And he laid his hands upon him, and gave him a charge.—NUM., ch. 27.

1096. —— **of Opinions.** *Barbarians.* ⁴ When the barbarians saw the *venomous* beast hang on his hand, they said.. No doubt this man is a murderer, whom, though he hath escaped the sea, yet vengeance suffereth not to live.. ⁶.. saw no harm come to him, they changed their minds, and said that he was god.—ACTS, ch. 28.

1097. —— **Great social.** *Job.* ⁷ When I went out to the gate through the city.. ⁸ The young men saw me, and hid themselves : and the aged arose, *and* stood up.. ⁹ The princes refrained talking.—JOB, ch. 29. ¹ But now *they that are* younger than I have me in derision, whose fathers I would have disdained to have set with the dogs of my flock.. ⁹ And now am I their song.. their byword. ¹⁰ They abhor me.. and spare not to spit in my face.—JOB, ch. 30.

1098. —— **A sudden.** *Saul.* ¹ Saul, yet breathing out threatenings and slaughter against the disciples of the Lord.. ⁶ And he trembling and astonished said, Lord, what wilt thou have me to do?—ACTS, ch. 9.

1099. —— **of Seasons.** *Regular.* [After the flood, God said,] ²¹ Neither will I again smite any more every thing living, as I have done.. ²² While the earth remaineth, seedtime and harvest, and cold and heat, and summer and winter, and day and night shall not cease.— GEN., ch. 8.

1100. —— **A surprising.** *Mordecai.* ¹⁵ Mordecai went out from the presence of the king in royal apparel of blue and white, and with a great crown of gold, and with a garment of fine linen and purple : and the city of Shushan rejoiced and was glad.—ESTHER, ch. 8.

1101. —— **Undesired.** *Aged.* [Being invited to go,] ³⁴ Barzillai said unto the king, How long have I to live, that I should go up with the king unto Jerusalem? ³⁵ I am this day fourscore years old.—2 SAM., ch. 19.

1102. CHANGES by Affliction. *Job's Friends.* ¹⁹ When they lifted up their eyes afar off, and knew him not, they lifted up their voice, and wept ; and they rent every one his mantle, and sprinkled dust upon their heads towards heaven.—JOB, ch. 2.

1103. —— **by Bereavement.** *Naomi.* ⁵ The woman was left of her two sons and her husband.. ²¹ I went out full, and the Lord hath brought me home again empty : why *then* call ye me Naomi, seeing.. the Almighty hath afflicted me.—RUTH, ch. 1.

1104. —— **Desolating.** *Job.* [After all his losses,] ²⁰ Job arose, and rent his mantle, and shaved his head, and fell down upon the ground,

and worshipped, ²¹ And ,said, Naked came I out of my mother's womb, and naked shall I return thither.—JOB, ch. 1.

1105. —— **of Spring-time.** *Flowers.* ¹¹ Lo, the winter is past, the rain is over *and* gone ; ¹² The flowers appear on the earth ; the time of the singing *of birds* is come, and the voice of the turtle is heard in our land ; ¹³ The fig tree putteth forth her green figs, and the vines *with* the tender grape give a *good* smell.—SOLOMON'S SONG, ch. 2.

1106. —— **Speedy spiritual.** *Jailer.* [To the would-be suicide,] ²⁸ Paul cried.. Do thyself no harm : for we are all here. ²⁹ Then he called for a light.. sprang in.. trembling, and fell down before Paul and Silas, ³⁰ And brought them out, and said, Sirs, what must I do to be saved?— ACTS, ch. 16.

See other illustrations under :

GROWTH.

Beautiful. Soul shall be as a well watered garden	3739
Continuous. Flourish like the palm tree.. fruit in	3740
Christian. Your faith groweth exceedingly	3741
Divine. Jesus increased in wisdom and stature	3742
Esteem. Samuel grew.. in favor with G. and man	3743
Fruit. Branch that beareth not he taketh away	3744
Grace. Like a tree planted by the rivers of water	3745
Imperceptible. First the blade, then the ear.. corn	3746
Inward. Leaven.. meal till the whole was leavened	3747
Outward. Becometh greater than all herbs	3748
Perfection. Path.. shineth more and more	3749
Stages. Blade.. ear.. full corn in the ear	3750
Strength. Clean hands shall be stronger and	3751
Spiritual. Child [J. B.].. grew and waxed strong	3752

INCREASE.

Miraculous. Five loaves and two fishes.. 5000 fed	4392
" Should I set this before a hundred	4393

IMPROVEMENT.

Adversity. God has furnished us less.. deserved	4363
Accountability. Whosoever hath [improved] to	4365
Necessary. These three years I come seeking	4366
Responsibility. Cast ye the unprofitable servant	4367

PERVERTER.

Famous. Jeroboam.. made Israel to sin, to	6108
Wicked. Elymas the sorcerer.. seeking to turn	6109
Perversion. Hezekiah brake in pieces the brazen	6110

RESTLESSNESS.

Care. He thought.. Thou fool, this night thy soul	7265
Fear. Would God it were morning	7266

SUBSTITUTE.

Inferior. Took away the shields of gold.. brazen	8418
Lord's. Every man a lamb.. for a house.. smote	8419
Official. Is not Aaron thy brother.. he can speak	8421
Personal. Became surety for the lad.. bear the	8422
Timely. Rain caught. offered him.. instead of his	8420

Assimilation. Leaven.. in three measures of meal	3678
Adversity. I was at ease.. He hath shaken me to	148
" All the city was moved.. Is this Naomi?	192
Conversion. Saul.. all said, Is not this he that	703
Contentment. Full and to be hungry.. abound	1642
Glorious. Sufferings.. not worthy to be compared	196
Interest. It is naught, saith the buyer.. he boasteth	641
Sudden. Sick of the palsy.. let down.. take up thy	824
Translation. Enoch walked with G.. G. took him	8880
Transfiguration. As he prayed.. his countenance	8882
" With open face, beholding.. are	8881
Vocation. Elisha.. left the oxen and ran after	176

See **CONVERSION.**

1107. CHAOS, Original. *Creation.* ² The earth was without form, and void ; and darkness *was* upon the face of the deep. And the Spirit of God moved upon the face of the waters. ³ And God said, Let there be light : and there was light.—GEN., ch. 1.

See other illustrations under :

CONFUSION.

Excitement. Some cried one thing, some another 1544
Public Opinion. Some say thou art John..Elias 1545
" Assembly was confused..knew 1546
Tongues. Confound their language..not 1547

1108. CHARACTER, An assumed. *Joseph.* ⁷ Joseph..knew them, but made himself strange ..and spake roughly ; and he said..Whence come ye? And they said, From the land of Canaan to buy food.—GEN., ch. 42.

1109. —— Decision of. *Daniel.* ⁸ Daniel purposed in his heart that he would not defile himself with the portion of the king's meat, nor with the wine which he drank : therefore he requested..that he might not defile himself.—DAN., ch. 1.

1110. —— disguised. *Chief Priests.* ²⁰ They watched *him*, and sent forth spies, which should feign themselves just men, that they might take hold of his words, that so they might deliver him unto..the governor.—LUKE, ch. 20.

1111. —— Deterioration of. *Demoniac.* ⁴⁵ Taketh with himself seven other spirits more wicked than himself, and they enter in and dwell there : and the last *state* of that man is worse than the first.—MAT., ch. 12.

1112. —— Dress indicates. *Prodigal.* ²² The father said to his servants, Bring forth the best robe, and put *it* on him ; and put a ring on his hand, and shoes on *his* feet.—LUKE, ch. 15.

1113. —— Deeds prove. *Blind Man*, [being healed, said,] ³² Since the world began was it not heard that any man opened the eyes of one that was born blind. ³³ If this man were not of God, he could do nothing.—JOHN, ch. 9.

1114. —— Failure of. *Adam.* ⁶ When the woman saw that the tree *was* good for food.. pleasant to the eyes..to be desired to make *one* wise, she took of the fruit thereof, and did eat, and gave also unto her husband.—GEN., ch. 3.

1115. —— Heroic. *Paul.* ¹² Besought him not to go up to Jerusalem. ¹³ Then Paul answered, What mean ye to weep and to break mine heart? for I am ready not to be bound only, but also to die at Jerusalem for the name the Lord Jesus.—ACTS, ch. 21.

1116. —— Judged by. *Eliab rejected.* ⁷ The Lord said unto Samuel, Look not on his countenance, or on the height of his stature ; because I have refused him : for *the* Lord *seeth* not as man seeth ; for man looketh on the outward appearance, but the Lord looketh on the heart. —1 SAM., ch. 16.

1117. —— misjudged. *By Murderers.* ⁵ Rechab and Baanah..came about the heat of the day to the house of Ish-bosheth, who lay on a bed at noon. ⁶..*as though* they would have fetched wheat.. ⁸ And they brought the head of Ish-bosheth unto David.—2 SAM., ch. 4. [They expected to please him, but he put them to death.]

1118. —— proved. *Abraham.* ¹ God did

tempt Abraham.. ¹⁶ By myself have I sworn, saith the Lord, for because thou..hast not withheld thy son, thine only *son.* ¹⁷ That in blessing I will bless thee.—GEN., ch. 22.

1119. —— Relapse of. *Backslider.* ²⁰ If after they have escaped the pollutions of the world ..they are again entangled therein, and overcome, the latter end is worse with them than the beginning.—2 PETER, ch. 2.

1120. —— Return of. *Apostate.* ²¹ It had been better for them not to have known the way of righteousness, than, after they have known *it*, to turn.. ²² But it is happened..The dog *is* turned to his own vomit again ; and, The sow that was washed to her wallowing in the mire. —2 PETER, ch. 2.

1121. —— Strength of. *Hebrew Worthies.* ¹⁸ But if not, be it known unto thee, O king, that we will not serve thy gods, nor worship the golden image which thou hast set up.— DAN., ch. 3.

1122. —— tested. *Adam.* ¹⁶ The Lord God commanded..Of every tree of the garden thou mayest freely eat : ¹⁷ But of the tree of the knowledge of good and evil, thou shalt not eat of it.— GEN., ch. 2.

1123. —— formed by Trial. *Israelites* ²⁹ Walked upon dry *land* in the midst of the sea ; and the waters *were* a wall unto them on their right hand, and on their left.—EX., ch. 14. [Bondmen's perilous route to freedom. Slaves to be a nation.]

1124. —— An unimpeachable. *Daniel.* ⁴ The presidents and princes sought to find occasion against Daniel concerning the kingdom ; but they could find none occasion nor fault ; forasmuch as he *was* faithful, neither was there any error.—DAN., ch. 6.

1125. —— verified. *Nicodemus* ² Came to Jesus by night, and said..Rabbi, we know that thou art a teacher come from God : for no man can do these miracles that thou doest, except God be with him.—JOHN, ch. 8.

1126. CHARACTERS differ. *Esau—Jacob.* ²⁷ The boys grew..Esau was a cunning hunter, a man of the field..Jacob *was* a plain man, dwelling in tents.—GEN., ch. 25.

1127. —— Mixed. *Wheat and Tares.* ²⁸ Wilt thou then that we go and gather them up? ²⁹ But he said, Nay ; lest while ye gather up the tares, ye root up also the wheat with them. ³⁰ Let both grow together until the harvest.— MAT., ch. 13.

1128. —— Opposite. *Two Creditors.* ³² O thou wicked servant, I forgave thee all that debt, because thou desiredst me.. ³³ Shouldest not thou also have had compassion on thy fellow servant, even as I had pity on thee? ³⁴ And his lord was wroth.—MAT., ch. 18.

1129. —— Separation of. *Ten Virgins* ¹ Took their lamps, and went forth to meet the bridegroom. ² And five of them were wise, and five *were* foolish.. ¹¹ Afterward came also the other virgins, saying, Lord, Lord, open to us.—MAT., ch. 25.

1130. —— unlike. *Two Sons.* ¹³ The younger son gathered all together, and took his journey into a far country, and there wasted his substance with riotous living..[The elder son said,] ²⁹ Lo, these many years do I serve thee, neither transgressed I at any time thy commandment.—LUKE, ch. 15.

See other illustrations under:

DISPOSITION.
Angry. Saul servants said, An evil spirit — 2413
Benevolent. Samaritan had compassion..bound — 2414
Curious. Levite came and looked on him and — 2415
Changed. Countenance of Laban was not..as b. — 2416
Giving. Every man that giveth willingly with — 2418
Indifferent. Priest when he saw him passed by — 2419
Religious. Ye men of Athens..ye are too — 2420

MORALITY.
Complete. All these..observed from my youth — 5561
False Zeal. They continued asking..went out one — 5562
Insufficient. I am not as other men are — 5563
Indispensable. Cease to do evil ; learn to do well — 5564
Without. Sons of B.—Judges, ch. 19 ; also Gen., ch. — 19

REPUTATION.
Acknowledged. Thy G. whom thou servest..will — 7160
Advantage. Been shown me, all thou hast done — 7161
Bad. Can any good thing come out of — 7162
Blotters. Herod feared John..holy and observed — 7163
Fearful. I have heard..much evil he hath done — 7164
Good. Cornelius..of good report among..Jews — 7165
Gaining. Let not mercy and truth forsake thee — 7166
Helpful. I have seen the son of Jesse..valiant — 7167
Jealous. I wrought for my name's sake..not be — 7168
Loss. Dead flies cause the ointment to stink — 7169
Official. Here I am ; witness against me — 7170
Posthumous. That men say not..a woman slew — 7171
Reviled. Clap their hands at thee and kiss — 7172
Unimpeachable. Could find none..as he..was — 7173
" Thou hast not defrauded, nor — 7174
Valuable. Good name is rather to be chosen than — 7175
Varied. Whom say the people..John..Elias..C. — 7176

Care. Should such a man as I flee ? — 4974
Divine. Proclaimed the L...merciful and — 3585
Discriminated. Abel offered a more excellent — 2363
Judged by. Man looketh on the outward — 474
Misjudged. Simon saw..H. G. was given he — 4454

1131. CHASTISEMENT of Children. *Proverb.* ²⁴ He that spareth his rod hateth his son : but he that loveth him chasteneth him betimes.—PROV., ch. 13.

1132. —— Fruits of. *Righteousness.* ¹¹ No chastening for the present seemeth to be joyous, but grievous : nevertheless, afterward it yieldeth the peaceable fruit of righteousness unto them which are exercised thereby.—HEB., ch. 12.

1133. —— for Good. *Parental.* ⁹ Fathers.. corrected *us*, and we gave *them* reverence : shall we not much rather be in subjection unto the Father of spirits, and live ? ¹⁰ For they..chastened *us* after their own pleasure ; but he for *our* profit.—HEB., ch. 12.

1134. —— in Love. *Solomon.* ¹¹ My son, despise not the chastening of the Lord ; neither be weary of his correction : ¹² For whom the Lord loveth he correcteth ; even as a father the son *in whom* he delighteth.—PROV., ch. 3.

See other illustrations under:

Children. Beat him with a rod..save his soul from — 1205
" Foolishness is in the heart of a child — 1172
See **ADVERSITY** and references.
See **PUNISHMENT** and references.

1135. CHASTITY commended. *Solomon.* ⁹ Lest thou give thine honour unto others, and thy years unto the cruel.. ¹¹ And thou mourn at the

last, when thy flesh and thy body are consumed, ¹² And say, How have I hated instruction, and my heart despised reproof.—PROV., ch. 5.

1136. —— Invincible. *Joseph.* [Potiphar's wife] ¹⁰ spake to Joseph day by day..he hearkened not unto her, to lie by her, *or* to be with her.—GEN., ch. 39.

1137. CHEATING in Trade. *Dealers.* ⁵ Making the ephah small, and the shekel great, and falsifying the balances by deceit ? ⁶ That we may buy the poor for silver, and the needy for a pair of shoes ; *yea*, and sell the refuse of the wheat ? —AMOS, ch. 8.

See **DECEPTION** and references

1138. CHEERFULNESS in Benevolence. *To needy Saints.* ⁵ That the same might be ready, as *a matter of* bounty, and not as *of* covetousness. ⁷ Every man according as he purposeth in his heart, *so let him give ;* not grudgingly, or of necessity : for God loveth a cheerful giver.— 2 COR., ch. 9.

1139. —— commended. *Proverb.* ¹³ A merry heart maketh a cheerful countenance : but by sorrow of the heart the spirit is broken. ¹⁵ All the days of the afflicted *are* evil : but he that is of a merry heart *hath* a continual feast.—PROV., ch. 15.

1140. —— Strange. *Haman.* ¹⁴ Said Zeresh his wife and all his friends..Let a gallows be made of fifty cubits high..that Mordecai may be hanged thereon : then go thou in merrily with the king unto the banquet. ¹⁵ And the thing pleased Haman.—ESTHER, ch. 5.

See other illustrations under:

COMFORT.
Adversity. Although the fig tree shall not blossom — 1379
Appreciated. Came to Elim..12 wells..[70] palm — 1380
Cruel. Esau doth comfort himself..to kill thee — 1381
Christians. Though thou wast angry..comfortest — 1382
Dangerous. Peter sat with the servants and — 1383
Experience. L. J. C..himself comfort your hearts — 1384
Fraternal. G. comforted us by the coming of Titus — 1385
Lonely. Jacob awaked..gate of heaven — 1386
Provision. Father..shall give you another com. — 1387
Short-lived. Jonah was exceeding glad of the g. — 1388
Zion. L. shall comfort Zion..voice of melody — 1389

ENCOURAGEMENT.
Angelic. Jacob went..angels of G. met him — 2632
Above. Let us run..looking to J. who for the joy — 2633
Affliction. Sufferings..not worthy to be compared — 2634
Example. Paul began to eat..all of good cheer — 2635
Fraternal. Whom when Paul saw he thanked God — 2636
in God. David encouraged himself in the L. — 2637
Hopeful. Bartimeus..be of good comfort..he — 2638
Past. Ye have seen..I bear ye up on eagles' wings — 2639
Substantial. Strengthened [builder's] hands with — 2640

JOY.
Builders. Ancient men wept..many shouted — 4732
Believers. Whom having not seen..joy unspeakable — 4733
Converts. Eat..with gladness of heart, praising G. — 4734
Conscience. Our rejoicing..testimony of our — 4735
Deliverance. Leaping up..leaping and praising — 4736
Exuberant. Rejoice with me, I have found the — 4737
Escape. Then was the king [Darius] exceeding — 4738
Excitement. Rhoda..opened not the gate for — 4739
Fear. Sore afraid..Bring you good tidings..joy — 4740
Giving. People rejoiced for that they offered — 4741
Hellish. Were glad and covenanted to give Judas — 4742
Irrepressible. Should hold their peace, the stones — 4743

Mother's. Mary kept all these things and pondered 4744
Overcoming. When Jacob saw the wagons..spirit 4745
Penitential. People wept..great mirth because 4746
Religious. David danced before the L. shouting 4747
Recovery. [At Samaria] Great joy in that city 4748
Success. [Walls erected] Joy of Jerusalem..afar 4749
Supreme. Not that the spirits are subject..names 4750
Song of. Hath put a new song in my mouth 4751
Weeping. Joseph could not refrain..wept aloud 4752
Want. Although the fig tree shall not blossom 4753
Worship. How amiable are thy tabernacles 4754

REJOICING.

Communion. This poor man cried..O taste and 6968
Conversion. There was great joy in that city 6969
Converts. [Jailer] rejoiced believing in G. with 6971
    "   I waited patiently. put a new song in 6972
    "   The eunuch went on his way rejoicing 6973
Duty. Thou shalt rejoice in every good thing. G. 6974
Deliverance. I will sing unto the L..triumphed 6975
    "   Jews had light, and gladness, and joy 9976
Great. At the descent of the mount of Olives 9978
Heavenly. Ransomed of the L. come to Z. with 9980
in Prison. At midnight Paul and Silas..sang praises 9981
in Persecutions. Rejoicing that they were counted 9982
Premature. [Amalekites] were eating and drink. 9983
in Reproach. Rejoice..and be exceeding glad 9885
in Tribulation. I am exceeding joyful in all our 9986
in Temptation. Count it all joy when ye fall into 9987
Victors. Praised their god..hearts were merry 9988

Refreshment. Came to Elim..12 wells..70 palm 6939

1141. CHILD blessed of God. *Samson.* ²⁴ The woman bare a son..and the child grew, and the Lord blessed him. ²⁵ And the Spirit of the Lord began to move him at times in the camp of Dan.—JUDGES, ch. 13.

1142. —— Dying. *David's.* ¹⁸ On the seventh day..the child died. And the servants of David feared to tell him..for they said, Behold, while the child was yet alive, we spake unto him, and he would not hearken unto our voice : how will he then vex himself.—2 SAM., ch. 12.

1143. —— —— *Shunammite's.* ²⁰ He sat on her knees till noon, and *then* died. ²¹ And she ..laid him on the bed of the man of God, and shut *the door* upon him, and went out.—2 KINGS, ch. 4. [See No. 1158.]

1144. —— A dutiful. *Jesus.* ⁵¹ He went down with them [his parents], and came to Nazareth, and was subject unto them.—LUKE, ch. 2.

1145. —— A guarded. *Moses.* ³ She took for him an ark of bulrushes..and put the child therein ; and she laid *it* in the flags by the river's brink. ⁴ And his sister stood afar off, to wit what would be done to him.—Ex., ch. 2.

1146. —— A holy. *John Baptist.* [The angel said to Zacharias,] ¹³ Thy wife Elisabeth shall bear thee a son.. ¹⁵..and he shall be filled with the Holy Ghost, even from his mother's womb. ¹⁶ And many of the children of Israel shall he turn to the Lord.—LUKE, ch. 1. [See No. 1153.]

1147. —— in Heaven, A. *David's.* ²³ But now he is dead, wherefore should I fast? can I bring him back again? I shall go to him, but he shall not return to me.—2 SAM., ch. 12. [See No. 1142.]

1148. —— Help from a. *Boy.* ²⁶ Samson said unto the lad that held him by the hand, Suffer me that I may feel the pillars whereupon the

house standeth, that I may lean upon them.— JUDGES, ch. 16. [He pulled the house down.]

1149. —— heard in Heaven, A. *Ishmael.* [Hagar] ¹⁶ went, and sat her down a good way off..for she said, Let me not see the death of the child. And she..lifted up her voice, and wept. ¹⁷ And God heard the voice of the lad.— GEN., ch. 21.

1150. —— brings Joy, A. *John.* ⁵⁷ Elisabeth's full time came..and she brought forth a son. ⁵⁸ And her neighbours and her cousins..rejoiced with her.—LUKE, ch. 1.

1151. —— A lost. *Jesus.* ⁴² When he was twelve years old.. ⁴³..the child Jesus tarried behind in Jerusalem ; and Joseph and his mother.. ⁴⁴..supposing him to have been in the company, went a day's journey ; and they sought him among *their* kinsfolk and acquaintance. ⁴⁵..they turned back again to Jerusalem, seeking him.— LUKE, ch. 2.

1152. —— Ministry of a. *Samuel.* ¹⁸ Samuel ministered before the Lord, *being* a child, girded with a linen ephod.—1 SAM., ch. 2.

1153. —— born in Old Age. *John.* ⁷ They both were *now* well stricken in years.. ¹³ But the angel said..Fear not, Zacharias : for thy prayer is heard ; and thy wife Elisabeth shall bear thee a son.—LUKE, ch. 1.

1154. —— early Piety of a. *Josiah.* ³ In the eighth year of his reign, while he was yet young, he began to seek after the God of David..and in the twelfth year he began to purge Judah and Jerusalem from the high places, and the groves, and the..images.—2 CHRON., ch. 34.

1155. —— resuscitated. *Widow's.* ²¹ He stretched himself upon the child three times.. and said, O Lord..let this child's soul come into him again. ²² And the Lord heard..Elijah ; and the soul of the child came into him again.— 1 KINGS, ch. 17.

1156. —— religious. *Obadiah.* [He said to Elijah,] ¹² I thy servant fear the Lord from my youth. ¹³..when Jezebel slew the prophets of the Lord..I hid a hundred men..by fifty in a cave, and fed them with bread and water.—1 KINGS, ch. 18.

1157. —— A sick. *Shunammite's.* ¹⁸ When the child was grown, it..went out to his father to the reapers. ¹⁹ And he said unto his father, My head, my head! And he said to a lad, Carry him to his mother.—2 KINGS, ch. 4. [See No. 1143.]

1158. —— A stolen. *Harlot's.* [Said to Solomon,] ¹⁹ This woman's child died in the night ; because she overlaid it. ²⁰ And she arose at midnight, and took my son from beside me, while thine handmaid slept..and laid her dead child in my bosom.—1 KINGS, ch. 3.

1159. —— Sayings of a. *Jesus.* ⁴⁹ He said unto them, How is it that ye sought me? wist ye not that I must be about my Father's business? ⁵¹..his mother kept all these sayings in her heart.—LUKE, ch. 2.

1160. —— A thoughtful. *Captive Maid.* ² She waited on Naaman's wife. ³ And she said unto her mistress, Would God my lord *were* with the prophet that *is* in Samaria! for he would recover him of his leprosy.—2 KINGS, ch. 5.

1161. —— An unfortunate. *Invalid.* ¹⁷ Master, I have brought unto thee my son, which hath a dumb spirit ; [18]..He teareth him ; and he foameth, and gnasheth with his teeth, and pineth away.—MARK, ch. 9.

1162. —— **A wonderful.** *John.* [Zacharias's tongue was loosed after the circumcision of his son John,] [66] All they that heard [his sayings], laid *them* up in their hearts, saying, What manner of child shall this be ! And the hand of the Lord was with him.—LUKE, ch. 1.

1163. —— **A wise.** *Jesus.* [46] After three days they found him in the temple, sitting in the midst of the doctors, both hearing them, and asking them questions. [47] And all that heard him were astonished at his understanding and answers.—LUKE, ch. 2. [See No. 1151.]

See other illustrations under :
Affecting. Babe [Moses] wept..she had compassion 107
Orphan. Esther was fair..father and mother 5932
Unwelcome. His daughter came to meet [Jephthah] 1936

1164. CHILDREN instructed by Age. *Joel.* [2] Hear this, ye old men..Hath this been in your days, or even in the days of your fathers ? [3] Tell ye your children of it, and *let* your children *tell* their children, and their children another generation.—JOEL, ch. 1.

1165. —— **abandoned.** *Israelites.* [18] Another king arose, which knew not Joseph. [19] The same dealt subtilely..and evil entreated our fathers, so that they cast out their young children, to the end they might not live.—ACTS, ch. 7.

1166. —— **a Blessing, Many.** *Arrows.* [4] As arrows *are* in the hand of a mighty man ; so *are* children of the youth. [5] Happy *is* the man that hath his quiver full of them : they shall not be ashamed, but they shall speak with the enemies in the gate.—Ps. 127.

1167. —— **Bereft of.** *Ephraim.* [21] Zabad.. Shuthelah..Ezer, and Elead..the men of Gath ..slew, because they came down to take away their cattle. [22] And Ephraim their father mourned many days, and his brethren came to comfort him.—1 CHRON., ch. 7.

1168. —— **Christian, Care of.** *Lambs.* [15] Simon, *son* of Jonas, lovest thou me more than these ? He saith unto him, Yea, Lord ; thou knowest that I love thee. He saith unto him, Feed my lambs.—JOHN, ch. 21.

1169. —— **controlled.** *Abraham's.* [19] I know him, that he will command his children and his household after him, and they shall keep the way of the Lord, to do justice and judgment.—GEN., ch. 18.

1170. —— **of Christians Remembered.** *Ishmael.* [13] Of the son of the bondwoman will I make a nation, because he *is* thy seed. [14] And Abraham..took bread, and a bottle of water, and gave *it* unto Hagar, putting *it* on her shoulder, and the child, and sent her away.—GEN., ch. 21.

1171. —— **Chastisement of.** *Solomon.* [24] He that spareth his rod hateth his son : but he that loveth him chasteneth him betimes.—PROV., ch. 13. [18] Chasten thy son while there is hope, and let not thy soul spare for his crying.—PROV., ch. 19.

1172. —— **Correction of.** *Proverb.* [15] Foolishness *is* bound in the heart of a child ; *but* the rod of correction shall drive it far from him.—PROV., ch. 22.

1173. —— **Tender Care for.** *Little.* [5] Whoso shall receive one such little child in my name receiveth me. [6] But whoso shall offend one of these little ones which believe in me, it were better for him that a millstone were hanged about his neck, and *that* he were drowned in the depth of the sea.—MAT., ch. 18.

1174. —— **Degenerate.** *Eli's.* [12] The sons of Eli *were* sons of Belial ; they knew not the Lord.. [17] Wherefore the sin of the young men was very great before the Lord : for men abhorred the offering of the Lord.—1 SAM., ch. 2.

1175. —— **Docility of.** *Solomon.* [8] My son, hear the instruction of thy father, and forsake not the law of thy mother : [9] For they *shall be* an ornament of grace unto thy head, and chains about thy neck.—PROV., ch. 1.

1176. —— **Diverse Characters of.** *Jacob—Esau.* [27] The boys grew..Esau was a cunning hunter, a man of the field ; and Jacob *was* a plain man, dwelling in tents.—GEN., ch. 25.

1177. —— **Sudden Death of.** *Job's.* [18] Thy sons and thy daughters *were* eating and drinking wine in their eldest brother's house : [19]..a great wind..smote the four corners of the house, and it fell upon the young men, and they are dead.—JOB, ch. 1.

1178. —— **dedicated.** *Command.* [12] Thou shalt set apart unto the Lord all that openeth the matrix ; [13]..and all the firstborn of man among thy children shalt thou redeem.—Ex., ch. 13.

1179. —— **Divine.** *Christians.* [2] Beloved, now are we the sons of God, and it doth not yet appear what we shall be : but we know that, when he shall appear, we shall be like him.—1 JOHN, ch. 3.

1180. —— **improperly educated.** *Jews'.* [23] Jews ..had married wives of Ashdod, of Ammon, *and* of Moab : [24] And their children spake half in the speech of Ashdod, and could not speak in the Jews' language.—NEH., ch. 13.

1181. —— **Gentleness with.** *Parental.* [4] Ye fathers, provoke not your children to wrath : but bring them up in the nurture and admonition of the Lord.—EPH., ch. 6.

1182. —— **of the Good.** *Timothy.* [5] When I call to remembrance the unfeigned faith that is in thee, which dwelt first in thy grandmother Lois, and thy mother Eunice.—2 TIM., ch. 1.

1183. —— **Gifts to.** *Abraham.* [5] Abraham gave all that he had unto Isaac. [6] But unto the sons of the concubines..Abraham gave gifts, and sent them away from Isaac his son.—GEN., ch. 25.

1184. —— **given by God.** *Gift.* [3] Lo, children *are* a heritage of the Lord : *and* the fruit of the womb *is his* reward.—Ps. 127.

1185. —— **to be imitated.** *Simplicity.* [2] Jesus called a little child unto him.. [3] And said..Except ye be converted, and become as little children, ye shall not enter into the kingdom of heaven.—MAT., ch. 18.

1186. —— **inherit Evil.** *Parental.* [5] I..am a jealous God, visiting the iniquity of the fathers upon the children unto the third and fourth *generation* of them that hate me.—Ex., ch. 20.

1187. —— **imitate Parents.** *Abijam.* [3] He walked in all the sins of his father, which he had done before him.—1 KINGS, ch. 15.

1188. —— —— *Impious.* [17] In the cities of Judah and in the streets of Jerusalem ? [18] The children gather wood, and the fathers kindle the fire, and the women knead *their* dough, to make cakes to the queen of heaven, and to pour out drink offerings unto other gods.—JER., ch. 7.

1189. —— Model. *Captives.* [Nebuchadnezzar ordered the selection of] [4] Children in whom *was* no blemish, but well favoured, and skilful in all wisdom, and cunning in knowledge, and understanding science, and such as *had* ability in them to stand in the king's palace, and whom they might teach the learning and the tongue of the Chaldeans.—DAN., ch. 1.

1190. —— murdered. *Ahab's.* [See No. 1196.]

1191. —— Mourning for. *Job.* [2] O that I were as *in* months past, as *in* the days *when* God preserved me ; [3] When his candle shined upon my head.. [5] When the Almighty *was* yet with me, *when* my children *were* about me.—JOB, ch. 29.

1192. —— neglected. *Proverb.* [15] The rod and reproof give wisdom : but a child left to *himself* bringeth his mother to shame.—PROV., ch. 29.

1193. —— born in Old Age. *Patriarch's.* [16] Abram *was* fourscore and six years old, when Hagar bare Ishmael.—GEN., ch. 16. [5] And Abraham was a hundred years old, when his son Isaac was born.—GEN., ch. 21.

1194. —— Parents to teach. *Law.* [9] Take heed to thyself..lest thou forget the things which thine eyes have seen, and lest they depart from thy heart all the days of thy life ; but teach them thy sons, and thy sons' sons.—DEUT., ch. 4.

1195. —— —— *Law.* [6] And these words, which I command thee this day.. [7]..thou shalt teach them diligently unto thy children, and shalt talk of them when thou sittest in thine house, and when thou walkest by the way, and when thou liest down, and when thou risest up.—DEUT., ch. 6.

1196. —— Parents' Sins on. *Ahab.* [20] Ahab said to Elijah, Hast thou found me, O mine enemy ? And he answered, I have found thee : because thou hast sold thyself to work evil.. [21] Behold, I will bring evil upon thee, and will take away thy posterity.—1 KINGS, ch. 21. [All were slain.]

1197. —— Parents involving. *Jews.* [25] Then answered all the people..His blood *be* on us, and on our children. [26] Then released he Barabbas ..and..scourged Jesus.—MAT., ch. 27.

1198. —— irresponsible for Parents. *Amaziah.* [5] He slew his servants which had slain the king his father. [6] But the children of the murderers he slew not : according unto..the law of Moses ..The fathers shall not be put to death for the children, nor the children be put to death for the fathers.—2 KINGS, ch. 14.

1199. —— Pride in numerous. *Haman.* [10] He sent and called for his friends, and Zeresh his wife. [11] And Haman told them of the glory of his riches, and the multitude of his children.—ESTHER, ch. 5.

1200. —— praising Jesus. *Hosanna.* [14] The blind and the lame came to him in the temple ; and he healed them. [15] And when the chief priests and scribes saw..the children crying.. Hosanna to the Son of David ; they were sore displeased.—MAT., ch. 21.

1201. —— The Promise to. *Pentecost.* [38] Peter said..Repent, and be baptized every one of you in the name of Jesus Christ for the remission of sins, and ye shall receive the gift of the Holy Ghost. [39] For the promise is unto you, and to your children.—ACTS, ch. 2.

1202. —— Privileges of. *Heirs.* [16] Spirit itself beareth witness with our spirit, that we are the children of God : [17] And if children, then heirs ; heirs of God, and joint heirs with Christ.—ROM., ch. 8.

1203. —— Religious. *Prophesy.* [3] I will pour my Spirit upon thy seed, and my blessing upon thine offspring.. [5] One shall say, I *am* the Lord's ; and another shall call *himself* by the name of Jacob.—ISA., ch. 44.

1204. —— resemble Parents. *Jews.* [30] If we had been in the days of our fathers, we would not have been partakers with them in the blood of the prophets. [31] Wherefore ye be witnesses unto yourselves, that ye are the children of them which killed the prophets.—MAT., ch. 23.

1205. —— saved by the Rod. *Solomon.* [13] Withhold not correction from the child : for *if* thou beatest him with the rod, he shall not die. [14] Thou shalt beat him with the rod, and shalt deliver his soul from hell.—PROV., ch. 23.

1206. —— rejoicing with Parents. *Walls.* [At the dedication of the walls,] [43] They offered great sacrifices, and rejoiced..with great joy : the wives also and the children rejoiced : so that the joy of Jerusalem was heard even afar off.—NEH., ch. 12.

1207. —— Relation of. *Heavenly.* [14] Jesus.. said..Suffer the little children to come unto me, and forbid them not ; for of such is the kingdom of God.—MARK, ch. 10.

1208. —— Jesus receives. *Infants.* [15] Brought unto him also infants, that he would touch them : but..*his* disciples..rebuked them. [16] But Jesus called them *unto him.*—LUKE, ch. 18.

1209. —— Second Family of. *Job.* [12] The Lord blessed the latter end of Job more than his beginning : for he had fourteen thousand sheep, and six thousand camels, and a thousand yoke of oxen, and a thousand she asses. [13] He had also seven sons and three daughters.—JOB, ch. 42.

1210. —— Parents to train. *Proverb.* [6] Train up a child in the way he should go : and when he is old, he will not depart from it.—PROV., ch. 22.

1211. —— sacrificed. *King Ahaz's.* [2] Made also molten images for Baalim. [3] Moreover he burnt incense in the valley of the son of Hinnom, and burnt his children in the fire, after the abominations of the heathen.—2 CHRON., ch. 28.

1212. —— stolen. *Of Shiloh.* [21] Behold, if the daughters of Shiloh come out to dance.. then come ye out of the vineyards, and catch you every man his wife..and go to the land of Benjamin.—JUDGES, ch. 21.

1213. —— Seventy. *Ahab's.* [1] Ahab had seventy sons in Samaria.. [6] *Were* with the great men of the city, which brought them up.

'..when the letter came..they took the king's sons, and slew..put their heads in baskets, and sent him them.—2 KINGS, ch. 10.

1214. —— **of Satan.** *Liars.* [44] Ye are of *your* father the devil, and the lusts of your father ye will do : he was a murderer from the beginning, and abode not in the truth.—JOHN, ch. 8.

1215. —— **Uncontrolled.** *Eli's.* [12] I will perform against Eli all *things* which I have spoken.. [13] For..I will judge his house for ever for the iniquity which he knoweth ; because his sons made themselves vile, and he restrained them not.—1 SAM., ch. 3. [See No. 1174.]

1216. —— **Unhappiness without.** *Hannah.* [8] Said Elkanah her husband to her, Hannah, why weepest thou? and why eatest thou not? and why is thy heart grieved? *am* not I better to thee than ten sons?—1 SAM., ch. 1.

1217. —— **of wicked Parents.** *Irreligious.* [7] The sons of Athaliah, that wicked woman, had broken up the house of God ; and also all the dedicated things of the house of the Lord did they bestow upon Baalim.—2 CHRON., ch. 24.

1218. CHILDHOOD dedicated. *Samuel.* [22] Hannah..said, unto her husband, *I will not go up* until the child be weaned, and *then* I will bring him, that he may appear before the Lord, and there abide for ever.—1 SAM., ch. 1.

1219. —— **Impressions of.** *Moses.* [24] By faith Moses..refused to be called the son of Pharaoh's daughter ; [25] Choosing rather to suffer affliction with the people of God, than to enjoy the pleasures of sin for a season.—HEB., ch. 11.

1220. —— **A pious.** *Josiah.* [1] Josiah *was* eight years old when he began to reign. [2] And he did *that which was* right in the sight of the Lord..and turned not aside to the right hand or to the left.—2 KINGS, ch. 22.

1221. —— **Trained in.** *Timothy.* [14] Continue thou in the things which thou hast learned.. knowing of whom thou hast learned *them;* [15] And that from a child thou hast known the holy Scriptures.—2 TIM., ch. 3.

See other illustrations under :

DAUGHTER.

Portion of. Caleb said, What wouldest thou?	1935
Unfortunate. Jephthah..daughter came to meet	1936

DAUGHTER IN LAW.

Faithful. Ruth said, Entreat me not to return	1937
Unwelcome. Were a grief of mind unto Isaac and	1938

FAMILY.

Affliction. Thy son liveth ; himself believed	3005
Alienation. Children shall rise up against their	3006
Bereaved. House fell upon the young men..dead	3007
Conversion. Jailer was baptized and all his	3008
Death. Miriam died..Aaron died..Moses died	3009
Exterminated. Jehu slew all that remained..of	3010
Good. Whosoever shall do the will of G..my	3011
Jars. Hannah's adversary..made her fret	3012
Numerous. Gideon had [70]..sons..many wives	3013
Prayer. When Aaron lighteth the lamps..burn	3014
" **for.** Job..rose up early..offered burnt	3015
Quarrel. Miriam and Aaron spake against..Moses	3016
" Cast out this bondwoman and her son	3017
Religion. As for me and my house, we will serve	3018
" Cornelius..feared G. with all his house	3019
Wicked. Children gather wood..offerings unto	3020
Worship. A lamb for a house	3021
Worshipped. He that loveth father..more than	3022

SON.

Affectionate. Joseph fell on his neck and wept	8177
Degenerate. Solomon's heart was not perfect..as	8178
Evil. Zedekiah [son of good Josiah]..hardened his	8179
Expelled. Abraham..gave Hagar..child and sent	8180
Firstborn. Sanctify unto me all the firstborn	8181
Healed. Nobleman saith, Come down ere my child	8182
Ingrate. Wasteth his father, and chaseth..mother	8183
" His lamp shall be put out in obscure	8184
Obedient. Abraham bound Isaac..laid him on the	8185
Penitent. I will go to my father..I have sinned	8186
Parent-like. Amon sacrificed unto all..father	8187
Parent-unlike. Manasseh built up..which his	8188
Rebellious. Son..will not obey..his father..stone	8189
Reformer. Asa..mother he removed..destroyed	8190
Sacrificed. Abraham took the knife to slay his son	8191
Scandalous. They spread Absalom a tent	8192
Son in Law. [Grasping] Jacob hath taken..was	8195
Unnatural. I will smite the king only..pleased	8193
Unfortunate. He foameth and gnasheth..pineth	8194

SONS.

Degenerate. Eli..heard what his sons did	8196
" Samuel..sons took bribes and	8197
Differ. [Two sons] The younger..Father give me	8198
" I will not..he went..I go, sir ; and went	8199
Rejected. Thy sons walk not in thy ways..make	8200

Comforting. Jacob mourned..sons and daughters	737
Desired. L. what wilt thou give me, seeing I go	6290
Murder. Pharaoh..every son that is born..river	4452
Massacre. Herod..slew all the children	4553
Spiritual. Babes in C..fed you with milk	605

See **YOUNG MEN** and **YOUTH.**

1222. CHOICE, The better. *Mary.* [41] Jesus ..said unto her, Martha, Martha, thou art careful and troubled about many things : [42] But one thing is needful ; and Mary hath chosen that good part, which shall not be taken away from her.—LUKE, ch. 10.

1223. —— **The decisive.** *Joshua,* [shortly before his death, said,] [15] If it seem evil unto you to serve the Lord, choose you this day whom ye will serve ; whether the gods which your fathers served..or the gods of the Amorites.. but as for me and my house, we will serve the Lord.—JOSH., ch. 24.

1224. —— **The desperate.** *Esther.* [16] Gather together all the Jews..and neither eat nor drink three days, night or day : I also and my maidens will fast likewise ; and so will I go in unto the king, which *is* not according to the law : and if I perish, I perish.—ESTHER, ch. 4.

1225. —— **A difficult.** *David.* [13] Gad came to David..and said..Shall seven years of famine come..or wilt thou flee three months before thine enemies..or that there be three days' pestilence in thy land?.. [14] And David said unto Gad, I am in a great strait.—2 SAM., ch. 24.

1226. —— **A dangerous.** *Sodom.* [10] Lot.. beheld all the plain of Jordan, that it *was* well watered every where..*even* as the garden of the Lord. [11] Then Lot chose him all the plain of Jordan..Lot dwelt in the cities of the plain, and pitched *his* tent toward Sodom.—GEN., ch. 13. [His wife became corrupted, his daughters shameless, himself impoverished in old age.]

1227. —— **of the Fruitful.** *Aaron's Rod.* [7] Moses laid up the rods before the Lord in the tabernacle.. [8] And..on the morrow..behold, the rod of Aaron..was budded, and brought forth buds, and bloomed blossoms, and yield almonds.—NUM., ch. 17.

1228. —— **The foolish.** *Broken Cisterns.*
[13] My people have committed two evils ; they have forsaken me the fountain of living waters, *and* hewed them out cisterns, broken cisterns, that can hold no water.—JER., ch. 2.

1229. —— **by the Heart.** *The Lord's.* [6] He looked on Eliab, and said, Surely the Lord's anointed *is* before him. [7] But the Lord sa²d unto Samuel, Look not on his countenance, or on the height of his stature ; because I have refused him : for *the Lord seeth* not as man seeth ; for man looketh on the outward appearance, but the Lord looketh on the heart.—1 SAM., ch. 16.

1230. —— **of Life or Death.** *Serpent.* [8] The Lord said unto Moses, Make thee a fiery serpent, and set it upon a pole ; and . . every one that is bitten, when he looketh upon it, shall live.—NUM., ch. 21.

1231. —— **of Murderers.** *Barabbas.* [18] They cried out all at once, saying, Away with this *man*, and release unto us Barabbas : [19] Who . . for murder, was cast into prison.—LUKE, ch. 23.

1232. —— **The neglected.** *Loss.* [18] O that thou hadst hearkened to my commandments ! then had thy peace been as a river, and thy righteousness as the waves of the sea : [19] Thy seed also had been as the sand.—ISA., ch. 48.

1233. —— **A pious.** *Moses.* [24] Moses . . refused to be called the son of Pharaoh's daughter ; [25] Choosing rather to suffer affliction with the people of God, than to enjoy the pleasures of sin for a season ; [26] Esteeming the reproach of Christ greater riches than the treasures in Egypt. —HEB., ch. 11.

1234. —— **of Piety.** *A Treasure.* [16] How much better *is it* to get wisdom than gold ! and to get understanding rather to be chosen than silver !—PROV., ch. 16.

1235. —— **A rebellious.** *Idolaters.* [17] We will certainly do whatsoever thing goeth forth out of our own mouth, to burn incense unto the queen of heaven, and to pour out drink offerings unto her, as we have done . . in the streets of Jerusalem : for *then* had we plenty of victuals, and were well, and saw no evil.—JER., ch. 44.

1236. —— **Responsibility of.** *Aged Moses.* [26] Behold, I set before you this day a blessing and a curse ; [27] A blessing, if ye obey the commandments of the Lord . . [28] And a curse, if ye will not obey the commandments of the Lord. —DEUT., ch. 11.

1237. —— **Results of.** *Religious.* [47] Because thou servedst not the Lord thy God with joyfulness, and with gladness of heart, for the abundance of all *things;* [48] Therefore shalt thou serve thine enemies . . in hunger, and in thirst, and in nakedness, and in want of all *things :* and he shall put a yoke of iron upon thy neck, until he have destroyed thee.—DEUT., ch. 28.

1238. —— **Saints are God's.** *Israelites.* [7] I will take you to me for a people, and I will be to you a God : and ye shall know that I *am* the Lord . . which bringeth you out from under the burdens of the Egyptians, [8] . . unto the land.— Ex., ch. 6.

1239. —— **Unexpected.** *David.* [10] Jesse made seven of his sons to pass before Samuel.

And Samuel said . . The Lord hath not chosen these. [11] . . Are here all *thy* children ? And he said, There remaineth yet the youngest . . he keepeth the sheep.—1 SAM., ch. 16.

1240. —— **A worldly.** *Young Ruler.* [21] Go *and* sell that thou hast, and give to the poor, and thou shalt have treasure in heaven : and come *and* follow me. [22] . . he went away sorrowful : for he had great possessions.—MAT., ch. 19.

Also see:
Dilemma. If we shall say from heaven . . or of men 2307
See **DECISION** *and references.*

1241. CHRIST, Advent of. *Bethlehem.* [Mary] [7] brought forth her firstborn son, and wrapped him in swaddling clothes, and laid him in a manger ; because there was no room for them in the inn.—LUKE, ch. 2.

1242. —— **Second Advent of.** *Clouds.* [30] They shall see the Son of man coming in the clouds of heaven with power and great glory. [31] And he shall send his angels with a great sound of a trumpet, and they shall gather together his elect.—MAT., ch. 24.

1243. —— **Appearings of.** *Three.* [26] Now once in the end of the world hath he appeared to put away sin by the sacrifice of himself. [24] [He has entered] heaven itself, now to appear in the presence of God for us : [28] . . and unto them that look for him shall he appear the second time without sin unto salvation.—HEB., ch. 9.

1244. —— **Access through.** *Speaketh.* [24] [Christians are come] to Jesus the mediator of the new covenant, and to the blood of sprinkling, that speaketh better things than *that of* Abel.—HEB., ch. 12.

1245. —— **Prior Claims of.** *Dead.* [21] Another of his disciples said . . Lord, suffer me first to go and bury my father. [22] But Jesus said . . Follow me ; and let the dead bury their dead.— MAT., ch. 8.

1246. —— **Claims the First.** *Firstborn.* [12] Thou shalt set apart unto the Lord all that openeth the matrix, and every firstling that cometh of a beast which thou hast. —EX., ch. 13.

1247. —— **The Corner Stone.** *Paul.* [20] Ye are built upon the foundation of the apostles and prophets, Jesus Christ himself being the chief corner *stone ;* [21] In whom all the building fitly framed together groweth unto a holy temple in the Lord : [22] In whom ye also are builded together for a habitation of God through the Spirit.—EPH., ch. 2.

1248. —— **Entrance by.** *Door.* [9] I am the door : by me if any man enter in, he shall be saved, and shall go in and out, and find pasture. —JOHN, ch. 10.

1249. —— **Our Example.** *Of Affection,* "Jesus loved Martha, Mary, and Lazarus." John 11 : 5.—*Of Affliction,* "Judas sought to betray him." Luke 22 : 6.—*Of Anger (just),* "with anger . . for the hardness of their hearts." Mark 3 : 5.—*Of dutiful Childhood,* "was subject unto them." Luke 2 : 51.—*Of comforting Others,* John 14.—*Of Compassion,* "weep not" (widow of Nain). Luke 7 : 13.—*Of spiritual Depression,* "why hast thou forsaken me." Mat. 27 : 46.—*Of Diligence,* "going about . . teaching . . preaching . . healing." Mat. 4 : 23. — *Of Disinterestedness,* "pleased not himself." Rom. 15 : 3.—*Of having* *some* Employment, "a carpenter." Mark 6 : 3.—*Of Fasting*, "forty days." Mat. 4 : 2.— *Of filial Affection*, "behold thy son." John 19 : 26. — *Of Forgiveness of Injuries*, "father, forgive them." Luke 23 : 34.— *Of Growth in Grace*, "increased in favour with God." Luke 2 : 52.— *Of Grief*, "exceeding sorrowful." Mark 14 : 34.—*Of Humility*, "made himself of no reputation." Phil. 2 : 7.— *Of Holiness*, "which of you convinceth me of sin?" John 8 : 46.—*Of Liberality* (in opinion), "forbid him not." Mark 9 : 39.—*Of Love to God*, "I love the Father." John 14 : 31.—*Of Meekness*, "when he was reviled, reviled not." 1 Peter 2 : 23.— *Of Patience*, "endured such contradiction." Heb. 12 : 3.— *Of Persecution*, "they took up stones to cast at him." John 8 : 59.— *Of Philanthropy*, "going about doing good." Acts 10 : 38. —*Of earnest Praying*, "offered up prayer..with strong crying and tears." Heb. 5 : 7.—*Of persistent Praying*, "all night in prayer." Luke 6 : 12.— *Of Prudence*, "render unto Cesar," etc. Mat. 22 : 21.— *Of Respect to the State*, "lest we offend..give unto them." Mat. 17 : 27.— *Of Spiritual Perplexity*, "now is my soul troubled." John 12 : 27.—*Of Self-denial*, "not to be ministered unto, but to minister." Mat. 20 : 28.— *Of Sympathy*, "Jesus wept" at Lazarus's grave. John 11 : 35.— *Of Teachableness*, "hearing the doctors." Luke 2 : 46.— *Of Temptation*, "to be tempted." Mat. 4 : 1.— *Of Thanksgiving*, "I thank thee, O Father." Mat. 11 : 25.— *Of Fidelity to Truth*, "born ..to bare witness to the truth." John 18 : 37.

1250. —— **The Foundation.** *Paul.* [11] Other foundation can no man lay than that is laid, which is Jesus Christ.—1 Cor., ch. 3.

1251. —— **Manifestation of.** *Indwelling.* [22] Judas saith..not Iscariot, Lord, how is it that thou wilt manifest thyself unto us, and not unto the world? [23] Jesus answered..If a man love me..my Father will love him, and we will come unto him, and make our abode with him. —John, ch. 14.

1252. —— **misunderstood.** *Crucifixion.* [46] About the ninth hour Jesus cried with a loud voice, saying, Eli, Eli, lama sabachthani?.. [47] Some.. when they heard *that*, said, This *man* calleth for Elias.—Mat., ch. 27.

1253. —— **Nourishment from.** *Paschal Lamb.* They shall eat the flesh in that night, roast with fire, and unleavened bread ; *and* with bitter *herbs*.—Ex., ch. 12.

1254. —— **Diverse Opinions of.** *At Jerusalem.* [12] There was much murmuring among the people concerning him: for some said, He is a good man : others said, Nay ; but he deceiveth the people.—John, ch. 7.

1255. —— **personated.** *The Weak.* [12] When ye sin so against the brethren, and wound their weak conscience, ye sin against Christ. [13] Wherefore, if meat make my brother to offend, I will eat no flesh while the world standeth.—1 Cor., ch. 8.

1256. —— **Representatives of.** *Christians.* [39] Or when saw we thee sick, or in prison, and came unto thee? [40] And the King shall answer ..Verily I say unto you, Inasmuch as ye have done *it* unto one of the least of these my brethren, ye have done *it* unto me.—Mat., ch. 25.

1257. —— **Receiving.** *Diverse Methods.* [38] Martha received him into her house. [39] ..Mary

..sat at Jesus' feet, and heard his word. [40] But Martha was cumbered about much serving.— Luke, ch. 10.

1258. —— **a Refiner.** *Fire.* [2] Who may abide the day of his coming? and who shall stand when he appeareth? for he is like a refiner's fire, and like fullers' soap : [3] And he shall sit *as* a refiner..of silver.—Mal., ch 3.

1259. —— **Rejection of.** *Parable.* [38] When the husbandmen saw the son, they said among themselves, This is the heir ; come, let us kill him, and let us seize on his inheritance.—Mat., ch. 21.

1260. —— **our Substitute.** *Atonement.* [4] Surely he hath borne our griefs, and carried our sorrows.. [5] ..he *was* wounded for our transgressions, he *was* bruised for our iniquities : the chastisement of our peace *was* upon him ; and with his stripes we are healed.—Isa., ch. 53.

1261. —— **a Stumblingblock.** *Paul.* [23] We preach Christ crucified, unto the Jews a stumblingblock, and unto the Greeks foolishness ; [24] But unto them which are called..Christ the power of God, and the wisdom of God.—1 Cor., ch. 1.

1262. —— **Slandered with.** *The Slandered.* [24] The disciple is not above *his* master, nor the servant above his lord. [25] ..If they have called the master of the house Beelzebub, how much more *shall they call* them of his household.— Mat., ch. 10.

1263. —— **Triumph of.** *Stone.* [42] Jesus saith..Did ye never read..the stone which the builders rejected, the same is become the head of the corner.. [44] And whosoever shall fall on this stone shall be broken : but on whomsoever it shall fall, it will grind him to powder.—Mat., ch. 21.

1264. —— **Voice of.** *Disciples.* [16] He that heareth you heareth me ; and he that despiseth you despiseth me ; and he that despiseth me despiseth him that sent me.—Luke, ch. 10.

1265. —— **the Way.** *To Nathanael.* [51] Hereafter ye shall see heaven open, and the angels of God ascending and descending upon the Son of man.—John, ch. 1.

See other illustrations under·

DIVINITY.

Asserted. Said G. was his F..equal with G.   2474
Acknowledged. I am he, they..fell to the ground   2475
Confessed. Thou art the C., the S. of the living G.   2476
Hatred. He ought to die..himself the S. of G.   2477
Manifested. What manner of man is this?..winds   2478
Professed. I and my F. are one..stones   2479

Abandoned. They all forsook him and fled   7
Divine. He arose and rebuked the wind and the   2833
Estimates. Stumblingblock..foolishness..power   1262

See JESUS.

1266. CHRISTS, False. *Jesus said,* [24] There shall arise false Christs, and false prophets, and shall shew great signs and wonders ; insomuch that, if *it were* possible, they shall deceive the very elect.—Mat., ch. 24.

1267. CHRISTIAN, Almost a. *Agrippa.* [27] King Agrippa, believest thou the prophets? I know that thou believest. [28] Then Agrippa said unto Paul, Almost thou persuadest me to be a Christian.—Acts, ch. 26.

1268. —— Epistles. *Heart.* ² Ye are our epistle written in our hearts, known and read of all men : ³.. *Ye are*..the epistle of Christ ministered by us, written not with ink, but with the Spirit of the living God ; not in tables of stone, but in fleshly tables of the heart.—2 Cor., ch. 3.

1269. —— The exemplary. *Bishop.* ⁷ A bishop must be blameless, as the steward of God ; not selfwilled, not soon angry, not given to wine, no striker, not given to filthy lucre ; ⁸ But a lover of hospitality, a lover of good men, sober, just, holy, temperate.—Titus, ch. 1.

1270. CHRISTIANS, Care for. *Sheep.* ¹⁵ I lay down my life for the sheep. ²⁸ And I give unto them eternal life ; and they shall never perish, neither shall any *man* pluck them out of my hand,—John, ch. 10.

1271. —— Childlike. *Child.* ¹⁶ Jesus called them *unto him*, and said, Suffer little children to come unto me..for of such is the kingdom of God. ¹⁷..Whosoever shall not receive the kingdom of God as a little child shall in no wise enter therein.—Luke, ch. 18.

1272. —— Carnal. *Corinthians.* ³ Whereas *there is* among you envying, and strife, and divisions, are ye not carnal, and walk as men ? ⁴ For while one saith, I am of Paul ; and another, I *am* of Apollos ; are ye not carnal ?— 1 Cor., ch. 3.

1273. —— True Greatness of. *The Least.* [Jesus said,] ²⁸ Among those that are born of women there is not a greater prophet than John the Baptist : but he that is least in the kingdom of God is greater than he.—Luke, ch. 7.

1274. —— Homeward bound. *Prophecy.* ¹⁰ The ransomed of the Lord shall return, and come to Zion with songs and everlasting joy upon their heads : they shall obtain joy and gladness, and sorrow and sighing shall flee away.—Isa., ch. 35.

1275. —— First named. *At Antioch.* [Paul and Barnabas for] ²⁶..a whole year they assembled themselves with the church, and taught much people. And the disciples were called Christians first in Antioch.—Acts, ch. 11.

1276. —— saved from Sin. *Delivered.* ⁸ He that committeth sin is of the devil ; for the devil sinneth from the beginning. For this purpose the Son of God was manifested, that he might destroy the works of the devil.—1 John, ch. 3.

1277. —— Visible. *Light.* ¹⁴ Ye are the light of the world. A city that is set on a hill cannot be hid. ¹⁵ Neither do men light a candle, and put it under a bushel, but on a candlestick ; and it giveth light unto all that are in the house.—Mat., ch. 5.

See other illustrations under:

BELIEVERS.
Joys. Though now ye see him not, yet believing 681
Possibilities. All things are possible to him that 682
Weak. Speak unto you..as unto babes in Christ 683

CONVERTS.
Counsel. Barnabas..exhorted them to cleave unto 1671
Duty. Woman went..and said, Come see 1667
Distinguished. Eunuch..went into the water 1668
Food. As new born babes desire..milk of the word 1672
Humble. Have any of the rulers or Pharisees 1673

Hypocrisy. Proselyte..twofold more the child of 1674
Influential. Believed..many honourable women 1675
Increase. Many believed..about 5000 men 1676
" Same day added..about 3000 souls 1677
Principle, No. Many became Jews..for fear of the 1678
Spurious. Simon..offered them money..give 1669
Steadfast. Continuing daily with one accord 1679
Superficial. Have no root in themselves 1680
Trial. Thou art his disciple, but we are Moses' 1670
Zeal. Made myself servant unto all 1681

CONVERSION.
Creation. New creature, old things passed away 1700
Conscious. Know we that we dwell in him..S. 1701
Changed. Made their feet fast..washed their 1702
Changes Life. Saul preached..Is not this he that 1703
Effort. Strive to enter in at the strait gate 1704
Evidence. Lydia..besought us..Come into my 1705
False. Simon saw..H. G. given..offered money 1706
Genuine. Set meat..rejoiced, believing in G. 1707
Heart Work. Out of the heart..evil thoughts 1708
Hasty. See here is water ; what doth hinder 1709
Inward. Pharisees make clean the outside of 1710
Mystery. Wind bloweth..canst not tell whence 1711
Necessity. Except a man be born of water and 1712
New Heart. God gave Saul another heart 1713
Negative. Reckon ye yourselves dead indeed unto 1714
Sudden. Called for a light..What must I do ? 1715
Superficial. When tribulation or persecution 1716
Wonderful. Suddenly there shined..voice..Saul 1717

CONVERSIONS.
Daily. L. added to the church daily..be saved 1718
Genuine. Confessed, showed their deeds..books 1719
Instrumental. Samaritans believed..for the saying 1720

DISCIPLINE.
Ancient. Separated from I. the mixed multitude 2337
Care. Nay..lest ye root up also the wheat 2338
Method. Tell him his fault..alone 2339
Primitive. Ananias and Sapphira..fell down 2340

DISCIPLESHIP.
Conditional. Lord, I will follow thee ; but 2331
Provisional. When I bow down..the L. pardon 2332
Postponed. Let me kiss my father..then I will 2333
Terms. Whosoever doth not bear his cross and 2334
Trials. Enough for the disciple to be as his master 2335
Unconditional. If any man..deny himself..cross 2336
Childlike. Except be converted and become as 1185
Divine. Now are ye the sons of G..shall be 1179
Godlikeness, Unconscious. Moses wist not that 3632
Happiness. Shall be like a tree planted by the 3633
Zionite. Who shall dwell..walketh..speaketh 1320

1278. CHRISTIANITY conserves. *Salt.* ¹³ Ye are the salt of the earth : but if the salt have lost his savour, wherewith shall it be salted ? it is thenceforth good for nothing, but..to be trodden under foot of men.—Mat., ch. 5.

1279. —— a Revolution. *Thessalonians.* ⁶ When they found them not, they drew Jason and certain brethren unto the rulers of the city, crying, These that have turned the world upside down are come hither also.—Acts, ch. 17.

See CHURCH *and* RELIGION.

1280. CHURCH, Admission to the. *Eunuch.* ³⁶ The eunuch said, See, *here is* water ; what doth hinder me to be baptized ? ³⁷ And Philip said, If thou believest with all thine heart, thou mayest. And he answered..I believe that Jesus Christ is the Son of God.—Acts, ch. 8.

1281. —— An abhorred. *Eli's Sons.* ¹³ The

priest's servant came .. with a fleshhook of three teeth in his hand ; ^{14} And he struck it into the pan, or kettle. .all that the fleshhook brought up the priest took for himself. ^{16}. .give it me now : and if not, I will take it by force. ^{17}. .the sin of the young men was very great . .for men abhorred the offering of the Lord.—1 Sam., ch. 2.

1282. —— **A backslidden.** *Deceived.* ^{30} A wonderful and horrible thing is committed in the land ; ^{31} The prophets prophesy falsely, and the priests bear rule by their means ; and my people love to have it so : and what will ye do in the end thereof?—Jer., ch. 5.

1283. —— **Commission of the.** *Ascension.* ^{19} Go ye therefore, and teach all nations, baptizing them in the name of the Father, and of the Son, and of the Holy Ghost : ^{20} Teaching them to observe all things whatsoever I have commanded you.—Mat., ch. 28.

1284. —— **Contributors for the.** *Jews.* ^{10} Bring ye all the tithes into the storehouse, that there may be meat in mine house, and prove me now herewith, saith the Lord of hosts, if I will not open you the windows of heaven, and pour you out a blessing, that there shall not be room enough to receive it.—Mal., ch. 3.

1285. —— **Corrupted, The.** *Apostolic.* ^{5} Why was not this ointment sold for three hundred pence, and given to the poor ? ^{6} This he said, not that he cared for the poor ; but because he was a thief, and had the bag.—John, ch. 12.

1286. —— —— *Tares.* ^{24} The kingdom of heaven is likened unto a man which sowed good seed in his field : ^{25} But while men slept, his enemy came and sowed tares among the wheat, and went his way.—Mat., ch. 13.

1287. —— **Divisions in the.** *Corinthian.* ^{3} Whereas there is among you envying, and strife, and divisions, are ye not carnal, and walk as men ? ^{4} For while one saith, I am of Paul ; and another, I am of Apollos ; are ye not carnal ?—1 Cor., ch. 3.

1288. —— **without Divisions.** *Jerusalem.* ^{32} Them them believed were of one heart and of one soul : neither said any of them that aught of the things which he possessed was his own : but they had all things common. ^{33} And with great power gave the apostles witness.—Acts, ch. 4.

1289. —— **An expensive.** *Tabernacle.* ^{24} All the gold that was. .in all the work of the holy place. .was twenty and nine talents, and seven hundred and thirty shekels. . ^{25} And the silver . .was a hundred talents, and a thousand seven hundred and threescore and fifteen shekels. . ^{29} And the brass of the offering was seventy talents, and two thousand and four hundred shekels.—Ex., ch. 38. [The entire cost was nearly one million dollars.]

1290. —— **Needless Fears of the.** *Saul.* ^{26} When Saul was come to Jerusalem, he assayed to join himself to the disciples : but they were all afraid of him, and believed not that he was a disciple.—Acts, ch. 9.

1291. —— **Fellowship of the.** *Invisible.* ^{22} Ye are come. .to an innumerable company of angels. ^{23} To the general assembly and church of the firstborn, which are written in heaven,

and to God the Judge of all, and to the spirits of just men made perfect.—Heb., ch. 12.

1292. —— **Gentleness with the.** *Shepherd.* ^{11} He shall feed his flock like a shepherd : he shall gather the lambs with his arm, and carry them in his bosom, and shall gently lead those that are with young.—Isa., ch. 40.

1293. —— **The ideal.** *Christ's.* ^{25} Christ. . loved the church, and gave himself for it ; ^{26} That he might sanctify and cleanse it. . ^{27} That he might present it to himself a glorious church, not having spot, or wrinkle, or any such thing ; but that it should be holy and without blemish. —Eph., ch. 5.

1294. —— **Iniquities in the.** *Jews.* ^{26} Among my people are found wicked men : they lay wait, as he that setteth snares ; they set a trap, they catch men. ^{28} They are waxen fat, they shine : yea, they overpass the deeds of the wicked : they judge not. .the cause of the fatherless, yet they prosper.—Jer., ch. 5.

1295. —— **Invitation of the.** *Come.* ^{29} Moses said unto Hobab. .Moses' father in law, We are journeying unto the place of which the Lord said, I will give it you : come thou with us, and we will do thee good : for the Lord hath spoken good concerning Israel.—Num., ch. 10.

1296. —— **Love works the.** *Church Erection.* ^{21} They came, every one whose heart stirred him up, and every one whom his spirit made willing, and they brought the Lord's offering to the work of the tabernacle.—Ex., ch. 35.

1297. —— **A mixed.** *Net.* ^{47} The kingdom of heaven is like unto a net, that was cast into the sea, and gathered of every kind : ^{48} Which, when it was full, they drew to shore and gathered the good into vessels, but cast the bad away.—Mat., ch. 13.

1298. —— **Opposition in the.** *Diotrephes.* ^{9} Diotrephes, who loveth to have the preeminence among them, receiveth us not. ^{10}. .prating against us with malicious words : and not content therewith, neither doth he himself receive the brethren, and forbiddeth them that would, and casteth them out of the church.—3 John.

1299. —— **Preservation by the.** *Sodom.* ^{32} Peradventure ten shall be found there. And he said, I will not destroy it for ten's sake.— Gen., ch. 18.

1300. —— **A prosperous.** *Palestine.* [Saul became a Christian,] ^{31} Then had the churches rest throughout all Judea and Galilee and Samaria, and were edified ; and walking in the fear of the Lord, and in the comfort of the Holy Ghost, were multiplied.—Acts, ch. 9.

1301. —— **Reformation in the.** *Jesus.* [Early and also late in his ministry,] ^{12} Jesus. .cast out all them that sold and bought in the temple, and overthrew the tables of the money changers, and the seats of them that sold doves, ^{13} And said. .It is written, My house shall be called the house of prayer ; but ye have made it a den of thieves.—Mat., ch. 21.

1302. —— **Support of the.** *Jews.* ^{32} We made ordinances. .to charge ourselves yearly with the third part of a shekel for the service of the house of our God ; ^{33} For the shewbread. .the continual meat offering. .the continual burnt offering .. sabbaths .. new moons. .set feasts. .holy things, and for the sin offerings.—Neh., ch. 10.

1303. —— A successful. *Jerusalem.* ⁴⁴ All that believed were together, and had all things common ; ⁴⁶ And they, continuing daily with one accord in the temple, and breaking bread from house to house.. ⁴⁷ Praising God, and having favour with all the people. And the Lord added to the church daily.—Acts, ch. 2.

1304. —— Unity of the. *A Body.* ²⁶ Whether one member suffer, all the members suffer with it ; or one member be honoured, all the members rejoice with it. ²⁷ Now ye are the body of Christ, and members in particular.—1 Cor., ch. 12.

1305. —— The true. *Proofs.* ²⁰ John the Baptist hath sent us unto thee, saying, Art thou he that should come? or look we for another ? ²² Then Jesus answering said.. tell John what things ye have seen and heard ; how that the blind see, the lame walk, the lepers are cleansed, the deaf hear, the dead are raised, to the poor the gospel is preached.—Luke, ch. 7.

1306. —— valuable to the State. *Egypt.* ⁴⁷ In the seven plenteous years the earth brought forth by handfuls. ⁴⁹ And Joseph gathered corn as the sand of the sea, very much, until he left numbering ; for *it was* without number.—Gen., ch. 41. [Pious Joseph revealed the future famine.]

1307. —— Unity in Variety. *Members.* ¹² All the members of that one body, being many, are one body : so also *is* Christ. ¹³ For by one Spirit are we all baptized into one body, whether *we be* Jew or Gentiles, whether *we be* bond or·free ; and have been all make to drink into one Spirit. —1 Cor., ch. 12.

1308. —— united in Spirit. *Philippians.* ²⁷ That .. I may hear of your affairs, that ye stand fast in one spirit, with one mind striving together for the faith of the gospel ; ²⁸ And in nothing terrified by your adversaries.—Phil., ch. 1.

1309. —— Women in the. *At Antioch.* ⁵⁰ The Jews stirred up the devout and honourable women, and the chief men of the city, and raised persecution against Paul and Barnabas, and expelled them out of their coasts.—Acts, ch. 13.

1310. —— —— First in Europe. [At Philippi,] ¹⁴ a certain woman named Lydia, a seller of purple.. which worshipped God, heard *us :* whose heart the Lord opened, that she attended unto the things which were spoken of Paul.— Acts, ch. 16. [Took him to her home.]

1311. —— Erection, Joy in. *Levites.* ¹¹ They sang together by course in praising.. the Lord ; because *he is* good, for his mercy *endureth* for ever toward Israel. And all the people shouted with a great shout, when they praised the Lord, because the foundation of the house of the Lord was laid.—Ezra, ch. 3.

1312. —— Erection opposed. *David.* ⁸ The word of the Lord came to me, saying.. thou shalt not build a house unto my name, because thou hast shed much blood upon the earth in my sight. ⁹ Behold, a son shall be born to thee, who shall be a man of rest.—1 Chron., ch. 22. [Solomon his son built it.]

1313. —— Erection proposed. *David.* ¹ When the king sat in his house, and the Lord had given him rest.. from all his enemies ; ² That the king said.. I dwell in a house of cedar, but the ark of God dwelleth within curtains.—2 Sam., ch. 7.

1314. CHURCHES, Destruction of. *Synagogues.* ⁶ They break down the carved work thereof at once with axes and hammers. ⁷ They have cast fire into thy sanctuary, they have defiled *by casting down* the dwellingplace of thy name to the ground. ⁸.. they have burned up all the synagogues of God in the land.—Ps. 74.

See other illustrations under :

CHRISTIANS.

Almost. Agrippa said unto Paul, Almost thou	1267
Care for. I lay down my life for the sheep	1268
Childlike. Suffer little children.. Of such	1269
Carnal. Whereas there is envying and strife	1270
Epistle. Ye are our epistle.. read of all	1271
Exemplary. Bishop must be blameless	1272
Greatness. Least in the kingdom.. greater	1273
Homeward. Come to Zion with songs	1274
First Named. First called Christians at Antioch	1275
Saved. He that committeth sin is of the devil	1276
Visible. Ye are the light of the world	1277

HOUSE OF GOD.

Abandoned. L. hath cast off his altar.. abhorred	4126
Closed. Ahaz shut up the doors	4127
Despoiled. Chaldees.. carried the pots, shovels	4128
Destroyed. Break down the carved work.. fire	4129
Expensive. [Costing £939,907,687, Jamieson]	4130
Gifts. Brought bracelets, earrings, and rings	4131
Given. Ahaz took away a portion.. king of A.	4132
Grandeur. D. said.. must be exceeding magnifical	4133
Neglected. Dwell in your ceiled houses.. waste	4134
Polluted. Manasseh built altars.. graven image	4135
Refuge. Adonijah feared.. horns of the altar	4136
Residence. Anna departed not from the temple	4137
Robbed. Shishak took.. treasures.. shields of gold	4138
" Ahaz cut in pieces the vessels.. altars	4139
Repairing. Jehoida took a chest.. beside the altar	4140

Attendance. Anna a prophetess.. departed not	225
Authority. If he neglect to hear the church	950
Corrupted. One is hungry, and another is drunken	2529
Caste. Man with gold ring.. poor man	1353
Failure. Thy disciples.. cast him out, and they	2870
Garden. Make her desert like garden	1389
Mixed. Tares are the children of the wicked one	4241
Prosperous. Same day were added 3000	1677
" Many.. believed.. about 5000	1676
Relation. [Gibeonites].. hewers of wood. for the	894

See **CHRISTIANITY, RELIGION.**

1315. CIRCUMSPECTION, Christian. *David.* ² I will behave myself wisely in a perfect way. Oh when wilt thou come unto me ? I will walk within my house with a perfect heart.—Ps. 101.

See other illustrations under

CAUTION.

Believers. Moses sent them to spy out the land	1548
Building. Lest not be able to finish	676
Eating. Put a knife to thy throat.. given to	1068
Forgetfulness. Take heed lest thou forget.. seen	3347
Fear. Howbeit no man speak openly.. for fear	3432
" Did not confess him lest.. put out	3433
Hearing. Increased.. 30.. 60.. 100 fold.. he that	1069
Hypocrisy. Beware of the scribes.. love greetings	321
Lack. Let about 3000.. smite Ai.. fled	1532
" I made as if they were beaten.. and fled	1522
Strife. Consulteth whether he be able to meet	677
Necessary. The simple believe every word	1070
Prudent. [Micah] saw they were too strong	1071
Wise. Fool uttereth all his mind.. wise	1072

PRUDENCE.

WATCHING.

WATCHFULNESS.

1316. CIRCUMSTANCES, Effect of. *Proverb.*
[23] The poor useth intreaties ; but the rich answereth roughly.—Prov., ch. 18.

1317. CITIES, Dangerous Class. *Thessalonica.*
[5] The Jews..moved with envy, took unto them certain lewd fellows of the baser sort, and gathered a company, and set all the city on an uproar, and assaulted the house of Jason.—Acts, ch. 17.

1318. —— Refuge in. *Manslayers.* [5] When a man goeth into the wood..and his hand fetcheth a stroke with the axe to cut down the tree, and the head slippeth from the helve, and lighteth upon his neighbour, that he die ; he shall flee unto one of those cities, and live.—Deut., ch. 19.

1319. CITIZEN, Law-abiding. *Paul.* [1] Let every soul be subject unto the higher powers.. the powers that be are ordained of God. [4] For he is the minister of God to thee for good. But if thou do that which is evil, be afraid ; for he beareth not the sword in vain : for he is the minister of God, a revenger to *execute* wrath upon him that doeth evil.—Rom., ch. 13.

1320. —— of Zion, A. *Christian.* [1] Lord, who shall abide in thy tabernacle? who shall dwell in thy holy hill? [2] He that walketh uprightly, and worketh righteousness, and speaketh the truth in his heart. [3] He that backbiteth not with his tongue, nor doeth evil to his neighbour,

nor taketh up a reproach against his neighbour. [4] In whose eyes a vile person is contemned, but he honoureth them that fear the Lord. *He that* sweareth to *his own* hurt, and changeth not. [5] *He that* putteth not out his money to usury, nor taketh reward against the innocent. He that doeth these *things* shall never be moved.—Ps. 15.

1321. CITY, A captured. *Jerusalem.* [1] Nebuchadnezzar king of Babylon came, he, and all his host, against Jerusalem..the famine prevailed.. [4] And the city was broken up, and all the men of war *fled* by night.—2 Kings, ch. 25.

1322. —— A doomed. *Jerusalem.* [Jesus] [41] beheld the city, and wept over it.. [42] Saying, If thou hadst known..the things *which belong* unto thy peace ! but now they are hid from thine eyes. [43] For..thine enemies shall cast a trench..and keep thee in on every side, [44] And shall lay thee even with the ground.—Luke, ch. 19.

1323. —— An excited. *Jerusalem.* [10] When he was come into Jerusalem, all the city was moved, saying, Who is this? [11] And the multitude said, This is Jesus the prophet of Nazareth. —Mat., ch. 21.

1324. —— The first. *Enoch.* [16] Cain..dwelt in the land of Nod, on the east of Eden. [17] ..and he builded a city, and called the name of the city, after the name of his son, Enoch.—Gen., ch. 4.

1325. —— Famine in the. *Samaria.* [3] There were four leprous men at the entering in of the gate : and they said..Why sit we here until we die? [4] If we say, We will enter into the city, then the famine *is* in the city, and we shall die there : and if we sit still here, we die also.—2 Kings, ch. 7.

1326. —— on Fire, A. *Ai.* [19] The ambush arose quickly..ran as soon as he had stretched out his hand : and they entered into the city, and took it, and hasted and set the city on fire. [20] And when the men of Ai looked behind them, they saw, and, behold, the smoke of the city ascended up to heaven.—Josh., ch. 8.

1327. —— A fallen. *Babylon.* [16] Alas, alas, that great city, that was clothed in fine linen, and purple, and scarlet, and decked with gold, and precious stones, and pearls ! [18] ..cried when they saw the smoke of her burning, saying, What *city is* like unto this great city !—Rev., ch. 18.

1328. —— The glorious. *New Jerusalem.* [18] The building of the wall of it was *of* jasper : and the city *was* pure gold, like unto clear glass. [19] And the foundations of the wall of the city *were* garnished with all manner of precious stones. [21] And the twelve gates *were* twelve pearls.—Rev., ch. 21.

1329. —— **The heavenly.** *New Jerusalem.* [2] I John saw the holy city, new Jerusalem, coming down from God out of heaven, prepared as a bride adorned for her husband.—Rev., ch. 21.

1330. —— **An idolatrous.** *Athens.* [16] While Paul waited..at Athens, his spirit was stirred in him, when he saw the city wholly given to idolatry.—Acts, ch. 17.

1331. —— **A joyful.** *Samaria.* [5] Philip went down to the city of Samaria, and preached Christ unto them. [6] And the people with one accord gave heed.. ˙..and many taken with palsies, and that were lame, were healed. [8] And there was great joy in that city.—Acts, ch. 8.

1332. —— **A mad.** *Jerusalem.* [27] They saw him in the temple, stirred up all the people, and laid hands on him, [28] Crying out, Men of Israel, help : [30] And all the city was moved, and the people ran together : and they took Paul, and drew him out..and forthwith the doors were shut. [31] And..they went about to kill him.— Acts, ch. 21.

1333. —— **preserved by the Church.** *Sodom.* [26] The Lord said, If I find in Sodom fifty righteous within the city, then I will spare all the place for their sakes.—Gen., ch. 18.

1334. —— **moved by a Revival, A.** *Antioch.* [43] When the congregation was broken up, many of the Jews and religious proselytes followed Paul and Barnabas ; who..persuaded them to continue in the grace of God. [44] And the next sabbath day came almost the whole city together to hear the word of God.—Acts, ch. 13.

1335. —— **Suburbs of the.** *Lord to Moses.* [2] Ye shall give *also* unto the Levites suburbs for the cities round about them. [3] And the cities shall they have to dwell in ; and the suburbs ..for their cattle, and for their goods.—Num., ch. 35.

1336. —— **A wasted.** *Jerusalem.* [3] Why should not my countenance be sad, when the city, the place of my fathers' sepulchres, *lieth* waste, and the gates thereof are consumed with fire ?—Neh., ch. 2.

1337. —— **A wicked.** *Sodom.* [13] The men of Sodom *were* wicked and sinners before the Lord exceedingly.—Gen., ch. 13.

Also see .

Joyful. Wives and children rejoiced..joy of   956

— **CIVILITY.** —— ——

See illustrations under :

POLITENESS.

Cultivated. May we know what this new doctrine   6232
Inculcated. Sit down in the lowest room   6233
Tender. Is your father well, the old man of whom   6234
Treacherous. Joab took Amasa..to kiss him   6235

1338. CLAIMS first, God's. *Firstlings.* [12] Thou shalt set apart unto the Lord all that openeth the matrix, and every firstling that cometh of a beast which thou hast ; the male *shall be* the Lord's. [13] ..and all the firstborn of man among thy children shalt thou redeem.—Ex., ch. 13.

1339. —— **first, The highest.** *Jesus.* [59] Follow me. But he said, Lord, suffer me first to go and bury my father. [60] Jesus said..Let the dead bury their dead ; but go thou and preach the kingdom of God.—Luke, ch. 9.

1340. —— **paramount, Christ's.** *Colt.* [30] Go ye into the village..at your entering ye shall find a colt tied, whereon yet never man sat : loose him, and bring *him hither.* [31] And if any man ask you, Why do ye loose *him?*..say unto him, Because the Lord hath need of him.—Luke, ch. 19.

See other illustrations under .

AUTHORITY.

Brothers. Family..sacrifice..brother commanded   584
Compared. Moses commanded..what sayest thou   585
False. I am a prophet..angel spake..lied   586
Obedience. All thou commandedst..will do   587
Power. I say unto one, Go, and he goeth   588
Questioned. By what authority doest thou these   589
Recognized. Scourge..drove them out of the t.   590
Supreme. Rebuked the wind and..calm   591

1341. CLAMOR, Success by. *Pilate.* [22] He said unto them the third time, Why, what evil hath he done ? I have found no cause of death in him : I will therefore chastise him, and let *him* go. [23] And they were instant with loud voices, requiring that he might be crucified.—Luke, ch. 23.

See other illustrations under :

MOB.

Bigots. Two hours cried out, Great is Diana   5487
Disturbance. Lewd fellows of the baser sort   5488
Murderous. City was moved..people ran..took   5489
Tumultuous. Left beating Paul..some cried one   5490
Trial by. Cried..loud voice..ran upon Stephen   5491
Workmen. By this craft we have our wealth   5492

SHOUTING.

Heaven. Voice of a great multitude..as many   7841
Idolatrous. Joshua heard the people as they   7842
Religious. Came a fire..all the people saw, they 7843
    "   Brought up the ark..with shouting and   7844
Stimulated. Philistines shouted against him..loosed 7845
Triumph. People shouted with a great shout   7846
Vain. Ark came into the camp..I. shouted   7847
Victory. People shouted when the priests blew the 7848
Weeping. Not discern the noise of joy from   7849

1342. CLASSES, Only two. *The Judgment.* [32] Before him shall be gathered all nations : and he shall separate them one from another, as a shepherd divideth *his* sheep from the goats : [33] And he shall set the sheep on his right hand, but the goats on the left.—Mat., ch. 25.

See other illustrations under ·

CASTE.

Abolished. G. hath shewed me..any man   1055
Egyptian. Egyptians..not eat bread with the   1056
Ignored. Ordained twelve. Simon the Canaanite   1057
Jewish. Thou being a Jew, askest drink of me   1058
No More. Great sheet..all manner of..beasts   1059
No Respect for. Smote the firstborn..throne   1060
Religious. Casting out devils..forbade him   1061
Super-religious. Have known..woman that   1062

Division. I will sever..my people..no flies be   2463

1343. CLEANSING, Blood of. *Sprinkling.* [8] Moses took the blood, and sprinkled *it* on the people, and said, Behold the blood of the covenant, which the Lord hath made with you.—Ex., ch. 24.

1344. —— **Blood.** *Christ's.* [13] If the blood of bulls and of goats, and the ashes of a heifer sprinkling the unclean, sanctifieth to the purifying of the flesh ; [14] How much more shall the blood of Christ.—Heb., ch. 9.

1345. —— **by Expulsion.** *Temple.* [14] [Jesus] found in the temple those that sold oxen and sheep and doves, and the changers of money sitting : ¹⁵ And when he had made a scourge of small cords, he drove them all out..and the sheep, and the oxen ; and poured out the changers' money, and overthrew the tables.—JOHN, ch. 2.

1346. —— **by Holy Fire.** *Isaiah.* ⁵ Woe *is* me ! for I am undone ; because I *am* a man of unclean lips..for mine eyes have seen..the Lord of hosts. ⁶ Then flew one of the seraphim unto me, having a live coal in his hand. ⁷ And he laid *it* upon my mouth, and said, Lo, this hath touched thy lips ; and thine iniquity is taken away, and thy sin purged.—ISA., ch. 6.

1347. —— **Heart.** *David.* ¹⁰ Create in me a clean heart, O God ; and renew a right spirit within me.—Ps. 51.

1348. —— **Spiritual.** *Hands.* ³ Who shall ascend into the hill of the Lord? or who shall stand in his holy place? ⁴ He that hath clean hands, and a pure heart.—Ps. 24.

1349. —— **Typical.** *Feet.* ⁹ Simon Peter saith ..Lord, not my feet only, but also *my* hands and *my* head. ¹⁰ Jesus saith..He that is washed needeth not save to wash *his* feet, but is clean every whit.—JOHN, ch. 13.

See other illustrations under :

PURITY.
Symbolized. Make a laver of brass..to wash   6813
Within. First cleanse within the cup   6814

SANCTIFICATION.
Firstborn. The males shall be the Lord's   7574
Sabbath. God blessed the seventh day..sanctified   7575

Disregarded. Drink..tables full of vomit   2523
     "   Sow that was washed..wallowing   4857
Divine. Though your sins be as scarlet..as snow   3356
External. Ye make clean the outside of the cup   2829
False. Shall I give the fruit of my body for the sin   3532
Inward. Ye make clean the outside of the cup   3855
Healthful. Clean hands shall be stronger and s.   3751
Honoured. Who shall ascend..clean hands   1348
Means. Washing of water by the word   4002
     "   Blood of J. C. his Son cleanseth us..sin   7948
Needed. All our righteousness..filthy rags—Isa. 64 : 6

— CLEMENCY. —— ——
See illustrations under :

MERCY.
Abused. When Pharaoh..thunders ceased   5339
Compassionate. L. saw the affliction of I...helper   5341
Conquerors. Captives..bands of Syria came no   5342
Divine. When the poor and needy seek water   5343
     "   L. the L. G. merciful and gracious   5344
     "   As a father pitieth his children, so the L.   5345
Deplored. I know thou art a gracious G..Jonah   5346
Entreated. Entreat the L. (for it is enough)   5348
Extension. Let it alone this year also, I will   5349
Gracious. To whom the king..golden sceptre   5350
Hope in. Let us fall into the hands of the L.   5352
Ignorant. Blasphemer..obtained mercy   5354
Limited. My S. shall not always strive with man   5355
Only. Let us fall unto..Syrians..shall but die   5356
Omitted. Priest passed on..Levite looked on   5357
Last Plea. Forgive..my sin only this once   5358
Power. Said Saul, I have sinned..Return my son   5359
Plea. Bartimeus..Thou s. of David have mercy on   5360
     "   [Publican] God be merciful to me a sinner   5361
Penitent. [Ninevites] Turned from..G. repented   5362
Reliance on. Forgive their sin, if not, blot me   5364
Reputation. Have heard..kings of I..merciful   5365
Suppliants. Sackcloth..ropes on their heads..to   5367
Success by. Two blind men followed..have m.   5368

1350. CLOTHES represent Character. *Prodigal.* ²² The father said to his servants, Bring forth the best robe, and put *it* on him ; and put a ring on his hand, and shoes on *his* feet.—LUKE, ch. 15.

1351. —— **Envy of.** *Jacob's Sons.* ³ Israel loved Joseph more than all his children, because he *was* the son of his old age : and he made him a coat of *many* colours. ⁴ And when his brethren saw that their father loved him more than all his brethren, they hated him, and could not speak peaceably unto him.—GEN., ch. 37.

1352. —— **Display of.** *Hypocrites.* ⁵ All their works they do for to be seen of men : they make broad their phylacteries, and enlarge the borders of their garments.—MAT., ch. 23.

1353. —— **Influence of.** *In Church.* ² If there come unto your assembly a man with a gold ring, in goodly apparel, and there come in also a poor man in vile raiment ; ³ And ye have respect to him that weareth the gay clothing, and say..Sit thou here in a good place ; and say to the poor, Stand thou there, or sit here under my footstool : ⁴ Are ye not then partial in yourselves?—JAMES, ch. 2.

1354. —— **mutilated.** *Insult.* ⁴ Hanun took David's servants, and shaved off the one half of their beards, and cut off their garments in the middle, even to their buttocks, and sent them away.—2 SAM., ch. 10.

1355. —— **Rending of.** *Grief.* ²⁹ Reuben returned unto the pit ; and, behold, Joseph *was* not in the pit ; and he rent his clothes. ³⁰ And he returned unto his brethren, and said, The child *is* not ; and I, whither shall I go?—GEN., ch. 37.

1356. —— **rent for a Sign.** *Grief.* ¹¹ David took hold on his clothes, and rent them ; and likewise all the men that *were* with him : ¹² And they mourned, and wept, and fasted until even, for Saul, and for Jonathan his son..because they were fallen by the sword.—2 SAM., ch. 1.

1357. —— **unwashed.** *In Grief.* ²⁴ Mephibosheth the son of Saul..had neither dressed his feet, nor trimmed his beard, nor washed his clothes, from the day the king departed until the day he came *again* in peace.—2 SAM., ch. 19.

1358. CLOTHING, Beautiful. *Priest's.* ⁴ A breastplate, and an ephod, and a robe, and a broidered coat, a mitre, and a girdle. ⁶..make the ephod *of* gold, *of* blue, and *of* purple, *of* scarlet, and fine twined linen, with cunning work. ³¹..make the robe of the ephod all *of* blue.—Ex., ch. 28.

1359. —— **Deception by.** *Gibeonites.* ⁴ Made as if they had been ambassadors, and took old sacks upon their asses, and wine bottles, old, and rent, and bound up ; ⁵ And old shoes and clouted upon their feet, and old garments upon them ; and all the bread of their provision was dry *and* mouldy. ⁶ And they went to Joshua.—JOSHUA, ch. 9. [They secured a treaty.]

1360. —— **Disguised by.** *False Prophets.* [Jesus said,] ¹⁵ Beware of false prophets, which come to you in sheep's clothing, but inwardly they are ravening wolves. ¹⁶ Ye shall know them by their fruits.—MAT., ch. 7.

1361. —— **The first.** *Leaves.* ⁷ They knew that they *were* naked ; and they sewed fig leaves together, and made themselves aprons. ²¹ Unto Adam also and to his wife did the Lord God make coats of skins.—GEN., ch. 3.

1362. —— **Gift of.** *To David.* ⁴ Jonathan stripped himself of the robe that *was* upon him, and gave it to David, and his garments, even to his sword, and to his bow, and to his girdle.—1 SAM., ch. 18.

1363. —— **annual Gift of.** *By Hannah.* ¹⁸ Samuel ministered before the Lord, *being* a child, girded with a linen ephod. ¹⁹ . . his mother made him a little coat, and brought *it* to him from year to year.—1 SAM., ch. 2.

1364. —— **Indestructible.** *Israelites.* ² Remember all the way which the Lord thy God led thee these forty years in the wilderness. ⁴ Thy raiment waxed not old upon thee.—DEUT., ch. 8.

1365. —— **Ornamental.** *Daughters of Zion.* ¹⁸ In that day the Lord will take away the bravery of *their* tinkling ornaments *about their feet*, and *their* cauls, and *their* round tires like the moon. ¹⁹ The chains, and the bracelets, and the mufflers. . ²⁰ The bonnets, and the ornaments of the legs, and the headbands, and the tablets, and the earrings. . ²¹ The rings, and nose jewels . . ²² The changeable suits of apparel, and the mantles, and the wimples, and the crisping pins. . ²³ The glasses, and the fine linen, and the hoods, and the vails.—ISA., ch. 3.

1366. —— **Plain.** *Baptist.* ⁴ John had his raiment of camel's hair, and a leathern girdle about his loins.—MAT., ch. 3.

1367. —— **preserved.** *Jesus.* ²³ The soldiers, when they had crucified Jesus, took his garments, and made four parts, to every soldier a part. . the coat was without seam, woven from the top throughout. ²⁴ They said . . Let us not rend it, but cast lots for it.—JOHN, ch. 19.

1368. —— **Showy.** *Paul.* ⁸ I will. . ⁹ . . that women adorn themselves in modest apparel, with shamefacedness and sobriety ; not with braided hair, or gold, or pearls, or costly array ; ¹⁰ But (which becometh women professing godliness) with good works.—1 TIM., ch. 2.

1369. —— **covers Sin.** *Dives.* ¹⁹ There was a certain rich man, which was clothed in purple and fine linen, and fared sumptuously every day. . ²³ And in hell he lifted up his eyes, being in torments, and seeth Abraham afar off, and Lazarus in his bosom.—LUKE, ch. 16.

1370. —— **Separate.** *The Sexes.* ⁵ The woman shall not wear that which pertaineth unto a man, neither shall a man put on a woman's garment : for all that do so *are* abomination unto the Lord.—DEUT., cb. 22.

1371. —— **Tasteful.** *Model Woman.* ²² She maketh herself coverings of tapestry ; her clothing *is* silk and purple.—PROV., ch. 31.

See other illustration under
JEWELRY.

Abundance. Weight of the golden earrings 1700 t.   4723
Badge. Clothed Daniel with scarlet. . chain   4724
Gifts. Bracelets and earrings and rings   4725
Snare. Gideon made an ephod thereof   4726

Angelic. Two men stood by them in white apparel   471
Benevolence. Widows showing the. . garments   3509
Bereavement. As a woman. . long time mourned   5606
Coveted. I saw a Babylonish garment, and coveted 8316

Christian. Women adorn themselves in modest   108
Embroidered. To Sisera a prey of divers colors of 8318
Mockery. They clothed him with purple. . crown   6600
Mourning. D. and men of I. clothed in   8534
Neglected. Mephibosheth. . nor trimmed his beard 3731
Promised. Clothed the grass. . much more you   9067
Regalia. Bring forth vestments for. . worshippers   6949

1372. CLOUD, God hidden in a. *Sinai* ¹⁶ The glory of the Lord abode upon mount Sinai, and the cloud covered it six days : and the seventh day he called unto Moses out of the midst of the cloud. ¹⁷ And the sight of the glory of the Lord *was* like devouring fire on the top of the mount.—EX., ch. 24.

1373. —— **An overshadowing.** *Transfiguration.* ³⁴ There came a cloud, and overshadowed them : and they feared as they entered into the cloud. ³⁵ And there came a voice out of the cloud, saying, This is my beloved Son : hear him.—LUKE, ch. 9.

1374. —— **The Pillar of.** *Tabernacle.* ³⁴ A cloud covered the tent. . and the glory of the Lord filled the tabernacle. ³⁸ For the cloud of the Lord *was* upon the tabernacle by day, and fire was on it by night, in the sight of all the house of Israel, throughout all their journeys. —EX., ch. 40.

See other illustrations under :
Baptismal. Baptized unto Moses in the cloud   638
Beatific. He was taken up. . cloud received him   3040
Brightened. I do set my bow in the cloud   7866
Ominous. Ariseth a cloud. . man's hand   6850
Overpowering. Priests could not stand to minister 6515

1375. COFFIN, The first mentioned. *Joseph's.* ²⁶ Joseph died, *being* a hundred and ten years old : and they embalmed him, and he was put in a coffin in Egypt.—GEN., ch. 50.

See other illustrations under :
BURIAL.

Denied. Bring out the bones of the kings. . spread   974
Life from. Touched the bones of Elisha, he revived 975
Living. Earth opened her mouth and swallowed   976
Mournful. David. . lifted up his voice. . grave of   977
Mysterious. Moses died. . no man knoweth his   978
Patriarchs. All the servants of Pharaoh. . elders   979
Perfumed. Filled with sweet odours. . spices   980

1376. COLD an Excuse. *Proverb.* ⁴ The sluggard will not plow by reason of the cold ; *therefore* shall he beg in harvest, and *have* nothing. —PROV., ch. 20.

See other illustrations under :
Considered. Taketh away a garment in c. weather 5378
Exposure. In cold and nakedness [Paul]   5424

1377. COLLECTION-BOX, The first. *For Building.* ⁹ Jehoiada the priest took a chest, and bored a hole in the lid of it, and set it beside the altar, on the right side. . and the priests that kept the door put therein all the money *that was* brought into the house of the LORD.—2 KINGS, ch. 12.

See other illustrations under :
CONTRIBUTIONS.

Abundant. [Temple] Offered willingly. . gold 5000 1657
Expenses. Charge ourselves yearly. . third part of 1658
for Jesus. Women. . healed. . ministered. . their   1659
for Levites. Firstfruits of corn, wine, oil, and   1660
Repairs. Chest. . set beside the altar. . right side   1661
Rebuilding. Chief of the fathers gave after their   1662
Various. Men and women. . blue, purple, scarlet   1663

1378. COLOR-LINE in Religion. *Ethiopian.*
[1] Miriam and Aaron spake against Moses because of the Ethiopian woman whom he had married : for he had married an Ethiopian woman.. [9] And the anger of the Lord was kindled against them ; and he departed.—Num., ch. 12.

1379. COMFORT in Adversity. *Habakkuk.*
[17] Although the fig tree shall not blossom, neither *shall* fruit *be* in the vines ; the labour of the olive shall fail, and the fields shall yield no meat ; the flock shall be cut off from the fold, and *there shall be* no herd in the stalls : [18] Yet I will rejoice in the Lord, I will joy in the God of my salvation.—Hab., ch. 3.

1380. —— An appreciated. *In the Wilderness.*
[27] They came to Elim, where *were* twelve wells of water, and threescore and ten palm trees : and they encamped there by the waters.—Ex., ch. 15.

1381. —— A cruel. *Esau's.* [42] These words of Esau..were told to Rebekah : and she sent and called Jacob..and said..Behold, thy brother Esau..doth comfort himself, *purposing* to kill thee.—Gen., ch. 27.

1382. —— The Christian's. *Divine.* [1] O Lord, I will praise thee : though thou wast angry with me, thine anger is turned away, and thou comfortedst me. [2] Behold, God *is* my salvation ; I will trust and not be afraid.—Isa., ch. 12.

1383. —— Dangerous. *Peter's.* [54] Peter followed him afar off, even into the palace of the high priest : and he sat with the servants, and warmed himself at the fire.—Mark, ch. 14.

1384. —— Experience of. *Everlasting.* [16] Now our Lord Jesus Christ himself, and God, even our Father which hath loved us, and hath given *us* everlasting consolation and good hope through grace, [17] Comfort your hearts, and stablish you in every good word and work.—2 Thess., ch. 2.

1385. —— Fraternal. *Paul.* [6] God, that comforteth those that are cast down, comforted us by the coming of Titus ; [7] And not by his coming only, but..when he told us your earnest desire, your mourning, your fervent mind toward me ; so that I rejoiced the more.—2 Cor., ch. 7.

1386. —— for the Lonely. *Angels near.* [16] Jacob awaked out of his sleep, and he said, Surely the Lord is in this place ; and I knew *it* not. [17] And he was afraid, and said, How dreadful *is* this place ! this *is* none other but the house of God, and this *is* the gate of heaven.—Gen., ch. 28.

1387. —— Provision for. *The Spirit.* [16] I will pray the Father, and he shall give you another Comforter, that he may abide with you for ever ; [17] *Even* the Spirit of truth ; whom the world cannot receive, because it seeth him not, neither knoweth him : but ye know him ; for he dwelleth with you, and shall be in you. [18] I will not leave you comfortless : I will come to you.—John, ch. 14.

1388. —— Short-lived. *Gourd.* [6] Jonah was exceeding glad of the gourd. [7] ..a worm when the morning rose the next day..smote the gourd that it withered. [8] ..when the sun did arise.. God prepared a vehement east wind ; and the sun beat upon the head of Jonah, that he fainted, and wished in himself to die.—Jonah, ch. 4.

1389. —— for Zion. *Promise.* [3] The Lord shall comfort Zion : he will comfort all her waste places ; and he will make her wilderness like Eden, and her desert like the garden of the Lord : joy and gladness shall be found therein, thanksgiving, and the voice of melody.—Isa., ch. 51.

See other illustrations under :

SYMPATHY.

Abundant. What mean ye to weep and break mine	8545
Bereavement. Much people..with her..he had	8546
" Many of the Jews came to Martha	8547
Distrusted. Thinkest thou that David..hath sent	8549
Eyes. Mine eye affected mine heart because of	8550
by Experience. Touched with the feeling..tempt	8551
Erring. Forgive..lest swallowed up with over	8552
" Count him not as an enemy, but..brother	8553
Forbidden. If any man lie in wait..eye shall not	8554
in Heaven. Not a high priest which can not be	8555
Ill-rewarded. Hanun shaved off one half of their	8556
for Jesus. Great company of people and women	8557
Manifested. [See Nos. 8547 and 8557]	
Offices. I was eyes to the blind, and feet..lame	8559
Power. Behold the babe wept, she had compassion	8560
Public. All the city was moved..Is this Naomi?	8561
Practical. Samaritan..went to him and bound up	8563
Power. What mean ye to weep and break mine	8564
Return. Weep not for me, but weep for yourselves	8565
Sentimental. Levite..looked on him and passed by	8566
Silent. Sat down upon the ground 7 days..none	8567
Tender. O that mine head were waters, and mine	8568
" Mine eye runneth down with rivers of	8569
" Saw her weeping..Jews also..Jesus wept	8570
Unshaken. I am ready not to be bound only, but	8571
Frail. Jonah was exceeding glad of the gourd	3404
Memory. I was eyes to the blind..feet	127
Vision. Jacob dreamed..ladder set up on the	5054

See **CHEERFULNESS** and references.

1390. COMFORTER, Reproof from the. *Spirit.*
[7] If I go not away, the Comforter will not come unto you ; but if I depart, I will send him unto you. [8] And when he is come, he will reprove the world of sin, and of righteousness, and of judgment.—John, ch. 16.

Also see :

Affliction. Child sick..David lay..elders..he would	31

1391. COMMANDMENT, The First. *Love.*
[28] Which is the first commandment of all ? [29] And Jesus answered him, The first of all the commandments is.. [30] Thou shalt love the Lord thy God with all thy heart, and with all thy soul, and with all thy mind, and with all thy strength.—Mark, ch. 12.

1392. —— ignored, The. *Strange Fire.* [1] Nadab and Abihu, the sons of Aaron, took either of them his censer, and put fire therein, and put incense thereon, and offered strange fire before the Lord, which he commanded them not. [2] And there went out fire from the Lord, and devoured them.—Lev., ch. 10.

1393. —— Nature obeys the. *Light.* [2] The earth was without form, and void ; and darkness *was* upon the face of the deep. And the Spirit of God moved upon the face of the waters. [3] And God said, Let there be light : and there was light.—Gen., ch. 1.

1394. —— The new. *Love.* [34] A new commandment I give unto you, That ye love one another ; as I have loved you, that ye also love one another. [35] By this shall all *men* know that ye are my disciples, if ye have love one to another.—JOHN, ch. 13.

1395. —— The smallest. *Birds.* [So called by the Jews.] [6] If a bird's nest chance to be before thee..and the dam sitting upon the young, or upon the eggs, thou shalt not take the dam with the young : [7] But thou shalt in any wise let the dam go, and take the young to thee ; that it may be well with thee, and *that* thou mayest prolong *thy* days.—DEUT., ch. 22.

1396. —— the Second. *Love.* [31] The second is like, *namely* this, Thou shalt love thy neighbour as thyself. There is none other commandment greater than these.—MARK, ch. 12.

1397. COMMANDMENTS kept. *Young Ruler.* [20] The young man saith unto him, All these things have I kept from my youth up : what lack I yet ?—MAT., ch. 19.

1398. —— test Character. *Obedience.* [3] Hereby we do know that we know him, if we keep his commandments. [4] He that saith, I know him, and keepeth not his commandments, is a liar.—1 JOHN, ch. 2.

1399. —— The Ten. *Decalogue.* [See Exodus 20 : 3-17.]

1400. —— Use of. *Lamp.* [23] For the commandment *is* a lamp ; and the law is light.—PROV., ch. 6.

See other illustrations under :

AUTHORITY.

Brother's. Our family hath a sacrifice..brother	584
Compared. Moses..commanded..what sayest thou	585
False. I am a prophet..angel spake..but he lied	586
Obedience. All thou commandest. will do	587
Power. I say unto one, Go, and he goeth	588
Questioned. By what authority doest thou these	589
Recognized. Scourge..drove them all out of the	590
Supreme. Rebuked the wind and the raging	591

LAW.

Appeal. Is it lawful..to scourge..a Roman ?	4900
Equality. Cut off..whether. a stranger or born	4901
" Think not that thou shalt escape..more	4902
Evasion. To justify himself..who is my neighbour	4903
Indifference. Nadab and Abihu..offered strange	4904
of Love. First commandment..love the Lord	4905
Misapplied. By our law he ought to die.. S. of G.	4906
Necessity. I will go..if I perish, I perish	4907
Protection. Said Paul, I stand at Cesar's	4908
Summary. Thou shalt love the L..do and live	4909
Superseded. Law..schoolmaster to bring us to C.	4910
Supremacy. Darius..set his heart on Daniel to	4911
Sumptuary. Fruit of the tree..ye shall not eat of it	4912
" Blood..whosoever eateth of it..cut off	4913
" Eat no manner of fat. of ox, or sheep	4914
" Ye shall eat..parteth the hoof..cud	4915
Transgressors. Not made for a righteous man	4916
Unobserved. Pay tithe of mint..omitted the	4917
Unchangeable. Law of the Medes and Persians	4918

See OBEDIENCE.

1401. COMMENDATION by Fruits. *Paul's.* [1] Do we begin again to commend ourselves ? or need we, as some *others,* epistles of commendation to you, or *letters* of commendation from you ? [2] Ye are our epistle written in our hearts, known and read of all men.—2 COR., ch. 3.

1402. —— Future. *Judgment.* [20] Lord, thou deliveredst unto me five talents : behold, I have gained beside them five talents more. [21] His lord

said.. Well done, *thou* good and faithful servant : thou hast been faithful over a few things, I will make thee ruler over many things : enter thou into the joy of thy lord.—MAT., ch. 25.

1403. —— A hurtful. *Damsel.* [At Philippi] [16] as we went to prayer, a certain damsel possessed with a spirit of divination met us, which brought her masters much gain by soothsaying : [17]..followed Paul and us, and cried, saying, These men are the servants of the most high God, which shew unto us the way of salvation.—ACTS, ch. 16. [Paul exorcised the evil spirit.]

See other illustrations under :

PRAISE.

Self. Let another praise thee..not thine own	6330
Praise. Loved the praise of men more than..of G.	6331
Dangerous. In all Israel..none so much to be	6332
Hypocrites. Love to pray..corners of the streets	6337
Unmerited. Doth he thank that servant ?	7376
Unexpected. This widow hath cast in more	7386
Worthy. Centurion..was worthy..built us a	688

1404. COMMERCE, Wealth from. *Tyrus.* [3] Thou hast said, I *am* a god, I sit *in* the seat of God, in the midst of the seas ; [4] With thy wisdom and with thine understanding thou hast gotten ..gold and silver into thy treasures : [5]..and by thy traffick hast thou increased thy riches, and thine heart is lifted up.—EZEK., ch. 28.

See BUSINESS and references.

1405. COMMUNISM, Christian. *Church at Jerusalem.* [44] All that believed were together, and had all things common ; [45] And sold their possessions and goods, and parted them .. as every man had need.—ACTS, ch. 2.

1406. —— —— *Jerusalem.* [32] Them that believed were of one heart and of one soul : neither said any *of them* that aught of the things which he possessed was his own : but they had all things common. [34] Neither was there any among them that lacked : for as many as were possessors of lands or houses sold them, and brought the prices of the things that were sold, [35] And laid *them* down at the apostles' feet : and distribution was made unto every man according as he had need.—ACTS, ch. 4.

1407. —— Jewish. *Fiftieth Year.* [10] Proclaim liberty throughout *all* the land unto all the inhabitants thereof : it shall be a jubilee unto you ; and ye shall return every man unto his possession.—LEV., ch. 25.

See other illustrations under

Jewish. Every seven years..every creditor..not	8149
Unfortunates. Every one that is in distress..debt	8153

1408. COMMUNION by Blood. *Sprinkled.* [8] Moses took the blood, and sprinkled *it* on the people, and said, Behold the blood of the covenant, which the Lord hath made with you.—EX., ch. 24.

1409. —— corrects Prejudice. *Nathanael.* [46] Nathanael said..Can there any good thing come out of Nazareth ? Philip saith..Come and see. [49] Nathanael answered..Rabbi, thou art the Son of God ; thou art the King of Israel.—JOHN, ch. 1.

1410. —— of Evil Doers. *Pharisees.* [10] Stretch forth thy hand. And he did so : and his hand was restored whole as the other. [11] And they were filled with madness ; and communed one with another what they might do to Jesus.— Luke, ch. 6.

1411. —— with God. *Friendship.* [23] Abraham believed God, and it was imputed unto him for righteousness : and he was called the friend of God.—James, ch. 2.

1412. —— Glorious. *Christian.* [22] To an innumerable company of angels, [23] To the general assembly and church of the firstborn which are written in heaven, and to God the Judge of all, and to the spirits of just men made perfect.— Heb., ch. 12.

1413. —— Invitation to. *Festal.* [20] Behold, I stand at the door, and knock : if any man hear my voice, and open the door, I will come in to him, and will sup with him, and he with me.— Rev., ch. 3.

1414. —— Mysterious. *Christian.* [22] Judas saith..not Iscariot, Lord, how is it that thou wilt manifest thyself unto us, and not unto the world ? [23] Jesus answered..If a man love me, he will keep my words : and my Father will love him, and we will come unto him, and make our abode with him.—John, ch. 14.

1415. —— in Old Age. *Abram.* [1] When Abram was ninety years old and nine, the Lord appeared..and said. I *am* the Almighty God ; walk before me, and be thou perfect.—Gen., ch. 17.

1416. —— Protracted. *Moses'.* [18] Moses went into the midst of the cloud..and Moses was in the mount forty days and forty nights.—Ex., ch. 24.

1417. —— Recorded. *Book.* [16] They that feared the Lord spake often one to another: and the Lord hearkened, and heard *it*, and a book of remembrance was written before him for them that feared the Lord.—Mal., ch. 3.

1418. —— strengthens. *Worship.* [30] Even the youths shall faint and be weary, and the young men shall utterly fall : [31] But they that wait upon the Lord shall renew *their* strength ; they shall mount up with wings as eagles ; they shall run, and not be weary ; *and* they shall walk, and not faint.—Isa., ch. 40.

1419. —— —— *Jesus said,* [19] If two of you shall agree on earth as touching any thing that they shall ask, it shall be done for them of my Father.. [20] For where two or three are gathered together in my name, there am I in the midst of them.—Mat., ch. 18.

1420. —— of Saints. *Fellow Citizens.* [19] Ye are no more strangers and foreigners, but fellow citizens with the saints, and of the household of God.—Eph., ch. 2.

1421. —— Walking in. *Enoch.* [22] Enoch walked with God after he begat Methuselah three hundred years.. [24] And Enoch walked with God : and he *was* not ; for God took him.—Gen., ch. 5. [9] Noah was a just man *and* perfect in his generations, *and* Noah walked with God.—Gen. ch. 6.

See other illustrations under :

UNION.

Buidling. Build..men of his place help 9099
Blessing. Cloven tongues..upon each of them 9100
with Christ. I am the vine, ye are the branches 9101
Constant. I will never leave thee..forsake thee 9102
in Charity. According to his ability..send relief 9103

Communistic. All that believed..all things 9104
in Communion. Him and his neighbor..eat 9105
Distress. Every one that was in distress..came 9106
Effect. If ye abide in me..ask what 9107
Eternal. Neither death nor life..separate 9108
Forces. Wilt thou go with me to battle ? 9109
Friends. Where thou lodgest, I will lodge 9110
Forbidden. Be hewers of wood and drawers 9111
Important. Wherefore discourage ye the heart 9112
Prayer. Moses' hands were heavy..A. and H. 9113
Perpetual. I am with you always..end of the w. 9114
Revival. Gathered themselves as one man 9115
Rejected. If a man abide not in me..burned 9116
Strength. If the Syrians be too strong..help me 9117
Two. Jonathan..armourbearer slew after him 9118
Unhallowed. Let us build with you..your G. 9119
Worship. All with one accord in one place 9120

UNITY.

by Creation. Made of one blood all nations of men 9121
Delightful. How pleasant it is..brethren in unity 9122
Dangerous. All people is one..nothing 9123
Diversity. Many members, yet but one body 9124
Dependence. Eye cannot say of the hand..no need 9125
Impracticable. Image..feet were of iron and clay 9126
Occupation. Because..of the same craft abode 9127
Prayer for. All may be one, as thou Father art in me 9128
Remarkable. Were of one heart..all things 9129
Spirit. By one spirit we are all baptized into one 9130
Suffering in. Whether one member suffer, all 9131

See FRIEND and FRIENDSHIP.
See UNION.

1422. COMMISSION to deliver. *Gideon.* [13] Now the Lord hath forsaken us, and delivered us into the hands of the Midianites. [14] And the Lord looked upon him, and said, Go in this thy might, and thou shalt save Israel from the hand of the Midianites : have not I sent thee? —Judges, ch. 6.

See other illustrations under:

CALL.

Apostleship. Follow me..[Levi] left all 1007
Children. L. called Samuel..here am I 1008
Dishonoured. Follow me..bury my father 1009
Earnestness. No man..looking back. is fit 1010
Instrumental. Take thee Joshua give him a 1011
Ministerial. Dwell with me..a priest. 10 shekels 1012
Obedience. Simon and Andrew..forsook the nets 1013
Preaching. Woe is unto me if I preach not 1014
Response. Whom shall I send..here am I 1015
Spirit. Thine ears..hear a word behind thee 1016
Sacrifice. He called..they left their father 1017
Vision. Come over into Macedonia..help 1018

Terrible. I persecuted them..commission..chief 7647

1423. COMPANIONS, Disgraceful. *Thieves.* [27] With him they crucify two thieves ; the one on his right hand, and the other on his left.— Mark, ch. 15.

1424. —— Ruinous. *Rehoboam's.* [10] The young men that were brought up with him spake ..Thus shalt thou answer the people..saying, Thy father made our yoke heavy, but make thou *it* somewhat lighter for us ; thus..say..My little *finger* shall be thicker than my father's loins. —2 Chron., ch. 10. [Result : the kingdom was divided.]

See other illustrations under:

ASSOCIATES.

Apostasy. Solomon loved many strange women 539
Beneficial. Ark..Noah went in and..his sons' wives 540

1425. COMPASSION, Appeal to. *A Father's.*
[17] Master, I have brought unto thee my son, which hath a dumb spirit ; [18] And wheresoever he taketh him, he teareth him ; and he foameth, and gnasheth with his teeth, and pineth away : [22] And ofttimes it hath cast him into the fire, and into the waters, to destroy him : but if thou canst do any thing, have compassion on us, and help us.—MARK, ch. 9.

1426. —— Active. *Jesus.* [35] Jesus went about all the cities and villages, teaching..and preaching..and healing every sickness and every disease among the people. [36] But when he saw the multitudes, he was moved with compassion on them, because they fainted, and were scattered abroad, as sheep having no shepherd.—MAT., ch. 9.

1427. —— A Brother's. *Joseph.* [18] His brethren..fell down before his face ; and they said, Behold, we *be* thy servants. [19] And Joseph said..Fear not.. [20]..as for you, ye thought evil against me ; *but* God meant it unto good..to save much people alive. [21] Now therefore fear ye not : I will nourish you, and your little ones. And he comforted them, and spake kindly unto them.—GEN., ch. 50.

1428. —— commended. *Good Samaritan.* [34] Went to *him*, and bound up his wounds, pouring in oil and wine, and set him on his own beast, and brought him to an inn, and took care of him. [35] Then said Jesus..Go, and do thou likewise.—LUKE, ch. 10.

1429. —— for Debtors. *The Insolvent.* [25] As he had not to pay, his lord commanded him to be sold, and his wife, and children, and all that he had.. [26] The servant..fell down..saying, Lord, have patience with me, and I will pay thee all. [27] Then the lord..was moved with compassion..and forgave him the debt.—MAT., ch. 18.

1430. —— denied. *The Insolvent.* [28] The same servant..found one of his fellow servants, which owed him a hundred pence : and he.. took *him* by the throat, saying, Pay me that thou owest. [29]..his fellow servant..besought him, saying, Have patience with me, and I will pay thee all. [30] And he would not : but..cast him into prison, till he should pay the debt.— MAT., ch. 18.

1431. —— for the Lowly. *For Bondmen.* [23] The children of Israel sighed by reason of the bondage, and they cried, and their cry came up unto God by reason of the bondage. [24] And God heard their groaning, and God remembered his covenant.—EX., ch. 2.

1432. —— Moved by. *The Lord.* [15] We have sinned : do thou unto us whatsoever seemeth good unto thee ; deliver us only, we pray thee, this day. [16] And they put away the strange gods from among them, and served the Lord : and his soul was grieved for the misery of Israel.—JUDGES, ch. 10.

1433. —— for the Penitent. *Prodigal.* [20] He arose, and came to his father. But when he was yet a great way off, his father saw him, and had compassion, and ran, and fell on his neck, and kissed him.—LUKE, ch. 15.

1434. —— Public. *Bethlehemites.* [19] When they were come to Bethlehem..all the city was moved about them, and they said, *Is* this Naomi ? [20] And she said..Call me not Naomi, call me Mara : for the Almighty hath dealt very bitterly with me.—RUTH, ch. 1.

1435. —— Patriotic. *Jesus.* [After denouncing the Pharisees, he said,] [37] O Jerusalem, Jerusalem, *thou* that killest the prophets, and stonest them which are sent unto thee, how often would I have gathered thy children together, even as a hen gathereth her chickens under *her* wings, and ye would not !—MAT., ch. 23.

1436. —— Practical. *Jesus.* [40] There came a leper to him, beseeching him, and kneeling down..and saying..If thou wilt, thou canst make me clean. [41] And Jesus, moved with compassion..touched him, and saith..I will ; be thou clean.—MARK, ch. 1.

1437. —— in Reproof. *Paul's.* [4] Out of much affliction and anguish of heart I wrote unto you with many tears ; not that ye should be grieved, but that ye might know the love which I have more abundantly unto you. [6] Sufficient to such a man *is* this punishment, which *was inflicted* of many. [7] So that contrariwise ye *ought* rather to forgive *him*, and comfort *him*, lest perhaps such a one should be swallowed up with overmuch sorrow.—2 COR., ch. 2.

1438. —— required. *Penalty.* [33] Shouldest not thou also have had compassion on thy fellow servant, even as I had pity on thee ? [34] And his lord was wroth, and delivered him to the tormentors, till he should pay all that was due unto him. [35] So likewise shall my heavenly Father do also unto you, if ye from your hearts forgive not every one his brother their trespasses. —MAT., ch. 18.

1439. —— Sensitive. *Jesus.* [15] We have not a high priest..which cannot be touched with the feeling of our infirmities ; but was in all points tempted like as *we are*, *yet* without sin.— HEB., ch. 4.

1440. —— **Unmoved by.** *Brothers of Joseph.* [21] We *are* verily guilty concerning our brother, in that we saw the anguish of his soul, when he besought us, and we would not hear ; therefore is this distress come upon us.—GEN., ch. 42.

1441. —— **Womanly.** *P r i n c e s s.* [5] The daughter of Pharaoh came down to wash *herself* at the river. . and when she saw the ark among the flags, she sent her maid to fetch it. [6]. . she saw the child : and, behold, the babe wept. And she had compassion on him, and said, This *is* one of the Hebrews' children.—EX., ch. 2.

1442. —— **Without.** *Soldiers.* [17] The king of the Chaldees. . slew their young men with the sword in the house of their sanctuary, and had no compassion upon young man or maiden, old man, or him that stooped for age.—2 CHRON., ch. 36.

See other illustrations under :

TENDERNESS.

Affectionate. I wrote unto you with many tears	8714
Bereavement. O my son Absalom, my son, my son	8715
Concealed. Joseph turned. . and wept	8716
Excessive. Joseph made haste. . sought where to	8717
Human. Her weeping, and the Jews weeping	8718
Animals. Lazarus. . full of sores. . dogs came and	6181
Wrong. If. . friend entice thee. . neither pity	6183
Wicked. Fain fill his belly. . husks. . no man gave	6185
Without. Nineveh spared. It displeased Jonah	6186

See SYMPATHY and references.

1443. COMPLAINERS, Unprincipled. *Primitive.* [16] These are murmurers, complainers, walking after their own lusts ; and their mouth speaketh great swelling *words*, having men's persons in admiration because of advantage.— JUDE.

1444. —— **punished.** *Israelites.* [5] *There is* no bread, neither *is there any* water ; and our soul loatheth this light bread. [6] And the Lord sent fiery serpents. . and they bit. . and much people of Israel died.—NUM., ch. 21.

1445. —— **Unreasonable.** *Labourers.* [10] When the first came, they supposed that they should have received more ; and they likewise received every man a penny. [11] And. . they murmured against the goodman of the house.—MAT., ch. 20.

1446. —— **Wicked.** *Ten Spies.* [37] Those men that did bring up the evil report upon the land, died by the plague before the Lord. [38] But Joshua. . and Caleb. . lived *still.*—NUM., ch. 14.

See other illustrations under :

Fastidious. Murmured. . eat and drink with	3088
Hypocritical. Why was not this ointment sold	3087
Malicious. John B. . hath a devil. . S. of man	3089

See BLAME and references.

1447. COMPOSURE, Holy. *Stephen.* [59] They stoned Stephen. . saying, Lord Jesus, receive my spirit. [60] And he kneeled down, and cried with a loud voice, Lord, lay not this sin to their charge. And when he had said this, he fell asleep.—ACTS, ch. 7.

1448. —— **Undisturbed.** *Peter.* [6] When Herod would have brought him forth, the same night Peter was sleeping between two soldiers, bound with two chains : and the keepers before the door kept the prison.—ACTS, ch. 12.

1449. COMPLAINTS redressed. *Greek.* [1] There arose a murmuring of the Grecians against the Hebrews, because their widows were neglected in the daily ministration.—ACTS, ch. 6. [Seven deacons were appointed to care for the poor.]

See BLAME and references.

1450. COMPREHENSION, Lack of. *Apostles'.* [Jesus said,] [33] They shall scourge *him*, and put him to death ; and the third day he shall rise again. [34]. . and this saying was hid from them, neither knew they the things which were spoken.—LUKE, ch. 18.

See other illustrations under :

MYSTERY.

Conversion. Nicodemus answered, How can these	5660
Marvellous. Sat. . according to his birthright. . men	5661
Strange. Why the bush is not consumed	5662
Stumbling. Eateth my flesh. . disciples went back	5664
Unsolved. No man knoweth his sepulchre. . this day	5663
Unexplainable. Thou knowest not now. . know	5665

1451. COMPROMISE, A dishonourable. *Rulers.* [42] Among the chief rulers. . many believed on him ; but because of the Pharisees they did not confess *him*, lest they should be put out of the synagogue : [43] For they loved the praise of men more than the praise of God.—JOHN, ch. 12.

1452. —— **The End of.** *Murder.* [24] And Pilate gave sentence that it should be as they required. [25] And he released. . him that for sedition and murder was cast into prison. . but he delivered Jesus to their will.—LUKE, ch. 23.

1453. —— **A Failure.** *Pharaoh.* [24] Pharaoh called unto Moses, and said, Go ye, serve the Lord ; only let your flocks and your herds be stayed : let your little ones also go with you. [26] Our cattle also shall go with us ; there shall not be a hoof be left behind.—EX., ch. 10.

1454. —— **A hurtful.** *Canaanites.* [55] If ye will not drive out the inhabitants of the land. . those which ye let remain of them *shall be* pricks in your eyes, and thorns in your sides, and shall vex you.—NUM., ch. 33.

1455. —— **Harmony by.** *At Antioch.* [2] They determined that Paul and Barnabas, and certain other of them, should go up to Jerusalem unto the apostles and elders about this question [of circumcision]. [Reply :] [28]. . It seemed good to the Holy Ghost, and to us, to lay upon you no greater burden than these necessary things ; [29] That ye abstain from meats offered to idols, and from blood, and from things strangled, and from fornication.—ACTS, ch. 15.

1456. —— **impossible.** *Mother's.* [24] And they brought a sword before the king. [25] And the king said, Divide the living child in two, and give half to the one, and half to the other. [26] Then spake the woman whose the living child *was.* . for her bowels yearned upon her son, and she said, O my lord, give her the living child.— 1 KINGS, ch. 3.

1457. —— **No.** *Pharaoh.* [8] Go, serve the Lord your God : *but* who *are* they that shall go? [9] And Moses said, We will go with our young and with our old, with our sons and with our daughters, with our flocks and with our herds will we go ; for we *must* hold a feast unto the Lord.—EX., ch. 10.

1458. —— **Unprincipled.** *Pilate's.* [16] I will therefore chastise him, and release *him.* [20] Pilate therefore, willing to release Jesus, spake again to them. [21] But they cried, saying, Crucify *him*, crucify him. ²² And he said..the third time, Why, what evil hath he done?—LUKE, ch. 23.

See other illustrations under:

DISSEMBLING.

Confession. Achan said..I saw..I took a wedge of 2424
Imitated. Other Jews dissembled likewise 2425
Inconsistency. If thou being a Jew, livest after the 2426
Rebuked. I withstood him to the face..separated 2427

1459. COMPULSION no Excuse. *Presumption.* ¹¹ Saul said, Because I saw that the people were scattered from me, and *that* thou camest not within the days appointed.. ¹² Therefore said I, The Philistines will come..and I have not made supplication unto the Lord : I forced myself therefore, and offered a burnt offering.—1 SAM., ch. 13. [He thereby lost his throne.]

1460. —— Financial. *Joab's.* ²⁸ Absalom dwelt two full years..and saw not the king's face. ²⁹ Therefore Absalom sent for Joab, to have sent him to the king ; but he would not come to him : and when he sent again..he would not come. ³⁰ Therefore he said, See.. Joab's field is near mine, and he hath barley there..And Absalom's servants set the field on fire.—2 SAM., ch. 14.

1461. CONCEIT, Religious. *Young Ruler.* ¹⁶ Good Master, what good thing shall I do, that I may have eternal life ? ²⁰ The young man saith..All these things have I kept from my youth up : what lack I yet ?—MAT., ch. 19.

See other illustrations under:

SELF-CONCEIT.

Hopeless. Wise in his own conceit..more hope of 7687
Poverty. He that is despised and hath a servant 7688

VANITY.

Forbidden. Be not ye called Rabbi, for one is your 9160
Punished. Hezekiah showed them all his precious 9161
" Haman arrayed Mordecai..and 9162
Religious. Enlarge the borders of their garments 9163
See PRIDE.

1462. CONCILIATION, A successful. *Jacob* ¹³ took..a present for Esau his brother ; ¹⁴ Two hundred she goats and twenty he goats, two hundred ewes and twenty rams, ¹⁵ Thirty milch camels with their colts, forty kine and ten bulls, twenty she asses and ten foals.—GEN.; ch. 32.

See other illustrations under:

PEACE.

Cost of. Menahem exacted..each man fifty shekels 6018
Contemned. What hast thou to do with peace? 6019
Commanded. Rebuked the wind..Peace, be still 6020
Disposition. Abram said..Let there be no strife 6021
Intercession. Sendeth an ambassador..conditions 6022
Insecure. Peace, peace, when there is no peace 6023
Kingdom of. Jesus stood in the midst..Peace be 6024
Jesus brings. The wolf shall dwell with the lamb 6025
Legacy. Peace I leave with you, my peace I give 6026
National. Given me rest on every side [David] 6027
Offering. What..the trespass offering..gold mice 6028
Pledge. The bow shall be seen in the cloud 6029
Plea. Shall the sword devour forever ? 6030
Purchased. Menahem gave Pul a thousand talents 6031
High Price. A tumult was made..I am innocent 6032
with Sin. I am come..to send a sword 6033
Tribute. Jehoash took all the hallowed things 6034
Typical. Every man under his own vine..fig tree 6035
Ten Years. Land was quiet..ten years 6036
Unstained. There shall not a man be put to death 6036
Universal. Nations..beat their swords into plow 6037

RECONCILIATION.

Noble. Esau ran to meet him and embraced 6905
Strange. The same day Pilate and Herod were 6906
Worship. Leave there thy gifts..first be reconciled 6907

Discretion. David behaved himself..name much 2365
Needless. Take the best fruits of the land to J. 6507
Pacification. Abigail made haste..200 loaves..cakes 398
Presents. Saw the ear-rings and bracelets..said 6511
Propitiatory. What shall be the trespass offering 6676
Warfare. Sendeth an ambassage desiring peace 2366

1463. CONCEALMENT by Appearances. *Joseph.* ⁷ Joseph saw his brethren, and he knew them, but made himself strange..and spake roughly..and he said..Whence come ye ? And they said, From the land of Canaan to buy food. —GEN., ch. 42.

1464. —— impossible. *Peter.* ⁶⁶ As Peter was beneath in the palace, there cometh one of the maids of the high priest : ⁶⁷ She looked upon him, and said, And thou also wast with Jesus of Nazareth. ⁶⁸ But he denied.—MARK, ch. 4.

1465. —— Unsuccessful. *Adam.* ⁸ Adam and his wife hid themselves from the presence of the Lord God amongst the trees of the garden. ⁹ And the Lord God called unto Adam..Where *art* thou ? ¹⁰ And he said, I heard thy voice.. and I was afraid, because I *was* naked ; and I hid myself.—GEN., ch. 3.

1466. —— —— Proverb. ¹³ He that covereth his sins shall not prosper : but whoso confesseth and forsaketh *them* shall have mercy.— PROV., ch. 28.

See other illustrations under:

DISGUISE.

Battle. Ahab said, I will disguise myself 2382
Failure. Ahijah said, Come in wife of Jeroboam 2383
Insufficient. Saul disguised himself [to visit witch] 2384
Penetrated. Is not the hand of Joab in this 2385

HIDDEN.

Cave. Obadiah took 200 prophets and hid 3966
Field. David hid himself in the field 3967
Graciously. King commanded to take Jeremiah 3968
House of God. Joash was hid..six years 3969
Housetop. Rahab. hid them with the..flax 3970
Infant. Ark..in the flags by the river brink 3971
Strangely. Took they up stones..Jesus hid himself 3972
Wilderness. Hide thyself..ravens to feed thee 3973

HIDING.

Difficult. Moses feared..Surely this is known 3974
Sinners. Adam, where art thou?..hid myself 3975
Sin. Set ye Uriah in the hottest battle..retire 3976
Talent. Received one..digged..hid his money 3977

MYSTERY.

Conversion. Nicodemus answered, how can 5660
Marvellous. Sat..according to his birthright 5661
Strange. Why the bush is not consumed 5662
Stumbling. Eateth my flesh..disciples went back 5663
Unsolved. No man knoweth his [Moses'] sepulchre 5664
Unexplainable. Thou knowest not now..know 5665

SECRET.

Difficult. Moses looked this way and that way 4645
Impossible. Elisha telleth the king..the words 4646
Woman's. If thou utter this our business [spies] 4644

TRICK.

Diplomatic. From a very far country are..come 8955
Hypocrites. Feign themselves just men..might 8956
Legerdemain. Magicians..rods became serpents 8957
Politicians. Shall ask a petition..save of the 8958

Exposed. Beware that thou pass not such a place 335
Vice. Adulterer waiteth for the twilight 111

1467. CONDUCT, Disposition affects. *Samaritan.* [Traveller was robbed, and nearly dead.] ³³ A certain Samaritan..when he saw him, he had compassion *on him*, ³⁴ And went to *him*, and bound up his wounds, pouring in oil and wine, and set him on his own beast, and brought him to an inn, and took care of him.—LUKE, ch. 10.

1468. —— observed. *David's.* ²⁹ Saul was yet the more afraid of David : and became David's enemy continually. ³⁰..David behaved himself more wisely than all the servants of Saul ; so that his name was much set by.—1 SAM., ch. 18.

1469. —— Strange. *Idolaters.* ⁷ The Lord said unto Moses..thy people, which thou broughtest out of the land of Egypt, have corrupted *themselves :* ⁸ They have turned aside quickly out of the way..they have made them a molten calf, and have worshipped it.—Ex., ch. 32.

See other illustrations under :

CONSISTENCY.

Apostolic. How holily and justly..we behaved 1588
Blameless. Be blameless and harmless..perverse 1589
Conscientious. I have lived in all good conscience 1590
Critics. Ought ye not to walk..reproach of the 1591
" Exercise myself..void of offence..toward 1592
Courageous. If not..we will not serve thy gods 1593
Exemplified. He took away the high places 1594
Fruit. Doth a fountain send forth..sweet..bitter 1595
Hypocrisy. Baptism of John, whence?..they 1596
Meekness. Bitter envying..descendeth not from 1597
Observed. Herod feared John..holy and observed 1598
Regarded. Giving no offence..ministry be not 1599
Separation. Ye can not drink the cup of the L. 1600

MAGNANIMITY.

Enemies. Shall there any man..be put to death 5164
Forgiveness. David's heart smote him..Saul's 5165
Fraternal. [Judah] became surety for the lad 5166
Gracious. Is not the whole land before thee 5167

WALK.

Consecrated. Put..blood upon the thumbs..great 9274
Holy. Enoch walked with G. 300 years 9275
Perfect. Noah..just man..perfect..walked with 9276
Saintly. Do justly, love mercy..walk..with thy G. 9277
See LIFE.

1470. CONDITION of Acceptance. *Uprightness.* ⁶ Wherewith shall I come before the Lord . ⁷ Will the Lord be pleased with thousands of rams, *or* with ten thousands of rivers of oil? shall I give my firstborn *for* my transgression, the fruit of my body *for* the sin of my soul? ⁸..what doth the Lord require of thee, but to do justly, and to love mercy, and to walk humbly with thy God?—MICAH, ch. 6.

1471. —— of Access. *Benjamin.* ²³ Except your youngest brother come down with you, ye shall see my face no more.—GEN., ch. 44.

1472. —— of Blessing. *See me.* ⁹ Elisha said ..let a double portion of thy spirit be upon me. ¹⁰ And he said, Thou hast asked a hard thing : *nevertheless*, if thou see me *when I am* taken from thee, it shall be so unto thee ; but if not, it shall not be so.—2 KINGS, ch. 2.

1473. —— A severe. *Right Eye.* ² Nahash the Ammonite answered them, On this *condition* will I make *a covenant* with you, that I may thrust out all your right eyes, and lay it *for* a reproach upon all Israel.—1 SAM., ch. 11.

1474. CONDITIONS ignored, Usual. *Water.* ¹⁶ Thus saith the Lord, Make this valley full of ditches. ¹⁷ For..Ye shall not see wind, neither shall ye see rain ; yet that valley shall be filled with water.—2 KINGS, ch. 3.

See other illustrations under :

AGREEMENT.

Fraudulent. Gibeonites did work willily..mouldy 266
Ignored. Received every man a penny..murmured 267
Refused. Let us pass through thy country 268

TERMS.

Acceptable. He that feareth him and worketh 8720
" Will the L. be pleased with thousands 8721
" Do justly, love mercy..walk humbly 8722

Conduct. The poor useth entreaties, the rich 1316

1475. CONDEMNATION, Cause of. *Pharisees.* [After rejecting the testimony of the restored blind man,] ⁴⁰*Some* of the Pharisees..heard these words, and said unto him, Are we blind also? ⁴¹ Jesus said..If ye were blind, ye should have no sin : but now ye say, We see ; therefore your sin remaineth.—JOHN, ch. 9.

1476. —— Future. *Neglectful.* ¹² Friend, how camest thou in hither not having a wedding garment? And he was speechless. ¹³ Then said the king to the servants, Bind him hand and foot, and take him away, and cast *him* into outer darkness ; there shall be weeping and gnashing of teeth.—MAT., ch. 22.

1477. —— of the Innocent. *Jesus.* ⁶ When the chief priests therefore and officers saw him, they cried out, saying, Crucify *him*, crucify *him*. Pilate saith unto them, Take ye him, and crucify *him :* for I find no fault in him.—JOHN, ch. 19.

1478. —— Qualification for. *Beam.* ⁴ How wilt thou say..Let me pull out the mote out of thine eye ; and, behold, a beam *is* in thine own eye? ⁵ Thou hypocrite, first cast out the beam out of thine own eye ; and then shalt thou see clearly to cast out the mote out of thy brother's eye.—MAT., ch. 7.

1479. —— Reason of. *Rejection.* ¹⁸ He that believeth not is condemned already, because he hath not believed in the name of the only begotten Son of God. ¹⁹ And this is the condemnation, that light is come into the world, and men loved darkness rather than light.—JOHN, ch. 3.

1480. —— Reversed. *One Talent.* ²⁴ Lord, I knew thee that thou art a hard man, reaping where thou hast not sown, and gathering where thou hast not strewed : ²⁵ And I was afraid, and went and hid thy talent in the earth.—MAT., ch. 25.

1481. —— An unjust. *Elihu's.* ² Then was kindled the wrath of Elihu..against Job was his wrath kindled, because he justified himself rather than God.—JOB, ch. 32.

1482. —— Unconscious. *David's.* ⁵ David's anger was greatly kindled..and he said to Nathan, *As* the Lord liveth, the man that has done this *thing* shall surely die : ⁶ And he shall restore the lamb fourfold.. ⁷ And Nathan said to David, Thou art the man.—2 SAM., ch. 12.

See other illustrations under :

AWAKENING.

Conscience. John the B. was risen from the dead 595
Fear. Centurion..feared greatly..was the S. of G. 596
Great. Into the house..all the people..read 597
General. All..Judea..Jerusalem..baptized 598

Sudden. Fell down..What must I do to be saved? 599
Trouble. Troubled the Egyptians..Let us flee 600
Truth. Paul reasoned..Felix trembled 601
Unexpected. We are verily guilty..our brother 602

SELF-CONDEMNATION.

Acknowledged. Convicted..went out one by one 7694
Future. Not having a wedding garment..speechless 7695
Sincere. We receive the due reward of our deeds 7696
Unexpected. He shall restore..thou art the man 7697

Hypocrites. Woe unto you..receive the greater 1897
See **BLAME** and references.

1483. CONDESCENSION of Jesus. *Example.*
[4] He riseth from supper, and laid aside his garments ; and took a towel, and girded himself. [5] After that he poureth water into a basin, and began to wash the disciples' feet, and to wipe *them* with the towel.—JOHN, ch. 13.

See **HUMILITY.**

1484. CONFESSION in Adversity. *Israelites.*
[14] Go and cry unto the gods which ye have chosen ; let them deliver you in the time of your tribulation. [15]..Israel said unto the Lord, We have sinned : do thou unto us whatsoever seemeth good unto thee ; deliver us only, we pray thee, this day. [16] And they put away the strange gods..and served the Lord : and his soul was grieved for the misery of Israel.—JUDGES, ch. 10.

1485. —— Acceptable. *Publican.* [13] The publican, standing afar off, would not lift up so much as *his* eyes unto heaven, but smote upon his breast, saying, God be merciful to me a sinner. [14]..this man went down to his house justified *rather* than the other.—LUKE, ch. 18.

1486. —— A costly. *Ephesians.* [19] Many.. which used curious arts brought their books together, and burned them before all *men* : and they counted the price of them..fifty thousand *pieces* of silver.—ACTS, ch. 19.

1487. —— The dual. *Reward.* [32] Whosoever..shall confess me before men, him will I confess also before my Father which is in heaven. [33] But whosoever shall deny me before men, him will I also deny before my Father.— MAT., ch. 10.

1488. —— Earnest. *Israelites.* [1] Were assembled with fasting, and with sackcloth, and earth upon them. [2] And..separated themselves from all strangers, and..confessed their sins, and the iniquities of their fathers. [3] and read in the book of the law..*one* fourth part of the day ; and *another* fourth part they confessed, and worshipped.—NEH., ch. 9.

1489. —— A forced. *Pharaoh.* [27] Pharaoh ..called for Moses and Aaron, and said..I have sinned this time : the Lord is righteous, and I and my people are wicked. [28] Entreat the Lord (for *it is* enough) that there be no *more* mighty thunderings and hail ; and I will let you go.— GEN., ch. 9.

1490. —— A fearless. *Daniel.* [10] When Daniel knew that the writing was signed, he went into his house ; and, his windows being open in his chamber toward Jerusalem, he kneeled upon his knees three times a day, and prayed ..as he did aforetime. [11] Then these men assembled, and found Daniel praying.— DAN., ch. 6.

1491. ——- of Faith. *Eunuch.* [36] The eunuch said, See, *here is* water ; what doth hinder me to be baptized ? [37] And Philip said, If thou believest with all thine heart, thou mayest. And he answered..I believe that Jesus Christ is the Son of God.—ACTS, ch. 8.

1492. —— Forgiveness by. *Proverb.* [13] He that covereth his sins shall not prosper : but whoso confesseth and forsaketh *them* shall have mercy.—PROV., ch. 28.

1493. —— The grand. *Peter.* [18] Whom say the people that I am ? [19] They..said, John the Baptist ; but some..Elias ; and others..that one of the old prophets is risen again. [20] He said unto them, But whom say ye that I am ? Peter answering said, The Christ of God.—LUKE, ch. 9.

1494. —— A genuine. *Thief.* [40] The other ..rebuked him, saying, Dost not thou fear God, seeing thou art in the same condemnation ? [41] And we indeed justly ; for we receive the due reward of our deeds : but this man hath done nothing amiss. [42] And he said unto Jesus, Lord, remember me when thou comest into thy kingdom.—LUKE, ch. 23.

1495. —— Honourable. *Shimei.* [19] Let not my lord..remember that which thy servant did perversely the day that my lord the king went out of Jerusalem, that the king should take it to his heart. [20]..I have sinned : therefore, behold, I am come the first this day of all the house of Joseph to go down to meet my lord the king.—2 SAM., ch. 19. [See 2 Sam., ch. 16.]

1496. —— Help in. *Martyrs.* [9] In the synagogues ye shall be beaten : and..be brought before rulers and kings for my sake, for a testimony against them.. [11]..Take no thought beforehand what ye shall speak, neither do ye premeditate : but whatsoever shall be given you in that hour, that speak ye : for it is not ye that speak, but the Holy Ghost.—MARK, ch. 13.

1497. —— Law of. *Jews.* [6] When a man or woman shall commit any sin.. [7] Then they shall confess their sin which they have done : and he shall recompense his trespass with the principal thereof, and add unto it the fifth *part* thereof, and give *it* unto him against whom he hath trespassed.—NUM., ch. 5.

1498. —— A late. *Achan.* [21] I saw among the spoils a goodly Babylonish garment, and two hundred shekels of silver, and a wedge of gold of fifty shekels weight, then I coveted them, and took them.—JOSH., ch. 7.

1499. —— A neglected. *Butler.* [8] Pharaoh told them his dream ; but *there was* none that could interpret.. [9] Then spake the chief butler ..I do remember my faults this day.. [12]..*there was* there with us..a Hebrew, servant to the captain of the guard..and he interpreted to us our dreams.—GEN., ch. 41. [He had promised to remember Joseph.]

1500. —— of National Sins. *Ezra.* [6] O my God, I am ashamed and blush to lift up my face to thee, my God : for our iniquities are increased over *our* head, and our trespass is grown up unto the heavens. [7] Since the days of our fathers *have* we *been* in a great trespass unto this day.—EZRA, ch. 9.

1501. —— necessary. *Prodigal.* [18] I will arise and go to my father, and will say unto him, Father, I have sinned against heaven, and before thee, [19] And am no more worthy to be called thy son : make me as one of thy hired servants. —LUKE, ch. 15.

1502. —— for Others. *The Pharisee* [11] Stood and prayed thus with himself, God, I thank thee, that I am not as other men *are*, extortioners, unjust, adulterers, or even as this publican.—LUKE, ch. 18.

1503. —— Pardon after. *Shimei.* [21] Abishai . . answered . . Shall not Shimei be put to death for this, because he cursed the Lord's anointed ? . . [23] . . The king said unto Shimei, Thou shalt not die.—2 SAM., ch. 19.

1504. —— in Prayer. *For Others.* [31] Moses . . said, Oh, this people have sinned a great sin, and have made them gods of gold. [32] Yet now, if thou wilt forgive their sin—; and if not, blot me, I pray thee, out of thy book which thou hast written.—Ex., ch. 32.

1505. —— Penitential. *Jews.* [4] John did . . preach the baptism of repentance for the remission of sins. [5] And there went out unto him all the land of Judea, and . . Jerusalem, and were all baptized . . confessing their sins.—MARK, ch.1.

1506. —— Prayerful. *Daniel.* [3] I set my face unto the Lord God, to seek by prayer and supplications, with fasting, and sackcloth, and ashes . . [5] We have sinned, and have committed iniquity, and have done wickedly, and have rebelled, even by departing from thy precepts and from thy judgments : [6] Neither have we hearkened unto thy . . prophets.—DAN., ch. 9.

1507. —— without Penitence. *Israelites.* [After rebelling with the ten spies,] [40] They rose up early in the morning . . saying, Lo, we . . will go up unto the place which the Lord hath promised : for we have sinned . . [44] . . nevertheless the ark . . of the Lord, and Moses, departed not out of the camp. [45] Then the Amalekites . . and the Canaanites . . smote them.—NUM., ch. 14.

1508. —— of Religion. *Mordecai.* [3] Then the king's servants . . said unto Mordecai, Why transgressest thou the king's commandment ? [4] . . When he hearkened not unto them . . they told Haman, to see whether Mordecai's matters would stand : for he had told them that he *was* a Jew. —ESTHER, ch. 3.

1509. —— required. *Israel.* [12] Return, thou backsliding Israel, saith the Lord ; *and* I will not cause mine anger to fall upon you : for I *am* merciful . . *and* I will not keep *anger* for ever. [13] Only acknowledge thine iniquity.—JER., ch. 3.

1510. —— restrained. *Rulers.* [42] Among the chief rulers . . many believed on him, but because of the Pharisees they did not confess *him*, lest they should be put out of the synagogue : [43] For they loved the praise of men more than the praise of God.—JOHN, ch. 12.

1511. —— A Traitor's. *Judas,* [3] When he saw that he was condemned, repented himself, and brought again the thirty pieces of silver to the chief priests and elders, [4] Saying, I have sinned in that I have betrayed the innocent blood.—MAT., ch. 27.

1512. —— of Transgression. *David.* [1] Have mercy upon me, O God, according to thy lovingkindness : according unto the multitude of thy tender mercies blot out my transgressions. [2] Wash me thoroughly from mine iniquity, and cleanse me from my sin. [3] For I acknowledge my transgressions : and my sin *is* ever before me. [4] Against thee, thee only, have I sinned, and done *this* evil in thy sight.—Ps. 51.

1513. —— Trouble brings. *Israelites.* [9] The children of Ammon passed over Jordan to fight also against Judah . . Benjamin, and . . Ephraim ; So that Israel was sore distressed. [10] . . Israel cried unto the Lord, saying, We have sinned against thee, both because we have forsaken our God, and also served Baalim.—JUDGES, ch. 10.

1514. —— Universal. *Of Jesus.* [9] God . . hath highly exalted him, and given him a name which is above every name : [10] That at the name of Jesus every knee should bow, of *things* in heaven, and *things* in earth, and *things* under the earth ; [11] And *that* every tongue should confess that Jesus Christ *is* Lord, to the glory of God the Father.—PHIL., ch. 2.

1515. —— An unavailing. *Achan* [20] Said, Indeed I have sinned against the Lord God of Israel, and thus and thus have I done : [25] And Joshua said, Why hast thou troubled us ? the Lord shall trouble thee this day. And all Israel stoned him with stones, and burned them with fire.—JOSH., ch. 7.

1516. —— A Wanderer's. *Lost.* [176] I have gone astray like a lost sheep : seek thy servant ; for I do not forget thy commandments.—Ps. 119.

1517. —— of Weakness. *Saul.* [19] Wherefore then didst thou not obey the voice of the Lord, but didst fly upon the spoil ? [24] And Saul said unto Samuel, I have sinned : for I have transgressed the commandment of the Lord . . because I feared the people, and obeyed their voice.—1 SAM., ch. 15.

See other illustrations under:

CONTRITION.

Accepted. Because thine heart was tender . . peace 1664
Annual. That ye may be clean from all your sins 1665
Bitter. Eat the flesh . . with bitter herbs 1666
See HUMILITY, PRAYER, REPENTANCE.

1518. CONFIDENCE, The Believer's. *David.* [1] The Lord *is* my shepherd ; I shall not want. [2] He maketh me to lie down in green pastures : he leadeth me beside the still waters. [3] He restoreth my soul : he leadeth me in the paths of righteousness for his name's sake. [4] Yea, though I walk through the valley of the shadow of death, I will fear no evil : for thou *art* with me, thy rod and thy staff they comfort me. [5] Thou preparest a table before me in the presence of mine enemies : thou anointest my head with oil, my cup runneth over. [6] Surely goodness and mercy shall follow me all the days of my life : and I will dwell in the house of the Lord for ever.—Ps. 23.

1519. —— A blind. *Micah.* [A wandering Levite came, and] [12] Micah consecrated the Levite ; and the young man became his priest, and was in the house of Micah. [13] Then said Micah, Now know I that the Lord will do me good, seeing I have a Levite to *my* priest.— JUDGES, ch. 17. [The Danites robbed him of his treasures and his priest.]

1520. —— without Caution. *Benjamites.* [After two successful battles, on the third day]

[32] The children of Benjamin said, They *are* smitten down before us, as at the first. But the children of Israel said, Let us flee, and draw them from the city unto the highways.—JUDGES, ch. 20. [They were destroyed.]

1521. —— **Disappointed,** *Ark.* [5] When the ark..of the Lord came into the camp, all Israel shouted with a great shout, so that the earth rang again.. [10] And the Philistines fought, and Israel was smitten, and they fled..and there was a very great slaughter ; for there fell..thirty thousand footmen. [11] And the ark of God was taken.—1 SAM., ch. 4.

1522. —— **False.** *Men of Ai.* [14] The king of Ai saw *it*..they hasted..and went out against Israel to battle, he and all his people..but he wist not that *there were* liers in ambush..behind the city. [15] And Joshua and all Israel made as if they were beaten before them, and fled.— JOSH., ch. 8. [The defenceless city was burned, and its army destroyed.]

1523. —— **for the Future.** *Paul.* [8] For we would not, brethren, have you ignorant of our trouble which came to us in Asia.. [9]..we had the sentence of death in ourselves..but..God.. [10]..delivered us from so great a death, and doth deliver : in whom we trust that he will yet deliver *us.*—2 COR., ch. 1.

1524. —— **An intelligent.** *Paul.* [12] I know whom I have believed, and am persuaded that he is able to keep that which I have committed unto him against that day.—2 TIM., ch. 1.

1525. —— **A joyful.** *David.* [19] Oh how great *is* thy goodness, which thou hast laid up for them that fear thee ; *which* thou hast wrought for them that trust in thee before the sons of men ! [20] Thou shalt hide them in the secret of thy presence from the pride of man : thou shalt keep them secretly in a pavilion from the strife of tongues.—Ps. 31.

1526. —— **Over.** *To Elisha.* [12] Hazael said, Why weepeth my lord ?..Because I know the evil that thou wilt do unto the children of Israel : their strong holds wilt thou set on fire, and their young men wilt thou slay with the sword, and wilt dash their children, and rip up their women with child. [13] And Hazael said, But what, *is* thy servant a dog, that he should do this great thing ?—2 KINGS, ch. 8. [He did it.]

1527. —— **in Time of Peril.** *Paul.* [See No. 1523.]

1528. —— **Piety begets.** *Joseph.* [Potiphar] [3] saw that the Lord *was* with him, and..made all that he did to prosper.. [4]..and he made him overseer over his house, and all *that* he had he put into his hand.. [22] And the keeper of the prison committed to Joseph's hand all the prisoners.. [23] The keeper..looked not to any thing *that was* under his hand : because the Lord was with him.—GEN., ch. 41.

1529. —— **Strong.** *Caleb and Joshua.* [8] If the Lord delight in us, then he will bring us into this land.. [9]..neither fear ye the people of the land ; for they *are* bread for us : their defence is departed from them, and the Lord *is* with us : fear them not. [10] But all..bade stone them with stones.—NUM., ch. 14.

1530. —— **in Self.** *Peter.* [37] Peter said.. Lord, why cannot I follow thee now ? I will lay down my life for thy sake.—JOHN, ch. 13.

1531. —— **Triumphant.** *In Adversity.* [17] Although the fig tree shall not blossom, neither *shall* fruit *be* in the vines ; the labour of the olive shall fail, and the fields shall yield no meat ; the flock shall be cut off from the fold, and *there shall be* no herd in the stalls : [18] Yet I will rejoice in the Lord, I will joy in the God of my salvation.—HAB., ch. 3.

1532. —— **Unwarranted.** *Israelites.* [3] Let not all the people go up ; but let about two or three thousand men go up and smite Ai ; *and* make not all the people to labour thither ; for they *are but* few. [4] So there went up..about three thousand men ; and they fled before the men of Ai. —JOSH., ch. 7.

1533. —— **An unfortunate.** *Proverb.* [19] Confidence in an unfaithful man in time of trouble *is like* a broken tooth, and a foot out of joint.— PROV., ch. 25.

1534. —— **Undermining.** *Rabshak-eh.* [20] Neither let Hezekiah make you trust in the Lord, saying, The Lord will surely deliver us, and this city shall not be delivered into the hand of the king of Assyria.. [33] Hath any of the gods of the nations delivered at all his land.. [34] Where *are* the gods of Hamath, and of Arpad ?..of Sepharvaim, Hena, and Ivah ? have they delivered Samaria out of mine hand ?— 2 KINGS, ch. 18.

1535. —— **A warranted.** *David.* [1] David spake..in the day *that* the Lord had delivered him out of the..hand of Saul : [2]..The Lord *is* my rock, and my fortress, and my deliverer : [3] The God of my rock ; in him will I trust : *he is* my shield, and the horn of my salvation, my high tower, and my refuge, my saviour.—2 SAM., ch. 22.

See other illustrations under :

ASSURANCE.

SELF-CONFIDENCE.

SELF-RIGHTEOUSNESS.

TRUST.

Providence. May boldly say, The L. is my helper 9021
Self. Philistine..saw David..disdained him 9022

Crushed. Haman thought..to whom..more than 2808
Proverb. Man wise in his own conceit..hope of 7698
See FAITH.

1536. CONFISCATION because of Absence.
The Shunammite [2] Went with her household, and
sojourned in the land of the Philistines seven
years. [3] ..The woman returned..and she went
forth to cry unto the king for her house and
..land. —2 KINGS, ch. 8.

1537. —— for Crime. *Haman's.* [He was
hanged for his wickedness.] [1] On that day did
the king Ahasuerus give the house of Haman
the Jews' enemy unto Esther the queen.—ES-
THER, ch. 8.

1538. —— Threat of. *Ezra.* [7] The priests
made proclamation throughout Judah..unto all
..of the captivity, that they should gather themselves..unto Jerusalem ; [8] And that whosoever
would not come within three days..all his substance should be forfeited.—EZRA, ch. 10.

1539. CONFLICT, respecting Duty. *Father or
Friend.* [16] Jonathan made *a covenant* with the
house of David..[17]..for he loved him as he loved
his own soul. [30] Then Saul's anger was kindled
against Jonathan, and he said..thou hast chosen
the son of Jesse to thine own confusion.—1
SAM., ch. 20.

1540. —— Preparation for. *Arms and Armour.*
[11] Put on the whole armour of God, that ye may
be able to stand against the wiles of the devil..
[16] Above all, taking the shield of faith, wherewith ye shall be able to quench all the fiery
darts of the wicked. [17] And take the helmet of
salvation, and the sword of the Spirit, which is
the word of God.—EPH., ch. 6.

1541. —— with Sin. *Paul.* [21] I find then a
law, that, when I would do good, evil is present
with me. [22] For I delight in the law of God after the inward man : [23] But I see another law
in my members, warring against the law of my
mind, and bringing me into captivity to the law
of sin.—ROM., ch. 7.

1542. —— of Truth. *Jesus.* [34] Think not
that I am come to send peace on earth : I came
not to send peace, but a sword. [35] For I am
come to set a man at variance against his father,
and the daughter against her mother, and the
daughter in law against her mother in law.
[36] And a man's foes *shall be* they of his own
household.—MAT., ch. 10.

1543. —— An unequal. *Benaiah.* [21] He slew
an Egyptian, a goodly man..but he went down
to him with a staff, and plucked the spear out of
the Egyptian's hand, and slew him with his own
spear.—2 SAM., ch. 23.

See other illustrations under :

BATTLE.
Ambuscade. Beware thou pass not such a place 334
Disarmed. No smith..lest Hebrews make swords 643
Hailstones. L. cast great stones from heaven 645
Lord's. When thou seest chariots, be not afraid 646
" L. saveth not with sword and spear 647
Needless. Need not to fight..stand still and see 644
Prayer. They cried to God in the battle 648

CONTEST.
Discouraging. I only am left, and they seek my 1655
Unequal. Goliath..whose height..helmet..mail 1656

CONTROVERSY.
Avoided. Our fathers worshipped..ye say 1652
Fatal. Cain talked with Abel..and slew him 1653
Holy. [At Athens] disputed Paul in the 1654

DISSENSIONS.
Doctrinal. P. and Barnabas had no small 2429
Perilous. Chief captain fearing lest P..pulled in 2430
Partisan. Every one of you saith, I am of..I of..I of 2431
Removed. [Explanation of the altar of witness.] 2432
Stubborn. Contention was so sharp..parted 2433

DIVISIONS.
Authors. L. hate..he that soweth discord among 2467
Harmful. Two men of the Hebrews strove together 2468
Harmonious. Body is not one member, but many 2469
Healed. From which if ye keep yourselves. well 2470
Party. I am of Paul..I am of Apollos 2471
Scandalous. I hear there be divisions..hungry 2472
Weakness. Kingdom divided against itself 2473

ENEMY
Aggressive. Saul breathing out threatening and 2643
Conquered. [King] Saul wept..rewarded me good 2644
Disarmed. [Benaiah] plucked the spear out of the 2645
Great. Men slept, his enemy sowed tares..wheat 2646
Jealous. Saul became David's enemy continually 2647
Routed. [Lepers] Camp of the Syrians..no man 2648
Suspected. It is false ; I fall not to the Chaldeans 2649
Spared. David..thou mayest do to him..skirt 2650
Weapons. Egyptians fled..L. overthrew 2651

ENEMIES.
Artful. Sent forth spies..feign themselves just 2652
Cross. Enemies of the cross..end is destruction 2653
Contempt. Laughed us to scorn..Will ye rebel? 2654
Disappointed. Our enemies were much cast down 2655
Dependence. No smith..lest the Hebrews make 2656
Favours. Enemy hunger, give him bread..coals 2657
Gospel. Perilous times shall come..covetous 2658
Help. We have sinned..deliver us only..this day 2659
Hidden. Adversaries said, They shall not know 2660
Intrigue. Hired counsellors..to frustrate their 2661
Kindness. Wouldest thou smite those..taken 2662
Malicious. Diotrephes..prating against us with 2663
Prayer. Make haste, O God, to help me [David] 2664
Successful. Made them to cease by force..work 2665
Sensitive. Children crying in the temple..sore 2666
Thwarted. Let the work alone..be not hindered 2667
Treatment. Love your enemies, bless them that 2668
Vexation. Grieved them exceedingly..seek the 2670
Unequal. Judah..could not drive out the 2669

FIGHTING.
Forbidden. Ye shall not fight your brethren..I. 3217
God. Mountain was full of chariots..fire 3218
for Jesus. Drew his sword, and struck a servant 3219

QUARREL.
Conjugal. It is better to dwell in a corner..woman 6828
Domestic. Sarah saw the son of Hagar mocking 6818
Destructive. Children of Ammon and Moab..slew 6819
Foolish. Wherefore didst thou not call us? 6820
Famished. What aileth thee?..hid her son 6821
Meddler. Who made thee a..judge over us? 6822
" Is like one that taketh a dog by the ears 6823
Matrimonial. Against Moses, because of the 6824
Overruled. Angel of G. called Hagar..lift up the 6825
Test. Say now Shibboleth, and he said, Sibboleth 6826
War from. We have no part in David..To your 6827

STRIFE.
Avoided. Go from us..mightier then we..Isaac 8378
Absence of. Isaac removed..and digged another 8379
Beginning. As when one letteth out water 8380
Cause of. As coals are..so is a contentious man 8381

Continued. Digged another well, and strove for 8382
Dishonour. An honour for a man to cease from 8383
Ended. Is not the whole land before thee? 8384
Occasion of. Their riches were more..dwell 8385
Prevention rewarded. All the land which thou 8386
Prosperity brings. Land was not able to bear 8387
Rebuked. Not from above..earthly, sensual 8388
Truth makes. I am not come to send peace, but a 8389
Wickedness of. Ungodly man diggeth up evil 8390
Words make. Where no wood is..fire goeth out 8391

WAR.

Art lost. Bent their swords into plowshares 9298
Art aids. Could not drive out..chariots of iron 9299
Civilized. Only the trees..not trees for meat 9300
Challenge. Set him on his father's throne and 9301
Dishonoured. David shed blood abundantly..not 9302
Exempt. Man..build a new house..lest another 9303
    "   Man..fearful and fainthearted..return 9304
    "   Man..betrothed a wife and not taken her 9305
Equipment. Put on the whole armour..may stand 9306
Flesh. Another law in my members, warring 9307
Insult. Hanun..cut off their garments..to the 9308
Levied. Of every tribe a thousand..send to the 9309
Lord in. Captain of the host of the L. am I now 9310
Merciless. Chaldees..had no compassion..old man 9311
Necessary. On this condition will I make a 9312
Prayer in. They cried to G. in the battle 9313
Ruin. Beat down the cities..stopped all the wells 9314
Readiness. Jabin..had 900 chariots of iron 9315
Truth. I came not to send peace, but a sword 9316

Spiritual. I will put enmity between thy seed and 450

1544. CONFUSION from Excitement. *Paul.*
[33] The chief captain..took him, and commanded
him to be bound with two chains ; and demanded who he was, and what he had done. [34] And
some cried one thing, some another, among the
multitude : and..he could not know the certainty for the tumult.—ACTS, ch. 21.

1545. —— of Public Opinion. *Jesus.* [13] He
asked his disciples, saying, Whom do men say
that I, the Son of man, am ? [14] And they said,
Some *say that thou art* John the Baptist ; some,
Elias ; and others, Jeremias, or one of the prophets.—MAT., ch. 16.

1546. —— Public. *Ephesus.* [29] The whole
city was filled with confusion : and having
caught..Paul's companions in travel, they rushed with one accord into the theatre.. [32] Some..
cried one thing, and some another : for the assembly was confused ; and the more part knew
not wherefore they were come together.—ACTS,
ch. 19.

1547. —— of Tongues. *Babel.* [7] Let us go
down, and there confound their language, that
they may not understand one another's speech.
[8] So the Lord scattered them abroad..and they
left off to build the city.—GEN., ch. 11.

See other illustrations under :
Calamities. L. turneth the earth upside down 4435
Chaotic. Earth was without form and void 1107
Success. With loud voices, requiring..crucified 1341

1548. CONQUEST, Preparation for. *Twelve*
Spies. [17] Moses sent them to spy out the land of
Canaan, and said .. go up into the mountain :
[18] And see the land, what it *is ;* and the people
that dwelleth therein, whether they *be* strong or
weak, few or many.—NUM., ch. 13. [Also if
cities were walled.]

1549. —— An unfortunate. *Ark.* [2] When

the Philistines took the ark of God, they brought
it into the house of Dagon, and set it by Dagon.
[3] And when they of Ashdod arose early on the
morrow, behold, Dagon *was* fallen upon his
face to the earth before the ark of the Lord.—
1 SAM., ch. 5. [The idol was broken, people
smitten with emerods, and terrified.]

1550. CONQUERORS welcomed. *David and*
Saul. [6] When David was returned from the
slaughter of the Philistine..the women came
out of all cities of Israel, singing and dancing,
to meet king Saul, with tabrets, with joy, and
with instruments of music. [7]..Answered *one*
another as they played, and said, Saul hath slain
his thousands, and David his ten thousands.
—1 SAM., ch. 18.

See other illustrations under :
CONFLICT.

Benaiah. Plucked the spear out of..Egyptian's hand 1543
Duty. Saul's anger..against Jonathan..David's 1539
Preparation. Put on the whole armour of God 1540
Sin. Law in my members warring..mind 1541
Truth. Not come to send peace, but a sword 1542

SUBJUGATION.

by Blindness. Saul arose..led him to Damascus 8405
Complete. No smith in all the land..make swords 8406

See VICTORY.

1551. CONSCIENCE awakened. *Joseph's*
Brethren. [Accused in Egypt of another offence,]
[21] They said one to another, We *are* verily guilty
concerning our brother, in that we saw the
anguish of his soul, when he besought us, and
we would not hear ; therefore is this distress
come upon us.—GEN., ch. 42.

1552. —— An alarmed. *Felix.* [24] He sent for
Paul, and heard him concerning the faith in
Christ. [25] And as he reasoned of righteousness,
temperance, and judgment to come, Felix trembled, and answered, Go thy way for this time ;
when I have a convenient season, I will call for
thee.—ACTS, ch. 24.

1553. —— for Appearances. *Eating.* [10] If any
man see thee which hast knowledge sit at meat
in the idol's temple, shall not the conscience of
him which is weak be emboldened to eat those
things which are offered to idols ; [11] And through
thy knowledge shall the weak brother perish, for
whom Christ died ?—1 COR., ch. 8.

1554. —— A bigoted. *Jews.* [10] The Jews..
said unto him that was cured, It is the sabbath
day : it is not lawful for thee to carry *thy* bed.—
JOHN, ch. 5.

1555. —— Conviction of. *Pharisees.* [7] He that
is without sin among you, let him first cast a
stone at her.. [9] And they which heard *it*, being
convicted by *their own* conscience, went out one
by one, beginning at the eldest, *even* unto the last :
and Jesus was left alone, and the woman.—JOHN,
ch. 8.

1556. —— A careful. *Paul.* [16] Herein do I
exercise myself, to have always a conscience void
of offence toward God, and *toward* men.—ACTS,
ch. 24.

1557. —— A charitable. *Paul.* [5] Now the
end of the commandment is charity out of a
pure heart, and *of* a good conscience, and *of* faith
unfeigned : [6] From which some having swerved
have turned aside unto vain jangling.—1 TIM.,
ch. 1.

1558. —— **A defiled.** *Impure.* [15] Unto the pure all things *are* pure : but unto them that are defiled and unbelieving *is* nothing pure ; but even their mind and conscience is defiled.— TITUS, ch. 1.

1559. —— **A distorted.** *Murderers of Jesus.* [Judas returned his reward.] [6] The chief priests took the silver pieces, and said, It is not lawful for to put them into the treasury, because it is the price of blood.—MAT., ch. 27.

1560. —— **Errors of.** *Jesus said,* [2] They shall put you out of the synagogues : yea, the time cometh, that whosoever killeth you will think that he doeth God service, [3] ..because they have not known the Father, nor me.—JOHN, ch. 16.

1561. —— **of Hypocrites.** *Pharisees.* [31] The Jews .. because it was the preparation, that the bodies should not remain upon the cross on the sabbath day..besought Pilate that their legs might be broken, and..be taken away.— JOHN, ch. 19.

1562. —— **Intimidation of.** *Pilate.* [7] By our law he ought to die, because he made himself the Son of God. [8] When Pilate therefore heard that saying, he was the more afraid. [12] And from thenceforth Pilate sought to release him.—JOHN, ch. 19.

1563. —— **A joy-giving.** *Paul.* [12] For our rejoicing is this, the testimony of our conscience, that in simplicity and godly sincerity, not with fleshly wisdom, but by the grace of God, we have had our conversation in the world, and more abundantly to you-ward.—2 COR., ch. 1.

1564. —— **A liberal.** *Food.* [25] Whatsoever is sold in the shambles, *that* eat, asking no question for conscience' sake : [27] If any..that believe not bid you *to a feast,* and ye be disposed to go ; whatsoever is set before you, eat, asking no question for conscience' sake.—1 COR., ch. 10.

1565. —— **a Light.** *Candle.* [27] The spirit of man *is* the candle of the Lord, searching all the inward parts of the belly.—PROV., ch. 20.

1566. —— **of Murderers.** *Pharisees.* [28] Then led they Jesus from Caiaphas unto the hall of judgment..and they themselves went not into the judgment hall, lest they should be defiled ; but that they might eat the passover.—JOHN, ch. 18.

1567. —— **A preserved.** *Paul.* [1] Paul, earnestly beholding the council, said, Men *and* brethren, I have lived in all good conscience before God until this day.—ACTS, ch. 23.

1568. —— **Power of.** *A Sadducee.* [14] King Herod heard *of* [Jesus]..he said, That John the Baptist was risen from the dead, and therefore mighty works do shew forth themselves in him. —MARK, ch. 6.

1569. —— **A perverted.** *Saul's.* [9] I verily thought with myself, that I ought to do many things contrary to the name of Jesus of Nazareth. [10] ..and many of the saints did I shut up in prison..and when they were put to death, I gave my voice against *them.* [11] And I punished them oft in every synagogue, and compelled *them* to blaspheme.—ACTS, ch. 26.

1570. —— **quickened.** *Israelites.* [18] The Lord sent thunder and rain that day : and all the people greatly feared the Lord and Samuel.

[19] And..said unto Samuel, Pray for thy servants ..that we die not : for we have added unto all our sins this evil, to ask us a king.—1 SAM., ch. 12.

1571. —— **a Reminder.** *Widow of Zarephath.* [Her son's] [17] sickness was so sore, that there was no breath left in him. [18] And she said unto Elijah, What have I to do with thee, O thou man of God ? art thou come unto me to call my sin to remembrance, and to slay my son ?—1 KINGS, ch. 17.

1572. —— **respected.** *Influence.* [28] If any man say unto you, This is offered in sacrifice unto idols, eat not for his sake that shewed it, and for conscience sake.. [29] Conscience, I say not thine own, but of the other.—1 COR., ch. 10.

1573. —— **A seared.** *Hot Iron.* [1] The spirit speaketh expressly, that in the latter times some shall depart from the faith, giving heed to seducing spirits, and doctrines of devils ; [2] Speaking lies in hypocrisy ; having their conscience seared with a hot iron.—1 TIM., ch. 4.

1574. —— **A sensitive.** *David.* [He had an opportunity to kill King Saul, intentional murderer, and was urged to do so.] [4] Then David arose, and cut off the skirt of Saul's robe privily. [5] ..afterward..David's heart smote him.. [6] And he said unto his men, The Lord forbid that I should..stretch forth mine hand against him, seeing he *is* the anointed of the Lord.—1 SAM., ch. 24.

1575. —— **A smiting.** *David's.* [10] David's heart smote him after that he had numbered the people. And David said..I have sinned greatly in that I have done : and now, I beseech thee, O Lord, take away the iniquity of thy servant ; for I have done very foolishly.—2 SAM., ch. 24.

1576. —— **A troublesome.** *Eliphaz said,* [20] The wicked man travaileth with pain all *his* days.. [21] A dreadful sound *is* in his ears : in prosperity the destroyer shall come upon him. [22] He believeth not that he shall return out of darkness, and he is waited for of the sword.— JOB, ch. 15.

1577. —— **A terrifying.** *Belshazzar.* [5] The king saw the part of the hand that wrote. [6] Then the king's countenance was changed, and his thoughts troubled him, so that the joints of his loins were loosed, and his knees smote one against another.—DAN., ch. 5.

1578. CONSCIENCES differ. *Eating.* [7] *There is* not in every man that knowledge : for some with conscience of the idol unto this hour eat it as a thing offered unto an idol ; and their conscience being weak is defiled. [8] But meat commendeth us not to God.—1 COR., ch. 8.

See other Illustrations under :

Examination. Searched the Scriptures..many b'd 1685
Heaven sent. Suddenly there shined a light 1686
Heartfelt. Pricked in their heart..[Pentecost] 1687
Necessary. Sprung up..no deepness of earth 1688
Prayer. Make me to know my transgression 1689
Resisted. Miracles before them..believed not 1690
Rational. When he came to himself..I will arise 1691
Sensitive. David's heart smote him..Saul's skirt 1692
Smiting. David's heart smote him..numbered 1693
Sudden. People saw it..fell..L. he is God 1694
Speechless. Beholding the man..healed..say n. 1695
Truth. Josiah..heard..the book of the..he rent 1696
Thorough. Digged deep..the foundation on a rock 1697
Transient. Centurion..earthquake..was the S. of 1698
Willing. Nathanael..Thou art the Son of God 1699

HARDNESS.

Adversity. In..his distress did Ahaz trespass more 3797
Heart. Looked..anger being grieved..hardness of 3798
Spiritual. We will certainly burn incense 3799

Cowardice. Adam and his wife hid themselves 3767
Reading. Baruch read the book..they were afraid 749
" Shaphan read it..king rent his clothes 752
" All the people wept when they heard 763

1579. CONSCRIPTION, Building by. *Temple.*
13 King Solomon raised a levy out of all Israel..
thirty thousand men. 14 And he sent them to
Lebanon, ten thousand a month by courses : a
month they were in Lebanon, *and* two months
at home.—1 KINGS, ch. 5.

1580. —— A peculiar. *Saul's.* 6 Saul when
he heard those tidings..his anger was kindled
greatly. 7 And he took a yoke of oxen, and
hewed in pieces, and sent *them* throughout
all the coasts of Israel..saying, Whosoever cometh not forth, after Saul and after Samuel, so
shall it be done unto his oxen..they came out
with one consent.—1 SAM., ch. 11.

1581. —— A sweeping. *Moabites.* 21 When
all the Moabites heard that the kings were come
up to fight against them, they gathered all that
were able to put on armour, and upward, and
stood in the border.—2 KINGS, ch. 3.

Also see :
Levy, the Lord's. What do ye loosing the colt ? 4944

1582. CONSECRATION, Covenant of. *Josiah's.*
3 The king..made a covenant..to walk after the
Lord, and to keep his commandments..with all
their heart and all *their* soul, to perform the
words..that were written in this book. And all
the people stood to the covenant.—2 KINGS, ch.
23.

1583. —— for Leadership. *Joshua.* 22 Moses
..took Joshua, and set him before Eleazar the
priest, and before all the congregation : 23 And
he laid his hands upon him, and gave him a
charge.—NUM., ch. 27.

1584. —— for Service. *Priest's.* 23 Moses took
of the blood of it, and put *it* upon the tip of Aaron's right ear, and upon the thumb of his right
hand, and upon the great toe of his right foot.—
LEV., ch. 8.

1585. —— Self-denying. *Women.* 8 He made
the laver..and the foot of it *of* brass, of the look-
ing-glasses of *the women*..which assembled at the
door of the tabernacle.—EX., ch. 38.

See other Illustrations under :

CONTRIBUTIONS.

Abundant. [Temple] Offered willingly..gold 5000 1657
Expenses. Charge ourselves yearly..third part 1658
for Jesus. Women..healed..ministered..their 1659

for Levites. Firstfruits of corn, wine, oil, and 1660
Repairs. Chest..set beside the altar..right side 1661
Rebuilding. Chief of the fathers gave after their 1662
Various. Men and women..blue, purple, scarlet 1663

DEDICATION.

Accepted. Fire came..consumed the sacrifices 2091
Heathen. Nebuchadnezzar sent..dedication of the 2092
Service. Vessels of..gold..did David dedicate 2093
Temple. Cloud filled the house..glory 3520

HOLINESS.

Acknowledged. Put off thy shoes..holy ground 3996
" Loose thy shoe..Joshua did so 3997
Alarming. Looked into the ark..who is able to 3998
Celebration. Cherubim..Holy, holy, holy is the L. 3999
Conspicuous. Holiness to the L...upon the 4000
Chosen. Shall be a peculiar treasure..holy nation 4001
Church. Glorious church not having spot..holy 4002
Prayer for. Be filled with all the fulness of God 4003
Perfect. Which of you convinceth me of sin ? 4004
Unapproachable. Let bounds..about the mount 4005
Universal. Upon the bells of the horses, Holiness 4006

PURITY.

Symbolized. Make a laver of brass to wash 6813
Within. First cleanse within the cup 6814

SURRENDER.

Absolute. I count all things but loss for..the 8503
Bodily. Yieldeth their bodies that..not serve any 8504
Christian. May know..fellowship of his sufferings 8505
Entire. One thing thou lackest, go..give to the 8506
Full. Whosoever..forsaketh not all..disciple 8507
Fear. We will do all that thou shalt bid us 8508
Moral. What things were gain to me, I counted 8509
Power. We have not used this power..lest we 8510
Resisted. When he saw him, the spirit tare him 8511
Sins. If thy right hand offend thee..cast it 8512
Sacrifice. Widow..cast in..all her living 8513
Undivided. Our cattle shall also go with us 8514
Weak. King Ahab said, My Lord, O King, I am 8515

Firstfruits. Man brought..20 loaves, and full ears 35
Healthful. Clean hands shall be stronger and 3751
Honoured. Who shall ascend..clean hands 1348
Means. Washing of water by the word 4002
" Blood of J. C. his son cleanseth us..sin 7948
Ordination. All night in prayer..chose twelve 5926

1586. CONSENT, A forced. *Pharaoh.* 30 There
was a great cry in Egypt : for *there was* not a
house where *there was* not one dead. 31 And he
called for Moses and Aaron by night, and said..
get you forth from among my people, both ye
and the children of Israel ; and go, serve the
Lord, as ye have said.—EX., ch. 12.

See other illustrations under :

AGREEMENT.

Fraudulent. Gibeonites did work wilily..mouldy 266
Ignored. Received every man a penny..murmured 267
Refused. Let us pass through thy country 268

WILLINGNESS.

Believe. Who is he..that I might believe ? 9595
Givers. Children of I. brought a willing offering 9596
Save. If thou wilt, thou canst..I will 9597
" This man receiveth sinners 9598

1587. CONSERVATISM, An unwise. *Jesus.*
36 No man putteth a piece of new garment upon
an old ; if otherwise..the piece that was *taken*
out of the new agreeth not with the old. 37 And
no man putteth new wine into old bottles ; else
the new wine will burst the bottles, and be
spilled, and the bottles shall perish.—LUKE,
ch. 5.

1588. CONSISTENCY, Apostolic. *Paul.* [10] Ye *are* witnesses, and God *also*, how holily and justly and unblameably we behaved ourselves among you that believe : [11] As ye know how we exhorted and comforted and charged every one of you, as a father *doth* his children.—1 THESS., ch. 2.

1589. —— **Blameless.** *Christians.* [14] Do all things without murmurings and disputings : [15] That ye may be blameless and harmless, the sons of God, without rebuke, in the midst of a crooked and perverse nation, among whom ye shine as lights in the world.—PHIL., ch. 2.

1590. —— **Conscientious.** *Paul.* [1] Paul, earnestly beholding the council, said, Men *and* brethren, I have lived in all good conscience before God until this day.—ACTS, ch. 23.

1591. —— **before Critics.** *Nehemiah.* [9] It *is* not good that ye do : ought ye not to walk in the fear of our God because of the reproach of the heathen our enemies? [10] I likewise, *and* my brethren, and my servants, might exact of them money and corn : I pray you, let us leave off this usury.—NEH., ch. 5.

1592. —— —— *Paul.* [See No. 1556.]

1593. —— **Courageous.** *Three Worthies.* [17] If it be *so*, our God whom we serve is able to deliver us from the burning fiery furnace, and he will deliver *us* out of thine hand, O king. [18] But if not, be it known unto thee, O king, that we will not serve thy gods, nor worship the golden image.—DAN., ch. 3.

1594. —— **exemplified.** *Reforms.* [3] The Lord was with Jehoshaphat, because he walked in the first ways of his father David.. [6] And his heart was lifted up in the ways of the Lord: moreover he took away the high places and groves out of Judah.—2 CHRON., ch. 17.

1595. —— **Fruit of.** *Christian.* [11] Doth a fountain send forth at the same place sweet *water* and bitter? [12] Can the fig tree, my brethren, bear olive berries? either a vine, figs? so *can* no fountain both yield salt water and fresh.—JAMES, ch. 3.

1596. —— **in Hypocrisy.** *Pharisees.* [25] The baptism of John, whence was it? from heaven, or of men? And they reasoned with themselves, saying, If we shall say, From heaven ; he will say unto us, Why did ye not then believe him? [26] But if we shall say, Of men ; we fear the people ; for all hold John as a prophet. [27] And they answered Jesus, and said, We cannot tell.—MAT., ch. 21.

1597. —— **in Meekness.** *Christian.* [14] If ye have bitter envying and strife in your hearts, glory not, and lie not against the truth. [15] This wisdom descendeth not from above, but *is* earthly, sensual, devilish.—JAMES, ch. 3.

1598. —— **Observed.** *John Baptist.* [20] Herod feared John, knowing that he was a just man and a holy, and observed him ; and..he did many things, and heard him gladly.—MARK, ch. 6.

1599. —— **regarded.** *Ministers.* [1] We then, *as* workers together *with him*, beseech *you* also that.. [3] Giving no offence in anything, that the ministry be not blamed : [4] But in all *things* approving ourselves as the ministers of God.—2 COR., ch. 6.

1600. —— **in Separation.** *Paul.* [20] The Gen-

tiles..sacrifice to devils, and not to God : and I would not that ye should have fellowship with devils. [21] Ye cannot drink the cup of the Lord, and the cup of devils : ye cannot be partakers of the Lord's table, and of the table of devils.—1 COR., ch. 10.

Also see :

Correspondence. No man seweth..new cloth on   1725

—— **CONSOLATION.** —— ——
See illustrations under :
Bereavement. I shall go to him   6902

SYMPATHY.

Refreshing Onesimus oft refreshed me   3460
Sorrowful. Comfort him..overmuch sorrow   8215
Unexpected. Lift up the lad..great nation   8230

1601. CONSPIRACY, Atrocious. *Abimelech.* [The men of Shechem] [4] gave him threescore and ten *pieces* of silver out of the house of Baal-berith, wherewith Abimelech hired vain and light persons, which followed him. [5] And he.. slew his brethren the sons of Jerubbaal, *being* threescore and ten persons, upon one stone.—JUDGES, ch. 9.

1602. —— **A Brother's.** *Absalom.* [28] When Amnon's heart is merry with wine, and when I say unto you, Smite Amnon ; then kill him, fear not..be courageous, and be valiant. [29] And the servants of Absalom did.—2 SAM., ch. 13.

1603. —— **in Court.** *Stephen.* [12] They stirred up the people..elders, and the scribes, and came..and caught him, and brought *him* to the council, [13] And set up false witnesses, which said, This man ceaseth not to speak blasphemous words against this holy place, and the law.—ACTS, ch. 6.

1604. —— **A desperate.** *Paul.* [12] Certain of the Jews banded together, and bound themselves under a curse, saying that they would neither eat nor drink till they had killed Paul. [13] And they were more than forty.—ACTS, ch. 23.

1605. —— **A defeated.** *Pharisees.* [15] The Pharisees..took counsel how they might entangle him in *his* talk.. [17]..Is it lawful to give tribute unto Cesar, or not? [18] But Jesus perceived their wickedness, and said.. [20]..penny..Render.. unto Cesar the things which are Cesar's ; and unto God the things that are God's.. [22]..they marvelled, and left him.—MAT., ch. 22.

1606. —— **Escape from.** *David.* [11] Saul..sent messengers unto David's house, to watch him, and to slay him in the morning : and Michal David's wife told him, saying, If thou save not thy life to night, to morrow thou shalt be slain.—1 SAM., ch. 19.

1607. —— **from Envy.** *Joseph.* [18] When they saw him..they conspired against him to slay him. [19]..Behold, this dreamer cometh. [20]..Let us slay him, and cast him into some pit, and we will say, Some evil beast hath devoured him, and we shall see what will become of his dreams.—GEN., ch. 37.

1608. —— **An Ingrate's.** *Absalom.* [10] Absalom sent spies throughout..Israel, saying, As soon as ye hear the sound of the trumpet..say, Absalom reigneth in Hebron. [11] And with Absalom went two hundred men out of Jerusalem.—2 SAM., ch. 15.

1609. —— **Infamous.** *Jezebel's.* [7] Dost thou now govern the kingdom of Israel? arise, *and* eat bread, and let thine heart be merry : I will give thee the vineyard of Naboth the Jezreelite. [15]..when Jezebel heard that Naboth was stoned.. Jezebel said to Ahab, Arise, take possession of the vineyard..which he refused to give thee for money.—1 KINGS, ch. 21.

1610. —— A political. *Babylon.* [4] The presidents and princes sought to find occasion against Daniel concerning the kingdom ; but they could find none occasion nor fault ; forasmuch as he *was* faithful, neither was there any error.—DAN., ch. 6.

1611. —— Joash. [20] His servants arose, and made a conspiracy, and slew Joash in the house of Millo, which goeth down to Silla. [21] For Jozachar..and Jehozabad..his servants, smote him, and he died ; and they buried..him in the city of David : and Amaziah his son reigned in his stead.—2 KINGS, ch. 12.

1612. —— A successful. *Samson.* [18] When Delilah saw that he had told her all his heart, she sent..for the lords of the Philistines, saying, Come up this once..Then the..Philistines came..and brought money in their hand. [21] The Philistines took him, and put out his eyes, and brought him down to Gaza, and bound him with fetters of brass.—JUDGES, ch. 16.

1613. —— against the Truth. *Ananias.* [1] Ananias, with Sapphira his wife, sold a possession, [2] And kept back *part* of the price, his wife also being privy *to it*, and brought a certain part, and laid *it* at the apostles' feet.—ACTS, ch. 5.

1614. —— The worst. *Rulers.* [4] Consulted that they might take Jesus by subtilty, and kill *him.* [5] But they said, Not on the feast *day*, lest there be an uproar among the people.—MAT., ch. 26.

See other illustrations under :
Dangerous. Ahithophel is among the conspirators 8871
Excused. I conspired..L. hath done—2 Kings 10 : 10
Punishment. Slew all that conspired—2 Kings 21 : 24
Political. They made a conspiracy—2 Kings 14 : 19
    "   Shullum..conspired..smote—2 Kings 15 : 10
    "   Jehu conspired against Joram—2 Kings 9 : 14
Suspected. All of you have conspired against me   473

1615. CONSTERNATION from Peril. *Persia.* [3] In every province, whithersoever the king's.. decree came, *there was* great mourning among the Jews, and fasting, and weeping, and wailing ; and many lay in sackcloth and ashes.—ESTHER, ch. 4.

See other illustrations under :
ALARM.
Conscience. Pray for thy servants..we die not 273
Death. Egyptians were urgent..we be all dead men 274
Failure. Chief priests..doubted..whereunto this 275
Manifestation. Belshazzar..countenance was 276
Preaching. Paul reasoned..Felix trembled 277
Reasonable. Esau cometh..400 men..Jacob 278
Superstitious. Jesus walking on the sea..troubled 279
Sinners'. Adam and his wife hid themselves 280
    " [At Sinai] Let not God speak with us..die 281
Sudden. Seeing the prison doors open..sword 282
Spiritual. Sirs, what must I do to be saved 283
Tempest. Entreat..be no more mighty thunderings 284
Unnecessary. My money is restored..heart failed 285

AGITATION.
Deception. Who art thou?..Esau..Isaac trembled 256
Diffuses. Disputed he in the synagogue. market 257
Deplored. [Israelites] Made. abhorred. slay us 258

General. [Philistines] Trembling in the host..field 259
Mount. Sinai..quaked greatly 260
Overcome. [At sepulchre] Keepers did shake 261
Physical. Belshazzar's thoughts troubled..knees 262
Terror. [Job's vision.] Trembling..my bones 263

DESPAIR.
Affliction. Let me not see the death of the child 2213
Anguish. Slay me, for anguish is come upon me 2214
Awaking. Wine was gone out..heart died within 2215
Deliverance. Been better for us to serve the Egyp. 2216
Needless. Widow..meal..oil..me and my son eat 2217

DISTRESS.
Cry of. Great cry..none like it, nor shall be 2437
Derided. They that see me, shoot out the lip 2438
Described. I was a derision to all my people 2439
Exasperation. What shall I do..people ready to 3440
Famine. Delicate women..shall eat..children 3441
Little Faith. Why are ye fearful..little faith..calm 3442
Friend. Gedaliah..took Jeremiah out of prison 3443
Great. Thrust right eyes..people wept 3444
Needless. Saul had adjured..food 3445
Refuge. Ahaz sacrificed unto the gods that smote 3446

TERROR.
Prostrating. Saul fell..all along on the ground 8723
Sinners. Belshazzar's..knees smote one against 8724
Sublime. Sinai .so terrible..I exceedingly fear 8725

1616. CONSULTATION, An evil. *Jews.* [3] Then assembled..the chief priests, and the scribes, and the elders..unto the palace of the high priest, who was called Caiaphas, [4] And consulted that they might take Jesus by subtilty, and kill *him*.—MAT., ch. 26.

See other illustrations under :
ADVICE.
Foolish. Said his wife..curse God and die 152
Good. Naaman's servants said, If the prophet had 153
Unfortunate. Let a gallows be made fifty cubits 154

COUNSEL.
Dying. I go..show thyself a man [David] 1746
Evil. Rehoboam consulted with the young men 1748
Friends. Let a gallows be made 50 cubits high 1740
Good. Rehoboam consulted with the old men 1749
Influential. David..the lords favor thee not 1750
Malicious. Come, let us take counsel together 1751
Neglected. Took not counsel of the L. 1741
Oracular. Counsel of Ahithophel..as..oracle of 1742
Opposing. Ahithophel said to Absalom..Hushai 1747
Payment. Saul to servant..what shall we bring 1744
Peace. Joab, hear the words..handmaid 1743
Rejection. Ahithophel saw..not followed 1745
Safety. In the multitude of counsellors..safety 1739
Unfortunate. Why sit we here until we die? 1738

1617. CONSUMPTION of the Flesh. *Job.* [8] Thou hast filled me with wrinkles *which* is a witness *against me :* and my leanness rising up in me beareth witness to my face.—JOB, ch. 16.

1618. CONTEMPT, A Bigot's. *Pharisee.* [11] The Pharisee stood and prayed thus with himself, God, I thank thee, that I am not as other men *are*, extortioners, unjust, adulterers, or even as this publican. [12] I fast twice in the week, I give tithes of all that I possess.—LUKE, ch. 18.

1619. —— A Critic's. *Michal.* [16] As the ark of the Lord came into the city of David, Michal Saul's daughter looked through a window, and saw king David leaping and dancing before the Lord ; and she despised him in her heart.—2 SAM., ch. 6.

1620. —— **for the Conceited.** *Thistle.*
[8] Amaziah sent messengers to Jehoash..king of
Israel, saying, Come, let us look one another in
the face. [9] And Jehoash..sent to Amaziah king
of Judah, saying, The thistle that *was* in Lebanon sent to the cedar that *was* in Lebanon,
saying, Give thy daughter to my son to wife :
and there passed by a wild beast..and trode
down the thistle.—2 KINGS, ch. 14.

1621. —— **disregarded.** *Nehemiah.* [19] When
Sanballat..and Tobiah..and Geshem..heard *it*,
they laughed us to scorn, and despised us, and
said, What *is* this thing, that ye do ? will ye rebel
against the king ? [20] Then answered I..The
God of heaven, he will prosper us ; therefore we
his servants will arise and build.—NEH., ch. 2.

1622. —— **An Enemy's.** *Goliath.* [42] He disdained him : for he was *but* a youth, and ruddy,
and of a fair countenance. [43] And the Philistine said, *Am* I a dog, that thou comest to me
with staves ? And the Philistine cursed David
by his gods.—1 SAM., ch. 17.

1623. —— **expressed.** *Sons of Belial.* [26] Saul
also went home to Gibeah ; and a band of men,
whose hearts God had touched. [27] But the children of Belial said, How shall this man save us ?
And they despised him, and brought him no
presents.—1 SAM., ch. 10.

1624. —— **Fraternal.** *For David.* [28] Eliab
his eldest brother heard..and he said, Why
camest thou down hither ? and with whom hast
thou left those few sheep in the wilderness ? I
know thy pride, and the naughtiness of thine
heart ; for thou art come down that thou mightest see the battle.—1 SAM., ch. 17.

1625. —— **for the Gospel.** *Marriage Supper.*
[4] Tell them which are bidden, Behold, I have
prepared my dinner : my oxen and *my* fatlings
are killed, and all things *are* ready : come unto
the marriage. [5] But they made light of *it*, and
went their ways, one to his farm, another to his
merchandise.—MAT., ch. 22.

1626. —— **for God.** *Idolatry.* [26] They, their
kings, their princes, and their priests, and their
prophets, [27] Saying to a stock, Thou *art* my father ; and to a stone, Thou hast brought me
forth : for they have turned *their* back unto me,
and not *their* face : but in the time of their
trouble they will say, Arise, and save us.—JER.,
ch. 2.

1627. —— **Insulting.** *Job.* [1] But now *they*
that are younger than I have me in derision,
whose fathers I would have disdained to have
set with the dogs of my flock.. [9] Now am I their
song, yea, I am their byword. [10] They abhor
me, they flee far from me, and spare not to spit
in my face.—JOB, ch. 30.

1628. —— **Malicious.** *Before Caiaphas.*
[67] Then did they spit in his face, and buffeted
him ; and others smote *him* with the palms of
their hands, [68] Saying, Prophesy unto us, thou
Christ, Who is he that smote thee ?—MAT., ch.
26.

1629. —— **for Others.** *Parable.* [9] He spake
this parable unto certain which trusted in themselves that they were righteous, and despised
others : [10] Two men went up into the temple to
pray ; the one a Pharisee, and the other a publican.—LUKE, ch. 18.

1630. —— **for Worship.** *Jews.* [13] Ye said

also, Behold, what a weariness *is it!* and ye
have snuffed at it..and ye brought *that which*
was torn, and the lame, and the sick ; thus
ye brought an offering : should I accept this
of your hand ? saith the Lord.—MAL., ch. 1.

See other illustrations under :

DESPISERS.

Others. Certain trusted in themselves..despised 2222
Privileges. Esau despised his birthright 2223
Sin. Trodden under foot the S. of G. 2224
Warning. I will laugh at your calamity 2225

INSULT.

Ignored. Despised him [Saul]..held his peace 4567
First. Thrust him [Jesus] out of the city..headlong 4568
Rewarded. Cut off their garments in the middle 4569
Stinging. To smite him on the mouth 4570

MOCKERY.

Blasphemous. Crown of thorns..reed..hail king 5494
of Truth. When they heard of the resurrection 5493

RIDICULE.

Doctrine. When they heard of the resurrection 7425
Fatal. Call for Samson that he may make us sport 7426
Failure. Not able to finish..begin to mock him 7427
Horrible. He saved others, let him save himself 7428
Impious. They laughed them to scorn and mocked 7429
" What will this babbler say [Athenians] 7430
Insulting. Cut off their garments..their buttocks 7431
Opposition. What do these feeble Jews? will they 7432
" If a fox go up, he shall break down 7433
Punishment. Children of Bethel..Go up, thou bald 7434
Royalty. Wearing the crown of thorns and purple 7435
Scornful. They laughed us to scorn and despised us 7436
Spirit. Mocking said,These men are full of new wine 7437
Trial. They reviled him and said, We are Moses' 7438

SCORN.

of Pride. [Haman] Scorn to lay hands on Mordecai 7618
Public. All clap their hands at thee and hiss 7619
Taunt. Who made thee a prince and a judge over 8592
Unbelief. She sleepeth..they laughed him to scorn 7620

PREJUDICE.

Alarmed. Deal wisely..any war..fight against us 6466
Blinded. When Moses is read the vail..their heart 6467
Children. Disciples rebuked them..Jesus called 6468
Custom. Disciples marvelled..talked with the w. 6469
Communion. Can any good..thou art the S. of G. 6470
Concession to. Paul circumcised him because 6471
Destructive. Rejected the counsel of God against 6472
National. How is it..being a Jew..Samaria 6473
" This fellow came..sojourn..needs be a 6474
Obstacle. We have found him..any good..Nazareth 6475
Obstinate. Stretch forth thine hand..might destroy 6476
Offended. Is not this the carpenter..? were offended 6477
Piety. Since we left off to burn incense..consumed 6478
Race. Spake against Moses..married an E. 6479
Removed. God hath showed..not call any..common 6480
Sectarian. Saw one casting out devils..forbade 6481
Super-religious. If a prophet..known..she is a 6482
Sinners. Murmured..guest with a man..a sinner 6483

Cruel. Mocked Jesus and smote him 4571
Knowledge. Born in sins, and dost thou teach us? 2788

1631. CONTENTION, Abundance brings.
Abram—Lot. [6] Their substance was great, so
that they could not dwell together. [7] And there
was a strife between the herdmen of Abram's
cattle and the herdmen of Lot's cattle.—GEN.,
ch. 13.

1632. —— **avoided.** *Esau.* [6] Esau took..
his cattle, and all his beasts, and all his sub-

stance..and went into the country from the face of his brother Jacob. ⁷ For their riches were more than that they might dwell together. —GEN., ch. 26.

1633. —— **Destructive.** *Paul.* ¹⁴ For all the law is fulfilled in one word, *even* in this ; Thou shalt love thy neighbour as thyself. ¹⁵ But if ye bite and devour one another, take heed that ye be not consumed one of another.—GAL., ch. 5.

1634. —— **Domestic.** *Proverb.* ⁹ *It is* better to dwell in a corner of the housetop, than with a brawling woman in a wide house. ¹⁹ *It is* better to dwell in the wilderness, than with a contentious and an angry woman.—PROV., ch. 21.

1635. —— **Foolish.** *Proverb.* ⁹ *If* a wise man contendeth with a foolish man, whether he rage or laugh, *there is* no rest.—PROV., ch. 29.

1636. —— —— *Corinth.* ¹¹ There are contentions among you. ¹² every one of you saith, I am of Paul ; and I of Apollos ; and I of Cephas ; and I of Christ. ¹³ Is Christ divided ? was Paul crucified for you ? or were ye baptized in the name of Paul ?—1 COR., ch. 1.

1637. —— **Meddling with.** *Proverb.* ¹⁷ He that passeth by, *and* meddleth with strife *belonging* not to him, *is like* one that taketh a dog by the ears.—PROV., ch. 26. ³ *It is* an honour for a man to cease from strife : but every fool will be meddling.—PROV., ch. 20.

1638. —— **Prevention of.** *Proverb.* ¹⁴ The beginning of strife *is as* when one letteth out water : therefore leave off contention, before it be meddled with.—PROV., ch. 17.

1639. —— **removed.** *Abram said,* ⁹ Separate thyself, I pray thee, from me : if *thou wilt take* the left hand, then I will go to the right ; or if *thou depart* to the right hand, then I will go to the left. ¹⁰ And Lot..beheld all the plain of Jordan.—GEN., ch. 13.

1640. —— **A sharp.** *Paul—Barnabas.* [In revisiting the churches,] ³⁷ Barnabas determined to take with them..Mark. ³⁸ But Paul thought not good to take him with them, who departed from them from Pamphylia, and went not with them to the work. ³⁹ And the contention was so sharp between them, that they departed asunder one from the other.—ACTS, ch. 15.

1641. —— **of a Woman.** *Proverb.* ¹⁵ A continual dropping in a very rainy day and a contentious woman are alike. ¹⁶ Whosoever hideth her hideth the wind.—PROV., ch. 27.

See other illustrations under :

1642. CONTENTMENT, Constant. *Paul.* ¹¹ Not that I speak in respect of want : for I have learned, in whatsoever state I am, *therewith* to be content. ¹² I know both how to be abased, and I know how to abound : every where and in all things I am instructed both to be full and to be hungry, both to abound and to suffer need.. ⁴³ I can do all things through Christ, which strengtheneth me.—PHIL., ch. 4.

1643. —— **Christian.** *Paul.* ⁵ *Let your* conversation *be* without covetousness ; *and be* content with such things as ye have : for he hath said, I will never leave thee, nor forsake thee. —HEB., ch. 13.

1644. —— **Godly.** *Paul.* ⁶ But godliness with contentment is great gain. ⁷ For we brought nothing into *this* world, *and it is* certain we can carry nothing out. ⁸ And having food and raiment, let us be therewith content.—1 TIM., ch. 6.

1645. —— **Home of.** *Jethro.* ²¹ Moses was content to dwell with the man : and he gave Moses Zipporah his daughter.—EX., ch. 1.

1646. —— **at Home.** *Barzillai.* ³³ David said unto Barzillai, Come thou over with me, and I will feed thee with me in Jerusalem.. ³⁵ I *am* this day fourscore years old : ³⁷ Let thy servant ..turn back again, that I may die in mine own city, *and be buried* by the grave of my father and of my mother.—2 SAM., ch. 19.

1647. —— **Lack of.** *Paul.* ⁹ They that will be rich fall into temptation and a snare, and *into* many foolish and hurtful lusts, which drown men in destruction and perdition. ¹⁰ For the love of money is the root of all evil : which while some coveted after, they have erred from the faith, and pierced themselves through with many sorrows.—1 TIM., ch. 6.

1648. —— **with Little.** *Proverb.* ¹⁶ Better *is* little with the fear of the Lord, than great treasure and trouble therewith. ¹⁷ Better *is* a dinner of herbs where love is, than a stalled ox and hatred therewith.—PROV., ch. 15. ⁸ Better *is* a little with righteousness, than great revenues without right.—PROV., ch. 16.

1649. —— **with Possessions.** *To Jacob.* ⁸ Said, What *meanest* thou by all this drove which I met? And he said, These *are* to find grace in the sight of my lord. ⁹ And Esau said, I have enough, my brother ; keep that thou hast. —GEN., ch. 33.

1650. —— **Perfect.** *David.* ¹ The Lord *is* my shepherd ; I shall not want. ² He maketh me to lie down in green pastures : he leadeth me beside the still waters.—PS. 23.

1651. —— **with Riches.** *Abram.* ²² Abram said to the king of Sodom, I have lifted up mine hand unto the Lord.. ²³ That I will not *take* from a thread even to a shoelatchet, and that I will not take any thing that *is* thine, lest thou shouldest say, I have made Abram rich.—GEN., ch. 14. [He had rescued the king and people out of the hands of their enemies.]

See other illustrations under:

PEACE.

Cost of. Menahem exacted..each man fifty shekels 6018
Contemned. What hast thou to do with peace? 6019
Commanded. Rebuked the wind..Peace be still 6020
Disposition. Abram said..Let there be no strife 6021
Intercession. Sendeth an ambassador..conditions 6022
Insecure. Peace, peace, when there is no peace 6023
Jesus brings. The wolf shall dwell with the lamb 6025
Kingdom of. Jesus stood in the midst..Peace be 6024
Legacy. Peace I leave with you, my peace I give 6026
National. Given me rest on every side [David] 6027
Offering. What..the trespass offering..gold mice 6028
Pledge. The bow shall be seen in the cloud 6029
Plea. Shall the sword devour forever? 6030
Purchased. Menahem gave Pul 1000 talents of 6031
High Price. A tumult was made..I am innocent 6032
with Sin. I am come..send a sword 6033
Tribute. Jehoash took all the hallowed things 6034
Typical. Every man under his own vine..fig tree 6035
Unstained. There shall not a man be put to death 6036
Universal. Nations..beat their swords into 6037
Ten Years. Land was quiet..ten years 6038

REST.

Enforced. Thick darkness in all the land of Egypt 7254
Faith. In..rest shall ye be saved 7255
Improved. Had the churches rest..walking 7256
Labour. G..rested on the seventh day 7257
No. Unclean spirit is gone..findeth none 7258
Soul. Take my yoke..ye shall find rest 7259
Without. Many were coming..no leisure 7260
" As a bird wandereth..so is a man 7261
" I am full of tossings to and fro 7262
Year of. Seventh year..rest unto the land 7263

See CONCILIATION.

1652. CONTROVERSY avoided. *Jesus.* [The Samaritan woman said,] [20] Our fathers worshipped in this mountain ; and ye say, that in Jerusalem is the place where men ought to worship. [21] Jesus saith unto her, Woman, believe me.; [23]..the true worshippers shall worship the Father in spirit and in truth.—JOHN, ch. 4.

1653. —— A fatal. *Cain.* [8] Cain talked with Abel..and..when they were in the field.. Cain rose up..and slew him.—GEN., ch. 4.

1654. CONTROVERSIALIST, A holy. *Paul.* [At Athens,] [17] Disputed he in the synagogue with the Jews, and with the devout persons, and in the market daily with them that met with him.—ACTS, ch. 17.

1655. CONTEST, A discouraging. *Elijah.* [13] What doest thou here, Elijah? [14] And he said, I have been very jealous for the Lord God of hosts : because the children of Israel have forsaken thy covenant, thrown down thine altars, and slain thy prophets..and I, *even* I only, am left ; and they seek my life.—1 KINGS, ch. 19.

1656. —— An unequal. *David with Goliath.* [4] There went out a champion..whose height *was* six cubits and a span. [5] And *he had* a helmet of brass..and he *was* armed with a coat of mail ; [6] And *he had* greaves of brass upon his legs, and a target of brass between his shoulders. [7] And the staff of his spear *was* like a weaver's beam ; and his spear's head *weighed* six hundred shekels of iron : and one bearing a shield went before him.—1 SAM., ch. 17. [David chose five smooth stones.]

See other illustrations under:

CHALLENGE.

Battle. I defy the armies of I. this day 1083
Champions. Let the young men play before us 1084
Prayer. Call ye on the name of your gods, and I 1085
War. Jehu wrote letters..fight for your master's 1086

Debate. Not able to resist the spirit and wisdom 2005
See CONFLICT and STRIFE.

—— CONTRAST. ——

See illustrations under:
Glorious. Beggar died..carried by the angels 370
Painful. Lame man..alms..gate called Beautiful 207
" Rich man..sumptuously..Lazarus at his 9292
Redemption. Equal with G..took..form of a s. 4184
Social. But now..have me in derision 146

1657. CONTRIBUTIONS, Abundant. *Solomon's Temple.* [6] The chief of the fathers and princes.. and the captains..with the rulers..offered willingly, [7] And gave..of gold five thousand talents and ten thousand drams, and of silver ten thousand talents, and of brass eighteen thousand talents, and one hundred talents of iron. [8] And ..*precious* stones.—1 CHRON., ch. 29.

1658. —— for Expenses. *Worship.* [32] We made ordinances..to charge ourselves yearly with the third part of a shekel for the service of the house of our God ; [33] For the shewbread.. the continual meat offering .. the continual burnt offering, of the sabbaths, of the new moons, for the set feasts, and for the holy *things*, and for the sin offerings..and *for* all the work of the house.—NEH., ch. 10. [About thirty-three cents.]

1659. —— for Jesus. *Women.* [Jesus was on a preaching tour, and] [2] Certain women, which had been healed of evil spirits and infirmities, Mary called Magdalene, out of whom went seven devils, [3] And Joanna the wife of Chuza Herod's steward, and Susanna, and many others..ministered unto him of their substance.—LUKE, ch. 8.

1660. —— for the Levites. *Tithes.* [5] The children of Israel brought in abundance the firstfruits of corn, wine, and oil, and honey, and of all the increase of the field ; and the tithe of all *things* brought they in abundantly. [6]..that dwelt in the cities of Judah, they also brought in the tithe of oxen and sheep.—2 CHRON., ch. 31.

1661. —— for Repairs. *Temple.* [9] Jehoiada the priest took a chest, and bored a hole in the lid of it, and set it beside the altar, on the right side..and the priests that kept the door put therein all the money *that was* brought.—2 KINGS, ch. 12.

1662. —— for Rebuilding. *Under Zerubbabel.* [68] *Some* of the chief of the fathers..offered freely ..[69] They gave after their ability unto the treasure of the work threescore and one thousand drams of gold, and five thousand pounds of silver, and one hundred priests' garments.—EZRA, ch. 2. [About $375,000.]

1663. —— Various. *Tabernacle.* [22] Both men and women..brought bracelets, and earrings, and rings, and tablets, all jewels of gold..[23] And every man, with whom was found blue, and purple, and scarlet, and fine linen, and goats' *hair*, and red skins of rams, and badgers' skins, brought *them*. [24]..silver and brass..and..shittim wood.—EX., ch. 35.

1664. CONTRITION accepted. *Josiah's.* ¹⁹ Because thine heart was tender, and thou hast humbled thyself before the Lord..and hast rent thy clothes, and wept before me ; I also have heard *thee*, saith the Lord. ²⁰ Behold therefore..thou shalt be gathered into thy grave in peace ; and thine eyes shall not see all the evil which I will bring upon this place.—2 KINGS, ch. 22.

1665. —— Annual. *Jewish.* ²⁹ *This* shall be a statute for ever..*that* in the seventh month, on the tenth *day*..ye shall afflict your souls, and do no work at all.. ³⁰ For on that day shall *the priest* make an atonement for you..*that* ye may be clean from all your sins.—LEV., ch. 16.

1666. —— Bitter. *Passover.* ⁸ They shall eat the flesh in that night, roast with fire, and unleavened bread ; *and* with bitter *herbs* they shall eat it.—Ex., ch. 12.

1667. CONVERT, Duty of a. *Samaritan.* ²⁸ The woman then left her waterpot, and went her way into the city, and saith to the men, ²⁹ Come, see a man, which told me all things that ever I did : is not this the Christ ? ³⁰ Then they..came unto him. ³⁹ And many of the Samaritans..believed on him for the saying of the woman.—JOHN, ch. 4.

1668. —— A distinguished. *Eunuch.* ²⁷ A eunuch of great authority under Candace queen of the Ethiopians, who had the charge of all her treasure, and had come to Jerusalem for to worship, ³⁸ And he commanded the chariot to stand still : and they went..into the water, both Philip and the eunuch ; and he baptized him.—ACTS, ch. 8.

1669. —— A spurious. *Simon.* ¹⁸ When Simon saw that through laying on of the apostles' hands the Holy Ghost was given, he offered them money, ¹⁹ Saying, Give me also this power. —ACTS, ch. 8.

1670. —— Trial of a. *Pharisees.* ²⁶ How opened he thine eyes ? ²⁷ He answered them, I have told you already, and ye did not hear : wherefore would ye hear *it* again ? will ye also be his disciples ? ²⁸ Then they reviled him, and said, Thou art his disciple ; but we are Moses' disciples. ³⁴..And they cast him out.—JOHN, ch. 9.

1671. CONVERTS, Counsel to. *Revival at Antioch.* ²² The church which was in Jerusalem.. sent forth Barnabas..as far as Antioch. ²³ Who, when he came, and had seen the grace of God, was glad, and exhorted them all, that with purpose of heart they would cleave unto the Lord. —ACTS, ch. 11.

1672. —— Food for. *Milk.* ² As newborn babes, desire the sincere milk of the word, that ye may grow thereby.—1 PET., ch. 2.

1673. —— from humble Life. *Jesus.* ⁴⁴ Some of them would have taken him ; but no man laid hands on him..Why have ye not brought him ? ⁴⁶ The officers answered, Never man spake like this man. ⁴⁷ Then answered..the Pharisees, Are ye also deceived ? ⁴⁸ Have any of the rulers or of the Pharisees believed on him?—JOHN, ch. 7.

1674. —— to Hypocrisy. *Pharisees.* ¹⁵ Woe unto you, scribes and Pharisees, hypocrites ! for ye compass sea and land to make one proselyte ; and when he is made, ye make him twofold more the child of hell than yourselves.—MAT., ch. 23.

1675. —— Influential. *Bereans.* ¹¹ These were more noble than those in Thessalonica, in that they received the word with all readiness of mind, and searched the Scriptures daily, whether those things were so. ¹² Therefore many of them believed ; also of honourable women which were Greeks, and of men, not a few.— ACTS, ch. 17.

1676. —— Increase of. *Five Thousand.* ⁴ Many of them which heard the word believed ; and the number of the men was about five thousand. —ACTS, ch. 4.

1677. —— —— *Three Thousand.* ⁴¹ They that gladly received his word were baptized : and the same day there were added *unto them* about three thousand souls. ⁴² And they continued steadfastly.—ACTS, ch. 2.

1678. —— without Principle. *Persians.* ¹⁷ In every city, whithersoever the king's..decree came, the Jews had joy and gladness, a feast and a good day. And many..became Jews ; for the fear of the Jews fell upon them.—ESTHER, ch. 8.

1679. —— Steadfast. *Jerusalem.* ⁴⁵ Sold their possessions and goods, and parted them to all *men*, as every man had need. ⁴⁶ And they, continuing daily with one accord in the temple, and breaking bread from house to house, did eat their meat with gladness and singleness of heart.—ACTS, ch. 2.

1680. —— Superficial. *Stony Ground.* ¹⁶ When they have heard the word, immediately receive it with gladness ; ¹⁷ And have no root in themselves, and so endure but for a time : afterward, when affliction or persecution ariseth for the word's sake, immediately they are offended.— MARK, ch. 4.

1681. —— Zeal for. *Paul.* ¹⁹ I made myself servant unto all, that I might gain the more. ²⁰ And unto the Jews I became as a Jew, that I might gain the Jews ; to them that are under the law, as under the law, that I might gain them that are under the law ; ²¹ To them that are without law, as without law. ²²..I am made all things to all *men*, that I might by all means save some.—1 COR., ch. 9.

See **CONVERSION** and references.

1682. CONVICTION, An awakening. *Dead.*
[13] All things that are reproved are made manifest by the light : for whatsoever doth make manifest is light. [14] Wherefore he saith, Awake thou that sleepest, and arise from the dead, and Christ shall give thee light.—EPH., ch. 5.

1683. —— **challenged.** *Aged Samuel.* [3] Behold, here I *am:* witness against me before the Lord, and before his anointed : whose ox have I taken? or whose ass have I taken? or whom have I defrauded? whom have I oppressed? or of whose hand have I received *any* bribe to blind mine eyes therewith? and I will restore it you.—1 SAM., ch. 12.

1684. —— **by Deeds.** *Widow of Zarephath.* [23] Elijah took the child . . down out of the chamber . . and delivered him unto his mother . . said, See, thy son liveth. [24] . . Now by this I know that thou *art* a man of God, *and* that the word of the Lord in thy mouth *is* truth.—1 KINGS, ch. 17.

1685. —— **from Examination.** *Bereans.* [11] They received the word with all readiness of mind, and searched the Scriptures daily, whether those things were so. [12] Therefore many of them believed ; also of honourable women which were Greeks, and of men, not a few.—ACTS, ch. 17.

1686. —— **Heaven sent.** *Saul.* [3] Suddenly there shined round about him a light from heaven : [4] And he fell to the earth, and heard a voice saying unto him, Saul, Saul, why persecutest thou me?—ACTS, ch. 9.

1687. —— **A heartfelt.** *Pentecost.* [37] When they heard *this,* they were pricked in their heart, and said unto Peter and to the rest of the apostles, Men *and* brethren, what shall we do? [38] Then Peter said . . Repent, and be baptized.—ACTS, ch. 2.

1688. —— **necessary.** *No Depth.* [5] Some fell upon stony places, where they had not much earth : and forthwith they sprung up, because they had no deepness of earth : [6] And when the sun was up, they were scorched ; and because they had no root, they withered away.—MAT., ch. 13.

1689. —— **Prayer under.** *Job.* [23] How many *are* mine iniquities and sins? make me to know my transgression and my sin. [24] Wherefore hidest thou thy face, and holdest me for thine enemy? [25] Wilt thou break a leaf driven to and fro? and wilt thou pursue the dry stubble? [26] For thou writest bitter things against me, and makest me to possess the iniquities of my youth. [27] Thou puttest my feet also in the stocks, and lookest narrowly unto all my paths ; thou settest a print upon the heels of my feet. [28] And he, as a rotten thing, consumeth, as a garment that is motheaten.—JOB, ch. 13.

1690. —— **resisted.** *Pharisees.* [Two days before Jesus' death, John says,] [37] Though he had done so many miracles before them, yet they believed not on him.—JOHN, ch. 12.

1691. —— **Rational.** *Prodigal.* [17] When he came to himself, he said, How many hired servants of my father's have bread enough and to spare, and I perish with hunger! [18] I will arise and go to my father.—LUKE, ch. 15.

1692. —— **Sensitiveness to.** *David.* [5] Afterwards David's heart smote him, because he had cut off Saul's skirt. [6] And he said unto his

men, The Lord forbid that I should do this thing unto my master, the Lord's anointed.—1 SAM., ch. 24.

1693. —— **Smiting.** *David.* [10] David's heart smote him after that he had numbered the people . . I have sinned greatly in that I have done : and now, I beseech thee, O Lord, take away the iniquity of thy servant ; for I have done very foolishly.—2 SAM., ch. 24.

1694. —— **Sudden.** *On Carmel.* [38] The fire of the Lord fell, and consumed the burnt sacrifice, and the wood, and the stones, and the dust, and licked up the water that *was* in the trench. [39] And when all the people saw *it,* they fell on their faces : and they said, The Lord, he *is* the God.—1 KINGS, ch. 18.

1695. —— **Speechless.** *Council.* [Peter had healed a lame man in the temple. Was arrested.] [14] And beholding the man which was healed standing with them, they could say nothing against it.—ACTS, ch. 4.

1696. —— **by the Truth.** *Josiah.* [10] Shaphan read it before the king. [11] And . . when the king had heard the words of the book of the law . . he rent his clothes.—2 KINGS, ch. 22.

1697. —— **Thorough.** *Digged Deep.* [48] He is like a man which built a house, and digged deep, and laid the foundation on a rock : and when the flood arose, the stream beat vehemently upon that house, and could not shake it ; for it was founded upon a rock.—LUKE, ch. 6.

1698. —— **Transient.** *At the Cross.* [54] When the centurion, and they that were with him, watching Jesus, saw the earthquake, and those things that were done, they feared greatly, saying, Truly this was the Son of God.—MAT., ch. 27.

1699. —— **A willing.** *Nathanael.* [48] Nathanael saith . . Whence knowest thou me? Jesus answered . . when thou wast under the fig tree, I saw thee. [49] Nathanael answered . . Rabbi, thou art the Son of God.—JOHN, ch. 1.

See other illustrations under :

AWAKENING.

1700. CONVERSION a Creation. *New Creature.* [17] Therefore if any man *be* in Christ, *he is* a new creature : old things are passed away ; behold, all things are become new.—2 COR., ch. 5.

1701. —— **Conscious.** *Spirit.* [13] Hereby know we that we dwell in him, and he in us, because he hath given us of his Spirit.—1 JOHN, ch. 4.

1702. —— **Changed by.** *Jailer.* [24] Thrust
them into the inner prison, and made their feet
fast in the stocks.—Acts, ch. 16. [See No. 1707.]

1703. —— **changes the Life.** *Saul.* [At
Damascus,] [20] He preached Christ in the synagogues, that he is the Son of God. [21] But all that
heard *him* were amazed, and said ; Is not this
he that destroyed them which called on this
name in Jerusalem, and came hither for that intent ?—Acts, ch. 9.

1704. —— **by Effort.** *Strait Gate.* [24] Strive
to enter in at the strait gate : for many..will
seek to enter in, and shall not be able.—Luke,
ch. 13.

1705. —— **Evidence of.** *Heart Opened.* [14] Lydia, a seller of purple..whose heart the Lord
opened, that she attended unto the things which
were spoken of Paul. [15] And when she was baptized, and her household, she besought *us*, saying, If ye have judged me to be faithful to the
Lord, come into my house, and abide *there.*—
Acts, ch. 16.

1706. —— **A false.** *Simon.* [18] When Simon
saw that through laying on of the apostles' hands
the Holy Ghost was given, he offered them
money, [19] Saying, Give me also this power, that
on whomsoever I lay hands, he may receive the
Holy Ghost.—Acts, ch. 8.

1707. —— **A genuine.** *Jailer.* [33] He took
them the same hour of the night, and washed
their stripes ; and was baptized, he and all his,
straightway. [34] And when he had brought them
into his house, he set meat before them, and
rejoiced, believing in God.—Acts, ch. 16. [See
No. 1715.]

1708. —— **a Heart-work.** *Cleansing.* [21] Out
of the heart of men, proceed evil thoughts, adulteries, fornications, murders, [22] Thefts, covetousness, wickedness, deceit, lasciviousness, an evil
eye, blasphemy, pride, foolishness.—Mark, ch.7.

1709. —— **a hasty.** *Eunuch.* [36] As they went
on *their* way..the eunuch said, See, *here is* water ; what doth hinder me to be baptized ? [37] And
Philip said, If thou believest with all thine
heart, thou mayest. And he answered..I believe that Jesus Christ is the Son of God.—Acts,
ch. 8.

1710. —— **Inward.** *Pharisees.* [38] The Pharisee..marvelled that he had not first washed before dinner. [39] And the Lord said..Now do ye
Pharisees make clean the outside of the cup and
the platter ; but your inward part is full of
ravening and wickedness.—Luke, ch. 11.

1711. —— **a Mystery.** *Wind.* [8] The wind
bloweth where it listeth, and thou hearest the
sound thereof, but canst not tell whence it
cometh, and whither it goeth : so is every one
that is born of the Spirit. [9] Nicodemus answered..How can these things be ?—John, ch. 3.

1712. —— **a Necessity.** *To Nicodemus.*
[5] Jesus answered, Verily, verily, I say unto thee,
Except a man be born of water and *of* the
Spirit, he cannot enter into the kingdom of God.
—John, ch. 3.

1713. —— **a new Heart.** *King Saul.* [9] When
he had turned his back to go from Samuel, God
gave him another heart.. [10]..and the Spirit of
God came upon him, and he prophesied.—1
Sam., ch. 10.

1714. —— **Negative and Positive.** *Paul.*
[11] Likewise reckon ye also yourselves to be dead
indeed unto sin, but alive unto God through
Jesus Christ our Lord.—Rom., ch. 6.

1715. —— **A sudden.** *Jailer.* [29] He called for
a light, and sprang in, and came trembling, and
fell down before Paul and Silas, [30] And brought
them out, and said, Sirs, what must I do to be
saved ? [31] And they said, Believe on the Lord
Jesus Christ.—Acts, ch. 16.

1716. —— **A superficial.** *"Not Root."* [20] He
that received the seed into stony places..is he
that heareth the word, and anon with joy receiveth it ; [21] Yet hath he not root in himself,
but dureth for a while : for when tribulation or
persecution ariseth because of the word, by and
by he is offended.—Mat., ch. 13.

1717. —— **A wonderful.** *Saul.* [3] Suddenly
there shined round about him a light from heav-
en : [4] And he fell to the earth, and heard a voice
saying..Saul, Saul, why persecutest thou me ?
[5] And he said, Who art thou, Lord? And the
Lord said, I am Jesus whom thou persecutest.—
Acts, ch. 9.

1718. CONVERSIONS daily. *Pentecost.* [41] They
that gladly received his word were baptized : and
the same day there were added *unto them* about
three thousand souls. [42]..And the Lord added to
the church daily such as should be saved.—Acts,
ch. 2.

1719. —— **Genuine.** *Ephesians.* [18] Many that
believed came, and confessed, and shewed their
deeds. [19] Many of them also which used curious arts brought their books together, and burned them before all *men :* and they counted the
price of them..fifty thousand *pieces* of silver.—
Acts, ch. 19. [About $10,000.]

1720. —— **Instrumental of.** *Woman.* [39] Many
of the Samaritans..believed on him for the saying of the woman, which testified, He told me
all that ever I did.—John, ch. 4.

See other illustrations under:

ACCEPTANCE.

Assurance. Would he have shewed us all these	53
Denied. Ye brought..torn, and the lame..sick	55
Evidence. There rose up fire out of the rock	56
Manifested. Burning lamp passed between those	57
of Piety. In every nation he that feareth..worketh	58
by Sacrifice. L. had respect unto A..offering	59
Terms. Do justly..love mercy..walk humbly	61

AWAKENING.

of Conscience. Herod said..J. B. was risen	595
Fear. Earthquake..this was the S. of G.	596
Great. All the people, both small and great	597
General. All the land of Judea..all baptized	598
Sudden. Came trembling..What must I do	599
Trouble. L..troubled the Egyptians..flee	600
Truth. Paul reasoned..Felix trembled	601
Unexpected. Our brother..therefore this distress	602

CHRISTIANS.

Almost. Agrippa said unto Paul, Almost thou	1267
Care for. I lay down my life for the sheep	1268
Childlike. Suffer little children..Of such is the	1269
Carnal. Whereas there is envying and strife	1270
Epistle. Ye are our epistle..read of all	1271
Exemplary. Bishop must be blameless	1272
Greatness. Least in the kingdom..greater	1273
Homeward. Come to Zion with songs	1274
First named. First called Christians at Antioch	1275

Saved. He that committeth sin is of the devil 1276
Visible. Ye are the light of the world 1277

JUSTIFICATION.

Difficulty. How then can man be justified with G. 4801
Penitents. [Publican] went down..justified 4802

Humane. Break every yoke..deal thy bread 3050
Humility. Him that is poor..contrite spirit 4149
Intention. Accepted according to that a man hath 735
Indispensable. Except ye be converted..not enter 7914
Preparation. Clean heart..teach..sinners con. 1485
Reasoning. Searched whether those things were 1685
Remarkable. Simon bewitched the people 8203
Saints. Take you for my people..your God 1238
Truth. Law of the L..converting the soul—Ps. 19 : 7
See REVIVAL and references.

1721. CONVERSATION, Impure. *Lot.* [6] Turning the cities of Sodom and Gomorrah into ashes.. [7]..delivered just Lot, vexed with the filthy conversation of the wicked : [8] For that righteous man dwelling among them, in seeing and hearing, vexed *his* righteous soul from day to day.— 2 PETER, ch. 2.

1722. —— Religious. *Law.* [6] These words ..shall be in thine heart : [7] And thou shalt.. talk of them when thou sittest in thine house, and when thou walkest by the way, and when thou liest down, and when thou risest up.— DEUT., ch. 6.

See other illustrations under :
SPEAKER.
Convincing. Never man spake like this man 8245
Engaging. Mary..sat at Jesus' feet and heard 8246
SPEAKING.
Evil. He that speaketh evil of his brother..of the 8241
Help. Filled with the H. S..gave them utterance 8242
for God. Say not I am a child..thou shalt..speak 8243
" Be not afraid of their faces..with thee 8244
SPEECH.
Assisted. I am not eloquent..with thy mouth 8247
" I can not speak..I shall send thee 8248
Appropriate. Apples of gold in pictures of silver 8249
Anointed. Tongues like..fire, it sat upon each 8250
Constrained. I am full of matter..constraineth 8251
Cautious. Be not rash with..mouth..hasty 8252
Confusion. L. did there confound the language 8253
Dangers of. Took counsel..entangle..speech 8254
Evidence. If..bridleth not his tongue..religion is 8255
Gift of. It shall be given you what ye shall speak 8256
Improved. Had an impediment..touched his 8257
Impossible. Not having a wedding garment 8258
Plainness. My speech was not with enticing 8259
Power of. Death and life..in the power of the 8260
Unrestrained. With flattering lips and a double 8261
Unentangled. Render unto Cesar..unto G..the 8262
Unguarded. Openeth wide his lips shall have 8263
Useless. Jesus answered Pilate to never a word 8264
" Herod questioned..answered him n. 8265
TONGUE.
Angry. Moses..spake unadvisedly with his lips 8830
Buyers. It is naught..then he boasteth 8831
Control. He that backbiteth not with his tongue 8832
" We put bits in the horses' mouths 8833
Foo'ish. The fool uttereth all his mind 8834
Hasty. Man hasty in his words..more..a fool 8835
Heart. Out of the abundance of the heart..speak 8836
Punished. We have sinned..spoken..away the 8837
Responsible. By thy words..justified..condemned 8838
Religious. Spake often..L. hearkened 8839
Untamed. Of beasts..tongue can no man tame 8840
Use of. Swift to hear, slow to speak 8841

Wise. If thou speak good words to them 8842
" Words of the wise are as goads 8843
Weapon. Let us smite him with the tongue 8844
Wicked. Tongue is a fire, a world of iniquity 8845
TONGUES.
Changed. Let us..confound their language 8846
" Amazed..How hear we..our own 8847
Differ. Wise man's mouth are gracious..fool 8848
Fire. Cloven tongues of fire..it sat upon each 8849
Restrained. King's commandment..Answer not 8850

Corrupted. Children could not speak in the 4896
Given. Every man heard them speak in his own 4897
Origin. Let us..confound their language 4898
Suppressed. Caleb stilled the people..we are 3128
Unfriendly. Brethren..not speak peaceably unto 3099

1723. CO-OPERATION needful. *Marriage.* [18] The Lord God said, *It is* not good that the man should be alone ; I will make him a help meet for him.—GEN., ch. 2.

See other illustrations under :
HELP.
Appeal. Come over into Macedonia and help 3925
" Help my Lord, O king..hid her son 3926
Angelic. [Gethsemane] An angel..from heaven 3937
Divine. I will be with thy mouth and teach 3928
" Let us flee from..Israel, the L. fighteth 3929
" Wherewith shall I save Israel..Gideon 3930
" King of Syria..more with us..him 3931
" Samuel..stone and called it Ebenezer 3938
Fraternal. Ye shall pass over before your 3927
Hurtful. Ahaz took a portion..he helped him not 3932
Injurious. Uzziah, when he was strong..heart 3933
Needed. If there be no man to serve us..will 3934
Provided. L. saw..saved them by..Jeroboam 3939
Reserved. Father..will give me twelve legions of 3935
Sought. [Canaanite woman] Send her away..L. 3936
Wanted. I have no man..to put me in 3940
Woman. I will make him a help meet 3941
HELPERS.
Builders. Whosoever remaineth..help him with 3942
Dependence. Aaron and Hur stayed up his hands 3943

1724. CORDIALITY, Lack of. *Jesus.* [44] Simon, Seest thou this woman ? I entered into thine house, thou gavest me no water for my feet : but she hath washed my feet with tears, and wiped *them* with the hairs of her head. [45] Thou gavest me no kiss : but this woman, since the time I came in, hath not ceased to kiss my feet. [46] My head with oil thou didst not anoint : but this woman hath anointed my feet with ointment.— LUKE, ch. 7.

See other illustrations under :
SINCERITY.
Consecration. Josiah made a covenant..burned 8025
Evil Doing. I thought I ought to..put to death 8026
Evidence. Brought their books..burned them 8027
Example. An Israelite in whom is no guile 8028
Heart. He that speaketh truth in his heart 8029
Lovable. All..have I kept..Jesus loved him 8030
Opinions. Rabbi, thou art the Son of God 8031
Positive. Thou knowest..that I love thee 8032
Proof. When..people saw it..said L., he is G. 8033
Reformation. Speak..the truth..execute..truth 8034

in Age. 110 years..children brought up on Joseph's 220
Domestic. Centurion's servant sick..very dear 158
Gratitude. I will shew kindness..for Jonathan's 4817
Kind. Depart..ye [Kenites] showed kindness 4825
Welcome. Well done, good and faithful servant 9490
See AFFECTION.
See LOVE and references.

1725. CORRESPONDENCE necessary. *Old and New.* [21] No man..seweth a piece of new cloth on an old garment ; else the new piece that filled it up taketh away from the old, and the rent is made worse. [22] And no man putteth new wine into old bottles ; else the new wine doth burst the bottles, and the wine is spilled, and the bottles will be marred : but new wine must be put into new bottles.—MARK, ch. 2.

See other illustrations under :

CONSISTENCY.

Apostolic. How holily and justly..we behaved	1588
Blameless. Be blameless and harmless..perverse	1589
Conscientious. I have lived in all good conscience	1590
Critics. Ought ye not to walk..reproach of the	1591
" Exercise myself..void of offence..toward	1592
Courageous. If not..we will not serve thy gods	1593
Exemplified. He took away the high places	1594
Fruit. Doth a fountain send forth..sweet..bitter	1595
Hypocrisy. Baptism of John when a..they	1596
Meekness. Bitter envying..descendeth not from	1597
Observed. Herod feared John..holy and observed	1598
Regarded. Giving no offence..ministry be not	1599
Separation. Ye cannot drink the cup of the L.	1600

1726. CORRUPTION from Associates. *Solomon.* [1] King Solomon loved many strange women, together with the daughter of Pharaoh, women of the Moabites, Ammonites, Edomites, Zidonians, *and* Hittites ; [3] And he had seven hundred wives, princesses, and three hundred concubines : and his wives turned away his heart.— 1 KINGS, ch. 11.

1727. —— by Avarice. *Achan.* [21] I saw among the spoils a goodly Babylonish garment, and two hundred shekels of silver, and a wedge of gold of fifty shekels weight, then I coveted them, and took them ; and..they *are* hid in the earth in..my tent.—JOSHUA, ch. 7.

1728. —— by Art. *Canaanites.* [51] When ye are passed over Jordan into the land of Canaan ; [52] Then ye shall drive out all the inhabitants.. before you, and destroy all their pictures, and destroy all their molten images.—NUM., ch. 33.

1729. —— by Fraud. *Primitive.* [4] False brethren unawares brought in..came in privily to spy out our liberty which we have in Christ Jesus, that they might bring us into bondage.— GAL., ch. 2.

1730. —— General. *Antediluvians.* [11] The earth also was corrupt before God ; and..filled with violence. [12] And God looked upon the earth.. for all flesh had corrupted his way upon the earth.—GEN., ch. 6.

1731. —— Moral. *Covetousness.* [10] Every one from the least even unto the greatest is given to covetousness, from the prophet even unto the priest every one dealeth falsely. [12] Were they ashamed when they had committed abomination ? nay, they were not at all ashamed, neither could they blush.—JER., ch. 8.

1732. —— Religious. *Calf.* [3] All the people brake off the golden earrings.. and brought *them* unto Aaron. [4] And he..fashioned it with a graving tool, after he had made it a molten calf : and they said, These *be* thy gods, O Israel, which brought thee up out of the land of Egypt.—EX., ch. 32.

1733. —— —— *Samaritans.* [29] Every nation made gods of their own, and put *them* in the houses of the high places which the Samaritans had made.. [30] And the men of Babylon

made Succoth-benoth, and the men of Cuth made Nergal, and the men of Hamath made Ashima, [31] And the Avites made Nibhaz and Tartak, and the Sepharvites burnt their children in fire to Adrammelech and Anammelech, the gods of Sepharvaim.—2 KINGS, ch. 17.

See other illustrations under :

BRIBERY.

Concealment. Gave large money..say ye..stole	930
Desecration. Ahaz took..out of the house..gave	931
Friendship. Entice him..give thee..1100 pieces of	932
Horrible. Covenanted with Judas for thirty	933
Official. Felix hoped that money..given of Paul	934
" Princes..every one loveth gifts	935

DEGRADATION.

Defilement. Out of the heart proceed evil thoughts	2118
Drink. Mighty man shall be humbled	2119
Food. Whatsoever goeth on the belly	2120
Morals. Sodomites	2121

DEPRAVITY.

Ancient. Every imagination of the thoughts	2188
Bestial. [Gibeathites] beset the house, and beat at	2189
Discovered. Woe is me..unclean lips..people	2190
Heathen. Changed the glory of..G. into an image	2191
Infectious. Daughters of Lot were with child	2192
Inherited. Ye are the children of them which	2193
Natural. L. looked down..all gone aside..filthy	2194

FRAUD.

Appearances. Gibeonites..took old sacks..old	3408
Commerce. Take thy bill..quickly..write fifty	3409
Demagogue. O that I were a judge..do justice	2171
Pious. Sons of the prophets, give..silver [Gehazi]	3410
Religious. His enemy..sowed tares among the	3411
Spiritual. Simon offered money..Holy Ghost	3412
Traitors. Whomsoever I shall kiss..is he	3413
Wages. Hire of the labourers kept..crieth	3414

TRICK.

Diplomatic. From a very far country are..come	8955
Hypocrites. Feign themselves just men..might	8956
Legerdemain. Magicians..rods became serpents	8957
Politicians. Shall ask a petition..save of thee	8958

1734. COST, Count the. *Disciple.* [19] A certain scribe came, and said unto him, Master, I will follow thee whithersoever thou goest. [20] And Jesus saith..The foxes have holes, and the birds of the air *have* nests ; but the Son of man hath not where to lay *his* head.—MAT., ch. 8.

1735. —— Counted the. *Ephesians.* [19] Many ..which used curious arts brought their books together, and burned them before all *men :* and they counted the price of them..fifty thousand *pieces* of silver.—ACTS, ch. 19. [About $10,000.]

1736. —— not counted. *Jesus.* [28] Which of you, intending to build a tower, sitteth not down first, and counteth the cost.. [29] Lest haply, after he hath laid the foundation, and is not able to finish *it*, all that behold *it* begin to mock him, [30] Saying, this man began to build, and was not able to finish.—LUKE, ch. 14.

1737. —— Sacrifice with. *David.* [22] Araunah said..take and offer up what *seemeth* good unto him : behold *here be* oxen for burnt sacrifice, and threshing instruments and *other* instruments of the oxen for wood. [24] And the king said..Nay ; but I will surely buy *it* of thee at a price : neither will I offer burnt offerings..of that which doth cost me nothing. So David bought the threshingfloor and the oxen for fifty shekels of silver. —2 SAM., ch. 24. [About $25.]

See other illustrations under:
PRICE.

Extortionate. Esau sold his birthright unto Jacob 6550
of Perfection. Go sell..give..follow me 6551

Contribution. I have given [$94,101,560] 3514
Estimated by. Widow..cast more in than all 711
Royalty. One day..ten fat oxen and twenty oxen 2807
Rebuilding. 61 drams of gold and 5000 pounds of 3532
Temple. [Costing nearly $4,700,000,000.] 4130
Vast. Gain the whole world. lose his own soul 8434

1738. COUNCIL of Unfortunates. *Four Lepers.*
[3] Why sit we here until we die ? [4] If we say, We will enter into the city, then the famine *is* in the city, and we shall die there : and if we sit still here, we die also..Let us fall unto the host of the Syrians: if they save us alive, we shall live ; and if they kill us, we shall but die.—2 KINGS, ch. 7.

1739. COUNSEL, Benefit in. *Proverb.* [14] Where no counsel *is*, the people fall : but in the multitude of counsellors *there is* safety.—PROV., ch. 11.

1740. —— of Friends, Evil. *Haman.* [14] Said Zeresh his wife and all his friends..Let a gallows be made of fifty cubits high, and to-morrow speak thou unto the king that Mordecai may be hanged thereon.—ESTHER, ch. 5.

1741. —— of God neglected. *Gibeonites.* [14] The men took of their victuals, and asked not *counsel* at the mouth of the Lord. [15] And Joshua made peace with them, and..a league..to let them live : and the princes..sware unto them. [16]..At the end of three days after..they heard that they *were* their neighbours.—JOSH., ch. 9.

1742. —— Oracular. *Ahithophel.* [23] The counsel of Ahithophel, which he counselled in those days, *was* as if a man had inquired at the oracle of God : so *was* all the counsel of Ahithophel both with David and with Absalom.—2 SAM., ch. 16.

1743. —— brings Peace. *Woman of Abel.* [16] Then cried a wise woman out of the city, Hear, hear ; say, I pray you, unto Joab, Come near hither, that I may speak with thee. [17]..Then she said..Hear the words of thine handmaid. And he answered, I do hear. [18] Then she spake, saying, They were wont to speak in old time, saying, They shall surely ask *counsel* at Abel : and so they ended *the matter.*—2 SAM., ch. 20. [Peace was procured.]

1744. —— Payment for. *Saul.* [7] Said Saul to his servant..what shall we bring the man ? for the bread is spent in our vessels, and *there is* not a present to bring to the man of God : what have we ? [8] And the servant answered..I have here at hand the fourth part of a shekel of silver. —1 SAM., ch. 9.

1745. —— Rejection of. *Ahithophel.* [14] Absalom and all the men of Israel said, The counsel of Hushai..*is* better than the counsel of Ahithophel ..[23] And when Ahithophel saw that his counsel was not followed, he saddled *his* ass..and gat him home to his..city, and put his household in order, and hanged himself.—2 SAM., ch. 17.

1746. COUNSELS of the Dying. *David.* [1] He charged Solomon his son, saying, [2] I go the way of all the earth : be thou strong therefore, and shew thyself a man ; [3] And keep the charge of the Lord thy God, to walk in his ways, to keep his statutes, and his commandments, and his judgments, and his testimonies.—1 KINGS, ch. 2.

1747. —— Opposing. *Ahithophel—Hushai.* [1] Ahithophel said unto Absalom, Let me now choose out twelve thousand men, and I will arise and pursue after David this night : [7] And Hushai said unto Absalom, The counsel that Ahithophel hath given is not good at this time. [11] Therefore I counsel that all Israel be generally gathered unto thee, from Dan even to Beer-sheba..and that thou go to battle in thine own person.—2 SAM., ch. 17.

1748. COUNSELLORS, Evil. *Young Men.* [8] He forsook the counsel of the old men..and consulted with the young men that were grown up with him.. [10]..unto this people that spake.. saying, Thy father made our yoke heavy, but make thou *it* lighter unto us ; thus shalt thou say..My little *finger* shall be thicker than my father's loins. [11]..I will add to your yoke : my father hath chastised you with whips, but I will chastise you with scorpions.—1 KINGS, ch. 12. [It divided the kingdom.]

1749. —— Good. *Old Men.* [6] King Rehoboam consulted with the old men, that stood before Solomon his father while he yet lived, and said, How do ye advise that I may answer this people ? [7] And they spake..If thou..wilt serve them.. and speak good words to them, then they will be thy servants for ever.—1 KINGS, ch. 12.

1750. —— Influential. *Philistines.* [6] Achish called David, and said..thou hast been upright ..I have not found evil in thee since the day of thy coming unto me unto this day : nevertheless the lords favor thee not. [7] Wherefore now return, and go in peace, that thou displease not the lords of the Philistines.—1 SAM., ch. 29.

1751. —— Malicious. *Enemies.* [1] When..our enemies heard that I had builded the wall, [2] Sanballat and Geshem sent unto me, saying, Come, let us meet together in *some one of* the villages in the plain of Ono. But they thought to do me mischief. [7] Come now therefore, and let us take counsel together.—NEH., ch. 6.

See other illustrations under:
ADMONITION.
Disregarded. Mordecai hearkened not unto them 102
Fraternal. If any man obey not..have no company 103
Incredible. One of you which calleth..betray me 104
ADVICE.
Foolish. Said his wife..curse God and die 152
Good. Naaman's servants said, If the prophet had 153
Unfortunate. Let a gallows be made fifty cubits 154
INSTRUCTION.
Better than Practice. They bid you..do, but do not 4541
Children. Teach them thy sons, and thy son's sons 4542
Course of. Nourishing them three years..might 4543
Humble. Apollos..Aquila and Priscilla..the way 4544
Important. Heareth the word, and understandeth 4545
Improvement by. Ornament of grace unto thy 4546
Personal. Aquila and Priscilla took him..and 4547
Public. Ezra..brought the law before the 4548
Private. There came many unto..his lodging 4549
Youthful. From a child thou hast known the Holy 4550
WARNING.
Additional. Lazarus..send him. I have five 9340
Destruction. [Scorners] I also will laugh at your 9317
Dream. Have nothing to do with that just man 9318
Dangers. Beware thou pass not such a place 9319
Despised. Get you out of this place..mocked 9320

Disobedience. If thine heart turn away..surely 9321
Doubted. Before the cock crow, thou shalt deny 9322
Example. Sodom and G. are set for an example 9323
"   Remember Lot's wife [Jesus] 9324
Experience. Alexander..did me much harm 9325
Faithful. Three years I ceased not to warn every 9326
Heedless. Sword come..blood on his own head 9327
Heeded. Noah being warned of God..prepared 9328
Historical. These things were our examples 9329
"   Did not Solomon..sin by these things 9330
Ignored. Abner said, Turn thee aside from 9331
Punishment. [Leprosy] Remember what the 9332
Preserved. Angel..Joseph..Herod will seek the 8333
Personal. Before the cock crow..deny me thrice 9334
Repeated. Moses..go down and charge the 9335
Saved. He that taketh warning shall deliver 9236
Solemn. All ye shall be offended..me this night 9337
Sorrowful. One of you shall betray me 9338
Wicked. Korah..fire devoured 250 men

Evil. Consulted how they might take J. 1617
Hired. [Samaritans] hired counsellors against them 961
Useful. Having made Blastus..their friend..peace 155

1752. COUNTRY the best. *Hadad.* [21] Hadad said to Pharaoh, Let me depart, that I may go to mine own country. [22] Then Pharaoh said.. But what hast thou lacked with me, that, behold, thou seekest to go to thine own country? And he answered, Nothing: howbeit let me go in any wise.—1 KINGS, ch. 11.

1753. —— **Customs of.** *Marriage.* [Jacob saw] [25] in the morning..it *was* Leah: and he said to Laban..did not I serve with thee for Rachel? wherefore then hast thou beguiled me? [26] And Laban said, It must not be so done in our country, to give the younger before the firstborn.—GEN., ch. 29.

1754. —— **Native, Love for.** *Jacob.* [25] When Rachel had borne Joseph .. Jacob said unto Laban, Send me away, that I may go unto mine own place, and to my country.—GEN., ch. 30.

1755. —— **Return to.** *Moses.* [18] Moses went..to Jethro his father in law, and said.. Let me go..and return unto my brethren which *are* in Egypt, and see whether they be yet alive. —Ex., ch. 4.

1756. —— —— **Surrender of.** *Abraham.* [1] Get thee out of thy country, and..kindred, and..thy father's house, unto a land that I will shew thee : [4] So Abram departed.—GEN., ch. 12.

See other illustrations under :

PATRIOTISM.

Absorbing. Why is thy countenance sad? 6005
Appeal. Fight for your brethren..houses 6006
Children. Wives also and the children rejoiced 6007
Dangerous. Ehud made him a dagger..two edges 6008
Deed. Moses..slew the Egyptian 6009
Generous. Were at my table 150 Jews besides 6010
Self-sacrificing. Forgive..if not blot me..out of 6013
Sacrifices. I..have not eaten the bread of the G. 6014
Sentiments. Moses said..Let me go..my brethren 6015

Temptations in. Jesus..in the wilderness to be 29

1757. COUNTENANCE, An angry. *Nebuchadnezzar.* [19] Then was Nebuchadnezzar full of fury, and the form of his visage was changed against Shadrach, Meshach, and Abed-nego : *therefore..* commanded that they should heat the furnace one seven times more than it was wont to be heated.—DAN., ch. 3.

1758. —— **Bold.** *Gadites.* [8] Gadites there separated themselves unto David into the hold to the wilderness, men of might, *and* men of war *fit* for the battle, that could handle shield and buckler, whose faces *were like* the faces of lions, and *were* as swift as the roes upon the mountains.—1 CHRON., ch. 12.

1759. —— **changed.** *Belshazzar's.* [5] Came forth fingers of a man's hand, and wrote..upon the plaister of the wall..and the king saw the part of the hand that wrote. [6] Then the king's countenance was changed, and his thoughts troubled him.—DAN., ch. 5.

1760. —— **An illuminated.** *Stephen's.* [15] All that sat in the council, looking steadfastly on him, saw his face as it had been the face of an angel.—ACTS, ch. 6.

1761. —— **Prayer-changed.** *Jesus.* [28] He took Peter and John and James, and went up into a mountain to pray. [29] And as he prayed, the fashion of his countenance was altered, and his raiment *was* white *and* glistering.—LUKE, ch. 9.

1762. —— **Power of the.** *A Friend's.* [17] Iron sharpeneth iron ; so a man sharpeneth the countenance of his friend.—PROV., ch. 27.

1763. —— **reveals the Heart.** *Cain's.* [5] Cain was very wroth, and his countenance fell. [6] And the Lord said..Why art thou wroth? and why is thy countenance fallen?—GEN., ch. 4.

1764. —— **A sad.** *Nehemiah.* [1] In the twentieth year of Artaxerxes the king..I took up the wine, and gave *it* unto the king. Now I had not been *beforetime* sad in his presence. [2] Wherefore the king said..Why *is* thy countenance sad, seeing that thou *art* not sick? this *is* nothing *else* but sorrow of heart.—NEH., ch. 2.

1765. —— **Sins upon the.** *Israel.* [9] The shew of their countenance doth witness against them ; and they declare their sin as Sodom, they hide *it* not. Woe unto their soul! for they have rewarded evil unto themselves.—ISA., ch. 3.

1766. —— **A sullen.** *Laban's.* [1] He heard the words of Laban's..sons, saying, Jacob hath taken away all that *was* our father's.. [2] And Jacob beheld the countenance of Laban, and, behold, it *was* not toward him as before.—GEN., ch. 31.

1767. —— **A shining.** *Moses'.* [29] When Moses came down from mount Sinai with the two tables of testimony..wist not that the skin of his face shone.. [30] And when Aaron and all..Israel saw Moses, behold, the skin of his face shone ; and they were afraid to come nigh him.—Ex., ch. 34.

1768. —— **A terrifying.** *Angel.* [Manoah] [6] then..came and told her husband, saying, A man of God came unto me, and his countenance *was* like the countenance of an angel of God, very terrible.—JUDGES, ch. 13.

Also see:

Expressive. Harlot..kissed him..impudent face 115
Unseen. Let him [Absalom] not see my face 44

1769. COURAGE in Old Age. *Caleb.* [10] Lo, I *am* this day fourscore and five years old..[12]..give me this mountain..for thou heardest in that day how the Anakim *were* there, and *that* the cities *were* great *and* fenced : if so be the Lord *will be* with me, then I shall be able to drive them out.—JOSH., ch. 14.

1770. —— **Absence of.** *Israelites.* [11] Three thousand men of Judah went to the top of the rock Etam, and said to Samson, Knowest thou not that the Philistines *are* rulers over us?.. [12]..We are come down to bind thee, that we may deliver thee into the hand of the Philistines. And Samson said..Swear..that ye will not fall upon me yourselves.—JUDGES, ch. 15. [Samson alone slew one thousand Philistines.]

1771. —— **Daring.** *Paul.* [The Ephesian mob rushed his companions into the theatre.] [30] When Paul would have entered in unto the people, the disciples suffered him not.—ACTS, ch. 19.

1772. —— **Faith inspires.** *David.* [37] David said..The Lord that delivered me out of the paw of the lion, and..of the bear, he will deliver me out of the hand of this Philistine. And Saul said unto David, Go, and the Lord be with thee. [45] Then said David to the Philistine, Thou comest to me with a sword, and with a spear, and with a shield : but I come to thee in the name of the Lord of hosts, the God of the armies of Israel, whom thou hast defied.—1 SAM., ch. 17.

1773. —— **Ground for.** *Hezekiah.* [7] Be strong and courageous, be not afraid nor dismayed for the king of Assyria, nor for all the multitude that *is* with him : for *there be* more with us than with him. [8] With him *is* an arm of flesh ; but with us *is* the Lord our God to help us, and to fight our battles. And the people rested themselves upon the words of Hezekiah.—2 CHRON., ch. 32.

1774. —— **God honouring.** *Caleb.* [30] Caleb stilled the people before Moses, and said, Let us go up at once, and possess it ; for we are well able to overcome it. [31] But the men that went up with him said, We be not able to go up against the people ; for they *are* stronger than we.— NUM., ch. 13.

1775. —— **Invincible, Pious.** *Joshua.* [5] There shall not any man be able to stand before thee all the days of thy life : as I was with Moses, *so* I will be with thee : I will not fail thee, nor forsake thee. [7] Only be thou strong and very courageous, that thou mayest observe to do according to all the law..turn not from it to the right hand or *to* the left, that thou mayest prosper withersoever thou goest.—JOSHUA, ch. 1.

1776. —— **Loss of.** *Israelites.* [7] When the men of Israel..on the other side Jordan, saw that the men of Israel fled, and that Saul and his sons were dead, they forsook the cities, and fled ; and the Philistines came and dwelt in them.— 1 SAM., ch. 31.

1777. —— **Moral.** *Jesus went before.* [32] They were..going up to Jerusalem ; and Jesus went before them : and they were amazed ; and as they followed, they were afraid. And he took again the twelve, and began to tell them.. [34]..they shall mock him, and shall scourge him, and shall spit upon him, and shall kill him.— MARK, ch. 10.

1778. —— —— *Paul.* [12] Both we, and they ..besought him not to go up to Jerusalem. [13] Then Paul answered, What mean ye to weep and to break mine heart? for I am ready not to be bound only, but also to die at Jerusalem for the name of the Lord Jesus.—ACTS, ch. 21.

1779. —— **Necessary.** *Joshua.* [3] Every place that the sole of your foot shall tread upon, that have I given unto you, as I said unto Moses.. [9]..Be strong and of a good courage ; be not afraid, neither be thou dismayed : for the Lord thy God *is* with thee whithersoever thou goest. —JOSH., ch. 1.

1780. —— **Patriotic.** *Nehemiah.* [14] I rose up, and said unto the nobles..rulers, and..people, Be not ye afraid of them : remember the Lord, *which is* great and terrible, and fight for your brethren, your sons, and your daughters, your wives, and your houses.—NEH., ch. 4.

1781. —— **to Rebuke.** *Paul.* [14] When I saw that they walked not uprightly..I said unto Peter before *them* all, If thou, being a Jew, livest after the manner of Gentiles, and not as do the Jews, why compellest thou the Gentiles to live as do the Jews?—GAL., ch. 2.

1782. —— **A Reformer's.** *Nehemiah.* [10] Shemaiah..said, Let us meet together..within the temple, and let us shut the doors..in the night will they come to slay thee. [11] And I said, Should such a man as I flee? and who *is there*, that, *being* as I *am*, would go into the temple to save his life? I will not go in.—NEH., ch. 6.

1783. —— **stimulated.** *Five Amorite Kings.* [24] Joshua called for all the men of Israel, and said unto the captains..Come near, put your feet upon the necks of these kings.. [25] And Joshua said..Fear not, nor be dismayed, be strong and of good courage : for thus shall the Lord do to all your enemies.—JOSH., ch. 10.

1784. —— **A Soldier's.** *Jonathan.* [6] Come, and let us go over unto the garrison of these uncircumcised : it may be that the Lord will work for us : for *there is* no restraint to the Lord to save by many or by few. [13] And Jonathan climbed up upon his hands and upon his feet, and his armourbearer after him : and they fell before Jonathan ; and his armourbearer slew after him. —1 SAM., ch. 14.

1785. —— **in Worship.** *Daniel.* [10] When Daniel knew that the writing was signed..his windows being open in his chamber toward Jerusalem, he kneeled upon his knees three times a day, and prayed..as he did aforetime. [11] Then these men assembled, and found Daniel praying.—DAN., ch. 6.

See other illustrations under :

BOLDNESS.

Angels urge. Brought them forth..speak in the	878
Apostolic. Whom ye put in prison are..in the	879
Believers. Three worthies..O, N. we are not	880
Brazen. Ahab said to Elijah, Art thou..troubleth	881
Innocence. With whom..be found, let him die	882
Influence. Saw the boldness of P. and J..took	883
Right. When thou seest..more than thou..not	884
Sinners. Jeroboam..served Baal..reared an altar	885
Shame. Absalom..tent upon the roof..concubines	886
Prayer. High priest touched..come boldly..throne	887
Venturesome. Peter, walked on the water to go to	888

HEROISM.

Christian. Bonds..abide me..none of these things	3959
Needless. Three mighty men brake through..well	3961
Numbers. Shamgar slew 600 with an ox-goad	3962
Patriotic. Jael..smote the nail into his..temples	3957
" Woman cast a stone upon Abimelech	3958

MANHOOD.

Aroused. Tell..I will do..I may not do   5199
Lost. Letters were sent..perish all Jews..drink   5200
Responsibility. He is of age..speak for himself   5201
Wanting. O King..I am thine, and all that I have   5202

MIGHTY MEN.

Adino. Mighty men whom David·had..chief   5332
Abishai. Chief among the three..against 300..slew 5336
Benaiah. Slew the lion-like men of Moab   5337
Eliezer. Smote the Philistines..hand clave to his 5333
Shammah. Stood in the midst..slew the Philistines 5334
Three. Brake through the host of the Philistines 5335

PERSEVERANCE.

Confident. Neither death nor life..separate me   6097
Exhortation. Barnabas exhorted..with purpose   6098
Encouragement. Can a woman forget her..child   6099
    "   Mountains shall depart..but my   6100
Help to. When..my foot slippeth..thy mercy held 6101
Prayer. This widow troubleth me, I will avenge   6102
Success by. I have fought a good fight..crown   6103
Test. If ye continue in my word, then..disciples 6104

Benaiah. Plucked the spear out of the Egyptian's 1543
Captains. [See Abner, Abishai, and Joab—1 and 2 Sam.]
Faith. He took his staff..five smooth stones   9443
Lord's. They cried, The sword of the L. and Gideon 8532
Ominous. David saw the angel, having a drawn   8534
    "   Joshua was by Jericho..stood a man   1021
Outfit. Take the sword of the S.,which is the word 8539
Useless. Peter..smote the high priest's servant   918

— COURTESY. —

See illustrations under :

HOSPITALITY.

Christian. Paul entered..a certain man's house   4098
Dangerous. Come home with me and eat..I may   4099
Forbidden. Diotrephes..forbiddeth them that   4100
Grateful. Mephibosheth shall eat at the king's   4101
Increase by. How shall I..before 100 men?   4102
Joyful. Zaccheus..haste..received him joyfully   4103
Odious. Baser sort..assaulted the house of Jason 4104
Preservation. Tarry all night, and wash your feet 4105
of Poor. Widow did according to the saying of E. 4106
Pagan. Barbarous people..received us every one   4107
Refused. Samaritans did not receive him   4108
Repaid. Shunammite..make a little chamber   4109
Reward. Abraham ran to meet them   4110
Treacherous. Pharisee besought him to dine with 4111
Unjust. Rich man..took the poor man's lamb   4112
Urgent. Lot pressed them greatly..his house   4113
    "   Urged him therefore, he lodged there again 4114
    "   They constrained him..sat at meat   4115
Woman's. Lydia..come into my house..constrained 4116
Willing. Ungirded his camels..set meat before him 4117
Wanting. Simon, thou gavest me no water to wash 4118

POLITENESS.

Cultivated. May we know what this new doctrine 6232
Inculcated. Sit down in the lowest room   6233
Tender. Is your father well, the old man of whom 6234
Treacherous. Joab took Amasa..to kiss him   6235

— COURTSHIP. —

Ancient. Loved the damsel..spoke kindly—Gen. 34 : 3
See MARRIAGE and WIFE.

1786. COVETOUSNESS abhorred. *Boast.*
[2] The wicked in *his* pride doth persecute the
poor.. [3] ..the wicked boasteth of his heart's desire, and blesseth the covetous, *whom* the Lord
abhorreth.—Ps. 10.

1787. —— alarmed. *Ephesians.* [24] Demetrius, a silversmith, which made silver shrines

for Diana, brought no small gain unto the craftsmen ; [25] Whom he called together..and said,
Sirs, ye know that by this craft we have our
wealth. [26] Moreover..throughout all Asia, this
Paul hath persuaded and turned away much
people. [29] And the whole city was filled with
confusion.—Acts, ch. 19.

1788. —— An Apostle's. *Judas.* [4] He went
his way, and communed with the chief priests
and captains, how he might betray him unto
them. [5] And they were glad, and covenanted
to give him money.—Luke, ch. 22.

1789. —— aroused. *Philippi.* [The evil
spirit being cast out of the soothsaying damsel,]
[19] Her masters saw that the hope of their gains
was gone, they caught Paul and Silas, and drew
them into the marketplace unto the rulers.—
Acts, ch. 16.

1790. —— Absence of. *Abram.* [22] Abram
said to the king of Sodom, I have lifted up
mine hand unto the Lord..the possessor of
heaven and earth, [23] That I will not *take* from
a thread even to a shoelatchet, and that I will
not take any thing that *is* thine, lest thou
shouldest say, I have made Abram rich.—Gen.,
ch. 14.

1791. —— in the Church. *Jews.* [10] Who is
there even among you that would shut the doors
for naught? neither do ye kindle *fire* on mine
altar for naught. I have no pleasure in you,
saith the Lord of hosts, neither will I accept an
offering at your hand.—Mal., ch. 1.

1792. —— Cruelty of. *Felix.* [26] Hoped also
that money should have been given him of Paul,
that he might loose him : wherefore he sent for
him the oftener, and communed with him.—
Acts, ch. 24.

1793. —— Caution against. *Heirs.* [13] Master, speak to my brother, that he divide the inheritance with me... [15] And he said..unto them,
Take heed, and beware of covetousness : for a
man's life consisteth not in the abundance of
the things which he possesseth.—Luke, ch. 12.

1794. —— Disobedience in. *Achan.* [21] I
saw among the spoils a goodly Babylonish garment, and two hundred shekels of silver, and a
wedge of gold of fifty shekels weight, then I
coveted them, and took them ; and, behold, they
are hid in the earth in..my tent.—Josh., ch. 7.
[Was stoned and burned.]

1795. —— forbidden. *Decalogue.* [17] Thou
shalt not covet thy neighbour's house, thou
shalt not covet thy neighbour's wife, nor his
manservant, nor his maidservant, nor his ox,
nor his ass, nor any thing that *is* thy neighbour's.—Ex., ch. 20.

1796. —— Fraud from. *Gehazi.* [20] Gehazi, the
servant of Elisha..said, Behold, my master hath
spared Naaman..in not receiving..that which
he brought : but..I will run after him, and take
somewhat of him. [22] ..My master hath sent me,
saying..there be come to me..two young men
of the sons of the prophets : give them, I pray
thee, a talent of silver, and two changes of garments.—2 Kings, ch. 5.

1797. —— Folly of. *Dives.* [19] I will say to my
soul, Soul, thou hast much goods laid up for
many years ; take thine ease, eat, drink, *and*
be merry. [20] But God said.. *Thou* fool, this night

thy soul shall be required of thee : then whose shall those things be.. ? [21] So *is* he that layeth up treasure for himself, and is not rich toward God.—LUKE, ch. 12.

1798. —— **begets Falsehood.** *Ananias.* [1] Ananias, with Sapphira his wife, sold a possession, [2] And kept back *part* of the price, his wife also being privy *to it*, and brought a certain part, and laid *it* at the apostles' feet.—ACTS, ch. 5.

1799. —— **Freedom from.** *Paul.* [33] I have coveted no man's silver, or gold, or apparel. [34] Yea, ye yourselves know, that these hands have ministered unto my necessities, and to them that were with me.—ACTS, ch. 20.

1800. —— **Inconsiderate.** *Lot.* [9] If *thou wilt take* the left hand, then I will go to the right ; or if *thou depart* to the right hand, then I will go to the left. [10] And Lot..beheld all the plain of Jordan, that it *was* well watered every where.. *even* as the garden of the Lord, like the land of Egypt.. [11] Then Lot chose him all the plain of Jordan.—GEN., ch. 13. [He lost all he had.]

1801. —— **Oppressive.** *Jews.* [6] I was very angry when I heard their cry.. [7]..and I rebuked the nobles, and the rulers, and said..Ye exact usury every one of his brother. And I set a great assembly against them. [8] And I said..We, after our ability, have redeemed our brethren the Jews, which were sold unto the heathen, and will ye even sell your brethren ?—NEH., ch. 5.

1802. —— **Overcome by.** *Saul.* [9] Saul and the people spared Agag, and the best of the sheep..oxen..fatlings..lambs, and all *that was* good, and would not utterly destroy them : but every thing *that was* vile and refuse, that they destroyed utterly.—1 SAM., ch. 15.

1803. —— **Overreaching.** *L a b a n .* [Jacob said,] [7] Your father hath deceived me, and changed my wages ten times ; but God suffered him not to hurt me.—GEN., ch. 31.

1804. —— **stigmatized.** *P a u l .* [11] I have written unto you not to keep company, if any man that is called a brother be a fornicator, or covetous, or an idolater, or a railer, or a drunkard, or an extortioner ; with such a one no not to eat.—1 COR., ch. 5.

1805. —— **Shameless.** *Jews.* [10] Every one from the least even unto the greatest is given to covetousness, from the prophet even unto the priest every one dealeth falsely. [12] Were they ashamed when they had committed abomination ? nay, they were not at all ashamed, neither could they blush.—JER., ch. 8.

1806. —— **Unhappiness from.** *Ahab.* [1] Naboth..had a vineyard, which *was* in Jezreel, hard by the palace of Ahab.. [3] And Naboth said to Ahab, The Lord forbid it me, that I should give the inheritance of my fathers unto thee. [4] And Ahab came into his house heavy and displeased.—1 KINGS, ch. 21.

See other illustrations under :

1807. COVENANT, A broken. *A t S i n a i .* [15] Moses..went down from the mount, and the two tables of the testimony *were* in his hand.. [19] And..as soon as..he saw the calf, and the dancing..Moses' anger waxed hot, and he cast the tables out of his hands, and brake them.—Ex., ch. 32.

1808. —— **in Blood.** *At Sinai.* [7] He took the book of the covenant, and read in the audience of the people : and they said, All that the Lord hath said will we do, and be obedient. [8] And Moses took the blood, and sprinkled *it* on the people, and said, Behold the blood of the covenant, which the Lord hath made with you.—Ex., ch. 24.

1809. —— **An evil.** *Judas.* [14] Judas Iscariot went unto the chief priests, [15] And said..What will ye give me, and I will deliver him unto you ? And they covenanted with him for thirty pieces of silver.—MAT., ch. 26.

1810. —— **of Friendship.** *David and Jonathan.* [17] Jonathan caused David to swear again, because he loved him : for he loved him as he loved his own soul. [42] And Jonathan said..Go in peace, forasmuch as we have sworn..The Lord be between me and thee, and between my seed and thy seed for ever.—1 SAM., ch. 20.

1811. —— **The People's.** *Josiah.* [2] Josiah read in their ears all the words of the book.. which was found in the house of the Lord. [3] And the king stood..made a covenant before the Lord, to walk after the Lord, and to keep his commandments..with all *their* heart and all *their* soul, to perform the words..that were written in this book. And all the people stood to the covenant.—2 KINGS, ch. 23.

1812. —— **perpetuated, The Lord's.** *Abram.* [1] When Abram was ninety years old and nine, the Lord appeared..and said..walk before me, and be thou perfect. [7] And I will establish my covenant between me and thee and thy seed after thee in their generations, for an everlasting covenant, to be a God unto thee and to thy seed after thee.—GEN., ch. 17.

1813. —— **Ratified.** *Abram.* [17] When the sun went down, and it was dark, behold a smoking furnace, and a burning lamp..passed between those pieces. [18] In the same day the Lord made a covenant with Abram, saying, Unto thy seed have I given this land.—GEN., ch. 15.

1814. —— **of Reformation.** *Jehoiada* [17] Made a covenant between the Lord and the king and the people, that they should be the Lord's people ; between the king also and the people. [18] And all the people of the land went into the house of Baal, and brake it down.—2 KINGS, ch. 11.

1815. —— **renewed.** *The People.* [28] The people..their wives, their sons, and their daughters, every one having knowledge, and having understanding ; [29] They clave to their brethren, their nobles, and entered into a curse, and into an oath, to walk in God's law.—NEH., ch. 10.

1816. —— **and Self-denial.** *Abram.* [1] Get thee out of thy country..unto a land that I will shew thee : [2] And I will make of thee a great nation, and I will bless thee.. [3] and in thee shall all families of the earth be blessed.—GEN., ch. 12.

1817. —— **Sign of.** *Bow.* [12] This *is* the token of the covenant which I make between me and you, and every living creature..for perpetual generations : [13] I do set my bow in the cloud, and it shall be for a token of a covenant between me and the earth.—GEN., ch. 9.

See other illustrations under :

AGREEMENT.
Fraudulent. As if they had been ambassadors   266
Ignored. Thou has made them equal unto us   267
Refused. Edom said, Thou shalt not pass   268

OATH.
Covenant. Ezra made chief priests..sware   5751
Casuistry. Swear by the temple it is nothing..by   1063
Conspirators. Bound ourselves with..curse..slain   5752
Obedience. Nobles entered..oath, to walk in God's 9248
Strange. Peter began to curse and swear   4631
Wicked. Herod..whatsoever thou shalt ask..give 5754

PROMISE.
Great. I send the promise of my Father upon you 6639
Royal. What is thy petition, queen Esther?..be   6640
   "   Whatsoever thou shalt ask..give it thee   6641
Regretted. King was..sorry ; yet for his oath's sake 6642

PROMISES.
Broken. I will let the people go..hardened   6643
   "   I will let you go..thunders were ceased   6644
   "   In haste..I have sinned..hardened   6645
False. Son go work..I will not..went   6646

VOW.
Despondency. I will not speak any more in his   9246
Inconsistent. Cursed be the man that eateth any   9247
Obedience. People entered into a curse, and into   9248
Observance. Better..shouldest not vow than..not 9249
Rash. Jephthah..whatsoever cometh..burnt   9250
Sailors. Took up Jonah and cast him..made vows 9251
Trouble. Hannah vowed..I will give him..L.   9252
   "   Jephthah came..his daughter came   9253
Teetotaller. Neither shall he drink any liquor of   9254

Benefit. G. heard their groaning and remembered 110
Better. He is the Mediator of a better c.—Heb. 8 : 6
Engraved. L. gave me the tables of the c.—Deut. 9 : 9
Perpetual. Let us join ourselves to the L. in—Jer. 50 : 5
Sinners. Your covenant with death—Isa. 28 : 18

1818. COWARDICE, Blemished by. *Peter.* [54] Took they him..into the high priest's house. And Peter followed afar off. [55] And when they had kindled a fire in the midst of the hall..Peter sat down among them.—LUKE, ch. 22.

1819. —— **Cruel.** *Herod.* [Herodias' daughter] [25] came in..unto the king..saying..give me..the head of John the Baptist. [26] And the king was exceeding sorry ; *yet* for his oath's sake, and for their sakes which sat with him, he would not reject her.—MARK, ch. 6.

1820. —— **Exemption by.** *In War.* [8] What man *is there that is* fearful and fainthearted? let him go and return unto his house, lest his brethren's heart faint as well as his heart.—DEUT., ch. 20.

1821. —— **of Guilt.** *Adam.* [8] They heard the voice of the Lord God walking in the garden in the cool of the day : and Adam and his wife

hid themselves..amongst the trees of the garden.
—GEN., ch. 3.

1822. —— **A Sinner's.** *Jeroboam.* [9] The king of Israel went, and the king of Judah, and the king of Edom : seven days' journey : and there was no water.. [10] And the king of Israel said, Alas ! that the Lord hath called these three kings together, to deliver them into the hand of Moab ! —2 KINGS, ch. 3.

1823. —— **A surprising.** *Elijah.* [2] Jezebel sent..saying, So let the gods do to *me*, and more also, if I make not thy life as the life of one of them by to morrow about this time. [3] And when he saw *that*, he arose, and went for his life.— 1 KINGS, ch. 19.

See other illustrations under :

INTIMIDATION.
Attempted. It is reported..thou thinkest to rebel 4629
Boastful. Let not Hezekiah deceive you..not be   4630
Fruit of. Peter denied it again..curse and swear   4631
Failure of. Should such a man as I flee !   4632
Moved by. Entice thy husband..lest we burn thee 4633
Unsuccessful. Hearken not unto him, nor consent 4634
Without. Opened the prison..go stand..and speak 4635
Woman's. So let the gods do..make thy life like   4636
Weakness. The garrison and the spoilers..trembled 4637

TIMIDITY.
Disciples. Nicodemus..came to Jesus by night   8816
   "   Joseph being a disciple, but secretly   8817
Friends. Good man, but no man spake openly   8818
Needless. Because of the money in our sacks   8819
Restrained. Were gathered..Peter knocked at the 8820

Military. Have feared the sword, I will bring the S. 8536
See FEAR.

1824. CREDENTIALS in Deeds. *Jesus.* [20] John Baptist hath sent us..Art thou he that should come ? or look we for another?.. [22] Then Jesus answering said Go your way, and tell John what things ye have seen and heard ; how that the blind see, the lame walk, the lepers are cleansed, the deaf hear, the dead are raised, to the poor the gospel is preached.—LUKE, ch. 7.

1825. —— **The highest.** *Fruit.* [7] Moses laid up the rods before the Lord in the tabernacle.. [8] ..on the morrow..behold, the rod of Aaron.. was budded, and brought forth buds, and bloomed blossoms, and yielded almonds.— NUM., ch. 17.

See other illustrations under :

AUTHORITY.
Brother's. My brother..commanded me to be   584
Compared. Moses commanded..what sayest thou   585
False. I am a prophet..he lied   586
Obedience. All..we will do..will go   587
Power. I say unto one, Go, and he goeth   588
Questioned. By what authority doest thou these   589
Recognized. Winds and water..obey him   591
Supreme. Drove them all out of the temple   590

Dominion. Fear of you..upon every beast of the 2490

1826. CREDITORS, Charity of. *Release.* [1] At the end of *every* seven years.. [2] ..Every creditor that lendeth *aught* unto his neighbour shall release *it* ; he shall not exact *it*..because it is called the Lord's release.—DEUT., ch. 15.

See other illustrations under :

BORROWING.
Distress. Have mortgaged our lands..buy corn   914
Forbidden. Owe no man anything, but to love   916

Ruin. Borrowed..spoiled the Egyptians 915
Servant. Borrower is servant of the lender 912
Trouble. Axe head fell into the water..borrowed 913

DEBTS.

Compromised. Take the bill..quickly, and write 2006
Forgiven. Every seven years..every creditor shall 2007
Miracle. Go sell the oil, and pay the debt 2009
Severity. Fellow servants took him by the throat 2008

DEBTORS.

Army. Every one that was in debt..gathered 2010
Destructive. Same servant [debtor] took him by 2011
Gratitude. To whom little is forgiven..loveth 2012
Insolvent. Have mortgaged our lands, vineyards 2013
Protected. When thou dost lend..not go into his 2014

Diverse. I forgave thee all..shouldest not thou 3351
Law. If a man borrow..make it good 7275

1827. CREDULITY of Unbelievers. *The Sad-ducee.* [Men were asking, Who is Jesus?] [16] When Herod heard *thereof*, he said, It is John, whom I beheaded : he is risen from the dead.—MARK, ch. 6.

See other illustrations under :

CONFIDENCE.

Believers. Though I walk through the valley 1518
Blind. Know I that the L..I have a priest 1519
Caution. They are smitten down..as at the first 1520
Disappointed. Ark came..I. shouted..ark taken 1521
False. King [of Ai] wist not..ambush 1522
Future. Doth deliver..trust he will deliver 1523
Intelligent. I know whom I have believed 1524
Joyful. How great is thy goodness..trust thee 1525
Over. Is thy servant a dog..do this? [Hazael] 1526
Peril. Have the sentence of death..we trust 1527
Piety begets. L. was with Joseph..into his hand 1528
Strong. L. delight in us..fear them not 1529
Self. Peter said..I will lay down my life 1530
Triumphant. Although the fig tree shall not b. 1531
Unwarranted. Let two or three thousand go 1532
Unfortunate. Confidence..like a broken tooth and 1533
Undermining. Neither let Hez. make you trust..L. 1534
Warranted. L. is my rock, fortress, deliverer 1535

PRESUMPTION.

Avoided. Better..he said, Come up hither ; than 6534
Daring. Egyptians pursued..midst of the sea 6535
Failure. Presumed to go..Amalekites smote them 6536
Future. Know not what shall be on the morrow 6537
Impatience. Because thou comest not..I offered 6538
Pride. Uzziah..burnt incense upon the altar 6539
Penalty. Come unto the king..not called..death 6540
Religious. Prophet that shall speak..not com'd 6541
Rebuked. Uzziah..censer in his hand..leprosy 6542
Sin. Trodden under foot the Son of God 6543
Success. Soul that doeth..presumptuously..cut off 6544
" Joshua made as if beaten..drawn away 6545
Temptation. On a pinnacle..cast thyself down 6546
Unholy. 250 princes..ye take too much upon you 6547

1828. CREMATION, Jewish. *Of Saul.* [12] All the valiant men..went all night, and took the body of Saul and the bodies of his sons from the wall of Beth-shan, and came to Jabesh, and burnt them there.—1 SAM., ch. 31.

1829. CRIME, Abetting. *To Ahimelech.* [13] Saul said..Why have ye conspired against me, thou and the son of Jesse, in that thou hast given him bread, and a sword, and hast inquired of God for him, that he should rise against me.— 1 SAM., ch. 22. [He slew him.]

1830. —— A Drunkard's. *Herod.* [21] Herod on his birthday made a supper to his lords.. [22] And

when..Herodias..danced, and pleased Herod and them that sat with him, [23]..he sware unto her, Whatsoever thou shalt ask of me, I will give *it* thee, unto the half of my kingdom. [24]..And she said, The head of John the Baptist. —MARK, ch. 6.

1831. —— Intemperance favors. *David.* [13] When David had called him, he did eat and drink before him ; and he made him drunk : and at even he went out to lie on his bed with the servants of his lord, but went not down to his house.—2 SAM., ch. 11. [Where David desired him to go.]

1832. —— and Wine. *Amnon.* [28] When Amnon's heart is merry with wine, and when I say..Smite Amnon ; then kill him, fear not..be courageous, and be valiant. [29] And the servants of Absalom did.—2 SAM., ch. 13.

1833. CRIMINAL, A shameful. *Unjust Steward.* [3] What shall I do ? for my lord taketh away from me the stewardship : I cannot dig ; to beg I am ashamed. [4] I am resolved what to do, that, when I am put out of the stewardship, they may receive me into their houses.—LUKE, ch. 16. [He fraudulently reduced the bills of debtors.]

1834. CRIMINALS, No Refuge for. *Sanctuary.* [28] Joab had turned after Adonijah..And Joab fled unto the tabernacle..and caught hold on the horns of the altar. [29]..Then Solomon sent Benaiah..saying, Go, fall upon him.—1 KINGS, ch. 2.

1835. —— Sanctuary for. *Adonijah.* [Having conspired to obtain the throne of his father, King David,] [50] Adonijah feared because of Solomon, and arose, and went. and caught hold on the horns of the altar.—1 KINGS, ch. 1.

See other illustrations under :

ARSON.

Dwellings. Nebuzaradan burned..every great 4384
Synagogues. Burned up all the synagogues in the 4129
Suicide. Zimri hath conspired..burned..house 6953
Temple. Nebuzaradan captain..burned the house 3235

BRIBERY.

Concealment. Gave large money unto the soldiers 930
Desecration. Ahaz took out of the house of the L. 931
Friendship. Entice him..may prevail against 932
Horrible. Judas said, What will you give me 933
Official. Felix hoped..money..of Paul 934
" Princes..loveth gifts..followeth after 935
" Samuel's sons..took bribes and perverted 100
Scorned. Shaketh his hand from holding of bribes 4051

CONSPIRACY.

Atrocious. Abimelech..slew his brethren..upon 1601
Brother's. When Amnon's heart is merry..kill him 1602
Court. Set up false witnesses [against Stephen] 1603
Desperate. Jews banded..under a curse..killed 1604
Defeated. How they might entangle him in his 1605
Escape. Saul sent messengers unto David's house 1606
Envy. When they saw Joseph..conspired against 1607
Ingrates. Absalom sent spies throughout..I. 1608
Infamous. I will give thee the vineyard of Naboth 1609
Political. Sought to find occasion against Daniel 1610
" Joash's servants..made a conspiracy 1611
Successful. Delilah..sent for the lords of the 1612
Against Truth. Ananias and S...kept back a part 1613
Worst. Consulted..take J. by subtilty and kill 1614

FRAUD.

Appearances. Gibeonites..took old sacks..old 3468
Commercial. Take thy bill..quickly..write fifty 3409

Demagogue. O that I were a judge..do justice   2171
Pious. Sons of the prophets give..silver [Gehazi]   3410
Religious. His enemy..sowed tares..wheat   3411
Spiritual. Simon offered money..Holy Ghost   3412
Traitor's. Whomsoever I shall kiss..is he   3413
Wages. Hire of the labourers kept..crieth   3414

GUILT.

Accumulated. Upon you may come all the   3766
Cowardice. Adam and his wife hid themselves   3767
Degrees. Two debtors; one owed 500 pence   3768
Panic. L. looked..through the cloud..troubled   3769

HANGING.

Ancient. Chief baker..him he hanged   7061
Accidental. Absalom's head caught hold of the   9946
Conspirators. Two chamberlains..hanged—Esth. 2 : 23
Deserved. They hanged Haman on the gallows   3787
Mortification. Ahithophel..hanged himself   8457
Remorse. Judas went out and hanged himself   5553
Retaliation. Seven sons of Saul they hanged   5724
Unjust. They hanged Haman's ten sons   3787

MURDER.

Attempted. Saul sought to smite David..slipped   5615
    " Led him to the brow of the hill..cast   5616
    " Jews watched the gates..to kill Saul   5617
    " Went about to kill Paul..Jerusalem   5618
Atrocious. Ish-bosheth lay on a bed at noon   5619
Avenged. Brought the head of Ish-bosheth unto   5620
Children. [Ahab's] Slew 70 persons..their heads   5621
Conspirators. When I say, Smite Amnon ; then   5622
Desire. Herodias would have killed John..could   5623
Escape from. Michal let David down through a   5624
Excuse. By our law he ought to die..S. of G.   5625
Fratricidal. Cain rose up against Abel   5626
Gain. Let us kill him..seize on his inheritance   5627
for Healing. Therefore..sought to slay him   5628
Intended. Saul thought to make David fall by P.   5629
of Jesus. Herod slew all the children   5630
Proposed. Esau hated Jacob..then will I slay   5632
Responsibility. The Just One..ye have been the   5633
Indirect. Letter to Joab..Set Uriah in..the hottest 5631
Suffocation. Hazael took a thick cloth..on his   5634
Stoning. Cast Stephen out of the city and stoned   5635

MURDERER.

Chosen. Away with this man..release Barabbas   5636
Children of. Nor children put to death for the   5637
Unknown. [Law respecting, Deut. 21 · 1-8]

ROBBERY.

Insolent. [Danites] Lay thy hand upon thy mouth 7457
Sacrilegious Shishak took away the treasures   7459
Spiritual. Will a man rob God..tithes and   7458

SUICIDE.

Imitated. Armourbearer..likewise fell upon his   8456
Mortification. Ahithophel..counsel was not   8457
Prevented. Keeper of the prison would have   8458
Soldiers. Saul took a sword, and fell upon it   8459
Traitor's. Judas went and hanged himself   8460

THEFT.

Abduction. When I rose in the morning..not my   8767
Confessed. Micah said the 1100 shekels..I took it   8768
Fear. Take thy bill..quickly write fifty   8769
Famished. Men do not despise a thief..hungry   8770
Improbable. Disciples came..stole him..we slept   8771
Justifiable Josheba took Joash..they hid him   8772
Kidnappers. Man be found stealing..brethren   8773

THIEF.

Killing. No blood be shed for him..sun be risen   8774
Office. Not that Judas cared for the poor..thief   8775

THIEVES.

Injuries. Thieves..stripped him and wounded   8776
Religious. Overthrew the tables..den of thieves   8777

Arson. We will burn thy house upon thee   503
Burglar. Found breaking up..sun be risen..blood   973
Compounded. Achan..stolen..dissembled   998
    " Peter denied [falsehood]..oath   810
Confiscation. House of Haman to the Jews   1537
    " Whosoever would not come within   1538
Fratricide. Abimelech slew his brethren, 70   3407
    " When I say, Smite Amnon ; then kill   5619
Misery. Our fathers cast out their children..not   897
Supposed. Jeremiah..thou fallest away to the C.   79
Wanton. They break down the carved work with   4129

1836. CRIPPLE, a royal. *Mephibosheth.*
[4] Jonathan, Saul s son, had a son *that was* lame
of *his* feet. He was five years old when the tidings came of Saul and Jonathan out of Jezreel,
and his nurse took him up..and..as she made
haste to flee..he fell, and became lame,—2 Sam.,
ch. 4.

See other illustrations under :

LAMENESS.

Disqualification. Not offer the bread of his God   4878
    " Lame..thou shalt not—Deut. 15 : 21
Healed. Never had walked..leaped and walked   4879
    " His feet and ankle bones received strength 4880
Want with. Laid daily at the gate..ask alms   4882

Benevolence. Feet was I to the lame [Job]   4827
Disqualifies. Lame..shalt not sacrifice it—Deut. 15 : 21
Sacrificed. Ye offer the lame for sacrifice   5848
Welcomed. Feast..call the poor..lame..blind   3756

1837. CRITICISM, Contemptuous. *Michal.*
[Having danced before the incoming of the ark
of God,] [20] David returned to bless his household. And Michal..came out..said, How glorious was the king of Israel to day, who uncovered
himself..in the eyes of the handmaids..as one
of the vain fellows shamelessly uncovereth himself.—2 Sam., ch. 6.

1838. —— Disparaging. *Sanballat* [2] Said,
What do these feeble Jews? will they fortify
themselves? will they sacrifice? will they make
an end in a day? will they revive the stones out
of the heaps of the rubbish which are burned?
[3] Now Tobiah the Ammonite *was* by him, and
he said, Even that which they build, if a fox go
up, he shall even break down their stone wall.
—Neh., ch. 4.

1839. —— of Enemies. *Nehemiah.* [9] It *is* not
good that ye do : ought ye not to walk in the
fear of our God because of the reproach of the
heathen our enemies? [10] I likewise, *and* my
brethren, and my servants, might exact of them
money and corn : I pray you, let us leave off this
usury.—Neh., ch. 5.

See other illustrations under :

ACCUSATION.

Astounding. [Concubine] No such deed done   2729
Bigotry. Withered hand..they watched..might   780
Confessed. Is not the hand of Joab..in this   2732
Evasion. Wherefore dealt ye so ill as to tell   2727
Fanaticism. His friends..said, He is beside   3036
Hypocritical. Why was not this sold..given   3088
Idleness. Make brick..ye are idle, ye are idle   4270
Malicious. Behold a gluttonous man, a wine   3089
    " Feigning themselves just men   1111
Reaction. Cast them [accusers] into the den of   439
Self. For my sake this great tempest [Jonah]   7205
Sinners. The woman..she gave me of the tree   4221

FAULTLESS.

Condemned. Pilate said..I find no fault in him   3085
Official. Sought occasion against Daniel..found   3086
   See **BLAME** and references.

1840. CROSS for Crucifixion, The. *Believers'.*
[24] They that are Christ's have crucified the flesh
with affections and lusts.—GAL., ch. 5.

1841. —— A compulsory. *Calvary.* [32] As they
came out, they found a man of Cyrene, Simon
by name : him they compelled to bear his cross.
—MAT., ch. 27.

1842. —— Death on the. *Jesus.* [17] He bearing his cross went forth into a place called *the
place* of a skull.. [18] Where they crucified him,
and two others with him, on either side one,
and Jesus in the midst.—JOHN, ch. 19.

1843. —— Glorying in the. *Paul.* [14] God
forbid that I should glory, save in the cross of
our Lord Jesus Christ, by whom the world is
crucified unto me, and I unto the world.—GAL.,
ch. 6.

1844. —— A heavy. *Rich Ruler.* [21] Jesus
beholding him loved him, and said..One thing
thou lackest : go thy way, sell whatsoever thou
hast, and give to the poor, and thou shalt have
treasure in heaven : and come, take up the
cross, and follow me. [22] And he was sad at that
saying, and went away grieved : for he had
great possessions.—MARK, ch. 10.

1845. —— the indispensable. *Disciple's.* [26] If
any *man* come to me, and hate not his father,
and mother, and wife, and children, and brethren, and sisters, yea, and his own life also, he
cannot be my disciple. [27] And whosoever doth
not bear his cross, and come after me, cannot
be my disciple.—LUKE, ch. 14.

1846. —— Opposite Views of the. *Paul.*
[17] Christ sent me .. to preach the gospel : not
with wisdom of words, lest the cross of Christ
should be made of none effect. [18] For the preaching of the cross is to them that perish, foolishness ; but unto us which are saved, it is the
power of God.—1 COR., ch. 1.

1847. CROSS-BEARING required. *Jesus.* [36] A
man's foes *shall be* they of his own household.
[37] He that loveth father or mother .. son or daughter more than me is not worthy of me.—MAT.,
ch. 10.

1848. CROSSNESS from Irritation. *Israelites.*
[Pharaoh pursued the people. They said to
Moses,] [12] We did tell thee in Egypt, saying,
Let us alone, that we may serve the Egyptians :
For *it had been* better for us to serve the Egyp-
tians, than that we should die in the wilderness.
—EX., ch. 14.

1849. —— Habitual. *Nabal.* [3] His wife
Abigail..*was* a woman of good understanding,
and of a beautiful countenance : but the man
was churlish and evil in his doings.. [10] And Nabal answered David's servants, and said, Who *is*
David? and who *is* the son of Jesse? there be
many servants nowadays that break away every
man from his master. [11] Shall I then take my
bread, and my water, and my flesh that I have
killed for my shearers, and give *it* unto men,
whom I know not whence they *be*?—1 SAM., ch.
25.

1850. —— of Prejudice. *Temple.* [15] When
the chief priests and scribes saw the wonderful

things that he did, and the children crying in
the temple, and saying, Hosanna to the Son of
David ; they were sore displeased.—MAT., ch.
21.

See other illustrations under :

JEALOUSY.

Crucified by. Pilate knew that for envy..delivered 4671
Disunion. Sheba blew a trumpet..we have no 4672
Free from. Enviest thou for my sake? Would God 4673
Fraternal. Elder son was angry, and would not go 4674
Implacable. Will not spare in the day of 4675
Local. Did not receive him because his face 4676
National. Are not Abana and Pharpar..better 4677
Polygamous. Bare no children..Rachel envied her 4678
Strife. We have more right in David than ye 4679
Success. Why wentest thou to fight..Midianites 4680
"   Saul was yet the more afraid of David 4681
Wounded. They have ascribed unto David ten 4682

Fretting. Fret not thyself because of evil doers 3416
Periodical. Saul..an evil spirit..troubleth him 2412
Sullen. Jacob beheld the countenance of Laban 2415
   See **ANGER** and references.

1851. CROWN, A costly. *Gold.* [29] David
gathered all the people..and went to Rabbah..
and took it. [30] And he took their king's crown
..the weight whereof *was* a talent of gold with
the precious stones : and it was *set* on David's
head.—2 SAM., ch. 12.

1852. —— Fighting for a. *Paul.* [7] I have
fought a good fight, I have finished *my* course,
I have kept the faith : [8] Henceforth there is laid
up for me a crown of righteousness, which the
Lord..shall give me at that day : and not to me
only, but unto all them also that love his appearing.—2 TIM., ch. 4.

1853. —— of Life. *After Trial.* [12] Blessed *is*
the man that endureth temptation : for when he
is tried, he shall receive the crown of life, which
the Lord hath promised to them that love him.
—JAMES, ch. 1.

1854. —— brings Sorrow, The. *David.*
[12] They mourned, and wept, and fasted until
even, for Saul, and for Jonathan his son. [25] How
are the mighty fallen in the midst of the battle !
O Jonathan, *thou wast* slain in thine high places.
[26] I am distressed for thee, my brother Jonathan :
very pleasant hast thou been unto me : thy love
to me was wonderful, passing the love of wom-
en.—2 SAM., ch. 1. [By their death David became the acknowledged king.]

1855. —— of Thorns. *Jesus.* [29] When they
had platted a crown of thorns, they put *it* upon
his head, and a reed in his right hand : and they
bowed the knee before him, and mocked him,
saying, Hail, King of the Jews !—MAT., ch. 27.

1856. CRUCIFIXION, Disgraced by. *Calvary.*
[33] There they crucified him, and the malefactors,
one on the right hand, and the other on the left.
[34] Then said Jesus, Father, forgive them ; for
they know not what they do.—LUKE, ch. 23.

See other illustrations under :

CROSS.

for Crucifixion. They that are Christ's have 1840
Compulsory. Simon..they compelled to bear the 1841
Death. Place of a skull..crucified him, and two 1842
Glorying. G. forbid that I should glory, save in 1843
Heavy. Take up the cross, and follow..grieved 1844
Indispensable. Whoso doth not bear his cross 1845
Opposite Views. To them that perish, foolishness 1846

1857. CRUELTY of Ambition. *Athaliah.*
[1] When Athaliah the mother of Ahaziah saw that
her son was dead, she arose and destroyed all
the seed royal. [2] But Jehosheba..took Joash
the son of Ahaziah..and they hid him..and his
nurse in the bedchamber from Athaliah, so that
he was not slain.—2 KINGS, ch. 11. [She expected the throne.]

1858. —— Brutal. *Jews.* [11] Smote of the
children of Seir ten thousand. [12] And *other* ten
thousand *left* alive did the children of Judah
carry away captive..and cast them down from
the top of the rock, that they all were broken
in pieces.—2 CHRON., ch. 25.

1859. —— Failure of. *Egyptians.* [10] Let us
deal wisely with them ; lest they multiply..they
join also unto our enemies, and fight against us,
and *so* get them up out of the land. [11]..they did
set over them taskmasters to afflict them with
their burdens. And they built for Pharaoh
treasure-cities, Pithom and Raamses. [12] But
the more they afflicted them, the more they
multiplied and grew.—Ex., ch. 1.

1860. —— Insulting. *Soldiers.* [17] They
clothed him with purple, and platted a crown
of thorns, and put it about his *head,* [18] And began to salute him, Hail, King of the Jews ! [19] And
they smote him on the head with a reed, and did
spit upon him, and bowing *their* knees worshipped him.—MARK, ch. 15.

1861. —— of wounded Pride. *Haman.*
[5] When Haman saw that Mordecai bowed not,
nor did him reverence, then was Haman full of
wrath. [6] And he thought scorn to lay hands on
Mordecai alone..wherefore Haman sought to destroy all the Jews.—ESTHER, ch. 3.

1862.—— Reward of. *Self.* [17] The merciful
man doeth good to his own soul : but *he that is
cruel* troubleth his own flesh.—PROV., ch. 11.

1863. —— Savage. *Nebuchadnezzar.* [6] The
king of Babylon slew the sons of Zedekiah in
Riblah before his eyes : also..all the nobles of
Judah. [7] Moreover he put out Zedekiah's eyes,
and bound him with chains, to carry him to
Babylon.—JER., ch. 39.

1864. —— in War. *David.* [Rabbah was
taken by Joab,] [31] And he . brought forth the
people..and put *them* under saws, and under
harrows of iron, and under axes of iron, and
made them pass through the brickkiln : and
thus did he unto all the cities of the children
of Ammon.—2 SAM., ch. 12.

See other illustrations under :
MASSACRE.
Intended. Letters were sent by posts..to destroy   5249
Infants. Herod..slew all the children..in B.   5250
Treacherous. Jehu said, Proclaim an assembly for 5251

Bondage. Egyptians made their lives better   895
Horrible. Galileans whose blood Pilate had mingled 137
Soldiers. Chaldees who slew..had no compassion   138
Well-intended. Our fathers cast out their children 897
   See MURDER.

1865. CULTURE an Adornment. *Proverb.*
[8] My son, hear the instruction of thy father, and
forsake not the law of thy mother : [9] For they
shall be an ornament of grace unto thy head, and
chains about thy neck.—PROV., ch. 1.

1866. CULTIVATION, Improvement by. *Fig
Tree.* [8] Lord, let it alone this year also, till I

shall dig about it, and dung *it :* [9] And if it bear
fruit, *well :* and if not, *then* after that thou shalt
cut it down.—LUKE, ch. 13.

See other illustrations under :
EDUCATION.
Monument. Children ask, What mean ye by these   2602
Neglected. Children spake half in the speech of   2603
Preparatory. Such as had ability in them..king's   2604

INSTRUCTION.
Better than Practice. Not move one of their fingers 4541
Children. Teach them [law] thy sons..sons' sons   4542
Course. Three years..might stand before the king 4543
Humble. A. and Priscilla..expounded unto   4544
Important. Heareth, and understandeth it not   4545
Improvement. Be an ornament of grace unto thy 4546
Personal. [See No. 4544.]
Public. Ezra brought the law..all that could hear 4548
Private. Came man to him [Paul] into his lodging 4549

REFINEMENT.
Affliction. I have refined thee..furnace of   6912
Fire. He is like a refiner's fire..purify sons of Levi 6913

1867. CURE for All, A. *Jesus.* [At Capernaum,] [40] When the sun was setting, all they that
had any sick with divers diseases brought them
unto him ; and he laid his hands on every one
of them, and healed them.—LUKE, ch. 4.

1868. —— for all Diseases. *Bethesda.* [4] An
angel went down at a certain season into the
pool, and troubled the water : whosoever then
first after..stepped in was made whole of whatsoever disease he had.—JOHN, ch. 5.

1869. —— A Faith. *Brazen Serpent.* [9] Moses
made a serpent of brass, and put it upon a pole
..if a serpent had bitten any man, when he beheld the serpent of brass, he lived.—NUM., ch.
21.

1870. —— Gratitude for. *"Ministered."* [38] Simon's wife's mother was taken with a great
fever ; and they besought him for her. [39] And
he stood over her, and rebuked the fever ; and
it left her : and immediately she arose and ministered unto them.—LUKE, ch. 4.

1871. —— by strange Means. *Clay.* [6] He
spat on the ground, and made clay of the spittle, and he anointed the eyes of the blind man
with the clay, [7] And said..Go, wash in the pool
of Siloam..He went his way therefore, and
washed, and came seeing.—JOHN, ch. 9.

1872. —— A progressive. *Blindness.* [23] And
when he had spit on his eyes, and put his hands
upon him, he asked him if he saw aught. [24] And
he looked up, and said, I see men as trees, walking. [25]..he put *his* hands again upon his eyes,
and made him look up ; and he was restored,
and saw every man clearly.—MARK, ch. 8.

1873. —— A threefold. *Jesus.* [22] Then was
brought unto him one possessed with a devil,
blind, and dumb : and he healed him, insomuch
that the blind and dumb both spake and saw.—
MAT., ch. 12.

1874. —— A wonderful. *Withered Hand.*
[5] Stretch forth thine hand. And he stretched *it*
out : and his hand was restored whole as the
other. [6] And the Pharisees..took counsel with
the Herodians..how they might destroy him.
—MARK, ch. 3.

See other illustrations under :
HEALTH.
Care. Fourteenth day fasting..take..for your   3847

Diet. Pulse to eat..end of ten days fairer and 3849
Temperance. Ye shall drink no wine..that ye may 3848
Water-cure. An angel troubled the water..made 9378

REMEDY.

Improbable. Anointed the eyes of the blind man 7058
Look. As Moses lifted up the serpent..S. of man 7059

Antidote. There is death in the pot..bring meal 452
Commissioned. Gave them power to cure—Luke 9 : 1
Impossible. Thy disciples they could not—Mat. 17 : 16

1875. CURIOSITY, A beneficial. *Zaccheus.*
³ He sought to see Jesus..and could not for the
press, because he was little of stature. ⁴ And he
ran before, and climbed up into a sycamore tree
to see him.. ⁵..Jesus..saw him, and said..Zac-
cheus, make haste, and come down; for to day I
must abide at thy house.—Luke, ch. 19.

1876. —— **at the Cross.** *Experiment.* ⁴⁸ One
of them ran, and took a sponge, and filled *it*
with vinegar, and put *it* on a reed, and gave him
to drink. ⁴⁹ The rest said, Let be, let us see
whether Elias will come to save him.—Mat., ch.
27.

1877. —— **Characteristic.** *Athenians.* ²¹ All
the Athenians, and strangers which were there,
spent their time in nothing else, but either to
tell or to hear some new thing.—Acts, ch. 17.

1878. —— **Dangers of.** *Sinai.* ²⁰ The Lord
called Moses *up* to the top of the mount.. ²¹ And
the Lord said unto Moses, Go down, charge the
people, lest they break through unto the Lord
to gaze, and many of them perish.—Ex., ch. 19.

1879. —— **rewarded.** *Burning Bush.* ³ I will
now turn aside, and see this great sight, why
the bush is not burnt. ⁴ And when the Lord
saw that he turned aside to see, God called unto
him out of the midst of the bush, and said,
Moses, Moses.—Ex., ch. 3.

1880. —— **Unhallowed.** *Philistines.* ¹⁹ He
smote the men of Bethshemesh, because they
had looked into the ark of the Lord..fifty thousand and threescore and ten men : and the people lamented.. ²⁰ And the men..said, Who is
able to stand before this holy Lord?—1 Sam.,
ch. 6.

1881. —— **Ungratified.** *Herod.* ⁸ When
Herod saw Jesus, he was exceeding glad : for
he was desirous to see him of a long *season,* because he had heard many things of him ; and
he hoped to have seen some miracle done by
him. ⁹ Then he questioned with him in many
words ; but he answered him nothing.—Luke,
ch. 23.

1882. CURSE, Abiding. *Jericho.* [After its cap-
ture,] ²⁶ Joshua adjured *them*..saying, Cursed *be*
the man before the Lord, that..buildeth this
city Jericho : he shall lay the foundation thereof in his firstborn, and in his youngest *son* shall
he set up the gates of it.—Josh., ch. 6. [Five
hundred and fifty years later,] ³⁴..did Hiel..
build Jericho : he laid the foundation thereof
in Abiram his firstborn, and set up the gates
thereof in his youngest *son* Segub.—1 Kings, ch.
16.

1883. —— **turned to Blessing, A.** *Balaam.*
[The Moabites] ² hired Balaam against them,
that he should curse them : howbeit our God
turned the curse into a blessing.—Neh., ch. 13.

1884. —— **upon Deceivers.** *Gibeonites.*

²² Joshua..spake..Wherefore have ye beguiled
us, saying, We *are* very far from you ; when ye
dwell among us ? ²³ Now therefore ye *are* cursed,
and there shall none of you be freed from being
bondmen, and hewers of wood and drawers of
water for the house of my God.—Josh., ch. 9.

1885. —— **The first.** *Serpent.* ¹⁴ Because
thou hast done this, thou *art* cursed above..
every beast..upon thy belly shalt thou go, and
dust shalt thou eat.. ¹⁵ And I will put enmity
between thee and the woman, and between thy
seed and her seed ; it shall bruise thy head,
and thou shalt bruise his heel.—Gen., ch. 3.

1886. —— **Money with a.** *Gehazi,* [by
fraud, obtained presents from Naaman. Elisha
said,] ²⁶ *Is it* a time to receive money, and to
receive garments, and oliveyards, and vineyards,
and sheep, and oxen, and menservants, and
maidservants ? ²⁷ The leprosy therefore of Naaman shall cleave unto thee, and unto thy seed
for ever. And he went out from his presence a
leper *as white* as snow.—2 Kings, ch. 5.

1887. —— **of Servitude, A.** *Canaan.* ²⁴ Noah
awoke from his wine, and knew what his younger
son had done unto him. ²⁵ And he said, Cursed
be Canaan ; a servant of servants shall he be
unto his brethren.—Gen., ch. 9.

1888. —— **Success a.** *The Chaldean.* ⁵ He
transgresseth by wine, *he is* a proud man, neither keepeth at home, who enlargeth his desire
as hell, and *is* as death, and cannot be satisfied
.. ⁶ Shall not all..take up..a taunting proverb
against him, and say, Woe to him that increaseth *that which is* not his ! how long ? and to him
that ladeth himself with thick clay.—Hab., ch. 2.

1889. —— **CURSES for the Disobedient.** *Moses.* ¹⁵ If thou wilt not hearken..to do all his
commandments..that all these curses shall
come upon thee.. ¹⁶ Cursed *shalt* thou be in
the city, and cursed *shalt* thou *be* in the field.
¹⁷ Cursed *shall be* thy basket and thy store.
¹⁸ Cursed *shall be* the fruit of thy body, and
the fruit of thy land, the increase of thy kine,
and the flocks of thy sheep. ¹⁹ Cursed *shalt*
thou *be* when thou comest in, and cursed *shalt*
thou *be* when thou goest out. ²⁰ The Lord shall
send upon thee cursing, vexation, and rebuke,
in all that thou settest thine hand unto for to
do.—Deut., ch. 28.

1890. —— **upon the Wicked.** *Jewish.* ¹⁴ The
Levites shall speak..unto all the men of Israel
with a loud voice, ¹⁵ Cursed *be* the man that
maketh *any* graven or molten image.. ¹⁶ Cursed
be he that setteth light by his father or his
mother.. ¹⁷ Cursed *be* he that removeth his
neighbour's landmark.. ¹⁸ Cursed *be* he that
maketh the blind to wander out of the way..
¹⁹ Cursed *be* he that perverteth the judgment of
the stranger, fatherless, and widow.. ²⁰ Cursed *be* he that lieth with his father's wife..with
any manner of beast..with his sister..with his
mother in law.. ²⁴ Cursed *be* he that smiteth his
neighbour secretly.. ²⁵ Cursed *be* he that taketh
reward to slay an innocent person.. ²⁶ Cursed *be*
he that confirmeth not *all* the words of this law
to do them. And all the people shall say, Amen.
—Deut., ch. 27.

1891. CURSING with Adversity. *David.*
⁵ Shimei..came forth, and cursed.. ⁶ And he
cast stones at David, and at all the servants..

[7] ..said Shimei..Come out, come out, thou bloody man, and thou man of Belial : [8] The Lord hath returned upon thee all the blood of the house of Saul, in whose stead thou hast reigned ; and the Lord hath delivered the kingdom into the hand of Absalom thy son.—2 SAM., ch. 16.

1892. —— Hire for. *Balaam.* [Balak said,] [6] Curse me this people ; for they *are* too mighty for me..*that* we may smite them, and *that* I may drive them out of the land. [7] And the elders of Moab and..of Midian departed with the rewards of divination..and spake unto him the words of Balak.—NUM., ch. 22.

1893. —— unresented. *David.* [9] Said Abishai..Why should this dead dog curse my lord the king ? let me go over..and take off his head. [11] Let him alone, and let him curse ; for the Lord hath bidden him. [12] It may be that the Lord will look on mine affliction, and..requite me for his cursing this day. [13] ..Shimei went along on the hill's side over against him, and cursed as he went, and threw stones at him, and cast dust.—2 SAM., ch. 16.

See other illustrations under :

BLASPHEMY.

Accused of. We stone thee not, but for blasphemy 801
Evidence of. High priest rent his clothes..spoken 802
Forbidden. Thou shalt not take the name..vain 803
Greatest. Word against the Son of man..be forgiven 804
Heedless. As the L. liveth, I will..take something 805
Habit. Stephen ceaseth not to speak blasphemous 806
Murdered. He ought to die..made himself the Son 807
No. Why..speak blasphemies ?..Who can forgive 808
Punishment. All that heard laid their hands..head 809
Strange. Peter began to curse and swear 810
Unpardonable. Blasphemy against the H. G..not 811

OATH.

Covenant. Put away all the wives..born of them 5751
Conspirators. Bound ourselves..eat nothing 5752
Foolish. Cursed be the man that eateth any food 5753
Wicked. Head of John..for his oath's sake 5754

1894. CUSTOMS, Attachment to. *Jews.* [Witnesses at the trial of Stephen said,] [14] We have heard him say, that this Jesus of Nazareth shall destroy this place, and shall change the customs which Moses delivered us.—ACTS, ch. 6.

1895. —— National. *J e w s .* [31] As Jacob passed over Penuel..he halted upon his thigh. [32] Therefore the children of Israel eat not *of* the sinew which shrank, which *is* upon the hollow of the thigh, unto this day.—GEN., ch. 32.

1896. —— Observance of. *Laban.* [25] In the morning, behold, it *was* Leah : and Jacob said to Laban..did not I serve with thee for Rachel ? wherefore then hast thou beguiled me ? [26] And Laban said, It must not be so done in our country, to give the younger before the firstborn.— GEN., ch. 29.

See other illustrations under :

HABIT.

Differs. Animals..darkness..wherein all beasts 3671
Prayer. Cornelius..prayed to G. always 3672
" 　Daniel..three times a day prayed 3673
" 　Evening, morning, *and noon will* I cry 3674
Worship. By river side, where prayer was wont 6395
" 　Offered burnt offerings..continually 6367
" 　As his custom was, Jesus went into the 9873
" 　Daniel prayed and gave thanks..as 8766

MANNERS.

Instruction in. Sit down in the lowest room 5207
Polite. May we know what this new doctrine is ? 5208
Rude. What will this babbler say ? [Athenians] 5209

—— **DAMAGE.** —— ——

See illustrations under :

Carelessness. He that kindleth the fire 7217
" 　　Dig a pit, and not cover it..give 7218
" 　　Ox hath used to push..not kept 7219
Divided. If one man's ox hurt another..divide 7227
Error. Taken..by false accusation, I restore 7267
Fear. Not pay tribute..endamage the revenue 8105
Irreparable. Enemy could not countervail the 5001
Lending. If a man borrow..hurt..make it good 7273
Neglect. Buildest a new house..battlement for 7216
Retaliation. Eye for eye, tooth for tooth, hand 7291
Theft. Deliver..money to keep..be stolen..pay 7272

INJURY.

Forgiveness. Father, forgive them, they know not 4498
Insulting. Samson's wife was given to his..friend 4496
Revenged. Samson caught 300 foxes..firebrands 4497

RETRIBUTION.

Angels. Kept not their first estate..chains 7292
Commenced. Jews had rule over them that hated 7293
" 　　G. rendered the wickedness of 7294
Fear. Therefore..[Joseph's] blood is required 7295
Inflicted. Cut off his thumbs and great toes 7296
" 　　Cast them [accusers] into the den of 7299
Natural. Barbarians..said..is a murderer 7297
Just. King said, Hang him [Haman] thereon 7298
Providential. Feared not the L..sent lions 7300
" 　　Smote all the firstborn..Egypt 7301
See CRIME.

1897. DAMNATION for Hypocrites. *Jews.* [14] Woe unto you, scribes and Pharisees, hypocrites ! for ye devour widows' houses, and for a pretence make long prayer : therefore ye shall receive the greater damnation.—MAT., ch. 23.

See other illustrations under :

CONDEMNATION.

Cause of. If ye were blind, ye should have no sin 1475
Future. How..not having a wedding garment 1476
Innocent. Pilate saith, Crucify him..no fault 1477
Others. First cast out the beam..own eye 1478
Reason of. Because..not believed in the..Son of 1479
Reversed. I knew thee..hard man..cast ye 1480
Unjust. Wrath of Elihu against Job..justified 1481
Unconscious. David said..shall surely die..thou 1482

HELL.

Affection in. Send Lazarus to my father's house 3922
Bottomless. He opened the bottomless pit 3923
Preparation of. Depart..fire prepared for the 3924

1898. DANCERS, Kidnapped. *Daughters of Shiloh.* [The elders said to the Benjamites,] [21] If the daughters of Shiloh come out to dance in dances, then come ye out of the vineyards, and catch you every man his wife..and go to the land of Benjamin.—JUDGES, ch. 21.

1899. DANCING, The first. *At Red Sea.* [20] Miriam the prophetess, the sister of Aaron, took a timbrel in her hand ; and all the women went out after her with timbrels and with dances. [21] And Miriam answered them, Sing ye to the Lord, for he hath triumphed gloriously : the horse and his rider hath he thrown into the sea.—EX., ch. 15.

1900. —— Idolatrous. *Calf.* [19] As soon as he ..saw the calf, and the dancing..Moses' anger waxed hot, and he cast the tables..and brake them beneath the mount.—Ex., ch. 32.

1901. —— Infatuation by. *Herod.* ²² When the daughter of..Herodias..danced, and pleased Herod and them that sat with him, the king said unto the damsel, Ask of me whatsoever thou wilt, and I will give *it* thee.—Mark, ch. 6.

1902. —— for Joy. *Women.* ⁶ When David was returned from the slaughter of the Philistine..the women came out of all cities of Israel, singing and dancing, to meet king Saul, with tabrets, with joy, and with instruments of music.—1 Sam., ch. 18.

1903. —— Religious. *David.* ¹³ When they that bare the ark of the Lord had gone six paces, he sacrificed oxen and fatlings. ¹⁴ And David danced before the Lord with all *his* might.. ¹⁵ So David and..Israel brought up the ark.. with shouting, and with the sound of the trumpet.—2 Sam., ch. 6.

See other illustrations under :

Festive. Amalekites were..eating, drinking, and 341
Unfortunate. [Jephthah] Only daughter came to 9253

1904. DANGER, Admonished of. *Asahel.* ²² Abner said again to Asahel, Turn thee aside from following me : wherefore should I smite thee to the ground.. ²³ Howbeit he refused..wherefore Abner with the hinder end of the spear smote him under the fifth *rib.*.and he fell down there, and died.—2 Sam., ch. 2.

1905. —— from Associates. *Lot.* ¹² Lot dwelt in the cities of the plain, and pitched *his* tent toward Sodom. ¹³ But the men of Sodom *were* wicked and sinners before the Lord exceedingly.—Gen., ch. 13.

1906. —— Appalled by. *Jesus.* ³² They were ..going up to Jerusalem ; and Jesus went before them : and they were amazed ; and as they followed, they were afraid. And he..began to tell them what things should happen unto him.—Mark, ch. 10.

1907. —— from Concealment. *Peter.* ⁶⁹ Peter sat without in the palace : and a damsel came.. saying, Thou also wast with Jesus of Galilee. ⁷⁰ But he denied before *them* all.—Mat., ch. 26.

1908. —— A common. *King Saul.* ²¹ Abiathar shewed David that Saul had slain the Lord's priests. ²² And David said.. ²³ Abide thou with me, fear not : for he that seeketh my life seeketh thy life : but with me thou *shalt be* in safeguard.—1 Sam., ch. 22.

1909. —— Escape from. *Damascus.* ²⁴ Their laying wait was known of Saul. And they watched the gates day and night to kill him. ²⁵ Then the disciples took him by night, and let *him* down by the wall in a basket.—Acts, ch. 9.

1910. —— of forgetting God. *Moses said,* ¹² Lest *when* thou hast eaten and art full, and hast built goodly houses, and dwelt *therein ;* ¹³ And *when* thy herds and thy flocks multiply, and thy silver and thy gold is multiplied, and all that thou hast is multiplied ; ¹⁴ Then thine heart be lifted up, and thou forget the Lord thy God.—Deut., ch. 8.

1911. —— Haste from. *Destruction.* ¹⁶ Then let them which be in Judea flee into the mountains : ¹⁷ Let him which is on the housetop not come down to take any thing out of his house :

¹⁸ Neither let him which is in the field return back to take his clothes.—Mat., ch. 24.

1912. —— intimidates. *Peter.* ²⁹ When Peter was come down out of the ship, he walked on the water, to go to Jesus. ³⁰ But when he saw the wind boisterous, he was afraid ; and beginning to sink, he cried, saying, Lord, save me.—Mat., ch. 14.

1913. —— Jesus sought in. *Storm.* ²³ There came down a storm of wind on the lake : and they were filled *with water*, and were in jeopardy. ²⁴ And they..awoke him, saying, Master, Master, we perish. Then he arose, and rebuked the wind and the raging of the water : and they ceased, and there was a calm.—Luke, ch. 8.

1914. —— in Prosperity. *Uzziah* ¹⁵ Made in Jerusalem engines, invented by cunning men, to be on the towers and upon the bulwarks, to shoot arrows and great stones..And his name spread far abroad ; for he was marvellously helped, till he was strong. ¹⁶ But when he was strong, his heart was lifted up to *his* destruction : for he..went into the temple of the Lord to burn incense.—2 Chron., ch. 26.

1915. —— Unsuspected. *Spiritual.* ⁶¹ Lord, I will follow thee ; but let me first go bid them farewell, which are at home.. ⁶². .Jesus said.. No man, having put his hand to the plough, and looking back, is fit for the kingdom of God.— Luke, ch. 9.

1916. —— Warnings of. *Elisha's.* ⁸ The king of Syria..took counsel with his servants, saying, In' such and such a place *shall be* my camp. ⁹ And the man of God sent unto the king of Israel, saying, Beware that thou pass not such a place ; for thither the Syrians are come down. ¹⁰ And the king of Israel..saved himself there, not once nor twice.—2 Kings, ch. 6.

See other illustrations under :

ALARM.

Conscience. Pray for thy servants..we die not 273
Death. Egyptians were urgent..we be all dead 274
Failure. Priests..doubted..whereunto this would 275
Manifestation. Belshazzar..countenance was 276
Preaching. Paul reasoned..Felix trembled 277
Reasonable. Esau cometh..400 men..Jacob 278
Superstitious. Jesus walking on the sea..troubled 279
Sinners. Adam and his wife hid themselves 280
" Let not God speak with us..die 281
Sudden. Seeing the prison doors open..sword 282
Spiritual. Sirs, what must I do to be saved ? 283
Tempest. Entreat..be no more mighty thunderings 284
Unnecessary. My money is restored..heart failed 285

AGITATION.

Deception. Who art thou ?..Esau..Isaac trembled 256
Diffuses. Disputed he in the synagogue..market 257
Deplored. [Israelites] Made..abhorred..slay us 258
General. [Philistines] Trembling in the host..field 259
Mount. Sinai..quaked greatly 260
Overcome. [At sepulchre] keepers did shake 261
Physical. Belshazzar's thoughts troubled..knees 262
Terror. [Job's vision.] Trembling..my bones 263

PERIL.

Assassins. Jews bound themselves. had killed 6057
Fasting. Fourteenth day ye have..continued 6058
Imminent. There is but a step between me and 6059
Prayer. Master, Master, we perish..rebuked the 6060
Sleeping. Jonah was fast asleep..Arise ; call upon 6061
Time. Egyptians marched after them..sore afraid 6062

Voluntary. The three brake through the host of 6063
"   **Sinful.** Shall I drink the blood of   6064
Many Perils. Thrice was I beaten with rods, once 6065

Beauty. Thou art a fair woman..E. will kill me   661
Responsibility. If a man open a pit..beast fall   1053
"   If corn consumed..he that   1025
"   Ox that used to push..pay ox for   1147

1917. DARKNESS of Adversity. *Jeremiah.* [1] I am the man *that* hath seen affliction by the rod of his wrath. [2] He hath led me, and brought *me* into darkness, but not *into* light.—LAM., ch. 3.

1918. —— **Beasts in.** *Awake.* [20] Thou makest darkness, and it is night : wherein all the beasts of the forest do creep *forth.* [21] The young lions roar after their prey, and seek their meat from God. [22] The sun ariseth, they gather themselves together, and lay them down in their dens.— Ps. 104.

1919. —— **Betrayed in.** *Jesus.* [3] Judas..having received a band *of men* and officers from the chief priests and Pharisees, cometh thither with lanterns and torches and weapons.—JOHN, ch. 18.

1920. —— **chosen.** *The Adulterer.* [15] The eye ..of the adulterer waiteth for the twilight, saying, No eye shall see me : and disguiseth *his* face. [15] In the dark they dig through houses, *which* they had marked for themselves in the daytime : they know not the light. [17] For the morning *is* to them even as the shadow of death : if *one* know *them, they are* in the terrors of the shadow of death.—JOB, ch. 24.

1921. —— **Dying in.** *Egypt.* [After the plague of darkness came the plague of death. See Ex., ch. 10.]

1922. —— **Deeds of.** *Evil Seed.* [25] While men slept, his enemy came and sowed tares among the wheat, and went his way. [26] But when the blade was sprung up, and brought forth fruit, then appeared the tares also.—MAT., ch. 13.

1923. —— **Future.** *The Wicked.* [5] The light of the wicked shall be put out, and the spark of his fire shall not shine. [6] The light shall be dark in his tabernacle, and his candle shall be put out with him.—JOB, ch. 18.

1924. —— **Hidden in.** *The Wicked.* [20] Every one that doeth evil hateth the light, neither cometh to the light, lest his deeds should be reproved. [21] But he that doeth truth cometh to the light, that his deeds may be made manifest, that they are wrought in God.—JOHN, ch. 3.

1925. —— **Hatred brings.** *Blindness.* [11] He that hateth his brother is in darkness, and walketh in darkness, and knoweth not whither he goeth, because that darkness hath blinded his eyes.—1 JOHN, ch. 2.

1926. —— **from Insects.** *Egypt.* [14] Locusts went up over all the land..very grievous *were they ;* before them there were no such locusts as they, neither after them.. [15] For they covered the face of the whole earth, so that the land was darkened.—Ex., ch. 10.

1927. —— **Light in.** *Sanctuary.* [13] The fire shall ever be burning upon the altar ; it shall never go out.—LEV., ch. 6. [38] The cloud of the Lord *was* upon the tabernacle by day, and fire was on it by night, in the sight of all the house of Israel, throughout all their journeys.—Ex., ch. 40.

1928. —— **Moral.** *Cause of.* [22] The light of the body is the eye : if therefore the eye be single, thy whole body shall be full of light. [23] But if thy eye be evil, thy whole body shall be full of darkness. If therefore the light that is in thee be darkness, how great *is* that darkness.— MAT., ch. 6.

1929. —— **Original.** *Creation.* [2] The earth was without form and void ; and darkness *was* upon the face of the deep. And the Spirit of God moved upon the face of the waters. [3] And God said, Let there be light.—GEN., ch. 1.

1930. DARKNESS, Plague of. *Egypt.* [22] Moses stretched forth his hand toward heaven ; and there was a thick darkness in all the land of Egypt.. [23] They saw not one another, neither rose any from his place for three days : but all the children of Israel had light in their dwellings.—Ex., ch. 10.

1931. —— **Punishment in.** *Angels.* [6] The angels which kept not their first estate, but left their own habitation, he hath reserved in everlasting chains under darkness unto the judgment of the great day.—JUDE.

1932. —— **Revelation in.** *At Sinai.* [20] Moses said..Fear not : for God is come to prove you, and that his fear may be before your faces.. [21] And the people stood afar off, and Moses drew near unto the thick darkness where God *was.*— Ex., ch. 20.

1933. —— **an unnatural.** *Crucifixion.* [45] From the sixth hour there was darkness over all the land unto the ninth hour. [46] And about the ninth hour Jesus cried with a loud voice, saying..My God, my God, why hast thou forsaken me ?—MAT., ch. 27.

1934. —— **for the Wicked.** *Stumble.* [15] Hear ye, and give ear ; be not proud.. [16] Give glory to the Lord your God, before he cause darkness, and before your feet stumble upon the dark mountains, and, while ye look for light, he turn it into the shadow of death, *and* make *it* gross darkness.—JER., ch. 13.

See other illustrations under:

MIDNIGHT.

Appeal at. Friend, lend me three loaves   5388
Songs. Feet fast..Paul and Silas..sang praises   5390

1935. DAUGHTER, Portion of. *Wedding.* [Achsah was married, and her father] [18] Caleb said unto her, What wouldest thou ? [19] Who answered, Give me a blessing : for thou hast given me a south land ; give me also springs of water. And he gave her the upper springs, and the nether springs.—JOSH., ch. 15.

1936. —— **An unfortunate.** *A Sacrifice.* [34] Jephthah came to..his house, and, behold, his daughter came out to meet him with timbrels and with dances : and she *was his* only child.. [35]..he rent his clothes, and said, Alas, my daughter ! thou hast brought me very low —JUDGES, ch. 11. [He had vowed to the Lord the first that should meet him on his return.]

1937. DAUGHTER IN LAW, Faithful. *Naomi's.* [16] Ruth said, Entreat me not..to return from following after thee : for whither thou goest, I will go ; and where thou lodgest, I will lodge : thy people *shall be* my people, and thy God my God : [17] Where thou diest, will I die, and there will I be buried : the Lord do so to me, and more also, *if aught* but death part thee and me. —RUTH, ch. 1.

1938. —— Unwelcome. *Esau's Wives.* [34] Esau was forty years old when he took to wife Judith.. the Hittite, and Bashemath..the Hittite: [35] Which were a grief of mind unto Isaac and to Rebekah. —GEN., ch. 26.

1939. DEAD, Apparently. *Youth.* [25] Thou dumb and deaf spirit, I charge thee, come out of him.. [26] And *the spirit* cried, and rent him sore, and came out of him : and he was as one dead ; insomuch that many said, He is dead. [27] But Jesus took him by the hand, and lifted him up ; and he arose.—MARK, ch. 9.

1940. —— Guarding the. *Seven Sons.* [9] The Gibeonites.. hanged them in the hill.. [10] And Rizpah..took sackcloth, and spread it for her upon the rock, from the beginning of harvest until water dropped upon them out of heaven, and suffered neither the birds of the air to rest on them by day, nor the beasts of the field by night.—2 SAM., ch. 21.

1941. —— and Living, Between. *Aaron.* [47] Aaron took..and ran into the midst of the congregation..and he put on incense, and made an atonement for the people. [48] And he stood between the dead and the living ; and the plague was stayed.—NUM., ch. 16.

1942. —— Mourning the. *David.* [33] The king was much moved, and went up to the chamber over the gate, and wept : and as he went, thus he said, O my son Absalom, my son, my son Absalom ! would God I had died for thee, O Absalom, my son, my son !—2 SAM., ch. 18.

1943. —— restored, The. *City of Nain.* [12] There was a dead man carried out, the only son of..a widow : and much people of the city was with her. [13] ..the Lord had compassion on her.. [14] And he came and touched the bier..And he said, Young man, I say unto thee, Arise. [15] And he that was dead sat up, and began to speak. And he delivered him to his mother.—LUKE, ch. 17.

1944. —— resuscitated, The. *Widow's Son.* [21] He stretched himself upon the child three times, and cried..O Lord my God, I pray thee, let this child's soul come into him again. [22] And the Lord heard the voice of Elijah..and he revived.—1 KINGS, ch. 17.

1945. —— Triumph over the. *Philistines.* [8] They found Saul.. [9] And they cut off his head ..and sent into the land of the Philistines round about, to publish *it in* the house of their idols, and among the people. [10] And they put his armour in the house of Ashtaroth : and they fastened his body to the wall of Beth-shan.—1 SAM., ch. 31.

1946. DEATH, Alarmed by. *Egyptians.* [33] The Egyptians were urgent upon the people, that they might send them out of the land in haste ; for they said, We *be* all dead *men.*—EX., ch. 12.

1947. —— Ascension in. *Elijah.* [11] As they still went on, and talked..behold, *there appeared* a chariot of fire, and horses of fire, and parted them both asunder ; and Elijah went up by a whirlwind into heaven.—2 KINGS, ch. 2.

1948. —— Abandoned to. *Ishmael.* [15] The water was spent..and she cast the child under one of the shrubs. [16] And she went..over against

him a good way off, as it were a bowshot : for she said, Let me not see the death of the child. And she..lifted up her voice, and wept.—GEN., ch. 21.

1949. —— Approach of. *Isaac.* [1] When Isaac was old, and his eyes were dim, so that he could not see, he called Esau.. [2] And he said, Behold now, I am old, I know not the day of my death. —GEN., ch. 27.

1950. —— Contentment in. *Jacob.* [29] Joseph ..went up to meet Israel his father, to Goshen ..and he fell on his neck, and wept on his neck a good while. [30] And Israel said..Now let me die, since I have seen thy face, because thou *art* yet alive.—GEN., ch. 46.

1951. —— Chosen Place of. *Barzillai, aged 86.* [David] [33] said unto Barzillai, Come thou over with me, and I will feed thee with me in Jerusalem. [Reply :] [37] Let thy servant.. turn back again, that I may die in mine own city, *and be buried* by the grave of my father and of my mother.—2 SAM., ch. 19.

1952. —— ignores Caste. *Tenth Plague.* [See No. 1976.] .

1953. —— from Delay. *Four Lepers.* [3] Why sit we here until we die? [4] If we say, We will enter into the city, then the famine *is* in the city, and we shall die there : and if we sit still here, we die also..let us fall unto the host of the Syrians : if they save us alive, we shall live ; and if they kill us, we shall but die.—2 KINGS, ch. 7.

1954. —— The Discouraged seek. *Elijah* [4] Went a day's journey into the wilderness, and ..sat down under a juniper tree : and he said..It is enough ; now, O Lord, take away my life ; for I *am* not better than my fathers.—1 KINGS, ch. 19.

1955. —— desired. *The Wicked.* [6] In those days shall men seek death, and shall not find it ; and shall desire to die, and death shall flee from them.—REV., ch. 9.

1956. —— —— *Jonah.* [2] O Lord, *was* not this my saying, when I was yet in my country? ..for I knew that thou *art* a gracious God, and merciful, slow to anger, and of great kindness, and repentest thee of the evil. [3] Therefore now, O Lord, take, I beseech thee, my life from me ; for *it is* better for me to die than to live.—JONAH, ch. 4. [He was angered because Nineveh was spared.]

1957. —— Destruction by. *Tree.* [7] There is hope of a tree, if it be cut down, that it will sprout again, and that the tender branch thereof will not cease. [8] Though the root thereof wax old in the earth, and the stock thereof die in the ground ; [9] *Yet* through the scent of water it will bud, and bring forth boughs like a plant. [10] But man dieth, and wasteth away : yea, man giveth up the ghost, and where *is* he ?—JOB, ch. 14.

1958. —— Escape from. *Jesus.* [56] If a man keep my saying, he shall never see death. [52] Then said the Jews unto him, Now we know that thou hast a devil.—JOHN, ch. 8.

1959. —— —— *First Resurrection.* [16] The Lord himself shall descend from heaven with a shout, with the voice of the archangel, and with the trump of God : and the dead in Christ shall rise first : [17] Then we which are alive *and* remain shall be caught up together with them in

the clouds, to meet the Lord in the air.—1
THESS., ch. 4.

1960. —— **The first.** *Abel.* ⁸ Cain talked
with Abel..and..when they were in the field..
Cain rose up against Abel his brother, and slew
him.—GEN., ch. 4.

1961. —— **of a Family.** *One Year.* [Miriam,
Aaron, and Moses. See Num., ch. 20 ; Deut., ch.
34.]

1962. —— **Faithful till.** *Ruth.* ¹⁴ And Orpah
kissed her mother in law ; but Ruth clave unto
her. ¹⁵ And she said.. ¹⁷..the Lord do so to me,
and more also, *if aught* but death part thee and
me.—RUTH, ch. 1.

1963. —— **in every House.** *Egyptians.*
³⁰ Pharaoh rose up in the night, he, and all his
servants, and all the Egyptians ; and there was
a great cry in Egypt : for *there was* not a house
where *there was* not one dead.—EX., ch. 12.

1964. —— **Humiliating.** *Abimelech.* ⁵³ A
certain woman cast a piece of a millstone upon
Abimelech's head, and all to brake his skull.
⁵⁴ Then he called hastily unto..his armourbearer,
and said..Draw thy sword, and slay me, that
men say not of me, A woman slew him. And
his young man thrust him through.—JUDGES,
ch. 9.

1965. —— **hastened.** *Two Thieves.* ³¹ The
Jews therefore..that the bodies should not remain upon the cross on the sabbath day..be-
sought Pilate that their legs might be broken, and
that they might be taken away. ³²..the soldiers
..brake the legs of the first, and of the other
which was crucified with him.—JOHN, ch. 19.

1966. —— **Influence after.** *Abel.* ⁴ By faith
Abel offered unto God a more excellent sacrifice than Cain, by which he obtained witness
that he was righteous, God testifying of his gifts :
and by it he being dead yet speaketh.—HEB.,
ch. 11.

1967. —— **by Divine Judgment.** *Ananias—
Sapphira.* ⁵ Ananias hearing these words fell
down, and gave up the ghost : and great fear
came on all.. ⁹..behold, the feet of them which
have buried thy husband *are* at the door, and
shall carry thee out. ¹⁰ Then fell she down..
and yielded up the ghost.—ACTS, ch. 5.

1968. —— **of Jesus.** *Calvary.* ⁴⁴ It was
about the sixth hour, and there was a darkness
over all the earth until the ninth hour. ⁴⁵ And
the sun was darkened, and the vail of the temple was rent in the midst. ⁴⁶ And when Jesus
had cried with a loud voice, he said, Father,
into thy hands I commend my spirit : and..
he gave up the ghost.—LUKE, ch. 23.

1969. —— **Longed for.** *The Afflicted.* ⁸ Oh
that I might have my request ; and that God
would grant *me* the thing that I long for !
⁹ Even that it would please God to destroy me ;
that he would let loose his hand, and cut me off.
—JOB, ch. 6.

1970. —— **on the Mount.** *Mount Hor.* ²⁸ Moses stripped Aaron of his garments, and put
them upon Eleazar his son ; and Aaron died
there in the top of the mount.—NUM., ch. 20.

1971. —— **merited.** *Ashael.* ²² Abner said
again to Asahel, Turn thee aside from following
me : wherefore should I smite thee to the
ground?.. ²³ Howbeit he refused to turn aside :

wherefore Abner with the hinder end of the
spear smote him under the fifth *rib.*—2 SAM.,
ch. 2.

1972. —— **Midst of.** *Aaron.* [See No. 1941.]

1973. —— **prevented, Needless.** *Jonathan.*
²⁴ Saul had adjured the people, saying, Cursed
be the man that eateth *any* food until evening,
that I may be avenged on mine enemies.. ⁴⁵ And
the people said unto Saul, Shall Jonathan die,
who hath wrought this great salvation in Israel ?
..there shall not one hair of his head fall to the
ground..So the people rescued Jonathan, that
he died not.—1 SAM., ch. 14.

1974. —— **Nearness to.** *A Step.* ³ David..
said, Thy father certainly knoweth that I have
found grace in thine eyes ; and he saith, Let
not Jonathan know this, lest he be grieved : but
truly, *as* the Lord liveth, and *as* thy soul liveth,
there is but a step between me and death.—1
SAM., ch. 20.

1975. —— **a Penalty.** *Adam.* ¹⁷ Because
thou hast..and hast eaten of the tree, of which
I commanded thee, saying, Thou shalt not eat
of it : cursed is the ground for thy sake. ¹⁹ In
the sweat of thy face shalt thou eat bread, till
thou return unto the ground..for dust thou *art*,
and unto dust shalt thou return.—GEN., ch. 3.

1976. —— **Plague of.** *The Tenth.* ²⁹ At midnight the Lord smote all the firstborn in the
land of Egypt, from the firstborn of Pharaoh
that sat on his throne unto the firstborn of the
captive that *was* in the dungeon ; and all the
firstborn of cattle.—EX., ch. 12.

1977. —— **Preparation for.** *Hezekiah.* ² In
those days was Hezekiah sick unto death. And
the prophet Isaiah..came..and said..Thus saith
the Lord, Set thine house in order ; for thou
shalt die, and not live.—2 KINGS, ch. 20. [His
life was spared in answer to prayer.]

1978. —— **preferred.** *Paul.* ²³ I am in a
strait betwixt two, having a desire to depart,
and to be with Christ ; which is far better :
²⁴ Nevertheless to abide in the flesh *is* more
needful for you.—PHIL., ch. 1.

1979. —— **prayed for.** *Job.* ¹³ Oh that thou
wouldest hide me in the grave, that thou wouldest keep me secret, until thy wrath be past, that
thou wouldest appoint me a set time, and remember me !—JOB, ch. 14.

1980. —— **preferred to Trouble.** *Moses.* ¹⁴ I
am not able to bear all this people alone, because *it is* too heavy for me. ¹⁵ And if thou
deal thus with me, kill me..out of hand, if I
have found favour in thy sight ; and let me not
see my wretchedness.—NUM., ch. 11.

1981. —— **Passage through.** *Jordan.* ¹⁵ As
..the feet of the priests that bare the ark were
dipped in the brim of the water.. ¹⁶..the waters
which came down from above stood *and* rose up
upon a heap.. ¹⁷ all the Israelites passed over
on dry ground.—JOSH., ch. 3.

1982. —— **a painful Sight.** *Ishmael.* [See
No. 1948.]

1983. —— **proven.** *Jesus.* ³³ When they
came to Jesus, and saw that he was dead already,
they brake not his legs : ³⁴ But one of the soldiers with a spear pierced his side, and forthwith came there out blood and water.—JOHN,
ch. 19.

1984. —— defeats Plans. *Rich Fool.* [19] I will say to my soul, 'Soul, thou hast much goods laid up for many years; take thine ease, eat, drink, *and* be merry. [20] But God said unto him, *Thou* fool, this night thy soul shall be required of thee: then whose shall those things be, which thou hast provided?—LUKE, ch. 12.

1985. —— Good Prospect in. *Paul.* [6] The time of my departure is at hand. [7] I have fought a good fight, I have finished *my* course, I have kept the faith: [8] Henceforth there is laid up for me a crown of righteousness, which the Lord..shall give me.—2 TIM., ch. 4.

1986. —— Penitence in. *Thief.* [41] We receive the due reward of our deeds: but this man hath done nothing amiss. [42] And he said unto Jesus, Lord, remember me when thou comest into thy kingdom.—LUKE, ch. 23.

1987. —— Remembered in. *Paul.* [26] When Jesus therefore saw his mother, and the disciple standing by, whom he loved, he saith unto his mother, Woman, behold thy son! [27] Then saith he to the disciple, Behold thy mother! And from that hour that disciple took her unto his own *home.*—JOHN, ch. 19.

1988. —— restores Friends. *David.* [22] While the child was yet alive, I fasted and wept.. [23] But now he is dead, wherefore should I fast? can I bring him back again? I shall go to him, but he shall not return to me.—2 SAM., ch. 12.

1989. —— Relief by. *Job.* [5] My flesh is clothed with worms and clods of dust; my skin is broken, and become loathsome. [14] Then thou scarest me with dreams, and terrifiest me through visions: [15] So that my soul chooseth strangling, *and* death rather than my life. [16] I loathe *it;* I would not live alway.—JOB, ch. 7.

1990. —— Summons of. *Moses.* [12] Get thee up into this mount Abarim, and see the land which I have given unto the children of Israel. [13] And when thou hast seen it, thou also shalt be gathered unto thy people.—NUM., ch. 27.

1991. —— petulantly solicited. *Jonah.* [8] The sun beat upon the head of Jonah, that he fainted, and wished in himself to die, and said, *It is* better for me to die than to live. [9] And God said to Jonah, Doest thou well to be angry for the gourd? And he said, I do well to be angry, *even* unto death.—JONAH, ch. 4.

1992. —— Silence of. *David's Child.* [18] On the seventh day..the child died. [19] ..when David saw that his servants whispered, David perceived that the child was dead.—2 SAM., ch. 12.

1993. —— Safety in. *David.* [4] Though I walk through the valley of the shadow of death, I will fear no evil: for thou *art* with me; thy rod and thy staff they comfort me.—PS. 23.

1994. —— Semblance of. *Child.* [See No. 1939.]

1995. —— a Sleep. *Stephen.* [See No. 1998.]

1996. —— Spiritual. *Dry Bones.* [1] The Lord, and set me down in the midst of the valley which *was* full of bones, [2] ..and, behold, *there were* very many in the open valley; and, lo, *they were* very dry.—EZEK., ch. 37.

1997. —— Testimony in. *Joshua.* [14] Behold, this day I *am* going the way of all the earth: and ye know in all your hearts and in all your souls, that not one thing hath failed of all the

good things which the Lord your God spake concerning you.—JOSH., ch. 23.

1998. —— in a Tumult. *Stephen.* [57] They cried out with a loud voice, and stopped their ears, and ran upon him with one accord, [58] And cast *him* out of the city, and stoned *him:* [60] And he kneeled down, and cried with a loud voice, Lord, lay not this sin to their charge. And when he had said this, he fell asleep.—ACTS, ch. 7.

1999. —— Triumph over. *The Christian.* [55] O death, where *is* thy sting? O grave, where *is* thy victory? [56] The sting of death *is* sin; and the strength of sin *is* the law. [57] But thanks *be* to God, which giveth us the victory through our Lord Jesus Christ.—1 COR., ch. 15.

2000. —— Universal. *Flood.* [17] I, do bring a flood of waters upon the earth, to destroy all flesh, wherein *is* the breath of life, from under heaven; *and* every thing that *is* in the earth shall die.—GEN., ch. 6.

2001. —— An unhappy. *Eli.* [17] Israel is fled before the Philistines..and thy two sons also, Hophni and Phinehas, are dead, and the ark of God is taken. [18] ..he fell from off the seat backward..and his neck brake, and he died: for he was an old man.—1 SAM., ch. 4.

2002. —— Victory by. *Samson.* [30] Let me die with the Philistines. And he bowed himself with *all his* might; and the house fell upon the lords, and upon all the people that *were* therein. So the dead which he slew at his death were more than *they* which he slew in his life.—JUDGES, ch. 16.

2003. —— parted, Waters of. *Elijah.* [7] With Elijah..they two stood by Jordan. [8] And Elijah took his mantle, and wrapped *it* together, and smote the waters, and they were divided hither and thither, so that they two went over on dry ground.—2 KINGS, ch. 2.

2004. —— Wailing by. *Egyptians.* [See No. 1963.]

See other illustrations under:

BEREAVEMENT.

MANSLAUGHTER.

MURDER.

Desire. Herodias would have killed John..could   5623
Escape from. Michal let David down through a   5624
Excuse. By our law he ought to die..S. of G.   5625
Fratricidal. Cain rose up against Abel   5626
Gain. Let us kill him..seize on his inheritance   5627
for Healing. Therefore..sought to slay him   5628
Intended. Saul thought to make David fall by   5629
Proposed. Esau hated Jacob..then will I slay   5632
Responsibility. The Just one..ye have been the   5633
**   "   of Jesus.** Herod slew all the   5630
Indirect. Letter to Joab..set Uriah in..the hottest 5631
Suffocation. Hazael took a thick cloth..on his   5634
Stoning. Cast Stephen out of the city, and stoned 5635

SUICIDE.

Imitated. Armourbearer saw that Saul was dead   8456
Mortification. Counsel was not followed..hanged 8457
Tratitor's. Cast down..silver..hanged himself   8460
Soldier's. Archers hit him..sore wounded..sword 8459

Affection. Jesus said..Woman, behold thy son   160
As Men only. Stripped Aaron of his garments   2564
Penalty. Aaron's sons..drink no wine..lest ye die   26

2005. DEBATE, Defeat in. *Jews* [9] Disputing with Stephen. [10] They were not able to resist the wisdom and the spirit by which he spake. —ACTS, ch. 6.

See other illustrations under :

CONTROVERSY.

Avoided. Our fathers worshipped..ye say   1652
Fatal. Cain talked with Abel..and slew him   1653
Holy. [At Athens] disputed Paul in the   1654

DISPUTE.

Foolish. Had disputed..who should be the   2422
Settled. Divide the living child in two   2423

DISSENSIONS.

Doctrinal. P. and Barnabas had no small   2429
Perilous. Chief captain fearing lest P...pulled in   2430
Partisan. Every one of you saith, I am of..I of..I of 2431
Removed. [Explanation of the altar of witness]   2432
Stubborn. Contention was so sharp..parted   2433

Protracted. Disputing daily..two years   2372

2006. —— DEBTS compromised. *Fraud.* [5] How much owest thou unto my lord? [6] And he said, An hundred measures of oil. And he said ..Take thy bill, and sit down quickly, and write fifty. [7] Then said he to another, And how much owest thou? And he said, An hundred measures of wheat. And he said..Take thy bill, and write fourscore.—LUKE, ch. 16.

2007. —— Forgiven. *Jubilee.* [1] At the end of *every* seven years.. [2]..Every creditor that lendeth *aught* unto his neighbour shall release *it*; he shall not exact *it* of his neighbour, or of his brother ; because it is called the Lord's release. —DEUT., ch. 15.

2008. —— Severity in collecting. *Forgiven Debtor.* [28] The same servant went out, and found one of his fellow servants, which owed him a hundred pence : and he laid hands on him, and took *him* by the throat, saying, Pay me that thou owest.—MAT., ch. 18.

2009. DEBTOR miraculously delivered. *Elisha.* [The creditor was about to take the widow's two sons for bondmen. Elisha commanded her to borrow vessels, which were miraculously filled with oil,] [7] And he said, Go, sell the oil, and pay thy debt, and live thou and thy children of the rest.—2 KINGS, ch. 4.

2010. DEBTORS, An Army of. *David.* [2] Every one *that was* in distress, and every one that *was* in debt, and every one *that was* discontented, gathered themselves unto him ; and he became a captain over them..about four hundred men. —1 SAM., ch. 22.

2011. —— forgiven. *Woman.* [46] My head with oil thou didst not anoint : but this woman hath anointed my feet with ointment. [47] Wherefore I say unto thee, Her sins, which are many, are forgiven ; for she loved much : but to whom little is forgiven, *the same* loveth little.—LUKE, ch. 7.

2012. —— Destroy each Other. *Parable.* [See No. 2008.]

2013. —— Insolvent. *Jews.* [1] There was a great cry of the people and of their wives against their brethren the Jews. [3] *Some*..said, We have mortgaged our lands, vineyards, and houses, that we might buy corn, because of the dearth. —NEH., ch. 5.

2014. —— protected. *Law.* [10] When thou dost lend thy brother any thing, thou shalt not go into his house to fetch his pledge. [11] Thou shalt stand abroad, and the man to whom thou dost lend shall bring out the pledge abroad unto thee.—DEUT., ch. 24.

See other illustrations under :

BORROWING.

Ruinous. Borrowed of the Egyptians..spoiled   915
Servant. Borrower is servant to the lender   912
Trouble. Axe head fell into the water..borrowed   913

LENDING.

Duty. Brethren..shalt surely lend him..his need   4940
Lord. As long as he liveth..lent unto the L.   4941
**   "   ** He that hath pity..lendeth unto the L.   4942

USURY.

Abolished. Let us leave off this usury   9146
Condemned. I was angry..ye exact usury   9147
Law. Not lend upon usury to thy brother   9148
Opportunity. Because of the dearth..borrowed   9149

Great. King take account..owed 10,000 talents   72
Mortgaged. Mortgaged our lands..vineyards   2013

2015. DECEPTION of Apostates. *Latter Times.* [1] The Spirit speaketh expressly, that in the latter times some shall depart from the faith, giving heed to seducing spirits, and doctrines of devils ; [2] Speaking lies in hypocrisy ; having their conscience seared with a hot iron.—1 TIM., ch. 4.

2016. —— An Assassin's. *Ehud* [19] Said, I have a secret errand unto thee, O king : who said, Keep silence. And all that stood by him went out from him. [21] And Ehud put forth his left hand, and took the dagger from his right thigh, and thrust it into his belly.—JUDGES, ch. 13.

2017. —— of Backsliders. *Proverb.* [14] The backslider in heart shall be filled with his own ways : and a good man *shall be satisfied* from himself.—PROV., ch. 14.

2018. —— A Brother's. *Jacob.* [19] Jacob said unto his father, I *am* Esau thy firstborn ; I have done according as thou badest me : arise, I pray thee, sit and eat of my venison, that thy soul may bless me.—GEN., ch. 27.

2019. —— A cruel. *Jacob's Sons.* [31] They took Joseph's coat, and killed a kid of the goats, and dipped the coat in the blood ; ³² . .and they brought *it* to their father ; and said, This have we found : know now whether it *be* thy son's coat or no.—GEN., ch. 37.

2020. —— Difficult. *Jacob.* ²² Jacob went near unto Isaac his father ; and he felt him, and said, The voice *is* Jacob's voice, but the hands *are* the hands of Esau.—GEN., ch. 27.

2021. —— discovered. *David* ¹⁹ Said, *Is not* the hand of Joab with thee in all this ? And the woman answered and said. .thy servant Joab, he bade me, and he put all these words in the mouth of thine handmaid.—2 SAM., ch. 14.

2022. —— of the Deceiver. *Jacob.* ²⁵ In the morning, behold, it *was* Leah : and he said to Laban. .did not I serve with thee for Rachel ? wherefore then hast thou beguiled me ?—GEN., ch. 29.

2023. —— hurts the Deceiver. *P r o v e r b.* ¹⁷ Bread of deceit *is* sweet to a man ; but afterwards his mouth shall be filled with gravel.—PROV., ch. 20.

2024. —— by Equivocation. *Abram.* ¹² The Egyptians shall see thee, that they shall say, This *is* his wife : and they will kill me. . ¹³ Say. . thou *art* my sister : that it may be well with me for thy sake.—GEN., ch. 12. [She was daughter to his father, but not to his mother.]

2025. —— Ineffective. *Blind Ahijah.* ² Jeroboam said to his wife. .disguise thyself, that thou be not known to be the wife of Jeroboam ; and get thee to. .Ahijah the prophet, which told me that *I should be* king over this people. ³. .go to him : he shall tell thee what shall become of the child.—1 KINGS, ch. 14.

2026. —— exposed. *Peter.* ⁷⁰ He denied it again. And a little after, they. .said again to Peter, Surely thou art *one* of them : for thou art a Galilean, and thy speech agreeth *thereto.* ⁷¹ But he began to curse and to swear, *saying,* I know not this man.—MARK, ch. 14.

2027. —— The first. *E v e* ⁶ Saw that the tree *was* good for food, and that it *was* pleasant to the eyes, and a tree to be desired to make *one* wise, she took. .and did eat, and gave also unto her husband. . ⁷ And the eyes of them both were opened.—GEN., ch. 3.

2028. —— Fear of. *Disciples.* ²⁶ When Saul was come to Jerusalem, he assayed to join himself to the disciples : but they were all afraid of him, and believed not that he was a disciple.—ACTS, ch. 9.

2029. —— for Gain. *Ananias.* ³ Peter said, Ananias, why hath Satan filled thine heart to lie to the Holy Ghost, and to keep back *part* of the price of the land ?—ACTS, ch. 5.

2030. —— of Hypocrites. *Pharisees.* ²³ Ye pay tithe of mint and anise and cummin, and have omitted the weightier *matters* of the law, judgment, mercy, and faith : these ought ye to have done, and not to leave the other undone. —MAT., ch. 23.

2031. —— Insincere. *Pilate.* ²⁴ When Pilate saw that he could prevail nothing, but *that* rather a tumult was made, he took water, and washed *his* hands before the multitude, saying, I am innocent of the blood of this just person. —MAT., ch. 27.

2032. —— impossible. *Elijah.* ³³ He put the

wood in order, and cut the bullock in pieces, and laid *him* on the wood, and said, Fill four barrels with water, and pour *it* on the burnt sacrifice, and on the wood. ³⁴ And he said, Do *it* the second time. .And he said, Do *it* the third time.— 1 KINGS, ch. 18.

2033. —— An ingenious. *Gibeonites.* ⁴ They . .made as if they had been ambassadors, and took old sacks upon their asses, and wine-bottles, old, and rent, and bound up ; ⁵ And old shoes and clouted. .and old garments upon them ; and all the bread. .was dry *and* mouldy. ⁶ And they went to Joshua.—JOSH., ch. 9.

2034 —— Justifiable. *By Michal.* ¹⁵ Saul sent the messengers *again* to see David, saying, Bring him up to me in the bed, that I may slay him. ¹⁶ And when the messengers were come in, behold, *there was* an image in the bed, with a pillow of goats' hair for his bolster.—1 SAM., ch. 19.

2035. —— Military. *Sisera to Jael.* ²⁰ He said unto her, Stand in the door of the tent, and it shall be, when any man doth come and inquire of thee, and say, Is there any man here ? that thou shalt say, No.—JUDGES, ch. 4.

2036. —— Overthrown by. *Moabites.* ²² The Moabites saw the water on the other side *as* red as blood : ²³ And they said, This *is* blood : the kings. .have smitten one another : now therefore, Moab, to the spoil. ²⁴ And when they came to the camp of Israel, the Israelites rose up and smote the Moabites, so that they fled before them.—2 KINGS, ch. 3.

2037. —— Perfidious. *Joab.* ⁹ Art thou in health, my brother ? And Joab took Amasa by the beard with the right hand to kiss him. ¹⁰ But Amasa took no heed to the sword that *was* in Joab's hand : so he smote him therewith in the fifth *rib.*—2 SAM., ch. 20.

2038. —— Preservation by. *Spies by Rahab.* ⁵ Whither the men went, I wot not : pursue after them quickly ; for ye shall overtake them. ⁶ But she had brought them up to the roof of the house, and hid them with the stalks of flax. —JOSH., ch. 2.

2039. —— Religious. *Scribes.* ⁴⁷ Which devour widows' houses, and for a shew make long prayers : the same shall receive greater damnation.—LUKE, ch. 20.

2040. —— repeated. *Delilah by Samson.* ¹⁵ She said unto him, How canst thou say, I love thee, when thine heart *is* not with me ? Thou hast mocked me these three times, and hast not told me wherein thy great strength *lieth.*—JUDGES, ch. 16.

2041. —— removed. *Parable of the Ewe Lamb.* ⁵ Davi's anger was greatly kindled. .and he said to Nathan, *As* the Lord liveth, the man that hath done this *thing* shall surely die : ⁶ And he shall restore the lamb fourfold. . ⁷ And Nathan said to David, Thou *art.*—2 SAM., ch. 12.

2042. —— Spiritual. *Laodiceans.* ¹⁷ Because thou sayest, I am rich, and increased with goods, and have need of nothing ; and knowest not that thou art wretched, and miserable, and poor, and blind, and naked : ¹⁸ I counsel thee to buy of me gold.—REV., ch. 3.

2043. —— A Sinner's. *Adam.* ⁹ The Lord God called unto Adam, and said. .Where *art* thou ? ¹⁰ And he said, I heard thy voice in the garden, and I was afraid, because I *was* naked ; and I hid myself.—GEN., ch. 3.

2044. —— **of the Self-willed.** *Saul.* ²¹ The people took of the spoil, sheep and oxen, the chief of the things which should have been utterly destroyed, to sacrifice unto the Lord.. ²² And Samuel said, Hath the Lord *as great* delight in burnt offerings and sacrifices, as in obeying the voice of the Lord ?—1 SAM., ch. 15.

2045. —— **taught.** *Rebekah.* ¹⁵ Rebekah took goodly raiment of..Esau, which *were* with her in the house, and put them upon Jacob.. ¹⁶ And ..the skins of the kids of the goats upon his hands, and upon the smooth of his neck.—GEN., ch. 27.

2046. —— **Unconscious.** *Graves.* ⁴⁴ Woe unto you, scribes and Pharisees, hypocrites ! for ye are as graves which appear not, and the men that walk over *them* are not aware *of them.*— LUKE, ch. 11.

2047. —— **in Wine.** *Proverb.* ¹ Wine *is* a mocker, strong drink *is* raging : and whosoever is deceived thereby is not wise.—PROV., ch. 20.

2048. —— **A woeful.** *Isaiah.* ²⁰ Woe unto them that call evil good, and good evil ; that put darkness for light, and light for darkness ; that put bitter for sweet, and sweet for bitter.— ISA., ch. 5.

See other illustrations under :

ASSASSINATION.
Foul. Joab..shed out [Amasa's]..bowels to the　523
Hired. When I say, Smite Amnon ; then kill him　524
Patriotic. Ehud took the dagger..thrust into　525
Revenge. Joab smote [Abner]..for Asahel his　526

DELUSION.
Destructive. Ahaz sacrificed unto the gods that　2168
Success. Our god hath delivered Samson..into　2169
Wicked. Lot seemed as one that mocked to his　2170

DISSEMBLING.
Confessed. I saw among the spoils..took　2424
Imitated. Barnabas..carried away with their d.　2425
Inconsistency. If thou, being a Jew..Gentiles to　2426
Rebuked. I withstood Peter to the face..blamed　2427

FALSEHOOD.
Agreement. Ananias kept back part..wife..privy　2985
Begets. My master hath sent me..went no whither　2986
Bribery. Say ye..stole him..they took the money　2987
Covering. Began to curse..I know not the man　2988
Folly. Ananias, was it not thine? and after it was　2989
Father. Your father the devil..no truth in him　2990
Impostor's. Jacob said to his father, The Lord　2992
Sacrilegious. An angel spake..Bring him back　2993
Saved by. David said to Abimelech, The king sent　2992
　　" 　　 Jonathan said, David..run to Bethlehem　2994
Shortlived. Lying tongue is but for a moment　2995
Statecraft. Garments and shoes, old..long journey　2996
Spirit of. I will be a lying spirit in..prophets　2997
Sin. Thou hast not lied unto men, but..G　2998
Victim. Joseph's master put him in prison　2999

FRAUD.
Appearances. Gibeonites..took old sacks..old　3468
Commerce. Take thy bill..quickly..write fifty　3409
Demagogue. Oh that I were a judge..do justice　2171
Pious. Sons of the prophets, give..silver [Gehazi]　3410
Religious. His enemy..sowed tares among the　3411
Spiritual. Simon offered money..Holy Ghost　3412
Traitors. Whomsoever I shall kiss..is he　3413
Wages. Hire of the labourers kept..crieth　3414

FLATTERY.
Danger. People gave a shout..voice of a god　3254
Failure. Herodians saying..regardest not..any　3255
Success. Ask a petition of any god..save thee　3256

INFATUATION.
Blind. Time of his distress did Ahaz trespass more　4455
Reproved. Knowest thou not yet..Egypt is　4456
Wicked. They were driven out from P.'s presence　4457
　　" 　　 Simon saw..H. G. was given, he offered　4458

MISTAKE.
Appearances. Eli thought she had been drunken　5468
Adversity. Bereaved..all these things are against　5469
Conscientious. I verily thought..I ought to do　5470
Corrected. There is death in the pot..bring meal　5471
Disastrous. The kings have smitten..Moab to the　5472
Glorious. She runneth..They have taken away　5473
Hearing. Eli, Eli, lama sabachthani..calleth for　5474
Infatuation. We will certainly burn incense..were　5475
Ignorance. In the resurrection, whose wife shall　5476
Man's. Samuel looked on Eliab..surely the L.'s　5477
Mortifying. King said to Haman..do so to Mord.　5478
Prejudice. I thought I ought..contrary to the　5479
Prosperity. Then had we plenty of victuals, and　5480
Serious. Altar of witness was supposed to be for　5481
Suspicion. David rather sent..to search the city　5482

SORCERY.
Captivating. Simon bewitched the people..all　8202
Curious Arts. [Ephesians] used curious arts..burn　908
Imposition. Magicians..cast down..rod..serpent　5162
Renounced. Simon himself believed..was bap'd.　8203
　　" 　　 [Ephesians] used curious arts　8204

TRICK.
Diplomatic. From a very far country are..come　8955
Hypocrites. Feign themselves just men..might　8956
Legerdemain. Magicians..rods became serpents　8957
Politicians. Shall ask a petition..save of thee　8958

Accusation. Abner came to deceive thee　8526
Concealed. Devour widows' houses..for a pretence　5548
Demagogue. Absalom..put forth his hand..kissed　2171
Error. There is a way that seemeth right..way of　2710
Friendly. David..go to Bethlehem..in the field　19
Method. By fair speeches deceive the—Rom. 16 : 18
Numbers. Number ye the people..why..this　6548
Process. Wax worse, deceiving and being—2 Tim. 3 : 13
Self-injurious. The wicked is snared by..his own　4947
Susceptibility. Adam was not deceived—1 Tim. 2 : 14
Stigmatized. Remember that deceiver said after　2054
Self. Let no man deceive himself—1 Cor. 3 : 18
　　" 　　 Deceiveth his own heart..religion is vain　8255
Spirits. L. said, Who shall deceive Ahab ?—1 Kings 22 : 30
Spiritual. If we say we have no sin, we d.　7948
Taunt. Are ye also deceived ?　7477
Unsuccessful. Hath deceived me and changed my　1804
Vice. Harlot..subtile of heart..kissed him　115
　　" 　　 Lips honeycomb..words smoother than oil　117
War. Elisha said, I will bring you to the man　829
Warning. Let not Hezekiah deceive you　2917
　　" 　　 Take heed that no man d..I am—Matt. 24 : 4

2049. DECEIVER, Accused as a. *Jesus.* ¹³ Pilate.. ¹⁴ Said..Ye have wrought this man unto me, as one that perverteth the people ; and, behold, I, having examined *him* before you, have found no fault in this man touching those things whereof ye accuse him.—LUKE, ch. 23.

2050. —— **A popular.** *Simon.* ⁹ Simon.. beforetime in the same city used sorcery, and bewitched the people of Samaria, giving out that himself was some great one : ¹⁰ To whom they all gave heed, from the least to the great-

est, saying, This man is the great power of God.
—Acts, ch. 8.

2051. —— **A reputed.** *Jesus.* [62] Pharisees came together unto Pilate, [63] Saying, Sir, we remember that that deceiver said, while he was yet alive, After three days I will rise again.—Mat., ch. 27.

2052. —— **Self-deceived, A.** *Simon.* [18] When Simon saw that through laying on of the apostles' hands the Holy Ghost was given, he offered them money, [19] Saying, Give me also this power.—Acts, ch. 8.

2053. —— **A Saint or a.** *Jesus.* [12] There was much murmuring among the people concerning him : for some said, He is a good man : others said, Nay ; but he deceiveth the people.—John, ch. 7.

See **DECEPTION** *and references.*

2054. DECEIT, Base. *Ishmael.* [Eighty men came,] [5] having their beards shaven, and their clothes rent, and having cut themselves, with offerings and incense in their hand, to bring *them* to the house of the Lord. [6] And Ishmael..went forth from Mizpah to meet them, weeping all along as he went : and..he said.. Come to Gedaliah.. [7]..when they came into the midst of the city..Ishmael..slew them, *and cast them* into the midst of the pit.—Jer., ch. 41.

2055. —— **Religious.** *Pharisees.* [15] The Pharisees..took counsel how they might entangle him in *his* talk. [16] And they sent..their disciples with the Herodians, saying, Master, we know that thou art true, and teachest the way of God in truth, neither carest thou for any *man :* for thou regardest not the person of men. [17] Tell us..Is it lawful to give tribute unto Cesar, or not ?—Mat., ch. 22.

2056. —— **Self-injurious.** *Proverb.* [17] Bread of deceit *is* sweet to a man ; but afterwards his mouth shall be filled with gravel.—Prov., ch. 20.

See **DECEPTION** *and references.*

2057. DECISION, An affectionate. *Ruth.* [16] Entreat me not to leave thee, *or* to return from following after thee : for whither thou goest, I will go ; and where thou lodgest, I will lodge : thy people *shall be* my people, and thy God my God.—Ruth, ch. 1.

2058. —— **A bold.** *Absalom.* [29] Absalom sent for Joab, to have sent him to the king ; but he would not come to him : and when he sent again the second time, he would not come. [30] Therefore he said unto his servants, See, Joab's field is near mine, and he hath barley there ; go and set it on fire.—2 Sam., ch. 14.

2059. —— **changed.** *Peter.* [8] Thou shalt never wash my feet. Jesus answered him, If I wash thee not, thou hast no part with me. [9] Simon Peter saith..Lord, not my feet only, but also *my* hands and *my* head.—John, ch. 13.

2060. —— **A Christian's.** *Jesus.* [24] No man can serve two masters : for either he will hate the one, and love the other ; or else he will hold to the one, and despise the other. Ye cannot serve God and mammon.—Mat., ch. 6.

2061. —— **A desperate.** *Esther.* [11] *There is* one law of his to put *him* to death, except such to whom the king shall hold out the golden sceptre, that he may live.. [16]..fast ye for me..

three days..I also and my maidens will fast likewise ; and so will I go in unto the king, which *is* not according to the law : and if I perish, I perish.—Esther, ch. 4.

2062. —— **A difficult.** *David.* [13] Gad came to David..and said..Shall seven years of famine come..or wilt thou flee three months before thine enemies..or that there be three days' pestilence in thy land?.. [14] And David said..I am in a great strait.—2 Sam., ch. 24.

2063. —— **by Evidence.** *Elijah.* [23] And I will dress the other bullock, and lay *it* on wood, and put no fire *under :* [24] And call ye on the name of your gods, and I will call on the name of the Lord : and the God that answereth by fire, let him be God. And all the people answered..it is well spoken.—1 Kings, ch. 18.

2064. —— **A final.** *Disciple.* [61] Lord, I will follow thee ; but let me first go bid them farewell, which are at home.. [62] And Jesus said.. No man, having put his hand to the plough, and looking back, is fit for the kingdom of God. —Luke, ch. 9.

2065. —— **A fixed.** *Three Hebrews.* [17] If it be *so,* our God whom we serve is able to deliver us from the burning fiery furnace, and he will deliver *us* out of thine hand, O king. [18] But if not, be it known unto thee, O king, that we will not serve thy gods, nor worship the golden image.—Dan., ch. 3.

2066. —— **A happy.** *The Prodigal.* [17] When he came to himself, he said, How many hired servants of my father's have bread enough and to spare, and I perish with hunger ! [18] I will arise and go to my father, and will say..Father, I have sinned.—Luke, ch. 15.

2067. —— **An heroic.** *Paul.* [12] Besought him not to go up to Jerusalem. [13] Then Paul answered, What mean ye to weep and to break mine heart? for I am ready not to be bound only, but also to die at Jerusalem for the name of the Lord Jesus.—Acts, ch. 21.

2068. —— **An immediate.** *Abram's Servant.* [49] Now, if ye will deal kindly and truly with my master, tell me : and if not, tell me ; that I may turn to the right hand, or to the left. [50] Then Laban and Bethuel answered..The thing proceedeth from the Lord.—Gen., ch. 24.

2069. —— **Important.** *Serpent of Brass.* [9] Moses made a serpent of brass, and put it upon a pole ; and..if a serpent had bitten any man when he beheld the serpent of brass, he lived. —Num., ch. 21.

2070. —— **An independent.** *Joshua.* [15] If it seem evil unto you to serve the Lord, choose you this day whom ye will serve ; whether..gods of the Amorites, in whose land ye dwell : but as for me and my house, we will serve the Lord. —Josh., ch. 24.

2071. —— **An ill-considered.** *Apostles.* [22] Jesus answered..Ye know not what ye ask. Are ye able to drink of the cup that I shall drink of, and to be baptized with the baptism that I am baptized with ? They say..We are able.—Mat., ch. 20.

2072. —— **manifested.** *Moses.* [After the golden calf was destroyed,] [26] Then Moses stood in the gate of the camp, and said, Who *is* on the Lord's side? *let him come* unto me.—Ex., ch. 32. [3000 idolaters slain.]

2073. —— **A modest.** *Guest.* ¹⁰ When thou art bidden, go and sit down in the lowest room ; that when he that bade thee cometh, he may say..Friend, go up higher : then shalt thou have worship in the presence of them that sit at meat with thee.—LUKE, ch. 14.

2074. —— **A premature.** *Builder.* ²⁸ For which of you, intending to build a tower, sitteth not down first, and counteth the cost.. ²⁹ Lest haply, after he hath laid the foundation, and is not able to finish it.—LUKE, ch. 14.

2075. —— **A ready.** *Paul.* ¹⁵ When it pleased God, who..called *me* by his grace, ¹⁶ To reveal his Son in me, that I might preach him among the heathen ; immediately I conferred not with flesh and blood.—GAL., ch. 1.

2076. —— **A resolute.** *Caleb.* ³⁰ Caleb stilled the people..and said, Let us go up at once, and possess it ; for we are well able to overcome it. ³¹ But the men..said..they *are* stronger than we.—NUM., ch. 3.

2077. —— **A rash.** *Ahasuerus.* ⁹ Let it be written that they may be destroyed : and I will pay ten thousand talents of silver..into the king's treasuries. ¹⁰ And the king took his ring from his hand, and gave it unto Haman..the Jews' enemy.—ESTHER, ch. 3.

2078. —— **in Religion.** *Mt. Carmel.* ²¹ Elijah ..said, How long halt ye between two opinions ? if the Lord *be* God, follow him : but if Baal, *then* follow him. And the people answered him not a word.—1 KINGS, ch. 18.

2079. —— **A speedy.** *The Eunuch.* ³⁶ They came unto a certain water : and the eunuch said, See, *here is* water ; what doth hinder me to be baptized ? ³⁷ And Philip said, If thou believest with all thine heart, thou mayest.—ACTS, ch. 8.

2080. —— **A serious.** *Aged Moses.* ²⁶ I set before you this day a blessing and a curse ; ²⁷ A blessing, if ye obey the commandments of the Lord your God.. ²⁸ And a curse, if ye will not obey the commandments of the Lord.—DEUT., ch. 11.

2081. —— **A selfish.** *Guest.* ⁸ When thou art bidden..to a wedding, sit not down in the highest room ; lest a more honourable man than thou be bidden of him ; ⁹ And he that bade thee ..say to thee, Give this man place ; and thou begin with shame to take the lowest room.— LUKE, ch. 14.

2082. —— **An unfortunate.** *Lot.* ⁹ Separate thyself, I pray thee, from me : if *thou wilt take* the left hand, then I will go to the right ; or if *thou depart* to the right hand, then I will go to the left. ¹⁰ And Lot lifted up his eyes, and beheld all the plain of Jordan, that it *was* well watered every where, before the Lord destroyed Sodom.—GEN., ch. 13.

2083. —— **Unavoidable.** *Jehu.* ³² Who *is* on my side ? who ? And there looked out to him two *or* three eunuchs. ³³ And he said, Throw her down. So they threw her down : and *some* of her blood was sprinkled on the wall, and on the horses : and he trode her under foot.— 2 KINGS, ch. 9. [So Jezebel died.]

2084. —— **A worldly.** *Young Ruler.* ²¹ Jesus said..If thou wilt be perfect, go *and* sell that thou hast, and give to the poor..*and* follow

me. ²²..he went away sorrowful : for he had great possessions.—MAT., ch. 19.

2085. —— **A wise.** *Four Lepers.* ⁴ If we say, We will enter into the city, then the famine *is* in the city, and we shall die there : and if we sit still here, we die also. Now therefore come, and let us fall unto the host of the Syrians : if they save us alive, we shall live ; and if they kill us, we shall but die.—2 KINGS, ch. 7.

2086. —— **A wavering.** *Wave.* ⁶ For he that wavereth is like a wave of the sea driven with the wind and tossed.—JAMES, ch. 1.

2087. —— **Youthful.** *Three Hebrews.* ⁸ Daniel purposed in his heart that he would not defile himself with the portion of the king's meat, nor with the wine which he drank : therefore he requested of the prince of the eunuchs that he might not defile himself.—DAN., ch. 1.

See other illustrations under

DETERMINATION.

Evil. As the L. liveth..I will not leave thee	2262
" We will certainly..burn incense to the queen	2260
Fixed. In every city bonds..none..move me	2261
Resolute. Absalom said..set it on fire	2263
Wanting. I will let him go..Pilate gave sentence	2264

JUDGE.

Bribery. Samuel's sons..took bribes, and	4760
Circuit. Samuel went from year to year in circuit	4756
Qualifications. He that is without sin among you	4757
Unjust. Crucify him ; I find no fault in him	4758
Unrighteous. Ananias commanded to smite him	4759
Rebellious. To your tents, O Israel	4643
Unconscious. King said..thyself hast decided it	7693
Wise. Divide the living child in two	490
" Render unto Cesar the things..are Cesar's	8602
See CHOICE.	

2088. DECORUM criticised. *Bartimeus.* ⁴⁷ When he heard that it was Jesus..he began to cry out, and say, Jesus, *thou* Son of David, have mercy on me. ⁴⁸ And many charged him that he should hold his peace : but he cried the more a great deal, *Thou* Son of David, have mercy on me.—MARK, ch. 10.

2089. —— **Want of.** *David.* ¹⁶ As the ark.. came into the city of David, Michal..looked through a window, and saw king David leaping and dancing before the Lord ; and she despised him in her heart.—2 SAM., ch. 6.

See other illustrations under :

MANNERS.

Instruction. Sit down in the lowest room	5207
Polite. May we know what this new doctrine is	5208
Rude. What will this babbler say ?	5209

2090. DECREE, A terrible. *Ahasuerus.* ¹⁰ The king took his ring from his hand, and gave it unto Haman..the Jews' enemy. ¹³ And the letters were sent by post into all the king's provinces, to destroy, to kill, and to cause to perish, all Jews, both young and old, little children and women.—ESTHER, ch. 3.

See other illustrations under :

Terrifying. Shall ask..of any god or man..lions	3256
Unexpected. Which speak anything against the G.	17

2091. DEDICATION accepted. *Tabernacle.* ²³ Moses and Aaron..came out, and blessed the people : and the glory of the Lord appeared.. ²⁴ And there came a fire out from before the Lord, and consumed upon the altar the burnt offering and the fat : *which* when all the people saw, they shouted, and fell on their faces.—LEV., ch. 9.

2092. —— A Heathen. *Golden Image.*
² Nebuchadnezzar..sent to gather together the princes, the governors, and the captains, the judges, the treasurers, the counsellors, the sheriffs, and all the rulers of the provinces, to come to the dedication of the image. ⁷..when all the people heard the sound of the cornet, flute, harp, sackbut, psaltery, and all kinds of music, all the people, the nations, and the languages, fell down *and* worshipped the golden image.—DAN., ch. 3.

2093. —— of Property. *David.* ¹⁰ *Joram* brought with him vessels of silver, and..of gold, and..of brass : ¹¹ Which also king David did dedicate unto the Lord, with the silver and gold that he had dedicated of all nations which he subdued.—2 SAM., ch. 8.

See other illustrations under :

CONSECRATION.
Covenant. All the people stood to the covenant 1584
Leadership. Took Joshua..laid hands upon him 1585
Service. Moses took of the blood..ear..thumb 1586
Self-denying. Made the laver..looking glasses 1587

DEVOTION.
Benevolent. Poor widow hath cast in more than 2269
Deceptive. I will lay down my life for thy sake 2270
Excessive. For the work of C..nigh unto death 2271
Expensive. Mary..pound of ointment..very c. 2272
Friendship. Ittai..whether in death or life..be 2273
Filial. Thy people shall be my..thy God my 2274
Fraternal. Priscilla and A..have for my life laid 2275
Hinderance. How can ye believe which receive 2276
Partial. Howbeit the high places were not r'd 2277
Rewarded. Followed me fully..into the land 2278
Religious. Great while before day..prayed 2279
Sublime. Lay not thine hand on the lad 2280
Unselfish. Forgive..if not, blot me 2281

Firstborn. Set apart unto the L..firstborn 1178
Childhood. Hannah said..appear before the L. 1218

2094. DEEDS, Authenticated by. *Jesus.* ³⁶ Say ye of him, whom the Father hath sanctified, and sent into the world, Thou blasphemest ; because I said, I am the Son of God ? ³⁷ If I do not the works of my Father, believe me not.—JOHN, ch. 10.

2095. —— evince Character. *Blind Man.* ³² Since the world began was it not heard that any man opened the eyes of one that was born blind. ³³ If this man were not of God, he could do nothing.—JOHN, ch. 9.

2096. —— Tested by. *Good Samaritan.* ³⁶ Which now of these three, thinkest thou, was neighbour unto him that fell among the thieves ? ³⁷ And he said, He that shewed mercy on him. Then said Jesus..Go, and do thou likewise.—LUKE, ch. 10.

2097. —— like Words. *Mt. Carmel.* ³⁹ When all the people saw *it*, they fell on their faces : and they said, The Lord, he *is* the God.. ⁴⁰ And Elijah said..Take the prophets of Baal ; let not one of them escape. And they took them..and slew them.—1 KINGS, ch. 18.

See other illustrations under :

ACTIVITY.
Astonishing. His friends..said, He is beside himself 92
Benevolent. Jesus went about all their cities 93
Spiritually. Mary hath chosen that good part 94

POWER.
Delegated. Why could we not cast him out 6312
Endowment. Filled..began to speak with other 6313
God gives. [Samson] L. blessed..Spirit began 6314
God only. [Peter] By our own power made 6315
Loss. [Samson] Shake myself..wist not L. was 6316
Might. Not by might, nor by power..great 6317
Promised. [Joshua] Not any able to stand 6318
Prayer. [Hezekiah] prayed Sennacherib..85,000 6319
Preaching. My speech..demonstration of the S. 6320
Ruling. Rebuked the wind, the raging water 6321
Spiritual. [Stephen] Not able to resist the 6322
Spirit. [Samson] Cords..upon his arms..as flax 6323
Sudden. [Joseph] No man lift up his hand or 6324
Tears. [Moses] Babe wept..had compassion on 6327
Temptation. All these will I give thee [Satan] 6325
Waiting. Wait for the promise..receive power 6329
Weakness. I am weak, though anointed [David] 6328

Differ. They fell before Jonathan..slew after 1784
Doubled. I am not able to bear all this people 453
Evidence in. Son liveth..by this I know..of God 1684
" Art come from God..could do them 1125
Presumed. James and John..can ye drink of the 477

See **WORK** and references.

2098. DEFEAT, Angered by. *Elihu.* ⁴ Now Elihu had waited till Job had spoken, because they *were* elder than he. ⁵ When Elihu saw that *there was* no answer in the mouth of *these* three men, then his wrath was kindled.—JOB, ch. 32.

2099. —— of Conspirators. *Pharisees.* ¹⁵ The Pharisees..took counsel how they might entangle him in *his* talk. ²¹..Then saith he unto them, Render therefore unto Cesar the things which are Cesar's ; and unto God the things that are God's. ²²..they marvelled, and left him.—MAT., ch. 22.

2100. —— Desperation from. *Jews.* ⁹ Disputing with Stephen. ¹⁰..they were not able to resist the wisdom and the spirit by which he spake. ¹¹ Then they suborned men, which said, We have heard him speak blasphemous words against Moses, and *against* God.—ACTS, ch. 6.

2101. —— A humiliating. *Israelites.* ⁵ The men of Ai smote of them about thirty and six men : for they chased them *from* before the gate..wherefore the hearts of the people melted, and became as water. ⁶ And Joshua rent his clothes, and fell to the earth upon his face before the ark of the Lord.—JOSH., ch. 7.

2102. —— predicted. *Israelites.* ¹⁵ Thus saith the Lord God..In returning and rest shall ye be saved ; in quietness and in confidence shall be your strength : and ye would not. ¹⁶ But ye said, No ; for we will flee upon horses ; therefore shall ye flee : and, We will ride upon the swift ; therefore shall they that pursue you be swift. ¹⁷ One thousand *shall flee* at the rebuke of one ; at the rebuke of five shall ye flee : till ye be left as a beacon upon the top of a mountain, and as an ensign on a hill.—ISA., ch. 30.

2103. —— A providential. *Babel.* ⁴ Let us build us a city, and a tower, whose top *may* reach unto heaven ; and let us make us a name, lest we be scattered abroad.. ⁹ Therefore is the name..Babel ; because the Lord did there confound the language of all the earth : and from thence..scatter them.—GEN., ch. 11.

See other illustrations under :

DISAPPOINTMENT.

Doubt. Heard..he was alive..seen..believed not   2315
in Gifts. Gave Hiram 20 cities..pleased him not   2316
Good. They have taken the L. out of the sepulchre 2318
Ignorance. Evil place ? no place of seed..figs   2319
Judgment. Thou hast taught in our streets   2320
Misjudged. We trusted..had been he..should have   2321
Maternal. Bare Cain..I have gotten a man of the   2322
Perplexing. Which of us is for the king of I. ?   2323
Religion. Since we left off to burn incense..for   2324
Unendurable. Ahithophel..counsel not followed   2325
Many Disappointments. Consider your ways   2326

FAILURE.

Avoiding. Intending to build a tower..first   2867
Cruelty. The more they afflicted them, the more   2868
Complaint. L. wherefore hast thou so evil   2869
Church. That they should cast him out..not   2870
Discouraging. Ye have..put a sword in their hand   2871
Disheartening. Have toiled all the night..taken   2872
Explained. This kind can come..by prayer   2873
Fear. We saw the giants..we were grasshoppers   2874
Irremediable. The door was shut..Lord came   2875
Ominous. If thou hast begun to fall..not prevail' 2876
Ridiculed. Mock him..began to build..not able   2878
Temporary. I know not the L., neither..let I. go   2879
        See BONDAGE and references.
        See VICTORY.

— DEFECT. —

See illustrations under :

BLEMISH.

Disqualifies. Let him not approach the altar   813
Without. Absalom..from the sole..without b.   814

FEEBLENESS.

Ashamed. I was ashamed to require..soldiers   3188
Age. Eli was 98 years old ; eyes were dim   3189
  "   David was old and stricken..gat no heat   3190

WEAKNESS.

Believers. Babes in Christ..not able to bare meat 9394
    "   Lest the people repent..return to   9395
Conscious. I am..weak, though anointed king   9396
Flesh. Moses' hands were heavy..stayed up his   9397
Instruments. L. sent flies..land was corrupted   9398
Moral. Peter separated..fearing them of the   9399
Personal. He that abideth in me bringeth forth   9400
Remembered. I was with you in weakness   9401
Submission. Ahab said, I am thine, and all that I 9402
Spiritless. All the kings..their heart melted   9403
    "   Ai smote..hearts of the people melted   9404

Overlooked. L. said unto Jehu..because..done   4350
        See DEFICIENCY and references.

2104. DEFENCE declined. *Jesus.* 12 When he
was accused of the chief priests and elders, he
answered nothing. 13 Then said Pilate..Hear-
est thou not how many things they witness
against thee ? 14 And he answered him to never
a word ; insomuch that the governor marvelled
greatly.—MAT., ch. 27.

2105. —— **An incomplete.** *Goliath.* 5 And *he
had* a helmet of brass..and he *was* armed with a
coat of mail ; and the weight..was five thousand
shekels of brass. 6 And *he had* greaves of brass
upon his legs, and a target of brass between his
shoulders. 7 And the staff of his spear *was* like
a weaver's beam..and one bearing a shield went
before him.—1 SAM., ch. 17. [He was killed by a
sling stone.]

2106. —— **A lawful.** *Jews.* 11 The king

granted the Jews..to gather themselves together,
and to stand for their life, to destroy..all.. that
would assault them, *both* little ones and women,
and *to take* the spoil of them for a prey.—Es-
THER, ch. 8.

2107. —— **A perilous.** *Of David.* 32 Jonathan
answered Saul his father, and said..Wherefore
shall he be slain ? what hath he done ? 33 And
Saul cast a javelin at him to smite him.—1 SAM.,
ch. 20.

2108. —— **Preparation for.** *Military.* 14 Uzziah prepared for ..all the host shields, and
spears, and helmets, and habergeons, and bows,
and slings *to cast* stones. 15 And he made in
Jerusalem engines, invented by cunning men,
to be on the towers and upon the bulwarks, to
shoot arrows and great stones.—2 CHRON., ch. 26.

2109. —— **Spiritual.** *Armour.* 14 Stand therefore, having your loins girt about with truth,
and having on the breastplate of righteousness ;
15 And your feet shod with the preparation of
the gospel of peace ; 16 Above all, taking the
shield of faith, wherewith ye shall be able to
quench all the fiery darts of the wicked. 17 And
take the helmet of salvation, and the sword of
the Spirit, which is the word of God.—EPH., ch.
6.

2110. —— **Unheard.** *Ephesians.* 33 Alexander beckoned with the hand, and would have
made his defence unto the people. 34 But when
they knew that he was a Jew, all with one voice
about the space of two hours cried out, Great *is*
Diana of the Ephesians.—ACTS, ch. 19.

2111. —— **by Weapons.** *First Invention.* 23 I
have slain a man to my wounding, and a young
man to my hurt. 24 If Cain shall be avenged
sevenfold, truly Lamech seventy and sevenfold.
—GEN., ch. 4. [I can slay a man for my hurt,
when he hurts me ; even a vigorous young man
for my wound, when he wounds me. If Cain
shall be avenged of God sevenfold, I will avenge
myself more—seventy times seven.]

See other illustrations under :

ARMOUR.

Defenceless. [Goliath] had a helmet of brass   494
Rejected. David girded his sword..I can not   495
Without. Neither sword nor spear   496

DELIVERER.

Great. Righteousness as a cloak, a helmet of   2134
Raised. [Ehud] I. cried..L. raised them up a   2135
Rewarded. Who killeth him [Goliath] the king   2136
Valiant. Shamgar slew..Philistines 600..delivered 2137

SAFETY.

Godly. He that keepeth thee will not slumber   7547
  "   The beloved..shall dwell between his s.   7548
  "   Hast thou not made a hedge about him   7549
  "   I will both lay me down in peace and sleep   7550
  "   He shall cover thee with his feathers   7551
Hiding. Jotham..was left ; for he hid himself   7552
Mutual. Except these abide in the ship..not be   7553
Supposed. Charging the jailer to keep them safely 7554

WEAPONS.

Faith. David chose him five smooth stones   9443
Rejected. Saul armed David..helmet..coat of   9444

Divine. L. is my rock..fortress..high tower   1535
Shield. Above all, taking the shield of faith   8669
        See DELIVERANCE.
        See PROTECTION.

2112. DEFERENCE to the Aged. *Elihu.*
[1] These three men ceased to answer Job, because he *was* righteous in his own eyes. [4] Now Elihu had waited till Job had spoken, because they *were* elder than he.—JOB, ch. 32.

2113. —— a wicked. *Herod.* [8] Give me here John the Baptist's head in a charger. [9] And the king was sorry : nevertheless for the oath's sake, and them which sat with him at meat, he commanded *it* to be given *her.*—MAT., ch. 14.

See other illustrations under :

POLITENESS.

Cultivated. May we know what this new doctrine	6232
Inculcated. Sit down in the lowest room..higher	6233
Treacherous Art thou in health, my brother?	6234
Tender Is. well, the old man of whom ye spake ?	6235

RESPECT.

Age. I am young, and ye are very old..mine	7206
Great. Young men hid themselves..aged arose	7207
Good. Herod feared John..observed him..did	7208

REVERENCE.

Attitude. He opened it..stood up..bowed their	7316
Affectionate. Stood at his feet behind him, weeping	7317
Age. Joseph brought in Jacob..blessed Pharaoh	7318
Careful. Put off thy shoes..holy ground	7319
Commanded. No man be seen throughout..mount	7320
Commends. Peter fell down at Jesus' knees	7321
Esteem. Mephibosheth was come..did reverence	7322
Joyous. Came a fire..people shouted and fell	7323
Manifested. Joshua fell on his face..did worship	7324
Necessary. Him that is poor and of a contrite	7325
" Men of Bethshemesh looked into the	7326
Preserved by. Third captain fell on his knees	7327
Unworthy of. The king's servants reverenced H.	7328
Word. Ezra opened the book..all the people stood	7329
Worthy. Sent his son..will reverence him	7330
Youthful. [Young ruler] came running, and	7331

2114. DEFIANCE, a bold. *Goliath.* [10] I defy the armies of Israel this day ; give me a man, that we may fight together.—1 SAM., ch. 17.

2115. —— An impious. *Belshazzar.* [2] Belshazzar, while he tasted the wine, commanded to bring the golden and silver vessels..taken out of the temple which *was* in Jerusalem ; that the king and his princes, his wives and his concubines, might drink therein.—DAN., ch. 5.

2116. —— A wicked. *Pharaoh.* [2] Who *is* the Lord, that I should obey his voice to let Israel go? I know not the Lord, neither will I let Israel go.—Ex., ch. 5.

See other illustrations under :

CHALLENGE.

Battle. I defy the armies of I. this day	1083
Champions. Let the young men play before us	1084
Prayer. Call ye on the name of your gods, and I	1085
War. Jehu wrote letters..fight for your master's	1086

OPPOSITION.

Malicious. Diotrephes..receiveth us not	5900
Ridicule. They laughed us to scorn	5901
Unmoved. G. of heaven he will prosper us	5902
Weakened by. Weakened the hands of the	5903

2117. DEFICIENCY, An unconscious. *Young Ruler.* [20] The young man saith . . All these things have I kept from my youth up : what lack I yet ? [21] Jesus said..go *and* sell that thou hast, and give to the poor..and come *and* follow me.— MAT., ch. 19.

See other illustrations under :

WANT.

A Blessing. I perish with hunger..my father	8286
Contentment. I have learned..to be content	8287
Degraded. We boiled my son..give thy son	8288
Frivolity. He that followeth vain persons	8289
near Luxury. Rich man..fared sumptuously	8290
to Plenty. Four lepers..did eat and drink	8291
Sin brings. Woman..brought to a piece of bread	8292

Financial. Began to build, and was not able to	2878
Moral. One thing thou lackest, sell..give..follow	2876
Proven. Weighed in the balance, and found	9293
See **DEFECT** and references.	

2118. DEFILEMENT, Origin of. *Heart.* [19] For out of the heart proceed evil thoughts, murders, adulteries, fornications, thefts, false witness, blasphemies : [20] These are *the things* which defile a man : but to eat with unwashen hands defileth not a man.—MAT., ch. 15.

See other illustrations under :

CLEANSING.

Blood. Moses..sprinkled it on all the people	1343
" If the blood of bulls..much more..Christ	1344
Expulsion. He drove them all out of the temple	1345
Fire. This [live coal] hath touched..sin purged	1346
Heart. Create in me a clean heart, O God	1347
Spiritual. Who shall stand in his holy place	1348

GUILT.

Accumulated. Upon you..all the righteous blood	3766
Cowardice. Adam and his wife hid	3767
Degrees. One owed 500 pounds, the other 50	3768
Panic. Egyptians said, Let us flee	3769
See **SIN** and **WICKEDNESS.**	

—— DEGENERATION. ——

See illustrations under :

Children. Sons of Eli were sons of Belial.	1174
Corruption. Jews had married wives of Ashdod	1180
Inheritance. Visiting the iniquity of the f. upon c.	1186
" Abijam walked in all the sins of his f.	1187
" Children gather wood..cakes to the	1188
Neglect. Child left to himself bringeth..shame	1192
Responsibility. His blood be upon us..our children	1198
Witnesses. Ye be w...children of them which	1199
See **DEGRADATION.**	

2119. DEGRADATION by Drink. *All Classes.* [11] Woe unto them that rise up early in the morning, *that* they may follow strong drink ; that continue until night, *till* wine inflame them ! [15] And the mean man shall be brought down, and the mighty man shall be humbled, and the eyes of the lofty shall be humbled.—ISA., ch. 5.

2120. —— in Food. *Law.* [42] Whatsoever goeth upon the belly, and..upon *all* four, or.. hath more feet among all creeping things that creep upon the earth, them ye shall not eat ; for they *are* an abomination.—LEV., ch. 11.

2121. —— of Morals. *Sodomites.*—GEN. 19 : 5. *Gibeathites.*—JUDGES 19 : 22.

2122. —— Mental. *Drink.* [7] The priest and the prophet have erred through strong drink, they are swallowed up of wine, they are out of the way through strong drink ; they err in vision, they stumble *in* judgment.—ISA., ch. 28.

See other illustrations under :

DEPRAVITY.

Ancient. Wickedness of man was great..every	2188
Bestial. Sons of Belial beset the house	2189
Discovered. Woe is me !..unclean lips	2190
Heathen. God gave them up to uncleanness	2191

Infectious. Both the daughters of Lot with child　2192
Inherited. Ye are..of them that killed the prophets 9193
Natural. All gone aside..filthy..none doeth g.　　9194
Unconscious. Is thy servant a dog..do this thing?　1526

2123. DELAY in Business, No. *Abraham's Servant.* ³³ There was set *meat* before him to eat : but he said, I will not eat, until I have told mine errand. And he said, Speak on. ³⁴ And he said, I *am* Abraham's servant.—GEN., ch. 24. [Rebekah was given him for Isaac's wife.]

2124. —— for Decency. *Ambassadors.* ⁴ Hanun took David's servants, and shaved off the one half of their beards, and cut off their garments in the middle, *even* to their buttocks, and sent them away. ⁵ ..the men were greatly ashamed : and the king said, Tarry at Jericho until your beards be grown, and *then* return.—2 SAM., ch. 10.

2125. —— A dangerous. *Burial.* ⁵⁹ Follow me. But he said, Lord, suffer me first to go and bury my father. ⁶⁰ Jesus said..Let the dead bury their dead ; but go thou and preach the kingdom of God.—LUKE, ch. 9.

2126. —— Evil of. *Samuel.* ¹¹ And Saul said, Because I saw that the people were scattered from me, and *that* thou camest not within the days appointed, and *that* the Philistines gathered themselves together at Michmash ; ¹² Therefore said I, The Philistines will come down now upon me to Gilgal, and I have not made supplication unto the Lord : I forced myself therefore, and offered a burnt offering.—1 SAM., ch. 13. [Saul lost his kingdom because of it.]

2127. —— Failure from. *Pool of Bethesda.* ⁴ An angel went down at a certain season into the pool, and troubled the water : whosoever then first after..stepped in was made whole of whatsoever disease he had.—JOHN, ch. 5.

2128. —— for Hinderances, No. *Bartimeus.* ⁴⁹ Be of good comfort, rise ; he calleth thee. ⁵⁰ And he, casting away his garment, rose, and came to Jesus.—MARK, ch. 10.

2129. —— Impatience from. *Sinai.* ¹ Moses delayed to come down out of the mount, the people gathered themselves together unto Aaron, and said..Up, make us gods, which shall go before us ; for *as for* this Moses, the man that brought us up out of the land of Egypt, we wot not what is become of him.—EX., ch. 32.

2130. —— A long. *Impotent Man.* ⁵ A certain man was there, which had an infirmity thirty and eight years. ⁷..Sir, I have no man, when the water is troubled, to put me into the pool : but while I am coming, another steppeth down before me.—JOHN, ch. 5.

2131. —— The Lord's. *Egypt.* ²² Moses..said, Lord, wherefore hast thou *so* evil entreated this people? why *is* it *that* thou hast sent me? ²³ For since I came to Pharaoh to speak in thy name, he hath done evil to this people ; neither hast thou delivered thy people at all.—EX., ch. 5.

2132. —— for Preparation. *Pentecost.* [Jesus] ⁴ commanded them that they should not depart from Jerusalem, but wait for the promise of the Father, which, *saith he*, ye have heard of me. —ACTS, ch. 1.

2133. —— Weariness from. *David.* ¹ How long wilt thou forget me, O Lord? for ever? how long wilt thou hide thy face from me?

² How long shall I take counsel in my soul, *having* sorrow in my heart daily? how long shall mine enemy be exalted over me?—Ps. 13.

See other illustrations under :

HINDERANCE.
Disobedience. Say nothing to any man..blaze　　3979
Natural. Let me..kiss my father..mother　　　3980
Provoking. Let us pass through thy country..not 3981
Removed. Angel..rolled back the stone..door　　3982
Riches. Deceitfulness of riches..choke the word 3983
"　　Easier for a camel..needle's eye than　　3984

HINDERANCES.
Care. Take heed lest..become a stumblingblock　3985
Malicious. People of the land hired counsellors　3986
Removed. I will eat no flesh while the world　　3987
Secular. I have bought..bought..married　　　3988
Social. Let me first go bid them farewell　　　3989
Selfish. Neither go in yourself, neither suffer ye 3990

HINDERING.
Fear. It is reported..Jews think to rebel　　　3991
Intrigue. Let us meet..in the plain of Ono　　3992

IDLENESS.
Accusation. No straw..ye are idle, ye are idle　4270
Ecstatic. Why stand ye gazing into heaven?　　4271
Needless. Why stand ye here all the day idle?　4272
Perishing. If we sit still here, we die also [lepers] 4273

LOITERERS.
Driven. Fire..consumed them in the uttermost　5052
Hastened. While he lingered, the men laid hold　5053

PROCRASTINATION.
Charity. Say not..to-morrow I will give when thou 6620
Fatal. Go thy way this time..convenient season　6621
Folly. Foolish said, Give us of your oil..gone out 6622
Loss. We will hear thee again..Paul departed　　6623
No. Suffer me first to go and bury my father　　6624

WAITING.
Calamity. Jonah sat..see what would..city　　9262
Eager. My soul waiteth..watch for the morning　9263
in Faith. Tell the stars..so shall thy seed be　9264
on God. Renew their strength..as eagles　　　9265
Patient. After one year, G. spake to Noah, Go forth 9267
for Power. Not depart from Jerusalem, but wait 9268
Rewarded. Simeon..waiting for the consolation　9269
Vigilant. Let your loins be girt..lights burning　9270
Weariness. Let me see the king's face..kill me　9271
Watching. When the fowls came..Abram drove　9272
for Work. When forty years were expired..an　9273

Diversion. If thou meet any man, salute him not 2454
Fatal. Virgins..went to buy..door was shut　　4899
Inexplicable. Neither hast thou delivered thy　2336
Late. While they went to buy, the bridegroom　4899
Perilous. Felix said, Go..when I have a more　1557

—— DELIGHT. —— ——
See illustrations under :
Friendship. Jonathan..delighted much in David　3694
Godly. His delight is in the law of the Lord　　5293
Lord's. Delightest not in burnt offering　　　7540
"　　Delighteth not in the strength of—Ps. 147 : 10
Redeemed. Shalt be called Hephzi-bah—Isa. 62 : 4

2134. DELIVERER, The great. *Jesus.* ¹⁶ He saw that *there was* no man, and wondered that *there was* no intercessor : therefore his arm brought salvation unto him ; and his righteousness, it sustained him. ¹⁷ For he put on righteousness as a breastplate, and a helmet of salvation upon his head ; and he put on the garments of vengeance *for* clothing, and was clad with zeal as a cloak.—ISA., ch. 59.

2135. —— raised up, A. *Ehud.* [15] When.. Israel cried unto the Lord, the Lord raised them up a deliverer, Ehud..a man lefthanded : and by him the children of Israel sent a present unto Eglon the king of Moab. [16] But Ehud made him a dagger which had two edges, of a cubit length ; and he did gird it under his raiment upon his right thigh.—JUDGES, ch. 3. [He stabbed the king. Israel broke the yoke of the Moabites.]

2136. —— rewarded. *Goliath.* [25] The man who killeth him, the king will enrich him with great riches, and will give him his daughter, and make his father's house free in Israel.—1 SAM., ch. 17.

2137. —— A valiant. *Shamgar.* [31] Shamgar ..slew of the Philistines six hundred men with an oxgoad : and he also delivered Israel.— JUDGES, ch. 3.

2138. DELIVERANCE appreciated. *Bartimeus.* [52] Jesus said..Go thy way : thy faith hath made thee whole. And immediately he received his sight, and followed Jesus in the way.— MARK, ch. 10.

2139. —— Completion of. *Lazarus.* [44] Came forth, bound hand and foot with graveclothes ; and his face was bound about with a napkin. Jesus saith..Loose him, and let him go.—JOHN, ch. 11.

2140. —— commemorated. *Purim.* [21] They should keep the fourteenth day of the month Adar, and the fifteenth day of the same, yearly, [24] Because Haman..the enemy of all the Jews, had devised..to destroy them, and had cast Pur, that *is*, the lot..to destroy them.—ESTHER, ch. 9.

2141. —— delayed. *From Pharaoh.* [See No. 2131.]

2142. —— from Despair. *At Red Sea.* [12] *It had been* better for us to serve the Egyptians, than that we should die in the wilderness. [13] And Moses said..Fear ye not, stand still, and see the salvation of the Lord..for the Egyptians whom ye have seen to day, ye shall see them again no more for ever.—Ex., ch. 14.

2143. —— in Extremity. *Abraham.* [12] Lay not thine hand upon the lad..for now I know that thou fearest God, seeing thou hast not withheld thy son, thine only *son*, from me. [13] ..lifted up his eyes..behold behind *him* a ram caught in a thicket by his horns : and Abraham ..offered him up for a burnt offering in the stead of his son.—GEN., ch. 22.

2144. —— Faith brings. *Distressed Father.* [23] If thou canst believe, all things *are* possible to him that believeth. [24] And straightway the father of the child cried out and said with tears, Lord, I believe ; help thou mine unbelief. [25] ..Jesus..rebuked the foul spirit.—MARK, ch. 9.

2145. —— False Hope of. *King Ahaz.* [22] In the time of his distress did he trespass yet more.. [23] For he sacrificed unto the gods of Damascus, which smote him : and he said, Because the gods of the kings of Syria help them, *therefore* will I sacrifice to them, that they may help me. But they were the ruin of him, and of all Israel.—2 CHRON., ch. 28.

2146. —— A great. *By Saul.* [2] Nahash..answered them, On this *condition* will I make a

covenant with you, that I may thrust out all your right eyes, and lay it *for* a reproach upon all Israel. [6] And the Spirit of God came upon Saul when he heard those tidings, and his anger was kindled greatly.—1 SAM., ch. 11. [He raised a victorious army, and won his crown.]

2147. —— by the Gospel. *Jesus.* [18] The Spirit of the Lord *is* upon me, because he hath anointed me to preach the gospel to the poor ; he hath sent me to heal the brokenhearted, to preach deliverance to the captives, and recovering of sight to the blind, to set at liberty them that are bruised.—LUKE, ch. 4.

2148. —— Hope of. *In Egypt.* [30] Aaron spake all the words..and did the signs in the sight of the people. [31] And the people believed : and when they heard that the Lord had visited the children of Israel, and..looked upon their affliction, then they bowed their heads and worshipped.—Ex., ch. 4.

2149. —— of the Innocent. *Daniel.* [22] My God hath sent his angel, and hath shut the lions' mouths, that they have not hurt me : forasmuch as before him innocency was found in me ; and also before thee, O king, have I done no hurt.—DAN., ch. 6.

2150. —— Incomplete. *Blind Man.* [23] When he had spit on his eyes, and put his hands upon him, he asked him if he saw aught. [24] And he looked up, and said, I see men as trees, walking.—MARK, ch. 8.

2151. —— A joyful. *Jews.* [11] The king granted the Jews..to stand for their life, to destroy.. all..that would assault them..and *to take* the spoil of them for a prey, [17] And in every province, and in every city..the Jews had joy and gladness, a feast and a good day. And many of the people..became Jews ; for the fear of the Jews fell upon them.—ESTHER, ch. 8.

2152. —— A miraculous. *Red Sea.* [21] Moses stretched out his hand over the sea ; and the Lord caused the sea to go *back* by a strong east wind, all that night, and made the sea dry *land*, and the waters were divided. [22] ..Israel went into the midst of the sea upon the dry *ground :* and the waters *were* a wall..on their right hand, and on their left.—Ex., ch. 14.

2153. —— Memorial of. *Passover.* [26] When your children shall say..What mean ye by this service? [27] ..ye shall say, It *is* the sacrifice of the Lord's passover, who passed over the houses of the children of Israel..when he smote the Egyptians.—Ex., ch. 12.

2154. —— by Money. *From King of Syria.* [8] Ahaz took the silver and gold that was found in the house of the Lord, and in..the king's house, and sent *it for* a present.. [9] And the king of Assyria hearkened unto him..went up against Damascus, and took it.—2 KINGS, ch. 16. [The Syrians raised the siege of Jerusalem.]

2155. —— Monument of. *Eben-ezer.* [11] The men of Israel went out of Mizpeh, and pursued the Philistines, and smote them.. [12] Then Samuel took a stone, and set *it* between Mizpeh and Shen, and called the name of it Eben-ezer, saying, Hitherto hath the Lord helped us.—1 SAM., ch. 7.

2156. —— A partial. *From King of Egypt.* [7] They have humbled themselves ; *therefore* I

will not destroy them, but I will grant them
some deliverance ; and my wrath shall not be
poured out upon Jerusalem by the hand of
Shishak.—2 Chron., ch. 12.

2157. —— **Publication of.** *Possessed Man.*
[18] He that had been possessed with the devil
prayed him that he might be with him. [19] Howbeit Jesus suffered him not, but saith..Go home
to thy friends, and tell them how great things
the Lord hath done for thee.—Mark, ch. 5.

2158. —— **Peril after.** *Samson.* [15] He found
a new jawbone of an ass..and took it, and slew
a thousand men therewith.. [18] And he was sore
athirst, and called on the Lord, and said, Thou
hast given this great deliverance into the hand
of thy servant : and now shall I die for thirst.—
Judges, ch. 15.

2159. —— **A perfect.** *Three Hebrews.* [27] The
princes, governors, and captains, and the king's
counsellors..saw these men, upon whose bodies
the fire had no power, nor was a hair of their
head singed, neither were their coats changed,
nor the smell of fire had passed on them.—Dan.,
ch. 3.

2160. —— **recognized.** *Nebuchadnezzar.* [28] Nebuchadnezzar..said, Blessed be the God of Shadrach, Meshach, and Abed-nego, who hath sent
his angel, and delivered his servants that trusted in him, and have changed the king's word,
and yielded their bodies, that they might not
serve nor worship any god, except their own
God.—Dan., ch. 3.

2161. —— **Spiritual.** *David.* [1] I waited patiently for the Lord ; and he inclined unto me,
and heard my cry. [2] He brought me up also out
of a horrible pit, out of the miry clay, and set
my feet upon a rock, *and* established my goings.
[3] And he hath put a new song in my mouth,
even praise unto our God.—Ps. 40.

2162. —— **from Trouble.** *David.* [9] Have mercy upon me, O Lord, for I am in trouble : mine
eye is consumed with grief, *yea*, my soul and
my belly.. [19] Oh how great *is* thy goodness, which
thou hast laid up for them that fear thee ; *which*
thou hast wrought for them that trust in thee
before the sons of men !—Ps. 31.

2163. —— **Unexpected.** *Red Sea.* [See No.
2152.]

2164. —— —— *Peter.* [6] When Herod would
have brought him forth, the same night Peter
was sleeping between two soldiers, bound with
two chains : and the keepers..kept the prison.
[7]..the angel of the Lord came upon *him*, and a
light shined in the prison : and he smote Peter
on the side, and raised him up..And his chains
fell off from *his* hands.—Acts, ch. 12.

2165. —— **Unequalled.** *Three Hebrews.* [29] I
make a decree, That every people..which speak
any thing amiss against the God of Shadrach,
Meshach, and Abed-nego, shall be cut in pieces,
and their houses shall be made a dunghill : because there is no other God that can deliver
after this sort.—Dan., ch. 3.

2166. —— **Work follows.** *Peter and John.*
[19] The angel of the Lord by night opened the
prison doors, and brought them forth, and said,
[20] Go, stand and speak in the temple to the people all the words of this life.—Acts, ch. 5.

See other illustrations under :

DEFENCE.

Declined. Jesus answered to him never a word 2104
Incomplete. Goliath had a helmet..coat of mail 2105
Lawful. King granted the Jews to stand for their 2106
Perilous. Jonathan said..Wherefore shall he be 2107
Preparation. Uzziah prepared..shields, spears 2108
Spiritual. Loins girt about with truth..breastplate 2109
Unheard. Alex. would have made his defence 2110
Weapons. I can slay a man for my hurt 2111

ESCAPE.

Assistance. Disciples by night ; let him down the 2712
Few. Noah, Shem, Ham, and Japheth..wives 2713
Hasty. David said, Arise, let us flee..from 2714
Miraculous. Jesus escaped out of their hand 2715
Any Means. Some on boards, some on broken 2716
Narrow. A great wind..I only am escaped 2717
No. They slew of Moab..escaped not a man 2718
Only One. Upon the priests, and slew 85 persons 2719
Strategy. Michal took an image..covered it 2721
Urging. While Lot lingered, the men laid hold 2722

REDEMPTION.

Blood. On the upper doorpost..I will pass over 6909
  "   Not redeemed with corruptible..blood of C. 6910
Power. The horse and his rider..cast into the sea 6911

SALVATION.

Brothers. His own brother Simon..brought him 7556
Belated. When once the master..shut to the door 7557
Difficulties. Strive to enter..many shall not be 7558
Emergency. I. shall go on dry ground..sea 7559
Free. Him that cometh..I will in no wise cast out 7560
  "   If any man thirst, let him come unto me 7561
Faith. Believe on the L. J. C. and thou shalt be 7562
  "   Whosoever believeth..should not perish 7563
by Few. No restraint to the L. to save by many or 7564
Gratitude. Fifth part unto Pharaoh..ha'st saved 7565
by Humanity. Angel said..call for Peter. he will 7566
Wonderful. Waters were a wall..right hand..left 7567
Waiting. Stand ye still and see the salvation 7568
One Way. Verily..I am the door of the sheep 7569
  See PROTECTION and PROVIDENCE.

2167. DELIBERATION necessary. *Building—
War.* [28] Which of you, intending to build a tower,
sitteth down not first, and counteth the cost,
whether he have *sufficient* to finish it ? [31] Or what
king, going to make war against another king, sitteth not down first, and consulteth whether he be
able with ten thousand to meet him that cometh
against him with twenty thousand?—Luke, ch.
14.

See other illustrations under :

REFLECTION.

Important. Whatsoever things are true..think on 6914
Painful. When Peter thought thereon, he wept 6915

2168. DELUSION, Destructive. *Ahaz.* [See No.
2145.]

2169. —— **from Success.** *Philistines.* [23] The
lords of the Philistines gathered..for to offer a
great sacrifice unto Dagon their god, and to rejoice : for they said, Our god hath delivered
Samson our enemy into our hand.—Judges, ch.
16.

2170. —— **of the Wicked.** *Lot's Sons in Law.*
[14] Lot went out, and spake unto his sons in law
..and said, Up, get you out of this place ; for
the Lord will destroy this city. But he seemed
as one that mocked unto his sons in law.—Gen.,
ch. 19.

See other illustrations under :
ERROR.
Sweeping. Barnabas also was carried away 2709
Sincere. There is a way that seemeth right..ways 2710
INFATUATION.
Blind. In the time of his distress did Ahaz trespass 4455
Reproved. Knowest thou not yet..Egypt is d. 4456
Wicked. They were driven out from Pharaoh's 4457
" Simon saw..H. G. was given, he offered 4458
INSANITY.
Exhibited. Hairs were grown like eagle's 4514
Feigned. David..feigned himself mad..spittle 4515
Moral. Pharaoh said.. see my face no more 4516
Occasional. Evil spirit from God came upon Saul 4517
Sinners. When he came to himself..bread 4518
So-called. His friends said..he is beside himself 4519
" Paul, thou art beside thyself..mad 4520
SORCERY.
Captivating. Simon bewitched the people..all 8202
Renounced. Simon himself believed..was bapt'd 8203
" [Ephesians] used curious arts 8204
WITCHCRAFT.
Abolished. Workers with familiar spirits..Josiah 9649
Famous. Seek me a woman..a familiar spirit 9647
Influential. They all gave heed..lest..greatest 9650
Curious Arts. [Ephesians] used curious arts..burn 908
Imposition. Magicians..cast down..rod..serpent 5162
See DECEPTION.

2171. DEMAGOGUE, Artful. *Absalom.*
² When any man that had a controversy came to the king for judgment, then Absalom..said..
³..See, thy matters *are* good and right ; but *there is* no man *deputed* of the king to hear thee. ⁴..Oh that I were made judge in the land, that every man which hath any suit or cause might come unto me, and I would do him justice ! ⁵ And ..when any man came nigh *to him* to do him obeisance, he put forth his hand, and took him, and kissed him.—2 SAM., ch. 15.
See other illustrations under :
POLITICS.
Condemned. We found this fellow..forbidding 6236
Influence. If thou let this man go..not Cesar's 6238
in Religion. Is it lawful to give tribute to Cesar? 6239

2172. DEMON within. *Unclean Spirit.* ²⁵ Jesus rebuked him, saying, Hold thy peace, and come out of him. ²⁶ And when the unclean spirit had torn him, and cried with a loud voice, he came out of him.—MARK, ch. 1.
See other illustrations under :
DEVIL.
Called a. Say we not well that thou hast a devil? 2266
Hypocrisy. Ye are of your father the devil 2267
Sold to. Ahab did sell himself to work wickedness 2268
SATAN.
Audacity. If thou be the S. of G. command..bread 7578
Bound. An angel..bound him a thousand years 7579
Children. Ye are of your father the devil..no 7580
Cunning. God doth know..your eyes shall be 7581
Doom. Cast him into the bottomless pit 7582
Delivered to. Hymeneas and Alex..delivered unto 7583
Enmity. I will put enmity between thee..woman 7584
Fall of. War in heaven..the dragon fought 7585
Filled. Ananias, why hath Satan filled thy heart 7586
Injurious. L. said..all that he hath..thy power 7587
Inspired by. Devil put into the heart of Judas 7588
Leader. After the sop, Satan entered into him 7589
Peril. The devil as a roaring lion..seeking 7590
Scripture. It is written, He shall give his angels 7591
Worshipper. Satan came also to present himself 7592

2173. DENIAL, Self-considerate. *David.*
¹⁶ The three mighty men brake through the host of the Philistines, and drew water out of the well of Beth-lehem..and brought *it* to David : nevertheless he..poured it out unto the Lord. ¹⁷ And he said, Be it far from me, O Lord, that I should do this : *is not this* the blood of the men that went in jeopardy of their lives ?—2 SAM., ch. 23.

2174. —— Self, for Others. *Eating.* ⁸ Neither, if we eat, are we the better ; neither, if we eat not, are we the worse. ⁹ But take heed lest by any means this liberty of yours become a stumblingblock to them that are weak. ¹³ Wherefore, if meat make my brother to offend, I will eat no flesh while the world standeth.—1 COR., ch. 8.

2175. —— Twofold. *Earth—Heaven.* ³³ Whosoever shall deny me before men, him will I also deny before my Father which is in heaven.—MAT., ch. 10.

2176. —— An unexpected. *Peter.* ⁵⁵ Peter sat down among them. ⁵⁶ But a certain maid.. earnestly looked upon him, and said, This man was also with him. ⁵⁷ And he denied him, saying, Woman, I know him not.—LUKE, ch. 22.
See other illustrations under :
SELF-DENIAL.
Abstinence. David would not drink thereof 7701
Bodily. I keep under my body lest..be a castaway 7702
Better. People complained..fire consumed them 7703
Costly. If thy right hand offend thee..cut it off 7704
Difficult. Young ruler went away grieved..great 7705
Decent. Put a knife to thy throat..given to a. 7706
Essential. Let him deny himself..take up his cross 7707
Marvellous. Get thee out of thy country..kindred 7708
" Moses refused to be called the son 7709
" Unto this present hour we both 7710
for Others. If meat make my brother to offend 7711
Patriotic. Twelve years..not eaten the bread of 7712
Positive. If..hate not his father..own life 7713
Rewarded. Ye also shall sit upon twelve thrones 7714
" Shall receive 100 fold..eternal life 7715
Saved by. Because strait is the gate and narrow 7716
Sabbath. If thou turn from doing thine own 7717
Service. Whosoever will be chief..be your servant 7718
Vow of. We will drink no wine..build..sow nor 7719
TEMPERANCE.
Advised. [Mother] drink no wine, nor strong 8659
Extreme. Neither liquor of grapes..moist or dried 8660
Eating. His dainties..are deceitful meat 8661
Hereditary. Our father commanded us..drink no 8662
Health. Proved them ten days..fairer and fatter 8663
Mastery. Striveth for mastery is temperate in all 8664
Piety. [J. B.] neither wine nor strong drink..H. G. 8665
Strength. [Mother of Samson] Drink no wine 8666
Refusal. Let us pass through thy country 6948

2177. DENUNCIATION, An appalling. *Simon.* ⁹ Then..Paul, filled with the Holy Ghost, set his eyes on him, ¹⁰ And said, O full of all subtilty and all mischief, *thou* child of the devil, *thou* enemy of all righteousness, wilt thou not cease to pervert the right ways of the Lord?—ACTS, ch. 13.

2178. —— of Hypocrites. *Jesus.* ²⁷ Woe unto you, scribes and Pharisees, hypocrites ! for ye are like unto whited sepulchres, which indeed appear beautiful outward, but are within full of dead *men's* bones, and of all uncleanness.

[33] *Ye* serpents, *ye* generation of vipers, how can ye escape the damnation of hell?—MAT., ch. 23.

See other illustrations under :

THREATENING.

Contemptible. Let fire..of the bramble..devour	8793
Intimidating. So let the gods do..make thy life	8792
Rash. I will chastise you with scorpions	8794
Repeated. Commanded them not to speak	8795
Terrible. Whosoever cometh not..be done unto	8796
Unfulfilled. I will give thy flesh unto the fowls	8797
Useless. [See 8798] They spake the word..with	8798
Unreasonable. King commanded to destroy the	8799

2179. DEPARTURE, A constrained. *Disciples.* [22] Jesus constrained his disciples to get into a ship, and to go before him unto the other side, while he sent the multitudes away.—MAT., ch. 14.

2180. —— in Haste. *Out of Egypt.* [33] The Egyptians were urgent..that they might send them out of the land in haste ; for they said, We *be* all dead *men*.—EX., ch. 12.

2181. —— for Safety. *Calamity.* [16] Then let them which be in Judea flee into the mountains : [17] Let him which is on the housetop not come down to take any thing out of his house : [18] Neither let him which is in the field return back to take his clothes.—MAT., ch. 24.

2182. —— A stolen. *Jacob.* [17] Jacob rose up, and set his sons and his wives upon camels ; [18] And he carried away all his cattle, and all his goods.. [20] And Jacob stole away unawares to Laban the Syrian.—GEN., ch. 31.

2183. —— An unexpected. *Four Lepers.* [5] When they were come to the uttermost part of the camp of Syria, behold, *there was* no man there. [6] For the Lord had made..the Syrians to hear..the noise of a great host : and they said one to another, Lo, the king of Israel hath hired against us the kings.—2 KINGS, ch. 7.

See other illustrations under :

ABANDONMENT.

Anger. Let me alone..wrath may wax hot	1
Blasphemers. Hymeneus and Alex..learn not to	2
Christ. Left house, or brethren..lands for my sake	3
Destruction. I will destroy from off the..earth	4
Home. Abram get thee..from thy father's house	5
Just. Go cry unto the gods which ye have chosen	6
Jesus. All the disciples forsook him, and fled	7
Merited. They hated knowledge..despised reproof	8
Sanctuary. L. abhorred his sanctuary	9
Surprising. The ark of God was taken	10
Transgressors. 3000 men fled before the men of Ai	11
Work. Mark..went not with them to the work	12
Unconscious. Samson wist not that the L. was	13

APOSTASY.

Angelic. Angels which kept not their first estate	461
Age. When Solomon was old..turned..other gods	462
Deception. Latter times..heed to seducing spirits	463
Enmity. Alexander..did me much evil	464
Hopeless. If we sin wilfully..no more sacrifice	465
Inconsiderate. Gave Esau pottage..despised his	466
Idolatrous. Ahab..served Baal, and worshipped	467
Prosperity. Jeshurun waxed fat, and kicked	468
Responsibility. Whoso shall offend..millstone	469
Shipwreck. Made shipwreck..Hymeneus..Alex.	470

DESERTION.

Ignorance. Drinketh my blood..disciples went	2204
Painful. At my first answer..all men forsook	2205
Prevented. Soldiers cut the ropes..boat..let her	2206

EXPULSION.

Ecclesiastic. If he neglect to hear the church	2821
Persecution. Jews..raised persecution against	2822
Sinners. Drove out the man..garden of Eden	2823
Vigorous. Jehoiada..I chased him from me	2824

FAREWELL.

Beatific. While he blessed them he was departed	3040
Glorious. Horses of fire..Elijah went up..into	3041
Loving. Naomi said, Turn again, my daughters	3042
Perilous. Let me first bid them farewell..at	3043
Sorrowful. All wept sore and fell on Paul's neck	3044

FORSAKING.

All. Flee into the mountains..not take anything	3378
Business. Ships to land, they forsook all and	3379
Duty. Jonah rose up to flee..going to Tarshish	3380
God. Amaziah. set them up to be his gods	3381
" But we will have a king over us..like all	3382
" Have despised the L..why came we forth	3383
" We have forsaken our God and followed	3384
" Forsaken..living waters, and hewed	3385
" Ahaz sacrificed unto the gods..which	3386
Office. Levi sitting at the receipt of custom..left	3388

FORSAKEN.

Friends. All the disciples forsook him and fled	3389
of God. [David] I cry in the daytime..hearest	3390
" [Saul] Bring me up Samuel..L. is	3391
" [Jesus] My God, my God, why hast	3392
" [Apparently] If the L. be with us, why	3393

FUGITIVE.

Criminal. Jacob..flee thou to Laban, my	3487
Infant. Take the young child..flee into Egypt	3488
Noble. Pharaoh sought to slay Moses..fled	3489
Protected. Not deliver unto his master the	3490
Return. [Onesimus] departed for a season	3491

SECESSION.

Political. If this city be builded..no portion on	7642
" I will chastise you with scorpions	7643

SEPARATION.

Drunkards. Not to keep company..not to eat	7758
Godly. Separated from I. all the mixed	7759
Impossible. Neither death nor life..able to	7764
Reason of. For they will turn away thy son	7778
Sorrowful. They kissed one another, and wept	7780
Spiritual. Fan is in his hand..wheat..chaff	7781
Sinners. Blessed..when they shall separate	7783
by Sin. As a shepherd divideth his sheep..goats	7789
" Your iniquities have separated..your	7784
Unavoidable. Ye cannot drink the cup of the L.	7787

WANDERING.

Corrected. Before I was afflicted, I went astray	9282
Invitation. Return unto me, and I will return	9280
Restoration. Lovest thou me?..Feed my sheep	9279
Search. Having a hundred sheep, if he lose one	9284
Unsatisfied. Dove found no rest for the..foot	9285
Wicked. I will be a swift witness against the	9281

See DEATH.

2184. DEPENDENCE cut off. *Straw.* [7] Ye shall no more give the people straw to make brick, as heretofore : let them go and gather straw for themselves. [8] And the tale of the bricks, which they did make heretofore, ye shall lay upon them.—EX., ch. 5.

2185. —— A doubtful. *Elijah.* [9] Arise, get thee to Zarephath..and dwell there : behold, I have commanded a widow woman there to sustain thee.—1 KINGS, ch. 17.

2186. —— Humiliating. *No Smith.* [19] There was no smith found throughout all the land of

Israel : for the Philistines said, Lest the Hebrews make *them* swords or spears : ²⁰ But all..went down to the Philistines, to sharpen every man his share, and his coulter, and his axe, and his mattock.—1 SAM., ch. 13.

2187. —— upon a Woman. *Deborah.* ⁸ Barak said unto her, If thou wilt go with me, *then* I will go : but if thou wilt not go with me, *then* I will not go. ⁹ And she said, I will..notwithstanding the journey..shall not be for thine honour ; for the Lord shall sell Sisera into the hand of a woman.—JUDGES, ch. 4.

See other illustrations under :

CONFIDENCE.

Believers. Though I walk through the valley	1518
Blind. Know I that the L..I have a priest	1519
Caution. They are smitten down..as at the first	1520
Disappointed. Ark came..I shouted..ark taken	1521
False. King [of Ai] wist not..ambush	1522
Future. Doth deliver..trust he will deliver	1523
Intelligent. I know whom I have believed	1524
Joyful. How great is thy goodness..trust thee	1525
Over. Is thy servant a dog..do this? [Hazael]	1526
Peril. Have the sentence of death..we trust	1527
Piety begets. L. was with Joseph..into his hand	1528
Strong. L. delight in us..fear them not	1529
Self. Peter said..I will lay down my life	1530
Triumphant. Although the fig tree shall not b.	1531
Unwarranted. Let two or three thousand go	1532
Unfortunate. Confidence..like a broken tooth and	1533
Undermining. Neither let Hez. make you trust..L.	1534
Warranted. L. is my rock, fortress, deliverer	1535

TRUST.

Active. Hezekiah clave to the L...rebelled against	9008
Courageous. Thou comest..I come..in the name	9009
Experience. L. who delivered me..the paw of the	9010
Egotists. Pharisee..I..I..I..I..I	9011
Fearless. Our G..is able to deliver us..furnace	9012
" Though I walk through the valley	9013
" The Lord is on my side, I will not fear	9014
Fixed. Though he slay me, yet will I trust	9015
Foolish. Bramble said..Put your trust in my s.	9016
Honoured. Cried to G. in the battle..trust in him	9017
" Angel smote..Assyrians, 185,000	9018
Ill-timed. Let us fetch the ark..it may save us	9020
Providence. May boldly say, The L. is my helper	9021
Self. Philistine..saw David..disdained him	9022

See **FAITH.**

2188. DEPRAVITY, Ancient. *Antediluvians.* ⁵ God saw that the wickedness of man *was* great in the earth, and *that* every imagination of the thoughts of his heart *was* only evil continually. ⁶ And it repented the Lord that he had made man on the earth, and it grieved him at his heart. —GEN., ch. 6.

2189. —— Bestial. *Gibeathites.* ²² The men of the city, certain sons of Belial, beset the house round about, *and* beat at the door, and spake to the..old man, saying, Bring forth the man that came into thine house.—JUDGES, ch. 19.

2190. —— discovered. *Isaiah.* ⁵ Woe *is* me ! for I am undone ; because I *am* a man of unclean lips, and I dwell in the midst of a people of unclean lips : for mine eyes have seen the King, the Lord of hosts.—ISA., ch. 6.

2191. —— of the Heathen. *Paul.* ²³ Changed the glory of the uncorruptible God into an image made like to corruptible man, and to birds, and fourfooted beasts, and creeping things.

²⁴ Wherefore God also gave them up to uncleanness.—ROM., ch. 1.

2192. —— infectious. *From Sodom.* ³⁶ Thus were both the daughters of Lot with child by their father.—GEN., ch. 19. [They were reared in Sodom.]

2193. —— inherited. *Pharisees.* ³¹ Ye be witnesses unto yourselves, that ye are the children of them which killed the prophets. ³³ *Ye* serpents, *ye* generation of vipers, how can ye escape the damnation of hell?—MAT., ch. 23.

2194. —— Natural. *Universal.* ¹ The fool hath said in his heart, *There is* no God. They are corrupt, they have done abominable works, *there is* none that doeth good. ² The Lord looked down from heaven upon the children of men, to see if there were any that did understand, *and* seek God. ³ They are all gone aside, they are *all* together become filthy: *there is* none that doeth good, no, not one.—Ps. 14.

See other illustrations under :

DEGRADATION.

Drink. Mighty man shall be humbled	2119
Food. Whatsoever goeth upon the belly..not eat	2120
Morals. [See Genesis 19 : 5 and Judges 19 : 22]	
Mental. Strong drink..stumble in judgment	2122

VICES.

Mental. Idolatry, witchcraft, hatred, variance	9188
Physical. Works of the flesh are..adultery	9189
Pleasures. As..lieth down in the midst of the sea	9190

See **SIN** and **WICKEDNESS.**

2195. DEPRECIATION, Self. *Jeremiah.* ⁶ Said I, Ah, Lord God ! behold, I cannot speak : for I *am* a child.. ¹⁰ See, I have this day set thee over the nations..to root out, and to pull down, and to destroy, and to throw down, to build, and to plant.—JER., ch. 1.

See other illustrations under :

FAULTS.

One. When my master..house of Rimmon	3083
Official. [Enemies] could find none..fault in	3086
Overlooked. Sins of Jehu..golden calves..done	4350
Unchurched. Neglect to hear the church..as a	3084

FAULTFINDERS.

Fastidious. Why do ye eat..with sinners	3087
Hypocritical. Why was not this..sold for 300	3088
Malicious. John B..he hath a devil..Son of man	3089

Discrimination. Abel offered..more excellent	2327

See **CRITICISM.**

2196. DEPRESSION, Overwhelming. *Jesus.* ⁴⁶ About the ninth hour Jesus cried with a loud voice, saying..My God, my God, why hast thou forsaken me?—MAT., ch. 27.

See other illustrations under :

DESPONDENCY.

Bereavement. Joseph is, without doubt, rent in	2226
Complaint. Since I came to Pharaoh..done evil	2227
Constitutional. Let us go..die with him	2230
Continued. My heart is smitten and withered like	2228
Cure. David was greatly distressed..spake of	2229
Difficulties. People was much discouraged	2231
Hope. Why art thou cast down, O my soul ?	2232
Hasty. Sun beat..Jonah fainted..wished to die	2233
Ill-timed. Handful of meal..little oil..die	2234
Loneliness. I only am left, and they seek my life	2235
Memories. By the rivers of Babylon we wept	2236
Overcare. If thou deal thus with me, kill me	2237
Public. Moses heard the people weeping..door	2238
Prayer. How long wilt thou forget me, O Lord	2239

Peril. Esau cometh..400 men..Jacob afraid   2240
Singular. Lord take away my life..not better   2242
Vows. L. make a reproach unto me..derision   2243
Without. Troubled on every side..not in despair   2244

DISAPPOINTMENT.

Doubt. Heard that he was alive..believed not   2315
Gifts. S. gave Hiram 20 cities..pleased him not   2316
Good. They have taken..Lord out of the S.   2317
Humiliating. Prison truly..shut..no man there   2318
Ignorance. No place of seed..figs..vines   2319
Judgment. Thou hast taught in our streets   2320
Misjudged. We trusted it had been he..saved I.   2321
Maternal. I have gotten a man [murderer] from L.   2322
Many. Sown much, and bring in little   2326
Perplexing. King of Syria sore troubled   2323
Religion. Have wanted all things..consumed   2324
Unendurable. Ahithophel..hanged himself   2325

DISCOURAGEMENT.

Contrast. But as for me, my feet were almost gone 2346
Defeat. Would to God we had been content   2347
Evildoers. I am..weak, though anointed king   2348
Failure. Neither hast thou delivered thy people   2349
    " We have toiled all the night, and taken   2350
Mismanagement. Men of Ai smote 36 men   2351
Ministerial. Some fell on stony ground..thorns   2352
Needless. They that be with us are more..with   2353
Overcome. He answered her not a word   2359
Reproved. Yet I have left me 7000 in I.   2354
Trials. I am not able to bear all this people..too 2355
Unbelief. Been better to have served the Egyptians 2356
Unreasonable. Wherefore have ye brought us out   2357
Without. We faint not..though our outward man   2358

DESPAIR.

Affliction. Let me not see the death of the child 2213
Anguish. Slay me, for anguish is come upon me   2214
Awaking. Wine was gone out..heart died within   2215
Deliverance. Been better for us to serve the Egyp. 2216
Needless. Widow..meal..oil..me and my son eat   2217

Melancholy. Evil spirit troubleth..cunning player 5318

2197. DERISION, Horrible. *Of Jesus.* [28] They stripped him, and put on him a scarlet robe. [29] And when they had platted a crown of thorns, they put *it* upon his head, and a reed in his right hand : and they bowed the knee before him, and mocked him, saying, Hail, King of the Jews ! [30] And they spit upon him, and took the reed, and smote him on the head.—MAT., ch. 27.

2198. —— Impious. *Passover Revival.* [10] The posts passed from city to city, through the country of Ephraim and Manasseh, even unto Zebulun : but they laughed them to scorn, and mocked them.—2 CHRON., ch. 30.

2199. —— punished. *Ishmael.* [9] Sarah saw the son of Hagar..mocking. [10] Wherefore she said unto Abraham, Cast out this bondwoman and her son..shall not be heir with my son, *even* with Isaac.—GEN., ch. 21.

2200. —— by Nickname. *Of Jesus.* [47] He that is of God heareth God's words : ye therefore hear *them* not, because ye are not of God. [48] Then answered the Jews, and said..Say we not well that thou art a Samaritan, and hast a devil?—JOHN, ch. 8.

2201. —— of Truth. *Pharisaic.* [Jesus taught the true use of wealth.] [14] The Pharisees also, who were covetous, heard all these things : and they derided him.—LUKE, ch. 16.

2202. —— by Unfortunates. *Two Thieves.* [43] He trusted in God ; let him deliver him now, if he will have him : for he said, I am the Son of God. [44] The thieves also, which were crucified with him, cast the same in his teeth.—MAT., ch. 27.

2203. —— of the Wicked. *David.* [6] I am a worm, and no man ; a reproach of men, and despised of the people. [7] All they that see me laugh me to scorn : they shoot out the lip, they shake the head, *saying*, [8] He trusted on the Lord *that* he would deliver him : let him deliver him, seeing he delighted in him.—Ps. 22.

See other illustrations under :

INSULT.

Ignored. Belial said, How shall this man save us 4567
Jesus. Thrust him out of the city..cast him   4568
Reward. Hanun shaved off one half their beards   4569
Stinging. Annas commanded them to smite   4570

INSULTS.

Cruel. Mocked Jesus..blindfolded, and struck   4576
Contemptuous. They that are younger have me in   4572

MOCKERY.

Blasphemous. Crown of thorns..reed..Hail, King   5494
of Truth. When they heard of the resurrection   5493

SCORN.

Pride. Haman thought scorn to..alone   7618
Public. All that pass by clap their hands at thee 7619
Sinners. They made light of it, and went   7621
Unbelief. They laughed him to scorn   7620

SCOFFERS..

Malicious. Spit in his face, and buffeted   7614
    " Mocked him..a gorgeous robe   7615

RIDICULE.

Doctrine. Heard of the resurrection..mocked   7425
Fatal. Call for Samson..sport..house fell   7426
Failure. Mock him..not able to finish   7427
Horrible. Mocking..he trusted in God..save him   7428
Impious. Laughed them to scorn   7429
    " What will this babbler say ?   7430
Insulting. Shaved off one half their beards   7431
Opposition. What do these feeble Jews   7432
    " If a fox go up..break down their wall   7433
Punishment. Go up, thou bald head..bears   7434
Royalty. Wearing the crown of thorns..purple   7435
Scornful. Laughed..will ye rebel against the king 7436
Spirit. Mocking, said..full of new wine   7437
Trial. Thou art his disciple, but we are Moses'   7438

Religion. The L. was made a reproach unto me   2243

2204. DESECRATION for Bribery. *Ahaz.* [21] For Ahaz took away a portion *out* of the house of the Lord, and *out* of the house of the king, and of the princes, and gave *it* unto the king of Assyria : but he helped him not.—2 CHRON., ch. 28.

2205. —— removed. *Temple.* [7] Eliashib did for Tobiah, in preparing him a chamber in the courts of the house of God. [8] And it grieved me sore : therefore I cast forth all the household stuff of Tobiah out of the chamber. [9] Then I commanded, and they cleansed the chambers : and thither brought I again the vessels of the house of God, with the meat offering and the frankincense.—NEH., ch. 13.

2206. —— Sacrilegious. *Belshazzar.* [2] Belshazzar, while he tasted the wine, commanded to bring the golden and silver vessels which.. Nebuchadnezzar had taken out of the temple which *was* in Jerusalem ; that the king and his princes, his wives and his concubines, might drink therein.—Dan., ch. 5. [An armless hand wrote on the wall the downfall of his throne.]

See other illustrations under :

PROFANATION.

Sanctuary. Those that sold oxen [first visit]   6626
    "   Sold and bought [last visit]   6627

2207. DESERTION in Ignorance. *Disciples.* [54] Whoso eateth my flesh, and drinketh my blood, hath eternal life ; and I will raise him up at the last day. [66] From that *time* many of his disciples went back, and walked no more with him. —John, ch. 6.

2208. —— A painful. *Paul at Rome.* [16] At my first answer no man stood with me, but all *men* forsook me : *I pray God* that it may not be laid to their charge.—2 Tim., ch. 4.

2209. —— prevented. *Sailors.* [31] Paul said to the centurion and to the soldiers, Except these abide in the ship, ye cannot be saved. [32] Then the soldiers cut off the ropes of the boat, and let her fall off.—Acts, ch. 27.

See other illustrations under :

Assumed. With whom hast thou left those few   1624
    "   Jeremiah..fallest away to the Chaldeans   79
    See DEPARTURE and references.

2210. DESIRE, The chief. *Bartimeus.* [51] Jesus..said..What wilt thou that I should do unto thee ? The blind man said unto him, Lord, that I might receive my sight.—Mark, ch. 10.

2211. —— An inconsiderate. *David.* [15] David longed, and said, Oh that one would give me drink of the water of the well of Beth-lehem, which *is* by the gate !—2 Sam., ch. 23. [Men risked their lives to get it.]

2212. —— for the Sanctuary. *David.* [1] How amiable *are* thy tabernacles, O Lord of hosts ! [2] My soul longeth, yea, even fainteth for the courts of the Lord : my heart and my flesh crieth out for the living God.—Ps. 84.

See other illustrations under :

AMBITION.

Impious. Diotrephes..loveth the pre-eminence   317
Fatal. Asahel refused to turn aside..Abner smote   318
Hypocrites. Scribes..love greetings..highest seats   321
Promotion. Brought you near him..Seek..priest   326
Reproved. [Disciples] had disputed which..great   320
Unsatisfied. [Haman] No man come in with the   332

COVETOUSNESS.

Abhorred. Blesseth the covetous whom the L.   1786
Alarmed. By this craft..our wealth..confusion   1787
Apostle. Judas went..to give him money   1788
Aroused. Damsel..masters saw..gains were gone   1789
Absence of. Abram said, I will not take..thread   1790
Church. Who would shut the doors for naught   1791
Cruelty. Felix hoped that money..of Paul   1792
Caution. Inheritance..take heed..beware of   1793
Disobedience. I saw among the spoils..took them   1794
Forbidden. Thou shalt not covet thy neighbour's   1795
Fraud. Gehazi..I will run and take..silver   1796
Folly. Soul, thou hast much goods..eat, drink   1797
Falsehood. Ananias with Sapphira..kept back   1798
Freedom. I have coveted no man's silver..Paul   1799
Inconsiderate. Well watered..Lot chose..plain of   1800
Oppressive. Ye exact usury..sell your brethren   1801
Overcome by. Saul and the people spared the best   1802
Overreaching. Laban..changed my wages ten   1803

Stigmatized. If any man that is called a brother   1804
Shameless. Given to covetousness..not..ashamed   1805
Unhappiness. Naboth had a vineyard..Ahab   1806
Greatest. That I might receive my sight   846

2213. DESPAIR in Affliction. *Hagar.* [15] She cast the child under one of the shrubs. [16] And she went..a good way off, as it were a bowshot : for she said, Let me not see the death of the child. And she..lifted up her voice, and wept. —Gen., ch. 21.

2214. —— Anguish of. *King Saul.* [9] Stand, I pray thee, upon me, and slay me : for anguish is come upon me, because my life *is* yet whole in me.—2 Sam., ch. 1.

2215. —— Awaking to. *Nabal.* [36] Nabal's heart..*was* very drunken : wherefore she told him nothing..until the morning light. [37]..when the wine was gone out of Nabal, and his wife had told him these things..his heart died within him, and he became *as* a stone.—1 Sam., ch. 25.

2216. —— Deliverance from. *At Red Sea.* [11] They said unto Moses..wherefore hast thou dealt thus with us, to carry us forth out of Egypt ? [12] *Is* not this the word that we did tell thee in Egypt, saying, Let us alone, that we may serve the Egyptians ? For *it had been* better for us to serve the Egyptians, than that we should die in the wilderness.—Ex., ch. 14. [The Lord opened a path in the sea.]

2217. —— Needless. *Widow of Zarephath.* [12] I have not a cake, but a handful of meal in a barrel, and a little oil in a cruse : and, behold, I *am* gathering two sticks, that I may go in and dress it for me and my son, that we may eat it, and die. [13] And Elijah said unto her, Fear not. —1 Kings, ch. 17.

See other illustrations under:

DESPONDENCY.

Bereavement. Joseph is, without doubt, rent in   2226
Complaint. Since I came to Pharaoh..done evil   2227
Constitutional. Let us go..die with him   2230
Continued. My heart is smitten and withered like   2228
Cure. David was greatly distressed..spake of   2229
Difficulties. People was much discouraged   2231
Prayer. How long wilt thou forget me, O Lord   2239
Hope. Why art thou cast down, O my soul   2232
Hasty. Sun beat..Jonah fainted..wished to die   2233
Illtimed. Handful of meal..little oil..die   2234
Loneliness. I only am left, and they seek my life   2235
Memories. By the rivers of Babylon we wept   2236
Overcare. If thou deal thus with me, kill me   2237
Public. Moses heard the people weeping..door   2238
Peril. Esau cometh..400 men..Jacob afraid   2240
Singular. Lord take away my life..not better   2242
Vows. L. made a reproach unto me..derision   2243
Without. Troubled on every side..not in despair   2244

DISAPPOINTMENT.

Doubt. Heard that he was alive..believed not   2315
Gifts. S. gave Hiram 20 cities..pleased him not   2316
Good. They have taken..Lord out of the s.   2317
Humiliating. Prison truly..shut..no man there   2318
Ignorance. No place of seed..figs..vines   2319
Judgment. Thou hast taught in our streets   2320
Misjudged. We trusted it had been he..saved I.   2321
Maternal. I have gotten a man [murderer] from   2322
Many. Sown much, and bring in little   2326
Perplexing. King of Syria sore troubled   2323
Religion. Have wanted all things..consumed   2324
Unendurable. Ahithophel..hanged himself   2325

DISTRESS.

Cry of. Great cry..none like it, nor shall be   2437
Derided. They that see me, shoot out the lip   2438
Described. I was a derision to all my people   2439
Exasperation. What shall I do..people ready to   3440
Famine. Delicate women..shall eat..children   3441
Friend. Gedaliah..took Jeremiah out of prison   3443
Great. Thrust..right eyes..people wept   3444
Little Faith. Why are ye fearful..little faith..calm   3442
Needless. Saul had abjured..food   3445
Refuge. Ahaz sacrificed unto the gods that smote   3446

REMORSE.

Needful. People that came..smote their breasts   7067
Prevented. Lest swallowed up with overmuch sor.   7068
Treachery. Judas..went and hanged himself   7069

Agony. My soul is exceeding sorrowful..unto death   264
Boldness. I will go in unto the king..if I perish   2218
Disappointment. Saw his counsel was not follow.   2325
Sacrifices. Took his eldest son..for burnt offering   2221

2218. DESPERATION, Boldness of. *Esther.*
¹⁶ Go, gather together all the Jews..and neither
eat nor drink three days, night or day : I also
and my maidens will fast likewise ; and so will
I go in unto the king, which *is* not according to
the law : and if I perish, I perish.—ESTHER, ch.
4.

2219. —— Effort of. *Four Lepers.* ³ Why sit
we here until we die? ⁴ If we say, We will enter
into the city, then the famine *is* in the city, and
we shall die there : and if we sit still here, we
die also..let us fall unto the host of the Syrians :
If they save us alive, we shall live ; and if they
kill us, we shall but die.—2 KINGS, ch. 7.

2220. —— A Sinner's. *King Saul.* ⁶ When
Saul inquired..the Lord answered him not..
⁷ Then said Saul unto his servants, Seek me a
woman that hath a familiar spirit, that I may go
to her, and inquire of her. And his servants said
to him, Behold, *there is* a woman that hath a familiar spirit at En-dor.—1 SAM., ch. 28.

2221. —— Sacrifices in. *Human Offering.*
²⁶ When the king of Moab saw that the battle
was too sore for him, he took with him seven
hundred men that drew swords, to brake through
..unto the king of Edom : but they could not.
²⁷ Then he took his eldest son that should have
reigned in his stead, and offered him *for* a
burnt offering upon the wall.—2 KINGS, ch. 3.

See other illustrations under :

DANGER.

Appalled. Jesus went before them..were amazed   1906
Escape. Disciples let him down by night in a basket   1909
Haste. Let them in Judea..flee to the mountains   1911
Intimidates. Peter saw..afraid, and beginning to   1912
Jesus. Storm..on the lake..Master, we perish   1913

DESPAIR.

Affliction. Let me not see the death of the child   2213
Anguish. Slay me, for anguish is come upon me   2214
Awaking. Wine was gone out..heart died within   2215
Deliverance. Been better for us to serve the E.   2216
Needless. Widow..meal..oil..me and my son eat   2217
See PERIL.

2222. DESPISERS of Others. *Pharisee.* ⁹ He
spake this parable unto certain which trusted in
themselves that they were righteous, and despised others : ¹⁰ Two men went up into the
temple to pray ; the one a Pharisee, and the
other a publican.—LUKE, ch. 18.

2223. —— of Privileges. *Esau.* ³⁴ Jacob gave
Esau bread and pottage of lentiles ; and he did

eat and drink, and rose up, and went his way.
Thus Esau despised *his* birthright.—GEN., ch.
25.

2224. —— Sin of. *Of Christ.* ²⁹ Of how much
sorer punishment, suppose ye, shall he be
thought worthy, who hath trodden under foot
the Son of God, and hath counted the blood of
the covenant, wherewith he was sanctified, an
unholy thing, and hath done despite unto the
Spirit of grace?—HEB., ch. 10.

2225. —— Warning to. *Of God.* ²⁴ Because
I have called, and ye refused ; I have stretched
out my hand, and no man regarded ; ²⁵ But ye
have set at nought all my counsel, and would
none of my reproof : ²⁶ I also will laugh at your
calamity ; I will mock when your fear cometh ;
²⁷ When your fear cometh as desolation, and
your destruction cometh as a whirlwind ; when
distress and anguish cometh upon you.—PROV.,
ch. 1.

See other illustrations under :

CONTEMPT.

Bigots. Pharisee prayed..I am not as other men   1618
Critics. Michal saw king David leaping..despised   1619
Conceited. Thistle..sent to the cedar..give thy   1620
Disregarded. The God of heaven will prosper us   1621
Enemy's. Am I a dog that thou comest..staves   1622
Expressed. Children of Belial..brought Saul no   1623
Fraternal. With whom hast thou left those few   1624
Gospel. Made light of it, and went their way   1625
for God. Have turned their back unto me..face   1626
Malicious. Did spit in his face, and buffeted   1628
Others. That they were righteous..despised others   1629
for Worship. Torn..the lame, and the sick..ye   1630

DERISION.

Horrible. Put on him a scarlet robe..crown   2197
Impious. Laughed them to scorn, and mocked   2198
Punished. Sarah saw the son of Hagar..mocking   2199
Nickname. Thou art a Samaritan, and hast a devil   2200
Truth. Pharisees who were covetous..derided   2201
Unfortunates. Thieves also..cast the same into   2202
Wicked. They shoot out the lip, and shake the   2203

INSULT.

Ignored. Despised him [Saul]..held his peace   4567
First. Thrust him [Jesus] out of the city..headlong   4568
Rewarded. Cut off their garments in the middle   4569
Stinging. To smite him on the mouth   4570

RIDICULE.

Doctrine. When they heard of the resurrection   7425
Fatal. Call for Samson, that he may make us sport   7426
Failure. Not able to finish..begin to mock him   7427
Horrible. He saved others, let him save himself   7428
Impious. They laughed them to scorn, and mocked   7429
"   What will this babbler say [Athenians]   7430
Insulting. Cut off their garments..their buttocks   7431
Opposition. What do these feeble Jews will they   7432
"   If a fox go up, he shall break down   7433
Punishment. Children of Bethel..Go up, thou bald   7434
Royalty. Wearing the crown of thorns and purple   7435
Scornful. They laughed us to scorn, and despised us   7436
Spirit. Mocking said,These men are full of new wine   7437
Trial. They reviled him and said, We are Moses'   7438

SCOFFERS.

Malicious. Prophesy unto us, thou Christ..who   7614
"   Herod arrayed him in a gorgeous robe   7615

SCORN.

of Pride. [Haman] Scorn to lay hands on Mordecai   7618
Public. All clap their hands at thee, and hiss   7619
Taunt. Who made thee a prince and a judge over   8592
Unbelief. She sleepeth..they laughed him to scorn   7620

2226. DESPONDENCY in Bereavement. *Jacob.*
[33] Joseph is without doubt rent in pieces. [34] And Jacob rent his clothes, and put sackcloth upon his loins, and mourned for his son many days. [35]..he refused to be comforted ; and he said, For I will go down into the grave unto my son mourning.—GEN., ch. 37.

2227. —— **Complaint in.** *Moses.* [22] Moses.. said, Lord, wherefore hast thou so evil entreated this people ? why is it that thou hast sent me ? [23] For since I came to Pharaoh to speak in thy name, he hath done evil to this people ; neither hast thou delivered thy people at all.—EX., ch. 5.

2228. —— **continued.** *Affliction.* [4] My heart is smitten, and withered like grass ; so that I forget to eat my bread.. [5] By reason of the voice of my groaning my bones cleave to my skin. [6] I am like a pelican of the wilderness : I am like an owl of the desert. [7] I watch, and am as a sparrow alone upon the housetop. [8] Mine enemies reproach me all the day ; and they that are mad against me are sworn against me. [9] For I have eaten ashes like bread, and mingled my drink with weeping.— Ps. 102.

2229. —— **Cure for.** *Prayer.* [3] The city..was burned with fire ; and their wives, and their sons, and their daughters, were taken captives. [6] And David was greatly distressed ; for the people spake of stoning him, because the soul of all the people was grieved, every man for his sons and for his daughters : but David encouraged himself in the Lord his God.—1 SAM., ch. 30.

2230. —— **Constitutional.** *Thomas.* [8] Master, the Jews of late sought to stone thee, and goest thou thither again ? [16] Then said Thomas..unto his fellow disciples, Let us also go, that we may die with him.—JOHN, ch. 11.

2231. —— **under Difficulties.** *Israelites.* [4] They journed from mount Hor by the way of the Red sea, to compass the land of Edom : and the soul of the people was much discouraged because of the way.—NUM., ch. 21.

2232. —— **Hope in.** *David.* [11] Why art thou cast down, O my soul? and why art thou disquieted within me ? hope thou in God : for I shall yet praise him, who is the health of my countenance, and my God.—Ps. 42.

2233. —— **Hasty.** *Jonah.* [6] The Lord God prepared a gourd..that it might be a shadow over his head, to deliver him from his grief. So Jonah was exceeding glad of the gourd. [7] But ..a worm..the next day..smote the gourd that it withered. [8]..and the sun beat upon the head of Jonah, that he fainted, and wished in himself to die, and said, It is better for me to die than to live.—JONAH, ch. 4.

2234. —— **Ill-timed.** *Widow of Z.* [12] I have not a cake, but a handful of meal in a barrel, and a little oil in a cruse : and, behold, I am gathering two sticks, that I may go in and dress it for me and my son, that we may eat it, and die.—1 KINGS, ch. 17. [Neither meal nor oil grew less.]

2235. —— **from Loneliness.** *Elijah.* [9] He came thither unto a cave, and lodged there ; and behold, the word of the Lord..What doest thou here, Elijah? [10] And he said, I have been very jealous for the Lord God of hosts : for the chil-

dren of Israel have forsaken thy covenant, thrown down thine altars, and slain thy prophets..and I, even I only, am left ; and they seek my life, to take it away.—1 KINGS, ch. 19.

2236. —— **Memories bring.** *Captives.* [1] By the rivers of Babylon, there we sat down, yea, we wept, when we remembered Zion. [2] We hanged our harps upon the willows in the midst thereof. [3] For there they that carried us away captive required of us a song.—Ps. 137.

2237. —— **from Overcare.** *Moses.* [14] I am not able to bear all this people alone, because it is too heavy for me. [15] And if thou deal thus with me, kill me..out of hand, if I have found favour in thy sight ; and let me not see my wretchedness.—NUM., ch. 11.

2238. —— **Public.** *Flesh-hungry.* [10] Moses heard the people weep throughout their families, every man in the door of his tent : and the anger of the Lord was kindled greatly ; Moses also was displeased.—NUM., ch. 11.

2239. —— **Prayer in.** *David.* [1] How long wilt thou forget me, O Lord? for ever? how long wilt thou hide thy face from me ? [2] How long shall I take counsel in my soul, having sorrow in my heart daily ? how long shall mine enemy be exalted over me ? [3] Consider and hear me, O Lord my God ; lighten mine eyes, lest I sleep the sleep of death.—Ps. 13.

2240. —— **from Peril.** *Jacob.* [6] The messengers returned to Jacob, saying, We came to thy brother Esau, and also he cometh to meet thee, and four hundred men with him. [7] Then Jacob was greatly afraid and distressed.—GEN., ch. 32. [He prayed all night.]

2241. —— **in Sickness.** *Hezekiah.* [10] I said in the cutting off of my days, I shall go to the gates of the grave : I am deprived of the residue of my years. [11] I said, I shall not see..the Lord, in the land of the living : I shall behold man no more with the inhabitants of the world. [12] Mine age is departed, and is removed from me as a shepherd's tent : I have cut off like a weaver my life : he will cut me off with pining sickness.—ISA., ch. 38.

2242. —— **Singular.** *Elijah.* [After the great success at Mount Carmel, he fled from Jezebel into the wilderness, and] [4] sat down under a juniper tree : and he..said, It is enough ; now, O Lord, take away my life ; for I am not better than my fathers.—1 KINGS, ch. 19.

2243. —— **Vows in.** *Jeremiah.* [7] I am in derision daily, every one mocketh me. [8]..the word of the Lord was made a reproach unto me, and a derision, daily. [9] Then I said, I will not make mention of him, nor speak any more in his name. But his word was in mine heart as a burning fire shut up in my bones, and I was weary with forbearing, and I could not stay.—JER., ch. 20.

2244. —— **Without.** *Paul.* [8] We are troubled on every side, yet not distressed ; we are perplexed, but not in despair.—2 COR., ch. 4.

See other illustrations under :

DESPAIR.
Affliction. Let me not see the death of the child 2213
Anguish. Slay me, for anguish is come upon me 2214
Awaking. Wine was gone out..heart died within 2215
Deliverance. Been better for us to serve the Egyp. 2216
Needless. Widow..meal..oil..me and my son eat 2217

DESPERATION.

Boldness. I will go in unto the king..if I perish   2218
Effort. Why sit we here till we die?   2219
Sinners. Saul inquired of the L..answered him   2220
Sacrifices. King of Moab took his eldest son   2221

DISCOURAGEMENT.

Contrast. But as for me, my feet were almost   2346
Defeat. Would to God we had been content..other 2347
Evildoers. I am..weak, though anointed king   2348
Failure. Neither hast thou delivered thy people   2349
   "   We have toiled all the night, and taken   2350
Mismanagement. Men of Ai smote 36 men   2351
Ministerial. Some fell on stony ground..thorns   2352
Needless. They that be with us are more..with   2353
Overcome. He answered her not a word   2359
Reproved. Yet I have left me 7000 in I.   2354
Trials. I am not able to bear all this people..too   2355
Unbelief. Been better to have served the Egyp'ns   2356
Unreasonable. Wherefore have ye brought us, out 2357
Without. We faint not..though our outward man 2358

DISTRESS.

Cry of. Great cry..none like it, nor shall be   2437
Derided. They that see me, shoot out the lip   2438
Described. I was a derision to all my people   2439
Exasperation. What shall I do..people ready to   2440
Famine. Delicate women..shall eat..children   2441
Little Faith. Why are ye fearful..little faith..calm 2442
Friend. Gedaliah..took Jeremiah out of prison   2443
Great. Thrust..right eyes..people wept   2444
Needless. Saul had adjured..food   2445
Refuge. Ahaz sacrificed unto the gods that smote   2446

DOUBT.

Adversity. Hearkened not unto Moses for anguish 2493
Disappointment. Disciples heard he was alive   2494
Forbidden. Consider the lilies..much'more..clothe 2495
Hurtful. Know..be hungry..get into the city   2496
Impossible. Fire..fell..licked..water..L. he is God 2497
Solved. If any man will do..know the doctrine   2498
Struggling. Say unto God, Do not condemn me   2499
Strong. Except I shall see..hands..not believe   2500
Snare. Discouraged..People is greater and taller   2501
Trouble. Life shall hang in doubt..none assurance 2502

LAMENTATION.

Adversity. Let the day perish wherein I was   4883
Fathers. O my son Absalom! my son, my son   4884
General. Thrust out right eyes..people..voices   4885
Ill-timed. Would to G. we had been content   4886
Jesus. O Jerusalem, Jerusalem..would I have   4887
for Jesus. Weep not for me, but weep for   4888
National. In every province..Jews..weeping and 4889
Tearful. Oh that my head were waters..fountain 4890

MOURNING.

Abstinence. [Abner assassinated] If I taste   5603
Bereavement. I am distressed for thee, my   5604
Beneficial. Better to go to the house of mourning 5605
Comfort. Asleep..sorrow not as others which   5598
Feigned. Be as a woman..long time mourned   5606
Good. Mary..told them. as they mourned and   5600
Genuine. Widows..weeping and showing   5601
Intense. David went up..wept..barefoot   5607
Joy. Jesus came and touched the bier   5608
Last. Thou mourn at the last..body consumed   5609
Time. Great and very sore lamentation   5610
Wicked. King wept at the grave of Abner   5611

REMORSE.

Needful. People that came..smote their breasts   7067
Prevented. Lest swallowed up with overmuch sor. 7068
Treachery. Judas..went and hanged himself   7069

Agony. My soul is exceeding sorrowful..unto death 264

Boldness. I will go in unto the king..if I perish   2218
Disappointment. Saw his counsel was not follow'd 2325
Ministerial. I will not speak any more in his name 9246
Mystery. Money..in sack..heart fainted   285
Sacrifices. Took his eldest son..for burnt offering 2221

2245. DESPOTISM, Royal. *Israel.* [Israel asked a king. Samuel premonished them of the burdens of royalty. Sons, daughters, fields, taxes, servants, animals, etc., would be taken for the king.] [18] And ye shall cry out in that day because of your king which ye shall have chosen you.—1 SAM., ch. 8.

See other illustrations under:

OPPRESSION.

Avarice. Buy the needy for a pair of shoes   5917
Deliverance. Hebrew..seventh year let him go   5918
Famine. Mortgaged our lands, vineyards, and   5919
Servants. Thou shalt not oppress a hired servant 5920
Slaves. Let there be more work laid upon the men 5921
Unendurable. Evil entreated our fathers..cast out 5922

Tyrannical. My father made your yoke heavy   9048

2246. DESTITUTION, Physical. *Paul.* [27] In weariness and painfulness, in watchings often, in hunger and thirst, in fastings often, in cold and nakedness.—2 COR., ch. 11.

2247. —— Pastoral. *Jews.* [34] Jesus..saw much people, and was moved with compassion toward them, because they were as sheep not having a shepherd : and he began to teach them. —MARK, ch. 6.

2248. —— Religious. *Israelites.* [Azariah said,] [2] The Lord *is* with you, while ye be with him ; and if ye seek him, he will be found of you ; but if ye forsake him, he will forsake you. [3] Now for a long season Israel *hath been* without the true God, and without a teaching priest, and without law.—2 CHRON., ch. 15.

See other illustrations under :

FAMINE.

Charity. Disciples determined to send relief   3023
Care. Shall eat bread by weight..water by   3024
Dying. Eaten no bread..three days..sick   3025
Distress. Delicate woman..children..eat then   3026
Exiled. Sojourn wherever thou canst..seven   3027
Escape. Abram went down into Egypt..famine   3028
Emigration. Elimelech went to sojourn in   3029
Inhumanity. Give thy son, that we may eat him   3030
Sin. I will break the staff of bread   3031
   "   Ye have forsaken the..L. and followed   3032
Seven Years. No bread..land of Canaan fainted   3033
Spiritual. I will send a famine..words of the L.   3034
Water. To kill us and our children..cattle   3035

POVERTY.

Affection. Entreat me not to leave thee [Ruth]   6291
Benevolence. Poor widow..two mites   6292
   "   Deep poverty abounded unto   6293
Born to. [Jesus] Sacrifice..two young pigeons   6294
Cause. Followeth vain persons..poverty enough   6295
   "   Be not among winebibbers..come to   6296
not a Crime. Poor man is better than a liar   6297
Dangers. Give me neither poverty nor riches   6298
Famine. We are many..take up corn for them   6299
Hinderance, No. King's son in law..I am a poor 6300
Inevitable. Famine prevailed..land became   6301
Known. She did cast in all her living   6302
to Plenty. Beggar..carried by the angels to   6303
Protection of. Left the poor of the land to be   6304
Sluggard. Will not plough..cold, therefore..beg 6305
   "   Little sleep, a little slumber, a little   6306

Suffering. In weariness and painfulness, in hunger 6307
and Riches. Beggar..at his gate..crumbs which 6308
Sin. Better is the poor that walketh uprightly 6309
Wealth in. There is that maketh himself poor 6310
Wealth. Better is the poor than..though he be 6311

WANT.

a Blessing. I perish with hunger..my father 8286
Contentment. I have learned..to be content 8287
Degraded. We boiled my son..give thy son 8288
Frivolity. He that followeth vain persons 8289
near Luxury. Rich man..fared sumptuously 8290
to Plenty. Four lepers..did eat and drink 8291
Sin brings. Woman..brought to a piece of bread 8292

Joyous. Although the fig tree shall not blossom 1379
See POOR.

2249. DESTRUCTION, Complete. *Egyptians.*
²⁸ The waters returned, and covered the chariots, and the horsemen, *and* all the host of Pharaoh that came into the sea after them ; there remained not so much as one of them.—Ex., ch. 14.

2250. —— by Fire. *In War.* ⁸ Nebuzar-adan, captain of the guard, a servant of the king of Babylon.. ⁹ .. he burnt the house of the Lord, and the king's house, and all the houses of Jerusalem, and every great *man's* house.—2 Kings, ch. 25.

2251. —— General. *Flood.* ²³ Every living substance was destroyed which was upon the face of the ground, both man, and cattle, and the creeping things, and the fowl of the heaven ; ..and Noah only remained *alive,* and they that *were* with him in the ark.—Gen., ch. 7.

2252. —— of the Grave. *Job.* ⁷ For there is hope of a tree, if it be cut down, that it will sprout again, and that the tender branch thereof will not cease. ⁸ Though the root thereof wax old in the earth, and the stock thereof die in the ground ; ⁹ *Yet* through the scent of water it will bud, and bring forth boughs like a plant. ¹⁰ But man dieth, and wasteth away : yea, man giveth up the ghost, and where *is* he ?—Job, ch. 14.

2253. —— Preserved from. *Israel.* ²⁶ The Lord saw the affliction of Israel, *that it was* very bitter : for *there was* not any shut up, nor any left, nor any helper for Israel. ²⁷ And the Lord said not that he would blot out the name of Israel from under heaven : but he saved them by the hand of Jeroboam.—2 Kings, ch. 14.

2254. —— Sudden. *Antediluvians.* ²⁷ They did eat, they drank, they married wives, they were given in marriage, until the day that Noe entered into the ark, and the flood came, and destroyed them all.—Luke, ch. 17.

2255. —— Unexpected. *Sodomites.* ²⁸ Likewise also as it was in the days of Lot ; they did eat, they drank, they bought, they sold, they planted, they builded ; ²⁹ But the same day that Lot went out of Sodom it rained fire and brimstone from heaven, and destroyed *them* all.—Luke, ch. 17.

2256. —— Vandals. *God's House.* ⁵ *A man* was famous according as he had lifted up axes upon the thick trees. ⁶ But now they break down the carved work thereof at once with axes and hammers. ⁷ They have cast fire into thy sanctuary. Ps. 74.

See other illustrations under :

CALAMITY.

Destructive. Wall fell upon 27,000 men that were 995
Feared. His strength shall be hunger bitten 1000
of God. Earth opened her mouth and swallowed 996
Hardened. I have smitten you with blasting 1001
Indiscriminating. The L. maketh the earth 1002
Misjudged. Tower in Siloam fell..think..they 1003
Predicted. Shall not be left one stone upon 997
Reflection. O that I were..days of my youth 1004
Sin. Taken the accursed thing..therefore could 998
Waiting. Jonah sat..see what would become 999

Arson. Nebuzar-adan burnt..all the houses 3235
Common. He that helpeth..is holpen, shall fall 293
Doom. Gather together first the tares..burn them 2492
Exterminating. Smite Amalek, and utterly destroy 2826
  " [Ahab's sons] Slew seventy 2827
Fire. L. rained upon Sodom and G. brimstone 3230
Forbidden. Only the trees..not for meat..destroy 9315
Shipwreck. Get to land..on broken pieces of the 7840
Wicked. In the lake which burneth with fire 3244
War. Moabites bent down their cities..felled good 9314

2257. DETECTIVE, A female. *Delilah.*
¹⁸ When Delilah saw that he had told her all his heart, she sent..for the lords of the Philistines, saying, Come up this once, for he hath shewed me all his heart. Then the lords .. brought money in their hand.—Judges, ch. 16.

2258. —— Impious. *Watch Jesus.* ² They watched him, whether he would heal him on the sabbath day ; that they might accuse him. ⁶ And the Pharisees..straightway took counsel with the Herodians..how they might destroy him.—Mark, ch. 3.

2259. DETECTION feared. *Moses.* ¹¹ He spied an Egyptian smiting a Hebrew, one of his brethren. ¹² And he looked this way and that way, and when he saw that *there was* no man, he slew the Egyptian, and hid him in the sand.—Ex., ch. 2.

See other illustrations under :

DISCOVERY.

Astounding. I am Joseph ; doth my father yet live 2360
Alarming. My money is restored in my sack 2361
Painful. Isaac trembled very exceedingly..Who 2362
Unexpected. Is not the hand of Joab..in this ? 2342

2260. DETERMINATION, An evil. *Idolatrous Jews.* ¹⁶ As for the word that thou hast spoken unto us in the name of the Lord, we will not hearken unto thee. ¹⁷ But we will certainly do whatsoever thing goeth forth out of our own mouth, to burn incense unto the queen of heaven.—Jer., ch. 44.

2261. —— Fixed. *Paul.* ²³ The Holy Ghost witnesseth in every city, saying that bonds and afflictions abide me. ²⁴ But none of these things move me, neither count I my life dear unto myself, so that I might finish my course with joy, and the ministry.—Acts, ch. 20.

2262. —— A fixed. *Shunammite.* [Her child was dead, and she came for the prophet Elisha. He said he would send Gehazi with his staff.] ³⁰ And the mother of the child said, As the Lord liveth, and *as* thy soul liveth, I will not leave thee. And he arose, and followed her.—2 Kings, ch. 4.

2263. —— A resolute. *Absalom.* ²⁹ Absalom sent for Joab..but he would not come to him.. the second time he would not come. ³⁰ Therefore he said unto his servants, See, Joab's field is near mine, and he hath barley there ; go and set it on fire. ³¹ Then Joab arose, and came to Absalom.—2 SAM., ch. 14.

2264. —— wanting. *Pilate.* ²² He said unto them the third time, Why, what evil hath he done? I have found no cause of death in him : I will therefore chastise him, and let *him* go. ²⁴ And Pilate gave sentence that it should be as they required.—LUKE, ch. 23.

See other illustrations under :

DESPERATION.

Boldness. I will go in unto the king..If I perish   2218
Effort. Why sit we here till we die ?   2219
Sinners. Saul inquired of the L..answered him   2220
Sacrifices. King of Moab took his eldest son   2221

HARDNESS.

Adversity. In his distress did Ahaz trespass more   3797
Heart. Looked..anger being grieved..hardness of   3798
Spiritual. We will certainly burn incense   3799

IMPENITENCE.

Affliction. Ahaziah said..Go inquire of Baal-zebub 4347
Hardened. Thou shalt die..He sent to arrest   4348

OBDURACY.

Defiant. Who is the L..let I. go   5755
Final. Pharaoh made ready his chariot..people   5756
Foolish. Ahaz in..distress did trespass more and   5757
Jewish. Thy neck is an iron sinew..brow brass   5758
Spiritual. If the mighty works..been done in Tyre 5759
Self-destructive. I know G. hath determined to   5760
Truth. Divers were hardened..spake evil   5761

OBSTINACY.

Provoking. The L. said..it is a stiffnecked people 5825
Rebuked. I..withstand thee..thy way is perverse   5826
Rebellious. People refused to obey the voice of   5827

PERSISTENCE.

Necessary. Aaron and Hur stayed up his hands   6067
Prayer. Let me go, for the day breaketh..will not 6068
Rewarded. As thy soul liveth, I will not leave thee 6069
Unchangeable. They spake daily..Mordecai   6070
Undiscouraged. Many charged Bartimeus..hold his 6071
"   Because of his importunity he will 6072

SELF-WILL.

Destructive. O Jerusalem, thou..ye would not   7731
Loss by. They presumed to go..smote them   7732
the Sacrifice. To obey is better than sacrifice   7734
Work. Simeon and Levi..self-will digged down   7735

STUBBORNNESS.

Punished. They mocked the messengers   8393
Sin. To obey is better than sacrifice   8394
"   We will certainly..burn incense   8395
"   Took Dagon and set him in his place again   8396

Changed. Why have ye not brought him?   1673
See DECISION.

2265. DETRACTION, Malicious. *Pharisees.* [Jesus healed two blind men, and cast out an evil spirit before the people,] ³³ And the multitudes marvelled, saying, It was never so seen in Israel. ³⁴ But the Pharisees said, He casteth out devils through the prince of the devils.—MAT., ch. 9.

See other illustrations under :

ACCUSATION.

Astounding. Why doth this man speak blasphemies 76
Fraudulent. The Hebrew..came in to mock me   77
False. Saul said..all..have conspired against me   78
"   Thou fallest away to the Chaldeans..in   79
Investigated. One of you..betray me..is it I ?   80

Meekness. Herod questioned..Jesus answered him 81
Misapplied. I have not troubled I., but thou   82
Malicious. Samaritans wrote [Ahasuerus] an   83
Resented. Abner said, Am I a dog's head..chargest 84
Sustained. Stephen..set up two false witnesses   85
Suppressed. Convicted by their own conscience   86
Unsustained. I have examined him. no fault   87
Withheld. Michael durst not bring..railing   88

BLAME.

Assumed. I will be surety for Benjamin..Judah   796
Benefactors. Ye have made..abhorred..Pharaoh   797
Misapplied. All..against Moses and Aaron   798
Others. How long shall this man be a snare?   799

SLANDER.

Antidote. They may by your good works..glorify 8101
Base. This fellow doth cast out devils by Beelzebub 8102
Disgraceful. We found this man a pestilent fellow 8103
Folly. He that uttereth a slander is a fool   8104
Hurtful. Then will they not pay tribute   8105
Impious. He saved others ; himself he cannot save 8106
Joyful. Blessed..men revile you..rejoice   8107
Loyalty. Ziba said..he abideth at Jerusalem   8108
Malicious. Diotrephes..prating against us   8109
Opposed. It is reported..be their king   8110
Refuted. If Satan cast out Satan..divided   8111
Rebels. The people is greater that we   8112
Sinners. Thou art an austere man   8113
Satan's. Touch all that he hath..will curse   8114
Secret. A whisperer separateth friends   8115
Unbelief. Would to G. we had died..by fleshpots 8116

Satan's. God doth know..ye shall be as gods   8117
See CRITICISM.

2266. DEVIL, Called a. *Jesus.* ⁴⁷ He that is of God heareth God's words : ye therefore hear *them* not, because ye are not of God. ⁴⁸ Then answered the Jews..Say we not well that thou.. hast a devil?—JOHN, ch. 8.

2267. —— Hypocrisy of the. *Pharisees.* ⁴⁴ Ye are of *your* father the devil, and the lusts of your father ye will do : he was a murderer from the beginning, and abode not in the truth.—JOHN, ch. 8.

2268. —— Sold to the. *Ahab.* ²⁵ There was none like unto Ahab, which did sell himself to work wickedness in the sight of the Lord, whom Jezebel his wife stirred up. ²⁶ And he did very abominably in following idols, according to all *things* as did the Amorites.—1 KINGS, ch. 21.

See other references under :

SATAN.

Audacity. If thou be the S. of G., command   7578
Bound. An angel..bound him a thousand years   7579
Children. Ye are of your father the devil..no truth 7580
Cunning. God doth know..your eyes shall be   7581
Doom. Cast him into the bottomless pit   7582
Delivered to. Hymeneas and Alex..delivered unto 7583
Enmity. I will put enmity between thee..woman   7584
Fall of. War in heaven..the dragon fought   7585
Filled. Ananias, why hath Satan filled thy heart   7586
Injurious. L. said..all that he hath..thy power   7587
Inspired by. Devil put into the heart of Judas   7588
Leader. After the sop, Satan entered into him   7589
Peril. The devil as a roaring lion..seeking   7590
Scripture. It is written, He shall give his angels   7591
Worshipper. Satan came also to present himself   7592

Delivered to. Hymeneus and Alex. I have..unto   13
Unclean. Jesus rebuked..came out of him   2172
See TEMPTATION and references.

2269. DEVOTION, Benevolent. *Widow.* [42] She threw in two mites.. [43].. this poor widow hath cast more in, than all they which have cast into the treasury : [44] For all *they* did cast in of their abundance ; but she of her want did cast in all that she had, *even* all her living.—MARK, ch. 12.

2270. —— A deceptive. *Peter.* [37] Peter said ..Lord, why cannot I follow thee now ? I will lay down my life for thy sake. [38] Jesus answered him, Wilt thou lay down thy life for my sake ?.. The cock shall not crow, till thou hast denied me thrice.—JOHN, ch. 13.

2271. —— Excessive. *Epaphroditus.* [30] For the work of Christ he was nigh unto death, not regarding his life, to supply your lack of service toward me.—PHIL., ch. 2.

2272. —— Expensive. *Ointment.* [3] Then took Mary a pound of ointment of spikenard, very costly, and anointed the feet of Jesus, and wiped his feet with her hair : and the house was filled with the odour of the ointment.—JOHN, ch. 12.

2273. —— Friendship's. *Ittai.* [20] Whereas thou camest *but* yesterday, should I this day make thee go up and down with us ? seeing I go whither I may, return thou, and take back thy brethren : mercy and truth *be* with thee. [21] And Ittai answered the king.. *As* the Lord liveth.. surely in what place my lord the king shall be, whether in death or life, even there also will thy servant be.—2 SAM., ch. 15.

2274. —— Filial. *Ruth.* [16] Entreat me not to leave thee, *or* to return from following after thee : for whither thou goest, I will go ; and where thou lodgest, I will lodge : thy people *shall be* my people, and thy God my God : [17] Where thou diest, will I die, and there will I be buried : the Lord do so to me, and more also, *if aught* but death part thee and me.—RUTH, ch. 1.

2275. —— Fraternal. *To Paul.* [3] Greet Priscilla and Aquila, my helpers in Christ Jesus : [4] Who have for my life laid down their own necks.—ROM., ch. 16.

2276. —— Hinderance to. *Pride.* [44] How can ye believe, which receive honour one of another, and seek not the honour that *cometh* from God only?—JOHN, ch. 5.

2277. —— Partial. *Amaziah.* [3] He did *that which was* right in the sight of the Lord, yet not like David his father : [4] Howbeit the high places were not taken away : as yet the people did sacrifice and burnt incense on the high places.—2 KINGS, ch. 14.

2278. —— rewarded. *Caleb.* [24] But my servant Caleb, because he had another spirit with him, and hath followed me fully, him will I bring into the land whereinto he went : and his seed shall possess it.—NUM., ch. 14.

2279. —— Religious. *Of Jesus.* [35] In the morning, rising up a great while before day, he went out, and departed into a solitary place, and there prayed.—MARK, ch. 1.

2280. —— Sublime. *Abraham.* [12] Lay not thine hand upon the lad.. for now I know that thou fearest God, seeing thou hast not withheld thy son, thine only *son* from me.—GEN., ch. 22.

2281. —— Unselfish. *Moses.* [Israel had made a golden calf.] [32] Yet now, if thou wilt forgive their sin—; and if not, blot me, I pray thee, out of thy book which thou hast written. —EX., ch. 32.

See other illustrations under :

CONSECRATION.

Covenant. All the people stood to the covenant	1584
Leadership. Took Joshua.. laid hands upon him	1585
Service. Moses took of the blood.. ear.. thumb	1586
Self-denying. Made the laver.. looking-glasses	1587
Affectionate. Peter saith.. dost thou wash my feet ?	579
Claimed. That loveth.. more than me is not worthy	580
Surpassing. I am in labors more abundant.. stripes	869

See PIETY, RELIGION, and references.

2282. DEVOTIONS, Midnight. *In Philippi's Jail.* [25] At midnight Paul and Silas prayed, and sang praises unto God : and the prisoners heard them.—ACTS, ch. 16.

See PRAISE, PRAYER, and WORSHIP.

2283. DEXTERITY, Left-handed. *Benjamites.* [16] *There were* seven hundred chosen men left-handed ; every one could sling stones at a hair *breadth*, and not miss.—JUDGES, ch. 20.

2284. DIET, for Health. *Four Hebrews.* [12] Prove thy servants, I beseech thee, ten days ; and let them give us pulse to eat, and water to drink. [15].. their countenances appeared fairer and fatter in flesh than all the children which did eat the portion of the king's meat.—DAN., ch. 1.

See other illustrations under :

APPETITE.

Control. Put a knife to thy throat if.. appetite	479
Dangers. We remember.. fish, cucumbers, melons	480
Heedless. [Pursuing Philistines] People were very	481
Sin. Who shall give us flesh ?.. be loathsome	482
Temptation. [Jesus] fasted 40 days.. afterward a	483
Unrestrained. At the point to die, what profit	484

ABSTINENCE.

Extreme. Nazarite.. wine.. strong drink.. moist	20
Excitement. Saul was three days.. eat or drink	21
Famishing. Found an Egyptian.. when he had eaten	22
Mourning. David sware.. If I taste bread	23
Necessitated. Desert place.. no leisure.. to eat	24
Passionate. Jonathan.. fierce anger.. eat no meat	25
Priestly. Not drink wine.. go into the tabernacle	26
Peril. Paul besought them to take meat [shipwreck]	27
Protracted. Moses.. 40 days.. neither eat.. drink	28
" Jesus.. 40 days.. afterward a hungered	29
Self-denying. David would not drink.. jeopardy	30
Sorrowful. Child sick.. David fasted.. lay.. on the	31
Total. [Rechabites] Drink no wine.. father com.	32

FOOD.

Animal. Every moving thing.. shall be meat for	3286
Better than. Esteemed the words.. more than my	3287
Cleansed. What G. had cleansed.. call not	3288
Costly. Jacob gave Esau bread and pottage and	3289
Chosen. Let them give us pulse to eat	3290
Daily. Give us this day our daily bread	3292
Diminished. [Sin] Given you cleanness of teeth	3293
Perilous. Jonathan.. taste a little honey.. must die	3312
Example. Conscience of him which is weak.. emb.	3294
Forbidden. Ye may eat of.. trees of the garden	3295
Favorite. I am old.. take me some venison.. I love	3296
Friendship. Isaac loved Esau because.. of his ven.	3297
Famine. Besieged Samaria.. ass's head.. 80 silver	3298
Freedom to gather. Neighbour's vineyard.. eat	3299
God honoured. Eat either bread nor.. until.. offer.	3300
God gives. Consider the ravens.. God feedeth them	3301
Heavenly. L. evermore give us of this bread	3302
Life-giving. Lest.. take.. tree of life, and live	3303
Miraculous. L. brought quails from the sea	3304
" Elijah.. ravens brought him bread	3305

Miraculous. Elijah..angel..cake baken on the   3306
    "   [5000 fed] Did all eat, and were filled   3307
    "   [100 fed] Twelve loaves of barley   3308
    "   [Manna] Did eat manna 40 years   3309
Necessity. Better than..honoureth himself and   3310
Natural. John..his meat was locusts and wild   3311
Prohibited. Life of the flesh is in the blood   3313
    "   Eat no..fat of ox, sheep, or goat   3314
Prudence. Fed you with milk, not with meat   3315
Promised. Trust in the L. and do good..be fed   3316
    "   He that walketh righteously..bread   3317
Restricted. Beasts..parteth the hoof..cheweth the   3318
Scarcity. Handful of meal..little oil..eat, and die   3319
Supplies. Solomon's provision for one day..20 oxen   3320
Spiritual. Labour..meet which endureth..life   3321
Scruples. Some with conscience of the idol..eat it   3322
Thanks. Jesus took bread, and blessed it, and   3323
    "   Jesus blessed and brake the loaves, and   3324
    "   [Paul shipwrecked] took bread, and gave   3325
Temptation in. Fasted 40 days..tempter came   3326
Weeping. Every man in the door of his tent   3327

HUNGER.

Appetizing. To the hungry soul, every bitter thing   4209
Demoralizes. Give thy son, that we may eat him   4210
Disappointment. Fig tree in the way..nothing but   4211
Fasting. Fasted 40 days..afterward a hungered   4212
Inconsiderate. People did eat them with the   4213
Impatience. What profit shall this birthright do   4214
Lawful. Sabbath..disciples began to pluck..corn   4215
Murmuring. When we sat by the fleshpots..full   4216
Overcome. I have meat to eat ye know not   4217
Removed. I am the bread of life..never hunger   4218
Subdued by. I will arise, and go to my father   4219
Temptation. Tempter came..stones be made   4220

2285. DIFFICULTIES, Doctrinal. *Disciples.*
56 He that eateth my flesh, and drinketh my
blood, dwelleth in me, and I in him.   60 Many
therefore of his disciples, when they had heard
this, said, This is a hard saying ; who can hear
it?—JOHN, ch. 6. [Many went back.]

2286. —— Despondency from. *Elijah.*   10 I
have been very jealous for the Lord..for the
children of Israel have forsaken thy covenant,
thrown down thine altars, and slain thy prophets..and I, *even* I only, am left ; and they seek
my life, to take it away.—1 KINGS, ch. 19.

2287. —— Discouragement from. *Israelites.*
4 They journeyed from mount Hor by the way
of the Red sea, to compass the land of Edom :
and the soul of the people was much discouraged because of the way.—NUM., ch. 21.

2288. —— increase Endeavours. *Bartimeus.*
[See No. 2297.]

2289. —— Faith removes. *Two Spies.*   8 If
the Lord delight in us, then he will bring us into this land, and give it us..   9 Only rebel not
ye against the Lord, neither fear ye the people
of the land : for they *are* bread for us : their defence is departed from them, and the Lord *is*
with us : fear them not.—NUM., ch. 14.

2290. —— feared. *Lion.*   13 The slothful *man*
saith, There is a lion without, I shall be slain in
the streets.—PROV., ch. 22.

2291. —— with God, No. *One Hundred Years
Old.*   13 The Lord said unto Abraham, Wherefore did Sarah laugh, saying, Shall I of a surety
bear a child, which am old ?   14 Is any thing too
hard for the Lord ?—GEN., ch. 18.

2292. —— God ignores. *Opened   Prison.*

5 Peter therefore was kept in prison : but prayer
was made without ceasing of the church unto
God for him..   7 And, behold, the angel of the
Lord came upon *him*, and a light shined in the
prison : and he smote Peter on the side, and
raised him up..And his chains fell off from *his*
hands.—ACTS, ch. 12.

2293. —— Help amid. *Divine.*   10 Moses said
..O my Lord, I *am* not eloquent..but I *am* slow
of speech, and of a slow tongue.   11 And the
Lord said..Who hath made man's mouth? or
who maketh the dumb, or deaf, or the seeing, or
the blind? have not I the Lord?—EX., ch. 4.

2294. —— magnified. *Ten Spies.*   32 The
land, through which we have gone to search it,
is a land that eateth up the inhabitants thereof ;
and all the people that we saw in it *are* men of
a great stature.   33 And there we saw the giants,
the sons of Anak..and we were in our own sight
as grasshoppers, and so we were in their sight.
—NUM., ch. 13.

2295. —— must be met. *Proverb.*   4 He that
observeth the wind shall not sow ; and he that
regardeth the clouds shall not reap.—ECCL., ch.
11.

2296. —— from Opposition. *Enemies.*   7 Heard
that the walls of Jerusalem were made up, *and*
that the breaches began to be stopped, then they
were very wroth,   8 And conspired all of them
together to come *and* to fight against Jerusalem,
and to hinder it.—NEH., ch. 4.

2297. —— overcome. *Blind Bartimeus.*
47 When he heard that it was Jesus of Nazareth,
he began to cry out..   48 And many charged him
that he should hold his peace : but he cried the
more a great deal, *Thou* Son of David, have mercy on me.—MARK, ch. 10.

2298. —— from Peril. *Building.*   16 The half
of my servants wrought in the work, and the
other half of them held both the spears, the
shields, and the bows, and the habergeons..
17 They which builded on the wall, and they that
bare burdens, with those that laded..with one
of his hands wrought in the work, and with the
other *hand* held a weapon.   18 ..every one had
his sword girded by his side, and *so* builded.—
NEH., ch. 4.

2299. —— Prayer removes. *Faith.*   22 Have
faith in God.   23 ..whosoever shall say unto this
mountain, Be thou removed, and be thou cast
into the sea ; and shall not doubt in his heart,
but shall believe that those things which he
saith shall come to pass ; he shall have whatsoever he saith.—MARK, ch. 11.

2300. —— in Prayer. *Jesus.*   45 He constrained his disciples to get into the ship, and to go
to the other side before unto Bethsaida, while
he sent away the people.   46 And when he had
sent them away, he departed into a mountain
to pray.—MARK, ch. 6.

2301. —— from Ridicule. *Sanballat.*   2 What
do these feeble Jews ? will they fortify themselves ? will they sacrifice ? will they make an
end in a day ? will they revive the stones out of
the heaps of the rubbish which are burned ?
3 Now Tobiah..said, Even that which they build,
if a fox go up, he shall even break down their
stone wall.—NEH., ch. 4.

2302. —— unexpectedly removed. *Stone.*
3 And they said..Who shall roll us away the

stone from the door of the sepulchre ? [4] And when they looked, they saw that the stone was rolled away : for it was very great.—MARK, ch. 16.

2303. —— **Self-sacrifice in.** *Jews.* [21] So we laboured in the work : and half of them held the spears from the rising of the morning till the stars appeared. [23] So neither I, nor my brethren, nor my servants, nor the men of the guard .. put off our clothes, *saving that* every one put them off for washing.—NEH., ch. 4.

2304. —— **A Seeker's.** *Zaccheus.* [3] He sought to see Jesus who he was ; and could not for the press, because he was little of stature. [4] And he ran before, and climbed up into a sycamore tree to see him ; for he was to pass that *way.*—LUKE, ch. 19.

2305. —— **unheeded.** *Samson.* [3] Samson.. arose at midnight, and took the doors of the gate of the city, and the two posts.. bar and all, and put *them* upon his shoulders, and carried them up to the top of a hill that *is* before Hebron.—JUDGES, ch. 16.

2306. —— **Zeal greater than.** *Palsy.* [4] When they could not come nigh unto him for the press, they uncovered the roof where he was : and when they had broken *it* up, they let down the bed wherein the sick of the palsy lay.— MARK, ch. 2. [Jesus healed his soul and body.]

See other illustrations under :

DESPONDENCY.

Bereavement. Joseph is, without doubt, rent in	2226
Complaint. Since I came to Pharaoh..done evil	2227
Constitutional. Let us go..die with him	2230
Continued. My heart is smitten and withered like	2228
Cure. David was greatly distressed..spake of	2229
Difficulties. People was much discouraged	2231
Hope. Why art thou cast down, O my soul?	2232
Hasty. Sun beat..Jonah fainted..wished to die	2233
Ill-timed. Handful of meal..little oil..die	2234
Loneliness. I only am left, and they seek my life	2235
Memories. By the rivers of Babylon we wept	2236
Overcare. If thou deal thus with me, kill me	2237
Prayer. How long wilt thou forget me, O Lord?	2239
Public. Moses heard the people weeping..door	2238
Peril. Esau cometh..400 men..Jacob afraid	2240
Singular. Lord take away my life..not better	2242
Vows. L. made a reproach unto me..derision	2243
Without. Troubled on every side..not in despair	2244

DETERMINATION.

Evil. We will certainly..burn incense to the	2260
Fixed. As the L. liveth..I will not leave thee	2262
" In every city bonds..none..move me	2266
Resolute. Absalom said..Set it on fire	2263
Wanting. I will let him go..Pilate gave sentence	2264

HINDERANCE.

Disobedience. Say nothing to any man..blaze	3979
Natural. Let me..kiss my father..mother	3980
Provoking. Let us pass through thy country..not	3981
Removed. Angel..rolled back the stone..door	3982
Riches. Deceitfulness of riches..choke the word	3983
" Easier for a camel..needle's eye than	3984

HINDERANCES.

Care. Take heed lest..become a stumblingblock	3985
Malicious. People of the land, hired counsellors	3986
Removed. I will eat no flesh while the world	3987
Secular. I have bought..bought..married	3988
Social. Let me first go bid them farewell	3989
Selfish. Neither go in yourselves, neither suffer ye	3990

HINDERING.

Fear. It is reported..Jews think to rebel	3991
Intrigue. Let us meet..in the plain of Ono	3992
Overcome by. Men rowed hard..but could not	7464

See DISCOURAGEMENT.

See TRIALS.

2307. DILEMMA, A Deceiver's. *Jews.* [25] The baptism of John, whence was it ? from heaven, or of men ? And they reasoned with themselves, saying, If we shall say, From heaven ; he will say unto us, Why did ye not then believe him ? [26] But if we shall say, Of men ; we fear the people ; for all hold John as a prophet. [27] And they answered Jesus.. We cannot tell.—MAT., ch. 21.

See other illustrations under :

CHOICE.

Better. Mary hath chosen that good part	1222
Decisive. Me and my house, we will serve	1223
Desperate. So will I go..if I perish, I perish	1224
Difficult. David said..I am in a great strait	1225
Dangerous. Lot chose..toward Sodom	1226
Fruitful. Rod of Aaron..budded..almonds	1227
Foolish. Hewed them out..broken cisterns	1228
Heart. L. looketh on the heart	1229
Life or Death. Fiery serpent..looketh on it..live	1230
Murderers. Release unto us Barabbas	1231
Neglected. O that thou hadst hearkened	1232
Pious. Moses..refused to be called	1233
of Piety. How much better..than to get gold	1234
Rebellious. We will certainly..burn incense	1235
Responsibility. Set before you..blessing and a	1236
Results. Therefore shalt thou serve..enemies	1237
Saints. I will take you..for a people	1238
Unexpected. Remaineth the youngest..feedeth	1239
Worldly. Went away sorrowful..great possessions	1240

2308. DILIGENCE, Lack of. *Denial of Faith.* [8] If any provide not for his own, and specially for those of his own house, he hath denied the faith, and is worse than an infidel.—1 TIM., ch. 5.

2309. —— **Success by.** *Business.* [29] Seest thou a man diligent in his business? he shall stand before kings ; he shall not stand before mean *men.*—PROV., ch. 22.

See other illustrations under :

CARES.

Burdensome. Martha was cumbered about much	1047
Disturbing. Abundance of the rich will not suffer	1048
Ministerial. Besides..the care of all the churches	1049
Wealth. What shall I do..I have no room	1050

INDUSTRY.

Active. Rebekah..let down her pitcher..hasted	4442
Benevolence. Showing the coats..Dorcas had	4443
Commended. Go to the ant, thou sluggard	4444
Domestic. [Model woman—Prov., ch. 31]	4445
Independent. Paul had gathered a bundle of sticks	4446
Jesus. Mighty works are wrought..this the	4447
Promotion. Solomon seeing..he was industrious	4448
Required. If any would not work, neither should	4449

LABOUR.

Advantage. Sleep of a labouring man is sweet..eat	4864
Curse. Thorns and thistles..sweat of thy face	4865
Commanded. Six days shalt thou labour	4866
Congenial. Put him into the garden..keep it	4867
Co-operative. One soweth, another reapeth	4868
Degradation. In the sweat of thy face	4869
Increase. No straw be given..tale of bricks	4870
Menial. Hewers of wood and drawers of water	4871
Motive. That..we may be accepted of him	4872

PERSEVERANCE.

Confident. Neither death nor life..separate me 6097
Exhortation. Barnabas exhorted..with purpose 6098
Encouragement. Can a woman forget her..child 6099
    "   Mountains shall depart..but my 6100
Help to. When..my foot slippeth..thy mercy held 6101
Prayer. Widow troubleth me, I will avenge her 6102
Success by. I have fought good fight..crown 6103
Test. If ye continue in my word, then..disciples 6104
   See WORK and references.

2310. DIRECTNESS commanded. *Joshua.* [7]Observe to do according to all the law..turn not from it *to* the right hand or *to* the left, that thou mayest prosper whithersoever thou goest. —Josh., ch. 1.

2311. —— God gives. *Kine.* [10] Shut up their calves at home : [11] And they laid the ark of the Lord upon the cart.. [12] And the kine took the straight way to the way of Beth-shemesh, *and* went..lowing as they went, and turned not aside *to* the right hand or *to* the left.—1 Sam., ch. 6.

  See other illustrations under :
APPLICATION.
Direct. Judas said, Master, is it I?..Thou hast said 487
Personal. Nathan said to David, Thou art the man 488
Unmistakable. Whom ye crucified..salvation in 489

Commanded. If thou meet any man, salute him 2454

2312. DISAGREEMENT in Quality. *New and Old.* [36]No man putteth a piece of a new garment upon an old ; if otherwise, then both the new maketh a rent, and the piece that was *taken* out of the new agreeth not with the old. [37] And no man putteth new wine into old bottles ; else the new wine will burst the bottles, and be spilled, and the bottles shall perish.—Luke, ch. 5.

2313. —— in Testimony. *Perjurers.* [55] The chief priests, and all the council, sought for witness against Jesus to put him to death ; and found none : [56] For many bare false witness against him, but their witness agreed not together.—Mark, ch. 14.

  See other illustrations under :
ANTAGONISM.
Spiritual. I will put enmity between thee 450
Truth. I am not come to send peace..sword 451
DIVISION.
Affections. Saul's anger was kindled against 2457
Brethren. Barnabas determined to take Mark 2458
Cruel. Divide the living child in two 2459
Doctrinal. Eateth my flesh..walked no more 2460
Divine. Elisha took the mantle of Elijah..parted 2461
Just. Shall his..tarrieth with the stuff 2462
Lord's. The land..my people dwell..no flies 2463
Misconception. Shall Christ come out of Galilee? 2464
Opinions. Some said, He is a good man 2465
by Truth. I came not to send peace..sword 2466
DIVISIONS.
Authors of. These six things doth the L. hate 2467
Harmful. Wherefore smitest thou thy fellow ? 2468
Harmonious. Body is not one member, but many 2469
Healed. Good..to lay upon you no greater burden 2470
Party. I am of Paul..I of Apollos..Cephas 2471
Scandalous. Come together, not for the better 2472
Weakness. Every kingdom divided against itself 2473
DISSENSIONS.
Doctrinal. Paul and Barnabas had no small 2429
Perilous. Sadducees..Pharisees..great dissension 2430
Removed. Altar of witness..God forbid that we 2432
Stubborn. Barnabas took Mark..Paul chose Silas 2433

Litigation. Fault among you..ye go to law 5050
  See CONFLICT and references.

2314. DISAFFECTION, Doctrinal. *Disciples.* [54] Whoso eateth my flesh, and drinketh my blood, hath eternal life ; and I will raise him up at the last day. [60] Many therefore of his disciples, when they had heard *this*, said, This is a hard saying ; who can hear it ? [66] From that *time* ..went back, and walked no more with him.— John, ch. 6.
  See other illustrations under .
DISAGREEMENT.
Grudge. Brother shall trespass..go tell him his 3753
Quality. No man putteth..a new garment on an 2312
Testimony. Against Jesus..witness agreed not 2313
DISPLEASURE.
False Piety. I hate your feast days..assemblies 2412
Holy. Jesus saw it, was much displeased..suffer 2411
HATRED.
Brother. If. say, I love God and hateth..is a liar 3828
Bitter. Brother shall betray brother..to death 3829
Commendable. Thou hatest the deeds of the 3830
Changed. Ready to die..for the L. Jesus 3831
Darkness. He that hateth his brother walketh 3832
Divine. Six things doth the L. hate 3833
Evil. Better is a dinner of herbs where love is 3834
Good. [Joseph's] brethren hated him..not speak 3835
Light. Every one that doeth evil hateth the light 3836
Manifested. When the days of mourning ended 3838
Silent. Absalom spake unto..Amnon..good nor 3840
Sinner's. Micaiah..I hate..doth not prophesy 3841
World. If the world hate you..it hated me before 3842
INDIGNATION.
Bigoted. Ruler answered with indignation 4415
Christian. Spirit was stirred..given to idolatry 4417
Contemptuous. Why camest thou? few sheep 4416
Excessive. Fire to come down..consume them 4418
Forgotten. Is thy servant a dog..do this? 4419
God gives. S. of G. came upon Saul..anger 4420
Hot. Saw the calf..Moses' anger waxed hot 4421
at Hypocrisy. Jesus looked on them with anger 4422
at Injustice. Elihu..wrath kindled..yet had con. 4423
Improper. Indignation..Why..waste of the 4424
Judgment. Remaineth..a certain fearful 4425
Murderous. When they heard..filled with wrath 4426
National. People arose as one man..to do to 4427
Natural. Ten heard it..moved with indignation 4428
Partisan. Sadducees..were filled with indignation 4429
Pride. Haman was full of indignation against M. 4430
Righteous. I may thrust out all your right eyes 4431
Religious. Against Job..because he justified 4432
at Sinners. David's anger was kindled..restore 4433
Severity. L. was wroth and..to tormentors 4434

2315. DISAPPOINTMENT, Doubt from. *Apostles.* [9] Mary Magdalene.. [10]..told them that had been with him, as they mourned and wept. [11]And they, when they had heard that he was alive, and had been seen of her, believed not.—Mark, ch. 16.

2316. —— in Gifts. *Hiram.* [11] King Solomon gave Hiram twenty cities in the land of Galilee. [12] And Hiram came out from Tyre to see the cities..and they pleased him not.—1 Kings, ch. 9.

2317. —— A good. *Mary.* [2] Then she runneth..to Simon Peter, and to the other disciple, whom Jesus loved, and saith..They have taken away the Lord out of the sepulchre, and we know not where they have laid him.—John, ch. 20.

2318. —— A humiliating. *Peter and John.*

22 The officers..returned.. **23** Saying, The prison truly found we shut with all safety, and the keepers standing without before the doors : but when we had opened, we found no man within. —ACTS, ch. 5.

2319. —— through Ignorance. *Desert of Zin.* **5** Wherefore have ye made us to come up out of Egypt, to bring us in unto this evil place? it *is* no place of seed, or of figs, or of vines, or of pomegranates ; neither *is* there any water.— NUM., ch. 20.

2320. —— at the Judgment. *The Rejected.* **26** We have eaten and drunk in thy presence, and thou hast taught in our streets. **27** But he shall say, I tell you, I know you not whence ye are ; depart from me, all *ye* workers of iniquity. **28** There shall be weeping and gnashing of teeth.—LUKE, ch. 13.

2321. —— Misjudged. *Disciples.* **20** The chief priests and our rulers delivered him to be condemned to death, and have crucified him. **21** But we trusted that it had been he which should have redeemed Israel.—LUKE, ch. 24.

2322. —— Maternal. *Eve.* **15** I will put enmity between thee and the woman, and between thy seed and her seed ; it shall bruise thy head, and thou shalt bruise his heel. **1**..she conceived, and bare Cain, and said, I have gotten a man from the Lord.—GEN., ch. 3 and 4. [This man bruised his brother's head.]

2323. —— A perplexing. *Syrian King.* **10** The man of God told him and warned him of, and saved himself there, not once nor twice. **11** Therefore the heart of the king of Syria was sore troubled..and he called his servants, and said.. Will ye not shew me which of us *is* for the king of Israel? **12** And one..said, None..Elisha, the prophet that *is* in Israel, telleth the king of Israel the words that thou speakest in thy bedchamber.—2 KINGS, ch. 6.

2324. —— in Religion. *Unconverted.* **18** Since we left off to burn incense to the queen of heaven, and to pour out drink offerings unto her, we have wanted all *things,* and have been consumed by the sword and by the famine.—JER., ch. 44.

2325. —— Unendurable. *Ahithophel.* **23** When Ahithophel saw that his counsel was not followed, he saddled *his* ass..and gat him home.. and put his household in order, and hanged himself.—2 SAM., ch. 17.

2326. DISAPPOINTMENTS, Many. *The Wicked.* **5** Thus saith the Lord of hosts ; Consider your ways. **6** Ye have sown much, and bring in little ; ye eat, but ye have not enough ; ye drink, but ye are not filled with drink ; ye clothe you, but there is none warm : and he that earneth wages, earneth wages *to put it* into a bag with holes.—HAG., ch. 1.

See other illustrations under :

DEFEAT.

Angered. Elihu saw..was no answer..wrath 2098
Conspirators. Entangle him..marvelled, and left 2099
Desperation. Not able to resist the wisdom and 2100
Humiliating. Men of Ai smote..Joshua rent 2101
Predicted. Will flee upon..horses, therefore shall 2102
Providential. L. did confound the language 2103

FAILURE.

Avoiding. First..counteth the cost..to finish 2867
Cruelty. More they afflicted them..grew 2868
Complaint. Why is it thou hast sent me? 2869

Church. Disciples..should cast him out..could 2870
Discouraging. Toiled all the night..taken nothing 2871
Disheartening. Put a sword in their hand to slay 2872
Explained. Why could not we cast him out? 2873
Fear. We were..as grasshoppers 2874
Irremediable. Went to buy..door was shut 2875
Ominous. Thou hast begun to fall..surely fall 2876
Providential. Confounded their language..left off 2877
Ridiculed. Mock him..began to build..not able 2878
Temporary. Pharaoh said..neither will I let I. go 2879

2327. DISCIPLES, Steadfast. *In the Word.* **31** Said Jesus to those Jews which believed on him, If ye continue in my word, *then* are ye my disciples indeed ; **32** And ye shall know the truth, and the truth shall make you free.—JOHN, ch. 8.

2328. —— Timid. *Joseph.* **38** Being a disciple of Jesus, but secretly for fear of the Jews, besought Pilate that he might take away the body of Jesus : and Pilate gave *him* leave.. **39** And there came also Nicodemus, (which at the first came to Jesus by night,) and brought a mixture of myrrh and aloes, about a hundred pounds *weight.*—JOHN, ch. 19.

2329. —— Willing. *John—Andrew.* **36** Behold the Lamb of God! **37** And the two disciples heard him speak, and they followed Jesus. **38** Then Jesus turned, and saw them following, and saith..What seek ye? They said..Rabbi.. where dwellest thou? **39** He saith..Come and see. They came..and abode with him that day ; for it was about the tenth hour.—JOHN, ch. 1.

See other illustrations under :

CHRISTIAN.

Almost. Almost thou persuadest me 1267
Care. I lay down my life for the sheep 1268
Childlike. Of such is the kingdom 1269
Carnal. Whereas there is..envying and strife 1270
Epistle. Ye are our epistle..read of all men 1271
Exemplary. Be blameless..not self willed..angry 1272
Greatness. Least..is greater than he [J. B.] 1273
Homeward. Come to Zion with songs 1274
Named. First called C. at Antioch 1275
Saved. He might destroy the works of the D. 1276
Visible. City..set upon a hill 1277

BELIEVERS.

Joys. Though now ye see him not,.yet believing, ye 681
Possibilities. All things are possible to him that 682
Weak. Speak unto you..as unto babes in Christ 683

CONVERTS.

Duty. Woman went..and saith, Come see 1667
Distinguished. Eunuch..went into the water 1668
Spurious. Simon..offered them money..give 1669
Trial. Thou art his disciple, but we are Moses' 1670
Counsel. Barnabas..exhorted them to cleave unto 1671
Food. As newborn babes desire..milk of the word 1672
Humble. Have any of the rulers or Pharisees 1673
Hypocrisy. Proselyte..twofold more the child of 1674
Influential. Believed..many honourable women 1675
Increase. Many believed..about 5000 men 1676
   "   Same day added..about 3000 souls 1677
Principle, No. Many became Jews..for fear of the 1678
Steadfast. Continuing daily with one accord 1679
Superficial. Have no root in themselves 1680
Zeal. Made myself servant unto all 1681

CONVERSION.

Creation. New creature, old things passed away 1700
Conscious. Know we that we dwell in him..S. 1701
Changed. Made their feet fast.. washed their 1702
Changes Life. Saul preached..Is not this he that 1703
Effort. Strive to enter in at the strait gate 1704

2330. DISCIPLESHIP, Abnegation of. *Jesus.*
[21] Another of his disciples said..Lord, suffer me first to go and bury my father. [22] But Jesus said..Follow me ; and let the dead bury their dead. —MAT., ch. 8.

2331. —— Conditional. *Jesus.* [61] Another also said, Lord, I will follow thee ; but let me first go bid them farewell, which are at home at my house.—LUKE, ch. 9.

2332. —— Provisional. *Naaman.* [17] Thy servant will henceforth offer neither burnt offering nor sacrifice unto other gods, but unto the Lord. [18]..when my master goeth into the house of Rimmon to worship there, and he leaneth on my hand..when I bow down myself in the house of Rimmon, the Lord pardon thy servant in this thing.—2 KINGS, ch. 5.

2333. —— postponed. *Elisha.* [19] Elijah passed by him, and cast his mantle upon him. [20] And he left the oxen, and ran after Elijah, and said, Let me, I pray thee, kiss my father and my mother, and *then* I will follow thee. And he said.. Go back again.—1 KINGS, ch. 19.

2334. —— Terms of. *Jesus.* [26] If any *man* come to me, and hate not his father, and mother, and wife, and children, and brethren, and sisters, yea, and his own life also, he cannot be my disciple. [27] And whosoever doth not bear his cross, and come after me, cannot be my disciple. —LUKE, ch. 14.

2335. —— Trials of. *Slander.* [25] It is enough for the disciple that he be as his master, and the servant as his lord. If they have called the master of the house Beelzebub, how much more *shall they call* them of his household.—MAT., ch. 10.

2336. —— Unconditional. *Jesus.* [23] Said to ..all, If any *man* will come after me, let him deny himself, and take up his cross daily, and follow me. [24] For whosoever will save his life shall lose it : but whosoever will lose his life for my sake, the same shall save it.—LUKE, ch. 9.

See other illustrations under :

DISCIPLINE.

LEADER.

2337. DISCIPLINE, Ancient. *Israelites.* [1] They read in the book of Moses..that the Ammonite and the Moabite should not come into the congregation of God for ever ; [2] Because they met not the children of Israel with bread and with water, but hired Balaam against them, that he should curse them.. [3]..when they had heard the law..they separated from Israel all the mixed multitude.—NEH., ch. 13.

2338. —— Care in. *Tares.* [28] The servants said..Wilt thou then that we go and gather them up ? [29] But he said, Nay ; lest while ye gather up the tares, ye root up also the wheat with them. [30] Let both grow together until the harvest : and..I will say to the reapers, Gather ye together first the tares, and bind them in bundles to burn them : but gather the wheat into my barn.—MAT., ch. 13.

2339. —— Method of. *Trespass.* [15] If thy brother shall trespass against thee, go and tell him his fault between thee and him alone.. [16] But if he will not hear *thee, then* take with thee one or two more, that in the mouth of two or three witnesses every word may be established.

[17] And if he shall neglect to hear them, tell *it* unto the church : but if he neglect to hear the church, let him be unto thee as a heathen man. —MAT., ch. 18.

2340. —— Primitive. *Ananias.* [1] Ananias, with Sapphira his wife, sold a possession..[10] Then fell she down straightway at his feet, and yielded up the ghost. And the young men..carrying *her* forth, buried *her* by her husband. [11] And great fear came upon all the church.—ACTS, ch. 5.

See other illustrations under :

CHASTISEMENT.

Children. He that spareth the rod hateth his son	1131
Fruits. It yieldeth the peaceable fruit of	1132
Good. Chastened us for their pleasure..our profit	1133
Love. Whom the L. loveth, he chasteneth	1134

SELF-CONTROL.

Lack. He that hath no rule over his own spirit	7698
Masterly. Belial said..He held his peace	7699
Resolute. Put a knife to thy throat..much	7700

SELF-DENIAL.

Abstinence. David would not drink thereof	7701
Bodily. I keep under my body lest..be a castaway	7702
Better. People complained..fire consumed them	7703
Costly. If thy right hand offend thee, cut it off	7704
Difficult. [Young ruler] went away grieved	7705
Decent. Put a knife to thy throat..given to	7706
Essential. Let him deny himself..take up his	7707
Marvellous. Get thee out of thy country..kindred	7708
" Moses refused to be called the son	7709
" Unto this present hour we both	7710
for Others. If meat make my brother to offend	7711
Patriotic. Twelve years..not eaten the bread	7712
Positive. If..hate not his father..own life	7713
Rewarded. Ye also shall sit upon 12 thrones	7714
" Shall receive 100 fold..eternal life	7715
Saved by. Because strait is the gate and narrow	7716
Sabbath. If thou turn from doing thine own	7717

TRAINING.

Early. Syrians brought a little maid..said	8876
" Moses when he was come to years refused	8877
" Samuel..shall be lent to the Lord	8878

Adornment. Shall be an ornament of grace	1867

See PUNISHMENT and TRIALS.

2341. DISCERNMENT, Imperfect. *Hypocrites.* [54] When ye see a cloud rise out of the west, straightway ye say, There cometh a shower ; and so it is. [55] And when *ye see* the south wind blow, ye say, There will be heat.. [56] *Ye* hypocrites, ye can discern the face of the sky and of the earth ; but how is it that ye do not discern this time?—LUKE, ch. 12.

See other illustrations under :

DISCRETION.

Necessary. King consulteth..war..or..peace	2366
Part of. Let not thy voice be heard..lose thy life	2367
Success. David said to Abigail..Blessed be the	2368
Safety. Paul perceived that one part were Saddu's	2369
Want of. As a jewel of gold in a swine's snout	2370
" Nabal said, Who is David?..his master	2371

PRUDENCE.

Age. Wherefore should thy servant be yet a burden	6774
Commended. Lord commended the unjust steward	6775
Example. Render unto Cesar..they marvelled and	6776
Preservation. Hold..lest angry fellows run upon	6777
" Joseph hearkened not..or to be with	6778
Resolutions. Intending to build a tower..counteth	6779

Discipline. Nay ; lest while ye gather up the tares	2338

Influence. Nor to drink wine..whereby thy	4460
Perception. Is not the hand of Joab..in this ?	95
Useless. Which..by taking thought, can add one	3333

2342. DISCLOSURE, Astounding. *Joseph.* [3] Joseph said..I *am* Joseph ; doth my father yet live ? And his brethren could not answer him ; for they were troubled at his presence.—GEN., ch. 45.

See other illustrations under :

DISCOVERY.

Alarming. My money is restored..heart failed	2360
Painful. Isaac trembled..Who ? where is he ?	2361
Unexpected. Is not the hand of Joab..in this ?	2362
Appalling. When saw we thee..in prison?..least	8502
Doubted. Told them..he was..seen, believed not	2320
Happy. Jesus saith unto her, Mary..master	9725
" [John] saith unto Peter, it is the Lord	3253
Judgment. We have eaten..I know not whence ye	2319
Strange. How is it thou wilt manifest thyself	5205
Unexpected. Come see a man..Is not this the C.	9741

2343. DISCONTENTMENT, A Foreigner's. *Hadad.* [21] Hadad said to Pharaoh, Let me depart, that I may go to mine own country. [22] Then Pharaoh said..But what hast thou lacked with me, that, behold, thou seekest to go to thine own country? And he answered, Nothing : howbeit let me go in any wise.—1 KINGS, ch. 11.

2344. —— of the Proud. *Haman.* [12] Yea, Esther the queen did let no man come in with the king unto the banquet that she had prepared but myself ; and to-morrow am I invited ..[13] Yet all this availeth me nothing, so long as I see Mordecai the Jew sitting at the king's gate.—ESTHER, ch. 5.

2345. —— Unity in. *David.* [2] Every one *that was* in distress, and..in debt, and..discontented, gathered themselves unto him ; and he became a captain over them..about four hundred men.—1 SAM., ch. 22.

See other illustrations under :

COMPLAINERS.

Punished. Our soul loatheth..bread..sent fiery	1445
Unreasonable. The first supposed..received more	1446
Unprincipled. These are..walking in their own	1447
Wicked. Did bring up an evil report..the plague	1448

DISAPPOINTMENT.

Doubt. Heard..he was alive..seen..believed not	2315
in Gifts. Gave Hiram 20 cities..pleased him not	2316
Good. They have taken the L. out of the sepulchre	2318
Ignorance. Evil place? no place of seed..figs	2319
Judgment. Thou hast taught in our streets	2320
Misjudged. We trusted..had been he..should have	2321
Maternal. Bare Cain..I have gotten a man of the	2322
Perplexing. Which of us is for the king of I. ?	2323
Religion. Since we left off to burn incense..for	2324
Unendurable. Ahithophel..counsel not followed	2325
Many Disappointments. Consider your ways	2326

FAULTFINDERS.

Fastidious. Why do ye eat..with sinners	3087
Hypocritical. Why was not this.. sold for 300 pence	3088
Malicious. John B..he hath a devil..Son of man	3089

MURMURING.

Disappointment. This evil place?..no place of figs	5639
Discouragement. People was much discouraged	5640
Distrust. Would G. that we had died in Egypt	5641
Fear. Did tell thee..been better serve the E.	5642
God. Hath not the potter power over the clay	5643
Mercenaries. These last have wrought but one	5644
Neglect. Murmuring of the Greeks against the	5645

Punished. Fire of the L. burnt them..uttermost 5646
Severity. What shall I do?..almost ready to stone 5647
Thirst. Three days..no water..bitter..what shall 5648

2346. DISCOURAGEMENT from Contrast. *David.* ² But as for me, my feet were almost gone ; my steps had well nigh slipped. ³ For I was envious at the foolish, *when* I saw the prosperity of the wicked. ⁴ For *there are* no bands in their death : but their strength *is* firm. ⁵ They *are* not in trouble *as other* men : neither are they plagued like *other* men. ¹³ Verily I have cleansed my heart *in* vain, and washed my hands in innocency.—Ps. 73.

2347. —— from Defeat. *At Ai.* ⁷ Joshua said, Alas ! O Lord God, wherefore hast thou at all brought this people over Jordan, to deliver us into the hand of the Amorites, to destroy us? would to God we had been content, and dwelt on the other side Jordan !—Josh., ch. 7.

2348. —— from Evildoers. *David's.* ³⁰ Joab and Abishai his brother slew Abner, because he had slain their brother Asahel at Gibeon in the battle. ³⁹ And I *am* this day weak, though anointed king ; and these men the sons of Zeruiah *be* too hard for me.—2 Sam., ch. 3.

2349. —— from Failure. *Moses.* ²² Lord, wherefore hast thou *so* evil entreated this people? why *is* it *that* thou hast sent me ? ²³ For since I came to Pharaoh to speak in thy name, he hath done evil to this people ; neither hast thou delivered thy people at all.—Ex., ch. 5.

2350. —— —— *Peter.* ⁴ He said unto Simon, Launch out into the deep, and let down your nets for a draught. ⁵ ..Master, we have toiled all the night, and have taken nothing : nevertheless, at thy word I will let down the net.—Luke, ch. 5.

2351. —— from Mismanagement. *At Ai.* ³ They returned to Joshua, and said..Let not all the people go up ; but let about two or three thousand men go up and smite Ai : ⁵ And the men of Ai smote of them about thirty and six men : for they chased them..and smote them.. wherefore the hearts of the people melted, and became as water.—Josh., ch. 7.

2352. —— Ministerial. *Parable.* ⁵ Some fell on stony ground, where it had not much earth ; and immediately it sprang up, because it had no depth of earth : ⁷ And some fell among thorns, and the thorns grew up, and choked it, and it yielded no fruit.—Mark, ch. 4.

2353. —— Needless. *Elisha's Servant* ¹⁵ was risen early, and gone forth, behold, a host compassed the city both with horses and chariots. And..said..Alas, my master ! how shall we do ? ¹⁶ And he answered, Fear not : for they that *be* with us *are* more than they that *be* with them.— 2 Kings, ch. 6.

2354. —— reproved. *Elijah.* ¹⁴ I, *even* I only, am left ; and they seek my life, to take it away. ¹⁵ And the Lord said..Go, return..to the wilderness of Damascus : and..anoint Hazael *to be* king over Syria : ¹⁶ And Jehu..*to be* king over Israel : and Elisha..*to be* prophet in thy room. ¹⁸ Yet I have left *me* seven thousand in Israel, all the knees which have not bowed unto Baal.—1 Kings, ch. 19.

2355. —— from Trials. *Moses.* ¹³ They weep unto me, saying, Give us flesh, that we may eat. ¹⁴ I am not able to bear all this people alone, because *it is* too heavy for me. ¹⁵ And if thou deal thus with me, kill me, I pray thee.—Num., ch. 11.

2356. —— from Unbelief. *At Red Sea.* ¹² It had been better for us to serve the Egyptians, than that we should die in the wilderness. ¹³ And Moses said unto the people, Fear ye not, stand still, and see the salvation of the Lord.. for the Egyptians whom ye have seen to day, ye shall see them again no more for ever.—Ex., ch. 14.

2357. —— Unreasonable. *Israelites.* ⁵ The people spake against God, and against Moses, Wherefore have ye brought us up out of Egypt to die in the wilderness? for *there is* no bread, neither *is there any* water ; and our soul loatheth this light bread. ⁶ And the Lord sent fiery serpents .. and much people of Israel died.— Num., ch. 21.

2358. —— without. *Paul.* ¹⁶ We faint not ; but though our outward man perish, yet the inward *man* is renewed day by day.—2 Cor., ch. 4.

2359. DISCOURAGEMENTS overcome. *Syrophenician.* ²² Have mercy on me..my daughter is grievously vexed with a devil. ²³ But he answered her not a word. And his disciples..besought him, saying, Send her away ; for she crieth after us. ²⁴ But he..said, I am not sent but unto the lost sheep of the house of Israel. ²⁵ Then came she..saying, Lord, help me. ²⁶ But he..said, It is not meet to take the children's bread, and to cast *it* to dogs. ²⁷ And she said, Truth, Lord : yet the dogs eat of the crumbs which fall from their masters' table. ²⁸ Then Jesus..said..O woman, great *is* thy faith : be it unto thee even as thou wilt.—Mat., ch. 15.

See other illustrations under :

DESPAIR.

Affliction. Let me not see the death of the child   2213
Anguish. Slay me, for anguish is come upon me   2214
Awaking. Wine was gone out..heart died within   2215
Deliverance. Been better for us to serve the Egyp. 2216
Needless. Widow..meal..oil..me and my son eat   2217

DESPERATION.

Boldness. I will go in unto the king..if I perish   2218
Effort. Why sit we here till we die?   2219
Sinners. Saul inquired of the L..answered him   2220
Sacrifices. King of Moab took his eldest son   2221

DESPONDENCY.

Bereavement. Joseph is, without doubt, rent in   2226
Complaint. Since I came to Pharaoh..done evil   2227
Constitutional. Let us go..die with him   2230
Continued. My heart is smitten and withered like 2228
Cure. David was greatly distressed..spake of   2229
Difficulties. People was much discouraged   2231
Hope. Why art thou cast down, O my soul   2232
Hasty. Sun beat..Jonah fainted..wished to die   2233
Ill-timed. Handful of meal..little oil..die   2234
Loneliness. I only am left, and they seek my life 2235
Memories. By the rivers of Babylon we wept   2236
Overcare. If thou deal thus with me, kill me   2237
Prayer. How long wilt thou forget me, O Lord?   2239
Public. Moses heard the people weeping..door   2238
Peril. Esau cometh..400 men..Jacob afraid   2240
Singular. Lord, take away my life..not better   2242
Vows. L. made a reproach upon me..derision   2243
Without. Troubled on every side..not in despair   2244

DISTRESS.

Cry of. Great cry..none like it, nor shall be   2437
Derided. They that see me, shoot out the lip   2438

Described. I was a derision to all my people 2439
Exasperation. What shall I do..people ready to 2440
Famine. Delicate woman..shall eat..children 2441
Little Faith. Why are ye fearful..little faith 2442
Friend. Gedaliah..took Jeremiah out of prison 2443
Great. Thrust right eyes..people wept 2444
Needless. Saul had adjured the people..food 2445
Refuge. Ahaz sacrificed unto the gods that smote 2446

FAILURE.

Avoiding. Intending to build a tower..first 2867
Cruelty. The more they afflicted them, the more 2868
Complaint. L. wherefore hast thou so evil 2869
Church. That they should cast him out..not 2870
Discouraging. Ye have..put a sword in their hand 2871
Disheartening. Have toiled all the night..taken 2872
Explained. This kind can come..by prayer 2873
Fear. We saw the giants..we were grasshoppers 2874
Irremediable. The door was shut..Lord open 2875
Ominous. If thou hast begun to fall..not prevail 2876
Ridiculed. Mock him..began to build..not able 2878
Temporary. I know not the L., neither..let I. go 2879
See DISAPPOINTMENT.

2360. **DISCOVERY, Alarming.** *Joseph's Brethren.* [28] My money is restored : and, lo, *it is* even in my sack : and their heart failed *them*, and they were afraid, saying one to another, What is this *that* God hath done unto us?—GEN., ch. 42.

2361. —— **Painful.** *Jacob.* [33] Isaac trembled very exceedingly, and said, Who? where *is* he that hath taken venison, and brought *it* me, and I have eaten of all before thou camest, and have blessed him?—GEN., ch. 27.

2362. —— **Unexpected.** *Widow of Tekoah.* [19] The king said, *Is not* the hand of Joab with thee in all this? And the woman answered..As thy soul liveth..none can turn to the right hand or to the left from aught that my lord the king hath spoken : for thy servant Joab, he bade me, and he put all these words in the mouth of thine handmaid.—2 SAM., ch. 14.

See other illustrations under :

INVENTION.

Musical. Jubal..handle the harp and the organ 4643
Inspired. Bezaleel..filled with the spirit..cunning 4644

INVENTORS.

Family. Jubal..harp..Tubal-cain..artificer in 4645
Valuable. Uzziah made..engines..he was strong 4646

Feared. Adulterer disguiseth his face..terrors 111
Spies. Moses sent them to spy out the land of 8274

2363. **DISCRIMINATION of Character.** *Divine.* [4] By faith Abel offered unto God a more excellent sacrifice than Cain, by which he obtained witness that he was righteous, God testifying of his gifts.—HEB., ch. 11.

See other illustrations under :

False. Swear by the temple, it is nothing; but..gold 2434
Reversed. Pay tithe of mint..omitted weightier 2425

2364. **DISCOURSE, Full of.** *Elihu.* [17] I also will shew mine opinion. [18] For I am full of matter ; the spirit within me constraineth me. [19] Behold, my belly *is* as wine *which* hath no vent ; it is ready to burst like new bottles. [20] I will speak, that I may be refreshed.—JOB, ch. 32.

See other illustrations under :

PREACHERS.

Called. Necessity is laid upon me..woe is unto me 6450
Duty. Preach the word..reprove rebuke, exhort 6451
Instructive. Ezra read..before those that could 6452

PREACHING.

Alarming. Paul reasoned..Felix trembled 6453
Forbidden. Commanded..not to speak at all 6454
Fruitful. Some a hundredfold, some sixty, some 6455
Hinderances. Care of this world..deceitfulness 6456
Ignorant. One heareth..understandeth it not 6457
Joyful. Shepherds..made known abroad the 6458
Masses. Went great multitudes with Jesus 6459
Opinions. Unto the Jews a stumblingblock 6460
Purpose. That we may present every man perfect 6461
Ridiculed. What will this babbler say? 6462
Strength. In demonstration of the spirit..power 6463

SERMON.

Long. Paul preached..until midnight 7790
to Women. By a river side..spake unto the 7791

SPEAKER.

Convincing. Never man spake like this man 8245
Engaging. Mary..sat at Jesus' feet and heard 8246

SPEAKING.

Evil. He that speaketh evil of his brother..of the 8241
Help. Filled with the H. S...gave them utterance 8242
for God. Say not I am a child..thou shalt..speak 8243
" Be not afraid of their faces..with thee 8244

SPEECH.

Assisted. I am not eloquent..with thy mouth 8247
" I can not speak..I shall send thee 8248
Appropriate. Apples of gold in pictures of silver 8249
Anointed. Tongues like..fire, it sat upon each 8250
Constrained. I am full of matter..constraineth me 8251
Cautious. Be not rash with thy mouth..hasty 8252
Confusion. L. did there confound the language 8253
Dangers of. Took counsel..entangled..speech 8254
Evidence. Bridleth not his tongue..religion is 8255
Gifts of. It shall be given you what ye shall speak 8256
Improved. Had an impediment..touched his 8257
Impossible. Not having a wedding garment 8258
Plainness. My speech was not with enticing 8259
Power of. Death and life..in the power of the 8260
Unrestrained. With flattering lips and a double 8261
Unentangled. Render unto Cesar..unto G..they 8262
Unguarded. Openeth wide his lips shall have 8263
Useless. Jesus answered Pilate to never a word 8264
" Herod questioned..answered him n. 8265

TONGUE.

Angry. Moses..spake unadvisedly with his lips 8830
Buyers. It is naught..then he boasteth 8831
Control. He that backbiteth not with his tongue 8832
" We put bits in the horses' mouths 8833
Foolish. The fool uttereth all his mind 8834
Hasty. Man hasty in his words..more..a fool 8835
Heart. Out of the abundance of the heart..speak 8836
Punished. We have sinned..spoken..away the 8837
Responsible. By thy words..justified..condemned 8838
Religious. Spake often..L. hearkened 8839
Untamed. Of beasts..tongue can no man tame 8840
Use of. Swift to hear, slow to speak 8841
Wise. If thou speak good words to them 8842
" Words of the wise are as goads 8843
Weapon. Let us smite him with the tongue 8844
Wicked. Tongue is a fire, a world of iniquity 8845

TONGUES.

Changed. Let us..confound their language 8846
" Amazed..How hear we..our own 8847
Differ. Wise man's mouth are gracious..fool 8848
Fire. Cloven tongues of fire..it sat upon each 8849
Restrained. King's commandment..Answer not 8850

WORD.

Divine. In the beginning was the word 9763
Important. Say now Shibboleth..said Sibboleth 9764
Only a. John saith, Behold the Lamb of God 9765

WORD OF GOD.

Limited. I cannot go beyond the word 9766
Effective. As the rain cometh..bread to the eater 9767
Hammer. Like a hammer that breaketh the rock 9768

WORDS.

Accountability. Every idle word..give account 9769
Cheerful. Heaviness in..heart good word..glad 9770
    "   Merry heart doeth good like medicine 9771
Effect. Words..as deep waters..flowing brook 9772
Kind. Pleasant words are as an honeycomb 9773
Listening. Spake often..L. hearkened and heard 9774
Overflow. Abundance of the heart..speaketh 9775
Proven. When Jacob saw the wagons..spirit 9776
Reliance. L...bid me come..on the water 9777

Corrupted. Children could not speak in the 4896
Given. Every man heard them speak in his own 4897
Irresistible. Not able to resist the wisdom and s. 96
Origin. Let us..confound their language 4898
Suppressed. Caleb stilled the people..we are 3128
Unfriendly. Brethren..not speak peaceably unto 3099

2365. DISCRETION, Friends by. *David.*
[30] The princes of the Philistines went forth : and
..David behaved himself more wisely than all
the servants of Saul ; so that his name was much
set by.—1 SAM., ch. 18.

2366. —— necessary. *War.* [31] What king,
going to make war..sitteth not down first, and
consulteth whether he be able with ten thousand
to meet him that cometh against him with
twenty thousand ? [32] Or else, while the other is
yet a great way off, he sendeth an ambassage,
and desireth conditions of peace.—LUKE, ch. 14.

2367. —— Part of. *Micah.* [25] Let not thy
voice be heard among us, lest angry fellows run
upon thee, and thou lose thy life, with the lives
of thy household. [26] And the children of Dan
went their way : and when Micah saw that they
were too strong for him, he..went back unto his
house.—JUDGES, ch. 18.

2368. —— Success by. *Nabal's Wife* [23] fell
before David on her face, and bowed herself to
the ground, [24] And fell at his feet, and said..
[32] And David said to Abigail, Blessed *be* the Lord
..which sent thee this day to meet me : [33] And
blessed *be* thy advice, and blessed *be* thou, which
hast kept me this day from coming to *shed*
blood, and from avenging myself.—1 SAM., ch.
25. [See No. 2371.]

2369. —— Safety by. *Paul.* [6] When Paul
perceived that the one part were Sadducees,
and the other Pharisees, he cried out in the
council, Men *and* brethren, I am a Pharisee, the
son of a Pharisee : of the hope and resurrection
of the dead I am called in question. [7] And
when he had so said, there arose a dissension
between the Pharisees and the Sadducees : and
the multitude was divided.—ACTS, ch. 23.

2370. —— Want of. *Proverb.* [Solomon
says,] [22] *As* a jewel of gold in a swine's snout, *so
is* a fair woman which is without discretion.—
PROV., ch. 11.

**2371. —— —— ** *Nabal.* [10] Who *is* David?
and who *is* the son of Jesse? there be many
servants nowadays that break away every man
from his master. [11] Shall I then take my bread,
and my water, and my flesh that I have killed
for my shearers, and give *it* unto men, whom I
know not whence they *be?*—1 SAM., ch. 25.

See other illustrations under :
CAUTION.

Believers. Moses sent them to spy out the land 1548
Building. Lest not be able to finish 676
Eating. Put a knife to thy throat..given to 1068
Forgetfulness. Take heed lest thou forget..seen 3347
Fear. Howbeit no man spake openly..for fear 3432
  "   Did not confess him lest..put out 3433
Hearing. Increased..30..60..100 fold..he that 1069
Hypocrisy. Beware of the scribes..love greetings 321
Lack. Let about 3000..smite Ai..fled 1532
  "   I made as if they were beaten..and fled 1522
Strife. Consulteth whether he be able to meet 677
Necessary. The simple believe every word 1070
Prudent. [Micah] saw they were too strong 1071
Wise. Fool uttereth all his mind..wise 1072

JUDGMENT.

Blindness. Hath blinded their eyes, and hardened 4763
Despondency. I, even I only am left..seek my life 4764
for Judgment. With what judgment ye judge 4771
Preparation. First cast out the beam..thine own 4773
Sincere. Let me be weighed in an even balance 4778

PRUDENCE.

Age. Wherefore should..be yet a burden 6774
Commended. Lord commended the unjust steward 6775
Example. Render unto Cesar..they marvelled 6776
Preservation. Hold..lest angry fellows..lose thy 6777
  "   Joseph hearkened not..or be with 6778
Resolutions. Intending to build..not able to finish 6779

THOUGHT.

Character. As he thinketh in his heart, so is he 8786
Evil. Every imagination of the thought..only evil 8787
Prompter. When they deliver you up, take no 8788
Subjects. Whatsoever things are true..honest 8789
  See WISDOM.

2372. DISCUSSION, A protracted. *Paul.*
[9] When divers were hardened, and believed not,
but spake evil of that way before the multitude,
he..separated the disciples, disputing daily in
the school of one Tyrannus. [10] And this continued by the space of two years.—ACTS, ch. 19.

See other illustrations under :
Doctrinal. Jews..disputing with Stephen..not 2005
Discourse. I am full of matter..constraineth me 2364
  See DEBATE.

2373. DISEASE, A chronic. 38 *Years.* [2] There
is at Jerusalem by the sheep *market* a pool,
which is called..Bethesda, having five porches.
[5] And a certain man was there, which had an
infirmity thirty and eight years.—JOHN, ch. 5.

2374. —— A painful. *Boils.* [7] So went Satan
forth..and smote Job with sore boils from the
sole of his foot unto his crown. [8] And he took
him a potsherd to scrape himself withal ; and
he sat down among the ashes.—JOB, ch. 2.

See other illustrations under :
CURE.

All Persons. Laid his hands on every one and heal 1867
All Diseases. Stepped in, was made whole of what 1868
Faith. When..beheld the serpent of brass, he lived 1869
Gratitude. She arose, and ministered unto them 1870
Means. Made clay of the spittle..anointed eyes 1871
Progressive. See men as trees walking..clearly 1872
Threefold. Possessed with a devil, blind and dumb 1873
Wonderful. Stretch forth thy hand..as the other 1874

SICKNESS.

Destructive. Elisha was sick..my father !..the 7852
Despondency. He will cut me off with pining 7853
Jesus in. Nobleman saith, Sir, come down ere my 7854

Overwork. Nigh unto death, not regarding his 7856
Punished. L. will make plagues..sore sickness 7857
Pretended. Saul sent..to take David, she said 7858
Reflections. I shall behold man no more 7859
Relieved. Simon's wife's mother..fever 7860
Sinners. Take a present..inquire. shall I recover 7861
Unimproved. [Hezekiah healed] Rendered not 7855
Wasting. My leanness..witness against me [Job] 7862

LAMENESS.
Disqualification. Not offer the bread of his God 4878
Lame. Thou shalt not sacrifice it—Deut. 15 : 21
Healed. Never had walked..leaped and walked 4879
" His feet and ancle bones received strength 4880
Royal. Jonathan hath a son..lame on his feet 4881
Want with. Laid daily at the gate..ask alms 4882

REMEDY.
Improbable. Anointed the eyes of the blind man 7058
Look. As Moses lifted up the serpent..S. of man 7059

Anxiety. Lazarus' sister sent unto Jesus, saying 7850
Boils.. Boils breaking forth with blains 6190
Effort. Nobleman went..besought..heal his son 7851
Pestilence. L. sent a pestilence upon I...died 6112
" Died in the plague, 14,700 9193
Ulcers. Lazarus was laid at his gate..sores 6181
See AFFLICTION.

2375. DISGRACE avenged. *Amnon.* [22] Absalom hated Amnon, because he had forced his sister Tamar. [28] ..when I say unto you, Smite Amnon ; then kill him, fear not..be courageous, and be valiant. [29] And the servants of Absalom did.—2 SAM., ch. 13.

2376. —— **of Drunkards.** *Filthy.* [1] Woe to the crown of pride, to the drunkards of Ephraim, whose glorious beauty *is* a fading flower.. [8] For all tables are full of vomit *and* filthiness, *so that there is* no place clean.—ISA., ch. 28.

2377. —— **Humiliating.** *One Half.* [4] Hanun took David's servants, and shaved off the one half of their beards, and cut off their garments in the middle, *even* to their buttocks, and sent them away.—2 SAM., ch. 10.

2378. —— **of the Innocent.** *Calvary.* [37] THIS IS JESUS THE KING OF THE JEWS. [38] Then were there two thieves crucified with him ; one on the right hand, and another on the left.—MAT., ch. 27.

2379. —— **Posthumous.** *Bones.* [1] Saith the Lord, they shall bring out the bones of the kings of Judah, and..of the inhabitants of Jerusalem, out of their graves : [2] And they shall spread them before the sun, and the moon, and all the host of heaven, whom they have loved, and..served..and whom they have worshipped : they shall not be gathered, nor be buried ; they shall be for dung upon..the earth.—JER., ch. 8.

2380. —— **Unendurable.** *Ahithophel.* [23] When Ahithophel saw that his counsel was not followed, he saddled *his* ass, and arose, and gat him home..and put his household in order, and hanged himself.—2 SAM., ch. 17.

See other illustrations under :

DISHONOUR.
Soldier's. That men say not, A woman slew him 2386
Reward. Entice him..give 1100 pieces of silver 2387

DISPARAGEMENT.
Ignoble. We were as grasshoppers in our own 2407
Provoked. L. had respect unto Abel..but unto Cain 2408

REPROACH.
Affliction. I was a reproach..especially among my 7128
Christ's. Away with such a fellow..not fit to live 7129
Cowardice. Should such a man as I flee? 7130
Fear. Many believed..not confess him..put out 7131
Intended. Thrust out right eyes..for a reproach 7132
Idolaters. Therefore I made thee a reproach and a 7133
Joy. Blessed are ye when men shall separate 7134
Neglect. Jerusalem lieth waste..be no more a r. 7135
Proverb. Thou shalt become a proverb and a r. 7136
Shame. For thy sake..shame hath covered my 7137
Unconscious. What have we spoken..vain to serve 7138
Welcomed. Esteeming the reproach of Christ 7139

SCANDAL.
Ministerial. Eli was very old..his sons..at the 7603
Public. Absalom spread a tent..father's concubine 7604

SHAME.
Criminal's. As the thief is ashamed when found 7827
Impossible. Dealeth falsely..were they ashamed? 7828
Rejoicing. That they were counted worthy 7829
for Shame. Ashamed of me..of him..be ashamed 7830
Sin. Eyes..opened..were naked..aprons 7831

SLANDER.
Antidote. They may by your good works..glorify 8101
Base. This fellow doth cast out devils by Beelzebub 8102
Disgraceful. We found this man a pestilent fellow 8103
Folly. He that uttereth a slander is a fool 8104
Hurtful. Then will they not pay tribute 8105
Impious. He saved others ; himself he cannot save 8106
Joyful. Blessed..men revile you..rejoice 8107
Loyalty. Ziba said..he abideth at Jerusalem 8108
Malicious. Diotrephes..prating against us 8109
Opposed. It is reported..be their king 8110
Refuted. If Satan cast out Satan..divided 8111
Rebels. The people is greater than we 8112
Sinners. Thou art an austere man 8113
Satan's. Touch all that he hath .will curse 8114
Secret. A whisperer separateth friends 8115
Unbelief. Would to G. we had died..by fleshpots 8116

Confessed. I am ashamed, and blush..my G. 4199
Defeat. Israel turned their backs..enemies 4200
National. No smith..in all the land of I. 4202
Painful. Haman..arrayed Mordecai..proclaimed 4203
" Begin with shame to take the lowest seat 4204
Sin. Sent him to feed swine..hunger 4206
Weakness. I was ashamed to require..soldiers 4208

2381. DISGUISE, A Brother's. *Joseph.* [7] Joseph saw his brethren, and he knew them, but made himself strange unto them, and spake roughly..and he said..Whence come ye? And they said, From the land of Canaan to buy food.—GEN., ch. 42.

2382. —— **Fighting in.** *Ahab.* [30] The king of Israel said unto Jehoshaphat, I will disguise myself and enter into the battle : but put thou on thy robes.. [34] And a *certain* man drew a bow at a venture, and smote the king of Israel between the joints of the harness.—1 KINGS, ch. 22.

2383. —— **Failure of.** *With Blind Priest.* [6] When Ahijah heard the sound of her feet, as she came in at the door..he said, Come in, thou wife of Jeroboam ; why feignest thou thyself *to* be another? for I *am* sent to thee *with* heavy tidings.—1 KINGS, ch. 14.

2384. —— **An insufficient.** *Saul.* [8] Saul disguised himself, and put on other raiment.. and two men with him, and they came to the woman by night : and he said, I pray thee, divine unto me by the familiar spirit. [12]..and the woman spake..Why hast thou deceived me? for thou *art* Saul.—1 SAM., ch. 28.

2385. —— **penetrated.** *Widow.* [19] The king said, *Is not* the hand of Joab with thee in all this? And the woman answered..none can turn to the right hand or to the left from aught that my lord the king hath spoken: for thy servant Joab, he bade me, and he put all these words in the mouth of thine handmaid.—2 SAM., ch. 14.

See other illustrations under:

CONCEALMENT.

Impossible. Thou wast with Jesus..Peter denied   1464
Unsuccessful. I was afraid, and hid myself [Adam]   1465
   "   He that covereth his sins shall not   1466

HIDDEN.

Cave. Obadiah took 200 prophets, and hid   3966
Field. David hid himself in the field   3967
Graciously. King commanded to take Jeremiah   3968
House of God. Joash was hid..six years   3969
Housetop. Rahab..hid them with the..flax   3970
Infant. Ark..in the flags by the river brink   3971
Strangely. Took they up stones..Jesus hid himself   3972
Wilderness. Hide thyself..ravens to feed thee   3973

HIDING.

Difficult. Moses feared..surely this is known   3974
Sinners. Adam, where art thou?..hid myself   3975
Sin. Set ye Uriah in the hottest battle..retire   3976
Talent. Received one..digged..hid..Lord's money   3977

SECRET.

Difficult. Moses looked this way and that way   4645
Impossible. Elisha telleth the king..the words   4646
Woman's. If thou utter this our business..spies   4644

TRICK.

Diplomatic. From a very far country are..come   8955
Hypocrites. Feign themselves just men..might   8956
Legerdemain. Magicians..rods became serpents   8957
Politicians. Shall ask a petition..save of thee   8958

Exposed. Beware that thou pass not such a place   335
Vice. Waiteth for the twilight..disguiseth his face   111

2386. DISHONOUR, A Soldier's. *Abimelech.* [53] A certain woman cast a piece of a millstone upon Abimelech's head, and all to break his skull. [54] Then he called hastily unto..his armourbearer, and said..Draw thy sword, and slay me, that men say not of me, A woman slew him.—JUDGES, ch. 9.

2387. —— **Reward of.** *Samson.* [5] The lords of the Philistines..said unto her, Entice him, and see wherein his great strength *lieth*, and by what *means* we may prevail against him, that we may bind him to afflict him : and we will give thee every one of us eleven hundred *pieces* of silver.—JUDGES, ch. 16.

See other illustrations under:

DISGRACE.

Avenged. Absalom hated Amnon..kill him   2375
Drunkards. Tables are full of vomit   2376
Humiliating. Cut off their garments..buttocks   2377
Innocent. Two thieves crucified with him   2378
Posthumous. Bones..be for dung on the earth   2379
Unendurable. Ahithophel..counsel..not followed   2380

2388. DISHONESTY, Avaricious. *Short Weight.* [4] O ye that swallow up the needy, even to make the poor of the land to fail, [5] Saying, When will the new moon be gone, that we may sell corn? and the sabbath, that we may set forth wheat,

making the ephah small, and the shekel great, and falsifying the balances by deceit? [6] That we may buy the poor for silver, and the needy for a pair of shoes; *yea*, and sell the refuse of the wheat?—AMOS, ch. 8.

2389. —— **toward God.** *Ananias.* [3] Peter said, Ananias, why hath Satan filled thine heart to lie to the Holy Ghost, and to keep back *part* of the price of the land? [4]..was it not thine own! and after it was sold, was it not in thine own power?..thou hast not lied unto men, but unto God.—ACTS, ch. 5.

See other illustrations under:

Shameless. I cannot dig; to beg I am ashamed   8344
See **DECEPTION.**

2390. DISINTERESTEDNESS in Love. *Christian.* [1] We then that are strong ought to bear the infirmities of the weak, and not to please ourselves. [2] Let every one of us please *his* neighbour for *his* good to edification. [3] For even Christ pleased not himself.—ROM., ch. 15.

2391. —— **Pious.** *Moses.* [27] There ran a young man..and said, Eldad and Medad do prophesy in the camp. [28] And Joshua..the servant of Moses..said, My lord Moses, forbid them. [29] And Moses said..Enviest thou for my sake? would God that all the Lord's people were prophets.—NUM., ch. 11.

See other illustrations under:

INDIFFERENCE.

Hearing. Foolish man who built..upon the sand   4405
Inconsiderate. Here is thy pound, which I have   4406
Provoking. Wrath because..have not hearkened   4407
Pitiless. Saw him, and passed by..other side   4408
Sin. I have sinned..What is that to us?   4409
Sinners. Made light of it, and went their ways   4410
Unbelievers. They did eat..until the day Noe   4411

INDIFFERENT.

Curse. Curse ye, Meroz..came not..help of the L.   4412
Woe. Woe unto them that are at ease   4413

UNSELFISHNESS.

Godly. Elisha said, I will receive none..refused   9132
Giving. Call the poor..they cannot recompense   9133
Manifested. I will not take from a thread to   9134
Official. Required not I the bread of the governor   9135
   "   Would G. that all..were prophets   9136
Popularity. He must increase, I must decrease   9137
Pious. I please all men in all things..be saved   9138
Religious. Daniel answered, Let thy gifts be to   9139
Rival. Jonathan..gave it to David..sword   9140
Rewarded. Because thou hast not asked..riches   9141
Wise. That I may discern between good and bad   9142

Neglect. What honour hath been done to M.   5696
Poor. When saw we thee ahungered..in prison?   5709
Ungrateful. Yet did not the chief butler remember   3096

2392. DISOBEDIENCE, Apostasy by. *Solomon.* [2] King Solomon loved many strange women, together with the daughter of Pharaoh, women of the Moabites, Ammonites, Edomites, Zidonians, *and* Hittites; [3] And he had seven hundred wives, princesses, and three hundred concubines: and his wives turned away his heart.—1 KINGS, ch. 11.

2393. —— **Curses upon.** *Moses.* [See Deut. 28 : 15-51.]

2394. —— **Dangerous.** *Ahab.* [The Lord gave him special help to conquer Benhadad king of Syria, and commanded his destruction. He spared and honoured him.] [42] Thus saith the Lord, Because thou hast let go out of *thy* hand a man whom I appointed to utter destruction, therefore thy life shall go for his life, and thy people for his people. ⁴³ And the king of Israel went to his house heavy and displeased. —1 KINGS, ch. 20.

2395. —— **Death from.** *Priests.* ¹ Nadab and Abihu, the sons of Aaron, took either of them his censer, and put fire therein, and put incense thereon, and offered strange fire before the Lord, which he commanded them not. ² And there went out fire from the Lord, and devoured them.—LEV., ch. 10.

2396. —— **through Fear.** *Joseph* ²¹ Took the young child and his mother, and came into the land of Israel. ²² But when he heard that Archelaus did reign in Judea..he was afraid to go thither : notwithstanding, being warned of God in a dream, he turned aside into the parts of Galilee.—MAT., ch. 2.

2397. —— **a Hindrance.** *Leper.* ⁴⁴ See thou say nothing to any man : but go thy way, shew thyself to the priest, and offer for thy cleansing those things which Moses commanded, for a testimony unto them. ⁴⁵ But he went out, and began to publish *it* much, and to blaze abroad the matter, insomuch that Jesus could no more openly enter into the city, but was without in desert places.—MARK, ch. 1.

2398. —— **A noble.** *Ahasuerus.* ¹⁰ On the seventh day, when the heart of the king was merry with wine, he commanded.. ¹¹ To bring Vashti the queen before the king with the crown royal, to shew the people and the princes her beauty : for she *was* fair to look on. ¹² But the queen Vashti refused to come.—ESTHER, ch. 1.

2399. —— **from Peril.** *King Saul.* ¹¹ Because I saw that the people were scattered from me, and *that* thou camest not within the days appointed, and *that* the Philistines gathered themselves together at Michmash ; ¹² Therefore said I, The Philistines will come..and I have not made supplication unto the Lord : I forced myself therefore, and offered a burnt offering. —1 SAM., ch. 13.

2400. —— **Penalty of.** *Temporal.* [See Lev. 26 : 15–38.]

2401. —— **Progressive.** *Israelites.* ³⁴ They did not destroy the nations, concerning whom the Lord commanded them : ³⁵ But were mingled among the heathen, and learned their works. ³⁶ And they served their idols : which were a snare unto them. ³⁷ Yea, they sacrificed their sons and their daughters unto devils, ³⁸..whom they sacrificed unto the idols of Canaan.—Ps. 106.

2402. —— **is Rebellion.** *King Saul.* ¹⁵ Saul said, They have brought them from the Amalekites : for the people spared the best of the sheep, and of the oxen, to sacrifice unto the Lord..and the rest we have utterly destroyed. ²² And Samuel said, Hath the Lord *as great* delight in burnt offerings and sacrifices as in obeying the voice of the Lord ? Behold, to obey *is* better than sacrifice, *and* to hearken than the fat of rams. ²³ For rebellion *is as* the sin of witchcraft, and stubbornness *is as* iniquity and idolatry. Because thou hast rejected the word of the Lord, he hath also rejected thee from *being* king.—1 SAM., ch. 15.

2403. —— **Results of.** *Israelites.* ² Ye shall make no league with the inhabitants of this land ; ye shall throw down their altars : but ye have not obeyed my voice.. ³..I will not drive them out from before you ; but they shall be *as thorns* in your sides, and their gods shall be a snare unto you. ⁴..when the Angel of the Lord spake these words..the people lifted up their voice, and wept.—JUDGES, ch. 2.

2404. —— **Rejection from.** *Israelites.* ⁷ The Lord said unto Moses, Go, get thee down ; for thy people..have corrupted *themselves* : ⁸ They have turned aside quickly out of the way which I commanded them : they have made them a molten calf.. ¹⁰ Now therefore let me alone, that my wrath may wax hot against them, and that I may consume them.—EX., ch. 32.

2405. —— **Unprofitable.** *Judah.* ²⁰ Them that had escaped from the sword carried he away to Babylon ; where they were servants.. ²¹..until the land had enjoyed her sabbaths : *for* as long as she lay desolate she kept sabbath, to fulfil threescore and ten years.—2 CHRON., ch. 36.

2406. —— **Warning against.** *National.* ²⁵ Shall corrupt *yourselves*, and make a graven image, *or* the likeness of any *thing*, and shall do evil in the sight of the Lord.. ²⁶ I call heaven and earth to witness against you this day, that ye shall soon utterly perish from off the land whereunto ye go over Jordan to possess it.. ²⁷ And the Lord shall scatter you among the nations, and ye shall be left few in number.—DEUT., ch. 4.

See other illustrations under :

INSUBORDINATION.

Intimidating. He could not answer Abner a word	4773
Soldiers. To translate the kingdom from..Saul	4774

OBDURACY.

Defiant. Who is the L. that I should obey ?	5755
Final. Why have we..let I. go from serving us	5756
Foolish. Ahaz..sacrificed unto the gods..smote	5757
Jewish. Thy neck is as an iron sinew, and thy	5758
Spiritual. Woe unto thee, Chorazin..if the mighty	5759
Self-destructive. I know that G. hath determined	5760
to Truth. Paul spake..three months..divers were	5761
Unfeeling. Past feeling have given themselves	5762
Wild. Balaam..went with the princes of Moab	5763

OBSTINACY.

Provoking. It is a stiffnecked people..consume	5825
Rebuked. Why..smitten thine ass these 3 times ?	5826
Rebellious. Nevertheless the people refused	5827

PERSISTENCE.

Necessary. Aaron and Hur held up his hands	6067
in Prayer. Let me go, for the day breaketh..I will	6068
Rewarded. I will not leave thee..he followed her	6069
Unchangeable. Mordecai bowed not, nor did him	6070
Undiscouraged. Charged him..he cried the more	6071
" Because of his importunity, he	6072

PROCRASTINATION.

Charity. Say not..go and come again	6620
Fatal. Paul reasoned..Felix trembled..time	6621
Folly. Give..our lamps are gone out	2622
Loss. We will hear thee again [Athenians]	2623
No. Suffer me first..to bury my father	2624

SELF-WILL.

Destructive. As a hen gathereth..ye would not	7731
Loss. Presumed to go up..Canaanites smote them	7732
Obstinate. We will certainly do whatsoever	7733
Sin. Rebellion is as the sin of witchcraft	7734
Work of. In their self-will they digged down a	7735

STUBBORNNESS.

Punished. They mocked..despised..therefore   8393
in Sin. To obey is better than sacrifice   8394
"   We will certainly..burn incense to the   8395
"   Took Dagon and set him in his place   8396

REBELLION.

Abominable. Rebellion is as the sin of   6874
Ingrates. Absalom sent spies..say Absalom   6875
Ill-government. Thy father made our yoke   6876
Jealousy. Ye take too much upon you [Korah]   6877
Mental. Not enter..ye rebelled against my word   6878
Sinners. We will not have this man to reign   6879
"   This is the heir ; come, let us kill him   6880
Tongue. Every kind of beasts..been tamed   6881
Uncontested. Ye shall not fight..return every man   6882
Vain. Sheba blew a trumpet..we have no part   6883
Will. How oft would I..but ye would not   6884
     See SIN and WICKED.

2407. DISPARAGEMENT, Ignoble. *Spies.*
[32] The land, through which we have gone to
search it..eateth up the inhabitants thereof ;
and all the people that we saw in it *are* men of
a great stature. [33] And there we saw the giants,
the sons of Anak..and we were in our own
sight as grasshoppers, and so we were in their
sight.—Num., ch. 13.

2408. —— Provoked by. *Cain.* [4] The Lord
had respect unto Abel and his offering.. [5] But
unto Cain and to his offering he.had not respect.
And Cain was very wroth, and his countenance
fell.—Gen., ch. 4.

See other illustrations under :

CRITICISM.

Contemptuous. Michal said..How glorious was the   1837
Disparaging. What do these feeble Jews?   1838
Enemies. Not good..because..reproach of the   1839

REPROACH.

Affliction. I was a reproach..especially among my   7128
Christ's. Away with such a fellow..not fit to live   7129
Cowardice. Should such a man as I flee?   7130
Fear. Many believed..not confess him..put out   7131
Intended. Thrust out right eyes..for a reproach   7132
Idolaters. Therefore I made thee a reproach and a   7133
Joy. Blessed are ye when men shall separate   7134
Neglect. Jerusalem lieth waste..be no more a r.   7135
Proverb. Thou shalt become a proverb and a r.   7136
Shame. For thy sake..shame hath covered my   7137
Unconscious. What have we spoken..vain to serve   7138
Welcomed. Esteeming the reproach of Christ   7139

SLANDER.

Antidote. They may by your good works..glorify   8101
Base. Doth cast out devils by Beelzebub   8102
Disgraceful. We found this man a pestilent   8103
Folly. He that uttereth a slander is a fool   8104
Hurtful. Then will they not pay tribute   8105
Impious. He saved others ; himself he cannot   8106
Joyful. Blessed..men revile you..rejoice   8107
Loyalty. Ziba said..he abideth at Jerusalem   8108
Malicious. Diotrephes..prating against us   8109
Opposed. It is reported..be their king   8110
Refuted. If Satan cast out Satan..divided   8111
Rebels. The people is greater than we   8112
Sinners. Thou art an austere man   8113
Satan's. Touch all that he hath..will curse   8114
Secret. A whisperer separateth friends   8115
Unbelief. Would to G. we had died..by fleshpots   8116

Satan's. G. doth know ye shall be as gods   8117

2409. DISPENSATIONS, Diverse. *Sinai—Sion.*
[18] Ye are not come unto the mount that might

be touched, and that burned with fire, nor unto
blackness, and darkness, and tempest, [22] But ye
are come unto mount Sion, and unto the city of
the living God, the heavenly Jerusalem, and to
an innumerable company of angels.—Heb., ch.
12.

2410. DISPLAY, Royal. *Ahasuerus.* [5] The
king made a feast..both unto great and small,
seven days, in the court of the garden.. [6] *Where
were* white, green, and blue *hangings*, fastened
with cords of fine linen and purple to silver
rings and pillars of marble : the beds *were of*
gold and silver, upon a pavement of red, and
blue, and white, and black marble. [7] And they
gave *them* drink in vessels of gold, (the vessels
being diverse one from another,) and royal wine
in abundance.—Esther, ch. 1.

See other illustrations under :

OSTENTATION.

Forbidden. Be not called Rabbi..are brethren   5933
"   Do not sound a trumpet before thee   5934
Purpose. Absalom prepared him chariots..50 men   5935
Prayer. Scribes..for a shew make long prayers   5936
Religious. To be seen..make broad their   5937

Dress. Scribes..desire to walk in long robes   476

2411. DISPLEASURE with Fraud. *Rejection.*
[21] I hate, I despise your feast days, and I will
not smell in your solemn assemblies. [22] Though
ye offer me burnt offerings and your meat offerings, I will not accept *them ;* neither will I regard the peace offerings of your fat beasts.
[23] Take thou away from me the noise of thy
songs ; for I will not hear the melody of thy
viols. [24] But let judgment run down as waters,
and righteousness as a mighty stream.—Amos,
ch. 5.

2412. —— A holy. *Jesus.* [13] Brought young
children ..that he should touch them ; and *his*
disciples rebuked those that brought *them.*
[14] But when Jesus saw *it*, he was much displeased, and said..Suffer the little children to come
unto me, and forbid them not ; for of such is the
kingdom of God.—Mark, ch. 10.

See other illustrations under :

HATRED.

Brother. If..say, I love God, and hateth..is a liar   3828
Bitter. Brother shall betray brother..to death   3829
Commendable. Thou hatest the deeds of the   3830
Changed. Ready to die..for the L. Jesus   3831
Darkness. He that hateth his brother walketh   3832
Divine. Six things doth the L. hate   3833
Evil. Better is a dinner of herbs where love is   3834
Good. [Joseph's] brethren hated him..not speak   3835
Light. Every one that doeth evil hateth the light   3836
Manifested. When the days of mourning ended   3838
Silent. Absalom spake unto..Amnon..good nor   3840
Sinner's. Micaiah..I hate..doth not prophesy   3841
World. If the world hate you..it hated me before   3842

INDIGNATION.

Bigoted. Ruler answered with indignation   4415
Christian. Spirit was stirred..given to idolatry   4417
Contemptuous. Why camest thou?..few sheep   4416
Excessive. Fire to come down..consume them   4418
Forgotten. Is thy servant a dog ..do this?   4419
God gives. S. of G. came upon Saul..anger   4420
Hot. Saw the calf..Moses' anger waxed hot   4421
at Hypocrisy. Jesus looked on them with anger   4422
at Injustice. Elihu..wrath kindled..yet had con.   4423
Improper. Indignation..Why..waste of the   4424
Judgment. Remaineth..a certain fearful   4425

Murderous. When they heard..filled with wrath 4426
National. People arose as one man..to do to 4427
Natural. Ten heard it..moved with indignation 4428
Partisan. Sadducees..were filled with indignation 4429
Pride. Haman was full of indignation against M. 4430
Righteous. I may thrust out all your right eyes 4431
Religious. Against Job..because he justified 4432
at Sinners. David's anger was kindled..restore 4433
Severity. L. was wroth, and..to tormentors 4434

OFFENCE.

Prejudice. Is not this the carpenter?..were 5834
Responsibility. Woe to that man by whom the 5835

RESENTMENT.

Cruel. Herod slew all the children..Bethlehem 7183
Indignant. Woman was fallen..hands on the 7184
of Self-seeking. Much displeased with James and 7185

SCORN.

of Pride. Haman..scorn to lay hands on Mordecai 7618
Public. All clap their hands at thee, and hiss, and 7619
Unbelief. She sleepeth..they laughed him to 7620

Taunt. Who made thee a prince and a judge over 8592
Doctrinal. Eateth my flesh..This is a hard saying 2326
See ANGER.
See CONFLICT and references.

2413. DISPOSITION, An angry. *Saul.* [15] Saul's servants said..Behold now, an evil spirit from God troubleth thee. [16]..to seek out a man, *who is* a cunning player on an harp : and..when the evil spirit from God is upon thee..he shall play with his hand, and thou shalt be well.—1 SAM., ch. 16.

2414. —— A benevolent. *Samaritan.* [33] When he saw him, he had compassion on *him,* [34] And went to *him,* and bound up his wounds, pouring in oil and wine, and set him on his own beast, and brought him to an inn, and took care of him. [35] And on the morrow when he departed, he took out two pence, and gave *them* to the host, and said..Take care of him : and whatsoever thou spendest more..I will repay thee.—LUKE, ch. 10.

2415. —— A curious. *Levite.* [32] And likewise a Levite, when he was at the place, came and looked on *him,* and passed by on the other side.—LUKE, ch. 10.

2416. —— Change in. *Laban.* [1] He heard the words of Laban's..sons, saying, Jacob hath taken away all that *was* our father's .. [2] And Jacob beheld the countenance of Laban, and, behold, it *was* not toward him as before.—GEN., ch. 31.

2417. —— Fixed. *Golden Calf.* [21] And Moses said unto Aaron, What did this people unto thee, that thou hast brought so great a sin upon them? [22] And Aaron said, Let not the anger of my lord wax hot : thou knowest the people that they *are set* on mischief.—EX., ch. 32.

2418. —— A giving. *Tabernacle.* [2] Speak unto the children of Israel, that they bring me an offering : of every man that giveth it willingly with his heart ye shall take my offering.—EX., ch. 25.

2419. —— An indifferent. *Priest.* [30] A certain *man* went down from Jerusalem to Jericho, and fell among thieves, which stripped him of his raiment, and wounded *him,* and departed, leaving *him* half dead. [31]..there came down a

certain priest that way ; and when he saw him he passed by on the other side.—LUKE, ch. 10.

2420. —— A religious. *Athenians.* [16] While Paul waited..at Athens, his spirit was stirred in him, when he saw the city wholly given to idolatry. [22] Then Paul stood in the midst of Mars' hill, and said, *Ye* men of Athens, I perceive that in all things ye are too superstitious [better rendered, "Ye are very devout"]. [23] For as I passed by, and beheld your devotions, I found an altar with this inscription, TO THE UNKNOWN GOD. Whom therefore ye ignorantly worship, him declare I unto you.—ACTS, ch. 17.

2421. DISPOSITIONS contrasted. *Mary—Martha.* [39] Mary..sat at Jesus' feet, and heard his word. [40] But Martha was cumbered about much serving..and said, Lord, dost thou not care that my sister hath left me to serve alone? bid her therefore that she help me.—LUKE, ch. 10.

See HEART and references.

2422. DISPUTE, A foolish. *Apostles.* [33] They came to Capernaum : and..he asked them, What was it that ye disputed among yourselves by the way? [34] But they held their peace : for by the way they had disputed among themselves, who *should be* the greatest.—MARK, ch. 9.

2423. —— wisely settled. *Solomon.* [24] Bring me a sword. And they brought a sword before the king. [25] And the king said, Divide the living child in two, and give half to the one, and half to the other. [26] Then spake the woman whose the living child *was.*—1 KINGS, ch. 3.

See other illustrations under:

DISSENSION.

Doctrinal. Except ye be circumcised..ye cannot be 2429
Perilous. Fearing lest Paul..pulled in pieces 2430
Partisan. I am of Paul, and I of Apollos 2431
Stubborn. Contention was sharp..departed 2432

CONTROVERSY.

Avoided. Our fathers worshipped..ye say 1652
Fatal. Cain talked with Abel..and slew him 1653
Holy. [At Athens] disputed Saul in the synagogue 1654

QUARREL.

Domestic. Sarah saw the son of Hagar mocking 6818
Destructive. Amnon and Moab..slew each other 6819
Foolish. Wherefore didst thou not call us?..burn 6820
Famished. What aileth thee?..hid her son 6821
Meddler. Who made thee a judge over us? 6822
" Is like one that taketh a dog by the ears 6823
Matrimonial. Against Moses, because of the 6824
Overruled. Angel of G. called to Hagar..lift up the 6825
Test. Say now Shibboleth, and he said, Sibboleth 6826
War from. We have no part in David..To your 6827
Woman. It is better to dwell in a corner 6828

STRIFE.

Avoided. Go from us..mightier than we..Isaac 8378
Absence of. Isaac removed..and digged another 8379
Beginning. As when one letteth out water 8380
Cause of. As coals are..so is a contentious man 8381
Continued. Digged another well, and strove for 8382
Dishonour. An honour for a man to cease from 8383
Ended. Is not the whole land before thee? 8384
Occasion of. Their riches were more..dwell 8385
Prevention rewarded. All the land which thou 8386
Prosperity brings. Land was not able to bear 8387
Rebuked. Not from above..earthly, sensual 8388
Truth makes. I am not come to send peace, but a 8389
Wickedness of. Ungodly man diggeth up evil..as 8390
Words make. Where no wood is..fire goeth out 8391

— DISSATISFACTION. —

See illustrations under:

in **Age.** Ye will take Benj..all these things are 9095
Covetous. Ahab..heavy and displeased 9096
Pride. All this availeth me nothing..see Mordecai 9097
Pleasure. Wine..houses..gardens..cattle..gold 6212
Royal. Neither were instruments of music brought 9098
Union in. Every one that was in distress..came 9099
Wealth. What shall I do..no room..build greater 6703

See DISCONTENTMENT and references.

2424. DISSEMBLING, Confession of. *Achan.*
[20] Achan answered Joshua..Indeed I have sinned.. [21] When I saw among the spoils a goodly Babylonish garment, and two hundred shekels of silver, and a wedge of gold of fifty shekels weight, then I coveted them, and took them.—JOSH., ch. 7.

2425. —— imitated. *Antiochians.* [13] The other Jews dissembled likewise with him ; insomuch that Barnabas also was carried away with their dissimulation. [14] But when I saw that they walked not uprightly according to the truth of the gospel, I said unto Peter before *them* all, If thou, being a Jew, livest after the manner of Gentiles, and not as do the Jews, why compellest thou the Gentiles to live as do the Jews?—GAL., ch. 2.

2426. —— Inconsistency of. *Peter.* [See next above.]

2427. —— rebuked. *Peter.* [11] When Peter was come to Antioch, I withstood him to the face, because he was to be blamed. [12] For before that certain came from James, he did eat with the Gentiles : but when they were come, he withdrew and separated himself, fearing them which were of the circumcision.—GAL., ch. 2.

2428. —— Vicious. *Proverbs.* [24] He that hateth dissembleth with his lips, and layeth up deceit within him ; [25] When he speaketh fair, believe him not : for *there are* seven abominations in his heart.—PROV., ch. 26.

See other illustrations under :

DISSIMULATION.

Detective. Samson told her .she sent for the lords 2257
Detectives. Watched him..that they might accuse 2258

FALSEHOOD.

Agreement. Ananias kept back part..wife..privy 2985
Begets. My master hath sent me..went no 2986
Bribery. Say ye..stole him..they took the money 2987
Covering. Began to curse..I know not the man 2988
Folly. Ananias, was it not thine? and after it was 2989
Father. 'Your father the devil..no truth in him 2990
Impostors. Jacob said to his father..the L. 2991
Saved by. David said to Ahimelech, The king sent 2992
" Jonathan said, David..run to Bethlehem 2994
Short-lived. Lying tongue is but for a moment 2995
Statecraft. Garments and shoes..old..long journey 2996
Sacrilegious. An angel spake..bring him back 2993
Spirit of. I will be a lying spirit in..prophets 2997
Sin. Thou hast not lied unto men, but..G. 2998
Victim. Joseph's master put him in prison 2999

INSINCERITY.

Blindness. Thou blind Pharisee, cleanse first 4521
Ceremonial. In the day of your fast ye find pleasure 4522
Covetous. Priests teach for hire..prophets..for 4523
Dilemma. No man can serve two masters ; either 4524
Fear. Baptism of John, whence was it ? 4525
Proven. Profess..know G., but in works deny him 4526
Reformers. Jehu departed not..the golden 4527
Reformation. Every nation made gods of their 4528
Seekers. To catch him in his words..master 4529

2429. DISSENSION, Doctrinal. *At Antioch.* [1] Certain men which came down from Judea taught..Except ye be circumcised after the manner of Moses, ye cannot be saved. [2] When therefore Paul and Barnabas had no small dissension and disputation with them, they determined that Paul and Barnabas, and certain other of them, should go up to Jerusalem unto the apostles and elders about this question.—ACTS, ch. 15.

2430. —— A perilous. *With Sadducees.* [9] The scribes *that were* of the Pharisees' part arose, and strove, saying, We find no evil in this man : but if a spirit or an angel hath spoken to him, let us not fight against God. [10] And when there arose a great dissension, the chief captain, fearing lest Paul should have been pulled in pieces of them, commanded the soldiers..to bring *him* into the castle.—ACTS, ch. 23.

2431. —— A partisan. *Corinthians.* [12] Every one of you saith, I am of Paul ; and I of Apollos ; and I of Cephas ; and I of Christ. [13] Is Christ divided? was Paul crucified for you? or were ye baptized in the name of Paul?—1 COR., ch. 1.

2432. —— A stubborn. *Mark.* [39] The contention was so sharp between them, that they departed asunder one from the other : and so Barnabas took Mark, and sailed unto Cyprus ; [40] And Paul chose Silas, and departed, being recommended by the brethren unto the grace of God.—ACTS, ch. 15.

See DISPUTE and references.

2433. DISTINCTION by Deeds. *David.* [57] As David returned from the slaughter of the Philistine, Abner..brought him before Saul with the head of the Philistine in his hand. [58] And Saul said..Whose son *art* thou, *thou* young man? And David answered, *I am* the son of thy servant Jesse the Beth-lehemite.—1 SAM., ch. 17.

See other illustrations under :

APPLAUSE.

Loved. Receive honour one of another 485
Temptation. On a pinnacle..cast thyself down 486

FAME.

Increasing. His fame spread abroad..about 3000
Military. Uzziah made..engines..to shoot 3001
Troublesome. Blaze abroad the matter..desert 3002
Unexpected. In the whole world..woman hath 3003
Wisdom. All the earth sought to Solomon 3004

HONOUR.

Age. Jacob blessed Pharaoh 4058
Appeal. L. was not able to bring..into the land 4059
Dishonour. Haman arrayed Mordecai..proclaimed 4060
Elders. Elihu had waited..were elder than he 4061
not Given. Not mine to give..for whom..prepared 4062
Given. Mephibosheth shall eat..as one..king's sons 4063
Protected. Wherefore should the Egyptians say 4064
Regarded. I was ashamed to require..soldiers 4065
Sale of. They covenanted with him..30 pieces 4066
Sudden. Pharaoh took off his ring..Joseph 4067
Seeking. How can ye believe which receive honour 4068
Service. Said unto the olive..Reign over us 4069
Special. Queen did let no man come..but myself 4070
Unexpected. Mordecai went out..in royal apparel 4071
Won. Abishai was chief of the three..300 slew them 4072

OFFICE.

Faithful. Because thou hast been faithful..ten 5851
Intrigue. Remember that I am your bone and 5852
Merit. Faithful over a few things..ruler over 5853
Seeking. Oh that I were made a judge in the land 5855
Trials. Wherefore..made us to come up out of E. ? 5856
Undesired. The fig tree said..should I forsake 5859

2434. DISTINCTIONS, False. *Pharisees.* [16] Woe unto you, *ye* blind guides, which say, Whosoever shall swear by the temple, it is nothing ; but whosoever shall swear by the gold of the temple, he is a debtor ! [17] *Ye* fools and blind : for whether is greater, the gold, or the temple that sanctifieth the gold ?—MAT., ch. 23.

2435. —— reversed. *Pharisees.* [23] Woe unto you, scribes and Pharisees, hypocrites ! for ye pay tithe of mint and anise and cummin, and have omitted the weightier *matters* of the law, judgment, mercy, and faith : these ought ye to have done, and not to leave the other undone. [24] *Ye* blind guides, which strain at a gnat, and swallow a camel.—MAT., ch. 23.

See other illustrations under :

HONOURS.

Abroad. No prophet is accepted in his own	4073
Brave. King will enrich..give him his daughter	4074
Many. Haman told them of the glory	4075
Posthumous. Widows weeping..shewing..Dorcas	4076
Service. Made Saul king [Ammonites subdued]	4077
Trials. I am..weak, though anointed king	4078

2436. DISTRESS of the Condemned. *In Persia.* [3] In every province, whithersoever the king's.. decree came, *there was* great mourning among the Jews, and fasting, and weeping, and wailing ; and many lay in sackcloth and ashes.—ESTHER, ch. 4.

2437. —— Great Cry of. *Egypt.* [5] All the firstborn in..Egypt shall die, from the firstborn of Pharaoh..even unto the firstborn of the maidservant..and..of beasts. [6] And there shall be a great cry throughout all the land of Egypt, such as there was none like it, nor shall be like it any more.—EX., ch. 11.

2438. —— derided. *David.* [7] All they that see me laugh me to scorn : they shoot out the lip, they shake the head, *saying,* [8] He trusted on the Lord *that* he would deliver him : let him deliver him, seeing he delighted in him.—PS. 22.

2439. —— described. *Jeremiah.* [14] I was a derision to all my people ; *and* their song all the day. [15] He hath filled me with bitterness, he hath made me drunken with wormwood. [16] He hath also broken my teeth with gravel stones, he hath covered me with ashes.—LAM., ch. 3.

2440. —— Exasperation of. *Israelites.* [3] The people murmured..Wherefore *is* this *that* thou hast brought us up out of Egypt to kill us and our children and our cattle with thirst ? [4] And Moses cried unto the Lord, saying, What shall I do unto this people ? they be almost ready to stone me.—EX., ch. 17.

2441. —— in Famine. *Disobedient.* [56] The tender and delicate woman among you, which would not adventure to set the sole of her foot upon the ground for delicateness and tenderness, her eyes shall be evil toward the husband of her bosom, and toward her son, and..daughter, [57]..and toward her children..for she shall eat them for want of all *things* secretly in the siege and straitness, wherewith thine enemy shall distress thee.—DEUT., ch. 28.

2442. —— from little Faith. *Disciples.* [24] There arose a great tempest in the sea..the ship was covered with the waves : but he was asleep. [25] And his disciples..awoke him, saying, Lord, save us ; we perish. [26] And he saith ..Why are ye fearful, O ye of little faith ? Then

he arose, and rebuked the winds and the sea ; and there was a great calm.—MAT., ch. 8.

2443. —— A Friend in. *Gedaliah.* [13] All the king of Babylon's princes ; [14]..sent, and took Jeremiah out of the court of the prison, and committed him unto Gedaliah..that he should carry him home : so he dwelt among the people. —JER., ch. 39.

2444. —— Great. *Blindness.* [2] Nahash the Ammonite answered them, On this *condition* will I make *a covenant* with you, that I may thrust out all your right eyes, and lay it *for* a reproach upon all Israel. [3] And the elders of Jabesh said ..Give us seven days' respite, that we may send messengers unto all the coasts of Israel : [4] Then came the messengers to Gibeah of Saul, and told the tidings..and all the people lifted up their voices, and wept.—1 SAM., ch. 11.

2445. —— A needless. *Israelites.* [The yoke of bondage was broken, and the Philistines were being pursued.] [24] The men of Israel were distressed that day : for Saul had adjured the people, saying, Cursed *be* the man that eateth *any* food until evening, that I may be avenged on mine enemies. So none of the people tasted *any* food.— 1 SAM., ch. 14. [Jonathan ate, and Saul proposed to kill him.]

2446. —— False Refuge in. *Ahaz.* [22] In the time of his distress did he trespass yet more against the Lord.. [23] For he sacrificed unto the gods of Damascus, which smote him : and he said, Because the gods of the kings of Syria help them, *therefore* will I sacrifice to them, that they may help me. But they were the ruin of him, and of all Israel.—2 CHRON., ch. 28.

See other illustrations under :

ALARM.

Conscience. Pray for thy servants..we die not	273
Death. Egyptians were urgent..we be all dead	274
Failure. Priests..doubted..whereunto this would	275
Manifestation. Belshazzar..countenance was	276
Preaching. Paul reasoned..Felix trembled	277
Reasonable. Esau cometh..400 men..Jacob	278
Superstitious. Jesus walking on the sea..troubled	279
S'ners. Adam and his wife hid themselves	280
" Let not God speak with us..die	281
Sudden. [Jailer] Seeing the prison doors open	282
Spiritual. [Jailer] Sirs, what must I do to be saved ?	283
Tempest. Entreat..be no more mighty thunder.	284
Unnecessary. My money is restored..heart failed	285

AGITATION.

Deception. Who art thou ?..Esau..Isaac trembled	256
Diffuses. Disputed he in the synagogue..market	257
Deplored. [Israelites] Made..abhorred..slay us	258
General. [Philistines] Trembling in the host..field	259
Mount. Sinai..quaked greatly	260
Overcome. [At sepulchre] keepers did shake	261
Physical. Belshazzar's thoughts troubled..knees	262
Terror. [Job's vision] Trembling..my bones	263

DESPAIR.

Affliction. Let me not see the death of the child	2213
Anguish. Slay me, for anguish is come upon me	2214
Awaking. Wine was gone out..heart died within	2215
Deliverance. Been better for us to serve the Egyp.	2216
Needless. Widow..meal..oil..me and my son eat	2217

LAMENTATION.

Adversity. Let the day perish wherein I was born	4883
Fathers. O my son Absalom ! my son, my son	4884
General. Thrust out right eyes..people..voices	4885
Ill-timed. Would to G. we had been content	4886

Jesus. O Jerusalem, Jerusalem..would I have   4887
for Jesus. Weep not for me, but weep for   4888
National. In every province..Jews..weeping and   4889
Tearful. Oh that my head were waters..fountain   4890

MOURNING.

Abstinence. [Abner assassinated] If I taste   5603
Bereavement. I am distressed for thee, my   5604
Beneficial. Better to go to the house of mourning   5605
Comfort. Asleep.. sorrow not as others which   5598
Feigned. Be as a woman..long time mourned   5606
Good. Mary..told them..as they mourned and   5600
Genuine. Widows..weeping and shewing   5601
Intense. David went up..wept..barefoot   5607
Joy. Jesus came and touched the bier   5608
Last. Thou mourn at the last..body consumed   5609
Time. Great and very sore lamentation   5610
Wicked. King wept at the grave of Abner   5611

TORTURE.

Hell. I am tormented in this flame   8852
Jesus. Crown of thorns..spit upon him..smote   8855
Prisoners. Elders of the city and thorns..briers   8853
    "   Put them under saws..harrows   8854

TRIBULATION.

Despair. Who shall be able to stand?   8946
Judgment. Sun..as sackcloth..stars fell..moved   8947
Joy in. I am exceeding joyful in all our   8948
Recompensed. White robes..out of great   8949
   See ADVERSITY, AFFLICTION, SUFFERING.

2447. DISTRIBUTION of Property. *Christians.*
³⁴ Neither was there any among them that lacked :
for as many as were possessors of lands or houses
sold them, and brought the prices of the things
that were sold, ³⁵ And laid *them* down at the
apostles' feet : and distribution was made unto
every man according as he had need.—ACTS,
ch. 4.

2448. DISTRUST in Adversity. *Bondmen.*
⁹ Moses spake so unto the children of Israel :
but they hearkened not unto Moses for anguish
of spirit, and for cruel bondage.—EX., ch. 6.

2449. —— of Evildoers. *Joseph's Brethren.*
¹⁸ The men were afraid, because they were
brought into Joseph's house ; and they said, Because of the money that was returned in our
sacks at the first time are we brought in ; that
he may seek occasion against us..and take us
for bondmen.—GEN., ch. 43.

2450. —— forbidden. *Jesus.* ²² Take no
thought for your life, what ye shall eat ; neither
for the body, what ye shall put on. ²³ The life
is more than meat, and the body *is more* than
raiment.—LUKE, ch. 12.

2451. —— Needless. *Lilies.* ²⁷ Consider the
lilies how they grow : they toil not, they spin
not ; and yet I say unto you, that Solomon in
all his glory was not arrayed like one of these.
²⁸ If then God so clothe the grass, which is to day
in the field, and to morrow is cast into the oven ;
how much more *will he clothe* you, O ye of little
faith?—LUKE, ch. 12.

2452. —— Persuasions to. *At Jerusalem.*
²⁸ Rab-shakeh..cried with a loud voice in the
Jews' language..saying, Hear the word of the
great king, the king of Assyria : ²⁹..Let not
Hezekiah deceive you : for he shall not be able
to deliver you out of his hand.—2 KINGS, ch. 18.

2453. —— Without. *Ravens.* ²⁴ Consider
the ravens : for they neither sow nor reap ; which
neither have storehouse nor barn ; and God

feedeth them : how much more are ye better
than the fowls?—LUKE, ch. 12.

   See other illustrations under :

DOUBT.

Adversity. They hearkened not..for anguish   2493
Disappointment. Told them..he was alive   2494
Forbidden. How much more will he clothe you   2495
Hurtful. King said, They know that we be hungry   2496
Impossible. Fire of the L. fell..licked up the w.   2497
Obedience. Do his will, he shall know of the d.   2498
Struggling. Hast thou eyes..seest thou as man   2499
Strong. Except I put my finger in the print   2500
Snare. People is great and taller than we   2501
Trouble. Would G. it were morning..were   2502

JEALOUSY.

Crucified by. Pilate knew that for envy they had   4671
Disunion. Sheba blew a trumpet..we have no God   4672
Free from. Enviest thou for my sake? Would God   4673
Fraternal. Elder son was angry, and would not go   4674
Implacable. Will not spare in the day of vengeance   4675
Local. Did not receive him because his face..J.   4676
National. Are not Abana and Pharpar..better   4677
Polygamous. Bare no children..Rachel envied her   4678
Strife. We have more right in David than ye   4679
Success. Why wentest thou to fight..Midianites ?   4680
    "   Saul was yet the more afraid of David   4681
Wounded. They have ascribed unto David ten   4682

SUSPICION.

Affected. Joseph knew his brethren..ye are spies   8516
Cruel. Why have ye conspired against me?   8517
Corrected. Fear not to take unto thee Mary   8518
Deterred by. What do these Hebrews here ?   8519
Evil. Cut off their garments in the middle   8520
Groundless. Which of us is for the king of I. ?   8521
Painful. Joseph will hate us..evil we did   8522
Removed. Fear not..G. meant it unto good   8523
Sagacious. Lest in the battle, he be an adversary   8524
Slanderous. Abner..came to deceive thee   8525
Unwarranted. David sent..to spy it out   8526
   See UNBELIEF.

2454. DIVERSION, No. *Elisha* ²⁹ Said to
Gehazi, Gird up thy loins, and take my staff in
thine hand, and go thy way . if thou meet any
man, salute him not ; and if any salute thee, answer him not again : and lay my staff upon the
face of the child.—2 KINGS, ch. 4.

   Also see :
Without. Kine took the straight way   4540

2455. DIVERSITY of Gifts. *Spiritual.* ⁸ To
one is given by the Spirit the word of wisdom ;
to another the word of knowledge.. ⁹ To another faith..to another the gifts of healing.. ¹⁰ To
another the working of miracles ; to another
prophecy : to another discerning of spirits ; to
another *divers* kinds of tongues ; to another the
interpretation of tongues.—1 COR., ch. 12.

2456. —— in Hearers. *Parable.* ⁴ When he
sowed, some *seeds* fell by the way side, and the
fowls came and devoured them up ; ⁵ Some fell
upon stony places ; ⁷ And some fell among
thorns ; ⁸ But other fell into good ground.—
MAT., ch. 13.

2457. DIVISION in Affections. *Jonathan.*
³⁰ Saul's anger was kindled against Jonathan,
and he said..Thou son of the perverse rebellious *woman*, do not I know that thou hast chosen
the son of Jesse.. ³² And Jonathan answered
Saul his father..Wherefore shall he be slain ?
what hath he done?—1 SAM., ch. 20.

2458. —— **of Brethren.** *Christians.* [37] Barnabas determined to take with them John, whose surname was Mark. [38] But Paul thought not good to take him with them, who departed from them from Pamphylia.. [39] And the contention was so sharp between them, that they departed asunder one from the other.—ACTS, ch. 15.

2459. —— **A cruel.** *Solomon.* [23] Then said the king, The one saith, This *is* my son that liveth, and thy son *is* the dead : and the other saith, Nay ; but thy son *is* the dead, and my son *is* the living. [25] And the king said, Divide the living child in two, and give half to the one, and half to the other.—1 KINGS, ch. 3.

2460. —— **Doctrines make.** *Disciples.* [56] He that eateth my flesh, and drinketh my blood, dwelleth in me, and I in him. [66] From that *time* many of his disciples went back, and walked no more with him.—JOHN, ch. 6.

2461. —— **A divine.** *Jordan.* [14] He took the mantle of Elijah that fell from him, and smote the waters, and said, Where *is* the Lord God of Elijah? And..they parted hither and thither : and Elisha went over.—2 KINGS, ch. 2.

2462. —— **A just.** *Soldiers.* [22] *Men* of Belial.. that went with David..said, Because they went not with us, we will not give them *aught* of the spoil that we have recovered. [24]..David said, As his part *is* that goeth down to the battle, so *shall* his part *be* that tarrieth by the stuff : they shall part alike.—1 SAM., ch. 30.

2463. —— **The Lord's.** *Egypt.* [22] I will sever in that day the land of Goshen, in which my people dwell, that no swarms of flies shall be there : to the end thou mayest know that I *am* the Lord in the midst of the earth.—EX., ch. 8.

2464. —— **from Misconceptions.** *Of Christ.* [40] Of a truth this is the Prophet. [41] Others said, This is the Christ. But some said, Shall Christ come out of Galilee? [42] Hath not the Scripture said, That Christ cometh of the seed of David, and out of the town of Bethlehem, where David was? [43] So there was a division among the people because of him.—JOHN, ch. 7.

2465. —— **of Opinions.** *Jesus.* [12] There was much murmuring among the people concerning him : for some said, He is a good man : others said, Nay ; but he deceiveth the people.—JOHN, ch. 7.

2466. —— **by Truth.** *Christ.* [34] Think not that I am come to send peace on earth : I came not to send peace, but a sword. [35] For I am come to set a man at variance against his father, and the daughter against her mother, and the daughter in law against her mother in law.—MAT., ch. 10.

2467. DIVISIONS, Authors of. *Hateful.* [16] These six *things* doth the Lord hate ; yea, seven *are* an abomination unto him : [17] A proud look, a lying tongue, and hands that shed innocent blood, [18] A heart that deviseth wicked imaginations, feet that be swift in running to mischief, [19] A false witness *that* speaketh lies, and he that soweth discord among brethren.—PROV., ch. 6.

2468. —— **Harmful.** *In Egypt.* [13] Two men of the Hebrews strove together : and he said to him that did the wrong, Wherefore smitest thou thy fellow? [14] And he said, Who made thee a prince and a judge over us? intendest thou to kill me, as thou killedst the Egyptian? And

Moses feared, and said, Surely this thing is known.—EX., ch. 2. [Enemies were multiplied, Israel was weakened, Moses was banished.]

2469. —— **Harmonious.** *Body.* [14] The body is not one member, but many. [15] If the foot shall say, Because I am not the hand, I am not of the body ; is it therefore not of the body? [16] And if the ear shall say, Because I am not the eye, I am not of the body ; is it therefore not of the body? [17] If the whole body *were* an eye, where *were* the hearing? If the whole were hearing, where *were* the smelling?—1 COR., ch. 12.

2470. —— **healed.** *At Antioch.* [28] It seemed good to the Holy Ghost, and to us, to lay upon you no greater burden than these necessary things ; [29] That ye abstain from meats offered to idols, and from blood, and from things strangled, and from fornication : from which if ye keep yourselves, ye shall do well. Fare ye well. —ACTS, ch. 15.

2471. —— **Party.** *At Corinth.* [3] Ye are yet carnal : for whereas *there is* among you envying, and strife, and divisions, are ye not carnal, and walk as men? [4] For while one saith, I am of Paul ; and another, I *am* of Apollos ; are ye not carnal?—1 COR., ch. 3.

2472. —— **Scandalous.** *Corinth.* [17] Ye come together not for the better, but for the worse. [18]..I hear that there be divisions among you; and I partly believe it. [21] For in eating every one taketh before *other* his own supper : and one is hungry, and another is drunken.—1 COR., ch. 11.

2473. —— **Weakness by.** *Kingdom.* [24] The Pharisees..said, This *fellow* doth not cast out devils, but by Beelzebub the prince of the devils. [25] And Jesus knew their thoughts, and said.. Every kingdom divided against itself is brought to desolation.—MAT., ch. 12.

See other illustrations under :

DISAGREEMENT.

Grudge. Brother shall trespass..tell him his fault	3753
Quality. No man putteth..new garment on an old	2312
Testimony. Against Jesus..witness agreed not	2313

DISSENSION.

Doctrinal. P. and Barnabas had no small	2429
Perilous. Chief captain, fearing lest P..pulled in	2430
Partisan. Every one of you saith, I am of..I of	2431
Removed. [Explanation of the altar of witness]	2432
Stubborn. Contention was so sharp..parted	2433

QUARREL.

Domestic. Sarah saw the son of Hagar mocking	6818
Destructive. Children of Ammon and Moab..slew	6819
Foolish. Wherefore didst thou not call us?	6820
Famished. What aileth thee?..hid her son	6821
Meddler. Who made thee a..judge over us?	6822
" Is like one that taketh a dog by the ears	6823
Matrimonial. Against Moses, because of the	6824
Overruled. Angel of G. called Hagar..lift up the	6825
Test. Say now Shibboleth, and he said, Sibboleth	6826
War from. We have no part in David..To your	6827
Woman. It is better to dwell in a corner..woman	6828

STRIFE.

Avoided. Go from us..mightier than we..Isaac	8378
Absence of. Isaac removed..and digged another	8379
Beginning. As when one letteth out water	8380
Cause of. As coals are..so is a contentious man	8381
Continued. Digged another well, and strove for	8382
Dishonour. An honour for a man to cease from s.	8383
Ended. Is not the whole land before thee?	8384

Occasion of. Their riches were more..dwell   8385
Prevention rewarded. All the land which thou   8386
Prosperity brings. Land was not able to bear   8387
Rebuked. Not from above..earthly, sensual   8388
Truth makes. I am not come to send peace, but a   8389
Wickedness of. Ungodly man diggeth up evil   8390
Words make. Where no wood is..fire goeth out   8391

SECTARIANISM.

Furious. Being exceedingly mad against them, I   7647
Reproved. Saw one casting out devils..forbid..not   7648

Side, which? Art thou for us or. adversaries   7863
"   Who is on the Lord's side?..Come   7864
See SEPARATION.

2474. DIVINITY of Christ. *Asserted.* [18] Therefore the Jews sought the more to kill him, because he not only had broken the sabbath, but said also, that God was his Father, making himself equal with God.—JOHN, ch. 5.   [He had healed an invalid on the sabbath.]

2475. —— —— *Acknowledged.* [5] Jesus saith ..I am *he*. And Judas also, which betrayed him, stood with them. [6] As soon then as he had said unto them, I am *he*, they went backward, and fell to the ground.—JOHN, ch. 18.

2476. —— —— *Confessed.* [13] Whom do men say that I, the Son of man, am? [14] And they said, Some *say that thou art* John the Baptist; some, Elias; and others, Jeremias, or one of the prophets. [15] He saith..But whom say ye that I am? [16] And Simon Peter answered..Thou art the Christ, the Son of the living God.—MAT., ch. 16.

2477. —— —— *Hatred of the Doctrine.* [6] Pilate saith..Take ye him, and crucify *him:* for I find no fault in him. [7] The Jews answered him, We have a law, and by our law he ought to die, because he made himself the Son of God.— JOHN, ch. 19.

2478. —— —— *Manifested.* [24] Master, Master, we perish. Then he arose, and rebuked the wind and the raging of the water: and they ceased, and there was a calm. [25] ..What manner of man is this! for he commandeth even the winds and water, and they obey him.—LUKE, ch. 8.

2479. —— —— *Professed.* [30] I and *my* Father are one. [31] Then the Jews took up stones again to stone him. [32] Jesus answered them..for which of those works do ye stone me? [33] The Jews answered him, saying, For a good work we stone thee not; but for blasphemy; and because that thou, being a man, makest thyself God.—JOHN, ch. 10.

2480. —— *of Man.* *Genealogy.* [23] Jesus himself began to be about thirty years of age, being (as was supposed) the son of Joseph, which was *the son* of Heli.. [38] Which was *the son* of Enos, which was *the son* of Seth, which was *the son* of Adam, which was *the son* of God.—LUKE, ch. 3.

2281. —— *to be Proved.* *Baal.* [31] Joash said unto all that stood against him, Will ye plead for Baal?..he that will plead for him, let him be put to death..if he *be* a god, let him plead for himself, because *one* hath cast down his altar.— JUDGES, ch. 6.

See other illustrations under:
INSPIRATION.
Art. To devise cunning works..carving of timber   4536
Duty. L. stirred up the spirit of Cyrus   4537
Emergency. It shall be given you in that hour   4538
See GOD.

2482. DIVORCE, Law of. *Christian.* [7] Why did Moses then command to give a writing of divorcement.. [8] ..Moses because of the hardness of your hearts suffered you to put away your wives: but from the beginning it was not so. [9] And I say unto you, Whosoever shall put away his wife, except *it be* for fornication, and shall marry another, committeth adultery: and whoso marrieth her which is put away doth commit adultery.—MAT., ch. 19.

2483. —— —— *Jewish.* [1] When a man hath taken a wife, and..she find no favour in his eyes, because he hath found some uncleanness in her; then let him write her a bill of divorcement, and give *it* in her hand, and send her out of his house. [2] And. she may go and be another man's *wife.*—DEUT., ch. 24.

2484. —— *Royal.* *Persian.* [11] To bring Vashti the queen before the king with the crown royal, to shew the people and the princes her beauty: for she *was* fair to look on. [12] But the queen Vashti refused.. [19] ..let it be written among the laws of the Persians and the Medes ..That Vashti come no more before king Ahasuerus; and let the king give her royal estate unto another.—ESTHER, ch. 1.

2485. DOCILITY, Filial. *Solomon.* [8] My son, hear the instruction of thy father, and forsake not the law of thy mother: [9] For they *shall be* an ornament of grace unto thy head, and chains about thy neck.—PROV., ch. 1.

See other illustrations under:
TEACHABLENESS.
Attitude. Mary sat at Jesus' feet..heard his word   8606
Characteristic. Received the word with..readiness   8607
Manifested. Eunuch desired Philip..sit with him   8608
Professed. All here present before G. to hear all   8609
Youthful. Found him in the temple. hearing them   8610

2486. DOCTRINE, Difficulties in. *Disciples.* [53] Except ye eat the flesh of the Son of man, and drink his blood, ye have no life in you. [60] Many therefore of his disciples, when they had heard *this*, said, This is a hard saying; who can hear it? [66] From that *time* many of his disciples went back, and walked no more with him. —JOHN, ch. 6.

2487. —— *Unauthorized.* *Pharisees.* [7] Howbeit in vain do they worship me, teaching *for* doctrines the commandments of men. [8] For laying aside the commandment of God, ye hold the tradition of men, *as* the washing of pots and cups.—MARK, ch. 7.

2488. DOERS of the Word. *Honoured.* [49] He stretched forth his hand toward his disciples, and said, Behold my mother and my brethren! [50] For whosoever shall do the will of my Father which is in heaven, the same is my brother, and sister, and mother.—MAT., ch. 12.

See other illustrations under:
ACTIVITY.
vs. Eloquence. I am not eloquent..take this rod   91
Astonishing. Not so much as eat..beside himself   92
Benevolent. Jesus went about..healing   93
vs. Spirituality. Martha was cumbered with much   94

DEEDS.
Authenticated. If I do not the works..believe not   2094
Evince. World began..not heard..opened eyes   2095
Test. Which of these three was neighbour   2096
Words. Said..Lord he is God..slew prophets   2097

EFFORT.

Concentrated. Fight neither small nor great 2605
Deliverance. Why sit we here till we die? 2606
Fruitless. The king laboured to deliver Daniel 2607
Humble. Jesus said..Loose him, and let him go 2608
Ill-considered. This man began to build..not able 2609
Personal. Have mercy on me..my daughter is 2610
Sphere. Witnesses..uttermost part of the earth 2611
Single. With the spear..I will not smite the 2612
Singleness. I determined not to know anything 2613
Union. They strengthened their hands with gold 2614
" Men and women brought bracelets and 2615
Unavailing. Earneth wages to put in a bag with 2616
Victory without. Stand still, and see. salvation 2617

Earnest. The kingdom of heaven..violent take it 9784
Evince. It..a great people..land of the giants 9811
Faith. Go shew..as they went, they were 2886
Gentleness. Youth drew not his sword, for he 9966
Industrious. She hasted..ran..drew for..camels 4442
Rewarded. Let not your hands be weak 9804
See WORK.

2489. DOMINION, Dream of. *Joseph.* 6 Hear, I pray you, this dream which I have dreamed : 7 For, behold, we *were* binding sheaves in the field, and, lo, my sheaf arose, and also stood upright ; and, behold, your sheaves stood round about, and made obeisance to my sheaf. 8 And his brethren said to him, Shalt thou indeed reign over us?—GEN., ch. 37.

2490. —— feared. *Animals.* 1 God blessed Noah and his sons, and..said.. 2..the fear of you and the dread of you shall be upon every beast of the earth, and upon every fowl of the air, upon all that moveth *upon* the earth, and upon all the fishes of the sea ; into your hand are they delivered.—GEN., ch. 9.

2491. —— Made for. *Adam.* 26 God said, Let us make man in our image, after our likeness : and let them have dominion over the fish of the sea, and over the fowl of the air, and over the cattle, and over all the earth, and over every creeping thing.—GEN., ch. 1.

See other illustrations under :

AUTHORITY.

Brief. Zimri hath conspired [seven days] 6953
Despotic. Ye shall cry out..because of your king 2245

GOVERNMENT.

Bad. Samuel's sons..after lucre..make us a king 3664
Commissioned. Let them have dominion..fish 3665
Method. Provide able men..truth..hating covet. 3666
Obedience. The powers that be are ordained of 3667
Revolt. I will chastise you..I. rebelled 3668
Support. Render..Cesar the things which are 3669
Vice. Lewd fellows of the baser sort..city in 3670

OFFICE.

Faithful. Because thou hast been faithful..ten 5851
Intrigue. Remember that I am your bone and 5852
Merit. Faithful over a few things..ruler over 5853
Seeking. Oh that I were made a judge in the land 5855
Trials. Wherefore..made us to come up out of E.? 5856
Undesired. The fig tree said..should I forsake 5859

RULER.

Born. Your sheaves stood round about..obeisance 7466
" Potiphar made him overseer over his house 7467
" Keeper committed to Joseph's hand all 7468
" Pharaoh made him ruler over all Egypt 7469
Foolish. Saul adjured..cursed be the man..eateth 7470
Pious. All these have I kept from my youth 7471
Ruled. Dost thou now govern the kingdom? 7472

Sinful. There was none like unto Ahab..wicked 7473
" As a roaring lion..so is a wicked ruler 7474
Unjust. A judge, which feared not G. nor regarded 7475

RULERS.

Guidance. Shall write a copy of this law 7476
Influence. Have any of the rulers..believed 7477
Many. Solomon's officers were..3300 7478
Qualifications. Men fear G., men of truth 7479
Responsibilities. Because thou hast..rejected thee 7480

Tribute. Menaham gave..1000 talents..to confirm 535

2492. DOOM of the Wicked. *Tares.* 30 Let both grow together until the harvest : and..I will say to the reapers, Gather ye together first the tares, and bind them in bundles to burn them : but gather the wheat into my barn.—MAT., ch. 13.

See other illustrations under :

HELL.

Affection in. Send Lazarus to my father's house 3922
Bottomless. Bottomless pit..smoke of a great 3923
Preparation of. Cursed..into fire prepared for the 3924
See PUNISHMENT.

2493. DOUBT in Adversity. *Bondmen.* 9 Moses spake so unto the children of Israel : but they hearkened not unto Moses for anguish of spirit, and for cruel bondage.—EX., ch. 6.

2494. —— from Disappointment. *Disciples.* 9 Mary Magdalene.. 10..she went and told them ..as they mourned and wept. 11 And they, when they had heard that he was alive, and had been seen of her, believed not.—MARK, ch. 16.

2495. —— forbidden. *Lilies.* 27 Consider the lilies how they grow : they toil not, they spin not ; and yet I say unto you, that Solomon in all his glory was not arrayed like one of these. 28 If then God so clothe the grass, which is to day in the field, and to morrow is cast into the oven ; how much more *will he clothe* you, O ye of little faith?—LUKE, ch. 12.

2496. —— Hurtful. *Israelites.* 12 The king arose in the night, and said unto his servants.. They know that we *be* hungry ; therefore are they gone out of the camp to hide themselves in the field, saying, When they come out of the city, we shall catch them alive, and get into the city.—2 KINGS, ch. 7. [Four lepers had said the Syrian camp is deserted.]

2497. —— impossible. 38 Then the fire of the Lord fell, and consumed the burnt sacrifice, and the wood, and the stones, and the dust, and licked up the water that *was* in the trench. 39 And when all the people saw *it*, they fell on their faces : And they said, The Lord he *is* the God.—1 KINGS, ch. 18.

2498. —— Obedience solves. *Jesus.* 16 Jesus answered..My doctrine is not mine, but his that sent me. 17 If any man will do his will, he shall know of the doctrine, whether it be of God, or *whether* I speak of myself.—JOHN, ch. 7.

2499. —— Struggling with. *Job.* 2 I will say unto God, Do not condemn me ; shew me wherefore thou contendest with me. 3 *Is it* good unto thee that thou shouldest oppress, that thou shouldest despise the work of thine hands, and shine upon the counsel of the wicked? 4 Hast thou eyes of flesh? or seest thou as man seeth? —JOB, ch. 10.

2500. —— Strong. *Thomas.* 25 The other disciples..said..We have seen the Lord. But he said. .Except I shall see in his hands the print of the nails, and put my finger into the print of the nails, and thrust my hand into his side. I will not believe.—JOHN, ch. 20.

2501. —— a Snare. *Moses said,* ²⁸ Whither shall we go up ? our brethren have discouraged our heart, saying, The people *is* greater and taller than we ; the cities *are* great and walled up to heaven ; and moreover, we have seen the sons of the Anakims there. ²⁹ Then I said. . Dread not, neither be afraid of them.—DEUT., ch. 1.

2502. —— Trouble from. *Moses.* ⁶⁶ Thy life shall hang in doubt before thee ; and thou shalt fear day and night, and shalt have none assurance of thy life : ⁶⁷ In the morning thou shalt say, Would God it were even ! and at even thou shalt say, Would God it were morning ! for the fear of thine heart wherewith thou shalt fear, and for the sight of thine eyes which thou shalt see.—DEUT., ch. 28.

See other illustrations under

INCREDULITY.

Disciples'. Words seemed to them as idle tales	4394
" [At Emmaus] Neither believed they	4395
Prayer. Gathered together praying [for Peter]	4396
Removed. Thomas, reach hither. .My Lord	4398
Unbelievers. Jews did not believe he had been	4397

SCRUPLES.

Hypocrites. Then led they Jesus. .themselves went	2628
Little. Pay tithe of mint, anise. .omit weightier	2629

SUSPICION.

Affected. Ye are spies ; to see the nakedness	8516
Cruel. Why have ye conspired against me ?	8517
Corrected. Joseph, fear not to take. .Mary	8518
Deterred. What do these Hebrews here ?	8519
Evil of. Hanun shaved off one half of their beards	8520
Groundless. Which of us is for the king of I.	8521
Painful. Joseph. .will hate us. .evil which we did	8522
Removed. Joseph said, Fear not	8523
Sagacious. Lest in the battle he be an adversary	8524
Unwarranted. Abner. .came to deceive thee	8525
" Hath not David sent. .to spy it out ?	8526

UNCERTAINTY.

Future. Thou hast much goods laid up. .years	9077
" We will buy and sell. .ye know not. .day	9078
" What is your life. .vapor	9079
Riches. Certainly make themselves wings ; they	9080

See UNBELIEF.

2503. DREAM, A comforting. *Exiled Jacob.* ¹² A ladder set up on the earth, and the top of it reached to heaven : and behold, the angels of God ascending and descending on it. ¹⁵. .I am with thee, and will keep thee in all *places* whither thou goest, and will bring thee again into this land.—GEN., ch. 28.

2504. —— Direction in a. *Joseph.* ²⁰ Behold, the angel of the Lord appeared unto him in a dream, saying, Joseph. .fear not to take unto thee Mary thy wife : for that which is conceived in her is of the Holy Ghost.—MAT., ch. 1.

2505. —— A delusive. *Hunger.* ⁸ As when a hungry man dreameth, and, behold, he eateth ; but he awaketh, and his soul is empty : or as when a thirsty man dreameth, and, behold, he drinketh ; but he awaketh, and, behold, *he is* faint, and his soul hath appetite : so shall the multitude of all the nations be, that fight against mount Zion.—ISA., ch. 29.

2506. —— A forgotten. *Nebuchadnezzar.* ⁵ The king answered. .the Chaldeans, The thing is gone from me : if ye will not make known unto me the dream, with the interpretation thereof, ye shall be cut in pieces, and your houses shall be made a dunghill.—DAN., ch. 2.

2507. —— A prophetic. *Nebuchadnezzar.* [See Dan. 2 : 36-45.]

2508. —— Preserved by a. *Babe.* ¹³ An angel of the Lord appeared to Joseph in a dream, saying, Arise, and take the young child and his mother, and flee into Egypt, and be thou there until I bring thee word ; for Herod will seek the young child to destroy him.—MAT., ch. 2.

2509. —— Reproved in a. *Abimelech.* ³ God came to Abimelech in a dream by night, and said. .Behold, thou *art but* a dead man, for the woman which thou hast taken ; for she *is* a man's wife.—GEN., ch. 20.

2510. —— Trouble from. *Pharaoh.* ⁷ The seven thin ears devoured the seven rank and full ears. And Pharaoh awoke, and, behold, *it was* a dream. ⁸. .in the morning. .his spirit was troubled ; and he sent and called for all the magicians of Egypt, and all the wise men.— GEN., ch. 41.

2511. —— A terrifying. *Daniel.* ⁷ I saw in the night visions, and behold a fourth beast, dreadful and terrible, and strong exceedingly ; and it had great iron teeth : it devoured and brake in pieces, and stamped the residue with the feet of it. .and it had ten horns.—DAN., ch. 7.

2512. —— verified, A. *Gideon.* ⁹ The same night, that the Lord said unto him, Arise, get thee down unto the host ; for I have delivered it into thine hand. ¹³ And when Gideon was come, behold, *there was* a man that told a dream unto his fellow, and said, Behold, I dreamed a dream, and, lo, a cake of barley bread tumbled into the host of Midian, and came unto a tent, and smote it that it fell, and overturned it, that the tent lay along. ¹⁴ And his fellow answered . .This is nothing else save the sword of Gideon. —JUDGES, ch. 7.

2513. —— Warning in a. *Pilate's Wife.* ¹⁹ When he was set down on the judgment seat, his wife sent unto him, saying, Have thou nothing to do with that just man : for I have suffered many things this day in a dream because of him.—MAT., ch. 27.

2514. DREAMS interpreted. *Joseph.* ¹² Joseph said. .This *is* the interpretation of it : The three branches *are* three days : ¹³ Yet within three days shall Pharaoh lift up thy head, and restore thee unto thy place : and thou shalt deliver Pharaoh's cup into his hand, after the former manner when thou wast his butler. ¹⁸ And Joseph. .said, This *is* the interpretation thereof : The three baskets *are* three days : ¹⁹ Yet within three days Pharaoh shall lift up thy head from off thee, and shall hang thee on a tree ; and the birds shall eat thy flesh.—GEN., ch. 40.

2515. —— Offensive. *Joseph.* ⁷ Behold, your sheaves stood round about, and made obeisance to my sheaf. ⁸ And his brethren said to him, Shalt thou indeed reign over us ? or shalt thou indeed have dominion over us ? And they hated him yet the more for his dreams.—GEN., ch. 37.

2516. —– **Terrific.** *Job.* ¹³ When I say.. my couch shall ease my complaint ; ¹⁴ Then thou scarest me with dreams, and terrifiest me through visions : ¹⁵ So that my soul chooseth strangling, *and* death rather than my life. ¹⁶ I loathe *it ;* I would not live alway.—Job, ch. 7.

See other illustrations under :

VISION.

Comforting. Stephen saw..Jesus standing	9225
of God. I saw also the L..on a throne	9226
" Woe is me, for I am undone..unclean	9227
Instructed. What G. hath cleansed..common	9228
Prepared for. I was fasting until..ninth hour	9229
Perfected. Restored, and saw every man clearly	9230
Spirit. A spirit passed.. hair of my flesh stood up	9231
Transforming. Moses wist not that..face shone	9232
" Beholding as in a glass..changed	9233
Trance. Peter fell into a trance .sheet knit.	9234

2517. DRIVING, Fast. *Jehu.* ¹⁶ Jehu rode in a chariot, and went to Jezreel ; for Joram lay there. And Ahaziah king of Judah was come down to see Joram. ¹⁷ And there stood a watchman on the tower in Jezreel. ²⁰ And the watchman told, saying..the driving *is* like the driving of Jehu the son of Nimshi ; for he driveth furiously.—2 Kings, ch. 9.

2518. DROUTH, Punishment by. *Israelites.* ¹ Elijah the Tishbite..said unto Ahab, *As* the Lord God of Israel liveth, before whom I stand, there shall not be dew nor rain these years, but according to my word.—1 Kings, ch. 17. [It was ended when the priests of Baal were slain.]

2519. DROWNING, Refuge in. *J e s u s.* ⁶ Whoso shall offend one of these little ones which believe in me, it were better for him that a millstone were hanged about his neck ; and *that* he were drowned in the depth of the sea.— Mat., ch. 18.

See other illustrations under :

Escape. Some on boards, some on broken pieces		2716
" Lord had prepared a great fish		3252
Feared. Mariners were afraid.. his god		8361
" Master, master, we perish		8359
" Mount up to the heaven..soul is melted		8362

2520. DRUNKARD, So called. *Jesus.* ²³ John the Baptist came neither eating bread nor drinking wine ; and ye say, He hath a devil. ³⁴ The Son of man is come eating and drinking ; and ye say, Behold a gluttonous man, and a winebibber.—Luke, ch. 7.

2521. —– **Folly of a.** *H e r o d.* ²² When the daughter of..Herodias came in and danced, and pleased Herod and them..the king.. ²³ He sware unto her, Whatsoever thou shalt ask of me, I will give *it* thee, unto the half of my kingdom.—Mark, ch. 6.

2522. DRUNKARDS, Curse upon. *By Moses.* ¹⁹ He bless himself in his heart, saying, I shall have peace, though I walk in the imagination of mine heart, to add drunkenness to thirst : ²⁰ The Lord will not spare him, but then the anger of the Lord and his jealousy shall smoke against that man, and all the curses that are written in this book shall lie upon him, and the Lord shall blot out his name from under heaven.—Deut., ch. 29.

2523. —– **Disgrace of.** *Ephraimites.* ⁷ The priest and the prophet have erred through strong drink..they err in vision, they stumble *in* judg-

ment. ⁸ For all tables are full of vomit *and* filthiness, *so that there is* no place *clean.*—Isa., ch. 28.

2524. —– **Maker of.** *Denounced.* ¹⁵ Woe unto him that giveth his neighbour drink, that puttest thy bottle to *him,* and makest *him* drunken also, that thou mayest look on their nakedness !—Hab., ch. 2.

2525. —– **Perdition for.** *Paul.* ⁹ Know ye not that the unrighteous shall not inherit the kingdom of God ? Be not deceived : neither fornicators, nor idolaters, nor adulterers, nor effeminate, nor abusers of themselves with mankind, ¹⁰ Nor thieves, nor covetous, nor drunkards..shall inherit the kingdom of God.—1 Cor., ch. 6.

2526. —– **Separation from.** *Paul.* ¹¹ I have written unto you not to keep company, if any man that is called a brother be a fornicator, or covetous, or an idolater, or a railer, or a drunkard, or an extortioner : with such a one no not to eat.—1 Cor., ch. 5.

2527. —– **Woe against.** *Dissipation.* ¹¹ Woe unto them that rise up early in the morning, *that* they may follow strong drink ; that continue until night, *till* wine inflame them ! ¹² And the harp and the viol, the tabret and pipe, and wine, are in their feasts : but they regard not the work of the Lord, neither consider the operation of his hands. ²² Woe unto *them that are* mighty to drink wine, and men of strength to mingle strong drink.—Isa., ch. 5.

2528. DRUNKENNESS, Battle lost by. *Syrian.* Ben-hadad *was* drinking himself drunk in the pavilions, he and..the thirty and two kings that helped him. ¹⁹ So these young men of the princes..came out of the city, and the army.. ²⁰ And they slew every one his man : and the Syrians fled.—1 Kings, ch. 20.

2529. —– **in the Church.** *Corinth.* ²¹ In eating every one taketh before *other* his own supper : and one is hungry, and another is drunken.—1 Cor., ch. 11.

2530. —– **The first.** *Noah.* ²⁰ Noah began *to be* a husbandman, and he planted a vineyard : ²¹ And he drank of the wine, and was drunken ; and he was uncovered within his tent.—Gen., ch. 9.

2531. —– **Shameful.** *Noah.* [Gen. 19 : 31-36.]

See other illustrations under :

INTEMPERANCE.

Avoiding. Look not on the wine when it is red	4584
Changed by. Nabal's heart was merry..was very	4587
Cruelty. Give me the head of John B..sorry	4588
Disarms. When Amnon's heart is merry with wine	4589
Dangers. Do not drink wine..into the tabernacle	4590
Degrades. Bring Vashti..shew the people her b.	4591
" Glorious beauty..shall be a fading	4592
Forgetfulness. Not for kings to drink wine..forget	4600
Poison of. Biteth like a serpent..an adder	4601
Profanity. Belshazzar tasted wine, commanded	4602
Shameless. King was merry with wine..bring	4603

WINE.

Changed. Wine..out of Nabal..heart died	9605
Mocker. Whosoever is deceived thereby is not	9608
Misled by. When it giveth his colour..moveth	9609
Poverty. Drunkard shall come to poverty..rags	9611
Sorrows. Who hath woe ? Who hath sorrow ?	9612

2532. DUELLIST, a Giant. *Goliath.* [8] Am not I a Philistine, and ye servants to Saul? choose you a man for you, and let him come down to me. [9] If he be able to fight w..th me, and to kill me, then will we be your servants : but if I prevail against him, and kill him, then shall ye be our servants.—1 Sam., ch. 17.

2533. DUMBNESS from Doubt. *Zacharias.* [18] Zacharias said unto the angel, Whereby shall I know this? for I am an old man, and my wife well stricken in years. [20] ..behold, thou shalt be dumb, and not able to speak, until the day that these things shall be performed, because thou believest not my words.—Luke, ch. 1.

2534. —— removed. *Zacharias.* (See above.) [The child was born,] [62] And they made signs to his father, how he would have him called. [63] And he asked for a writing table, and wrote, saying, His name is John. And they marvelled all. [64] And his mouth was opened immediately and his tongue *loosed*, and he spake, and praised God.—Luke, ch. 1.

2535. DUTY abandoned. *One Talent.* [24] Lord, I knew thee that thou art a hard man, reaping where thou hast not sown, and gathering where thou hast not strewed : [25] And I was afraid, and went and hid thy talent in the earth : lo, *there* thou hast *that is* thine. [26] ..*Thou* wicked and slothful servant.—Mat., ch. 25.

2536. —— Angels urge to. *Peter and John.* [19] The angel of the Lord by night opened the prison doors, and brought them forth, and said, [20] Go, stand and speak in the temple to the people all the words of this life.—Acts, ch. 5.

2537. —— Compassion a. *Samaritan.* [33] When he saw him, he had compassion *on him.* [34] And went to *him*, and bound up his wounds, pouring in oil and wine, and set him on his own beast, and brought him to an inn, and took care of him. [37] Then said Jesus unto him, Go, and do thou likewise.—Luke, ch. 10.

2538. —— A delightful. *Moses' Mother.* [7] Said his sister..Shall I go and call to thee a nurse of the Hebrew women, that she may nurse the child for thee? [8] And Pharaoh's daughter said..Go. And the maid went and called the child's mother.—Ex., ch. 2.

2539. —— The first. *Love God.* [25] A certain lawyer stood up..saying, Master, what shall I do to inherit eternal life? [26] He said unto him, What is written in the law?.. [27] And he answering said, Thou shalt love the Lord thy God with all thy heart, and with all thy soul, and with all thy strength, and with all thy mind ; and thy neighbour as thyself. [28] And he said ..Thou hast answered right : this do, and thou shalt live.—Luke, ch. 10.

2540. —— Faithfulness to. *Agabus* [11] Took Paul's girdle, and bound his own hands and feet, and said, Thus saith the Holy Ghost, So shall the Jews at Jerusalem bind the man that owneth this girdle, and shall deliver *him* into the hands of the Gentiles. [12] We..besought him not to go up.. [13] Then Paul answered, What mean ye to weep and to break mine heart? for I am ready not to be bound only, but also to die at Jerusalem for the name of the Lord Jesus.—Acts, ch. 21.

2541. —— A grievous. *Young Ruler.* [21] Jesus beholding him loved him, and said.

One thing thou lackest : go thy way, sell whatsoever thou hast, and give to the poor, and thou shalt have treasure in heaven : and come, take up the cross, and follow me. [22] And he was sad at that saying, and went away grieved : for he had great possessions.—Mark, ch. 10.

2542. —— Hesitation in. *Looking Back.* [61] Another..said, Lord, I will follow thee : but let me first go bid them farewell, which are at home at my house. [62] ..Jesus said..No man, having put his hand to the plough, and looking back, is fit for the kingdom of God.—Luke, ch. 9.

2543. —— —— Lot's Wife. [17] Escape for thy life ; look not behind thee, neither stay thou in all the plain ; escape to the mountain, lest thou be consumed. [26] But his wife looked back ..and she became a pillar of salt.—Gen., ch. 19.

2544. —— intimated. *Ark returned.* [14] The cart came into the field of Joshua, a Beth-shemite, and stood there, where *there was* a great stone : and they clave the wood of the cart, and offered the kine a burnt offering unto the Lord. —1 Sam., ch. 6.

2545. —— Instruction in. *Cornelius.* [4] Angel said, [5] ..send men to Joppa, and call for..Peter : [6] He lodgeth with one Simon a tanner, whose house is by the sea side : he shall tell thee what thou oughtest to do.—Acts, ch. 10.

2546. —— The most important. *Scribe.* [28] Which is the first commandment of all? [29] And Jesus answered him, The first of all the commandments is.. [30] ..thou shalt love the Lord thy God with all thy heart, and with all thy soul, and with all thy mind, and with all thy strength : this is the first commandment. [31] And the second is like, *namely* this, Thou shalt love thy neighbour as thyself.—Mark, ch. 12.

2547. —— vs. Money. *Amaziah.* [7] O king, let not the army of Israel go with thee ; for the Lord is not with Israel, *to wit, with* all the children of Ephraim. [9] And Amaziah said..But what shall we do for the hundred talents which I have given to the army of Israel? And the man of God answered, The Lord is able to give thee much more than this.—2 Chron., ch. 25.

2548. —— manifested. *Following the Ark.* [3] When ye see the ark of the covenant..and.. the Levites bearing it, then ye shall..go after it. [15] And as they..were come unto Jordan, and the feet of the priests that bare the ark were dipped in the brim of the water (Jordan overfloweth all his banks all the time of harvest,) [16] That the waters which came down from above stood *and* rose up upon a heap.—Josh., ch. 3.

2549. —— Mistaking. *Saul.* [9] I verily thought with myself, that I ought to do many things contrary to the name of Jesus of Nazareth. [10] Which thing I also did in Jerusalem : and many of the saints did I shut up in prison.— Acts, ch. 26.

2550. —— Only our. *Obedience.* [9] Doth he thank that servant because he did the things that were commanded him? I trow not. [10] So likewise ye, when ye shall have done all those things which are commanded you, say, We are unprofitable servants : we have done that which was our duty to do.—Luke, ch. 17.

2551. —— performed. *Abram.* [4] So Abram departed..and Lot went with him : and Abram *was* seventy and five years old when he departed out of Haran. ⁷ And the Lord appeared..and said, Unto thy seed will I give this land : and there builded he an altar unto the Lord.—GEN., ch. 12.

2552. —— **Protection in.** *Jewish Feasts.* ²⁴ Neither shall any man desire thy land, when thou shalt go up to appear before the Lord.. thrice in the year.—Ex., ch. 34.

2553. —— **Prospered in.** *Samuel.* ¹⁹ Samuel grew, and the Lord was with him, and did let none of his words fall to the ground.—1 SAM., ch. 3.

2554. —— **of the Rich.** *Paul.* ¹⁷ Charge them that are rich in this world, that they be not highminded, nor trust in uncertain riches, but in the living God.. ¹⁸ That they do good, that they be rich in good works, ready to distribute, willing to communicate.—1 TIM., ch. 6.

2555. —— **Reward of.** *Abraham.* ¹⁰ Abraham stretched forth his hand, and took the knife to slay his son. ¹⁸ And in thy seed shall all the nations of the earth be blessed ; because thou hast obeyed my voice.—GEN., ch. 22.

2556. —— **Safety in.** *Prophet.* ⁴ When king Jeroboam heard the saying of the man of God, which had cried against the altar in Beth-el..he put forth his hand from the altar, saying, Lay hold on him. And his hand..dried up, so that he could not pull it in again.—1 KINGS, ch. 13.

2557. —— **will be shown.** *Saul.* ⁶ He trembling and astonished said, Lord, what wilt thou have me to do ? And the Lord *said* unto him, Arise, and go into the city, and it shall be told thee what thou must do.—ACTS, ch. 9.

2558. —— **A trying.** *Abraham.* ² Take now thy son, thine only *son* Isaac, whom thou lovest, and get thee into the land of Moriah ; and offer him there for a burnt offering upon one of the mountains which I will tell thee of.—GEN., ch. 22.

2559. —— **The whole.** *Solomon.* ¹³ Let us hear the conclusion of the whole matter : Fear God, and keep his commandments : for this *is* the whole *duty* of man.—ECCL., ch. 12.

2560. —— **Daily.** *Temple.* ³⁸ Thou shalt offer upon the altar ; two lambs of the first year day by day continually. ³⁹ The one lamb thou shalt offer in the morning ; and the other lamb thou shalt offer at even.—Ex., ch. 29.

2561. —— **the first.** *Jesus.* ²³ Woe unto you, scribes and Pharisees, hypocrites ! for ye pay tithe of mint and anise and cummin, and have omitted the weightier *matters* of the law, judgment, mercy, and faith : these ought ye to have done, and not to leave the other undone. ²⁴ Ye blind guides, which strain at a gnat, and swallow a camel.—MAT., ch. 23.

2562. DUTIFUL, Blessings on the. *Prosperity.* ² Unto you that fear my name shall the Sun of righteousness arise with healing in his wings ; and ye shall go forth, and grow up as calves of the stall. ³ And ye shall tread down the wicked ; for they shall be ashes under the soles of your feet.—MAL., ch. 4.

See other illustrations under:

ACCOUNTABILITY.

Humility. We are unprofitable servants..our duty 8479
See **OBEDIENCE** and **RESPONSIBILITY.**

2563. DWARF rejected, The. *Law.* ²⁰ A dwarf, or that hath a blemish in his eye, or be scurvy, or scabbed.. ²¹..shall come nigh to offer the offerings of the Lord made by fire : he hath a blemish ; he shall not come nigh to offer the bread of his God.—LEV., ch. 21.

2564. DYING on the Mount. *Aaron.* ²⁷ And they went up into mount Hor in the sight of all the congregation. ²⁸ And Moses stripped Aaron of his garments, and put them upon Eleazar his son ; and Aaron died there in the top of the mount.—NUM., ch. 20.

2565. —— **a painful Sight.** *Hagar.* ¹⁴ In the wilderness of Beer-sheba. ¹⁵ And the water was spent in the bottle, and she cast the child under one of the shrubs. ¹⁶ And she went, and sat her down..a good way off, as it were a bowshot : for she said, Let me not see.the death of the child. And she..lift up her voice, and wept.—GEN., ch. 21.

2566. —— **Soul forgotten in.** *Saul.* ³ He was sore wounded of the archers. ⁴ Then said Saul unto his armourbearer, Draw thy sword, and thrust me through therewith ; lest these uncircumcised come and thrust me through, and abuse me. But his armourbearer would not ; for he was sore afraid. Therefore Saul took a sword, and fell upon it.—1 SAM., ch. 31.

2567. —— **Words of the.** *David.* ² I go the way of all the earth : be thou strong therefore, and shew thyself a man ; ³ And keep the charge of the Lord..to walk in his ways, to keep his statutes..that thou mayest prosper in all that thou doest.—1 KINGS, ch. 2.

See **DEATH.**

2568. EARNESTNESS of Angels. *Lot.* ¹⁶ While he lingered, the men laid hold upon his hand, and upon the hand of his wife, and..his two daughters ; the Lord being merciful unto him : and they brought him forth, and set him without the city.—GEN., ch. 19.

2569. —— **Bold.** *Fire.* ²⁹ Absalom sent for Joab, to have sent him to the king ; but he would not come to him..the second time, he would not come. ³⁰ Therefore he said unto his servants, See, Joab's field is near mine, and he hath barley there ; go and set it on fire.—2 SAM., ch. 14.

2570. —— **checked.** *Young Ruler.* ¹⁷ There came one running, and kneeled to him, and asked him, Good Master, what shall I do that I may inherit eternal life?.. ²¹..give to the poor, and thou shalt have treasure in heaven : and come, take up the cross, and follow me. ²² And he was sad at that saying, and went away grieved : for he had great possessions.—MARK, ch. 10.

2571. —— **chosen.** *Lappeth.* ⁵ Every one that lappeth of the water with his tongue, as a dog lappeth, him shalt thou set by himself ; likewise every one that boweth down upon his knees to drink. ⁷ And the Lord said unto Gideon, By the three hundred men that lapped will I save you, and deliver the Midianites into thine hand : and let all the *other* people go every man unto his place.—Judges, ch. 7.

2572. —— **in Hospitality.** *Lot.* [1] There came two angels..and Lot sat in the gate of Sodom : and..rose up to meet them ; and he bowed himself with his face toward the ground ; [3] And he pressed upon them greatly ; and they..entered into his house ; and he made them a feast.— Gen., ch. 19.

2573. —— **important.** *Murmurers.* [47] Aaron took as Moses commanded, and ran into the midst of the congregation ; and, behold, the plague was begun..and'he put on incense, and made an atonement for the people. [48] And he stood between the dead and the living ; and the plague was stayed.—Num., ch. 16.

2574. —— **Influence of.** *Borrower.* [5] Which of you shall have a friend, and shall go unto him at midnight, and say..Friend, lend me three loaves : Trouble me not : the door is now shut, and my children are with me in bed ; I cannot rise and give thee. [8]..Though he will not rise and give him, because he is his friend, yet because of his importunity he will rise and give him as many as he needeth.—Luke, ch. 11.

2575. —— **Lack of.** *Joash.* [18] He said, Take the arrows..Smite upon the ground. And he smote thrice, and stayed. [19] And the man of God was wroth with him, and said, Thou shouldest have smitten five or six times ; then hadst thou smitten Syria till thou hadst consumed *it :* whereas now thou shalt smite Syria *but* thrice. —2 Kings, ch. 13.

2576. —— **rewarded.** *Bethesda.* [4] An angel went down at a certain season into the pool, and troubled the water ; whosoever then first after the troubling of the water stepped in, was made whole of whatsoever disease he had.— John, ch. 5.

2577. —— **Safety by.** *Lot.* [17] When they had brought them forth..he said, Escape for thy life ; look not behind thee, neither stay thou in all the plain : escape to the mountain, lest thou be consumed.—Gen., ch. 19.

2578. —— —— *Bartimeus.* [47] *Thou* Son of David, have mercy on me. [48] And many charged him that he should hold his peace : but he cried the more a great deal, *Thou* Son of David, have mercy on me. [49] And Jesus stood still, and commanded him to be called..Be of good comfort, rise ; he calleth thee.—Mark, ch. 10.

2579. —— **A Seeker's.** *Palsy.* [3] They come.. bringing one sick of the palsy, which was borne of four. [4] And when they could not come nigh unto him for the press, they uncovered the roof where he was : and when they had broken *it* up, they let down the bed wherein the sick of the palsy lay.—Mark, ch. 2.

See other illustrations under :

2580. EARTHQUAKE, Battle with. *Philistines.* [15] There was trembling in the host, in the field, and among all the people : the garrison, and the spoilers, they also trembled, and the earth quaked : so it was a very great trembling. —1 SAM., ch. 14.

2581. —— **Deliverance by.** *Paul and Silas.* [26] Suddenly there was a great earthquake, so that the foundations of the prison were shaken : and immediately all the doors were opened, and every one's bands were loosed.—ACTS, ch. 16.

2582. —— **A destructive.** *Korah.* [31] The ground clave asunder that *was* under them : [32] And the earth opened her mouth, and swallowed them up, and their houses, and all the men that *appertained* unto Korah, and all *their* goods.—NUM., ch. 16.

2583. —— **A responsive.** *Calvary.* [50] Jesus, when he had cried again with a loud voice, yielded up the ghost. [51] And, behold, the vail of the temple was rent in twain from the top to the bottom ; and the earth did quake, and the rocks rent.—MAT., ch. 27.

2584. —— **at Sinai.** *Moses.* [18] Mount Sinai was altogether on a smoke, because the Lord descended upon it in fire : and the smoke thereof ascended as the smoke of a furnace, and the whole mount quaked greatly.—EX., ch. 19.

2585. —— —— *Elijah.* [11] After the wind an earthquake ; *but* the Lord *was* not in the earthquake : [12] And after the earthquake a fire. —1 KINGS, ch. 19.

2586. EASE, Care for. *Loan of Bread.* [See No. 2574.]

2587. —— **of Indifference.** *Jews.* [8] If ye offer the blind for sacrifice, *is it* not evil ? and if ye offer the lame and sick, *is it* not evil ? offer it now unto thy governor ; will he be pleased with thee, or accept thy person ?—MAL., ch. 1.

2588. —— **vainly promised.** *Dives.* [18] And there will I bestow all my fruits and my goods. [19] And I will say..Soul, thou hast much goods laid up for many years ; take thine ease, eat, drink, *and* be merry. [20] But God said unto him, Thou fool, this night thy soul shall be required. —LUKE, ch. 12.

2589. —— **Religious.** *In Zion.* [1] Woe to them *that are* at ease in Zion, and trust in the mountain of Samaria, *which are* named chief of the nations, to whom the house of Israel came. —AMOS, ch. 6.

See other illustrations under :

INDIFFERENCE.
Hearing. Foolish man who built..upon the sand 4405
Inconsiderate. Here is thy pound which I have 4406
Provoking. Wrath because..have not hearkened 4407
Pitiless. Saw him and passed by..other side 4408
Sin. I have sinned..What is that to us? 4409
Sinners. Made light of it, and went their ways 4410
Unbelievers. They did eat..until the day Noe 4411

INDIFFERENT.
Curse. Curse ye, Meroz..came not..help of the L. 4412
Woe. Woe unto them that are at ease in Zion 4413

INDOLENCE.
Exhibited. I went by the field of the slothful 4436
Excuse. There is a lion without..I shall be slain 4437
Perfect. Hand..not so much as bring it to his 4438
Shame. Sleepeth in harvest..causeth shame 4439
Wasteful. Slothful in his work..a great waster 4440

LEISURE.
Without. They had no leisure so much as to eat 4938
" They could not so much as eat bread 4939

SLUGGARD.
Reproved. Go to the ant, thou sluggard 8145
Vexatious. As smoke to the eyes, so is the sluggard 8146
" Way of the slothful..full of thorns 8147

Neglect. What honour hath been done to Mordecai 5696
Poor. When saw we thee a hungered..in prison 5709
Ungrateful. Yet did not the chief butler remember 3096

2590. EATING, Bigotry limits. *Pharisees.* [1] Then drew near unto him all the publicans and sinners for to hear him. [2] And the Pharisees and scribes murmured, saying, This man receiveth sinners, and eateth with them.— LUKE, ch. 15.

2591. —— **Conscientious.** *Paul.* [13] If any of them that believe not bid you *to a feast*, and ye be disposed to go ; whatsoever is set before you, eat, asking no question for conscience' sake. [28] But if any man say unto you, This is offered in sacrifice unto idols, eat not for his sake that shewed it, and for conscience' sake.—1 COR., ch. 10.

2592. —— **Considerate.** *Paul.* [13] If meat make my brother to offend, I will eat no flesh while the world standeth, lest I make my brother to offend.—1 COR., ch. 8.

2593. —— **Caste in.** *Egyptian.* [32] They set on for him by himself, and for them by themselves, and for the Egyptians, which did eat with him, by themselves : because the Egyptians might not eat bread with the Hebrews ; for that *is* an abomination unto the Egyptians.— GEN., ch. 43.

2594. —— **prevented.** *Jesus.* [20] The multitude cometh together again, so that they could not so much as eat bread. [21] And when his friends heard *of it*, they went out to lay hold on him : for they said, He is beside himself.— MARK, ch. 3.

2595. —— **by Grief.** *Hannah.* [6] Her adversary also provoked her sore, for to make her fret.. [7] ..he did so year by year, when she went up to the house of the Lord..therefore she wept, and did not eat.—1 SAM., ch. 1.

2596. —— **restricted.** *Eden.* [16] Of every tree of the garden thou mayest freely eat : [17] But of the tree of the knowledge of good and evil, thou shalt not eat of it : for in the day that thou eatest thereof thou shalt surely die. —GEN., ch. 2.

2597. —— **Separation.** *Paul.* [11] I have written unto you not to keep company, if any man that is called a brother be a fornicator, or covetous, or an idolater, or a railer, or a drunkard, or an extortioner ; with such a one no not to eat. —1 COR., ch. 5.

2598. —— **Trial in.** *Judas.* [18] As they sat and did eat, Jesus said, Verily I say unto you, One of you which eateth with me shall betray me.—MARK, ch. 14.

2599. —— **No Time for.** *Jesus.* [31] Come ye yourselves apart into a desert place, and rest a while : for there were many coming and going, and they had no leisure so much as to eat.— MARK, ch. 6.

See other illustrations under:

ABSTINENCE.

Extreme. Nazarite..wine..strong drink..moist   20
Excitement. Saul was three days..eat or drink   21
Famishing. Found an Egyptian..when he had eaten 22
Mourning. David sware..if I taste bread   23
Necessitated. Desert place..no leisure..to eat   24
Passionate. Jonathan..fierce anger..eat no meat   25
Priestly. Not drink wine..go into the tabernacle   26
Peril. Paul besought them to take meat [shipwreck] 27
Protracted. Moses..40 days..neither eat..drink   28
    "   Jesus..40 days..afterward a hungered   29
Self-denying. David would not drink..jeopardy   30
Sorrowful. Child sick..David fasted..lay..on the   31
Total. [Rechabites] Drink no wine..father com.   32

APPETITE.

Control. Put a knife to thy throat if..appetite   479
Dangers. We remember fish, cucumbers, melons   480
Heedless. [Pursuing Philistines,] people were faint 481
Sin. Who shall give us flesh?..be [loathsome]   482
Temptation. [Jesus] fasted 40 days..afterward   483
Unrestrained. At the point to die, what profit   484

FAMINE.

Charity. Disciples determined to send relief   3023
Care. Shall eat bread by weight..water by   3024
Dying. Eaten no bread..three days..sick   3025
Distress. Delicate woman..children..eat them   3026
Exiled. Sojourn wherever thou canst..seven   3027
Escape. Abram went into Egypt..famine   3028
Emigration. Elimelech went to sojourn in..famine 3029
Inhumanity. Give thy son, that we may eat him   3030
Sin. I will break the staff of bread   3031
  " Ye have forsaken the..L. and followed   3032
Seven Years. No bread..land of Canaan fainted   3033
Spiritual. I will send a famine..words of the L.   3034
Water. To kill us and our children..cattle   3035

FEAST.

Ancient. Sarah..made cakes..Abraham..calf   3172
Birthday. Herod on his birthday made a supper   3173
Charitable. Call the poor, the lame..blind   3174
Complimentary. At Bethany..they made Jesus a 3175
    "   Levi made Jesus a great feast   3176
Death. Job's sons and daughters..brother's house 3177
Ended sadly. Merry with wine..smite Amnon   3178
Farewell. Elisha..oxen, and slew them..people   3179
Great. Solomon offered 22,000 oxen and 120,000 s. 3180
Idolatrous. [Calf] People..eat..drink..rose up to 3181
Impious. Belshazzar made a feast to a thousand   3182
Joyous. [Tabernacles] Seven days shall dwell in 3183
Marriage. Jesus and his disciples were called   3184
National. Three times..keep a feast unto me..year 3186
Royal. Ahasuerus made a feast at Shushan   3185

FOOD.

Animal. Every moving thing..shall be meat for   3286
Better than. Esteemed the words..more than my 3287
Cleansed. What G. had cleansed..call not   3288
Costly. Jacob gave Esau bread and pottage and 3289
Chosen. Let them give us pulse to eat..water   3290
Daily. Give us this day our daily bread   3292
Diminished. [Sin] Given you cleanness of teeth   3293
Perilous. Jonathan..taste a little honey..must die 3312
Example. Conscience of him which is weak..emb. 3294
Forbidden. Ye may eat of..trees of the garden   3295
Favorite. I am old..take me some venison..I love 3296
Friendship. Isaac loved Esau because..of his ven. 3297
Famine. Besieged Samaria..ass's head..80 silver 3298
Freedom to gather. Neighbour's vineyard..eat   3299
God honoured. Eat either bread nor..until..offer. 3300
God gives. Consider the ravens..God feedeth them 3301
Heavenly. L. evermore give us of this bread   3302

Life-giving. Lest..take..tree of life, and live   3303
Miraculous. L. brought quails from the sea   3304
    "   Elijah..ravens brought him bread   3305
    "   Elijah..angel..cake baken on the   3306
    "   [5000 fed] Did all eat, and were filled 3307
    "   [100 fed] Twelve loaves of barley   3308
    "   [Manna] Did eat manna 40 years   3309
Necessity. Better than..honoureth himself and   3310
Natural. John..his meat was locusts and wild   3311
Prohibited. Life of the flesh is in the blood   3313
    "   Eat no..fat of ox, sheep, or goat   3314
Prudence. Fed you with milk, not with meat   3315
Promised. Trust in the L. and do good..be fed   3316
    "   He that walketh righteously..bread   3317
Restricted. Beasts..parteth the hoof..cheweth the 3318
Scarcity. Handful of meal..little oil..eat, and die 3319
Supplies. Solomon's provision for one day..20 oxen 3320
Spiritual. Labour..meat which endureth..life   3321
Scruples. Some with conscience of the idol..eat it 3322
Thanks. Jesus took bread, and blessed it, and   3323
    "   Jesus blessed and brake the loaves, and 3324
    "   [Paul shipwrecked] took bread, and gave 3325
Temptation in. Fasted 40 days..tempter came   3326
Weeping. Every man in the door of his tent   3327

HUNGER.

Appetizing. To the hungry soul every bitter..sweet 4209
Disappointment. Fig tree in the way..nothing   4211
Lawful. Sabbath..disciples began to pluck..corn 4215
Murmuring. When we sat by the fleshpots..full 4216
Overcome. I have meat to eat ye know not of   4217
Removed. I am the bread of life..never hunger   4218
Subdued by. I will arise, and go to my father   4219
Temptation. Tempter came..stones be made   4220

HOSPITALITY.

Christian. Paul entered..a certain man's house   4098
Dangerous. Come home..and eat..I may not   4099
Forbidden. Diotrephes..forbiddeth them that   4100
Grateful. Mephibosheth shall eat at the king's   4101
Increase by. How shall I..before 100 men?   4102
Joyful. Zaccheus..haste..received him joyfully   4103
Odious. Baser sort..assaulted the house of Jason 4104
Preservation. Tarry all night, and wash your feet 4105
of Poor. Widow did according to the saying of E. 4106
Pagan. Barbarous people..received us every one 4107
Refused. Samaritans did not receive him   4108
Repaid. Shunammite..make a little chamber   4109
Reward. Abraham ran to meet them   4110
Treacherous. Pharisee brought him to dine with 4111
Unjust. Rich man..took the poor man's lamb   4112
Urgent. Lot pressed them greatly..his house   4113
    "   Urged him, therefore he lodged there   4114
    "   They constrained him..sat at meat   4115
Woman's. Lydia..came into my house..constrain'd 4116
Willing. Ungirded his camels..set meat before him 4117
Wanting. Simon, thou gavest me no water to wash 4118

TEMPERANCE.

Advised. Drink no wine, nor strong drink   8659
Eating. His dainties..are deceitful meat   8661
Health. Proved them ten days..fairer and fatter 8663
Hereditary. Our father commanded us..drink   8662
Mastery. Striveth for mastery is temperate   8664
Piety. [J. B.] Neither wine nor strong drink   8660
Strength. [Mother of Samson] Drink no wine   8660

Criticised. Behold, a gluttonous man, and a wine 3577

2600. ECONOMY in Food. *Jesus.* [Five thousand people.] [12] When they were filled, he said unto his disciples, Gather up the fragments that remain, that nothing be lost.—JOHN, ch. 6.

2601. ——— False. *Apostles.* [3] A woman having an alabaster box of ointment of spikenard very precious ; and she brake the box, and poured *it* on his head. ⁴ And there were some..said, Why was this waste of the ointment made? ⁵ For it might have been sold for more than three hundred pence, and have been given to the poor.—MARK, ch. 14.

See other illustrations under :

Excessive. There is that scattereth..yet increaseth 4367
See **MONEY.**

2602. EDUCATION by Monuments. *Stones.* ⁶ When your children ask *their fathers* in time to come, saying, What *mean* ye by these stones? ⁷ Then ye shall answer them, That the waters of Jordan were cut off before the ark of the covenant of the Lord.—JOSH., ch. 4.

2603. —— neglected. *Nehemiah.* ²³ In those days also saw I Jews *that* had married wives of Ashdod, of Ammon, *and* of Moab : ²⁴ And their children spake half in the speech of Ashdod, and could not speak in the Jews' language, but according to the language of each people.—NEH., ch. 13.

2604. —— Preparatory. *Four Hebrews.* ³ The king spake unto Ashpenaz..that he should bring *certain*..of the king's seed, and of the princes ; ⁴ Children in whom *was* no blemish, but well favoured, and skilful in all wisdom, and cunning in knowledge, and understanding science, and such as *had* ability in them to stand in the king's palace, and whom they might teach the learning and the tongue of the Chaldeans.—DAN., ch. 1.

See other illustrations under :

INSTRUCTION.
Better than Practice. Not move one of their f's. 4541
Children. Teach them [law] thy sons..sons' sons 4542
Course. Three years..might stand before the king 4543
Humble. A. and Priscilla..expounded unto Apollos 4544
Important. Heareth, and understandeth it not 4545
Improvement. Be an ornament of grace unto thy 4546
Personal. [See No. 4544.]
Public. Ezra brought the law..all that could hear 4548
Private. Came man to him [Paul] into his lodging 4549

KNOWLEDGE.
Adamic. Gave names to all cattle..fowl..beast 4853
Detrimental. Man is come to know good and evil 4854
Forbidden. Tree of the knowledge..shalt not eat 4855
Faith to. Believe not because of thy saying..heard 4856
Guilt. Better for them not to have known the way 4857
Grace. Perceived they were unlearned men 4858
Ignorance. I go bound in the spirit..not knowing 4859
Responsibility. Known that the ox hath used to 4860
Spiritual. I know that my Redeemer liveth 4861
Temptation. Woman saw..tree..make one wise 4862
Used. Whosoever heareth..taketh not warning 4863

SCHOOL.
Christianity. Paul..disputing daily in the school 7605
Gospel. In every house they ceased not..teach 7606
Home. These words..teach..in thine house 7607
Synagogue. Jesus went..teaching in their's. 7608

LEARNING.
Profound. Moses was learned in all the wisdom 4931
Superior. Jews marvelled..how knoweth this man 4932
Worship. Came wise men from the east..worship 4933

STUDY.
Bible. Eunuch..sitting in his chariot read Esaias 8397
Commended. These were more noble..searched 8398
Beneficial. Hearts burn..opened to us the 8399
Wearisome. Much study is a weariness to the flesh 8400

TEACHER.
Authoritative. Jesus taught them as one having 8611
Art. Bezaleel..carving..he may teach 8612
Great. Jesus went about..teaching in..synagogues 8613
Home. Thou shalt teach them..in thine house 8614
Necessary. Understandest thou..? How can I 8615
Prepared. Come up..mount..that thou mayest 8616
Spirit. When they bring you..H. G. shall teach 8617

TEACHING.
Culture. Ornament of grace unto thy head 1865
Divine. G. hath shewed me..not call..common 8618
Ministerial. In the temple they ceased not to teach 8619

2605. EFFORT, Concentrated. *On Ahab.* ³¹ The king of Syria commanded his thirty and two captains..over his chariots, saying, Fight neither with small nor great, save only with the king of Israel.—1 KINGS, ch. 22.

2606. —— Delivering. *Four Lepers.* ³ Why sit we here until we die? ⁴ If we say, We will enter into the city, then the famine *is* in the city, and we shall die there : and if we sit still here, we die also. Now therefore come, and let us fall unto the host of the Syrians : if they save us alive, we shall live ; and if they kill us, we shall but die.—2 KINGS, ch. 7. [The Syrians fled before them.]

2607. —— Fruitless. *Darius.* ¹⁴ The king ..was sore displeased with himself, and set *his* heart on Daniel to deliver him : and he laboured till the going down of the sun to deliver him. —DAN., ch. 6.

2608. —— Humble. *Loose the Napkin.* ⁴⁴ He that was dead came forth, bound hand and foot with graveclothes ; and his face was bound about with a napkin. Jesus saith..Loose him, and let him go.—JOHN, ch. 11.

2609. —— Ill-considered. *Building.* ²⁸ Which of you, intending to build a tower, sitteth not down first, and counteth the cost..? ²⁹ Lest haply, after he hath laid the foundation, and is not able to finish *it*, all that behold *it* begin to mock him, ³⁰ Saying, This man began to build, and was not able to finish.—LUKE, ch. 14.

2610. —— Personal. *Me..My Daughter.* ²² Behold, a woman of Canaan came..and cried unto him, saying, Have mercy on me, O Lord *thou* Son of David ; my daughter is grievously vexed with a devil.—MAT., ch. 15.

2611. —— Sphere of. *Christian.* ⁸ Ye shall be witnesses unto me both in Jerusalem, and in all Judea, and in Samaria, and unto the uttermost part of the earth. ⁹ And when he had spoken these things, while they beheld, he was taken up.—ACTS, ch. 1.

2612. —— A single. *King Saul.* ⁸ Said Abishai to David..let me smite him, I pray thee, with the spear even to the earth at once, and I will not *smite* him the second time.—1 SAM., ch. 26.

2613. —— Singleness of. *Paul.* ¹ Came not with excellency of speech or of wisdom, declaring unto you the testimony of God. ² For I determined not to know any thing among you, save Jesus Christ, and him crucified.—1 COR., ch. 2.

2614. —— Union in. *In Babylon.* ⁵ Then rose up the chief of the fathers of Judah and Benjamin, and the priests, and the Levites, with all *them* whose spirit God had raised, to go up to build the house of the Lord which *is* in Jerusalem. ⁶ And all they that *were* about them strengthened their hands with vessels of silver, with gold, with goods, and with beasts, and with precious things, besides all *that* was willingly offered.—EZRA, ch. 1.

2615. —— *Tabernacle.* ²² They came, both men and women, as many as were willing hearted, *and* brought bracelets, and earrings, and rings, and tablets, all jewels of gold : and every man that offered, *offered* an offering of gold unto the Lord.—Ex., ch. 35.

2616. —— **Unavailing.** *Disobedient.* ⁵ Thus saith the Lord of hosts ; Consider your ways. ⁶ Ye have sown much, and bring in little ; ye eat, but ye have not enough ; ye drink, but ye are not filled with drink ; ye clothe you, but there is none warm ; and he that earneth wages, earneth wages *to put it* into a bag with holes.— HAG., ch. 1.

2617. —— **Victory without.** *Moabites and Ammonites.* ¹⁷ Ye shall not *need* to fight in this *battle :* set yourselves, stand ye *still,* and see the salvation of the Lord with you, O Judah and Jerusalem : fear not, nor be dismayed. — 2 CHRON., ch. 20.

See other illustrations under :
MEANS.
Defence. Hezekiah..built up the walls..made   5255
Escape. They let him down the wall in a basket   5256
Heroic. Soldiers cut off the ropes of the boat   5257
Ingenious. Ark of bulrushes..pitch..stood   5258
Insignificant. Touched he their eyes..eyes were   5259
Not neglected. Take a lump of figs..laid it on the   5260
Prayer. We made our prayer..set a watch..day   5261
Prudential. Jesus..would not walk in Jewry   5262
Strange. Moses..rod of God..held up his hand   5263
"   Sound of the trumpet..people shouted   5264
Use of. Think on me when it shall be well with thee   5265
Unworthy. If I make not thy life..went for his   5266

DETERMINATION.
Evil. We will certainly..burn incense to the queen   2260
Fixed. In every city bonds..none..move me   2261
"   As the L. liveth..I will not leave thee   2262
Resolute. Absalom said..set it on fire   2263
Wanting. I will let him go..Pilate gave sentence   2264
See WORK and references.

2618. ELOQUENCE, Better than. *In Midian.* ¹⁰ Moses said..O my Lord, I *am* not eloquent.. but I *am* slow of speech, and of a slow tongue. ¹¹ And the Lord said..Who hath made man's mouth ? or who maketh the dumb, or deaf, or the seeing, or the blind ? have not I the Lord ? ¹². .I will be with thy mouth, and teach thee what thou shalt say.—Ex., ch. 4.

2619. —— **Ministerial.** *Apollos.* ²⁴ A certain Jew named Apollos, born at Alexandria, an eloquent man, *and* mighty in the scriptures, came to Ephesus.—ACTS, ch. 18

See other illustrations under :
SPEAKER.
Convincing. Never man spake like this man   8245
Engaging. Mary..sat at Jesus' feet, and heard   8246

SPEAKING.
Evil. He that speaketh evil of his brother..of the   8241
Help. Filled with the H. S..gave them utterance   8242
for God. Say not I am a child..thou shalt..speak   8243
"   Be not afraid of their faces..with thee   8244

SPEECH.
Assisted. I am not eloquent..with thy mouth   8247
"   I can not speak..I shall send thee   8243
Appropriate. Apples of gold in pictures of silver   8249
Anointed. Tongues like..fire, it sat upon each   8250
Constrained. I am full of matter..constraineth me 8251
Cautious. Be not rash with thy mouth..hasty   8252
Confusion. L. did there confound the language   8253
Dangers of. Took counsel..entangled..speech   8254
Evidence. Bridleth not his tongue..religion is   8255
Gifts of. It shall be given you what ye shall speak   8256
Improved. Had an impediment..touched his   8257
Impossible. Not having a wedding garment   8258
Plainness. My speech was not with enticing   8259
Power of. Death and life..in the power of the   8260
Unrestrained. With flattering lips and a double   8261
Unentangled. Render unto Cesar..unto G..they   8262
Unguarded. Openeth wide his lips shall have   8263
Useless. Jesus answered Pilate to never a word   8264
"   Herod questioned..answered him n.   8265

Effective. Paul reasoned..Felix trembled   6453
Irresistible. Not able to resist the..spirit   96
Spiritual. My preaching..demonstration..power   6463

2620. EMIGRATION from Famine. *Shunammite.* ¹ The Lord hath called for a famine ; and it shall also come upon the land seven years. ² And the woman..did after the saying of the man of God..and sojourned in the land of the Philistines seven years.—2 KINGS, ch. 8.

2621. —— **An immense.** *From Egypt.* ³⁷ The children of Israel journeyed..about six hundred thousand on foot *that were* men, beside children. ³⁸ And a mixed multitude went up also with them ; and flocks, and herds, *even* very much cattle.—Ex., ch. 12.

See other illustrations under :
BANISHMENT.
Paradise. He drove out the man   629
Punishment. Will not do the law..to banishment   630

CAPTIVES.
Compassion. I have heard..groaning..bondage   1022
Kindness. Gave them to eat..feeble upon asses   1024
Mercy. Shalt not smite..set bread..go   1025
Mourning. By the rivers of Babylon..we wept   1026
Songless. How shall we sing..strange land   1027
Return. Come to Zion with songs..joy and   1028
Sin. Walked in the sins of..until removed   1029
"   L. strengthened..Moab against I...done evil   1030
Unexpected. David and his men..wives..captives   1031
Victorious. Found a jawbone..slew 1000 men   1023

EXILE.
Command. [Abram] Get thee out of thy country   2802
Criminal. David mourned..Absalom fled   2803
Infant. Take the young child..mother..Egypt   2804
Necessary. Flee..to Laban my brother, to Haran   2805
Painful. Sold Joseph to the Ishmaelites..into E.   2806

FOREIGNER.
Despised. My master hath spared Naaman this S.   3331
Discrimination. Every creditor..of a foreigner   3332
Homesick. Hadad said to Pharaoh, Let me depart 3333
Ineligible. King over thee..not set a stranger   3334

FOREIGNERS.
Increase. Israel were fruitful..increased   3335
Jealousy. War, they join also unto our enemies   3336
Liberality to. One law shall be..homeborn   3347

Safety. Pharaoh sought to slay Moses..fled   3489

2622. EMOTION exhibited. *Josiah.* ¹⁰ Shaphan read it before the king. ¹¹ And..when the king had heard the words of the book of the law..he rent his clothes.—2 Kings, ch. 22.

2623. —— Irrepressible. *Joseph.* [30] Joseph made haste ; for his bowels did yearn upon his brother : and he sought *where* to weep ; and he entered into *his* chamber, and wept there. [31] And he washed his face, and went out, and refrained himself.—Gen., ch. 43.

2624. —— in Worship. *Jews.* [9] Nehemiah.. and Ezra the priest the scribe, and the Levites.. said unto all the people, This day *is* holy unto the Lord your God ; mourn not, nor weep. For all the people wept, when they heard the words of the law.—Neh., ch. 8.

2625. EMOTIONS changed. *Disciples.* [20] He shewed unto them *his* hands and his side. Then were the disciples glad, when they saw the Lord. —John, ch. 20.

2626. —— Mixed. *Jews.* [12] Ancient men, that had seen the first house, when the foundation of this house was laid before their eyes, wept with a loud voice ; and many shouted aloud for joy : [13] So that the people could not discern the noise of the shout of joy from the noise of the weeping of the people.—Ezra, ch. 3.

2627. —— —— To the Marys. [7] Go quickly, and tell his disciples that he is risen from the dead ; and behold, he goeth before you into Galilee ; there shall ye see him.. [8] And they departed quickly from the sepulchre with fear and great joy.—Mat., ch. 28.

2628. —— Opposite. *At Jerusalem.* [38] Blessed *be* the King that cometh in the name of the Lord : Peace in heaven, and glory in the highest. [39] And some of the Pharisees..said..Master, rebuke thy disciples. [40] And he answered.. I tell you, that if these should hold their peace, the stones would immediately cry out.—Luke, ch. 19.

See other illustrations under :

AGITATION.

Deception. Who art thou?..Esau..Isaac trembled ... 256
Diffuses. Disputed he in the synagogue..market ... 257
Deplored. [Israelites] Made..abhorred..slay us ... 258
General. [Philistines] Trembling in the host..field ... 259
Mount. Sinai..quaked greatly ... 260
Overcome. [At sepulchre] Keepers did shake ... 261
Physical. Belshazzar's thoughts troubled..knees ... 262
Terror. [Job's vision] Trembling..my bones ... 263

ALARM.

Conscience. Pray for thy servants..we die not ... 273
Death. Egyptians were urgent..we be all dead ... 274
Failure. Priests..doubted..whereunto this would ... 275
Manifestation. Belshazzar..countenance was ... 276
Preaching. Paul reasoned..Felix trembled ... 277
Reasonable. Esau cometh..400 men..Jacob ... 278
Superstitious. Jesus walking on the sea..troubled ... 279
Sinners. Adam and his wife hid themselves ... 280
" Let not God speak with us..die ... 281
Sudden. Seeing the prison doors open..sword ... 282
Spiritual. Sirs, what must I do to be saved? ... 283
Tempest. Entreat..be no more mighty thunderings ... 284
Unnecessary. My money is restored..heart failed ... 285

FEELING.

Compassionate. Samaritan..had compassion ... 3191
Past. Could not believe..hardened their heart ... 3192
Without. Levite looked..passed by on the other ... 3193

FEELINGS.

Concealed. Joseph wept..washed his face, and ... 3194
Control. Joseph turned himself about and wept ... 3195
Music. How shall we sing..in a strange land ... 3196
Responsive. Jesus was moved with compassion ... 3197
Strong. Jesus wept ... 3198
Suppressed. Haman was full of indignation ... 3199

TEARS.

Affectionate. I wrote unto you with many tears ... 8620
Bereavement. Mary weeping..Jews weeping ... 8621
" Where have ye laid him?..how he ... 8622
Constant. Mine eye trickleth down, and ceaseth ... 8623
Desired. O that mine..eyes a fountain of tears ... 8624
Disregarded. Chasten thy son..not spare for his ... 8625
End of. G. shall wipe away all tears ... 8626
Grateful. She hath washed my feet with tears ... 8627
Night. Water my couch with tears ... 8628
Precious. Put thou my tears into thy bottle ... 8629
Patriotic. Jesus beheld the city, and wept over it ... 8630
Power. The babe wept..she had compassion ... 8631
" Samson's wife wept before him ... 8632
Parting. Wept one with another..David exceeded ... 8633
Penitential. When Peter thought thereon, he wept ... 8634
Transient. Saul lifted up his voice, and wept ... 8635

See REJOICING *and* WEEPING.

2629. EMPLOYMENT Honoured. *Jesus.* [3] Is not this the carpenter, the son of Mary, the brother of James, and of Joses, and of Juda, and Simon ? and are not his sisters here with us?— Mark, ch. 6.

2630. —— in Innocence. *Eden.* [28] Replenish the earth, and subdue it : and have dominion over the fish of the sea, and over the fowl of the air, and over every living thing.—Gen., ch. 1. [15] And the Lord God took the man, and put him into the garden of Eden to dress it and to keep it.—Gen., ch. 2.

See other illustrations under:

BUSINESS.

Capacity [Pharaoh to Joseph] None so discreet ... 985
Diligence. Man diligent in business..stand before ... 986
Frauds. Take thy bill, quickly..write fifty ... 988
Spiritual. [Stewards] Men..honest..full of H. S. ... 991
Success. Joseph gathered up all the money ... 993
Talent. The feebler [cattle] were Laban's ... 994

INDUSTRY.

Active. Rebekah..let down their pitcher..hasted ... 4442
Benevolence. Shewing the coats..Dorcas had m. ... 4443
Commended. Go to the ant, thou sluggard ... 4444
Domestic. [Model woman—Prov., ch. 31] ... 4445
Independent. Paul had gathered a bundle of sticks ... 4446
Jesus. Mighty works are wrought..the carpenter ... 4447
Promotion. Solomon seeing..he was industrious ... 4448
Required. If any would not work, neither should ... 4449

LABOUR.

Advantage. Sleep of a labouring man is sweet..eat ... 4864
Curse. Thorns and thistles..sweat of thy face ... 4865
Commanded. Six days shalt thou labour ... 4866
Congenial. Put him into the garden..keep it ... 4867
Co-operative. One soweth, another reapeth ... 4868
Degradation. In the sweat of thy face ... 4869
Increase. No straw be given..tale of bricks ... 4870
Menial. Hewers of wood and drawers of water ... 4871
Motive. That..we may be accepted of him ... 4872

BUILDER.

Jotham. Built cities in the mountains..castles, and ... 953
Unsuccessful. Laid the foundation..not able ... 954
Visionary. I will pull down my barns and build ... 955

ENGRAVING.

Inspired. Bezaleel..in cutting of stones..carving	2671
Lord's. Tables..writing of G. graven upon the	2672
Law. Set thee up great stones..plaster..write	2673

MECHANIC.

Apostle. [Paul and Aquila] were tentmakers	5268
Christ. Is not this the carpenter?..offended	5269
Expert. Hiram..worker in brass..came to S.	5270
Independence. Not be chargeable..wrought	5272
Lost. No smith..lest Hebrews make swords	5277
Original. Tubal Cain an instructor of..artificer	5271
Opposition. Alexander the coppersmith did..harm	5273
" Called workmen of like occupation	5274
Renown. Not any..hew timber..like Sidonians	5276

2631. ENCAMPMENT, An immense. *Israelites.*
[37] The children of Israel journeyed..about six
hundred thousand on foot *that were* men, beside
children. [38] And a mixed multitude went up
also with them ; and flocks, and herds, *even* very
much cattle.—Ex., ch. 12. [See No. 2621.]

2632. ENCOURAGEMENT, Angelic. *Jacob.*
[1] Jacob went on his way, and the angels of God
met him. [2] And..he said, This *is* God's host :
and he called the name of that place Mahanaim.
—Gen., ch. 32.

2633. —— from Above. *Jesus.* [1] Let us run
with patience the race that is set before us,
[2] Looking unto Jesus the author and finisher of
our faith ; who for the joy that was set before
him endured the cross, despising the shame.—
Heb., ch. 12.

2634. —— in Affliction. *Paul.* [17] If so be
that we suffer with *him*, that we may be also
glorified together. [18] For I reckon that the sufferings of this present time *are* not worthy *to be
compared* with the glory which shall be revealed
in us.—Rom., ch. 8.

2635. —— from Example. *Shipwrecked.*
[33] This day is the fourteenth day that ye have
tarried and continued fasting.. [35] And..he took
bread, and gave thanks to God in presence of
them all ; and when he had broken *it*, he began to eat. [36] Then were they all of good cheer,
and they also took *some* meat.—Acts, ch. 27.

2636. —— Fraternal. *Paul.* [14] We found
brethren, and were desired to tarry with them
seven days : and so we went toward Rome,
[15] And from thence, when the brethren heard of
us, they came to meet us as far as Appii Forum,
and the Three Taverns ; whom when Paul saw,
he thanked God, and took courage.—Acts, ch.
28.

2637. —— in God. *Ziklag.* [3] David and his
men came to the city, and, behold, *it was* burned
with fire ; and their wives, and their sons, and
their daughters, were taken captives. [6] And David was greatly distressed ; for the people spake
of stoning him, because the soul of all the people was grieved,·every man for his sons and for
his daughters : but David encouraged himself
in the Lord his God.—1 Sam., ch. 30.

2638. —— Hopeful. *Bartimeus.* [49] Jesus..
commanded him to be called. And they call
the blind man, saying unto him, Be of good
comfort, rise ; he calleth thee. [50] And he, casting away his garment, rose, and came to Jesus.
—Mark, ch. 10.

2639. —— from the Past. *Moses.* [4] Ye have
seen what I did unto the Egyptians, and how I

bare you on eagles' wings, and brought you unto
myself. [5] Now therefore, if ye will obey my voice
indeed, and keep my covenant, then ye shall be a
peculiar treasure unto me above all people.—
Ex., ch. 19.

2640. —— Substantial. *Rebuilding the Temple.*
[6] All they that ·*were* about them strengthened
their hands with vessels of silver, with gold,
with goods, and with beasts, and with precious
things, besides all *that* was willingly offered.—
Ezra., ch. 1.

Religious. David danced before the L..shouting 4747
Recovery. [At Samaria] Great joy in that city 4748
Success. [Walls erected] Joy of Jerusalem..afar 4749
Supreme. Not that the spirits are subject..names 4750
Song of. Hath put a new song in my mouth 4751
Weeping. Joseph could not refrain..wept aloud 4752
Want. Although the fig tree shall not blossom 4753
Worship. How amiable are they tabernacles 4754

REJOICING.
Communion. This poor man cried..O taste and see 6968
Conversion. There was great joy in that city 6969
Converts. [Jailer] rejoiced, believing in G. with 6971
"   I waited patiently..put a new song in 6972
"   The eunuch went on his way rejoicing 6973
Duty. Thou shalt rejoice in every good thing..G. 6974
Deliverance. I will sing unto the L..triumphed 6975
"   Jews had light, and gladness, and 6976
Great. At the descent of the mount of Olives 6978
Heavenly. Ransomed of the L..come..with songs 6980
in Prison. At midnight Paul and Silas..sang 6981
in Persecutions. Rejoicing that they were counted 6982
Premature. [Amalekites] were eating and drinking 6983
in Reproach. Rejoice..be exceeding glad..reward 6985
in Tribulation. I am exceeding joyful in all our 6986
in Temptation. Count it all joy when ye fall into 6987
Victors. Praised their god..hearts were merry 6988

2641. ENCUMBRANCES, Removal of. *Fig Tree.* ⁷ Said he unto the dresser of his vineyard, Behold, these three years I come seeking fruit on this fig tree, and find none : cut it down ; why cumbereth it the ground ?—LUKE, ch. 13.´

See other illustrations under :

HINDERANCE.
Disobedience. Say nothing to any man..blaze 3979
Natural. Let me..kiss my father..mother 3980
Provoking. Let us pass through thy country 3981
Removed. Angel..rolled back the stone..door 3982
Riches. Deceitfulness of riches..choke the word 3983
"   Easier for a camel..needle's eye than 3984

HINDERANCES.
Care. Take heed lest..become a stumblingblock 3985
Malicious. People of the land hired counsellors 3986
Removed. I will eat no flesh while the world 3987
Secular. I have bought..bought..married 3988
Social. Let me first go bid them farewell 3989
Selfish. Neither go in yourself, neither suffer ye 3990

HINDERING.
Fear. It is reported..Jews think to rebel 3991
Intrigue. Let us meet..in the plain of Ono 3992

2642. ENDURANCE rewarded. *Jesus.* ¹³ Ye shall be hated of all *men* for my name's sake : but he that shall endure unto the end, the same shall be saved.—MARK, ch. 13.

See other illustrations under :

FORBEARANCE.
Divine. A king shall reign..G. was your king 3328
"   I come seeking fruit, and find none 3329
Pious. David..hast rewarded me good..killedst 3330

PATIENCE.
Divine. Last of all, he sent his son 5994
Example. Consider him that endureth such 5995
Labour. This year also..I will dig about it 5996
Maintained. Come out, thou bloody man..of B. 5997
Needful. Fret not thyself in any wise to do evil 5998
Picture of. The husbandman waiteth..hath long 5999
Rewarded. He brought me out of the miry clay 6000
Refused. Have patience, and I will pay..would not 6001
Trial of. They despised Saul..he held his peace 6002
Without. Why should this dead dog curse my lord 6003
Waiting. Have need of patience..after ye have 6004

RESIGNATION.
Bereavement. David was comforted concerning 7192
Inevitable. If I be bereaved of my children, I am 7193
Pious. L. gave, and the L. hath taken away 7194
"   David said..Let him do as seemeth good 7195
Submission. When he would not be persuaded 7196

SUFFERING.
for Christ. [Paul and Silas] Laid many stripes 8448
Faithful. Were stoned..sawn asunder, were 8449
Subdued. Bit the people..died, therefore..we 8451
Support. Sufferings of this present time not 8450

SUFFERINGS.
Apostolic. [Paul] Five times.,stripes..thrice 8452
Chosen. Moses..choosing rather to suffer..than 8453
Recompensed. Moses..had respect unto the r. 8454
Sacred. Remove this cup..not my will [Jesus] 8455

TRIAL.
Character. Saw the Egyptians dead..feared the L. 8914
"   Waters were a wall unto them 8915
Faith. Trial of your faith..more precious than g. 8916
Impenitence. Thy sons..as a wild bull in a net 8917
Life. God commanded..Thou shalt not eat 8918
Mock. Witness against Jesus to put..death 8919
Proportioned. Led them not..was near..lest 8920
Severe. Take now thy son..Isaac..burnt offering 8922
Stubbornness. Ahaz..trespass yet more 8921

TRIALS.
Business. Day the drought consumed me..frost 8923
Backsliding. Who shall give us flesh to eat 8924
Blessing. Blessed are ye when men shall revile 8925
"   I am exceeding joyful in all our 8948
Comfort. David encouraged himself in his G. 8926
Confidence. I am persuaded..be able to separate 8927
Darkness. I cry out of wrong, but I am not heard 8930
after Deliverance From the Red Sea..no water 8929
Despair. There was a great earthquake..sun 8946
Encouragement. Work out..far more exceeding 8931
Follow. Three days in the wilderness..no water 8929
Hope. I know that my Redeemer liveth 8932
"   Why art thou cast down, O my soul ? 8933
Joyful. Took joyfully the spoiling of your goods 8935
Multiplied. All my inward friends abhorred me 8936
"   In labours more abundant..stripes 8940
Overburdened. Burden of all this people on me 8937
Recompensed. These..came out of great 8949
Rest. Came to Elim..12 wells..70 palm trees 8938
Severe. In labours..stripes..prison..deaths 8940
"   In weariness, painfulness..in watchings 8942
"   We hunger and thirst, and are naked 8939
"   In perils of waters..robbers..heathen 8941
Use. Nations which the L. left to prove I. 8943
"   Branch that beareth not fruit..purgeth it 8944
Victory. In all..more than conquerors 8945
Winnow. When affliction or persecution ariseth 8928

2643. ENEMY, An aggressive. *Saul.* ¹ Saul, yet breathing out threatenings and slaughter.. ² And desired..letters to Damascus to the synagogues, that if he found any of this way, whether they were men or women, he might bring them bound unto Jerusalem.—ACTS, ch. 9.

2644. —— conquered by Kindness. *Saul.* [See above.] ¹⁶ When David had made an end of speaking these words unto Saul..Saul said, *Is* this thy voice, my son David? And Saul lifted up his voice, and wept. ¹⁷ And he said to David, Thou *art* more righteous than I : for thou hast rewarded me good, whereas I have rewarded thee evil.—1 SAM., ch. 24.

2645. —— Disarmed by an. *Benaiah.* ²¹ The

Egyptian had a spear in his hand ; but he went down to him with a staff, and plucked the spear out of the Egyptian's hand, and slew him with his own spear.—2 SAM., ch. 23.

2646. —— **The great.** *Satan.* [24] The kingdom of heaven is likened unto a man which sowed good seed in his field : [25] But while men slept, his enemy came and sowed tares among the wheat, and went his way.—MAT., ch. 13.

2647. —— **A jealous.** *Saul.* [28] Saul saw..that the Lord *was* with David, and *that* Michal Saul's daughter loved him. [29] And Saul was yet the more afraid of David ; and Saul became David's enemy continually.—1 SAM., ch. 18.

2648. —— **routed, An.** *By Four Lepers.* [10] We came to the camp of the Syrians, and, behold, *there was* no man there, neither voice of man, but horses tied, and asses tied, and the tents as they *were*.—2 KINGS, ch. 7.

2649. —— **A suspected.** *Jeremiah.* [13] When he was in the gate of Benjamin, a captain of the ward *was* there, whose name *was* Irijah..saying, Thou fallest away to the Chaldeans. [14] Then said Jeremiah, It *is* false ; I fall not away to the Chaldeans. But he hearkened not to him : So Irijah took Jeremiah, and brought him to the princes.—JER., ch. 37.

2650. —— **spared, An.** *King Saul.* [3] Saul went in to cover his feet : and David and his men remained in the sides of the cave. [4] And the men of David said..thou mayest do to him as it shall seem good unto thee. Then David arose, and cut off the skirt of Saul's robe privily.—1 SAM., ch. 24.

2651. —— **Weapons from.** *Egyptians.* [27] Moses stretched forth his hand over the sea, and the sea returned to his strength when the morning appeared ; and the Egyptians fled against it ; and the Lord overthrew the Egyptians in the midst of the sea.—EX., ch. 14. [The Lord gave them the arms of the Egyptians.]

2652. ENEMIES, Artful. *Priests and Scribes.* [20] Sent forth spies, which shoul feign themselves just men, that they might take hold of his words, that so they might deliver him unto the power and authority of the governor.—LUKE, ch. 20.

2653. —— **of the Cross.** *Paul.* [18] They *are* the enemies of the cross of Christ : [19] Whose end *is* destruction, whose God *is their* belly, and *whose* glory *is* in their shame, who mind earthly things.—PHIL., ch. 3.

2654. —— **Contempt of.** *Heathen.* [19] They laughed us to scorn, and despised us, and said, What *is* this thing that ye do? will ye rebel against the king? [20] Then answered I..The God of heaven, he will prosper us ; therefore we his servants will arise and build.—NEH., ch. 2.

2655. —— **disappointed.** *Heathen.* [16] When all our enemies heard *thereof*, and all the heathen that *were* about us saw *these things*, they were much cast down in their own eyes : for they perceived that this work was wrought of our God.—NEH., ch. 6.

2656. —— **Dependence on.** *Philistines.* [19] There was no smith found throughout all the land of Israel : for the Philistines said, Lest the Hebrews make *them* swords or spears : [20] But all the Israelites went down to the Philistines, to

sharpen every man his share, and his coulter, and his axe, and his mattock.—1 SAM., ch. 13.

2657. —— **Favours for.** *Food and Water.* [21] If thine enemy be hungry, give him bread to eat ; and if he be thirsty, give him water to drink : [22] For thou shalt heap coals of fire upon his head, and the Lord shall reward thee.—PROV., ch. 25.

2658. —— **Gospel.** *Last Times.* [1] In the last days perilous times shall come. [2] For men shall be lovers of their own selves, covetous, boasters, proud, blasphemers, disobedient to parents, unthankful, unholy. [3] Without natural affection, trucebreakers, false accusers, incontinent, fierce, despisers of those that are good, [4] Traitors, heady, highminded, lovers of pleasures more than lovers of God.—2 TIM., ch. 3.

2659. —— **Help against.** *Ammonite Oppressors.* [15] We have sinned : do thou unto us whatsoever seemeth good unto thee ; deliver us only, we pray thee, this day. [16] And they put away the strange gods from among them, and served the Lord : and his soul was grieved for the misery of Israel.—JUDGES, ch. 10.

2660. —— **Hidden.** *Heathen.* [11] Our adversaries said, They shall not know, neither see, till we come in the midst among them, and slay them, and cause the work to cease.—NEH., ch. 4.

2661. —— **Intrigue of.** *Rebuilding the Temple.* [4] The people of the land weakened the hands of the people of Judah, and troubled them in building, [5] And hired counsellors against them, to frustrate their purpose, all the days of Cyrus king of Persia.—EZRA, ch. 4.

2662. —— **Kindness to.** *Syrians.* [22] Elisha answered, Thou shalt not smite *them:* wouldest thou smite those whom thou hast taken captive with thy sword and with thy bow? set bread and water before them, that they may eat and drink, and go to their master.—2 KINGS, ch. 6.

2663. —— **Malicious.** *Diotrephes.* [9] Diotrephes, who loveth to have the preeminence among them, receiveth us not.. [13]..prating against us with malicious words : and not content therewith, neither doth he himself receive the brethren, and forbiddeth them that would, and casteth *them* out of the church.—3 JOHN.

2664. —— **Prayer against.** *David.* [1] Make haste, O God, to deliver me ; make haste to help me, O Lord. [2] Let them be ashamed and confounded that seek after my soul.—Ps. 70.

2665. —— **Successful.** *Heathen.* [23] Rehum and Shimshai the scribe, and their companions, they went up in haste to Jerusalem unto the Jews, and made them to cease by force and power. [24] Then ceased the work of the house of God.—EZRA, ch. 4.

2666. —— **Sensitive.** *Priests.* [15] When the chief priests and scribes saw the wonderful things that he did, and the children crying in the temple..Hosanna to the Son of David ; they were sore displeased.—MAT., ch. 21.

2667. —— **thwarted.** *Darius.* [7] Let the work of this house of God alone ; let the governor of the Jews and the elders of the Jews build this house of God.. [8] Moreover I make a decree..that of the king's goods, *even* of the tribute beyond the river, forthwith expenses be given unto these men, that they be not hindered.—EZRA, ch. 6.

2668. —— **Treatment of.** *Christ.* [43] Ye have heard that it hath been said, Thou shalt love thy neighbour and hate thine enemy. [44] But I say unto you, Love your enemies, bless them that curse you, do good to them that hate you, and pray for them which despitefully use you, and persecute you.—MAT., ch. 5.

2669. —— **Unequal to.** *Philistines.* [19] The Lord was with Judah; and he drave out *the inhabitants of* the mountain; but could not drive out the inhabitants of the valley, because they had chariots of iron.—JUDGES, ch. 1.

2670. —— **Vexation of.** *Nehemiah.* [10] When Sanballat the Horonite, and Tobiah..the Ammonite, heard *of it*, it grieved them exceedingly that there was come a man to seek the welfare of the children of Israel.—NEH., ch. 2.

See other illustrations under:

ANTAGONISM.
Spiritual. I will put enmity between..thy seed and 450
Truth. I came not to send peace, but a sword 451

HATRED.
Brother. If..say, I love God and hateth..is a liar 3828
Bitter. Brother shall betray brother..to death 3829
Commendable. Thou hatest the deeds of the N. 3830
Changed. Ready to die..for the L. Jesus 3831
Darkness. He that hateth his brother walketh 3832
Divine. Six things doth the L. hate 3833
Evil. Bitter is a dinner of herbs when love is 3834
Good. [Joseph's] brethren hated him..not speak 3835
Light. Every one that doeth evil hateth the light 3836
Manifested. When the days of mourning ended 3838
Silent. Absalom spake unto..Amnon..good nor b. 3840
Sinner's. Micaiah..I hate..doth not prophesy 3841
World. If the world hate you..it hated me before 3842
Displeasure. Brought young children..disciples 2412
" I hate your feast days..let judgment 2411
Enmity. Citizens hated him..will not have..reign 2676
Estrangement. Younger son..journey into a far 2725
Jealousy. Ten heard it..much displeased with 7185

RETALIATION.
Cowardly. Joab took Abner aside..smote him 7289
Disallowed. Been said, An eye for an eye 7290
Jewish. Life shall go for life, eye for eye 7291

REVENGE.
Avoided. Flee thou to Laban..brother's fury turn 7304
Brother's. When I say, Smite Amnon; then kill 7305
" Joab smote Abner..for the blood of 7306
Best. If thine enemy be hungry, give him bread 7307
Frustrated. Haman was come..Hang Mordecai 7308
Ignored. Spake against Moses..M. cried unto the 7309
" Shall not Shimei be put to death? 7310
Justifiable. Philistines burnt her..S. smote them 7311
Nursed. Absalom spake neither good nor bad 7312
Proposed. Then will I slay my brother Jacob 7313
Price. That they may be destroyed..I will pay 7314
Prayer. O L. G., strengthen me..avenged of the P. 7315

VENGEANCE.
Averted. Let not my lord regard..Nabal 9169
" Kept me..from coming to shed blood 9170
Blood. Cain said..every one that findeth me..slay 9171
Call. Stoned [Zachariah]..in house of the L. 9172
Divine. To me belongeth vengeance and 9173
" If I whet my glittering sword 9174
Declined. Not a man be put to death [Saul] 9175
Fear. Joseph will peradventure hate us 9176
with God. My G., think thou upon Tobiah 9177
Inappropriate. I forgave thee..shouldest thou not 9178

Mistaken. Command fire..to consume them 9179
Monstrous. Haman thought scorn..Mordecai 9180
Prohibited. If ye from your hearts forgive not 9182
Undesired. Behold the head of Ish-bosheth 9183
for Vengeance. David commanded..slew them 9184
See **WAR** and references.

2671. ENGRAVER, An inspired. *Bezaleel.* [31] He hath filled him with the spirit of God..in all manner of workmanship; [32] And to devise curious works, to work in gold, and in silver, and in brass, [33] And in the cutting of stones, to set *them*, and in carving of wood, to make any manner of cunning work.—EX., ch. 35.

2672. ENGRAVING, The Lord's. *Law.* [16] The tables *were* the work of God, and the writing *was* the writing of God, graven upon the tables.—EX., ch. 32.

2673. —— **of the Law.** *Great Stones.* [2] On the day when ye shall pass over Jordan unto the land..thou shalt set thee up great stones, and plaster them with plaster: [3] And thou shalt write upon them all the words of this law.—DEUT., ch. 27.

See other illustrations under:

WRITING.
Alarming. King saw the part of the hand that 9926
Perishable. Jesus..wrote on the ground 9927
Tenderness. I wrote unto you with many tears 9928

2674. ENJOYMENT, Beauty for. *Eden.* [8] The Lord God planted a garden eastward in Eden; and there he put the man whom he had formed. [9] And out of the ground made the Lord God to grow every tree that is pleasant to the sight, and good for food.—GEN., ch. 2.

2675. —— **Prospective.** *Dives.* [18] This will I do: I will pull down my barns, and build greater; and there will I bestow all my fruits and my goods. [19] And I will say to my soul, Soul, thou hast much goods laid up for many years; take thine ease, eat, drink, *and* be merry.—LUKE, ch. 12.

See other illustrations under:

AMUSEMENT.
Curiosity. Spend their time to..hear some new thing 336
Dangerous. Daughters of Shiloh come out to dance 337
an End. Much goods..many years..be merry 338
Fatal. Philistines called for Samson..made sport 339
Idolatrous. Moses saw the calf, and the dancing 340
Perilous. Amalekites were eating, drinking, danc'g 341
Royal. Herod made a supper..danced, and pleased 342
Sorrow. Herod was exceeding sorry 343

PLEASURE.
Business first. I will not eat..told mine errand 6206
Bitter. Benhadad was drinking himself drunk 6207
Brief. Eat..until it come out at your nostrils 6215
Deceptive. Jezebel said to Ahab, Arise, take 6223
End. Soul, thou hast much goods..eat, drink 6209
Expensive. He that loveth pleasure shall be a poor 6208
False. Forsaken..fountain..broken cisterns 6216
Ingrates. I will smite the king..pleased Absalom 6210
Moderation. Hast thou found honey?..vomit 6211
Poisoned. Yet all this availeth me nothing 6217
Rejected. King went to his palace..fasting 6219
Renounced. Moses..choosing..rather than the p. 6218
Ruinous. Wasted his substance in riotous living 6220
Sin. They drank wine, and praised the gods 6221
" The hatred wherewith he hated her was 6222
Temptation. People sat down to eat..drink..play 6213
" The tree..was pleasant to the eyes 6212
Unsatisfying. My heart, I will prove thee with 6214

HAPPINESS.

Failure. Some coveted after [money]..pierced 3788
Possessors. Blessed are [See Beatitudes] 3789
Pardon. Blessed are they whose iniquities are f. 3790
Postponed. I will pull down..build..take thy ease 3791
Present. It is good..to enjoy the good..his labour 3792
Poisoned. All this..nothing..sitting at the..gate 3793
Perfect. G. shall wipe away all tears 3794
Rule. Eschew evil, and do good..seek peace 3795
Riches. What shall I do, because I have no room 3796

Condition. As vinegar upon nitre, so..singeth 5378
Lawful. It is good to eat..drink..enjoy the good 3792

2676. ENMITY, Contemptuous. *Parable.* [13] He called his ten servants, and delivered them ten pounds, and said..Occupy till I come. [14] But his citizens hated him, and sent a message after him, saying, We will not have this *man* to reign over us.—LUKE, ch. 19.

2677. —— An undying. *Serpent.* [14] Upon thy belly shalt thou go, and dust shalt thou eat all the days of thy life : [15] And I will put enmity between thee and the woman, and between thy seed and her seed ; it shall bruise thy head, and thou shalt bruise his heel.—GEN., ch. 3.

See ENEMIES *and references.*

2678. ENTERPRISE, Wide-awake. *Proverb.* [13] Love not sleep, lest thou come to poverty ; open thine eyes, *and* thou shalt be satisfied with bread.—PROV., ch. 20.

See ACTIVITY *and references.*

2679. ENTHUSIASM, Brief. *Rootless.* [20] He that received the seed into stony places, the same is he that heareth the word, and anon with joy receiveth it ; [21] Yet hath he not root in himself, but dureth for a while : for when tribulation or persecution ariseth because of the word, by and by he is offended.—MAT., ch. 13.

2680. —— in Benevolence. *Jesus.* [19] And they went into a house. [20] And the multitude cometh together again, so that they could not so much as eat bread. [21] And when his friends heard *of it*, they went out to lay hold on him : for they said, He is beside himself.—MARK, ch. 3.

2681. —— Contempt for. *Michal.* [16] As the ark of the Lord came into the city of David, Michal Saul's daughter looked through a window, and saw king David leaping and dancing before the Lord : and she despised him in her heart.—2 SAM., ch. 6.

2682. —— misunderstood. [See No. 2680.]

2683. —— Public. *Galileans,* [14] When they had seen the miracle that Jesus did, said, This is of a truth that Prophet that should come into the world. [15] When Jesus therefore perceived that they would come and take him by force, to make him a king, he departed again into a mountain himself alone.—JOHN, ch. 6. [Five thousand had been fed.]

See other illustrations under :

EARNESTNESS.

Angelic. [Lot] While he lingered..laid hold 2568
Bold. Second time..Joab's field..set it on fire 2569
Checked. Running and kneeled..master what 2570
Chosen. Every one that lappeth of the water 2571
Hospitality. [Lot] Pressed upon them greatly 2572
Important. Aaron ran..plague begun..incense 2573
Influence. Because of his importunity, he will 2574
Lack. [Joash] Should have smitten 5 or 6 times 2575

Rewarded. Whoso first after the troubling 2576
Safety. Look not behind..escape to the mount 2577
"   [Bartimeus] cried the more a great deal 2578
Seeking. Uncovered the roof..broke it..down 2579

EXCITEMENT.

Abstinence. Saul rose from the earth..neither did 2777
Creating. [Stephen's enemies] stirred up the 2778
Ecstasy. Peter said..it is good for us to be here 2779
Evildoers. They were instant with loud voices 2780
General. Multitude cometh..could not eat 2781
Needless. Israel..to go up to war against 2782
Public. City was moved..This is Jesus 2783
Trembling. [Jailer] came trembling..what must 2784
Wild. Some cried one thing, some another 2785

FANATICISM.

Accused. His friends said..He is beside himself 3036
Fickle. Would have done sacrifice..stoned Paul 3037
Genuine. Two hours cried out, Great is Diana 3038
Idolatry. They cried out, and cut themselves 3039

ZEAL.

Age. [Caleb, 85 years] Give me this..Anakim 9974
Affecting. Many..afoot out of all cities..out went 9975
Acknowledged. [Epaphras] laboring fervently 9976
Affectionate. Brought spices very early in the m. 9977
Desirable. Good to be zealously affected always 9981
Excelling. Priests were too few..Levites did 9983
Energetic. [Nehemiah] contend..cursed..hair 9984
Holy. Behold the men ye put in prison..teaching 9989
Hurtful. Say nothing..he began to blaze abroad 9991
Ministerial. Three years..I warned every one 10000
Misunderstood. [Jesus] Friends said, He is beside 9997
Prosperous. [Hezekiah] In every work..with 10005
Rewarded. Give my covenant..he was zealous 10013
Reformers. I chased him from me [Nehemiah] 10009
Reformation. Made a scourge..drove them out 10012
Sudden. Service..set in order..done suddenly 10016
Seeker's. [Zaccheus] ran before, climbed..tree 10020
"   Made haste, came down, received 10014
Testify. Left her waterpot..come see a man 10022
Unwavering. None of these things move me 10025
Working. From the rising..morning..till the stars 10026

2684. ENTREATY, A heart-breaking. *At Cesarea.* [12] When we heard these things, both we, and they of that place, besought him not to go up.. [13] Then Paul answered, What mean ye to weep and to break mine heart ? for I am ready not to be bound only, but also to die at Jerusalem for the name of the Lord Jesus.—ACTS, ch. 21.

2685. —— An urgent. *Nobleman.* [47] When he heard that Jesus was come..into Galilee, he went..and besought him that he would come down, and heal his son ; for he was at the point of death. [48] Then said Jesus..Except ye see signs and wonders, ye will not believe. [49] The nobleman saith..Sir, come down ere my child die.—JOHN, ch. 4.

See other illustrations under :

IMPORTUNITY.

Desperate. I will not let thee go, except thou bless 4358
Power of. Because of his importunity..give him 4359
Prayer. I will..lest she weary me [unjust judge] 4360
Tested. He answered her not a word 4361
Undiscouraged. Many charged Bartimeus..hold his 4362
Wearying. Delilah pressed Samson daily..words 4363

INTERCESSION.

Denied. I will not return with thee..L. rejected 4616
Effect. Let it alone this year also 4617
Friendly. Wherefore then wilt thou slay David 4618
"   Wilt thou not spare the place for fifty 4619

Limit. I will not destroy it for ten's sake..L. went 4620
Needless. They came near to the steward of J. 4621
Needed. Take your flocks..and bless me also 4622
Obtained. I have sinned..Samuel turned again 4623
Penitential. I have transgressed..pardon my sin 4624
Rewarded. Forgive..if not blot me..cleft of the r. 4625
Resented. Moses and Aaron..get you unto your 4626

PERSUASION.

Excuse. Because thou hast hearkened unto..wife 6106
Ineffective. Paul would not be persuaded, we 6107

PETITION.

Denied. Serve alone..bid her..help me [Martha] 6114
Rejected. Get you unto your burdens [Pharaoh] 6115
" I will chastise you with scorpions 6116

PLEA.

Affecting. We are sold, I and my people [Esther] 6201
Patriotism. How can I endure to see the evil..my 6202
See PRAYER.

2686. ENVY of Brethren. *Joseph's Brethren.* [9] Behold, I have dreamed a dream more ; and, behold, the sun and the moon and the eleven stars made obeisance to me.. [11] And his brethren envied him ; but his father observed the saying. —GEN., ch. 37.

2687. —— A Brother's. *Elder Son.* [28] He was angry, and would not go in : therefore came his father out, and entreated him [29] And he..said to *his* father, Lo, these many years do I serve thee, neither transgressed I at any time thy commandment ; and yet thou never gavest me a kid, that I might make merry with my friends.— LUKE, ch. 15.

2688. —— leads to Crime. *Crucifixion.* [Pilate] [10] knew that the chief priests had delivered him for envy. [11] But the chief priests moved the people, that he should rather release Barabbas.— MARK, ch. 15.

2689. —— of the Covetous. *King Ahab.* [2] Give me thy vineyard, that I may take it for a garden of herbs, because it *is* near unto my house : and I will give thee for it a better vineyard than it ; *or*..the worth of it in money.. [4] And Ahab came into his house heavy and displeased because.. Naboth..said, I will not give thee the inheritance of my fathers. And he laid him down upon his bed, and turned away his face, and would eat no bread.—1 KINGS, ch. 21.

2690. —— Dangers of. *David.* [3] I was envious at the foolish, *when* I saw the prosperity of the wicked. [4] For *there are* no bands in their death : but their strength *is* firm. [5] They *are* not in trouble *as other* men ; neither are they plagued like *other* men. [16] When I thought to know this, it *was* too painful for me ; [17] Until I went into the sanctuary of God ; *then* understood I their end.—Ps. 73.

2691. —— Distress from. *Rachel.* [1] When Rachel saw that she bare Jacob no children, Rachel envied her sister ; and said unto Jacob, Give me children, or else I die.—GEN., ch. 30.

2692. —— Folly of. *Proverb.* [2] For wrath killeth the foolish man, and envy slayeth the silly one.—JOB, ch. 5.

2693. —— Inspired by. *Thessalonians.* [5] The Jews which believed not, moved with envy, took unto them certain lewd fellows of the baser sort, and gathered a company, and set all the city on an uproar, and assaulted the house of Jason, and sought to bring them out to the people.—ACTS, ch. 17.

2694. —— Manifested. *Laban's Sons.* [1] Jacob hath taken away all that *was* our father's ; and of *that* which *was* our father's hath he gotten all this glory. [2] And Jacob beheld the countenance of Laban, and, behold, it *was* not toward him as before.—GEN., ch. 31.

2695. —— Ministerial. *Paul.* [16] Some indeed preach Christ even of envy and strife ; and some also of good will : [16] The one preach Christ of contention, not sincerely, supposing to add affliction to my bonds : [17] But the other of love.— PHIL., ch. 1.

2696. —— Murder from. *Cain.* [5] Unto Cain and to his offering he had not respect. And Cain was very wroth, and his countenance fell. [6] And the Lord said unto Cain, Why art thou wroth ? and why is thy countenance fallen ?—GEN., ch. 4.

2697. —— of Office. *Aaron and Miriam.* [2] Hath the Lord indeed spoken only by Moses ? hath he not also spoken by us ? And the Lord heard *it.* [3] Now the man Moses *was* very meek, above all the men which *were* upon the face of the earth.—NUM., ch. 12.

2698. —— punished. *Song of Korah.* [3] They gathered..against Moses and against Aaron, and said.. *Ye take* too much upon you, seeing all the congregation *are* holy, every one of them, and the Lord *is* among them : wherefore then lift ye up yourselves above the congregation ?—NUM., ch. 16. [An earthquake swallowed them.]

2699. —— Poisoned by. *King Saul.* [7] The women answered *one another* as they played, and said, Saul hath slain his thousands, and David his ten thousands. [8] And Saul was very wroth.. and he said, They have ascribed unto David ten thousands, and to me they have ascribed *but* thousands : and *what* can he have more but the kingdom ? [9] And Saul eyed David from that day and forward.—1 SAM., ch. 18.

2700. —— of Prosperity. *Isaac.* [13] The man waxed great, and went forward, and grew until he became very great : [14] For he had possession of flocks, and possession of herds, and great store of servants : and the Philistines envied him.—GEN., ch. 26.

2701. —— Promotion fires. *Daniel.* [3] The king thought to..set him over the whole realm. [4] Then the president and princes sought to find occasion against Daniel concerning the kingdom ; but they could find none occasion nor fault.—DAN., ch. 6.

2702. —— Rottenness of. *Solomon.* [30] A sound heart *is* the life of the flesh : but envy the rottenness of the bones.—PROV., ch. 14.

2703. —— Relentless. *Solomon.* [4] Wrath *is* cruel, and anger *is* outrageous ; but who *is* able to stand before envy ?—PROV., ch. 27.

2704. —— of the Successful. *David.* [7] Rest in the Lord, and wait patiently for him : fret not thyself because of him who prospereth in his way, because of the man who bringeth wicked devices to pass.—Ps. 37.

2705. —— and Strife. *Every Evil.* [16] Where envying and strife *is*, there *is* confusion and every evil work.—JAMES, ch. 3.

2706. —— Unchristian. *Corinthians.* [3] Whereas *there is* among you envying, and strife, and divisions, are ye not carnal, and walk as men ? [4] For while one saith, I am of Paul ; and another,

I *am* of Apollos ; are ye not carnal?—1 Cor., ch. 3.

2707. EQUIVOCATION through Fear. *Abraham.* [11] Because I thought, Surely the fear of God *is* not in this place ; and they will slay me for my wife's sake. [12] And yet indeed *she is* my sister ; she *is* the daughter of my father, but not the daughter of my mother.—Gen., ch. 20.

2708. —— Hypocrites'. *Priests.* [Respecting John,] [25] If we shall say, From heaven ; he will say unto us, Why did ye not then believe him? [26] But if we shall say, Of men ; we fear the people ; for all hold John as a prophet. [27] And they answered Jesus..We cannot tell.—Mat., ch. 21.

See other illustrations under :

DISSEMBLING.

Confession. Achan said..I saw..I took a wedge of 2424
Imitated. Other Jews dissembled likewise   2425
Inconsistency. If thou, being a Jew..livest after 2426
Rebuked. I withstood him to the face..separated   2427

EVASION.

Answer by. Is it well with the child?..It is well 2726
Impossible. Asked us..Have ye another brother?   2727
by Silence. Let no man know these words   2728

Prevarication. Who hath opened his eyes, we   6549

2709. ERROR, Sweeping. *Peter* [12] separated himself, fearing them which were of the circumcision. [13] And the other Jews dissembled likewise with him ; insomuch that Barnabas also was carried away with their dissimulation.—Gal., ch. 2.

2710. —— Sincere. *Solomon.* [12] There is a way which seemeth right unto a man ; but the end thereof *are* the ways of death.—Prov., ch. 14.

2711. ERRING, Sympathy for. *Christians.* [14] If any man obey not our word by this epistle, note that man, and have no company with him, that he may be ashamed. [15] Yet count *him* not as an enemy, but admonish *him* as a brother.—2 Thess., ch. 3.

See other illustrations under :

HERESY.

Test. To the law and the testimony..this word   3946
Tested by. They which are approved..manifested   3947

HERESIES.

Corruption. Perverse disputings of men of corrupt 3948
Pride. If any man teach otherwise..He is proud   3949

HERETIC.

Rejection. After the first and second admonition 3951
So-called. After the way which they call heresy   3952

HERETICS.

Errors. Saying the resurrection is past   3953
Primitive. [Sadducees] In the resurrection..whose 3954

STUMBLING.

at Truth. This is a hard saying..many went back   8401
Stumblingblock. Christ crucified unto the Jews   8402
   "   Liberty of yours, become a   8403
   "   Whoso shall offend one..better   8404

WANDERING.

Corrected. Before I was afflicted, I went astray 9282
Invitation. Return unto me, and I will return   9280
Restoration. Lovest thou me?..Feed my sheep   9279
Search. Having a hundred sheep, if he lose one   9284
Unsatisfied. Dove found no rest for the..foot   9285
Wicked. I will be a swift witness against the   9281
   See DECEPTION and IGNORANCE.

2712. ESCAPE, Assistance to. *Saul.* [23] The Jews took counsel to kill him : [24]..and they watched the gates day and night to kill him. [25] Then the disciples took him by night, and let *him* down by the wall in a basket.—Acts, ch. 9.

2713. —— of a Few. *Flood.* [12] The rain was upon the earth forty days and forty nights. [13] In the selfsame day entered Noah, and Shem, and Ham, and Japheth..and Noah's wife, and the three wives of his sons with them, into the ark.—Gen., ch. 7.

2714. —— A hasty. *David.* [14] David said unto all his servants that *were* with him at Jerusalem, Arise, and let us flee ; for we shall not *else* escape from Absalom : make speed to depart, lest he overtake us suddenly.—2 Sam., ch. 16.

2715. —— Miraculous. *Jesus.* [At Jerusalem] [39] They sought again to take him ; but he escaped out of their hand.—John, ch. 10.

2716. —— by any Means. *Shipwreck.* [43] The centurion..commanded that they which could swim should cast *themselves* first *into the sea,* and get to land : [44] And the rest, some on boards, and some on *broken pieces* of the ship..they escaped all safe on land.—Acts, ch. 27.

2717. —— A narrow. *Job's Servant.* [19] There came a great wind from the wilderness, and smote the four corners of the house, and it fell upon the young men, and they are dead ; and I only am escaped.—Job, ch. 1.

2718. —— No. *Israelites.* [29] They slew of Moab at that time about ten thousand men, all lusty, and all men of valour ; and there escaped not a man.—Judges, ch. 3.

2719. —— of One only. *King Saul* [18] said to Doeg, Turn thou, and fall upon the priests.. and he fell upon the priests, and slew on that day fourscore and five persons that did wear a linen ephod.—1 Sam., ch. 22. [Abiathar alone escaped.]

2720. —— from Prison. *Peter and John.* [18] Laid their hands on the apostles, and put them in the common prison. [19] But the angel of the Lord by night opened the prison doors, and brought them forth.—Acts, ch. 5.

2721. —— by Strategy. *David.* [12] Michal let David down through a window : and he..escaped. [13] And Michal took an image, and laid *it* in the bed, and put a pillow of goats' *hair* for his bolster, and covered *it* with a cloth. [14] And when Saul sent messengers to take David, she said, He *is* sick.—1 Sam., ch. 19.

2722. —— by Urging. *Lot.* [16] While he lingered, the men laid hold upon his hand, and upon the hand of his wife, and upon the hand of his two daughters ; the Lord being merciful unto him : and they brought him forth, and set him without the city.—Gen., ch. 19.

See other illustrations under :

DEPARTURE.

Constrained. Jesus constrained his disciples..ship 2179
Haste. Egyptians were urgent..be all dead men   2180
Safety. In Judea flee to the mountains   2181
Stolen. Jacob stole away unawares to Laban   2182
Unexpected. Camp of Syria..was no man there   2183

FUGITIVE.

Criminal. Jacob..flee thou to Laban, my uncle   3487
Infant. Take the young child..flee into Egypt   3488

Noble. Pharaoh sought to slay Moses..fled 3489
Protected. Not deliver unto his master the s. 3490
Return. [Onesimus] departed for a season 3491

Danger. All the disciples forsook him, and fled 3389
Duty. Jonah..to flee. going to Tarshish 3380
Prevented. Soldiers cut the ropes..boat..let her 2206

2723. ESSENTIALS overlooked. *Pharisees.*
42 Woe unto you, Pharisees : for ye tithe mint
and rue and all manner of herbs, and pass over
judgment and the love of God : these ought ye
to have done, and not to leave the other undone.
—LUKE, ch. 11.

Also see :
One Need. One thing is needful..Mary hath 5693

2724. ESTATE, A contested. *To Jesus.* 13 Master, speak to my brother, that he divide the inheritance with me. 14 And he said unto him,
Man, who made me a judge or a divider over
you?—LUKE, ch. 12.

See other illustrations under :

CONFISCATION.

Absence. Shunammite..in land of Philistines seven 1536
Crime. Give the house of Haman unto Esther 1537
Threat. Come within 3 days..substance forfeited 1538

LAND.

Conveyance. Subscribed the evidence..witnesses 4891
Cursed. Therefore is your land a desolation 4892
First Purchase. Field of Ephron..in Machpelah 4893
Prohibited. Thou shalt have no inheritance 4894
    "   [Rechabites] Neither have we 4895

2725. ESTRANGEMENT, Wilful. *Prodigal.*
13 Not many days after, the younger son gathered
all together, and took his journey into a far
country, and there wasted his substance with
riotous living.—LUKE, ch. 15.

See other illustrations under :

DISTRUST.

Adversity. They hearkened not unto Moses for 2448
Evildoers. Money..in our sacks..seek occasion 2449
Forbidden. Take no thought..what ye shall eat 2450
Needless. Consider the lilies how they grow 2451
Persuasions. Let not Hezekiah deceive you 2452
Without. Ravens neither sow nor reap..G. feedeth 2453

DIVISIONS.

Authors. L. hate..he that soweth discord among 2467
Harmful. Two men of the Hebrews strove together 2468
Harmonious. Body is not one member, but many 2469
Healed. From which if ye keep yourselves..well 2470
Party. I am of Paul..I am of Apollos 2471
Scandalous. I hear there be divisions..hungry 2472
Weakness. Kingdom divided against itself 2473

DISPLEASURE.

False Piety. I hate your feast days..assemblies 2412
Holy. Jesus saw it, was much displeased..suffer 2411

DISSENSIONS.

Doctrinal. P. and Barnabas had no small 2429
Perilous. Chief captain, fearing lest P..pulled in 2430
Partisan. Every one of you saith, I am of..I of 2431
Removed. [Explanation of the altar of witness] 2432
Stubborn. Contention was so sharp..parted 2433

SEPARATION.

Drunkards. Not to keep company..not to eat 7758
Godly. Separated from I. all the mixed multitude 7759
Impossible. Neither death nor life..able to s. 7764
Reason of. For they will turn away thy son 7778
Sorrowful. They kissed one another, and wept 7780
Spiritual. Fan in his hand..wheat..chaff 7781
Sinners. Blessed..when they shall separate 7783

by Sin. As a shepherd divideth his sheep..goats 7789
    "   Your iniquities have separated..your 7784
Unavoidable. Ye cannot drink the cup of the L. 7787

Doctrinal. Eateth my flesh..disciples went back 2326

2726. EVASION, Answer by. *Shunammite.*
25 When the man of God saw her afar off..he
said to Gehazi..Behold, *yonder is* that Shunammite : 26 Run now..and say unto her, *Is it* well
with thee? *is it* well with thy husband? *is it*
well with the child? And she answered, It *is*
well.—2 KINGS, ch. 4. [Her son was dead.]

2727. —— impossible. *Joseph.* 6 Israel said,
Wherefore dealt ye *so* ill with me, *as* to tell the
man whether ye had yet a brother ? 7 And they
said, The man asked us straitly of our state,
and of our kindred, saying, *Is* your father yet
alive? have ye *another* brother?—GEN., ch. 43.

2728. —— by Silence. *Jeremiah.* [He predicted the overthrow of the king.] 24 Then said
Zedekiah unto Jeremiah, Let no man know of
these words, and thou shalt not die.. 27 Then
came all the princes unto Jeremiah..and he told
them according to all these words that the king
had commanded. So they left off speaking with
him : for the matter was not perceived.—JER.,
ch. 38.

See other illustrations under :

EQUIVOCATION.

Fear. She is my sister..daughter of my father 2707
Hypocrites. Fear the people..John for a prophet 2708

2729. EVIDENCE, Astounding. *Against Gibeathites.* [A Levite's concubine was outraged and
killed.] 29 He took a knife, and laid hold on his
concubine, and divided her, *together* with her
bones, into twelve pieces, and sent her into all
the coasts of Israel. 30..all that saw it said,
There was no such deed done nor seen from the
day that the children of Israel came up out of
the land of Egypt unto this day : consider of
it, take advice, and speak *your minds.*—JUDGES,
ch. 19. 11 So all the men of Israel were gathered
against the city, knit together as one man.—
JUDGES, ch. 20.

2730. —— Circumstantial. *Joseph.* [Poti-
phar's wife said,] 17 The Hebrew servant..came
in unto me to mock me : 18 And..as I lifted up
my voice and cried..he left his garment with
me, and fled out.—GEN., ch. 39.

2731. —— Confirmatory. *Peter.* 70 He denied
it again. And a little after, they that stood by
said again to Peter, Surely thou art *one* of them :
for thou art a Galilean, and thy speech agreeth
thereto.—MARK, ch. 14.

2732. —— —— *Woman of Tekoah.* 19 The
king said, *Is not* the hand of Joab with thee in
all this ? And the woman answered.. *As* thy soul
liveth..none can turn to the right hand or to
the left from aught that my lord the king hath
spoken : for thy servant Joab, he bade me, and
he put all these words in the mouth of thine
handmaid.—2 SAM., ch. 14.

2733. —— —— *Healing.* 13 When they saw
the boldness of Peter and John, and perceived
that they were unlearned and ignorant men, they
marvelled ; and they took knowledge of them,
that they had been with Jesus. 14 And beholding the man which was healed standing with
them, they could say nothing against it.—ACTS
ch. 4.

2734. —— in Deeds. *Jesus.* [37] If I do not the works of my Father, believe me not. [38] But if I do, though ye believe not me, believe the works ; that ye may know, and believe, that the Father *is* in me, and I in him.—JOHN, ch. 10.

2735. —— Divine. *Jesus.* [20] They said, John Baptist hath sent us unto thee, saying, Art thou he that should come ? or look we for another ? [22]..Go your way, and tell John what things ye have seen and heard ; how that the blind see, the lame walk, the lepers are cleansed, the deaf hear, the dead are raised, to the poor the gospel is preached.—LUKE, ch. 7.

2736. —— Fraudulent. *Gibeonites.* [4] Made as if they had been ambassadors, and took old sacks upon their asses, and wine bottles, old, and rent, and bound up ; [5] And old shoes and clouted..and old garments..and all the bread of their provision was dry *and* mouldy. [6] And they went to Joshua.—JUDGES, ch. 9.

2737. —— False. *Priests and Council* [59] sought false witness against Jesus, to put him to death ; [60] But found none : yea, though many false witnesses came, *yet* found they none. At the last came two false witnesses, [61] And said, This *fellow* said, I am able to destroy the temple of God, and to build it in three days.—MAT., ch. 26.

2738. —— of Innocence. *David.* [35] David sware, saying, So do God to me, and more also, if I taste bread, or aught else, till the sun be down. [37]..and all Israel understood that day that it was not of the king to slay Abner.— 2 SAM., ch. 3.

2739. —— The Lord's. *Philistines.* [10] Took two milch kine, and tied them to the cart, and shut up their calves at home : [12] And the kine took the straight way to the way of Beth-shem-esh, *and* went along the highway, lowing as they went, and turned not aside *to* the right hand or *to* the left.—1 SAM., ch. 13.

2740. —— misconstrued. *Jesus.* [4] Those eighteen, upon whom the tower in Siloam fell, and slew them, think ye that they were sinners above all men that dwelt in Jerusalem ?—LUKE, ch. 13.

2741. —— Mistaken. *Pharisees.* [51] If a man keep my saying, he shall never see death. [52] Then said the Jews unto him, Now we know that thou hast a devil.—JOHN, ch. 8.

2742. —— manufactured. *Joseph's Coat.* [31] They took Joseph's coat, and killed a kid of the goats, and dipped the coat in the blood ; [32]..and they brought *it* to their father ; and said, This have we found : know now whether it be thy son's coat or no.—GEN., ch. 37.

2743. —— Practical. *Thomas.* [27] Reach hither thy finger, and behold my hands ; and reach hither thy hand, and thrust *it* into my side ; and be not faithless, but believing. [28] And Thomas answered..My Lord and my God.—JOHN, ch. 20.

2744. —— rejected. *Jonah.* [38] The Pharisees answered, saying, Master, we would see a sign from thee..[40]..as Jonas was three days and three nights in the whale's belly ; so shall the Son of man be three days and three nights in the heart of the earth.—MAT., ch. 12.

2745. —— Satisfying. *Samaritans.* [41] Many more believed because of his own word ; [42] And

said unto the woman, Now we believe, not because of thy saying : for we have heard *him* ourselves, and know that this is indeed the Christ. —JOHN, ch. 4.

2746. —— Suggestive. *Dagon Fallen.* [3] They took Dagon, and set him in his place again. [4]..early on the morrow morning, behold, Dagon *was* fallen upon his face to the ground before the ark of the Lord ; and the head of Dagon and both the palms of his hands *were* cut off upon the threshold ; only *the stump of* Dagon was left to him.—1 SAM., ch. 5.

2747. —— of Sincerity. *Ephesians.* [19] Many of them also which used curious arts brought their books together, and burned them before all *men :* and they counted the price..fifty thousand *pieces* of silver.—ACTS, ch. 19.

2748. —— by Trial. *Daniel.* [12] Prove thy servants..ten days ; and let them give us pulse to eat, and water to drink. [13] Then let our countenances be looked upon..and the countenance of the children that eat of the portion of the king's meat : and as thou seest, deal.—DAN., ch. 1.

2749. —— Unexplainable. *Silver Cup.* [11] They speedily took down every man his sack to the ground.. [12] And he searched, *and* began at the eldest, and left at the youngest : and the cup was found in Benjamin's sack. [13] Then they rent their clothes..and returned to the city.— GEN., ch. 44.

2750. —— unsuppressed. *Disobedience.* [13] Saul said..I have performed the commandment of the Lord. [14] And Samuel said, What *meaneth* then this bleating of the sheep in mine ears, and the lowing of the oxen which I hear ?—1 SAM., ch. 15.

2751. —— understood. *Sanhedrim.* [See No. 2733.]

SIGN.

Beautiful. My bow in the cloud..for a token 7866
Cheering. We have seen his star in the east 7867
Dumbness. Be dumb..because thou believest not 7868
Encouraging. Ariseth a little cloud out of the sea 7869
Gifts. Tongues are for a sign 7870
Grief. Jacob rent his clothes..sackcloth 7871
Influenced by. If they say thus..we will go up 7872
Lord's. Shadow go backward ten degrees 7873
Protecting. Blood shall be..for a token 7874
Purity. Riband of blue..look..remember 7875
Preserved. Aaron's rod..kept for a token 7876
Summer. Fig tree..putteth forth leaves 7877
Traitor's. Gave them a sign..I kiss..he 7878

SIGNS.

Celestial. Lights in the firmament..signs 7879
Converted by. Simon believed..wondered..signs 7880
Desired. Adulterous generation seeketh after 7881
Evidence. Rod..became a serpent..leprous 7882
" Except ye see signs..not believe 7883
Intrigue. Winketh with his eyes..fingers 7884
Overlooked. Discern the face of the sky..this time 7885
Required. Jews require a sign, Greeks..wisdom 7886
Test. Wringed the dew out of the fleece 7887
Weather. It will be fair..sky is red 7888

TEST.

Benevolence. One thing thou lackest..go sell..give 8726
Character. Ye shall not eat of it [tree] lest ye die 8727
Diet. Give us pulse to eat, and water to drink 8728
Exact. It was at the same hour..Jesus said..son 8729
Lord's. Man's rod whom I shall choose, shall be 8730
Needful. Girded his sword..I have not proved 8731
Obedience. That saith, I know him, and keepeth 8732
Password. Say now Shibboleth..said Sibboleth 8733
Prayer. Call ye upon the name of your gods, and I 8734
Question. Certain lawyer..tempted him, saying 8735
Severe. Take now..thine only son..burnt offering 8736
Trials. To know whether they would hearken 8737
" That they which are approved..made m. 8738

TRIAL.

Mock. Sought for witness against Jesus 8919
Fruitless. Having examined him..found no fault 90

Conquest. If..great people get thee..land of the 6663
Faith. Except ye..signs and wonders..not believe 680
Identification. Upon whom thou shalt see the S. 4269
See WITNESS and TESTIMONY.

2752. EVIL, Appearance of. *Tax.* [27] Lest we
should offend them, go thou to the sea, and cast
a hook, and take up the fish that first cometh
up ; and when thou hast opened his mouth,
thou shalt find a piece of money : that take, and
give unto them for me and thee.—MAT., ch. 17.

2753. —— Freedom from. *Jesus.* [20] Pilate
therefore, willing to release Jesus, spake again
to them. [21] But they cried, saying, Crucify *him,*
crucify him. [22] And he said unto them the third
time, Why, what evil hath he done?—LUKE, ch.
23.

2754. —— overruled. *Joseph's Brethren.*
[19] Joseph said unto them, Fear not : for *am* I in
the place of God ? [20] But as for you, ye thought
evil against me ; *but* God meant it unto good..
to save much people alive.—GEN., ch. 50.

2755. —— temporarily permitted. *Tares.*
[29] Nay ; lest while ye gather up the tares, ye
root up also the wheat with them. [30] Let both
grow together until the harvest : and..I will say
to the reapers, Gather ye together first the tares,
and bind them in bundles to burn them : but
gather the wheat into my barn.—MAT., ch. 13.

2756. —— repaid with Good. *David* [9] said
to Saul, Wherefore hearest thou men's words,
saying, Behold, David seeketh thy hurt ? [10] Behold, this day..the Lord had delivered thee to
day into mine hand in the cave : and *some* bade
me kill thee : but *mine eye* spared thee.—1 SAM.,
ch. 24.

2757. —— The Root of. *Money.* [9] They that
will be rich fall into temptation and a snare,
and *into* many foolish and hurtful lusts, which
drown men in destruction and perdition. [10] For
the love of money is the root of all evil : which
while some coveted after, they have erred from
the faith, and pierced themselves through with
many sorrows.—1 TIM., ch. 6.

See other illustrations under :

INJURY.

Forgiveness. Father, forgive them, they know not 4498
Insulting. Samson's wife was given to his..friend 4496
Revenged. Samson caught 300 foxes..firebrands 4497
See CRIME, SIN, and WICKED.

2858. EXAMPLE, Encouragement by. *Calm-
ness.* [33] While the day was coming on, Paul besought *them* all to take meat, saying, This day is
the fourteenth that ye have..continued fasting. [35] And..he took bread, and gave thanks to
God in presence of them all ; and..he began to
eat. [36] Then were they all of good cheer, and
they also took *some* meat.—ACTS, ch. 27.

2759. —— Following. *Ruth.* [16] Ruth said,
Entreat me not to leave thee..for whither thou
goest, I will go ; and where thou lodgest, I will
lodge : thy people *shall be* my people, and thy
God my God : [17] Where thou diest, will I die,
and there will I be buried.—RUTH, ch. 1.

2760. —— Hindered by. *Pharisees.* [13] Woe
unto you, scribes and Pharisees, hypocrites !
for ye shut up the kingdom of heaven against
men : for ye neither go in *yourselves,* neither
suffer ye them that are entering, to go in.—MAT.,
ch. 23.

2761. —— for Imitation. *Washing Feet.* [14] If
I then, *your* Lord and Master, have washed
your feet ; ye also ought to wash one another's
feet. [15] For I have given you an example, that
ye should do as I have done to you.—JOHN, ch.
13.

2762. —— Instruction by. [See No. 2761.]

2763. —— Inferior. *Pharisees.* [3] All therefore whatsoever they bid you observe, *that* observe and do ; but do not ye after their works :
for they say, and do not. [4] For they bind heavy
burdens and grievous to be borne, and lay *them*
on men's shoulders ; but they *themselves* will not
move them with one of their fingers.—MAT., ch.
23.

2764. —— Justification by. *Disciples.* [1] Jesus went on the sabbath day through the corn ;
and his disciples were a hungered, and began
to pluck the ears of corn, and to eat. [2] ..the
Pharisees saw it..Behold, thy disciples do that
which is not lawful.. [3] But he said unto them,
Have ye not read what David did, when he was
a hungered, and they that were with him ;
[4] How he entered into the house of God, and
did eat the shewbread..only for the priests ?—
MAT., ch. 12.

2765. —— a Light. *Christ.* [15] Neither do
men light a candle, and put it under a bushel,
but on a candlestick ; and it giveth light unto

all that are in the house. [16] Let your light so shine before men, that they may see your good works, and glorify your Father.—MAT., ch. 5.

2766. —— The Lord's. *Slander.* [24] The disciple is not above *his* master, nor the servant above his lord. [25] It is enough for the disciple that he be as his master, and the servant as his lord. If they have called the master of the house Beelzebub, how much more *shall they call* them of his household?—MAT., ch. 10.

2767. —— Ministerial. *Minister.* [12] Let no man despise thy youth ; but be thou an example of the believers, in word, in conversation, in charity, in spirit, in faith, in purity.—1 TIM., ch. 4.

2768. —— Observation of. *Paul.* [9] Those things, which ye have both learned, and received, and heard, and seen in me, do : and the God of peace shall be with you.—PHIL., ch. 4.

2769. —— in Prayer. *Lord's Prayer.* [1] As he was praying..when he ceased, one of his disciples said unto him, Lord, teach us to pray, as John also taught his disciples. [2] And he said unto them, When ye pray, say, Our Father which art in heaven.—LUKE, ch. 11.

2770. —— in public Life. *Vashti.* [17] *This* deed of the queen shall come abroad unto all women, so that they shall despise their husbands in their eyes, when it shall be reported. The king Ahasuerus commanded Vashti the queen to be brought in before him, but she came not.—ESTHER, ch. 1.

2771. —— Teaching by. *Paul.* [8] Neither did we eat any man's bread for nought ; but wrought with labour and travail night and day, that we might not be chargeable to any of you : [9] Not because we have not power, but to make ourselves an example unto you.—2 THESS., ch. 3.

2772. EXAMPLES, Warning by. *Israelites.* [9] Neither let us tempt Christ, as some of them also tempted, and were destroyed of serpents. [10] Neither murmur ye, as some of them also murmured, and were destroyed of the destroyer. [11] Now all these things happened unto them for ensamples : and they are written for our admonition.—1 COR., ch. 10.

See other illustrations under :

IMITATION.

Benevolence. Samaritan had comp'n..do likewise   4333
Childhood. Humble himself as this little child   4334
Sacrilegious. Whosoever shall make like [incense]   4335

Precedent. David entered..did eat the shewbread   6464

2773. EXAMINATION, A brutal. *Paul.* [24] The chief captain commanded him to be brought into the castle, and bade that he should be examined by scourging ; that he might know wherefore they cried so against him.—ACTS, ch. 22.

2774. —— of Doctrines. *Bereans.* [11] These were more noble than those in Thessalonica, in that they received the word with all readiness of mind, and searched the Scriptures daily, whether those things were so. [12] Therefore many of them believed ; also of honourable women which were Greeks, and of men, not a few.—ACTS, ch. 17.

2775. —— of Self. *Apostles.* [18] As they.. did eat, Jesus said..One of you which eateth with me shall betray me. [19] And they began to

be sorrowful, and to say unto him one by one, *Is it I?*—MARK, ch. 14.

2776. —— A vindicating. *Pilate.* [14] Ye have brought this man unto me, as one that perverteth the people ; and, behold, I, having examined *him* before you, have found no fault in this man touching those things whereof ye accuse him. [15] No, nor yet Herod.—LUKE, ch. 23.

See other illustrations under :

ACCOUNTABILITY.

Future. Likened unto..king..take account of his s.   72
for Gifts. Called his servants, and delivered..pounds   73
Minute. Every idle word..shall give account   74
Personal. Give an account of thy stewardship   75

INVESTIGATION.

Fruitless. Against Daniel they could find none   4647
Secret. Went I. up in the night, and viewed the W.   4648

TEST.

Benevolence. One thing thou lackest..go sell..give   8726
Character. Ye shall not eat of it [tree] lest ye die   8727
Diet. Give us pulse to eat, and water to drink   8728
Exact. It was at the same hour..Jesus said..son   8729
Lord's. Man's rod whom I shall choose, shall be   8730
Needful. Girded his sword..I have not proved their   8731
Obedience. That saith, I know him, and keepeth   8732
Password. Say now, Shibboleth..said Sibboleth   8733
Prayer. Call ye upon the name of your gods, and I   8734
Question. Certain lawyer..tempted him, saying   8735
Severe. Take now..thine only son..burnt offering   8736
Trials. To know whether they would hearken   8737
"   That they which are approved..made   8738

TRIAL.

Mock. Sought for witness against Jesus   8919
Fruitless. Having examined him..found no fault   90

2777. EXCITEMENT, Abstinence by. *Saul.* [8] Saul arose from the earth..they led him by the hand, and brought *him* into Damascus. [9] And he was three days without sight, and neither did eat nor drink.—ACTS, ch. 9.

2778. —— Creating. *Stephen's Enemies.* [11] They suborned men, which said, We have heard him speak blasphemous words against Moses, and *against* God. [12] And they stirred up the people, and the elders, and the scribes.. and brought *him* to the council.—ACTS, ch. 6.

2779. —— of Ecstasy. *Transfiguration.* [33] Peter said unto Jesus, Master, it is good for us to be here : and let us make three tabernacles ; one for thee, and one for Moses, and one for Elias : not knowing what he said.—LUKE, ch. 9.

2780. —— of Evildoers. *Murderers.* [22] Pilate said..I will therefore chastise him, and let *him* go. [23] And they were instant with loud voices, requiring that he might be crucified.— LUKE, ch. 23.

2781. —— Public. *At Capernaum.* [19] They went into a house. [20] And the multitude cometh together again, so that they could not so much as eat bread. [21] And when his friends heard *of it*, they went out to lay hold on him : for they said, He is beside himself.—MARK, ch. 3.

2782. —— Needless. *Monument.* [10] When they came..in the land of Canaan, the children of Reuben and..of Gad and the half tribe of Manasseh built there an altar by Jordan.. [12] And when the children of Israel heard *of it*, the whole congregation..gathered themselves together at Shiloh, to go up to war against them. —Josh., ch. 22. [They were pleased when informed of its religious design.]

2783. —— *Last Visit.* [10] When he was come into Jerusalem, all the city was moved, saying, Who is this? [11] And the multitude said, This is Jesus the prophet of Nazareth.—Mat., ch. 21.

2784. —— **Trembling with.** *Jailer.* [28] Paul cried..Do thyself no harm : for we are all here. [29] Then he called for a light, and sprang in, and came trembling, and fell down before Paul and Silas, [30] And brought them out, and said, Sirs, what must I do to be saved?—Acts, ch. 16.

2785. —— **A wild.** *Paul's Enemies.* [34] Some cried one thing, some another, among the multitude : and when he could not know the certainty for the tumult, he commanded him to be carried into the castle.—Acts, ch. 21.

See other illustrations under :

AGITATION.
Deception. Who art thou ?..Esau..Isaac trembled 256
Diffuses. Disputed he in the synagogue..market 257
Deplored. [Israelites] Made..abhorred..slay us 258
General. [Philistines] Trembling in the host..field 259
Mount. Sinai..quaked greatly 260
Overcome. [At sepulchre] Keepers did shake 261
Physical. Belshazzar's thoughts troubled..knees 262
Terror. [Job's vision] Trembling..my bones 263

EMOTION.
Changed. Jesus showed them his hands..disciples 2625
Exhibited. Shaphan read it..the king rent his 2622
Irrepressible. Joseph made haste..sought where 2623
Mixed. Ancient men..seen the first..wept 2626
" From the sepulchre with fear and great 2627
Opposite. If these should hold their peace 2628
Worship. Mourn not..they heard..law 2624

Cause. Eli sat..watching..his heart trembled for 444
Restless. Would God it were even !..would morn. 7266
Spiritual. It shall bruise thy head..bruise his 451
Sleepless. Darius..sleep went from him..early to 458
Sickness. Nobleman besought him..come..ere 459
Strong. Jesus..groaned in the spirit, and was 3198
Suppressed. Haman was full of indignation 3199
Truth. Not come to send peace, but a sword 450
Vexations. Delilah..pressed him daily..urged 9187

2786. EXCLUSIVENESS reproved. *John said,* [38] Master, we saw one casting out devils in thy name..and we forbade him, because he followeth not us. [39] But Jesus said, Forbid him not : for there is no man which shall do a miracle in my name, that can lightly speak evil of me.— Mark, ch. 9.

See other illustrations under :

CASTE.
Abolished. G. hath showed me..any man..unclean 1055
Egyptian. Egyptians..not eat bread with the H. 1056
Ignored. Ordained twelve..Simon the Canaanite 1057
Jewish. Thou, being a Jew..askest drink of me 1058
No More. Great sheet..all manner of..beasts 1059
No Respect for. Smote the firstborn..throne 1060
Religious. Casting out devils..Forbade him 1061
Super-religious. Have known..woman that 1062

Division. I will sever..my people..no flies be there 2463

2787. EXCOMMUNICATION avoided. *Caution.* [21] Who hath opened his eyes, we know not : he is of age ; ask him : he shall speak for himself. [22] These *words* spake his parents, because they

feared the Jews : for the Jews had agreed already, that if any man did confess that he was Christ, he should be put out of the synagogue. —John, ch. 9.

2788. —— **by Bigots.** *Ex-Blind Man.* [33] If this man were not of God, he could do nothing. [34] They answered..Thou wast altogether born in sins, and dost thou teach us ? And they cast him out.—John, ch. 9.

2789. —— **feared.** *Pharisees.* [42] Among the chief rulers also many believed on him ; but because of the Pharisees they did not confess *him*, lest they should be put out of the synagogue : [43] For they loved the praise of men more than the praise of God.—John, ch. 12.

2790. —— **Method of.** *Christian.* [15] If thy brother shall trespass against thee, go and tell him his fault between thee and him alone : if he shall hear thee, thou hast gained thy brother. [16] But if he will not hear *thee, then* take with thee one or two more, that in the mouth of two or three witnesses every word may be established. [17] And if he shall neglect to hear them, tell *it* unto the church : but if he neglect to hear the church, let him be unto thee as a heathen man. —Mat., ch. 18.

2791. —— **Schismatic.** *Diotrephes.* [9] Diotrephes, who loveth to have the preeminence among them, receiveth us not. [10] ..prating against us with malicious words : and not content therewith, neither doth he himself receive the brethren, and forbiddeth them that would, and casteth *them* out of the church.—3 John.

See other illustrations under :

DISCIPLINE.
Ancient. Separated from l. the mixed multitude 2337
Care. Nay..lest ye root up also the wheat 2338
Primitive. Ananias and Sapphira..fell down 2340

SEPARATION.
Drunkards. Not to keep company..not to eat 7758
Godly. Separated from I. all the mixed multitude 7759
Impossible. Neither death nor life..able to s. 7764
Reason of. For they will turn away thy son 7778
Sorrowful. They kissed one another, and wept 7780
Spiritual. Fan is in his hand..wheat..chaff 7781
Sinners. Blessed..when they shall separate 7783
by Sin. As a shepherd•divideth his sheep..goats 7786
" Your iniquities have separated..your 7784
Unavoidable. Ye cannot drink the cup of the L. 7787

2792. EXCUSE for Disobedience, No. *King Saul.* [15] The people spared the best of the sheep and of the oxen, to sacrifice unto the Lord..the rest we have utterly destroyed. [22] And Samuel said, Hath the Lord as *great* delight in burnt offerings and sacrifices, as in obeying the voice of the Lord? Behold, to obey *is* better than sacrifice, *and* to hearken than the fat of rams. —1 Sam., ch. 15. [God had commanded a total destruction.]

2793. —— **A false.** *Jonathan.* [27] Wherefore cometh not the son of Jesse to meat, neither yesterday, nor to day ? [28] And Jonathan answered Saul, David earnestly asked *leave* of me *to go* to Beth-lehem.—1 Sam., ch. 20. [He was near by.]

2794. —— **The Idler's.** *Solomon.* [13] The slothful *man* saith, There is a lion without, I shall be slain in the streets.—Prov., ch. 22.

2795. —— **An inadequate.** *Golden Calf.*

²¹ Moses said unto Aaron, What did this people unto thee, that thou hast brought so great a sin upon them ?   ²³..they said unto me, Make us gods, which shall go before us : for *as for* this Moses..we wot not what is become of him.—Ex., ch. 32.

2796. EXCUSES of Cavillers. *Sabbath.* ²³If a man on the sabbath day receive circumcision, that the law of Moses should not be broken ; are ye angry at me, because I have made a man every whit whole on the sabbath day?—John, ch. 7.

2797. —— Feeble. *Parable.* ⁵ Friend, lend me three loaves ; ⁶ For a friend of mine in his journey is come to me, and I have nothing to set before him : ⁷ And he from within shall answer and say, Trouble me not : the door is now shut, and my children are with me in bed ; I cannot rise and give thee?—Luke, ch. 11.

2798. —— for Indolence. *Solomon.* ¹⁶ The sluggard *is* wiser in his own conceit than seven men that can render a reason.—Prov., ch. 26.

2799. —— Loss from. *Moses.* ¹⁰ O my Lord, I *am* not eloquent, neither heretofore, nor since thou hast spoken unto thy servant ; but I *am* slow of speech, and of a slow tongue. ¹⁴ And the anger of the Lord was kindled against Moses.—Ex., ch. 4.

2800. —— Worldly. *Invited Guests.* ¹⁸ They all with one *consent* began to make excuse. The first said..I have bought a piece of ground, and I must needs go and see it : I pray thee have me excused. ¹⁹ And another said, I have bought five yoke of oxen, and I go to prove them : I pray thee have me excused. ²⁰ And another said, I have married a wife, and therefore I cannot come.—Luke, ch. 14.

See other illustrations under :

EXPLANATION.
False. Say ye, His disciples..stole him..we slept   2819
Hereafter. What I do thou knowest not now   2820

PARDON.
Unexpected. Woman..neither do I condemn thee   5950
Wise. There shall not a man be put to death   5951
See FORGIVENESS.

2801. EXHIBITION declined. *Vashti.* ¹⁰ On the seventh day, when the heart of the king was merry with wine, he commanded.. ¹¹ To bring Vashti the queen..to shew the people and the princes her beauty.. ¹² But the queen Vashti refused to come.—Esther, ch. 1.

See other illustrations under :

APPEARANCES.
Conceal. Joseph made himself strange unto them   474
Evil. Lest we should offend..take up a fish   475
False. Walk in long robes, and love greetings   476
Hurtful. Be emboldened to eat those things   477
Uncertain. Man looketh on the outward   478

MANIFESTATION.
of Jesus. We will come unto him, and make our   5205
Piety. Because thou hast not withheld thy son   5206

Display. Ahasuerus the king make a feast   2409
Public. [Commands] Write them..on the posts   6289

2802. EXILE commanded. *Abram.* ¹ Get thee out of thy country, and from thy kindred, and from thy father's house, unto a land that I will shew thee : ² And I will make of thee a great nation.—Gen., ch. 12.

2803. —— A Criminal's. *Absalom.* ³⁷ David

mourned for his son every day.   ³⁸ So Absalom fled, and went to Geshur, and was there three years.   ³⁹..David .. was comforted concerning Amnon, seeing he was dead.—2 Sam., ch. 12.

2804. —— An Infant. *Jesus.* ¹³ Angel of the Lord appeareth to Joseph in a dream, saying, Arise, and take the young child and his mother, and flee into Egypt, and be thou there until I bring thee word : for Herod will seek the young child to destroy him.—Mat., ch. 2.

2805. —— necessary. *Jacob.* ⁴² Rebekah ..sent and called Jacob..and said..Behold, thy brother Esau..doth comfort himself, *purposing* to kill thee. ⁴³..flee thou to Laban my brother to Haran.—Gen., ch. 27.

2806. —— A painful. *Joseph.* ²⁸ Lifted up Joseph out of the pit, and sold Joseph to the Ishmaelites for twenty *pieces* of silver : and they brought Joseph into Egypt.—Gen., ch. 37.

See other illustrations under :

BANISHMENT.
Paradise. He drove out the man..garden of Eden   629
Punishment. Whosoever will not do the law   630
Persecution. Paul and Barnabas, and expelled   2922

EMIGRATION.
Famine. Shunammite..land of the Philistines   2620
Immense. 600,000 on foot..besides children   2621

FOREIGNER.
Despised. My master hath spared Naaman this   3331
Discrimination. Every creditor..of a foreigner   3332
Homesick. Hadad said to Pharaoh, Let me depart   3333
Ineligible. King over them..not set a stranger.   3334

FOREIGNERS.
Increase. Israel were fruitful, and increased   3335
Jealousy. War, they join also unto our enemies   3336
Liberality to. One law shall be..homeborn   3347

Mourning. By the rivers of Babylon..we wept   1026
Songless. How shall we sing the L.'s song?   1028
Sin. Walked in the sins..until removed   1029
"   I..did evil..L. sold them..of the Philistines   384

2807. EXPECTATION crushed. *Haman.* ⁶ The king said unto him, What shall be done unto the man whom the king delighteth to honour? Now Haman thought in his heart, To whom would the king delight to do honour more than to myself?.. ¹⁰ Then the king said to Haman, Make haste, *and* take the apparel and the horse, as thou hast said, and do even so to Mordecai the Jew.—Esther, ch. 6.

See other illustrations under :

ASSURANCE.
Believers. I know that my Redeemer liveth   557
Fall. I am persuaded that neither death, nor life   558
Heavenly. We know if..earthly house be dissolved   559
Inferential. If..would not..received..offering   560
Impudent. Bramble said to the trees..my shadow   561
Personal. I know whom I have believed   562
Victors. Who shall separate us from the love of C.?   563

CONFIDENCE.
Believers. Though I walk through the valley   1518
Blind. Know I that the L..I have a priest   1519
Caution. They are smitten down..as at the first   1520
Disappointed. Ark came..I. shouted..ark taken   1521
False. King [of Ai] wist not..ambush   1522
Future. Doth deliver..trust he will deliver   1523
Intelligent. I know whom I have believed   1524
Joyful. How great is thy goodness..trust thee   1525
Over. Is thy servant a dog..do this? [Hazael]   1526
Peril. Have the sentence of death..we trust   1527

Piety begets. L. was with Joseph..into his hand 1528
Strong. L. delight in us..fear them not 1529
Self. Peter said..I will lay down my life 1530
Triumphant. Although the fig tree shall not b. 1531
Unwarranted. Let two or three thousand go..Ai 1532
Unfortunate. Confidence..like a broken tooth and 1533
Undermining. Neither let Hez. make you trust..L. 1534
Warranted. L. is my rock, fortress, deliverer 1535

HOPE.

Abandoned. Martha saith..He hath been dead 4 4083
Deferred. While I am coming, another steppeth 4084
Deceptive. Think not..thou shalt escape in the 4085
Grave. My change come..I will answer thee 4086
Forlorn. Ark came into the camp, all I. shouted 4087
Ill-founded. The ark of God is taken by P. 4088
Joyful. Let the king and Haman come..glad 4089
Living. Begotten us..lively hope..inheritance 4090
Trials. We are..perplexed, but not cast down 4091
Triumphant. I am persuaded that neither..s. 4092

TRUST.

Active. Hezekiah clave to the L..rebelled against 9008
Courageous. Thou comest..I come..in the name 9009
Experience. L. who delivered me..the paw of..lion 9010
Egotists. Pharisee..I..I..I..I..I 9011
Fearless. Our G..is able to deliver us..furnace 9012
"   Though I walk through the valley 9013
"   The Lord is on my side, I will not fear 9014
Fixed. Though he slay me yet, will I trust 9015
Foolish. Bramble said..put your trust in my s. 9016
Honoured. Cried to G. in the battle..trust in him 9017
"   Angel smote..Assyrians, 185,000 9018
Ill-timed. Let us fetch the ark..it may save us 9020
Providence. May boldly say, The L. is my helper 9021
Self. Philistine..saw David..disdained him 9022

2808. EXPEDIENCY, Influenced by. *Paul.*
[11] If we have sown unto you spiritual things, *is
it* a great thing if we shall reap your carnal
things ? [12] If others be partakers of *this* power
over you, *are* not we rather ? Nevertheless we
have not used this power ; but suffer all things,
lest we should hinder the gospel of Christ.—1
Cor., ch. 8.

2809. EXPEDIENT, A strange. *Absent Jesus.*
[7] Nevertheless I tell you the truth ; It is expedient for you that I go away : for if I go not
away, the Comforter will not come unto you ;
but if I depart, I will send him unto you.—
John, ch. 16.

See other illustrations under :

MEANS.

Defence. Hezekiah..built up the walls..made 5255
Escape. They let him down the wall in a basket 5256
Heroic. Soldiers cut off the ropes of the boat 5257
Ingenious. Ark of bulrushes..pitch..stood 5258
Insignificant. Touched he their eyes..eyes were 5259
not Neglected. Take a lump of figs..laid it on the 5260
Prayer. We made our prayer..set a watch..day 5261
Prudential. Jesus..would not walk in Jewry 5262
Strange. Moses..rod of God..held up his hand 5263
"   Sound of the trumpet..people shouted 5264
Use of. Think on me when it shall be well with thee 5265
Unworthy. If I make not thy life..went for his 5266

2810. EXPENSE of Royalty. *Provisions.*
[22] Solomon's provision for one day was thirty
measures of fine flour, and threescore measures
of meal, [23] Ten fat oxen, and twenty oxen out
of the pastures, and a hundred sheep, besides
harts, and roebucks, and fallow-deer, and fatted
fowl.—1 Kings, ch. 4.

See other illustrations under :

COST.

Count. Master, I will follow thee whithersoever 1734
Counted. Gathered books, and burned..50,000 p. 1735
not Counted. Began to build, and was not able 1736
Sacrifice. Nay, but I will surely buy it 1737

GIFTS.

Valuable. Bring me a morsel of meal..but a 3531
Rebuilding. 61,000 drams of gold, and 5000 pounds 3532

PRICE.

Extortion. Esau sold his birthright unto Jacob 6550
of Perfection. Go sell..give..follow me 6551

Valued. Widow..cast more in than all 711
Contribution. I have given [$94,101,560] 3514
Temple. [Costing nearly $4,700,000,000] 4130

2811. EXPERIENCE, Confident. *Paul.* [12] I
am not ashamed ; for I know whom I have believed, and am persuaded that he is able to keep
that which I have committed unto him against
that day.—2 Tim., ch. 1.

2812. —— Growth in. *Rod budded.* [5] The
man's rod, whom I shall choose, shall blossom..
[8]..on the morrow Moses went into the tabernacle of witness ; and, behold, the rod of Aaron
..was budded, and brought forth buds, and
bloomed blossoms, and yielded almonds.—Num.,
ch. 17.

2813. —— Religious. *David.* [1] I will bless
the Lord at all times : his praise *shall* continually *be* in my mouth. [2] My soul shall make her
boast in the Lord : the humble shall hear there-
of, and be glad. [3] Oh magnify the Lord with
me, and let us exalt his name together. [4] I
sought the Lord, and he heard me, and delivered
me from all my fears.—Ps. 34.

2814. —— Typified. *Three Feasts.* [[a] The
passover, the atonement ; a way of escape opened. [b] Pentecost, firstfruits ; new birth, every-
thing new. [c] Tabernacles, ingathering, memorial of the wilderness, indicating the finally
perfected transformation to which we journey.]
[15] Thou shalt keep the feast of unleavened
bread : thou shalt eat unleavened bread seven
days..in..for in it thou camest out from Egypt :
and none shall appear before me empty : [16] And
the feast of harvest, the firstfruits of thy labours, which thou hast sown in the field : and
the feast of ingathering, *which is* in the end of
the year, when thou hast gathered in thy labours
out of the field.—Ex., ch. 23.

2815. —— Testimony of. *Paul.* [Paul's
conversion.—Acts, ch. 26.]

2816. —— Sympathetic. *High Priest.* [15] We
have not a high priest which cannot be touched
with the feeling of our infirmities ; but was in
all points tempted like as *we are*, *yet* without sin.
[16] Let us therefore come boldly unto the throne
of grace.—Heb., ch. 4.

See other illustrations under :

COMMUNION.

Invitation. I stand at the door..open..I will c. 1413
Mysterious. We will come..make our abode with 1414
Recorded. They that feared the L..book of r. 1417
Saints. No more..foreigners, but fellow citizens 1420
Walking. Enoch walked with God..God took 1421

CONVERSION.

Creation. New creature, old things passed away 1700
Conscious. Know we that we dwell in him..S. 1701
Changed. Made their feet fast..washed their s. 1702

Changes Life. Saul preached..Is not this he that	1703
Effort. Strive to enter in at the strait gate	1704
Evidence. Lydia..besought us..Come into my	1705
False. Simon saw..H. G. given..offered money	1706
Genuine. Set meat..rejoiced, believing in G.	1707
Heart Work. Out of the heart..evil thoughts	1708
Hasty. See here is water ; what doth hinder	1709
Inward. Pharisees make clean the outside of	1710
Mystery. Wind bloweth..canst not tell whence	1711
Necessity. Except a man be born of water and	1712
New Heart. God gave Saul another heart	1713
Negative. Reckon ye yourselves dead indeed unto	1714
Sudden. Called for a light. What must I do ?	1715
Superficial. When tribulation or persecution	1716
Wonderful. Suddenly there shined..voice..Saul	1717

HISTORY.

Unwritten. The world itself could not contain the	3994
Warning. Some murmured..written for our	3995
See **TRIAL.**	

2817. EXPERIMENT, A dietetic. *Four Hebrews.* [12] Prove thy servants.. ten days ; and let them give us pulse to eat, and water to drink. [13] Then let our countenances be looked upon before thee, and the countenance of the children that eat of the portion of the king's meat.—DAN., ch. 1.

2818. —— Faith's. *Peter.* [29] He walked on the water, to go to Jesus. [30] But when he saw the wind boisterous, he was afraid ; and beginning to sink, he cried, saying, Lord, save me.—MAT., ch. 14.

See other illustrations under :

TEST.

Benevolence. One thing thou lackest..go sell..give	8726
Character. Ye shall not eat of it [tree] lest ye die	8727
Diet. Give us pulse to eat, and water to drink	8728
Exact. It was at the same hour..Jesus said..son	8729
Lord's. Man's rod whom I shall choose, shall b.	8730
Needful. Girded his sword..I have not proved their	8731
Obedience. That saith, I know him, and keepeth	8732
Password. Say now, Shibboleth..said Sibboleth	8733
Prayer. Call ye upon the name of your gods	8734
Question. Certain lawyer..tempted him, saying	8735
Severe. Take now..thine only son..burnt offering	8736
Trials. To know whether they would hearken	8737
" That they which are approved..made m.	8738

TOUCH.

Healing. She came behind, and touched	8856
" Laid the sick in the streets..might	8857

TRIAL.

Character. Saw the Egyptians dead..feared the L.	8914
" Midst of the sea..Waters were a wall	8915
Faith. More precious than gold..tried in the fire	8916
Impenitence. Thy sons..as a wild bull in a net	8917
Life. But of the tree..shalt not eat	8918
Mock. Council sought for witness against Jesus	8919
Proportioned. G. led them not..way of the P.	8920
Stubbornness. In the time of his distress..trespass	8921

VENTURE.

Believers. Went into the midst of the sea..waters	9185
Shot. Drew a bow at a venture and smote the	9186
See **EXPERIENCE.**	

2819. EXPLANATION, A false. *Chief Priests.* [12] Gave large money unto the soldiers, [13] Saying, Say ye, His disciples came by night, and stole him *away* while we slept.—MAT., ch. 28.

2820. EXPLANATIONS hereafter. *Lord's Doing.* [6] Peter saith unto him, Lord, dost thou wash my feet ? [7] Jesus answered..What I do

thou knowest not now ; but thou shalt know hereafter.—JOHN, ch. 13.

See other illustrations under :

EXCUSE.

Disobedience. Spared the best of the sheep..to	2792
False. Wherefore cometh not..[David] to meat	2793
Idlers. Lion without, I shall be slain	2794
Inadequate. Make us gods..as for this Moses	2795

EXCUSES.

Caviller's. Angry..made a man..whole on the s.	2796
Feeble. The door is now shut..in bed..cannot	2797
Indolence. Sluggard is wiser..render a reason	2798
Loss. I am slow of speech..anger of the Lord	2799
Worldly. I have bought a piece of ground..oxen	2800

ILLUSTRATION.

Allegory. Abraham had two sons..an allegory	4321
Effective. Pharisees make clean the outside of the	4322
Nature. Like a grain of mustard seed..groweth	4323
Striking. Who is my neighbour..fell among thieves	4324

INSTRUCTION.

Better than Practice. Not move one of their fingers	4541
Children. Teach them [law] thy sons..sons' sons	4542
Course. Three years..might stand before the king	4543
Humble. A. and Priscilla..expounded unto	4544
Important. Heareth, and understandeth it not	4545
Improvement. Be an ornament of grace unto thy	4546
Personal. [See No. 4544.]	
Public. Ezra brought the law..all that could hear	4548
Private. Came man to him [Paul] into his lodging	4549

2821. EXPULSION, Ecclesiastical. *Method.* [17] If he shall neglect to hear them, tell *it* unto the church : but if he neglect to hear the church, let him be unto thee as a heathen man.—MAT., ch. 18.

2822. —— by Persecution. *From Antioch.* [50] The Jews stirred up the devout and honourable women, and the chief men of the city, and raised persecution against Paul and Barnabas, and expelled them out of their coasts. [51] But they shook off the dust of their feet against them.—ACTS, ch. 13.

2823. —— of Sinners. *Paradise.* [24] He drove out the man : and he placed at the east of the garden of Eden cherubim, and a flaming sword which turned every way, to keep the way of the tree of life.—GEN., ch. 3.

2824. —— A vigorous. *Nehemiah.* [27] Shall we then hearken unto you to do all this great evil, to transgress against our God in marrying strange wives? [28] And *one* of the sons of Joiada ..*was* son in law to Sanballat the Horonite : therefore I chased him from me.—NEH., ch. 13.

See other illustrations under :

EXCOMMUNICATION.

Avoided. His parents..feared the Jews..put out	2787
Bigots. Dost thou teach us ? and they cast him	2788
Feared. Did not confess him, lest they should be	2789
Method. If he neglect to hear the church..heathen	2790
Schismatic. Diotrephes..casteth them out of the	2791

EXILE.

Command. [Abram] Get thee out of thy country	2802
Criminal. David mourned for [Amnon]..Absalom	2803
Infant. Take the young child..mother..Egypt	2804
Necessary. Flee..to Laban my brother, to Haran	2805
Painful. Sold Joseph to the Ishmaelites..into E.	2806

Mourning. By the rivers of Babylon..we wept	1029
Return. Return to Zion with songs	1028
Noble. Pharaoh sought to slay Moses..fled	3489

Punishment. Whosoever will not do the law..b. 630
Spiritual. Fan is in his hand..wheat..chaff 7781
Sinners. Blessed..when they shall separate 7883
by Sin. As a shepherd divided his sheep..goats 7789
"   Your iniquities have separated 7784

2825. EXTERMINATION, Bloody. *Amalek.*
[2] Thus saith the Lord of hosts, I remember *that*
which Amalek did to Israel, how he laid *wait* for
him in the way, when he came up from Egypt.
[3] Now go and smite Amalek, and utterly destroy
all that they have, and..slay both man and
woman, infant and suckling, ox and sheep, camel and ass.—1 SAM., ch. 15.

2826. —— **of the Wicked.** *A h a b ' s   S o n s.*
[6] Now the king's sons, *being* seventy persons,
were with the great men of the city, which
brought them up.   [7]..when the letter came to
them .. slew seventy persons, and put their
heads in baskets, and sent him *them* to Jezreel.
—2 KINGS, ch. 10.

See other illustrations under:

CALAMITY.
Destructive. Wall fell upon 27,000 men that were 995
of God. Earth opened her mouth, and swallowed 996
Hardened. I have smitten you with blasting 1001
Indiscriminating. The L. maketh the earth 1002
Misjudged. Tower in Siloam fell, think..they 1003
Predicted. Shall not be left one stone upon 997
Waiting. Jonah sat..see what would become 999

CRUELTY.
Captives. Joab put them under saws..harrows 1864
"   Judah cast [10,000 men of Sier] from the 1858
Maternal. Athaliah..destroyed all the seed royal 1857

MASSACRE.
Intended. Letters were sent by post..to destroy 5249
Infants. Herod..slew all the children..in Bethlehem 5250
Treacherous. Jehu said, Proclaim an assembly for 5251

2827. EXTERNALS overestimated. *Pharisee.*
[38] He marvelled that he had not first washed before dinner.   [39] And the Lord said unto him,
Now do ye Pharisees make clean the outside of
the cup and the platter ; but your inward part is
full of ravening and wickedness.—LUKE, ch. 11.

See other illustrations under:

APPEARANCES.
Conceal. Joseph..spake roughly..whence come 474
Evil. Lest we should offend..fish..mouth..money 475
False. Scribes..shew, make long prayers 476
Hurtful. If..see thee..at meat in the idol's temple 477
Uncertain. Look not on his countenance..heart 478

DISGUISE.
Battle. Ahab said, I will disguise myself 2382
Failure. Ahijah said, Come in, wife of Jeroboam 2383
Insufficient. Saul disguised himself [to visit witch] 2384
Penetrated. Is not the hand of Joab in this ? 2385

Display. Ahasuerus..court..white, green and blue 2409
Deception. Israel made as if beaten..Ai 6544
Fashion. Ahaz went to Damascus..fashion..altar 290
Formalist. I fast..I give tithes of all 3376
Hypocrites. Ye devour widows' houses, and for a 6548
Lip-service. This people draweth nigh..with 5049
Overstrained. Pay tithe of mint..have omitted 4936
Public. If any man see thee at meat in the idol's 1558
Quibbles. Swear by the temple, it is nothing..gold 4937

2828. EXTORTION, Extraordinary. *J a c o b .*
[30] Feed me, I pray thee, with that same red *pot-*
tage ; for I *am* faint..   [31] And Jacob said, Sell
me this day thy birthright.   [32] And Esau said, Be-

hold, I *am* at the point to die : and what profit
shall this birthright do to me?—GEN., ch. 25.

2829. —— **Pious.** *Pharisees.*   [25] Woe unto
you, scribes and Pharisees, hypocrites ! for ye
make clean the outside of the cup and of the
platter, but within they are full of extortion
and excess.—MAT., ch. 23.

2830. —— **rebuked.** *By Nehemiah.*   [4] We
have borrowed money for the king's tribute, *and*
that upon our lands and vineyards.   [5]..now our
flesh *is* as the flesh of our brethren, our children as their children : and lo, we bring into
bondage our sons and our daughters..   [13] Also
I shook my lap, and said, So God shake out
every man from his house, and from his labour,
that performeth not this promise.—NEH., ch. 5.

2831. EXTORTIONERS, Separation from. *Paul.*
[11] Now I have written unto you not to keep company, if any man that is called a brother be a
fornicator, or covetous, or an idolater, or a
railer, or a drunkard, or an extortioner ; with
such a one no not to eat.—1 COR., ch. 5.

See other illustrations under:

AVARICE.
Falsehood. Ananias with Sapphira..kept back 592
Oppression. Swallow up the needy..make the poor 593
Victim. Were glad..covenanted to give Judas 594

USURY.
Abolished. I pray you, let us leave off this usury 9146
Condemned. I was very angry..great assembly 9147
Law. Unto a stranger thou mayest lend upon usury 9148
Opportunity. That we might buy corn because of 9149

2832. EXTRAVAGANCE regretted. *H e r o d .*
[25] Give me..in a charger the head of John the
Baptist.   [26] And the king was exceeding sorry ;
yet for his oath's sake, and for their sakes 'which
sat with him, he would not reject her.—MARK,
ch. 1.

See other illustrations under:

CRUELTY.
Captives. Joab put them under saws..harrows 1864
"   Judah cast [10,000 men of Sier] from the 1858
Maternal. Athaliah..destroyed all the seed royal 1857

FANATICISM.
Accused. His friends said..He is beside himself 3036
Fickle. Would have done sacrifice..stoned Paul 3037
Genuine. Two hours cried out, Great is Diana 3038
Idolatry. They cried out, and cut themselves 3039

MASSACRE.
Intended. Letters were sent by post..to destroy 5249
Infants. Herod..slew all the children..in Bethlehem 5250
Treacherous. Jehu said, Proclaim an assembly for 5251

Assumed. Why was this waste of..ointment made 9341
Bravado. I will give thy flesh to the fowls [Goliath] 920
Display. Solomon made 200 targets of beaten gold 7390
"   Solomon's drinking vessels were of gold 7396
Prodigality. Wasted his substance in riotous 6625
Royalty. Solomon's provision for one day was 2807
Vanity. I builded me houses..gardens, orchards 7422
Wealth. Rich man..fared sumptuously every day 7382

2833. EXTREMITY, Christ in. *Sea.*   [23] As
they sailed, he fell asleep : and there came down
a storm of wind on the lake ; and they were
filled *with water,* and were in jeopardy.   [24] And
they..awoke him, saying, Master, Master, we
perish.   Then he arose, and rebuked the wind
and the raging of the water : and they ceased,
and there was a calm.—LUKE, ch. 8.

2834. —— **Deliverance in.** *Abraham.* [13] Abraham..looked, and behold, behind *him* a ram caught in a thicket by his horns..took the ram and offered him up for a burnt offering in the stead of his son.—GEN., ch. 22.

2835. —— **Help in.** *Food.* [See below.] [13] And Elijah said unto her, Fear not..make me thereof a little cake first..and after make for thee and for thy son. [14] For thus saith the Lord God of Israel, The barrel of meal shall not waste, neither shall the cruse of oil fail.—1 KINGS, ch. 17.

2836. —— **The last.** *Widow of Zarephath.* [12] I have not a cake, but a handful of meal in a barrel, and a little oil in a cruse : and, behold, I *am* gathering two sticks, that I may go in and dress it for me and my son, that we may eat it, and die.—1 KINGS, ch. 17.

2837. —— **A reversed.** *Haman.* [11] Then took Haman the apparel and the horse, and arrayed Mordecai, and brought him on horseback through the street of the city, and proclaimed before him, Thus shall it be done unto the man whom the king delighteth to honour.—ESTHER, ch. 6.

2838. —— **An unexpected.** *Abhorred of Pharaoh.* [20] They met Moses and Aaron..as they came forth from Pharaoh : [21]..said unto them, The Lord look upon you, and judge ; because ye have made our savour to be abhorred in the eyes of Pharaoh, and in the eyes of his servants, to put a sword in their hand to slay us.—Ex., ch. 5.

2839. —— **Victorious in.** *At Red Sea.* [13] Moses said..Fear ye not, stand still, and see the salvation of the Lord..for the Egyptians whom ye have seen to day, ye shall see them again no more for ever. [14] The Lord shall fight for you, and ye shall hold your peace. [30]..and Israel saw the Egyptians dead upon the sea shore.—Ex., ch. 14.

See other illustrations under :

DESPERATION.

Boldness. I will go in unto the king..if I perish	2218
Effort. Why sit we here till we die ?	2219
Sinners. Saul inquired of the L...answered him	2220
Sacrifices. King of Moab took his eldest son	2221

FAMINE.

Charity. Disciples determined to send relief	3023
Care. Shall eat bread by weight..water by	3024
Dying. Eaten no bread..three days..sick	3025
Distress. Delicate woman..children..eat them	3026
Exiled. Sojourn wherever thou canst..seven	3027
Escape. Abram went down into Egypt..famine	3028
Emigration. Elimelech went to sojourn in	3029
Inhumanity. Give thy son, that we may eat him	3030
Sin. I will break the staff of bread	3031
" Ye have forsaken the..L. and followed	3032
Seven Years. No bread..land of Canaan fainted	3033
Spiritual. I will send a famine..words of the L.	3034
Water. To kill us and our children..cattle	3035

PERIL.

Assassins. Jews bound themselves..had killed	6057
Fasting. Fourteenth day ye have..continued f.	6058
Imminent. There is but a step between me and d.	6059
Prayer. Master, we perish..rebuked the wind	6060
Sleeping. Jonah was fast asleep..Arise, call..God	6061
Time. Egyptians marched after them..sore afraid	6062
Voluntary. The three brake through the host of P.	6063
" Sinful. Shall I drink the blood of these	6064
Many Perils. Thrice was I beaten with rods, once	6065

2840. EXTREMES in Superstition. *Melitans.* [4] When the barbarians saw the *venomous* beast hang on his hand, they said among themselves, No doubt this man is a murderer, whom, though he hath escaped the sea, yet vengeance suffereth not to live. [5] And he shook off the beast into the fire, and felt no harm. [6]..but after they had looked a great while, and saw no harm come to him, they changed their minds, and said that he was a god.—ACTS, ch. 28.

See other illustrations under :

Meet. Beggar at his gate..crumbs..rich man's	6303
Separate. Beggar died..angels..rich man..hell	5156

2841. EYE, Guidance by the. *Discipline.* [8] I will instruct thee and teach thee in the way which thou shalt go : I will guide thee with mine eye. [9] Be ye not as the horse, *or* as the mule, *which* have no understanding : whose mouth must be held in with bit and bridle.—Ps. 32.

2842. —— **Guarding the.** *Christ.* [28] Whosoever looketh on a woman to lust after her hath committed adultery with her already in his heart.—MAT., ch. 5.

2843. —— **affects the Heart, The.** *Jesus.* [35] Healing every sickness and every disease among the people. [36]..when he saw the multitudes, he was moved with compassion on them, because they fainted, and were scattered abroad, as sheep having no shepherd.—MAT., ch. 9.

2844. —— **Importance of the.** *Jesus.* [22] The light of the body is the eye : if therefore thine eye be single, thy whole body shall be full of light. [23] But if thine eye be evil, thy whole body shall be full of darkness. If therefore the light that is in thee be darkness, how great *is* that darkness !—MAT., ch. 6.

2845. —— **Power of the.** *Trial of Christ.* [60] Peter said, Man, I know not what thou sayest. And immediately, while he yet spake, the cock crew. [61] And the Lord turned, and looked upon Peter. And Peter remembered..how he had said unto him, Before the cock crow, thou shalt deny me thrice. [62] And Peter went out, and wept bitterly.—LUKE, ch. 22.

2846. —— **The spiritual.** *Single.* [34] The light of the body is the eye : therefore when thine eye is single, thy whole body also is full of light ; but when *thine eye* is evil, thy body also *is* full of darkness. [35] Take heed therefore. that the light which is in thee be not darkness.—LUKE, ch. 11.

2847. EYES blinded, Spiritual. *Heathen.* [17] Gentiles walk, in the vanity of their mind, [18] Having the understanding darkened, being alienated from the life of God through the ignorance that is in them, because of the blindness of their heart.—EPH., ch. 4.

2848. —— **dimmed by Age.** *Isaac.* [1] When Isaac..was old, and his eyes were dim, so that he could not see, he called Esau..My son, go out to the field, and take me *some* venison.—GEN., ch. 27.

2849. —— **dazzled.** *Saul.* [11] I could not see for the glory of that light, being led by the hand..I came into Damascus.—ACTS, ch. 22.

2850. —— **Danger through the.** *At Sinai.* [21] Go down, charge the people, lest they break through unto the Lord to gaze, and many of them perish.—Ex., ch. 19.

2851. —— **Divinely enlightened.** *Hagar.*
[19] God opened her eyes, and she saw a well of water ; and she went, and filled the bottle with water, and gave the lad drink.—GEN., ch. 21.

2852. —— **Extinguishment of.** *Reproach.*
[1] The men of Jabesh said unto Nahash, Make a covenant with us, and we will serve thee. [2] And Nahash the Ammonite answered them, On this *condition* will I make a *covenant* with you, that I may thrust out all your right eyes, and lay it *for* a reproach upon all Israel.—1 SAM., ch. 11.

2853. —— —— *Samson.* [21] The Philistines took him, and put out his eyes, and brought him down to Gaza, and bound him with fetters of brass ; and he did grind in the prison house.—JUDGES, ch. 16.

2854. —— **holden, The.** *To Emmaus.* [15] While they communed *together* and reasoned, Jesus himself drew near, and went with them. [16] But their eyes were holden that they should not know him.—LUKE, ch. 24.

2855. —— **for the Invisible.** *At Dothan.* [17] Elisha prayed, and said, Lord, I pray thee, open his eyes, that he may see. And the Lord opened the eyes of the young man ; and he saw : and, behold, the mountain *was* full of horses and chariots of fire round about Elisha.— 2 KINGS, ch. 6.

2856. —— **Imperfect.** *Jesus.* [23] When he had spit on his eyes, and put his hands upon him, he asked him if he saw aught. [24] . .said, I see men as trees, walking.—MARK, ch. 8.

2857. —— **perfected.** *Jesus.* [26] After that he put *his* hands again upon his eyes, and made him look up ; and he was restored, and saw every man clearly.—MARK, ch. 8.

2858. —— **restored.** *Ananias said,* [17] Brother Saul, the Lord, *even* Jesus. .hath sent me, that thou mightest receive thy sight, and be filled with the Holy Ghost. [18] And immediately there fell from his eyes as it had been scales : and he received sight forthwith.—ACTS, ch. 9.

2859. —— **smitten.** *By Angels.* [10] Put forth their hand, and pulled Lot into the house to them, and shut to the door. [11] And they smote the men that *were* at the door of the house with blindness, both small and great : so that they wearied themselves to find the door.—GEN., ch. 19.

2860. —— **Temptation through.** *Abram.* [11] He said unto Sarai his wife, Behold now, I know that thou *art* a fair woman. . [12] Therefore. .when the Egyptians shall see thee, that they shall say, This *is* his wife: and they will kill me, but they will save thee alive.—GEN., ch. 12.

2861. —— —— *Eve.* [6] When the woman saw that the tree *was* good for food, and that it *was* pleasant to the eyes, and a tree to be desired to make one wise.—GEN., ch. 3.

2862. —— **unimpaired by Age.** *Moses.* [7] Moses *was* a hundred and twenty years old when he died : his eye was not dim.—DEUT., ch. 34.

2863. —— **unveiled.** *Christian's.* [16] The vail shall be taken away. [18] . .we all, with open face beholding as in a glass the glory of the Lord, are changed into the same image from glory to glory, *even* as by the Spirit of the Lord.—2 COR., ch. 3.

2864. —— **unsatisfied.** *Solomon.* [20] Hell and destruction are never full ; so the eyes of man are never satisfied.—PROV., ch. 27.

2865. —— **Weak.** *Vail.* [13] Moses. .put a vail over his face, that the children of Israel could not steadfastly look to the end of that which is abolished : [14] But their minds were blinded.—2 COR., ch. 3.

See other illustrations under :

APPEARANCES.

Conceal. Joseph made himself strange unto them 474
Evil. Lest we should offend. .take up a fish 475
False. Walk in long robes, and love greetings 476
Hurtful. Be emboldened to eat those things 477
Uncertain. Man looketh on the outward 478

BLIND.

Believing. Believe ye that I am able to do this? 827
Delivered. Made clay of the spittle. .anointed the 828
Led. Follow me. .led them to Samaria 829
Restored. When he had spit on his eyes. .restored 830

BLINDNESS.

Age. Isaac was old. .eyes were dim 831
Affecting. Slew the sons. .before his eyes. .put out 832
Brightness. I could not see for the glory. .light 833
Bondage. P. put out Samson's eyes. .prison 834
Bigots. Thou hast a devil. .Abraham is dead 835
Disqualifies. Let him not offer the bread of his G. 836
Inflicted. Angels smote the men. .at the door 837
Infirmity. Ahijah could not see. .eyes were set 838
Judicial. He hath blinded their eyes and hardened 839
Leadership. Woe unto you, ye blind guides... 840
Protected. Not put a stumblingblock before the b. 841
Prejudice. Moses put a vail. .remaineth the same 842
Relief. Bartimeus said, L. .my sight. .thy faith 843
Ruin. Are hid from thine eyes. .days shall come 844
Removed. L. open the eyes of these men. .Samaria 845
Satan. Knowest thou not yet. .E. is destroyed? 846
Spiritual. Understanding darkened. .blindness of 847
Unconscious. Pharisees said, Are we blind also? 848
Visitation. There fell upon Elymas a mist. .darkness 849

LOOK.

Life. When he beheld the serpent of brass, he l. 5056
Reproof. L. turned and looked upon Peter 5057
Trouble. L. looked through. .troubled the Egyp'ns 5058

SEEING.

Partial. Woman saw that the tree was good for f. 7654
Proof. G. hath given one to sit on my throne. .eyes 7655
Unsatisfactory. Eye is not satisfied with seeing 7656
Vexatious. Lot. .wicked. .seeing and hearing 7657

VANITY.

Forbidden. Be not called rabbi. .are brethren 9160
Humbled. Haman arrayed Mordecai. .proclaimed 9162
Punished. Hezekiah showed them all. .silver 9161
Religious. To be seen. .garments. .love greetings 9163

Adornment. Women adorn themselves. .not with 108
Concealment. Adulterer waiteth. .twilight. .no eye 111
Display. Ahasuerus made a feast. .hangings 2409

2866. FACE an Index, The. *Nehemiah.* [1] I took up the wine, and gave *it* unto the king. Now I had not been *beforetime* sad in his presence. [2] Wherefore the king said unto me, Why *is* thy countenance sad, seeing thou *art* not sick? this *is* nothing *else* but sorrow of heart.—NEH., ch. 2.

See other illustrations under :

COUNTENANCE.

Angry. Nebuchadnezzar was full of wrath 1757
Bold. [Gadites] Faces were like the faces of lions 1758
Changed. Belshazzar's countenance was changed 1759

Illuminated. Stephen's face, as it had been the 1760
Prayer changed. Countenance was altered 1761
Power. Iron sharpeneth iron..countenance of his 1762
Reveals. Cain..Why is thy countenance fallen? 1763
Sad. Why is thy countenance sad?..sorrow of 1764
Sins. Countenance doth witness..sin of Sodom 1765
Sullen. Jacob beheld the countenance of Laban 1766
Shining. Moses wist not that..his face shone 1767
Terrifying. Angel..his countenance was..very t. 1768

Withdrawn. Let Absalom not see my face 46

2867. FAILURE, Avoiding. *Building.*
[28] Which of you, intending to build a tower,
sitteth not down first, and counteth the cost,
whether he have *sufficient* to finish *it*? [29] Lest
haply, after he hath laid the foundation, and is
not able to finish *it*, all that behold *it* begin to
mock him, [30] Saying, This man began to build,
and was not able to finish.—LUKE, ch. 14.

2868. —— of Cruelty. *Egyptians.* [11] Therefore they did set over them taskmasters to afflict
them with their burdens.. [12] But the more they
afflicted them, the more they multiplied and
grew.—Ex., ch. 1.

2869. —— Complaint in. *Moses.* [22] Lord,
wherefore hast thou so evil entreated this people? why is it that thou hast sent me? [23] For
since I came to Pharaoh to speak in thy name,
he hath done evil to this people ; neither hast
thou delivered thy people at all.—Ex., ch. 5.

2870. —— of the Church. *Evil Spirit.*
[18] Wheresoever he taketh him, he teareth him ;
and he foameth, and gnasheth with his teeth,
and pineth away : and I spake to thy disciples
that they should cast him out ; and they could
not—MARK, ch. 9.

2871. —— Discouraging. *Israelites.* [19] Ye
shall not minish *aught* from your bricks of your
daily task. [20] And they met Moses and Aaron..
as they came forth from Pharaoh : [21] And they
said..ye have made our savour to be abhorred
in the eyes of Pharaoh, and in the eyes of his
servants, to put a sword in their hand to slay
us.—Ex., ch. 5.

2872. —— A disheartening. *Fishers.* [4] Let
down your nets for a draught. [5] And Simon..
said..Master, we have toiled all the night, and
have taken nothing : nevertheless at thy word I
will let down the net.—LUKE, ch. 5.

2873. —— explained. *The Church.* [28] When
he was come into the house, his disciples asked
him privately, Why could not we cast him out?
[29] And he said unto them, This kind can come
forth by nothing, but by prayer and fasting.—
MARK, ch. 9.

2874. —— through Fear. *Spies.* [32] Is a
land that eateth up the inhabitants thereof ;
and all the people..*are* men of a great stature.
[33] And there we saw the giants, the sons of Anak
..and we were in our own sight as grasshoppers,
and so we were in their sight.—NUM., ch. 13.
[35]..in this wilderness..they shall die.—NUM.,
ch. 14.

2875. —— An irremediable. *Foolish Virgins.*
[10] While they went to buy, the bridegroom came ;
and they that were ready went in with him to
the marriage : and the door was shut. [11] Afterward came also the other virgins, saying, Lord,
lord, open to us.—MAT., ch. 25.

2876. —— An ominous. *Haman.* [13] Haman

told Zeresh his wife and all his friends every
thing that had befallen him. Then said his wise
men and Zeresh..unto him, If Mordecai *be* of
the seed of the Jews, before whom thou hast
begun to fall, thou shalt not prevail against
him, but shalt surely fall before him.—ESTHER,
ch. 6.

2877. —— A providential. *Babel.* [7] Let us
go down, and there confound their language,
that they may not understand one another's
speech. [8] So the Lord scattered them abroad
from thence upon the face of all the earth : and
they left off to build the city.—GEN., ch. 11.

2878. —— ridiculed. *Unfinished.* [See No.
2867.]

2879. —— A temporary. *Moses.* [1] Thus
saith the Lord God of Israel, Let my people go
..[2] And Pharaoh said, Who *is* the Lord, that I
should obey his voice to let Israel go? I know
not the Lord, neither will I let Israel go.—Ex.,
ch. 5.

See other illustrations under :

DEFEAT.

Angered. Elihu saw..was no answer..wrath 2098
Conspirators. Entangle him..marvelled, and left 2099
Desperation. Not able to resist the wisdom and 2100
Humiliating. Men of Ai smote..Joshua rent 2101
Predicted. Will flee upon..horses, therefore shall 2102
Providential. L. did confound the language 2103

DISAPPOINTMENT.

Doubt. Heard that he was alive..believed not 2315
Gifts. S. gave Hiram 20 cities..pleased him not 2316
Good. They have taken..Lord out of the s. 2317
Humiliating. Prison truly..shut..no man there 2318
Ignorance. No place of seed..figs..vines 2319
Judgment. Thou hast taught in our streets 2320
Misjudged. We trusted it had been he..saved I. 2321
Maternal. I have gotten a man [murderer] from 2322
Many. Sown much, and bring in little 2326
Perplexing. King of Syria sore troubled 2323
Religion. Have wanted all things..consumed 2324
Unendurable. Ahithophel..hanged himself 2325

DISCOURAGEMENT.

Contrast. But as for me, my feet were almost gone 2346
Defeat. Would to God we had been content 2347
Evildoers. I am..weak, though anointed king 2348
Failure. Neither hast thou delivered thy people 2349
  "   We have toiled all the night, and taken 2350
Mismanagement. Men of Ai smote 36 men 2351
Ministerial. Some fell on stony ground..thorns 2352
Needless. They that be with us are more..with 2353
Overcome. He answered her not a word 2359
Reproved. Yet I have left me 7000 in I. 2354
Trials. I am not able to bear all this people..too 2355
Unbelief. Been better to have served the Egyptians 2356
Unreasonable. Wherefore have ye brought us out 2357
Without. We faint not..though our outward man 2358

INSOLVENCY.

Confessed. Have patience with me, I will pay 4534
Forgiven. Had nothing to pay, he frankly forgave 4535

LOSS.

Absence. Thomas..was not with them when Jesus 5063
Authority. I called my servant, he gave me no a. 5064
Accidental. Axe head fell into the water..alas 5065
Delay. While I am coming, another steppeth in 5066
Discovery. Found him not..found him in the t. 5067
Irreparable. The ark of God was taken by the P. 5068
Irrecoverable. If the salt hath lost its savour 5069
Ignorance. Heareth the word..understandeth..not 5070

of Losses. Gain the whole world, and lose his own 5071
Love. I have somewhat against thee..repent 5072
Profit and. What is a man advantaged if..lose h. 5073
Zeal. Thou shouldest have smitten five or six times 5074

LOSSES.
Accountability. I bear the loss, whether stolen or 5075
Restored. L. blessed the latter end of Job more 5076

OMISSION.
Cursed. Curse ye, Meroz..came not up to the help 5875
Deception. If any man be a hearer..and not a doer 5876
Great. When saw we thee a hungered..not minister 5877
Inexcusable. These shall go..everlasting punish't 5878
Nobles. Put not their necks to the work of the L. 5879
Sin. Ye pay tithe of mint..omitted weighter 5880
 See NEGLECT.

2880. **FAINT, yet pursuing.** *Four Hundred.*
[10] David pursued, he and four hundred men :
for two hundred abode behind, which were so
faint that they could not go over the brook Besor.
[18] And David recovered all that the Amalekites
had carried away.—1 SAM., ch. 30.

2881. —— **Strength for the.** *Eagles.* [30] Even
the youths shall faint and be weary, and the
young men shall utterly fall : [31] But they that
wait upon the Lord shall renew *their* strength ;
they shall mount up with wings as eagles ; they
shall run, and not be weary ; *and* they shall walk,
and not faint.—ISA., ch. 40.

2882. **FAINTING from Hunger.** *Pursuing
Philistines.* [24] The men of Israel were distressed
that day : for Saul had adjured the people, saying, Cursed *be* the man that eateth *any* food until
evening, that I may be avenged on mine enemies.
So none of the people tasted *any* food.—1 SAM.,
ch. 14.

2883. —— **Preserved from.** *David.* [12] False
witnesses are risen up against me, and such as
breathe out cruelty. [13] *I had fainted,* unless I
had believed to see the goodness of the Lord in
the land of the living. [14] Wait on the Lord : be
of good courage, and he shall strengthen thine
heart : wait, I say, on the Lord.—Ps. 27.

2884. —— —— *R e n e w e d.* [16] For which
cause we faint not ; but though our outward man
perish, yet the inward *man* is renewed day by
day.—2 COR., ch. 4.

2885. —— **a Weakness.** *Adversity.* [10] *If* thou
faint in the day of adversity, thy strength *is*
small.—PROV., ch. 24.

 See other illustrations under :

WEAK.
Care. Whoso shall offend one of these little ones 9391
 " Take heed..stumblingblock to them..weak 9392
Help. If there be no man to save us, we will 9393

WEAKNESS.
Believers. Babes in Christ..not able to bare meat 9394
 " Lest the people repent..return to 9395
Conscious. I am..weak, though anointed king 9396
Flesh. Moses' hands were heavy..stayed up his 9397
Instruments. L. sent flies..land was corrupted 9398
Moral. Peter separated..fearing them of the 9399
Personal. He that abideth in me bringeth forth 9400
Remembered. I was with you in weakness 9401
Submission. Ahab said, I am thine, and all that I 9402
Spiritless. All the kings..their heart melted 9403
 " Ai smote..hearts of the people melted 9404
 See DESPONDENCY and references.

2886. **FAITH with Action.** *Ten Lepers.*
[13] Lifted up *their voices,* and said, Jesus, Master,
have mercy on us. [14] And..he said unto them,
Go shew yourselves unto the priests. And..as
they went, they were cleansed.—LUKE, ch. 17.

2887. —— **Armour of.** *Breastplate.* [8] Let us,
who are of the day, be sober, putting on the
breastplate of faith and love ; and for a helmet,
the hope of salvation.—1 THESS., ch. 5.

2888. —— **Basis of.** *Paul.* [4] My preaching
was not with enticing words of man's wisdom,
but in demonstration of the Spirit and of power :
[5] That your faith should not stand in the wisdom
of men, but in the power of God.—1 COR., ch. 2.

2889. —— **Bible inspires.** *Bereans.* [11] Were
more noble than those in Thessalonica, in that
they received the word with all readiness of
mind, and searched the Scriptures daily, whether
those things were so. [12] Therefore many of them
believed.—ACTS, ch. 17.

2890. —— **Boundless.** *Martha.* [22] I know,
that even now, whatsoever thou wilt ask of God,
God will give *it* thee. [23] Jesus saith unto her,
Thy brother shall rise again.—JOHN, ch. 11.

2891. —— **benefited by Trial.** *J o y.* [2] My
brethren, count it all joy when ye fall into divers
temptations ; [3] Knowing *this,* that the trying of
your faith worketh patience. [4] But let patience
have *her* perfect work, that ye may be perfect
and entire, wanting nothing.—JAMES, ch. 1.

2892. —— **Condition of.** *Sceptics.* [39] They
that passed by reviled him, wagging their heads,
[40] And saying, Thou that destroyest the temple,
and buildest *it* in three days, save thyself. If
thou be the Son of God, come down from the
cross.—MAT., ch. 27.

2893. —— **confessed.** *In Egypt.* [30] Aaron
spake all the words..and did the signs in the
sight of the people. [31] And the people believed :
and when they heard that the Lord had visited
the children of Israel, and that he had looked
upon their affliction, then they bowed their
heads and worshipped.—EX., ch. 4.

2894. —— **confirmed.** *Samaritans.* [41] Many
more believed because of his own word ; [42] And
said unto the woman, Now we believe, not because of thy saying : for we have heard *him* ourselves, and know that this is indeed the Christ.
—JOHN, ch. 4.

2895. —— **Conditioned by.** *Eunuch.* [36] See,
here is water ; what doth hinder me to be baptized ? [37] And Philip said, If thou believest with
all thine heart, thou mayest. And he answered
and said, I believe that Jesus Christ is the Son
of God.—ACTS, ch. 8.

2896. —— **Courageous.** *Five Stones.* [40] He took
his staff in his hand, and chose him five smooth
stones out of the brook, and put them in a
shepherd's bag..and his sling *was* in his hand :
and he drew near to the Philistine. [45] Then said
David..Thou comest to me with a sword, and
with a spear, and with a shield : but I come to
thee in the name of the Lord.—1 SAM., ch. 17.

2897. —— **conquers Death.** *To Martha.* [39] He
hath been *dead* four days. [40] Jesus saith unto
her, Said I not unto thee, that, if thou wouldest
believe, thou shouldest see the glory of God ?
[43] And..he cried with a loud voice, Lazarus,
come forth.—JOHN, ch. 11.

2898. —— **distant Object of.** *Christ.* [24] Christ
is not entered into the holy places made with

hands, *which are* the figures of the true ; but into heaven itself, now to appear in the presence of God for us.—HEB. ch. 9.

2899. —— **A dead.** *Without Works.* [15] If a brother or sister be naked, and destitute of daily food, [16] And one of you say unto them, Depart in peace, be *ye* warmed and filled ; notwithstanding ye give them not..what *doth it* profit ? [17] Even so faith, if it hath not works, is dead.—JAMES, ch. 2.

2900. —— **No Difficulties with.** *Aged Abram.* [5] Look now toward heaven, and tell the stars, if thou be able to number them : and he said unto him, So shall thy seed be. [6] And he believed in the Lord.—GEN., ch. 15.

2901. —— **Degrees of.** *P e t e r.* [See Nos. 2911 and 2973.]

2902. —— **A defective.** *Disables.* [19] Then came the disciples to Jesus apart, and said, Why could not we cast him out ? [20] And Jesus said unto them, Because of your unbelief.—MAT., ch. 17.

2903. —— **removes Difficulties.** *Mountains.* [20] Jesus said..If ye have faith as a grain of mustard seed, ye shall say unto this mountain, Remove hence to yonder place ; and it shall remove : and nothing shall be impossible unto you.—MAT., ch. 17.

2904. —— **An evangelical.** *A b e l.* [3] Cain brought of the fruit of the ground an offering unto the Lord. [4] And Abel, he also brought of the firstlings of his flock and of the fat thereof. And the Lord had respect unto Abel and to his offering.—GEN., ch. 4.

2905. —— **by Evidence.** *Wine.* [11] This beginning of miracles did Jesus in Cana of Galilee, and manifested forth his glory ; and his disciples believed on him.—JOHN, ch. 2.

2906. —— **exemplified.** *Law.* [3] If his offering *be* a burnt sacrifice of the herd..he shall offer it of his own voluntary will at the door of the tabernacle. [4] And he shall put his hand upon the head of the burnt offering ; and it shall be accepted for him to make atonement for him. [5] And he shall kill the bullock before the Lord.—LEV., ch. 1.

2907. —— **Effort of.** *Withered Hand.* [13] Then saith he to the man, Stretch forth thine hand. And he stretched *it* forth ; and it was restored whole, like as the other.—MAT., ch. 12.

2908. —— **encouraged.** *Cloud.* [44] He said, Behold, there ariseth a little cloud out of the sea, like a man's hand. And he said, Go up, say unto Ahab, Prepare *thy chariot,* and get thee down, that the rain stop thee not.—1 KINGS, ch. 18.

2909. —— **faltering.** *Abraham.* [11] He said unto Sarai his wife, Behold now, I know that thou *art* a fair woman.. [12] Therefore..when the Egyptians shall see thee..they shall say, This *is* his wife : and they will kill me, but they will save thee alive. [13] Say..thou *art* my sister.—GEN., ch. 12.

2910. —— **and Fear.** *Spies.* [Caleb said,] [9] Only rebel not ye against the Lord, neither fear ye the people of the land ; for they *are* bread for us : their defence is departed from them, and the Lord *is* with us : fear them not. [10] But all the congregation bade stone them with stones.—NUM., ch. 14.

2911. —— **A failing.** *Peter.* [See No. 2973.] [30] When he saw the wind boisterous, he was afraid ; and beginning to sink, he cried, saying, Lord, save me. [31] And immediately Jesus.. caught him, and said..O thou of little faith, wherefore didst thou doubt ?—MAT., ch. 14.

2912. —— **Healed by.** *Forty Years Lame.* [16] Through faith in his name, hath made this man strong, whom ye see and know : yea, the faith which is by him hath given him this perfect soundness in the presence of you all.—ACTS, ch. 8.

2913. —— **honoured.** *Nobleman.* [49] Sir, come down ere my child die. [50] Jesus saith..Go thy way ; thy son liveth. And the man believed the word that Jesus had spoken unto him, and went his way. [51]..his servants met him, and told *him,* saying, Thy son liveth.—JOHN, ch. 4.

2914. —— **Healing by.** *Leper.* [12] A man full of leprosy..fell on *his* face, and besought him, saying, Lord, if thou wilt, thou canst make me clean. [13] And he put forth *his* hand, and touched him, saying, I will ; be thou clean..the leprosy departed.—LUKE, ch. 5.

2915. —— **A humble.** *Centurion's.* [6] Lord, trouble not thyself ; for I am not worthy that thou shouldest enter under my roof : [7] Wherefore neither thought I myself worthy to come unto thee ; but say in a word, and my servant shall be healed.—LUKE, ch. 7.

2916. —— **An imperfect.** *S u b s t i t u t e f o r.* [17] Abraham fell upon his face, and laughed, and said in his heart, Shall *a child* be born unto him that is a hundred years old? and shall Sarah, that is ninety years old, bear ? [18] And Abraham said unto God, Oh that Ishmael might live before thee !—GEN., ch. 18.

2917. —— **Intimidation of.** *Assyrians against Jerusalem.* [28] Rab-shakeh stood and cried with a loud voice..Hear the word of the great king, the king of Assyria : [29]..Let not Hezekiah deceive you : for he shall not be able to deliver you out of his hand : [30] Neither let Hezekiah make you trust in the Lord.—2 KINGS, ch. 18.

2918. —— **indispensable.** *Only Son.* [22] And ofttimes it hath cast him into the fire, and into the waters, to destroy him : but if thou canst do any thing, have compassion on us, and help us. [23] Jesus said..If thou canst believe, all things *are* possible to him that believeth. [24]..the father of the child cried out, and said with tears, Lord, I believe ; help thou mine unbelief.—MARK, ch. 9.

2919. —— **inspires Courage.** *Israelites.* [7] Be strong and courageous, be not afraid nor dismayed for the king of Assyria, nor for all the multitude that *is* with him : for *there be* more with us than with him. [8] With him *is* an arm of flesh ; but with us *is* the Lord our God to help us, and to fight our battles. And the people rested themselves upon the words of Hezekiah. —2 CHRON., ch. 32.

2920. —— **A living.** *With Works.* [18] A man may say, Thou hast faith, and I have works : shew me thy faith without thy works, and I will shew thee my faith by my works.—JAMES, ch. 2.

2921. —— **Lessons of.** *Flowers.* [27] Consider the lilies how they grow : they toil not, they spin not ; and yet I say unto you, that Solomon in all his glory was not arrayed like one of these.

28 If then God so clothe the grass, which is to day in the field, and to morrow is cast into the oven ; how much more *will he clothe* you, O ye of little faith ?—LUKE, ch. 12.

2922. —— **Lack of.** *Lot.* 17 Escape for thy life ; look not behind thee, neither stay thou in all the plain ; escape to the mountain, lest thou be consumed. 20 Behold now, this city *is* near to flee unto, and it *is* a little one : O, let me escape thither, (*is* it not a little one ?) and my soul shall live.—GEN., ch. 19.

2923. —— —— *Disciples.* 14 Afterward he appeared unto the eleven, as they sat at meat, and upbraided them with their unbelief, and hardness of heart, because they believed not them which had seen him after he was risen.—MARK, ch. 16.

2924. —— **only a Look.** *Brazen Serpent.* [See No. 2944.]

2925. —— **by Miracles.** *Disciples.* 11 This beginning of miracles did Jesus in Cana of Galilee, and manifested forth his glory ; and his disciples believed on him. 23 ..in Jerusalem at the passover .. many believed in his name, when they saw the miracles which he did.—JOHN, ch. 2.

2926. —— **A mixed.** *Evil Spirit.* 23 If thou canst believe, all things *are* possible to him that believeth. 24 And straightway the father of the child cried out, and said with tears, Lord, I believe ; help thou mine unbelief.—MARK, ch. 9.

2927. —— **measures Success.** *Blind Men.* 27 Two blind men followed him, crying .. *Thou* Son of David, have mercy on us. 28 And when he was come into the house, the blind men came to him : and Jesus saith .. Believe ye that I am able to do this ? They said unto him, Yea, Lord. 29 Then touched he their eyes, saying, According to your faith be it unto you.—MAT., ch. 9.

2928. —— **with Mystery.** *Paul.* 7 Into the second *went* the high priest alone once every year, not without blood, which he offered for himself, and *for* the errors of the people : 8 The Holy Ghost this signifying, that the way into the holiest of all was not yet made manifest.—HEB., ch. 9.

2929. —— **Obedient.** *Net.* 4 Launch out into the deep, and let down your nets for a draught. 5 And Simon answering said .. Master, we have toiled all the night, and have taken nothing : nevertheless at thy word I will let down the net. 6 And .. they inclosed a great multitude of fishes : and their net brake.—LUKE, ch. 5.

2930. —— **omnipotent.** *Mountain.* 21 Jesus answered .. If ye have faith, and doubt not, ye shall not only do this which is done to the fig tree, but also if ye shall say unto this mountain, Be thou removed, and be thou cast into the sea ; it shall be done. 22 And all things, whatsoever ye shall ask in prayer, believing, ye shall receive. —MAT., ch. 21.

2931. —— **a Protection.** *Daniel.* 23 Daniel was taken up out of the den, and no manner of hurt was found upon him, because he believed in his God.—DAN., ch. 6.

2932. —— **Power of.** *Mustard Seed.* 5 The apostles said .. Increase our faith. 6 And the Lord said, If ye had faith as a grain of mustard seed, ye might say unto this sycamine tree, Be thou plucked up by the root, and be thou planted in the sea ; and it should obey you.—LUKE, ch. 17.

2933. —— **A profitless.** *Wavering.* 6 Let him ask in faith, nothing wavering : for he that wavereth is like a wave of the sea driven with the wind and tossed. 7 For let not that man think that he shall receive any thing of the Lord.—JAMES, ch. 1.

2934. —— **A perfect.** *Abraham.* 17 By faith Abraham, when he was tried, offered up Isaac .. his only begotten *son.* 18 Of whom it was said, That in Isaac shall thy seed be called : 19 Accounting that God *was* able to raise *him* up, even from the dead.—HEB., ch. 11.

2935. —— **A proven.** *Abram.* 11 The angel of the Lord called unto him out of heaven, and said, Abraham, Abraham : and he said, Here *am* I. 12 And he said, Lay not thine hand upon the lad .. for now I know that thou fearest God, seeing thou hast not withheld thy son, thine only *son,* from me.—GEN., ch. 22.

2936. —— **Practical.** *With Works.* 19 Thou believest that there is one God ; thou doest well : the devils also believe, and tremble. 20 But wilt thou know, O vain man, that faith without works is dead ?—JAMES, ch. 2.

2937. —— **Possibilities of.** *Evil Spirit.* 23 Jesus said unto him, If thou canst believe, all things *are* possible to him that believeth. 24 And straightway the father of the child cried out, and said with tears, Lord, I believe ; help thou mine unbelief.—MARK, ch. 9.

2938. —— **A rootless.** *Rock.* 13 They on the rock .. when they hear, receive the word with joy ; and these have no root, which for a while believe, and in time of temptation fall away.—LUKE, ch. 8.

2939. —— **Results strengthen.** *Red Sea.* 30 Israel saw the Egyptians dead upon the sea shore. 31 .. and the people feared the Lord, and believed the Lord, and his servant Moses.—EX., ch. 14.

2940. —— **Results of.** *History.* [See Heb., ch. 11.]

2941. —— **A resting.** *Moabites Slain.* 17 Ye shall not *need* to fight in this *battle :* set yourselves, stand ye *still,* and see the salvation of the Lord with you, O Judah and Jerusalem : fear not, nor be dismayed .. 24 behold. they *were* dead bodies fallen to the earth, and none escaped.—2 CHRON., ch. 20.

2942. —— —— *At the Red Sea.* [See No. 2839.] Stand still and see.

2943. —— **A ready.** *Nathanael.* 48 When thou wast under the fig tree, I saw thee. 49 Nathanael answered .. him, Rabbi, Thou art the Son of God ; thou art the King of Israel. 50 Jesus answered .. Because I said .. I saw thee under the fig tree, believest thou ? thou shalt see greater things than these.—JOHN, ch. 1.

2944. —— **Saved by.** *Serpent.* 8 The Lord said unto Moses, Make thee a fiery serpent, and set it upon a pole : and it shall come to pass, that every one that is bitten, when he looketh upon it, shall live.—NUM., ch. 21.

2945. —— **Sustaining.** *David.* 13 *I had fainted,* unless I had believed to see the goodness of the Lord in the land of the living.

[14] Wait on the Lord : be of good courage, and he shall strengthen thine heart : wait, I say, on the Lord.—Ps. 27.

2946. —— Shield of. *Paul.* [16] Above all, taking the shield of faith, wherewith ye shall be able to quench all the fiery darts of the wicked. —Eph., ch. 6.

2947. —— Salvation by. *Jesus.* [16] God so loved the world, that he gave his only begotten Son, that whosoever believeth in him should not perish, but have everlasting life.—John, ch. 2.

2948. —— —— *Philippian Jailer.* [31] And they said, Believe on the Lord Jesus Christ, and thou shalt be saved, and thy house.—Acts, ch. 16.

2949. —— strengthened. *Disciples.* [20] Then said the Jews, Forty and six years was this temple in building, and wilt thou rear it up in three days? [21] But he spake of the temple of his body. [22] When therefore he was risen from the dead, his disciples remembered that he had said this unto them ; and they believed the scripture, and the word which Jesus had said. —John, ch. 2.

2950. —— Stability by. *David.* [1] They that trust in the Lord *shall be* as mount Zion, *which* cannot be removed, *but* abideth forever. [2] *As* the mountains *are* round about Jerusalem, so the Lord *is* round about his people from henceforth even forever.—Ps. 125.

2951. —— Sustaining. *Walked on the Water.* [See No. 2973.]

2952. —— without Sight. *Thomas.* [29] Thomas, because thou hast seen me, thou hast believed : blessed *are* they that have not seen, and *yet* have believed.—John, ch. 20.

2953. —— Superior. *Centurion.* [9] Jesus ..marvelled at him, and turned him about, and said unto the people that followed him, I say unto you, I have not found so great faith, no, not in Israel.—Luke, ch. 7.

2954. —— A simple. *Touch the Hem.* [47] When the woman saw that she was not hid, she came trembling, and falling down before him, she declared unto him before all the people for what cause she had touched him, and how she was healed immediately.—Luke, ch. 8.

2955. —— surmounting Obstacles. *Canaanite.* He answered her not a word..Send her away.. Lost sheep .. Children's bread .. Great is thy faith. [See No. 2359.]

2956. —— A sham. *Simon.* [13] When he was baptized, he continued with Philip..beholding the miracles.. [18] And when Simon saw that through laying on of the apostles' hands the Holy Ghost was given, he offered them money, [19] Saying, give me also this power.— Acts, ch. 8.

2957. —— Simplicity of. *Naaman.* [13] And his servants .. said, My father, *if* the prophet had bid thee *do some* great thing, wouldest thou not have done *it?* how much rather then, when he saith to thee, Wash, and be clean ? [14] Then went he down, and dipped himself seven times in Jordan..and his flesh came again like unto the flesh of a little child.—2 Kings, ch. 5.

2958. —— with Sacrifice. *Widow of Zarephath.* [13] Go and..make me thereof a little cake first..and after make for thee and for thy son. [14] For thus saith the Lord God of Israel, The barrel of meal shall not waste, neither shall the cruse of oil fail.—1 Kings, ch. 17.

2959. —— Touch of. *Healing.* [20] Behold, a woman..with an issue of blood twelve years, came behind *him*, and touched the hem of his garment : [21] For she said within herself, If I may but touch his garment, I shall be whole.— Mat., ch. 9.

2960. —— Trial of. *Red' Sea.* [22] The children of Israel went into the midst of the sea upon the dry *ground :* and the waters *were* a wall unto them on their right hand, and on their left.—Ex., ch. 14.

2961. —— A tempted. *Paul.* [13] There hath no temptation taken you but such as is common to man : but God *is* faithful, who will not suffer you to be tempted above that ye are able ; but will with the temptation also make a way to escape, that ye may be able to bear *it.*—1 Cor., ch. 10.

2962. —— A timid. *Pharisees.* [42] Among the chief rulers also many believed on him ; but because of the Pharisees they did not confess *him*, lest they should be put out of the synagogue.—John, ch. 12.

2963. —— Their united. *Palsy.* [4] When they could not come nigh unto him for the press, they uncovered the roof where he was : and..they let down the bed wherein the sick of the palsy lay. [5] When Jesus saw their faith, he said..Son, thy sins be forgiven thee. [11]..Arise, and take up thy bed, and go thy way into thine house.—Mark, ch. 2.

2964. —— gives Utterance. *Paul.* [13] We having the same spirit of faith, according as it is written, I believed, and therefore have I spoken ; we also believe, and therefore speak. —2 Cor., ch. 4.

2965. —— An unuttered. *Mary.* [37] Jesus sat at meat in the Pharisee's house, brought an alabaster box of ointment, [38] And stood at his feet behind *him* weeping, and began to wash his feet with tears, and did wipe *them* with the hairs of her head, and kissed his feet, and anointed *them* with the ointment.—Luke, ch. 7.

2966. —— unshaken. *Death.* [49] There cometh one from the ruler of the synagogue's *house*, saying to him, Thy daughter is dead ; trouble not the Master. [50] But when Jesus heard *it*, he answered..Fear not : believe only, and she shall be made whole.—Luke, ch. 8.

2967. —— A visible. *Working.* [2] They brought to him a man sick of the palsy, lying on a bed : and Jesus seeing their faith said unto the sick of the palsy ; Son, be of good cheer ; thy sins be forgiven thee.—Mat., ch. 9.

2968. —— A valueless. *"Without Works."* [See No. 2936.]

2969. —— precedes Victory. *Jericho.* [20] So the people shouted when *the priests* blew the trumpets..and the people shouted with a great shout..the wall fell down flat, so that the people went up..every man straight before him, and they took the city.—Josh., ch. 6. [They shouted while the walls were firm.]

2970. —— Venturing all. *Abram.* [1] Get thee out of thy country, and from thy kindred, and from thy father's house, unto the land that I will shew thee : ² And I will make of thee a great nation.—GEN., ch. 12.

2971. —— **Weakness of.** *Impediment.* ¹⁷ God led them not *through* the way of the land of the Philistines, although that *was* near ; for God said, Lest peradventure the people repent when they see war, and they return to Egypt.—EX., ch. 13.

2972. —— **Victory by.** *Moabites.* ¹⁷ Ye shall not *need* to fight in this *battle :* set yourselves, stand ye *still,* and see the salvation of the Lord with you, O Judah and Jerusalem : fear not, nor be dismayed ; to morrow go out against them : for the Lord *will be* with you. ¹⁸ And Jehoshaphat bowed his head with *his* face to the ground.—2 CHRON., ch. 20.

2973. —— **Venturing.** *Peter.* ²⁸ Lord, if it be thou, bid me come unto thee on the water. ²⁹ And he said, Come. And when Peter was come down out of the ship, he walked on the water, to go to Jesus.—MAT., ch. 14.

See other illustrations under :

ASSURANCE.

Believers. I know that my Redeemer liveth	557
Full. Neither death nor life..separate us	558
Heavenly. If our earthly house be dissolved	559
Inferential. If to kill us..would not receive	560
Impudent. Bramble said..put your trust in	561
Personal. I know..he is able to keep	562
Victor's. Who shall separate us from..C.	563

CONFIDENCE.

Believers. Though I walk through the valley	1518
Blind. Know I that the L..I have a priest	1519
Caution. They are smitten down..as at the first	1520
Disappointed. Ark came..I shouted..ark taken	1521
False. King [of Ai] wist not..ambush	1522
Future. Doth deliver..trust he will deliver	1523
Intelligent. I know whom I have believed	1524
Joyful. How great is thy goodness..trust thee	1525
Over. Is thy servant a dog?..do this [Hazael]	1526
Peril. Have the sentence of death..we trust	1527
Piety begets. L. was with Joseph..into his hand	1528
Strong. L. delight in us..fear them not	1529
Self. Peter said..I will lay down my life	1530
Triumphant. Although the fig tree shall not b.	1531
Unwarranted. Let two or three thousand go..Ai	1532
Unfortunate. Confidence..like a broken tooth and	1533
Undermining. Neither let Hez. make you trust..L.	1534
Warranted. L. is my rock, fortress, deliverer	1535

EVIDENCE.

Astounding. Divided her..twelve pieces sent	2729
Circumstantial. Potiphar's wife..left his garment	2730
Confirmatory. Thou art one..thy speech agreeth	2731
Confirmed. Is not the hand of Joab in this?	2732
Convincing. Man..healed standing..say nothing	2733
Deeds. If I do not the works..believe me not	2734
Divine. Tell John..blind see, the lame walk	2735
Fraudulent. Gibeonites..old shoes..old garments	2736
False. Sought false witness..two false witnesses	2737
Innocence. So do God..if I taste bread..sun be	2738
Lord's. Kine took the straight way..lowing	2739
Misconstrued. Tower..fell..sinners above all	2740
Mistaken. Keep my saying..never see death	2741
Manufactured. Took Joseph's coat..dipped in	2742
Practical. Reach hither thy hand, and thrust it	2743
Rejected. We would seek a sign..Jonas was three	2744
Satisfying. Now we believe..heard him ourselves	2745
Suggestive. Dagon was fallen..before the ark of	2746
Sincerity. Used curious arts..their books..burned	2747

Trial. Ten days..give us pulse to eat..looked upon	2748
Unexplainable. Cup was found in Benjamin's sack	2749
Unsuppressed. What meaneth then this bleating	2750
Understood. Saw the boldness..with Jesus	2751

PRESUMPTION.

Daring. Egyptians went..midst of the sea	6535
Failure. Presumed to go up. Amalekites smote	6536
Future. Know not what shall be..morrow	6537
Impatience. Because..people scattered..I offered	6538
Pride. Uzziah..heart lifted up..burn incense	6539
Penalty. Death, except..king hold out..sceptre	6540
Religious. Prophet that shall presume to speak	6541
Rebuke. Uzziah..leprosy..priests thrusting out	6542
Sin. Much sorer punishment..under foot..blood	6543
" Doeth aught presumptuously..cut off	6545
Success. Israel made as if..beaten..Ai..drawn	6544
Temptation Setteth him on a pinnacle..cast	6546
Unholy. Ye take too much upon you [Korah]	6547

TRUST.

Active. Hezekiah clave to the L..rebelled against	9008
Courageous. Thou comest..I come..in the name	9009
Experience. L. who delivered me..the paw of the	9010
Egotists. Pharisee..I..I..I..I..I	9011
Fearless. Our G..is able to deliver us..furnace	9012
" Though I walk through the valley	9013
" The Lord is on my side, I will not fear	9014
Fixed. Though he slay me, yet will I trust	9015
Foolish. Bramble said..Put your trust in my s.	9016
Honoured. Cried to G. in the battle..trust in him	9017
" Angel smote..Assyrians, 185,000	9018
Ill-timed. Let us fetch the ark..it may save us	9020
Providence. May boldly say, The L. is my helper	9021
Self. Philistine..saw David..disdained him	9022

Boastful. [Goliath] I will give thy flesh to the fowl 920

2974. FAITHFUL, Angels guard the. *At Dothan.* ¹⁷ Elisha prayed..And the Lord opened the eyes of the young man ; and he saw : and, behold, the mountain *was* full of horses and chariots of fire round about Elisha.—2 KINGS, ch. 6.

2975. FAITHFULNESS blessed. *Servant.* ⁴⁶ Blessed *is* that servant, whom his lord when he cometh shall find so doing.—MAT., ch. 24.

2976. —— **Constant.** *Altar.* ¹² The priest shall burn wood on it every morning, and lay the burnt offering in order upon it ; and he shall burn thereon the fat of the peace offerings. ¹³ The fire shall ever be burning upon the altar ; it shall never go out.—LEV., ch. 6.

2977. —— **in Despondency.** *Thomas.* ¹⁶ Let us also go, that we may die with him. ¹⁷ Then when Jesus came, he found that he had *lain* in the grave four days already.—JOHN, ch. 11.

2978. —— **honoured.** *Three Hebrews.* ²⁹ I make a decree, That every people, nation, and language, which speak any thing amiss against the God of Shadrach, Meshach, and Abed-nego, shall be cut in pieces, and their houses shall be made a dunghill ; because there is no other God that can deliver after this sort.—DAN., ch. 3.

2979. —— *Ministerial.* [See 2 Cor. 4 : 1-11.]

2980. —— **to the Truth.** *Ministerial.* ¹³ The messenger..to call Micaiah spake..Behold now, the words of the prophets *declare* good unto the king with one mouth : let thy word, I pray thee, be like the word of one of them, and speak *that which is* good. ¹⁴ And Micaiah said, As the Lord liveth, what the Lord saith unto me, that will I speak.—1 KINGS, ch. 22.

2981. —— Primitive. *Persecuted.* [1] There was a great persecution against the church which was at Jerusalem ; and they were all scattered abroad throughout the regions of Judea and Samaria, except the apostles.—Acts, ch. 8.

2982. —— by Principle. *Least.* [10] He that is faithful in that which is least is faithful also in much : and he that is unjust in the least is unjust also in much. [11] If therefore ye have not been faithful in the unrighteous mammon, who will commit to your trust the true *riches?*—Luke, ch. 16.

2983. —— rewarded. *Elisha.* [9] Elijah said unto Elisha, Ask what I shall do for thee, before I be taken away from thee. And Elisha said, I pray thee, let a double portion of thy spirit be upon me. [10] And he said, Thou hast asked a hard thing : *nevertheless,* if thou see me *when I am* taken from thee, it shall be so unto thee ; but if not, it shall not be *so.*—2 Kings, ch. 2.

2984. —— Religious. *Vows.* [4] When thou vowest a vow unto God, defer not to pay it ; for *he hath* no pleasure in fools : pay that which thou hast vowed. [5] Better *is it* that thou shouldest not vow, than that thou shouldest vow and not pay.—Eccl., ch. 5.

See other illustrations under :

HONESTY.

Accredited. My master wotteth not what is with	4043
Acknowledged. Samuel..thou hast not defrauded	4044
Commended. Hath not oppressed..usury..iniquity	4045
Happiness. Better is little with righteousness	4046
Ignored. It is naught, saith the buyer..boasteth	4047
Official. Gift doth blind the eyes of the wise	4048
Payment. Go sell the oil and pay the debt	4049
Rare. Seek..if there be any..the truth	4050
Reward. Shaketh his hand from holding bribes	4051
Restitution. If I have taken..restore fourfold	4052
Trained. All these have I observed from my y.	4053
Test. The money that was. in your sacks..carry	4054
Trade. Not have..divers weights, a great and s.	4055
" Divers weights, and divers measures	4056
Trusted. They delivered the money to..workmen	4057

SINCERITY.

Consecration. Josiah made a covenant..burned	8025
Evildoing. I thought I ought to..put to death	8026
Evidence. Brought their books..burned them	8027
Example. An Israelite in whom is no guile	8028
Heart. He that speaketh truth in his heart	8029
Lovable. All..have I kept..Jesus loved him	8030
Opinions. Rabbi, thou art the Son of God	8031
Positive. Thou knowest that I love thee	8032
Proof. When..people saw it..L. he is G.	8033
Reformation. Speak..the truth..execute..truth	8034

STEADFASTNESS.

Converts. 3000..continued steadfastly in f.	8337
Determined. Till I die, I will not remove mine	8338
Duty. Josiah..turned not aside to the right..left	8339
Integrity. I kept myself from mine iniquity	8340
Principle. Daniel purposed..not defile himself	8341
Religious. We will not serve thy gods, nor worship	8342
Seen. Satan, hast thou considered..Job?	8343

2985. FALSEHOOD, Agreement in. *Ananias.* [1] Ananias, with Sapphira his wife, sold a possession, [2] And kept back *part* of the price..and brought a certain part, and laid *it* at the apostles' feet. [9] Then Peter said unto her, How is it that ye have agreed together to tempt the Spirit of the Lord? behold, the feet of them which have buried thy husband *are* at the door, and shall carry thee out.—Acts, ch. 5.

2986. —— begets Falsehood. *Gehazi.* [21] So Gehazi followed after Naaman.. [22] And he said ..My master hath sent me, saying..give them, I pray thee, a talent of silver, and two changes of garments. [25] But he went in, and stood before his master. And Elisha said .. Whence *comest thou,* Gehazi ? And he said, Thy servant went no whither. [26] And he said unto him..*Is it* a time to receive money, and to receive garments ?—2 Kings, ch. 5.

2987. —— by Bribery. *Soldiers.* [13] Say ye, His disciples came by night, and stole him *away* while we slept.. [15] So they took the money, and did as they were taught.—Mat., ch. 28.

2988. —— covering Falsehood. *Peter.* [70] He denied it again. And a little after, they that stood by said again to Peter, Surely thou art *one* of them : for thou art a Galilean, and thy speech agreeth *thereto.* [71] But he began to curse and to swear, *saying,* I know not this man of whom ye speak.—Mark, ch. 14.

2989. —— Folly of. *Ananias.* [3] Peter said, Ananias, why hath Satan filled thine heart to lie to the Holy Ghost, and to keep back *part* of the price of the land ? [4] While it remained, was it not thine own ? and after it was sold, was it not in thine own power?..thou hast not lied unto men, but unto God.—Acts, ch. 5.

2990. —— The Father of. *Devil.* [44] Ye are of *your* father the devil..he was a murderer from the beginning, and..there is no truth in him. When he speaketh a lie, he speaketh of his own ; for he is a liar, and the father of it.—John, ch. 8.

2991. —— An Impostor's. *Jacob.* [20] Isaac said ..How *is it* that thou hast found *it* so quickly, my son ? And he said, Because the Lord thy God brought *it* to me.—Gen., ch. 27.

2992. —— Saved by. *David.* [2] David said unto Ahimelech the priest, The king hath commanded me a business, and hath said unto me, Let no man know any thing of the business whereabout I send thee.—1 Sam., ch. 21. [He obtained a sword.]

2993. —— Sacrilegious. *False Prophet.* [The Lord sent a prophet to speak against the idolatrous altar at Bethel.] [17] It was said to me by the word of the Lord, Thou shalt eat no bread nor drink water there, nor turn again to go by the way that thou camest. [18] He said unto him, I *am* a prophet also as thou *art ;* and an angel spake unto me by the word of the Lord, saying, Bring him back with thee into thine house, that he may eat bread and drink water. *But* he lied unto *him.*—1 Kings, ch. 13.

2994. —— By Jonathan. [6] If thy father at all miss me, then say, David earnestly asked *leave* of me that he might run to Bethlehem his city : for *there is* a yearly sacrifice there for all the family.—1 Sam., ch. 20. [He was near by.]

2995. —— Shortlived. *Moment.* [19] The lip of truth shall be established for ever : but a lying tongue *is* but for a moment.—Prov., ch. 12.

2996. —— of Statecraft. *Gibeonites.* [11] Make ye a league with us. [12] This our bread we took hot *for* our provision out of our houses on the day we came forth..but now, behold, it is dry, and it is mouldy : [13] And these bottles of wine, which we filled, were new ; and, behold, they be rent : and these our garments and our shoes are become old by reason of the very long journey. —JOSH., ch. 9.

2997. —— **Spirits of.** *Micaiah.* [20] And the Lord said, Who shall persuade Ahab, that he may go up and fall at Ramoth-gilead?.. [21] And there came forth a spirit, and stood before the Lord, and said, I will persuade him. [22] And the Lord said unto him, Wherewith ? And he said, I will go forth, and I will be a lying spirit in the mouth of all his prophets.—1 KINGS, ch. 22. [See context.]

2998. —— **Sin of.** *Ananias.* [See No. 2989.]

2999. —— **Victim of.** *Potiphar's Wife.* [18] I lifted up my voice and cried..he left his garment with me, and fled out.. [20] And Joseph's master..put him into the prison.—GEN., ch. 39.

See DECEPTION *and references.*

3000. FAME of Jesus. *Exorcist.* [He rebuked an unclean spirit.] [28] Immediately his fame spread abroad throughout all the region round about Galilee.—MARK, ch. 1.

3001. —— **Military.** *Uzziah.* [15] He made in Jerusalem engines, invented by cunning men, to be on the towers and upon the bulwarks, to shoot arrows and great stones withal. And his name spread far abroad.—2 CHRON., ch. 26.

3002. —— **A troublesome.** *Jesus.* [45] He went out, and began to publish *it* much, and to blaze abroad the matter, insomuch that Jesus could no more openly enter into the city, but was without in desert places : and they came to him from every quarter.—MARK, ch. 1.

3003. —— **Unexpected.** *Jesus said,* [13] Wheresoever this gospel shall be preached in the whole world, *there* shall also this, that this woman hath done, be told for a memorial of her.—MAT., ch. 26.

3004. —— **for Wisdom.** *Solomon.* [1] When the queen of Sheba heard of the fame of Solomon concerning the name of the Lord, she came to prove him with hard questions. [24] And all the earth sought to Solomon, to hear his wisdom, which God had put in his heart.—1 KINGS, ch. 10.

See other illustrations under :

AMBITION.

Impious. Diotrephes..loveth the pre-eminence	317
Fatal. Asahel refused to turn aside..Abner smote	318
Hypocrites. Scribes..love greetings..highest seats	321
Promotion. Brought you near him..Seek..priest	326
Reproved. [Disciples] had disputed which..great	320
Unsatisfied. [Haman] No man came in with the	332

HONOURS.

Abroad. No prophet is accepted in his own country	4073
Brave. King will enrich..give him his daughter	4074
Many. Haman told them of the glory	4075
Posthumous. Widows weeping..shewing..Dorcas	4076
Service. People..made Saul king..Ammonites	4077
Trials. I am..weak, though anointed king	4078

GREATNESS.

Ambition. Disciples had disputed..who should be	3707
Doing Good. If any man desire to be first..servant	3708
Humility. As this little child..is greatest in the	3709
Proof. Sayest thou art great..drive out..Canaanites	3710
Service. Whosoever..will be chiefest, shall be	3711

Tarnished. Naaman captain, was a great man	3712
Temptation. If thou be the S. of G..cast thyself	486
Woodsman. Was famous as he lifted up axes	4129

3005. FAMILY Affliction. *Saved in.* [52] Yesterday at the seventh hour the fever left him. [53] So the father knew that *it was* at the same hour, in the which Jesus said unto him, Thy son liveth : and himself believed, and his whole house.—JOHN, ch. 4.

3006. —— **Alienation.** *Jesus.* [12] Now the brother shall betray the brother to death, and the father the son ; and children shall rise up against *their* parents, and shall cause them to be put to death.—MARK, ch. 13.

3007. —— **A bereaved.** *Job's.* [19] There came a great wind from the wilderness, and smote the four corners of the house, and it fell upon the young men, and they are dead ; and I only am escaped.. [20] Then Job..fell down upon the ground, and worshipped.—JOB, ch. 1.

3008. —— **conversion.** *Philippian Jailer.* [32] They spake unto him the word of the Lord, and to all that were in his house. [33] And he.. washed *their* stripes ; and was baptized, he and all his, straightway. [34]..he set meat before them, and rejoiced, believing in God with all his house.—ACTS, ch. 16. [Lydia was the first woman, and the jailer was the first man who were converted in Europe. Both brought their households into the church with themselves.]

3009. —— **Death destroys.** *Moses, Aaron, Miriam.* [21] The people abode in Kadesh ; and Miriam died there, and was buried there. [22] And the children of Israel..came unto mount Hor. [28]..and Aaron died there in the top of the mount. —NUM., ch. 20. [1] Moses went up..to the top of Pisgah..and the Lord shewed him all the land. [5] So Moses..died there in the land of Moab.—DEUT., ch. 34.

3010. —— **exterminated, A.** *Ahab's.* [11] Jehu slew all that remained of the house of Ahab in Jezreel, and all his great men, and his kinsfolks, and his priests, until he left him none remaining.—2 KINGS, ch. 10.

3011. —— **of the Good.** *Christians.* [32] Behold, thy mother and thy brethren without seek for thee. [33] And he answered..Who is my mother, or my brethren ? [34] And he looked..on them which sat about him, and said, Behold my mother and my brethren ! [35] For whosoever shall do the will of God, the same is my brother, and my sister, and mother.—MARK, ch. 3.

3012. —— **Jars.** *Elkanah's.* [Peninnah and Hannah were his wives. Peninnah] [6] Her adversary also provoked her sore..to make her fret, because the Lord had shut up her womb. [7]..when she went up to the house of the Lord, so she provoked her ; therefore she wept, and did not eat.—1 SAM., ch. 1. [She became the mother of Samuel.]

3013. —— **A numerous.** *Gideon.* [30] Gideon had threescore and ten sons of his body begotten : for he had many wives. [31] And his concubine..she also bare him a son, whose name he called Abimelech.—JUDGES, ch. 8.

3014. —— **Prayer.** *Tabernacle.* [7] Aaron shall burn thereon sweet incense every morning : when he dresseth the lamps, he shall burn incense upon it. [8] And when Aaron lighteth the lamps at even, he shall burn incense upon it, a perpetual incense before the Lord throughout your generations.—Ex., ch. 30.

3015. —— Prayer for. *Job.* ⁵ When the days of *their* feasting were gone about. . Job sent and sanctified them, and rose up early in the morning, and offered burnt offerings *according* to the number of them all : for Job said, It may be that my sons have sinned.—Job, ch. 1.

3016. —— Quarrel. *Against Moses.* ¹ Miriam and Aaron spake against Moses because of the Ethiopian woman whom he had married. . ² And they said, Hath the Lord indeed spoken only by Moses? hath he not spoken also by us? —Num., ch. 12.

3017. —— Quarrel overruled. *Hagar.* ¹⁰ Cast out this bondwoman and her son. .shall not be heir with my son, *even* with Isaac. ¹⁷. .and the angel of God called to Hagar out of heaven. . What aileth thee, Hagar? fear not ; for God hath heard the voice of the lad.—Gen., ch. 21.

3018. —— Religion. *Joshua.* ¹⁵ If it seem evil unto you to serve the Lord, choose you this day whom ye will serve ; whether the gods which your father served. .or the gods of the Amorites, in whose land ye dwell : but as for me and my house, we will serve the Lord.— Josh., ch. 24.

3019. —— —— *Cornelius.* ¹ There was a certain man in Cesarea. .Cornelius, a centurion . .² A devout *man*, and one that feared God with all his house.—Acts, ch. 10.

3020. —— A wicked. *Jews.* ¹⁷ Seest thou not what they do in. .the streets of Jerusalem? ¹⁸ The children gather wood, and the fathers kindle the fire, and the women knead *their* dough, to make cakes to the queen of heaven, and to pour out drink offerings unto other gods. —Jer., ch. 7.

3021. —— Worship. *Jewish.* ³ Shall take to them every man. .a lamb for an house : ⁴ And if the household be too little for the lamb, let him and his neighbour next unto his house take *it* according to the number of souls.—Ex., ch. 12.

3022. —— worshipped. *Jesus said,* ³¹ He that loveth father or mother more than me is not worthy of me : and he that loveth son or daughter more than me is not worthy of me.—Mat., ch. 10.

See other illustrations under

ADOPTION.

Attraction. Mordecai brought up Esther. .was fair 105
Grateful. Mephibosheth. .as one of the king's sons 106
Sympathy. She brought Moses unto Pharaoh's 107

DAUGHTER.

Portion of. Caleb said, What wouldest thou? 1935
Unfortunate. Jephthah. .daughter came to meet 1936

DAUGHTER IN LAW.

Faithful. Ruth said, Entreat me not to return 1937
Unwelcome. Were a grief of mind unto Isaac and 1938

FATHER.

Beloved. Joseph fell on his neck, and wept 3071
Bereaved. O my son Absalom ! my son, my son 3072
Compassionate. A great way off, his father saw 3073
Kind. Much more shall your Father. .give good 3074
Liars. Ye are of your father the devil. .he is a liar 3075

FATHERLESS.

Advocate. Their Redeemer is mighty. .plead their 3076
Protected. Shall not afflict any. .fatherless child 3077

HOME.

Age. Barzillai said. .How long have I to live ? 4023
Blessed. L. blessed the Egyptian's house for 4024
Bible. Thou shalt write them upon. .house 4025
Dismal. David escaped to the cave. .brethren 4026
Dangerous. Bid them farewell which are at home 4027
Godly. As for me and my house. .serve the L. 4028
Heavenly. Father's house are many mansions 4029
Influence. Hired servants in my father's house 4030
Longing. Go unto mine own place and to my 4031
Not at. Peter sat down among them 4032
Providence. Barrel of meal wasted not 4033
Protected. Strike the lintel. .two side posts with 4034
Pious. First findeth his own brother Simon. .to 4035
Reformation. His mother Asa removed. .her idol 4036
Religious. Cornelius feared G. with all his house 4037
Sanctity. Slain. .in his own house, upon his bed 4038
Testimony at. Go home to thy friends, and tell 4039
Weaned of. God hath made me forget. .father's 4040

MOTHER.

Ambitious. Grant these my two sons may sit 5570
Anxious. Rebekah said, I am weary of my life 5571
Brutalized. We boiled my son. .Give thy son 5572
Cruel. Athaliah the mother of. .slew the seed 5573
Careful. Made Samuel a little coat. .every year 5574
Care for. Behold thy mother [Jesus to John] 5575
Distress. Let me not see the death of the child 5576
Ingenious. Took an ark of bulrushes, and daubed 5577
in Israel. I am one of them that are peaceable 5578
Revengeful. What shall I ask ?. .The head of John 5579
Robbery of. 1100 shekels of silver. .I took it 5580
True. Give her the living child, in no wise slay it 5581
Wicked. Rebekah put the skins upon his hands 5582
    "   Maachah his mother. .made an idol 5583

MOTHER IN LAW.

Beloved. Ruth said, Entreat me not to leave thee 5584
Tender. L. deal kindly with you, as ye have. .Naomi 5585
Vexed. [Esau's wives] were a grief of mind unto 5586

SON.

Affectionate. Joseph fell on his neck, and wept 8177
Degenerate. Solomon's heart was not perfect. .as 8178
Evil. Zedekiah [son of good Josiah]. .hardened his 8179
Expelled. Abraham. .gave Hagar. .child, and sent 8180
Firstborn. Sanctify me unto all the firstborn 8181
Healed. Nobleman saith, Come down ere my child 8182
Ingrate. Wasteth his father, and chaseth. .mother 8183
    "   His lamp shall be put out in obscure 8184
Obedient. Abraham bound Isaac. .laid him on the 8185
Penitent. I will go to my father. .I have sinned 8186
Parent-like. Amon sacrificed unto all. .father 8187
Parent-unlike. Manasseh built up. .which his 8188
Rebellious. Son. .will not obey. .his father. .stone 8189
Reformer. Asa. .mother he removed. .destroyed 8190
Sacrificed. Abraham took the knife to slay his son 8191
Scandalous. They spread Absalom a tent 8192
Son in Law. [Grasping] Jacob hath taken. .was 8195
Unnatural. I will smite the king only. .pleased 8193
Unfortunate. He foameth and gnasheth. .pineth 8194

SONS.

Degenerate. Eli. .heard what his sons did 8196
    "   Samuel. .sons took bribes and 8197
Differ. [Two sons] The younger. .Father, give me 8198
    "   I will not. .he went. .I go, sir ; and went 8199
Rejected. Thy sons walk not in thy ways. .make 8200

Comforting. Jacob mourned. .sons and daughters 737
Converted. Lydia was baptized, and her 4142
Excuse. It is good for the present distress so to be 606
Establishment. Betrothed. .let him return, lest he 749

Division. Isaac loved Esau, and R. loved J. 4789
Desired. L., what wilt thou give me, seeing I go 6290
Importance. It is not good for man to be alone 607
Murder. Pharaoh..every son that is born..river 4452
Massacre. Herod..slew all the children 4553
Religion. Jailer..baptized he and all his 637
" David said..family hath a sacrifice 19
Salvation. Unbelieving husband is sanctified by the 550
" [Six apostles were three pairs of..] 551
Surrendered. He that loveth father or mother 3022
Spiritual. Babes in C..fed you with milk 605
Union. Where thou lodgest will I lodge 581
See CHILD, WIDOW, WIFE, YOUTH.

3023. FAMINE, Charity in. *Antiochians.*
[29] Then the disciples, every man according to
his ability, determined to send relief unto the
brethren which dwelt in Judea : [30]..and sent it
to the elders by the hands of Barnabas and Saul.
—ACTS, ch. 11.

3024. —— Care in. *Prophecy.* [16] Son of man,
behold, I will break the staff of bread in Jerusalem : and they shall eat bread by weight, and
with care ; and they shall drink water by measure, and with astonishment.—EZEK., ch. 4.

3025. —— Dying of. *Aamlekite.* [11] They
found an Egyptian in the field, and brought him
to David, and gave him bread, and he did eat ;
and they made him drink water ; [12] And they
gave him a piece of cake of figs, and two clusters
of raisins : and when he had eaten, his spirit
came again to him : for he had eaten no bread,
nor drunk *any* water, three days and three
nights. [13] And David said unto him, To whom
belongest thou ? and whence *art* thou ? And he
said, I *am* a young man of Egypt, servant to an
Amalekite ; and my master left me, because three
days agone I fell sick.—1 SAM., ch. 30.

3026. —— Distress in. *Cannibals.* [55] In the
straitness, wherewith thine enemies shall distress thee.. [56] The tender and delicate woman
among you, which would not adventure to set
the sole of her foot upon the ground for delicateness and tenderness, her eye shall be evil
toward the husband of her bosom, and toward
her son, and toward her daughter, [57]And toward
her young one..and..her children..for she
shall eat them for want of all *things* secretly in
the siege.—DEUT., ch. 28.

3027. —— Exiled by. *Shunammite.* [1] Spake
Elisha unto the woman, whose son he had restored to life, saying, Arise, and go..and sojourn
wheresoever thou canst sojourn : for the Lord
hath called for a famine..upon the land seven
years. [2] And the woman..with her household..
sojourned in the land of the Philistines seven
years.—2 KINGS, ch. 8.

3028. —— Escape from. *Abram.* [10] There
was a famine in the land : and Abram went
down into Egypt to sojourn there ; for the famine *was* grievous in the land.—GEN., ch. 12.

3029. —— Emigration from. *Elimelech.*
[1] There was a famine in the land. And a certain
man of Bethlehem-judah went to sojourn in the
country of Moab, he, and his wife, and his two
sons.—RUTH, ch. 1.

3030. —— Inhumanity in. *Samaria.* [28] The
king said unto her, What aileth thee ? And she
answered, This woman said unto me, Give thy
son, that we may eat him to-day, and we will eat

my son to-morrow. [29] So we boiled my son, and
did eat him : and I said unto her on the next
day, Give thy son, that we may eat him : and
she hath hid her son.—2 KINGS, ch. 6.

3031. —— Sin causes. *Prophecy.* [13] Son of
man, when the land sinneth against me by trespassing grievously, then will I stretch out mine
hand upon it, and will break the staff of the
bread thereof and will send famine upon it,
and will cut off man and beast from it.—EZEK.,
ch. 14.

3032. —— —— Three Years. [1] Go, shew thyself unto Ahab : and I will send rain upon the
earth. [17]..when Ahab saw Elijah..Ahab said..
Art thou he that troubleth Israel ? [18] I have not
troubled Israel ; but thou, and thy father's
house, in that ye have forsaken the commandments of the Lord, and thou hast followed
Baalim.—1 KINGS, ch. 18.

3033. —— Seven Years of. *Egypt.* [13] *There
was* no bread in all the land, for the famine
was very sore, so that the land of Egypt and *all*
the land of Canaan fainted.—GEN., ch. 47.

3034. —— A spiritual. *Israel.* [11] I will send
a famine in the land, not a famine of bread, nor
a thirst for water, but of hearing the words
of the Lord : [12] And they shall wander from
sea to sea, and from the north even to the east,
they shall run to and fro to seek the word of
the Lord, and shall not find *it.*—AMOS, ch. 8.

3035. —— A Water. *Wilderness.* [2] The people did chide with Moses, and said, Give us water that we may drink.. [3]..and the people..
said, Wherefore *is* this *that* thou hast brought us
up out of Egypt, to kill us and our children and
our cattle with thirst ?—EX., ch. 17.

See other illustrations under :

APPETITE.

Control. Put a knife to thy throat if..appetite 479
Dangers. We remember fish, cucumbers, melons 480
Heedless. [Pursuing Philistines,] people were very 481
Sin. [Israelites] Who shall give us flesh ? 482
Temptation. [Jesus] fasted 40 days..afterward a h. 483
Unrestrained. At the point to die, what profit 484

ABSTINENCE.

Extreme. Nazarite..wine..strong drink..moist 20
Excitement. Saul was three days..eat or drink 21
Famishing. Found an Egyptian..when he had eaten 22
Mourning. David sware..If I taste bread 23
Necessitated. Desert place..no leisure..to eat 24
Passionate. Jonathan..fierce anger..eat no meat 25
Priestly. Not drink wine..go into the tabernacle 26
Peril. Paul besought them to take meat [shipwreck] 27
Protracted. Moses..40 days..neither eat..drink 28
" Jesus..40 days..afterwards a hungered 29
Self-denying. David would not drink..jeopardy 30
Sorrowful. Child sick..David fasted..lay..on the g. 31
Total. [Rechabites] We will drink no wine..father c. 32

HUNGER.

Appetizing. To the hungry soul..every bitter thing 4209
Demoralizes. Give thy son, that we may eat him 4210
Disappointment. Fig tree in the way..nothing but 4211
Fasting. Fasted 40 days..afterward a hungered 4212
Inconsiderate. People did eat them with the blood 4213
Impatience. What profit shall this birthright do 4214
Lawful. Sabbath..disciples began to pluck..corn 4215
Murmuring. When we sat by the fleshpots..full 4216
Overcome. I have meat to eat ye know not 4317
Removed. I am the bread of life..never hunger 4218

Subdued by. I will arise and go to my father   4219
Temptation. Tempter came..stones be made   4220

Misinterpreted. Since we left off..queen of heaven 136

3036. FANATICISM, Accused of. *At Capernaum.* [19] And they went into a house. [20] And the multitude cometh..so that they could not so much as eat bread. [21] And when his friends heard *of it*, they went out to lay hold on him : for they said, He is beside himself.—MARK, ch. 3.

3037. —— Fickle. *At Lystra.* [11] When the people saw what Paul had done, they lifted up their voices, saying..The gods are come down to us in the likeness of men. [12] And they called Barnabas, Jupiter; and Paul, Mercurius, because he was the chief speaker. [13] Then the priest of Jupiter..brought oxen and garlands..and would have done sacrifice with the people.. [19] And there came thither *certain* Jews from Antioch and Iconium, who persuaded the people, and, having stoned Paul, drew *him* out of the city, supposing he had been dead.—ACTS, ch. 14.

3038. —— Genuine. *Ephesians.* [32] Some therefore cried one thing, and some another ; for the assembly was confused ; and the more part knew not wherefore they were come together. [33] ..Alexander beckoned with the hand, and would have made his defence.. [34] But when they knew that he was a Jew, all with one voice about the space of two hours cried out, Great is Diana of the Ephesians.—ACTS, ch. 19.

3039. —— of Idolaters. *Carmel.* [27] Elijah mocked them, and said, Cry aloud : for he *is* a god ; either he is talking, or he is pursuing, or he is in a journey, *or* peradventure he sleepeth, and must be awaked. [28] And they cried aloud, and cut themselves .. with knives and lancets, till the blood gushed out.—1 KINGS, ch. 18.

See other illustrations under :

INFATUATION.
Blind. In the time of his distress did Ahaz trespass 4455
Reproved. Knowest thou not yet..Egypt is d.   4456
Wicked. They were driven out from Pharaoh's   4457
"   Simon saw..H. G. was given, he offered 4458

INSANITY.
Exhibited. Hairs were grown like eagle's feathers 4514
Feigned. David..feigned himself mad..spittle   4515
Moral. Pharaoh said..see my face no more   4516
Occasional. Evil spirit from God came upon Saul 4517
Sinners. When he came to himself..bread   4518
"   Paul, thou art beside thyself..mad   4520

ZEAL.
Age. [Caleb 85 years] Give me this..Anakim   9974
Affecting. Many..afoot out of all cities..out went 9975
Acknowledged. [Epaphras] laboring fervently   9976
Affectionate. Brought spices very early in the m. 9977
Desirable. Good to be zealously affected always 9981
Excelling. Priests were too few..Levites did   9983
Energetic. [Nehemiah,] contend..cursed..smote 9984
Holy. Behold the men ye put in prison..teaching 9989
Hurtful. Say nothing..he began to blaze abroad 9991
Ministerial. Three years..I warned every one 10000
Misunderstood. [Jesus] Friends said, He is beside 9997
Prosperous. [Hezekiah] In every work..with   10005
Rewarded. Give my covenant..he was zealous 10013
Reformers. I chased him from me [Nehemiah] 10009
Reformation. Made a scourge..drive them out 10012
Sudden. Device..set in order..done suddenly 10016

Seeker's. [Zaccheus] ran before, climbed..tree 10020
"   Made haste, came down, received   10014
Testify. Left her waterpot..come see a man   10022
Unwavering. None of these things move me   10025
Weatherwise. When ye see a cloud rise..shower 2341
See ENTHUSIASM.

3040. FAREWELL, A beatific. *Jesus.* [50] He led them out as far as to Bethany, and he lifted up his hands, and blessed them. [51] And..while he blessed them, he was parted from them.—LUKE, ch. 24. [9] ..When he had spoken these things, while they beheld, he was taken up ; and a cloud received him out of their sight.—ACTS, ch. 1.

3041. —— A glorious. *Elijah.* [11] Behold, *there appeared* a chariot of fire, and horses of fire, and parted them both asunder ; and Elijah went up by a whirlwind into heaven. [12] And Elisha saw *it*, and he cried, My father, my father, the chariot of Israel, and the horsemen thereof ! And he saw him no more.—2 KINGS, ch. 2.

3042. —— A loving. *Orpah.* [10] Surely we will return with thee unto thy people. [11] And Naomi said, Turn again, my daughters : why will ye go with me?.. [14] And they lifted up their voice, and wept again : and Orpah kissed her mother in law ; but Ruth clave unto her.—RUTH, ch. 1.

3043. —— A perilous. *Looking back.* [61] Lord, I will follow thee ; but let me first go bid them farewell, which are at home at my house. [62] ..Jesus said..No man, having put his hand to the plough, and looking back, is fit for the kingdom of God.—LUKE, ch. 9.

3044. —— A sorrowful. *Ephesians.* [36] He kneeled down, and prayed with them all. [37] And they all wept sore, and fell on Paul's neck, and kissed him. [38] Sorrowing most of all..that they should see his face no more. And they accompanied him unto the ship.—ACTS, ch. 20.

Also see :
Address. Joshua..this day going..way of all   239
See ABANDONMENT.

3045. FARMER called. *Elisha.* [19] Elisha.. *was* ploughing *with* twelve yoke *of oxen* before him..and Elijah passed by him, and cast his mantle upon him. [20] And he left the oxen, and ran after Elijah.—1 KINGS, ch. 19.

3046. —— by Choice. *King Uzziah.* [10] He built towers in the desert, and digged many wells : for he had much cattle, both in the low country, and in the plains ; husbandmen *also*, and vinedressers in the mountains, and in Carmel : for he loved husbandry.—2 CHRON., ch. 26.

3047. —— Deliverance by a. *Gideon.* [11] Gideon threshed wheat by the winepress, to hide *it* from the Midianites. [12] And the angel of the Lord appeared..and said..The Lord *is* with thee, thou mighty man of valour.—JUDGES, ch. 6.

3048. —— A selfish. *The Rich Fool.* [18] This will I do : I will pull down my barns, and build greater ; and there will I bestow all my fruits and my goods. [19] And I will say to my soul, Soul, thou hast much goods laid up for many years ; take thine ease, eat, drink, *and* be merry.—LUKE, ch. 12.

3049. FARMING forbidden. *Rechabites.* [8] Thus have we obeyed the voice of Jonadab the son of

Rechab our father in all that he hath charged us.. ⁹..neither have we vineyard, nor field, nor seed.—Jer., ch. 35.

See other illustrations under:

3050. FAST, An acceptable. *Reformation.* ⁶ *Is* not this the fast that I have chosen? to loose the bands of wickedness, to undo the heavy burdens, and to let the oppressed go free, and that ye break every yoke? ⁷ *Is it* not to deal thy bread to the hungry, and that thou bring the poor that are cast out to thy house? when thou seest the naked, that thou cover him?—Isa., ch. 58.

3051. —— **A false.** *Formal.* ³ Wherefore have we fasted, *say they*, and thou seest not?.. Behold, in the day of your fast ye find pleasure, and exact all your labours. ⁴ Behold, ye fast for strife and debate, and to smite with the fist of wickedness : ye shall not fast as *ye do this* day, to make your voice to be heard on high.—Isa., ch. 58.

3052. —— **forty Days.** *Moses.* ²⁸ He was there with the Lord forty days and forty nights ; he did neither eat bread, nor drink water. And He wrote upon the tables..the ten commandments.—Ex., ch. 34.

3053. —— **A genuine.** *Jews.* ¹ The children of Israel were assembled with fasting, and with sackclothes, and earth upon them. ² And..separated themselves from all strangers, and stood and confessed their sins, and the iniquities of their fathers. ³ And they stood up in their place, and read in the book of the law of the Lord their God one fourth part of the day ; and *an-other* fourth part they confessed, and worshipped. —Neh., ch. 9.

3054. —— **A mournful.** *Ninevites.* ⁶ The king of Nineveh..laid his robe from him, and covered *him* with sackcloth, and sat in ashes. ⁷ And..published through Nineveh..saying, Let neither man nor beast, herd nor flock, taste any thing : let them not feed, nor drink water : ⁸ But let man and beast be covered with sackcloth, and cry mightily unto God : yea, let them turn every one from his evil way.—Jonah, ch. 3.

3055. —— **A prolonged.** *Sailors.* ³³ Paul be-

sought *them* all to take meat, saying, This day is the fourteenth day that ye have tarried and continued fasting, having taken nothing. ³⁴..for this is for your health.—Acts, ch. 27.

3056. FASTING in Anxiety. *Darius* ¹⁸ passed the night fasting : neither were instruments of music brought before him : and his sleep went from him. ¹⁹..very early in the morning..went in haste unto the den of lions. ²⁰ And when he came to the den, he cried with a lamentable voice unto Daniel.—Dan., ch. 6.

3057. —— **in Affliction.** *David.* ¹⁵ The child that Uriah's wife bare unto David..was very sick. ¹⁶ David therefore besought God for the child ; and David fasted, and went in, and lay all night upon the earth. ¹⁷ And the elders of his house..*went* to him, to raise him up from the earth : but he would not, neither did he eat bread with them.—2 Sam., ch. 12.

3058. —— **in Bereavement.** *Israelites.* ¹² All the valiant men..went all night, and took the body of Saul and the bodies of his sons from the wall of Bethshan, and..burnt them.. ¹³ And they took their bones, and buried *them* under a tree at Jabesh, and fasted seven days.—1 Sam., ch. 31.

3059. —— **in Defeat.** *Israelites.* ²⁵ Benjamin went forth against them..the second day, and destroyed..of the children of Israel again eighteen thousand men ; all these drew the sword. ²⁶ Then all the children of Israel, and all the people..came unto the house of God. and wept, and sat there before the Lord, and fasted that day until even, and offered burnt offerings and peace offerings before the Lord.—Judges, ch. 20.

3060. —— **Habitual.** *Anna.* ³⁶ Anna, a prophetess.. ³⁷..*was* a widow of about fourscore and four years, which departed not from the temple, but served *God* with fastings and prayers night and day.—Luke, ch. 2.

3061. —— **Meaning of.** *Christians.* ¹⁸ Why do the disciples of John and of the Pharisees fast, but thy disciples fast not? ¹⁹ And Jesus said unto them, Can the children of the bride-chamber fast, while the bridegroom is with them?.. ²⁰ But the days will come, when the bridegroom shall be taken away from them, and then shall they fast.—Mark, ch. 2.

3062. —— **in Peril.** *Israelites* ⁶ drew water, and poured *it* out before the Lord, and fasted on that day, and said there, We have sinned against the Lord.. ⁷ And when the Philistines heard that the children of Israel were gathered together to Mizpeh, the lords..went up against Israel.—1 Sam., ch. 7.

3063. —— **and Prayer.** *Jews.* ³ In every province, whithersoever the king's..decree came, *there was* great mourning among the Jews, and fasting, and weeping, and wailing ; and many lay in sackcloth and ashes.. ¹⁵ Then Esther bade *them* return Mordecai *this answer.* ¹⁶ Go, gather together all the Jews that are present in Shushan, and fast ye for me, and neither eat nor drink three days, night or day : I also and my maidens will fast likewise ; and so will I go in unto the king, which *is* not according to the law ; and if I perish, I perish.—Esther, ch. 4.

3064. —— **in Preparation.** *Ezra.* ⁶ Ezra ..went into the chamber of Johanan..and..he did eat no bread, nor drink water : for he mourned because of the transgression of them that had been carried away.—Ezra, ch. 10.

3065. —— **in Penitence.** *King Ahab.* ²⁵ There was none like unto Ahab, which did sell himself to work wickedness..whom Jezebel his wife stirred up. ²⁶ And he did very abominably in following idols..as did the Amorites.. ²⁷ And ..when Ahab heard those words..he rent his clothes, and put sackcloth upon his flesh, and fasted, and lay in sackcloth, and went softly.—1 Kings, ch. 21.

3066. —— **Patriotic.** *Nehemiah.* ⁴ When I heard these words..I sat down and wept, and mourned *certain* days, and fasted, and prayed before the God of heaven.—Neh., ch. 1.

3067. —— **Sincere.** *Jesus said,* ¹⁶ When ye fast, be not as the hypocrites, of a sad countenance : for they disfigure their faces, that they may appear unto men to fast. Verily, I say unto you, They have their reward. ¹⁷ But thou, when thou fastest, anoint thy head, and wash thy face ; ¹⁸ That thou appear not unto men, to fast, but unto thy Father, which is in secret : and thy Father, which seeth in secret, shall reward thee openly.—Mark, ch. 6.

3068. —— **Vision after.** *Daniel.* ³ I ate no pleasant bread, neither came flesh nor wine in my mouth, neither did I anoint myself at all, till three whole weeks were fulfilled.—Dan., ch. 10. [A glorious vision followed.]

3069. —— **Vision during.** *Cornelius.* ³⁰ Four days ago I was fasting until this hour ; and at the ninth hour I prayed in my house, and, behold, a man stood before me in bright clothing. ³¹ And said, Cornelius, thy prayer is heard, and thine alms are had in remembrance in the sight of God.—Acts, ch. 10.

See other illustrations under :

HUNGER.

Appetizing. To the hungry soul every bitter	4209
Disappointment. Fig tree in the way..nothing	4211
Lawful. Sabbath..disciples began to pluck..corn	4215
Murmuring. When we sat by the fleshpots..full	4216
Overcome. I have meat to eat ye know not of	4217
Removed. I am the bread of life..never hunger	4218
Subdued by. I will arise and go to my father	4219
Temptation. Tempter came..stones be made	4220

Devil's. Neither eat nor drink till they had killed 1604
See **ABSTINENCE.**

3070. FATHER, Alienated. *David.* ²⁴ The king said, Let him turn to his own house, and let him not see my face. So Absalom returned to his own house, and saw not the king's face.—1 Sam., ch. 14.

3071. —— **Beloved.** *Israel.* ²⁹ Joseph made ready his chariot, and went up to meet Israel his father, to Goshen, and presented himself unto him ; and he fell on his neck, and wept on his neck a good while.—Gen., ch. 46.

3072. —— **Bereaved.** *David.* ³³ The king was much moved, and went up to the chamber over the gate, and wept : and as he went, thus he said, O my son Absalom ! my son, my son Absalom ! would God I had died for thee, O Absalom, my son, my son !—2 Sam., ch. 18.

3073. —— **The compassionate.** *Prodigal.* ²⁰ He arose, and came to his father. But when he was yet a great way off, his father saw him,

and had compassion, and ran, and fell on his neck, and kissed him.—Luke, ch. 15.

3074. —— **The kind.** *"Much More."* ⁹ What man is there of you, whom if his son ask bread, will he give him a stone ? ¹⁰ Or if he ask a fish, will he give him a serpent ? ¹¹ If ye then, being evil, know how to give good gifts unto your children, how much more shall your Father which is in heaven give good things to them that ask him ?—Mat., ch. 7.

3075. —— **The Liar's.** *Satan.* ⁴⁴ Ye are of your father the devil, and the lusts of your father ye will do : he was a murderer from the beginning, and abode not in the truth, because there is no truth in him. When he speaketh a lie, he speaketh of his own : for he is a liar, and the father of it.—John, ch. 8.

See other illustrations under :

ADOPTION.

Attraction. Mordecai..brought up Esther..beautiful	105
Grateful. Mephibosheth shall eat as..king's sons	106
Sympathy. Babe wept..became her son	107

3076. FATHERLESS, Advocate of. *Proverb.* ¹⁰ Enter not into the fields of the fatherless : ¹¹ For their Redeemer *is* mighty ; he shall plead their cause with thee.—Prov., ch. 23.

3077. —— **protected.** *Jewish Law.* ²² Ye shall not afflict any widow, or fatherless child. ²³ If thou afflict them in any wise, and they cry at all unto me, I will surely hear their cry ; ²⁴ And my wrath shall wax hot, and I will kill you with the sword ; and your wives shall be widows, and your children fatherless.—Ex., ch. 22.

3078. FATIGUE of Indifference. *Jews.* ¹² Ye say, The table of the Lord is polluted ; and the fruit thereof, *even* his meat, *is* contemptible. ¹³ Ye said also, Behold, what a weariness *is it !* and ye have snuffed at it, saith the Lord of hosts ; and ye brought *that which was* torn, and the lame, and the sick : thus ye brought an offering.—Mal., ch. 1.

3079. —— **Overcome by.** *After Amalekites.* ¹⁰ David pursued, he and four hundred men ; for two hundred abode behind, which were so faint that they could not go over the brook Besor.—1 Sam., ch. 30.

3080. —— **from Overwork.** *Apostles.* ³⁰ The apostles..told him all things, both what they had done, and what they had taught. ³¹ And he said unto them, Come ye yourselves apart into a desert place, and rest a while : for there were many coming and going, and they had no leisure so much as to eat.—Mark, ch. 6.

3081. —— **Sleep from.** *Disciples.* ⁴⁰ He cometh unto the disciples, and findeth them asleep, and saith unto Peter, What, could ye not watch with me one hour ? ⁴¹ Watch and pray, that ye enter not into temptation : the spirit indeed *is* willing, but the flesh *is* weak.—Mat., ch. 26.

3082. —— **A Traveller's.** *Jesus.* ⁵ Then cometh he to a city of Samaria, which is called Sychar.. ⁶ Now Jacob's well was there. Jesus therefore, being wearied with *his* journey, sat thus on the well.—John, ch. 4.

See other illustrations under :

FAINTING.

Hunger. I. were distressed..none..tasted food	2882
Preserved. I had fainted unless I had believed	2883
" Our outward man perish, yet the	2884
Weakness. If thou faint..thy strength is small	2885

WEAKNESS.

Believers. Babes in Christ..not able to bare meat 9394
"   Lest the people repent..return to 9395
Conscious. I am..weak, though anointed king. 9396
Flesh. Moses' hands were heavy..stayed up his 9397
Instruments. L. sent flies..land was corrupted 9398
Moral. Peter separated..fearing them of the 9399
Personal. He that abideth in me bringeth forth 9400
Remembered. I was with you in weakness 9401
Submission. Ahab said, I am thine, and all that I 9402
Spiritless. All the kings..their heart melted 9403
"   Ai smote..hearts of the people melted 9404

Prayer. Moses' hands were heavy..stayed up 9450
Saviour's. Laid the cross that he might bear it 8557
Strength. Wait upon the L..run and not be weary 2881
Weariness. Thou layest the burden of all..on me 9448

3083. FAULT, But One. *Naaman.* ¹⁷ Thy servant will henceforth offer neither burnt offering nor sacrifice unto other gods, but unto the Lord. ¹⁸ In this thing the Lord pardon thy servant, *that* when my master goeth into the house of Rimmon to worship there, and he leaneth on my hand..when I bow down myself in the house of Rimmon, the Lord pardon thy servant in this thing.—2 KINGS, ch. 5.

3084. FAULTS, Correction of. *Christians.* ¹⁵ If thy brother shall trespass against thee, go and tell him his fault between thee and him alone : if he shall hear thee, thou hast gained thy brother. ¹⁶ But if he will not hear *thee, then* take with thee one or two more, that in the mouth of two or three witnesses every word may be established. ¹⁷ And if he shall neglect to hear them, tell *it* unto the church : but if he neglect to hear the church, let him be unto thee as a heathen man.—MAT., ch. 18.

See other illustrations under :

ERROR.

Sweeping. Barnabas also was carried away 2709
Sincere. There is a way that seemeth right..ways 2710

FOLLY.

Anger. Nabal answered, Who is David? 3262
Ashamed. Held their peace..who should be the g. 3263
Backsliders. Forsaken..living waters..broken 3264
Ecclesiastical. Whether is greater, the gift or the 3265
Inseparable. Bray a fool in a mortar..not depart 3266
Indifference. Heareth..doeth not..build upon the 3267
Idolaters. Mouths, but they speak not ; eyes..see 3268
"   Warm himself..maketh a graven image 3269
Natural. Ostrich..G. hath deprived her of wisdom 3270
Neglect. Foolish.. took no oil with them 3271
Worldly. I will pull down..build..eat, drink 3272
Youth. Rehoboam forsook the counsel of the old 3273

3085. FAULTLESS, Condemnation of the. *Pilate.* ⁴ Pilate..Behold, I bring him forth to you, that ye may know that I find no fault in him. ⁵ Then came Jesus forth, wearing the crown of thorns, and the purple robe.—JOHN, ch. 19.

3086. —— Official. *Daniel.* ³ Daniel was preferred above the presidents and princes, because an excellent spirit *was* in him ; and the king thought to set him over the whole realm. ⁴ Then the presidents and princes sought to find occasion against Daniel concerning the kingdom ; but they could find none occasion nor fault ; forasmuch as he *was* faithful.—DAN., ch. 6.

See other illustrations under :

INNOCENT.

Mediation. Ye shall not see my face except your 4502
Punishment by. He..without sin cast the first stone 4503

INNOCENCE.

Avenged. Murderers..David..cut off their hands 4505
Boldness. With whomsoever..it be found, let him 4506
Betrayed. I have betrayed innocent blood..Judas 4507
Convincing. All understood..it was not of the king 4508
Conduct of. Some bade me kill thee..mine eye 4509
False. Pilate washed his hands..I am innocent 4510
Proved. G. shut the lions' mouths..innocency 4511
Protected. Should I not spare..not discern..right 4512

PERFECTION.

Aim. Not turn aside to the right..or to the left 6051
Object. That we may present every man perfect 6052
Price. Go sell..give..come, and follow me 6053
Proposed. Let us go on unto perfection, not laying 6054
Required. Abram..walk before me, and be thou 6055
Service. He that hath a blemish shall not approach 6056

3087. FAULTFINDERS, Fastidious. *Pharisees.* ²⁹ Levi made..a great feast..and there was a great company of publicans, and of others that sat down with them. ³⁰ But the scribes and Pharisees murmured against his disciples, saying, Why do ye eat and drink with publicans and sinners?—LUKE, ch. 5.

3088. —— Hypocritical. *Judas.* ⁵ Why was not this ointment sold for three hundred pence, and given to the poor? ⁶ This he said, not that he cared for the poor ; but because he was a thief, and had the bag, and bare what was put therein.—JOHN, ch. 12.

3089. —— Malicious. *Jews.* ³³ John the Baptist came neither eating bread nor drinking wine ; and ye say, He hath a devil. ³⁴ The Son of man is come eating and drinking ; and ye say, Behold, a gluttonous man, and a winebibber, a friend of publicans and sinners.—LUKE, ch. 7.

See BLAME and references.

3090. FAVOUR besought. *Pharaoh.* ³⁰ Not a house where *there was* not one dead. ³¹ And he called for Moses and Aaron by night, and said, Rise up, *and* get you forth from among my people..and go, serve the Lord, as ye have said. ³² Also take your flocks and your herds, as ye have said, and be gone ; and bless me also.—Ex., ch. 12.

3091. —— Divine. *Promise.* ⁴ Ye have seen what I did unto the Egyptians, and *how* I bare you on eagles' wings, and brought you unto myself. ⁵ Now therefore, if ye will obey my voice indeed, and keep my covenant, then ye shall be a peculiar treasure unto me above all people.—Ex., ch. 19.

3092. —— evinced. *Ruth.* ¹⁴ Boaz said..At mealtime come thou hither, and eat of the bread, and dip thy morsel in the vinegar. And she sat beside the reapers : and he reached her parched *corn,* and she did eat, and was sufficed, and left. ¹⁵..Boaz commanded his young men, saying, Let her glean even among the sheaves, and reproach her not : ¹⁶ And let fall also *some* of the handfuls of purpose for her.—RUTH, ch. 2.

3093. —— indicated. *Ahasuerus.* ² The king held out to Esther the golden sceptre that *was* in his hand. So Esther drew near, and touched the top of the sceptre. ³ Then said the king.. What wilt thou, queen Esther? and what *is* thy request?—ESTHER, ch. 5.

3094. —— refused. *Edom.* ¹⁸ Edom said.. Thou shalt not pass by me, lest I come out against thee with the sword. [19]And the children of Israel said..We will go by the highway : and if I and my cattle drink of thy water, then I will pay for it : I will only, without *doing* any thing *else*, go through on my feet. [20]And he said, Thou shalt not go through.—NUM., ch. 20.

See other illustrations under :

ACCEPTANCE.
Assurance. Would he have shewed us all these   53
Denied. Ye brought..torn and the lame..sick   55
Evidence. There rose up fire out of the rock   56
Manifested. Burning lamp passed between those   57
of Piety. In every nation he that feareth..worketh   58
by Sacrifice. L. had respect unto Abel..offering   59
Terms. Do justly..love mercy..walk humbly   61

See GRACE.

3095. FAVOURS compensated. *Chief Butler.* [14]But think on me when it shall be well with thee..and make mention of me unto Pharaoh, and bring me out of this house : [15]For indeed I was stolen away out of the land of the Hebrews. —GEN., ch. 40.

3096. —— forgotten. *Chief Butler.* [See above.] [23]Yet did not the chief butler remember Joseph, but forgat him.—GEN., ch. 40.

3097. —— remembered. *Chief Butler.* [9]Then spake the chief butler unto Pharaoh, saying, I do remember my faults this day : [12]And there *was* there with us a young man, a Hebrew, servant to the captain of the guard ; and we told him, and he interpreted to us our dreams.— GEN., ch. 41.

See other illustrations under :

BENEFACTORS.
Censured. Ye have made our savour to be abhorred 685
  "   We did tell thee in Egypt..Let us alone   686
Honoured. He received his sight, and followed   687
Remembered. He was worthy..built us a   688
Slandered. All murmured..Ye have killed the   689

GIFTS.
Diversity. To one is given..spirit..wisdom [Paul]   3537
  "   To one..five talents..according to   3538
for Jesus. [Magi] presented him gifts ; gold and   3543
Lesser. I give you power to tread on serpents   3541
Withheld. Will a man rob God ? Yet ye have   4550

KINDNESS.
Appreciated. Barzillai..I will feed thee in J.   4808
Animals. Rebekah..I will draw for thy camels   4809
Bereavement. In the choice of our sepulchres, bury 4810
Brethren. Waken poor ; thou shalt relieve him   4811
Conquerors. Saul..Is this thy voice..David..wept   4812
Christians. Disciples..relief unto brethren..Judea 4814
Captives. Clothed naked..shod them..eat and   4815
Father. If ye..know how to give..much more..F.   4816
Gratitude. Mephibosheth..kindness for Jonathan's   4817
Insulted. David sent to comfort him..cut   4819
Inopportune. Ahab..because thou hast let go   4820
Loan. Hath pity..lendeth to the Lord   4821
Providential. Boaz unto Ruth..abide here   4822
Prosperity. I delivered the poor that cried [Job]   4823
Prisoner. Jeremiah put these..rags under..arms   4824
Remembered. Lest I destroy you, for ye showed   4825
Rewarded. Rahab..hid them with the flax..saved   4826
Substitutional. I was eyes to the blind..feet [Job] 4827
Servant. Centurion's servant who was dear to him   4828
Strangers. Drink my lord..wasted..gave him   4829
Timely. Barzillai brought beds..flour..butter..to   4830
Unexpected. Shall I smite them?..Let bread   4831
Widow. Harvest..forgot a sheaf..be for the   4832

PRESENT.
Bloody. Put their [70] heads in baskets..to Jehu   6503
Conciliatory. It is a present unto my lord Esau   6504
Deceptive. I. sent a present unto Eglon..a dagger   6505

PRESENTS.
Affection. Jonathan gave David..his garments   6506
Conciliatory. A present..honey..nuts   6507
Declined. I have enough, my brother [Esau to J.]   6508
Favour. Hazael took a present..40 camels' burden   6509
Gratitude. Receive my present..thou wast pleased   6510
Influence. When he saw the earring and bracelets   6511

Fraternal. To Benjamin he gave 300 pieces of   5988

See BENEVOLENCE.

3098. FAVORITISM denied. *Jesus.* [20]Then came..the mother of Zebedee's children with her sons, worshipping *him*, and desiring a certain thing of him. [21]..What wilt thou ? She saith..Grant that these my two sons may sit, the one on thy right hand, and the other on the left, in thy kingdom. [22]But Jesus answered.. Ye know not what ye ask.—MAT., ch. 20.

3099. —— hurtful. *Jacob.* [3]Israel loved Joseph more than all his children, because he *was* the son of his old age : and he made him a coat of *many* colours. [4]And when his brethren saw that their father loved him more..they hated him, and could not speak peaceably unto him.— GEN., ch. 37.

See other illustrations under :

PARTIALITY.
Complaint. There arose a murmuring of the G.   5985
Improper. Weareth gay clothing..sit thou here   5986
Justifiable. But to Benjamin he gave 300 pieces   5988
Surprising. Benjamin's mess was five times as   5989

3100. FEAR, Agitation from. *Job.* [14]Fear came upon me, and trembling, which made all my bones to shake. [15]Then a spirit passed before my face ; the hair of my flesh stood up : [16]It stood still, but I could not discern the form thereof.—JOB, ch. 4.

3101. —— of an Angel. *Manoah.* [20]When the flame went up toward heaven from off the altar ..the angel of the Lord ascended in the flame of the altar : and Manoah and his wife looked on *it*, and fell on their faces to the ground.. [22]And Manoah said unto his wife, We shall surely die, because we have seen God.—JUDGES, ch. 13.

3102. —— —— *Gideon.* [21]There rose up fire out of the rock, and consumed the flesh and the unleavened cakes.. [22]And when Gideon perceived that he *was* an angel of the Lord, Gideon said, Alas, O Lord God ! for because I have seen an angel of the Lord face to face.— JUDGES, ch. 6.

3103. —— —— *Mary's.* [29]When she saw *him*, she was troubled at his saying, and cast in her mind what manner of salutation this should be. [30]And the angel said..Fear not, Mary : for thou hast found favour with God.—LUKE, ch. 1.

3104. —— —— *Soldier's.* [3]His countenance was like lightning, and his raiment white as snow : [4]And for fear of him the keepers did shake, and became as dead *men*.—MAT., ch. 28.

3105. —— —— *The Marys'.* [5]Entering into the sepulchre, they saw a young man sitting on the right side, clothed in a long white garment ; and they were affrighted. [6]And he saith unto them, Be not affrighted.—MARK, ch. 16.

3106. —— —— *Shepherds'.* ⁹ And they were sore afraid. ¹⁰ And the angel said..Fear not : for, behold, I bring you good tidings of great joy, which shall be to all people.—LUKE, ch. 2.

3107. —— abandoned. *Nehemiah.* ¹⁰ I came unto the house of Shemaiah..who *was* shut up ; and he said, Let us meet together in the house of God..and let us shut the doors of the temple : for they will come to slay thee ; yea, in the night will they come.. ¹¹ And I said, should such a man as I flee ? and who *is there*, that, *being* as I *am*, would go into the temple to save his life ? I will not go in.—NEH., ch. 6.

3108. —— Converts through. *Persians.* ¹⁷ In every province..whithersoever the king's..decree came, the Jews had joy and gladness, a feast and a good day. And many of the people of the land became Jews ; for the fear of the Jews fell upon them.—ESTHER, ch. 8.

3109. —— The Conspirators'. *Adonijah's Friends.* ⁴¹ Adonijah and all the guests..heard *it* as they had made an end of eating. And when Joab heard the sound of the trumpet, he said, Wherefore *is this* noise of the city being in an uproar ? ⁴⁹ And all the guests that *were* with Adonijah were afraid, and rose up, and went every man his way.—1 KINGS, ch. 1.

3110. —— contagious. *Soldier.* ⁸ Moses said, the officers shall speak..What man *is there that is* fearful and fainthearted ? let him go and return unto his house, lest his brethren's heart faint as well as his heart.—DEUT., ch. 20.

3111. —— Conscientious. *Pilate.* ⁷ By our law he ought to die, because he made himself the Son of God. ⁸ When Pilate therefore heard that saying, he was the more afraid ; ⁹ And went again into the judgment hall, and saith unto Jesus, Whence art thou ? But Jesus gave him no answer.—JOHN, ch. 19.

3112. —— God disarms. *Moses.* ² When ye are come nigh unto the battle..the priest shall.. ³..shall say unto them, Hear, O Israel..let not your hearts faint, fear not, and do not tremble, neither be ye terrified because of them ; ⁴ For the Lord your God *is* he that goeth with you, to fight for you.—DEUT., ch. 20.

3113. —— A Dreamer's. *Midianite.* ¹³ There *was* a man that told a dream unto his fellow, and said..a cake of barley bread tumbled into the host of Midian, and came unto a tent, and smote it that it fell, and overturned it.. ¹⁴ And his fellow answered..This *is* nothing else save the sword of Gideon..*for* into his hand hath God delivered Midian.—JUDGES, ch. 7.

3114. —— distrusts God. *At Red Sea.* ¹² For *it had been* better for us to serve the Egyptians, than that we should die in the wilderness. ¹³ And Moses said..Fear ye not, stand still, and see the salvation of the Lord..for the Egyptians whom ye have seen to day, ye shall see them again no more for ever.—EX., ch. 14.

3115. —— of Disapproval. *Saul.* ⁹ Saul and the people spared Agag, and the best of the sheep..oxen..fatlings, and the lambs, and all *that was* good, and would not utterly destroy them : but every thing *that was* vile and refuse, that they destroyed utterly. ²⁴ And Saul said unto Samuel, I have sinned : for I have transgressed the commandment of the Lord..I feared the people, and obeyed their voice.—1 SAM., ch. 15.

3116. —— Disqualified by. *Israelites.* ² The Lord said unto Gideon, The people that *are* with thee *are* too many for me to give the Midianites into their hands, lest Israel vaunt themselves against me, saying, Mine own hand hath saved me. ³ Now..Whosoever *is* fearful and afraid, let him return..And there returned..twenty and two thousand ; and there remained ten thousand. —JUDGES, ch. 7.

3117. —— Demoralizing. *Israelites.* ⁵ The Philistines gathered..thirty thousand chariots, and six thousand horsemen, and people as the sand which *is* on the sea shore in multitude.. ⁶ When the men of Israel saw that they were in a strait, (for the people were distressed,) then the people did hide themselves in caves, and in thickets, and in rocks, and in high places, and in pits.—1 SAM., ch. 13.

3118. —— Disobedience through. *King Saul.* ¹¹ Samuel said, What hast thou done ? And Saul said, Because I saw that the people were scattered from me, and *that* thou camest not within the days appointed, and *that* the Philistines gathered themselves together at Michmash ; ¹² Therefore said I, The Philistines will come down now upon me to Gilgal, and I have not made supplication unto the Lord : I forced myself therefore, and offered a burnt offering.—1 SAM., ch. 13. [It cost him the kingdom.]

3119. —— Diverted through. *I s r a e l i t e s.* ¹⁷ God led them not *through* the way of the land of the Philistines, although that *was* near ; for God said, Lest peradventure the people repent when they see war, and they return to Egypt : ¹⁸ But God led the people about, *through* the way of the wilderness.—EX., ch. 13.

3120. —— Disturbing. *Last Journey.* ³² They were..going up to Jerusalem ; and Jesus went before them : and they were amazed ; and as they followed, they were afraid. And he took again the twelve, and began to tell them what things should happen unto him.—MARK, ch. 10.

3121. —— The Evildoers'. *Sons of Jacob.* ¹⁵ Their father was dead, they said, Joseph will peradventure hate us, and will certainly requite us all the evil which we did unto him. ¹⁶ And they sent a messenger unto Joseph, saying, Thy father did command before he died, saying, ¹⁷ So shall ye say unto Joseph, Forgive.—GEN., ch. 50.

3122. —— Excessive. *Transfiguration.* ⁵ A bright cloud overshadowed them : and behold a voice out of the cloud, which said, This is my beloved Son, in whom I am well pleased ; hear ye him. ⁶ And when the disciples heard *it*, they fell on their face, and were sore afraid. ⁷ And Jesus came and touched them, and said, Arise, and be not afraid.—MAT., ch. 17.

3123. —— Ensnaring. *Proverb.* ²⁵ The fear of man bringeth a snare : but whoso putteth his trust in the Lord shall be safe.—PROV., ch. 29.

3124. —— no Excuse. *Saul.* [See No. 3118.]

3125. —— Exiled by. *Joseph.* ¹⁹ Herod was dead, behold, an angel of the Lord appeareth in a dream to Joseph in Egypt, ²⁰ Saying, Arise, and take the young child and his mother, and go into the land of Israel : for they are dead which sought the young child's life.—MAT., ch. 2.

3126. —— of an Enemy. *G o l i a t h.* ¹⁰ The Philistine said, I defy the armies of Israel this day ; give me a man, that we may fight together.

[11] When Saul and all Israel heard those words of the Philistine, they were dismayed, and greatly afraid.—1 SAM., ch. 17.

3127. —— **of the Elements.** *Israelites.* [17] He shall send thunder and rain ; that ye may perceive..your wickedness *is* great, which ye have done..in asking you a king. [18] Samuel called unto the Lord, and the Lord sent thunder and rain that day : and all the people greatly feared the Lord and Samuel.—1 SAM., ch. 12.

3128. —— **Failure through.** *Israelites.* [30] Caleb stilled the people..and said, Let us go up at once, and possess it ; for we are well able to overcome it. [31] But the men that went up with him said, We be not able to go up against the people ; for they *are* stronger than we.— NUM., ch. 13.

3129. —— **Cripple's Faith.** *Peter.* [29] When Peter was come down out of the ship, he walked on the water, to go to Jesus. [30] But when he saw the wind boisterous, he was afraid ; and beginning to sink, he cried, saying, Lord, save me.— MAT., ch. 14.

3130. —— **of the Good.** *Herod.* [20] Herod feared John, knowing that he was a just man and a holy, and observed him ; and when he heard him, he did many things, and heard him gladly.—MARK, ch. 6.

3131. —— **Glad Tidings received with.** *Zacharias.* [11] There appeared unto him an angel of the Lord, standing on the right side of the altar of incense. [12] And when Zacharias saw *him,* he was troubled, and fear fell upon him. [13] But the angel said..Fear not, Zacharias ; for thy prayer is heard ; and thy wife Elisabeth shall bear thee a son, and thou shalt call his name John.— LUKE, ch. 1.

3132. —— —— *Shepherds.* [See No. 3106.]

3133. —— **Helpless through.** *Enemies.* [3] When all the kings of the Amorites..and..of the Canaanites..heard that the Lord had dried up the waters of Jordan from before the children of Israel, until we were passed over..their heart melted, neither was there spirit in them any more.—JOSH., ch. 5.

3134. —— **Ill-timed.** *Women.* [8] And they went out quickly, and fled from the sepulchre ; for they trembled and were amazed : neither said they any thing to any *man;* for they were afraid.—MARK, ch. 16.

3135. —— **through Ignorance.** *At Dothan.* [15] A host compassed the city..And his servant said..Alas, my master ! how shall we do ? [16] And he answered, Fear not : for they that *be* with us *are* more than they that *be* with them. [17] And Elisha prayed..And the Lord opened the eyes of the young man ; and he saw : and, behold, the mountain *was* full of horses and chariots of fire round about Elisha.—2 KINGS, ch. 6.

3136. —— **Insincerity through.** *Jews.* [25] The baptism of John, whence was it ? from heaven, or of men ? And they reasoned with themselves, saying, If we shall say, From heaven ; he will say unto us, Why did ye not then believe him ? [26] But if we shall say, Of men ; we fear the people ; for all hold John as a prophet. [27] And they answered Jesus..We cannot tell.—MAT., ch. 21.

3137. —— **Infected with.** *Ten Spies Report.* [28] The people *be* strong..the cities *are* walled,

and very great ; and moreover we saw the children of Anak there. [29] The Amalekites dwell in the land of the south : and the Hittites, and the Jebusites, and the Amorites, dwell in the mountains : and the Canaanites dwell by the sea, and by the coast of Jordan.—NUM., ch. 13. [1] The congregation said unto them, Would God that we had died in the land of Egypt !—NUM., ch. 14.

3138. —— **of God's Majesty.** *Sinai.* [18] All the people saw the thunderings, and the lightnings, and the noise of the trumpet, and the mountain smoking ; and..they removed, and stood afar off. [19] And they said unto Moses, Speak thou with us, and we will hear : but let not God speak with us, lest we die.—EX., ch. 20.

3139. [" Fear not " is repeated nearly eighty times in the Word of God.]

3140. —— **Needless.** *Lord to Joshua.* [9] Be strong and of a good courage ; be not afraid, neither be thou dismayed : for the Lord thy God *is* with thee whithersoever thou goest.—JOSH., ch. 1.

3141. —— **Panic from.** *At Red Sea.* [24] The Lord looked..through the pillar of fire and of the cloud, and troubled the host of the Egyptians, [25] And took off their chariot wheels, that they drave them heavily : so that the Egyptians said, Let us flee from the face of Israel ; for the Lord fighteth for them.—EX., ch. 14.

3142. —— **Punished through.** *Idolaters.* [36] I will send a faintness into their hearts in the lands of their enemies ; and the sound of a shaken leaf shall chase them ; and they shall flee, as fleeing from a sword ; and they shall fall when none pursueth. [37] And they shall fall one upon another..and ye shall have no power to stand before your enemies.—LEV., ch. 26.

3143. —— **Prostrating.** *"Saul fell..no Strength."* [19] The Lord will also deliver Israel with thee into the hand of the Philistines : and to morrow *shalt* thou and thy sons *be* with me.. shall deliver the host of Israel into the hand of the Philistines. [20] Then Saul fell straightway all along on the earth, and was sore afraid, because of the words of Samuel : and there was no strength in him ; for he had eaten no bread all the day, nor all the night.—1 SAM., ch. 28.

3144. —— **Precaution of.** *Disciples.* [19] The same day at evening, being the first *day* of the week, when the doors were shut where the disciples were assembled for fear of the Jews, came Jesus and stood in the midst.—JOHN, ch. 20.

3145. —— **Religious.** *Pentecost.* [41] About three thousand souls. [42] ..continued steadfastly in the apostles' doctrine and fellowship, and in breaking of bread, and in prayers. [43] And fear came upon every soul.—ACTS, ch. 2.

3146. —— **Jesus removes.** *Walking the Sea.* [50] They all saw him, and were troubled. And immediately he..saith unto them, Be of good cheer : it is I ; be not afraid. [51] And he went ..into the ship ; and the wind ceased : and they were sore amazed in themselves beyond measure, and wondered.—MARK, ch. 6.

3147. —— **Restraint of.** *Parents.* [21] Who hath opened his eyes, we know not : he is of age ; ask him : he shall speak for himself. [22] ..they feared the Jews : for the Jews had agreed already, that if any man did confess that he was Christ, he should be put out of the synagogue.—John, ch. 9.

3148. —— —— *Believers.* ⁴² Among the chief rulers also many believed on him ; but because of the Pharisees they did not confess *him*, lest they should be put out of the synagogue.—John, ch. 12.

3149. —— —— *Joseph.* ³⁸ After this Joseph of Arimathea, being a disciple of Jesus, but secretly for fear of the Jews, besought Pilate that he might take away the body of Jesus : and Pilate gave *him* leave.—John, ch. 19.

3150. —— **Restless through.** *Israelites.* ⁶⁵ Among these nations shalt thou find no ease, neither shall the sole of thy foot have rest : but ¹ the Lord shall give thee there a trembling heart, and failing of eyes, and sorrow of mind : ⁶⁶ And thy life shall hang in doubt before thee ; and thou shalt fear day and night, and shalt have none assurance of thy life : ⁶⁷ In the morning thou shalt say, Would God it were even ! and at even thou shalt say, Would God it were morning !—Deut., ch. 28.

3151. —— **Fugitives through.** *Disciples.* ⁵⁶ Then all the disciples forsook him, and fled. ⁵⁷ And they. .led *him* away to Caiaphas the high priest, where the scribes and the elders were assembled. ⁵⁸ But Peter followed him afar off. .and went in, and sat with the servants, to see the end.—Mat., ch. 26.

3152. —— **A sacred.** *Jacob.* ¹⁶ Jacob awaked out of his sleep, and he said, Surely the Lord is in this place ; and I knew *it* not. ¹⁷ And he was afraid, and said, How dreadful *is* this place ! this *is* none other but the house of God, and this *is* the gate of heaven.—Gen., ch. 28.

3153. —— **Surrender of.** *Ammon and Moab.* ¹⁷ Ye shall not *need* to fight in this *battle :* set yourselves, stand ye *still*, and see the salvation of the Lord with you, O Judah and Jerusalem : fear not, nor be dismayed ; to morrow go out against them : for the Lord *will be* with you.—2 Chron., ch. 20.

3154. —— **A slavish.** *Sinner's.* ¹⁴ The sinners in Zion are afraid ; fearfulness hath surprised the hypocrites. Who among us shall dwell with the devouring fire ? who among us shall dwell with everlasting burnings ?—Isa., ch. 33.

3155. —— **Sacrifice through.** *King Ahaz.* ²³ Because the gods of the kings of Syria help them, *therefore* will I sacrifice to them, that they may help me. But they were the ruin of him, and of all Israel.—2 Chron., ch. 28.

3156. —— **The Sinner's.** *Adam.* ⁸ They heard the voice of the Lord God walking in the garden in the cool of the day : and Adam and his wife hid themselves from the presence of the Lord God amongst the trees.—Gen., ch. 2.

3157. —— **Servile.** *One Talent.* ²⁰ Lord, behold, *here is* thy pound, which I have kept laid up in a napkin : ²¹ For I feared thee, because thou art an austere man : thou takest up that thou layedst not down, and reapest that thou didst not sow.—Luke, ch. 19.

3158. —— **from Suspicion.** *Disciples.* ²⁶ When Saul was come to Jerusalem, he assayed to join himself to the disciples : but they were all afraid of him, and believed not that he was a disciple.—Acts, ch. 9.

3159. —— **restrains Testimony.** *At Jerusalem.* ¹² There was much murmuring among the people concerning him : for some said, He is a good man : others said, Nay ; but he deceiveth the people. ¹³ Howbeit no man spake openly of him for fear of the Jews.—John, ch. 7.

3160. —— **of a Tempest.** *Pharaoh.* ²³ Moses stretched forth his rod toward heaven : and the Lord sent thunder and hail, and the fire ran along upon the ground. . ²⁴ So there was hail, and fire mingled with the hail, very grievous, such as there was none like it in all the land. . ²⁸ Entreat the Lord (for *it is* enough) that there be no *more* mighty thunderings and hail ; and I will let you go.—Ex., ch. 9.

3161. —— **through Unbelief.** *Tempest.* ²⁴ Master, we perish. Then he arose, and rebuked the wind and the raging of the water : and they ceased, and there was a calm. ²⁵ And he said. . Where is your faith ? And they being afraid wondered, saying one to another, What manner of man is this ! for he commandeth even the winds and water, and they obey him.—Luke, ch. 8.

3162. —— **An unreasonable.** *Gadarenes.* ¹⁵ They come to Jesus, and see him that was possessed with the devil, and had the legion, sitting, and clothed, and in his right mind ; and they were afraid. ¹⁶ And they that saw *it* told them. .concerning the swine.—Mark, ch. 5.

3163. —— **Unmanned by.** *Israelites.* ⁵ The men of Ai. .they chased them *from* before the gate *even* unto Shebarim, and smote them in the going down : wherefore the hearts of the people melted, and became as water.—Josh., ch. 7.

3164. —— **Victims of.** *Said Rahab,* ¹⁰ We have heard how the Lord dried up the water of the Red sea for you. .and what ye did unto the two kings of the Amorites. .Sihon and Og, whom ye utterly destroyed. ¹¹ And. .our hearts did melt, neither did there remain any more courage in any man.—Josh., ch. 2.

3165. —— **Weakened by.** *Peter.* ¹² Before that certain came from James, he did eat with the Gentiles : but when they were come, he withdrew and separated himself, fearing them which were of the circumcision. ¹³ And the other Jews dissembled likewise with him.—Gal., ch. 2.

3166. —— **to Worship.** *David.* ²⁹ The tabernacle of the Lord, which Moses made in the wilderness, and the altar of the burnt offering, *were* at that season in the high place at Gibeon. ³⁰ But David could not go before it to inquire of God : for he was afraid because of the sword of the angel of the Lord.—1 Chron., ch. 21.

3167. FEARS of Old Age. *Jacob.* ³⁸ My son shall not go down with you ; for his brother is dead, and he is left alone : if mischief befall him by the way. .then shall ye bring down my gray hairs with sorrow to the grave.—Gen., ch. 42.

3168. —— **Restrained by.** *Enemies.* ¹⁸ The scribes and chief priests heard *it*, and sought how they might destroy him : for they feared him, because all the people was astonished at his doctrine.—Mark, ch. 11.

3169. —— **Victorious.** *Caleb said,* ⁹ Rebel not ye against the Lord, neither fear ye the people of the land ; for they *are* bread for us : their defence is departed from them, and the Lord *is* with us : fear them not. [10] But all the congregation bade stone them with stones.—Num., ch. 14.

3170. FEARFUL, but Faithful. *Thomas.* [8] *His* disciples say .. Master, the Jews of late sought to stone thee ; and goest thou thither again ? [16] Then said Thomas..unto his fellow-disciples, Let us also go, that we may die with him.—John, ch. 11.

3171. —— Punished, The. *Talents.* [25] I was afraid, and went and hid thy talent in the earth : lo, *there* thou hast *that is* thine. [30]..cast ye the unprofitable servant into outer darkness : there shall be weeping and gnashing of teeth.—Mat., ch. 25.

See other illustrations under :

AGITATION.

Deception. Who art thou?..Esau..Isaac trembled 256
Diffuses. Disputed he in the synagogue..market 257
Deplored. [Israelites] Made. abhorred..slay us 258
General. [Philistines] Trembling in the host..field 259
Mount. Sinai..quaked greatly 260
Overcome. [At sepulchre] Keepers did shake 261
Physical. Belshazzar's thoughts troubled..knees 262
Terror. [Job's vision] Trembling..my bones 263

ALARM.

Conscience. Pray for thy servants..we die not 273
Death. Egyptians were urgent..we be all dead 274
Failure. Priests..doubted..whereunto this would 275
Manifestation. Belshazzar..countenance was 276
Preaching. Paul reasoned..Felix trembled 277
Reasonable. Esau cometh..400 men..Jacob 278
Superstitious. Jesus walking on the sea..troubled 279
Sinners. Adam and his wife hid themselves 280
" Let not God speak with us..die 281
Sudden. Seeing the prison doors open..sword 282
Spiritual. Sirs, what must I do to be saved 283
Tempest. Entreat..be no more mighty thunderings 284
Unnecessary. My money is restored..heart failed 285

DANGER.

Appaied. Jesus went before them..amazed 1906
Escape. Disciples let him down by night in a 1909
Haste. Let them in Judea..flee to the mountains 1911
Intimidates. Peter saw..afraid, and beginning to 1912
Jesus. Storm..on the lake..Master, we perish 1913

DESPONDENCY.

Bereavement. Joseph is, without doubt, rent in 2226
Complaint. Since I came to Pharaoh..done evil 2227
Constitutional. Let us go..die with him 2230
Continued. My heart is smitten and withered like 2228
Cure. David was greatly distressed..spake of 2229
Difficulties. People was much discouraged 2231
Hope. Why art thou cast down, O my soul 2232
Hasty. Sun beat..Jonah fainted..wished to die 2233
Ill-timed. Handful of meal..little oil..die 2234
Loneliness. I only am left, and they seek my life 2235
Memories. By the rivers of Babylon we wept 2236
Overcare. If thou deal thus with me, kill me 2237
Prayer. How long wilt thou forget me, O Lord ? 2239
Public. Moses heard the people weeping..door 2238
Peril. Esau cometh..400 men..Jacob afraid 2240
Singular. Lord, take away my life..not better 2242
Vows. L. made a reproach unto me..derision 2243
Without. Troubled on every side..not in despair 2244

INTIMIDATION.

Attempted. It is reported..thou thinkest to rebel 4629
Boastful. Let not Hezekiah deceive you..not be 4630
Fruit of. Peter denied it again..curse and swear 4631
Failure of. Should such a man as I flee ! 4632
Moved by. Entice thy husband..lest we burn thee 4633

Unsuccessful. Hearken not unto him, nor consent 4634
Without. Opened the prison..go stand..and speak 4635
Woman's. So let the gods do..make thy life like 4636
Weakness. The garrison and the spoilers..trembled 4637

Cause. Eli sat..watching..his heart trembled for 444
Restless. Would God it were even !..would 7266
Sacred. We shall surely die..have seen God 603
Sickness. Nobleman besought him..come..ere 459
Sinners. L. looked..E. said, Let us flee 600
Sleepless. Darius..sleep went from him..early to 458
Sudden. Jailer..came trembling..fell down 599
Truth. Not come to send peace, but a sword 450
Unexpected. Therefore is this distress come upon us 601

3172. FEAST, An ancient. *To Three Angels.* [6] Abraham hastened..unto Sarah, and said, Make ready quickly three measures of fine meal, knead *it*, and make cakes upon the hearth. [7] And Abraham ran unto the herd, and fetched a calf tender and good, and gave *it* unto a young man ; and he hasted to dress it. [8] And he took butter, and milk, and the calf which he had dressed, and set *it* before them ; and he stood by them under the tree, and they did eat.—Gen., ch. 18.

3173. —— A birthday. *Herod.* [21] Herod on his birthday made a supper to his lords, high captains, and chief *estates* of Galilee ; [22] The daughter of the said Herodias .. danced, and pleased Herod and them that sat with him.—Mark, ch. 6.

3174. —— A charitable. *Jesus said,* [12] When thou makest..a supper, call not thy friends.. brethren..kinsmen..rich neighbours ; lest they also bid thee again, and a recompense be made thee. [13] But..call the poor, the maimed, the blind : [14] And thou shalt be blessed ; for they cannot recompense thee : for thou shalt be recompensed at the resurrection.—Luke, ch. 14.

3175. —— Complimentary. *By Lazarus.* [1] Jesus..came to Bethany, where Lazarus was ..whom he raised from the dead. [2] There they made him a supper ; and Martha served : but Lazarus was one of them that sat at the table with him.—John, ch. 12.

3176. —— —— To Jesus. [29] Levi made him a great feast in his own house ; and there was a great company of publicans, and of others that sat down with them.—Luke, ch. 5.

3177. —— Death at. *Job's Sons.* [18] Thy sons and thy daughters *were* eating and drinking wine in their eldest brother's house : [19]..there came a great wind from the wilderness, and smote the four corners of the house, and it fell upon the young men, and they are dead.—Job, ch. 1.

3178. —— sadly ended, A. *Murder.* [23] Absalom had sheepshearers in Baal-hazor..and.. invited all the king's sons. [28] Now Absalom had commanded his servants, saying, Mark ye now when Amnon's heart is merry with wine, and when I say unto you, Smite Amnon ; then kill him, fear not..be courageous, and be valiant. [29] And the servants of Absalom did..Then all the king's sons arose..gat him up upon his mule, and fled.—2 Sam., ch. 13.

3179. —— A farewell. *Elisha.* [After receiving his prophetic call,] [21] he returned..took a yoke of oxen, and slew them, and boiled their flesh with the instruments of the oxen, and gave unto the people, and they did eat. Then he arose, and went after Elijah, and ministered unto him.—1 Kings, ch. 19.

3180. —— **A great.** *Dedication.* [5] King Solomon offered a sacrifice of twenty and two thousand oxen, and a hundred and twenty thousand sheep. So the king and all the people dedicated the house of God.—2 Chron., ch. 7.

3181. —— **An idolatrous.** *Golden Calf.* [6] They rose up early..and offered burnt offerings, and brought peace offerings ; and the people sat down to eat and to drink, and rose up to play.—Ex., ch. 32.

3182. —— **An impious.** *Belshazzar.* [1] Belshazzar the king made a great feast to a thousand of his lords.. [3] Then they brought the golden vessels that were taken out of the temple ..at Jerusalem ; and the king and his princes, his wives and his concubines, drank in them. [4] They drank wine, and praised the gods.—Dan., ch. 5.

3183. —— **A joyous.** *Tabernacles.* [39] When ye have gathered in the fruit of the land.. [40] And ye shall take..on the first day the boughs of goodly trees, branches of palm trees, and the boughs of thick trees, and willows of the brook ; and ye shall rejoice before the Lord your God seven days. [42] ..seven days all that are Israelites born shall dwell in booths.—Lev., ch. 23.

3184. —— **A marriage.** *At Cana.* [2] Both Jesus was called, and his disciples, to the marriage. [9] ..the ruler of the feast had tasted the water that was made wine, and knew not whence it was,—John, ch. 2.

3185. —— **A royal.** *Ahasuerus.* [5] The king made a feast..in Shushan..both unto great and small, seven days, in the court of the garden of the king's palace ; [6] *Where were* white, green, and blue *hangings*, fastened with cords of fine linen and purple to silver rings and pillars of marble : the beds *were of* gold and silver, upon a pavement of red, and blue, and white, and black marble. [7] And they gave *them* drink in vessels of gold (the vessels being diverse..), and royal wine in abundance.. [8] And the drinking *was* according to the law ; none did compel : for so the king had appointed..that they should do according to every man's pleasure.—Esther, ch. 1.

3186. FEASTS, National. *Three.* [14] Three times thou shalt keep a feast unto me in the year. [15] ..the feast of unleavened bread : thou shalt eat unleavened bread seven days..in it thou camest out from Egypt.. [16] And the feast of harvest, the firstfruits of thy labours..in the field : and the feast of ingathering..when thou hast gathered in thy labours out of the field.—Ex., ch. 23.

3187. FEASTING, Affection from. *Isaac.* [28] Isaac loved Esau, because he did eat of *his* venison : but Rebekah loved Jacob.—Gen., ch. 25.

See other illustrations under :

EATING.

Bigotry. This man receiveth sinners, and eateth 2590
Conscientious. Sacrifice to idols..eat not 2591
Considerate. If meat make my brother to offend 2592
Caste. [Joseph] They sat on for him by himself 2593
Prevented. [Jesus] Multitude cometh..not eat 2594
" [Grief] Hannah..fret..wept..not eat 2595
Restricted. Tree of the knowledge..not eat of it 2596
Separation. Brother..fornicator, covetous..not 2597
Trial. One..which eateth with me shall betray me 2598

FOOD.

Animal. Every moving thing..shall be meat for 3286
Better than. Esteemed the words..more than my 3287
Cleansed. What G. had cleansed..call not 3288
Costly. Jacob gave Esau bread and pottage and 3289
Chosen. Let them give us pulse to eat..water 3290
Daily. Give us this day our daily bread 3292
Diminished. [Sin] Given you cleanness of teeth 3293
Example. Conscience of him which is weak..emb. 3294
Forbidden. Ye may eat of..trees of the garden 3295
Favorite. I am old..take me some venison..I love 3296
Friendship. Isaac loved Esau because..of his ven. 3297
Famine. Besieged Samaria..ass's head..80 silver 3298
Freedom to gather. Neighbour's vineyard..eat 3299
God honoured. Eat either bread nor..until..offer. 3300
God gives. Consider the ravens..God feedeth them 3301
Heavenly. L. evermore give us of this bread 3302
Life-giving. Lest..take..tree of life, and live 3303
Miraculous. L. brought quails from the sea 3304
" Elijah..ravens brought him bread 3305
" Elijah..angel..cake baken on the 3306
" [5000 fed] Did all eat, and were filled 3307
" [100 fed] Twelve loaves of barley 3308
" [Manna] Did eat manna 40 years 3309
Necessity. Better than..honoureth himself and 3310
Natural. John..his meat was locusts and wild 3311
Perilous. Jonathan..taste a little honey..must die 3312
Prohibited. Life of the flesh is in the blood 3313
" Eat no..fat of ox, sheep, or goat 3314
Prudence. Fed you with milk, not with meat 3315
Promised. Trust in the L. and do good..be fed 3316
" He that walketh righteously..bread 3317
Restricted. Beasts..parteth the hoof..cheweth the 3318
Scarcity. Handful of meal..little oil..eat, and die 3319
Supplies. Solomon's provision for one day..20 oxen 3320
Spiritual. Labour..meat which endureth..life 3321
Scruples. Some with conscience of the idol..eat it 3322
Thanks. Jesus took bread, and blessed it, and 3323
" Jesus blessed and brake the loaves 3324
" [Paul shipwrecked] took bread, and gave 3325
Temptation in. Fasted 40 days..tempter came 3326
Weeping. Every man in the door of his tent 3327

Festival. David dealt to every one..cake..wine 3209
Preparation. M. may be hanged..go merrily..unto 154
Perpetual. A merry heart hath a continual feast 1139
Select. Let the king and Haman come to the 4089
Sorrowful. One of you..betray me..sorrowful..Is 88

3188. FEEBLENESS, Ashamed of. *Ezra.* [22] I was ashamed to require of the king a band of soldiers and horsemen to help us..because we had spoken unto the king, saying, The hand of our God *is* upon all them for good that seek him ; but his power and his wrath *is* against all them that forsake him.—Ezra, ch. 8.

3189. —— **of Age.** *Eli.* [15] Eli was ninety and eight years old ; and his eyes were dim, that he could not see.—1 Sam., ch. 4.

3190. —— —— *David.* [1] King David was old *and* stricken in years ; and they covered him with clothes, but he gat no heat.—1 Kings, ch. 1.

See other illustrations under :

FAINT.

Pursuing. David pursued, he and 400..200 so faint 2880
Strength. Wait upon the L..run, and not be weary 2881

FAINTING.

Hunger. I. were distressed..none..tasted food 2882
Preserved. I had fainted unless I had believed 2883
" Our outward man perish, yet the 2884
Weakness. If thou faint..thy strength is small 2885

FATIGUE.

o' Indifference. Table of the L..Behold what a   3078
Overcome. 200 were so faint they could not go   3079
Overwork. Come..into a desert place, and rest   3080
Sleep. He cometh..disciples, and findeth them   3081
Travellers. Jesus being wearied..sat thus on the   3082

WEAK.

Care for. Offend one of these little ones..hanged   9391
  "   Take heed lest..a stumblingblock   9392
Help. If there be no man to save us, we will come   9393

WEAKNESS.

Believers. Fed you with milk..not able to bear it   9394
  "   Repent when they see war, and return   9395
Conscious. I am this day weak, though.. king   9396
Flesh. Moses' hands were heavy..stayed up his h.   9397
Instruments. Lice..flies..land was corrupted   9398
Moral. Peter separated himself, fearing them   9399
Personal. Abide in me..without me..nothing   9400
Remembered. I was with you in weakness   9401
Submission. I am thine, and all that I have   9402
Spiritless. Their hearts melted, neither..any s.   9403
  "   Hearts..melted and became as water   9404

Care. Brethren, comfort the feeble—1 Thess. 5 : 14
Destroyed. Amalekites smote all..feeble—Deut. 25 : 18
Death. Abner dead, Ish-bosheth's..feeble—2 Sam. 4 : 1
Despised. What do these feeble Jews?   7429
Exempt. Not one feeble person among their tribes 6723
Fear. Angel rolled back the stone.. as dead men   261
Weariness. Thou layest the burden of all.. on me   9448

3191. FEELING, Compassionate. *Samaritan.*
[See No. 3193.] ³³ But a certain Samaritan, as
he journeyed, came where he was ; and when
he saw him, he had compassion *on him.*—LUKE,
ch. 12.

3192. —— Past. *Jews.* ³⁹ They could not
believe, because.. ⁴⁰ He hath blinded their eyes,
and hardened their heart ; that they should not
see with *their* eyes, nor understand with *their*
heart, and be converted.—JOHN, ch. 12.

3193. —— Without. *Levite.* ³⁰ Jesus..said,
A certain *man*..fell among thieves, which stripped him of his raiment, and wounded *him*..
leaving *him* half dead. ³²..a Levite, when he
was at the place, came and looked *on him,* and
passed by on the other side.—LUKE, ch. 12.

3194. FEELINGS concealed. *For Benjamin.*
³⁰ Joseph made haste ; for his bowels did yearn
upon his brother : and he sought *where* to weep ;
and he entered into *his* chamber, and wept
there. ³¹ And he washed his face, and went out,
and refrained himself, and said, Set on bread.—
GEN., ch. 43.

3195. —— Control of. *For his Brethren.*
²³ They knew not that Joseph understood *them ;*
for he spake unto them by an interpreter. ²⁴And
he turned himself about from them, and wept ;
and returned to them again.—GEN., ch. 42.

3196. —— in Music. *Captives.* ³ They that
carried us away captive required of us a song ;
and they that wasted us *required of us* mirth,
saying, Sing us *one* of the songs of Zion. ⁴ How
shall we sing the Lord's song in a strange land ?
—Ps. 137.

3197. —— Responsive. *Jesus.* ³³ The people
saw them departing..and ran afoot thither out
of all cities, and outwent them, and came together unto him. ³⁴ And Jesus..was moved with
compassion toward them, because they were as
sheep not having a shepherd : and he began to
teach them.—MARK, ch. 6.

3198. —— Strong. *For Lazarus.* ³³ When
Jesus..saw her weeping, and the Jews also
weeping..he groaned in the spirit, and was
troubled, ³⁴ And said, Where have ye laid him ?
They say unto him, Lord, come and see. ³⁵ Jesus wept.—JOHN, ch. 11.

3199. —— suppressed. *Haman.* ⁹ Then went
Haman forth..joyful and with a glad heart : but
when Haman saw Mordecai in the king's gate,
that he stood not up, nor moved for him, he was
full of indignation.. ¹⁰ Nevertheless Haman refrained himself.—ESTHER, ch. 5.

See other illustrations under :

ANGUISH.

Bereavement. Let her alone, for her soul is vexed   416
Bitter. Esau cried..Bless me, even me also !   417

AGITATION.

Deception. Who art thou ?..Esau.. Isaac trembled   256
Diffuses. Disputed he in the synagogue..market   257
Deplored. [Israelites] Made..abhorred..slay us   258
General. [Philistines] Trembling in the host..field   259
Mount. Sinai..quaked greatly   260
Overcome. [At sepulchre] keepers did shake   261
Physical. Belshazzar's thoughts troubled..knees   262
Terror. [Job's vision] Trembling.. my bones   263

EMOTION.

Changed. Jesus showed them his hands..disciples 2625
Exhibited. Shaphan read it..the king rent his   2622
Irrepressible. Joseph made haste..sought where   2623
Mixed. Ancient men..seen the first..wept   2626
  "   From the sepulchre with fear and great   2627
Opposite. If these should hold their peace   2628
Worship. Mourn not..they heard..law   2624

TERROR.

Prostrating. Saul fell..all along on the ground   8723
Sinners. Belshazzar's..knees smote one against   8724
Sublime. Sinai.. so terrible..I exceedingly fear   8725

Expressed. Woman..box of ointment..at his feet   170
Overwhelming. O, my son Absalom, my son, my   163
Sympathy. High priest..touched with a feeling of 6348
See REJOICING, SYMPATHY, WEEPING.

3200. FEET consecrated. *Priests'.* ²⁴ He
brought Aaron's sons, and Moses put of the
blood upon the tip of their right ear, and upon
the thumbs of their right hands, and upon the
great toes of their right feet.—LEV., ch. 8.

3201. —— Hallowing. *Bush.* ⁵ Draw not
nigh hither : put off thy shoes from off thy
feet ; for the place whereon thou standest *is*
holy ground.—Ex., ch. 3.

See other illustrations under :

LAMENESS.

Disqualification. Not offer the bread of his God   4878
  "   Lame..thou shalt not—Deut. 15 : 21
Healed. Never had walked..leaped and walked   4879
  "   His feet and ankle bones received strength 4880
Want with. Laid daily at the gate..ask alms   4882

WALK.

Holy. Enoch walked with G. 300 years   9275
Perfect. Noah..just man..perfect..walked with   9276
Saintly. Do justly, love mercy..walk..with thy G. 9277

Benevolence. Feet was I to the lame [Job]   4827
of Majesty. Saw the G. of I..under his feet   50
Hallowing. Take off thy shoes from thy feet   7324
Kissing. Woman..a sinner..ointment..kissed his   170
Neglected. Mephibosheth had not dressed his feet 5697
Prepared. Your feet shod with the preparation of 2109
Sacrificed. Ye offer the lame for sacrifice   5848

Swift. Asahel was as light of foot as a wild roe 7482
"   He maketh my feet like hinds' feet   6977
Tripped. Youth arise..push away my feet—Job 30 : 12
Worship. She kissed his feet, and anointed them 7317

3202. FELLOWSHIP, Fraternal. *A n a n i a s .*
[17] Putting his hands on him said, Brother Saul,
the Lord, *even* Jesus, that appeared unto thee
in the way as thou camest, hath sent me, that
thou mightest receive thy sight, and be filled
with the Holy Ghost.—ACTS, ch. 9.

3203. —— Grand. *Christian.* [22] Ye are
come unto mount Sion, and unto..the heavenly
Jerusalem, and to an innumerable company of
angels, [23] To the general assembly and church
of the firstborn, which are written in heaven,
and to God the Judge of all, and to the spirits
of just men made perfect, [24] And to Jesus the
mediator of the new covenant.—HEB., ch. 12.

3204. —— invited. *Jethro.* [29] Moses said
unto Hobab..the Midianite, Moses' father in
law, We are journeying unto the place of which
the Lord said, I will give it you : come thou
with us, and we will do thee good : for the Lord
hath spoken good concerning Israel.—NUM., ch.
10.

3205. —— Primitive. *Communistic.* [44] All
that believed were together, and had all things
common ; [45] And sold their possessions and
goods, and parted them..as every man had
need.—ACTS, ch. 2.

3206. —— prohibited. *Vicious.* [11] I have
written unto you not to keep company, if any
man that is called a brother be a fornicator, or
covetous, or an idolater, or a railer, or a drunkard, or an extortioner ; with such a one no not
to eat.—1 COR., ch. 5.

3207. -—— refused. *Simon Magus.* [19] Give
me also this power, that on whomsoever I lay
hands, he may receive the Holy Ghost. [20] But
Peter said..Thy money perish with thee, because thou hast thought that the gift of God
may be purchased with money. [21] Thou hast
neither part nor lot in this matter : for thy heart
is not right in the sight of God.—ACTS, ch. 8.

3208. —— Safety by. *Disciples.* [23] There
came down a storm of wind on the lake ; and
they were filled *with water*, and were in jeopardy.
[24] And they..awoke him, saying, Master, master,
we perish. Then he arose, and rebuked the
wind and the raging of the water : and they
ceased.—LUKE, ch. 8.

See other illustrations under :

COMMUNION.

Blood. Moses..sprinkled it on the people   1408
Corrects. Can any good thing come..? Come..see 1409
Evildoers. Filled with madness..communed..do 1410
God. Abraham..was called the friend of God   1411
Invitation. I stand at the door..open..I will   1413
Mysterious. We will come..make our abode with 1414
Old Age. Abram [at 99]..walk before me..be perfect 1415
Protracted. Moses was in the mount forty days   1416
Recorded. They that feared the L..book of   1417
Strengthens. Mount up with wings as eagles..run 1418
"   If two of you shall agree on earth   1419
Saints. No more..foreigners, but fellow citizens   1420
Walking. Enoch walked with God..God took   1421

Christian. Continued in the apostle's doctrine,and 7347
Divine. Our fellowship is with the F.—1 John 1 : 3
Means. If we walk in the light..have fellowship 5036
See FRIEND and FRIENDSHIP.

3209. FESTIVAL, A Church. *Bringing in the
Ark.* [18] As soon as David had made an end of
offering burnt offerings and peace offerings, he
blessed the people in the name of the Lord of
hosts. [19] And he dealt..as well to the women
as men, to every one a cake of bread, and a good
piece *of flesh*, and a flagon *of wine*.—2 SAM.,
ch. 6.

See FEAST.

3210. FEW, Influence of a. *Three Hundred.*
[3] There remained ten thousand. [4] And the Lord
said unto Gideon, The people *are* yet *too* many.
[8] So the people took victuals in their hand, and
their trumpets : and he sent all *the rest of* Israel
every man unto his tent, and retained those
three hundred men.—JUDGES, ch. 7. [The Midianites were destroyed.]

See other illustrations under :

NUMBERS.

Danger. Lest I. vaunt..my own hand saved me 5744
Despised. Jonathan said unto his armourbearer 5745
Disparity. I. like two little flocks of kids   5746
"   L. it is nothing with thee, whether with 5747
Invisible. Mountain was full of horses..fire   5748
Pride. David's heart smote him after he had n. 5749

ONE.

Care. Martha was cumbered..Mary..one thing   5883
for God. Moses stood..Who is on the Lord's side? 5884
with God. I, even I only..Baal's prophets 450 men 5885
"   I come to thee in the name of the L. of 5886
vs. 1000. Samson..slew a thousand men   5887
Power of. [Evil] Sheba hath lifted up his hand 5888
Victory. Shamgar slew 600..delivered I.   5889

3211. FICKLENESS, Burdensome. *Seventy
Elders.* [17] Shall bear the burden of the people
with thee, that thou bear it not thyself alone.
[18] And say thou..ye shall eat flesh : for ye have
wept in the ears of the Lord, saying, Who shall
give us flesh to eat? for *it was* well with us in
Egypt?—NUM., ch. 11.

3212. —— of Purpose. *Apostates.* [16] These
..which are sown on stony ground ; who, when
they have heard the word, immediately receive
it with gladness ; [17] And have no root in themselves, and so endure but for a time : afterward,
when affliction or persecution ariseth for the
word's sake, immediately they are offended.—
MARK, ch. 4.

3213. —— Superstitious. *"Gods are come..
stoned."* [11] And when the people saw what Paul
had done, they lifted up their voices..The gods
are come down to us in the likeness of men.
[12] And they called Barnabas, Jupiter ; and Paul,
Mercurius, because he was the chief speaker.
[18]..scarce restrained they the people, that they
had not done sacrifice unto them.. [19] And there
came thither *certain* Jews from Antioch and
Iconium, who persuaded the people, and, having stoned Paul, drew *him* out of the city, supposing he had been dead.—ACTS, ch. 14.

See CHANGE and references.

3214. FIDELITY required. *Buried Talent.*
[26] His Lord answered.. *Thou* wicked and slothful servant, thou knewest that I reap where I
sowed not, and gather where I have not strewed.
[27] Thou oughtest therefore to have put my
money to the exchangers, and *then* at my coming I should have received mine own with usury.
[28] Take therefore the talent from him.—MAT.,
ch. 25.

3215. —— **tested.** *Three Hebrews.* ²⁸ Neb-uchadnezzar spake..Blessed be the God of Sha-drach, Meshach, and Abed-nego, who hath sent his angel, and delivered his servants that trusted in him..and yielded their bodies, that they might not serve nor worship any god, except their own God.—DAN., ch. 3.

3216. —— **Want of.** *Unjust Steward.* ⁵ How much owest thou unto my lord? ⁶ And he said, A hundred measures of oil. And he said unto him, Take thy bill, and sit down quickly, and write fifty. ⁷ Then said he to another, And how much owest thou? And he said, A hundred measures of wheat. And he said unto him.. write fourscore.—LUKE, ch. 16.

See other illustrations under :

FAITHFULNESS.

Blessed is that servant whom his lord..so doing	2975
Constant. The fire shall ever be burning upon the	2976
Despondency. Let us also go..may die with him	2977
Honoured. I make a decree..speak..against the G.	2978
Ministerial. [See 2 Cor. 4 : 1–11]	2979
Primitive. All scattered abroad..except the a.	2981
Principle. Faithful in that which is least..also in	2982
Rewarded. If thou see me when I am taken..be	2983
Truth. What the L. saith unto me, that I will s.	2980

INTEGRITY.

Acknowledged. Thou art more righteous than I	4575
Conscious. The L. be judge, between me and thee	4576
Delight. The integrity of the upright shall guide	4577
Fixed. Till I die I will not remove mine integrity	4578
False. Is thy servant a dog..do this?	4579
Observed. God said, I know thou didst this	4580
Official. Witness..whom have I defrauded?	4581
Steadfast. L. said..Job holdeth fast his integrity	4582

See HONESTY.

3217. FIGHTING forbidden. *To Rehoboam and Israel.* ²⁴ Ye shall not go up, nor fight against your brethren the children of Israel : return every man to his house ; for this thing is from me. They hearkened therefore to the word of the Lord, and returned.—1 KINGS, ch. 12.

3218. —— **against God.** *Syrians.* ¹⁷ The Lord opened the eyes of the young man..and, behold, the mountain *was* full of horses and chariots of fire round about Elisha. ¹⁸ Elisha prayed unto the Lord, and said, Smite this peo-ple, I pray thee, with blindness. And he smote them.. ¹⁹ And Elisha said unto them, This *is* not the way, neither *is* this the city : follow me, and I will bring you to the man whom ye seek. But he led them to Samaria.—2 KINGS, ch. 6.

3219. —— **for Jesus.** *Ill-timed.* ⁵⁰ They.. laid hands on Jesus, and took him. ⁵¹ And, be-hold, one of them which were with Jesus..drew his sword, and struck a servant of the high priest, and smote off his ear. ⁵² Then said Jesus, Put up again thy sword .. they that take the sword shall perish with the sword.—MAT., ch. 26.

See WAR and references.

3220. FINANCE, Plan of. *Paul.* ¹ Concern-ing the collection for the saints, as I have given order to the churches of Galatia, even so do ye. ² Upon the first *day* of the week let every one of you lay by him in store, as God hath prospered him, that there be no gatherings when I come. —1 COR., ch. 16.

3221. —— **Simplicity in.** *Repairing the Tem-ple.* ⁹ Jehoiada the priest took a chest, and

bored a hole in the lid of it, and set it beside the altar, on the right side..and the priests that kept the door put therein all the money *that was* brought into the house of the Lord.—2 KINGS, ch. 12.

See other illustrations under :

COST.

Count. I will follow thee..not where to lay his h.	1734
Counted. Burned their books before all men	1735
not Counted. This man began to build, and was not	1736
Sacrifice. Neither will I offer..cost me nothing	1737

CONTRIBUTIONS.

Abundant. [Temple] offered willingly..gold 5000	1657
Expenses. Charge ourselves yearly..third part of	1658
for Jesus. Women..healed..ministered..their	1659
for Levites. Firstfruits of corn, wine, oil, and	1660
Repairs. Chest..set beside the altar..right side	1661
Rebuilding. Chief of the fathers gave after their	1662
Various. Men and women..blue, purple, scarlet	1663

PRICE.

Extortionate. Esau sold his birthright unto Jacob	6550
of Perfection. Go sell..give..follow me	6551

TAX.

Burdensome. That which thou puttest on me I	8595
Collector. Levi sitting at the receipt of custom	8596

TAXATION.

Exempted. Ministers..not be lawful to impose	8597
" King will make his house free in Israel	8598
Endangered. Then will they not pay tribute	8599
Eminence by. He shall stand up..a raiser of taxes	8600
Foreign. Jehoiakim..according to his taxation	8601
Lawful. Render unto Cesar the things..are Cesar's	8602
Oppressive. We have borrowed money for the	8603
Succession. Make..this heavy yoke lighter	8604
Universal. Joseph also went up..to be taxed with	8605

TRIBUTE.

Sheep. King of Moab rendered..100,000 lambs	8952
Useless. Ahaz took a portion..but he helped..not	8954
Contribution. I have given [$34,101,560]	3514
Estimated by. Widow..cast more in than all	711
Royalty. One day..ten fat oxen and twenty oxen	2807
Rebuilding. 61 drams of gold and 5000 pounds of	3532
Revenue. The weight of gold that came to Solomon	7316
Royalty. Solomon's provision for one day was	2807
Temple. [Costing nearly $4,700,000,000]	4130
Vast. Gain the whole world..lose his own soul	8434

See MONEY.

3222. FIRE, Ascension in. *Angel.* ¹⁹ *The angel* did wondrously ; and Manoah and his wife looked on. ²⁰ For..when the flame went up toward heaven from off the altar..the angel of the Lord ascended in the flame.—JUDGES, ch. 13.

3223. —— **Answered by.** *David.* ²⁵ David gave to Ornan for the place six hundred shekels of gold by weight. ²⁶ And David built there an altar..and offered burnt offerings and peace of-ferings, and called upon the Lord ; and he an-swered him from heaven by fire upon the altar of burnt offering.—1 CHRON., ch. 21.

3224. —— **Baptism of.** *Pentecost.* ³ There appeared unto them cloven tongues like as of fire, and it sat upon each of them.—ACTS, ch. 2.

3225. —— **Chariots of.** *At Dothan.* ¹⁷ Elisha prayed, and said, Lord, I pray thee, open his eyes, that he may see. And the Lord opened the eyes of the young man ; and he saw : and, behold, the mountain *was* full of horses and chariots of fire round about Elisha.—2 Kings, ch. 6.

3226. —— **A constant.** *Altar.* ¹² The priest shall burn wood on it every morning, and lay the burnt offering in order upon it ; and he shall burn thereon the fat of the peace offerings. ¹³ The fire shall ever be burning upon the altar ; it shall never go out.—Lev., ch. 6.

3227. —— **Consigned to.** *Perdition.* ⁴⁹ At the end of the world : the angels shall come forth, and sever the wicked from among the just, ⁵⁰ And shall cast them into the furnace of fire : there shall be wailing and gnashing of teeth.—Mat., ch. 3.

3228. —— **Descending.** *Carmel.* ³⁷ That this people may know that thou *art* the Lord God, and *that* thou hast turned their heart back again. ³⁸ Then the fire of the Lord fell, and consumed the burnt sacrifice, and the wood, and the stones, and the dust, and licked up the water that *was* in the trench.—1 Kings, ch. 18.

3229. —— **Descending in.** *Sinai.* ¹⁸ The Lord descended upon it in fire : and the smoke thereof ascended as the smoke of a furnace, and the whole mount quaked greatly. ¹⁹..the voice of the trumpet sounded long, and waxed louder and louder.—Ex., ch. 19.

3230. —— **Destructive.** *Sodom.* ²⁴ The Lord rained upon Sodom and upon Gomorrah brimstone and fire from the Lord out of the heaven : ²⁵ And he overthrew those cities, and all the plain, and all the inhabitants..and that which grew upon the ground.—Gen., ch. 19.

3231. —— —— *By Moses in Egypt.* ²³ Moses stretched forth his rod toward heaven : and the Lord sent thunder and hail, and the fire ran along upon the ground.—Ex., ch. 9.

3232. —— —— *Azariah.* ¹³ The third captain..fell on his knees before Elijah, and besought him..O man of God, I pray thee, let my life, and the life of these fifty thy servants, be precious in thy sight. ¹⁴ Behold, there came fire down from heaven, and burnt up the two captains of the former fifties with their fifties.—2 Kings, ch. 1.

3233. —— —— *Korah.* ³⁵ There came out a fire from the Lord, and consumed the two hundred and fifty men that offered incense.—Num., ch. 16.

3234. —— **Departure in.** *Elijah.* ¹¹ They still went on, and talked..behold, *there appeared* a chariot of fire, and horses of fire, and parted them both asunder ; and Elijah went up by a whirlwind into heaven.—2 Kings, ch. 2.

3235. —— **Destruction by.** *Jerusalem.* ⁸ Nebuzar-adan, captain..of the king of Babylon.. ⁹..burnt the house of the Lord, and the king's house, and all the houses of Jerusalem, and every great *man's* house.—2 Kings, ch. 25.

3236. —— **evinces Favour.** *Gideon.* ²¹ The angel of the Lord put forth the end of the staff that *was* in his hand, and touched the flesh and the unleavened cakes ; and there rose up fire out of the rock, and consumed the flesh and the unleavened cakes.—Judges, ch. 6.

3237. —— **A false.** *Nadab and Abihu.* ¹ Took either of them his censer, and put fire therein, and put incense thereon, and offered strange fire before the Lord, which he commanded them not. ² And there went out fire from the Lord, and devoured them.—Lev., ch. 10.

3238. —— **Guarded by.** *Tabernacle.* ³⁸ The cloud of the Lord *was* upon the tabernacle by day, and fire was on it by night, in the sight of all the house of Israel, throughout all their journeys.—Ex., ch. 40.

3239. —— **Glorious.** *Sinai.* ¹⁷ The glory of the Lord *was* like devouring fire on the top of the mount in the eyes of the children of Israel. ¹⁸ And Moses went into the midst of the cloud. —Ex., ch. 24.

3240. —— **A holy.** *At Dedication.* ²⁴ There came a fire out from before the Lord, and consumed upon the altar the burnt offering and the fat : *which* when all the people saw, they shouted, and fell on their faces.—Lev., ch. 9.

3241. —— —— *Temple.* ¹ When Solomon had made an end of praying, the fire came down from heaven, and consumed the burnt offering and the sacrifices.. ² And the priests could not enter..because the glory of the Lord had filled the Lord's house.—2 Chron., ch. 7.

3242. —— **Lord not in.** *Elijah at Sinai.* ¹² After the earthquake a fire ; *but* the Lord *was* not in the fire : and after the fire a still small voice.—1 Kings, ch. 19.

3243. —— **Powerless.** *Three Hebrews.* ²⁶ Shadrach, Meshach, and Abed-nego, came forth of the midst of the fire. ²⁷ And the princes, governors, and captains, and the king's counsellors, being gathered together, saw these men, upon whose bodies the fire had no power, nor was a hair of their head singed, neither were their coats changed, nor the smell of fire had passed on them.—Dan., ch. 3.

3244. —— **of Perdition.** *Lake.* ⁸ The fearful, and unbelieving, and the abominable, and murderers, and whoremongers, and sorcerers, and idolaters, and all liars, shall have their part in the lake which burneth with fire and brimstone : which is the second death.—Rev., ch. 21.

3245. —— **Preparation by.** *Lips.* ⁵ Woe *is* me ! for I am undone ; because I *am* a man of unclean lips, and I dwell in the midst of a people of unclean lips : for mine eyes have seen the King, the Lord of hosts. ⁶ Then flew one of the seraphims..having a live coal in his hand..from off the altar : ⁷ And he laid *it* upon my mouth, and said, Lo, this hath touched thy lips ; and thine iniquity is taken away, and thy sin purged. ⁸ Also I heard the voice of the Lord, saying, Whom shall I send..Then said I, *Here am* I ; send me.—Isa., ch. 6.

3246. —— **A refining.** *Christ.* ² He *is* like a refiner's fire, and like fullers' soap : ³ And he shall sit *as* a refiner and purifier of silver : and he shall purify the sons of Levi, and purge them as gold and silver, that they may offer unto the Lord an offering in righteousness.—Mal., ch. 3.

3247. —— **in the Sanctuary.** *Tabernacle.* [See No. 3226.]

3248. —— **a Test.** *Carmel.* ²⁴ Call ye on the name of your gods, and I will call on the name of the Lord : and the God that answereth by fire, let him be God. And all the people answered ..It is well spoken.—1 Kings, ch. 18.

3249. —— **Unconsuming.** *By Horeb.* ² The angel of the Lord appeared unto him in a flame of fire out of the midst of a bush..and behold, the bush burned with fire, and the bush *was* not consumed. ³ And Moses said, I will now turn aside, and see this great sight, why the bush is not burnt.—Ex., ch. 3.

See other illustrations under :

Affliction. I have chosen thee in the furnace of   211
Arson. We will burn thine house upon thee   503
Dwellings. Nebuzar-adan burned..every great   4384
Malicious. Samson caught 300 foxes..burned   4383
Punishment. Fire of the L. burned them in the   5646
Synagogues. Burned up all the synagogues in the   4129
Temple. Nebuzar-adan captain..burned the house 3235

3250. FISH, A great Catch. *Gennesaret:* ⁵ Simon..said..Master, we have toiled all the night, and have taken nothing : nevertheless at thy word I will let down the net. ⁶ And..they inclosed a great multitude of fishes : and their net brake.—LUKE, ch. 5.

3251. —— Service by. *For Jesus.* ²⁷ Lest we should offend them, go thou to the sea, and cast a hook, and take up the fish that first cometh up ; and when thou hast opened his mouth, thou shalt find a piece of money : that take, and give unto them for me and thee.—MAT., ch. 17.

3252. —— Saved by a. *Jonah.* ¹⁰ The Lord spake unto the fish, and it vomited out Jonah upon the dry *land.*.And Jonah was in the belly of the fish three days and three nights. ¹⁷ Now the Lord had prepared a great fish to swallow up Jonah.—JONAH, chs. 1 and 2.

3253. FISHES, Suggestion by. *Gennesaret.* ⁶ They cast therefore, and now they were not able to draw it for the multitude of fishes. ⁷ Therefore that disciple whom Jesus loved saith unto Peter, It is the Lord.—JOHN, ch. 21.

Also see:

Dominion. Have dominion over fish of the sea   3664
Fondness for. We remember the fish..eat in Egypt 480

3254. FLATTERY, Dangerous. *Herod.* ²¹ Herod, arrayed in royal apparel, sat upon his throne, and made an oration unto them. ²² And the people gave a shout, *saying, It is* the voice of a god, and not of a man. ²³ And immediately the angel of the Lord smote him, because he gave not God the glory : and he was eaten of worms, and gave up the ghost.—ACTS, ch. 12.

3255. —— Failure of. *Pharisees.* ¹⁶ Sent ..their disciples with the Herodians, saying, Master, we know that thou art true, and teachest the way of God in truth, neither carest thou for any *man :* for thou regardest not the person of men. ¹⁷..Is it lawful to give tribute unto Cesar, or not ?—MAT., ch. 22.

3256. —— Success by. *Daniel's Enemies.* ⁷ All the presidents of the kingdom, the governors, and the princes, the counsellors, and the captains, have consulted together..to make a firm decree, that whosoever shall ask a petition of any god or man for thirty days, save of thee, O king, he shall be cast into the den of lions. ⁸ Now, O king, establish the decree.—DAN., ch. 6.

See other illustrations under:

PRAISE.

Dangerous. None so much praised as Absalom   6332
Love of. Loved the praise of men more   6336
"   Love to pray..to be seen of men   6337
Self. Let another praise thee, not..own lips   6341

Politics. He shall obtain the kingdom by flatteries 8600

3257. FLESH, Weakness of. *Garden.* ³⁹ O my Father, if it be possible, let this cup pass from me.. ⁴⁰ And he cometh .. and findeth them asleep, and saith unto Peter, What, could ye not watch with me one hour ? ⁴¹ The spirit indeed *is* willing, but the flesh *is* weak.—MAT., ch. 26.

3258. —— Works of. *Evil.* ¹⁹ The works of the flesh are manifest, which are *these ;* Adultery, fornication, uncleanness, lasciviousness, ²⁰ Idolatry, witchcraft, hatred, variance, emulations, wrath, strife, seditions, heresies, ²¹ Envyings, murders, drunkenness, revellings, and such like ..they which do such things shall not inherit the kingdom of God.—GAL., ch. 5.

See other illustrations under :

Devotion. They that are after the flesh do mind   9855
Dangerous. If ye live after the flesh ye shall—Rom. 8 : 13
Epistle. Not in stone, but in fleshly tables of the   903
Health. Sound heart is the life of the flesh   2698
Inferior. With him is an arm of flesh..God   1773
Sickening. Eat..mouth..out at the nostrils   6215
Supremacy. He that soweth to the flesh—Gal. 6 : 8
Weariness. Much study is a weariness to the flesh 8400

3259. FLIES, Plague of. *Egypt.* ²⁴ There came a grievous swarm of flies into the house of Pharaoh, and *into* his servants' houses, and into all the land of Egypt : the land was corrupted by reason of the swarm of flies.—Ex., ch. 8.

3260. FLOWERS, Beauty of. *Jesus said,* ²⁷ Consider the lilies how they grow : they toil not, they spin not ; and yet..Solomon in all his glory was not arrayed like one of these.—LUKE, ch. 12.

3261. —— teach Faith. *Jesus said,* ²⁸ If then God so clothe the grass, which is to day in the field, and to morrow is cast into the oven ; how much more *will he clothe* you, O ye of little faith ? ²⁹ And seek not ye what ye shall eat, or what ye shall drink, neither be ye of doubtful mind,—LUKE, ch. 12.

See other illustrations under :

Architectural. House..was carved—1 Kings 6 : 18
Coveted. Hard by the palace..for a garden of herbs 3503
Eden. G. planted a garden..pleasant to the sight   3506
Man. He cometh forth as a flower..cut down   5017
"   As a flower of the field, so he flourish—Ps. 103 : 15
"   Whose glorious beauty is a fading—Isa. 18 : 28
Signal. Flowers appear on the earth, time of sing. 8462

3262. FOLLY of Anger. *Nabal.* ³ *Was* churlish and evil in his doings. ¹⁰ And Nabal answered David's servants..Who *is* David ?..there be many servants nowadays that break away every man from his master. ¹¹ Shall I then take my bread, and my water, and my flesh that I have killed for my shearers, and give *it* unto men, whom I know not whence they *be ?*—1 SAM., ch. 25.

3263. —— Ashamed of. *Disciples.* ³³ He came to Capernaum : and..he asked them, What was it that ye disputed among yourselves by the way ? ³⁴ But they held their peace..they had disputed..who *should* be the greatest.—MARK, ch. 9.

3264. —— of Backsliders. *Broken Cisterns.* ¹³ My people have committed two evils : they have forsaken me the fountain of living waters, *and* hewed them out cisterns, broken cisterns, that can hold no water.—JER., ch. 2.

3265. —— Ecclesiastical. *Pharisees.* ¹⁸ Whosoever shall swear by the altar, it is nothing ;

but whosoever sweareth by the gift that is upon it, he is guilty. ¹⁹ *Ye* fools and blind : for whether *is* greater, the gift, or the altar that sanctifieth the gift ?—MAT., ch. 23.

3266. —— **Inseparable.** *Proverb.* ²² Though thou shouldest bray a fool in a mortar among wheat with a pestle, *yet* will not his foolishness depart from him.—PROV., ch. 27.

3267. —— **of Indifference.** *Builder.* ²⁶ Every one that heareth these sayings of mine, and doeth them not, shall be likened unto a foolish man, which built his house upon the sand : ²⁷ And the rain descended, and the floods came, and the winds blew, and beat upon that house ; and it fell : and great was the fall of it.—MAT., ch. 7.

3268. —— **of Idolaters.** *Idols.* ⁴ Their idols *are* silver and gold, the work of men's hands. ⁵ They have mouths, but they speak not : eyes have they, but they see not : ⁶ They have ears, but they hear not : noses have they, but they smell not : ⁷ They have hands, but they handle not : feet have they, but they walk not : neither speak they through their throat. ⁸ They that make them are like unto them ; *so is* every one that trusteth in them.—Ps. 115.

3269. —— —— *Wood.* ¹⁴ He planteth an ash, and the rain doth nourish *it.* ¹⁵ Then shall it be for a man to burn : for he will take thereof, and warm himself ; yea, he kindleth *it,* and baketh bread ; yea, he maketh a god, and worshippeth *it ;* he maketh it a graven image, and falleth down thereto.—ISA., ch. 44.

3270. —— **Natural.** *Ostrich.* ¹⁴ Which leaveth her eggs in the earth, and warmeth them in the dust, ¹⁵ And forgetteth that the foot may crush them, or that the wild beast may break them. ¹⁷ Because God hath deprived her of wisdom.—JOB, ch. 39.

3271. —— **of Neglect.** *Five Virgins.* ² Five of them were wise, and five *were* foolish. ³ They that *were* foolish took their lamps, and took no oil with them : ⁴ But the wise took oil in their vessels with their lamps.—MAT., ch. 25.

3272. —— **of the Worldly.** *Rich Fool.* ¹⁷ What shall I do, because I have no room where to bestow my fruits ? ¹⁸ . . I will pull down my barns, and build greater ; and there will I bestow all my fruits and my goods. ¹⁹ And I will say to my soul, Soul, thou hast much goods laid up for many years ; take thine ease, eat, drink, *and* be merry.—LUKE, ch. 12.

3273. —— **of Youth.** *Rehoboam.* ⁸ He forsook the counsel of the old men . . and consulted with the young men that were grown up with him . . ¹³ And the king answered the people roughly.— 1 KINGS, ch. 12. [Ten tribes seceded.]

See other illustrations under:

FLATTERY.

Dangerous. Herod . . was eaten of worms	3254
Failure. Herodians saying . . thou art true	3255
Successful. Ask . . save of thee, O king . . lions	3256

PRESUMPTION.

Avoided. Better . . he said, Come up hither ; than	6534
Daring. Egyptians pursued . . midst of the sea	6535
Failure. Presumed to go . . Amalekites smote them	6536
Future. Know not what shall be on the morrow	6537
Impatience. Because thou comest not . . I offered	6538
Pride. Uzziah . . burnt incense upon the altar	6539

Penalty. Come unto the king . . not called . . death	6540
Religious. Prophet that shall speak . . not com'd	6541
Rebuked. Uzziah . . censer in his hand . . leprosy	6542
Sin. Trodden under foot the Son of God	6543
Success. Soul that doeth . . presumptuously . . cut off	6544
" Joshua made as if beaten . . drawn away	6545
Temptation. On a pinnacle . . cast thyself down	6546
Unholy. 250 princes . . ye take too much upon you	6547

Adulterer. Fire in his bosom . . lacketh understanding	113
Anger. He that is hasty of spirit exalteth—Prov. 14 : 29	
Atheism. The fool hath said in his heart, there is no	570

3274. FOLLOWING to Deliverance. *Peter.* ⁹ He went out, and followed him ; and wist not that it was true which was done by the angel ; but thought he saw a vision. ¹⁰ When they were past the first and the second ward, they came unto the iron gate that leadeth unto the city ; which opened to them of his own accord : and they went out, and passed on through one street ; and forthwith the angel departed from *him.*—ACTS, ch. 12.

3275. —— **A faithful.** *Elisha.* ¹⁹ He departed thence, and found Elisha . . ploughing *with* twelve yoke *of oxen* before him . . and Elijah passed by him, and cast his mantle upon him. ²⁰ And he left the oxen, and ran after Elijah.— 1 KINGS, ch. 19.

3276. —— **the Leader.** *Armourbearer.* ¹³ Jonathan climbed up upon his hands and upon his feet, and his armourbearer after him : and they fell before Jonathan ; and his armourbearer slew after him.—1 SAM., ch. 14.

3277. —— **the Multitude.** *Hushai.* ¹⁷ Absalom said to Hushai . . why wentest thou not with thy friend ? ¹⁸ And Hushai said . . Nay ; but whom the Lord, and this people, and all the men of Israel, choose, his will I be, and with him will I abide.—2 SAM., ch. 16.

3278. —— **with Trembling.** *Israelites.* ⁶ When the men of Israel saw that they were in a strait . . then the people did hide themselves in caves, and in thickets, and in rocks, and in high places, and in pits. ⁷ And *some* . . went over Jordan to . . Gilead. As for Saul, he *was* yet in Gilgal, and all the people followed him trembling. —1 SAM., ch. 13.

3279. —— **Unwilling.** *Israelites.* ¹⁸ Sanctify yourselves against to morrow, and ye shall eat flesh : for ye have wept in the ears of the Lord, saying, Who shall give us flesh to eat ? for *it was* well with us in Egypt.—NUM., ch. 11.

3280. —— **Jesus afar off.** *Peter.* ⁵³ They led Jesus away to the high priest . . ⁵⁴ And Peter followed him afar off, even into the palace of the high priest : and he sat with the servants, and warmed himself at the fire.—MARK, ch. 14.

3281. —— —— **The Delivered.** *Bartimeus.* ⁵¹ The blind man said . . Lord, that I might receive my sight. ⁵² And Jesus said . . Go thy way ; thy faith hath made thee whole. And immediately he received his sight, and followed Jesus in the way.—MARK, ch. 10.

3282. —— —— **by forsaking All.** *Peter.* ¹⁰ Jesus said unto Simon, Fear not ; from henceforth thou shalt catch men. ¹¹ And when they had brought their ships to land, they forsook all, and followed him.—LUKE, ch. 5.

3283. —— —— **with Fear.** *Disciples.* ³² They were in the way going up to Jerusalem ; and Jesus went before them : and they were amazed ; and as they followed, they were afraid. And he took again the twelve, and began to tell them what things should happen unto him.—MARK, ch. 10.

3284. —— —— **from a Word.** *Andrew and John.* ³⁵ John stood.. ³⁶ And looking upon Jesus as he walked, he said, Behold the Lamb of God ! ³⁷ And the two disciples heard him speak, and they followed Jesus.—JOHN, ch. 1.

3285. —— —— **willingly.** *Matthew.* ¹⁴ As he passed by, he saw Levi..sitting at the receipt of custom, and said unto him, Follow me. And he arose and followed him.—MARK, ch. 2.

See other illustrations under :

3286. FOOD, Animals for. *After the Deluge.* ² The fear of you..shall be upon every beast of the earth, and upon every fowl of the air, upon all that moveth *upon* the earth, and upon all the fishes of the sea : into your hand are they delivered. ³ Every moving thing that liveth shall be meat for you.—GEN., ch. 9.

3287. —— **Better than.** *Job.* ¹¹ His way have I kept, and not declined. ¹² Neither have I gone back from the commandment of his lips ; I have esteemed the words of his mouth more than my necessary *food.*—JOB, ch. 23.

3288. —— **cleansed of God.** *Vision.* ¹⁴ Peter said, Not so, Lord ; for I have never eaten any thing that is common or unclean. ¹⁵ And the voice *spake*..the second time, What God hath cleansed, *that* call not thou common. ¹⁶ This was done thrice : and the vessel was received up again into heaven.—ACTS, ch. 10.

3289. —— **Costly.** *Esau.* ³³ He sold his birthright unto Jacob. ³⁴ Then Jacob gave Esau bread and pottage of lentiles ; and he did eat and drink, and rose up, and went his way. Thus Esau despised *his* birthright.—GEN., ch. 25.

3290. —— **Choice of plain.** *Four Hebrews.*

¹¹ Said Daniel.. ¹² Prove thy servants, I beseech thee, ten days ; and let them give us pulse to eat, and water to drink. ¹³ Then let our countenances be looked upon before thee, and the countenance of the children that eat of the portion of the king's meat : and as thou seest, deal with thy servants.—DAN., ch. 1.

3291. —— **Caution in eating.** *Solomon.* ¹ When thou sittest to eat with a ruler, consider diligently what *is* before thee : ² And put a knife to thy throat if thou *be* a man given to appetite. ³ Be not desirous of his dainties : for they *are* deceitful meat.—PROV., ch. 23.

3292. —— **Daily.** *Prayer.* ¹¹ Give us this day our daily bread.—MAT., ch. 6.

3293. —— **Diminished.** *Drought.* ⁶ I also have given you cleanness of teeth in all your cities, and want of bread..yet have ye not returned unto me, saith the Lord. ⁷ And also I have withholden the rain from you, when *there were* yet three months to the harvest : and I caused it to rain upon one city, and caused it not to rain upon another city.—AMOS, ch. 4.

3294. —— **Example in.** *Paul.* ¹⁰ If any man see thee which hast knowledge sit at meat in the idol's temple, shall not the conscience of him which is weak be emboldened to eat those things which are offered to idols ; ¹³ Wherefore, if meat make my brother to offend, I will eat no flesh while the world standeth, lest I make my brother to offend.—1 COR., ch. 8.

3295. —— **Forbidden.** *Eden.* ² We may eat of the fruit of the trees of the garden : ³ But of the fruit of the tree which *is* in the midst of the garden, God hath said, Ye shall not eat of it, neither shall ye touch it, lest ye die.—GEN., ch. 3.

3296. —— **Favorite.** *Jacob.* ² I am old, I know not the day of my death : ³..take, I pray thee, thy weapons, thy quiver and thy bow, and go out to the field, and take me *some* venison ; ⁴ And make me savoury meat, such as I love.—GEN., ch. 27.

3297. —— **Friendship by.** *Isaac.* ²⁸ Isaac loved Esau, because he did eat of *his* venison : but Rebekah loved Jacob.—GEN., ch. 25.

3298. —— **in Famine.** *Samaria.* ²⁴ Benhadad king of Syria gathered all his host, and went up, and besieged Samaria. ²⁵ And there was a great famine in Samaria..until an ass's head was *sold* for fourscore *pieces* of silver, and the fourth part of a cab of dove's dung for five *pieces* of silver.—2 KINGS, ch. 6.

3299. —— **Freedom to gather.** *Law.* ²⁴ Into thy neighbour's vineyard, then thou mayest eat grapes thy fill at thine own pleasure ; but thou shalt not put *any* in thy vessel. ²⁵ When thou comest into the standing corn of thy neighbour, then thou mayest pluck the ears with thine hand ; but thou shalt not move a sickle.—DEUT., ch. 23.

3300. —— **Honouring God with.** *Firstfruits.* ¹⁴ Ye shall eat neither bread, nor parched corn, nor green ears, until the selfsame day that ye have brought an offering unto your God : *it shall be* a statute for ever.—LEV., ch. 23.

3301. —— **God gives.** *Ravens.* ²⁴ Consider the ravens : for they neither sow nor reap ; which neither have storehouse nor barn ; and

God feedeth them : how much more are ye better than the fowls?—LUKE, ch. 12.

3302. —— **from Heaven.** *Jesus.* [32] Jesus said..Moses gave you not that bread from heaven ; but my Father giveth you the true bread from heaven. [34] Then said they..Lord, evermore give us this bread. [35] And Jesus said..I am the bread of life : he that cometh to me shall never hunger ; and he that believeth on me shall never thirst.—JOHN, ch. 6.

3303. —— **Life-giving.** *Eden.* [22] The Lord God said..lest he put forth his hand, and take also of the tree of life, and eat, and live forever : [23] Therefore the Lord God sent him forth from the garden of Eden.—GEN., ch. 3.

3304. —— **miraculously given.** *Quails.* [31] There went forth a wind from the Lord, and brought quails from the sea, and let *them* fall by the camp, as it were a day's journey on this side, and..on the other side..and as it were two cubits *high* upon..the earth.—NUM., ch. 11.

3305. —— *Elijah.* [6] The ravens brought him bread and flesh in the morning, and..in the evening ; and he drank of the brook [Cherith].—1 KINGS, ch. 17.

3306. —— *Elijah.* [5] Slept under a juniper tree, behold, then an angel touched him, and said..Arise *and* eat. [6] *There was* a cake baken on the coals, and a cruse of water at his head. And he did eat and drink, and laid him down again.—1 KINGS, ch. 19.

3307. —— *Five Thousand.* [41] When he had taken the five loaves .. blessed, and brake the loaves, and *gave* them to his disciples to set before them ; and the two fishes divided he among them all. [42] And they did all eat, and were filled. [43] And they took up twelve baskets full of the fragments.—MARK, ch. 6.

3308. —— —— *One Hundred.* [42] There came a man from Baal-shalisha, and brought the man of God bread of the firstfruits, twenty loaves of barley, and full ears of corn in the husk thereof. And he said, Give unto the people.. [43] And his servitor said, What, should I set this before a hundred men? He said again, Give the people, that they may eat : for thus saith the Lord, They shall eat, and shall leave *thereof*.—2 KINGS, ch. 4. [It was so.]

3309. —— *Manna.* [14] *There lay* a small round thing, *as* small as the hoar frost on the ground. [15] And..they said one to another, It *is* manna : for they wist not what it *was*. And Moses said..This *is* the bread which the Lord hath given you to eat.. [35]..did eat manna forty years, until they came to a land inhabited.—EX., ch. 16.

3310. —— **a Necessity.** *Proverb.* [9] *He that* is despised, and hath a servant, *is* better than he that honoureth himself, and lacketh bread.—PROV., ch. 12.

3311. —— **Natural.** *Baptist.* [4] John had his raiment of camel's hair, and a leathern girdle about his loins ; and his meat was locusts and wild honey.—MAT., ch. 3.

3312. —— **Perilous.** *Jonathan.* [27] Jonathan heard not when his father charged the people with the oath.. [43]..Jonathan..said, I did but taste a little honey with the end of the rod that *was* in mine hand, *and*, lo, I must die.—1 SAM., ch. 14.

3313. —— **prohibited.** *Blood.* [11] The life of the flesh *is* in the blood ; and I have given it to you upon the altar to make an atonement for your souls : for it *is* the blood *that* maketh an atonement for the soul. [12] Therefore I said.. No soul of you shall eat blood, neither shall any stranger that sojourneth among you.—LEV., ch. 17.

3314. —— —— *Fat.* [23] Ye shall eat no manner of fat, of ox, or of sheep, or of goat.. [25] For whosoever eateth the fat of the beast, of which men offer an offering made by fire unto the Lord, even the soul that eateth *it* shall be cut off from his people.—LEV., ch. 7.

3315. —— **Prudence with.** *Paul.* [1] I, brethren, could not speak unto you as unto spiritual, but as unto carnal, *even* as unto babes in Christ. [2] I have fed you with milk, and not with meat : for hitherto ye were not able *to bear it*, neither yet now are ye able.—1 COR., ch. 3.

3316. —— **Promise of.** *Christian.* [3] Trust in the Lord, and do good ; *so* shalt thou dwell in the land, and verily thou shalt be fed.—PS. 37.

3317. —— —— *Christian.* [15] He that walketh righteously, and speaketh uprightly ; he that despiseth the gain of oppressions, that shaketh his hands from holding of bribes, that stoppeth his ears from hearing of blood, and shutteth his eyes from seeing evil ; [16] He shall dwell on high ; his place of defence *shall be* the munitions of rocks : bread shall be given him ; his waters *shall be* sure.—ISA., ch. 33.

3318. —— **restricted.** *Law.* [2] These *are* the beasts which ye shall eat.. [3] Whatsoever parteth the hoof, and is clovenfooted, *and* cheweth the cud, among the beasts, that shall ye eat. —LEV., ch. 11. [See from 2 to 22 verses.]

3319. —— **Scarcity of.** *Widow of Zarephath.* [12] I have not a cake, but a handful of meal in a barrel, and a little oil in a cruse : and, behold, I *am* gathering two sticks, that I may go in and dress it for me and my son, that we may eat it, and die.—2 KINGS, ch. 17.

3320. —— **Royal Supplies of.** *Solomon's.* [22] Solomon's provision for one day was thirty measures of fine flour, and threescore measures of meal, [23] Ten fat oxen, and twenty oxen out of pastures, and a hundred sheep, besides harts, and roebucks, and fallow deer, and fatted fowl. —1 KINGS, ch. 4.

3321. —— **Spiritual.** *Everlasting.* [26] Ye seek me, not because ye saw the miracles, but because ye did eat of the loaves, and were filled. [27] Labour not for the meat which perisheth, but for that meat which endureth unto everlasting life, which the Son of man shall give unto you. —JOHN, ch. 6.

3322. —— **Scruples respecting.** *Paul.* [7] Some with conscience of the idol unto this hour eat *it* as a thing offered unto an idol ; and their conscience being weak is defiled. [8] But meat commendeth us not to God : for neither, if we eat, are we the better ; neither, if we eat not, are we the worse.—1 COR., ch. 8.

3323. —— **Thanks for.** *At Emmaus.* [30] As he sat at meat with them, he took bread, and blessed *it*, and brake, and gave to them. [31] And their eyes were opened, and they knew him.— LUKE, ch. 24.

3324. —— —— *Wilderness.* [See No. 3307.]

3325. —— **Shipwrecked.** *Paul.* [35] He took bread, and gave thanks to God in presence of them all ; and when he had broken *it*, he began to eat. [36] Then were they all of good cheer, and they also took *some* meat.—ACTS, ch. 27.

3326. —— **Temptation in.** *Jesus.* [2] When he had fasted forty days and forty nights, he was afterward a hungered. [3] And when the tempter came to him, he said, If thou be the Son of God, command that these stones be made bread.—MAT., ch. 4.

3327. —— **Weeping for.** *Israelites.* [Being weary of manna,] [10] Moses heard the people weep throughout their families, every man in the door of his tent : and the anger of the Lord was kindled greatly ; Moses also was displeased. —NUM., ch. 11.

See other illustrations under:

APPETITE.

Control. Put a knife to thy throat, if..appetite	479
Dangers. We remember fish, cucumbers, melons	480
Heedless. [Pursuing Philistines,] people were faint	481
Sin. Who shall give us flesh?..be [loathsome]	482
Temptation. [Jesus] fasted 40 days..afterward	483
Unrestrained. At the point to die, what profit	484

FAMINE.

Charity. Disciples determined to send relief	3022
Care. Shall eat bread by weight..water by	3024
Dying. Eaten no bread..three days..sick	3025
Distress. Delicate woman..children..eat them	3026
Exiled. Sojourn wherever thou canst..seven	3027
Escape. Abram went down into Egypt..famine	3028
Emigration. Elimelech went to sojourn in..famine	3029
Inhumanity. Give thy son, that we may eat him	3030
Sin. I will break the staff of bread	3031
" Ye have forsaken the..L. and followed	3032
Seven Years. No bread..land of Canaan fainted	3033
Spiritual. I will send a famine..words of the L.	3034
Water. To kill us and our children..cattle	3035

FEAST.

Ancient. Sarah..made cakes..Abraham..calf	3172
Birthday. Herod on his birthday made a supper	3173
Charitable. Call the poor, the lame..blind	3174
Complimentary. At Bethany..they made Jesus a	3175
" Levi made Jesus a great feast	3176
Death. Job's sons and daughters..brother's house	3177
Ended sadly. Merry with wine..smite Amnon	3178
Farewell. Elisha..oxen, and slew them..people	3179
Great. Solomon offered 22,000 oxen and 120,000 s.	3180
Idolatrous. [Calf] People..eat..drink..rose up to	3181
Impious. Belshazzar made a feast to a thousand	3182
Joyous. [Tabernacles] Seven days shall dwell in	3183
Marriage. Jesus and his disciples were called	3184
National. Three times..keep a feast unto me..year	3186
Royal. Ahasuerus made a feast at Shushan	3185

HUNGER.

Appetizing. To the hungry soul every bitter..sweet	4209
Disappointment. Fig tree in the way..nothing	4211
Lawful. Sabbath..disciples began to pluck..corn	4215
Murmuring. When we sat by the fleshpots..full	4216
Overcome. I have meat to eat ye know not of	4217
Removed. I am the bread of life..never hunger	4218
Subdued by. I will arise, and go to my father	4219
Temptation. Tempter came..stones be made	4220

TEMPERANCE.

Advised. Drink no wine, nor strong drink	8659
Eating. His dainties..are deceitful meat	8661
Health. Proved them ten days..fairer and fatter	8663

Hereditary. Our father commanded us..drink	8662
Mastery. Striveth for mastery is temperate	8664
Piety. [J. B.] Neither wine nor strong drink	8665
Strength. [Mother of Samson] Drink no wine	8666

Charity. Lazarus..feed with the crumbs which fell	431
Complaint. No water..loathsome..this light bread	1415
Commissary. Solomon had 12 officers..provided	6815
Deceived by. Took of their victuals, and did not	1741
Disposition. Better is a dinner of herbs where love	3834
Degrading. Serpent..upon thy belly..dust..eat	419
Hurtful. Eating pottage..death in the pot	452
Spiritual. I am the door..find pasture	47

See **FASTING.**

3328. FORBEARANCE, Divine. *When Rejected.* [12] When..Nahash the king..of Ammon came against you, ye said unto me, Nay ; but a king shall reign over us : when the Lord your God *was* your king. [22] ..the Lord will not forsake his people for his great name's sake : because it hath pleased the Lord to make you his people. —1 SAM., ch. 12.

3329. —— —— *Limited.* [7] Behold, these three years I come seeking fruit on this fig tree, and find none : cut it down ; why cumbereth it the ground ? [8] ..Lord, let it alone this year also, till I shall dig about it, and dung *it :* [9] And if it bear fruit, *well :* and if not, *then* after that thou shalt cut it down.—LUKE, ch. 13.

3330. —— **Pious.** *David's.* [16] Saul lifted up his voice, and wept. [17] And he said to David, Thou *art* more righteous than I : for thou hast rewarded me good, whereas I have rewarded thee evil. [18] ..when the Lord had delivered me into thine hand, thou killedst me not. [19] For if a man find his enemy, will he let him go well away ?—1 SAM., ch. 24 :

See other illustrations under:

PATIENCE.

Divine. Last of all he sent his son..they will r.	5994
Example of. Consider him that endured such	5995
Labour of. Let it alone this year also..I shall dig	5996
Maintained. Mighty men were..thou bloody man	5997
Needful. Rest in the L...fret not thyself..wicked	5998
Picture of. Husbandman waiteth for the precious	5999
Rewarded. I waited patiently for the L...heard	6000
Tested. Have patience..I will pay thee all	6001
" Belial..despised him, and brought no p.	6002
Without. Should this dead dog curse my lord	6003
Waiting. Need of p. after that ye have done the	6004

See **MERCY.**

3331. FOREIGNER, Despised. *"This Syrian."* [20] Gehazi, the servant of Elisha..said, Behold, my master hath spared Naaman this Syrian, in not receiving at his hands that which he brought : but, *as* the Lord liveth, I will run after him, and take somewhat of him.—2 KINGS, ch. 5.

3332. —— **Discrimination against.** *Debtors.* [2] Every creditor that lendeth *aught* unto his neighbour shall release *it;* he shall not exact.. of his brother ; because it is called the Lord's release. [3] Of a foreigner thou mayest exact *it* again.—DEUT., ch. 15.

3333. —— **Homesick.** *Hadad.* [21] When Hadad heard..that David..and..Joab..[were] dead, Hadad said to Pharaoh, Let me depart, that I may go to mine own country. [22] Then Pharaoh said..But what hast thou lacked with me, that, behold, thou seekest to go to thine own country? And he answered, Nothing : howbeit let me go in any wise.—1 KINGS, ch. 11.

3334. —— **Ineligibility of.** *King.* ¹⁵ Thou shalt in any wise set *him* king over thee, whom the Lord thy God shall choose : *one* from among thy brethren..thou mayest not set a stranger over thee.—DEUT., ch. 17.

3335. —— **Prejudice against.** *Sodomites.* ⁹ They said, Stand back..This one *fellow* came in to sojourn, and he will needs be a judge : now will we deal worse with thee than with them. And they pressed sore upon..Lot, and came near to break the door.—GEN., ch. 19.

3336. —— **Increase of.** *In Egypt.* ⁷ The children of Israel were fruitful, and increased abundantly, and multiplied, and waxed exceeding mighty ; and the land was filled with them. —EX., ch. 1.

3337. —— **Jealousy against.** *Pharaoh.* ⁹ The children of Israel *are* more and mightier than we : ¹⁰ Come on, let us deal wisely with them ; lest they multiply, and..when there falleth out any war, they join also unto our enemies, and fight against us, and *so* get them up out of the land. ¹¹ Therefore they did set over them taskmasters.—EX., ch. 1.

3338. —— **Liberality to.** *Passover.* ⁴⁸ When a stranger..will keep the passover to the Lord, let all his males be circumcised, and then let him come near and keep it ; and he shall be as one that is born in the land.. ⁴⁹ One law shall be to him that is homeborn, and unto the stranger that sojourneth among you.—EX., ch. 12.

See other illustrations under :

EXILE.

Commanded. Get thee out of thy country 2802
Criminal. Absalom fled to Geshur..three years 2803
Infant. Joseph..flee into Egypt..young child 2804
Necessary. Flee thou to Laban my brother 2805
Painful. Sold Joseph..into Egypt. 2806

STRANGERS.

Hospitality. Wash your feet and rest yourselves 8365
Lonely. Sat him down in a street in the city 8364

Abolished. Ye are no more..foreigners..but 1420
Discrimination. Of a foreigner thou mayest exact 2006
Excluded. Foreigner..shall not eat thereof—Ex. 12 : 45

3339. FORETHOUGHT, Necessary. *Builder.* ²⁸ Which of you, intending to build a tower, sitteth not down first, and counteth the cost, whether he have *sufficient* to finish *it* ? ²⁹ Lest haply, after he hath laid the foundation, and is not able to finish *it*, all that behold *it* begin to mock him, ³⁰ Saying, This man began to build, and was not able to finish.—LUKE, ch. 14.

3340. —— —— *Soldier.* ³¹ What king, going to make war..sitteth not down first, and consulteth whether he be able with ten thousand to meet him..with twenty thousand ? ³² Or else, while the other is yet a great way off, he sendeth an ambassage, and desireth conditions of peace.—LUKE, ch. 14.

3341. —— **Useless.** *Stature.* ²⁵ Which of you with taking thought can add to his stature one cubit ? ²⁶ If ye then be not able to do that thing which is least, why take ye thought for the rest ? —LUKE, ch. 12.

See other illustrations under :

CAUTION.

Believers. Moses sent them to spy out the land 1548
Building. Lest not be able to finish 676
Eating. Put a knife to thy throat..given to 1068

Forgetfulness. Take heed lest thou forget..seen 3347
Fear. Howebit no man speak openly..for fear 3432
" Did not confess him lest..put out 3433
Hearing. Increased..30..60..100 fold..he that 1069
Hypocrisy. Beware of the scribes..love greetings 321
Lack. Let about 3000..smite Ai..fled 1532
" I made as if they were beaten..and fled 1522
Necessary. The simple believe every word 1070
Prudent. [Micah] saw they were too strong 1071
Strife. Consulteth whether he be able to meet 677
Wise. Fool uttereth all his mind..wise 1072

FUTURE.

God's Will. If the L. will, we shall live and do this 3494
Ignorance. If thou hadst known..hid from thine 3495
Piety. Let me first go and bid them farewell 3496
Presuming. I will pull down my barns..ease, eat 3497
Uncertainty. Boast not..of to-morrow..knowest 3498
Unseen. God said, Thou fool, this night thy soul 3499

PREPARATION.

Anointing. Samuel..anointed David in the midst 6486
Appreciated. Blessed are those servants..find w. 6487
Blood. Upon the tip of the right ear of Aaron 6488
Blessing. Elijah repaired the altar..broken down 6489
Conquest. Moses sent them to spy out..Canaan 6490
Fire. Lo this [live coal] hath touched thy lips 6491
for Heaven. Let your loins be girt about..lights 6492
in Heaven. [Mansions.] I go to prepare a place for 6493
Lord. The crooked shall be made straight 6494
Materials. For the house of the L. 100,000 talents 6495
Mind. Opened he their understanding..scriptures 6496
Neglecting. Took no oil in their vessels 6497
Prayer. Continued all night..chose twelve 6498
Prepared. Be given unto them for whom p. 6499
Strength. Went in the strength of that meat 40 days 6500
Training. [Hebrews.] no blemish, well favoured 6501
Want of. How..not having a wedding garment 6502

PRUDENCE.

Age. How long have I to live that I should go 6774
Commended. Lord commended the unjust steward 6775
Example. Render unto Cesar the things which 6776
Preserved. Lest angry fellows..lose thy life 6777
" Joseph hearkened not..or to be with 6778
Resolutions. Not able to finish..mock him 6779

WATCHING.

Affectionate. His sister stood..see what would 9342
Constant. Thief would come..have watched 9343
Dead. Rizpah..suffered neither the birds 9344
Failure. Asleep..could ye not watch..one hour 9345
Hinderances. Take heed..lest..overcharged 9346
Malicious. Watched..whether he would heal on 9347
Prayerful. Fowls came..Abram drove them away 9348
" Made our prayer..set a watch 9349
" Anna..fastings and prayers..night and 9350
" Jesus..mountain to pray..all night 9351
Vigilant. Watch..lest coming suddenly..you 9352
and Watched. Compassed about..cloud of 9353
World. Herod feared John..observed him 9354

WATCHFULNESS.

Luck. Foolish said..Our lamps are gone out 9355
Necessary. Be sober, be vigilant..roaring lion 9356
Personal. Blessed are those servants..find 9357
Rewarded. Watch..every one over against his own 9358

Caution. Take heed..lest thou forget [Moses] 4542
" Take heed to thyself..teach thy sons 1191
Ignorance. Word..understandeth it not..cometh 4545

3342. FORGETFULNESS in Adversity. *Job.* ¹⁶ I called my servant, and he gave *me* no answer ; I entreated him with my mouth. ¹⁷ My breath is strange to my wife, though I entreated

for the children's *sake* of mine own body. [18] Yea,
young children despised me ; I arose, and they
spake against me.   [19] All my inward friends abhorred me : and they whom I loved are turned
against me.—Job, ch. 19.

3343. —— **of God.** *Aged Moses said,*
[9] Take heed to thyself..lest thou forget the
things which thine eyes have seen, and lest they
depart from thy heart all the days of thy life :
but teach them thy sons, and thy sons' sons ;
[10] *Specially* the day that thou stoodest before the
Lord thy God in Horeb, when the Lord said..
I will make them hear my words, that they may
learn to fear me all the days..and *that* they may
teach their children.—Deut., ch. 4.

3344. —— —— *Warning.* [10] When the
Lord thy God shall have brought thee into the
land..to give thee great and goodly cities, which
thou buildest not, [11] And houses full of all good
things, which thou filledst not, and wells digged,
which thou diggedst not, vineyards and olive
trees, which thou plantedst not ; when thou
shalt have eaten and be full ; [12] *Then* beware
lest thou forget the Lord.—Deut., ch. 8.

3345. —— —— *In Prosperity.* [15] Jeshurun
waxed fat, and kicked : thou art waxen fat, thou
art grown thick, thou art covered *with fatness ;*
then he forsook God *which* made him, and lightly esteemed the Rock of his salvation. [16] They
provoked him to jealousy with strange *gods.*—
Deut., ch. 32.

3346. —— —— *In Wealth.* [13] When thy
herds and thy flocks..and thy silver and thy
gold..and all that thou hast is multiplied ;
[14] Then thine heart be lifted up, and thou forget the Lord thy God.—Deut., ch. 8.

3347. —— **of the Sanctuary.** *David.* [5] If I
forget thee, O Jerusalem, let my right hand forget *her* cunning. [6] If I do not remember thee,
let my tongue cleave to the roof of my mouth ;
if I prefer not Jerusalem above my chief joy.—
Ps. 137.

3348. —— **Religious.** *Prophet.* [8] Said unto
the king, If thou wilt give me half thine house,
I will not go in with thee, neither will I eat
bread nor drink water in this place : [9] For so
was it charged me by the word of the Lord. [A
false prophet deceived him.] [19] So he went
back with him, and did eat bread in his house,
and drank water.—1 Kings, ch. 13.

3349. —— **Spiritual.** *Mirror.* [23] If any be a
hearer of the word, and not a doer, he is like
unto a man beholding his natural face in a glass :
[24] For he beholdeth himself, and goeth his way,
and straightway forgetteth what manner of man
he was.—James, ch. 1.

See other illustrations under :

3350. FORGIVENESS removes Anger. *Covered.*
[2] Thou hast forgiven the iniquity of thy people ;
thou hast covered all their sin.. [3] Thou hast
taken away all thy wrath : thou hast turned *thyself* from the fierceness of thine anger.—Ps. 85.

3351. —— **of Brethren.** *Parable.* [32] O thou
wicked servant, I forgave thee all that debt, because thou desiredst me : [33] Shouldest not thou
also have had compassion on thy fellow servant,
even as I had pity on thee ? [34] And his lord
was wroth.—Mat., ch. 18.

3352. —— **a Blotting-out.** *Cloud.* [21] Thou
art my servant : O Israel, thou shalt not be forgotten of me. [22] I have blotted out, as a thick
cloud, thy transgressions, and, as a cloud, thy
sins.—Isa., ch. 44.

3353. —— **Christ-like.** *Prisoner Paul.* [16] At
my first answer no man stood with me, but all
men forsook me : *I pray God* that it may not be
laid to their charge.—2 Tim., ch. 4.

3354. —— **commanded.** *Jesus.* [44] Love your
enemies, bless them that curse you, do good to
them that hate you, and pray for them which despitefully use you, and persecute you ; [45] That
ye may be the children of your Father..for he
maketh his sun to rise on the evil and on the
good, and sendeth rain on the just and on the
unjust.—Mat., ch. 5.

3355. —— **a Covering.** *David.* [1] Blessed *is*
he *whose* transgression *is* forgiven, *whose* sin *is*
covered.—Ps. 32.

3356. —— **a cleansing.** *Snow.* [18] Come now,
let us reason together, saith the Lord : though
your sins be as scarlet, they shall be as white as
snow ; though they be red like crimson, they
shall be as wool.—Isa., ch. 1.

3357. —— **a Casting away.** *Behind.* [17] Behold, for peace I had great bitterness ; but thou
hast in love to my soul *delivered it* from the pit
of corruption : for thou hast cast all my sins behind thy back.—Isa., ch. 38.

3358. —— **discharges Debt.** *Parable.* [24] One
was brought..which owed him ten thousand
talents. [25]..he had not to pay, his lord commanded him to be sold, and his wife, and children, and all that he had.. [26] The servant therefore fell down..Lord, have patience with me,
and I will pay thee all. [27] Then the lord..was
moved with compassion..forgave him the debt.
—Mat., ch. 18.

3359. —— **Generous.** *Of Jacob.* [4] Esau ran
to meet him, and embraced him, and fell on his
neck, and kissed him : and they wept.—Gen.,
ch. 33.

3360. —— **Gratitude for.** *Two Debtors.*
[41] There was a certain creditor which had two
debtors : the one owed five hundred pence, and
the other fifty. [42] And when they had nothing
to pay, he frankly forgave them both. Tell me
therefore, which of them will love him most ?
[43] Simon answered..I suppose that *he*, to whom
he forgave most..Thou hast rightly judged.—
Luke, ch. 7.

3361. —— —— *Woman.* ⁴⁴ Simon, seest thou this woman? I entered into thine house, thou gavest me no water for my feet : but she hath washed my feet with tears, and wiped *them* with the hairs of her head. ⁴⁵ Thou gavest me no kiss : but this woman, since the time I came in, hath not ceased to kiss my feet. ⁴⁶ My head with oil thou didst not anoint : but this woman hath anointed my feet with ointment. ⁴⁷ Wherefore..Her sins, which are many, are forgiven ; for she loved much : but to whom little is forgiven, *the same* loveth little.—LUKE, ch. 7.

3362. —— **Glory of.** *Proverb.* ¹¹ The discretion of a man deferreth his anger ; and *it is* his glory to pass over a transgression.—PROV., ch. 19.

3363. —— **Intercession for.** *Moses.* ³¹ Moses returned..and said, Oh, this people have sinned a great sin, and have made them gods of gold. ³² Yet now, if thou wilt forgive their sin— ; and if not, blot me, I pray thee, out of thy book which thou hast written.—Ex., ch. 32.

3364. —— **Magnanimous.** *Joseph's.* ³ I am Joseph ; doth my father yet live? And his brethren could not answer him ; for they were troubled at his presence. ⁴..Come near to me, I pray you. And they came near. And he said, I *am* Joseph your brother, whom ye sold into Egypt. ⁵ Now therefore be not grieved, nor angry with yourselves, that ye sold me hither : for God did send me before you to preserve life.— GEN., ch. 45.

3365. —— **Model of.** *Jesus.* ³⁴ Father, forgive them : for they know not what they do. And they parted his raiment, and cast lots.— LUKE, ch. 23.

3366. —— **A Martyr's.** *Stephen.* ⁵⁹ They stoned Stephen, calling upon *God,* and saying, Lord Jesus, receive my spirit. ⁶⁰ And he kneeled down, and cried with a loud voice, Lord, lay not this sin to their charge.—ACTS, ch. 7.

3367. —— **Policy in.** *Paul.* ¹⁰ To whom ye forgive any thing, I *forgive* also : for if I forgave any thing, to whom I forgave *it,* for your sakes *forgave I it* in the person of Christ ; ¹¹ Lest Satan should get an advantage of us : for we are not ignorant of his devices.—2 COR., ch. 2.

3368. —— **A royal.** *Solomon's.* ⁵¹ Behold, Adonijah..hath caught hold on the horns of the altar, saying, Let king Solomon swear unto me to day that he will not slay his servant with the sword. ⁵² And Solomon said, If he will shew himself a worthy man, there shall not a hair of him fall to the earth.—1 KINGS, ch. 1.

3369. —— **required.** *Jesus said* [See No. 3370], ³⁵ So likewise shall my heavenly Father do also unto you, if ye from your hearts forgive not every one his brother their trespasses.— MAT., ch. 18.

3370. —— —— *Jesus said,* ²⁵ When ye stand praying, forgive, if ye have aught against any ; that your Father also which is in heaven may forgive you your trespasses. ²⁶ But if ye do not forgive, neither will your Father which is in heaven forgive your trespasses.—MARK, ch. 11.

3371. —— **refused.** *Eli.* ¹³ Because his sons made themselves vile, and he restrained them not. ¹⁴..therefore I have sworn..that the iniquity of Eli's house shall not be purged with sacrifice nor offering for ever.—1 SAM., ch. 3.

3372. —— **a Separation.** *East from West.* ¹¹ As the heaven is high above the earth, *so* great is his mercy toward them that fear him. ¹² As far as the east is from the west, *so* far hath he removed our transgressions from us.—Ps. 103.

See other illustrations under :

ACCEPTANCE.

Assurance. Would he have shewed us all these	53
Denied. Ye brought..torn, and the lame..sick	55
Evidence. There rose up fire out of the rock	56
Manifested. Burning lamp passed between those	57
of Piety. In every nation he that feareth..worketh	58
by Sacrifice. L. had respect unto A..offering	59
Terms. Do justly..love mercy..walk humbly	61

JUSTIFICATION.

Difficulty. How then can man be justified with G.	4801
Penitents. [Publican] went down..justified	4802

PARDON.

Conditioned. If ye do not forgive, neither will	5949
Unexpected. Woman..neither do I condemn..sin	5950
Wise. There shall not a man be put to death	5951

RECONCILIATION.

Noble. Esau ran to meet him, and embraced	6905
Strange. The same day Pilate and Herod were	6906
Worship. Leave there thy gifts..first be reconciled	6907

Compassionate. His father saw..ran..neck	157
Enemies. Judah took the captives..clothed..eat	1024
" Thou shalt not smite. set bread..send	1025
Tender. Ye ought to forgive him lest..swallowed	182

See **MERCY.**

3373. **FORMALIST, Prayer of a.** *Pharisee.* ¹¹ Prayed thus with himself, God, I thank thee, that I am not as other men *are,* extortioners, unjust, adulterers, or even as this publican. ¹² I fast twice in the week, I give tithes of all that I possess.—LUKE, ch. 18.

3374. **FORMALITY, Failure of.** *Gehazi.* ³¹ Gehazi..laid the staff upon the face of the child ; but *there was* neither voice, nor hearing. Wherefore he went..saying, The child is not awaked. ³² And when Elisha was come..the child was dead, *and* laid upon his bed. ³³ He..shut the door upon them twain, and prayed.. ³⁴..and lay upon the child, and put his mouth upon his mouth, and his eyes upon his eyes, and his hands upon his hands : and he stretched himself upon the child ; and the flesh of the child waxed warm.—2 KINGS, ch. 4.

3375. —— **Heartless.** *Jews.* ¹³ Ye said also, Behold, what a weariness *is it!* and ye have snuffed at it, saith the Lord of hosts ; and ye brought *that which was* torn, and the lame, and the sick ; thus ye brought an offering : should I accept this of your hand?—MAL., ch. 1.

3376. —— **Lip.** *Jesus said,* ⁶ Esaias prophesied of you hypocrites..This people honoureth me with *their* lips, but their heart is far from me. ⁷ Howbeit in vain do they worship me, teaching *for* doctrines the commandments of men.—MARK, ch. 7.

See **HYPOCRISY.**

3377. **FORSAKING All.** *Abram.* ¹ Get thee out of thy country, and from thy kindred, and from thy father's house, unto a land that I will shew thee.. ⁴ So Abram departed, as the Lord had spoken unto him..and Abram *was* seventy and five years old.—GEN., ch. 12.

3378. —— —— *Safety by.* ¹⁶ Then let them which be in Judea flee into the mountains :

[17] Let him which is on the housetop not come down to take any thing out of his house : [18] Neither let him which is in the field return back to take his clothes.—MAT., ch. 24.

3379. —— Business. *Apostles.* [9] He was astonished . . at the draught of the fishes. . [10] And so *was* also James, and John . . which were partners with Simon. And Jesus said unto Simon, Fear not ; from henceforth thou shalt catch men. [11] And when they had brought their ships to land, they forsook all, and followed him.—LUKE, ch. 5.

3380. —— Duty. *Jonah.* [3] Jonah rose up to flee . . from the presence of the Lord, and went down to Joppa ; and he found a ship going to Tarshish : so he paid the fare thereof, and went down into it.—JONAH, ch. 1.

3381. —— God. *Amaziah.* [14] After that Amaziah was come from the slaughter of the Edomites . . he brought the gods of the children of Seir, and set them up *to be* his gods, and bowed down himself before them, and burned incense unto them. [15] Wherefore the anger of the Lord was kindled against Amaziah.—2 CHRON., ch. 25.

3382. —— —— For a King. [18] The Lord will not hear you in that day. [19] Nevertheless, the people refused to obey the voice of Samuel ; and they said, Nay ; but we will have a king over us ; [20] That we also may be like all the nations.—1 SAM., ch. 18.

3383. —— —— By Murmuring. [18] The Lord will give you flesh, and ye shall eat . . [20] . . be loathsome unto you : because that ye have despised the Lord . . and have wept before him, saying, Why came we forth out of Egypt?—NUM., ch. 11.

3384. —— —— Regretted. [10] The children of Israel cried unto the Lord, saying, We have sinned against thee, both because we have forsaken our God, and also served Baalim.—JUDGES, ch. 10.

3385. —— —— Folly of. [13] For my people have committed two evils ; they have forsaken me the fountain of living waters, *and* hewed them out cisterns, broken cisterns, that can hold no water.—JER., ch. 2.

3386. —— —— In Trouble. [22] In the time of his distress did he trespass yet more against the Lord : this *is that* king Ahaz. [23] For he sacrificed unto the gods of Damascus, which smote him : and he said, Because the gods of the kings of Syria help them, *therefore* will I sacrifice to them, that they may help me. But they were the ruin of him, and of all Israel.—2 CHRON., ch. 28.

3387. —— Jesus. *Disciples.* [56] He that eateth my flesh, and drinketh my blood, dwelleth in me, and I in him . . [66] From that *time* many of his disciples went back, and walked no more with him.—JOHN, ch. 6.

3388. —— Office. *Matthew.* [27] He went forth, and saw a publican, named Levi, sitting at the receipt of custom : and he said . . Follow me. [28] And he left all, rose up, and followed him.—LUKE, ch. 5.

3389. FORSAKEN by Friends. *Jesus.* [56] Then all the disciples forsook him, and fled. [57] And they led *him* away to Caiaphas the high priest, where the scribes and the elders were assembled.—MAT., ch. 26.

3390. —— of God. *David.* [1] My God, my God, why hast thou forsaken me ? *why art thou* so far from helping me, *and from* the words of my roaring ? [2] O my God, I cry in the daytime, but thou hearest not ; and in the night season, and am not silent.—Ps. 22.

3391. —— —— King Saul. [11] Said the woman, Whom shall I bring up unto thee ? And he said, Bring me up Samuel . . [16] Then said Samuel, Wherefore then dost thou ask of me, seeing the Lord is departed from thee, and is become thine enemy ?—1 SAM., ch. 28.

3392. —— —— Jesus. [45] From the sixth hour there was darkness over all the land unto the ninth hour. [46] And about the ninth hour Jesus cried with a loud voice, saying, Eli, Eli, lama sabachthani ? that is to say, My God, my God, why hast thou forsaken me?—MAT., ch. 27.

3393. —— —— Apparently. [13] Gideon said . . O my Lord, if the Lord be with us, why then is all this befallen us ? and where *be* all his miracles which our fathers told us of, saying, Did not the Lord bring us up from Egypt ?—JUDGES, ch. 6.

See other illustrations under :

3394. FORWARDNESS, Brave. *Peter.* [28] Peter . . said, Lord, if it be thou, bid me come unto thee on the water. [29] And he said, Come. And when Peter was come down out of the ship, he walked on the water, to go to Jesus.—MAT., ch. 14.

3395. —— **checked.** *Peter.* ⁴ They ran both together : and the other disciple did outrun Peter, and came first to the sepulchre.—JOHN, ch. 20.

3396. —— **Failure in.** *Peter.* ³⁰ But when he saw the wind boisterous, he was afraid ; and beginning to sink, he cried, saying, Lord, save me. ³¹ And immediately Jesus stretched forth *his* hand, and caught him.—MAT., ch. 14.

3397. —— **Hazardous.** *Peter.* ⁵¹ Drew his sword, and struck a servant of the high priest, and smote off his ear. ⁵² Then said Jesus..Put up again thy sword.—MAT., ch. 26.

See other illustrations under :

LEADERSHIP.

Divine. L. went before them..pillar of cloud, fire	4924
Failure. Went ill with Moses..spake unadvisedly	4925
Loved. Diotrephes loveth to have the preeminence	4926
Rejected. Let us make a captain..return into E.	4928
Trials. People chode with Moses..Why have ye	4927

ZEAL.

Age. [Caleb, 85 years] Give me this..Anakim	9974
Affecting. Many..afoot out of all cities..out went	9975
Acknowledged. [Epaphras] labouring fervently	9976
Affectionate. Brought spices very early in the	9977
Desirable. Good to be zealously affected always	9981
Excelling. Priests were too few..Levites did	9983
Energetic. [Nehemiah] contend..cursed	9984
Holy. Behold the men ye put in prison..teaching	9989
Hurtful. Say nothing..he began to blaze abroad	9991
Misunderstood. [Jesus] Friends said, He is	9997
Ministerial. Three years..I warned every one	10000
Prosperous. [Hezekiah] In every work..with	10005
Reformers. I chased him from me [Nehemiah]	10009
Reformation. Made a scourge..drove them out	10012
Rewarded. Give my covenant..he was zealous	10013
Seeker's. Made haste, came down, received	10014
" [Zaccheus] ran before, climbed..tree	10020
Sudden. Service..set in order..done suddenly	10016
Testify. Left her waterpot..come see a man	10022
Unwavering. None of these things move me	10025
Working. From the rising..morning..till the stars	10026

See **COURAGE.**

3398 FOUNDATION, Insecure. *Sand.* ⁴⁹ He that heareth, and doeth not, is like a man that without a foundation built a house upon the earth; against which the stream did beat vehemently, and immediately it fell ; and the ruin of that house was great.—LUKE, ch. 6.

3399. —— **Only.** *Jesus.* ¹⁰ Let every man take heed how he buildeth thereupon. ¹¹ For other foundation can no man lay than that is laid, which is Jesus Christ.—1 COR., ch. 3.

3400. —— **Spiritual.** *Jesus.* ²⁰ [Ye] are built upon the foundation of the apostles and prophets, Jesus Christ himself being the chief corner *stone ;* ²¹ In whom all the building fitly framed together groweth unto a holy temple in the Lord : ²² In whom ye also are builded together for a habitation of God through the Spirit.—EPH., ch. 2.

3401. —— **Second Temple.** *Celebration of.* ¹⁰ They set the priests in their apparel with trumpets, and the Levites the sons of Asaph with cymbals, to praise the Lord, after the ordinance of David.. ¹¹ And they sang together by course in praising and giving thanks unto the Lord ; because *he is* good, for his mercy *endureth* for ever toward Israel. And all the people shouted with a great shout, when they praised the Lord,

because the foundation of the house of the Lord was laid.—EZRA, ch. 3.

3402. —— **Uses of.** *Various.* ¹² If any man build upon this foundation gold, silver, precious stones, wood, hay, stubble ; ¹³ Every man's work shall be made manifest : for the day shall declare it .. and the fire shall try every man's work.—1 COR., ch. 3.

See other illustrations under :

Costly. Brought great stones..costly..hewed	7478
Failure. Hath laid the foundation..not able to	2331
Glorious. First f. jasper ; the second sapphire	1328
Secure. Digged deep, and laid the f. upon a rock	1697
Without. Man without a foundation built a house	3398

3403. FOUNDER, A celebrated. *Hiram.* ¹⁴ He *was* a widow's son..and his father *was*..a worker in brass : and he was filled with wisdom, and understanding, and cunning to work all works in brass. And he came to king Solomon, and wrought all his work.—1 KINGS, ch. 7.

—— FOUNTAIN. —— ——

See illustrations under :

Attraction. I. pitched by a fountain in J.—1 Sam. 29 : 1	
Discovery. Angel..found Hagar a fountain—Gen. 16 : 7	
Forsaken. Have forsaken fountain..broken c.	6216
Sorrow. O that mine eyes were a fountain of tears	5143

3404. FRAILTY of Comfort. *Jonah.* ⁶ So Jonah was exceeding glad of the gourd. ⁷..A worm..smote the gourd that it withered. ⁸..God prepared a vehement east wind ; and the sun beat upon the head of Jonah..he fainted, and wished in himself to die.—JONAH, ch. 4.

See other illustrations under :

FEEBLENESS.

Ashamed. I was ashamed to require..soldiers	3188
Age. Eli was 98 years old ; eyes were dim	3189
" David was old and stricken..gat no heat	3190

WEAKNESS.

Believers. Babes in Christ..not able to bare meat	9394
" Lest the people repent..return to Egypt	9395
Conscious. I am..weak, though anointed king	9396
Flesh. Moses' hands were heavy..stayed up..hands	9397
Instruments. L. sent flies..land was corrupted	9398
Moral. Peter separated..fearing them of the	9399
Personal. He that abideth in me bringeth forth	9400
Remembered. I. was with you in weakness	9401
Submission. Ahab said, I am thine, and all that I	9402
Spiritless. All the kings..their heart melted	9403
" Ai smote..hearts of the people melted	9404

3405. FRATERNITY, Primitive. *Ananias.* ¹⁷ Ananias..entered into the house : and putting his hands on him, said, Brother Saul, the Lord..hath sent me, that thou mightest receive thy sight, and be filled with the Holy Ghost.—ACTS, ch. 9.

See other illustrations under :

BRETHREN.

Compassion. Have had compassion on thy fellow	921
Dangerous. In perils among false brethren [Paul]	922
Encouragement. Brethren came to meet us..took	923
Forgiveness. How oft..forgive him ?..70 times 70	924
False. Come in privily to spy out our liberty	925
Love. He that loveth not knoweth not God	926
" Ought to lay down our lives for the brethren	927
Spurious. Let both grow together until the harvest	928
Unity. How pleasant..to dwell together in unity !	929

FELLOWSHIP.

Fraternal. Brother Saul..the Lord sent me	3202
Grand. Ye are come unto..angels..just men	3203

Invited. Come thou with us and we will..good   3204
Primitive. Were together, and had all things   3205
Prohibited. Not to keep company..not to eat   3206
Refused. Thou hast neither part nor lot   3207
Safety. Master, we perish..he rebuked the wind   3208

FRIENDSHIP.

Ardent. No rest because I found not Titus   3450
Benefit. As iron sharpeneth iron, so..countenance 3451
Covenant. Jonathan made a covenant with D.   3453
Fictitious. Art thou in health, my brother?   3454
for Christ. Presented gifts..gold, frankincense   3452
Gifts. Jonathan stripped himself..gave to David   3455
Inseparable. As the L. liveth..not leave thee   3457
Insulted. Samson's wife was given to..used as a   3456
    "   In what place..the king..servant be   3458
Law. That hath friends, must show himself f.   3459
Proven. Onesimus oft refreshed me and was not   3460
Questioned. Jonadab..is thine heart right as my   3461
Treacherous. Whomsoever I shall kiss, the same   3462
    "   Took him aside..smote..Abner   3463
Unexpected. When he had made an end of   3464

Companions. Young men that were brought up   1460
    See UNION and UNITY.

3406. FRATRICIDE, The first. *Cain.* [5] Unto
Cain and to his offering he had not respect. And
Cain was very wroth, and his countenance fell.
[8] And Cain talked with Abel his brother : and..
when they were in the field .. Cain rose up
against Abel his brother, and slew him.—GEN.,
ch. 4.

3407. —— A terrible. *Gideon's Sons.* [4] Abimelech hired vain and light persons, which followed him. [5] And he went unto his father's house
at Ophrah, and slew his brethren..threescore
and ten persons, upon one stone.—JUDGES, ch.
9.

Also see :

Avenging. When I say, Smite Amnon..kill   5622
Proposed. Esau hated Jacob..then will I slay   5632

3408. FRAUD by Appearances. *Gibeonites.*
[4] Made as if they had been ambassadors, and
took old sacks upon their asses, and wine bottles,
old, and rent, and bound up ; [5] And old shoes
and clouted..and old garments upon them ; and
all the bread of their provision was dry *and*
mouldy. [6] And they went to Joshua.—JOSH.,
ch. 9.

3409. —— Commercial. *Unjust Steward.* [5] He
called..his lord's debtors..and said..How much
owest thou.. [6] And he said, A hundred measures of oil. And he said..Take thy bill, and
sit down quickly, and write fifty. [7]..to another,
And how much owest thou? And he said, A
hundred measures of wheat, And he said..write
fourscore.—LUKE, ch. 16.

3410. —— A pious. *Gehazi.* [22] My master
hath sent me, saying..there be come to me..
two young men of the sons of the prophets :
give them..a talent of silver, and two changes
of garments. [23] And Naaman said..take two
talents.—2 KINGS, ch. 5.

3411. —— Religious. *Tares.* [25] While men
slept, his enemy came and sowed tares among
the wheat, and went his way. [26] But when the
blade was sprung up, and brought forth fruit,
then appeared the tares also.—MAT., ch. 13.

3412. —— A spiritual. *Simon Magus.*
[18] When Simon saw that through laying on of

the apostles' hands the Holy Ghost was given,
he offered them money, [19] Saying, Give me also
this power, that on whomsoever I lay hands, he
may receive the Holy Ghost.—ACTS, ch. 8.

3413. —— A Traitor's. *Judas.* [48] Whomsoever I shall kiss, that same is he ; hold him
fast. [49] And forthwith he came to Jesus, and
said, Hail, Master ; and kissed him.—MAT., ch.
26.

3414. —— in Wages. *Crieth out.* [4] The hire
of the labourers who have reaped down your
fields, which is of you kept back by fraud,
crieth : and the cries of them..are entered into
the ears of the Lord of Sabaoth. [5] Ye have lived
in pleasure.—JAMES, ch. 5.

See other illustrations under :

IMPOSTOR.

Called. Others said, Nay..he deceiveth the people 4352
Punished. Elemas the sorcerer..thou shalt be blind 4353
Treated as. Herod..arrayed him in a gorgeous robe 4354

IMPOSTORS.

Exposed. Seven sons of Sceva..fled out..wounded   4355
Punished. Hewers of wood and drawers of water   4356

TRICK.

Diplomatic. From a very far country are..come   8955
Hypocrites. Feign themselves just men..might   8956
Legerdemain. Magicians..rods became serpents   8957
Politicians. Shall ask a petition..save of thee   8958

Innocent. Whom have I defrauded? [Samuel]   7174
Religious. I am a prophet..angel spake..he lied   586
Unresented. Rather suffer yourselves..defrauded   4794

3415. FREEDOM, Birthright of. *Christians.*
[22] Abraham had two sons, the one by a bondmaid, the other by a free woman. [23] But he
who was of the bondwoman was born after the
flesh ; but he *of the free* woman *was* by promise.
[28] Now we, brethren, as Isaac was, are the children of promise.—GAL., ch. 4.

See other illustrations under :

CHOICE.

Better. Mary hath chosen that good part   1222
Decisive. Me and my house, we will serve   1223
Desperate. So will I go..if I perish, I perish   1224
Difficult. David said..I am in a great strait   1225
Dangerous. Lot chose..toward Sodom   1226
Fruitful. Rod of Aaron..budded..almonds   1227
Foolish. Hewed them out..broken cisterns   1228
Heart. L. looketh on the heart   1229
Life or Death. Fiery serpent..looketh on it..live 1230
Murderers. Release unto us Barabbas   1231
Neglected. O that thou hadst hearkened   1232
Pious. Moses..refused to be called   1233
of Piety. How much better..than to get gold   1234
Rebellious. We will certainly..burn incense   1235
Responsibility. Set before you..blessing and a   1236
Results. Therefore shalt thou serve..enemies   1237
Saints. I will take you..for a people   1238
Unexpected. Remaineth the youngest..feedeth   1239
Worldly. Went away sorrowful..great possessions   1240

INDEPENDENCE.

Exhibited. These hands have ministered unto my   4400
Financial. I will not take from a thread..shoelatchet 4401
Opinion. Me and my house, we will serve the L.   4402
Youthful. Father, give me the portion of goods   4403

LIBERTY.

Choice. Father give..he divided unto them   4962
Common. Casting out devils..Forbid him not   4963
not License. Take heed lest..liberty..stumbling   4964

SELF-WILL.

Destructive. O Jerusalem, thou..ye would not   7731
Loss by. They presumed to go..smote them   7732
the Sacrifice. To obey is better than sacrifice   7734
Work. Simeon and Levi..self-will digged down   7735

Liberation. Hebrew servant in the seventh year   5918
Reward. Let him go free for his tooth's sake—Ex. 5 : 27
"   Make his father's house free in Israel   8598
Spiritual. If the S. make you free..free—John 8 : 36.
    See DECISION.

3416. FRETTING forbidden. *Proverb.* [19] Fret
not thyself because of evil *men*, neither be thou
envious of the wicked ; [20] For there shall be no
reward to the evil *man ;* the candle of the wicked shall be put out.—PROV., ch. 24.
  See other illustrations under :

COMPLAINERS.

Punished. Our soul loatheth..bread..sent fiery   1445
Unreasonable. The first supposed..received more   1446
Unprincipled. These are..walking in their own   1447
Wicked. Did bring up an evil report..the plague   1448

CROSSNESS.

Irritation. Let us alone that we may serve the   1849
Habitual. Nabal was churlish and evil in his doings 1849
Prejudice. Children crying, Hosannah..sore d.   1850

DISCONTENTMENT.

Foreigners. Hadad..to Pharaoh, Let me depart   2343
Proud. All this availeth me nothing..see Mordecai 2344
Unity in. Every one that was discontented..unto   2345

FAULTFINDERS.

Fastidious. Why do ye eat..with sinners   3087
Hypocritical. Why was not this..sold for 300 pence 3088
Malicious. John B..he hath a devil..Son of man   3089

MURMURING.

Disappointment. This evil place?..no place of figs 5639
Discouragement. People was much discouraged   5640
Distrust. Would G. that we had died in Egypt   5641
Fear. Did tell thee..been better serve the E.   5642
God. Hath not the potter power over the clay   5643
Mercenaries. These last have wrought but one   5644
Neglect. Murmuring of the Greeks against the   5645
Punished. Fire of the L. burnt them..uttermost   5646
Severity. What shall I do?..almost ready to stone 5647
Thirst. Three days..no water..bitter..what shall 5648

Domestic. Hannah's adversary made her to fret   3012
Evildoers. Fret not thyself because of evil men   9526
Fretting. She urged him..soul was vexed unto   443
Peevishness. To me they have ascribed but   6038

3417. FRIEND at Court. *Obadiah.* [3] Ahab
called Obadiah, which *was* the governor of *his*
house. Now Obadiah feared the Lord greatly :
[4] For it was *so*, when Jezebel cut off the prophets
of the Lord, that Obadiah took a hundred
prophets, and hid them by fifty in a cave, and
fed them with bread and water.—1 KINGS, ch. 18.

3418. —— —— *Blastus.* [20] Herod was highly
displeased with them of Tyre and Sidon : but
they came with one accord to him, and, having
made Blastus the king's chamberlain their
friend, desired peace.—ACTS, ch. 12.

3419. —— **A distrusted.** *Disciple.* [38] Master,
we saw one casting out devils in thy name..and
we forbade him, because he followeth not us.
[39] But Jesus said, Forbid him not : for there is
no man which shall do a miracle in my name,
that can lightly speak evil of me.—MARK, ch. 9.

3420. —— **A feeble.** *Loan.* [5] Which of you
shall have a friend, and..at midnight..say..

Friend, lend me three loaves ; [6] For a friend of
mine in his journey is come to me, and I have
nothing to set before him : [7] And he from within
shall answer and say, Trouble me not : the door
is now shut, and my children are with me in
bed ; I cannot rise and give thee ?—LUKE, ch.
11.

3421. —— **A godly.** *Jehoshaphat.* [13] The king
of Israel said..the Lord hath called these three
kings together, to deliver them into the hand of
Moab. [14] And Elisha said..were it not that I regard the presence of Jehoshaphat the king of
Judah, I would not look toward thee, nor see
thee.—2 KINGS, ch. 3.

3422. —— **A genuine.** *Samaritan.* [33] When
he saw him, he had compassion on *him*, [34] And
went to *him*, and bound up his wounds, pouring
in oil and wine, and set him on his own beast,
and brought him to an inn, and took care of him.
—LUKE, ch. 10.

3423. —— **An interceding.** *Jonathan.*
[4] Jonathan spake good of David unto Saul his
father, and said..Let not the king sin against
his servant, against David ; because he hath not
sinned against thee, and because his works *have
been* to theeward very good.—1 SAM., ch. 19.

3424. —— **An irresolute.** *Pilate.* [12] From
thenceforth Pilate sought to release him : but
the Jews cried out, saying, If thou let this man
go, thou art not Cesar's friend.—JOHN, ch. 19.

3425. —— **An intimate.** *John.* [23] Now there
was leaning on Jesus' bosom one of his disciples,
whom Jesus loved.—JOHN, ch. 13.

3426. —— **A loving.** *Covenant.* [16] Jonathan
made *a covenant* with the house of David, *saying,*
Let the Lord even require *it* at the hand of
David's enemies. [17] And Jonathan caused David
to swear again, because he loved him : for he
loved him as he loved his own soul.—1 SAM., ch.
20.

3427. —— **needed.** *Pious.* [17] Elisha prayed,
..And the Lord opened the eyes of the young
man ; and he saw : and, behold, the mountain
was full of horses and chariots of fire round
about Elisha.—2 KINGS, ch. 6.

3428. —— **A useful.** *A Spy.* [37] Hushai David's friend came into the city.—2 SAM., ch. 15.
[14] And Absalom and all the men of Israel said,
The counsel of Hushai..*is* better than the counsel of Ahithophel. For the Lord had appointed
to defeat the good counsel of Ahithophel, to the
intent that the Lord might bring evil upon Absalom.—2 SAM., ch. 17.

3429. —— **A wavering.** *Pilate.* [20] Pilate
therefore, willing to release Jesus, spake again
to them. [21] But they cried, saying, Crucify *him,*
crucify him. [22] And he said..the third time,
Why, what evil hath he done..I will therefore
chastise him, and let *him* go. [23] And they were
instant with loud voices, requiring that he might
be crucified. And..prevailed.—LUKE, ch. 23.

3430. FRIENDS, Ardent. *"Knit."* [3] The soul
of Jonathan was knit with the soul of David, and
Jonathan loved him as his own soul. [4] And
Jonathan stripped himself of the robe that *was*
upon him, and gave it to David, and his garments, even to his sword, and to his bow, and
to his girdle.—1 SAM., ch. 18.

3431. —— **Abuse of.** *Hanun.* [3] Hath not

David *rather* sent his servants unto thee, to search the city, and to spy it out.. [4] Wherefore Hanun..shaved off the one half of their beards, and cut off their garments in the middle, *even* to their buttocks, and sent them away.—2 SAM., ch. 10.

3432. —— Cautious. *Disciples.* [12] There was much murmuring among the people concerning him : for some said, He is a good man : others said, Nay ; but he deceiveth the people. [13] Howbeit no man spake openly of him for fear of the Jews.—JOHN, ch. 7.

3433. —— Compromising. *Rulers.* [42] Among the chief rulers also many believed on him ; but because of the Pharisees they did not confess *him*, lest they should be put out of the synagogue : [43] For they loved the praise of men more than the praise of God.—JOHN, ch. 12.

3434. —— First Duty to. *Converts.* [19] Go home to thy friends, and tell them how great things the Lord hath done for thee, and hath had compassion on thee. [20] And he departed, and began to publish in Decapolis how great things Jesus had done for him : and all *men* did marvel.—MARK, ch. 5.

3435. —— in Distress. *Jeremiah.* [11] Nebuchadrezzar..gave charge concerning Jeremiah to Nebuzar-adan the captain of the guard, saying, [12]..look well to him, and do him no harm ; but do unto him even as he shall say unto thee.—JER., ch. 39.

3436. —— Devoted. *Paul's.* [3] Greet Priscilla and Aquila, my helpers in Christ Jesus : [4] Who have for my life laid down their own necks.—ROM., ch. 16.

3437. —— Interference of. *Jesus.* [20] The multitude cometh together again, so that they could not so much as eat bread. [21] And when his friends heard *of it*, they went out to lay hold on him : for they said, He is beside himself.—MARK, ch. 3.

3438. —— overlooked. *David.* [5] And Joab came into the house to the king, and said, Thou hast shamed this day the faces of all thy servants, which this day have saved thy life, [6] In that thou lovest thine enemies, and hatest thy friends..for this day I perceive, that if Absalom had lived, and all we had died this day, then it had pleased thee well. [7] Now therefore arise, go forth, and speak comfortably unto thy servants. —2 SAM., ch. 19.

3439. —— Post-mortem. *Joseph.* [51] Who also himself waited for the kingdom of God. [52]..went unto Pilate, and begged the body of Jesus. [53] And he took it down, and wrapped it in linen, and laid it in a sepulchre that was hewn in stone. —LUKE, ch. 23.

3440. —— —— *Men of Jabesh-Gilead.* [12] Valiant men..went all night, and took the body of Saul and the bodies of his sons from the wall of Beth-shan, and came to Jabesh, and burnt them there.—1 SAM., ch. 31. [The Philistines had dishonoured them.]

3441. —— Persuasions of. *Paul.* [12] When we heard these things, both we, and they of that place, besought him not to go up to Jerusalem. [13] Then Paul answered, What mean ye to weep and to break mine heart ? for I am ready not to be bound only, but also to die at Jerusalem for the name of the Lord Jesus.—ACTS, ch. 13.

3442. —— Response of. *Proverbs.* [17] Iron sharpeneth iron ; so a man sharpeneth the countenance of his friend. [19] As in water face *answereth* to face, so the heart of man to man.— PROV., ch. 27.

3443. —— Reclamation of. *Proverb.* [19] A brother offended *is harder to be won* than a strong city : and *their* contentions *are* like the bars of a castle.—PROV., ch. 18.

3444. —— Secret. *Joseph.* [38] Joseph of Arimathea, being a disciple of Jesus, but secretly for fear of the Jews, besought Pilate that he might take away the body of Jesus.—JOHN, ch. 19.

3445. —— separated. *Finally.* [41] David arose out of *a place* toward the south, and fell on his face to the ground, and bowed himself three times : and they kissed one another, and wept one with another, until David exceeded. [42] And Jonathan said to David, Go in peace.—1 SAM., ch. 20.

3446. —— Trouble makes. *David.* [2] Every one *that was* in distress..in debt, and..discontented, gathered themselves unto him ; and he became a captain over them..about four hundred men.—1 SAM., ch. 22.

3447. —— amid Trouble. *Fleeing from Absalom.* [27] Shobi..and Machir..and Barzillai.. [28] Brought beds, and basins, and earthen vessels, and wheat, and barley, and flour, and parched *corn*, and beans, and lentiles, and parched *pulse*, [29] And honey, and butter, and sheep, and cheese of kine, for David, and for the people..in the wilderness.—2 SAM., ch. 17.

3448. —— Wealth makes. *Proverb.* [20] The poor is hated even of his own neighbour : but the rich *hath* many friends.—PROV., ch. 14.

3449. —— Winning. *Proverb.* [24] A man *that hath* friends must shew himself friendly ; and there is a friend *that* sticketh closer than a brother.—PROV., ch. 18.

See other illustrations under :

ASSOCIATES.

Apostasy. Solomon loved many strange women	539
Beneficial. Ark..Noah went in, and..his sons' wives	540
Corrupt. Mingled among the heathen and learned	541
Dangerous. Lot..pitched his tent toward Sodom	542
Forbidden. Called a brother..be a fornicator	543
" If any man obey not our word	544
Hurtful. Inhabitants..priests in your eyes	545
Intolerable. Lot, vexed with the filthy conversation	546
Ill-chosen. Peter sat with the servants and warmed	547
Influence. Make no friendship with an angry man	548
Likeness. Sons of G..daughters of men..wives	549
Saved by. Unbelieving husband is sanctified by	550
" [Three pairs of brothers among 12 apostles]	551
Uncorrupted. Wickedness. great in..earth..but	552
Worthy. Three Hebrews gave them pulse	553

ASSOCIATIONS.

Happy. Happy..that hear thy wisdom	554
Helpful. Were it not that I regard Jehoshaphat	555

BENEFACTORS.

Censured. Ye have made..abhorred in the eyes of	685
" Let us alone, that we may serve the E.	686
Honoured. He received his sight..followed Jesus	687
Remembered. Worthy..hath built us a synagogue	688
Slandered. Ye have killed the people of the Lord	689

SOCIETY.

Changed. Now they that are younger..in derision	8150

Conservator. Ye are the salt of the earth 8151
Influence. He that walketh with wise men shall 8152
Miserable. Every one that was in distress..gather 8153
Needful. It is not good for man to be alone 8154
Respect of. Young men..hid themselves, and the 8155

Chosen. Twelve with him, and certain women 295
Condemned. This man receiveth sinners and eateth 778
Forsaken by. All my inward friends abhorred me 8936
Restored. I shall go to him, but he shall not return 736
Ruinous. Taketh seven other..more wicked than 1112
See BRETHREN and BROTHER.

3450. FRIENDSHIP, Ardent. *Paul.* [13] I had
no rest in my spirit, because I found not Titus
my brother ; but taking my leave of them, I
went from thence into Macedonia.—2 Cor., ch.
2.

3451. —— Benefit of. *Proverb.* [17] Iron
sharpeneth iron ; so a man sharpeneth the
countenance of his friend.—Prov., ch. 27.

3452. —— for Christ. *Magi.* [10] When they
saw the star, they rejoiced with exceeding great
joy. [11] And when . they saw the young child
with Mary his mother, and fell down, and worshipped him : and when they had opened their
treasures, they presented unto him gifts ; gold,
and frankincense, and myrrh.—Mat., ch. 2.

3453. —— Covenant of. *David and Jonathan.*
[16] Jonathan made *a covenant* with the house of
David, *saying,* Let the Lord even require *it* at
the hand of David's enemies. [17] And Jonathan
caused David to swear again, because he loved
him : for he loved him as he loved his own soul.
—1 Sam., ch. 20.

3454. —— A fictitious. *Joab.* [9] Joab said
to Amasa, *Art* thou in health, my brother ? And
Joab took Amasa by the beard with the right
hand to kiss him. [10] But Amasa took no heed
to the sword that *was* in Joab's hand : so he
smote him therewith in the fifth *rib.*—2 Sam.,
ch. 20.

3455. —— Gifts of. *Jonathan.* [4] Jonathan
stripped himself of the robe that *was* upon him,
and gave it to David, and his garments, even to
his sword, and to his bow, and to his girdle.—
1 Sam., ch. 18.

3456. —— insulted. *Samson's.* [20] Samson's
wife was *given* to his companion, whom he had
used as his friend.—Judges, ch. 14.

3457. —— Inseparable. *Elisha.* [1] When
the Lord would take up Elijah into heaven by a
whirlwind, that.. [2]..Elijah said unto Elisha,
Tarry here..for the Lord hath sent me to Beth-
el. And Elisha said..*As* the Lord liveth, and
as thy soul liveth, I will not leave thee.—2
Kings, ch. 2.

3458. —— —— *David said,* [19] Wherefore
goest thou also with us ? return to ·thy place,
and abide with the king : for thou *art* a stranger,
and also an exile. [21] And Ittai answered..*As*
the Lord liveth, and *as* my lord the king liveth,
surely in what place my lord the king shall be,
whether in death or life, even there also will thy
servant be.—2 Sam., ch. 15.

3459. —— Law of. *Proverb.* [See No.
3449.]

3460. —— proven. *Onesiphorus.* [16] He oft
refreshed me, and was not ashamed of my chain :
[17] But, when he was in Rome, he sought me out
very diligently, and found *me.*—2 Tim., ch. 1.

3461. —— questioned. *Jehu.* [15] Jehonadab
..*coming* to meet him : and he saluted him, and
said to him, Is thine heart right, as my heart *is*
with thy heart ? And Jehonadab answered, It
is. If it be, give *me* thine hand. And he gave
him his hand ; and he took him up to him into
the chariot.—2 Kings, ch. 10.

3462. —— Treacherous. *Judas.* [48] Gave
them a sign, saying, Whomsoever I shall kiss,
that same is he ; hold him fast. [49] And forthwith he came to Jesus, and said, Hail, Master ;
and kissed him.—Mat., ch. 26.

**3463. —— ** *Joab.* [27] When Abner was
returned to Hebron, Joab took him aside in
the gate to speak with him quietly, and smote
him there under the fifth *rib.*—2 Sam., ch. 3.

3464. —— Unexpected. *Rivals.* [1] When he
had made an end of speaking unto Saul..the
soul of Jonathan was knit with the soul of David, and Jonathan loved him as his own soul.—
1 Sam., ch. 18.

See other illustrations under :

FAVOUR.

Besought. Go serve the L..bless me also 3090
Divine. I bare you on eagles' wings 3091
Evinced. Let her glean even among the sheaves 3092
Indicated. King held out to Esther the golden 3093
Refused. Edom said, Thou shalt not pass by me 3094

FAVOURS.

Compensated. Think on me when it..be well with 3095
Forgotten. Yet did not the chief butler remember 3096
Remembered. There was a Hebrew..interpreted 3097

FAVORITISM.

Denied. Grant that..my two sons may sit..kingdom 3098
Hurtful. Israel loved Joseph more than all his c. 3099

FELLOWSHIP.

Fraternal. Brother Saul, the L. even J..sent me 3202
Invited. Come..with us, and we will do thee good 3204
Primitive. Believed had all things common 3205
Prohibited. If any man..called a brother..eat 3206
Refused. Thy money perish with thee..thy heart 3207
Safety. Master, Master, we perish..calm 3208

KINDNESS.

Appreciated. Barzillai..I will feed thee in 4808
Animals. Rebekah..I will draw for thy camels 4809
Bereavement. In the choice of our sepulchres, bury 4810
Brethren. Waken poor ; thou shalt relieve him 4811
Conquerors. Saul. is this thy voice..David..wept 4812
Christians. Disciples..relief unto brethren..Judea 4814
Captives. Clothed naked..shod them..eat and 4815
Father. If ye..know how to give..much more..F. 4816
Gratitude. Mephibosheth..kindness for Jonathan's 4817
Insulted. David sent to comfort him..cut 4819
Inopportune. Ahab..because thou hast let go 4820
Loan. Hath pity..lendeth to the Lord 4821
Providential. Boaz unto Ruth..abide here 4822
Prosperity. I delivered the poor that cried [Job] 4823
Prisoner. Jeremiah put these..rags under..arms 4824
Remembered. Lest I destroy you, for ye showed 4825
Rewarded. Rahab..hid them with the flax..saved 4826
Substitutional. I was eyes to the blind..feet [Job] 4827
Servant. Centurion's servant who was dear to him 4828
Strangers. Drink my lord..wasted..gave him 4829
Timely. Barzillai brought beds..flour..butter..to 4830
Unexpected. Shall I smite them ?..Let bread 4831
Widow. Harvest..forgot a sheaf..be for thee 4832

Deceptive. Felix sent for him oftener [bribe-seeking] 984
See AFFECTION, LOVE, and SYMPATHY.

3465. FRIVOLITY brings Want. *Proverb.*
[19] He that tilleth his land shall have plenty of bread : but he that followeth after vain *persons* shall have poverty enough.—Prov., ch. 28.

See other illustrations under :

TRIFLES.

Blinded by. Blind guides..strain at a gnat..camel 8959
Comparatively. Samson took the doors of the gate 8960
Magnified. Pay tithes of mint..omitted..truth   8961
   "   Why..eat with unwashen hands?   8962

3466. FROGS, Plague of. *Second.* [3] The river shall bring forth frogs abundantly, which shall go up and come into thine house, and into thy bed-chamber, and upon thy bed, and into the house of thy servants, and upon thy people, and into thine ovens, and into thy kneadingtroughs.—Ex., ch. 8.

3467. FRUGALITY, Excessive. *Proverb.*
[24] There is that scattereth, and yet increaseth ; and *there is* that withholdeth more than is meet, but *it tendeth* to poverty.—Prov., ch. 11.

See other illustrations under :

ECONOMY.

Food. Gather up the fragments..nothing be lost   2600
False. Why was this waste of the ointment   2601

3468. FRUIT commends. *Paul.* [1] Need we, as some *others*, epistles of commendation to you, or *letters* of commendation from you? [2] Ye are our epistle written in our hearts, known and read of all men.—2 Cor., ch. 3.

3469. —— Choice by. *Almond-rod.* [See No. 3471.]

3470. —— expected. *Parable.* [34] When the time of the fruit drew near, he sent his servants to the husbandmen, that they might receive the fruits of it.—Mat., ch. 21.

3471. —— God gives. *Rod.* [5] The man's rod, whom I shall choose, shall blossom [8] And ..on the morrow Moses went into the tabernacle..the rod of Aaron for the house of Levi was budded, and brought forth buds, and bloomed blossoms, and yielded almonds.—Num., ch. 17.

3472. —— Good. *Zaccheus.* [8] Behold, Lord, the half of my goods I give to the poor ; and if I have taken any thing from any man by false accusation, I restore *him* fourfold.—Luke, ch. 19.

3473. —— Lack of. *Fig Tree.* [19] When he saw a fig tree in the way, he came to it, and found nothing thereon, but leaves only, and said unto it, Let no fruit grow on thee henceforward forever. And presently the fig tree withered away.—Mat., ch. 21.

3474. —— in Old Age. *David.* [5] Solomon my son *is* young and tender, and the house *that is* to be builded for the Lord *must be* exceeding magnifical, of fame and of glory throughout all countries : I will *therefore* now make preparation for it. So David prepared abundantly before his death.—1 Chron., ch. 22.

3475. —— —— *Abram.* [1] When Abram was ninety years old and nine, the Lord appeared to Abram, and said..I *am* the Almighty God ; walk before me, and be thou perfect.—Gen., ch. 17.

3476. —— the Object. *Fig Tree.* [8] Lord, let it alone this year also, till I shall dig about it, and dung *it :* [9] And if it bear fruit, *well :* and if not, *then* after that thou shalt cut it down.—Luke, ch. 13.

3477. —— Proved by. *Piety.* [18] A good tree cannot bring forth evil fruit, neither *can* a corrupt tree bring forth good fruit.. [20] Wherefore by their fruits ye shall know them.—Mat., ch. 7.

3478. —— a Sign. *Good and Bad.* [3] Said the Lord unto me, What seest thou, Jeremiah? And I said, Figs ; the good figs, very good ; and the evil, very evil, that cannot be eaten, they are so evil.—Jer., ch. 24. [Israel was the good figs, and Judah the bad.]

3479. —— of Repentance. *John Baptist.* [8] Bring forth therefore fruits worthy of repentance, and begin not to say within yourselves, We have Abraham to *our* father.. [9] And now also the axe is laid unto the root of the trees : every tree therefore which bringeth not forth good fruit is hewn down, and cast into the fire.—Luke, ch. 3.

3480. FRUITS of the Spirit. *Graces.* [22] The fruit of the spirit is love, joy, peace, longsuffering, gentleness, goodness, faith, [23] Meekness, temperance.—Gal., ch. 5.

3481. FRUIT TREES preserved. *Law.* [19] When thou shalt besiege a city a long time, in making war against it to take it, thou shalt not destroy the trees thereof by forcing an axe against them : for thou mayest eat of them, and thou shalt not cut them down (for the tree of the field *is* man's *life*) to employ *them* in the siege.—Deut., ch. 20.

See other illustrations under :

Attractive. Come to Elim..12 wells..70 palm trees 1380
Conditioned. Fell into good ground..beareth fruit 6455
Discipleship. Bear much fruit, so shall ye be my d. 3569
First. Twenty loaves of barley and full ears of corn 35
Gift. I have given you every tree wherein is—Gen. 1 : 29
Hindered. Thorns choked it..it yielded no fruit   5427
Means. He purgeth it that it may..more fruit   8944
Offering. Take of the firstfruits of the earth..L. 7023
Prohibited. Nazarite..not eat moist grapes, nor   20
Refreshing. [Famished slave] Cake of figs..raisins 22
Sacrifice. Cain brought of the fruit of the ground 850
Useless. If it bear fruit well, if not, cut it down   ..5910

   See **WORKS.**

3482. FRUITFULNESS, Christian. *Garden.* [11] The Lord shall guide thee continually, and satisfy thy soul in drought, and make fat thy bones : and thou shalt be like a watered garden, and like a spring of water, whose waters fail not.—Isa., ch. 58.

3483. —— indispensable. *Taketh Away.* [1] I am the true vine, and my Father is the husbandman. [2] Every branch in me that beareth not fruit he taketh away : and every *branch* that beareth fruit, he purgeth it, that it may bring forth more fruit.—John, ch. 15.

3484. —— Means of. *"Add to Faith."* [5] Giving all diligence, add to your faith virtue.. knowledge.. [6]..temperance..patience..godliness ; [7]..brotherly kindness..charity. [8] For if these things be in you, and abound, they make *you that ye shall* neither *be* barren nor unfruitful in the knowledge of our Lord Jesus Christ.—2 Peter, ch. 1.

3485. —— Source of. *In Christ.* [5] He that abideth in me, and I in him, the same bringeth forth much fruit.—John, ch. 15.

3486. —— Varied. *"Good Ground."* [20] These are they which are sown on good ground ; such as hear the word, and receive *it*, and bring forth fruit, some thirtyfold, some sixty, and some a hundred.—MARK, ch. 3.

See DEEDS.

3487. FUGITIVE, A Criminal. *Jacob.* [42] Behold, thy brother Esau..doth comfort himself, *purposing* to kill thee. [43] Now therefore, my son, obey my voice ; and arise, flee thou to Laban my brother to Haran.—GEN., ch. 27.

3488. —— An Infant. *Jesus.* [13] Angel of the Lord appeareth to Joseph in a dream, saying, Arise, and take the young child and his mother, and flee into Egypt, and be thou there until I bring thee word : for Herod will seek the young child to destroy him. [14] ..he took the young child and his mother by night, and departed.—MAT., ch. 2.

3489. —— A noble. *Moses.* [14] Intendest thou to kill me, as thou killedst the Egyptian ? And Moses feared, and said, Surely this thing is known. [15] Now when Pharaoh heard this thing, he sought to slay Moses. But Moses fled..and dwelt in the land of Midian.—EX., ch. 2.

3490. —— protected. *Slave.* [15] Thou shalt not deliver unto his master the servant which is escaped from his master unto thee : [16] He shall dwell with thee, *even* among you, in that place which he shall choose in one of thy gates, where it liketh him best : thou shalt not oppress him.—DEUT., ch. 23.

3491. —— Return of. *Onesimus.* [15] Perhaps he therefore departed for a season, that thou shouldest receive him for ever ; [16] Not now as a servant, but above a servant, a brother beloved. —PHILEMON.

See other illustrations under :

from Duty. Jonah rose up to flee..to Tarshish	3380
Disciples. All forsook him, and fled	7
False. Let us flee, and draw them from..city	1067
Female. I flee from my mistress [Hagar]	8417
Maimed. Mephibosheth..nurse made haste to flee	65
Scattered. Men of war fled by night..scattered	501
Transgressors. 3000 men fled before the men of Ai	11
Unexpected. Camp of Syria..was no man there	2183

3492. FUNERAL, Joyful. *At Nain.* [13] When the Lord saw her, he had compassion on her, and said .. Weep not. [14] And he came and touched the bier : and they that bare *him* stood still. And he said, Young man, I say unto thee, Arise. [15] And he that was dead sat up, and began to speak,—LUKE, ch. 7.

See other illustrations under :

BURIAL.

Denied. Bring out the bones of the kings..spread	974
Life from. Touched the bones of Elisha, he revived	975
Living. Earth opened her mouth and swallowed	976
Mournful. David..lifted up his voice..grave of	977
Mysterious. Moses died..no man knoweth his	978
Patriarchs. All the servants of Pharaoh..elders	979
Perfumed. Asa's grave..filled with sweet odours	980

GRAVE.

Chosen. Bury me with my fathers in the cave	3703
First Bargain. Cave of Machpelah..money..worth	3704
Longed for. O that thou couldest hide me in the g.	3705

Crematory. Valiant men..body of Saul..sons..burnt 1828

3493. FURNITURE, Plain. *Prophet's Chamber.* [10] Let us make a little chamber, I pray thee, on the wall ; and let us set for him there a bed, and a table, and a stool, and a candlestick :

and it shall be, when he cometh to us, that he shall turn in thither.—2 KINGS, ch. 4.

—— Extraordinary. *Bedstead.* [11] Only Og king of Bashan remained of the remnant of giants ; behold, his bedstead *was* a bedstead of iron..nine cubits *was* the length thereof, and four cubits the breadth of it.—DEUT., ch. 3.

See other illustrations under :

Luxurious. Beds of gold and silver	3640
Royal. Sol. made a throne of ivory..overlaid..best	3647

3494. FUTURE by God's Will. *Plans.* [13] Go to now, ye that say, To day or to morrow we will go into such a city, and continue there a year, and buy and sell, and get gain : [14] Whereas ye know not what *shall be* on the morrow. For what *is* your life ? It is even a vapour, that appeareth for a little time, and then vanisheth away. [15] For that ye *ought* to say, If the Lord will, we shall live, and do this, or that.—JAMES, ch. 4.

3495. —— Ignorance of. *Jerusalem.* [41] He beheld the city, and wept over it, [42] Saying, If thou hadst known, even thou, at least in this thy day, the things *which belong* unto thy peace ! but now they are hid from thine eyes.—LUKE, ch. 19.

3496. —— Piety in the. *Disciple.* [61] Lord, I will follow thee ; but let me first go bid them farewell, which are at home at my house. [62] And Jesus said..No man, having put his hand to the plough, and looking back, is fit for the kingdom of God.—LUKE, ch. 9.

3497. —— Presuming the. *Rich Fool.* [17] What shall I do, because I have no room where to bestow my fruits ? [18] And he said, This will I do : I will pull down my barns, and build greater.. [19] And I will say..Soul, thou hast much goods laid up for many years ; take thine ease, eat, drink, *and* be merry.—LUKE, ch. 12.

3498. —— Uncertainty of the. *Proverb.* [1] Boast not thyself of to morrow ; for thou knowest not what a day may bring forth.— PROV., ch. 27.

3499. —— Unseen. *Rich Fool.* [20] God said unto him, Thou fool, this night thy soul shall be required of thee : then whose shall those things be, which thou hast provided ?—LUKE, ch. 12. [See No. 3497.]

See other illustrations under :

ACCOUNTABILITY.

Future. King which would take account..servants	72
Gifts. Ten pounds..occupy till I come	73
Minute. Every idle word..give account	74
Personal. Give account of thy stewardship	75

FORETHOUGHT.

Necessary. Intending to build..first counteth the	3339
" Consulteth whether he be able with	3340
Useless. Which..with taking thought can add one	3341

PROPHECY.

Gift. Spirit..unto the 70 elders..did prophesy	6672
Involuntary. Spirit..was upon Saul..prophesied	6673
Revival. I prophesied..bones came together	6674
Spiritual. These are not drunken..prophesy	6675

3500. FUTURE LIFE, Affection in the. *" In Torment."* [28] I have five brethren ; that he may testify unto them, lest they also come into this place of torment.—LUKE, ch. 16.

See HEAVEN and HELL.

3501. GALLANTRY, Timely. *Moses.* [18] Reuel their father, he said, How *is it that* ye are come so soon to day ? [19] And they said, An Egyptian delivered us out of the hand of the shepherds, and also drew *water* enough for us, and watered the flock.—Ex., ch. 2.

See other illustrations under:

COURAGE.

Age. [Caleb 85 years] Give me this mt..Anakim 1769
Absent. 3000 men..said to Samson..may deliver 1770
Daring. Paul would have entered..suffered him n. 1771
Faith. L. that delivered me. lion. this Philistine 1772
Ground. With him..arm of flesh but with us..Lord 1773
Honouring. Let us go up at once and possess it 1774
Invincible. Not any..able to stand before thee 1775
Lost Men of Israel fled..forsook the cities 1776
Moral. Jesus went before them..amazed 1777
"   I am ready..bound and also to die 1778
Necessary. Be strong and of good courage 1779
Patriotic. Fight for your brethren, sons, wives 1780
Rebuke. I said unto Peter before them all 1781
Reformers. Should such a man as I flee? 1782
Stimulated. Put your feet..necks of these kings 1783
Soldier's. Jonathan climbed up..hands and feet 1784
Worship. Daniel knew..writing was signed 1785

HEROISM.

Christian. Bonds..abide me..none of these things 3959
Needless. Three mighty men brake through..well 3961
Numbers. Shamgar slew 600 with an ox-goad 3962
Patriotic. Jael..smote the nail into his..temples 3957
"   Woman cast a stone upon Abimelech 3958

3502. GARDEN, Agony in. *Jesus.* [42] Father, if thou be willing, remove this cup from me: nevertheless, not my will, but thine, be done.. [44] And being in an agony he prayed more earnestly : and his sweat was as it were great drops of blood falling down to the ground.—Luke, ch. 22. [See No. 3504.]

3503. —— Coveted. *Ahab.* [1] Naboth..had a vineyard .. in Jezreel, hard by the palace of Ahab king of Samaria. [2] And Ahab spake..Give me thy vineyard, that I may have it for a garden of herbs, because it *is* near unto my house : and I will give thee for it a better vineyard than it.—1 Kings, ch. 21.

3504. —— A familiar. *Gethsemane.* [1] He went forth with his disciples over the brook Cedron, where was a garden, into the which he entered, and his disciples. [2] And Judas also.. knew the place : for Jesus ofttimes resorted thither with his disciples.—John, ch. 18.

3505. —— The Lord's. *Eden.* [8] The Lord God planted a garden eastward in Eden ; and there he put the man whom he had formed. [9] And out of the ground made..to grow every tree that is pleasant to the sight, and good for food.—Gen., ch. 2.

3506. —— A sacred. *Jesus.* [41] In the place where he was crucified there was a garden ; and in the garden a new sepulchre, wherein was never man yet laid. [42] There laid they Jesus.—John, ch. 19.

3507. GARDENER, The first. *Adam.* [15] The Lord God took the man, and put him into the garden of Eden to dress it and to keep it.—Gen., ch. 2. [See No. 3505.]

See other illustrations under:

AGRICULTURE.

Benevolence. Let Ruth glean among the sheaves 678
Bountiful Harvest. Seven plenteous years 1306

Discouragements. Although the fig tree shall not 1379
Danger. Noah began to be a husbandman 236
Dangers. Samson..300 foxes..burnt shocks of c. 438
Growth. Blade..ear..full corn in the ear 3750
Indispensable. Every branch..beareth not..sway 3483
Indolence. I went by the field of the slothful 4436
Misplaced. No place for seed..figs..vines 5639
Plenty. Land of wheat..barley..vines..fig trees 6224
Poor. Nebuzar-adan left the poor to be 6304
Prosperous. What shall I do?..no room..fruits 3272
Skill in. Fig tree..let it alone this year, I will dig 642
Type. Flourish like the palm..fruit..age 3340
"   Like a tree planted by the rivers 3745
"   Becometh greater than all herbs 3748
"   Soul shall be as a well-watered garden 3739
Vanity. I planted me gardens and orchards 7396
Varied. Bring forth fruit, some 30..60..100 fold 3486

FARMER.

Choice. King Uzziah..loved husbandry 3046
Deliverance. Gideon threshed wheat by the wine 3047
Enterprising. Elisha was plowing with 12 yoke of 3045
Selfish. I will pull down my barns..Soul, take thy 3048

Church. Her desert like the garden of the L...joy 1389
Mistaken. She supposing he..the gardener—John 20 : 5
Prohibition. [Rechabites] neither have we vineyard 3049

3508. GARMENT, A gorgeous. *Priests.* [4] These *are* the garments which they shall make ; a breastplate, and an ephod, and a robe, and a broidered coat, a mitre, and a girdle..holy garments for Aaron. and his sons.. [5] And they shall take gold, and blue, and purple, and scarlet, and fine linen.—Ex., ch. 28.

3509. GARMENTS, Benevolence in. *Dorcas.* [39] Peter..went with them..into the upper chamber : and all the widows stood by him weeping, and shewing the coats and garments which Dorcas made, while she was with them.—Acts, ch. 9.

See other illustrations under:

CLOTHES.

Character. Bring forth the best robe..a ring 1350
Display. Make broad their phylacteries and 1352
Envy. Israel made him a coat of many colours 1351
Influence. Sit thou here in a good place 1353
Mutilated. Hanun cut off their garments in the m. 1354
Rending. Reuben returned unto the pit..rent his 1355
"   David took hold on his clothes..rent 1356
Unwashed. Mephibosheth..nor washed his clothes 1357

CLOTHING.

Beautiful. [High priest's] A robe and a broidered 1358
Deception. Old shoes and clouted..old garments 1359
Disguised. False prophets..in sheep's clothing 1360
First. Sewed fig leaves together..coats of skins 1361
Gift. Jonathan stripped himself..gave..David 1362
"   His mother made Samuel a little coat 1363
Indestructible. 40 years..raiment 'waxed not old 1364
Ornamental. Chains and bracelets and mufflers 1365
Plain. Raiment of camel's hair and a leathern 1366
Preserved. Let us not rend it, but cast lots for it 1367
Showy. Women adorn themselves in modest 1368
Sins. [Dives] was clothed in purple and fine linen 1369
Separate. Neither shall a man put on a woman's 1370
Tasteful. [Model woman] clothing is silk and 1371

Attractive. Achan..saw a goodly Babylonish g. 8316
Abandoned. Bartimeus..casting away his garment 8431
Exchange. Neither a man put on a woman's g. 7822
Omitted. Man had not on a wedding garment 5710
Royal. Mordecai..apparel of blue..white..purple 1100
"   Herod arrayed him in a gorgeous robe 1108
Testifying. She caught J. by his garment ; he left 8678
Unmixed. Neither a garment mingled of linen and 7785

3510. GENERATION, An evil. *Proverbs.* [11] *There is* a generation *that* curseth their father, and doth not bless their mother. [12] *There is* a generation *that are* pure in their own eyes, and *yet* is not washed from their filthiness. [13] *There is* a generation, O how lofty are their eyes ! and their eyelids are lifted up. [14] *There is* a generation, whose teeth *are as* swords, and their jaw teeth *as* knives, to devour the poor from off the earth, and the needy from *among* men.—PROV., ch. 30.

3511. GENEROSITY to the Afflicted. *Ephron said,* [11] The field give I thee, and the cave that *is* therein..in the presence of the sons of my people give it I thee : bury thy dead. [12] And Abraham bowed down himself before the people of the land.—GEN., ch 23.

3512. —— Excessive. *Building Tabernacle.* [5] The people bring much more than enough for the service of the work.. [6] And Moses..proclaimed throughout the camp, saying, Let neither man nor woman make any more work for the offering of the sanctuary. So the people were restrained.—EX., ch. 36.

3513. —— A forgiving. *Esau.* [8] What *meanest* thou by all this drove which I met? And he said, *These are* to find grace in the sight of my lord. [9] And Esau said, I have enough, my brother ; keep that thou hast unto thyself.—GEN., ch. 33.

3514. —— Royal. *David.* [3] I have..gold and silver, *which* I have given to the house of my God, over and above all that I have prepared for the holy house, [4] *Even* three thousand talents of gold, of the gold of Ophir, and seven thousand talents of refined silver, to overlay the walls of the houses *withal :* [5] The gold for *things* of gold, and the silver for *things* of silver.—1 CHRON., ch. 29. [Gold, $82,125,000 ; silver, $11,976,560 ; total, $94,101,560.]

See GIFTS and references.

3515. GENTLENESS in Youth. *Gideon.* [20] Said unto Jether his firstborn, Up, *and* slay them. But the youth drew not his sword : for he feared, because he *was* yet a youth. [21] Then Zebah and Zalmunna said, Rise thou, and fall upon us : for as the man *is, so is* his strength. And Gideon arose, and slew.—JUDGES, ch. 8.

See other illustrations under :

MEEKNESS.

TENDERNESS.

3516. GIANT, Armed. *Goliath.* [4] There went out a champion out of the camp of the Philistines, named Goliath, of Gath, whose height *was* six cubits and a span. [5] And *he had* a helmet of brass upon his head, and he *was* armed with a coat of mail ; and the weight of the coat *was* five thousand shekels of brass.—1 SAM., ch. 17.

3517. —— A royal. *Og.* [11] Only Og king of Bashan remained of the remnant of giants ; behold, his bedstead *was* a bedstead of iron.. nine cubits *was* the length thereof, and four cubits the breadth of it.—DEUT., ch. 3.

3518. GIANTS, Celebrated. *Philistines.* [16] Ishbi-benob, which *was* of the sons of the giant, the weight of his spear *weighed* three hundred *shekels* of brass..thought to have slain David.. [18] ..then Sibbechai..slew Saph, which *was* of the sons of the giant. [19] ..Elhanan..slew *the brother of* Goliath the Gittite, the staff of whose spear *was* like a weaver's beam. [20] And there was yet a battle in Gath, where was a man of *great* stature, that had on every hand six fingers, and on every foot six toes, four and twenty in number.. [21] And when he defied Israel, Jonathan..the brother of David slew him. —2 SAM., ch. 21.

3519. GIFT for Art, A. *Bezaleel.* [31] He hath filled him with the spirit of God, in wisdom, in understanding, and in knowledge, and in all manner of workmanship ; [32] And to devise curious works, to work in gold, and in silver, and in brass, [33] And in the cutting of stones, to set *them,* and in carving of wood, to make any manner of cunning work.—EX., ch. 35.

3520. —— accepted. *Dedication.* [10] When the priests were come out of the holy *place*..the cloud filled the house of the Lord, [11] So that the priests could not stand to minister because of the cloud ; for the glory of the Lord had filled the house.—1 KINGS, ch. 8.

3521. —— better than Gold. *Health.* [6] Peter said, Silver and gold have I none ; but such as I have give I thee : In the name of Jesus Christ of Nazareth, rise up and walk.—ACTS, ch. 3.

3522. —— to Counsellor. *Saul said,* [7] The bread is spent in our vessels, and *there is* not a present to bring to the man of God : what have we? [8] And the servant answered..Behold, I have here at hand the fourth part of a shekel of silver : *that* will I give to the man of God, to tell us our way.—1 SAM., ch. 9.

3523. —— of Children. *Reward.* [3] Lo, children *are* a heritage of the Lord : *and* the fruit of the womb *is his* reward.—PS. 127.

3524. —— A farewell. *Elijah's.* [9] Elijah said unto Elisha, Ask what I shall do for thee, before I be taken away from thee. And Elisha said, I pray thee, let a double portion of thy spirit be upon me.—2 KINGS, ch. 2.

3525. —— A ghastly. *Herodias' Daughter.* [25] She came..with haste unto the king. saying, I will that thou give me by and by in a charger the head of John the Baptist.—MARK, ch. 10.

3526. —— Hypocrisy in a. *King Saul.* [20] Michal Saul's daughter loved David : and they told Saul, and the thing pleased him. [21] And Saul said, I will give him her, that she may be a snare to him, and that the hand of the Philistines may be against him.—1 Sam., ch. 18.

3527. —— **Influence of a.** *Proverb.* [16] A man's gift maketh room for him, and bringeth him before great men.—Prov., ch. 18.

3528. —— **An impossible.** *James and John.* [37] Grant unto us that we may sit, one on thy right hand, and the other on thy left hand, in thy glory.. [40] But to sit on my right hand and on my left hand is not mine to give ; but *it shall be given to them* for whom it is prepared.—Mark, ch. 10.

3529. —— **The unspeakable.** *Jesus.* [16] For God so loved the world, that he gave his only begotten Son, that whosoever believeth in him should not perish, but have everlasting life.—John, ch. 3. [15] Thanks be unto God for his unspeakable gift.—2 Cor., ch. 9.

3530. —— **An unaccepted.** *David.* [23] Lo, I give *thee* the oxen *also* for burnt offerings, and the threshing instruments for wood, and the wheat for the meat offering ; I give it all. [24] And king David said to Ornan, Nay ; but I will verily buy it for the full price : for I will not take *that* which *is* thine for the Lord, nor offer burnt offerings without cost.—1 Chron., ch. 21.

3531. —— **A valuable.** *Widow of Zarephath.* [11] Bring me, I pray thee, a morsel of bread in thine hand. [12] And she said . . I have.. but a handful of meal in a barrel, and a little oil in a cruse : and, behold, I *am* gathering two sticks, that I may.. dress it for me and my son, that we may eat it, and die.—1 Kings, ch. 17.

3532. GIFTS, No cleansing by. *Sin.* [7] Will the Lord be pleased with thousands of rams, *or* with ten thousands of rivers of oil ? shall I give my firstborn *for* my transgression, the fruit of my body *for* the sin of my soul ?—Micah, ch. 6.

3533. —— **to Children.** *Abraham.* [5] Abraham gave all that he had unto Isaac. [6] But unto the sons of the concubines.. Abraham gave gifts.—Gen., ch. 25.

3534. —— **Contemptible.** *Religious.* [18] Thou shalt not bring the hire of a whore, or the price of a dog, into the house of the Lord thy God for any vow : for even both these *are* abomination unto the Lord.—Deut., ch. 23.

3535. —— **declined.** *Daniel.* [11] Daniel answered.. Let thy gifts be to thyself, and give thy rewards to another ; yet I will read the writing unto the king, and make known to him the interpretation.—Dan., ch. 5.

3536. —— —— *Esau.* [See No. 3513.]

3537. —— **Diversity in.** *Spiritual.* [8] To one is given by the Spirit the word of wisdom ; to another the word of knowledge.. [9] To another faith.. the gifts of healing.. [10].. the working of miracles .. prophecy .. discerning of spirits .. *divers* kinds of tongues ; to another the interpretation of tongues : [11] But all these worketh that one and the selfsame Spirit, dividing to every man severally as he will.—1 Cor., ch. 12.

3538. —— **differ.** *Parable.* [15] Unto one he gave five talents, to another two, and to another one ; to every man according to his several ability.—Mat., ch. 25.

3539. —— **Disappointment in.** *Hiram.* [12] Hiram came out from Tyre to see the cities which Solomon had given him ; and they pleased him not.—1 Kings, ch. 9.

3540. —— **Festival.** *David's.* [Bringing the ark to Zion.] [19] He dealt among all the people.. as well to the women as men, to every one a cake of bread, and a good piece of *flesh*, and a flagon of *wine*.—2 Sam., ch. 6.

3541. —— **less than Grace.** *Jesus said,* [19] I give unto you power to tread on serpents and scorpions, and over all the power of the enemy ; and nothing shall by any means hurt you. [20] Notwithstanding, in this rejoice not, that the spirits are subject unto you ; but rather rejoice, because your names are written in heaven.—Luke, ch. 10.

3542. —— **of Gratitude.** *Midianites slain.* [49] They said unto Moses, Thy servants have taken the sum of the men of war which *are* under our charge, and there lacketh not one man of us. [50] We have therefore brought an oblation for the Lord, what every man hath gotten, of jewels of gold, chains, and bracelets, rings, earrings, and tablets, to make an atonement for our souls.—Num., ch. 31.

3543. —— **for Jesus.** *Magi.* [11] When they were come into the house, they saw the young child with Mary his mother, and fell down, and worshipped him : and when they had opened their treasures, they presented unto him gifts ; gold, and frankincense, and myrrh.—Mat., ch. 2.

3544. —— **Rule for.** *Rebuilding.* [68] Offered freely for the house of God to set it up in his place : [69] They gave after their ability unto the treasure of the work threescore and one thousand drams of gold, and five thousand pounds of silver, and one hundred priests.—Ezra, ch. 2.

3545. —— **Supported by.** *Law.* [20] The Lord spake unto Aaron, Thou shalt have no inheritance in their land.. I *am* thy part and thine inheritance among the children of Israel. [21].. I have given the children of Levi all the tenth in Israel for an inheritance, for their service.—Num., ch. 18.

3546. —— **Thanksgiving.** *Feast of Purim.* [22] The days wherein the Jews rested from their enemies, and the month which was turned unto them from sorrow to joy, and from mourning into a good day : that they should make them days of feasting and joy, and of sending portions one to another, and gifts to the poor.—Esther, ch. 9.

3547. —— **Trouble from.** *In Sacks.* [27] As one of them opened his sack to give his ass provender in the inn, he espied his money.. [28] And he said.. My money is restored.. their heart failed *them*, and they were afraid, saying one to another, What *is* this *that* God hath done unto us ?—Gen., ch. 42.

3548. —— **Value of.** *Two Mites.* [43] This poor widow hath cast more in, than all they which have cast into the treasury : [44] For all *they* did cast in of their abundance ; but she of her want did cast in all that she had, *even* all her living.—Mark, ch. 12.

3549. —— **Various.** *For Tabernacle.* [23] Every man, with whom was found blue, and purple, and scarlet, and fine linen, and goats' hair, and red skins of rams, and badgers' skins, brought *them.* ²⁴..an offering of silver and brass..and.. shittim wood for any work of the service.. ²⁵ And all the women..did spin with their hands, and brought..of blue, and of purple, *and* of scarlet, and of fine linen.. ²⁷ And the rulers brought onyx stones, and stones to be set, for the ephod, and for the breastplate ; ²⁸ And spice, and oil for the light, and for the anointing oil, and for the sweet incense.—Ex., ch. 35.

3550. —— withheld. *Robbery.* ⁸ Will a man rob God ? Yet ye have robbed me. But ye say, Wherein have we robbed thee ? In tithes and offerings. ⁹ Ye *are* cursed with a curse : for ye have robbed me, *even* this whole nation.—MAL., ch. 3.

3551. GIVERS, Disposition makes. *Building Tabernacle.* ²¹ Every one whose heart stirred him up, and every one whom his spirit made willing, *and* they brought the Lord's offering to the work of the tabernacle..and for all his service, and for the holy garments.—Ex., ch. 35.

3552. —— Grateful. *Women.* ² Certain women, which had been healed of evil spirits and infirmities, Mary called Magdalene, out of whom went seven devils, ³ And Joanna the wife of Chuza Herod's steward, and Susanna, and many others..ministered unto him of their substance. —LUKE, ch. 8.

3553. —— Happy. *Building Temple.* ⁹ Then the people rejoiced, for that they offered willingly, because with perfect heart they offered willingly to the Lord : and David the king also rejoiced with great joy.—1 CHRON., ch. 29.

3554. —— Lovely. *Cheerful.* ⁷ Every man according as he purposeth in his heart, *so let him give ;* not grudgingly, or of necessity : for God loveth a cheerful giver.—2 COR., ch. 9.

3555. GIVING, Royal. *Araunah.* ²³ All these *things* did Araunah, *as* a king, give unto the king.. ²⁴ And the king said..Nay ; but I will surely buy *it* of thee at a price : neither will I offer burnt offerings..of that which doth cost me nothing. So David bought the threshing-floor and the oxen for fifty shekels of silver.— 2 SAM., ch. 24.

See other illustrations under :

CONTRIBUTIONS.
Abundant. [Temple] Offered willingly..gold 5000 1657
Expenses. Charge ourselves yearly..third part 1658
for Jesus. Women..healed..ministered..their 1659
for Levites. Firstfruits of corn..wine, oil, and 1660
Repairs. Chest..set beside the altar..right side 1661
Rebuilding. Chief of the fathers gave after their 1662
Various. Men and women..blue, purple, scarlet 1663

GENEROSITY.
Royal. [David's] 3000 talents of gold..70,000 silver 3514
Tabernacle Builders. People..much more than 3511

KINDNESS.
Appreciated. Barzillai. I will feed thee in Jeru'm 4808
Animals. Rebekah..I will draw for thy camels 4809
Bereavement. In the choice of our sepulchres..bury 4810
Brethren. Waxen poor ; thou shalt relieve him 4811
Conquerors. Saul. is this thy voice, David?..wept 4812
to Christians. A cup of cold water only..his r. 4813
Christians. Disciples..relief unto brethren..Judea 4814
Captives. Clothed naked..shod them..eat 4815
Father. If ye know how to give..much more..F. 4816
Gratitude. Mephibosheth..kindness for Jonathan's 4817

Heathen. Barbarous people shewed..kindness 4818
Insulted. David sent to comfort him..cut beards 4819
Inopportune. Ahab..because thou hast let go 4820
Loan. Hath pity..lendeth to the L. 4821
Providential. Boaz unto Ruth..abide here 4822
Prosperity. I delivered the poor that cried [Job] 4823
Prisoner. Jeremiah put these rags..under arms 4824
Remembered. Lest I destroy you, for ye showed 4825
Rewarded. Rahab hid them with flax..saved 4826
Substitutional. I was eyes to the blind..feet [Job] 4827
Servant. Centurion's servant was dear to him 4828
Strangers. Drink, my lord..hasted..gave him 4829
Timely. Barzillai brought beds..flour..butter 4830
Unexpected. Shall I smite them?..set bread 4831
Widow. Harvest..forgot a sheaf..be for the w. 4832

LIBERALITY.
Benevolent. Much entreaty, that we would receive 4949
Commended. Thine heart shalt not be grieved 4950
Denominational. He followeth not us ; and we f. 4952
Pagan. He hath built us a synagogue 4954
Rule. Poor widow hath cast in more than all 4955
Returned. Liberal soul shall be made fat 4956
Return. Give, and it shall be given unto you 4957
Royal. Every one a loaf..flesh..wine 4958
Ungrudging. Thine heart shall not be grieved 4960

MAGNANIMITY.
Enemies. Shall there any man..be put to death 5164
Forgiveness. David's heart smote him..Saul's 5165
Fraternal. [Judah] became surety for the lad 5166
Gracious. Is not the whole land before thee 5167

OFFERING.
Accepted. Five came..consumed upon the altar 5836
Best. Do justly, love mercy..walk humbly with 5937
Humble. Samuel took a sucking lamb..L. heard 5938

OFFERINGS.
Abominable. Sacrifice of the wicked is an a. 5839
Forbidden. I will hide mine eyes..hands full of 5840
Ministerial. Offer up..even a tenth part of the t. 5841
Many. Solomon offered 22,000 oxen..120,000 sheep 5842
Rejected. To what purpose is the multitude of 5843
Scrutinized. Jesus sat over against the treasury 5844
Unworthy. If ye offer the lame and sick, is it not 5845
Voluntary. Freewill offering..for the house of 5846
Willing. The stuff they had was..too much 5847

TALENTS.
Accountability. Five talents, I have gained..five 8582
Faithful. Well done, good and faithful servant 8583
Hidden. I was afraid, and went and hid thy talent 8584
Improvement. Give it unto him that hath ten 8585
Increase. Traded..and made them other five 8586
Numerous. David..cunning in playing..war 8587
Unused. I hid thy talent in the earth 8588
Unimproved. Cast..unprofitable servant into 8589

Friendship. J. stripped himself..robe .sword..save 1342
for All. Called his ten servants. delivered unto 1073
Power. Will the son of Jesse give..fields and 78
See BENEVOLENCE.

3556. GLORY in the Cross. *Paul.* ¹⁴ God forbid that I should glory, save in the cross of our Lord Jesus Christ, by whom the world is crucified unto me, and I unto the world.—GAL., ch. 6.

3557. —— on the Countenance. *Moses.* ²⁹ When Moses came down from mount Sinai with the two tables of testimony..Moses wist not that the skin of his face shone while he talked with him.—Ex., ch. 34.

3558. —— —— *Stephen.* ¹⁵ All that sat in

the council, looking steadfastly on him, saw his face as it had been the face of an angel.—ACTS, ch. 6.

3559. —— A dazzling. *Saul.* [3] He came near Damascus : and suddenly there shined round about him a light from heaven : [9] And he was three days without sight, and neither did eat nor drink.—ACTS, ch. 9.

3560. —— Excluded by. *Cloud.* [35] Moses was not able to enter.. because the cloud abode thereon, and the glory of the Lord filled the tabernacle.—EX., ch. 40.

3561. —— —— Temple. [10] When the priests were come out of the holy *place*.. the cloud filled the house of the Lord, [11] So that the priests could not stand to minister because of the cloud : for the glory of the Lord had filled the house. —1 KINGS, ch. 8.

3562. —— of God. *Sidereal.* [1] The heavens declare the glory of God ; and the firmament sheweth his handywork. [2] Day unto day uttereth speech, and night unto night sheweth knowledge. [3] *There is* no speech nor language, *where* their voice is not heard.—Ps. 19.

3563. —— —— Mount Sinai. [9] Then went up Moses, and Aaron, Nadab, and Abihu, and seventy of the elders of Israel : [10] And they saw the God of Israel ; and *there was* under his feet as it were a paved work of a sapphire stone, and as it were the body of heaven in *his* clearness.— EX., ch. 24.

3564. —— —— Revelation of. [18] I beseech thee, shew me thy glory.. [22].. while my glory passeth by.. I will put thee in a cleft of the rock, and will cover thee with my hand while I pass by : [23] And I will take away mine hand, and thou shalt see my back parts ; but my face shall not be seen.—EX., ch. 33.

3565. —— —— Symbol of Cloud. [42] They looked toward the tabernacle of the congregation : and, behold, the cloud covered it, and the glory of the Lord appeared.—NUM., ch. 16.

3566. —— in God only. *Wise.* [23] Let not the wise *man* glory in his wisdom, neither let the mighty *man* glory in his might, let not the rich *man* glory in his riches : [24] But let him that glorieth glory in this, that he understandeth and knoweth me, that I *am* the Lord which exercise lovingkindness, judgment, and righteousness, in the earth : for in these *things* I delight. —JER., ch. 9.

3567. —— to God only. *Increase.* [6] I have planted, Apollos watered ; but God gave the increase. [7] So then neither is he that planteth any thing, neither he that watereth ; but God that giveth the increase.—1 COR., ch. 3.

3568. —— God demands. *Herod.* [21] Herod, arrayed in royal apparel, sat upon his throne, and made an oration unto them. [22] And the people gave a shout, *saying, It is* the voice of a god, and not of a man. [23] And immediately the angel of the Lord smote him, because he gave not God the glory : and he was eaten of worms, and gave up the ghost.—ACTS, ch. 12.

3569. —— from good Deeds. *Fruitfulness.* [8] Herein is my Father glorified, that ye bear much fruit ; so shall ye be my disciples.—JOHN, ch. 15.

3570. —— not in Man. *"All Yours."* [21] Let no man glory in men : for all things are yours ; [22] Whether Paul, or Apollos, or Cephas, or the world, or life, or death, or things present, or things to come ; all are yours ; [23] And ye are Christ's ; and Christ is God's.—1 COR., ch. 3.

3571. —— of Nature. *Lilies.* [27] Consider the lilies how they grow : they toil not, they spin not ; and yet I say unto you, that Solomon in all his glory was not arrayed like one of these. —LUKE, ch. 12.

3572. —— revealed. *Transfiguration.* [29] As he prayed, the fashion of his countenance was altered, and his raiment *was* white *and* glittering.—LUKE, ch. 9.

3573. —— Transient. *Human.* [24] All flesh *is* as grass, and all the glory of man as the flower of grass. The grass withereth, and the flower thereof falleth away.—1 PETER, ch. 1.

3574. —— in Trials. *Paul.* [30] If I must needs glory, I will glory of the things which concern mine infirmities.—2 COR., ch. 11.

3575. —— a transforming. *Grace.* [18] We all, with open face beholding as in a glass the glory of the Lord, are changed into the same image from glory to glory, *even* as by the Spirit of the Lord.—2 COR., ch. 3.

See other illustrations under :

FAME.

Increasing. His fame spread abroad.. about		3000
Military. Uzziah made.. engines.. to shoot		3001
Troublesome. Blaze abroad the matter.. desert		3002
Unexpected. In the whole world.. woman hath		3003
Wisdom. All the earth sought to Solomon		3004

HONOUR.

Age. Jacob blessed Pharaoh		4058
Appeal. L. was not able to bring.. into the land		4059
Dishonour. Haman arrayed Mordecai.. and		4060
Elders. Elihu had waited.. were elder than he		4061
Given. Mephibosheth shall eat.. as one.. king's sons		4063
Not given. Not mine to give.. for whom.. prepared		4062
Protected. Wherefore should the Egyptians say		4064
Regarded. I was ashamed to require.. soldiers		4065
Sale of. They covenanted with him.. 30 pieces		4066
Sudden. Pharaoh took off his ring.. Joseph		4067
Seeking. How can ye believe which receive honour		4068
Service. Said unto the olive.. Reign over us		4069
Special. Queen did let no man come.. but myself		4070
Unexpected. Mordecai went out.. in royal apparel		4071
Won. Abishai was chief of the three.. 300 slew		4072

3576. GLORYING in God. *Diadem.* [5] In that day shall the Lord of hosts be for a crown of glory, and for a diadem of beauty, unto the residue of his people.—ISA., ch. 28.

See other illustrations under :

BOASTING.

Folly. Seest thou a man wise.. own conceit		7698
Glorious. Are they Hebrews? So am I.. more		869
Inoffensive. If I have boasted.. I am not ashamed		870
Prayer. Pharisee.. I am not as other men		871
Prevented. People are too many.. lest vaunt		872
Rebuked. Lord, I will lay down my life		873

3577. GLUTTON, Called a. *Jesus.* [34] The Son of man is come eating and drinking ; and ye say, Behold, a gluttonous man, and a winebibber, a friend of publicans and sinners ! [35] But wisdom is justified of all her children.—LUKE, ch. 7.

See other illustrations under :

Cautioned. Put a knife to thy throat.. dainties		479
Reaction. Come out at your nostrils.. loathsome		482

3578. GOD Angry with Sinners. *Calf-worship-pers.* [9] The Lord said unto Moses, I have seen this people, and behold, it *is* a stiffnecked people : [10] Now therefore let me alone, that my wrath may wax hot against them, and that I may consume them.—Ex., ch. 32.

3579. —— Ability of. *"Too Hard."* [27] I *am* the Lord, the God of all flesh : is there any thing too hard for me ? [28]..Behold, I will give this city into the hand of the Chaldeans, and into the hand of Nebuchadrezzar king of Babylon, and he shall take it.—Jer., ch. 32.

3580. —— Awe of. *Moses.* [2] The Angel of the Lord appeared unto him in a flame of fire out of the midst of a bush.. [6] And Moses hid his face ; for he was afraid to look upon God.—Ex., ch. 3.

3581. —— Acceptance with. *Abel.* [4] By faith Abel offered unto God a more excellent sacrifice than Cain, by which he obtained witness that he was righteous, God testifying of his gifts.—Heb., ch. 11.

3582. —— Human Appearance of. *To Abram.* [1] The Lord appeared unto him in the plains of Mamre : and he sat in the tent door in the heat of the day ; [2]..lo, three men stood by him : and when he saw *them*, he ran to meet them..and bowed himself toward the ground.—Gen., ch. 18.

3583. —— Abandoned by. *Delilah said,* [20] The Philistines *be* upon thee, Samson. And he awoke out of his sleep, and said, I will go out as at other times before, and shake myself. And he wist not that the Lord was departed from him. [21] But the Philistines took him, and put out his eyes.—Judges, ch. 16.

3584. —— Bold Access to. *Christ.* [14] Seeing then that we have a great high priest, that is passed into the heavens, Jesus the Son of God, let us hold fast *our* profession.. [16] Let us therefore come boldly unto the throne of grace, that we may obtain mercy, and find grace to help in time of need.—Heb., ch. 4.

3585. —— Character of. *At Sinai.* [6] The Lord passed by before him, and proclaimed, The Lord, The Lord God, merciful and gracious, longsuffering, and abundant in goodness and truth, [7] Keeping mercy for thousands, forgiving iniquity and transgression and sin, and that will by no means clear *the guilty ;* visiting the iniquity of the fathers upon the children, and upon the children's children, unto the third and to the fourth *generation.*—Ex., ch. 34.

3586. —— not counselled. *Gibeonites' Trick.* [12] This our bread we took hot..out of our houses ..but now..it is mouldy : [13] And these bottles of wine..*were* new, and behold they be rent : and these our garments and our shoes are become old by reason of the very long journey. [14] And the men took of their victuals, and asked not *counsel* at the mouth of the Lord.—Josh., ch. 9.

3587. —— defeated, Cause of. *By Philistines.* [5] When the ark..of the Lord came into the camp, all Israel shouted with a great shout, so that the earth rang again.. [10] And the Philistines fought, and Israel was smitten, and they fled..a very great slaughter.. [11] And the ark of God was taken.—1 Sam., ch. 4.

3588. —— The Door to. *Jesus.* [9] I am the

door : by me if any man enter in, he shall be saved, and shall go in and out, and find pasture. —John, ch. 10.

3589. —— despised, Power of. *Rab-shakeh said,* [30] Neither let Hezekiah make you trust in the Lord, saying, The Lord will surely deliver us, and this city shall not be delivered into the hand of the king of Assyria.. [33] Hath any of the gods of the nations delivered at all his land out of the hand of the king of Assyria?—2 Kings, ch. 18.

3590. —— distrusted. *Forbidden Fruit.* [6] When the woman saw that the tree *was* good for food, and..pleasant to the eyes, and..to be desired to make *one* wise, she took..and did eat, and gave also unto her husband.—Gen., ch. 3.

3591. —— The first for. *Harvest.* [14] Ye shall eat neither bread, nor parched corn, nor green ears, until the selfsame day that ye have brought an offering unto your God : *It shall be* a statute for ever..in all your dwellings.—Lev., ch. 23.

3592. —— Firstborn for. *All.* [12] Thou shalt set apart unto the Lord all that openeth the matrix, and every firstling that cometh of a beast which thou hast ; the male *shall be* the Lord's. [13] And every firstling of an ass thou shalt redeem with a lamb..and all the firstborn of man among thy children shalt thou redeem.—Ex., ch. 13.

3593. —— honoured first. *Proverb.* [9] Honour the Lord with thy substance, and with the firstfruits of all thine increase : [10] So shall thy barns be filled with plenty, and thy presses shall burst out with new wine.—Prov., ch. 3.

3594. —— First. Building for. *Altar.* [2] Then stood up Jeshua..and his brethren the priests, and Zerubbabel..and his brethren, and builded the altar of the God of Israel, to offer burnt offerings.—Ezra, ch. 3.

3595. —— obeyed first. *At Jerusalem.* [28] Did not we straitly command you that ye should not teach in this name? and, behold, ye have filled Jerusalem with your doctrine, and intend to bring this man's blood upon us. [29] Then Peter and the *other* apostles answered..We ought to obey God rather than men.—Acts, ch. 5.

3596. —— Fidelity honours. *Three Hebrews.* [28] Nebuchadnezzar spake..Blessed *be* the God.. who hath sent his angel, and delivered his servants that trusted in him..yielded their bodies, that they might not serve nor worship any god, except their own God. [29] Therefore I make a decree, That every people, nation, and language, which speak any thing amiss against the God.. shall be cut in pieces, and their houses shall be made a dunghill ; because there is no other God that can deliver after this sort.—Dan., ch. 3.

3597. —— Fleeing from. *Jonah.* [3] Jonah rose up to flee unto Tarshish from the presence of the Lord, and went down to Joppa ; and he found a ship going to Tarshish : so he paid the fare thereof, and went down into it.—Jonah, ch. 1.

3598. —— Forsaken by. *Jesus.* [45] From the sixth hour there was darkness over all the land unto the ninth hour. [46] And about the ninth hour Jesus cried with a loud voice, saying, Eli, Eli, lama sabachthani? that is to say, My God, my God, why hast thou forsaken me?—Mat., ch. 27.

3599. —— **Visible Glory of.** *At Sinai.* [9] Went up Moses, and Aaron, Nadab, and Abihu, and seventy of the elders of Israel ; [10] And they saw the God of Israel : and *there was* under his feet as it were a paved work of a sapphire stone, and as it were the body of heaven in *his* clearness.— Ex., ch. 24.

3600. —— **Glorious Knowledge of.** *"Knoweth me."* [23] Thus saith the Lord, Let not the wise *man* glory in his wisdom, neither let the mighty *man* glory in his might, let not the rich *man* glory in his riches : [24] But let him that glorieth glory in this, that he understandeth and knoweth me, that I *am* the Lord which exercise lovingkindness, judgment, and righteousness, in the earth : for in these *things* I delight, saith the Lord.—Jer., ch. 9.

3601. —— **All Gifts from.** *Proverb.* [12] The hearing ear, and the seeing eye, the Lord hath made even both of them.—Prov., ch. 20.

3602. —— **honours the Faithful.** *Three Hebrews.* [27] The princes, governors, and captains, and the king's counsellors. . saw these men, upon whose bodies the fire had no power, nor was a hair of their head singed, neither were their coats changed, nor the smell of fire had passed on them. . [30] Then the king promoted Shadrach, Meshach, and Abed-nego, in the province of Babylon.—Dan., ch. 3.

3603. —— **Intercourse with.** *Jacob.* [12] He dreamed, and behold a ladder set up on the earth, and the top of it reached to heaven : and behold the angels of God ascending and descending on it. [13] And, behold, the Lord stood above it.—Gen., ch. 28.

3604. —— **longingly desired.** *David.* [1] As the hart panteth after the water brooks, so panteth my soul after thee, O God. [2] My soul thirsteth for God, for the living God : when shall I come and appear before God ?—Ps. 42.

3605. —— **less than Gold.** *Pharisees.* [16] Whosoever shall swear by the temple, it is nothing ; but whosoever shall swear by the gold of the temple, he is a debtor ! [17] *Ye* fools and blind : for whether is greater, the gold, or the temple that sanctifieth the gold?—Mat., ch. 23.

3606. —— **Manifestation of.** *"Back Part."* [20] Thou canst not see my face : for there shall no man see me, and live. [21] . .Behold, *there is* a place by me, and thou shalt stand upon a rock. . [22] I will put thee in a cleft of the rock, and will cover thee with my hand while I pass by : [23] And I will take away mine hand, and thou shalt see my back parts ; but my face shall not be seen.—Ex., ch. 33.

3607. —— **Mercy of.** *To Ninevites.* [1] It displeased Jonah exceedingly, and he was very angry. [2] And he prayed. .O Lord, *was* not this my saying, when I was yet in my country ? Therefore I fled before unto Tarshish : for I knew that thou *art* a gracious God, and merciful, slow to anger, and of great kindness, and repentest thee of the evil.—Jonah, ch. 4.

3608. —— **misjudged.** *Destructive.* [21] Then Manoah knew that he *was* an angel. . [22] And Manoah said unto his wife, We shall surely die, because we have seen God. [23] But his wife said . .If the Lord were pleased to kill us, he would not have received a burnt offering.—Judges, ch. 13.

3609. —— **Nearness of.** *Unconscious.* [16] Jacob awaked out of his sleep, and he said, Surely the Lord is in this place ; and I knew *it* not. [17] And he was afraid, and said, How dreadful *is* this place ! this *is* none other but the house of God, and this *is* the gate of heaven.— Gen., ch. 28.

3610. —— **near to All.** *Paul at Athens.* [27] That they should seek the Lord, if haply they might feel after him, and find him, though he be not far from every one of us : [28] For in him we live, and move, and have our being.—Acts, ch. 17.

3611. —— **Omnipotence of.** *"Hangeth the Earth."* [6] He stretcheth out the north over the empty place, *and* hangeth the earth upon nothing.—Job, ch. 26.

3612. —— **Omniscience of.** *David.* [2] Thou knowest my downsitting and mine uprising ; thou understandest my thought afar off. [3] Thou compassest my path and my lying down, and art acquainted *with* all my ways. [4] For *there is* not a word in my tongue, *but* lo, O Lord, thou knowest it altogether.—Ps. 139.

3613. —— **Omnipresence of.** *David.* [7] Whither shall I go from thy Spirit ? or whither shall I flee from thy presence ? [8] If I ascend up into heaven, thou *art* there : if I make my bed in hell, behold, thou *art there.* [9] *If* I take the wings of the morning, *and* dwell in the uttermost parts of the sea ; [10] Even there shall thy hand lead me, and thy right hand shall hold me.—Ps. 139.

3614. —— **Presence of.** *Dispels Fear.* [2] Jacob. And he said, Here *am* I. [3] And he said, I *am* God, the God of thy father : fear not to go down into Egypt ; for I will there make of thee a great nation. [4] I will go down with thee into Egypt ; and I will also surely bring thee up *again.*—Gen., ch. 46.

3615. —— **revealed.** *To a Child.* [9] Samuel went and lay down in his place. [10] And the Lord . .called as at other times, Samuel, Samuel. Then Samuel answered, Speak ; for thy servant heareth.—1 Sam., ch. 3.

3616. —— **Reverence for.** *At Sinai.* [21] Moses, Go down, charge the people, lest they break through unto the Lord to gaze, and many of them perish. [22] And let the priests also, which come near to the Lord, sanctify themselves, lest the Lord break forth upon them.—Ex., ch. 19.

3617. —— **rejected.** *Ahaziah.* [6] Thus saith the Lord, *Is it* not because *there is* not a God in Israel, *that* thou sendest to inquire of Baal-zebub the god of Ekron ? therefore thou shalt not come down from that bed on which thou art gone up, but shalt surely die.—2 Kings, ch. 1.

3618. —— **Remaining with.** *"Forty Days."* [18] Moses went into the midst of the cloud. .and Moses was in the mount forty days and forty nights.—Ex., ch. 24.

3619. —— **Supremacy of.** *Dagon.* [4] Dagon *was* fallen upon his face to the ground before the ark of the Lord ; and the head of Dagon and both the palms of his hands *were* cut off upon the threshold ; only *the stump of* Dagon was left to him.—1 Sam., ch. 5.

3620. —— **Sufficiency in.** *Sun.* [11] The Lord God *is* a sun and shield : the Lord will give grace and glory : no good *thing* will he withhold from them that walk uprightly.—Ps. 84.

3621. —— **seen by the Purified.** *S i n a i .*
[8] Moses took the blood, and sprinkled *it* on the people. [9] . . went up Moses, and Aaron, Nadab, and Abihu, and seventy of the elders of Israel ; [10] And they saw the God of Israel.—Ex., ch. 24.

3622. —— **Tithes for.** *Animals.* [32] Concerning the tithe of the herd, or of the flock, *even* the tenth whatsoever passeth under the rod, the tenth shall be holy unto the Lord. [33] He shall not search whether it be good or bad, neither shall he change it.—Lev., ch. 27.

3623. —— —— *Abraham.* [1] This Melchisedec, king of Salem, priest of the most high God, who met Abraham returning from the slaughter of the kings, and blessed him ; [2] To whom also Abraham gave a tenth part of all.—Heb., ch. 7.

3624. —— **The true.** *Dagon.* [3] They took Dagon, and set him in his place again. [4] . . on the morrow morning, behold, Dagon *was* fallen. —1 Sam., ch. 5. [See No. 3619.]

3625. —— **Terms of.** *P i e t y .* [8] He hath shewed thee, O man, what *is* good ; and what doth the Lord require of thee, but to do justly, and to love mercy, and to walk humbly with thy God ?—Micah, ch. 6.

3626. —— **unlimited.** *" Hills."* [23] The servants of the king of Syria said . . Their gods *are* gods of the hills ; therefore they were stronger than we ; but let us fight against them in the plain, and surely we shall be stronger than they. —1 Kings, ch. 20. [Were defeated again.]

3627. —— **The unsearchable.** *J o b .* [See Job, 38th chapter entire.]

3628. —— **An unknown.** *Athenians.* [23] As I passed by, and beheld your devotions, I found an altar with this inscription, TO THE UNKNOWN GOD. Whom therefore ye ignorantly worship, him declare I unto you.—Acts, ch. 17.

3629. —— **New Way to.** *Mt. Sion.* [18] For ye are not come unto the mount . . that burned with fire, nor unto blackness, and darkness, and tempest . . [22] But ye are come unto mount Sion, and unto the city of the living God, the heavenly Jerusalem, and to an innumerable company of angels, [23] To the general assembly and church of the firstborn, which are written in heaven, and to God the Judge of all, and to the spirits of just men made perfect, [24] And to Jesus the mediator of the new covenant, and to the blood of sprinkling, that speaketh better things than *that of* Abel.—Heb., ch. 12.

3630. —— **Wrestling with.** *Jacob.* [24] Jacob was left alone ; and there wrestled a man with him until the breaking of the day . . [28] And he said, Thy name shall be called no more Jacob, but Israel : for as a prince hast thou power with God and with men, and hast prevailed.—Gen., ch. 32.

See other illustrations under :

DIVINITY.

Asserted. Said G. was his F. . equal with G.   2474
Acknowledged. I am he, they . . fell to the ground   2475
Confessed. Thou art the C., the S. of the living G.   2476
Hatred. He ought to die . . himself the S. of G.   2477
Manifested. What manner of man is this? . . winds   2478
Professed. I and my F. are one . . stones   2479

See PROVIDENCE.

3631. **GODS of this World.** *On Carmel.* [27] At noon . . Elijah mocked them, and said, Cry aloud : for he *is* a god : either he is talking, or he is pursuing, or he is in a journey, *or* peradventure he sleepeth, and must be awaked.—1 Kings, ch. 18.

See other illustrations under :

IDOL.

Chosen. Go thy way, sell whatever thou hast, and   4274
Self. I am a god, I sit in the seat of G.   4275
State Religion. Made two calves of gold . . thy gods   4276

IDOLATRY.

Folly. They have ears, but they hear not   4277
"   Manufacture of. [See Isa. 44 : 9-17]   4278
"   Gods of the people which could not deliver   4279
Sanctuary. Set a graven image in the . . house   4280
Sacrifices. People break off the golden earrings   4281
Unreasonableness. Ought not to think . . like unto   4282

IDOLATER.

Punished. Slay every man his brother . . 3000 men   4283
Strange. Solomon . . burnt incense and sacrificed   4284

Powerless. Have any of the gods delivered   1534

3632. GODLIKENESS, Unconscious. *Moses.*
[29] When Moses came down from mount Sinai with the two tables of testimony in Moses' hand . . Moses wist not that the skin of his face shone while he talked with him.—Ex., ch. 34.

3633. GODLY, Happiness of the. *Tree.* [3] He shall be like a tree planted by the rivers of water, that bringeth forth his fruit in his season : his leaf also shall not wither ; and whatsoever he doeth shall prosper.—Ps. 1.

See other illustrations under :

CHRISTIANS.

Almost. Agrippa said unto Paul, Almost thou   1267
Care for. I lay down my life for the sheep   1268
Childlike. Suffer little children . . Of such is the   1269
Carnal. Whereas there is envying and strife   1270
Epistle. Ye are our epistle . . read of all   1271
Exemplary. Bishop must be blameless   1272
First named. First called Christians at Antioch   1275
Greatness. Least in the kingdom . . greater   1273
Homeward. Come to Zion with songs   1274
Saved. He that committeth sin is of the devil   1276
Visible. Ye are the light of the world   1277

RIGHTEOUSNESS.

Benefits. Prolongeth days . . hope of the righteous   7444
Discarded. If any . . might trust in the flesh, I more   7445
False. Say not . . for my righteousness the L. hath   7446
Flattery. Pharisee . . prayed thus with himself   7447

See PIETY and RELIGION.

3634. GOLD in Architecture. *Temple.* [21] Solomon overlaid the house within with pure gold : and he made a partition by the chains of gold before the oracle ; and he overlaid it with gold. [22] And the whole house . . also the whole altar that *was* by the oracle he overlaid with gold.— 1 Kings, ch. 6.

3635. —— **Abundance of.** *Solomon.* [14] The weight of gold that came to Solomon in one year was six hundred threescore and six talents of gold, [16] . . Solomon made two hundred targets *of* beaten gold : six hundred *shekels* of gold went to one target. [17] And *he made* three hundred shields *of* beaten gold ; three pounds of gold went to one shield.—1 Kings, ch. 10.

3636. —— **The best.** *Grace.* [17] Because

thou sayest, I am rich, and increased with goods, and have need of nothing; and knowest not that thou art wretched, and miserable, and poor, and blind, and naked : [18] I counsel thee to buy of me gold tried in the fire, that thou mayest be rich.—Rev., ch. 3.

3637. —— **Better than.** *Lame Beggar.* [5] He ..expecting to receive something of them. [6] Then Peter said, Silver and gold have I none ; but such as I have give I thee : In the name of Jesus Christ of Nazareth rise up and walk.— Acts, ch. 3.

3638. —— **City of.** *Heaven.* [18] The building of the wall of it was *of* jasper : and the city *was* pure gold, like unto clear glass.—Rev., ch. 21.

3639. —— **The first mentioned.** *Eden.* [10] A river went out of Eden to water the garden.. and became into four heads.. [11] The name of the first is Pison ; it compasseth the land of Havilah where there is gold.—Gen., ch. 2.

3640. —— **Furniture of.** *Ahasuerus.* [6] The beds *were of* gold and silver, upon a pavement of red, and blue, and white, and black marble. [7] And they gave *them* drink in vessels of gold.. being diverse one from another..and royal wine in abundance.—Esther, ch. 1.

3641. —— **imported.** *By Solomon.* [27] The servants of Solomon.. [28]..came to Ophir, and fetched from thence gold, four hundred and twenty talents.—1 Kings, ch. 9.

3642. —— **Image of.** *Idol.* [1] Nebuchadnezzar the king made an image of gold, whose height *was* threescore cubits, *and* the breadth thereof six cubits : he set it up in the plain of Dura.—Dan., ch. 3.

3643. —— **more than God.** *Pharisees.* [16] Whosoever shall swear by the temple, it is nothing ; but whosoever shall swear by the gold of the temple, he is a debtor ! [17] Ye fools and blind : for whether is greater, the gold, or the temple that sanctifieth the gold.—Mat., ch. 25.

3644. —— **Offerings of.** *For Tabernacle.* [22] Both men and women, as many as were willing hearted..brought bracelets, and earrings, and rings, and tablets, all jewels of gold : and every man that offered, *offered* an offering of gold unto the Lord.—Ex., ch. 35.

3645. —— **prohibited.** *Women.* [3] Whose adorning, let it not be that outward *adorning* of plaiting the hair, and of wearing of gold, or of putting on of apparel.—1 Peter, ch. 3.

3646. —— **for Trespass.** *Philistine's.* [7] Take two milch kine..and tie the kine to the cart.. [8] And take the ark of the Lord, and lay it upon the cart ; and put the jewels of gold, which ye return him *for* a trespass offering, in a coffer by the side thereof ; and send it away.—1 Sam., ch. 6.

3647. —— **Throne of.** *Solomon.* [18] The king made a great throne of ivory, and overlaid it with the best gold.—1 Kings, ch. 10.

3648. —— **Spoils of.** *Gideon's.* [26] The weight of the golden earrings..was a thousand and seven hundred *shekels* of gold ; besides ornaments, and collars, and purple raiment that *was* on the kings of Midian, and besides the chains that *were* about their camels' necks.— Judges, ch. 8.

See other illustrations under :

AVARICE.

Falsehood. Ananias with S. kept back part	592
Oppression. Making the ephah small and the shekel	593
Victim. Judas communed..betray.. money	594

COVETOUSNESS.

Abhorred. Blesseth the covetous whom the L.	1786
Alarmed. By this craft..our wealth..confusion	1787
Apostle. Judas went..to give him money	1788
Aroused. Damsel..masters saw..gains were gone	1789
Absence of. Abram said, I will not take..thread	1790
Church. Who would shut the doors for naught	1791
Cruelty. Felix hoped that money..of Paul	1792
Caution. Inheritance..take heed..beware of	1793
Disobedience. I saw among the spoils..took them	1794
Forbidden. Thou shalt not covet thy neighbour's	1795
Fraud. Gehazi..I will run and take..silver	1796
Folly. Soul, thou hast much goods..eat, drink	1797
Falsehood. Ananias with Sapphira..kept back	1798
Freedom. I have coveted no man's silver..Paul	1799
Inconsiderate. Well watered..Lot chose..plain of	1800
Oppressive. Ye exact usury..sell your brethren	1801
Overcome by. Saul and the people spared the best	1802
Overreaching. Laban..changed my wages ten	1803
Stigmatized. If any man that is called a brother	1804
Shameless. Given to covetousness..not..ashamed	1805
Unhappiness. Naboth had a vineyard..Ahab	1806

JEWELRY.

Abundance. Weight of the golden earrings 1700 t.	4723
Badge. Clothed Daniel with scarlet..chain	4724
Gifts. Bracelets and earrings and rings	4725
Snare. Gideon made an ephod thereof	4726

See **MONEY, RICHES, WEALTH.**

3649. GOOD or Bad. *Baskets of Figs.* [3] Said the Lord..What seest thou, Jeremiah ? And I said, Figs ; the good figs, very good ; and the evil, very evil, that cannot be eaten, they are so evil.—Jer., ch. 24.

3650. —— **Hatred of the.** *Joseph.* [4] When his brethren saw that their father loved him more than all his brethren, they hated him, and could not speak peaceably unto him.—Gen., ch. 37.

3651. —— **mixed with Bad.** *Tares.* [28] The servants said..Wilt thou then that we go and gather them up ? [29] But he said, Nay ; lest while ye gather up the tares, ye root up also the wheat with them. [30] Let both grow together until the harvest .. I will say to the reapers, Gather ye together first the tares, and bind them in bundles to burn them : but gather the wheat into my barn.—Mat., ch. 13.

3652. —— **Omission of.** *Dives.* [19] There was a certain rich man, which was clothed in purple and fine linen and fared sumptuously every day ..[23] And in hell he lifted up his eyes, being in torments.—Luke, ch. 16.

3653. GOODNESS, Commendation of. *Proverb.* [3] Let not mercy and truth forsake thee : bind them about thy neck ; write them upon the table of thine heart : [4] So shalt thou find favour and good understanding in the sight of God and man.—Prov., ch. 3.

3654. —— **distrusted.** *Eve.* [4] The serpent said unto the woman, Ye shall not surely die : [5] For God doth know that in the day ye eat thereof, then your eyes shall be opened ; and ye shall be as gods, knowing good and evil.—Gen., ch. 3.

3655. —— **Divine.** *To Saints.* [7] The angel of the Lord encampeth round about them that fear him, and delivereth them. [8] O taste and see that the Lord *is* good : blessed *is* the man *that* trusteth in him. [9] O fear the Lord, ye his saints : for *there is* no want to them that fear him. [10] The young lions do lack, and suffer hunger : but they that seek the Lord shall not want any good thing.—Ps. 34.

3656. —— **Pride in.** *Pharisee.* [11] God, I thank thee, that I am not as other men *are*, extortioners, unjust, adulterers, or even as this publican. [12] I fast twice in the week, I give tithes of all that I possess.—Luke, ch. 18.

3657. —— **reveals Glory.** *Moses' Prayer.* [18] I beseech thee, shew me thy glory. [19] And he said, I will make all my goodness pass before thee, and I will proclaim the name of the Lord before thee ; and will be gracious to whom I will be gracious, and will shew mercy on whom I will shew mercy.—Ex., ch. 33.

3658. —— **no Shield.** *John.* [19] Herodias had a quarrel against him, and would have killed him ; but she could not : [20] For Herod feared John, knowing that he was a just man and a holy, and observed him.—Mark, ch. 6.

3659. —— **Tribute to.** *Proverb.* [19] The evil bow before the good ; and the wicked at the gates of the righteous.—Prov., ch. 14.

3660. —— **Unconscious.** *Moses.* [29] And it came to pass, when Moses came down from mount Sinai with the two tables of testimony in Moses' hand, when he came down from the mount, that Moses wist not that the skin of his face shone while he talked with him.—Ex., ch. 34.

See other illustrations under:

KINDNESS.

Appreciated. Barzillai..I will feed thee in Jeru'm 4808
Animals. Rebekah..I will draw water for thy c. 4809
Bereavement. In the choice of our sepulchres bury 4810
Brethren. Waxen poor..thou shalt relieve him 4811
Conquerors. Saul..is this thy voice, David?..wept 4812
to Christians. A cup of cold water only..his r. 4813
Christians. Disciples..relief unto brethren..Judea 4814
Captives. Clothed naked..shod them..eat 4815
Father. If ye know how to give..much more your 4816
Gratitude. Mephibosheth..kindness for Jonathan's 4817
Heathen. Barbarous people shewed..kindness 4818
Insulted. David sent to comfort him..cut off 4819
Inopportune. Ahab..because thou hast let go 4820
Loan. Hath pity, lendeth to the Lord 4821
Providential. Boaz unto Ruth..abide here 4822
Prosperity. I delivered the poor that cried 4823
Prisoner. Jeremiah..put these rags..under arms 4824
Remembered. Lest I destroy you..for ye showed 4825
Rewarded. Rahab hid them with the flax..saved 4826
Substitutional. I was eyes to the blind..feet..poor 4827
Servant. Centurion's servant, who was dear to him 4828
Strangers. Drink my lord..hasted..gave him 4829
Timely. Barzillai brought beds..flour..butter 4830
Unexpected. Shall I smite them..set bread 4831
Widow. Harvest..forgot a sheaf..for the poor 4832

SYMPATHY.

Abundant. What mean ye to weep and break mine 8545
Bereavement. Much people..with her..he had 8546
" Many of the Jews came to Martha 8547
Distrusted. Thinkest thou that David..hath sent 8549
Eyes. Mine eye affected mine heart, because of 8550
by Experience. Touched with the feeling 8551

Erring. Forgive..lest swallowed up with 8552
" Count him not as an enemy, but..a brother 8553
Forbidden. If any man lie in wait..eye shall not 8554
in Heaven. Not a high priest, which cannot be 8555
Ill-rewarded. Hanun shaved off one half of their 8556
for Jesus. Great company of people and women 8557
Manifested. [See Nos. 8547, 8557.]
Offices. I was eyes to the blind, and feet..lame 8559
Power. Behold the babe wept. She had compassion 8560
Public. All the city was moved..Is this Naomi? 8561
Practical. Samaritan..went to him and bound up 8563
Power. What mean ye to weep and..break mine 8564
Return. Weep not for me, but weep for yourselves 8565
Sentimental. Levite..looked on him and passed by 8566
Silent. Sat down upon the ground 7 days..none 8567
Tender. O that mine head were waters, and mine 8568
" Mine eye runneth down with rivers of 8569
" Saw her weeping..Jews also..Jesus wept 8570
Unshaken. I am ready not to be bound only, but 8571

Enemies. Love your enemies, bless them that 6121
Liberal. As we have opportunity..do good..all 6125

See BENEVOLENCE, MERCY, PIETY.

3661. GOSPEL of Deliverance. *In Egypt.* [30] Moses..did the signs. [31] And the people believed : and when they heard that the Lord had visited the children of Israel, and that he had looked upon their affliction, then they bowed their heads and worshipped.—Ex., ch. 4.

3662. —— **of Glad Tidings.** *Advent.* [10] Fear not : for, behold, I bring you good tidings of great joy, which shall be to all people. [11] For unto you is born this day in the city of David a Saviour, which is Christ the Lord.—Luke, ch. 2.

3663. —— **honoured.** *Paul.* [15] As much as in me is, I am ready to preach the gospel to you that are at Rome also. [16] For I am not ashamed of the gospel of Christ : for it is the power of God unto salvation to every one that believeth. —Rom., ch. 1.

Also see:

Tidings. Tell John..blind see..lame walk..deaf 1305
Welcomed. They that gladly rec'd the word..3000 1677
See GRACE.

3664. GOVERNMENT, Bad. *Revolution.* [3] His sons..turned aside after lucre, and took bribes, and perverted judgment. [4] Then all the elders of Israel..came to Samuel.. [5] And said..Behold, thou art old, and thy sons walk not in thy ways : now make us a king to judge us like all the nations.—1 Sam., ch. 8.

3665. —— **Commissioned for.** *Man.* [26] Let us make man in our image, after our likeness : and let them have dominion over the fish of the sea, and over the fowl of the air, and over the cattle, and over all the earth, and over every creeping thing.—Gen., ch. 1.

3666. —— **Method in.** *Jethro said,* [21] Thou shalt provide out of all the people able men, such as fear God, men of truth, hating covetousness ; and place *such* over them, *to be* rulers of thousands, *and* rulers of hundreds, rulers of fifties, and rulers of tens : [22] And let them judge the people at all seasons..every great matter they shall bring unto thee.—Ex., ch. 18.

3667. —— **Obedience to.** *"Higher Power."* [1] Let every soul be subject unto the higher powers. For there is no power but of God : the powers that be are ordained of God. [2] Whosoever therefore resisteth the power, resisteth the ordinance of God.—Rom., ch. 13.

3668. —— **Revolt against.** *Young Rehoboam.*
[18] After the counsel of the young men, saying,
My father made your yoke heavy, and I will
add to your yoke : my father *also* chastised you
with whips, but I will chastise you with scorpions. [19] So Israel rebelled against the house of
David unto this day.—1 KINGS, ch. 12.

3669. —— **Support of.** *Tribute.* [17] Is it lawful to give tribute unto Cesar, or not ?.. [20] And
he saith.. Whose *is* this image and superscription ? [21] They say..Cesar's. Then saith he..
Render therefore unto Cesar the things which are
Cesar's.—MAT., ch. 22.

3670. —— **Vice endangers.** *Thessalonica.*
[5] The Jews..moved with envy, took unto them
certain lewd fellows of the baser sort, and gathered a company, and set all the city on an uproar, and assaulted the house of Jason.—ACTS,
ch. 17.

See other illustrations under :

ADMINISTRATION.
Change. There arose a king..knew not Joseph 99
Rejected. Now make us a king to judge us 100
   " Let us make a captain..return into E. 101

AUTHORITY.
Brother's. My brother..commanded me to be 584
Compared. Moses commanded..what sayest thou 585
False. I am a prophet..he lied 586
Obedience. All..we will do..will go 587
Power, I say unto one, Go, and he goeth 588
Questioned. By what authority doest thou these 589
Recognized. Winds and water..obey him 591
Supreme. Drove them out all of the temple 590

COMMANDMENT.
First. Thou shalt love the Lord 1391
Ignored. Nadab and Abihu..offered strange fire 1392
Nature. God said, Let there be light..was light 1393
New. Love one another 1394
Smallest. [So called] Bird's nest..not take dam 1395
Second. Love thy neighbour as thyself 1396
Kept. All these have I kept from my youth 1397
Test. We do know that we..love if we keep his 1398
Ten [Exodus 20 : 3-17.]
Use. Thy commandment is a lamp 1400

JUDGE.
Bribery. Samuel's sons..took bribes 4760
Circuit. Samuel went from year to year in circuit 4756
Qualifications. He that is without sin among you 4757
Unjust. Crucify him ; I find no fault in him 4758
Unrighteous. Ananias commanded to smite him 4759

LAW.
Appeal. Is it lawful..to scourge..a Roman ? 4900
Equality. Cut off..whether..a stranger or born 4901
   " Think not that thou shalt escape..more 4902
Evasion. To justify himself..who is my neighbour 4903
Indifference. Nadab and Abihu..offered strange 4904
of Love. First commandment..love the Lord 4905
Misapplied. By our law he ought to die..S. of G. 4906
Necessity. I will go..if I perish, I perish 4907
Protection. Said Paul, I stand at Cesar's 4908
Summary. Thou shalt love the L..do and live 4909
Superseded. Law..schoolmaster to bring us to C. 4910
Supremacy. Darius..set his heart on Daniel to 4911
Sumptuary. Fruit of the tree..ye shall not eat of it 4912
   " Blood..whosoever eateth of it..cut off 4913
   " Eat no manner of fat, of ox, or sheep 4914
   " Ye shall eat..parteth the hoof..cud 4915
Transgressors. Not made for a righteous man 4916
Unobserved. Pay tithe of mint..omitted the 4917
Unchangeable. Law of the Medes and Persians 4918

OFFICE.
Faithful. Because thou hast been faithful..ten 5851
Intrigue. Remember that I am your bone 5852
Merit. Faithful over a few things..ruler over 5853
Seeking. Oh that I were made a judge in the land 5855
Trials. Wherefore..made us to come up out of E.? 5856
Undesired. The fig tree said..should I forsake 5859

OFFICEHOLDER.
Blameless. Sought to find occasion against Daniel 5860
   " Of whose hand have I received any b. 5861
Dishonest. Not that Judas cared for the poor 5863
Prayer. I am but a little child, I know not 5862

OFFICERS.
Church. First apostles, secondarily prophets 5864
Qualifications. Look out seven men of honest r. 5865
   " Deacons must be grave..not greedy 5866
   " Bishop must be..not given to wine 5867
Responsibility. Because those..rejected thee 5868
   " Provide able men..of truth 5869
Selection. Over the king's treasures was Azmaveth 5870
Unconverted. Have any of the rulers..believed on 5871

RULER.
Born. Your sheaves made obeisance to my sheaf 7466
   " Potiphar..made him overseer..all that he 7467
   " Keeper of the prison committed to Joseph's 7468
   " [Enthroned.] Cried before him, Bow the knee 7469
Foolish. Cursed. that eateth..until evening 7470
Pious. Have kept commands from my youth up 7471
Ruled. Jezebel his wife said..Dost thou now 7472
Sinful. Ahab did sell himself to work wickedness 7473
   " As a roaring lion..is a wicked ruler 7474
Unjust. Feared not God, neither regarded man 7475

RULERS.
Guidance. Book..shall be with him..read 7476
Influence. Have any of the rulers..believed on 7477
Many. Besides the chief of Sol.'s officers..3300 7478
Qualifications. Provide able men..fear G..of truth 7479

SECESSION.
Political. I will chastise you with scorpions 7643
Predicted. If this city be builded..no portion on 7642

STATE.
Appeal. I refuse not to die..but I appeal to Cesar 8321
Endangered. [Ignorance] With Absalom went men 8322
   " [Vice] Jews took..lewd fellows 8323
Honours. Mordecai wrote..sealed with the king's 8324
   " Gave Daniel many great gifts..ruler over 8325
Majesty. Magistrates..feared when they heard 8326
Men. When Saul saw any strong man..took him 8327
Protection. Is it lawful..to scourge a..Roman 8328
Protector. Egypt was famished..Joseph opened 8329
Support. Is it lawful to give tribute unto Cesar ? 8330

STATESMANSHIP.
Evil. Jeroboam made priests of the lowest 8331
Poor. Rehoboam forsook the counsel of the old 8332

TREASON.
Justifiable. Athaliah rent her clothes, and cried 8902
Spiritual. Wherefore lift ye up yourselves above 8903
   " The earth opened..Korah..went down 8904

Assessment. Menahem gave Pul..1000 talents of 535
Changed. Ye said..a king..when the L..was your 4487
Demagogue. Oh that I were made a judge in the 6237
Failure. No power to him that went out, nor..came 144
Gracious. Shall Saul reign over I..not a man be 1108
Officiousness. Disciples rebuked them..Jesus 5872
Rebellion. [Seven days] Zimri hath conspired 6953
Support. Abimelech..gave him 70 pieces of silver 1601
Tyrannical. I will chastise you with scorpions 9048

3671. GRACE assimilative. *Leaven.* [See No. 3678.]

3672. —— **Advancement in.** *Child Jesus.* [52] Jesus increased in wisdom and stature, and in favour with God and man.—LUKE, ch. 2.

3673. —— **All of.** *Paul.* [9] I am the least of the apostles, that am not meet to be called an apostle, because I persecuted the church of God. [10] But by the grace of God I am what I am : and his grace which *was bestowed* upon me was not in vain.—1 COR., ch. 15.

3674. —— **accessible.** *Brazen Serpent.* [8] The Lord said unto Moses, Make thee a fiery serpent, and set it upon a pole : and..every one that is bitten, when he looketh upon it, shall live.—NUM., ch. 21.

3675. —— **better than Gifts.** *Apostles.* [19] I give unto you power to tread on serpents and scorpions, and over all the power of the enemy ; and nothing shall by any means hurt you. [20] Notwithstanding, in this rejoice not, that the spirits are subject unto you ; but rather rejoice, because your names are written in heaven.—LUKE, ch. 10.

3676. —— **Conquests of.** *Canaanites.* [22] Thy God will put out those nations before thee by little and little : thou mayest not consume them at once, lest the beasts of the field increase upon thee. [23] But the Lord thy God shall deliver them unto thee, and shall destroy them with a mighty destruction, until they be destroyed. —DEUT., ch. 7.

3677. —— **A Day of.** *Fig Tree.* [8] Let it alone this year also, till I shall dig about it, and dung *it :* [9] And if it bear fruit, *well :* and if not, *then* after that thou shalt cut it down.—LUKE, ch. 13.

3678. —— **Diffusive.** *Leaven.* [20] Whereunto shall I liken the kingdom of God ? [21] It is like leaven, which a woman took and hid in three measures of meal, till the whole was leavened.—LUKE, ch. 13.

3679. —— **Dishonoured.** *Corinthians.* [20] *This* is not to eat the Lord's supper. [21] For in eating every one taketh before *other* his own supper : and one is hungry, and another is drunken. [22] What ! have ye not houses to eat and to drink in ? or despise ye the church of God.—1 COR., ch. 11.

3680. —— **Free.** *Water.* [6] I will stand before thee there upon the rock in Horeb ; and thou shalt smite the rock, there shall come water out of it, that the people may drink. And Moses did so.—EX., ch. 17.

3681. —— **Growth in.** *Aaron's Rod.* [8] Moses went into the tabernacle..the rod of Aaron ..was budded, and brought forth buds, and bloomed blossoms, and yielded almonds.— NUM., ch. 17.

3682. —— **Invitation of.** *" Come."* [17] The Spirit and the bride say, Come. And let him that heareth say, Come. And let him that is athirst come. And whosoever will, let him take the water of life freely.—REV., ch. 22.

3683. —— **Indwelling.** *Well.* [13] Jesus.. said unto her, Whosoever drinketh of this water shall thirst again : [14] But whosoever drinketh of the water that I shall give him shall never thirst ; but..shall be in him a well of water springing up into everlasting life.—JOHN, ch. 4.

3684. —— **Means of.** *Pentecost.* [41] They that gladly received his word, were baptized.. there were added *unto them* about three thousand souls. [42] And they continued steadfastly in the apostles' doctrine and fellowship, and in breaking of bread, and in prayers.—ACTS, ch. 2.

3685. —— **Absence from.** [21] Then said Jesus to them again, Peace *be* unto you.. [24] But Thomas, one of the twelve, called Didymus, was not with them when Jesus came.—JOHN, ch. 20.

3686. —— **only.** *Unprofitable Servants.* [9] Doth he thank that servant because he did the things that were commanded him ? I trow not. [10] So likewise ye, when ye shall have done all those things which are commanded you, say, We are unprofitable servants : we have done that which was our duty to do.—LUKE, ch. 17.

3687. —— **Rewarded by.** *Parable.* [9] They came that *were hired* about the eleventh hour, they received every man a penny. [10] But when the first came, they supposed that they should have received more ; and they likewise received every man a penny.—MAT., ch. 20.

3688. —— **boldly sought.** *Paul.* [15] We have not a high priest which cannot be touched with the feeling of our infirmities ; but was in all points tempted like as *we are, yet* without sin. [16] Let us therefore come boldly unto the throne of grace, that we may obtain mercy, and find grace to help in time of need.—HEB., ch. 4.

3689. —— **transforms.** *Jacob.* [16] Jacob awaked out of his sleep, and he said, Surely the Lord is in this place ; and I knew *it* not. [17] And he was afraid, and said, How dreadful *is* this place ! this *is* none other but the house of God, and this *is* the gate of heaven.—GEN., ch. 28.

3690. —— **Test of.** *Naaman.* [10] Elisha sent a messenger..saying, Go and wash in Jordan seven times, and thy flesh shall come again to thee, and thou shalt be clean. [11] But Naaman was wroth.—2 KINGS, ch. 5.

3691. —— **Unfailing.** *Manna.* [35] Did eat manna forty years, until they came to a land inhabited..unto the borders of the land of Canaan.—EX., ch. 16.

3692. —— **for Work.** *Paul.* [10] But I laboured more abundantly than they all : yet not I, but the grace of God which was with me.—1 COR., ch. 15. [See No. 3673.]

See other illustrations under :
FAVOUR.

Evinced. Boaz commanded the young men, Let   3092
Indicated. The king held out to Esther the sceptre 3093
Resented. Jacob loved Joseph..coat of many   3008

No Changes. Not eloquent, neither heretofore nor   91
See GOODNESS and references.

3693. GRACES, Addition of. *Christian.* [5] Giving all diligence, add to your faith virtue ; and to virtue, knowledge ; [6] And to knowledge, temperance ; and to temperance, patience ; and to patience, godliness ; [7] And to godliness, brotherly kindness ; and to brotherly kindness, charity. [8] For if these things be in you, and abound.. ye *shall* neither *be* barren nor unfruitful in the knowledge of our Lord Jesus Christ.—2 PETER, ch. 1.

3694. GRATITUDE, Appeal to. *Jonathan.* [1] Saul spake to..all his servants, that they should kill David. [2] But Jonathan Saul's son delighted much in David: and Jonathan told David. [4] And Jonathan spake good of David unto Saul his father, and said.. [5] For he did put his life in his hand, and slew the Philistine, and the Lord wrought a great salvation for all Israel: thou sawest it, and didst rejoice: Wherefore then wilt thou sin against innocent blood, and slay David without a cause?—1 SAM., ch. 19.

3695. —— **for Deliverance.** *Undemonized.* [19] Go home to thy friends, and tell them how great things the Lord hath done for thee.. [20] And he departed, and began to publish in Decapolis how great things Jesus had done for him: and all men did marvel.—MARK, ch. 5.

3696. —— **Evidences of.** *Women.* [2] Certain women, which had been healed of evil spirits and infirmities, Mary called Magdalene, out of whom went seven devils, [3] And Joanna the wife of Chuza Herod's steward, and Susanna, and many others, which ministered unto him of their substance.—LUKE, ch. 8.

3697. —— **forgotten.** *Butler.* [9] Then spake the chief butler unto Pharaoh, saying, I do remember my faults this day.. [12]..there was there with us a young man, a Hebrew, servant to the captain of the guard..and he interpreted to us our dreams.—GEN., ch. 41.

3698. —— **Kindness inspires.** *David.* [6] David said, Mephibosheth.. [7]..Fear not: for I will surely shew thee kindness for Jonathan thy father's sake, and will restore thee all the land of Saul thy father; and thou shalt eat bread at my table continually.—2 SAM., ch. 9.

3699. —— **Office of.** *Joseph.* [13] Within three days shall Pharaoh..restore thee unto thy place; and thou shalt deliver Pharaoh's cup into his hand, after the former manner when thou wast his butler. [14] But think on me when it shall be well with thee..and make mention of me unto Pharaoh, and bring me out of this house. —GEN., ch. 40.

3700. —— **for Pardon.** *Woman.* [37] A woman in the city, which was a sinner..brought an alabaster box of ointment, [38] And stood at his feet behind him weeping, and began to wash his feet with tears, and did wipe them with the hairs of her head, and kissed his feet, and anointed them with the ointment.—LUKE, ch. 7.

3701. —— **Rare.** *Leper.* [12] Ten men that were lepers, which stood afar off: [13]..said, Jesus, Master, have mercy on us.. [17] And Jesus answering said, Were there not ten cleansed? but where are the nine? [18] There are not found that returned to give glory to God, save this stranger.—LUKE, ch. 17.

3702. —— **Unutterable.** *Lame Man.* [11] As the lame man which was healed held Peter and John, all the people ran together unto them in the porch that is called Solomon's, greatly wondering.—ACTS, ch. 3.

See other illustrations under:

THANKOFFERINGS.

Many. Solomon sacrificed sheep and oxen..not 8760
Valuable. All the gold of the offering..16,750 shek. 8761

THANKS.

Earnest. Fell..at his feet, giving him thanks 8762
Food. When he had given thanks, he distributed 8763
Maternal. [Hannah for a son—See 1 Sam., ch. 2]
Perilous. Daniel knew the writing was sealed 8766
Sincere. Paul took bread, and gave thanks to God 8764

3703. GRAVE, A chosen. *Jacob.* [29] I am to be gathered unto my people: bury me with my fathers in the cave that is in the field of Ephron the Hittite, [30]..in Machpelah.—GEN., ch. 49.

3704. —— **First Bargain for a.** *Abraham.* [8] Entreat for me to Ephron.. [9] That he may give me the cave of Machpelah..for as much money as it is worth..for a possession of a burying place amongst you.—GEN., ch. 23.

3705. —— **Longed for.** *Job.* [13] O that thou wouldest hide me in the grave, that thou wouldest keep me secret, until thy wrath be past, and thou wouldest appoint me a set time, and remember me!—JOB, ch. 14.

3706. —— **A perfumed.** *Asa's.* [14] They buried him in his own sepulchres, which he had made for himself in the city of David, and laid him in the bed which was filled with sweet odours and divers kinds of spices prepared by the apothecaries' art: and they made a very great burning for him.—2 CHRON., ch. 16.

See other illustrations under:

BURIAL.

Denied. Bring out the bones of the kings..spread 974
Life from. Touched the bones of Elisha, he revived 975
Living. Earth opened her mouth and swallowed 976
Mournful. David..lifted up his voice..grave of 977
Mysterious. Moses died..no man knoweth his 978
Patriarchs. All the servants of Pharaoh..elders 979

Desecrated. Spread the bones of the kings of J. 974

3707. GREATNESS, Ambition for. *Apostles.* [33] What was it that ye disputed among yourselves by the way? [34] But they held their peace ..they had disputed among themselves, who should be the greatest.—MARK, ch. 9.

3708. —— **in doing Good.** *Apostles.* [35] And he sat down, and called the twelve, and saith unto them, If any man desire to be first, the same shall be last of all, and servant of all.— MARK, ch. 9. [See No. 3707.]

3709. —— **Humility in.** *Childlike.* [4] Whosoever therefore shall humble himself as this little child, the same is greatest in the kingdom of heaven.—MAT., ch. 18.

3710. —— **Proof of.** *Power.* [17] Joshua spake unto..Ephraim and to Manasseh, saying, Thou art a great people, and hast great power: thou shalt not have one lot only: [18] But the mountain shall be thine; for it is a wood, and thou shalt cut it down..for thou shalt drive out the Canaanites, though they have iron chariots, and though they be strong.—JOSH., ch. 17.

3711. —— **by Service.** *Jesus.* [44] Whosoever of you will be the chiefest, shall be servant of all. [45] For even the Son of man came not to be ministered unto, but to minister, and to give his life a ransom for many.—MARK, ch. 10.

3712. —— **tarnished.** *Leper.* [1] Naaman, captain of the host of the king of Syria, was a great man with his master, and honourable, because by him the Lord had given deliverance unto Syria: he was also a mighty man in valour, but he was a leper.—2 KINGS, ch. 5.

See other illustrations under:

AMBITION.

Fatal. Ashael refused to turn aside..Abner smote 318
Hypocrites. Scribes..love greetings..highest seats 321
Impious. Diotrephes..loveth the pre-eminence 317

Promotion. Brought you near him..Seek..priest 326
Reproved. [Disciples] had disputed which..great 320
Unsatisfied. [Haman] No man come in with thee 332

FAME.

Increasing. His fame spread abroad..about 3000
Military. Uzziah made..engines..to shoot 3001
Troublesome. Blaze abroad the matter..desert 3002
Unexpected. In the whole world..woman hath 3003
Wisdom. All the earth sought to Solomon 3004

HONOUR.

Age. Jacob blessed Pharaoh 4058
Appeal. L. was not able to bring..into the land 4059
Dishonour. Haman arrayed Mordecai..and pro. 4060
Elders. Elihu had waited..were elder than he 4061
not Given. Not mine to give..for whom..prepared 4062
Given. Mephibosheth shall eat..as one..king's sons 4063
Protected. Wherefore should the Egyptians say 4064
Regarded. I was ashamed to require..soldiers 4065
Sale of. They covenanted with him..30 pieces 4066
Sudden. Pharaoh took off his ring..Joseph 4067
Seeking. How can ye believe which receive honour 4068
Service. Said unto the olive..Reign over us 4069
Special. Queen did let no man come..but myself 4070
Unexpected. Mordecai went out..in royal apparel 4071
Won. Abishai was chief of the three..300 slew them 4072

HONOURS.

Abroad. No prophet is accepted in his own 4073
Brave. King will enrich..give him his daughter 4074
Many. Haman told them of the glory 4075
Posthumous. Widows weeping..shewing..Dorcas 4076
Service. Made Saul king [Ammonites subdued] 4077
Trials. I am..weak, though anointed king 4078

MAJESTY.

Overcoming. I am he..they fell to the ground 5168
Royal. When the queen of Sheba had seen 5169
Terrific. Mount that burned..blackness 5170

vs. Goodness. David..not build..much blood 859

3713. GREED, Ministerial. *Eli's Sons.*
[12] *Were* sons of Belial ; they knew not the Lord.
[13] And the priest's custom.. *was, that,* when any
man offered sacrifice, the priest's servant came,
while the flesh was in seething, with a fleshhook
of three teeth.. [14] And he struck *it* into the pan,
or kettle..all that the fleshhook brought up the
priest took for himself.—1 SAM., ch. 2.

See other illustrations under :

AVARICE.

Falsehood. Ananias with Sapphira..kept back part 592
Oppression. Swallow up the needy..make the poor 593
Victim. Were glad..covenanted to give Judas m. 594

COVETOUSNESS.

Abhorred. Blesseth the covetous whom the L. 1786
Alarmed. By this craft..our wealth..confusion 1787
Apostle. Judas went..to give him money 1788
Aroused. Damsel..masters saw..gains were gone 1789
Absence of. Abram said, I will not take..thread 1790
Church. Who would shut the doors for naught 1791
Cruelty. Felix hoped that money..of Paul 1792
Caution. Inheritance..take heed. beware of 1793
Disobedience. I saw among the spoils..took them 1794
Forbidden. Thou shalt not covet thy neighbour's 1795
Fraud. Gehazi..I will run and take..silver 1796
Folly. Soul, thou hast much goods..eat, drink 1797
Falsehood. Ananias with Sapphira..kept back 1798
Freedom. I have coveted no man's silver..Paul 1799
Inconsiderate. Well watered..Lot chose..plain of 1800
Oppressive. Ye exact usury..sell your brethren 1801
Overcome by. Saul and the people spared the best 1802
Overreaching. Laban..changed my wages ten 1803

Stigmatized. If any man that is called a brother 1804
Shameless. Given to covetousness..not..ashamed 1805
Unhappiness. Naboth had a vineyard..Ahab 1806

SELFISHNESS.

Appeal. As long as [David] liveth, thou shalt not 7736
Ministerial. Thou shalt give it..I will take it by f. 7737
Misery. All this..nothing so long as I see Mordecai 7738
Overreaching. Do even so to Mordecai the Jew 7739
Outrageous. The rich man..took the poor man's 7740
Provision. Call not thy rich..lest they also bid thee 7741
Rebuked. But a certain Samaritan..had compas'on 7742
Revealed. Went away grieved..had great poss'ns 7743
Wealth. What shall I do..bestow my fruits?..my 7744

3714. GRIEF, An angry. *Jonathan.* [33] Jonathan knew that it was determined of his father
to slay David. [34] So Jonathan arose from the
table in fierce anger, and did eat no meat..for
he was grieved for David.—1 SAM., ch. 20.

3715. —— Abstinence in. *David.* [15] The
Lord struck the child that Uriah's wife bare..
and it was very sick. [16] David therefore besought God for the child ; and David fasted,
and went in, and lay all night upon the earth.
[17]..neither did he eat bread.—2 SAM., ch. 12.

3716. —— in Affliction. *Jairus.* [22] One of
the rulers of the synagogue, Jairus by name..
fell at his feet, [23] And besought him greatly,
saying, My little daughter lieth at the point of
death : *I pray thee,* come and lay thy hands on
her, that she may be healed.—MARK, ch. 5.

3717. —— Bitter. *Esau's.* [38] Hast thou but
one blessing, my father ? bless me, *even* me also,
O my father. And Esau lifted up his voice, and
wept.—GEN., ch. 27.

3718. —— of Bereavement. *Mary.* [31] Jews
then which were with her in the house, and
comforted her, when they saw Mary, that she
rose up hastily and went out, followed her, saying, She goeth unto the grave to weep there.—
JOHN, ch. 11.

3719. —— —— *Jesus.* [33] When Jesus therefore saw her weeping, and the Jews also weeping which came with her, he groaned in the
spirit, and was troubled.. [35] Jesus wept.—JOHN,
ch. 11.

3720. —— —— *David and People.* [11] Then
David took hold on his clothes, and rent them ;
and likewise all the men that *were* with him :
[12] And they mourned, and wept, and fasted until even, for Saul, and for Jonathan.—2 SAM.,
ch. 1.

3721. —— —— *Joseph.* [1] Joseph fell upon
his father's face, and wept upon him, and kissed
him. [2] And Joseph commanded the physicians
to embalm his father.—GEN., ch. 50.

3722. —— —— *Job.* [20] Then Job arose,
and rent his mantle, and shaved his head, and
fell down upon the ground, and worshipped.—
JOB, ch. 1.

3723. —— from Distrust. *Peter.* [17] Peter
was grieved because he said unto him the third
time, Lovest thou me ? And he said unto him,
Lord, thou knowest all things ; thou knowest
that I love thee.—JOHN, ch. 21.

3724. —— Divine. *Antediluvians.* [5] God
saw that the wickedness of man *was* great..and
that every imagination of the thoughts of his
heart *was* only evil continually. [6]..and it
grieved him at his heart.—GEN., ch. 6.

3725. —— **Effect of.** *David's.* ² The victory that day was *turned* into mourning..for the people heard say that day how the king was grieved for his son. ³ And the people gat them by stealth that day into the city, as people being ashamed steal away when they flee in battle. ⁴ But the king..cried with a loud voice, O my son Absalom! O Absalom, my son, my son!— 2 SAM., ch. 19.

3726. —— **Fraternal.** *Reuben.* ²⁹ Reuben returned..behold, Joseph *was* not in the pit ; and he rent his clothes. ³⁰ And he returned unto his brethren, and said, The child *is* not ; and I, whither shall I go?—GEN., ch. 37.

3727. —— **A Husband's.** *For Michal.* ¹⁵ And Ish-bosheth sent, and took her from *her* husband, *even* from Phaltiel.. ¹⁶ And her husband went with her along weeping behind her to Bahurim.—2 SAM., ch. 3. [She was David's wife by prior marriage.]

3728. —— **Irrational.** *Ziklag.* [Taken by Philistines.] ² *It was* burned with fire ; and their wives..sons..daughters, were taken captives. ⁴ Then David and the people that *were* with him lifted up their voice and wept, until they had no more power to weep.—1 SAM., ch. 30.

3729. —— **of Jealousy.** *Enemies'.* ¹⁰ When Sanballat..and Tobiah..heard *of it*, it grieved them exceedingly that there was come a man to seek the welfare of the children of Israel. ¹¹ So I came to Jerusalem.—NEH., ch. 2.

3730. —— **from Marriage.** *Rebekah.* ³⁴ Esau was forty years old when he took to wife Judith ..the Hittite, and Bashemath ..the Hittite : ³⁵ Which were a grief of mind unto Isaac and to Rebekah.—GEN., ch. 26.

3731. —— **Neglect in.** *Absalom against David.* ²⁴ Mephibosheth the son of Saul came down to meet the king, and had neither dressed his feet, nor trimmed his beard, nor washed his clothes, from the day the king departed until the day he came *again* in peace.—2 SAM., ch. 19.

3732. —— **Patriotic.** *Ezra.* ² They have taken of their daughters for themselves, and for their sons : so that the holy seed have mingled themselves with the people of *those* lands : yea, the hand of the princes and rulers hath been chief in this trespass. ³ And when I heard this thing, I rent my garment and my mantle, and plucked off the hair of my head and of my beard, and sat down astonied.—EZRA, ch. 9.

3733. —— **reproved.** *David's.* [See No. 3725.] ⁵ Joab..said, Thou hast shamed this day the faces of all thy servants, which this day have saved thy life, and the lives of thy sons..thy daughters.. ⁶..I perceive, that if Absalom had lived, and all we had died this day, then it had pleased thee well. ⁷ Now..speak comfortably unto thy servants : for I swear by the Lord, if thou go not forth, there will not tarry one with thee this night.—2 SAM., ch. 19.

3734. —— **Solicitous.** *Dumb Spirit.* ²⁰ They brought him unto him : and when he saw him, straightway the spirit tare him ; and he fell on the ground, and wallowed foaming. ²¹ And he asked his father, How long is it ago since this came unto him? And he said, Of a child. ²² And ofttimes it hath cast him into the fire, and into the waters, to destroy him : but if thou canst do

any thing, have compassion on us, and help us. —MARK, ch. 9.

3735. —— **Silence in.** *Job's Friends.* ¹² When they lifted up their eyes afar off, and knew him not, they lifted up their voice and wept ; and they rent every one his mantle, and sprinkled dust upon their heads toward heaven. ¹³ So they sat down with him upon the ground seven days and seven nights, and none spake a word unto him : for they saw that *his* grief was very great. —JOB, ch. 2.

3736. —— **Show of.** *Ashes.* ⁷ Smote Job with sore boils from the sole of his foot unto his crown. ⁸ And he took him a potsherd to scrape himself withal ; and he sat down among the ashes.—JOB, ch. 2.

3737. —— **Unutterable.** *Shunammite.* [Her child was dead.] ²⁷ When she came to the man of God to the hill, she caught him by the feet : but Gehazi came near to thrust her away. And the man of God said, Let her alone ; for her soul *is* vexed within her : and the Lord hath hid *it* from me, and hath not told me.—2 KINGS, ch. 4.

See other illustrations under:

Intense. David wept as he went..head covered 5607
Joy for. Touched the bier..gave him to his mother 5608
Last. Mourn at the last..hated instruction 5609
Time. [For Jacob] Great company..very sore 5610
Wicked. David..lifted up his voice and wept 5611

TEARS.

Affectionate. I wrote unto you with many tears 8620
Bereavement. Mary weeping..Jews weeping 8621
"　　　Where have ye laid him..how he 8622
Constant. Mine eye trickleth down..ceaseth not 8623
Desired. O that mine..eyes a fountain of tears 8624
Disregarded. Chasten thy son..not spare for his 8625
End of. God shall wipe away all tears 8626
Grateful. She hath washed my feet with tears 8627
Night. Water my couch with tears 8628
Precious. Put thou my tears into thy bottle 8629
Patriotic. Jesus beheld the city, and wept over it 8630
Power. The babe wept..she had compassion 8631
"　　Samson's wife wept before him 8632
Parting. Wept one with another..David exceeded 8633
Penitential. When Peter thought thereon, he wept 8634
Transient. Saul lifted up his voice and wept 8635

Overwhelming. Made mention..Eli fell..brake 149
See AFFLICTION, MOURNERS, SORROW, WEEPING.

3738. GROANS, God hears. *In Egypt.* [5] I have also heard the groaning of the children of Israel, whom the Egyptians keep in bondage ; and I have remembered my covenant.—Ex., ch. 6.

3739. GROWTH, A beautiful. *Garden.* [12] They shall come and sing in the height of Zion, and shall flow together to the goodness of the Lord, for wheat, and for wine, and for oil, and for the young of the flock and of the herd ; and their soul shall be as a watered garden ; and they shall not sorrow any more at all.—Jer., ch. 31.

3740. —— Continuous. *Old Age.* [12] The righteous shall flourish like the palm tree : he shall grow like a cedar in Lebanon. [13] Those that be planted in the house of the Lord shall flourish in the courts of our God. [14] They shall still bring forth fruit in old age.—Ps. 92.

3741. —— Christian. *Thessalonians.* [3] We are bound to thank God always for you, brethren, as it is meet, because that your faith groweth exceedingly, and the charity of every one of you all toward each other aboundeth.—2 Thess., ch. 1.

3742. —— Divine. *Child Jesus.* [52] Jesus increased in wisdom and stature, and in favour with God and man.—Luke, ch. 2.

3743. —— in Esteem. *Samuel.* [26] The child Samuel grew on, and was in favour both with the Lord, and also with men.—1 Sam., ch. 2.

3744. —— Fruit the End of. *Vine.* [2] Every branch in me that beareth not fruit he taketh away : and every *branch* that beareth fruit, he purgeth it, that it may bring forth more fruit.—John, ch. 15.

3745. —— in Grace. *Tree.* [3] He shall be like a tree planted by the rivers of water, that bringeth forth his fruit in his season : his leaf also shall not wither ; and whatsoever he doeth shall prosper.—Ps. 1.

3746. —— Imperceptible. *Corn.* [27] The seed should spring and grow up, he knoweth not how. [28] For the earth bringeth forth fruit of herself ; first the blade, than the ear, after that the full corn in the ear.—Mark, ch. 4.

3747. —— Inward. *Leaven.* [20] The kingdom of God ? [21] It is like leaven, which a woman took and hid in three measures of meal, till the whole was leavened.—Luke, ch. 13.

3748. —— Outward. *The Kingdom of Heaven.* [31] *It is* like a grain of mustard seed, which..is less than all the seeds that be in the earth : [32] But.. it groweth up, and becometh greater than all herbs, and shooteth out great branches ; so that the fowls of the air may lodge under the shadow of it.—Mark, ch. 4.

3749. —— toward Perfection. *Light.* [18] The path of the just *is* as the shining light, that shineth more and more unto the perfect day.—Prov., ch. 4.

3750. —— Stages of. *Blade—Ear—Corn.* [See No. 3746.]

3751. —— in Strength. *Clean Hands.* [9] The righteous also shall hold on his way, and he that hath clean hands shall be stronger and stronger.—Job, ch. 17.

3752. —— Spiritual. *John Baptist.* [80] The child grew, and waxed strong in spirit, and was in the deserts till the day of his shewing unto Israel.—Luke, ch. 1.

See other illustrations under :

IMPROVEMENT.

or Loss. Whosoever hath not [improved]..taken 4365
"　　Three years..seeking fruit..why c. 4366

INCREASE.

Miraculous. Blessed and brake the loaves..5000 4398
"　　Should I set this before a hundred 4399

PROGRESS.

Christian. Path of the just..shineth more and 6631
Hindered. L..took off their chariot wheels..drave 6632
Spiritual. See men as trees walking..clearly 6334
Time. When thou hearest a sound of a going in 6333

VEGETATION.

Beginning. G. said, Let the earth bring forth 9164
Development. First the blade, then the ear..corn 9165
Mystery. Seed should..grow..knowest not how 9166

3753. GRUDGES forbidden. *Jesus said,* [15] If thy brother shall trespass against thee, go and tell him his fault between thee and him alone : if he shall hear thee, thou hast gained thy brother. [16] But if he will not hear *thee, then* take with thee one or two more.. [17] And if he shall neglect to hear them, tell *it* unto the church.—Mat., ch. 18.

See HATRED and references.

3754. GUARD, A terrifying. *Cherubim.* [24] He drove out the man : and he placed at the east of the garden of Eden cherubim, and a flaming sword which turned every way, to keep the way of the tree of life.—Gen., ch. 3.

3755. GUARDIANS, Destructive. *Of Ahab's Children.* [6] He wrote a letter the second time to them, saying, If ye *be* mine..take ye the heads of the men your master's sons, and come to me to Jezreel by to morrow this time. Now the king's sons, *being* seventy persons, *were* with the great men of the city, which brought them up. [7] ..they took the king's sons, and slew seventy persons.—2 Kings, ch. 10.

See other illustrations under :

WATCHING.

Affectionate. Moses..sister stood afar off, to wit 9342
Constant. If the good man of the house had k. 9343

Dead. Rizpah..from the beginning of harvest till 9344
Failure. Disciples, and findeth them asleep 9345
Hinderances. Overcharged with surfeiting..cares 9346
Malicious. Watched him whether he would heal 9347
Prayer. When the fowls came..Abram drove them 9348
    " We made our prayer..and set a watch 9349
    " Anna..fastings and prayers night and day 9350
    " Jesus..continued all night in prayer to G. 9351
Vigilant. Watch..lest coming suddenly he find 9352
Watched. Compassed about..cloud of witnesses 9353
World's. Herod feared John..observed him 9854

WATCHFULNESS.

Lack. Foolish virgins..said, Give us of your oil 9855
Necessary. Be vigilant..the devil as a roaring lion 9856
Personal. Appointed watches..every one..against 9857
Rewarded. Blessed are those servants..shall find 9858
    See **PROTECTION.**

3756. GUESTS, Mercy's. *Poor.* [12] When thou makest a dinner or a supper, call not thy friends, nor thy brethren, neither thy kinsmen, nor *thy* rich neighbours ; lest they also bid thee again, and a recompense be made thee. [13] But when thou makest a feast, call the poor, the maimed, the lame, the blind : [14] And thou shalt be blessed. —LUKE, ch. 14.

See other illustrations under :

HOSPITALITY.

Christian. Paul entered..a certain man's house 4098
Dangerous. Come home with me, and eat..I may 4099
Forbidden. Diotrephes..forbiddeth them that 4100
Grateful. Mephibosheth shall eat at the king's 4101
Increase by. How shall I..before 100 men ? 4102
Joyful. Zaccheus..haste..received him joyfully 4103
Odious. Baser sort..assaulted the house of Jason 4104
Preservation. Tarry all night, and wash your feet 4105
of Poor. Widow did according to the saying of E. 4106
Pagan. Barbarous people..received us every one 4107
Refused. Samaritans did not receive him 4108
Repaid. Shunammite..make a little chamber 4109
Reward. Abraham ran to meet them 4110
Treacherous. Pharisee besought him to dine with 4111
Unjust. Rich man..took the poor man's lamb 4112
Urgent. Lot pressed them greatly..his house 4113
    " Urged him therefore, he lodged there again 4114
    " They constrained him..sat at meat 4115
Woman's. Lydia..come into my house..constrained 4116
Willing. Ungirded his camels..set meat before him 4117
Wanting. Simon, thou gavest me no water to wash 4118

3757. GUIDE, A divine. *Pillar.* [21] The Lord went before them by day in a pillar of a cloud, to lead them the way ; and by night in a pillar of fire, to give them light ; to go by day and night.—Ex., ch. 13.

3758. —— A human. *Eyes.* [Moses to Jethro.] [31] Leave us not, I pray thee ; forasmuch as thou knowest how we are to encamp in the wilderness, and thou mayest be to us instead of eyes.—NUM., ch. 10.

3759. —— necessary, A. *Spiritual.* [30] Understandest thou what thou readest ? [31] And he said, How can I, except some man should guide me ? And he desired Philip that he would come up and sit with him.—ACTS, ch. 8.

3760. GUIDES, Blind. *Pharisees.* [16] Woe unto you, *ye* blind guides ! which say, Whosoever shall swear by the temple, it is nothing ; but whosoever shall swear by the gold of the temple, he is a debtor. [17]..for whether is greater, the gold, or the temple that sanctifieth the gold ?— MAT., ch. 23.

3761. GUIDANCE, Divine. *Kine.* [10] Took two milch kine, and tied them to the cart, and shut up their calves at home : [11] And they laid the ark of the Lord upon the cart.. [12] And the kine took the straight way to the way of Beth-shemesh ..lowing as they went, and turned not aside *to* the right hand or *to* the left.—1 SAM., ch. 6.

3762. —— explained. *Circuitous.* [17] God led them not *through* the way of the land of the Philistines, although that *was* near : for God said, Lest peradventure the people repent when they see war, and they return to Egypt : [18] But ..*through* the way of the wilderness.—Ex., ch. 13.

3763. —— Gentle. *Eye.* [8] I will instruct thee and teach thee in the way which thou shalt go : I will guide thee with mine eye. [9] Be ye not as the horse, *or* as the mule, *which* have no understanding : whose mouth must be held in with bit and bridle.—Ps. 32.

3764. —— promised. *Solomon.* [5] Trust in the Lord with all thine heart ; and lean not unto thine own understanding. [6] In all thy ways acknowledge him, and he shall direct thy paths. —PROV., ch. 3.

3765. —— Waiting for. *Cloud.* [37] If the cloud were not taken up, then they journeyed not till the day that it was taken up.—Ex., ch. 40.

See other illustrations under :

FOLLOWING.

Deliverance. Peter followed him..angel departed 3274
Faithful. Elisha left the oxen and ran after Elijah 3275
Leader. Jonathan..his armourbearer slew after 3276
Multitude. Whom all the men of I. choose, his will 3277
Trembling. All the people did follow Saul with t. 3278
Unwilling. Who shall give us flesh to eat ?..in E. 3279

FOLLOWING JESUS.

Afar off. Peter followed afar off..warmed himself 3280
Delivered. He received his sight and followed J. 3281
Forsaking. Brought their ships to land..forsook all 3282
Fear. Jesus went before them..amazed..afraid 3283
a Word. Behold the Lamb of G..followed Jesus 3284
Willingly. Levi..arose and followed him 3285

LEADER.

Always. Jesus went before them..amazed 4914
Blind. Smote them with blindness..he led them 4920
Bold. Ehud made him a dagger..present unto 4921
Unwise. Jonathan heard not when his father 4922
Zion's. Congregation be not as sheep..no shepherd 4923

LEADERSHIP.

Failure. Went ill with Moses..spake unadvisedly 4924
Loved. Diotrephes, who loveth to have 4925
Trials. People chode with Moses..why have ye 4926
Rejected. Let us make a captain and return to E. 4927

3766. GUILT, Accumulated. *Jews.* [35] That upon you may come all the righteous blood shed upon the earth, from the blood of righteous Abel unto the blood of Zacharias..whom ye slew between the temple and the altar.—MAT., ch. 23.

3767. —— Cowardice of. *Garden.* [8] They heard the voice of the Lord God walking in the garden in the cool of the day : and Adam and his wife hid themselves from the presence of the Lord God amongst the trees of the garden. —GEN., ch. 3.

3768. —— Degrees in. *Debtors.* [41] There was a certain creditor, which had two debtors : the one owed five hundred pence, and the other fifty.

[42] And when they had nothing to pay he frankly forgave them both.—Luke, ch. 7.

3769. —— Panic from. *Egyptians.* [24] The Lord looked unto the host of the Egyptians through the pillar of fire and of the cloud, and troubled the host of the Egyptians, [25] And took off their chariot wheels, that they drave them heavily : so that the Egyptians said, Let us flee from the face of Israel.—Ex., ch. 14.

See other Illustrations under :

AWAKENING.

Conscience. John the B. was risen from the dead	595
Fear. Centurion..feared greatly..was the S. of G.	596
Great. Into the house..all the people..read	597
General. All Judea..Jerusalem..baptized	598
Sudden. Fell down..What must I do to be savèd?	599
Trouble. Troubled the Egyptians..Let us flee	600
Truth. Paul reasoned..Felix trembled	601
Unexpected. We are verily guilty..our brother	602

CONDEMNATION.

Cause of. If ye were blind, ye should have no sin	1475
Future. How..not having a wedding garment	1476
Innocent. Pilate saith, Crucify him..no fault	1477
Others. First cast out the beam..own eye	1478
Reason of. Because..not believed in the..Son of	1479
Reversed. I knew thee..hard man..cast ye	1480
Unjust. Wrath of Elihu against Job..justified	1481
Unconscious. David said..shall surely die..Thou	1482

CONVICTION.

Awakening. Made manifest by the light..Awake	1682
Deeds. By this I know thou art..man of God	1684
Examination. Searched the Scriptures..many b'd	1685
Heaven sent. Suddenly there shined a light	1686
Heartfelt. Pricked in their heart [Pentecost]	1687
Necessary. Sprung up..no deepness of earth	1688
Prayer. Make me to know my transgression	1689
Resisted. Miracles before them..believed not	1690
Rational. When he came to himself..I will arise	1691
Sensitive. David's heart smote him..Saul's skirt	1692
Smiting. David's heart smote him..numbered	1693
Sudden. People saw it..fell..L. he is God	1694
Speechless. Beholding the man..healed..say n.	1695
Truth. Josiah..heard..the brook of the..he rent	1696
Thorough. Digged deep..the foundation on a rock	1697
Transient. Centurion..earthquake..was the S. of	1698
Willing. Nathanael..Thou art the Son of God	1699

HARDNESS.

Adversity. In..his distress did Ahaz trespass more	3797
Heart. Looked..anger being grieved..hardness of	3798
Spiritual. We will certainly burn incense	3799

REMORSE.

Needful. People that came..smote their breasts	7067
Prevented. Lest swallowed up with overmuch sor.	7068
Treachery. Judas..went and hanged himself	7069

WICKEDNESS.

Climax. This is the heir ; let us kill him	9532
Delusive. Manasseh..dealt with familiar spirits	9533
Desperation. Pharaoh said, Get thee from me	9534
Depravity. Josiah brake down the houses..S.	9535
Exceeding. Ahab did more to provoke the L. than	9536
Flagrant. They beat one and killed another, and	9537
Heart. Evil man out of the evil treasure bringeth	9538
Natural. Every imagination..was only evil	9539
Paternal. Manasseh made his son pass through f.	9540
Royal. Manasseh reared up altars at Bethel..built	9541

Confessed. Cast the first stone..went out	1560
Cowardice. Adam and his wife hid themselves	3767
Reading. Baruch read the book..they were afraid	749
" Shaphan read it..king rent his clothes	752
" All the people went when they heard	763

See **CRIME, EVIDENCE, PUNISHMENT.**

3770. HABIT of Prayer. *Cornelius.* [2] *A* devout man, and one that feared God with all his house, which gave much alms to the people, and prayed to God always.—Acts, ch. 10.

**3771. —— —— ** *Daniel.* [10] When Daniel knew that the writing was signed, he went into his house ; and, his windows being open in his chamber toward Jerusalem, he kneeled upon his knees three times a day, and prayed, and gave thanks before his God, as he did aforetime.—Dan., ch. 6.

**3772. —— —— ** *David.* [16] As for me.. [17] Evening, and morning, and at noon, will I pray, and cry aloud : and he shall hear my voice.—Ps. 55.

3773. HABITS, Bondage to. *Bad.* [Like Egyptian bondage.] [14] They made their lives bitter with hard bondage, in mortar, and in brick, and in all manner of service in the field : all their service, wherein they made them serve, *was* with rigour.—Ex., ch. 1.

3774. —— differ. *Animals.* [20] Thou makest darkness, and it is night : wherein all the beasts of the forest do creep *forth.* [21] The young lions roar after their prey, and seek their meat from God. [22] The sun ariseth, they gather themselves together, and lay them down in their dens. [23] Man goeth forth unto his work and to his labour until the evening.—Ps. 104.

See other illustrations under :

CUSTOMS.

Attachment. Have heard him say..change the c.	1894
National. I. eat not of the sinew that shrank	1895
Observance. It must not be so done in one country	1896

3775. HAIL, Plague of. *Seventh.* [23] The Lord sent thunder and hail, and the fire ran along upon the ground.. [24]..and fire mingled with the hail, very grievous, such as there was none like it in all the land of Egypt since it became a nation. [25] And the hail smote..all that *was* in the field, both man and beast ; and..every herb of the field, and brake every tree.—Ex., ch. 9.

3776. HAIR, Appropriate. *Paul.* [14] Doth not even nature itself teach you, that, if a man have long hair, it is a shame unto him ? [15] But if a woman have long hair, it is a glory to her : for *her* hair is given her for a covering.—1 Cor., ch. 11.

3777. —— of Age. *Jacob.* [38] My son shall not go down with you ; for his brother is dead and he is left alone : if mischief befall him..then shall ye bring down my gray hairs with sorrow to the grave.—Gen., ch. 42.

3778. —— Loss of. *" Clean."* [40] The man whose hair is fallen off his head, he *is* bald ; *yet* is he clean.—Lev., ch. 13.

3779. —— Luxuriant. *Absalom's.* [26] It..at every year's end..he polled *it* ; because *the hair* was heavy on him, therefore he polled it, he weighed the hair of his head at two hundred shekels.—2 Sam., ch. 14.

3780. —— pulled. *Nehemiah.* [25] I contended with them, and cursed them, and smote certain of them, and plucked off their hair, and made them swear by God, *saying,* Ye shall not give your daughters unto their sons, nor take their daughters unto your sons, or for your yourselves.—Neh., ch. 13.

3781. HAND, Cure of the. *Withered.* [5] Stretch
forth thine hand. And he stretched it out : and
his hand was restored whole as the other. [6] And
the Pharisees went forth, and straightway took
counsel with the Herodians against him, how
they might destroy him.—MARK, ch. 3.

3782. —— Consecrated. *Blood.* [24] He brought
Aaron's sons, and Moses put of the blood upon
the tip of their right ear, and upon the thumbs
of their right hands, and upon the great toes of
their right feet.—LEV., ch. 8.

3783. —— A mysterious. *Belshazzar.* [4] They
drank wine, and praised the gods of gold, and
of silver, of brass, of iron, of wood, and of stone.
[5] In the same hour came forth fingers of a man's
hand, and wrote over against the candlestick
upon the plaster of the wall of the king's palace.
—DAN., ch. 5.

3784. HANDS, Equality in. *David's Soldiers.*
[2] *They were* armed with bows, and could use both
the right hand and the left in *hurling* stones and
shooting arrows out of a bow, *even* of Saul's
brethren of Benjamin.—1 CHRON., ch. 12.

3785. —— Laying on of. *Sick.* [40] When the
sun was setting, all they that had any sick with
divers diseases brought them unto him ; and he
laid his hands on every one of them, and healed
them.—LUKE, ch. 4.

3786. —— less than Heart. *Pharisees.* [5] Why
walk not thy disciples according to the tradition
of the elders, but eat bread with unwashen
hands ? [6] He answered..Well hath Esaias prophesied of you hypocrites, as it is written, This
people honoureth me with *their* lips, but their
heart is far from me.—MARK, ch. 7.

3787. HANGING deserved. *Haman.* [14] Then
said Zeresh his wife and all his friends..Let a
gallows be made of fifty cubits high, and to morrow speak thou unto the king that Mordecai
may be hanged thereon.. [10] So they hanged Haman on the gallows that he had prepared for
Mordecai. Then was the king's wrath pacified..
[14] And they hanged Haman's ten sons.—ESTHER,
chs. 5 and 7.

3788. HAPPINESS, Failure of. *"Many Sorrows."* [10] The love of money is the root of all
evil : which while some coveted after, they have
erred from the faith, and pierced themselves
through with many sorrows.—1 TIM., ch. 6.

3789. —— Possessors of. *"Blessed are."* [See
Sermon on the Mount, MAT. 5 : 1, 12.]

3790. —— of Pardon. *"Blessed."* [7] Blessed
are they whose iniquities are forgiven, and
whose sins are covered. [8] Blessed *is* the man to
whom the Lord will not impute sin.—ROM., ch.
4.

3791. —— postponed. *Rich Fool.* [See No.
3796.]

3792. —— present. *Earthly.* [18] *It is* good and
comely *for one* to eat and to drink, and to enjoy
the good of all his labour that he taketh under
the sun all the days of his life, which God giveth
him : for it *is* his portion.—ECCL., ch. 5.

3793. —— poisoned. *Pride..* [12] Haman said
..Esther the queen did let no man come in with
the king unto the banquet..but myself ; and to
morrow am I invited.. [13] Yet all this availeth
me nothing, so long as I see Mordecai the Jew
sitting at the king's gate.—ESTHER, ch. 5.

3794. —— Perfect. *Heaven.* [16] They shall
hunger no more, neither thirst any more ; neither shall the sun light on them, nor any heat.
[17] For the Lamb which is in the midst of the
throne shall feed them, and shall lead them unto living fountains of waters : and God shall
wipe away all tears from their eyes.—REV., ch. 7.

3795. —— Rule for. *Piety.* [10] He that will
love life, and see good days, let him refrain his
tongue from evil, and his lips that they speak
no guile : [11] Let him eschew evil, and do good ;
let him seek peace, and ensue it.—1 PETER, ch. 3.

3796. —— in Riches, No. *Rich Fool.* [17] What
shall I do, because I have no room where to bestow my fruits ? [18] ..I will pull down my barns,
and build greater.. [19] And I will say to my soul,
Soul, thou hast much goods laid up for many
years ; take thine ease, eat, drink, *and* be merry.
—LUKE, ch. 12.

Possessions. Esau said, I have enough, my brother 1649
Perfect. L. is my shepherd, I shall not want 1650
Riches. I will not take from a thread to a shoe-l. 1651

ENJOYMENT.

for Beauty. L. G. planted..every tree..pleasant to 2674
Prospective. I will pull down..I will say..be merry 2675

JOY.

Builders. Ancient men wept..many shouted 4732
Believers. Whom having not seen..joy unspeak'e 4733
Converts. Eat..with gladness of heart, praising G. 4734
Conscience. Our rejoicing..testimony of our c. 4735
Deliverance. Leaping up..leaping and praising 4736
Exuberant. Rejoice with me, I have found the 4737
Escape. Then was the king [Darius] exceeding 4738
Excitement. Rhoda..opened not the gate for g. 4739
Fear. Sore afraid..bring you good tidings..joy 4740
Giving. People rejoiced for that they offered 4741
Hellish. Were glad, and covenanted to give Judas 4742
Irrepressible. Should hold their peace, the stones 4743
Mother's. Mary kept all these things and pondered 4744
Overcoming. When Jacob saw the wagons..spirit 4745
Penitential. People wept..great mirth because 4746
Religious. David danced before the L., shouting 4747
Recovery. [At Samaria] Great joy in that city 4748
Success. [Walls erected] Joy of Jerusalem..afar 4749
Supreme. Not that the spirits are subject..names 4750
Song of. Hath put a new song in my mouth 4751
Weeping. Joseph could not refrain..wept aloud 4752
Want. Although the fig tree shall not blossom 4753
Worship. How amiable are thy tabernacles 4754

PLEASURE.

Business first. I will not eat..told mine errand 6206
Bitter. Benhadad was drinking himself drunk 6207
Brief. Eat..until it come out at your nostrils 6215
Deceptive. Jezebel said to Ahab, Arise, take 6223
End. Soul, thou hast much goods..eat, drink 6209
Expensive. He that loveth pleasure shall be a poor 6208
False. Forsaken..fountain..broken cisterns 6216
Ingrates. I will smite the king..pleased Absalom 6210
Moderation. Hast thou found honey?..vomit 6211
Rejected. King went to his palace..fasting 6219
Renounced. Moses choosing affliction..rather than 6218
Ruinous. Wasted his substance in riotous living 6220
Sin. They drank wine, and praised the gods 6221
"   The hatred wherewith he hated her was 6222
Temptation. The people sat down to eat..drink 6213
"   The tree..was pleasant to the eyes 6212
Unsatisfying. My heart, I will prove thee with 6214

REJOICING.

Communion. This poor man cried..O taste and 6968
Conversion. There was great joy in that city 6969
Converts. [Jailer] rejoiced believing in G. with 6971
"   I waited patiently..put a new song in 6972
"   The eunuch went on his way rejoicing 6973
Duty. Thou shalt rejoice in every good thing..G. 6974
Deliverance. I will sing unto the L...triumphed 6975
"   Jews had light, and gladness, and joy 6976
Great. At the descent of the mount of Olives 6978
Heavenly. Ransomed of the L...come to Z. with 6980
in Prison. At midnight Paul and Silas..sang praises 6981
in Persecutions. Rejoicing that they were counted 6982
Premature. [Amalekites] were eating and drink. 6983
in Reproach. Rejoice..and be exceeding glad 6985
in Tribulation. I am exceeding joyful in all our 6986
in Temptation. Count it all joy when ye fall into 6987
Victors. Praised their god..hearts were merry 6988

Merriment. As..he that singeth songs to a heavy 5378
Refreshment. Came to Elim..12..wells..70 palm 6939

3797. HARDNESS in Adversity. *Ahaz.* [22] In

the time of his distress did he trespass yet more against the Lord : this *is that* king Ahaz. [23] For he sacrificed unto the gods of Damascus, which smote him.—2 CHRON., ch. 28.

3798. —— **of Heart.** *Pharisees.* [2] They watched him, whether he would heal him on the sabbath day ; that they might accuse him.. [5] And when he had looked round about on them with anger, being grieved for the hardness of their hearts, he saith unto the man, Stretch forth thy hand..And his hand was restored.—MARK, ch. 3.

3799. —— **Spiritual.** *Jews in Egypt.* [17] We will certainly..burn incense unto the queen of heaven, and to pour out drink offerings unto her, as we have done, we, and our fathers..in the streets of Jerusalem : for *then* had we plenty of victuals, and were well, and saw no evil.—JER., ch. 44.

<small>See other illustrations under :</small>

HARDNESS.

Adversity. In his distress did Ahaz trespass more 3797
Heart. Looked..anger being grieved..hardness of 3798
Spiritual. We will certainly burn incense 3799

HATRED.

Brother. If..say, I love God and hateth..is a liar 3828
Bitter. Brother shall betray brother..to death 3829
Commendable. Thou hatest the deeds of the 3830
Changed. Ready to die..for the L. Jesus 3831
Darkness. He that hateth his brother walketh 3832
Divine. Six things doth the L. hate 3833
Evil. Better is a dinner of herbs where love is 3834
Good. [Joseph's] brethren hated him..not speak 3835
Light. Every one that doeth evil hateth the light 3836
Manifested. When the days of mourning ended 3838
Silent. Absalom spake unto..Amnon..good nor 3840
Sinner's. Micaiah..I hate..doth not prophesy 3841
World. If the world hate you..it hated me before 3842

IMPENITENCE.

Affliction. Ahaziah said..Go inquire of Baal-zebub 4347
Hardened. Thou shalt die..He sent to arrest 4348

INGRATITUDE.

Beneficiaries. Ten cleansed? Where are the nine? 4485
Confessed. What hath been done to Mordecai? 4486
Deliverance. Ye said..a king, when the L...was 4487
Royal. Some bade me kill thee..mine eye spared 4488
Vengeance. When he died, he said, L. look upon it 4480

OBDURACY.

Defiant. Who is the L...let I. go 5755
Final. Pharaoh made ready his chariot..people 5756
Foolish. Ahaz in..distress did trespass more and 5757
Jewish. Thy neck is as an iron sinew..brow brass 5758
Spiritual. If the mighty works..been done in Tyre 5759
Self-destructive. I know G. hath determined to 5760
Truth. Divers were hardened..spake evil 5761

OBSTINACY.

Provoking. The L. said..it is a stiffnecked people 5825
Rebuked. I..withstand thee..thy way is perverse 5826
Rebellious. People refused the voice of the 5827

SELF-WILL.

Destructive. O Jerusalem, thou..ye would not 7731
Loss by. They presumed to go..smote them 7732
the Sacrifice. To obey is better than sacrifice 7734
Work. Simeon and Levi..self-will digged down 7735

STUBBORNNESS.

Punished. They mocked the messengers 8393
Sin. To obey is better than sacrifice 8394
"   We will certainly..burn incense 8395
"   Took Dagon and set him in his place again 8396

3800. HARDSHIPS, Increase of. *"No straw."*
[10] Thus saith Pharaoh, I will not give you straw.
[11] Go ye, get you straw where ye can find it : yet not aught of your work shall be diminished.
—Ex., ch. 5.

See other illustrations under :
TRIBULATION.
Despair. Who shall be able to stand?	8946
Judgment. Sun..as sackcloth..stars fell..moved	8947
Joy in. I am exceeding joyful in all our t.	8948
Recompensed. White robes..out of great	8949

See **ADVERSITY** and **TRIAL.**

3801. HARLET described. *"Impudent face."*
[11] She *is* loud and stubborn ; her feet abide not in her house : [12] Now *is she* without, now in the streets, and lieth in wait at every corner. [14] *I have* peace offerings with me.—Prov., ch. 7.

3802. —— Peril of. *Hell.* [26] For she hath cast down many wounded : yea, many strong *men* have been slain by her. [27] Her house *is* the way to hell, going down to the chambers of death.—Prov., ch. 7.

See other illustrations under :
ADULTERY.
Accusation. After this manner did Joseph	109
" Ishbosheth to Abner, My father's con.	110
Concealment. No eye shall see me	111
Divorce. Whosoever shall put away his wife	112
Destructive. Can a man take fire in his bosom	113
Incipient. Whosoever looketh on a woman	114

ADULTERESS.
Arts. She caught him and kissed him	115
Destructive. Her house inclineth unto death	116
Deception. Lips..drop as a honeycomb	117
Pardoned. Neither do I condemn thee	118

3803. HARVEST, Abundant. *Egypt.* [48] He gathered up all the food of the seven years..and laid up the food in the cities..[49] And Joseph gathered corn as the sand of the sea, very much, until he left numbering ; for *it was* without number.—Gen., ch. 41.

3804. —— Firstfruits of. *For God.* [10] When ye be come into the land..and shall reap the harvest thereof, then ye shall bring a sheaf of the firstfruits of your harvest unto the priest : [11] And he shall wave the sheaf before the Lord, to be accepted for you.—Lev., ch. 23.

3805. —— The Great. *End of the World.* [37] He that soweth the good seed is the Son of man ; [38] The field is the world ; the good seed are the children of the kingdom ; but the tares are the children of the wicked *one ;* [39] The enemy that sowed them is the devil ; the harvest is the end of the world ; and the reapers are the angels.—Mat., ch. 13.

3806. —— Gleaning in. *Ruth.* [8] Said Boaz.. Hearest thou not, my daughter ? Go not to glean in another field, neither go from hence, but abide here fast by my maidens.—Ruth, ch. 2.

3807. —— Prayer in. *Spiritual.* [37] The harvest truly *is* plenteous, but the labourers *are* few ; [38] Pray ye therefore the Lord of the harvest, that he will send forth labourers into his harvest.—Mat., ch. 9.

3808. —— Promise of. *Ever.* [21] Neither will I again smite any more every thing living, as I have done. [22] While the earth remaineth, seed-time and harvest, and cold and heat, and summer and winter, and day and night shall not cease.—Gen., ch. 8.

3809. —— The Poor Man's. *Gleanings.* [22] When ye reap the harvest of your land, thou shalt not make clean riddance of the corners of thy field when thou reapest, neither shalt thou gather any gleaning of thy harvest : thou shalt leave them unto the poor, and to the stranger.—Lev., ch. 23.

3810. —— Sowing for. *Grain.* [24] Doth the ploughman plough all day to sow? doth he open and break the clods of his ground ? [25] When he hath made plain the face thereof, doth he not cast abroad the fitches, and scatter the cummin, and cast in the principal wheat and the appointed barley and the rye in their place ?—Isa., ch. 28.

3811. —— Secret of the. *Measure.* [6] He which soweth sparingly shall reap also sparingly ; and he which soweth bountifully shall reap also bountifully.—2 Cor., ch. 9.

3812. HARVEST-TIME, Spiritual. *Now.* [35] Say not ye, There are yet four months, and *then* cometh harvest?..Lift up your eyes, and look on the fields ; for they are white already to harvest. [36] And he that reapeth receiveth wages, and gathereth fruit unto life eternal : that both he that soweth and he that reapeth may rejoice together.—John, ch. 4.

See other illustrations under :
FRUIT.
Commends. The man's rod that I shall choose	3469
Expected. Sent his servants..might receive	3470
God gives. Tabernacle..rod of Aaron..yielded	3471
Lack. Saw a fig tree..nothing but leaves	3473
Object. If it bear fruit well..if not..cut it down	3476
Preserved. In making war..not destroy the trees	3481
Repentance. Bringeth not..good fruit..cast..fire	3479
Sign. Figs ; the good figs very good..bad, very	3478

FRUITFULNESS.
Christian. L. shall make thee..well watered gar.	3482
Indispensable. Every branch that beareth not f.	3483
Means of. If these be in you and abound	3484
Source. Abideth in me..bringeth forth much f.	3485
Varied. Some thirtyfold, some 60, and some	3486

3813. HASTE, Attack in. *Counselled.* [1] Ahithophel said unto Absalom, Let me now choose out twelve thousand men, and I will arise and pursue after David this night : [2]..While he *is* weary and weak handed, and will make him afraid.—2 Sam., ch. 17.

3814. —— Anxious. *Darius.* [18] His sleep went from him. [19] Then the king arose very early in the morning, and went in haste unto the den of lions. [20] And when he came to the den, he cried with a lamentable voice unto Daniel.—Dan., ch. 6.

3815. —— in Alarm. *Mary.* [1] Cometh Mary Magdalene early, when it was yet dark, unto the sepulchre, and seeth the stone taken away from the sepulchre. [2] Then she runneth, and cometh to Simon Peter, and to the other disciple.—John, ch. 20.

3816. —— A careful. *Passover.* [11] Thus shall ye eat it ; *with* your loins girded, your shoes on your feet, and your staff in your hand : and ye shall eat it in haste ; it *is* the Lord's passover. [12] For I will pass through the land of Egypt this night, and will smite all the firstborn..both man and beast.—Ex., ch. 12.

3817. —— **Departure in.** *Israelites.* 33 The Egyptians were urgent upon the people, that they might send them out of the land in haste ; for they said, We be all dead men.—Ex., ch. 12.

3818. —— **Escape in.** *Destruction.* 16 Then let them which be in Judea flee into the mountains : 17 Let him which is on the housetop not come down to take any thing out of his house : 18 Neither let him which is in the field return back to take his clothes.—Mat., ch. 24.

3819. —— **for Help.** *Shunammite.* 24 She saddled an ass, and said to her servant, Drive, and go forward ; slack not thy riding for me, except I bid thee.—2 Kings, ch. 4. [Elisha restored her child.]

3820. —— **Joyful.** *From a Tree.* 5 Jesus.. looked up, and saw him, and said..Zaccheus, make haste, and come down ; for to day I must abide at thy house. 6 And he made haste, and came down, and received him joyfully.—Luke, ch. 19.

3821. —— —— *Manoah's Wife.* 9 The angel of God came again unto the woman as she sat in the field : but Manoah her husband was not with her. 10 And the woman made haste, and ran, and shewed her husband, and said..Behold, the man hath appeared unto me.—Judges, ch. 13.

3822. —— **to Jesus.** *Peter.* 7 That disciple whom Jesus loved saith unto Peter, It is the Lord. Now when Simon Peter heard that it was the Lord, he girt his fisher's coat unto him, (for he was naked,) and did cast himself into the sea.—John, ch. 21.

3823. —— **for Riches.** *Proverb.* 20 He that maketh haste to be rich shall not be innocent.. 22 He that hasteth to be rich hath an evil eye, and considereth not that poverty shall come upon him.—Prov., ch. 28.

3824. —— **A strange.** *Syrians.* [Four lepers approached them.] 6 The kings of the Egyptians..come upon us. 7 Wherefore they arose and fled in the twilight, and left their tents, and their horses, and their asses, even the camp as it was, and fled for their life.—2 Kings, ch. 7.

3825. —— **A stealthy.** *Jacob.* 20 Jacob stole away unawares to Laban the Syrian, in that he told him not that he fled.—Gen., ch. 31.

3826. —— **to Save.** *Plague.* 46 Take a censer, and put fire therein from off the altar, and put on incense, and go quickly unto the congregation, and make an atonement for them : for there is wrath gone out from the Lord ; the plague is begun. 47 And Aaron..ran into the midst of the congregation.—Num., ch. 16.

3827. —— **to be Saved.** *Lot.* 17 When they had brought them forth abroad..he said, Es cape for thy life ; look not behind thee, neither stay thou in all the plain ; escape to the mountain, lest thou be consumed.—Gen., ch. 19.

See other illustrations under :
Driving. The driving is like the driving of Jehu 2517
Hearers. Ran afoot thither out of all cities 9975
Running. Asahel was as light of foot as a wild roe 7482
Revival. Hezekiah rejoiced..thing was done sud. 10016

3828. HATRED of a Brother. *Unchristian.* 20 If a man say, I love God, and hateth his brother, he is a liar : for he that loveth not his

brother whom he hath seen, how can he love God whom he hath not seen ?— 1 John, ch. 4.

3829. —— **Bitter.** *Religious.* 12 The brother shall betray the brother to death, and the father the son ; and children shall rise up against their parents, and shall cause them to be put to death. 13 And ye shall be hated of all men for my name's sake.—Mark, ch. 13.

3830. —— **A commendable.** *Ephesians.* 4 Nevertheless I have somewhat against thee, because thou hast left thy first love. 5..repent, and do the first works ; or else I..will remove thy candlestick.. 6 But this thou hast, that thou hatest the deeds of the Nicolaitans, which I also hate.—Rev. ch. 2.

3831. —— **changed.** *Saul the Persecutor.* 13 Paul answered, What mean ye to weep and to break mine heart ? for I am ready not to be bound only, but also to die at Jerusalem for the name of the Lord Jesus.—Acts, ch. 21.

3832. —— **brings Darkness.** *Spiritual.* 9 He that saith he is in the light, and hateth his brother, is in darkness even until now.—1 John, ch. 2.

3833. —— **Divine.** *Seven Things.* 16 These six things doth the Lord hate ; yea, seven are an abomination unto him : 17 A proud look, a lying tongue, and hands that shed innocent blood, 18 A heart that deviseth wicked imaginations, feet that be swift in running to mischief, 19 A false witness that speaketh lies, and he that soweth discord among brethren.—Prov., ch. 6.

3834. —— **Evil of.** *Proverb.* 17 Better is a dinner of herbs where love is, than a stalled ox and hatred therewith.—Prov., ch. 15.

3835. —— **of the Good.** *Joseph.* 3 Israel loved Joseph more than all his children, because he was the son of his old age : and he made him a coat of many colours. 4 And when his brethren saw that their father loved him more..they hated him, and could not speak peaceably unto him.—Gen., ch. 37.

3836. —— **of Light.** *Evil - doer's.* 20 For every one that doeth evil hateth the light, neither cometh to the light, lest his deeds should be reproved. 21 But he that doeth truth cometh to the light, that his deeds may be made manifest, that they are wrought in God. —John, ch. 3.

3837. —— **Manifested.** *Dust.* 13 As David and his men went by the way, Shimei went along on the hill's side over against him, and cursed as he went, and threw stones at him, and cast dust.—2 Sam., ch. 16.

3838. —— **Merited.** *Esau's.* 41 Esau hated Jacob because of the blessing wherewith his father blessed him : and Esau said in his heart, The days of mourning for my father are at hand ; then will I slay my brother Jacob.—Gen., ch. 27.

3839. —— **Proud.** *Haman.* 5 When Haman saw that Mordecai bowed not, nor did him reverence, then was Haman full of wrath. 6 And he thought scorn to lay hands on Mordecai alone..sought to destroy all the Jews that were throughout the whole kingdom—Esther, ch. 3.

3840. —— **Silent.** *Absalom.* 22 Absalom spake unto his brother Amnon neither good nor bad : for Absalom hated Amnon, because he had forced his sister Tamar.—2 Sam., ch. 13.

3841. —— Sinner's. *Ahab.* ⁸ The king of
Israel said unto Jehoshaphat, *There is* yet one
man, Micaiah..by whom we may inquire of the
Lord : but I hate him ; for he doth not prophesy
good concerning me, but evil.—1 KINGS, ch. 22.

3842. —— by the World. *Disciples.* ¹⁸ If the
world hate you, ye know that it hated me before *it hated* you. ¹⁹ If ye were of the world,
the world would love his own ; but because ye
are not of the world, but I have chosen you out
of the world, therefore the world hateth you.—
JOHN, ch. 15.

3843. —— Watchful. *Herodias.* ¹⁸ John
had said unto Herod, It is not lawful for thee
to have thy brother's wife. ¹⁹ Therefore Herodias had a quarrel against him, and would
have killed him ; but she could not.—MARK,
ch. 6.

See other illustrations under :

ENEMY.

Aggressive. Saul breathing out threatening	2643
Conquered. [King] Saul wept..rewarded me good	2644
Disarmed. [Benaiah] plucked the spear out of the	2645
Great. Men slept, his enemy sowed tares..wheat	2646
Jealous. Saul became David's enemy continually	2647
Routed. [Lepers] Camp of the Syrians..no man	2648
Suspected. It is false ; I fall not to the Chaldeans	2649
Spared. David..thou mayest do to him..skirt	2650
Weapons. Egyptians fled..L. overthrew	2651

ENEMIES.

Artful. Sent forth spies..feign themselves just	2652
Cross. Enemies of the cross..end is destruction	2653
Contempt. Laughed us to scorn..Will ye rebel ?	2654
Disappointed. Our enemies were much cast down	2655
Dependence. No smith..lest the Hebrews make	2656
Favours. Enemy hunger, give him bread..coals	2657
Gospel. Perilous times shall come..covetous	2658
Help. We have sinned..deliver us only..this day	2659
Hidden. Adversaries said, They shall not know	2660
Intrigue. Hired counsellors..to frustrate their	2661
Kindness. Wouldest thou smite those..taken	2662
Malicious. Diotrephes..prating against us with	2663
Prayer. Make haste, O God, to help me [David]	2664
Successful. Made them to cease by force..work	2665
Sensitive. Children crying in the temple..sore	2666
Thwarted. Let the work alone..be not hindered	2667
Treatment. Love your enemies, bless them that	2668
Unequal. Judah..could not drive out	2669
Vexation. Grieved them exceedingly..seek the w.	2670

ENMITY.

Contemptuous. Not have this man to reign over us	2676
Undying. Seed..shall bruise thy head..his heel	2677

FIGHTING.

Forbidden. Ye shall not fight your brethren..I.	3217
God. Mountain was full of chariots..fire	3218
for Jesus. Drew his sword, and struck a servant	3219

QUARREL.

Conjugal. It is better to dwell in a corner..woman	6828
Domestic. Sarah saw the son of Hagar mocking	6818
Destructive. Children of Ammon and Moab..slew	6819
Foolish. Wherefore didst thou not call us ?	6820
Famished. What aileth thee?..hid her son	6821
Meddler. Who made thee a..judge over us ?	6822
" Is like one that taketh a dog by the ears	6823
Matrimonial. Against Moses, because of the	6824
Overruled. Angel of G. called Hagar..lift up the	6825
Test. Say now Shibboleth, and he said, Sibboleth	6826
War from. We have no part in David..To your t.	6827

RETALIATION.

Cowardly. Joab took Abner aside..smote him	7289
Disallowed. Been said, An eye for an eye	7290
Jewish. Life shall go for life, eye for eye	7291

REVENGE.

Avoided. Flee thou to Laban..brother's fury turn	7304
Brother's. When I say, Smite Amnon, then kill	7305
" Joab smote Abner..for the blood of	7306
Best. If thine enemy be hungry, give him bread	7307
Frustrated. Haman was come..Hang Mordecai	7308
Ignored. Spake against Moses..M. cried unto the	7309
" Shall not Shimei be put to death?	7310
Justifiable. Philistines burnt her..S. smote them	7311
Nursed. Absalom spake neither good nor bad	7312
Proposed. Then will I slay my brother Jacob	7313
Price. That they may be destroyed..I will pay	7314
Prayer. O L. G. strengthen me..avenged of the P.	7315

STRIFE.

Avoided. Go from us..mightier than we..Isaac	8378
Absence of. Isaac removed..and digged another	8379
Beginning. As when one letteth out water	8380
Cause of. As coals are..so is a contentious man	8381

VENGEANCE.

Averted. Let not my lord regard..Nabal	9169
" Kept me..from coming to shed blood	9170
Blood. Cain said..every one that findeth me..stay	9171
Call. Stoned [Zachariah]..in house of the L.	9172
Divine. To me belongeth vengeance and r.	9173
" If I whet my glittering sword	9174
Declined. Not a man be put to death [Saul]	9175
Fear. Joseph will peradventure hate us	9176
with God. My G., think thou upon Tobiah	9177
Inappropriate. I forgave thee..shouldst thou not	9178
Mistaken. Command fire..to consume them	9179
Monstrous. Haman thought scorn..Mordecai	9180
Prohibited. If ye from your hearts forgive not	9182
for Vengeance. David commanded..slew them	9184
Undesired. Behold the head of Ishbosheth	9183

Displeasure. I hate your feast days..let judgment	2411
Enmity. Citizens hated him..will not have..reign	2676
Estrangement. Younger son..journey into a far	2725
See ANGER.	

3844. HAUGHTINESS, Cruel. *Haman.* ⁵ Saw
that Mordecai bowed not, nor did him reverence,
then was Haman full of wrath. ⁶ And he thought
scorn to lay hands on Mordecai alone..sought
to destroy all the Jews.—ESTHER, ch. 3.

3845. —— humbled. *Zion.* ¹⁶ Because the
daughters of Zion are haughty, and walk with
stretched forth necks and wanton eyes, walking
and mincing *as* they go, and making a tinkling
with their feet : ¹⁷ Therefore the Lord will smite
with a scab the crown of the head.. ²⁴..instead
of sweet smell there shall be stink ; and instead of a girdle a rent ; and instead of well set
hair baldness ; and instead of a stomacher a
girding of sackcloth ; *and* burning instead of
beauty.—ISA., ch. 3.

See other illustrations under :

BOASTING.

Glorious. Are they Hebrews? So am I	869
Inoffensive. Our boasting..is found a truth	870
Prayer. I am not as other men..I..I	871
Prevented. With these are too many..vaunt	872
Rebuked. I will lay down my life..deny me	873

Bravado. I will give thy flesh unto the fowls	920
See PRIDE and references.	

3846. HEALER, The great. *Jesus.* [40] Now when the sun was setting, all they that had any sick with divers diseases brought them unto him ; and he laid his hands on every one of them, and healed them.—LUKE, ch. 4.

3847. HEALTH, Care for. *Shipwrecked.* [33] This day is the fourteenth day that ye have tarried and continued fasting, having taken nothing. [34] Wherefore I pray you to take *some* meat ; for this is for your health.—ACTS, ch. 27.

3848. —— Temperance promotes. *Rechabites.* [1] Jonadab the son of Rechab our father commanded us, saying, Ye shall drink no wine, *neither* ye, nor your sons for ever : that ye may live many days.—JER., ch. 35.

3849. —— diet. *Young Hebrews.* [15] At the end of ten days their countenances appeared fairer and fatter in flesh than all the children which did eat the portion of the king's meat. [16] Thus Melzar took away. . their meat, and the wine. . and gave them pulse.—DAN., ch. 1.

See other illustrations under :

CURE.

All Persons. Laid his hands on every one and heal 1867
All Diseases. Stepped in, was made whole of what 1868
Faith. When. . beheld the serpent of brass, he lived 1869
Gratitude. She arose, and ministered unto them 1870
Means. Made clay of the spittle. . anointed eyes 1871
Progressive. See men as trees walking. . clearly 1872
Threefold. Possessed with a devil, blind and dumb 1873
Wonderful. Stretch forth thy hand. . as the other 1874

REMEDY.

Improbable. Anointed the eyes of the blind man 7058
Look. As Moses lifted up the serpent. . S. of man 7059
See AFFLICTION and DISEASE.

3850. HEART, Altar of the. *Fire.* [12] The fire upon the altar shall be burning in it ; it shall not be put out : and the priest shall burn wood on it every morning, and lay the burnt offering in order upon it.—LEV., ch. 6.

3851. —— a Book, The. *Epistles.* [3] Ye are manifestly declared to be the epistle of Christ ministered by us, written not with ink, but with the Spirit of the living God ; not in tables of stone, but in fleshy tables of the heart.—2 COR., ch. 3.

3852. —— in Bereavement. *Cry of.* [One dead in every house.] [33] The Egyptians were urgent. . that they might send them out of the land in haste ; for they said, We *be* all dead men.—EX., ch. 12.

3853. —— Change of. *Saul.* [9] When he had turned his back to go from Samuel, God gave him another heart. . [10] And when they came thither to the hill, behold, a company of prophets met him ; and the Spirit of God came upon him, and he prophesied among them.—1 SAM., ch. 10.

3854. —— Chosen by the. *David.* [7] The Lord said unto Samuel, Look not on his countenance, or on the height of his stature ; because I have refused him : for *the Lord seeth* not as man seeth ; for man looketh on the outward appearance, but the Lord looketh on the heart. [Eliab was passed by and David chosen.]—1 SAM., ch. 16.

3855. —— to be cleansed. *Platter.* [29] Now do ye Pharisees make clean the outside of the cup and the platter ; but your inward part is full of ravening and wickedness.—LUKE, ch. 11.

3856. —— Convicting. *David's.* [5] David's heart smote him, because he had cut off Saul's skirt. [6] And he said unto his men, The Lord forbid that I should do this thing unto my master, the Lord's anointed, to stretch forth mine hand against him.—1 SAM., ch. 24.

3857. —— Controlling. *Keep Words.* [23] If a man love me, he will keep my words : and my Father will love him, and we will come unto him, and make our abode with him.—JOHN, ch. 14.

3858. —— Deceitfulness of. *Ruler.* [20] Master, all these have I observed from my youth. [21] Then Jesus. . loved him, and said. . One thing thou lackest : go thy way, sell whatsoever thou hast, and give to the poor. . and come, take up the cross, and follow me. [22] And he was sad at that saying, and went away grieved : for he had great possessions.—MARK, ch. 10.

3859. —— Deception of the. *Solomon says,* [26] He that trusteth in his own heart is a fool : but whoso walketh wisely, he shall be delivered.—PROV., ch. 28.

3860. —— Divided. *"Looking Back."* [61] Lord, I will follow thee ; but let me first go bid them farewell, which are at home at my house. [62] And Jesus said. . No man, having put his hand to the plough, and looking back, is fit for the kingdom of God.—LUKE, ch. 9.

3861. —— Evil. *From Youth.* [21] And the Lord smelled a sweet savour ; and the Lord said in his heart, I will not again curse the ground any more for man's sake ; for the imagination of man's heart *is* evil from his youth : neither will I again smite any more every thing living, as I have done.—GEN., ch. 8.

3862. —— —— Fountain. [21] From within, out of the heart of men, proceed evil thoughts, adulteries, fornications, murders, [22] Thefts, covetousness, wickedness, deceit, lasciviousness, an evil eye, blasphemy, pride, foolishness.—MARK, ch. 7.

3863. —— Hardness of. *Spies.* [2] They watched him, whether he would heal him on the sabbath day ; that they might accuse him. [5] And when he had looked. . with anger, being grieved for the hardness of their hearts, he saith unto the man, Stretch forth thine hand.—MARK, ch. 3.

3864. —— Largeness of. *Gift.* [29] God gave Solomon wisdom and understanding exceeding much, and largeness of heart, even as the sand that *is* on the sea shore.—1 KINGS, ch. 4.

3865. —— misleads the Head. *Simon Magus.* [19] Give me also this power, that on whomsoever I lay hands, he may receive the Holy Ghost. [20] But Peter said. . Thy money perish with thee, because thou hast thought that the gift of God may be purchased with money. [21] . . thy heart is not right in the sight of God.—ACTS, ch. 8.

3866. —— melted. *Water.* [5] The men of Ai smote. . about thirty and six men : for they chased them *from* before the gate. . and smote them in the going down : wherefore the hearts of the people melted, and became as water.—JOSH., ch. 7.

3867. —— Obdurate. *Pharaoh's.* [11] Pharaoh

also called the wise men and the sorcerers..
they also did in like manner with their enchantments. ¹² For they cast down every man
his rod, and they became serpents : but Aaron's
rod swallowed up their rods. ¹³ And he hardened Pharaoh's heart.—Ex., ch. 7.

3868. —— Offerings. *Building Tabernacle.*
²² They..brought bracelets, and earrings, and
rings, and tablets, all jewels of gold : and every
man that offered, *offered* an offering of gold unto
the Lord. ²⁹ The children of Israel brought a
willing offering unto the Lord, every man and
woman, whose heart made them willing.—Ex.,
ch. 35.

3869. —— Prejudiced. *Vailed.* ¹⁵ Even unto this day, when Moses is read, the vail is upon their heart. ¹⁶ Nevertheless, when it shall
turn to the Lord, the vail shall be taken away.
—2 Cor., ch. 3.

3870. —— revealed. *C o u n t e n a n c e .* ¹³ A
merry heart maketh a cheerful countenance :
but by sorrow of the heart the spirit is broken.
—Prov., ch. 15.

3871. —— —— Nehemiah. ¹ I had not been
beforetime sad in his presence. ² Wherefore the
king said unto me, Why *is* thy countenance sad,
seeing thou *art* not sick? this *is* nothing *else*
but sorrow of heart. Then I was very sore
afraid.—Neh., ch. 2.

3872. —— Divers states of. *Sower.* ⁶ Because they had no root, they withered away.
⁷ And some fell among thorns ; and the thorns
sprung up, and choked them : ⁸ but others fell
into good ground, and brought forth fruit, some
a hundredfold, some sixtyfold, some thirtyfold.
—Mat., ch. 13.

3873. —— The stony. *Seed.* ⁵ Some fell on
stony ground, where it had not much earth ;
and immediately it sprang up, because it had
no depth of earth : ⁶ But when the sun was up,
it was scorched ; and because it had no root, it
withered away.—Mark, ch. 4.

3874. —— Seeking. *Finding.* ¹³ Ye shall
seek me, and find *me,* when ye shall search for
me with all your heart.—Jer., ch. 29.

3875. —— Type of. *Bitter.* ²³ When they
came to Marah, they could not drink of the waters of Marah ; for they *were* bitter.. ²⁵ and the
Lord shewed him a tree, *which* when he had
cast into the waters, the waters were made
sweet.—Ex., ch. 15.

3876. —— Wicked. *Vipers.* ³⁴ O generation
of vipers, how can ye, being evil, speak good
things ? for out of the abundance of the heart,
the mouth speaketh.—Mat., ch. 12.

3877. —— warmed. *By the Word.* ³² Did
not our heart burn within us, while he talked
with us by the way, and while he opened to us
the Scriptures?—Luke, ch. 24.

3878. —— Word in the. *L a w .* ⁶ These
words..shall be in thine heart : ⁷ And thou shalt
teach them diligently unto thy children, and
shalt talk of them when thou sittest in thine
house, and when thou walkest by the way, and
when thou liest down, and when thou risest up.
—Deut., ch. 6.

3879. —— Worshipper without. *Jews.* ¹³ Ye
said also, Behold, what a weariness *is it !* and ye
have snuffed at it, saith the Lord of hosts ; and

ye brought *that which was* torn, and the lame,
and the sick ; thus ye brought an offering.—
Mal., ch. 1.

See other illustrations under :

HARDNESS.
Adversity. In his distress did Ahaz trespass more 3797
Heart. Looked..anger being grieved..hardness of 3798
Spiritual. We will certainly burn incense   3799

INTENTION.
Accepted. Abraham..offered up his only begotten   4604
Approved. Whereas it was in thine heart to build   4605
Abandoned. Pilate sought to release him   4606
Commended. Poor widow..cast more in than   4607
Crime. If he thrust him suddenly without enmity   4608
Fixes guilt. If any man hate..lie in wait..smite   4609
Honoured. She hath done what she could   4610
Misjudged. All of you have conspired against me   4611
Sincere. Abraham..took the knife to slay his son   4612
Superior. Beyond their power they were willing   4613
Unexecuted. Peter having a sword..cut off his ear 4614
Unprotected by. Put..hand to the ark..oxen shook   4615

MOTIVE.
Labour. We labour..may be accepted of him   5587
Unsanctified. People spared the best..to sacrifice 5588

MOTIVES.
Inferior. Ye seek me..because ye did eat..loaves   5589
Suspicion. Urged him till he was ashamed, he said 5590
Worldly. Peter..thou savourest..things that be of 5591

OBDURACY.
Defiant. Who is the L. that I should obey ?   5755
Final. Why have we..let I. go from serving us   5756
Foolish. Ahaz..sacrificed unto the gods..smote   5757
Jewish. Thy neck is as an iron sinew   5758
Spiritual. Woe unto thee, Chorazin..if the mighty 5759
Self-destructive. I know that G. hath determined   5760
to Truth. Paul spake..three months..divers were   5761
Unfeeling. Past feeling have given themselves   5762
Wild. Balaam..went with the princes of Moab   5763

OBSTINACY.
Provoking. It is a stiffnecked people..consume   5825
Rebuked. Why..smitten thine ass these 3 times?   5826
Rebellious. Nevertheless the people refused   5827

SINCERITY.
Consecration. Josiah made a covenant..burned   8025
Evil-doing. I thought I ought to..put to death   8026
Evidence. Brought their books..burned them   8027
Example. An Israelite in whom is no guile   8028
Heart. He that speaketh truth in his heart   8029
Lovable. All..have I kept..Jesus loved him   8030
Opinions. Rabbi, thou art the Son of God   8031
Positive. Thou knowest..that I love thee   8032
Proof. When..people saw it..said L., he is G.   8033
Reformation. Speak..the truth .execute..truth   8034

STUBBORNNESS.
Punished. They mocked..despised..therefore   9393
in Sin. To obey is better than sacrifice   9394
"   We will certainly..burn incense to thee   9395
"   Took Dagon and set him in his place   9396

3880. HEARER, An eager. *M a r y .* ³⁹ She
had a sister called Mary, which also sat at Jesus'
feet, and heard his word.—Luke, ch. 10.

3881. —— A listless. *Adulteress.* ⁶ This
they said, tempting him, that they might have
to accuse him. But Jesus stooped down, and
with *his* finger wrote on the ground, *as though he
heard them not.* ⁷ So when they continued asking
him, he lifted up himself, and said..He that is
without sin among you, let him first cast a stone
at her.—John, ch. 8.

3882. —— **A prepared.** *Blood.* ²⁰ Take of his blood, and put *it* upon the tip of the right ear of Aaron, and upon the tip of the right ear of his sons.—Ex., ch. 29.

3883. —— **An unprofited.** *Herod.* ²⁰ Herod feared John, knowing that he was a just man and an holy, and observed him : and when he heard him, he did many things, and heard him gladly.—Mark, ch. 6.

3884. HEARERS, Attentive. *Revival.* ³ He read therein .. before the water gate from the morning until midday, before the men and the women, and those that could understand ; and the ears of all the people *were attentive* unto the book of the law.—Neh., ch. 8.

3885. —— **Angry.** *Stephen's.* ⁵⁷ Then they cried out with a loud voice, and stopped their ears, and ran upon him with one accord, ⁵⁸ And cast *him* out of the city, and stoned *him.*—Acts, ch. 7.

3886. —— **Captious.** *Critics.* ²² Is not this Joseph's son ? ²³ And he said..Ye will surely say unto me this proverb, Physician, heal thyself : whatsoever we have heard done in Capernaum, do also here in thy country. ²⁴..No prophet is accepted in his own country.—Luke, ch. 4.

3887. —— **Divided.** *Opinions.* ¹⁹ There was a division therefore again among the Jews for these sayings. ²⁰ And many of them said, He hath a devil, and is mad ; why hear ye him ? ²¹ Others said, These are not the words of him that hath a devil. Can a devil open the eyes of the blind ?—John, ch. 10.

3888. —— **Eager.** *Jesus.* ³² They departed into a desert place by ship privately. ³³ And the people saw them departing..and ran afoot thither out of all cities, and outwent them, and came together unto him.—Mark, ch. 6.

3889. —— **Good.** *At Cornelius' House.* ³³ Now therefore are we all here present before God, to hear all things that are commanded thee of God. —Acts, ch. 10.

3890. —— **Good and Bad.** *Athenians.* ³² Some mocked : and others said, We will hear thee again of this *matter*.. ³⁴ Howbeit certain men clave unto him, and believed : among the which *was* Dionysius the Areopagite, and a woman named Damaris.—Acts, ch. 17.

3891. —— **Investigating.** *Bereans.* ¹¹ These were more noble than those in Thessalonica, in that they received the word with all readiness of mind, and searched the Scriptures daily, whether those things were so. ¹² Therefore many of them believed.—Acts, ch. 17.

3892. —— **Quality of.** *Chief Men.* ⁴⁷ Then answered them the Pharisees, Are ye also deceived ? ⁴⁸ Have any of the rulers or of the Pharisees believed on him ?—John, ch. 7. [See No. 3893.]

3893. —— **Spellbound.** *Officers.* ⁴⁴ Some of them would have taken him ; but no man laid hands on him. ⁴⁵ Then came the officers to the chief priests and Pharisees ; and they said unto them, Why have ye not brought him ? ⁴⁶ The officers answered, Never man spake like this man.—John, ch. 7.

3894. —— **Unwilling.** *" Itching Ears."* ³ The time will come when they will not endure sound doctrine ; but after their own lusts shall they heap to themselves teachers, having itching ears ; ⁴ And they shall turn away *their* ears from the truth, and shall be turned unto fables.—2 Tim., ch. 4.

3895. —— **Various.** *Sower.* ⁴ Some *seeds* fell by the wayside, and the fowls came and devoured them up : ⁵ Some fell upon stony places, where they had not much earth.. ⁶..they withered away. ⁷ And some fell among thorns..choked them : ⁸ But others fell into good ground, and brought forth fruit, some an hundredfold, some sixtyfold, some thirtyfold.—Mat., ch. 13.

3896. —— **Work for.** *St. James.* ²³ If any be a hearer of the word, and not a doer, he is like unto a man beholding his natural face in a glass : ²⁴ For he beholdeth himself, and goeth his way, and straightway forgetteth what manner of man he was.—James, ch. 1.

3897. HEARING precedes Believing. *Israelites.* ³⁰ Aaron spake all the words which the Lord had spoken unto Moses, and did the signs in the sight of the people. ³¹ And the people believed. —Ex., ch. 4.

3898. —— **Indifferent.** *Punishment.* ²⁶ Every one that heareth..and doeth them not, shall be likened unto a foolish man, which built his house upon the sand : ²⁷ And the rain descended, and the floods came, and the winds blew, and beat upon that house ; and it fell : and great was the fall of it.—Mat., ch. 7.

3899. —— **Mistakes in.** *Crucifixion.* ⁴⁶ About the ninth hour Jesus cried with a loud voice, saying, Eli, Eli, lama sabachthani ?.. ⁴⁷ Some of them that stood there, when they heard *that*, said, This *man* calleth for Elias.—Mat., ch. 27.

3900. HEAVEN, Assurance of. *" We know."* ¹ We know that, if our earthly house of *this* tabernacle were dissolved, we have a building of God, a house not made with hands, eternal in the heavens.—2 Cor., ch. 5.

3901. —— **Barricaded.** *Hypocrisy.* ¹³ Woe unto you, scribes and Pharisees, hypocrites ! for ye shut up the kingdom of heaven against men : for ye neither go in *yourselves*, neither suffer ye them that are entering to go in.—Luke, ch. 11.

3902. —— **Bliss of.** *" Living Fountains."* ¹⁵ Therefore are they before the throne of God, an l serve him day and night in his temple : and he that sitteth on the throne shall dwell among them. ¹⁶ They shall hunger no more, neither thirst any more ; neither shall the sun light on them, nor any heat. ¹⁷ For the Lamb..shall feed them, and shall lead them unto living fountains of waters : and God shall wipe away all tears from their eyes.—Rev., ch. 7.

3903. —— **a Country.** *"Better."* ¹⁶ They desire a better *country*, that is, a heavenly : wherefore God is not ashamed to be called their God : for he hath prepared for them a city.—Heb., ch. 11.

3904. —— **a City.** *Jerusalem.* ²² Ye are come unto mount Zion, and unto the city of the living God, the heavenly Jerusalem.—Heb., ch. 12.

3905. —— —— **Vision.** [See description. —Rev., ch. 21.]

3906. —— **Conveyance to.** *Elijah.* ¹¹ As they still went on, and talked, that, behold, *there* appeared a chariot of fire, and horses of fire, and parted them both asunder ; and Elijah went up by a whirlwind into heaven.—2 Kings, ch. 2.

3907. —— **Deliverance of.** *"No Crying."* [3] And they shall be his people, and God himself shall be with them, *and be their God.* [4] And God shall wipe away all tears from their eyes ; and there shall be no more death, neither sorrow, nor crying, neither shall there be any more pain : for the former things are passed away.—REV., ch. 21.

3908. —— **Exclusion from.** *"Works of the Flesh."* [19] Adultery, fornication, uncleanness, lasciviousness, [20] Idolatry, witchcraft, hatred, variance, emulations, wrath, strife, seditions, heresies, [21] Envyings, murders, drunkenness, revellings, and such like..they which do such things shall not inherit the kingdom of God.—GAL., ch. 5.

3909. —— **Grandeur of.** *Gold.* [21] The twelve gates *were* twelve pearls ; every several gate was of one pearl : and the street of the city *was* pure gold, as it were transparent glass.—REV., ch. 21.

3910. —— **the Holy of Holies.** *Mount Hor.* [Aaron went up dressed to enter the Holy of Holies.] [28] Moses stripped Aaron of his garments, and put them upon Eleazar his son ; and Aaron died there in the top of the mount.—NUM., ch. 20.

3911. —— **an Inheritance.** *Christians.* [4] An inheritance incorruptible, and undefiled, and that fadeth not away, reserved in heaven for you, [5] Who are kept by the power of God through faith unto salvation.—1 PETER, ch. 1.

3912. —— **Mansions in.** *Father's House.* [2] In my Father's house are many mansions.—JOHN, ch. 14.

3913. —— **near by.** *Crucifixion.* [42] Lord, remember me when thou comest into thy kingdom. [43] And Jesus said..Verily I say unto thee, To day shalt thou be with me in paradise. —LUKE, ch. 23.

3914. —— **Preparation in.** *Place.* [2] I go to prepare a place for you. [3] And if I go and prepare a place for you, I will come again, and receive you unto myself ; that where I am, *there* ye may be also.—JOHN, ch. 14.

3915. —— —— *Kingdom.* [34] Then shall the King say unto them on his right hand, Come, ye blessed of my Father, inherit the kingdom prepared for you from the foundation of the world.—MAT., ch. 25.

3916. —— **Praises of.** *Saints.* [2] And I saw as it were a sea of glass mingled with fire : and them that had gotten the victory..stand on the sea of glass, having the harps of God. [3] And they sing the song of Moses..and the song of the Lamb, saying, Great and marvellous *are* thy works, Lord God Almighty ; just and true *are* thy ways, thou King of saints.—REV., ch. 15.

3917. —— **Recognition in.** *David.* [21] Said his servants..thou didst fast and weep for the child, *while it was* alive ; but when the child was dead, thou didst rise and eat bread. [22] And he said..[23] Now he is dead, wherefore should I fast ? can I bring him back again ? I shall go to him, but he shall not return to me.—2 SAM , ch. 12.

3918. —— **seen afar.** *Land of Promise.* [12] The Lord said unto Moses, Get thee up into this mount Abarim, and see the land..[13] And

when thou hast seen it, thou also shalt be gathered unto thy people, as Aaron thy brother was gathered.—NUM., ch. 27.

3919. —— **Sight of.** *Stephen.* [55] Being full of the Holy Ghost, looked up steadfastly into heaven, and saw the glory of God...[56] And said, Behold, I see the heavens opened and the Son of man standing on the right hand of God.—ACTS, ch. 7.

3920. —— **on this Side.** *Land of Promise.* [Two and a half tribes entered into rest "this side" of Jordan.] [1] Reuben and..Gad had a very great multitude of cattle : and when they saw the land of Jazer, and the land of Gilead.. a place for cattle.. [5] Wherefore, said they..let this land be given unto thy servants for a possession, *and* bring us not over Jordan.—NUM., ch. 32.

3921. —— **Thoughts absorbed in.** *Ascension.* [10] Men stood by them in white apparel. [11] Which also said, Ye men of Galilee, why stand ye gazing up into heaven ?—ACTS, ch. 1.

See other illustrations under:

PARADISE.

Near. To day shalt thou be..in paradise   5947
Unspeakable. Was caught up..heard unspeakable 5948

3922. HELL, Affection in. *Dives.* [27] I pray thee, therefore, father, that thou wouldest send him to my father's house. [28] For I have five brethren ; that he may testify unto them, lest they also come into this place of torment.—LUKE, ch. 16.

3923. —— **Bottomless.** *Pit.* [2] He opened the bottomless pit ; and there arose a smoke out of the pit, as the smoke of a great furnace ; and the sun and the air were darkened by reason of the smoke of the pit.—REV., ch. 9.

3924. —— **Preparation of.** *For Devils.* [41] Then shall he say also unto them on the left hand, Depart from me, ye cursed, into everlasting fire, prepared for the devil and his angels.—MAT., ch. 25.

Also see

Torment. In hell he lifted up his eyes, being   8852

3925. HELP, Appeal for. *Macedonia.* [9] A vision appeared to Paul in the night ; There stood a man of Macedonia, and prayed him, saying, Come over into Macedonia, and help us. —ACTS, ch. 16.

3926. —— **Cry for.** *Siege of Samaria.* [26] And as the king of Israel was passing by upon the wall, there cried a woman unto him, saying, Help, my lord, O king ..[28]..This woman said unto me, Give thy son, that we may eat him to day, and we will eat my son to morrow. [29] So we boiled my son, and did eat him : and I said unto her on the next day, Give thy son, that we may eat him : and she hath hid her son.—2 KINGS, ch. 6.

3927. —— **Fraternal.** *Two and a half Tribes.* [14] Your wives, your little ones, and your cattle, shall remain in the land which Moses gave you on this side Jordan ; but ye shall pass before your brethren armed, all the mighty men of valor, and help them.—JOSH., ch. 1.

3928. —— **from God.** *Moses.* [10] Moses said ..O my Lord, I *am* not eloquent..but I *am* slow of speech, and of a slow tongue. [11] And the Lord said..Who hath made man's mouth ?

or who maketh the dumb, or deaf, or the seeing, or the blind? have not I the Lord? ¹² Now therefore go, and I will be with thy mouth, and teach thee what thou shalt say.—Ex., ch. 4.

3929. —— —— *Red Sea.* ²⁴ The Lord looked..through the pillar of fire..and troubled the host of the Egyptians, ²⁵ And took off their chariot wheels, that they drave them heavily: so that the Egyptians said, Let us flee from the face of Israel; for the Lord fighteth for them.—Ex., ch. 14.

3930. —— —— *Gideon.* ¹⁵ O my Lord, wherewith shall I serve Israel? behold, my family *is* poor in Manasseh, and I *am* the least in my father's house. ¹⁶ And the Lord said.. Surely I will be with thee, and thou shalt smite the Midianites as one man.—Judges, ch. 6.

3931. —— —— *Judah.* ⁷ Be not afraid nor dismayed for the king of Assyria, nor for all the multitude that *is* with him: for *there be* more with us than with him. ⁸ With him *is* an arm of flesh; but with us *is* the Lord our God to help us, and to fight our battles. And the people rested themselves upon the words of Hezekiah.—2 Chron., ch. 32.

3932. —— *Hurtful.* *Ahaz.* ²⁰ Tilgath-pilneser king of Assyria came unto him, and distressed him, but strengthened him not. ²¹ For Ahaz took away a portion *out* of the house of the Lord, and *out* of..of the king, and of the princes, and gave it..but he helped him not.—2 Chron., ch. 28.

3933. —— *an Injury.* *Uzziah.* ¹⁶ When he was strong, his heart was lifted up to *his* destruction: for he transgressed..and went into the temple of the Lord to burn incense upon the altar of incense.—2 Chron., ch. 26.

3934. —— *needed.* *Reproach.* ² And Nahash..answered them, On this *condition* will I make *a covenant* with you, that I may thrust out all your right eyes, and lay it *for* a reproach upon all Israel. ³ And the elders of Jabesh said ..Give us seven days' respite..and then, if *there be* no man to save us, we will come out to thee. [Saul became a deliverer.]—1 Sam., ch. 11.

3935. —— *reserved.* *Angels.* ⁵¹ Smote off his ear. ⁵² Then said Jesus..Put up again thy sword into his place ..⁵³ Thinkest thou that I cannot now pray to my Father, and he shall presently give me more than twelve legions of angels?—Mat., ch. 26.

3936. —— *earnestly sought.* *"Help me."* [Canaanite woman. Daughter sick.] ²³ He answered her not a word. And his disciples.. saying, Send her away; for she crieth after us. ²⁴ But he answered..I am not sent but unto the lost sheep of the house of Israel. ²⁵ Then came she and worshipped him, saying, Lord, help me.—Mat., ch. 15.

3937. HELPER, An angelic. *Garden.* ⁴³ There appeared an angel unto him from heaven, strengthening him. ⁴⁴ And being in an agony he prayed more earnestly: and his sweat was as it were great drops of blood.—Luke, ch. 22.

3938. —— *The Lord our.* *Eben-ezer.* ¹¹ The men of Israel went out of Mizpeh, and pursued the Philistines, and smote them.. ¹² Then Samuel took a stone..and called the name of it

Eben-ezer, saying, Hitherto hath the Lord helped us.—1 Sam., ch. 7.

3939. —— *provided, A.* *Jeroboam.* ²⁶ The Lord saw the affliction of Israel, *that it was* very bitter: for *there was* not any shut up, nor any left, nor any helper.. ²⁷ And the Lord said not that he would blot out the name of Israel..he saved them by the hand of Jeroboam.—2 Kings, ch. 14.

3940. —— *Want of a.* *At Bethesda.* [Thirty-eight years' waiting.] ⁷ The impotent man answered him, Sir, I have no man, when the water is troubled, to put me into the pool: but while I am coming, another steppeth down before me.—John, ch. 5.

3941. —— *Woman, A.* *Eve.* ¹⁸ The Lord God said, It *is* not good that the man should be alone; I will make him a help meet for him.—Gen., ch. 2.

3942. HELPERS in Building. *Temple.* ⁴ Whosoever remaineth..let the men of his place help him with silver, and with gold, and with goods, and with beasts, besides the freewill offering for the house of God that *is* in Jerusalem.—Ezra, ch. 1.

3943. —— *Dependence on.* *Against Amalek.* ¹¹ When Moses held up his hand..Israel prevailed: and when he let down his hand, Amalek prevailed. ¹² But Moses' hands *were* heavy.. and Aaron and Hur stayed up his hands, the one on the one side, and the other on the other side ..until the going down of the sun. ¹³ And Joshua discomfited Amalek.—Ex., ch. 17.

3944. HELPLESS spared, The. *Syrians.* ²¹ The king of Israel said unto Elisha, when he saw them, My father, shall I smite *them?*.. ²² And he answered..wouldest thou smite those whom thou hast taken captive with thy sword and with thy bow? set bread and water before them.. ²³..and they went to their master. So the bands of Syria came no more into the land of Israel.—2 Kings, ch. 6.

3945. —— *welcomed, All.* *By David.* ² Every one *that was* in distress, and..in debt, and..discontented, gathered themselves unto him; and he became a captain over..about four hundred men.—1 Sam., ch. 22.

See UNION.

3946. HERESY, Test of. *Word.* ¹⁹ When they shall say unto you, Seek unto them that have familiar spirits, and unto wizards that peep and that mutter: should not a people seek unto their God?.. ²⁰ to the law and to the testimony: if they speak not according to this word, *it is* because *there is* no light in them.—Isa., ch. 8.

3947. —— *Tested by.* *Corinthians.* ¹⁸ When ye come together in the church, I hear that there be divisions among you; and I partly believe it. ¹⁹ For there must be also heresies among you, that they which are approved may be made manifest among you.—1 Cor., ch. 11.

3948. HERESIES from Corruption. *Primitive.* ⁵ Perverse disputings of men of corrupt minds, and destitute of the truth, supposing that gain is godliness: from such withdraw thyself. —1 Tim., ch. 6.

3949. —— *from Pride.* *Primitive.* ³ If any man teach otherwise, and consent not to wholesome words, *even* the words of our Lord Jesus

Christ, and to the doctrine which is according to godliness ; [4] He is proud, knowing nothing, but doting about questions and strifes of words, whereof cometh envy, strife, railings, evil surmisings.—1 TIM., ch. 6.

3950. —— Teachers of. *Primitive.* [1] There shall be false teachers among you, who privily shall bring in damnable heresies, even denying the Lord that brought them, and bring upon themselves swift destruction. [2] And many shall follow their pernicious ways ; by reason of whom the way of truth shall be evil spoken of. — 2 PETER, ch. 2.

3951. HERETIC, Rejection of. *Paul.* [10] A man that is a heretic, after the first and second admonition, reject ; [11] Knowing that he that is such is subverted, and sinneth, being condemned of himself.—TITUS, ch. 3.

3952. —— So-called. *Paul.* [14] I confess unto thee, that after the way which they call heresy, so worship I the God of my fathers, believing all things which are written in the law and in the prophets.—ACTS, ch. 24.

3953. HERETICS, Errors of. *Hymeneus.* [17] Hymeneus and Philetus ; [18] Who concerning the truth have erred, saying that the resurrection is past already ; and overthrow the faith of some.—2 TIM., ch. 2.

3954. —— Primitive. *Sadducees.* [20] Now there were seven brethren : and the first took a wife.. [21] And the second took her..and the third likewise. [22] And the seven had her..last of all the woman died also. [23] In the resurrection therefore .. whose wife shall she be?—MARK, ch. 12.

See other illustrations under :

DELUSION.

Destructive. Ahaz sacrificed unto the gods that   2168
Success. Our god hath delivered Samson..into   2169
Wicked. Lot seemed as one that mocked to his   2170

3955. HERO, Christian. *Paul.* [12] We and they of that place, besought him not to go up to Jerusalem. [13] Then Paul answered, What mean ye to weep, and to break my heart? for I am ready not to be bound only, but also to die at Jerusalem for the name of the Lord Jesus.—ACTS, ch. 21.

3956. HEROES, Chosen. *David's mighty Men.* [See 2 Sam., ch. 23.]

3957. HEROINE, A patriotic. *Sisera Hidden.* [21] Then Jael Heber's wife took a nail in the tent, and took a hammer in her hand, and went softly unto him, and smote the nail into his temples, and fastened it into the ground : for he was fast asleep and weary.—JUDGES, ch. 4.

3958. —— —— *Abimelech.* [52] Abimelech came unto the tower and fought against it, and went hard unto the door of the tower to burn it with fire. [53] And a certain woman cast a piece of a millstone upon Abimelech's head, and all to brake his skull.—JUDGES, ch. 9.

3959. HEROISM, Christian. *Paul's.* [23] The Holy Ghost witnesseth in every city, saying, that bonds and afflictions abide me. [24] But none of these things move me, neither count I my life dear unto myself, so that I might finish my course with joy, and the ministry which I have received of the Lord Jesus.—ACTS, ch. 20.

3960. —— Daring. *Jonathan.* [13] Jonathan

climbed up upon his hands and upon his feet, and his armour-bearer after him : and they fell before Jonathan ; and his armour-bearer slew after him.—1 SAM., ch. 14.

3961. —— Needless. *Mighty Men.* [15] David longed, and said, Oh that one would give me drink of the water of the well of Beth-lehem.. [16] And the three mighty men brake through the host of the Philistines..took *it*, and brought *it* to David..poured it out unto the Lord.—2 SAM., ch. 23.

3962. —— against Numbers. *Shamgar.* [31] Shamgar the son of Anath, which slew of the Philistines six hundred men with an oxgoad : and he also delivered Israel.—JUDGES, ch. 3.

3963. —— Youthful. *David.* [32] David said to Saul, Let no man's heart fail because of him ; thy servant will go and fight with this Philistine. [33] And Saul said..Thou art not able..to fight with him : for thou *art but* a youth, and he a man of war from his youth.—1 SAM., ch. 17.

See other illustrations under :

BOLDNESS.

Angels urge. Brought them forth..speak in the t.   878
Apostolic. Whom ye put in prison are..in the t.   879
Believers. Three worthies..O, N. we are not   880
Brazen. Ahab said to Elijah, Art thou..troubleth   881
Innocence. With whom..be found, let him die   882
Influence. Saw the boldness of P. and J..took   883
Right. When thou seest..more than thou..not   884
Sinners. Jeroboam..served Baal..reared an altar   885
Shame. Absalom..tent upon the roof..concubines   886
Prayer. High priest touched..come boldly..throne   887
Venturesome. Peter walked on the water to go to   888

COURAGE.

Absence. 3000 men said. P. are rulers over us   1770
Daring. Paul would have entered   1771
Faith inspires. I come..in the name of the Lord   1772
Ground. With him..arm of flesh..us the Lord   1773
Honouring. Caleb said, Let us go up at once   1774
Invincible. Not any man be able..before thee   1775
Los?. Israel fled..forsook the cities   1776
Moral. Jesus went before them..amazed   1777
"   I am ready..to die at Jerusalem   1778
Necessary. Every place..feet shall tread..unto   1779
Patriotic. Fight for your daughters..wives   1780
to Rebuke. I said unto Peter before them all   1781
Reformer's. Should such a man as I flee ?   1782
Stimulated. Put your feet upon the necks..kings   1783
Soldier's. Jonathan climbed..slew   1784
in Worship. Daniel knew..kneeled   1785

MIGHTY MEN.

Adino. Mighty men whom David had..chief   5332
Abishai. Chief among the three..against 300..slew 5336
Benaiah. Slew the lion-like men of Moab   5337
Eliezer. Smote the Philistines..hand clave to his   5333
Shammah. Stood in the midst..slew the Philistines 5334
Three. Brake through the host of the Philistines   5335

Benaiah. Plucked the spear out of the Egyptian's   1543
Captains. [See Abner, Abishai, and Joab—1 and 2 Sam.]
Faith. He took his staff..five smooth stones   9443
Lord's. They cried, The sword of the L. and Gideon 8532
Outfit. Take the sword of the S., which is the word 8539
Useless. Peter..smote the high priest's servant   918

3964. HESITATION in Duty. *"Looking Back."* [61] Lord, I will follow thee ; but let me first go bid them farewell, which are at home at my house. [62] And Jesus said..No man, having put his hand to the plough, and looking back, is fit for the kingdom of God.—LUKE, ch. 9.

3965. —— punished. *The Hindermost.*
[1] When the people complained, it displeased the Lord..and his anger was kindled ; and the fire of the Lord burnt among them, and consumed *them that were* in the uttermost parts of the camp. —NUM., ch. 11.

See other illustrations under :

DELAY.

Business. I will not eat until..told my errand	2123
Decency. Tarry at Jericho until your beards are	2124
Dangerous. Let the dead bury..but go thou and	2125
Evil. Thou camest not within the time..burnt	2126
Failure. Whoso stepped in first..made whole	2127
Hinderances. Casting away his garment..came to	2128
Impatience. Moses..we wot not what has become	2129
Long. Man was there..infirmity..38 years	2130
Lord's. Neither hast thou delivered thy people	2131
Preparation. Wait for the promise of the Father	2132
Weariness. How long wilt thou forget me, O L.	2133

HINDERANCE.

Disobedience. Say nothing to any man..blaze	3979
Natural. Let me..kiss my father..mother	3980
Provoking. Let us pass through thy country	3981
Removed. Angel..rolled back the stone..door	3982
Riches. Deceitfulness of riches..choke the word	3983
" Easier for a camel..needle's eye than	3984

HINDERANCES.

Care. Take heed lest..become a stumblingblock	3985
Loss. Reuben was returned..Joseph was not in the	4404
Loiterers. While Lot lingered the men laid hold	5053
Malicious. People of the land hired counsellors	3986
Removed. I will eat no flesh while the world	3987
Secular. I have bought..bought..married	3988
Social. Let me first go bid them farewell	3989
Selfish. Neither go in yourselves, neither suffer ye	3990

IDLENESS.

Accusation. No straw..ye are idle, ye are idle	4270
Ecstatic. Why stand ye gazing into heaven?	4271
Needless. Why stand ye here all the day idle?	4272
Perishing. If we sit still here, we die also [lepers]	4273

LOITERERS.

Driven. Fire..consumed them in the uttermost	5052
Hastened. While he lingered, the men laid hold	5053

PROCRASTINATION.

Charity. Say not..to-morrow I will give when thou	6620
Fatal. Go thy way this time..convenient season	6621
Folly. Foolish said, Give us of your oil..gone out	6622
Loss. We will hear thee again..Paul departed	6623
No. Suffer me first to go and bury my father	6624

WAITING.

Calamity. Jonah sat..see what would..city	9262
Eager. My soul waiteth..watch for the morning	9263
in Faith. Tell the stars..so shall thy seed be	9264
on God. Renew their strength..as eagles	9265
Patient. After one year, G. spake to Noah, Go forth	9267
for Power. Not depart from Jerusalem, but wait	9268
Rewarded. Simeon..waiting for the consolation	9269
Vigilant. Let your loins be girt..lights burning	9270
Weariness. Let me see the king's face..kill me	9271
Watching. When the fowls came..Abram drove	9272
for Work. When forty years were expired..an	9273

Diversion. If thou meet any man, salute him not	2454
Fatal. Virgins..went to buy..door was shut	4899
Inexplicable. Neither hast thou delivered thy	2336
Late. While they went to buy, the bridegroom	4899
Perilous. Felix said, Go..when I have a more	1557

3966. HIDDEN in a Cave. *Prophets.* [4] When Jezebel cut off the prophets of the Lord..Obadiah took a hundred prophets, and hid them by fifty in a cave, and fed them with bread and water.—1 KINGS, ch. 18.

3967. —— in the Field. *David.* [24] David hid himself in the field : and when the new moon was come, the king sat him down to eat meat.—1 SAM., ch. 20. [Saul sought to kill him.]

3968. —— Graciously. *Baruch.* [26] The king commanded Jerahmeel..and Seraiah..and Shelemiah to take Baruch the scribe and Jeremiah the prophet : but the Lord hid them.--JER., ch. 36.

3969. —— in the House of God. *Joash.* [11] Jehoshabeath..took Joash..and stole him from among the king's sons that were slain, and put him and his nurse in a bedchamber. [12] And he was with them hid in the house of God six years.—2 CHRON., ch. 22.

3970. —— on the Housetop. *Two Spies.* [6] Rahab had brought them up to the roof of the house, and hid them with the stalks of flax, which she had laid in order upon the roof.— JOSH., ch 2.

3971. —— An Infant. *Moses.* [2] He *was* a goodly *child.* [3] And when she could not longer hide him, she took for him an ark of bulrushes, and daubed it with slime and with pitch, and put the child therein ; and she laid *it* in the flags by the river's brink.—EX., ch. 2.

3972. —— Strangely. *Jesus.* [58] Before Abraham was, I am. [59] Then took they up stones to cast at him : but Jesus hid himself, and went out of the temple, going through the midst of them, and so passed by.—JOHN, ch. 8.

3973. —— in the Wilderness. *Elijah.* [3] Hide thyself by the brook Cherith, that *is* before Jordan. [4] Thou shalt drink of the brook ; and I have commanded the ravens to feed thee there. —1 KINGS, ch. 17.

3974. HIDING, A difficult. *Manslaughter.* [13] Wherefore smitest thou thy fellow ? [14] And he said, Who made thee a prince and a judge over us ? intendest thou to kill me, as thou killedst the Egyptian ? And Moses feared, and said, Surely this thing is known.—EX., ch 2.

3975. —— of Sinners. *Adam.* [9] The Lord God called unto Adam..Where *art* thou ? [10] And he said, I heard thy voice in the garden, and I was afraid because I *was* naked ; and I hid myself.—GEN., ch, 3.

3976. —— Sin with Sin. *David.* [14] David wrote a letter to Joab, and sent *it* by the hand of Uriah. [15] Saying, Set ye Uriah in the forefront of the hottest battle, and retire ye from him, that he may be smitten, and die.—2 SAM., ch. 11.

3977. —— Talent. *One.* [18] He that had received one went and digged in the earth, and hid his lord's money. [19] After a long time the lord of those servants cometh, and reckoneth with them.--MAT., ch. 25.

3978. —— Unsuccessful. *Five Kings.* [22] Then said Joshua, Open the mouth of the cave, and bring out these five kings. [23] And they did so ..the king of Jerusalem, the king of Hebron, the king of Jarmuth, the king of Lachish, *and* the king of Eglon.—JOSH., ch. 10.

See other illustrations under :
CONCEALMENT.
Impossible. Thou wast with Jesus..Peter denied 1464
Unsuccessful. I was afraid, and hid myself [Adam] 1465
   "   He that covereth his sins shall not 1466

DISCOVERY.
Astounding. I am Joseph ; doth my father yet live 2360
Alarming. My money is restored in my sack 2361
Painful. Isaac trembled very exceedingly..Who 2362
Unexpected. Is not the hand of Joab..in this ? 2342

DISGUISE.
Battle. Ahab said, I will disguise myself 2382
Failure. Ahijah said, Come in, wife of Jeroboam 2383
Insufficient. Saul disguised himself [to visit witch] 2384
Penetrated. Is not the hand of Joab in this? 2385

EVASION.
Answer by. Is it well with the child?..It is well 2726
Impossible. Asked us..Have ye another brother 2727
by Silence. Let no man know these words 2728

MYSTERY.
Conversion. Nicodemus answered, How can 5660
Marvellous. Sat..according to his birthright 5661
Strange. Why the bush is not consumed 5662
Stumbling. Eateth my flesh..disciples went back 5663
Unsolved. No man knoweth his [Moses'] sepulchre 5664
Unexplainable. Thou knowest not now..know 5665

SECRET.
Difficult. Moses looked this way and that way 4645
Impossible. Elisha telleth the king..the words 4646
Woman's. If thou utter this our business..spies 4644

TRICK.
Diplomatic. From a very far country are..come 8955
Hypocrites. Feign themselves just men..might 8956
Legerdemain. Magicians..rods became serpents 8957
Politicians. Shall ask a petition..save of thee 8958

3979. HINDERANCE, Disobedience a. *Leper.*
[43] He straitly charged him.. [44] See thou say nothing to any man .. [45] But he went out, and began to publish it much, and to blaze abroad the matter, insomuch that Jesus could no more openly enter into the city, but was without in desert places.—MARK, ch. 1.

3980. —— Natural. *Elisha.* [20] He left the oxen and ran after Elijah, and said, Let me, I pray thee, kiss my father and my mother, and *then* I will follow thee.—1 KINGS, ch. 19.

3981. —— Provoking. *King of Edom.* [17] Let us pass, I pray thee, through the country : we will not pass through the fields, or through the vineyards, neither will we drink *of* the water of the wells : we will go by the king's *high* way, we will not turn to the right hand nor to the left, until we have passed thy borders. [18] And Edom said ..Thou shalt not pass by me, lest I come out against thee with the sword.—NUM., ch. 20. [On Canaan route.]

3982. —— removed. *"Stone."* [1] As it began to dawn toward the first *day* of the week, came Mary Magdalene and the other Mary to see the sepulchre. [2] And behold, there was a great earthquake ; for the angel of the Lord descended from heaven, and came and rolled back the stone from the door.—MAT., ch. 28.

3983. —— Riches in. *"Thorns."* [18] These are they which are sown among thorns ; such as hear the word, [19] And the cares of this world, and the deceitfulness of riches, and the lusts of other things entering in choke the word, and it becometh unfruitful.—MARK, ch. 4.

3984. —— —— Young Ruler. [24] How hardly shall they that have riches enter into the kingdom of God ! [25] For it is easier for a camel to go through a needle's eye than for a rich man to enter into the kingdom of God.—LUKE, ch. 18.

3985. HINDERANCES, Cause of. *Eating.*
[8] Meat commendeth us not to God : for neither, if we eat, are we the better ; neither, if we eat not, are we the worse. [9] But take heed lest by any means this liberty of yours become a stumblingblock to them that are weak.—1 COR., ch. 8.

3986. —— Malicious. *Rebuilding Temple.*
[4] The people of the land weakened the hands of the people of Judah, and troubled them in building, [5] And hired counsellors against them, to frustrate their purposes.—EZRA, ch. 4.

3987. —— Removal of. *Eating.* [13] If meat make my brother to offend, I will eat no flesh while the world standeth, lest I make my brother to offend.—1 COR. ch. 8.

3988. —— Secular. *Great Supper.* [18] I have bought a piece of ground, and I must needs go and see it : I pray thee have me excused.. [19] I have bought five yoke of oxen, and I go to prove them : I pray thee have me excused.. [20] I have married a wife, and therefore I cannot come.—LUKE, ch. 14.

3989. —— Social. *Disciple.* [61] Lord, I will follow thee ; but let me first go bid them farewell which are at home at my house.—LUKE, ch. 9.

3990. —— Selfish. *Pharisees.* [13] Woe unto you, scribes and Pharisees, hypocrites ! for ye shut up the kingdom of heaven against men ; for ye neither go in *yourselves*, neither suffer ye them that are entering to go in.—MAT., ch. 23.

3991. —— by Fear. *Enemies.* [6] It is reported among the heathen, and Gashmu saith *it*, *that* thou and the Jews think to rebel ; for which cause thou buildest the wall, that thou mayest be their king.—NEH., ch. 6.

3992. —— by Intrigue. *Enemies.* [2] Sanballat and Geshem sent unto me, saying, Come, let us meet together in *some one of* the villages in the plain of Ono. But they thought to do me mischief. [3] And I sent..saying, I *am* doing a great work, so that I cannot come down.—NEH., ch. 6.

See other illustrations under :
DISCOURAGEMENT.
Contrast. But as for me, my feet were almost 2346
Defeat. Would to God, we had been content..other 2347
Evil-doers. I am..weak, though anointed king 2348
Failure. Neither hast thou delivered thy people 2349
   "   We have toiled all the night and taken 2350
Mismanagement. Men of Ai smote 36 men 2351
Ministerial. Some fell on stony ground..thorns 2352
Needless. They that be with us are more..with 2353
Overcome. He answered her not a word 2359
Reproved. Yet I have left me 7000 in I. 2354
Trials. I am not able to bear all the people..too 2355
Unbelief. Been better to have served the Egyp'ns 2356
Unreasonable. Wherefore have ye brought us out 2357
Without. We faint not..though our outward man 2358

DESPONDENCY.
Bereavement. Joseph is, without doubt, rent in 2226
Complaint. Since I came to Pharaoh..done evil 2227
Constitutional. Let us go..die with him 2230
Continued. My heart is smitten and withered like 2228

Cure. David was greatly distressed..spake of 2229
Difficulties. People was much discouraged 2231
Hope. Why art thou cast down, O my soul? 2232
Hasty. Sun beat..Jonah fainted..wished to die 2233
Ill-timed. Handful of meal..little oil..die 2234
Loneliness. I only am left, and they seek my life 2235
Memories. By the rivers of Babylon we wept 2236
Overcare. If thou deal thus with me, kill me 2237
Prayer. How long wilt thou forget me, O Lord? 2239
Public. Moses heard the people weeping..door 2238
Peril. Esau cometh..400 men..Jacob afraid 2240
Singular. Lord take away my life..not better 2242
Vows. L. made a reproach unto me..derision 2243
Without. Troubled on every side..not in despair 2244

PERSISTENCE.

Necessary. Aaron and Hur stayed up his hands 6067
Prayer. Let me go, for the day breaketh..will not 6068
Rewarded. As thy soul liveth, I will not leave thee 6069
Unchangeable. They spake daily..Mordecai 6070
Undiscouraged. Many charged Bartimeus..hold his 6071
" Because of his importunity he will 6077

3993. HIRELING, Selfishness of a. *"Fleeth."*
[12] He that is a hireling, and not the shepherd, whose own the sheep are not, seeth the wolf coming, and leaveth the sheep, and fleeth ; and the wolf catcheth them.—John, ch. 10.

See other illustrations under :

SERVANT.

Christian. But if when ye do well and suffer for it 7799
Deceitful. I will run after Naaman and take Gehazi 7800
Lord's. Moses the servant of the Lord 7801
Men. Made myself servant of all..gain the more 7802
Only. Hireling fleeth because he is a hireling 7803
Oppression. Shalt not oppress a..servant 7804
Unprofitable. We are unprofitable..duty to do 7805

WAGES.

Back. Borrow..jewels of silver..gold and raiment 9255
Changed. Your father [Laban] changed my wages 9256
Daily. The wages..shall not abide with thee 9257
" At his day thou shalt give him his hire 9258
Others. These last have wrought but one hour..us 9259
Unimportant. Take this child..will give thee wages 9260

3994. HISTORY, Unwritten. *Of Jesus.*
[25] There are also many other things which Jesus did, the which, if they should be written every one, I suppose that even the world itself could not contain the books that should be written.—John, ch. 21.

3995. —— Warning of. *Israelites.* [10] Neither murmur ye, as some of them also murmured, and were destroyed.. [11] Now all these things happened unto them for ensamples : and they are written for our admonition—1 Cor., ch. 10.

3996. HOLINESS, Acknowledgment of. *"Shoes."* [4] God called unto him out of the midst of the bush, and said, Moses, Moses. And he said, Here am I. [5] And he said, Draw not nigh hither : put off thy shoes from off thy feet, for the place whereon thou standest is holy ground. —Ex., ch. 4.

3997. —— —— Shoes. [15] The captain of the Lord's host said unto Joshua, Loose thy shoe from off thy foot ; for the place whereon thou standest is holy. And Joshua did so.—Josh., ch. 5.

3998. —— Alarming. *Philistines.* [19] He smote the men of Beth-shemesh, because they had looked into the ark of the Lord, even..fifty thousand and threescore and ten men : and the people lamented.. [20] And the men of Beth-shemesh said, Who is able to stand before this holy Lord God?—1 Sam., ch. 6.

3999. —— Celebration of. *Cherubim.* [2] Above it stood the seraphim : each one had six wings ; with twain he covered his face, and with twain he covered his feet, and with twain he did fly. [3] And one cried unto another..Holy, holy, holy is the Lord of hosts : the whole earth is full of his glory.—Isa., ch. 6.

4000. —— Conspicuous. *Mitre.* [36] Thou shalt make a plate of pure gold, and grave upon it.. HOLINESS TO THE LORD. [37] And thou shalt put it on a blue lace, that it may be..upon the forefront of the mitre.. [38] And it shall be upon Aaron's forehead.—Ex., ch. 28.

4001. —— Chosen for. *The Church.* [5] If ye will obey my voice indeed, and keep my covenant, then ye shall be a peculiar treasure unto me above all people.. [6] And ye shall be unto me a kingdom of priests, and an holy nation.— Ex., ch. 19.

4002. —— of the Church. *"Glorious."* [25] Christ also loved the church, and gave himself for it ; [26] That he might sanctify and cleanse it with the washing of water by the word, [27] That he might present it to himself a glorious church, not having spot, or wrinkle, or any such thing ; but that it should be holy and without blemish.— Eph., ch. 5.

4003. —— Prayer for. *Paul.* [17] That ye, being rooted and grounded in love, [18] May be able to comprehend with all saints what is the breadth, and length, and depth, and height ; [19] And to know the love of Christ, which passeth knowledge, that ye might be filled with all the fulness of God.—Eph., ch. 3.

4004. —— Perfect. *Jesus.* [45] Because I tell you the truth, ye believe me not. [46] Which of you convinceth me of sin ? And if I say the truth, why do ye not believe me?—John, ch. 8.

4005. —— Unapproachable. *Sinai.* [23] Moses said unto the Lord, The people cannot come up to mount Sinai : for thou chargedst us, saying, Set bounds about the mount, and sanctify it.— Ex., ch. 19.

4006. —— Universal. *"Bells."* [20] In that day shall there be upon the bells of the horses, HOLINESS UNTO THE LORD ; and the pots in the Lord's house shall be like the bowls before the altar. [21] Yea, every pot in Jerusalem and in Judah shall be holiness unto the Lord.— Zech., ch. 14.

See other illustrations under :

CLEANSING.

Blood. Moses..sprinkled it on all the people 1343
" If the blood of bulls..much more..Christ 1344
Expulsion. He drove them all out of the temple 1345
Fire. This [live coal] hath touched..sin purged 1346
Heart. Create in me a clean heart, O God 1347
Spiritual. Who shall stand in his holy place 1348

PURITY.

Symbolized. Make a laver of brass to wash 6813
Within. First cleanse within the cup 6814

SANCTIFICATION.

First Born. Thou shalt set apart unto the L. 7374
Sabbath. G. blessed the seventh day and sanctified 7375

SURRENDER.

Absolute. I count all things but loss for..the 8503

Bodily. Yieldeth their bodies that..not serve any 8504
Christian. May know..fellowship of his sufferings 8505
Entire. One thing thou lackest, go..give to the 8506
Full. Whosoever..forsaketh not all..disciple 8507
Fear. We will do all that thou shalt H. bid us 8508
Moral. What things were gain to me, I counted 8509
Power. We have not used this power..lest we 8510
Resisted. When he saw him, the spirit tare him 8511
Sins. If thy right hand offend thee..cast it 8512
Sacrifice. Widow..cast in..all her living 8513
Undivided. Our cattle shall also go with us 8514
Weak. King Ahab said, My Lord, O King, I am 8515

Healthful. Clean hands shall be stronger and 3751
Honoured. Who shall ascend..clean hands 1348
Means. Washing of water by the word 4002
"	Blood of J. C. his son cleanseth us..sin 7948
Ordination. All night in prayer..chose twelve 5926

4007. HOLY SPIRIT, Changes. *Saul.* ¹⁰ A
company of prophets met him ; and the Spirit
of God came upon him, and he prophesied
among them. ¹¹..when all that knew him beforetime saw that..then the people said one to
another, What *is* this *that* is come unto the son
of Kish ? *Is* Saul also among the prophets?—1
SAM., ch. 10.

4008. —— dishonoured. *Simon Magus.* ¹⁸ And
when Simon saw that through laying on of the
apostles' hands the Holy Ghost was given, he
offered them money, ¹⁹ Saying, Give me also
this power, that on whomsoever I lay hands, he
may receive the Holy Ghost.—ACTS, ch. 8.

4009. —— Evidence by. *Discipleship.* ¹² If we
love one another, God dwelleth in us, and his
love is perfected in us. ¹³ Hereby know we that
we dwell in him, and he in us, because he hath
given us of his Spirit.—1 JOHN, ch. 4.

4010. —— Freeness of. *Jesus said.* ¹³ If ye
then, being evil, know how to give good gifts
unto your children ; how much more shall *your*
heavenly Father give the Holy Spirit to them
that ask him ?—LUKE, ch. 11.

4011. —— Gift of. *Jesus.* ²¹ Peace *be* unto
you : as *my* Father hath sent me, even so send
I you. ²² And when he had said this, he breathed on *them,* and saith unto them, Receive ye the
Holy Ghost.—JOHN, ch. 20.

4012. —— grieved. *Antediluvians.* ⁵ God
saw that the wickedness of man *was* great in the
earth, and *that* every imagination of the thoughts
of his heart *was* only evil continually. ⁶ And it
repented the Lord that he had made man..and
it grieved him at his heart.—GEN., ch. 6.

4013. —— Ignorance of. *At Ephesus.* ¹ Finding certain disciples, ² He said unto them, Have
ye received the Holy Ghost since ye believed?
And they said..We have not so much as heard
whether there be any Holy Ghost.—ACTS, ch. 19.

4014. —— Light by. *Paul.* ¹⁷ Brother Saul,
the Lord, *even* Jesus, that appeared unto thee..
hath sent me, that thou mightest receive thy
sight, and be filled with the Holy Ghost. ¹⁸ And
immediately there fell from his eyes as it had
scales : and he received sight forthwith.—ACTS,
ch. 9.

4015. —— Mystery of. *New Birth.* ⁷ Marvel
not that I said unto thee, Ye must be born
again. ⁸ The wind bloweth where it listeth, and
thou hearest the sound thereof, but canst not
tell whence it cometh, and whither it goeth : so

is every one that is born of the Spirit. ⁹ Nicodemus answered .. How can these things be?—
JOHN, ch. 3.

4016. —— Prayer for. *Jesus.* ¹⁶ I will pray
the Father, and he shall give you another Comforter, that he may abide with you for ever ;
¹⁷ *Even* the Spirit of truth..know him ; for he
dwelleth with you, and shall be in you.—JOHN,
ch. 14.

4017. —— Promise of. *Pentecost.* ⁴ Commanded them that they should not depart from
Jerusalem, but wait for the promise of the Father.. ⁵ For John truly baptized with water : but
ye shall be baptized with the Holy Ghost not
many days hence.—ACTS, ch. 1.

4018. —— Symbol of. *Dove.* ²¹ Jesus also
being baptized, and praying, the heaven was
opened, ²² And the Holy Ghost descended in a
bodily shape like a dove upon him.—LUKE,
ch. 3.

4019. —— Speech by. *Moses.* ¹⁰ O my Lord,
I *am* not eloquent..I *am* slow of speech, and of
a slow tongue. ¹¹ And the Lord said..Who hath
made man's mouth ? or who maketh the dumb,
or deaf, or the seeing, or the blind ? have not I
the Lord ? ¹² Now therefore go, and I will be
with thy mouth, and teach thee what thou shalt
say.—EX., ch. 4.

4020. —— Taught by the. *Moses.* [See No.
4019.]

4021. —— Temple of. *Body.* ¹⁶ Know ye
not that ye are the temple of God, and *that* the
Spirit of God dwelleth in you? ¹⁷ If any man
defile the temple of God, him shall God destroy;
for the temple of God is holy, which *temple* ye
are.—1 COR., ch. 3.

4022. —— unexpected. *Mystery.* [See No.
4007.]
See SPIRIT.

4023. HOME, in Age. *Eighty Years Old.*
³² He *was* a very great man. ³³..Come thou over
with me, and I will feed thee with me in Jerusalem. ³⁴ And Barzillai said unto the king, How
long have I to live, that I should go up with the
king unto Jerusalem ?—2 SAM., ch. 19.

4024. —— Piety blesses the. *Potiphar.*
⁵ From the time *that* he had made him overseer
in his house, and over all that he had..the Lord
blessed the Egyptian's house for Joseph's sake.
—GEN., ch. 39.

4025. —— Bible in the. *Law.* ⁶ And these
words..shall be in thine heart : ⁷ And thou shalt
teach them diligently unto thy children, and
shalt talk of them when thou sittest in thine
house, and when thou walkest by the way, and
when thou liest down, and when thou risest up.
⁹ And thou shalt write them upon the posts of
thy house, and on thy gates.—DEUT., ch. 6.

4026. —— A dismal. *Cave.* ¹ David..es-
caped to the cave Adullam : and when his brethren and all his father's house heard *it,* they went
down thither.—1 SAM., ch. 22.

4027. —— A dangerous. *"Looking back."*
⁶¹ Lord, I will follow thee ; but let me first go
bid them farewell, which are at home at my
house. ⁶² And Jesus said..No man, having put
his hand to the plough, and looking back, is fit
for the kingdom of God.—LUKE, ch. 9.

4028. —— Godly. *Joshua said,* ¹⁵ Choose

you this day whom ye will serve ; whether the gods..that *were* on the other side of the flood, or the gods of the Amorites, in whose land ye dwell : but as for me and my house, we will serve the Lord.—JOSHUA, ch. 24.

4029. —— Heavenly. *Mansions.* [2] In my Father's house are many mansions : if *it were* not *so,* I would have told you. I go to prepare a place for you. [3] And if I go and prepare a place for you, I will come again, and receive you unto myself ; that where I am, *there* ye may be also. —JOHN, ch. 14.

4030. —— Influence of. *Prodigal.* [17] When he came to himself, he said, How many hired servants of my father's have bread enough and to spare, and I perish with hunger ! [18] I will arise and go to my father.—LUKE, ch. 15.

4031. —— Longing for. *Jacob and Laban.* [25] Jacob said unto Laban, Send me away, that I may go unto mine own place, and to my country. [26] Give *me* my wives and my children, for whom I have served thee, and let me go.—GEN., ch. 30.

4032. —— Not at. *Peter.* [54] Brought him into the high priest's house. And Peter followed afar off. [55] And when they had kindled a fire in the midst of the hall, and were set down together, Peter sat down among them.—LUKE, ch. 22.

4033. —— Providence in the. *Widow of Zarephath.* [15] Did according to the saying of Elijah : and she, and he, and her house, did eat *many* days. [16] *And* the barrel of meal wasted not, neither did the cruse of oil fail, according to the word of the Lord.—1 KINGS, ch. 17.

4034. —— protected. *The Passover.* [22] And ye shall take a bunch of hyssop, and dip *it* in the blood that *is* in the basin, and strike the lintel and the two side posts with the blood.. [23] For the Lord will pass through to smite the Egyptians ; and when he seeth the blood..the Lord will pass over the door, and will not suffer the destroyer to come in unto your houses to smite *you.*—EX., ch. 12.

4035. —— A pious. *Andrew.* [41] He first findeth his own brother Simon, and saith..We have found the Messias, which is, being interpreted, the Christ. [42] And he brought him to Jesus.—JOHN, ch. 1.

4036. —— Reformation at. *Asa.* [13] Maachah his mother..he removed from *being* queen, because she had made an idol in a grove ; and Asa destroyed her idol, and burnt *it* by the brook Kidron.—1 KINGS, ch. 15.

4037. —— A religious. *Cornelius.* [1] Cornelius, a centurion.. [2] *A* devout *man,* and one that feared God with all his house, which gave much alms to the people, and prayed to God always. —ACTS, ch. 10.

4038. —— Sanctity of. *David said,* [10] Told me, saying, Behold, Saul is dead, thinking to have brought good tidings, I .. slew him in Ziklag, who *thought* that I would have given him a reward for his tidings : [11] How much more, when wicked men have slain a righteous person in his own house upon his bed ?—2 SAM., ch. 4.

4039. —— Testimony at. *The Delivered.* [18] He that had been possessed with the devil prayed him that he might be with him. [19] Howbeit Jesus suffered him not, but saith..Go home to

thy friends, and tell them how great things the Lord hath done for thee.—MARK, ch. 5.

4040. —— Weaned of. *Joseph.* [51] Joseph called the name of the firstborn Manasseh : For God, *said he,* hath made me forget all my toil, and all my father's house. [52] And the name of the second called he Ephraim : For God hath caused me to be fruitful in the land of my affliction.—GEN., ch. 41. [High honours, yet land of affliction.]

4041. HOME-SICKNESS, A Foreigner's. *Hadad.* [21] Hadad said to Pharaoh, Let me depart, that I may go to mine own country. [22] Then Pharaoh said..But what hast thou lacked with me, that, behold, thou seekest to go to thine own country ? And he answered, Nothing : howbeit let me go in any wise.—1 KINGS, ch. 11.

4042. HOMES, Bad. *Lot's Daughters.* [30] And Lot went up out of Zoar, and dwelt in the mountains, and his two daughters with him ; for he feared to dwell in Zoar : and he dwelt in a cave, he and his two daughters.—See Gen., ch. 19, 30-36.

See other illustrations under :

HOSPITALITY.

Christian. Paul entered..a certain man's house	4008
Dangerous. Come home..and eat..I may not	4099
Forbidden. Diotrephes..forbiddeth them that	4100
Grateful. Mephibosheth shall eat at the king's	4101
Increase by. How shall I..before 100 men?	4102
Joyful. Zaccheus..haste..received him joyfully	4103
Odious. Baser sort..assaulted the house of Jason	4104
Preservation. Tarry all night, and wash your feet	4105
of Poor. Widow did according to the saying of E.	4106
Pagan. Barbarous people..received us every one	4107
Refused. Samaritans did not receive him	4108
Repaid. Shunammite..make a little chamber	4109
Reward. Abraham ran to meet them	4110
Treacherous. Pharisee brought him to dine with	4111
Unjust. Rich man..took the poor man's lamb	4112
Urgent. Lot pressed them greatly..his house	4113
" Urged him, therefore he lodged there	4114
" They constrained him..sat at meat	4115
Woman's. Lydia..came into my house..constrain'd	4116
Willing. Ungirded his camels..set meat before him	4117
Wanting. Simon, thou gavest me no water to wash	4118

RESIDENCE.

Chosen. It is good for us to be here..make three	7186
Divine. We will come and make our abode in him	7187
Known. Peter..he lodgeth with one Simon a tanner	7188

Abandoned. Abram..get thee out..thy father's	5
Adopted. Behold thy mother..took her to his	160
Contention. Better to dwell in a corner of the h.	1634
Heart. We will come and make our abode with	1252
Hinderances. [Job's wife said] Dost thou retain	152
Pious. Teach them..when thou sittest..house	753
Protected. Slain a righteous person in his own house	855
" When thou dost lend..not go into his h.	2314
Religion. But Israel had light in their dwellings	2029
Saving. Send Lazarus to my father's house	168
Sorrowful. Great cry in E...not a house..one dead	274

See FAMILY and references.

4043. HONESTY, Accredited. *Joseph.* [8] Said unto his master's wife, Behold, my master wotteth not what *is* with me in the house, and he hath committed all that he hath to my hand ; [9] *There is* none greater in this house than I ; neither hath he kept back any thing from me but thee.—GEN., ch. 39.

4044. —— **acknowledged.** *Samuel said,*
[3] Whose ox have I taken? or whose ass have
I taken? or whom have I defrauded? whom
have I oppressed? or of whose hand have I
received *any* bribe to blind mine eyes therewith? and I will restore it you. [4] And they
said, Thou hast not defrauded us..neither hast
thou taken aught of any man's hand.—1 Sam.,
ch. 12.

4045. —— **commended.** *"Just."* [7] Hath
not oppressed any..hath spoiled none by violence, hath given his bread to the hungry, and
hath covered the naked with a garment; [8] He
that hath not given forth upon usury..*that* hath
withdrawn his hand from iniquity, hath executed
true judgment between man and man, [9] Hath
walked in my statutes, and hath kept my judgments, to deal truly; he *is* just, he shall surely
live, saith the Lord God.—Ezek., ch. 18.

4046. —— **Happiness from.** *Proverb.* [7] When
a man's ways please the Lord, he maketh even
his enemies to be at peace with him. [8] Better
is a little with righteousness, than great revenues
without right.—Prov., ch. 16.

4047. —— **ignored.** *Deception.* [14] *It is* naught,
it is naught, saith the buyer: but when he is
gone his way, then he boasteth.—Prov., ch. 20.

4048. —— **Official.** *Jewish Officers.* [19] Thou
shalt not wrest judgment; thou shalt not respect persons, neither take a gift: for a gift doth
blind the eyes of the wise, and pervert the words
of the righteous.—Deut., ch. 16.

4049. —— **in Payment.** *Widow's Oil.* [1] My
husband is dead; and..thy servant did fear the
Lord; and the creditor is come to take..my
two sons to be bondmen.. [6] *There is* not a vessel
more. And the oil stayed. [7] ..The man of God
..said, Go, sell the oil, and pay thy debt, and
live thou and thy children of the rest.—2 Kings,
ch. 4.

4050. —— **rare.** *In Jerusalem.* [1] Run ye
to and fro through the streets of Jerusalem..
and seek in the broad places thereof, if ye can
find a man, if there be *any* that executeth judgment, that seeketh the truth; and I will pardon
it.—Jer., ch. 5.

4051. —— **Reward of.** *"Dwell on high."*
[15] He that walketh righteously, and speaketh uprightly; he that despiseth the gain of oppressions, that shaketh his hands from holding of
bribes, that stoppeth his ears from hearing of
blood, and shutteth his eyes from seeing evil;
[16] He shall dwell on high; his place of defence
shall be the munitions of rocks: bread shall be
given him; his waters *shall be* sure.—Isa., ch. 33.

4052. —— **by Restitution.** *Zaccheus.* [8] Behold, Lord, the half of my goods I give to the
poor; and if I have taken any thing from any
man by false accusation, I restore *him* fourfold.
—Luke, ch. 19.

4053. —— **Trained to.** *Young Ruler.* [19] Thou
knowest the commandments, Do not commit
adultery, Do not kill, Do not steal, Do not bear
false witness, Defraud not, Honour thy father
and mother. [20] And he answered..Master, all
these have I observed from my youth.—Mark,
ch. 10.

4054. —— **Test of.** *Joseph's Brethren.* [12] The
money that was brought again in the mouth of

your sacks, carry *it* again in your hand; peradventure it *was* an oversight.—Gen., ch. 43.

4055. —— **in Trade.** *Law.* [13] Thou shalt
not have in thy bag divers weights, a great and
a small: [14] ..in thine house divers measures, a
great and a small: [15] *But* thou shalt have a perfect and just weight, a perfect and just measure
shalt thou have.—Deut., ch. 25.

4056. —— —— *Proverb.* [10] Divers weights,
and divers measures, both of them *are* alike
abomination to the Lord.—Prov., ch. 20.

4057. —— **Trusted.** *Builders.* [15] They reck-
oned not with the men, into whose hand they
delivered the money to be bestowed on workmen: for they dealt faithfully. [Repairing the
temple.]—2 Kings, ch. 12.

See other illustrations under:

FAITHFULNESS.

Blessed. Is that servant whom his lord..so doing	2975
Constant. The fire shall ever be burning upon the	2976
Despondency. Let us also go that we may die with	2977
Honoured. I make a decree..speak..against the G.	2978
Ministerial. See 2 Cor. 4:1-11.	2979
Primitive. All scattered abroad..except the a.	2981
Principle. Faithful in that which is least..also in	2982
Rewarded. If thou see me when I am taken..be so	2983
Truth. What the L. saith unto me, that I will speak	2980

INTEGRITY.

Acknowledged. Thou art more righteous than I	4575
Conscious. The L. be judge between me and thee	4576
Delight. The integrity of the upright shall guide	4577
Fixed. Till I die I will not remove mine integrity	4578
False. Is thy servant a dog..do this?	4579
Observed. God said, I know thou didst this	4580
Official. Witness..whom have I defrauded?	4581
Steadfast. L. said..Job holdeth fast his integrity	4582

SINCERITY.

Consecration. Josiah made a covenant..burned	8025
Evildoing. I thought I ought to..put to death	8026
Evidence. Brought their books..burned them	8027
Example. An Israelite in whom is no guile	8028
Heart. He that speaketh truth in his heart	8029
Lovable. All..have I kept...Jesus loved him	8030
Opinions. Rabbi, thou art the Son of God	8031
Positive. Thou knowest that I love thee	8032
Proof. When..people saw it..L. he is G.	8033
Reformation. Speak..the truth..execute..truth	8034

See HONOUR.

4058. HONOUR to Age. *Jacob.* [7] Joseph
brought in Jacob his father, and set him before Pharaoh: and Jacob blessed Pharaoh.—
Gen., ch. 47.

4059. —— **Appeal to.** *Moses said,* [15] *If*
thou shalt kill *all* this people as one man, then
the nations..will speak, saying, [16] Because the
Lord was not able to bring this people into the
land which he sware unto them, therefore he
hath slain them in the wilderness.—Num., ch.
14.

4060. —— **and Dishonour.** *Haman.* [11] Haman
..arrayed Mordecai, and brought him on horseback through the street of the city, and proclaimed before him, Thus shall it be done unto
the man whom the king delighteth to honour.—
Esther, ch. 6.

4061. —— **for Elders.** *Elihu.* [4] Elihu had
waited till Job had spoken, because they *were*
elder than he.—Job, ch. 32.

4062. —— **not a Gift.** *James and John.*
[37] Grant unto us that we may sit, one on thy right hand, and the other on thy left hand, in thy glory. [40]..not mine to give ; but *it shall be given to them* for whom it is prepared.—MAT., ch. 10.

4063. —— **honourably given.** *To Mephibosheth.* [1] David said, Is there yet any that is left of the house of Saul, that I may shew him kindness for Jonathan's sake?.. [3] And Ziba said.. Jonathan hath yet a son, *which is* lame on *his* feet..he shall eat at my table as one of the king's sons.—2 SAM., ch. 9.

4064. —— **protected, Divine.** *Moses said,* [12] Wherefore should the Egyptians .. say, For mischief did he bring them out, to slay them in the mountains, and to consume them.. [14] And the Lord repented of the evil which he thought to do unto his people.—Ex., ch. 32.

4065. —— **regarded, Divine.** *Ezra said,* [22] I was ashamed to require of the king a band of soldiers and horsemen to help us against the enemy in the way : because we had spoken unto the king, saying, The hand of our God *is* upon all them for good that seek him.—EZRA, ch. 8.

4066. —— **Sale of.** *Judas.* [15] What will ye give me, and I will deliver him unto you ? And they covenanted with him for thirty pieces of silver.—MAT., ch. 26.

4067. —— **Surprising.** *Joseph.* [41] See, I have set thee over all the land of Egypt. [42] And Pharaoh took off his ring from his hand, and put it upon Joseph's hand, and arrayed him in vestures of fine linen, and put a gold chain about his neck ; [43] And he made him to ride in the second chariot..and they cried before him, Bow the knee.—GEN., ch. 41.

4068. —— **Seeking.** *Jews.* Jesus said, [44] How can ye believe, which receive honour one of another, and seek not the honour that *cometh* from God only?—JOHN, ch. 5.

4069. —— **of Service.** *Olive-tree.* [8] The trees went forth *on a time* to anoint the king over them ; and they said unto the olive tree, Reign thou over us. [9] But the olive tree said .. Should I leave my fatness, wherewith by me they honour God and man, and go to be promoted over the trees ?—JUDGES, ch. 9.

4070. —— **Special.** *Haman.* [11] How he had advanced him above the princes .. [12] .. Yea, Esther the queen did let no man come in with the king unto the banquet that she had prepared but myself.—ESTHER, ch. 5.

4071. —— **Unexpected.** *Mordecai.* [15] Mordecai went out from the presence of the king in royal apparel of blue and white, and with a great crown of gold, and with a garment of fine linen and purple : and the city of Shushan rejoiced.—ESTHER, ch. 8.

4072. —— **won by Merit.** *Abishai.* [20] Abishai..he was chief of the three : for lifting up his spear against three hundred, he slew *them*.. [21] Of the three, he was more honourable than the two ; for he was their captain : howbeit he attained not to the *first* three.—1 CHRON., ch. 11.

See other illustrations under :

AMBITION.

Impious. Diotrephes..loveth the pre-eminence   317
Fatal. Asahel refused to turn aside..Abner smote   318
Hypocrites. Scribes..love greetings..highest seats   321

Promotion. Brought you near him..Seek..priest   326
Reproved. [Disciples] had disputed which..great   320
Unsatisfied. [Haman] No man came in with the   332

GREATNESS.

Ambition. Disciples had disputed..who should be   3707
Doing Good. If any man desire to be first..servant   3708
Humility. As this little child..is greatest in the   3709
Proof. Sayest thou art great..drive out..Canaanites   3710
Service. Whosoever..will be chiefest, shall be   3711
Tarnished. Naaman captain, was a great man   3712

JUSTICE.

Avenging. G. rendered the wickedness of   4788
Compensating. Isaac loved Esau..Rebekah loved   4789
Deferred. Resist not evil..let him have thy cloak   4790
Equality. An eye for an eye, a tooth for a tooth   4791
Impartial. Ye shall hear the small as well as the   4792
Indignant. They hanged Haman..king's wrath   4793
Improper. Utterly at fault..go to law one with   4794
Insulted. Thou art not Cesar's friend..Pilate   4795
at Last. Borrowed of the Egyptians jewels of silver   4796
Overtaken. Samuel hewed Agag in pieces before   4797
Penalty. Let seven..of his sons be delivered..hang   4798
Parental. Fathers, provoke not your children to   4799
Retributive. Cut off his thumbs and toes..as I have   4800

Temptation. If thou be the S. of G..cast thyself   486
Utmost. Women..wash his feet with tears..hair   170
Woodsman. Was famous as he lifted up axes   4129

See **CHARACTER.**

4073. HONOURS from Abroad. *"Own Country."*
[23] Ye will surely say unto me this proverb, Physician, heal thyself : whatsoever we have heard done in Capernaum, do also here in thy country. [24] And he said..No prophet is accepted in his own country.—LUKE, ch. 4.

4074. —— **to the Brave.** *Of Goliath.*
[25] The man who killeth him, the king will enrich him with great riches, and will give him his daughter, and make his father's house free in Israel.—1 SAM., ch. 7.

4075. —— **Too many.** *Haman.* [10] He sent ..for his friends, and Zeresh his wife. [11] And Haman told them of the glory of his riches, and the multitude of his children, and all *the things* wherein the king had promoted him..above the princes.—ESTHER, ch. 5.

4076. —— **Posthumous.** *Dorcas.* [39] Then Peter arose..they brought him into the upper chamber : and all the widows stood by him weeping, and shewing the coats and garments which Dorcas made, while she was with them. —ACTS, ch. 9.

4077. —— **by Service.** *Royal.* [Saul delivered Israel from the Ammonites.] [15] All the people..made Saul king before the Lord in Gilgal..they sacrificed..before the Lord ; and there Saul and all the men of Israel rejoiced greatly.—1 SAM., ch. 11.

4078. —— **bring Trials.** *King David.*
[Lately crowned.] [30] So Joab and Abishai.. slew Abner, because he had slain their brother Asahel at Gibeon in the battle.. [39]..I am this day weak, though anointed king..the sons of Zeruiah *be* too hard for me : the Lord shall reward the doer of evil according to his wickedness.—2 SAM., ch. 3.

See other illustrations under :

FAME.

Increasing. His fame spread abroad..about   3000
Military. Uzziah made..engines..to shoot   3001

Troublesome. Blaze abroad the matter..desert   3002
Unexpected. In the whole world..woman hath   3003
Wisdom. All the earth sought to Solomon   3004

GLORY.

Cross. God forbid that I should glory save..cross   3556
Countenance. Moses wist not that..his face shone   3557
    "   Saw Stephen's face as it had been   3558
Dazzling. There shined about him a light from   3559
Excluded. Moses was not able to enter..tabernacle 3560
    "   Priests could not stand to minister   3561
Glory of God. Heavens declare the glory of G.   3562
    "   Under his feet..paved work of   3563
    "   While my glory passeth by..cover   3564
    "   Tabernacle..cloud covered it and   3565
    "   The L. of hosts be for a crown of   3576
God only. Let not the wise glory in his wisdom   3566
to God. Neither is he that planteth any thing..God 3567
    "   Herod..gave not G. the glory..eaten of   3568
Good Deeds. Herein is my Father glorified..much   3569
Man. Let no man glory in men..ye are Christ's   3570
Nature. Lilies..Solomon..not arrayed like..these   3571
Revealed. As he prayed..his countenance was   3572
Transient. All flesh is grass..flower thereof   3573
Trials. I will glory in my infirmities   3574
Transforming. Beholding..the glory of G..changed 3575

OFFICE.

Faithful. Because thou hast been faithful..ten   5851
Intrigue. Remember that I am your bone and   5852
Merit. Faithful over a few things..ruler over   5853
Seeking. Oh that I were made a judge in the land 5855
Trials. Wherefore..made us to come up out of E. ? 5858
Undesired. The fig tree said..should I forsake   5859

Deeds. Before Saul, with the head of the Philistine 2433
Precedence. He must increase but I must decrease 6465

4079. HONOURING God. *Boldly.* [15] And if it seem evil unto you to serve the Lord, choose you this day whom ye will serve ; whether the gods which your fathers served that *were* on the other side of the flood, or the gods of the Amorites, in whose land ye dwell : but as for me and my house, we will serve the Lord.—JOSH., ch. 24.

4080. —— —— *First of All.* [2] Zerubbabel ..and his brethren..builded the altar..to offer burnt offerings thereon.—EZRA., ch. 3. [They built the altar before building the walls of Jerusalem.]

4081. —— —— *In Every Place.* [At Sichem.] [7] There builded he an altar unto the Lord, who appeared unto him. [8] And he removed..unto a mountain on the east of Beth-el, and pitched his tent..and here he builded an altar.—GEN., ch. 12.

4082. —— —— *By Gifts.* [20] Jacob vowed a vow, saying, If God will be with me, and will keep me in this way that I go.. [21]..then shall the Lord be my God : [22]..of all that thou shalt give me I will surely give the tenth unto thee.—GEN., ch. 28.

See other illustrations under :

REVERENCE.

Attitude. He opened it..stood up..bowed their   7316
Affectionate. Stood at his feet behind him, weeping 7317
Careful. Put off thy shoes..holy ground   7319
Commanded. No man be seen throughout..mount 7320
Commends. Peter fell down at Jesus' knees   7321
Joyous. Came a fire..people shouted and fell   7323
Manifested. Joshua fell on his face..did worship   7324
Necessary. Him that is poor and of a contrite   7325

Necessary. Men of Bethshemesh looked into the   7326
Word. Ezra opened the book..all the people stood 7329
Worthy. Sent his son..will reverence him   7330
Youthful. [Young ruler] came running, and   7331

4083. HOPE abandoned. *Lazarus Dead.* [39] Jesus said, Take ye away the stone. Martha.. saith unto him, Lord, by this time he stinketh : for he hath been *dead* four days.—JOHN, ch. 11.

4084. —— deferred. *At Bethesda.* [5] Had an infirmity thirty and eight years. [6]..Jesus saith unto him, Wilt thou be made whole ? [7] The impotent man answered him, Sir, I have no man, when the water is troubled, to put me into the pool : but while I am coming, another steppeth down before me.—JOHN, ch. 5.

4085. —— A deceptive. *Queen Esther.* [13] Mordecai commanded to answer Esther, Think not with thyself that thou shalt escape in the king's house, more than all the Jews.—ESTHER, ch. 4.

4086. —— beyond the Grave. *Live Again.* [14] If a man die, shall he live *again?* all the days of my appointed time will I wait, till my change come. [15] Thou shalt call, and I will answer thee : thou wilt have a desire to the work of thine hands.—JOB, ch. 14.

4087. —— A forlorn. *Ark.* [5] When the ark ..came into the camp, all Israel shouted with a great shout, so that the earth rang again. [6]..the Philistines..said, What *meaneth* the noise of this great shout in the camp of the Hebrews ?—1 SAM., ch. 4.

4088. —— Ill-founded. *Sinners.* [See above.] [17] And the messenger..said, Israel is fled before the Philistines, and there hath been also a great slaughter..and thy two sons also, Hophni and Phinehas, are dead, and the ark of God is taken. —1 SAM., ch. 4.

4089. —— Joyful. *Haman.* [8] Let the king and Haman come to the banquet that I shall prepare for them.. [9] Then went Haman forth that day joyful and with a glad heart.—ESTHER, ch. 5.

4090. —— A living. *"Begotten."* [3] Blessed *be* the God and Father of our Lord Jesus Christ, which according to his abundant mercy hath begotten us again unto a lively hope by the resurrection of Jesus Christ from the dead, [4] To an inheritance incorruptible.—1 PETER, ch. 1.

4091. —— amid Trials. *Paul.* [8] We are troubled on every side, yet not distressed ; *we are* perplexed, but not in despair.—2 COR., ch. 4.

4092. —— Triumphant. *Paul.* [38] I am persuaded, that neither death, nor life, nor angels, nor principalities, nor powers, nor things present, nor things to come, [39] Nor height, nor depth, nor any other creature, shall be able to separate us from the love of God, which is in Christ Jesus our Lord.—ROM., ch. 8.

See other illustrations under :

ASSURANCE.

Believers. I know that my Redeemer liveth   557
Full. Neither death nor life..separate us   558
Heavenly. If our earthly house be dissolved   559
Inferential. If to kill us..would not receive   560
Impudent. Bramble said..put your trust in   561
Personal. I know..he is able to keep   562
Victor's. Who shall separate us from..C.   563

CONFIDENCE.

Believers. Though I walk through the valley 1518
Blind. Know I that the L...I have a priest 1519
Caution. They are smitten down..as at the first 1520
Disappointed. Ark came..I. shouted..ark taken 1521
False. King [of Ai] wist not..ambush 1522
Future. Doth deliver..trust he will deliver 1523
Intelligent. I know whom I have believed 1524
Joyful. How great is thy goodness..trust thee 1525
Over. Is thy servant a dog?..do this [Hazael] 1526
Peril. Have the sentence of death..we trust 1527
Piety begets. L. was with Joseph..into his hand 1528
Strong. L. delight in us..fear them not 1529
Self. Peter said..I will lay down my life 1530
Triumphant. Although the fig tree shall not b. 1531
Unwarranted. Let two or three thousand go..Ai 1532
Unfortunate. Confidence..like a broken tooth and 1533
Undermining. Neither let Hez. make you trust..L. 1534
Warranted. L. is my rock, fortress, deliverer 1535

DESIRE.

Chief. L. that I might receive my sight 2210
Longing. Give me drink of..well of Bethlehem 2211
Sanctuary. My soul longeth..for the courts of the 2212

TRUST.

Active. Hezekiah clave to the L...rebelled against 9008
Courageous. Thou comest..I come..in the name 9009
Experience. L. who delivered me..the paw of..lion 9010
Egotists. Pharisee..I..I,.I..I..I 9011
Fearless. Our G..is able to deliver us..furnace 9012
" Though I walk through the valley 9013
" The Lord is on my side, I will not fear 9014
Fixed. Though he slay me, yet will I trust 9015
Foolish. Bramble said..put your trust in my s. 9016
Honoured. Cried to G. in the battle..trust in him 9017
" Angel smote..Assyrians, 185,000 9018
Ill-timed. Let us fetch the ark..it may save us 9020
Providence. May boldly say, The L. is my helper 9021
Self. Philistine..saw David..disdained him 9022

Adversity. The Lord will not cast off for ever [Jer.] 133
Crushed. Haman..do even so to Mordecai the Jew 2808
Persistent. Man was there [pool of B.]..infirmity 38

4093. HORSES forbidden. *Israelites.* [16] He shall not multiply horses..nor cause the people to return to Egypt, to the end that he should multiply horses..Ye shall henceforth return no more that way.—DEUT., ch. 17.

4094. —— **of Fire.** *Elijah.* [11] Behold, *there appeared* a chariot of fire, and horses of fire, and parted them both asunder ; and Elijah went up by a whirlwind into heaven.—2 KINGS, ch. 2.

4095. —— **Many.** *Solomon's.* [26] Solomon had forty thousand stalls of horses for his chariots, and twelve thousand horsemen. [28] Barley also and straw for the horses and dromedaries brought they.—1 KINGS, ch. 4.

4096. —— **Sacred.** *Josiah.* [11] He took away the horses that the kings of Judah had given to the sun, at the entering in of the house of the Lord..burned the chariots of the sun with fire.—2 KINGS, ch. 23.

4097. —— **White.** *Heaven.* [13] His name is called The Word of God. [14] And the armies *which were* in heaven followed him upon white horses, clothed in fine linen, white and clean.—REV., ch. 19.

Also see :
Fast. The driving is like the driving of Jehu 3517

4098. HOSPITALITY, Christian. *Paul.* [7] Entered into a certain *man's* house, named Justus, *one* that worshipped God, whose house joined hard to the synagogue.—ACTS, ch. 18.

4099. —— **Dangerous.** *Lying Prophet.* [15] Come home with me, and eat bread. [16] And he said, I may not..go in with thee .. [17] For it was said to me by the word of the Lord, Thou shalt eat no bread nor drink water there, nor turn again to go by the way that thou camest.—1 KINGS, ch. 13. [He accepted and was slain.]

4100. —— **forbidden.** *Diotrephes.* [9] Diotrephes, who loveth to have the preeminence among them, receiveth us not. [10] ..Neither doth he himself receive the brethren, and forbiddeth them that would, and casteth *them* out of the church.—JOHN, ch. 3.

4101. —— **Grateful.** *David.* [1] David said, Is there yet any that is left of the house of Saul, that I may shew him kindness for Jonathan's sake? [11] Then said Ziba unto the king, According to all that my lord the king hath commanded his servant, so shall thy servant do. As for Mephibosheth, *said the king,* he shall eat at my table, as one of the king's sons.—2 SAM., ch. 9.

4102. —— **Increase by.** *To Elisha.* [42] A man from Baal shali-sha..brought the man of God.. twenty loaves of barley, and full ears of corn in the husk thereof. And he said, Give unto the people.. [43] And his servitor said, What, should I set this before a hundred men?.. [44] So he set *it* before them, and they did eat, and left *thereof.*—2 KINGS, ch. 4.

4103. —— **Joyful.** *To Jesus.* [5] Zaccheus, make haste, and come down ; for to day I must abide at thy house. [6] And he made haste..and received him joyfully.—LUKE, ch. 19.

4104. —— **Odious.** *To Paul.* [At Thessalonica.] [5] The Jews..took unto them certain lewd fellows of the baser sort, and gathered a company, and set all the city on an uproar, and assaulted the house of Jason, and sought to bring them out to the people.—ACTS, ch. 17.

4105. —— **Preservation by.** *Lot.* [See No. 4113.]

4106. —— **of the Poor.** *Widow.* [15] And she went and did according to the saying of Elijah.. [16] *And* the barrel of meal wasted not, neither did the cruse of oil fail, according to the word of the Lord.—1 KINGS, ch. 17.

4107. —— **Pagan.** *To Paul after Shipwreck.* [1] The island was called Melita. [2] And the barbarous people shewed us no little kindness : for they kindled a fire, and received us every one, because of the present rain, and because of the cold.—ACTS, ch. 28.

4108. —— **refused.** *Jesus.* [52] Sent messengers..entered into a village of the Samaritans, to make ready for him. [53] And they did not receive him, because his face was as though he would go to Jerusalem.—LUKE, ch. 9.

4109. —— **repaid.** *Shunammite.* [10] Let us make a little chamber, I pray thee, on the wall ; and let us set for him there a bed, and a table, and a stool, and a candlestick..he shall turn in thither.—2 KINGS, ch. 4. [When her only son was dead, Elisha restored him..alive.]

4110. —— **Reward of.** *Abraham.* [1] He sat in the tent door in the heat of the day ; [2] ..and, lo, three men stood by him : and..he ran to meet them..and bowed himself toward the ground, [3] And said, My Lord, if now I have found favour in thy sight, pass not away, I pray thee, from thy servant.—GEN., ch. 18. ["Angels unawares."]

4111. —— **Treacherous.** *Pharisees.* [37] A certain Pharisee besought him to dine with him.. [53] And..the scribes and the Pharisees began to urge *him* vehemently, and to provoke him to speak of many things : [54] Laying wait for him, and seeking to catch something out of his mouth, that they might accuse him.—LUKE, ch. 11.

4112. —— **Unjust.** *Nathan said,* [4] There came a traveller unto the rich man, and he spared to take of his own flock and of his own herd, to dress for the wayfaring man that was come unto him ; but took the poor man's lamb. —2 SAM., ch. 12.

4113. —— **Urgent.** *Lot's.* [2] Behold now, my lords, turn in..and tarry all night, and wash your feet, and ye shall rise up early, and go on your ways. And they said, Nay ; but we will abide in the street all night. [3] And he pressed upon them greatly ; and they..entered into his house ; and he made them a feast.—GEN., ch. 19.

4114. —— —— *Bethlehemite.* [7] When the man rose up to depart, his father in law urged him : therefore he lodged there again. [8] And he arose early in the morning on the fifth day to depart : and the damsel's father said, Comfort thine heart, I pray thee. And they tarried until afternoon, and they did eat.—JUDGES, ch. 19.

4115. —— —— *At Emmaus.* [28] He made as though he would have gone further. [29] But they constrained him, saying, Abide with us ; for it is toward evening, and the day is far spent.. [30] ..as he sat at meat with them, he took bread, and blessed *it*, and brake, and gave to them. [31] And their eyes were opened, and they knew him.—LUKE, ch. 24.

4116. —— **A Woman's.** *Lydia.* [15] When she was baptized..she besought *us*, saying, If ye have judged me to be faithful to the Lord, come into my house, and abide *there.* And she constrained us.—ACTS, ch. 16.

4117. —— **Willing.** *Laban's.* [32] He ungirded his camels, and gave straw and provender..and water to wash his feet... [33] And there was set *meat* before him to eat.—GEN., ch. 24.

4118. —— **Wanting.** *Pharisee's.* [44] Simon, Seest thou this woman ? I entered into thine house, thou gavest me no water for my feet : but she hath washed my feet with tears, and wiped *them* with the hairs of her head. [45] Thou gavest me no kiss : but this woman, since the time I came in, hath not ceased to kiss my feet. [46] My head with oil thou didst not anoint : but this woman hath anointed my feet with ointment.—LUKE, ch. 7.

See other illustrations under :

FEAST.

4119. HOSTAGE, A Brother for. *Simeon.* [18] Joseph said..the third day, This do, and live ; *for* I fear God : [19] If ye *be* true *men*, let one of your brethren be bound in the house of your prison : go ye, carry corn for the famine of your houses.—GEN., ch. 42.

4120. HOSTAGES, Sons for. *Reuben's.* [37] Reuben spake unto his father, saying, Slay my two sons, if I bring him not to thee : deliver him into my hand, and I will bring him to thee again.—GEN., ch. 42.

See other illustrations under :

SURETY.

See CAPTIVITY.

4121. HOUSE of Ivory. *Ahab's.* [39] The acts of Ahab, and all that he did, and the ivory house which he made, and all the cities that he built, *are* they not written in..the Chronicles?—1 KINGS, ch. 22.

4122. —— **An illfounded.** *Sand.* [26] A foolish man, which built his house upon the sand : [27] And the rain descended, and the floods came, and the winds blew, and beat upon that house ; and it fell : and great was the fall of it.—MAT., ch. 7.

4123. —— **Mansion.** *Father's.* [2] In my Father's house are many mansions : if *it were* not *so,* I would have told you. I go to prepare a place for you.—JOHN, ch. 14.

4124. —— **necessary, New.** *Prophet's Sons.* [1] Said unto Elisha, Behold now, the place where we dwell with thee is too strait for us. [2] Let us go..unto Jordan, and take thence every man a beam, and let us make us a place there, where we may dwell. And he answered, Go ye.—2 KINGS, ch. 6.

4125. —— **Temporary.** *Booth.* [5] Jonah went out of the city, and sat on the east side of the city, and there made him a booth, and sat under it in the shadow, till he might see what would become of the city.—JONAH, ch. 4.

4126. —— **of God.** *Abandoned.* [7] The Lord hath cast off his altar, he hath abhorred his sanctuary, he hath given up into the hand of the enemy the walls of her palaces ; they have made a noise in the house of the Lord, as in the day of a solemn feast.—LAM., ch. 2.

4127. —— —— *Discovered.* [16] Jacob awaked out of his sleep, and he said, Surely the Lord is in this place ; and I knew it not. [17] And he was afraid, and said, How dreadful is this place !

this is none other but the house of God, and this is the gate of heaven.—GEN., ch. 28.

4128. —— —— *Despoiled.* [By Nebuchadnezzar.] [13] The pillars of brass..and the bases, and the brazen sea..did the Chaldees break in pieces, and carried the brass of them to Babylon. [14] And the pots..shovels..snuffers..spoons, and all the vessels of brass wherewith they ministered, took they away. [15] And the firepans, and the bowls, *and* such things as *were* of gold.—2 KINGS, ch. 25.

4129. —— —— *Destroyed.* [5] *A man* was famous according as he had lifted up axes upon the thick trees. [6] But now they break down the carved work thereof at once with axes and hammers. [7] They have cast fire into thy sanctuary.. [8]..they have burned up all the synagogues of God in the land.—Ps. 74.

4130. —— —— *Expensive.* [Costing £939,-907,687, or $4,699,538,435.—JAMIESON.]

4131. —— —— *Gifts for.* [22] Both men and women, as many as were willing hearted.. brought bracelets, and earrings, and rings, and tablets, all jewels of gold : and every man that offered *offered* an offering of gold unto the Lord. [23] And every man, with whom was found blue, and purple, and scarlet, and fine linen, and goats' *hair*, and red skins of rams, and badgers' skins, brought *them.*—Ex., ch. 35.

4132. —— —— *Given in Bribery.* [20] Tilgathpilneser, king of Assyria, came unto him, and distressed him, but strengthened him not. [21] For Ahaz took away a portion *out* of the house of the Lord..and gave *it*..but he helped him not.—2 CHRON., ch. 28.

4133. —— —— *Grandeur of Temple.* [5] David said, Solomon my son *is* young and tender, and the house *that is* to be builded for the Lord *must* be exceeding magnifical, of fame and of glory throughout all countries..So David prepared abundantly before his death.—1 CHRON., ch. 22.

4134. —— —— *Neglected.* [2] This people say, The time is not come, the time that the Lord's house should be built. [3] Then came the word of the Lord by Haggai the prophet, saying, [4] *Is* it time for you, O ye, to dwell in your ceiled houses, and this house *lie* waste?—HAGGAI, ch. 1.

4135. —— —— *Polluted.* [5] Manasseh built altars for all the host of heaven in the two courts of the house of the Lord.. [7] And he set a graven image of the grove that he had made in the house.—2 KINGS, ch. 21.

4136. —— —— *Refuge in.* [50] Adonijah feared because of Solomon, and arose, and went, and caught hold of the horns of the altar. —1 KINGS, ch. 1.

4137. —— —— *Residence in.* [36] There was one Anna, a prophetess.. [37]..a widow of about fourscore and four years, which departed not from the temple, but served *God* with fastings and prayers night and day.—LUKE, ch. 2.

4138. —— —— *Robbed.* [25] Shishak king of Egypt came up against Jerusalem : [26] And he took away the treasures of the house of the Lord..and he took away all the shields of gold which Solomon had made.—1 KINGS, ch. 14.

4139. —— —— *Robbed for Idols.* [24] Ahaz gathered together the vessels..and cut in pieces the vessels..and shut up the doors of the house

of the Lord, and he made him altars in every corner of Jerusalem. [25] And in every several city of Judah he made high places to burn incense unto other gods.—2 CHRON., ch. 28.

4140. —— —— *Repairing.* [9] Jehoiada the priest took a chest, and bored a hole in the lid of it, and set it beside the altar..and the priests that kept the door put therein all the money *that was* brought into the house of the Lord.. [11] And they gave the money, being told into the hands of them that did the work.—2 KINGS, ch. 12.

4141. HOUSES, Prohibited. *Rechabites.* [8] Our father..hath charged us, to drink no wine all our days, we, our wives, our sons, nor our daughters ; [9] Nor to build houses for us to dwell in.. [10] But we have dwelt in tents.—JER., ch. 35.

4142. HOUSEHOLD, A converted. *Lydia.* [15] When she was baptized, and her household, she besought *us*, saying, If ye have judged me to be faithful to the Lord, come into my house, and abide *there.* And she constrained us.—ACTS, ch. 16.

See other illustrations under :

RESIDENCE.

Burning. We will burn thine house over thine head 503
   "   Nebuzaradan..burned..every great man's 4884
Prohibited. Neither shall ye build house..dwell in 961

SANCTUARY.

Criminals. Adonijah..caught hold on the horns of 7571
   "   Solomon sent Benaiah..Go, fall upon 7572
Help in. My feet were almost gone..too painful 7573

TEMPLE.

Chosen. L. dwelleth not in temples made with 8654
Construction. He was seven years in building it 8655
   "   Forty and six years was this temple 8656
Glorious. The whole house was overlaid with gold 8657
Human. Ye are the temple of G..If any man defile 8658
Silent. There was neither hammer..heard in the 8659

Cares. Martha was cumbered about much serving 94
Destruction. Decree..speak against the G..dunghill 17

— HUMANITY. —— ——

See illustrations under :

COMPASSION.

Appeal. Son..spirit teareth him..have compassion 1423
Active. Jesus went about all the cities..healing 1424
Brother's. Joseph said, Fear not..comforted them 1425
Commended. [Good Samaritan] Go thou and do 1426
Debtors. To be sold and his wife..had compassion 1427
Denied. Took him by the throat..pay me 1428
Lowly. Israel sighed..G. heard the groaning 1429
Moved. We have sinned..grieve for the misery of 1430
Penitent. While..a great way off..compassion 1431
Public. City was moved..Is this Naomi ? 1432
Patriotic. O Jerusalem..how often..ye would not 1433
Practical. Leper..Jesus..with compassion 1434
Reproof. Forgive him and comfort him 1435
Required. Shouldest thou not have..on thy fellow 1436
Sensitive. Not a high priest which cannot be 1437
Unmoved. [Joseph] We saw the anguish..would 1438
Womanly. Daughter of Pharaoh..babe wept..had 1439
Without. Chaldees..had no compassion..old 1440

Exhibited. Samaritan..bound up his wounds 728
   "   I delivered the poor that cried..none to 708
See SYMPATHY.

4143. HUMILITY, in Adversity. *Conspiracy of Absalom.* [30] David went up by the ascent of *mount* Olivet, and wept..and had his head covered, and he went barefoot : and all the people ..covered every man his head, and they went up, weeping.—2 SAM., ch. 15.

4144. —— **Apostolical.** *Peter.* ²⁵ Cornelius met him, and fell down at his feet, and worshipped *him.* ²⁶ But Peter took him up, saying, Stand up ; I myself also am a man.—ACTS, ch. 10.

4145. —— —— *Peter said,* ¹² Ye men of Israel, why marvel ye at this ? or why look ye so earnestly on us, as though by our own power or holiness we had made this man to walk ?— ACTS, ch. 3.

4146. —— *Paul.* ¹¹ When the people saw what Paul had done, they lifted up their voices, saying..The gods are come down to us in the likeness of men. ¹³ Then the priest of Jupiter..brought oxen and garlands unto the gates, and would have done sacrifice with the people. ¹⁴ ..Barnabas and Paul rent their clothes, and ran in among the people, crying out, ¹⁵ And saying, Sirs, why do ye these things ? We also are men of like passions with you.— ACTS, ch. 14.

4147. —— —— *Paul.* ⁸ Unto me, who am less than the least of all saints, is this grace given, that I should preach among the Gentiles the unsearchable riches of Christ.—EPH., ch. 3.

4148. —— **in Adversity.** *Manasseh.* ¹¹ The king of Assyria, which took Manasseh..bound him with fetters, and carried him to Babylon. ¹² And when he was in affliction, he besought the Lord his God, and humbled himself greatly before the God of his fathers. ¹³ ..he was entreated of him.—2 CHRON., ch. 33.

4149. —— **Acceptable.** *"Contrite."* ² To this man will I look, *even to him that is* poor and of a contrite spirit, and trembleth at my word.—ISA., ch. 66.

4150. —— **assists Faith.** *Centurion.* ⁶ When he was now not far from the house, the centurion sent friends to him, saying..Lord, trouble not thyself ; for I am not worthy that thou shouldest enter under my roof : ⁷ Wherefore neither thought I myself worthy to come unto thee : but say in a word, and my servant shall be healed.—LUKE, ch. 7.

4151. —— **Angelic.** *Manoah said,* ¹⁵ I pray thee, let us..ready a kid for thee. ¹⁶ The angel of the Lord said unto Manoah, Though thou detain me, I will not eat of thy bread : and if thou wilt offer a burnt offering, thou must offer it unto the Lord.—JUDGES, ch. 13.

4152. —— **Absence of.** *"Thou art."* ²⁰ Another came, saying, Lord, behold, *here is* thy pound, which I have kept laid up in a napkin : ²¹ For I feared thee, because thou art an austere man.—LUKE, ch. 19.

4153. —— —— *Scribes.* ⁴⁶ Beware of the scribes, which desire to walk in long robes, and love greetings in the markets, and the highest seats in the synagogues, and the chief rooms at feasts.—LUKE, ch. 20.

4154. —— **Additional.** *David.* ¹¹ David said to Abishai..Behold, my son..seeketh my life : how much more now *may this* Benjamite *do it ?* let him alone, and let him curse. ¹³ ..Shimei went along on the hill's side over against him,

and cursed as he went, and threw stones at him, and cast dust.—2 SAM., ch. 16.

4155. —— **Childlike.** *Jeremiah.* ⁵ I ordained thee a prophet unto the nations. ⁶ Then said I, Ah, Lord God ! behold, I cannot speak : for I *am* a child. ⁷ But the Lord said..Say not, I *am* a child : for thou shalt go to all that I shall send thee, and whatsoever I command thee thou shalt speak.—JER., ch. 1.

4156. —— **Conspicuous.** *Baptist.* ¹⁶ I indeed baptize you with water ; but one mightier than I cometh, the latchet of whose shoes I am not worthy to unloose : he shall baptize you with the Holy Ghost and with fire.—LUKE, ch. 3.

4157. —— **Confession of.** *Baptist.* ²⁸ I am not the Christ, but that I am sent before him. ²⁹ He that hath the bride is the bridegroom : but the friend of the bridegroom..rejoiceth greatly because of the bridegroom's voice : this my joy therefore is fulfilled. ³⁰ He must increase, but I *must* decrease.—JOHN, ch. 3.

4158. —— **Condescending.** *Divine.* ¹⁷ The angel of God called to Hagar out of heaven, and said..What aileth thee, Hagar ? fear not ; for God hath heard the voice of the lad where he *is.*—GEN.,ch. 21. [The first appearance of the angel of the Lord was to an outcast female slave.]

4159. —— **Devotional.** *Publican.* ¹³ The publican, standing afar off, would not lift up so much as *his* eyes unto heaven, but smote upon his breast, saying, God be merciful to me a sinner. ¹⁴ ..this man went down to his house justified *rather* than the other.—LUKE, ch. 18.

4160. —— **Complete.** *Canaanite woman.* ²⁵ Lord, help me. ²⁶ But he answered and said, It is not meet to take the children's bread and to cast *it* to dogs. ²⁷ And she said, Truth, Lord : yet the dogs eat of the crumbs which fall from their masters' table.—MAT., ch. 15.

4161. —— **Display of.** *Peter.* ⁸ Peter saith ..Thou shalt never wash my feet. Jesus answered him, If I wash thee not, thou hast no part with me.—JOHN, ch. 13.

4162. —— **Example of.** *Jesus.* ⁴ Took a towel, and girded himself. ⁵ After that he poureth water into a basin, and began to wash the disciples' feet, and to wipe *them*..the towel. —JOHN, ch. 13.

4163. —— **Greatness by.** *Child.* ² Jesus called a little child..and set him in the midst of them, ³ And said..Except ye be converted, and become as little children, ye shall not enter into the kingdom of heaven. ⁴ Whosoever..shall humble himself as this little child, the same is greatest in the kingdom of heaven.—MAT., ch. 18.

4164. —— **Honoured.** *Abram.* ³ Abram fell on his face : and God talked with him, saying, ⁴ ..my covenant *is* with thee, and thou shalt be a father of many nations.—GEN , ch. 17.

4165. —— **before Honour.** *Proverb.* ¹² Before destruction the heart of man is haughty ; and before honour *is* humility.—PROV., ch. 18.

4166. —— **in Heaven.** *"Covered Face."* ² The seraphim : each one had six wings ; with twain he covered his face, and with twain..his feet, and with twain he did fly.—ISA., ch. 6.

4167. —— **Incarnate.** *Jesus.* ⁷ She brought forth her firstborn son, and wrapped him in

swaddling clothes, and laid him in a manger.
—LUKE, ch. 2.

4168. —— **Intellectual.** *David.* ¹ Lord, my heart is not haughty, nor mine eyes lofty : neither do I exercise myself in great matters, or in things too high for me. ² Surely I have behaved and quieted myself, as a child that is weaned of his mother.—Ps. 131.

4169. —— **Impulsive.** *Peter.* ⁸ He fell down at Jesus' knees, saying, Depart from me ; for I am a sinful man, O Lord. ⁹ For he was astonished, and all that were with him, at the draught of the fishes.—LUKE, ch. 5.

4170. —— **Joyful.** *Apostles.* ⁴⁰ And when they had..beaten *them,* they commanded that they should not speak in the name of Jesus, and let them go. ⁴¹ And they departed from the presence of the council, rejoicing that they were counted worthy to suffer for his name.—ACTS, ch. 5.

4171. —— **for Leadership.** *Gideon.* ¹⁴ Thou shalt save Israel from the hand of the Midianites : have not I sent thee? ¹⁵ And he said.. O my Lord, wherewith shall I save Israel? behold, my family *is* poor in Manasseh, and I *am* the least in my father's house. ¹⁶ And the Lord said..Surely I will be with thee.—JUDGES, ch. 6.

4172. —— **manifested.** *Baptist.* ¹³ Then cometh Jesus..unto John, to be baptized of him. ¹⁴ But John forbade him, saying, I have need to be baptized of thee, and comest thou to me ?— MAT., ch. 3.

4173. —— **mitigates Punishment.** *Rehoboam.* ⁵ Ye have forsaken me, and therefore have I also left you in the hand of Shishak. ⁶ Whereupon the princes of Israel and the king humbled themselves ; and they said, The Lord *is* righteous.— —2 CHRON., ch. 12. [God gave "some deliverance."]

4174. —— **Ministerial.** *Paul.* ⁷ Neither is he that planteth any thing, neither he that watereth ; but God that giveth the increase.—1 COR., ch. 3.

4175. —— **in Prayer.** *Abraham.* ²⁷ Abraham..said, Behold now, I have taken upon me to speak unto the Lord, which *am but* dust and ashes : ²⁸ Peradventure there shall lack five of the fifty righteous.—GEN., ch. 18.

4176. —— —— *Jacob.* ⁹ Jacob said, O God of my father Abraham, and God of my father Isaac.. ¹⁰ I am not worthy of the least of all the mercies, and of all the truth, which thou hast shewed unto thy servant ; for with my staff I passed over this Jordan : and now I am become two bands.—GEN., ch. 32.

4177. —— **Penitential.** *Pardon.* ¹⁴ If my people..shall humble themselves, and pray, and seek my face, and turn from their wicked ways ; then will I hear from heaven, and will forgive their sin.—2 CHRON., ch. 7.

4178. —— **Preservation by.** *From Darkness.* ¹⁶ Give glory to the Lord your God, before he cause darkness, and before your feet stumble upon the dark mountains, and, while ye look for light, he turn it into the shadow of death, *and* make *it* gross darkness. ¹⁷ But if ye will not hear it, my soul shall weep in secret places for *your* pride.—JER., ch. 13.

4179. —— —— *Captain.* ¹³ The third captain..fell on his knees before Elijah, and be-

sought him..O man of God, I pray thee, let my life, and the life of these fifty thy servants, be precious in thy sight. ¹⁴ Behold, there came fire down from heaven, and burnt up the two captains of the former fifties with their fifties. —2 KINGS, ch. 1.

4180. —— **Public.** *Young Ruler.* ¹⁷ Into the way, there came one running, and kneeled to him, and asked him, Good Master, what shall I do that I may inherit eternal life?—MARK, ch. 5.

4181. —— **Royal.** *Solomon.* ⁵ In Gibeon the Lord appeared to Solomon in a dream by night..said, Ask what I shall give thee. ⁷ And now, O Lord my God, thou hast made thy servant king..and I *am but* a little child : I know not *how* to go out or come in. ⁹ Give therefore thy servant an understanding heart to judge thy people, that I may discern between good and bad.—1 KINGS, ch. 3.

4182. —— **required.** *" Walk Humbly."* ⁷ Will the Lord be pleased with thousands of rams, *or* with ten thousands of rivers of oil? shall I give..the fruit of my body *for* the sin of my soul? ⁸..what doth the Lord require of thee, but to do justly, and to love mercy, and to walk humbly with thy God?—MICAH, ch. 6.

4183. —— **regarded.** *Josiah.* ²⁷ Because thine heart was tender, and thou didst humble thyself before God, when thou heardest his words against this place..and didst rend thy clothes, and weep before me ; I have even heard *thee* also, saith the Lord.—2 CHRON., ch. 34.

4184. —— **Surpassing.** *Jesus.* ⁶ Thought it not robbery to be equal with God : ⁷ But made himself of no reputation, and took upon him the form of a servant, and was made in the likeness of men : ⁸..He humbled himself, and became obedient unto death, even the death of the cross.—PHILIP., ch. 2.

4185. —— **Surprise of.** *Saul:* ²⁰ On whom *is* all the desire of Israel ? *Is it* not on thee.. ²¹ And Saul answered..Am not I a Benjamite, of the smallest of the tribes of Israel? and my family the least of all the families of the tribe of Benjamin? wherefore then speakest thou so to me ?—1 SAM., ch. 9.

4186. —— **Saved by.** *Ahab.* ²⁸ The word of the Lord came to Elijah.. ²⁹ Seest thou how Ahab humbleth himself before me ? because he humbleth himself before me, I will not bring the evil in his days : *but* in his son's days.—1 KINGS, ch. 21.

4187. —— —— *Hezekiah.* ²⁶ Hezekiah humbled himself for the pride of his heart, *both* he and the inhabitants of Jerusalem, so that the wrath of the Lord came not upon them in the days of Hezekiah. ²⁷ And Hezekiah had exceeding much riches and honour : and he made himself treasuries for silver, and for gold, and for precious stones, and for spices, and for shields, and for all manner of pleasant jewels ; ²⁸ Storehouses also for the increase.—2 CHRON., ch. 32.

4188. —— **in Social Life.** *Feast.* ¹⁰ When thou art bidden, go and sit down in the lowest room ; that when he that bade thee cometh, he may say..Friend, go up higher : then shalt thou have worship in the presence of them that sit at meat with thee.—LUKE, ch. 14.

4189. —— **Self-abhorring.** *Job.* [5] I have heard of thee by the hearing of the ear ; but now mine eye seeth thee : [6] Wherefore I abhor *myself*, and repent in dust and ashes.—Job, ch. 42.

4190. —— **in Service.** *"Thy Pound."* [15] He commanded these servants to-be called..to whom he had given the money, that he might know how much every man had gained by trading. [16] Then came the first, saying, Lord, thy pound hath gained ten pounds.—Luke, ch. 19.

4191. —— **Suitable.** *Prodigal.* [18] I will arise and go to my father, and will say..Father, I have sinned against heaven, and before thee, [19] And am no more worthy to be called thy son : make me as one of thy hired servants.—Luke, ch. 15.

4192. —— **in Supplication.** *"Kneeled."* [40] There came a leper .. beseeching him, and kneeling down..and saying..If thou wilt, thou canst make me clean. [41] And Jesus, moved with compassion, put forth *his* hand, and touched him.—Mark, ch. 1.

4193. —— **in Self-judgment.** *"Unprofitable."* [9] Doth he thank that servant because he did the things that were commanded him ? I trow not. [10] So likewise ye, when ye shall have done all those things which are commanded you, say, We are unprofitable servants : we have done that which was our duty to do.—Luke, ch. 17.

4194. —— **Teachable.** *Mary.* [39] She had a sister called Mary, which also sat at Jesus' feet, and heard his word.—Luke, ch. 10.

4195. —— **Unambitious.** *Saul.* [22] The Lord answered, Behold, he hath hid himself among the stuff. [23] And they ran and fetched him thence : and..he was higher than any..from his shoulders and upward. [24] And Samuel said to all the people, See ye him whom the Lord hath chosen, that *there is* none like him among all the people ? And all the people shouted..God save the king.—1 Sam., ch. 10.

4196. —— **of Worth.** *Olive Tree Parable.* [8] The trees went forth *on a time* to anoint a king over them ; and they said unto the olive tree, Reign thou over us. [9] But the olive .. unto them, Should I leave my fatness, wherewith by me they honour God and man, and go to be promoted over the trees?—Judges, ch. 9.

4197. —— **Want of.** *Bramble.* [15] The bramble said unto the trees, If in truth ye anoint me king over you, *then* come *and* put your trust in my shadow ; and if not, let fire come out of the bramble, and devour the cedars of Lebanon.—Judges, ch. 9.

See other illustrations under :

MODESTY.

Endangered. Saul..there was not a goodlier	5497
Enjoined. Sit not down in the highest room	5498
Ministerial. I have need to be baptized of thee	5499
Preserved. Am I not a Benjamite..smallest of	5500
Punished. [Vashti] Let the king give her royal	5501
Womanly. Bring Vashti..show her beauty	5502

| Christian. I made myself servant to all..gain the | 1681 |

4198. HUMILIATION accepted. *Nineveh.* [7] Published through Nineveh by the decree of the king..Let neither man nor beast, herd nor flock, taste any thing : let them not feed, nor drink water : [8] But let man and beast be covered with sackcloth, and cry mightily unto God : yea, let them turn every one from his evil way.. [9] Who can tell *if* God will turn and repent.—Jonah, ch. 3.

4199. —— **confessed.** *Ezra.* [6] Said, O my God, I am ashamed and blush to lift up my face to thee, my God : for our iniquities are increased over *our* head, and our trespass is grown up unto the heavens. [7] Since the days of our fathers *have* we *been* in a great trespass unto this day.—Ezra, ch. 9.

4200. —— **from Defeat.** *Joshua.* [Israel fled from the men of Ai.] [8] O Lord, what shall I say, when Israel turneth their backs before their enemies ! [9] For the Canaanites and all the inhabitants of the land shall hear *of it.*—Josh., ch. 7.

4201. —— **exhibited.** *Job.* [8] He took him a potsherd to scrape himself withal ; and he sat down among the ashes. [9] Then said his wife.. Dost thou still retain thine integrity? curse God, and die.—Job, ch. 2.

4202. —— **National.** *"No Smith."* [19] There was no smith found throughout all the land of Israel : for the Philistines said, Lest the Hebrews make *them* swords or spears : [20] But all ..went down to the Philistines, to sharpen every man his share, and his coulter, and his axe, and his mattock.—1 Sam., ch. 13.

4203. —— **of Pride.** *Haman.* [11] Then took Haman the apparel and the horse, and arrayed Mordecai, and brought him on horseback through the street of the city, and proclaimed before him, Thus shall it be done unto the man whom the king delighteth to honour.—Esther, ch. 6.

4204. —— **A painful.** *Wedding.* [8] When.. to a wedding, sit not down in the highest room ; lest a more honourable man than thou be bidden of him ; [9] And he that bade thee and him..say to thee, Give this man place ; and thou begin with shame to take the lowest room.—Luke, ch. 14.

4205. —— **Sincerity in.** *Warning.* [16] When ye fast, be not, as the hypocrites, of a sad countenance : for they disfigure their faces, that they may appear unto men to fast. [17] But.. when thou fastest, anoint thine head, and wash thy face ; [18] That thou appear not unto men to fast, but unto thy Father.—Mat., ch. 6.

4206. —— **by Sin.** *Prodigal.* [15] He sent him into his fields to feed swine. [16] And he would fain have filled his belly with the husks that the swine did eat : and no man gave.. [17]..he said, How many hired servants of my father's have bread enough and to spare, and I perish with hunger !—Luke, ch. 15.

4207. —— **Use of.** *Paul.* [7] Lest I should be exalted above measure through the abundance of the revelations, there was given to me a thorn in the flesh, the messenger of Satan to buffet me, lest I should be exalted above measure.—2 Cor., ch. 12.

4208. —— **by Weakness.** *Ezra.* [22] For I was ashamed to require of the king a band of soldiers and horsemen to help us against the enemy in the way : because we had spoken unto the king, saying, The hand of our God *is* upon all them for good that seek him ; but his power and his wrath *is* against all them that forsake him. ²³ So we fasted, and besought our God for this : and he was entreated of us.—EZRA, ch. 8.

4209. HUNGER, Appetizing. *Proverb.* ⁷ The full soul loatheth an honeycomb ; but to the hungry soul every bitter thing is sweet.—PROV., ch. 27.

4210. —— demoralizes. *Siege of Samaria.* ²⁹ So we boiled my son, and did eat him : and I said unto her on the next day, Give thy son, that we may eat him : and she hath hid her son.—2 KINGS, ch. 6.

4211. —— Disappointment in. *Jesus.* ¹⁸ In the morning, as he returned into the city, he hungered. ¹⁹ And when he saw a fig tree in the way, he came to it, and found nothing thereon but leaves.—MAT., ch. 21.

4212. —— from Fasting. *Jesus.* ² When he had fasted forty days and forty nights, he was afterward ahungered.—MAT., ch. 4.

4213. —— Inconsiderate. *"Blood."* ³¹ They smote the Philistines that day from Michmash to Aijalon : and the people were very faint. ³² And the people flew upon the spoil, and took sheep, and oxen, and calves, and slew *them* on the ground : and the people did eat *them* with the blood.—1 SAM., ch. 14.

4214. —— Impatience from. *Esau.* ³⁰ Esau said..Feed me..with that same red *pottage ;* for I *am* faint.. ³¹ And Jacob said, Sell me this day thy birthright. ³² And Esau said, Behold, I *am* at the point to die : and what profit shall this birthright do to me? ³³..and he sold his birthright unto Jacob.—GEN., ch. 25.

4215. —— Lawful to appease. *Sabbath.* ¹ Jesus went on the sabbath day through the corn : and his disciples were ahungered, and began to pluck the ears of corn, and to eat.—MAT., ch. 12.

4216. —— Murmuring from. *Wilderness.* ³ Would to God we had died by the hand of the Lord in the land of Egypt, when we sat by the flesh pots, *and* when we did eat bread to the full ; for ye have brought us forth into this wilderness, to kill this whole assembly with hunger.—EX., ch. 16.

4217. —— overcome. *Zeal.* [Disciples returned to Jacob's well with food.] ³¹ His disciples prayed him, saying, Master, eat. ³² But he said..I have meat to eat that ye know not of.—JOHN, ch. 4.

4218. —— removed. *Bread of Life.* ³⁵ Jesus said..I am the bread of life : he that cometh to me shall never hunger ; and he that believeth on me shall never thirst.—JOHN, ch. 6.

4219. —— Subdued by. *Prodigal.* ¹⁶ And he would fain have filled his belly with the husks that the swine did eat : and no man gave unto him. ¹⁷ And when he came to himself, he said, How many hired servants of my father's have bread enough and to spare, and I perish with hunger ! ¹⁸ I will arise and go to my father.—LUKE, ch. 15.

4220. —— Temptation with. *Jesus.* [See above.] ³ When the tempter came to him, he said, If thou be the Son of God, command that these stones be made bread.—MAT. ch. 4.

FAST.

Acceptable. Is not this the fast that I have chosen 3050
False. Ye fast for strife and debate..pleasure 3051
Forty days. Moses did neither eat bread nor drink 3052
Genuine. Israel..stood and confessed their sins 3053
Mournful. King of Nineveh..covered himself with 3054
Prolonged. Paul besought them all to take meat 3055

FASTING.

Anxiety. Darius passed the night fasting..sleep 3056
Affliction. David fasted..lay all night upon the 3057
Bereavement. Valiant men [buried Saul]..fasted 3058
Defeat. I. wept and sat..fasted till even 3059
Habitual. Anna..served G. with fastings..night 3060
Meaning. Why do..thy disciples fast not? 3061
Peril. Fasted..we have sinned against the L. 3062
   " Jews..fasting and weeping and wailing 3063
Preparation. Ezra went into the chamber..fasted 3064
Penitence. Ahab..rent his clothes..fasted..went 3065
Patriotic. I sat down and wept..fasted and prayed 3066
Sincere. Appear not unto men to fast..thy Father 3067
Vision. I ate no pleasant bread..three whole 3068
   " I was fasting..man..in bright clothing 3069

Sacrament. Worse..one is hungry and another is 40

4221. HUSBAND, An accusing. *Adam.* ¹² The man said, The woman whom thou gavest *to be* with me, she gave me of the tree, and I did eat.—GEN., ch. 3.

4222. —— Agreement with. *Jacob.* ¹⁴ Rachel and Leah answered..*Is there* yet any portion or inheritance for us in our father's house? ¹⁵ Are we not counted of him strangers? for he hath sold us.. ¹⁶..all the riches which God hath taken from our father, that *is* ours, and our children's : now then, whatsoever God hath said unto thee, do.—GEN., ch. 31.

4223. —— betrayed. *Samson.* ¹⁶ Samson's wife wept before him, and said, Thou dost but hate me, and lovest me not : thou hast put forth a riddle unto..my people, and hast not told *it* me. And he said..Behold, I have not told *it* my father nor my mother, and shall I tell *it* thee? ¹⁷ And she wept before him the seven days, while their feast lasted : and..on the seventh day..he told her, because she lay sore upon him, and she told the riddle.—JUDGES, ch. 14.

4224. —— Claim upon. *Wife.* ²³ Adam said, This *is* now bone of my bones, and flesh of my flesh : she shall be called Woman, because she was taken out of man. ²⁴ Therefore shall a man leave his father and his mother, and cleave unto his wife : and they shall be one flesh.—GEN., ch. 2.

4225. —— corrupted. *Joram.* ¹⁸ He walked ..as did the house of Ahab ; for the daughter of Ahab was his wife : and he did evil in the sight of the Lord.—2 KINGS, ch. 8.

4226. —— badly counselled. *Haman.* ¹⁴ Said Zeresh his wife and all his friends..Let a gallows be made of fifty cubits high, and to morrow speak thou unto the king that Mordecai may be hanged thereon..and he caused the gallows to be made.—ESTHER, ch. 5.

4227. —— counselled to Sin. *Job.* ⁹ Then said his wife unto him, Dost thou still retain thine integrity? curse God, and die. ¹⁰ But he said unto her, Thou speakest as one of the foolish women speaketh. What? shall we receive good at the hand of God, and shall we not re-ceive evil? In all this did not Job sin with his lips.—JOB, ch. 2.

4228. —— Grief of. *Michal.* ¹⁵ Ishbosheth ..took her from *her* husband, *even* from Phaltiel .. ¹⁶ And her husband went with her along weeping behind her to Bahurim. Then said Abner unto him. Go, return. And he returned. —2 SAM., ch. 3.

4229. —— A noble. *Elkanah.* ⁸ Said Elkanah her husband to her, Hannah, why weepest thou? and why eatest thou not? and why is thy heart grieved? *am* not I better to thee than ten sons?—1 SAM., ch. 1.

4230. —— Rule of. *Adam.* ¹⁶ Unto the woman he said..in sorrow thou shalt bring forth children ; and thy desire *shall be* to thy husband, and he shall rule over thee.—GEN., ch. 3.

4231. —— —— Persians. [Vashti rebelled against her royal husband.] ²² He sent letters into all the king's provinces..that every man should bear rule in his own house, and that *it* should be published.—ESTHER, ch. 1.

4232. —— ridiculed. *David.* ²⁰ David returned to bless his household. And Michal.. came out to meet David, and said, How glorious was the king of Israel to day, who uncovered himself..in the eyes of the handmaids of his servants, as one of the vain fellows shamelessly uncovereth himself.—2 SAM., ch. 6.

4233. —— saved. *David.* ¹¹ Saul also sent messengers..to watch him, and to slay him in the morning : and Michal David's wife told him, saying, If thou save not thy life to night, to morrow thou shalt be slain. ¹² So Michal let David down through a window : and he went, and fled, and escaped. ¹³ And Michal took an image, and laid *it* in the bed.—1 SAM., ch. 19.

4234. —— An unworthy. *Nabal.* ³ The name of the man *was* Nabal, and the name of his wife Abigail ; and *she was* a woman of good understanding, and of a beautiful countenance : but the man *was* churlish and evil in his doings. —1 SAM., ch. 25.

4235. HUSBANDS, Five. *At Jacob's Well.* ¹⁷ Jesus said..Thou hast well said. I have no husband : ¹⁸ For thou hast had five husbands, and he whom thou now hast, is not thy husband.—JOHN, ch. 4.

4236. —— Two. *Saul's Daughter.* ¹⁴ David sent messengers to Ish-bosheth Saul's son, saying, Deliver *me* my wife Michal, which I espoused to me for a hundred foreskins of the Philistines. ¹⁵ And Ish-bosheth sent, and took her from *her* husband, *even* from Phaltiel.—2 SAM., ch. 3.

4237. HYPOCRITE, An expert. *Jacob.* ¹⁹ Jacob said unto his father, I *am* Esau thy first-born ; I have done according as thou badest me : arise, I pray thee, sit and eat of my venison, that thy soul may bless me.—GEN., ch. 27.

4238. —— Hope of. " *Spider's Web.*" ¹¹ Can the rush grow up without mire? can the flag grow without water? ¹² Whilst it *is* yet in his greenness, *and* not cut down, it withereth before any *other* herb. ¹³ So *are* the paths of all that forget God ; and the hypocrite's hope shall perish : ¹⁴ Whose hope shall be cut off, and whose trust *shall be* a spider's web.—JOB, ch. 8.

4239. HYPOCRITES characterized. *Pharisees.* ²³ Woe unto you, scribes and Pharisees, hypocrites ! for ye pay tithe of mint and anise and cummin, and have omitted the weightier *matters* of the law, judgment, mercy, and faith. —MAT., ch. 23.

4240. —— in the Church. *Tares.* [38] The field is the world..the tares are the children of the wicked *one;* [39] The enemy that sowed them is the devil ; the harvest is the end of the world ; and the reapers are the angels. [40] As therefore the tares are gathered and burned in the fire.— MAT., ch. 13.

4241. —— The Chief of. *Judas.* [47] Judas, one of the twelve, went before them, and drew near unto Jesus to kiss him. [48] But Jesus said ..Judas, betrayest thou the Son of man with a kiss ?—LUKE, ch. 22.

4242. —— cut off. *Israelites.* [20] Ye dissembled in your hearts, when ye sent me unto the Lord..saying, Pray for us unto the Lord our God.. [22] Now therefore know certainly that ye shall die by the sword, by the famine, and by the pestilence, in the place whither ye desire to go.—JER., ch. 42.

4243. —— Condemnation of. *Harlots.* [31] The publicans and the harlots go into the kingdom of God before you. [32] For John came unto you in the way of righteousness, and ye believed him not ; but the publicans and the harlots believed him : and ye, when ye had seen *it,* repented not afterward..ye might believe him.— MAT., ch. 21.

4244. —— Disguised. *Wolves.* [15] Beware of false prophets, which come to you in sheep's clothing, but inwardly they are ravening wolves. [16] Ye shall know them by their fruits.—MAT., ch. 7.

4245. —— described. *Scribes.* [46] Beware of the scribes, which desire to walk in long robes, and love greetings in the markets, and the highest seats in the synagogues, and the chief rooms at feasts ; [47] Which devour widows' houses, and for a shew make long prayers : the same shall receive greater damnation.—LUKE, ch. 20.

4246. —— silenced. *Adulterers.* [7] He that is without sin among you, let him first cast a stone at her. [8] And again he stooped down, and wrote on the ground. [9] And they which heard *it,* being convicted by *their own* conscience, went out one by one, beginning at the eldest, *even* unto the last.—JOHN, ch. 8.

4247. HYPOCRISY in Benevolence. *Judas.* [5] Why was not this ointment sold for three hundred pence, and given to the poor ? [6] This he said, not that he cared for the poor ; but because he was a thief, and had the bag.—JOHN, ch. 12.

4248. —— A Conspirator's. *Absalom.* [7] Absalom said unto the king, I pray thee, let me go and pay my vow, which I have vowed unto the Lord, in Hebron .. [12] And the conspiracy was strong ; for the people increased continually with Absalom.—2 SAM., ch. 15.

4249. —— Concealment of. *Graves.* [44] Woe unto you, scribes and Pharisees, hypocrites ! for ye are as graves which appear not, and the men that walk over *them* are not aware *of them.* —LUKE, ch. 11.

4250. —— Conservative. *Peter.* [12] Before that certain came from James, he did eat with the Gentiles : but when they were come, he withdrew and separated himself, fearing them which were of the circumcision. [13] And the other Jews dissembled likewise with him.. Barnabas also was carried away with their dissimulation.—GAL., ch. 2.

4251. —— despised. *Jews.* [21] I hate, I despise your feast days, and I will not smell in your solemn assemblies. [22] Though ye offer me burnt offerings, and your meat offerings, I will not accept *them* ; neither will I regard the peace offerings of your fat beasts. [23] Take thou away from me the noise of thy songs ; for I will not hear the melody of thy viols. [24] But let judgment run down as waters, and righteousness as a mighty stream.—AMOS, ch. 5.

4252. —— denounced. *Woe.* [14] Woe unto you, scribes and Pharisees, hypocrites ! for ye devour widows' houses, and for a pretence make long prayer : therefore ye shall receive the greater damnation. [15] Woe unto you, scribes and Pharisees, hypocrites ! for ye compass sea and land to make one proselyte ; and when he is made, ye make him twofold more the child of hell than yourselves.—MAT., ch. 23. [See No. 4239.]

4253. —— discovered. *Ananias.* [3] Peter said, Ananias, why hath Satan filled thine heart to lie to the Holy Ghost, and to keep back *part* of the price of the land?—ACTS, ch. 5.

4254. —— Fear of. *Paul.* [26] When Saul was come to Jerusalem, he assayed to join himself to the disciples : but they were all afraid of him, and believed not that he was a disciple. —ACTS, ch. 9.

4255. —— falsely charged. *Eliphaz to Job.* [5] But now it is come upon thee, and thou faintest .. [6] *Is* not *this* thy fear, thy confidence, thy hope, and the uprightness of thy ways ? [7] Remember, I pray thee, who *ever* perished, being innocent ? or where were the righteous cut off ? —JOB, ch. 4.

4256. —— in Fault-finding. *"Mote."* [4] How wilt thou say to thy brother, Let me pull out the mote out of thine eye ; and, behold, a beam *is* in thine own eye ? [5] Thou hypocrite, first cast out the beam out of thine own eye ; and then shalt thou see clearly to cast out the mote out of thy brother's eye.—MAT., ch. 7.

4257. —— Heartless. *Pharisees.* [6] Well hath Esaias prophesied of you hypocrites, as it is written, This people honoureth me with *their* lips, but their heart is far from me. [7] Howbeit in vain do they worship me, teaching *for* doctrine the commandments of men.—MARK, ch. 7.

4258. —— Outwardness of. *Pots and Cups.* [8] Laying aside the commandment of God, ye hold the tradition of men, *as* the washing of pots and cups : and many other such like things ye do. [9] And he said unto them, Full well ye reject the commandment of God, that ye may keep your own tradition.—MARK, ch. 7.

4259. —— Official. *Pilate.* [24] When Pilate saw that he could prevail nothing, but *that* rather a tumult was made, he took water, and washed *his* hands before the multitude, saying, I am innocent of the blood of this just person : see ye *to it.*—MAT., ch. 27.

4260. —— **Prevalence of.** *Latter Times.* [1] The Spirit speaketh expressly, that in the latter times some shall depart from the faith, giving heed to seducing spirits, and doctrines of devils ; [2] Speaking lies in hypocrisy ; having their conscience seared with a hot iron.—1 TIM., ch. 4.

4261. —— **Pharisaic.** *Tribute.* [15] The Pharisees..they might entangle him in *his* talk. [16] Sent..their disciples with the Herodians, saying, Master, we know that thou..teachest the way of God in truth, neither carest thou for any *man*..[17] Tell us, therefore, What thinkest thou ? Is it lawful to give tribute unto Cesar, or not ? [18]..Why tempt ye me, *ye* hypocrites ?—MAT., ch. 22.

4262. —— **punished.** *Ananias.* [8] Peter answered..Tell me whether ye sold the land for so much ? And she said, Yea, for so much. [9] Then Peter said..How is it that ye have agreed together to tempt the Spirit of the Lord ? behold, the feet of them which have buried thy husband *are* at the door, and shall carry thee out. [10] Then fell she down straightway.—ACTS, ch. 5.

4263. —— **Revengeful.** *Joab.* [9] Joab said to Amasa, *Art* thou in health, my brother ? And Joab took Amasa by the beard with the right hand to kiss him. [10] Amasa took no heed to the sword that *was* in Joab's hand : so he smote him therewith in the fifth *rib*, and shed out his bowels to the ground.—2 SAM., ch. 20.

4264. —— **rebuked.** *Sabbath.* [15] *Thou* hypocrite, doth not each one of you on the sabbath loose his ox or *his* ass from the stall, and lead *him* away to watering ? [16] And ought not this woman, being a daughter of Abraham, whom Satan hath bound, lo, these eighteen years, be loosed from this bond on the sabbath day ? [17] And..all his adversaries were ashamed.—LUKE, ch. 13.

4265. —— **Royal.** *Herod.* [7] Herod, when he had privily called the wise men, inquired of them diligently what time the star appeared. [8] And he sent them to Bethlehem, and said, Go and search diligently for the young child ; and when ye have found *him*, bring me word again, that I may come and worship him also.—MAT., ch. 2.

4266. —— **Shameful.** *Jacob.* [16] She put the skins of the kids of the goats upon his hands, and upon the smooth of his neck : [17] And she gave the savoury meat .. [20] And Isaac said unto his son, How *is it* that thou hast found *it* so quickly, my son ? And he said, Because the Lord thy God brought *it* to me.—GEN., ch. 27.

4267. —— **Zeal in.** *Children.* [25] Then answered all the people, and said, His blood *be* on us, and on our children. [26] Then released he Barabbas unto them : and when he had scourged Jesus, he delivered *him* to be crucified. —MAT., ch. 27.

See other illustrations under :

IMPOSTOR.

Called. Others said, Nay..he deceiveth the people 4352
Punished. Elymas the sorcerer..thou shalt be   4353
Treated as. Herod..arrayed him in a gorgeous   4354

IMPOSTORS.

Exposed. Seven sons of Sceva..fled out..wounded 4355
Punished. Hewers of wood and drawers of water 4356

INCONSISTENCY.

Blot. Solomon loved the L..only he burned incense 4387
Hypocritical. Strain at a gnat and swallow a camel 4388
Inward. Ye make clean the outside of the cup   4389
Rebuked. Make this fellow return..be an ad'y   4390
Shocking. Whited sepulchres..full of dead men's 4391

FRAUD.

Appearances. Gibeonites took old sacks..old   3468
Commerce. Take thy bill..quickly..write fifty   3409
Demagogue. Oh that I were a judge..do justice   2171
Pious. Sons of the prophets, give..silver [Gehazi] 3410
Religious. His enemy..sowed tares among the   3411
Spiritual. Simon offered money..Holy Ghost   3412
Traitors. Whomsoever I shall kiss..is he   3413
Wages. Hire of the labourers kept..crieth   3414

SORCERY.

Captivating. Simon bewitched the people..all   8202
Curious Arts. [Ephesians] used curious arts..burn 908
Imposition. Magicians..cast down..rod..serpent 5162
Renounced. Simon himself believed..was bap'd.   8203
    "   [Ephesians] used curious arts   8204

TRICK.

Diplomatic. From a very far country are..come   8955
Hypocrites. Feign themselves just men..might   8956
Legerdemain. Magicians..rods became serpents   8957
Politicians. Shall ask a petition..save of thee   8958
  See DECEPTION.

4268. ICONOCLAST, A pious. *Josiah.* [See 2 Kings, ch. 23.]

4269. IDENTIFICATION, Spiritual. *Dove.* [33] I knew him not : but he that sent me to baptize with water, the same said unto me, Upon whom thou shalt see the Spirit descending and remaining on him, the same is he which baptizeth with the Holy Ghost.—JOHN, ch. 1.

Also see :
Convincing. Thomas, reach hither thy finger..my 2743

4270. IDLENESS, Accusation of. *Pharaoh.* [16] There is no straw given unto thy servants, and they say to us, Make brick : and behold, thy servants *are* beaten ; but the fault *is* in thine own people. [17] But he said, Ye *are* idle, *ye are* idle : therefore ye say, Let us go, *and* do sacrifice to the Lord.—EX., ch. 5.

4271. —— **Ecstatic.** *Ascension.* [10] While they looked steadfastly toward heaven as he went up, behold, two men stood by them in white apparel ; [11] Which also said, Ye men of Galilee, why stand ye gazing up into heaven ?—ACTS, ch. 1.

4272. —— **Needless.** *Eleventh Hour.* [6] About the eleventh hour he..found others standing idle, and saith..Why stand ye here all the day idle ? [7] They say..Because no man hath hired us. He saith..Go ye also into the vineyard.—MAT., ch. 20.

4273. —— **Perishing in.** *Four Lepers.* [3] Why sit we here until we die ? [4] If we say, We will enter into the city, then the famine *is* in the city, and we shall die there : and if we sit still here, we die also..let us fall unto the host of the Syrians : if they save us alive, we shall live ; and if they kill us, we shall but die.—2 KINGS, ch. 7.

See other illustrations under :

INDIFFERENT.

Curse. Curse ye, Meroz..came not..help of the L. 4412
Woe. Woe unto them that are at ease in Zion   4413

INDOLENCE.

Exhibited. I went by the field of the slothful   4436
Excuse. There is a lion without..I shall be slain   4437
Perfect. Hand..not so much as bring it to his   4438
Shame. Sleepeth in harvest..causeth shame   4439
Wasteful. Slothful in his work..a great waster   4440

SLUGGARD.

Reproved. Go to the ant, thou sluggard   8145
Vexatious. As smoke to the eyes, so is the sluggard 8146
   "   Way of the slothful..full of thorns   8147

4274. IDOL, The chosen. *Young Ruler.* [21] One thing thou lackest : go thy way, sell whatsoever thou hast, and give to the poor, and thou shalt have treasure in heaven : and come, take up the cross, and follow me. [22] And he was sad at that saying, and went away grieved : for he had great possessions.—MARK, ch. 10.

4275. IDOLATRY, Folly of. *Powerless.* [4] Their idols *are* silver and gold, the work of men's hands. [5] They have mouths, but they speak not : eyes have they, but they see not : [6] They have ears, but they hear not : noses have they, but they smell not : [7] They have hands, but they handle not : feet have they, but they walk not : neither speak they through their throat. [8] They that make them are like unto them ; *so is* every one that trusteth in them.—Ps. 115.

4276. —— —— *Manufacture.* [See Isaiah, ch. 44 : 9-17.]

4277. —— —— *To Amaziah.* [15] He sent unto him a prophet, which said..Why hast thou sought after the gods of the people, which could not deliver their own people out of thine hand? —2 CHRON., ch. 25.

4278. —— of Self. *Prince of Tyrus.* [2] Thus saith the Lord God ; Because thine heart *is* lifted up, and thou hast said, I *am* a god, I sit *in* the seat of God, in the midst of the seas ; and yet thou *art* a man, and not God.—EZEK., ch. 28.

4279. —— the State Religion. *Jeroboam.* [28] The king took counsel, and made two calves *of* gold, and said unto them, It is too much for you to go up to Jerusalem : behold thy gods, O Israel, which brought thee up out of the land of Egypt. [29] And he set the one in Bethel, and the other..in Dan.—1 KINGS, ch. 12.

4280. —— in the Sanctuary. *Manasseh.* [7] He set a graven image of the grove..in the house..in Jerusalem, which I have chosen out of all the tribes of Israel, will I put my name for ever.—1 KINGS, ch. 21.

4281. —— Sacrifices for. *Calf.* [3] All the people brake off the golden earrings which *were* in their ears, and brought *them* unto Aaron. [4] And he received *them* at their hand, and fashioned it with a graving tool, after he had made it a molten calf.—EX., ch. 32.

4282. —— Unreasonableness of. *Paul said,* [28] In him we live, and move, and have our being ; as certain also of your own poets have said, For we are also his offspring. [29] Forasmuch then as we are the offspring of God, we ought not to think that the Godhead is like unto gold, or silver, or stone, graven by art and man's device.—ACTS, ch. 17.

4283. IDOLATER, A strange. *Solomon.* [7] Then did Solomon build a high place for Chemosh, the abomination of Moab..and for Molech, the abomination of the children of Ammon. [8] And likewise did he for all his strange wives, which burnt incense and sacrificed unto their gods.— 1 KINGS, ch. 11.

4284. IDOLATERS punished. *At Sinai.* [27] Thus saith the Lord..Put every man his sword by his side, *and* go in and out from gate to gate throughout the camp, and slay every man his brother, and every man his companion, and every man his neighbour. [28] And the children of Levi did..and there fell..about three thousand men.—EX., ch. 32.

Also see :

Folly. Cry aloud..peradventure he sleepeth   3631
Iconoclast. Pious Josiah.—See 2 Kings, ch. 23.

4285. IGNORANCE, Blind. *Gentiles.* [17] Gentiles walk, in the vanity of their minds, [18] Having the understanding darkened, being alienated from the life of God through the ignorance that is in them, because of the blindness of their heart.—EPH., ch. 4.

4286. —— The Backslider's. *Samson.* [20] She said, The Philistines *be* upon thee, Samson. And he awoke out of his sleep, and said, I will go out as at other times before, and shake myself. And he wist not that the Lord was departed from him.—JUDGES, ch. 16.

4287. —— Biblical. *Sadducees.* [See No. 4295.]

4288. —— Conscientious. *Persecutors.* [2] They shall put you out of the synagogues : yea, the time cometh, that whosoever killeth you will think that he doeth God service.—JOHN, ch. 16.

4289. —— Criminal. *Peter said,* [17] I wot that through ignorance ye did *it*, as *did* also your rulers.. [19] Repent ye therefore, and be converted.—ACTS, ch. 3.

4290. —— Dangers of. *Conspiracy.* [11] With Absalom went two hundred men out of Jerusalem, *that were* called ; and they went in their simplicity, and they knew not any thing.—2 SAM., ch. 15.

4291. —— —— *At Thessalonica.* [5] The Jews ..moved with envy, took unto them certain lewd fellows of the baser sort, and gathered a company, and set all the city on an uproar, and assaulted the house of Jason, and sought to bring them out to the people.—ACTS, ch. 17.

4292. —— The Doubter's. *"The Way."* [4] Whither I go ye know, and the way ye know. [5] Thomas saith..Lord, we know not whither thou goest ; and how can we know the way ?— JOHN, ch. 14.

4293. —— Disappointment by. *Wilderness of Zin.* [5] Wherefore have ye made us to come up out of Egypt, to bring us in unto this evil place? it *is* no place of seed, or of figs, or of vines, or of pomegranates ; neither *is* there any water to drink.—NUM., ch. 20.

4294. —— by Darkness. *Hatred.* [11] He that hateth his brother is in darkness, and walketh in darkness, and knoweth not whither he goeth, because that darkness hath blinded his eyes.—1 JOHN, ch. 2.

4295. —— Errors from. *Sadducees.* [28] Whose wife shall she be of the seven ? for they all had her. [29] Jesus answered..Ye do err, not knowing the Scriptures, nor the power of God. [30] For in the resurrection they neither marry, nor are given in marriage, but are as the angels of God in heaven.—MAT., ch. 22.

4296. —— **False.** *Proverb.* [12] If thou sayest, Behold, we knew it not ; doth not he that pondereth the heart consider *it ?* and he that keepeth thy soul, doth *not* he know *it ?* and shall *not* he render to *every* man according to his works ?—Prov., ch. 24.

4297. —— —— *Peter.* [67] When she saw Peter warming himself, she looked upon him, and said, And thou also wast with Jesus of Nazareth. [68] But he denied, saying, I know not, neither understand I what thou sayest.—Mark, ch. 14.

4298. —— **Intentional.** *Selfish.* [13] Whoso stoppeth his ears at the cry of the poor, he also shall cry himself, but shall not be heard.—Prov., ch. 21.

4299. —— **Ignorant of.** *Pharisees.* [40] *Some* of the Pharisees..heard these words, and said ..Are we blind also ? [41] Jesus said..If ye were blind, ye should have no sin : but now ye say, We see ; therefore your sin remaineth.—John, ch. 9.

4300. —— **of Jesus.** *Apostles.* [3] That night they caught nothing. [4] But when the morning was now come, Jesus stood on the shore ; but the disciples knew not that it was Jesus.—John, ch. 20.

4301. —— **Justification of.** *Ahimelech.* [He helped David when escaping from Saul.] [14] Ahimelech answered the king..who *is so* faithful..as David, which is the king's son in law, and goeth at thy bidding, and is honourable in thine house ? [15] Did I then begin to inquire of God for him ? be it far from me : let not the king impute *any* thing unto his servant..for thy servant knew nothing of all this, less or more. —1 Sam., ch. 22.

4302. —— **and Knowledge.** *Ox.* [29] But if the ox were wont to push with his horn in time past, and it hath been testified to his owner, and he hath not kept him in, but that he hath killed a man or a woman ; the ox shall be stoned, and his owner also shall be put to death.—Ex., ch. 21.

4303. —— **Loss by.** *Word.* [19] When any one heareth the word of the kingdom, and understandeth *it* not, then cometh the wicked *one*, and catcheth away that which was sown in his heart. This is he which received seed by the way-side.—Mat., ch. 13.

4304. —— **manifested.** *At Jacob's Well.* [10] Jesus answered and said unto her, If thou knewest the gift of God, and who it is that saith to thee, Give me to drink ; thou wouldest have asked of him, and he would have given thee living water. [11] The woman saith unto him, Sir, thou hast nothing to draw with, and the well is deep : from whence then hast thou that living water ?—John, ch. 4.

4305. —— **Mitigation of.** *Paul.* [12] I thank Christ Jesus our Lord..that he counted me faithful, putting me into the ministry ; [13] Who was before a blasphemer, and a persecutor, and injurious : but I obtained mercy, because I did *it* ignorantly in unbelief.—1 Tim., ch. 1.

4306. —— —— *Gentiles.* [30] And the times of this ignorance God winked at ; but now commandeth all men every where to repent : [31] Because he hath appointed a day..judge the world. —Acts, ch. 17.

4307. —— **of Opportunity.** *Jerusalem.* [43] Thine enemies shall cast a trench..and compass thee round, and keep thee in on every side, [44] And shall lay thee even with the ground, and thy children within thee ; and they shall not leave in thee one stone upon another ; because thou knewest not the time of thy visitation.—Luke, ch. 19.

4308. —— **Poisoned through.** *" Gourds."* [39] One went out into the field to gather herbs, and found a wild vine, and gathered thereof wild gourds his lap full, and came and shred *them* into the pot of pottage : for they knew *them* not. [40] ..as they were eating of the pottage..they cried out, and said..*there is* death in the pot.— 2 Kings, ch. 4.

4309. —— **of Privilege.** *Woman of Samaria.* [10] Jesus..said..If thou knewest the gift of God, and who it is that saith to thee, Give me to drink, thou wouldest have asked of him, and he would have given thee living water. [11] The woman saith..Sir, thou hast nothing to draw with, and the well is deep : from whence then hast thou that living water ?—John, ch. 4.

4310. —— **A pretended.** *Joseph's Coat.* [32] They sent the coat of *many* colours..to their father ; and said, This have we found : know now whether it *be* thy son's coat or no. [33] And he knew it, and said, It *is* my son's coat ; an evil beast hath devoured him.—Gen., ch. 37.

4311. —— **in Prayer.** *Mother of John and James.* [21] Grant that these my two sons may sit, the one on thy right hand, and the other on the left, in thy kingdom. [22] But Jesus answered..Ye know not what ye ask. Are ye able to drink of the cup that I shall drink of ?—Mat., ch. 20.

4312. —— **Sorrow from.** *Two Angels.* [13] Woman, why weepest thou ? She saith unto them, Because they have taken away my Lord, and I know not where they have laid him.— John, ch. 20.

4313. —— **Spiritual.** *At Ephesus.* [1] Finding certain disciples, [2] He said..Have ye received the Holy Ghost since ye believed ? And they said..We have not so much as heard whether there be any Holy Ghost. [3] And he said..Unto what then were ye baptized ? And they said, Unto John's baptism.—Acts, ch. 19.

4314. —— **Superstitious.** *Heathen.* [4] When the barbarians saw the *venomous* beast hang on his hand, they said..No doubt this man is a murderer, whom, though he hath escaped the sea, yet vengeance suffereth not to live.—Acts, ch. 28.

4315. —— **Sins of.** *Sacrifice.* [27] If any one of the common people sin through ignorance, while he doeth *somewhat against* any of the commandments of the Lord..and be guilty ; [28] Or if his sin..come to his knowledge ; then he shall bring his offering, a kid of the goats, a female without blemish.—Lev., ch. 4.

4316. —— **of Transgression.** *Robbery.* [7] Ye are gone away from mine ordinances, and have not kept *them*. Return unto me, and I will return unto you, saith the Lord of hosts. But ye said, Wherein shall we return ? [8] Will a man rob God ? Yet ye have robbed me. But ye say, Wherein have we robbed thee ? In tithes and offerings.—Mal., ch. 3.

4317. —— **A temporary.** *Disciples.* ³³ They shall scourge him, and put him to death ; and the third day he shall rise again. ³⁴ And they understood none of these things : and this saying was hid from them.—LUKE, ch. 18.

4318. —— **Unrelieved.** *Ascension.* ⁶ They asked..Lord, wilt thou at this time restore again the kingdom to Israel ? ⁷ And he said..It is not for you to know the times or the seasons, which the Father hath put in his own power. —ACTS, ch. 1.

4319. —— **in Worship.** *At Athens.* [See No. 4320.]

4320. —— **of the Wise.** *Athenians.* ²² Then Paul stood in the midst of Mars' hill, and said, Ye men of Athens, I perceive that in all things ye are too superstitious. ²³ For as I passed by, and beheld your devotions, I found an altar with this inscription, TO THE UNKNOWN GOD. Whom therefore ye ignorantly worship, him declare I unto you.—ACTS, ch. 17.

See other illustrations under :

ERROR.
Sweeping. Barnabas also was carried away 2709
Sincere. There is a way that seemeth right..ways 2710

FOLLY.
Anger. Nabal answered, Who is David 3262
Ashamed. Held their peace..who should be the g. 3263
Backsliders. Forsaken..living waters..hewn 3264
Ecclesiastical. Whether is greater the gift or the 3265
Inseparable. Bray a fool in a mortar..not depart 3266
Indifference. Heareth..doeth not..built upon the 3267
Idolaters. Mouths but they speak not ; eyes..see 3268
" Warm himself..maketh a graven image 3269
Natural. Ostrich..G. hath deprived her of wisdom 3270
Neglect. Foolish..took no oil with them 3271
Worldly. I will pull down..build..eat, drink 3272
Youth. Rehoboam forsook the counsel of the old 3273

INFATUATION.
Blind. In the time of his distress did Ahaz trespass 4455
Reproved. Knowest thou not yet..Egypt is d. 4456
Wicked. They were driven out from Pharaoh's 4457
" Simon saw..H. G. was given, he offered 4458

MISTAKE.
Appearances. Eli thought she had been drunken 5468
Adversity. Bereaved..all these things are against 5469
Conscientious. I verily thought..I ought to do 5470
Corrected. There is death in the pot..bring meal 5471
Disastrous. The kings have smitten..Moab to the 5472
Glorious. She runneth..They have taken away 5473
Hearing. Eli, Eli, lama sabachthani..calleth for 5474
Infatuation. We will certainly burn incense..were 5475
Ignorance. In the resurrection, whose wife shall 5476
Man's. Samuel looked on Eliab..surely the L.'s 5477
Mortifying. King said to Haman..do so to Mor. 5478
Prejudice. I thought I ought..contrary to the 5479
Prosperity. Then had we plenty of victuals, and 5480
Serious. Altar of witness was supposed to be for 5481
Suspicion. David rather sent..to search the city 5482

SUPERSTITION.
Credulous. The gods are come..in the likeness of 8475
Fatal. Their gods are the gods of the hills 8476
Grievous. We also are men of like passions 8477
Ignorance. Changed their minds..he is a God 8478
Mistake. Viper fastened on Paul's hand..murderer 8479

Conjectured. If. were a prophet would have k. 1062
Dangerous. With A. went men..knew not anything 8322
Hopeless. Dost thou teach us?..cast him out 2788
Temporary. Third day he shall rise..saying was 1443

4321. ILLUSTRATION by Allegory. *Paul.* ²² Abraham had two sons, the one by a bondmaid, the other by a free woman. ²³ But he who was of the bondwoman was born after the flesh ; but he of the free woman was by promise. ²⁴ Which things are an allegory : for these are the two covenants.—GAL., ch. 4.

4322. —— **Effective.** *Pharisees.* ³⁷ Certain Pharisee besought him to dine with him : and he..sat down to meat. ³⁸..the Pharisee..marvelled that he had not first washed before dinner. ³⁹ And the Lord said..Now do ye Pharisees make clean the outside of the cup and the platter ; but your inward part is full of ravening and wickedness.—LUKE, ch. 11.

4323. —— **from Nature.** *Jesus.* ³⁰ Whereunto shall we liken the kingdom of God?.. ³¹ It is like a grain of mustard seed, which..is less than all the seeds that be in the earth : ³² But when it is sown, it groweth up, and becometh greater than all herbs, and shooteth out great branches ; so that the fowls of the air may lodge under the shadow of it.—MARK, ch. 4.

4324. —— **A striking.** *Good Samaritan.* ²⁹ He, willing to justify himself, said..And who is my neighbour ? ³⁰ And Jesus..said, A certain man went down from Jerusalem to Jericho, and fell among thieves, which stripped him of his raiment, and wounded him, and departed, leaving him half dead.—LUKE, ch. 10.

4325 IMAGE, A golden. *Idol.* ¹ Nebuchadnezzar the king made an image of gold, whose height was threescore cubits, and the breadth thereof six cubits : he set it up..in the province of Babylon.—DAN., ch. 3.

4326. —— **God's.** *Man.* ²⁶ Let us make man in our image, after our likeness : and let them have dominion..over all the earth.. ²⁷ So God created man in his own image, in the image of God created he him.—GEN., ch. 1.

4327. —— **A mysterious.** *Dream.* ³¹ This great image, whose brightness was excellent, stood before thee ; and the form thereof was terrible. ³² This image's head was of fine gold, his breast and his arms of silver, his belly and his thighs of brass, ³³ His legs of iron, his feet part of iron and part of clay.—DAN., ch. 2.

4328. —— **in the Temple.** *Manasseh.* ⁷ He set a graven image of the grove that he had made in the house..in Jerusalem, which I have chosen out of all the tribes of Israel, will I put my name for ever.—2 KINGS, ch. 21.

4329. IMAGES, Broken. *By Josiah.* ¹³ And the high places that were before Jerusalem.. which Solomon had builded for Ashtoreth.. and for Chemosh..and for Milcom..did the king defile. ¹⁴ And he brake in pieces the images, and cut down the groves, and filled their places with the bones of men.—2 KINGS, ch. 23.

4330. —— **Destruction of.** *Canaanites.* ⁵² Then ye shall drive out all the inhabitants of the land from before you, and destroy all their pictures, and destroy all their molten images.—NUM., ch. 33.

See other illustrations under

Divine. Let us make man in our image 2491
Iconoclast. Pious Josiah [See 2 Kings, ch. 23.]

See **IDOLATER.**

4331. IMAGERY, Grand. *David.* ² The Lord is my rock, and my fortress, and my deliverer ; ³ The God of my rock ; in him will I trust : he is my shield, and the horn of my salvation, my high tower, and my refuge, my saviour.—2 SAM., ch. 22.

4332. IMAGINATION, Wicked. *Antediluvians.* ⁵ God saw that the wickedness of man *was* great in the earth, and *that* every imagination of the thoughts of his heart *was* only evil continually. —GEN., ch. 6.

See other illustrations under :

DREAM.

Comforting. Ladder..angels descending on it	2503
Direction. Fear not to take unto thee Mary	2504
Delusive. Hungry man..and behold he eateth	2505
Forgotten. The thing is gone from me [Neb.]	2506
Interpreted. The three branches are three days	2514
Offensive. Your sheaves made obeisance to my	2515
Prophetic. [See Daniel 2 : 26-45.]	
Preserved. Joseph..take the young child and flee	2508
Reproof. G. came to Abimelech in a dream	2509
Trouble. Seven thin ears devoured the seven rank	2510
Terrifying. Fourth beast..iron teeth, it devoured	2511
Verified. This is..the sword of Gideon	2512
Warning. I have suffered in a dream [Pilate's wife]	2513

POEM.

Oldest. I will sing unto the L..he hath triumphed	6226
Songs. Solomon's..songs were 1005	6227

SUBLIMITY.

Descriptive. G. said. Let there be light	8407
Poetic. With the blast of thy nostrils the waters	8408

4333. IMITATION in Benevolence. *"Do Likewise."* ³³ A certain Samaritan .. when he saw him, he had compassion *on him,* ³⁴ And went to *him,* and bound up his wounds, pouring in oil and wine..Then said Jesus..Go, and do thou likewise.—LUKE, ch. 10. [Also see No. 4324.]

4334. —— of Childhood. *"Greatest."* ⁴ Whosoever therefore shall humble himself as this little child, the same is greatest in the kingdom of heaven.—MAT., ch. 18.

4335. —— Sacrilegious. *Incense.* ³⁷ As for the perfume which thou shalt make, ye shall not make to yourselves according to the composition thereof : it shall be unto thee holy for the Lord. ³⁸ Whosoever shall make like unto that, to smell thereto, shall even be cut off from his people. —EX., ch. 30.

4336. —— Unholy. *Exorcists.* ¹² The evil spirits went out of them. ¹³ Then certain of the vagabond Jews, exorcists, took upon them to call over them which had evil spirits the name of the Lord Jesus, saying, We adjure you by Jesus whom Paul preacheth.—ACTS, ch. 19.

4337. —— Vicious. *Lying.* ⁴⁴ Ye are of *your* father the devil, and the lusts of your father ye will do : he was a murderer from the beginning, and abode not in the truth, because there is no truth in him. When he speaketh a lie, he speaketh of his own : for he is a liar, and the father of it.—JOHN, ch. 8

See other illustrations under :

DISGUISE.

Battle. Ahab said, I will diguise myself	2382
Failure. Ahijah said, Come in, wife of Jeroboam	2383
Insufficient. Saul disguised himself [to visit witch]	2384
Penetrated. Is not the hand of Joab in this?	2385

EXAMPLE.

Encouragement. Paul..in presence of them all	2758
Following. Whither thou goest, I will go..lodge	2759
Hindered. Neither go in yourselves, neither	2760
Imitation. If I..have washed your feet..another's	2761
Instruction. If I then your L...ye also ought	2762
Inferior. Not move them with one of their fingers	2763
Justification. Read what David did when h.	2764
Light. Let your light so shine..good works	2765
Lord's. Disciple is not above his master	2766
Ministerial. Be thou [Timothy] an example	2767
Observation. Those things..seen in me, do	2768
Prayer. When ye pray say, Our Father which	2769
Public Life. This deed of the queen shall..abroad	2770
Teaching. We wrought..to make ourselves an e.	2771
Warning. All these things happened..for our	2772

RESEMBLANCE.

Desired. Let a double portion of thy spirit be	7186
Parental. Ye are of your father the devil	7182

4338. IMPATIENCE, Advice of. *Jesus' Brethren.* ² The Jews' feast of tabernacles was at hand. ³ His brethren therefore said..Depart hence, and go into Judea, that thy disciples also may see the works.. ⁵ For neither did his brethren believe in him.—JOHN, ch. 7.

4339. —— Counsels of. *Job's Wife.* ⁹ Dost thou still retain thine integrity? curse God, and die. ¹⁰ But he said..Thou speakest as one of the foolish women speaketh.—JOB, ch. 2.

4340. —— Foolish. *Golden Calf.* ¹ When the people saw that Moses delayed to come down out of the mount..Up, make us gods, which shall go before us ; for *as for* this Moses, the man that brought us up out of the land of Egypt, we wot not what is become of him. ² And Aaron said unto them, Break off the golden earrings.—EX., ch. 32. [Three thousand executed.]

4341. —— from Hunger. *Esau.* ³² Esau said, Behold, I *am* at the point to die : and what profit shall this birthright do to me? ³³ ..and he sold his birthright unto Jacob. ³⁴ Then Jacob gave Esau bread and pottage of lentiles.—GEN., ch. 25.

4342. —— and Patience. *David.* ⁶ He cast stones at David, and at all the servants..and all the mighty men *were* on his right hand and on his left. ⁷ And thus said Shimei when he cursed, Come out, come out, thou bloody man, and thou man of Belial.. ⁹ Then said Abishai.. Why should this dead dog curse my lord the king? let me go over, I pray thee, and take off his head.. ¹¹ And David said..Behold, my son ..seeketh my life : how much more now *may* this Benjamite do *it?* let him alone, and let him curse.—2 SAM., ch. 16.

4343. —— punished. *Moses.* ¹⁰ Hear now, ye rebels ; must we fetch you water out of this rock? ¹¹ And Moses..smote the rock twice : and the water came out abundantly.. ¹² And the Lord spake..Because ye believed me not, to sanctify me in the eyes of the children of Israel, therefore ye shall not bring this congregation into the land which I have given them.—NUM., ch. 20.

4344. —— leads to Sin. *Saul.*—1 SAM., ch. 13. [The Lord took the kingdom from him.]

4345. —— Unwise. *Rachel.* ¹ She bare Jacob no children, Rachel envied her sister ;

and said unto Jacob, Give me children, or else I die. [18]..as her soul was in departing, (for she died,]..she called his name Ben-oni : but his father called him Benjamin.—GEN., ch. 30.

4346. —— from **Weariness.** *Moses.* [13] They weep unto me, saying, Give us flesh, that we may eat. [14] I am not able to bear all this people alone, because *it is* too heavy for me. [15] And if thou deal thus with me, kill me, I pray thee, out of hand, if I have found favour in thy sight ; and let me not see my wretchedness.—NUM., ch. 11.

See other illustrations under :

COMPLAINERS.
Punished. Our soul loatheth..bread..sent fiery 1445
Unreasonable. The first supposed..received more 1446
Unprincipled. These are..walking in their own 1447
Wicked. Did bring up an evil report..the plague 1448

CROSSNESS.
Habitual. Nabal was churlish and evil in his 1849
Irritation. Let us alone that we may serve the 1848
Prejudice. Children crying, Hosannah.. sore dis. 1850

DISCONTENTMENT.
Foreigners. Hadad..to Pharaoh, Let me depart 2343
Proud. All this availeth me nothing..see M. 2344
Unity in. Every one that was discontented..unto 2345

IRRITABILITY.
Fretting. Fret not thyself because of evil doers 3416
Prejudice. Children crying..Hosannah..sore 1850
Peevish. To me they have ascribed but thousands 6039

MURMURING.
Disappointment. This evil place?..no place of figs 5639
Discouragement. People was much discouraged 5640
Distrust. Would G. that we had died in Egypt 5641
Fear. Did tell thee..been better serve the E. 5642
God. Hath not the potter power over the clay 5643
Mercenaries. These last have wrought but one 5644
Neglect. Murmuring of the Greeks against the 5645
Punished. Fire of the L. burnt them..uttermost 5646
Severity. What shall I do?..almost ready to stone 5647
Thirst. Three days..no water..bitter..what shall 5648

Fretting. Fret not thyself because of evil doers 3416
" Hannah..adversary provoked..make 2595

4347. **IMPENITENCE in Affliction.** *Ahaziah.* [2] Ahaziah fell down through a lattice in his upper chamber..and was sick : and he sent messengers, and said unto them, Go, inquire of Baal-zebub the god of Ekron whether I shall recover of this disease.—2 KINGS, ch. 1.

4348. —— **Hardened.** *Ahaziah.* [See above.] [6] Thus saith the Lord, *Is it* not because *there is* not a God in Israel, *that* thou sendest to inquire of Baal-zebub the god of Ekron? therefore thou ..shalt surely die. [7] And he said..What manner of man *was he* which came up to meet you, and told you these words? [8] And they answered him, *He was* a hairy man, and girt..about his loins. And he said, It *is* Elijah the Tishbite.— 2 KINGS, ch. 1. [He sent soldiers to arrest Elijah. Fire consumed them.]

See other illustrations under:

HARDNESS.
Adversity. In his distress did Ahaz trespass more 3797
Heart. Looked..anger being grieved..hardness 3798

OBDURACY.
Defiant. Who is the L. that I should obey? 5755
Final. Why have we..let I. go from serving us 5756
Foolish. Ahaz..sacrificed unto the gods..smote 5757

Jewish. Thy neck is as an iron sinew, and thy 5758
Spiritual. Woe unto thee, Chorazin..if the mighty 5759
Self-destructive. I know that G. hath determined 5760
to Truth. Paul spake..three months..divers were 5761
Unfeeling. Past feeling have given themselves 5762
Wild. Balaam..went with the princes of Moab 5763

OBSTINACY.
Provoking. It is a stiffnecked people..consume 5825
Rebuked. Why..smitten thine ass these 3 times? 5826
Rebellious. Nevertheless the people refused 5827

SELF-WILL.
Destructive. As a hen gathereth..ye would not 7731
Loss. Presumed to go up..Canaanites smote them 7732
Obstinate. We would certainly do whatsoever 7733
Sin. Rebellion is as the sin of witchcraft 7734
Work of. In their self-will they digged down a 7735

STUBBORNNESS.
Punished. They mocked..despised..therefore 8393
in Sin. To obey is better than sacrifice 8394
" We will certainly..burn incense to the 8395
" Took Dagon and set him in his place 8396

4349. **IMPERTINENCE rebuked.** *Peter.* [21] Be killed, and be raised again the third day. [22] Then Peter..began to rebuke him, saying, Be it far from thee, Lord : this shall not be unto thee. [23] But he turned, and said unto Peter, Get thee behind me, Satan : thou art an offence unto me : for thou savourest not the things that be of God, but those that be of men.—JOHN, ch. 19.

See other illustrations under :

OFFICIOUSNESS.
Mistaken. Disciples rebuked..J..much displeased 5872
Rebuked. Gehazi came to thrust her away 5873

4350. **IMPERFECTION overlooked.** *Jehu.* [29] *From* the sins of Jeroboam..Jehu departed not from them, *to wit,* the golden calves that *were* in Beth-el, and..Dan. [30] And the Lord said unto Jehu, Because thou hast done well in executing *that which is* right in mine eyes, *and* hast done unto the house of Ahab according to all that *was* in mine heart, thy children of the fourth *generation* shall sit on the throne of Israel.—2 KINGS, ch. 10. [The calves were symbols of Jehovah the true God.]

4351. —— **rejected.** *Priesthood.* [17] That hath *any* blemish, let him not approach to offer the bread of his God. [18]..a blind man, or a lame, or he that hath a flat nose, or any thing superfluous, [19] Or a man that is brokenfooted, or brokenhanded, [20] Or crookbacked, or a dwarf, or that hath a blemish in his eye, or be scurvy, or scabbed.—LEV., ch. 21.

See other illustrations under :

BLEMISH.
Disqualifies. Let him not approach the altar 813
Without. Absalom..from the sole..without b. 814

ERROR.
Sweeping. Barnabas also was carried away 2709
Sincere. There is a way that seemeth right..ways 2710

FAULTS.
Fastidious. Why do ye eat..with sinners? 3089
Faultfinder. Why..not sold for 300 pence..poor 3087
" J. B..hath a devil..son..gluttonous 3088
Official. Enemies could find none..fault..in Daniel 3086
One. When my master..house of Rimmon..lean 3083
Overlooked. Sins of Jehu..golden calves..done 4350
Unchurched. Neglect to hear the church..heathen 3084

FEEBLENESS.

Ashamed. I was ashamed to require..soldiers   3188
Age. Eli was 98 years old ; eyes were dim   3189
 "   David was old and stricken..gat no heat   3190

INCONSISTENCY.

Blot. Sol. loved the Lord..burnt incense   4387
Hypocritical. Pay tithe of mint..omit..mercy   4388
Inward. Make clean the outside of the cup   4389
Rebuked. Philistines said..be an adversary   4390
Shocking. Appear beautiful..full of..bones   4391

INFIRMITY.

Age. Can I discern what I eat or drink..hear   4464
 "   David was old..clothes..gat no heat   4465
 "   Keepers of the house shall tremble..bow   4466
 "   Moses 120 years..eye was not dim   4467
Overlooked. Temptation..in my flesh ye despised   4463

WEAKNESS.

Believers. Babes in Christ..not able to bear meat 9394
 "   Lest the people repent..return to   9395
Conscious. I am..weak, though anointed king   9396
Flesh. Moses' hands were heavy..stayed up his   9397
Instruments. L. sent flies..land was corrupted   9398
Moral. Peter separated..fearing them of the   9399
Personal. He that abideth in me bringeth forth   9400
Remembered. I was with you in weakness   9401
Submission. Ahab said, I am thine, and all that I 9402
Spiritless. All the kings..their heart melted   9403
 "   Ai smote..hearts of the people melted   9404

Baldness. He is bald, yet he is clean   627
Drunkards. Tables are full of vomit and filthiness 2376
Humiliating. Hanun..shaved off half their beards   2377
Ridiculed. Go up, thou bald head   628
Soldier's. That men say not a woman slew him   2386
Young Ruler. All..observed..one thing thou l.   4876

See BLAME *and references.*

4352. **IMPOSTOR, Called an.** *Jesus.* [12] Some said, He is a good man : others said, Nay ; but he deceiveth the people.—JOHN, ch. 7. [At feast of the Passover.]

4353. —— **punished.** *Elymas.* [At Paphos.] [8] Elymas the sorcerer..withstood them, seeking to turn away the deputy from the faith. [9] Then Saul..said.. [11]..the hand of the Lord *is* upon thee, and thou shalt be blind, not seeing the sun for a season. And immediately there fell on him a mist and a darkness ; and he went about seeking some to lead him by the hand.—ACTS, ch. 13.

4354. —— **Treated as an.** *Jesus.* [11] Herod with his men of war set him at nought, and mocked *him*, and arrayed him in a gorgeous robe, and sent him again to Pilate.—LUKE, ch. 23.

4355. **IMPOSTORS exposed.** *Sons of Sceva.* [14] There were seven sons of *one* Sceva..chief of the priests, which did so. [15] And the evil spirit answered..Jesus I know, and Paul I know ; but who are ye? [16] And the man in whom the evil spirit was, leaped on them, and overcame them ..so that they fled out of that house naked and wounded.—ACTS, ch. 19. [They tried to exorcise evil spirits in the name of Jesus.]

4356. —— **punished.** *Gibeonites.* [22] Joshua called for them..Wherefore have ye beguiled us, saying, We *are* very far from you ; when ye dwell among us? [23]..ye *are* cursed, and there shall none of you be freed from being bondmen, and hewers of wood and drawers of water for the house of my God.—JOSH., ch. 9. [They came

with old clothes and mouldy bread, as if long on the way.]

4357. **IMPOSITION, A conjugal.** *Jacob.* [25] In the morning, behold, it *was* Leah : and he said to Laban, What *is* this thou hast done unto me? did not I serve with thee for Rachel? wherefore then hast thou beguiled me?—GEN., ch. 29.

<small>See other illustrations under :</small>

FALSEHOOD.

Agreement. Ananias kept back part..wife..privy   2985
Begets. My master hath sent me..went no   2986
Bribery. Say ye..stole him..they took the money   2987
Covering. Began to curse..I know not the man   2988
Folly. Ananias, was it not thine? and after it was 2989
Father. Your father the devil..no truth in him   2990
Impostors. Jacob said to his father..the L.   2991
Saved by. David said to Ahimelech, The king sent   2992
 "   Jonathan said, David..run to Bethlehem   2994
Short-lived. Lying tongue is but for a moment   2995
Statecraft. Garments and shoes..old..long journey 2996
Sacrilegious. An angel spake..bring him back   2993
Spirit of. I will be a lying spirit in..prophets   2997
Sin. Thou hast not lied unto men, but..G.   2998
Victim. Joseph's master put him in prison   2999

FRAUD.

Appearances. Gibeonites..took old sacks..old   3408
Commercial. Take thy bill..quickly..write fifty   3409
Demagogue. O that I were a judge..do justice   2171
Pious. Sons of the prophets give..silver [Gehazi] 3410
Religious. His enemy..sowed tares..wheat   3411
Spiritual. Simon offered money..Holy Ghost   3412
Traitor's. Whomsoever I shall kiss..is he   3413
Wages. Hire of the labourers kept..crieth   3414

TRICK.

Diplomatic. From a very far country are..come   8955
Hypocrites. Feign themselves just men..might   8956
Legerdemain. Magicians..rods became serpents   8957
Politicians. Shall ask a petition..save of thee   8958

See DECEPTION *and* HYPOCRISY.

4358. **IMPORTUNITY, Desperate.** *Jacob.* [25] When he saw that he prevailed not..he touched the hollow of his thigh ; and the..thigh was out of joint, as he wrestled with him. [26] And he said, Let me go, for the day breaketh. And he said, I will not let thee go, except thou bless me. —GEN., ch. 32.

4359. —— **Power of.** *Prayer.* [7] Trouble me not : the door is now shut, and my children are with me in bed ; I cannot rise and give thee? [8]..Though he will not rise and give him, because he is his friend, yet because of his importunity he will rise and give him as many as he needeth. —LUKE, ch. 11.

4360. —— **in Prayer.** "*Unjust Judge.*" [3] There was a widow in that city..saying, Avenge me of mine adversary. [4] And he would not for a while : but afterward he said within himself, Though I fear not God, nor regard man ; [5] Yet because this widow troubleth me, I will avenge her, lest by her continual coming she weary me. —LUKE, ch. 18.

4361. —— **tested.** *Canaanite.* [24] He answered..I am not sent but unto the lost sheep of the house of Israel. [25] Then came she..saying, Lord, help me. [26] But he answered..It is not meet to take the children's bread, and to cast *it* to dogs. [27] And she said, Truth, Lord : yet the dogs eat of the crumbs which fall.. [28] Then Jesus answered..her, O woman, great *is* thy faith : be it unto thee even as thou wilt.—MAT., ch. 15.

4362. —— **undiscouraged.** *Blind Bartimeus.*
[46] Sat by the highway side begging. [47] ..he began to cry out, and say, Jesus, *thou* Son of David, have mercy on me. [48] And many charged him that he should hold his peace : but he cried the more a great deal, Thou Son of David, have mercy on me.—Mark, ch. 10.

4363. —— **Wearying by.** *Delilah.* [16] When she pressed him daily with her words, and urged him, *so* that his soul was vexed unto death ; [17]..he told her all his heart..There hath not come a razor upon mine head ; for I *have been* a Nazarite..if I be shaven, then my strength will go from me.—Judges, ch. 16.

See other illustrations under :

INTERCESSION.

Denied. I will not return with thee..L. rejected	4616
Effect. Let it alone this year also	4617
Friendly. Wherefore then wilt thou slay David	4618
" Wilt thou not spare the place for fifty	4619
Limit. I will not destroy it for ten's sake..L. went	4620
Needless. They came near to the steward of J.	4621
Needed. Take your flocks..and bless me also	4622
Obtained. I have sinned..Samuel turned again	4623
Penitential. I have transgressed..pardon my sin	4624
Rewarded. Forgive..if not blot me..cleft of the r.	4625
Resented. Moses and Aaron..get you unto your	4626

4364. IMPROVEMENT by Adversity. *Jews.*
[13] After all that is come upon us for our evil deeds..seeing that thou our God hast punished us less than our iniquities *deserve*, and hast given us *such* deliverance as this ; [14] Should we again break thy commandments, and join in affinity with the people of these abominations ?—Ezra, ch. 9.

4365. —— **or Loss.** *Jesus said,* [11] It is given unto you to know the mysteries of the kingdom of heaven, but to them it is not given. [12] For whosoever hath, to him shall be given, and he shall have more abundance : but whosoever hath not, from him shall be taken away even that he hath.—Mat., ch. 13.

4366. —— **necessary.** *Fig Tree.* [6] He came and sought fruit thereon, and found none. [7] Then said he unto the dresser..Behold, these three years I come seeking fruit on this fig tree, and find none : cut it down ; why cumbereth it the ground ?—Luke, ch. 13.

4367. —— **Responsibility for.** *Talent.* [28] Take therefore the talent from him, and give *it* unto him which hath ten talents. [29]..but from him that hath not, shall be taken away even that which he hath. [30] And cast ye the unprofitable servant into outer darkness : there shall be weeping and gnashing of teeth.—Mat., ch. 25.

See other illustrations under :

GROWTH.

Beautiful. Soul shall be as a well watered garden	3739
Continuous. Flourish like the palm tree..fruit in	3740
Christian. Your faith groweth exceedingly	3741
Divine. Jesus increased in wisdom and stature	3742
Esteem. Samuel grew..in favour with G. and man	3743
Fruit. Branch that beareth not he taketh away	3744
Grace. Like a tree planted by the rivers of water	3745
Imperceptible. First the blade, then the ear..corn	3746
Inward. Leaven..meal till the whole was leavened	3747
Outward. Becometh greater than all herbs	3748
Perfection. Path..shineth more and more	3749
Stages. Blade..ear..full corn in the ear	3750
Strength. Clean hands shall be stronger and	3751
Spiritual. Child [J. B.]..grew and waxed strong	3752

INCREASE.

Miraculous. Five loaves and two fishes..5000 fed	4392
" Should I set this before a hundred	4393

PROGRESS.

Christian. Path..shineth more and more	6631
Hindered. Chariot wheels..they drave them heavily	6632
Spiritual. See men as trees..saw clearly	6634
Time for. When thou hearest a sound..trees	6633

TEACHABLENESS.

Attitude. Mary sat at Jesus' feet..heard his word	8606
Characteristic. Received the word with..readiness	8607
Manifested. Eunuch desired Philip..sit with him	8608
Professed. All here present before G. to hear all	8609
Youthful. Found him in the temple..hearing them	8610

Culture. Ornament of grace unto thy head	1865
Cultivation. Let it alone..till I shall dig about it	1867
Mending. Piece of a new garment upon an old	5338
Without. Fed not with meat, hitherto..nor yet now	605

4368. IMPRUDENCE, Dangerous. *Hezekiah.*
[12] King of Babylon, sent letters and a present unto Hezekiah : for he..had been sick. [13] And Hezekiah ..shewed them all..his precious things, the silver, and the gold, and the spices, and the precious ointment, and *all* the house of his armour, and all that was found in his treasures : there was nothing..in all his dominion, that Hezekiah shewed them not.—2 Kings, ch. 20. [All were captured.]

See other illustrations under :

DESPERATION.

Boldness. I will go in unto the king..If I perish	2218
Effort. Why sit we here till we die ?	2219
Sinners. Saul inquired of the L...answered him	2220
Sacrifices. King of Moab took his eldest son	2221

IMPULSE.

Affectionate. Peter..cast himself into the sea	4374
Dangers. Peter..smote the high priest's servant	4375
Rash. Master, I will follow..foxes..birds	4376

RASHNESS.

Answering. Are ye able to drink of the cup ?	6851
Courageous. Peter..drew his sword..smote off his	6852
Drunkards. Ask of me whatever thou wilt..Herod	6853
Decree. Let it be written [all Jews]..may be d.	6854
Enterprise. Sitteth not down first and counteth	6855
Hunger. To die, and what profit..birthright do me ?	6856
Heedless. See thou say nothing to any..publish it	6857
Ignorance. With whomsoever thou findest thy	6858
Judgment. David to Ziba..thine are all M.	6859
Needless. With [whom]..found..let him die	6860
Perilous. Mighty men brake through the host	6861
Ruler's. I will chastise you with scorpions	6862
Responsibility. Answereth a matter before he h.	6863
Reproof. Eli said, How long wilt thou be drunken	6864
Vowing. Saul had adjured the people, cursed	6865
Youth. Asahel..wherefore should I smite thee	6866
Zeal. Slay my two sons if I bring him not	6867

4369. IMPURITY, Holiness reveals. The Cherubim. *Vision.* [3] One cried unto another, and said, Holy, holy, holy, *is* the Lord of hosts : the whole earth *is* full of his glory.. [5] Then said I, Woe *is* me ! for I am undone ; because I *am* a man of unclean lips, and I dwell in the midst of a people of unclean lips : for mine eyes have seen the King, the Lord of hosts.— Isa., ch. 6.

See other illustrations under :

CLEANSING.

Blood. Sprinkled it on the people	1343
" If the blood of bulls..much more..blood of	1344

by Expulsion. Jesus made a scourge..drove them 1345
Holy Fire. Live coal..upon my mouth..cleansed 1346
Heart. Create in me a clean heart 1347
Spiritual. Who shall ascend..clean hands 1348
Typical. Needeth not save to wash his feet 1349

DEPRAVITY.
Ancient. Wickedness of man was great..every 2188
Bestial. Sons of Belial beset the house 2189
Discovered. Woe is me !..unclean lips 2190
Heathen. God gave them up to uncleanness 2191
Infectious. Both the daughters of Lot with child 2192
Inherited. Ye are..of them that killed the prophets 2193
Natural. All gone aside..filthy..none doeth g. 2194
Unconscious. Is thy servant a dog..do this thing? 1526

GUILT.
Accumulated. Upon you..all the righteous blood 3766
Cowardice. Adam and his wife hid 3767
Degrees. One owed 500 pounds, the other 50 3768
Panic. Egyptians said, Let us flee 3769
See SIN and WICKEDNESS.

4370. IMPRESSIONS, Abiding. *Early.* [24] By
faith Moses, when he was come to years, refused to be called the son of Pharaoh's daughter ; [25] Choosing rather to suffer affliction with
the people of God, than to enjoy the pleasures
of sin for a season.—HEB., ch. 11.

4371. —— Superficial. *Stony Ground.*
[16] These are .. sown on stony ground ; who,
when they have heard the word, immediately
receive it with gladness ; [17] And have no root in
themselves, and so endure but for a time : afterward, when affliction or persecution ariseth for
the word's sake, immediately they are offended.
—MARK, ch. 4.

4372. —— Transient. *At Sinai.* [18] All the
people saw the thunderings, and the lightnings,
and the noise of the trumpet, and the mountain
smoking..and stood afar off. [19] And they said
unto Moses, Speak thou with us, and we will
hear : but let not God speak with us, lest we
die.—Ex., ch. 20. [Soon they made the golden
calf.]
See other illustrations under :

AWAKENING.
of Conscience. Herod said..J. B. was risen 595
Fear. Earthquake..this was the S. of G. 596
Great. All the people, both small and great 597
General. All the land of Judea..all baptized 598
Sudden. Came trembling..What must I do 599
Trouble. L..troubled the Egyptians..flee 600
Truth. Paul reasoned..Felix trembled 601
Unexpected. Our brother..therefore this distress 602

EMOTION.
Changed. Jesus shewed them his hands..disciples 2625
Exhibited. Shaphan read it..the king rent his 2622
Irrepressible. Joseph made haste..sought where 2623
Mixed. Ancient men..seen the first..wept 2626
 " From the sepulchre with fear and great 2627
Opposite. If these should hold their peace 2628
Worship. Mourn not..they heard..law 2624

EXCITEMENT.
Abstinence. Saul rose from the earth..neither did 2777
Creating. [Stephen's enemies] stirred up the 2778
Ecstasy. Peter said..it is good for us to be here 2779
 vildoers. They were instant with loud voices 2780
General. Multitude cometh..could not eat 2781
Needless. Israel..to go up to war against 2782
Public. City was moved..this is Jesus 2783
Trembling. [Jailer] came trembling..what must 2784
Wild. Some cried one thing, some another 2785

SENSES.
Impressed. People saw the thunderings..lest we 7745
Impaired. Can thy servant taste..hear 7746
 " That look out of the windows be d. 7747
Use of. Jacob felt him..smelled..his raiment 7748
See FEELINGS.

4373. IMPRISONMENT of the Innocent. *Joseph.* [19] When his master heard the words of
his wife..saying, After this manner did thy servant to me..his wrath was kindled. [20]..put
him into the prison.—GEN., ch. 39.
See other illustrations under :
Speedy. Not do the law..judgment be executed 630
 See CAPTIVITY and references.

4374. IMPULSE, An affectionate. *Peter.*
[7] Now when Simon Peter heard that it was the
Lord, he girt *his* fisher's coat *unto him*, for he
was naked, and did cast himself into the sea.
[8] And the other disciples came in a little ship.—
JOHN, ch. 21.

4375. —— Dangers of. *Peter.* [10] Simon
Peter having a sword drew it, and smote the
high priest's servant, and cut off his right ear.
—JOHN, ch. 18.

4376. —— A rash. *Disciple.* [19] A certain
scribe..said..Master, I will follow thee whithersoever thou goest. [20] And Jesus saith .. The
foxes have holes, and the birds of the air *have*
nests ; but the Son of man hath not where to
lay *his* head.—MAT., ch. 8.
See other illustrations under :
Vexation. Delilah pressed him daily..told her all 4363
 See RASHNESS and references.

4377. IMPUDENCE, Self-confessed. *Accusers.*
[An adulteress was brought.] [7] When they continued asking him, he..said..He that is without
sin among you, let him first cast a stone at her.
[8] And again he stooped down, and wrote on the
ground. [9] And they..being convicted by *their
own* conscience, went out one by one..and Jesus was left alone, and the woman. — JOHN,
ch. 8.
See other illustrations under :

INSOLENCE.
Added. [Danite robbers] said unto Micah, What 4530
Fraternal. With whom hast thou left those few 4531
Friends. Hanun cut off the garments in the 3431
Injustice. There is no straw..ye are idle 4532
Resented. Whatsoever is pleasant in thine eyes 4533

Shameless. Were they ashamed..neither could 7831

4378. INCARNATION, Divine. *Jesus.*
[34] Said Mary unto the angel, How shall this be,
seeing I know not a man? [35] And the angel
answered..The Holy Ghost shall come upon
thee, and the power of the Highest shall over-
shadow thee : therefore also that holy thing that
shall be born of thee shall be called the Son of
God.—LUKE, ch. 1.
Also see :
Advent. Mary brought forth her first-born son 122

4379. INCEST, A Brother's. *Amnon.* [12] Nay,
my brother, do not force me ; for no such thing
ought to be done in Israel : do not thou this
folly. [13] And I, whither shall I cause my shame
to go ? and as for thee. thou shalt be as one of
the fools in Israel.—2 SAM., ch. 13.

4380. —— in the Church. *Corinth.* [1] It is
reported commonly *that there is* fornication

among you, and such fornication as is not so much as named among the Gentiles, that one should have his father's wife .. mourned.—1 Cor., ch. 5.

4381. —— **Shameful.** *Lot.* ²⁶ Thus were both the daughters of Lot with child by their father.—Gen., ch. 19.

4382. INCENSE, Idolatrous. *Israelites.* ⁴ Hezekiah..brake in pieces the brazen serpent that Moses had made..the children of Israel did burn incense to it.—2 Kings, ch. 18.

4383. INCENDIARY, Ingenious. *Samson.* ⁴ Samson..caught three hundred foxes..and put a firebrand in the midst between two tails. ⁵ And..he let *them* go into the standing corn of the Philistines, and burnt up both the shocks, and also the standing corn, with the vineyards *and* olives.—Judges, ch. 15.

4384. —— **A sacrilegious,** *Temple.* ⁸ Nebuzar-adan, captain of the guard..of the king of Babylon.. ⁹ ..burnt the house of the Lord, and the king's house, and all the houses of Jerusalem, and every great *man's* house. —2 Kings, ch. 25.

See other illustrations under :
Arson. We will burn thy house upon thee 503
Dwellings. Nebuzar-adan..burnt every great man's 4384
Synagogues. Burned up all the synagogues in the 4129

4385. INCONGRUITY, Economic. *Old Bottles.* ³⁷ No man putteth new wine into old bottles ; else the new wine will burst the bottles, and be spilled, and the bottles shall perish.—Luke, ch. 5.

4386. —— **Remedial.** *Clay.* ⁶ He spat on the ground, and made clay of the spittle, and he anointed the eyes of the blind man with the clay, ⁷ And said..Go, wash in the pool of Siloam..He went his way therefore, and washed, and came seeing.—John, ch. 9.

See HYPOCRISY.

4387. INCONSISTENCY a Blot. *Solomon.* ³ Solomon loved the Lord, walking in the statutes of David his father : only he sacrificed and burnt incense in high places.—1 Kings, ch. 3.

4388. —— **Hypocritical.** *Gnat.* ²³ Woe unto you, scribes and Pharisees, hypocrites ! for ye pay tithe of mint and anise and cummin, and have omitted the weightier *matters* of the law, judgment, mercy, and faith.. ²⁴ *Ye* blind guides, which strain at a gnat, and swallow a camel.— Mat., ch. 23.

4389. —— **Inward.** *Platter.* ²⁵ Woe unto you, scribes and Pharisees, hypocrites ! for ye make clean the outside of the cup and of the platter, but within they are full of extortion and excess. ²⁶ *Thou* blind Pharisee, cleanse first that *which is* within the cup and platter.—Mat., ch. 23.

4390. —— **rebuked.** *David's.* ⁴ The princes of the Philistines were wroth with him ; and ..said..Make this fellow return..and let him not go down with us to battle, lest in the battle he be an adversary to us : for wherewith should he reconcile himself unto his master? *should it* not *be* with the heads of these men?—1 Sam., ch. 29.

4391. —— **Shocking.** *Bones.* ²⁷ Woe unto you, scribes and Pharisees, hypocrites ! for ye

are like unto whited sepulchres, which indeed appear beautiful outward, but are within full of dead *men's* bones, and of all uncleanness. ²⁸ Even so ye also outwardly appear righteous unto men, but within ye are full of hypocrisy and iniquity.—Mat., ch. 23.

See other illustrations under :
INCONGRUITY.
Economic. No man putteth new wine into old 4385
Remedial. Anointed the eyes of the blind man 4386

4392. INCREASE, A miraculous. *Five Loaves.* ⁴¹ He looked up to heaven, and blessed, and brake the loaves, and gave *them* to his disciples to set before them ; and the two fishes divided he among them all. ⁴² And they did all eat, and were filled. ⁴³ And they took up twelve baskets full of the fragments, and of the fishes. ⁴⁴ And they..were about five thousand men.—Mark, ch. 6.

4393. —— —— *Twenty Loaves.* [To Elisha.] ⁴³ His servitor said, What, should I set this before a hundred men ? He said again, Give the people, that they may eat : for thus saith the Lord, They shall eat, and shall leave *thereof.* ⁴⁴ ..And they did eat, and left *thereof.*—2 Kings, ch. 4.

See other illustrations under :
GROWTH.
Beautiful. Soul shall be as a well watered garden .. 3739
Continuous. Flourish like the palm tree..fruit in .. 3740
Christian. Your faith groweth exceedingly 3741
Divine. Jesus increased in wisdom and stature 3742
Esteem. Samuel grew..in favour with G. and man 3743
Fruit. Branch that beareth not he taketh away 3744
Grace. Like a tree planted by the rivers of water .. 3745
Imperceptible. First the blade, then the ear..corn 3746
Inward. Leaven..meal till the whole was leavened 3747
Outward. Becometh greater than all herbs 3748
Perfection. Path..shineth more and more 3749
Stages. Blade..ear..full corn in the ear 3750
Strength. Clean hands shall be stronger and 3751
Spiritual. Child [J. B.]..grew and waxed strong .. 3752

HARVEST.
Abundant. Joseph gathered corn..without num. .. 3803
First Fruits. Bring a sheaf of the first fruits 3804
Great. The field is the world..reapers the angels 3805
Gleaning. [Boaz to Ruth] Glean not in another .. 3806
Prayer. That he will send forth labourers 3807
Promise. While earth remaineth, seed time and .. 3808
Poor Man's. Not make clean the corners..poor .. 3809
Sewing. Plowman..open and break the clods 3810
Secret. He which soweth sparingly shall reap also 3811

Gospel. Left houses or brethren..hundredfold now .. 3

4394. INCREDULITY, Disciples'. *Resurrection.* ⁹ Returned from the sepulchre, and told all these things.. ¹⁰ It was Mary Magdalene, and Joanna, and Mary *the mother* of James, and other *women that were* with them, which told these things unto the Apostles. ¹¹ And their words seemed to them as idle tales, and they believed them not.—Luke, ch. 21.

4395. —— —— *At Emmaus.* ¹² He appeared in another form unto two of them, as they walked, and went into the country. ¹³ And they went and told *it* unto the residue : neither believed they them.—Mark, ch. 16.

4396. —— **Determined.** *Thomas.* ²⁵ Said.. Except I shall see in his hands the print of the nails, and put my finger into the print of the nails, and thrust my hand into his side, I will not believe.—John, ch. 20.

4397. —— **with Prayer.** *Disciples.* [12] Where many were gathered together praying. [13] And as Peter knocked..a damsel came to hearken, named Rhoda. [14] And..she opened not the gate for gladness, but ran in, and told how Peter stood before the gate. [15] And they said..Thou art mad. But she constantly affirmed that it was even so. Then said they, It is his angel.—Acts, ch. 12.

4398. —— **removed.** *Thomas.* [Eight days after.] [27] Thomas, Reach hither thy finger, and behold my hands; and reach hither thy hand, and thrust *it* into my side; and be not faithless, but believing. [28] And Thomas answered..My Lord and my God.—John, ch. 20.

4399. —— **of Unbelievers.** *Jews.* [18] The Jews did not believe..that he had been blind, and received his sight, until they called the parents .. [19] And they asked them, saying, Is this your son, who ye say was born blind? how then doth he now see?—John, ch. 9.

See other illustrations under:

DISTRUST.
Adversity. They hearkened not unto Moses for   2448
Evildoers. Money..in our sacks..seek occasion   2449
Forbidden. Take no thought..what ye shall eat   2450
Needless. Consider the lilies how they grow   2451
Persuasions. Let not Hezekiah deceive you   2452
Without. Ravens neither sow nor reap..G. feedeth 2453

DOUBT.
Adversity. They hearkened not..for anguish   2493
Disappointment. Told them..he was alive   2494
Forbidden. How much more will he clothe you   2495
Hurtful. King said, They know that we be hungry 2496
Impossible. Fire of the L. fell..licked up the w. 2497
Obedience. Do his will, he shall know of the d. 2498
Struggling. Hast thou eyes..seest thou as man   2499
Strong. Except I put my finger in the print   2500
Snare. People is great and taller than we   2501
Trouble. Would G. it were morning..were   2502
See UNBELIEF.

4400. **INDEPENDENCE exhibited.** *Paul.* [34] Yea..these hands have ministered unto my necessities, and to them that were with me. [35] I have shewed you all things, how that so labouring ye ought to support the weak.—Acts, ch. 20.

4401. —— **Financial.** *Abram.* [22] Abram said to the king of Sodom, I have lifted up mine hand unto the Lord.. [23] That I will not *take* from a thread even to a shoelatchet, and that I will not take any thing that *is* thine, lest thou shouldest say, I have made Abram rich.—Gen., ch. 14.

4402. —— **of Opinion.** *Joshua.* [15] If it seem evil unto you to serve the Lord, choose you this day whom ye will serve; whether the gods..that *were* on the other side of the flood, or the gods of the Amorites..but as for me and my house, we will serve the Lord. [16] And the people answered and said, God forbid that we should forsake the Lord, to serve other gods.—Josh., ch. 24.

4403. —— **Youthful.** *Prodigal.* [11] A certain man had two sons: [12] And the younger..said to *his* father, Father, give me the portion of goods that falleth *to me.* And he divided unto them *his* living.—Luke, ch. 15.

See other illustrations under:

LIBERTY.
Choice. Father give..He divided unto them   4962
Common. Casting out devils..Forbid him not   4963
not License. Take heed lest..liberty..stumbling 4964

REBELLION.
Abominable. Rebellion is as the sin of witchcraft 6874
Ingrates. Absalom sent spies..say Absalom   6875
Ill-government. Thy father made our yoke   6876
Jealousy. Ye take too much upon you [Korah]   6877
Mental. Not enter..ye rebelled against my word   6878
Sinners. We will not have this man to reign   6879
   "   This is the heir; come, let us kill him   6880
Tongue. Every kind of beasts..been tamed   6881
Uncontested. Ye shall not fight..return every man 6882
Vain. Sheba blew a trumpet..we have no part   6883
Will. How oft would I..but ye would not   6884

SELF-WILL.
Destructive. As a hen gathereth..ye would not   7731
Loss. Presumed to go up..Canaanites smote them   7732
Obstinate. We will certainly do whatsoever   7733
Sin. Rebellion is as the sin of witchcraft   7734
Work of. In their self-will they digged down a wall 7735
                                                 ────
Birthright. Abraham had two sons..by a free w.   3415
Financial. These hands have ministered..my   537

4404. **INDECISION, Loss by.** *Reuben.* [29] Reuben returned..and, behold, Joseph *was* not in the pit; and he rent his clothes. [30] And he returned unto his brethren, and said, The child *is* not; and I, whither shall I go?—Gen., ch. 37.

See other illustrations under:

HESITATION.
Discipleship. I will follow thee, but   3964
Punished. Fire of the L. burnt..uttermost parts 3965
                                                 ────
Sad. Pilate sought to release..delivered he him 4662

4405. **INDIFFERENCE in Hearing.** *Sand.* [26] Every one that heareth these sayings of mine, and doeth them not, shall be likened unto a foolish man, which built his house upon the sand: [27] And the rain descended, and the floods came, and the winds blew, and beat upon that house; and it fell: and great was the fall of it.—Mat., ch. 7.

4406. —— **Inconsiderate.** *Pound.* [20] Lord, behold, *here is* thy pound, which I have kept laid up in a napkin.—Luke, ch. 19.

4407. —— **Provoking.** *Josiah said,* [13] Great *is* the wrath of the Lord that is kindled against us, because our fathers have not hearkened unto the words of this book.—2 Kings, ch. 22.

4408. —— **Pitiless.** *Priest.* [30] A certain man..fell among thieves, which stripped him of his raiment, and wounded *him,* and departed, leaving *him* half dead. [31] ..there came down a certain priest that way; and when he saw him, he passed by on the other side.—Luke, ch. 10.

4409. —— **to Others' Sin.** *Judas.* [3] Brought again the thirty pieces of silver to the chief priests and elders, [4] Saying, I have sinned in that I have betrayed the innocent blood. And they said, What *is that* to us? see thou *to that.*—Mat., ch. 27.

4410. —— **of Sinners.** *Feast.* [4] Tell them which are bidden, Behold, I have prepared my dinner: my oxen and *my* fatlings *are* killed, and all things *are* ready: come unto the marriage. [5] But they made light of *it,* and went their ways, one to his farm, another to his merchandise.—Mat., ch. 22.

4411. —— **Unbelievers'.** *Flood.* [26] As it was in the days of Noe, so shall it be also in the days of the Son of man. [27] They did eat, they drank, they married wives, they were given in marriage, until the day that Noe entered into the ark, and the flood came, and destroyed them all.—LUKE, ch. 17.

4412. INDIFFERENT, Curse upon. *Deborah said,* [23] Curse ye Meroz, said the angel of the Lord, curse ye bitterly the inhabitants thereof; because they came not to the help of the Lord, to the help of the Lord against the mighty.—JUDGES, ch. 5.

4413. —— **Woe upon the.** *At Ease.* [1] Woe to them *that are* at ease in Zion, and trust in the mountain of Samaria, *which are* named chief of the nations, to whom the house of Israel came! [3] Ye that put far away the evil day.—AMOS, ch. 6.

See other illustrations under :

CARELESSNESS.
Fire. He that kindleth the fire..restitution 1051
Presumptions. If it be known that the ox..used 1052
Responsibility. If a man shall open a pit and not 1053

EASE.
Care for. Trouble me not..in bed, I cannot arise 2586
Indifference. If ye offer the lame and sick is it not 2587
Promised. Soul thou hast much goods..take thine 2588
Religious. Woe unto them that are at ease in Zion 2589

FORGETTING.
God. When thou shalt have eaten and be full 3342
" Jeshurun waxed fat and kicked 3343
" When thy silver and thy gold..is multiplied 3344
Sanctuary. If I forget..Jerusalem..hand..cunning 3345

FORGETFULNESS.
Adversity. Whom I loved have turned against me 3346
Caution. Take heed..lest thou forget..thine eyes 3347
of God. Have eaten..full, beware..forget the L. 3342
" Jeshurun..lightly esteemed the rock 3343
" When silver and gold is multiplied..forget 3344
Religious. I will not go..He went back with him 3348
Sanctuary. If I forget thee, O Jerusalem..tongue 3345
Spiritual. Face in a glass..straightway forgetteth 3349

NEUTRALITY.
Advised. Refrain from these men, and let them 5720
Disagreeable. Because thou art lukewarm..spue 5721
Impossible. Fall on this stone be broken..it shall 5722
No. He that is not against us is on our side 5723
Punished. Lived sumptuously..in hell torments 5724
Silent. If the L. be G. follow him..not a word 5725
Unreasonable. If the L. be G. follow him, but if 5726
Wanting. One basket had very good figs..the other 5727

Adversity. I called my servants..no answer [Job] 3346
Continued. Mordecai hearkened not unto them 102
See NEGLECT.

4414. INDIGNITY, Humiliating. *Prince said,* [3] Thinkest thou that David doth honour thy father, that he hath sent comforters unto thee? hath not David *rather* sent his servants ..to spy.. [4] Wherefore Hanun took David's servants, and shaved off the one half of their beards, and cut off their garments in the middle, *even* to their buttocks, and sent them away.—2 SAM., ch. 10.

See other illustrations under :

CONTEMPT.
Bigots. I am not as other men..as this publican 1618
Critics. Michal saw David..despised him in her 1619
Conceited. The thistle..to the cedar..Give thy d. 1620

Disregarded. They laughed us to scorn and 1621
Enemy's. The Philistine disdained him..but a y. 1622
Expressed. How shall this man [Saul] save us? 1623
Fraternal. With whom hast thou left those few s. 1624
Gospel. They made light of it..one to his farm 1625
God. Saying to a stock, Thou art my father 1626
Insulting. They spare not to spit in my face 1627
Malicious. They did spit in his face and buffeted 1628
Others. Parable..that they were righteous and 1629
Worship. Behold what a weariness is it? 1630

DERISION.
Horrible. Put on him a scarlet robe..crown 2197
Impious. Laughed them to scorn, and mocked 2198
Punished. Sarah saw the son of Hagar..mocking 2199
Nickname. Thou art a Samaritan, and hast a devil 2200
Truth. Pharisees who were covetous..derided 2201
Unfortunates. Thieves also..cast the same into 2202
Wicked. They shoot out the lip, and shake the 2203

INSULT.
Ignored. Despised him [Saul]..held his peace 4567
First. Thrust him [Jesus] out of the city..headlong 4568
Rewarded. Cut off their garments in the middle 4569
Stinging. To smite him on the mouth 4570

RIDICULE.
Doctrine. When they heard of the resurrection 7425
Fatal. Call for Samson, that he may make us sport 7426
Failure. Not able to finish..begin to mock him 7427
Horrible. He saved others, let him save himself 7428
Impious. They laughed them to scorn, and mocked 7429
" What will this babbler say [Athenians] 7430
Insulting. Cut off their garments..their buttocks 7431
Opposition. What do these feeble Jews? will they 7432
" If a fox go up, he shall break down 7433
Punishment. Children of Bethel..Go up, thou bald 7434
Royalty. Wearing the crown of thorns and purple 7435
Scornful. They laughed us to scorn, and despised us 7436
Spirit. Mocking said, These men are full of new 7437
Trial. They reviled him and said, We are Moses' 7438

SCOFFERS.
Malicious. Prophesy unto us, thou Christ..who 7614
" Herod arrayed him in a gorgeous robe 7615

SCORN.
of Pride. [Haman] Scorn to lay hands on Mordecai 7618
Public. All clap their hands at thee, and hiss 7619
Taunt. Who made thee a prince and a judge over 8592
Unbelief. She sleepeth..they laughed him to scorn 7620

4415. INDIGNATION, Bigoted. *Ruler.* [13] He laid *his* hands on her : and immediately she was made straight, and glorified God. [14] And the ruler of the synagogue answered with indignation, because that Jesus had healed on the sabbath day.—LUKE, ch. 13. [She was bent over for eighteen years.]

4416. —— **Contemptuous.** *Eliab.* [28] Eliab his eldest brother heard..and Eliab's anger was kindled against David, and he said, Why camest thou down hither? and with whom hast thou left those few sheep in the wilderness? I know thy pride, and the naughtiness of thine heart; for thou art come down that thou mightest see the battle.—1 SAM., ch. 17.

4417. —— **Christian.** *At Idolatry.* [16] While Paul waited for them at Athens, his spirit was stirred in him, when he saw the city wholly given to idolatry.—ACTS, ch. 17.

4418. —— **Excessive.** *At Samaritans.* [54] When his disciples James and John saw *this*, they said, Lord, wilt thou that we command fire to come down from heaven, and consume them, even as

Elias did ?   [55] But he turned, and rebuked them, and said, Ye know not what manner of spirit ye are of.—LUKE, ch. 9. [Samaritans were inhospitable.]

4419. —— **Forgotten.** *Hazael.* [12] The evil that thou wilt do unto the children of Israel : their strong holds wilt thou set on fire, and their young men wilt thou slay with the sword, and wilt dash their children, and rip up their women with child. [13] And Hazael said, But what, *is* thy servant a dog, that he should do this great thing?—2 KINGS, ch. 8. [He did it.]

4420. —— **God gives.** *Saul.* [See No. 4431.]

4421. —— **Hot.** *Moses.* [19] As soon as..he saw the calf, and the dancing..Moses' anger waxed hot, and he cast the tables out of his hands, and brake them beneath the mount. [20] And he took the calf..and burnt *it* in the fire, and ground *it* to powder, and strewed *it* upon the water, and made the children of Israel drink of *it.*—EX., ch. 32.

4422. —— **at Hypocrisy.** *Jesus.* [3] He saith unto the man which had the withered hand, Stand forth. [5] And when he had looked round about on them with anger, being grieved for the hardness of their hearts, he saith..Stretch forth thine hand.—MARK, ch. 3.

4423. —— **at Injustice.** *Elihu.* [See No. 4432.] [3] Against his three friends was his wrath kindled, because they had found no answer, and *yet* had condemned Job.—JOB, ch. 32.

4424. —— **Improper.** *Ointment.* [3] In the house of Simon the leper, as he sat at *meat,* there came a woman having an alabaster box of ointment of spikenard very precious ; and she brake the box, and poured *it* on his head. [4] And there were some that had indignation within themselves, and said, Why was this waste of the ointment made ?—MARK, ch. 14. [Equal to $45. Judas sold his Lord for one third the amount.]

4425. —— **at the Judgment.** *Devouring.* [26] If we sin wilfully after that we have received the knowledge of the truth, there remaineth no more sacrifice for sins, [27] But a certain fearful looking for of judgment and fiery indignation, which shall devour the adversaries.—HEB., ch. 10.

4426. —— **Murderous.** *At Nazareth.* [27] Many lepers were in Israel in the time of Elisha..and none of them was cleansed, saving Naaman the Syrian. [28] And all they in the synagogue, when they heard these things, were filled with wrath, [29] And rose up, and thrust him out of the city, and led him unto the brow of the hill, whereon their city was built, that they might cast him down headlong.—LUKE, ch. 4.

4427. —— **National.** *Gibeans.* [They committed a fatal outrage on a woman.] [7] There was no such deed done nor seen..unto this day : consider of it, take advice, and speak *your minds.* [8] And all the people arose as one man, saying, We will not any *of us* go to his tent, neither will we any *of us* turn into his house.. [9]..this..we will do to Gibeah ; *we will go up* by lot against it.—JUDGES, ch. 20.

4428. —— **A natural.** *Mother of James and John.* [21] What wilt thou? She saith..Grant that these my two sons may sit, the one on thy right hand, and the other on the left, in thy kingdom. [24] And when the ten heard *it,* they

were moved with indignation against the two brethren.—MAT., ch. 20.

4429. —— **Partisan.** *At Jerusalem.* [17] The high priest rose up, and all..is..of the Sadducees, and were filled with indignation, [18] And laid their hands on the apostles, and put them in the common prison.—ACTS, ch. 5.

4430. —— **of Pride.** *Haman.* [9] Then went Haman forth that day joyful and with a glad heart : but when Haman saw Mordecai in the king's gate, that he stood not up, nor moved for him, he was full of indignation against Mordecai. [10] Nevertheless Haman refrained himself.—ESTHER, ch. 5.

4431. —— **Righteous.** *Saul's.* [2] Nahash the Ammonite answered them, On this *condition* will I make *a covenant* with you, that I may thrust out all your right eyes, and..lay it *for* a reproach upon all Israel.. [6] And the Spirit of God came upon Saul when he heard those tidings, and his anger was kindled greatly.—1 SAM., ch. 11.

4432. —— **Religious.** *Elihu.* [2] Against Job was his wrath kindled, because he justified himself rather than God.—JOB, ch. 32.

4433. —— **at Others' Sins.** *David.* [5] David's anger was greatly kindled against the man ; and he said to Nathan, *As* the Lord liveth, the man that hath done this *thing* shall surely die : [6] And he shall restore the lamb fourfold.—2 SAM., ch. 12.

4434. —— **at Severity.** *Parable.* [The merciless servant.] [33] Shouldest not thou also have had compassion on thy fellow servant, even as I had pity on thee ? [34] And his lord was wroth, and delivered him to the tormentors, till he should pay all that was due unto him.—MAT., ch. 18.

See other illustrations under :

RESENTMENT.

Cruel. Herod slew all the children..Bethlehem   7183
Indignant. Woman was fallen..hands on the   7184
of Self-seeking. Much displeased with James and   7185

SCORN.

of Pride. Haman..scorn to lay hands on Mordecai 7618
Public. All clap their hands at thee, and hiss, and   7619
Unbelief. She sleepeth..they laughed him to   7620

Controlled. Nevertheless Haman refrained himself 4430
   See **ANGER** and references.

4435. INDISCRIMINATION in Calamities. *National.* [1] The Lord maketh the earth empty, and maketh it waste, and turneth it upside down, and scattereth abroad the inhabitants thereof. [2] And it shall be, as with the people, so with the priest ; as with the servant, so with his master ; as with the maid, so with her mistress ; as with the buyer, so with the seller ; as with the lender, so with the borrower ; as with the taker of usury, so with the giver of usury to him.—ISA., ch. 24.

4436. INDOLENCE exhibited. *Husbandman.* [30] I went by the field of the slothful, and by the vineyard of the man void of understanding ; [31] And, lo, it was all grown over with thorns, *and* nettles had covered the face thereof, and the stone wall thereof was broken down.—PROV., ch. 24.

4437. —— **Excuse of.** *Proverb.* [13] The slothful *man* saith, *There is* a lion without, I shall be slain in the streets.—PROV., ch. 22.

4438. —— **Perfect.** *Proverb.* [24] A slothful man hideth his hand in *his* bosom, and will not so much as bring it to his mouth again.—PROV., ch. 19.

4439. —— **Shame from.** *Poverty.* [4] He becometh poor that dealeth *with* a slack hand : but the hand of the diligent maketh rich. [5] He that gathereth in summer *is* a wise son : *but* he that sleepeth in harvest *is* a son that causeth shame. —PROV., ch. 10.

4440. —— **Wasteful.** *Proverb.* [9] He also that is slothful in his work is brother to him that is a great waster.—PROV., ch. 18.

See other Illustrations under :

IDLENESS.

Accusation. No straw..ye are idle, ye are idle 4270
Ecstatic. Why stand ye gazing into heaven ? 4271
Needless. Why stand ye here all the day idle ? 4272
Perishing. If we sit still here we die also [lepers] 4273

SLUGGARD.

Reproved. Go to the ant, thou sluggard 8145
Vexatious. As smoke to the eyes, so is the sluggard 8146
" Way of the slothful..full of thorns 8147

4441. INDULGENCE, Parental. *Eli.* [13] Because his sons made themselves vile, and he restrained them not. [14]..therefore I have sworn ..that the iniquity of Eli's house shall not be purged with sacrifice nor offering for ever.—1 SAM., ch. 2.

See other illustrations under :

FAVOUR.

Evinced. Boaz commanded the young men, Let 3092
Indicated. The king held out to Esther the 3093
Resented. Jacob loved Joseph..coat of many 3098

KINDNESS.

Appreciated. Barzillai..I will feed thee in J. 4808
Animals. Rebekah..I will draw for thy camels 4809
Bereavement. In the choice of our sepulchres, bury 4810
Brethren. Waken poor ; thou shalt relieve him 4811
Conquerors. Saul..is this thy voice..David..wept 4812
Christians. Disciples..relief unto brethren..Judea 4814
Captives. Clothed naked..shod them..eat and 4815
Father. If ye..know how to give..much more..F. 4816
Gratitude. Mephibosheth..kindness for Jonathan's 4817
Insulted. David sent to comfort him..cut 4819
Inopportune. Ahab..because thou hast let go 4820
Loan. Hath pity..lendeth to the Lord 4821
Providential. Boaz unto Ruth..abide here 4822
Prosperity. I delivered the poor that cried [Job] 4823
Prisoner. Jeremiah put these..rags under..arms 4824
Remembered. Lest I destroy you, for ye shewed 4825
Rewarded. Rahab..hid them with the flax..saved 4826
Substitutional. I was eyes to the blind..feet [Job] 4827
Servant. Centurion's servant who was dear to him 4828
Strangers. Drink my lord..wasted..gave him 4829
Timely. Barzillai brought beds..flour..butter..to 4830
Unexpected. Shall I smite them ?..Let bread 4831
Widow. Harvest..forgot a sheaf..be for thee 4832

PARTIALITY.

Complaint. There arose a murmuring of the 5985
Improper. Weareth gay clothing..sit thou here 5986
Justifiable. But to Benjamin he gave 300 pieces of 5988
Surprising. Benjamin's mess was five times as 5989

4442. INDUSTRY, Active. *Rebekah.* [18] She hasted, and let down her pitcher upon her hand, and gave him drink. [19] And when she had done giving him drink.. [20]..she hasted, and emptied her pitcher into the trough, and ran again unto

the well to draw *water*, and drew for all his camels.—GEN., ch. 24.

4443. —— **Benevolent.** *Dorcas.* [39] Peter.. went with them..and all the widows stood by him weeping, and shewing the coats and garments which Dorcas made, while she was with them.—ACTS, ch. 9.

4444. —— **commended.** *Parable.* [6] Go to the ant, thou sluggard ; consider her ways, and be wise : [7] Which having no guide, overseer, or ruler, [8] Provideth her meat in the summer, *and* gathereth her food in the harvest ?—PROV., ch. 6.

4445. —— **Domestic.** *Model Woman.*— PROV., ch. 31.

4446. —— **Independent.** *Paul.* [2] The barbarous people shewed us no little kindness : for they kindled a fire, and received us every one, because of the present rain, and because of the cold. [3]..Paul had gathered a bundle of sticks, and laid *them* on the fire.—ACTS, ch. 28.

4447. —— **Jesus'.** *At Nazareth.* [2] What wisdom *is* this which is given unto him, that even such mighty works are wrought by his hands ? [3] Is not this the carpenter?— MARK, ch. 6.

4448. —— **Promotion by.** *Jeroboam.* [28] Jeroboam *was* a mighty man of valour : and Solomon seeing the young man that he was industrious, he made him ruler over all the charge of the house of Joseph.—1 KINGS, ch. 11.

4449. —— **required.** *Christians.* [10] This we commanded you, that if any would not work, neither should he eat. [11] For we hear that there are some which walk among you disorderly, working not at all, but are busybodies. — 2 THESS., ch. 3.

See other illustrations under :

ACTIVITY.

Astonishing. Jesus..could not so much as eat bread 92
Benevolent. Jesus went..all the cities and villages 93
vs. Eloquence. Slow of speech..do signs 91
vs. Spirituality. Mary sat..feet..Martha..cumbered 94

BUILDER.

Jotham. Built cities in the mountains..castles, and 953
Unsuccessful. Laid the foundation..not able 954
Visionary. I will pull down my barns and build 955

BUSINESS.

Capacity. [Pharaoh to Joseph] None so discreet 985
Diligence. Man diligent in business..stand before 986
Frauds. Take thy bill, quickly..write fifty 988
Spiritual. [Stewards] Men..honest..full of H. S. 991
Success. Joseph gathered up all the money 993
Talent. [Cattle] The feebler were Laban's 994

DILIGENCE.

Lack. Provide not for his own..worse..infidel 2308
Success. Seest thou a man diligent in his business 2309

ENGRAVING.

Inspired. Bezaleel..in cutting of stones..carving 2671
Lord's. Tables..writing of G. graven upon the 2672
Law. Set thee up great stones..plaster..write 2673

EMPLOYMENT.

Honoured. Is not this the carpenter..? 2629
Innocence. The earth..subdue..dominion..Eden 2630

LABOUR.

Advantage. Sleep of a labouring man is sweet..eat 4864
Curse. Thorns and thistles..sweat of thy face 4865
Commanded. Six days shalt thou labour 4866

Congenial. Put him into the garden..keep it — 4867
Co-operative. One soweth, another reapeth — 4868
Degradation. In the sweat of thy face — 4869
Increase. No straw be given..tale of bricks — 4870
Menial. Hewers of wood and drawers of water — 4871
Motive. That..we may be accepted of him — 4872

MECHANIC.

Apostle. [Paul and Aquila] were tentmakcrs — 5268
Christ. Is not this the carpenter?..offended — 5269
Expert. Hiram..worker in brass..came to S. — 5270
Independence. Not be chargeable, wrought — 5272
Lost. No smith..lest Hebrews make swords — 5277
Original. Tubal Cain an instructor of every artifice 5271
Opposition. Alexander the coppersmith did..harm 5273
    "   Called workmen of like occupation — 5274
Renown. Not any..hew timber..like Sidonians — 5276

Occupation. Thy servant's trade hath been about — 5830
Offensive. Every shepherd is an abomination unto 5831
See WORK.

4450. INFANT, Accidental Death of. *"Over-laid."* [19] This woman's child died in the night ; because she overlaid it.—1 KINGS, ch. 3,

4451. INFANTS for Jesus. *"Touch them."* [See No. 4454.]

4452. —— Murder of. *Hebrews'.* [22] Pharaoh charged all his people, saying, Every son that is born ye shall cast into the river, and every daughter ye shall save alive.—Ex., ch. 1.

4453. —— Massacre of. *Herod.* [16] Herod, when he saw that he was mocked of the wise men, was exceeding wroth, and sent forth, and slew all the children that were in Bethlehem, and in all the coasts thereof, from two years old and under.—MAT., ch. 2.

4454. —— Regard for. *Jesus.* [15] They brought..infants, that he would touch them : but when *his* disciples saw *it,* they rebuked them. [16] But Jesus called them *unto him,* and said, Suffer little children to come unto me, and forbid them not : for of such is the kingdom of God.—LUKE, ch. 18.

See other illustrations under :
Spiritual. Babes in Christ ; I have fed you with — 605
Sympathy. Babe wept..she had compassion — 107
See CHILD and CHILDREN.

4455. INFATUATION, Blind. *Ahaz.* [21] Ahaz took away a portion *out* of the house of the Lord, and..of the king, and of the princes, and gave *it* unto the king of Assyria : but he helped him not. [22] And in the time of his distress did he trespass yet more against the Lord.—2 CHRON., ch. 28.

4456. —— reproved. *Pharaoh.* [7] Pharaoh's servant said unto him, How long shall this man be a snare unto us ? let the men go, that they may serve the Lord their God : knowest thou not yet that Egypt is destroyed?—Ex., ch. 10.

4457. —— of the Wicked. *Pharaoh.* [10] I will let you go, and your little ones : look *to it ;* for evil *is* before you. [11] Not so : go now ye *that are* men, and serve the Lord ; for that ye did desire. And they were driven out from Pharaoh's presence.—Ex., ch. 10. [After seven plagues.]

**4458. —— —— ** *Simon.* [18] When Simon saw that through laying on of the apostles' hands the Holy Ghost was given, he offered them money.—ACTS, ch. 8.

See other illustrations under :
DELUSION.

Destructive. Ahaz sacrificed unto the gods that — 2168
Success. Our god hath delivered Samson..into — 2169
Wicked. Lot seemed as one that mocked to his — 2170

INSANITY.

Exhibited. Hairs were grown like eagle's — 4514
Feigned. David..feigned himself mad..spittle — 4515
Moral. Pharaoh said..see my face no more — 4516
Occasional. Evil spirit from God came upon Saul — 4517
Sinners. When he came to himself..bread — 4518
So-called. His friends said, he is beside himself — 4519
    "   Paul, thou art beside thyself..mad — 4520

Curious Arts. [Ephesians] used curious arts..burn 908
Imposition. Magicians..cast down..rod..serpent 5162

4459. INFERENCE, A mistaken. *Apostles.* [After resurrection of Jesus.] [6] When they.. were come together, they asked of him, saying, Lord, wilt thou at this time restore again the kingdom to Israel? [7] And he said..It is not for you to know the times or the seasons.— ACTS, ch. 1.

4460. —— A wrong. *Naaman.* [7] *Am* I God, to kill and to make alive, that this man doth send unto me to recover a man of his leprosy ? Wherefore consider, I pray you, and see how he seeketh a quarrel against me. [8]..when Elisha ..had heard that the king of Israel had rent his clothes, that he sent to the king, saying..let him come now to me, and he shall know that there is a prophet in Israel.—2 KINGS, ch. 5.

4461. —— A warranted. *Miracle.* [6] They were not able to draw it for the multitude of fishes. [7] Therefore that disciple whom Jesus loved saith unto Peter, It is the Lord.—JOHN, ch. 21.

4462. INFERENCES differ. *At Jerusalem.* [28] Father, glorify thy name. Then came there a voice from heaven, *saying,* I have both glorified *it,* and will glorify *it* again. [29] The people ..said that it thundered : others said, An angel spake to him.—JOHN, ch. 12.

See other illustrations under :
MISTAKE.

Appearances. Eli thought she had been drunken — 5468
Adversity. Bereaved..all these things are against — 5469
Conscientious. I verily thought..I ought to do — 5470
Corrected. There is death in the pot..bring meal — 5471
Disastrous. The kings have smitten..Moab to the — 5472
Glorious. She runneth..They have taken away — 5473
Hearing. Eli, Eli, lama sabachthani..calleth for — 5474
Infatuation. We will certainly burn incense..were 5475
Ignorance. In the resurrection, whose wife shall — 5476
Man's. Samuel looked on Eliab..surely the L.'s — 5477
Mortifying. King said to Haman..do so to Mord. — 5478
Prejudice. I thought I ought. contrary to the — 5479
Prosperity. Then had we plenty of victuals, and — 5480
Serious. Altar of witness was supposed to be for — 5481
Suspicion. David rather sent..to search the city — 5482

Erroneous. Why doth this man speak blasphemies? 6873

4463. INFIRMITY overlooked. *Paul's.* [13] Ye know how through infirmity of the flesh I preach- ed the gospel unto you at the first. [14] And my temptation which was in my flesh ye despised not, nor rejected ; but received me as an angel of God, *even* as Christ Jesus.—GAL., ch. 4.

4464. INFIRMITIES of Age. *Barzillai.* [Da- vid asked him to go to Jerusalem and live.]

[34] Can I discern between good and evil? can thy servant taste what I eat or what I drink? can I hear any more the voice of singing men and singing women? wherefore then should thy servant be yet a burden unto my lord the king?—2 SAM., ch. 19.

4465. —— —— *David.* [1] King David was old *and* stricken in years ; and they covered him with clothes, but he gat no heat.—1 KINGS, ch. 1.

4466. —— —— *Described.* [3] In the day when the keepers of the house shall tremble, and the strong men shall bow themselves, and the grinders cease because they are few, and those that look out of the windows be darkened, [4] And the doors shall be shut in the streets, when the sound of the grinding is low, and he shall rise up at the voice of the bird, and all the daughters of music shall be brought low ; [5] Also *when* they shall be afraid of *that which is* high, and fears *shall be* in the way, and the almond tree shall flourish, and the grasshopper shall be a burden, and desire shall fail : because man goeth to his long home, and the mourners go about the streets.—ECCL., ch. 12.

4467. —— —— *Without.* [7] Moses *was* a hundred and twenty years old when he died : his eye was not dim, nor his natural force abated.—DEUT., ch. 34.

See other illustrations under :

FAINT.
Pursuing. David pursued, he and 400..200 so faint 2880
Strength. Wait upon the L..run, and not be weary 2881

FAINTING.
Hunger. I. were distressed..none..tasted food 2882
Preserved. I had fainted unless I had believed 2883
" Our outward man perish, yet the 2884
Weakness. If thou faint..thy strength is small 2885

FATIGUE.
of Indifference. Table of the L..Behold what a 3078
Overcome. 200 were so faint they could not go 3079
Overwork. Come..into a desert place, and rest 3080
Sleep. He cometh..disciples, and findeth them 3081
Travellers. Jesus being wearied..sat thus on the 3082

FEEBLENESS.
Ashamed. I was ashamed to require..soldiers 3188
Age. Eli was 98 years old ; eyes were dim 3189

WEAK.
Care for. Offend one of these little ones..hanged 9391
" Take heed lest..a stumblingblock 9392
Help. If there be no man to save us, we will come 9393

WEAKNESS.
Believers. Fed you with milk..not able to bear it 9394
" Repent when they see war, and return 9395
Conscious. I am this day weak, though..king 9396
Flesh. Moses' hands were heavy..stayed up his h. 9397
Instruments. Lice..flies..land was corrupted 9398
Moral. Peter separated himself, fearing them 9399
Personal. Abide in me..without me..nothing 9400
Remembered. I was with you in weakness 9401
Submission. I am thine, and all that I have 9402
Spiritless. Their hearts melted, neither..any s. 9403
" Hearts..melted and became as water 9404

Care. Brethren, comfort the feeble—1 Thess. 5 : 14
Destroyed. Amalekites smote all..feeble—Deut. 25 : 18
Death. Abner dead, Ish-bosheth's..feeble—2 Sam. 4 : 1
Despised. What do these feeble Jews? 7429
Disqualifies. Any blemish let him not approach the 813
Exempt. Not one feeble person among their tribes 6723
Fear. Angel rolled back the stone..as dead men 261

One. One thing thou lackest..sell..give..cross 4876
" When my master goeth..Rimmon to worship 3083
Overlooked. Jehu..thou hast done well..in part 4351
Weariness. Thou layest the burden of all..on me 9448
Without. Absalom..from the sole..without blemish 814

4468. INFLUENCE bequeathed. *Elijah.* [14] He took the mantle of Elijah that fell from him, and smote the waters, and said, Where *is* the Lord God of Elijah? And..they parted hither and thither : and Elisha went over.—2 KINGS, ch. 2.

4469. —— Care for. *Eating.* [20] All things indeed *are* pure ; but *it is* evil for that man who eateth with offence. [21] *It is* good neither to eat flesh, nor to drink wine, nor *any thing* whereby thy brother stumbleth, or is offended, or is made weak.—ROM., ch. 14.

4470. —— of Example. *Prayer.* [1] As he was praying in a certain place, when he ceased, one of his disciples said..Lord, teach us to pray, as John also taught his disciples.—LUKE, ch. 11.

4471. —— felt. *Baptist's.* [20] Herod feared John, knowing that he was a. just man and a holy, and observed him ; and when he heard him, he did many things, and heard him gladly. —MARK, ch. 6.

4472. —— of Leaders. *"Rulers."* [48] Have any of the rulers or of the Pharisees believed on him ? [49] But this people who knoweth not the law are cursed.—JOHN, ch. 7.

4473. —— Parental. *Rechab.* [5] I set before the sons of the house of the Rechabites pots full of wine, and cups, and I said..Drink ye wine. [6] But they said, We will drink no wine : for..our father commanded us, saying, Ye shall drink no wine, *neither* ye, nor your sons for ever.—JER., ch. 35.

4474. —— Posthumous. *Abel.* [4] By faith Abel offered unto God a more excellent sacrifice than Cain, by which he obtained witness that he was righteous, God testifying of his gifts : and by it he being dead yet speaketh.—HEB., ch. 11.

4475. —— —— *Elisha.* [20] The Moabites invaded the land.. [21]..as they were burying a man..they spied a band *of men ;* and they cast the man into the sepulchre of Elisha : and when the man..touched the bones of Elisha, he revived, and stood up on his feet.—2 KINGS, ch. 13.

4476. —— Pernicious. *Pharisees.* [13] Woe unto you, scribes and Pharisees, hypocrites ! for ye shut up the kingdom of heaven against men : for ye neither go in *yourselves*, neither suffer ye them that are entering to go in.—MAT., ch. 23.

4477. —— Personal. *Shunammite's Child.* [The prophet's rod had failed.] [33] Elisha..shut the door upon them twain, and prayed unto the Lord. [34]..and lay upon the child, and put his mouth upon his mouth, and his eyes upon his eyes, and his hands upon his hands : and he stretched himself upon the child ; and the flesh of the child waxed warm.—2 KINGS, ch. 4.

4478. —— Responsibility for. *Offend.* [6] But whoso shall offend one of these little ones which believe in me, it were better for him that a millstone were hanged about his neck, and *that* he were drowned in the depth of the sea.—MAT., ch. 18.

4479. —— regarded. *In War.* [8] The officers
..shall say, What man *is there that is* fearful and
fainthearted ? let him go and return unto his
house, lest his brethren's heart faint as well as
his heart.—DEUT., ch. 20.

4480. —— of Rank. *Vashti.* [17] The king
Ahasuerus commanded Vashti the queen to be
brought in before him, but she came not. [18] *Likewise* shall the ladies of Persia and Media say..
which have heard of the deed of the queen.
Thus *shall there arise* too much contempt and
wrath.—ESTHER, ch. 1.

4481. —— Supernatural. *Kine.* [10] The men
..took two milch-kine, and tied them to the
cart, and shut up their calves at home : [11] And
they laid the ark of the Lord upon the cart..
[12] And the kine took the straight way to..Beth-
shemesh, *and* went along the highway, lowing
as they went, and turned not aside *to* the right
hand or *to* the left.—1 SAM., ch. 6.

4482. —— Survival of. *Dorcas.* [39] Peter
..went with them. When he was come, they
brought him into the upper chamber : and all
the widows stood by him weeping, and shewing
the coats and garments which Dorcas made,
while she was with them.—ACTS, ch. 9.

See other illustrations under :

DOMINION.

Dream. Your sheaves..made obeisance to my   2489
Feared. The fear of you shall be upon every beast 2490
Made for. Let us make..dominion over..all the   2491

LEADERSHIP.

Failure. Went ill with Moses..spake unadvisedly 4924
Loved. Diotrephes, who loveth to have the   4925
Rejected. Let us make a captain and return to E. 4927
Trials. People chode with Moses..Why have ye   4926

PERSUASION.

Excuse. Because thou hast hearkened unto..wife 6106
Ineffective. Paul would not be persuaded, we   6107

POWER.

Delegated. Why could we not cast him out   6312
Endowment. Filled..began to speak with other   6313
God gives. [Samson] L. blessed..Spirit began   6314
God only. [Peter] By our own power, made   6315
Loss. [Samson] Shake myself..wist not that the L. 6316
Might. Not by might, nor by power..great   6317
Promised. [Joshua] Not any able to stand   6318
Prayer. [Hezekiah] prayed Sennacherib..85,000 6319
Preaching. My speech..demonstration of the S. 6320
Ruling. Rebuked the wind, the raging water   6321
Spiritual. [Stephen] Not able to resist the   6322
Spirit. [Samson] Cords..upon his arms..as flax 6323
Sudden. [Joseph] No man lift up his hand or   6324
Tears. [Moses] Babe wept..had compassion on   6327
Temptation. All these will I give thee [Satan] 6325
Waiting. Wait for the promise..receive power   6329
Weakness. I am weak, though anointed [David]   6328

See GOVERNMENT and references.

4483. INGENUITY by Inspiration. *Bezaleel.*
[35] Hath he filled with wisdom of heart, to work
all manner of work, of the engraver, and of the
cunning workman, and of the embroiderer, in
blue, and in purple, in scarlet, and in fine linen,
and of the weaver, *even* of them that do any
work.—Ex., ch. 35.

4484. —— A Mother's. *Moses'.* [3] When
she could not longer hide him, she took for him
an ark of bulrushes, and daubed it with slime
and with pitch, and put the child therein ; and

she laid *it* in the flags by the river's brink. [4] And
his sister stood afar off, to wit what would be
done to him.—Ex., ch. 2.

See other illustrations under :

ART.

Architect. [Bezaleel] Filled with the spirit..to 506
Music. [David] Cunning in playing..man of war   71
War. [Uzziah] Made engines..invented by   508

INVENTION.

Musical. Jubal..handle the harp and the organ 4643
Inspired. Bezaleel..filled with the spirit..cunning 4644

INVENTORS.

Family. Jubal..harp..Tubal-cain..artificer in 4645
Valuable. Uzziah made..engines..he was strong 4646

4485. INGRATITUDE of Beneficiaries. *Nine
Lepers.* [15] One of them, when he saw that he
was healed, turned back, and with a loud voice
glorified God, [16] And fell down on *his* face at his
feet, giving him thanks : and he was a Samaritan. [17] And Jesus .. said, Were there not ten
cleansed ? but where *are* the nine ?—LUKE, ch. 17.

4486. —— confessed. *To Mordecai.* [1] On
that night could not the king sleep, and..the
chronicles .. were read before the king. [2] And
it was found written, that Mordecai had told of
..two of the king's chamberlains..who sought
to lay hand on the king Ahasuerus. [3] And the
king said, What honour and dignity hath been
done to Mordecai for this?..There is nothing
done for him.—ESTHER, ch. 6.

4487. —— after Deliverance. *Dethrone God.*
[12] When ye saw that Nahash the king of the
children of Ammon came against you, ye said
unto me, Nay ; but a king shall reign over us :
when the Lord your God *was* your king.—1 SAM.,
ch. 12.

4488. —— Royal. *Saul.* [9] David said to
Saul, Wherefore hearest thou men's words, saying, Behold, David seeketh thy hurt ? [10] Behold
..the Lord had delivered thee to day into mine
hand in the cave : and *some* bade *me* kill thee :
but *mine eye* spared thee.—1 SAM., ch. 24.

4489. —— Vengeance for. *Zechariah.* [22] Joash
the king remembered not the kindness which
Jehoiada his father had done to him, but slew
his son. And when he died, he said, The Lord
look upon *it* and require *it.*—2 CHRON., ch. 24.

See other illustrations under :

Confessed. I have rewarded thee evil [King Saul] 8635
Neglect. Were not ten cleansed ? but where are the 3701
Reminded. D. did put his life in his hand..slew 3694

4490. INHERITANCE, Tendency of. *Proverb.*
[22] A good *man* leaveth an inheritance to his children's children : and the wealth of the sinner
is laid up for the just.—PROV., ch. 13.

4491. —— Uncertainty of. *Solomon.* [18] I
hated all my labour which I had taken under
the sun : because I should leave it unto the
man that shall be after me. [19] And who knoweth whether he shall be a wise *man* or a fool ?
yet shall he have rule over all my labour wherein
I have laboured.—ECCL., ch. 2.

See other illustrations under :

Renounced. Moses refused to be called the son 8201
Spiritual. The spirit of Elijah doth rest on Elisha 4935

4492. INHOSPITALITY, Provoking. *Samaritans.* [53] They did not receive him, because his
face was as though he would go to Jerusalem.
[54] ..James and John..said, Lord, wilt thou that

we command fire to come down from heaven, and consume them, even as Elias did ?—LUKE, ch. 9.

See other illustrations under :

Fraudulent. Pharisee besought him to dine..catch 4111
" Rich man..took the poor man's lamb 4112
Indifference. Simon, I entered thy house..no w. 4118
Malicious. Diotrephes, neither doth he receive the 4100

4493. INIQUITY, Great. *Pharisees.* [27] Hypocrites ! for ye are like unto whited sepulchres, which indeed appear beautiful outward, but are within full of dead *men's* bones, and of all uncleanness. [28] Even so ye also outwardly appear righteous unto men, but within ye are full of hypocrisy and iniquity.—MAT., ch. 23.

4494. —— Hidden. *Pharisees.* [25] Ye make clean the outside of the cup and of the platter, but within they are full of extortion and excess. —MAT., ch. 23.

4495. INIQUITIES in the Church. *Corruption.* [26] Among my people are found wicked *men :* they lay wait, as he that setteth snares ; they set a trap, they catch men. [27] As a cage is full of birds, so *are* their houses full of deceit .. [28] They are waxen fat, they shine : yea, they overpass the deeds of the wicked.—JER., ch. 5.

See other illustrations under :

DEPRAVITY.

Ancient. Every imagination of the thoughts 2188
Bestial. [Gibeathites] beset the house, and beat at 2189
Discovered. Woe is me..unclean lips..people 2190
Heathen. Changed the glory of..G. into an image 2191
Infections. Daughters of Lot were with child 2192
Inherited. Ye are the children of them which 2193
Natural. L. looked down..all gone aside..filthy 2194

EVIL.

Appearance. Lest we should offend them..money 2752
Freedom. Pilate said..third time..What evil hath 2753
Overruled. Ye thought evil..G. meant it unto 2754
Permitted. Lest while ye gather..tares ye root up 2755
Repaid. Good. David said to Saul..mine eye spared 2756
Root. Love of money is the root of all evil 2757

GUILT.

Accumulated. Upon you may come all the 3766
Cowardice. Adam and his wife hid themselves 3767
Degrees. Two debtors ; one owed 500 pence 3768
Panic. L. looked..through the cloud..troubled 3769

VICES.

Mental. Idolatry, witchcraft, hatred, variance 9188
Physical. Works of the flesh are..adultery 9189
Pleasures. As..lieth down in the midst of the sea 9190

Impurity. Woe is me for I am .a man of unclean 4369
See SIN, SINNERS, WICKED.

4496. INJURY, An insulting. *Samson.* [20] Samson's wife was *given* to his companion, whom he had used as his friend. [2] And her father said, I verily thought thou hadst utterly hated her ; therefore I gave her to thy companion : *is* not her younger sister fairer than she ?—JUDGES, chs. 14 and 15.

4497. —— revenged. *Firebrands.* [See No. 4383.]

4498. INJURIES, Forgiveness of. *Jesus.* [34] Then said Jesus, Father, forgive them ; for they know not what they do.—LUKE, ch. 23.

See other illustrations under :

INSULT.

Ignored. Belial said, How shall this man save us 4567

Jesus. Thrust him out of the city..cast him 4568
Reward. Hanun shaved off one half their beards 4569
Stinging. Annas commanded them to smite 4570

INSULTS.

Cruel. Mocked Jesus..blindfolded, and struck 4576
Contemptuous. They that are younger have me in 4572

MOCKERY.

Blasphemous. Crown of thorns..reed..Hail, King 5494
of Truth. When they heard of the resurrection 5493

RIDICULE.

Doctrine. Heard of the resurrection..mocked 7425
Fatal. Call for Samson..sport..house fell 7426
Failure. Mock him..not able to finish 7427
Horrible. Mocking..he trusted in God..save him 7428
Impious. Laughed them to scorn 7429
" What will this babbler say ? 7430
Insulting. Shaved off one half their beards 7431
Opposition. What do these feeble Jews 7432
" If a fox go up..break down their wall 7433
Punishment. Go up, thou bald head..bears 7434
Royalty. Wearing the crown of thorns..purple 7435
Scornful. Laughed..will ye rebel against the king 7436
Spirit. Mocking, said..full of new wine 7437
Trial. Thou art his disciple, but we are Moses' 7438

SCORN.

Pride. Haman thought scorn to..alone 7618
Public. All that pass by clap their hands at thee 7619
Sinners. They made light of it, and went 7621
Unbelief. They laughed him to scorn 7620

SCOFFERS.

Malicious. Spit in his face, and buffeted 7614
" Mocked him..a gorgeous robe 7615

Hospitality. Lewd fellows..assaulted the house of 5453
Odium. Ye have made..to be abhorred in the eyes 5833
Religion. The L. was made a reproach unto me 2243
See INJUSTICE.

4499. INJUSTICE, Indignation at. *David.* [4] There came a traveller unto the rich man, and he spared to take of his own flock..to dress for the wayfaring man..but took the poor man's lamb, and dressed it for the man.. [5] And David's anger was greatly kindled..and he said to Nathan, *As* the Lord liveth, the man that hath done this *thing* shall surely die : [6] And..restore the lamb fourfold.—2 SAM., ch. 12.

4500. —— Official. *Unjust Judge.* [5] Yet because this widow troubleth me, I will avenge her, lest by her continual coming she weary me. [6] And the Lord said, Hear what the unjust judge saith.—LUKE, ch. 18.

4501. —— —— Pilate. [14] I, having examined *him*..have found no fault in this man touching those things whereof ye accuse him : [15] No, nor yet Herod : for I sent you to him ; and, lo, nothing worthy of death is done unto him. [16] I will therefore chastise him, and release *him*.—LUKE, ch. 23.

See other illustrations under :

FAVORITISM.

Denied. Grant that..my two sons may sit 3098
Hurtful. Israel loved Joseph more than all his 3099

PERSECUTOR.

Arrested. Saul, Saul : why persecutest thou me 6077
Lawless. Lewd fellows of the baser sort..assaulted 6078
Prayer. Father, forgive them, they know not what 6079
" L. lay not this sin to their charge 6080
Unbelieving. Servants and entreated them 6081

PERSECUTION.

Adversity. Come out, thou bloody man..Shimei to 6082
Associated. Chief priests consulted..put Lazarus 6083
Born to. He that was born after the flesh 6084
Blessed. They that were scattered abroad went 6085
Escape. In a basket was I let down by the wall 6086
Honoured. Rejoiced that they were..worthy to 6087
Juvenile. Sarah saw the son of Hagar..mocking 6088
Joy in. Paul and Silas sung praises at midnight 6089
Overruled. Men..were come..great number 6090
Painful. Laid many stripes on..feet..stocks 6091
Promised. Receive a hundredfold..with persecu'n 6092
    "   I am come to set a man at variance 6093
Slavery. Thy servants are beaten, but the fault is 6094
Subtile. We shall not find any occasion..except 6095
Unmoved. None of these things move me 6096

SLANDER.

Antidote. They may by your good works..glorify 8101
Base. Doth cast out devils by Beelzebub 8102
Disgraceful. We found this man a pestilent 8103
Folly. He that uttereth a slander is a fool 8104
Hurtful. Then will they not pay tribute 8105
Impious. He saved others ; himself he cannot 8106
Joyful. Blessed..men revile you..rejoice 8107
Loyalty. Ziba said..he abideth at Jerusalem 8108
Malicious. Diotrephes..prating against us 8109
Opposed. It is reported..be their king 8110
Refuted. If Satan cast out Satan..divided 8111
Rebels. The people is greater than we 8112
Sinners. Thou art an austere man 8113
Satan's. Touch all that he hath..will curse 8114
Secret. A whisperer separateth friends 8115
Unbelief. Would to G. we had died..by fleshpots 8116

See **CRIME** and references.

4502. INNOCENT, Mediation of the. *Benjamin.* [3] Judah spake..The man did solemnly protest unto us, saying, Ye shall not see my face, except your brother *be* with you. [5]..if thou wilt not send *him*, we will not go down.—GEN., ch. 43.

4503. —— Punishment by the. *Adulteress.* [3] The scribes and Pharisees brought..a woman taken in adultery : and..set her in the midst, [7] So when they continued asking him..and said ..He that is without sin among you, let him first cast a stone at her.—JOHN, ch. 8.

4504. —— Punishment of the. *Jesus.* [See No. 4510.]

4505. INNOCENCE avenged. *Ish-bosheth.* [11] Wicked men have slain a righteous person in his own house upon his bed? shall I not therefore now require his blood of your hand.. [12] And David commanded his young men, and they slew them, and cut off their hands and their feet, and hanged *them* up over the pool in Hebron.—2 SAM., ch. 4.

4506. —— Boldness of. *Joseph's Brethren.* [9] With whomsoever of thy servants it be found, both let him die, and we also will be my lord's bondmen. [11] Then they speedily took down.. and opened every man his sack.—GEN., ch. 44.

4507. —— betrayed. *Judas.* [3] Repented himself, and brought again the thirty pieces of silver to the chief priests and elders, [4] Saying, I have sinned in that I have betrayed the innocent blood.—MAT., ch. 27.

4508. —— Convincing. *D a v i d.* [31] David said to Joab, and to all the people..Rend your clothes, and gird you with sackcloth, and mourn before Abner. And king David *himself* followed the bier. [32]..and the king lifted up his voice, and wept at the grave of Abner ; and all the people wept. [37] For all..understood that day that it was not of the king to slay Abner.—2 SAM., ch. 3.

4509. —— Conduct of. *David.* [Saul sought to kill him.] [10] This day thine eyes have seen how that the Lord had delivered thee to day into mine hand in the cave : and *some* bade *me* kill thee : but *mine eye* spared thee.—1 SAM., ch. 24.

4510. —— A false. *Pilate.* [24] When Pilate saw that he could prevail nothing, but *that* rather a tumult was made, he took water, and washed *his* hands before the multitude, saying, I am innocent of the blood of this just person : see ye *to it.*—MAT., ch. 27.

4511. —— proved. *Daniel.* [22] My God hath sent his angel, and hath shut the lions' mouths, that they have not hurt me : forasmuch as before him innocency was found in me ; and also before thee, O king, have I done no hurt.—DAN., ch. 6.

4512. —— Protected by. *Nineveh.* [11] Should not I spare Nineveh, that great city, wherein are more than sixscore thousand persons that cannot discern between their right hand and their left hand.—JONAH, ch. 4.

4513. —— vindicated. *J e s u s.* [See No. 4510.

See other illustrations under :

FAULTLESS.

Condemned. Pilate said..I find no fault in him 3085
Official. Sought occasion against Daniel..found 3086

INTEGRITY.

Acknowledged. Thou art more righteous than I 4575
Conscious. The L. be judge, between me and thee 4576
Delight. The integrity of the upright shall guide 4577
Fixed. Till I die I will not remove mine integrity 4578
False. Is thy servant a dog..do this? 4579
Observed. God said, I know thou didst this 4580
Official. Witness..whom have I defrauded? 4581
Steadfast. L. said..Job holdeth fast his integrity 4582

PURITY.

Symbolized. Make a laver of brass..to wash 6813
Within. First cleanse within the cup 6814

RIGHTEOUSNESS.

Benefits. Prolongeth days..hope of the righteous 7444
Discarded. If any..might trust in the flesh, I more 7445
False. Say not..for my righteousness the L. hath 7446
Flattery. Pharisee..prayed thus with himself 7447

Commended. Turn not to the right..left..from 6908

4514. INSANITY exhibited. *Nebuchadnezzar.* [33] Nebuchadnezzar..was driven from men, and did eat grass as oxen, and his body was wet with the dew of heaven, till his hairs were grown like eagles' *feathers*, and his nails like birds' *claws*. [34] And at the end of the days I Nebuchadnezzar lifted up mine eyes unto heaven, and mine understanding returned unto me, and I blessed the Most High.—DAN., ch. 4.

4515. —— feigned. *David.* [13] He changed his behaviour before them, and feigned himself mad in their hands, and scrabbled on the doors of the gate, and let his spittle fall down upon his beard. [14] Then said Achish..Lo, ye see the man is mad : wherefore *then* have ye brought him to me ?—1 SAM., ch. 21.

4516. —— **Moral.** *Pharaoh.* [27] The Lord hardened Pharaoh's heart, and he would not let them go. [28] And Pharaoh said..Get thee from me, take heed to thyself, see my face no more ; for in *that* day thou seest my face thou shalt die. —Ex., ch. 10.

4517. —— **Occasional.** *Saul.* [10] The evil spirit from God came upon Saul, and he prophesied in the midst of the house : and David played with his hand.. [11] And Saul cast the javelin ; for he said, I will smite David even to the wall *with it.* And David avoided out of his presence twice.—1 Sam., ch. 18.

4518. —— **The Sinner's.** *Prodigal.* [17] When he came to himself, he said, How many hired servants of my father's have bread enough and to spare, and I perish with hunger ! [18] I will arise and go to my father.—Luke, ch. 15.

4519. —— **So-called.** *Jesus.* [19] And they went into a house. [20] And the multitude cometh together again, so that they could not so much as eat bread. [21] And when his friends heard *of it,* they went out to lay hold on him : for they said, He is beside himself.—Mark, ch. 3.

4520. —— —— *Paul.* [24] Festus said with a loud voice, Paul, thou art beside thyself ; much learning doth make thee mad. [25] But he said, I am not mad, most noble Festus ; but speak forth the words of truth and soberness.—Acts, ch. 26.

See other illustrations under :

DELUSION.
Destructive. Ahaz..sacrificed..gods that smote 2168
Success. Philistines..sacrifice unto Dagon 2169
Wicked. Lot..seemed as one that mocked 2170

FANATICISM.
Accused. His friends said..He is beside himself 3036
Fickle. Would have done sacrifice..stoned Paul 3037
Genuine. Two hours cried out, Great is Diana 3038
Idolatry. They cried out, and cut themselves 3039

INFATUATION.
Blind. In the time of his distress did Ahaz trespass 4455
Reproved. Knowest thou not yet..Egypt is d. 4456
Wicked. They were driven out from Pharaoh's 4457
" Simon saw..H. G. was given, he offered 4458

LUNACY.
Diabolic. In the tombs crying and cutting himself 5154
Moral. [Gadarenes] Began to pray him to depart 5155

Stigmatized. Thou hast a devil ; who goeth to kill 5160

4521. INSINCERITY, Blindness of. *Pharisees.* [26] *Thou* blind Pharisee, cleanse first that *which is* within the cup and platter, that the outside of them may be clean also.—Mat., ch. 23.

4522. —— **Ceremonial.** *Fasting.* [3] Wherefore have we fasted, *say they,* and thou seest not ? ..Behold, in the day of your fast ye find pleasure, and exact all your labours. [4] Behold, ye fast for strife and debate, and to smite with the fist of wickedness.—Isa., ch. 58.

4523. —— **of the Covetous.** *Officials.* [11] The heads thereof judge for reward, and the priests thereof teach for hire, and the prophets thereof divine for money : yet will they lean upon the Lord, and say, *Is* not the Lord among us ? none evil can come upon us.—Micah, ch. 3.

4524. —— **Dilemma from.** *Two Masters.* [24] No man can serve two masters : for either he will hate the one, and love the other ; or else he will hold to the one, and despise the other. Ye cannot serve God and mammon.—Mat., ch. 6.

4525. —— **through Fear.** *Priests.* [25] The baptism of John, whence was it ? from heaven, or of men ? And they reasoned with themselves, saying, If we shall say, From heaven ; he will say unto us, Why did ye not then believe him ? [26] But if we shall say, Of men ; we fear the people ; for all hold John as a prophet. [27] And they answered Jesus, and said, We cannot tell.— Mat., ch. 21.

4526. —— **proven.** *Fruit.* [16] They profess that they know God ; but in works they deny *him,* being abominable, and disobedient, and unto every good work reprobate.—Titus, ch. 1.

4527. —— **A Reformer's.** *Jehu.* [27] They brake down the image of Baal, and brake down the house of Baal, and made it a draught house unto this day. [29] Howbeit, *from* the sins of Jeroboam..Jehu departed not from after them, *to wit,* the golden calves that *were* in Beth-el, and that *were* in Dan.—2 Kings, ch. 10.

4528. —— **in Reformation.** *Samaritans.* [28] Then one of the priests whom they had carried away from Samaria came and dwelt in Beth-el, and taught them how they should fear the Lord. [29] Howbeit every nation made gods of their own, and put *them* in the houses of the high places which the Samaritans had made.—2 Kings, ch. 17.

4529. —— **of Seekers.** *Tribute.* [13] And they send unto him certain..to catch him in *his* words. [14] And..they say unto him, Master, we know that thou art true, and carest for no man ; for thou regardest not the person of men, but teachest the way of God in truth : Is it lawful to give tribute to Cesar, or not ?—Mark, ch. 12.

See other illustrations under :

DISGUISE.
Battle. Ahab said, I will disguise myself 2382
Failure. Ahijah said, Come in, wife of Jeroboam 2383
Insufficient. Saul disguised himself [to visit witch] 2384
Penetrated. Is not the hand of Joab in this ? 2385

DISSIMULATION.
Detective. Samson told her..she sent for the lords 2257
Detectives. Watched him..that the mighty accuse 2258

FALSEHOOD.
Agreement. Ananias kept back part..wife..privy 2985
Begets. My master hath sent me..went no w. 2986
Bribery. Say ye..stole him..they took the money 2987
Covering. Began to curse..I know not the man 2988
Folly. Ananias, was it not thine ? and after it was 2989
Father. Your father the devil..no truth in him 2990
Impostors. Jacob said to his father..the L. 2991
Saved by. David said to Ahimelech, the king sent 2992
" Jonathan said David..run to Bethlehem 2994
Short-lived. Lying tongue is but for a moment 2995
Statecraft. Garments and shoes..old..long journey 2996
Sacrilegious. An angel spake..bring him back 2993
Spirit of. I will be a lying spirit in..prophets 2997
Sin. Thou hast not lied unto men, but..G. 2998
Victim. Joseph's master put him in prison 2999

FLATTERY.
Danger. People gave a shout..voice of a god 3254
Failure. Herodians saying..regardest not..any 3255
Success. Ask a petition of any god..save thee 3256

FRAUD.
Appearances. Gibeonites..took old sacks..old 3408

Commerce. Take thy bill..quickly..write fifty   3409
Pious. Sons of the prophets, give..silver [Gehazi]   3410
Religious. His enemy..sowed tares among the   3411
Spiritual. Simon offered money..Holy Ghost   3412
Traitors. Whomsoever I shall kiss..is he   3413
Wages. Hire of the labourers kept..crieth   3414

TRICK.

Diplomatic. From a very far country are..come   8955
Hypocrites. Feign themselves just men..might   8956
Legerdemain. Magicians..rods became serpents   8957
Politicians. Shall ask a petition..save of thee   8958

Demagogue. O that I were a judge..do justice   2171
See DECEPTION.

4530. INSOLENCE, Added. *Danites.* [Robbed him of his household gods. His neighbours pursued.] [23] And they cried unto the children of Dan. And they turned their faces, and said unto Micah, What aileth thee, that thou comest with such a company?—JUDGES, ch. 18.

4531. —— Fraternal. *Eliab.* [28] Eliab his eldest brother heard when he spake unto the men ; and Eliab's anger was kindled against David, and he said, Why camest thou down hither? and with whom hast thou left those few sheep in the wilderness?–1 SAM., ch. 17.

4532. —— with Injustice. *Pharaoh.* [16] There is no straw given..and they say to us, Make brick : and, behold, thy servants *are* beaten ; but the fault *is* in thine own people. [17] But he said, Ye *are* idle, ye *are* idle : therefore ye say, Let us go *and* do sacrifice to the Lord.—Ex., ch. 5.

4533. —— resented. *Ahab.* [4] Said, My lord, O king, according to thy saying, I *am* thine, and all that I have. [5] And the messengers came again, and said, Thus speaketh Ben-hadad, saying, Although I have sent unto thee, saying, Thou shalt deliver me thy silver, and thy gold, and thy wives, and thy children ; [6] Yet I will send my servants unto thee to morrow about this time, and they shall search thine house, and the houses of thy servants ; and..whatsoever is pleasant in thine eyes, they shall..take *it* away.—1 KINGS, ch. 20. [Ahab resolved to fight.]

See other illustrations under :
CONTEMPT.

Bigots. Pharisee prayed..I am not as other men   1618
Critics. Michal saw king David leaping—despised   1619
Conceited. Thistle..sent to the cedar..give thy   1620
Disregarded. The God of heaven will prosper us   1621
Enemy's. Am I a dog that thou comest..staves   1622
Expressed. Children of Belial..brought Saul no   1623
Fraternal. With whom hast thou left those few   1624
Gospel. Made light of it, and went their way   1625
for God. Have turned their back unto me..face   1626
Malicious. Did spit in his face, and buffeted   1628
Others. That they were righteous..despised others   1629
for Worship. Torn..the lame, and the sick..ye   1630

DERISION.

Horrible. Put on him a scarlet robe..crown   2197
Impious. Laughed them to scorn and mocked   2198
Nickname. Thou art a Samaritan, and hast a devil   2200
Punished. Sarah saw the son of Hagar mocking   2199
Truth. Pharisees who were covetous..derided   2201
Unfortunates. Thieves also..cast the same into   2202
Wicked. They shoot out the lip, and shake the   2203

INSULT.

Ignored. Despised him [Saul]..held his peace   4567
First. Thrust him [Jesus] out of the city..headlong   4568
Rewarded. Cut off their garments in the middle   4569
Stinging. To smite him on the mouth   4570

RIDICULE.

Doctrine. When they heard of the resurrection   7425
Fatal. Call for Samson that he may make us sport   7426
Failure. Not able to finish..begin to mock him   7427
Horrible. He saved others, let him save himself   7428
Impious. They laughed them to scorn and mocked   7429
"   What will this babbler say [Athenians]   7430
Insulting. Cut off their garments..their buttocks   7431
Opposition. What do these feeble Jews? will they   7432
"   If a fox go up, he shall break down   7433
Punishment. Children of Bethel..Go up, thou bald   7434
Royalty. Wearing the crown of thorns and purple   7435
Scornful. They laughed us to scorn and despised us   7436
Spirit. Mocking said,These men are full of new wine   7437
Trial. They reviled him and said, We are Moses'   7438

SCOFFERS.

Malicious. Prophesy unto us, thou Christ..who   7614
"   Herod arrayed him in a gorgeous robe   7615

SCORN.

of Pride. [Haman] Scorn to lay hands on Mordecai   7618
Public. All clap their hands at thee and hiss   7619
Unbelief. She sleepeth..they laughed him to scorn   7620

Taunt. Who made thee a prince and a judge over   8592

4534. INSOLVENCY confessed. *Merciless Servant.* [29] His fellow servant fell down at his feet, and besought him, saying, Have patience with me, and I will pay thee all. [30] And he would not : but went and cast him into prison, till he should pay the debt.—MAT., ch. 18.

4535. —— forgiven. *Parable.* [41] A certain creditor..had two debtors : the one owed him five hundred pence, and the other fifty. [42] And when they had nothing to pay, he frankly forgave them both. Tell me therefore, which of them will love him most?—LUKE, ch. 7.

See other illustrations under :
BORROWING.

Distress. Have mortgaged our lands..buy corn   914
Forbidden. Owe no man anything, but to love   916
Ruin. Borrowed..spoiled the Egyptians   915
Servant. Borrower is servant of the lender   912
Trouble. Axe head fell into the water..borrowed   913

DEBTS.

Compromised. Take thy bill..quickly, and write   2006
Forgiven. Every seven years..every creditor shall   2007
Miracle. Go sell the oil, and pay the debt   2009
Severity. Fellow servants took him by the throat   2008

DEBTORS.

Army. Every one that was in debt gathered   2010
Destructive. Same servant [debtor] took him by   2011
Gratitude. To whom little is forgiven..loveth   2012
Insolvent. Have mortgaged our lands, vineyards   2013
Protected. When thou dost lend..not go into his   2014

4536. INSPIRATION for Art. *Bezaleel.* [3] I have filled him with the spirit of God.. [4] To devise cunning works, to work in gold, and in silver, and in brass, [5] And in cutting of stones, to set *them*, and in carving of timber, to work in all manner of workmanship.—Ex., ch. 31.

4537. —— for Duty. *Cyrus.* [1] The Lord stirred up the spirit of Cyrus king of Persia, that he made a proclamation throughout all his kingdom, [2] ..he hath charged me to build him a house at Jerusalem.—EZRA, ch. 1.

4538. —— for Emergency. *Persecution.* [11] When they shall..deliver you up, take no thought beforehand what ye shall speak, neither do ye premeditate : but whatsoever shall be given you in that hour, that speak ye : for it is not ye that speak, but the Holy Ghost.—MARK, ch. 13.

See other illustrations under:

ENTHUSIASM.

Brief. With joy receiveth..not root	2679
Benevolence. They said, He is beside himself	2680
Contempt. Michal saw king David leaping	2681
Misunderstood. He is beside himself	2682
Public. Take him by force, to make him king	2683

PROPHECY.

Gift. Spirit..unto the 70 elders..did prophesy	6672
Involuntary. Spirit..was upon Saul..prophesied	6673
Revival. I prophesied..bones came together	6674
Spiritual. These are not drunken..prophesy	6675

4539. INSTINCT of Animals. *Various.* [See JOB, ch. 39.]

4540. —— **overruled.** *Kine.* ¹⁰ The men ..took two milch kine, and tied them to the cart, and shut up their calves at home : ¹¹ And they laid the ark of the Lord upon the cart.. ¹² And the kine took the straight way to the way of Beth-shemesh, *and* went along the highway, lowing as they went, and turned not aside *to* the right hand or *to* the left ; and the lords of the Philistines went after them.—1 SAM., ch. 6.

Also see :

| Changed. Lord..shut the lions' mouths | 437 |
| Overruled. Ravens brought him [Elijah] bread | 427 |

4541. INSTRUCTION better than Practice. *Pharisees.* ³ All therefore whatsoever they bid you observe, *that* observe and do ; but do not ye after their works : for they say, and do not. ⁴ For they bind heavy burdens and grievous to be borne, and lay *them* on men's shoulders ; but they *themselves* will not move them with one of their fingers.—MAT., ch. 23.

4542. —— **of Children.** *Moses.* [Farewell address.] ⁹ Only take heed to thyself..lest thou forget the things which thine eyes have seen, and lest they depart from thy heart..but teach them thy sons, and thy sons' sons ; ¹⁰ *Specially* the day that thou stoodest before the Lord..in Horeb.—DEUT., ch. 4.

4543. —— **Course of.** *Hebrews.* ⁴ Children in whom *was* no blemish, but well favoured, and skilful in all wisdom, and cunning in knowledge, and understanding science, and such as *had* ability.. ⁵..so nourishing them three years, that at the end thereof they might stand before the king.—DAN., ch. 1.

4544. —— **Humble.** *Apollos.* ²⁴ Apollos..an eloquent man, *and* mighty in the Scriptures, came to Ephesus. ²⁵ This man was instructed in the way of the Lord ; and being fervent in the spirit, he spake and taught diligently the things of the Lord, knowing only the baptism of John. ²⁶..whom when Aquila and Priscilla had heard, they..expounded unto him the way of God more perfectly.—ACTS, ch. 18.

4545. —— **Important.** *Word.* ¹⁹ When any one heareth the word..and understandeth *it* not, then cometh the wicked one, and catcheth away that which was sown in his heart. This is he which received seed by the way side.—MAT., ch. 13.

4546. —— **Improvement by.** *Proverb.* ⁸ My son, hear the instruction of thy father, and forsake not the law of thy mother : ⁹ For they *shall*

be an ornament of grace unto thy head, and chains about thy neck.—PROV., ch. 1.

4547. —— **Personal.** *Apollos.* [See No. 4544.]

4548. —— **Public.** *Israelites.* ² Ezra the priest brought the law before the congregation both of men and women, and all that could hear with understanding.—NEH., ch. 8.

4549. —— **Private.** *Paul.* ²³ There came many to him into *his* lodging ; to whom he expounded and testified the kingdom of God, persuading them concerning Jesus, both out of the law of Moses, and *out of* the prophets, from morning till evening.—ACTS, ch. 28.

4550. —— **Youthful.** *Timothy.* ¹⁵ From a child thou hast known the holy Scriptures, which are able to make thee wise unto salvation.—2 TIM., ch. 3.

See other illustrations under :

DISCIPLESHIP.

Conditional. Lord, I will follow thee ; but	2331
Provisional. When I bow down..the L. pardon	2332
Postponed. Let me kiss my father..then I will	2333
Terms. Whosoever doth not bear his cross and	2334
Trials. Enough for the disciple to be as his master	2335
Unconditional. If any man..deny himself..cross	2336

SCHOOL.

Christianity. Paul..disputing daily in the school	7605
Gospel. In every house they ceased not..teach	7606
Home. These words..teach..in thine house	7607
Synagogue. Jesus went..teaching in their s.	7608

STUDY.

Bible. Eunuch..sitting in his chariot read Esaias	8397
Commended. These were more noble..searched	8398
Beneficial. Hearts burn..opened to us the	8399
Wearisome. Much study is a weariness to the flesh	8400

TEACHABLENESS.

Attitude. Mary sat at Jesus' feet..heard his word	8606
Characteristic. Received..word with all readiness	8607
Manifested. Eunuch desired Philip..sit with him	8608
Professed. All here present before G. to hear all	8609
Youthful. Found him in the temple..hearing	8610

TEACHER.

Authoritative. Jesus taught them as one having	8611
Art. Bezaleel..carving..he may teach	8612
Great. Jesus went about..teaching in..synagogues	8613
Home. Thou shalt teach them..in thine house	8614
Necessary. Understandest thou..? How can I	8615
Prepared. Come up. mount..that thou mayest	8616
Spirit. When they bring you..H. G. shall teach	8617

TEACHING.

Divine. G. hath shewed me..not call..common	8618
Ministerial. In the temple they ceased not to teach	8619
Despised. Mourn at the last..how have I hated	8930

See DISCOURSE, INTELLIGENCE, and references.

4551. INSTRUMENT contemned. *Jordan.* ¹¹ Naaman was wroth, and went away, and said, Behold, I thought, He will surely come out to me..and call on..his God, and strike his hand over the place, and recover the leper. ¹² *Are* not Abana and Pharpar, rivers of Damascus, better than all the waters of Israel ?—2 KINGS, ch. 5.

4552. —— **A disdained.** *Young David.* ²⁸ Eliab his eldest brother heard when he spake unto the men ; and Eliab's anger was kindled against David, and he said, Why camest thou down hither ? and with whom hast thou left those few sheep in the wilderness ? I know thy pride, and the naughtiness of thine heart ; for thou art come down that thou mightest see the battle.—1 Sam., ch. 17.

4553. —— A destroying. *Red Sea.* [See No. 4557.] ²⁸ The waters returned, and covered..all the host of Pharaoh that came into the sea after them : there remained not so much as one of them.—Ex., ch. 14.

4554. —— A humiliating. *Naaman.* ¹⁰ Elisha sent a messenger unto him, saying, Go and wash in Jordan seven times, and thy flesh shall come again to thee, and thou shalt be clean.—2 Kings, ch. 5.

4555. —— Insignificant. *Jaw-bone.* ¹⁴ The Philistines shouted against him : and the Spirit of the Lord came mightily upon him, and the cords that *were* upon his arms became as flax that was burnt with fire.. ¹⁵ And he found a new jawbone of an ass..and slew a thousand men therewith.—Judges, ch. 15.

4556. —— A strange. *Brazen Serpent.* ⁹ Moses made a serpent of brass, and put it upon a pole..if a serpent had bitten any man when he beheld the serpent of brass, he lived.—Num., ch. 21.

4557. —— A saving. *Red Sea.* ²² The children of Israel went into the midst of the sea upon the dry *ground :* and the waters *were* a wall unto them on their right hand, and on their left.—Ex., ch. 14.

4558. —— A sinful. *Woman.* ⁴¹ Many more believed because of his own word ; ⁴² And said unto the woman, Now we believe, not because of thy saying : for we have heard *him* ourselves, and know that this is indeed the Christ, the Saviour of the world.—John, ch. 4.

4559. —— A strange. *Fish.* ¹⁷ The Lord had prepared a great fish to swallow up Jonah. And Jonah was in the belly of the fish three days and three nights.. ¹⁰ And the Lord spake unto the fish, and it vomited out Jonah upon the dry *land.*—Jonah, chs. 1 and 2.

4560. INSTRUMENTS, Feeble. *Four Lepers.* ⁶ The Lord had made the host of the Syrians to hear a noise of chariots, and..horses, *even* the noise of a great host : and they said..Lo, the king of Israel hath hired against us the kings of the Hittites, and..of the Egyptians.. ⁷..left their tents, and their horses, and their asses,. even the camp as it *was,* and fled for their life. —2 Kings, ch. 7.

4561. —— Men are God's. *Cornelius.* ¹³ An angel in his house..said..Send men to Joppa, and call for Simon, whose surname is Peter ; ¹⁴ Who shall tell thee words, whereby thou and all thy house shall be saved.—Acts, ch. 10.

4562. —— Insignificant. *Stones.* ⁵⁰ David prevailed over the Philistine with a sling and with a stone, and smote the Philistine, and slew him ; but *there was* no sword in the hand of David.—1 Sam., ch. 17.

4563. —— only. *Apostles.* ¹² Peter..answered..Ye men of Israel, why marvel ye at this ? or why look ye so earnestly on us, as though by our own power or holiness we had made this man to walk?—Acts, ch. 3.

4564. —— Quality of. *Soldiers.* ⁶ Jonathan said to the young man that bare his armour, Come, and let us go over unto..these uncircum-

cised : it may be that the Lord will work for us : for *there is* no restraint to the Lord to save by many or by few. ¹³ And Jonathan climbed up upon his hands and upon his feet, and his armourbearer after him : and they fell before Jonathan ; and his armourbearer slew after him. ¹⁴..about twenty men.—2 Sam., ch. 14.

4565. —— Weak. *Plagues.* ³⁰ Their land brought forth frogs in abundance, in the chambers of their kings. ³¹ He spake, and there came divers sorts of flies, *and* lice.. ³² He gave them hail for rain, *and* flaming fire in their land. ³³ He smote their vines also and their fig-trees ; and brake the trees.. ³⁴ He spake, and the locusts came, and caterpillars, and that without number, ³⁴ And did eat up all the herbs.—Ps. 105.

4566. INSTRUMENTALITY, Waiting. *Moses.* ²⁸ Wilt thou kill me, as thou didst the Egyptian yesterday ? ²⁹ Then fled Moses at this saying, and was a stranger in the land of Madian, where he begat two sons.—Acts, ch. 7. [Forty years God waited till his return, and then delivered Israel.]

See other illustrations under :

AGENT.

Necessary. Go forward, but lift thou up thy rod 249
Simple. Go wash..I thought..come..stand..call 250

AGENCY.

Boastful. Shall the axe boast itself against him ? 251
Indirect. I have occasioned the death..father's 252
Seeming. Tree cast into the waters..made sweet 253
Strange. Made clay of the spittle..anointed the 254

MEANS.

Defence. Hezekiah..built up the walls..made 5255
Escape. They let him down the wall in a basket 5256
Heroic. Soldiers cut off the ropes of the boat 5257
Ingenious. Ark of bulrushes..pitch..stood 5258
Insignificant. Touched he their eyes..eyes were 5259
not Neglected. Take a lump of figs..laid it on the 5260
Prayer. We made our prayer..set a watch..day 5261
Prudential. Jesus..would not walk in Jewry 5262
Strange. Moses..rod of God..held up his hand 5263
 " Sound of the trumpet..people shouted 5264
Use of. Think on me when it shall be well with thee 5265
Unworthy. If I make not thy life..went for his 5266

UTENSILS.

Desecrated. Cyrus brought the vessels..house of 9150
Restored. Bring up with..captivity..to Jerusalem 9151
Valuable. 30 charges of gold, 1000 charges of silver 9152

Benefactor. More blessed to give than to receive 704
 See WEAPONS and references.

4567. INSULT ignored. *King Saul.* ²⁷ The children of Belial said, How shall this man save us ? And they despised him, and brought him no presents. But he held his peace. [He having conquered their national enemies, the Ammonites.] ¹²..The people said..Who *is* he that said, Shall Saul reign over us ? bring the men, that we may put them to death. ¹³ And Saul said, There shall not a man be put to death this day : for to day the Lord hath wrought salvation in Israel.—1 Sam., chs. 10 and 11.

4568. —— Jesus' first. *At Nazareth.* ²⁸ All they in the synagogue, when they heard these things, were filled with wrath, ²⁹ And rose up, and thrust him out of the city, and led him unto the brow of the hill, (whereon their city was built,) that they might cast him down headlong. —Luke, ch. 4.

4569. —— **Rewarded by.** *Ammonite King.*
[David's sympathizers were taken for spies.]
⁴ Wherefore Hanun..and shaved off the one
half of their beards, and cut off their garments
in the middle, *even* to their buttocks, and sent
them away.—2 SAM., ch. 10.

4570. —— **A stinging.** *Paul.* ² The high
priest Ananias commanded them..to smite him
on the mouth. ³ Then said Paul unto him, God
shall smite thee, *thou* whited wall: for sittest
thou to judge me after the law, and commandest
me to be smitten contrary to the law?—ACTS,
ch. 23.

4571. **INSULTS, Crue** ̄ *Trial of Jesus.* ⁶³ The
men that held Jesus mocked him, and smote
him. ⁶⁴ And when they had blindfolded him,
they struck him on the face, and asked him,
saying, Prophesy, who is it that smote thee?—
LUKE, ch. 22. ⁶⁵ And some began to spit on
him..and the servants did strike him with the
palms of their hands.—MARK, ch. 14.

4572. —— **Contemptuous.** *Job.* ¹ But now
they that are younger than I have me in derision,
whose fathers I would have disdained to have
set.with the dogs of my flock. ⁹ And now am I
their song, yea, I am their byword. ¹⁰ They abhor me, they flee far from me, and spare not to
spit in my face.—JOB, ch. 30.

Also see:
Accusation. Hebrew servant came in to mock me   77
   See INSOLENCE and references.

4573. **INSUBORDINATION, Intimidated by.**
Ish-bosheth. [See No. 4574.] ¹¹ He could not
answer Abner a word again, because he feared
him.—2 SAM., ch. 3.

4574. —— **A Soldier's.** *Abner.* [Being
charged by Saul's son with dishonour, he said,]
⁹ So do God to Abner, and more also, except, as
the Lord hath sworn to David, even so I do to
him; ¹⁰ To translate the kingdom from the house
of Saul, and to set up the throne of David.—2
SAM., ch. 3. [He went over to David.]

See other illustrations under:

DISOBEDIENCE.

IRREVERENCE.

REBELLION.

SECESSION.

4575. **INTEGRITY acknowledged.** *David's.*
[See below.] ¹⁶ Saul lifted up his voice, and
wept. ¹⁷ And he said to David, Thou *art* more
righteous than I: for thou hast rewarded me
good, whereas I have rewarded thee evil.—1
SAM., ch. 24.

4576. —— **Conscious.** *David.* [Having permitted Saul to escape unharmed, he said,]
¹³ Wickedness proceedeth from the wicked: but
mine hand shall not be upon thee." ¹⁵ The Lord
therefore be judge, and judge between me and
thee, and see, and plead my cause, and deliver
me out of thine hand.—1 SAM., ch. 24.

4577. —— **Delight in.** *Divine.* ¹ A false
balance *is* abomination to the Lord: but a just
weight *is* his delight. ³ The integrity of the upright shall guide them.. ⁵..but the wicked shall
fall by his own wickedness.—PROV., ch. 11.

4578. —— **Fixed.** *Job.* ⁵ Till I die I will
not remove mine integrity from me. ⁶ My righteousness I hold fast, and will not let it go: my
heart shall not reproach *me* so long as I live.—
JOB, ch. 27.

4579. —— **False.** *Hazael.* ¹² Their strong
holds wilt thou set on fire, and their young men
..slay with the sword, and wilt dash their children, and rip up their women with child. ¹³ And
Hazael said, But what, *is* thy servant a dog, that
he should do this great thing? ¹⁵..on the morrow..he took a thick cloth, and dipped *it* in
water, and spread *it* on his face, so that he died:
and Hazael reigned in his stead.—2 KINGS,
ch. 8.

4580. —— **observed.** *King Abimelech.* ⁶ God
said unto him in a dream, Yea, I know that thou
didst this in the integrity of thy heart; for I
also withheld thee from sinning against me:
therefore suffered I thee not to touch her. ⁷ Now
therefore restore the man *his* wife.—GEN., ch.
20.

4581. —— **Official.** *Samuel the Judge.* ³ Witness against me before the Lord..whose ox have
I taken? or whose ass have I taken? or whom
have I defrauded? whom have I oppressed? or
of whose hand have I received *any* bribe to blind
mine eyes therewith? and I will restore it you.
⁴ And they said, Thou hast not defrauded us.—
1 SAM., ch. 12.

4582. —— **Steadfast.** *Job.* ³ The Lord said
unto Satan, Hast thou considered my servant
Job, that *there is* none like him in the earth, a
perfect and an upright man,one that feareth God,
and escheweth evil? and still he holdeth fast
his integrity, although thou movedst me against
him, to destroy him without cause.—JOB, ch. 2.

   See HONOUR and references.

4583. **INTELLIGENCE, Responsibility of.**
Blood. ⁴ Whosoever heareth the sound of the
trumpet, and taketh not warning; if the sword

come, and take him away, his blood shall be upon his own head.—Ezek., ch. 33.

See other illustrations under:

ADVICE.

Foolish. Said his wife..curse God and die   152
Good. Naaman's servants said, If the prophet had   153
Unfortunate. Let a gallows be made fifty cubits   154

COUNSEL.

Dying. I go..show thyself a man [David]   1746
Evil. Rehoboam consulted with the young men   1748
Friends. Let a gallows be made 50 cubits high   1740
Good. Rehoboam consulted with the old men   1749
Influential. David..the lords favour thee not   1750
Malicious. Come, let us take counsel together   1751
Neglected. Took not counsel of the L.   1741
Oracular. Counsel of Ahithophel..as..oracle of   1742
Opposing. Ahithophel said to Absalom..Hushai   1747
Payment. Saul to servant..what shall we bring   1744
Peace. Joab, hear the words..handmaid   1743
Rejection. Ahithophel saw..not followed   1745
Safety. In the multitude of counsellors..safety   1739
Unfortunate. Why sit we here until we die?   1738

DISCRETION.

Necessary. King consulteth..war..or..peace   2366
Part of. Let not thy voice be heard..lose thy life   2367
Success. David said to Abigail..Blessed be thy   2368
Safety. Paul perceived that one part were Saddu's   2369
Want of. As a jewel of gold in a swine's snout   2370
    "   Nabal said, Who is David?..his master   2371

EDUCATION.

Monument. Children ask, What mean ye by these   2602
Neglected. Children spake half in the speech of   2603
Preparatory. Such as had ability in them..king's   2604

INSTINCT.

Animals. [Various. See Job, ch. 39.]   4539
Overruled. Kine took the straight way to B.   4540

KNOWLEDGE.

Adamic. Gave names to all cattle..fowl..beast   4853
Detrimental. Man is come to know good and evil   4854
Forbidden. Tree of the knowledge..shalt not eat   4855
Faith to. Believe not because of thy saying..heard   4856
Guilt. Better for them not to have known the way   4857
Grace. Perceived they were unlearned men   4858
Ignorance. I go bound in the spirit..not knowing   4859
Responsibility. Know that the ox hath used to   4860
Spiritual. I know that my Redeemer liveth   4861
Temptation. Woman saw..tree..make one wise   4862
Used. Whosoever heareth..taketh not warning   4863

LEARNING.

Profound. Moses was learned in all the wisdom   4931
Superior. Jews marvelled..how knoweth this man   4932
Worship. Came wise men from the east..worship   4933

LIGHT.

Christian. But I. had light in their dwellings   5029
Conversion. There fell from his eyes as..scales   5030
Condemnation. Behold a greater than Solomon is   5031
Commanded. Let there be light ; and there was   5032
Dazzling. Saul was three days without sight   5033
Deeds. Let your light so shine..good deeds   5034
Exposure. Every one that doeth evil hateth the   5035
Fellowship. If we walk in the light..have   5036
Hatred. Men loved darkness..deeds were evil   5037
Improvement. Walk while ye have the light   5038
and Love. He that hateth his brother is in darkness   5039
of Life. I am the light of the world..light of life   5040
Responsibility. More tolerable for the land of s.   5041
Sinning. If ye were blind, ye should have no sin   5042
Transforming. Moses wist not that..face shone   5043
Waiting for. Saw not..neither rose..three days   5044
Withdrawn. There shall no sign be given..Jonas   5045

MEMORY.

Perdition. Send Lazarus to my..five brethren   5319
Painful. I am the least..apostles..I persecuted   5320

NEWS.

Bad. Eli said..hide it not from me   5728
  " More. While he was yet speaking, another   5729
  " Unrewarded. Thinking to have brought good   5730
  " Withheld. Samuel feared to shew Eli the   5731
  "   " Servants feared to tell..child was   5732
Confirmation. Thomas, reach hither thy finger   5733
Doubted. Syrians..gone out of the camp to hide   5734
  " Mary went and told..believed not   5735
Important. Sent letters by..mules..camels   5736
Refreshing. As cold waters to a thirsty soul   5737

READING.

Effective. All the people answered, Amen   6869
Instructive. Ears of all the people were attentive   6870
Pious. Eunuch..sitting in his chariot read   6871

REMEMBRANCE.

Book. Was written before him of them that feared   7060
Late. I do remember my faults this day..chief   7061
Perpetual. This is my body..in remembrance of   7062
Painful. When Peter thought thereon, he wept   7063
Stimulated. Wherefore I put thee in remembrance   7064
of Sins. How thou provokedst the L. ..in the   7065
Ungrateful. Yet did not the chief butler remember   3066

SCIENTIST.

First. Whatsoever Adam called..creature..name   7610
Famous. Solomon spake of trees..beasts..fowl   7611
Tribute. Wise men came..opened their treasures   7612
Worshippers. Have seen his star..come to worship   7613

THOUGHT.

Character. As he thinketh in his heart, so is he   8786
Evil. Every imagination of the thought..only evil   8787
Prompter. When they deliver you up, take no   8788
Subjects. Whatsoever things are true..honest   8789

TRUTH.

Agitation spreads. Disputed he in the synagogue   9032
Blood with. Spoken..sprinkled..book..all the   9033
Convicts. Paul reasoned..Felix trembled   9034
Conspiracy. Have agreed together to tempt the S.   9035
Conflict. On whomsoever it shall fall..grind him   9036
Effects. Some mocked..some..hear thee again   9037
Freedom. Truth shall make you free   9038
Inquiry. Pilate saith..What is truth?   9039
Power. King had heard..rent his clothes   9040
Ridiculed. Heard of the resurrection..mocked   9041
Resisted. Hard for thee to kick against the pricks   9042
Standard. [False] Teaching for doctrines the c.   9043
Stumbling. Because I tell you the truth ye   9044
  " From that time many went back   9045
Whole. Samuel..What..? hide it not from me   9046
Warfare. Not come to send peace..sword   9047

Tidings feared. Angel said..Fear not..good tidings   8802

See EDUCATION, REASONING.

4584. INTEMPERANCE, Avoiding. *Look not.* [31] Look not thou upon the wine when it is red, when it giveth his colour in the cup, *when* it moveth itself aright.—Prov., ch. 23.

4585. —— Battle lost by. *Benhadad.* [16] Benhadad *was* drinking himself drunk in the pavilions, he and..the thirty and two kings that helped him. [19] So these young men of the princes..came out of the city, and the army.. [20] And they slew every one his man : and the Syrians fled.—1 Kings, ch. 20.

4586. —— in the Church. *Corinthians.* [20] When ye come together therefore into one place, *this* is not to eat the Lord's supper. [21] For in eating every one taketh before *other* his own supper : and one is hungry, and another is drunken.—1 Cor., ch. 11.

4587. —— **Changed by.** *Nabal.* [3] The man *was* churlish, and evil in his doings.. [10] And Nabal answered David's servants, and said, Who *is* David?.. [36]. he held a feast in his house, like the feast of a king ; and Nabal's heart *was* merry within him, for he *was* very drunken.—1 Sam., ch. 25. [His wife pacified David.]

4588. —— **Cruelty of.** *Murder.* [25] She came in straightway with haste..saying, I will that thou give me by and by in a charger the head of John the Baptist. [26] And the king was exceeding sorry.—Mark, ch. 6.

4589. —— **Disarmed by.** *Amnon.* [28] Absalom had commanded his servants, saying, Mark ye now when Amnon's heart is merry with wine, and when I say unto you, Smite Amnon ; then kill him.. [29] And the servants of Absalom did.. Then all the king's sons arose, and every man gat him up upon his mule, and fled.—2 Sam., ch. 13.

4590. —— **Dangers of.** *Priests.* [8] The Lord spake unto Aaron, saying, [9] Do not drink wine nor strong drink, thou, nor thy sons with thee, when ye go into the tabernacle..lest ye die : *it shall be* a statute for ever.—Lev., ch. 10.

4591. —— **Degradation by.** *Vashti.* [See No. 4603.]

4592. —— —— *Drunkards.* [3] The crown of pride, the drunkards of Ephraim, shall be trodden under feet : [4] And the glorious beauty, which *is* on the head of the fat valley, shall be a fading flower, *and* as the hasty fruit before the summer ; which *when* he that looketh upon it ..seeth, while it is yet in his hand he eateth it up.—Isa., ch. 28.

4593. —— **Forgetfulness by.** *"Law."* [See No. 4600.]

4594. —— **The first.** *Noah.* [20] Noah began *to be* a husbandman, and he planted a vineyard : [21] And he drank of the wine, and was drunken ; and he was uncovered within his tent.—Gen., ch. 9.

4595. —— **Folly of.** *Herod.* [21] Herod on his birthday made a supper to his lords..of Galilee ; [22] And when the daughter of..Herodias came in, and danced, and pleased Herod and them that sat with him, the king said unto the damsel, Ask of me whatsoever thou wilt, and I will give *it* thee.—Mark, ch. 6.

4596. —— **facilitates Crime.** *Uriah.* [To conceal his crime with Bathsheba,] [13] When David had called him..he made him drunk : and at even he went out to lie on his bed..but went not down to his house.—2 Sam., ch. 11.

4597. —— **Injuries from.** *Proverb.* [29] Who hath woe ? who hath sorrow ? who hath contentions ? who hath babbling ? who hath wounds without cause ? who hath redness of eyes ? [30] They that tarry long at the wine ; they that go to seek mixed wine.—Prov., ch. 23.

4598. —— **Kingdom lost by.** *Elah King of Judah* [9] His servant Zimri, captain of half *his* chariots, conspired against him, as he was in Tirzah, drinking himself drunk.. [10] And Zimri

went in and..killed him..and reigned in his stead.—1 Kings, ch. 16.

4599. —— **Obduracy in.** *Ahasuerus.* [The Jews were to be massacred.] [15] The posts went out, being hastened by the king's commandment, and the decree was given..And the king and Haman sat down to drink ; but the city Shushan was perplexed.—Esther, ch. 3.

4600. —— **of Officials.** *"Pervert."* [4] O Lemuel, *it is* not for kings to drink wine ; nor for princes strong drink : [5] Lest they drink, and forget the law, and pervert the judgment.—Prov., ch. 31.

4601. —— **Poison of.** *"Stingeth."* [See No. 4584.] [32] At the last it biteth like a serpent, and stingeth like an adder.—Prov., ch. 23.

4602. —— **Profanity with.** *Belshazzar.* [1] Belshazzar..made a great feast to a thousand of his lords, and drank wine.. [2]..while he tasted the wine, commanded to bring the golden and silver vessels which..Nebuchadnezzar had taken out of the temple which *was* in Jerusalem ; that the king, and his princes, his wives, and his concubines, might drink therein.—Dan., ch. 5.

4603. —— **Shameless.** *Ahasuerus.* [10] On the seventh day, when the heart of the king was merry with wine, he commanded..the seven chamberlains.. [11] To bring Vashti the queen before the king with the crown royal, to shew the people and the princes her beauty : for she *was* fair to look on.—Esther, ch. 1.

See other illustrations under :

DRUNKARDS.

Called. Behold [Jesus] a gluttonous man and a	2520
Curse. L. will not spare him..blot out his name	2522
Disgrace. Err in vision, they stumble in judgment	2523
Maker. Woe..giveth his neighbour drink	2524
Perdition. Drunkards..shall not inherit the	2525
Separation. Not to keep company if any..is a d.	2526
Woe. Woe unto them that..mighty to drink wine	2527

WINE.

Dangers. Noah..planted a vineyard..wine	9607
Medicinal. Drink..wine for..thine often infirmities	9610
Sacramental. Melchizedek..brought forth bread	9613

See TEMPERANCE.

4604. INTENTION accepted. *Offering Isaac.* [17] By faith Abraham, when he was tried, offered up Isaac : and he that had received the promises offered up his only begotten *son.*—Heb., ch. 11.

4605. —— **approved.** *David's.* [18] The Lord said unto David my father, Whereas it was in thine heart to build a house unto my name, thou didst well that it was in thine heart.—1 Kings, ch. 8.

4606. —— **abandoned.** *Pilate.* [12] Pilate sought to release him : but the Jews cried out, saying, If thou let this man go, thou art not Cesar's friend.. [16] Then delivered he him therefore unto them to be crucified.—John, ch. 19.

4607. —— **commended.** *Benevolence.* [43] This poor widow hath cast more in, than all they which have cast into the treasury : [44] For all *they* did cast in of their abundance ; but she of her want did cast in all that she had, *even* all her living.—Mark, ch. 12.

4608. —— **Crime from.** *Law.* [22] If he thrust him suddenly without enmity, or have cast upon him any thing without laying of wait, [23] Or with any stone, wherewith a man may die, seeing *him* not..and *was* not his enemy, neither sought his harm : [24] Then the congregation shall judge between the slayer and the revenger of blood.—Num., ch. 35.

4609. —— **fixes Guilt.** *Law.* [11] If any man hate his neighbour, and lie in wait for him.. and smite him mortally..and fleeth into one of these cities ; [13] Thine eye shall not pity him, but thou shalt put away *the guilt of* innocent blood from Israel.—Deut., ch. 19.

4610. —— **honoured.** *"Spikenard."* [8] She hath done what she could : she is come aforehand to anoint my body to the burying. [9]..Wheresoever this gospel shall be preached throughout the whole world, *this* also that she hath done shall be spoken of for a memorial of her.—Mark, ch. 14.

4611. —— **misjudged.** *King Saul.* [7] Hear now, ye Benjamites ; will the son of Jesse give every one of you fields..*and* make you all captains.. [8] That all of you have conspired against me.—1 Sam., ch. 22.

4612. —— **A sincere.** *Abraham.* [10] Abraham stretched forth his hand, and took the knife to slay his son. [11] And the Angel of the Lord called unto him out of heaven.—Gen., ch. 22.

4613. —— **Superior.** *Macedonians.* [3] For to *their* power..and beyond *their* power *they were* willing of themselves ; [4] Praying us with much entreaty that we would receive the gift, and *take upon us* the fellowship of the ministering to the saints.—2 Cor., ch. 8.

4614. —— **unexecuted.** *Garden.* [10] Simon Peter having a sword drew it, and smote the high priest's servant, and cut off his right ear. —John, ch. 18. [He aimed at the head.]

4615. —— **Unprotected by.** *Disobedient.* [6] Uzzah put forth *his hand* to the ark of God, and took hold of it : for the oxen shook *it*. [7] And the anger of the Lord was kindled against Uzzah, and God smote him there for *his* error ; and there he died by the ark of God.—2 Sam., ch. 6.

See other illustrations under :

MOTIVE.
Labour. Labour that..we may be accepted of him   5587
Unsanctified. People spared the best..to sacrifice   5588

MOTIVES.
Inferior. Ye seek me because..did eat of the loaves   5589
Suspected. Urged him till he was ashamed..send   5590
Worldly. Savourest not the things that be of God   5591

PRINCIPLE.
Ignored. Then had we plenty of victuals..well   6595
Policy. Let us deal wisely..lest they multiply   6593
Without. People became Jews..for fear of the   6594

SINCERITY.
Consecration. Josiah made a covenant..burned   8025
Evildoing. I thought I ought to..put to death   8026
Evidence. Brought their books..burned them   8027
Example. An Israelite in whom is no guile   8028
Heart. He that speaketh truth in his heart   8029
Lovable. All..have I kept..Jesus loved him   8030
Opinions. Rabbi, thou art the Son of God   8031
Positive. Thou knowest that I love thee   8032
Proof. When..people saw it..L. he is G.   8033
Reformation. Speak..the truth..execute..truth   8034

4616. INTERCESSION denied. *Samuel.* [See No. 4624.] [26] I will not return with thee : for thou hast rejected the word of the Lord, and the Lord hath rejected thee from being king over Israel. [27] And as Samuel turned about to go away, he laid hold upon the skirt of his mantle, and it rent.—1 Sam., ch. 15.

4617. —— **Effect of.** *Fig Tree.* [7] These three years I come seeking fruit on this fig tree, and find none : cut it down ; why cumbereth it the ground ? [8]..Lord, let it alone this year also, till I shall dig about it, and dung *it:* [9] And if it bear fruit, *well :* and if not, *then* after that thou shalt cut it down.—Luke, ch. 13.

4618. —— **Friendly.** *Jonathan said,* [5] He did put his life in his hand, and slew the Philistine, and the Lord wrought a great salvation for all Israel : thou sawest *it*, and didst rejoice : wherefore then wilt thou sin against innocent blood, to slay David without a cause ? [6]..Saul sware, *As* the Lord liveth, he shall not be slain.—1 Sam., ch. 19.

4619. —— —— **Abraham.** [23] Wilt thou also destroy the righteous with the wicked ? [24] Peradventure there be fifty righteous within the city : wilt thou also destroy and not spare the place for the fifty righteous that *are* therein ?— Gen., ch. 18.

4620. —— **Limit to.** *Abraham* [32] said, Oh let not the Lord be angry, and I will speak yet but this once : Peradventure ten shall be found there. And he said, I will not destroy *it* for ten's sake. [33] And the Lord went his way.—Gen., ch. 18.

4621. —— **A needless.** *Joseph's Brethren.* [19] They came near to the steward of Joseph's house, and they communed with him at the door of the house, [20] And said, O sir, we came indeed down at the first time to buy food.— Gen., ch. 43.

4622. —— **needed.** *Pharaoh.* [32] Take your flocks and your herds, as ye have said, and be gone ; and bless me also.—Ex., ch. 12.

4623. —— **obtained.** *King Saul.* [30] I have sinned : *yet* honour me now, I pray thee, before ..Israel, and turn again with me, that I may worship the Lord thy God. [31] So Samuel turned again after Saul..Saul worshipped the Lord.— 1 Sam., ch. 15.

4624. —— **Penitential.** *King Saul.* [24] Saul said unto Samuel, I have sinned : for I have transgressed the commandment..because I feared the people, and obeyed their voice. [25] Now therefore, I pray thee, pardon my sin, and turn again with me, that I may worship the Lord.— 1 Sam., ch. 15.

4625. —— **rewarded.** *Moses.* [32] Yet now, if thou wilt forgive their sin—; and if not, blot me, I pray thee, out of thy book.. [22]..while my glory passeth by..I will put thee in a cleft of the rock, and will cover thee with my hand.—Ex., chs. 32, 33.

4626. —— **resented.** *Pharaoh.* [4] The king of Egypt said..Wherefore do ye, Moses and Aaron, let the people from their works ? get you unto your burdens.—Ex., ch. 5.

See other illustrations under :

ADVOCATE.
Friendly. Made Blastus..their friend, desiring   155
Sinners. We have an advocate with the Father   156

ENTREATY.

Heart-breaking. What mean ye to..break mine   2684
Urgent. Come down 'ere my child die   2685

MEDIATOR.

Diplomatic. Made Blastus the king's chamberlain   5279
Female. Woman of Abel..His head shall be thrown 5280
Great. He is the mediator of the N. T.   5281
Present. Now to appear in the presence of G. for 5282
Required. Not see my face, except your brother 5283
Wanted. Speak thou..but let not G. speak with us 5284

MEDIATION.

Double. Thee a god to Pharaoh..Aaron thy p.   5285
Effectual. Aaron stood between the dead and   5286
Moses. Moses returned the words..unto the L.   5287
Righteous. I regard the presence of Jehoshaphat 5288
Transgressors. Moses besought the L...L. repented 5289
See **PRAYER.**

4627. INTEREST, Watchful. *Stephen* [56] said,
Behold, I see the heavens opened, and the Son of
man standing on the right hand of God. [57] Then
they cried out with a loud voice, and stopped
their ears, and ran upon him.—ACTS, ch. 7. [A
posture of readiness for action.]

See **USURY.**

4628. INTERFERENCE, A strange. *Relatives.*
[20] The multitude cometh together again, so that
they could not so much as eat bread. [21] And
when his friends heard *of it,* they went out to
lay hold on him : for they said, He is beside
himself.—MARK, ch. 3.

See other illustrations under :

Meddler. Meddleth with strife..taketh a dog by   5278
Officious. Disciples rebuked those that brought   7852

4629. INTIMIDATION attempted. *Nehemiah.*
[Sanballat wrote,] [6] It is reported among the
heathen, and Gashmu saith *it, that* thou and the
Jews think to rebel ; for which cause thou
buildest the wall, that thou mayest be their
king.. [7] And thou hast also appointed prophets
to preach of thee at Jerusalem, saying, *There is*
a king in Judah : and now shall it be reported
to the king..Come now therefore, and let us
take counsel together. [9] For they all made us
afraid, saying, Their hands shall be weakened
from the work.—NEH., ch. 6.

4630. —— Boastful. *At Samaria.* [28] Rab-
shakeh stood and cried with a loud voice..Hear
the word of the great king, the king of Assyria :
[29]..Let not Hezekiah deceive you : for he shall
not be able to deliver you out of his hand.—2
KINGS, ch. 18.

4631. —— Fruit of. *Peter.* [69] A maid..be-
gan to say..This is one of them. [70] And he denied it again. And a little after..Surely thou
art *one* of them.. [71] But he began to curse and
to swear, *saying,* I know not this man.—MARK,
ch. 14.

4632. —— Failure of. *Nehemiah.* [10] Shemaiah..said, Let us meet together in the house of
God..and let us shut the doors..for they will
come to slay thee ; yea, in the night.. [11] And I
said, Should such a man as I flee? and who *is
there,* that, *being* as I *am,* would go into the temple to save his life? I will not go in.—NEH.,
ch. 6.

4633. —— Moved by. *Delilah.* [15] On the
seventh day..they said unto Samson's wife,
Entice thy husband, that he may declare unto

us the riddle, lest we burn thee and thy father's
house with fire.—JUDGES, ch. 14.

4634. —— Unsuccessful. *Ahab.* [6] My servants..shall search thy house, and the houses of
thy servants ; and..whatsoever is pleasant in
thy eyes, they shall..take *it* away. [8] And all the
elders and all the people said unto him, Hearken
not *unto him,* nor consent.—1 KINGS, ch. 20.

4635. —— Without. *Peter and John.* [19] The
angel of the Lord by night opened the prison
doors, and brought them forth, and said, [20] Go,
stand and speak in the temple to the people all
the words of this life.—ACTS, ch. 5.

4636. —— A Woman's. *Elijah.* [2] Jezebel
sent a messenger unto Elijah, saying, So let the
gods do *to me,* and more also, if I make not thy
life as the life of one of them by to morrow
about this time. [3]..he arose, and went for his
life.—1 KINGS, ch. 19.

4637. —— Weakness of. *Philistines.* [14] That
first slaughter, which Jonathan and his armourbearer made, was about twenty men.. [15] And
there was trembling in the host, in the field,
and among all the people : the garrison, and the
spoilers, they also trembled, and the earth
quaked : so it was a very great trembling.—1
SAM., ch. 14.

See other illustrations under :

AGITATION.

Deception. Who art thou ?..Esau..Isaac trembled   256
Diffuses. Disputed he in the synagogue..market   257
Deplored. [Israelites] Made..abhorred..slay us   258
General. [Philistines] Trembling in the host..field   259
Mount. Sinai..quaked greatly   260
Overcome. [At sepulchre] keepers did shake   261
Physical. Belshazzar's thoughts troubled..knees   262
Terror. [Job's vision] Trembling..my bones   263

ALARM.

Conscience. Pray for thy servants..we die not   273
Death. Egyptians were urgent..we be all dead   274
Failure. Priests..doubted..whereunto this would   275
Manifestation. Belshazzar..countenance was   276
Preaching. Paul reasoned..Felix trembled   277
Reasonable. Esau cometh..400 men..Jacob   278
Superstitious. Jesus walking on the sea..troubled   279
Sinners. Adam and his wife hid themselves   280
     "   Let not God speak with us..die   281
Sudden. Seeing the prison doors open..sword   282
Spiritual. Sirs, what must I do to be saved   283
Tempest. Entreat..be no more mighty thunderings 284
Unnecessary. My money is restored..heart failed   285

COWARDICE.

Blemish. Peter followed afar off   1819
Cruel. For their sakes which sat..not reject   1820
Exemption. Fainthearted..return unto his house 1821
Guilt. Adam and his wife hid themselves   1822
Sinners. Jeroboam said..Alas ! that the Lord   1823
Surprising. Jezebel sent..Elijah went for his life 1824

DANGER.

Appalled. Jesus went before them..amazed   1906
Escape. Disciples let him down by night in a   1909
Haste. Let them in Judea..flee to the mountains 1911
Intimidates. Peter saw..afraid, and beginning to 1912
Jesus. Storm..on the lake..Master, we perish   1913

TERROR.

Prostrating. Saul fell..all along on the ground   8723
Sinners. Belshazzar's..knees smote one against   8724
Sublime. Sinai..so terrible..I exceedingly fear   8725

TIMIDITY.

Disciples. Nicodemus..came to Jesus by night 8816
    "   Joseph being a disciple, but secretly 8817
Friends. Good man, but no man spake openly 8818
Needless. Because of the money in our sacks 8819
Restrained. Were gathered..Peter knocked at the 8820
    See FEAR and references.

4638. INTRIGUE, A Mother's. *R e b e k a h.*
[6] I heard thy father speak unto Esau thy brother, saying, [7] Bring me venison.. [16] And she
put the skins of the kids..upon his hands, and
upon the smooth of his neck : [11] And she gave
the savoury meat and the bread, which she had
prepared, into the hand of her son Jacob.—
GEN., ch. 27.

4639. —— for Office. *Shechemites.* [3] Their
hearts inclined to follow Abimelech.. [4] And
they gave him threescore and ten *pieces* of silver
out of the house of Baalberith, wherewith Abimelech hired vain and light persons, which followed him.—JUDGES, ch. 9. [He became king
of Israel.]

4640. —— by Signs. *Proverb.* [12] A naughty
person, a wicked man, walketh with a froward
mouth. [13] He winketh with his eyes, he speaketh with his feet, he teacheth with his fingers.
—PROV., ch. 6.

4641. —— Successful. *Gibeonite Neighbours.*
[12] This our bread we took hot..but now, behold, it is dry, and it is mouldy : [13] And these
bottles of wine..*were* new ; and, behold, they
be rent : and these our garments and our shoes
are become old by reason of the very long journey.—JOSH., ch. 9.

4642. —— Unsuccessful. *A t J e r u s a l e m.*
[2] That Sanballat and Geshem sent unto me,
saying, Come, let us meet together in *some one
of* the villages in the plain of Ono. But they
thought to do me mischief. [3] And I sent..say-
ing, I *am* doing a great work, so that I cannot
come down.—NEH., ch. 6.

    See other illustrations under :

CONSPIRACY.

Atrocious. Abimelech hired..light persons 1601
Brother's. When Amnon's heart is merry..kill 1602
Court. Set up false witnesses 1603
Desperate. Bound themselves under a curse 1604
Defeated. Took counsel how they might entangle 1605
Escape. Saul sent..David's house..slay 1606
Envy. Let us..slay..cast into some pit 1607
Ingrate's. Say Absalom reigneth in Hebron 1608
Infamous. I will give thee the vineyard of Naboth 1609
Political. Sought to find occasion against Daniel 1610
    "   Servants..made a c..slew Joash 1611
Successful. Philistines came..brought money 1612
against Truth. Ananias and Sapphira 1613
Worst. Consulted that they might take Jesus by s. 1614

STRATAGEM.

Battle. Joshua saw that the ambush had taken the 8366
Success. Joab's field..set it on fire 8367
Subtile. Joseph's coat..dipped in the blood 8424

Dangerous. Ahithophel is among the conspirators 8871
Excused. I conspired..L. hath done—2 Kings 10 : 9-10
Punishment. Slew all that conspired—2 Kings 21 : 24
Political. They made a conspiracy—2 Kings 14 : 19
    "   Shallum..conspired..smote—2 Kings 15 : 10
    "   Jehu conspired against Joram—2 Kings 9 : 14
Suspected. All of you have conspired against me 473
    See TRICK.

4643. INVENTION, First Musical. *Jubal.*
[See No. 4645.]

4644. —— Inspiration for. *Bezaleel.* [3] I have
filled him with the spirit of God..in all manner
of workmanship, [4] To devise cunning works, to
work in gold, and in silver, and in brass, [5] And
in cutting of stones, to set *them*, and in carving
of timber.—Ex., ch. 31.

4645. INVENTORS, Family of. *Lamech's.*
[21] Jubal : he was the father of all such as handle
the harp and organ. [22] And Zillah, she also
bare Tubal-cain, an instructor of every artificer
in brass and iron.—GEN., ch. 4.

4646. —— Value of. *"Engines."* [14] Uzziah
prepared..shields, and spears, and helmets, and
habergeons, and bows, and slings *to cast* stones.
[15] And he made in Jerusalem engines, invented
by cunning men, to be on the towers and upon
the bulwarks, to shoot arrows and great stones
withal. And his name spread far abroad ; for
he was marvellously helped, till he was strong.
—2 CHRON., ch. 26.

    Also see :
Mother's. She took for him an ark of bulrushes 4484
Protected by. Could not drive out..chariots of iron 507

4647. INVESTIGATION, A fruitless. *Daniel.*
[4] The presidents and princes sought to find occasion against Daniel concerning the kingdom ;
but they could find none occasion nor fault ;
forasmuch as he *was* faithful.—DAN., ch. 6.

4648. —— Secret. *Nehemiah.* [15] Then went
I up in the night by the brook, and viewed the
wall..and *so* returned. [16] And the rulers knew
not whither I went, or what I did ; neither had
I as yet told *it* to the Jews, nor to the priests.
—NEH., ch. 2.

    See other illustrations under :

DISCOVERY.

Alarming. My money is restored..heart failed 2360
Painful. Isaac trembled..Who? where is he ? 2361
Unexpected. Is not the hand of Joab..in this ? 2362

EXAMINATION.

Brutal. Paul should be examined by scourging 2773
Doctrines. [Bereans] searched..whether those 2774
Self. One of you..shall betray me..Is it I 2775
Vindicating. I have examined..found no fault 2776

Appalling. When saw we thee..in prison?..least 8502
Challenged. Whom have I defrauded..oppressed 1683
Criminal. Pilate said, I have examined him 87
Declined. Herod questioned..answered nothing 81
Doubted. Told them..he was..seen, believed not 2320
Financial. King would take account of his s. 72
    "   Steward..I hear of thee..give account 75
Happy. Jesus saith unto her, Mary..master 9725
    "   [John] saith unto Peter, It is the Lord 3253
Judgment. We have eaten..I know not whence ye 2319
Strange. How is it thou wilt manifest thyself 5205
Unexpected. Come see a man..Is not this the C. 9741
Unsuccessful. One..betray..one by one, is it I ? 80
    See EVIDENCE and references.

4649. INVITATION, Bountiful. *Pharaoh's.*
[18] Take your father, and your households, and
come unto me : and I will give you the good of
the land of Egypt, and ye shall eat the fat of the
land.—GEN., ch. 45.

4650. —— to Benevolence. *Building Tabernacle.* [5] Take ye from among you an offering
unto the Lord : whosoever *is* of a willing heart
..gold, and silver, and brass, [6] And blue, and

purple, and scarlet, and fine linen, and goats' hair, ⁸ And oil for the light, and spices for anointing oil, and for the sweet incense.—Ex., ch. 35.

4651. —— The Christian. *" Come."* ⁴⁵ We have found him, of whom Moses in the law, and the prophets, did write, Jesus of Nazareth.. ⁴⁶ And Nathanael said unto him, Can there any good thing come out of Nazareth? Philip saith unto him, Come and see.—John, ch. 1.

4652. —— The Divine. *" Come."* ¹ Ho, every one that thirsteth, come ye to the waters, and he that hath no money ; come ye, buy, and eat ; yea, come, buy wine and milk without money and without price.—Isa., ch. 55.

4653. —— The Gospel. *" Feast."* ² The kingdom of heaven is like unto a certain king, which made a marriage for his son, ³ And sent forth his servants to call them that were bidden to the wedding : and they would not come.—Mat., ch. 22.

4654. —— of Grace. *" Say, Come."* ¹⁷ The Spirit and the bride say, Come. And let him that heareth say, Come. And let him that is athirst come. And whosoever will, let him take the water of life freely.—Rev., ch. 22.

4655. —— Heavenward. *Moses'.* ²⁹ Moses said unto Hobab..Moses' father in law, We are journeying unto the place of which the Lord said, I will give it you : come thou with us, and we will do thee good : for the Lord hath spoken good concerning Israel. ³⁰ And he said..I will not go.—Num., ch. 10.

4656. —— A pressing. *" Knock."* ²⁰ Behold, I stand at the door, and knock : if any man hear my voice, and open the door, I will come in to him, and will sup with him, and he with me.—Rev., ch. 3.

4657. —— solicited. *Peter.* ²⁷ It is I ; be not afraid. ²⁸ And Peter answered him and said, Lord, if it be thou, bid me come unto thee on the water. ²⁹ And he said, Come.—Mat., ch. 14.

See other illustrations under :

CALL.

Apostleship. Follow me.. [Levi] left all	1007
Children. L. called Samuel..here am I	1008
Dishonoured. Follow me..bury my father	1009
Earnestness. No man..looking back..is fit	1010
Instrumental. Take thee Joshua..give him a	1011
Ministerial. Dwell with me..a priest..10 shekels	1012
Obedience. Simon and Andrew..forsook the nets	1013
Preaching. Woe is unto me if I preach not	1014
Response. Whom shall I send..here am I	1015
Spirit. Thine ears..hear a word behind thee	1016
Sacrifice. He called..they left their father	1017
Vision. Come over into Macedonia..help	1018

PROMISE.

Great. I send the promise of my Father upon you	6639
Royal. What is thy petition, queen Esther?..be	6640
" Whatsoever thou shalt ask..give it thee	6641
Regretted. King was..sorry ; yet for his oath's sake	6642

4658. IRON, First Use of. *Lamech's.* ²² Zillah, she..bare Tubal-cain, an instructor of every artificer in brass and iron.. ²³ And Lamech said unto his wives, Adah and Zillah..I have slain a man to my wounding, and a young man to my hurt. ²⁴ If Cain shall be avenged sevenfold, truly Lamech seventy and sevenfold.—Gen., ch. 4, [These verses have been rendered thus :

I can slay a man for my hurt, when he hurts me, or even a vigorous young man for my wound when he wounds me. If Cain shall be avenged of God sevenfold, I will avenge myself more— seventy times seven. Lamech rejoiced over the invention of arms.]

4659. IRONY, Horrible. *" King."* ³⁷ Over his head his accusation written, THIS IS JESUS THE KING OF THE JEWS.. ⁴² He saved others ; himself he cannot save.—Mat., ch. 27.

4660. —— Rebuke of. *Elijah's.* ²⁷ Elijah mocked them, and said, Cry aloud : for he *is* a god ; either he is talking, or he is pursuing, or he is in a journey, *or* peradventure he sleepeth, and must be awaked. ²⁸ And they cried aloud, and cut themselves..with knives and lancets, till the blood gushed out.—1 Kings, ch. 18.

See other illustrations under :

MOCKERY.

Blasphemous. Crown of thorns..reed..Hail, King	5494
of Truth. When they heard of the resurrection	5493

RIDICULE.

Doctrine. Heard of the resurrection..mocked	7425
Fatal. Call for Samson..sport..house fell	7426
Failure. Mock him..not able to finish	7427
Horrible. Mocking..he trusted in God..save him	7428
Impious. Laughed them to scorn	7429
" What will this babbler say?	7430
Insulting. Shaved off one half their beards	7431
Opposition. What do these feeble Jews	7432
" If a fox go up..break down their wall	7433
Punishment. Go up, thou bald head..bears	7434
Royalty. Wearing the crown of thorns..purple	7435
Scornful. Laughed..will ye rebel against the king	7436
Spirit. Mocking, said..full of new wine	7437
Trial. Thou art his disciple, but we are Moses'	7438

SCOFFERS.

Malicious. Spit in his face, and buffeted	7614
" Mocked him..a gorgeous robe	7615

SCORN.

Pride. Haman thought scorn to..alone	7618
Public. All that pass by clap their hands at thee	7619
Sinners. They made light of it, and went	7621
Unbelief. They laughed him to scorn	7620

4661. IRRESOLUTION in Religion. *" Farewell."* ⁶¹ Lord, I will follow thee ; but let me first go bid them farewell, which are at home.. ⁶² And Jesus said..No man, having put his hand to the plough, and looking back, is fit for the kingdom of God.—Luke, ch. 9.

4662. —— A sad. *Pilate.* ¹² Pilate sought to release him : but the Jews cried out, saying, If thou let this man go, thou art not Cesar's friend.. ¹⁶ Then delivered he him therefore unto them to be crucified.—John, ch. 19.

See HESITATION and references.

4663. IRREVERENCE from Curiosity. *Ark.* ¹⁹ He smote the men of Beth-shemesh, because they had looked into the ark of the Lord..fifty thousand and threescore and ten men.—1 Sam., ch. 6.

4664. —— Heedless. *Uzzah.* ⁶ Uzzah put forth *his hand* to the ark of God, and took hold of it ; for the oxen shook *it.* ⁷ And the anger of the Lord was kindled against Uzzah ; and God smote him there for *his* error ; and there he died.—2 Sam., ch. 6.

4665. —— punished. *Nadab and Abihu.* ¹ Took either of them his censer, and put fire therein, and put incense thereon, and offered strange fire before the Lord, which he commanded them not. ². .fire from the Lord. .devoured them.—Lev., ch. 10.

4666. —— Presumptuous. *King Saul* ⁸ Tarried seven days, according to the set time that Samuel *had appointed :* but Samuel came not to Gilgal ; and the people were scattered from him. ⁹ And Saul said, Bring hither a burnt offering to me, and peace offerings. And he offered the burnt offering.—1 Sam., ch. 13. [It cost him his kingdom.]

4667. —— reproved. *Saul's Destroyer* ¹³ Answered, I am. .an Amalekite. ¹⁴ And David said . .How wast thou not afraid to stretch forth thine hand to destroy the Lord's anointed ? ¹⁵ And David called one of the young men, and said, Go near, *and* fall upon him. .he died.— 2 Sam., ch. 1.

4668. —— Rebellious. *Sinners.* ³⁷ They will reverence my son. ³⁸. .the husbandmen. . said among themselves, This is the heir ; come, let us kill him, and let us seize on his inheritance. ³⁹ And they caught him, and cast *him* out of the vineyard, and slew *him.*—Mat., ch. 21.

See other illustrations under :

BLASPHEMY.

Accused of. We stone thee not, but for blasphemy   801
Evidence of. High priest rent his clothes. .spoken   802
Forbidden. Thou shalt not take the name. .vain   803
Greatest. Word against the Son of man..be forgiven 804
Heedless. As the L. liveth, I will. .take something   805
Habit. Stephen ceaseth not to speak blasphemous   806
Murdered. He ought to die. .made himself the Son   807
No. Why. .speak blasphemies ?. .Who can forgive   808
Punishment. All that heard laid their hands. .head 809
Strange. Peter began to curse and swear   810
Unpardonable. Blasphemy against the H. G. .not   811

DESECRATION.

Bribery. Ahaz took. .out of the house of the L.   2204
Removed. I cast forth all the household stuff   2205
Sacrilegious. That his concubines might drink   2206

PROFANATION.

Sanctuary. Those that sold oxen. .first visit   6626
    "   Sold and bought. .Last visit   6627

SACRILEGE.

Presumptuous. They brought the golden vessels   7544
Priestly. Men abhorred the offering of the L.   7545
Unintended. Uzzah put forth his hand. .ark   7546

4669. IRRITATION by Disappointment. *Israelites.* ¹² *Is* not this the word that we did tell thee in Egypt, saying, Let us alone, that we may serve the Egyptians ? For *it had been* better for us to serve the Egyptians, than that we should die in the wilderness.—Ex., ch. 14.

4670. IRRITABILITY, A Drunkard's. *Nabal.* ³ The man *was* churlish and evil in his doings. . ³⁶ And Abigail came to Nabal ; and, behold, he held a feast in his house, like the feast of a king ; and Nabal's heart *was* merry within him, for he *was* very drunken.—1 Sam., ch. 25.

See IMPATIENCE and references.

4671. JEALOUSY, Crucified by. *Jesus.* ¹⁷ Pilate said . .Whom will ye that I release unto you ? Barabbas, or Jesus which is called Christ ? ¹⁸ For he knew that for envy they had delivered him.—Mat., ch. 27.

4672. —— Disunion by. *Israel.* ¹ There hap-

pened to be there a man of Belial, whose name *was* Sheba. .he blew a trumpet, and said, We have no part in David. .every man to his tents, O Israel. ² So every man of Israel went up from after David, *and* followed Sheba. .but the men of Judah clave unto their king.—2 Sam., ch. 20.

4673. —— Free from. *Moses.* ²⁸ Joshua. .said, My lord Moses, forbid them. ²⁹ And Moses said . .Enviest thou for my sake ? would God that all the Lord's people were prophets, *and* that the Lord would put his Spirit upon them.—Num., ch. 11.

4674. —— Fraternal. *Elder Son.* ²⁸ He was angry, and would not go in : therefore came his father out, and entreated him. ²⁹ And he answering said. .Lo, these many years do I serve thee, neither transgressed I at any time thy commandment ; and yet thou never gavest me a kid, that I might make merry with my friends.—Luke, ch. 15.

4675. —— Implacable. *Proverb.* ³⁴ Jealousy *is* the rage of a man : therefore he will not spare in the day of vengeance. ³⁵ He will not regard any ransom ; neither will he rest content, though thou givest many gifts.—Prov., ch. 6.

4676. —— Local. *Samaritans.* ⁵² Jesus sent messengers before his face : and they went, and entered into a village of the Samaritans, to make ready for him. ⁵³ And they did not receive him, because his face was as though he would go to Jerusalem.—Luke, ch. 9.

4677. —— National. *Naaman.* ¹² *Are* not Abana and Pharpar, rivers of Damascus, better than all the waters of Israel ? may I not wash in them, and be clean ? So he turned and went away in a rage.—2 Kings, ch. 5.

4678. —— Polygamous. *Rachel.* ¹ When Rachel saw that she bare Jacob no children, Rachel envied her sister ; and said unto Jacob, Give me children, or else I die.—Gen., ch. 30.

4679. —— incites Strife. *Advice.* [After the overthrow of Absalom,] ⁴³ The men of Israel answered the men of Judah. .We have ten parts in the king, and we have also more *right* in David than ye : why then did ye despise us, that our advice should not be first had in bringing back our king ? And the words of the men of Judah were fiercer than the words of the men of Israel.—2 Sam., ch. 19.

4680. —— of Success. *Ephraimites.* ¹ Why hast thou served us thus, that thou calledst us not, when thou wentest to fight with the Midianites ? And they did chide with him sharply. ² And he said unto them, What have I done now in comparison of you ? *Is* not the gleaning of the grapes of Ephraim better than the vintage of Abi-ezer ?—Judges, ch. 8.

4681. —— Success begets. *King Saul* ²⁸ Knew that the Lord *was* with David, and *that* Michal Saul's daughter loved him. ²⁹ And Saul was yet the more afraid of David ; and Saul became David's enemy continually.—1 Sam., ch. 18.

4682. —— Wounded. *King Saul.* ⁸ Saul was very wroth. .and he said, They have ascribed unto David ten thousands, and to me they have ascribed *but* thousands : and *what* can he have more but the kingdom ? ⁹ And Saul eyed David from that day and forward.—1 Sam., ch. 18.

See other illustrations under:

RIVALRY.

Apostles. There was a strife..which should be *g.*   7450
Place. The ten..were moved with indignation   7451
Reproved. Ye call me Master..washed your feet   7452

SUSPICION.

Affected. Ye are spies; to see the nakedness   8516
Cruel. Why have ye conspired against me?   8517
Corrected. Joseph, fear not to take..Mary   8518
Deterred. What do these Hebrews here?   8519
Evil of. Hanun shaved off one half of their beards   8520
Groundless. Which of us is for the king of I.   8521
Painful. Joseph..will hate us..evil which we did   8522
Removed. Joseph said, Fear not   8523
Sagacious. Lest in the battle he be an adversary   8524
Unwarranted. Abner..came to deceive thee   8525
    "   Hath not David sent..to spy it out? 8526

See ENVY and references.

4683. JESUS the Avenger. *Armour.* ¹⁶ He saw that *there was* no man, and wondered that *there was* no intercessor: therefore his arm brought salvation unto him; and his righteousness, it sustained him. ¹⁷ For he put on righteousness as a breastplate, and a helmet of salvation upon his head; and he put on the garments of vengeance *for* clothing, and was clad with zeal as a cloak.—ISA., ch. 59.

4684. —— Affection of. *Natural.* ⁵ Jesus loved Martha, and her sister, and Lazarus.—JOHN, ch. 11.

4685. —— our Advocate. *"With the Father."* ¹ If any man sin, we have an advocate with the Father, Jesus Christ the righteous: ² And he is the propitiation for our sins.—1 JOHN, ch. 2.

4686. —— All for. *"Every Creature."* [See No. 4712.]

4687. —— the Beloved Son. *Baptism.* ¹⁶ The heavens were opened..and he saw the Spirit of God descending like a dove, and lighting upon him: ¹⁷ And lo a voice from heaven, saying, This is my beloved Son, in whom I am well pleased.—MAT., ch. 3.

4688. —— with his Church. *Commission.* ¹⁹ Go..teach all nations, baptizing them.. ²⁰ Teaching them to observe all things whatsoever I have commanded you: and, lo, I am with you alway, *even* unto the end of the world.—MAT., ch. 28.

4689. —— the Conqueror. *"White Horses."* [See above.] ¹⁴ The armies *which were* in heaven followed him upon white horses, clothed in fine linen, white and clean. ¹⁵ And out of his mouth goeth a sharp sword, that with it he should smite the nations; and he shall rule them with a rod of iron: and' he treadeth the winepress of the fierceness and wrath of Almighty God. ¹⁶ And he hath on *his* vesture and on his thigh a name written, KING OF KINGS, AND LORD OF LORDS.—REV., ch. 19.

4690. —— called Lord. *First.* [Jesus unborn, Elisabeth saluted Mary.] ⁴² She spake out with a loud voice, and said, Blessed *art* thou among women, and blessed *is* the fruit of thy womb. ⁴³ And whence *is* this to me, that the mother of my Lord should come to me?—LUKE, ch. 1.

4691. —— crowded out. *"No Room."* ⁷ She brought forth her firstborn son..and laid him in a manger; because there was no room for them in the inn.—LUKE, ch. 2.

4692. —— the Defence. *"Standard."* ¹⁹ When the enemy shall come in like a flood, the Spirit of the Lord shall lift up a standard against him. —ISA., ch. 59.

4693. —— Divine. *Trial.* ⁷ Jews answered him, We have a law, and by our law he ought to die, because he made himself the Son of God. ⁸ When Pilate therefore heard that saying, he was the more afraid.—JOHN, ch. 19.

4694. —— discovered. *At Emmaus.* ³⁰ He took bread, and blessed *it,* and brake, and gave to them. ³¹ And their eyes were opened, and they knew him; and he vanished.. ³² And they said..Did not our heart burn within us, while he talked..and while he opened to us the Scriptures?—LUKE, ch. 24.

4695. —— despised. *In Representatives.* ¹⁶ He that heareth you heareth me; and he that despiseth you despiseth me; and he that despiseth me despiseth him that sent me.—LUKE, ch. 10.

4696. —— dismissed. *Gadarenes.* ¹⁵ They come to Jesus, and see him that was possessed with the devil, and had the legion, sitting, and clothed, and in his right mind; and they were afraid. ¹⁶ And they that saw *it* told them how it befell to him..and *also* concerning the swine. ¹⁷ And they began to pray him to depart out of their coasts.—MARK, ch. 5.

4697. —— discarded. *For Barabbas.* ²⁴ Pilate.. ²⁵..released..him that for sedition and murder was cast into prison, whom they had desired; but he delivered Jesus to their will.—LUKE, ch. 23.

4698. —— disguised. *Near Emmaus.* ¹² He appeared in another form unto two of them, as they walked, and went into the country. ¹³ And they went and told *it* unto the residue: neither believed they them.—MARK, ch. 16.

4699. —— disturbed by. *"Knock..Voice."* ²⁰ Behold, I stand at the door, and knock: if any man hear my voice, and open the door, I will come in to him.—REV., ch. 3.

4700. —— expedites Effort. *Disciples.* [They laboured eight or nine hours in rowing three miles and a half.] ²¹ They willingly received him into the ship: and immediately the ship was at the land whither they went.—JOHN, ch. 6.

4701. —— in Glory. *Amid the Candlesticks.* ¹⁴ His head and *his* hairs *were* white like wool, as white as snow; and his eyes *were* as a flame of fire; ¹⁵ And his feet like unto fine brass, as if they burned in a furnace; and his voice as the sound of many waters. ¹⁶ And he had in his right hand seven stars: and out of his mouth went a sharp two-edged sword: and his countenance *was* as the sun shineth in his strength. ¹⁷ And when I saw him, I fell at his feet as dead.—REV., ch. 1.

4702. —— our High Priest. *Unchangeable.* ²³ They truly were many priests, because they were not suffered to continue by reason of death: ²⁴ But this *man,* because he continueth ever, hath an unchangeable priesthood.—HEB., ch. 7.

4703. —— on High. *Stephen saw.* ⁵⁵ Looked up steadfastly into heaven, and saw the glory of God, and Jesus standing on the right hand of God.—ACTS, ch. 7.

4704. —— **our Intercessor.** *"Ever liveth."* [See No. 4702.] [25] Wherefore he is able also to save them to the uttermost that come unto God by him, seeing he ever liveth to make intercession for them.—Heb., ch. 7.

4705. —— **the King.** *Cross.* [19] Pilate wrote a title, and put *it* on the cross..JESUS OF NAZARETH THE KING OF THE JEWS.. [21] Then said the chief priests..to Pilate, Write not, The King of the Jews ; but that he said, I am King of the Jews. [22] Pilate answered, What I have written I have written.—John, ch. 19.

4706. —— **Life in.** *To Martha.* [25] Jesus said..I am the resurrection, and the life : he that believeth in me, though he were dead, yet shall he live : [26] And whosoever liveth and believeth in me shall never die. Believest thou this ?—John, ch. 11.

4707. —— **mistaken.** *Prophet only.* [13] He asked his disciples, saying, Whom do men say that I, the Son of man, am? [14] And they said, Some *say that thou art* John the Baptist ; some, Elijah ; and others, Jeremiah, or one of the prophets.—Mat., ch. 16.

4708. —— **mobbed.** *Pharisees.* [58] Before Abraham was, I am. [59] Then took they up stones to cast at him : but Jesus hid himself, and went out of the temple, going through the midst of them.—John, ch. 8.

4709. —— **nicknamed.** *"Samaritan."* [48] The Jews..said unto him, Say we not well that thou art a Samaritan, and hast a devil ?—John, ch. 8.

4710. —— **Offerings for.** *Magi.* [11] They saw the young child with Mary his mother, and fell down, and worshipped him : and..they presented unto him gifts ; gold, and frankincense, and myrrh.—Mat., ch. 2.

4711. —— **personated.** *Persecuted.* [7] I fell unto the ground, and heard a voice saying unto me, Saul, Saul, why persecutest thou me ? [8] And I answered, Who art thou, Lord ? And he said ..I am Jesus of Nazareth, whom thou persecutest.—Acts, ch. 22.

4712. —— **Praise to.** *In Heaven.* [11] I heard the voice of many angels round about the throne, and the beasts, and the elders.. [12] Saying with a loud voice, Worthy is the Lamb that was slain to receive power, and riches, and wisdom, and strength, and honour, and glory, and blessing. [13] And every creature..in heaven..earth, and under the earth, and..sea, and all that are in them, heard I saying, Blessing, and honour, and glory, and power, *be* unto him that sitteth upon the throne, and unto the Lamb for ever and ever.—Rev., ch. 5.

4713. —— **Patience of.** *"Stand at the Door."* [See No. 4699.]

4714. —— **Reception of.** *Child.* [5] Whoso shall receive one such little child in my name receiveth me.—Mat., ch. 18.

4715. —— **Representatives of.** *Disciples.* [40] He that receiveth you receiveth me ; and he that receiveth me receiveth him that sent me.—Mat., ch. 10.

4716. —— **rejected.** *Samaritans.* [See No. 4676.]

4717. —— **Saved by.** *Lake Gennesaret.* [29] Peter..walked on the water, to go to Jesus. [30] But when he saw the wind boisterous, he was afraid ;

and beginning to sink, he cried, saying, Lord, save me. [31] And immediately Jesus stretched forth *his* hand, and caught him.—Mat., ch. 14.

4718. —— **unrecognized.** *Resurrection.* [15] Jesus saith..Woman, why weepest thou ? whom seekest thou? She, supposing him to be the gardener, saith..Sir, if thou have borne him hence, tell me where thou hast laid him, and I will take him away. [16] Jesus saith..Mary. She turned herself, and saith..Rabboni.—John, ch. 20.

4719. —— **understood.** *Son of God.* [See No. 4707.] [15] But whom say ye that I am ? [16]..Peter answered..Thou art the Christ, the Son of the living God.—Mat., ch. 16.

4720. —— **the Warrior.** *"Judge and make War."* [11] I saw heaven opened, and behold a white horse ; and he that sat upon him *was* called Faithful and True, and in righteousness he doth judge and make war. [12] His eyes *were* as a flame of fire, and on his head *were* many crowns ; and he had a name written, that no man knew, but he himself. [13] And he *was* clothed with a vesture dipped in blood : and his name is called The Word of God.—Rev., ch. 19.

4721. —— **welcomed.** *In Bereavement.* [20] Martha, as soon as she heard that Jesus was coming, went and met him : but Mary sat *still* in the house.—John, ch. 11.

Also see:
Coming to. Peter walked on the water to go to J.   888
See CHRIST.

4722. JEWELS, The Lord's. *Age of Sceptics.* [16] They that feared the Lord spake often one to another : and the Lord hearkened, and heard *it*, and a book of remembrance was written before him for them that feared the Lord, and that thought upon his name. [17] And they shall be mine, saith the Lord of hosts, in that day when I make up my jewels.—Mal., ch. 3.

4723. JEWELRY, Abundance of. *Gideon's Men* [25] Spread a garment, and did cast therein every man the earrings of his prey. [26] And the weight of the golden earrings..was a thousand and seven hundred *shekels* of gold ; besides ornaments, and collars, and purple raiment that *was* on the kings of Midian, and besides the chains ..about their camels' necks.—Judges, ch. 8.

4724. —— **a Badge.** *Chain.* [29] Then commanded Belshazzar, and they clothed Daniel with scarlet, and *put* a chain of gold about his neck, and made a proclamation concerning him, that he should be the third ruler in the kingdom.—Dan., ch. 5.

4725. —— **given to God.** *Building Tabernacle.* [22] Men and women, as many as were willing hearted..brought bracelets, and earrings, and rings, and tablets, all jewels of gold : and ..*offered* an offering of gold unto the Lord.—Ex., ch. 35.

4726. —— **a Snare.** *Gideon.* [See No. 4723.] [27] Gideon made an ephod thereof, and put it in his city..and all Israel went thither a whoring after it: which thing became a snare unto Gideon, and to his house.—Judges, ch. 8.

Also see:
Adorning. Women..not with gold or pearls..array   108
Borrowed. Borrowed of the E. jewels of gold   915
Foundation of. First jasper ; the second sapphire 1328
Precious. Breastplate..four rows of stones   8348

4727. JOURNEY arrested. *Israelites.* [17] Let us pass, I pray thee, through thy country : we will not pass through the fields, or..vineyards, neither..drink..of the wells : we will go by the king's *high* way, we will not turn to the right hand nor to the left, until we have passed thy borders. [18] And Edom said..Thou shalt not pass by me, lest I come out against thee with the sword.—Num., ch. 20.

4728. —— The Christian's. *Abram.* [1] Get thee out of thy country, and from thy kindred ..unto a land that I will shew thee : [2] And I will make of thee a great nation, and I will bless thee, and make thy name great ; and thou shalt be a blessing.—Gen., ch. 12.

4729. —— Preparation for. *Elijah.* [7] The angel of the Lord came again the second time, and touched him, and said, Arise *and* eat, because the journey *is* too great for thee. [8] And he arose, and did eat and drink, and went in the strength of that meat forty days and forty nights unto Horeb.—1 Kings, ch. 19.

4730. —— A sad. *Sacrifice of Isaac.* [3] Abraham rose up early in the morning, and saddled his ass, and took two of his young men with him, and Isaac his son, and clave the wood for the burnt offering..and went unto the place of which God had told him.—Gen., ch. 22.

4731. —— to Zion, The. *The Ransomed.* [4] Say to them *that are* of a fearful heart, Be strong, fear not : behold, your God will come *with* vengeance, *even* God *with* a recompense ; he will come and save you.. [6] Then shall the lame *man* leap as a hart, and the tongue of the dumb sing : for in the wilderness shall waters break out, and streams in the desert.. [8] And a highway shall be there, and a way, and it shall be called The way of holiness ; the unclean shall not pass over it ; but it *shall be* for those : the wayfaring men, though fools, shall not err *therein.* [9] No lion shall be there, nor *any* ravenous beast shall go up thereon, it shall not be found there ; but the redeemed shall walk *there :* [10] And the ransomed of the Lord shall return, and come to Zion with songs and everlasting joy upon their heads : they shall obtain joy and gladness, and sorrow and sighing shall flee away.—Isa., ch. 35.

See other illustrations under :

EMIGRATION.

EXILE.

4732. JOY of Builders. *Temple.* [12] Many of the..ancient men, that had seen the first house, when the foundation of this house was laid before their eyes, wept with a loud voice ; and many shouted aloud for joy : [13] So that the people could not discern the noise of the shout of joy from the noise of the weeping of the people.—Ezra, ch. 3.

4733. —— of Believers. *"Unspeakable."* [8] Whom having not seen, ye love ; in whom, though now ye see *him* not, yet believing, ye rejoice with joy unspeakable and full of glory : [9] Receiving the end of your faith, *even* the salvation of *your* souls.—1 Peter, ch. 1.

4734. —— The Convert's. *At Jerusalem.* [46] They, continuing daily with one accord in the temple, and breaking bread from house to house, did eat their meat with gladness and singleness of heart, [47] Praising God, and having favour with all the people.—Acts, ch. 2.

4735. —— of Conscience. *Paul.* [12] Our rejoicing is this, the testimony of our conscience, that in simplicity and godly sincerity, not with fleshly wisdom, but by the grace of God, we have had our conversation in the world, and more abundantly to you-ward.—2 Cor., ch. 1.

4736. —— of Deliverance. *Lame Man.* [7] Peter took him by the right hand, and lifted *him* up : and immediately his feet and ankle bones received strength. [8] And he leaping up stood, and walked, and entered with them into the temple, walking, and leaping, and praising God.—Acts, ch. 3.

4737. —— Exuberant. *Conversion.* [9] When she hath found *it*, she calleth *her* friends and *her* neighbours together, saying, Rejoice with me ; for I have found the piece which I had lost. [10] Likewise..there is joy in the presence of the angels of God over one sinner that repenteth.—Luke, ch. 15.

4738. —— of Escape. *Darius.* [23] Then was the king exceeding glad for him, and commanded that they should take Daniel up out of the den.—Dan., ch. 6.

4739. —— Excitement of. *Rhoda's.* [14] When she knew Peter's voice, she opened not the gate for gladness, but ran in, and told how Peter stood before the gate.—Acts, ch. 12.

4740. —— rather than Fear. *To Shepherds.* [9] They were sore afraid. [10] And the angel said ..Fear not : for, behold, I bring you good tidings of great joy, which shall be to all people.—Luke, ch. 2.

4741. —— of Giving. *For Temple.* [9] The people rejoiced, for that they offered willingly, because with perfect heart they offered willingly to the Lord : and David the king also rejoiced with great joy.—1 Chron., ch. 29.

4742. —— A hellish. *Murderers.* [5] They were glad, and covenanted to give him money. [6] And he promised, and sought opportunity to betray him..in the absence of the multitude.—Luke, ch. 22.

4743. —— Irrepressible. *At Jerusalem.* [39] Some of the Pharisees..said..Master, rebuke thy disciples. [40] And he answered..I tell you that, if these should hold their peace, the stones would immediately cry out.—Luke, ch. 19.

4744. —— The Mother's. *Mary.* [18] All.. wondered at those things which were told them by the shepherds. [19] But Mary kept all these things, and pondered *them* in her heart.—Luke, ch. 2.

4745. —— Overcoming. *Israel.* [27] They told him all the words of Joseph..and when he saw the wagons which Joseph had sent to carry him, the spirit of Jacob their father revived.— GEN., ch. 45.

4746. —— **Penitential.** *Israelites.* ⁹ This day *is* holy unto the Lord your God ; mourn not, nor weep. For all the people wept, when they heard the words of the law.. ¹²..went their way to eat, and to drink, and to send portions, and to make great mirth, because they had understood the words that were declared unto them. —NEH., ch. 8.

4747. —— **Religious.** *Bringing the Ark.* ¹⁴ David danced before the Lord with all *his* might.. ¹⁵ So David and all the house of Israel brought up the ark of the Lord with shouting, and with the sound of the trumpet.—2 SAM., ch. 6. [It had been away nearly fifty years.]

4748. —— **of Recovery.** *Philip at Samaria.* ⁷ Unclean spirits, crying with loud voice, came out of many that were possessed..and many taken with palsies, and that were lame, were healed. ⁸ And there was great joy in that city. —ACTS, ch. 8.

4749. —— **of Success.** *Walls erected.* ⁴² The singers sang loud.. ⁴³ Also that day they offered great sacrifices, and rejoiced : for God had made them rejoice with great joy : the wives also and the children rejoiced : so that the joy of Jerusalem was heard even afar off.—NEH., ch. 12.

4750. —— **The supreme.** *To the Seventy.* ²⁰ In this rejoice not, that the spirits are subject unto you ; but rather rejoice, because your names are written in heaven.—LUKE, ch. 10.

4751. —— **Song of.** *David's.* ¹ I waited patiently for the Lord, and he inclined unto me, and heard my cry. ² He brought me up also out of a horrible pit, out of the miry clay, and set my feet upon a rock, *and* established my goings. ³ And he hath put a new song in my mouth, *even* praise unto our God.—Ps. 40.

4752. —— **Weeping for.** *Joseph.* ¹ Joseph could not refrain himself..he cried, Cause every man to go out from me. And there stood no man with him, while Joseph made himself known unto his brethren. ² And he wept aloud. —GEN., ch. 45.

4753. —— **amid Want.** *"In God."* ¹⁷ Although the fig tree shall not blossom, neither *shall* fruit *be* in the vines ; the labour of the olive shall fail, and the fields shall yield no meat ; the flock shall be cut off from the fold, and *there shall be* no herd in the stalls : ¹⁸ Yet I will rejoice in the Lord, I will joy in the God of my salvation.—HAB., ch. 3.

4754. —— **in Worship.** *David.* ¹ How amiable *are* thy tabernacles, O Lord of hosts ! ² My soul longeth, yea, even fainteth for the courts of the Lord : my heart and my flesh crieth out for the living God.—Ps. 84.

See other illustrations under :

CHEERFULNESS.
Benevolence. Lord loveth a cheerful giver   1138
Commended. Merry heart hath a continual feast   1139
Strange. Let a gallows be made..pleased Haman   1140

REJOICING.
Communion. This poor man cried..O taste and   3968
Conversion. There was great joy in that city   3969
Converts. [Jailer] rejoiced, believing in G. with   6971
    "   I waited patiently..put a new song in   6972

Converts. The eunuch went on his way rejoicing   6973
Duty. Thou shalt rejoice in every good thing..G.   6974
Deliverance. I will sing unto the L...triumphed   6975
    "   Jews had light, and gladness, and joy   6976
Great. At the descent of the mount of Olives   6978
Heavenly. Ransomed of the L...come to Z. with   6980
in Prison. At midnight Paul and Silas..sang praises   6981
in Persecutions. Rejoicing that they were counted   6982
Premature. [Amalekites] were eating and drink.   6983
in Reproach. Rejoice..be exceeding glad   6985
in Tribulation. I am exceeding joyful in all our   6986
in Temptation. Count it all joy when ye fall into   6987
Victors. Praised their god..hearts were merry   6988

SHOUTING.
Heaven. Voice of a great multitude..as many   7841
Idolatrous. Joshua heard the people as they   7842
Religious. Came a fire..all the people saw, they   7843
    "   Brought up the ark..with shouting and   7844
Stimulated. Philistines shouted against him..loosed   7845
Triumph. People shouted with a great shout   7846
Vain. Ark came into the camp..I. shouted   7847
Victory. People shouted when the priests blew the   7848
Weeping. Not discern the noise of joy from   7849

SINGING.
Difficult. They that..captive required of us a song   8035
Easy. Ransomed..return..come to Z. with songs   8036
Victory by. When they began to sing..the L. set   8037

Brief. Jonah was exceeding glad of the gourd   1387
Conscience. Our rejoicing..simplicity and godly   1568
Overcoming. Joseph made haste where to weep   164
    "   Joseph went up to meet his father   165

See **ENJOYMENT** and references.

4755. JUBILEE, Year of. *Law.* ¹⁰ Proclaim liberty throughout *all* the land unto all the inhabitants thereof : it shall be a jubilee unto you ; and ye shall return every man unto his possession, and..unto his family. ¹¹ A jubilee shall that fiftieth year be unto you : ye shall not sow, neither reap.—LEV., ch. 25.

4756. JUDGE, A Circuit. *Samuel.* ¹⁶ He went from year to year in circuit to Beth-el, and Gilgal, and Mizpeh, and judged Israel in all those places. ¹⁷ And his return *was* to Ramah ; for there *was* his house.—1 SAM., ch. 7.

4757. —— **Qualification of a.** *Innocence.* ⁴ Master, this woman was taken in adultery.. ⁵ Now Moses..commanded us, that such should be stoned : but what sayest thou ?.. ⁷..He that is without sin among you, let him first cast a stone at her.—JOHN, ch. 8.

4758. —— **An unjust.** *Pilate.* ⁶ Pilate saith unto them, Take ye him, and crucify *him* : for I find no fault in him.—JOHN, ch. 19.

4759. —— **An unrighteous.** *Ananias.* ¹ Men *and* brethren, I have lived in all good conscience before God until this day. ² And the high priest Ananias commanded..to smite him on the mouth. ³ Then said Paul .. God shall smite thee, *thou* whited wall : for sittest thou to judge me after the law, and commandest me to be smitten contrary to the law ?—ACTS, ch. 23.

4760. JUDGES, Bribery of. *Samuel's Sons* ² *Were* judges in Beersheba. ³ And his sons walked not in his ways, but turned aside after lucre, and took bribes, and perverted judgment. —1 SAM., ch. 8.

4761. JUDGMENT, Awards at the. *Jesus said,* ⁴⁴ Lord, when saw we thee a hungered, or athirst, or a stranger, or naked, or sick, or in prison, and did not minister unto thee ? ⁴⁵ Then shall he answer..Inasmuch as ye did *it* not to one of the least of these, ye did *it* not to me.—MAT., ch. 25.

4762. —— Accountability at the. *"Pounds."* ¹⁵ When he was returned..he commanded these servants to be called..that he might know how much every man had gained by trading. ¹⁶ Then came the first, saying, Lord, thy pound hath gained ten pounds. ¹⁷ And he said..Well, thou good servant.—LUKE, ch. 19.

4763. —— Blindness a. *Of Jews.* ⁴⁰ He hath blinded their eyes, and hardened their heart ; that they should not see with *their* eyes, nor understand with *their* heart, and be converted, and I should heal them.—JOHN, ch. 12.

4764. —— in Despondency. *Elijah.* ¹⁷ The children of Israel have forsaken thy covenant, thrown down thine altars, and slain thy prophets with the sword ; and I, *even* I only, am left ; and they seek my life, to take it away. ¹⁸ Yet I have left *me* seven thousand in Israel..which have not bowed unto Baal.—1 KINGS, ch. 19.

4765. —— Disappointment at the. *" Know you not."* ²⁶ We have eaten and drunk in thy presence, and thou hast taught in our streets. ²⁷ But he shall say..I know you not whence ye are ; depart from me, all *ye* workers of iniquity. ²⁸ There shall be weeping and gnashing of teeth. —LUKE, ch. 13.

4766. —— Discoveries at the. *"Saw thee."* [See No. 4761.]

4767. —— Effect of. *"Afraid."* [See No. 4769.] ⁹ David was afraid of the Lord that day, and said, How shall the ark of the Lord come to me ?—2 SAM., ch. 6.

4768. —— Humiliating. *Herod.* ²¹ Herod, arrayed in royal apparel, sat upon his throne, and made an oration.. ²² And the people gave a shout, *saying, It is* the voice of a god, and not of a man. ²³ And immediately the angel of the Lord smote him, because he gave not God the glory : and he was eaten of worms and gave up the ghost.—ACTS, ch. 12.

4769. —— upon the Heedless. *Uzzah.* ⁶ Uzzah put forth *his hand* to the ark of God, and took hold of it ; for the oxen shook *it.* ⁷ And the anger of the Lord was kindled against Uzzah, and God smote him there for *his* error.—2 SAM., ch. 6.

4770. —— Individual. *" Garment."* ¹¹ When the king came in to see the guests, he saw there a man which had not on a wedding garment : ¹² And he saith..Friend, how camest thou in hither, not having a wedding garment ? And he was speechless.—MAT., ch. 22.

4771. —— for Judgment. *Christ said,* ² With what judgment ye judge, ye shall be judged : and with what measure ye mete, it shall be measured to you again.—MAT., ch. 7.

4772. —— the Lord's. *Eliab.* ⁷ The Lord said unto Samuel, Look not on his countenance, or on the height of his stature ; because I have refused him : for *the Lord seeth* not as man seeth ; for man looketh on the outward appearance, but the Lord looketh on the heart.—1 SAM., ch. 16.

4773. —— Preparation for. *" Beam."* [See No. 4771.] ⁴ How wilt thou say to thy brother, Let me pull out the mote out of thine eye ; and,

behold, a beam *is* in thine own eye ? ⁵ Thou hypocrite, first cast out the beam out of thine own eye ; and then shalt thou see clearly to cast out the mote out of thy brother's eye.— MAT., ch. 7.

4774. —— Preparation for. *Paul at Athens.* ³⁰ The times of this ignorance God winked at ; but now commandeth all men every where to repent : ³¹ Because he hath appointed a day, in the which he will judge the world.—ACTS, ch. 17.

4775. —— repeated. *Sapphira.* [See No. 4780.] ⁹ Then Peter said unto her, How is it that ye have agreed together to tempt the Spirit of the Lord ? behold, the feet of them which have buried thy husband *are* at the door, and shall carry thee out. ¹⁰ Then fell she down..and yielded up the ghost.—ACTS, ch. 5.

4776. —— Swift. *Miriam.* ¹ Miriam and Aaron spake against Moses because of the Ethiopian woman whom he had married.. ² And they said, Hath the Lord indeed spoken only by Moses ? hath he not spoken also by us ?.. ¹⁰ And the cloud departed.. Miriam *became* leprous, *white* as snow.—NUM., ch. 12.

4777. —— Surprising. *Belshazzar.* ²⁵ This *is* the writing that was written,: MENE, MENE, TEKEL, UPHARSIN. ²⁶ This *is* the interpretation of the thing : MENE ; God hath numbered thy kingdom, and finished it. ²⁷ TEKEL ; Thou art weighed in the balances, and art found wanting. ²⁸ PERES ; Thy kingdom is divided, and given to the Medes and Persians.—DAN., ch. 5.

4778. —— Sincerity. *Balance.* ⁵ If I have walked with vanity, or if my foot hath hasted to deceit ; ⁶ Let me be weighed in an even balance, that God may know mine integrity. ⁷ If my step hath turned out of the way, and mine heart walked after mine eyes, and if any blot hath cleaved to mine hands.—JOB, ch. 31. ⁵ Also when he had opened the third seal..I beheld, and lo a black horse ; and he that sat on him had a pair of balances in his hand. ⁶ And I heard a voice..say, A measure of wheat for a penny, and three measures of barley for a penny ; and *see* thou hurt not the oil and the wine. —REV., ch. 6.

4779. —— Sermon on the. *Paul's.* ²⁵ As he reasoned of righteousness, temperance, and judgment to come, Felix trembled.—ACTS, ch. 24.

4780. —— A terrifying. *Ananias.* ³ Peter said, Ananias, why hath Satan filled thine heart to lie to the Holy Ghost, and to keep back *part* of the price of the land ?.. ⁵ And Ananias hearing these words fell down, and gave up the ghost ; and great fear came on all.—ACTS, ch. 5.

See other illustrations under :

CHOICE.

4781. JUDGMENT-DAY, Commotions of. *"Sixth Seal."* [12] There was a great earthquake ; and the sun became black as sackcloth of hair, and the moon became as blood ; [13] And the stars of heaven fell unto the earth, even as a fig tree casteth her untimely figs, when she is shaken of a mighty wind. [14] And the heaven departed as a scroll when it is rolled together ; and every mountain and island were moved out of their places.—REV., ch. 6.

4782. —— Escape from. *"Hide."* [See No. 4785.]

4783. —— Gathering at. *"Gave up their Dead."* [13] The sea gave up the dead which were in it ; and death and hell delivered up the dead which were in them : and they were judged every man according to their works.—REV., ch. 20.

4784. —— Records for. *"Books."* [See Nos. 4783, 4786.]

4785. —— Terrors of. *Sinners.* [15] The kings of the earth .. great men .. rich men .. chief captains..mighty men..bond man, and every free man, hid themselves in the dens and in the rocks of the mountains ; [16] And said to the mountains and rocks, Fall on us, and hide us from the face of him that sitteth on the throne, and from the wrath of the Lamb : [17] For the great day of his wrath is come ; and who shall be able to stand?—REV., ch. 6.

4786. —— Vision of the. *"White Throne."* [11] I saw a great white throne, and him that sat on it, from whose face the earth and the heaven fled away ; and there was found no place for them. [12] And I saw the dead, small and great, stand before God ; and the books were opened : and another book was opened, which is *the book* of life : and the dead were judged out of those things which were written in the books, according to their works.—REV., ch. 20.

4787. JUDGMENTS misinferred. *Calamity.* [4] Those eighteen, upon whom the tower in Siloam fell, and slew them, think ye that they were sinners above all men that dwelt in Jerusalem ? [5] I tell you, Nay : but, except ye repent, ye shall all likewise perish.—LUKE, ch. 13.

Also see :
Weeping. Depart..there shall be weeping   4770

4788. JUSTICE, Avenging. *Siege of Thebez.* [52] Abimelech..went hard unto the door of the tower to burn it with fire. [53] And a certain woman cast a piece of a millstone upon Abimelech's head, and all to brake his skull.. [56] Thus God rendered the wickedness of Abimelech, which he did unto his father, in slaying his seventy brethren.—JUDGES, ch. 9.

4789. —— Compensating. *Family.* [28] Isaac loved Esau, because he did eat of *his* venison : but Rebekah loved Jacob.—GEN., ch. 25.

4790. —— deferred. *Gospel.* [See No. 4791.] [39] Resist not evil : but whosoever shall smite thee on thy right cheek, turn to him the other also. [40] And if any man will sue thee at the law, and take away thy coat, let him have *thy* cloak also.—MAT., ch. 5.

4791. —— Equality in. *Law.* [38] Ye have heard that it hath been said, An eye for an eye, and a tooth for a tooth.—MAT., ch. 5.

4792. —— Impartial. *Moses said,* [16] I charged your judges..saying, Hear *the causes* between your brethren, and judge righteously between *every* man and his brother, and the stranger.. [17] Ye shall not respect persons in judgment ; *but* ye shall hear the small as well as the great ; ye shall not be afraid of the face of man ; for the judgment *is* God's.—DEUT., ch. 1.

4793. —— Indignant. *Haman.* [10] They hanged Haman on the gallows that he had prepared for Mordecai. Then was the king's wrath pacified.—ESTHER, ch. 7.

4794. —— improperly sought. *Corinthians.* [7] There is utterly a fault among you, because ye go to law one with another. Why do ye not rather take wrong ? Why do ye not rather *suffer yourselves to* be defrauded ?—1 COR., ch. 6.

4795. —— insulted. *"In the Judgment Seat."* [12] Pilate sought to release him : but the Jews cried out, saying, If thou let this man go, thou art not Cesar's friend : whosoever maketh himself a king speaketh against Cesar. [13] When Pilate therefore heard that saying, he brought Jesus forth, and sat down in the judgment seat.—JOHN, ch. 19.

4796. —— at Last. *"Spoiled."* [35] They borrowed of the Egyptians jewels of silver, and jewels of gold, and raiment : [36] And the Lord gave the people favour in the sight of the Egyptians, so that they lent unto them *such things as* *they required.* And they spoiled the Egyptians. —Ex., ch. 12.

4797. —— **Overtaken by.** *Agag.* ³² Bring ye hither to me Agag the king of the Amalekites ..And Agag said, Surely the bitterness of death is past. ³³ And Samuel said, As thy sword hath made women childless, so shall thy mother be childless among women. And Samuel hewed Agag in pieces before the Lord in Gilgal.—1 SAM., ch. 15.

4798. —— **Penalty of.** *Capital.* ⁵ The man that consumed us, and that devised against us *that* we should be destroyed from remaining in any of the coasts of Israel, ⁶ Let seven men of his sons be delivered unto us, and we will hang them up unto the Lord in Gibeah of Saul, *whom* the Lord did choose. And the king said, I will give *them.*—2 SAM., ch. 21.

4799. —— **Parental.** *Paul.* ⁴ Ye fathers, provoke not your children to wrath.—EPH., ch. 6.

4800. —— **Retributive.** *Adoni-bezek.* ⁶ Adoni-bezek fled..caught him, and cut off his thumbs and his great toes. ⁷ And Adoni-bezek said, Threescore and ten kings, having their thumbs and their great toes cut off, gathered *their meat* under my table : as I have done, so God hath requited me.—JUDGES, ch. 1.

See other illustrations under:

FAITHFULNESS.

Blessed is that servant whom his lord..so doing 2975
Constant. The fire shall ever be burning upon the 2976
Despondency. Let us also go..may die with him 2977
Honoured. I make a decree..speak..against the G. 2978
Ministerial. [See 2 Cor. 4 : 1-11.] 2979
Truth. What the L. saith unto me..that I will s. 2980
Primitive. All scattered abroad..except the a. 2981
Principle. Faithful in that which is least..also in 2982
Rewarded. If thou see me when I am taken..be 2983

HONESTY.

Accredited. My master wotteth not what is with 4043
Acknowledged. Samuel..thou hast not defrauded 4044
Commended. Hath not oppressed..usury..iniquity 4045
Happiness. Better is little with righteousness 4046
Ignored. It is naught, saith the buyer..boasteth 4047
Official. Gift doth blind the eyes of the wise 4048
Payment. Go sell the oil and pay the debt 4049
Rare. Seek..if there be any..the truth 4050
Reward. Shaketh his hand from holding bribes 4051
Restitution. If I have taken..restore fourfold 4052
Trained. All these have I observed from my y. 4053
Test. The money that was..in your sacks..carry 4054
Trade. Not have..divers weights, a great and s. 4055
   Divers weights, and divers measures 4056
Trusted. They delivered the money to..workmen 4057

Speedy. Not obey the law..executed speedily 630
Abandoned. Pilate said, Take ye him..no fault 1477
   See INTEGRITY.

4801. JUSTIFICATION, Difficulty of. *Bildad said,* ⁴ How then can man be justified with God? · or how can he be clean *that is* born of a woman? ⁵ Behold even to the moon, and it shineth not ; yea, the stars are not pure in his sight. ⁶ How much less man, *that is* a worm? and the son of man, *which is* a worm.—JOB, ch. 25.

4802. —— **for Penitents.** *Publican.* ¹³ The publican, standing afar off, would not lift up so much as *his* eyes unto heaven, but smote upon his breast, saying, God be merciful to me a sin-

ner. ¹⁴ I tell you, this man went down to his house justified *rather* than the other.—LUKE, ch. 18.

4803. —— **by Precedent.** *Jesus said,* ³ Have ye not read what David did, when he was a hungered, and they that were with him ; ⁴ How he entered into the house of God, and did eat the shewbread, which was not lawful for him to eat, neither for them which were with him, but only for the priests?—MAT., ch. 12.

4804. —— **by Sophistry.** *A Lawyer.* [Quoting the law.] ²⁷ Thou shalt love the Lord thy God with all thy heart, and with all thy soul, and with all thy strength, and with all thy mind ; and thy neighbour as thyself. ²⁸ And he said.. this do, and thou shalt live. ²⁹ But he, willing to justify himself, said unto Jesus, And who is my neighbour?—LUKE, ch. 10.

See other illustrations under :

ACCEPTANCE.

Assurance. Would he have shewed us all these 53
Denied. Ye brought..torn and the lame..sick 55
Evidence. There rose up fire out of the rock 56
Manifested. Burning lamp passed between those 57
of Piety. In every nation he that feareth..worketh 58
by Sacrifice. L. had respect unto Abel..offering 59
Terms. Do justly love mercy..walk humbly 61

CONVERSION.

Creation. New creature, old things passed away 1700
Conscious. Know we that we dwell in him..S. 1701
Changed. Made their feet fast..washed their s. 1702
Changes Life. Saul preached..Is not this he that 1703
Effort. Strive to enter in at the strait gate 1704
Evidence. Lydia..besought us..Come into my 1705
False. Simon saw..H. G. given..offered money 1706
Genuine. Set meat..rejoiced, believing in G. 1707
Heart Work. Out of the heart..evil thoughts 1708
Hasty. See, here is water ; what doth hinder 1709
Inward. Pharisees make clean the outside of 1710
Mystery. Wind bloweth..canst not tell whence 1711
Necessity. Except a man be born of water and 1712
New Heart. God gave Saul another heart 1713
Negative. Reckon ye yourselves dead indeed unto 1714
Sudden. Called for a light. What must I do ? 1715
Superficial. When tribulation or persecution 1716
Wonderful. Suddenly there shined..voice..Saul 1717

EXCUSE.

Disobedience. Spared the best of the sheep..to 2792
False. Wherefore cometh not..[David] to meat 2793
Idlers. Lion without, I shall be slain 2794
Inadequate. Make us gods..as for this Moses 2795

EXCUSES.

Caviller's. Angry..made a man..whole on the s. 2796
Feeble. The door is now shut..in bed..cannot 2797
Indolence. Sluggard is wiser..render a reason 2798
Loss. I am slow of speech..anger of the Lord 2799
Worldly. I have bought a piece of ground..oxen 2800

4805. KIDNAPPERS, Crime of. *Law.* ⁷ If a man be found stealing any of his brethren.. and maketh merchandise of him, or selleth him ; then that thief shall die.—DEUT., ch. 24.

4806. —— **of Wives.** *Daughters of Shiloh.* ²³ The children of Benjamin did so, and took *them* wives, according to their number, of them that danced, whom they caught.—JUDGES, ch. 21.

4807. KINDNESS, Almsgiving. *Cornelius.* ² A devout *man,* and one that feared God with all his house, which gave much alms to the people, and prayed to God always.—ACTS, ch. 10.

4808. —— **appreciated.** *By David.* [He returned victorious ; see No. 4830.] [33] The king said unto Barzillai, Come thou over with me, and I will feed thee with me in Jerusalem.—2 SAM., ch. 19.

4809. —— **to Animals.** *Rebekah.* [See No. 4829.] [19] When she had done giving him drink, she said, I will draw *water* for thy camels also, until they have done drinking. [20] And she hasted. —GEN., ch. 24.

4810. —— **to the Bereaved.** *Sepulchre.* [5] The children of Heth answered Abraham.. [6]..thou *art* a mighty prince among us : in the choice of our sepulchres bury thy dead ; none of us shall withhold from thee his sepulchre.—GEN., ch. 23.

4811. —— **to Brethren.** *Law.* [35] If thy brother be waxen poor, and fallen in decay with thee ; then thou shalt relieve him : yea, *though he be* a stranger, or a sojourner.—LEV., ch. 25.

4812. —— **conquers.** *David said,* [11] See the skirt of thy robe in my hand : for in that I cut off the skirt of thy robe, and killed thee not, know thou and see that *there is* neither evil nor transgression in mine hand..yet thou huntest my soul to take it.. [16]..Saul said, Is this thy voice, my son David? And Saul lifted up his voice, and wept.—1 SAM., ch. 24.

4813. —— **to Christians.** *Jesus said,* [42] Whosoever shall give to drink unto one of these little ones a cup of cold *water* only in the name of a disciple, verily I say unto you, he shall in no wise lose his reward.—MAT., ch. 10.

4814. —— —— *From Antioch.* [29] Then the disciples, every man according to his ability, determined to send relief unto the brethren which dwelt in Judea.—ACTS, ch. 11.

4815. —— **to Captives.** *To Judah.* [15] The men..took the captives, and with the spoil clothed all that were naked among them, and arrayed them, and shod them, and gave them to eat and to drink, and anointed them, and carried all the feeble of them upon asses, and brought them to Jericho.—2 CHRON., ch. 28.

4816. —— **of "our Father."** *"Much More."* Jesus said, [11] If ye then, being evil, know how to give good gifts unto your children, how much more shall your Father which is in heaven give good things to them that ask him?—MAT., ch. 7.

4817. —— —— **from Gratitude.** *Mephibosheth.* [7] David said unto him, Fear not.. for I will surely shew thee kindness for Jonathan thy father's sake, and will restore thee all the land of Saul thy father ; and thou shalt eat bread at my table continually.—2 SAM., ch. 9.

4818. —— **Heathen.** *At Malta.* [2] The barbarous people shewed us no little kindness : for they kindled a fire, and received us every one, because of the present rain, and because of the cold.—ACTS, ch. 28.

4819. —— **insulted.** *In Bereavement.* [12] David sent to comfort him by the hand of his servant for his father.. [13] Hath not David *rather* sent..to search the city, and to spy it out..? [4] Wherefore Hanun..shaved off the one half of their beards, and cut off their garments in the middle, *even* to their buttocks, and sent them away.—2 SAM., ch. 10.

4820. —— **Inopportune.** *Benhadad Captured.* [34] Ahab..made a covenant with him, and sent

him away.. [42]..Thus saith the Lord, Because thou hast let go out of *thy* hand a man whom I appointed to utter destruction, therefore thy life shall go for his life, and thy people for his people.—1 KINGS, ch. 20.

4821. —— **a Loan.** *Proverb.* [17] He that hath pity upon the poor lendeth unto the Lord ; and that which he hath given will he pay him again. —PROV., ch. 19.

4822. —— **A providential.** *Boaz.* [8] Boaz unto Ruth..my daughter? Go not to glean in another field..but abide here fast by my maidens : [9] Let thine eyes *be* on the field that they do reap, and go thou after them : have I not charged the young men that they shall not touch thee? and when thou art athirst..drink of *that* which the young men have drawn.—RUTH, ch. 2. [He proved to be a kinsman and became a husband.]

4823. —— **in Prosperity.** *Job.* [12] I delivered the poor that cried, and the fatherless, and *him that had* none to help him. [13] The blessing of him that was ready to perish came upon me : and I caused the widow's heart to sing for joy. —JOB, ch. 29.

4824. —— **to a Prisoner.** *To Jeremiah.* [12] Ebed-melech the Ethiopian said unto Jeremiah, Put now *these* old cast clouts and rotten rags under thine armholes under the cords.. [13] So they drew up Jeremiah with cords, and took him up out of the dungeon.—JER., ch. 38.

4825. —— **remembered.** *Saul said,* [6] Go, depart..from among the Amalekites, lest I destroy you with them : for ye shewed kindness to all the children of Israel, when they came up out of Egypt. So the Kenites departed from among the Amalekites.—1 SAM., ch. 15.

4826. —— **rewarded.** *To Rahab.* [6] She had brought them up to the roof of the house, and hid them with the stalks of flax.. [18] Behold, *when* we come into the land, thou shalt bind this line of scarlet thread in the window which thou didst let us down by : and..bring..all thy father's household home unto thee.—JOSH., ch. 2. [All were saved.]

4827. —— **Substitutional.** *Job.* [15] I was eyes to the blind, and feet *was* I to the lame. [16] I *was* a father to the poor : and the cause *which* I knew not I searched out. [17] And I brake the jaws of the wicked, and plucked the spoil out of his teeth.—JOB, ch. 29.

4828. —— **to a Servant.** *Centurion.* [2] A certain centurion's servant, who was dear unto him, was sick, and ready to die. [3] And when he heard of Jesus, he sent unto him the elders of the Jews, beseeching him that he would come and heal.—LUKE, ch. 7.

4829. —— **to Strangers.** *Rebekah.* [To Abraham's servant.] [18] Drink, my lord : and she hasted, and let down her pitcher upon her hand, and gave him drink.—GEN., ch. 24.

4830. —— **Timely.** *Barzillai.* [Fleeing from Absalom.] [28] Brought beds, and basins, and earthen vessels, and wheat, and barley, and flour, and parched *corn*, and beans, and lentiles, and parched *pulse*, [29] And honey, and butter, and sheep, and cheese of kine, for David, and for the people that *were* with him, to eat : for they said, The people is hungry, and weary, and thirsty, in the wilderness.—2 SAM., ch. 17.

4831. —— **An unexpected.** *To Syrians.* [21] The king of Israel said unto Elisha, when he saw them, My father, shall I smite *them?* shall I smite *them?* [22] And he answered, Thou shalt not smite *them*: wouldest thou smite those whom thou hast taken captive with thy sword and with thy bow? set bread and water before them..and go to their master.—2 Kings, ch. 6.

4832. —— **to the Widow.** *Law.* [19] When thou cuttest down thine harvest in thy field, and hast forgot a sheaf in the field, thou shalt not go again to fetch it: it shall be for the stranger, for the fatherless, and for the widow: that the Lord thy God may bless thee in all the work of thine hands.—Deut., ch. 29.

See other illustrations under:

COMPASSION.

Appeal. Son..spirit teareth him..have compassion	1423
Active. Jesus went about all the cities..healing	1424
Brother's. Joseph said, Fear not..comforted them	1425
Commended. [Good Samaritan] Go thou and do	1426
Debtors. To be sold and his wife..had compassion	1427
Denied. Took him by the throat..Pay me	1428
Lowly. Israel sighed..G. heard the groaning	1429
Moved. We have sinned..grieve for the misery of	1430
Penitent. While..a great way off..compassion	1431
Public. City was moved..Is this Naomi?	1432
Patriotic. O Jerusalem..how often..ye would not	1433
Practical. Leper..Jesus..with compassion	1434
Reproof. Forgive him and comfort him	1435
Required. Shouldest thou not have..on thy fellow	1436
Sensitive. Not a high priest which cannot be	1437
Unmoved. [Joseph] We saw the anguish..would	1438
Womanly. Daughter of Pharaoh..babe wept..had	1439
Without. Chaldees..had no compassion..old	1440

FAVOUR.

Besought. Go serve the L..bless me also	3090
Divine. I bear you on eagles' wings	3091
Evinced. Let her glean even among the sheaves	3092
Indicated. King held out to Esther the golden	3093
Refused. Edom said, Thou shalt not pass by me	3094

FAVOURS.

Compensated. Think on me when it..be well with	3095
Forgotten. Yet did not the chief butler remember	3096
Remembered. There was a Hebrew..interpreted	3097

GENEROSITY.

Afflicted. The field give I thee and the cave..bury	3511
Excessive. So the people were restrained from	3512
Forgiving. Esau said, I have enough, my brother	3513
Royal. [David's gift for the temple, $94,000,000]	3514

GRACE.

Assimilative. Leaven..whole was leavened	3671
Advancement. Jesus increased..wisdom..stature	3672
All of. By the grace of G. I am what I am	3673
Accessible. That is bitten, when he looketh..live	3674
Better. Tread on serpents..rejoice..names written	3675
Conquest. Put out those nations..little by little	3676
Day of. Let it alone this year also	3677
Diffusive. Leaven hid in three measures meal	3678
Dishonoured. One is hungry and another is drunken	3679
Free. Smite the rock..people may drink	3680
Growth. Rod of Aaron budded..blossoms	3681
Invitation. Spirit and the bride say, Come	3682
Indwelling. In him a well of water springing up	3683
Means. Continued steadfastly..doctrine	3684
" Thomas was not with them when J. came	3685
Only. Unprofitable servants..done..our duty to do	3686
Reward. Likewise received every man a penny	3687
Sought. Come boldly to the throne of grace	3688
Transforms. This..house of G..gate..heaven	3689

Tested. Go wash in Jordan..Naaman was wroth	3690
Unfailing. Eat manna..until they came to..Canaan	3691
Work. I laboured..yet not I, but the grace of G.	3692

TENDERNESS.

Affectionate. I wrote unto you with many tears	8714
Bereavement. O my son Absalom, my son, my son	8715
Concealed. Joseph turned..and wept	8716
Excessive. Joseph made haste..sought where to	8717
Human. Her weeping, and the Jews weeping	8718

Impressive. I will draw water for thy camels also 429

See **BENEVOLENCE** and references.

4833. **KING of Animals.** *Leviathan.* [19] Out of his mouth go burning lamps, *and* sparks of fire leap out. [20] Out of his nostrils goeth smoke, as *out* of a seething pot or caldron. [21] His breath kindleth coals, and a flame goeth out of his mouth.. [33] Upon earth there is not his like, who is made without fear.—Job, ch. 41.

4834. —— **Burdens of a.** *Samuel said,* [13] And he will take your daughters *to be* confectionaries ..cooks, and..bakers. [14] And he will take your fields..vineyards..oliveyards, *even* the best *of them*, and give *them* to his servants. [15] And he will take the tenth of your seed, and of your vineyards, and give to his officers, and to his servants. [16] And he will take your menservants ..maidservants, and your goodliest young men, and your asses, and put *them* to his work. [17] He will take the tenth of your sheep: and we shall be his servants.—1 Sam., ch. 8.

4835. —— **in Burlesque.** *Soldiers.* [28] Put on him a scarlet robe. [29] And when they had platted a crown of thorns, they put *it* upon his head, and a reed in his right hand: and they bowed the knee before him, and mocked him, saying, Hail, King of the Jews! [30] And they spit upon him, and took the reed, and smote him on the head.—Mat., ch. 27.

4836. —— **A cruel.** *At Rabbah.* [31] He brought forth the people that *were* therein, and put *them* under saws, and under harrows of iron, and under axes of iron, and made them pass through the brickkiln: and thus did he unto.. the children of Ammon. So David..returned unto Jerusalem.—2 Sam., ch. 12.

4837. —— **Seven Days a.** *Zimri.* [15] Did Zimri reign seven days in Tirzah.. [16] And the people *that were* encamped heard say, Zimri hath conspired, and hath also slain the king: wherefore all Israel made Omri, the captain of the host, king over Israel.—1 Kings, ch. 16.

4838. —— **Goodly.** *Saul.* [2] A choice young man, and a goodly: and *there was* not among the children of Israel a goodlier person than he: from his shoulders and upward *he was* higher than any of the people.—1 Sam., ch. 9.

4839. —— **A helpless.** *Darius.* [14] The king, when he heard *these* words, was sore displeased with himself, and set *his* heart on Daniel to deliver him: and he laboured till the going down of the sun.—Dan., ch. 6.

4840. —— **The last.** *Jewish.* [The Babylonians] [7] Slew the sons of Zedekiah before his eyes, and put out the eyes of Zedekiah, and bound him with fetters of brass, and carried him to Babylon.—2 Kings, ch. 25.

4841. —— **of all Nations.** *Jesus.* [19] Pilate wrote a title, and put *it* on the cross. And the writing was, JESUS OF NAZARETH THE KING

OF THE JEWS. ²⁰..and it was written in Hebrew, *and* Greek, *and* Latin.—JOHN, ch. 19.

4842. —— of the Jews. *Bramble Chosen.*
³ The trees went forth *on a time* to anoint a king
over them ; and they said unto the olive tree,
Reign thou over us. ⁹ But the olive tree said..
Should I leave my fatness, wherewith by me
they honour God and man, and go to be promoted over the trees?—JUDGES, ch. 9.

4843. —— An unhappy. *Zimri.* [See No.
4837.] ¹⁷ Omri went up..and all Israel with him,
and they besieged Tirzah. ¹⁸..when Zimri saw
that the city was taken..he went into the palace
..and burnt the king's house over him with
fire.—1 KINGS, ch. 16.

4844. —— The universal. *Jesus.* ¹¹ From
the rising of the sun even unto the going down
of the same, my name *shall be* great among the
Gentiles ; and in every place incense *shall be*
offered unto my name, and a pure offering.—
MAL., ch. 1.

4845. —— A wicked. *Manasseh.* ² He did
..evil..after the abominations of the heathen..
³ For he built up again the high places which
Hezekiah his father had destroyed, and he reared up altars for Baal, and made a grove..and
worshipped all the host of heaven.—2 KINGS,
ch. 21.

4846. —— A youthful. *"Eight Years."*
¹ Josiah *was* eight years old when he began to
reign, and he reigned thirty and one years in
Jerusalem.—2 KINGS, ch. 22.

4847. —— —— *"Sixteen."* ³ Sixteen years
old *was* Uzziah when he began to reign, and he
reigned fifty and 'two years in Jerusalem.—2
CHRON., ch. 26.

4848. KINGSHIP declined. *Gideon.* ²² The
men of Israel said unto Gideon, Rule thou over
us, both thou, and thy son, and thy son's son
also : for thou hast delivered us from the hand
of Midian. ²³ And Gideon said..I will not rule
over you, neither shall my son rule over you :
the Lord shall rule over you.—JUDGES, ch. 8.

4849. —— —— *Jesus.* ¹⁵ When Jesus therefore perceived that they would come and take
him by force, to make him a king, he departed
again into a mountain himself alone.—JOHN,
ch. 6.

See other illustrations under:

DOMINION.

Dream of. Your sheaves..made obeisance to my　2489
Feared. Dread of you..upon every beast　　　2490
Made for. Have dominion over the fish..fowl　　2491

4850. KISS, A filial. *Elisha.* ¹⁹ Elijah..
cast his mantle upon him. ²⁰ And he left the
oxen, and ran after Elijah, and said, Let me, I
pray thee, kiss my father and my mother, and
then I will follow thee. And he said unto him,
Go back again.—1 KINGS, ch. 19.

4851. —— Treacherous. *Joab.* ⁹ Joab said
to Amasa, *Art* thou in health, my brother? And
Joab took Amasa by the beard with the right
hand to kiss him. ¹⁰ But Amasa took no heed
to the sword that *was* in Joab's hand : so he
smote him therewith in the fifth *rib.*—2 SAM.,
ch. 20.

4852. —— —— *Judas.* ⁴⁸ Gave them a sign,
saying, Whomsoever I shall kiss, that same is
he ; hold him fast. ⁴⁹ And forthwith he came

to Jesus, and said, Hail, Master ; and kissed
him.—MAT., ch. 26.

See other illustrations under :

Adoring. A woman which was a sinner..kissed his　170
Demagogue's. Absalom..took him and kissed him　161
Deceitful. The kisses of an enemy are deceitful　5149
Farewell. Orpah kissed her mother in law, but Ruth 166
Parental. His father..fell on his neck and kissed　157

4853. KNOWLEDGE, Adamic. *Animals.*
¹⁹ The Lord God formed every beast of the field,
and every fowl of the air ; and brought *them*
unto Adam to see what he would call them..
²⁰ And Adam gave names to all cattle, and to the
fowl of the air, and to every beast of the field.
—GEN., ch. 2.

4854. —— A detrimental. *Of Evil.* ²² Behold, the man is become as one of us, to know
good and evil : and now, lest he put forth his
hand, and take also of the tree of life, and eat,
and live for ever : ²³ Therefore the Lord God
sent him forth.—GEN., ch. 3.

4855. —— A forbidden. *Tree.* ¹⁷ But of the
tree of the knowledge of good and evil, thou shalt
not eat of it : for in the day that thou eatest
thereof thou shalt surely die.—GEN., ch. 2.

4856. —— From Faith to. *Samaritans*
⁴² Said unto the woman, Now we believe, not
because of thy saying : for we have heard *him*
ourselves, and know that this is indeed the
Christ, the Saviour of the world.—JOHN, ch. 4.

4857. —— increases Guilt. *Peter.* ²¹ It had
been better for them not to have known the way
of righteousness, than, after they have known
it, to turn from the holy commandment delivered unto them. ²² But it is happened unto
them according to the true proverb, The dog *is*
turned to his own vomit again ; and, The sow
that was washed to her wallowing in the mire.—2
PETER, ch. 2.

4858. —— less than Grace. *Apostles.* ¹³ When
they saw the boldness of Peter and John, and
perceived that they were unlearned and ignorant
men, they marvelled ; and they took knowledge
of them, that they had been with Jesus.—ACTS,
ch. 4.

4859. —— with Ignorance. *Paul.* ²² I go
bound in the spirit unto Jerusalem, not knowing the things that shall befall me there : ²³ Save
that the Holy Ghost witnesseth in every city,
saying that bonds and afflictions abide me.
²⁴ But none of these things move me.—ACTS,
ch. 20.

4860. —— Responsibility for. *Law.* ³⁶ If it
be known that the ox hath used to push in time
past, and his owner hath not kept him in ; he
shall surely pay.—EX., ch. 21.

4861. —— Spiritual. *Job.* ²⁵ I know *that*
my Redeemer liveth, and *that* he shall stand at
the latter *day* upon the earth : ²⁶ And *though* after my skin *worms* destroy this *body,* yet in my
flesh shall I see God : ²⁷ Whom I shall see for
myself, and mine eyes shall behold, and not another.—JOB, ch. 19.

4862. —— Temptation in. *Eden.* ⁵ God
doth know that in the day ye eat thereof, then
your eyes shall be opened ; and ye shall be as
Gods, knowing good and evil. ⁶ And when the
woman saw that the tree *was*..a tree to be desired to make *one* wise, she took of the fruit
thereof.—GEN., ch. 3.

4863. —— **to be used.** *Warning.* [4] Whosoever heareth the sound of the trumpet, and taketh not warning ; if the sword come, and take him away, his blood shall be upon his own head.—EZEK., ch. 33.

See other illustrations under :

Hidden. This saying was hid from them 1443
Influence. If any man see thee which hast k. sit 477
Joy. Happy are the people that hear thy wisdom 554
Responsibility. Through thy knowledge..weak 477
Value. How much better is it to get wisdom than 1234
Withheld. Ye have taken away the key of 9092
See INTELLIGENCE and references.

4864. LABOUR, Advantage of. *Sleep.* [12] The sleep of a labouring man *is* sweet, whether he eat little or much : but the abundance of the rich will not suffer him to sleep.—ECCL., ch. 5.

4865. —— **Curse of.** *Adam's.* [18] Thorns also and thistles shall it bring forth to thee ; and thou shalt eat the herb of the field : [19] In the sweat of thy face shalt thou eat bread, till thou return unto the ground..for dust thou *art*, and unto dust shalt thou return.—GEN., ch. 3.

4866. —— **commanded.** *L a w .* [9] Six days shalt thou labour, and do all thy work.—EX., ch. 20.

4867. —— **Congenial.** *Horticulture.* [15] The Lord God took the man, and put him into the garden of Eden to dress it and to keep it.—GEN., ch. 2.

4868. —— **Co-operative.** *Christian.* [37] Jesus said..herein is that saying true, One soweth, and another reapeth. [38] I sent you to reap that whereon ye bestowed no labour : other men laboured, and ye are entered into their labours.—JOHN, ch. 4.

4869. —— **Degradation of.** *"Sweat."* [19] In the sweat of thy face shalt thou eat bread, till thou return unto the ground ; for out of it wast thou taken : for dust thou *art*, and unto dust shalt thou return.—GEN., ch. 3.

4870. —— **Increase of.** *In Egypt.* [18] Go therefore now, *and* work ; for there shall no straw be given you, yet shall ye deliver the tale of bricks. [19] And the officers of the children of Israel did see *that* they *were* in evil *case*.—EX., ch. 5.

4871. —— **Menial.** *Gibeonites.* [22] Joshua called for them..Wherefore have ye beguiled us, saying, We *are* very far from you ; when ye dwell among us ? [23] Now therefore ye *are* cursed, and there shall none of you be freed from being bondmen, and hewers of wood and drawers of water for the house of my God.—JOSH., ch. 9.

4872. —— **Motive for.** *Paul.* [9] Wherefore we labour, that, whether present or absent, we may be accepted of him.—2 COR., ch. 5.

4873. LABOURER, Jesus a. *Carpenter.* [2] He began to teach in the synagogue : and many hearing *him* were astonished, saying, From whence hath this *man* these things ? and what wisdom *is* this which is given unto him, that even such mighty works are wrought by his hands ? [3] Is not this the carpenter ?—MARK, ch. 6.

4874. LABOURERS, Need of. *Harvest.* [36] When he saw the multitudes, he was moved with compassion..because they fainted, and were scattered abroad, as sheep having no shepherd. [37] Then saith he unto his disciples, The harvest truly *is* plenteous, but the labourers *are* few ; [38] Pray ye therefore the Lord of the harvest, that he will send forth labourers into his harvest.—MAT., ch. 9.

4875. —— **Reward of.** *"Wages."* [35] Look on the fields ; for they are white already to harvest. [36] And he that reapeth receiveth wages, and gathereth fruit unto life eternal : that both he that soweth and he that reapeth may rejoice together.—JOHN, ch. 4.

See other illustrations under :

INDUSTRY.

Active. Rebekah..let down her pitcher..hasted 4442
Benevolence. Showing the coats..Dorcas had 4443
Commended. Go to the ant, thou sluggard 4444
Domestic. [Model woman—Prov., ch. 31.] 4445
Independent. Paul had gathered a bundle of sticks 4446
Jesus. Mighty works are wrought..this the 4447
Promotion. Solomon seeing..he was industrious 4448
Required. If any would not work, neither should 4449

MECHANIC.

Apostle. [Paul and Aquila] were tentmakers 5268
Christ. Is not this the carpenter ?..offended 5269
Expert. Hiram..worker in brass..came to S. 5270
Independence. Not be chargeable..wrought 5272
Lost. No smith..lest Hebrews make swords 5277
Original. Tubal Cain an instructor of..artificer 5271
Opposition. Alexander the coppersmith did..harm 5273
" Called workmen of like occupation 5274
Renown. Not any..hew timber..like Sidonians 5276
Foolish. Earneth wages to put in a bag with holes 2616
See SERVANT, WORK.

4876. LACK, A single. *Young Ruler.* [20] Master, all these have I observed from my youth. [21] Then Jesus beholding him loved him, and said unto him, One thing thou lackest : go thy way, sell whatsoever thou hast, and give to the poor..and come, take up the cross, and follow me.—MARK, ch. 10.

See other illustrations under :

BLEMISH.

Disqualifies. Let him not approach the altar 813
Without. Absalom..from the sole..without b. 814

LOSS.

Absence. Thomas..was not with them when Jesus 5063
Authority. I called my servant, he gave me no a. 5064
Accidental. Axe head fell into the water..alas 5065
Delay. While I am coming, another steppeth in 5066
Discovery. Found him not..found him in the t. 5067
Irreparable. The ark of God was taken by the P. 5068
Irrecoverable. If the salt hath lost its savour 5069
Ignorance. Heareth the word..understandeth..not 5070
of Losses. Gain the whole world, and lose his own 5071
Love. I have somewhat against thee..repent 5072
Profit and. What is a man advantaged if..lose h. 5073
Zeal. Thou shouldest have smitten five or six times 5074

LOSSES.

Accountability. I bear the loss, whether stolen or 5075
Restored. L. blessed the latter end of Job more 5076

OMISSION.

Cursed. Curse ye, Meroz..came not up to the help 5875
Deception. If any man be a hearer..and not a doer 5876
Great. When saw we thee a hungered..not minister 5877
Inexcusable. These shall go..everlasting punish't 5878
Nobles. Put not their necks to the work of the L. 5879
Sin. Ye pay tithe of mint..omitted weightier 5880

4877. LAMENESS from Accident. *Mephibosheth.* ⁴ He was five years old when the tidings came of Saul and Jonathan out of Jezreel, and his nurse took him up, and fled : and..as she made haste to flee..he fell, and became lame.—2 SAM., ch. 4.

4878. —— Disqualified by. *Priesthood.* ¹⁷ Whosoever *he be* of thy seed in their generations that hath *any* blemish, let him not approach to offer the bread of his God. ¹⁸..a blind man, or a lame, or he that hath a flat nose, or any thing superfluous.—LEV., ch. 21.

4879. —— healed. *Cripple.* ⁸ There sat a certain man at Lystra, impotent in his feet, being a cripple from his mother's womb, who never had walked : ⁹ The same heard Paul speak : who steadfastly beholding him, and perceiving that he had faith to be healed, ¹⁰ Said with a loud voice, Stand upright on thy feet. And he leaped and walked.—ACTS, ch. 14.

4880. —— —— At Beautiful Gate. ⁶ Peter said, Silver and gold have I none ; but such as I have give I thee : In the name of Jesus Christ of Nazareth rise up and walk. ⁷ And he took him by the right hand, and lifted *him* up : and immediately his feet and ankle bones received strength. ⁸ And he leaping up stood, and walked, and entered with them into the temple, walking, and leaping, and praising God.—ACTS, ch. 3.

4881. —— Royal. *Mephibosheth.* ³ The king said, *Is* there not yet any of the house of Saul, that I may shew the kindness of God unto him ? And Ziba said..Jonathan hath yet a son, *which is* lame on *his* feet.—2 SAM., ch. 9.

4882. —— Want with. *Cripple.* [See No. 4880.] ² A certain man lame from his mother's womb was carried, whom they laid daily at the gate of the temple which is called Beautiful, to ask alms of them that entered into the temple.—ACTS, ch. 3.

Also see:

Royal. Asa was diseased in his feet.—1 Kings 15 : 23.

4883. LAMENTATION in Adversity. *Job.* ³ Let the day perish wherein I was born, and the night *in which* it was said, There is a man child conceived. ⁴ Let that day be darkness ; let not God regard it from above, neither let the light shine upon it.—JOB, ch. 3.

4884. —— A Father's. *David's.* ³³ The king was much moved, and went up to the chamber over the gate, and wept : and as he went, thus he said, O my son Absalom ! my son, my son Absalom ! would God I had died for thee, O Absalom, my son, my son !—2 SAM., ch. 18.

4885. —— General. *Israelites.* ² Nahash the Ammonite answered them, On this *condition* will I make *a* covenant with you, that I may thrust out all your right eyes, and lay it *for* a reproach upon all Israel. ⁴..and all the people lifted up their voices, and wept.—1 SAM., ch. 11.

4886. —— Ill-timed. *Near Ai.* ⁷ Would to God we had been content, and dwelt on the other side Jordan ! ⁸ O Lord, what shall I say, when Israel turneth their backs before their enemies !—JOSH., ch. 7.

4887. —— of Jesus. *Jerusalem.* ³⁷ O Jerusalem, Jerusalem, *thou* that killest the prophets, and stonest them which are sent unto thee, how

often would I have gathered thy children together, even as a hen gathereth her chickens under *her* wings, and ye would not ! ³⁸ Behold, your house is left unto you desolate.—MAT., ch. 23.

4888. —— for Jesus. *Crucifixion.* ²⁷ There followed him a great company of people, and of women, which also bewailed and lamented him. ²⁸ But Jesus..said, Daughters of Jerusalem, weep not for me, but weep for yourselves, and for your children.—LUKE, ch. 23.

4889. —— National. *In Persia.* ³ And in every province, whithersoever the king's..decree came, *there was* great mourning among the Jews, and fasting, and weeping, and wailing ; and many lay in sackcloth and ashes.—ESTHER, ch. 4.

4890. —— Tearful. *Jeremiah.* ¹ Oh that my head were waters, and mine eyes a fountain of tears, that I might weep day and night for the slain of the daughter of my people !—JEREMIAH, ch. 9.

See **MOURNING** and references.

4891. LAND, Conveyance of. *Mode.* ⁹ And I bought the field of Hanameel..and weighed him..seventeen shekels of silver. ¹⁰ And I subscribed the evidence, and sealed *it*, and took witnesses.. ¹¹ So I took the evidence of the purchase, *both* that which was sealed *according to* the law and custom, and that which was open.—JER., ch. 32.

4892. —— cursed by Sin. *Israelites.* ²¹ The incense that ye burned in the cities of Judah, and in the streets of Jerusalem, ye and your fathers.. ²²..the Lord could no longer bear, because of the evil of your doings, *and* because of the abominations which ye have committed : therefore is your land a desolation, and an astonishment, and a curse, without an inhabitant, as at this day.—JER., ch. 44.

4893. —— The first Purchase of. *Cemetery.* ¹⁶ Abraham weighed to Ephron the silver, which he had named in the audience of the sons of Heth, four hundred shekels of silver, current *money* with the merchant. ¹⁷ And the field of Ephron, which *was* in Machpelah..and the cave which *was* therein, and all the trees that *were* in the field, that *were* in all the borders round about, were made sure ¹ᵇ Unto Abraham.—GEN., ch. 23.

4894. —— prohibited. *Priests.* ²⁰ The Lord spake unto Aaron, Thou shalt have no inheritance in their land, neither shalt thou have any part among them : I *am* thy part and thine inheritance.—NUM., ch. 18.

4895. —— —— Rechabites. ⁸ Thus have we obeyed the voice of..our father in all that he hath charged us, to drink no wine.. ⁹ Nor to build houses for us to dwell in ; neither have we vineyard, nor field, nor seed : ¹⁰ But we have dwelt in tents.—JER., ch. 35.

Also see:

Estate. Speak to my brother..divide..inheritance. 2724
Examination. We passed through to search it   413

4896. LANGUAGE corrupted. *Hebrew.* ²³ Saw I Jews *that* had married wives of Ashdod, of Ammon, *and* of Moab : ²⁴ And their children spake half in the speech of Ashdod, and could not speak in the Jews' language, but according to the language of each people.—NEH., ch. 13.

4897. —— given. *Pentecost.* ⁶ The multitude .. were confounded, because that every man heard them speak in his own language. [7] And they .. marvelled, saying .. Behold, are not all these which speak Galileans? [8] And how hear we every man in our own tongue, wherein we were born?—ACTS, ch. 2.

4898. LANGUAGES, Origin of. *Babel.* [6] Behold, the people *is* one, and they have all one language ; and this they begin to do ; and now nothing will be restrained from them, which they have imagined to do. [7] Go to, let us go down, and there confound their language, that they may not understand one another's speech.—GEN., ch. 11.

See other illustrations under:

CONVERSATION.

Impure. Lot vexed with the filthy conversation   1721
Religious. Talk of them when thou sittest   1722

See DISCOURSE and references.

4899. LATE, Too Late. *Foolish Virgins.* [8] The foolish said unto the wise, Give us of your oil ; for our lamps are gone out. [9] But the wise answered .. *Not so ;* lest there be not enough for us and you.. [10] And while they went to buy, the bridegroom came ; and they that were ready went in with him to the marriage : and the door was shut.—MAT., ch. 25.

See DELAY and references.

4900. LAW, Appeal to. *Paul.* [24] The chief captain .. brought into the castle, and bade that he should be examined by scourging ; that he might know wherefore they cried so against him. [25] And as they bound him with thongs, Paul said unto the centurion that stood by, Is it lawful for you to scourge a man that is a Roman, and uncondemned?—ACTS, ch. 22.

4901. —— Equality before the. *Passover.* [19] Seven days shall there be no leaven found in your houses : for whosoever eateth that which is leavened .. shall be cut off from the congregation of Israel, whether he be a stranger, or born in the land.—Ex., ch. 12.

4902. —— —— *Queen Esther.* [13] Mordecai .. to .. Esther, Think not with thyself that thou shalt escape in the king's house, more than all the Jews. [14] For if thou altogether holdest thy peace at this time, *then* shall there enlargement and deliverance arise to the Jews from another place ; but thou and thy father's house shall be destroyed.—ESTHER, ch. 4.

4903. —— Evasion of. *A Lawyer.* [See No. 4909.] [29] But he, willing to justify himself, said unto Jesus, And who is my neighbour?—LUKE, ch. 10.

4904. —— Indifference to. *Common Fire.* [1] Nadab and Abihu .. took either of them his censer .. and offered strange fire before the Lord .. [2] And there went out fire from the Lord, and devoured them.—LEV., ch. 10.

4905. —— of Love. *First Commandment.* [28] Which is the first commandment of all? [29] And Jesus answered him .. [30] .. thou shalt love the Lord thy God with all thy heart, and with all thy soul, and with all thy mind, and with all thy strength.—MARK, ch. 12.

4906. —— misapplied. *Pilate said,* [6] I find no fault in him. [7] The Jews answered him, We have a law, and by our law he ought to die, because he made himself the Son of God.—JOHN, ch. 19.

4907. —— Necessity knows no. *Esther.* [16] Neither eat nor drink three days, night or day : I also and my maidens will fast likewise ; and so will I go in unto the king, which *is* not according to the law : and if I perish, I perish. —ESTHER, ch. 4.

4908. —— Protection of. *Paul.* [9] Festus, willing to do the Jews a pleasure, answered Paul, and said, Wilt thou go up to Jerusalem, and there be judged of these things before me? [10] Then said Paul, I stand at Cesar's judgment-seat, where I ought to be judged.—ACTS, ch. 25.

4909. —— Summary of. *A Lawyer said,* [27] Thou shalt love the Lord thy God with all thy heart, and with all thy soul, and with all thy strength, and with all thy mind ; and thy neighbour as thyself. [28] And he said unto him, Thou hast answered right : this do, and thou shalt live.—LUKE, ch. 10.

4910. —— superseded, The. *By Faith.* [24] The law was our schoolmaster *to bring us* unto Christ, that we might be justified by faith. [25] But after that faith is come, we are no longer under a schoolmaster.—GAL., ch. 3.

4911. —— Supremacy of. *Over Royalty.* [See No. 4918.] [14] Then the king .. was sore displeased with himself, and set *his* heart on Daniel to deliver him : and he laboured till the going down of the sun to deliver him.—DAN., ch. 6.

4912. —— Sumptuary. *In Eden.* [2] The woman said unto the serpent, We may eat of the fruit of the trees of the garden : [3] But of the fruit of the tree which *is* in the midst of the garden, God hath said, Ye shall not eat of it, neither shall ye touch it, lest ye die.—GEN., ch. 3.

4913. —— —— "Blood." [13] And whatsoever man .. catcheth any beast or fowl that may be eaten ; he shall even pour out the blood thereof, and cover it with dust. [14] .. for the life of all flesh *is* the blood thereof : whosoever eateth it shall be cut off.—LEV., ch. 17.

4914. —— —— "Fat." [23] Speak unto the children of Israel, saying, Ye shall eat no manner of fat, of ox, or of sheep, or of goat.—LEV., ch. 7.

4915. —— —— "Unclean." [2] These *are* the beasts which ye shall eat.. [3] Whatsoever parteth the hoof, and is clovenfooted, *and* cheweth the cud.—LEV., ch. 11. [See entire chapter.]

4916. —— for Transgressors. *Paul.* [9] The law is not made for a righteous man, but for the lawless and disobedient, for the ungodly and for sinners, for unholy and profane, for murderers of fathers and murderers of mothers, for manslayers, [10] For whoremongers, for them that defile themselves with mankind, for menstealers, for liars, for perjured persons.—1 TIM., ch. 1.

4917. —— Unobserved, The greater. *Pharisees.* [23] Woe unto you, scribes and Pharisees, hypocrites! for ye pay tithe of mint and anise and cummin, and have omitted the weightier *matters* of the law, judgment, mercy, and faith. —MAT., ch. 23.

4918. —— An unchangeable. *Persian.* [15] The law of the Medes and Persians *is*, That no decree nor statute which the king establisheth may be changed. [16] Then the king commanded,

and they brought Daniel, and cast *him* into the
den of lions.—DAN., ch. 6.

See other Illustrations under :
COMMANDMENTS.
Kept. All these..I kept from my youth up   1397
Test. Hereby we do know that we know him   1398
Ten. [Decalogue]   1399
Use. Is a lamp, and the law is light   1400
LEGALITY.
Overstrained. We strain at a gnat and swallow a   4936
Quibbles. Swear by the temple it is nothing..gold 4937
Litigation. A fault among you..ye go to law   5050
POLITICS.
Condemned. We found this fellow..forbidding   6236
Demagogue. Oh that I were made a judge   6237
Influence. If thou let this man go..not Cesar's   6238
in Religion. Is it lawful to give tribute to Cesar ? 6239
Ring. Sought to find occasion against D.   6240

Decree. To destroy all Jews..both young and old   2090
Respected. Speaketh evil of the law judgeth the   1081
Sin. Law in my members warring..law of my mind   1541
Unrepealable. Drink no wine..statute forever   26
See GOVERNMENT and references.

4919. LEADER, Always a. *Jesus.* [32] Going up
to Jerusalem ; and Jesus went before them :
and they were amazed ; and as they followed,
they were afraid.   And he took again the twelve,
and began to tell them what things should
happen unto him.—MARK, ch. 10.

4920. —— of the Blind. *The Syrians.* [18] He
smote them with blindness.. [19] And Elisha said
unto them, This *is* not the way, neither *is* this
the city : follow me, and I will bring you to the
man whom ye seek.   But he led them to Samaria.
—2 KINGS, ch. 6.

4921. —— A bold. *Ehud.* [16] Ehud made
him a dagger which had two edges, of a cubit
length ; and he did gird it under his raiment
upon his right thigh. [17] And he brought the
present unto Eglon king of Moab.—JUDGES,
ch. 3. [He killed the king.]

4922. —— An unwise. *King Saul* [com-
manded his army to fast.] [26] When the people
were come into the wood, behold, the honey
dropped ; but no man put his hand to his
mouth : for the people feared the oath. [27] But
Jonathan heard not when his father charged the
people with the oath.—1 SAM., ch. 14. [Also
people ate blood from hunger.]

4923. —— Zion's. *Moses' Request.* [16] Let the
Lord..set a man over the congregation, [17] Which
may go out before them, and which may go in
before them, and which may lead them out, and
which may bring them in ; that the congregation of the Lord be not as sheep which have no
shepherd.—NUM., ch. 27.

4924. LEADERSHIP, Divine. *Cloud.* [21] The
Lord went before them by day in a pillar of a
cloud, to lead them the way ; and by night in a
pillar of fire, to give them light ; to go by day
and night.—Ex., ch. 13.

4925. —— Failure in. *Moses.* [32] They angered *him* also at the waters of strife, so that it
went ill with Moses for their sakes : [33] Because
they provoked his spirit, so that he spake unadvisedly with his lips.—Ps. 106.

4926. —— Loved. *Diotrephes.* [9] Diotrephes,
who loveth to have the preeminence among

them, receiveth us not. [10] ..neither doth he
himself receive the brethren, and forbiddeth
them that would, and casteth *them* out of the
church.—JOHN, ch. 3.

4927. —— Trials of. *Moses.* [3] The people
chode with Moses..saying, Would God that we
had died when our brethren died before the
Lord ! [4] And why have ye brought up the congregation..into this wilderness, that we and
our cattle should die there ?—NUM., ch. 20.

4928. —— rejected. *Near Canaan.* [4] Let us
make a captain, and let us return into Egypt.
[5] Then Moses and Aaron fell on their faces before all the assembly..of Israel.—NUM., ch. 14.

See other illustrations under :
DISCIPLES.
Steadfast. If ye continue in my word..my disciples 2327
Timid. Nicodemus first came to Jesus by night   2328
Willing. Come and see.   They came and abode   2329
FORWARDNESS.
Brave. Lord, bid me come unto thee on the water   3394
Checked. Other disciple did outrun Peter   3395
Failure. When he saw the wind boisterous..afraid 3396
Hazardous. [Peter] drew his sword..smote off his 3397
GUIDE.
Blind. Woe unto you, ye blind guides   3760
Divine. By day in a pillar of cloud..night..fire 3757
Human. Leave us not..be to us instead of eyes   3758
Necessary. How can I, except some..guide me   3759
GUIDANCE.
Divine. The kine took the straight way..B.   3761
Explained. Lest peradventure..see war and they   3762
Gentle. I will guide thee with mine eye   3763
Promised. Acknowledge him..direct thy paths   3764
Waiting. If the cloud were not taken up   3765
MIGHTY MEN.
Adino. Mighty men whom David had..chief   5332
Abishai. Chief among the three..against 300..slew 5336
Benaiah. Slew the lion-like men of Moab   5337
Eliezer. Smote the Philistines..hand clave to his 5333
Shammah. Stood in the midst..slew the Philistines 5334
Three. Brake through the hosts of the Philistines 5335

Rejected. Children of Belial..How shall this man 1623
Spirit. Jesus was led by the S..wilderness   29
See FOLLOWING.

4929. LEAGUE, A fraternal. *Covenant.*
[16] Jonathan made *a covenant* with the house of
David.. [17] And Jonathan caused David to swear
again, because he loved him : for he loved him
as he loved his own soul.—1 SAM., ch. 20.

4930. —— A fraudulent. *Gibeonites.*
[13] These bottles of wine, which we filled, *were*
new ; and, behold, they be rent : and these our
garments and our shoes are become old by
reason of the very long journey.. [15] And Joshua
made peace with them, and made a league with
them, to let them live.. [16] ..at the end of three
days..they heard that they *were* their neighbours.—JOSH., ch. 9.

See other illustrations under :
ALLIANCE.
Contaminating. Ahaz went to Damascus..fashion   290
Dangerous. Make [David] return..in the battle   291
Failure. Egyptians are men, and not God   293
Forbidden. Woe..go down to Egypt for help   292
Treacherous. Gibeonites..Joshua..league with the 294
COVENANT.
Broken. Moses saw the calf..cast the tables   1807
Blood. Moses took the blood and sprinkled   1808

Evil. What will ye give me?..30 pieces of silver 1809
Friendship. Jonathan caused David to sware 1810
People's. All the people stood to the covenant 1811
Perpetuated. Walk before me..thy seed after thee 1812
Ratified. Burning lamp passed between the pieces 1813
Reformation. Made a covenant..be the Lord's 1814
Renewed. Clave to their brethren..curse 1815
Self-denial. Get thee out of thy country..be 1816
Sign. Set my bow in the clouds..token 1817
See UNION.

4931. LEARNING, Profound. *Moses.* [22] Moses was learned in all the wisdom of the Egyptians, and was mighty in words and in deeds.—ACTS, ch. 7.

4932. —— Superior. *Jesus.* [14] About the midst of the feast Jesus went up into the temple, and taught. [15] And the Jews marvelled, saying, How knoweth this man letters, having never learned?—JOHN, ch. 7.

4933. —— Worship from. *Magi.* [1] Now when Jesus was born in Bethlehem..there came wise men from the east to Jerusalem, [2] Saying, Where is he that is born King of the Jews? for we have seen his star in the east, and are come to worship him.—MAT., ch. 2.

See other illustrations under:
Useful. I have learned..to be content 8287
See EDUCATION, INTELLIGENCE, and references.

4934. LEFT-HANDED Skill. *Benjamites.* [15] The children of Benjamin were numbered.. twenty and six thousand men that drew sword, besides the inhabitants of Gibeah, which were numbered seven hundred chosen men. [16]..every one could sling stones at a hair *breadth*, and not miss.—JUDGES, ch. 20.

4935. LEGACY, The best. *Spirit of Elijah.* [14] He took the mantle of Elijah that fell from him, and smote the waters, and said, Where is the Lord God of Elijah? And when he also had smitten the waters, they parted hither and thither: and Elisha went over. [15] And when the sons of the prophets..saw him, they said, The spirit of Elijah doth rest on Elisha.—2 KINGS, ch. 2.

See other illustrations under:
INHERITANCE.
Tendency. The wealth of the sinner is laid up for 4490
Uncertainty. I should leave it unto..that followeth 4491

4936. LEGALITY overstrained. *Pharisees.* [23] Woe unto you, scribes and Pharisees, hypocrites! for ye pay tithe of mint and anise and cummin, and have omitted the weightier *matters* of the law, judgment, mercy, and faith.. [24] *Ye* blind guides, which strain at a gnat, and swallow a camel.—MAT., ch. 23.

4937. —— Quibbles of. *Pharisees.* [16] Woe unto you, *ye* blind guides, which say, Whosoever shall swear by the temple, it is nothing; but whosoever shall swear by the gold of the temple, he is a debtor!—MAT., ch. 23.

See other illustrations under:
LAW.
Appeal. Is it lawful..to scourge..a Roman? 4900
Equality. Cut off..whether..a stranger or born 4901
"   Think not that thou shalt escape..more 4902
Evasion. To justify himself..who is my neighbour 4903
Indifference. Nadab and Abihu..offered strange 4904
of Love. First commandment..love the Lord 4905
Misapplied. By our law he ought to die..S. of G. 4906

Necessity. I will go..if I perish, I perish 4907
Protection. Said Paul, I stand at Cesar's 4908
Summary. Thou shalt love the L..do and live 4909
Superseded. Law..schoolmaster to bring us to C. 4910
Supremacy. Darius..set his heart on Daniel to 4911
Sumptuary. Fruit of the tree..ye shall not eat of it 4912
"   Blood..whosoever eateth of it..cut off 4913
"   Eat no manner of fat, of ox, or sheep 4914
"   Ye shall eat..parteth the hoof..cud 4915
Transgressors. Not made for a righteous man 4916
Unobserved. Pay tithe of mint..omitted the 4917
Unchangeable. Law of the Medes and Persians 4918

4938. LEISURE, Without. *Jesus said,* [31] Come ye yourselves apart into a desert place, and rest a while: for there were many coming and going, and they had no leisure so much as to eat.—MARK, ch. 6.

4939. —— —— *Jesus.* [20] The multitude cometh together again, so that they could not so much as eat bread. [21] And when his friends heard *of it*, they went out to lay hold on him: for they said, He is beside himself.—MARK, ch. 3.

See other illustrations under:
DELAY.
Business. Not eat, until I have done mine errand 2123
Decency. Shaved..one half their beards..Tarry 2124
Dangerous. Suffer me first to go and bury my f. 2125
Evil. Because..thou camest not within the days 2126
Failure. First after stepped in was made whole 2127
Hinderance. Casting away his garment..came to J. 2128
Impatience. As for this Moses..we wot not 2129
Long. Man..an infirmity 38 years 2130
Lord's. Neither hast thou delivered thy people 2131
Preparation. Wait for the promise of the F. 2132
Weariness. How long wilt thou forget me? 2133

EASE.
Care for. Trouble me not..the door is now shut 2586
Indifference. If ye offer the lame and sick 2587
Promised. Then..Saul take thine ease, eat 2588
Religious. Woe to them that are at ease in Z. 2589

IDLENESS.
Accusation. No straw..ye are idle, ye are idle 4270
Ecstatic. Why stand ye gazing into heaven? 4271
Needless. Why stand ye here all the day idle? 4272
Perishing. If we sit still here we die also..four 4273

LOITERERS.
Driven. Fire..consumed them in the uttermost 5052
Hastened. While he lingered, the men laid hold 5053

PROCRASTINATION.
Charity. Say not..to morrow I will give when thou 6620
Fatal. Go thy way this time..convenient season 6621
Folly. Foolish said, Give us of your oil..gone out 6622
Loss. We will hear thee again..Paul departed 6623
No. Suffer me first to go and bury my father 6624

WAITING.
Calamity. Jonah sat..see what would..city 9262
Eager. My soul waiteth..watch for the morning 9263
in Faith. Tell the stars..so shall thy seed be 9264
on God. Renew their strength..as eagles 9265
Patient. After one year, G. spake to Noah, Go forth 9267
for Power. Not depart from Jerusalem, but wait 9268
Rewarded. Simeon..waiting for the consolation 9269
Vigilant. Let your loins be girt..lights burning 9270
Weariness. Let me see the king's face..kill me 9271
Watching. When the fowls came..Abram drove 9272
for Work. When forty years were expired..an 9273
Inexplicable. Neither hast thou delivered thy 2336

Religion. It is too much for thee to go up to J. 9876

4940. LENDING a Duty. *Law.* [7] If there be among you a poor man of one of thy brethren ..thou shalt not harden thine heart, nor shut thine hand from thy poor brother : [8] But thou shalt open thine hand wide unto him, and shalt surely lend him sufficient for his need.—DEUT., ch. 15.

4941. —— to the Lord. *Mother of Samuel.* [27] For this child I prayed ; and the Lord hath given me my petition which I asked of him : [28] Therefore ..as long as he liveth he shall be lent to the Lord.—1 SAM., ch. 1.

4942. —— —— Gifts. [17] He that hath pity upon the poor lendeth unto the Lord ; and that which he hath given will he pay him again.—PROV., ch. 19.

See DEBTOR *and references.*

4943. LETTER, A faithful. *Paul.* [8] Though I made you sorry with a letter, I do not repent, though I did repent : for I perceive that the same epistle hath made you sorry, though *it were* but for a season. [9] Now I rejoice, not that ye were made sorry, but that ye sorrowed to repentance.—2 COR., ch. 7.

See other illustrations under :

MESSAGE.

Rejected. Hezekiah ..wrote letters ..come to the	5379
Received. Divers ..humbled themselves and came	5380
Shameful. David wrote a letter to Joab ..by Uriah	5382
Terrible. Letters were sent ..destroy all Jews	5386

4944. LEVY, The Lord's. *Colt.* [5] What do ye, loosing the colt? [6] And they said unto them even as Jesus had commanded : and they let them go. [7] And they brought the colt to Jesus, and cast their garments on him ; and he sat upon him.—MARK, ch. 11.

See other illustrations under :

CONSCRIPTION.

Building. Solomon raised a levy ..sent ..Lebanon	1551
Peculiar. So shall it be done unto his oxen ..Saul	1552
Sweeping. Moabites.. gathered all ..able to put	1553

TAXATION.

Burdensome. King of Assyria appointed 300 talents	8595
Collector. Levi sitting at the receipt of custom	8596
Exempt. Ministers of this house of God	8597
"　　The man who killeth [Goliath] ..house	8598
Endangered. If ..be builded ..endamage the rev.	8599
Eminence. He shall stand up ..a raiser of taxes	8600
Foreign. According to the commandment of P.	8601
Lawful. Render unto Caesar the things which are	8602
Oppressive. We have borrowed money for the	8603
Secession. Thy father made our yoke grievous	8604
Universal. All the world ..Joseph also went ..to be	8605
Assessment. Each man fifty shekels of silver	535
Draft. Of every tribe a thousand shall ye send	9309

4945. LIAR, Religious. " *Prophet.*" [18] I am a prophet also as thou *art* ; and an angel spake unto me by the word of the Lord, saying, Bring him back with thee into thine house, that he may eat bread and drink water. *But* he lied unto him. [19] So he went back with him.—1 KINGS, ch. 13.

4946. —— Satan a. *Jesus said,* [44] When he speaketh a lie, he speaketh of his own : for he is a liar, and the father of it.—JOHN, ch. 8.

4947. —— Self-injurious. *Proverb.* [13] The wicked is snared by the transgression of *his* lips.—PROV., ch. 12.

4948. LIARS, Religious. *Disobedient.* [4] He that saith, I know him, and keepeth not his commandments, is a liar, and the truth is not in him.—1 JOHN, ch. 2.

See other illustrations under :

SLANDER.

Antidote. They may by your good works ..glorify	8101
Base. This fellow doth cast out devils by Beelzebub	8102
Disgraceful. We found this man a pestilent fellow	8103
Folly. He that uttereth a slander is a fool	8104
Hurtful. Then will they not pay tribute	8105
Impious. He saved others ; himself he cannot save	8106
Joyful. Blessed ..men revile you ..rejoice	8107
Loyalty. Ziba said ..he abideth at Jerusalem	8108
Malicious. Diotrephes ..prating against us	8109
Opposed. It is reported ..be their king	8110
Refuted. If Satan cast out Satan ..divided	8111
Rebels. The people is greater than we	8112
Sinners. Thou art an austere man	8113
Satan's. Touch all that he hath ..will curse	8114
Secret. A whisperer separateth friends	8115
Unbelief. Would to G. we had died ..by fleshpots	8116
Religious. I know him, and keep not his c ..is a liar	1398

See DECEPTION *and references.*

See HYPOCRISY.

4949. LIBERALITY, Benevolent. *Macedonians.* [3] To *their* power ..yea, and beyond *their* power *they* were willing of themselves ; [4] Praying us with much entreaty that we would receive the gift, and *take upon us* the fellowship of the ministering to the saints.—2 COR., ch. 8.

4950. —— commanded. *Poor Brother.* [10] Thou shalt surely give him, and thine heart shall not be grieved when thou givest unto him : because that for this thing the Lord thy God shall bless thee in all thy works, and in all that thou puttest thine hand unto. [11] For the poor shall never cease out of the land.—DEUT., ch. 15.

4951. —— Christian. *Eating.* [2] One believeth that he may eat all things : another, who is weak, eateth herbs. [3] Let not him that eateth despise him that eateth not ; and let not him which eateth not judge him that eateth.—ROM., ch. 14.

4952. —— Denominational. "*Casting out Devils.*" [38] John answered ..Master, we saw one casting out devils in thy name, and he followeth not us ; and we forbade him, because he followeth not us. [39] But Jesus said, Forbid him not. —MARK, ch. 9.

4953. —— of Opinion. *Sabbath.* [23] He went through the corn fields on the sabbath day ; and his disciples began, as they went, to pluck the ears of corn. [24] And the Pharisees said.. [27] And he said unto them, The sabbath was made for man, and not man for the sabbath.—MARK, ch. 2.

4954. —— Pagan. *Centurion.* [3] That he would come and heal his servant. [4] And when they came to Jesus, they besought him instantly, saying, That he was worthy for whom he should do this : [5] For he loveth our nation, and he hath built us a synagogue. [6] Then Jesus went with them.—LUKE, ch. 7.

4955. —— Rule of. *Remainder.* [43] Verily I say unto you, That this poor widow hath cast more in, than all they which have cast into the treasury : [44] For all *they* did cast in of their abundance ; but she of her want did cast in all that she had, *even* all her living.—MARK, ch. 12.

4956. —— **Reward of.** *"Made Fat."* [25] The liberal soul shall be made fat : and he that watereth shall be watered also himself.—Prov., ch. 11.

4957. —— **Return from.** *"Given You."* [38] Give, and it shall be given unto you ; good measure, pressed down, and shaken together, and running over. shall men give into your bosom. For with the same measure that ye mete withal it shall be measured to you again. —Luke, ch. 6.

4958. —— **Royal.** *David.* [The ark was returned.] [3] He dealt to every one of Israel, both man and woman, to every one a loaf of bread, and a good piece of flesh, and a flagon *of wine.* —1 Chron., ch. 16.

4959. —— **of Sentiment.** *Moses.* [27] There ran a young man, and told Moses, and said, Eldad and Medad do prophesy in the camp. [28] And Joshua..said, My lord Moses, forbid them. [29] And Moses said unto him, Enviest thou for my sake ? would God that all the Lord's people were prophets, *and* that the Lord would put his Spirit upon them.—Num., ch. 11.

4960. —— **Ungrudging.** *Law.* [See No. 4950.]

See other illustrations under :

BENEFACTORS.

Censured. Ye have made our savour to be abhorred 685
"   We did tell thee in Egypt..Let us alone 686
Honoured. He received his sight, and followed 687
Remembered. He was worthy..built us a 688
Slandered. All murmured..Ye have killed the 689

CONTRIBUTIONS.

Abundant. [Temple] Offered willingly..gold 5000 1657
Expenses. Charge ourselves yearly..third part of 1658
for Jesus. Women..healed..ministered..their 1659
for Levites. Firstfruits of corn, wine, oil, and 1660
Repairs. Chest..set beside the altar..right side 1661
Rebuilding. Chief of the fathers gave after their 1662
Various. Men and women..blue, purple, scarlet 1663

GENEROSITY.

Royal. [David's] 3000 talents of gold..70,000 silver 3514
Tabernacle Builders. People..much more than 3511

MAGNANIMITY.

Enemies. Shall there any man..be put to death 5164
Forgiveness. David's heart smote him..Saul's 5165
Fraternal. [Judah] became surety for the lad 5166
Gracious. Is not the whole land before thee 5167

In Poverty. Deep poverty abounded unto..liberality 727
See BENEVOLENCE and references.

4961. LIBERTY, Common. *Doing Good.* [38] John answered him..Master, we saw one casting out devils in thy name, and he followeth not us ; and we forbade him, because he followeth not us. [39] But Jesus said, Forbid him not. —Mark, ch. 9.

4962. —— **of Choice.** *Prodigal.* [12] The younger of them said to *his* father, Father, give me the portion of goods that falleth *to me.* And he divided unto them *his* living.—Luke, ch. 15.

4963. —— **not License.** *Eating.* [8] Meat commendeth us not to God : for neither, if we eat, are we the better ; neither, if we eat not, are we the worse. [9] But take heed lest by any means this liberty of yours become a stumbling-block to them that are weak.—1 Cor., ch. 8.

See other illustrations under :

INDEPENDENCE.

Exhibited. These hands have ministered unto my 4400
Financial. Not take from a thread..shoelatchet 4401
Opinion. Me and my house, we will serve the L. 4402
Youthful. Father, give me the portion of goods 4403

SELF-WILL.

Destructive. O Jerusalem, thou..ye would not 7731
Loss by. They presumed to go..smote them 7732
the Sacrifice. To obey is better than sacrifice 7734
Work. Simeon and Levi..self-will digged down 7735

Birthright. Abraham had two sons..bondmaid 3415
Liberation. Hebrew servant in the seventh year 5918
Reward. Let him go free for his tooth's sake—Ex. 5 : 27
"   Make his father's house free in I. 8598
Spiritual. If the S. make you free..free—John 8 : 36.
See DELIVERANCE.

4964. LICE, Plague of. *Plague.* [17] Aaron stretched out his hand with his rod, and smote the dust of the earth, and it became lice in man, and in beast ; throughout all the land of Egypt. —Ex., ch. 8.

4965. LIFE, Book of. *"Lamb's."* [27] There shall in no wise enter into it any thing that defileth, neither *whatsoever* worketh abomination, or *maketh* a lie : but they which are written in the Lamb's book of life.—Rev., ch. 21.

4966. —— **Consummation of.** *Simeon.* [28] Took ..him up in his arms, and blessed God, and said, [29] Lord, now lettest thou thy servant depart in peace, according to thy word : [30] For mine eyes have seen thy salvation.—Luke, ch. 2.

4967. —— **above Circumstances.** *Wealth.* [15] Beware of covetousness : for a man's life consisteth not in the abundance of the things which he possesseth. [16] And he spake a parable..saying, The ground of a certain rich man brought forth plentifully.—Luke, ch. 12.

4968. —— **Condition of.** *Esther said,* [11] All the king's servants..do know, that whosoever, whether man or woman, shall come unto the king into the inner court, who is not called, *there is* one law of his to put *him* to death, except such to whom the king shall hold out the golden sceptre.—Esther, ch. 4.

4969. —— **Cessation of.** *"Tree cut down."* [7] There is hope of a tree, if it be cut down, that it will sprout again, and that the tender branch thereof will not cease. [8] Though the root thereof wax old in the earth, and the stock thereof die in the ground ; [9] *Yet* through the scent of water it will bud, and bring forth boughs like a plant. [10] But man dieth, and wasteth away : yea, man giveth up the ghost, and where *is* he?— Job, ch. 14.

4970. —— **less than Character.** *Nehemiah's.* [10] I came unto the house of Shemaiah..who *was* shut up ; and he said, Let us meet..in the temple, and let us shut the doors .. for they will come to slay thee ; yea, in the night will they come to slay thee. [11] And I said, Should such a man as I flee ? and who *is there,* that, *being* as I *am,* would go into the temple to save his life ? I will not go in.—Neh., ch. 6.

4971. —— **compensated.** *Lazarus.* [22] The beggar died, and was carried by the angels into Abraham's bosom : the rich man also died, and was buried ; [23] And in hell he lifted up his eyes, being in torment.—Luke, ch. 16.

4972. —— Dilemma in. *Unjust Steward.*
[3] The steward said within himself, What shall I do? for my lord taketh away from me the stewardship : I cannot dig ; to beg I am ashamed. —LUKE, ch. 16.

4973. —— worse than Death. *In Egypt.*
[18] Another king arose, which knew not Joseph. [19] The same dealt subtilely..and evil entreated our fathers, so that they cast out their young children, to the end they might not live.—ACTS, ch. 7.

4974. —— from Spiritual Death. *Prodigal.*
[23] Bring hither the fatted calf, and kill *it ;* and let us eat, and be merry : [24] For this my son was dead, and is alive again.—LUKE, ch. 15.

4975. —— Destruction of. *Flood.* [23] Every living substance was destroyed..both man, and cattle, and the creeping things, and the fowl of the heaven..and Noah only remained *alive,* and they that *were* with him in the ark.—GEN., ch. 7.

4976. —— Desire for. *Esau.* [31] Jacob said, Sell me this day thy birthright. [32] And Esau said, Behold, I *am* at the point to die : and what profit shall this birthright do to me?—GEN., ch. 25.

4977. —— evasive. *"Shadow."* [See No. 5017.]

4978. —— Requisites for Eternal. *A Lawyer,* [27] Answering said, Thou shalt love the Lord thy God with all thy heart, and with all thy soul, and with all thy strength, and with all thy mind ; and thy neighbour as thyself. [28] And he said unto him, Thou hast answered right : this do, and thou shalt live.—LUKE, ch. 10.

4979. —— Possessors of eternal. *Jesus said,* [24] He that heareth my word, and believeth on him that sent me, hath everlasting life, and shall not come into condemnation ; but is passed from death unto life.—JOHN, ch. 5.

4980. —— Loss of eternal. *Eden.* [22] Behold, the man is become as one of us, to know good and evil : and now, lest he put forth his hand, and take also of the tree of life, and eat, and live for ever : [24] So he drove out the man. —GEN., ch. 3.

4981. —— Enjoyment of. *Solomon.* [18] It is good and comely *for one* to eat and to drink, and to enjoy the good of all his labour that he taketh under the sun all the days of his life, which God giveth him : for it *is* his portion.—ECCL., ch. 5.

4982. —— evaporated. *Sea.* [11] As the waters fail from the sea, and the flood decayeth and drieth up ; [12] So man lieth down, and riseth not ; till the heavens *be* no more.—JOB, ch. 14.

4983. —— Exposure of. *"Mighty Men."* [16] The three mighty men brake through the host of the Philistines, and drew water out of the well of Beth-lehem..and brought *it* to David : nevertheless he would not drink thereof, but poured it out unto the Lord. [17] And he said, Be it far from me, O Lord, that I should do this : *is not this* the blood of the men that went in jeopardy of their lives?—2 SAM., ch. 23.

4984. —— embittered. *In Egypt.* [13] The Egyptians made the children of Israel to serve with rigour : [14] And they made their lives bitter with hard bondage, in mortar, and in brick, and in all manner of service in the field.—EX., ch. 5.

4985. —— Frailty of. *"Grass."* [5] In the morning *they are* like grass *which* groweth up. [6] In the morning it flourisheth, and groweth up ; in the evening it is cut down, and withereth.— Ps. 90.

4986. —— Foolish. *Dives.* [18] I will pull down my barns, and build greater ; and there will I bestow all my fruits and my goods. [19] And I will say to my soul, Soul, thou hast much goods laid up for many years ; take thine ease, eat, drink, *and* be merry.—LUKE, ch. 12.

4987. —— Forsaking all for. *Syrians.* [6] The Lord had made the host of the Syrians to hear ..the noise of a great host : and they said..Lo, the king of Israel hath hired against us the kings .. [7] Wherefore they..left their tents, and their horses, and their asses, even the camp as it *was,* and fled for their life.—2 KINGS, ch. 7.

4988. —— The future. *Marriage.* [23] In the resurrection, whose wife shall she be of the seven ? for they all had her. [30]..in the resurrection they neither marry, nor are given in marriage, but are as the angels of God in heaven.— MAT., ch. 22.

4989. —— given for the Truth. *John Baptist.* [18] John had said unto Herod, It is not lawful for thee to have thy brother's wife. [19] Therefore Herodias had a quarrel against him, and would have killed him.. [28]..brought his head in a charger..and the damsel gave it to her mother. —MARK, ch. 6.

4990. —— Gifts of. *Wisdom—Knowledge.* [26] *God* giveth to a man that *is* good in his sight wisdom, and knowledge, and joy : but to the sinner he giveth travail, to gather and to heap up, that he may give to *him that is* good before God. —ECCL., ch. 2.

4991. —— Haste in saving. *"Aaron ran."* [47] Aaron..ran into the midst of the congregation ; and, behold, the plague was begun among the people : and he put on incense, and made an atonement for the people. [48] And he stood between the dead and the living ; and the plague was stayed.—NUM., ch. 16.

4992. —— Inequalities in. *Dives—Lazarus.* [19] Was clothed in purple and fine linen, and fared sumptuously every day : [20] And there was a certain beggar named Lazarus, which was laid at his gate, full of sores, [21] And desiring to be fed with the crumbs.—LUKE, ch. 16.

4993. —— exhibits the Heart. *Solomon.* [4] His heart was not perfect with the Lord his God, as *was* the heart of David his father. [5] For Solomon went after Ashtoreth the goddess of the Zidonians.—1 KINGS, ch. 11.

4994. —— A higher. *Mary.* [41] Martha, Martha, thou art careful and troubled about many things : [42] But one thing is needful ; and Mary hath chosen that good part, which shall not be taken away from her.—LUKE, ch. 10.

4995. —— Joys of. *Solomon.* [19] Every man also to whom God hath given riches and wealth, and hath given him power to eat thereof, and to take his portion, and to rejoice in his labour ; this *is* the gift of God.—ECCL., ch. 5.

4996. —— Jeopardy of. *David said,* [3] Thy father certainly knoweth that I have found grace in thine eyes ; and he saith, Let not Jonathan know this, lest he be grieved : but truly, *as* the Lord liveth, and *as* thy soul liveth, *there is* but a step between me and death.—1 Sam., ch. 20. [King Saul sought to kill him.]

4997. —— Limits of. *Fourscore.* ¹⁰ The days of our years *are* threescore years and ten ; and if by reason of strength *they* be fourscore years, yet *is* their strength labour and sorrow ; for it is soon cut off, and we fly away.—Ps. 90.

4998. —— for Life. *Jehu said,* ²³ Search.. that there be here with you none..but the worshippers of Baal only. ²⁴ And when they went in to offer sacrifices and burnt offerings, Jehu appointed fourscore men without, and said, *If* any of the men..*he that letteth him go,* his life *shall be* for the life of him.—2 Kings, ch. 10.

4999. —— Loathing of. *Job.* ¹³ When I say, My bed shall comfort me, my couch shall ease my complaint ; ¹⁴ Then thou scarest me with dreams, and terrifiest me through visions : ¹⁵ So that my soul chooseth strangling, *and* death rather than my life. ¹⁶ I loathe *it* ; I would not live alway : let me alone ; for may days *are* vanity.—Job, ch. 7.

5000. —— lengthened by Prayer. *Hezekiah's.* ⁵ Thus saith the Lord..I have heard thy prayer, I have seen thy tears : behold, I will heal thee : on the third day thou shalt go up unto the house of the Lord. ⁶ And I will add unto thy days fifteen years.—2 Kings, ch. 20.

5001. —— limited. *Hananiah.* ¹⁶ Thus saith the Lord ; Behold, I will cast thee from off the face of the earth : this year thou shalt die, because thou hast taught rebellion against the Lord.—Jer., ch. 28.

5002. —— Presumption of. *" Know not."* ¹³ Go to now, ye that say, To day or to morrow we will go into such a city, and continue there a year, and buy and sell, and get gain : ¹⁴ Whereas ye know not what *shall be* on the morrow. For what *is* your life? It is even a vapour, that appeareth for a little time, and then vanisheth away.—James, ch. 4.

5003. —— perishable. *" Dust."* ¹⁹ Them that dwell in houses of clay, whose foundation *is* in the dust, *which* are crushed before the moth? ²⁰ They are destroyed from morning to evening.—Job, ch. 4.

5004. —— Plea for. *Esther.* ³ Esther.. said, If I have found favour in thy sight, O king, and if it please the king. let my life be given me at my petition, and my people at my request : ⁴ For we are sold, I and my people, to be destroyed..But if we had been sold for bondmen and bondwomen, I had held my tongue, although the enemy could not countervail the king's damage.—Esther, ch. 7.

5005. —— Promise of. *Proverb.* ¹ My son, forget not my law ; but let thine heart keep my commandments : ² For length of days, and long life, and peace, shall they add to thee.—Prov., ch. 3.

5006. —— a Pilgrimage. *Jacob.* ⁹ And Jacob said unto Pharaoh, The days of the years of my pilgrimage *are* a hundred and thirty years : few and evil have the days of the years of my life been.—Gen., ch. 47.

5007. —— Review of. *Jacob.* ⁹ Jacob said unto Pharaoh, The days of the years of my pilgrimage *are* a hundred and thirty years : few and evil have the days of the years of my life been. —Gen., ch. 47.

5008. —— Reversals in. *Job.* ² Oh that I were as *in* months past, as *in* the days *when* God preserved me ; ⁶ When I washed my steps with butter, and the rock poured me out rivers of oil : ⁸ The young men saw me, and hid themselves : and the aged arose, *and* stood up.—Job, ch. 29. [He was derided in adversity.]

5009. —— regretted. *Job.* ³ Let the day perish wherein I was born.. ⁹ Let the stars of the twilight thereof be dark ; let it look for light, but *have* none ; neither let it see the dawning of the day : ¹⁰ Because it shut not..nor hid sorrow from mine eyes. ¹¹ Why died I not from the womb?—Job, ch. 3.

5010. —— restored. *Shunammite's Child.* ³⁴ Elisha went up, and lay upon the child, and put his mouth upon his mouth, and his eyes upon his eyes, and his hands upon his hands : and he stretched himself upon the child ; and the flesh of the child waxed warm. ³⁵ Then he ..walked in the house to and fro ; and went up, and stretched himself upon him : and the child sneezed seven times, and..opened his eyes.—2 Kings, ch. 4.

5011. —— —— Jairus' Daughter. ⁴⁰ He taketh the father and the mother of the damsel, and them that were with him, and entereth in where the damsel was lying. ⁴¹ And he took the damsel by the hand, and said..Talitha cumi ; which is..Damsel, (I say unto thee,) arise. ⁴² And straightway the damsel arose.—Mark, ch. 5.

5012. —— —— Lazarus. ⁴³ He cried with a loud voice, Lazarus, come forth. ⁴⁴ And he that was dead came forth, bound hand and foot with graveclothes ; and his face was bound about with a napkin. Jesus saith..Loose him, and let him go.—John, ch. 11.

5013. —— —— Widow's Son. ¹³ He had compassion on her, and said..Weep not. ¹⁴ And he came and touched the bier..And he said, Young man, I say unto thee, Arise. ¹⁵ And he that was dead sat up, and began to speak.— Luke, ch. 7.

5014. —— —— Dorcas. ³⁹ All the widows stood by him weeping, and shewing the coats and garments which Dorcas made. ⁴⁰ But Peter ..kneeled down, and prayed ; and turning *him* to the body said, Tabitha, arise. And she opened her eyes : and when she saw Peter, she sat up.—Acts, ch. 9.

5015. —— Religion a new. *To Nicodemus.* ³ Jesus answered..Verily, verily, I say unto thee, Except a man be born again, he cannot see the kingdom of God.—John, ch. 3.

5016. —— Success in. *Sinner's.* [See No. 4986.]

5017. —— Swiftness of. *" Shuttle."* ⁶ My days are swifter than a weaver's shuttle, and are spent without hope. ⁷ O remember that my life *is* wind.—Job, ch. 7.

5018. —— Selling all for. *Egyptians.* ²⁰ The Egyptians sold every man his field, because the famine prevailed over them : so the land became Pharaoh's.—Gen., ch. 47. [Also their money and cattle.]

5019. —— commended, Social. *Passover.* ³ They shall take..a lamb for a house : ⁴ And if the household be too little for the lamb, let him and his neighbour next unto his house take *it*.—Ex., ch. 12.

5020. —— **a Trial.** *Eden.* [16] Of every tree of the garden thou mayest freely eat : [17] But of the tree of the knowledge of good and evil, thou shalt not eat of it : for in the day that thou eatest thereof thou shalt surely die.—GEN., ch. 2.

5021. —— **of Trouble.** *Job.* [1] Man *that is* born of a woman *is* of few days, and full of trouble. [2] He cometh forth like a flower, and is cut down : he fleeth also as a shadow, and continueth not.—JOB, ch. 14.

5022. —— **Tired of.** *Elijah.* [He fled from Jezebel.] [4] And sat down under a juniper tree : and he requested for himself that he might die ; and said, It is enough ; now, O Lord, take away my life ; for I *am* not better than my fathers.—1 KINGS, ch. 19.

5023. —— **typified.** *Christian.* [11] Thus shall ye eat it ; *with* your loins girded, your shoes on your feet, and your staff in your hand : and ye shall eat it in haste ; it *is* the Lord's passover. [13] . .and when I see the blood, I will pass over you, and the plague shall not. .destroy *you*, when I smite the land of Egypt.—EX., ch. 12.

5024. —— **Uncertainty of.** *" Watch."* [34] *For the Son of man is* as a man taking a far journey, who. .gave authority to his servants, and to every man his work, and commanded the porter to watch. [35] Watch ye therefore : for ye know not when the master of the house cometh, at even, or at midnight, or at the cockcrowing, or in the morning.—MARK, ch. 13.

5025. —— **Union in.** *Interwoven.* [30] When I come to thy servant my father, and the lad *be* not with us ; seeing that his life is bound up in the lad's life ; [31] . .he will die : and thy servants shall bring down the gray hairs of thy servant our father with sorrow to the grave.—GEN., ch. 44.

5026. —— **Various Values of.** *David.* [2] The king said. .I will surely go forth with you myself also. [3] But the people answered, Thou shalt not go forth : for if we flee away, they will not care for us ; neither if half of us die, will they care for us. .thou art worth ten thousand of us.—2 SAM., ch. 18.

5027. —— **Weariness of.** *Job.* [2] As a servant earnestly desireth the shadow, and as a hireling looketh for *the reward* of his work ; [3] So am I made to possess months of vanity, and wearisome nights are appointed to me. [4] When I lie down, I say, When shall I arise, and the night be gone? and I am full of tossings to and fro until the dawning of the day.—JOB, ch. 7.

5028. —— **by the Word.** *Satan said,* [3] If thou be the Son of God, command that these stones be made bread. [4] But he answered. .It is written, Man shall not live by bread alone, but by every word that proceedeth out of the mouth of God.—MAT., ch. 3.

5029. LIGHT for the Christian. *In Egypt.* [22] There was a thick darkness in all the land of Egypt three days : [23] They saw not one another, neither rose any from his place for three days : but all the children of Israel had light in their dwellings.—EX., ch. 10.

5030. —— **Conversion brings.** *Paul.* [17] Ananias went. .and putting his hands on him said, Brother Saul, the Lord, *even* Jesus. .hath sent me, that thou mightest receive thy sight, and be filled with the Holy Ghost. [18] And immediately there fell from his eyes as it had been scales.—ACTS, ch. 9.

5031. —— **Condemnation for.** *Pharisees.* [42] The queen of the south shall rise up in the judgment with this generation, and shall condemn it : for she came from the uttermost parts of the earth to hear the wisdom of Solomon ; and behold, a greater than Solomon *is* here.—MAT., ch. 12.

5032. —— **commanded.** *Creation.* [3] God said, Let there be light : and there was light.—GEN., ch. 1.

5033. —— **Dazzling.** *Paul.* [3] He came near Damascus : and suddenly there shined round about him a light from heaven. .[9] And he was three days without sight, and neither did eat nor drink.—ACTS, ch. 9.

5034. —— **of Deeds.** *Candle.* [15] Neither do men light a candle, and put it under a bushel, but on a candlestick ; and it giveth light unto all that are in the house. [16] Let your light so shine before men, that they may see your good works, and glorify your Father.—MAT., ch. 5.

5035. —— **Exposure by.** *Evil Deeds.* [20] Every one that doeth evil hateth the light, neither cometh to the light, lest his deeds should be reproved. [21] But he that doeth truth cometh to the light, that his deeds may be made manifest, that they are wrought in God.—JOHN, ch. 3.

5036. —— **Fellowship in.** *" Walk in."* [6] If we say that we have fellowship with him, and walk in darkness, we lie, and do not the truth : [7] But if we walk in the light, as he is in the light, we have fellowship one with another, and the blood of Jesus Christ his Son cleanseth us from all sin.—1 JOHN, ch. 1.

5037. —— **Hatred of.** *Evil-doers.* [18] He that believeth not is condemned already, because he hath not believed in the name of the only begotten Son of God. [19] And this is the condemnation, that light is come into the world, and men loved darkness rather than light, because their deeds were evil.—JOHN, ch. 3.

5038. —— **Improvement by.** *Walk.* [Two days before his death.] [35] Yet a little while is the light with you. Walk while ye have the light, lest darkness come upon you : for he that walketh in darkness knoweth not whither he goeth. [36] While ye have light, believe in the light, that ye may be the children of light.—JOHN, ch. 12.

5039. —— **and Love.** *Christian.* [9] He that saith he is in the light, and hateth his brother, is in darkness even until now. [10] He that loveth his brother abideth in the light, and there is none occasion of stumbling in him. [11] But he that hateth his brother is in darkness, and walketh in darkness, and knoweth not whither he goeth, because that darkness hath blinded his eyes.—1 JOHN, ch. 2.

5040. —— of Life. *Jesus.* [12] I am the light of the world : he that followeth me shall not walk in darkness, but shall have the light of life.—JOHN, ch. 8.

5041. —— Responsibility for. *Jesus said,* [23] Thou, Capernaum, which art exalted unto heaven, shalt be brought down to hell : for if the mighty works, which have been done in thee, had been done in Sodom, it would have remained until this day. [24]..it shall be more tolerable for the land of Sodom in the day of judgment, than for thee.—MAT., ch. 11.

5042. —— Sinning against. *Pharisees.* [40] Are we blind also ? [41] Jesus said..If ye were blind, ye should have no sin : but now ye say, We see ; therefore your sin remaineth.—JOHN, ch. 9.

5043. —— Transforming. *Moses' Face.* [29] When Moses came down from mount Sinai with the two tables of testimony..Moses wist not that the skin of his face shone while he talked with him.—EX., ch. 34.

5044. —— Waiting for. *In Egypt.* [See No. 5029.]

5045. —— withdrawn. *Scribes and Pharisees.* [38] Master, we would see a sign from thee. [39] But he answered..An evil and adulterous generation seeketh after a sign, and there shall no sign be given to it, but the sign of the prophet Jonas.—MAT., ch. 12.

See other illustrations under :
SUN.
Arrested. Sun, stand thou still upon Gibeon 8464
Gifts to. Horses..the kings of Judah had given to 8465
Healing. Shall the Sun of Righteousness arise with 8466
Outshone. A light..above the brightness of the 8467
Symbol. The righteous shine forth as the sun 8468
" The Lord God is a Sun and a Shield 8469

Inner. Spirit of man is the candle of the Lord 1570

5046. LIGHTNING, Alarmed by. *Pharaoh.* [27] I have sinned this time : the Lord *is* righteous, and I and my people *are* wicked. [28] Entreat the Lord (for *it is* enough) that there be no *more* mighty thunderings and hail ; and I will let you go.—EX., ch. 9.

5047. —— Destruction by. *Job's Sheep.* [16] The fire of God is fallen from heaven, and hath burned up the sheep, and the servants..I only am escaped.—JOB, ch. 1.

5048. —— Terrific. *In Egypt.* [23] The Lord sent thunder and hail, and the fire ran along upon the ground..upon the land of Egypt. [24] So there was hail, and fire mingled with the hail, very grievous.—EX., ch. 9.

5049. —— —— *Sinai.* [16] On the third day in the morning, that there were thunders and lightnings, and a thick cloud upon the mount, and the voice of the trumpet exceeding loud ; so that all the people that *was* in the camp trembled.—EX., ch. 19.

5050. LITIGATION condemned. *Christian.* [7] There is utterly a fault among you, because ye go to law one with another. Why do ye not rather take wrong? Why do ye not rather *suffer yourselves* to be defrauded?—1 COR., ch. 6.

See **LAW** and references.

5051. LITTLE, but Wise. *Animals.* [24] There be four *things which are* little upon the earth, but they *are* exceeding wise : [25] The ants.. [26] The conies.. [27] The locusts.. [28] The spider.—PROV., ch. 30.

See other illustrations under :
TRIFLES.
Blinded by. Blind guides..strain at a gnat..camel 8959
Comparatively. Samson took the doors of the gate 8960
Magnified. Pay tithes of mint..omitted..truth 8961
" Why..eat with unwashen hands? 8962

5052. LOITERERS driven. *From Sinai.* [1] When the people complained..the Lord heard *it ;* and his anger was kindled ; and the fire of the Lord..consumed *them that were* in the uttermost parts of the camp.—NUM., ch. 11.

5053. —— hastened. *Lot.* [16] While he lingered, the men laid hold upon his hand, and.. his wife, and..his two daughters ; the Lord being merciful unto him : and they..set him without the city.—GEN., ch. 19.

See **PROCRASTINATION** and references.

5054. LONELINESS, Comfort in. *Jacob.* [An exiled wanderer.] [11] He took of the stones..for his pillows, and lay down in that place to sleep. [12] And he dreamed, and behold a ladder set up on the earth, and the top of it reached to heaven : and..the angels of God ascending and descending on it. [13] And..the Lord stood above it.—GEN., ch. 28.

5055. —— Despondency in. *Elijah.* [13] What doest thou here, Elijah ? [14] And he said, I have been very jealous for the Lord..because the children of Israel have forsaken thy covenant, thrown down thine altars, and slain thy prophets..and I, *even* I only, am left ; and they seek my life, to take it away.—1 KINGS, ch. 19.

See other illustrations under :
DESERTION.
Ignorance. Eateth my flesh..disciples went back 2207
Painful. At my first answer..all men forsook me 2208
Prevented. Soldiers cut off the ropes of the boat 2209
SOLITUDE.
Hurtful. It is not good..man should be alone 8173
Prayer. Jesus went up..mountain to pray..alone 8174
Rest. Come ye..into a desert place and rest 8175
Strange. Camp of the Syrians..no man there 8176

5056. LOOK, Life in a. *Israelites.* [9] Moses made a serpent of brass, and put it upon a pole ..if a serpent had bitten any man, when he beheld the serpent of brass, he lived.—NUM., ch. 21.

5057. —— of Reproof. *Trial of Jesus.* [61] The Lord turned, and looked upon Peter. And Peter remembered..how he had said unto him, Before the cock crow, thou shalt deny me thrice. [62] And Peter went out, and wept bitterly.—LUKE, ch. 22.

5058. —— Trouble from a. *Egyptians.* [24] The Lord looked unto..the Egyptians through the pillar of fire..and troubled the host of the Egyptians, [25] And took off their chariot wheels, that they drave them heavily : so that the Egyptians said, Let us flee..for the Lord fighteth for them.—EX., ch. 14.

5059. LOOKING to the Blood. *Passover.* [In conspicuous places.] [7] They shall take of the blood, and strike *it* on the two side posts and on the upper door post of the houses.—EX., ch. 12.

5060. —— back. *Lot's Wife.* [11] Escape for thy life ; look not behind thee, neither stay thou in all the plain ; [26] But his wife looked l k from behind him, and she became a pillar o⅃ salt.—Gen., ch. 19.

5061. —— —— *Disciple.* [61] One said, Lord, I will follow thee ; but let me first go bid them fa⅃ well, which are at home. . [62] And Jesus said . .No man, having put his hand to the plough, and looking back, is fit for the kingdom of God. —Luke, ch. 9.

5062. —— to Jesus. *Peter.* [30] When he saw the wind boisterous, he was afraid ; and beginning to sink, he cried, saying, Lord, save me. [31] And immediately Jesus stretched forth *his* hand, and caught him.—Mat., ch. 14.

See other illustrations under :

OBSERVATION.

Difficult. Zaccheus. .climbed. .tree to see Jesus   5822
Unfeeling. Looked on him and passed. .other side 5823

SEEING.

Partial. Woman saw that. .tree was good for food 7679
Proof. L. given one. .mine eyes even seeing it   7680
Unsatisfactory. Eye is not atisfied with seeing 7681
Vexatious. Lot. .seeing and hearing vexed. .soul 7682

5063. LOSS by Absence. *Thomas.* [24] Thomas, one of the twelve. .was not with them when Jesus came.—John, ch. 20. [He remained one week in unhappy doubt.]

5064. —— of Authority. *Job.* [15] They that dwell in mine house, and my maids, count me for a stranger : I am an alien in their sight. [16] I called my servant, and he gave *me* no answer ; I entreated him with my mouth.--Job, ch. 19.

5065. —— by Accident. *Son of Prophets.* [5] As one was felling a beam, the axe head fell into the water : and he cried, and said, Alas, master ! for it was borrowed. [6] And the man of God. .cut down a stick, and cast *it* in thither ; and the iron did swim.—2 Kings, ch. 6.

5066. —— by Delay. *At Bethesda.* [7] The impotent man answered him, Sir, I have no man, when the water is troubled, to put me into the pool : but while I am coming, another steppeth down before me.—John, ch. 5.

5067. —— Discovery of. *Joseph and Mary.* [45] When they found him not, they turned back again to Jerusalem, seeking him. [46] And. .after three days they found him in the temple, sitting in the midst of the doctors.—Luke, ch. 2.

5068. —— An irreparable. *Ark of God.* [10] The Philistines fought, and Israel was smitten, and they fled. . [11] And the ark of God was taken. . when the man came into the city, and told *it*, all the city cried out.—1 Sam., ch. 4.

5069. —— An irrecoverable. *Saltness.* [50] Salt *is* good : but if the salt have lost his saltness, wherewith will ye season it ?—Mark, ch. 9.

5070. —— by Ignorance. *Parable of the Sower.* [19] When any one heareth the word of the kingdom, and understandeth *it* not, then cometh the wicked one, and catcheth away that which was sown in his heart. This is he which received seed by the way side.—Mat., ch. 13.

5071. —— of Losses, The. *The Soul.* [26] What is a man profited, if he shall gain the whole world, and lose his own soul ? or what shall a man give in exchange for his soul ?—Mat., ch. 16.

5072. —— of Love. *Ephesian Church.* [4] Nevertheless I have *somewhat* against thee, because thou hast left thy first love. [5] Remember therefore from whence thou art fallen, and repent, and do the first works ; or else I will come unto thee.—Rev., ch. 2.

5073. —— Profit and. *The Soul.* [25] What is a man advantaged, if he gain the whole world, and lose himself, or be cast away ?—Luke, ch. 9.

5074. —— by lack of Zeal. *Elisha to Joash.* [18] Smite upon the ground. And he smote thrice, and stayed. [19] And the man of God was wroth with him, and said, Thou shouldest have smitten five or six times ; then hadst thou smitten Syria till thou hadst consumed *it :* whereas now thou shalt smite Syria *but* thrice.—2 Kings, ch. 13.

5075. LOSSES, Accountability for. *Jacob to Laban.* [39] That which was torn *of beasts* I brought not unto thee ; I bare the loss of it ; of my hand didst thou require it, *whether* stolen by day, or stolen by night.—Gen., ch. 31.

5076. —— restored. *Job.* [12] The Lord blessed the latter end of Job more than his beginning : for he had fourteen thousand sheep, and six thousand camels, and a thousand yoke of oxen, and a thousand she asses. [13] He had also seven sons and three daughters.—Job, ch. 42.

5077. LOST Bible, A. *Reign of Josiah.* [8] Hilkiah the high priest said unto Shaphan the scribe, I have found the book of the law in the house of the Lord. .and he read it.—2 Kings, ch. 22.

5078. —— to the Good. *Prodigal.* [13] The younger son gathered all together, and took his journey into a far country, and there wasted his substance with riotous living.—Luke, ch. 15.

5079. —— Penitence of the. *Prodigal.* [18] I will arise and go to my father, and will say unto him, Father, I have sinned against heaven, and before thee, [19] And am no more worthy to be called thy son : make me as one of thy hired servants.—Luke, ch. 15.

5080. —— Reflections of the. *Prodigal.* [17] When he came to himself, he said, How many hired servants of my father's have bread enough and to spare, and I perish with hunger !—Luke, ch. 15.

5081. —— restored, The. *Joseph.* [27] When he saw the wagons which Joseph had sent to carry him, the spirit of Jacob their father revived. [28] And Israel said, *It is* enough ; Joseph my son *is* yet alive : I will go and see him before I die.—Gen., ch. 45.

5082. —— Recovery of the. *Prodigal.* [22] Bring forth the best robe, and put *it* on him ; and put a ring on his hand, and shoes on *his* feet : [23] And bring hither the fatted calf, and kill *it* ; and let us eat, and be merry : [24] For this my son was dead, and is alive again ; he was lost, and is found.—Luke, ch. 15.

5083. —— Restoration of the. *Law.* [1] Thou shalt not see thy brother's ox or his sheep go astray, and hide thyself from them : thou shalt in any case bring them again unto thy brother. [2] And if thy brother *be* not nigh unto thee, or if thou know him not, then thou shalt bring it unto thine own house, and it shall be with thee until thy brother seek after it.—Deut., ch. 22.

5084. —— Seeking the. *Unconscious.* [8] What woman having ten pieces of silver, if she lose one piece, doth not light a candle, and sweep the house, and seek diligently till she find *it?*—Luke, ch. 15.

5085. —— —— *Conscious.* [4] What man of you, having a hundred sheep, if he lose one of them, doth not leave the ninety and nine in the wilderness, and go after that which is lost, until he find it?—Luke, ch. 15.

5086. —— from Unbelief. *Jesus said,* [16] He that believeth and is baptized, shall be saved ; but he that believeth not, shall be damned.—Mark, ch. 16.

See other illustrations under :

DEFEAT.

Angered. Elihu saw..was no answer..wrath 2098
Conspirators. Entangle him..marvelled, and left 2099
Desperation. Not able to resist the wisdom and 2100
Humiliating. Men of Ai smote..Joshua rent 2101
Predicted. Will flee upon..horses, therefore shall 2102
Providential. L. did confound the language 2103

DISAPPOINTMENT.

Doubt. Heard that he was alive..believed not 2315
Gifts. S. gave Hiram 20 cities..pleased him not 2316
Goo! . They have taken..Lord out of the s. 2317
Humiliating. Prison truly..shut..no man there 2318
Ignorance. No place of seed..figs..vines 2319
Judgment. Thou hast taught in our streets 2320
Misjudged. We trusted it had been he..saved I. 2321
Maternal. I have gotten a man [murderer] from 2322
Many. Sown much, and bring in little 2326
Perplexing. King of Syria sore troubled 2323
Religion. Have wanted all things .consumed 2324
Unendurable. Ahithophel..hanged himself 2325

FAILURE.

Avoiding. Intending to build a tower..first 2867
Cruelty. The more they afflicted them, the more 2868
Complaint. L. wherefore hast thou so evil 2869
Church. That they should cast him out..not 2870
Discouraging. Ye have..put a sword in their hand 2871
Disheartening. Have toiled all the night..taken 2872
Explained. This kind can come..by prayer 2873
Fear. We saw the giants..we were grasshoppers 2874
Irremediable. The door was shut..Lord open 2875
Ominous. If thou hast begun to fall..not prevail 2876
Ridiculed. Mock him..began to build..not able 2878
Temporary. I know not the L., neither..let I. go 2879

5087. LOT, Condemned by. *Achan.* [17] He brought the family of Judah ; and he took the family of the Zarhites : and he brought the family of the Zarhites man by man ; and Zabdi was taken : [18] And he brought his household man by man ; and Achan..was taken.—Josh., ch. 7.

5088. —— —— *Sailors said,* [7] Come, and let us cast lots, that we may know for whose cause this evil *is* upon us. So they cast lots, and the lot fell upon Jonah.—Jonah, ch. 1.

5089. —— Called by. *Zacharias.* [9] According to the custom of the priest's office, his lot was to burn incense when he went into the temple of the Lord.—Luke, ch. 1.

5090. —— Division by. *Canaan.* [54] Ye shall divide the land by lot for an inheritance among your families ; *and* to the more ye shall give the more inheritance, and to the fewer ye shall give the less inheritance.—Num., ch. 33.

5091. —— Gambling by. *At the Cross.* [23] The soldiers, when they had crucified Jesus, took his garments, and made four parts, to every soldier a part ; and also *his* coat.. [24] They said ..Let us not rend it, but cast lots for it, whose it shall be.—John, ch. 19.

5092. —— with Prayer. *Apostles.* [23] Appointed two, Joseph..and Matthias. [24] And they prayed..Thou, Lord, which knowest the hearts of all *men,* show whether of these two thou hast chosen, [25] That he may take part of this ministry and apostleship, from which Judas by transgression fell.. [26] And they gave forth their lots ; and the lot fell upon Matthias.—Acts, ch. 1.

5093. LOVE, Absorbed by. *Mary.* [40] Bid her ..that she help me. [41] And Jesus answered.. Martha, Martha, thou art careful and troubled about many things : [42] But one thing is needful ; and Mary hath chosen that good part, which shall not be taken away from her.—Luke, ch. 10.

5094. —— one Another. *"Knoweth God."* [7] Beloved, let us love one another : for love is of God ; and every one that loveth is born of God, and knoweth God. [8] He that loveth not, knoweth not God ; for God is love.—1 John, ch. 4.

5095. —— kills Bigotry. *Moses to Jethro.* [A Midianite.] [32] If thou go with us, yea, it shall be, that what goodness the Lord shall do unto us, the same will we do unto thee.—Num., ch. 10.

5096. —— A Brother's. *Aaron's.* [14] *Is* not Aaron the Levite thy brother ? I know that he can speak well. And also, behold, he cometh forth to meet thee : and when he seeth thee, he will be glad in his heart.—Ex., ch. 4.

5097. —— for the Church. *Joel.* [17] Let the priests, the ministers of the Lord, weep between the porch and the altar, and let them say, Spare thy people, O Lord, and give not thine heritage to reproach, that the heathen should rule over them : wherefore should they say..Where *is* their God?—Joel, ch. 2.

5098. —— Compassion of. *Jesus.* [37] O Jerusalem, Jerusalem, *thou* that killest the prophets, and stonest them which are sent unto thee, how often would I have gathered thy children together, even as a hen gathereth her chickens under *her* wings, and ye would not !—Mat., ch. 23.

5099. —— a Compensation. *Proverb.* [17] Better *is* a dinner of herbs where love is, than a stalled ox and hatred therewith.—Prov., ch. 15.

5100. —— works the Church. *Tabernacle.* [21] Every one whose heart stirred him up, and every one whom his spirit made willing, brought the Lord's offering to the work of the tabernacle..and for all his service, and for the holy garments. [22]..both men and women.. brought bracelets, and earrings, and rings, and tablets, all jewels of gold.—Ex., ch. 35.

5101. —— the great Duty. *To a Lawyer.* [37] Jesus said..Thou shalt love the Lord thy God with all thy heart, and with all thy soul, and with all thy mind. [38] This is the first and great commandment. [39] And the second *is* like unto it, Thou shalt love thy neighbour as thyself.— Mat., ch. 22.

5102. —— shows Discipleship. *Jesus said,* [34] A new commandment I give unto you, That ye love one another ; as I have loved you, that ye also love one another. [35] By this shall all *men* know that ye are my disciples, if ye have love one to another.—JOHN, ch. 13.

5103. —— Devotion of. *Galatians.* [15] I bear you record, that, if *it had been* possible, ye would have plucked out your own eyes, and have given them to me.—GAL., ch. 4.

5104. —— Destitute of. *David.* [4] I looked on *my* right hand, and beheld, but *there was* no man that would know me : refuge failed me ; no man cared for my soul. [5] I cried unto thee, O Lord : I said, Thou *art* my refuge.—Ps. 42.

5105. —— Effects of. *" No Fear."* [18] There is no fear in love ; but perfect love casteth out fear : because fear hath torment. He that feareth, is not made perfect in love. [20] If a man say, I love God, and hateth his brother, he is a liar. —1 JOHN, ch. 4.

5106. —— Evidence in. *Loveth his Brother.* [10] He that loveth his brother abideth in the light, and there is none occasion of stumbling in him. [11] But he that hateth his brother is in darkness, and walketh in darkness, and knoweth not whither he goeth, because that darkness hath blinded his eyes.—1 JOHN, ch. 2.

5107. —— of Enemies. *Command.* [43] It hath been said, Thou shalt love thy neighbour, and hate thine enemy. [44] But I say unto you, Love your enemies, bless them that curse you, do good to them that hate you, and pray for them which despitefully use you, and persecute you. —MAT., ch. 5.

5108. —— Fraternal. *Christian.* [16] Hereby perceive we the love *of* God, because he laid down his life for us : and we ought to lay down *our* lives for the brethren. [17] But whoso hath this world's goods, and seeth his brother have need, and shutteth up his bowels *of* compassion from him, how dwelleth the love of God in him ? —1 JOHN, ch. 3.

5109. —— of Friendship. *David.* [25] O Jonathan, *thou wast* slain in thine high places. [26] I am distressed for thee, my brother Jonathan : very pleasant hast thou been unto me : thy love to me was wonderful, passing the love of women. —2 SAM., ch. 1.

5110. —— of God. *Distinguishing.* [4] What is man, that thou art mindful of him ?.. [5] For thou hast made him a little lower than the angels, and hast crowned him with glory and honour. [6] Thou madest him to have dominion over the works of thy hands ; thou hast put all *things* under his feet.—Ps. 8.

5111. —— *Not forgetful.* [15] Can a woman forget her sucking child..yea, they may forget, yet will I not forget thee. [16] Behold, I have graven thee upon the palms of *my* hands ; thy walls *are* continually before me.—ISA., ch. 49.

5112. —— *For Sinners.* [16] God so loved the world, that he gave his only begotten Son, that whosoever believeth in him should not perish, but have everlasting life.—JOHN, ch. 3.

5113. —— *Remarkable.* [1] Behold what manner of love the Father hath bestowed upon us, that we should be called the sons of God.. [2] Beloved, now are we the sons of God, and it doth not yet appear what we shall be : but we know that, when he shall appear, we shall be like him.—1 JOHN, ch. 3.

5114. —— —— *The Seeking.* The lost sheep ..The lost coin..The lost son. [See Luke, ch. 15.]

5115. —— —— *The Receiving.* [20] He arose, and came to his father. But when he was yet a great way off, his father saw him, and had compassion, and ran, and fell on his neck, and kissed him.—LUKE, ch. 15.

5116. —— —— *The Honouring.* [See No. 5082.] [19] Am no more worthy to be called thy son : make me as one of thy hired servants. [22] But the father said to his servants, Bring forth the best robe, and put *it* on him ; and put a ring on his hand, and shoes on *his* feet : [23] And bring hither the fatted calf, and kill *it ;* and let us eat, and be merry.—LUKE, ch. 15.

5117. —— to God. *Command.* [5] Thou shalt love the Lord thy God with all thine heart, and with all thy soul, and with all thy might. [6] And these words..shall be in thine heart.—DEUT., ch. 6.

5118. —— better than Hatred. *Proverbs.* [12] Hatred stirreth up strifes : but love covereth all sins [18] He that hideth hatred *with* lying lips, and he that uttereth a slander, *is* a fool. —PROV., ch. 10.

5119. —— Imperfect. *Solomon.* [3] Solomon loved the Lord..only he sacrificed and burnt incense in high places.—1 KINGS, ch. 3.

5120. —— An inseparable. *Ruth.* [16] Entreat me not to leave thee..for whither thou goest, I will go ; and where thou lodgest, I will lodge : thy people *shall be* my people, and thy God my God : [17] Where thou diest, will I die, and there will I be buried : the Lord do so to me, and more also, *if aught* but death part thee and me. —RUTH, ch. 1.

5121. —— Life in. *Lawyer said,* [25] Master, what shall I do to inherit eternal life ? [26] He said..What is written in the law ?.. [27] And he answering said, Thou shalt love the Lord thy God with all thy heart, and with all thy soul, and with all thy strength, and with all thy mind ; and thy neighbour as thyself. [28] And he said..this do, and thou shalt live.—LUKE, ch. 10.

5122. —— Loss of. *Ephesians.* [4] I have *somewhat* against thee, because thou hast left thy first love. [5] Remember therefore from whence thou art fallen, and repent, and do the first works ; or else I will come unto thee quickly, and will remove thy candlestick out of his place, except thou repent.—REV., ch. 2.

5123. —— A Lover's. *Jacob.* [20] Jacob served seven years for Rachel ; and they seemed unto him *but* a few days, for the love he had to her.—GEN., ch. 29.

5124. —— Labour of. *Five Months.* [David took seven of Saul's descendants..Gibeonites hung them.] [10] And Rizpah..took sackcloth, and spread it for her upon the rock, from the beginning of harvest until the water dropped upon them out of heaven, and suffered neither the birds of the air to rest on them by day, nor the beasts of the field by night.—2 SAM., ch. 21.

5125. —— Memorial of. *Mary.* [8] She hath done what she could : she is come aforehand to anoint my body to the burying. [9]..Wheresoever this gospel shall be preached throughout the whole world, *this* also that she hath done shall be spoken of for a memorial of her.—MARK, ch. 14.

5126. —— **Mission of.** *John said,* [54] Command fire to come down from heaven, and consume them, even as Elias did ? [55] But he turned, and rebuked them, and said, Ye know not what manner of spirit ye are of. [56] For the Son of man is not come to destroy men's lives, but to save *them.*—LUKE, ch. 9.

5127. —— **A Mother's.** *Of Moses.* [2] She hid him three months. [3] And when she could not longer hide him, she took for him an ark of bulrushes, and daubed it with slime and with pitch, and put the child therein ; and she laid *it* in the flags by the river's brink.—EX., ch. 2.

5128. —— **of Money.** *"Root of all Evil."* [10] The love of money is the root of all evil : which while some coveted after, they have erred from the faith, and pierced themselves through with many sorrows. [11]..O man of God, flee these things.—1 TIM., ch. 6.

5129. —— **More than natural.** *Spiritual.* [35] I am come to set a man at variance against his father, and the daughter against her mother ..[37] He that loveth father or mother more than me is not worthy of me : and he that loveth son or daughter more than me is not worthy of me. —MAT., ch. 10.

5130. —— **Nobility of.** *Judah.* [33] Let thy servant abide instead of the lad a bondman to my lord ; and let the lad go up with his brethren. [34] For how shall I go up to my father, and the lad *be* not with me.—GEN., ch. 44.

5131. —— **Philanthropic.** *Law of.* [30] Thou shalt love the Lord thy God with all thy heart, and with all thy soul, and with all thy mind, and with all thy strength : this *is* the first commandment. [31] And the second is like, *namely* this, Thou shalt love thy neighbour as thyself. There is none other commandment greater than these.—MARK, ch. 12.

5132. —— **Perfection of.** *"His Love."* [12] If we love one another, God dwelleth in us, and his love is perfected in us.—1 JOHN, ch. 4.

5133. —— **A pretended.** *Assassin's.* [9] Joab said to Amasa, *Art* thou in health, my brother ? And Joab took Amasa by the beard with the right hand to kiss him. [10] But Amasa took no heed to the sword that *was* in Joab's hand : so he smote him therewith in the fifth *rib.*—2 SAM., ch. 20.

5134. —— **Reason for.** *"Loved us."* [10] Herein is love, not that we loved God, but that he loved us, and sent his Son *to be* the propitiation for our sins. [11] Beloved, if God so loved us, we ought also to love one another.—1 JOHN, ch. 4.

5135. —— **Rule for.** *"Forgiven much."* [46] My head with oil thou didst not anoint : but this woman hath anointed my feet with ointment. [47] Wherefore..her sins, which are many, are forgiven ; for she loved much : but to whom little is forgiven, *the same* loveth little.—LUKE, ch. 7.

5136. —— **Superiority of.** *"Greatest of these is Charity."* [See 1 Cor., 13.]

5137. —— **better than Sacrifice.** *A Scribe said,* [33] To love him with all the heart, and

with all the understanding, and with all the soul, and with all the strength, and to love *his* neighbour as himself, is more than all whole burnt offerings and sacrifices. [34]..Jesus..said ..Thou art not far from the kingdom of God.— MARK, ch. 12.

5138. —— **before Sacrifice.** *Reconciliation.* [23] If thou bring thy gift to the altar, and there rememberest that thy brother hath aught against thee ; [24] Leave there thy gift before the altar, and go thy way ; first be reconciled to thy brother, and then come and offer thy gift.—MAT., ch. 5.

5139. —— **Sincere.** *Peter's.* [17] Simon, *son* of Jonas, lovest thou me ? Peter was grieved because he said unto him the third time, Lovest thou me ? And he said..Lord, thou knowest all things ; thou knowest that I love thee.— JOHN, ch. 21.

5140. —— **Service of.** *Samaritan.* [33] He had compassion *on him,* [34] And went to *him,* and bound up his wounds, pouring in oil and wine, and set him on his own beast, and brought him to an inn, and took care of him. [35]..when he departed, he took out two pence, and gave *them* to the host.—LUKE, ch. 10.

5141. —— **Self-abnegating.** *Paul's.* [3] I could wish that myself were accursed from Christ for my brethren, my kinsmen according to the flesh.—ROM., ch. 9.

5142. —— **Standard of.** *"As I have loved you."* [See No. 5102.]

5143. —— **Sorrows of.** *Jeremiah.* [1] Oh that my head were waters, and mine eyes a fountain of tears, that I might weep day and night for the slain of the daughter of my people.—JER., ch. 9.

5144. —— **Strength of.** *"Cannot quench."* [6] Set me as a seal upon thine heart..for love *is* strong as death.. [7] Many waters cannot quench love, neither can the floods drown it : if a man would give all the substance of his house for love, it would utterly be contemned.—SOLOMON'S SONG, ch. 8.

5145. —— **Test of.** *"In Death."* [14] We know that we have passed from death unto life, because we love the brethren. He that loveth not *his* brother, abideth in death.—1 JOHN, ch. 3.

5146. —— **in the Tongue.** *Deeds.* [18] Let us not love in word, neither in tongue, but in deed and in truth. [19] And hereby we know that we are of the truth, and shall assure our hearts before him.—1 JOHN, ch. 3.

5147. —— **A Traitor's.** *Judas.* [48] Whomsoever I shall kiss, that same is he ; hold him fast. [49]..he came to Jesus, and said, Hail, Master ; and kissed him.—MAT., ch. 26.

5148. —— **unites to God.** *St. John says,* [16] We have known and believed the love that God hath to us. God is love : and he that dwelleth in love, dwelleth in God, and God in him. —1 JOHN, ch. 4.

5149. —— **Unmanifested.** *Proverb.* [5] Open rebuke *is* better than secret love. [6] Faithful *are* the wounds of a friend ; but the kisses of an enemy *are* deceitful.—PROV., ch. 27.

5150. —— **for the Unlovely.** *Jesus said,* [46] For if ye love them which love you, what reward have ye ? do not even the publicans the same ? [47] And if ye salute your brethren only, what do ye more *than others?* do not even the publicans so ?—Mat., ch. 5.

5151. —— **Work of.** *"Built."* [4] When they came to Jesus, they besought him instantly, saying, That he was worthy for whom he should do this : [5] For he loveth our nation, and he hath built us a synagogue.—Luke, ch. 7.

See other illustrations under :

KINDNESS.

Appreciated. Barzillai..I will feed thee in Jeru'm	4808
Animals. Rebekah..I will draw for thy camels	4809
Bereavement. In the choice of our sepulchres..bury	4810
Brethren. Waxen poor ; thou shalt relieve him	4811
Conquerors. Saul..is this thy voice, David?..wept	4812
to Christians. A cup of cold water only..his r.	4813
Christians. Disciples..relief unto brethren..Judea	4814
Captives. Clothed naked..shod them..eat	4815
Father. If ye know how to give..much more..F.	4816
Gratitude. Mephibosheth..kindness for Jonathan's	4817
Heathen. Barbarous people shewed..kindness	4818
Insulted. David sent to comfort him..cut beards	4819
Inopportune. Ahab..because thou hast let go	4820
Loan. Hath pity..lendeth to the L.	4821
Providential. Boaz unto Ruth..abide here	4822
Prosperity. I delivered the poor that cried [Job]	4823
Prisoner. Jeremiah put these rags..under arms	4824
Remembered. Lest I destroy you, for ye showed	4825
Rewarded. Rahab hid them with flax..saved	4826
Substitutional. I was eyes to the blind..feet [Job]	4827
Servant. Centurion's servant was dear to him	4828
Strangers. Drink, my lord..hasted..gave him	4829
Timely. Barzillai brought beds..flour..butter	4830
Unexpected. Shall I smite them?..set bread	4831
Widow. Harvest..forgot a sheaf..be for the w.	4832

KISS.

Filial. Let me kiss my father	4850
Treacherous. Joab took Amasa..to kiss him	4851
" Whomsoever I shall kiss..is he	4852

PHILANTHROPY.

Creditable. Jeremiah is like to die for hunger	6118
Divine. Jesus went about..teaching..preaching	6119
" Went about doing good..healing all	6120
Inculcated. Bless them that curse you, do good	6121
Noble. Samaritan had compassion..care	6122
Practical. Take this child..nurse it for me..wages	6123
Pious. Barnabas sold it..brought the money	6124
Preference. Do good unto all, especially..faith	6125
Revival. Sold their possessions..every man	6126

See AFFECTION, BENEVOLENCE.

5152. LOYALTY undermined. *Absalom.* [5] When any man came nigh *to him* to do him obeisance, he put forth his hand, and took him, and kissed him. [6] And on this manner did Absalom..all Israel that came to the king for judgment : so Absalom stole the hearts of the men. —2 Sam., ch. 15.

See other illustrations under :

PATRIOTISM.

Absorbing. Why is thy countenance sad ?	6005
Appeal. Fight for your brethren..houses	6006
Children. Wives also and the children rejoiced	6007
Dangerous. Ehud made him a dagger..two edges	6008
Deed. Moses..slew the Egyptian	6009
Generous. Were at my table 150 Jews besides	6010
Self-sacrificing. Forgive..if not, blot me..out of	6013
Sacrifices. I..have not eaten the bread of the G.	6014
Sentiments. Moses said..Let me go..my brethren	6015

5153. LUKEWARMNESS spewed out. *Laodiceans.* [15] I know thy works, that thou art nei-

ther cold nor hot : I would thou wert cold or hot. [16] So then because thou art lukewarm, and neither cold nor hot, I will spew thee out of my mouth.—Rev., ch. 3.

See other illustrations under :

EASE.

Care for. Trouble me not..the door is shut	2586
Indifference. Ye offer the lame and sick	2587
Promised. Then..Soul, take thine ease	2588
Religious. Woe unto them that are at ease in Zion	2589

INDIFFERENCE.

Hearing. Foolish man who built..upon the sand	4405
Inconsiderate. Here is thy pound which I have	4406
Provoking. Wrath because..have not hearkened	4407
Pitiless. Saw him, and passed by..other side	4408
Sin. I have sinned..What is that to us?	4409
Sinners. Made light of it, and went their ways	4410
Unbelievers. They did eat..until the day Noe	4411

5154. LUNACY, Diabolic. *Gadarene.* [5] Always, night and day, he was in the mountains, and in the tombs, crying, and cutting himself with stones.—Mark, ch. 5.

5155. —— **Moral.** *Gadarenes.* [16] They that saw *it* told them how it befell to him that was possessed with the devil, and *also* concerning the swine. [17] And they began to pray him to depart out of their coasts.—Mark, ch. 5.

See other illustrations under :

MADMAN.

Esteemed. Paul..thou art beside thyself	5160
Stigmatized. Who goeth about to kill thee..hast a	5162
See INSANITY and references.	

5156. LUXURY to Torment, From. *Dives.* [22] The beggar died, and was carried by the angels into Abraham's bosom : the rich man also died, and was buried ; [23] And in hell he lifted up his eyes, being in torments, and seeth Abraham afar off, and Lazarus in his bosom.—Luke, ch. 16.

5157. LUXURIES, Trade in. *Babylon.* [12] The merchandise of gold, and silver, and precious stones, and of pearls, and fine linen, and purple, and silk, and scarlet, and all thyine wood, and all manner vessels of ivory, and..of most precious wood, and of brass, and iron, and marble, [13] And cinnamon, and odours, and ointments, and frankincense, and wine, and oil, and fine flour, and wheat, and beasts, and sheep, and horses, and chariots, and slaves, and souls of men.—Rev., ch. 18.

5158. —— **Indifferent in.** *Beds of Ivory.* [3] Ye that put far away the evil day, and cause the seat of violence to come near ; [4] That lie upon beds of ivory, and stretch themselves upon their couches, and eat the lambs out of the flock, and the calves out of the midst of the stall ; [5] That chant to the sound of the viol, *and* invent to themselves instruments of music, like David ; [6] That drink wine in bowls, and anoint themselves with the chief ointments : but they are not grieved for the affliction of Joseph.—Amos, ch. 6.

5159. —— **Uncorrupted by.** *Moses.* [24] By faith Moses..refused to be called the son of Pharaoh's daughter ; [25] Choosing rather to suffer affliction with the people of God, than to enjoy the pleasures of sin for a season ; [26] Esteeming the reproach of Christ greater riches than the treasures in Egypt.—Heb., ch. 11.

See other illustrations under:

FEAST.

Ancient. Sarah..made cakes..Abraham..calf   3172
Birthday. Herod on his birthday made a supper   3173
Charitable. Call the poor, the lame..blind   3174
Complimentary. At Bethany..they made Jesus a   3175
     Levi made Jesus a great feast   3176
Death. Job's sons and daughters..brother's house   3177
Ended sadly. Merry with wine..smite Amnon   3178
Farewell. Elisha..oxen, and slew them .people   3179
Great. Solomon offered 22,000 oxen and 120,000 s.   3180
Idolatrous. [Calf] People..eat..drink..rose up to   3181
Impious. Belshazzar made a feast to a thousand   3182
Joyous. [Tabernacles] Seven days shall dwell in   3183
Marriage. Jesus and his disciples were called   3184
National. Three times..keep a feast unto me..year   3186
Royal. Ahasuerus made a feast at Shushan   3185

5160. MADMAN, Esteemed a. *Paul.* [24] Festus said with a loud voice, Paul, thou art beside thyself; much learning doth make thee mad. [25] But he said, I am not mad, most noble Festus; but speak forth the words of truth and soberness.—Acts, ch. 26.

5161. —— stigmatized. *Jesus.* [Six months before his murder.] [19] Why go ye about to kill me? [20] The people answered .. Thou hast a devil: who goeth about to kill thee?—John, ch. 7.

See other illustrations under:

LUNACY.

Diabolic. In the tombs crying and cutting himself   5154
Moral. [Gadarenes] began to pray him to depart   5155
See INSANITY and references.

5162. MAGIC, Imposition of. *Egyptian.* [11] The magicians of Egypt. [12]..cast down every man his rod, and they became serpents: but Aaron's rod swallowed up their rods.—Ex., ch. 7.

See other illustrations under:

SORCERY.

Captivating. Simon..all gave heed..great power   8202
Renounced. Simon himself believed..baptized   8203
     "   Ephesians brought their books..burned 8204

WITCHCRAFT.

Abolished. Workers with familiar spirits..Josiah   9649
Consoling. Thy words have upholden him that   145
Doubters. Go into Judea, that thy disciples also   4338
Famous. Seek me a woman..a familiar spirit   9647
Influential. They all gave heed..least..greatest   9650
Appreciated. D. said to Abigail, Blessed be thee   2368
Commendation. [Hurtful]. These men are the   6896

5163. MAGNANIMITY, Apostolic. *Paul.* [28] Agrippa said unto Paul, Almost thou persuadest me to be a Christian. [29] And Paul said, I would to God, that not only thou, but also all that hear me this day, were both almost, and altogether such as I am, except these bonds.—Acts, ch. 26.

5164. —— to Enemies. *David.* [After Absalom's rebellion.] [21] Abishai..said, Shall not Shimei be put to death for this, because he cursed the Lord's anointed? [22] And David said, What have I to do with you, ye sons of Zeruiah, that ye should this day be adversaries unto me? shall there any man be put to death this day in Israel?—2 Sam., ch. 19.

5165. —— in Forgiveness. *David.* [5] David's heart smote him, because he had cut off Saul's skirt. [6] And he said unto his men, The Lord forbid that I should do this thing unto my master, the Lord's anointed, to stretch forth mine hand against him.—1 Sam., ch. 24.

5166. —— Fraternal. *Judah.* [32] Thy servant became surety for the lad..saying, If I bring him not unto thee, then I shall bear the blame to my father for ever. [33] Now therefore, I pray thee, let thy servant abide instead of the lad a bondman to my lord.—Gen., ch. 44.

5167. —— Gracious. *Abraham.* [8] Abram said unto Lot, Let there be no strife, I pray thee, between me and thee, and between my herdmen and thy herdmen; for we *be* brethren. [9] *Is* not the whole land before thee? separate thyself, I pray thee, from me: if *thou wilt take* the left hand, then I will go to the right; or if *thou depart* to the right hand, then I will go to the left.—Gen., ch. 13.

See other illustrations under:

GENEROSITY.

Afflicted. The field give I..bury thy dead   3511
Forgiving. Esau said, I have enough   3513
Royal. [David's] 3000 talents of gold..70,000 silver   3514
Tabernacle Builders. People..much more than   3512

LIBERALITY.

Benevolent. Much entreaty that we would receive   4949
Commended. Thine heart shall not be grieved   4950
Denominational. He followeth not us; and we f.   4952
Pagan. He hath built us a synagogue   4954
Rule. Poor widow hath cast in more than all   4955
Reward. Liberal soul shall be made fat   4956
Return. Give, and it shall be given unto you   4957
Royal. Every one a loaf..flesh..wine   4958
Ungrudging. Thine heart shall not be grieved   4960

5168. MAJESTY, Overcoming. *In Gethsemane.* [4] Whom seek ye? [5] They answered him, Jesus of Nazareth. Jesus saith unto them, I am *he*. And Judas..stood with them. [6] As soon then as he had said unto them, I am *he*, they went backward, and fell to the ground.—John, ch. 18.

5169. —— Royal. *Solomon.* [4] When the queen of Sheba had seen all Solomon's wisdom, and the house that he had built, [5] And the meat of his table, and the sitting of his servants, and the attendance of his ministers, and their apparel, and his cupbearers, and his ascent by which he went up unto the house of the Lord; there was no more spirit in her.—1 Kings, ch. 10.

5170. —— Terrific. *Sinai.* [18] Ye are not come unto the mount that might be touched, and that burned with fire, nor unto blackness, and darkness, and tempest, [19] And the sound of a trumpet, and the voice of words; which *voice* they..entreated that the word should not be spoken to them any more.—Heb., ch. 12.

See other illustrations under:

AWE.

Alarming. We shall surely die..have seen G.   603
Painful. Alas..I have seen an angel   604

LIGHTNING.

Alarm. Entreat the L. ..no more mighty t.   5046
Destruction. Fire of G. is fallen..burned up the s.   5047
Terrific. Fire ran along upon the ground   5048
     "   Thunders and lightnings and a thick cloud 5049

Glory of God. There shined about him a light from   3559
     "   Moses was not able to enter..t.   3560
     "   Priests could not stand to minister   3561
     "   Heavens declare the glory of God   3562
     "   Under his feet..paved work of a   3563
     "   While my glory passeth by..cover   3564
     "   Tabernacle..cloud covered it and   3565

5171. MAJORITY with God. *Against Syrians.*
[15] Alas, my master! how shall we do? [16] And he answered, Fear not: for they that *be* with us *are* more than they *be* with them. [17] And Elisha prayed..And the Lord opened the eyes of the young man; and he saw: and, behold, the mountain *was* full of horses and chariots of fire round about Elisha.—2 Kings, ch. 6.

5172. MAJORITIES, Fearless of. *Battle.*
When thou goest out to battle against thine enemies, and seest horses, and chariots, *and* a people more than thou, be not afraid of them: for the Lord thy God *is* with thee.—Deut., ch. 20.

See other illustrations under:

NUMBERS.

Danger. Lest I. vaunt..my own hand saved me	5744
Despised. Jonathan said unto his armourbearer	5745
Disparity. I. like two little flocks of kids	5746
" L. it is nothing with thee, whether with	5747
Invisible. Mountain was full of horses..fire	5748
Pride. David's heart smote him after he had n.	5749

ONE.

Care. Martha was cumbered..Mary..one thing	5883
for God. Moses stood..Who is on the Lord's side?	5884
with God. I, even I only..Baal's prophets 450 men	5885
" I come to thee in the name of the L. of	5886
vs. 1000. Samson..slew a thousand men	5887
Power of. [Evil] Sheba hath lifted up his hand	5888
Victory. Shamgar slew 600..delivered I.	5889

5173. MALFORMATION, Physical. *Giant.*
[20] A battle in Gath, where was a man of *great* stature, that had on every hand six fingers, and on every foot six toes.—2 Sam., ch. 21.

5174. MALIGNANCY, Scornful. *Haman.*
[5] Saw that Mordecai bowed not..then was Haman full of wrath. [6] And he thought scorn to lay hands on Mordecai alone..wherefore Haman sought to destroy all the Jews that *were* throughout the whole kingdom of Ahasuerus.—Esther, ch. 3.

5175. MALICE, Pharisaic. *At Capernaum.*
[10] Stretch forth thy hand. And he did so: and his hand was restored whole as the other. [11] And they were filled with madness; and communed one with another what they might do to Jesus.—Luke, ch. 6.

See other illustrations under:

Accusation. [Samaritans] wrote him..against Judah 83
Shameless. Soldiers..spit in his face and buffeted 1628

See ENEMIES and references.

5176. MAN like Beast. *"One Breath."*
[19] That which befalleth the sons of men befalleth beasts; even one thing befalleth them: as the one dieth, so dieth the other; yea, they have all one breath; so that a man hath no preeminence above a beast.—Eccl., ch. 3.

5177. —— **above Cattle.** *Companion.* [20] Adam gave names to all cattle, and to the fowl of the air, and to every beast of the field; but for Adam there was not found a help meet for him.—Gen., ch. 2.

5178. —— **Care for.** *"Ravens."* [24] Consider the ravens: for they neither sow nor reap; which neither have storehouse nor barn; and God feedeth them: how much more are ye better than the fowls?—Luke, ch. 12.

5179. —— **chosen.** *God rejected.* [6] The thing displeased Samuel, when they said, Give us a king to judge us.. [7] And the Lord said unto Samuel, Hearken unto the voice of the people ..for they have not rejected thee, but they have rejected me, that I should not reign over them. —1 Sam., ch. 8.

5180. —— **Dignity of.** *"Little lower than Angels."* [4] What is man, that thou art mindful of him? and the son of man, that thou visitest him? [5] For thou hast made him a little lower than the angels, and hast crowned him with glory and honour.—Ps. 8.

5181. —— **Depreciation of.** *Gadarenes.*
[16] They that saw it told them how it befell to him that was possessed with the devil, and also concerning the swine. [17] And they began to pray him to depart out of their coasts.—Mark, ch. 5.

5182. —— **Dominion of.** *Creation.* [28] God said unto them..and have dominion over the fish of the sea, and over the fowl of the air, and over every living thing that moveth upon the earth. —Gen., ch. 1.

5183. —— —— *After Flood.* [2] The dread of you shall be upon every beast of the earth, and upon every fowl of the air, upon all that moveth *upon* the earth, and upon all the fishes of the sea; into your hand are they delivered.—Gen., ch. 9.

5184. —— —— *Qualification.* [6] Thou madest him to have dominion over the works of thy hands; thou hast put all *things* under his feet: [7] All sheep and oxen, yea, and the beasts of the field; [8] The fowl of the air, and the fish of the sea, *and* whatsoever passeth through the paths of the seas.—Ps. 8.

5185. —— **Divine Extraction of.** *"Son of God."* [38] Which was *the* son of Enos, which was *the* son of Seth, which was *the* son of Adam, which was *the* son of God.—Luke, ch. 3.

5186. —— **Esteem for.** *Healing.* [11] What man..shall have one sheep, and if it fall into a pit on the sabbath day, will he not lay hold on it, and lift *it* out? [12] How much then is a man better than a sheep?—Mark, ch. 3.

5187. —— **A tall.** *Saul.* [2] Saul, a choice young man, and a goodly: and *there was* not..a goodlier person than he: from his shoulders and upward he *was* higher than any of the people.—1 Sam., ch. 9.

5188. —— **A lawless.** *Ishmael.* [12] He will be a wild man; his hand *will be* against every man, and every man's hand against him.—Gen., ch. 16.

5189. —— **A little.** *Zaccheus.* [2] Zaccheus, which was the chief among the publicans, and he was rich. [3] And he sought to see Jesus who he was; and could not for the press, because he was little of stature.—Luke, ch. 19.

5190. —— **Mortality of.** *"So dieth."* [See No. 5176.]

5191. —— **The model.** *Godly.* [1] Lord, who shall abide in thy tabernacle? who shall dwell in thy holy hill? [2] He that walketh uprightly, and worketh righteousness, and speaketh the truth in his heart. [See 15th Psalm in full.]

5192. —— **Origin of.** *Adam—Eve.* [7] The Lord God formed man *of* the dust of the ground, and breathed into his nostrils the breath of life; and man became a living soul. [18] And the Lord ..*It is* not good that the man should be alone;

I will make him a help meet for him. ^{21} And.. caused a deep sleep to fall upon Adam..and he took one of his ribs, and closed up the flesh instead thereof. ^{22} And the rib..made he a woman. —GEN., ch. 2.

5193. —— **for Society.** *Creation.* [See No. 5192.]

5194. —— **Superiority of.** *" Upward."* ^{20} All go unto one place ; all are of the dust, and all turn to dust again. ^{21} Who knoweth the spirit of man that goeth upward, and the spirit of the beast that goeth downward to the earth ?—ECCL., ch. 3.

5195. —— **A sincere.** *Nathanael.* ^{47} Jesus saw Nathanael coming to him, and saith of him, Behold an Israelite indeed, in whom is no guile ! —JOHN, ch. 1.

5196. —— **A spotless.** *Job.* ^{8} The Lord said unto Satan, Hast thou considered my servant Job, that *there is* none like him in the earth, a perfect and an upright man, one that feareth God, and escheweth evil ?—JOB, ch. 1.

5197. —— **Trust in.** *" Cursed."* ^{5} Saith the Lord ; Cursed *be* the man that trusteth in man, and maketh flesh his arm, and whose heart departeth from the Lord.—JER., ch. 17.

5198. —— **An unfaithful.** *Proverb.* ^{19} Confidence in an unfaithful man in time of trouble *is like* a broken tooth, and a foot out of joint.— PROV., ch. 25.

See other illustrations under :

CITIZEN.
Christian. Walketh uprightly and speaketh the t. 1320
Law-abiding. The powers that be are ordained of G. 1319

Nobility of. I should not call any man common 1055
See MEN.

5199. MANHOOD aroused. *Ahab's.* [See No. 5202]. ^{6} My servants..shall search thine house, and the houses of thy servants ; and.. whatsoever is pleasant in thine eyes, they shall.. take *it* away.. ^{9} Wherefore he said unto the messengers of Ben-hadad, Tell my lord the king, All that thou didst send for to thy servant at the first I will do : but this thing I may not do. —1 KINGS, ch. 20.

5200. —— **Lost.** *Haman.* ^{13} The letters were sent by posts into all the king's provinces ..to cause to perish, all Jews, both young and old, little children and women, in one day. ^{15}..And the king and Haman sat down to drink. —ESTHER, ch. 3.

5201. —— **Responsibility of.** *" Of Age."* ^{20} His parents answered..We know that this is our son, and that he was born blind : ^{21} But by what means he now seeth, we know not ; or who hath opened his eyes, we know not : he is of age ; ask him : he shall speak for himself.— JOHN, ch. 9.

5202. —— **wanting.** *To Ahab.* ^{2} Thus saith Ben-hadad, ^{3} Thy silver and thy gold *is* mine ; thy wives also and thy children, *even* the goodliest, *are* mine. ^{4} And the king of Israel answered and said, My lord, O king, according to thy saying, I *am* thine, and all that I have.— 1 KINGS, ch. 20.

See other illustrations under :

COURAGE.
Age. [Caleb, 85 years] Give me this mt..Anakim 1769
Absent. 3000 men..said to Samson..may deliver 1770

Daring. Paul would have entered..suffered him 1771
Faith. L. that delivered me..lion..this Philistine 1772
Ground. With him..arm of flesh, but with us..Lord 1773
Honouring. Let us go up at once and possess it 1774
Invincible. Not any..able to stand before thee 1775
Lost. Men of I. fled..forsook the cities 1776
Moral. Jesus went before them..amazed 1777
" I am ready..bound and also to die 1778
Necessary. Be strong and of good courage 1779
Patriotic. Fight for your brethren, sons, wives 1780
Rebuke. I said unto Peter before them all 1781
Reformer's. Should such a man as I flee ? 1782
Stimulated. Put your feet..necks of these kings 1783
Soldier's. Jonathan climbed up..hands and feet 1784
Worship. Daniel knew..writing was signed 1785

HEROISM.
Christian. Bonds..abide me..none of these things 3959
Needless. Three mighty men brake through..well 3961
Numbers. Shamgar slew 600 with an ox goad 3962
Patriotic. Jael..smote the nail into his..temples 3957
" Woman cast a stone upon Abimelech 3958
See CHARACTER.

5203. MANAGEMENT, Bad. *Tower.* ^{28} Which of you, intending to build a tower, sitteth not down first, and counteth the cost, whether he have *sufficient* to finish *it* ? ^{29} Lest haply, after he hath laid the foundation, and is not able to finish *it*, all that behold *it* begin to mock him, ^{30} Saying, This man began to build, and was not able to finish.—LUKE, ch. 14.

5204. —— **Skilful.** *Miriam said,* ^{7} Shall I go and call to thee a nurse of the Hebrew women, that she may nurse the child for thee ? ^{8} And Pharaoh's daughter said to her, Go. And the maid went and called the child's mother.—EX., ch. 2.

See other illustrations under :

PRUDENCE.
Age. Wherefore should..be yet a burden 6774
Commended. Lord commended the unjust steward 6775
Example. Render unto Cesar..they marvelled 6776
Preservation. Hold..lest angry fellows..lose thy 6777
" Joseph hearkened not..or be with 6778
Resolutions. Intending to build..not able to finish 6779
See GOVERNMENT and references.

5205. MANIFESTATION of Jesus. *Within.* ^{22} Lord, how is it that thou wilt manifest thyself unto us, and not unto the world ? ^{23} Jesus answered..If a man love me, he will keep my words : and my Father will love him, and we will come unto him, and make our abode with him.—JOHN, ch. 14.

5206. —— **of Piety.** *Abraham.* ^{16} Because thou..hast not withheld thy son, thine only *son*, ^{17} That in blessing I will bless thee, and in multiplying I will multiply thy seed as the stars of the heaven.—GEN., ch. 22.

See other illustrations under :

APPEARANCES.
Conceal. Joseph made himself strange unto them 474
Evil. Lest we should offend..take up a fish 475
False. Walk in long robes, and love greetings 476
Hurtful. Be emboldened to eat those things 477
Uncertain. Man looketh on the outward 478

Beauty. Bring Vashti to show..her beauty 2801
Grandeur. Ahasuerus..made a feast..white, green 2409
Pretence. Devour widows' houses..for pretence..p. 6548
See HYPOCRISY.

5207. MANNERS, Instruction in. *Modesty.*
[10] Go and sit down in the lowest room ; that when he that bade thee cometh, he may say unto thee, Friend, go up higher : then shalt thou have worship in the presence of them that sit at meat with thee.—LUKE, ch. 14.

5208. —— Polite. *Athenians.* [19] May we know what this new doctrine, whereof thou speakest, *is ?* [20] For thou bringest certain strange things to our ears : we would know therefore what these things mean.—ACTS, ch. 17.

5209. —— Rude. *Athenians.* [18] What will this babbler say? other some, He seemeth to be a setter forth of strange gods : because he preached unto them Jesus, and the resurrection. —ACTS, ch. 17.

See other illustrations under :

CUSTOMS.

Attachment. Heard..change the customs which M. 1894
National. Israel eat not of the sinew..unto this d. 1895
Observance. Must not be so done in our country 1896

HABIT.

Differs. Animals..darkness..wherein all beasts 3671
Prayer. Cornelius..prayed to G. always 3672
   "   Daniel..three times a day prayed 3673
   "   Evening, morning, *and noon will* I cry 3674
Worship. By river side, where prayer was wont 6395
   "   Offered burnt offerings..continually 6367
   "   As his custom was, Jesus went into the 9873
   "   Daniel prayed and gave thanks..as 8766

MODESTY.

Endangered. Saul a choice young man 5497
Enjoined. Sit not down in the highest room 5498
Ministerial. I have need..baptized of thee 5499
Preserved. Am not I..of the smallest..tribes 5500
Punished. Vashti came no more before the king 5501
Womanly. Queen Vashti refused to come 5502

POLITENESS.

Cultivated. May we know what this new doctrine 6232
Inculcated. Sit down in the lowest room 6233
Tender. Is your father well, the old man of whom 6234
Treacherous. Joab took Amasa..to kiss him 6235

Deception. Joseph made himself strange..spake r. 474

5210. MANSIONS, Heavenly. *"Many."* [2] In my father's house are many mansions..I go to prepare a place for you. [3] And if I go and prepare a place for you, I will come again, and receive you unto myself ; that where I am, *there* ye may be also.—JOHN, ch. 14.

5211. MANSLAUGHTER, Accidental. *Law.* [See Num., 35 : 9–29.]

5212. —— Defensive. *Of Asahel.* [22] Abner said again to Asahel, Turn thee aside from following me : wherefore should I smite thee to the ground?..[23] Howbeit he refused to turn aside : wherefore Abner with the hinder end of the spear smote him under the fifth *rib.*—2 SAM., ch. 2.

5213. —— Justifiable. *Thief.* [2] If a thief be found breaking up, and be smitten that he die, *there shall* no blood *be shed* for him. [3] If the sun be risen upon him, *there shall be* blood *shed* for him.—EX., ch. 22.

5214. —— Pardonable. *Accident.* [5] When a man goeth into the wood..and his hand fetcheth a stroke with the axe to cut down the tree, and the head slippeth from the helve, and

lighteth upon his neighbour, that he die ; he shall flee unto one of those cities, and live.— DEUT., ch. 19.

5215. —— Solicited. *Saul said,* [9] Stand, I pray thee, upon me, and slay me : for anguish is come upon me, because my life *is* yet whole in me. [10] So I..slew him, because I was sure that he could not live.—2 SAM., ch. 1.

5216. —— Unjustifiable. *"Sun risen."* [See No. 5213.]

See MURDER and references.

5217. MARINERS, Distress of the. *Storm.* [23] They that go down to the sea in ships, that do business in great waters ; [24] These see the works of the Lord..[25] For he commandeth, and raiseth the stormy wind, which lifteth up the waves thereof. [26] They mount up to the heaven, they go down again to the depths : their soul is melted because of trouble.—Ps. 107.

—— Mourning of. *Babylon.* [17] And every shipmaster, and all the company in ships, and sailors, and as many as trade by sea, stood afar off, [18] And cried when they saw the smoke of her burning, saying, What *city is* like unto this great city ! [19] And they cast dust on their heads, and cried, weeping and wailing, saying, Alas, alas, that great city, wherein were made rich all that had ships in the sea by reason of her costliness ! for in one hour is she made desolate.—REV., ch. 18.

5218. —— Deliverance of. *Prayer.* [27] They reel to and fro, and stagger like a drunken man, and are at their wit's end. [28] Then they cry unto the Lord in their trouble, and he bringeth them out of their distresses.—Ps. 107.

See other illustrations under :

SHIPWRECK.

Perils by. Thrice I suffered shipwreck [Paul] 7839
Saved in. Some on boards, and some on broken 7840

Helpless. When the ship was caught..let her drive 8411
Navy. Solomon made a navy of ships..shipmen 5689
Needed. Except these abide in the ship..not be s. 5329
Prayer. Master, Master, we perish 7631

5219. MARRIAGE, Forbidden. *By Apostates.* [1] The Spirit speaketh expressly, that in the latter times some shall depart from the faith, giving heed to seducing spirits, and doctrines of devils ; [3] Forbidding to marry.—1 TIM., ch. 4.

5220. —— Feast at. *Cana.* [See John, ch. 2.]

5221. —— A good. *Ruth.* [13] So Boaz took Ruth, and she was his wife..and she bare a son.. [17] ..and they called his name Obed : he *is* the father of Jesse, the father of David.—RUTH, ch. 4. [She was a Moabitess, reared an idolater.]

5222. —— An ill-mated. *Abigail.* [3] The man *was* Nabal, and..his wife Abigail ; and *she was* a woman of good understanding, and of a beautiful countenance : but the man *was* churlish and evil in his doings.—1 SAM., ch. 25.

5223. —— An incestuous. *Herod.* [17] Laid hold upon John, and bound him in prison for Herodias' sake, his brother Philip's wife ; for he had married her. [18] For John had said unto Herod, It is not lawful for thee to have thy brother's wife.—MARK, ch. 6.

5224. —— for Life. *Jesus said,* [5] For this cause shall a man leave father and mother, and shall cleave to his wife : and they twain shall be one flesh ? ⁶..What therefore God hâth joined together, let not man put asunder.—MAT., ch. 19.

5225. —— **A mixed.** *Joseph.* ⁴⁵ Pharaoh.. gave him to wife Asenath the daughter of Potipherah priest of On.—GEN., ch. 47.

5226. —— **Needful.** *In Paradise.* ⁸ The Lord God planted a garden eastward in Eden ; and there he put the man whom he had formed. ¹⁸ And..said, *It is* not good that the man should be alone ; I will make him a help meet for him. —GEN., ch. 2.

5227. —— **A near.** *Half-sister.* [To king Abimelech,] ¹¹ Abraham said, Because I thought ..they will slay me for my wife's sake. ¹² And yet indeed *she is* my sister ; she *is* the daughter of my father, but not the daughter of my mother. —GEN., ch. 20.

5228. —— **Protection by.** *Lot's Sons.* ¹² The men said unto Lot, Hast thou here any besides ? son in law..bring *them* out of this place : ¹³ For we will destroy this place.—GEN., ch. 19.

5229. —— **Ruined by.** *S a m s o n .* ¹⁵ How canst thou say, I love thee, when thine heart *is* not with me ? Thou hast mocked me these three times, and hast not told me wherein thy great strength *lieth.* ¹⁶..when she pressed him daily with her words, and urged him, *so* that his soul was vexed unto death ; ¹⁷..He told her all his heart.—JUDGES, ch. 16.

5230. —— **resented.** *Relatives.* ¹ Miriam and Aaron spake against Moses because of the Ethiopian woman whom he had married.—NUM., ch. 12.

5231. —— **A sinful.** *Ahab.* ³¹ As if it had been a light thing for him to walk in the sins of Jeroboam..he took to wife Jezebel the daughter of Ethbaal king of the Zidonians, and went and served Baal.—1 KINGS, ch. 16.

5232. —— **Trouble from.** *Rebekah.* ⁴⁶ Rebekah said to Isaac, I am weary of my life because of the daughters of Heth : if Jacob take a wife of the daughters of Heth, such as these *which are* of the daughters of the land, what good shall my life do me ?—GEN., ch. 27.

5233. —— **Undesirable.** *Paul.* ⁸ I say therefore to the unmarried and widows, It is good for them if they abide even as I. ²⁶ I suppose therefore that this is good for the present distress.— 1 COR., ch. 7.

5234. —— **An unequal.** *Moses.* ²¹ Moses was content to dwell with the man : and he gave Moses Zipporah his daughter.—EX., ch. 2.

5235. —— **An unsought.** *David's.* ²³ Saul's servants spake those words..And David said, Seemeth it to you a light thing to be a king's son in law, seeing that I *am* a poor man, and lightly esteemed ?—1 SAM., ch. 18.

5236. —— **Without.** *In Heaven.* ²⁹ Ye do err, not knowing the Scriptures, nor the power of God. ³⁰ For in the resurrection they neither marry, nor are given in marriage, but are as the angels of God.—MAT., ch. 22.

5237. MARRIAGES, Broken. *Jews.* ³ Let us make a covenant with our God to put away all the wives, and such as are born of them, according to the counsel of my lord, and of those that tremble at the commandment of our God ; and let it be done according to the law.—EZRA, ch. 10.

5238. —— **Corrupting.** *" Sons of God."*

¹ When men began to multiply on the face of the earth.. ²..the sons of God saw the daughters of men that they *were* fair ; and they took them wives.. ³ And the Lord said, My Spirit shall not always strive with man.—GEN., ch. 6.

5239. —— **Irreligious.** *Canaanites.* ³ Neither shalt thou make marriages with them.. ⁴ For they will turn away thy son from following me, that they may serve other gods : so will the anger of the Lord be kindled against you, and destroy thee suddenly.—DEUT., ch..7.

5240. —— —— *M i x e d .* . ¹ The people of Israel, and the priests, and the Levites, have not separated themselves from the people of the lands.. ² For they have taken of their daughters for themselves, and for their sons : so that the holy seed have mingled themselves with the people of *those* lands.—EZRA, ch. 9.

5241. —— **Prosperity by.** *Unmixed.* ¹² Give not your daughters unto their sons, neither take their daughters unto your sons, nor seek their peace or their wealth for ever : that ye may be strong, and eat the good of the land, and leave *it* for an inheritance to your children for ever. —EZRA, ch. 9.

5242. —— **rebuked.** *Irreligious.* ²³ Saw I Jews *that* had married wives of Ashdod, of Ammon, *and* of Moab : ²⁴ And their children spake half in the speech of Ashdod, and could not speak in the Jews' language, but according to the language of each people. ²⁵ And I contended with them, and cursed.—NEH., ch. 13.

5243. —— **Rape.** *B e n j a m i t e s .* ²¹ If the daughters of Shiloh come out to dance in dances, then come ye out of the vineyards, and catch you every man his wife of the daughters.— JUDGES, ch. 21. [They did so.]

5244. —— **Unwise.** *Solomon.* ³ Solomon he had seven hundred wives, princesses, and three hundred concubines : and his wives turned away his heart. ⁴..when Solomon was old.. after other gods.—1 KINGS, ch. 11.

5245. MARRIED, Privilege of the. *L a w .* ⁵ When a man hath taken a new wife, he shall not go out to war, neither shall he be charged with any business : *but* he shall be free at home one year, and shall cheer up his wife.—DEUT., ch. 24.

See other illustrations under :

5246. MARTYR, A brave. *John.* [18] John had said unto Herod, It is not lawful for thee to have thy brother's wife.. [27]..the king sent an executioner..and he went and beheaded him in the prison.—Mar[.], ch. 6.

5247. —— The first. *Abel.* [4] Abel, he also brought of the firstlings of his flock..And the Lord had respect unto Abel and to his offering : [5] But unto Cain and to his offering he had not respect. And Cain was very wroth.. [8] And Cain talked with Abel his brother : and..when they were in the field..Cain..slew him.—Gen., ch. 4.

5248. —— The saintly. *Stephen.* [59] They stoned Stephen, calling upon *God*, and saying, Lord Jesus, receive my spirit. [60] And he kneeled down, and cried with a loud voice, Lord, lay not this sin to their charge.—Acts, ch. 7.

See PERSECUTION.

5249. MASSACRE, An intended. *Haman's.* [13] The letters were sent by posts into all the king's provinces, to destroy, to kill, and to cause to perish all Jews, both young and old, little children and women in one day..and *to take* the spoil of them for a prey.—Esther, ch. 3.

5250. —— of Infants. *Herod's.* [16] Herod, when he saw that he was mocked of the wise men, was exceeding wroth..and slew all the children that were in Bethlehem, and in all the coasts thereof, from two years old and under.—Mat., ch. 2.

5251. —— A treacherous. *Of Baalites.* [20] Jehu said, Proclaim a solemn assembly for Baal.. [25] And..as soon as he had made an end of offering the burnt offering, that Jehu said.. to the captains, Go in, *and* slay them ; let none come forth.—2 Kings, ch. 10.

See MURDER and references.

5252. MASSES, Bible for the. *Stones.* [4] When ye be gone over Jordan..ye shall set up these stones..in mount Ebal, and thou shalt plaster them with plaster.. [8] And thou shalt write upon the stones all the words of this law very plainly. —Deut., ch. 27.

5253. —— The neglected. *Jesus Moved.* [33] The people saw them departing..and ran afoot thither out of all cities, and outwent them, and came together unto him. [34] And Jesus..was moved with compassion toward them, because they were as sheep not having a shepherd : and he began to teach.—Mark, ch. 6.

See other illustrations under :

ASSEMBLY.

MOB.

POPULARITY.

PEOPLE.

5254. MATERIALISTS, Jewish. *Sadducees.* [8] The Sadducees say that there is no resurrection, neither angel, nor spirit.—Acts, ch. 23:

5255. MEANS for Defence. *Hezekiah.* [4] Stopped all the fountains, and the brook that ran through the midst of the land, saying, Why should the kings of Assyria come, and find much water ? [5] And he strengthened himself, and built up all the wall that was broken, and raised *it* up to the towers, and another wall without, and repaired Millo..and made darts and shields in abundance.—2 Chron., ch. 32.

5256. —— Escape by any. *Paul.* [24] And they watched the gates day and night to kill him. [25] Then the disciples took him by night, and let *him* down by the wall in a basket.—Acts, ch. 9.

5257. —— Heroic. *Shipwreck.* [30] As the shipmen were about to flee..they had let down the boat into the sea, under colour as though they would have cast anchors out of the foreship. [31] Paul said to the centurion and to the soldiers, Except these abide in the ship, ye cannot be saved. [32] Then the soldiers cut off the ropes of the boat, and let her fall off.—Acts, ch. 27.

5258. —— Ingenious. *Ark.* [3] When she could not longer hide him, she took for him an ark of bulrushes, and daubed it with slime and with pitch, and put the child therein ; and she laid *it* in the flags by the river's brink. [4] And his sister stood afar off.—Ex., ch. 2.

5259. —— Insignificant. *Blind Men.* [28] Believe ye that I am able to do this ? They said unto him, Yea, Lord. [29] Then touched he their eyes, saying, According to your faith be it unto you. [30] And their eyes were opened.—Mat., ch. 9.

5260. —— not neglected. *Hezekiah.* [6] I will add unto thy days fifteen years ; and I will deliver thee and this city.. [7] And Isaiah said, Take a lump of figs. And they..laid *it* on the boil, and he recovered.—2 Kings, ch. 20.

5261. —— with Prayer. *Samaritans* [8] Conspired all of them together to come *and* to fight against Jerusalem, and to hinder it. [9] Nevertheless we made our prayer unto our God, and set a watch against them day and night.—Neh., ch. 4.

5262. —— **Prudential.** *Jesus.* [1] After these things Jesus walked in Galilee : for he would not walk in Jewry, because the Jews sought to kill him.—JOHN, ch. 7.

5263. —— **Strange.** *Prayer.* [9] Moses said unto Joshua..to morrow I will stand on the top of the hill with the rod of God in mine hand. [11]..when Moses held up his hand..Israel prevailed : and when he let down his hand, Amalek prevailed.—EX., ch. 17.

5264. —— —— *At Jericho.* [20] When the people heard the sound of the trumpet, and the people shouted with a great shout..the wall fell down flat, so that..every man straight before him, and they took the city.—JOSHUA, ch. 6.

5265. —— **Use of.** *Joseph to the Butler.* [14] Think on me when it shall be well with thee.. and make mention of me unto Pharaoh, and bring me out of this house : [15] For indeed..have I done nothing that they should put me into the dungeon.—GEN., ch. 40.

5266. —— **Unworthy.** *Flight.* [2] Jezebel sent a messenger unto Elijah, saying, So let the gods do *to me*, and more also, if I make not thy life as the life of one of them by to morrow about this time. [3]..he arose, and went for his life.—1 KINGS, ch. 19.

See other illustrations under :

AGENCY.

Boastful. Axe boast..against him that heweth? 251
Indirect. I have occasioned the death of all 252
Seeming. Tree..cast into the waters..made sweet 253
Strange. Clay of the spittle..anointed the eyes 254
Twofold. Ark of bulrushes..Pharaoh's daughter c. 255

INSTRUMENT.

Disdained. Eliab..anger was kindled..left the 4552
Destroying. Waters returned..covered the host 4553
Feeble. Syrians to hear the noise of chariots 4560
Gods. Angel said..call for Peter..he shall tell 4561
Insignificant. Samson..jaw bone of an ass 4555
" David prevailed over the Philistine 4562
Only. Why marvel..as though by our own power 4563
Quality. Philistines..fell before Jonathan 4564
Simple. When he beheld the serpent of brass he 4556
Saving. Red sea..waters were a wall unto them 4557
Sinful. We believe, not because of thy saying 4558
Strange. L. prepared a great fish to swallow Jonah 4559
Weak. [Plagues] frogs..flies..lice..hail 4565
Waiting. Then fled Moses..land of Madian 4566

5267. MEASURE of Benevolence. *"Two Mites."* [43] This poor widow hath cast more in, than all they which have cast into the treasury : [44] For all *they* did cast in of their abundance ; but she of her want did cast in all..all her living.—MARK, ch. 12.

5268. MECHANIC, An apostolical. *Paul.* [2] Found a certain Jew named Aquila..with his wife Priscilla.. [3] And because he was of the same craft, he abode with them, and wrought : (for by their occupation they were tentmakers.) —ACTS, ch. 18.

5269. —— **A divine.** *Jesus.* [3] Is not this the carpenter, the son of Mary .. of James, and Joses, and of Judas, and Simon? and are not his sisters here with us? And they were offended at him.—MARK, ch. 6.

5270. —— **A distinguished.** *Hiram.* [14] He *was* a widow's son..and his father *was* a man of Tyre, a worker in brass : and he was filled with wisdom, and understanding, and cunning to work all works in brass. And he came to king Solomon, and wrought all his work.—1 KINGS, ch. 7.

5271. —— **The first.** *Jubal.* [21] Jubal..was the father of all such as handle the harp and organ. [22] And..Tubalcain, an instructor of every artificer in brass and iron.—GEN., ch. 4.

5272. —— **An independent.** *Paul.* [8] Neither did we eat any man's bread for nought ; but wrought with labour and travail night and day, that we might not be chargeable to any of you : [9] Not because we have not power, but to make ourselves an ensample.—2 THESS., ch. 3.

5273. —— **Opposition of a.** *Alexander.* [14] Alexander the coppersmith did me much evil.. [15] Of whom be thou ware also ; for he hath greatly withstood our words.—2 TIM., ch. 4.

5274. MECHANICS enraged. *At Ephesus.* [24] Demetrius, a silversmith, which made silver shrines for Diana, brought no small gain unto the craftsmen ; [25] Whom he called together with the workmen of like occupation, and said, Sirs, ye know that by this craft we have our wealth.. [28] And when they heard *these sayings*, they were full of wrath, and cried out, saying, Great *is* Diana of the Ephesians.—ACTS, ch. 19.

5275. —— **Slaves for.** *Israelites.* [14] They made their lives bitter with hard bondage, in mortar, and in brick, and in all manner of service in the field : all their service..*was* with rigour,—EX., ch. 1.

5276. —— **Superior.** *Sidonians.* [6] Solomon said, Hew me cedar trees out of Lebanon ; and my servants shall be with thy servants..for thou knowest that *there is* not among us any that can skill to hew timber like unto the Sidonians.—1 KINGS, ch. 5.

5277. —— **Without.** *Israelites.* [19] There was no smith found throughout all the land of Israel : for the Philistines said, Lest the Hebrews make *them* swords or spears : [20] But all.. went down to the Philistines, to sharpen every man his share, and his coulter, and his axe, and his mattock.—1 SAM., ch. 13.

See other illustrations under :

BUILDER.

Jothan. Built cities in the mountains..castles and 953
Unsuccessful. Laid the foundation..not able 954
Visionary. I will pull down my barns and build 955

BUILDERS.

Joyful. Walls completed..wives and children r. 956
" [Temple] Ancient men..wept..many s. 957
Stupendous. [Babel] Tower whose top may reach 959
Volunteer. [Temple] Who is there..let him go up 958

BUILDING.

Glorious. [Temple] Solomon built..cedar..gold 960
Hindered. People of the land..weakened the hands 961
Necessitated. Jerusalem..waste..gates burned 962
Outgrown. Elisha..the place..dwell..too strait 963
Prevented. Confound their language..left off to 964
Prohibited. [Rechabites] Neither..build house 965
Revival after. Ezra had prayed..people wept..very 966
Spiritual. Built upon the foundation..corner-stone 967

5278. MEDDLER, A foolish. *Proverb.* [17] He that passeth by, *and* meddleth with strife *belonging* not to him, *is like* one that taketh a dog by the ears.—PROV., ch. 26.

See other illustrations under :

Intercessor. Wherefore do ye Moses and A. let the 4626
Strange. Friends went out..He is beside himself   4627
Officious. Disciples rebuked those that brought t.   5872
      "   Gehazi came near to thrust her away   5873

5279. MEDIATOR, A diplomatic. *Blastus.*
[20] Herod was highly displeased with them of
Tyre and Sidon : but they came with one accord to him, and having made Blastus the king's
chamberlain their friend, desired peace ; because their country was nourished by the king's
country.—ACTS, ch. 12.

5280. —— A female. *Woman of Abel.* [21] A
man of mount Ephraim, Sheba..hath lifted up
his hand against..David : deliver him only,
and I will depart from the city. And the woman said unto Joab, Behold, his head shall be
thrown to thee over the wall.—2 SAM., ch. 20.

5281. —— The great. *Jesus.* [15] He is the
mediator of the new testament, that by means
of death, for the redemption of the transgressions *that were* under the first testament, they
which are called might receive the promise of
eternal inheritance.—HEB., ch. 9.

5282. —— The present. *Jesus.* [24] Christ is
not entered into the holy places made with
hands, *which are* the figures of the true ; but
into heaven itself, now to appear in the presence
of God for us.—HEB., ch. 9.

5283. —— required. *Benjamin.* [3] Judah
spake..The man did solemnly protest unto us,
saying, Ye shall not see my face, except your
brother be with you.—GEN., ch. 43.

5284. —— wanted, A. *At Sinai.* [18] All the
people saw the thunderings, and the lightnings,
and the noise of the trumpet, and the mountain
smoking : and..they moved, and stood afar off.
[19] And they said unto Moses, Speak thou with
us, and we will hear : but let not God speak
with us, lest we die.—EX., ch. 20.

5285. MEDIATION, A double. *Moses and
Aaron.* [1] I have made thee a god to Pharaoh ;
and Aaron thy brother shall be thy prophet.
[2] Thou shalt speak all that I command thee ;
and Aaron thy brother shall speak unto Pharaoh, that he send the children of Israel out of
his land.—EX., ch. 7.

5286. —— Effectual. *Rebellion of Korah.*
[47] Aaron..ran into the midst of the congregation ; and, behold, the plague was begun among
the people : and he put on incense, and made
an atonement for the people. [48] And he stood
between the dead and the living ; and the
plague was stayed.—NUM., ch. 16.

5287. —— of Moses. *At Sinai.* [7] Moses..
called for the elders of the people, and laid before their faces all these words which the Lord
commanded him. [8] And all the people answered together, and said, All that the Lord
hath spoken we will do. And Moses returned
the words of the people unto the Lord.—EX.,
ch. 19.

5288. —— of the Righteous. *To King Jehoram.* [14] Elisha said, As the Lord of hosts liveth,
before whom I stand, surely, were it not that I
regard the presence of Jehoshaphat the king of
Judah, I would not look toward thee, nor see
thee.—2 KINGS, ch. 3. [They were soon to fight
the Moabites.]

5289. —— for Transgressors. *Moses.* [The
golden calf was made.] [10] Now therefore let me
alone, that my wrath may wax hot against them,
and that I may consume them : and I will make
of thee a great nation. [11] And Moses besought
the Lord.. [14] And the Lord repented of the evil
which he thought to do unto his people.—EX.,
ch. 32.

See **INTERCESSION.**

5290. MEDITATION, Awakened by. *Peter.*
[72] And the second time the cock crew. And Peter
called to mind the word that Jesus said unto
him, Before the cock crow twice, thou shalt deny
me thrice. And when he thought thereon, he
wept.—MARK, ch. 14.

5291. —— Food for. *Word.* [16] Thy words
were found, and I did eat them ; and thy word
was unto me the joy and rejoicing of mine
heart : for I am called by thy name, O Lord
God of hosts.—JER., ch. 15.

5292. —— Hour of. *Isaac.* [63] Isaac went
out to meditate in the field at the eventide :
and he lifted up his eyes, and saw, and, behold,
the camels *were* coming.—JER., ch. 24.

5293. —— Habitual. *Godly.* [2] His delight
is in the law of the Lord ; and in his law doth
he meditate day and night. [3] And he shall be
like a tree planted by the rivers of water, that
bringeth forth his fruit in his season ; his leaf
also shall not wither ; and whatsoever he doeth
shall prosper.—PS. 1.

5294. —— Ill-timed. *Rich Fool.* [17] He
thought within himself, saying, What shall I do,
because I have no room where to bestow my
fruits?.. [20] But God said unto him, *Thou* fool,
this night thy soul shall be required of thee :
then whose shall those things be which thou
hast provided?—LUKE, ch. 12.

5295. —— Instruction by. *"Sheet."* [19] While
Peter thought on the vision, the Spirit said..
Behold, three men seek thee. [20] ..go with them,
doubting nothing : for I have sent them. [21] Then
Peter went down to the men which were sent..
from Cornelius.—ACTS, ch. 10.

5296. —— Love of. *David.* [97] O how love
I thy law! it *is* my meditation all the day..
[148] Mine eyes prevent the *night* watches, that I
might meditate in thy word.—PS. 119.

5297. —— Prayerful. *David.* [14] Let..the
meditation of my heart, be acceptable in thy
sight, O Lord.—PS. 19.

5298. —— Religious. *To Joshua.* [8] This
book of the law shall not depart out of thy
mouth ; but thou shalt meditate therein day
and night, that thou mayest observe to do according to all that is written therein : for then
thou shalt make thy way prosperous.—JOSH.,
ch. 1.

See other illustrations under :

FORETHOUGHT.

Necessary. Intending to build..first counteth the   3339
      "   Consulteth whether he be able with   3340
Useless. Which..with taking thought can add one 3341

REFLECTION.

Important. Whatsoever things are true..honest   6914
Painful. When Peter thought thereon, he wept   6915

THOUGHT.

Character. As he thinketh in his heart, so is he   8786
Evil. Every imagination of the thoughts..only evil 8787

Prompter. Take no thought..it shall be given 8788
Subject. Whatsoever things are pure..lovely 8789

THOUGHTFULNESS.

Enjoined. Virtue..praise..think on these things 8790
Timely. Cock crew..he thought thereon..wept 8791

5299. MEEKNESS in Adversity. *Hezekiah.* [6] Shall be carried to Babylon: nothing shall be left, saith the Lord. [7]..Thy sons..shall they take away; and they shall be eunuchs in the palace of the king of Babylon. [8] Then said Hezekiah to Isaiah, Good *is* the word of the Lord which thou hast spoken.—ISA., ch. 39.

5300. —— with Courage. *Jeremiah.* [14] As for me, behold, I *am* in your hand: do with me as seemeth good and meet unto you. [15] But know ye for certain, that if ye put me to death, ye shall surely bring innocent blood upon yourselves, and upon this city..for of a truth the Lord hath sent me unto you to speak all these words.—JER., ch. 26.

5301. —— Divine. *Jesus.* [23] Who, when he was reviled, reviled not again; when he suffered, he threatened not; but committed *himself* to him that judgeth righteously.—1 PETER, ch. 2.

5302. —— Forgiveness in. *Peter.* [21] Then came Peter to him, and said, Lord, how oft shall my brother sin against me, and I forgive him? till seven times? [22] Jesus saith unto him, I say not unto thee, Until seven times: but, Until seventy times seven.—MAT., ch. 18.

5303. —— Glory of. *"Acceptable to God."* [See No. 5304.] [20] For what glory *is it,* if when ye be buffeted for your faults, ye shall take it patiently? but if, when ye do well, and suffer *for it,* ye take it patiently, this *is* acceptable with God.—1 PETER, ch. 2.

5304. —— under Injury. *Servants.* [18] Servants, *be* subject to *your* masters with all fear; not only to the good and gentle, but also to the froward. [19] For this *is* thankworthy, if a man for conscience toward God endure grief, suffering wrongfully.—1 PETER, ch. 2.

5305. —— Model. *Jesus.* [35] The rulers also ..derided *him,* saying, He saved others; let him save himself, if he be Christ, the chosen of God. [36] And the soldiers also mocked him.—LUKE, ch. 23.

5306. —— A Martyr's. *Stephen.* [59] They stoned Stephen, calling upon *God,* and saying, Lord Jesus, receive my spirit. [60] And he kneeled down, and cried with a loud voice, Lord, lay not this sin to their charge.—ACTS, ch. 7.

5307. —— an Ornament. *Christian.* [3] Whose adorning, let in not be that outward *adorning* of plaiting the hair, and of wearing of gold, or.. apparel; [4] But *let it be* the hidden man of the heart..*even the ornament* of a meek and quiet spirit, which is in the sight of God of great price.—1 PETER, ch. 3.

5308. —— Provocation of. *Jews.* [18] They cried out all at once, saying, Away with this *man,* and release unto us Barabbas: [19] (Who for a certain sedition..and for murder, was cast into prison.)—LUKE, ch. 23.

5309. —— Remarkable. *Isaac.* [19] Isaac's servants digged in the valley, and found there a well of springing water. [20] And the herdmen of Gerar did strive with Isaac's herdmen, saying,

The water *is* ours.. [21] And they digged another well, and strove for that also.. [22] And he removed from thence, and digged.—GEN., ch. 26.

5310. —— required. *Jesus said,* [38] It hath been said, An eye for an eye, and a tooth for a tooth: [39] But I say unto you, That ye resist not evil: but whosoever shall smite thee on thy right cheek, turn to him the other also. [40] And if any man will sue thee at the law, and take away thy coat, let him have *thy* cloak also.—MAT., ch. 5.

5311. —— Royal. *David.* [David fled from Absalom.] [6] He cast stones at David, and at all the servants of king David..and all the mighty men *were* on his right hand and on his left. [7]..said Shimei when he cursed, Come out, come out, thou bloody man, and thou man of Belial.—2 SAM., ch. 16. [David did not resent it.]

5312. —— unprovoked. *Moses.* [1] Miriam and Aaron spake against Moses because of the Ethiopian woman whom he had married.. [2] And they said, Hath the Lord indeed spoken only by Moses? hath he not spoken also by us?.. [3] (Now the man Moses *was* very meek, above all the men which *were* upon the face of the earth.)—NUM., ch. 12.

5313. —— Want of. *Proverb.* [28] He that *hath* no rule over his own spirit *is like* a city *that is* broken down, *and* without walls.—PROV., ch. 25.

5314. —— more than Wrath. *Moses.* [11] Went out unto his brethren, and looked on their burdens: and he spied an Egyptian smiting a Hebrew.. [12] And he looked this way and that way, and when he saw that *there was* no man, he slew the Egyptian, and hid him in the sand.—EX., ch. 2. [25] For he supposed his brethren would have understood how that God by his hand would deliver them; but they understood not. —ACTS, ch. 7. [Forty years later, in another spirit, he delivered Israel.]

5315. —— Want of. *Bramble.* [15] The bramble said unto the trees, If in truth ye anoint me king over you, *then* come *and* put your trust in my shadow; and if not, let fire come out of the bramble, and devour the cedars of Lebanon.—JUDGES, ch. 9.

See other illustrations under:

CONTRITION.

Accepted. Because thine heart was tender..peace 1664
Annual. That ye may be clean from all your sins 1665
Bitter. Eat the flesh..with bitter herbs 1666

DISCIPLESHIP.

Conditional. Lord, I will follow thee; but 2331
Provisional. When I bow down..the L. pardon 2332
Postponed. Let me kiss my father..then I will 2333
Terms. Whosoever doth not bear his cross and 2334
Trials. Enough for the disciple to be as his master 2335
Unconditional. If any man..deny himself..cross 2336

TEACHABLENESS.

Attitude. Mary sat at Jesus' feet 8606
Characteristic. Rec'd the Word..searched the S. 8607
Manifested. How can I, except some one teach me 8608
Professed. We are all here..to hear all things 8609
Youthful. Found him in the temple..hearing 8610

Abasement. We were in our own sight as grasshop. 7686
Soldiers. David's heart smote him..L. forbid 1579
See **HUMILITY, HUMILIATION,** and references.

5316. MEETING, A joyful. *Lost Son.* [29] Joseph made ready his chariot, and went up to meet Israel his father, to Goshen..and he fell on his neck, and wept on his neck a good while. [30] And Israel said..Now let me die, since I have seen thy face.—GEN., ch. 46.

5317. —— A protracted. *Ten Days.* [13] They went up into an upper room, where abode both Peter, and James, and.. [14] These all continued with one accord in prayer and supplication, with the women, and Mary the mother of Jesus, and with his brethren.—ACTS, ch. 1.

See other illustrations under:

ASSEMBLY.

Eager. Could not so much as eat bread	527
Evil. Assembled..consulted..take Jesus..death	528
Great. All the people..small and great..read	529
Important. All I..prophets of Baal 450..grove 400	530
Nobility. At the dedication of the image	531
Nations. Shall be gathered all nations	532
Persistent. Many ran out..outwent them	533
Pious. All the people gathered..as one man	534

MOB.

Bigots. Two hours cried out, Great is Diana	5487
Disturbance. Lewd fellows of the baser sort	5488
Murderous. City was moved..people ran..took	5489
Tumultuous. Left beating Paul..some cried one	5490
Trial by. Cried..loud voice..ran upon Stephen	5491
Workmen. By this craft we have our wealth	5492

5318. MELANCHOLY, Music for. *Saul.* [15] Behold now, an evil spirit from God troubleth thee. [16] Let..thy servants..seek out a man, *who is* a cunning player on a harp: and..when the evil spirit from God is upon thee..he shall play..and thou shalt be well.—1 SAM., ch. 16.

See DESPONDENCY and references.

5319. MEMORY in Perdition. *Dives.* [27] I pray thee..send him to my father's house: [28] For I have five brethren; that he may testify unto them, lest they also come into this place of torment.—LUKE, ch. 16.

5320. —— A painful. *Paul.* [9] I am the least of the apostles, that am not meet to be called an apostle, because I persecuted the church of God.—1 COR., ch. 15.

See other illustrations under:

FORGETFULNESS.

Adversity. Whom I loved have turned against me	3346
Caution. Take heed..lest thou forget..thine eyes	3347
of God. Have eaten..full, beware..forget the L.	3342
" Jeshurun..lightly esteemed the rock	3343
" When silver and gold is multiplied..forget	3344
Religious. I will not go..He went back with him	3348
Sanctuary. If I forget thee, O Jerusalem..tongue	3345
Spiritual. Face in a glass..straightway forgetteth	3349

REMEMBRANCE.

Book. Was written before him of them that feared	7060
Late. I do remember my faults this day..chief	7061
Perpetual. This is my body..in remembrance of	7062
Painful. When Peter thought thereon, he wept	7063
Stimulated. Wherefore I put thee in remembrance	7064
of Sins. How thou provokedst the L..in the	7065
Ungrateful. Yet did not the chief butler remember	3096

Refreshed. Do this in remembrance of me	868

See MEMORIAL.

5321. MEMORIAL, Benevolence, a. *Cornelius.* [3] He saw in a vision..an angel of God..saying unto him, Cornelius. [4] ..Thy prayers and thine alms are come up for a memorial before God.—ACTS, ch. 10.

5322. —— of Deliverance. *Redemption.* [14] When thy son asketh thee in time to come, saying, What *is* this?..thou shalt say..By strength of hand the Lord brought us out from Egypt, from the house of bondage: [15] And.. when Pharaoh would hardly let us go..the Lord slew all the firstborn in the land of Egypt.. therefore I sacrifice to the Lord all that openeth the matrix, being males; but all the firstborn of my children I redeem.—EX., ch. 13.

5323. —— of Food. *Manna.* [33] Moses said unto Aaron, Take a pot, and put an omer full of manna therein, and lay it up before the Lord, to be kept for your generations.—EX., ch. 16.

5324. —— of Love. *Mary.* [8] She hath done what she could..she is come aforehand to anoint my body to the burying. [9] ..Wheresoever this gospel shall be preached throughout the whole world, *this* also that she hath done shall be spoken of for a memorial of her.—MARK, ch. 14.

5325. —— Stones for. *Jordan.* [9] Joshua set up twelve stones in the midst of Jordan, in the place where the feet of the priests which bare the ark of the covenant stood: and they are there unto this day.—JOSH., ch. 4.

5326. —— of Victory. *Ebenezer.* [11] The men of Israel..pursued the Philistines, and smote them.. [12] Then Samuel took a stone, and set *it* between Mizpeh and Shen, and called the name of it Eben-ezer, saying, Hitherto hath the Lord helped us.—1 SAM., ch. 7.

5327. —— —— Sword. [9] Ahimelech said, The sword of Goliath the Philistine, whom thou slewest..*is here* wrapped in a cloth behind the ephod: if thou wilt take that, take *it*.. And David said, *There is* none like that; give it me.—1 SAM., ch. 21.

See other illustrations under:

Monument. Jacob set up a pillar..Rachel's grave	5560
Relic. Hezekiah brake in pieces the brazen serpent	6998

See MEMORY.

5328. MEN, The greatest. *Believers.* [28] Among those that are born of women there is not a greater prophet than John the Baptist: but he that is least in the kingdom of God is greater than he.—LUKE, ch. 7.

5329. —— Indispensable. *Sailors.* [31] Paul said to the centurion and to the soldiers, Except these abide in the ship, ye cannot be saved. [32] Then the soldiers cut off the ropes of the boat, and let her fall off.—ACTS, ch. 27.

5330. —— Picked. *Saul's Army.* [52] There was sore war against the Philistines all the days of Saul: and when Saul saw any strong man, or any valiant man, he took him unto him.—1 SAM., ch. 14.

5331. —— Simple. *Absalom's Army.* [11] With Absalom went two hundred men out of Jerusalem, *that were* called; and they went in their simplicity, and they knew not any thing.—2 SAM., ch. 15.

5332. —— Mighty. *Adino.* [8] These *be* the names of the mighty men whom David had: The Tachmonite..chief among the captains; the same *was* Adino the Eznite: *he lifted up his spear* against eight hundred, whom he slew at one time. —2 SAM., ch. 23.

5333. —— —— *Eleazer.* [9] The men of Israel were gone away : [10] He arose, and smote the Philistines until his hand was weary, and his hand clave unto the sword : and the Lord wrought a great victory that day.—2 SAM., ch. 23.

5334. —— —— *Shammah.* [11] And after him *was* Shammah..where was a piece of ground full of lentiles ; and the people fled from the Philistines. [12] But he stood in the midst of the ground, and defended it, and slew the Philistines.—2 SAM., ch. 23.

5335. —— —— *Exploit.* [15] David longed.. Oh that one would give me..of the well of Beth-lehem which *is* by the gate ! [16] And the three mighty men brake through the host of the Philistines, and drew water out of the well of Beth-lehem..and brought *it* to David.—2 SAM., ch. 23.

5336. —— —— *Abishai.* [18] Abishai, the brother of Joab..was chief among three. And he lifted up his spear against three hundred, *and* slew *them..* [19] Was he not most honourable of three ? therefore he was their captain : howbeit he attained not unto the *first* three.—2 SAM., ch. 23.

5337. —— —— *Benaiah.* [20] Benaiah..he slew two lionlike men of Moab : he went down also and slew a lion in the midst of a pit in time of snow. [21] And he slew an Egyptian, a goodly man.. he went down to him with a staff, and plucked the spear out of the Egyptian's hand, and slew him with his own spear.—2 SAM., ch. 23.

See other illustrations under :

GIANTS.

Four. Ishbi-benob..Sibbechai..Elhanan 3518
Military. Goliath..six cubits and a span 3516
Royal. Og king of Bashan..bedstead..nine cubits 3517

MASSES.

Bible. Set up these stones..plaster..write very p. 5252
Neglected. Jesus was moved..not having a sheph. 5253

PEOPLE.

Feared. Sought to destroy him..could not..p. 6047
 " Would have..death..feared the multitude 6048
Offering. A kid of the goats, a female 6049
 See MAN.

5338. MENDING, Loss by. *Garment.* [36] No man putteth a piece of a new garment upon an old ; if otherwise, then both the new maketh a rent, and the piece that was *taken* out of the new agreeth not with the old.—LUKE, ch. 5.

See other illustrations under :

Tools. Went down to the Philistines to sharpen 5559
Repairs. Priests take..repair the breaches of the h. 7071

5339. MERCY abused. *Pharaoh.* [34] When Pharaoh saw that the rain and the hail and the thunders were ceased, he sinned yet more, and hardened his heart, he and his servants. [35]..neither would he let the children of Israel go.—Ex., ch. 9.

5340. —— **Compassionate.** *Jesus.* [37] O Jerusalem, Jerusalem, *thou* that killest the prophets, and stonest them which are sent unto thee, how often would I have gathered thy children together, even as a hen gathereth her chickens under *her* wings, and ye would not.—MAT., ch. 23.

5341. —— —— *" Helper."* [26] The Lord saw the affliction of Israel, *that it was* very bitter :

for *there was* not any shut up, nor any left, nor any helper for Israel. [27] And the Lord said not that he would blot out the name of Israel from under heaven : but he saved them by the hand of Jeroboam.—2 KINGS, ch. 14.

5342. —— **conquers.** *To King of Israel.* [22] Elisha answered..wouldest thou smite those whom thou hast taken captive with thy sword?.. set bread and water before them, that they may eat and drink, and go to their master. [23]..So the bands of Syria came no more into the land of Israel.—2 KINGS, ch. 6.

5343. —— **Divine.** *Sufferers.* [17] When the poor and needy seek water, and *there is* none, *and* their tongue faileth for thirst, I the Lord will hear them, *I* the God of Israel will not forsake them. [18] I will open rivers in high places, and fountains in the midst of the valleys : I will make the wilderness a pool of water, and the dry land springs of water.—ISA., ch. 41.

5344. —— —— *Proclamation.* [6] The Lord ..proclaimed, The Lord, The Lord God, merciful and gracious, longsuffering, and abundant in goodness and truth, [7] Keeping mercy for thousands, forgiving iniquity and transgression and sin, and that will by no means clear *the guilty.* —Ex., ch. 34.

5345. —— —— *Fatherly.* [13] Like as a father pitieth *his* children, *so* the Lord pitieth them that fear him. [14] For he knoweth our frame ; he remembereth that we *are* dust.—Ps. 103.

5346. —— **deplored.** *Jonah said,* [The Ninevites were spared.] [2] *Was* not this my saying, when I was yet in my country ? Therefore I fled before unto Tarshish : for I knew that thou *art* a gracious God, and merciful, slow to anger, and of great kindness, and repentest thee of the evil. [3] Therefore now, O Lord, take, I beseech thee, my life from me ; for *it is* better for me to die than to live.—JONAH, ch. 4.

5347. —— **desired.** *By Recipients.* [See No. 5351.] [28] One of his fellow-servants, which owed him a hundred pence : and he laid hands on him, and took *him* by the throat, saying, Pay me that thou owest. [29] And his fellow-servant fell down at his feet, and besought him, saying, Have patience with me, and I will pay thee all. [30] And he would not : but went and cast him into prison, till he should pay the debt.—MAT., ch. 18.

5348. —— **entreated.** *Pharaoh.* [27] I have sinned this time : the Lord *is* righteous, and I and my people *are* wicked. [28] Entreat the Lord (for *it is* enough) that there be no *more* mighty thunderings and hail ; and I will let you go, and ye shall stay no longer.—Ex., ch. 9.

5349. —— **Extension of.** *Fig Tree.* [7] These three years I come seeking fruit on this fig tree, and find none : cut it down ; why cumbereth it the ground ? [8] And he..said..Lord, let it alone this year also, till I shall dig about it, and dung *it :* [9] And if it bear fruit, *well :* and if not, *then* after that thou shalt cut it down.—LUKE, ch. 13.

5350. —— **Gracious.** *Esther said,* [11] Whosoever, whether man or woman, shall come unto the king into the inner court, who is not called, *there is* one law of his to put *him* to death, except such to whom the king shall hold out the golden sceptre, that he may live.—ESTHER, ch. 4.

5351. —— **granted.** *To Unfortunates.* ²⁵ Forasmuch as he had not to pay, his lord commanded him to be sold, and his wife and children, and all that he had.. ²⁶ The servant..Lord, have patience with me, and I will pay thee all. ²⁷ Then the lord..was moved with compassion, and loosed him, and forgave him the debt.—MAT., ch. 18.

5352. —— **Hope in.** *David's.* ¹³ Shall seven years of famine come..or wilt thou flee three months before thine enemies..or that there be three days' pestilence in thy land?.. ¹⁴ And David said unto Gad, I am in a great strait : let us fall now into the hand of the Lord ; for his mercies *are* great : and let me not fall into the hand of man. ¹⁵ So the Lord sent a pestilence.—2 SAM., ch. 24.

5353. —— **Ill-timed.** *Ahab's.* [A prophet] ⁴² Said unto him, Thus saith the Lord, Because thou hast let go out of *thy* hand a man whom I appointed to utter destruction, therefore thy life shall go for his life, and thy people for his people.—1 KINGS, ch. 20.

5354. —— **for the Ignorant.** *Paul.* ¹³ Who was before a blasphemer, and a persecutor, and injurious : but I obtained mercy, because I did *it* ignorantly in unbelief.—1 TIM., ch. 1.

5355. —— **limited.** *Antediluvians.* ³ My Spirit shall not always strive with man, for that he also *is* flesh : yet his days shall be a hundred and twenty years.—GEN., ch. 6.

5356. —— **only.** *Four Lepers.* [At siege of Samaria.] ⁴ Let us fall unto the host of the Syrians : if they save us alive, we shall live ; and if they kill us, we shall but die.—2 KINGS, ch. 7.

5357. —— **omitted.** *Parable.* ³⁰ Fell among thieves, which stripped him..leaving *him* half dead. ³¹..there came down a certain priest..he passed by on the other side. ³² And likewise a Levite..looked *on him*, and passed by on the other side.—LUKE, ch. 10.

5358. —— **Last Plea for.** *Pharaoh.* ¹⁷ Forgive, I pray thee, my sin only this once, and entreat the Lord..that he may take away from me this death only.. ¹⁹ And the Lord turned a mighty strong west wind which took away the locusts.—EX., ch. 10.

5359. —— **Power of.** *Saul.* ¹² David took the spear and the cruse of water from Saul's bolster ; and they gat them away, and no man saw *it*, nor knew *it*, neither awaked : for they *were* all asleep.. ²¹ Then said Saul, I have sinned : return, my son David ; for I will no more do thee harm, because my soul was precious in thine eyes this day : behold, I have played the fool.—1 SAM., ch. 26.

5360. —— **Earnest Plea for.** *Bartimeus.* ⁴⁸ Many charged him that he should hold his peace ; but he cried the more a great deal, *Thou Son of David, have mercy on me.* ⁴⁹ And Jesus stood still.—MARK, ch. 10.

5361. —— **the Sinner's Plea.** *Publican.* ¹³ Would not lift up so much as *his* eyes unto heaven, but smote upon his breast, saying, God be merciful to me a sinner. ¹⁴ I tell you, this man went down to his house justified *rather* than the other.—LUKE, ch. 18.

5362. —— **for the Penitent.** *Ninevites.* ⁷ Let neither man nor beast, herd nor flock, taste any thing.. ⁸ But let man and beast be covered with sackcloth, and cry mightily unto God : yea, let them turn every one from his evil way, ¹⁰ And God saw their works, that they turned from their evil way ; and God repented of the evil.—JONAH, ch. 3.

5363. —— **Practical.** *Samaritan.* [See No. 5357.] ³⁴ Bound up his wounds, pouring in oil and wine, and set him on his own beast, and brought him to an inn, and took care of him. ³⁵..when he departed, he took out two pence, and gave *them* to the host.—LUKE, ch. 10.

5364. —— **Reliance on.** *Calf.* ³¹ Moses.. said, Oh, this people have sinned a great sin, and have made them gods of gold. ³² Yet now, if thou wilt, forgive their sin : and if not, blot me, I pray thee, out of thy book which thou hast written.—EX., ch. 32.

5365. —— **Reputation for.** *"Kings."* [Benhadad was defeated and secreted,] ³¹ And his servants said unto him, Behold now, we have heard that the kings of the house of Israel *are* merciful kings : let us, I pray thee, put sackcloth on our loins, and ropes upon our heads, and go out to the king of Israel : peradventure he will save thy life.—1 KINGS, ch. 20.

5366. —— **required.** *Mutual.* [See No. 5351.] ³² Then his lord..said..O thou wicked servant, I forgave thee all that debt, because thou desiredst me : ³³ Shouldest not thou also have had compassion on thy fellow servant, even as I had pity on thee ? ³⁴ And his lord was wroth, and delivered him to the tormentors, till he should pay all.—MAT., ch. 18.

5367. —— **Suppliants for.** *Confession.* [See No. 5365.] ³² So they girded sackcloth on their loins, and *put* ropes on their heads, and came to the king of Israel, and said, Thy servant Benhadad saith, I pray thee, let me live. And he said, *Is* he yet alive ? he *is* my brother.—1 KINGS, ch. 20.

5368. —— **Success by.** *Blind Men.* ²⁷ Two blind men followed him, crying, and saying, *Thou Son of David, have mercy on us.* ²⁸..Jesus saith ..Believe ye that I am able to do this ? They said..Yea, Lord. ²⁹ Then touched he their eyes, saying, According to your faith be it unto you. —MAT., ch. 9.

5369. —— **Throne of.** *"Throne of Grace."* ¹⁵ We have not a high priest which cannot be touched with the feeling of our infirmities ; but was in all points tempted like as *we are, yet* without sin. ¹⁶ Let us therefore come boldly unto the throne of grace, that we may obtain mercy, and find grace to help in time of need.—HEB., ch. 4.

5370. MERCIES remembered. *Israelites.* ² Thou shalt remember all the way which the Lord thy God led thee these forty years in the wilderness, to humble thee, *and* to prove thee, to know what *was* in thine heart, whether thou wouldest keep his commandments, or no. ³ And he..fed thee with manna.—DEUT., ch. 8.

See other illustrations under :

COMPASSION.

Denied. Took him by the throat..pay me 1428
Lowly. Israel sighed..heard the groaning 1429
Moved. We have sinned..grieved for the misery of 1430
Penitent. While..a great way off..compassion 1431
Public. City was moved..Is this Naomi? 1432
Patriotic. O Jerusalem..how often..ye would not 1433
Practical.Leper..Jesus..with compassion touched 1434
Reproof. Forgive him and comfort him 1435
Required. Shouldest thou not have..on thy fellow 1436
Sensitive. Not a high priest which cannot be touch. 1437
Unmoved. Joseph. We saw the anguish..would 1438
Womanly. Daughter of Pharaoh..babe wept..had 1439
Without. Chaldees..had no compassion..old 1440

FORBEARANCE.

Divine. A king shall reign..G. was your king 3328
" I come seeking fruit, and find none 3329
Pious. David..hast rewarded me good..killedst 3330
See FORGIVENESS.

5371. MERCHANTS, Mourning of. *Babylon.*
[15] The merchants of these things, which were
made rich by her, shall stand afar off for the
fear of her torment, weeping and wailing,
[16] And saying, Alas, alas, that great city, that
was clothed in fine linen, and purple, and scarlet, and decked with gold, and precious stones,
and pearls ! [17] For in one hour so great riches
is come to nought.—REV., ch. 18.

5372. —— Ruin of. *Babylon.* [11] The merchants..shall weep and mourn over her ; for no
man buyeth their merchandise any more : [12] The
merchandise of gold, and silver, and precious
stones, and of pearls, and fine linen, and purple, and silk, and scarlet, and all thyine wood,
and all manner vessels of ivory, and all manner
vessels of most precious wood, and of brass, and
iron, and marble, [13] And cinnamon, and odours,
and ointments, and frankincense, and wine,
and oil, and fine flour, and wheat, and beasts,
and sheep, and horses, and chariots, and slaves,
and souls of men.—REV., ch. 18.

5373. MERCHANDISE misplaced. *Temple.*
[15] And when he had made a scourge of small
cords, he drove them all out of the temple, and
the sheep, and the oxen ; and poured out the
changers' money, and overthrew the tables.—
JOHN, ch. 2.

See other illustrations under :

TRADE.

Beneficial. Let them trade..substance be ours 8858
Beating down. It is naught, it is naught..then he b. 8859
Dishonesty. Making the ephah small and the shek. 8860
" A false balance is an abomination to 8861
" Prophet unto the priest, every one d. 8862
Lawful. Might know how much..gained by trad. 8863
Luxuries. Merchandise of precious stones..silks 8864
Protection. Our craft is in danger to be set at n. 8865
Sabbath. Brought fish..ware and sold on the sab. 8866
" Corrected. If ye do..I will lay hands on 8867
Tricks. Shalt not have divers weights, a great 8868
Union. Demetrius a silversmith..called the work. 8869

5374. MERCENARIES, Complaint of. *Parable.*
[10] When the first came, they supposed that they
should have received more ; and they likewise
received every man a penny. [11] And..they murmured.. [12] Saying, These last have wrought *but*
one hour, and thou hast made them equal unto
us, which have borne the burden and heat of
the day.—MAT., ch. 20.

See MONEY, WAGES.

5375. MERIT disclaimed. *Apostles.* [11] As
the lame man which was healed held Peter and
John, all the people ran together unto them..
greatly wondering. [12] And when Peter saw *it*,
he answered..Ye men of Israel, why marvel
ye at this ? or why look ye so earnestly on us,
as though by our own power or holiness we had
made this man to walk?—ACTS, ch. 3.

5376. —— honoured. *Daniel.* [3] Daniel was
preferred above the presidents and princes, be
cause an excellent spirit *was* in him ; and the
king thought to set him over the whole realm.
—DAN., ch. 6.

5377. —— unappreciated. *Enemies.* [4] The
presidents and princes sought to find occasion
against Daniel concerning the kingdom ; but
they could find none occasion nor fault ; forasmuch as he *was* faithful, neither was there any
error.. [5] Then said these men, We shall not
find any occasion against this Daniel, except..
concerning the law of his God.—DAN., ch. 6.

See other illustrations under :

GOODNESS.

Commendation. Mercy and truth..find favour..G. 3653
Distrusted. Serpent said..G. doth know..be as g. 3654
Divine. Angel..campeth round about them 3655
Pride. I am not as other men are..I fast 3656
Reveals. Show me thy glory..my goodness 3657
no Shield. Herod feared John..just and a holy 3658
Tribute. The evil bow before the good 3659
Unconscious. Moses wist not..face shone 3660

DEEDS.

Authenticated. If I do not the works..believe not 2094
Evince. World began..not heard..opened eyes 2095
Test. Which of these three was neighbour 2096
Words. Said..Lord he is God..slew prophets 2097

WORTH.

Estimated. He was worthy for whom he should do 9923
Promotion. Cunning in playing..man of war..p. 9924
Without. I am not worthy..come to thee 9925
See CHARACTER.

5378. MERRIMENT, Ill-timed. *Proverb.*
[20] *As* he that taketh away a garment in cold
weather, *and as* vinegar upon nitre, so *is* he that
singeth songs to a heavy heart.—PROV., ch. 25.

See HAPPINESS and references.

5379. MESSAGE rejected, A. *To Passover.*
[1] Hezekiah sent to all Israel and Judah..that
they should come to the house of the Lord at
Jerusalem, to keep the passover.. [10] So the
posts passed from city to city, through the
country of Ephraim and Manasseh..but they
laughed them to scorn, and mocked them.—2
CHRON., ch. 30.

5380. —— received, A. *To Passover.*
[11] Nevertheless, divers of Asher and Manasseh
and of Zebulun humbled themselves, and came
to Jerusalem. [12] Also in Judah the hand of God
was to give them one heart to do the commandment of the king.—2 CHRON., ch. 30.

5381. MESSENGER, A fictitious. *Ehud.* [The
assassinator of king Eglon.] [20] He was sitting
in a summer parlour, which he had for himself
alone : and Ehud said, I have a message from
God unto thee. And he arose out of *his* seat.
[22] And the haft also went in after the blade ; and
the fat closed upon the blade, so that he could
not draw the dagger out of his belly.—JUDGES,
ch. 3.

5382. —— **A fated.** *Uriah.* [14] David wrote a letter to Joab, and sent *it* by the hand of Uriah, [15]..saying, set ye Uriah in the forefront of the hottest battle, and retire ye from him, that he may be smitten, and die.—2 SAM., ch. 11.

5383. —— **A prepared.** *Isaiah.* [6] Then flew one of the seraphim unto me, having a live coal in his hand, *which* he had taken with the tongs from off the altar : [7] And he laid *it* upon my mouth, and said, Lo, this hath touched thy lips ; and thine iniquity is taken away, and thy sin purged. [8] Also I heard the voice of the Lord, saying, Whom shall I send, and who will go for us? Then said I, Here *am* I ; send me.—ISA., ch. 6.

5384. —— **without a Message.** *Ahimaaz said,* [After the defeat of Absalom,] [22] Let me, I pray thee, also run after Cushi. And Joab said, Wherefore wilt thou run, my son, seeing that thou hast no tidings ready ? [29] And the king said, Is the young man Absalom safe? And Ahimaaz answered..I saw a great tumult, but I knew not what *it was.*—2 SAM., ch. 18.

5385. MESSENGERS, Convenient. *Raven— Dove.* [7] He sent forth a raven, which went forth to and fro, until the waters were dried up from off the earth. [8] Also he sent forth a dove.. [9] But the dove found no rest for the sole of her foot.—GEN., ch. 8.

5386. —— **for Destruction.** *In Persia.* [13] The letters were sent by posts into all the king's provinces, to destroy..all Jews, both young and old, little children and women, in one day..and *to take* the spoil of them for a prey.—ESTHER, ch. 3.

5387. —— **Glad.** *Joseph's Brethren.* [13] Ye shall tell my father of all my glory in Egypt, and of all that ye have seen ; and ye shall haste and bring down my father hither. [14] And he fell upon his brother Benjamin's neck, and wept. —GEN., ch. 45.

See other illustrations under :

NEWS.

WRITING.

5388. MIDNIGHT, Appeal at. *Bread.* [5] Which of you shall have a friend, and shall go unto him at midnight, and say unto him, Friend, lend me three loaves ; [6] For a friend of mine in his journey is come to me, and I have nothing to set before him ?—LUKE, ch. 11.

5389. —— **Alarm at.** *In Egypt.* [30] Pharaoh rose up in the night, he..and all the Egyptians ; and there was a great cry in Egypt : for *there was* not a house where *there was* not one dead. [31] And he called for Moses and Aaron by night, and said, Rise up, *and* get you forth from among

my people. [33] And the Egyptians were urgent.. for they said, We *be* all dead *men.*—EX., ch. 12.

5390. —— **Songs at.** *Philippi Prison.* [24] Who ..thrust them into the inner prison, and made their feet fast in the stocks. [25] And at midnight Paul and Silas prayed, and sang praises unto God : and the prisoners heard them.—ACTS, ch. 16.

Also see :

5391. Mind and Body, Both. *Daniel and Others.* [4] Children in whom *was* no blemish, but well favoured, and skilful in all wisdom, and cunning in knowledge, and understanding science, and such as *had* ability in them to stand in the king s palace, and whom they might teach the learning and the tongue of the Chaldeans.— DAN., ch. 1.

5392. —— **of Christ.** *Humility.* [5] Let this mind be in you, which was also in Christ Jesus : [6] Who, being in the form of God, thought it not robbery to be equal with God : [7] But made himself of no reputation, and took upon him the form of a servant, and was made in the likeness of men.—PHIL., ch. 2.

5393. MINDS differ. *Mary vs. Martha.* [39] Mary, which also sat at Jesus' feet, and heard his word. [40] But Martha was cumbered about much serving.—LUKE, ch. 10.

5394. MIND, Opening the. *Resurrection Eve.* [45] Then opened he their understanding, that they might understand the Scriptures, [46] And said..Thus it is written, and thus it behooved Christ to suffer, and to rise from the dead the third day.—LUKE, ch. 24.

Also see :
   See **INTELLIGENCE.**

5395. MINISTRY of Angels. *Peter and John.* [19] The angel of the Lord by night opened the prison doors, and brought them forth, and said, [20] Go, stand and speak in the temple to the people all the words of this life.—ACTS, ch. 5.

5396. —— *Secondary.* [4] Cornelius looked on him, he was afraid, and said, What is it, Lord? And he said..Thy prayers and thine alms are come up for a memorial before God. [5] And now send men to Joppa, and call for..Peter : [6]..he shall tell thee what thou oughtest to do.—ACTS, ch. 10.

5397. —— **Burden of.** *Paul.* [13] What is it wherein ye were inferior to other churches, except *it* be that I myself was not burdensome to you? forgive me this wrong.—2 COR., ch. 12.

5398. —— **Christ's.** *Support.* [2] Certain women, which had been healed of evil spirits and infirmities, Mary called Magdalene, out of whom went seven devils, [3] And Joanna the wife of Chuza Herod's steward, and Susanna, and many others, which ministered unto him of their substance.—LUKE, ch. 12.

5399. —— **Covetous.** *Eli's Sons.* [15] The priest's servant..said to the man that sacrificed, Give flesh to roast for the priest ; for he will not have sodden flesh of thee, but raw. [16] And *if* any man said..Let them not fail to burn the fat presently, and *then* take *as much* as thy soul desireth ; then he would answer him, *Nay ;* but thou shalt give *it me* now : and if not, I will take *it* by force. [17] Wherefore the sin of the young men was very great before the Lord : for men abhorred the offering of the Lord.—1 SAM., ch. 2.

5400. —— **Call to the.** *Aaron.* [27] The Lord said to Aaron, Go into the wilderness to meet Moses.. [28] And Moses told Aaron all the words of the Lord who had sent him, and all the signs which he had commanded him. [29] And Moses and Aaron went.—Ex., ch. 4.

5401. —— **A courageous.** *Micaiah.* [26] Take Micaiah, and carry him back unto Amon the governor of the city.. [27] And say, Thus saith the king, Put this *fellow* in the prison, and feed him with bread of affliction and with water of affliction, until I come in peace. [28] And Micaiah said, If thou return at all in peace, the Lord hath not spoken by me. And he said, Hearken, O people, every one of you.—1 KINGS, ch. 22.

5402. —— **Devotion to the.** *Paul.* [1] I came to you..not with excellency of speech or of wisdom, declaring unto you the testimony of God. [2] For I determined not to know anything among you, save Jesus Christ, and him crucified.—1 COR., ch. 2.

5403. —— **A faithful.** *M i c a i a h.* [13] The messenger..spake..the words of the prophets *declare* good unto the king with one mouth : let thy word, I pray thee, be like the word of one of them, and speak *that which is* good. [14] And Micaiah said, *As* the Lord liveth, what the Lord saith unto me, that will I speak.—1 KINGS, ch. 22.

5404. —— **Joy in the.** *Paul.* [13] Ye know how through infirmity of the flesh I preached the gospel unto you at the first. [14] And my temptation which was in my flesh ye despised not, nor rejected ; but received me as an angel of God, *even* as Christ Jesus.—GAL., ch. 4.

5405. —— **Portion for.** *Sons of Eli.* [13] The priest's custom..*was, that,* when any man offered sacrifice, the priest's servant came, while the flesh was in seething, with a fleshhook of three teeth in his hand ; [14] And he struck *it* into the pan, or kettle..all that the fleshhook brought up the priest took for himself.—1 SAM., ch. 2.

5406. —— **Preparation for.** *Isaiah.* [See No. 5383.]

5407. —— —— *Jeremiah.* [6] Then said I, Ah, Lord God ! behold, I cannot speak : for I *am* a child. [7] .Say not, I *am* a child : for thou shalt go to all that I shall send thee, and whatsoever I command thee thou shalt speak. [8] Be not afraid of their faces : for I *am* with thee.. [9] Then the Lord put forth his hand, and touched my mouth.—JER., ch. 1.

5408. —— **Proof of.** *Widow of Zarephath.* [23] Elijah took the child, and brought him down out of the chamber..and delivered him unto his mother : and Elijah said, See, thy son liveth. [24] And the woman said..Now by this I know that thou *art* a man of God.—1 KINGS, ch. 17.

5409. —— **Promise to the.** *"Rain."* [10] As the rain cometh down, and the snow from heaven, and returneth not thither, but watereth the earth, and maketh it bring forth and bud, that it may give seed to the sower, and bread to the eater : [11] So shall my word be that goeth forth out of my mouth.—ISA., ch. 55.

5410. —— **Qualifications of.** *Bishop.* [7] A bishop must be blameless, as the steward of God ; not selfwilled, not soon angry, not given to wine, no striker, not given to filthy lucre ; [8] But a lover of hospitality, a lover of good men, sober, just, holy, temperate ; [9] Holding fast the faithful word.—TITUS, ch. 1.

5411. —— **Self-supported.** *Paul.* [33] I have coveted no man's silver, or gold, or apparel. [34] Yea, ye yourselves know, that these hands have ministered unto my necessities, and to them that were with me.—ACTS, ch. 20.

5412. —— **Support of.** *L a w.* [21] I have given the children of Levi all the tenth in Israel for an inheritance, for their service..of the tabernacle of the congregation.—NUM., ch. 18.

5413. —— —— *Reasonable.* [7] Who goeth a warfare any time at his own charges ? who planteth a vineyard, and eateth not of the fruit thereof ? or who feedeth a flock, and eateth not of the milk of the flock ? [9] For it is written in the law of Moses, Thou shalt not muzzle the mouth of the ox that treadeth out the corn. Doth God take care for oxen ?—1 COR., ch. 9.

5414. —— —— *Gospel.* [13] Do ye not know that they which minister about holy things live *of the things* of the temple ? and they which wait at the altar are partakers with the altar ? [14] Even so hath the Lord ordained that they which preach the gospel should live of the gospel.—1 COR., ch. 9.

5415. —— **A spiritual.** *Apostles.* [See No. 5416.] [4] But we will give ourselves continually to prayer, and to the ministry of the word.—ACTS, ch. 6.

5416. —— **undiverted.** *"S e r v e Tables."* [2] It is not reason that we should leave the word of God, and serve tables. [3] Wherefore, brethren, look ye out among you seven men..whom we may appoint over this business.—ACTS, ch. 6.

5417. —— **Work of.** *Jeremiah.* [10] See, I have this day set thee over the nations and over the kingdoms, to root out, and to pull down, and to destroy, and to thrown down, to build, and to plant.—JER., ch. 1.

5418. MINISTER, A bold. *John.* [18] John had said unto Herod, It is not lawful for thee to have thy brother's wife. [19] Therefore Herodias had a quarrel against him, and would have killed him.—MARK, ch. 6.

5419. —— **A consistent.** *Paul.* [10] Ye *are* witnesses, and God *also,* how holily and justly and unblamably we behaved ourselves among you that believe.—1 THESS., ch. 2.

5420. —— **called away.** *Micah's.* [See No. 5423. Danites] [19] Said unto him, Hold thy peace, lay thine hand upon thy mouth, and go with us, and be to us a father and a priest : *is it* better for thee to be a priest unto the house of one man, or that thou be a priest unto a tribe and a family in Israel ? [20] And the priest's heart was glad.—JUDGES, ch. 18.

5421. —— **Loss of a.** *Micah's.* [See No. 5420. His friends pursued,] [23] And they cried unto the children of Dan. And they turned their faces, and said unto Micah, What aileth thee, that thou comest with such a company ? [24] And he said, Ye have taken away my gods which I made, and the priest..and what have I more? and what *is* this *that* ye say unto me, What aileth thee?—JUDGES, ch. 18.

5422. —— A respected. *J o h n .* ²⁰ Herod feared John, knowing that he was a just man and a holy, and observed him ; and when he heard him, he did many things, and heard him gladly.—MARK, ch. 6.

5423. —— A settled. *A Levite.* ⁹ Micah said unto him, Whence comest thou ? And he said..I am a Levite of Bethlehem-judah, and I go to sojourn where I may find *a place.* ¹⁰ And Micah said..Dwell with me, and be unto me a father and a priest, and I will give thee ten *shekels* of silver by the year, and a suit of apparel, and thy victuals.—JUDGES, ch. 17.

5424. MINISTERS, Cares of. *P a u l .* ²⁷ In weariness and painfulness, in watchings often, in hunger and thirst, in fastings often, in cold and nakedness. ²⁸ Beside those things that are without, that which cometh upon me daily, the care of all the churches.—2 COR., ch. 11.

5425. —— dependent. *The Apostles.* ⁹ Provide neither gold, nor silver, nor brass in your purses ; ¹⁰ Nor scrip for *your* journey, neither two coats, neither shoes, nor yet staves : for the workman is worthy of his meat.—MAT., ch. 10.

5426. —— differ. *" More Upright."* [See No. 5429.] ³⁴ Wherefore their brethren the Levites did help them, till the work was ended, and until the *other* priests had sanctified themselves : for the Levites *were* more upright in heart to sanctify themselves than the priests.— 2 CHRON., ch. 29.

5427. —— Discouragements of. *" Sower."* Seed fell by the .. wayside .. and on .. stony ground..and..among thorns.—[See Mark 4 :4-7.]

5428. —— Encouragement of. *" Fr u i t ."* ⁸ Other fell on good ground, and did yield fruit that sprang up and increased ; and brought forth, some thirty, and some sixty, and some a hundred.—MARK, ch. 4.

5429. —— Too few. *In Revival.* ³² The number of the burnt offerings, which the congregation brought, was threescore and ten bullocks, a hundred rams, *and* two hundred lambs.. ³³ And the consecrated things *were* six hundred oxen and three thousand sheep. ³⁴ But the priests were too few, so that they could not flay all the burnt offerings.—2 CHRON., ch. 29.

5430. —— only Instruments. *Paul.* ⁵ Who then is Paul, and who *is* Apollos, but ministers by whom ye believed.. ⁶ I have planted, Apollos watered ; but God gave the increase. ⁷ So then neither is he that planteth any thing, neither he that watereth ; but God that giveth the increase.—1 COR., ch. 3.

5431. —— Intemperate. *Strong Drink.* [See No. 5434.]

5432. —— but Men. *" I am a Man."* ²⁵ As Peter was coming in, Cornelius met him, and fell down at his feet, and worshipped *him.* ²⁶ But Peter took him up, saying, Stand up ; I myself also am a man.—ACTS, ch. 10.

5433. —— neglected. *J e w i s h .* [See No. 5436.] ⁴ The diseased have ye not strengthened, neither have ye healed that which was sick, neither have ye bound up *that which was* broken,

neither have ye brought again that which was driven away, neither have ye sought that which was lost ; but with force and with cruelty have ye ruled them. ⁵ And they were scattered, because *there is* no shepherd.—EZEK., ch. 34.

5434. —— Recreant. *Jewish.* ¹⁰ His watchmen *are* blind : they are all ignorant, they *are* all dumb dogs, they cannot bark ; sleeping, lying down, loving to slumber. ¹¹ Yea, *they are* greedy dogs *which* can never have enough, and they *are* shepherds *that* cannot understand : they all look to their own way, every one for his gain, from his quarter. ¹² Come ye, *say they,* I will fetch wine, and we will fill ourselves with strong drink ; and to morrow shall be as this day, *and* much more abundant.—ISA., ch. 56.

5435. —— Evil Sons of. *E l i ' s .* [See No. 5440.] ¹³ Because his sons made themselves vile, and he restrained them not. ¹⁴ And therefore I have sworn..that the iniquity of Eli's house shall not be purged with sacrifice and offering for ever.—1 SAM., ch. 3.

5436. —— Self-seeking. *" Feed Themselves."* ² Woe *be* to the shepherds of Israel that do feed themselves ! should not the shepherds feed the flocks ? ³ Ye eat the fat, and ye clothe you with the wool, ye kill them that are fed : *but* ye feed not the flock.—EZEK., ch. 34.

5437. —— —— *" His G a i n ."* [See No. 5434.]

5438. —— untaxed. *Artaxerxes' Decree.* ²⁴ Any of the priests and Levites, singers, porters, Nethinim, or ministers of this house of God, it shall not be lawful to impose toll, tribute, or custom, upon them.—EZRA, ch. 7.

5439. —— Useless. *" Dumb Dogs."* [See No. 5434.]

5440. —— Wicked. *Eli's Sons.* ²² Eli was very old, and heard all that his sons did..and how they lay with the women that assembled *at* the door of the tabernacle.—1 SAM., ch. 2.

See other illustrations under :

CALL.

MESSENGER.

MESSENGERS.

PREACHERS.

PREACHING.

Alarming. Paul reasoned..Felix trembled		6453
Forbidden. Commanded..not to speak at all		6454
Fruitful. Some a hundredfold, some sixty, some		6455
Hinderances. Care of this world..deceitfulness		6456
Ignorant. One heareth..understandeth it not		6457
Joyful. Shepherds..made known abroad the		6458
Masses. Went great multitudes with Jesus		6459
Opinions. Unto the Jews a stumblingblock		6460
Purpose. That we may present every man perfect		6461
Ridiculed. What will this babbler say?		700
Strength. In demonstration of the spirit..power		6463

PRIEST.

Chosen. Sanctify unto me all the firstborn		6590
Exodus. Priests..left..came to Judah		6591

SERMON.

Long. Paul preached..until midnight		7790
to Women. By a river side..spake unto the		7791

Sacrifices. Ministers left their possessions..came to 6591
Travelling. Jesus went throughout every city and 700
Youthful. Samuel ministered before the Lord 172
See REVIVAL.

5441. MINORITY, A noble. *Joshua and Caleb* said, [7] The land, which we passed through to search it, *is* an exceeding good land. [10] But all the congregation bade stone them with stones.—NUM., ch. 14.

See other illustrations under:

NUMBERS.

Danger. Lest I. vaunt..my own hand saved me		5744
Despised. Jonathan said unto his armourbearer		5745
Disparity. I. like two little flocks of kids		5746
" L. it is nothing with thee, whether with		5747
Invisible. Mountain was full of horses..fire		5748
Pride. David's heart smote him after he had n.		5749

ONE.

Care. Martha was cumbered..Mary..one thing		5883
for God. Moses stood..Who is on the Lord's side?		5884
with God. I, even I only..Baal's prophets 450 men		5885
" I come to thee in the name of the L. of		5886
vs. 1000. Samson..slew a thousand men		5887
Power of. [Evil] Sheba hath lifted up his hand		5888
Victory. Shamgar slew 600..delivered I.		5889

5442. MIRACLE, Astonishing. " *Walking on the Sea.*" [25] In the fourth watch of the night Jesus went unto them, walking on the sea. [26] And when the disciples saw him walking on the sea, they were troubled, saying, It is a spirit ; and they cried out for fear.—MAT., ch. 14.

5443. —— Authenticated by. *Widow of Zarephath.* [23] Elijah said, See, thy son liveth. [24] And the woman said..Now by this I know that thou *art* a man of God, *and* that the word of the Lord in thy mouth *is* truth.—1 KINGS, ch. 17.

5444. —— Convinced by. *Naaman.* [15] Returned to the man of God, he and all his company..and stood before him : and he said, Behold, now I know that *there is* no God in all the earth, but in Israel.—2 KINGS, ch. 5.

5445. —— Money by. *Tribute.* [Jesus to Peter.] [27] Lest we should offend them, go thou to the sea, and cast a hook, and take up the fish that first cometh up ; and when thou hast opened his mouth, thou shalt find a piece of money : that take, and give unto them for me and thee.—MAT., ch. 17.

5446. —— No needless. " *Manna.*" [12] The manna ceased on the morrow after they had eaten of the old corn of the land ; neither had the children of Israel manna any more.—JOSH., ch. 5.

5447. —— of Salvation. " *Eye of Needle.*" [25] It is easier for a camel to go through the eye of a needle, than for a rich man to enter into the kingdom of God. [26] ..Who then can be saved ? [27] ..Jesus..saith, With men *it is* impossible, but not with God : for with God all things are possible.—MARK, ch. 10.

5448. —— Office of. *Nicodemus.* [2] Rabbi, we know that thou art a teacher come from God : for no man can do these miracles that thou doest, except God be with him.—JOHN, ch. 3.

5449. —— Moral Power of. " *Believed not.*" [37] Though he had done so many miracles before them, yet they believed not on him.—JOHN, ch. 12.

5450. —— —— After creating Bread. [30] What sign shewest thou then, that we may see, and believe thee? what dost thou work? [31] Our fathers did eat manna in the desert.—JOHN, ch. 6.

5451. —— for Unbelievers. " *Tongues.*" [22] Tongues are for a sign, not to them that believe, but to them that believe not : but prophesying *serveth* not for them that believe not, but for them which believe.—1 COR., ch. 14.

See other illustrations under:

PROPHECY.

Gift. Spirit..unto the 70 elders..did prophesy		6672
Involuntary. Spirit..was upon Saul..prophesied		6673
Revival. I prophesied..bones came together		6674
Spiritual. These are not drunken..prophesy		6675

Demanded. Except ye..wonders, ye will not b. 9762
Ineffective. Though he had done so many m. 1690
Value of. Saw the earthquake..was the Son of G. 1698

5452. MIRTH impossible. *At Babylon.* [3] They that carried us away captive required of us a song ; and they that wasted us *required of us* mirth, *saying,* Sing us *one* of the songs of Zion. [4] How shall we sing the Lord's song in a strange land ?—Ps. 137.

See MERRIMENT and references.

5453. MISCHIEF, Makers of. *At Thessalonica.* [5] Jews which believed not, moved with envy, took unto them certain lewd fellows of the baser sort, and gathered a company, and set all the city on an uproar, and assaulted the house of Jason, and sought to bring them out to the people.—ACTS, ch. 17.

See other illustrations under:

INJURY.

Forgiveness. Father, forgive them, they know not		4498
Insulting. Samson's wife was given to his. friend		4496
Revenged. Samson caught 300 foxes..firebrands		4497

TALEBEARER.

Flattering. Revealeth secrets..flattereth with his l.		8578
Strife. Where there is no talebearer strife ceaseth		8579
Tattling. He that repeateth..separateth very f.		8580
Wounds. Words of a talebearer are as wounds		8581

See MISFORTUNE.

5454. MISERY, Brutalizing. *In Egypt.* [18] Another king arose, which knew not Joseph. [19] The same..evil entreated our fathers, so that they cast out their young children, to the end they might not live.—ACTS, ch. 7.

See other illustrations under :

ANGUISH.

Bereavement. Let her alone, for her soul is vexed   416
Bitter. Esau cried..Bless me, even me also !   417

CRUELTY.

Ambition. Athaliah..destroyed all the seed royal   1857
Captives. Judah cast [10,000 men of Sier] from the   1858
Failure. More they afflicted them..grew   1859
Insulting. Purple..crown of thorns..Hail King   1860
Pride. Mordecai bowed not..H. was full of wrath   1861
Reward. Cruel..troubleth his own flesh   1862
Savage. Slew the sons of Z..before his eyes   1863
War. Joab put them under saws..harrows   1864

DESPAIR.

Affliction. Let me not see the death of the child   2213
Anguish. Slay me, for anguish is come upon me   2214
Awaking. Wine was gone out..heart died within   2215
Deliverance. Been better for us to serve the Egyp.   2216
Needless. Widow..meal..oil..me and my son eat   2217

DESPERATION.

Boldness. I will go in unto the king..If I perish   2218
Effort. Why sit we here till we die ?   2219
Sacrifices. King of Moab took his eldest son   2221
Sinners. Saul inquired of the L...answered him   2220

DISTRESS.

Cry of. Great cry..none like it, nor shall be   2437
Derided. They that see me, shoot out the lip   2438
Described. I was a derision to all my people   2439
Exasperation. What shall I do..people ready to   2440
Famine. Delicate woman..shall eat..children   2441
Friend. Gedaliah..took Jeremiah out of prison   2443
Great. Thrust..right eyes..people wept   2444
Little Faith. Why are ye fearful..little faith   2442
Needless. Saul had adjured the people..food   2445
Refuge. Ahaz sacrificed unto the gods that smote   2446

SUFFERING.

for Christ. [Paul and Silas] Laid many stripes   8448
Faithful. Were stoned..sawn asunder, were   8449
Subdued. Bit the people..died, therefore..we   8451
Support. Sufferings of this present time not   8450

SUFFERINGS.

Apostolic. [Paul] Five times..stripes..thrice   8452
Chosen. Moses..choosing rather to suffer..than   8453
Recompensed. Moses..had respect unto the r.   8454
Sacred. Remove this cup..not my will [Jesus]   8455

TORTURE.

Hell. I am tormented in this flame   8852
Jesus. Crown of thorns..spit upon him..smote   8855
Prisoners. Elders of the city and thorns..briers   8853
     "   Put them under saws..harrows   8854

TRIBULATION.

Despair. Who shall be able to stand?   8946
Joy in. I am exceeding joyful in all our   8948
Judgment. Sun..as sackcloth..stars fell..moved   8947
Recompensed. White robes..out of great   8949

Bondage. Egyptians made their lives bitter   895
Forgotten. It was well with us in Egypt   482
Horrible. Galileans whose blood Pilate had mingled   137
Soldiers. Chaldees who slew..had no compassion   138
Well-intended. Our fathers cast out their children   897

See ADVERSITY and references.

5455. MISFORTUNE misinterpreted. *Syrians.*
²³ The servants of the king of Syria said..Their
gods *are* gods of the hills ; therefore they were
stronger than we ; but let us fight against them
in the plain, and surely we shall be stronger
than they.—1 KINGS, ch. 20.

5456. —— —— *"Tower fell."* ⁴ Those

---

eighteen, upon whom the tower in Siloam fell,
and slew them, think ye that they were sinners
above all men that dwelt in Jerusalem ? ⁵ I tell
you, Nay : but, except ye repent, ye shall all
likewise perish.—LUKE, ch. 13.

5457. —— **not understood.** *Gideon.* ¹³ If
the Lord be with us, why then is all this befallen
us ? and where *be* all his miracles which our fathers told us of, saying, Did not the Lord bring
us up from Egypt? but now the Lord hath forsaken us, and delivered us into the hands of the
Midianites.—JUDGES, ch. 6.

See other illustrations under :

ACCIDENT.

Destructive. Wall fell upon 27,000 men   62
Fatal. Child died..she overlaid it   63
Impossible. Calves at home..kine took the straight   64
Lameness. Nurse made haste to flee, he fell   65
Loss. Axe head fell into the water   66
Misjudged. Think ye they were sinners above   67
Pardonable. Cast upon him..without laying in wait   68
Unpunished. Axe..head slippeth from the helve   69

CALAMITY.

of God. Earth opened her mouth, and swallowed   996
Hardened. I have smitten you with blasting   1001
Indiscriminating. The L. maketh the earth   1002
Predicted. Shall not be left one stone upon   997
Waiting. Jonah sat..see what would become   999

DISAPPOINTMENT.

Doubt. Heard that he was alive..believed not   2315
Gif.s. S. gave Hiram 20 cities..pleased him not   2316
Good. They have taken..Lord out of the s.   2317
Humiliating. Prison truly. shut..no man there   2318
Ignorance. No place of seed..figs..vines   2319
Judgment. Thou hast taught in our streets   2320
Misjudged. We trusted it had been he..saved I.   2321
Maternal. I have gotten a man [murderer] from   2322
Many. Sown much, and bring in little   2326
Perplexing. King of Syria sore troubled   2323
Religion. Have wanted all things..consumed   2324
Unendurable. Ahithophel..hanged himself   2325

DISCOURAGEMENT.

Contrast. But as for me, my feet were almost   2346
Defeat. Would to God we had been content..other   2347
Evildoers. I am..weak, though anointed king   2348
Failure. Neither hast thou delivered thy people   2349
     "   We have toiled all the night, and taken   2350
Mismanagement. Men of Ai smote 36 men   2351
Ministerial. Some fell on stony ground..thorns   2352
Needless. They that be with us are more..with   2353
Overcome. He answered her not a word   2359
Reproved. Yet I have left me 7000 in I.   2354
Trials. I am not able to bear all this people..too   2355
Unbelief. Been better to have served the Egyp'ns   2356
Unreasonable. Wherefore have ye brought us, out   2357
Without. We faint not..though our outward man   2358

DISTRESS.

Cry of. Great cry..none like it, nor shall be   2437
Derided. They that see me, shoot out the lip   2438
Described. I was a derision to all my people   2439
Exasperation. What shall I do..people ready to   2440
Famine. Delicate women..shall eat..children   2441
Little Faith. Why are ye fearful..little faith..calm   2442
Friend. Gedaliah..took Jeremiah out of prison   2443
Great. Thrust..right eyes..people wept   2444
Needless. Saul had adjured..food   2445
Refuge. Ahaz sacrificed unto the gods that smote   2446

FAILURE.

Avoiding. First..counteth the cost..to finish   2867
Cruelty. More they afflicted them..grew   2868

Complaint. Why is it thou hast sent me? 2869
Church. Disciples..should cast him out..could n. 2870
Discouraging. Toiled all the night..taken nothing 2871
Disheartening. Put a sword in their hand to slay 2872
Explained. Why could not we cast him out? 2873
Fear. We were..as grasshoppers 2874
Irremediable. Went to buy..door was shut 2875
Ominous. Thou hast begun to fall..surely fall 2876
Providential. Confounded their language..left off 2877
Ridiculed. Mock him..began to build..not able 2878
Temporary. Pharaoh said..neither will I let I. go 2879

Superstition. Who did sin..born blind 203
See ADVERSITY and references.

5458. MISIMPROVEMENT punished. *Parable.* [28] Take therefore the talent from him, and give it unto him which hath ten talents. [29] For unto every one that hath shall be given, and he shall have abundance : but from him that hath not shall be taken away even that which he hath. [30] And cast ye the unprofitable servant into outer darkness.—MAT., ch. 25.

See other illustrations under :
IDLENESS.
Accusation. No straw..ye are idle, ye are idle 4270
Ecstatic. Why stand ye gazing into heaven? 4271
Needless. Why stand ye here all the day idle? 4272
Perishing. If we sit still here, we die also [lepers] 4273
INDOLENCE.
Exhibited. I went by the field of the slothful 4436
Excuse. There is a lion without..I shall be slain 4437
Perfect. Hand..not so much as bring it to his 4438
Shame. Sleepeth in harvest..causeth shame 4439
Wasteful. Slothful in his work..a great waster 4440
LOITERERS.
Driven. Fire..consumed them in the uttermost 5052
Hastened. While he lingered, the men laid hold 5053
OMISSION.
Cursed. Curse ye Meroz..came not up to the help 5875
Deception. If any man be a hearer..and not a doer 5876
Great. When saw we thee ahungered..not minister 5877
Inexcusable. These shall go..everlasting punish't 5878
Nobles. Put not their necks to the work of the L. 5879
Sin. Ye pay tithe of mint..omitted weightier 5880
PROCRASTINATION.
Charity. Say not..to morrow I will give when thou 6620
Fatal. Go thy way this time..convenient season 6621
Folly. Foolish said, Give us of your oil..gone out 6622
Loss. We will hear thee again..Paul departed 6623
No. Suffer me first to go and bury my father 6624
SLUGGARD.
Reproved. Go to the ant, thou sluggard 8145
Vexatious. As smoke to the eyes, so is the sluggard 8146
" Way of the slothful..full of thorns 8147
See NEGLECT and references.

5459. MISREPRESENTATION of Benefactors. *Israelites.* [20] They met Moses and Aaron..as they came forth from Pharaoh : [21] And they said ..The Lord look upon you, and judge ; because ye have made our savour to be abhorred in the eyes of Pharaoh, and in the eyes of his servants, to put a sword in their hand to slay us.—Ex., ch. 5.

See other illustrations under :
SLANDER.
Antidote. They may by your good works..glorify 8101
Base. This fellow doth cast out devils by Beelzebub 8102
Disgraceful. We found this man a pestilent fellow 8103
Folly. He that uttereth a slander is a fool 8104

Hurtful. Then will they not pay tribute 8105
Impious. He saved others ; himself he cannot save 8106
Joyful. Blessed..men revile you..rejoice 8107
Loyalty. Ziba said..he abideth at Jerusalem 8108
Malicious. Diotrephes..prating against us 8109
Opposed. It is reported..be their king 8110
Refuted. If Satan cast out Satan..divided 8111
Rebels. The people is greater than we 8112
Sinners. Thou art an austere man 8113
Satan's. Touch all that he hath..will curse 8114
Secret. A whisperer separateth friends 8115
Unbelief. Would to G. we had died..by fleshpots 8116
See DECEPTION and references.

5460. MISSION of the Church. *Commission.* [19] Go ye therefore, and teach all nations, baptizing them in the name of the Father, and of the Son, and of the Holy Ghost : [20] Teaching them to observe all things whatsoever I have commanded you : and, lo, I am with you alway.—MAT., ch. 28.

5461. —— **first, Home.** *At Ascension.* [8] Ye shall receive power, after that the Holy Ghost is come upon you : and ye shall be witnesses unto me both in Jerusalem, and in all Judea, and in Samaria, and unto the uttermost part of earth.—ACTS, ch. 1.

5462. MISSIONS, Success of. *Universal.* [11] From the rising of the sun even unto the going down of the same, my name *shall be* great among the Gentiles ; and in every place incense *shall be* offered unto my name, and a pure offering.—MAL., ch. 1.

5463. MISSIONARY, A foreign. *Jonah.* [1] The word of the Lord came unto Jonah..saying, [2] Arise, go to Nineveh, that great city, and cry against it ; for their wickedness is come up before me.—JONAH, ch. 1.

5464. —— **A successful.** *Jonah.* [4] Jonah began to enter into the city a day's journey, and he cried..Yet forty days, and Nineveh shall be overthrown. [5] So the people of Nineveh believed God, and proclaimed a fast, and put on sackcloth, from the greatest of them even to the least.—JONAH, ch. 3.

5465. —— **wanted, A.** *Dives.* [27] I pray thee..wouldest send him to my father's house : [28] For I have five brethren ; that he may testify unto them, lest they also come into this place of torment.—LUKE, ch. 16.

5466. MISSIONARIES, A Cry for. *Vision.* [9] A vision appeared to Paul in the night ; There stood a man of Macedonia, and prayed him, saying, Come over into Macedonia, and help us. [10] And..immediately we endeavoured to go.—ACTS, ch. 16.

5467. —— **First Christian.** *Paul and Barnabas.* [2] As they ministered to the Lord, and fasted, the Holy Ghost said, Separate me Barnabas and Saul for the work whereunto I have called them.. [4] So they, being sent forth by the Holy Ghost, departed unto Seleucia ; and from thence they sailed to Cyprus.—ACTS, ch. 13.

5468. MISTAKE from Appearances. *Mother of Samuel.* [13] Only her lips moved, but her voice was not heard : therefore Eli thought she had been drunken. [14] And Eli said..How long wilt thou be drunken? put away thy wine from thee. [15] And Hannah answered..No, my lord, I am a woman of a sorrowful spirit : I have drunk neither wine nor strong drink, but have poured out my soul before the Lord.—1 Sam., ch. 1.

5469. —— **in Adversity.** *Jacob.* ³⁶ Me have ye bereaved *of my children:* Joseph *is* not, and Simeon *is* not, and ye will take Benjamin *away:* all these things are against me.—Gen., ch. 42.

5470. —— **A conscientious.** *Persecutors.* ² They shall put you out of the synagogues : yea, the time cometh, that whosoever killeth you will think that he doeth God service. ³ And these things will they do unto you, because they have not known the Father, nor me.—John, ch. 16.

5471. —— **corrected.** *Poison.* ³⁹ One went out into the field to gather herbs, and found a wild vine, and gathered thereof wild gourds his lap full, and came and shred *them* into the pot of pottage : for they knew *them* not. ⁴⁰..*there is* death in the pot.. ⁴¹ But he said, Then bring meal. And he cast *it* into the pot..And there was no harm in the pot.—2 Kings, ch. 4.

5472. —— **A disastrous.** *Moabites.* ²² The sun shone upon the water, and the Moabites saw the water on the other side *as* red as blood : ²³ And they said, This *is* blood : the kings are surely slain, and they have smitten one another : now therefore, Moab, to the spoil. ²⁴ And when they came to the camp..the Israelites rose up and smote the Moabites, so that they fled.—2 Kings, ch. 3.

5473. —— **A glorious.** *Mary.* ² She runneth, and cometh to Simon Peter, and to the other disciple, whom Jesus loved, and saith.. They have taken away the Lord out of the sepulchre, and we know not where they have laid him.—John, ch. 20.

5474. —— **in Hearing.** *Crucifixion.* ⁴⁶ Eli, Eli, lama sabachthani ? that is to say, My God, my God, why hast thou forsaken me ? ⁴⁷ Some of them that stood there, when they heard *that,* said, This *man* calleth for Elias.—Mat., ch. 27.

5475. —— **from Infatuation.** *Idolaters.* ¹⁷ We will certainly..burn incense unto the queen of heaven..pour out drink offerings unto her, as we have done, we, and our fathers, our kings, and our princes, in the cities of Judah, and in the streets of Jerusalem : for *then* had we plenty of victuals, and were well, and saw no evil.—Jer., ch. 44.

5476. —— **from Ignorance.** *Sadducees.* ²⁸ In the resurrection, whose wife shall she be of the seven ? for they all had her. ²⁹ Jesus answered ..Ye do err, not knowing the Scriptures, nor the power of God. ³⁰ For in the resurrection they neither marry, nor are given in marriage, but are as the angels of God.—Mat., ch. 22.

5477. —— **Man's.** *Choice for King.* ⁶ He looked on Eliab, and said, Surely the Lord's anointed *is* before him. ⁷ But the Lord said unto Samuel, Look not on his countenance, or on the height of his stature ; because I have refused him : for the Lord *seeth* not as man seeth ; for man looketh on the outward appearance, but the Lord looketh on the heart.—1 Sam., ch. 16.

5478. —— **A mortifying.** *Haman's.* ⁶ So Haman came in. And the king said.. What shall be done unto the man whom the king delighteth to honour ? Now Haman thought in his heart, To whom would the king delight to do honour

more than to myself?.. ¹⁰ Then the king said to Haman, Make haste, *and* take the apparel and the horse, as thou hast said, and do even so to Mordecai the Jew.—Esther, ch. 6.

5479. —— **through Prejudice.** *Paul.* ⁹ I verily thought with myself, that I ought to do many things contrary to the name of Jesus of Nazareth. ¹⁰..and many of the saints did I shut up in prison..and when they were put to death, I gave my voice against *them.*—Acts, ch. 26.

5480. —— **from Prosperity.** *"Plenty."* [See No. 5475.]

5481. —— **A serious.** *Altar of Witness.* ²² The Lord God of gods, he knoweth, and Israel he shall know ; if *it be* in rebellion, or if in transgression against the Lord, (save us not this day,) ²³ That we have built us an altar to turn from following the Lord, or if to offer thereon burnt offering or meat offering, or if to offer peace offerings thereon, let the Lord himself require *it.*—Josh., ch. 22. [A war was prevented.]

5482. —— **from Suspicion.** *Hanun.* ³ The princes of the children of Ammon said unto Hanun their lord, Thinkest thou that David doth honour thy father, that he hath sent comforters unto thee ? hath not David *rather* sent his servants unto thee, to search the city, and to spy it out, and to overthrow it?—2 Sam., ch. 10. [He mutilated their beards and garments.]

5483. —— **A Zealot's.** *Irijah.* ¹⁴ Said Jeremiah, *It is* false ; I fall not away to the Chaldeans. But he hearkened not to him : so Irijah took Jeremiah, and brought him to the princes. ¹⁵ Wherefore the princes were wroth with Jeremiah, and smote him, and put him in prison.—Jer., ch. 37.

See other illustrations under :

DISAPPOINTMENT.

Doubt. Heard..he was alive..seen..believed not   2315
in Gifts. Gave Hiram 20 cities..pleased him not   2316
Good. They have taken the L. out of the sepulchre   2318
Ignorance. Evil place ? no place of seed..figs   2319
Judgment. Thou hast taught in our streets   2320
Misjudged. We trusted..had been he..should have   2321
Maternal. Bare Cain..I have gotten a man of the   2322
Perplexing. Which of us is for the king of Israel ?   2323
Religion. Since we left off to burn incense..for   2324
Unendurable. Ahithophel..counsel not followed   2325
Many Disappointments. Consider your ways   2326

ERROR.

Sweeping. Barnabas also was carried away   2709
Sincere. There is a way that seemeth right..ways   2710

FOLLY.

Anger. Nabal answered, Who is David ?   3262
Ashamed. Held their peace..who should be the g.   3263
Backsliders. Forsaken..living waters..broken   3264
Ecclesiastical. Whether is greater, the gift or the   3265
Inseparable. Bray a fool in a mortar..not depart   3266
Indifference. Heareth..doeth not..build upon the   3267
Idolaters. Mouths, but they speak not ; eyes..see   3268
"   Warm himself..maketh a graven image   3269
Natural. Ostrich..G. hath deprived her of wisdom   3270
Neglect. Foolish..took no oil with them   3271
Worldly. I will pull down..build..eat, drink   3272
Youth. Rehoboam forsook the counsel of the old   3273

5484. MISUSE of Privileges. *Nadab and Abihu.* ¹ Took either of them his censer, and put fire therein, and put incense thereon, and offered strange fire before the Lord.. ² And there went out fire from the Lord, and devoured them.—LEV., ch. 10.

See other illustrations under :

ABUSE.

Mercy. Pharaoh saw..thunders were ceased..hard. 39
Privileges. Come together, not for the better..worse 40
Religious. Brazen serpent..burn incense to it 41

CRUELTY.

Ambition. Athaliah destroyed all the seed royal 1857
Brutal. Ten thousand..cast down..top of a rock 1858
Failure. More they afflicted them..grew 1859
Insulting. Purple..crown of thorns..Hail ! 1860
Pride. Mordecai bowed not..H. full of wrath 1861
Reward. Troubleth his own flesh 1862
Savage. Slew the sons..before his eyes 1863
War. Put them under saws..harrows 1864

INJURY.

Forgiveness. Father, forgive them, they know not 4498
Insulting. Samson's wife was given to his..friend 4496
Revenged. Samson caught 300 foxes..firebrands 4497

INSULT.

Ignored. Belial said, How shall this man save us 4567
Jesus. Thrust him out of the city..cast him 4568
Reward. Hanun shaved off one half their beards 4569
Stinging. Ananias commanded them to smite 4570

INSULTS.

Cruel. Mocked Jesus..blindfolded, and struck 4576
Contemptuous. They that are younger have me in 4572

See DISPARAGEMENT and references.

5485. MISUNDERSTANDINGS of Christians.
Primitive. ¹ When the number of the disciples was multiplied, there arose a murmuring of the Grecians against the Hebrews, because their widows were neglected in the daily ministration.—ACTS, ch. 6.

See IGNORANCE, MISTAKE, and references.

5486. MIXING, An unwise. *New with Old.*
³⁷ No man putteth new wine into old bottles ; else the new wine will burst the bottles, and be spilled, and the bottles shall perish. ³⁸ But new wine must be put into new bottles ; and both are preserved.—LUKE, ch. 5.

See SEPARATION and references.

5487. MOB of Bigots. *" Jew."* [See No. 5492.]

5488. —— Disturbance from a. *At Thessalonica.* ⁵ Jews which believed not, moved with envy, took unto them certain lewd fellows of the baser sort, and gathered a company, and set all the city on an uproar, and assaulted the house of Jason, and sought to bring them out to the people.—ACTS, ch. 17.

5489. —— A murderous. *At Jerusalem.*
³⁰ All the city was moved, and the people ran together : and they took Paul, and drew him out of the temple : and forthwith the doors were shut. ³¹ And as they went about to kill him, tidings came unto the chief captain..that all Jerusalem was in an uproar.—ACTS, ch. 21.

5490. —— A tumultuous. *At Jerusalem.*
³² They saw the chief captain and the soldiers, they left beating of Paul. ³³ Then the chief captain..commanded *him* to be bound with two chains ; and demanded who he was, and what he had done. ³⁴ And some cried one thing, some another.—ACTS, ch. 21.

5491. —— Trial by a. *Stephen.* ⁵⁴ When they heard these things, they were cut to the heart, and they gnashed on him with *their* teeth.. ⁵⁷ Then they cried out with a loud voice, and stopped their ears, and ran upon him with one accord, ⁵⁸ And cast *him* out of the city, and stoned *him*.—ACTS, ch. 7.

5492. —— Workmen's. *Ephesian.* ²⁵ With the workmen of like occupation, and said, Sirs, ye know that by this craft we have our wealth. ²⁶..not alone at Ephesus, but almost throughout all Asia, this Paul hath persuaded and turned away much people, saying that they be no gods, which are made with hands.. ³⁴ But when they knew that he was a Jew, all with one voice about the space of two hours cried out, Great *is* Diana of the Ephesians.—ACTS, ch. 19.

5493. MOCKERS of Truth. *Athenians.*
³² When they heard of the resurrection of the dead, some mocked.—ACTS, ch. 17.

5494. MOCKERY, Blasphemous. *Soldiers.*
²⁹ When they had platted a crown of thorns, they put *it* upon his head, and a reed in his right hand : and they bowed the knee before him, and mocked him, saying, Hail, King of the Jews !—MAT., ch. 27.

See other illustrations under :

DERISION.

Horrible. Put on him a scarlet robe..crown 2197
Impious. Laughed them to scorn and mocked them 2198
Nickname. Thou art a Samaritan and hast a devil 2200
Punished. Sarah saw the son of Hagar mocking 2199
Truth. Pharisees who were covetous..derided him 2201
Unfortunates. Thieves also..cast the same into his 2202
Wicked. They shoot out the lip and shake the head 2203

RIDICULE.

Doctrine. When they heard of the resurrection 7425
Fatal. Call for Samson that he may make us sport 7426
Failure. Not able to finish..begin to mock him 7427
Horrible. He saved others, let him save himself 7428
Impious. They laughed them to scorn and mocked 7429
   " What will this babbler say ? [Athenians] 7430
Insulting. Cut off their garments..their buttocks 7431
Opposition. What do these feeble Jews? will they 7432
   " If a fox go up, he shall break down 7433
Punishment. Children of Bethel..Go up, thou bald 7434
Royalty. Wearing the crown of thorns and purple 7435
Scornful. They laughed us to scorn and despised us 7436
Spirit. Mocking said, These men are full of new wine 7437
Trial. They reviled him, and said, We are Moses' 7438

SCOFFERS.

Malicious. Spit in his face and buffeted 7614
   " Mocked him..a gorgeous robe 7615

SCORN.

of Pride. [Haman] Scorn to lay hands on Mordecai 7618
Public. All clap their hands at thee and hiss 7619
Taunt. Who made thee a prince and a judge over 8592
Unbelief. She sleepeth..they laughed him to scorn 7620

5495. MODERATION in Pleasure. *Proverb.*
¹⁶ Hast thou found honey ? eat so much as is sufficient for thee, lest thou be filled therewith, and vomit it. ¹⁷ Withdraw thy foot from thy neighbour's house ; lest he be weary of thee, and *so* hate thee.—PROV., ch. 25.

5496. —— Safety in. *Little by Little.* ²² The Lord thy God will put out those nations before thee by little and little : thou mayest not consume them at once, lest the beasts of the field increase upon thee.—DEUT., ch. 7.

See other illustrations under :

PRUDENCE.

See CONTENTMENT.

5497. MODESTY endangered. *Saul.* ² Saul, a choice young man, and a goodly : and *there was* not among the children of Israel a goodlier person than he : from his shoulders and upward *he was* higher than any of the people.—1 SAM., ch. 9.

5498. —— enjoined. *At a Wedding Feast.* ⁸ Sit not down in the highest room ; lest a more honourable man than thou be bidden of him ; ⁹ And he that bade thee and him come and say to thee, Give this man place ; and thou begin with shame to take the lowest room.—LUKE, ch. 14.

5499. —— Ministerial. *John.* ¹³ Then cometh Jesus from Galilee to Jordan unto John, to be baptized of him. ¹⁴ But John forbade him, saying, I have need to be baptized of thee, and comest thou to me ?—MAT., ch. 3.

5500. —— preserved. *Saul.* [See No. 5497.] ²⁰ On whom *is* all the desire of Israel ? *Is it* not on thee.. ? ²¹.. Saul answered.. *Am* not I a Benjamite, of the smallest of the tribes of Israel ? and my family the least of all the families of the tribe of Benjamin ? wherefore then speakest thou so to me ?—1 SAM., ch. 9.

5501. —— Punished for. *Vashti.* [See No. 5202.] ¹⁹ If it please the king, let there go a royal commandment from him.. That Vashti come no more before king Ahasuerus ; and let the king give her royal estate unto another that is better that she.—ESTHER, ch. 1.

5502. —— Womanly. *Vashti.* ¹⁰ The king commanded.. ¹¹ To bring Vashti the queen before the king with the crown royal, to shew the people and the princes her beauty : for she *was* fair to look on. ¹² But the queen Vashti refused to come.—ESTHER, ch. 1.

See HUMILITY and references.

5503. MONEY, Alarm at. *Joseph's Brethren.* ²⁷ As one of them opened his sack to give his ass provender in the inn, he espied his money.. ²⁸ And he said unto his brethren, My money is restored ; and lo, *it is* even in my sack : and their heart failed *them,* and they were afraid, saying one to another, What *is* this *that* God hath done unto us ?—GEN., ch. 42.

5504. —— Abominable. *Joseph's Brethren.* ²⁸ There passed by Midianites merchantmen ; and they drew.. Joseph out of the pit, and sold Joseph to the Ishmaelites for twenty *pieces* of silver : and they brought Joseph into Egypt.—GEN., ch. 37.

5505. —— Accountability for. *Parable.* ¹⁵ When he was returned.. he commanded these servants to be called.. to whom he had given the money, that he might know how much every man had gained by trading. ¹⁶ Then came the first, saying, Lord, thy pound hath gained ten pounds.—LUKE, ch. 19.

5506. —— Bribe. *Judges.* ¹ When Samuel was

old.. he made his sons judges over Israel. ³ And his sons walked not in his ways, but turned aside after lucre, and took bribes, and perverted judgment.—1 SAM., ch. 8.

5507. —— Blood. *Judas* ³ Repented himself, and brought again the thirty pieces of silver to the chief priests and elders, ⁴ Saying, I have sinned in that I have betrayed the innocent blood. And they said, What *is that* to us ? see thou *to that.* ⁵ And he cast down the pieces of silver.—MAT., ch. 27.

5508. —— Best Use of. *Parable.* ⁸ The Lord commended the unjust steward, because he had done wisely.. ⁹ And I say unto you, Make to yourselves friends of the mammon of unrighteousness ; that, when ye fail, they may receive you into everlasting habitations.—LUKE, ch. 16.

5509. —— Box for. *"Beside the Altar."* ⁹ Jehoiada the priest took a chest, and bored a hole in the lid of it, and set it beside the altar, on the right side as one cometh into the house of the Lord : and the priests that kept the door put therein all the money *that was* brought.—2 KINGS, ch. 12.

5510. —— buys Place. *Proverb.* ¹⁶ A man's gift maketh room for him, and bringeth him before great men.—PROV., ch. 18.

5511. —— buys Friends. *Unjust Steward.* ⁴ When I am put out of the stewardship, they may receive me into their houses. ⁵ So he called every one of his lord's debtors.. and said unto the first, How much owest thou unto my lord ? ⁶ And he said, A hundred measures of oil. And he said.. Take thy bill, and sit down quickly, and write fifty.—LUKE, ch. 16.

5512. —— buys Men. *The Jews* ¹² Gave large money unto the soldiers, ¹³ Saying, Say ye, His disciples came by night, and stole him *away* while we slept.—MAT., ch. 28.

5513. —— Better than. *Blood of Christ.* ¹⁸ Ye know that ye were not redeemed with corruptible things, *as* silver and gold.. ¹⁹ But with the precious blood of Christ.—1 PETER, ch. 1.

5514. —— with a Curse. *Gehazi said,* ²² My master hath sent me, saying.. there be come to me.. two young men of the sons of the prophets : give them, I pray thee, a talent of silver, and two changes of garments. ²³ And Naaman said .. take two talents.. ²⁷ The leprosy therefore of Naaman shall cleave unto thee, and unto thy seed for ever. And he went out.. a leper *as while* as snow.—2 KINGS, ch. 5.

5515. —— Cursed by. *Chaldeans.* ⁶ Woe to him that increaseth *that which is* not his ! how long ? and to him that ladeth himself with thick clay ! ⁷ Shall they not rise up suddenly that shall bite thee, and awake that shall vex thee ?—HAB., ch. 2.

5516. —— Corrupted by. *Priests.* ¹⁰ They build up Zion with blood, and Jerusalem with iniquity. ¹¹ The heads thereof judge for reward, and the priests thereof teach for hire, and the prophets thereof divine for money : yet will they lean upon the Lord, and say, *Is* not the Lord among us ? none evil can come upon us.—MICAH, ch. 3.

5517. —— —— Ministers. ¹⁰ There are many unruly and vain talkers and deceivers, specially they of the circumcision : ¹¹.. who subvert whole houses, teaching things which they ought not, for filthy lucre's sake.—Titus, ch. 1.

5518. —— **Choice of.** *Young Ruler.* ²¹ Jesus . .loved him, and said. .One thing thou lackest : go thy way, sell whatsoever thou hast, and give to the poor, and thou shalt have treasure in heaven : and come, take up the cross, and follow me. ²² And he. .went away grieved : for he had great possessions.—Mark, ch. 10.

5519. —— **declined.** *Naaman.* ¹⁵ Behold, now I know that *there is* no God in all the earth, but in Israel : now therefore. .take a blessing of thy servant. ¹⁶ But he said, *As* the Lord liveth, before whom I stand, I will receive none. And he urged him to take *it;* but he refused.—2 Kings, ch. 5.

5520. —— **disregarded.** *Amaziah.* ⁶ Hired . .men of valour out of Israel. . ⁷ But there came a man of God to him, saying, O king, let not the army of Israel go with thee ; for the Lord *is* not with Israel, ⁹. .Amaziah said. .But what shall we do for the hundred talents which I have given to the army of Israel ? And the man of God answered, The Lord is able to give thee much more than this.—2 Chron., ch. 25.

5521. —— **devoted.** *Primitive Church.* ³⁶ Joses. .surnamed Barnabas, (which is, being interpreted, The son of consolation,) a Levite . . ³⁷ Having land, sold *it,* and brought the money, and laid *it* at the apostles' feet.—Acts, ch. 4.

5522. —— **Eagerness for.** *"Snare."* ⁹ They that will be rich fall into temptation and a snare, and *into* many foolish and hurtful lusts, which drown men in destruction and perdition.—1 Tim., ch. 6.

5523. —— **Evil of.** *Root.* ¹⁰ The love of money is the root of all evil : which while some coveted after, they have erred from the faith, and pierced themselves through with many sorrows. —1 Tim., ch. 6.

5524. —— **for a Grave.** *About* $225. ⁴ I am a stranger. .give me a possession of a burying-place with you, that I may bury my dead out of my sight. . ¹⁶. .and Abraham weighed to Ephron . .four hundred shekels of silver, current *money.* —Gen., ch. 23.

5525. —— **Greed for.** *Judas.* ¹⁴ One of the twelve, called Judas Iscariot, went unto the chief priests, ¹⁵ And said. .What will ye give me, and I will deliver him unto you ? And they covenanted with him for thirty pieces of silver. —Mat., ch. 26.

5526. —— **freely given.** *Repairs.* ⁴ All the money that cometh into any man's heart to bring into the house of the Lord, ⁵ Let the priests take *it* to them, every man of his acquaintance : and let them repair the breaches of the house.—2 Kings, ch. 12.

5527. —— **Independence of.** *To King of Sodom.* ²³ I will not *take* from a thread even to a shoe-latchet. .lest thou shouldest say, I have made Abram rich : ²⁴ Save only that which the young men have eaten, and the portion of the men which went with me.—Gen., ch. 14.

5528. —— **Influence of.** *Partiality.* ² If there come unto your assembly a man with a gold ring, in goodly apparel, and there come in

also a poor man in vile raiment ; ³ And ye have respect to him that weareth the gay clothing, and say. .Sit thou here in a good place ; and say to the poor, Stand thou there, or sit here under my footstool : ⁴ Are ye not then partial ?—James, ch. 2.

5529. —— **Intrusion of.** *His first Visit.* ¹⁴ Found in the temple those that sold oxen and sheep and doves, and the changers of money sitting : ¹⁵ And when he had made a scourge of small cords, he drove them all out. .and poured out the changers' money, and overthrew the tables.—John, ch. 2.

5530. —— **Lost with.** *Dives.* ¹⁹ There was a certain rich man, which was clothed in purple and fine linen, and fared sumptuously every day : ²². .the rich man also died, and was buried ; ²³ And in hell he lifted up his eyes, being in torments.—Luke, ch. 16.

5531. —— **Misery from.** *Judas.* ¹⁸ Purchased a field with the reward of iniquity ; and falling headlong, he burst asunder in the midst, and all his bowels gushed out.—Acts, ch. 1.

5532. —— **Monopoly of.** *Famine.* ¹⁴ Joseph gathered up all the money that was found in the land of Egypt, and. .Canaan, for the corn which they bought : and Joseph brought the money into Pharaoh's house.—Gen., ch. 47.

5533. —— **the Motive.** *At Ephesus.* ¹⁸ Paul . .said to the spirit, I command thee in the name of Jesus Christ to come out of her. And he came out. . ¹⁹ And when her masters saw that the hope of their gains was gone, they caught Paul and Silas, and drew *them* into the market-place unto the rulers.—Acts, ch. 16.

5534. —— —— *"Diana."* [See No. 5558.]

5535. —— **Pride with.** *Hezekiah.* [See No. 5544.]

5536. —— **powerless.** *Balaam.* ¹⁶ Thus saith Balak. .Let nothing, I pray thee, hinder thee from coming unto me : ¹⁷ For I will promote thee. .I pray thee, curse me this people. ¹⁸ And Balaam answered. .If Balak would give me his house full of silver and gold, I cannot go beyond the word of the Lord my God, to do less or more.—Num., ch. 22.

5537. —— **Payment in.** *Naaman.* ⁵ The king of Syria said, Go. .I will send a letter unto the king of Israel. And he. .took with him ten talents of silver, and six thousand *pieces* of gold, and ten changes of raiment.—2 Kings, ch. 5.

5538. —— **Perishing with.** *Simon.* [See No. 5548.] ²⁰ Peter said. .Thy money perish with thee, because thou hast thought that the gift of God may be purchased with money. ²¹ Thou hast neither part nor lot in this matter : for thy heart is not right in the sight of God.—Acts, ch. 8.

5539. —— **Pressure for.** *Tribute.* [See No. 5554.] ¹⁵ Hezekiah gave *him* all the silver that was found in the house of the Lord, and in the treasures of the king's house. ¹⁶. .Hezekiah cut off *the gold from* the doors of the temple. .and *from* the pillars which Hezekiah. .had overlaid, and gave it to the king of Assyria.—2 Kings, ch. 18.

5540. —— **Revenue of.** *Solomon's.* ¹⁴ The weight of gold that came to Solomon in one year was six hundred threescore and six talents of gold, 15 Besides *that he had* of the merchantmen, and of the traffick of the spice merchants, and of all the kings of Arabia, and of the governors of the country.—1 KINGS, ch. 10.

5541. —— **Return for.** *Paid.* [See No. 5520.]

5542. —— **returned.** *"Found."* 21 When we came to the inn..we opened our sacks, and, behold, *every* man's money *was* in the mouth of his sack..and we have brought it again in our hand.—GEN., ch. 43.

5543. —— **Reintrusion of.** *His last Visit.* 12 Cast out all them that sold and bought in the temple, and overthrew the tables of the money changers, and the seats of them that sold doves, 13 And said..It is written, My house shall be called the house of prayer ; but ye have made it a den of thieves.—MAT., ch. 21.

5544. —— **a Snare.** *Hezekiah.* 12 Berodach-baladan..king of Babylon, sent letters and a present unto Hezekiah..[who] had been sick. 13 And Hezekiah..shewed them all the house of his precious things, the silver, and the gold, and the spices, and the precious ointment, and *all* the house of his armour, and all that was found in his treasures.. 17 Behold, the days come, that all ..shall be carried unto Babylon.—2 KINGS, ch. 20.

5545. —— **Sacrifice of.** *Ephesus.* 19 Many of them also which used curious arts brought their books together, and burned them before all *men :* and they counted the price of them, and found *it* fifty thousand *pieces* of silver.—ACTS, ch. 19.

5546. —— **Sinning for.** *Balaam.* 15 Balaam ..loved the wages of unrighteousness ; 16 But was rebuked for his iniquity : the dumb ass speaking with man's voice forbade the madness of the prophet.—2 PETER, ch. 2.

5547. —— **Sold for.** *Samson.* 5 The lords of the Philistines..said unto her, Entice him, and see wherein his great strength *lieth*, and by what *means* we may prevail against him, that we may bind him to afflict him : and we will give thee every one of us eleven hundred *pieces* of silver.—JUDGES, ch. 16.

5548. —— **for Simony.** *Simon Magus.* 18 When Simon saw that through laying on of the apostles' hands the Holy Ghost was given, he offered them money, 19 Saying, Give me also this power, that on whomsoever I lay hands, he may receive the Holy Ghost.—ACTS, ch. 8.

5549. —— **scrutinized.** *In Temple.* 41 Jesus sat over against the treasury, and beheld how the people cast money into the treasury : and many that were rich cast in much. 42 And there came a certain poor widow, and she threw in two mites.—MARK, ch. 12. [His last visit.]

5550. —— **Life saved by.** *Ten Men.* 8 Ten men were found among them that said unto Ishmael, Slay us not : for we have treasures in the field, of wheat, and of barley, and of oil, and of honey. So he forbare.—JER., ch. 41.

5551. —— **Seeking for.** *Lost Coin.* 8 What woman having ten pieces of silver, if she lose one piece, doth not light a candle, and sweep the house, and seek diligently till she find *it ?* —LUKE, ch. 15.

5552. —— **Tainted.** *Judas'.* 5 The chief priests took the silver pieces, and said, It is not lawful for to put them into the treasury, because

it is the price of blood. 7 And they took counsel, and bought with them the potter's field, to bury strangers.—MAT., ch. 27.

5553. —— **thrown away.** *Judas.* 5 He cast down the pieces of silver in the temple..and went and hanged himself.—MAT., ch. 27.

5554. —— **Heavy Tribute.** $1,755,000. 14 Hezekiah king of Judah sent to the king of Assyria to Lachish, saying, I have offended ; return from me : that which thou puttest on me will I bear. And the king of Assyria appointed..three hundred talents of silver and thirty talents of gold.—2 KINGS, ch. 18.

5555. —— **Uninfluenced by.** *Simon.* [See No. 5548.]

5556. —— **Weakness of.** *Judas.* [See No. 5553.]

5557. —— **Waiting for.** *Bribe.* 26 He hoped also that money should have been given him of Paul, that he might loose him : wherefore he sent for him the oftener, and communed with him. 27 But after two years Porcius Festus came into Felix' room.—ACTS, ch. 24.

5558. MONEY-POWER aroused. *Silversmiths.* 27 Not only this our craft is in danger to be set at nought ; but also that the temple of the great goddess Diana should be despised, and her magnificence should be destroyed, whom all Asia and the world worshippeth. 28..they were full of wrath, and cried out, saying, Great *is* Diana of the Ephesians.—ACTS, ch. 19.

See other illustrations under :

AVARICE.

Falsehood. Ananias with Sapphira..kept back	592
Oppression. Swallow up the needy..make the poor	593
Victim. Were glad..covenanted to give Judas	594

COST.

Count. I will follow thee..not where to lay his h.	1734
Counted. Burned their books before all men	1735
not Counted. This man began to build, and was not	1736
Sacrifice. Neither will I offer..cost me nothing	1737

COVETOUSNESS.

Abhorred. Blesseth the covetous whom the L.	1786
Alarmed. By this craft..our wealth..confusion	1787
Apostle. Judas went..to give him money	1788
Aroused. Damsel..masters saw..gains were gone	1789
Absence of. Abram said, I will not take..thread	1790
Church. Who would shut the doors for naught	1791
Cruelty. Felix hoped that money..of Paul	1792
Caution. Inheritance..take heed..beware of	1793
Disobedience. I saw among the spoils..took them	1794
Forbidden. Thou shalt not covet thy neighbour's	1795
Fraud. Gehazi..I will run and take..silver	1796
Folly. Soul, thou hast much goods..eat, drink	1797
Falsehood. Ananias with Sapphira..kept back	1798
Freedom. I have coveted no man's silver..Paul	1799
Inconsiderate. Well watered..Lot chose..plain of	1800
Oppressive. Ye exact usury..sell your brethren	1801
Overcome by. Saul and the people spared the best	1802
Overreaching. Laban..changed my wages ten	1803
Stigmatized. If any man that is called a brother	1804
Shameless. Given to covetousness..not..ashamed	1805
Unhappiness. Naboth had a vineyard..Ahab	1806

FINANCE.

Plan. First day of the week..every one	3220
Simplicity. Chest..hole in the lid	3221

SIMONY.

Crime. Offered them money..give me this power	7912
Scorn. Thy money perish with thee	7913

TREASURES.

Cross. Esteeming the reproach of C. greater riches 8884
Discovery. Selleth all..buyeth that field 8885
Forsaken. Regard not your stuff..land of Egypt 8886
Heaven. Go..sell..give..have treasures in heaven 8887
Insecure. Moth and rust..thieves break through 8888
Restored. All the vessels of gold and silver, 5400 8889
Secure. Lay up..treasures in heaven 8890
Watched. Jesus sat over against the treasury 8891

USURY.

Abolished. I pray you, let us leave off this usury 9146
Condemned. I was very angry..great assembly 9147
Law. Unto a stranger thou mayest lend upon usury 9148
Opportunity. That we might buy corn because of 9149

WAGES.

Back. Borrow jewels of silver..gold..raiment 9255
Changed. Laban..changed my wages ten times 9256
Daily. Not abide with thee all night 9257
  " At his day..give him his hire 9258
Others. Thou hast made them equal..us 9259
Unimportant. Take this child..give thee wages 9260
Withheld. Hire..kept back..crieth 9261

Convenience. If the way be too long..turn it into 8821
Dishonesty. Judas..was a thief and had the bag 8892
Mercenary. The first supposed..have received 5374
Monopolist. Joseph gathered all the m. in E. 993
See RICHES, WEALTH.

5559. MONOPOLY of Weapons. *Philistines.*
[19] There was no smith found throughout all the
land of Israel : (for the Philistines said, Lest
the Hebrews make *them* swords or spears :)
[20] But all the Israelites went down to the Philistines, to sharpen every man his share, and his
coulter, and his axe, and his mattock.—1 SAM.,
ch. 13.

5560. MONUMENT, The first. *Grave.* [20] Jacob set a pillar upon her grave : that *is* the pillar of Rachel's grave unto this day.—GEN., ch.
35.

See other illustrations under :

MEMORIAL.

Benevolence. Alms are come up for a memorial 5321
Deliverance. When thy son asketh thee, What is 5322
Food. Omar full of manna..kept for your 5323
Love. Throughout the whole world..memorial of 5324
Stones. Joshua set up twelve stones in..Jordan 5325
Victory. Samuel took a stone and set it..Ebenezer 5326
  " Sword of Goliath..behind the ephod 5327

5561. MORALITY, Complete. *Young Ruler.*
[19] Thou knowest the commandments, Do not
commit adultery, Do not kill, Do not steal, Do
not bear false witness, Defraud not, Honour thy
father and mother. [20] And he answered..all
these have I observed from my youth. [21] Then
Jesus..said..One thing thou lackest.—MARK,
ch. 10.

5562. —— False Zeal for. *Adulterers.* [7] When
they continued asking him, he..said..He that
is without sin among you, let him first cast a
stone at her. [9] And they..being convicted by
their own conscience, went out one by one, beginning at the eldest, *even* unto the last : and
Jesus was left alone, and the woman.—JOHN,
ch. 8.

5563. —— insufficient. *Negative.* [11] The
Pharisee stood and prayed thus with himself,
God, I thank thee, that I am not as other men
are, extortioners, unjust, adulterers, or even as
this publican.—LUKE, ch. 18.

5564. —— indispensable. *"Do Well."* [15] Ye
make many prayers, I will not hear : your hands
are full of blood. [16] Wash ye, make you clean ;
put away the evil of your doings from before
mine eyes ; cease to do evil ; [17] Learn to do
well ; seek judgment, relieve the oppressed,
judge the fatherless, plead for the widow.—ISA.,
ch. 1.

5565. —— Without. *"Sons of Belial."*
[See Judges, ch. 19 ; also Sodomites, Gen., ch.
19.]
See other illustrations under :

CONDUCT.

Disposition. Samaritan had compassion 1467
Observed. David behaved himself..much set by 1468
Strange. Turned aside quickly..calf and worship 1469

HONESTY.

Accredited. My master wotteth not what is with 4043
Acknowledged. Samuel..thou hast not defrauded 4044
Commended. Hath not oppressed..usury..iniquity 4045
Happiness. Better is little with righteousness 4046
Ignored. It is naught, saith the buyer..boasteth 4047
Official. Gift doth blind the eyes of the wise 4048
Payment. Go sell the oil and pay the debt 4049
Rare. Seek..if there be any..the truth 4050
Reward. Shaketh his hands from holding of bribes 4051
Restitution. If I have taken..restore fourfold 4052
Trained. All these have I observed from my y. 4053
Test. The money that was..in your sacks..carry 4054
Trade. Not have..divers weights, a great and a s. 4055
  " Divers weights, and divers measures 4056
Trusted. They delivered the money to..workmen 4057

RIGHTEOUSNESS.

Benefits. Prolongeth days..hope of the righteous 7444
Discarded. If any..might trust in the flesh, I more 7445
False. Say not..for my righteousness the L. hath 7446
Flattery. Pharisee..prayed thus with himself 7447
See CHARACTER.

5566. MORTALITY of Man. *"Grass."* [24] For
all flesh *is* as grass, and all the glory of man as
the flower of grass. The grass withereth, and
the flower thereof falleth away.—1 PETER, ch. 1.

5567. —— remembered. *Eighty Years Old.*
[34] Barzillai said..How long have I to live, that I
should go up with the king unto Jerusalem ?
[35] I *am* this day fourscore years old : *and* can I
discern between good and evil ? can thy servant
taste what I eat or what I drink ? can I hear
any more ?—2 SAM., ch. 19.

See BEREAVEMENT, DEATH.

5568. MORTIFICATION of Pride. *Fatal.*
[23] When Ahithophel saw that his counsel was
not followed, he saddled *his* ass..and gat him
home..and put his household in order, and
hanged himself.—2 SAM., ch. 16.

See other illustrations under ·

SHAME.

Criminal's. As the thief is ashamed when found 7827
Impossible. Dealeth falsely..were they ashamed? 7828
Rejoicing. That they were counted worthy 7829
for Shame. Ashamed of me..of him..be ashamed 7830
Sin. Eyes..opened..were naked..aprons 7831
See HUMILIATION and references.

5569. MORTGAGES, Irredeemable. *Jews.*
[3] We have mortgaged our lands, vineyards, and
houses, that we might buy corn, because of the
dearth. [5] ..and, lo..*some* of our daughters are
brought into bondage *already* : neither *is it* in
our power *to redeem* them.—NEH., ch. 5.

See DEBT.

5570. MOTHER, An ambitious. *"Right Hand."* [21] Grant that these my two sons may sit, the one on thy right hand, and the other on the left, in thy kingdom. [22] But Jesus answered..Ye know not what ye ask.—MAT., ch. 20.

5571. —— **An anxious.** *Rebekah.* [46] Rebekah said to Isaac, I am weary of my life because of the daughters of Heth : if Jacob take a wife..such as these *which are* of the daughters of the land, what good shall my life do me?— GEN., ch. 27.

5572. —— **Brutalized.** *Siege of Samaria.* [29] So we boiled my son, and did eat him : and I said unto her on the next day, Give thy son, that we may eat him : and she hath hid her son. —2 KINGS, ch. 6.

5573. —— **A cruel.** *Athaliah.* [1] Athaliah the mother of Ahaziah saw that her son was dead, she arose and destroyed all the seed royal. —2 KINGS, ch. 11. [She became queen.]

5574. —— **Careful.** *Samuel's.* [18] Samuel ministered before the Lord, *being* a child.. [19]..his mother made him a little coat, and brought it to him from year to year, when she came up with her husband, to offer the yearly sacrifice. —1 SAM., ch. 2.

5575. —— **Care for.** *Jesus crucified.* [26] When Jesus therefore saw his mother, and the disciple standing by, whom he loved, he saith unto his mother, Woman, behold thy son ! [27] Then saith he to the disciple, Behold thy mother ! And from that hour that disciple took her unto his own *home.*—JOHN, ch. 19.

5576. —— **Distress of a.** *Hagar.* [15] She cast the child under one of the shrubs. [16]..and sat her down over against *him* a good way off ..for she said, Let me not see the death of the child. And she..lifted up her voice, and wept. —GEN., ch. 21.

5577. —— **An ingenious.** *Moses'.* [3] When she could not longer hide him, she took for him an ark of bulrushes, and daubed it with slime and with pitch, and put the child therein ; and she laid *it* in the flags by the river's brink.— EX., ch. 2.

5578. —— **in Israel, A.** *At Abel.* [19] I am one *of them that are* peaceable *and* faithful in Israel : thou seekest to destroy a city and a mother in Israel.. [21]..Sheba..hath lifted up his hand against the king, *even* against David : deliver him only, and I will depart from the city. And the woman said unto Joab, Behold, his head shall be thrown to thee over the wall. —2 SAM., ch. 20.

5579. —— **A revengeful.** *Herodias.* [24] She went forth, and said unto her mother, What shall I ask ? And she said, The head of John the Baptist.—MARK, ch. 6.

5580. —— **Robbery of a.** *By Micah.* [2] He said unto his mother, The eleven hundred *shekels* of silver that were taken from thee, about which thou cursedst, and spakest of also in mine ears..I took it.—JUDGES, ch. 17.

5581. —— **The true.** *Solomon.* [25] The king said, Divide the living child in two, and give half to the one, and half to the other. [26] Then spake the woman whose the living child *was..* O my lord, give her the living child, and in no wise slay it. But the other said, Let it be nei-

ther mine nor thine. *but* divide .*it.*—1 KINGS, ch. 3.

5582. —— **A wicked.** *Rebekah.* [15] Rebekah took goodly raiment of her eldest son Esau.. and put then upon Jacob her younger son : [16] And she put the skins of the kids of the goats upon his hands, and upon the smooth of his neck.— GEN., ch. 27.

5583. —— —— *Reproved.* [By Asa.] [13] Maachah his mother, even her he removed from *being* queen, because she had made an idol in a grove.—1 KINGS, ch. 15.

5584. MOTHER IN LAW, A beloved. *Naomi.* [16] And Ruth said, Entreat me not to leave thee ..for whither thou goest, I will go ; and where thou lodgest, I will lodge : thy people *shall be* my people, and thy God my God : [17] Where thou diest, will I die, and there will I be buried : the Lord do so to me, and more also, *if aught* but death part thee and me.—RUTH, ch. 1.

5585. —— **A tender.** *Naomi.* [7] On the way to return unto the land of Judah. [8]..Naomi said unto her two daughters in law, Go, return each to her mother's house : the Lord deal kindly with you, as ye have dealt with the dead, and with me. [14] And they lifted up their voice, and wept again.—RUTH, ch. 1.

5586. —— **A vexed.** *Rebekah.* [34] Esau was forty years old when he took to wife Judith.. the Hittite, and Bashemath .. the Hittite : [35] Which were a grief of mind unto Isaac and to Rebekah.—GEN., ch. 26.

5587. MOTIVE to Labour. *Paul.* [9] Wherefore we labour, that, whether present or absent, we may be accepted of him.—2 COR., ch. 5.

5588. —— **Unsanctified.** *Excuse.* [3] Smite Amalek, and utterly destroy all that they have.. [15] And Saul said..the people spared the best of the sheep and of the oxen, to sacrifice unto the Lord.. [22] And Samuel said, Hath the Lord *as great* delight in burnt offerings and sacrifices, as in obeying the voice of the Lord? Behold, to obey *is* better than sacrifice, *and* to hearken than the fat of rams.—1 SAM., ch. 15.

5589. MOTIVES, Inferior. *"Did eat."* [26] Jesus answered..Ye seek me, not because ye saw the miracles, but because ye did eat of the loaves, and were filled.—JOHN, ch. 6.

5590. —— **suspected.** *Elisha's.* [16] They said ..Behold now..fifty strong men ; let them go, we pray thee, and seek thy master : lest peradventure the Spirit of the Lord hath taken him up, and cast him upon some mountain, or into some valley. And he said, Ye shall not send. [17] And when they urged him till he was ashamed, he said, Send.—2 KINGS, ch. 2. [The successor to Elijah.]

5591. —— **Worldly.** *Rebuke.* [22] Peter..began to rebuke him, saying, Be it far from thee, Lord : this shall not be unto thee. [23] But he turned, and said unto Peter, Get thee behind me, Satan ; thou art an offence unto me : for thou savourest not the things that be of God, but those that be of men.—MAT., ch. 16.

See SINCERITY and references.

5592. MOUNTAIN of Deliverance. *Lot.* [17] Escape for thy life ; look not behind thee, neither stay thou in all the plain ; escape to the mountain, lest thou be consumed.—GEN., ch. 19.

5593. —— **on Fire.** *Sinai.* [18] Mount Sinai was altogether on a smoke, because the Lord descended upon it in fire : and the smoke thereof ascended as the smoke of a furnace, and the whole mount quaked greatly.—Ex., ch. 19.

5594. —— **Temptation in the.** *Jesus.* [8] The devil taketh him up into an exceeding high mountain, and sheweth him all the kingdoms of the world, and the glory of them ; [9] And saith ..All these things will I give thee, if thou wilt fall down and worship me.—Mat., ch. 4.

5595. —— **View from.** *Nebo.* [1] Moses went up from the plains of Moab unto the mountain of Nebo, to the top of Pisgah, that *is* over against Jericho : and the Lord shewed him all the land. —Deut., ch. 34.

5596. —— **of Vision.** *Transfiguration.* [1] Jesus taketh Peter, James, and John his brother, and bringeth them up into a high mountain apart, [2] And was transfigured before them : and his face did shine as the sun, and his raiment was white as the light. [3] And, behold..Moses and Elias talking with him.—Mat., ch. 17.

5597. MOUNTAINS, Emblematic. *Providence.* [1] They that trust in the Lord *shall be* as mount Zion, *which* cannot be removed, *but* abideth for ever. [2] *As* the mountains *are* round about Jerusalem, so the Lord *is* round about his people from henceforth even for ever.—Ps. 125.

Also see:

Accessible. Ye are not come to the mount..burned 45

5598. MOURNERS, Comfort for. *"Asleep."* [13] I would not have you to be ignorant, brethren, concerning them which are asleep, that ye sorrow not, even as others which have no hope. [14] ..them also which sleep in Jesus will God bring with him.—1 Thess., ch. 4.

5599. —— **delighted.** *At Emmaus.* [30] As he sat at meat with them, he took bread, and blessed *it*, and brake, and gave to them. [31] And their eyes were opened, and they knew him ; and he vanished.—Luke, ch. 24.

5600. —— **Good News for.** *Resurrection.* [9] When *Jesus* was risen..he appeared first to Mary Magdalene, out of whom he had cast seven devils. [10] *And* she went and told them that had been with him, as they mourned and wept.— Mark, ch. 16.

5601. —— **Genuine.** *For Dorcas.* [39] Peter arose and..they brought him into the upper chamber : and all the widows stood by him weeping, and shewing the coats and garments which Dorcas made, while she was with them. —Acts, ch. 9.

5602. —— **Weeping of.** *Captives.* [1] By the rivers of Babylon, there we sat down, yea, we wept, when we remembered Zion. [2] We hanged our harps upon the willows in the midst thereof.—Ps. 137.

5603. MOURNING, Abstinence in. *Abner assassinated.* [See No. 5611.] [34] All the people wept again over him. [35] And when all the people came to cause David to eat meat while it was yet day, David sware, saying, So do God to me, and more also, If I taste bread, or aught else, till the sun be down.—2 Sam., ch. 3.

5604. —— **in Bereavement.** *David.* [26] I am distressed for thee, my brother Jonathan : very pleasant hast thou been unto me : thy love to

me was wonderful, passing the love of women. [27] How are the mighty fallen.—2 Sam., ch. 1.

5605. —— **beneficial.** *Proverb.* [2] *It is* better to go to the house of mourning, than to go to the house of feasting : for that *is* the end of all men ; and the living will lay *it* to his heart. [3] Sorrow *is* better than laughter.—Eccl., ch. 7.

5606. —— **feigned.** *"A wise Woman."* [2] Joab ..said unto her, I pray thee, feign thyself to be a mourner, and put on now mourning apparel, and anoint not thyself with oil, but be as a woman that had a long time mourned for the dead : [3] And come to the king.—2 Sam., ch. 14.

5607. —— **Intense.** *Escaping from Absalom.* [30] David went up by the ascent of *mount* Olivet, and wept as he went up, and had his head covered, and he went barefoot : and all the people that *was* with him covered every man his head, and they went up, weeping as they went up.— 2 Sam., ch. 15.

5608. —— **Joy for.** *At Nain.* [14] He came and touched the bier..And he said, Young man, I say unto thee, Arise. [15] And he that was dead sat up, and began to speak. And he delivered him to his mother.—Luke, ch. 7.

5609. —— **at the Last.** *Solomon.* [11] Thou mourn at the last, when thy flesh and thy body are consumed, [12] And say, How have I hated instruction, and my heart despised reproof ; [13] And have not obeyed the voice of my teachers. —Prov., ch. 5.

5610. —— **Time of.** *For Jacob.* [9] There went up with him both chariots and horsemen : and it was a very great company. [10] And they came to the threshingfloor of Atad, which *is* beyond Jordan, and there they mourned with a great and very sore lamentation.. [11] And when.. the Canaanites ..they said, This *is* a grievous mourning to the Egyptians.—Gen., ch. 50.

5611. —— **The Wicked bring.** *Joab the Assassin.* [32] The king lifted up his voice, and wept at the grave of Abner ; and all the people wept. [33] And the king lamented over Abner, and said, Died Abner as a fool dieth?—2 Sam., ch. 3.

See other illustrations under :

ANGUISH.

Bereavement. Let her alone, for her soul is vexed 416
Bitter. Esau cried..Bless me, even me also ! 417

DESPAIR.

Affliction. Let me not see the death of the child 2213
Anguish. Slay me, for anguish is come upon me 2214
Awaking. Wine was gone out..heart died within 2215
Deliverance. Been better for us to serve the Egyp. 2216
Needless. Widow..meal..oil..me and my son eat 2217

DESPONDENCY.

Bereavement. Joseph is, without doubt, rent in 2226
Complaint. Since I came to Pharaoh..done evil 2227
Constitutional. Let us go..die with him 2230
Continued. My heart is smitten and withered like 2228
Cure. David was greatly distressed..spake of 2229
Difficulties. People was much discouraged 2231
Hope. Why art thou cast down, O my soul 2232
Hasty. Sun beat..Jonah fainted..wished to die 2233
Ill-timed. Handful of meal..little oil..die 2234
Loneliness. I only am left, and they seek my life 2235
Memories. By the rivers of Babylon we wept 2236
Overcare. If thou deal thus with me, kill me 2237
Prayer. How long wilt thou forget me, O Lord ? 2239
Public. Moses heard the people weeping..door 2238

Peril. Esau cometh..400 men..Jacob afraid 2240
Singular. Lord, take away my life..not better 2242
Vows. L. made a reproach unto me..derision 2243
Without. Troubled on every side..not in despair 2244

DISAPPOINTMENT.

Doubt. Heard..he was alive..seen..believed not 2315
in Gifts. Gave Hiram 20 cities..pleased him not 2316
Good. They have taken the L. out of the sepulchre 2318
Ignorance. Evil place? no place of seed..figs 2319
Judgment. Thou hast taught in our streets 2320
Misjudged. We trusted..had been he..should have 2321
Maternal. Bare Cain..I have gotten a man of the 2322
Perplexing. Which of us is for the king of I.? 2323
Religion. Since we left off to burn incense..for 2324
Unendurable. Ahithophel..counsel not followed 2325
Many Disappointments. Consider your ways 2326

HUMILIATION.

Accepted. Let man and beast be covered..sackc. 4198
Confessed. I am ashamed and blush..my G. 4199
Defeat. I. turneth their backs before their enemies 4200
Exhibited. Job sat down among the ashes 4201
National. No smith..in all the land of I. 4202
Pride. Haman..arrayed Mordecai..and proclaimed 4203
Painful. Thou begin with shame to take the lowest 4204
Sincerity. When thou fastest..wash thy face 4205
Sin. Sent him to feed swine..hunger 4206
Use. Lest I should be exalted..thorn in the flesh 4207
Weakness. I was ashamed to require..soldiers 4208

LAMENTATION.

Adversity. Let the day perish wherein I was born 4883
Father's. O my son Absalom! my son, my son 4884
General. Thrust out right eyes..people..voices 4885
Ill-timed. Would to G. we had been content 4886
Jesus. O Jerusalem, Jerusalem..would I have 4887
for Jesus. Weep not for me, but weep for 4888
National. In every province..Jews..weeping and 4889
Tearful. Oh that my head were waters..fountain 4890

REMORSE.

Needful. People that came..smote their breasts 7067
Prevented. Lest swallowed up with overmuch sor. 7068
Treachery. Judas..went and hanged himself 7069

TEARS.

Affectionate. I wrote unto you with many tears 8620
Bereavement. Mary weeping..Jews weeping 8621
" Where have ye laid him?..how he 8622
Constant. Mine eye trickleth down, and ceaseth 8623
Desired. O that mine..eyes a fountain of tears 8624
Disregarded. Chasten thy son..not spare for his 8625
End of. G. shall wipe away all tears 8626
Grateful. She hath washed my feet with tears 8627
Night. Water my couch with tears 8628
Precious. Put thou my tears into thy bottle 8629
Patriotic. Jesus beheld the city, and wept over it 8630
Power. The babe wept..she had compassion 8631
" Samson's wife wept before him 8632
Parting. Wept one with another..David exceeded 8633
Penitential. When Peter thought thereon, he wept 8634
Transient. Saul lifted up his voice, and wept 8635

TRIBULATION.

Despair. Who shall be able to stand? 8946
Judgment. Sun..as sackcloth..stars fell..moved 8947
Joy in. I am exceeding joyful in all our 8948
Recompensed. White robes..out of great 8949

Agony. My soul is exceeding sorrowful..unto death 264
Boldness. I will go in unto the king..If I perish 2218
Disappointment. Saw his counsel was not follow. 2325
Sacrifices. Took his eldest son..for burnt offering 2221
See GRIEF, BEREAVEMENT, REPENTANCE,
       SORROW, WEEPING.

5612. MOUTH shows the Heart. *Word.* [34] O generation of vipers, how can ye, being evil, speak good things? for out of the abundance of the heart the mouth speaketh..[36]..every idle word that men shall speak, they shall give account thereof in the day of judgment. [37] For by thy words thou shalt be justified, and..condemned.—MAT., ch. 12.

See DISCOURSE and references.

5613. MULTITUDE, Following the. *The Spy.* [17] Why wentest thou not with thy friend? [18] And Hushai said unto Absalom, Nay; but whom the Lord, and this people, and all the men of Israel, choose, his will I be, and with him will I abide. —2 SAM., ch. 16.

See other illustrations under:

ARMY.

Great. [Uzziah's army] 37,500 men 497
Impressed. When Saul saw any strong man, he 498
Strange. Every one..in distress, debt, discontent 499
Standing. Saul chose 3000..the rest..his tent 500
Scattered. [Zedekiah's] Chaldees pursued..army 501
See MASSES and references.

5614. MUNITIONS of War. *Uzziah.* [14] Uzziah prepared..shields, and spears, and helmets, and habergeons, and bows, and slings *to cast* stones. [15] And he made in Jerusalem engines, invented by cunning men, to be on the towers and upon the bulwarks, to shoot arrows and great stones withal.—2 CHRON., ch. 26.

See other illustrations under:

ARMOUR.

Defenceless. [Goliath] had a helmet of brass 494
Rejected. David girded his sword..I can not 495
Without. Neither sword nor spear 496

WEAPONS.

Faith. David chose him five smooth stones 9443
Rejected. Saul armed David..helmet..coat of 9444

Divine. L. is my rock..fortress..high tower 1535
Shield. Above all, taking the shield of faith 8669

5615. MURDER attempted. *Of David.* [10] Saul sought to smite David..but he slipped away out of Saul's presence, and he smote the javelin into the wall: and David fled, and escaped that night.—1 SAM., ch. 19.

5616. —— —— At Nazareth. [28] All they in the synagogue, when they heard these things, were filled with wrath, [29] And rose up, and thrust him out of the city, and led him unto the brow of the hill whereon their city was built, that they might cast him down headlong. [30] But he, passing through the midst of them, went his way.—LUKE, ch. 4.

5617. —— —— Of Paul. [23] The Jews took counsel to kill him: [24] But their laying wait was known of Saul. And they watched the gates day and night to kill him. Then the disciples took him by night, and let *him* down by the wall in a basket.—ACTS, ch. 9.

5618. —— —— Of Paul. [31] As they went about to kill him, tidings came unto the chief captain of the band, that all Jerusalem was in an uproar: [32] Who immediately took soldiers and centurions, and ran down unto them.— ACTS, ch. 21.

5619. —— An atrocious. *Of Ishbosheth.* [5] Rechab and Baanah..came about the heat of the day to the house of Ishbosheth, who lay on a bed at noon. [6] ..as though they would have fetched wheat ; and they smote him under the fifth rib.—2 Sam., ch. 4.

5620. —— avenged. Of Ishbosheth. [8] They brought the head of Ishbosheth unto David.. and said..Behold the head of..the son of Saul thy enemy.. [11] How much more, when wicked men have slain a righteous person in his own house upon his bed ? shall I not therefore now require his blood of your hand, and take you away from the earth ?—2 Sam., ch. 4.

5621. —— of Children. Ahab's. [5] He that was over the city, the elders also, and the bringers up of the children, sent to Jehu, saying, We are thy servants, and will do all that thou shalt bid us.. [7] ..when the letter came to them..they took the king's sons, and slew seventy persons, and put their heads in baskets, and sent him them to Jezreel.—2 Kings, ch. 10.

5622. —— by Conspirators. Of Amnon. [28] When Amnon's heart is merry with wine, and when I say unto you, Smite Amnon ; then kill him, fear not : have not I commanded you ? be courageous, and be valiant. [29] And the servants of Absalom did.—2 Sam., ch. 13.

5623. —— Desire to. John Baptist. [19] Herodias had a quarrel against him, and would have killed him ; but she could not.—Mark, ch. 6.

5624. —— Escape from. David's. [11] Saul also sent messengers unto David's house, to watch him, and to slay him in the morning : and Michal David's wife told him, saying, If thou save not thy life to night, to morrow thou shalt be slain. [12] So Michal let David down through a window : and he..escaped.—1 Sam., ch. 19.

5625. —— Excuse for. Crucifixion. [6] Pilate saith..Take ye him, and crucify him : for I find no fault in him. [7] The Jews answered him, We have a law, and by our law he ought to die, because he made himself the Son of God.—John, ch. 19.

5626. —— Fratricidal. Abel. [8] Cain talked with Abel his brother : and..when they were in the field..Cain rose up against Abel his brother, and slew him.—Gen., ch. 4.

5627. —— for Gain. Parable. [38] The husbandmen..said among themselves, This is the heir ; come, let us kill him, and let us seize on his inheritance. [39] And they caught him, and cast him out of the vineyard, and slew him.—Mat., ch. 21.

5628. —— for Healing. Jews. [15] The man ..told the Jews that it was Jesus, which had made him whole. [16] And therefore did the Jews persecute Jesus, and sought to slay him, because he had done these things on the sabbath day.—John, ch. 5.

5629. —— intended. Of David. [25] Saul said, Thus shall ye say to David, The king desireth not any dowry, but a hundred foreskins of the Philistines, to be avenged of the king's enemies. But Saul thought to make David fall by the hand of the Philistines.—1 Sam., ch. 18.

5630. —— —— Of Jesus. [16] Herod, when he saw that he was mocked of the wise men, was exceeding wroth, and sent forth, and slew all the children that were in Bethlehem, and in all the coasts thereof, from two years old and under.—Mat., ch. 2.

5631. —— Indirect. Of Uriah. [14] David wrote a letter to Joab, and sent it by the hand of Uriah. [15] ..saying, Set ye Uriah in the forefront of the hottest battle, and retire ye from him, that he may be smitten, and die.—2 Sam., ch. 11.

5632. —— proposed. Of Jacob. [41] Esau hated Jacob because of the blessing wherewith his father blessed him : and Esau said in his heart, The days of mourning for my father are at hand ; then will I slay my brother Jacob.—Gen., ch. 27.

5633. —— Responsibility for. Indirect. [Stephen said,] [52] Which of the prophets have not your fathers persecuted ? and they have slain them which shewed before of the coming of the Just One ; of whom ye have been now the betrayers and murderers.—Acts, ch. 7.

5634. —— by Suffocation. Hazael. [15] He took a thick cloth, and dipped it in water, and spread it on his face, so that he died : and Hazael reigned in his stead.—2 Kings, ch. 8.

5635. —— by Stoning. Stephen. [57] Then they cried out with a loud voice, and stopped their ears, and ran upon him with one accord, [58] And cast him out of the city, and stoned him.—Acts, ch. 7.

5636. MURDERER chosen by Murderers. Barabbas. [18] They cried out all at once, saying, Away with this man, and release unto us Barabbas : [19] (Who, for a certain sedition made in the city, and for murder, was cast into prison.)—Luke, ch. 23.

5637. MURDERERS, Children of. Amaziah. [5] He slew his servants which had slain the king his father. [6] But the children of the murderers he slew not : according unto that which is written in the book of the law of Moses..saying, The fathers shall not be put to death for the children, nor the children be put to death for the fathers.—2 Kings, ch. 14.

5638. MURDERER, The unknown. The Law. [See Deut. 21 : 1–8.]

See other illustrations under :

ASSASSINATION.

Foul. Joab..shed out [Amasa's]..bowels to the	523
Hired. When I say, Smite Amnon ; then kill him	524
Patriotic. Ehud took the dagger..thrust into	525
Revenge. Joab smote [Abner]..for Asahel his	526

FRATRICIDE.

First. In the field, Cain..against Abel slew him	3406
Terrible. Ahimelech..slew his [70] brethren	3407

MANSLAUGHTER.

Accidental. [See Numbers 35 : 9–29.]	
Defensive. Abner said, Turn..why should I smite	5211
Justifiable. If the thief..be smitten..no blood be	5212
Pardonable. Axe head slippeth from the helve..	5213
Solicited. Slay me, for anguish is come upon me	5214
Unjustifiable. If the sun be risen..shall be blood	5215

MASSACRE.

Intended. Letters were sent by post..to destroy	5249
Infants. Herod..slew all the children..in Bethlehem	5250
Treacherous. Jehu said, Proclaim an assembly for	5251

SUICIDE.

Imitated. Armourbearer saw that Saul was dead	8456
Mortification. Counsel was not followed..hanged	8457
Traitor's. Cast down..silver..hanged himself	8460
Soldier's. Archers hit him..sore wounded..sword	8459

5639. MURMURING from Disappointment. *At Zin.* ⁵ Wherefore have ye made us to come up out of Egypt, to bring us in unto this evil place? it *is* no place of seed, or of figs, or of vines, or of pomegranates ; neither *is* there any water to drink.—Num., ch. 20.

5640. —— **from Discouragement.** "*T h e Way.*" ⁴ Journeyed from mount Hor by the way of the Red Sea, to compass the land of Edom : and the soul of the people was much discouraged because of the way. ⁵ And the people spake against God, and against Moses, Wherefore have ye brought us up out of Egypt to die in the wilderness?—Num., ch. 21.

5641. —— **from Distrust.** *Ten Spies.* ³² They brought up an evil report of the land which they had searched.. ¹..and the people wept that night. ² And..murmuring against Moses and against Aaron : and the whole congregation said unto them, Would God that we had died in the land of Egypt !—Num., chs. 13 and 14.

5642. —— **from Fear.** *At Red Sea.* ¹² Is not this the word that we did tell thee in Egypt, saying, Let us alone, that we may serve the Egyptians? For *it had been* better for us to serve the Egyptians, than that we should die in the wilderness.—Ex., ch. 14.

5643. —— **against God.** *Potter.* ²⁰ O man, who art thou that repliest against God? Shall the thing formed say to him that formed *it*, Why hast thou made me thus? ²¹ Hath not the potter power over the clay, of the same lump to make one vessel unto honour, and another unto dishonour?—Rom., ch. 9.

5644. —— **of Mercenaries.** *Parable.* ¹¹ They murmured against the goodman of the house, ¹² Saying, These last have wrought *but* one hour, and thou hast made them equal unto us, which have borne the burden and heat of the day.—Mat., ch. 20.

5645. —— **at Neglect.** *Grecian W i d o w s.* ¹ When the number of the disciples was multiplied, there arose a murmuring of the Grecians against the Hebrews, because their widows were neglected in the daily ministration.—Acts, ch. 6.

5646. —— **punished.** *At Sinai.* ¹ *When* the people complained, it displeased the Lord..and his anger was kindled ; and the fire of the Lord burnt among them, and consumed *them that were* in the uttermost parts of the camp.—Num., ch. 11.

5647. —— **Severity in.** *In Wilderness.* ³ The people thirsted there for water ; and . . murmured against Moses..Wherefore *is* this *that* thou hast brought us up out of Egypt, to kill us and our children and our cattle with thirst? ⁴ And Moses cried unto the Lord, saying, What shall I do unto this people? they be almost ready to stone me.—Ex., ch. 17.

5648. —— **from Thirst.** *Israelites.* ²² They went three days in the wilderness, and found no water. ²³..they could not drink of the waters of Marah, for they *were* bitter.. ²⁴ And the people murmured against Moses, saying, What shall we drink?—Ex., ch. 15.

See BLAME *and references.*

5649. MUSIC, Aid of. "*Hand of the Lord came.*" [Elisha said,] ¹⁵ Bring me a minstrel.. when the minstrel played..the hand of the Lord came upon him.—2 Kings, ch. 3.

5650. —— **Cured by.** *Melancholy.* ²³ When the *evil* spirit from God was upon Saul..David took a harp, and played with his hand : so Saul was refreshed, and was well, and the evil spirit departed from him.—1 Sam., ch. 16.

5651. —— **Instruments of.** *Invention.* ²¹ Jubal : he was the father of all such as handle the harp and organ.—Gen., ch. 4.

5652. —— **undesired.** *Darius.* ¹⁷ A stone was brought, and laid upon the mouth of the den.. ¹⁸ Then the king went to his palace, and passed the night fasting: neither were instruments of music brought before him.—Dan., ch. 6.

5653. —— **for Joy.** *Prodigal.* ²⁵ Now his elder son was in the field : and as he came and drew nigh to the house, he heard music and dancing.—Luke, ch. 15.

5654. —— **for Liberty.** *Captives in Babylon.* [See No. 5602.]

5655. —— **Power of.** "*Another Man.*" ⁵ When thou art come thither to the city..thou shalt meet a company of prophets coming down from the high place with a psaltery, and a tabret, and a pipe, and a harp, before them ; and they shall prophesy : ⁶ And the Spirit of the Lord will come upon thee, and thou shalt prophesy with them, and shalt be turned into another man.—1 Sam., ch. 10.

5656. ——— **prostituted.** *To Intemperance.* ¹² The harp and the viol, the tabret and pipe, and wine, are in their feasts : but they regard not the work of the Lord, neither consider the operation of his hands. ¹³ Therefore my people are gone into captivity, because *they* have no knowledge : and their honourable men *are* famished, and their multitude dried up with thirst.—Isa., ch. 5.

5657. —— **Variety of.** *To Jerusalem.* ⁴ Accompanying the ark of God.. ⁵..David and all the house of Israel played before the Lord on all manner of *instruments made of* fir wood, even on harps, and on psalteries, and on timbrels, and on cornets, and on cymbals.—2 Sam., ch. 6.

5658. —— **in Worship.** *Instrumental.* ³ Praise him with the sound of the trumpet : praise him with the psaltery and harp. ⁴ Praise him with the timbrel and dance : praise him with stringed instruments and organs. ⁵ Praise him upon the loud cymbals : praise him upon the high sounding cymbals.—Ps. 150.

5659. MUSICIAN, A skilful. *David.* ¹⁸ Then answered one of the servants..Behold, I have seen a son of Jesse the Beth-lehemite, *that is* cunning in playing.—1 Sam., ch. 16.

See other illustrations under:

SINGING.

Difficult. How can we sing..in a strange land ?   8035
Easy. Come to Zion with songs   8036
Victory. When they began to sing..L. set ambush. 8037

5660. MYSTERY of Conversion. "*Born again.*" ⁷ Ye must be born again. ⁸ The wind bloweth where it listeth, and thou hearest the sound thereof, but canst not tell whence it cometh, and whither it goeth : so is every one that is born of the Spirit. ⁹ Nicodemus answered and said unto him, How can these things be?—John, ch. 3.

5661. —— **A marvellous.** *Joseph's Brethren.* ³³ They sat before him, the firstborn according to his birthright, and the youngest according to his youth : and the men marvelled one at another.—Gen., ch. 43.

5662. —— **A strange.** *Burning Bush.* ³ Moses said, I will now turn aside, and see this great sight, why the bush is not burnt.—Ex., ch. 3.

5663. —— **An unsolved.** *Burial of Moses.* ⁶ He buried him in a valley in the land of Moab, over against Beth-peor : but no man knoweth of his sepulchre unto this day.—Deut., ch. 34.

5664. MYSTERIES, Stumbling at. *" Went back."* ⁵⁶ He that eateth my flesh, and drinketh my blood, dwelleth in me, and I in him. ⁶⁶ From that *time* many of his disciples went back, and walked no more with him.—John, ch. 6.

5665. —— **Unexplainable.** *Washing Feet.* ⁷ Jesus answered..What I do thou knowest not now ; but thou shalt know hereafter. ⁸ Peter saith ..Thou shalt never wash my feet.—John, ch. 13.

See other illustrations under :

NATURE.
Creation. In the beginning G. created the heaven 5680
Grace. Man come to me and hate not his father 5681
Mystery. Seed should spring..knoweth not how 5682
Overruled. Took two milch kine..calves shut up 5683
Religion of. Left not himself without witness..did 5684
Superior. Lilies..Solomon in all his glory was not 5685
Teaching. Nature itself teach you..long hair 5686
Supernatural. Voice from heaven saying..it thun. 5687
Naturalist. Solomon spake of trees..from the c. 5688

RIDDLE.
Wedding. Out of the eater came forth meat 7421
See **GRACE.**

5666. NAME, A changed. *Abraham.* ⁵ Neither shall thy name any more be called Abram, but thy name shall be Abraham ; for a father of many nations have I made thee.—Gen., ch. 17.

5667. —— **A glorified.** *By Jesus.* [See No. 5687.]

5668. —— **A good.** *David's.* ³⁰ The princes of the Philistines went forth : and..David behaved himself more wisely than all the servants of Saul ; so that his name was much set by.—1 Sam., ch. 18.

5669. —— —— *Cornelius.* ²² A just man, and one that feareth God, and of good report among all the nation of the Jews, was warned from God by a holy angel to send for thee.—Acts, ch. 10.

5670. —— —— *Ananias.* ¹² Ananias, a devout man according to the law, having a good report of all the Jews which dwelt *there,* ¹³ Came ..and said unto me, Brother Saul, receive thy sight.—Acts, ch. 22.

5671. —— **A new.** *Israel.* ²⁸ Thy name shall be called no more Jacob, but Israel : for as a prince hast thou power with God and with men, and hast prevailed.—Gen., ch. 32.

5672. —— **refused.** *Angel.* ¹⁷ Manoah said unto the angel of the Lord, What *is* thy name, that when thy sayings come to pass we may do thee honour ? ¹⁸ ..Why askest thou thus after my name, seeing it *is* secret ?—Judges, ch. 13.

5673. NAMES, Bestowment of. *By Adam.* ¹⁹ The Lord God formed every beast of the field, and every fowl of the air ; and brought *them* unto Adam to see what he would call them : and whatsoever Adam called every living creature, that *was* the name thereof.—Gen., ch. 1.

5674. —— **known.** *To Jesus.* ⁵ When Jesus came to the place, he looked up, and saw him, and said..Zaccheus, make haste, and come down ; for to day I must abide at thy house.—Luke, ch. 19.

5675. —— **New.** *Hebrews.* ⁷ The prince of the eunuchs gave names : for he gave unto Daniel *the name* of Belteshazzar ; and to Hananiah, of Shadrach ; and to Mishael, of Meshach ; and to Azariah, of Abed-nego.—Dan., ch. 1.

5676. —— **Wonderful.** *Of Jesus.* ⁶ For unto us a child is born, unto us a son is given : and the government shall be upon his shoulder : and his name shall be called Wonderful, Counsellor, The mighty God, The everlasting Father, The Prince of Peace.—Isa., ch. 9.

5677. —— **written in Heaven.** *The Seventy.* ²⁰ In this rejoice not, that the spirits are subject unto you ; but rather rejoice, because your names are written in heaven.—Luke, ch. 10.

See other illustrations under :

FAME.
Increasing. His fame spread abroad..about 3000
Military. Uzziah made..engines..to shoot 3001
Troublesome. Blaze abroad the matter..desert 3002
Unexpected. In the whole world..woman hath 3003
Wisdom. All the earth sought to Solomon 3004

REPUTATION.
Acknowledged. Thy G. whom thou servest..will 7160
Advantage. Been shown me, all thou hast done 7161
Bad. Can any good thing come out of 7162
Blotless. Herod feared John..holy and observed 7163
Fearful. I have heard..much evil he hath done 7164
Good. Cornelius..of good report among..Jews 7165
Gaining. Let not mercy and truth forsake thee 7166
Helpful. I have seen the son of Jesse..valiant 7167
Jealous. I wrought for my name's sake..not be 7168
Loss. Dead flies cause the ointment to stink 7169
Official. Here I am ; witness against me 7170
Posthumous. That men say not..a woman slew 7171
Reviled. Clap their hands at thee and hiss 7172
Unimpeachable. Could find none..as he..was 7173
"   Thou hast not defrauded, nor 7174
Valuable. Good name is rather to be chosen than 7175
Varied. Whom say the people..John..Elias..C. 7176

5678. NARCOTIC refused, A. *Crucifixion.* ²³ They gave him to drink wine mingled with myrrh : but he received *it* not.—Mark, ch. 15.

5679. NATIONS, Birth of. *In Crisis.* ²⁹ The children of Israel walked upon dry *land* in the midst of the sea ; and the waters *were* a wall unto them on their right hand, and on their left. ³⁰ Thus the Lord saved Israel..and Israel saw the Egyptians dead upon the sea shore.—Ex., ch. 14.

5680. NATURE from God. *Creation.* ¹ In the beginning God created the heaven and the earth.—Gen., ch. 1.

5681. —— **less than Grace.** *Love less.* ²⁵ There went great multitudes with him : and he turned, and said.. ²⁶ If any *man* come to me, and hate not his father, and mother, and wife, and children, and brethren, and sisters, yea, and his own life also, he cannot be my disciple.—Luke, ch. 14.

5682. —— **Mystery of.** *Processes.* ²⁷ The seed should spring and grow up, he knoweth not how. ²⁸ For the earth bringeth forth fruit of herself ; first the blade, then the ear, after that the full corn in the ear.—Mark, ch. 4.

5683. —— **overruled.** *Instinct.* [10] And the men..took two milch kine, and tied them to the cart, and shut up their calves at home : [11] And they laid the ark of the Lord upon the cart.. [12] And the kine took the straight way to..Bethshemesh, *and* went along the highway, lowing as they went.—1 Sam., ch. 6.

5684. —— **Religion of.** *At Lystra.* [17] He left not himself without witness, in that he did good, and gave us rain from heaven, and fruitful seasons, filling our hearts with food and gladness.—Acts, ch. 14.

5685. —— **Superiority of.** *Above Art.* [27] Consider the lilies how they grow : they toil not, they spin not ; and yet I say unto you, that Solomon in all his glory was not arrayed like one of these.—Luke, ch. 12.

5686. —— **Teaching of.** *Hair.* [14] Doth not even nature itself teach you, that, if a man have long hair, it is a shame unto him ? [15] But if a woman have long hair, it is a glory to her : for *her* hair is given her for a covering.—1 Cor., ch. 11.

5687. NATURAL, Supernatural for. *Jesus prayed,* [28] Father, glorify thy name. Then came there a voice from heaven, *saying,* I have both glorified *it,* and will glorify *it* again. [29] The people therefore that stood by, and heard *it,* said that it thundered : others said, An angel spake to him.—John, ch. 12.

See other illustrations under :

DEPRAVITY.

Ancient. Every imagination of the thoughts 2188
Bestial. [Gibeathites] beset the house, and beat at 2189
Discovered. Woe is me..unclean lips..people 2190
Heathen. Changed the glory of..G. into an image 2191
Infectious. Daughters of Lot were with child 2192
Inherited. Ye are the children of them which 2193
Natural. L. looked down..all gone aside..filthy 2194

FLESH.

Weakness. The spirit indeed is willing..flesh is w. 3257
Works. Works of the flesh are these, Adultery 3258

5688. NATURALIST, A royal. *Solomon.* [33] He spake of trees, from the cedar tree that *is* in Lebanon even unto the hyssop that springeth out of the wall : he spake also of beasts, and of fowl, and of creeping things, and of fishes. [34] And there came of all people to hear the wisdom of Solomon.—1 Kings, ch. 4.

5689. NAVY, Mercantile. *About* $13,000,000. [26] King Solomon made a navy of ships..on the shore of the Red Sea.. [27] And Hiram sent..shipmen that had knowledge of the sea, with the servants of Solomon. [28] And they came to Ophir, and fetched from thence gold, four hundred and twenty talents.—1 Kings, ch. 9.

See other illustrations under :

MARINER.

Distress. Their soul is melted because of trouble 5217
Deliverance. They cry unto the L..he delivereth 5218

SHIPS.

Building. The ark shall be 300 cubits..50..30 7838
Shipwreck. Some on boards, and some on broken 7839
" Thrice I suffered shipwreck..[Paul] 7840
Wealth by. Ophir..they fetched from thence gold 7837

5690. NEARNESS to God. *Degrees in.* [9] Then went up Moses, and Aaron, Nadab, and Abihu, and seventy of the elders of Israel ; [10] And they saw the God of Israel.. [13]..Moses went up into the mount of God. [14] And he said unto the elders, Tarry ye here for us, until we come again unto you.—Ex., ch. 24.

See other illustrations under :

ACCESS.

Bold. A high priest..touched..come with boldness 42
Conditioned. Except your youngest brother come 43
Denied. Let Absalom not see my face..David 44
Improved. Not come unto the mount..that burned 45
Prohibited. Come unto the king..not called..death 46
Provision. I am the door of the sheep 47
Restricted. Set bounds around the mount 48
Preparation. Moses sprinkled..the hook and all the 49
after " Then went up Moses and Aaron, N. 50
See COMMUNION.

5691. NECESSITY knows no Law. *Tribute.* [See No. 5539.]

5692. NECESSITIES cared for. *Clothing.* [21] Unto Adam also and to his wife did the Lord God make coats of skins, and clothed them.— Gen., ch. 3.

5693. NEED, The One. *Mary.* [40] Hath left me to serve alone ? bid her therefore that she help me. [41] And Jesus answered..Martha, Martha, thou art careful, and troubled about many things : [42] But one thing is needful ; and Mary hath chosen that good part, which shall not be taken away from her.—Luke, ch. 10.

5694. NEEDS, Supply of. *Felt first.* [3] Ye have brought us forth into this wilderness, to kill this whole assembly with hunger. [4] Then said the Lord unto Moses, Behold, I will rain bread from heaven for you.—Ex., ch. 16.

5695. —— —— **From Father.** [29] Seek not ye what ye shall eat, or what ye shall drink, neither be ye of doubtful mind. [30] For all these things do the nations of the world seek after : and your Father knoweth that ye have need of these things.—Luke, ch. 12.

See other illustrations under :

WANT.

A Blessing. I perish with hunger..my father 8286
Contentment. I have learned..to be content 8287
Degraded. We boiled my son..give thy son 8288
Frivolity. He that followeth vain persons..poverty 8289
near Luxury. Rich man..fared sumptuously..L. 8290
to Plenty. Four lepers..did eat and drink..carried 8291
Sin brings. Woman..brought to a piece of bread 8292

5696. NEGLECT acknowledged. *Ahasuerus.* [2] It was found written, that Mordecai had told of Bigthana and Teresh, two of the king's chamberlains, the keepers of the door, who sought to lay hand on the king Ahasuerus. [3] And the king said, What honour and dignity hath been done to Mordecai for this ? Then said the king's servants..There is nothing done for him.—Esther, ch. 6.

5697. —— **of Dress.** *Mephibosheth.* [24] Mephibosheth the son of Saul came down to meet the king, and had neither dressed his feet, nor trimmed his beard, nor washed his clothes, from the day the king departed until the day he came *again* in peace.—2 Sam., ch. 19.

5698. —— **Excuse for.** *One Talent.* [24] Lord, I knew thee that thou art a hard man, reaping where thou hast not sown, and gathering where thou hast not strewed : [25] And I was afraid, and went and hid thy talent in the earth.—Mat., ch. 25.

5699. —— **Folly of.** *Ten Virgins.* [3] They that *were* foolish took their lamps, and took no oil with them : [4] But the wise took oil in their vessels with their lamps.—MAT., ch. 25.

5700. —— **made good.** *To Mordecai.* [11] Then took Haman the apparel and the ,horse, and arrayed Mordecai, and brought him on horseback through the street of the city, and proclaimed before him, Thus shall it be done unto the man whom the king delighteth to honour.—ESTHER, ch. 6.

5701. —— **of God.** *Samaritans.* [25] At the beginning of their dwelling there, *that* they feared not the Lord, therefore the Lord sent lions among them which slew *some* of them.—2 KINGS, ch. 17.

5702. —— **of God's House.** *Punished.* [2] This people say, The time is not come..that the Lord's house should be built.. [6] Ye have sown much, and bring in little ; ye eat, but ye have not enough ; ye drink, but ye are not filled with drink ; ye clothe you, but there is none warm ; and he that earneth wages, earneth wages *to put it* into a bag with holes.—HAG., ch. 1.

5703. —— **of the Gospel.** *"Made Light."* [4] Behold, I have prepared my dinner : my oxen and *my* fatlings *are* killed, and all things *are* ready : come unto the marriage. [5] But they made light of *it*, and went their ways, one to his farm, another to his merchandise.—MAT., ch. 22.

5704. —— **of God's Service.** *Tithes.* [10] Bring ye all the tithes into the storehouse, that there may be meat in mine house, and prove me now herewith, saith the Lord of hosts, if I will not open you the windows of heaven, and pour you out a blessing, that *there shall* not *be* room enough *to receive it.*—MAL., ch. 3.

5705. —— **Heedless.** *A Prophet* [39] Cried unto the king..Thy servant went out into the midst of the battle ; and, behold, a man.. brought a man unto me, and said, Keep this man : if by any means he be missing, then shall thy life be for his life, or else thou shalt pay a talent of silver. [40] And as thy servant was busy here and there, he was gone. And the king of Israel said..So *shall* thy judgment *be ;* thyself hast decided *it.*—1 KINGS, ch. 20.

5706. —— **Important.** *Pharisees.* [23] Woe unto you, scribes and Pharisees, hypocrites ! for ye pay tithe of mint and anise and cummin, and have omitted the weightier *matters* of the law, judgment, mercy, and faith : these ought ye to have done, and not to leave the other un- done. [24] *Ye* blind guides, which strain at a gnat, and swallow a camel.—MAT., ch. 23.

5707. —— **Loss by.** *Ten Virgins.* [10] They that were ready went in with him to the mar- riage : and the door was shut. [11] Afterward came also the other virgins, saying, Lord, Lord, open to us. [12] But he answered..Verily..I know you not.—MAT., ch. 25.

5708. —— **punished.** *Talent.* [28] Take there- fore the talent from him, and give *it* unto him which hath ten talents.. [30] And cast ye the un- profitable servant into outer darkness : there shall be weeping and gnashing of teeth.—MAT., ch. 25.

5709. —— **of the Poor.** *Punished.* [44] Lord, when saw we thee ahungered, or athirst, or a stranger, or naked, or sick, or in prison, and did not minister unto thee ? [45]..Inasmuch as ye did *it* not to one of the least of these, ye did *it* not to me. [46] And these shall go away into ever- lasting punishment.—MAT., ch. 25.

5710. —— **of Preparation.** *Garment.* [12] Friend, how camest thou in hither not having a wedding garment ? And he was speechless. [13] Then said the king to the servants, Bind him hand and foot..and cast *him* into outer darkness ; there shall be weeping and gnashing of teeth.—MAT., ch. 22.

5711. —— **Parental.** *Eli's Sons.* [13] Because his sons made themselves vile, and he restrained them not. [14]..therefore I have sworn..that the iniquity of Eli's house shall not be purged with sacrifice nor offering for ever.—1 SAM., ch. 3.

5712. —— **Ruin by.** *Proverb.* [30] I went by the field of the slothful, and by the vineyard of the man void of understanding ; [31] And, lo, it was all grown over with thorns, *and* nettles had covered the face thereof, and the stone wall thereof was broken down.—PROV., ch. 24.

5713. —— **Responsibility for.** *Builders.* [8] When thou buildest a new house, then thou shalt make a battlement for thy roof, that thou bring not blood upon thine house, if any man fall from thence.—DEUT., ch. 22.

5714. —— **of the Unfaithful.** *Pound.* [20] Lord, behold, *here is* thy pound, which I have kept laid up in a napkin : [21] For I feared thee, be- cause thou art an austere man.—LUKE, ch. 19.

5715. —— **Unfeeling.** *"Passed by."* [30] Fell among thieves, which stripped him of his rai- ment, and wounded *him*, and departed, leaving *him* half dead. [31]..there came..priest that way ; and..he passed by on the other side. [32] And likewise a Levite..looked *on him*, and passed by on the other side.—LUKE, ch. 10.

5716. —— **A Witness's.** *Law.* [1] If a soul sin, and hear the voice of swearing, and *is* a witness, whether he hath seen or known *of it ;* if he do not utter *it*, then he shall bear his iniq- uity.—LEV., ch. 5.

See other illustrations under :

CARELESSNESS.

Fire. He that kindled..make restitution	1051
Presumptuous. Known that the ox used to push	1052
Responsibility. Open a pit and not cover it	1053

FAILURE.

Avoiding. First..counted the cost..to finish	2867
Cruelty. More they afflicted them..grew	2868
Complaint. Why is it thou hast sent me ?	2869
Church. Disciples..should cast him out..could	2870
Discouraging. Toiled all the night..taken nothing	2871
Disheartening. Put a sword in their hand to slay	2872
Explained. Why could not we cast him out ?	2873
Fear. We were..as grasshoppers	2874
Irremediable. Went to buy..door was shut	2875
Ominous. Thou hast begun to fall..surely fall	2876
Providential. Confounded their language..left off	2877
Ridiculed. Mock him..began to build..not able	2878
Temporary. Pharaoh said..neither will I let I. go	2879

FORGETFULNESS.

Adversity. Whom I loved have turned against me	3346
Caution. Take heed..lest thou forget..thine eyes	3347
of God. Have eaten..full, beware..forget the L.	3342
" Jeshurun..lightly esteemed the Rock	3343
" When silver and gold is multiplied..forget	3344

Religious. I will not go..he went back with him   3348
Sanctuary. If I forget thee, O Jerusalem..tongue   3345
Spiritual. Face in a glass..straightway forgetteth   3349

INDIFFERENCE.

Hearing. Foolish man who built..upon the sand   4405
Inconsiderate. Here is thy pound which I have   4406
Provoking. Wrath because..have not hearkened   4407
Pitiless. Saw him and passed by..other side   4408
Sin. I have sinned..What is that to us?   4409
Sinners. Made light of it and went their ways   4410
Unbelievers. They did eat..until the day Noe   4411

INDIFFERENT.

Curse. Curse ye Meroz..came not..help of the L.   4412
Woe. Woe unto them that are at ease in Zion   4413

LOITERERS.

Driven. Fire..consumed them in the uttermost   5052
Hastened. While he lingered, the men laid hold   5053

PROCRASTINATION.

Charity. Say not..to-morrow I will give when thou   6620
Fatal. Go thy way this time..convenient season   6621
Folly. Foolish said, Give us of your oil..gone out   6622
Loss. We will hear thee again..Paul departed   6623
No. Suffer me first to go and bury my father   6624

Neglect. What honour hath been done to Mordecai   5696
Poor. When saw we thee ahungered..in prison   5709
Ungrateful. Yet did not the chief butler remember   3096

5717. NEIGHBOUR, Who is my? *Good Samaritan.* [36] Which now of these three, thinkest thou, was neighbour unto him that fell among the thieves? [37] And he said, He that shewed mercy on him. Then said Jesus..Go, and do thou likewise.—LUKE, ch. 10.

5718. NEIGHBOURS in Bereavement. *Lazarus.* [19] Many of the Jews came to Martha and Mary, to comfort them concerning their brother.—JOHN, ch. 11.

5719. —— Vexatious. *Lot.* [7] Vexed with the filthy conversation of the wicked : [8] For that righteous man dwelling among them, in seeing and hearing, vexed *his* righteous soul from day to day with *their* unlawful deeds.—2 PETER, ch. 2.

5720. NEUTRALITY advised. *Gamaliel.* [38] Refrain from these men, and let them alone ; for if this counsel or this work be of men, it will come to nought : [39] But if it be of God, ye cannot overthrow it ; lest haply ye be found even to fight against God. [40] And to him they agreed.—ACTS, ch. 5.

5721. —— disagreeable. *"Lukewarm."* [15] I know thy works, that thou art neither cold nor hot : I would thou wert cold or hot. [16] So then because thou art lukewarm, and neither cold nor hot, I will spew thee out of my mouth.—REV., ch. 3.

5722. —— impossible. *Stone.* [42] Jesus saith ..Did ye never read in the Scriptures, The stone which the builders rejected, the same is become the head of the corner?.. [44] And whosoever shall fall on this stone shall be broken : but on whomsoever it shall fall, it will grind him to powder. —MAT., ch. 21.

5723. —— No. *Jesus said,* [39] For there is no man which shall do a miracle in my name, that can lightly speak evil of me. [40] For he that is not against us is on our part.—MARK, ch. 9.

5724. —— punished. *Dives.* [19] There was a certain rich man, which was clothed in pur-

ple and fine linen, and fared sumptuously every day.. [23] And in hell he lifted up his eyes, being in torments.—LUKE, ch. 16. [He was neutral in religion.]

5725. —— Silent. *"Answered not."* [20] Ahab ..gathered the prophets together unto mount Carmel. [21] And Elijah..said, How long halt ye between two opinions? if the Lord *be* God, follow him : but if Baal, *then* follow him. And the people answered him not a word.—1 KINGS, ch. 18.

5726. —— Unreasonable. *At Carmel.* [See No. 5725.]

5727. —— wanting. *Figs.* [2] One basket had very good figs, *even* like the figs *that are* first ripe : and the other basket *had* very naughty figs, which could not be eaten, they were so bad. —JER., ch. 24.

See other illustrations under :

INDIFFERENCE.

Hearing. Foolish man who built..upon the sand   4405
Inconsiderate. Here is thy pound, which I have   4406
Provoking. Wrath because..have not hearkened   4407
Pitiless. Saw him, and passed by..other side   4408
Sin. I have sinned..What is that to us?   4409
Sinners. Made light of it, and went their ways   4410
Unbelievers. They did eat..until the day Noe   4411

INDIFFERENT.

Curse. Curse ye Meroz..came not..help of the L.   4412
Woe. Woe unto them that are at ease   4413

Caste. Jews have no dealings with the Samaritans   1058
Poor. When saw we thee ahungered..in prison?   5709
Ungrateful. Yet did not the chief butler remember   3096

5728. NEWS declared, Bad. *To Eli.* [See No. 5731.] [16] Then Eli called Samuel.. [17] ..What is the thing that *the* Lord hath said unto thee? I pray thee hide *it* not from me : God do so to thee, and more also, if thou hide *any* thing from me of all the things that he said unto thee. [18] And Samuel told him every whit.—1 SAM., ch. 3.

5729. —— More bad. *Job's Losses.* [14] And there came a messenger unto Job, and said, The oxen were ploughing, and the asses feeding beside them : [15] And the Sabeans fell *upon them,* and took them away ; yea, they have slain the servants with the edge of the sword ; and I only am escaped alone to tell thee. [16] While he was yet speaking, there came also another, and said, The fire of God is fallen from heaven, and hath burned up the sheep, and the servants, and consumed them ; and I only am escaped alone to tell thee.—JOB, ch. 1.

5730. —— unrewarded, Bad. *David.* [10] When one told me, saying, Behold, Saul is dead, thinking to have brought good tidings, I took hold of him, and slew him in Ziklag, who *thought* that I would have given him a reward for his tidings. —2 SAM., ch. 4.

5731. —— withheld, Bad. *From Eli.* [11] The Lord said to Samuel, Behold, I will do a thing in Israel, at which both the ears of every one that heareth it shall tingle.. [15] And Samuel lay until the morning..And Samuel feared to shew Eli the vision.—1 SAM., ch. 3.

**5732. —— —— ** *From David.* [18] On the seventh day..the child died. And the servants of David feared to tell him..for they said, Behold, while the child was yet alive, we spake unto him, and he would not hearken unto our voice : how will he then vex himself, if we tell him that the child is dead ?—2 SAM., ch. 12.

5733. —— Confirmation of. *Thomas.* 27 Thomas, Reach hither thy finger, and behold my hands; and reach hither thy hand, and thrust *it* into my side ; and be not faithless, but believing. 28 And Thomas answered .. My Lord and my God.—JOHN, ch. 20.

5734. —— doubted. *By four Lepers.* 12 The king arose in the night, and said unto his servants, I will now shew you what the Syrians have done to us. They know that *we be* hungry ; therefore are they gone out of the camp, to hide themselves in the field, saying, When they come out of the city, we shall catch them alive, and get into the city.—2 KINGS, ch. 7.

5735. —— doubted, Good. *Resurrection.* 10 Mary went and told them..as they mourned and wept. 11 And they, when they had heard that he was alive, and had been seen of her, believed not.—MARK, ch. 16.

5736. —— Important. *Haste.* 10 He wrote in the king Ahasuerus' name, and sealed *it* with the king's ring, and sent letters by posts on horseback, *and* riders on mules, camels, *and* young dromedaries : 11 Wherein the king granted the Jews which *were* in every city to gather themselves together, and to stand for their life.—ESTHER, ch. 7.

5737. —— refreshing, Good. *Proverb.* 25 As cold waters to a thirsty soul, so *is* good news from a far country.—PROV , ch. 25.

See other illustrations under :

REPORT.

Evil. We saw the giants, the sons of Anak	7122
False. Not suppose..slain all the king's sons	7123
Intimidating. It is reported among the heathen	7124
Manufactured. Say ye, His disciples stole him a.	7125
Offensive. Joseph brought..his father their evil r.	7126
Terrorizing. As we heard..our hearts did melt	7127

SLANDER.

Antidote. They may by your good works..glorify	8101
Base. This fellow doth cast out devils by Beelzebub	8102
Disgraceful. We found this man a pestilent fellow	8103
Folly. He that uttereth a slander is a fool	8104
Hurtful. Then will they not pay tribute	8105
Impious. He saved others ; himself he cannot	8106
Joyful. Blessed..men revile you..rejoice	8107
Loyalty. Ziba said..he abideth at Jerusalem	8108
Malicious. Diotrephes..prating against us	8109
Opposed. It is reported..be their king	8110
Refuted. If Satan cast out Satan..divided	8111
Rebels. The people is greater than we	8112
Sinners. Thou art an austere man	8113
Satan's. Touch all that he hath..will curse	8114
Secret. A whisperer separateth friends	8115
Unbelief. Would to G. we had died..by fleshpots	8116

TALEBEARER.

Flattering. Meddle not with him that flattereth	8578
Strife. No talebearer, the strife ceaseth	8579
Tattling. Repeateth a matter separateth very f.	8580
Wounds. Words of the talebearer are as wounds	8581

Good Tidings. I bring you good tidings of great joy 8803
See **MESSAGE.**

5738. NIGHT of Bereavement. *In Egypt.* 27 At midnight the Lord smote all the firstborn in the land of Egypt, from the firstborn of Pharaoh that sat on his throne unto the firstborn of the

captive that *was* in the dungeon ; and all the firstborn of cattle.—Ex., ch. 12.

5739. —— Escape in the. *Joseph.* 14 He took the young child and his mother by night, and departed into Egypt.—MAT., ch. 2.

5740. —— Investigation by. *Nehemiah.* 12 I arose in the night, I and some few men with me ; neither told I *any* man what my God had put in my heart to do..and viewed the walls of Jerusalem, which were broken down.—NEH., ch. 2.

5741. —— of Prayer. *Jesus.* 12 He went out into a mountain to pray, and continued all night in prayer to God.—LUKE, ch. 6.

5742. —— Songs in the. *Philippian Jailer.* 24 Thrust them into the inner prison, and made their feet fast in the stocks. 25 And at midnight Paul and Silas prayed, and sang praises unto God : and the prisoners heard them.—ACTS, ch. 16.

See other illustrations under :

DARKNESS.

Adversity. He brought me into darkness [Job]	1917
Beasts. Wherein all the beasts of the forest do c.	1918
Betrayed. Judas..cometh thither with lanterns	1919
Chosen. The..adulterer waiteth the twilight..see	1920
Dying in. [After the plague of darkness came..d.]	1921
Deeds. While men slept his enemy..sowed tares	1922
Future. Light of the wicked shall be put out	1923
Hidden in. Neither cometh to the light lest..r.	1924
Hatred. He that hateth his brother is in darkness	1925
Insects. Locusts went up..land was darkened	1926
Light. Tabernacle..fire was on it by night	1927
Moral. If..light that is in thee be darkness..great	1928
Original. Darkness was upon the face of the waters	1929
Plague. Thick darkness over all the land of E.	1930
Punishment. Angels which kept not their first e.	1931
Revelation. Moses drew near..darkness where G.	1932
Unnatural. From the sixth hour there was dark	1933
Wicked. Hear..before you stumble on the dark m.	1934

MIDNIGHT.

Appeal at. Friend, lend me three loaves	5388
Alarm. Pharaoh rose up in the night..get you forth	5389
Songs. Paul and Silas sang..prisoners heard them	5390
Watch-night. Paul preached..until midnight	9359

Work. People..all that night..gathered the quails 38

5743. NUISANCE, A general. *Frogs.* 3 The river shall bring forth frogs abundantly, which shall go up and come into thine house, and into thy bedchamber, and upon thy bed, and into the house of thy servants, and upon thy people, and into thine ovens, and into thy kneading-troughs.—Ex., ch. 8.

5744. NUMBERS, Danger in. *32,000.* 2 The Lord said unto Gideon, The people that *are* with thee *are* too many for me to give the Midianites into their hands, lest Israel vaunt themselves against me, saying, Mine own hand hath saved me.. 8..and he sent all the *rest of* Israel every man unto his tent, and retained those three hundred men.—JUDGES, ch. 7.

5745. —— despised. *The Philistines.* 12 The men of the garrison answered..Come up to us, and we will shew you a thing. And Jonathan said unto his armourbearer, Come up after me : for the Lord hath delivered them into the hand of Israel.—1 SAM., ch. 14.

5746. —— Disparity in. *"Kids."* 27 The children of Israel were numbered, and were all

present, and went against them : and..pitched
before them like two little flocks of kids ; but
the Syrians filled the country.—1 KINGS, ch. 20.

5747. —— —— At Mareshah. ¹¹ Asa..said,
Lord; *it is* nothing with thee to help, whether
with many, or with them that have no power :
help us, O Lord our God ; for we rest on thee,
and in thy name we go against this multitude..
¹² So the Lord smote the Ethiopians before Asa.
—2 CHRON., ch. 14.

5748. —— Invisible. *At Dothan.* ¹⁷ Elisha
prayed..open his eyes, that he may see. And
the Lord opened the eyes of the young man ;
and he saw : and, behold, the mountain *was* full
of horses and chariots of fire round about
Elisha.—2 KINGS, ch. 6.

5749. —— Pride in. *David.* ¹⁰ David's
heart smote him after that he had numbered the
people. And David said..I have sinned greatly
in that I have done : and now, I beseech thee,
O Lord, take away the iniquity of thy servant ;
for I have done very foolishly.—2 SAM., ch. 24.

5750. —— Quality, not. *Joshua said,* ⁹ The
Lord hath driven out from before you great nations and strong : but *as for* you, no man hath
been able to stand before you unto this day.
¹⁰ One man of you shall chase a thousand.—
NUM., ch. 23.

5751. OATH, A Covenant. *Jews.* ³ Let us
make a covenant with our God to put away all
the wives, and such as are born of them..and
let it be done according to the law. ⁵ Then arose
Ezra, and made the chief priests, the Levites,
and all Israel, to swear that they should do according to this word. And they sware.—EZRA,
ch. 10.

5752. —— Conspirators'. *At Jerusalem.*
¹⁴ They came to the chief priests and elders,
and said, We have bound ourselves under a
great curse, that we will eat nothing until we
have slain Paul.—ACTS, ch. 23.

5753. —— A foolish. *Saul's.* [Philistines
were fleeing.] ²⁴ The men of Israel were distressed that day : for Saul had adjured the people, saying, Cursed *be* the man that eateth *any*
food until evening, that I may be avenged on
mine enemies.—1 SAM., ch. 14.

5754. —— A wicked. *Herod's Murder of
John.* ²² When the daughter of the said Herodias
came in, and danced, and pleased Herod and
them that sat with him, the king said unto the
damsel, Ask of me whatsoever thou wilt, and I
will give *it* thee. ²³ And he sware unto her,
Whatsoever thou shalt ask of me, I will give *it*
thee, unto the half of my kingdom. ²⁴ And she
went forth, and said unto her mother, What
shall I ask ? And she said, The head of John
the Baptist.—MARK, ch. 6.

5755. OBDURACY, Defiant. *Pharaoh.* ² Pharaoh said, Who *is* the Lord, that I should obey
his voice to let Israel go ? I know not the Lord,
neither will I let Israel go.—EX., ch. 5.

5756. —— Final. *Pharaoh.* ⁵ The heart of
Pharaoh and of his servants was turned against
the people, and they said, Why have we done
this, that we have let Israel go from serving us ?
⁶ And he made ready his chariot, and took his
people with him.—EX., ch. 14.

5757. —— Foolish. *Ahaz.* ²² In the time
of his distress did he trespass yet more against
the Lord : this *is that* king Ahaz. ²³ For he sacrificed unto the gods of Damascus, which smote
him : and he said, Because the gods of the kings
of Syria help them, *therefore* will I sacrifice to
them, that they may help me. But they were
the ruin of him, and of all Israel.—2 CHRON.,
ch. 28.

5758. —— Jewish. *Brow Brass.* ⁴ Because
I knew that thou *art* obstinate, and thy neck *is*
an iron sinew, and thy brow brass ; ⁵ I have
even from the beginning declared *it* to thee.—
ISA., ch. 48.

5759. —— Spiritual. *Jesus said,* ²¹ Woe
unto thee, Chorazin ! woe unto thee, Bethsaida !

for if the mighty works, which were done in you, had been done in Tyre and Sidon, they would have repented long ago in sackcloth and ashes.—MAT., ch. 11.

5760. —— **Self-destructive.** *Amaziah.* [16] As he talked with him..*the king* said..Art thou made of the king's counsel? forbear; why shouldest thou be smitten? Then the prophet forbare, and said, I know that God hath determined to destroy thee, because thou hast done this, and hast not hearkened unto my counsel. —2 CHRON., ch. 25.

5761. —— **against Truth.** *Ephesians.* [8] He went into the synagogue, and spake boldly for the space of three months, disputing and persuading the things concerning the kingdom of God. [9] But when divers were hardened, and believed not, but spake evil of that way before the multitude, he departed from them, and separated the disciples.—ACTS, ch. 19.

5762. —— **Unfeeling.** *Gentiles.* [19] Who being past feeling have given themselves over unto lasciviousness, to work all uncleanness with greediness.—EPH., ch. 4.

5763. —— **Mild.** *Baalam.* [21] Baalam rose up in the morning, and saddled his ass, and went with the princes of Moab. [22] And God's anger was kindled because he went: and.the angel of the Lord stood in the way for an adversary.—NUM., ch. 22.

See other illustrations under :

HARDNESS.
Adversity. In his distress did Ahaz trespass more 3797
Heart. Looked..anger being grieved..hardness 3798

IMPENITENCE.
Affliction. Ahaziah said..Go inquire of Baal-zebub 4347
Hardened. Thou shalt die..He sent to arrest 4348

OBSTINACY.
Provoking. It is a stiffnecked people..consume 5825
Rebuked. Why..smitten thine ass these 3 times? 5826
Rebellious. Nevertheless the people refused 5827

SELF-WILL.
Destructive. As a hen gathereth..ye would not 7731
Loss. Presumed to go up..Canaanites smote them 7732
Obstinate. We will certainly do whatsoever 7733
Sin. Rebellion is as the sin of witchcraft 7734
Work of. In their self-will they digged down a 7735

STUBBORNNESS.
Punished. They mocked..despised..therefore 8393
in Sin. To obey is better than sacrifice 8394
" We will certainly..burn incense to the 8395
" Took Dagon and set him in his place 8396

Calamities. Smitten you with..not returned 1001
Insane. Let the men go..E. is destroyed 799
See IMPENITENCE.

5764. OBEDIENCE, Blessings of. *To Israel.* [22] If thou shalt indeed obey his voice, and do all that I speak; then I will be an enemy unto thine enemies, and an adversary unto thine adversaries. [23] For mine Angel shall go before thee.—EX., ch. 23. [See verses 20–33.]

5765. —— **Blessings in.** *Many.* [3] Blessed *shalt* thou *be* in the city, and blessed *shalt* thou *be* in the field. [4] Blessed *shall be* the fruit of thy body..of thy ground..of thy cattle, the increase of thy kine, and the flocks of thy sheep. [5] Blessed *shall be* thy basket and thy store.— DEUT., ch. 28. [See chapter.]

5766. —— **Continued.** *Rechabites.* [18] Because ye have obeyed the commandment of Jonadab your father.. [19] Therefore thus saith the Lord of hosts, the God of Israel ; Jonadab the son of Rechab shall not want a man to stand before me for ever.—JER., ch. 35.

5767. —— **Complete.** *Joshua.* [15] As the Lord commanded Moses his servant, so did Moses command Joshua, and so did Joshua ; he left nothing undone of all that the Lord commanded Moses.—JOSH., ch. 11.

5768. —— **Cured by.** *Naaman.* [14] Then went he down, and dipped himself seven times in Jordan, according to the saying of the man of God : and his flesh came again like unto the flesh of a little child, and he was clean.—2 KINGS, ch. 5.

5769. —— **Conditional.** *Pharaoh.* [28] I will let you go, that ye may sacrifice to the Lord your God in the wilderness ; only ye shall not go very far away : entreat for me.—EX., ch. 8.

5770. —— *Pharaoh.* [24] Go ye, serve the Lord ; only let your flocks and your herds be stayed : let your little ones also go with you. —EX., ch. 10.

5771. —— **Delight in.** *Jesus.* [32] I have meat to eat that ye know not of. [33] Therefore said the disciples one to another, Hath any man brought him *aught* to eat? [34] Jesus saith..My meat is to do the will of him that sent me, and to finish his work.—JOHN, ch. 4.

5772. —— **in Discouragement.** *Peter.* [5] Simon answering, said..Master, we have toiled all the night, and have taken nothing ; nevertheless, at thy word I will let down the net.—LUKE, ch. 5.

5773. —— **solves Doubt.** *Jesus said,* [17] If any man will do his will, he shall know of the doctrine, whether it be of God, or *whether* I speak of myself.—JOHN, ch. 7.

5774. —— **Difficult.** *Gideon.* [25] The Lord said .. Take thy father's young bullock.. and throw down the altar of Baal that thy father hath, and cut down the grove that *is* by it : [26] And build an altar unto the Lord..upon the top of this rock.. [27] Then Gideon took ten men ..and *so* it was, because he feared his father's household, and the men of the city, that he could not do *it* by day, that he did *it* by night. —JUDGES, ch. 6.

5775. —— **essential.** *House on Rock.* [46] Why call ye me, Lord, Lord, and do not the things which I say ? [47] Whosoever cometh to me, and heareth my sayings, and doeth them, I will shew you to whom he is like.—LUKE, ch. 6.

5776. —— **Exact.** *To Joshua.* [5] I will not fail thee, nor forsake thee. [7] Only be thou strong and very courageous, that thou mayest observe to do according to all the law, which Moses my servant commanded thee : turn not from it *to* the right hand or *to* the left, that thou mayest prosper whithersoever thou goest.— JOSH., ch. 1.

5777. —— **of Elements.** *On Gennesaret.* [25] Where is your faith ? And they being afraid wondered, saying one to another, What manner of man is this ! for he commandeth even the winds and water, and they obey him.—LUKE, ch. 8.

5778. —— **Full.** *Marriage Feast.* [3] The mother of Jesus saith .. They have no wine. [4] Jesus saith..Woman, what have I to do with thee? mine hour is not yet come. [5] His mother saith unto the servants, Whatsoever he saith unto you, do *it*.—JOHN, ch. 2.

5779. —— —— *Saved by.* [22] Thus did Noah ; according to all that God commanded him, so did he.—GEN., ch. 6.

5780. —— —— *Pharaoh.* [25] Moses said.. [26] Our cattle also shall go with us ; there shall not a hoof be left behind ; for thereof must we take to serve the Lord our God.—Ex., ch. 10.

5781. —— **Faithful.** *Paul's.* [19] O king Agrippa, I was not disobedient unto the heavenly vision : [20] But shewed first unto them of Damascus, and at Jerusalem, and throughout all the coasts of Judea, and *then* to the Gentiles, that they should repent.—ACTS, ch. 26.

5782. —— **Filial.** *Jacob.* [7] Jacob obeyed his father and his mother, and was gone to Padan-aram.—GEN., ch. 28.

5783. —— —— *Ornament.* [8] My son, hear the instruction of thy father, and forsake not the law of thy mother : [9] For they *shall be* an ornament of grace unto thy head, and chains about thy neck.—PROV., ch. 1.

5784. —— —— *Queen Esther.* [20] For Esther did the commandment of Mordecai, like as when she was brought up with him.—ESTHER, ch. 2.

5785. —— —— *"Tie them."* [20] My son, keep thy father's commandment, and forsake not the law of thy mother : [21] Bind them continually upon thine heart, *and* tie them about thy neck.—PROV., ch. 6.

5786. —— **False.** *Saul.* [20] Saul said unto Samuel, Yea, I have obeyed the voice of the Lord..and have brought Agag the king of Amalek, and have utterly destroyed the Amalekites. [21] But the people took of the spoil, sheep and oxen, the chief of the things which should have been utterly destroyed, to sacrifice unto the Lord.—1 SAM., ch. 15.

5787. —— **Fickle.** *At Sinai.* [8] They have turned aside quickly out of the way which I commanded them : they have made them a molten calf, and have worshipped it, and have sacrificed thereunto, and said, These *be* thy gods, O Israel.—Ex., ch. 32.

5788. —— **from Gratitude.** *Aged Moses said,* [7] The Lord did not set his love upon you, nor choose you, because ye were more in number than any people ; for ye *were* the fewest of all people : [8] But because the Lord loved you.. [11] Thou shalt therefore keep the commandments, and the statutes, and the judgments..to do them. —DEUT., ch. 7.

5789. —— **to God rather than Man.** *Apostles.* [11] They..commanded them not to speak at all nor teach in the name of Jesus. [19] But Peter and John answered..Whether it be right in the sight of God to hearken unto you more than unto God, judge ye.—ACTS, ch. 4.

5790. —— —— *Apostles.* [28] Did not we straitly command you that ye should not teach in this name? and, behold, ye have filled Jerusalem with your doctrine, and intend to bring this man's blood upon us. [29] Then Peter

and the *other* apostles answered..We ought to obey God rather than men.—ACTS, ch. 5.

5791. —— **General.** *Solomon's.* [3] Solomon loved the Lord, walking in the statutes of David his father : only he sacrificed and burnt incense in high places. [4] And the king went to Gibeon to sacrifice there ; for that *was* the great high place : a thousand burnt offerings did Solomon offer upon that altar.--1 KINGS, ch. 3.

5792. —— **indispensable.** *"Do well."* [15] And when ye spread forth your hands, I will hide mine eyes from you ; yea, when ye make many prayers, I will not hear : your hands are full of blood. [16] Wash ye, make you clean ; put away the evil of your doings from before mine eyes ; cease to do evil ; [17] Learn to do well ; seek judgment, relieve the oppressed, judge the fatherless, plead for the widow.—ISA., ch. 1.

5793. —— **Late.** *Israelites.* [40] They rose up early in the morning, and gat them up into the top of the mountain, saying, Lo, we *be here*, and will go up unto the place which the Lord hath promised : for we have sinned. [41] And Moses said, Wherefore now do ye transgress the commandment of the Lord? but it shall not prosper. —NUM., ch. 14.

5794. —— **National.** *Aged Samuel said,* [24] Only fear the Lord, and serve him in truth with all your heart : for consider how great *things* he hath done for you. [25] But if ye shall still do wickedly, ye shall be consumed, both ye and your king.—1 SAM., ch. 12.

5795. —— **of Nature.** *Creation.* [3] God said, Let there be light : and there was light.—GEN., ch. 1.

5796. —— **Painful.** *Husband's.* [14] David sent messengers to Ish-bosheth Saul's son, saying, Deliver *me* my wife Michal, which I espoused to me for a hundred foreskins of the Philistines. [15] And Ish-bosheth sent, and took her from *her* husband, *even* from Phaltiel.. [16] And her husband went with her along weeping behind her to Bahurim. Then said Abner unto him, Go, return. And he returned.--2 SAM., ch. 3.

5797. —— **vs. Profession.** *Parable.* [28] A certain man had two sons ; and he came to the first, and said, Son, go work to day in my vineyard. [29] He answered..I will not ; but afterward he repented, and went. [30] And he came to the second, and said likewise. And he answered..I *go*, sir ; and went not.—MAT., ch. 21.

5798. —— **Perfect.** *Command.* [32] Ye shall observe to do therefore as the Lord your God hath commanded you : ye shall not turn aside to the right hand or to the left. [33] Ye shall walk in all the ways which the Lord your God hath commanded you, that ye may live, and *that it may be* well with you, and *that* ye may prolong *your* days in the land which ye shall possess.— DEUT., ch. 5.

5799. —— **Prosperity by.** *God said,* [3] If ye ..keep my commandments, and do them ; [4] Then I will give you rain in due season, and the land shall yield her increase, and the trees of the field shall yield their fruit.—LEV., ch. 26. [See verses 3-13.]

5800. —— —— *Moses said,* [13] If ye shall hearken diligently unto my commandments.. to love the Lord..to serve him with all your heart and with all your soul, [14] That I will give *you* the rain of your land in his due season, the first rain and the latter rain, that thou mayest gather in thy corn, and thy wine, and thine oil. —Deut., ch. 11.

5801. —— **Protection by.** *Israelites.* [4] Ye have seen what I did unto the Egyptians, and *how* I bare you on eagles' wings, and brought you unto myself. [5] Now therefore, if ye will obey my voice indeed, and keep my covenant, then ye shall be a peculiar treasure unto me above all people.—Ex., ch. 19.

5802. —— **Pledge of.** *At Sinai.* [7] Moses.. called for the elders..and laid before their faces all these words which the Lord commanded him. [8] And all the people answered together, and said, All that the Lord hath spoken we will do. And Moses returned the words of the people unto the Lord.—Ex., ch. 19.

5803. —— **No Peril in.** *" On the Water."* [28] Peter..said, Lord, if it be thou, bid me come unto thee on the water. [29] And he said, Come. And when Peter was come down out of the ship, he walked on the water, to go to Jesus.—Mat., ch. 14.

5804. —— **qualified.** *Naaman.* [18] In this thing the Lord pardon thy servant, *that* when my master goeth into the house of Rimmon to worship there, and he leaneth on my hand, and I bow myself in the house of Rimmon.—2 Kings, ch. 5.

5805. —— **Rule for.** *Aged Samuel said,* [14] If ye will fear the Lord, and serve him..and not rebel against the commandment of the Lord; then shall both ye and also the king that reigneth over you continue following the Lord.—1 Sam., ch. 12.

5806. —— **required.** *For Heaven.* [21] Not every one that saith unto me, Lord, Lord, shall enter into the kingdom of heaven; but he that doeth the will of my Father which is in heaven. [22] Many will say to me in that day, Lord, Lord, have we not prophesied?—Mat., ch. 7.

5807. —— **rewarded.** *In Canaan.* [Caleb said,] [8] My brethren that went up with me made the heart of the people melt : but I wholly followed the Lord my God. [10] And now, behold, the Lord hath kept me alive, as he said, these forty and five years.—Josh., ch. 14.

5808. —— **Reluctant.** *At Sinai.* [1] When the people complained, it displeased the Lord.. and his anger was kindled ; and the fire of the Lord..consumed *them that were* in the uttermost parts of the camp.—Num., ch. 10.

5809. —— **better than Sacrifice.** *Saul.* [8] And he tarried seven days, according to the set time that Samuel *had appointed :* but Samuel came not to Gilgal ; and the people were scattered from him. [9] And Saul said, Bring hither a burnt offering to me, and peace offerings. And he offered the burnt offering. [13] And Samuel said to Saul, Thou hast done foolishly : thou hast not kept the commandment of the Lord thy God, which he commanded thee : for now would the Lord have established thy kingdom upon Israel for ever.—1 Sam., ch. 13.

5810. —— —— *Saul.* [15] Saul said, They have brought them from the Amalekites : for the people spared the best of the sheep and of the oxen, to sacrifice unto the Lord thy God.

[22] And Samuel said, Hath the Lord *as great* delight in burnt offerings and sacrifices, as in obeying the voice of the Lord? Behold, to obey *is* better than sacrifice, *and* to hearken than the fat of rams.—1 Sam., ch. 15.

5811. —— **Success by.** *Caleb.* [24] My servant Caleb, because he had another spirit with him, and hath followed me fully, him will I bring into the land whereinto he went ; and his seed shall possess it.—Num., ch. 14.

5812. —— **Self-sacrificing.** *Widow.* [15] She went and did according to the saying of Elijah : and she, and he, and her house, did eat *many* days. [16] *And* the barrel of meal wasted not.—1 Kings, ch. 17.

5813. —— **Partial.** *Herod.* [20] Herod feared John, knowing that he was a just man and a holy, and observed him ; and when he heard him, he did many things, and heard him gladly. —Mark, ch. 6.

5814. —— **Saved by.** *Noah* [7] Went in, and his sons, and his wife, and his sons' wives with him, into the ark, because of the waters of the flood.—Gen., ch. 7.

5815. —— **Test of.** *In Eden.* [3] Of the fruit of the tree which *is* in the midst of the garden, God hath said, Ye shall not eat of it, neither shall ye touch it, lest ye die.—Gen., ch. 3.

5816. —— —— *Savage.* [Jehu to exterminate Ahab's family.] [6] He wrote.. If ye *be* mine..take ye the heads of the men your master's sons, and come to me to Jezreel by to-morrow this time. Now the king's sons, *being* seventy persons, *were* with the great men of the city, which brought them up.—2 Kings, ch. 10.

5817. —— **A willing.** *Disciple.* [14] He saw Levi the *son* of Alpheus sitting at the receipt of custom, and said..Follow me. And he arose and followed him.—Mark, ch. 2.

5818. —— **of Wives.** *" Subjection."* [1] Likewise, ye wives, *be* in subjection to your own husbands ; that, if any obey not the word, they also may without the word be won by the conversation of the wives.—1 Peter, ch. 2.

5819. —— **Wonderful.** *Abraham.* [16] By myself have I sworn..because thou hast done this thing, and hast not withheld thy son, thine only son, [17] That in blessing I will bless thee, and in multiplying I will multiply thy seed as the stars of the heaven, and as the sand which *is* upon the sea shore.—Gen., ch. 22.

See other illustrations under :

AUTHORITY.

SUBMISSION.

Punishment. Eli said, It is the L. let him do   8416
Providence. Return tc thy mistress and submit   8417

SURRENDER.

Absolute. I count all things but loss for..the   8503
Bodily. Yieldeth their bodies that..not serve any   8504
Christian. May know..fellowship of his sufferings   8505
Entire. One thing thou lackest, go..give to the   8506
Full. Whosoever..forsaketh not all..disciple   8507
Fear. We will do all that thou shalt bid us   8508
Moral. What things were gain to me, I counted   8509
Power. We have not used this power..lest we   8510
Resisted. When he saw him, the spirit tare him   8511
Sins. If thy right hand offend thee..cast it   8512
Sacrifice. Widow..cast in..all her living   8513
Undivided. Our cattle shall also go with us   8514
Weak. King Ahab said, My Lord, O King, I am   8515

Conditional. Go serve the L..but who shall go?   1452
   "   Go, only let your flocks be stayed   1448
Promised. All that thou commandest us we will do   587
   See DUTY.

5820. OBJECTORS silenced. *The Rulers.*
[13] When they saw the boldness of Peter and
John, and perceived that they were unlearned
and ignorant men, they marvelled ; and they took
knowledge of them, that they had been with
Jesus. [14] And beholding the man which was
healed standing with them, they could say nothing against it.—ACTS, ch. 4.

5821. OBJECTIONS, False. *Jesus said,* [33] John
the Baptist came neither eating bread nor
drinking wine ; and ye say, He hath a devil.
[34] The Son of man is come eating and drinking ;
and ye say, Behold, a gluttonous man, and a
winebibber.--LUKE, ch. 7.

See other illustrations under :

COMPLAINERS.

Punished. Our soul loatheth..bread..sent fiery   1445
Unreasonable. The first supposed..received more   1446
Unprincipled. These are..walking in their own   1447
Wicked. Did bring up an evil report..the plague   1448

CROSSNESS.

Irritation. Let us alone that we may serve the   1848
Habitual. Nabal was churlish and evil in his doings   1849
Prejudice. Children crying, Hosannah..sore d.   1850

DISCONTENTMENT.

Foreigners. Hadad..to Pharaoh, Let me depart   2343
Proud. All this availeth me nothing..see Mordecai   2344
Unity in. Every one that was discontented..unto   2345

FAULTFINDERS.

Fastidious. Why do ye eat..with sinners   3087
Hypocritical. Why was not this..sold for 300 pence   3088
Malicious. John B..he hath a devil..Son of man   3089

MURMURING.

Disappointment. This evil place?..no place of figs   5639
Discouragement. People was much discouraged   5640
Distrust. Would G. that we had died in Egypt   5641
Fear. Did tell thee..been better serve the E.   5642
God. Hath not the potter power over the clay   5643
Mercenaries. These last have wrought but one   5644
Neglect. Murmuring of the Greeks against the   5645
Punished. Fire of the L. burnt them..uttermost   5646
Severity. What shall I do?..almost ready to stone   5647
Thirst. Three days..no water..bitter..what shall   5648

Domestic. Hannah's adversary made her to fret   3012
Evildoers. Fret not thyself because of evil men   9526
Fretting. She urged him..soul was vexed unto   443
Peevishness. To me they have ascribed but   6038
   See HINDERANCE and references.

5822. OBSERVATION, Difficult. *Zaccheus.*
[3] He sought to see Jesus who he was ; and could
not for the press, because he was little of
stature. [4] And he ran before, and climbed up
into a sycamore tree to see him ; for he was to
pass that *way*.—LUKE, ch. 19.

5823. —— **Unfeeling.** *Parable.*   [30] Fell
among thieves..leaving *him* half dead, [31]..there
came down a certain priest that way ; and when
he saw him, he passed by on the other side.
[32] And likewise a Levite..came and looked *on*
him, and passed by on the other side.—LUKE,
ch. 10.

See other illustrations under :

APPEARANCES.

Conceal. Joseph made himself strange unto them   474
Evil. Lest we should offend..take up a fish   475
False. Walk in long robes, and love greetings   476
Hurtful. Be emboldened to eat those things   477
Uncertain. Man looketh on the outward   478

LOOK.

Life. When he.beheld the serpent of brass, he l.   5056
Reproof. L. turned and looked upon Peter   5057
Trouble. L. looked through..troubled the Egyp'ns   5058

LOOKING.

Blood. Strike it on the..door post of the houses   5059
Back. Escape for thy life..look not behind   5060
   "   Put his hand to the plow and looking back   5061
Jesus. Beginning to sink..L. save me   5062

SEEING.

Partial. Women saw that the tree was good for f.   7654
Proof. G. hath given one to sit on my throne..eyes   7655
Unsatisfactory. Eye is not satisfied with seeing   7656
Vexatious. Lot..wicked..seeing and hearing   7657

VANITY.

Forbidden. Be not called Rabbi..are brethren   9160
Humbled. Haman arrayed Mordecai..proclaimed   9162
Punished. Hezekiah showed them all..silver   9161
Religious. To be seen..garments..love greetings   9163

Adornment. Women adorn themselves..not with   108
Concealment. Adulterer waiteth..twilight..no eye   111
Display. Ahasuerus made a feast..hangings   2409

5824. OBSTACLE, Affection an. *Elisha said,*
[20] Let me, I pray thee, kiss my father and my
mother, and *then* I will follow thee. And he said
unto him, Go back again : for what have I done
to thee ? [21] And he returned back from him.
—1 KINGS, ch. 19.

   See HINDERANCE and references.

5825. OBSTINACY, Provoking. *Calf-Wor-*
shippers.   [9] The Lord said unto Moses, I have
seen this people, and, behold, it *is* a stiffnecked
people : [10] Now therefore let me alone, that my
wrath may wax hot against them, and that I
may consume them.—EX., ch. 32.

5826. —— **rebuked.** *Balaam.*   [32] The angel
of the Lord said unto him, Wherefore hast thou
smitten thine ass these three times? Behold, I
went out to withstand thee, because *thy* way is
perverse before me.—NUM., ch. 22.

5827. —— **Rebellious.** *King Wanted.*   [18] Ye
shall cry out in that day because of your king
which ye shall have chosen you ; and the Lord
will not hear you.. [19] Nevertheless the people
refused to obey the voice of Samuel ; and they
said, Nay ; but we will have a king over us ;
[20]..like all the nations.—1 SAM., ch. 8.

See other illustrations under :
DETERMINATION.
Evil. We will certainly..burn incense to the 2260
Fixed. As the L. liveth..I will not leave thee 2262
" In every city bonds..none..move me 2266
Resolute. Absalom said..Set it on fire 2263
Wanting. I will let him go..Pilate gave sentence 2264
PERSISTENCE.
Necessary. Aaron and Hur held up his hands 6067
in Prayer. Let me go, for the day breaketh..I will 6068
Rewarded. I will not leave thee..he followed her 6069
Unchangeable. Mordecai bowed not, nor did him 6070
Undiscouraged. Charged him..he cried the more 6071
" Because of his importunity, he 6072
WILL.
Rebellious. How often would I..ye would not 9593
" We will certainly..burn incense..queen 9594
See OBDURACY and references.

5828. OBSTRUCTIONIST, A malicious. *Diotrephes.* ⁹ Diotrephes, who loveth to have the preeminence among them, receiveth us not. ¹⁰..neither doth he himself receive the brethren, and forbiddeth them that would, and casteth *them* out of the church.—3 JOHN.

5829. OBSTRUCTIONISTS, Religious. *Pharisees.* ¹³ Woe unto you, scribes and Pharisees, hypocrites ! for ye shut up the kingdom of heaven against men : for ye neither go in *yourselves,* neither suffer ye them that are entering to go in.—MAT., ch. 23.

See other illustrations under :
HINDERANCE.
Disobedience. Say nothing to any man..blaze 3979
Natural. Let me..kiss my father..mother 3980
Provoking. Let us pass through thy country 3981
Removed. Angel..rolled back the stone..door 3982
Riches. Deceitfulness of riches..choke the word 3983
" Easier for a camel..needle's eye than 3984
HINDERANCES.
Care. Take heed lest..become a stumblingblock 3985
Malicious. People of the land hired counsellors 3986
Removed. I will eat no flesh while the world 3987
Secular. I have bought..bought..married 3988
Social. Let me first go bid them farewell 3989
Selfish. Neither go in yourself, neither suffer ye 3990
HINDERING.
Fear. It is reported..Jews think to rebel 3991
Intrigue. Let us meet..in the plain of Ono 3992

5830. OCCUPATION, An inherited. *Shepherds.* ³³ When Pharaoh..shall say, What *is* your occupation ? ³⁴..ye shall say, Thy servants' trade hath been about cattle from our youth even until now, both we, *and* also our fathers..ye may dwell in the land of Goshen ; for every shepherd *is* an abomination unto the Egyptians. —GEN., ch. 46.

5831. —— An offensive. *Shepherds.* [See Nos. 5830 and 5834.]

See other illustrations under :
TRADE.
Dishonesty. Making the ephah and the shekel 8860
" False balance is an abomination to 8861
" Every one dealeth falsely 8862
Lawful. How much..gained by trading 8663
Luxuries. Merchandise of gold..odours..wine 8664
Protection. Our craft is in danger..wealth 8865
Sabbath. Brought fish and..ware 8866
" If ye do so..I will lay hands on 8867
Tricks. Divers weights a great and a small 8868
Union. Called..workmen of like occupation 8869
See EMPLOYMENT and references.

5832. ODDNESS, A convenient. *"Left Hand."* ²⁰ Ehud said, I have a message from God unto thee.. ²¹ And Ehud put forth his left hand, and took the dagger from his right thigh, and thrust it into his belly.—JUDGES, ch. 3.

5833. ODIUM, Undeserved. *To Moses and Aaron.* ²¹ The Lord look upon you, and judge ; because ye have made our savour to be abhorred in the eyes of Pharaoh, and in the eyes of his servants, to put a sword in their hand to slay us.—Ex., ch. 5.
See DISGRACE and references.

5834. OFFENCE from Prejudice. *Carpenter.* ² Such mighty works are wrought by his hands ? ³ Is not this the carpenter, the son of Mary.. And they were were offended at him.—MARK, ch. 6.

5835. OFFENCES, Responsibility for. *"Woe."* ⁷ Woe unto the world because of offences ! for it must needs be that offences come ; but woe to that man by whom the offence cometh !—MAT., ch. 18.

See other illustrations under :
CRIME.
Abetting. Why have ye conspired against me 1829
Drunkard's. Ask of me..I will give you 1830
Intemperance. David..made [Uriah] drunk 1831
Wine. Smite Amnon, then kill him 1832
CRIMINALS.
no Refuge. Solomon sent Benaiah..fall on him 1835
Sanctuary. Adonijah..took hold of the..altar 1834
Shameful. I can not dig ; to beg I am ashamed 1833
INJURY.
Forgiveness. Father, forgive them, they know not 4498
Insulting. Samson's wife was given to his..friend 4496
Revenged. Samson caught 300 foxes..firebrands 4497
INSULT.
Ignored. Despised him [Saul]..held his peace 4567
First. Thrust him [Jesus] out of the city..headlong 4568
Rewarded. Cut off their garments in the middle 4569
Stinging. To smite him on the mouth 4570

Avoided. Lest they should be offended..fish 475
See RESENTMENT and references.

5836. OFFERING accepted. *Tabernacle.* ²⁴ There came a fire out from before the Lord, and consumed upon the altar the burnt offering and the fat : *which* when all the people saw, they shouted, and fell on their faces.—LEV., ch. 9.

5837. —— The best. *Heart.* ⁷ Will the Lord be pleased with thousands of rams, *or* with ten thousands of rivers of oil ? shall I give my firstborn *for* my transgression?.. ⁸..what doth the Lord require of thee, but to do justly, and to love mercy, and to walk humbly with thy God ? —MICAH, ch. 6.

5838. —— A humble. *Little Lamb.* ⁹ Samuel took a sucking lamb, and offered *it for* a burnt offering wholly unto the Lord : and Samuel cried unto the Lord for Israel ; and the Lord heard him.—1 SAM., ch. 7.

5839. OFFERINGS, Abominable. *Wicked.* ⁸ The sacrifice of the wicked *is* an abomination to the Lord : but the prayer of the upright *is* his delight.—PROV., ch. 15.

5840. —— forbidden. *Heartless.* ¹³ Bring no more vain oblations ; incense is an abomination unto me ; the new moons and sabbaths, the calling of assemblies, I cannot away with ;

it is iniquity, even the solemn meeting. ¹⁵ And when ye spread forth your hands, I will hide mine eyes from you ; yea, when ye make many prayers, I will not hear : your hands are full of blood.—Isa., ch. 1.

5841. —— **Ministerial.** *" One Tenth."* ²⁶ Thus speak unto the Levites..When ye take of the children of Israel the tithes which I have given you from them for your inheritance, then ye shall offer up a heave offering of it for the Lord, *even* a tenth *part* of the tithe.—Num., ch. 18.

5842. —— **Many.** *Dedication of Temple.* ⁶⁵ Solomon offered a sacrifice of peace offerings, ..two and twenty thousand oxen, and a hundred and twenty thousand sheep.—1 Kings, ch. 8.

5843. —— **rejected.** *Heartless.* ¹¹ To what purpose *is* the multitude of your sacrifices unto me? saith the Lord : I am full of the burnt offerings of rams, and the fat of fed beasts ; and I delight not in the blood of bullocks, or of lambs, or of he goats.—Isa., ch. 1.

5844. —— **scrutinized.** *" Two Mites."* ⁴¹ And Jesus sat over against the treasury, and beheld how the people cast money into the treasury : and many that were rich cast in much. ⁴² And there came a certain poor widow, and she threw in two mites, which make a farthing. ⁴³ And he called *unto him* his disciples.—Mark, ch. 12.

5845. —— **Unworthy.** *" Maimed."* ⁸ If ye offer the blind for sacrifice, *is it* not evil ? and if ye offer the lame and sick, *is it* not evil ? offer it now unto thy governor ; will he be†pleased with thee, or accept thy person ? saith the Lord of hosts.—Mal., ch. 1.

5846. ‑—— **Voluntary.** *Artaxerxes said,* ¹³ I make a decree, that all they of the people of Israel..in my realm, which are minded of their own freewill to go up to Jerusalem, go with thee.. ¹⁶ And all the silver and gold that thou canst find in all the province of Babylon, with the freewill offering of the people..offering willingly for the house of their God which *is* in Jerusalem.—Ezra, ch. 1.

5847. —— **Willing.** *Tabernacle.* ⁶ Moses gave commandment..throughout the camp, saying, Let neither man nor woman make any more work for the offering of the sanctuary. So the people were restrained from bringing. ⁷ For the stuff they had was sufficient..and too much.—Ex., ch. 36.

See **GENEROSITY** and references.

See **SACRIFICE** and references.

5848. OFFICE, Burdens of. *David.* [Joab assassinated Abner.] ³⁹ I *am* this day weak, though anointed king ; and these men the sons of Zeruiah *be* too hard for me.—2 Sam., ch. 3.

5849. —— **declined.** *Gideon.* ²² The men of Israel said..Rule thou over us, both thou, and thy son, and thy son's son also : for thou hast delivered us from the hand of Midian. ²³ And Gideon said..I will not rule over you, neither shall my son..the Lord shall rule over you.—Judges, ch. 8.

5850. —— **Examination for.** *Deacons.* ¹⁰ Let these also first be proved ; then let them use the office of a deacon, being *found* blameless.—1 Tim., ch. 3.

5851. —— **The Faithful for.** *" Ten Cities."* ¹⁶ Lord, thy pound hath gained ten pounds.

¹⁷..Well, thou good servant because thou hast been faithful in a very little, have thou authority over ten cities.—Luke, ch. 19.

5852. —— **Intrigue for.** *Abimelech.* ² Whether *is* better for you, either that all the *sons* of Jerubbaal, *which are* threescore and ten persons, reign over you, or that one reign over you? remember also that I *am* your bone and your flesh. ³ And his mother's brethren spake of him in the ears of all the men of Shechem all these words. —Judges, ch. 9.

5853. —— **by Merit.** *" Been Faithful."* ²⁰ I have gained beside them five talents more. ²¹ His lord said..Well done, *thou* good and faithful servant : thou hast been faithful over a few things, I will make thee ruler over many things. —Mat., ch. 25.

5854. —— **Petition for.** *James and John.* ³⁵ James and John.. ³⁷..Grant unto us that we may sit, one on thy right hand, and the other on thy left hand, in thy glory.—Mark, ch. 10.

5855. OFFICE-SEEKING, A Demagogue. *Absalom.* ⁴ Oh that I were made judge in the land, that every man which hath any suit or cause might come unto me, and I would do him justice ! ⁵..when any man came nigh *to him* to do him obeisance, he put forth his hand, and took him, and kissed him.—2 Sam., ch. 15.

5856. —— **Trials of.** *At Zin.* ⁵ Wherefore have ye made us to come up out of Egypt..unto this evil place? it *is* no place of seed, or of figs, or of vines, or of pomegranates ; neither *is* there any water to drink. ⁶ And Moses and Aaron went..unto the door of the tabernacle.. and they fell upon their faces : and the glory of the Lord appeared unto them.—Num.. ch. 20.

5857. —— **unsought.** *Saul.* ²² He hath hid himself among the stuff. ²³ And they ran and fetched him thence : and..he was higher than any of the people from his shoulders and upward. ²⁴ And Samuel said..See ye him whom the Lord hath chosen..And all the people shouted..God save the king.—1 Sam., ch. 10.

5858. —— —— *David.* ¹¹ Are here all *thy* children? And he said, There remaineth yet the youngest, and, behold, he keepeth the sheep. And Samuel said unto Jesse, Send and fetch him ..¹²..Now he *was* ruddy, *and* withal of a beautiful countenance, and goodly to look to. And the Lord said, Arise, anoint him.—1 Sam., ch. 16.

5859. —— **Undesired.** *" Fig Tree."* ¹⁰ The trees said to the fig tree, Come thou, *and* reign over us. ¹¹ But the fig tree said..Should I forsake my sweetness, and my good fruit, and go to be promoted over the trees?—Judges, ch. 9.

5860. OFFICE-HOLDER, A blameless. *Daniel.* ³ The king thought to set him over the whole realm. ⁴ Then the presidents and princes sought to find occasion against Daniel concerning the kingdom ; but they could find none occasion nor fault ; forasmuch as he *was* faithful.—Dan., ch. 6.

5861. —— —— *Samuel.* ³ Behold, here I *am :* witness against me before the Lord..whose ox have I taken? or whose ass have I taken? or whom have I defrauded? whom have I oppressed? or of whose hand have I received *any* bribe to blind mine eyes therewith? and I will restore it you. ⁴ And they said, Thou hast not defrauded us.—1 Sam., ch. 12.

5862. —— **A dishonest.** *Judas.* 5 Why was not this ointment sold for three hundred pence, and given to the poor? 6 This he said, not that he cared for the poor ; but because he was a thief, and had the bag.—JOHN, ch. 12.

5863. OFFICE-HOLDER'S Prayer. *Solomon.* 7 O Lord my God, thou hast made thy servant king..and I *am but* a little child : I know not *how* to go out or come in. 9 Give therefore thy servant an understanding heart to judge thy people, that I may discern between good and bad : for who is able to judge this thy so great a people ?—1 KINGS, ch. 3.

5864. OFFICERS, Church. *Various.* 28 God hath set some in the church, first apostles, secondarily prophets, thirdly teachers, after that miracles, then gifts of healings, helps, governments, diversities of tongues.—1 COR., ch. 12.

5865. —— **Qualifications of.** *Deacons.* 3 Brethren, look ye out among you seven men of honest report, full of the Holy Ghost and wisdom, whom we may appoint over this business.—ACTS, ch. 6.

5866. —— —— *Deacons.* 8 Likewise *must* the deacons be grave, not double-tongued, not given to much wine, not greedy of filthy lucre ; 9 Holding the mystery of the faith in a pure conscience.—1 TIM., ch. 3.

5867. —— —— *Bishop.* 2 A bishop then must be blameless, the husband of one wife, vigilant, sober, of good behaviour, given to hospitality, apt to teach ; 3 Not given to wine, no striker, not greedy of filthy lucre ; but patient, not a brawler, not covetous.—1 TIM., ch. 3.

5868. —— **Responsibility of.** *Saul.* 21 The people took of the spoil, sheep and oxen, the chief of the things which should have been utterly destroyed, to sacrifice unto the Lord.. 23..Because thou hast rejected the word of the Lord, he hath also rejected thee from *being* king. —1 SAM., ch. 15.

5869. —— —— *Jethro said,* 21 Thou shalt provide..able men, such as fear God, men of truth, hating covetousness ; and place *such* over them, *to be* rulers of thousands, *and* rulers of hundreds, rulers of fifties, and rulers of tens. —EX., ch. 18.

5870. —— **Selection of.** *David's.* 25 Over the king's treasures *was* Azmaveth..and over the storehouses in the fields, in the cities, and in the villages, and in the castles, *was* Jehonathan.—1 CHRON., ch. 27.

5871. —— **unconverted.** *Evidence.* 47 Then answered them the Pharisees, Are ye also deceived? 48 Have any of the rulers or of the Pharisees believed on him ?—JOHN, ch. 7.

See other illustrations under:

ADMINISTRATION.

Change. There arose a king..knew not Joseph	99
Rejected. Now make us a king to judge us	100
" Let us make a captain..return unto	101

AUTHORITY.

Brother's. My brother..commanded me to be	584
Compared. Moses commanded..what sayest thou	585
False. I am a prophet..he lied	586
Obedience. All..we will do..will go	587
Power. I say unto one, Go, and he goeth	588
Questioned. By what authority doest thou these	589
Recognized. Winds and water..obey him	591
Supreme. Drove them all out of the temple	590

JUDGE.

Bribery. Samuel's sons..took bribes and	4760
Circuit. Samuel went from year to year in circuit	4756
Qualifications. He that is without sin among you	4757
Unjust. Crucify him ; I find no fault in him	4758
Unrighteous. Ananias commanded to smite him	4759

PROMOTION.

Avoided. Behold, Saul hath hid himself among the	6647
Desirable. Go up higher ; then shalt thou have w.	6648
Envied. Princes sought..occasion against Daniel	6649
Eagerness. Better..that thou be a priest unto a t.	6650
Honourable. Better..said..come up hither..put l.	6651
Merit. D. was preferred..because an excellent s.	6652
Means. When thou art bidden, sit..lowest room	6653
Piety. Can we find such a one..Spirit of G. is?	6654
Requested. We may sit, one on thy right hand	6655
Sought. Diotrephes loveth to have the preeminence	6656
" Ye shall be as gods, knowing good from e.	6657
Unsought. There remaineth yet the youngest..s.	6658
Unsatisfying. Haman told..the king had promoted	6659
" Seek ye the priesthood also	6660
Worthy. Only in the throne will I be greater than	6661

RULER.

Born. Your sheaves made obeisance to my sheaf	7466
" Potiphar..made him overseer..all that he	7467
" Keeper of the prison committed to Joseph's	7468
" [Enthroned] Cried before him, Bow the k.	7469
Foolish. Cursed..that eateth..until evening	7470
Pious. Have kept from my youth up	7471
Ruled. Jezebel his wife said..Dost thou now	7472
Sinful. Ahab did sell himself to work wickedness	7473
" As a roaring lion..is a wicked ruler	7474
Unjust. Feared not God, neither regarded man	7475

RULERS.

Guidance. Book..shall be with him..read	7476
Influence. Have any of the rulers..believed on	7477
Many. Besides the chief of Sol.'s officers..3300	7478
Qualifications. Provide able men..fear G..of truth	7479
Responsibility. Because..L. hath rejected thee	7480

STATESMANSHIP.

Evil. Jeroboam made priests of the lowest of the	8331
Poor. Rehoboam forsook the counsel of the old	8332

Application. Mother of Z. children..two sons	322
Discharged. Thou mayest no longer be steward	75
Eagerness. Oh that I were made a judge	161
Happy. Mordecai wrote..sealed with the king's r.	8324
Hope. Will the son of Jesse..make you all captains?	78
Ineligible. King..mayest not set a stranger	3337
Love. Disputed among themselves..greatest	331
Malicious. Diotrephes loveth..preeminence	317
Responsibility. Ahaz..ruin of him and all I.	140
Religious. Eunuch of great authority..charge of her	352
Rejected. Moses..make another captain	101
Self-promoted. Adonijah exalted himself..king	302
Taskmaster. Let them go and gather straw	8593
Undesired. Saul hid himself among the stuff	333

5872. OFFICIOUSNESS, Mistaken. *Disciples.* 13 They brought young children to him, that he should touch them ; and *his* disciples rebuked those that brought *them.* 14 But when Jesus saw *it,* he was much displeased, and said..Suffer the little children to come.—MARK, ch. 10.

5873. —— **rebuked.** *Shunammite.* 27 When she came to the man of God..she caught him by the feet : but Gehazi came near to thrust her away. And the man of God said, Let her alone ; for her soul *is* vexed within her : and the Lord hath hid *it* from me.—2 KINGS, ch. 4. [Her child was dead.]

See other illustrations under :
Impertinence. L..this shall not be..behind me, S. 4347
Meddler. Like one that taketh a dog by the ears 5278

5874. OLD better than New. *At Matthew's Feast.* ³⁹ No man also having drunk old *wine* straightway desireth new ; for he saith, The old is better.—LUKE, ch. 5.

See other illustrations under :

AGE.

Blessed. L. blessed the latter end of Job more   150
Blindness in. Isaac was old..eyes were dim   834
"   Ahijah..his eyes were set by..age   840
Children of. Israel loved Joseph more..of old age   177
Counsels of. I set before you a blessing..curse   1236
Cruelty to. Chaldeans..no compassion for age   1440
Disregarded. They that are younger than I..derision 146
Emotions. Ancient men..shouted..wept   2626
Fears. My son shall not go down..mischief   241
Paternity in. Z. and E..well stricken in years..son 1153
"   Abram was 100 years old..Isaac born 1193
Pleasures of. Wherefore..a burden unto..the king   237
Reflections. Ancient men had seen the first house   957
Respected. Elihu waited till Job had spoken..elder 4061
Revealed. Sat according to his birthright.marvelled 5661

5875. OMISSION, Cursed for. *Deborah sang,* ²³ Curse ye Meroz, said the angel of the Lord, curse ye bitterly the inhabitants thereof ; because they came not to the help of the Lord, to the help of the Lord against the mighty.—JUDGES, ch. 5.

5876. —— Deception by. *"Forgetteth."* ²² Be ye doers of the word, and not hearers only, deceiving your own selves. ²³ For if any be a hearer of the word, and not a doer, he is like unto a man beholding his natural face in a glass : ²⁴..and goeth his way, and straightway forgetteth what manner of man he was.—JAMES, ch. 1.

5877. —— A great. *"Did it not."* ⁴⁴ Lord, when saw we thee a hungered, or athirst, or a stranger, or naked, or sick, or in prison, and did not minister unto thee ? ⁴⁵..Inasmuch as ye did *it* not to one of the least of these, ye did *it* not to me. ⁴⁶ And these shall go away into everlasting punishment.—MAT., ch. 25.

5878. —— An inexcusable. *The Judgment.* [See No. 5877.]

5879. —— The Nobles'. *Building Wall.* ⁵ But their nobles put not their necks to the work of their Lord. ⁶ Moreover the old gate repaired Jehoiada.—NEH., ch. 3.

5880. —— Sin of. *"Weightier Matters."* ²³ Woe unto you, scribes and Pharisees, hypocrites ! for ye pay tithe of mint and anise and cummin, and have omitted the weightier *matters* of the law, judgment, mercy, and faith.—MAT., ch. 23.

See other illustrations under :

UNFAITHFULNESS.

Disqualifies. Not good to take Mark..went not   9091
Hinderance. Entered not..were entering ye h.   9092
Surprise. Lord..shall come..when he looked not   9089
Slander. I feared thee..an austere man   9090
See NEGLECT and references.

5881. OMNIPOTENCE in Creation. *Job.* ⁷ He stretcheth out the north over the empty place, *and* hangeth the earth upon nothing.—JOB, ch. 26. [See chap.]

Also see :

Ruling. Jesus rebuked the wind..water   6321

5882. OMNISCIENCE, Confession of. *David.* ¹ O Lord, thou hast searched me, and known me. ² Thou knowest my downsitting and mine uprising ; thou understandest my thought afar off.—Ps. 139. [See chapter.]

5883. ONE great Care. *Martha.* ⁴⁰ Martha was cumbered about much serving..and said, Lord, dost thou not care that my sister hath left me to serve alone ? bid her therefore that she help me. ⁴¹ And Jesus answered..Martha, thou art careful and troubled about many things : ⁴² But one thing is needful ; and Mary hath chosen that good part.—LUKE, ch. 10.

5884. —— for God. *Moses.* [A golden calf was made.] ²⁵ When Moses saw that the people *were* naked..²⁶ Then Moses stood in the gate of the camp, and said, Who *is* on the Lord's side ? *let him come* unto me. And all the sons of Levi gathered..unto him.—Ex., ch. 32.

5885. —— with God. *Elijah.* ²² I, *even* I only, remain a prophet of the Lord ; but Baal's prophets *are* four hundred and fifty men..²⁴ And call ye on the name of your gods, and I will call on the name of the Lord : and the God that answereth by fire, let him be God.—1 KINGS, ch. 18.

5886. —— —— *David.* ⁴⁵ To the Philistine, Thou comest to me with a sword, and with a spear, and with a shield : but I come to thee in the name of the Lord of hosts, the God of the armies of Israel, whom thou hast defied.—1 SAM., ch. 17.

5887. —— Action of. *Samson.* ¹⁴ The Philistines shouted against him : and the Spirit of the Lord came mightily upon him, and the cords that *were* upon his arms became as flax that was burnt with fire, and his bands loosed..¹⁵ And he found a new jawbone of an ass..and took it, and slew a thousand men.—JUDGES, ch. 15.

5888. —— Evil of. *At Abel.* ²¹ Sheba..hath lifted up his hand..against David : deliver him only, and I will depart from the city..²² ..They cut off the head of Sheba..and cast *it* out to Joab. And he blew a trumpet, and they retired from the city.—2 SAM., ch. 20.

5889. —— Victory by. *Shamgar.* ³¹ Shamgar ..slew of the Philistines six hundred men with an oxgoad : and he also delivered Israel.—JUDGES, ch. 3.

5890. OPINION, Control of. *Achish.* ⁶ Achish called David, and said..thy going out and thy coming in with me in the host *is* good in my sight : for I have not found evil in thee since the day of thy coming unto me..nevertheless the lords favour thee not. ⁷ Wherefore now return..that thou displease not the lords of the Philistines.—1 SAM., ch. 29.

5891. —— Change of. *Paul.* ⁴ No doubt this man is a murderer, whom, though he hath escaped the sea, yet vengeance suffereth not to live. ⁵ And he shook off the beast into the fire, and felt no harm. ⁶ Howbeit they looked when he should have swollen, or fallen down dead suddenly : but after they had looked a great while, and saw no harm come to him, they changed their minds, and said that he was a god.—ACTS, ch. 28.

5892. —— Preconceived. *Naaman.* ¹¹ I thought, He will surely come out..and call on the name of the Lord..and strike his hand over the place, and recover the leper. ¹² *Are* not

Abana and Pharpar, rivers of Damascus, better than all the waters of Israel?—2 KINGS, ch. 5.

5893. OPINIONS concealed. *Believers.* [See No. 5894.]

5894. —— divided. *Public.* 12 Some said, He is a good man : others said, Nay ; but he deceiveth the people. 13 Howbeit no man spake openly of him for fear of the Jews.—JOHN, ch. 7.

5895. —— Diverse. *Of Paul.* 5 We have found this man a pestilent *fellow*, and a mover of sedition among all the Jews throughout the world, and a ringleader of the sect of the Nazarenes : 6 Who also hath gone about to profane the temple ∴ 16..herein do I exercise myself, to have always a conscience void of offence toward God, and *toward* men.—ACTS, ch. 24.

**5896. —— ** *Of Christ.* 40 Many of the people..said, Of a truth this is the Prophet. 41 Others said, This is the Christ, But some said, Shall Christ come out of Galilee ? 42 Hath not the Scripture said, That Christ cometh..out of the town of Bethlehem, where David was ? 43 So there was a division among the people.—JOHN, ch. 7.

5897. —— Opposite. *Cloud.* 20 It came between the camp of the Egyptians and the camp of Israel ; and it was a cloud and darkness *to them*, but it gave light by night *to these*.—Ex., ch. 14.

5898. —— prejudiced. *Job's Friends.* [Elihu.] 3 Against his three friends was his wrath kindled, because they had found no answer, and *yet* had condemned Job.—JOB, ch. 32.

5899. —— Undecided. *At Carmel.* 21 Elijah ..said, How long halt ye between two opinions ? if the Lord *be* God, follow him : but if Baal, *then* follow him. And the people answered him not a word.—1 KINGS, ch. 18.

See other illustrations under :

BELIEF.
Conviction. Searched the scriptures daily whether 679
Signs. Except ye see signs..not believe 680

INFERENCE.
Differ. Voice from heaven..it thundered 4462
Mistaken. Wilt thou at this time restore the kingd. 4459
Wrong. See how he seeketh a quarrel against me 4460
Warranted. Disciple saith to Peter, It is the L. 4461

JUDGMENT.
Blindness. Hath blinded their eyes, and hardened 4763
Despondency. I, even I only, am left..seek my life 4764
for Judgment. With what judgment ye judge 4771
Preparation. First cast out the beam..thine own 4773
Sincere. Let me be weighed in an even balance 4778

SENTIMENTS.
Changed. Wondered at the gracious words..wrath 7753
Divided. Part held with the Jews and part..apos. 7754

Defied. Rehoboam..answered the people roughly 448
Insincere. If we shall say from heaven..of men 446
Public. We fear the people 446
Premature. He that answereth..before he heareth 445
Rule. [King Saul] I feared the people 1516
See MISTAKE and references.

5900. OPPOSITION, Malicious. *Diotrephes.* 9 Diotrephes, who loveth to have the preeminence among them, receiveth us not. 10 Wherefore, if I come, I will remember his deeds which he doeth, prating against us with malicious words : and not content therewith, neither doth he himself receive the brethren, and forbiddeth

them that would, and casteth *them* out of the church.—3 JOHN, ch. 1.

5901. —— by Ridicule. *Builders.* 19 When Sanballat the Horonite, and Tobiah the servant, the Ammonite, and Geshem the Arabian, heard *it*, they laughed us to scorn, and despised us, and said, What *is* this thing that ye do ? will ye rebel against the king ? 20 Then answered I.. The God of heaven, he will prosper us ; therefore.we his servants will arise and build.—NEH., ch. 2.

5902. —— Unmoved by. *Nehemiah.* [See No. 5901.]

5903. —— Weakened by. *Jews.* 4 The people of the land weakened the hands of the people of Judah, and troubled them in building, 5 And hired counsellors against them, to frustrate their purpose.—EZRA, ch. 4.

See other illustrations under :

HINDERANCE.
Disobedience. Say nothing to any man..blaze 3979
Natural. Let me..kiss my father..mother 3980
Provoking. Let us pass through thy country 3981
Removed. Angel..rolled back the stone..door 3982
Riches. Deceitfulness of riches..choke the word 3983
" Easier for a camel..needle's eye than 3984

HINDERANCES.
Care. Take heed lest..become a stumblingblock 3985
Malicious. People of the land hired counsellors 3986
Removed. I will eat no flesh while the world 3987
Secular. I have bought..bought..married 3988
Social. Let me first go bid them farewell 3989
Selfish. Neither go in yourself, neither suffer ye 3990

HINDERING.
Fear. It is reported. Jews think to rebel 3991
Intrigue. Let us meet..in the pain of Ono 3992

INSUBORDINATION.
Intimidating. He could not answer Abner a word 4773
Soldiers. To translate the kingdom from..Saul 4774

OBDURACY.
Defiant. Who is the L..let I. go 5755
Final. Pharaoh made ready his chariot..people 5756
Foolish. Ahaz in..distress did trespass more and 5757
Jewish. Thy neck is an iron sinew..brow brass 5758
Spiritual. If the mighty works..been done in Tyre 5759
Self-destructive. I know G. hath determined to 5760
Truth. Divers were hardened..spake evil 5761

OBSTINACY.
Provoking. The L. said..it is a stiffnecked people 5825
Rebuked. I..withstand thee..thy way is perverse 5826
Rebellious. People refused to obey the voice of 5827

REBELLION.
Abominable. Rebellion is as the sin of 6874
Ingrates. Absalom sent spies..say Absalom 6875
Ill-government. Thy father made our yoke 6876
Jealousy. Ye take too much upon you [Korah] 6877
Mental. Not enter..ye rebelled against my word 6878
Sinners. We will not have this man to reign 6879
" This is the heir ; come, let us kill him 6880
Tongue. Every kind of beasts..been tamed 6881
Uncontested. Ye shall not fight..return every man 6882
Vain. Sheba blew a trumpet..we have no part 6883
Will. How oft would I..but ye would not 6884

STUBBORNNESS.
Punished. They mocked the messengers 8393
Sin. To obey is better than sacrifice 8394
" We will certainly..burn incense 8395
" Took Dagon and set him in his place again 8396

Official. Take too much upon you..why lift ye up 330
Subdued. Enemies of the Jews hoped to have prey 1092
See PERSECUTION.

5904. OPPORTUNITY in Extremity. *Widow of Zarephath.* 15 She went and did according to the saying of Elijah : and she, and he, and her house, did eat *many* days. 16 *And* the barrel of meal wasted not, neither did the cruse of oil fail. —1 KINGS, ch. 17.

5905. —— A favourable. *Eunuch.* 36 They came unto a certain water : and the eunuch said, See, *here is* water ; what doth hinder me to be baptized ? 37 And Philip said, If thou believest with all thine heart, thou mayest. . I believe that Jesus Christ is the Son of God.— ACTS, ch. 8.

5906. —— improved. *Blind Men.* 31 The multitude rebuked them, because they should hold their peace : but they cried the more, saying, Have mercy on us, O Lord, *thou* Son of David. 32 And Jesus stood still, and called them. —MAT., ch. 20.

5907. —— —— Quails. 31 There went forth a wind from the Lord, and brought quails from the sea, and let *them* fall by the camp. 32 And the people stood up all that day, and all *that* night, and all the next day, and they gathered the quails.—NUM., ch. 11.

5908. —— The last. *Offering Isaac.* 10 Abraham stretched forth his hand, and took the knife to slay his son. 11 And the Angel of the Lord called unto him out of heaven, and said, Abraham, Abraham.—GEN., ch. 22.

5909. —— A lost. *Young Ruler.* 21 If thou wilt be perfect, go *and* sell that thou hast, and give to the poor, and thou shalt have treasure in heaven : and come *and* follow me. 22 But when the young man heard that saying, he went away sorrowful : for he had great possessions. —MAT., ch. 19.

5910. —— limited. *Fig Tree.* 8 Lord, let it alone this year also, till I shall dig about it, and dung *it :* 9 And if it bear fruit, *well :* and if not, *then* after that thou shalt cut it down.— LUKE, ch. 13.

5911. —— Neglect of. *Ahab.* [Benhadad had been spared and honoured.] 40 As thy servant was busy here and there, he was gone. . 42 . . Thus saith the Lord, Because thou hast let go out of *thy* hand a man whom I appointed to utter destruction, therefore thy life shall go for his life, and thy people for his people. 43 And the king of Israel went to his house heavy and displeased.—1 KINGS, ch. 20.

5912. —— passed. *Fig Tree.* 19 When he saw a fig tree in the way, he came to it, and found nothing thereon, but leaves only, and said unto it, Let no fruit grow on thee henceforward for ever. And presently the fig tree withered away.—MAT., ch. 21.

5913. —— Readiness for. *Miriam.* 7 Shall I go and call to thee a nurse of the Hebrew women, that she may nurse the child for thee ? 8 And Pharaoh's daughter said to her, Go. And the maid went and called the child's mother.— EX., ch. 2.

5914. —— sought. *Judas.* 15 What will ye give me, and I will deliver him unto you ? And they covenanted with him for thirty pieces of silver. 16 And from that time he sought opportunity to betray him.—MAT., ch. 26.

5915. —— A special. *Mordecai to Esther.* 14 If thou altogether holdest thy peace at this time, *then* shall there enlargement and deliverance arise to the Jews from another place ; but thou and thy father's house shall be destroyed : and who knoweth whether thou art come to the kingdom for *such* a time as this ?—ESTHER, ch. 5.

5916. —— unperceived. *Jerusalem.* 41 He beheld the city, and wept over it, 42 Saying, If thou hadst known, even thou, at least in this thy day, the things *which belong* unto thy peace ! but now they are hid from thine eyes.—LUKE, ch. 19.

See other illustrations under :
PRIVILEGES.

Appreciated. It is good for us to be here. . 3 taber. 6613
Ignorance. If thou knewest. . thou wouldest have 6614
Responsibility. L. was angry with Solomon. . a. 6615
Reduced. Word of the L. was precious in those d. 6616
Removed. Famine. . of hearing the words of the L. 6617
Unimproved. These three years I come seeking f. 6618

Discovered. Reconcile himself. . with the heads of 290
See RESPONSIBILITY.

5917. OPPRESSION of Avarice. *Jews.* 5 Making the ephah small, and the shekel great, and falsifying the balances by deceit ? 6 That we may buy the poor for silver, and the needy for a pair of shoes ; *yea,* and sell the refuse of the wheat ?—AMOS, ch. 8.

5918. —— Deliverance from. *Jubilee.* 12 If thy brother, a Hebrew. . be sold unto thee, and serve thee six years ; then in the seventh year thou shalt let him go free from thee. 13 And. . thou shalt not let him go away empty.—DEUT., ch. 15.

5919. —— in Famine. *Jews.* 3 Some. . said, We have mortgaged our lands, vineyards, and houses, that we might buy corn, because of the dearth. 4 There were also that said, We have borrowed money for the king's tribute.—NEH., ch. 5.

5920. —— of Servants. *Law.* 14 Thou shalt not oppress a hired servant *that is* poor and needy, *whether he be* of thy brethren, or of thy strangers that *are* in thy land.—DEUT., ch. 24.

5921. —— of Slaves. *In Egypt.* 8 The tale of the bricks, which they did make heretofore. . ye shall not diminish. . for they *be* idle ; therefore they cry, saying, Let us go *and* sacrifice to our God. 9 Let there more work be laid upon the men.—EX., ch. 5.

5922. —— unendurable. *In Egypt.* 19 The same. . evil entreated our fathers, so that they cast out their young children, to the end they might not live.—ACTS, ch. 7.

See other illustrations under :
CRUELTY.

Captives. Joab put them under saws. . harrows 1864
 " Judah cast [10,000 men of Sier] from the 1858
Maternal. Athaliah. . destroyed all the seed royal 1857
See PRISONER and PERSECUTION.

5923. ORDER out of Chaos. *Creation.* 2 The earth was without form, and void ; and darkness *was* upon the face of the deep. And the Spirit of God moved upon the face of the waters. 3 And God said, Let there be light : and there was light.—GEN., ch. 1.

5924. —— in the Church. *Corinth.* 31 Ye may all prophesy one by one, that all may learn, and all may be comforted. 32 And the spirits of the prophets are subject to the prophets. 33 For

God is not *the author* of confusion, but of peace.
—1 COR., ch. 14.

5925. —— **regarded.** 5000 *fed.* [39] He commanded them to make all sit down by companies upon the green grass. [40] And they sat down in ranks, by hundreds, and by fifties.—MARK, ch. 6.

See other illustrations under :

SYSTEM.
Benevolence. Half of my goods I give to the poor 8572
Condemned. Surely wear thyself out..too heavy 8573
Lack. Murmuring..Grecian widows were neglected 8574
Necessary. Look out 7 men..appoint over this b. 8575
Relief by. Provide..rulers of hundreds..fifties 8576
Worship. Jacob vowed..the tenth unto thee 8577

5926. ORDINATION, Apostolic. *By Jesus.* [12] He went out into a mountain to pray, and continued all night in prayer to God. [13] And when it was day, he called *unto him* his disciples : and of them he chose twelve, whom also he named apostles.—LUKE, ch. 6.

5927. —— **End of.** *Apostles.* [14] He ordained twelve, that they should be with him, and that he might send them forth to preach, [15] And to have power to heal sicknesses, and to cast out devils.—MARK, ch. 3.

See other illustrations under :

Consecration. Moses took of the blood..Aaron's r. 586
Leadership. Moses took Joshua..laid his hands on 585

5928. ORNAMENTS, Female. *Christian.* [3] Whose adorning, let it not be that outward *adorning* of plaiting the hair, and of wearing of gold, or of putting on of apparel ; [4] But *let it be* the hidden man of the heart.. *even the ornament* of a meek and quiet spirit, which is in the sight of God of great price.—1 PETER, ch. 3.

5929. —— **Inspiration for.** *For Tabernacle.* [31] He hath filled him with the spirit of God.. [32] ..to devise curious works, to work in gold, and in silver, and in brass, [33] And in the cutting of stones, to set *them,* and in carving of wood, to make any manner of cunning work.—Ex., ch. 35.

5930. —— **Sacrifice of.** *At Sinai.* [3] All the people brake off the golden earrings .. and brought *them* unto Aaron. [4] And he..fashioned it with a graving tool, after he had made it a molten calf : and they said, These *be* thy gods. Ex., ch. 32.

5931. —— **Stripped of.** *Jews.* [16] Because the daughters of Zion are haughty, and walk with stretched forth necks and wanton eyes, walking and mincing *as* they go, and making a tinkling with their feet . [18] In that day the Lord will take away the bravery of *their* tinkling ornaments *about their feet,* and *their* cauls, and *their* round tires like the moon.—ISA., ch. 3. [See chapter.]

See other illustrations under :

JEWELRY.
Abundance. Weight of the golden earrings 1700 t. 4723
Badge. Clothed Daniel with scarlet..chain 4724
Gifts. Bracelets and earrings and rings. 4725
Snare. Gideon made an ephod thereof 4726

Architecture. Carved..palm-trees..open flowers 492
of Vice. Decked my bed with tapestry..perfumed 517

5932. ORPHAN, Adopted. *Esther.* [7] He brought up..Esther, his uncle's daughter..and the maid *was* fair and beautiful ; whom Morde-

cai, when her father and mother were dead, took for his own daughter.—ESTHER, ch. 2.

Also see :

Adopted. Mephibosheth..as one of the king's sons 106

5933. OSTENTATION forbidden. *Christians.* [8] Be not ye called Rabbi : for one is your Master, *even* Christ ; and all ye are brethren. [9] And call no *man* your father..for one is your Father, which is in heaven. [10] Neither be ye called masters : for one is your Master, *even* Christ.—MAT., ch. 23.

5934. —— —— *"Before Men."* [2] When thou doest *thine* alms, do not sound a trumpet before thee, as the hypocrites do in the synagogues and in the streets, that they may have glory of men. Verily I say unto you, They have their reward. [3] But when thou doest alms, let not thy left hand know what thy right hand doeth.—MAT., ch. 6.

5935. —— **for a Purpose.** *Absalom.* [1] Absalom prepared him chariots and horses, and fifty men to run before him.—2 SAM., ch. 15.

5936. —— **in Prayer.** *Scribes.* [47] Which devour widows' houses, and for a shew make long prayers : the same shall receive greater damnation.—LUKE, ch. 20.

5937. —— **Religious.** *Pharisees.* [5] All their works they do for to be seen of men : they make broad their phylacteries, and enlarge the borders of their garments, [6] And love the uppermost rooms at feasts, and the chief seats in the synagogues, [7] And greetings in the markets, and to be called of men, Rabbi.—MAT., ch. 23.

See other illustrations under :

Display. Ahasuerus made a feast..garden 2409
Hypocrites. For a shew make long prayers 476
" I fast, I give, I..I..I 3376

5938. —— **OSTRACISM, A blessed.** *Jesus* said, [22] Blessed are ye, when men shall hate you, and when they shall separate you *from their company,* and shall reproach *you,* and cast out your name as evil, for the Son of man's sake. [23] ..leap for joy : for, behold, your reward *is* great in heaven.—LUKE, ch. 6.

See other illustrations under :

CASTE.
Abolished. G. hath shewed me..any man..unclean 1055
Egyptian. Egyptians..not eat bread with the H. 1056
Ignored. Ordained twelve..Simon the Canaanite 1057
Jewish. Thou, being a Jew..askest drink of me 1058
No More. Great sheet..all manner of..beasts 1059
No Respect for. Smote the firstborn..throne 1060
Religious. Casting out devils..Forbade him 1061
Super-religious. Have known..woman that 1062

5939. OVERWORK, Sickness from. *Epaphroditus.* [30] For the work of Christ he was nigh unto death, not regarding his life, to supply your lack of service toward me.—PHIL., ch. 2.

5940. PACIFICATION, Gifts for. *Esau.* [17] When Esau..asketh thee, saying, Whose *art* thou?. and whither goest thou? and whose *are* these before thee ? [18] Then thou shalt say, *They be* thy servant Jacob's ; it *is* a present sent unto my lord Esau..he *is* behind us.—GEN., ch. 32.

See other illustrations under :

Christian. [Hebrew *vs.* Greek widows.] 1453
Intercessor. Herod..highly displeased..Blastus 155
Noble. Joseph said, Fear not..G. meant it unto g. 1435
See **FORGIVENESS** and references.

5941. PANIC, Death makes a. *In Egypt.*
[33] The Egyptians were urgent upon the people,
that they might send them out of the land in
haste ; for they said, We *be* all dead *men.*—Ex.,
ch. 12.

5942. —— A disastrous. *At Red Sea.* [24] The
Lord looked..through the pillar of fire and of
the cloud, and troubled the host of the Egyptians, [25] And took off their chariot wheels, that
they drave them heavily : so that the Egyptians
said, Let us flee from the face of Israel ; for the
Lord fighteth for them.—Ex., ch. 14.

5943. —— A marvellous. *Four Lepers.* [6] The
Lord had made the host of the Syrians to hear a
noise of chariots, and a noise of horses, *even* the
noise of a great host : and they said..Lo, the
king of Israel hath hired against us the kings of
the Hittites, and..of the Egyptians.. [7] Wherefore they..fled in the twilight, and left their
tents, and their horses, and their asses, even
the camp as it *was*, and fled for their life.—2
Kings, ch. 7.

5944. —— from Reports. *In Jericho.* [Rahab
said,] [9] I know..your terror is fallen upon us,
and that all the inhabitants of the land faint
because of you. [10] For we have heard how the
Lord dried up the water of the Red sea.—Josh.,
ch. 2.

5945. —— from Surprise. *Midianites.* [20] The
three companies blew the trumpets, and brake
the pitchers, and held the lamps in their left
hands, and the trumpets in their right hands to
blow *withal :* and they cried, The sword of the
Lord, and of Gideon. [21] And they stood..round
about the camp : and all the host ran, and cried,
and fled.—Judges, ch. 7.

See other illustrations under :

TERROR.

Prostrating. Saul fell..all along on the ground   8723
Sinners. Belshazzar's..knees smote one against   8724
Sublime. Sinai..so terrible..I exceedingly fear   8725

War. All the host ran and cried and fled   8492
   See FEAR and references.

5946. PARADOX, A strong. *Spiritually dead.*
[21] Another of his disciples said..Lord, suffer me
first to go and bury my father. [22] But Jesus said
..Follow me ; and let the dead bury their dead.
—Mat., ch. 8.

5947. PARADISE near by. *To Thief.* [42] Lord,
remember me when thou comest into thy kingdom. [43] And Jesus said unto him, Verily I say
unto thee, To day shalt thou be with me in
paradise.—Luke, ch. 23.

5948. —— Unspeakable. *P a u l.* [4] He was
caught up into paradise, and heard unspeakable
words, which it is not lawful for a man to utter.
—2 Cor., ch. 12.

   See HEAVEN.

5949. PARDON, Conditioned. *Forgiveness.*
[25] When ye stand praying, forgive, if ye have
aught against any ; that your Father also which
is in heaven may forgive you your trespasses.
[26] But if ye do not forgive, neither will your
Father..forgive your trespasses.—Mark, ch. 11.

5950. —— Unexpected. *Adulteress.* [10] Woman,
where are those thine accusers ? hath no man
condemned thee ? [11] She said, No man, Lord.
And Jesus said unto her, Neither do I condemn
thee : go, and sin no more.—John, ch. 8.

5951. —— A wise. *Ammonites defeated.*
[12] The people said unto Samuel, Who *is* he that
said, Shall Saul reign over us ? bring the men,
that we may put them to death. [13] And Saul
said, There shall not a man be put to death this
day : for to day the Lord hath wrought salvation in Israel.—1 Sam., ch. 11.

   See FORGIVENESS and references.

5952. PARENT, An angry. *Saul.* [30] Saul's
anger was kindled against Jonathan, and he said
..Thou son of the perverse rebellious *woman,*
do not I know that thou hast chosen the son of
Jesse to thine own confusion ?—1 Sam., ch. 20.

5953. —— Ambitious. *Z e b e d e e ' s W i f e.*
[20] Came to him the mother of Zebedee's children
with her sons, worshipping *him,* and desiring a
certain thing.. [21]..She saith..Grant that these
my two sons may sit, the one on thy right hand,
and the other on the left, in thy kingdom.—
Mat., ch. 20.

5954. —— An affectionate. *David.* [38] Absalom fled..to Geshur, and was there three years.
[39] And *the soul of* king David longed to go forth
unto Absalom : for he was comforted concerning
Amnon, seeing he was dead.—2 Sam., ch. 13.

5955. —— bereaved, A. *David.* [33] The king
was much moved, and went up to the chamber
over the gate, and wept : and as he went, thus
he said, O my son Absalom ! my son, my son
Absalom ! would God I had died for thee, O
Absalom, my son, my son !—2 Sam., ch. 18.

5956. —— Distress of a. *D u m b S p i r i t.*
[22] Ofttimes it hath cast him into the fire, and
into the waters, to destroy him : but if thou
canst do any thing, have compassion on us, and
help us.—Mark, ch. 9.

5957. —— A forgiving. *Prodigal Son.* [21] Father, I have sinned against heaven, and in thy
sight, and am no more worthy to be called thy
son. [22] But the father said..Bring forth the best
robe, and put *it* on him ; and put a ring on his
hand, and shoes on *his* feet.—Luke, ch. 15.

5958. —— A governing. *Abraham.* [19] I know
him, that he will command his children and his
household after him, and they shall keep the
way of the Lord, to do justice and judgment.—
Gen., ch. 18.

5959. —— A heedless. *Jephthah.* [30] Jephthah
vowed..If thou shalt without fail deliver the
children of Ammon into my hands, [31]..whatso-
ever cometh forth of the doors of my house to
meet me, when I return in peace..I will offer it
up for a burnt offering. [34]..and behold, his
daughter came out to meet him with timbrels
and with dances..*his* only child.—Judges, ch. 11.

5960. —— Instruction of a. *Samson's Mother.*
[12] Manoah said..How shall we order the child,
and *how* shall we do unto him ? [13] And the angel
of the Lord said unto Manoah, Of all that I said
unto the woman let her beware.—Judges, ch.
13.

5961. —— Influence of. *Rechab.* [6] We will
drink no wine : for Jonadab the son of Rechab
our father commanded us, saying, Ye shall drink
no wine, *neither* ye, nor your sons for ever.—
Jer., ch. 35.

5962. —— A pious. *Samuel's Mother.* [11] She
vowed..O Lord of hosts, if thou wilt indeed look
on the affliction of thine handmaid, and remem-

ber me, and not forget thine handmaid, but wilt give unto thine handmaid a man child, then I will give him unto the Lord all the days of his life, and there shall no razor come upon his head.—1 Sam., ch. 1.

5963. —— **Respect for.** *Esau's.* [41] Esau hated Jacob because..his father blessed him : and Esau said in his heart, The days of mourning for my father are at hand ; then will I slay my brother Jacob.—Gen., ch. 27.

5964. —— **Responsibility of.** *Vows.* [3] If a woman..vow a vow unto the Lord, and bind *herself* by a bond, *being* in her father's house in her youth ; [4] And her father hear her vow, and her bond..and her father shall hold his peace. —Num., ch. 30.

5965. —— **Sons like.** *Athaliah.* [7] The sons of Athaliah, that wicked woman, had broken up the house of God ; and also all the dedicated things..did they bestow upon Baalim. — 2 Chron., ch. 24.

5966. PARENTS' Piety, Benefits from. *David's.* [12] Thou shalt sleep with thy fathers, I will set up thy seed after thee..and I will establish his kingdom. [13] He shall build a house for my name, and I will establish the throne of his kingdom for ever.—2 Sam., ch. 7.

5967. —— —— *To Jeroboam.* [35] I will take the kingdom out of his son's hand, and will give it unto thee, *even* ten tribes. [36] And unto his son will I give one tribe, that David my servant may have a light alway before me in Jerusalem.—1 Kings, ch. 11.

5968. —— **to correct.** *Proverb.* [15] The rod and reproof give wisdom : but a child left *to himself* bringeth his mother to shame.. [17] Correct thy son, and he shall give thee rest : yea, he shall give delight unto thy soul. —Prov., ch. 29.

5969. —— **Care for.** *David.* [3] He said unto the king of Moab, Let my father and my mother, I pray thee, come forth, *and be* with you, till I know what God will do for me.—1 Sam., ch. 22.

5970. —— **Children of wicked.** *At Beth-el.* [23] Elisha went..unto Beth-el : and..there came forth little children out of the city, and mocked him..Go up, thou bald-head.. [24] And he.. cursed them in the name of the Lord. And there came forth two she-bears out of the wood, and tare forty and two children of them.—2 Kings, ch. 2.

5971. —— **Esteem for.** *Proverb.* [6] Children's children *are* the crown of old men ; and the glory of children *are* their fathers.—Prov., ch. 17.

5972. —— **Example of.** *Abijam.* [A golden calf was set up at Bethel.] [3] He walked in all the sins of his father, which he had done before him : and his heart was not perfect with the Lord his God.—1 Kings, ch. 15.

5973. —— **followed.** *Example.* [30] If we had been in the days of our fathers, we would not have been partakers with them in the blood of the prophets. [31] Wherefore ye be witnesses unto yourselves, that ye are the children of them which killed the prophets. [32] Fill ye up then the measure of your fathers.—Mat., ch. 23.

5974. —— —— *Amaziah.* [3] He did *that which was* right in the sight of the Lord, yet not like David his father : he did according to all

things as Joash his father did. [4] Howbeit the high places were not taken away.—2 Kings, ch. 14.

5975. —— **Honour for.** *Fifth Command.* [12] Honour thy father and thy mother : that thy days may be long upon the land which the Lord thy God giveth thee.—Ex., ch. 20.

5976. —— **involving Children.** "*Blood upon.*" [24] Pilate..took water, and washed *his* hands before the multitude, saying, I am innocent of the blood of this just person : see ye *to it.* [25] Then answered all the people, and said, His blood *be* on us, and on our children.—Mat., ch. 27.

5977. —— **to be just.** "*Provoke not.*" [4] Ye fathers, provoke not your children to wrath : but bring them up in the nurture and admonition of the Lord.—Eph., ch. 6.

5978. —— **Partiality of.** *Unhappy.* [27] The boys grew : and Esau was a cunning hunter, a man of the field ; and Jacob *was* a plain man, dwelling in tents. [28] And Isaac loved Esau, because he did eat of *his* venison : but Rebekah loved Jacob.—Gen., ch. 25.

5979. —— **punished.** *Eli.* [11] The ark of God was taken ; and the two sons of Eli, Hophni and Phinehas, were slain. [18]..when he made mention of the ark of God..he fell from off the seat backward by the side of the gate, and his neck brake, and he died.—1 Sam., ch. 4.

5980. —— **Responsibility of.** *Eli's.* [11] The Lord said to Samuel, Behold, I will do a thing in Israel, at which both the ears of every one that heareth it shall tingle.. [13]..I will judge his house for ever for the iniquity which he knoweth ; because his sons made themselves vile, and he restrained them not.—1 Sam., ch. 3.

5981. —— —— *Limited.* [2] His disciples asked..who did sin, this man, or his parents, that he was born blind ? [3] Jesus answered, Neither hath this man sinned, nor his parents : but that the works of God should be made manifest in him.—John, ch. 9.

5982. —— **Sins of.** *Idols.* [5] Thou shalt not bow down thyself to them, nor serve them : for I the Lord thy God *am* a jealous God, visiting the iniquity of the fathers upon the children unto the third and fourth *generation* of them that hate me.—Ex., ch. 20.

5983. —— —— *Ahab's.* [20] Ahab said to Elijah, Hast thou found me, O mine enemy ? And he answered, I have found *thee :* because thou hast sold thyself to work evil in the sight of the Lord. [21] Behold, I will bring evil upon thee, and will take away thy posterity. — 1 Kings, ch. 21.

5984. —— **to teach.** *The Law.* [6] These words..shall be in thine heart : [7] And thou shalt teach them diligently unto thy children, and shalt talk of them when thou sittest in thine house, and when thou walkest by the way, and when thou liest down, and when thou risest up.—Deut., ch. 6.

See other illustrations under :

ADOPTION.

FATHER.

Beloved. Joseph fell on his neck, and wept 3071
Bereaved. O my son Absalom! my son, my son 3072
Compassionate. A great way off, his father saw 3073
Kind. Much more shall your Father..give good 3074
Liars. Ye are of your father the devil..he is a liar 3075

MOTHER.

Ambitious. Grant these my two sons may sit 5570
Anxious. Rebekah said, I am weary of my life 5571
Brutalized. We boiled my son..Give thy son 5572
Cruel. Athaliah the mother of..slew the seed 5573
Careful. Made Samuel a little coat..every year 5574
Care for. Behold thy mother [Jesus to John] 5575
Distress. Let me not see the death of the child 5576
Ingenious. Took an ark of bulrushes, and daubed 5577
in Israel. I am one of them that are peaceable 5578
Revengeful. What shall I ask? The head of John 5579
Robbery of. 1100 shekels of silver..I took it 5580
True. Give her the living child, in no wise slay it 5581
Wicked. Rebekah put the skins upon his hands 5582
　　　Maachah his mother..made an idol 5583

MOTHER IN LAW.

Beloved. Ruth said, Entreat me not to leave thee 5584
Tender. L. deal kindly with you, as ye have..Naomi 5585
Vexed. [Esau's wives] were a grief of mind unto 5586

Abandoned. Left father and mother for my sake 3
　" 　Abram..get thee out..thy father's 5
Respected. Days of mourning for my father are at 947

5985. PARTIALITY, Complaint against.
Grecians. [1] There arose a murmuring of the
Grecians against the Hebrews, because their
widows were neglected in the daily ministration.
—Acts, ch. 6.

5986. —— Improper. *Wealth.* [3] Ye have respect to him that weareth the gay clothing, and
say..Sit thou here in a good place; and say to
the poor, Stand thou there, or sit here under my
footstool: [4] Are ye not then partial in yourselves?—James, ch. 2.

5987. —— Justifiable. *Joseph's.* [He had
revealed himself.] [22] To all of them he gave
each man changes of raiment; but to Benjamin
he gave three hundred *pieces* of silver, and five
changes of raiment.—Gen., ch. 45.

5988. —— manifested. *Jacob.* [3] Israel loved
Joseph more than all his children, because he
was the son of his old age: and he made him a
coat of *many* colours. [4] And when his brethren
saw that their father loved him more..they
hated him, and could not speak peaceably unto
him.—Gen., ch. 37.

5989. —— Surprising. *Joseph's House.* [34] He
..sent messes unto them from before him: but
Benjamin's mess was five times so much as any
of theirs. And they drank, and were merry
with him.—Gen., ch. 43.

See other illustrations under:

FAVORITISM.

Denied. Grant that..my two sons may sit..kingdom 3098
Hurtful. Israel loved Joseph more than all his c. 3099

Partisan. I am of Paul..I of Apollos 5985

5990. PARTING, A beatific. *Ascension.* [50] He
lifted up his hands, and blessed them. [51] And..
while he blessed them, he was parted from
them, and carried up into heaven.—Luke, ch. 24.

See other illustrations under:

ABSENCE.

Detrimental. Thomas was not with them when Jesus 18
Excused. Our family hath a sacrifice 19
See ABANDONMENT and references.

5991. PARTISANS, Religious. *At Corinth.*
[11] There are contentions among you. [12] Now
this I say, that every one of you saith, I am of
Paul; and I of Apollos; and I of Cephas; and
I of Christ. [13] Is Christ divided?—1 Cor., ch. 1.

See STRIFE and references.

5992. PAST, Memory of the. *Job.* [2] O that
I were as *in* months past, as *in* the days *when*
God preserved me; [3] When his candle shined
upon my head, *and when* by his light I walked
through darkness; [4] As I was in the days of my
youth, when the secret of God *was* upon my
tabernacle.—Job, ch. 29.

5993. PASSION, Conquest of. *Proverb.* [32] He
that is slow to anger *is* better than the mighty;
and he that ruleth his spirit than he that taketh
a city.—Prov., ch. 16.

5994. PATIENCE, Divine. *Wicked Husbandmen.* [35] The husbandmen took his servants, and
beat one, and killed another, and stoned another.
[36] Again, he sent other servants more than the
first: and they did unto them likewise. [37] But
last of all he sent unto them his son, saying,
They will reverence my son.—Mat., ch. 21.

5995. —— Exemplar of. *Jesus.* [3] Consider
him that endured such contradiction of sinners
against himself, lest ye be wearied and faint in
your minds. [4] Ye have not yet resisted unto
blood, striving against sin.—Heb., ch. 12.

5996. —— Labour of. *Fig Tree.* [8] Lord, let
it alone this year also, till I shall dig about it,
and dung *it:* [9] And if it bear fruit, *well:* and if
not, *then* after that thou shalt cut it down.—
Luke, ch. 13.

5997. —— maintained. *Absalom's Rebellion.*
[6] He cast stones at David, and at all the servants..and all the mighty men *were* on his right
hand and on his left. [7] And thus said Shimei
when he cursed, Come out, come out, thou
bloody man, and thou man of Belial.—2 Sam.,
ch. 16.

5998. —— needful. *"Fret not."* [7] Rest in
the Lord, and wait patiently for him: fret not
thyself because of him who prospereth in his
way, because of the man who bringeth wicked
devices to pass. [8] Cease from anger, and forsake wrath: fret not thyself in any wise to do
evil.—Ps. 37.

5999. —— Picture of. *"Husbandman."* [7] Be
patient therefore, brethren, unto the coming of
the Lord. Behold, the husbandman waiteth
for the precious fruit of the earth, and hath
long patience for it, until he receive the early
and latter rain. [8] Be ye also patient.—James,
ch. 5.

6000. —— rewarded. *Seeker's.* [1] I waited
patiently for the Lord: and he inclined unto me,
and heard my cry. [2] He brought me up also out
of a horrible pit, out of the miry clay, and set
my feet upon a rock, *and* established my goings.
[3] And he hath put a new song in my mouth,
even praise unto our God.—Ps. 40.

6001. —— tested. *Creditor.* [28] The same servant..found one of his fellow servants, which
owed him a hundred pence: and he..took *him*
by the throat, saying, Pay me that thou owest.
[29] And his fellow servant fell down at his feet..
saying, Have patience with me, and I will pay
thee all. [30] And he would not: but..cast him
into prison.—Mat., ch. 18.

6002. —— —— *Saul the King.* ²⁷ The children of Belial said, How shall this man save us? And they despised him, and brought him no presents. But he held his peace.—1 SAM., ch. 10.

6003. —— **Without.** *Abishai.* [See No. 5997.] ⁹ Then said Abishai..Why should this dead dog curse my lord the king? let me go over, I pray thee, and take off his head. ¹⁰ And the king said, What have I to do with you, ye sons of Zeruiah? so let him curse, because the Lord hath said unto him, Curse.—2 SAM., ch. 16.

6004. —— **in Waiting.** *For Promise.* ³⁵ Cast not away therefore your confidence, which hath great recompense of reward. ³⁶ For ye have need of patience, that, after ye have done the will of God, ye might receive the promise.—HEB., ch. 10.

See other illustrations under :

FORBEARANCE.

Divine. A king shall reign..G. was your king 3328
" I come seeking fruit, and find none..this 3329
Pious. David..hast rewarded me good..killedst 3330

MEEKNESS.

Adversity. Good is the word the L. hast spoken 5299
Courage. I am in your hand..but know ye 5300
Divine. When he was reviled, reviled not again 5301
Forgiveness. How oft shall I forgive him ?..70 times 5302
Glory. When ye do well, and suffer for it 5203
Injury. If a man..endure grief, suffering 5304
Model. He saved others ; let him save himself 5305
Martyrs. L. lay not this sin to their charge 5306
Ornament. The ornament of a meek..spirit 5307
Provocation.Away with this man..release Barabbas 5308
Resentless. Isaac..removed from thence 5309
Required. Smite thee on thy right cheek..other 5310
Royal. Shimei cast stones at David..bloody man 5311
Unprovoked. Moses was very meek, above all men 5312
Want of. Like a city that is broken down 5313
Wrath. How that G. by his hand would deliver 5314

PERSEVERANCE.

Confident. Neither death nor life..separate me 6097
Exhortation. Barnabas exhorted..with purpose 6098
Encouragement. Can a woman forget her..child 6099
" Mountains shall depart..but my 6100
Help to. When..thy foot slippeth..thy mercy held 6101
Prayer. Widow troubleth me, I will avenge her 6102
Success by. I have fought a good fight..crown 6103
Test. If ye continue in my word, then..disciples 6104

RESIGNATION.

Bereavement. David was comforted concerning A. 7192
Inevitable. If I be bereaved of my children, I am 7193
Pious. L. gave, and the L. hath taken away 7194
" David said..Let him do as seemeth good 7195
Submission. When he would not be persuaded 7196

SELF-CONTROL.

Lack. He that hath no rule over his own spirit 7698
Masterly. Belial said..He held his peace 7699
Resolute. Put a knife to thy throat..much 7700

SUBMISSION.

Bereavement. Fire devoured them..Aaron held 8409
" David arose from the earth 8410
Circumstances. Ship was caught..let her drive 8411
Difficult. Not my feet only..hands..head 8412
Example. If this cup may not pass..thy will 8413
Humiliating. Sackcloth..ropes on their heads 8414
Painful. Take also your brother [Benjamin] 8415
Punishment. Let him do what seemeth him good 8416

SUFFERING.

for Christ. [Paul and Silas] laid many stripes 8448
Faithful. Were stoned..sawn asunder, were 8449
Subdued. Bit the people..died, therefore..we 8451
Support. Sufferings of this present time not w. 8450

SUFFERINGS.

Apostolic. [Paul] Five times..stripes..thrice 8452
Chosen. Moses..choosing rather to suffer..than 8453
Recompensed. Moses..had respect unto the r. 8454
Sacred. Remove this cup..not my will [Jesus] 8455

6005. PATRIOTISM, Absorbing. *Nehemiah.* ² Why *is* thy countenance sad, seeing thou *art* not sick? this *is* nothing *else* but sorrow of heart. Then I was very sore afraid, ³ And said..Let the king live for ever : why should not my countenance be sad, when the city, the place of my fathers' sepulchres, *lieth* waste, and the gates thereof are consumed with fire?—NEH., ch. 2.

6006. —— **Appeal to.** *Nehemiah.* ¹¹ Our adversaries said, They shall not know, neither see, till we come in the midst among them, and slay them, and cause the work to cease.. ¹⁴..Be not ye afraid of them : remember the Lord..and fight for your brethren, your sons, and your daughters, your wives, and your houses.—NEH., ch. 4.

6007. —— **of Children.** *Walls built.* ⁴³ That day they offered great sacrifices, and rejoiced : for God had made them rejoice with great joy : the wives also and the children rejoiced : so that the joy of Jerusalem was heard even afar off.—NEH., ch. 12.

6008. —— **A dangerous.** *Assassin.* ¹⁴ The children of Israel served Eglon..eighteen years. ¹⁶ But Ehud made him a dagger which had two edges, of a cubit length ; and he did gird it under his raiment upon his right thigh. ¹⁷ And he brought the present unto Eglon king of Moab [and killed him].—JUDGES, ch. 3.

6009. —— **Deed of.** *Moses.* ¹¹ When Moses was grown..he went out unto his brethren, and looked on their burdens : and he spied an Egyptian smiting a Hebrew.. ¹² And he looked this way and that way, and when he saw that *there was* no man, he slew the Egyptian, and hid him in the sand.—Ex., ch. 2.

6010. —— **Generous.** *Nehemiah.* ¹⁷ *There were* at my table a hundred and fifty of the Jews and rulers, besides those that came unto us from among the heathen.. ¹⁸ Now *that* which was prepared *for me* daily *was* one ox *and* six choice sheep ; also fowls..and once in ten days store of all sorts of wine : yet for all this required not I the bread of the governor, because the bondage was heavy upon this people.—NEH., ch. 5.

6011. —— **Longing of.** *Jacob.* ²⁵ When Rachel had borne Joseph..Jacob said unto Laban, Send me away, that I may go unto..my country.—GEN., ch. 30.

6012. —— **Survival of.** *Hadad.* ²¹ Hadad said..Let me..go to mine own country. ²² Then Pharaoh said..But what hast thou lacked with me, that, behold, thou seekest to go to thine own country? And he answered, Nothing : howbeit let me go in any wise.—1 KINGS, ch. 11.

6013. —— **self-sacrificing.** *Moses* ³¹ Said, Oh, this people have sinned a great sin, and have made them gods of gold. ³² Yet now, if thou wilt forgive their sin— ; and if not, blot me, I pray thee, out of thy book which thou hast written.—Ex., ch. 32.

6014.—— **Sacrifices of.** *Nehemiah.* ¹⁴ I and my brethren have not eaten the bread of the governor. ¹⁵ But the former governors..were chargeable unto the people, and had taken of them bread and wine, besides forty shekels of silver ; yea, even their servants bare rule over the people : but so did not I, because of the fear of God.—Neh., ch. 5.

6015.—— **Sentiments of.** *Moses.* ¹⁸ Moses went..to Jethro his father in law, and said.. Let me go, I pray thee, and return unto my brethren which *are* in Egypt, and see whether they be yet alive.—Ex., ch. 4.

6016. PASTOR, Need of a. *No Shepherd.* ³⁶ When he saw the multitudes, he was moved with compassion on them, because they fainted, and were scattered abroad, as sheep having no shepherd.—Mat., ch. 9.

See MINISTER and references.

6017. PAYMENT, Prompt. *Proverb.* ²⁸ Say not unto thy neighbour, Go, and come again, and to morrow I will give : when thou hast it by thee.—Prov., ch. 3.

See other illustrations under :

REWARD.

Abundant. Entered..Simon's..ship..of fishes	7369
Benevolence. Call the poor..recompensed at the	7370
Delayed. What..hath been done to Mordecai for	7371
Declined. Not take from a thread to a shoelatchet	7372
Dishonour. Entice him..give thee 1100 pieces of s.	7373
Future. Moses..had respect unto the recompense	7374
Gracious. Give me to drink..Is not this the Christ	7375
Grace. Unprofitable servants..done our duty	7376
Labourers. He that reapeth receiveth wages	7377
Treachery. Judas cast down the pieces of silver	7378

WAGES.

Back. Borrow jewels of silver..gold	9255
Changed. [Laban] changed my wages ten times	9256
Daily. Not abide with thee all night	9257
" Neither shall the sun go down on it	9258
Others. Made them equal unto us	9259
Unimportant. Take this child..give thee wages	9260
Withheld. Hire of the labourers..crieth	9261

Recompense. Receive a hundredfold now	0904

6018. PEACE, Cost of. *About* $27. ²⁰ Menahem exacted the money of Israel, *even* of all the mighty men of wealth, of each man fifty shekels of silver, to give to the king of Assyria. So the king of Assyria..stayed not there in the land.—2 Kings, ch. 15.

6019.—— **contemned.** *Jehu.* ¹⁷ Joram said, Take a horseman, and send to meet them, and let him say, Is it peace ? ¹⁸ So there went one on horseback to meet them, and said, Thus saith the king, Is it peace ? And Jehu said, What hast thou to do with peace ? turn thee behind me.— 2 Kings, ch. 8.

6020.—— **commanded.** *By Jesus.* ³⁹ He arose, and rebuked the wind, and said unto the sea, Peace, be still. And the wind ceased, and there was a great calm.—Mark, ch. 4.

6021.—— **Disposition for.** *Abram.* ⁸ Abram said unto Lot, Let there be no strife, I pray thee..we *be* brethren. ⁹ *Is* not the whole land

before thee ? separate thyself, I pray thee, from me : if *thou wilt take* the left hand, then I will go to the right ; or if *thou depart* to the right hand, then I will go to the left.—Gen., ch. 13.

6022.—— **Intercession for.** *Ambassage.* ³¹ What king, going to make war against another king, sitteth not down first, and consulteth whether he be able with ten thousand to meet.. him with twenty thousand ? ³² Or else, while the other is yet a great way off, he sendeth an ambassage, and desireth conditions of peace.— Luke, ch. 14.

6023.—— **Insecure.** *"Healed Slightly."* ¹⁰ From the least even unto the greatest is given to covetousness, from the prophet even unto the priest every one dealeth falsely. ¹¹ For they have healed the hurt of the daughter of my people slightly, saying, Peace, peace ; when *there is* no peace.—Jer., ch. 8.

6024.—— **Jesus brings.** *Resurrection.* ²⁵ After eight days again his disciples were within, and Thomas with them : *then* came Jesus, the doors being shut, and stood in the midst, and said, Peace *be* unto you.—John, ch. 20.

6025.—— **Kingdom of.** *Messiah's.* ⁶ The wolf also shall dwell with the lamb, and the leopard shall lie down with the kid ; and the calf and the young lion and the fatling together ; and a little child shall lead them. ⁷ And the cow and the bear shall feed ; their young ones shall lie down together : and the lion shall eat straw like the ox.—Isa., ch. 11.

6026.—— **Legacy of.** *Christ's.* ²⁷ Peace I leave with you, my peace I give unto you : not as the world giveth, give I unto you. Let not your heart be troubled, neither let it be afraid. —John, ch. 14.

6027.—— **National.** *Solomon.* ⁴ My God hath given me rest on every side, *so that there is* neither adversary nor evil occurrent. ⁵ And, behold, I purpose to build a house unto the name of the Lord.—1 Kings, ch. 5.

6028.—— **Offering for.** *Sinner's.* ¹² The men that died not were smitten with the emerods : and the cry of the city went up to heaven.. ⁴ Then said they, What *shall be* the trespass offering which we shall return to him ? They answered, Five golden emerods, and five golden mice, *according to* the number of the lords of the Philistines.—1 Sam., chs. 5, 6.

6029.—— **Pledge of.** *Rainbow.* ¹⁴ When I bring a cloud over the earth..the bow shall be seen in the cloud : ¹⁵ And I will remember my covenant, which *is* between me and you and every living creature of all flesh ; and the waters shall no more become a flood to destroy all flesh.— Gen., ch. 9.

6030.—— **Plea for.** *Abner's.* ²⁶ Shall the sword devour for ever ? knowest thou not that it will be bitterness in the latter end ? how long shall it be then, ere thou bid the people return from following their brethren ? ²⁷ And Joab said ..unless thou hadst spoken, surely then in the morning the people had gone up every one from following his brother.—2 Sam., ch. 2.

6931.—— **purchased.** *About* $1,811,000. ¹⁹ Pul the king of Assyria came against the land : and Menahem gave Pul a thousand talents of silver, that his hand might be with him to confirm the kingdom in his hand.—2 Kings, ch. 15.

6032. —— **High Price of.** *Pilate.* ²⁴ When Pilate saw that he could prevail nothing, but *that* rather a tumult was made, he took water, and washed *his* hands before the multitude, saying, I am innocent of the blood of this just person : see ye *to it.*—MAT., ch. 27.

6333. —— **with Sin, No.** *"Sword."* ³⁴ Think not that I am come to send peace on earth : I came not to send peace, but a sword.—MAT., ch. 10.

6034. —— **Tribute for.** *Hazael.* ¹⁸ Jehoash king of Judah took all the hallowed things that ..his fathers, kings of Judah, had dedicated.. and all the gold *that was* found in the treasures of the house of the Lord, and in the king's house, and sent *it* to Hazael king of Syria : and he went away from Jerusalem.—2 KINGS, ch. 12.

6035. —— **Typical.** *"Own Vine."* ²⁵ Judah and Israel dwelt safely, every man under his vine and under his fig tree, from Dan even to Beersheba, all the days of Solomon.—1 KINGS, ch. 4.

6036. —— **Untarnished.** *Saul.* ¹² The people said unto Samuel, Who *is* he that said, Shall Saul reign over us? bring the men, that we may put them to death. ¹³ And Saul said, There shall not a man be put to death this day : for to day the Lord hath wrought salvation in Israel:—1 SAM., ch. 11.

6037. —— **Universal.** *Millennium.* ⁴ He shall judge among the nations..and they shall beat their swords into ploughshares, and their spears into pruninghooks : nation shall not lift up sword against nation, neither shall they learn war any more.—ISA., ch. 9.

6038. —— **Ten Years of.** *In Judah.* ¹ Asa ..reigned..In his days the land was quiet ten years. ² And Asa did *that which was* good and right in the eyes of the Lord.—2 CHRON., ch. 14.

See other illustrations under :

ACCEPTANCE.

Assurance. Would he have shewed us all these	53
Denied. Ye brought..torn, and the lame..sick	55
Evidence. There rose up fire out of the rock	56
Manifested. Burning lamp passed between those	57
of Piety. In every nation he that feareth..worketh	58
by Sacrifice. L. had respect unto A..offering	59
Terms. Do justly..love mercy..walk humbly	60

RECONCILIATION.

Noble. Esau ran to meet him, and embraced	6905
Strange. The same day Pilate and Herod were	6906
Worship. Leave there thy gifts..first be reconciled	6907

6039. PEEVISHNESS, Jealous. *Saul.* ⁷ The women answered *one another* as they played, and said, Saul hath slain his thousands, and David his ten thousands. ⁸ And Saul was very wroth.. and he said, They have ascribed unto David ten thousands, and to me they have ascribed *but* thousands : and *what* can he have more but the kingdom?—1 SAM., ch. 18.

6040. —— **Natural.** *Nabal.* ³ The man *was* Nabal, and the name of his wife Abigail ; and *she was* a woman of good understanding, and of a beautiful countenance : but the man *was* churlish and evil in his doings.—1 SAM., ch. 25.

6041. PENITENCE, Blessedness of. *Beatitude.* ³ Blessed *are* the poor in spirit : for theirs is the kingdom of heaven. ⁴ Blessed *are* they that

mourn : for they shall be comforted.—MAT., ch. 5.

6042. —— **regarded.** *Josiah.* ²⁷ Because thine heart was tender, and thou didst humble thyself before God, when thou heardest his words against this place..and humbledst thyself before me, and didst rend thy clothes, and weep before me ; I have even heard *thee* also, saith the Lord. ²⁸ Behold..thou shalt be gathered to thy grave in peace.—2 CHRON., ch. 34.

6043. —— —— *Ahab.* ²⁹ Seest thou how Ahab humbleth himself before me? because he humbleth himself before me, I will not bring the evil in his days : but .in his son's days will I bring the evil upon his house.—1 KINGS, ch. 21.

6044. —— **True.** *Publican.* ¹³ The publican, standing afar off, would not lift up so much as *his* eyes unto heaven, but smote upon his breast, saying, God be merciful to me a sinner. ¹⁴ I tell you, this man went down to his house justified *rather* than the other.—LUKE, ch. 18.

6045. —— **Tears of.** *Peter.* ⁷² The second time the cock crew. And Peter called to mind the word that Jesus said..Before the cock crow twice, thou shalt deny me thrice. And when he thought thereon, he wept.—MARK, ch. 14.

See other illustrations under :

Revival. Great multitude..wept sore	966
Rebellious. We will go..for we have sinned..ark	1507
Sad. We have sinned..Saul was grieved for I.	1430
" Voice was heard..weeping and supplicating	614
Truth. All the people wept when they heard..the l.	763

6046. PENURY, Benevolence in. *Widow.* ⁴³ This poor widow hath cast more in, than all they which have cast into the treasury : ⁴⁴ For all *they* did cast in of their abundance ; but she of her want did cast in all that she had, *even* all her living.—MARK, ch. 12.

See POOR and references.

6047. PEOPLE feared. *At Jerusalem.* ⁴⁷ Taught daily in the temple. But the chief priests and the scribes and the chief of the people sought to destroy him, ⁴⁸ And could not find what they might do : for all the people were very attentive to hear him.—LUKE, ch. 19.

6048. —— —— *King Herod.* ⁴ John said unto him, It is not lawful for thee to have her. ⁵ And when he would have put him to death, he feared the multitude, because they counted him as a prophet.—MAT., ch. 14.

6049. —— **Offering for the.** *Law.* ²⁸ If his sin, which he hath sinned, come to his knowledge ; then he shall bring his offering, a kid of the goats, a female without blemish, for his sin. —LEV., ch. 4. [See verses 27–31.]

See other illustrations under :

MASSES.

Bible. Set up these stones..write plainly..law	5252
Neglected. Sheep not having a shepherd	5253

MEN.

Greatest. He that is least in the kingdom..is gr.	5328
Indispensable. Except these [sailors] abide in the	5329
Picked. Saul saw any strong man..took him	5330
Simple. 200..their simplicity..knew not anything	5331

See MAN and WOMAN.

6050. PERFUME, A sacred. *Inimitable.* ³⁴ The Lord said unto Moses, Take unto thee sweet spices, stacte, and onycha, and galbanum ; *these* sweet spices with pure frankincense : of each shall there be a like *weight :* ³⁵ Whosoever shall make like unto that, to smell thereto, shall even be cut off from his people.—Ex., ch. 30.

6051. PERFECTION, Aim at. *In Obedience.* ³² Ye shall observe to do therefore as the Lord your God hath commanded you : ye shall not turn aside to the right hand or to the left. ³³ Ye shall walk in all the ways which the Lord your God hath commanded you, that ye may live, and *that it may be* well with you, and *that* ye may prolong *your* days in the land.—Deut., ch. 5.

6052. —— the Object. *Of Preaching.* ²⁸ Whom we preach, warning every man, and teaching every man in all wisdom ; that we may present every man perfect in Christ Jesus : ²⁹ Whereunto I also labour, striving according to his working, which worketh in me mightily.—Col., ch. 1.

6053. —— Price of. *Young Ruler.* ²⁰ All these things have I kept from my youth up : what lack I yet ? ²¹ Jesus said unto him, If thou wilt be perfect, go *and* sell that thou hast, and give to the poor, and thou shalt have treasure in heaven : and come *and* follow me.—Mat., ch. 19.

6054. —— proposed. *"Leaving Principles."* ¹ Therefore leaving the principles of the doctrine of Christ, let us go on unto perfection ; not laying again the foundation of repentance from dead works, and of faith toward God.—Heb., ch. 6.

6055. —— required. *"Walk before Me."* ¹ When Abram was ninety years old and nine, the Lord appeared to Abram, and said unto him, I *am* the Almighty God ; walk before me, and be thou perfect. ² And I will make my covenant between me and thee.—Gen., ch. 17.

6056. —— Service in. *Altar.* ¹⁸ He..that hath a blemish, he shall not approach : a blind man, or a lame, or he that hath a flat nose, or any thing superfluous, ¹⁹ Or a man that is brokenfooted, or brokenhanded, ²⁰ Or crookbacked, or a dwarf, or that hath a blemish in his eye, or be scurvy, or scabbed.—Lev., ch. 21.

See other illustrations under :

FAULTLESS.

INNOCENT.

INNOCENCE.

HOLINESS.

6057. PERIL from Assassins. *At Jerusalem.* ¹² Certain of the Jews banded together, and bound themselves under a curse, saying that they would neither eat nor drink till they had killed Paul. ¹³ And they were more than forty which had made this conspiracy.—Acts, ch. 23.

6058. —— Fasting in. *Shipwrecked.* ³³ Paul besought *them* all to make meat, saying, This day is the fourteenth day that ye have tarried and continued fasting.. ³⁴ Wherefore I pray you to take *some* meat ; for this is for your health. —Acts, ch. 27.

6059. —— Imminent. *"A Step."* ¹ David fled from Naioth..and came and said before Jonathan, What have I done? what *is* mine iniquity? and what *is* my sin before thy father, that he seeketh my life?.. ³..truly, *as* the Lord liveth, and *as* thy soul liveth, *there* is but a step between me and death.—1 Sam., ch. 20.

6060. —— Praying in. *Sea of Galilee.* ²³ There came down a storm of wind on the lake : and they were filled *with water,* and were in jeopardy. ²⁴ And they..awoke him, saying, Master, Master, we perish. Then he arose, and rebuked the wind.—Luke, ch. 8.

6061. —— Sleeping in. *Jonah* ⁵ Was fast asleep. ⁶ So the shipmaster.. said unto him, What meanest thou, O sleeper? arise, call upon thy God, if so be that God will think upon us, that we perish not.—Jonah, ch. 1.

6062. —— Time of. *At Red Sea.* ¹⁰ When Pharaoh drew nigh, the children of Israel lifted up their eyes, and behold, the Egyptians marched after them ;·and they were sore afraid : and..cried out unto the Lord.—Ex., ch. 14.

6063. —— Voluntary. *Three Captains.* ¹⁷ David..said, Oh that one would give me drink of the water of the well of Beth-lehem, that *is* at the gate ! ¹⁸ And the three brake through the host of the Philistines, and drew water out of the well of Beth-lehem, that *was* by the gate ..ar.d brought *it* to David : but David..poured it out to the Lord.—1 Chron., ch. 11.

6064. —— —— *Sin of.* [See No. 6063.] ¹⁹ And said, My God forbid it me, that I should do this thing : shall I drink the blood of these men that have put their lives in jeopardy? for with *the jeopardy of* their lives they brought it : therefore he would not drink it.—1 Chron., ch. 11.

6065. PERILS, Many. *Paul.* ²⁵ Thrice was I beaten with rods, once was I stoned, thrice I suffered shipwreck, a night and a day I have been in the deep ; ²⁶ *In* journeyings often, *in* perils of waters, *in* perils of robbers, *in* perils by *mine own* countrymen, *in* perils by the heathen, *in* perils.in the city, *in* perils in the wilderness, *in* perils in the sea, *in* perils among false brethren.—2 Cor., ch. 11.

See other illustrations under :

ALARM.

Spiritual. Sirs, what must I do to be saved? 283
Tempest. Entreat..be no more mighty thunderings 284
Unnecessary. My money is restored..heart failed 285

BOLDNESS.

Angels urge. Brought them forth..speak in the 878
Apostolic. Whom ye put in prison are..in the t. 879
Believers. O. N. we are not careful 880
Brazen. Ahab said to Elijah. Art thou..troubleth 881
Innocence. With whom..be found, let him die 882
Influence. Saw the boldness of P. and J..took 883
Right. When thou seest..more than thou..not 884
Sinners. Jeroboam..served Baal..reared an altar 885
Shame. Absalom..tent upon the roof..concubines 886
Prayer. High priest touched..come boldly..throne 887
Venturesome. Peter walked on the water to go to 888

COURAGE.

Age. [Caleb, 85 years] Give me this mt..Anakim 1769
Absent. 3000 men..said to Samson..may deliver 1770
Daring. Paul would have entered..suffered him n. 1771
Faith. L. that delivered me..lion..this Philistine 1772
Ground. With him..arm of flesh, but with us..Lord 1773
Honouring. Let us go up at once and possess it 1774
Invincible. Not any..able to stand before thee 1775
Lost. Men of Israel fled..forsook the cities 1776
Moral. Jesus went before them..amazed 1777
" I am ready..bound and also to die 1778
Necessary. Be strong and of good courage 1779
Patriotic. Fight for your brethren, sons, wives 1780
Rebuke. I said unto Peter before them all 1781
Reformers. Should such a man as I flee? 1782
Stimulated. Put your feet..necks of these kings 1783
Soldier's. Jonathan climbed up..hands and feet 1784
Worship. Daniel knew..writing was signed 1785

DANGER.

Appalled. Jesus went before them..amazed 1906
Escape. Disciples let him down by night in a b. 1909
Haste. Let them in Judea..flee to the mountains 1911
Intimidates. Peter saw..afraid, and beginning to 1912
Jesus. Storm..on the lake..Master, we perish 1913

HEROISM.

Christian. Bonds..abide me..none of these things 3959
Needless. Three mighty men brake through..well 3961
Numbers. Shamgar slew 600 with an oxgoad 3962
Patriotic. Jael..smote the nail into his..temples 3957
" Woman cast a stone upon Abimelech 3958

Agitation. [Philistines] Trembling in the host..f. 259
" [At sepulchre] Keepers did shake 261
" Belshazzar's thoughts troubled..knees 262
" [Job's vision] Trembling..my bones 263
Bravery. Should such a man as I flee? 4632
Daring. Let us go..die with him 2230
Despondency. D. was greatly distressed..stoning 2229
" I only am left..seek my life 2235
Enemy. Esau cometh..400 men..Jacob afraid 2240
Forebodings. Have sentence of death in ourselves 1527
Failure. Peter denied it again..curse..swear 4631
Hope. Why art thou cast down 2232
Sacred. We shall surely die..seen God 603
Sinners. L. looked..Egyptians said, Let us flee 600
Threat. So let the gods do..make thy life 4636
Watching. Eli sat watching..heart trembled 444
Weakness. Garrison and the spoilers trembled 4637

6066. PERPLEXITY from Success. *At Ekron.*
[11] All the lords of the Philistines..said, Send
away the ark of the God of Israel..to his own
place, that it slay us not, and our people : for
there was a deadly destruction throughout all
the city ; the hand of God was very heavy there.
—1 SAM., ch. 5.

See other illustrations under :

DESPERATION.

Boldness. I will go in unto the king..if I perish 2218
Effort. Why sit we here till we die ? 2219
Sinners. Saul inquired of the L..answered him n. 2220
Sacrifices. King of Moab took his eldest son 2221

Dilemma. The baptism of John, whence was it ? 2307
See **DIFFICULTIES** and **TROUBLE.**

6067. PERSISTENCE necessary. *"Stayed up his Hands."* [12] Moses' hands *were* heavy ; and they took a stone, and put *it* under him, and he sat thereon ; and Aaron and Hur stayed up his hands, the one on the one side, and the other on the other side ; and his hands were steady until the going down of the sun. [13] And Joshua discomfited Amalek.—EX., ch. 17.

6068. —— in Prayer. *Jacob.* [26] Let me go, for the day breaketh. And he said, I will not let thee go, except thou bless me. [27] And he said ..What *is* thy name. And he said, Jacob. [28] And he said, Thy name shall be called no more Jacob, but Israel : for as a prince hast thou power with God and with men, and hast prevailed.—GEN., ch. 32.

6069. —— rewarded. *The Shunammite.* [29] He said to Gehazi..take my staff in thy hand, and go thy way..and lay my staff upon the face of the child. [30] And the mother of the child said, *As* the Lord liveth, and *as* thy soul liveth, I will not leave thee. And he arose, and followed her. —2 KINGS, ch. 4.

6070. —— Unchangeable. *Mordecai.* [2] Mordecai bowed not, nor did *him* reverence. [3] Then the king's servants, which *were* in the king's gate, said unto Mordecai, Why transgressest thou the king's commandment ? [4]..they spake daily unto him, and he hearkened not.—ESTHER, ch. 3.

6071. —— Undiscouraged. *Bartimeus.* [48] Many charged him that he should hold his peace : but he cried the more a great deal, *Thou* Son of David, have mercy on me. [49] And Jesus stood still, and commanded him to be called. —MARK, ch. 10.

6072. —— —— *"Importunity."* [5] Which of you shall have a friend, and..at midnight..say unto him, Friend, lend me three loaves.. [7]..Trouble me not : the door is now shut, and my children are with me in bed ; I cannot rise and give thee. [8]..Though he will not rise and give him, because he is his friend, yet because of his importunity he will rise and give him as many as he needeth.—LUKE, ch. 11.

See other illustrations under :

DETERMINATION.

Evil. As the L. liveth..I will not leave thee 2262
" We will certainly..burn incense to the queen 2260
Fixed. In every city bonds..none..move me 2261
Resolute. Absalom said..set it on fire 2263
Wanting. I will let him go..Pilate gave sentence 2264

PERSEVERANCE.

Confident. Neither death nor life..separate me 6097
Exhortation. Barnabas exhorted..with purpose 6098
Encouragement. Can a woman forget her..child 6099
" Mountains shall depart..but my 6100
Help to. When..my foot slippeth..thy mercy held 6101
Prayer. Widow troubleth me, I will avenge her 6102
Success by. I have fought a good fight..crown 6103
" Delilah pressed him daily..told her 6104
Test. If ye continue in my word, then..disciples 6105
See **DISOBEDIENCE** and references.

6073. PERSON, Character more than. *Vision of Sheet.* [34] Then Peter..said, Of a truth, I perceive that God is no respecter of persons : [35] But in every nation he that feareth him, and worketh righteousness, is accepted with him.—Acts, ch. 10.

6074. PERSONS not respected. *Plague of Death.* [29] At midnight the Lord smote all the firstborn in the land of Egypt, from the firstborn of Pharaoh that sat on his throne unto the firstborn of the captive that *was* in the dungeon ; and all the firstborn of cattle.—Ex., ch. 12.

6075. —— Respect for. *Clothing.* [3] And ye have respect to him that weareth the gay clothing, and say unto him, Sit thou here in a good place, and say to the poor, Stand thou there, or sit here under my footstool : [4] Are ye not then partial ?—James, ch. 2.

6076. —— —— *Prejudice.* [1] Miriam and Aaron spake against Moses because of the Ethiopian woman whom he had married.. [10]..Miriam *became* leprous, *white* as snow.—Num., ch. 12.

6077. PERSECUTOR arrested, A. *Saul.* [4] He fell to the earth, and heard a voice saying.. Saul, Saul, why persecutest thou me ? [5] And he said, Who art thou, Lord ? And the Lord said, I am Jesus whom thou persecutest : *it is* hard for thee to kick against the pricks. [6] And he trembling and astonished said, Lord, what wilt thou have me to do ?—Acts, ch. 9.

6078. PERSECUTORS Lawless. *At Thessalonica.* [5] The Jews..moved with envy, took unto them certain lewd fellows of the baser sort, and gathered a company, and set all the city on an uproar, and assaulted the house of Jason, and sought to bring them out to the people.—Acts, ch. 17.

6079. —— Prayer for. *On the Cross.* [34] Then said Jesus, Father, forgive them ; for they know not what they do.—Luke, ch. 23.

6080. —— —— *Stephen.* [59] They stoned Stephen, calling upon *God,* and saying, Lord Jesus, receive my spirit. [60] And he kneeled down, and cried with a loud voice, Lord, lay not this sin to their charge. And when he had said this, he fell asleep.—Acts, ch. 7.

6081. —— Unbelieving. *Wedding Feast.* [5] They made light of *it,* and went their ways, one to his farm, another to his merchandise : [6] And the remnant took his servants, and entreated *them* spitefully, and slew *them.*—Mat., ch. 22.

6082. PERSECUTION in Adversity. *Shimei.* [Fleeing from Absalom,] [5] Shimei..cursed still as he came. [6] And he cast stones at David, and at all the servants of king David..and all the mighty men *were* on his right hand and on his left. [7] And thus said Shimei..Come out, come out, thou bloody man, and thou man of Belial. —2 Sam., ch. 16.

6083. —— Associated in. *Lazarus.* [10] The chief priests consulted that they might put Lazarus also to death ; [11] Because that by reason of him many of the Jews went away, and believed on Jesus.—John, ch. 12.

6084. —— Born to. *" Flesh."* [See No. 6088.] [29] He that was born after the flesh persecuted him *that was born* after the Spirit, even so *it is* now.—Gal., ch. 4.

6085. —— Blessed. *" Scattered."* [1] There was a great persecution against the church..at Jerusalem ; and they were all scattered abroad throughout the regions of Judea and Samaria, except the apostles. [4]..They that were scattered abroad went every where preaching the word. —Acts, ch. 8.

6086. —— Escape from. *Paul.* [32] In Damascus the governor..kept the city of the Damascenes with a garrison, desirous to apprehend me : [33] And through a window in a basket was I let down by the wall, and escaped his hands.— 2 Cor., ch. 11.

6087. —— Honoured by. *Apostles.* [40] When they had called the apostles, and beaten *them,* they commanded that they should not speak in the name of Jesus, and let them go. [41] And they departed from..the council, rejoicing that they were counted worthy to suffer shame for his name.—Acts, ch. 5.

6088. —— Juvenile. *Ishmael.* [8] Abraham made a great feast the *same* day that Isaac was weaned. [9] And Sarah saw the son of Hagar the Egyptian..mocking.—Gen., ch. 21.

6089. —— Joy in. *Paul and Silas.* [See No. 6091.] [25] At midnight Paul and Silas prayed, and sang praises unto God : and the prisoners heard them,—Acts, ch. 16.

6090. —— overruled. *At Antioch.* [20] Some of them were men of Cyprus and Cyrene, which, when they were come to Antioch, spake unto the Grecians, preaching the Lord Jesus. [21] And the hand of the Lord was with them : and a great number believed, and turned unto the Lord.— Acts, ch. 11.

6091. —— Painful. *At Philippi.* [23] When they had laid many stripes upon them, they cast *them* into prison, charging the jailer to keep them safely : [24] Who..thrust them into the inner prison, and made their feet fast in the stocks. —Acts, ch. 16.

6092. —— promised. *" With Persecution."* [29] There is no man that hath left house, or brethren, or sisters, or father, or mother, or wife, or children, or lands, for my sake, and the gospel's, [30] But he shall receive a hundredfold now in this time, houses, and brethren, and sisters, and mothers, and children, and lands, with persecutions ; and in the world to come eternal life.—Mark, ch. 10.

6093. —— —— *" Own Household."* [34] Think not that I am come to send peace on earth : I came not to send peace, but a sword. [35] For I am come to set a man at variance against his father, and the daughter against her mother.. [36] And *a* man's foes *shall be* they of his own household.—Mat., ch. 10.

6094. —— in Slavery. *Pharaoh.* [16] There is no straw given..and they say to us, Make brick : and, behold, thy servants *are* beaten ; but the fault *is* in thine own people. [17] But he said, Ye *are* idle, ye *are* idle : therefore *ye* say, Let us go *and* do sacrifice to the Lord.—Ex., ch. 5.

6095. —— Subtile. *Of Daniel.* [5] Then said these men, We shall not find any occasion against this Daniel, except we find *it* against him concerning the law of his God. [6] Then these presidents and princes..said..King Darius, live for ever. [7]..make a firm decree, that whosoever shall ask a petition of any god or man for thirty days, save of thee, O king, he shall be cast into the den of lions.—Dan., ch. 6.

6096. —— **Unmoved by.** *Paul.* [22] I go bound in the spirit unto Jerusalem, not knowing the things that shall befall me there : [23] Save that the Holy Ghost witnesseth in every city, saying that bonds and afflictions abide me. [24] But none of these things move me, neither count I my life dear unto myself.—Acts, ch. 20.

Also see :

Recompensed. Receive a hundredfold now..life   6092

6097. PERSEVERANCE, Confident. *P a u l .* [38] I am persuaded, that neither death, nor life, nor angels, nor principalities, nor powers, nor things present, nor things to come, [39] Nor height, nor depth, nor any other creature, shall be able to separate us from the love of God, which is in Christ Jesus our Lord.—Rom., ch. 8.

6098. —— **Exhortation to.** *Barnabas.* [22] They sent forth Barnabas, that he should go as far as Antioch. [23] Who, when he came, and had seen the grace of God, was glad, and exhorted them all, that with purpose of heart they would cleave unto the Lord.—Acts, ch. 11.

6099. —— **Encouragement to.** *Not Forgotten.* [14] Zion said, The Lord hath forsaken me.. [15] Can a woman forget her sucking child, that she should not have compassion on the son of her womb ? yea, they may forget, yet will I not forget thee. [16] Behold, I have graven thee upon the palms of *my* hands ; thy walls *are* continually before me.—Isa., ch. 49.

6100. —— *For Zion.* [7] For a small moment have I forsaken thee ; but with great mercies will I gather thee. [8] In a little wrath I hid my face from thee for a moment ; but with everlasting kindness will I have mercy on thee, saith the Lord thy Redeemer. [10] For the mountains shall depart, and the hills be removed ; but my kindness shall not depart from thee, neither shall the covenant of my peace be removed.—Isa., ch. 54.

6101. —— **Help to.** *Meditation.* [18] When I said, My foot slippeth ; thy mercy, O Lord, held me up. [19] In the multitude of my thoughts within me thy comforts delight my soul.—Ps. 94.

6102. —— **in Prayer.** *" Unjust Judge."* [4] He would not for a while : but afterward he said within himself, Though I fear not God, nor regard man ; [5] Yet because this widow troubleth me, I will avenge her, lest by her continual coming she weary me.—Luke, ch. 18.

6103. —— **Success by.** *Paul.* [7] I have fought a good fight, I have finished *my* course, I have kept the faith : [8] Henceforth there is laid up for me a crown of righteousness, which the Lord, the righteous judge, shall give me at that day.—2 Tim., ch. 4.

6104. —— —— *Delilah.* [16] When she pressed him daily with her words, and urged him, *so* that his soul was vexed unto death ; [17] That he told her all his heart, and said unto her, There hath not come a razor upon my head ; for I *have* been a Nazarite unto God.—Judges, ch. 16.

6105. —— **Test of.** *Discipleship.* [30] Many believed on him. [31] Then said Jesus..If ye continue in my word, *then* are ye my disciples indeed.—John, ch. 8.

See other illustrations under :

FAITHFULNESS.

Blessed is that servant whom his lord..so doing   2975
Constant. The fire shall ever be burning upon the   2976
Despondency. Let us also go..may die with him   2977
Honoured. I make a decree. speak..against the G.   2978
Ministerial. [See 2 Cor. 4 : 1-11.]   2979
Primitive. All scattered abroad..except the apos.   2981
Principle. Faithful in that which is least..also in   2982
Rewarded. If thou see me when I am taken..be   2983
Truth. What the L. saith unto me, that I will s.   2980

IMPORTUNITY.

Desperate. I will not let thee go, except thou bless 4358
Power of. Because of his importunity..give him   4359
Prayer. I will..lest she weary me [unjust judge]   4360
Tested. He answered her not a word   4361
Undiscouraged. Many charged Bartimeus..hold his 4362
Wearying. Delilah pressed Samson daily..words   4363

STEADFASTNESS.

Converts. 3000..continued steadfastly in f.   8337
Determined. Till I die, I will not remove mine i.   8338
Duty. Josiah..turned not aside to the right..left   8339
Integrity. I kept myself from mine iniquity   8340
Principle. Daniel purposed..not defile himself   8341
Religious. We will not serve thy gods, nor worship 8342
Seen. Satan, hast thou considered..Job ?   8343

Endurance. He that endureth to the end..saved   2642
See DIFFICULTIES.

6106. PERSUASION no Excuse. *Adam.* [17] Because thou hast hearkened unto the voice of thy wife, and hast eaten of the tree, of which I commanded thee, saying, Thou shalt not eat of it : cursed *is* the ground for thy sake ; in sorrow shalt thou eat *of* it all the days of thy life.— Gen., ch. 3.

6107. —— **ineffective.** *Paul.* [12] We, and they of that place, besought him not to go up to Jerusalem. [13] Then Paul answered, What mean ye to weep and to break mine heart ? for I am ready not to be bound only, but also to die at Jerusalem for the name of the Lord Jesus. [14] And when he would not be persuaded, we ceased, saying, The will of the Lord be done.— Acts, ch. 21.

See other illustrations under :

ENCOURAGEMENT.

Angelic. Jacob went..angels of G. met him   2632
Above. Let us run..looking to J. who for the joy   2633
Affliction. Sufferings..not worthy to be compared 2634
Example. Paul began to eat..all of good cheer   2635
Fraternal. Whom when Paul saw he thanked God 2636
in God. David encouraged himself in the Lord   2637
Hopeful. Bartimeus..be of good comfort..he   2638
Past. Ye have seen..I bear ye up on eagles' wings 2639
Substantial. Strengthened [builder's] hands with 2640

ENTREATY.

Heart-breaking. What mean ye to weep..break m. 2684
Urgent. Come down ere my child die   2685

INVITATION.

Bountiful. Come unto me and I will give..good   4649
Benevolence. Whosoever is of willing heart..gold 4650
Christian. Any good thing..Nazareth ?..come and 4651
Divine. Ho, every one that thirsteth..no money   4652
Gospel. Marriage for his son..bidden to the wed.   4653
Grace. Spirit and the bride say, Come   4654
Heavenward. Come thou with us, and we will do   4655
Pressing. I stand at the door and knock..voice   4656
Solicited. Bid me come unto thee upon the water   4657

!INTERCESSION.

Denied. I will not return with thee..L. rejected 4616
Effect. Let it alone this year also 4617
Friendly. Wherefore then wilt thou slay David 4618
    `..` Wilt thou not spare the place for fifty 4619
Limit. I will not destroy it for ten's sake..L. went 4620
Needless. They came..to the steward of Joseph 4621
Needed. Take your flocks..and bless me also 4622
Obtained. I have sinned..Samuel turned again 4623
Penitential. I have transgressed..pardon my sin 4624
Rewarded. Forgive..if not, blot me..cleft of the r. 4625
Resented. Moses and Aaron..get you unto your 4626

PETITION.

Denied. Serve alone..bid her..help me [Martha] 6114
Rejected. Get you unto your burdens [Pharaoh] 6115
    `..` I will chastise you with scorpions 6116

PLEA.

Affecting. We are sold, I and my people [Esther] 6201
Patriotism. How can I endure to see the evil..my 6202

6108. PERVERTER, A famous. *"Made Israel sin."* [26] Jeroboam the son of Nebat, and in his sin wherewith he made Israel to sin, to provoke the Lord..to anger with their vanities.—1 KINGS, ch. 16.

6109. —— A wicked. *Elymas.* [8] Elymas the sorcerer..withstood them, seeking to turn away the deputy from the faith.—ACTS, ch. 13.

6110. PERVERSION of Good. *"Brazen Serpent."* [4] He removed the high places, and brake the images, and cut down the groves, and brake in pieces the brazen serpent that Moses had made : for unto those days the children of Israel did burn incense to it : and he called it Nehushtan.—2 KINGS, ch. 18.

See other illustrations under :

HERESY.

Test. To the law and the testimony this word 3946
Tested by. They which are approved..manifested 3947

HERESIES.

Corruption. Perverse disputings of men of corrupt 3948
Pride. If any man teach otherwise..he is proud 3949

HERETIC.

Rejection. After the first and second admonition 3951
So-called. After the way which they call heresy 3952

HERETICS.

Errors. Saying the resurrection is past already 3953
Primitive. [Sadducees] In the resurrection..whose 3954

OBSTRUCTIONIST.

Malicious. Diotrephes..forbiddeth them that w. 5828
Religious. Neither go in yourselves, neither suffer 5829

STUMBLING.

at Truth. This is a hard saying..many went back 8401
Stumblingblock. Christ crucified unto the Jews 8402
    `..` Liberty of yours, become a s. 8403
    `..` Whoso shall offend one..better 8404

6111. PESTILENCE, Choice of. *David.* [13] Shall seven years of famine come..or wilt thou flee three months before thine enemies..or that there be three days' pestilence in thy land? [14] And David said unto Gad, I am in a great strait : let us fall now into the hand of the Lord ; for his mercies *are* great : and let me not fall into the hand of man.—2 SAM., ch. 24.

6112. —— Punishment by. *Israel.* [See No. 6111.] [15] So the Lord sent a pestilence upon Israel from the morning even to the time appointed : and there died of the people from Dan even to Beer-sheba seventy thousand men.—2 SAM., ch. 24.

Also see:

Destroying. There died of the plague 14,700   6193

6113. PET, Domestic. *"Lamb."* [3] The poor man had nothing, save one little ewe lamb, which he had bought and nourished up : and it grew up together..with his children ; it did eat of his own meat, and drank of his own cup, and lay in his bosom, and was unto him as a daughter.—2 SAM., ch. 12.

6114. PETITION denied. *Martha's.* [40] Lord, dost thou not care that my sister hath left me to serve alone ? bid her therefore that she help me. [41] And Jesus answered and said unto her, Martha, Martha, thou art careful and troubled about many things : [42] But one thing is needful ; and Mary hath chosen that good part, which shall not be taken away from her.—LUKE, ch. 10.

6115. ——. —— *Rehoboam.* [4] Make thou the grievous service of thy father, and his heavy yoke which he put upon us, lighter, and we will serve thee.. [14]..My father made your yoke heavy, and I will add to your yoke : my father *also* chastised you with whips, but I will chastise you with scorpions.—1 KINGS, ch. 12.

6116. —— rejected. *By Pharaoh.* [3] The God of the Hebrews hath met with us : let us go, we pray thee, three days' journey into the desert, and sacrifice unto the Lord our God ; lest he fall upon us with pestilence, or with the sword. [4] And the king of Egypt said..Wherefore do ye, Moses and Aaron, let the people from their works? get you unto your burdens.—Ex., ch. 5.

See PRAYER and references.

6117. PHARISEES, Hypocrisy of. *Jesus said,* [42] Woe unto you, Pharisees ! for ye tithe mint and rue and all manner of herbs, and pass over judgment and the love of God : these ought ye to have done, and not to leave the other undone. —LUKE, ch. 11. [See context.]

Also see:

Hindering. Ye shut up the kingdom..against men 8239
Proselyters. Ye compass sea and land to make one 8237

6118. PHILANTHROPY, Creditable. *Prison.* [8] Ebed-melech .. spake to the king, saying, [9]..these men have done evil in all that they have done to Jeremiah the prophet, whom they have cast into the dungeon ; and he is like to die for hunger in the place where he is : for *there is* no more bread in the city.—JER., ch. 38.

6119. —— Divine. *Jesus.* [35] Jesus went about all the cities and villages, teaching in their synagogues, and preaching the gospel of the kingdom, and healing every sickness and every disease among the people.—MAT., ch. 9.

6120. —— —— Of Jesus. [38] God anointed Jesus of Nazareth with the Holy Ghost and with power : who went about doing good, and healing all that were oppressed of the devil ; for God was with him.—ACTS, ch. 10.

6121. —— inculcated. *Enemies.* [43] Ye have heard that it hath been said, Thou shalt love thy neighbour, and hate thine enemy. [44] But I say unto you, Love your enemies, bless them that curse you, do good to them that hate you, and pray for them which despitefully use you, and persecute you.—MAT., ch. 5.

6122. —— Noble. *Samaritan.* [33] A certain

Samaritan. .had compassion *on him*, [34] And went to *him*, and bound up his wounds, pouring in oil and wine, and set him on his own beast, and brought him to an inn, and took care of him. —LUKE, ch. 10.

6123. —— **Practical.** *Moses.* [9] Pharaoh's daughter said. .Take this child away, and nurse it for me, and I will give *thee* thy wages. And the woman took the child, and nursed it. —EX., ch. 2.

6124. —— **Pious.** *Barnabas.* [36] Barnabas, (which is, being interpreted, The son of consolation,). . [37] Having land, sold *it*, and brought the money, and laid *it* at the apostles' feet.— ACTS, ch. 4.

6125. —— **Preference in.** *To Believers.* [10] As we have therefore opportunity, let us do good unto all *men*, especially unto them who are of the household of faith.—GAL., ch. 6.

6126. —— **Revival of.** *Communistic.* [44] All that believed were together, and had all things common ; [45] And sold their possessions and goods, and parted them to all *men*, as every man had need.—ACTS, ch. 2.

See BENEVOLENCE and LOVE.

6127. PHILOSOPHER, A converted. *At Athens.* [32] When they heard of the resurrection of the dead, some mocked : and others said, We ·will hear thee again of this *matter*. . [34] Howbeit certain men clave unto him, and believed : among the which *was* Dionysius the Areopagite.—ACTS, ch. 17.

6128. —— **A proverbial.** *S o l o m o n .* [32] He spake three thousand proverbs : and his songs were a thousand and five.—1 KINGS, ch. 4.

6129. PHYSICIAN, The Great. *Jesus.* [9] He spake to his disciples, that a small ship should wait on him because of the multitude, lest they should throng him. [10] For he had healed many ;, insomuch that they pressed upon him for to touch him, as many as had plagues.—MARK, ch. 3.

6130. —— —— *Jesus went. .healing every sickness.* [See No. 6119.]

6131. —— —— *Jesus.* [40] Now when the sun was setting, all they that had any sick with divers diseases brought them unto him ; and he laid his hands on every one of them, and healed them.—LUKE, ch. 4.

6132. —— **Unsuccessful.** *" Nothing bettered."* [25] A certain woman . . had an issue of blood twelve years, [26] And had suffered many things of many physicians, and had spent all that she had, and was nothing bettered, but rather grew worse.—MARK, ch. 5.

6133. —— **wrongly sought.** *King Asa.* [12] Asa . .was diseased in his feet, until his disease *was* exceeding *great:* yet in his disease he sought not to the Lord, but to the physicians.—2 CHRON., ch. 16.

See DISEASE and references.

6134. PICTURES, Destruction of. *Canaanites.* [52] Ye shall drive out all the inhabitants of the land from before you, and destroy all their pictures, and destroy all their molten images.— NUM., ch. 33.

6135. PIETY acknowledged. *Joseph's.* [21] The Lord was with Joseph. .and gave him favour in the sight of the keeper of the prison. [22] And the

keeper of the prison committed to Joseph's hand all the prisoners that *were* in the prison ; and whatsoever they did there, he was the doer *of it.* —GEN., ch. 39.

6136. —— **Assurance from.** *Micah.* [12] Micah consecrated the Levite ; and the young man became his priest, and was in the house of Micah. [13] Then said Micah, Now know I that the Lord will do me good, seeing I have a Levite to *my* priest.—JUDGES, ch. 17.

6137. —— **in Old Age.** *P r o v e r b .* [31] The hoary head *is* a crown of glory, *if* it be found in the way of righteousness.—PROV., ch. 16.

6138. —— —— *Anna.* [37] She *was* a widow of about fourscore and four years, which departed not from the temple, but served *God* with fastings and prayers night and day.—LUKE, ch. 2.

6139. —— —— *E n o c h .* [22] Enoch walked with God after he begat Methuselah three hundred years. . [24] And Enoch walked with God : and he *was* not : for God took him. —GEN., ch. 5.

6140. —— —— *Abram.* [1] When Abram was ninety years old and nine, the Lord appeared to Abram, and said unto him, I *am* the Almighty God ; walk before me, and be thou perfect.— GEN., ch. 17.

6141. —— **begets Confidence.** *Joseph.* [4] Joseph found grace in his sight, and he served him : and he made him overseer over his house, and all *that* he had he put into his hand. [6]. .he knew not aught he had, save the bread which he did eat.—GEN., ch. 39.

6142. —— **Consistent.** *" Blameless."* [1] Priest named Zacharias . . and his wife . . Elisabeth. [6]. .they were both righteous before God, walking in all the commandments and ordinances of the Lord blameless.—LUKE, ch. 1.

6143. —— **a Cloak for Sin.** *Long Prayers.* [14] Woe unto you, scribes and Pharisees, hypocrites ! for ye devour widows' houses, and for a pretence made long prayer : therefore ye shall receive the greater damnation.—MAT., ch. 23.

6144. —— —— *Herod.* [8] And he sent them to Bethlehem, and said, Go and search diligently for the young child ; and when ye have found *him*, bring me word again, that I may come and worship him also. --MAT., ch. 2.

6145. —— **Decision of.** *D a n i e l .* [8] Daniel purposed in his heart that he would not defile himself with the portion of the king's meat, nor with the wine which he drank : therefore he requested of the prince of the eunuchs that he might not defile himself.—DAN., ch. 1.

6146. —— **Devotional.** *J e s u s .* [35] In the morning, rising up a great while before day, he went out and departed into a solitary place, and there prayed. [36] And Simon, and they that were with him, followed after him.—MARK, ch. 1.

6147. —— **amid Depravity.** *Noah.* [9] Noah was a just man *and* perfect in his generations, *and* Noah walked with God. . [11] The earth also was corrupt before God ; and the earth was filled with violence.—GEN., ch. 6.

6148. —— **disparaged.** *By Contrast.* [14] Ye have said, It *is* vain to serve God : and what profit *is it* that we have kept his ordinance, and that we have walked mournfully before the Lord of hosts ? [15] And now we call the proud happy ;

yea, they that work wickedness are set up ; yea, *they that* tempt God are even delivered.—MAL., ch. 3.

6149. —— —— *By Contrast.* ² But as for me, my feet were almost gone ; my steps had well nigh slipped. ³ For I was envious at the foolish, *when* I saw the prosperity of the wicked. ⁴ For *there are* no bands in their death : but their strength *is* firm. ⁵ They *are* not in trouble *as other* men ; neither are they plagued like *other* men.—Ps. 73. [See Psalm.]

6150. —— **Exhortation to.** *Early.* ¹ Remember now thy Creator in the days of thy youth, while the evil days come not, nor the years draw nigh, when thou shalt say, I have no pleasure in them ; ² While the sun, or the light, or the moon, or the stars, be not darkened, nor the clouds return after the rain.—ECCL., ch. 12. [See verses 3–7.]

6151. —— **Evidence of.** *Fruit.* ¹⁵ Beware of false prophets, which come to you in sheep's clothing, but inwardly they are ravening wolves. ¹⁶ Ye shall know them by their fruits. Do men gather grapes of thorns, or figs of thistles ?—MAT., ch. 7.

6152. —— **Energetic.** *King Hezekiah.* ⁴ He removed the high places, and brake the images, and cut down the groves, and brake in pieces the brazen serpent that Moses had made : for unto those days the children of Israel did burn incense to it : and he called it Nehushtan.—2 KINGS, ch. 18.

6153. —— **Extraordinary.** *Hezekiah.* ⁵ He trusted in the Lord God of Israel ; so that after him was none like him among all the kings of Judah, nor *any* that were before him. ⁶ For he clave to the Lord, *and* departed not from following him, but kept his commandments.. ⁷ And the Lord was with him : *and* he prospered whithersoever he went forth.—2 KINGS, ch. 18.

6154. —— **Early.** *Josiah.* ¹ Josiah *was* eight years old when he began to reign.. ² And he did *that which was* right in the sight of the Lord, and walked in all the way of David his father, and turned not aside to the right hand or to the left.—2 KINGS, ch. 22.

6155. —— **Exulting.** *Virgin Mary.* ⁴⁶ Mary said, My soul doth magnify the Lord, ⁴⁷ And my spirit hath rejoiced in God my Saviour.—LUKE, ch. 1.

6156. —— **exalted.** *By Contrast.* [See No. 6149.] ¹⁸ Surely thou didst set them in slippery places : thou castedst them down into destruction. ¹⁹ How are they *brought* into desolation, as in a moment ! they are utterly consumed with terrors. ²⁰ As a dream when *one* awaketh.—Ps. 73. [See Psalm.]

6157. —— **A false.** "*Went not.*" ²⁸ A *certain* man had two sons ; and he came to the first, and said, Son, go work to day in my vineyard. ²⁹ He answered.. I will not ; but afterwards he repented, and went. ³⁰.. the second.. said, I *go,* sir ; and went not.—MAT., ch. 21.

6158. —— **Fruit of.** "*Blessed the Work.*" ⁹ Then Satan answered the Lord, and said, Doth Job fear God for naught ? ¹⁰ Hast not thou made a hedge about him, and about his house, and about all that he hath on every side ? thou hast blessed the work of his hands, and his substance is increased in the land.—JOB, ch. 1.

6159. —— **for Government.** *Rulers.* ²¹ Thou shalt provide out of all the people able men, such as fear God, men of truth, hating covetousness ; and place *such* over them, *to be* rulers of thousands, *and* rulers of hundreds, rulers of fifties, and rulers of tens : ²² And let them judge the people at all seasons.—Ex., ch. 18.

6160. —— **Inward and Outward.** *Hand and Heart.* ³ Who shall ascend into the hill of the Lord ? or who shall stand in his holy place ? ⁴ He that hath clean hands, and a pure heart.—Ps. 24.

6161. —— **lost in Old Age.** *Solomon.* ⁴ When Solomon was old.. his wives turned away his heart after other gods : and his heart was not perfect with the Lord.—1 KINGS, ch. 11.

6162. —— **the best Legacy.** *Mantle of Elijah.* ⁹ Elijah said unto Elisha, Ask what I shall do for thee, before I be taken away from thee. And Elisha said, I pray thee, let a double portion of thy spirit be upon me.. ¹⁴ And he took the mantle of Elijah that fell from him, and smote the waters, and said, Where *is* the Lord God of Elijah ? And.. they parted hither and thither.—2 KINGS, ch. 2.

6163. —— **Maternal.** *Hannah.* ¹¹ She vowed ..O Lord of hosts, if thou wilt indeed look on the affliction of thine handmaid, and remember me, and.. wilt give unto thine handmaid a man child ; then I will give him unto the Lord all the days of his life.—1 SAM., ch. 1.

6164. —— **An Office-holder's.** *Daniel.* ⁴ The presidents and princes sought to find occasion against Daniel concerning the kingdom ; but they could find none.. forasmuch as he *was* faithful.. ⁵ Then said these men, We shall not find any occasion.. except we find *it* against him concerning the law of his God.—DAN., ch. 6.

6165. —— —— *Obadiah.* ³ Ahab called Obadiah, which *was* the governor of *his* house. (Now Obadiah feared the Lord greatly : ⁴.. when Jezebel cut off the prophets of the Lord.. Obadiah took a hundred prophets, and hid them by fifty in a cave, and fed them with bread and water.) —1 KINGS, ch. 18.

6166. —— —— *Nehemiah.* ² Why is thy countenance sad, seeing thou *art* not sick ? this *is* nothing *else* but sorrow of heart. Then I was very sore afraid, ³ And said unto the king, Let the king live for ever : why should not my countenance be sad, when the city, the place of my fathers' sepulchres, *lieth* waste, and the gates thereof are consumed with fire ?—NEH., ch. 2.

6167. —— **Only outward.** *Pharisees.* ²⁵ Woe unto you, scribes and Pharisees, hypocrites ! for ye make clean the outside of the cup and of the platter, but within they are full of extortion and excess.—MAT., ch. 23.

6168. —— **Preservation by.** *Wisdom.* ¹⁰ When wisdom entereth into thine heart, and knowledge is pleasant unto thy soul ; ¹¹ Discretion shall preserve thee, understanding shall keep thee : ¹² To deliver thee from the way of the evil *man,* from the man that speaketh froward things ; ¹³ Who leave the paths of uprightness, to walk in the ways of darkness.—PROV., ch. 2.

6169. —— **Prosperity by.** *Isaac.* ¹² Isaac sowed in that land, and received in the same year a hundredfold : and the Lord blessed him.

[13] And the man waxed great, and went forward, and grew until he became very great.—GEN., ch. 26.

6170. —— —— *Job.* [9] Satan answered the Lord..Doth Job fear God for naught? [10] Hast not thou made a hedge about him, and about his house, and about all that he hath on every side? thou hast blessed the work of his hands, and his substance is increased in the land.—JOB, ch. 1.

6171. —— —— *Proverb.* [9] Honour the Lord with thy substance, 'and with the firstfruits of all thine increase : [10] So shall thy barns be filled with plenty, and thy presses shall burst out with new wine.—PROV., ch. 3.

6172. —— —— *Obed-edom.* [12] It was told king David, saying, The Lord hath blessed the house of Obed-edom, and all that *pertaineth* unto him, because of the ark of God.—2 KINGS, ch. 18.

6173. —— Promotion by. *Joseph.* [38] Can we find *such a one* as this *is*, a man in whom the spirit of God *is*? [39] And Pharaoh said unto Joseph, Forasmuch as God hath shewed thee all this, *there is* none so discreet and wise as thou *art:* [40] Thou shalt be over my house, and according unto thy word shall all my people be ruled : only in the throne will I be greater than thou.—GEN., ch. 41.

6174. —— Paternal. *Job* [5] Rose up early in the morning, and offered burnt offerings *according* to the number of them all : for Job said, It may be that my sons have sinned, and cursed God in their hearts. Thus did Job continually.. [8] And the Lord said unto Satan, Hast thou considered my servant Job, that *there is* none like him in the earth, a perfect and an upright man, one that feareth God and escheweth evil?—JOB, ch. 1.

6175. —— Primitive. *At Jerusalem.* [42] They continued steadfastly in the apostles' doctrine and fellowship, and in breaking of bread, and in prayers.. [45] And sold their possessions and goods, and parted them to all *men*, as every man had need.—ACTS, ch. 2.

6176. —— Pharisaic. *Prayer.* [11] Pharisee stood and prayed thus with himself, God, I thank thee, that I am not as other men *are*, extortioners, unjust, adulterers, or even as this publican.—LUKE, ch. 18.

6177. —— Repelled by. *The Wicked.* [30] When Aaron and all the children of Israel saw Moses, behold, the skin of his face shone ; and they were afraid to come nigh him.—EX., ch. 34.

6178. —— Unrighteous. *Hateful.* [21] I hate, I despise your feast days, and I will not smell in your solemn assemblies. —AMOS, ch. 5. [See more at No. 7539.]

See other illustrations under :

6179. PILLAGE of Sanctuary. *Nebuchadnezzar.* [13] The house of the Lord, did the Chaldees break in pieces, and carried the brass of them to Babylon. [14] And the pots..shovels..snuffers..spoons, and all the vessels of brass wherewith they ministered, took they away. [15] And the firepans..bowls, *and* such things as *were* of gold, *in* gold, and of silver, *in* silver, the captain of the guard took away.—2 KINGS, ch. 25.

6180. —— —— *Shishak.* [25] Shishak king of Egypt came up against Jerusalem : [26] And he took away the treasures of the house of the Lord, and.. of the king's house he even took away all : and he took away all the shields of gold which Solomon had made.—1 KINGS, ch. 14.

See other illustrations under :

6181. PITY of Animals. *Dogs.* [20] A certain beggar named Lazarus.. was laid at his gate, full of sores, [21] And desiring to be fed with the crumbs which fell from the rich man's table : moreover the dogs came and licked his sores.—LUKE, ch. 16.

6182. —— Divine. *Paternal.* [13] Like as a father pitieth *his* children, *so* the Lord pitieth them that fear him. [14] For he knoweth our frame ; he remembereth that we *are* dust.—Ps. 103.

6183. —— Injustice in. *Seducers.* [6] If thy brother, the son of thy mother, or thy son, or thy daughter, or the wife of thy bosom, or thy friend, which *is* as thine own soul, entice thee secretly, saying, Let us go and serve other gods.. [8] Thou shalt not consent unto him, nor hearken unto him ; neither shall thine eye pity him, neither shalt thou spare, neither shalt thou conceal him : [9] But thou shalt surely kill him.—DEUT., ch. 13.

6184. —— Womanly. *Pharaoh's Daughter.* [5] When she saw the ark among the flags, she sent her maid to fetch it. [6] And when she had opened *it*, she saw the child : and, behold, the babe wept. And she had compassion on him,

and said, This *is one* of the Hebrews' children.
—Ex., ch. 2.

6185. —— **of the Wicked.** *Prodigal.* [14] When
he had spent all, there arose a mighty famine in
that land ; and he began to be in want. [15] And
he..joined himself to a citizen..and he sent
him into his fields to feed swine. [16] And he
would fain have filled his belly with the husks
that the swine did eat : and no man gave unto
him.—Luke, ch. 15.

6186. —— **Without.** *Jonah.* [10] God saw their
works, that they turned from their evil way ;
and God repented of the evil, that he had said
that he would do unto them ; and he did *it* not.
—Jonah, ch. 3. [1] But it displeased Jonah exceedingly, and he was very angry. [2] And he..said
..O Lord, *was* not this my saying, when I was
yet in my country?—Jonah, ch. 4.

6187. —— —— *Five Kings of Canaan.*
[24] Joshua called for all the men of Israel, and
said unto the captains of the men of war which
went with him, Come near, put your feet upon
the necks of these kings. And they came near,
and put their feet upon the necks of them.
[25] And Joshua said unto them, Fear not, nor be
dismayed, be strong and of good courage.—
Josh., ch. 10.

6188. —— —— *"Robbed, and half dead."*
[31] A certain priest..when he saw him, he passed
by on the other side. [32] And likewise a Levite
..came and looked *on him*, and passed by on the
other side.—Luke, ch. 10.

See SYMPATHY and references.

6189. PLAGUE of Blood. *The First.* [20] All the
waters that *were* in the river were turned to
blood. [21] And the fish that *was* in the river
died ; and the river stank, and the Egyptians
could not drink of the water of the river ; and
there was blood throughout all the land of
Egypt.—Ex., ch. 7.

6190. —— **of Boils.** *The Sixth.* [8] Take to you
handfuls of ashes of the furnace, and let Moses
sprinkle it toward the heaven in the sight of
Pharaoh. [9] And it shall become small dust in
all the land of Egypt, and shall be a boil breaking forth *with* blains upon man, and upon beast.
—Ex., ch. 9.

6191. —— **of Darkness.** *The Ninth.* [22] There
was a thick darkness in all the land of Egypt
three days : [23] They saw not one another, neither
rose any from his place for three days : but all
the children of Israel had light in their dwellings.
—Ex., ch. 10.

6192. —— **of Death.** *The Tenth.* [29] At midnight the Lord smote all the firstborn in the
land of Egypt, from the firstborn of Pharaoh
that sat on his throne unto the firstborn of the
captive that *was* in the dungeon ; and all the
firstborn of cattle. [30] And Pharaoh rose up in
the night, he, and all his servants, and all the
Egyptians ; and there was a great cry in Egypt :
for *there was* not a house where *there was* not one
dead.—Ex., ch. 12.

6193. —— **Destructive.** *For Murmuring.*
[49] They that died in the plague were fourteen
thousand and seven hundred, besides them that
died about the matter of Korah.—Num., ch. 16.

6194. —— **of Frogs.** *The Second.* [3] The river
shall bring forth frogs abundantly, which shall
go up and come into thine house, and into thy
bedchamber, and upon thy bed, and into the
house of thy servants, and upon thy people, and
into thine ovens, and into thy kneadingtroughs :
[4] And the frogs shall come up both on thee, and
upon thy people, and upon all thy servants.—
Ex., ch. 8.

6195. —— **of Flies.** *The Fourth.* [24] There came
a grievous swarm of flies into the house of Pharaoh, and *into* his servants' houses, and into all
the land of Egypt : the land was corrupted by
reason of the swarm of flies.—Ex., ch. 8.

6196. —— **of Hail.** *The Seventh.* [24] There was
hail, and fire mingled with the hail, very grievous, such as there was none like it in all the
land of Egypt since it became a nation. [25] And
the hail smote..all that *was* in the field, both
man and beast ; and the hail smote every herb
of the field, and brake every tree of the field.
[26] Only in the land of Goshen.—Ex., ch. 9.

6197. —— **of Locusts.** *The Eighth.* [15] They
covered the face of the whole earth, so that the
land was darkened ; and they did eat every herb
of the land, and all the fruit of the trees which
the hail had left : and there remained not any
green thing in the trees, or in the herbs of the
field, through all the land of Egypt.—Ex., ch. 10.

6198. —— **of Lice.** *The Third.* [17] Aaron
stretched out his hand with his rod, and smote
the dust of the earth, and it became lice in man,
and in beast ; all the dust of the land became lice
throughout all the land of Egypt.—Ex., ch. 8.

6199. —— **of Murrain.** *The Fifth.* [5] The hand
of the Lord is upon thy cattle which *is* in the
field, upon the horses, upon the asses, upon the
camels, upon the oxen, and upon the sheep :
there shall be a very grievous murrain. [7] And
Pharaoh sent, and, behold, there was not one of
the cattle of the Israelites dead.—Ex., ch. 9.

See other illustrations under :

PESTILENCE.

Chosen. Shall 7 yrs. of famine..flee..or..pestilence ? 6111
Punished by. From morn. till eve. there died 70,000 6112

6200. PLAN, Man's. *Naaman.* [12] Abana
and Pharpar..may I not wash in them, and be
clean ? So he turned and went away in a rage.
[13] And his servants..said, My father, *if* the
prophet had bid thee *do some* great thing, wouldest thou not have done *it?* how much rather
then, when he saith to thee, Wash, and be clean ?
—2 Kings, ch. 5.

6201. PLANS defeated, Man's. *Babel.* [4] Go to,
let us build us a city, and a tower, whose top
may reach unto heaven ; and let us make us a
name, lest we be scattered abroad.. [7] Go to, let
us go down, and there confound their language,
that they may not understand one another's
speech. [8] So the Lord scattered them abroad.
—Gen., ch. 11.

See other illustrations under :

MANAGEMENT.

Bad. Intending to build..sitteth not..and counteth 5203
Skilful. Shall I go and call to thee a nurse?..Miriam 5204

STRATAGEM.

Battle. Joshua saw that the ambush had taken the 8366
Success. Joab's field..set it on fire 8367
Subtile. Joseph's coat..dipped in the blood 8424

SYSTEM.

Benevolence. Half of my goods I give to the poor 8572
Condemned. Thou wilt surely wear away 8573

Lack of. Grecians..widows..neglected in the daily 8574
Necessary. Seven men..appoint over this matter 8575
Relief by. Rulers of thousands..hundreds..fifties 8576
Worship. I will..give the tenth unto thee 8577

6202. PLEA, An affecting. *Queen Esther.*
[3] Esther the queen..said, If I have found favour in thy sight, O king, and if it please the king, let my life be given me at my petition, and my people at my request : [4] For we are sold, I and my people, to be destroyed, to be slain, and to perish.—ESTHER, ch. 7.

6203. —— of Patriotism. *Queen Esther.* [6] For how can I endure to see the evil that shall come unto my people? or how can I endure to see the destruction of my kindred? [7] Then the king Ahasuerus said unto Esther the queen and to Mordecai the Jew.. [8] Write ye also for the Jews, as it liketh you, in the king's name, and seal *it* with the king's ring.—ESTHER, ch. 8.

6204. PLEADING, Importunate. *Canaanite.*
[24] But he..said, I am not sent but unto the lost sheep of the house of Israel. [25] Then came she and worshipped him, saying, Lord, help me. [26] But he answered..It is not meet to take the children's bread, and to cast *it* to dogs. [27] And she said, Truth, Lord : yet the dogs eat of the crumbs which fall from their masters' table. [28] Then Jesus..said unto her, O woman, great *is* thy faith : be it unto thee even as thou wilt.—MAT., ch. 15.

6205. —— in Prayer. *Moses.* [15] If thou shalt kill *all* this people as one man, then the nations which have heard the fame of thee will speak, saying, [16] Because the Lord was not able to bring this people into the land which he sware unto them, therefore he hath slain them in the wilderness. [17] And now, I beseech thee, let the power of my Lord be great.—NUM., ch. 14.

See other illustrations under :

IMPORTUNITY.

Desperate. I will not let thee go, except thou bless 4358
Power of. Because of his importunity..give him 4359
Prayer. I will..lest she weary me [unjust judge] 4360
Tested. He answered her not a word 4361
Undiscouraged. Many charged [Bartimeus]..hold 4362
Wearying. Delilah pressed Samson daily..words 4363
See PERSUASION and references.

6206. PLEASURE, Business before. *A t L a - ban's.* [33] There was set *meat* before him to eat : but he said, I will not eat, until I have told mine errand. And he said, Speak on. [34] And he said, I *am* Abraham's servant.—GEN., ch. 24.

6207. —— Bitter end of. *King Benhadad.* [16] Ben-hadad *was* drinking himself drunk in the pavilions, he and..the thirty and two kings that helped him. [17] And the young men of the princes of the provinces went out first.. [20] And they slew every one his man : and the Syrians fled ; and Israel pursued them : and Ben-hadad the king of Syria escaped on a horse.—1 KINGS, ch. 20.

6208. —— Expensive. *Proverb.* [17] He that loveth pleasure *shall be* a poor man : he that loveth wine and oil shall not be rich.—PROV., ch. 21.

6209. —— the End. *Rich Fool.* [19] I will say to my soul, Soul, thou hast much goods laid up for many years ; take thine ease, eat, drink, *and*

be merry. [20] But God said unto him, *Thou* fool, this night thy soul shall be required of thee : then whose shall those things be, which thou hast provided ?—LUKE, ch. 12.

6210. —— An Ingrate's. *Absalom.* [1] Ahithophel said..I will arise and pursue after David this night : [2] And I will come upon him while he *is* weary and weak handed, and will make him afraid : and all the people that *are* with him shall flee ; and I will smite the king only : [4] And the saying pleased Absalom well. —2 SAM., ch. 17.

6211. —— Moderation in. *Satiety.* [16] Hast thou found honey? eat so much as is sufficient for thee, lest thou be filled therewith, and vomit it. [17] Withdraw thy foot from thy neighbour's house ; lest he be weary of thee, and *so* hate thee.—PROV., ch. 25.

6212. —— Temptation in. *P a r a d i s e.* [6] When the woman saw that the tree *was* good for food, and that it *was* pleasant to the eyes.. she took of the fruit thereof, and did eat ; and gave also unto her husband.—GEN., ch. 3.

6213. —— —— Golden Calf made. [6] They rose up early on the morrow, and offered burnt offerings, and brought peace offerings ; and the people sat down to eat and to drink, and rose up to play.—EX., ch. 32.

6214. —— Unsatisfying. *Solomon.* [1] I said in mine heart, Go to now, I will prove thee with mirth ; therefore enjoy pleasure..vanity..[3]..wine ..houses..vineyards, gardens..orchards..pools of water..servants..cattle..silver..gold..singers..musical instruments..my wisdom remained ..whatsoever mine eyes desired.. [11] Then I looked on all the works that my hands had wrought, and on the labour that I had laboured to do : and, behold, all *was* vanity and vexation of spirit, and *there was* no profit under the sun. —ECCL., ch. 2.

6215. PLEASURES, Brief. *Murmurers for Flesh.* [19] Ye shall not eat one day, nor two days, nor five days, neither ten days, nor twenty days ; [20] *But* even a whole month, until it come out at your nostrils, and it be loathsome unto you : because that ye have despised the Lord..saying, Why came we forth out of Egypt?—NUM., ch. 11.

6216. —— False. *Backsliders.* [12] Be astonished, O ye heavens, at this.. [13] For my people have committed two evils ; they have forsaken me the fountain of living waters, *and* hewed them out cisterns, broken cisterns, that can hold no water.—JER., ch. 2.

6217. —— poisoned. *Haman.* [11] Haman told them of the glory of his riches, and the multitude of his children, and all *the things* wherein the king had promoted him.. [12] Haman said.. Esther the queen did let no man come in with the king unto the banquet..but myself ; and to morrow am I invited..with the king. [13] Yet all this availeth me nothing, so long as I see Mordecai the Jew sitting at the king's gate.—ESTHER, ch. 5.

6218. —— renounced. *Moses.* [24] By faith Moses..refused to be called the son of Pharaoh's daughter ; [25] Choosing rather to suffer affliction with the people of God, than to enjoy the pleasures of sin for a season ; [26] Esteeming the reproach of Christ greater riches than the treasures in Egypt : for he had respéct unto the recompense of the reward.—HEB., ch. 11.

6219. —— rejected. *Darius.* ¹⁸ The king went to his palace, and passed the night fasting : neither were instruments of music brought before him : and his sleep went from him. ¹⁹ Then the king arose very early in the morning, and went in haste unto the den of lions.—DAN., ch. 6.

6220. —— Ruinous. *Prodigal.* ¹³ The younger son gathered all together, and took his journey into a far country, and there wasted his substance in riotous living.—LUKE, ch. 15. [See No. 6185.]

6221. —— of Sin. *Sacrilege.* ³ The king and his princes, his wives and his concubines, drank in them. ⁴ They drank wine, and praised the gods of gold, and of silver, of brass, of iron, of wood, and of stone. ⁵ In the same hour came forth fingers of a man's hand, and wrote over against the candlestick upon the plaster of the wall.—DAN., ch. 5.

6222. —— —— Reversed. ⁴ Why *art* thou, *being* the king's son, lean from day to day?.. And Amnon said..I love Tamar, my brother Absalom's sister.. ¹⁵ Then Amnon hated her exceedingly ; so that the hatred wherewith he hated her *was* greater than the love wherewith he had loved her. And Amnon said unto her, Arise, be gone.—2 SAM., ch. 13.

6223. —— —— Deceptive. ¹⁵ When Jezebel heard that Naboth was stoned. Jezebel said to Ahab, Arise, take possession of the vineyard of Naboth .. which he refused to give thee for money.. ¹⁶..Ahab rose up to go down to the vineyard of Naboth the Jezreelite, to take possession of it. ²⁷ And..when Ahab heard those words..he rent his clothes, and put sackcloth upon his flesh, and fasted, and lay in sackcloth, and went softly.—1 KINGS, ch. 21.

See other illustrations under :

SHOUTING.

Heaven. Voice of a great multitude..as many w.   7841
Idolatrous. Joshua heard the people as they s.   7842
Religious. Came a fire..all the people saw, they s. 7843
    "   Brought up the ark..with shouting and 7844
Stimulated. Philistines shouted against him..loosed 7845
Triumph. People shouted with a great shout   7846
Vain. Ark came into the camp..I. shouted   7847
Victory. People shouted when the priests blew the 7848
Weeping. Not discern the noise of joy from s.   7849

SINGING.

Difficult. They that..captive required of us a song 8035
Easy. Ransomed..return..come to Z. with songs   8036
Victory by. When they began to sing..the L. set   8037

SATISFACTION.

Fulness. L. now lettest thou thy servant depart in 7593
Inward. A good man shall be satisfied from him.   7594

Worldly. Daughter of H. danced..pleased Herod   790
    See HAPPINESS and references.

6224. PLENTY, Land of. *Canaan.* ⁷ Thy God bringeth thee into a good land, a land of brooks of water, of fountains and depths that spring out of valleys and hills ; ⁸ A land of wheat, and barley, and vines, and fig trees, and pomegranates ; a land of oil olive, and honey ; ⁹ A land wherein thou shalt eat bread without scarceness, thou shalt not lack any *thing* in it ; a land whose stones *are* iron, and out of whose hills thou mayest dig brass.—DEUT., ch. 8.

6225. —— to Poverty, From. *Dives.* ¹⁹ There was a certain rich man, which was clothed in purple and fine linen, and fared sumptuously every day.. ²²..also died, and was buried ; ²³ And in hell he lifted up his eyes, being in torments.. ²⁴ And he cried..Father Abraham, have mercy on me, and send Lazarus, that he may dip the tip of his finger in water, and cool my tongue ; for I am tormented in this flame.—LUKE, ch. 16.

6226. POEM, The oldest. *At Red Sea.* ¹ I will sing unto the Lord, for he hath triumphed gloriously : the horse and his rider hath he thrown into the sea. ² The Lord *is* my strength and song, and he is become my salvation : he *is* my God, and I will prepare him a habitation ; my father's God, and I will exalt him. ³ The Lord *is* a man of war : the Lord *is* his name.—Ex., ch. 15. [See chapter.]

6227. POET, A voluminous. *Solomon.* ³ His fame was in all nations round about.. ³² And he spake three thousand proverbs : and his songs were a thousand and five.—1 KINGS, ch. 4.

6228. POISON, Antidote for. *"Death in the Pot."* ³⁹ One went..to gather herbs and found a wild vine, and gathered thereof wild gourds his lap full, and came and shred *them* into the pot of pottage : for they knew *them* not. ⁴⁰..They cried out..O *thou* man of God, *there is* death in the pot. And they could not eat *thereof.* ⁴¹ But he said, Then bring meal. And he cast *it* into the pot ; and he said, Pour out for the people, that they may eat. And there was no harm in the pot.—2 KINGS, ch. 4.

6229. POLICY before Principle. *Egyptians.* ⁹ Behold, the..children of Israel *are* more and mightier than we. ¹⁰ Come on, let us deal wisely with them, lest they multiply, and .. when there falleth out any war, they join also unto our enemies,.and fight against us, and *so* get them up out of the land.—Ex., ch. 1.

See other illustrations under :

DISCRETION.

Necessary. King consulteth..war..or..peace   2366
Part of. Let not thy voice be heard..lose thy life   2367
Success. David said to Abigail..Blessed be thy   2368
Safety. Paul perceived that one part were Saddu's 2369
Want of. As a jewel of gold in a swine's snout   2370
    "   Nabal said, Who is David?..his master   2371

PLAN.

Man's. May I not wash in them and be clean   6200
Defeated. Let us build..tower..reach unto heaven 6201

PRUDENCE.

Age. Wherefore should thy servant be yet a burden 6774
Commended. Lord commended the unjust steward 6775
Example. Render unto Cesar..they marvelled and 6776
Preservation. Hold..lest angry fellows run upon t. 6777
    "   Joseph hearkened not..or to be with 6778
Resolutions. Intending to build a tower..counteth 6779

Discipline. Nay ; lest while ye gather up the tares 2338
Influence. Nor to drink wine..whereby..stumbleth 4469
Perception. Is not the hand of Joab in this ?   95
Useless. Which..by taking thought, can add one   3333

6230. POLYGAMIST, The first. *Lamech.* ¹⁹ Lamech took unto him two wives : the name of the one *was* Adah, and the name of the other Zillah.—GEN., ch. 4.

6231. POLYGAMY, Destructive. *Solomon.* ³ He had seven hundred wives, princesses, and three hundred concubines : and his wives turned away his heart.—1 KINGS, ch. 11.

6232. POLITENESS, Cultivated. *Stoics and Epicureans.* ¹⁹ They..brought him unto Areopagus, saying, May we know what this new doctrine, whereof thou speakest, *is?* ²⁰ For thou bringest certain strange things to our ears : we would know therefore what these things mean. —ACTS, ch. 17.

6233. —— **inculcated.** *As Guests.* ¹⁰ When thou art bidden, go and sit down in the lowest room ; that when he that bade thee cometh, he may say unto thee, Friend, go up higher ; then shalt thou have worship in the presence of them that sit at meat with thee.—LUKE, ch. 14.

6234. —— **a Mask.** *Joab.* ⁹ Joab said to Amasa, *Art* thou in health, my brother? And Joab took Amasa by the beard with the right hand to kiss him. ¹⁰ But Amasa took no heed to the sword that *was* in Joab's hand : so he smote him therewith in the fifth *rib.*—2 SAM., ch. 20.

6235. —— **Tender.** *Joseph.* ²⁷ *Is* your father well, the old man of whom ye spake? *Is* he yet alive?—GEN., ch. 43.

6236. POLITICS, Condemnation of. *Jesus.* ² We found this *fellow* perverting the nation, and forbidding to give tribute to Cesar, saying that he himself is Christ a King. ³ And Pilate asked him, saying, Art thou the King of the Jews? And he answered him and said, Thou sayest *it.* —LUKE, ch. 23.

6237. —— **Devices in.** *Absalom.* ⁴ Oh that I were made judge in the land, that every man which hath any suit or cause might come unto me, and I would do him justice! ⁵..when any man came nigh *to him* to do him obeisance, he put forth his hand, and took him, and kissed him.—2 SAM., ch. 15.

6238. —— **Influence of.** *Pilate.* ¹² Pilate sought to release him : but the Jews cried out, saying, If thou let this man go, thou art not Cesar's friend : whosoever maketh himself a king speaketh against Cesar. ¹³ When Pilate therefore heard that saying, he brought Jesus forth, and sat down in the judgment seat.—JOHN, ch. 12.

6239. POLITICS in Religion. *Tribute.* ¹⁵ The Pharisees..took counsel how they might entangle him in *his* talk. ¹⁶ And they sent..their disciples with the Herodians, saying.. ¹⁷..What thinkest thou? Is it lawful to give tribute unto Cesar, or not?—MAT., ch. 22.

6240. POLITICIANS, Plot of. *Against Daniel.* ³ Then this Daniel was preferred above the presidents and princes, because an excellent spirit *was* in him ; and the king thought to set him over the whole realm. ⁴ Then the presidents and princes sought to find occasion against Daniel concerning the kingdom ; but they could find none occasion nor fault.. ⁵ Then said these men, We shall not find any occasion against this Daniel, except we find *it* against him concerning the law of his God.—DAN., ch. 6.

See **GOVERNMENT** and references.

6241. POOR, Angels honour the. *Lazarus.* ²² The beggar died, and was carried by the angels into Abraham's bosom.—LUKE, ch. 16.

6242. —— **Great Benevolence to the.** *Zac-*

cheus. ⁸ Zaccheus stood, and said unto the Lord ; Behold, Lord, the half of my goods I give to the poor.—LUKE, ch. 19.

6243. —— —— *Job.* ¹⁵ I was eyes to the blind, and feet *was* I to the lame. ¹⁶ I *was* a father to the poor : and the cause *which* I knew not I searched out. ¹⁷ And I brake the jaws of the wicked, and plucked the spoil out of his teeth.—JOB, ch. 29.

6244. —— —— *Antiochians.* ²⁸ Great dearth throughout all the world..in the days of Claudius Cesar. ²⁹ Then the disciples, every man according to his ability, determined to send relief unto the brethren which dwelt in Judea : ³⁰ Which also they did..by the hands of Barnabas and Saul.—ACTS, ch. 11.

6245. —— —— *Dorcas.* ³⁶ There was at Joppa a certain disciple named..Dorcas : this woman was full of good works and almsdeeds which she did.—ACTS, ch. 9.

6246. —— —— *Grecians.* ²⁵ I go unto Jerusalem to minister unto the saints. ²⁶ For it hath pleased them of Macedonia and Achaia to make a certain contribution for the poor saints which are at Jerusalem.—ROM., ch. 15.

6247. —— —— *Primitive Church.* ¹ When the number of the disciples was multiplied, there arose a murmuring of the Grecians against the Hebrews, because their widows were neglected in the daily ministration.—ACTS, ch. 6.

6248. —— **Ever with the.** *Church.* ⁸ The poor always ye have with you ; but me ye have not always.—JOHN, ch. 12.

6249. —— **chosen.** *Gideon.* ¹⁴ Go in this thy might, and thou shalt save Israel from the hand of the Midianites : have not I sent thee? ¹⁵ And he said..O my Lord, wherewith shall I save Israel? behold, my family *is* poor in Manasseh, and I am the least in my father's house. —JUDGES, ch. 6.

6250. —— **God's care of the.** *Oil increased.* ¹ One of the wives of the sons of the prophets spake unto Elisha..my husband is dead ; and ..did fear the Lord : and the creditor is come to take..my two sons to be bondmen.. ⁷..And he said, Go, sell the oil, and pay thy debt, and live thou and thy children of the rest.—2 KINGS, ch. 4.

6251. —— **Eagerness of the.** *Bartimeus.* ⁴⁶ Blind Bartimeus..sat by the highway side begging. ⁴⁷ And when he heard that it was Jesus of Nazareth, he began to cry out and say, Jesus, *thou* Son of David, have mercy on me. ⁴⁸ And many charged him that he should hold his peace, but he cried the more a great deal.— MARK, ch. 10.

6252. —— **enriched, The.** *Jacob.* ¹⁰ I am not worthy of the least of all the mercies.. which thou hast shewed unto thy servant ; for with my staff I passed over this Jordan ; and now I am become two bands.—GEN., ch. 32.

6253. —— **Extortions from the.** *Rich Men.* ⁴ O ye that swallow up the needy, even to make the poor of the land to fail.. ⁵ Saying, When will the new moon be gone, that we may sell corn? and the sabbath, that we may set forth wheat, making the ephah small, and the shekel great, and falsifying the balances by deceit? ⁶ That we may buy the poor for silver, and the needy for a pair of shoes ; *yea*, and sell the refuse of the wheat ?—Amos, ch. 8.

6254. —— **forgotten, The.** *Deliverer.* [14] There came a great king. .and besieged it, and built great bulwarks against it. [15] Now there was found in it a poor wise man, and he by his wisdom delivered the city ; yet no man remembered that same poor man.—Eccl., ch. 9.

6255. —— **Gospel for the.** *At Nazareth.* [17] He found the place where it was written, [18] The Spirit of the Lord *is* upon me, because he hath anointed me to preach the gospel to the poor ; he hath sent me to heal the brokenhearted, to preach deliverance to the captives, and recovering of sight to the blind.—Luke, ch. 4.

6256. —— —— *" Great Supper."* [20] And another said, I have married a wife : and therefore I cannot come. [21]. .Then the master of the house being angry, said to his servant, Go out quickly into the streets and lanes of the city, and bring in hither the poor, and the maimed, and the halt, and the blind.—Luke, ch. 14.

6257. —— **Hospitality of the.** *Widow of Zarephath.* [12] I have not a cake, but a handful of meal in a barrel, and a little oil in a cruse : and, behold, I *am* gathering two sticks, that I may go in and dress it for me and my son, that we may eat it, and die. [13] And Elijah said. .Fear not ; go *and* do as thou hast said : but make me thereof a little cake first.—1 Kings, ch. 17.

6258. —— **Homeless.** *Jesus.* [20] The foxes have holes, and the birds of the air *have* nests ; but the Son of man hath not where to lay *his* head.—Mat., ch. 8.

6259. —— **Indifference to the.** *Dives.* [20] There was a certain beggar named Lazarus, which was laid at his gate, full of sores, [21] And desiring to be fed with the crumbs which fell from the rich man's table : moreover the dogs came and licked his sores.—Luke, ch. 16.

6260. —— **Investment for the.** *Proverb.* [17] He that hath pity upon the poor lendeth unto the Lord ; and that which he hath given will he pay him again.—Prov., ch. 19.

6261. —— —— *Proverb.* [27] He that giveth unto the poor shall not lack : but he that hideth his eyes *shall have* many a curse.—Prov., ch. 28.

6262. —— **oppressed.** *" One little Ewe Lamb."* [4] There came a traveller unto the rich man, and he spared to take of his own flock. .to dress for the wayfaring man. .but took the poor man's lamb, and dressed it for the man.—2 Sam., ch. 12.

6263. —— **Provision for the.** *Law.* [28] At the end of three years thou shalt bring forth all the tithe of thine increase the same year, and shalt lay *it* up within thy gates : [29] And the Levite, (because he hath no part nor inheritance with thee,) and the stranger, and the fatherless, and the widow, which *are* within thy gates, shall come, and shall eat and be satisfied ; that the Lord thy God may bless thee in all the work of thine hand which thou doest.—Deut., ch. 14.

6264. —— —— *Law.* [19] When thou cuttest down thine harvest. .and hast forgot a sheaf. . thou shalt not go again to fetch it. . [20] When thou beatest thine olive tree, thou shalt not go over the boughs again. . [21] When thou gatherest the grapes of thy vineyard, thou shalt not glean

it afterward : it shall be for the stranger, for the fatherless, and for the widow.—Deut., ch. 24.

6265. —— **remembered.** *In Rejoicing.* [22] As the days wherein the Jews rested from their enemies, and the month which was turned unto them from sorrow to joy, and from mourning into a good day : that they should make them days of feasting and joy, and of sending portions one to another, and gifts to the poor.—Esther, ch. 9.

6266. —— **God remembers the.** *Not Forgotten.* [18] The needy shall not always be forgotten : the expectation of the poor shall *not* perish for ever. —Ps. 9.

6267. —— —— *"Sighing."* [5] For the oppression of the poor, for the sighing of the needy, now will I arise, saith the Lord ; I will set *him* in safety *from him that* puffeth at him.— Ps. 12.

6268. —— **Reminded by the.** *" Thou wast."* [See No. 6264.] [22] Thou shalt remember that thou wast a bondman in the land of Egypt : therefore I command thee to do this thing.— Deut., ch. 24.

6269. —— **Rewards from the.** *Job.* [12] Because I delivered the poor that cried, and the fatherless, and *him that had* none to help him. [13] The blessing of him that was ready to perish came upon me : and I caused the widow's heart to sing for joy.—Job, ch. 29.

6270. —— **Rejection of the.** *Proverb.* [13] Whoso stoppeth his ears at the cry of the poor, he also shall cry himself, but shall not be heard.— Prov., ch. 21.

See other illustrations under :

6271. POPULARITY a Burden. *Jesus.* [31] Come ye yourselves apart into a desert place, and rest a while : for there were many coming and going, and they had no leisure so much as to eat. [32] And they departed into a desert place by ship privately. [33] And the people saw them departing, and many knew him, and ran afoot thither out of all cities, and outwent them, and came together unto him.—Mark, ch. 6.

6272. —— **courted.** *Herod.* [1] Herod the king stretched forth *his* hands to vex certain of the church. [2] And he killed James the brother of John with the sword. [3] And because he saw it pleased the Jews, he proceeded further to take Peter also.—Acts, ch. 12.

6273. —— **A Demagogue's.** *"Stole the Hearts."* [4] Absalom said. .Oh that I were made judge in the land, that every man which hath any suit or cause might come unto me, and I would do him justice ! [5] And it was *so*, that when any man came nigh *to him* to do him obeisance, he put forth his hand, and took him, and kissed him. —2 Sam., ch. 15.

6274. —— **A Deceiver's.** *Simon Magus.* [9] There was a certain man, called Simon, which . .used sorcery, and bewitched the people of Samaria, giving out that himself was some great one : [10] To whom they all gave heed, from the least to the greatest, saying, This man is the great power of God.—Acts, ch. 8.

6275. —— Early. *David's.* [30] The princes of the Philistines went forth : and..David behaved himself more wisely than all the servants of Saul ; so that his name was much set by.—1 SAM., ch. 18.

6276. —— Envy of. *At Antioch.* [44] The next sabbath day came almost the whole city together to hear the word of God. [45] But when the Jews saw the multitudes, they were filled with envy, and spake against those things which were spoken by Paul, contradicting and blaspheming. —ACTS, ch. 13.

6277. —— An honourable. *Solomon.* [33] He spake also of beasts, and of fowl, and of creeping things, and of fishes. [34] And there came of all people to hear the wisdom of Solomon, from all kings of the earth, which had heard of his wisdom.—1 KINGS, ch. 4.

6278. —— Love of. *Rulers.* [42] Among the chief rulers..many believed on him ; but because of the Pharisees they did not confess *him*, lest they should be put out of the synagogue : [43] For they loved the praise of men more than the praise of God.—JOHN, ch. 12.

6279. —— Loss of. *Jesus.* [54] Whoso eateth my flesh, and drinketh my blood, hath eternal life ; and I will raise him up at the last day. [60] Many therefore of his disciples..said, This is an hard saying ; who can hear it ?.. [66] From that *time* many of his disciples went back, and walked no more with him.—JOHN, ch. 6.

6280. —— Sacrifice to. *Felix.* [27] After two years Porcius Festus came into Felix' room : and Felix, willing to shew the Jews a pleasure, left Paul bound.—ACTS, ch. 24.

6281. —— The Saviour's. *By Deeds.* [8] From Jerusalem..Idumea, and *from* beyond Jordan ; and they about Tyre and Sidon, a great multitude, when they had heard what great things he did, came unto him.—MARK, ch. 3.

6282. —— undesired. *By Jesus.* [44] See thou say nothing to any man : but go thy way, shew thyself to the priest, and offer for thy cleansing ..[45] But he went out, and began to publish *it* much, and to blaze abroad the matter, insomuch that Jesus could no more openly enter into the city, but was without in desert places : and they came to him from every quarter.—MARK, ch. 1.

See other illustrations under :
FAME.

Increasing. His fame spread abroad about	3000
Military. Uzziah made..engines..to shoot	3001
Troublesome. Blaze abroad the matter..desert	3002
Unexpected. In the whole world..woman hath	3003
Wisdom. All the earth sought to Solomon	3004

Appearance of. Hired vain..persons..followed him	169
Harmful. I am of Paul..I of Apollos	1636
Price. Saul..transgressed..feared the people	1497
Sought. Lest..put out the s...praise of m.	1510

6283. POPULATION, Increase of. *In Egypt.* [7] The children of Israel were fruitful, and increased abundantly, and multiplied, and waxed exceeding mighty ; and the land was filled with them.—EX., ch. 1.

Also see :
Reduced. Wild beasts..make you few in number	435

6284. POSITION, Love of. *Scribes.* [46] Beware of the scribes, which desire to walk in long robes, and love greetings in the markets, and

the highest seats in the synagogues, and the chief rooms at feasts.—LUKE, ch. 20.

6285. —— not a Gift. *Preparation for.* [40] But to sit on my right hand and on my left hand is not mine to give ; but *it shall be given to them* for whom it is prepared.—MARK, ch. 10.

6286. —— Petition for. *James and John.* [37] They said..Grant unto us that we may sit, one on thy right hand, and the other on thy left hand, in thy glory.—MARK, ch. 10.

See other illustrations under :
PROMOTION.

Avoided. Saul..hath hid himself..stuff	6647
Desirable. May say..Friend, go up higher	6648
Envied. Princes sought to find occasion against D.	6649
Eagerness. Better..be priest unto a tribe	6650
Honourable. Better be said..come up hither	6651
by Merit. Daniel was preferred above..princes	6652
Means of. Sit down in the lowest room	6653
Piety brings. Can we find such a one ?	6654
Requested. That we may sit..hand in glory	6655
Sought. Diotrephes loveth to have the preeminence	6656
" Your eyes shall be opened..be as gods	6659
Unsought. The youngest..he [David] keepeth the	6660
Unsatisfying. All this..nothing so long as I see M.	6661

Seeking. Levite..seeking to find a place	8100

6287. POSSESSION, Condition of. *Merit.* [3] Every place that the sole of your foot shall tread upon, that have I given unto you, as I said unto Moses. [4] From the wilderness and this Lebanon even unto..the river Euphrates. —JOSH., ch. 1.

6288. POSSESSIONS, Extensive. *Christians.* [21] For all things are yours ; [22] Whether Paul, or Apollos, or Cephas, or the world, or life, or death, or things present, or things to come ; all are yours.—1 COR., ch. 3.

See **WEALTH.**

6289. POSTERS, Biblical. *Commands.* [9] Thou shalt write them upon the posts of thy house, and on thy gates. [5] And thou shalt love the Lord thy God with all thine heart, and with all thy soul, and with all thy might.—DEUT., ch. 6.

6290. POSTERITY desired. *Abram.* [2] Lord God, what wilt thou give me, seeing I go childless, and the steward of my house is Eliezer of Damascus ? [5] And he..Look now toward heaven, and tell the stars, if thou be able to number them : and he said unto him, So shall thy seed be.—GEN., ch. 15.

6291. POVERTY, Affection with. *Ruth.* [16] Entreat me not to leave thee, *or* to return..for whither thou goest, I will go ; and where thou lodgest, I will lodge : thy people *shall be* my people, and thy God my God : [17] Where thou diest, will I die, and there will I be buried : the Lord do so to me, and more also, *if aught* but death part thee and me.—RUTH, ch. 1.

6292. —— Benevolence with. *"Two Mites."* [41] Many that were rich cast in much. [42] And there came a certain poor widow, and she threw in two mites, which make a farthing.—MARK, ch. 12.

6293. —— —— *Macedonians.* [2] In a great trial of affliction, the abundance of their joy and their deep poverty abounded unto the riches of their liberality. [3] For to *their* power, I bear record, yea, and beyond *their* power *they were* willing of themselves ; [4] Praying us with much entreaty that we would receive the gift.--2 Cor., ch. 8.

6294. —— **Born to.** *Jesus.* [22] They brought him to Jerusalem, to present *him* to the Lord ; [24] And to offer a sacrifice according to that which is said in the law of the Lord, A pair of turtledoves, or two young pigeons.—Luke, ch. 2. [This was the offering of persons in moderate poverty.]

6295. —— **Cause of.** *Idleness.* [19] He that tilleth his land shall have plenty of bread : but he that followeth after vain *persons* shall have poverty enough.—Prov., ch. 28.

6296. —— *Proverb.* [20] Be not among winebibbers ; among riotous eaters of flesh : [21] For the drunkard and the glutton shall come to poverty : and drowsiness shall clothe *a man* with rags.—Prov., ch. 23.

6297. —— **Consolation in.** *Proverb.* [22] A poor man *is* better than a liar.—Prov., ch. 19.

6298. —— **Dangers of.** *Prayer of Agur.* [8] Give me neither poverty nor riches ; feed me with food convenient for me : [9] Lest I be full, and deny *thee*, and say, Who *is* the Lord ? or lest I be poor, and steal, and take the name of my God *in vain.*—Prov., ch. 30.

6299. —— **from Famine.** *At Jerusalem.* [1] There was a great cry of the people and of their wives against their brethren the Jews.. [3] *Some*..said, We have mortgaged our lands, vineyards, and houses, that we might buy corn, because of the dearth.—Neh., ch. 5.

6300. —— **no Hinderance.** *David.* [22] Saul commanded his servants, *saying*, Commune with David secretly, and say, Behold, the king hath delight in thee, and all his servants love thee : now therefore be the king's son in law. [23]..David said, Seemeth it to you a light thing to be a king's son in law, seeing that I *am* a poor man, and lightly esteemed ?—1 Sam., ch. 18.

6301. —— **inevitable.** *Egyptians.* [20] Joseph bought all the land of Egypt for Pharaoh ; for the Egyptians sold every man his field, because the famine prevailed over them : so the land became Pharaoh's.—Gen., ch. 47.

6302. —— **known.** *Jesus.* [43] This poor widow hath cast more in, than all they which have cast into the treasury : [44] For all *they* did cast in of their abundance ; but she of her want did cast in all that she had, *even* all her living. —Mark, ch. 13.

6303. —— **to Plenty, From.** *Lazarus.* [20] There was a certain beggar..laid at his gate, full of sores, [21] And desiring to be fed with the crumbs which fell from the rich man's table : moreover the dogs came and licked his sores. [22]..the beggar died, and was carried by the angels into Abraham's bosom.—Luke, ch. 16.

6304. —— **Protected by.** *Not Captives.* [11] The rest of the people that were left in the city, and the fugitives that fell away to the king of Babylon, with the remnant of the multitude, did Nebuzar-adan the captain of the guard carry away. [12] But..left of the poor of the land to be vinedressers and husbandmen.—2 Kings, ch. 25.

6305. —— **of the Sluggard.** *Proverb.* [4] The sluggard will not plough by reason of the cold ; *therefore* shall he beg in harvest, and *have* nothing.—Prov., ch. 20.

6306. —— —— *Proverb.* [10] Yet a little sleep, a little slumber, a little folding of the hands to sleep : [11] So shall thy poverty come as one that travelleth, and thy want as an armed man.—Prov., ch. 6.

6307. —— **Suffering from.** *Paul.* [27] In weariness and painfulness, in watchings often, in hunger and thirst, in fastings often, in cold and nakedness.—2 Cor., ch. 11.

6308. —— **and Riches.** *Lazarus—Dives.* [19] There was a certain rich man, which was clothed in purple and fine linen, and fared sumptuously every day.—Luke, ch. 16. [See No. 6303.]

6309. —— **better than Sin.** *Proverb.* [See Nos. 6297 and 6311.]

6310. —— **Wealth in.** *Proverb.* [7] There is that maketh himself rich, yet *hath* nothing : there, is that maketh himself poor, yet *hath* great riches.—Prov., ch. 13.

6311. —— **better than Wealth.** *Proverb.* [6] Better *is* the poor man that walketh in his uprightness, than *he that is* perverse in *his* ways, though he *be* rich.—Prov., ch. 28.

See other Illustrations under :

BEGGAR.

Blind. Bartimeus..sat by the highway side begging	670
Changed. The beggar..was carried by the angels	671
Fraudulent. My master hath sent me..talent	672
Devout. Joseph..begged the body of Jesus	673
Undeserving. Sluggard..will beg in harvest	674

Joy in. Abundance of their joy..deep poverty	6293

See **POOR.**

6312. POWER delegated to Faith. *Exorcising.* [19] Then came the disciples..and said, Why could not we cast him out ? [20] And Jesus said..Because of your unbelief : for..if ye have faith as a grain of mustard seed, ye shall say unto this mountain, Remove hence to yonder place ; and it shall remove : and nothing shall be impossible unto you.—Mat., ch. 17.

6313. —— **Endowment of.** *Pentecost.* [1] They were all with one accord in one place. [2] And suddenly there came a sound from heaven as of a rushing mighty wind, and it filled all the house where they were sitting. [3] And there appeared unto them cloven tongues like as of fire, and it sat upon each of them. [4] And they were all filled with the Holy Ghost, and began to speak with other tongues, as the Spirit gave them utterance.—Acts, ch. 2.

6314. —— **God given.** *Samson.* [24] The woman bare a son, and called his name Samson : and the child grew, and the Lord blessed him. [25] And the Spirit of the Lord began to move him at times in the camp of Dan.—Judges, ch. 13.

6315. —— **from God only.** *Peter.* [11] As the lame man which was healed held Peter and John, all the people ran..greatly wondering. [12] And when Peter saw *it*, he answered..Ye men of Israel, why marvel ye at this ? or why look ye so earnestly on us, as though by our own power or holiness we had made this man to walk ?— Acts, ch. 3.

6316. —— **Loss of.** *Samson.* [20] She said, The Philistines be upon thee, Samson. And he awoke out of his sleep, and said, I will go out as at other times before, and shake myself. And he wist not that the Lord was departed from him.

[21]..the Philistines..put out his eyes..and bound him with fetters of brass ; and he did grind in the prison house.—JUDGES, ch. 16.

6317. —— Might or. *Spirit.* [6] This *is* the word of the Lord unto Zerubbabel, saying, Not by might, nor by power, but by my Spirit, saith the Lord of hosts. [7] Who *art* thou, O great mountain ? before Zerubbabel *thou shalt become* a plain : and he shall bring forth the headstone *thereof* with shoutings, *crying*, Grace, grace unto it.—ZECH., ch. 4.

6318. —— promised. *To Joshua.* [5] There shall not any man be able to stand before thee all the days of thy life : as I was with Moses, so I will be with thee : I will not fail thee, nor forsake thee. [6] Be strong and of a good courage.—JOSH., ch. 1.

6319. —— in Prayer. *Hezekiah.* [20] Then Isaiah..sent to Hezekiah, saying, Thus saith the Lord .. *That* which thou hast prayed to me against Sennacherib king of Assyria I have heard. [35] And..that night .. the angel of the Lord.. smote in the camp of the Assyrians a hundred fourscore and five thousand.—ISA., ch. 37.

6320. —— in Preaching. *Paul's.* [3] I was with you in weakness, and in fear, and in much trembling. [4] And my speech and my preaching *was* not with enticing words of man's wisdom, but in demonstration of the Spirit and of power. —1 COR., ch. 2.

6321. —— Ruling. *Tempest.* [23] There came down a storm of wind on the lake ; and they were filled *with water*, and were in jeopardy. [24] And they..awoke him, saying, Master, Master, we perish. Then he arose, and rebuked the wind, and the raging of the water : and they ceased, and there was a calm.—LUKE, ch. 8.

6322. —— Spiritual. *Stephen.* [9] Disputing with Stephen. [10] And they were not able to resist the wisdom and the spirit by which he spake. —ACTS, ch. 6.

6323. —— Spirit brings. *Samson at Lehi.* [14] The Philistines shouted against him : and the Spirit of the Lord came mightily upon him, and the cords that *were* upon his arms became as flax that was burnt with fire, and his bands loosed.. [15] And he found a new jawbone of an ass..and took it, and slew a thousand men therewith.—JUDGES, ch. 15.

6324. —— suddenly acquired. *Joseph.* [44] Pharaoh said unto Joseph, I *am* Pharaoh, and without thee shall no man lift up his hand or foot in all the land of Egypt.—GEN., ch. 41.

6325. —— Temptation in. *Of Jesus.* [8] The devil taketh him up into an exceeding high mountain, and sheweth him all the kingdoms of the world, and the glory of them ; [9] And saith.. All these things will I give thee, if thou wilt fall down and worship me.—MAT., ch. 4.

6326. —— for Testimony. *The Witnesses.* [See No. 6329.]

6327. —— in Tears. *Pharaoh's Daughter.* [5] When she saw the ark among the flags, she sent her maid to fetch it.. [6] And when she had opened *it*..behold, the babe wept. And she had compassion on him.—Ex., ch. 2.

6328. —— Weakness with. *King David.* [Joab had assassinated Abner.] [38] A prince and a great man fallen this day in Israel ?.. [39] And I am this day weak, though anointed king ; and these men the sons of Zeruiah *be* too hard for me.—2 SAM., ch. 3.

6329. —— Waiting for. *At Ascension.* [4] He commanded them that they should not depart from Jerusalem, but wait for the promise of the Father.. [8]..ye shall receive power, after that the Holy Ghost is come upon you : and ye shall be witnesses .. unto the uttermost part of the earth.—ACTS, ch. 1.

See other illustrations under:

AUTHORITY.

Brother's. My brother..commanded me to be there	584
Compared. Moses commanded..what sayest thou	585
False. I am a prophet..he lied	586
Obedience. All..we will do..will go	587
Power. I say unto one, Go, and he goeth	588
Questioned. By what authority doest thou these t.	589
Recognized. Winds and water..obey him	591
Supreme. Drove them all out of the temple	590

INFLUENCE.

Bequeathed. Elisha took the mantle..waters	4468
Care. Neither to eat flesh..drink wine..further	4469
Example. L. teach us to pray..as John	4470
Felt. Herod feared John..knowing that..just	4471
Leaders. Have any of the rulers believed	4472
Personal. Elisha lay upon the child..mouth upon	4477
Parental. Will drink no wine..our father	4473
Posthumous. G. testifying..gifts..yet speaketh	4474
" Touched the bones of Elisha	4475
Pernicious. Pharisees neither go in..nor suffer	4476
Regarded. Fearful and faint-hearted ?..return	4479
Responsibility. Offend..little ones..better	4478
Rank. Ladies have heard..deed of the queen	4480
Supernatural. Ark on the cart..two cows	4481
Sorrowful. Showing the coats..garments which D.	4482

STRENGTH.

from Above. Elijah went..strength of that meat	8368
Natural. I will lay down my life for thy sake	8369
Physical. Samson rent [the lion]..as he would..a	8370
" With the jaw-bone..slew a thousand m.	8371
" Samson..took the doors..of the city	8372
" Samson bowed himself..house fell	8374
Secret of. If I be shaven, then..become weak	8375
Unimpaired. 85 years old..strength now for war	8376
Worship. Wait on the L. renew their strength	8377

6330. PRAISE from All. *Creation's.* [7] Praise the Lord from the earth, ye dragons, and all deeps : [8] Fire, and hail ; snow, and vapour ; stormy wind fulfilling his word : [9] Mountains, and all hills ; fruitful trees, and all cedars.—Ps. 184. [See Psalm.]

6331. —— for Deliverance. *At Red Sea.* [1] Then sang Moses and the children of Israel this song unto the Lord, and spake, saying, I will sing unto the Lord, for he hath triumphed gloriously : the horse and his rider hath he thrown into the sea. [2] The Lord *is* my strength and song, and he is become my salvation.—Ex., ch. 15.

6332. —— Dangers of. *Absalom.* [25] In all Israel there was none to be so much praised as Absalom for his beauty : from the sole of his foot even to the crown of his head there was no blemish in him.—2 SAM., ch. 14.

6333. —— Fulness of. *David's.* [1] Bless the Lord, O my soul : and all that is within me, *bless* his holy name. [22] Bless the Lord, all his works in all places of his dominion : bless the Lord, O my soul.—Ps. 103. [See Psalm.]

6334. —— **Irrepressible.** *Triumphal Entry.*
[38] Blessed *be* the King that cometh in the name of the Lord : peace in heaven, and glory in the highest. [39] And some of the Pharisees..said.. Master, rebuke thy disciples. [40] And he answered ..if these should hold their peace, the stones would immediately cry out.—Luke, ch. 19.

6335. —— **with Instruments.** *Organs.*
[3] Praise him with the sound of the trumpet : praise him with the psaltery and harp. [4] Praise him with the timbrel and dance : praise him with 'ringed instruments and organs.—Ps. 150.

6336. —— **Love of.** *Preferred.* [42] And I knew that thou hearest me always : but because of the people which stand by I said *it*, that they may believe that thou hast sent me. [43] And when he thus had spoken, he cried with a loud voice, Lazarus, come forth.—John, ch. 11.

6337. —— —— *Hypocrites.* [5] The hypo-crites..they love to pray standing in the syna-gogues and in the corners of the streets, that they may be seen of men.—Mat., ch. 6.

6338. —— **Offensive.** *Priest's.* [15] When the chief priests and scribes saw the wonderful things that he did, and the children crying in the temple, and saying, Hosanna to the Son of David ; they were sore displeased.—Mat., ch. 21.

6339. —— **Offering of.** *David's.* [30] I will praise the name of God with a song, and will magnify him with thanksgiving. [31] *This* also shall please the Lord better than an ox *or* bul-lock that hath horns and hoofs.—Ps. 69.

6340. —— **Reasons for.** *Divine.* [1] Praise ye the Lord : for *it is* good to sing praises unto our God ; for *it is* pleasant ; *and* praise is comely. [2] The Lord doth build up Jerusalem : he gather-eth together the outcasts of Israel. [3] He healeth the broken in heart, and bindeth up their wounds.—Ps. 147. [See Psalm.]

6341. —— **of Self.** *Proverb.* [2] Let another man praise thee, and not thine own mouth ; a stranger, and not thine own lips.—Prov., ch. 27.

See other illustrations under :

Victory. Women came singing..dancing to meet S.　1902
Withheld. No prophet is without honour save..own　4073
See **WORSHIP.**

6342. PRAYER more than answered. *Solomon.*
[11] Because thou..hast not asked for thyself long life ; neither hast asked riches for thyself, nor hast asked the life of thine enemies ; but..un-derstanding to discern judgment ; [13]..I have also given thee that which thou hast not asked, both riches, and honour.—1 Kings, ch. 3.

6343. —— **Agreement in.** *Promise.* [19] If two of you shall agree on earth as touching any thing that they shall ask, it shall be done for them of my Father which is in heaven. [20] For where two or three are gathered together in my name, there am I in the midst of them.—Mat., ch. 18.

6344. —— **strangely answered.** *"Serpent."*
[7] Moses prayed for the people. [8] And the Lord said..Make thee a fiery serpent, and set it upon a pole ; and..every one that is bitten, when he looketh upon it, shall live.—Num., ch. 21. [He gave a cure, but left the serpents.]

6345. —— **unexpectedly answered.** *Rhoda.*
[14] When she knew Peter's voice, she opened not the gate for gladness, but ran in, and told how Peter stood before the gate. [15] And they said.. Thou art mad. But she constantly affirmed that it was even so. Then said they, It is his angel. —Acts, ch. 12.

6346. —— **Benevolence with.** *Cornelius.*
[4] The angel..said unto him, Thy prayers and thy alms are come up for a memorial before God. [5] And now send men to Joppa, and call for *one* Simon, whose surname is Peter.—Acts, ch. 10.

6347. —— **Boldness by.** *Disciples.* [31] And they were all filled with the Holy Ghost, and they spake the word of God with boldness. [32] And the multitude of them that believed were of one heart and of one soul.—Acts, ch. 4.

6348. —— **Boldness in.** *High Priest.* [15] We have not a high priest which cannot be touched with the feeling of our infirmities ; but was in all points tempted like as *we are*, *yet* without sin. [16] Let us therefore come boldly unto the throne of grace, that we may obtain mercy, and find grace to help in time of need.—Heb., ch. 4.

6349. —— **turns the Battle.** *Israelites.* [20] The Hagarites were delivered into their hand, and all that *were* with them : for they cried to God in the battle, and he was entreated of them ; because they put their trust in him.—1 Chron., ch. 5.

6350. —— **Boasting in.** *Pharisee.* [11] God, I thank thee, that I am not as other men *are*, ex-tortioners, unjust, adulterers, or even as this publican. [12] I fast twice in the week, I give tithes of all that I possess.—Luke, ch. 18.

6351. —— **Comfort in.** *"When in the Cave."*
[1] With my voice unto the Lord did I make my supplication. [2] I poured out my complaint before him ; I shewed before him my trouble. [3] When my spirit was overwhelmed within me, then thou knewest my path.—Ps. 142.

6352. —— **Constant.** *Cornelius.* [2] *A* devout man, and one that feared God with all his house, which gave much alms to the people, and prayed to God always.—Acts, ch. 10.

6353. —— Closet. *Secret.* 6 When thou prayest, enter into thy closet, and when thou hast shut thy door, pray to thy Father. . and thy Father which seeth in secret shall reward thee openly.—MAT., ch. 6.

6354. —— Deliverance by. *At Dothan.* 18 When they came down to him, Elisha prayed unto the Lord. . Smite this people, I pray thee, with blindness. And he smote them with blindness.—2 KINGS, ch. 6. [The Syrians were blinded and captured.]

6355. —— denied. *Moses.* 25 I pray thee, let me go over, and see the good land that *is* beyond Jordan, that goodly mountain, and Lebanon. 26 But the Lord was wroth with me for your sakes, and would not hear me : and the Lord said unto me, Let it suffice thee ; speak no more unto me of this matter.—DEUT., ch. 3.

6356. —— defeated. *Transgression.* 37 Saul asked counsel of God, Shall I go down after the Philistines ? wilt thou deliver them into the hand of Israel ? But he answered him not that day. 38 And Saul said, Draw ye near hither, all the chief of the people ; and know and see wherein this sin hath been this day.—1 SAM., ch. 14.

6357. —— End of. *Acceptance.* 1 When Solomon had made an end of praying, the fire came down from heaven, and consumed the burnt offering and the sacrifices. . 2 And the priests could not enter. . because the glory of the Lord had filled the Lord's house.—2 CHRON., ch. 7.

6358. —— Encouragement to. *Jesus said,* 9 What man is there of you, whom if his son ask bread, will he give him a stone ? 10 Or if he ask a fish, will he give him a serpent? 11 If ye then, being evil, know how to give good gifts unto your children, how much more shall your Father which is in heaven give good things to them that ask him.—MAT., ch. 7.

6359. —— Elevation in. *Jacob.* 11 Deliver me, I pray thee, from the hand of my brother. . Esau : for I fear him, lest he will come and smite me, *and* the mother with the children. . 29 And Jacob. . said, Tell *me*, I pray thee, thy name. And he said, Wherefore *is* it *that* thou dost ask after my name ? And he blessed him there.—GEN., ch. 32.

6360. —— Early. *Jesus.* 35 In the morning, rising up a great while before day, he went out, and departed into a solitary place, and there prayed.—MARK, ch. 1.

6361. —— with Effort. *Elisha.* 32 The child was dead, *and* laid upon his bed. 33 He. . shut the door upon them twain, and prayed unto the Lord. 34 And he. . lay upon the child, and put his mouth upon his mouth, and his eyes upon his eyes, and his hands upon his hands : and he stretched himself upon the child ; and the flesh of the child waxed warm.—2 KINGS, ch. 4.

6362. —— Earnestness in. *Tears.* 7 In the days of his flesh, when he had offered up prayers and supplications with strong crying and tears unto him that was able to save him from death, and was heard in that he feared.—HEB., ch. 5.

6363. —— —— *Gethsemane.* 43 There appeared an angel unto him from heaven, strengthening him. 44 And being in an agony he prayed more earnestly : and his sweat was as it were great drops of blood falling down to the ground. —LUKE, ch. 22.

6364. —— —— *Bartimeus.* 47 When he heard that it was Jesus of Nazareth, he began to cry out, and say, Jesus, *thou* Son of David, have mercy on me. 48 And many charged him that he should hold his peace : but he cried the more a great deal, Thou Son of David, have mercy on me.—MARK, ch. 10.

6365. —— Efficiency of. *Moses.* 13 If I have found grace in thy sight, shew me now thy way, that I may know thee, that I may find grace in thy sight : and consider that this nation *is* thy people. 14 And he said, My presence shall go *with thee.*—Ex., ch. 33.

6366. —— Frequent. *Jesus.* 44 He left them, and went away again, and prayed the third time, saying the same words.—MAT., ch. 26.

6367. —— Family. *Job.* 5 When the days of *their* feasting were gone about. . Job sent and sanctified them, and rose up early in the morning, and offered burnt offerings *according* to the number of them all : for Job said, It may be that my sons have sinned. . Thus did Job continually.—JOB, ch. 1.

6368. —— inspired by Fear. *Israelites.* 12 The Zidonians. . the Amalekites, and the Maonites, did oppress you ; and ye cried to me, and I delivered you out of their hand. 13 Yet have ye forsaken me, and served other gods : wherefore I will deliver you no more.—JUDGES, ch. 10.

6369. —— Forgiveness with. *Jesus said,* 24 What things soever ye desire, when ye pray, believe that ye receive *them,* and ye shall have *them.* 25 And when ye stand praying, forgive, if ye have aught against any : that your Father also which is in heaven may forgive you your trespasses. 26 But if ye do not forgive, neither will your Father which is in heaven forgive your trespasses.—MARK, ch. 11.

6370. —— Fraternal. *Paul.* 9 God is my witness, whom I serve with my spirit in the gospel of his Son, that without ceasing I make mention of you always in my prayers ; 13 Making request, if by any means now at length I might. . by the will of God to come unto you.— ROM., ch. 1.

6371. —— for Friends. *Job.* 10 The Lord turned the captivity of Job, when he prayed for his friends : also the Lord gave Job twice as much as he had before.—JOB, ch. 42.

6372. —— for Guidance. *In Ordaining.* 23 Appointed two, Joseph called Barsabas. . and Matthias. 24 And they prayed, and said, Thou, Lord, which knowest the hearts of all *men*, shew whether of these two thou hast chosen.—ACTS, ch. 1.

6373. —— House of. *The Church.* 12 Jesus went into the temple of God, and cast out all them that sold and bought in the temple, and overthrew the tables of the money changers, and the seats of them that sold doves, 13 And said. . It is written, My house shall be called the house of prayer ; but ye have made it a den of thieves.—MAT., ch. 21.

6374. —— Hinderances to. *Jesus.* 31 Come ye yourselves apart into a desert place, and rest a while : for there were many coming and going, and they had no leisure so much as to eat.

[22] And they departed into a desert place by ship privately .. [46] And when he had sent them away, he departed into a mountain to pray.—MARK, ch. 6.

6375. —— **for Help in Prayer.** *Canaanite.* My daughter..help me. [See No. 6381.]

6376. —— **for Helpers.** *Jesus said* [37] Unto his disciples, The harvest truly *is* plenteous, but the labourers *are* few ; [38] Pray ye therefore the Lord of the harvest, that he will send forth labourers into his harvest.—MAT., ch. 9.

6377. —— **with Humiliation.** *Manasseh.* [12] When Manasseh was in affliction, he besought the Lord his God, and humbled himself greatly.. [13]..and he was entreated of him, and heard his supplication, and brought him again to Jerusalem into his kingdom.—2 CHRON., ch. 33.

6378. —— **Instruction in.** *By Jesus.* [1] As he was praying in a certain place, when he ceased, one of his disciples said..Lord, teach us to pray, as John also taught his disciples. [2] And he said ..When ye pray, say, Our Father which art in heaven.—LUKE, ch. 11.

6379. —— **Incense of.** *Zacharias.* [10] The whole multitude of the people were praying without at the time of incense. [11] And there appeared unto him an angel of the Lord standing on the right side of the altar of incense.— LUKE, ch. 1.

6380. —— **Intercession in.** *Moses.* [31] Oh, this people have sinned a great sin, and have made them gods of gold. [32] Yet now, if thou wilt forgive their sin— ; and if not, blot me, I pray thee, out of thy book which thou hast written. —Ex., ch. 32.

6381. —— **Importunity in.** *Canaanite.* [22] Have mercy on me, O Lord, *thou* son of David ; my daughter is grievously vexed with a devil. [23] But he answered her not a word. And his disciples came..saying, Send her away ; for she crieth after us. [24] But he answered..I am not sent but unto the lost sheep of the house of Israel. [25] Then came she and worshipped him, saying, Lord, help me.—MAT., ch. 15. [See more at No. 6204.]

6382. —— —— *"Three Loaves."* [6] A friend of mine in his journey is come to me, and I have nothing to set before him ? [7] And he from within shall answer..Trouble me not : the door is now shut, and my children are with me in bed ; I cannot rise and give thee. [8] Though he will not rise and give him, because he is his friend, yet because of his importunity he will rise and give him as many as he needeth.—LUKE, ch. 11.

6383. —— —— *Of Moses.* [15] If thou shalt kill *all* this people as one man, then the nations which have heard the fame of thee will speak, saying, [16] Because the Lord was not able to bring this people into the land which he sware unto them, therefore he hath slain them in the wilderness. [17] And now, I beseech thee, let the power of my Lord be great.—NUM., ch. 14.

6384. —— **Ignorance in.** *John's Mother.* [21] She saith..Grant that these my two sons may sit, the one on thy right hand, and the other on the left, in thy kingdom. [22] But Jesus answered ..Ye know not what ye ask. Are ye able to drink of the cup that I shall drink of ?—MAT., ch. 20.

6385. —— **Insincerity in.** *Israelites.* [14] They have not cried unto me with their heart, when they howled upon their beds : they assemble themselves for corn and wine, *and* they rebel against me.—HOSEA, ch. 7.

6386. —— **Justification by.** *Publican.* [See No. 6403.]

6387. —— **The Model.** *Lord's.* [9] After this manner therefore pray ye : Our Father which art in heaven, Hallowed be thy name.—MAT., ch. 6.

6388. —— **Midday.** *Peter.* [See No. 6394.]

6389. —— **Morn. and Eve.** *Tabernacle.* [6] Thou shalt put it before the vail that *is* by the ark of the testimony, before the mercy seat that *is* over the testimony, where I will meet with thee. [7] And Aaron shall burn thereon sweet incense every morning : when he dresseth the lamps, he shall burn incense upon it.—Ex., ch. 30.

6390. —— **of Mariners.** *Storm.* [27] They reel to and fro, and stagger like a drunken man, and are at their wit's end. [28] Then they cry unto the Lord in their trouble, and he bringeth them out of their distresses.—Ps. 107. [See Psalm.]

6391. —— **for Others.** *Intercessory.* [23] God forbid that I should sin against the Lord in ceasing to pray for you : but I will teach you the good and the right way : [24] Only fear the Lord, and serve him in truth with all your heart. —1 SAM., ch. 12.

6392. —— **Privilege of.** *Solomon.* [5] In Gibeon the Lord appeared to Solomon in a dream by night : and God said, Ask what I shall give thee. —1 KINGS, ch. 3.

6393. —— **Preparation for.** *Reformation.* [15] When ye make many prayers, I will not hear : your hands are full of blood. [16] Wash ye, make you clean ; put away the evil of your doings from before mine eyes ; cease to do evil ; [17] Learn to do well ; seek judgment, relieve the oppressed, judge the fatherless, plead for the widow.—ISA., ch. 1.

6394. —— **Place of.** *At Joppa.* [9] Peter went up upon the housetop to pray about the sixth hour : [10] And he became very hungry.—ACTS, ch. 10.

6395. —— —— *At Philippi.* [13] On the sabbath we went out of the city by a river side, where prayer was wont to be made..and spake unto the women which resorted *thither.*—ACTS, ch. 16.

6396. —— —— *Strange.* [1] Then Jonah prayed unto the Lord his God out of the fish's belly, [2] And said, I cried by reason of mine affliction unto the Lord, and he heard me : out of the belly of hell cried I.—JONAH, ch. 2.

6397. —— **Power in.** *Peter out of Prison.* [31] When they had prayed, the place was shaken where they were assembled together ; and they were all filled with the Holy Spirit, and they spake the word of God with boldness. [32]..them that believed were of one heart and of one soul. —ACTS, ch. 4.

6398. —— **Persistent.** *"Steady."* [12] Moses' hands *were* heavy..and Aaron and Hur stayed up his hands, the one on the one side, and the other on the other side ; and his hands were steady until the going down of the sun. [13] And Joshua discomfited Amalek and his people with the edge of the sword.—Ex., ch. 17.

6399. —— Protracted. *Jesus.* [12] He went out into a mountain to pray, and continued all night in prayer to God. [13] And when it was day, he called *unto him* his disciples : and of them he chose twelve, whom also he named apostles.—LUKE, ch. 6.

6400. —— Power of. *Intercessory.* [32] Oh, let not the Lord be angry, and I will speak yet but this once : Peradventure ten shall be found there. And he said, I will not destroy *it* for ten's sake.—GEN., ch. 18.

6401. —— Pleading in. *Moses.* [See Nos. 6380, 6383, 6437.]

6402. —— Perseverance in. *Unjust Judge.* [3] A widow..came..saying, Avenge me of mine adversary. [4] And he would not for a while : but afterward he said within himself, Though I fear not God, nor regard man ; [5] Yet because this widow troubleth me, I will avenge her, lest by her continual coming she weary me.—LUKE, ch. 18.

6403. —— Penitence in. *Publican.* [13] The publican, standing afar off, would not lift up so much as *his* eyes unto heaven, but smote upon his breast, saying, God be merciful to me 'a sinner. [14] I tell you, this man went down to his house justified rather than the other.—LUKE, ch. 18.

6404. —— evil Persistence in. *Israel.* [6] The thing displeased Samuel, when they said, Give us a king to judge us : and Samuel prayed unto the Lord.—1 SAM., ch. 8. [9] O Israel, thou hast destroyed thyself.. [10] I will be thy king : where *is any other* that may save thee in all thy cities ? and thy judges of whom thou saidst, Give me a king and princes ? [11] I gave thee a king in my anger, and took *him* away in my wrath.—HOSEA, ch. 13.

6405. —— Regular. *David.* [16] As for me, I will call upon God ; and the Lord shall save me. [17] Evening, and morning, and at noon, will I pray, and cry aloud : and he shall hear my voice.—Ps. 55.

6406. —— Revengeful. *Samson.* [27] *There were* upon the roof about three thousand men and women, that beheld while Samson made sport. [28] And Samson..said, O Lord God, remember me, I pray thee, and strengthen me, I pray thee, only this once, O God, that I may be at once avenged of the Philistines for my two eyes.—JUDGES, ch. 16.

6407. —— Revived by. *Hannah.* [13] Hannah, she spake in her heart ; only her lips moved, but her voice was not heard.. [15] And Hannah answered and said, No, my lord, I *am* a woman of a sorrowful spirit.. [18] So the woman went her way, and did eat, and her countenance was no more *sad.*—1 SAM., ch. 1.

6408. —— for physical Relief. *Jeroboam.* [See No. 6418.]

6409. —— rejected. *Saul's.* [5] When Saul saw the host of the Philistines, he was afraid, and his heart greatly trembled. [6] And when Saul inquired of the Lord, the Lord answered him not, neither by dreams, nor by Urim, nor by prophets.—1 SAM., ch. 28.

6410. —— —— *Saul.* [25] I pray thee, pardon my sin, and turn again with me, that I may worship the Lord. [26] And Samuel said unto Saul, I will not return with thee : for thou hast rejected the word of the Lord, and the Lord hath rejected thee.—1 SAM., ch. 15.

6411. —— Rescued by. *At Philippi.* [24] Their feet fast in the stocks. [25] And at midnight Paul and Silas prayed, and sang praises unto God : and the prisoners heard them. [26] And suddenly there was a great earthquake, so that the foundations of the prison were shaken : and immediately all the doors were opened, and every one's bands were loosed.—ACTS, ch. 16.

6412. —— refused. *Wanderer's.* [10] Thus saith the Lord..Thus have they loved to wander, they have not refrained their feet, therefore the Lord doth not accept them ; he will now remember their iniquity, and visit their sins. [11] Then said the Lord unto me, Pray not for this people for *their* good.—JER., ch. 14.

6413. —— —— *" Thorn in the Flesh."* [8] For this thing I besought the Lord thrice, that it might depart from me. [9] And he said unto me, My grace is sufficient for thee : for my strength is made perfect in weakness.—2 COR., ch. 12.

6414. —— Successful. *Elijah.* [42] Elijah went up to the top of Carmel ; and he cast himself down upon the earth, and put his face between his knees, [44] And..at the seventh time..he said. Behold, there ariseth a little cloud out of the sea, like a man's hand. And he said..say unto Ahab, Prepare *thy chariot,* and get thee down, that the rain stop thee not.—1 KINGS, ch. 18.

6415. —— Secret. *Gethsemane.* [36] Then cometh Jesus with them unto..Gethsemane, and saith unto the disciples, Sit ye here, while I go and pray yonder.—MAT., ch. 26.

6416. —— A short. *Peter's.* [29] When Peter was come down out of the ship, he walked on the water, to go to Jesus. [30] But when he saw the wind boisterous, he was afraid ; and beginning to sink, he cried, saying, Lord, save me.—MAT., ch. 14.

6417. —— solicited. *Simon Magus.* [23] I perceive that thou art in the gall of bitterness, and in the bond of iniquity. [24] Then answered Simon..Pray ye to the Lord for me, that none of these things which ye have spoken come upon me.—ACTS, ch. 8.

6418. —— —— *Jeroboam.* [4] His hand, which he put forth against him, dried up, so that he could not pull it in again to him.. [6] And the king ..said..pray for me, that my hand may be restored me again. And the man of God besought the Lord, and the king's hand was restored him again.—1 KINGS, ch. 13.

6419. —— in Sickness. *Hezekiah.* [5] I have heard thy prayer, I have seen thy tears : behold, I will heal thee : on the third day thou shalt go up unto the house of the Lord. [6] And I will add unto thy days fifteen years ; and I will deliver thee and this city out of the hand of the king of Assyria.—2 KINGS, ch. 20.

6420. —— Supremacy of. *Elijah.* [17] Elias was a man subject to like passions as we are, and he prayed earnestly that it might not rain : and it rained not on the earth by the space of three years and six months. [18] And he prayed again, and the heaven gave rain.—JAMES, ch. 5.

6421. —— Succour by. *Poor.* [17] *When* the poor and needy seek water, and *there is* none, *and* their tongue faileth for thirst, I the Lord will hear them, I..will not forsake them. [18] I will open rivers in high places, and fountains in the midst of the valleys : I will make the wilderness a pool of water, and the dry land springs of water.—Isa., ch. 41.

6422. —— **Sorrow removed by.** *Hagar.* [15] She cast the child under one of the shrubs. [16]..and sat..a good way off, as it were a bowshot : for she said, Let me not see the death of the child. And she..lifted up her voice, and wept. [17] And God heard the voice of the lad.—Gen., ch. 21.

6423. —— *Hannah.* [See No. 6407.]

6424. —— **vs. the Sword.** *Hezekiah prayed,* [16] Lord, bow down thine ear, and hear : open, Lord, thine eyes, and see : and hear the words of Sennacherib, which hath sent him to reproach the living God.. [35]..the angel of the Lord went out, and smote in the camp of the Assyrians a hundred fourscore and five thousand. —2 Kings, ch. 19.

6425. —— **A Sceptic's.** *Thief.* [39] One of the malefactors which were hanged railed on him, saying, If thou be Christ, save thyself and us. —Luke, ch. 23.

6426. —— **Transformation by.** *Jesus* [28] Took Peter and John and James, and went up into a mountain to pray. [29] And as he prayed, the fashion of his countenance was altered, and his raiment *was* white *and* glistering.—Luke, ch. 9.

6427. —— **Unintimidated in.** *Daniel.* [10] When Daniel knew that the writing was signed, he went into his house ; and, his windows being open in his chamber toward Jerusalem, he kneeled upon his knees three times a day, and prayed, and gave thanks before his God, as he did aforetime.—Dan., ch. 6.

6428. —— **Union in.** *Moses.* [See No. 6398.]

6429. —— **Union in.** *Church.* [5] Peter..was kept in prison : but prayer was made without ceasing of the church unto God for him.. [7] And, behold, the angel of the Lord came upon *him,* and a light shined in the prison : and he smote Peter on the side, and raised. him up, saying, Arise up quickly. And his chains fell off from *his* hands.—Acts, ch. 12.

6430. —— **unanswered.** *At Carmel.* [26] Called on the name of Baal from morning even until noon, saying, O Baal, hear us. But *there was* no voice, nor any that answered. And they leaped upon the altar which was made.—1 Kings, ch. 18.

6431. —— —— *Pharisee.* [See No. 6403.]

6432. —— —— *David.* [16] Besought God for the child ; and David fasted, and went in, and lay all night upon the earth. [18] And..on the seventh day..the child died.—2 Sam., ch. 12.

6433. —— **Unavailing.** *Saints'.* [13] Son of man, when the land sinneth against me by trespassing grievously, then will I..break the staff of the bread..and will send famine upon it, and will cut off man and beast from it : [14] Though these three men, Noah, Daniel, and Job, were in it, they should deliver *but* their own souls by their righteousness.—Ezek., ch. 14.

6434. —— **Vigilance in.** *Samuel.* [10] The word of the Lord unto Samuel.. [11] It repenteth me that I have set up Saul *to be* king : for he is turned back from following me, and hath not performed my commandments. And it grieved

Samuel ; and he cried unto the Lord all night. —1 Sam., ch. 15.

6435. —— —— *Jacob.* [24] Jacob was left alone ; and there wrestled a man with him until the breaking of the day.. [26] And he said, Let me go, for the day breaketh. And he said, I will not let thee go, except thou bless me.—Gen., ch. 32.

6436. —— **withholds Vengeance.** *Calf made.* [10] Now therefore let me alone, that my wrath may wax hot against them, and that I may consume them : and I will make of thee a great nation. [11] And Moses besought the Lord.—Ex., ch. 32.

6437. —— —— *Spies' evil Report.* [19] Pardon, I beseech thee, the iniquity of this people according unto the greatness of thy mercy, and as thou hast forgiven this people, from Egypt even until now. [20] And the Lord said, I have pardoned according to thy word.—Num., ch. 14.

6438. —— **for Victory.** *Asa.* [11] Asa..said, Lord, *it is* nothing with thee to help, whether with many, or with them that have no power : help us, O Lord our God ; for we rest on thee, and in thy name we go against this multitude. O Lord, thou *art* our God ; let not man prevail against thee. [12] So the Lord smote the Ethiopians before Asa.—2 Chron., ch. 14.

6439. —— **witnessed.** *Jesus.* [48] Nathanael saith..Whence knowest thou me ? Jesus answered..Before that Philip called thee, when thou wast under the fig tree, I saw thee.—John, ch. 1.

6440. —— **Wonderful.** *Paul's.* [14] For this cause I bow my knees unto the Father of our Lord Jesus Christ, [15] Of whom the whole family in heaven and earth is named, [16] That he would grant you.—Eph., ch. 3.

6441. —— **Waiting in.** *Jesus.* [23] When he had sent the multitudes away, he went up into a mountain apart to pray : and when the evening was come, he was there alone.—Mat., ch. 14.

6442. —— **Whispered.** *Hannah.* [12] As she continued praying before the Lord..Eli marked her mouth. [13] Now Hannah, she spake in her heart ; only her lips moved, but her voice was not heard ; therefore Eli thought she had been drunken.—1 Sam., ch. 1.

6443. —— **tested.** *At Carmel.* [23] Let them choose one bullock..and cut it in pieces, and lay *it* on wood, and put no fire *under :* and I will dress the other bullock, and lay *it* on wood, and put no fire *under :* [24] And call ye on the name of your gods, and I will call on the name of the Lord : and the God that answereth by fire, let him be God.—1 Kings, ch. 18.

6444. —— —— *The Nobleman.* [52] Then inquired he..the hour when he began to amend. And they said..Yesterday at the seventh hour the fever left him. [53] So the father knew that *it was* at the same hour, in the which Jesus said ..Thy son liveth : and himself believed, and his whole house.—John, ch. 4.

6445. —— —— *Gideon's.* [37] I will put a fleece of wool in the floor ; *and* if the dew be on the fleece only, and *it be* dry upon all the earth *besides,* then shall I know that thou wilt save Israel by mine hand, as thou hast said. [38] And it was so : for he..wringed the dew out of the fleece, a bowl full of water.—Judges, ch. 6.

6446. PRAYERS helpful. *Peter released.* [See No. 6429.]

6447. —— solicited. *Saints.* [27] Pharaoh sent..for Moses and Aaron, and said..I have sinned this time : the Lord *is* righteous, and I and my people *are* wicked. [28] Entreat the Lord (for *it is* enough) that there be no *more* mighty thunderings and hail ; and I will let you go.—Ex., ch. 9.

6448. —— for Show. *Pharisees.* [47] Which devour widows' houses, and for a shew make long prayers : the same shall receive greater damnation.—Luke, ch. 20.

6449. —— Useless. *Baalites.* [27] At noon.. Elijah mocked them, and said, Cry aloud : for he *is* a god ; either he is talking, or he is pursuing, or he is in a journey, *or* peradventure he sleepeth, and must be awaked. [28] And they cried aloud, and cut themselves after their manner with knives and lancets, till the blood gushed out upon them.—1 Kings, ch. 18.

See other illustrations under :

ENTREATY.
Heart-breaking. What mean ye to..break mine h. 2684
Urgent. Come down ere my child die   2682

INTERCESSION.
Denied. I will not return with thee..L. rejected   4616
Effect. Let it alone this year also   4617
Friendly. Wherefore then wilt thou slay David   4618
"   Wilt thou not spare the place for fifty   4619
Limit. I will not destroy it for ten's sake..L. went 4620
Needless. They came near to the steward of J.   4621
Needed. Take your flocks..and bless me also   4622
Obtained. I have sinned..Samuel turned again   4623
Penitential. I have transgressed..pardon my sin   4624
Rewarded. Forgive..if not blot me..cleft of the r. 4625
Resented. Moses and Aaron..get you unto your   4626

MEDIATION.
Double. Thee a god to Pharaoh..Aaron thy p.   5285
Effectual. Aaron stood between the dead and living 5286
Moses. Moses returned the words unto the L.   5287
Righteous. I regard the presence of Jehoshaphat 5288
Transgressors. Moses besought the L..L. repented 5289

MEDIATOR.
Diplomatic. Made Blastus the king's chamberlain 5279
Female. Woman of Abel, His head shall be thrown 5280
Great. He is the mediator of the N. T.   5281
Present. Now to appear in the presence of G. for 5282
Required. Not see my face except your brother   5283
Wanted. Speak thou..but let not G. speak with us 5284

PERSUASION.
Excuse. Because thou hast hearkened unto..wife 6106
Ineffective. Paul would not be persuaded, we   6107

PETITION.
Denied. Serve alone..bid her..help me [Martha] 6114
Rejected. Get you unto your burdens [Pharaoh]   6115
"   I will chastise you with scorpions   6116

PLEA.
Affecting. We are sold, I and my people [Esther] 6201
Patriotism. How can I endure to see the evil..my 6205

Hinderance. As we went to prayer..damsel met us 1403
See WORSHIP.

6450. PREACHERS called. *Paul.* [16] Though I preach the gospel, I have nothing to glory of : for necessity is laid upon me ; yea, woe is unto me, if I preach not the gospel ! [17] For if I do this thing willingly, I have a reward : but if against my will, a dispensation *of the gospel* is committed unto me.—1 Cor., ch. 9.

6451. —— Duty of. *Paul.* [2] Preach the word ; be instant in season, out of season ; reprove, rebuke, exhort with all longsuffering and doctrine.—2 Tim., ch. 4.

6452. —— Instructive. *Ezra.* [3] He read therein before the street..from the morning until midday, before the men and the women, and those that could understand ; and the ears of all the people *were* attentive unto the book of the law.—Neh., ch. 8.

6453. PREACHING, Alarming. *"Trembled."* [25] As he reasoned of righteousness, temperance, and judgment to come, Felix trembled, and answered, Go thy way for this time ; when I have a convenient season, I will call for thee.—Acts, ch. 24.

6454. —— forbidden. *Peter and John.* [17] That it spread no further among the people, let us straitly threaten them, that they speak henceforth to no man in this name. [18] And they.. commanded them not to speak at all, nor teach in the name of Jesus. [19] But Peter and John answered..Whether it be right in the sight of God to hearken unto you more than unto God, judge ye. [20] For we cannot but speak the things which we have seen and heard.—Acts, ch. 4.

6455. —— Fruitful. *"Hundredfold."* [23] He that received seed into the good ground is he that heareth the word, and understandeth *it ;* which also beareth fruit, and bringeth forth, some a hundredfold, some sixty, some thirty.— Mat., ch. 13.

6456. —— Hinderances in. *Riches.* [22] He also that received seed among the thorns is he that heareth the word ; and the care of this world, and the deceitfulness of riches, choke the word, and he becometh unfruitful.—Mat., ch. 13.

6457. —— to the Ignorant. *"Understandeth it not."* [19] When any one heareth the word of the kingdom, and understandeth *it* not, then cometh the wicked *one,* and catcheth away that which was sown in his heart. This is he which received seed by the way side.—Mat., ch. 13.

6458. —— Joyful. *Shepherds.* [17] When they had seen *it,* they made known abroad the saying which was told them concerning this child. —Luke, ch. 2.

6459. —— to Masses. *Beyond Jordan.* [25] There went great multitudes with him : and he turned, and said.. [26] If any *man* come to me, and hate not his father, and mother, and wife, and children, and brethren, and sisters, yea, and his own life also, he cannot be my disciple.—Luke, ch. 14.

6460. —— Opinions of. *Contrary.* [23] We preach Christ crucified, unto the Jews a stumblingblock, and unto the Greeks foolishness ; [24] But unto them which are called, both Jews and Greeks, Christ the power of God, and the wisdom of God.—1 Cor., ch. 1.

6461. —— Purpose in. *Perfection.* [28] Whom we preach, warning every man, and teaching every man in all wisdom ; that we may present every man perfect in Christ Jesus : [29] Whereunto I also labour, striving according to his working, which worketh in me mightily.—Col., ch. 1.

6462. —— ridiculed. *At Athens.* [18] Certain philosophers of the Epicureans, and of the Stoics, encountered him. And some said, What will this babbler say?—ACTS, ch. 17.

6463. —— **Strength in.** *Paul.* [3] I was with you in weakness, and in fear, and in much trembling. [4] And my speech and my preaching *was* not with enticing words of man's wisdom, but in demonstration of the Spirit and of power.—1 COR., ch. 2.

See other illustrations under:

SERMON.

Long. Paul preached..until midnight	7790
to Women. By a river side..spake unto the w.	7791

SPEAKER.

Convincing. Never man spake like this man	8245
Engaging. Mary..sat at Jesus' feet and heard	8246

UTTERANCE.

Deficient. I am not eloquent..slow of speech	9153
Gift. I will be with thy mouth and teach	9154
" All filled with the H. G..speak	9155

Eloquence. Apollos..an eloquent man and mighty 2619
See MINISTERS and references.

6464. PRECEDENT, Use of. *Holy Bread.* [2] Thy disciples do that which is not lawful to do upon the sabbath day. [3] But he said..Have ye not read what David did, when he was a hungered, and they that were with him ; [4] How he entered into the house of God, and did eat the shewbread, which was not lawful for him to eat, neither for them which were with him, but only for the priests?—MAT., ch. 12.

See other illustrations under:

EXAMPLE.

Encouragement. Paul..in presence of them all	2758
Following. Whither thou goest, I will go..lodge	2759
Hindered. Neither go in yourselves, neither suf.	2760
Imitation. If I..have washed your feet..another's	2761
Instruction. If I then your L..ye also ought	2762
Inferior. Not move them with one of their fingers	2763
Justification. Read what David did when h.	2764
Light. Let you light so shine..good works	2765
Lord's. Disciple is not above his master	2766
Ministerial. Be thou [Timothy] an example	2767
Observation. Those things..seen in me, do	2768
Prayer. When ye pray say, Our Father which art	2769
Public Life. This deed of the queen shall..abroad	2770
Teaching. We wrought..to make ourselves an e.	2771
Warning. All these things happened..for our	2772

6465. PRECEDENCE, Yielding. *John Baptist.* [28] Ye yourselves bear me witness, that I said, I am not the Christ, but that I am sent before him. [30] He must increase, but I *must* decrease.—JOHN, ch. 3.

6466. PREJUDICE, Alarm from. *Egyptians.* [9] He said unto his people, Behold..Israel *are* more and mightier than we. [10] Come on, let us deal wisely with them, lest they multiply, and it come to pass, that, when there falleth out any war, they join also unto our enemies, and fight against us, and *so* get them up out of the land. —EX., ch. 1.

6467. —— **Blindness of.** *" Vail."* [15] Even unto this day, when Moses is read, the vail is upon their heart. [16] Nevertheless when it shall turn to the Lord, the vail shall be taken away. —2 COR., ch. 3.

6468. —— **against Children.** *Disciples.* [15] They brought..infants, that he would touch them : but when *his* disciples saw *it*, they rebuked them. [16] But Jesus called them..and

said, Suffer little children to come unto me, and forbid them not ; for of such is the kingdom of God.—LUKE, ch. 18.

6469. —— **of Custom.** *Samaritan Woman.* [27] His disciples..marvelled that he talked with the woman : yet no man said, What seekest thou ? or, Why talkest thou with her?—JOHN, ch. 4.

6470. —— **Communion removes.** *Nathanael.* [48] Nathanael saith..Whence knowest thou me ? [49] Nathanael answered..Rabbi, thou art the Son of God ; thou art the King of Israel.—JOHN, ch. 1.

6471. —— **Concession to.** *Paul's.* [1] Then came he to Derbe and Lystra..a certain disciple was there, named Timotheus, the son of a certain woman, which was a Jewess, and believed ; but his father *was* a Greek.. [3] Him would Paul have to go forth with him ; and took and circumcised him because of the Jews which were in those quarters : for they knew all that his father was a Greek.—ACTS, ch. 16.

6472. —— **Destructive.** *Pharisees.* [29] All the people that heard *him*, and the publicans, justified God, being baptized with the baptism of John. [30] But the Pharisees and lawyers rejected the counsel of God against themselves, being not baptized of him.—LUKE, ch. 7.

6473. —— **National.** *Samaritan.* [9] Saith the woman of Samaria..How is it that thou, being a Jew, askest drink of me, which am a woman of Samaria ? for the Jews have no dealings with the Samaritans.—JOHN, ch. 4.

6474. —— —— *Sodomites.* [9] This one *fellow* came in to sojourn, and he will needs be a judge : now will we deal worse with thee, than with them. And they pressed sore upon the man, *even* Lot, and came near to break the door. —GEN., ch. 19.

6475. —— **an Obstacle.** *Philip saith,* [45] We have..him, of whom Moses in the law, and the prophets, did write, Jesus of Nazareth, the son of Joseph. [46] And Nathanael said..Can there any good thing come out of Nazareth ? Philip saith unto him, Come and see.—JOHN, ch. 1.

6476. —— **Obstinate.** *Jewish.* [5] He saith unto the man, Stretch forth thine hand. And he stretched *it* out : and his hand was restored whole as the other. [6] And the Pharisees went forth, and straightway took counsel with the Herodians against him, how they might destroy him.—MARK, ch. 3.

6477. —— **Offended.** *The Carpenter.* [3] Is not this the carpenter, the son of Mary, the brother of James, and Joses, and of Juda, and Simon ? and are not his sisters here with us ? And they were offended at him.—MARK, ch. 6.

6478. —— **against Piety.** *In Egypt.* [17] We will certainly..burn incense unto the queen of heaven, and to pour out drink offerings unto her, as we have done, we, and our fathers..in the cities of Judah..for *then* had we plenty of victuals, and were well, and saw no evil. [18] But since we left off to burn incense to the queen of heaven, and to pour out drink offerings unto her, we have wanted all *things*, and have been consumed by the sword and by the famine.— JER., ch. 44.

6479. —— **Race.** *Ethiopian.* [1] Miriam and Aaron spake against Moses because of the Ethiopian woman whom he had married : for he had married an Ethiopian woman.—Num., ch. 12.

6480. —— **removed.** *Peter.* [28] Ye know how that it is an unlawful thing for a man that is a Jew to keep company, or come unto one of another nation ; but God hath shewed me that I should not call any man common or unclean. [29] Therefore came I *unto you.*—Acts, ch. 10.

6481. —— **Sectarian.** *John's.* [38] John answered him, saying, Master, we saw one casting out devils in thy name, and he followeth not us : and we forbade him, because he followeth not us. [39] But Jesus said, Forbid him not : for there is no man which shall do a miracle in my name, that can lightly speak evil of me.—Mark, ch. 9.

6482. —— **Super-religious.** *Pharisee.* [38] Did wipe *them* with the hairs of her head, and kissed his feet, and anointed *them* with the ointment. [39] Now when the Pharisee which had bidden him saw *it*, he spake within himself, saying, This man, if he were a prophet, would have known who and what manner of woman *this is* that toucheth him : for she is a sinner.—Luke, ch. 7.

6483. —— **against Sinners.** *Pharisees.* [5] Zaccheus..to day I must abide at thy house. [6] And he made haste, and came down, and received him joyfully. [7]..they all murmured, saying, That he was gone to be guest with a man that is a sinner.—Luke, ch. 19.

6484. —— **An unhappy.** *Priests.* [14] The blind and the lame came to him in the temple ; and he healed them. [15] And when the chief priests and scribes saw the wonderful things that he did, and the children crying in the temple, and saying, Hosanna to the son of David ; they were sore displeased.—Mat., ch. 21.

Also see :

Disaffection. Eateth my flesh..disciples went back 2326

6485. PREMEDITATION needless. *Witnesses.* [11] When they shall .. deliver you up, take no thought beforehand what ye shall speak, neither do ye premeditate : but whatsoever shall be given you in that hour, that speak ye : for it is not ye that speak, but the Holy Ghost.—Mark, ch. 13.

See other illustrations under :

ACCOUNTABILITY.

Future. King which would take account..servants 72
Gifts. Ten pounds..occupy till I come 73
Minute. Every idle word..give account 74
Personal. Give account of thy stewardship 75

FORETHOUGHT.

Necessary. Intending to build..first counteth the 3339
" Consulteth whether he be able with 3340
Useless. Which..with taking thought can add one 3341

6486. PREPARATION by anointing. *David.* [11] The youngest .. keepeth the sheep. And Samuel said unto Jesse, Send and fetch him.. [12]..he *was* ruddy, *and* withal of a beautiful countenance, and goodly to look to. And the Lord said, Arise, anoint him : for this *is* he. [13] Then Samuel took the horn of oil, and anointed him in the midst of his brethren : and the Spirit of the Lord came upon David from that day.—1 Sam., ch. 16.

6487. —— **appreciated.** *Honours.* [37] Blessed *are* those servants, whom the lord when he com-

eth shall find watching..he shall gird himself, and make them to sit down to meat, and..serve them.—Luke, ch. 12.

6488. —— **by Blood.** *Priests.* [20] Then shalt thou kill the ram, and take of his blood, and put *it* upon the tip of the right ear of Aaron, and upon the tip of the right ear of his sons, and upon the thumb of their right hand, and upon the great toe of their right foot, and sprinkle the blood upon the altar.—Ex., ch. 29.

6489. —— **for a Blessing.** *At Carmel.* [30] Elijah said..Come near unto me. And all the people came..And he repaired the altar of the Lord *that was* broken down.—1 Kings, ch. 18.

6490. —— **for Conquest.** *Spies.* [17] Moses sent them to spy out the land of Canaan, and said.. [18]..see the land, what it *is*; and the people that dwelleth therein, whether they *be* strong or weak, few or many.—Num., ch. 13.

6491. —— **by Fire.** *Isaiah's.* [5] Woe *is* me ! for I am undone ; because I *am* a man of unclean lips..for mine eyes have seen the King, the Lord of hosts. [6] Then flew one of the seraphims ..having a live coal in his hand..from off the altar : [7] And he laid *it* upon my mouth, and said, Lo, this hath touched thy lips ; and thine iniquity is taken away, and thy sin purged.—Isa., ch. 6.

6492. —— **for Heaven.** *"Lights burning."* [35] Let your loins be girded about, and *your* lights burning ; [36] And ye yourselves like unto men that wait for their lord, when he will return from the wedding ; that, when he cometh and knocketh, they may open unto him immediately.—Luke, ch. 12.

6493. —— **in Heaven.** *"Place."* [2] In my Father's house are many mansions : if *it were* not *so*, I would have told you. I go to prepare a place for you. [3] And if I go and prepare a place for you, I will come again, and receive you unto myself ; that where I am, *there* ye may be also.—John, ch. 14.

6494. —— **for the Lord.** *"Make straight."* [4] Prepare ye the way of the Lord, make his paths straight. [5] Every valley shall be filled, and every mountain and hill shall be brought low ; and the crooked shall be made straight, and the rough ways *shall be* made smooth ; [6] And all flesh shall see the salvation of God.—Luke, ch. 3.

6495. —— **of Materials.** *Temple.* [14] In my trouble I have prepared for the house of the Lord a hundred thousand talents of gold, and a thousand thousand talents of silver ; and of brass and iron without weight ; for it is in abundance : timber also and stone have I prepared.—1 Chron., ch. 22.

6496. —— **of Mind.** *Divine.* [45] Then opened he their understanding, that they might understand the Scriptures. [46] And said .. Thus it is written, and thus it behooved Christ to suffer, and to rise from the dead the third day.—Luke, ch. 24.

6497. —— **Neglecting.** *Foolish Virgins.* [3] They that *were* foolish took their lamps, and took no oil with them : [4] But the wise took oil in their vessels with their lamps.—Mat., ch. 25.

6498. —— **by Prayer.** *Apostles.* [12] He went out into a mountain to pray, and continued all night in prayer to God. [13] And when it was day, he called *unto him* his disciples : and of them he chose twelve, whom also he named apostles.—LUKE, ch. 6.

6499. —— for the Prepared. *John's Mother.* [21] She saith..Grant that these my two sons may sit, the one on thy right hand, and the other on the left, in thy kingdom. [23]..to sit on my right hand, and on my left, is not mine to give, but *it shall be given to them* for whom it is prepared of my Father.—MAT., ch. 20.

6500. —— of Strength. *Angel to Elijah.* [7] Arise *and* eat ; because the journey *is* too great for thee. [8] And he arose, and did eat and drink, and went in the strength of that meat forty days and forty nights unto Horeb.—1 KINGS, ch. 19.

6501. —— by Training. *Courtiers.* [3] Bring *certain* of the children of Israel, and of the king's seed, and of the princes ; [4]..in whom *was* no blemish, but well favoured, and skilful in all wisdom, and cunning in knowledge, and understanding science, and such as *had* ability in them to stand in the king's palace, and whom they might teach the learning and the tongue of the Chaldeans.—DAN., ch. 1.

6502. —— Want of. *"Wedding Garment."* [12] Friend, how camest thou in hither not having a wedding garment? And he was speechless. [13] Then said the king..Bind him hand and foot, and take him away, and cast *him* into outer darkness ; there shall be weeping and gnashing of teeth.—MAT., ch. 22.

See other illustrations under :

FOUNDATION.

Only. Other foundation can no man lay	3399
2d Temple. People shouted..because..was laid	3401
Various Uses. Build on..gold..wood..stubble	3402

Access after. Moses..elders..saw G...feet	50
Communion. Moses..sprinkled the book and all the	49
Service. S. of G. came upon Saul..prophecy	444

See PREMEDITATION and references.

6503. PRESENT, A bloody. *To Jehu.* [7] When the letter came to them..they took the king's sons, and slew seventy persons, and put their heads in baskets, and sent him *them* to Jezreel.—JUDGES, ch. 3.

6504: —— A conciliatory. *Jacob's.* [17] He commanded the foremost, saying, When Esau my brother meeteth thee, and asketh..Whose *art* thou? and whither goest thou? and whose *are* these before thee? [18] Then thou shalt say, *They* be thy servant Jacob's ; it *is* a present sent unto my lord Esau.—GEN., ch. 32.

6505. —— A deceptive. *Ehud.* [15] By him the children of Israel sent a present unto Eglon the king of Moab. [16] But Ehud made him a dagger which had two edges, of a cubit length ; and he did gird it under his raiment upon his right thigh.—JUDGES, ch. 3.

6506. PRESENTS, Conciliatory. *Jacob's.* [11] Take of the best fruits in the land in your vessels, and carry down the man a present, a little balm, and a little honey, spices and myrrh, nuts and almonds : [12] And take double money in your hand ; and the money that was brought again in the mouth of your sacks.—GEN., ch. 43.

6507. —— declined. *Jacob's.* [9] Esau said, I have enough, my brother ; keep that thou hast unto thyself. [8] And he said, What *meanest* thou by all this drove which I met? And he said,

These are to find grace in the sight of my lord.—GEN., ch. 33.

6508. —— of Friendship. *Jonathan's.* [3] He loved him as his own soul. [4] And Jonathan stripped himself of the robe..and gave it to David, and his garments, even to his sword, and to his bow, and to his girdle.—1 SAM., ch. 18.

6509. —— for Favour. *To Elisha.* [9] Hazael ..took a present with him, even of every good thing of Damascus, forty camels' burden, and ..said, Thy son Ben-hadad king of Syria hath sent me to thee, saying, Shall I recover of this disease?—2 KINGS, ch. 8.

6510. —— from Gratitude. *Jacob's.* [See No. 6507.] [10] Jacob said, Nay, I pray thee..receive my present at my hand : for therefore I have seen thy face, as though I had seen the face of God, and thou wast pleased with me. [11]..because God hath dealt graciously with me, and because I have enough. And he urged him, and he took *it*.—GEN., ch. 33.

6511. —— Influence of. *Rebekah's Brother.* [30] When he saw the earring, and bracelets upon his sister's hands, and when he heard the words of Rebekah.. [31]..he said, Come in, thou blessed of the Lord ; wherefore standest thou without? for I have prepared the house, and room for the camels.—GEN., ch. 24.

See other illustrations under :

PRICE.

Extortion. Esau sold his birthright unto Jacob	6550
of Perfection. Go sell..give..follow me	6551

Annual. Samuel ministered..mother..little cost	172
Contribution. I have given [\$94,101.560]	3514
Temple. [Costing nearly \$4,700,000,000.]	4130
Valued. Widow..cast more in than all..treasury	711

See GIFT, GIFTS, GIVERS, and references.

6512. PRESENCE acknowledged. *To Saul.* [18] One of the servants..said, Behold, I have seen a son of Jesse the Beth-lehemite, *that* is cunning in playing, and a mighty valiant man, and a man of war, and prudent in matters, and a comely person, and the Lord *is* with him.—1 SAM., ch. 16.

6513. —— conditioned. *Covetous Achan.* [12] Turned *their* backs before their enemies, because they were accursed : neither will I be with you any more, except ye destroy the accursed from among you.—JOSH., ch. 7.

6514. —— Effect of. *To Joshua.* [5] There shall not any man be able to stand before thee all the days of thy life : as I was with Moses, *so* I will be with thee ; I will not fail thee, nor forsake thee.—JOSH., ch. 1.

6515. —— indicated. *Dedication.* [10] When the priests were come out of the holy *place*..the cloud filled the house of the Lord, [11] So that the priests could not stand to minister because of the cloud : for the glory of the Lord had filled the house of the Lord.—1 KINGS, ch. 8.

6516. —— indispensable. *To Moses.* [14] My presence shall go *with thee*, and I will give thee rest. [15] And he said..If thy presence go not *with me*, carry us not up hence.—EX., ch. 33.

6517. —— of Jesus. *Calms.* [51] He went up unto them into the ship ; and the wind ceased : and they were sore amazed in themselves beyond measure, and wondered.—MARK, ch. 6.

6518. —— —— *Near.* [13] Mary said..they have taken away my Lord, and I know not where they have laid him. [14] And when she had thus said, she turned herself back, and saw Jesus standing, and knew not that it was Jesus. —JOHN, ch. 20.

6519. —— —— *Unconscious of.* [Walking to Emmaus.] [15] While they communed *together* and reasoned, Jesus himself drew near, and went with them. [16] But their eyes were holden that they should not know him.—LUKE, ch. 24.

6520. —— —— *Evidenced.* [See No. 6519.] [32] They said one to another, Did not our heart burn within us, while he talked with us by the way, and while he opened to us the scriptures? —LUKE, ch. 24.

6521. —— misjudged. *At Sinai.* [12] After the earthquake a fire; *but* the Lord *was* not in the fire: and after the fire a still small voice. [13]..when Elijah heard *it*..he wrapped his face in his mantle, and went out, and stood in the entering in of the cave. And, behold, *there came* a voice unto him.—1 KINGS, ch. 19.

6522. —— manifested. *Cloud.* [15] On the day that the tabernacle was reared up the cloud covered the tabernacle..and at even there was ..the appearance of fire, until the morning. [16] So it was alway.—NUM., ch. 9.

6523. —— questioned. *Jehovah's.* [6] I will stand before thee there upon the rock in Horeb; and thou shalt smite the rock, and there shall come water out of it, that the people may drink. And Moses did so in the sight of the elders of Israel. [7] And he called the name of the place Massah, and Meribah, because of the chiding of the children of Israel, and because they tempted the Lord, saying, Is the Lord among us, or not?—EX., ch. 17.

6524. —— Sign of. *"Sound."* [24] When thou hearest the sound of a going in the tops of the mulberry trees..then thou shalt bestir thyself: for then shall the Lord go out before thee, to smite the host of the Philistines. [25] And David did so..and smote the Philistines from Geba until thou come to Gazer.—2 SAM., ch. 5.

6525. —— Undiscovered. *Samuel.* [6] The Lord called yet again, Samuel: and Samuel arose and went to Eli, and said, Here *am* I; for thou didst call me. And he answered, I called not, my son: lie down again.—1 SAM., ch. 3.

6526. —— withdrawn. *Israelites.* [42] Go not up, for the Lord *is* not among you.. [43] For the Amalekites and the Canaanites *are* there before you, and ye shall fall by the sword: because ye are turned away from the Lord, therefore the Lord will not be with you.—NUM., ch. 14.

Also see:

Divine. Be not afraid..L. thy G. is with thee   582

6527. PRESERVATION by Association. *To King Jehoram.* [14] Elisha said, As the Lord of hosts liveth, before whom I stand, surely, were it not that I regard the presence of Jehoshaphat the king of Judah, I would not look toward thee, nor see thee.—2 KINGS, ch. 3.

6528. —— by Concealment. *Rahab.* [4] The women took the two men, and hid them, and said thus, There came men unto me, but I wist not whence they *were;* [5] And..*about the time of*

shutting of the gate, when it was dark..the men went out.—JOSH., ch. 2.

6529. —— by the Church. *The Wicked.* [24] Peradventure there be fifty righteous within the city: wilt thou also destroy and not spare the place for the fifty righteous that *are* therein? —GEN., ch. 18.

6530. —— Miraculous. *Raiment.* [4] Thy raiment waxed not old upon thee, neither did thy foot swell, these forty years.—DEUT., ch. 8.

6531. —— by Obedience. *At Zarephath.* [15] She, and he, and her house, did eat *many* days. [16] *And* the barrel of meal wasted not, neither did the cruse of oil fail, according to the word of the Lord, which he spake by Elijah.—1 KINGS, ch. 17.

6532. —— Remarkable. *Elijah.* [3] Get thee hence..and hide thyself by the brook Cherith.. [4]..thou shalt drink of the brook; and I have commanded the ravens to feed thee there.—1 KINGS, ch. 17.

6533. —— Wonderful. *Furnace.* [27] The king's counsellors..saw these men, upon whose bodies the fire had no power, nor was a hair of their head singed, neither were their coats changed, nor the smell of fire had passed on them.—DAN., ch. 3.

See other illustrations under :

GUIDANCE.

Divine. The kine took the straight way..to B.   3761
Explained. Lest peradventure..see war and they   3762
Gentle. I will guide thee with mine eye   3763
Promised. Acknowledge him..direct thy paths   3764
Waiting. If the cloud were not taken up   3765

SAFETY.

Godly. He that keepeth thee will not slumber   7547
"   The beloved..shall dwell between his s.   7548
"   Hast thou not made a hedge about him   7549
"   I will both lay me down in peace and sleep 7550
"   He shall cover thee with his feathers   7551
Hiding. Jotham..was left; for he hid himself   7552
Mutual. Except these abide in the ship..not be   7553
Supposed. Charging the jailer to keep them safely 7554
See DELIVERANCE and references.

6534. PRESUMPTION avoided. *Proverb.* [7] Better *it is* that it be said unto thee, Come up hither; than that thou shouldest be put lower in the presence of the prince whom thine eyes have seen.—PROV., ch. 25.

6535. —— Daring. *At Red Sea.* [23] The Egyptians pursued, and went in after them to the midst of the sea, *even* all Pharaoh's horses, his chariots.—EX., ch. 14.

6536. —— Failure from. *Israelites.* [44] They presumed to go up unto the hill top; nevertheless the ark of the covenant of the Lord, and Moses, departed not out of the camp. [45] Then the Amalekites..and the Canaanites which dwelt in that hill..smote them.—NUM., ch. 13.

6537. —— Future. *"To Morrow."* [13] Go to now, ye that say, To day or to morrow we will go into such a city, and continue there a year, and buy and sell, and get gain: [14] Whereas ye know not what *shall be* on the morrow. For what *is* your life? It is even a vapour, that appeareth for a little time, and then vanisheth away.—JAMES, ch. 4.

6538. —— from Impatience. *Saul.* [11] Saul said, Because I saw that the people were scattered from me, and *that* thou camest not within the days appointed, and *that* the Philistines gathered themselves together at Michmash : [12] Therefore said I, The Philistines will come down now upon me to Gilgal, and I have not made supplication unto the Lord : I forced myself therefore, and offered a burnt offering.—1 SAM., ch. 13.

6539. —— **from Pride.** *King Uzziah.* [15] His name spread far abroad ; for he was marvellously helped, till he was strong. [16] But when he was strong, his heart was lifted up to *his* destruction : for he transgressed..and went into the temple of the Lord to burn incense upon the altar of incense.—2 CHRON., ch. 26.

6540. —— **Penalty for.** *Esther said,* [11] All ..the people..do know, that whosoever, whether man or woman, shall come unto the king into the inner court, who is not called, *there is* one law of his to put *him* to death, except such to whom the king shall hold out the golden sceptre, that he may live.—ESTHER, ch. 4.

6541. —— **Religious.** *Law.* [20] The prophet, which shall presume to speak a word in my name, which I have not commanded him to speak, or that shall speak in the name of other gods..shall die.—DEUT., ch. 18.

6542. —— **rebuked.** *King Uzziah.* [19] Had a censer in his hand to burn incense : and while he was wroth with the priests, the leprosy even rose up in his forehead..in the house of the Lord, from beside the incense altar. [20] And Azariah the chief priest, and all the priests, looked upon him..and they thrust him out from thence ; yea, himself hasted also to go out, because the Lord had smitten him.—2 CHRON., ch. 26.

6543. —— **Sin of.** *No Mercy.* [28] He that despised Moses' law died without mercy under two or three witnesses : [29] Of how much sorer punishment, suppose ye, shall he be thought worthy, who hath trodden under foot the Son of God, and hath counted the blood of the covenant, wherewith he was sanctified, an unholy thing, and hath done despite unto the Spirit of grace ?—HEB., ch. 11.

6544. —— —— *Law.* [27] If any soul sin through ignorance, then he shall bring a..sin offering. [30] But the soul that doeth *aught* presumptuously, *whether he be* born in the land, or a stranger, the same reproacheth the Lord ; and that soul shall be cut off from among his people. [31] Because he hath despised the word of the Lord.—NUM., ch. 15.

6545. —— **from Success.** *Ai.* [15] Joshua and all Israel made as if they were beaten before them, and fled by the way of the wilderness. [16] And all the people that *were* in Ai were called together to pursue after them..and were drawn away from the city.—JOSH., ch. 8.

6546. —— **Temptation to.** *Jesus.* [5] The devil taketh him up into the holy city, and setteth him on a pinnacle of the temple, [6] And saith.. If thou be the Son of God, cast thyself down : for it is written, He shall give his angels charge concerning thee : and in *their* hands they shall bear thee up.—MAT., ch. 4.

6547. —— **Unholy.** *Sons of Korah.* [2] Two hundred and fifty princes..men of renown : [3] ..gathered themselves together against Moses

and against Aaron, and said unto them, *Ye take* too much upon you, seeing all the congregation *are* holy, every one of them, and the Lord *is* among them.—NUM., ch. 16.

See other illustrations under :

CONFIDENCE.

Believers. Though I walk through the valley..d.		1518
Blind. Know I that the L...I have a priest		1519
Caution. They are smitten down..as at the first		1520
Disappointed. Ark came..I. shouted..ark taken		1521
False. King [of Ai] wist not..ambush		1522
Future. Doth deliver..trust he will deliver		1523
Intelligent. I know whom I have believed		1524
Joyful. How great is thy goodness..trust thee		1525
Over. Is thy servant a dog ?..do this [Hazael]		1526
Peril. Have the sentence of death..we trust		1527
Piety begets. L. was with Joseph..into his hand		1528
Strong. L. delight in us..fear them not		1529
Self. Peter said..I will lay down my life		1530
Triumphant. Although the fig tree shall not b.		1531
Unwarranted. Let two or three thousand go..Ai		1532
Unfortunate. Confidence..like a broken tooth		1533
Undermining. Neither let Hez. make you trust..L.		1534
Warranted. L. is my rock, fortress, deliverer		1535

SELF-CONCEIT.

Hopeless. Wise in his own conceit..more hope of		7687
Poverty. He that is despised and hath a servant		7688

SELF-CONFIDENCE.

Boasting. L. said to Gideon..too many..vaunt		7694
Rebuked. I will lay down my life..denied me		7695

SELF-RIGHTEOUSNESS.

Caution. Speak not in thine heart..my		7724
Correct·d. Remember how thou provokedst the		7725
Failure. This man went..justified rather..other		7726
Mistake. Thou hast said..I am clean in thine		7727
Offensive. Stand by thyself ; come not..holier		7728
Recital. I am not as other men are, extortioners		7729
Unlawful. Walketh..after their own thoughts		7730

Ambition. Seek ye the priesthood also ?		330
" Thistle..to the cedar of Lebanon		328

6548. PRETENCE, Religious. *Pharisees.* [14] Woe unto you, scribes and Pharisees, hypocrites ! for ye devour widows' houses, and for a pretence make long prayer : therefore ye shall receive the greater damnation.—MAT., ch. 23.

See other illustrations under :

EXCUSE.

Disobedience. Spared the best of the sheep..to		2792
False. Wherefore cometh not..[David] to meat		2793
Idlers. Lion without..I shall be slain		2794
Inadequate. Make us gods..as for this Moses		2795

EXCUSES.

Caviller's. Angry..made a man..whole on the S.		2796
Feeble. The door is now shut..in bed..cannot		2797
Indolence. Sluggard is wiser..render a reason		2798
Loss. I am slow of speech..anger of the Lord		2799
Worldly. I have bought a piece of ground..oxen		2800

PROFESSION.

Only. Not every one that sayeth L.		6629
Worthless. Son, go work..I go sir, and went not		6630

Conceal. Joseph..spake roughly..whence come		474
Deception. Israel made as if beaten..Ai		6544
Formalist. I fast..I give tithes of all		3376
Lip-service. This people draweth nigh..with		5049
Overstrained. Pay tithe of mint..have omitted		4936
Quibbles. Swear by the temple, it is nothing..gold		4937

6549. PREVARICATION through Fear. *Parents.* [21] By what means he now seeth, we know

not ; or who hath opened his eyes, we know not..
[22]..because they feared the Jews : for the Jews
had agreed already, that if any man did confess
that he was Christ, he should be put out of the
synagogue.—JOHN, ch. 9.

See other illustrations under :

DISSEMBLING.

Confession. Achan said..I saw..I took a wedge of 2424
Imitated. Other Jews dissembled likewise 2425
Inconsistency. If thou, being a Jew..livest after 2426
Rebuked. I withstood him to the face..separated 2427

EQUIVOCATION.

Fear. I thought..they will slay me..[wife's sake] 2707
Hypocrites. If we shall say from heaven 2708

EVASION.

Answer by. Is it well with the child?..It is well 2726
Impossible. Asked us..Have ye another brother? 2727
by Silence. Let no man know these words 2728
See DECEPTION.

6550. PRICE, Extortioner's. *Jacob.* [33] Jacob
said, Swear to me this day ; and he sware unto
him : and he sold his birthright unto Jacob.
[34] Then Jacob gave Esau bread and pottage of
lentiles ; and he did eat and drink.—GEN., ch. 25.

6551. —— of Perfection. *Young Ruler.* [21] Jesus beholding him loved him..One thing thou
lackest..sell whatsoever thou hast, and give to
the poor..and come, take up the cross, and follow me.—MARK, ch. 10.

See other illustrations under :

COST.

Count. Master, I will follow thee whithersoever 1734
Counted. Gathered books, and burned..50,000 p. 1735
not Counted. Began to build, and was not able 1736
Sacrifice. Nay, but I will surely buy it 1737

EXTORTION.

Extraordinary. I am faint..Sell me..thy birthright 2828
Pious. Pharisees..full of extortion and excess 2829
Rebuked. Shook my lap..So G. shake out 2830
Separation. If any brother..be covetous..extor. 2831

6552. PRIDE, Contemptible. *Bramble.* [15] The
bramble said unto the trees, If in truth ye
anoint me king over you, *then* come *and* put your
trust in my shadow ; and if not, let fire come
out of the bramble, and devour the cedars of
Lebanon.—JUDGES, ch. 9.

6553. —— conquered. *Naaman.* [12] *Are* not
Abana and Pharpar, rivers of Damascus, better
than all the waters of Israel ? may I not wash
in them, and be clean ? So he turned and went
away in a rage.. [14] Then went he down, and
dipped himself seven times in Jordan.—2 KINGS,
ch. 5.

6554. —— Charged with. *David.* [28] Eliab
his eldest brother heard when he spake unto the
men..and he said, Why camest thou down
hither ? and with whom hast thou left those few
sheep in the wilderness ? I know thy pride, and
the naughtiness of thine heart.—1 SAM., ch. 17.

6555. —— Cowardice of. *Herod.* [Herodias'
daughter asked him to kill John.] [26] The king
was exceeding sorry ; *yet* for his oath's sake, and
for their sakes which sat with him, he would
not reject her.—MARK, ch. 6.

6556. —— Conceited. *Hopeless.* [12] Seest
thou a man wise in his own conceit? *there is*
more hope of a fool than of him.—PROV., ch. 26.

6557. —— Cruelty of. *Haman.* [5] When

Haman saw that Mordecai bowed not..then was
Haman full of wrath. [6] And he thought scorn
to lay hands on Mordecai alone..wherefore Haman sought to destroy all the Jews that *were*
throughout the whole kingdom of Ahasuerus.—
ESTHER, ch. 3.

6558. —— Deifying. *Prince of Tyrus.* [2] Son
of man, say unto the prince of Tyrus..thine
heart *is* lifted up, and thou hast said, I *am* a
god, I sit *in* the seat of God, in the midst of the
seas ; yet thou *art* a man, and not God.—EZEK.,
ch. 28. [See No. 6575.]

6559. —— Disdainful. *Pharaoh.* [2] Pharaoh
said, Who *is* the Lord, that I should obey his
voice to let Israel go? I know not the Lord,
neither will I let Israel go.—EX., ch. 5.

6560. —— Downfall of. *Haman.* [11] Then
took Haman the apparel and the horse, and arrayed Mordecai, and brought him on horseback
through the street of the city, and proclaimed
before him, Thus shall it be done unto the man
whom the king delighteth to honour.—ESTHER,
ch. 6.

6561. —— A Father's. *Haman.* [10] Sent and
called for his friends, and Zeresh his wife.
[11] And Haman told them of the..multitude of
his children, and all *the things* wherein the king
had promoted him.—ESTHER, ch. 5.

6562. —— humbled. *David.* [See No. 6568.]
[10] David's heart smote him after that he had
numbered the people. And David said unto the
Lord, I have sinned greatly in that I have done..
[15] So the Lord sent a pestilence upon Israel..
and there died of the people from Dan even to
Beer-sheba seventy thousand men.—2 SAM., ch.
24.

6563. —— Humiliation of. *Divine.* [10] Enter
into the rock, and hide thee in the dust, for fear
of the Lord, and for the glory of his majesty.
[11] The lofty looks of man shall be humbled,
and the haughtiness of men shall be bowed
down ; and the Lord alone shall be exalted.—
ISA., ch. 2.

6564. —— —— Women. [16] The Lord saith,
Because the daughters of Zion are haughty, and
walk with stretched forth necks and wanton
eyes, walking and mincing *as* they go, and making a tinkling with their feet : [17] Therefore the
Lord will smite them.—ISA., ch. 3.

6565. —— Hatefulness of. *One of Six.*
[16] These six *things* doth the Lord hate ; yea,
seven *are* an abomination unto him : [17] A proud
look, a lying tongue, and hands that shed innocent blood, [11] A heart that deviseth wicked
imaginations, feet that be swift in running to
mischief, [12] A false witness *that* speaketh lies,
and he that soweth discord among brethren.—
PROV., ch. 6.

6566. —— Insulting. *Joash.* [9] Joash the
king of Israel sent to Amaziah king of Judah,
saying, The thistle that *was* in Lebanon sent to
the cedar that *was* in Lebanon, saying, Give thy
daughter to my son to wife : and there passed
by a wild beast..and trode down the thistle.—2
KINGS, ch. 14.

6567. —— prevents Instruction. *Pharisees.*
[32] Since the world began was it not heard that
any man opened the eyes of one that was born
blind. [33] If this man were not of God, he could
do nothing. [34] They answered..Thou wast al-

together born in sins, and dost thou teach us? And they cast him out.—JOHN, ch. 9.

6568. —— in Numbers. *David.* [2] Go now through all the tribes of Israel, from Dan even to Beersheba, and number ye the people.. [3] And Joab said..the Lord thy God add unto the people, how many soever they be, a hundred fold, and that the eyes of my Lord the king may see *it :* but why doth my lord the king delight in this thing?—2 SAM., ch. 24.

6569. —— overreaching. *Haman.* [See No. 6557.] [8] Let the royal apparel be brought which the king *useth* to wear, and the horse that the king rideth upon, and the crown royal which is set upon his head : [9] And let this apparel and horse be delivered to the hand of one of the king's most noble princes, that they may array the man *withal* whom the king delighteth to honour, and bring him on horseback through the street of the city, and proclaim before him. —ESTHER, ch. 6.

6570. —— Peril of. *Proverb.* [18] Pride *goeth* before destruction, and a haughty spirit before a fall. [19] Better *it is to be* of an humble spirit with the lowly, than to divide the spoil with the proud.—PROV., ch. 16.

6571. —— Punishment of. *"Eat Grass."* [31] While the word *was* in the king's mouth, there fell a voice from heaven, *saying,* O king Nebuchadnezzar, to thee it is spoken ; The kingdom is departed from thee. [32] And they shall drive thee from men, and thy dwelling *shall be* with the beasts of the field : they shall make thee to eat grass as oxen.—DAN., ch. 4.

6572. —— Presumption of. *Uzziah.* [15] He made in Jerusalem engines, invented by cunning men, to be on the towers and upon the bulwarks, to shoot arrows and great stones withal. And his name spread far abroad.. [16] But when he was strong, his heart was lifted up to *his* destruction : for he..went into the temple.. to burn incense upon the altar.—2 CHRON., ch. 26.

6573. —— Profane. *Holy Vessels.* [22] O Belshazzar, hast not humbled thine heart, though thou knewest all this ; [23] But hast lifted up thyself against the Lord of heaven ; and they have brought the vessels of his house before thee, and thou and thy lords, thy wives and thy concubines, have drunk wine in them.—DAN., ch. 5.

6574. —— prevented. *Paul.* [7] Lest I should be exalted above measure through the abundance of the revelations, there was given to me a thorn in the flesh, the messenger of Satan to buffet me.—2 COR., ch. 12.

6575. —— —— *Herod.* [22] The people gave a shout, *saying, It is* the voice of a god, and not of a man. [23] And immediately the angel of the Lord smote him, because he gave not God the glory : and he was eaten of worms, and gave up the ghost.—ACTS, ch. 12.

6576. —— Poison of. *Haman.* [9] Then went Haman forth that day joyful and with a glad heart : but when Haman saw Mordecai in the king's gate, that he stood not up, nor moved for him, he was full of indignation against Mordecai.—ESTHER, ch. 5.

6577. —— Philosophic. *At Athens.* [18] Certain philosophers of the Epicureans, and of the Stoics, encountered him. And some said, What will this babbler say?—ACTS, ch. 17.

6578. —— Quarrelsome. *Proverb.* [10] Only by pride cometh contention : but with the well devised *is* wisdom.—PROV., ch. 13.

6579. —— and Revenge. *Pharaoh.* [5] The heart of Pharaoh and of his servants was turned against the people, and they said, Why have we done this, that we have let Israel go from serving us ? [6] And he made ready his chariot.—EX., ch. 14.

6580. —— in Riches. *Prince of Tyrus.* [See No. 6558.] [4] With thy wisdom and with thine understanding thou hast gotten thee..gold and silver into thy treasures : [5] By thy great wisdom *and* by thy traffick hast thou increased thy riches, and thine heart is lifted up because of thy riches.—EZEK., ch. 28.

6581. —— Religious. *Pharisee* [11] Stood and prayed thus with himself, God, I thank thee, that I am not as other men *are,* extortioners, unjust, adulterers, or even as this publican.— LUKE, ch. 18.

6582. —— of Success. *Forbidden.* [17] Thou say in thine heart, My power and the might of *mine* hand hath gotten me this wealth.. [14] Then thine heart be lifted up, and thou forget the Lord thy God, which brought thee..from the house of bondage.—DEUT., ch. 8.

6583. —— —— *Nebuchadnezzar* [30] Said, Is not this great Babylon, that I have built for the house of the kingdom by the might of my power, and for the honour of my majesty?—DAN., ch. 4.

6584. —— Self-conceit of. *Haman.* [6] Haman came in. And the king said..What shall be done unto the man whom the king delighteth to honour? Now Haman thought in his heart, To whom would the king delight to do honour more than to myself?—ESTHER, ch. 6.

6585. —— in Treasures. *Hezekiah* [13] Shewed them all..of his precious things, the silver, and the gold, and the spices, and the precious ointment, and *all* the house of his armour, and all that was found in his treasures : there was nothing..in all his dominion, that Hezekiah shewed them not.—2 KINGS, ch. 20.

6586. —— Worldly. *Israelites.* [19] The people refused to obey the voice of Samuel ; and they said, Nay ; but we will have a king over us ; [20] That we also may be like all the nations.—1 SAM., ch. 8.

6587. —— and Want. *Proverb.* [9] He that is despised, and hath a servant, *is* better than he that honoureth himself, and lacketh bread.— PROV., ch. 12.

6588. —— Wounded. *Haman.* [12] To morrow am I invited unto her also with the king. [13] Yet all this availeth me nothing, so long as I see Mordecai the Jew sitting at the king's gate.— ESTHER, ch. 5.

See other illustrations under :

SELF-CONCEIT.

Hopeless. Wise in his own conceit..more hope of　**7687**
Poverty. He that is despised and hath a servant　**7688**

SELF-CONFIDENCE.

Boasting. L. said to Gideon..too many..vaunt　**7694**
Rebuked. I will lay down my life..denied me　**7695**

SELF-RIGHTEOUSNESS.

Caution. Speak not in thine heart..my right's   7724
Corrected. Remember how thou provokedst the   7725
Failure. This man went..justified rather..other   7726
Mistake. Thou hast said..I am clean in thine   7727
Offensive. Stand by thyself ; come not..I am holier   7728
Recital. I am not as other men are, extortioners   7729
Unlawful. Walketh..after their own thoughts   7730

Conceit. All these have I kept from my youth   1461

6589. PRIEST, The chosen. *Firstborn.* ² Sanctify unto me all the firstborn, whatsoever openeth the womb among the children of Israel, *both* of man and of beast : it *is* mine.—Ex., ch. 13.

6590. —— Salaried. *Levite.* ¹⁰ Micah said.. Dwell with me, and be unto me a father and a priest, and I will give thee ten *shekels* of silver by the year, and a suit of apparel, and thy victuals. So the Levite went in.—Judges, ch. 17. [About $6 a year.]

6591. PRIESTS, Exodus of. *To Rehoboam.* ¹³ The priests and the Levites that *were* in all Israel resorted to him out of all their coasts. ¹⁴ For the Levites left their suburbs and their possession, and came to Judah and Jerusalem. —2 Chron., ch. 11.

6592. —— Temperance of. *Law.* ⁹ Do not drink wine nor strong drink, thou, nor thy sons with thee, when ye go into the tabernacle..lest ye die : *it shall be* a statute forever throughout your generations.—Lev., ch. 10.

See MINISTERS *and references.*

6593. PRINCIPLE, Policy before. *"Deal wisely."* ¹⁰ Let us deal wisely with them ; lest they multiply, and..when there falleth out any war, they join also unto our enemies, and fight against us, and *so* get them up out of the land. ¹¹ Therefore they did set over them taskmasters to afflict them with their burdens.—Ex., ch. 1.

6594. —— Without. *Persians.* ¹⁷ Whithersoever the king's commandment and his decree came, the Jews had joy and gladness, a feast and a good day. And many of the people of the land became Jews ; for the fear of the Jews fell upon them.—Esther, ch. 8.

6595. PRINCIPLES ignored. *Jews in Egypt.* ¹⁷ *Then* had we plenty of victuals, and were well, and saw no evil. ¹⁸ But since we left off to burn incense to the queen of heaven, and to pour out drink offerings unto her, we have wanted all *things*, and have been consumed by the sword and by the famine.—Jer., ch. 44.

See other illustrations under :

MOTIVE.

Labour. Labour that..we may be accepted of him   5587
Unsanctified. People spared the best..to sacrifice   5588

MOTIVES.

Inferior. Ye seek me because..did eat of the loaves   5589
Suspected. Urged him till he was ashamed..Send   5590
Worldly. Savourest not the things that be of God   5591

PRINCIPLE.

Ignored. Then had we plenty of victuals..well   6595
Policy. Let us deal wisely..lest they multiply   6593
Without. People became Jews..for fear of the J.   6594

SINCERITY.

Consecration. Josiah made a covenant..burned   8025
Evildoing. I thought I ought to..put to death   8026
Evidence. Brought their books..burned them   8027
Example. An Israelite in whom is no guile   8028

Heart. He that speaketh truth in his heart   8029
Lovable. All..have I kept..Jesus loved him   8030
Opinions. Rabbi, thou art the Son of God   8031
Positive. Thou knowest that I love thee   8032
Proof. When..people saw it..L. he is G.   8033
Reformation. Speak..the truth..execute..truth   8034

See CHARACTER *and references.*

6596. PRISON Delivery. *At Jerusalem.* ¹⁸ Laid their hands on the apostles, and put them in the common prison. ¹⁹ But the angel of the Lord by night opened the prison doors, and brought them forth, and said, ²⁰ Go, stand and speak in the temple.—Acts, ch. 5.

6597. —— emptied. *Guarding.* ²² When the officers came, and found them not in the prison, they returned.. ²³ Saying, The prison truly found we shut with all safety, and the keepers standing without before the doors : but..we found no man within.—Acts, ch. 5.

6598. —— Joy in. *At Philippi.* ²³ When they had laid many stripes upon them, they cast *them* into prison.. ²⁵ And at midnight Paul and Silas prayed, and sang praises unto God : and the prisoners heard them.—Acts, ch. 16.

6599. —— Open. *At Philippi.* [See above.] ²⁶ Suddenly there was a great earthquake, so that the foundations of the prison were shaken : and immediately all the doors were opened, and every one's bands were loosed.—Acts, ch. 16.

6600. PRISONER abused. *Jesus.* ¹⁷ They clothed him with purple, and platted a crown of thorns, and put it about his *head*, ¹⁸ And began to salute him, Hail, King of the Jews ! ¹⁹ And they smote him on the head with a reed, and did spit upon him, and bowing *their* knees worshipped him.—Mark, ch. 15.

6601. —— aided. *Peter.* ⁵ Was kept in prison : but prayer was made without ceasing of the church unto God for him.. ⁷..the angel of the Lord came upon *him*, and a light shined in the prison : and he smote Peter on the side, and raised him up, saying, Arise up quickly. And his chains fell off from *his* hands.—Acts, ch. 12.

6602. —— Alarming. *Felix.* ²⁵ As he reasoned of righteousness, temperance, and judgment to come, Felix trembled, and answered, Go thy way for this time ; when I have a convenient season, I will call for thee.—Acts, ch. 24.

6603. —— Blameless. *John.* ¹⁷ Herod himself had sent forth and laid hold upon John, and bound him in prison for Herodias' sake, his brother Philip's wife : for he had married her.—Mark, ch. 6.

**6604. —— —— ** *Peter.* ³ Because he saw it pleased the Jews, he proceeded further to take Peter also.. ⁴ And when he had apprehended him, he put *him* in prison.—Acts, ch. 12.

6605. —— Dangerous. *Samson.* ²¹ The Philistines took him, and put out his eyes, and brought him down to Gaza, and bound him with fetters of brass ; and he did grind in the prison house. ²² Howbeit the hair of his head began to grow again.—Judges, ch. 16.

6606. —— by Error. *Jeremiah.* ¹³ When he was in the gate of Benjamin, a captain of the ward *was* there, whose name *was* Irijah..and he took Jeremiah the prophet, saying, Thou fallest away to the Chaldeans.. ¹⁵ Wherefore the princes were wroth..and smote him, and put him in prison.—JER., ch. 37.

6607. —— **The first.** *Joseph .* [20] Joseph's master took him, and put him into the prison, a place where the king's prisoners *were* bound.—GEN., ch. 39.

6608. —— **outraged.** *Felix.* [26] He hoped also that money should have been given him of Paul, that he might loose him : wherefore he sent for him the oftener, and communed with him.—ACTS, ch. 24.

6609. —— **Sympathy for.** *Ebed-Melech.* [See No. 6606.] [6] In the dungeon *there was* no water, but mire : so Jeremiah sunk in the mire.. [9] My lord the king, these men have done evil in all that they have done to Jeremiah..he is like to die for hunger..for *there is* no more bread in the city.—JER., ch. 38.

6610. —— **Tenderness to.** *Ebed-Melech.* [11] So Ebed-Melech took the men with him..and took ..old cast clouts and old rotten rags, and let them down by cords into the dungeon to Jeremiah. [12] And Ebed-Melech the Ethiopian said ..Put now *these*..under thine armholes under the cords.. [13] So they drew up Jeremiah with cords.—JER., ch. 38.

See other illustrations under :

BONDS.

Broken. New ropes..Samson brake them..thread   889
Innocence. The Jews took Jesus and bound him   890
Imprisonment. Left beating Paul..bound..two c.   891
Resting in. Peter was sleeping between two soldiers   892
Strength. Bound Samson with fetters..did grind   893

BONDAGE.

Degrading. Hewers of wood and drawers of water   894
Rigorous. Get you straw..not aught..diminished   895
Unendurable. Our fathers cast out..children..not   897
Wealth. Rich young ruler was sad and went   896

CAPTIVES.

Compassion. I have heard..groaning..bondage   1022
Kindness. Gave them to eat..feeble upon asses   1024
Mercy. Shalt not smite..set bread..go   1025
Mourning. By the rivers of Babylon..we wept   1026
Return. Come to Zion with songs..joy and g.   1028
Sin. Walked in the sins of..until removed   1029
   " L. strengthened..Moab against I..done evil   1030
Songless. How shall we sing..strange land   1027
Unexpected. David and his men..wives..captives   1031
Victorious. Found a jawbone..slew 1000 men   1023

HOSTAGE.

Brother. Let one of your brethren be bound..p.   4119
Sons. Slay my two sons if I bring him not   4120

——

Labour. Samson..did grind in prison   6605

6611. PRIVACY difficult. *Jesus.* [31] Come ye yourselves apart into a desert place, and rest a while : for there were many coming and going, and they had no leisure so much as to eat. —MARK, ch. 6.

6612. —— **for Sin.** *Judas.* [4] He went his way, and communed with the chief priests and captains, how he might betray him unto them. —LUKE, ch. 22.

See other illustrations under :

CONCEALMENT.

Impossible. Thou wast with Jesus..Peter denied   1464
Unsuccessful. I was afraid, and hid myself [Adam]   1465
   " He that covereth his sins shall not   1466

HIDDEN.

Cave. Obadiah took 200 prophets, and hid..cave   3966
Field. David hid himself in the field   3967
Graciously. King commanded to take Jeremiah   3968
House of God. Joash was hid..six years   3969
Housetop. Rahab..hid them with the..flax   3970
Infant. Ark..in the flags by the river brink   3971
Strangely. Took they up stones..Jesus hid himself   3972
Wilderness. Hide thyself..ravens to feed thee   3973

HIDING.

Difficult. Moses feared..surely this is known   3974
Sinners. Adam, where art thou?..hid myself   3975
Sin. Set ye Uriah in the hottest battle..retire   3976
Talent. Received one..digged..hid..Lord's money   3977

SECRET.

Difficult. Moses looked this way and that way   4645
Impossible. Elisha telleth the king..the words   4646
Woman's. If thou utter this our business..spies   4644

6613. PRIVILEGES appreciated. *Transfiguration.* [33] As they departed from him, Peter said unto Jesus, Master, it is good for us to be here : and let us make three tabernacles ; one for thee, and one for Moses, and one for Elias.—LUKE, ch. 9.

6614. —— **Ignorance of.** *Samaritan.* [10] Jesus..said unto her, If thou knewest the gift of God, and who it is that saith to thee, Give me to drink ; thou wouldest have asked of him, and he would have given thee living water.—JOHN, ch. 4.

6615. —— **Responsibility for.** *"Twice."* [9] The Lord was angry with Solomon, because his heart was turned from the Lord God of Israel, which had appeared unto him twice, [10] And had commanded him concerning this thing, that he should not go after other gods.—1 KINGS, ch. 11.

6616. —— **reduced.** *Vision.* [1] The child Samuel ministered unto the Lord before Eli. And the word of the Lord was precious in those days ; *there was* no open vision.—1 SAM., ch. 3.

6617. —— **removed.** *Religious.* [11] Behold, the days come, saith the Lord God, that I will send a famine in the land, not a famine of bread, nor a thirst for water, but of hearing the words of the Lord.—AMOS, ch. 8.

6618. —— **unimproved.** *Fig Tree.* [7] Behold, these three years I come seeking fruit on this fig tree, and find none : cut it down ; why cumbereth it the ground?—LUKE, ch. 13.

See other illustrations under :

LIBERTY.

Choice. Father give..He divided..his living   4962
Common. Casting out devils..Forbid him not   4963
not License. Take heed lest..liberty..stumbling   4964

RIGHTS.

Affirmed. Let them come themselves and fetch us   7440
   " Take heed..this man is a Roman   7441
Belittled. Thus Esau despised his birthright   7442
Surrender. Not used this power..lest..hinder   7443

6619. PROCESSION, Sorrowful. *To Calvary.* [27] There followed him a great company of people, and of women, which also bewailed and lamented him. [28] But Jesus turning unto them, said, Daughters of Jerusalem, weep not for me, but weep for yourselves, and for your children. —LUKE, ch. 23.

6620. PROCRASTINATION of Charity. *Proverb.* [27] Withhold not good from them to whom it is due, when it is in the power of thine hand to do *it*. ²⁸ Say not unto thy neighbour, Go, and come again, and to morrow I will give ; when thou hast it by thee.—Prov., ch. 3.

6621. —— **A fatal.** *Felix.* ²⁵ As he reasoned of righteousness, temperance, and judgment to come, Felix trembled, and answered, Go thy way for this time ; when I have a convenient season, I will call for thee. ²⁶ He hoped also that money should have been given him of Paul, that he might loose him.—Acts, ch. 24.

6622. —— **Folly of.** *Virgins.* ⁸ The foolish said unto the wise, Give us of your oil ; for our lamps are gone out.—Mat., ch. 25.

6623. —— **Loss by.** *At Athens.* ³² When they heard of the resurrection of the dead, some mocked : and others said, We will hear thee again of this *matter*. ³³ So Paul departed from among them.—Acts, ch. 17.

6624. —— **No.** *" Bury the Dead."* ²¹ Another of his disciples said..Lord, suffer me first to go and bury my father. ²² But Jesus said.. Follow me ; and let the dead bury their dead.— Mat., ch. 8.

See other illustrations under :

EASE.

Care for. Trouble me not..in bed, I cannot arise 2586
Indifference. If ye offer the lame and sick is it not 2587
Promised. Soul, thou hast much goods..take thine 2588
Religious. Woe unto them that are at ease in Zion 2589

HESITATION.

Discipleship. I will follow thee, but 3964
Punished. Fire of the L. burnt..uttermost parts 3965

WAITING.

Calamity. Jonah sat..see what would..city 9262
Eager. My soul waiteth..watch for the morning 9263
in Faith. Tell the stars..so shall thy seed be 9264
on God. Renew their strength..as eagles 9265
Patient. After one year, G. spake to Noah, Go forth 9267
for Power. Not depart from Jerusalem, but wait 9268
Rewarded. Simeon..waiting for the consolation 9269
Vigilant. Let your loins be girt..lights burning 9270
Weariness. Let me see the king's face..kill me 9271
Watching. When the fowls came..Abram drove 9272
for Work. When forty years were expired 9273

Inexplicable. Neither hast thou delivered thy p. 2336
Sad. Pilate sought to release..delivered he him 4662
See **DELAY** and references.

6625. PRODIGALITY, Ruin from. *Younger Son.* ¹³ Took his journey into a far country, and there wasted his substance with riotous living. ¹⁴ And when he had spent all, there arose a mighty famine..and he began to be in want. —Luke, ch. 15.

Also see :
Extravagance. Ask me..I will give it..head of J. 2832

6626. PROFANATION of the Sanctuary. *Money Making.* [On Jesus' first visit,] ¹⁴ Found in the temple those that sold oxen, and sheep, and doves, and the changers of money, sitting : ¹⁵ And when he had made a scourge of small cords, he drove them all out..and poured out the changers' money, and overthrew the tables : ¹⁶ And said..make not my Father's house an house of merchandise.—John, ch. 2.

6627. —— —— *His Last Visit.* ¹² Jesus went into the temple of God, and cast out all them that sold and bought in the temple, and

overthrew the tables of the money changers, and the seats of them that sold doves, ¹³ And said..It is written, My house shall be called the house of prayer ; but ye have made it a den of thieves.—Mat., ch. 21.

See other illustrations under :

BLASPHEMY.

Accused of. We stone thee not, but for blasphemy 801
Evidence of. High priest rent his clothes..spoken 802
Forbidden. Thou shalt not take the name..vain 803
Greatest. Word against the Son of man..be forgiven 804
Heedless. As the L. liveth, I will..take something 805
Habit. Stephen ceaseth not to speak blasphemous 806
Murdered. He ought to die..made himself the Son 807
No. Why..speak blasphemies?..Who can forgive 808
Punishment. All that heard laid their hands..head 809
Strange. Peter began to curse and swear 810
Unpardonable. Blasphemy against the H. G..not 811

DESECRATION.

Bribery. Ahaz took..out of the house of the L. 2204
Removed. I cast forth all the household stuff 2205
Sacrilegious. That his..concubines might drink t. 2206

SACRILEGE.

Presumptuous. They brought the golden vessels 7544
Priestly. Men abhorred the offering of the L. 7545
Unintended. Uzzah put forth his hand..ark 7546

6628. PROFITS forgotten. *Peter.* ⁸ When Simon Peter saw *it*, he fell down at Jesus' knees, saying, Depart from me ; for I am a sinful man, O Lord. ⁹ For he was astonished..at the draught of the fishes.—Luke, ch. 5.

6629. PROFESSION only. *Lord, Lord!* ²¹ Not every one that saith unto me, Lord, Lord, shall enter into the kingdom of heaven ; but he that doeth the will of my Father.. ²² Many will say to me in that day, Lord, Lord, have we not prophesied in thy name?.. ²³ And then will I profess unto them, I never knew you : depart from me, ye that work iniquity.—Mat., ch. 7.

6630. —— **Worthless.** *" Went not."* ²⁸ A *certain* man had two sons ; and he came to the first, and said, Son, go work to day in my vineyard. ²⁹ He answered..I will not ; but afterward he repented, and went. ³⁰..the second.. said, I *go* sir ; and went not. ³¹ Whether of them twain did the will of *his* father?—Mat., ch. 21.

Also see :
Pretence. For a pretence make long prayers 6548

6631. PROGRESS, Christian. *" Shineth."* ¹⁸ The path of the just *is* as the shining light, that shineth more and more unto the perfect day. ¹² The way of the wicked *is* as darkness : they know not at what they stumble.—Prov., ch. 4.

6632. —— **hindered.** *Egyptians.* ²⁴ The Lord looked..through the pillar of fire and of the cloud, and troubled the host of the Egyptians, ²⁶ And took off their chariot wheels, that they drave them heavily : so that the Egyptians said, Let us flee from the face of Israel ; for the Lord fighteth for them.—Ex., ch. 14.

6633. —— **Time for.** *" Sound of a Going."* ²⁴ When thou hearest the sound of a going in the tops of the mulberry trees, that then thou shalt bestir thyself : for then shall the Lord go out before thee, to smite the host of the Philistines.—2 Sam., ch. 5.

6634. PROGRESSION, Spiritual. *"Again."*
[24] He looked up, and said, I see men as trees,
walking. [25] After that he put *his* hands again
upon his eyes, and made him look up ; and he
was restored, and saw every man clearly. —
MARK, ch. 8.

See other illustrations under :

ADVANCE.

Faith. Go forward..but lift thou up the rod	119
Signal. When thou hearest a sound..trees	120
" If they say..we will go up	121

IMPROVEMENT.

Adversity. God has furnished us less..deserved	4363
Accountability. Whosoever hath [improved] to h.	4365
Necessary. These three years I come seeking f.	4366
Responsibility. Cast ye the unprofitable servant	4367

See PROMOTION.

6635. PROHIBITION of Blood. *Law.* [14] The
blood of it *is* for the life thereof : therefore..
Ye shall eat the blood of no manner of flesh..
whosoever eateth it shall be cut off.—LEV., ch.
17.

6636. —— of Fruit. *Paradise.* [11] Hast thou
eaten of the tree, whereof I commanded thee
that thou shouldest not eat? [12] And the man
said, The woman..she gave me of the tree, and
I did eat.—GEN., ch. 3.

6637. —— of Flesh. *Law.* [2] These *are* the
beasts which ye shall eat.. [3] Whatsoever parteth the hoof, and is clovenfooted, *and* cheweth
the cud, among the beasts, that shall ye eat.—
LEV., ch. 11. [See chapter.]

6638. —— of Fat. *Law.* [23] Speak unto the
children of Israel, saying, Ye shall eat no manner of fat, of ox, or of sheep, or of goat.—LEV.,
ch. 7.

See ABSTINENCE and references.

6639. PROMISE, The great. *At Ascension.*
[49] Behold, I send the promise of my Father upon
you : but tarry ye in the city of Jerusalem, until ye be endued with power from on high.—
LUKE, ch. 24.

6640. —— A royal. *Ahasuerus.* [2] The king
said..on the second day at the banquet of wine,
What *is* thy petition, queen Esther? and it shall
be granted thee : and what *is* thy request? and
it shall be performed, *even* to the half of the
kingdom.—ESTHER, ch. 7.

6641. —— —— *Herod.* [23] He sware unto
her, Whatsoever thou shalt ask of me, I will
give *it* thee, unto the half of my kingdom.
[24] And she..said unto her mother, What shall I
ask? And she said, The head of John the Baptist.—MARK, ch. 6.

6642. —— regretted, A. *Herod.* [26] The king
was exceeding sorry, *yet* for his oath's sake, and
for their sakes which sat with him, he would
not reject her.—MARK, ch. 6.

6643. PROMISES broken. *Pharaoh.* [8] Intreat the Lord, that he may take away the frogs
..and I will let the people go, that they may do
sacrifice unto the Lord.. [15] But when Pharaoh
saw that there was respite, he hardened his
heart, and hearkened not unto them.—EX., ch. 8.

6644. —— —— *Pharaoh.* [28] Intreat the
Lord (for *it is* enough) that there be no *more*
mighty thunderings and hail : and I will let you
go, and ye shall stay no longer.. [34] And when

Pharaoh saw that the rain and the hail and the
thunders were ceased, he sinned yet more, and
hardened his heart.—EX., ch. 9.

6645. —— —— *Pharaoh.* [15] There remained
not any green thing in the trees, or in the herbs
of the field.. [16] Then Pharaoh called for Moses
and Aaron in haste ; and he said, I have sinned..
[35] And the heart of Pharaoh was hardened,
neither would he let the children of Israel go.—
EX., ch. 9.

6646. —— —— Parable. [28] A *certain* man
had two sons ; and he came to the first, and
said, Son, go work to day in my vineyard. [29] He
..said, I will not ; but afterward he repented,
and went. [30] And..the second..said, I *go*, sir ;
and went not.—MAT., ch. 21.

See other illustrations under :

ASSURANCE.

Believers. I know that my Redeemer liveth	557
Full. Neither death nor life..separate us	558
Heavenly. If our earthly house be dissolved	559
Inferential. If to kill us..would not receive	560
Impudent. Bramble said..put your trust in my	561
Personal. I know..he is able to keep	562
Victor's. Who shall separate us from..love of C.	563

BARGAIN.

Bad. Feed me..sold his birthright	640
Tricks. It is naught, saith the buyer..boasteth	641

See COVENANT and references.

6647. PROMOTION avoided. *Saul.* [22] Behold,
he hath hid himself among the stuff. [23] And
they ran and fetched him thence : and..he was
higher than any of the people from his shoulders and upward. [24] And Samuel said..See ye
him whom the Lord hath chosen, that *there is*
none like him?.. And all the people shouted,
and said, God save the king.—1 SAM., ch. 10.

6648. —— desirable. *Guest.* [10] Sit down in
the lowest room ; that when he that bade thee
cometh, he may say unto thee, Friend, go up
higher : then shalt thou have worship in the
presence of them that sit at meat with thee.—
LUKE, ch. 14.

6649. —— envied. *Daniel's.* [4] Then the
presidents and princes sought to find occasion
against Daniel concerning the kingdom ; but
they could find none occasion nor fault ; forasmuch as he *was* faithful.—DAN., ch. 6.

6650. —— Eagerness for. *Daniel's.* [18] Then
said the priest..What do ye? [19] ..Hold thy
peace, lay thine hand upon thy mouth, and go
with us, and be to us a father and a priest : *is it*
better for thee to be a priest unto the house of
one man, or that thou be a priest unto a tribe?
—JUDGES, ch. 19.

6651. —— Honourable. *Proverb.* [6] Put not
forth thyself in the presence of the king, and
stand not in the place of great men : [7] For better
it is that it be said unto thee, come up hither ;
than that thou shouldest be put lower in the
presence of the prince whom thine eyes have
seen.—PROV., ch. 25.

6652. —— by Merit. *Daniel.* [8] Daniel was
preferred above the presidents and princes, because an excellent spirit *was* in him ; and the
king thought to set him over the whole realm.—
DAN., ch. 6.

6653. —— Means of. *Humility.* [See No.
6648.]

6654. —— **Piety brings.** *Joseph.* [See No. 6661.]

6655. —— **requested.** *James and John.* [37] Grant unto us that we may sit, one on thy right hand, and the other on thy left hand, in thy glory. [38] But Jesus said..Ye know not what ye ask.—MARK, ch. 10.

6656. —— **sought.** *Diotrephes.* [9] Diotrephes, who loveth to have the preeminence among them, receiveth us not. [10] Wherefore, if I come, I will remember his deeds which he doeth, prating against us with malicious words. 3. JOHN,

6657. —— —— *Eden.* [4] The serpent said unto the woman, Ye shall not surely die : [5] For God doth know that in the day ye eat thereof, then your eyes shall be opened, and ye shall be as gods, knowing good and evil.—GEN., ch. 3.

6658. —— **unsought.** *David.* [11] There remaineth yet the youngest.. he keepeth the sheep. And Samuel said unto Jesse, Send and fetch him.. [12] ..he *was* ruddy, *and* withal of a beautiful countenance, and goodly to look to. And the Lord said, Arise, anoint him ; for this *is* he.—1 SAM., ch. 16.

6659. —— **Unsatisfying.** *Haman.* [11] Haman told them of the glory of his riches, and the multitude of his children, and all *the things* wherein the king had promoted him, and how he had advanced him above the princes.. [12] ..to morrow am I invited unto her also with the king. [13] Yet all this availeth me nothing, so long as I see Mordecai the Jew sitting at the king's gate.—ESTHER, ch. 5.

6660. —— —— *Levites.* [8] And Moses said unto Korah.. [9] *Seemeth it but* a small thing unto you, that the God of Israel hath separated you from the congregation..to bring you near to himself to do the service of the tabernacle..and to stand before the congregation to minister unto them ? [10] ..and seek ye the priesthood also ?—NUM., ch. 16.

6661. —— **A worthy.** *Joseph.* [38] Pharaoh said unto his servants, Can we find *such a one* as this *is*, a man in whom the Spirit of God *is ?* [40] Thou shalt be over my house, and according unto thy word shall all my people be ruled : only in the throne will I be greater than thou. —GEN., ch. 41.

See other illustrations under :

GROWTH.

Beautiful. Soul shall be as a well watered garden	3739
Continuous. Flourish like the palm tree..fruit in	3740
Christian. Your faith groweth exceedingly	3741
Divine. Jesus increased in wisdom and stature	3742
Esteem. Samuel grew..in favour with G. and man	3743
Fruit. Branch that beareth not he taketh away	3744
Grace. Like a tree planted by the rivers of water	3745
Imperceptible. First the blade, then the ear..corn	3746
Inward. Leaven..meal till the whole was leavened	3747
Outward. Becometh greater than all herbs	3748
Perfection. Path..shineth more and more perfect	3749
Stages. Blade..ear..full corn in the ear	3750
Strength. Clean hands shall be stronger and S.	3751
Spiritual. Child [J. B.]..grew and waxed strong	3752

IMPROVEMENT.

Adversity. God has punished us less..deserved	4363
Accountability. Whosoever hath [improved] to	4365
Necessary. These three years I come seeking	4366
Responsibility. Cast ye the unprofitable servant	4367

POSITION.

Love. Love..the highest seats in the synagogues	2284
Gift. To sit on my right hand..not mine to give	2285
Petition. We may sit one on thy right hand	2286

PROGRESS.

Christian. Path..shineth more and more	6631
Hindered. Chariot wheels..they drave them heavily	6632
Time for. When thou hearest a sound..trees	6633
Spiritual. See men as trees..saw clearly	6634

Brief. Haman told how the the king had p.   6561

6662. PROOF in Deeds. *Jesus.* [37] If I do not the works of my Father, believe me not. [38] But if I do, though ye believe not me, believe the works ; that ye may know, and believe, that the Father *is* in me, and I in him.—JOHN, ch. 10.

6663. —— **of Strength.** *Conquest.* [14] The children of Joseph spake..Why hast thou given me but..one portion to inherit, seeing I *am* a great people.. [15] And Joshua answered them, If thou *be* a great people, *then* get thee up to the wood *country*, and cut down for thyself there in the land of the Perizzites and of the giants, if mount Ephraim be too narrow for thee.—JOSH., ch. 17.

6664. —— **by Trial.** *Young Hebrews.* [12] Prove thy servants, I beseech thee, ten days ; and let them give us pulse to eat, and water to drink. [13] Then let our countenances be looked upon before thee, and the countenance of the children that eat of the portion of the king's meat : and as thou seest, deal with thy servants.—DAN., ch. 1.

Also see :

Identification. Upon whom..the S. descending   4269
Indisputable. When they saw the boldness of P. and 883

See EVIDENCE and references.

See WITNESS and TESTIMONY.

6665. PROPERTY, Confiscation of. *Haman's.* [7] The king Ahasuerus said..I have given Esther the house of Haman, and him they have hanged upon the gallows, because he laid his hand upon the Jews.—ESTHER, ch. 8.

6666. —— **Life more than.** *Dives.* [15] Take heed, and beware of covetousness : for a man's life consisteth not in the abundance of the things which he possesseth. [16] And he spake a parable..saying, The ground of a certain rich man brought forth plentifully.—LUKE, ch. 12.

6667. —— **Restoration of.** *The Shunammite.* [3] At the seven years' end..the woman returned out of the land of the Philistines : and she went forth to cry unto the king for her house and for her land. [6] ..So the king appointed..Restore all that *was* hers, and all the fruits of the field since the day that she left the land, even until now.—2 KINGS, ch. 8.

6668. —— **Surrender of.** *Christians.* [32] The multitude of them that believed were of one heart and of one soul : neither said any..that aught of the things which he possessed was his own ; but they had all things common.—ACTS, ch. 4.

6669. —— **Selfish Use of.** *Dives.* [17] He thought within himself, saying, What shall I do, because I have no room where to bestow my fruits ? [18] ..I will pull down my barns, and build greater ; and there will I bestow all my fruits and my goods. [19] And I will say to my soul, Soul, thou hast much goods laid up for many years ; take thine ease, eat, drink, *and* be merry.—LUKE, ch. 12.

6670. —— **Transfer of.** *Laban's.* [1] He heard the words of Laban's sons, saying, Jacob hath taken away all that *was* our father's ; and of *that* which *was* our father's hath he gotten all this glory.—GEN., ch. 31.

6671. —— **by Violence.** *Parable.* [38] When the husbandmen saw the son, they said among themselves, This is the heir ; come, let us kill him, and let us seize on his inheritance. [39] And they caught him, and cast *him* out of the vineyard, and slew *him.*—MAT., ch. 21.

Also see :

Estate. Speak..that he divide the inheritance　2724
Possession. Every place..your foot shall tread u.　6287
　　See MONEY, RICHES, WEALTH.

6672. PROPHECY, Gift of. *Seventy Elders.* [25] The Lord came down in a cloud..and took of the spirit that *was* upon him, and gave *it* unto the seventy elders : and..when the spirit rested upon them, they prophesied.—NUM., ch. 11.

6673. —— **Involuntary.** *King Saul.* [23] The Spirit of God was upon him also, and he went on, and prophesied, until he came to Naioth in Ramah. [24] And he stripped off his clothes also, and prophesied before Samuel in like manner, and lay down naked all that day and all that night. Wherefore they say, *Is* Saul also among the prophets?—1 SAM., ch. 19.

6674. —— **Revival by.** *Vision.* [7] As I prophesied, there was a noise, and behold a shaking, and the bones came together, bone to his bone. [8]..the sinews and the flesh came up upon them, and the skin covered them above : but *there was* no breath in them. [9] Then said he unto me, Prophesy unto the wind.—EZEK., ch. 37.

6675. —— **Spiritual.** *Pentecost.* [15] For these are not drunken, as ye suppose, seeing it is *but* the third hour of the day. [16] But this is that which was spoken by the prophet Joel ; [17]..in the last days, saith God, I will pour out of my Spirit upon all flesh : and your sons and your daughters shall prophesy.—ACTS, ch. 2.

See other illustrations under :

WARNING.

Additional. Lazarus..send him..I have five　9340
Destruction. [Scorners] I also will laugh at your.　9317
Dream. Have nothing to do with that just man　9318
Dangers. Beware thou hast not such a place　9319
Despised. Get you out of this place..secured　9320
Disobedience. If thine heart turn away..surely　9321
Doubted. Before the cock crow, thou shalt deny　9322
Example. Sodom and G. are set for an example　9323
　"　Remember Lot's wife　9324
Experience. Alexander..did me much harm　9325
Faithful. Three years I ceased not to warn every　9326
Heedless. Sword come..blood on his own head　9327
Heeded. Noah being warned of God..prepared　9328
Historical. These things were our examples　9329
　"　Did not Solomon..sin by these things　9330
Ignored. Abner said, Turn thee aside to thy r.　9331
Punishment. [Leprosy] Remember what the L.　9332
Preserved. Angel..Joseph..Herod will seek the c.　9333
Repeated. Moses..go down and charge the p.　9334
Saved. He that heareth warning shall deliver..soul　9336
Solemn. All ye shalt be offended..me this night　9337
Sorrowful. One of you shall betray me　9338

6676. PROPITIATION, A vain. *Return of Ark.* [4] Then said they, What *shall be* the trespass offering which we shall return to him ? They answered, Five golden emerods, and five golden mice, *according to* the number of the lords of the Philistines : for one plague *was* on you all, and on your lords.—1 SAM., ch. 6.

See other illustrations under :

ATONEMENT.

Accepted. L. had respect unto Abel　571
Blood. It is the blood that maketh atonement　572
Death. Aaron stood between the dead..living　573
Justice. His head shall be thrown to thee　574
Omitted. Cain brought of the fruit of the ground　575

RECONCILIATION.

Noble. Esau ran to meet him and embraced　6905
Strange. The same day Pilate and Herod were　6906
Worship. Leave there thy gifts..first be reconciled 6907

Gifts. Jacob's present..unto my lord Esau　5940

6677. PROSPERITY with Adversity. *In Egypt.* [10] Let us deal wisely with them ; lest they multiply, and..when there falleth out any war, they join also unto our enemies and..*so* get them up out of the land. [11] Therefore they did set over them taskmasters to afflict them.. [12] But the more they afflicted them, the more they multiplied and grew.—EX., ch. 1.

6678. —— **Apostasy by.** *Jeshurun.* [15] Jeshurun waxed fat, and kicked..then he forsook God *which* made him, and lightly esteemed the Rock of his salvation.—DEUT., ch. 32.

6679. —— **with the Bible.** *To Joshua.* [8] This book of the law shall not depart out of thy mouth ; but thou shalt meditate therein day and night, that thou mayest observe to do according to all that is written therein : for then thou shalt make thy way prosperous, and then thou shalt have good success.—JOSH., ch. 1.

6680. —— **Displeasure from.** *Enemies.* [10] When Sanballat the Horonite, and Tobiah the servant, the Ammonite, heard *of it*, it grieved them exceedingly that there was come a man to seek the welfare of the children of Israel.—NEH., ch. 2.

6681. —— **dedicated.** *David.* [10] Joram brought with him vessels of silver, and vessels of gold, and vessels of brass : [11] Which also king David did dedicate unto the Lord, with the silver and gold that he had dedicated of all nations which he subdued.—2 SAM., ch. 8.

6682. —— **destruction of.** *Aged Moses.* [15] If thou wilt not hearken..to do all his commandments..that all these curses shall come upon thee.. [16] Cursed *shalt* thou *be* in the city, and cursed *shalt* thou *be* in the field. [17] Cursed *shall be* thy basket and thy store.—DEUT., ch. 28. [See chapter.]

6683. —— **Dangers of.** *Pride.* [13] When thy herds and thy flocks multiply, and thy silver and thy gold is multiplied, and all that thou hast is multiplied ; [14] Then thine heart be lifted up, and thou forget the Lord thy God, which brought thee..from the house of bondage.—DEUT., ch. 8.

6684. —— —— *Uzziah.* [15] As long as he sought the Lord, God made him to prosper. [16] But when he was strong, his heart was lifted up to *his* destruction : for he transgressed..and went into the temple of the Lord to burn incense upon the altar.—2 CHRON., ch. 26.

6685. —— **A delusive.** *Rich Fool.* [See No. 6703.] [20] God said.. *Thou* fool, this night thy soul shall be required of thee : then whose shall those things be, which thou hast provided ? [21] So *is* he that layeth up treasure for himself, and is not rich toward God.—LUKE, ch. 12.

6686. —— **envied.** *Isaac.* [14] He had possession of the flocks, and possession of herds, and great store of servants : and the Philistines envied him. [15] For all the wells which his father's servants had digged in the days of Abraham his father, the Philistines had stopped them, and filled them with earth.—GEN., ch. 26.

6687. —— **A false.** *Sinners.* [3] I was envious of the foolish, *when* I saw the prosperity of the wicked. [4] For *there are* no bands in their death : but their strength *is* firm. [5] They *are* not in trouble *as other* men ; neither are they plagued like *other* men. [7] Their eyes stand out with fatness : they have more than heart could wish.—Ps. 73.

6688. —— **Improvement of.** *King Asa* [7] Said unto Judah, Let us build these cities, and make.. walls and towers, gates and bars, *while* the land *is* yet before us; because we have sought the Lord our God.. and he hath given us rest on every side. So they built and prospered. —2 CHRON., ch. 14.

6689. —— —— *Solomon.* [4] My God hath given me rest on every side, *so that there is* neither adversity nor evil occurrent. [5] And, behold, I purpose to build a house unto the name of the Lord.—1 KINGS, ch. 5.

6690. —— **by Obedience.** *Moses said,* [1] All these blessings shall come on thee, and overtake thee, if thou shalt hearken unto the voice of the Lord thy God.. [3] Blessed *shalt* thou *be* in the city, and blessed *shalt* thou *be* in the field. —DEUT., ch. 28. [See chapter.]

6691. —— —— *Aged Joshua said,* [15] As all good things are come upon you, which the Lord your God promised you; so shall the Lord bring upon you all evil things, until he have destroyed you from off this good land which the Lord your God hath given you.—JOSH., ch. 23.

6692. —— **Piety favours.** *Abram.* [2] Abram *was* very rich in cattle, in silver, and in gold.— GEN., ch. 13.

6693. —— —— *King Jotham.* [3] He built the high gate of the house of the Lord, and on the wall of Ophel he built much. [4] Moreover he built cities in the mountains of Judah, and in the forests he built castles and towers.. [6] So Jotham became mighty, because he prepared his ways before the Lord.—2 CHRON., ch. 27.

6694. —— —— *Isaac.* [12] Isaac sowed in that land, and received in the same year a hundredfold : and the Lord blessed him. [13] And the man waxed great, and went forward, and grew until he became very great : [14] For he had possession of flocks, and.. herds, and great store of servants.—GEN., ch. 26.

6695. —— —— *Joseph.* [2] The Lord was with Joseph, and he was a prosperous man ; and he was in the house of his master the Egyptian. —GEN., ch. 39.

6696. —— —— *Obed-edom.* [11] The ark of the Lord continued in the house of Obed-edom the Gittite three months : and the Lord blessed Obed-edom, and all his household.—2 SAM., ch. 6.

6697. —— —— *King Uzziah.* [9] He did that *which was* right in the sight of the Lord.. [5] And he sought God in the days of Zechariah, who had understanding in the visions of God : and as long as he sought the Lord, God made him to prosper.—2 CHRON., ch. 26.

6698. —— —— *Job.* [9] Satan answered the Lord.. Doth Job fear God for nought ? [10] Hast not thou made a hedge about him, and about his house, and about all that he hath on every side ? thou hast blessed the work of his hands, and his substance is increased in the land.— JOB, ch. 1.

6699. —— —— *Solomon.* [21] All king Solomon's drinking vessels *were of* gold, and all the vessels of the house of the forest of Lebanon *were of* pure gold ; none *were of* silver : it was nothing accounted of in the days of Solomon.. [22] For the kings had at sea a navy of Tharshish with the navy of Hiram : once in three years came the navy of Tharshish, bringing gold, and silver, ivory, and apes, and peacocks. [23] So king Solomon exceeded all the kings of the earth for riches and for wisdom.—1 KINGS, ch. 10.

6700. —— **Reflections in.** *" Ark of God."* [1] When the king sat in his house, and the Lord had given him rest round about from all his enemies ; [2] That the king said unto Nathan the prophet, See now, I dwell in a house of cedar, but the ark of God dwelleth within curtains.— 2 SAM., ch. 7.

6701. —— **A secure.** *Balaam said,* [7] The king of Moab hath brought me from Aram, out of the mountains of the east, *saying,* Come, curse me Jacob, and come, defy Israel. [8] How shall I curse, *whom* God hath not cursed ? or how shall I defy, *whom* the Lord hath not defied ?—NUM., ch. 23.

6702. —— **Strife with.** *Lot.* [6] The land was not able to bear them, that they might dwell together : for their substance was great.. [7] And there was a strife between the herdmen of Abram's cattle and.. of Lot's cattle.—GEN., ch. 13.

6703. —— **Selfishness in.** *Rich Fool.* [17] What shall I do, because I have no room where to bestow my fruits ? [18] And he said.. I will pull down my barns, and build greater.. [19] And I will say to my soul, Soul, thou hast much goods laid up for many years ; take thine ease, eat, drink, *and* be merry.—LUKE, ch. 12.

6704. —— **Trouble from.** *Rich Fool.* [See No. 6703.]

See other illustrations under :

Church. Walking in the fear.. multiplied   1300
Forsaken. Oxen.. asses.. sheep.. camels.. sons   148
Mysterious. The more they afflicted.. more grew   6676
Returned. Job had sheep.. camels   150
Past. Then were we well, and saw no evil   5775
    See **HAPPINESS, SUCCESS, RICHES, WEALTH.**

6705. PROSTRATION, Involuntary. *Gethsemane.* [3] Judas then, having received a band *of men* and officers.. cometh thither with lanterns and torches and weapons.. [6] As soon then as he had said unto them, I am *he*, they went backward, and fell to the ground.—JOHN, ch. 18.

6706. —— A Sinner's. *Saul.* ³ Near Damascus : and suddenly there shined round about him a light from heaven : ⁴ And he fell to the earth, and heard a voice saying..Saul, Saul, why persecutest thou me ?—ACTS, ch. 9.

6707. —— from Terror. *King Saul.* [Said the ghost of Samuel,] ¹⁹ To morrow *shalt* thou and thy sons *be* with me : the Lord also shall deliver the host of Israel into the hand of the Philistines. ²⁰ Then Saul fell..on the earth, and was sore afraid, because of the words of Samuel : and there was no strength in him ; for he had eaten no bread all the day, nor all the night.— 1 SAM., ch. 28.

See other illustrations under :

REVERENCE.

Commends. Peter fell down at Jesus' knees   7321
Joyous. Came a fire..people shouted and fell   7323
Manifested. Joshua fell on his face..did worship   7324
Youthful. [Young ruler] came running, and   7331

6708. PROTECTION by Art. *Canaanites.* ¹⁹ Judah..could not drive out the inhabitants of the valley, because they had chariots of iron.— JUDGES, ch. 1.

6709. —— by Alliance. *Abiathar.* ²¹ Abiathar shewed David that Saul had slain the Lord's priests. ²² And David said..I knew..when Doeg the Edomite *was* there, that he would surely tell Saul : I have occasioned *the death* of all the persons of thy father's house. ²³ Abide thou with me, fear not : for he that seeketh my life seeketh thy life : but with me thou *shalt be* in safeguard.—1 SAM., ch. 22.

6710. —— by Blood. *Passover.* ¹³ The blood shall be to you for a token upon the houses where ye *are :* and when I see the blood, I will pass over you, and the plague shall not be upon you to destroy *you*, when I smite the land of Egypt.—EX., ch. 12.

6711. —— Constant. *Israel.* ¹ I have redeemed thee, I have called *thee* by thy name ; thou *art* mine. ² When thou passest through the waters, I *will be* with thee ; and through the rivers, they shall not overflow thee : when thou walkest through the fire, thou shalt not be burned.—ISA., ch. 43.

6712. —— Defensive. *Hedge.* ⁹ Then Satan answered the Lord..Doth Job fear God for nought ? ¹⁰ Hast not thou made a hedge about him, and about his house, and about all that he hath on every side ?—JOB, ch. 1.

6713. —— in Duty. *Prophet.* ⁴ When king Jeroboam heard..the man of God, which had cried against the altar in Beth-el..he put forth his hand from the altar, saying, Lay hold on him. And his hand..dried up, so that he could not pull it in again to him.—1 KINGS, ch. 13.

6714. —— Divine. *Elijah.* ⁹ The king sent unto him a captain of fifty with his fifty..and he spake..Thou man of God, the king hath said, Come down. ¹⁰ And Elijah answered..If I *be* a man of God,then let fire come down from heaven, and consume thee and thy fifty..consumed him and his fifty.—2 KINGS, ch. 1.

6715. —— —— From Syrians. ¹⁶ Fear not : for they that *be* with us *are* more than they that be with them. ¹⁷ And Elisha prayed..And the Lord opened the eyes of the young man ; and he saw : and, behold, the mountain was full of horses and chariots of fire round about Elisha. —2 KINGS, ch. 6.

6716. —— —— Jacob's Dream. ¹⁵ I *am* with thee, and will keep thee in all *places* whither thou goest, and will bring thee again into this land ; for I will not leave thee.—GEN., ch. 28.

6717. —— —— From Lions. ²¹ Then said Daniel..O king, live for ever. ²² My God hath sent his angel, and hath shut the lions' mouths, that they have not hurt me : forasmuch as..innocency was found in me.—DAN., ch. 6.

6718. —— —— From Fire. ²⁷ The princes, governors, and captains, and the king's counsellors..saw these men, upon whose bodies the fire had no power, nor was a hair of their head singed, neither were their coats changed, nor the smell of fire had passed on them.—DAN., ch. 3.

6719. —— —— Happy. ⁴ He shall cover thee with his feathers, and under his wings shalt thou trust : his truth *shall be thy* shield and buckler. ⁵ Thou shalt not be afraid for the terror by night ; *nor* for the arrow *that* flieth by day. Ps. 91.

6720. —— —— Shield. ¹ The word of the Lord came unto Abram in a vision, saying, Fear not, Abram : I *am* thy shield, *and* thy exceeding great reward.—GEN., ch. 15.

6721. —— —— Proverb. ¹⁰ The name of the Lord *is* a strong tower : the righteous runneth into it, and is safe.—PROV., ch. 18.

6722. —— —— Laban said, ²⁷ Wherefore didst thou flee away secretly..and didst not tell me, that I might have sent thee away with mirth, and with songs, with tabret, and with harp ? ²⁹ It is in the power of my hand to do you hurt : but the God of your father spake unto me yesternight, saying, Take thou heed that thou speak not to Jacob, either good or bad.—GEN., ch. 31.

6723. —— Intervening. *Cloud.* ²⁰ It came between the camp of the Egyptians and the camp of Israel ; and it was a cloud and darkness *to them*, but it gave light by night *to these :* so that the one came not near the other all the night.—EX., ch. 14.

6724. —— of the Obedient. *Feasts.* ²⁴ Neither shall any man desire thy land, when thou shalt go up to appear before the Lord thy God thrice in the year.—EX., ch. 34.

6725. —— Promised. *In Battle.* ¹ When thou goest out to battle against thine enemies, and seest horses, and chariots, *and* a people more than thou, be not afraid of them : for the Lord thy God *is* with thee.—DEUT., ch. 20.

6726. —— Remarkable. *Cloud.* ³⁷ He brought them forth also with silver and gold : and *there was* not one feeble *person* among their tribes. ³⁹ He spread a cloud for a covering ; and fire to give light in the night.—Ps. 105.

6727. —— of Saints. *Angelic.* [Also see No. 6715.] ¹³ Behold, *he is* in Dothan. ¹⁴ Therefore sent he thither horses, and chariots, and a great host : and they came by night, and compassed the city about.—2 KINGS, ch. 6.

6728. —— **Tender.** *Jesus said,* ³⁷ O Jerusalem, Jerusalem, *thou* that killest the prophets, and stonest them which are sent unto thee, how often would I have gathered thy children together, even as a hen gathereth her chickens under *her* wings, and ye would not!—Mat., ch. 23.

6729. —— **Trust in.** *Daniel.* ¹⁶ We *are* not careful to answer thee in this matter. ⁴⁷ If it be *so,* our God whom we serve is able to deliver us from the burning fiery furnace, and he will deliver *us* out of thine hand, O king.—Dan., ch. 3.

6730. —— **A vain.** *Goliath.* ⁵ He had a helmet of brass upon his head, and he *was* armed with a coat of mail; and the weight of the coat *was* five thousand shekels of brass. ⁶ And *he had* greaves of brass upon his legs, and a target of brass between his shoulders.—1 Sam., ch. 17.

See other illustrations under:

REFUGE.

Christian's. His children shall have a place of r.   6940
Cities. Appoint..for you cities of refuge   6941
Fearless. G. is one refuge..present help   6942
Faith's. When my father and my mother forsake   6443
Fleeing. Flee unto one of those cities   6444
Lord. Hezekiah prayed..angel smote   6445
Safe. Name of the L. is a strong tower   6446
Sanctuary. Adonijah..caught hold..altar   6447

Divine. Thou shalt hide them in the secret p.   1525
See DELIVERANCE and references.

6731. PROTEST unheeded. *Samuel's.* ¹¹ This will be the manner of the king that shall reign over you: He will take your sons..for his chariots, and *to be* his horsemen; and *some* shall run before his chariots.. ¹⁹ Nevertheless, the people refused to obey the voice of Samuel; and they said, Nay; but we will have a king over us; ²⁰ That we also may be like all the nations.—1 Sam., ch. 8.

6732. PROVIDENCE in Affliction. *Hagar.* ¹⁷ What aileth thee, Hagar? fear not; for God hath heard the voice of the lad where he *is.* ¹⁸ Arise, lift up the lad, and hold him in thine hand; for I will make him a great nation. ¹⁹ And God opened her eyes, and she saw a well of water.—Gen., ch. 21.

6733. —— **Acknowledgment of.** *Proverb.* ⁵ Trust in the Lord with all thine heart; and lean not unto thine own understanding. ⁶ In all thy ways acknowledge him, and he shall direct thy paths.—Prov., ch. 3.

6734. —— **Bounty of.** *Food.* ¹⁴ He causeth the grass to grow for the cattle, and herb for the service of man: that he may bring forth food out of the earth; ¹⁵ And wine *that* maketh glad the heart of man, *and* oil to make *his* face to shine, and bread which strengtheneth man's heart.—Ps. 104.

6735. —— **Confidence in.** *"Boldly say."* ⁵ *Be* content with such things as ye have: for he hath said, I will never leave thee, nor forsake thee. ⁶ So that we may boldly say, The Lord *is* my helper, and I will not fear what man shall do unto me.—Heb., ch. 13.

6736. —— **Care of.** *Jacob.* ²⁰ Jacob vowed ..If God will be with me, and will keep me in this way that I go, and will give me bread to eat, and raiment to put on, ²¹ So that I come again to my father's house in peace; then shall the Lord be my God: ²².. and of all that thou shalt give me I will surely give the tenth unto thee.—Gen., ch. 28.

6737. —— **Commitment to.** *Esther.* ¹⁶ Gather together all the Jews *that are* present in Shushan, and fast ye for me, and neither eat nor drink three days, night or day: I also and my maidens will fast likewise: and so will I go in unto the king, which *is* not according to the law; and if I perish, I perish.—Esther, ch. 4.

6738. —— **A directing.** *Saints.* ²³ The steps of a *good* man are ordered by the Lord: and he delighteth in his way. ²⁴ Though he fall, he shall not be utterly cast down: for the Lord upholdeth *him with* his hand.—Ps. 37.

6739. —— **Dependence on.** *Keeper.* ¹ Except the Lord build the house, they labour in vain that build it: except the Lord keep the city, the watchman waketh *but* in vain.—Ps. 127.

6740. —— **disclosed.** *Joseph.* ⁴ I *am* Joseph your brother, whom ye sold into Egypt. ⁵ Now therefore be not grieved, nor angry with yourselves, that ye sold me hither: for God did send me before you to preserve life.—Gen., ch. 45.

6741. —— **Delays of.** *Sinner.* ¹² Though a sinner do evil a hundred times, and his *days* be prolonged, yet surely I know that it shall be well with them that fear God.. ¹³ But it shall not be well with the wicked, neither shall he prolong his days, *which are* as a shadow.—Eccl., ch. 8.

6742. —— **Deterred by.** *Laban.* ²⁷ Wherefore didst thou flee away secretly, and steal away from me; and didst not tell me, that I might have sent thee away with mirth, and with songs, with tabret, and with harp?.. ²⁹ It is in the power of my hand to do you hurt: but the God of your father spake unto me yesternight, saying, Take thou heed that thou speak not to Jacob either good or bad.—Gen., ch. 31.

6743. —— **Dependence on.** *Apostles.* ⁹ Provide neither gold, nor silver, nor brass in your purses; ¹⁰ Nor scrip for *your* journey, neither two coats, neither shoes, nor yet staves: for the workman is worthy of his meat. ¹¹ And into whatsoever city or town ye shall enter, inquire who in it is worthy; and there abide till ye go thence.—Mat., ch. 10.

6744. —— **Fighting.** *Gamaliel.* ³⁸ Refrain from these men, and let them alone: for if this counsel or this work be of men, it will come to naught: ³⁹ But if it be of God, ye cannot overthrow it; lest haply ye be found even to fight against God.—Acts, ch. 5.

6745. —— **Interfering.** *"Frustrateth."* ²⁴ I *am* the Lord that maketh all *things;* that stretcheth forth the heavens alone; that spreadeth abroad the earth by myself; ²⁵ That frustrateth the tokens of the liars, and maketh diviners mad; that turneth wise *men* backward, and maketh their knowledge foolish; ²⁶ That confirmeth the word of his servant.—Isa., ch. 44.

6746. —— **Interpretation of.** *Sons of Jacob.* ²⁸ And he said unto his brethren, My money is restored; and.. in my sack: and their heart failed *them,* and they were afraid, saying one to another, What *is* this *that* God hath done unto us?—Gen., ch. 42.

6747. —— **Increase from.** *Elisha.* [42] Twenty loaves of barley, and full ears of corn in the husk thereof.. [43] and his servitor said, What, should I set this before a hundred men?.. They shall eat, and shall leave *thereof*. [44] So he set *it* before them, and they did eat, and left *thereof*, according to the word of the Lord.—2 KINGS, ch. 4.

6748. —— **Instruments of.** *Boasting.* [15] Shall the axe boast itself against him that heweth therewith? *or* shall the saw magnify itself against him that shaketh it? as if the rod should shake *itself* against them that lift it up, *or* as if the staff should lift up *itself*, *as if it were* no wood. —ISA., ch. 10.

6749. —— **Strange Instruments of.** *Ravens.* [3] Hide thyself by the brook Cherith, that *is* before Jordan. [4] And..thou shalt drink of the brook; and I have commanded the ravens to feed thee there.—1 KINGS, ch. 17.

6750. —— **Indiscriminating.** *Temporary.* [14] There be just *men*, unto whom it happeneth according to the work of the wicked; again, there be wicked *men*, to whom it happeneth according to the work of the righteous: I said that this also *is* vanity.—ECCL., ch. 8.

6751. —— **Leading of.** *Israel.* [9] The Lord's portion *is* his people; Jacob *is* the lot of his inheritance. [10] He found him in a desert land, and in the waste howling wilderness; he led him about, he instructed him, he kept him as the apple of his eye.—DEUT., ch. 32.

6752. —— **misconstrued.** *David.* [7] Thus said Shimei when he cursed, Come out, come out, thou bloody man, and thou man of Belial: [8] The Lord hath returned upon thee all the blood of the house of Saul, in whose stead thou hast reigned; and the Lord hath delivered the kingdom into the hand of Absalom thy son.—2 SAM., ch. 16.

6753. —— **Opposing.** *Balaam.* [21] Balaam.. saddled his ass, and went with the princes of Moab. [22] And God's anger was kindled because he went: and the angel of the Lord stood in the way for an adversary against him.—NUM., ch. 22.

6754. —— **Overruling.** *Babel.* [4] Let us build us a city, and a tower, whose top *may reach* unto heaven; and let us make us a name, lest we be scattered.. [6] ..now nothing will be restrained from them, which they have imagined to do. [7] Go to, let us go down, and there confound their language, that they may not understand one another's speech.—GEN., ch. 11.

6755. —— **Proof of.** *Wall finished.* [16] When all our enemies heard *thereof*, and all the heathen that *were* about us saw *these things*, they were much cast down in their own eyes: for they perceived that this work was wrought of our God. —NEH., ch. 6.

6756. —— **A remarkable.** *Captive.* [2] The Syrians..had brought away captive out of the land of Israel a little maid; and she waited on Naaman's wife. [3] And she said unto her mistress, Would God my lord *were* with the prophet that *is* in Samaria! for he would recover him of his leprosy.—2 KINGS, ch. 5.

6757. —— **Refuge in.** *Aged Moses said,* [26] *There is* none like unto the God of Jeshurun, *who* rideth upon the heaven in thy help, and in his excellency on the sky. [27] The eternal God *is* thy refuge, and underneath *are* the everlasting arms.—DEUT., ch. 33.

6758. —— **Reproof of.** *Elymas.* [8] Elymas the sorcerer..withstood them, seeking to turn away the deputy from the faith.. [11] ..the hand of the Lord *is* upon thee, and thou shalt be blind, not seeing the sun for a season. And immediately there fell on him a mist and a darkness; and he went about seeking some to lead him by the hand.—ACTS, ch. 13.

6759. —— **Sustaining.** *Manna.* [35] The children of Israel did eat manna forty years, until they came to a land inhabited..until they came unto the borders of the land of Canaan.—EX., ch. 16.

6760. —— —— *At Zarephath.* [15] She..did according to the saying of Elijah: and she, and he, and her house, did eat *many* days. [16] *And* the barrel of meal wasted not, neither did the cruse of oil fail, according to the word of the Lord.—1 KINGS, ch. 17.

6761. —— **Selection by.** *A Wife.* [13] I stand *here* by the well of water; and the daughters of the men of the city come out to draw water: [14] ..the damsel to whom I shall say, Let down thy pitcher, I pray thee,·that I may drink; and she shall say, Drink, and I will give thy camels drink also: *let the same be* she *that* thou hast appointed for thy servant Isaac.—GEN., ch. 24.

6762. —— **Trust in.** *Lilies.* [27] Consider the lilies how they grow: they toil not, they spin not; and yet..Solomon in all his glory was not arrayed like one of these. [28] If then God so clothe the grass, which is to day in the field, and to morrow is cast into the oven; how much more *will he clothe* you, O ye of little faith?— LUKE, ch. 12.

6763. —— **Sinner's Trust in.** .*Saul.* [7] It was told Saul that David was come to Keilah. And Saul said, God hath delivered him into mine hand; for he is shut in, by entering into a town that hath gates and bars. [8] And Saul called all the people together..to Keilah, to besiege David and his men.—1 SAM., ch. 23.

6764. —— **A timely.** *Offering Isaac.* [10] Took the knife to slay his son. [11] And the Angel of the Lord called unto him out of heaven.. [13] ..and behold behind *him* a ram caught in a thicket by his horns: and Abraham..offered him up for a burnt offering in the stead of his son.—GEN., ch. 22.

6765. —— **Unfailing.** *Saints.* [25] I have been young, and *now* am old; yet have I not seen the righteous forsaken, nor his seed begging bread. —PS. 37.

6766. —— **Upholding.** *Eagle.* [11] As an eagle stirreth up her nest, fluttereth over her young, spreadeth abroad her wings, taketh them, beareth them on her wings: [12] *So* the Lord alone did lead him.—DEUT., ch. 32.

6767. —— **Working with.** *Esther.* [13] Mordecai commanded to answer Esther, Think not with thyself that thou shalt escape in the king's house, more than all the Jews. [14] For if thou altogether holdest thy peace at this time, *then* shall their enlargement and deliverance arise to the Jews from another place..and who knoweth, whether thou art come to the kingdom for *such* a time as this?—ESTHER, ch. 4.

6768. —— **Withholding.** *Manna.* [12] The manna ceased on the morrow after they had eaten of the old corn of the land ; neither had the children of Israel manna any more ; but they did eat of the fruit of the land of Canaan. —Josh., ch. 5.

6769. PROVIDENCES, Succession of. *In Wilderness.* [12] Marvellous things did he in the sight of their fathers.. [13] He divided the sea, and caused them to pass through ; and he made the waters to stand as a heap. [14] In the daytime also he led them with a cloud, and all the night with a light of fire.—Ps. 78. [See chapter.]

6770. —— **misinterpreted.** *Calamities.* [4] Those eighteen, upon whom the tower in Siloam fell, and slew them, think ye that they were sinners above all men that dwelt in Jerusalem? [5]..Nay ; but, except ye repent, ye shall all likewise perish.—Luke, ch. 13.

See PROTECTION.

6771. PROVISIONS, Abundant. *Solomon's.* [22] Solomon's provision for one day was thirty measures of fine flour, and threescore measures of meal, [23] Ten fat oxen, and twenty oxen out of the pastures, and a hundred sheep, besides harts, and roebucks, and fallow deer, and fatted fowl.—1 Kings, ch. 4.

Also see:
Purveyors. Solomon had 12 officers who   6815
See FOOD and references.

6772. PROVOCATION forbidden. *To Children.* [4] Ye fathers, provoke not your children to wrath : but bring them up in the nurture and admonition of the Lord.—Eph., ch. 6.

6773. —— **Severe.** *Paul.* [2] The high priest Ananias commanded them..to smite him on the mouth. [3] Then said Paul..God shall smite thee, *thou* whited wall : for sittest thou to judge me after the law, and commandest me to be smitten contrary to the law?—Acts, ch. 23.

6774. PRUDENCE in Age. *Eighty Years.* [34] Barzillai said..How long have I to live, that I should go up with the king unto Jerusalem? [35] I *am* this day fourscore years old : *and* can I discern between good and evil ? can thy servant taste what I eat or what I drink ? can I hear any more the voice of singing men and singing women? wherefore then should thy servant be yet a burden unto my lord.—2 Sam., ch. 19.

6775. —— **commended.** *Steward.* [7] How much owest thou ? And he said, A hundred measures of wheat. And he said..Take thy bill, and write fourscore. [8] And the lord commended the unjust steward, because he had done wisely.— Luke, ch. 16.

6776. —— **Example of.** *Jesus.* [17] What thinkest thou ? Is it lawful to give tribute unto Cesar, or not?..[21]..Render therefore unto Cesar the things which are Cesar's ; and unto God the things that are God's. [22] When they had heard *these words*, they marvelled, and left him.— Mat., ch. 22.

6777. —— **Preserved by.** *Micah.* [25] The children of Dan said unto him, Let not thy voice be heard among us, lest angry fellows run upon thee, and thou lose thy life, with the lives of thy household. [26]..and when Micah saw that they *were* too strong for him, he..went back unto his house.—Judges, ch. 18.

6778. —— **Preservation by.** *Joseph.* [9] How then can I do this great wickedness, and sin against God? [10] And..as she spake to Joseph day by day..he hearkened not unto her..*or* to be with her.—Gen., ch. 39.

6779. —— **in Resolutions.** *Tower.* [28] Which of you, intending to build a tower, sitteth not down first, and counteth the cost, whether ye have *sufficient* to finish *it*? [29] Lest haply, after he hath laid the foundation, and is not able to finish *it*, all that behold *it* begin to mock him.—Luke, ch. 14.

See other illustrations under:

DISCRETION.
Necessary. King consulteth..war..or..peace		2366
Part of. Let not thy voice be heard..lose thy life		2367
Success. David said to Abigail..Blessed..advice		2368
Safety. Paul perceived..part..Sadducees..other		2369
Want of. As a jewel of gold in a swine's snout		2370
" Nabal said, Who is David?..his master		2371

ECONOMY.
Food. Gather up the fragments..nothing be lost		2600
False. Why was this waste of the ointment		2601

See FORETHOUGHT and references.
See WISDOM.

6780. PULPIT, The first. *Ezra's.* [4] Ezra the scribe stood upon a pulpit of wood, which they had made for the purpose.. [5] And Ezra opened the book in the sight of all the people..and when he opened it, all the people stood up.— Neh., ch. 8.

6781. PUNISHMENT of Angels. *"In Chains."* [6] The angels which kept not their first estate, but left their own habitation, he hath reserved in everlasting chains under darkness unto the judgment of the great day.—Jude.

6782. —— **by Blindness.** *Elymas.* [10] O full of all subtilty and all mischief, *thou* child of the devil, *thou* enemy of all righteousness, wilt thou not cease to pervert the right ways of the Lord ? [11] And now, behold, the hand of the Lord *is* upon thee, and thou shalt be blind, not seeing the sun for a season. And immediately there fell on him a mist and a darkness ; and he went about seeking some to lead him by the hand.— Acts, ch. 13.

6783. —— **Barbarous.** *David.* [3] He brought out the people that *were* in it, and cut *them* with saws, and with harrows of iron, and with axes. Even so dealt David with all the cities of the children of Ammon.—1 Chron., ch. 20.

6784. —— **by Conscience.** *"Sound."* [20] The wicked man travaileth with pain all *his* days, and the number of years is hidden to the oppressor. [21] A dreadful sound *is* in his ears : in prosperity the destroyer shall come upon him. —Job, ch. 15.

6785. —— **Choice in.** *David's.* [13] Shall seven years of famine come?..or wilt thou flee three months before thine enemies..? or that there be three days' pestilence in thy land? now advise, and see what answer I shall return to him that sent me. [14] And David said unto Gad, I am in a great strait : let us fall now into the hand of the Lord ; for his mercies *are* great : and let me not fall into the hand of man.—2 Sam., ch. 24.

6786. —— **Curses for.** *Rebellious.* [20] The Lord shall send upon thee cursing, vexation, and rebuke, in all that thou settest thine hand unto for to do..until thou perish quickly; because of the wickedness of thy doings, whereby thou hast forsaken me.—Deut., ch. 28. [See chapter.]

6787. —— Devoted to. *In Egypt.* [8] They rebelled..and would not hearken unto me: they did not every man cast away the abominations of their eyes, neither did they forsake the idols of Egypt: then I said, I will pour out my fury upon them.—Ezek., ch. 20.

6788. —— of Drunkards. *Parents.* [20] Shall say unto the elders of his city, This our son *is* stubborn and rebellious, he will not obey our voice; *he is* a glutton, and a drunkard. [21] And all the men of the city shall stone him.—Deut., ch. 21.

6789. —— for Disobedience. *Afflictions.* [15] If ye shall despise my statutes, or if your soul abhor my judgments, so that ye will not do all my commandments, *but* that ye break my covenant: [16]..I will even appoint over you terror, consumption, and the burning ague, that shall consume the eyes, and cause sorrow of heart: and ye shall sow your seed in vain, for your enemies shall eat it.—Lev., ch. 6.

6790. —— Humility in. *After Captivity.* [13] After all that is come upon us for our evil deeds..seeing that thou our God hast punished us less than our iniquities *deserve*.. [14] Should we again break thy commandments, and join in affinity with the people of these abominations? —Ezra, ch. 9.

6791. —— by Irritation. *Canaanites.* [55] If ye will not drive out the inhabitants of the land.. then..those which ye let remain of them *shall be* pricks in our eyes, and thorns in your sides, and shall vex you.—Num., ch. 33.

6792. —— in Kind. *Death.* [22] Pharaoh charged all his people, saying, Every son that is born ye shall cast in the river, and every daughter ye shall save alive.—Ex., ch. 1. [30] Pharaoh rose up in the night, he..and all the Egyptians; and there was a great cry in Egypt: for *there was* not a house where *there was* not one dead.—Ex., ch. 12.

6793. —— —— *Joab.* [31] The king said..Do as he hath said, and fall upon him, and bury him; that thou mayest take away the innocent blood, which Joab shed, from me..[32]..to wit, Abner..captain of the host of Israel, and Amasa ..captain of the host of Judah. [33] Their blood shall therefore return upon the head of Joab.— 1 Kings, ch. 2.

6794. —— Knowledge grades. *Uzzah.* [6] Uzzah put forth *his hand* to the ark of God, and took hold of it; for the oxen shook *it.* [7] And the anger of the Lord was kindled against Uzzah, and God smote him there for *his* error; and there he died by the ark.—2 Sam., ch. 6. [The Philistines were not killed because of their ignorance. Uzzah was a Levite.]

6795. —— limited. *Law.* [See No. 2802.] [3] Forty stripes he may give him, *and* not exceed: lest, *if* he should exceed..these with many stripes, then thy brother should seem vile unto thee.—Deut., ch. 25.

6796. —— Misfortune not. *Affliction.* [2] His disciples asked..Master, who did sin, this man, or his parents, that he was born blind? [3] Jesus answered, Neither hath this man sinned, nor his parents: but that the works of God should be made manifest in him.—John, ch. 9.

6797. —— Opportunity grades. *Capernaum.* [23] Thou, Capernaum, which art exalted unto heaven, shalt be brought down to hell: for if the mighty works, which have been done in thee, had been done in Sodom, it would have remained until this day. [24] But..it shall be more tolerable for the land of Sodom in the day of judgment, than for thee.—Mat., ch. 11.

6798. —— Overzeal for. *Jews.* [32] Many good works have I shewed you from my Father; for which of those works do ye stone me? [33] The Jews answered..For a good work we stone thee not; but for blasphemy; and because that thou, being a man, makest thyself God.—John, ch. 10.

6799. —— Preparation for. *The Wicked.* [8] They that plough iniquity, and sow wickedness, reap the same. [9] By the blast of God they perish, and by the breath of his nostrils are they consumed.—Job, ch. 4.

6800. —— by the Public. *Sabbath-breaker.* [32] In the wilderness, they found a man that gathered sticks upon the sabbath day. [35] And the Lord said unto Moses, The man shall be surely put to death: all the congregation shall stone him.—Num., ch. 15.

6801. —— Rule for. *Like Offense.* [24] They brought those men which had accused Daniel, and they cast *them* into the den of lions, them, their children, and their wives; and the lions ..brake all their bones in pieces or ever they came at the bottom of the den.—Dan., ch. 6.

6802. —— by Stripes. *Corporeal.* [2] If the wicked man *be* worthy to be beaten..the judge shall cause him to lie down, and to be beaten before his face, according to his fault, by a certain number.—Deut., ch. 25. [See No. 6795.]

6803. —— for Sin. *Israelites.* [5] I will therefore put you in remembrance..that the Lord, having saved the people out of the land of Egypt, afterward destroyed them that believed not.— Jude.

6804. —— of Satan. *Lake of Fire.* [10] The devil that deceived them was cast into the lake of fire and brimstone, where the beast and the false prophet *are*, and shall be tormented day and night for ever and ever.—Rev., ch. 20.

6805. —— by Torment. *Hell.* [22] The rich man also died.. [23] And in hell he lift up his eyes, being in torments.. [24] And he cried.. Father Abraham, have mercy on me, and send Lazarus, that he may dip the tip of his finger in water, and cool my tongue; for I am tormented in this flame.—Luke, ch. 16.

6806. —— Unmerciful. *Philistines.* [5] When he had set the brands on fire, he let *them* go into the standing corn of the Philistines..the vineyards *and* olives. [6] Then the Philistines said, Who hath done this? And they answered, Samson, the son in law of the Timnite, because he had taken his wife, and given her to his companion..Philistines came up, and burnt her and her father with fire.—Judges, ch. 15.

6807. —— of the Unsaved. *Hell.* [10] He shall be tormented with fire and brimstone in the presence of the holy angels, and in the presence of the Lamb: [11] And the smoke of their torment ascendeth up for ever and ever : and they have no rest day nor night, who worship the beast and his image.—Rev. ch. 14.

6808. —— **of Vanity.** *Herod.* ²¹ Upon a set day Herod, arrayed in royal apparel, sat upon his throne, and made an oration.. ²² And the people gave a shout, *saying, It is* the voice of a god, and not of a man. ²³ And immediately the angel of the Lord smote him.—Acts, ch. 12.

6809. —— **of the Wicked.** *Torment.* ¹² Friend, how camest thou in hither, not having a wedding-garment? And he was speechless. ¹³ Then said the king to the servants, Bind him hand and foot, and take him away, and cast *him* into outer darkness : there shall be weeping and gnashing of teeth.—Mat., ch. 22.

6810. —— **a Warning.** *"A Sign."* ¹⁰ The earth opened her mouth, and swallowed them up together with Korah, when that company died, what time the fire devoured two hundred and fifty men : and they became a sign.—Num., ch. 26.

See other illustrations under :

CHASTISEMENT.
Children. He that spareth the rod hateth his son 1131
Fruits. It yieldeth the peaceable fruit of r. 1132
Good. Chastened us for their pleasure..our profit 1133
Love. Whom the L. loveth, he chasteneth 1134

DISCIPLINE.
Ancient. Separated from I. the mixed multitude 2337
Care. Nay..lest ye root up also the wheat 2338
Method. Tell him his fault..alone 2339
Primitive. Ananias and Sapphira..fell down 2340

RETALIATION.
Cowardly. Joab took Abner aside..smote him 7289
Disallowed. Been said, An eye for an eye 7290
Jewish. Life shall go for life, eye for eye 7291

RETRIBUTION.
Angels. Reserved in everlasting chains 7292
Commenced. Jews had rule over them that hated 7293
" Thus G. rendered the w. of Abime. 7294
Fear of. Ye would not hear ?..his blood is required 7295
Inflicted. Adoni-bezek fled..cut off his thumbs 7296
Natural. Vengeance suffereth not to live 7297
Just. King said, Hang Haman thereon 7298
" Cast them into the den of lions 7299
Providential. L. sent lions among them 7300
" At midnight L. smote the firstborn 7301

REVENGE.
Avoided. Flee thou to Laban..brother's fury turn 7304
Brother's. When I say, Smite Amnon ; then kill 7305
" Joab smote Abner..for the blood of 7306
Best. If thine enemy be hungry, give him bread 7307
Frustrated. Haman was come..Hang Mordecai 7308
Ignored. Spake against Moses..M. cried unto the 7309
" Shall not Shimei be put to death ? 7310
Justifiable. Philistines burnt her..S. smote them 7311
Nursed. Absalom spake neither good nor bad 7312
Proposed. Then will I slay my brother Jacob 7313
Price. That they may be destroyed..I will pay 7314
Prayer. O L. G., strengthen me..avenged of the P. 7315

STONING.
Covetousness. I. stoned Achan with stones 8349
Innocent. Men of Belial witnessed..stoned Naboth 8350
Intended. Jews took up stones again to stone him 8351
Persecutors. Stoned Paul, drew him out of the city 8352
" Out of the city..they stoned Stephen 8353
Reproof. They conspired against Zachariah..ston. 8354
Revenge. Shimei..cast stones at David..bloody 8355

VENGEANCE.
Averted. Let not my lord regard..Nabal 9169
" Kept me..from coming to shed blood 9170
Blood. Cain said..every one that findeth me..slay 9171
Call. Stoned [Zachariah]..in the house of the L. 9172
Divine. To me belongeth vengeance and r. 9173
" If I whet my glittering sword 9174
Declined. Not a man be put to death [Saul] 9175
Fear. Joseph will peradventure hate us 9176
with God. My G., think thou upon Tobiah 9177
Inappropriate. I forgave thee..shouldest thou not 9178
Mistaken. Command fire..to consume them 9179
Monstrous. Haman thought scorn..Mordecai 9180
Prohibited. If ye from your hearts forgive not e. 9182
Undesired. Behold the head of Ish-bosheth 9183
for Vengeance. David commanded..slew them 9184

Innocent. I find no fault in him..take ye him 90
See CRIMINAL and references.

6811. PURIFICATION, Difficult. *Of the Church.* ²⁸ Wilt thou then that we go and gather them up ? ²⁹ But he said, Nay ; lest while ye gather up the tares, ye root up also the wheat with them. ³⁰ Let both grow together until the harvest.—Mat., ch. 13.

6812. PURITY by Refining. *Refiner's Fire.* ² He *is* like a refiner's fire, and like fullers' soap : ³ And he shall sit *as* a refiner and purifier of silver : and he shall purify the sons of Levi, and purge them as gold and silver.—Mal., ch. 3.

6813. —— **symbolized.** *Laver.* ¹⁸ Thou shalt also make a laver of *brass*..to wash *withal :* and thou shalt put it between the tabernacle..and the altar, and thou shalt put water therein. ¹⁹ For Aaron and his sons shall wash their hands and their feet thereat : ²⁰ When they go into the tabernacle.—Ex., ch. 30.

6814. —— **within.** *Platter.* ²⁶ Thou blind Pharisee, cleanse first that *which is* within the cup and platter, that the outside of them may be clean also. ²⁷..ye are like unto whited sepulchres, which indeed appear beautiful outward, but are within full of dead *men's* bones, and of all uncleanness. ²⁸ Even so ye also outwardly appear righteous unto men, but within ye are full of hypocrisy and iniquity.—Mat., ch. 23.

See other illustrations under :

CLEANSING.
Blood. Sprinkled it on the people 1343
" If the blood of bulls..much more..blood of 1344
by Expulsion. Jesus made a scourge..drove them 1345
Holy Fire. Live coal..upon my mouth..cleansed 1346
Heart. Create in me a clean heart 1348
Spiritual. Who shall ascend..clean hands 1347
Typical. Needeth not save to wash his feet 1349

CONSECRATION.
Covenant. All the people stood to the covenant 1584
Leadership. Took Joshua..laid hands upon him 1585
Service. Moses took of the blood..ear..thumb 1586
Self-denying. Made the laver..looking-glasses 1587

DEDICATION.
Accepted. Fire came..consumed the sacrifices 2091
Heathen. Nebuchadnezzar sent..dedication of the 2092
Service. Vessels of..gold..did David dedicate 2093
Temple. Cloud filled the house..glory 3520

HOLINESS.
Acknowledged. Put off thy shoes..holy ground 3996
" Loose thy shoe..Joshua did so 3997
Alarming. Looked into the ark..who is able to 3998
Celebration. Cherubim..Holy, holy, holy is the L. 3999

Conspicuous. Holiness to the L..upon the b. 4000
Chosen. Shall be a peculiar treasure..holy nation 4001
Church. Glorious church not having spot..holy 4002
Prayer for. Be filled with all the fulness of God 4003
Perfect. Which of you convinceth me of sin? 4004
Unapproachable. Set bounds..about the mount 4005
Universal. Upon the bells of the horses, Holiness 4006

REFINEMENT.

Affliction. I have refined thee..furnace of 6912
Fire. He is like a refiner's fire..purify sons of Levi 6913

SANCTIFICATION.

Firstborn. Thou shalt set apart unto the Lord 7574
Sabbath. G. blessed the seventh day and sanctified 7575

SINCERITY.

Consecration. Josiah made a covenant..burned 8025
Evildoing. I thought I ought to..put to death 8026
Evidence. Brought their books..burned them 8027
Example. An Israelite in whom is no guile 8028
Heart. He that speaketh truth in his heart 8029
Lovable. All..have I kept..Jesus loved him 8030
Opinions. Rabbi, thou art the Son of God 8031
Positive. Thou knowest that I love thee 8132
Proof. When..people saw it..L. he is God 8033
Reformation. Speak..the truth..execute..truth 8034

Healthful. Clean hands shall be stronger and 3751
Honoured. Who shall ascend..clean hands..heart 1348
Means. Washing of water by the word 4002
" Blood of J. C. his Son cleanseth us..sin 7948

6815. PURVEYORS, Royal. *Solomon's.* [7] Solomon had twelve officers..which provided victuals for the king and his household : each man his month in a year made provision.—1 KINGS, ch. 4.

6816. PURPOSE, Unchangeable. *Darius.* [15] Know, O king, that the law of the Medes and Persians is, That no decree nor statute which the king establisheth may be changed. [16] Then the king commanded, and they brought Daniel, and cast him into the den of lions.—DAN., ch. 6.

See other illustrations under :

INTENTION.

Accepted. Abraham..offered up his only begotten 4604
Approved. Whereas it was in thine heart to build 4605
Abandoned. Pilate sought to release him 4606
Commended. Poor widow..cast more in than all 4607
Crime. If he thrust him suddenly without enmity 4608
Fixes Guilt. If any man hate..lie in wait..smite 4609
Honoured. She hath done what she could 4610
Misjudged. All you have conspired against me 4611
Sincere. Abraham..took the knife to slay his son 4612
Superior. Beyond their power they were willing 4613
Unexecuted. Peter having a sword..cut off his ear 4614
Unprotected by. Put..hand to the ark..oxen shook 4615

MOTIVE.

Labour. We labour..may be accepted of him 5587
Unsanctified. People spared the best..to sacrifice 5588

MOTIVES.

Inferior. Ye seek me..because ye did eat..loaves 5589
Suspicion. Urged him till he was ashamed, he said 5590
Worldly. Peter..thou savourest..things that be of 5591

WILL.

Rebellious. I would have gathered..ye would not 9593
" We will certainly do 9594
See DETERMINATION and references.
See DECISION.

6817. QUALIFICATION for Office. *Jethro* said, [21] Thou shalt provide out of all the people, able men, such as fear God, men of truth, hating covetousness ; and place *such* over them *to be* rulers of thousands, *and* rulers of hundreds, rulers of fifties, and rulers of tens.—EX., ch. 18.

6818. QUARREL, Domestic. *Hagar's Son.* [9] Sarah saw the son of Hagar..which she had borne unto Abraham, mocking [10] Wherefore she said unto Abraham, Cast out this bondwoman and her son.—GEN., ch. 21.

6819. —— Destructive. *Ammonites.* [23] The children of Ammon and Moab stood up against the inhabitants of mount Seir, utterly to slay and destroy *them :* and when they had made an end of the inhabitants of Seir, every one helped to destroy another.—2 CHRON., ch. 20.

6820. —— Foolish. *A slight.* [1] The men of Ephraim gathered .. and said unto Jephthah, Wherefore passedst thou over to fight against the children of Ammon, and didst not call us to go with thee? we will burn thy house upon thee with fire.—JUDGES, ch. 12.

6821. —— of the Famished. *"In Famine."* [28] The king said..What aileth thee? And she answered, This woman said unto me, Give thy son, that we may eat him to day, and we will eat my son to morrow. [29] So we boiled my son, and did eat him : and I said unto her on the next day, Give thy son, that we may eat him : and she hath hid her son.—2 KINGS, ch. 6.

6822. —— Meddling with a. *Moses.* [13] Two men of the Hebrews strove together : and he said to him that did the wrong, Wherefore smitest thou thy fellow? [14] And he said, Who made thee a prince and a judge over us? intendest thou to kill me, as thou killedst the Egyptian? And Moses feared.—EX., ch. 2.

6823. —— *Proverb.* [17] He that passeth by, *and* meddleth with strife *belonging* not to him, *is like* one that taketh a dog by the ears. —PROV., ch. 26.

6824. —— Matrimonial. *Moses.* [1] Miriam and Aaron spake against Moses because of the Ethiopian woman whom he had married.. [2] And they said, Hath the Lord indeed spoken only by Moses? hath he not spoken also by us?—NUM., ch. 12.

6825. —— overruled. *Ishmael.* [See No. 6818.] [18] Arise, lift up the lad, and hold him in thine hand ; for I will make him a great nation. —GEN., ch. 21.

6826. —— Test in. *Shibboleth.* [See No. 5820.] [5] The men of Gilead said..Art thou an Ephraimite? If he said, Nay ; [6] Then said they ..Say now, Shibboleth : and he said, Sibboleth ; for he could not frame to pronounce *it* right. Then they..slew him at the passages of Jordan : and there fell..of the Ephraimites, forty and two thousand.—JUDGES, ch. 12.

6827. —— War from a. *Sheba.* [Judah had brought David to Jerusalem.] [1] A man of Belial, whose name *was* Sheba..blew a trumpet, and said, We have no part in David.. [2] So every man of Israel went up from after David, *and* followed Sheba..but the men of Judah clave unto their king.—2 SAM., ch. 20.

6828. QUARRELS, Conjugal. *Proverb.* [9] It is better to dwell in a corner of the housetop, than with a brawling woman in a wide house.. [19] It is better to dwell in the wilderness, than with a contentious and an angry woman.—PROV., chs. 21 and 22.

6829. QUARTER, No. *Five Kings.* 24 Joshua called for all the men of Israel, and said unto the captains. . Come near, put your feet upon the necks of these kings. And they came near, and put their feet upon the necks of them.— Josh., ch. 10.

See CONTENTION and references.

6830. QUESTION, An alarming. *Sinners.* 8 Adam and his wife hid themselves from the presence of the Lord God amongst the trees of the garden. 9 And the Lord God called unto Adam, and said. . Where *art* thou?—GEN., ch. 3.

6831. —— An embarrassing. *To Peter.* 15 So when they had dined, Jesus saith to Simon Peter, Simon, *son* of Jonas, lovest thou me more than these? He saith unto him, Yea, Lord; thou knowest that I love thee.—JOHN, ch. 21.

6832. —— A fearful. *Disciples.* 31 The Son of man is delivered into the hands of men, and they shall kill him; and after that he is killed, he shall rise the third day. 32 But they understood not that saying, and were afraid to ask him.—MARK, ch. 9.

6833. —— The great. *"What shall I do?"* 25 A certain lawyer. . tempted him, saying, Master, what shall I do to inherit eternal life? 26 He said. . What is written in the law? how readest thou?—LUKE, ch. 10.

6834. —— —— *Philippian Jailer.* 30 Brought them out, and said, Sirs, what must I do to be saved? 31 And they said, Believe on the Lord Jesus Christ, and thou shalt be saved, and thy house.—ACTS, ch. 16.

6835. —— A startling. *At Sinai.* 12 After the earthquake a fire; *but* the Lord *was* not in the fire: and after the fire a still small voice. 13 . . when Elijah heard *it*. . he wrapped his face in his mantle, and went out, and stood in the entering in of the cave. And, behold, *there came* a voice . . What doest thou here, Elijah?—1 KINGS, ch. 19.

6836. —— The Soul's. *Pentecost.* 37 When they heard *this*, they were pricked in their heart, and said unto Peter and to the rest of the apostles, Men *and* brethren, what shall we do? 38 Then Peter said. . Repent, and be baptized.— ACTS, ch. 2.

6837. —— A trying. *Isaac's.* 7 He said, Behold the fire and the wood: but where is the lamb for a burnt offering? 8 And Abraham said, My son, God will provide himself a lamb.— GEN., ch. 22.

6838. QUESTIONERS silenced. *By Jesus.* 24 I also will ask you one thing, which if ye tell me, I in like wise will tell you by what authority I do these things. 25 The baptism of John, whence was it? from heaven, or of men? And they reasoned. . If we shall say, From heaven; he will say unto us, Why did ye not then believe him? 26 But if we shall say, Of men; we fear the people; for all hold John as a prophet. 27 And they answered . . We cannot tell.—MAT., ch. 21.

6839. QUESTIONS, Test. *Queen of Sheba.* 2 She came to Jerusalem with a very great train, with camels that bare spices, and very much gold, and precious stones. . 3 And Solomon told her all her questions: there was not *any* thing hid from the king, which he told her not.—1 KINGS, ch. 10.

6840. —— withheld. *From Jesus.* 28 One of the scribes came, and having heard them reasoning together, and perceiving that he had answered them well, asked him, Which is the first commandment of all?. . 34 And when Jesus saw that he answered discreetly, he said. . Thou art not far from the kingdom of God. And no man after that durst ask him *any question.*—MARK, ch. 12.

6841. QUOTATIONS, Use of. *Paul.* [At Athens.] 28 For in him we live, and move, and have our being; as certain also of your own poets have said, For we are also his offspring.— ACTS, ch. 17.

6842. RADICALISM, Religious. *Hezekiah.* 4 He removed the high places, and brake the images, and cut down the groves, and brake in pieces the brazen serpent that Moses had made: for unto those days the children of Israel did burn incense to it.—2 KINGS, ch. 18.

6843. —— Teaching. *Jesus.* 11 Not that which goeth into the mouth defileth a man; but that which cometh out. . 12 Then came his disciples, and said. . Knowest thou that the Pharisees were offended, after they heard this saying? 13 But he answered . . Every plant, which my heavenly Father hath not planted, shall be rooted up.—MAT., ch. 15.

Also see:

Extreme. Barbarians said. . is a murderer. . god   2840
    See RASHNESS.

6844. RAID, Successful. *Amalekites.* 1 When David and his men were come to Ziklag on the third day. . the Amalekites had. . smitten Ziklag, and burned it with fire; 2 And had taken the women captives. . they slew not any, either great or small, but carried *them* away.—1 SAM., ch. 30.

6845. RAIN of Bread. *Manna.* 4 I will rain bread from heaven for you; and the people shall. . gather a certain rate every day, that I may prove them, whether they will walk in my law, or no.—EX., ch. 16.

6846. —— Destructive. *Brimstone.* 24 The Lord rained upon Sodom and upon Gomorrah brimstone and fire from the Lord out of heaven; 25 And he overthrew those cities, and all the plain.—GEN., ch. 19.

6847. —— of Hail. *Plague of.* 22 The Lord said unto Moses, Stretch forth thine hand toward heaven, that there may be hail in all the land of Egypt, upon man, and upon beast, and upon every herb of the field.—EX., ch. 9.

6848. —— Long. *Flood.* 4 Yet seven days, and I will cause it to rain upon the earth forty days and forty nights; and every living substance that I have made will I destroy from off the face of the earth.—GEN., ch. 7.

6849. —— Promised. *"First and Latter."* 14 I will give *you* the rain of your land in his due season, the first rain and the latter rain, that thou mayest gather in thy corn, and thy wine, and thine oil.—DEUT., ch. 11.

6850. —— Prayer for. *Elijah.* [After a drought of three years,] 42 Ahab went up to eat and to drink. And Elijah went up to the top of Carmel; and he cast himself down upon the earth, and put his face between his knees. . 44 And . . at the seventh time. . he said, Behold, there ariseth a little cloud out of the sea, like a man's hand. And he said..say unto Ahab..get thee down, that the rain stop thee not.—1 KINGS, ch. 18.

See other illustrations under :

STORM.

Alarming. Entreat the L..be no more mighty t. 8356
Destructive. L. cast down great stones from h. 8357
Exigency. Undergirding the ship..lightened 8358
Mastered. He arose and rebuked the wind..calm 8359
Prayer. Arise, call upon thy god..we perish not 8360
Sea. Great wind..ship was like to be broken 8361
　" 　 Mount up to the heaven, they go down to the 8362
　" 　 They reel to and fro, and stagger..drunken 8363

Terrifying. Pharaoh saw that the rain..hail..ceased 40

6851. RASHNESS in Answering. *James and John.* [They asked for positions of honour.] 22 Are ye able to drink of the cup that I shall drink of, and to be baptized with the baptism that I am baptized with? They say..We are able.—MAT., ch. 20.

6852. —— Courageous. *Peter.* 51 One of them which were with Jesus stretched out *his* hand, and drew his sword, and struck a servant of the high priest, and smote off his ear.—MAT., ch. 26.

6853. —— A Drunkard's. *Herod.* 21 Herod on his birthday made a supper to his lords.. 22 And when the daughter of..Herodias..danced, and pleased Herod and them that sat with him, the king said unto the damsel, Ask of me whatsoever thou wilt, and I will give *it* thee.—MARK, ch. 6.

6854. —— Decree in. *Ahasuerus.* 9 Let it be written that they may be destroyed : and I will pay ten thousand talents of silver..to bring *it* into the king's treasuries. 10 And the king took his ring from his hand, and gave it unto Haman.—ESTHER, ch. 3.

6855. —— in Enterprise. *Tower.* 28 Which of you, intending to build a tower, sitteth not down first, and counteth the cost, whether he have *sufficient* to finish *it*? 29 Lest haply, after he hath laid the foundation, and is not able to finish *it*, all that behold *it* begin to mock him.— LUKE. ch. 14.

6856. —— from Hunger. *Esau.* 30 Feed me ..with that same red *pottage;* for I *am* faint.. 31 And Jacob said, Sell me this day thy birthright. 32 And Esau said, Behold, I *am* at the point to die : and what profit shall this birthright do to me?—GEN., ch. 25.

6857. —— Heedless. *Healed Leper.* 44 See thou say nothing to any man : but go thy way, shew thyself to the priest, and offer for thy cleansing.. 45 But he..began to publish *it* much..insomuch that Jesus could no more openly enter into the city.—MARK, ch. 1.

6858. —— in Ignorance. *Jacob.* 32 With whomsoever thou findest thy gods, let him not live : before our brethren discern thou what *is* thine with me, and take *it* to thee. For Jacob knew not that Rachel had stolen them.—GEN., ch. 31.

6859. —— in Judgment. *David.* 4 Said the king to Ziba, Behold, thine *are* all that *pertained* unto Mephibosheth. And Ziba said, I humbly beseech thee *that* I may find grace in thy sight, my lord, O king.—2 SAM., ch. 16. [Mephibosheth had not deserted David, as he supposed.]

6860. —— Needless. *In Benjamin's Sack.* 8 Behold, the money, which we found in our sacks' mouths, we brought again unto thee..how then should we steal out of thy lord's house silver or gold? 9 With whomsoever..it be found, both let him die, and we also will be my lord's bondmen.—GEN., ch. 44.

6861. —— Perilous. *Three Mighty Men.* 15 Oh that one would give me drink of the water of the well of Beth-lehem, which *is* by the gate ! 16 And the three mighty men brake through the host of the Philistines..and took *it*, and brought *it* to David : nevertheless he would not drink thereof, but poured it out unto the Lord.— 2 SAM., ch. 23.

6862. —— A Ruler's. *Rehoboam.* 10 My little *finger* shall be thicker than my father's loins. 11 And now whereas my father did lade you with a heavy yoke, I will add to your yoke : my father hath chastised you with whips, but I will chastise you with scorpions.—1 KINGS, ch. 12. [The ten tribes seceded.]

6863. —— in Responding. *Proverb.* 13 He that answereth a matter before he heareth *it*, it *is* folly and shame unto him.—PROV., ch. 18.

6864. —— in Reproof. *Eli.* 13 Hannah, she spake in her heart ; only her lips moved, but her voice was not heard : therefore Eli thought she had been drunken. 14 And Eli said unto her, How long wilt thou be drunken? put away thy wine from thee. 15 And Hannah answered ..I *am* a woman of a sorrowful spirit.—1 SAM., ch. 1.

6865. —— in Vowing. *Saul's.* 23 When they heard that the Philistines fled, even they also followed hard after them in the battle. 24 And the men of Israel were distressed that day : for Saul had adjured the people, saying, Cursed *be* the man that eateth *any* food until evening.—1 SAM., ch. 14.

6866. —— of Youth. *Asahel.* 22 Abner said again to Asahel, Turn thee aside from following me : wherefore should I smite thee to the ground?.. 23 Howbeit he refused to turn aside : wherefore Abner with the hinder end of the spear smote him under the fifth rib.—2 SAM., ch. 2. [Abner, a veteran captain.]

6867. —— from Zeal. *Benjamin.* 37 Reuben spake unto his father, saying, Slay my two sons, if I bring him not to thee : deliver him into my hand, and I will bring him to thee again. —GEN. ch. 42.

See other illustrations under :

ENTHUSIASM.

Brief. With joy receiveth..not root 2679
Benevolence. They said, He is beside himself 2680
Contempt. Michal saw king David leaping..d. 2681
Misunderstood. He is beside himself 2682
Public. Take him by force, to make him king 2683

FANATICISM.

Accused. His friends said..He is beside himself 3036
Fickle. Would have done sacrifice..stoned Paul 3037
Genuine. Two hours cried out, Great is Diana 3038
Idolatry. They cried out, and cut themselves 3039

INFATUATION.

Blind. In the time of his distress did Ahaz trespass 4455
Reproved. Knowest thou not yet..Egypt is d. 4456
Wicked. They were driven out from Pharaoh's 4457
　" 　 Simon saw..H. G. was given, he offered 4458

Imprudence. Hezekiah..shewed them..all his t. 4368

6868. RATIONALISM, Religious. *Cain.*
² Cain was a tiller of the ground. ³ And..Cain brought of the fruit of the ground an offering unto the Lord.—GEN., ch. 4.

See other illustrations under:

INCREDULITY.

6869. READING. Effective. *Law.* [See No. 6870.] ⁵ Ezra opened the book in the sight of all the people..and when he opened it, all the people stood up : ⁶ And Ezra blessed the Lord, the great God. And all the people answered, Amen, Amen, with lifting up their hands : and they bowed their heads, and worshipped the Lord with *their* faces to the ground.—NEH., ch. 8.

6870. —— An instructive. *Law.* ² Ezra the priest brought the law before the congregation both of men and women, and all that could hear with understanding.. ³ And he read therein.. from the morning until midday..and the ears of all the people *were attentive.*—NEH., ch. 8.

6871. —— Pious. *Eunuch.* ²⁷ A man of Ethiopia, a eunuch of great authority under Candace queen of the Ethiopians, who had the charge of all her treasure, and had come to Jerusalem for to worship, ²⁸ Was returning, and sitting in his chariot read Esaias the prophet.—ACTS, ch. 8.

See other illustrations under:

BIBLE.

BOOK.

BOOKS.

6872. REASON degraded. *By Bondage.* ³ The children of Israel said..Would to God we had died by the hand of the Lord in the land of Egypt, when we sat by the fleshpots, *and* when we did eat bread to the full.—EX., ch. 16.

6873. REASONING with Prejudice. *Scribes.* ⁵ When Jesus saw their faith, he said unto the sick of the palsy, Son, thy sins be forgiven thee. ⁶ But there were certain of the scribes sitting there, and reasoning in their hearts, ⁷ Why doth this *man* thus speak blasphemies? who can forgive sins but God only?—MARK, ch. 2.

See other illustrations under:

INFERENCE.

MEDITATION.

See **INTELLIGENCE** and references.

6874. REBELLION, Abominable. *Religious.* ¹⁵ Saul said..the people spared the best of the sheep and of the oxen, to sacrifice unto the Lord.. ²² And Samuel said, Hath the Lord *as great* delight in burnt offerings and sacrifices, as in obeying the voice of the Lord? Behold, to obey *is* better than sacrifice, *and* to hearken than the fat of rams. ²³ For rebellion *is as* the sin of witchcraft, and stubbornness *is as* iniquity and idolatry.—1 SAM., ch. 15.

6875. —— The Ingrate's. *Absalom.* ⁴ Oh that I were made judge in the land, that every man which hath any suit or cause might come unto me, and I would do him justice! ⁵..when any man came nigh *to him* to do him obeisance, he put forth his hand, and took him, and kissed him.. ¹⁰ But Absalom sent spies throughout all the tribes of Israel, saying, As soon as ye hear the sound of the trumpet, then ye shall say, Absalom reigneth in Hebron.—2 SAM., ch. 15.

6876. —— From Ill-government. *Ten Tribes.* ⁴ Thy father made our yoke grievous : now therefore make thou the grievous service of thy father..lighter, and we will serve thee.. ¹⁶ So when all Israel saw that the king hearkened not unto them, the people answered the king, saying, What portion have we in David?..to your tents, O Israel : now see to thine own house, David.—1 KINGS, ch. 12. [The kingdom was divided.]

6877. —— from Jealousy. *Korah.* ³ They gathered..against Moses and against Aaron, and said.. *Ye take* too much upon you, seeing all the congregation *are* holy, every one of them, and the Lord *is* among them : wherefore then lift ye up yourselves above the congregation of the Lord?—Num., ch. 16.

6878. —— Mental. *Aaron.* ²⁴ Aaron shall be gathered unto his people : for he shall not enter into the land which I have given unto the children of Israel, because ye rebelled against my word at the water of Meribah.—Num., ch. 20.

6879, —— The Sinner's. *Parable.* ¹³ He called his ten servants, and delivered them ten pounds, and said unto them, Occupy till I come. ¹⁴ But his citizens hated him, and sent a message after him, saying, We will not have this *man* to reign over us.—Luke, ch. 19.

6880. —— *Parable.* ³⁷ Last of all he sent unto them his son, saying, They will reverence my son. ³⁸ But when the husbandmen saw the son, they said among themselves, This is the heir ; come, let us kill him, and let us seize on his inheritance.—Mat., ch. 21.

6881. —— of Tongue. *"Tame."* ⁷ Every kind of beasts, and of birds, and of serpents, and of things in the sea, is tamed, and hath been tamed of mankind : ⁸ But the tongue can no man tame ; *it is* an unruly evil, full of deadly poison.—James, ch. 3.

6882. —— Uncontested. *Ten Tribes.* ²³ Judah and Benjamin, and to the remnant of the people, saying, ²⁴ Thus saith the Lord, Ye shall not go up, nor fight against your brethren the children of Israel : return every man to his house ; for this thing is from me. They hearkened.. and returned.—1 Kings, ch. 12.

6883. —— Disunion by. *Israel.* ¹ There happened to be there a man of Belial, whose name *was* Sheba..he blew a trumpet, and said, We have no part in David..every man to his tents, O Israel. ² So every man of Israel went up from after David, *and* followed Sheba..but the men of Judah clave unto their king.—2 Sam., ch. 20.

6884. —— of Will. *Jews.* ³⁷ O Jerusalem, Jerusalem, *thou* that killest the prophets, and stonest them which are sent unto thee, how often would I have gathered thy children together, even as a hen gathereth her chickens under *her* wings, and ye would not !—Mat., ch. 23.

See other illustrations under :

INSUBORDINATION.

Intimidating. He could not answer Abner a word 4773
Soldiers. To translate the kingdom from..Saul 4774

SELF-WILL.

Destructive. As a hen gathereth..ye would not 7731
Loss. Presumed to go up..Canaanites smote them 7732
Obstinate. We will certainly do whatsoever 7733
Sin. Rebellion is as the sin of witchcraft 7734
Work of. In their self-will they digged down a w. 7735

———

Obstinate. Rebelled..would not hearken..pour out 201

6885. REBUKE, A Brother's. *Eliab.* ²⁸ Eliab his eldest brother heard when he spake unto the men ; and Eliab's anger was kindled against David, and he said, Why camest thou down hither ? and with whom hast thou left those few sheep in the wilderness ? I know thy pride, and the naughtiness of thine heart.—1 Sam., ch. 17.

6886. —— a Duty. *Trespass.* ³ If thy brother trespass against thee, rebuke him ; and if he repent, forgive him. ⁴ And if he trespass against thee seven times in a day, and seven times in a day turn again to thee, saying, I repent ; thou shalt forgive him.—Luke, ch. 17.

6887. —— Energetic. *Nehemiah.* ²⁷ Shall we then..do all this great evil, to transgress against our God in marrying strange wives ? ²⁸ And *one* of the sons of Joiada..*was* son in law to Sanballat the Horonite : therefore I chased him from me.—Neh., ch. 13.

6888. —— better than Flattery. *Proverb.* ²³ He that rebuketh a man afterwards shall find more favour than he that flattereth with the tongue.—Prov., ch. 28.

6889. —— Insulting. *Ananias.* ¹ Paul, earnestly beholding the council, said, Men *and* brethren, I have lived in all good conscience before God until this day. ² And the high priest Ananias commanded them..to smite him on the mouth.—Acts, ch. 23.

6890. —— Moderation in. *St. Michael.* ⁹ Michael the archangel, when contending with the devil he disputed about the body of Moses, durst not bring against him a railing accusation, but said, The Lord rebuke thee.—Jude.

6891. —— for Rebukers. *Disciples.* ¹³ They brought young children to him, that he should touch them ; and *his* disciples rebuked those that brought *them.* ¹⁴ But when Jesus saw *it,* he was much displeased, and said..Suffer the little children to come unto me.—Mark, ch. 10.

6892. —— Significant. *Extortioners.* [Nehemiah said,] ¹³ I shook my lap, and said, So God shake out every man from his house, and from his labour, that performeth not this promise, even thus be he shaken out, and emptied. And all the congregation said, Amen.—Neh., ch. 5.

6893. —— Terrible. *Elymas the Sorcerer.* ⁹ Paul, filled with the Holy Ghost, set his eyes on him, ¹⁰ And said, O full of all subtilty and all mischief, *thou* child of the devil, *thou* enemy of all righteousness, wilt thou not cease to pervert the right ways of the Lord ? ¹¹..behold, the hand of the Lord *is* upon thee, and thou shalt be blind.—Acts, ch. 13.

6894. —— Wife's. *Michal.* ¹⁶ As the ark of the Lord came into the city of David, Michal.. saw king David leaping and dancing before the Lord ; and she despised him in her heart.. ²⁰ How glorious was the king of Israel to day, who uncovered himself..in the eyes of the handmaids of his servants, as one of the vain fellows shamelessly uncovereth himself !—2 Sam., ch. 6.

See other illustrations under :

Fitting. Dost not thou fear G.?..we..this man 1494
See REPROOF and references.

6895. RECEPTION, Discouraging. *Paul's.* ²⁶ When Saul was come to Jerusalem, he essayed to join himself to the disciples : but they were all afraid of him, and believed not that he was a disciple.—Acts, ch. 9.

See other illustrations under :

ACCEPTANCE.

Assurance. Would he have shewed us all these 53
Denied. Ye brought..torn and the lame..sick 55
Evidence. There rose up fire out of the rock 56
Manifested. Burning lamp passed between those 57

of Piety. In every nation he that feareth..worketh 58
by Sacrifice. L. had respect unto A..offering 59
Terms. Do justly..love' mercy..walk humbly 61

Compassionate. His father saw..ran..neck 157
Enemies. Judah took the captives..clothed..eat 1024
" Thou shalt not smite..set bread..send 1025

6896. RECOMMENDATION, A hurtful.
At Philippi. [16] A certain damsel possessed with a spirit of divination met us, which brought her masters much gain by soothsaying : [17] The same followed Paul and us, and cried, saying, These men are the servants of the most high God, which shew unto us the way of salvation.—Acts, ch. 16.

See other illustrations under :
ADVICE.
Foolish. Said his wife..curse God and die 152
Good. Naaman's servants said, If the prophet had 153
Unfortunate. Let a gallows be made fifty cubits 154

ADVOCATE.
Friendly. Made Blastus their friend..peace 155
Sinners. Advocate with the Father 156

COMMENDATION.
Fruits. Ye are our epistle of commendation 1401
Future. Well done, good and faithful servant 1402
Hurtful. These..are servants of the most high God 1403

COUNSEL.
Dying. [David said,] I go..shew thyself a man 1746
Evil. Rehoboam consulted with the young men 1748
Friends. Let a gallows be made 50 cubits high 1740
Good. Rehoboam consulted with the old men 1749
Influential. David..the lords favour thee not 1750
Malicious. Come, let us take counsel together 1751
Neglected. Took not counsel of the Lord 1741
Oracular. Counsel of Ahithophel..as..oracle of 1742
Opposing. Ahithophel said to Absalom..Hushai 1747
Payment. Saul to servant..what shall we bring 1744
Peace. Joab, hear the words..handmaid 1743
Rejection. Ahithophel saw..not followed..h. 1745
Safety. In the multitude of counsellors..safety 1739
Unfortunate. Why sit we here until we die? 1738

6897. RECOVERY, A full.
David's. [18] David recovered all that the Amalekites had carried away.. [19] And there was nothing lacking to them, neither small nor great, neither sons nor daughters, neither spoil, nor any *thing.*--1 Sam., ch. 30.

6898. —— ——
Job. [12] The Lord blessed the latter end of Job more than his beginning : for he had fourteen thousand sheep, and six thousand camels, and a thousand yoke of oxen, and a thousand she asses. [13] He had also seven sons and three daughters.—Job, ch. 42.

6899. —— Joy of.
Parable. [4] What man of you, having a hundred sheep, if he lose one of them, doth not leave the ninety and nine in the wilderness, and go after that which is lost, until he find it? [5] And when he hath found *it,* he layeth *it* on his shoulders, rejoicing.—Luke, ch. 15.

6900. —— Use of.
From Sickness. [38] Simon's wife's mother was taken with a great fever.. [39] And he stood over her, and rebuked the fever ; and it left her : and immediately she arose and ministered unto them.—Luke, ch. 4.

See other illustrations under :
CURE.
All Persons. Laid his hands on every one and heal. 1867
All Diseases. Stepped in, was made whole of what 1868

Faith. When..beheld the serpent of brass, he lived 1869
Gratitude. She arose, and ministered unto them 1870
Means. Made clay of the spittle..anointed eyes 1871
Progressive. See men as trees walking..clearly 1872
Threefold. Possessed with a devil, blind and dumb 1873
Wonderful. Stretch forth thy hand..as the other 1874

REMEDY.
Improbable. Anointed the eyes of the blind man 7058
Look. As Moses lifted up the serpent..S. of man 7059

RESTORATION.
Property. Leave off this usury..we will restore t. 7274
Spiritual. Bring forth the best robe..ring..shoes 7275

RESTITUTION.
Gains. I give to the poor, if I have taken 7267
Imperative. Thief..if he hath nothing..be sold 7268
Loss. If a man dig a pit..ox fall therein 7269
" Ox hath used to push in times past 7270
" He that kindleth the fire..make restitution 7271
" If the thief be found..pay double 7272
" If a man borrow..make it good 7273

6901. RECOGNITION, Difference in.
John first. [3] That night they caught nothing. [4] But when the morning was now come, Jesus stood on the shore ; but the disciples knew not that it was Jesus.. [6] ..they were not able to draw it for the multitude of fishes. [7] Therefore that disciple whom Jesus loved saith unto Peter, It is the Lord.—John, ch. 21.

6902. —— in Heaven.
David. [23] Now he is dead, wherefore should I fast ? can I bring him back again ? I shall go to him, but he shall not return to me. [24] And David comforted Bathsheba his wife.—2 Sam., ch. 12.

6903. —— Without.
Jacob's Sons. [3] Joseph's ten brethren went down to buy corn in Egypt.. [8] And Joseph knew his brethren, but they knew not him.—Gen., ch. 42.

Also see :
Avoided. No eye shall see ; and disguiseth his face 111
Identification. Upon whom thou shalt see the S. 4269

6904. RECOMPENSE for Sacrifices.
Here—Hereafter. [29] There is no man that hath left house, or brethren, or sisters, or father, or mother, or wife, or children, or lands, for my sake, and the gospel's, [30] But he shall receive a hundredfold now in this time, houses, and brethren, and sisters, and mothers, and children, and lands, with persecutions ; and in the world to come eternal life.—Mark, ch. 10.

See REWARD and references.

6905. RECONCILIATION, A noble.
With Jacob. [4] Esau ran to meet him, and embraced him, and fell on his neck, and kissed him : and they wept.—Gen., ch. 33.

6906. —— Strange.
Pilate—Herod. [11] Herod with his men of war..mocked *him,* and arrayed him in a gorgeous robe, and sent him again to Pilate. [12] And the same day Pilate and Herod were made friends together ; for before they were at enmity.—Luke, ch. 23.

6907. —— before Worship.
Jesus said, [23] If thou bring thy gift to the altar, and there rememberest that thy brother hath aught against thee ; [24] Leave there thy gift before the altar, and go thy way ; first be reconciled to thy brother, and then come and offer thy gift.—Mat., ch. 5.

6908. RECTITUDE commended. *Proverb.*
²⁵ Let thine eyes look right on, and let thine
eyelids look straight before thee. ²⁶ Ponder the
path of thy feet, and let all thy ways be established. ²⁷ Turn not to the right hand nor to
the left : remove thy foot from evil.—Prov.,
ch. 4.

See RIGHTEOUSNESS and references.

6909. REDEMPTION by Blood. *Passover.*
⁷ They shall take of the blood, and strike *it* on
the two side posts and on the upper doorpost..
¹³..for a token upon the houses where ye *are :*
and when I see the blood, I will pass over you,
and the plague shall not be upon you.—Ex., ch.
12.

6910. —— —— *"Precious."* ¹⁸ Ye know
that ye were not redeemed with corruptible
things, *as* silver and gold, from your vain conversation *received* by tradition from your fathers ;
¹⁹ But with the precious blood of Christ, as of a
lamb without blemish.—1 Peter, ch. 1.

6911. —— by Power. *Israel.* ¹ Sang Moses
and the children of Israel..I will sing unto the
Lord, for he hath triumphed gloriously : the
horse and his rider hath he thrown into the sea..
⁴ Pharaoh's chariots and his host hath he cast
into the sea : his chosen captains also are drowned in the Red sea.—Ex., ch. 15.

6912. REFINEMENT by Affliction. *Furnace.*
¹⁰ I have refined thee, but not with silver ; I
have chosen thee in the furnace of affliction.—
Isa., ch. 48.

6913. —— by Fire. *A Refiner.* ² Who may
abide the day of his coming ? and who shall
stand when he appeareth ? for he *is* like a refiner's fire.. ³..he shall sit *as* a refiner and purifier of silver : and he shall purify the sons of
Levi, and purge them as gold and silver, that
they may offer unto the Lord an offering in
righteousness.—Mal., ch. 3.

6914. REFLECTION, Important. *Christian.*
⁸ Whatsoever things are true, whatsoever things
are honest, whatsoever things *are* just, whatsoever things *are* pure, whatsoever things *are* lovely,
whatsoever things *are* of good report ; if *there be*
any virtue, and if *there be* any praise, think on
these things.—Phil., ch. 4.

6915. —— Painful. *Peter.* ⁷² The second
time the cock crew. And Peter called to mind
the word that Jesus said unto him, Before the
cock crow twice, thou shalt deny me thrice.
And when he thought thereon, he wept.—Mark,
ch. 14.

6916. REFORM denied. *By Rehoboam.* [See
No. 6918.] ¹³ The king answered the people
roughly, and forsook the old men's counsel that
they gave him ; ¹⁴ And spake to them after the
counsel of the young men, saying, My father

made your yoke heavy, and I will add to your yoke : my father *also* chastised you with whips, but I will chastise you with scorpions.—1 KINGS, ch. 12.

6917. —— **in Earnest.** *Sabbath Observance.* [19] When the gates of Jerusalem began to be dark before the sabbath, I commanded that the gates should be shut, and charged that they should not be opened till after the sabbath : and *some* of my servants set I at the gates, *that* there should no burden be brought in on the sabbath day. [20] So the merchants and sellers of all kind of ware lodged without Jerusalem once or twice. —NEH., ch. 13.

6918. —— **requested.** *Political.* [3] Israel came, and spake unto Rehoboam, saying, [4] Thy father made our yoke grievous : now therefore make thou the grievous service of thy father, and his heavy yoke which he put upon us, lighter, and we will serve thee.—1 KINGS, ch. 12.

6919. —— **or Rebellion.** *Ten Tribes.* [See Nos. 6918 and 6916.] [16] When all Israel saw that the king hearkened not unto them, the people answered the king, saying, What portion have we in David ?. .to your tents, O Israel : now see to thine own house, David.—1 KINGS, ch. 12. [Ten tribes seceded.]

6920. —— **Thorough.** *"Old Bottles."* [37] No man putteth new wine into old bottles ; else the new wine will burst the bottles, and be spilled, and the bottles shall perish. [38] But new wine must be put into new bottles ; and both are preserved.—LUKE, ch. 5.

6921. REFORMER, A divine. *Jesus.* [15] When he had made a scourge of small cords, he drove them all out of the temple, and the sheep, and the oxen ; and poured out the changers' money, and overthrew the tables ; [16] And said. .Take these things hence ; make not my Father's house a house of merchandise.—JOHN, ch. 2.

6922. —— **A great.** *Ezra.* [10] Ye have transgressed, and have taken strange wives, to increase the trespass of Isaael. [11] Now therefore make confession unto the Lord . . and do his pleasure : and separate yourselves from the people of the land, and from the strange wives.— EZRA, ch. 10.

6923. —— **A royal.** *Asa.* [12] He took away the sodomites out of the land, and removed all the idols that his fathers had made. [13] And also Maachah his mother, even her he removed from *being* queen, because she had made an idol in a grove ; and Asa destroyed her idol, and burnt *it* by the brook Kidron.—1 KINGS, ch. 15.

6924. —— **A pretended.** *Absalom.* [3] Absalom said. .See, thy matters *are* good and right ; but *there is* no man *deputed* of the king to hear thee. [4]. .Oh that I were made judge in the land, that every man which hath any suit or cause might come unto me, and I would do him justice !—2 SAM., ch. 15.

6925. —— **A vigorous.** *Nehemiah.* [23] Saw I Jews *that* had married wives of Ashdod, of Ammon, *and* of Moab : [24] And their children spake half in the speech of Ashdod, and could not speak in the Jews' language, but according to the language of each people. [25] And I contended with them, and cursed them, and smote certain of them, and plucked off their hair, and made

them swear by God, *saying*, Ye shall not give your daughters unto their sons.—NEH., ch. 13.

6926. REFORMATION with Confession. *Ezra.* [1] When Ezra had prayed, and. .confessed, weeping and casting himself down before the house of God, there assembled. .a very great congregation of men and women and children : for the people wept very sore.—EZRA, ch. 10.

6927. —— **Covenant for.** *Made Oath.* [30] We would not give our daughters unto the people of the land, nor take their daughters for our sons : [31] And *if* the people of the land bring ware or any victuals on the sabbath day to sell, *that* we would not buy it.—NEH., ch. 10.

6928. —— **A determined.** *Nehemiah.* [7] I came to Jerusalem, and understood of the evil that Eliashib did for Tobiah, in preparing him a chamber in the courts of the house of God. [8] And it grieved me sore : therefore I cast forth all the household stuff of Tobiah out of the chamber.—NEH., ch. 13.

6929. —— **Failure of.** *"Vomit."* [21] It had been better for them not to have known the way of righteousness, than, after they have known *it*, to turn from the holy commandment delivered unto them. [22] But it is happened unto them according to the true proverb, The dog *is* turned to his own vomit again ; and, The sow that was washed to her wallowing in the mire.—2 PETER, ch. 2.

6930. —— **indispensable.** *Israelites.* [15] When ye spread forth your hands, I will hide mine eyes from you ; yea, when ye make many prayers, I will not hear : your hands are full of blood. [16] Wash ye, make you clean ; put away the evil of your doings from before mine eyes ; cease to do evil ; [17] Learn to do well ; seek judgment, relieve the oppressed, judge the fatherless, plead for the widow.—ISA., ch. 1.

6931. —— **necessary.** *Samuel said,* [23] God forbid that I should sin against the Lord in ceasing to pray for you : but I will teach you. . the right way : [24] Only fear the Lord, and serve him in truth with all your heart : for consider how great *things* he hath done for you. [25] But if ye shall still do wickedly, ye shall be consumed, both ye and your king.—1 SAM., ch. 12.

6932. —— **A penitential.** *Israelites.* [15] The children of Israel said unto the Lord, We have sinned : do thou unto us whatsoever seemeth good unto thee ; deliver us only, we pray thee, this day. [16] And they put away the strange gods from among them, and served the Lord : and his soul was grieved for the misery of Israel.— JUDGES, ch. 10.

6933. —— **A real.** *King Jehoiada.* [17] Jehoiada made a covenant between the Lord and the king and the people, that they should be the Lord's people ; between the king also and the people. [18] And all the people of the land went into the house of Baal, and brake it down ; his altars and his images brake they in pieces thoroughly, and slew Mattan the priest of Baal before the altars.—2 KINGS, ch. 11.

6934. —— **with Repentance.** *John Baptist.* [7] Saw many of the Pharisees and Sadducees come to his baptism, he said unto them, O generation of vipers, who hath warned you to flee from the wrath to come ? [8] Bring forth therefore fruits meet for repentance.—MAT., ch. 3.

6935. —— **A radical.** *Hezekiah.* [4] He removed the high places, and brake the images, and cut down the groves, and brake in pieces the brazen serpent that Moses had made : for unto those days the children of Israel did burn incense to it.—2 KINGS, ch. 18.

6936. —— **Truth brings.** *Josiah.* [2] He read in their ears all the words of the book of the covenant which was found in the house of the Lord.. [4] ..to bring forth out of the temple of the Lord all the vessels that were made for Baal, and for the grove, and for all the host of heaven : and he burned them.—2 KINGS, ch. 23.

6937. —— **Transient.** *Saul.* [16] When David had made an end of speaking..Saul said, Is this thy voice, my son David..and wept. [17] And he said to David, Thou *art* more righteous than I : for thou hast rewarded me good, whereas I have rewarded thee evil.—1 SAM., ch. 24.

6938. —— **wanted.** *Not Fasting.* [6] *Is* not this the fast that I have chosen ? to loose the bands of wickedness, to undo the heavy burdens, and to let the oppressed go free, and that ye break every yoke ? [7] *Is it* not to deal thy bread to the hungry, and that thou bring the poor that are cast out to thy house ? when thou seest the naked, that thou cover him ?—ISA., ch. 58.

See other illustrations under :

CONVERSION.

Creation. New creature, old things passed away	1700
Conscious. Know we that we dwell in him..S.	1701
Changed. Made their feet fast..washed their	1702
Changes Life. Saul preached..Is not this he that	1703
Effort. Strive to enter in at the strait gate	1704
Evidence. Besought us..come into my house	1705
False. Simon saw..H. G. given..offered money	1706
Genuine. Set meat..rejoiced, believing in G.	1707
Heart-work. Out of the heart..evil thoughts	1708
Hasty. See, here is water ; what doth hinder	1709
Inward. Pharisees make clean the outside of the	1710
Mystery. Wind bloweth..canst not tell whence	1711
Necessity. Except a man be born of water and the	1712
New Heart. God gave Saul another heart	1713
Negative. Reckon ye yourselves dead indeed unto	1714
Sudden. Called for a light..what must I do ?	1715
Superficial. When tribulation or persecution	1716
Wonderful. Suddenly there shined..voice..Saul	1717

REGENERATION.

Mystery. Wind bloweth..canst not tell whence	6951
Necessity. Except..he cannot enter the kingdom	6950

RESTITUTION.

Gains. If taken..wrongfully..I restore fourfold	7267
Imperative. Thief..full restitution..sold	7268
Loss. Owner of the pit..make it good	7269
" Ox hath used to push..ox for ox	7270
" He that kindled the fire..restitution	7271
" Stuff to keep..thief pay double	7272
" Owner be with it..not make it good	7273

Called. I have set thee to root out..pull down	2195
Difficult. None that go in to her return again	116
Transient. Sow that was washed..wallowing in the	613

See REPENTANCE and references.

6939. REFRESHMENT for the Weary. *Wilderness.* [27] They came to Elim, where *were* twelve wells of water, and threescore and ten palm trees : and they encamped there by the waters.—Ex., ch. 15.

6940. REFUGE, The Christian's. *Proverb.*

[26] In the fear of the Lord *is* strong confidence : and his children shall have a place of refuge.—PROV., ch. 14.

6941. —— **Cities of.** *Six.* [2] Appoint out for you cities of refuge.. [3] That the slayer that killeth *any* person unawares *and* unwittingly may flee thither.—JOSH., ch. 20.

6942. —— **Faith's.** *David's.* [1] God *is* our refuge and strength, a very present help in trouble. [2] Therefore will not we fear, though the earth be removed, and though the mountains be carried into the midst of the sea ; [3] *Though* the waters thereof roar *and* be troubled, *though* the mountains shake with the swelling thereof.—Ps. 46.

6943. —— —— *The Lord.* [10] When my father and mother forsake me, then the Lord will take me up.—Ps. 27.

6944. —— **Fleeing for.** *Manslayer.* [5] When a man goeth into the wood..to hew wood, and his hand fetcheth a stroke with the axe to cut down the tree, and the head slippeth from the helve, and lighteth upon his neighbour, that he die : he shall flee unto one of those cities, and live.—DEUT., ch. 19.

6945. —— **in Prayer.** *Prayer.* [14] Hezekiah received the letter..of the messengers, and read it : and Hezekiah went up into the house of the Lord, and spread it before the Lord. [15] And Hezekiah prayed.. [35] And..that night..the angel of the Lord went out, and smote in the camp of the Assyrians a hundred fourscore and five thousand.—2 KINGS, ch. 19.

6946. —— **Safe.** *Tower.* [10] The name of the Lord *is* a strong tower : the righteous runneth into it, and is safe.—PROV., ch. 18.

6947. —— **Sanctuary.** *Adonijah.* [51] It was told Solomon..Adonijah feareth king Solomon : for, lo, he hath caught hold on the horns of the altar, saying, Let king Solomon swear unto me to day that he will not slay his servant.. [52] And Solomon said, If he will shew himself a worthy man, there shall not a hair of him fall to the earth..but if wickedness shall be found in him, he shall die.—1 KINGS, ch. 1.

See SAFETY and references.

6948. REFUSAL, An unwise. *To Canaan.* [17] Let us pass, I pray thee, through thy country : we will not pass through the fields, or..vineyards, neither will we drink *of* the water of the wells : we will go by the king's *high* way, we will not turn to the right hand nor to the left.. [18] And Edom said..Thou shalt not pass by me.—NUM., ch. 20.

See other illustrations under :

DENIAL.

Considerate. David would not drink thereof	2173
Others. Become a stumblingblock to others	2174
Twofold. Deny me..will I also deny	2175
Unexpected. Peter denied him..I know him not	2176

PROHIBITION.

Blood. Ye shall eat the blood of..no flesh	6635
Fat. Ye shall eat no manner of fat	6638
Flesh. Whatsoever parteth the hoof..shall ye eat	6637
Fruit. Tree..I commanded thee..not eat ?	6636

REJECTION.

Acclamation. They were instant with loud voices	6957
Anger. Command fire to come down and consume	6956
Authority. Diotrephes..neither..receive the b.	6955

Conditional. Ye shall not see my face except 6958
Disobedient. Thou hast rejected..L. hath rejected 6959
God. Rejected your God..set a king over us 6960
" Inquire of Baal-zebub the god of Ekron 6961
Jealousy. Samaritans did not receive him..go to J. 6962
Moses. Who made thee a ruler and a judge over 6963
Rebellious. This is the heir ; let us kill him..seize 6964
Sin. He that believeth not is condemned already 6965
Treason. Korah went down alive into the pit 6966
Worldly. Swine..pray him to depart..their coasts 6967

6949. REGALIA, The fatal. *Baalites.* ²¹ Jehu sent..and all the worshippers of Baal came, so that there was not a man left that came not.. and the house of Baal was full from one end to another. ²² And he said unto him that *was* over the vestry, Bring forth vestments for all the worshippers of Baal... ²⁴..Jehu said to the guard and to the captains, Go in, *and* slay them ; let none come forth.—2 KINGS, ch. 10.

6950. REGENERATION, Mystery of. *"Wind."* ⁸ The wind bloweth where it listeth, and thou hearest the sound thereof, but canst not tell whence it cometh, and whither it goeth : so is every one that is born of the Spirit. ⁹ Nicodemus answered..How can these things be?—JOHN, ch. 3.

6951. —— Necessity of. *To Nicodemus.* ⁵ Jesus answered, Verily, verily, I say unto thee, Except a man be born of water and *of* the Spirit, he cannot enter into the kingdom of God.—JOHN, ch. 3.

See CONVERSION and references.

6952. REGRETS, Vain. *Herod's.* ²⁵ I will that thou give me by and by in a charger the head of John the Baptist. ²⁶ And the king was exceeding sorry ; *yet* for his oath's sake, and for their sakes which sat with him, he would not reject her.—MARK, ch. 6.

See other illustrations under :
REMORSE.
Needful. People that came..smote their breasts 7067
Prevented. Lest swallowed up with overmuch sor. 7068
Treachery. Judas..went and hanged himself 7069
See REPENTANCE and GUILT.

6953. REIGN, A short. *Seven Days.* ¹⁶ The people *that were* encamped heard say, Zimri hath conspired, and hath also slain the king : wherefore all Israel made Omri, the captain of the host, king over Israel that day in the camp. ¹⁷ And Omri..besieged Tirzah. ¹⁸ And..when Zimri saw that the city was taken..he went into the palace..and burnt the king's house over him with fire.—1 KINGS, ch. 16.

See other illustrations under :
DOMINION.
Dream. Your sheaves made obeisance to my s. 2489
Feared. The fear of you shall be upon every beast 2490
Made for. Let us make..dominion over..all 2491
KING.
of Animals. [Leviathan] not his like 4833
Burdens. Take your sons and daughters 4834
Burlesque. Scarlet robe..crown of thorns 4835
Cruel. Under harrows..axes of iron 4836
Goodly. Saul..not a goodlier person 4838
Helpless. Set his heart on D. to deliver 4839
Last. Zedekiah..carried him to Babylon 4840
of Nations. Written in Hebrew, Greek, Latin 4841
of Trees. To the olive, Reign over us 4842
Unhappy. Zimri..went into the palace..burnt 4843

Universal. From the rising of the sun 4844
Wicked. Manasseh..did evil 4845
Youthful. Josiah was eight years old 4846
" Sixteen years old was Uzzah 4847
KINGSHIP.
Declined. Gideon said, I will not reign 4848
" By force to make him a king..departed 4849

Long. David reigned..forty years 228
See GOVERNMENT and references.

6954. REJECTED chosen, The. *"Stone."* ¹⁰ By him doth this man stand here before you whole. ¹¹ This is the stone which was set at nought of you builders, which is become the head of the corner.—ACTS, ch. 4.

6955. REJECTION of Authority. *Diotrephes.* ⁹ I wrote unto the church : but Diotrephes, who loveth to have the preeminence among them, receiveth us not. ¹⁰..prating against us with malicious words : and not content therewith, neither doth he himself receive the brethren, and forbiddeth them that would, and casteth *them* out of the church.—3 JOHN.

6956. —— Anger at. *James and John* [See No. 6962.] ⁵⁴ When his disciples James and John saw *this*, they said, Lord, wilt thou that we command fire to come down from heaven, and consume them, even as Elias did ? ⁵⁵ But he..rebuked them, and said, Ye know not what manner of spirit ye are of.—LUKE, ch. 9.

6957. —— by Acclamation. *Jews.* ²⁰ Pilate therefore, willing to release Jesus, spake again to them.. ²³ And they were instant with loud voices, requiring that he might be crucified : and the voices of them and of the chief priests prevailed.—LUKE, ch. 23.

6958. —— Conditional. *Joseph.* ² Go again, buy us a little food. ³ And Judah spake..saying, The man did solemnly protest unto us, saying, Ye shall not see my face, except your brother *be* with you.—GEN., ch. 43.

6959. —— of the Disobedient. *Israelites.* ²¹ The people took of the spoil, sheep and oxen, ..which should have been utterly destroyed, to sacrifice unto the Lord.. ²² And Samuel said, Hath the Lord *as great* delight in burnt offerings and sacrifices, as in obeying the voice of the Lord ? Behold, to obey *is* better than sacrifice, *and* to hearken than the fat of rams. ²³ For rebellion *is as* the sin of witchcraft, and stubbornness *is as* iniquity and idolatry. Because thou hast rejected the word of the Lord, he hath also rejected thee from *being* king.—1 SAM., ch. 15.

6960. —— of God. *For a King.* ¹⁹ Ye have this day rejected your God, who himself saved you out of all your adversities and your tribulations ; and ye have said unto him, *Nay*, but set a king over us.—1 SAM., ch. 10.

6961. —— —— *Punished*. ² Ahaziah fell down through a lattice in his upper chamber that *was* in Samaria, and was sick : and he sent messengers, and said..Go, inquire of Baal-zebub the god of Ekron whether I shall recover.. ⁴..thus saith the Lord, Thou shalt not come down from that bed..but shalt surely die.—2 KINGS, ch. 1.

6962. —— from Jealousy. *Samaritans.* ⁵² Sent messengers before his face : and they went..into a village of the Samaritans, to make ready for him. ⁵³ And they did not receive him, because his

face was as though he would go to Jerusalem.—
LUKE, ch. 9.

6963. —— **of Minister.** *Hebrew.* [27] He that
did his neighbour wrong thrust him away, saying, Who made thee a ruler and a judge over
us ? [28] Wilt thou kill me, as thou didst the
Egyptian yesterday ? [29] Then fled Moses..in the
land of Madian.—ACTS, ch. 7.

6964. —— **Rebellious.** *Parable.* [37] Last of
all he sent..his son, saying, They will reverence
my son. [38] But when the husbandmen saw the
son, they said among themselves, This is the
heir ; come, let us kill him, and let us seize on
his inheritance.—MAT., ch. 21.

6965. —— **Sin of.** *Of Christ.* [16] God so loved
the world, that he gave his only begotten Son,
that whosoever believeth in him should not perish, but have everlasting life.. [18] He that believeth on him is not condemned : but he that
believeth not is condemned already, because he
hath not believed in the name of the only begotten Son of God.—JOHN, ch. 3.

6966. —— **Treason in.** *Korah.* [28] Moses said,
Hereby ye shall know that the Lord hath sent
me to do all these works ; for *I have not done
them* of mine own mind.. [33] They, and all that
appertained to them, went down alive into the
pit, and the earth closed upon them.—NUM.,
ch. 16.

6967. —— **Worldly.** *Gadarenes.* [16] They
that saw *it* told them how it befell to him that
was possessed with the devil, and *also* concerning the swine. [17] And they began to pray him
to depart out of their coasts.—MARK, ch. 5.

See other illustrations under :

REBELLION.

Abominable. Rebellion is as the sin of witchcraft	6874
Ingrates. Absalom sent spies..say Absalom	6875
Ill-government. Thy father made our yoke	6876
Jealousy. Ye take too much upon you [Korah]	6877
Mental. Not enter..ye rebelled against my word	6878
Sinners. We will not have this man to reign	6879
" This is the heir ; come, let us kill him	6880
Tongue. Every kind of beasts..been tamed	6881
Uncontested. Ye shall not fight..return every man	6882
Vain. Sheba blew a trumpet..we have no part	6883
Will. How oft would I..but ye would not	6884

RESISTANCE.

Prohibited. If any..take away thy coat..cloak	7197
Prompt. We gave place by subjection, no, not for	7198
Spirit. My Spirit shall not always strive	7199
" It is hard for thee to kick against the pricks	7200

See ABANDONMENT and references.

6968. REJOICING, Communion brings. *David.*
[6] This poor man cried, and the Lord heard *him*,
and saved him out of all his troubles. [8] O taste
and see that the Lord *is* good : blessed *is* the
man *that* trusteth in him.—Ps. 34.

6969. —— **Conversion brings.** *Samaria.*
[5] Philip went down to the city of Samaria, and
preached Christ unto them. [6] And the people
with one accord gave heed.. [8] And there was
great joy in that city.—ACTS, ch. 8.

6970. —— **Conscience gives.** *Paul.* [12] Our
rejoicing is this, the testimony of our conscience,
that in simplicity and godly sincerity, not with
fleshly wisdom, but by the grace of God, we have
had our conversation in the world.—2 COR.,
ch. 1.

6971. —— **A Convert's.** *Jailer.* [33] He took
them the same hour of the night, and washed
their stripes ; and was baptized, he and all his,
straightway. [34] And when he had brought them
into his house, he set meat before them, and rejoiced, believing in God with all his house.—
ACTS, ch. 16.

6972. —— —— *David.* [1] I waited patiently for the Lord ; and he inclined unto me, and
heard my cry. [2] He brought me up also out
of an horrible pit, out of the miry clay, and set
my feet upon a rock, *and* established my goings.
[3] And he hath put a new song in my mouth,
even praise unto our God.—Ps. 40.

6973. —— —— *Eunuch.* [38] He commanded the chariot to stand still ; and they went down
both into the water, both Philip and the eunuch ;
and he baptized him. [39] ..the eunuch saw him
no more : and he went on his way rejoicing.—
ACTS, ch. 8.

6974. —— **a Duty.** *The Law.* [11] Thou shalt
rejoice in every good *thing* which the Lord thy
God hath given unto thee, and unto thine house,
thou, and the Levite, and the stranger that *is*
among you.—DEUT., ch. 26.

6975. —— **for Deliverance.** *Israelites at Red
Sea.* [1] Then sang Moses and the children of Israel..I will sing unto the Lord, for he hath triumphed gloriously : the horse and his rider hath
he thrown into the sea. [2] The Lord *is* my strength
and song, and he is become my salvation.—EX.,
ch. 15.

6976. —— —— *Haman overthrown.* [16] The
Jews had light, and gladness, and joy, and
honour. [17] And in every province, and in every
city, whithersoever the king's commandment
and his decree came, the Jews had joy and gladness, a feast and a good day.—ESTHER, ch. 8.

6977. —— **in God.** *In Adversity.* [17] Although
the fig tree shall not blossom, neither *shall* fruit
be in the vines ; the labour of the olive shall fail,
and the fields shall yield no meat ; the flock
shall be cut off from the fold, and *there shall be*
no herd in the stalls : [18] Yet I will rejoice in the
Lord, I will joy in the God of my salvation.
[19] The Lord God *is* my strength, and he will
make my feet like hinds' *feet*, and he will make
me to walk upon mine high places.—HAB., ch. 3.

6978. —— **A great.** *King Jesus.* [37] When
he was. at the descent of the mount of Olives,
the whole multitude of the disciples began to
rejoice and praise God with a loud voice for all
the mighty works that they had seen ; [38] Saying,
Blessed *be* the King that cometh in the name of
the Lord : peace in heaven, and glory in the
highest.—LUKE, ch. 19.

6979. —— **in Gifts.** *For Temple.* [9] Then
the people rejoiced, for that they offered willingly, because with perfect heart they offered
willingly to the Lord : and David the king also
rejoiced with great joy.—1 CHRON., ch. 29.

6980. —— **Heavenly.** *In Zion.* [10] The ransomed of the Lord shall return, and come to
Zion with songs and everlasting joy upon their
heads : they shall obtain joy and gladness, and
sorrow and sighing shall flee away.—ISA., ch. 35.

6981. —— **in Prison.** *Paul and Silas.*
[24] Thrust them into the inner prison, and made
their feet fast in the stocks. [25] And at midnight
Paul and Silas prayed, and sang praises unto

God : and the prisoners heard them.—ACTS, ch. 16.

6982. —— in Persecutions. *Peter and John.*
[40] When they had called the apostles, and beaten *them,* they commanded that they should not speak in the name of Jesus, and let them go. [41] And they departed from the presence of the council, rejoicing that they were counted worthy to suffer shame for his name.—ACTS, ch. 5.

6983. —— Premature. *Amalekites.* [16] *They were* spread abroad. . eating and drinking, and dancing, because of all the great spoil that they had taken out of the land of the Philistines, and . . of Judah. [17] And David smote them from the twilight even unto the evening of the next day : and there escaped not a man of them, save four hundred young men, which rode upon camels. —1 SAM., ch. 30.

6984. —— Religious. *D a v i d.* [14] David danced, before the Lord with all *his* might ; and David *was* girded with a linen ephod. [15] So David. . brought up the ark of the Lord with shouting, and with the sound of the trumpet.—2 SAM., ch. 6.

6985. —— in Reproach. *Christian.* [22] Blessed are ye, when men shall hate you, and when they shall separate you *from their company,* and shall reproach *you,* and cast out your name as evil, for the Son of man's sake. [23] Rejoice ye in that day, and leap for joy : for, behold, your reward *is* great in heaven.—LUKE, ch. 7.

6986. —— in Tribulation. *Paul.* [4] I am filled with comfort, I am exceeding joyful in all our tribulation. [5] For, when we were come into Macedonia, our flesh had no rest, but we were troubled on every side ; without *were* fightings, within *were* fears. [6] Nevertheless God, that comforteth those that are cast down, comforted us by the coming of Titus.—2 COR., ch. 7.

6987. —— in Temptation. *Christians.* [2] My brethren, count it all joy when ye fall into divers temptations ; [3] Knowing *this,* that the trying of your faith worketh patience. [4] But let patience have *her* perfect work, that ye may be perfect and entire, wanting nothing.—JAMES, ch. 1.

6988. —— of Victors. *Philistines.* [24] When the people saw him, they praised their god : for they said, Our god hath delivered into our hands our enemy, and the destroyer of our country, which slew many of us. [25] And. . when their hearts were merry. . they said, Call for Samson, that he may make us sport.—JUDGES, ch. 16.

See JOY and references.

6989. RELAPSE, Spiritual. *Unclean Spirit.* [44] He saith, I will return into my house from whence I came out ; and when he is come, he findeth *it* empty, swept, and garnished. [45] Then goeth he, and taketh with himself seven other spirits more wicked than himself, and they enter in and dwell there : and the last *state* of that man is worse than the first.—MAT., ch. 12.

See other illustrations under :
Character. If again entangled. . latter end is worse 1119
    " Taketh seven other spirits more wicked 1112
    " Sow returned to her wallowing in the 1120
See BACKSLIDING and references.

6990. RELATIVE, Claims of a. *Abimelech.* [2] Whether *is* better for you, either that all the sons of Jerubbaal, *which are* threescore and ten

persons, reign over you, or that one reign over you ? remember also that I *am* your bone and your flesh. [3] . . all the men of Shechem. . their hearts inclined to follow Abimelech ; for they said, He *is* our brother.—JUDGES, ch. 9.

6991. RELATIVES, Fear of. *Gideon.* [25] Take thy father's young bullock. and throw down the altar of Baal that thy father hath, and cut down the grove that *is* by it : [26] And build an altar unto the Lord. . [27] Then Gideon took ten men. . and *so* it was, because he feared his father's household, and the men of the city, that he could not do *it* by day, that he did *it* by night. —JUDGES, ch. 6.

6992. —— Hinderance of. *Disciple.* [59] Follow me, But he said, Lord, suffer me first to go and bury my father. [60] Jesus said. . Let the dead bury their dead ; but go thou and preach the kingdom of God.—LUKE, ch. 9.

6993. —— Interference of. *Moses.* [1] Miriam and Aaron spake against Moses because of the Ethiopian woman whom he had married.—NUM., ch. 12.

6994. —— —— *Jesus.* [20] The multitude cometh together again, so that they could not so much as eat bread. [21] And when his friends heard *of it,* they went out to lay hold on him : for they said, He is beside himself.—MARK, ch. 3.

6995. —— The Lord's. *" Whosoever.''* [46] *His* mother and his brethren stood without, desiring to speak with him. . [49] And he stretched forth his hand toward his disciples, and said, Behold my mother and my brethren ! [50] For whosoever shall do the will of my Father. . the same is my brother, and sister, and mother.—MAT., ch. 12.

6996. —— Persecution from. *P r e d i c t i o n.* [12] Now the brother shall betray the brother to death, and the father the son ; and children shall rise up against *their* parents, and shall cause them to be put to death. . but he that shall endure unto the end, the same shall be saved. —MARK, ch. 13.

6997. —— Saved by. *A p o s t l e s.* [40] One of the two which heard John speak. . was Andrew. . [41] He first findeth his own brother Simon and saith unto him, We have found the Messias, which is, being interpreted, the Christ. [42] And he brought him to Jesus.—JOHN, ch. 1.

See other illustrations under :

UNCLE.
Gracious. Abram said unto Lot. . no strife   9081
    " Laban. . kissed him. . to his house   9082
Respected. Esther did the commandment of Mor. 9083

Helpful. Mordecai brought up Esther his uncle's d. 105
Posterity desired. I go childless, and the steward 6290
See FAMILY and references.

6998. RELIC, Worship of. *Hezekiah.* [4] He removed the high places, and brake the images, and cut down the groves, and brake in pieces the brazen serpent that Moses had made : for unto those days the children of Israel did burn incense to it.—2 KINGS, ch. 18.

6999. RELIGION, Approximating. *S c r i b e.* [33] To love him with all the heart, and with all the understanding, and with all the soul, and with all the strength, and to love *his* neighbour as himself, is more than all whole burnt offerings and sacrifices. [34] . . Jesus. . said unto him,

Thou art not far from the kingdom.—MARK, ch. 12.

7000. —— **of Appearances.** *"Show."* [46] Beware of the scribes, which desire to walk in long robes, and love greetings in the markets, and the highest seats in the synagogues, and the chief rooms at feasts ; [47] Which devour widows' houses, and for a shew make long prayers : the same shall receive greater damnation.— LUKE, ch. 20.

7001. —— **Blessings of.** *Proverbs.* [13] Happy *is* the man *that* findeth wisdom, and the man *that* getteth understanding : [14] For the merchandise of it *is* better than the merchandise of silver, and the gain thereof than fine gold. [15] She *is* more precious than rubies.—PROV., ch. 3. [See chapter.]

7002. —— **for Children.** *Law.* [9] Keep thy soul diligently, lest thou forget the things which thine eyes have seen, and lest they depart from thy heart all the days of thy life : but teach them thy sons, and thy sons' sons.—DEUT., ch. 4.

7003. —— **the first Concern.** *Jesus said,* [29] Seek not ye what ye shall eat, or what ye shall drink, neither be ye of doubtful mind. [30]..your Father knoweth that ye have need of these things. [31] But rather seek ye the kingdom of God, and all these things shall be added unto you.—LUKE, ch. 12.

7004. —— **Deceit in.** *Pharisees* [15] Took counsel how they might entangle him in *his* talk. [16] And they sent..their disciples with the Herodians, saying, Master, we know that thou art true, and teachest the way of God in truth, neither carest thou for any *man.*—MAT., ch. 22.

7005. —— **Corrupted.** *For the Calf.* [5] Aaron made proclamation, and said, To morrow is a feast to the Lord. [6] And they..offered burnt offerings, and brought peace offerings ; and the people sat down to eat and to drink, and rose up to play.—Ex., ch. 32.

7006. —— **Caste in.** *Ethiopian.* [1] Miriam and Aaron spake against Moses because of the Ethiopian woman whom he had married.—NUM., ch. 12. [Miriam became a leper.]

7007. —— **Conceit in.** *Young Ruler.* [20] The young man saith..all these things have I kept from my youth up : what lack I yet ?—MAT., ch. 19.

7008. —— **Contempt for.** *Athenians.* [18] Certain philosophers of the Epicureans, and of the Stoics, encountered him. And some said, What will this babbler say? other some, He seemeth to be a setter forth of strange gods : because he preached unto them Jesus, and the resurrection. —ACTS, ch. 17.

7009. —— **Contrasted.** *Light—Darkness.* [18] The path of the just *is* as the shining light, that shineth more and more unto the perfect day. [19] The way of the wicked *is* as darkness : they know not at what they stumble.—PROV., ch. 4.

7010. —— **Deliberation in.** *Tower.* [27] Whosoever doth not bear his cross, and come after me, cannot be my disciple. [28] For which of you, intending to build a tower, sitteth not down first, and counteth the cost, whether he have *sufficient* to finish *it* ? [29] Lest haply, after he hath laid the foundation, and is not able to fin-

ish *it*, all that behold *it* begin to mock him.— LUKE, ch. 14.

7011. —— **Disgraced.** *Eli's Sons.* [16] If any man said..Let them not fail to burn the fat presently, and *then* take *as much* as thy soul desireth ; then he would answer him, Nay ; but thou shalt give *it* me now : and if not, I will take *it* by force. [17] Wherefore the sin of the young men was very great..for men abhorred the offering of the Lord.—1 SAM., ch. 2.

7012. —— **a Cloak.** *Absalom.* [8] Thy servant vowed a vow while I abode at Geshur in Syria, saying, If the Lord shall bring me again indeed to Jerusalem, then I will serve the Lord. [9] And the king said..Go in peace. So he..went to Hebron. [10] But Absalom sent spies throughout all the tribes of Israel, saying..ye shall say, Absalom reigneth in Hebron.—2 SAM., ch. 15.

7013. —— **Destitution of.** *Reign of Asa.* [3] For a long season Israel *hath been* without the true God, and without a teaching priest, and without law. [4] But when they in their trouble did turn unto the Lord God of Israel, and sought him, he was found of them.—2 CHRON., ch. 15.

7014. —— **despised.** *Jews.* [7] Ye offer polluted bread upon mine altar ; and ye say, Wherein have we polluted thee ? In that ye say, The table of the Lord *is* contemptible. [8] And if ye offer the blind for sacrifice, *is it* not evil ? and if ye offer the lame and sick, *is it* not evil ? offer it now unto thy governor ; will he be pleased with thee ?—MAL., ch. 1.

7015. —— **of Externals.** *Platter.* [38] He marvelled that he had not first washed before dinner. [39] And the Lord said..Now do ye Pharisees make clean the outside of the cup and the platter ; but your inward part is full of ravening and wickedness.—LUKE, ch. 11.

7016. —— **made easy.** *New Kingdom.* [See No. 7040.] [28] Jeroboam said unto them, It is too much for you to go up to Jerusalem.—1 KINGS, ch. 12.

7017. —— **ennobling.** *Crown.* [7] Wisdom *is* the principal thing ; *therefore* get wisdom.. [8] Exalt her, and she shall promote thee : she shall bring thee to honour, when thou dost embrace her. [9] She shall give to thine head an ornament of grace : a crown of glory shall she deliver to thee.—PROV., ch. 4.

7018. —— **Enthusiasm in.** *David.* [14] David danced before the Lord with all *his* might ; and David *was* girded with a linen ephod. [15] So.. all the house of Israel brought up the ark of the Lord with shouting, and with the sound of the trumpet.—2 SAM., ch. 6.

7019. —— **Excitement in.** *At Capernaum.* [20] The multitude cometh together again, so that they could not so much as eat bread. [21] And when his friends heard *of it*, they went out to lay hold on him : for they said, He is beside himself.—MARK, ch. 3.

7020. —— **Family.** *Isaac.* [25] He builded an altar there, and called upon the name of the Lord, and pitched his tent there : and there Isaac's servants digged a well.—GEN., ch. 26.

7021. —— —— *Job.* [5] When the days of *their* feasting were gone..Job sent and sanctified them, and rose up early in the morning, and offered burnt offerings *according* to the number of them all : for Job said, It may be that my sons have sinned..Thus did Job continually.—Job, ch. 1.

7022. —— **The First for.** "*Firstborn.*" [11] It shall be when the Lord shall bring thee into the land of the Canaanites.. [12] That thou shalt set apart unto the Lord..every firstling that cometh of a beast which thou hast ; the male *shall be* the Lord's.. [14]..and all the firstborn of man among thy children shalt thou redeem.—Ex., ch. 13.

7023. —— —— *First Fruits.* [2] Thou shalt take of the first of all the fruit of the earth.. and shall put *it* in a basket, and shalt go unto the place which the Lord thy God shall choose to place his name there. [3]..And thou shalt set it before the Lord thy God.—Deut., ch. 26.

7024. —— **Fickleness in.** *At Lystra.* [11] The gods are come down to us in the likeness of men. [12] And they called Barnabas, Jupiter ; and Paul, Mercurius, because he was the chief speaker. [13] Then the priest of Jupiter..brought oxen and garlands unto the gates, and would have done sacrifice with the people.. [19]..*certain* Jews from Antioch and Iconium, who persuaded the people, and, having stoned Paul, drew *him* out of the city, supposing he had been dead.—Acts, ch. 14.

7025. —— **Folly in.** *Vows.* [4] When thou vowest a vow unto God, defer not to pay it ; for *he hath* no pleasure in fools : pay that which thou hast vowed. [5] Better *is it* that thou shouldest not vow, than that thou shouldest vow and not pay.—Eccl., ch. 5.

7026. —— **Hypocrisy in.** *Jacob.* [20] Isaac said unto his son, How *is it* that thou hast found *it* so quickly, my son ? And he said, Because the Lord thy God brought *it* to me.—Gen., ch. 27.

7027. —— **Hindered.** *Excuse.* [18] They all with one *consent* began to make excuse. The first said..I have bought a piece of ground, and I must needs go and see it.. [19] And another said, I have bought five yoke of oxen, and I go to prove them.. [20] And another said, I have married.—Luke, ch. 14.

7028. —— **Hidden.** *Peter.* [67] When she saw Peter warming himself, she looked upon him, and said, And thou also wast with Jesus of Nazareth.—Mark, ch. 14.

7029. —— **in the Home.** *Proverb.* [1] Better *is* a dry morsel, and quietness therewith, than an house full of sacrifices *with* strife.—Prov., ch. 17.

7030. —— **Invitation of.** "*Come.*" [29] Moses said unto Hobab..Moses' father in law, We are journeying unto the place of which the Lord said, I will give it you : come thou with us, and we will do thee good : for the Lord hath spoken good concerning Israel.—Num., ch. 10.

7031. —— —— "*Bride saith, Come.*" [17] The Spirit and the bride say, Come. And let him that heareth say, Come. And let him that is athirst come. And whosoever will, let him take the water of life freely.—Rev., ch. 22.

7032. —— **Joyous.** *Three Thousand.* [46] They, continuing daily with one accord in the temple, and breaking bread from house to house, did eat their meat with gladness and singleness of heart, [47] Praising God, and having favour with all the people. And the Lord added to the church daily such as should be saved.—Acts, ch. 2.

7033. —— **The chief Joy.** *Captives.* [5] If I forget thee, O Jerusalem, let my right hand forget *her cunning.* [6] If I do not remember thee, let my tongue cleave to the roof of my mouth ; if I prefer not Jerusalem above my chief joy.—Ps. 137.

7034. —— —— *Registered.* [19] I give unto you power to tread on serpents and scorpions, and over all the power of the enemy : and nothing shall by any means hurt you. [20] Notwithstanding in this rejoice not, that the spirits are subject unto you ; but rather rejoice, because your names are written in heaven.—Luke, ch. 10.

7035. —— **A liberal.** *Samaritan's.* [29] Every nation made gods of their own, and put *them* in the houses of the high places which the Samaritans had made..in their cities wherein they dwelt.—2 Kings, ch. 17.

7036. —— **a Life.** "*Born.*" [6] That which is born of the flesh is flesh, and that which is born of the Spirit is spirit. [7] Marvel not that I said unto thee, Ye must be born again.—John, ch. 3.

7037. —— **Life in.** *Proverb.* [20] My son, attend to my words ; incline thine ear unto my sayings. [21] Let them not depart from thine eyes ; keep them in the midst of thine heart. [22] For they *are* life unto those that find them, and health to all their flesh.—Prov., ch. 4.

7038. —— **Lukewarmness in.** *Laodiceans.* [15] I know thy works, that thou art neither cold nor hot : I would thou wert cold or hot. [16] So then, because thou art lukewarm, and neither cold nor hot, I will spew thee out of my mouth.—Rev., ch. 3.

7039. —— **Loss in.** *No Vision.* [1] The child Samuel ministered unto the Lord before Eli. And the word of the Lord was precious in those days ; *there was* no open vision.—1 Sam., ch. 3.

7040. —— **A mercenary.** "*Loaves.*" [26] Ye seek me, not because ye saw the miracles, but because ye did eat of the loaves, and were filled.—John, ch. 6.

7041. —— **necessary.** *For the State.* [26] Jeroboam said in his heart.. [27] If this people go up to do sacrifice in the house of the Lord at Jerusalem, then shall the heart of this people turn again unto..Rehoboam king of Judah, and they shall kill me.. [28] Whereupon the king..made two calves *of* gold. [29] And he set the one in Beth-el, and the other..in Dan.—1 Kings, ch. 12.

7042. —— **for every Place.** *In Canaan.* [7] The Lord appeared unto Abram, and said, Unto thy seed will I give this land : and there builded he an altar unto the Lord, who appeared unto him.—Gen., ch. 12.

7043. —— **Pleasurable.** *Proverb.* [16] Length of days *is* in her right hand ; *and* in her left hand riches and honour. [17] Her ways *are* ways of pleasantness, and all her paths *are* peace. [18] She is a tree of life to them that lay hold upon her : and happy *is* every one that retaineth her.—Prov., ch. 3.

7044. —— **Price of.** *"Selleth All."* [44] The kingdom of heaven is like unto treasure hid in a field ; the which when a man hath found he hideth, and for joy thereof goeth and selleth all that he hath, and buyeth that field.—MAT., ch. 13.

7045. —— **a Pearl.** *"Great Price."* [45] The kingdom of heaven is like unto a merchantman, seeking goodly pearls : [46] Who, when he had found one pearl of great price, went and sold all that he had, and bought it.—MAT., ch. 13.

7046. —— **Practical.** *Parable.* [28] A *certain* man had two sons ; and he came to the first, and said, Son, go work to day in my vineyard. [29] He answered..I will not ; but afterward he repented, and went. [30]..the second..said, I *go*, sir ; and went not. [31] Whether of them twain did the will of *his* father ? They say unto him, The first. —MAT., ch. 21.

7047. —— **a Pretext.** *Silversmiths.* [27] Not only this our craft is in danger to be set at naught ; but also that the temple of the great goddess Diana should be despised, and her magnificence should be destroyed.. [28] And..they were full of wrath, and cried out..Great *is* Diana of the Ephesians.—ACTS, ch. 19.

7048. —— **Pure.** *"Unspotted."* [27] Pure religion and undefiled before God and the Father is this, To visit the fatherless and widows in their affliction, *and* to keep himself unspotted from the world.—JAMES, ch. 1.

7049. —— **of Robbers.** *Danites.* [19] They said..Hold thy peace, lay thine hand upon thy mouth, and go with us, and be to us a father and a priest : *is it* better for thee to be a priest unto the house of one man, or that thou be a priest unto a tribe..in Israel ? [20] And the priest's heart was glad, and he..went in the midst of the people. [21] So they turned and departed, and put [stolen] little ones and the cattle and the carriage before them.—JUDGES, ch. 18.

7050. —— **of Self-denial.** *"Strait Gate."* [13] Enter ye in at the strait gate : for wide *is* the gate, and broad *is* the way, that leadeth to destruction, and many there be which go in thereat : [14] Because strait *is* the gate, and narrow *is* the way, which leadeth unto life, and few there be that find it.—MAT., ch. 7.

7051. —— **Selfishness in.** *Eli's Sons.* [28] I give unto the house of thy father all the offerings made by fire of the children of Israel ? [29] Wherefore kick ye at my sacrifice and at mine offering..and honourest thy sons above me, to make yourselves fat with the chiefest of all the offerings of Israel my people ?—1 SAM., ch. 2.

7052. —— **Security by.** *Proverb.* [23] Then shalt thou walk in thy way safely, and thy foot shall not stumble. [24] When thou liest down, thou shalt not be afraid : yea, thou shalt lie down, and thy sleep shall be sweet. [25] Be not afraid of sudden fear, neither of the desolation of the wicked.—PROV., ch. 3.

7053. —— **Transient.** *"No Root."* [16] These are they likewise which are sown on stony ground : who, when they have heard the word, immediately receive it with gladness ; [17] And have no root in themselves, and so endure but for a time : afterward, when affliction or persecution ariseth for the word's sake, immediately they are offended.—MARK, ch. 4.

7054. —— **A vain.** *Unruly.* [26] If any man among you seem to be religious, and bridleth not his tongue, but deceiveth his own heart, this man's religion *is* vain.—JAMES, ch. 1.

7055. —— **Welfare in.** *Isaac's.* [12] Isaac sowed in that land, and received in the same year an hundredfold : and the Lord blessed him.. [14] For he had possession of flocks, and possession of herds, and great store of servants : and the Philistines envied him.—GEN., ch. 26.

7056. —— **Worldliness in.** *Ahaz.* [10] King Ahaz went to Damascus to meet Tiglath-pileser king of Assyria, and saw an altar..and..sent to Urijah the priest the fashion of the altar, and the pattern of it.. [11] And Urijah..built an altar according to all that king Ahaz had sent.—2 KINGS, ch. 16.

See other illustrations under :

BELIEVERS.

Joys. Though now ye see him not..yet believing, ye	681
Possibilities. All things are possible to him that	682
Weak. Speak unto you..as unto babes in Christ	683

CHRISTIANS.

Almost. Agrippa said unto Paul, Almost thou	1267
Care for. I lay down my life for the sheep	1268
Childlike. Suffer little children..Of such	1269
Carnal. Whereas there is envying and strife	1270
Epistle. Ye are our epistle..read of all	1271
Exemplary. Bishop must be blameless	1272
Greatness. Least in the kingdom..greater	1273
Homeward. Come to Zion with songs	1274
First Named. First called Christians at Antioch	1275
Saved. He that committeth sin is of the devil	1276
Visible. Ye are the light of the world	1277

CHRISTIANITY.

Conserves. Ye are the salt of the earth	1278
Revolution. These that have turned the world	1279

CONVERTS.

Duty. Woman went..and saith, Come see	1667
Distinguished. Eunuch..went into the water	1668
Spurious. Simon..offered them money..give	1669
Trial. Thou art his disciple, but we are Moses'	1670
Counsel. Barnabas..exhorted them to cleave unto	1671
Food. As newborn babes desire..milk of the word	1672
Humble. Have any of the rulers or Pharisees	1673
Hypocrisy. Proselyte..twofold more the child of	1674
Influential. Believed..many humble women	1675
Increase. Many believed..about 5000 men	1676
" Same day added..about 3000 souls	1677
Principle. No. Many became Jews..for fear of the	1678
Steadfast. Continuing daily with one accord	1679
Superficial. Have no root in themselves	1680
Zeal. Made myself servant unto all	1681

CONVERSION.

Creation. New creature, old things passed away	1700
Conscious. Know we that we dwell in him..S.	1701
Changed. Made their feet fast..washed their	1702
Changes Life. Saul preached..Is not this he that	1703
Effort. Strive to enter in at the strait gate	1704
Evidence. Besought us..come into my house	1705
False. Simon saw..H. G. given..offered money	1706
Genuine. Set meat..rejoiced, believing in G.	1707
Heart-work. Out of the heart..evil thoughts	1708
Hasty. See here is water ; what doth hinder	1709
Inward. Pharisees make clean the outside of the	1710
Mystery. Wind bloweth..canst not tell whence	1711
Necessity. Except a man be born of water and the	1712
New Heart. God gave Saul another heart	1713
Negative. Reckon ye yourselves dead indeed unto	1714

Sudden. Called for a light..what must I do? 1715
Superficial. When tribulation or persecution 1716
Wonderful. Suddenly there shined..voice..Saul 1717

CONVERSIONS.

Daily. L. added to the church daily..be saved 1718
Genuine. Confessed, showed their deeds..books 1719
Instrumental. Samaritans believed for the saying 1720

SALVATION.

Brothers. His own brother Simon..brought him 7556
Belated. When once the master..shut to the door 7557
Difficulties. Strive to enter..many shall not be 7558
Emergency. I. shall go on dry ground..sea 7559
Free. Him that cometh..I will in no wise cast out 7560
"   If any man thirst, let him come unto me 7561
Faith. Believe on the L. J. C. and thou shalt be 7562
"   Whosoever believeth..should not perish 7563
by Few. No restraint to the L. to save by many or 7564
Gratitude. Fifth part unto Pharaoh..hast saved 7565
by Humanity. Angel said..call for Peter..he will 7566
Wonderful. Waters were a wall..right hand..left 7567
Waiting. Stand ye still and see the salvation 7568
One Way. Verily..I am the door of the sheep 7569

Belittled. Pay tithe of mint..omit..mercy 1064
Childlike. Except..be converted and become as 1185
Divine. Now are ye the sons of G..shall be 1179
Godlikeness. [Unconscious] Moses wist not that 3632
Happiness. Shall be like a tree planted by the 3633
Heartfelt. Servest not..with gladness 1237
Joyous. Come to Zion with songs and everlasting j. 1274
Mask. Our family hath a sacrifice 19
Secular Ends. Because gods of Syrians help, I will s. 140
Transforms. Make her desert like the garden of 1389
Unsecular. Although the fig tree..not blossom 142
Zionite. Who shall dwell..walketh..speaketh 1320

7057. RELUCTANCE manifested. *"Looking back."*

[61] Lord, I will follow thee ; but let me first go bid them farewell, which are at home at my house. [62] And Jesus said unto him, No man, having put his hand to the plough, and looking back, is fit for the kingdom of God.—LUKE, ch. 9.

See HESITATION.

7058. REMEDY, An improbable. *"Clay."*

[6] He spat on the ground, and made clay of the spittle, and he anointed the eyes of the blind man with the clay, [7] And said..Go wash in the pool of Siloam.. He went his way therefore, and washed, and came seeing.—JOHN, ch. 9.

7059. —— for Sin. *Look.*

[14] Moses lifted up the serpent in the wilderness, even so must the Son of man be lifted up : [15] That whosoever believeth in him should not perish, but have eternal life.—JOHN, ch. 3.

See other illustrations under :

CURE.

All Persons. Laid his hands on every one and heal. 1867
All Diseases. Stepped in, was made whole of what 1868
Faith. When..beheld the serpent of brass, he lived 1869
Gratitude. She arose, and ministered unto them 1870
Means. Made clay of the spittle..anointed eyes 1871
Progressive. See men as trees walking..clearly 1872
Threefold. Possessed with a devil, blind and dumb 1873
Wonderful. Stretch forth thy hand..as the other 1874

PHYSICIAN.

Great. He healed many..pressed to touch him 6129
"   He went about all the cities..healing 6130
"   Hands on every one..healed them 6131
Unsuccessful. Woman suffered..of many phys'ns 6132
Wrongly Sought. Sought not to the L. but..phys. 6133

7060. REMEMBRANCE, Book of. *"Mine."*

[16] They that feared the Lord spake often one to another : and the Lord hearkened, and heard *it*, and a book of remembrance was written before him for them that feared the Lord, and that thought upon his name. [17] And they shall be mine, saith the Lord of hosts, in that day when I make up my jewels.—MAL., ch. 3.

7061. —— A late. *Of Joseph.*

[9] Spake the chief butler unto Pharaoh, saying, I do remember my faults this day.. [12]..*there was.* a Hebrew, servant..and we told him, and he interpreted to us our dreams.. [13] And..as he interpreted to us, so it was ; me he restored unto mine office, and him he hanged.—GEN., ch. 41. [He had promised to remember him.]

7062. —— perpetuated. *Eucharist.*

[19] He took bread, and gave thanks, and brake *it*, and gave unto them, saying, This is my body which is given for you : this do in remembrance of me.—LUKE, ch. 22.

7063. —— A painful. *Peter.*

[71] He began to curse and to swear, *saying*, I know not this man of whom ye speak. [72] And the second time the cock crew. And Peter called to mind the word that Jesus said unto him, Before the cock crow twice, thou shalt deny me thrice. And when he thought thereon, he wept.—MARK, ch. 14.

7064. —— Stimulated. *Paul.*

[5] I call to remembrance the unfeigned faith that is in thee, which dwelt first in thy grandmother Lois, and thy mother Eunice ; and I am persuaded that in thee also. [6] Wherefore I put thee in remembrance, that thou stir up the gift of God, which is in thee.—2 TIM., ch. 1.

7065. —— of Sins. *Israel.*

[7] Remember, *and* forget not, how thou provokedst the Lord thy God to wrath in the wilderness : from the day that thou didst depart out of the land of Egypt, until ye came unto this place, ye have been rebellious against the Lord.—DEUT., ch. 9.

See other illustrations under :

MEMORY.

Perdition. Send Lazarus to my..five brethren 5319
Painful. I am the least..apostles..I persecuted 5320

MEMORIAL.

Benevolence. Alms are come up for a memorial 5321
Deliverance. When thy son asketh thee, What is 5322
Food. Omer full of manna..kept for your 5323
Love. Throughout the whole world..memorial of 5324
Stones. Joshua set up 12 stones in..Jordan 5325
Victory. Samuel took a stone and set it..Ebenezer 5326
"   Sword of Goliath..behind the ephod 5327
See REMORSE, below.

7066. REMNANT saved. *Little.*

[12] Thus saith the Lord ; As the shepherd taketh out of the mouth of the lion two legs, or a piece of an ear ; so shall the children of Israel be taken out that dwell in Samaria in the corner of a bed, and in Damascus *in* a couch.—AMOS, ch. 3.

7067. REMORSE, Fitting. *Crucifixion.*

[47] When the centurion saw what was done, he glorified God, saying, Certainly this was a righteous man. [48] And all the people that came together to that sight, beholding the things which were done, smote their breasts, and returned.—LUKE, ch. 23.

7068. —— prevented. *The Erring.*

[5] If any have caused grief.. [6] Sufficient to such a man *is*

this punishment, which *was afflicted* of many.
[7] So that contrariwise ye *ought* rather to forgive
him, and comfort *him*, lest perhaps such a one
should be swallowed up with overmuch sorrow.
—2 Cor., ch. 2.

7069. —— **for Treachery.** *Judas.* [4] I have
sinned in that I have betrayed the innocent
blood. And they said, What *is that* to us? see
thou *to that.* [5] And he cast down the pieces of
silver in the temple, and departed, and went
and hanged himself.—Mat., ch. 27.

See REPENTANCE and references.

7070. RENUNCIATION of the World. *Moses.*
[25] Choosing rather to suffer affliction with the
people of God, than to enjoy the pleasures of
sin for a season ; [26] Esteeming the reproach of
Christ greater riches than the treasures in Egypt.
—Heb., ch. 11.

See other illustrations under :
REJECTION.

Authority. Neither receiveth the brethren..forbid.	6955
Anger. Command fire to come..consume	6956
Acclamation. Instant with loud voices..crucified	6957
Conditional. Not see my face except your brother	6958
Disobedient. Because..rejected thee from being k.	6959
of God. Rejected your G..set a king over	6960
" Go inquire of B. the god of Ekron	6961
Jealousy. Because his face..toward J.	6962
Minister. Who made thee a ruler..over us	6963
Rebellious. This if the heir..let us kill	6964
Sin of. Believeth not..is condemned already	6965
Treason. All..went down into the pit	6966
Worldly. Pray him to depart out..coasts	6967

7071. REPAIRS of Temple. *"Breaches."*
[4] Jehoash said to the priests, All the money of
the dedicated things that is brought into the
house of the Lord..the money that every man
is set at, *and* all the money that cometh into any
man's heart to bring.. [5] Let the priests take *it*
..and let them repair the breaches of the house.
—2 Kings, ch. 12.

Also see :

Important. Elijah repaired [at Carmel] the altar	301
Mending. Piece of a new garment upon an old	5338

7072. REPARATION demanded. *At Philippi.*
[37] Being Romans, and have cast *us* into prison ;
and now do they thrust us out privily? nay
verily ; but let them come themselves and fetch
us out. [38] And the serjeants told these words
unto the magistrates : and they feared, when
they heard that they were Romans. [39] And they
came and besought them, and brought *them* out.
—Acts, ch. 16.

7073. —— **intended.** *Oversight.* [12] Take
double money in your hand ; and the money
that was brought again in the mouth of your
sacks, carry *it* again in your hand ; peradventure
it *was* an oversight.—Gen., ch. 43.

See other illustrations under :
RESTITUTION.

Cains. By false accusation..r. fourfold	6267
Imperative. Thief..make full restitution..be sold	6268
Loss. Pit..ox or ass fall therein	6269
" Ox .used to push in times past	6270
" He that kindleth the fire make r.	6271
" Thief..pay double	6272
" Borrow..surely make it good	6273

RESTORATION.

Property. Lands, vineyards, and olive yards	7274
Spiritual. Put a ring on his hand	7275

7074. REPENTANCE for All. *" Ye repent."*
[4] Those eighteen, upon whom the tower in
Siloam fell, and slew them, think ye that they
were sinners above all men that dwelt in Jerusalem? [5] I tell you, Nay : but, except ye repent,
ye shall all likewise perish.—Luke, ch. 13.

7075. —— —— *Pentecost.* [37] Men *and*
brethren, what shall we do? [38] Then Peter said
..Repent, and be baptized every one of you in
the name of Jesus Christ for the remission of
sins, and ye shall receive the gift of the Holy
Ghost.—Acts, ch. 2.

7076. —— **acceptable.** *" Repented and went."*
[28] But what think ye? A *certain* man had two
sons ; and he came to the first, and said, Son,
go work to day in my vineyard. [29] He answered
and said, I will not ; but afterward he repented,
and went.—Mat., ch. 21.

7077. —— **in Adversity.** *Moses said,* [30] When
thou art in tribulation..if thou turn to the Lord
thy God, and shalt be obedient unto his voice ;
[31] (For the Lord thy God *is* a merciful God ;)
he will not forsake thee, neither destroy thee,
nor forget the covenant of thy fathers, which he
sware unto them.—Deut., ch. 4.

7078. —— —— *"Distressed."* [9] The
children of Ammon passed over Jordan to fight
also against Judah, and..Benjamin, and..Ephra-
im ; so that Israel was sore distressed. [10] And
the children of Israel cried unto the Lord, saying, We have sinned against thee, both because
we have forsaken our God, and also served
Baalim.—Judges, ch. 10.

7079. —— —— *Saul.* [8] God hath delivered
thy enemy into thy hand this day : now therefore let me smite him, I pray thee, with the
spear even to the earth at once, and I will not
smite him the second time. [9] And David said to
Abishai, Destroy him not.. [21] Then said Saul, I
have sinned : return, my son David ; for I will
no more do thee harm, because my soul was
precious in thine eyes this day : behold, I have
played the fool, and have erred exceedingly.—
1 Sam., ch. 26.

7080. —— **in Affliction.** *Egyptians.* [32] Be-
gone ; and bless me also. [33] And the Egyptians
were urgent upon the people, that they might
send them out of the land in haste ; for they
said, We *be* all dead *men.*—Ex., ch. 12.

7081. —— **Call to.** *Jesus.* [12] When Jesus
had heard that John was cast into prison, he
departed into Galilee ; [13] ..and dwelt in Capernaum.. [17] From that time Jesus began to preach,
and to say, Repent : for the kingdom of heaven
is at hand.—Mat., ch. 4.

7082. —— —— *Dives in Torment.* [27] I pray
thee therefore, Father, that thou wouldest send
Lazarus to my father's house.. [31] And he said..
If they hear not Moses and the prophets, neither
will they be persuaded, though one rose from
the dead.—Luke, ch. 16.

7083. —— **Change of.** *Jailer.* [32] They spake
unto him the word of the Lord.. [33] And he took
them the same hour of the night, and washed
their stripes ; and was baptized, he and all his,
straightway.—Acts, ch. 16.

7084. —— **for Coldness.** *Ephesians.* [4] I have
somewhat against thee, because thou hast left
thy first love. [5] Remember therefore from
whence thou art fallen, and repent, **a**nd do the

first works ; or else I will. .remove thy candlestick out of his place.—REV., ch. 2.

7085. —— Delay for. *Fig Tree.* ⁷ These three years I come seeking fruit on this fig tree, and find none : cut it down ; why cumbereth it the ground ? ⁸ And he. .said. .Lord, let it alone this year also, till I shall dig about it, and dung *it :* ⁹ And if it bear fruit, *well :* and if not, *then* after that thou shalt cut it down.—LUKE, ch. 10.

7086. —— Effectual. *D e l i v e r a n c e came.* ⁸ Cease not to cry unto the Lord our God for us, that he will save us out of the hand of the Philistines. ⁹ And Samuel took a sucking lamb, and offered *it for* a burnt offering wholly unto the Lord : and Samuel cried unto the Lord for Israel ; and the Lord heard him.—1 SAM., ch. 7.

7087. —— Effects of. *Corinthians.* ¹¹ Behold this selfsame thing, that ye sorrowed after a godly sort, what carefulness it wrought in you, yea, *what* clearing of yourselves, yea, *what* indignation, yea. *what* fear, yea, *what* vehement desire, yea, *what* zeal, yea, *what* revenge !—2 COR., ch. 7.

7088. —— Encouragement to. *"I will return."* ⁷ Return unto me, and I will return unto you, saith the Lord of hosts. But ye said, Wherein shall we return?.. ¹⁰ Bring ye all the tithes into the storehouse, that there may be meat in mine house, and prove me now.—MAL., ch. 3.

7089. —— Fruits of. *Books burned.* ¹⁸ Many that believed came, and confessed, and shewed their deeds. ¹⁹ Many. .which used curious arts brought their books together, and burned them before all *men :* and they counted the price of them, and found *it* fifty thousand *pieces* of silver. —ACTS, ch. 19.

7090. —— Feeling. *Revival.* ⁹ All the men of Judah and Benjamin gathered. .unto Jerusalem within three days. .and all the people sat in the street of the house of God, trembling because of *this* matter, and for the great rain.— EZRA, ch. 10.

7091. —— through Fear. *Pharaoh.* ²⁷ Pharaoh sent, and called for Moses and Aaron, and said. .I have sinned this time : the Lord *is* righteous, and I and my people *are* wicked. ²⁸ Entreat the Lord (for *it is* enough) that there be no *more* mighty thunderings and hail ; and I will let you go.—EX., ch. 9.

7092. —— the Gate. *Strait.* ¹³ Enter ye in at the strait gate : for wide *is* the gate, and broad *is* the way, that leadeth to destruction, and many there be which go in thereat : ¹⁴ Because strait *is* the gate, and narrow *is* the way, which leadeth unto life, and few there be that find it.—MAT., ch. 7.

7093. —— A hearty. *Backsliders.* ²⁸ There ye shall serve gods, the work of men's hands, wood and stone, which neither see, nor hear, nor eat, nor smell. ²⁹ But if from thence thou shalt seek the Lord thy God, thou shalt find *him,* if thou seek him with all thy heart.—DEUT., ch. 4.

7094. —— Invitation to. *Zion.* ¹² Turn ye *even* to me with all your heart, and with fasting, and with weeping, and with mourning : ¹³ And rend your heart, and not your garments, and turn unto the Lord your God : for he *is* gracious and merciful, slow to anger, and of great kindness. and repenteth him of the evil.—JOEL, ch. 2.

7095. —— from a Look. *Peter.* ⁶¹ The Lord turned, and looked upon Peter. And Peter remembered the word of the Lord, how he had said unto him, Before the cock crow, thou shalt deny me thrice. ⁶² And Peter went out, and wept bitterly.—LUKE, ch. 22.

7096. —— Late. *Thief.* ⁴⁰ The other. .rebuked him, saying, Dost not thou fear God, seeing thou art in the same condemnation ? ⁴¹ And we indeed justly ; for we receive the due reward of our deeds : but this man hath done nothing amiss. ⁴² And he said unto Jesus, Lord, remember me when thou comest into thy kingdom.—LUKE, ch. 23.

7097. —— Life by. *To Israel.* ¹⁴ When I say unto the wicked, Thou shalt surely die ; if he turn from his sin, and do that which is lawful and right ; ¹⁵ *If* the wicked restore the pledge, give again that he had robbed, walk in the statutes of life, without committing iniquity ; he shall surely live, he shall not die.—EZEK., ch. 33.

7098. —— Ministry of. *John.* ¹ In those days came John the Baptist, preaching in the wilderness of Judea, ² And saying, Repent ye ; for the kingdom of heaven is at hand.—MAT., ch. 3.

7099. —— Oath of. *Judah.* ¹² They entered into a covenant to seek the Lord God. .with all their heart. . ¹³ That whosoever would not seek the Lord. .should be put to death, whether small or great, whether man or woman. ¹⁴ And they sware unto the Lord with a loud voice, and with shouting, and with trumpets, and with cornets. —2 CHRON., ch. 15.

7100. —— Proof of. *Chorazin.* ²¹ Woe unto thee, Chorazin !. .Bethsaida ! for if the mighty works, which were done in you, had been done in Tyre and Sidon, they would have repented long ago in sackcloth and ashes.—MAT., ch. 11.

7101. —— —— *Publicans.* ¹² Then came also publicans to be baptized, and said. .Master, what shall we do ? ¹³ And he said. .Exact no more than that which is appointed you.—LUKE, ch. 3.

7102. —— —— *Soldiers.* ¹⁴ The soldiers likewise demanded. .And what shall we do ? And he said. .Do violence to no man, neither accuse *any* falsely ; and be content with your wages.—LUKE, ch. 3.

7103. —— passed. *Day of.* ¹³ Because his sons made themselves vile, and he restrained them not. ¹⁴ . .therefore I have sworn. .that the iniquity of Eli's house shall not be purged with sacrifice nor offering for ever.—1 SAM., ch. 3.

7104. —— Partial. *Judah.* ⁵ Thus saith the Lord, Ye have forsaken me, and therefore have I also left you in the hand of Shishak. . ⁷ They have humbled themselves ; *therefore* I will not destroy them, but I will grant them some deliverance.—2 CHRON., ch. 12.

7105. —— —— *Beneficial.* ²⁷ Put sackcloth upon his flesh, and fasted, and lay in sackcloth, and went softly. ²⁸ And the word of the Lord came to Elijah. . ²⁹ . .humbleth himself before me, I will not bring the evil in his days : *but* in his son's days.—1 KINGS, ch. 21.

7106. —— checked by Pride. *"For their Sakes."* [See No. 7117.]

7107. —— Reformatory. *David.* [5] David did *that which was* right in the eyes of the Lord, and turned not aside from any *thing* that he commanded him all the days of his life, save only in the matter of Uriah the Hittite.—1 KINGS, ch. 15.

7108. —— —— *Pharisees.* [7] When he saw many of the Pharisees and Sadducees come to his baptism, he said..O generation of vipers, who hath warned you to flee from the wrath to come? [8] Bring forth therefore fruits meet for repentance.—MAT., ch. 3.

7109. —— —— *Israelites.* [3] Samuel spake.. saying, If ye do return unto the Lord with all your hearts, *then* put away the strange gods and Ashtaroth from among you, and prepare your hearts unto the Lord, and serve him only : and he will deliver you out of the hand of the Philistines.—1 SAM., ch. 7.

7110. —— refused. *Israel.* [6] I also have given you cleanness of teeth in all your cities, and want of bread in all your places : yet have ye not returned unto me, saith the Lord.— AMOS, ch. 4. [See chapter.]

7111. —— not Restoration. *"All is thine."* [30] As soon as this thy son was come, which hath devoured thy living with harlots, thou hast killed for him the fatted calf. [31] And he said.. Son, thou art ever with me, and all that I have is thine.—LUKE, ch. 15. [No redivision of the property.]

7112. —— Results of. *Golden Calf destroyed.* [6] They caused it to be proclaimed throughout the camp, saying, Let neither man nor woman make any more work for the offering of the sanctuary. So the people were restrained from bringing. [7] For the stuff they had was sufficient..and too much.—EX., ch. 36.

7113. —— refused. *Jews in Egypt.* [16] We will not hearken unto thee. [17] But we will certainly..burn incense unto the queen of heaven, and to pour out drink offerings unto her, as we have done.—JER., ch. 44.

7114. —— Saved by. *Ninevites.* [7] Let them not feed, nor drink water. [8] But let man and beast be covered with sackcloth, and cry mightily unto God : yea, let them turn every one from his evil way.. [9] Who can tell *if* God will turn and repent, and turn away from his fierce anger, that we perish not? [10] And God saw..and God repented of the evil.—JONAH, ch. 3.

7115. —— for Sins. *Of Ignorance.* [17] Brethren, I wot that through ignorance ye did *it*, as *did* also your rulers.. [19] Repent ye therefore, and be converted, that your sins may be blotted out. —ACTS, ch. 3.

7116. —— Surrender in. *Saul.* [5] The Lord said, I am Jesus whom thou persecutest : *it is* hard for thee to kick against the pricks. [6] And he trembling and astonished said, Lord, what wilt thou have me to do?—ACTS, ch. 9.

7117. —— Superficial. *Herod.* [25] Give me by and by in a charger the head of John the Baptist. [26] And the king was exceeding sorry ; *yet* for his oath's sake, and for their sakes which sat with him, he would not reject her.—MARK, ch. 6.

7118. —— —— *Saul.* [16] Saul said, Is this thy voice, my son David ? And Saul lifted up his voice, and wept. [17] And he said to David, Thou *art* more righteous than I : for thou hast rewarded me good, whereas I have rewarded thee evil.—1 SAM., ch. 24. [A transient feeling.]

7119. —— Unavailing. *Esau.* [16] Esau, who for one morsel of meat sold his birthright. [17] For ye know how that afterward, when he would have inherited the blessing, he was rejected : for he found no place of repentance, though he sought it carefully with tears.—HEB., ch. 12.

7120. —— —— *Judas.* [3] When he saw that he was condemned, repented himself, and brought again the thirty pieces of silver to the chief priests and elders, [4] Saying, I have sinned in that I have betrayed the innocent blood. And they said, What *is that* to us? see thou *to that.*—MAT., ch. 27.

7121. —— for Worldliness. *Laodiceans.* [17] Because thou sayest, I am rich, and increased with goods, and have need of nothing ; and knowest not that thou art wretched, and miserable, and poor, and blind, and naked : [18] I counsel thee to buy of me gold tried in the fire, that thou mayest be rich ; and white raiment, that thou mayest be clothed, and *that* the shame of thy nakedness do not appear ; and anoint thine eyes with eye-salve, that thou mayest see. [19] ..be zealous therefore, and repent.—REV., ch. 3.

See other Illustrations under :

AWAKENING.

Conscience. John the B. was risen from the dead	595
Fear. Centurion..feared greatly..was the S. of G.	596
Great. Into the house..all the people..read	597
General. All Judea..Jerusalem..baptized	598
Sudden. Fell down..what must I do to be saved ?	599
Trouble. Troubled the Egyptians..Let us flee	600
Truth. Paul reasoned..Felix trembled	601
Unexpected. We are verily guilty..our brother	602

CONTRITION.

Accepted. Because thine heart was tender..peace	1664
Annual. That ye may be clean from all your sins	1665
Bitter. Eat the flesh..with bitter herbs	1666

CONVICTION.

Awakening. Made manifest by the light..Awake	1682
Deeds. By this I know thou art..man of God	1684
Examination. Searched the Scriptures..many b'd	1685
Heaven sent. Suddenly there shined a light	1686
Heartfelt. Pricked in their heart [Pentecost]	1687
Necessary. Sprung up..no deepness of earth	1688
Prayer. Make me to know my transgression	1689
Resisted. Miracles before them..believed not	1690
Rational. When he came to himself..I will arise	1691
Sensitive. David's heart smote him..Saul's skirt	1692
Smiting. David's heart smote him..numbered	1693
Sudden. People saw it..fell..L. he is God	1694
Speechless. Beholding the man..healed..say n.	1695
Truth. Josiah..heard..the brook of the..he rent	1696
Thorough. Digged deep..the foundation on a rock	1697
Transient. Centurion..earthquake..was the S. of	1698
Willing. Nathanael..Thou art the Son of God	1699

HARDNESS.

Adversity. In..his distress did Ahaz trespass more	3797
Heart. Looked..anger being grieved..hardness of	3798
Spiritual. We will certainly burn incense	3799

IMPENITENCE.

Affliction. Ahaziah said..go inquire of Baal-zebub	4347
Hardened. Thou shalt die..He sent to arrest	4348

OBDURACY.

Defiant. Who is the L. that I should obey ? 5755
Final. Why have we..let I. go from serving us 5756
Foolish. Ahaz..sacrificed unto the gods..smote 5757
Jewish. Thy neck is an iron sinew, and thy 5758
Spiritual. Woe unto thee, Chorazin..if the mighty 5759
Self-destructive. I know that G. hath determined 5760
to Truth. Paul spake..three months..divers were 5761
Unfeeling. Past feeling have given themselves 5762
Wild. Balaam..went with the princes of Moab 5763

OBSTINACY.

Provoking. It is a stiffnecked people..consume 5825
Rebuked. Why..smitten thine ass these 3 times? 5826
Rebellious. Nevertheless the people refused 5827

PENITENCE.

Blessedness. Blessed are they that mourn 6041
Regarded. Because thine heart was tender 6042
    " Ahab humbleth himself..not bring the 6043
True. Would not lift so much as his eyes..smote 6044
Tears of. Peter..when he thought thereon, he w. 6045

REMORSE.

Needful. People that came..smote their breasts 7067
Prevented. Lest swallowed up with overmuch sor. 7068
Treachery. Judas..went and hanged himself 7069

STUBBORNNESS.

Punished. They mocked..despised..therefore 9393
Sin. To obey is better than sacrifice 9394
    " We will certainly..burn incense to thee 9395
    " Took Dagon and set him in his place 9396

Regrets. Vain. Herod was exceeding sorry 6950
Superficial. Go..serve the L...bless me also 208
    See CONSCIENCE, REFORM, and REFORMATION.

7122. REPORT, Evil. *Ten Spies.* ³² The land, through which we have gone to search it.. eateth up the inhabitants thereof ; and all the people that we saw in it *are* men of a great stature. ³³ And there we saw the giants, the sons of Anak..and we were in our own sight as grasshoppers, and so we were in their sight.—Num., ch. 13.

7123. —— False. *David.* ³¹ The king arose, and tare his garments, and lay on the earth ; and all his servants stood by with their clothes rent. ³² And Jonadab..David's brother..said, Let not my lord suppose *that* they have slain all the young men the king's sons ; for Amnon only is dead.—2 Sam., ch. 13.

7124. —— for Intimidation. *Sanballat.* ⁶ It is reported among the heathen, and Gashmu saith *it, that* thou and the Jews think to rebel : for which cause thou buildest the wall, that thou mayest be their king.—Neh., ch. 6.

7125. —— Manufactured. *Priests.* ¹³ Say ye, His disciples came by night, and stole him *away* while we slept. ¹⁴ And if this come to the governor's ears, we will persuade him, and secure you. —Mat., ch. 28.

7126. —— Offensive. *Jacob's Sons.* ² Joseph, *being* seventeen years old, was feeding the flock with his brethren..and Joseph brought unto his father their evil report.—Acts, ch. 7.

7127. —— Terrorizing. *Rahab said,* ¹¹ As soon as we had heard *these things,* our hearts did melt, neither did there remain any more courage in any man, because of you : for the Lord your God, he *is* God in heaven above, and in earth beneath.—Josh., ch. 2.

Also see :
Rumor. Syrians fled in the twilight 7481
Tradition. Making the word of G. of none effect 8870
    See REPUTATION and references.

7128. REPROACH with Affliction. *David.* ¹⁰ My life is spent with grief, and my years with sighing : my strength faileth because of mine iniquity, and my bones are consumed. ¹¹ I was a reproach among all mine enemies, but especially among my neighbours.—Ps. 31.

7129. —— of Christ. *Paul.* ²² They gave him audience unto this word, and *then* lifted up their voices, and said, Away with such a *fellow* from the earth : for it is not fit that he should live. ²³ And as they cried out, and cast off *their* clothes, and threw dust into the air.—Acts, ch. 22.

7130. —— Cowardice a. *Shemaiah said,* ¹⁰ Let us meet together..within the temple, and let us shut the doors..in the night will they come to slay thee. ¹¹ And I said, Should such a man as I flee? and who *is there,* that, *being* as I *am,* would go into the temple to save his life ! I will not go in.—Neh., ch. 6.

7131. —— Fear of. *Disciples.* ⁴² Among the chief rulers also many believed on him ; but because of the Pharisees they did not confess *him,* lest they should be put out of the synagogue.— John, ch. 12.

7132. —— Intended. *Nahash the Ammonite.* ² On this *condition* will I make a *covenant* with you, that I may thrust out all your right eyes, and lay it *for* a reproach upon all Israel.—1 Sam., ch. 11.

7133. —— of Idolaters. *Jews.* ⁴ Thou art become guilty in thy blood that thou hast shed ; and hast defiled thyself in thine idols which thou hast made..therefore have I made thee a reproach unto the heathen, and a mocking to all countries.—Ezek., ch. 22.

7134. —— Joy in. *Christians.* ²² Blessed are ye, when men shall hate you, and when they shall separate you *from their company,* and shall reproach *you,* and cast out your name as evil, for the Son of man's sake. ²³ Rejoice ye in that day, and leap for joy : for, behold, your reward *is* great in heaven.—Luke, ch. 6.

7135. —— of Neglect. *" Walls."* ¹⁷ Ye see the distress that we *are* in, how Jerusalem lieth waste, and the gates thereof are burned with fire : come, and let us build up the wall of Jerusalem, that we be no more a reproach.—Neh., ch. 2.

7136. —— Proverb of. *Jews.* ³⁷ Thou shalt become an astonishment, a proverb, and a byword, among all nations whither the Lord shall lead thee.—Deut., ch. 28.

7137. —— Shame of. *David.* ⁷ Because for thy sake I have borne reproach ; shame hath covered my face. ⁸ I am become a stranger unto my brethren, and an alien unto my mother's children.—Ps. 69.

7138. —— Unconscious. *" What ?"* ¹³ Your words have been stout against me, saith the Lord. Yet ye say, What have we spoken so much against thee ? ¹⁴ Ye have said, It *is* vain to serve God : and what profit *is it* that we have kept his ordinance.—Mal., ch. 3.

7139. —— welcomed. *Moses.* ²⁶ Esteeming

the reproach of Christ greater riches than the treasures in Egypt : for he had respect unto the recompense of the reward.—HEB., ch. 11.

See other illustrations under :

DISGRACE.

Avenged. Smite Amnon ; then kill him, fear not 2375
Drunkards. Tables are full of vomit and filthiness 2376
Humiliating. Hanun cut off their garments 2377
Innocent. This is Jesus the king of the Jews 2378
Posthumous. Bring out the bones of the kings 2379
Unendurable. Ahithophel..his counsel not followed 2380

DISHONOUR.

Soldier's. That men say not, A woman slew him 2386
Reward. Entice him..give 1100 pieces of silver 2387

DISPARAGEMENT.

Ignoble. We were as grasshoppers in our own 2407
Provoked. L. had respect unto Abel..but unto Cain 2408

REMORSE.

Needful. People that came..smote their breasts 7067
Prevented. Lest swallowed up with overmuch sor. 7068
Treachery. Judas..went and hanged himself 7069

SCANDAL.

Ministerial. Eli was very old..his sons..at the 7603
Public. Absalom spread a tent..father's concubine 7604

SHAME.

Criminal's. As the thief is ashamed when found 7827
Impossible. Dealeth falsely..were they ashamed? 7828
Rejoicing. That they were counted worthy 7829
for Shame. Ashamed of me..of him..be ashamed 7830
Sin. Eyes..opened..were naked..aprons 7831

SLANDER.

Antidote. They may by your good works..glorify 8101
Base. This fellow doth cast out devils by Beelzebub 8102
Disgraceful. We found this man a pestilent f. 8103
Folly. He that uttereth a slander is a fool 8104
Hurtful. Then will they not pay tribute 8105
Impious. He saved others ; himself he cannot s. 8106
Joyful. Blessed..men revile you..rejoice..glad 8107
Loyalty. Ziba said..he abideth at Jerusalem 8108
Malicious. Diotrephes..prating against us 8109
Opposed. It is reported..be their king 8110
Refuted. If Satan cast out Satan..divided 8111
Rebels. The people is greater than we 8112
Sinners Thou art an austere man 8113
Satan's. Touch all that he hath..will curse 8114
Secret. A whisperer separateth friends 8115
Unbelief. Would to G. we had died..by fleshpots 8116

Confessed. I am ashamed, and blush..my God 4199
Defeat. Israel turned their backs..enemies 4200
National. No smith..In all the land of Israel 4202
Painful. Haman..arrayed Mordecai..proclaimed 4203
    " Begin with shame to take the lowest seat 4204
Sin. Sent him to feed swine..perish with h. 4206
Weakness. I was ashamed to require..soldiers 4208

7140. REPROOF appreciated. *Wise Man.* [10] A reproof entereth more into a wise man than a hundred stripes into a fool.—PROV., ch. 17.

7141. —— accepted. *In Revival.* [11] Make confession unto the Lord..and do his pleasure : and separate yourselves from the people of the land, and from the strange wives. [12] Then all the congregation..said with a loud voice, As thou hast said, so must we do.—EZRA, ch. 10.

7142. —— —— *David.* [10] The sword shall never depart from thine house ; because thou hast despised me, and hast taken the wife of Uriah the Hittite to be thy wife.. [13] And David saith unto Nathan, I have sinned against the

Lord. And Nathan said unto David, The Lord also hath put away thy sin ; thou shalt not die. —2 SAM., ch. 12.

7143. —— —— *Abimelech.* [25] Abraham reproved Abimelech because of a well of water, which Abimelech's servants had violently taken away. [26] And Abimelech said, I wot not who hath done this thing : neither didst thou tell me, neither yet heard I *of it,* but to day.—GEN., ch. 21.

7144. —— Angered by. *Stephen's.* [54] When they heard these things, they were cut to the heart, and they gnashed on him with *their* teeth. —ACTS, ch. 7.

7145. —— Christian. *Method of.* [15] If thy brother shall trespass against thee, go and tell him his fault between thee and him alone : if he shall hear thee, thou hast gained thy brother. [16] But if he will not hear *thee, then* take with thee one or two more, that in the mouth of two or three witnesses every word may be established. —MAT., ch. 18.

7146. —— A disagreeable. *Paul.* [See No. 7149.]

7147. —— from the Good. *David.* [5] Let the righteous smite me ; *it shall be* a kindness : and let him reprove me ; *it shall be* an excellent oil, *which* shall not break my head.—Ps. 141.

7148. —— of Hypocrisy. *Jesus.* [8] This people draweth nigh unto me with their mouth, and honoureth me with *their* lips ; but their heart is far from me.—MAT., ch. 15.

7149. —— Love after. *Peter.* [11] When Peter was come to Antioch, I withstood him to the face, because he was to be blamed.—GAL., ch. 2. [15] Account *that* the longsuffering of our Lord *is* salvation ; even as our beloved brother Paul also according to the wisdom given unto him hath written unto you.—2 PETER, ch. 3.

7150. —— A mild. *"Jesus looked."* [61] The Lord turned and looked upon Peter. And Peter remembered..how he had said unto him, Before the cock crow, thou shalt deny me thrice. [62] And Peter went out, and wept bitterly.— LUKE, ch. 22.

7151. —— Personal. *Nathan.* [6] He shall restore the lamb fourfold, because he did this thing, and because he had no pity. [7] And Nathan said to David, Thou *art* the man.—2 SAM., ch. 12.

7152. —— Prudence in. *Gold.* [11] A word fitly spoken *is like* apples of gold in pictures of silver. [12] *As* an earring of gold, and an ornament of fine gold, *so is* a wise reprover upon an obedient ear.—PROV., ch. 25.

7153. —— Stinging. *Simony.* [20] Peter said unto him, Thy money perish with thee, because thou hast thought that the gift of God may be purchased with money. [21] Thou hast neither part nor lot in this matter : for thy heart is not right in the sight of God. [22] Repent therefore.—ACTS, ch. 8.

7154. —— Sharp. *"Behind me, Satan."* [22] Peter..began to rebuke him, saying, Be it far from thee, Lord : this shall not be unto thee. [23] But he turned, and said unto Peter, Get thee behind me, Satan : thou art an offence unto me : for thou savourest not the things that be of God, but those that be of men.—MAT., ch. 16.

7155. —— Sarcastic. *Saul spared.* [7] David and Abishai came..by night : and, behold, Saul lay sleeping within the trench, and his spear stuck in the ground at his bolster.. [15] And David said to Abner, *Art* not thou a *valiant* man? and who *is* like to thee in Israel? wherefore then hast thou not kept thy lord the king? for there came one of the people in to destroy the king thy lord.—1 SAM., ch. 26.

7156. —— A sensible. *Joab's.* [4] The king covered his face, and the king cried with a loud voice, O my son Absalom! O Absalom, my son, my son! [5] And Joab..to the king..said, Thou hast shamed this day the faces of all thy servants, which this day have saved thy life.. [6] ..if Absalom had lived, and all we had died this day, then it had pleased thee well. [7] Now therefore arise, go forth, and speak comfortably unto thy servants.—2 SAM., ch. 19.

7157. —— Unwelcome. *"A Blot."* [7] He that reproveth a scorner getteth to himself shame : and he that rebuketh a wicked *man getteth* himself a blot. [8] Reprove not a scorner, lest he hate thee : rebuke a wise man, and he will love thee.—PROV., ch: 9.

7158. —— Vigorous. *Mixed Marriages.* [24] Their children spake half in the speech of Ashdod, and could not speak in the Jews' language, but according to the language of each people. [25] And I contended with them, and cursed them, and smote certain of them, and plucked off their hair.—NEH., ch. 13.

7159. —— Welcomed. *Proverb.* [23] He that rebuketh a man, afterwards shall find more favour than he that flattereth with the tongue.—PROV., ch. 28.

See other illustrations under :

REBUKE.

Brother's. Why camest thou down hither? Eliab	6885
Duty. If thy brother trespass..rebuke him	6886
Energetic. I chased him from me..Neh.	6887
Flattery. He that rebuketh shall find more favour	6888
Insulting. Ananias com'd..smite him on..mouth	6889
Moderation. Michael..not bring a railing accusa'n	6890
Rebukers. Suffer the little children to come unto	6891
Significant. I shook my lap..So G. shake out	6892
Terrible. O full of all subtilty..child of the devil	6893
Wife's. How glorious was the king..shamelessly	6894

Mother's. Mary..son why hast thou dealt with us t.	456
Separation. Have no company with him..eat	103

See BLAME and references.

7160. REPUTATION acknowledged. *"Servest continually."* [16] They brought Daniel, and cast *him* into the den of lions. *Now* the king..said unto Daniel, Thy God whom thou servest continually, he will deliver thee.—DAN., ch. 6.

7161. —— Advantage of. *Husband gained.* [11] Boaz answered..It hath fully been shewed me, all that thou hast done unto thy mother in law since the death of thy husband : and *how* thou hast left thy father and thy mother, and the land of thy nativity, and art come unto a people which thou knewest not heretofore. [12] The Lord recompense thy work.—RUTH, ch. 2.

7162. —— A bad. *Nazareth.* [45] We have found him of whom Moses in the law, and the prophets, did write, Jesus of Nazareth.. [46] And Nathanael said unto him, Can there any good thing come out of Nazareth? Philip saith unto him, Come and see.—JOHN, ch. 1.

7163. —— Blameless. *John.* [20] Herod feared John, knowing that he was a just man and a holy, and observed him ; and when he heard him, he did many things, and heard him gladly. —MARK, ch. 6.

7164. —— A fearful. *Saul.* [13] Ananias answered, Lord, I have heard by many of this man, how much evil he hath done to thy saints at Jerusalem : [14] And here he hath authority from the chief priests, to bind all that call on thy name.—ACTS, ch. 9.

7165. —— A good. *Messengers.* [22] Cornelius the centurion, a just man, and one that feareth God, and of good report among all the nation of the Jews, was warned from God.—ACTS, ch. 10.

7166. —— Gaining a. *Proverb.* [3] Let not mercy and truth forsake thee : bind them about thy neck ; write them upon the table of thine heart ; [4] So shalt thou find favour and good understanding in the sight of God.—PROV., ch. 3.

7167. —— Helpful. *David.* [18] Behold, I have seen a son of Jesse..*that is* cunning in playing, and a mighty valiant man, and a man of war, and prudent in matters, and a comely person, and the Lord *is* with him.—1 SAM., ch. 16.

7168. —— Jealous of. *The Lord.* [9] I wrought for my name's sake, that it should not be polluted before the heathen, among whom they *were,* in whose sight I made myself known unto them, in bringing them forth out of..Egypt. —EZEK., ch. 20.

7169. —— Loss of. *Proverb.* [1] Dead flies cause the ointment of the apothecary to send forth a stinking savour : *so doth* a little folly him that is in reputation for wisdom *and* honour.—ECCL., ch. 10.

7170. —— Official. *Judges.* [See Nos. 7173, 7174.]

7171. —— Posthumous. *At Thebez.* [53] A certain woman cast a piece of a millstone upon Abimelech's head.. [54] Then he called hastily unto the young man his armourbearer, and said ..Draw thy sword, and slay me, that men say not of me, A woman slew him.—JUDGES, ch. 9.

7172. —— reviled. *Zion.* [15] All that pass by clap *their* hands at thee ; they hiss and wag their head at the daughter of Jerusalem, *saying, Is* this the city that *men* call The perfection of beauty, The joy of the whole earth?—LAM., ch. 2.

7173. —— Unimpeachable. *Daniel.* [4] The presidents and princes sought to find occasion against Daniel concerning the kingdom ; but they could find none occasion nor fault ; forasmuch as he *was* faithful.—DAN., ch. 6.

7174. —— —— *Samuel.* [2] I am old and grayheaded..and I have walked before you from my childhood unto this day. [3] Behold, here I *am :* witness against me before the Lord, and before his anointed : whose ox have I taken? or whose ass have I taken? or whom have I defrauded? whom have I oppressed? or of whose hand have I received *any* bribe to blind mine eyes therewith? and I will restore it you. [4] And they said, Thou hast not defrauded us, nor oppressed us, neither hast thou taken aught of any man's hand.—1 SAM., ch. 12.

7175. —— **Valuable.** *Proverb.* [1] A *good* name *is* rather to be chosen than great riches, *and* loving favour rather than silver and gold.— Prov., ch. 22.

7176. —— **Varied.** *Jesus.* [18] Whom say the people that I am? [19] They answering said, John the Baptist; but some *say*, Elias; and others *say*, that one of the old prophets has risen again. [20] He said..But whom say ye that I am? Peter answering said, The Christ of God.—Luke, ch. 9.

See other illustrations under:

FAME.

Increasing. His fame spread abroad..about 3000
Military. Uzziah made..engines..to shoot 3001
Troublesome. Blaze abroad the matter..desert 3002
Unexpected. In the whole world..woman hath 3003
Wisdom. All the earth sought to Solomon 3004

HONOURS.

Abroad. No prophet is accepted in his own 4073
Brave. King will enrich..give him his daughter 4074
Many. Haman told them of the glory 4075
Posthumous. Widows weeping..shewing..Dorcas 4076
Service. Made Saul king [Ammonites subdued] 4077
Trials. I am..weak, though anointed king 4078

REPORT.

Evil. Land..eateth up the inhabitants 7122
False. Amnon only is dead 7123
Intimidation. Jews think to rebel 7124
Manufactured. Say, His disciples..stole 7125
Offensive. Joseph brought..their evil report 7126
Terrorizing. Had heard..our hearts did melt 7127

TALEBEARER.

Flattering. Revealeth secrets..flattereth with his l. 8578
Strife. Where there is no talebearer strife ceaseth 8579
Tattling. He that repeateth..separateth very f. 8580
Wounds. Words of a talebearer are as wounds 8581

Careful. That ye may be blameless..shine as lights 1589
Preserved. Build up the wall..no more a reproach 962
Value. Look out seven men..honest report 5865
See **CHARACTER** and references.

7177. REPRESENTATIVES, Divine. *"My Brethren."* [37] Lord, when saw we thee a hungered, and fed *thee?* or thirsty, and gave *thee* drink? [38] When saw we thee a stranger, and took *thee* in? or naked, and clothed *thee?*—Mat., ch. 25.

7178. —— **Honoured with.** *"Receiveth me."* [40] He that receiveth you receiveth me, and he that receiveth me receiveth him that sent me.. [42] And whosoever shall give to drink unto one of these little ones a cup of cold *water* only in the name of a disciple..he shall in no wise lose his reward.—Mat., ch. 10.

7179. —— **Identity with.** *The Seventy sent.* [16] He that heareth you heareth me; and he that despiseth you despiseth me; and he that despiseth me despiseth him that sent me.—Luke, ch. 10.

7180. REQUEST, A great. *Office.* [20] Then came to him the mother of Zebedee's children with her sons, worshipping *him*, and desiring a certain thing.. [23]..to sit on my right hand, and on my left, is not mine to give, but *it shall be given to them* for whom it is prepared of my Father.—Mat., ch. 20.

See **PETITION** and references.

7181. RESEMBLANCE desired. *Likeness.* [9] Elijah said unto Elisha, Ask what I shall do for thee, before I be taken away from thee. And Elisha said, I pray thee, let a double portion of thy spirit be upon me.—2 Kings, ch. 2.

7182. —— **Parental.** *Devil.* [44] Ye are of *your* father the devil, and the lusts of your father ye will do. He was a murderer from the beginning, and abode not in the truth, because there is no truth in him.—John, ch. 8.

See other illustrations under:

IMITATION.

Benevolence. Samaritan..go thou and do likewise 4333
Childhood. Humble himself as this little child 4334
Sacrilegious. The perfume..ye shall not make..h. 4335
Unholy. Vagabond Jews..We adjure you by Jesus 4336
Vicious. Ye are of your father the devil..will do 4337

REPRESENTATIVES.

Divine. When saw we the a stranger..naked? 7177
Honoured. He that receiveth you, receiveth me 7178
Identity. He that heareth you, heareth me 7179

7183. RESENTMENT, Cruel. *Herod's.* [10] Herod, when he saw that he was mocked of the wise men, was exceeding wroth..and slew all the children that were in Bethlehem..from two years old and under.—Mat., ch. 2.

7184. —— **Indignant.** *"Sons of Belial."* [27] Behold, the woman his concubine was fallen down *at* the door of the house, and her hands *were* upon the threshold.—Judges, ch. 19. [8] And all the people arose as one man, saying, We will not any *of us* go to his tent, neither..into his house. [9] But now this..we will do to Gibeah; *we will go up* by lot against it.—Judges, ch. 20.

7185. —— **of Self-seeking.** *Apostles.* [See No. 7180.] [41] And when the ten heard *it*, they began to be much displeased with James and John.—Mark, ch. 10.

See other illustrations under:

SCOFFERS.

Malicious. Spit in his face, and buffeted 7614
  " Mocked him..a gorgeous robe 7615

SCORN.

Pride. Haman thought scorn to..alone 7618
Public. All that pass by clap their hands at thee 7619
Sinners. They made light of it, and went 7621
Unbelief. They laughed him to scorn 7620
See **ANGER** and references.

7186. RESIDENCE, A chosen. *Transfiguration.* [33] As they departed from him, Peter said unto Jesus, Master, it is good for us to be here: and let us make three tabernacles; one for thee, and one for Moses, and one for Elias.—Luke, ch. 9.

7187. —— **Divine.** *The Heart.* [23] If a man love me, he will keep my words: and my Father will love him, and we will come unto him, and make our abode with him.—John, ch. 14.

7188. —— **Knowledge of.** *To Cornelius.* [5] Send men to Joppa, and call for..Peter: [6] He lodgeth with one Simon a tanner, whose house is by the sea side; he shall tell thee what thou oughtest to do.—Acts, ch. 10.

See other illustrations under:

HOME.

Age. Barzillai said..How long have I to live? 4023
Blessed. L. blessed the Egyptian's house for 4024
Bible. Thou shalt write them upon..house 4025
Dismal. David escaped to the cave..brethren 4026
Dangerous. Bid them farewell which are at home 4027

Godly. As for me and my house..serve the L. 4028
Heavenly. Father's house are many mansions 4029
Influence. Hired servants in my father's house 4030
Longing. Go unto mine own place and to my 4031
Not at. Peter sat down among them 4032
Providence. Barrel of meal wasted not 4033
Protected. Strike the lintel..two side posts with 4034
Pious. First findeth his own brother Simon..to 4035
Reformation. His mother Asa removed..her idol 4036
Religious. Cornelius feared G. with all his house 4037
Sanctity. Slain..in his own house, upon his bed 4038
Testimony at. Go home to thy friends, and tell 4039
Weaned of. God hath made me forget..father's 4040

7189. RESERVES concealed. *At Ai.* [11] All
the people..of war that *were* with him..came
before the city, and pitched on the north side
of Ai : now *there was* a valley between them and
Ai. [12] And he took about five thousand men,
and set them to lie in ambush.—Josh., ch. 8.

7190. —— Many. *At Gethsemane.* [53] Thinkest thou that I cannot now pray to my Father,
and he shall presently give me more than twelve
legions of angels ?—Mat., ch. 26.

7191. —— No. *At Ai.* [17] There was not
a man left in Ai or Beth-el, that went not out
after Israel : and they left the city open, and
pursued after Israel. [8]..And Joshua stretched
out the spear that *he had* in his hand toward
the city.—Josh., ch. 8.

Also see :
Remnant. Mouth of the l..piece of an ear 7066

7192. RESIGNATION to Bereavement. *David.*
[38] So Absalom fled, and went to Geshur, and
was there three years. [39] And *the soul of* king
David longed to go forth unto Absalom : for he
was comforted concerning Amnon, seeing he
was dead.—2 Sam., ch. 13.

7193. —— to the Inevitable. *Jacob.* [13] Take
also your brother, and arise, go again unto the
man : [14] And God Almighty give you mercy before the man, that he may send away your other
brother, and Benjamin. If I be bereaved *of my
children,* I am bereaved.—Gen., ch. 43.

7194. —— Pious. *Job.* [20] Job arose, and
rent his mantle, and shaved his head, and fell
down upon the ground, and worshipped, [21] And
said..the Lord gave, and the Lord hath taken
away ; blessed be the name of the Lord.—Job,
ch. 1.

7195. —— —— *David.* [25] The king said
unto Zadok, Carry back the ark of God into the
city : if I shall find favour in the eyes of the
Lord, he will bring me again, and shew me *both*
it, and his habitation : [26] But if he thus say, I
have no delight in thee ; behold, *here am* I, let
him do to me as seemeth good unto him.—2
Sam., ch. 15.

7196. —— Submissive. *Jerusalem bound.*
[14] When he would not be persuaded, we ceased,
saying, The will of the Lord be done.—Acts,
ch. 21.

See other illustrations under :

PATIENCE.

Divine. Last of all he sent his son 5994
Example. Consider him that endureth such 5995
Labour. This year also..I will dig about it 5996
Maintained. Come out, thou bloody man..of B 5997
Needful. Fret not thyself in any wise to do evil 5998
Picture of. The husbandman waiteth..hath long 5999
Rewarded. He brought me out of the miry clay 6000

Refused. Have patience, and I will pay..would not 6001
Trial of. They despised Saul..he held his peace 6002
Without. Why should this dead dog curse my lord 6003
Waiting. Have need of patience..after ye have 6004

SUBMISSION.

Bereavement. [Sons slain] Aaron held his peace 8409
" David arose..washed..did eat 8410
to Circumstances. Could not bear up..let her drive 8411
Difficult. Thou shalt never wash my feet 8412
Example. If this cup may not..thy will be done 8413
Humiliating. Sackcloth..ropes on their heads 8414
Painful. Take also your brother..unto the man 8415
Punishment. Eli said..It is the Lord 8416
Providence. Angel said, Return to thy mistress 8417

SURRENDER.

Absolute. I count all things but loss..win Christ 8503
Bodily. Yielded their bodies..not serve any god 8504
Christian. Fellowship of his sufferings 8505
Entire. Go thy way, sell..give..follow me 8506
Full. Forsaketh not all that he hath..disciple 8507
Fear. We will do all that thou shalt bid 8508
Moral. What things were gain to me, those I 8509
Power. We have not used this power..hinder 8510
Resisted. Straightway the spirit tare him and he 8511
Sins. Right hand offend thee, cut it off 8512
Sacrifice. She cast in all that she had 8513
Undivided. Cattle also..not a hoof left 8514
Weak. I am thine and all that I have..Ahab 8515

7197. RESISTANCE prohibited. *"Other
Cheek."* [39] Resist not evil : but whosoever shall
smite thee on thy right cheek, turn to him the
other also. [40] And if any man will sue thee at
the law, and take away thy coat, let him have
thy cloke also.—Mat., ch. 5.

7198. —— Prompt. *Paul.* [4] False brethren
unawares brought in, who came in privily to
spy out our liberty which we have in Christ
Jesus, that they might bring us into bondage :
[5] To whom we gave place by subjection, no, not
for an hour.—Gal., ch. 2.

7199. —— Spiritual. *Long.* [3] The Lord said,
My spirit shall not always strive with man, for
that he also *is* flesh : yet his days shall be a
hundred and twenty years.. [5] And God saw that
the wickedness of man *was* great in the earth,
and *that* every imagination of the thoughts of
his heart *was* only evil continually.—Gen., ch. 6.

7200. —— —— *Saul.* [5] He said, Who art
thou, Lord? And the Lord said, I am Jesus
whom thou persecutest : *it is* hard for thee to
kick against the pricks.—Acts, ch. 9.

7201. —— —— *Constant.* [Stephen to his
murderers.] [51] Ye stiffnecked and uncircumcised in heart and ears, ye do always resist the
Holy Ghost : as your fathers *did,* so *do* ye.—
Acts, ch. 7.

See other illustrations under :

DEFENCE.

Declined. Jesus answered to him never a word 2104
Incomplete. Goliath had a helmet..coat of mail 2105
Lawful. King granted the Jews to stand for their 2106
Perilous. Jonathan said..Wherefore shall he be 2107
Preparation. Uzziah prepared..shields, spears 2108
Spiritual. Loins girt about with truth..breastplate 2109
Unheard. Alex. would have made his defence 2110
Weapons. I can slay a man for my hurt 2111

FIGHTING.

Forbidden. Ye shall not fight your brethren..I 3217
God. Mountain was full of chariots..fire 3218
for Jesus. Drew his sword, and struck a servant 3219

HINDERANCE.

Disobedience. Say nothing to any man..blaze 3979
Natural. Let me..kiss my father..mother 3980
Provoking. Let us pass through thy country 3981
Removed. Angel..rolled back the stone..door 3982
Riches. Deceitfulness of riches..choke the word 3983
   "   Easier for a camel..needle's eye than 3984

HINDERANCES.

Care. Take heed lest..become a stumblingblock 3985
Loss. Reuben was returned..Joseph was not in the 4404
Loiterers. While Lot lingered the men laid hold 5053
Malicious. People of the land hired counsellors 3986
Removed. I will eat no flesh while the world 3987
Secular. I have bought..bought..married 3988
Social. Let me first go bid them farewell 3989
Selfish. Neither go in yourselves, neither suffer ye 3990

HINDERING.

Fear. It is reported..Jews think to rebel 3991
Intrigue. Let us meet..in the plain of Ono 3992
   See OPPOSITION.

7202. RESOLUTION, Forgotten. "*Went back.*"
[16] I may not return with thee..neither will I
eat bread nor drink water.. [17] For it was said
to me by..the Lord, Thou shalt eat no bread
nor drink water there, nor turn again to go by
the way that thou camest. [18] ..*But* he lied unto
him. [19] So he went back with him, and did eat
bread in his house, and drank water.—1 KINGS,
ch. 13.

7203. —— Unchangeable. *Paul.* [23] The Holy
Ghost witnesseth in every city, saying that
bonds and afflictions abide me. [24] But none of
these things move me, neither count I my life
dear unto myself, so that I might finish my
course with joy.—ACTS, ch. 20.

7204. —— —— Three Hebrews. [17] If it be
so, our God whom we serve is able to deliver
us from the burning fiery furnace, and he will
deliver *us* out of thine hand, O king. [18] But if
not, be it known unto thee, O king, that we will
not serve thy gods, nor worship the golden
image.—DAN., ch. 3.

   See other illustrations under :

BOLDNESS.

Angels urge. Brought them forth..speak in the t. 878
Apostolic. Whom ye put in prison are..in the t. 879
Believers. [Three worthies] O. N. we are not 880
Brazen. Ahab said to Elijah, Art thou..troubleth 881
Innocence. With whom..be found, let him die 882
Influence. Saw the boldness of P. and J...took 883
Right. When thou seest..more than thou..not 884
Sinners. Jeroboam..served Baal..reared an altar 885
Shame. Absalom..tent upon the roof..concubines 886
Prayer. High priest touched..come boldly..throne 887
Venturesome. Peter walked on the water to go to 888

COURAGE.

Absence. 3000 men said..P. are rulers over us 1770
Daring. Paul would have entered 1771
Faith inspires. I come..in the name of the Lord 1772
Ground. With him..arm of flesh..us the Lord 1773
Honouring. Caleb said, Let us go up at once 1774
Invincible. Not any man be able..before thee 1775
Loss. Israel fled..forsook the cities 1776
Moral. Jesus went before them..amazed 1777
   "   I am ready..to die at Jerusalem 1778
Necessary. Every place..feet shall tread..unto 1779
Patriotic. Fight for your daughters..wives 1780
to Rebuke. I said unto Peter before them all 1781
Reformer's. Should such a man as I flee ? 1782
Stimulated. Put your feet upon the necks..kings 1783

Soldier's. Jonathan climbed..slew 1784
in Worship. Daniel knew..kneeled 1785

DESPERATION.

Boldness. I will go in unto the king..if I perish 2218
Effort. Why sit we here till we die ? 2219
Sinners. Saul inquired of the L..answered him n. 2220
Sacrifices. King of Moab took his eldest son 2221

PERSEVERANCE.

Confident. Neither death nor life..separate me 6097
Exhortation. Barnabas exhorted..with purpose 6098
Encouragement. Can a woman forget her..child 6099
   "   Mountains shall depart..but my 6100
Help to. When..my foot slippeth..thy mercy held 6101
Prayer. Widow troubleth me, I will avenge her 6102
Success by. I have fought a good fight..crown 6103
Test. If ye continue in my word, then..disciples 6104
   See DECISION and references.

7205. RESORT, The last. *Sailor's.* [12] Take me
up, and cast me forth into the sea ; so shall the
sea be calm unto you : for I know that for my
sake this great tempest *is* upon you. [13] Nevertheless the men rowed hard to bring *it* to the
land ; but they could not : [14] Wherefore they
cried..O Lord, we beseech thee, let us not
perish for this man's life.—JONAH, ch. 1.

   Also see :

Prayer. River side where prayer was wont 7791
Water-cure. Angel went down..troubled the water 9378
Watering-place. J. was baptizing in Enon..much 9380

7206. RESPECT for Age. *Elihu.* [6] Elihu..
said, I *am* young, and ye *are* very old ; wherefore I was afraid, and durst not shew you mine
opinion. [7] I said, Days should speak, and
multitude of years should teach wisdom.—JOB,
ch. 32.

7207. —— for the Great. *Job.* [7] When I went
out to the gate through the city, *when* I prepared my seat in the street ! [8] The young men
saw me, and hid themselves : and the aged
arose, *and* stood up. [9] The princes refrained
talking.—JOB, ch. 29.

7208. —— for the Good. "*Holy.*" [20] Herod
feared John, knowing that he was a just man
and an holy. and observed him ; and when he
heard him, he did many things, and heard him
gladly.—MARK, ch. 6.

   See other illustrations under :

DEFERENCE.

Aged. Elihu had waited..were elder than he 2112
Wicked. Herod was sorry, nevertheless..sake 2113

REVERENCE.

Attitude. He opened it..stood up..bowed their 7316
Affectionate. Stood at his feet behind him, weeping 7317
Careful. Put off thy shoes..holy ground 7319
Commanded. No man be seen throughout..mount 7320
Commends. Peter fell down at Jesus' knees 7321
Joyous. Came a fire..people shouted and fell 7322
Manifested. Joshua fell on his face..did worship 7324
Necessary. Him that is poor and of a contrite 7325
   "   Men of Bethshemesh looked into the 7326
Word. Ezra opened the book..all the people stood 7329
Worthy. Sent his son..will reverence him 7330
Youthful. [Young ruler] came running, and 7331
   See HONOURS.

7209. RESPONSES in Worship. "*Amen!*"
[5] Ezra opened the book in the sight of all the
people..and..all the people stood up : [6] And
Ezra blessed the Lord, the great God. And all
the people answered, Amen, Amen, with lifting

up their hands : and they bowed their heads, and worshipped the Lord with *their* faces to the ground.—NEH., ch. 8.

7210. —— Heavenly. *Vision.* ² The seraphim : each one had six wings ; with twain he covered his face, and with twain he covered his feet, and with twain he did fly. ³ And one cried unto another, and said, Holy, holy, holy, *is* the Lord of hosts : the whole earth *is* full of his glory.—ISA., ch. 6.

See other illustrations under :

ANSWER.

Hasty. Answereth before he heareth..folly   445
Insincere. Baptism of John, whence was it?   446
Ill-considered. Can ye drink of the cup that I   447
Unwise. King..answered the people roughly   448
Wise. Render..unto Cesar the things..Cesar's   449

7211. RESPONSIBILITY assumed. *Jews.* [See No. 7225.] ²⁵ Then answered all the people, and said, His blood *be* on us, and on our children.—MAT., ch. 27.

7212. —— —— *Financial.* [The good Samaritan,] ³⁵ When he departed, he took out two pence, and gave *them* to the host, and said.. Take care of him ; and whatsoever thou spendest more, when I come again, I will repay thee. —LUKE, ch. 10.

7213. —— —— *Self-defence.* [See No. 7252.] ²³ Howbeit he refused to turn aside : wherefore Abner with the hinder end of the spear smote him under the fifth *rib*..and he fell down there, and died.—2 SAM., ch. 2.

7214. —— acknowledged. *Samaritan.* ³³ A certain Samaritan, as he journeyed, came where he was..he had compassion *on him*, ³⁴ And went to *him*, and bound up his wounds, pouring in oil and wine, and set him on his own beast, and brought him to an inn, and took care of him.—LUKE, ch. 10.

7215. —— Alppied. *Nathan said*, ⁹ Thou hast killed Uriah the Hittite..and hast taken his wife *to be* thy wife, and hast slain him with the sword of the children of Ammon.—2 SAM., ch. 12.

7216. —— of Builders. *Battlement.* ⁸ When thou buildest a new house, then thou shalt make a battlement for thy roof, that thou bring not blood upon thine house, if any man fall from thence.—DEUT., ch. 22.

7217. —— for Carelessness. *Fire.* ⁶ If fire break out, and catch in thorns, so that the stacks of corn, or the standing corn, or the field, be consumed *therewith;* he that kindled the fire shall surely make restitution.—EX., ch. 22.

7218. —— —— *Pit.* ³³ If a man shall dig a pit, and not cover it, and an ox or an ass fall therein ; ³⁴ The owner of the pit shall make *it* good, *and* give money unto the owner of them ; and the dead *beast* shall be his.—EX., ch. 21.

7219. —— —— *Cattle.* ³⁶ If it be known that the ox hath used to push in time past, and his owner hath not kept him in ; he shall surely pay ox for ox ; and the dead shall be his own. —EX., ch. 21.

7220. —— confessed. *Jonah.* ¹² He said unto them, Take me up, and cast me forth into the sea ; so shall the sea be calm unto you : for I know that for my sake this great tempest *is* upon you.—JONAH, ch. 1.

7221. —— Conscious of. *Sailors.* ¹³ The men rowed hard to bring *it* to the land ; but they could not : for the sea wrought, and was tempestuous against them. ¹⁴ Wherefore they cried unto the Lord, and said, We beseech thee, O Lord, we beseech thee, let us not perish for this man's life, and lay not upon us innocent blood. —JONAH, ch. 1.

7222. —— Charged with. *Ahab.* ¹⁷ When Ahab saw Elijah..Ahab said unto him, *Art* thou he that troubleth Israel? ¹⁸ And he answered, I have not troubled Israel ; but thou, and thy father's house, in that ye have forsaken the commandments of the Lord, and thou hast followed Baalim.—1 KINGS, ch. 18.

7223. —— Cleared of. *Paul.* ²⁵ Ye shall see my face no more. ²⁶ Wherefore I take you to record this day, that I *am* pure from the blood of *all* men. ²⁷ For I have not shunned to declare unto you all the counsel of God.—ACTS, ch. 20.

7224. —— Christian. *"Occupy."* ¹² A certain nobleman went into a far country to receive for himself a kingdom, and to return. ¹³ And he called his ten servants, and delivered them ten pounds, and said unto them, Occupy till I come.—LUKE, ch. 19.

7225. —— disclaimed. *Pilate.* ²⁴ When Pilate saw that he could prevail nothing, but *that* rather a tumult was made, he took water, and washed *his* hands before the multitude, saying, I am innocent of the blood of this just person : see ye *to it*.—MAT., ch. 27.

7226. —— distributed. *Calf made.* ³⁵ The Lord plagued the people, because they made the calf, which Aaron made.—EX., ch. 32.

7227. —— divided. *Law.* ³⁵ If one man's ox hurt another's, that he die ; then they shall sell the live ox, and divide the money of it ; and the dead *ox* also they shall divide.—EX., ch. 21.

7228. —— —— discharged. *At Ephesus.* ²⁰ I kept back nothing that was profitable *unto you*..and have taught you publicly, and from house to house, ²¹ Testifying both to the Jews, and also to the Greeks, repentance toward God, and faith toward our Lord Jesus Christ.—ACTS, ch. 20.

7229. —— —— *Watchman.* ³ If..he blow the trumpet, and warn the people ; ⁴ Then whosoever heareth the sound of the trumpet, and taketh not warning ; if the sword come, and take him away, his blood shall be upon his own head.—EZEK., ch. 33.

7230. —— evaded. *"Other Side."* ³⁰ Leaving *him* half dead. ³¹ And by chance there came down a certain priest that way : and when he saw him, he passed by on the other side. ³² And likewise a Levite..came and looked *on him*, and passed by on the other side.—LUKE, ch. 10.

7231. —— Freed from. *At Corinth.* ⁵ Paul was pressed in the spirit, and testified to the Jews *that* Jesus *was* Christ. ⁶ And when they opposed themselves, and blasphemed, he shook *his* raiment, and said..Your blood *be* upon your own heads ; I *am* clean : from henceforth I will go unto the Gentiles.—ACTS, ch. 18.

7232. —— feared. *Council.* ²⁸ Did not we straitly command you that ye should not teach in this name? and, behold, ye have filled Jerusalem with your doctrine, and intend to bring this man's blood upon us.—ACTS, ch. 5.

7233. —— **Indirect.** *Stephen said,* [52] Which of the prophets have not your fathers persecuted? and they have slain them which shewed before of the coming of the Just One ; of whom ye have been now the betrayers and murderers. —ACTS, ch. 7.

7234. —— **for Injury.** *" Woe."* [7] Woe unto the world because of offences ! for it must needs be that offences come ; but woe to that man by whom the offence cometh !—MAT., ch. 18.

7235. —— **for Improvement.** *Talent.* [28] Take therefore the talent from him.. [29] For unto every one that hath shall be given, and he shall have abundance : but from him that hath not shall be taken away even that which he hath. [30] And cast ye the unprofitable servant into outer darkness.—MAT., ch. 25.

7236. —— **for Knowledge.** *Backsliders.* [20] For if after they have escaped the pollutions of the world..they are again entangled therein, and overcome, the latter end is worse with them than the beginning. [21] For it had been better for them not to have known the way of righteousness, than, after they have known *it*, to turn from the holy commandment.—2 PETER, ch. 2.

7237. —— **Ministerial.** *Plague stayed.* [46] Moses said unto Aaron, Take a censer, and put fire therein from off the altar, and put on incense, and go quickly unto the congregation, and make an atonement for them : for..the plague is begun.—NUM., ch. 16.

7238. —— —— *Watchman.* [8] When I say unto the wicked, O wicked *man*, thou shalt surely die ; if thou dost not speak to warn the wicked from his way, that wicked *man* shall die in his iniquity ; but his blood will I require at thine hand.—EZEK., ch. 33.

7239. —— —— *Loose.* [19] I will give unto thee the keys of the kingdom of heaven : and whatsoever thou shalt bind on earth shall be bound in heaven ; and whatsoever thou shalt loose on earth shall be loosed in heaven.—MAT., ch. 16.

7240. —— **of Manhood.** *Blind Man.* [22] His parents .. feared the Jews : for the Jews had agreed already, that if any man did confess that he was Christ, he should be put out of the synagogue. [23] Therefore said his parents, He is of age ; ask him.—JOHN, ch. 9.

7241. —— **misplaced.** *Providence.* [32] The earth opened her mouth, and swallowed them up, and their houses, and all the men that *appertained* unto Korah, and all *their* goods.. [41] But on the morrow all the congregation..murmured against Moses and against Aaron, saying, Ye have killed the people.—NUM., ch. 16.

7242. —— **Minute.** *Words.* [36] Every idle word that men shall speak, they shall give account thereof in the day of judgment. [37] For by thy words thou shalt be justified, and by thy words thou shalt be condemned.—MAT., ch. 12.

7243. —— **Overwhelming.** *Moses.* [11] Thou layest the burden of all this people upon me ? [12] Have I conceived all this people ? have I begotten them, that thou shouldest say unto me, Carry them in thy bosom, as a nursing father beareth the sucking child, unto the land which

thou swarest unto their fathers ? [13] Whence should I have flesh to give ?—NUM., ch. 11.

7244. —— **for Offences.** *Drowned.* [5] Whoso shall receive one such little child in my name receiveth me. [6] But whoso shall offend one of these little ones which believe in me, it were better for him that a millstone were hanged about his neck, and *that* he were drowned in the depth of the sea.—MAT., ch. 18.

7245. —— **for Others.** *" Keeper."* [9] The Lord said unto Cain, Where *is* Abel thy brother ? And he said, I know not : *Am* I my brother's keeper ? [10] And he said, What hast thou done ? the voice of thy brother's blood crieth unto me from the ground.—GEN., ch. 4.

7246. —— **Parental.** *Eli's.* [Adulterers ..covetous.] [13] Will judge his house for ever for the iniquity which he knoweth ; because his sons made themselves vile, and he restrained them not.—1 SAM., ch. 3.

7247. —— **Strict.** *A Prophet.* [Ahab let Ben-hadad go.] [42] Said unto him, Thus saith the Lord, Because thou hast let go out of *thy* hand a man whom I appointed to utter destruction, therefore thy life shall go for his life, and thy people for his people.—1 KINGS, ch. 20.

7248. —— **for Servants.** *Arson.* [31] Joab arose, and came to Absalom unto *his* house, and said..Wherefore have thy servants set my field on fire ?—2 SAM., ch. 14.

7249. —— **for Success.** *" Tread upon."* [25] There shall no man be able to stand before you : *for* the Lord your God shall lay the fear of you and the dread of you upon all the land that ye shall tread upon.—DEUT., ch. 11.

7250. —— **A terrible.** *Haman.* [9] If it please the king, let it be written that they may be destroyed : and I will pay ten thousand talents of silver..to bring *it* into the king's treasuries.—ESTHER, ch. 3.

7251. —— **Unintended.** *David's.* [21] Saul had slain the Lord's priests. [22] And David said unto Abiathar, I knew..when Doeg the Edomite *was* there, that he would surely tell Saul : I have occasioned *the death* of all the persons of thy father's house. [23] Abide thou with me.— 1 SAM., ch. 22.

7252. —— **Warning of.** *Unheeded.* [18] Asahel *was as* light of foot as a wild roe. [19] And Asahel pursued after Abner.. [22] And Abner said again to Asahel, Turn thee aside from following me : wherefore should I smite thee to the ground ?— 2 SAM., ch. 2.

7253. RESPONSIBILITIES, Various. *Talents.* [15] Unto one he gave five talents, to another two. and to another one ; to every man according to his several ability ; and straightway took his journey.—MAT., ch. 25.

See other illustrations under :

ACCOUNTABILITY.

Future. King which would take account..servants 72
Gifts. Ten pounds..occupy till I come 73
Personal. Give account of thy stewardship 75

7254. REST, An enforced. *Darkness.* [22] Moses stretched forth his hand toward heaven ; and there was a thick darkness in all the land of Egypt three days : [23] They saw not one another, neither rose any from his place for three days. —EX , ch. 12.

7255. —- of Faith. *Quietness.* [15] Thus saith the Lord..In returning and rest shall ye be saved ; in quietness and in confidence shall be your strength : and ye would not. [16] But ye said, No ; for we will flee upon horses ; therefore shall ye flee : and. We will ride upon the swift ; therefore shall they that pursue you be swift.—Isa., ch. 30.

7256. —— Improved. *"Edified."* [31] Then had the churches rest throughout all Judea and Galilee and Samaria, and were edified ; and walking in the fear of the Lord, and in the comfort of the Holy Ghost, were multiplied.—Acts, ch. 9.

7257. —— after Labour. *Creation.* [1] The heavens and the earth were finished, and all the host of them. [2] And on the seventh day God ended his work which he had made ; and he rested on the seventh day.—Gen., ch. 2.

7258. —— No. *Dry Places.* [43] When the unclean spirit is gone out of a man, he walketh through dry places, seeking rest, and findeth none.—Mat., ch. 12. [20] The bed is shorter than that a man can stretch himself on it : and the covering narrower than that he can wrap himself in it.—Isa., ch. 28.

7259. —— of Soul. *In Jesus.* [28] Come unto me, all ye that labour and are heavy laden, and I will give you rest. [29] Take my yoke upon you, and learn of me ; for I am meek and lowly in heart : and ye shall find rest unto your souls.— Mat., ch. 11.

7260. —— without. *Jesus.* [31] Come ye yourselves apart into a desert place, and rest a while : for there were many coming and going, and they had no leisure so much as to eat. [32] And they departed into a desert place by ship privately.—Mark, ch. 6.

7261. —— —— *Wanderer.* [8] As a bird that wandereth from her nest, so is a man that wandereth from his place.—Prov., ch. 27.

7262. —— —— *Afflicted.* [4] When I lie down, I say, When shall I arise, and the night be gone? and I am full of tossings to and fro unto the dawning of the day.—Job, ch. 7.

7263. —— Year of. *"Seventh."* [3] Six years thou shalt sow thy field, and six years thou shalt prune thy vineyard, and gather in the fruit thereof ; [4] But in the seventh year shall be a sabbath of rest unto the land, a sabbath for the Lord : thou shalt neither sow thy field, nor prune thy vineyard.—Lev., ch. 25.

See other illustrations under :

CONTENTMENT.

Constant. In whatsoever state I am..to be content 1642
Christian. Be content with such things as ye have 1643
Godly. Having food and raiment let us be..content 1644
Home. Moses was content to dwell with the man 1645
at Home. That I may die in mine own city 1646
Lack. They that will be rich fall into..a snare 1647
Little. Better is little with..than great treasure 1648
Possessions. Esau said, I have enough, my brother 1649
Perfect. L. is my shepherd, I shall not want 1650
Riches. I will not take from a thread to a shoe-l. 1651

LEISURE.

Without. They had no leisure so much as to eat 4938
   "   They could not so much as eat bread 4939

Vacation. Come..into a desert place and rest 9156
   See SLEEP and references.

7264. RESTLESSNESS from Care. *"Abundance."* [12] The sleep of a labouring man is sweet, whether he eat little or much : but the abundance of the rich will not suffer him to sleep.— Eccl., ch. 5.

7265. —— —— *Rich Fool.* [16] The ground of a certain rich man brought forth plentifully : [17] And he thought. .What shall I do, because I have no room where to bestow my fruits?.. [20] But God said..Thou fool, this night thy soul shall be required of thee : then whose shall those things be?— Luke, ch. 12.

7266. —— from Fear. *The Disobedient.* [66] Thy life shall hang in doubt before thee ; and thou shalt fear day and night, and shalt have none assurance of thy life : [67] In the morning thou shalt say, Would God it were even ! and at even thou shalt say, Would God it were morning.—Deut., ch. 28.

See other illustrations under :

AGITATION.

Deception. Who art thou?..Esau..Isaac trembled 256
Diffuses. Disputed he in the synagogue..market 257
Deplored. [Israelites] Made..abhorred..slay us 258
General. [Philistines] Trembling in the host..field 259
Mount. Sinai..quaked greatly 260
Overcome. [At sepulchre] Keepers did shake 261
Physical. Belshazzar's thoughts troubled..knees 262
Terror. [Job's vision] Trembling..my bones 263

ANXIETY.

Burdensome. Give us flesh..I am not able to bear 453
God's Curse. Eli's heart trembled for the ark of 454
Forbidden. Take no thought..consider the ravens 455
Parental. [Mary said,] Son, why hast thou dealt 456
Relief. When they deliver you up, take no thought 457
Sleepless. Darius..sleep passed from him 458
Sickness. Come down ere my child die 459

7267. RESTITUTION of Gains. *Zaccheus.* [8] Behold, Lord, the half of my goods I give to the poor ; and if I have taken any thing from any man by false accusation, I restore him fourfold.—Luke, ch. 19.

7268. —— Imperative. *Theft.* [2] If a thief be found breaking up, and be smitten that he die, there shall no blood be shed for him. [3] If the sun be risen upon him, there shall be blood shed for him ; for he should make full restitution : if he have nothing, then he shall be sold for his theft.—Ex., ch. 22.

7269. —— for Loss. *By Carelessness.* [33] And if a man shall open a pit, or if a man shall dig a pit, and not cover it, and an ox or an ass fall therein ; [34] The owner of the pit shall make it good, and give money unto the owner of them ; and the dead beast shall be his.—Ex., ch. 21.

7270. —— —— *By Neglect.* [35] And if one man's ox hurt another's, that he die ; then they shall sell the live ox, and divide the money of it ; and the dead ox also they shall divide. [36] Or if it be known that the ox hath used to push in time past, and his owner hath not kept him in ; he shall surely pay ox for ox ; and the dead shall be his own.—Ex., ch. 21.

7271. —— —— *By Fire.* [6] If fire break out, and catch in thorns, so that the stacks of corn, or the standing corn, or the field, be consumed therewith ; he that kindled the fire shall surely make restitution.—Ex., ch. 22.

7272. —— —— *By Theft.* [7] If a man shall

deliver unto his neighbour money or stuff to keep, and it be stolen out of the man's house ; if the thief be found, let him pay double.—Ex., ch. 22.

7273. —— —— *By Lending.* [14] If a man borrow *aught* of his neighbour, and it be hurt, or die, the owner thereof *being* not with it, he shall surely make *it* good. [15] *But* if the owner thereof *be* with it, he shall not make *it* good : if it *be* an hired *thing*, it came for his hire.—Ex., ch. 22.

See other illustrations under :
REPARATION.

Demanded. Let them come and fetch us out 7072
Intended. Take double money..an oversight 7073

7274. RESTORATION of Property. *At Jerusalem.* [10] Let us leave off this usury. [11] Restore, I pray you, to them, even this day, their lands, their vineyards, and their oliveyards, and their houses, also the hundredth *part* of the money, and of the corn, the wine, and the oil, that ye exact of them. [12] Then said they, We will restore *them.*—NEH., ch. 5.

7275. —— **Spiritual.** *P r o d i g a l.* [22] The father said to his servants, Bring forth the best robe, and put *it* on him ; and put a ring on his hand, and shoes on *his* feet.—LUKE, ch. 15.

See other illustrations under :
RESURRECTION.

Announced. All..in their graves..come forth 7278
Bodies. Sown a natural body, it is raised a spiritual 7279
Difficulties. Whose wife shall she be of the seven? 7280
Denied. When they heard of the resurrection..m. 7281
"　　Sadducees say..no..neither angel 7282
Foretold. Them that sleep in the dust of the e. 7283
Faith, Ancient. The dead are raised even Moses s. 7284
"　　"　　Thy dead men shall live..arise 7285
"　　"　　I will ransom them from the..grave 7286
Marriage. Neither marry, nor are given in mar. 7288
See RECOVERY and references.

7276. RESULTS, Discouraging. *His last Year.* [13] Whom do men say that I, the Son of man, am ? [14] And they said, Some *say that thou art* John the Baptist ; some, Elias ; and others, Jeremias, or one of the prophets.—MAT., ch. 16.

7277. —— **Evidence by.** *Law.* [21] How shall we know the word which the Lord hath not spoken ? [22] When a prophet speaketh in the name of the Lord, if the thing follow not, nor come to pass, that *is* the thing which the Lord hath not spoken..thou shalt not be afraid of him.—DEUT., ch. 18.

Also see :
Commend. Ye are our epistle..known 401

7278. RESURRECTION, Announcement of. *Jesus.* [28] The hour is coming, in the which all that are in the graves shall hear his voice, [29] And shall come forth ; they that have done good, unto the resurrection of life ; and they that have done evil, unto the resurrection of damnation.—JOHN, ch. 5.

7279. —— **Bodies.** *Spiritual.* [42] It is sown in corruption, it is raised in incorruption : [43] It is sown in dishonour, it is raised in glory : it is sown in weakness, it is raised in power : [44] It is sown a natural body, it is raised a spiritual body.—1 COR., ch. 15.

7280. —— **Difficulties representing.** *" Whose Wife."* [See No. 7287.]

7281. —— **Denied.** *At A t h e n s.* [32] When they heard of the resurrection of the dead, some mocked : and others said, We will hear thee again of this *matter.*—ACTS, ch. 17.

7282. —— —— *Sadducees.* [7] There arose a dissension between the Pharisees and the Sadducees : and the multitude was divided. [8] For the Sadducees say that there is no resurrection, neither angel, nor spirit.—ACTS, ch. 23.

7283. —— **foretold.** *" A w a k e."* [2] Many of them that sleep in the dust of the earth shall awake, some to everlasting life, and some to shame *and* everlasting contempt. And they that be wise shall shine as the brightness of the firmament.—DAN., ch. 12.

7284. —— **Ancient Faith in.** *Moses.* [37] That the dead are raised, even Moses shewed at the bush, when he calleth the Lord the God of Abraham..Isaac, and..Jacob. [38] For he *is* not a God of the dead, but of the living.—LUKE, ch. 20.

7285. —— —— *Isaiah.* [19] Thy dead *men* shall live, *together with* my dead body shall they arise. Awake and sing, ye that dwell in dust : for thy dew *is as* the dew of herbs, and the earth shall cast out the dead—ISA., ch. 26.

7286. —— —— *H o s e a.* [14] I will ransom them from the power of the grave ; I will redeem them from death : O death, I will be thy plagues ; O grave, I will be thy destruction.—HOSEA, ch. 13.

7287. —— **and Marriage.** *As Angels.* [27] Last of all the woman died also. [28] Therefore in the resurrection whose wife shall she be of the seven ? for they all had her.. [30] For in the resurrection they neither marry, nor are given in marriage, but are as the angels.—MAT., ch. 22.

7288. —— **recompenses.** *" Blessed."* [13] When thou makest a feast, call the poor, the maimed, the lame, the blind : [14] And thou shalt be blessed ; for they cannot recompense thee : for thou shalt be recompensed at the resurrection of the just.—LUKE, ch. 12.

7289. RETALIATION, Cowardly. *J o a b.* [27] When Abner was returned to Hebron, Joab took him aside in the gate to speak with him quietly, and smote him there under the fifth *rib*, that he died, for the blood of Asahel his brother. —2 SAM., ch. 3.

7290. —— **disallowed.** *" Resist not."* [38] It hath been said, An eye for an eye, and a tooth for a tooth : [39] But I say unto you, That ye resist not evil : but whosoever shall smite thee on thy right cheek, turn to him the other also.— MAT., ch. 5.

7291. —— **Jewish.** *" Eye for Eye."* [20] Those which remain shall hear, and fear, and shall henceforth commit no more any such evil among you. [21] And thine eye shall not pity ; *but* life *shall go* for life, eye for eye, tooth for tooth, hand for hand, foot for foot.—DEUT., ch. 19.

See REVENGE and references.

7292. RETRIBUTION for Angels. *In Darkness.* [6] The angels which kept not their first estate, but left their own habitation, he hath reserved in everlasting chains under darkness unto the judgment of the great day.—JUDE.

7293. —— **commenced.** *In Persia.* [1] When the king's commandment..drew near to be put in execution, in the day that the enemies of the

Jews hoped to have power over them..it was turned to the contrary, that the Jews had rule over them that hated them.—ESTHER, ch. 9.

7294. —— —— *Slew seventy Brothers.* ⁵³ A certain woman cast a piece of a millstone upon Abimelech's head, and all to brake his skull. ⁵⁶ Thus God rendered the wickedness of Abimelech, which he did unto his father, in slaying his seventy brethren.—JUDGES, ch. 9.

7295. —— **Fear of.** *Joseph's Brethren.* ²² Reuben answered..Spake I not unto you, saying, Do not sin against the child ; and ye would not hear? therefore, behold, also his blood is required.—GEN., ch. 42.

7296. —— **Faith in.** *Natural.* ⁴ When the barbarians saw the *venomous* beast hang on his hand, they said among themselves, No doubt this man is a murderer, whom, though he hath escaped the sea, Yet vengeance suffereth not to live.—ACTS, ch. 28.

7297. —— **inflicted.** *Providential.* ⁶ Adonibezek fled ; and they pursued after him, and caught him, and cut off his thumbs and his great toes. ⁷ And Adonibezek said, Threescore and ten kings, having their thumbs and their great toes cut off, gathered *their meat* under my table : as I have done, so God hath requited me.—JUDGES, ch. 1.

7298. —— **Justifiable.** *Haman's.* ⁹ Harbonah, one of the chamberlains, said..Behold also the gallows fifty cubits high..made for Mordecai, who had spoken good for the king, standeth in the house of Haman. Then the king said, Hang him thereon.—ESTHER, ch. 7.

7299. —— —— *Daniel's Foes.* ²⁴ They brought those men who had accused Daniel, and they cast *them* into the den of lions, them, their children, and their wives ; and the lions ..brake all their bones in pieces.—DAN., ch. 6.

7300. —— **Providential.** *In Samaria.* ²⁵ At the begining of their dwelling there..they feared not the Lord : therefore the Lord sent lions among them which slew some of them.—2 KINGS, ch. 17.

7301. —— —— *In Egypt.* ²⁹ At midnight the Lord smote all the firstborn in the land of Egypt, from the firstborn of Pharaoh that sat on his throne unto the firstborn of the captive that *was* in the dungeon.—EX., ch. 12.

See RETALIATION *and references.*

7302. RETURN, A sad. *Joseph's Brethren.* ¹² He searched, *and* began at the eldest, and left at the youngest : and the cup was found in Benjamin's sack. ¹³ Then they rent their clothes, and laded every man his ass, and returned to the city.—GEN., ch. 44.

See RESTORATION *and references.*

7303. REVELRY, Impious. *Belshazzar.* ³ They brought the golden vessels that were taken out of the temple..at Jerusalem ; and the king and his princes, his wives and his concubines, drank in them. ⁴ They drank wine, and praised the gods of gold, and of silver, of brass.—DAN., ch. 5.

See other illustrations under :

AMUSEMENT.

Curiosity. Spend their time to..hear some new t. 336
Dangerous. Daughters of Shiloh come out to dance 337
an End. Much goods..many years..be merry 338
Fatal. Philistines called for Samson..made sport 339

Idolatrous. Moses saw the calf and the dancing 340
Perilous. Amalekites were eating, drinking, dancing 341
Royal. Herod made a supper..danced, and pleased 342
Sorrow. Herod was exceeding sorry 343

7304. REVENGE avoided. *Jacob.* ⁴² Esau.. doth comfort himself, *purposing* to kill thee. ⁴³ Now therefore, my son..flee thou to Laban my brother, to Haran ; ⁴⁴ And tarry with him a few days, until thy brother's fury turn away.— GEN., ch. 27.

7305. —— **A Brother's.** *Absalom.* ²⁸ When I say unto you, Smite Amnon ; then kill him, fear not..be courageous.. ²⁹ And the servants of Absalom did..Then all the king's sons arose, and..gat him up upon his mule, and fled.—2 SAM., ch. 13.

7306. —— —— *Joab.* ²⁷ And when Abner was returned to Hebron, Joab took him aside in the gate to speak with him quietly, and smote him there under the fifth *rib*, that he died, for the blood of Asahel his brother.—2 SAM., ch. 3.

7307. —— **The best.** *Kindness.* ²¹ If thine enemy be hungry, give him bread to eat ; and if he be thirsty, give him water to drink : ²² For thou shalt heap coals of fire upon his head, and the Lord shall reward thee.—PROV., ch. 25.

7308. —— **frustrated.** *Haman.* ⁴ The king said, Who *is* in the court? Now Haman was come..to speak unto the king to hang Mordecai on the gallows that he had prepared for him.— ESTHER, ch. 6.

7309. —— **ignored.** *Moses.* ¹ Miriam and Aaron spake against Moses because of the Ethiopian woman whom he had married.. ¹³ And Moses cried unto the Lord, saying, Heal her now, O God, I beseech thee.—NUM., ch. 12. [Of leprosy inflicted.]

7310. —— —— *By David.* [Shimei cursed and cast stones when David fled from Absalom.] ²¹ Abishai..said, Shall not Shimei be put to death for this, because he cursed the Lord's anointed ? ²² And David said, What have I to do with you, ye sons of Zeruiah, that ye should this day be adversaries unto me ?—2 SAM., ch. 19.

7311. —— **Justifiable.** *Samson.* ⁶ The Philistines came up, and burnt her and her father with fire. ⁷ And Samson said..Though ye have done this, yet will I be avenged of you, and after that I will cease. ⁸ And he smote them hip and thigh with a great slaughter.—JUDGES, ch. 15.

7312. —— **nursed.** *Absalom.* ²² Absalom spake unto his brother Amnon neither good nor bad : for Absalom hated Amnon, because he had forced his sister Tamar. ²³..after two full years ..Absalom had sheepshearers in Baalhazor..and Absalom invited all the king's sons. —2 SAM., ch. 13. [See No. 7305.]

7313. —— **proposed.** *Esau.* ⁴¹ Esau hated Jacob because..his father blessed him : and Esau said in his heart, The days of mourning for my father are at hand ; then will I slay my brother Jacob.—GEN., ch. 27.

7314. —— **Price for.** *Haman.* ⁹ Let it be written that they may be destroyed : and I will pay ten thousand talents of silver..into the king's treasuries.—ESTHER, ch. 3.

7315. —— **Prayer for.** *Samson.* ²⁷ *There were* upon the roof about three thousand men and

women, that beheld while Samson made sport.
^{28} And Samson..said, O Lord God..strengthen
me, I pray thee, only this once, O God, that I
may be at once avenged of the Philistines for
my two eyes. ^{29} And Samson took hold of the
two middle pillars upon which the house stood.
—JUDGES, ch. 16.

See other illustrations under:

RESENTMENT.

Cruel. Herod slew all the children..Bethlehem 7183
Indignant. Woman was fallen..hands on the t. 7184
of Self-Seeking. Much displeased with James and 7185

RETALIATION.

Cowardly. Joab took Abner aside..smote him 7289
Disallowed. Been said, An eye for an eye 7290
Jewish. Life shall go for life, eye for eye 7291

VENGEANCE.

Averted. Let not my lord regard..Nabal 9169
"   Kept me..from coming to shed blood 9170
Blood. Cain said..every one that findeth me..slay 9171
Call. Stoned [Zachariah] in house of the Lord 9172
Divine. To me belongeth vengeance and rec. 9173
"   If I whet my glittering sword 9174
Declined. Not a man be put to death [Saul] 9175
Fear. Joseph will peradventure hate us 9176
with God. My G., think thou upon Tobiah 9177
Inappropriate. I forgave thee..shouldest thou not 9178
Mistaken. Command fire..to consume them 9179
Monstrous. Haman thought scorn..Mordecai 9180
Prohibited. If ye from your hearts forgive not 9182
for Vengeance. David commanded..slew them 9184
Undesired. Behold the head of Ish-bosheth 9183

See PUNISHMENT.
See RETRIBUTION above.

7316. REVERENCE, Attitudes of. *Bound.*
^{5} Ezra opened the book in the sight of all the
people ; (for he was above all the people ;) and
when he opened it, all the people stood up :
^{6} And Ezra blessed the Lord, the great God.
And all the people answered, Amen, Amen, with
lifting up their hands : and they bowed their
heads, and worshipped the Lord with *their* faces
to the ground.—NEH., ch. 8.

7317. —— Affectionate. *Magdalene.* ^{7} Jesus
sat at meat in the Pharisee's house, brought an
alabaster box of ointment.. ^{38} And stood at his
feet behind *him* weeping, and began to wash his
feet with tears, and did wipe *them* with the hairs
of her head, and kissed his feet, and anointed
them with the ointment.—LUKE, ch. 7.

7318. —— for Age. *Pharaoh's.* ^{7} Joseph
brought in Jacob his father, and set him before Pharaoh : and Jacob blessed Pharaoh.—
GEN., ch. 47.

7319. —— Careful. *"Shoes off!"* ^{4} God
called unto him out of the midst of the bush,
and said, Moses, Moses ! And he said, Here *am*
I. ^{5} And he said, Draw not nigh hither : put
off thy shoes from off thy feet ; for the place
whereon thou standest *is* holy ground.—Ex.,
ch. 3.

7320. —— commanded. *Flocks.* ^{3} No man
shall come up with thee, neither let any man
be seen throughout all the mount ; neither let
the flocks nor herds feed before that mount.—
Ex., ch. 34.

7321. —— commends. *Peter.* ^{8} When Simon
Peter saw *it*, he fell down at Jesus' knees, saying, Depart from me ; for I am a sinful man, O

Lord.. ^{10}..And Jesus said unto Simon..from
henceforth thou shalt catch men.—LUKE, ch. 5.

7322. —— of Esteem. *Mephibosheth.* ^{6} When
Mephibosheth, the son of Jonathan..was come
unto David, he fell on his face, and did reverence.—2 SAM., ch. 9.

7323. —— Joyous. *"Shouted..fell."* ^{24} There
came a fire out from before the Lord, and consumed upon the altar the burnt offering and
the fat : *which* when all the people saw, they
shouted, and fell on their faces.—LEV., ch. 22.

7324. —— manifested. *Joshua.* ^{14} As captain of the host of the Lord am I now come.
And Joshua fell on his face to the earth, and
did worship, and said unto him, What saith my
lord unto his servant ? ^{15}..Loose thy shoe from
off thy foot ; for the place whereon thou standest
is holy.—JOSH., ch. 5.

7325. —— necessary. *Sacrifices.* ^{1} The
heaven *is* my throne, and the earth *is* my footstool.. ^{2}..but to this *man* will I look, *even* to
him that is poor and of a contrite spirit, and
trembleth at my word. ^{3} He that killeth an ox
is as if he slew a man ; he that sacrificeth a
lamb, *as if* he cut off a dog's neck.—ISA., ch. 66.

**7326. —— —— ** *Philistines.* ^{19} The men of
Beth-shemesh, because they had looked into
the ark of the Lord, even he smote of the people
fifty thousand and threescore and ten men.—1
SAM., ch. 6.

7327. —— Preserved by. *Soldiers.* ^{13} The
third captain of fifty went up..and fell on his
knees before Elijah..and said..O man of God,
I pray thee, let my life, and the life of these
fifty thy servants, be precious in thy sight.—2
KINGS, ch. 1.

7328. —— Unworthy of. *The Agagite.* ^{2} All
the king's servants, that *were* in the king's gate,
bowed, and reverenced Haman ; for the king
had so commanded concerning him. But Mordecai bowed not, nor did *him* reverence.—ES-
THER, ch. 3.

7329. —— for the Word. *"When he opened
it, all the people stood up."* [See No. 7316.]

7330. —— Worthy of. *Parable.* ^{35} The husbandmen took his servants, and beat one, and
killed another, and stoned another. ^{36} Again,
he sent other servants.. ^{37} But last of all he
sent unto them his son, saying, They will reverence my son.—MAT., ch. 21.

7331. —— Youthful. *Young Ruler.* ^{17} When
he was gone forth into the way, there came one
running, and kneeled to him, and asked him,
Good Master, what shall I do that I may inherit
eternal life?—MARK, ch. 10.

See other illustrations under:

AWE.

Alarming. We..die..have seen God 603
Painful. Alas, O L. G...have seen an angel 604

PROSTRATION.

Involuntary. I am he..they fell to the ground 6705
Sinners. Saul fell to the earth..Saul, Saul 6706

of God. Moses hid his face..look upon G. 3580
Prostration. Angel ascended..M..and wife fell 349

See WORSHIP.

7332. REVENUE, Royal. *Solomon.* ^{14} The
weight of gold that came to Solomon in one
year was six hundred threescore and six talents

of gold, ¹⁵ Besides *that he had* of the merchant-men, and of the traffick of the spice merchants, and of all the kings of Arabia.—1 KINGS, ch. 10.

7333. REVELATION sufficient. *Dives.* ³⁰ He said, Nay, father Abraham : but if one went unto them from the dead, they will repent. ³¹ And he said..If they hear not Moses and the prophets, neither will they be persuaded, though one rose from the dead.—LUKE, ch. 16.

7434. REVIVAL, Bible Reading in. *K i n g Josiah said,* ¹³ Go ye, inquire of the Lord for me, and for the people, and for all Judah, concerning the words of this book that is found : for great *is* the wrath of the Lord that is kindled against us, because our fathers have not hearkened unto the words of this book.—2 KINGS, ch. 22.

7335. —— Call for a. *"Proclamation."* ⁷ They made proclamation throughout Judah and Jerusalem..that they should gather..unto Jerusalem ; ⁸ And that whosoever would not come within three days, according to the counsel of the princes and the elders, all his substance should be forfeited, and himself separated from the congregation.—EZRA, ch. 10.

7336. —— Changes in. *By the Spirit.* ¹⁵ Until the spirit be poured upon us from on high, and the wilderness be a fruitful field, and the fruitful field be counted for a forest. ¹⁶ Then judgment shall dwell in the wilderness, and righteousness remain in the fruitful field.—ISA., ch. 32.

7337. —— A continued. *At Jerusalem.* [Temple purified, priests reconsecrated.] ²¹ The children of Israel..kept the feast of unleavened bread seven days with great gladness : and the Levites and the priests praised the Lord day by day, *singing* with loud instruments unto the Lord.. ²³ And the whole assembly took counsel to keep other seven days : and they kept *other* seven days with gladness. ²⁴ For Hezekiah king of Judah did give to the congregation a thousand bullocks and seven thousand sheep ; and the princes gave to the congregation a thousand bullocks and ten thousand sheep : and a great number of priests sanctified themselves. — 2 CHRON., ch. 30.

7338. —— Commotion in. *"Shaking."* [See No. 7355.] ⁷ So I prophesied as I was commanded : and as I prophesied, there was a noise, and behold a shaking, and the bones came together, bone to his bone.—EZEK., ch. 37.

7339. —— Eagerness for a. *"Amen."* [See No. 7354.] ⁵ Ezra opened the book in the sight of all the people..and when he opened it, all the people stood up : ⁶ And Ezra blessed the Lord, the great God. And all the people answered Amen, Amen, with lifting up their hands : and they bowed their heads, and worshipped the Lord with *their* faces to the ground. —NEH., ch. 8.

7340. —— Fruit of. *Pentecost.* ⁴⁴ All that believed were together, and had all things common ; ⁴⁵ And sold their possessions and goods, and parted them to all *men*, as every man had need.—ACTS, ch. 2.

7341. —— Families in. [See No. 7334.] *"Small and Great."* ² The king went up into the house of the Lord, and all the men of Judah and all the inhabitants of Jerusalem..and all the people, both small and great : and he read in their ears all the words of the book of the covenant.—2 KINGS, ch. 23.

7342. —— A famous. *"Great Joy."* [See No. 7337.] ²⁵ All the congregation of Judah, with the priests and the Levites, and all..that came out of the land of Israel, and the strangers that dwelt in Judah, rejoiced. ²⁶ So there was great joy in Jerusalem : for since the time of Solomon..*there was* not the like in Jerusalem.—2 CHRON., ch. 30.

7343. —— A genuine. *Jewish.* ³¹ Hezekiah ..said, Now ye have consecrated yourselves unto the Lord, come near and bring sacrifices and thank offerings into the house of the Lord. And the congregation brought in sacrifices and thank offerings ; and as many as were of a free heart, burnt offerings.—2 CHRON., ch. 29.

7344. —— A general. *Antioch.* ⁴³ When the congregation was broken up, many of the Jews and religious proselytes followed Paul and Barnabas : who..persuaded them to continue in the grace of God. ⁴⁴ And the next sabbath day came almost the whole city together to hear the word of God.—ACTS, ch. 13.

7345. —— —— *Samaria.* ⁵ Philip went down to the city of Samaria, and preached Christ unto them. ⁶ And the people with one accord gave heed unto those things which Philip spake, hearing and seeing the miracles which he did.. ⁸ And there was great joy in that city.— ACTS, ch. 8.

7346. —— Irregularity in. *"Levites helped."* [See No. 7343.] ³⁴ The priests were too few, so that they could not flay all the burnt offerings : wherefore their brethren the Levites did help them, till the work was ended, and until the *other* priests had sanctified themselves : for the Levites *were* more upright in heart to sanctify themselves than the priests.—2 CHRON., ch. 29.

7347. —— Ingathering by. *Primitive.* [See No. 7363]. ⁴¹ The same day there were added unto *them* about three thousand souls. ⁴² And they continued steadfastly in the apostles' doctrine and fellowship, and in breaking of bread, and in prayers.—ACTS, ch. 2.

7348. —— —— *Jerusalem.* ⁴ Many of them which heard the word believed ; and the number of the men was about five thousand.—ACTS, ch. 4.

7349. —— Joy of. *Jewish.* [See No. 7346.] ³⁵ The burnt offerings *were* in abundance, with the fat of the peace offerings, and the drink offerings for *every* burnt offering. So the service of the house of the Lord was set in order. ³⁶ And Hezekiah rejoiced, and all the people, that God had prepared the people : for the thing was *done* suddenly.—2 CHRON., ch. 29.

7350. —— —— *Pentecost.* ⁴⁶ They, continuing daily with one accord in the temple, and breaking bread from house to house, did eat their meat with gladness and singleness of heart, ⁴⁷ Praising God, and having favour with all the people. And the Lord added to the church daily such as should be saved.—ACTS, ch. 2.

7351. —— Liberality in. *Jewish.* [See No. 7343.] ³² The number of the burnt offerings, which the congregation brought, was threescore and ten bullocks, an hundred rams, *and* two hundred lambs.. [33] And the consecrated things *were* six hundred oxen and three thousand sheep. —2 CHRON., ch. 29.

7352. —— **Means of.** *"Put Away."* [3] Samuel spake.. If ye do return unto the Lord with all your hearts, *then* put away the strange gods, and Ashtaroth, from among you, and prepare your hearts unto the Lord, and serve him only: and he will deliver you out of the hand of the Philistines.—1 SAM., ch. 7.

7353. —— **Mourning for a.** *Temple rebuilt.* [1] When Ezra had prayed, and when he had confessed, weeping and casting himself down before the house of God, there assembled unto him out of Israel a very great congregation of men and women and children: for the people wept very sore.. [6] Then Ezra rose up.. and went into the chamber of Johanan.. he did eat no bread, nor drink water: for he mourned because of the transgression of them that had been carried away.—EZRA, ch. 10.

7354. —— **A Meeting for.** *At Jerusalem.* [2] Ezra the priest brought the law before the congregation both of men and women, and all that could hear with understanding.. [3] And he read therein.. from the morning until midday.. and the ears of all the people *were attentive* unto the book of the law.—NEH., ch. 8.

7355. —— **Need of.** *"Dry Bones."* [1] Hand of the Lord was upon me.. and set me down in the midst of the valley which *was* full of bones, [2] And caused me to pass by them round about: and, behold, *there were* very many in the open valley; and, lo, *they were* very dry.—EZEK., ch. 37.

7356. —— **Preparation for a.** *Made straight.* [4] Prepare ye the way of the Lord, make his paths straight. [5] Every valley shall be filled, and every mountain and hill shall be brought low; and the crooked shall be made straight, and the rough ways *shall be* made smooth; [6] And all flesh shall see the salvation of God.— LUKE, ch. 3.

7357. —— —— *Elijah.* [30] He repaired the altar of the Lord *that was* broken down. [31] And Elijah took twelve stones, according to the number of the tribes of the sons of Jacob.. [32] And with the stones he built an altar.—1 KINGS, ch. 18.

7358. —— **Preaching.** *At Capernaum.* [2] Straightway many were gathered together, insomuch that there was no room to receive *them*, no, not so much as about the door: and he preached the word unto them.—MARK, ch. 2.

7359. —— **by Preaching.** *Prophesy.* [4] Prophesy upon these bones, and say unto them, O ye dry bones, hear the word of the Lord. [5] Thus saith the Lord God unto these bones; Behold, I will cause breath to enter into you, and ye shall live.—EZEK., ch. 37.

7360. —— **Remarkable.** *The Baptist.* [5] Then went out to him Jerusalem, and all Judea, and all the region round about Jordan, [6] And were baptized of him in Jordan, confessing their sins.—MAT., ch. 3.

7361. —— **Readiness for.** *"Great Rain."* [See No. 7353.] [9] Then all the men of Judah and Benjamin gathered themselves together unto Jerusalem within three days.. and all the people sat in the street of the house of God, trembling because of *this* matter, and for the great rain.— EZRA, ch. 10.

7362. —— **Reclaimed by.** *"Bones.. Army."* [See No. 7359.] [10] So I prophesied as he commanded me, and the breath came into them, and they lived, and stood up upon their feet, an exceeding great army.—EZEK., ch. 37.

7363. —— **A sudden.** *Pentecost.* [37] When they heard *this*, they were pricked in their heart, and said unto Peter and to the rest of the apostles, Men *and* brethren, what shall we do? [38] Then Peter said.. Repent, and be baptized.. and ye shall receive the gift of the Holy Ghost.—ACTS, ch. 2.

7364. —— **By the Truth.** *"Gave the Sense."* [See No. 7354.] [7] The Levites, caused the people to understand the law: and the people *stood* in their place. [8] So they read in the book in the law of God distinctly, and gave the sense, and caused *them* to understand the reading.— NEH., ch. 8.

7365. —— **Unity in a.** *"All.. loud Voice."* [See No. 7361.] [11] Make confession unto the Lord God of your fathers, and do his pleasure: and separate yourselves from the people of the land, and from the strange wives. [12] Then all the congregation answered and said with a loud voice, As thou hast said, so must we do.—EZRA, ch. 10.

7366. —— **Vows in.** *"Stood to the Covenant."* [3] The king stood by a pillar, and made a covenant before the Lord, to walk after the Lord, and to keep his commandments.. with all *their* heart and all *their* soul, to perform the words of this covenant that were written in this book. And all the people stood to the covenant.—2 KINGS, ch. 23.

See other illustrations under:

CONVERTS.

CONVERSION.

Sudden. Called for a light..What must I do ? 1715
Superficial. When tribulation or persecution 1716
Wonderful. Suddenly there shined..voice..Saul 1717

CONVERSIONS.

Daily. L. added to the church daily..be saved 1718
Genuine. Confessed, showed their deeds..books 1719
Instrumental. Samaritans believed..for the saying 1720

Refreshment. Came to Elim..12 wells..70 palm t's 6639
See REPENTANCE and references.

7367. REVILING, Abusive. *Paul.* [22] They gave him audience unto this word, and *then* lifted up their voices, and said, Away with such a *fellow* from the earth : for it is not fit that he should live. [23]..they cried out..and threw dust into the air.—ACTS, ch. 22.

7368. REVOLUTION, Christianity a. *At Thessalonica.* [5] The Jews..moved with envy, took unto them certain lewd fellows of the baser sort ..and set all the city on an uproar, and assaulted the house of Jason.. [6] And when they found them not, they drew Jason and certain brethren unto the rulers of the city, crying, These that have turned the world upside down are come hither also.—ACTS, ch. 17.

See other illustrations under :
REBELLION.
Abominable. Rebellion is as the sin of a. 6874
Ingrates. Absalom sent spies..say Absalom 6875
Ill-government. Thy father made our yoke 6876
Jealousy. Ye take too much upon you [Korah] 6877
Mental. Not enter..ye rebelled against my word 6878
Sinners. We will not have this man to reign 6879
" This is the heir, come, let us kill him 6880
Tongue. Every kind of beasts..been tamed 6881
Uncontested. Ye shall not fight..return every man 6882
Vain. Sheba blew a trumpet..we have no part 6883
Will. How oft would I..but ye would not 6884

7369. REWARD, Abundant. *Peter's.* [3] He entered into one of the ships, which was Simon's, and prayed him that he would thrust out a little from the land. And he sat down, and taught the people out of the ship.. [5]..nevertheless at thy word I will let down the net. [6] And when they had this done, they inclosed a great multitude of fishes.—LUKE, ch. 5.

7370. —— for Benevolence. *At Resurrection.* [12] Said .. to him that bade him, When thou makest a dinner or a supper, call not thy friends, nor thy brethren, neither thy kinsmen, nor *thy* rich neighbours ; lest they also bid thee again, and a recompense be made thee. [13] But..call the poor, the maimed, the lame, the blind : [14] And thou shalt be blessed..thou shalt be recompensed at the resurrection of the just.—LUKE, ch. 14.

7371. —— delayed. *Mordecai.* [2] It was found written, that Mordecai had told of Bigthana and Teresh, two of the king's chamberlains, the keepers of the door, who sought to lay hand on the king Ahasuerus. [3] And the king said, What honour and dignity hath been done to Mordecai for this ? Then said the king's servants..There is nothing done for him.—ESTHER, ch. 6.

7372. —— declined. *Abram.* [22] Abram said to the king of Sodom, I have lifted up mine hand unto the Lord.. [23] That I will not *take* from a thread even to a shoelatchet, and that I will not take any thing that *is* thine, lest thou shouldest say, I have made Abram rich.—GEN., ch. 14.

7373. —— for Dishonour. *Delilah.* [*] The lords of the Philistines..said unto her, Entice him, and see wherein his great strength *lieth*, and by what *means*..we may bind him to afflict him : and we will give thee every one of us eleven hundred *pieces* of silver.—JUDGES, ch. 16.

7374. —— Future. *Moses.* [26] Esteeming the reproach of Christ greater riches than the treasures in Egypt : for he had respect unto the recompense of the reward.—HEB., ch. 11.

7375. —— Gracious. *Woman.* [7] There cometh a woman of Samaria to draw water : Jesus saith..Give me to drink.. [28] The woman then left her waterpot, and went her way into the city, and saith to the men, [29] Come, see a man which told me all things that ever I did : is not this the Christ ?—JOHN, ch. 4.

7376. —— by Grace. *Servants.* [9] Doth he thank that servant because he did the things that were commanded him ? I trow not. [10] So likewise ye, when ye shall have done all..say, We are unprofitable servants : we have done that which was our duty to do.—LUKE, ch. 17.

7377. —— The Labourer's. *"Fruit."* [35] Lift up your eyes, and look on the fields ; for they are white already to harvest. [36] And he that reapeth receiveth wages, and gathereth fruit unto life eternal : that both he that soweth and he that reapeth may rejoice together.—JOHN, ch. 4.

7378. —— of Treachery. *Judas.* [4] I have sinned in that I have betrayed the innocent blood. And they said, What *is that* to us? see thou *to that.* [5] And he cast down the pieces of silver in the temple, and departed, and went and hanged himself.—MAT., ch. 27.

See other illustrations under :
RETRIBUTION.
Angels. Reserved in everlasting chains 7292
Commenced. Jews had rule over them 7293
" Millstone upon Abimelech's head 7294
Fear. Reuben spake..his blood is required 7295
Faith in. Barbarians said..he is a murderer 7296
Inflicted. Adoni-bezek..cut off his thumbs and 7297
Just. King said, Hang Haman thereon 7298
" Lions brake their bones 7299
Providential. Lord sent lions among them 7300
" Lord smote the firstborn 7301

REVENGE.
Avoided. Flee thou to Laban..brother's fury turn 7304
Brother's. When I say, Smite Amnon, then kill 7305
" Joab smote Abner..for the blood of 7306
Best. If thine enemy be hungry, give him bread 7307
Frustrated. Haman was come..Hang Mordecai 7308
Ignored. Spake against Moses..M. cried unto the 7309
" Shall not Shimei be put to death ? 7310
Justifiable. Philistines burnt her..S. smote them 7311
Nursed. Absalom spake neither good nor bad 7312
Proposed. Then will I slay my brother Jacob 7313
Price. That they may be destroyed..I will pay 7314
Prayer. O L. G. strengthen me..avenged of the P. 7315

WAGES.
Back. Borrow..jewels of silver..gold and raiment 9255
Changed. Your father [Laban] changed my wages 9256
Daily. The wages..shall not abide with thee 9257
" At his day thou shalt give him his hire 9258
Others. These last have wrought but one hour..us 9259
Unimportant. Take this child..will give thee wages 9260

7379. RICH, Benevolence of the. *Zaccheus.* [8] Lord, the half of my goods I give to the poor ;

and if I have taken any thing from any man by false accusation, I restore *him* fourfold.—LUKE, ch. 19.

7380. —— **Duty of the.** *"Do Good."* [18] That they do good, that they be rich in good works, ready to distribute, willing to communicate ; [19] Laying up in store for themselves a good foundation against the time to come, that they may lay hold on eternal life.—1 TIM., ch. 6.

7381. —— **Hospitality of the.** *Zaccheus.* [5] Zaccheus, make haste, and come down ; for to day I must abide at thy house. [6] And he made haste, and came down, and received him joyfully.—ACTS, ch. 19.

7382. —— **Indifference of the.** *Dives.* [19] There was a certain rich man, which..fared sumptuously every day : [20] And there was a certain beggar named Lazarus, which was laid at his gate, full of sores, [21] And desiring to be fed with the crumbs.—LUKE, ch. 16.

7383. —— **Oppression of the.** *" Buy."* [6] That we may buy the poor for silver, and the needy for a pair of shoes ; *yea,* and sell the refuse of the wheat?—AMOS, ch. 8.

7384. —— **Peril by the.** *Young Ruler.* [22] He was sad at that saying, and went away grieved : for he had great possessions. [23] And Jesus.. saith..How hardly shall they that have riches enter into the kingdom of God !—MARK, ch. 10.

7385. —— **Robbery by the.** *Parable.* [2] The rich *man* had exceeding many flocks and herds : [3] But the poor *man* had nothing, save one little ewe lamb, which he had bought and nourished up : and it grew up..with his children..The rich man..spared to take of his own flock..to dress for the wayfaring man that was come..but took the poor man's lamb.—2 SAM., ch. 12.

7386. —— **surpassed, The.** *" Two Mites."* [43] This poor widow hath cast more in, than all they which have cast into the treasury : [44] For all *they* did cast in of their abundance ; but she of her want did cast in all that she had, *even* all her living.—MARK, ch. 12.

7387. RICHES, Advantage of. *" Distribute."* [See No. 7380.]

7388. —— **Cost of.** *Jacob.* [40] *Thus* I was ; in the day the drought consumed me, and the frost by night ; and my sleep departed from mine eyes. [41] Thus have I been twenty years in thy house.—GEN., ch. 31.

7389. —— **Care of.** *Dives.* [17] He thought within himself, saying, What shall I do, because I have no room where to bestow my fruits ? [18] And he said, This will I do : I will pull down my barns, and build greater.—LUKE, ch. 12.

7390. —— **Display of.** *Solomon's.* [16] King Solomon made two hundred targets *of* beaten gold : six hundred *shekels* of gold went to one target. [17] And *he made* three hundred shields *of* beaten gold ; three pounds of gold went to one shield : and the king put them in the house of the forest of Lebanon.—1 KINGS, ch. 10.

7391. —— —— *Solomon's.* [18] The king made a great throne of ivory, and overlaid it with the best gold. [19] The throne had six steps, and the top of the throne *was* round behind : and *there were* stays on either side .. and two lions stood beside the stays. [20] And twelve lions stood there on the one side and on the

other upon the six steps : there was not the like made in any kingdom.—1 KINGS, ch. 10.

7392. —— **Dangers in.** *The King.* [16] He shall not multiply horses to himself.. [17] Neither shall he multiply wives to himself, that his heart turn not away : neither shall he greatly multiply to himself silver and gold.—DEUT., ch. 17.

7393. —— **Despised.** *Moses.* [24] By faith Moses..refused to be called the son of Pharaoh's daughter ; [25] Choosing rather to suffer affliction with the people of God, than to enjoy the pleasures of sin for a season ; [26] Esteeming the reproach of Christ greater riches than the treasures in Egypt.—HEB., ch. 11.

7394. —— **Deceptive.** *Proverb.* [7] There is that maketh himself rich, yet *hath* nothing : *there is* that maketh himself poor, yet *hath* great riches.—PROV., ch. 13.

7395. —— **Discontent with.** *Haman.* [11] Haman told them of the glory of his riches, and.. his children, and..the king had promoted him.. [13] Yet all this availeth me nothing, so long as I see Mordecai the Jew sitting at the king's gate. —ESTHER, ch. 5.

7396. —— **Extravagance with.** *Solomon.* [21] All king Solomon's drinking vessels *were of* gold, and all the vessels of the house of the forest of Lebanon *were of* pure gold ; none *were of* silver : it was nothing accounted of in the days of Solomon.—1 KINGS, ch. 10.

7397. —— **Great.** *Solomon's.* [14] The weight of gold that came to Solomon in one year was six hundred threescore and six talents of gold, [15] Besides *that he had* of the merchantmen, and of the traffick of the spice merchants, and of all the kings of Arabia, and of the governors of the country.—1 KINGS, ch. 10.

7398. —— **Hurtful.** *" Kept."* [13] There is a sore evil..*namely,* riches kept for the owners thereof to their hurt. [14] But those riches perish by evil travail : and he begetteth a son, and *there is* nothing in his hand. [15] As he came forth.. naked shall he return.—ECCL., ch. 5.

7399. —— **Hasty.** *Proverb.* [20] A faithful man shall abound with blessings : but he that maketh haste to be rich shall not be innocent.. [22] He that hasteth to be rich *hath* an evil eye, and considereth not that poverty shall come upon him.—PROV., ch. 28.

7400. —— **Increase of.** *Jacob.* [10] I am not worthy of the least of all the mercies..which thou hast shewed unto thy servant ; for with my staff I passed over this Jordan ; and now I am become two bands. [11] Deliver me, I pray thee, from the hand of..Esau.—GEN., ch. 32.

7401. —— **Ill-gotten.** *Ahab's.* [19] Thus saith the Lord, Hast thou killed, and also taken possession?..In the place where dogs licked the blood of Naboth shall dogs lick thy blood, even thine. [20] And Ahab said to Elijah, Hast thou found me, O mine enemy?—1 KINGS, ch. 21.

7402. —— **Misled by.** *Dives.* [19] I will say to my soul, Soul, thou hast much goods laid up for many years ; take thine ease, eat, drink, *and* be merry.—LUKE, ch. 12.

7403. —— **Overgrowth of.** *" Thorns."* [18] These are they which are sown among thorns ; such as hear the word, [19] And the cares of this world, and the deceitfulness of riches, and the lusts of other things entering in, choke the word, and it becometh unfruitful.—MARK, ch. 4.

7404. —— **an Obstacle.** *Young Ruler.* ²² Yet lackest thou one thing : sell all that thou hast, and distribute unto the poor, and thou shalt have treasure in heaven : and come, follow me. ²³ And when he heard this, he was very sorrowful ; for he was very rich.—LUKE, ch. 18.

7405. —— **Poverty with.** *Laodiceans.* ¹⁶ So then because thou art lukewarm, and neither cold nor hot, I will spew thee out of my mouth. ¹⁷ Because thou sayest, I am rich, and increased with goods, and have need of nothing ; and knowest not that thou art wretched, and miserable, and poor, and blind, and naked.—REV., ch. 3.

7406. —— **Pride from.** *Tyre.* ² Son of man, say unto the prince of Tyrus..Because thine heart *is* lifted up, and thou hast said, I *am* a god, I sit *in* the seat of God, in the midst of the seas.. ⁵..by thy traffick hast thou increased thy riches, and thine heart is lifted up because of thy riches.—EZEK., ch. 28.

7407. —— **restored.** *Job.* ¹² The Lord blessed the latter end of Job more than his beginning : for he had fourteen thousand sheep, and six thousand camels, and a thousand yoke of oxen, and a thousand she asses. ¹³ He had also seven sons and three daughters.—JOB, ch. 42.

7408. —— **for the Eye.** *" Beholding."* ¹¹ When goods increased. they are increased that eat them : and what good *is there* to the owners thereof, saving the beholding *of them* with their eyes ?—ECCL., ch. 5.

7409. —— **Separation by.** *Jacob — Esau.* ⁶ Esau took his wives..and all the persons of his house, and his cattle..and all his substance ..and went into the country from the face of his brother Jacob. ⁷ For their riches were more than that they might dwell together ; and the land..could not bear..their cattle.—GEN., ch. 36.

7410. —— **Surrender of.** *Dives.* ²⁰ But God said unto him, *Thou* fool, this night thy soul shall be required of thee : then whose shall those things be, which thou hast provided ?—LUKE, ch. 12.

7411. —— **A Sinner's.** *Gehazi's.* ²⁶ *Is it* a time to receive money, and to receive garments, and oliveyards, and vineyards, and sheep, and oxen, and menservants, and maidservants ? ²⁷ The leprosy therefore of Naaman shall cleave unto thee, and unto thy seed for ever.—2 KINGS, ch. 5.

7412. —— **transformed.** *"Treasure in Heaven."* [See No. 7404.]

7413. —— **Unjust.** *" Fraud."* ⁴ The hire of the labourers who have reaped down your fields, which is of you kept back by fraud, crieth ; and the cries of them which have reaped are entered into the ears of the Lord of Sabaoth.— JAMES, ch. 5.

7414. —— **Unsatisfying.** *" Beholding."* ¹⁰ He that loveth silver shall not be satisfied with silver ; nor he that loveth abundance with increase : this *is* also vanity. ¹¹ When goods increase, they are increased that eat them : and what good *is there* to the owners thereof, saving

the beholding *of them* with their eyes ?—ECCL., ch. 5.

7415. —— **unchosen.** *Solomon.* ¹¹ Because thou hast asked this thing, and hast not asked for thyself long life ; neither..riches..nor..the life of thine enemies ; but hast asked for thyself understanding to discern judgment.. ¹³ I have also given thee that which thou hast not asked, both riches, and honour.—1 KINGS, ch. 3.

7416. —— **undesired.** *Agur.* ⁸ Give me neither poverty nor riches ; feed me with food convenient for me : ⁹ Lest I be full, and deny *thee*, and say, Who *is* the Lord? or lest I be poor, and steal and take the name of my God *in vain*.—PROV., ch. 30.

7417. —— **Uncertain.** *Wings.* ⁵ Wilt thou set thine eyes upon that which is not? for *riches* certainly make themselves wings ; they fly away as an eagle toward heaven.—PROV., ch. 23.

7418. —— **Undesirable.** *Proverb.* ⁸ Better *is* a little with righteousness than great revenues without right.—PROV., ch. 16.

7419. —— **Unessential.** *Dives.* ¹⁵ Take heed, and beware of covetousness : for a man's life consisteth not in the abundance of the things which he possesseth. ¹⁶ And he spake a parable ..The ground of a certain rich man brought forth plentifully.—LUKE, ch. 12.

7420. —— **Unhappiness with.** *Nabal* ² *Was* very great, and he had three thousand sheep, and a thousand goats.. ³..the name of his wife Abigail ; and *she was* a woman of good understanding, and of a beautiful countenance : but the man *was* churlish and evil in his doings.—1 SAM., ch. 25.

7421. —— **unenjoyed.** *Vanity.* ¹ There is an evil which..*is* common among men : ² A man to whom God hath given riches, wealth, and honour, so that he wanteth nothing for his soul of all that he desireth, yet God giveth him not power to eat thereof, but a stranger eateth it : this *is* vanity.—ECCL., ch. 6.

7422. —— **Vanity of.** *Solomon.* ⁴ I made me great works ; I builded me houses ; I planted me vineyards : ⁵ I made me gardens and orchards, and I planted trees in them of all *kind of* fruits.—[See Eccl. 2 : 4–11.]

7423. —— **and Wickedness.** *Woe.* ¹ Go to now, *ye* rich men, weep and howl for your miseries that shall come upon *you.* ² Your riches are corrupted, and your garments are motheaten. ³ Your gold and silver is cankered ; and the rust of them shall be a witness against you, and shall eat your flesh as it were fire.—JAMES, ch. 5.

See other illustrations under :

GOLD.

Architecture. S. overlaid the house with pure gold	3634
Abundance. Weight of gold that came to S. in	3635
Best. Buy of me gold tried in the fire	3636
Better. Silver and gold have I none, such as I have	3637
City. City was pure gold like unto glass	3638
First. Land of Havilah, where there is gold	3639
Furniture. Beds of gold and silver..vessels	3640
Imported. Came to Ophir and fetched thence	3641
Image. Image of gold whose height was 60 cubits	3642
More. Swear by the temple it is nothing..but gold	3643
Offerings. Brought bracelets and earrings..of gold	3644
Prohibited. Not..wearing of gold or putting on of	3645
Trespass. Jewels of gold..by the side thereof	3646

POSSESSIONS.

Condition. Every place..your foot shall tread 6287
Extensive. Whether things present or things to 6288

TREASURE.

Cross. Moses..esteeming the reproach of C. 8884
Discovery. Treasure hid in a field 8885

TREASURES.

Forsaken. Regard not your stuff..E. is yours 8886
in Heaven. Sell..give..have treasures in h. 8887
Insecure. Moth..rust..thieves 8888
Restored. Brought up from the captivity 8889
Secure. Lay up..in heaven 8890

Greater. Esteeming the reproach of C...riches of E. 195
See MONEY *and* WEALTH.

7424. RIDDLE, Difficult. *Samson's.* [14] Out of the eater came forth meat, and out of the strong came forth sweetness. And they could not in three days expound the riddle.. [18] And the men of the city said unto him on the seventh day before the sun went down, What *is* sweeter than honey? and what *is* stronger than a lion. —JUDGES, ch. 14.

7425. RIDICULE of Doctrine. *At Mars' Hill.* [32] When they heard of the resurrection of the dead, some mocked.—ACTS, ch. 17.

7426. —— Fatal. *Samson.* [25] When their hearts were merry..they said, Call for Samson, that he may make us sport.. [30] And Samson said, Let me die with the Philistines. And he bowed himself with *all his* might; and the house fell upon the lords, and upon all the people.— JUDGES, ch. 16.

7427. —— of Failure. *Tower-builder.* [29] Lest haply, after he hath laid the foundation, and is not able to finish *it*, all that behold *it* begin to mock him, [30] Saying, This man began to build, and was not able to finish.—LUKE, ch. 14.

7428. —— Horrible. *Trial of Christ.* [41] The chief priests mocking *him*, with the scribes and elders, said, [42] He saved others; himself he cannot save. If he be the King of Israel, let him now come down from the cross, and we will believe him. [43] He trusted in God; let him deliver him now, if he will have him: for he said, I am the Son of God. [44] The thieves also..cast the same in his teeth.—MAT., ch. 27.

7429. —— Impious. *Ephraimites.* [Hezekiah sent messengers calling Israel to the passover.] [10] They laughed them to scorn, and mocked them. [11] Nevertheless, divers of Asher and Manasseh and of Zebulun humbled themselves, and came to Jerusalem.—2 CHRON., ch. 30.

7430. —— —— At Athens. [18] Certain philosophers of the Epicureans, and of the Stoics, encountered him. And some said, What will this babbler say? other some, He seemeth to be a setter forth of strange gods: because he preached unto them Jesus, and the resurrection. —ACTS, ch. 17.

7431. —— Insulting. *Mutilation.* [2] David sent to comfort him by the hand of his servants for his father.. [4] Hanun took David's servants, and shaved off the one half of their beards, and cut off their garments in the middle, *even to* their buttocks, and sent them away.—2 SAM., ch. 10.

7432. —— Opposition by. *Wall-builders.* [2] He spake before his brethren and the army of

Samaria, and said, What do these feeble Jews? will they fortify themselves? will they sacrifice? will they make an end in a day? will they revive the stones out of the heaps of the rubbish. —NEH., ch. 4.

7433. —— —— Of Work. [3] Tobiah the Ammonite *was* by him, and he said, Even that which they build, if a fox go up, he shall even break down their stone wall.—NEH., ch. 4.

7434. —— Punishment for. *Bethel Children.* [23] Said unto him, Go up, thou bald head.. [24] And he turned back..and cursed them in the name of the Lord. And there came forth two she bears out of the wood, and tare forty and two children of them.—2 KINGS, ch. 2.

7535. —— of Royalty. *Pilate's Hall.* [5] Then came Jesus forth, wearing the crown of thorns, and the purple robe. And *Pilate* saith..Behold the man.—JOHN, ch. 19.

7436. —— Scornful. *Wall-builders.* [19] When Sanballat the Horonite, and Tobiah the servant, the Ammonite, and Geshem the Arabian, heard *it*, they laughed us to scorn, and despised us, and said, What *is* this thing that ye do? will ye rebel against the king?—NEH., ch. 2.

7437. —— of the Spirit. *Pentecost.* [12] Were all amazed, and were in doubt, saying one to another, What meaneth this? [13] Others mocking said, These men are full of new wine.— ACTS, ch. 2.

7438. —— Trial by. *Blind Son.* [28] They reviled him, and said, Thou art his disciple; but we are Moses' disciples. [29] We know that God spake unto Moses: *as for this fellow*, we know not from whence he is.—JOHN, ch. 9.

See other illustrations under:

DERISION.

Horrible. Put on him a scarlet robe..crown 2197
Impious. Laughed them to scorn and mocked 2198
Nickname. Thou art a Samaritan, and hast a devil 2200
Punished. Sarah saw the son of Hagar mocking 2199
Truth. Pharisees who were covetous..derided 2201
Unfortunates. Thieves also..cast the same into 2202
Wicked. They shoot out the lip, and shake the 2203

INSULT.

Ignored. Despised him [Saul]..held his peace 4567
First. Thrust him [Jesus] out of the city..headlong 4568
Rewarded. Cut off their garments in the middle 4569
Stinging. To smite him on the mouth 4570

IRONY.

Horrible. This is Jesus the king of the Jews 4659
Rebuke. Cry aloud, for he is a god 4660

MOCKERY.

Blasphemous. Crown of thorns..reed..Hail, King 5494
of Truth. When they heard of the resurrection 5493

SARCASM.

Brother's. With whom hast thou left those few s. 7576
Wife's. How glorious was the king of I. to-day? 7577

SCOFFERS.

Malicious. Prophesy unto us, thou Christ..who 7614
" Herod arrayed him in a gorgeous robe 7615

SCORN.

of Pride. [Haman] Scorn to lay hands on Mordecai 7618
Public. All clap their hands at thee and hiss 7619
Unbelief. She sleepeth..they laughed him to scorn 7620

Taunt. Who made thee a prince and a judge over 8590

7439. RIGHT, Boldness for the. *Battle.*
[1] When thou goest out to battle against thine enemies, and seest horses, and chariots, *and* a people more than thou, be not afraid of them : for the Lord thy God *is* with thee.—DEUT., ch. 20.

7440. RIGHTS affirmed. *Civil.* [37] Paul said.. They have beaten us openly uncondemned, being Romans, and have cast *us* into prison ; and now do they thrust us out privily? nay verily ; but let them come themselves and fetch us out.—ACTS, ch. 16. [Done at Philippi.]

7441. —— —— *At Jerusalem.* [25] As they bound him with thongs, Paul said..Is it lawful for you to scourge a man that is a Roman, and uncondemned? [26] When the centurion heard *that*, he went and told the chief captain, saying, Take heed what thou doest ; for this man is a Roman.—ACTS, ch. 22.

7442. —— Belittled. *Esau.* [34] Jacob gave Esau bread and pottage of lentiles ; and he did eat and drink, and rose up, and went his way. Thus Esau despised *his* birthright.—GEN., ch. 25.

7443. —— Surrender of. *Pay.* [11] If we have sown unto you spiritual things, *is it* a great thing if we shall reap your carnal things? [12] ..Nevertheless we have not used this power : but suffer all things, lest we should hinder the gospel of Christ.—1 COR., ch. 9.

See other illustrations under :

LIBERTY.

Choice. Father give..he divided unto them   4962
Common. Casting out devils..Forbid him not   4963
not License. Take heed lest..liberty..stumbling   4964

7444. RIGHTEOUSNESS, Benefits of. *Proverb.* [27] The fear of the Lord prolongeth days : but the years of the wicked shall be shortened. [28] The hope of the righteous *shall be* gladness : but the expectation of the wicked shall perish. —PROV., ch. 10.

7445. —— Discarded. *Legal.* [4] If any other man thinketh that he hath whereof he might trust in the flesh, I more : [5] Circumcised the eighth day, of the stock of Israel, *of* the tribe of Benjamin, a Hebrew of the Hebrews ; as touching the law, a Pharisee ; [6] Concerning zeal, persecuting the church ; touching the righteousness which is in the law, blameless. [7] But what things were gain to me, those I counted loss for Christ.—PHIL., ch. 3.

7446. —— False. *Boast.* [4] Speak not thou in thine heart..saying, For my righteousness the Lord hath brought me in to possess this land : but for the wickedness of these nations the Lord doth drive them out from before thee. —DEUT., ch. 9.

7447. —— Flattery of. *Pharisee.* [11] The Pharisee..prayed thus with himself, God, I thank thee, that I am not as other men *are*, extortioners, unjust, adulterers, or even as this publican. [12] I fast twice in the week, I give tithes of all that I possess.—LUKE, ch. 18.

7448. —— observed. *Noah's.* [1] Come thou and all thy house into the ark : for thee have I seen righteous before me in this generation. —GEN., ch. 7.

See other illustrations under :

FAULTLESS.

Condemned. Pilate said..I find no fault in him   3085
Official. Sought occasion against Daniel..found   3086

HOLINESS.

Acknowledged. Put off thy shoes..holy ground   3996
     "   Loose thy shoe..Joshua did so   3997
Alarming. Looked into the ark..who is able to   3998
Celebration. Cherubim..Holy, holy, holy is the L.   3999
Conspicuous. Holiness to the L..upon the d.   4000
Chosen. Shall be a peculiar treasure..holy nation   4001
Church. Glorious church not having spot..holy   4002
Prayer for. Be filled with all the fulness of God   4003
Perfect. Which of you convinceth me of sin?   4004
Unapproachable. Let bounds..about the mount   4005
Universal. Upon the bells of the horses, Holiness   4006
     See PIETY and references.

7449. RISING, Early. *Jesus.* [35] In the morning, rising up a great while before day, he ..departed into a solitary place, and there prayed. [36] And Simon and they that were with him, followed after him.—MARK, ch. 1.

7450. —— —— *Apostles.* [24] There was also a strife among them, which of them should be accounted the greatest.--LUKE, ch. 22.

7451. RIVALRY for Place. *James and John.* [23] To sit on my right hand, and on my left, is not mine to give, but *it shall be given to them* for whom it is prepared of my Father. [24] And when the ten heard *it*, they were moved with indignation against the two brethren.—MAT., ch. 20.

7452. —— reproved. *Serving.* [After above.] [13] Ye call me Master and Lord : and ye say well ; for *so* I am. [14] If I then, *your* Lord and Master, have washed your feet ; ye also ought to wash one another's feet.—JOHN, ch. 13.

7453. RIVER, The first mentioned. *Eden.* [10] A river went out of Eden to water the garden ; and from thence it was parted, and became into four heads.—GEN., ch. 2.

7454. —— of Life. *Heaven.* [1] He shewed me a pure river of water of life, clear as crystal, proceeding out of the throne of God and of the Lamb. [2] In the midst of the street of it, and on either side of the river, *was there* the tree of life, which bare twelve *manner of* fruits, *and* yielded her fruit every month : and the leaves of the tree *were* for the healing of the nations.— REV., ch. 22.

7455. —— —— *On Earth.* [4] *There is* a river, the streams whereof shall make glad the city of God, the holy *place* of the tabernacles of the Most High.—PS. 46.

7456. —— of Salvation. *"To swim in."* [3] The man that had the line..measured a thousand cubits, and he brought me through the waters ; the waters *were* to the ankles. [4] Again he measured a thousand..the waters *were* to the knees. Again he measured a thousand .. the waters *were* to the loins. [5] Afterward he measured a thousand ; *and it was* a river that I could not pass over : for the waters were risen, waters to swim in.--EZEK., ch. 47.

7457. ROBBERY, Insolent. *Danites.* [18] Went into Micah's house, and fetched the carved image, the ephod, and the teraphim, and the molten image. Then said the priest unto them, What do ye? [19] And they said unto him, Hold thy peace, lay thine hand upon thy mouth, and go with us.-- JUDGES, ch. 18.

7458. —— Spiritual. *Offerings.* [8] Will a man rob God? Yet ye have robbed me. But ye say, Wherein have we robbed thee? In tithes and offerings. ⁹ Ye *are* cursed with a curse : for ye have robbed me, *even* this whole nation.—MAL., ch. 3.

7459. —— Sacrilegious. *Shishak.* ²⁶ He took away the treasures of the house of the Lord, and the treasures of the king's house. .and. .the shields of gold which Solomon had made.—2 KINGS, ch. 14.

See other illustrations under :

THEFT.

Abduction. When I rose in the morning..not my 8767
Confessed. Micah said the 1100 shekels..I took it 8768
Fear. Take thy bill..quickly write fifty 8769
Famished. Men do not despise a thief..hungry 8770
Improbable. Disciples came..stole him..we slept 8771
Justifiable. Josheba took Joash..they hid him 8772
Kidnappers. Man be found stealing..brethren 8773

7460. ROCK of Punishment. *Seirites.* ¹² Other ten thousand *left* alive did the children of Judah carry away captive, and brought them unto the top of the rock, and cast them down from the top of the rock, that they all were broken in pieces.—2 CHRON., ch. 25.

7461. —— of Salvation. *Christ.* ³¹ Their rock *is* not as our Rock, even our enemies themselves *being* judges.—DEUT., ch. 32.

7462. —— —— " *Higher than I.*" ² From the end of the earth will I cry unto thee, when my heart is overwhelmed : lead me to the rock *that* is higher than I. ³ For thou hast been a shelter for me, *and* a strong tower from the enemy.—Ps. 61.

Also see:

Precious Stones. Breastplate..four rows 4348

7463. ROWING, Hard. *Tempest.* ¹³ The men rowed hard to bring *it* to the land ; but they could not : for the sea wrought, and was tempestuous against them.—JONAH, ch. 1.

7464. RUDENESS, Inconsiderate. *To Shunammite.* ²⁷ When she came to the man of God ..she caught him by the feet : but Gehazi came near to thrust her away. And the man of God said, Let her alone ; for her soul *is* vexed within her : and the Lord hath hid *it* from me.—2 KINGS, ch. 4.

See other illustrations under :

INSULT.

Ignored. Belial said, How shall this man save us 4567
Jesus. Thrust him out of the city..cast him 4568
Reward. Hanun shaved off one half their beards 4569
Stinging. Ananias commanded them to smite 4570

INSULTS.

Cruel. Mocked Jesus..blindfolded, and struck 4576
Contemptuous. They that are younger have me in 4572

INSOLENCE.

Added. [Danite robbers] said unto Micah, What 4530
Fraternal. With whom hast thou left those few 4531
Injustice. There is no straw..ye are idle 4532
Resented. Whatsoever is pleasant in thine eyes 4533

Friends. Hanun cut off the garments in the 3431

7465. RUIN by Losses. *Laban.* ⁴³ The man increased exceedingly, and had much cattle, and maidservants, and menservants, and camels, and asses. ¹ And he heard the words of Laban's sons, saying, Jacob hath taken away all that *was* our father's.—GEN., chs. 30, 31.

See other illustrations under :

CALAMITY.

Destructive. Wall ːell upon 27,000 men that were 995
of God. Earth opened her mouth, and swallowed 996
Hardened. I have smitten you with blasting 1001
Indiscriminating. The L. maketh the earth 1002
Misjudged. Tower in Siloam fell, think..they 1003
Predicted. Shall not be left one stone upon a. 997
Waiting. Jonah sat..see what would become 990

CRUELTY.

Captives. Joab put them under saws..harrows 1864
" Judah cast [10,000 men of Seir] from the 1858
Maternal. Athaliah..destroyed all the seed royal 1857

DESTRUCTION.

Flood. They ate..drank..married..destroyed 2254
" Every living..man..cattle..fowl 2256
Grave. Hope of a tree if it be cut down 2258
Israelites. The affliction of I. was very bitter 2253
Losses. Riches certainly make themselves wings 9080
Red Sea. Waters returned..covered the chariots 2257
Sodom. They bought..sold..planted..builded 2255

EXTERMINATION.

Bloody. Smite Amalek..man, woman..infant 2825
of Wicked. Slew [Ahab's sons]..seventy persons 2826

MASSACRE.

Intended. Letters were sent by post..to destroy 5249
Infants. Herod..slew all the children..in Bethlehem 5250
Treacherous. Jehu said, Proclaim an assembly for 5251

Spiritual. Alex. and Hymeneus..made shipwreck 470

7466. RULER, A born. *Joseph.* ⁷ We *were* binding sheaves in the field, and, lo, my sheaf arose, and also stood upright ; and, behold, your sheaves stood round about, and made obeisance to my sheaf.. ⁸ And his brethren said to him, Shalt thou indeed reign over us ?—GEN., ch. 37.

**7467. —— —— ** *With Potiphar.* ⁴ Joseph found grace in his sight, and he served him : and he made him overseer over his house, and all *that* he had he put into his hand.—GEN., ch. 39.

**7468. —— —— ** *In Prison.* ²² The keeper of the prison committed to Joseph's hand all the prisoners that *were* in the prison ; and whatsoever they did there, he was the doer *of it.*—GEN., ch. 39.

**7469. —— —— ** *Enthroned.* ⁴² Pharaoh took off his ring from his hand, and put it upon Joseph's hand, and arrayed him in vestures of fine linen, and put a gold chain about his neck ; ⁴³ And he made him to ride in the second chariot which he had ; and they cried before him, Bow the knee : and he made him *ruler* over all the land of Egypt.—GEN., ch. 41.

7470. —— A foolish. *Saul.* ²⁴ The men of Israel were distressed that day : for Saul had adjured the people, saying, Cursed *be* the man that eateth *any* food until evening, that I may be avenged on mine enemies.. ³⁰ How much more, if haply the people had eaten freely to day of the spoil of their enemies which they found? for had there not been now a much greater slaughter among the Philistines ?—1 SAM., ch. 14. [Captivity was broken, and Philistines fleeing.]

7471. —— A pious. *Rich.* ¹⁸ A certain ruler asked him, saying, Good Master, what shall I do to inherit eternal life ?.. ²⁰ Thou knowest the commandments.. ²¹ And he said, All these have I kept from my youth up.—LUKE, ch. 18.

7472. —— **ruled.** *Ahab.* [6] He answered, I will not give thee my vineyard. [7] And Jezebel his wife said unto him, Dost thou now govern the kingdom of Israel? arise, *and* eat bread, and let thine heart be merry : I will give thee the vineyard of Naboth the Jezreelite.—1 KINGS, ch. 21.

7473. —— **A sinful.** *Ahab.* [25] There was none like unto Ahab, which did sell himself to work wickedness in the sight of the Lord, whom Jezebel his wife stirred up. [26] And he did very abominably in following idols..as did the Amorites.—1 KINGS, ch. 21.

7474. —— —— **Proverb.** [15] *As* a roaring lion, and a ranging bear ; *so is* a wicked ruler over the poor people.—PROV., ch. 28.

7475. —— **An unjust.** *Parable.* [2] There was in a city a judge, which feared not God, neither regarded man.—LUKE, ch. 18.

7476. RULERS, Guidance for. *Bible.* [18] When he sitteth upon the throne of his kingdom..he shall write him a copy of this law in a book out of *that which is* before the priests, the Levites : [19] And it shall be with him, and he shall read therein all the days of his life.—DEUT., ch. 17.

7477. —— **Influence of.** *Example.* [45] Why have ye not brought him ? [46] The officers answered, Never man spake like this man. [47] Then answered them the Pharisees, Are ye also deceived ? [48] Have any of the rulers or of the Pharisees believed on him?—JOHN, ch. 7.

7478. —— **Many.** *Solomon's.* [15] Solomon had threescore and ten thousand that bare burdens, and fourscore thousand hewers in the mountains ; [16] Beside the chief of Solomon's officers which *were* over the work, three thousand and three hundred.. [17]..they brought great stones, costly stones, *and* hewed stones, to lay the foundation of the house.—1 KINGS, ch. 5.

7479. —— **Qualifications of.** *Jethro said,* [21] Thou shalt provide out of all the people able men, such as fear God, men of truth, hating covetousness ; and place *such* over them, *to be* rulers of thousands, *and* rulers of hundreds, rulers of fifties, and rulers of tens.—EX., ch. 18.

7480. —— **Responsibility of.** *Saul.* [23] Because thou hast rejected the word of the Lord, he hath also rejected thee from *being* king. [24] And Saul said unto Samuel, I have sinned : for I have transgressed the commandment of the Lord, and thy words : because I feared the people, and obeyed their voice.—1 SAM., ch. 15.

See other illustrations under :
Ambitious. Diotrephes desireth the preeminence 317
Bible. Sitteth upon the throne..copy of this law 772
Wise. None so wise..thy word all my people be r. 985
See **GOVERNMENT** and references.

7481. RUMOR, A demoralizing. *Syrian.* [6] The Lord had made..the Syrians to hear a noise of chariots..of horses, *even* the noise of a great host : and they said..Lo, the king of Israel hath hired against us the kings of the Hittites, and the kings of the Egyptians, to come upon us. [7] Wherefore they arose and fled in the twilight, and left .even the camp as it *was*, and fled for their life.—2 KINGS, ch. 7.

7482. RUNNER, A swift. *Asahel.* [18] There were three sons of Zeruiah there, Joab, and Abishai, and Asahel : and Asahel *was* as light of foot as a wild roe. [19] And Asahel pursued after Abner.—2 SAM., ch. 2.

7483. SABBATH not desecrated. *Invalid.* [10] The Jews therefore said unto him that was cured, It is the sabbath day ; it is not lawful for thee to carry *thy* bed. [11]..He that made me whole..said unto me, Take up thy bed, and walk.—JOHN, ch. 5.

7484. —— **financiering.** *Benevolence.* [1] Concerning the collection for the saints, as I have given order to the churches of Galatia, even so do ye. [2] Upon the first *day* of the week let every one of you lay by him in store, as *God* hath prospered him.—1 COR., ch. 16.

7485. —— **A gloomy.** *Joseph's Tomb.* [See No. 7495.]

7486. —— **divinely honoured.** *Creation.* [2] He rested on the seventh day from all his work which he had made. [3] And God blessed the seventh day, and sanctified it.—GEN., ch. 2.

7487. —— **Law of.** *Decalogue.* [8] Remember the sabbath day, to keep it holy.—Ex. 20 : 8-10.

7488. —— **for Man.** *Food.* [23] On the sabbath day ; and his disciples began, as they went, to pluck the ears of corn. [24] And the Pharisees said..Behold, why do they on the sabbath day that which is not lawful ?.. [27] And he said..The sabbath was made for man, and not man for the sabbath.—MARK, ch. 2.

7489. —— **and Necessity.** *Accident.* [11] What man shall..have one sheep, and if it fall into a pit on the sabbath day, will he not lay hold on it, and lift *it* out ? [12] How much then is a man better than a sheep ? Wherefore it is lawful to do well on the sabbath days.—MAT., ch. 12.

7490. —— **Neglect of the.** *Jews.* [19] They burnt the house of God, and brake down the wall of Jerusalem, and burnt all the palaces thereof with fire, and destroyed all the goodly vessels thereof. [20] And them that had escaped from the sword carried he away to Babylon ; where they were servants.. [21] To fulfil the word of the Lord by the mouth of Jeremiah, until the land had enjoyed her sabbaths : *for* as long as she lay desolate she kept sabbath, to fulfil threescore and ten years.—2 CHRON., ch. 36.

7491. —— **Observers of.** *" Ride upon the high places."* [13] If thou turn away thy foot from the sabbath, *from* doing thy pleasure.—ISA., ch. 58. [See chapter.]

7492. —— **Preparation for the.** *Manna.* [22] On the sixth day they gathered twice as much bread, two omers for one *man :* and all the rulers of the congregation came and told Moses.—EX., ch. 16.

7493. —— **protected.** *Vigorously.* [20] The merchants and sellers of all kind of ware lodged without Jerusalem once or twice. [21] Then I.. said..Why lodge ye about the wall ? if ye do *so* again, I will lay hands on you. From that time forth came they no *more* on the sabbath.—NEH., ch. 13.

7494. —— **restraint.** *Traffic.* [19] When the gates of Jerusalem began to be dark before the sabbath, I commanded that the gates should be shut..not be opened till after the sabbath : and *some* of my servants set I at the gates, *that* there should no burden be brought in.. [20] So the merchants and sellers of all kind of ware lodged without Jerusalem once or twice.—NEH., ch. 13.

7495. —— **Rest on the.** *Women* [55] Beheld the sepulchre, and how his body was laid. [56] And they returned, and prepared spices and ointments ; and rested the sabbath day according to the commandment.—Luke, ch. 23.

7496. —— **Regard for the.** *Oath.* [31] If the people of the land bring ware or any victuals on the sabbath day to sell, *that* we would not buy it of them on the sabbath, or on the holy day.—Neh., ch. 10.

7497. —— —— *By Murderers.* [15] The man departed, and told the Jews that it was Jesus, which had made him whole. [16] And therefore did the Jews persecute Jesus, and sought to slay him, because he had done these things on the sabbath day.—John, ch. 5.

7498. —— **Work.** *At Capernaum Synagogue.* [2] They watched him, whether he would heal him on the sabbath day ; that they might accuse him. [3] And he said unto the man which had the withered hand, Stand forth. [4] And he saith unto them, Is it lawful to do good on the sabbath days, or to do evil? to save life, or to kill? but they held their peace.—Mark, ch. 3.

7499. —— **False Zeal for the.** *Hypocrites.* [15] *Thou* hypocrite, doth not each one of you on the sabbath loose his ox or *his* ass from the stall, and lead *him* away to watering ? [16] And ought not this woman, being a daughter of Abraham, whom Satan hath bound, lo, these eighteen years, be loosed from this bond on the sabbath day? —Luke, ch. 13.

7500. SACRIFICE, Apostolical. *Paul.* [11] Even unto this present hour we both hunger, and thirst, and are naked, and are buffeted, and have no certain dwellingplace ; [12] And labour, working with our own hands : being reviled, we bless ; being persecuted, we suffer it : [13] Being defamed, we entreat : we are made as the filth of the world, *and are* the offscouring of all things unto this day.—1 Cor., ch. 4.

7501. —— **Better than.** *Proverb.* [3] To do justice and judgment *is* more acceptable to the Lord than sacrifice.—Prov., ch. 21.

7502. —— **Blessing by.** *" Tithes."* [10] Bring ye all the tithes into the storehouse, that there may be meat in mine house, and prove me now herewith, saith the Lord of hosts, if I will not open you the windows of heaven, and pour you out a blessing, that *there shall* not *be room* enough *to receive it.*—Mal., ch. 3.

7503. —— **Benevolence a.** *Macedonians.* [2] In a great trial of affliction, the abundance of their joy and their deep poverty abounded unto the riches of their liberality.—2 Cor., ch. 8.

7504. —— **Consumed with.** *Galileans.* [1] There were present at that season some that told him of the Galileans, whose blood Pilate had mingled with their sacrifices.—Luke, ch. 13.

7505. —— **A costless.** *David.* [24] The king said unto Araunah, Nay ; but I will surely buy *it* of thee at a price : neither will I offer burnt offerings unto the Lord my God of that which doth cost me nothing. So David bought the threshingfloor and the oxen for fifty shekels of silver.—2 Sam., ch. 24.

7506. —— **of Children.** *Heathenish.* [2] Ahaz.. made also molten images for Baalim. [3] Moreover he burnt incense in the valley of the son of Hinnom, and burnt his children in the fire,

after the abominations of the heathen.—2 Chron., ch. 28.

7507. —— **Cheerful.** *Disciples.* [34] Ye had compassion of me in my bonds, and took joyfully the spoiling of your goods, knowing in yourselves that ye have in heaven a better and an enduring substance.—Heb., ch. 10.

7508. —— **for Discipleship.** *Matthew.* [27] He went forth, and saw a publican, named Levi, sitting at the receipt of custom : and he said unto him, Follow me. [28] And he left all, rose up, and followed him.—Luke, ch. 5.

7509. —— —— *Apostles.* [10] James, and John..which were partners with Simon. And Jesus said unto Simon, Fear not ; from henceforth thou shalt catch men. [11] And when they had brought their ships to land, they forsook all, and followed him.—Luke, ch. 5.

7510. —— **Daily.** *Jewish.* [38] Thou shalt offer upon the altar ; two lambs of the first year day by day continually. [39] The one lamb thou shalt offer in the morning ; and the other..at even.—Ex., ch. 29.

7511. —— **estimated.** *" Two Mites."* [43] This poor widow hath cast more in, than all they which have cast into the treasury : [44] For all *they* did cast in of their abundance ; but she of her want did cast in all that she had, *even* all her living.—Mark, ch. 12.

7512. —— **The first.** *Cain—Abel.* [3] Cain brought of the fruit of the ground an offering unto the Lord. [4] And Abel, he also brought of the firstlings of his flock and of the fat thereof. And the Lord had respect unto Abel and to his offering.—Gen., ch. 4.

7513. —— **A great.** *Dedication.* [5] King Solomon offered a sacrifice of twenty and two thousand oxen, and an hundred and twenty thousand sheep : so the king and all the people dedicated the house of God.—2 Chron., ch. 7.

7514. —— **Gain by.** *Treasure.* [44] The kingdom of heaven is like unto treasure hid in a field ; the which when a man hath found, he hideth, and for joy thereof goeth and selleth all that he hath, and buyeth that field.—Mat., ch. 13.

7515. —— —— *Pearl.* [45] The kingdom of heaven is like unto a merchantman, seeking goodly pearls : [46] Who, when he had found one pearl of great price, went and sold all that he had, and bought it.—Mat., ch. 13.

7516. —— **Human.** *Moabite.* [26] When the king of Moab saw that the battle was too sore for him, he took with him seven hundred men that drew swords, to break through *even* unto the king of Edom : but they could not. [27] Then he took his eldest son that should have reigned in his stead, and offered him *for* a burnt offering upon the wall.—2 Kings, ch. 3.

7517. —— **intimated.** *Return of Ark.* [14] The cart came into the field of Joshua..and stood there, where *there was* a great stone : and they clave the wood of the cart, and offered the kine a burnt offering unto the Lord. [15] And the Levites took down the ark of the Lord.—1 Sam., ch. 6.

7518. —— **an Investment.** *" Treasure in Heaven."* [See No. 7528.]

7519. —— **Irreverent.** *Jews.* [3] That offereth an oblation, *as if he offered* swine's blood ;

he that burneth incense, *as if* he blessed an idol. Yea, they have chosen their own ways, and their soul delighteth in their abominations. —Isa., ch. 66.

7520. —— **necessary.** *"Strait Gate."* [13] Enter ye in at the strait gate : for wide *is* the gate, and broad *is* the way, that leadeth to destruction, and many there be which go in thereat : [14] Because strait *is* the gate, and narrow *is* the way, which leadeth unto life, and few there be that find it.—Mat., ch. 7.

7521. —— **Pecuniary.** *At Ephesus.* [18] Many that believed came, and confessed, and shewed their deeds. [19] Many..which used curious arts brought their books together, and burned them before all *men :* and they counted the price of them, and found *it* fifty thousand *pieces* of silver. —Acts, ch. 19.

7522. —— **Prosperity by.** *Proverb.* [9] Honour the Lord with thy substance, and with the firstfruits of all thine increase : [10] So shall thy barns be filled with plenty, and thy presses shall burst out with new wine.—Prov., ch. 3.

7523. —— **of Property.** *Disciples.* [34] As many as were possessors of lands or houses sold them, and brought the prices.. [35] And laid *them* down at the apostles' feet : and distribution was made unto every man according as he had need. —Acts, ch. 4.

7524. —— **of Praise.** *Better.* [30] I will praise the name of God with a song, and will magnify him with thanksgiving. [31] *This* also shall please the Lord better than an ox *or* bullock that hath horns and hoofs.—Ps. 69.

7525. —— **refused.** *Jews.* [8] Will a man rob God? Yet ye have robbed me. But ye say, Wherein have we robbed thee? In tithes and offerings. [9] Ye *are* cursed with a curse : for ye have robbed me, *even* this whole nation. [10] Bring ye all the tithes into the storehouse..and prove me now herewith.—Mal., ch. 3.

7526. —— **of Self.** *Jesus.* [31] Come ye yourselves apart into a desert place, and rest a while : for there were many coming and going, and they had no leisure so much as to eat.—Mark, ch. 6.

7527. —— **Tested by.** *Abraham's.* [6] Abraham took the wood of the burnt offering, and laid *it* upon Isaac his son ; and he took the fire in his hand, and a knife ; and they went both of them together.—Gen., ch. 22.

7528. —— **withheld.** *Young Ruler.* [22] Sell all that thou hast, and distribute unto the poor, and thou shalt have treasure in heaven : and come, follow me. [23] And when he heard this, he was very sorrowful : for he was very rich.—Luke, ch. 18.

7529. —— **Waiting by.** *Abram.* [10] He.. divided them in the midst, and laid each piece one against another ; but the birds divided he not. [11] And when the fowls came down upon the carcasses, Abram drove them away.. [17]..when the sun went down, and it was dark, behold a smoking furnace, and a burning lamp that passed between those pieces.— Gen., ch. 15.

7530. SACRIFICES blemished. *Unaccepted.* [19] Ye *shall offer* at your own will a male without blemish, of the beeves, of the sheep, or of the goats. [20] *But* whatsoever hath a blemish, *that* shall ye not offer : for it shall not be acceptable. —Lev., ch. 22.

7531. —— **begrudged.** *Jews.* [10] Who *is there* even among you that would shut the doors *for nought ?* neither do ye kindle *fire* on mine altar for nought. I have no pleasure in you, saith the Lord of hosts, neither will I accept an offering at your hand.—Mal., ch. 1. [See chapter.]

7532. —— **Diabolical.** *Apostates.* [17] They sacrificed unto devils, not to God ; to gods whom they knew not, to new *gods that* came newly up, whom your fathers feared not.—Deut., ch. 32.

7533. —— **Love more than.** *A Scribe said,* [33] To love him with all the heart, and with all the understanding, and with all the soul, and with all the strength, and to love *his* neighbour as himself, is more than all whole burnt offerings and sacrifices.—Mark, ch. 12.

7534. —— **Numerous.** *Temple begun.* [21] They sacrificed sacrifices..and offered burnt offerings unto the Lord, on the morrow after that day, *even* a thousand bullocks, a thousand rams, *and* a thousand lambs, with their drink offerings, and sacrifices in abundance for all Israel : [22] And did eat and drink before the Lord on that day with great gladness.—1 Chron., ch. 29.

7535. —— **rewarded.** *Christian.* [29] There is no man that hath left house, or brethren, or sisters, or father, or mother, or wife, or children, or lands, for my sake, and the gospel's, [30] But he shall receive a hundredfold now in this time, houses, and brethren, and sisters, and mothers, and children, and lands, with persecutions ; and in the world to come eternal life.—Mat., ch. 10.

7536. —— **rejected.** *Wicked.* [21] I hate, I despise your feast days, and I will not smell in your solemn assemblies. [See Amos 5 : 22-24.]

7537. —— —— *Wicked.* [19] They have not hearkened unto my words, nor to my law, but rejected it. [20] To what purpose cometh there to me incense from Sheba, and the sweet cane from a far country ? your burnt offerings *are* not acceptable, nor your sacrifices sweet unto me.—Jer., ch. 6.

7538. —— —— *Reluctant.* [13] Ye said also, Behold, what a weariness *is it!* and ye have snuffed at it, saith the Lord of hosts ; and ye brought *that which was* torn, and the lame, and the sick ; thus ye brought an offering : should I accept this of your hand?—Mal., ch. 1.

7539. —— **Personal.** *"Bodies."* [1] I beseech you therefore, brethren, by the mercies of God, that ye present your bodies a living sacrifice, holy, acceptable unto God, *which is* your reasonable service.—Rom., ch. 12.

7540. —— **Unavailing.** *Heartless.* [11] To what purpose *is* the multitude of your sacrifices unto me ? saith the Lord : I am full of the burnt offerings of rams, and the fat of fed beasts ; and I delight not in the blood of bullocks, or of lambs, or of he goats.—Isa., ch. 1. [16] For thou desireth not sacrifice ; else would I give *it :* thou delightest not in burnt offering. [17] The sacrifices of God *are* a broken spirit : a broken and a contrite heart, O God, thou wilt not despise. —Ps. 51.

7541. —— —— *Eli's.* [13] Because his sons made themselves vile, and he restrained them not. [14] And therefore I have sworn unto the house of Eli, that the iniquity of Eli's house shall not be purged with sacrifice nor offering for ever.—1 Sam., ch. 3.

7542. —— **Willing.** *Tabernacle.* [21] They came, every one whose heart stirred him up, and every one whom his spirit made willing, *and* they brought the Lord's offering to the work of the tabernacle.—Ex., ch. 35.

7543. —— —— *Joyful.* [5] If I forget thee, O Jerusalem, let my right hand forget *her cunning.* [6] If I do not remember thee, let my tongue cleave to the roof of my mouth ; if I prefer not Jerusalem above my chief joy.—Ps. 137.

See other illustrations under :

ATONEMENT.

Accepted. Abel brought..of his flock..L. had r.	571
Blood of. It is the blood that maketh atonement	572
Death stayed. Aaron..made atonement..plague	573
Justice. Sheba..his head shall be thrown	574
Omitted. Cain brought of the fruit of the g.	575
Sorrow. My soul is exceeding sorrowful	576
Sufferings. My God, Why hast thou forsaken?	577

OFFERING.

Accepted. Fire came..consumed upon the altar	5836
Best. Do justly, love mercy..walk humbly with	5837
Humble. Samuel took a sucking lamb..L. heard	5838

OFFERINGS.

Abominable. Sacrifice of the wicked is an a.	5839
Forbidden. I will hide mine eyes..hands full of	5840
Ministerial. Offer up..even a tenth part of the t.	5841
Many. Solomon offered 22,000 oxen..120,000 sheep	5842
Rejected. To what purpose is the multitude of	5843
Scrutinized. Jesus sat over against the treasury	5844
Unworthy. If ye offer the lame and sick, is it not	5845
Voluntary. Freewill offering..for the house of	5846
Willing. The stuff they had was..too much	5847

SELF-DENIAL.

Abstinence. David would not drink thereof	7701
Bodily. I keep under my body lest..be a castaway	7702
Better. People complained..fire consumed them	7703
Costly. If thy right hand offend thee, cut it off	7704
Difficult. [Young ruler] went away grieved	7705
Decent. Put a knife to thy throat..given to	7706
Essential. Let him deny himself..take up his c.	7707
Marvellous. Get thee out of thy country..kindred	7708
" Moses refused to be called the son	7709
" Unto this present hour we both h.	7710
for Others. If meat make my brother to offend	7711
Patriotic. Twelve years..not eaten the bread	7712
Positive. If..hate not his father..own life	7713
Rewarded. Ye also shall sit upon 12 thrones	7714
" Shall receive 100 fold..eternal life	7715
Saved by. Because strait is the gate and narrow	7716
Sabbath. If thou turn from doing thine own p.	7717

SURRENDER.

Recompense. Receive a hundredfold..eternal life	3
Renunciation. Moses, choosing rather to suffer	7070

REDEMPTION.

Blood. On the upper door post..I will pass over	6909
" Not redeemed with corruptible..blood of C.	6910
Power. The horse and his rider..cast into the sea	6911

Ministerial. Priests left their possessions	6591
Poor. Widow cast in two mites	34
Property. Possessors of houses..lands sold	1406
Sinners. Break off the g. earrings..molten calf	511

See BLOOD.

7544. SACRILEGE, Presumptuous. *Belshazzar.* [3] Then they brought the golden vessels that were taken out of the temple..which *was* at Jerusalem : and the king and his princes, his wives and his concubines, drank in them.—Dan., ch. 5.

7545. —— **Priestly.** *Eli's Sons.* [16] If any man said..Let them not fail to burn the fat presently, and *then* take as much as thy soul desireth ; then he would answer him, Nay *;* but thou shalt give *it* me now : and if not, I will take *it* by force. [17] Wherefore the sin of the young men was very great before the Lord : for men abhorred the offering of the Lord.—1 Sam., ch. 2.

7546. —— **Unintended.** *Uzzah.* [6] Uzzah put forth *his* hand to the ark of God, and took hold of it ; for the oxen shook *it.* [7] And the anger of the Lord was kindled against Uzzah, and God smote him there for *his* error ; and there he died.—2 Sam., ch. 6.

Also see :

Church. Manasseh built altars for all..in the h..L. 305
See PROFANATION and references.

7547. SAFETY of the Godly. *"Keepeth."* [3] He will not suffer thy foot to be moved : he that keepeth thee will not slumber. [4] Behold, he that keepeth Israel shall neither slumber nor sleep.—Ps. 121. [See chapter.]

7548. —— —— *Moses said,* [12] Benjamin.. The beloved of the Lord shall dwell in safety by him ; *and the Lord* shall cover him all the day long, and he shall dwell between his shoulders.—Deut., ch. 33.

7549. —— —— *"Hedge."* [9] Satan answered the Lord, and said, Doth Job fear God for nought ? [10] Hast not thou made a hedge about him, and about his house, and about all that he hath on every side ?—Job, ch. 1.

7550. —— —— *Sleep.* [8] I will both lay me in peace, and sleep : for thou, Lord, only makest me dwell in safety.—Ps. 4.

7551. —— —— *"Cover."* [3] Surely he shall deliver thee from the snare of the fowler, *and* from the noisome pestilence. [4] He shall cover thee with his feathers, and under his wings shalt thou trust : his truth *shall be thy* shield and buckler.—Ps. 91.

7552. —— **by Hiding.** *Jotham.* [5] Abimelech went unto his father's house at Ophrah, and slew his brethren the sons of Jerubbaal, *being* threescore and ten persons, upon one stone.. yet Jotham the youngest son..was left : for he hid himself.—Judges, ch. 9.

7553. —— **Mutual.** *Sailors.* [30] As the shipmen were about to flee out of the ship, when they had let down the boat into the sea, under colour as though they would have cast anchors out of the foreship, [31] Paul said to the centurion and to the soldiers, Except these abide in the ship, ye cannot be saved.—Acts, ch. 27.

7554. —— **supposed.** *Jailer.* [23] When they had laid many stripes upon them, they cast *them* into prison, charging the jailer to keep them safely : [24] Who..thrust them into the inner prison, and made their feet fast in the stocks. —Acts, ch. 16.

See SALVATION and references.

7555. SALT a Corrective. *At Jericho.* [21] He went forth unto the spring of the waters, and cast the salt in there, and said, Thus saith the Lord, I have healed these waters ; there shall not be from hence any more death or barren *land.* [22] So the waters were healed..according to the saying of Elisha.—2 Kings, ch. 2.

7556. SALVATION by a Brother. *Peter.* [41] He first findeth his own brother Simon, and saith ..We have found the Messias, which is, being interpreted, the Christ.—JOHN, ch. 1.

7557. —— belated. *Door shut.* [25] When once the master of the house is risen up, and hath shut to the door, and ye begin to stand without, and to knock at the door, saying, Lord, Lord, open unto us ; and he shall answer..I know you not whence ye are.—LUKE, ch. 13.

7558. —— Difficulties of. *" Strive."* [23] Lord, are there few that be saved ? And he said.. [24] Strive to enter in at the strait gate : for many, I say unto you, will seek to enter in, and shall not be able.—LUKE, ch. 13.

7559. —— in Emergency. *Red Sea.* [15] Wherefore criest thou unto me ? speak unto the children of Israel, that they go forward : [16] But lift thou up thy rod, and stretch out thine hand over the sea, and divide it..Israel shall go on dry *ground* through the midst of the sea.—Ex., ch. 14.

7560. —— free. *" Him that cometh."* [35] And Jesus said..I am the bread of life : he that cometh to me shall never hunger.. [37] All that the Father giveth me shall come to me ; and him that cometh to me I will in no wise cast out.—JOHN, ch. 6.

7561. —— —— *" Rivers."* [37] In the last day, that great *day* of the feast, Jesus stood and cried, saying, If any man thirst, let him come unto me, and drink. [38] He that believeth on me, as the Scripture hath said, out of his belly shall flow rivers of living water.—JOHN, ch. 7.

7562. —— by Faith. *Jailer* [29] Came trembling, and fell down before Paul and Silas, [30] And brought them out, and said, Sirs, what must I do to be saved ? [31] And they said, Believe on the Lord Jesus Christ, and thou shalt be saved.—ACTS, ch. 16.

7563. —— —— Whosoever. [14] Moses lifted up the serpent in the wilderness, even so must the Son of man be lifted up : [15] That whosoever believeth in him should not perish, but have eternal life.—JOHN, ch. 3.

7564. —— by Few. *Jonathan.* [6] Jonathan said to the young man that bare his armour, Come, and let us go over unto the garrison of these uncircumcised : it may be that the Lord will work for us : for *there is* no restraint to the Lord to save by many or by few.—1 SAM., ch. 14. [Twenty years of tribute ended.]

7565. —— Gratitude for. *Joseph said,* [24] Ye shall give the fifth *part* unto Pharaoh, and four parts shall be your own, for seed of the field, and for your food, and for them of your households, and for food for your little ones. [25] And they said, Thou hast saved our lives.—GEN., ch. 47.

7566. —— by Humanity. *Angel said,* [5] Now send men to Joppa..and call for..Peter : [6] He lodgeth with one Simon a tanner, whose house is by the sea side : he shall tell thee what thou oughtest to do.—ACTS, ch. 10.

7567. —— A wonderful. *Red Sea.* [22] The children of Israel went into the midst of the sea upon the dry *ground :* and the waters *were* a wall unto them on their right hand, and on their left.—Ex., ch. 14.

7568. —— by Waiting. *The Nations.* [17] Ye shall not *need* to fight in this *battle :* set yourselves, stand ye *still,* and see the salvation of the Lord with you, O Judah and Jerusalem : fear not, nor be dismayed ; to morrow go out against them : for the Lord *will be* with you. [18] And Jehoshaphat bowed his head.—2 CHRON., ch. 20.

7569. -—— One Way of. *Door.* [7] Verily, verily, I say unto you, I am the door of the sheep.—JOHN, ch. 10.

See other illustrations under :

DELIVERANCE.

Appreciated. Received his sight and followed J.		2138
Delayed. Came to Pharaoh..neither..delivered		2142
Extremity. Behold a ram caught in a thicket		2143
Faith brings. Father of the child..help..unbelief		2144
Great. S. of G. came upon Saul..anger kindled		2146
Gospel. Preach deliverance to the captives..blind		2147
Hope. People believed..L. had visited his people		2148
Innocent. Shut the lions' mouths..not hurt me		2149
Miraculous. Waters were a wall..right..left hand		2152
Memori l. Say..passed over the houses of..I.		2153
Monument. Samuel took a stone..Ebenezer		2155
Perfect. Neither the smell of fire had passed		2159
Recognized. Blessed be the God..sent his angel		2160
Spiritual. Out of a horrible pit..miry clay		2161
Trouble. Oh, how great is thy goodness..laid up		2162
Unexpected. Peter was sleeping between two s.		2164
Unequalled. No other G. that can deliver after		2165

PRESERVATION.

by Associates. Were it not that I regard Jehosh.		6527
Conce²lment. Woman took the two men and hid		6528
by Church. Spare the place for 50 righteous		6529
Miraculous. Raiment waxed not old for 40 yrs.		6530
by Obedience. Meal wasted not..oil fail		6531
Remarkable. Commanded the ravens to feed thee		6532
Wonderful. Fire had no power..hair..singed		6533

REFUGE.

Christians. Lord is a strong tower		6940
Cities. Killeth any..unawares flee thither		6941
Fearless. Though the earth be removed		6942
Faith's. When..forsake me, the L. take me		6943
Fleeing. Axe slippeth..flee..cities		6944
Prayer. H. prayed..angel..smote..Assyrians		6945
Safe. Name of the L. is a strong tower		6946
Sanctuary. Adonijah feared..caught hold on the		6947

SOULS.

Destroyers. Make him twofold more the child of		8237
Eager. I made myself servant..gain the more		8238
Hindering. Neither suffer ye them..to enter		8239
Mistake. Soul..eat, drink, and be merry		8234
Starved. Cares..riches..choke the word		8235
Winning. I am made all things to all men..save		8240
Yearning. Oh that I knew where I might find him		8236

Any Way. Some on boards..some on broken p.		7840
False Hope. Ark came..I. shouted..ark taken		1549
Lord's Way. L. saveth not with sword and spear		647
Security. He is my refuge and fortress		7649

7570. SANCTIMONY, Pharisaic. *Prayer.* [11] The Pharisee..prayed thus with himself, God, I thank thee, that I am not as other men *are,* extortioners, unjust, adulterers, or even as this publican. [12] I fast twice in the week. I give tithes of all that I possess.—LUKE, ch. 18.

See HYPOCRISY.

7571. SANCTUARY for Criminals. *Temple.* [51] It was told Solomon..Adonijah feareth king Solomon ; for, lo, he hath caught hold on the horns of the altar, saying, Let king Solomon swear unto me to day that he will not slay his servant.—1 KINGS, ch. 1.

7572. —— —— *Tabernacle.* [29] It was told king Solomon that Joab was fled unto the tabernacle..by the altar. Then Solomon sent Benaiah the son of Jehoiada, saying, Go, fall upon him.—1 KINGS, ch. 2.

7573. —— **Help in the.** *Envy of the Wicked.* [2] As for me, my feet were almost gone ; my steps had well nigh slipped.. [16] When I thought to know this, it *was* too painful for me ; [17] Until I went into the sanctuary of God ; *then* understood I their end.—Ps. 73.

See other illustrations under :

HOUSE OF GOD.

Abandoned. L. hath cast off his altar..abhorred		4126
Closed. Ahaz shut up..doors..made high places		4127
Despoiled. Chaldees..carried the pots, shovels		4128
Destroyed. Break down the carved work..cast		4129
Expensive. Costing £939,907,687 [Jamieson]		
Given for Bribery. Ahaz took away a portion		4132
Grandeur. David said..must be exceeding m.		4133
Neglected. Dwell in your ceiled houses, and this		4134
Robbed. Shishak took..treasures..shields of gold		4138
" Ahaz..cut in pieces the vessels		4139
Repairing. Jehoiada took a chest and bored a hole		4140

7574. SANCTIFICATION of the Firstborn. *Priests.* [12] Thou shalt set apart unto the Lord all that openeth the matrix, and every firstling that cometh of a beast which thou hast ; the males *shall be* the Lord's.—Ex., ch. 12.

7575. —— **of the Sabbath.** *Creation.* [3] God blessed the seventh day, and sanctified it : because that in it he had rested from all his work which God created and made.—GEN., ch. 2.

See other illustrations under :

CONSECRATION.

Covenant. All the people stood to the covenant	1584
Leadership. Took Joshua..laid hands upon him	1585
S·rvice. Moses took of the blood..ear..thumb	1586
Self-denying. Made the laver..looking glasses	1587

DEVOTION.

Benevolent. Poor widow hath cast in more than	2269
Deceptive. I will lay down my life for thy sake	2270
Excessive. For the work of C..nigh unto death	2271
Expensive. Mary..pound of ointment..very c.	2272
Friendship. Ittai..whether in death or life..be	2273
Filial. Thy people shall be my..thy God my	2274
Fraternal. Priscilla and A..have for my life laid	2275
Hinderance. How can ye believe which receive	2276
Partial. Howbeit the high places were not r'd	2277
Rewarded. Followed me fully..into the land	2278
Religious. Great while before day..prayed	2279
Sublime. Lay not thine hand on the lad	2280
Unselfish. Forgive..if not, blot me	2281

HOLINESS.

Acknowledged. Put off thy shoes..holy ground	3996
" Loose thy shoes..Joshua did so	3997
Alarming. Looked into the ark..Who is able to s.?	3998
Celebration. Cherubim..Holy, holy, holy is the L.	3999
Conspicuous. Holiness to the L..upon the foref.	4000
Chosen. Shall be a peculiar treasure..holy nation	4001
Church. Glorious church not having spot..holy	4002
Prayer for Be filled with all the fulness of God	4003
Perfect. Which of you convinceth me of sin ?	4004
Unapproachable. Set bounds about the mount	4005
Universal. Upon the bells of the horses, Holiness	4006

PURITY.

Symbolized. Make a laver of brass to wash	6813
Within. First cleanse within the cup	6814

SURRENDER.

Absolute. I count all things but loss for..the k.	8503
Bodily. Yielded their bodies that..not serve any g.	8504
Christian. May know..fellowship of his s.	8505
Entire. One thing thou lackest go..give to the p.	8506
Fall. Whosoever..forsaketh not all. disciple	8507
Fear. We will do all that thou shalt bid us	8508
Moral. What things were gain to me I counted l.	8509
Power. We have not used this power..lest we	8510
Resisted. When he saw him, the spirit tare him	8511
Sins. If thy right hand offend thee..cut it off	8512
Sacrifice. Widow..cast in ..all her living	8513
Undivided. Our cattle shall also go with us	8514
Weak. King Ahab said, My Lord, O King, I am t.	8515

Childhood. Hannah said..appear before the L.	1218

7576. SARCASM, A Brother's. *Eliab.* [28] Eliab's anger was kindled against David, and he said, Why camest thou down hither ? and with whom hast thou left those few sheep in the wilderness ? I know thy pride, and the naughtiness of thine heart ; for thou art come down that thou mightest see the battle.—1 SAM., ch. 17.

7577. —— **A Wife's.** *Michal.* [20] David returned to bless his household. And Michal.. came out to meet David, and said, How glorious was the king of Israel to day, who uncovered himself to day in the eyes of the handmaids.. as one of the vain fellows shamelessly uncovereth himself !—2 SAM., ch. 6.

7578. SATAN, Audacity of. *Temptation.* [3] When the tempter came to him, he said, If thou be the Son of God, command that these stones be made bread.—MAT., ch. 4.

7579. —— **bound.** *Thousand Years.* [1] I saw an angel come down from heaven, having the key of the bottomless pit and a great chain in his hand. [2] And he laid hold on the dragon, that old serpent, which is the devil, and Satan, and bound him a thousand years.—REV., ch. 20.

7580. —— **Children of.** *Pharisees.* [44] Ye are of *your* father the devil, and the lusts of your father ye will do : he was a murderer from the beginning, and abode not in the truth, because there is no truth in him..he is a liar, and the father of it.—JOHN, ch. 8.

7581. —— **Cunning of.** *Fall.* [4] The serpent said unto the woman, Ye shall not surely die : [5] For God doth know that in the day ye eat thereof, then your eyes shall be opened, and ye shall be as gods, knowing good and evil.—GEN., ch. 3.

7582. —— **Doom of.** *Hell.* [3] And cast him into the bottomless pit, and shut him up, and set a seal upon him, that he should deceive the nations no more, till the thousand years should be fulfilled : and after that he must be loosed a little season.—REV., ch. 20.

7583. —— **Delivered to.** *Apostates.* [19] Have made shipwreck : [20] Of whom is Hymeneus and Alexander ; whom I have delivered unto Satan, that they may learn not to blaspheme.—1 TIM., ch. 1.

7584. —— **Enmity of.** *Eden.* [15] I will put enmity between thee and the woman, and between thy seed and her seed ; it shall bruise thy head, and thou shalt bruise his heel.—GEN., ch. 3.

7585. —— Fall of. *War in Heaven.* 7 There was war in heaven : Michael and his angels fought against the dragon ; and the dragon fought and his angels, 8 And prevailed not ; neither was their place found any more in heaven.—REV., ch. 12.

7586. —— Filled by. *Ananias.* 3 Peter said, Ananias, why hath Satan filled thine heart to lie to the Holy Ghost, and to keep back *part* of the price of the land.—ACTS, ch. 5.

7587. —— Injurious. *To Job.* 11 Put forth thine hand now, and touch all that he hath, and he will curse thee to thy face. 12 And the Lord said unto Satan, Behold, all that he hath *is* in thy power ; only upon himself put not forth thine hand.—JOB, ch. 1.

7588. —— Inspired by. *Judas.* 2 Supper being ended, the devil having now put into the heart of Judas Iscariot, Simon's *son*, to betray him.—JOHN, ch. 13.

7589. —— Leadership of. *Judas.* 27 After the sop Satan entered into him. Then said Jesus unto him, That thou doest, do quickly.—JOHN, ch. 13.

7590. —— Peril from. *" Lion."* 8 Be sober, be vigilant ; because your adversary the devil, as a roaring lion, walketh about, seeking whom he may devour.—1 PETER, ch. 5.

7591. —— quoting Scripture. *To Jesus.* 6 If thou be the Son of God, cast thyself down : for it is written, He shall give his angels charge concerning thee : and in *their* hands they shall bear thee up, lest at any time thou dash thy foot against a stone.—MAT., ch. 4.

7592. —— at Worship. *"Came also."* 1 There was a day when the sons of God came to present themselves before the Lord, and Satan came also among them to present himself before the Lord.—JOB, ch. 2.

See other illustrations under :
DEVIL.

Called a. Say we not well that thou hast a devil? 2266
Hypocrisy. Ye are of your father the devil 2267
Sold to. Ahab did sell himself to work wickedness 2268

Delivered to. Hymeneus and Alex..I have d. 2
Demonized. Hold thy peace and come out of him 2172
See TEMPTER and TEMPTATION.

7593. SATISFACTION, Fulness of. *Simeon.* 28 Then took he him up in his arms, and blessed God, and said, 29 Lord, now lettest thou thy servant depart in peace, according to thy word : 30 For mine eyes have seen thy salvation.—LUKE, ch. 2.

7594. —— Inward. *Proverb.* 14 The backslider in heart shall be filled with his own ways : and a good man *shall be satisfied* from himself.—PROV., ch. 14.

See other illustrations under :
CONTENTMENT.

Constant. In whatsoever state I am..to be content 1642
Christian. Be content with such things as ye have 1643
Godly. Having food and raiment, let us be..content 1644
Home. Moses was content to dwell with the man 1645
at Home. That I may die in mine own city 1646
Lack. They that will be rich fall into..a snare 1647
Little. Better is little with..than great treasure 1648

Possessions. Esau said, I have enough, my brother 1649
Perfect. L. is my shepherd, I shall not want 1650
Riches. I will not take from a thread to a shoe-l. 1651
See HAPPINESS.

7595. SAVED, Many. *In Heaven.* 9 I beheld, and, lo, a great multitude, which no man could number, of all nations, and kindreds, and people, and tongues, stood before the throne.—REV., ch. 7.

7596. SAVING Men. *Peril.* 47 Aaron..ran into the midst of the congregation ; and, behold, the plague was begun..and he put on incense, and made an atonement for the people. 48 And he stood between the dead and the living ; and the plague was stayed.—NUM., ch. 16.

7597. —— Devoted to. 19 I made myself servant unto all, that I might gain the more. 20 And unto the Jews I became as a Jew, that I might gain the Jews ; to them that are under the law, as under the law, that I might gain them that are under the law.—1 COR., ch. 9.

7598. —— Zeal in. 15 When the morning arose, then the angels hastened Lot, saying, Arise, take thy wife, and thy two daughters, which are here ; lest thou be consumed in the iniquity of the city.—GEN., ch. 19.

7599. —— Property. *Swine.* 13 Two thousand ..were choked in the sea. 14 And they that fed the swine fled, and told *it* in the city, and in the country. And they went out to see what it was that was done. 17 And they began to pray him to depart out of their coasts.—MARK, ch. 5.

7600. —— Self with Others. *Esther.* 13 Mordecai commanded to answer Esther, Think not with thyself that thou shalt escape in the king's house, more than all the Jews.—ESTHER, ch. 4.

7601. SAVIOUR needed, A. *Enemies.* 2 Nahash the Ammonite answered them, On this *condition* will I make a covenant with you, that I may thrust out all your right eyes, and lay it *for* a reproach upon all Israel. 3 And the elders of Jabesh said..Give us seven days' respite..and then, if *there be* no man to save us, we will come out to thee.—1 SAM., ch. 11.

See other illustrations under :
DELIVERER.

Great. Righteousness as a cloak, a helmet of 2134
Raised. [Ehud] I. cried..L. raise them up a 2135
Rewarded. Who killeth him [Goliath] the king 2136
Vailant. Shamgar slew..Philistines 600..delivered 2137
See CHRIST, JESUS.
See SALVATION and references.

7602. SAYINGS treasured. *Mary.* 49 How is it that ye sought me? wist ye not that I must be about my Father's business? 50 And they understood not the saying which he spake unto them. 51 ..But his mother kept all these sayings in her heart.—LUKE, ch. 2.

7603. SCANDAL, Ministerial. *Eli's Sons.* 22 Eli was very old, and heard all that his sons did unto all Israel ; and how they lay with the women..*at* the door of the tabernacle.—1 SAM., ch. 2.

7604. —— A public. *Absalom.* 22 They spread Absalom a tent upon the top of the house ; and Absalom went in unto his father's concubines in the sight of all Israel.—2 SAM., ch. 16.
See REPROACH and references.

7605. SCHOOL, Christianity in the. *At Ephesus.* [9] He departed from them, and separated the disciples, disputing daily in the school of one Tyrannus. [10]..by the space of two years.—ACTS, ch. 19.

7606. —— The Gospel. *"Every House."* [42] Daily in the temple, and in every house, they ceased not to teach and preach Jesus Christ.—ACTS, ch. 5.

7607. —— The Home. *" Children."* [6] These words, which I command thee.. [7]..thou shalt teach them diligently unto thy children, and shalt talk of them when thou sittest in thine house, and when thou walkest by the way, and when thou liest down, and when thou risest up.—DEUT., ch. 6.

7608. —— The Synagogue. *Jesus.* [23] Jesus went about all Galilee, teaching in their synagogues, and preaching the gospel of the kingdom.—MAT., ch. 4.

See other illustrations under :

DISCIPLESHIP.
Conditional. Lord, I will follow thee ; but	2331
Provisional. When I bow down..the L. pardon	2332
Postponed. Let me kiss my father..then I will	2333
Terms. Whosoever doth not bear his cross and	2334
Trials. Enough for the disciple to be as his master	2335
Unconditional. If any man..deny himself..cross	2336

EDUCATION.
Monument. Children ask, What mean ye by these	2602
Neglected. Children spake half in the speech of	2603
Preparatory. Such as had ability in them..kings	2604

INSTRUCTION.
Better than Practice. They bid you..do, but do not	4541
Children. Teach them thy sons, and thy sons' sons	4542
Course of. Nourishing them three years..might	4543
Humble. Apollos..Aquila and Priscilla..expounded	4544
Important. Heareth the word, and understandeth	4545
Improvement by. Ornament of grace unto thy	4546
Personal. Aquila and Priscilla took him..and	4547
Public. Ezra..brought the law before the	4548
Private. There came many unto..his lodging	4549
Youthful. From a child thou hast known the Holy	4550

KNOWLEDGE.
Adamic. Gave names to all cattle..fowl..beast	4853
Detrimental. Man is come to know good and evil	4854
Forbidden. Tree of the knowledge..shalt not eat	4855
Faith to. Believe not because of thy saying..heard	4856
Guilt. Better for them not to have known the way	4857
Grace. Perceived they were unlearned men	4858
Ignorance. I go bound in the spirit..not knowing	4859
Responsibility. Known that the ox hath used to	4860
Spiritual. I know that my Redeemer liveth	4861
Temptation. Woman saw..tree..make one wise	4862
Used. Whosoever heareth..taketh not warning	4863

LEARNING.
Profound. Moses was learned in all the wisdom	4931
Superior. Jews marvelled..how knoweth this man	4932
Worship. Came wise men from the east..worship	4933

TEACHABLENESS.
Attitude. Mary sat at Jesus' feet..heard his word	8606
Characteristic. Received..word with all readiness	8607
Manifested. Eunuch desired Philip..sit with him	8608
Professed. All here present before G. to hear all	8609
Youthful. Found him in the temple..hearing	8610

TEACHER.
Authoritative. Jesus taught them as one having	8611
Art. Bezaleel..carving..he may teach	8612
Great. Jesus went about..teaching in..synagogues	8613

Home. Thou shalt teach them..in thine house	8614
Necessary. Understandest thou..? How can I	8615
Prepared. Come up..mount..that thou mayest	8616
Spirit. When they bring you..H. G. shall teach	8617

TEACHING.
Divine. G. hath showed me..not call..common	8618
Ministerial. In the temple they ceased not to teach	8619

STUDY.
Bible. Eunuch..sitting in his chariot read Esaias	8397
Commended. These were more noble..searched	8398
Beneficial. Hearts burn..opened to us the	8399
Wearisome. Much study is a weariness to the flesh	8400

See INTELLIGENCE.

7609. SCHISM, Hurtful. *Body.* [15] If the foot shall say, Because I am not the hand, I am not of the body ; is it therefore not of the body ? [16] And if the ear shall say, Because I am not the eye, I am not of the body ; is it therefore not of the body?—1 COR., ch., 12.

See DIVISIONS and references.

7610. SCIENTIST, The first. *Adam.* [19] The Lord God formed every beast of the field, and every fowl of the air, and brought *them* unto Adam to see what he would call them ; and whatsoever Adam called every living creature, that *was* the name thereof.—GEN., ch. 2.

7611. —— A famous. *Solomon.* [33] He spake of trees, from the cedar tree that *is* in Lebanon, even unto the hyssop that springeth out of the wall : he spake also of beasts, and of fowl, and of creeping things, and of fishes.—1 KINGS, ch. 4.

7612. SCIENTISTS, Tributes of. *Magi.* [10] When they saw the star, they rejoiced with exceeding great joy. [11]..they saw the young child with Mary his mother, and fell down, and worshipped him : and when they had opened their treasures, they presented unto him gifts ; gold, and frankincense, and myrrh.—MAT., ch. 2.

7613. —— Worshipping. *Magi.* [1] When Jesus was born in Bethlehem..there came wise men from the east to Jerusalem, [2] Saying, Where is he that is born King of the Jews ? for we have seen his star in the east, and are come to worship him.—MAT., ch. 2.

7614. SCOFFERS, Malicious. *Caiaphas' Court.* [67] They spit in his face, and buffeted him ; and others smote *him* with the palms of their hands, [68] Saying, Prophesy unto us, thou Christ, Who is he that smote thee?—MAT., ch. 26.

7615. —— —— *Herod's Court.* [11] Herod with his men of war set him at nought, and mocked *him*, and arrayed him in a gorgeous robe, and sent him again to Pilate.—LUKE, ch. 23.

7616. —— —— *Pilate's Court.* [28] They stripped him, and put on him a scarlet robe. [29] And when they had platted a crown of thorns, they put *it* upon his head, and a reed in his right hand : and they bowed the knee before him, and mocked him, saying, Hail, King of the Jews ! [30] And they spit upon him, and took the reed, and smote him on the head.—MAT., ch. 27.

7617. —— —— *Crucifixion.* [39] They that passed by reviled him, wagging their heads, [40] And saying, Thou that destroyest the temple, and buildest *it* in three days, save thyself. If thou be the Son of God, come down from the cross.—MAT., ch. 27.

See other illustrations under :

DERISION.

Horrible. Put on him a scarlet robe..crown 2197
Impious. Laughed them to scorn, and mocked 2198
Punished. Sarah saw the son of Hagar..mocking 2199
Nickname. Thou art a Samaritan, and hast a devil 2200
Truth. Pharisees who were covetous..derided 2201
Unfortunates. Thieves also..cast the same into 2202
Wicked. They shoot out the lip, and shake the 2203

RIDICULE.

Doctrine. When they heard of the resurrection 7425
Fatal. Call for Samson, that he may make us sport 7426
Failure. Not able to finish..begin to mock him 7427
Horrible. He saved others, let him save himself 7428
Impious. They laughed them to scorn, and mocked 7429
" What will this babbler say [Athenians] 7430
Insulting. Cut off their garments..their buttocks 7431
Opposition. What do these feeble Jews ? will they 7432
" If a fox go up, he shall break down 7433
Punishment. Children of Bethel..Go up, thou bald 7434
Royalty. Wearing the crown of thorns and purple 7435
Scornful. They laughed us to scorn, and despised us 7436
Spirit. Mocking said,These men are full of new wine 7437
Trial. They reviled him and said, We are Moses' 7438

7618. SCORN of Pride. *Haman.* ⁵ When Haman saw that Mordecai bowed not, nor did him reverence, then was Haman full of wrath. ⁶ And he thought scorn to lay hands on Mordecai alone ; for they had shewed him the people of Mordecai.—ESTHER, ch. 3.

7619. —— Public. *Jerusalem.* ¹⁵ All that pass by clap *their* hands at thee ; they hiss and wag their head at the daughter of Jerusalem, *saying, Is* this the city that *men* call The perfection of beauty, The joy of the whole earth?—LAM., ch. 2.

7620. —— of Unbelief. *Jairus' Daughter.* ⁵² All wept, and bewailed her : but he said, Weep not ; she is not dead, but sleepeth. ⁵³ And they laughed him to scorn, knowing that she was dead. ⁵⁴ And he..took her by the hand, and called, saying, Maid, arise.—LUKE, ch. 8.

7621. SCORNERS of the Gospel. *"Made Light."* ⁴ My oxen and *my* fatlings *are* killed, and all things *are* ready : come unto the marriage. ⁵ But they made light of *it*, and went their ways, one to his farm, another to his merchandise. ⁶ And the remnant took his servants ..and slew *them.*—MAT., ch. 22.

See other illustrations under :

CONTEMPT.

Bigots. Pharisee prayed..I am not as other men 1618
Critics. Michal saw king David leaping..despised 1619
Conceited. Thistle..sent to the cedar..give thy 1620
Disregarded. The God of heaven will prosper us 1621
Enemy's. Am I a dog that thou comest..staves 1622
Expressed. Children of Belial..brought Saul no 1623
Fraternal. With whom hast thou left those few 1624
Gospel. Made light of it, and went their way 1625
for God. Have turned their back unto me..face 1626
Malicious. Did spit in his face, and buffeted 1628
Others. That they were righteous..despised others 1629
for Worship. Torn..the lame, and the sick..ye 1630

See RIDICULE.

7622. SCOURGE, Use of. *In Temple.* ¹⁵ When he had made a scourge of small cords, he drove them all out of the temple, and the sheep, and the oxen ; and poured out the changers' money, and overthrew the tables ; ¹⁶ And said..make not my Father's house a house of merchandise. —JOHN, ch. 2.

7623. SCRIPTURE, Adding to. *Woe.* ¹⁸ I testify unto every man that heareth the words of the prophecy of this book, If any man shall add unto these things, God shall add unto him the plagues that are written in this book.—REV., ch. 22.

7624. —— Diminishing. *Woe.* ¹⁹ If any man shall take away from the words of the book of this prophecy, God shall take away his part out of the book of life, and out of the holy city, and *from* the things which are written in this book.—REV., ch. 22.

7625. SCRIPTURES, Efficacy of. *"Rain."* ¹⁰ As the rain cometh down, and the snow from heaven, and returneth not thither, but watereth the earth, and maketh it bring forth and bud, that it may give seed to the sower, and bread to the eater : ¹¹ So shall my word be.—ISA., ch. 55.

7626. —— Opening of. *At Emmaus.* ³² They said..Did not our heart burn within us, while he talked with us by the way, and while he opened to us the Scriptures?—LUKE, ch. 24.

7627. —— regarded. *By Murderers.* ³¹ The Jews therefore, because it was the preparation, that the bodies should not remain upon the cross on the sabbath day, (for that sabbath day was a high day,) besought Pilate that their legs might be broken, and *that* they might be taken away.—JOHN, ch. 19.

See BIBLE.

7628. SCRUPLES of Hypocrites. *Murderers.* ²⁸ Then led they Jesus from Caiaphas unto the hall of judgment..and they themselves went not into the judgment hall, lest they should be defiled ; but that they might eat the passover. —JOHN, ch. 18.

7629. —— Little. *Tithes.* ²³ Woe unto you, scribes and Pharisees, hypocrites ! for ye pay tithe of mint and anise and cummin, and have omitted the weightier *matters* of the law, judgment, mercy, and faith.—MAT., ch. 23.

See CONSCIENCE and references.

7630. SEA calmed. *Gennesaret.* ²⁴ They came to him, and awoke him, saying, Master, Master, we perish. Then he arose, and rebuked the wind and the raging of the water : and they ceased, and there was a calm.—LUKE, ch. 8.

7631. —— divided, The. *Red Sea.* ²² And the children of Israel went into the midst of the sea upon the dry *ground:* and the waters *were* a wall unto them on their right hand, and on their left.—EX., ch. 14.

7632. —— Destruction by the. *Red Sea.* ²⁸ The waters returned, and covered the chariots, and the horsemen, *and* all the host of Pharaoh that came into the sea after them ; there remained not so much as one of them.—EX., ch. 14.

7633. —— of Glass. *Revelation.* ² I saw as it were a sea of glass mingled with fire : and them that had gotten the victory over the beast ..stand on the sea of glass, having the harps of God.—REV., ch. 15.

7634. —— Tempestuous. *Waves.* ²⁵ He commandeth, and raiseth the stormy wind, which lifteth up the waves thereof. ²⁶ They mount up to the heaven, they go down again to the depths : their soul is melted because of trouble.—Ps. 107.

7635. SEASIDE Meeting. *Successful.* [8] When Simon Peter saw *it*, he fell down at Jesus' knees, saying, Depart from me ; for I am a sinful man, O Lord. [9] For he was astonished, and all that were with him, at the draught of the fishes.. [10]..Jesus said unto Simon, Fear not ; from henceforth thou shalt catch men. [11] And when they had brought their ships to land, they forsook all, and followed him.—LUKE, ch. 5.

7636. —— Worship by. *Jesus.* [1] He began again to teach by the sea side : and there was gathered unto him a great multitude, so that he entered into a ship, and sat in the sea ; and the whole multitude was by the sea on the land.— MARK, ch. 4.

7637. SEAMEN, Distress of. *"Reel."* [27] They reel to and fro, and stagger like a drunken man, and are at their wit's end. [28] Then they cry unto the Lord in their trouble, and he bringeth them out of their distresses. [29] He maketh the storm a calm.—Ps. 107.

See other illustrations under :

MARINERS.

Distress. Soul is melted because of trouble	5217
Mourning. Every shipmaster..cried	5217
Prayer. Cry unto the L. in their trouble	5218

SHIPWRECK.

Perils by. Thrice I [Paul] suffered shipwreck	7839
Saved in. Some on boards, and some on broken	7840

Prayer. Master, we perish	7631

7638. SEARCH, Unsuccessful. *For Elijah.* [16] Lest peradventure the Spirit of the Lord hath taken him up, and cast him upon some mountain, or into some valley. And he said, Ye shall not send. [17] And when they urged him till he was ashamed, he said, Send. They sent therefore fifty men ; and they sought three days, but found him not.—2 KINGS, ch. 2.

See EVIDENCE.

7639. SEASON, Out of. *Parable.* [5] Which of you shall have a friend, and shall go unto him at midnight, and say unto him, Friend, lend me three loaves ; [7] And he from within shall answer..Trouble me not : the door is now shut, and my children are with me in bed ; I cannot rise and give thee.—LUKE, ch. 11.

7640. SEASONS, Certainty of the. *Changes.* [21] Neither will I again smite any more every thing living, as I have done. [22] While the earth remaineth, seedtime and harvest, and cold and heat, and summer and winter, and day and night shall not cease.—GEN., ch. 8.

7641. —— Changes of. *Summer.* [11] For, lo, the winter is past, the rain is over *and* gone ; [12] The flowers appear on earth ; the time of the singing *of birds* is come, and the voice of the turtle is heard in our land ; [13] The fig tree putteth forth her green figs, and the vines *with* the tender grape give a *good* smell.—SOLOMON'S SONG, ch. 2.

See other illustrations under :

SUMMER.

Approach. The winter is past, the rain is over		8462
" Fig tree..putteth forth leaves..s.		8463

7642. SECESSION predicted. *Enemies.* [16] We certify the king that, if this city be builded *again*, and the walls thereof set up, by this means thou shalt have no portion on this side the river. —EZRA, ch. 4.

7643. —— Political. *Rehoboam* [14] Spake to them after the counsel of the young men, saying, My father made your yoke heavy, and I will add to your yoke : my father *also* chastised you with whips, but I will chastise you with scorpions. [16] So when all Israel saw that the king hearkened not unto them, the people answered..What portion have we in David?..to your tents, O Israel.—1 KINGS, ch. 12.

7644. SECRET, A Woman's. *Spies to Rahab.* [20] If thou utter this our business, then we will be quit of thine oath which thou hast made us to swear.—JOSH., ch. 2.

7645. SECRECY, Difficult. *Manslaughter.* [12] He looked this way and that way, and when he saw that *there was* no man, he slew the Egyptian, and hid him in the sand. [13] And when he went out the second day.. [14] And he said..intendest thou to kill me, as thou killedst the Egyptian? And Moses feared, and said, Surely this thing is known.—Ex., ch. 2.

7646. —— impossible. *Of Plans.* [11] The heart of the king of Syria was sore troubled.. and he called his servants, and said..which of us *is* for the king of Israel ? [12] And one of his servants said, None, my lord, O king : but Elisha, the prophet..telleth the king of Israel the words that thou speakest in thy bedchamber. —2 KINGS, ch. 6.

See other illustrations under :

HIDDEN.

Cave. Obadiah took 200 prophets and hid in a c.	3966
Field. David hid himself in the field	3967
Graciously. King commanded to take Jeremiah	3968
House of God. Joash was hid..six years	3969
Housetop. Rahab..hid them with the..flax	3970
Infant. Ark..in the flags by the river brink	3971
Strangely. Took they up stones..Jesus hid himself	3972
Wilderness. Hid thyself..ravens to feed thee	3973

HIDING.

Difficult. Moses feared..Surely this is known	3974
Sinners. Adam, where art thou?..hid myself	3975
Sin. Set ye Uriah in the hottest battle..retire	3976
Talent. Received one..digged..hid his money	3977

MYSTERY.

Conversion. Nicodemus answered, How can these	5660
Marvellous. Sat..according to his birthright..men	5661
Strange. Why the bush is not consumed	5662
Stumbling. Eateth my flesh..disciples went back	5664
Unsolved. No man knoweth his sepulchre..this day	5663
Unexplainable. Thou knowest not now..know	5665

7647. SECTARIAN, A furious. *Saul.* [11] I punished them oft in every synagogue, and compelled *them* to blaspheme ; and being exceedingly mad against them, I persecuted *them* even unto strange cities. [12] Whereupon as I went to Damascus with authority and commission from the chief priests.—ACTS, ch. 26.

7648. SECTARIANISM reproved. *John said,* [38] We saw one casting out devils in thy name, and he followeth not us : and we forbade him, because he followeth not us. [39] But Jesus said, Forbid him not.—MARK, ch. 9.

Also see :

Partisans. I am of Paul, and I of Apollos	5985
Schism. If the foot shall say..I am not the hand	7609

7649. SECURITY of the Godly. *Fortress.* [1] He that dwelleth in the secret place of the Most High shall abide under the shadow of the

Almighty. ² I will say of the Lord, *He is* my refuge and my fortress : my God ; in him will I trust.—Ps. 91. [See chapter.]

See SAFETY.

7650. SEED, According to the. *Eliphaz said,* ⁸ They that plough iniquity, and sow wickedness, reap the same. ⁹ By the blast of God they perish.—Job, ch. 4.

7651. —— Accidental. *"By Way Side."* ¹⁹ When any one heareth the word of the kingdom, and understandeth *it* not, then cometh the wicked one, and catcheth away that which was sown in his heart, This is he which received seed by the way side.—Mat., ch. 13.

7652. —— Growth of. *"Mystery."* ²⁷ The seed should spring and grow up, he knoweth not how. ²⁸ For the earth bringeth forth fruit of herself ; first the blade, then the ear, after that the full corn in the ear.—Mark, ch. 4.

7653. —— A little. *Mustard.* ³¹ The kingdom of heaven is like to a grain of mustard seed.. ³²..the least of all seeds : but when it is grown, it is the greatest among herbs, and becometh a tree, so that the birds..lodge in the branches.—Mat., ch. 13.

7654. SEEING, Partial. *Eve.* ⁶ When the woman saw that the tree *was* good for food, and that it *was* pleasant to the eyes, and a tree to be desired to make *one* wise, she took of the fruit thereof, and did eat.—Gen., ch. 3.

7655. —— Proof by. *Jonathan.* ⁴⁸ Blessed *be* the Lord God of Israel, which hath given *one* to sit on my throne this day, mine eyes even seeing *it.* ⁴⁹ And all the guests that *were* with Adonijah were afraid, and rose up, and went every man his way.—1 Kings, ch. 1.

7656. —— unsatisfactory. *Proverb.* ⁸ All things *are* full of labour ; man cannot utter *it* : the eye is not satisfied with seeing, nor the ear filled with hearing.—Eccl., ch. 1.

7657. —— vexatious. *Lot.* ⁷ Delivered just Lot, vexed with the filthy conversation of the wicked : ⁸ (For that righteous man dwelling among them, in seeing and hearing, vexed *his* righteous soul from day to day.)—2 Peter, ch. 2.

See other illustrations under :

VISION.

Comforting. Stephen saw..Jesus standing	9225
of God. I saw also the Lord .on a throne	9226
" Woe is me, for I am undone..unclean l.	9227
Instructed. What G. hath cleansed..common	9228
Prepared for. I was fasting until..ninth hour	9229
Perfected. Restored, and saw every man clearly	9230
Spirit. A spirit passed..hair of my flesh stood up	9231
Transforming. Moses wist not that..face shone	9232
" Beholding as in a glass..changed	9233
Trance. Peter fell into a trance..sheet knit.	9234

See EYE *and references.*

7658. SEEKER, A determined. *Jacob.* ²⁵ The hollow of Jacob's thigh was out of joint, as he wrestled with him. ²⁶ And he said, Let me go, for the day breaketh. And he said, I will not let thee go, except thou bless me.—Gen., ch. 32.

7659. —— An earnest. *David.* ¹ O God, thou *art* my God ; early will I seek thee : my soul thirsteth for thee, my flesh longeth for thee in a dry and thirsty land, where no water is ; ² To see thy power and thy glory, so *as* I have seen thee in the sanctuary.—Ps. 63.

7660. —— —— David. ¹ As the heart panteth after the water brooks, so panteth my soul after thee, O God. ² My soul thirsteth for God, for the living God : when shall I come and appear before God ?—Ps. 42.

7661. —— A hopeful. *David.* ¹⁰ *As* with a sword in my bones, mine enemies reproach me ; while they say daily unto me, Where *is* thy God ? ¹¹ Why art thou cast down, O my soul? and why art thou disquieted within me ? hope thou in God : for I shall yet praise him, *who is* the health of my countenance, and my God.—Ps. 42.

7662. —— A rich. *Zaccheus.* ² A man named Zaccheus, which was the chief among the publicans, and he was rich. ³ And he sought to see Jesus who he was.—Luke, ch. 19.

7663. —— A sad. *David.* ³ My tears have been my meat day and night, while they continually say unto me, Where *is* thy God ? ⁴ When I remember these *things*, I pour out my soul in me : for I had gone with the multitude, I went with them to the house of God, with the voice of joy and praise.—Ps. 42.

7664. SEEKERS, False. *"Loaves."* ²⁵ When they had found him on the other side of the sea, they said .. Rabbi, when camest thou hither ? ²⁶ Jesus..said..Ye seek me, not because ye saw the miracles, but because ye did eat of the loaves, and were filled.—John, ch. 6.

7665. —— —— Disciples. ²⁴ There arose a great tempest in the sea, insomuch that the ship was covered with the waves : but he was asleep. ²⁵ And his disciples..awoke him, saying, Lord, save us : we perish.—Mat., ch. 8.

7666. SEEKING, Continuous. *Anna.* ³⁷ She *was* a widow of about fourscore and four years, which departed not from the temple, but served God with fastings and prayers night and day.—Luke, ch. 2.

7667. —— in Distress. *Moses.* ³ Thou hast brought us up out of Egypt, to kill us and our children and our cattle with thirst ? ⁴ And Moses cried unto the Lord, saying, What shall I do unto this people ? they be almost ready to stone me.—Ex., ch. 17.

7668. —— Determined. *"Roof."* ⁴ When they could not come nigh unto him for the press, they uncovered the roof where he was : and when they had broken *it* up, they let down the bed wherein the sick of the palsy lay.—Mark, ch. 2.

7669. —— Earnestness in. *Bartimeus.* [See No. 7675.] ⁴⁹ They call the blind man, saying unto him, Be of good comfort, rise ; he calleth thee. ⁵⁰ And he, casting away his garment, rose, and came to Jesus.—Mark, ch. 10.

7670. —— —— *"Sweep."* ¹ What woman having ten pieces of silver, if she lose one piece, doth not light a candle, and sweep the house, and seek diligently till she find *it* ?—Luke, ch. 15.

7671. —— in Haste. *Shepherds.* ¹⁵ Let us now go even unto Bethlehem, and see this thing ..which the Lord hath made known unto us. ¹⁶ And they came with haste, and found Mary, and Joseph, and the babe lying in a manger.—Luke, ch. 2.

7672. —— in Humility. *Daniel.* ³ I set my

face unto the Lord God, to seek by prayer and supplications, with fasting, and sackcloth, and ashes : ⁴ And I prayed unto the Lord my God, and made my confession.—DAN., ch. 9.

7673. —— **heartily.** *Successful.* ¹² Then.. ye shall go and pray unto me, and I will hearken unto you. ¹³ And ye shall seek me, and find me, when ye shall search for me with all your heart.—JOB, ch. 29.

7674. —— **intensely.** *Jesus.* ⁷ In the days of his flesh, when he had offered up prayers and supplications with strong crying and tears unto him that was able to save him from death, and was heard in that he feared.—HEB., ch. 7.

7675. —— **Irrepressible.** *Bartimeus.* ⁴⁷ When he heard that it was Jesus of Nazareth, he began to cry out, and say, Jesus, *thou* Son of David, have mercy on me. ⁴⁸ And many charged him that he should hold his peace : but he cried the more a great deal, *Thou* Son of David, have mercy on me.—MARK, ch. 10. [See No. 7669.]

7676. —— **longingly.** *In Adversity.* ³ Oh that I knew where I might find him ! *that* I might come *even* to his seat ! ⁴ I would order *my* cause before him, and fill my mouth with arguments. —JOB, ch. 23.

7677. —— **Piety first.** *Jesus said,* ²⁹ Seek not ye what ye shall eat or what ye shall drink, neither be ye of doubtful mind. ³¹ But rather seek ye the kingdom of God ; and all these things shall be added unto you.—LUKE, ch. 12.

7678. —— **prompted.** *In Samaria.* ²⁶ He hath sent lions among them, and, behold, they slay them, because they know not the manner of the God of the land. ²⁷ Then the king of Assyria commanded, saying, Carry thither one of the priests whom ye brought from thence.. and let him teach them the manner of the God of the land.—2 KINGS, ch. 17.

7679. —— **Persistent.** *Humility.* ²⁴ Wherefore hidest thou thy face, *and* forgettest our affliction and our oppression ? ²⁵ For our soul is bowed down to the dust : our belly cleaveth unto the earth. ²⁶ Arise for our help, and redeem us, for thy mercies' sake.—Ps. 44.

7680. —— **repeated.** *Paul.* ⁷ There was given to me a thorn in the flesh, the messenger of Satan to buffet me, lest I should be exalted above measure. ⁸ For this thing I besought the Lord thrice, that it might depart from me.—2 COR., ch. 12.

7681. —— **Relatives.** *For Jesus.* ⁴⁰ One of the two which heard John *speak*..was Andrew, Simon Peter's brother. ⁴¹ He first findeth his own brother Simon, and saith..We have found the Messias.—JOHN, ch. 1.

7682. —— **for Sinners.** *Jesus.* ¹² They that be whole need not a physician, but they that are sick. ¹³..For I am not come to call the righteous, but sinners to repentance.—MAT., ch. 9.

Also see :
Unsuccessful. 50 men sought..3 days [for M.'s b.] 7630

7683. SELF, Unmindful of. *Jesus.* ²⁷ There followed him a great company of people, and of women, which also bewailed and lamented him. ²⁸ But Jesus turning unto them said, Daughters of Jerusalem, weep not for me, but weep for yourselves.—MAT., ch. 27.

7684. —— —— *Jesus.* ²⁰ And the multitude cometh together again, so that they could not so much as eat bread. ²¹ And when his friends heard *of it*, they went out to lay hold on him : for they said, He is beside himself.— —MARK, ch. 4.

7685. SELF-ABASEMENT rewarded. *Publican.* ¹³ The publican, standing afar off, would not lift up so much as *his* eyes unto heaven, but smote upon his breast, saying, God be merciful to me a sinner. ¹⁴ I tell you, this man went down to his house justified.—LUKE, ch. 18.

7686. —— **Unworthy.** *Spies.* ³³ We saw the giants, the sons of Anak..and we were in our own sight as grasshoppers, and so we were in their sight.—NUM., ch. 13.

See HUMILITY.

7687. SELF-CONCEIT, Hopeless. *Proverb.* ¹² Seest thou a man wise in his own conceit ? *there is* more hope of a fool than of him.—PROV., ch. 26. ² Let another man praise thee, and not thine own mouth ; a stranger, and not thine own lips.—PROV., ch. 27.

7688. —— **Poverty and.** *Proverb.* ⁹ *He that is* despised, and hath a servant, *is* better than he that honoureth himself, and lacketh bread.— PROV., ch. 12.

See PRIDE.

7689. SELF-CONFIDENCE, Boasting. *Israelites.* ² The Lord said unto Gideon, The people that *are* with thee *are* too many for me to give the Midianites into their hands, lest Israel vaunt themselves against me, saying, Mine own hand hath saved me.—JUDGES, ch. 7.

7690. —— **False.** *Hazael.* ¹² I know the evil that thou wilt do unto the children of Israel : their strong holds wilt thou set on fire, and their young men wilt thou slay with the sword, and wilt dash their children, and rip up their women with child. ¹³ And Hazael said, But what, *is* thy servant a dog, that he should do this great thing?—2 KINGS, ch. 8.

7691. —— **Rebuked.** *Peter.* ³⁷ Lord, why cannot I follow thee now ? I will lay down my life for thy sake. ³⁸..Wilt thou lay down thy life for my sake ? Verily, verily, I say unto thee, The cock shall not crow, till thou hast denied me thrice.—JOHN, ch. 13.

See other illustrations under :
PRESUMPTION.

Avoided. Better..he said, Come up hither ; than	6534
Daring. Egyptians pursued..midst of the sea	6535
Failure. Presumed to go..Amalekites smote them	6536
Future. Know not what shall be on the morrow	6537
Impatient. Because thou comest not..I offered	6538
Pride. Uzziah..burnt incense upon the altar	6539
Penalty. Come unto the king..not called..death	6540
Religious. Prophet that shall speak..not com'd.	6541
Rebuked. Uzziah..censer in his hand..leprosy	6542
Sin. Trodden under foot the Son of God	6543
Success. Soul that doeth..presumptuously..cut off	6544
" Joshua made as if beaten..drawn away	6545
Temptation. On a pinnacle..cast thyself down	6546
Unholy. 250 princes..ye take too much upon you	6547

See SELF-RIGHTEOUSNESS below.

7692. SELF CONDEMNATION acknowledged. *King Ahab.* ⁴⁰ As thy servant was busy here and there, he was gone. And the king of Israel said ..So *shall* thy judgment *be* ; thyself hast decided *it.* [42]..Thus saith the Lord, Because thou hast let go out of *thy* hand a man whom I appointed to utter destruction, therefore thy life shall go for his life, and thy people for his people.—1 KINGS, ch. 20.

7693. —— —— *Pharisees.* [7] He that is without sin among you, let him first cast a stone at her.. [9] And they..being convicted by *their own* conscience, went out one by one, beginning at the eldest, *even* unto the last : and Jesus was left alone, and the woman.—JOHN, ch. 8.

7694. —— *Future.* " *Speechless.*" [12] Friend, how camest thou in hither not having a wedding garment? And he was speechless.—MAT., ch. 22.

7695. —— *Sincere. Thief.* [40] The other answering rebuked him, saying, Dost not thou fear God, seeing thou art in the same condemnation ? [41] And we indeed justly ; for we receive the due reward of our deeds : but this man hath done nothing amiss.—LUKE, ch. 24.

7696. —— *Unexpected. David.* [6] He shall restore the lamb fourfold, because he did this thing, and because he had no pity. [7] And Nathan said to David, *Thou art* the man.—2 SAM., ch. 12.

See CONSCIENCE.

7697. SELF-CONTROL, Lack of. *Proverb.* [28] He that *hath* no rule over his own spirit *is like* a city *that is* broken down, *and* without walls.—PROV., ch. 25.

7698. —— *Masterly. Saul.* [26] Saul also went home to Gibeah ; and there went with him a band of men, whose hearts God had touched. [27] But the children of Belial said, How shall this man save us? And they despised him, and brought him no presents. But he held his peace.—1 SAM., ch. 10.

7699. —— *Resolute. Eating.* [2] Put a knife to thy throat, if thou *be* a man given to appetite. [3] Be not desirous of his dainties : for they *are* deceitful meat.—PROV., ch. 23.

See TEMPERANCE.

7700. SELF-DEFENCE, Lawful. *In Persia.* [11] The king granted the Jews which *were* in every city to gather themselves together, and to stand for their life, to destroy, to slay..the people and province that would assault them, *both* little ones and women, and *to take* the spoil of them for a prey.—ESTHER, ch. 8.

Also see:
Valorous. Slew him with his own spear   9159

7701. SELF-DENIAL in Abstinence. *David.* [16] The three mighty men brake through the host of the Philistines, and drew water out of the well of Beth-lehem, that *was* by the gate..and brought *it* to David : nevertheless he would not drink thereof, but poured it out unto the Lord.—2 SAM., ch. 23.

7702. —— *Bodily. Paul.* [27] I keep under my body, and bring *it* into subjection : lest that by any means, when I have preached to others, I myself should be a castaway.—1 COR., ch. 9.

7703. —— *better. Loiterers.* [1] *When* the people complained, it displeased the Lord..and his anger was kindled ; and the fire of the Lord ..consumed *them that were* in the uttermost parts of the camp.—NUM., ch. 11.

7704. —— *Costly. Jesus said,* [30] If thy right hand offend thee, cut it off, and cast *it* from thee : for it is profitable for thee that one of thy members should perish, and not *that* thy whole body should be cast into hell.—MAT., ch. 5.

7705. —— *difficult. Young Ruler.* [1] One thing thou lackest..sell whatsoever thou hast, and give to the poor, and thou shalt have treasure in heaven ; and come, take up the cross, and follow me. [22]..went away grieved : for he had great possessions.—MARK, ch. 10.

7706. —— *Decent. Eating.* [1] When thou sittest to eat with a ruler, consider diligently what *is* before thee : [2] And put a knife to thy throat, if thou *be* a man given to appetite.—PROV., ch. 23.

7707. —— *essential. " Cross."* [23] If any *man* will come after me, let him deny himself, and take up his cross daily, and follow me. [24] For whosoever will save his life shall lose it : but whosoever will lose his life for my sake, the same shall save it.—LUKE, ch. 9.

7708. —— *Marvellous. Abram.* [1] The Lord had said unto Abram, Get thee out of thy country, and from thy kindred, and from thy father's house, unto a land that I will shew thee.—GEN., ch. 12.

7709. —— —— *Moses.* [24] By faith Moses, when he was come to years, refused to be called the son of Pharaoh's daughter ; [25] Choosing rather to suffer affliction with the people of God, than to enjoy the pleasures of sin for a season.—HEB., ch. 11.

7710. —— —— *Paul.* [11] Even unto this present hour we both hunger, and thirst, and are naked. [See No. 7526.]

7711. —— *for Others. Paul.* [13] If meat make my brother to offend, I will eat no flesh while the world standeth, lest I make my brother to offend.—1 COR., ch. 8.

7712. —— *Patriotic. Nehemiah.* [14] Twelve years, I and my brethren have not eaten the bread of the governor. [15] But the former governors.. were chargeable unto the people, and had taken of them bread and wine, besides forty shekels of silver.—NEH., ch. 5.

7713. —— *Positive. Christian.* [26] If any *man* come to me, and hate not his father, and mother, and wife, and children, and brethren, and sisters. yea, and his own life also, he cannot be my disciple. [27] And whosoever doth not bear his cross, and come after me, cannot be my disciple.—LUKE, ch. 14.

7714. —— *rewarded. Future.* [27] We have forsaken all, and followed thee ; what shall we have therefore ? [28] And Jesus said..in the regeneration when the Son of man shall sit in the throne of his glory, ye also shall sit upon twelve thrones, judging the twelve tribes of Israel.—MAT., ch. 19.

7715. —— —— *" Hundredfold."* [29] Every one that hath forsaken houses, or brethren, or sisters, or father, or mother, or wife, or children, or lands, for my name's sake, shall receive a hundredfold, and shall inherit everlasting life.—MAT., ch. 19.

7716. —— *Saved by. " Strait Gate."* [13] Enter ye in at the strait gate : for wide *is* the gate, and broad *is* the way, that leadeth to destruction, and many there be which go in thereat : ¹⁴ Because strait *is* the gate, and narrow *is* the way, which leadeth unto life, and few there be that find it.—Mat., ch. 7.

7717. —— **Sabbath.** *Rewarded.* ¹³ If thou turn away thy foot from the sabbath, *from* doing thy pleasure on my holy day ; and call the sabbath a delight, the holy of the Lord, honourable ; and shalt honour him, not doing thine own ways, nor finding thine own pleasure, nor speaking *thine own* words : ¹⁴ Then shalt thou delight thyself in the Lord.—Isa., ch. 58.

7718. —— **Service of.** *"To Minister."* ²⁷ Whosoever will be chief among you, let him be your servant : ²⁸ Even as the Son of man came not to be ministered unto, but to minister, and to give his life a ransom.—Mat., ch. 20.

7719. —— **Vow of.** *Rechabites.* ⁶ We will drink no wine : for Jonadab..our father commanded us, saying, Ye shall drink no wine, *neither* ye, nor your sons forever : ⁷ Neither shall ye build house, nor sow seed, nor plant vineyard.—Isa., ch. 35.

See SELF-CONTROL.

7720. SELF-EXAMINATION, Benefits of. *Corinthians.* ¹¹ Ye sorrowed after a godly sort, what carefulness it wrought in you, yea, *what* clearing of yourselves, yea, *what* indignation, yea, *what* fear, yea, *what* vehement desire, yea, *what* zeal, yea, *what* revenge ! In all *things* ye have approved yourselves to be clear in this matter. —2 Cor., ch. 7.

7721. —— **overlooked.** *"Beam."* ³ Why beholdest thou the mote that is in thy brother's eye, but considerest not the beam that is in thine own eye.—Mat., ch. 7.

7722. —— **Prayerful.** *David.* ²³ Search me, O God, and know my heart: try me, and know my thoughts : ²⁴ And see if *there be any* wicked way in me, and lead me in the way everlasting. —Ps. 139.

7723. —— **Personal.** *Apostles.* ²¹ As they did eat, he said..one of you shall betray me. ²² And they were exceeding sorrowful, and began every one of them to say unto him, Lord, is it I?—Mat., ch. 26.

7724. SELF-RIGHTEOUSNESS cautioned against. *Israelites.* ² A people great and tall, the children of the Anakim..*of whom* thou hast heard *say*, Who can stand before the children of Anak !.. ⁴ Speak not thou in thine heart.. saying, For my righteousness the Lord hath brought me in to possess this land : but for the wickedness of these nations the Lord doth drive them out from before thee.—Deut., ch. 9.

7725. —— **corrected.** *"Remember."* ⁶ God giveth thee not this good land to possess it for thy righteousness ; for thou *art* a stiffnecked people. ⁷ Remember, *and* forget not, how thou provokedst the Lord thy God to wrath in the wilderness : from the day that thou didst depart out of the land of Egypt, until ye came unto this place, ye have been rebellious.—Deut., ch. 9.

7726. —— **Failure of.** *Pharisee.* ¹³ And the publican, standing afar off, would not lift up so much as *his* eyes unto heaven, but smote upon his breast, saying, God be merciful to me a sin-

ner. ¹⁴ I tell you, this man went down to his house justified *rather* than the other.— Luke, ch. 18.

7727. —— **Mistake of.** *Zophar said,* ⁴ Thou hast said, My doctrine *is* pure, and I am clean in thine eyes. ⁵ But oh that God would speak, and open his lips against thee ; ⁶ And that he would shew thee the secrets of wisdom, that *they are* double to that which is ! Know therefore that God exacteth of thee *less* than thine iniquity *deserveth.*—Job, ch. 11.

7728. —— **Offensive.** *Smoke.* ⁵ Stand by thyself, come not near to me ; for I am holier than thou. These *are* a smoke in my nose, a fire that burneth all the day.—Isa., ch. 65.

7729. —— **Recital of.** *Pharisee.* ¹¹ Pharisee ..prayed thus with himself, God, I thank thee, that I am not as other men *are*, extortioners, unjust, adulterers, or even as this publican. ¹² I fast twice in the week, I give tithes of all that I possess.—Luke, ch. 18.

7730. —— **Unlawful.** *Jewish.* ² I have spread out my hands all the day unto a rebellious people, which walketh in a way *that was* not good, after their own thoughts ; ³ A people that provoketh me to anger continually to my face ; that sacrificeth in gardens, and burneth incense upon altars of brick.—Isa., ch. 65.

7731. SELF-WILL, Destructive. *Jews.* ³⁷ O Jerusalem, Jerusalem, *thou* that killest the prophets, and stonest them which are sent unto thee, how often would I have gathered thy children together, even as a hen gathereth her chickens under *her* wings, and ye would not ! ³⁸ Behold, your house is left unto you desolate. —Mat., ch. 23.

7732. —— **Loss by.** *Israel.* ⁴⁴ They presumed to go up unto the hill top : nevertheless the ark of the covenant of the Lord, and Moses, departed not out of the camp. ⁴⁵ Then the Amalekites..and the Canaanites which dwelt in that hill..smote them.—Num., ch. 14.

7733. —— **Obstinate.** *Jews.* ¹⁵ All the people that dwelt in the land of Egypt, in Pathros, answered Jeremiah, saying, ¹⁶..we will not hearken unto thee. ¹⁷ But we will certainly do whatsoever thing goeth forth out of our own mouth, to burn incense unto the queen of heaven.—Jer., ch. 44.

7734. —— **Sin of.** *King Saul.* [Saul had disobediently spared animals of Amalek for sacrifice.] ²² Behold, to obey *is* better than sacrifice, *and* to hearken than the fat of rams. ²³ For rebellion *is as* the sin of witchcraft, and stubbornness *is as* iniquity and idolatry.—1 Sam., ch. 15.

7735. —— **Work of.** *Simeon and Levi.* ⁶ O my soul, come not thou into their secret ; unto their assembly, mine honour, be not thou united : for in their anger they slew a man, and in their selfwill they digged down a wall. ⁷ Cursed *be* their anger, for *it was* fierce ; and their wrath, for it was cruel.—Gen., ch. 49.

See WILL and references.

7736. SELFISHNESS, Appeal to. *Jonathan.* ³¹ For as long as the son of Jesse liveth upon the ground, thou shalt not be established, nor thy kingdom. Wherefore now send and fetch him unto me, for he shall surely die. ³² And

Jonathan answered Saul his father, and said unto him, Wherefore shall he be slain? what hath he done?—1 Sam., ch. 20.

7737. —— **Ministerial.** *Eli's Sons.* [16] And if any man said unto him, Let them not fail to burn the fat presently, and then take as much as thy soul desireth ; then he would answer him, *Nay;* but thou shalt give it me now, and if not, I will take it by force. [17] Wherefore the sin of the young men was very great before the Lord : for men abhorred the offering of the Lord.—1 Sam., ch. 2.

7738. —— **Misery of.** *Haman.* [11] Haman told them of the glory of his riches, and the multitude of his children, and..the king had promoted him.. [13] Yet all this availeth me nothing, so long as I see Mordecai the Jew sitting at the king's gate.—Esther, ch. 5.

7739. —— **Overreaching.** *Haman.* [6] Haman thought in his heart, To whom would the king delight to do honour more than to myself?.. [10] Then the king said to Haman.. take the apparel and the horse, as thou hast said, and do even so to Mordecai the Jew..let nothing fail of all that thou hast spoken.—Esther, ch. 6.

7740. —— **Outrageous.** *Parable.* [2] The rich man had exceeding many flocks and herds : [3] But the poor man had nothing, save one little ewe lamb, which he had bought and nourished up : and it grew up..with his children ; [4] And there came a traveller unto the rich man, and he spared..his own flock..but took the poor man's lamb, and dressed it for the man.—2 Sam., ch. 12.

7741. —— **Provision for.** *Feast.* [12] When thou makest a dinner or a supper, call not thy friends, nor thy brethren, neither thy kinsmen, nor thy rich neighbours ; lest they also bid thee again, and a recompense be made thee.—Luke, ch. 14.

7742. —— **rebuked.** *Good Samaritan.* [Wounded by robbers, a priest and Levite passed him by on "the other side."] [33] But a certain Samaritan, as he journeyed, came where he was : and when he saw him, he had compassion on him.—Luke, ch. 10. [See chapter.]

7743. —— **revealed.** *Young Ruler.* [22] And he was sad at that saying, and went away grieved: for he had great possessions. [23] And Jesus.. saith unto his disciples, How hardly shall they that have riches enter into the kingdom of God ! —Mark, ch. 10.

7744. —— **with Wealth.** *"Fool."* [17] What shall I do, because I have no room where to bestow my fruits ? [18] And he said, This will I do : I will pull down my barns, and build greater.. [19] And I will say to my soul, Soul, thou hast much goods laid up for many years ; take thine ease, eat, drink, and be merry.—Luke, ch. 12.

See other illustrations under :

AVARICE.

Falsehood. Ananias with Sapphira..kept back part 592
Oppression. Swallow up the needy..make the poor 593
Victim. Were glad..covenanted to give Judas m. 594

COVETOUSNESS.

Abhorred. Blesseth the covetous whom the L. 1786
Alarmed. By this craft..our wealth..confusion 1787
Apostle. Judas went..to give him money 1788
Aroused. Damsel..masters saw..gains were gone 1789

Absence of. Abram said, I will not take..thread 1790
Church. Who would shut the doors for naught 1791
Cruelty. Felix hoped that money..of Paul 1792
Caution. Inheritance..take heed..beware of 1793
Disobedience. I saw among the spoils..took them 1794
Forbidden. Thou shalt not covet thy neighbour's 1795
Fraud. Gehazi..I will run and take..silver 1796
Folly. Soul, thou hast much goods..eat, drink 1797
Falsehood. Ananias with Sapphira..kept back 1798
Freedom. I have coveted no man's silver..Paul 1799
Inconsiderate. Well watered..Lot chose..plain of 1800
Oppressive. Ye exact usury..sell your brethren 1801
Overcome by. Saul and the people spared the best 1802
Overreaching. Laban..changed my wages ten 1803
Stigmatized. If any man that is called a brother 1804
Shameless. Given to covetousness..not..ashamed 1805
Unhappiness. Naboth had a vineyard..Ahab 1806

Greed. All that the fleshhooks brought up 3713
Success. The feebler were Laban's..stronger J. 994

7745. SENSES impressed, Only. *Sinai.* [18] All the people saw the thunderings, and the lightnings, and the noise of the trumpet, and the mountain smoking : and..they removed, and stood afar off. [19] And they said unto Moses, Speak thou with us, and we will hear : but let not God speak with us, lest we die.—Ex., ch. 20. [Afterward the golden calf.]

7746. —— **impaired.** *Barzillai.* [34] How long have I to live, that I should go up with the king unto Jerusalem ? [35] I am this day fourscore years old : and can I discern between good and evil ? can thy servant taste what I eat or what I drink ? can I hear any more the voice of singing ?—2 Sam., ch. 19.

7747. —— **Description.** [3] When the keepers of the house shall tremble, and the strong men shall bow themselves, and the grinders cease because they are few, and those that look out of the windows be darkened.—Eccl., ch. 12. [See chapter.]

7748. SENSES, Use of. *Five.* [22] Jacob went near unto Isaac his father ; and he felt him, and said, The voice is Jacob's voice, but the hands are the hands of Esau. [27] And he came near, and kissed him : and he smelled the smell of his raiment, and blessed him.—Gen., ch. 27.

Also see :

to the Heart. Thunder..lightnings..Let not G. s. 281
" P. said, It is enough that there be no 284

7749. SENSITIVENESS from Prejudice. *Priests.* [15] When the chief priests and scribes saw the wonderful things that he did, and the children crying in the temple, and saying, Hosanna to the Son of David ; they were sore displeased.—Mat., ch. 21.

See other illustrations under :

CROSSNESS.

Habitual. Nabal was churlish and evil in his 1849
Irritation. Let us alone, that we may serve the 1848
Prejudice. Children crying, Hosanna..sore dis. 1850

IRRITABILITY.

Fretting. Fret not thyself because of evildoers 3416
Peevish. To me they have ascribed but thousands 6039

7750. SENTENCE, An unjust. *Pilate.* [6] Pilate saith..Take ye him, and crucify him : for I find no fault in him.—John, ch. 19.

7751. SENTIMENT divided. *Public.* [At Iconium,] [4] The multitude of the city was divided : and part held with the Jews, and part with the apostles.—ACTS, ch. 14.

7752. —— **Changed.** *At Nazareth.* ²² All.. wondered at the gracious words which proceeded out of his mouth. And they said, Is not this Joseph's son? ²⁸ And all they in the synagogue, when they heard these things, were filled with wrath, ²⁹..and thrust him out of the city, and led him unto the brow of the hill whereon their city was built, that they might cast him down headlong.—LUKE, ch. 4.

See OPINIONS.

7753. SENSUALIST, A rich. *Dives.* ¹⁹ I will say to my soul, Soul, thou hast much goods laid up for many years ; take thine ease, eat, drink, *and* be merry.—LUKE, ch. 12.

See other illustrations under :

APPETITE.

Control. Put a knife to thy throat, if..appetite   479
Dangers. We remember fish, cucumbers, melons   480
Heedless. [Pursuing Philistines,] people were faint 481
Sin. Who shall give us flesh?..be [loathsome]   482
Temptation. [Jesus] fasted 40 days..afterward   483
Unrestrained. At the point to die, what profit   484

ADULTERY.

Accusation. After this manner did Joseph   109
  "   Ishbosheth to Abner, My father's con. 110
Concealment. No eye shall see me   111
Divorce. Whosoever shall put away his wife   112
Destructive. Can a man take fire in his bosom   113
Incipient. Whosoever looketh on a woman   114

ADULTERESS.

Arts. She caught him and kissed him   115
Destructive. Her house inclineth unto death   116
Deception. Lips..drop as an honeycomb   117
Pardoned. Neither do I condemn thee   118

7754. SEPARATION from Christ, No. *Mary.* ³⁸ Martha received him into her house. ³⁹ And she had a sister called Mary, which also sat at Jesus' feet, and heard his word.. ⁴² But one thing is needful ; and Mary hath chosen that good part, which shall not be taken away from her.—LUKE, ch. 10.

7755. —— **declined.** *Ruth.* ¹⁶ Ruth said, Entreat me not to leave thee, *or* to return from following after thee : for whither thou goest, I will go : and where thou lodgest, I will lodge : thy people *shall be* my people, and thy God my God : ¹⁷ Where thou diest, will I die, and there will I be buried.—RUTH, ch. 1.

7756. —— **Desirable.** *Jeremiah.* ² Oh that I had in the wilderness a lodging place of wayfaring men ; that I might leave my people, and go from them ! for they *be* all adulterers, an assembly of treacherous men.—JER., ch. 9.

7757. —— **deferred.** *"End."* ⁴⁷ The kingdom.of heaven is like unto a net, that was cast into the sea, and gathered of every kind : ⁴⁸ Which, when it was full, they drew to shore, and sat down, and gathered the good into vessels, but cast the bad away. ⁴⁹ So shall it be at the end of the world : the angels shall come forth, and sever the wicked from among the just.—MAT., ch. 13.

7758. —— **from Drunkards.** *"Not to eat."* [See No. 7770.]

7759. —— **an Evidence.** *Religious.* ¹⁶ Wherein shall it be known here that I and thy people have found grace in thy sight? *is it* not in that

thou goest with us? So shall we be separated, I and thy people, from all the people that *are* upon the face of the earth.—EX., ch. 32.

7760. —— **effected.** *Shechaniah* ² Said unto Ezra, We have trespassed against our God, and have taken strange wives of the people of the land : yet now there is hope in Israel concerning this thing. ³ Now therefore let us make a covenant with our God to put away all the wives, and such as are born of them.—EZRA, ch. 10.

7761. —— **feared.** *Babel.* ⁴ They said, Go to, let us build us a city, and a tower, whose top *may reach* unto heaven ; and let us make us a name, lest we be scattered abroad upon the face of the whole earth.—GEN., ch. 11.

7762. —— **A glorious.** *Elijah.* ¹¹ As they still went on, and talked..behold, *there appeared* a chariot of fire, and horses of fire, and parted them both asunder : and Elijah went up by a whirlwind into heaven.—2 KINGS, ch. 2.

7763. —— **A godly.** *Jews.* ¹ They read in the book of Moses in the audience of the people..that the Ammonite and the Moabite should not come into the congregation of God for ever.. ³..when they had heard the law.. they separated from Israel all the mixed multitude.—NEH., ch. 13.

7764. —— **impossible.** *Paul.* ³⁸ I am persuaded, that neither death, nor life, nor angels, nor principalities, nor powers, nor things present, nor things to come, ³⁹ Nor height, nor depth, nor any other creature, shall be able to separate us from the love of God, which is in Christ Jesus our Lord.—ROM., ch. 8.

7765. —— **ignored.** *Solomon.* ² Of the nations *concerning* which the Lord said..Ye shall not go in to them, neither shall they come in unto you : *for* surely they will turn away your heart after their gods : Solomon clave unto these in love.—1 KINGS, ch. 11.

7766. —— —— *"Sons of God."* ² The sons of God saw the daughters of men that they *were* fair ; and they took them wives of all which they chose.—GEN., ch. 6. [The flood followed.]

7767. —— **An impressive.** *At Sanai.* ¹⁸ And all the people saw the thunderings, and the lightnings, and the noise of the trumpet, and the mountain smoking..they removed, and stood afar off.—EX., ch. 20.

7768. —— **at the Judgment.** *"Tares."* ²⁹ Nay ; lest while ye gather up the tares, ye root up also the wheat with them. ³⁰ Let both grow together until the harvest: and..I will say to the reapers, Gather ye together first the tares, and bind them in bundles to burn them : but gather the wheat unto my barn.—MAT., ch. 13.

7769. —— **made.** *Egypt.* ²² I will sever in that day the land of Goshen, in which my people dwell, that no swarms of flies shall be there.—EX., ch. 8.

7770. —— **from Misers.** *"Covetous."* ¹¹ I have written unto you not to keep company, if any man that is called a brother be a fornicator, or covetous, or an idolater, or a railer, or a drunkard, or an extortioner ; with such a one no not to eat.—1 COR., ch. 5.

7771. —— **neglected.** *From Egypt.* ⁴ The

mixed multitude that *was* among them fell a lusting : and the children of Israel also wept again, and said, Who shall give us flesh to eat ? [5] We remember the fish, which we did eat in Egypt freely ; the cucumbers, and the melons, and the leeks, and the onions, and the garlic. —NUM., ch. 11.

7772. —— —— *Jews.* [1] *Even* of the Canaanites, the Hittites, the Perizzites, the Jebusites, the Ammonites, the Moabites, the Egyptians, and the Amorites. [2] For they have taken of their daughters for themselves, and for their sons : so that the holy seed have mingled themselves with the people of *those* lands.—EZRA, ch. 9.

7773. —— —— *" Thorns."* [55] If ye will not drive out the inhabitants of the land from before you ; then..those which ye let remain of them *shall be* pricks in your eyes, and thorns in your sides, and shall vex you in the land wherein ye dwell. [56] Moreover..I shall do unto you, as I thought to do unto them.—NUM., ch. 33.

7774. —— *Canaanites* [35] Were mingled among the heathen, and learned their works. [36] And they served their idols : which were a snare unto them. [37] Yea, they sacrificed their sons and their daughters unto devils.—Ps. 106.

7775. —— **Overscrupulous.** *P h a r i s e e s.* [2] The Pharisees and scribes murmured, saying, This man receiveth sinners, and eateth with them.—LUKE, ch. 15.

7776. —— **Reverential.** *At Sinai.* [11] The third day the Lord will come down in the sight of all the people.. [12] And thou shalt set bounds unto the people round about, saying, Take heed to yourselves, *that ye* go *not* up into the mount ..whosoever toucheth the mount shall be surely put to death.—Ex., ch. 19.

7777. —— **required.** *P r e j u d i c e.* [26] Moses said, It is not meet so to do ; for we shall sacrifice the abomination of the Egyptians to the Lord our God..before their eyes, and will they not stone us ?—Ex., ch. 8.

7778. —— **Reason of.** *Moses said,* [3] Neither shalt thou make marriages with them ; thy daughter thou shalt not give unto his son, nor his daughter shalt thou take unto thy son. [4] For they will turn away thy son from following me, that they may serve other gods.—DEUT., ch. 7.

7779. —— **A sorrowful.** *N a o m i.* [14] They lifted up their voice, and wept again : and Orpah kissed her mother in law ; but Ruth clave unto her.—RUTH, ch. 1.

7780. —— *David.* [41] David..fell on his face to the ground, and bowed himself three times : and they kissed one another, and wept one with another, until David exceeded. [42] And Jonathan said to David, Go in peace.—1 SAM., ch. 20.

7781. —— **Spiritual.** *Fan.* [17] Whose fan *is* in his hand, and he will thoroughly purge his floor, and will gather the wheat into his garner ; but the chaff he will burn with fire unquenchable.—LUKE, ch. 3.

7782. —— **Significant.** *Clean and Unclean.* [See Lev., ch. 11.]

7783. —— **of Sinners.** *Beatitude.* [22] Blessed are ye, when men shall hate you, and when they shall separate you *from their company,* and shall reproach *you,* and cast out your name as evil, for the Son of man's sake. [23] Rejoice ye in that day, and leap for joy : for, behold, your reward is great in heaven.—LUKE, ch. 6.

7784. —— **by Sin.** *From God.* [1] The Lord's hand is not shortened, that it cannot save ; neither his ear heavy, that it cannot hear : [2] But your iniquities have separated between you and your God, and your sins have hid *his* face from you, that he will not hear.—ISA., ch. 59.

7785. —— **taught.** *Law.* [19] Thou shalt not let thy cattle gender with a diverse kind : thou shalt not sow thy field with mingled seed : neither shall a garment mingled with linen and woollen come upon thee.—LEV., ch. 19.

7786. —— *Law.* [10] Thou shalt not plough with an ox and an ass together. [11] Thou shalt not wear a garment of divers sorts, *as* of woollen and linen together.—DEUT., ch. 22.

7787. —— **unavoidable.** *Corinthians.* [20] I would not that ye should have fellowship with devils. [21] Ye cannot drink the cup of the Lord, and the cup of devils : ye cannot be partakers of the Lord's table, and of the table of devils. —1 COR., ch. 10.

7788. —— **from the World.** *The Angel said,* [2] Ye shall make no league with the inhabitants of this land ; ye shall throw down their altars : but ye have not obeyed my voice ; why have ye done this ?—JUDGES, ch. 2.

7789. —— —— *" Sheep"—" Goats."* [31] Then shall he sit upon the throne of his glory : [32] And before him shall be gathered all nations : and he shall separate them..as a shepherd divideth *his* sheep from the goats.—MAT., ch. 25.

See other illustrations under :

ABANDONMENT.

Anger. Let me alone..wrath may wax hot	1
Blasphemers. Hymeneus and Alex..learn not to b.	2
Christ. Left house, or brethren..lands for my sake	3
Destruction. I will destroy from off the..earth	4
Just. Go cry unto the gods which ye have chosen	6
Merited. They hated knowledge..despised reproof	8
Sanctuary. Lord abhorred his sanctuary	9
Surprising. The ark of God was taken	10
Transgressors. 3000 men fled before the men of Ai	11
Unconscious. Samson wist not that the L. was d.	13
Work. Mark..went not with them to the work	12

DEPARTURE.

Stolen. Jacob stole away unawares to Laban	2182
Unexpected. Camp of Syria..was no man there	2183

DESERTION.

Ignorance. Drinketh my blood..disciples went b.	2207
Painful. At my first answer..all men forsook me	2208
Prevented. Soldiers cut the ropes..boat..let her	2209

FAREWELL.

Beatific. While he blessed them he was parted	3040
Glorious. Horses of fire..Elijah went up..into	3041
Loving. Naomi said, Turn again, my daughters	3042
Perilous. Let me first bid them farewell..at	3043
Sorrowful. All wept sore and fell on Paul's neck	3044

FORSAKING.

All. Flee into the mountains..not take anything	3378
Business. Ships to land, they forsook all and f.	3379
Duty. Jonah rose up to flee..going to Tarshish	3380

God. Amaziah..set them up to be his gods　3381
" But we will have a king over us..like all　3382
" Have despised the L...why came we forth　3383
" We have forsaken our God and followed　3384
" Forsaken..living waters and hewed b.　3385
" Ahaz sacrificed unto the gods..which s.　3386
Office. Levi sitting at the receipt of custom..left　3388

FORSAKEN.

Friends. All the disciples forsook him and fled　3389
Of God. [David] I cry in the daytime..hearest　3390
" [Saul] Bring me up Samuel..L. is　3391
" [Jesus] My God, my God, why hast t.　3392
" [Apparently] If the L. be with us, why　3393

FUGITIVE.

Criminal. Jacob..flee thou to Laban, my b.　3487
Infant. Take the young child..flee into Egypt　3488
Noble. Pharaoh sought to slay Moses..fled　3489
Protected. Not deliver unto his master the　3490
Return. [Onesimus] departed for a season　3491

SECESSION.

Political. If this city be builded..no portion on　7642
" I will chastise you with scorpions　7643

Misconstrued. Jeremiah went to separate [arrested] 79

7790. SERMON, A long. *Paul.* [7] Paul preached unto them, ready to depart on the morrow; and continued his speech until midnight.—Acts, ch. 20.

7791. —— to Women. *At Philippi.* [13] On the sabbath we went out of the city by a river side, where prayer was wont to be made; and we sat down, and spake unto the women which resorted *thither.*—Acts, ch. 16.

See MINISTRY.

7792. SERPENT, An evil. *Satan.* [2] The woman said unto the serpent, We may eat of the fruit of the trees of the garden: [3] But of the fruit of the tree which *is* in the midst of the garden.. [4] And the serpent said..Ye shall not surely die.—Gen., ch. 3.

7793. —— A healing. *Brass.* [9] Moses made a serpent of brass, and put it upon a pole; and ..if a serpent had bitten any man, when he beheld the serpent of brass, he lived.—Num., ch. 21.

7794. —— A harmless. *Paul.* [5] And he shook off the beast into the fire, and felt no harm. [6] Howbeit they looked when he should have swollen, or fallen down dead suddenly: but after they..saw no harm come to him, they changed their minds, and said that he was a god. —Acts, ch. 28.

7795. —— A Rod. *Aaron's.* [10] Aaron cast down his rod before Pharaoh, and before his servants, and it became a serpent.—Ex., ch. 7.

7796. —— The stinging. *Cup.* [31] Look not thou upon the wine when it is red, when it giveth his colour in the cup, *when* it moveth itself aright. [32] At the last it biteth like a serpent, and stingeth like an adder.—Prov., ch. 23.

7797. SERPENTS, Plague of. *Wilderness.* [5] *There is* no bread, neither *is there any* water; and our soul loatheth this light bread. [6] And the Lord sent fiery serpents among the people, and they bit the people; and much people of Israel died.—Num., ch. 21.

7798. SERVANT, Affection for a. *Centurion's.* [2] A certain centurion's servant, who was dear unto him, was sick, and ready to die. [3] And

when he heard of Jesus, he sent unto him the elders of the Jews, beseeching him that he would come and heal his servant.—Luke, ch. 7.

7799. —— The Christian. *Meek.* [20] For what glory *is it,* if, when ye be buffeted for your faults, ye shall take it patiently? but if, when ye do well, and suffer *for it,* ye take it patiently, this *is* acceptable with God.—1 Peter, ch. 2.

7800. —— A deceitful. *Gehazi.* [20] The servant of Elisha..said, Behold, my master hath spared Naaman this Syrian, in not receiving at his hands that which he brought: but, *as* the Lord liveth, I will run after him, and take somewhat of him.—2 Kings, ch. 5.

7801. —— The Lord's. *Moses.* [1] After the death of Moses, the servant of the Lord..the Lord spake unto Joshua the son of Nun, Moses' minister.—Josh., ch. 1.

7802. —— of Men. *Paul.* [19] Though I be free from all *men,* yet have I made myself servant unto all, that I might gain the more. [20] And unto the Jews I became as a Jew, that I might gain the Jews; to them that are under the law, as under the law, that I might gain them.—1 Cor., ch. 9.

7803. —— Only a. *Shepherd.* [12] Shepherd, whose own the sheep are not, seeth the wolf coming, and leaveth the sheep, and fleeth; and the wolf catcheth them.. [13] The hireling fleeth, because he is a hireling, and careth not for the sheep.—John, ch. 10.

7804. SERVANTS, Oppression of. *Law.* [14] Thou shalt not oppress a hired servant *that is* poor and needy, *whether he be* of thy brethren, or of thy strangers.. [15] At his day thou shalt give *him* his hire, neither shall the sun go down upon it; for he *is* poor, and setteth his heart upon it: lest he cry against thee unto the Lord. —Deut., ch. 24.

7805. —— Unprofitable. *Duty only.* [8] Afterward thou shalt eat and drink? [9] Doth he thank that servant because he did the things that were commanded him? I trow not. [10] So likewise ye, when ye shall have done all those things which are commanded you, say, We are unprofitable servants: we have done that which was our duty to do.—Luke, ch. 17.

7806. SERVICE from all. *Christian.* [26] He that is greatest among you, et him be as the younger; and he that is chief, ε, he that doth serve. [27] For whether *is* greater, he that sitteth at meat, or he that serveth? *is* not he that sitteth at meat? but I am among you as he that serveth.—Luke, ch. 22.

7807. —— Consecrated. *Priests.* [23] Moses took of the blood of it, and put *it* upon the tip of Aaron's right ear, and upon the thumb of his right hand, and upon the great toe of his right foot.—Lev., ch. 8. [Also his sons.]

7808. —— Distinction by. *David's.* [57] As David returned from the slaughter of the Philistine, Abner took him, and brought him before Saul with the head of the Philistine in his hand.—1 Sam., ch. 17.

7809. —— dishonoured. *God's.* [8] If ye offer the blind for sacrifice, *is it* not evil? and if ye offer the lame and sick, *is it* not evil? offer it now unto thy governor; will he be pleased with thee, or accept thy person? saith the Lord of hosts.—Mal., ch. 1.

7810. SERVICES, Diverse. *David said,* ²⁴ As his part *is* that goeth down to the battle, so *shall* his part *be* that tarrieth by the stuff : they shall part alike.—1 SAM., ch. 30.

7811. SERVICE, Earnestness in. *Tabernacle Builders.* ²² They came, both men and women, as many as were willing-hearted, *and* brought bracelets, and ear-rings, and rings, and tablets, all jewels of gold : and every man that offered, *offered* an offering of gold unto the Lord.—Ex., ch. 35.

7812. —— Excused from. *Mary.* ⁴⁰ Lord, dost thou not care that my sister hath left me to serve alone ? bid her therefore that she help me.. ⁴².. Mary hath chosen that good part, which shall not be taken away from her.—LUKE, ch. 10.

7813. —— Hardships of. *Laban's.* ³⁹ That which was torn *of beasts* I brought not unto thee ; I bare the loss of it ; of my hand didst thou require it, *whether* stolen by day, or stolen by night. ⁴⁰.. in the day the drought consumed me, and the frost by night, and my sleep departed from mine eyes. ⁴¹ Thus have I been twenty years.—GEN., ch. 31.

7814. —— Half-hearted. *Irksome.* ¹³ Ye said also, Behold, what a weariness *is it!* and ye have snuffed at it, saith the Lord of hosts ; and ye brought *that which was* torn, and the lame, and the sick ; thus ye brought an offering : should I accept this of your hand ?—MAL., ch. 1.

7815. —— neglected. *God's.* ⁸ Will a man rob God?..robbed me. But ye say, Wherein have we robbed thee ? In tithes and offerings. ⁹ Ye *are* cursed with a curse : for ye have robbed me, *even* this whole nation. ¹⁰ Bring ye all the tithes into the storehouse, that there may be meat in mine house, and prove me now herewith. —MAL., ch. 3.

7816. —— An outward. *Naaman.* ¹⁸ When my master goeth into the house of Rimmon to worship there, and he leaneth on my hand, and I bow myself in the house of Rimmon..the Lord pardon thy servant in this thing. ¹⁹ And he said unto him, Go in peace.—2 KINGS, ch. 5.

7817. —— One or Other. *Moses said,* ⁴⁷ Because thou servedst not the Lord thy God with joyfulness..for the abundance of all *things;* ⁴⁸ Therefore shalt thou serve thine enemies..in hunger, and in thirst, and in nakedness, and in want of all *things:* and he shall put a yoke of iron upon thy neck, until he have destroyed thee.—DEUT., ch. 28.

7818. —— Pay for. *God's.* ¹⁰ Who *is there* even among you that would shut the doors *for nought?* neither do ye kindle *fire* on mine altar for nought. I have no pleasure in you, saith the Lord of hosts, neither will I accept an offering at your hand.—MAL., ch. 1.

7819. —— rewarded. *" Cup."* ⁴¹ Whosoever shall give you a cup of water to drink in my name, because ye belong to Christ.. he shall not lose his reward.—MARK, ch. 9.

See other illustrations under :

HELP.

Appeal. Come over into Macedonia and help	3925
" Help my Lord, O king..hid her son	3926
Angelic. [Gethsemane] An angel..from heaven	3927
Divine. I will be with thy mouth and teach	3928
" Let us flee from..Israel, the L. fighteth	3929
" Wherewith shall I save Israel..Gideon	3930

Divine. King of Syria..more with us..him	3931
" Samuel..stone and called it Ebenezer	3938
Fraternal. Ye shall pass over before your b.	3927
Hurtful. Ahaz took a portion..he helped him not	3932
Injurious. Uzziah, when he was strong..heart	3933
Needed. If there be no man to save us..will	3934
Provided. L. saw..saved them by..Jeroboam	3939
Reserved. Father..will give me twelve legions of	3935
Sought. [Canaanite woman] Send her away..L.	3936
Wanted. I have no man..to put me in	3940
Woman. I will make him a help meet	3941

HELPERS.

Builders. Whosoever remaineth..help him with	3942
Dependence. Aaron and Hur stayed up his hands	3943

LABOUR.

Advantage. Sleep of a labouring man is sweet..eat	4864
Curse. Thorns and thistles..sweat of thy face	4865
Commanded. Six days shalt thou labour and do	4866
Congenial. Put him into the garden..keep it,	4867
Co-operative. One soweth, another reapeth	4868
Degradation. In the sweat of thy face	4869
Increase. No straw be given..tale of bricks	4870
Menial. Hewers of wood and drawers of water	4871
Motive. That..we may be accepted of him	4872

WAGES.

Back. Borrow..jewels of silver..gold and raiment	9255
Changed. Your father [Laban] changed my wages	9256
Daily. The wages..shall not abide with thee	9257
" At his day thou shalt give him his hire	9258
Others. These last have wrought but one hour..us	9259
Unimportant. Take this child..will give thee wages	9260
Christ's. Give you a cup of water because	725
" Unto one of the least..unto me	713
Hireling. He that is a hireling..leaveth the sheep	3993
Independence. These hands..my necessities	537
Overpaid. Made them equal unto us..born..heat	267

7820. SERVITUDE, Degraded by. *At Red Sea.* ¹² *Is* not this the word that we did tell thee in Egypt, saying, Let us alone, that we may serve the Egyptians ? For *it had been* better for us to serve the Egyptians, than that we should die in the wilderness.—Ex., ch. 14.

7821. —— Rigorous. *Egyptian.* ¹⁴ They made their lives bitter with hard bondage, in mortar, and in brick, and in all manner of service in the field : all their service.. *was* with rigour.—Ex., ch. 2.

See BONDAGE and references.

7822. SEXES, Distinction of. *Dress.* ⁵ The woman shall not wear that which pertaineth unto a man, neither shall a man put on a woman's garment : for all that do so *are* abomination unto the Lord.—DEUT., ch. 22.

7823. —— unlike. *Hair.* ¹⁴ Doth not even nature itself teach you, that, if a man have long hair, it is a shame unto him ? ¹⁵ But if a woman have long hair, it is a glory to her : for *her* hair is given her for a covering.—1 COR., ch. 11.

7824. SEVERITY, Merciless. *Creditor.* ²⁸ The same servant went out, and found one of his fellow servants, which owed him a hundred pence : and he laid hands on him, and took *him* by the throat, saying, Pay me that thou owest. —MAT., ch. 18.

See other illustrations under :

CRUELTY.

Ambition. [Athaliah] saw her son was dead	1857
Brutal. 10,000 men..did Judah..cast from the r.	1858

Failure. Egyptians set taskmakers to afflict t.   1859
Insulting. Herod's soldiers smote him..spit on h.   1860
Pride. Mordecai bowed not..Haman sought to   1861
Reward. He that is cruel troubleth his own flesh   1862
Savage. Slew..the sons of Hezekiah before his e.   1863
War. [Joab] put them under saws..harrows of i.   1864

TORTURE.

Hell. I am tormented in this flame   8852
Prisoners. Elders of the city and thorns..briers   8853
   "   Put them under saws..harrows   8854
Jesus. Crown of thorns..spit upon him..smote   8855

VENGEANCE.

Averted. Let not my lord regard..Nabal   9169
   "   Kept me..from coming to shed blood   9170
Blood. Cain said..every one that findeth me..stay   9171
Call. Stoned [Zachariah]..in house of the L.   9172
Divine. To me belongeth vengeance and r.   9173
   "   If I whet my glittering sword   9174
Declined. Not a man be put to death [Saul]   9175
Fear. Joseph will peradventure hate us   9176
with God. My G., think thou upon Tobiah   9177
Inappropriate. I forgave thee..shouldest thou not   9178
Mistaken. Command fire..to consume them   9179
Monstrous. Haman thought scorn..Mordecai   9180
Prohibited. If ye from your hearts forgive not   9182
for Vengeance. David commanded..slew them   9184
Undesired. Behold the head of Ish-bosheth   9183

7825. SHADOW reversed. *Dial.* 8 Hezekiah said unto Isaiah, What *shall be* the sign that the Lord will heal me, and that I shall go up into the house of the Lord the third day? 11 And Isaiah the prophet cried unto the Lord : and he brought the shadow ten degrees backward, by which it had gone down in the dial of Ahaz.—2 KINGS, ch. 20.

7826. SHAME from Abuse. *Messengers.* 4 The men were greatly ashamed : and the king said, Tarry at Jericho until your beards be grown, and *then* return.—2 SAM., ch. 10.

7827. —— A Criminal's. *Idolaters.* 26 As the thief is ashamed when he is found, so is the house of Israel ashamed ; they, their kings, their princes, and their priests, and their proph-ets. 27 Saying to a stock, Thou *art* my father.—JER., ch. 2.

7828. —— impossible. *Obdurate.* 10 For ev-ery one from the least even unto the greatest is given to covetousness, from the prophet even unto the priest every one dealeth falsely. 12 Were they ashamed when they had committed abomination ? nay, they were not at all ashamed, neither could they blush.—JER., ch. 8.

7829. —— Rejoicing in. *Apostles.* 41 They departed from the presence of the council, re-joicing that they were counted worthy to suffer shame for his name.—ACTS, ch. 5.

7830. —— for Shame. *Judgment.* 20 Who-soever shall be ashamed of me, and of my words, of him shall the Son of man be ashamed, when he shall come in his own glory, and *in his* Father's, and of the holy angels.—LUKE, ch. 9.

7831. —— Sin causes. *In Eden.* 7 The eyes of them both were opened, and they knew that they *were* naked ; and they sewed fig leaves to-gether, and made themselves aprons. — GEN., ch. 3.

Also see :

Odium. Ye have made..to be abhorred before P.   5833
See DISGRACE and references.

7832. SHEPHERD, The first. *Abel.* 2 Abel was a keeper of sheep, but Cain was a tiller of the ground.—GEN., ch. 4.

7833. —— A faithful. *Jacob.* 39 That which was torn *of beasts*..I bare the loss of it ; of my hand didst thou require it, *whether* stolen by day, or stolen by night. 40 *Thus* I was ; in the day the drought consumed me, and the frost by night ; and my sleep departed from mine eyes.—GEN., ch. 31.

7834. —— The good. *Jesus.* 11 I am the good shepherd : the good shepherd giveth his life for the sheep.—JOHN, ch. 10.

7835. —— A great. *King Mesha.* 4 Mesha king of Moab was a sheepmaster, and rendered unto the king of Israel a hundred thousand lambs, and a hundred thousand rams, with the wool.—2 KINGS, ch. 3.

7836. SHEPHERDS, Unfaithful. *Priests.* 2 Woe be to the shepherds of Israel that do feed them-selves ! should not the shepherds feed the flocks ? 3 Ye eat the fat, and ye clothe you with the wool, and ye kill them that are fed : *but* ye feed not the flock.—EZEK., ch. 34.

Also see :

Needed. Jesus was moved..sheep having no s.   6016
See MINISTERS and MINISTRY.

7837. SHIPS, Wealth by. *Solomon's.* 26 King Solomon made a navy of ships in Ezion-geber.. on the shore of the Red sea.. 28 And they came to Ophir, and fetched from thence gold, four hundred and twenty talents, and brought *it* to king Solomon.—1 KINGS, ch. 9.

7838. —— Builder, The first. *Noah.* 15 The length of the ark *shall be* three hundred cubits, the breadth of it fifty cubits, and the height of it thirty cubits.—GEN., ch. 6.

7839. SHIPWRECK, Perils from. *Paul.* 25 Thrice was I beaten with rods, once was I stoned, thrice I suffered shipwreck.—2 COR., ch. 11.

7840. —— Saved in. *Paul.* 43 The centuri-on, willing to save Paul, kept them from *their* purpose ; and commanded that they which could swim should cast *themselves* first *into the* sea, and get to land : 44 And the rest, some on boards, and some on *broken pieces* of the ship.. they escaped all safe to land.—ACTS, ch. 27.

See MARINERS.

7841. SHOUTING in Heaven. *"Alleluia !"* 6 I heard as it were the voice of a great multi-tude, and as the voice of many waters, and as the voice of mighty thunderings, saying, Alle-luia : for the Lord God omnipotent reigneth.—REV., ch. 19.

7842. —— Idolatrous. *Golden Calf.* 17 When Joshua heard the noise of the people as they shouted, he said unto Moses, There is a noise of war in the camp.—EX., ch. 32.

7843. —— Religious. *Dedication.* 24 There came a fire out from before the Lord, and con-sumed upon the altar the burnt offering and the fat : *which* when all the people saw, they shouted, and fell on their faces.—LEV., ch. 9.

7844. —— —— Bringing the Ark. 14 David danced before the Lord with all *his* might.. 15 So David and all the house of Israel brought up the ark of the Lord with shouting, and with the sound of the trumpet.—2 SAM., ch. 6.

7845. —— **Stimulated by.** *Samson.* [14] The Philistines shouted against him : and the Spirit of the Lord came mightily upon him, and the cords that *were* upon his arms became as flax that was burnt with fire, and his bands loosed from off his hands.—JUDGES, ch. 15. [He slew a thousand men.]

7846. —— **of Triumph.** *Builders.* [11] They sang together by course in praising and giving thanks unto the Lord ; because *he is* good, for his mercy *endureth* for ever toward Israel. And all the people shouted with a great shout, when they praised the Lord, because the foundation of the house of the Lord was laid.—EZRA, ch. 3.

7847. —— **Vain.** *Ark lost.* [5] When the ark of the covenant of the Lord came into the camp, all Israel shouted with a great shout, so that the earth rang again.—1 SAM., ch. 4.

7848. —— **for Victory.** *At Jericho.* [20] The people shouted when *the priests* blew with the trumpets..when the people heard the sound of the trumpet, and the people shouted with a great shout..the wall fell down flat.—JOSH., ch. 6.

7849. —— **and Weeping.** *Builders.* [12] Ancient men, that had seen the first house, when the foundation of this house was laid before their eyes, wept with a loud voice ; and many shouted aloud for joy : [13] So that the people could not discern the noise of the shout of joy from the noise of the weeping of the people ; for the people shouted with a loud shout, and the noise was heard afar off.—EZRA, ch. 3.

Also see :

Relief. I. shouted with a great shout..ark of G. 10

See REJOICING and references.

7850. SICK, Anxiety for the. *Lazarus.* [3] His sisters sent unto him, saying, Lord, behold, he whom thou lovest is sick.—JOHN, ch. 11.

7851. —— —— *Nobleman.* [47] When he heard that Jesus was come out of Judea into Galilee, he went unto him, and besought him that he would come down, and heal his son : for he was at the point of death.—JOHN, ch. 4.

7852. SICKNESS, Distressing. *Mortal.* [14] Elisha was fallen sick of his sickness whereof he died. And Joash the king of Israel came down unto him, and wept over his face, and said, O my father, my father ! the chariot of Israel, and the horsemen thereof.—2 KINGS, ch. 13.

7853. —— **Despondency in.** *Hezekiah.* [12] Mine age is departed, and is removed from me as a shepherd's tent : I have cut off like a weaver my life : he will cut me off with pining sickness : from day *even* to night wilt thou make an end of me.—ISA., ch. 38.

7854. —— **Jesus in.** *Sought.* [47] When he heard that Jesus was come out of Judea into Galilee, he went unto him, and besought him that he would come down, and heal his son : for he was at the point of death.. [49] The nobleman saith unto him, Sir, come down ere my child die.—JOHN, ch. 4.

7855. —— **misimproved.** *Hezekiah.* [24] Hezekiah was sick to the death, and prayed unto the Lord : and he..gave him a sign. [25] But Hezekiah rendered not again according to the benefit *done* unto him ; for his heart was lifted up.—2 CHRON., ch. 32.

7856. —— **from Overwork.** *Epaphroditus.* [30] For the work of Christ he was nigh unto death, not regarding his life, to supply your lack of service toward me.—PHIL., ch. 2.

7857. —— **Punished by.** *Disobedient.* [58] If thou wilt not observe to do all..that are written in this book, that thou mayest fear this glorious and fearful name, THE LORD THY GOD ; [59] Then the Lord will make thy plagues wonderful..even great plagues, and of long continuance, and sore sicknesses, and of long continuance. —DEUT., ch. 28.

7858. —— **Pretended.** *David.* [12] Michal let David down through a window : and he went, and fled, and escaped.. [14] And when Saul sent messengers to take David, she said, He *is* sick. —1 SAM., ch. 19.

7859. —— **Reflections in.** *Hezekiah.* [10] I said in the cutting off of my days, I shall go to the gates of the grave : I am deprived of the residue of my years. [11] I said, I shall not see the Lord, *even* the Lord, in the land of the living : I shall behold man no more with the inhabitants of the world.—ISA., ch. 38.

7860. —— **relieved.** *By Jesus.* [28] Simon's wife's mother was taken with a great fever ; and they besought him for her. [39] And he stood over her, and rebuked the fever : and it left her : and immediately she arose and ministered unto them.—LUKE, ch. 4.

7861. —— **Restoration from.** *Ben-hadad.* [7] Elisha came to Damascus ; and Ben-hadad the king of Syria was sick.. [8] And the king said unto Hazael, Take a present in thine hand, and go, meet the man of God, and inquire of the Lord by him, saying, Shall I recover of this disease ?—2 KINGS, ch. 8.

7862. —— **Wasting.** *Wrinkles.* [8] Thou hast filled me with wrinkles, *which* is a witness *against me :* and my leanness rising up in me beareth witness to my face.—JOB, ch. 16.

See other illustrations under :

CURE.

All Persons. Laid his hands on every one and heal 1867
All Diseases. Stepped in, was made whole of what 1868
Faith. When..beheld the serpent of brass he lived 1869
Gratitude. She arose and ministered unto them 1870
Means. Made clay of the spittle..anointed eyes 1871
Progressive. See men as trees walking..clearly 1872
Threefold. Possessed with a devil, blind and dumb 1873
Wonderful. Stretch forth thy hand..as the other 1874

DISEASE.

Chronic. Certain man..had an infirmity 38 years 2773
Painful. Satan..smote Job with sore boils 2774

PESTILENCE.

Choice. Shall three days' pestilence in thy land ? 6111
Punishment. L. sent a pestilence..70,000 men 6112

REMEDY.

Improbable. Anointed the eyes of the blind man 7058
Look. As Moses lifted up the serpent..S. of man 7059

Abandoned in. My master left me..fell sick 3025
Anxiety. Lazarus' sister sent unto Jesus, saying 7850
Boils. Boils breaking forth with blains 6190
Effort. Noblemen went..besought..heal his son 7851
Feared. He will cut himself off with pining sickness 2241
Pestilence. Died in the plague, 14,700 9193
Relapse. Last state is worse than the first 6989
Ulcers. Lazarus was laid at his gate..sores 6181

See RECOVERY.

7863. SIDE, Which. *Angel of God.* [13] When Joshua was by Jericho..he lifted up his eyes and looked, and, behold, there stood a man over against him with his sword drawn in his hand : and Joshua went unto him, and said unto him, *Art* thou for us, or for our adversaries ?—Josh., ch. 5.

7864. —— —— *Calf made.* [25] When Moses saw that the people *were* naked.. [26] Then Moses stood in the gate of the camp, and said, Who *is* on the Lord's side ? *let him come* unto me.—Ex., ch. 32.

See DIVISIONS and references.

7865. SIGHT, Walking by. *Israelites.* [3] Would to God we had died by the hand of the Lord in the land of Egypt, when we sat by the fleshpots, *and* when we did eat bread to the full ; for ye have brought us forth into this wilderness, to kill this whole assembly with hunger.—Ex., ch. 16.

7866. SIGN, A beautiful. *Rainbow.* [13] I do set my bow in the cloud, and it shall be for a token of a covenant between me and the earth. —Gen., ch. 9.

7867. —— A cheering. *Star.* [1] There came wise men from the east to Jerusalem, [2] Saying, Where is he that is born King of the Jews? for we have seen his star in the east, and are come to worship him.—Mat., ch. 2.

7868. —— Dumbness a. *Zacharias.* [20] Thou shalt be dumb, and not able to speak, until the day that these things shall be performed, because thou believest not my words, which shall be fulfilled in their season.—Luke, ch. 1.

7869. —— Encouraging. *Mount Carmel.* [44] At the seventh time..he said, Behold, there ariseth a little cloud out of the sea, like a man's hand. And he said, Go up, say unto Ahab, Prepare *thy chariot,* and get thee down, that the rain stop thee not.—1 Kings, ch. 18.

7870. —— Gifts for a. *"Tongues."* [22] Tongues are for a sign, not to them that believe, but to them that believe not : but prophesying *serveth* not for them that believe not, but for them which believe.—1 Cor., ch. 14.

7871. —— Influential. *Jonathan.* [9] If they say thus unto us, Tarry until we come to you ; then we will stand still in our place, and will not go up unto them. [10] But if they say thus, Come up unto us ; then we will go up : for the Lord hath delivered them into our hand ; and this *shall be* a sign unto us.—1 Sam., ch. 14.

7872. —— The Lord's. *Shadow—Backward.* [See No. 7825.]

7873. —— A protecting. *"Blood."* [13] The blood shall be to you for a token upon the houses where ye *are:* and when I see the blood, I will pass over you..when I smite the land of Egypt. —Ex., ch. 12.

7874. —— of Purity. *Blue Ribband.* [38] Their generations, and that they put upon the fringe of the borders a ribband of blue : [39]..for a fringe, that ye may look upon it, and.. [40] remember, and do all my commandments, and be holy unto your God.—Num., ch. 15.

7875. —— A preserved. *Aaron's Rod.* [10] The Lord said unto Moses, Bring Aaron's rod again before the testimony, to be kept for a token against the rebels.—Num., ch. 17.

7876. —— of Summer, A. *Verdure.* [32] Learn a parable of the fig tree ; When his branch is yet tender, and putteth forth leaves, ye know that summer *is* nigh.—Mat., ch. 24.

7877. —— A Traitor's. *Judas.* [48] He that betrayed him gave them a sign, saying, Whomsoever I shall kiss, the same is he : hold him fast.—Mat., ch. 26.

7878. SIGNS, Celestial. *Planets.* [14] God said, Let there be lights in the firmament of the heaven to divide the day from the night ; and let them be for signs, and for seasons, and for days, and years : [15] And let them be for lights in the firmament.—Gen., ch. 1.

7879. —— Converted by. *Simon Magus.* [13] Simon himself believed also : and when he was baptized, he continued with Philip, and wondered, beholding the miracles and signs which were done.—Acts, ch. 8.

7880. —— desired. *Jews.* [38] Master, we would see a sign from thee. [39] But he answered..An evil and adulterous generation seeketh after a sign ; and there shall no sign be given to it, but the sign of the prophet Jonas.—Mat., ch. 12.

7881. —— Evidence by. *Moses' Rod.* [3] He cast it on the ground and it became a serpent : and Moses fled from before it.. [6] And he put his hand into his bosom : and when he took it out, behold, his hand *was* leprous as snow. [7] And he said, Put thine hand into thy bosom again. And he put his hand into his bosom again ; and plucked it out..and, behold, it was turned again as his *other* flesh.—Ex., ch. 4.

7882. —— of Grief. *For Joseph.* [34] Jacob rent his clothes, and put sackcloth upon his loins, and mourned for his son many days.— Gen., ch. 37.

7883. —— Evidence in. *Nobleman's.* [46] There was a certain nobleman, whose son was sick at Capernaum. [48] Then said Jesus unto him, Except ye see signs and wonders, ye will not believe.—John, ch. 4.

7884. —— Intrigue by. *Wicked.* [12] A naughty person, a wicked man, walketh with a froward mouth. [13] He winketh with his eyes, he speaketh with his feet, he teacheth with his fingers. —Prov., ch. 6.

7885. —— overlooked. *Jews.* [54] When ye see a cloud rise out of the west, straightway ye say, There cometh a shower ; and so it is. [55] And when *ye see* the south wind blow, ye say, There will be heat ; and it cometh to pass. [56] *Ye* hypocrites, ye can discern the face of the sky and of the earth ; but how is it that ye do not discern this time ?—Luke, ch. 12.

7886. —— required. *By Jews.* [21] It pleased God by the foolishness of preaching to save them that believe. [22] For the Jews require a sign, and the Greeks seek after wisdom.—1 Cor., ch. 1.

7887. —— Test. *Gideon's Fleece.* [38] He rose up early on the morrow, and thrust the fleece together, and wringed the dew out of the fleece, a bowl full of water. [39] And Gideon said unto God, Let not thine anger be hot against me, and I will speak but this once..let it now be dry only upon the fleece, and upon all the ground let there be dew.—Judges, ch. 6.

7888. —— **Weather.** *Jesus said,* [2] When it is evening, ye say, *It will be* fair weather : for the sky is red. [3] And in the morning, *It will be* foul weather to day : for the sky is red and lowering. O *ye* hypocrites, ye can discern the face of the sky ; but can ye not *discern* the signs of the times ?—Mat., ch. 16.

Also see :

Dishonour. Judas gave them a sign..kiss   169
Signal. At the sound of the cornet..image   2092
   " People shouted when..blew the trumpets 7848
   See EVIDENCE and references.

7889. SIGNAL to Advance. *"A Going."* [24] When thou hearest the sound of a going in the tops of the mulberry trees..then thou shalt bestir thyself : for then shall the Lord go out before thee, to smite the host of the Philistines.— 2 Sam., ch. 5.

7890. —— **Conspirator's.** *Kiss.* [49] And forthwith he came to Jesus, and said, Hail, Master ; and kissed him. [50] And Jesus said unto him, Friend, wherefore art thou come ? Then came they, and laid hands on Jesus, and took him.— Mat., ch. 26.

See SIGN.

7891. SILENCE of Awe. *Manoah's Wife.* [6] The woman came and told her husband, saying, A man of God came unto me, and his countenance *was* like the countenance of an angel of God, very terrible : but I asked him not whence he *was*, neither told he me his name.—Judges, ch. 13.

7892. —— **Criminal.** *To Esther.* [14] If thou altogether holdest thy peace at this time, *then* shall there enlargement and deliverance arise to the Jews from another place ; but thou and thy father's house shall be destroyed : and who knoweth whether thou art come to the kingdom for *such* a time as this ?—Esther, ch. 4.

7893. —— **of Conviction.** *At Capernaum.* [3] He saith unto the man which had the withered hand, Stand forth. [4] And he saith unto them, Is it lawful to do good on the sabbath days, or to do evil? to save life, or to kill? But they held their peace.—Mark, ch. 3.

7894. —— **Construction in.** *Temple.* [7] The house, when it was in building, was built of stone made ready before it was brought thither : so that there was neither hammer nor axe *nor* any tool of iron heard in the house, while it was in building.—1 Kings, ch. 6.

—— **of Desolation.** *Babylon.* [22] And the voice of harpers, and musicians, and of pipers, and trumpeters, shall be heard no more at all in thee ; and no craftsman, of whatsoever craft *he be*, shall be found any more in thee : and the sound of a millstone shall be heard no more at all in thee : [23] And the light of a candle shall shine no more at all in thee : and the voice of the bridegroom and of the bride shall be heard no more at all in thee : for thy merchants were the great men of the earth ; for by thy sorceries were all nations deceived.—Rev., ch. 18.

7895. —— **Difficult.** *Leper.* [44] See thou say nothing to any man : but go thy way, shew thyself to the priests, and offer for thy cleansing.. [45] But he went out, and began to publish *it* much, and to blaze abroad the matter.—Mark, ch. 1.

7896. —— —— *King Saul.* [27] The children of Belial said, How shall this man save us ? And they despised him, and brought him no presents. But he held his peace.—1 Sam., ch. 10.

7897. —— —— *Bartimeus.* [48] Many charged him that he should hold his peace : but he cried the more a great deal, *Thou* Son of David, have mercy on me. [49] And Jesus..commanded him to be called.—Mark, ch. 10.

7898. —— **A dangerous.** *Four Lepers.* [9] We do not well : this day *is* a day of good tidings, and we hold our peace : if we tarry till the morning light, some mischief will come upon us : now therefore come, that we may go and tell the king's household.—2 Kings, ch. 7.

7899. —— **A discouraging.** *" Not a Word."* [22] A woman of Canaan..cried unto him, saying, Have mercy on me, O Lord, *thou* son of David ; my daughter is grievously vexed with a devil. [23] But he answered her not a word.—Mat., ch. 15.

7900. —— **of Fear.** *Ish-bosheth.* [8] Then was Abner very wroth for the words of Ish-bosheth, and said, *Am* I a dog's head, which against Judah do shew kindness this day unto the house of Saul thy father? [11] And he could not answer Abner a word again, because he feared him. —2 Sam., ch. 3.

7901. —— **in Grief.** *Job's Friends* [12] Wept ; and they rent every one his mantle, and sprinkled dust upon their heads toward heaven. [13] So they sat down with him upon the ground seven days and seven nights, and none spake a word unto him : for they saw that *his* grief was very great.—Job, ch. 2.

7902. —— **impossible.** *Apostles.* [40] When they had called the apostles, and beaten *them*, they commanded that they should not speak in the name of Jesus, and let them go. [42] And daily in the temple, and in every house, they ceased not to teach and to preach Jesus Christ.—Acts, ch. 5.

7903. —— **Importance of.** *"Keepeth his Soul."* [23] Whoso keepeth his mouth and his tongue, keepeth his soul from troubles.—Prov., ch. 21.

7904. —— **of Meekness.** *Before Herod.* [9] Then he questioned with him in many words ; but he answered him nothing. [10] And the chief priests and scribes stood and vehemently accused him. —Luke, ch. 23.

7905. —— **Noncommittal.** *Mt. Carmel.* [21] Elijah..said, How long halt ye between two opinions ? if the Lord *be* God, follow him : but if Baal, *then,* follow him. And the people answered him not a word.—1 Kings, ch. 18.

7906. —— **Orderly.** *At Jericho.* [10] Joshua had commanded the people, saying, Ye shall not shout, nor make any noise with your voice, neither shall *any* word proceed out of your mouth, until the day I bid you shout ; then shall ye shout.—Josh., ch. 6.

7907. —— **Speech useless.** *Before Pilate.* [4] Pilate asked him again, saying, Answerest thou nothing ? behold how many things they witness against thee. [5] But Jesus yet answered nothing ; so that Pilate marvelled.—Mark, ch. 15.

7908. —— **Safety in.** *Proverb.* [7] A fool's mouth *is* his destruction, and his lips *are* the snare of his soul. [8] The words of a talebearer *are* as wounds, and they go down into the innermost parts of the belly.—Prov., ch. 18.

7909. —— **of Women.** *Paul.* [11] Let the woman learn in silence with all subjection. [12] But I suffer not a woman to teach, nor to usurp authority over the man, but to be in silence.—1 TIM., ch. 2.

7910. —— **Wisdom of.** *Proverb.* [28] Even a fool, when he holdeth his peace, is counted wise : *and* he that shutteth his lips *is esteemed* a man of understanding.—PROV., ch. 17.

7911. —— **Weary of.** *Jeremiah.* [8] Because the word of the Lord was made a reproach unto me, and a derision, daily. [9] Then I said, I will not make mention of him, nor speak any more in his name. But *his word* was in mine heart as a burning fire shut up in my bones, and I was weary with forbearing, and I could not *stay.*—JER., ch. 20.

Also see :

Doubt. Zach..be dumb..because thou believest n. 2553

7912. SIMONY, Crime of. *Simon Magus.* [18] When Simon saw that through laying on of the apostles' hands the Holy Ghost was given, he offered them money, [19] Saying, Give me also this power, that on whomsoever I lay hands, he may receive the Holy Ghost.—ACTS, ch. 8.

7913. —— **Scorn of.** *Peter.* [20] Thy money perish with thee, because thou hast thought that the gift of God may be purchased with money. [21] Thou hast neither part nor lot in this matter : for thy heart is not right in the sight of God.—ACTS, ch. 8.

7914. SIMPLICITY, Necessity of. *Child.* [3] Except ye be converted, and become as little children, ye shall not enter into the kingdom of heaven.—MAT., ch. 18.

See other illustrations under :

FOLLY.

Anger Nabal answered, Who is David	3262
Ashamed. Held their peace..who should be the g.	3263
Backsliders. Forsaken..living waters..hewn	3264
Ecclesiastical. Whether is greater the gift or the	3265
Inseparable. Bray a fool in a mortar..not depart	3266
Indifference. Heareth..doeth not..built upon the	3267
Idolaters. Mouths, but they speak not ; eyes..see	3268
" Warm himself..maketh a graven image	3269
Natural. Ostrich..G. hath deprived her of wisdom	3270
Neglect. Foolish..took no oil with them	3271
Worldly. I will pull down..build..eat, drink	3272
Youth. Rehoboam forsook the counsel of the old	3273

See SINCERITY.

7915. SIN from Anger. *Moses.* [10] Hear now, ye rebels ; must we fetch you water out of this rock ? [11] And Moses lifted up his hand, and with his rod he smote the rock twice.—NUM., ch. 20.

7916. —— **attractive.** *Eve.* [6] When the woman saw that the tree *was* good for food, and that it *was* pleasant to the eyes, and a tree to be desired to make *one* wise.—GEN., ch. 3.

7917. —— **advertised.** *Judah.* [9] The shew of their countenance doth witness against them ; and they declared their sin as Sodom, they hide *it* not. Woe unto their soul !—ISA., ch. 3.

7918. —— **Atonement for.** *Abel.* [4] Abel, he also brought of the firstlings of his flock and of the fat thereof. And the Lord had respect unto Abel and to his offering.—GEN., ch. 4.

7919. —— **abhorred.** *"Unclean."* [5] Woe is me ! for I am undone ; because I *am* a man of unclean lips, and I dwell in the midst of a people of unclean lips : for mine eyes have seen the King, the Lord of hosts.—ISA., ch. 6.

7920. —— **Boldness in.** *Ahab.* [29] Ahab.. reigned over Israel in Samaria twenty and two years. [30] And Ahab..did evil in the sight of the Lord above all that *were* before him.—1 KINGS, ch. 16.

7921. —— *Absalom.* [20] Said Absalom to Ahithophel, Give counsel.. [21] And Ahithophel said unto Absalom, Go in unto thy father's concubines, which he hath left to keep the house : and all Israel shall hear that thou art abhorred of thy father : then shall the hands of all that *are* with thee be strong.—2 SAM., ch. 16.

7922. —— **Bitterness after.** *Adultery.* [3] For the lips of a strange woman drop *as* an honeycomb, and her mouth *is* smoother than oil : [4] But her end is bitter as wormwood, sharp as a twoedged sword. [5] Her feet go down to death ; her steps take hold on hell.—PROV., ch. 5.

7923. —— **Bitterness for.** *"Bitter Herbs."* [7] They shall take of the blood, and strike *it* on the two side posts and on the upper door post of the houses.. [8] And they shall eat the flesh in that night, roast with fire, and unleavened bread ; *and* with bitter *herbs.*—EX., ch. 12.

7924. —— **defeats the Church.** *Achan.* [See No. 8024.]

7925. —— **Counselled to.** *Absalom.* [See No. 7921.]

7926. —— **Cowards by.** *Proverb.* [1] The wicked flee when no man pursueth : but the righteous are bold as a lion.—PROV., ch. 28.

7927. —— **Calamity from.** *At Ai.* [13] There is an accursed thing in the midst of thee, O Israel : thou canst not stand before thine enemies, until ye take away the accursed thing from among you.—JOSH., ch. 7. [See No. 8012.]

7928. —— —— *Jews.* [6] I also have given you cleanness of teeth in all your cities, and want of bread in all your places : yet have ye not returned unto me, saith the Lord.—AMOS, ch. 4.

7929. —— **Curses the Land.** *Israel.* [9] I have smitten you with blasting and mildew ; when your gardens and your vineyards and your fig trees and your olive trees increased, the palmerworm devoured *them :* yet have ye not returned unto me, saith the Lord.—AMOS, ch. 4.

7930. —— **Captivity to.** *Paul.* [14] We know that the law is spiritual : but I am carnal, sold under sin. [15] For that which I do, I allow not : for what I would, that do I not ; but what I hate, that do I.—ROM., ch. 7.

7931. —— **Conflict with.** *Paul.* [18] To will is present with me ; but how to perform that which is good I find not. [19] For the good that I would, I do not : but the evil which I would not, that I do.—ROM., ch. 7.

7932. —— **Consciousness of.** *Job.* [5] I have heard of thee by the hearing of the ear ; but now mine eye seeth thee : [6] Wherefore I abhor *myself,* and repent in dust and ashes.—JOB, ch. 42.

7933. —— **not covered.** *Gehazi.* [25] Elisha said..Whence *comest thou,* Gehazi ? And he said, Thy servant went no whither. [26] And he said.. Went not mine heart *with thee,* when the man turned again from his chariot to meet thee ? *Is* *it* a time to receive money, and to receive garments, and oliveyards, and vineyards, and sheep, and oxen, and menservants, and maidservants? [27] The leprosy therefore of Naaman shall cleave unto thee.—2 KINGS, ch. 5.

7934. —— —— *Judah's.* [1] The sin of Judah is written with a pen of iron, and with the point of a diamond : *it is* graven upon the table of their heart, and upon the horns of your altars. —JER., ch. 17.

7935. —— covered with Sin. *David.* [14] David wrote a letter to Joab, and sent *it* by the hand of Uriah. [15]..saying, Set ye Uriah in the forefront of the hottest battle, and retire ye from him, that he may be smitten, and die.—2 SAM., ch. 11.

7936. —— A costly. *Haman.* [9] If it please the king, let it be written that they may be destroyed : and I will pay ten thousand talents of silver to the hands of those that have the charge of the business.—ESTHER, ch. 3. [About $15,-000,000.]

7937. —— Contrition for. *On Atonement Day.* [29] Whatsoever soul *it be* that shall not be afflicted in that same day, he shall be cut off from among his people.—LEV., ch. 23.

7938. —— Conscious of. *"Went out."* [3] The scribes and Pharisees brought unto him a woman taken in adultery ; [5] Now Moses in the law commanded us, that such should be stoned : but what sayest thou? [7]..He that is without sin among you, let him first cast a stone at her. [9] And they..being convicted by *their own* conscience, went out one by one, beginning at the eldest, *even* unto the last.—JOHN, ch. 8.

7939. —— Consequences of. *"Burned."* [27] Can a man take fire in his bosom, and his clothes not be burned? [28] Can one go upon hot coals, and his feet not be burned? [32] Whoso committeth adultery with a woman lacketh understanding : he *that* doeth it destroyeth his own soul.—PROV., ch. 6.

7940. —— Causing to. *Others.* [21] *It is* good neither to eat flesh, nor to drink wine, nor *any thing* whereby thy brother stumbleth, or is offended, or is made weak.—ROM., ch. 14.

7941. —— —— *Jeroboam.* [25] Omri wrought evil in the eyes of the Lord, and did worse than all that *were* before him. [26]..and in his sin wherewith he made Israel to sin.—1 KINGS, ch. 16.

7942. —— —— *Responsibility.* [6] Whoso shall offend one of these little ones which believe in me, it were better for him that a millstone were hanged about his neck, and *that* he were drowned in the depth of the sea.—MAT., ch. 18.

7943. —— —— *Eve.* [6] She took of the fruit thereof, and did eat, and gave also unto her husband with her ; and he did eat.—GEN., ch. 3.

7944. —— Drought from. *Rain.* [7] I have withholden the rain from you, when *there were* yet three months to the harvest : and I caused it to rain upon one city, and caused it not to rain upon another city.. [8] So two *or* three cities wandered unto one city, to drink water ; but they were not satisfied : yet have ye not returned unto me, saith the Lord.—AMOS, ch. 4. [See No. 7929.]

7945. —— Degradation in. *"Vomit."* [22] It is happened unto them according to the true proverb, The dog *is* turned to his own vomit again ; and, The sow that was washed to her wallowing in the mire.—2 PETER, ch. 2.

7946. —— disowned. *In Eden.* [12] The woman whom thou gavest *to be* with me, she gave me of the tree, and I did eat. [13] And the Lord God said unto the woman, What *is* this *that* thou hast done? And the woman said, The serpent beguiled me.—GEN., ch. 3.

7947. —— Destruction in. *Sodom.* [14] Lot went out, and..said, Up, get you out of this place ; for the Lord will destroy this city. But he seemed as one that mocked unto his sons in law.—GEN., ch. 19.

7948. —— Deliverance from. *"Cleanse."* [7] If we walk in the light, as he is in the light, we have fellowship one with another, and the blood of Jesus Christ his Son cleanseth us from all sin. [8] If we say that we have no sin, we deceive ourselves, and the truth is not in us.—1 JOHN, ch. 1.

7949. —— denied. *"Liar."* [9] If we confess our sins, he is faithful and just to forgive us *our* sins, and to cleanse us from all unrighteousness. [10] If we say that we have not sinned, we make him a liar, and his word is not in us.—1 JOHN, ch. 1.

7950. —— Enormity of. *"Stonest."* [37] O Jerusalem, Jerusalem, *thou* that killest the prophets, and stonest them which are sent unto thee, how often would I have gathered thy children together, even as a hen gathereth her chickens under *her* wings, and ye would not !—MAT., ch. 23.

7951. —— Evidence of. *Saul's.* [13] I have performed the commandment of the Lord. [14] And Samuel said, What *meaneth* then this bleating of the sheep in mine ears, and the lowing of the oxen which I hear?—1 SAM., ch. 15.

7952. —— by Excess. *"Smote twice."* [See No. 7915.]

7953. —— Exclusion by. *Aaron.* [24] Aaron shall be gathered unto his people : for he shall not enter into the land which I have given unto the children of Israel, because ye rebelled against my word at the water of Meribah.—NUM., ch. 20.

7954. —— expensive. *Prodigal.* [13] The younger son gathered all together, and took his journey into a far country, and there wasted his substance with riotous living. [14] And when he had spent all, there arose a mighty famine..and he began to be in want.—LUKE, ch. 15.

7955. —— Effects of. *Grave.* [19] So doth the grave *those which* have sinned. [20] The womb shall forget him ; the worm shall feed sweetly on him ; he shall be no more remembered ; and wickedness shall be broken as a tree.—JOB, ch. 24.

7956. —— Folly of. *David's.* [10] David's heart smote him after that he had numbered the people. And David said..I have sinned greatly..I beseech thee, O Lord, take away the iniquity of thy servant ; for I have done very foolishly.—2 SAM., ch. 24,

7957. —— Forfeited by. *Canaan.* [11] He smote the rock twice : and the water came out abundantly.. [12] And the Lord spake unto Moses and

Aaron, Because ye believed me not, to sanctify me in the eyes of the children of Israel, therefore ye shall not bring this congregation into the land.—NUM., ch. 20.

7958. The fatal. *Unpardonable.* [32] Whosoever speaketh against the Holy Ghost, it shall not be forgiven him, neither in this world, neither in the *world* to come.—MAT., ch. 12.

7959. —— —— *Presumption.* [30] The soul that doeth *aught* presumptuously, *whether he be* born in the land, or a stranger, the same reproacheth the Lord; and that soul shall be cut off from among his people.—NUM., ch. 15.

7960. —— against God, All. *Murmurers.* [7] What *are* we, that ye murmur against us? [8] And Moses said .. the Lord shall give you in the evening flesh to eat, and in the morning bread to the full..what *are* we? your murmurings *are* not against us, but against the Lord.—EX., ch. 16.

7961. —— offensive to God. *Joseph.* [9] There *is* none greater in this house than I; neither hath he kept back any thing from me but thee, because thou *art* his wife: how then can I do this great wickedness, and sin against God?—GEN., ch. 39.

7962. —— angers God. *Calf-Worship.* [8] They have turned aside quickly..they have made them a molten calf, and have worshipped it, and have sacrificed thereunto, and said, These *be* thy gods, O Israel, which have brought thee up out of the land of Egypt. [10] Now therefore let me alone, that my wrath may wax hot against them, and that I may consume them.— EX., ch. 32.

7963. —— grieves God. *Antediluvians.* [5] God saw that the wickedness of man *was* great in the earth, and *that* every imagination of the thoughts of his heart *was* only evil continually. [6] And it repented the Lord that he had made man on the earth, and it grieved him at his heart.—GEN., ch. 6.

7964. —— Gifts for. *Many.* [7] Will the Lord be pleased with thousands of rams, *or* with ten thousands of rivers of oil? shall I give my firstborn *for* my transgression, the fruit of my body *for* the sin of my soul?—MICAH, ch. 6.

7965. —— Hurt of. *"Pricks."* [4] Saul, Saul, why persecutest thou me? [5] And he said, Who art thou, Lord? And the Lord said, I am Jesus whom thou persecutest: *it is* hard for thee to kick against the pricks.—ACTS, ch. 9.

7966. —— from Haste. *Saul.* [11] Thou camest not within the days appointed, and..the Philistines gathered themselves together at Michmash; [12] Therefore said I, The Philistines will come down now upon me to Gilgal, and I have not made supplication unto the Lord: I forced myself therefore, and offered a burnt offering. —1 SAM., ch. 13.

7967. —— —— At Sinai. [1] When the people saw that Moses delayed to come down out of the mount, the people gathered..unto Aaron, and said..Up, make us gods, which shall go before us; for *as for* this Moses, the man that brought us up out of the land of Egypt, we wot not what is become of him.—EX., ch. 33.

7968. —— Hiding. *Proverb.* [13] He that covereth his sins shall not prosper: but whoso confesseth and forsaketh *them* shall have mercy. —PROV., ch. 28.

7969. —— —— *Adam.* [8] Amongst the trees of the garden. [9] And the Lord God called unto Adam..Where *art* thou? [10] And he said, I heard thy voice in the garden, and I was afraid, because I *was* naked; and I hid myself.—GEN., ch. 3.

7970. —— Humiliation for. *Ahab.* [27] When Ahab heard those words..he rent his clothes, and put sackcloth upon his flesh, and fasted, and lay in sackcloth, and went softly.—1 KINGS, ch. 21.

7971. —— in the Heart. *"Tablet."* [See No. 7934.]

7972. —— Influence for. *Ahithophel.* [See No. 7921.] [23] The counsel of Ahithophel..*was* as if a man had inquired at the oracle of God: so *was* all the counsel of Ahithophel both with David and with Absalom.—2 SAM., ch. 16.

7973. —— by Impatience. *"Ye Rebels."* [See No. 7915.]

7974. —— Irremediable. *Hence Captivity.* [15] The Lord God..sent to them by his messengers, rising up betimes, and sending; because he had compassion on his people.. [16] But they mocked the messengers of God, and despised his words, and misused his prophets, until the wrath of the Lord arose against his people, till *there was* no remedy.—2 CHRON., ch. 36.

7975. —— indelible. *"Diamond."* [See No. 7934.]

7976. —— Jesus reveals. *To Peter.* [8] Simon Peter saw *it*, he fell down at Jesus' knees, saying, Depart from me; for I am a sinful man, O Lord. [9] For he was astonished..at the draught of the fishes which they had taken.—LUKE, ch. 5.

7977. —— Knowledge by. *In Eden.* [7] The eyes of them both were opened, and they knew that they *were* naked; and they sewed fig leaves together, and made themselves aprons.—GEN., ch. 3.

7978. —— Look of. *Jesus said,* [28] That whosoever looketh on a woman to lust after her hath committed adultery with her already in his heart.—MAT., ch. 5.

7979. —— Loathing of. *Job.* [4] Behold, I am vile; what shall I answer thee? I will lay mine hand upon my mouth. [5] Once have I spoken; but I will not answer: yea, twice; but I will proceed no further.—JOB, ch. 40.

7980. —— Leadership in. *Ahaziah* [51] Reigned two years over Israel. [52] And he did evil in the sight of the Lord, and walked in the way of his father, and..his mother, and in the way of Jeroboam the son of Nebat, who made Israel to sin.—1 KINGS, ch. 22.

7981. —— of public Men. *Saul.* [See No. 7951.] [22] To obey *is* better than sacrifice, *and* to hearken than the fat of rams. [23] For rebellion *is as* the sin of witchcraft, and stubbornness *is as* iniquity and idolatry. Because thou hast rejected the word of the Lord, he hath also rejected thee from *being* king.—1 SAM., ch. 15.

7982. —— Misery from. *Prodigal.* [17] How many hired servants of my father have bread enough and to spare, and I perish with hunger! [18] I will arise and go to my father, and will say unto him, Father, I have sinned.—LUKE, ch. 15.

7983. —— —— *Oppressors.* [16] They put away the strange gods from among them, and served the Lord : and his soul was grieved for the misery of Israel. [17] Then the children of Ammon were. .encamped in Gilead.—Judges, ch. 10.

7984. —— and Misfortune. *Blindness.* [2] His disciples asked. : Master, who did sin, this man, or his parents, that he was born blind ? [3] Jesus answered, Neither hath this man sinned, nor his parents : but that the works of God should be made manifest in him.—John, ch. 3.

7985. —— Marred by. *Solomon.* [3] Solomon loved the Lord, walking in the statutes of David his father : only he sacrificed and burnt incense in high places.—1 Kings, ch. 3.

7986. —— Natural. *Birth.* [5] Behold, I was shapen in iniquity ; and in sin did my mother conceive me.—Ps. 51.

7987. —— Only one. *David.* [5] David did *that which was* right in the eyes of the Lord, and turned not aside from any *thing* that he commanded him all the days of his life, save only in the matter of Uriah the Hittite.—1 Kings, ch. 15.

7988. —— Obduracy in. *Jews.* [10] I have sent among you the pestilence after the manner of Egypt : your young men have I slain with the sword, and have taken away your horses ; and I have made the stink of your camps to come up unto your nostrils : yet have ye not returned unto me, saith the Lord.—Amos, ch. 4.

7989. —— Offering for the People. *" Kid" or "Lamb."* [29] He shall lay his hand upon the head. . and say the sin offering. . [30] And the priest shall take of the blood thereof with his finger, and put it upon the horns of the altar of burnt offering, and shall pour out all the blood thereof at the bottom of the altar.—Lev., ch. 4.

7990. —— Plausible. *Saul.* [See No. 7951.] [21] The people took of the spoil, sheep and oxen, the chief of the things, which should have been utterly destroyed, to sacrifice unto the Lord. —1 Sam., ch. 15.

7991. —— by Pride. *" Must we."* [See No. 7915.]

7992. —— Perils in. *Proverb.* [27] Can a man take fire in his bosom, and his clothes not be burned ? [28] Can one go upon hot coals, and his feet not be burned ?—Prov., ch. 6.

7993. —— —— *Adulterers.* [22] He goeth after her straightway, as an ox goeth to the slaughter, or as a fool to the correction of the stocks ; [23] Till a dart strike through his liver ; as a bird hasteth to the snare, and knoweth not that it *is* for his life.—Prov., ch. 7.

7994. —— Pleasures of. *The Adulteress.* [16] She saith to him, [17] Stolen waters are sweet, and bread *eaten* in secret is pleasant. [18] But he knoweth not that the dead *are* there ; *and that* her guests *are* in the depths of hell.—Pnov., ch. 9.

7995. —— —— *Deception.* [17] Bread of deceit *is* sweet to a man ; but afterwards his mouth shall be filled with gravel.—Prov., ch. 20.

7996. —— —— *Poverty.* [17] He that loveth pleasure *shall be* a poor man : he that loveth wine and oil shall not be rich.—Prov., ch. 21.

7997. —— of Presumption. *Korah.* [2] Two hundred and fifty princes. .men of renown :

[3]. .gathered themselves together against Moses and against Aaron, and said. . *Ye take* too much upon you, seeing all the congregation *are* holy, every one of them, and the Lord *is* among them : wherefore then lift ye up yourselves above the congregation ?—Num., ch. 16.

7998. —— Permeated with. *Nature.* [5] The whole head is sick, and the whole heart faint. [6] From the sole of the foot even unto the head *there is* no soundness in it ; *but* wounds, and bruises, and putrifying sores : they have not been closed, neither bound up, neither mollified with ointment.—Isa., ch. 1.

7999. —— Purified from. *" Blood."* [19] When Moses had spoken every precept to all the people. .he took the blood of calves and of goats, with water, and scarlet wool, and hyssop, and sprinkled both the book and all the people.— Heb., ch. 9.

8000. —— —— *" No Remission."* [21] He sprinkled likewise with blood both the tabernacle, and all the vessels of the ministry. [22] And almost all things are by the law purged with blood ; and without shedding of blood is no remission.—Heb., ch. 9.

8001. —— a Reproach. *National.* [34] Righteousness exalteth a nation : but sin *is* a reproach to any people.—Prov., ch. 14.

8002. —— feared, Reproach of. *Nehemiah.* [12] Sanballat had hired him. [13]. .that I should be afraid, and do so, and sin, and *that* they might have *matter* for an evil report, that they might reproach me.—Neh., ch. 6.

8003. —— Responsibility in. *Ahithophel.* [See No. 7972.]

8004. —— National Ruin by. *King Ahaz.* [23] He sacrificed unto the gods of Damascus, which smote him : and he said, Because the gods of the kings of Syria help them, *therefore* will I sacrifice to them, that they may help me. But they were the ruin of him, and of all Israel. —2 Chron.,ch. 28.

8005. —— —— *Jerusalem.* [19] Judah kept not the commandments of the Lord. .but walked in the statutes of Israel which they made. [20] And the Lord rejected all the seed of Israel, and afflicted them, and delivered them into the hand of spoilers, until he had cast them out of his sight.—2 Kings, ch. 17.

8006. —— Wicked Ruler's. *King Ahab.* [17] When Ahab saw Elijah. .Ahab said. . *Art* thou he that troubleth Israel ? [18] And he answered, I have not troubled Israel ; but thou, and thy father's house, in that ye have forsaken the commandments of the Lord, and thou hast followed Balaam.—1 Kings, ch. 18.

8007. —— Removal of. *" Walk."* [8] He.hath shewed thee, O man, what *is* good ; and what doth the Lord require of thee, but to do justly, and to love mercy, and to walk humbly with thy God.—Micah, ch. 6.

8008. —— —— *By Fire.* [6] Then flew one of the seraphim unto me, having a live coal in his hand, *which* he had taken. .from off the altar : [7] And he laid *it* upon my mouth, and said, Lo, this hath touched thy lips ; and thine iniquity is taken away.—Isa., ch. 6.

8009. —— —— *By Blood.* [13] If the blood of bulls and of goats, and the ashes of a heifer sprinkling the unclean, sanctifieth to the purifying of the flesh ; [14] How much more shall the blood of Christ, who through the eternal Spirit offered himself without spot to God, purge your conscience from dead works to serve the living God?—HEB., ch. 9.

8010. —— Remaining. *Hurtful.* [55] If ye will not drive out the inhabitants of the land from before you ; then..those which ye let remain of them *shall be* pricks in your eyes, and thorns in your sides, and shall vex you.—NUM., ch. 33.

8011. —— returning. *Self.* [15] He made a pit, and digged it, and is fallen into the ditch *which* he made. [16] His mischief shall return upon his own head, and his violent dealing shall come down upon his own pate.—Ps. 7.

8012. —— leads to Sin. *Achan's.* [See No. 8024.] [10] And the Lord said unto Joshua, Get thee up ; wherefore liest thou thus upon thy face? [11] Israel hath sinned, and they have also transgressed my covenant which I commanded them : for they have even taken of the accursed thing, and have also stolen, and dissembled also, and they have put *it* even among their own stuff.—JOSH., ch. 7.

8013. —— Separation by. *Jews.* [1] The Lord's hand is not shortened, that it cannot save ; neither his ear heavy, that it cannot hear : [2] But your iniquities have separated between you and your God, and your sins have hid *his* face from you, that he will not hear.—ISA., ch. 59.

8014. —— Servitude in. *To Moab.* [12] The Lord strengthened Eglon the king of Moab against Israel, because they had done evil.. [13] ..went and smote Israel, and possessed the city of palm trees. [14] So the children of Israel served Eglon..eighteen years.—JUDGES, ch. 3.

8015. —— surrendered. *Any Cost.* [30] If thy right hand offend thee, cut it off, and cast *it* from thee : for it is profitable for thee that one of thy members should perish, and not *that* thy whole body should be cast into hell.—MAT., ch. 5.

8016. —— Saved from. *"Born of God."* [9] Whosoever is born of God doth not commit sin ; for his seed remaineth in him : and he cannot sin, because he is born of God.—1 JOHN, ch. 3.

8017. —— typified. *Serpents.* [5] Wherefore have ye brought us up out of Egypt to die in the wilderness? for *there is* no bread, neither *is there any* water ; and our soul loatheth this light bread. [6] And the Lord sent fiery serpents among the people, and they bit the people ; and much people of Israel died.—NUM., ch. 21.

8018. —— The unpardonable. *Holy Ghost.* [28] All sins shall be forgiven unto the sons of men, and blasphemies wherewith soever they shall blaspheme : [29] But he that shall blaspheme against the Holy Ghost hath never forgiveness, but is in danger of eternal damnation.—MARK, ch. 3.

8019. —— unwashed. *Pilate.* [24] When Pilate saw that he could prevail nothing, but *that* rather a tumult was made, he took water, and washed *his* hands before the multitude, saying, I am innocent of the blood of this just person : see ye *to it.*—MAT., ch. 27.

8020. —— Unpolluted by. *"Without Sin."* [15] We have not a high priest which cannot be touched with the feeling of our infirmities ; but was in all points tempted like as *we are,* yet without sin.—HEB., ch. 4.

8021. —— Wretchedness in. *Bondage.* [24] Oh wretched man that I am ! who shall deliver me from the body of this death? [25] I thank God through Jesus Christ our Lord.—ROM., ch. 7.

8022. —— Wilful. *Hopeless.* [26] If we sin wilfully after that we have received the knowledge of the truth, there remaineth no more sacrifice for sins, [27] But a certain fearful looking for of judgment and fiery indignation, which shall devour the adversaries.—HEB., ch. 10.

8023. —— Washing. *Typical.* [9] Simon Peter saith..Lord, not my feet only, but also *my* hands and *my* head. [10] Jesus saith..He that is washed needeth not save to wash *his* feet, but is clean every whit.—JOHN, ch. 13.

8024. —— Weakness from. *At Ai.* [11] They have even taken of the accursed thing, and have also stolen, and dissembled also, and they have put *it* even among their own stuff. [12] Therefore the children of Israel could not stand before their enemies.—JOSH., ch. 7.

See other illustrations under :

DEPRAVITY.

Ancient. Every imagination of the thoughts	2188
Bestial. [Gibeathites] beset the house, and beat at	2189
Discovered. Woe is me..unclean lips..people	2190
Heathen. Changed the glory of..G. into an image	2191
Infectious. Daughters of Lot were with child	2192
Inherited. Ye are the children of them which	2193
Natural. L. looked down..all gone aside..filthy	2194

EVIL.

Appearance. Lest we should offend them..money	2752
Freedom. Pilate said..third time..What evil hath	2753
Overruled. Ye thought evil..G. meant it unto	2754
Permitted. Lest while ye gather..tares ye root up	2755
Repaid with Good. David said to Saul..mine eye s.	2756
Root. Love of money is the root of all evil	2757

GUILT.

Accumulated. Upon you may come all the	3766
Cowardice. Adam and his wife hid themselves	3767
Degrees. Two debtors ; one owed 500 pence	3768
Panic. L. looked..through the cloud..troubled	3769

INIQUITY.

Church. My people..overpass the deeds of the w.	4495
Great. Within full of..all uncleanness	4493
Hidden. Ye make clean the outside..but within	4494

VICES.

Mental. Idolatry, witchcraft, hatred, variance	9188
Physical. Works of the flesh are..adultery	9189
Pleasures. As..lieth down in the midst of the sea	9190

Alarm. Adam..his wife..hid themselves	280
Beginning. Whoso looketh upon..to lust	114
Changes. Angels which kept not their first	461
Discovery. Ahab said to E., Hast thou found me?	1196
Original. Eve..saw that the tree was good..pleas.	329
Renewed. Pharaoh..thunders ceased..sinned yet m.	30
Reproof. Without sin..cast the first stone	86
Supposed. Did this man sin, or his p.	203
Troubles. Travaileth in pain..dreadful sound	1581
" Art thou come to call my sin, to remem.	1576
Wilful. If ye sin wilfully..knowledge	465

See **CONFESSION** and references.
See **REPENTANCE** and references.
See **SINNER** and **WICKEDNESS.**

8025. SINCERITY of Consecration. *Josiah.*
³ The king stood by a pillar, and made a covenant before the Lord, to walk after the Lord.
⁴..cast forth out of the temple of the Lord all the vessels that were made for Baal, and for the grove, and for all the host of heaven : and he burned them.—2 Kings, ch. 23.

8026. —— in Evil Doing. *Saul.* ⁹ I verily thought..that I ought to do many things contrary to the name of Jesus of Nazareth. ¹⁰..and when they were put to death, I gave my voice against *them.* ¹¹ And I punished them oft in every synagogue, and compelled *them* to blaspheme..being exceedingly mad against them, I persecuted *them* even unto strange cities.—Acts, ch. 26.

8027. —— Evidence of. *Ephesians.* ¹⁹ Many ..which used curious arts, brought their books together, and burned them before all *men ;* and they counted the price of them, and found *it* fifty thousand *pieces* of silver. ²⁰ So mightily grew the word of God, and prevailed.—Acts, ch. 19.

8028. —— Example of. *Nathanael.* ⁴⁷ Behold an Israelite indeed, in whom is no guile ! ⁴⁸ Nathanael saith..Whence knowest thou me? Jesus answered..Before that Philip called thee, when thou wast under the fig tree, I saw thee.—John, ch. 1.

8029. —— of Heart. *Godly.* ¹ Lord, who shall abide in thy tabernacle? who shall dwell in thy holy hill ? ² He that walketh uprightly, and worketh righteousness, and speaketh the truth in his heart.—Ps. 15.

8030. —— Lovable. *Young Ruler.* ¹⁶ Good Master, what good thing shall I do, that I may have eternal life?..²⁰ The young man saith.. All these things have I kept from my youth up : what lack I yet?—Mat., ch. 19. ²¹ Jesus beholding him loved him.—Mark, ch. 10.

8031. —— in Opinions. *Nathanael.* [See No. 8028.] ⁴⁹ Nathanael answered..Rabbi, thou art the Son of God ; thou art the King of Israel. ⁵⁰ Jesus answered..Because I said..I saw thee under the fig tree, believest thou? thou shalt see greater things than these.—John, ch. 1.

8032. —— Positive. *Peter.* ¹⁷ He saith.. the third time, Simon, *son* of Jonas, lovest thou me? Peter was grieved, because he said unto him the third time, Lovest thou me? And he said unto him, Lord, thou knowest all things ; thou knowest that I love thee.—John, ch. 21.

8033. —— Proof of. *At Carmel.* ³⁹ When all the people saw *it*, they fell on their faces : and they said, The Lord, he *is* the God.. ⁴⁰ And Elijah said..Take the prophets of Baal ; let not one of them escape. And they took them : and Elijah brought them down to the brook Kishon, and slew them there.—1 Kings, ch. 18.

8034. —— in Reformation. *Good Works.* ¹⁶ Speak ye every man the truth to his neighbour ; execute the judgment of truth and peace in your gates : ¹⁷ And let none of you imagine evil in your hearts against his neighbour ; and love no false oath : for all these *are things* that I hate, saith the Lord.—Zech., ch. 8.

See other illustrations under :
HONESTY.
Accredited. My master wotteth not what is with 4043
Acknowledged. Samuel..thou hast not defrauded 4044

Commended. Hath not oppressed..usury..iniquity 4045
Happiness. Better is little with righteousness 4046
Ignored. It is naught, saith the buyer..boasteth 4047
Official. Gift doth blind the eyes of the wise 4048
Payment. Go sell the oil and pay the debt 4049
Rare. Seek..if there be any..the truth 4050
Reward. Shaketh his hands from holding bribes 4051
Restitution. If I have taken..restore fourfold 4052
Trained. All these have I observed from my y. 4053
Test. The money that was..in your sacks..carry 4054
Trade. Not have..divers weights, a great and s. 4055
  "   Divers weights, and divers measures 4056
Trusted. They delivered the money to..workmen 4057

INTEGRITY.
Acknowledged. Thou art more righteous than I 4575
Conscious. The L. be judge between me and thee 4576
Delight. The integrity of the upright shall guide 4577
Fixed. Till I die I will not remove mine integrity 4578
False. Is thy servant a dog..do this ? 4579
Observed. God said, I know thou didst this 4580
Official. Witness..whom have I defrauded ? 4581
Steadfast. L. said..Job holdeth fast his integrity 4582

INTENTION.
Accepted. Abraham..offered up his only begotten 4604
Approved. Whereas it was in thine heart to build 4605
Abandoned. Pilate sought to release him 4606
Commended. Poor widow..cast more in than 4607
Crime. If he thrust him suddenly without enmity 4608
Fixes Guilt. If any man hate..lie in wait..smite 4609
Honoured. She hath done what she could 4610
Misjudged. All of you have conspired against me 4611
Sincere. Abraham..took the knife to slay his son 4612
Superior. Beyond their power they were willing 4613
Unexecuted. Peter having a sword..cut off his ear 4614
Unprotected by. Put..hand to the ark..oxen shook 4615

MOTIVE.
Labour. We labour..may be accepted of him 5587
Unsanctified. People spared the best..to sacrifice 5588
MOTIVES.
Inferior. Ye seek me..because ye did eat..loaves 5589
Suspicion. Urged him till he was ashamed, he said 5590
Worldly. Peter..thou savourest..things that be of 5591

Simplicity. Except ye become as little children 7914

8035. SINGING, Difficult. *Captives.* ² We hanged our harps upon the willows.. ³ For there they that carried us away captive required of us a song ; and they that wasted us *required of us* mirth, *saying,* Sing us *one* of the songs of Zion. ⁴ How shall we sing the Lord's song in a strange land?—Ps. 137.

8036. —— Easy. *Delivered.* ¹⁰ The ransomed of the Lord shall return, and come to Zion with songs and everlasting joy upon their heads : they shall obtain joy and gladness, and sorrow and sighing shall flee away.—Isa., ch. 35.

8037. —— Victory by. *Battle.* ²² When they began to sing and to praise, the Lord set ambushments against the children of Ammon, Moab, and mount Seir. ²³ For the children of Ammon and Moab stood up against..Seir, utterly to..destroy *them :* and when they had made an end of the inhabitants of Seir, every one helped to destroy another.—2 Chron., ch. 20.

Also see :
Love of. Solomon..his songs were 1005   583
  See **MUSIC.**

8038. SINNING in Prayer. *Pharisee.* ¹¹ God, I thank thee, that I am not as other men *are,* extortioners, unjust, adulterers, or even as this publican. [12] I fast twice in the week, I give tithes of all that I possess.—Luke, ch. 18.

8039. —— **by Proxy.** *Israelites.* [35] The Lord plagued the people, because they made the calf, which Aaron made.—Ex., ch. 32.

8040. —— **Preserved from.** *Abimelech.* [6] God said unto him in a dream, Yea, I know that thou didst this in the integrity of thy heart ; for I also withheld thee from sinning against me : therefore suffered I thee not to touch her. —Gen., ch. 20.

8041. —— **for Reward.** *Balaam.* [6] Curse me this people ; for they *are* too mighty for me : [7] And the elders of Moab and the elders of Midian departed with the rewards of divination in their hand ; and they came unto Balaam, and spake unto him the words of Balak.—Num., ch. 22.

8042. —— —— *Balaam.* [14] Having eyes full of adultery, and that cannot cease from sin ; beguiling unstable souls : a heart they have exercised with covetous practices ; cursed children : [15] Which have forsaken the right way.. following the way of Balaam *the son* of Bosor, who loved the wages of unrighteousness.—2 Peter, ch. 2.

8043. SINNER, The blinded. *"Darkened."* [18] Having the understanding darkened, being alienated from the life of God through the ignorance that is in them, because of the blindness of their heart : [19] Who being past feeling. —Eph., ch. 4.

8044. —— **The dying.** *Stumbling.* [16] Give glory to the Lord your God, before he cause darkness, and before your feet stumble upon the dark mountains, and, while ye look for light, he turn it into the shadow of death, *and* make *it* gross darkness.—Jer., ch. 13.

8045. —— **A deteriorating.** *Apostate.* [44] He findeth *it* empty, swept, and garnished. [45] Then goeth he, and taketh with himself seven other spirits more wicked than himself, and they enter in and dwell there : and the last *state* of that man is worse than the first.—Mat., ch. 12.

8046. —— **A grateful.** *Woman.* [38] Began to wash his feet with tears, and did wipe *them* with the hairs of her head, and kissed his feet, and anointed *them* with the ointment. [39]..when the Pharisee..saw *it*, he spake within himself, saying, This man, if he were a prophet, would have known who and what manner of woman *this is* that toucheth him ; for she is a sinner.—Luke, ch. 7.

8047. —— **An insane.** *Prodigal.* [17] When he came to himself, he said, How many hired servants of my father's have bread enough and to spare, and I perish with hunger !—Luke, ch. 15.

8048. —— **Overthrown.** *"Powder."* [44] Whosoever shall fall on this stone shall be broken : but on whomsoever it shall fall, it will grind him to powder.—Mat., ch. 21.

8049. —— **An obdurate.** *Zedekiah.* [13] He also rebelled against king Nebuchadnezzar, who had made him swear by God : but he stiffened his neck, and hardened his heart from turning unto the Lord God of Israel.—2 Chron., ch. 36. [He was a son of pious Josiah.]

8050. —— **A persistent.** *Amon.* [22] Amon

sacrificed unto all the carved images which Manasseh his father had made, and served them ; [23] And humbled not himself before the Lord, as Manasseh..had humbled himself ; but Amon trespassed more and more.—2 Chron., ch. 33.

8051. —— **A reclaimed.** *Prodigal.* [20] He arose, and came to his father. But when he was yet a great way off, his father saw him, and had compassion, and ran, and fell on his neck, and kissed him.—Luke, ch. 16.

8052. —— **The stupid.** *"Sheep."* [4] What man of you, having a hundred sheep, if he lose one of them, doth not leave the ninety and nine in the wilderness, and go after that which is lost, until he find it ?—Luke, ch. 15.

8053. —— **The sleeping.** *"Awake."* [14] Awake thou that sleepest, and arise from the dead, and Christ shall give thee light.—Eph., ch. 5.

8054. —— **The stricken.** *Gehazi.* [27] The leprosy therefore of Naaman shall cleave unto thee, and unto thy seed for ever. And he went out from his presence a leper *as white* as snow.—2 Kings, ch. 5.

8055. —— **A surpassing.** *King Ahab.* [30] Ahab ..did evil in the sight of the Lord above all that *were* before him. [31]..as if it had been a light thing for him to walk in the sins of Jeroboam.. he took to wife Jezebel the daughter of Ethbaal king of the Zidonians, and went and served Baal, and worshipped him. [32] And he reared up an altar for Baal.—1 Kings, ch. 16.

8056. —— —— *Jezebel.* [See Nos. 8055 and 8057.]

8057. —— **A sold.** *Ahab.* [25] There was none like unto Ahab, which did sell himself to work wickedness in the sight of the Lord, whom Jezebel his wife stirred up. [26] And he did very abominably in following idols.—1 Kings, ch. 21.

8058. SINNERS, All. *Natural.* [9] Jews and Gentiles, that they are all under sin : [10] As it is written, There is none righteous, no, not one : [11] There is none that understandeth, there is none that seeketh after God. [12] They are all gone out of the way, they are together become unprofitable ; there is none that doeth good, no, not one.—Rom., ch. 3.

8059. —— **against Sinners.** *Pharisees.* [13] Woe unto you, scribes and Pharisees, hypocrites ! for ye shut up the kingdom of heaven against men : for ye neither go in *yourselves*, neither suffer ye them that are entering to go in. —Mat., ch. 23.

8060. —— —— *On Earth.* [22] Then was brought unto him one possessed with a devil, blind, and dumb : and he healed him.. [23] And all the people were amazed, and said, Is not this the Son of David ? [24] But when the Pharisees heard *it*, they said, This *fellow* doth not cast out devils, but by Beelzebub the prince of the devils.—Mat., ch. 12.

8061. —— —— *At Judgment.* [41] The men of Nineveh shall rise in judgment with this generation, and shall condemn it : because they repented at the preaching of Jonas ; and, behold, a greater than Jonas *is* here.—Mat., ch. 12.

8062. —— **Abandoned.** *"Glory in..Shame."* [See No. 8086.]

8063. —— **Alarm of.** *Egyptians.* [24] The Lord

looked..through the pillar of fire and of the cloud,.and troubled the host of the Egyptians, ²⁵ And took off their chariot wheels, that they drave them heavily : so that the Egyptians said, Let us flee from the face of Israel ; for the Lord fighteth for them.—Ex., ch. 14.

8064. —— **Adversity for.** *Famine.* ⁶ I also have given you cleanness of teeth in all your cities, and want of bread in all your places : yet have ye not returned unto me, saith the Lord. —Amos, ch. 4.

8065. —— **Contemning.** *One Talent.* ²⁴ Lord, I knew thee that thou art a hard man, reaping where thou hast not sown, and gathering where thou hast not strewed : ²⁵ And I was afraid, and went and hid thy talent in the earth.—Mat., ch. 25.

8066. —— **Captivity for.** *Jews.* ¹⁶ The wrath of the Lord arose against his people, till there was no remedy. ¹⁷ Therefore he brought upon them the king of the Chaldees, who slew their young men with the sword in the house of their sanctuary, and had no compassion upon young man or maiden, old man, or him that stooped for age.—2 Chron., ch. 36.

8067. —— **Defeat of.** *Proverb.* [See No. 8084.]

8068. —— **Exceeding.** *Sodomites.* ¹³ The men of Sodom were wicked and sinners before the Lord exceedingly.—Gen., ch. 13.

8069. —— **enlightened.** *Of Capernaum.* ²³ Thou, Capernaum, which are exalted unto heaven, shalt be brought down to hell : for if the mighty works, which have been done in thee, had been done in Sodom, it would have remained until this day. ²⁴..it shall be more tolerable for the land of Sodom in the day of judgment, than for thee.—Mat., ch. 11.

8070. —— **End of.** *Punishment.* ¹³ My people are gone into captivity, because they have no knowledge : and their honourable men are famished, and their multitude dried up with thirst. ¹⁴ Therefore hell hath enlarged herself, and opened her mouth without measure : and their glory, and their multitude, and their pomp, and he that rejoiceth, shall descend into it.—Isa., ch. 5.

8171. —— —— *Punishment.* ²³ Which justify the wicked for reward, and take away the righteousness of the righteous from him ! ²⁴ Therefore as the fire devoureth the stubble, and the flame consumeth the chaff, so their root shall be as rottenness, and their blossom shall go up as dust.—Isa., ch. 5.

8072. —— **The greatest.** *"Blood..under Foot."* ²⁹ Of how much sorer punishment, suppose ye, shall he be thought worthy, who hath trodden under foot the Son of God, and hath counted the blood of the covenant, wherewith he was sanctified, an unholy thing, and hath done despite unto the Spirit of grace?—Heb., ch. 10.

8073. —— **Helpless.** *Bethesda Pool.* ⁷ The impotent man answered him, Sir, I have no man, when the water is troubled, to put me into the pool : but while I am coming, another steppeth down before me.—John, ch. 5.

8074. —— **Indifference of.** *Feast.* ⁴ I have prepared my dinner : my oxen and my fatlings are killed, and all things are ready : come unto the marriage. ⁵ But they made light of it, and went their ways, one to his farm, another to his merchandise.—Mat., ch. 22.

8075. —— **Irrational.** *Pharaoh.* ²² And the waters were a wall unto them on their right hand, and on their left. ²³ And the Egyptians pursued, and went in after them to the midst of the sea.—Ex., ch. 14.

8076. —— **Ridicule from.** *Hence Captivity.* ¹⁶ They mocked the messengers of God, and despised his words, and misused his prophets, until the wrath of the Lord arose against his people, till there was no remedy.—2 Chron., ch. 36.

8077. —— **Repentance for.** *"Ye repent."* ¹ Told him of the Galileans, whose blood Pilate had mingled with their sacrifices. ² And Jesus answering said..Suppose ye that these Galileans were sinners above all the Galileans, because they suffered such things? ³ I tell you, Nay : but, except ye repent, ye shall all likewise perish.—Luke, ch. 13.

8078. —— **Remembrance of.** *Moses said,* ⁷ Remember, and forget not, how thou provokedst the Lord thy God to wrath in the wilderness : from the day that thou didst depart out of the land of Egypt..ye have been rebellious against the Lord.—Deut., ch. 9. [See chapter.]

8079. —— **Salvation for.** *Only.* ¹¹ When the Pharisees saw it, they said unto his disciples, Why eateth your master with publicans and sinners ? ¹² But when Jesus heard that, he said.. They that be whole need not a physician, but they that are sick.—Mat., ch. 9.

8080. —— **Separation from.** *Pharisee.* [See No. 8046.]

8081. —— **Transformed.** *Magdalene.* ⁴⁴ Simon, Seest thou this woman? I entered into thy house, thou gavest me no water for my feet : but she hath washed my feet with tears, and wiped them with the hairs of her head. ⁴⁵ Thou gavest me no kiss : but this woman, since the time I came in, hath not ceased to kiss my feet. —Luke, ch. 7.

8082. —— **Violent.** *Ancient.* ¹³ Their tongues they have used deceit ; the poison of asps is under their lips : ¹⁴ Whose mouth is full of cursing and bitterness : ¹⁵ Their feet are swift to shed blood : ¹⁶ Destruction and misery are in their ways.—Rom., ch. 3.

8083. —— **Varieties of.** *Parable.* ["Coin," unconsciously lost. "Sheep," consciously lost. "Son," degradingly lost.]—Luke, ch. 15.

8084. —— **Wealth of.** *Proverb.* ²² A good man leaveth an inheritance to his children's children : and the wealth of the sinner is laid up for the just.—Prov., ch. 13.

8085. —— **The worst.** *Hypocrites.* ⁴⁶ Beware of the scribes, which desire to walk in long robes, and love greetings in the markets, and the highest seats in the synagogues, and the chief rooms at feasts : ⁴⁷ Which devour widows' houses, and for a shew make long prayers : the same shall receive greater damnation.—Luke, ch. 20.

8086. —— **Weeping over.** *Paul.* ¹⁸ (For many walk..whom I have told you often, and now tell you even weeping, that they are the enemies of the cross of Christ : ¹⁹ Whose end is destruction, whose God *is their* belly, and *whose* glory *is* in their shame, who mind earthly things.) PHIL., ch. 3.

8087. —— False Zeal of. *Pharisees.* [3] The scribes and Pharisees brought unto him a woman taken in adultery ; and when they had set her in the midst, [4] They say unto him, Master.. [5]..Moses in the law commanded us, that such should be stoned : but what sayest thou?—JOHN, ch. 8.

8088. SINS known to Jesus. *Samaritan.* [17] Jesus said unto her.. [18]..thou hast had five husbands ; and he whom thou now hast is not thy husband : in that saidst thou truly. [19] The woman saith unto him, Sir, I perceive that thou art a prophet.—JOHN, ch. 4.

8089. —— against Light. *Jesus.* [20] Then began he to upbraid the cities wherein most of his mighty works were done, because they repented not : [21] Woe unto thee, Chorazin ! woe unto thee Bethsaida ! for if the mighty works, which were done in you, had been done in Tyre and Sidon, they would have repented long ago.—MAT., ch. 11.

8090. —— Ministerial. *Eli's Sons* [12] Were sons of Belial ; they knew not the Lord. [13]..when any man offered sacrifice, the priest's servant came, while the flesh was in seething, with a fleshhook of three teeth in his hand ; [14] And he struck *it* into the pan, or kettle, or caldron, or pot ; all that the fleshhook brought up the priest took for himself.—1 SAM., ch. 2.

8091. —— Misjudgment of. *Pillar of Fire.* [20] Between the camp of the Egyptians and the camp of Israel, and it was a cloud and darkness *to them,* but it gave light by night *to these.* —EX., ch. 14.

8092. —— Misjudged. *Calamities.* [4] Those eighteen, upon whom the tower in Siloam fell, and slew them, think ye that they were sinners above all men that dwelt in Jerusalem ? [5] I tell you, Nay : but, except ye repent, ye shall all likewise perish.—LUKE, ch. 13.

8093. —— Misleading. *Woe !* [20] Woe unto them that call evil good, and good evil ; that put darkness for light, and light for darkness ; that put bitter for sweet, and sweet for bitter ! [21] Woe unto *them that are* wise in their own eyes, and prudent in their own sight !—ISA., ch. 5.

8094. SINS, Others'. *Irresponsible for.* [5] As soon as the kingdom was confirmed in his hand ..he slew his servants which had slain the king his father. [6] But the children of the murderers he slew not : according unto that which is written in the book of the law of Moses..The fathers shall not be put to death for the children, nor the children..for the fathers ; but every man shall be put to death for his own sin.—2 KINGS, ch. 14.

8095. —— Power over. *Questioned.* [5] When Jesus saw their faith, he said unto the sick of the palsy, Son, thy sins be forgiven thee. [6] But there were certain of the scribes sitting there, and reasoning in their hearts.. [7] Why doth this *man* thus speak blasphemies ? who can forgive sins but God only?—MARK, ch. 2.

**8096. —— —— ** *Proven.* [See No. 8095.] [10] That ye may know that the Son of man hath power on earth to forgive sins, (he saith to the sick of the palsy,) [11] I say unto thee, Arise, and take up thy bed, and go thy way.—MARK, ch. 2.

See SIN and references.

8097. SISTER brought to Jesus. *Mary.* [28] She went her way, and called Mary her sister secretly, saying, The Master is come, and calleth for thee. [29] As soon as she heard *that,* she arose quickly, and came unto him.—JOHN, ch. 11.

8098. —— A dutiful. *Miriam.* [4] His sister stood afar off, to wit what would be done to him. [7] Then said his sister to Pharaoh's daughter, Shall I go and call to thee a nurse of the Hebrew women.. [8] And Pharaoh's daughter said ..Go, And the maid..called the child's mother. —EX., ch. 2.

8099. SISTERS, Diverse. *Mary—Martha.* [38] Martha received him into her house. [39] And she had a sister called Mary, which also sat at Jesus' feet, and heard his word. [40] But Martha was cumbered about much serving.—LUKE, ch. 10.

8100. SITUATION, Seeking a. *Levite.* [8] The man departed out of the city from Beth-lehem-judah to sojourn where he could find *a place :* and he came to mount Ephraim to the house of Micah.—JUDGES, ch. 17. [Who employed him as his priest.]

8101. SLANDER, Antidote for. *"Good Works."* [12] Having your conversation honest among the Gentiles : that, whereas they speak against you as evil doers, they may by *your* good works, which they shall behold, glorify God in the day of visitation.—1 PETER, ch. 2.

8102. —— A base. *Pharisees.* [22] Then was brought..one possessed with a devil, blind, and dumb : and he healed him, insomuch that the blind and dumb both spake and saw. [23] And all the people were amazed, and said, Is not this the Son of David ? [24]..the Pharisees..said, This *fellow* doth not cast out devils, but by Beelzebub the prince of the devils.—MAT., ch. 12.

8103. —— Disgraceful. *Paul.* [5] We have found this man *a* pestilent *fellow,* and a mover of sedition among all the Jews throughout the world, and a ringleader of the sect of the Nazarenes : [6] Who also hath gone about to profane the temple.—ACTS, ch. 24.

8104. —— Folly of. *Proverb.* [18] He that hideth hatred *with* lying lips, and he that uttereth a slander, *is* a fool. [19] In the multitude of words there wanteth not sin.—PROV., ch. 10.

8105. —— A hurtful. *Rebellion.* [12] Be it known unto the king, that the Jews which..are come unto Jerusalem, building the rebellious and the bad city.. [13]..if this city be builded, and the walls set up *again, then* will they not pay toll, tribute, and custom, and *so* thou shalt endamage the revenue of the kings.—EZRA, ch. 4.

8106. —— Impious. *Calvary.* [41] The chief priests mocking *him,* with the scribes and elders, said, [42] He saved others ; himself he cannot save.—MAT., ch. 27.

8107. —— of Loyalty. *Ziba's.* [3] The king said, And where *is* thy master's son ? And Ziba said..Behold, he abideth at Jerusalem : for he said, To day shall the house of Israel restore me the kingdom of my father. [4] Then said the king to Ziba, Behold, thine *are* all that *pertained* unto Mephibosheth.—2 SAM., ch. 16.

8108. —— **Joyful under.** *Jesus said,* ¹¹ Blessed are ye, when *men* shall revile you, and persecute *you,* and shall say all manner of evil against
you falsely, for my sake. ¹² Rejoice. and be exceeding glad : for great *is* your reward in heav-
en.—MAT., ch. 5.

8109. —— **Malicious.** *Diotrephes.* ⁹ I wrote
unto the church : but Diotrephes, who loveth to
have the preeminence among them, receiveth us
not. ¹⁰ Wherefore, if I come, I will remember
his deeds which he doeth, prating against us
with malicious words.—3 JOHN.

8110. —— **Opposed by.** *Nehemiah.* ⁵ Then
sent Sanballat his servant..the fifth time with
an open letter.. ⁶ Wherein *was* written, It is reported among the heathen, and Gashmu saith
it, that thou and the Jews think to rebel..thou
buildest the wall, that thou mayest be their
king.—NEH., ch. 6.

8111. —— **refuted.** *By Jesus.* [See No.
8102.] ²⁵ Jesus knew their thoughts, and said
..Every kingdom divided against itself is
brought to desolation ; and every..house divid-
ed against itself shall not stand : ²⁶ And if Satan
cast out Satan, he is divided against himself ;
how shall then his kingdom stand?—MAT.,
ch. 12.

8112. —— **of Rebels.** *Israelites.* ²⁷ Because
the Lord hated us, he hath brought us forth out
of the land of Egypt, to deliver us into the hand
of the Amorites, to destroy us. ²⁸ Whither shall
we go up? our brethren have discouraged our
heart, saying, The people *is* greater and taller
than we.—DEUT., ch. 1.

8113. —— **of Sinners.** *Talent.* ²⁰ Behold,
here is thy pound, which I have kept laid up in
a napkin : ²¹ For I feared thee, because thou art
an austere man : thou takest up that thou layedst not down, and reapest that thou didst not
sow.—LUKE,. ch. 19.

8114. —— **Satanic.** *Job.* ¹⁰ Hast not thou
made a hedge about him, and about his house,
and about all that he hath on every side?..and
his substance is increased in the land. ¹¹ But
put forth thine hand now, and touch all that he
hath, and he will curse thee to thy face.—JOB,
ch. 1.

8115. —— **Secret.** *Whisperer.* ²⁸ A froward
man soweth strife ; and a whisperer separateth
chief friends.—PROV., ch. 16.

8116. —— **from Unbelief.** *Israelites.* ³ Would
to God we had died by the hand of the Lord in
the land of Egypt, when we sat by the fleshpots, *and* when we did eat bread to the full ;
for ye have brought us forth into this wilderness, to kill this whole assembly with hunger.
--Ex., ch. 16.

8117. SLANDERER, Satan a. *Eden.* ⁵ God
doth know that in the day ye eat thereof, then
your eyes shall be. opened, and ye shall be as
gods, knowing good and evil.—GEN., ch. 3. [As
if unwilling to promote their welfare.]

8118. SLANDERERS punished. *Israelites.*
³² Your carcasses, they shall fall in this wilder-
ness. ³³ And your children shall wander in the
wilderness forty years, and bear your whore-
doms, until your carcasses be wasted in the
wilderness.—NUM., ch. 14.

See other illustrations under :

TALEBEARER.

Flattery. Meddle not with him that flattereth	8578
Strife. Where no talebearer the strife ceaseth	8579
Tattling. Repeateth a matter separateth very f.	8580
Wounds. Words of the t. are as wounds	8581
Expected. If they have called the master..Beelz.	1263

8119. SLAUGHTER of Captives. *Amaziah.*
¹² Ten thousand *left* alive did the children of Ju-
dah carry away captive..and cast them down
from the top of the rock, that they all were broken in pieces.—2 CHRON., ch. 25.

See other illustrations under :

MANSLAUGHTER.

Accidental. [See Jewish law—Num. 35 : 9-29.]	
Defensive. He refused..Abner smote him	5212
Justifiable. Thief..be smitten that he die	5213
Pardonable. Axe..head slippeth..upon his n.	5214
Solicited. Stand..upon me and slay me [Saul]	5215
Unjustifiable. If the sun be risen upon him	5216

See MASSACRE.

8120. SLAVE, Sale of a. *Joseph.* ¹ Potiphar,
an officer of Pharaoh..bought him of the hands
of the Ishmaelites, which had brought him down
thither.—GEN., ch. 39.

8121. SLAVERY, Egyptian. *Brickmakers.*
¹³ Fulfil your works, *your* daily tasks, as when
there was straw. ¹⁴ And the officers of the children of Israel, which Pharaoh's taskmasters had
set over them, were beaten, *and* demanded,
Wherefore have ye not fulfilled your task in
making brick?—Ex., ch. 5.

See BONDAGE and references.

8122. SLEEP, Abstinence from. *David.* ³ Surely I will not come into..my house, nor go up into
my bed ; ⁴ I will not give sleep to mine eyes, *or*
slumber to mine eyelids, ⁵ Until I find out a
place for the Lord, a habitation for the mighty
God of Jacob.—Ps. 132.

8123. —— **Beneficial.** *Adam's.* ²¹ The Lord
God caused a deep sleep to fall upon Adam, and
he slept : and he took one of his ribs, and closed
up the flesh instead thereof ; ²² And the rib..
made he a woman, and brought her unto the
man.—GEN., ch. 2.

8124. —— **Caution against.** *"Watch."* ³⁴ *For
the Son of man is* as a man taking a far journey,
who left his house, and gave authority to his
servants, and to every man his work, and commanded the porter to watch.—MARK, ch. 13.

8125. —— **Comforting.** *Jacob's.* ¹⁶ Jacob
awaked out of his sleep, and he said, Surely the
Lord is in this place ; and I knew *it* not. ¹⁷ And
he was afraid, and said, How dreadful *is* this
place ! this *is* none other but the house of God,
and this *is* the gate of heaven.—GEN., ch. 28.

8126. —— **disturbed.** *Proverb.* ¹² The sleep
of a labouring man *is* sweet, whether he eat little or much : but the abundance of the rich will
not suffer him to sleep.—ECCL., ch. 5.

8127. —— —— *Rich Fool.* ¹⁷ He thought
within himself, saying, What shall I do, because
I have no room where to bestow my fruits?
²⁰ But God said unto him, *Thou* fool, this night
thy soul shall be required of thee : then whose
shall those things be, which thou hast provided?
—LUKE, ch. 12.

8128. —— **Dangerous.** *Samson.* ¹⁹ She made
him sleep upon her knees and she called for a

man, and she caused him to shave off the seven locks of his head, and she began to afflict him, and his strength went from him.—JUDGES, ch. 16.

8129. —— —— *Unconscious.* [12] David took the spear and the cruse of water from Saul's bolster ; and they gat them away, and no man saw *it*, nor knew *it*, neither awaked : for they *were* all asleep.—1 SAM., ch. 26.

8130. —— **Defenceless in.** *"Tares."* [24] The kingdom of heaven is likened unto a man which sowed good seed in his field : [25] But while men slept, his enemy came and sowed tares among the wheat, and went his way.—MAT., ch. 13.

8131. —— **Death a.** *Stephen.* [59] They stoned Stephen, calling upon *God*, and saying, Lord Jesus, receive my spirit. [60] And he kneeled down, and cried with a loud voice, Lord, lay not this sin to their charge. And when he had said this, he fell asleep.—ACTS, ch. 7.

8132. —— **Heavy with.** *Transfiguration.* [32] Peter and they were with him were heavy with sleep : and when they were awake, they saw his glory, and the two men that stood with him.—LUKE, ch. 9.

8133. —— **impossible.** *Ahasuerus.* [1] On that night could not the king sleep, and he commanded to bring the book of records of the chronicles ; and they were read before the king.—ESTHER, ch. 6.

8134. —— —— *Darius* [18] Passed the night fasting : neither were instruments of music brought before him : and his sleep went from him. [19] Then the king arose very early in the morning, and went in haste unto the den of lions.—DAN., ch. 6.

8135. —— **Irresistible.** *Gethsemane.* [40] He cometh unto the disciples, and findeth them asleep, and saith unto Peter, What, could ye not watch with me one hour?—MAT., ch. 26.

8136. —— **Overcome by.** *Eutychus.* [9] There sat in a window a certain young man named Eutychus, being fallen into a deep sleep : and as Paul was long preaching, he..fell down from the third loft, and was taken up dead.—ACTS, ch. 20.

8137. —— **A pretended.** *Guard.* [12] They gave large money unto the soldiers, [13] Saying, Say ye, His disciples came by night, and stole him *away* while we slept.—MAT., ch. 28.

8138. —— **Refreshing.** *Poor Man.* [See No. 8126.]

8139. —— **in a Storm.** *Jesus.* [23] As they sailed, he fell asleep : and there came down a storm of wind on the lake ; and they were filled *with water*, and were in jeopardy.—LUKE, ch. 8.

8140. —— —— *Jonah.* [5] The mariners were afraid, and cried every man unto his god, and cast forth the wares that *were* in the ship into the sea, to lighten *it* of them. But Jonah was gone down into the sides of the ship ; and he lay, and was fast asleep.—JONAH, ch. 1.

8141. —— **of the Sick.** *Job.* [4] When I lie down, I say, When shall I arise, and the night be gone? and I am full of tossings to and fro unto the dawning of the day.—JOB, ch. 7.

8142. —— **A troubled.** *Eliphaz.* [15] A spirit passed before my face ; the hair of my flesh stood up : [16] It stood still, but I could not dis-

cern the form thereof : an image *was* before mine eyes, *there was* silence, and I heard a voice.—JOB, ch. 4.

8143. —— **Undisturbed.** *Peter.* [6] When Herod would have brought him forth, the same night Peter was sleeping between two soldiers, bound with two chains ; and the keepers before the door kept the prison.—ACTS, ch. 12.

8144. —— **Vision in.** *Abraham.* [12] When the sun was going down, a deep sleep fell upon Abram ; and, lo, a horror of great darkness fell upon him. [13] And he said unto Abram..thy seed shall be a stranger in a land *that is* not theirs, and shall serve them..four hundred years.—GEN., ch. 15.

See other illustrations under :

DREAM.

Comforting. Ladder..angels descending on it	2503
Direction. Fear not to take unto thee Mary	2504
Delusive. Hungry man..and behold he eateth	2505
Forgotten. The thing is gone from me [Neb.]	2506
Interpreted. The three branches are three days	2514
Offensive. Your sheaves made obeisance to my s.	2515
Prophetic. [See Daniel 2 : 26-45.]	
Preserved. Joseph..take the young child and flee	2508
Reproof. G. came to Abimelech in a dream	2509
Trouble. Seven thin ears devoured the seven rank	2510
Terrifying. Fourth beast..iron teeth, it devoured	2511
Verified. This is..the sword of Gideon	2512
Warning. I have suffered in a dream [Pilate's wife]	2513
Preparation. I will both lay me down in peace	7551

8145. **SLUGGARD reproved.** *Ant.* [6] Go to the ant, thou sluggard ; consider her ways, and be wise : [7] Which having no guide, overseer, or ruler, [8] Provideth her meat in the summer, *and* gathereth her food in the harvest.—PROV., ch. 6.

8146. —— **Vexatious, The.** *Smoke.* [26] As vinegar to the teeth, and as smoke to the eyes, so *is* the sluggard to them that send him.—PROV., ch. 10.

8147. —— —— *Proverb.* [19] The way of the slothful *man is* as a hedge of thorns : but the way of the righteous *is* made plain.—PROV., ch. 15.

See other illustrations under :

EASE.

Care for. Trouble me not..in bed, I cannot arise	2586
Indifference. If ye offer the lame and sick, is it not	2587
Promised. Soul, thou hast much goods..take thine	2588
Religious. Woe unto them that are at ease in Zion	2589

IDLENESS.

Accusation. No straw..ye are idle, ye are idle	4270
Ecstatic. Why stand ye gazing into heaven?	4271
Needless. Why stand ye here all the day idle?	4272
Perishing. If we sit still here, we die also [lepers]	4273

INDOLENCE.

Exhibited. I went by the field of the slothful	4436
Excuse. There is a lion without..I shall be slain	4437
Perfect. Hand..not so much as bring it to his h.	4438
Shame. Sleepeth in harvest..causeth shame	4439
Wasteful. Slothful in his work..a great waster	4440

LOITERERS.

Driven. Fire..consumed them in the uttermost	5052
Hastened. While he lingered, the men laid hold	5053

8148. **SOCIALISM, Christian.** *Jerusalem.* [44] All that believed were together, and had all things common ; [45] And sold their possessions and goods, and parted them to all *men*, as every man had need.—ACTS, ch. 2.

8149. —— **Jewish.** *Law.* [1] At the end of *every* seven years thou shalt make a release. [2] And this *is* the manner of the release : Every creditor that lendeth *aught* unto his neighbour shall release it ; he shall not exact *it*. .because it is called the Lord's release.—Deut., ch. 15.

8150. SOCIETY changed. *Job.* [1] Now *they that are* younger than I have me in derision, whose fathers I would have disdained to have set with the dogs of my flock.—Job, ch. 30.

8151. —— **Conservator of.** *The Church.* [13] Ye are the salt of the earth : but if the salt have lost his savour, wherewith shall it be salted ? it is thenceforth good for nothing, but to be cast out, and to be trodden under foot of men.—Mat., ch. 5.

8152. —— **Influence of.** *Assimilation.* [20] He that walketh with wise *men* shall be wise : but a companion of fools shall be destroyed.—Prov., ch. 13.

8153. —— **Miserable.** *David's.* [2] Every one that was in distress, and. .in debt, and. .discontented, gathered themselves unto him ; and he became a captain over them : and there were with him about four hundred men.—1 Sam., ch. 22.

8154. —— **Needful.** *Eden.* [18] The Lord God said, *It is* not good that the man should be alone : I will make him a help meet for him.—Gen., ch. 2.

8155. —— **Respect of.** *Job.* [8] The young men saw me, and hid themselves : and the aged arose, *and* stood up. [9] The princes refrained talking, and laid *their* hand on their mouth.—Job, ch. 29.

8156. SOCIABILITY, Devotional. *Record.* [16] Then they that feared the Lord spake often one to another : and the Lord hearkened, and heard *it*, and a book of remembrance was written before him for them that feared the Lord, and that thought upon his name.—Mal., ch. 3.

8157. —— **interdicted.** *Samaritan.* [9] Then saith the woman of Samaria. .How is it that thou, being a Jew, askest drink of me, which am a woman of Samaria? for the Jews have no dealings with the Samaritans.—John, ch. 4.

8158. —— **Primitive.** *Christian.* [46] They, continuing daily with one accord in the temple, and breaking meat from house to house, did eat their bread with gladness and singleness of heart.—Acts, ch. 2.

8159. —— **rewarded.** *Jewels.* [See No. 8156.] [17] They shall be mine, saith the Lord of hosts, in that day when I make up my jewels ; and I will spare them, as a man spareth his own son that serveth him.—Mal., ch. 3.

8160. —— **Religious.** *Passover.* [4] If the household be too little for the lamb, let him and his neighbour next unto his house take *it* according to the number of the souls.—Ex., ch. 12.

See FRIENDS, FRIENDSHIP, *and references.*

8161. SOLDIER, A brave. *Jonathan.* [13] Jonathan climbed up upon his hands and upon his feet, and his armourbearer after him : and they fell before Jonathan ; and his armourbearer slew after him.—1 Sam., ch. 14.

8162. —— **The Christian.** *Free.* [3] Endure hardness, as a good soldier of Jesus Christ. [4] No man that warreth entangleth himself with the affairs of *this* life ; that he may please him who hath chosen him to be a soldier.—2 Tim., ch. 2.

8163. —— **A magnanimous.** *David.* [4] The men of David said. .Behold the day of which the Lord said. .Behold, I will deliver thine enemy into thine hand, that thou mayest do to him as it shall seem good unto thee. Then David arose, and cut off the skirt of Saul's robe privily.—1 Sam., ch. 24.

8164. —— **A pious.** *Cornelius was* [1] A centurion of the band called the Italian *band*, [2] *A* devout *man*, and one that feared God with all his house, which gave much alms. .and prayed to God always.—Acts, ch. 10.

8165. —— —— *Joshua.* [11] The Lord spake unto Moses face to face, as a man speaketh unto his friend. And he turned again into the camp ; but his servant Joshua, the son of Nun, a young man, departed not out of the tabernacle.—Ex., ch. 33.

8166. —— **Pride of a.** *Abimelech.* [54] He called hastily unto the young man his armourbearer. .Draw thy sword, and slay me, that men say not of me, A woman slew him. And his young man thrust him through.—Judges, ch. 9.

8167. —— **A Volunteer.** *David.* [32] David said to Saul, Let no man's heart fail because of him ; thy servant will go and fight with this Philistine.—1 Sam., ch. 17.

8168. SOLDIERS, Bribery of. *Guard.* [12] When they were assembled with the elders, and had taken counsel, they gave large money unto the soldiers, [13] Saying, Say ye, His disciples came by night, and stole him *away* while we slept.—Mat., ch. 28.

8169. —— **Extraordinary.** *Benjamites.* [1] They *were* among the mighty men, helpers of the war. [2] *They were* armed with bows, and could use both the right hand and the left in *hurling* stones and *shooting* arrows out of a bow, *even* of Saul's brethren of Benjamin.—1 Chron., ch. 12. Also— *David's.* [8] These *be* the names of the mighty men whom David had : The Tachmonite, that sat in the seat, chief among the captains ; the same *was* Adino the Eznite ; *he lifted up his spear* against eight hundred, whom he slew at one time.—2 Sam., ch. 23. [See chapter.]

8170. —— —— *Gadites.* [8] Of the Gadites there separated themselves unto David. .men of might, *and* men of war *fit* for the battle, that could handle shield and buckler, whose faces *were like* the faces of lions, and *were* as swift as the roes upon the mountains.—1 Chron., ch. 12.

8171. —— **Hired.** *Amaziah.* [6] He hired also a hundred thousand mighty men of valour out of Israel for a hundred talents of silver.—2 Chron., ch. 25.

Also see :

Aged. [Caleb 85 yrs. old] So is my strength for war 243
Conscientious. David's heart smote him   1579
Conscription. Gathered all that were able to put   1581
Divine. Stood a man. .sword drawn   1021
Obedience. Centurion. .I say go, and he goeth   588
See WAR *and references.*

8172. SOLITUDE hurtful. *Eden.* [8] The Lord God planted a garden eastward in Eden ; and there he put the man whom he had formed

..¹⁸ And..said, *It is* not good that the man should be alone : I will make him a help meet. —GEN., ch. 2.

8173. —— for Prayer. *Jesus.* ²³ When he had sent the multitudes away, he went up into a mountain apart to pray : and when the evening was come, he was there alone.—MAT., ch. 14.

8174. —— for Rest. *Apostles.* ³⁰ The apostles gathered themselves together unto Jesus, and told him all things, both what they had done, and what they had taught. ³¹ And he said unto them, Come ye yourselves apart into a desert place, and rest a while.—MARK, ch. 6.

8175. —— A strange. *Four Lepers.* ⁵ They rose up in the twilight, to go unto the camp of the Syrians : and when they were come to the uttermost part..behold; *there was* no man there. —2 KINGS, ch. 7.

See other illustrations under:
LONELINESS.
Comfort in. Jacob dreamed, and behold a ladder   5054
Despondency. I, even I only, am left..seek my life 5055

Rest. Come ye..into a desert place and rest   7260
Religious. Eli..his heart trembled for the ark of G. 454

8176. SON, Affectionate. *Joseph.* ²⁹ Joseph made ready his chariot, and went up to meet Israel his father, to Goshen, and presented himself unto him ; and he fell on his neck, and wept on his neck a good while.—GEN., ch. 46.

8177. —— Degenerate. *Solomon.* ⁴ When Solomon was old..his wives turned away his heart after other gods : and his heart was not perfect with the Lord his God, as *was* the heart of David his father.—1 KINGS, ch. 11.

8178. —— Evil. *Zedekiah.* [Son of good Josiah.] ¹² He did *that which was* evil in the sight of the Lord his God, *and* humbled not himself.. ¹³..he stiffened his neck, and hardened his heart from turning unto the Lord God. —2 CHRON., ch. 36.

8179. —— expelled. *Ishmael.* ¹⁴ Abraham rose up early in the morning, and took bread, and a bottle of water, and gave *it* unto Hagar, putting *it* on her shoulder, and the child, and sent her away : and she..wandered in the wilderness of Beer-sheba.—GEN., ch. 21.

8180. —— Firstborn. *Priest.* ² Sanctify unto me all the firstborn, whatsoever openeth the womb among the children of Israel, *both* of man and of beast : it *is* mine.—EX., ch. 14.

8181. —— healed. *Nobleman's.* ⁴⁹ The nobleman saith..Sir, come down ere my child die. ⁵⁰ Jesus saith..Go thy way ; thy son liveth. And the man believed the word that Jesus had spoken.—JOHN, ch. 4.

8182. —— Ingrate. *"Shame."* ²⁶ He that wasteth *his* father, *and* chaseth away *his* mother, *is* a son that causeth shame, and bringeth reproach.—PROV., ch. 19.

8183. —— —— End of. ²⁰ Whoso curseth his father or his mother, his lamp shall be put out in obscure darkness.—PROV., ch. 20.

8184. —— Hopeful. *Cain.* ¹ Adam knew Eve his wife ; and she conceived, and bare Cain, and said, I have gotten a man from the Lord.— GEN., ch. 4. [But Cain became a fratricide.]

8185. —— An obedient. *Isaac.* [See No. 8191.]

8186. —— Penitent. *Prodigal.* ¹⁸ I will arise and go to my father, and will say unto him, Father, I have sinned against heaven, and before thee, ¹⁹ And am no more worthy to be called thy son : make me as one of thy hired servants.—LUKE, ch. 15.

8187. —— like Parent. *Amon.* ²² He did *that which was* evil in the sight of the Lord.. for Amon sacrificed unto all the carved images which Manasseh his father had made, and served them.—2 CHRON., ch. 33.

8188. —— unlike Parent. *Manasseh.* ³ He built up again the high places which Hezekiah his father had destroyed ; and he reared up altars for Baal, and made a grove.—2 KINGS, ch. 21.

8189. —— Rebellious. *Law.* ¹⁸ If a man have a stubborn and rebellious son, which will not obey the voice of his father, or..his mother, and *that* when they have chastened him, will not hearken unto them ; ²¹..all the men of his city shall stone him..that he die.—DEUT., ch. 21.

8190. —— Reformed by a. *Maachah.* ¹³ Maachah his mother, even her he removed from *being* queen, because she had made an idol in a grove ; and Asa destroyed her idol, and burnt *it* by the brook Kidron.—1 KINGS, ch. 15.

8191. —— sacrificed. *Isaac.* ⁹ Abraham built an altar there, and laid the wood in order, and bound Isaac his son, and laid him on the altar upon the wood. ¹⁰ And Abraham..took the knife to slay his son.—GEN., ch. 22.

8192. —— Scandalous. *Absalom.* ²² They spread Absalom a tent upon the top of the house ; and Absalom went in unto his father's concubines in the sight of all Israel.—2 SAM., ch. 16.

8193. —— Unnatural. *Absalom.* ¹ Ahithophel said..Let me now choose out twelve thousand men, and I will arise and pursue after David this night : ² And I will come upon him while he *is* weary and weak handed, and will make him afraid..I will smite the king only.. ⁴ And the saying pleased Absalom well.—2 SAM., ch. 17.

8194. —— Unfortunate. *"Dumb Spirit."* ¹⁸ Wheresoever he taketh him he teareth him ; and he foameth, and gnasheth with his teeth, and pineth away.—MARK, ch. 9.

8195. SONS, Degenerate. *Eli's.* ²² Eli was very old, and heard all that his sons did unto all Israel ; and how they lay with the women that assembled *at* the door of the tabernacle.— 1 SAM., ch. 3.

8196. —— —— *Samuel's.* ¹ When Samuel was old..he made his sons judges of Israel.. ³ And his sons walked not in his ways, but turned aside after lucre, and took bribes, and perverted judgment.—1 SAM., ch. 8.

8197. —— differ. *Adam's.* ³ Cain brought of the fruit of the ground an offering unto the Lord. ⁴ And Abel, he also brought of the firstlings of his flock and of the fat thereof. And the Lord had respect unto Abel and to his offering : ⁵ But unto Cain..not respect. And Cain was very wroth.—GEN., ch. 4.

8198. —— —— *Parable.* ¹¹ A certain man had two sons : ¹² And the younger of them said to *his* father, Father, give me the portion of goods that falleth *to me*.—LUKE, ch. 15.

8199. —— —— *Parable.* 28 Son, go work to day in my vineyard. 29 He answered and said, I will not ; but afterward he repented, and went. 30..the second..said, I *go*, sir ; and went not.—MAT., ch. 21.

8200. —— rejected, Wicked. *Samuel's.* [See No. 8196.] 5 Behold, thou art old, and thy sons walk not in thy ways : now make us a king to judge us like all the nations. 6 But the thing displeased Samuel, when they said, Give us a king to judge us.—1 SAM., ch. 8.

8201. SONSHIP renounced. *Moses.* 24 By faith Moses, when he was come to years, refused to be called the son of Pharaoh's daughter ; 26 Esteeming the reproach of Christ greater riches than the treasures in Egypt.—HEB., ch. 11.

See other illustrations under :

ADOPTION.

Attraction. Mordecai..brought up Esther..beautiful 105
Grateful. Mephibosheth shall eat as..king's sons 106
Sympathy. Babe wept..became her son 107

INHERITANCE.

Tendency. The wealth of the sinner is laid up for 4490
Uncertainty. I should leave it unto..that followeth 4491

8202. SORCERY, Captivating. *Simon Magus.* 9 Simon, which..used sorcery, and bewitched the people of Samaria.. 10 To whom they all gave heed, from the least to the greatest, saying, This man is the great power of God.—ACTS, ch. 8.

8203. —— renounced. *Simon.* 13 Then Simon himself believed also : and when he was baptized, he continued with Philip, and wondered, beholding the miracles and signs which were done.—ACTS, ch. 8.

8204. —— —— *Ephesians.* 19 Many of them also which used curious arts brought their books together, and burned them before all *men* : and they counted the price of them, and found *it* fifty thousand *pieces* of silver.—ACTS, ch. 19.

See other illustrations under :

SPIRITS.

Appearance. Saints which slept arose..appeared 8304
Communication. Neither will they be..though one 8305
Familiar. Workers with familiar spirits..wizards 8306
Seducing. Latter times..giving heed to seducing s. 8307
"   Manasseh..dealt with familiar spirits a. 8308

WITCHCRAFT.

Abolished. Workers with familiar spirits..put a. 9649
Work of. The woman saw Samuel, she cried..loud 9648

Magi. Magicians..rod..became serpents 5162

8205. SORROW, The atoning. *Calvary.* 46 And about the ninth hour Jesus cried with a loud voice, saying, Eli, Eli, lama sabachthani ? that is to say, My God, my God, why hast thou forsaken me ?—MAT., ch. 27.

8206. —— —— *Garden.* 37 He took with him Peter, and the two sons of Zebedee, and began to be sorrowful and very heavy. 38 Then saith he unto them, My soul is exceeding sorrowful, even unto death.—MAT., ch. 26.

8207. —— Affecting. *David.* 30 David went up by the ascent of *mount* Olivet, and wept as he went up, and had his head covered, and he went barefoot : and all the people that *was* with him covered every man his head, and they went up, weeping as they went up.—2 SAM., ch. 15.

8208. —— in Age. *Jacob.* 38 My son shall not go down with you ; for his brother is dead, and he is left alone : if mischief befall him by the way in the which ye go, then shall ye bring down my gray hairs with sorrow to the grave.—GEN., ch. 42.

8209. —— of Bereavement. *Jesus.* 33 When Jesus therefore saw her weeping, and the Jews also weeping which came with her, he groaned in the spirit, and was troubled, 34 And said, Where have ye laid him ? They say unto him, Lord, come and see. 35 Jesus wept.—JOHN, ch. 11.

8210. —— betrayed. *Nehemiah's.* 1 I had not been *beforetime* sad in his presence. 2 Wherefore the king said unto me, Why *is* thy countenance sad, seeing thou *art* not sick? this *is* nothing *else* but sorrow of heart. Then I was very sore afraid.—NEH., ch. 2.

8211. —— Benefits of. *Heart.* 2 It *is* better to go to the house of mourning, than to go to the house of feasting : for that *is* the end of all men ; and the living will lay *it* to his heart. 3 Sorrow *is* better than laughter : for by the sadness of the countenance the heart is made better.—ECCL., ch. 7.

8212. —— Cause of. *Sin.* 16 Unto the woman he said, I will greatly multiply thy sorrow and thy conception ; in sorrow thou shalt bring forth children ; and thy desire *shall be* to thy husband, and he shall rule over thee.—GEN., ch. 3.

8213. —— Constant. *Amnon dead.* 37 David mourned for his son every day. 38 So Absalom fled, and went to Geshur, and was there three years.—2 SAM., ch. 13.

8214. —— considered. *Abram's.* 10 Ephron the Hittite answered Abraham in the audience ..of all that went in at the gate of his city, saying, 11..the field give I thee, and the cave that *is* therein, I give it thee..bury thy dead.—GEN., ch. 23.

8215. —— compassionated. *Penitent.* 7 Ye *ought* rather to forgive *him*, and comfort *him*, lest perhaps such a one should be swallowed up with overmuch sorrow.—2 COR., ch. 2.

8216. —— The Disciples'. *To Emmaus.* 16 Their eyes were holden that they should not know him. 17 And he said..What manner of communications *are* these that ye have one to another, as ye walk, and are sad ?—LUKE, ch. 24.

8217. —— Domestic. *Hannah.* 9 Eli the priest sat upon a seat by a post of the temple of the Lord. 10 And she *was* in bitterness of soul, and prayed unto the Lord, and wept sore.—1 SAM., ch. 1.

8218. —— Distressing. *Esther.* 3 Esther spake yet again before the king, and fell down at his feet, and besought him with tears to put away the mischief of Haman..that he had devised against the Jews.—ESTHER, ch. 8.

8219. —— A Father's. *David.* 33 Went up to the chamber over the gate, and wept : and as he went, thus he said, O my son Absalom ! my son, my son Absalom ! would God I had died for thee, O Absalom, my son, my son !—2 SAM., ch. 18.

8220. —— Healer of. *Jesus.* 18 The spirit of the Lord *is* upon me, because he hath anointed

me to preach the gospel to the poor ; he hath
sent me to heal the broken-hearted, to preach
deliverance to the captives, and recovering of
sight to the blind, to set at liberty them that
are bruised.—Luke, ch. 4.

8221. —— **Joy after.** *Affliction.* [See Lam.,
ch. 3.]

8222. —— **Judgment.** *" Hide us."* ¹⁶ Said
to the mountains and rocks, Fall on us, and
hide us from the face of him that sitteth on the
throne, and from the wrath of the Lamb : ¹⁷ For
the great day of his wrath is come.—Rev., ch. 6.

8223. —— —— **Parable.** ²⁷ Depart from
me, all *ye* workers of iniquity. ²⁸ There shall be
weeping and gnashing of teeth, when ye shall
see Abraham, and Isaac, and Jacob, and all
the prophets, in the kingdom of God, and you
yourselves thrust out.—Luke, ch. 13.

8224. —— **by Neglect.** *Talent.* ²⁵ I was
afraid, and went and hid thy talent in the earth :
lo, *there* thou hast *that is* thine. ³⁰..cast ye the
unprofitable servant into outer darkness : there
shall be weeping and gnashing of teeth.—Mat.,
ch. 25.

8225. —— **Prostrating.** *David.* ¹⁶ David
therefore besought God for the child ; and David
fasted, and went in, and lay all night upon the
earth. ¹⁷ And the elders of his house arose,
and went to him, to raise him up from the earth :
but he would not, neither did he eat bread with
them.—2 Sam., ch. 12.

8226. —— **A profitable.** *Corinthians.* ¹¹ Ye
sorrowed after a godly sort, what carefulness it
wrought in you, yea, *what* clearing of yourselves,
yea, *what* indignation, yea, *what* fear, yea, *what*
vehement desire, yea, *what* zeal, yea, *what* revenge ! In all *things* ye have approved yourselves to be clear in this matter.—2 Cor., ch. 7.

8227. —— **A profitless.** *Herod.* ²⁵ I will that
thou give me by and by in a charger the head
of John the Baptist. ²⁶ And the king was exceeding sorry ; *yet* for his oath's sake, and for
their sakes which sat with him, he would not
reject her.—Mark, ch. 6.

8228. —— **Royal.** *David.* [Lately crowned.]
²⁵ How are the mighty fallen in the midst of the
battle ! O Jonathan, *thou wast* slain in thine high
places. ²⁶ I am distressed for thee, my brother
Jonathan : very pleasant hast hast thou been
unto me : thy love to me was wonderful, passing the love of women.—2 Sam., ch. 1.

8229. —— **relieved.** *Prayer.* ¹² [Hannah]
as she continued praying before the Lord..Eli
marked her mouth. ¹⁸ So the woman went her
way, and did eat, and her countenance was no
more *sad.*—1 Sam., ch. 1.

8230. —— —— *Hagar.* ¹⁷ The angel of God
called to Hagar out of heaven..What aileth thee,
Hagar? fear not ; for God hath heard the voice
of the lad where he *is.* ¹⁸ Arise, lift up the lad
..for I will make him a great nation. ¹⁹ And
God opened her eyes, and she saw a well of
water.—Gen., ch. 21.

8231. —— **from Suspicion.** *Apostles.* ¹⁸ One
of you which eateth with me shall betray me.
¹⁹ And they began to be sorrowful, and to say
unto him one by one, *Is* it I? and another *said,
Is* it I?—Mark, ch. 14.

8232. —— **Sin brings.** *Prodigal.* ¹⁷ When he
came to himself, he said, How many hired serv-

ants of my father's have bread enough and to
spare, and I perish with hunger !—Luke, ch. 15.

8233. —— **Worldly.** *Young Ruler.* ²² Sell all
that thou hast, and distribute unto the poor,
and thou shalt have treasure in heaven : and
come, follow me. ²³ And when he heard this,
he was very sorrowful : for he was very rich.
—Luke, ch. 18.

See other illustrations under :

DISAPPOINTMENT.

Doubt. Heard that he was alive..believed not	2315
in Gifts. S. gave Hiram 20 cities..pleased him not	2316
Good. They have taken..L. out of the sepulchre	2317
Humiliating. Prison truly..shut..no man there	2318
Ignorance. No place of seed..figs..vines	2319
Judgment. Thou hast taught in our streets	2320
Misjudged. We trusted it had been he..saved I.	2321
Maternal. I have gotten a man [murderer] from L.	2322
Many. Sown much, and bring in little	2326
Perplexing. King of Syria sore troubled	2323
Religion. Have wanted all things..consumed	2324
Unendurable. Ahithophel..hanged himself	2325

DESPAIR.

Affliction. Let me not see the death of the child	2213
Anguish. Slay me, for anguish is come upon me	2214
Awaking. Wine was gone out..heart died within	2215
Deliverance. Been better for us to serve the Egyp.	2216
Kindness. Widow..meal..oil..me and my son eat	2217

DESPONDENCY.

Bereavement. Joseph is, without doubt, rent in p.	2226
Complaint. Since I came to Pharaoh..done evil	2227
Constitutional. Let us go..die with him	2230
Continued. My heart is smitten and withered like	2228
Cure. David was greatly distressed..spake of s.	2229
Difficulties. People was much discouraged	2231
Hasty. Sun beat..Jonah fainted..wished to die	2233
Hope. Why art thou cast down, O my soul	2232
Ill-timed. Handful of meal..little oil..die	2234
Loneliness. I only am left, and they seek my life	2235
Memories. By the rivers of Babylon we wept	2236
Over-care. If thou deal thus with me, kill me	2237
Peril. Esau cometh..400 men..Jacob afraid	2240
Prayer. How long wilt thou forget me, O L.	2239
Public. Moses heard the people weeping..door	2238
Singular. Lord take away my life..not better	2242
Vows. L. made a reproach unto me..derision	2243
Without. Troubled on every side..not in despair	2244

DISTRESS.

Cry of. Great cry..none like it, nor shall be	2437
Derided. They that see me, shoot out the lip	2438
Described. I was a derision to all my people	2439
Exasperation. What shall I do..people ready to s.	3440
Famine. Delicate women..shall eat..children	3341
Friend. Gedaliah..took Jeremiah out of prison	3443
Great. Thrust..right eyes..people wept	3444
Little Faith. Why are ye fearful..little faith..calm	3442
Needless. Saul had adjured..food	3445
Refuge. Ahaz sacrificed unto the gods that smote	3446

See **ADVERSITY** and references.

See **AFFLICTION, GRIEF,** and references.

8234. SOUL, Mistake respecting the. *Stomach.*
¹⁹ I will say to my soul, Soul, thou hast much
goods laid up for many years ; take thine ease,
eat, drink, *and* be merry.—Luke, ch. 12.

8235. —— **starved.** *Riches.* ¹⁸ These are they
which are sown among thorns ; such as hear the
word, ¹⁹ And the cares of this world, and the
deceitfulness of riches, and the lusts of other
things entering in, choke the word, and it becometh unfruitful.—Mark, ch. 4.

8236. —— **Yearning of the.** *For God.* [3] Oh that I knew where I might find him ! *that I* might come *even* to his seat ! [4] I would order *my* cause before him, and fill my mouth with arguments.—Job, ch. 23.

8237. SOULS, Destroyers of. *Hypocrites.* [25] Woe unto you, scribes and Pharisees, hypocrites ! for ye compass sea and land to make one proselyte ; and when he is made, ye make him twofold more the child of hell than yourselves.—Mat., ch. 23.

8238. —— **Eager for.** *Paul.* [19] Yet have I made myself servant unto all, that I might gain the more. [20] And unto the Jews I became as a Jew, that I might gain the Jews ; to them that' are under the law, as under the law, that I might gain them that are under the law.—1 Cor., ch. 9.

8239. —— **Hindering.** *Pharisees.* [13] Woe unto you, scribes and Pharisees, hypocrites ! for ye shut up the kingdom of heaven against men : for ye neither go in *yourselves*, neither suffer ye them that are entering to go in.—Mat., ch. 23.

8240. —— **Winning.** *Paul.* [22] To the weak became I as weak, that I might gain the weak : I am made all things to all *men*, that I might by all means save some. [23] And this I do for the gospel's sake.—1 Cor., ch. 9.

See SALVATION, SPIRIT, *and references.*

8241. SPEAKING, Evil. *Judge.* [11] Speak not evil one of another, brethren. He that speaketh evil of *his* brother, and judgeth his brother, speaketh evil of the law, and judgeth the law : but if thou judge the law, thou art not a doer of the law, but a judge.—James, ch. 4.

8242. —— **for God.** *Timid.* [6] Ah, Lord God ! behold, I cannot speak : for I *am* a child. [7] . .Say not, I *am* a child : for thou shalt go to all that I shall send thee, and whatsoever I command thee thou shalt speak.—Jer., ch. 1.

8243. —— —— *Fearless.* [8] Be not afraid of their faces : for I *am* with thee to deliver thee, saith the Lord. [9] Then the Lord put forth his hand, and touched my mouth. And the Lord said. .Behold I have put my words in thy mouth. —Jer., ch. 1.

8244. —— **Help for.** *Spirit.* [3] There appeared unto them cloven tongues like as of fire, and it sat upon each of them. [4] And they were all filled with the Holy Ghost, and began to speak with other tongues, as the Spirit gave them utterance.—Acts, ch. 2.

8245. SPEAKER, Convincing. *Jesus.* [45] Came the officers to the chief priests and Pharisees ; and they said unto them, Why have ye not brought him ? [46] The officers answered, Never man spake like this man.—John, ch. 7.

8246. —— **Engaging.** *Jesus.* [38] Martha received him into her house. [39] And she had a sister called Mary, which also sat at Jesus' feet, and heard his word.—Luke, ch. 10.

8247. SPEECH assisted. *Moses.* [10] O my Lord, I *am* not eloquent, neither heretofore, nor since thou hast spoken unto thy servant ; but I *am* slow of speech, and of a slow tongue. [12] . .go, and I will be with thy mouth, and teach thee what thou shalt say.—Ex., ch. 4.

8248. —— —— *Jeremiah.* [See No. 8243.]

8249. —— **Appropriate.** *"Apples of Gold."* [11] A word fitly spoken *is like* apples of gold in pictures of silver.—Prov., ch. 25.

8250. —— **Anointed.** *Pentecost.* [See No. 8244.]

8251. —— **constrained.** *Elihu said,* [17] *I said,* I will answer also my part ; I also will shew mine opinion. [18] For I am full of matter ; the spirit within me constraineth' me.—Job, ch. 32.

8252. —— **Cautious.** *"Words be few."* [2] Be not rash with thy mouth, and let not thine heart be hasty to utter *any* thing before God : for God *is* in heaven, and thou upon earth : therefore let thy words be few.—Eccl., ch. 5.

8253. —— **Confusion of.** *Babel.* [9] Therefore is the name of it called Babel ; because the Lord did there confound the language of all the earth : and from thence did the Lord scatter them abroad upon the face of all the earth.—Gen., ch. 11.

8254. —— **Dangers of.** *Bridle.* [2] In many things we offend all. If any man offend not in word, the same *is* a perfect man, *and* able also to bridle the whole body.—James, ch. 3.

8255. —— **Evidence by.** *"Bridleth not."* [26] If any man among you seem to be religious, and bridleth not his tongue, but deceiveth his own heart, this man's religion is vain.—James, ch. 1.

8256. —— **Gift of.** *Witness.* [18] Ye shall be brought before governors and kings for my sake, for a testimony. . [19] But when they deliver you up, take no thought how or what ye shall speak : for it shall be given you in that same hour what ye shall speak. [20] For it is not ye that speak, but the Spirit of your Father—Mat., ch. 10.

8257. —— **improved.** *Impediment.* [32] They bring. .one that was deaf, and had an impediment in his speech ; and they beseech him to put his hand upon him. [33] And he. .put his fingers into his ears, and he spit, and touched his tongue.—Mark, ch. 7.

8258. —— **impossible.** *At Judgment.* [12] Friend, how camest thou in hither not having a wedding garment ? And he was speechless.— Mat., ch. 22.

8259. —— **Plainness of.** *Paul.* [4] My speech and my preaching *was* not with enticing words of man's wisdom, but in demonstration of the Spirit and of power.—1 Cor., ch. 2.

8260. —— **Power of.** *"Death"—"Life."* [21] Death and life *are* in the power of the tongue : and they that love it shall eat the fruit thereof. —Prov., ch. 18.

8261. —— **unrestrained.** *Deceitful.* [2] They speak vanity every one with his neighbour : *with* flattering lips *and* with a double heart do they speak. [3] The Lord shall cut off all flattering lips, *and* the tongue that speaketh proud things.—Ps. 12.

8262. —— **unentangled.** *Jesus.* [15] The Pharisees. .took counsel how they might entangle him in *his* talk. [21] Render therefore unto Cesar the things which are Cesar's ; and unto God the things that are God's. [22] . .they marvelled, and left him.—Mat., ch. 22.

8263. —— **Unguarded.** *Proverb.* [3] He that keepeth his mouth keepeth his life : *but* he that openeth wide his lips shall have destruction.— Prov., ch. 13.

8264. —— **useless.** *Pilate's Court.* ¹² When he was accused of the chief priests and elders, he answered nothing. ¹³ Then said Pilate..Hearest thou not how many things they witness against thee? ¹⁴ And he answered him to never a word ; insomuch that the governor marvelled greatly.—MAT., ch. 27.

8265. —— —— *Herod's Court.* ⁹ He questioned with him in many words ; but he answered him nothing. ¹⁰ And the chief priests and scribes stood and vehemently accused him.—LUKE, ch. 23.

See other illustrations under :
ELOQUENCE.
Better than. I will be with thy mouth ! to Moses 2618
Ministerial. Apollos an eloquent man and mighty 2619
LANGUAGE.
Corrupted. Children spake half in the speech of A. 4896
Given. How hear we every man in our own tongue 4897
Origin. Let us..confound their language..not 4898
TALEBEARER.
Flattery. Meddle not with him that flattereth 8578
Strife. Where no talebearer the strife ceaseth 8579
Tattling. Repeateth a matter..separateth very 8580
Wounds. Words of the t. are as wounds 8581
UTTERANCE.
Deficient. O my L. I am not eloquent 9153
Gift. I will be with thy mouth 9154
" Spake with other tongues..S. gave 9155
WORD.
Divine. In the beginning was the word 9763
Important. Say now Shibboleth..said Sibboleth 9764
Only a. John saith, Behold the Lamb of God 9765
WORDS.
Accountability. Every idle word..give account 9769
Cheerful. Heaviness in..heart..good word..glad 9770
" Merry heart doeth good like medicine 9771
Effect. Words..as deep waters..flowing brook 9772
Kind. Pleasant words are as an honeycomb 9773
Listening. Spake often..L. hearkened and heard 9774
Overflow. Abundance of the heart..speaketh 9775
Proven. When Jacob saw the wagons..spirit r. 9776
Reliance. L... bid me come to thee..on the water 9777

Corrupted. Children could not speak in the l. 4896
Delightful. All wondered at the gracious words 7753
Given. Every man heard them speak in his own t. 4897
Irresistible. Not able to resist the wisdom and s. 96
Origin. Let us..confound their language 4898
Suppressed. Caleb stilled the people..we are a. 3128
" Decree..speak anything against the God 9
Talking vs. Doing. Aaron..mouth..take thou the 8591
Unfriendly. Brethren..not speak peaceably unto 3099

8266. SPIES, Accusation. *Jacob's Sons.* ¹⁶ Send one of you, and let him fetch your brother, and ye shall be kept in prison, that your words may be proved, whether *there be any* truth in you : or else by the life of Pharaoh surely ye *are* spies.—GEN., ch. 42.

8267. —— **in the Church.** *At Jerusalem.* ⁴ Because of false brethren unawares brought in, who came in privily to spy out our liberty which we have in Christ Jesus, that they might bring us into bondage : ⁵ To whom we gave pl..ce by subjection, no, not for an hour.—GAL., ch. 2.

8268. —— **disguised.** *Jesus.* ²⁰ They watched *him,* and sent forth spies, which should feign themselves just men, that they might take hold of his words, that so they might deliver him unto..the governor.—LUKE, ch. 20.

8269. —— **entertained.** *Rahab.* ¹ Joshua.. sent out of Shittim two men to spy secretly, saying, Go view the land, even Jericho. And they ..came into a harlot's house, named Rahab, and lodged there.—JOSH., ch. 2.

8270. —— **intimidated.** *Ten.* ³² And they brought up an evil report..saying, The land.. eateth up the inhabitants thereof ; and all the people that we saw in it *are* men of a great stature. ³³ And there we saw the giants, the sons of Anak..we were in our own sight as grasshoppers, and so we were in their sight.—NUM., ch. 13.

8271. —— **Political.** *Absalom's.* ¹⁰ Absalom sent spies throughout all the tribes of Israel, saying, As soon as ye hear the sound of the trumpet, then ye shall say, Absalom reigneth in Hebron.—2 SAM., ch. 15.

8272. —— **Suspected.** *Hanun.* ³ The princes ..of Ammon said unto Hanun their lord, Thinkest thou that David doth honour thy father, that he hath sent comforters unto thee? hath not David *rather* sent his servants unto thee, to search the city, and to spy it out, and to overthrow it?—2 SAM., ch. 10.

8273. —— —— *Sympathizers.* [See above.] ⁴ Wherefore Hanun took David's servants, and shaved off the one half of their beards, and cut off their garments in the middle, *even* to their buttocks, and sent them away.—2 SAM., ch. 10.

8274. —— **Service of.** *Canaan.* ¹⁷ Moses sent them to spy out the land of Canaan, and said.. ¹⁸..see the land, what it *is ;* and the people that dwelleth therein, whether they *be* strong or weak, few or many.—NUM., ch. 13.

8275. —— **Watchful.** *Daniel.* ¹⁰ When Daniel knew that the writing was signed, he went into his house ; and, his windows being open in his chamber toward Jerusalem, he kneeled.. three times a day, and prayed, and gave thanks before his God, as he did aforetime. ¹¹ Then these men assembled, and found Daniel praying.--DAN., ch. 6.

See other illustrations under :
DETECTIVES.
Female. Delilah said..Come up..he hath shown 2257
Impious. They watched him whether he would h. 2258
Unknown. Moses looked this way and that..slew 2259
Invisible. Elisha sent unto the king..S. are come 334

8276. SPIRIT by Anointing. *David.* ¹³ Samuel took the horn of oil, and anointed him in the midst of his brethren : and the Spirit of the Lord came upon David from that day forward. —1 SAM., ch. 16.

8277. —— **breathed.** *On Apostles.* ²² He breathed on *them,* and saith unto them, Receive ye the Holy Ghost : ²³ Whosesoever sins ye remit, they are remitted unto them , *and* whosesoever *sins* ye retain, they are retained.—JOHN, ch. 20.

8278. —— **Baptism of.** *Jesus.* ¹⁶ Jesus, when he was baptized, went up straightway out of the water : and lo, th heavens were opened unto him, and he saw the Spirit of God descending like a dove, and lighting upon him.—MAT., ch. 3.

8279. —— **Choice of the.** *Eliab.* ⁷ The Lord said unto Samuel, Look not on his countenance, or on the height of his stature ; because I have refused him : for *the Lord seeth* not as man seeth ; for man looketh on the outward appearance, but the Lord looketh on the heart.—1 SAM., ch. 16.

8280. —— —— *David.* ¹¹ There remaineth yet the youngest, and behold, he keepeth the sheep. And Samuel said unto Jesse, Send and fetch him.. ¹².. Now he *was* ruddy, *and* withal of a beautiful countenance, and goodly to look to. And the Lord said, Arise, anoint him : for this *is* he.—1 SAM., ch. 16.

8281. —— Demonstration of the. *Pentecost.* ⁶ When this was noised abroad, the multitude came together, and were confounded, because that every man heard them speak in his own language. ⁷ And they were amazed and marvelled.—ACTS, ch. 2.

8282. —— Evil. *Saul.* ¹⁴ The Spirit of the Lord departed from Saul.. ¹⁵ And Saul's servants said unto him, Behold now, an evil spirit from God troubleth thee.—1 SAM., ch. 16.

8283. —— Filled with the. *Pentecost.* ³ And there appeared unto them cloven tongues like as of fire, and it sat upon each of them. ⁴ And they were all filled with the Holy Ghost, and began to speak.—ACTS, ch. 2.

8284. —— Fruit by. *Pentecost.* ⁴¹ They that gladly received his word were baptized : and the same day there were added *unto them* about three thousand souls.—ACTS, ch. 2.

8285. —— Flesh weakens the. *Gethsemane.* ⁴⁰ Findeth them asleep, and saith unto Peter, What, could ye not watch with me one hour? ⁴¹ Watch and pray, that ye enter not into temptation : the spirit indeed *is* willing, but the flesh *is* weak.—MAT., ch. 26.

8286. —— Fruits of the. *Graces.* ²²˙The fruit of the Spirit is love, joy, peace, longsuffering, gentleness, goodness, faith, ²³ Meekness, temperance : against such there is no law.—GAL., ch. 5.

8287. —— A familiar. *Witch of En-dor.* ⁷ Said Saul unto his servants, Seek me a woman that hath a familiar spirit, that I may go to her, and inquire of her. And his servants said.. Behold, *there is* a woman.. at En-dor.—1 SAM., ch. 28.

8288. —— Fear of a. *Visible.* ⁴⁸ He cometh unto them.. and would have passed by them. ⁴⁹ But when they saw him walking upon the sea, they supposed it had been a spirit, and cried out.—MARK, ch. 6.

8289. —— —— *Needless.* ³⁶ Jesus himself stood in the midst of them, and saith.. Peace *be* unto you. ³⁷ But they were terrified and affrighted, and supposed that they had seen a spirit.—LUKE, ch. 24.

8290. —— Ignorant of the. *Ephesians.* ¹ Paul.. came to Ephesus : and finding certain disciples, ² He said.. Have ye received the Holy Spirit since ye believed? And they said.. We have not so much as heard whether there be any Holy Spirit.—ACTS, ch. 19.

8291. —— Incorporeal. *Resurrection.* ³⁹ Behold my hands and my feet, that it is I myself : handle me, and see ; for a spirit hath not flesh and bones, as ye see me have.—LUKE, ch. 24.

8292. —— Loss of. *Samson.* ²⁰ Said, The Philistines *be* upon thee, Samson. And he awoke out of his sleep, and said, I will go out as at other times before, and shake myself. And he wist not the Lord was departed from him.—JUDGES, ch. 16.

8293. —— misjudged. *Pentecost.* ¹¹ Cretes and Arabians, we do hear them speak in our tongues the wonderful works of God. ¹³ Others mocking said, These men are full of new wine.—ACTS, ch. 2.

8294. —— Moved by the. *Samson.* ²⁴ Samson.. grew, and the Lord blessed him. ²⁵ And the Spirit of the Lord began to move him at times in the camp of Dan.—JUDGES, ch. 13.

8295. —— Might by the. *Samson.* ¹⁴ The Philistines shouted against him : and the Spirit of the Lord came mightily upon him, and the cords that *were* upon his arms became as flax that was burnt with fire, and his bands loosed from off his hands. ¹⁵ And he found a new jawbone of an ass.. and took it, and slew a thousand men.—JUDGES, ch. 15.

8296. —— Promise of. *"Last Days."* ¹⁶ This.. was spoken by the prophet Joel ; ¹⁷.. in the last days, saith God, I will pour out of my Spirit upon all flesh : and your sons and your daughters shall prophesy.—ACTS, ch. 2.

8297. Power of the. *" Bones live."* ⁹ Come from the four winds, O breath, and breathe upon these slain, that they may live. ¹⁰ So I prophesied as he commanded me, and the breath came into them, and they lived, and stood up upon their feet, an exceeding great army.—EZEK., ch. 37.

8298. —— Resistless, The. *Stephen.* ¹⁰ They were not able to resist the wisdom and the spirit by which he spake. ¹¹ Then they suborned men, which said, We have heard him speak blasphemous words against Moses, and *against* God.—ACTS, ch. 6.

8299. —— Sent by the. *Peter.* ¹⁹ While Peter thought on the vision, the Spirit said.. Behold, three men seek thee. ²⁰ Arise therefore, and get thee down, and go with them, doubting nothing : for I have sent them.—ACTS, ch. 10.

8300. —— Symbol of the. *Dove.* [See No. 8278.]

8301. —— —— *Fire.* ²¹ The Lord went before them by day in a pillar of a cloud, to lead them the way ; and by night in a pillar of fire, to give them light ; to go by day and night.—EX., ch. 13.

8302. —— Vision of a. *Job.* ¹⁴ Fear came upon me, and trembling, which made all my bones to shake. ¹⁵ Then a spirit passed before my face ; the hair of my flesh stood up : ¹⁶ It stood still, but I could not discern the form thereof : an image *was* before mine eyes, *there was* silence, and I heard a voice.—JOB, ch. 4.

8303. —— for Workers. *Bezaleel.* ³ I have filled him with the spirit of God, in wisdom.. and in all manner of workmanship, ⁴ To devise cunning works, to work in gold, and in silver, and in brass, ⁵ And in cutting of stones, to set *them*, and in carving of timber.—EX., ch. 31.

See other illustrations under :

HOLY SPIRIT.

Grieved. It repented the L...grieved..at his h.   4012
Ignorance. We have not..heard..be any H. G.   4013
Light. Be filled..fell from Saul's eyes..scales   4014
Mystery. Wind bloweth..canst not tell whence   4015
Prayer. I will pray the Father..give you..the S.   4016
Promise. Wait for the promise of the Father   4017
Symbol. H. G. descended..like a dove   4018
Speech. I will be with thy mouth   4019
Taught. Go, and I will teach thee what..say   4020
Temple. Ye are the temple..S. of G. dwelleth in y.   4021
Wonderful. What is this that is come unto [Saul]?   4022

See SOUL and references.

8304. SPIRITS, Appearance of. *At Crucifixion.*
[52] The graves were opened ; and many bodies of
the saints which slept arose, [53]..after his resurrection, and went into the holy city, and appeared unto many.—MAT., ch. 27.

8305. —— Communication with. *Dives.*
[30] Nay, father Abraham : but if one went unto
them from the dead, they will repent. [31] And
he said..If they hear not Moses and the prophets, neither will they be persuaded, though one
rose from the dead.—LUKE, ch. 16.

8306. —— Familiar. *"Put away."* [24] The
workers with familiar spirits, and the wizards,
and the images, and the idols, and all the abominations that were spied in the land of Judah
and in Jerusalem, did Josiah put away.—2
KINGS, ch. 23.

8307. —— Seducing. *"Latter Times."* [1] In
the latter times some shall depart from the faith,
giving heed to seducing spirits, and doctrines of
devils ; [2] Speaking lies in hypocrisy ; having
their conscience seared with a hot iron ; [3] Forbidding to marry.—1 TIM., ch. 4.

8308. —— —— *Manasseh.* [6] He made his
son pass through the fire..and used enchantments, and dealt with familiar spirits and wizards : he wrought much wickedness in the sight
of the Lord.—2 KINGS, ch. 21.

See ANGELS.

8309. SPIRITUALITY, Ignorance of. *Samaritan.* [11] The woman saith..Sir, thou hast nothing to draw with, and the well is deep : from
whence hast thou that living water ? [12] Art
thou greater than our father Jacob, which gave
us the well?—JOHN, ch. 4.

8310. —— by Separation. *Apostles.* [2] It is
not reason that we should leave the word of
God, and serve tables. [3] 'ook ye out among
you seven men of honest report, full of the Holy
Ghost and wisdom, whom we may appoint over
this business. [4] But we will give ourselves continually to prayer, and to the ministry of the
word.—ACTS, ch. 6.

8311. —— and Activity. *Mary—Martha.*
[40] Lord..my sister hath left me to serve alone?
bid her therefore that she help me. [41] And Jesus answered..Martha, thou art careful and
troubled about many things : [42] But one thing is
needful ; and Mary hath chosen that good part,
which shall not be taken away from her.—
LUKE, ch. 10.

8312. —— Importance of. *Salt.* [50] Salt *is*
good : but if the salt have lost his saltness,
wherewith will ye season it ? Have salt in yourselves, and have peace one with another.—
MARK, ch. 9.

8313. —— vs. Locality. *Samaritan.* [20] Our

fathers worshipped in this mountain ; and ye
say, that in Jerusalem is the place where men
ought to worship.. [24] God *is* a Spirit : and they
that worship him must worship *him* in spirit
and in truth.—JOHN, ch. 4.

See PIETY.

8314. SPOILS abundant. *Moabites..Ammonites.*
[25] When Jehoshaphat and his people..found..
both riches with the dead bodies, and precious
jewels, which they stripped off for themselves,
more than they could carry away : and they
were three days in gathering of the spoil, it was
so much.—2 CHRON., ch. 20.

8315. —— From Hagarites. [21] They
took away their cattle ; of their camels fifty
thousand, and of sheep two hundred and fifty
thousand, and of asses two thousand, and of
men a hundred thousand.—1 CHRON., ch. 5.

8316. —— coveted. *Achan.* [21] I saw among
the spoils a goodly Babylonish garment, and
two hundred shekels of silver, and a wedge of
gold of fifty shekels weight, then I coveted them,
and took them ; and, behold, they *are* hid in the
earth in the midst of my tent.—JOSH., ch. 7.

8317. —— declined. *Abram.* [21] Take the
goods to thyself. [22] And Abram said to the
king of Sodom, I have lifted up mine hand unto
the Lord.. [23] That I will not *take* from a thread
even to a shoelatchet, and that I will not take
any thing that *is* thine, lest thou shouldest say,
I have made Abram rich.—GEN., ch. 14.

8318. —— Expectation of. *Women said,*
[30] Have they not sped? have they *not* divided
the prey ; to every man a damsel *or* two ; to Sisera a prey of divers colours, a prey of divers colours of needlework, of divers colours of needlework on both sides, *meet* for the necks of *them
that take* the spoil?—JUDGES, ch. 5.

8319. —— forbidden. *At Jericho.* [18] Keep
yourselves from the accursed thing, lest ye make
yourselves accursed, when ye take of the accursed
thing, and make the camp of Israel a curse, and
trouble it.—JOSH., ch. 6.

See other illustrations under :

PILLAGE.

Jerusalem. Shishak took away the treasures   6180
Temple. Chaldeans carried to Babylon..gold   6179

Booty. 675,000 sheep, 72,000 beeves..61,000 asses   911
Dangerous. Amalekites..eating..drinking..danc'g   341

8320. SPY, A skilful. *Hushai.* [14] Absalom
and all the men of Israel said, The counsel of
Hushai..*is* better than the counsel of Ahithophel. For the Lord had appointed to defeat
the good counsel of Ahithophel, to..bring evil
upon Absalom.—2 SAM., ch. 17.

See SPIES.

8321. STATE, Appeal to the. *Paul.* [11] I refuse not to die : but if there be none of these
things whereof these accuse me, no man may
deliver me unto them. I appeal unto Cesar.
[12] Then Festus, when he had conferred with the
counsel, answered, Hast thou appealed unto
Cesar? unto Cesar shalt thou go.—ACTS, ch. 25.

8322. —— endangered. *By Ignorance.*
[11] With Absalom went two hundred men out of
Jerusalem, *that were* called ; and they went in
their simplicity, and they knew not any thing.
—2 SAM., ch. 15.

8323. —— —— *By Vice, at Thessalonica.* ⁵ The Jews..moved with envy, took unto them certain lewd fellows of the baser sort, and gathered a company, and set all the city on an uproar, and assaulted the house of Jason.—Acts, ch. 17.

8324. —— Honoured by the. *Secretary.* ⁹ It was written according to all that Mordecai commanded unto the Jews, and to the..rulers of the provinces.. ¹⁰ And he wrote in the king Ahasuerus' name, and sealed *it* with the king's ring.—Esther, ch. 8.

8325. —— —— *Prime Minister.* ⁴⁸ The king made Daniel a great man, and gave him many great gifts, and made him ruler over the whole province of Babylon, and chief of the governors over all the wise *men* of Babylon.—Dan., ch. 2

8326. —— Majesty of the. *At Philippi.* ³⁷ Paul said..They have beaten us openly uncondemned, being Romans, and have cast *us* into prison ; and now do they thrust us out privily ? nay verily ; but let them come themselves and fetch us out. ³⁸ And the sergeants told these words unto the magistrates : and they feared, when they heard that they were Romans.—Acts, ch. 16.

8327. —— Best Men for the. *Saul.* ⁵² There was sore war against the Philistines all the days of Saul : and when Saul saw any strong man, or any valiant man, he took him unto him.—1 Sam., ch. 14.

8328. —— Protection from the. *Paul.* ²⁵ As they bound him with thongs, Paul said unto the centurion that stood by, Is it lawful for you to scourge a man that is a Roman, and uncondemned?—Acts, ch. 22.

8329. —— Protector of the. *The Church.* ⁵⁵ When..Egypt was famished, the people cried to Pharaoh for bread : and Pharaoh said..Go unto Joseph ; what he saith you, do. ⁵⁶ And the famine was over all the face of the earth : an⁻ Joseph opened all the storehouses.—Gen., ch. 41.

8330. —— Support of. *Duty.* ¹⁷ Tell us therefore, What thinkest thou ? Is it lawful to give tribute unto Cesar, or not? ²¹..Render therefore unto Cesar the things which are Cesar's : and unto God the things that are God's.—Mat., ch. 22.

See other illustrations under :

NATIVE COUNTRY.

Best. Pharaoh let me depart..mine own country 1752
Customs. It must not be so done in our country 1753
Love. Jacob said..I may go..to my country 1754
Return. Moses said, Let me go..unto my brethren 1755
Surrendered. Abram, get thee out of thy country 1756

8331. STATESMANSHIP, Evil. *Jeroboam.* ²⁶ And Jeroboam said in his heart, Now shall the kingdom return to the house of David : ²⁷ If this people go up to do sacrifice in the house of the Lord at Jerusalem.. ³¹ And he made a house of high places, and made priests of the lowest of the people which were not of the sons of Levi. —1 Kings, ch. 12.

8332. —— Poor. *Rehoboam.* ⁸ He forsook the counsel of the old men, which they had given him, and consulted with the young men that were grown up with him, *and* which stood before him.—1 Kings, ch. 11. [The kingdom was divided.]

See other illustrations under :

PATRIOTISM.

Absorbing. Why is thy countenance sad ? 6005
Appeal. Fight for your brethren..houses 6006
Children. Wives also and the children rejoiced 6007
Dangerous. Ehud made him a dagger..two edges 6008
Deed. Moses..slew the Egyptian 6009
Generous. Were at my table 150 Jews besides 6010
Self-sacrificing. Forgive..if not blot me..out of 6013
Sacrifices. I..have not eaten the bread of the G. 6014
Sentiments. Moses said..Let me go..my brethren 6015

POLITICS.

Condemned. We found this fellow..forbidding 6236
Demagogue. O that I were made a judge 6237
Influence. If thou let this man go..not Cesar's 6238
in Religion. Is it lawful to give tribute to Cesar ? 6239
Ring. Sought to find occasion against Daniel 6240
See GOVERNMENT and references.

8333. STATURE, High. *King Saul.* ² Saul, a choice young man, and a goodly : and *there was* not among the children of Israel a goodlier person than he : from his shoulders and upward *he was* higher than any of the people.—1 Sam., ch. 9.

8334. —— Low. *Zaccheus.* ³ He sought to see Jesus who he was ; and could not for the press, because he was little of stature. ⁴ And he ran before, and climbed up into a sycamore tree to see him ; for he was to pass that *way.*—Luke, ch. 19.

8335. STABILITY of Character. *Godly.* ² He that walketh uprightly, and worketh righteousness, and speaketh the truth in his heart. ³ *He that* backbiteth not with his tongue, nor doeth evil to his neighbour, nor taketh up a reproach against his neighbour. ⁵ *He that* putteth not out his money to usury, nor taketh reward against the innocent. He that doeth these *things* shall never be moved.—Ps. 15. [See chapter.]

8636. —— *Faith gives.* ¹ They that trust in the Lord *shall be* as mount Zion, *which* cannot be removed, *but* abideth for ever. ² *As* the mountains *are* round about Jerusalem, so the Lord *is* round about his people from henceforth even for ever.—Ps. 125.

See other illustrations under :

FOUNDATION.

Only. Other foundation can no man lay 3399
Second Temple. People shouted..because..was 3401
Various Uses. Build on..gold..wood..stubble 3402

Rock. Their rock is not like our rock..judges 7461
See STEADFASTNESS.

8337. STEADFASTNESS of Converts. *Jerusalem.* ⁴¹ There were added *unto them* about three thousand souls. ⁴² And they continued steadfastly in the apostles' doctrine and fellowship, and in breaking of bread, and in prayers.—Acts, ch. 2.

8338. —— Determined. *Job.* ⁵ Till I die I will not remove my integrity from me. ⁶ My righteousness I hold fast, and will not let it go : my heart shall not reproach *me* so long as I live. —Job, ch. 27.

8339. —— to Duty. *King Josiah.* ² He did *that which was* right in the sight of the Lord, and walked in all the way of David..and turned not aside to the right hand or to the left.—2 Kings, ch. 22.

8340. —— in Integrity. *David.* ²¹ I have kept the ways of the Lord, and have not wickedly departed from my God. ²² For all his judgments *were* before me, and I did not put away his statutes from me. ²³ I was also upright before him, and I kept myself from mine iniquity. —Ps. 18.

8341. —— to Principle. *Daniel.* ⁸ Daniel purposed in his heart that he would not defile himself with the .. king's meat, nor with the wine which he drank : therefore he requested of the prince of the eunuchs that he might not defile himself.—DAN., ch. 1.

8342. —— Religious. *Three Hebrews.* ¹⁷ Our God whom we serve is able to deliver us from the burning fiery furnace, and he will deliver *us* out of thine hand, O king. ¹⁸ But if not, be it known unto thee, O king, that we will not serve thy gods, nor worship the golden image which thou hast set up.—DAN., ch. 3.

8343. —— seen. *Job's.* ³ The Lord said unto Satan, Hast thou considered my servant Job, that *there is* none like him in the earth, a perfect and an upright man, one that feareth God, and escheweth evil ? and still he holdeth fast his integrity, although thou movedst me against him, to destroy him without cause.— JOB, ch. 2.

See other illustrations under :

FAITHFULNESS.

Blessed. Is that servant whom his lord..so doing 2975
Constant. The fire shall ever be burning upon the 2976
Despondency. Let us also go that we may die with 2977
Honoured. I make a decree..speak..against the G. 2978
Ministerial. [See 2 Cor. 4 : 1-11.]　　　　　　2979
Primitive. All scattered abroad..except the a.　2981
Principle. Faithful in that which is least..also in 2982
Rewarded. If thou see me when I am taken..be so 2983
Truth. What the L. saith unto me, that I will speak 2980

PERSEVERANCE.

Confident. Neither death nor life..separate me　6097
Exhortation. Barnabas exhorted..with purpose　6098
Encouragement. Can a woman forget her..child　6099
　　　　"　　　Mountains shall depart..but my 6100
Help to. When..my foot slippeth..thy mercy held 6101
Prayer. This widow troubleth me, I will avenge 6102
Success by. I have fought a good fight..crown　6103
Test. If ye continue in my word, then..disciples 6104

Endeavour. He that endureth to the end..saved　2642

8344. STEALING, Shameless. *Steward.* ³ Cannot dig ; to beg I am ashamed. ⁴ I am resolved what to do, that, when I am put out of the stewardship, they may receive me into their houses. —LUKE, ch. 16.

See THEFT and references.

8345. STEWARDS, Christian. *At Jerusalem.* ³² The multitude of them that believed were of one heart and of one soul : neither said any *of them* that aught of the things which he possessed was his own ; but they had all things common. —ACTS, ch. 4.

8346. STEWARDSHIP, Christian. *Parable.* ¹² A certain nobleman went into a far country to receive for himself a kingdom.. ¹³ And he called his ten servants, and delivered them ten pounds, and said unto them, Occupy till I come. —LUKE, ch. 19.

8347. —— withdrawn. *Unjust Steward.* ¹ A steward..was accused..that he had wasted his goods. ²..How is it that I hear this of thee?

give an account of thy stewardship ; for thou mayest be no longer steward.—LUKE, ch. 16.

See **RESPONSIBILITY** and references.

8348. STONES, Precious. *Breastplate.* ¹⁷ Four rows of stones : *the first* row *shall be* a sardius, a topaz, and a carbuncle.. ¹⁸ And the second row *shall be* an emerald, a sapphire, and a diamond. ¹⁹ And the third row a ligure, an agate, and an amethyst. ²⁰ And the fourth row a beryl, and an onyx, and a jasper : they shall be set in gold.— Ex., ch. 28.

8349. STONING for Covetousness. *Achan.* ²⁵ Joshua said, Why hast thou troubled us ? the Lord shall trouble thee this day. And all Israel stoned him with stones, and burned them with fire.—JOSH., ch. 7.

8350. —— the Innocent. *Naboth.* ¹³ Men of Belial witnessed..against Naboth, in the presence of the people, saying, Naboth did blaspheme God and the king. Then they carried him forth out of the city, and stoned him.—1 KINGS, ch. 21.

8351. —— intended. *Of Jesus.* ³⁰ I and *my* Father are one. ³¹ Then the Jews took up stones again to stone him.. ³⁹ Therefore they sought again to take him ; but he escaped out of their hand.—JOHN, ch. 10.

8352. —— by Persecutors. *At Lystra.* ¹⁹ Jews from Antioch and Iconium, who persuaded the people, and, having stoned Paul, drew *him* out of the city, supposing he had been dead.—ACTS, ch. 14.

8353. —— —— Stephen. ⁵⁸ Cast *him* out of the city, and stoned *him :* and the witnesses laid down their clothes at a young man's feet, whose name was Saul. ⁵⁹ And they stoned Stephen, calling upon *God,* and saying, Lord Jesus, receive my spirit.—ACTS, ch. 7.

8354. —— for Reproof. *Zechariah.* ²⁰ The Spirit of God came upon Zechariah..the priest ..Thus saith God, Why transgress ye the commandments of the Lord, that ye cannot prosper ? because ye have forsaken the Lord, he hath also forsaken you. ²¹ And they conspired against him, and stoned him.—2 CHRON., ch. 24.

8355. —— for Revenge. *Absalom's Rebellion.* ⁵ Shimei..he came forth, and cursed still as he came. ⁶ And he cast stones at David, and at all the servants of king David : and..all the mighty men *were* on his right hand and on his left.—2 SAM., ch. 16.

8356. STORM, Alarming. *Egypt.* ²³ Moses stretched forth his rod toward heaven : and the Lord sent thunder and hail, and the fire ran along upon the ground.. ²⁸ Entreat the Lord (for *it is* enough) that there be no *more* mighty thunderings and hail ; and I will let you go. —Ex., ch. 9.

8357. —— Destructive. *Amorites.* ¹¹ As they fled from before Israel, *and* were in the going down to Beth-horon .. the Lord cast down great stones from heaven upon them unto Azekah, and they died : *they were* more which died with hailstones than..Israel slew with the sword.—JOSH., ch. 10.

8358. —— Exigencies in a. *Paul.* ¹⁷ They used helps, undergirding the ship ; and fearing lest they should fall into the quicksands, strake sail, and so were driven. ¹⁸ And we being exceedingly tossed with a tempest, the next *day* they lightened the ship ; ¹⁹ And the third *day* we cast out with our own hands the tackling of the ship.—ACTS, ch. 27. [See chapter.]

8359. —— mastered. *Jesus.* ²⁴ They came to him, and awoke him, saying, Master, Master, we perish. Then he arose, and rebuked the wind and the raging of the water : and they ceased, and there was a calm.—LUKE, ch. 8.

8360. —— Prayer in. *Jonah.* ⁶ The shipmaster came to him, and said..What meanest thou, O sleeper ? arise, call upon thy God, if so be that God will think upon us, that we perish not.—JONAH, ch. 1.

8361. —— at Sea. *Peril.* ⁴ The Lord sent out a great wind..and there was a mighty tempest in the sea, so that the ship was like to be broken. ⁵ Then the mariners were afraid, and cried every man unto his god, and cast forth the wares that *were* in the ship into the sea, to lighten *it.*—JONAH, ch. 1.

8362. —— —— *Terrifying.* ²⁵ He commandeth, and raiseth the stormy wind, which lifteth up the waves thereof. ²⁶ They mount up to the heaven, they go down again to the depths : their soul is melted because of trouble.—Ps. 107.

8363. —— —— *Sailors.* ²⁷ They reel to and fro, and stagger like a drunken man, and are at their wit's end. ²⁸ Then they cry unto the Lord in their trouble, and he bringeth them out of their distresses.—Ps. 107.

See other illustrations under :

8364. STRANGER, A lonely. *A Levite.* ¹⁵ They turned aside..to lodge in Gibeah : and..he sat him down in a street of the city : for *there was* no man that took them into his house to lodging.—JUDGES, ch. 19.

8365. STRANGERS, Hospitality to. *Abram.* ⁴ Let a little water, I pray you, be fetched, and wash your feet, and rest yourselves under the tree : ⁵ And I will fetch a morsel of bread, and comfort ye your hearts ; after that ye shall pass on.—GEN., ch. 18.

See FOREIGNER.

8366. STRATAGEM in Battle. *At Ai.* ²¹ When Joshua..saw that the ambush had taken the city, and that the smoke of the city ascended, then they turned again, and slew the men of Ai. ²² And the other issued out of the city against them ; so they were in the midst of Israel, some on this side, and some on that side..they let none of them remain or escape.—JOSH., ch. 8.

8367. —— Success by. *Absalom's.* ²⁹ He sent again the second time, he would not come. ³⁰ Therefore he said unto his servants, See, Joab's field is near mine, and he hath barley there ; go and set it on fire. And Absalom's servants set the field on fire.—2 SAM., ch. 14.

Also see:

8368. STRENGTH from Above. *Elijah.* ⁷ The angel of the Lord came again the second time, and touched him, and said, Arise *and* eat ; because the journey *is* too great for thee. ⁸ And he arose, and did eat and drink, and went in the strength of that meat forty days and forty nights unto Horeb the mount of God.—1 KINGS, ch. 19.

8369. —— Natural. *Peter.* ³⁷ Lord, why cannot I follow thee now ? I will lay down my life for thy sake. ³⁸ Jesus answered him, Wilt thou lay down thy life for my sake ?..The cock shall not crow, till thou hast denied me thrice.—JOHN, ch. 13.

8370. —— Physical. *Samson.* ⁵ Samson.. came to the vineyards of Timnath : and, behold, a young lion roared against him. ⁶ And the Spirit of the Lord came mightily upon him, and he rent him as he would have rent a kid, and *he had* nothing in his hand.—JUDGES, ch. 14.

8371. —— —— *Samson.* ¹⁵ He found a new jaw-bone of an ass..and took it, and slew a thousand men therewith. ¹⁶ And Samson said, With the jaw-bone of an ass, heaps upon heaps, with the jaw of an ass have I slain a thousand men.—JUDGES, ch. 15.

8372. —— —— *Gazites.* ² They compassed *him* in, and laid wait for him all night in the gate of the city..saying, In the morning when it is day we shall kill him. ³ And Samson.. arose at midnight, and took the doors of the gate of the city, and the two posts, and went away with them, bar and all.—JUDGES, ch. 16.

8373. —— —— *Secret of.* ¹⁷ If I be shaven, then my strength will go from me, and I shall become weak, and be like any *other* man. ¹⁸ And when Delilah saw that he had told her all his heart, she sent and called for the lords of the Philistines.—JUDGES, ch. 16.

8374. —— —— *Samson.* ²⁹ Samuel took hold of the two middle pillars upon which the house stood..³⁰ And Samson said, Let me die with the Philistines. And he bowed himself with *all his* might ; and the house fell upon the lords, and upon all the people that *were* therein. So the dead which he slew at his death were more than *they* which he slew in his life.—JUDGES, ch. 16.

8375. —— tested. *Peter.* ²⁵ Simon Peter stood and warmed himself. They said..Art not thou also *one* of his disciples ? He denied *it*, and said, I am not.—JOHN, ch. 18.

8376. —— unimpaired. *Caleb.* ¹⁰ I am this

day fourscore and five years old. [11] As yet I *am as* strong this day as *I was* in the day that Moses sent me : as my strength *was* then, even so *is* my strength now, for war, both to go out, and to come in. [12] Now therefore give me this mountain..for thou heardest in that day how the Anakim *were* there, and *that* the cities *were* great *and* fenced.—JOSH., ch. 14.

8377. —— **from Worship.** *Renew.* [31] They that wait upon the Lord shall renew *their* strength ; they shall mount up with wings as eagles ; they shall run, and not be weary ; *and* they shall walk, and not faint.—ISA., ch. 40.

See other illustrations under :

POWER.

Delegated. Why could we not cast him out ?	6312
Endowment. Filled..began to speak with other	6313
God gives. [Samson] L. blessed..Spirit began	6314
God only. [Peter] By our own power made	6315
Loss. [Samson] shake myself..wist not that the L.	6316
Might. Not by might, nor by power..great mt.	6317
Promised. [Joshua] Not any able to stand before	6318
Prayer. [Hezekiah] prayed Sennacherib..185,000	6319
Preaching. My speech..demonstration of the S.	6320
Ruling. Rebuked the wind, the raging water	6321
Spiritual. [Stephen] Not able to resist the w.	6322
Spirit. [Samson] Cords..upon his arms..as flax	6323
Sudden. [Joseph] No man lift up his hand or f.	6324
Tears. [Moses] Babe wept..had compassion on	6327
Temptation. All these will I give thee [Satan]	6325
Waiting. Wait for the promise..receive power	6329
Weakness. I am weak, though anointed [David]	6328

VIGOUR.

Age. Moses..120..nor natural force abated	9220
" [Caleb 85 yrs] I am as strong..for war	9221
" " Give me this mt..able to drive them	9222

Utilized. Samson did grind in his prison 834

8378. STRIFE avoided. *Isaac.* [15] All the wells ..digged in the days of Abraham his father, the Philistines had..filled them with earth. [16] And Abimelech said unto Isaac, Go from us ; for thou art much mightier than we. [17] And Isaac departed thence.—GEN., ch. 26.

8379. —— **Absence of.** *Isaac.* [See above.] [22] He removed from thence, and digged another well ; and for that they strove not : and he called the name of it Rehoboth ; and he said, For now the Lord hath made room for us, and we shall be fruitful in the land.—GEN., ch. 26.

8380. —— **Beginning of.** *Proverb.* [14] The beginning of strife *is as* when one letteth out water : therefore leave off contention, before it be meddled with.—PROV., ch. 17.

8381. —— **Cause of.** *Proverb.* [21] *As* coals *are* to burning coals, and wood to fire ; so *is* a contentious man to kindle strife. [22] The words of a talebearer *are* as wounds, and they go down into the innermost parts of the belly.—PROV., ch. 26.

8382. —— **continued.** *Philistines.* [19] Isaac's servants digged in the valley, and found there a well of springing water. [20] And the herdmen of Gerar did strive..saying, The water *is* ours : and he called the name of the well Esek ; because they strove with him. [21] And they digged another well, and strove for that also : and he called the name of it Sitnah.—GEN., ch. 26.

8383. —— **Dishonour in.** *Proverb.* [3] *It is an*

honour for a man to cease from strife : but every fool will be meddling.—PROV., ch. 20.

8384. —— **ended.** *Abram.* [9] *Is* not the whole land before thee ? separate thyself, I pray thee, from me : if *thou wilt take* the left hand, then I will go the right ; or if *thou depart* to the right hand, then I will go to the left.—GEN., ch. 13.

8385. —— **Occasion for.** *Esau.* [6] Esau took his wives, and his sons, and his daughters.. and all his substance..and went into the country from the face of his brother Jacob. [7] For their riches were more than that they might dwell together ; and the land..could not bear them because of their cattle.—GEN., ch. 36.

8386. —— **prevented.** *Reward.* [14] The Lord said unto Abram, after that Lot was separated from him, Lift up now thine eyes, and look.. northward, and southward, and eastward, and westward. [15] For all the land which thou seest, to thee will I give it, and to thy seed for ever. —GEN., ch. 13.

8387. —— **Prosperity brings.** *Abram—Lot.* [5] Lot also..had flocks, and herds, and tents. [6] And the land was not able to bear them..for their substance was great, so that they could not dwell together. [7] And there was a strife between the herdmen of Abram's cattle and the herdmen of Lot's cattle.—GEN., ch. 13.

8388. —— **rebuked.** *Christians.* [14] But if ye have bitter envying and strife in your hearts, glory not, and lie not against the truth. [15] This wisdom descendeth not from above, but *is* earthly, sensual, devilish. [16] For where envying and strife *is*, there *is* confusion and every evil work.—JAMES, ch. 3.

8389. —— **Truth makes.** *Jesus said,* [34] Think not that I am come to send peace on earth : I came not to send peace, but a sword. [35] For I am come to set a man at variance against his father, and the daughter against her mother.— MAT., ch. 10.

8390. —— **Wickedness of.** *Fire.* [27] An ungodly man diggeth up evil : and in his lips *there is* as a burning fire. [28] A froward man soweth strife : and a whisperer separateth chief friends.—PROV., ch. 16.

8391. —— **Words make.** *Talebearer.* [20] Where no wood is, *there* the fire goeth out : so where *there is* no talebearer, the strife ceaseth.—PROV., ch. 26.

See other illustrations under :

SIDE.

Which ? Art thou for us, or for our adversaries ? 7863
" Who is on the Lord's side ?..come unto me 7864
See CONFLICT and references.

8392. STRUGGLE, Deliverance by. *Demon bound.* [20] They brought him unto him : and when he saw him, straightway the spirit tare him ; and he fell on the ground, and wallowed foaming.—MARK, ch. 9.

8393. STUBBORNNESS punished. *Captivity.* [16] They mocked the messengers of God, and despised his words, and misused his prophets, until the wrath of the Lord arose against his people, till *there was* no remedy. [17] Therefore he brought upon them the king of the Chaldees, who slew them.—2 CHRON., ch. 36.

8394. —— **in Sin.** *Saul.* [22] Behold, to obey *is* better than sacrifice, *and* to hearken than the fat of rams. ²³ For rebellion *is as* the sin of witchcraft, and stubbornness *is as* iniquity and idolatry.—1 SAM., ch. 15.

8395. —— —— *Jews in Egypt.* ¹⁷ We will certainly do whatsoever thing goeth forth out of our own mouth, to burn incense unto the queen of heaven.—JER., ch. 44.

8396. —— —— *Philistines.* ³ They took Dagon, and set him in his place again.. ⁴ Early on the morrow morning, behold, Dagon *was* fallen upon his face to the ground before the ark of the Lord ; and the head of Dagon and both the palms of his hands *were* cut off.—1 SAM., ch. 5.

See other illustrations under :

HARDNESS.
Adversity. In his distress did Ahaz trespass more ... 3797
Heart. Looked..anger being grieved..hardness ... 3798

OBDURACY.
Defiant. Who is the L. that I should obey? ... 5755
Final. Why have we..Let I. go from serving us ... 5756
Foolish. Ahaz..sacrificed unto the gods..smote ... 5757
Jewish. Thy neck is as an iron sinew, and thy ... 5758
Spiritual. Woe unto thee, Chorazin..if the mighty ... 5759
Self-destructive. I know that G. hath determined ... 5760
to Truth. Paul spake..three months..divers were ... 5761
Unfeeling. Past feeling have given themselves ... 5762
Wild. Balaam..went with the princes of Moab ... 5763

OBSTINACY.
Provoking. It is a stiffnecked people..consume ... 5825
Rebuked. Why..smitten thine ass these 3 times? ... 5826
Rebellious. Nevertheless the people refused ... 5827

SELF-WILL.
Destructive. As a hen gathereth..ye would not ... 7731
Loss. Presumed to go up..Canaanites smote them ... 7732
Obstinate. We would certainly do whatsoever ... 7733
Sin. Rebellion is as the sin of witchcraft ... 7734
Work of. In their self-will they digged down a w. ... 7735

8397. STUDY, Bible. *Eunuch.* ²⁷ A eunuch of great authority under Candace queen of the Ethiopians, who had the charge of all her treasure, and had come to Jerusalem for to worship, ²⁸ Was returning, and sitting in his chariot read Esaias the prophet.—ACTS, ch. 8.

8398. —— —— *Bereans commended.* ¹¹ These were more noble than those in Thessalonica, in that they received the word with all readiness of mind, and searched the Scriptures daily, whether those things were so.—ACTS, ch. 17.

8399. —— —— *Benefits.* ³² They said one to another, Did not our heart burn within us, while he talked with us by the way, and while he opened to us the Scriptures ?—LUKE, ch. 24.

8400. —— **Wearisome.** *To the Flesh.* ¹² My son, be admonished : of making many books *there is* no end ; and much study *is* a weariness of the flesh.—ECCL., ch. 12.

See SCHOOL and references.

8401. STUMBLING at Truth. *Disciples.* ⁶⁰ Many therefore of his disciples, when they had heard *this,* said, This is a hard saying; who can hear it? ⁶⁶ From that *time* many of his disciples went back, and walked no more with him. —JOHN, ch. 6.

8402. STUMBLINGBLOCK, Christ a. *Prejudice.* ²³ We preach Christ crucified, unto the Jews a stumblingblock, and unto the Greeks foolishness.—1 COR., ch. 1.

8403. —— **Liberty a.** *Example.* ⁸ Meat commendeth us not to God : for neither, if we eat, are we the better ; neither, if we eat not, are we the worse. ⁹ But take heed lest by any means this liberty of yours become a stumblingblock to them that are weak.—1 COR., ch. 8.

8404. STUMBLINGBLOCKS responsible. " *Offend* ".. *cause to sin.* ⁶ Whoso shall offend one of these little ones which believe in me, it were better for him that a millstone were hanged about his neck, and *that* he were drowned in the depth of the sea.—MAT., ch. 18.

See ERROR and references.

8405. SUBJUGATION by Blindness. *Saul.* ⁸ Saul arose from the earth ; and when his eyes were opened, he saw no man : but they led him by the hand, and brought *him* into Damascus.— ACTS, ch. 9.

8406. —— **Complete.** *To Philistines.* ¹⁹ There was no smith found throughout all the land of Israel : for the Philistines said, Lest the Hebrews make *them* swords or spears : ²⁰ But all the Israelites went down to the Philistines to sharpen every man his share, and his coulter, and his axe, and his mattock.—1 SAM., ch. 13.

See other illustrations under :

CONQUEST.
Preparation for. [Twelve] to spy out the land of C. ... 1548
Unfortunate. Philistines took the ark of G. ... 1549

See SUBMISSION.

8407. SUBLIMITY, Descriptive. *Creation.* ² The earth was without form, and void ; and darkness *was* upon the face of the deep. And the Spirit of God moved upon the face of the waters. ³ And God said, Let there be light : and there was light.—GEN., ch. 1.

8408. —— **Poetic.** *Deliverance.* ⁸ With the blast of thy nostrils the waters were gathered together, the floods stood upright as a heap, *and* the depths were congealed in the heart of the sea.—EX., ch. 15. [See chapter.]

8409. SUBMISSION in Bereavement. *Aaron's Sons.* ² There went out fire from the Lord, and devoured them, and they died before the Lord. ³ Then Moses said unto Aaron, This *is it* that the Lord spake, saying, I will be sanctified in them that come nigh me, and before all the people' I will be glorified. And Aaron held his peace.—LEV., ch. 10.

8410. —— *Child Dead.* ¹⁹ And they said, He is dead. ²⁰ Then David arose from the earth, and washed, and anointed *himself,* and changed his apparel, and came into the house of the Lord, and worshipped : then he came to his own house ; and when he required, they set bread before him, and he did eat.—2 SAM., ch. 12.

8411. —— **to Circumstances.** *Sailors.* ¹⁴ Not long after there arose against it a tempestuous wind, called Euroclydon. ¹⁵ And when the ship was caught, and could not bear up into the wind, we let *her* drive.—ACTS, ch. 27.

8412. —— **difficult.** *Washing Feet.* ⁸ Peter saith..Thou shalt never wash my feet. Jesus answered him, If I wash thee not, thou hast no part with me. ⁹ Simon Peter saith..Lord, not my feet only, but also *my* hands and *my* head. —JOHN, ch. 13.

8413. —— **Example of.** *Jesus.* ⁴² He went

away again the second time, and prayed, saying, O my Father, if this cup may not pass away from me, except I drink it, thy will be done.—MAT., ch. 26.

8414. —— **Humiliating.** *Syrians.* [32] They girded sackcloth on their loins, and *put* ropes on their heads, and came to the king of Israel, and said, Thy servant Benhadad saith, I pray thee, let me live.—2 KINGS, ch. 20.

8415. —— **Painful.** *Jacob.* [11] If *it must be so* now, do this ; take of the best fruits in the land in your vessels, and carry down the man a present, a little balm, and a little honey, spices and myrrh, nuts and almonds : [13] Take also your brother, and arise, go again unto the man.—GEN., ch. 43.

8416. —— **to Punishment.** *Eli.* [13] I will judge his house for ever for the iniquity which he knoweth ; because his sons made themselves vile, and he restrained them not. [18] And Samuel told him every whit, and hid nothing from him. And he said, It *is* the Lord : let him do what seemeth him good.—1 SAM., ch. 3.

8417. —— **to Providence.** *Hagar.* [8] Hagar ..whence camest thou ? and whither wilt thou go? And she said, I flee from the face of my mistress Sarai. [9] And the angel of the Lord said unto her, Return to thy mistress, and submit thyself under her hands.—GEN., ch. 16.

See other illustrations under :

PATIENCE.
Divine. Last of all, he sent his son　　　　5994
Example. Consider him that endureth such　　5995
Labour. This year also..I will dig about it　　5996
Maintained. Come out, thou bloody man..of B.　5997
Needful. Fret not thyself in any wise to do evil　5998
Picture of. The husbandman waiteth..hath long　5999
Rewarded. He brought me out of the miry clay　6000
Refused. Have patience, and I will pay..would not 6001
Trial of. They despised Saul..he held his peace　6002
Without. Why should this dead dog curse my lord 6003
Waiting. Have need of patience..after ye have　6004

RESIGNATION.
Bereavement. David was comforted concerning　7192
Inevitable. If I be bereaved of my children, I am　7193
Pious. L. gave, and the L. hath taken away　　7194
　" 　David said..Let him do as seemeth good　7195
Submission. When he would not be persuaded, we 7196

SUFFERING.
for Christ. [Paul and Silas] Laid many stripes　8448
Faithful. Were stoned..sawn asunder, were　　8449
Subdued. Bit the people..died, therefore..we　8451
Support. Sufferings of this present time not　　8450

SUFFERINGS.
Apostolic. Five times..stripes..thrice..shipwreck 8452
Chosen. Moses..choosing rather to suffer..than　8453
Recompensed. Moses..had respect unto the　　8454
Sacred. Remove this cup..not my will [Jesus]　8455

SURRENDER.
Absolute. I count all things but loss for..the k.　8503
Bodily. Yieldeth their bodies that..not serve any 8504
Christian. May know..fellowship of his sufferings 8505
Entire. One thing thou lackest..sell..give..follow 8506
Full. Whosoever..forsaketh not all..disciple　　8507
Fear. We will do all that thou shalt bid us　　8508
Moral. What things were gain to me, I counted l.　8509
Power. We have not used this power..lest we　　8510
Resisted. When he saw him, the spirit tare him　8511
Sins. If thy right hand offend thee..cast it　　8512

Sacrifice. Widow..cast in..all her living　　8513
Undivided. Our cattle shall also go with us　　8514
Weak. King Ahab said, My Lord, O King, I am　8515

Sorrowful. If I am bereaved, I am bereaved　　743
　See SUBJUGATION.

8418. SUBSTITUTE, An inferior. *Shields.* [26] He took away all the shields of gold which Solomon had made. [27] And king Rehoboam made in their stead brazen shields, and committed *them* unto the hands of the chief of the guard, which kept the door of the king's house. —1 KINGS, ch. 14.

8419. —— **The Lord's.** *For Firstborn.* [28] They shall take to them every man a lamb, according to the house of *their* fathers, a lamb for an house : [29] ..at midnight the Lord smote all the firstborn in the land of Egypt.—EX., ch. 12.

8420. —— **A timely.** *Sacrifice.* [13] Abraham lifted up his eyes, and looked, and behold behind *him* a ram caught in a thicket by his horns ..and offered him up for a burnt offering in the stead of his son.—GEN., ch. 22.

8421. SUBSTITUTION, Official. *Aaron.* [12] Go, and I will be with thy mouth, and teach thee what thou shalt say. [13] And he said, O my Lord, send, I pray thee, by the hand *of him whom* thou wilt send. [14] And the anger of the Lord was kindled against Moses, and he said, *Is* not Aaron the Levite thy brother? I know that he can speak well.—EX., ch. 4.

8422. —— **Personal.** *Judah.* [32] Thy servant became surety for the lad unto my father, saying, If I bring him not unto thee, then I shall bear the blame to my father for ever. [33] ..let thy servant abide instead of the lad a bondman to my lord ; and let the lad go up with his brethren.—GEN. ch. 44.

8423. SUBSIDY, Holy Things for. *From Temple.* [8] Ahaz took the silver and gold that was found in the house of the Lord, and in the treasures of the king's house, and sent *it for* a present to the king of Assyria. [9] And the king of Assyria hearkened unto him..went up against Damascus, and took it.—2 KINGS, ch. 16.

See other illustrations under :

TRIBUTE.
Sheep. King of Moab rendered..100,000 lambs　8952
Useless. Ahaz took a portion..but he helped..not 8954
　See TAX.

8424. SUBTLETY, Deception by. *Jacob's Sons.* [31] They took Joseph's coat, and killed a kid of the goats, and dipped the coat in the blood ; [32] And they sent the coat of *many* colours..to their father ; and said, This have we found : know now whether it *be* thy son's coat or no.— GEN., ch. 37.

See other illustrations under :

TRICK.
Diplomatic. From a very far country are..come　8955
Hypocrites. Feign themselves just men..might　8956
Legerdemain. Magicians..rods became serpents　8957
Politicians. Shall ask a petition..save of thee　8958

8425. SUCCESS, Business. *Jacob.* [43] The man increased exceedingly, and had much cattle, and maidservants, and menservants, and camels, and asses.—GEN., ch. 30.

8426. —— —— *Change.* [9] Jacob said, O God of my father Abraham, and ..Isaac, the Lord which saidst unto me, Return unto thy country..

[10]..with my staff I passed over this Jordan ; and now I am become two bands.—GEN., ch. 32.

8427. —— —— *Joseph.* [57] All countries came into Egypt to Joseph for to buy *corn;* because that the famine was so sore in all lands.— GEN., ch. 41.

8428. —— **Deluded by.** *Benjamites.* [32] The children of Benjamin said, They *are* smitten down before us, as at the first. But the children of Israel said, Let us flee, and draw them from the city unto the highways.—JUDGES, ch. 20.

8429. —— **Dangers of.** *Three Hundred.* [2] The Lord said unto Gideon, The people that *are* with thee *are* too many for me to give the Midianites into their hands, lest Israel vaunt themselves against me, saying, Mine own hand hath saved me.—JUDGES, ch. 7.

8430. —— **Determination for.** *Palsy.* [4] When they could not come nigh unto him for the press, they uncovered the roof where he was: and when they had broken *it* up, they let down the bed wherein the sick of the palsy lay.— MARK, ch. 2.

8431. —— **by Earnestness.** *Bartimeus.* [48] Many charged him that he should hold his peace : but he cried the more a great deal, Thou Son of David, have mercy on me.. [50] And he, casting away his garment, rose, and came to Jesus.—MARK, ch. 10.

8432. —— **Enemies from.** *Nehemiah.* [7] When Sanballat, and Tobiah, and the Arabians, and the Ammonites, and the Ashdodites, heard that the walls of Jerusalem were made up, *and* that the breaches began to be stopped, then they were very wroth, [8] And conspired all of them together to come *and* to fight against Jerusalem, and to hinder it.—NEH., ch. 4.

8433. —— **Faith measures.** *Blind Men.* [28] The blind men came to him : and Jesus saith..Believe ye that I am able to do this? They said.. Yea, Lord. [29] Then touched he their eyes, saying, According to your faith be it unto you.— MAT., ch. 9.

8434. —— **Failure of.** *Lost Soul.* [26] What is a man profited, if he shall gain the whole world, and lose his own soul? or what shall a man give in exchange for his soul?—MAT., ch. 16.

8435. —— **from God only.** *Preaching.* [6] I have planted, Apollos watered ; but God gave the increase. [7] So then neither is he that planteth any thing, neither he that watereth ; but God that giveth the increase.—1 COR., ch. 3.

8436. —— **by God's Blessing.** *Rod.* [8] On the morrow Moses went into the tabernacle.. and, behold, the rod of Aaron for the house of Levi was budded, and brought forth buds, and bloomed blossoms, and yielded almonds.—NUM., ch. 17.

8437. —— **Guided by.** *Sinners.* [17] *Then* had we plenty of victuals, and were well, and saw no evil. [18] But since we left off to burn incense to the queen of heaven, and to pour out drink offerings unto her, we have wanted all *things.*— JER., ch. 44.

8438. —— **Humility in.** *David.* [14] David behaved himself wisely in all his ways ; and the Lord *was* with him. [15] Wherefore when Saul saw that he behaved himself very wisely, he was afraid of him. [16] But all Israel and Judah loved David, because he went out and came in before them.—1 SAM., ch. 18.

8439. —— **Humiliation in.** *Israelites.* [3] The people gat them by stealth that day into the city, as people being ashamed steal away when they flee in battle. [4] But the king covered his face, and the king cried with a loud voice, O my son Absalom ! O Absalom, my son, my son !— 2 SAM., ch. 19.

8440. —— **Ministerial.** *Pentecost.* [41] They that gladly received his word were baptized : and the same day there were added *unto them* about three thousand souls.—ACTS, ch. 2.

8441. —— **Piety favours.** *Joshua.* [8] This book of the law shall not depart out of thy mouth ; but thou shalt meditate therein day and night, that thou mayest observe to do according to all that is written therein : for then thou shalt make thy way prosperous, and then thou shalt have good success.—JOSH., ch. 1.

8442. —— —— *Jotham.* [2] He did *that which was* right in the sight of the Lord, according to all that his father Uzziah did.. [4] Moreover he built cities in the mountains of Judah, and in the forests he built castles and towers.—2 CHRON., ch. 27.

8443. —— **promotes Selfishness.** *Spoil.* [22] *Men* of Belial..said, Because they went not with us, we will not give them *aught* of the spoil that we have recovered, save to every man his wife and his children.. [23] Then said David, Ye shall not do so.. [24]..as his part *is* that goeth down to the battle, so *shall* his part *be* that tarrieth by the stuff : they shall part alike.—1 SAM., ch. 30. [All had been lost.]

8444. —— **Strife from.** *Servants.* [5] Lot also, which went with Abram, had flocks, and herds, and tents, [6] And the land was not able to bear them, that they might dwell together : for their substance was great, so that they could not dwell together. [7] And there was a strife.—GEN., ch. 13.

8445. —— **Trouble from.** *Ark captured.* [11] The lords of the Philistines..said, Send away the ark of the God of Israel, and let it go again to his own place, that it slay us not, and our people : for there was a deadly destruction throughout all the city ; the hand of God was very heavy there.—1 SAM., ch. 5.

See PROSPERITY and VICTORY.

8446. SUCCESSION, Ministerial. *At Corinth.* [6] I have planted, Apollos watered ; but God gave the increase.—1 COR., ch. 3.

8447. —— **Official.** *Joshua.* [2] Moses my servant is dead ; now therefore arise, go over this Jordan, thou, and all this people, unto the land which I do give to them.—JOSH., ch. 1.

8448. SUFFERING for Christ. *At Philippi.* [23] When they had laid many stripes upon them, they cast *them* into prison, charging the jailer to keep them safely : [24] Who..thrust them into the inner prison, and made their feet fast in the stocks.—ACTS, ch. 16.

8449. —— **Faithful in.** *Martyrs.* [36] Others had trial of *cruel* mockings and scourgings, yea, moreover of bonds and imprisonment : [37] They were stoned, they were sawn asunder, were tempted, were slain with the sword : they wandered about in sheepskins and goatskins ; being destitute, afflicted, tormented.. [39] And these all, having obtained a good report through faith.—HEB., ch. 11.

8450. —— **Support under.** "*Glory.*" ¹⁷ If so be that we suffer with *him*, that we may be also glorified together. ¹⁸ For I reckon that the sufferings of this present time *are* not worthy *to be compared* with the glory which shall be revealed in us.—ROM., ch. 8.

8451. —— **Subdued by.** *Israelites.* The Lord sent fiery serpents among the people, and they bit the people ; and much people of Israel died. ⁷ Therefore the people..said, We have sinned, for we have spoken against the Lord, and against thee.—NUM., ch. 21.

8452. SUFFERINGS, Apostolic. *Paul.* ²⁴ Of the Jews five times received I forty *stripes* save one. ²⁵ Thrice was I beaten with rods, once was I stoned, thrice I suffered shipwreck, a night and a day I have been in the deep.—2 COR., ch. 11.

8453. —— **chosen.** *Moses* ²⁴ Refused to be called the son of Pharaoh's daughter ; ²⁵ Choosing rather to suffer affliction with the people of God, than to enjoy the pleasures of sin for a season.—HEB., ch. 11.

8454. —— **recompensed.** *Moses.* [See No. 8453.] ²⁶ Esteeming the reproach of Christ greater riches than the treasures in Egypt : for he had respect unto the recompense of the reward.—HEB., ch. 11.

8455. —— **Sacred.** *Garden.* ⁴² Father, if thou be willing, remove this cup from me : nevertheless, not my will, but thine, be done.. ⁴⁴ And being in an agony he prayed more earnestly : and his sweat was as it were great drops of blood falling down to the ground.—LUKE, ch. 22.

See other illustrations under :
CRUELTY.
Ambition. [Athaliah] saw her son was dead 1857
Brutal. 16,000 men..did Judah..cast from the r. 1858
Failure. Egyptians set taskmasters to afflict 1859
Insulting. Herod's soldiers smote him..spit on 1860
Pride. Mordecai bowed not..Haman sought to 1861
Reward. He that is cruel troubleth his own flesh 1862
Savage. Slew..the sons of Hezekiah before his e. 1863
War. [Joab] put them under saws..harrows of i. 1864
TORTURE.
Hell. I am tormented in this flame 8852
Jesus. Crown of thorns..spit upon him..smote 8855
Prisoners. Elders of the city and thorns..briers 8853
"   Put them under saws..harrows 8854
TRIALS.
Business. Day the drought consumed me..frost 8923
Backsliding. Who shall give us flesh to eat 8924
Blessing. Blessed are ye when men shall revile y. 8925
"   I am exceeding joyful in all our t. 8948
Comfort. David encouraged himself in his G. 8926
Confidence. I am persuaded..be able to separate 8927
Darkness. I cry out of wrong, but I am not heard 8930
after Deliverance. From the Red Sea..no water 8929
Despair. There was a great earthquake..sun 8946
Encouragement. Work out..far more exceeding 8931
Follow. Three days in the wilderness..no water 8929
Hope. I know that my Redeemer liveth 8932
"   Why art thou cast down, O my soul? 8933
Joyful. Took joyfully the spoiling of your goods 8935
Multiplied. All my inward friends abhorred me 8936
"   In labours more abundant..stripes 8940
Overburdened. Burden of all this people on me 8937

Recompensed. These..came out of great t. 8949
Rest. Came to Elim..12 wells..70 palm trees 8938
Severe. In labours..stripes..prison..deaths 8940
"   In weariness, painfulness.. in watchings 8942
"   We hunger and thirst, and are naked 8939
"   In perils of waters..robbers..heathen 8941
Use. Nations which the L. left to prove Israel 8943
"   Branch that beareth not fruit..purgeth it 8944
Victory. In all..more than conquerors..loved 8945
Winnow. When affliction or persecution ariseth 8928

Bribery. Entice him..where his great strength lieth 932
Dangerous. [Babel] This they begin to do..nothing 964
See ADVERSITY, AFFLICTION, GRIEF.

8456. SUICIDE imitated. *Armourbearer.* [See No. 8459.] ⁵ When his armourbearer saw that Saul was dead, he fell likewise upon his sword, and died with him.—1 SAM., ch. 31.

8457. —— **from Mortification.** *Ahithophel.* ²³ When Ahithophel saw that his counsel was not followed, he saddled *his* ass..and gat him home to his house, to his city, and put his household in order, and hanged himself.—2 SAM., ch. 17.

8458. —— **prevented.** *At Philippi.* ²⁷ The keeper of the prison awaking out of his sleep, and seeing the prison doors open, he drew out his sword, and would have killed himself, supposing that the prisoners had been fled. ²⁸ But Paul cried with a loud voice, saying, Do thyself no harm : for we are all here.—ACTS, ch. 16.

8459. —— **A Soldier's.** *Saul.* ³ Archers hit him ; and he was sore wounded.. ⁴ Then said Saul unto his armourbearer, Draw thy sword, and thrust me through therewith ; lest these uncircumcised come and thrust me through, and abuse me. But his armourbearer would not, for he was sore afraid. Therefore Saul took a sword, and fell upon it.—1 SAM., ch. 31.

8460. —— **A Traitor's.** *Judas.* ⁵ He cast down the pieces of silver in the temple, and departed, and went and hanged himself.—MAT., ch. 27.

Also see :
Royal. Zimri..servants conspired..burnt..house 6953

8461. SULLENNESS from Envy. *Laban.* ¹ Of that which *was* our father's hath he gotten all this glory. ² And Jacob beheld the countenance of Laban, and, behold, it *was* not toward him as before.—GEN., ch. 31.

8462. SUMMER, Approach of. *Flowers.* ¹¹ For, lo, the winter is past, the rain is over *and* gone ; ¹² The flowers appear on the earth ; the time of the singing *of birds* is come, and the voice of the turtle is heard in our land.—SONG OF SOLOMON, ch. 2.

8463. —— —— *Leaves.* ³² Learn a parable of the fig tree ; When his branch is yet tender, and putteth forth leaves, ye know that summer *is* nigh.—MAT., ch. 24.

8464. SUN arrested, The. *Joshua* ¹² Said in the sight of Israel, Sun, stand thou still upon Gibeon ; and thou, Moon, in the valley of Ajalon. ¹³ And the sun stood still, and the moon stayed, until the people had avenged themselves upon their enemies.—JOSH., ch. 10.

8465. —— **Gifts to the.** *Idolatrous.* ¹¹ Josiah took away the horses that the kings of Judah had given to the sun, at the entering in of the house of the Lord..and burned the chariots of the sun with fire.—2 Kings, ch. 23.

8466. —— A healing. *Of Righteousness.* ² Unto you that fear my name shall the Sun of righteousness arise with healing in his wings.— Mal., ch. 4.

8467. —— outshone, The. *Paul said,* ¹³ At midday, O king, I saw in the way a light from heaven, above the brightness of the sun, shining round about me.—Acts, ch. 26.

8468. —— a Symbol. *Christian.* ⁴³ Then shall the righteous shine forth as the sun in the kingdom of their father.—Mat., ch. 13.

8469. —— —— *God.* ¹¹ The Lord God *is* a sun and shield : the Lord will give grace and glory : no good *thing* will he withhold from them that walk uprightly.—Ps. 84.

8470. SUPEREROGATION, Works of. *None.* ⁸ Make ready wherewith I may sup, and gird thyself, and serve me, till I have eaten and drunken ; ⁹ Doth he thank that servant..I trow not. ¹⁰ So likewise ye, when ye shall have done all those things which are commanded you, ¹¹..We are unprofitable servants : we have done that which was our duty to do.—Luke, ch. 17.

8471. SUPERIORITY claimed. *Peter.* ³³ Peter .Though all *men* shall be offended because of thee, *yet* will I never be offended. ³⁴ Jesus said unto him, Verily I say unto thee, that this night, before the cock crow, thou shalt deny me thrice. —Mat., ch. 26.

8472. —— manifested. *To Egyptians.* ¹² They cast down every man his rod, and they became serpents : but Aaron's rod swallowed up their rods.—Ex., ch. 7.

8473. —— —— *Rod budded.* ⁸ On the morrow Moses went into the tabernacle of witness ; and, behold, the rod of Aaron for the house of Levi was budded, and brought forth buds, and bloomed blossoms, and yielded almonds.—Num., ch. 17.

8474. —— unclaimed. *Peter.* ¹⁵ When they had dined, Jesus saith..Simon, *son* of Jonas, lovest thou me more than these ? He saith unto him, Yea, Lord ; thou knowest that I love thee. —John, ch. 21.

8475. SUPERSTITION, Credulous. *Lystrians.* ¹¹ The gods are come down to us in the likeness of men. ¹² And they called Barnabas, Jupiter ; and Paul, Mercurius, because he was the chief speaker. ·¹³ Then the priest of Jupiter..brought oxen and garlands unto the gates, and would have done sacrifice with the people.—Acts, ch. 14.

8476. —— A fatal. *Syrians.* ²³ The servants of the king of Syria said unto him, Their gods *are* gods of the hills ; therefore they were stronger than we ; but let us fight against them in the plain, and surely we shall be stronger than they.—1 Kings, ch. 20.

8477. —— A grievous. *Lystrians.* ¹⁴ Barnabas and Paul..rent their clothes, and ran in among the people, crying out, ¹⁵ And saying, Sirs, why do ye these things ? We also are men of like passions with you, and preach unto you that ye should turn from these vanities unto the living God.—Acts, ch. 14.

8478. —— from Ignorance. *Paul* ⁵ Shook off the beast into the fire, and felt no harm.

⁶ Howbeit they looked when he should have swollen, or fallen down dead suddenly : but after they had looked a great while, and saw no harm come to him, they changed their minds, and said that he was a god.—Acts, ch. 28.

8479. —— Mistake of. *Barbarians.* ³ A viper out of the heat..fastened on his hand. ⁴ And when the barbarians saw the *venomous* beast hang on his hand, they said among themselves, No doubt this man is a murderer.—Acts, ch. 28.

See other illustrations under :
WITCHCRAFT.
Abolished. Workers with familiar spirits..Josiah 9649
Famous. Seek me a woman..a familiar spirit 9647
Influential. They all gave heed..lest..greatest 9650

Divine. Dagon was fallen with his face toward the 1549

8480. SUPPRESSION impossible. *Bartimeus.* ⁴⁸ Many charged him that he should hold his peace ; but he cried the more, a great deal, Jesus thou Son of David, have mercy on me.— Mark, ch. 10.

See CONCEALMENT.

8481. SURETY, Brother's. *Additional.* ⁸ Judah said..Send the lad with me, and we will arise and go ; that we may live, and not die, both we, and thou, *and* also our little ones. ⁹ I will be surety for him.—Gen., ch. 43.

8482. —— —— *Joseph said,* ¹⁹ If ye *be* true *men,* let one of your brethren be bound in the house of your prison : go ye, carry corn for the famine of your houses : ²⁰ But bring your youngest brother.—Gen., ch. 42.

8483. —— Dangerous. *Proverb.* ¹⁵ He that is surety for a stranger shall smart *for it* : and he that hateth suretiship is sure.—Prov., ch. 11.

8484. —— Folly of. *Proverb.* ¹ My son, if thou be surety for thy friend, *if* thou hast stricken thy hand with a stranger, ² Thou art snared with the words of thy mouth, thou art taken with the words of thy mouth.—Prov., ch. 6.

8485. —— offered. *Reuben.* ³⁷ Slay my two sons, if I bring him not to thee : deliver him into my hand, and I will bring him to thee again. ³⁸ And he said, My son shall not go down with you.—Gen., ch. 42.

8486. —— A painful. *Simon.* ²⁴ He turned himself about from them, and wept ; and returned to them again. and communed with them, and took from them Simeon, and bound him before their eyes.—Gen., ch. 42.

8487. —— A precious. *Jesus.* ²² By so much was Jesus made a surety of a better testament. —Heb., ch. 7.

8488. SURPRISE, Appalling. *Haman.* ⁶ Haman thought in his heart, To whom would the king delight to do honour more than to myself ?.. ¹⁰ Then the king said to Haman, Make haste, *and* take the apparel and the horse, as thou hast said, and do even so to Mordecai the Jew..let nothing fail of all that thou hast spoken.— Esther, ch. 6.

8489. —— Astonishing. *Escape.* ²⁵ Behold, the men whom ye put in prison are standing in the temple, and teaching the people. — Acts, ch. 5.

8490. —— in Choice. *David.* ¹¹ Samuel said unto Jesse, Are here all *thy* children ? And he

said, There remaineth yet the youngest, and,
behold, he keepeth the sheep.. ¹²And he sent,
and brought him in. Now he *was* ruddy, *and*
withal of a beautiful countenance, and goodly
to look to. And the Lord said, Arise, anoint
him : for this *is* he.—1 Sam., ch. 16.

8491. —— of Conspirators. *A d o n i j a h' s
Friends.* ⁴³Jonathan answered..Adonijah, Verily our lord king David hath made Solomon
king.. ⁴⁹And all the guests that *were* with
Adonijah were afraid, and rose up, and went
every man his way.—1 Kings, ch. 1.

8492. —— Conquest by. *Gideon.* ²⁰They
cried, The sword of the Lord, and of Gideon.
²¹And they stood every man in his place round
about the camp : and all the host ran, and cried,
and fled. ²²And the three hundred blew the
trumpets, and the Lord set every man's sword
against his fellow.—Judges, ch. 7.

8493. —— Family. *Jesse's.* ¹ Go, I will
send thee to Jesse the Beth-lehemite : for I have
provided me a king among his sons. ² And
Samuel said, How can I go? if Saul hear *it*, he
will kill me.—1 Sam., ch. 16.

8494. —— Great. *Mordecai,* ¹⁵ Mordecai
went out from the presence of the king in royal
apparel of blue and white, and with a great
crown of gold, and with a garment of fine linen
and purple : and the city of Shushan rejoiced.
—Esther, ch. 8.

8495. —— Needless. *Antediluvians.* ²⁷They
did eat, they drank, they married wives, they
were given in marriage, until the day that Noe
entered into the ark, and the flood came, and
destroyed them all.—Luke, ch. 17.

8496. —— Providential. *J o s e p h .* ⁴ I am
Joseph your brother, whom ye sold into Egypt.
⁵..be not grieved, nor angry with yourselves,
that ye sold me hither : for God did send me
before you to preserve life.—Gen., ch. 45.

8497. —— from Rejection. *Eliab.* ⁶ He looked
on Eliab, and said, Surely the Lord's anointed *is*
before him. ⁷ But the Lord said unto Samuel,
Look not on his countenance, or on the height
of his stature ; because I have refused him :
for *the Lord seeth* not as a man seeth ; for man
looketh on the outward appearance, but the
Lord looketh on the heart.—1 Sam., ch. 16.

8498. —— Speechless. *Brothers.* ² He wept
aloud : and the Egyptians and the house of
Pharaoh heard. ³ And Joseph said..I *am* Joseph ; doth my father yet live? And his brethren
could not answer him ; for they were troubled
at his presence.—Gen., ch. 45.

8499. —— of the Worldly. *Sodomites.* ²⁸ As
it was in the days of Lot ; they did eat, they
drank, they bought, they sold, they planted,
they builded ; ²⁹ But the same day that Lot
went out of Sodom it rained fire and brimstone
from heaven, and destroyed *them* all.—Luke,
ch. 17.

8500. —— The World's. *Second Advent.* ²⁶ As
it was in the days of Noe, so shall it be also in
the days of the Son of man.. ³⁰ Even thus shall
it be in the day when the Son of man is revealed.
—Luke, ch. 17.

8501. SURPRISES at the Judgment. *Righteous.*
³⁷ Lord, when saw we thee an hungered, and
fed *thee?* or thirsty, and gave *thee* drink?.. ⁴⁰ In-

asmuch as ye have done *it* unto one of the least
of these my brethren, ye have done *it* unto me.
—Mat., ch. 25.

8502. —— —— Sinners. ⁴⁴ Then shall they
also answer him, saying, Lord, when saw we
thee.. ⁴⁵ Then shall he answer them..Inasmuch
as ye did *it* not to one of the least of these, ye
did *it* not to me.—Mat., ch. 25.

See other illustrations under :

AMAZEMENT.

Great. Winds ceased..sore amazed   307
Natural. Rebuked the wind and the raging w.   308

ASTONISHMENT.

Mystery. Nebuchadnezzar..was astonished..I   565
Sacred. Angel ascended in the flame of the altar   566
Speech. All amazed..how hear we our own t.   567

AWAKENING.

Conscience. John the B. was risen from the dead   595
Fear. Centurion..feared greatly..was the S. of G.   596
Great. Into the house..all the people..read   597
General. All..Judea..Jerusalem..baptized   598
Sudden. Fell down..What must I do to be saved?   599
Trouble. Troubled the Egyptians..Let us flee   600
Truth. Paul reasoned..Felix trembled   601
Unexpected. We are verily guilty..our brother   602

Reading. Baruch read the book..they were afraid   749
  "   Shaphan read it..king rent his clothes   752
  "   All the people wept when they heard   763

8503. SURRENDER, Absolute. *P a u l .* ⁸ I
count all things *but* loss for the excellency of the
knowledge of Christ Jesus my Lord : for whom
I have suffered the loss of all things, and do
count them *but* dung, that I may win Christ.—
Phil., ch. 3.

8504. —— Bodily. *H e b r e w s .* ²⁸ Then
Nebuchadnezzar..said, Blessed *be* the God of
Shadrach, Meshach, and Abed-nego, who hath
sent his angel, and delivered his servants that
trusted in him, and have changed the king's
word, and yielded their bodies, that they might
not serve nor worship any god, except their own
God.—Dan., ch. 3.

8505. —— Christian. *Its Object.* ¹⁰ That I
may know him, and the power of his resurrection, and the fellowship of his sufferings, being
made conformable unto his death.—Phil., ch. 3.

8506. —— Entire. *Young Ruler.* ²¹ One thing
thou lackest : go thy way, sell whatsoever thou
hast, and give to the poor, and thou shalt have
treasure in heaven : and come, take up the
cross, and follow me. ²² And he was sad.—
Mark, ch. 10.

8507. —— —— Of All. ³³ Whosoever he be
of you that forsaketh not all that he hath, he
cannot be my disciple.—Luke, ch. 14.

8508. —— through Fear. *Rulers of Jezreel.*
⁵ He that *was* over the city, the elders also, and
the bringers up *of the children,* sent to Jehu, saying, We *are* thy servants, and will do all that
thou shalt bid us ; we will not make any king :
do thou *that which is* good in thine eyes.—2
Kings, ch. 10.

8509. —— Moral. *Paul.* ⁴ If any other man
thinketh that he hath whereof he might trust in
the flesh, I more.. ⁷ But what things were gain
to me, those I counted loss for Christ.—Phil.,
ch. 3.

8510. —— of Power. *Paul.* ¹² If others be
partakers of *this* power over you, *are* not we

rather? Nevertheless we have not used this power ; but suffer all things, lest we should hinder the gospel of Christ.—1 Cor., ch. 9.

8511. —— **resisted.** *Foul Spirit.* [20] And when he saw him [Jesus], straightway the spirit tare him ; and he fell on the ground, and wallowed foaming.—Mark, ch. 9.

8512. —— **of Sins.** *Disciples.* [30] If thy right hand offend thee, cut it off, and cast it from thee : for it is profitable for thee that one of thy members should perish, and not *that* thy whole body should be cast into hell.—Mat., ch. 6.

8513. —— **in Sacrifice.** "*Two Mites.*" [41] This poor widow hath cast more in, than all they which have cast into the treasury.. [44] For all *they* did cast in of their abundance ; but she of her want did cast in all that she had, *even* all her living.—Mark, ch. 9.

8514. —— **Undivided.** *Pharaoh.* [24] Go ye, serve the Lord ; only let your flocks and your herds be stayed.. [26] Our cattle also shall go with us ; there shall not a hoof be left behind.—Ex., ch. 10.

8515. —— **A weak.** *Ahab.* [2] Thus saith Ben-hadad, [3] Thy silver and thy gold *is* mine ; thy wives also and thy children, *even* the goodliest, *are* mine. [4] And the king of Israel answered ..My lord, O king, according to thy saying, I *am* thine, and all that I have.—1 Kings, ch. 20.

See other Illustrations under:

DEFEAT.

See RESIGNATION and references.

8516. SUSPICION affected. *Joseph.* [8] Joseph knew his brethren, but they knew not him. [9]..Ye *are* spies ; to see the nakedness of the land ye are come. [10] And they said..Nay, my lord, but to buy food.—Gen., ch. 42.

8517. —— **Cruel.** *Saul's.* [13] Why have ye conspired against me, thou and the son of Jesse, in that thou hast given him bread, and a sword, and hast inquired of God for him, that he should rise against me, to lie in wait, as at this day? [14] Then Ahimelech answered the king..who *is* so faithful among all thy servants as David.—1 Sam., ch. 22. [Saul killed him.]

8518. —— **corrected.** *Joseph.* [19] Joseph her husband, being a just *man*, and not willing to make her a public example, was minded to put her away privily. [20]..the angel of the Lord appeared unto him in a dream, saying, Joseph, thou son of David, fear not to take unto thee Mary thy wife : for that which is conceived in her is of the Holy Ghost.—Mat., ch. 1.

8519. —— **Deterred by.** *David.* [2] David and his men passed on in the rearward with Achish. [3] Then said the princes of the Philistines, What *do* these Hebrews *here?* And Achish said..*Is* not this David, the servant of Saul the king of Israel, which hath been with me..these years, and I have found no fault with him.—1 Sam., ch. 29.

8520. —— **Evil of.** *Hanun.* [See No. 8526.] [4] Wherefore Hanun took David's servants, and shaved off the one half of their beards, and cut

off their garments in the middle, *even* to their buttocks, and sent them away.—2 Sam., ch. 10.

8521. —— **Groundless.** *King of Syria.* [11] The heart of the king of Syria was sore troubled for this thing ; and he called his servants, and said.. Will ye not shew me which of us *is* for the king of Israel ? [12] And one..said, None, my lord, O king : but Elisha, the prophet.—2 Kings, ch. 6.

8522. —— **Painful.** *Brothers'.* [15] When Joseph's brethren saw that their father was dead, they said, Joseph will peradventure hate us, and will certainly requite us all the evil which we did unto him.—Gen., ch. 50.

8523. —— **removed.** *Joseph.* [19] Joseph said unto them, Fear not : for *am* I in the place of God ? [20] But as for you, ye thought evil against me ; *but* God meant it unto good, to bring to pass, as *it is* this day, to save much people alive. —Gen., ch. 50.

8524. —— **Sagacious.** *Philistines.* [4] The princes of the Philistines were wroth..said unto him, Make this fellow return..and let him not go down with us to battle, lest in the battle he be an adversary to us : for wherewith should he reconcile himself unto his master ? *should it* not *be* with the heads of these men ?—1 Sam., ch. 29.

8525. —— **Unwarranted.** *Joab said,* [25] Abner the son of Ner..came to deceive thee, and to know thy going out and thy coming in, and to know all that thou doest.—2 Sam., ch. 3. [He came to surrender to David.]

8526. —— —— *Hanun's.* [2] Said David, I will shew kindness unto Hanun the son of Nahash, as his father shewed kindness unto me. And David sent to comfort him by the hand of his servants for his father. [3]..hath not David *rather* sent his servants unto thee, to search the city, and to spy it out, and to overthrow it?—2 Sam., ch. 10.

See other illustrations under:

DISTRUST.

DOUBT.

JEALOUSY.

8527. SUSTENANCE, A precarious. *Elijah.*
[6] The ravens brought him bread and flesh in the morning, and bread and flesh in the evening ; and he drank of the brook.—1 Kings, ch. 17.

8528. —— **Royal.** *Solomon.* [22] Solomon's provision for one day was thirty measures of fine flour, and threescore measures of meal, [23] Ten fat oxen, and twenty oxen out of the pastures, and a hundred sheep, besides harts, and roebucks, and fallow deer, and fatted fowl. —1 Kings, ch. 4.

See FOOD.

8529. SWEAT of Blood. *Jesus.* [44] Being in an agony he prayed more earnestly : and his sweat was as it were great drops of blood falling down to the ground.—Luke, ch. 22.

8530. —— **of Toil.** *Curse.* [18] Thorns also and thistles shall it bring forth to thee ; and thou shalt eat the herb of the field : [19] In the sweat of thy face shalt thou eat bread, till thou return unto the ground.—Gen., ch. 3.

8531. SWORD, A flaming. *Eden.* [24] He drove out the man : and he placed at the east of the garden of Eden cherubim, and a flaming sword which turned every way, to keep the way of the tree of life.—Gen., ch. 3.

8532. —— **The Lord's.** *Lord and Gideon.* [20] And the three companies blew the trumpets, and brake the pitchers, and held the lamps in their left hands, and the trumpets in their right hands to blow *withal :* and they cried, The sword of the Lord, and of Gideon. [21] And they stood every man in his place round about the camp : and all the host ran, and cried, and fled. —Judges, ch. 7.

8533. —— **Memorial.** *Goliath.* [9] The priest said, The sword of Goliath the Philistine, whom thou slewest..it *is here* wrapped in a cloth behind the ephod : if thou wilt take that, take it : for *there is* none save that here. And David said, *There is* none like that ; give it me.—1 Sam., ch. 21.

8534. —— **Ominous.** *Drawn.* [15] The angel of the Lord stood by the threshingfloor of Ornan the Jebusite. [16] And David..saw the angel of the Lord stand between the earth and the heaven, having a drawn sword in his hand stretched out over Jerusalem. Then David and the elders *of Israel, who were* clothed in sackcloth, fell upon their faces.—1 Chron., ch. 21.

8535. —— —— *Entering Canaan.* [13] Joshua was by Jericho..behold, there stood a man over against him with his sword drawn in his hand : and Joshua went unto him, and said unto him, *Art* thou for us, or for our adversaries?—Josh., ch. 5.

8536. —— **for Punishment.** *Fear.* [8] Ye have feared the sword ; and I will bring a sword upon you, saith the Lord God.—Ezek., ch. 11.

8537. —— **rejected, The.** *Peter's.* [51] Struck a servant of the high priest, and smote off his ear. [52] Then said Jesus..Put up again thy sword into his place : for all they that take the sword shall perish with the sword.—Mat., ch. 26.

8538. —— **of the Spirit.** *"Word of God."* [17] Take the helmet of salvation, and the sword of the Spirit, which is the word of God.—Eph., ch. 6.

8539. —— —— *Effective.* [12] The word of God *is* quick, and powerful, and sharper than any twoedged sword, piercing even to the dividing asunder of soul and spirit, and of the joints and marrow, and *is* a discerner of the thoughts and intents of the heart.—Heb., ch. 4.

8540. —— **The sharpest.** *Wicked.* [4] The sons of men, whose teeth *are* spears and arrows, and their tongue a sharp sword.—Ps. 57.

8541. —— —— *Proverb.* [18] There is that speaketh like the piercings of a sword : but the tongue of the wise *is* health.—Prov., ch. 12.

8542. SWORDS, Fallen. *Benjamites.* [46] All which fell that day of Benjamin were twenty and five thousand men that drew the sword ; all these *were* men of valour.—Judges, ch. 20.

8543. —— **necessary.** *Ploughshares.* [10] Beat your ploughshares into swords, and your pruninghooks into spears : let the weak say, I *am* strong.—Joel, ch. 3.

8544. —— **transformed.** *Ploughshares.* [4] He shall judge among the nations, and shall rebuke many people : and they shall beat their swords into ploughshares, and their spears into pruninghooks : nation shall not lift up sword against nation, neither shall they learn war any more. —Isa., ch. 2.

Also see :
Manufacture. No smith..make them swords

8545. SYMPATHY abundant. *At Cesarea.* [12] When we heard these things, both we, and they of that place, besought him not to go up to Jerusalem. [13] Then Paul answered, What mean ye to weep and to break mine heart ? for I am ready not to be bound only, but also to die at Jerusalem for the name of the Lord Jesus.— Acts, ch. 21.

8546. —— **in Bereavement.** *Jesus.* [12] There was a dead man carried out, the only son of his mother, and she was a widow : and much people of the city was with her. [13] And when the Lord saw her, he had compassion on her, and said unto her, Weep not.—Luke, ch. 7.

8547. —— —— *Martha and Mary.* [19] Many of the Jews came to Martha and Mary, to comfort them concerning their brother.—John, ch. 11.

8548. —— **Deed of.** *Moses.* [24] Seeing one *of them* suffer wrong, he defended *him,* and avenged him..and smote the Egyptian : [25] For he supposed his brethren would have understood how that God by his hand would deliver them ; but they understood not.—Acts, ch. 7. [A taskmaster scourging a slave.]

8549. —— **distrusted.** *David's.* [3] The princes of the children of Ammon said unto Hanun their lord, Thinkest thou that David doth honour thy father, that he hath sent comforters unto thee ? hath not David *rather* sent his servants unto thee, to search the city, and to spy it out, and to overthrow it ?—2 Sam., ch. 10. [David's messengers were shamefully abused. See No. 8556.]

8550. —— **by the Eye.** *Jeremiah.* [51] Mine eye affecteth mine heart, because of all the daughters of my city.—Lam., ch. 3.

8551. —— **from Experience.** *Jesus.* [See No. 8555.]

8552. —— **for the Erring.** *Brotherly.* [6] Sufficient to such a man *is* this punishment, which *was inflicted* of many. ⁷ So that contrariwise ye ought rather to forgive *him*, and comfort *him*, lest perhaps such a one should be swallowed up with overmuch sorrow. ⁸ Wherefore I beseech you that ye would confirm *your* love toward him. —2 Cor., ch. 2.

8553. —— —— *Brotherly.* ¹⁴ If any man obey not our word by this epistle, note that man, and have no company with him, that he may be ashamed. ¹⁵ Yet count *him* not as an enemy, but admonish *him* as a brother. — 2 Thess., ch. 3.

8554. —— forbidden. *Murderer.* ¹¹ If any man hate his neighbour, and lie in wait for him ..and smite him mortally..and fleeth into one of these cities : ¹² Then the elders of his city shall..deliver him into the hand of the avenger of blood, that he may die. ¹³ Thine eye shall not pity him.—Deut., ch. 19.

8555. —— in Heaven. *Jesus.* ¹⁵ We have not a high priest which cannot be touched with the feeling of our infirmities ; but was in all points tempted like as *we are, yet* without sin. ¹⁶ Let us therefore come boldly unto the throne of grace, that we may obtain mercy, and find grace to help in time of need.—Heb., ch. 4.

8556. —— ill-rewarded. *Hanun.* ⁴ Wherefore Hanun took David's servants, and shaved off the one half of their beards, and cut off their garments in the middle, *even* to their buttocks, and sent them away.—2 Sam., ch. 10.

8557. —— for Jesus. *Women.* ²⁶ They laid the cross, that he might bear *it* after Jesus. ²⁷ And there followed him a great company of people, and of women, which also bewailed and lamented him.—Luke, ch. 23.

8558. —— manifested. *Job's Friends.* [See No. 8567.]

8559. —— Offices of. *Job.* ¹⁵ I was eyes to the blind, and feet *was* I to the lame. ¹⁶ I *was* a father to the poor : and the cause *which* I knew not I searched out. ¹⁷ And I brake the jaws of the wicked, and plucked the spoil out of his teeth.—Job, ch. 29.

8560. —— Power of. *Pharaoh's Daughter.* ⁶ When she had opened *it*, she saw the child : and, behold, the babe wept. And she had compassion on him, and said, This *is one* of the Hebrews' children.—Ex., ch. 2.

8561. —— Public. *Naomi.* ¹⁹ When they were come to Beth-lehem .. all the city was moved about them, and they said, *Is* this Naomi ? ²⁰ And she said..Call me not Naomi, call me Mara : for the Almighty hath dealt very bitterly with me. ²¹ I went out full, and the Lord hath brought me home again empty.—Ruth, ch. 1.

8562. —— —— Widows. [See Nos. 8546, 8561.]

8563. —— Practical. *Samaritan.* ³³ A certain Samaritan..came where he was ; and when he saw him he had compassion on *him*, ³⁴ And went to *him*, and bound up his wounds, pouring in oil and wine, and set him on his own beast, and brought him to an inn, and took care of him.— Luke, ch. 10.

8564. —— Power of. *On Paul.* [See No. 8545.]

8565. —— Return of. *Jesus.* ²⁸ Jesus turning unto them said, Daughters of Jerusalem,

weep not for me, but weep for yourselves, and for your children. ²⁹ For, behold, the days are coming.—Luke, ch. 23.

8566. —— Sentimental. *Wounded Man.* ³² Likewise a Levite, when he was at the place, came and looked on *him*, and passed by on the other side.—Luke, ch. 10.

8567. —— Silent. *Job's Friends.* ¹² They lifted up their voice, and wept ; and they rent every one his mantle, and sprinkled dust upon their heads toward heaven. ¹³ So they sat down with him upon the ground seven days and seven nights, and none spake a word unto him : for they saw that *his* grief was very great.—Job, ch. 3.

8568. —— Tender. *Jeremiah.* ¹ Oh that my head were waters, and mine eyes a fountain of tears, that I might weep day and night for the slain of the daughter of my people !—Jer., ch. 9.

8569. —— —— *Weeping.* ⁴⁸ Mine eye runneth down with rivers of water for the destruction of the daughter of my people. ⁴⁹ Mine eye trickleth down, and ceaseth not, without any intermission, ⁵⁰ Till the Lord look down, and behold from heaven.—Lam., ch. 3.

8570. —— Touched with. *Jesus.* ³² Mary.. fell down at his feet, saying unto him, Lord if thou hadst been here, my brother had not died. ³³ When Jesus therefore saw her weeping, and the Jews also weeping which came with her, he groaned in the spirit, and was troubled.—John, ch. 11.

8571. —— Unshaken by. *Paul.* [See No. 8545.]

See other illustrations under :

COMPASSION.

Appeal. Son..spirit teareth him..have compassion 1423
Active. Jesus went about all the cities..healing 1424
Brother's. Joseph said, Fear not..comforted them 1425
Commended. [Good Samaritan] Go thou and do l. 1426
Debtors. To be sold and his wife..had compassion 1427
Denied. Took him by the throat..Pay me..owest 1428
Lowly. Israel sighed..G. heard the groaning 1429
Moved. We have sinned..grieve for the misery of 1430
Penitent. While..a great way off..compassion 1431
Public. City was moved..Is this Naomi? 1432
Patriotic. O Jerusalem..how often..ye would not 1433
Practical. Leper..Jesus..moved with compassion 1434
Reproof. Forgive him and comfort him 1435
Required. Shouldest thou not have..on thy fellow 1436
Sensitive. Not a high priest which cannot be t. 1437
Unmoved. [Joseph] We saw the anguish..would 1438
Womanly. Daughter of Pharaoh..babe wept..had 1439
Without. Chaldees..had no compassion..old 1440

TENDERNESS.

Affectionate. I wrote unto you with many tears 8714
Bereavement. O my son Absalom, my son, my son 8715
Concealed. Joseph turned..and wept 8716
Excessive. Joseph made haste..sought where to w. 8717
Human. Her weeping, and the Jews weeping..J. 8718

Controlled. Chasten..let not thy soul spare for 1171
Dishonour. Jonathan was grieved for D..shame 25
Exhibited. Samaritan..bound up his wounds 728
    " I delivered the poor that cried..none to 708
See PITY.

8572. SYSTEM, Benevolent. *Zaccheus.* ⁸ Zaccheus stood, and said unto the Lord ; Behold, Lord, the half of my goods I give to the poor.— Luke, ch. 19.

8573. —— condemned. *Moses.* [16] When they have a matter, they come unto me, and I judge between one and another, and I do make *them* know the statutes of God, and his laws. [17] And Moses' father in law said . . The thing that thou doest *is* not good. [18] Thou wilt surely wear away, both thou, and this people that *is* with thee : for this thing *is* too heavy for thee. —Ex., ch. 18.

8574. —— Lack of. *Benevolence.* [1] When the number of the disciples was multiplied, there arose a murmuring of the Grecians against the Hebrews, because their widows were neglected in the daily ministration.—Acts, ch. 6.

8575. —— necessary. *Deacons.* [3] Brethren, look ye out among you seven men of honest report, full of the Holy Ghost and wisdom, whom we may appoint over this business. [4] But we will give ourselves continually to prayer, and to the ministry of the word.—Acts, ch. 6.

8576. —— Relief by. *Hobab's.* [21] Thou shalt provide out of all the people, able men, such as fear God, men of truth, hating covetousness ; and place *such* over them *to be* rulers of thousands, *and* rulers of hundreds, rulers of fifties, and rulers of tens : [22] And let them judge the people at all seasons . . every great matter they shall bring unto thee.—Ex., ch. 18.

8577. —— in Worship. *Jacob.* [20] Jacob vowed a vow, saying, If God will be with me, and will keep me in this way that I go . . of all that thou shalt give me I will surely give the tenth unto thee.—Gen., ch. 28.

See other illustrations under :

ORDER.

Chaos. Earth was without form and void   5923
Church. Ye may all prophesy one by one   5924
Regarded. Make all sit down by companies   5925

8578. TALEBEARER, The flattering. *Proverb.* [19] He that goeth about *as* a talebearer revealeth secrets : therefore meddle not with him that flattereth with his lips.—Prov., ch. 20.

8579. —— Strife by the. *Proverb.* [20] Where no wood is, *there* the fire goeth out : so where *there is* no talebearer, the strife ceaseth.—Prov., ch. 26.

8580. —— The tattling. *Proverb.* [9] He that covereth a transgression seeketh love ; but he that repeateth a matter separateth *very* friends.—Prov., ch. 17.

8581. —— Wounds of the. *Proverb.* [22] The words of a talebearer *are* as wounds, and they go down into the innermost parts of the belly. —Prov., ch. 26.

See SLANDER.

8582. TALENTS, Accountability for. *Future.* [19] After a long time the lord of those servants cometh, and reckoneth with them. [20] And so he that had received five talents came and brought other five talents, saying, Lord, thou deliveredst unto me five talents : behold, I have gained beside them five talents more.—Mat., ch. 25.

8583. —— faithfully used. *"Ruler."* [21] Well done, *thou* good and faithful servant : thou hast been faithful over a few things, I will make thee ruler over many things : enter thou into the joy of thy lord.—Mat., ch. 25.

8584. —— hidden in Fear. *One Talent.*

[24] Lord, I knew thee that thou art a hard man, reaping where thou hast not sown, and gathering where thou has not strewed : [25] And I was afraid, and went and hid thy talent in the earth. —Mat., ch. 25.

8585. —— Improvement of. *Rewarded.* [28] Take therefore the talent from him, and give *it* unto him which hath ten talents. [29] For unto every one which hath shall be given, and he shall have abundance.—Mat., ch. 25.

8586. —— Increase of. *Gained.* [16] He that had received the five talents went and traded with the same, and made *them* other five talents. [17] And likewise he that *had received* two, he also gained other two.—Mat., ch. 25.

8587. —— Numerous. *David.* [18] Cunning in playing, and a mighty valiant man, and a man of war, and prudent in matters, and a comely person, and the Lord *is* with him.—1 Sam., ch. 16.

8588. —— Unused. *"Hid."* [See No. 8584.]

8589. —— unimproved. *Punished.* [26] His lord answered . . Thou wicked and slothful servant . . [30] And cast ye the unprofitable servant into outer darkness : there shall be weeping and gnashing of teeth.—Mat., ch. 25.

8590. —— Various. *Parable.* [15] Unto one he gave five talents, to another two, and to another one ; to every man according to his several ability ; and straightway took his journey. —Mat., ch. 25.

See other illustrations under :

DEXTERITY.

Slingers. 700 left-handed . . sling stones at a hair   2283
Soldiers. Could use both the right hand and the   3784

GIFTS.

Diversity. To one is given . . spirit . . wisdom [Paul]   3537
"   To one . . five talents . . according to . . a   3538
Lesser. I give you power to tread on serpents   3541

INVENTORS.

Family. [Jubal] Handle harp and organ   4645
Weapon. I can slay a man for my hurt [Lamech]   4658

8591. TALKING—Doing. *Aaron—Moses.* [16] He shall be thy spokesman unto the people . . he shall be to thee instead of a mouth, and thou shalt be to him instead of God. [17] And thou shalt take this rod in thy hand, wherewith thou shalt do signs.—Ex., ch. 4.

See SPEECH and references.

8592. TAUNT, Alarming. *A Hebrew.* [13] Wherefore smitest thou thy fellow? [14] And he said, Who made thee a prince and a judge over us? intendest thou to kill me, as thou killedst the Egyptian? And Moses feared, and said, Surely this thing is known.—Ex., ch. 2.

See other illustrations under :

CONTEMPT.

Bigots. Pharisee prayed . . I am not as other men   1618
Critics. Michal saw king David leaping . . despised   1619
Conceited. Thistle . . sent to the cedar . . give thy d.   1620
Disregarded. The God of heaven will prosper us   1621
Enemy's. Am I a dog that thou comest . . staves   1622
Expressed. Children of Belial . . brought Saul no p.   1623
Fraternal. With whom has thou left those few s.   1624
Gospel. Made light of it, and went their way   1625
for God. Have turned their back unto me . . face   1626
Malicious. Did spit in his face, and buffeted   1628
Others. That they were righteous . . despised others   1629
for Worship. Torn . . the lame, and the sick . . ye   1630

DERISION.

Horrible. Put on him a scarlet robe..crown 2197
Impious. Laughed them to scorn and mocked 2198
Nickname. Thou art a Samaritan, and hast a devil 2200
Punished. Sarah saw the son of Hagar mocking 2199
Truth. Pharisees who were covetous..derided 2201
Unfortunates. Thieves also..cast the same into 2202
Wicked. They shoot out the lip, and shake the h. 2203

MOCKERY.

Blasphemous. Crown of thorns..reed..Hail, King 5494
of Truth. When they heard of the resurrection 5493

See RIDICULE.

8593. TASKMASTERS, Exacting. *Egyptian.*
⁷ Ye shall no more give the people straw to make brick, as heretofore : let them go and gather straw for themselves. ⁸ And the tale of the bricks..ye shall not diminish *aught* thereof.—Ex., ch. 5.

See OPPRESSION and references.

8594. TASTES differ. *Parental.* ²⁸ Isaac loved Esau, because he did eat of *his* venison : but Rebekah loved Jacob.—GEN., ch. 25.

8595. TAX, A burdensome. *Tribute.* ¹⁴ Hezekiah king of Judah sent to the king of Assyria to Lachish, saying, I have offended ; return from me : that which thou puttest on me will I bear. And the king of Assyria appointed.. three hundred talents of silver and thirty talents of gold.—2 KINGS, ch. 18.

8596. TAX COLLECTOR, A converted. *Levi.* ²⁷ He went forth, and saw a publican, named Levi, sitting at the receipt of custom : and he said unto him, Follow me. ²⁸ And he left all, rose up, and followed him.—LUKE, ch. 5.

8597. TAXATION, Exempted from. *Ministers.* ²⁴ We certify you, that, touching any of the priests and Levites, singers, porters, Nethinim, or ministers of this house of God, it shall not be lawful to impose toll, tribute, or custom, upon them.—EZRA, ch. 7.

8598. —— —— *Goliath.* ²⁵ The man who killeth him, the king will enrich him with great riches, and will give him his daughter, and make his father's house free in Israel.—1 SAM., ch. 17.

8599. —— endangered. *Rebuilding Jerusalem.* ¹³ Be it known now unto the king, that, if this city be builded, and the walls set up *again*, *then* will they not pay toll, tribute, and custom, and *so* thou shalt endamage the revenue. —EZRA, ch. 4.

8600. —— Eminence by. *Heliodorus.* ²⁰ Then shall stand up in his estate a raiser of taxes *in* the glory of the kingdom : but within few days he shall be destroyed, neither in anger, nor in battle. ²¹ And in his estate shall stand up a vile person, to whom they shall not give the honour of the kingdom : but he shall come in peaceably, and obtain the kingdom by flatteries.—DAN., ch. 11.

8601. —— Foreign. *Israel.* ³⁵ Jehoiakim.. taxed the land to give the money according to the commandment of Pharaoh : he exacted the silver and the gold of the people of the land, of every one according to his taxation.—2 KINGS, ch. 23.

8602. —— lawful. *Cesar's.* ²¹ Render therefore unto Cesar the things which are Cesar's ;

and unto God the things that are God's.—MAT., ch. 22.

8603. —— Oppressive. *Jews.* ⁴ We have borrowed money for the king's tribute, *and that* upon our lands and vineyards.—NEH., ch. 5.

8604. —— Secession because of. *Israel.* ³ Spake unto Rehoboam, saying, ⁴ Thy father made our yoke grievous : now therefore make thou the grievous service of thy father, and his heavy yoke which he put upon us, lighter, and we will serve thee.—1 KINGS, ch. 12. [He refused, and the kingdom was divided.]

8605. —— Universal. *"All the World."* ⁴ Joseph also went up from Galilee, out of the city of Nazareth..unto..Bethlehem, (because he was of the house of lineage of David,) ⁵ To be taxed with Mary his espoused wife, being great with child.—LUKE, ch. 2.

See other illustrations under :

TITHES.

Exchanged. If..be too long..turn it into money 8821
First. Abraham gave a tenth part of all 8822
Lord's. Passeth under the rod, the tenth..L. 8823
Ministry. The tithe of thine increase..the Levite 8824
Poor. The tithe of thine increase..the poor eat 8825
Substitute. Pay tithes of mint..omitted mercy 8826
Tithed. Offer up..a tenth of the tithe 8827
Unaccepted. I fast..I give tithes of all that I pos. 8828

TRIBUTE.

Sheep. King of Moab rendered..100,000 lambs 8952
Useless. Ahaz took a portion..but he helped..not 8954

Assessment. Menaham exacted..of each man 50 s. 535
Subsidy. Ahaz took [holy things]..sent it to the k. 8423

8606. TEACHABLENESS, Attitude of. *Mary.* ³⁸ Martha received him into her house. ³⁹ And she had a sister called Mary, which also sat at Jesus' feet, and heard his word.—LUKE, ch. 10.

8607. —— Characteristic. *Bereans.* ¹¹ These were more noble than those in Thessalonica, in that they received the word with all readiness of mind, and searched the Scriptures daily, whether those things were so.—ACTS, ch. 10.

8608. —— manifested. *Eunuch.* ³⁰ Understandest thou what thou readest ? ³¹ And he said, How can I, except some man should guide me ? And he desired Philip that he would come up and sit with him.—ACTS, ch. 8.

8609. —— professed. *Cornelius.* ³³ I sent to thee ; and thou hast well done that thou art come. Now therefore are we all here present before God, to hear all things that are commanded thee of God.—ACTS, ch. 10.

8610. —— Youthful. *Jesus.* ⁴⁶ After three days they found him in the temple, sitting in the midst of the doctors, both hearing them, and asking them questions.—LUKE, ch. 2.

8611. TEACHER, An authoritative. *Jesus.* ²¹ They went into Capernaum ; and straightway on the sabbath day he entered into the synagogue and taught. ²² And they were astonished at his doctrine : for he taught them as one that had authority, and not as the scribes.—MARK, ch. 1.

8612. —— of Art. *Bezaleel.* ³³ In the cutting of stones, to set *them*, and in carving of wood, to make any manner of cunning work. ³⁴ And he hath put in his heart that he may teach, *both* he, and Aholiab.—EX., ch. 35.

8613. —— **The great.** *Jesus.* [23] Jesus went about all Galilee, teaching in their synagogues. —MAT., ch. 4.

8614. —— **Home.** *Parent.* [7] Thou shalt teach them diligently unto thy children, and shalt talk of them when thou sittest in thine house, and when thou walkest by the way, and when thou liest down, and when thou risest up. —DEUT., ch. 6.

8615. —— **necessary, A.** *Eunuch.* [30] Philip ran thither to *him*, and heard him read the prophet Esaias, and said, Understandest thou what thou readest? [31] And he said, How can I, except some man should guide me?—ACTS, ch. 8.

8616. —— **A prepared.** *Moses.* [12] Come up to me into the mount, and be there : and I will give thee tables of stone, and a law, and commandments which I have written ; that thou mayest teach them.—EX., ch. 24.

8617. —— **The Spirit a.** *Present.* [11] When they bring you unto the synagogues, and *unto* magistrates, and powers, take ye no thought how or what thing ye shall answer, or what ye shall say : [12] For the Holy Ghost shall teach you in the same hour what ye ought to say. —LUKE, ch. 12.

8618. —— **Divine.** *Peter.* [28] Ye know how that it is an unlawful thing for a man that is a Jew to keep company, or come unto one of another nation ; but God hath shewed me that I should not call any man common or unclean.— ACTS, ch. 10.

8619. —— **Ministerial.** *Apostles.* [42] Daily in the temple, and in every house, they ceased not to teach and preach Jesus Christ.—ACTS, ch. 5.

Also see :

Art. Tubal Cain an instructor..brass and iron   5271
Bible. Levites read in the book..gave the sense   770
and Preaching. Jesus went teaching..and preaching 93
Rejected. Dost thou teach us..cast him out   2788
by Torture. Took the elders and thorns   8853
Zealous. Men put in prison..teaching in the temple 879
    See EDUCATION and references.

8620. TEARS, Affectionate. *Paul.* [4] Out of much affliction and anguish of heart I wrote unto you with many tears ; not that ye should be grieved, but that ye might know the love which I have more abundantly unto you.—2 COR., ch. 2.

8621. —— **in Bereavement.** *For Lazarus.* [33] When Jesus therefore saw her weeping, and the Jews also weeping which came with her, he groaned in the spirit, and was troubled.—JOHN, ch. 11.

8622. —— —— *For Lazarus.* [34] Where have ye laid him ? They said unto him, Lord, come and see. [35] Jesus wept. [36] Then said the Jews, Behold how he loved him !—JOHN, ch. 11.

8623. —— **Constant.** *Jeremiah.* [48] Mine eye runneth down with rivers of water for the destruction of the daughter of my people. [49] Mine eye trickleth down, and ceaseth not, without any intermission.—1 LAM., ch. 3.

8624. —— **desired.** *Jeremiah.* [1] Oh that my head were waters, and mine eyes a fountain of tears, that I might weep day and night for the slain of the daughter of my people !—JER., ch. 9.

8625. —— **disregarded.** *Punishment.* [18] Chas-

ten thy son while there is hope, and let not thy soul spare for his crying.—PROV., ch. 19.

8626. —— **An End of.** *Heaven.* [17] The Lamb which is in the midst of the throne shall feed them, and shall lead them unto living fountains of waters : and God shall wipe away all tears from their eyes.—REV., ch. 7.

8627. —— **Grateful.** *Sinner's.* [44] Simon, Seest thou this woman ? I entered into thine house, thou gavest me no water for my feet : but she hath washed my feet with tears, and wiped *them* with the hairs of her head.—LUKE, ch. 7.

8628. —— **in the Night.** *David.* [6] I am weary with my groaning ; all the night make I my bed to swim ; I water my couch with my tears.—PS. 6.

8629. —— **Precious.** *David.* [8] Thou tellest my wanderings ; put thou my tears into thy bottle : *are they* not in thy book ?—PS. 56.

8630. —— **Patriotic.** *For Jerusalem.* [41] When he was come near, he beheld the city, and wept over it, [42] Saying, If thou hadst known, even thou, at least in this thy day, the things *which belong* unto thy peace ! but now they are hid from thine eyes.—LUKE, ch. 19.

8631. —— **Power of.** *Infants.* [5] She saw the ark among the flags, she sent her maid to fetch it. [6] And when she had opened *it*, she saw the child : and, behold, the babe wept. And she had compassion on him.—EX., ch. 2.

8632. —— —— *Woman's.* [16] Samson's wife wept before him, and said, Thou dost but hate me, and lovest me not : thou hast put forth a riddle unto the children of my people, and hast not told *it* me.—JUDGES, ch. 14.

8633. —— **Parting.** *David and Jonathan.* [41] David arose out of *a place* toward the south, and fell on his face to the ground, and bowed himself three times : and they kissed one another, and wept one with another, until David exceeded.—1 SAM., ch. 20.

8634. —— **Penitential.** *Peter.* [72] The cock crew. And Peter called to mind the word that Jesus said..Before the cock crow twice, thou shalt deny me thrice. And when he thought thereon, he wept.—MARK, ch. 14.

8635. —— **Transient.** *Saul's.* [16] *Is* this thy voice, my son David ? And Saul lifted up his voice, and wept. [17] And he said to David, Thou *art* more righteous than I : for thou hast rewarded me good, whereas I have rewarded thee evil. —1 SAM., ch. 24. [He soon sought David's life again.]

See other illustrations under :

MOURNERS.

Abstinence. [Abner assassinated] If I taste   5603
Bereavement. I am distressed for thee, my b.   5604
Beneficial. Better to go to the house of mourning 5605
Comfort. Asleep..sorrow not as others which   5598
    See GRIEF and references.

8636. TEMPORALITIES, Advice in. *Ahijah's.* [3] He shall tell thee what shall become of the child. [4] And Jeroboam's wife..went to Shiloh, and came to the house of Ahijah. But Ahijah could not see..by reason of his age.—1 KINGS, ch. 14.

8637. —— **God consulted.** *Hezekiah.* [8] The king said unto Hazael, Take a present in thine hand, and go, meet the man of God, and inquire of the Lord by him, saying, Shall I recover of this disease ?—2 Kings, ch. 8.

8638. —— —— *Zedekiah.* ² Inquire, I pray thee, of the Lord for us ; for Nebuchadrezzar king of Babylon maketh war against us ; if so be that the Lord will deal with us according to all his wondrous works, that he may go up from us. ³ Then said Jeremiah unto them, Thus shall ye say to Zedekiah.—Jer., ch. 21.

8639. —— —— *To Micah.* ² The children of Dan sent of their family five men from their coasts, men of valour..to spy out the land.. ⁵ And they said unto him, Ask counsel, we pray thee, of God, that we may know whether our way which we go shall be prosperous.—Judges, ch. 18.

8640. —— —— *In War.* ¹⁸ The children of Israel..went up to the house of God, and asked counsel of God, and said, Which of us shall go up first to the battle against the children of Benjamin ? And the Lord said, Judah *shall go up* first.—Judges, ch. 20.

8641. —— —— *Saul said,* ⁶ *There is* in this city a man of God, and *he is* an honourable man ; all that he saith cometh surely to pass : now let us go thither ; peradventure he can shew us our way that we should go.—1 Sam., ch. 9.

8642. —— —— *In War.* ² David inquired of the Lord, saying, Shall I go and smite these Philistines? And the Lord said unto David, Go.—1 Sam., ch. 23.

8643. —— —— *Israelites.* ¹ After the death of Joshua..the children of Israel asked the Lord, saying, Who shall go up for us against the Canaanites first, to fight against them ?—Josh., ch. 1.

8644. —— —— *Josiah to Hilkiah.* ¹³ Inquire of the Lord for me..and for all Judah, concerning the words of this book that is found : for great *is* the wrath of the Lord that is kindled against us, because our fathers have not hearkened unto the words of this book.—2 Kings, ch. 22.

8645. —— **Divine Supremacy in.** *"Good—Evil."* ⁷ The king of Israel said unto Jehoshaphat, *There is* yet one man, by whom we may inquire of the Lord : but I hate him ; for he never prophesied good unto me, but always evil.—2 Chron., ch. 18.

8646. —— **Direction in.** *Trust.* ⁵ Trust in the Lord with all thine heart ; and lean not unto thine own understanding. ⁶ In all thy ways acknowledge him, and he shall direct thy paths.—Prov., ch. 3.

8647. —— **Enlargement of.** *Prayer for.* ¹⁰ Jabez called on the God of Israel, saying, Oh that thou wouldest bless me indeed, and enlarge my coast, and that thine hand might be with me, and that thou wouldest keep *me* from evil, that it may not grieve me ! And God granted him that which he requested.—1 Chron., ch. 4.

8648. —— **Neglecting God in.** *Saul.* ¹³ So Saul died for his transgression which he committed against the Lord, *even* against the word of the Lord, which he kept not, and also for asking *counsel* of *one that had* a familiar spirit, to inquire *of it.*—1 Chron., ch. 10.

8649. —— —— *Gibeonites.* ¹³ Our shoes are become old by reason of the very long journey. ¹⁴ And the men took of their victuals, and asked not *counsel* at the mouth of the Lord.. ¹⁵ And Joshua made peace with them.—Josh., ch. 9.

8650. —— **Prayer in.** *Abraham's Servant.* ¹⁴ The damsel to whom I shall say, Let down thy pitcher, I pray thee, that I may drink ; and she shall say, Drink, and I will give thy camels drink also : *let the same be* she *that* thou hast appointed for thy servant Isaac.—Gen., ch. 24.

8651. —— —— *Nehemiah.* ¹¹ O Lord, I beseech thee, let now thine ear be attentive to the prayer of thy servant, and to the prayer of thy servants, who desire to fear thy name : and prosper, I pray thee, thy servant this day, and grant him mercy in the sight of this man. For I was the king's cupbearer.—Neh., ch. 1.

8652. —— —— *Moses.* ¹⁷ Let the beauty of the Lord our God be upon us : and establish thou the work of our hands upon us ; yea, the work of our hands establish thou it.—Ps. 90.

8653. —— **Withdrawn from.** *Apostles.* ² It is not reason that we should leave the word of God, and serve tables. ³ Wherefore, brethren, look ye out among you seven men..whom we may appoint over this business.—Acts, ch. 6.

See PROPERTY.

8654. TEMPLE, The chosen. *Heart.* ²³ As I passed by, and beheld your devotions, I found an altar with this inscription, TO THE UNKNOWN GOD. ²⁴ God that made the world and all things therein, seeing that he is Lord of heaven and earth, dwelleth not in temples made with hands.—Acts, ch. 17.

8655. —— **Construction of.** *Seven Years.* ³⁸ Was he seven years in building it.—1 Kings, ch. 6.

8656. —— —— *Forty-six.* ²⁰ Said the Jews, Forty and six years was this temple in building, and wilt thou rear it up in three days ?—John, ch. 2.

8657. —— **Human.** *Body.* ¹⁶ Know ye not that ye are the temple of God, and *that* the Spirit of God dwelleth in you ? ¹⁷ If any man defile the temple of God, him shall God destroy ; for the temple of God is holy, which *temple* ye are. —1 Cor., ch. 3.

8658. —— **Silent.** *Glorious.* ⁷ The house.. was built of stone made ready before it was brought thither : so that there was neither hammer nor axe *nor* any tool of iron heard in the house, while it was in building.. ²² The whole house he overlaid with gold, until he had finished all the house : also the whole altar that *was* by the oracle he overlaid with gold.—1 Kings, ch. 6.

See other illustrations under :

HOUSE OF GOD.

Abandoned. L. hath cast off his altar..abhorred	4126
Closed. Ahaz shut up the doors	4127
Despoiled. Chaldees..carried the pots, shovels	4128
Destroyed. Break down the carved work..fire	4129
Expensive. [Costing £939,907,687—Jamieson]	4130
Gifts. Brought bracelets, earrings, and rings	4131
Given. Ahaz took away a portion..king of As.	4132
Grandeur. D. said..must be exceeding magnifical	4133
Neglected. Dwell in your ceiled houses..waste	4134
Polluted. Manasseh built altars..graven image	4135
Refuge. Adonijah feared..horns of the altar	4136

Residence. Anna departed not from the temple 4137
Robbed. Shishak took..treasures..shields of gold 4138
"   Ahaz cut in pieces the vessels..altars 4139
Repairing. Jehoiada took a chest..beside the altar 4140

SANCTUARY.

Criminals. Adonijah..caught hold on the horns of 7571
"   Solomon sent Benaiah..Go, fall upon 7572
Help in. My feet were almost gone..too painful 7573

8659. TEMPERANCE advised. *Angel said,* [To Samson's mother,] ⁷ Thou shalt..bear a son ; and now drink no wine nor strong drink, neither eat any unclean *thing:* for the child shall be a Nazarite to God from the womb to the day of his death.—JUDGES, ch. 13.

8660. —— Extreme. *Nazarite.* ³ He shall separate *himself* from wine and strong drink, and shall drink no vinegar of wine, or vinegar of strong drink, neither shall he drink any liquor of grapes, nor eat moist grapes, or dried. ⁴ All the days of his separation shall he eat nothing that is made of the vine tree, from the kernels even to the husk.—NUM. ch. 6.

8661. —— in Eating. *Appetite.* ¹ When thou sittest to eat with a ruler, consider diligently what *is* before thee : ² And put a knife to thy throat, if thou *be* a man given to appetite. ³ Be not desirous of his dainties : for they *are* deceitful meat.—PROV., ch. 23.

8662. —— Hereditary. *Rechabites.* ⁶ We will drink no wine : for Jonadab the son of Rechab our father commanded us, saying, Ye shall drink no wine, *neither* ye, nor your sons for ever.—JER., ch. 35.

8663. —— promotes Health. *Hebrews.* ¹⁴ Proved them ten days. ¹⁵ And at the end of ten days their countenances appeared fairer and fatter in flesh than all the children which did eat the portion of the king's meat. ¹⁶ Thus Melzar took away the portion of their meat, and the wine..and gave them pulse.—DAN., ch. 1.

8664. —— Mastery by. *Athlete.* ²⁴ So run, that ye may obtain. ²⁵ And every man that striveth for the mastery is temperate in all things.—1 COR., ch. 9.

8665. —— and Piety. *Baptist.* ¹⁵ He shall be great in the sight of the Lord, and shall drink neither wine nor strong drink ; and he shall be filled with the Holy Ghost, even from his mother's womb.—LUKE, ch. 1.

8666. —— Strength by. *Samson.* [A Nazarite. See No. 8659.]

See INTEMPERANCE and references.

8667. TEMPTER, A bold. *Satan.* ¹ Then was Jesus led up of the Spirit into the wilderness to be tempted of the devil. ² And when he had fasted forty days and forty nights, he was afterward a hungered.—MAT., ch. 4.

8668. —— vanquished. *By Bible.* ¹⁰ Get thee hence, Satan : for it is written, Thou shalt worship the Lord thy God, and him only shalt thou serve. ¹¹ Then the devil leaveth him, and, behold, angels came and ministered unto him. —MAT., ch. 4.

8669. —— —— *Means.* ¹⁶ Above all, taking the shield of faith, wherewith ye shall be able to quench all the fiery darts of the wicked. ¹⁷ And take the helmet of salvation, and the sword of the Spirit, which is the word of God. —EPH., ch. 6.

8670. TEMPTATION avoided. *Rechabites* ⁶ Said, We will drink no wine : for Jonadab the son of Rechab our father commanded us.—JER., ch. 35.

8671. —— in Ambition. *Eve.* ⁴ The serpent said unto the woman, Ye shall not surely die : ⁵ For God doth know that in the day ye eat thereof, then your eyes shall be opened, and ye shall be as gods.—GEN., ch. 3.

8672. —— in Appetite. *Israelites.* ³ Would to God we had died by the hand of the Lord in the land of Egypt, when we sat by the flesh-pots, *and* when we did eat bread to the full ; for ye have brought us forth into this wilderness, to kill this whole assembly with hunger.—EX., ch. 16.

8673. —— with Affliction. *Job.* ⁸ He sat down among the ashes. ⁹ Then said his wife unto him, Dost thou still retain thine integrity ? curse God, and die. ¹⁰ But he said unto her, Thou speakest as one of the foolish women speak. —JOB, ch. 2.

8674. —— from Applause. *Jesus.* Cast thyself down..bear thee up. [See No. 8691.]

8675. —— in Beauty. *Sarah.* ¹¹ When he was come near to enter into Egypt..he said unto Sarai his wife, Behold now, I know that thou *art* a fair woman to look upon : ¹²..they shall say, This *is* his wife : and they will kill me, but they will save thee alive.—GEN., ch. 12.

8676. —— —— *"Sons of God."* ² The sons of God saw the daughters of men that they *were* fair ; and they took them wives of all which they chose.—GEN., ch. 6.

8677. —— Buffeted by. *"Thorn."* ⁷ Lest I should be exalted above measure through the abundance of the revelations, there was given to me a thorn in the flesh, the messenger of Satan to buffet me, lest I should be exalted above measure.—2 COR., ch. 12.

8678. —— A concealed. *Hypocrites.* ¹⁷ Is it lawful to give tribute unto Cesar, or not ? ¹⁸ But Jesus perceived their wickedness, and said, Why tempt ye me, ye hypocrites ? ¹⁹ Shew me the tribute money.—MAT., ch. 22.

8679. —— —— *Jesus.* ⁵³ The scribes and the Pharisees began to urge *him* vehemently, and to provoke him to speak of many things : ⁵⁴ Laying wait for him, and seeking to catch something out of his mouth, that they might accuse him.—LUKE, ch. 11.

8680. —— in Dominion. *Jesus.* ⁸ Again, the devil taketh him up into an exceeding high mountain, and sheweth him all the kingdoms of the world, and the glory of them ; ⁹ And saith ..All these things will I give thee, if thou wilt fall down and worship me.—MAT., ch. 4.

8681. —— Exposure to. *Peter.* ⁵⁵ Peter sat down among them. ⁵⁶ But a certain maid beheld him as he sat by the fire, and earnestly looked upon him, and said, This man was also with him.—LUKE, ch. 22.

8682. —— through the Eyes. *David.* ² In an eveningtide..David arose from off his bed, and walked upon the roof of the king's house : and ..saw a woman washing herself ; and the woman *was* very beautiful to look upon.—2 SAM., ch. 11.

8683. —— —— [Also see Nos. 8676, 8680, 8684, 8689, 8695.]

8684. —— The first. *Eden.* [6] When the woman saw that the tree *was* good for food, and that it *was* pleasant to the eyes, and a tree to be desired to make one wise, she took of the fruit. —GEN., ch. 3.

8685. —— in the Flesh. *Paul.* [14] My temptation which was in my flesh ye despised not, nor rejected ; but received me as an angel of God, *even* as Christ Jesus.—GAL., ch. 4.

8686. —— in Hunger. *Jesus.* [3] When the tempter came to him, he said, If thou be the Son of God, command that these stones be made bread. [4] But he answered. . It is written, Man shall not live by bread alone, but by every word that proceedeth out of the mouth of God. —MAT., ch. 4.

8687. —— Heaviness from. *Hope.* [6] Wherein ye greatly rejoice, though now for a season, if need be, ye are in heaviness through manifold temptations.—1 PETER, ch. 1.

8688. —— in Money. *" Root."* [10] The love of money is the root of all evil : which while some coveted after, they have erred from the faith, and pierced themselves through with many sorrows.—1 TIM., ch. 6.

8689. —— offered. *From Bablyon.* [13] Hezekiah hearkened unto them, and showed them all the house of his precious things, the silver, and the gold, and the spices, and the precious ointment, and *all* the house of his armour, and all that was found in his treasures. . in his house . . in all his dominion.—2 KINGS, ch. 20. [Babylonians captured them.]

8690. —— in Office. *Balaam.* [17] I will promote thee unto very great honour, and I will do whatsoever thou sayest unto me : come therefore, I pray thee, curse me this people.—NUM., ch. 22.

8691. —— to Presumption. *Jesus.* [5] Then the devil : . setteth him on a pinnacle of the temple, [6] And saith . . If thou be the Son of God, cast thyself down : for it is written, He shall give his angels charge concerning thee : and in *their* hands they shall bear thee up.—MAT., ch. 4.

8692. —— after Pardon. *Illustration.* [22] Moses brought Israel from the Red sea . . and they went three days in the wilderness, and found no water. [23] And when they came to Marah, they could not drink of the waters . . for they *were* bitter.—Ex., ch. 15.

8693. —— Prayer against. *At Gethsemane.* [40] When he was at the place, he said unto them, Pray that ye enter not into temptation.—LUKE, ch. 22.

8694. —— Proved by. *Manna.* [4] I will rain bread from heaven for you ; and the people shall go out and gather a certain rate every day, that I may prove them, whether they will walk in my law, or no.—Ex., ch. 16.

8695. —— prevented. *Canaanite.* [52] Ye shall drive out all the inhabitants of the land from before you, and destroy all their pictures, and destroy all their molten images, and quite pluck down all their high places.—NUM., ch. 33.

8696. —— resisted. *Joseph.* [10] She spake to Joseph day by day . . he hearkened not unto her . . or to be with her . . [12] And she caught him by his garment, saying, Lie with me : and he left his garment in her hand, and fled, and got him out.—GEN., ch. 39.

8697. —— —— *Proverb.* [10] My son, if sinners entice thee, consent thou not. [15] My son, walk not thou in the way with them ; refrain thy foot from their path.—PROV., ch. 1.

8698. —— —— *" Devil."* [7] Submit yourselves therefore to God. Resist the devil, and he will flee from you.—JAMES, ch. 4.

8699. —— repeated. *" Day by day."* [See No. 8696.]

8700. —— removed. *Horses.* [The king] [16] Shall not multiply horses to himself, nor cause the people to return to Egypt, to the end that he should multiply horses.—DEUT., ch. 17.

8701. —— not removed. *Grace.* [8] For this thing I besought the Lord thrice, that it might depart from me. [9] And he said unto me, My grace is sufficient for thee : for my strength is made perfect in weakness. Most gladly therefore will I rather glory in my infirmities, that the power of Christ may rest upon me.—2 COR., ch. 12.

8702. —— Remembered. *At Rephidim.* [6] Thou shalt smite the rock, and there shall come water out of it, that the people may drink. And Moses did, so in the sight of the elders of Israel. [7] And he called the name of the place Massah, and Meribah, because of the chiding of the children of Israel, and because they tempted the Lord, saying, Is the Lord among us or not ? —Ex., ch. 17. [Marginal reading—" Place of temptation."]

8703. —— A studied. *Gehazi.* [20] Gehazi, the servant of Elisha . . said, Behold, my master hath spared Naaman this Syrian, in not receiving at his hands that which he brought : but, *as* the Lord liveth, I will run after him, and take somewhat of him.—2 KINGS, ch. 5.

8704. —— Weakness in. *Canaan-bound.* [17] God led them not *through* the way of the land of the Philistines, although that *was* near ; for God said, Lest peradventure the people repent when they see war, and they return to Egypt.— Ex., ch. 13.

8705. TEMPTATIONS. Numerous. *Jesus.* [15] We have not a high priest which cannot be touched with the feeling of our infirmities ; but was in all points tempted like as *we are*, *yet* without sin.—HEB., ch. 4.

8706. —— necessary. *Sift.* [19] There must be also heresies among you, that they which are approved may be made manifest among you.— 1 COR., ch. 11.

8707. —— Rejoicing in. *Patience.* [2] My brethren, count it all joy when ye fall into divers temptations ; [3] Knowing *this*, that the trying of your faith worketh patience. [4] But let patience have *her* perfect work, that ye may be perfect. —JAMES, ch. 1.

8708. —— Self-imposed. *Canaanites.* [55] But if ye will not drive out the inhabitants of the land from before you ; then . . those which ye let remain of them *shall be* pricks in your eyes, and thorns in your sides, and shall vex you in the land.—NUM., ch. 33.

8709. —— Successive. *Jesus.* [See Nos. 8668, 8680, 8691.]

8710. —— Victim of. *Job.* [8] The Lord said unto Satan, Hast thou considered my servant Job, that *there is* none like him in the earth, a perfect and an upright man, one that feareth God, and escheweth evil ? ⁹ Then Satan answered..Doth Job fear God for nought ?—Job, ch. 1.

8711. —— **in Wealth.** *" Snare."* ⁹ They that will be rich fall into temptation and a snare, and *into* many foolish and hurtful lusts, which drown men in destruction and perdition. —1 Tim., ch. 6.

8712. —— **of Youth.** *" Entice."* [See No. 8697.]

See other illustrations under :

DEVIL.

Hypocrisy. Ye are of your father the devil   2267
Sold to. Ahab did sell himself to work w.   2268

SATAN.

Audacity. If thou be the S. of G., command   7578
Bound. An angel..bound him a thousand years   7579
Children. Ye are of your father the devil..no truth 7580
Cunning. God doth know..your eyes shall be o.   7581
Doom. Cast him into the bottomless pit   7582
Delivered to. Hymeneas and Alex..delivered unto 7583
Enmity. I will put enmity between thee..woman 7584
Fall of. War in heaven..the dragon fought   7585
Filled. Ananias, why hath Satan filled thy heart 7586
Injurious. L. said..all that he hath..thy power 7587
Inspired by. Devil put into the heart of Judas 7588
Leader. After the sop, Satan entered into him 7589
Peril. The devil as a roaring lion..seeking w.   7590
Scripture. It is written, He shall give his angels 7591
Worshipper. Satan came also to present himself 7592

Continuous. Spake to Joseph day by day   77
Resisted. I set before..Rechabites pots of wine   32
    See TRIALS and references.

8713. TENANTS, Abusive. *Parable.* ³⁴ He sent his servants to the husbandmen, that they might receive the fruits of it. ³⁵ And the husbandmen took his servants, and beat one, and killed another, and stoned another.—Mat., ch. 21.

8714. TENDERNESS in Bereavement. *David.* ³³ The king was much moved, and went up to the chamber over the gate, and wept : and as he went, thus he said, O my son Absalom ! my son, my son Absalom ! would God I had died for thee, O Absalom, my son, my son !—2 Sam., ch. 18.

8715. —— **concealed.** *Joseph.* ²³ They knew not that Joseph understood *them ;* for he spake unto them by an interpreter. ²⁴ And he turned himself about from them, and wept ; and returned..and took from them Simeon, and bound him before their eyes.—Gen., ch. 42.

8716. —— **to the Erring.** *Paul.* ⁴ Out of much affliction and anguish of heart I wrote unto you with many tears ; not that ye should be grieved, but that ye might know the love which I have more abundantly unto you.—2 Cor., ch. 2.

8717. —— **Excessive.** *Joseph.* ³⁰ Joseph made haste ; for his bowels did yearn upon his brother : and he sought *where* to weep ; and he entered into *his* chamber, and wept there.— Gen., ch. 43.

8718. —— **Human.** *Jesus.* ³³ When Jesus therefore saw her weeping, and the Jews also weeping which came with her, he groaned in the spirit, and was troubled, ³⁴ And said, Where have ye laid him ? They say unto him, Lord, come and see. ³⁵ Jesus wept.—John, ch. 11.

See other illustrations under :

SYMPATHY.

Abundant. What mean ye to weep and break mine 8545
Bereavement. Much people..with her..he had   8546
   "   Many of the Jews came to Martha 8547
Distrusted. Thinkest thou that David..hath sent 8549
Eyes. Mine eye affected mine heart, because of 8550
by Experience. Touched with the feeling of o.   8551
Erring. Forgive..lest swallowed up with..s.   8552
   "   Count him not as an enemy, but..a brother 8553
Forbidden. If any man lie in wait..eye shall not 8554
in Heaven. Not a high priest, which cannot be t.   8555
Ill-rewarded. Hanun shaved off one half of their 8556
for Jesus. Great company of people and women 8557
Manifested. [See Nos. 8547, 8557.]
Offices. I was eyes to the blind, and feet..lame 8559
Power. Behold the babe wept. She had compassion 8560
Public. All the city was moved..Is this Naomi?   8561
Practical. Samaritan..went to him and bound up 8563
Power. What mean ye to weep and break mine 8564
Return. Weep not for me, but weep for yourselves 8565
Sentimental. Levite..looked on him and passed by 8566
Silent. Sat down upon the ground 7 days..none 8567
Tender. O that mine head were waters, and mine 8568
   "   Mine eye runneth down with rivers of 8569
   "   Saw her weeping..Jews also..Jesus wept 8570
Unshaken. I am ready not to be bound only, but 8571

Gentleness. Drew not his sword..yet a youth   3515
    See KINDNESS and references.

8719. TENDENCIES, Evil. *Calf made.* ²² Aaron said, Let not the anger of my lord wax hot : thou knowest the people, that they *are set* on mischief.—Ex., ch. 32.

8720. TERMS, Acceptable. *Peter said,* ³⁴ God is no respecter of persons : ³⁵ But in every nation he that feareth him, and worketh righteousness, is accepted with him.—Acts, ch. 10.

8721. —— —— **Not formal.** ⁷ Will the Lord be pleased with thousands of rams, *or* with ten thousands of rivers of oil? shall I give my firstborn *for* my transgression, the fruit of my body *for* the sin of my soul ?—Micah, ch. 6.

8722. —— —— **Inward.** ⁸ He hath shewed thee, O man, what *is* good ; and what doth the Lord require of thee, but to do justly, and to love mercy, and to walk humbly with thy God ? —Micah, ch. 6.

See other illustrations under :

CONDITIONS.

Acceptance. What doth the L. require?..do   1470
Access. Except your youngest brother come   1471
Blessing. If thou shalt see me..taken..it shall   1472
Severe. This condition..I may thrust out..right e. 1473

8723. TERROR, Prostrating. *Saul.* ¹⁹ To morrow *shalt* thou and thy sons be with me : the Lord also shall deliver the host of Israel into the hand of the Philistines. ²⁰ Then Saul fell straightway all along on the earth, and was sore afraid, because of the words of Samuel : and there was no strength in him ; for he had eaten no bread all the day, nor all the night.— 1 Sam., ch. 28.

8724. —— **A Sinner's.** *Belshazzar.* ⁵ The king saw the part of the hand that wrote. ⁶ Then the king's countenance was changed, and his thoughts troubled him, so that the joints of his loins were loosed, and his knees smote one against another. ⁷ The king cried aloud to bring in the astrologers.—Dan., ch. 5.

8725. TERRORS, Divine. *Sinai.* [21] So terrible was the sight, *that* Moses said, I exceedingly fear and quake.—HEB., ch. 12.

See FEAR *and references.*

8726. TEST, Benevolence a. *Young Ruler.* [21] Jesus beholding him loved him, and said unto him, One thing thou lackest: go thy way, sell whatsoever thou hast, and give to the poor, and thou shalt have treasure in heaven..and follow me. [22] And he was sad at that saying, and went away grieved.—MARK, ch. 10.

8727. —— of Character. *Tree.* [3] Of the fruit of the tree which *is* in the midst of the garden, God hath said, Ye shall not eat of it, neither shall ye touch it, lest ye die.—GEN., ch. 3.

8728. —— Dietetic. *Young Hebrews.* [12] Prove thy servants..ten days; and let them give us pulse to eat, and water to drink. [13] Then let our countenances be looked upon before thee, and the countenance of the children that eat of the portion of the king's meat: and as thou seest, deal with us.—DAN., ch. 1.

8729. —— Exact. *Nobleman.* [52] Inquired he of them the hour when he began to amend. And they said..Yesterday at the seventh hour the fever left him. [53] So the father knew that *it was* at the same hour, in the which Jesus said unto him, Thy son liveth: and himself believed, and his whole house.—JOHN, ch. 4.

8730. —— The Lord's. *Fruit.* [5] The man's rod, whom I shall choose, shall blossom: and I will make to cease from me the murmurings of the children of Israel, whereby they murmur against you.—NUM., ch. 17.

8731. —— needful. *Saul's Armour.* [39] David girded his sword upon his armour, and he assayed to go; for he had not proved *it.* And David said unto Saul, I cannot go with these; for I have not proved *them.* And David put them off him.—1 SAM., ch. 17.

8732. —— Obedience a. *Commandments.* [4] He that saith, I know him, and keepeth not his commandments, is a liar, and the truth is not in him.—1 JOHN, ch. 2.

8733.] —— Password for. *Shibboleth.* [See No. 6820.] [5] And the Gileadites took the passages of Jordan before the Ephraimites: and it was so, that when those Ephraimites which were escaped said, Let me go over, that the men of Gilead said unto him, Art thou an Ephraimite? If he said, Nay; [6] Then said they unto him, Say now Shibboleth: and he said Sibboleth: for he could not frame to pronounce *it* right. Then they took him, and slew him at the passages of Jordan: and there fell at that time of the Ephraimites forty and two thousand.—JUDGES, ch. 12.

8734. —— A Prayer. *Mount Carmel.* [24] Call ye on the name of your gods, and I will call on the name of the Lord: and the God that answereth by fire, let him be God. And all the people answered and said, It is well spoken.—1 KINGS, ch. 18.

8735. —— A Question. *Lawyer.* [25] A certain lawyer stood up, and tempted him, saying, Master, what shall I do to inherit eternal life?—LUKE, ch. 10.

8736. —— A severe. *Abraham.* [2] Take now thy son, thine only *son* Isaac, whom thou lovest, and get thee into the land of Moriah; and offer him there for a burnt offering upon one of the mountains which I will tell thee of.—GEN., ch. 22.

8737. —— by Trials. *Enemies.* [4] They were to prove Israel by them, to know whether they would hearken unto the commandments of the Lord, which he commanded their fathers by the hand of Moses.—JUDGES, ch. 3.

8738. —— Heresies. [19] There must be also heresies among you, that they which are approved may be made manifest among you.—1 COR., ch. 11.

8739. TESTS repeated. *Water.* [Water wanted at Rephidim, and also at Kadesh.—NUM., ch. 20.]

Also see:
Adversity. All that he hath is in thy power . . . 212
See EVIDENCE *and references.*
See TEMPTATION.

8740. TESTAMENT, A bloody. *At Sinai.* [19] When Moses had spoken every precept..he took the blood of calves and of goats, with water, and scarlet wool, and hyssop, and sprinkled both the book and all the people, [20] Saying, This *is* the blood of the testament which God hath enjoined.—HEB., ch. 9.

8741. —— The Lord's. *Blood.* [23] He took the cup, and when he had given thanks, he gave *it* to them: and they all drank of it. [24] And he said unto them, This is my blood of the new testament, which is shed for many.—MARK, ch. 14.

8742. TESTIMONY of Assurance. *"My Presence."* [13] If I have found grace in thy sight, shew me now thy way, that I may know thee, that I may find grace in thy sight: and consider that this nation *is* thy people. [14] And he said, My presence shall go *with thee*, and I will give thee rest.—EX., ch. 33.

8743. —— Altar of. *Beyond Jordan.* [28] It shall be, when they should *so* say to us or to our generations in time to come, that we may say *again*, Behold the pattern of the altar of the Lord, which our fathers made, not for burnt offerings, nor for sacrifices; but it *is* a witness between us and you.—JOSH., ch. 22.

8744. —— Ark of. *Tabernacle.* [16] Thou shalt put into the ark the testimony which I shall give thee. [17] And thou shalt make a mercy seat *of* pure gold.—EX., ch. 25.

8745. —— Convincing. *Peter.* [16] Peter continued knocking: and when they had opened *the door*, and saw him, they were astonished.—ACTS, ch. 12.

8746. —— of Deeds. *Jesus.* [4] Go and shew John again those things which ye do hear and see: [5] The blind receive their sight, and the lame walk, the lepers are cleansed, and the deaf hear, the dead are raised up, and the poor have the gospel preached to them.—MAT., ch. 11.

8747. —— Humble. *Little Maid.* [2] The Syrians..had brought away captive out of the land of Israel a little maid; and she waited on Naaman's wife. [3] And she said unto her mistress, Would God my lord *were* with the prophet that is in Samaria! for he would recover him of his leprosy.—2 KINGS, ch. 5.

8748. —— Irrepressible. *"Loosed."* [35] His

ears were opened, and the string of his tongue was loosed, and he spake plain. ³⁶ And he charged them that they should tell no man : but the more he charged them, so much the more a great deal they published *it.*—Mark, ch. 7.

8749. —— **Incredible.** *Mary.* ¹⁰ She went and told them that had been with him, as they mourned and wept. ¹¹ And they, when they had heard that he was alive, and had been seen of her, believed not.—Mark, ch. 16.

8750. —— —— *Peter.* ¹³ As Peter knocked at the door of the gate, a damsel came to hearken, named Rhoda. ¹⁴ And when she knew Peter's voice, she opened not the gate for gladness, but ran in, and told how Peter stood before the gate. ¹⁵ And they said..Thou art mad.—Acts, ch. 12.

8751. —— **incomplete.** *Moses said,* ¹² Thou sayest unto me, Bring up this people : and thou hast not let me know whom thou wilt send with me. Yet thou hast said, I know thee by name, and thou hast also found grace in my sight.— Ex., ch. 33.

8752. —— **of Life.** *"Works I do."* ²⁴ If thou be the Christ, tell us plainly. ²⁵ Jesus answered them, I told you, and ye believed not : the works that I do in my Father's name, they bear witness of me. ²⁶ But ye believe not, because ye are not of my sheep.—John, ch. 10.

8753. —— **Limit of.** *"We know..we know not."* ²⁰ His parents answered..We know that this is our son, and that he was born blind : ²¹ But by what means he now seeth, we know not.—John, ch. 9.

8754. —— **perverted.** *"His Angel."* [See No. 8758.]

8755. —— **Positive.** *"I see."* ²⁵ Whether he be a sinner *or no,* I know not : one thing I know, that, whereas I was blind, now I see.— John, ch. 9.

8756. —— **rejected.** *Of Stephen.* ⁵⁷ They cried out with a loud voice, and stopped their ears, and ran upon him with one accord. ⁵⁸ And cast *him* out of the city, and stoned *him.*—Acts, ch. 7.

8757. —— **An unwelcome.** *Damsel.* ¹⁷ Followed Paul and us, and cried, saying, These men are the servants of the most high God, which shew unto us the way of salvation. ¹⁸ And this did she many days. But Paul, being grieved, turned and said to the spirit, I command thee in the name of Jesus Christ to come out of her.— Acts, ch. 16.

8758. —— **unshaken.** *Rhoda's.* [See No. 8750.] ¹⁵ But she constantly affirmed that it was even so. Then said they, It is his angel.—Acts, ch. 12.

8759. —— **useless.** *Jesus.* ⁴ Pilate asked him again, saying, Answerest thou nothing ? behold how many things they witness against thee. ⁵ But Jesus yet answered nothing ; so that Pilate marvelled.—Mark, ch. 15.

Also see:

See EVIDENCE and references.
See WITNESSES.

8760. THANKOFFERINGS, Many. *Dedication.* ⁵ King Solomon, and all the congregation of Is-

rael that were assembled unto him, *were* with him before the ark, sacrificing sheep and oxen, that could not be told nor numbered for multitude.—1 Kings, ch. 8.

8761. —— **Valuable.** *For Preservation.* ⁵² All the gold of the offering that they offered up to the Lord, of the captains. of thousands, and of the captains of hundreds, was sixteen thousand seven hundred and fifty shekels : ⁵³ For the men of war had taken spoils, every man for himself [about $439,345].—Num., ch. 31.

8762. THANKS, Earnest. *Leper.* ¹⁵ One of them, when he saw that he was healed, turned back, and with a loud voice glorified God. ¹⁶ And fell down on *his* face at his feet, giving him thanks : and he was a Samaritan.—Luke, ch. 17.

8763. —— **for Food.** *Five Thousand fed.* ¹¹ Jesus took the loaves ; and when he had given thanks, he distributed to the disciples, and the disciples to them that were set down ; and likewise of the fishes as much as they would.—John, ch. 6.

8764. —— **Sincere.** *Shipwrecked.* ³⁵ When he had thus spoken, he took bread, and gave thanks to God in presence of them all ; and when he had broken *it,* he began to eat.—Acts, ch. 27.

8765. THANKSGIVING, Maternal. *Hannah.* [See 1 Sam., ch. 2.]

8766. —— **Perilous.** *Daniel.* ¹⁰ When Daniel knew that the writing was signed, he went into his house ; and, his windows being open in his chamber toward Jerusalem, he kneeled.. three times a day, and prayed, and gave thanks before his God, as he did aforetime.—Dan., ch. 6.

See other illustrations under :
THANKS.
See GRATITUDE.

8767. THEFT by Abduction. *Babe.* ²¹ When I rose in the morning to give my child suck, behold, it was dead : but when I had considered it in the morning, behold, it was not my son, which I did bear.—1 Kings, ch. 3.

8768. —— **confessed.** *Micah.* ² The eleven hundred *shekels* of silver that were taken from thee, about which thou cursedst, and spakest of also in mine ears, behold, the silver *is* with me ; I took it. And his mother said, Blessed *be thou* of the Lord, my son.—Judges, ch. 17.

8769. —— **through Fear.** *Unjust Steward.* ⁵ He called every one of his lord's debtors *unto him,* and said unto the first, How much owest thou unto my lord ? ⁶ And he said, A hundred measures of oil. And he said..Take thy bill, and sit down quickly, and write fifty.—Luke, ch. 16.

8770. —— **of the Famished.** *Bread.* ³⁰ Men do not despise a thief, if he steal to satisfy his soul when he is hungry ; ³¹ But *if* he be found, he shall restore sevenfold ; he shall give all the substance of his house.—Prov., ch. 6.

8771. —— **An improbable.** *Body of Jesus.*

[12] They gave large money unto the soldiers, [13] Saying, Say ye, His disciples came by night, and stole him *away* while we slept.—MAT., ch. 28.

8772. —— **A justifiable.** *Abduction.* [1] When Athaliah the mother of Ahaziah saw that her son was dead, she arose and destroyed all the seed royal. [2] But Jehosheba, the daughter of king Joram, sister of Ahaziah, took Joash the son of Ahaziah, and stole him from among the king's sons *which were* slain ; and they hid him. —2 KINGS, ch. 11.

8773. —— **Kidnapper's.** *Law.* [7] If a man be found stealing any of his brethren of the children of Israel, and maketh merchandise of him, or selleth him ; then that thief shall die.—DEUT., ch. 24.

8774. THIEF, Killing a. *Law.* [2] If a thief be found breaking up, and be smitten that he die, *there shall* no blood *be shed* for him. [3] If the sun be risen upon him, *there shall be* blood *shed* for him.—Ex., ch. 22.

8775. —— **in Office.** *Judas.* [5] Why was not this ointment sold for three hundred pence, and given to the poor ? [6] This he said, not that he cared for the poor ; but because he was a thief, and had the bag.—JOHN, ch. 12.

8776. THIEVES, Injuries from. *Parable.* [30] A certain *man* went down from Jerusalem to Jericho, and fell among thieves, which stripped him of his raiment, and wounded *him*, and departed, leaving *him* half dead.—LUKE, ch. 10.

8777. —— **Religious.** *Jesus* [12] Overthrew the tables of the money changers, and the seats of them that sold doves, [13] And said unto them, It is written, My house shall be called the house of prayer ; but ye have made it a den of thieves. —MAT., ch. 21.

8778. —— **slain.** *Cattle.* [21] Zabad his son, and Shuthelah his son, and Ezer, and Elead, whom the men of Gath *that were* born in *that* land slew, because they came down to take away their cattle.—1 CHRON., ch. 7.

See other illustrations under:

DISHONESTY.

Avaricious. Buy the poor for a pair of shoes 2388
toward God. Ananias..why keep back part of the 2389

KIDNAPPERS.

Crime. Selleth him ; then that thief shall die 4805
Wives. Children of Benjamin did so..wives 4806

PILLAGE.

Jerusalem. Shishak took away the treasure 6180
Temple. Chaldeans carried to Babylon..gold 6179

ROBBERY.

Insolent. Lay thy hand upon thy mouth 7457
Sacrilegious. Shishak took away the treasures 7459
Spiritual. Will a man rob God..tithes and 7458

Apparent. [Joseph's cup] It be found, let him die 882
Shameless. I cannot dig ; to beg I am ashamed 5344
Stripped. Stripped him of his raiment..half dead 722

8779. THIRST of the Dying. *Jesus* [28] Saith, I thirst. [29]..and they filled a sponge with vinegar, and put *it* upon hyssop, and put *it* to his mouth. [30] When Jesus therefore had received the vinegar, he said, It is finished.—JOHN, ch. 19.

8780. —— **A famishing.** *Samson's.* [19] God clave a hollow place that *was* in the jaw, and there came water thereout ; and when he had

drunk, his spirit came again, and he revived.— JUDGES, ch. 15.

8781. —— **No more.** *Living Fountains.* [17] The Lamb which is in the midst of the throne shall feed them, and shall lead them unto living fountains of waters.—REV., ch. 7.

8782. —— **Relief for.** *At Rephidim.* [5] Go on before the people, and take with thee of the elders of Israel ; and thy rod, wherewith thou smotest the river. . [6] Behold, I will stand before thee there upon the rock in Horeb : and thou shalt smite the rock, and there shall come water.—Ex., ch. 17.

8783. —— **Spiritual.** *Jesus said,* [14] Whosoever drinketh of the water that I shall give *him* shall never thirst ; but the water. shall be in him a well of water springing up into everlasting life. [15] The woman saith..Sir, give me this water, that I thirst not.—JOHN, ch. 4.

Also see:

Perishing. Made him drink..nor drunk 3 days 22
Special. Water out of the well of Beth-lehem 2211

8784. THORNS, Crowned with. *Jesus.* [1] Pilate therefore took Jesus, and scourged him. [2] And the soldiers platted a crown of thorns, and put *it* on his head.—JOHN, ch. 19.

8785. —— **Punished with.** *Gideon.* [16] He took the elders of the city, and thorns of the wilderness, and briers, and with them he taught the men of Succoth.—JUDGES, ch. 8.

8786. THOUGHT makes Character. *Proverb.* [7] For as he thinketh in his heart, so *is* he : Eat and drink, saith he to thee ; but his heart *is* not with thee.—PROV., ch. 23.

8787. —— **Evil.** *Antediluvians.* [5] God saw that the wickedness of man *was* great in the earth, and *that* every imagination of the thoughts of his heart *was* only evil continually.—GEN., ch. 6.

8788. —— **Prompter of.** *Spirit.* [19] But when they deliver you up, take no thought how or what ye shall speak : for it shall be given you in that same hour what ye shall speak. [20] For it is not ye that speak, but the Spirit of your Father which speaketh in you.—MAT., ch. 10.

8789. —— **Subjects of.** *Pure.* [8] Whatsoever things are true, whatsoever things *are* honest, whatsoever things *are* just, whatsoever things *are* pure, whatsoever things *are* lovely, whatsoever things *are* of good report ; if *there be* any virtue, and if *there be* any praise, think on these things.—PHIL., ch. 4.

8790. THOUGHTFULNESS enjoined. *Paul.* [See above.]

8791. —— **Prompted.** *Peter.* [72] The second time the cock crew. And Peter called to mind the word that Jesus said unto him, Before the cock crow twice, thou shalt deny me thrice. And when he thought thereon, he wept.—MARK, ch. 14.

See other illustrations under :

FORETHOUGHT.

Necessary. Intending to build..first counteth the 3339
"   Consulteth whether he be able with 3340
Useless. Which..with taking thought can add one 3341

MEDITATION.

Awakened by. When he [Peter] thought thereon 5290
Food. Thy words..did eat them 5291
Hour. Isaac went out to m..eventide 5292

Habitual. In his law..day and night　　　　　5293
Ill-timed. What shall I do..fruits..thy soul　　5294
Instruction. While Peter thought on the vision..S. 5295
Love of. Mine eyes prevent the night watches　5296
Prayerful. Meditation of my heart be acceptable　5297
Religious. Meditate therein day and night　　5298

Astonishing. Jesus in the midst..astonished at his 1163
　See **CARES** and references.
　See **INTELLIGENCE** and references.

8792. THREAT, An intimidating. *Jezebel.*
² Jezebel sent a messenger unto Elijah, saying,
So let the gods do *to me*, and more also, if I
make not thy life as the life of one of them by
to morrow about this time.—1 KINGS, ch. 19.

8793. THREATENING, A contemptible. *Bramble.* ¹⁵ The bramble said unto the trees, If in
truth ye anoint me king over you, *then* come *and*
put your trust in my shadow ; and if not, let
fire come out of the bramble, and devour the
cedars of Lebanon.—JUDGES, ch. 9.

8794. —— A rash. *Rehoboam's.* ¹¹ Whereas
my father did lade you with a heavy yoke, I
will add to your yoke : my father hath chastised
you with whips, but I will chastise you with
scorpions.—1 KINGS, ch. 12. [Ten tribes seceded.]

8795. —— repeated. *Apostles.* ¹⁸ They
called them, and commanded them not to speak
at all nor teach in the name of Jesus.. ²¹ So
when they had further threatened them, they
let them go.—ACTS, ch. 4.

8796. —— A terrible. *Saul's.* ⁷ He took a
yoke of oxen, and hewed them in pieces, and
sent *them* throughout all the coasts of Israel by
the hands of messengers, saying, Whosoever
cometh not forth after Saul and after Samuel, so
shall it be done unto his oxen..they came out
with one consent.—1 SAM., ch. 11.

8797. —— unfulfilled. *Goliath* ⁴³ Cursed
David by his gods. ⁴⁴ And the Philistine said
to David, Come to me, and I will give thy flesh
unto the fowls of the air, and to the beasts of
the field.—1 SAM., ch. 17.

8798. —— A useless. *Apostles.* [See No.
8795.] ³¹ When they had prayed, the place was
shaken where they were assembled together ;
and they were all filled with the Holy Ghost,
and they spake the word of God with boldness.
—ACTS, ch. 4.

8799. —— An unreasonable. *Nebuchadnezzar.* ¹¹ *It is* a rare thing that the king requireth,
and there is none other that can shew it..except
the gods, whose dwelling is not with flesh.
¹² For this cause the king was angry and very
furious, and commanded to destroy all the wise
men of Babylon.—DAN., ch. 2.

　See other illustrations under :
DENUNCIATION.
Appalling. Full of all subtilty..child of the devil　2177
Hypocrites. How can ye escape the damnation of 2178
　See **ADMONITION.**

8800. THRONE, A magnificent. *Solomon's.*
¹⁷ Made a great throne of ivory, and overlaid it
with pure gold. ¹⁸ And *there were* six steps to
the throne, with a footstool of gold.. ¹⁹ And
twelve lions stood there on the one side and
on the other upon the six steps.—2 CHRON.,
ch. 9.

8801. THUNDER, Alarming. *Rebellion.*
¹⁸ Samuel called unto the Lord ; and the Lord
sent thunder and rain that day : and all the
people greatly feared the Lord and Samuel.
¹⁹ And..said unto Samuel, Pray for thy servants
..that we die not : for we have added unto all
our sins *this* evil, to ask us a king.—1 SAM., ch.
12.

　See other illustrations under :
LIGHTNING.
Alarm. Entreat the L..no more mighty thunderings 5046
Destruction. Fire of G. is fallen..burned up the s. 5047
Terrific. Fire ran along upon the ground　　　5048
　　" 　Thunders and lightnings, and a thick c. 5049

8802. TIDINGS, Fearing good. *Shepherds.*
Lo, the angel of the Lord came upon them,
and the glory of the Lord shone round about
them : and they were sore afraid. ¹⁰ And the
angel said unto them, Fear not ; for behold, I
bring you good tidings of great joy.—LUKE, ch. 2.

　See other illustrations under :
NEWS.
Bad. Eli said..hide it not from me　　　　　5728
　" **More.** While he was yet speaking, another　5729
　" **Unrewarded.** Thinking to have brought good 5730
　" **Withheld.** Samuel feared to shew Eli the　5731
　" 　" 　Servants feared to tell..child was 5732
Confirmation. Thomas, reach hither thy finger　5733
Doubted. Syrians..gone out of the camp to hide　5734
　" 　Mary went and told..believed not　5735
Important. Sent letters by..mules..camels　　5736
Refreshing. As cold waters to a thirsty soul　　5737

8803. TIME, The acceptable. *"Visitation."*
⁴⁴ And shall lay thee even with the ground, and thy
children within thee ; and they shall not leave
in thee one stone upon another ; because thou
knewest not the time of thy visitation.—LUKE,
ch. 19.

8804. —— Beginning of. *Creation.* ¹ In the
beginning God created the heaven and the
earth.—GEN., ch. 1.

8805. —— extended. *Fig Tree.* ⁸ Lord, let
it alone this year also, till I shall dig about it,
and dung *it :* ⁹ And if it bear fruit, *well :* and if
not, *then* after that thou shalt cut it down.—
LUKE, ch. 13.

8806. —— The end of. *"No longer."* ⁵ The
angel which I saw stand upon the sea and upon
the earth lifted up his hand to heaven, ⁶ And
sware by him that liveth for ever and ever, who
created heaven, and the things that therein are,
and the earth, and the things that therein are,
and the sea, and the things which are therein,
that there should be time no longer.—REV., ch.
10.

8807. —— The Lord's. *Deliverance.* ²² Moses..said, Lord, wherefore hast thou so evil entreated this people ? why *is it that* thou hast sent
me ? ²³ For since I came to Pharaoh to speak
in thy name, he hath done evil to this people ;
neither hast thou delivered thy people at all.—
Ex., ch. 5.

8808. —— Mitigation of. *Esau's Anger.*
⁴⁴ Tarry with him a few days, until thy brother's
fury turn away.. ⁴⁵..and he forget *that* which
thou hast done to him.—GEN., ch. 27.

8809. —— —— Bereavement. ³⁸ Absalom
fled .. to Geshur, and was there three years.
³⁹ And *the soul of* king David longed to go forth

unto Absalom : for he was comforted concerning Amnon, seeing he was dead.—2 SAM., ch. 13.

8810. —— **The only.** *Bethesda.* ⁴ An angel went down at a certain season into the pool, and troubled the water : whosoever then first after the troubling of the water stepped in was made whole of whatsoever disease he had. ⁵ And a certain man was there, which had an infirmity thirty and eight years.—JOHN, ch. 5.

8811. —— **procrastinated.** *Felix.* ²⁵ As he reasoned of righteousness, temperance, and judgment to come, Felix trembled, and answered, Go thy way for this time ; when I have a convenient season, I will call for thee.—ACTS, ch. 24.

8812. —— **provided.** *All Things.* ¹ To every thing there is a season, and a time to every purpose under the heaven : ² A time to be born, and a time to die ; a time to plant, and a time to pluck up *that which is* planted.—ECCL., ch. 3. [See chapter.]

8813. —— **Spending.** *Athenians.* ²¹ All the Athenians, and the strangers which were there, spent their time in nothing else, but either to tell or to hear some new thing.—ACTS, ch. 17.

See other illustrations under :

AGE.

Blessed. L. blessed the latter end of Job more	150
Blindness in. Isaac was old..eyes were dim	834
" Ahijah..his eyes were set by..age	840
Cruelty to. Chaldeans..no compassion for age	1440
Children of. Israel loved Joseph more..of old age	177
Counsels of. I set before you a blessing..curse	1236
Disregarded. They that are younger than I..derision	146
Emotions. Ancient men..shouted..wept	2626
Fears. My son shall not go down..mischief	241
Pleasures of. Wherefore..a burden unto..the king	237
Paternity in. L. and E..well stricken in years..son	1153
" Abram was 100 years old..Isaac born	1193
Respected. Elihu waited till Job had spoken..elder	4061
Revealed. Sat according to his birthright..marvelled	5661
Reflections. Ancient men had seen the first house	957

FUTURE.

God's Will. If the L. will, we shall live and do this	3494
Ignorance. If thou hadst known..hid from thine	3495
Piety. Let me first go and bid them farewell	3496
Presuming. I will pull down my barns..ease, eat	3497
Uncertainty. Boast not..of to morrow..knowest	3498
Unseen. God said, Thou fool, this night thy soul	3499

YEAR.

Changed. This month shall be..the beginning of	9929
Jubilee. Fiftieth year proclaim liberty..possessions	9930
Rest. Seventh year..rest unto the land	9931
Burden of Years. I am this day fourscore years old	9932
Past. O that I were as in months past	5992

8814. TIMES, Bad. *Israel.* ⁵ In those times there was no peace to him that went out, nor to him that came in, but great vexations *were* upon all the inhabitants of the countries. ⁶ And nation was destroyed of nation, and city of city. —2 CHRON., ch. 15.

8815. —— **Signs of.** *Last.* ¹ The Spirit speaketh expressly, that in the latter times some shall depart from the faith, giving heed to seducing spirits, and doctrines of devils ; ² Speaking lies in hypocrisy, having their conscience seared with a hot iron : ³ Forbidding to marry, *and commanding* to abstain from meats.—1 TIM., ch. 4.

8816. TIMIDITY, Disciple's. *Nicodemus.* ¹ There was a man of the Pharisees, named Nicodemus, a ruler of the Jews : ² The same came to Jesus by night.—JOHN, ch. 3.

8817. —— —— *Joseph.* ³⁸ Joseph of Arimathea, being a disciple of Jesus, but secretly for fear of the Jews, besought Pilate that he might take away the body of Jesus.—JOHN, ch. 19.

8818. —— **of Friends.** *Believers.* ¹² Some said, He is a good man : others said, Nay ; but he deceiveth the people. ¹³ Howbeit no man spake openly of him for fear of the Jews.—JOHN, ch. 7.

8819. —— **Needless.** *Brethren.* ¹⁸ The men were afraid, because they were brought into Joseph's house ; and they said, Because of the money that was returned in our sacks..are we brought in ; that he may seek occasion against us..and take us for bondmen, and our asses.— GEN., ch. 43.

8820. —— **Restrained by.** *Rhoda.* ¹² Many were gathered together, praying. ¹³ And as Peter knocked at the door of the gate, a damsel came to hearken, named Rhoda.—ACTS, ch. 12.

See INTIMIDATION and references.

8821. TITHES exchanged. *"Too Far."* ²⁴ If the way be too long for thee..to carry it ; *or* if the place be too far from thee, which the Lord thy God shall choose to set his name there, when the Lord thy God hath blessed thee ; ²⁵ Then shalt thou turn *it* into money, and bind up the money in thine hand, and shalt go unto the place which the Lord thy God shall choose. —DEUT., ch. 14. [There buy..eat..rejoice.]

8822. —— **The first.** *Abram's to Melchisedec.* ¹ Melchisedec, king of Salem, priest of the most high God, who met Abraham returning from the slaughter of the kings, and blessed him ; ² To whom also Abraham gave a tenth part of all.— HEB., ch. 7.

8823. —— **The Lord's.** *Tenth.* ³² Concerning the tithe of the herd, or of the flock, *even* the tenth shall be holy unto the Lord.—LEV., ch. 27.

8824. —— **for Ministry.** *Levites.* ²⁸ At the end of three years thou shalt bring forth all the tithe of thine increase the same year, and shalt lay *it* up within thy gates : ²⁹ And the Levite, (because he hath no part nor inheritance with thee) and the stranger, and the fatherless, and the widow, which *are* within thy gates, shall come, and shall eat and be satisfied.—DEUT., ch. 14.

8825. —— **for the Poor.** *Law.* [See above.]

8826. —— **substituted.** *For Piety.* ²³ Woe unto you, scribes and Pharisees, hypocrites ! for ye pay tithe of mint, and anise, and cummin, and have omitted the weightier *matters* of the law, judgment, mercy, and faith.—MAT., ch. 23.

8827. —— **tithed.** *Levites.* ²⁶ When ye take of the children of Israel the tithes which I have given you from them for your inheritance, then ye shall offer up a heave offering of it for the Lord, *even* a tenth *part* of the tithe.—NUM., ch. 18.

8828. —— **unaccepted.** *Pharisee.* ¹¹ God, I thank thee, that I am not as other men *are*, extortioners, unjust, adulterers, or even as this publican. ¹² I fast twice in the week, I give tithes of all that I possess.—LUKE, ch. 18.

See TAXES and references.

8829. TITLES, Ambition for. "*Rabbi.*" ⁶ Who love greetings in the markets, and to be called of men, Rabbi, Rabbi. ⁸ But be not ye called Rabbi : for one is your Master, *even* Christ ; and all ye are brethren.—MAT., ch. 23.

8830. TONGUE, An angry. *Moses.* ³² They angered *him* also at the waters of strife, so that it went ill with Moses for their sakes : ³³ Because they provoked his spirit, so that he spake unadvisedly with his lips.—Ps. 106.

8831. —— **A Buyer's.** *Proverb.* ¹³ It is naught, *it is* naught, saith the buyer : but when he is gone his way, then he boasteth.—PROV., ch. 20.

8832. —— **Control of.** "*Backbiteth not.*" ¹ Lord, who shall abide in thy tabernacle ? who shall dwell in thy holy hill ? ² He that walketh uprightly, and worketh righteousness, and speaketh the truth in his heart. ³ *He that* backbiteth not with his tongue, nor doeth evil to his neighbour, nor taketh up a reproach against his neighbour.—Ps. 15.

8833. —— —— *Bridle.* ³ We put bits in the horses' mouths, that they may obey us ; and we turn about their whole body. ⁴ Behold also the ships, which, though *they be* so great, and *are* driven of fierce winds, yet are they turned about with a very small helm, whithersoever the governor listeth. ⁵ Even so the tongue.—JAMES, ch. 3.

8834. TONGUES changed. *Babel.* ⁷ Go to, let us go down, and there confound their language, that they may not understand one another's speech. ⁸ So the Lord scattered them abroad.—GEN., ch. 11.

8835. —— —— *Pentecost.* ⁷ They were all amazed and marvelled, saying one to another, Behold, are not all these which speak Galileans ? ⁸ And how hear we every man in our own tongue, wherein we were born ?—ACTS, ch. 2.

8836. —— **Foolish.** *Proverb.* ¹¹ A fool uttereth all his mind : but a wise *man* keepeth it in till afterwards.—PROV., ch. 29.

8837. —— **A hasty.** *Proverb.* ²⁰ Seest thou a man *that is* hasty in his words ? *there is* more hope of a fool than of him.—PROV., ch. 29.

8838. —— **shows the Heart.** *Overflow.* ³⁴ O generation of vipers, how can ye, being evil, speak good things ? for out of the abundance of the heart the mouth speaketh.—MAT., ch. 12.

8839. —— **punished.** *Serpents.* ⁷ The people came to Moses, and said, We have sinned, for we have spoken against the Lord, and against thee ; pray unto the Lord, that he take away the serpents from us.—NUM., ch. 21.

8840. —— **responsible.** *Judgment.* ³⁶ Every idle word that men shall speak, they shall give account thereof in the day of judgment. ²⁷ For by thy words thou shalt be justified, and by thy words thou shalt be condemned.—MAT., ch. 12.

8841. —— **A religious.** "*Jewels.*" ¹⁶ Then they that feared the Lord spake often one to another : and the Lord hearkened, and heard *it*, and a book of remembrance was written before him for them that feared the Lord, and that

thought upon his name. ¹⁷ And they shall be mine, saith the Lord of hosts, in that day when I make up my jewels.—MAL., ch. 3.

8842. —— **untamed.** *Wild.* ⁷ Every kind of beasts, and of birds, and of serpents, and of things in the sea, is tamed, and hath been tamed, of mankind : ⁸ But the tongue can no man tame.—JAMES, ch. 3.

8843. —— **Use of.** "*Slow.*" ¹⁹ My beloved brethren, let every man be swift to hear, slow to speak, slow to wrath.—JAMES, ch. 1.

8844. —— **A wise.** *To Rehoboam.* ¹ If thou be kind to this people, and please them, and speak good words to them, they will be thy servants for ever.. ⁸ But he forsook the counsel which the old men gave him.—2 CHRON., ch. 10. [Rough answers divided the kingdom.]

8845. —— —— "*Nails.*" ¹¹ The words of the wise *are* as goads, and as nails fastened *by* the masters of assemblies, *which* are given from one shepherd.—ECCL., ch. 12.

8846. —— **a Weapon.** "*Smite.*" ¹⁸ Come, and let us devise devices against Jeremiah ; for the law shall not perish from the priest, nor counsel from the wise, nor the word from the prophet. Come, and let us smite him with the tongue, and let us not give heed to any of his words.— JER., ch. 18.

8847. —— **A wicked.** "*Defileth.*" ⁶ The tongue *is* a fire, a world of iniquity : so is the tongue among our members, that it defileth the whole body, and setteth on fire the course of nature ; and it is set on fire of hell.—JAMES, ch. 3.

8848. TONGUES differ. "*Bite.*" ¹¹ Surely the serpent will bite without enchantment ; and a babbler is no better. ¹² The words of a wise man's mouth *are* gracious ; but the lips of a fool will swallow up himself.—ECCL., ch. 10.

8849. —— **of Fire.** *Pentecost.* ³ There appeared unto them cloven tongues like as of fire, and it sat upon each of them. ⁴ And they were all filled with the Holy Ghost, and began to speak with other tongues, as the Spirit gave them utterance.—ACTS, ch. 2.

8850. —— **restrained.** *Rab-shakeh.* ³⁵ Who *are* they among all the gods of the countries, that have delivered their country out of mine hand, that the Lord should deliver Jerusalem out of mine hand ? ³⁶ But the people held their peace, and answered him not a word : for the king's commandment was, saying, Answer him not.—2 KINGS, ch. 18.

Also see :
Power of. Soft tongue breaketh the bone　　5733
See SPEECH and references.

8851. TOMB, A perfumed. *Asa's.* ¹⁴ They buried him in his own sepulchres, which he had made for himself in the city of David, and laid him in the bed which was filled with sweet odours and divers kinds *of spices* prepared by the apothecaries' art : and they made a very great burning for him.—2 CHRON., ch. 16.

See other illustrations under :
BURIAL.
Denied. Bring out the bones of the kings..spread　974
Life from. Touched the bones of Elisha..he revived 975
Living. Earth opened her mouth and swallowed　976
Mournful. David..lifted up his voice..grave of A.　977

Mysterious. Moses died. . no man knoweth his s. 978
Patriarchs. All the servants of Pharaoh. . elders 979
Perfumed. Filled with sweet odours. . spices 980

GRAVE.

Chosen. Bury me with my fathers in the cave 3703
First Bargain. Care of Machpelah. . money as it is 3704
Longed for. O that thou wouldest hide me in the g. 3705

8852. TORMENTS of Perdition. *Dives.* ²³ In hell he lifted up his eyes, being in torments. . ²⁴ And he cried. . Father Abraham, have mercy on me, and send Lazarus, that he may dip the tip of his finger in water, and cool my tongue : for I am tormented in this flame.—LUKE, ch. 16.

8853. TORTURE of Prisoners. *By Gideon.* ¹⁶ He took the elders of the city, and thorns of the wilderness, and briers, and with them he taught the men of Succoth.—JUDGES, ch. 8.

8854. —— —— *By David.* ³¹ He brought forth the people that *were* therein, and put *them* under saws, and under harrows of iron, and under axes of iron, and made then pass through the brickkiln : and thus did he unto all the cities of the children of Ammon.—2 SAM., ch. 12.

8855. —— —— *Soldiers.* ²⁸ They stripped him, and put on him a scarlet robe. ²⁹ And when they had platted a crown of thorns, they put *it* upon his head, and a reed in his right hand : and they bowed the knee before him, and mocked him, saying, Hail ! King of the Jews ! ³⁰ And they spit upon him, and took the reed, and smote him on the head.—MAT., ch. 27.

See other illustrations under :

CRUELTY.

Ambition. Athaliah destroyed all the seed royal 1857
Brutal. Ten thousand. . cast down. . top of a rock 1858
Failure. More they afflicted them. . grew 1859
Insulting. Purple. . crown of thorns. . Hail ! 1860
Pride. Mordecai bowed not. . Haman full of wrath 1861
Reward. Troubleth his own flesh 1862
Savage. Slew the sons. . before his eyes 1863
War. Put them under saws. . harrows 1864

HELL.

Affection in. Send Lazarus to my father's house 3922
Bottomless. Bottomless pit. . smoke of a great 3923
Preparation of. Cursed. . into fire prepared for the 3924
See GRIEF and references.

8856. TOUCH, A healing. *Of Jesus.* ²⁵ A certain woman, which had an issue of blood twelve years, ²⁶ And had suffered many things of many physicians, and had spent all that she had, and was nothing bettered, but rather grew worse, ²⁷. . came in the press behind, and touched his garment.—MARK, ch. 5.

8857. —— —— *Of Jesus.* ⁵⁶ Whithersoever he entered, into villages, or cities, or country, they laid the sick in the streets, and besought him that they might touch if it were but the border of his garment : and as many as touched him were made whole.—MARK, ch. 6.

8858. TRADE, Beneficial. *With Jacob.* ²⁰ Hamor and Shechem his son. . communed with the men of their city, saying, ²¹ These men *are* peaceable with us ; therefore let them dwell in the land, and trade therein ; for the land, behold, *it is* large enough for them. . ²³ Shall not their cattle and their substance and every beast of theirs *be* ours ?—GEN., ch. 34.

8859. —— **Beating down in.** *Proverb.* ¹⁴ *It is* naught, *it is* naught, saith the buyer : but

when he is gone his way, then he boasteth.—PROV., ch. 20.

8860. —— **Dishonesty in.** *"Falsifying."* ⁵ Making the ephah small, and the shekel great, and falsifying the balances by deceit ? ⁶ That we may buy the poor for silver, and the needy for a pair of shoes ; *yea,* and sell the refuse of the wheat.—AMOS, ch. 8.

8861. —— —— *Short Weight.* ¹ A false balance *is* abomination to the Lord ; but a just weight *is* his delight.—PROV., ch. 11.

8862. —— —— *"Dealeth falsely."* ¹¹ For every one from the least even unto the greatest is given to covetousness, from the prophet even unto the priest every one dealeth falsely.—JER., ch. 8.

8863. —— **Lawful.** *Parable.* ¹⁵ When he was returned, having received the kingdom, then he commanded these servants to be called. . to whom he had given the money, that he might know how much every man had gained by trading.—LUKE, ch. 19.

8864. —— **in Luxuries.** *Arrested.* ¹² The merchandise of gold, and silver, and precious stones, and of pearls, and fine linen, and purple, and silk, and scarlet, and all thyine wood, and all manner vessels of ivory, and all manner vessels of most precious wood, and of brass, and iron, and marble, ¹³ And cinnamon, and odours, and ointments, and frankincense, and wine, and oil, and fine flour, and wheat, and beasts, and sheep, and horses, and chariots, and slaves, and souls of men.—REV., ch. 18.

8865. —— **Protection of.** *Silversmiths.* ²⁶ Saying that they be no gods, which are made with hands : ²⁷ So that not only this our craft is in danger to be set at nought ; but also that the temple of the great goddess Diana.—ACTS, ch. 19.

8866. —— **Sabbath.** *Merchandise.* ¹⁶ There dwelt men of Tyre also therein, which brought fish, and all manner of ware, and sold on the sabbath unto the children of Judah, and in Jerusalem.—NEH., ch. 13.

8867. —— —— *Corrected.* ²⁰ So the merchants and sellers of all kind of ware lodged without Jerusalem once or twice. ²¹ Then I testified against them. . Why lodge ye about the wall ? if ye do *so* again, I will lay hands on you. From that time forth came they no *more* on the sabbath.—NEH., ch. 13.

8868. —— **Tricks in.** *Forbidden.* ¹³ Thou shalt not have in thy bag divers weights, a great and a small : ¹⁴ Thou shalt not have in thine house divers measures, a great and a small.—DEUT., ch. 25.

8869. TRADE-UNION, Power of. *Silversmiths.* ²⁴ A certain *man* named Demetrius, a silversmith, which made silver shrines for Diana, brought no small gain unto the craftsmen ; ²⁵ Whom he called together with the workmen of like occupation, and said, Sirs, ye know that by this craft we have our wealth.—ACTS, ch. 19.

See other illustrations under :

BUSINESS.

Capacity. [Pharaoh to Joseph] None so discreet 985
Diligence. Man diligent in business. . stand before 986
Frauds. Take thy bill, quickly. . write fifty 988
Spiritual. [Stewards] Men. . honest. . full of H. S. 991
Success. Joseph gathered up all the money 993
Talent. [Cattle] The feebler were Laban's 994

MERCHANTS.

Babylon. Merchants..weep and mourn for her　5371
Intruders. Drove them all out of the temple　5372

8870. TRADITION, Inferior. *Pharisees.*
[13] Making the word of God of none effect
through your tradition, which ye have delivered :
and many such like things do ye.—Mark, ch. 7.

8871. TRAITOR, A conspiring. *Ahithophel.*
[31] *One* told David, saying, Ahithophel *is* among
the conspirators with Absalom. And David said,
O Lord, I pray thee, turn the counsel of Ahithophel into foolishness.—2 Sam., ch. 15.

8872. —— A defeated. *Ahithophel.* [23] When
Ahithophel saw that his counsel was not followed, he saddled *his* ass..and gat him home..
and put his household in order, and hanged
himself.—2 Sam., ch. 16.

8873. —— Repentance of a. *Judas.* [3] Judas,
which had betrayed him, when he saw that he
was condemned, repented himself, and brought
again the thirty pieces of silver to the chief
priests and elders.—Mat., ch. 27.

8874. —— Remorse of. *Judas.* [4] I have
sinned in that I have betrayed the innocent
blood. And they said, What *is that* to us ? see
thou *to that.* [5] And he cast down the pieces of
silver in the temple..and went and hanged himself.—Mat., ch. 27.

8875. —— suspected, A. *By Defeat.* [10] The
king of Israel sent to the place which the man
of God..warned him of, and saved himself there,
not once nor twice. [11] Therefore the heart of
the king of Syria was sore troubled for this
thing ; and he called his servants, and said..
Will ye not shew me which of us *is* for the king
of Israel ?—2 Kings, ch. 6.

See other illustrations under :

TREASON.

Justifiable. Athaliah rent her clothes, and cried　8902
Spiritual. Wherefore lift ye up yourselves above　8903
　　　　" 　The earth opened..Korah..went down　8904

8876. TRAINING, Early. *Maid.* [2] The Syrians had gone out by companies, and had
brought away captive out of the land of Israel a
little maid ; and she waited on Naaman's wife.
[3] And she said unto her mistress, Would God
my lord *were* with the prophet that *is* in Samaria ! for he would recover him of his leprosy.
—2 Kings, ch. 5.

8877. —— —— *Moses.* [24] By faith Moses,
when he was come to years, refused to be called
the son of Pharaoh's daughter ; [25] Choosing
rather to suffer affliction with the people of God,
than to enjoy the pleasures of sin for a season :
[26] Esteeming the reproach of Christ greater
riches than the treasures in Egypt : for he had
respect unto the recompense of the reward.—
Heb., ch. 11.

8878. —— —— *Samuel.* [27] For this child I
prayed ; and the Lord hath given me my petition.. [28] Therefore also I have lent him to the
Lord ; as long as he liveth he shall be lent to
the Lord.—1 Sam., ch. 1.

See EDUCATION and references.

8879. TRANCE, A heavenly. *Paul's.* [3] I
knew such a man, whether in the body, or out
of the body, I cannot tell : God knoweth ; [4] How
that he was caught up into paradise, and heard
unspeakable words, which it is not lawful for a
man to utter.—2 Cor., ch. 12.

8880. TRANSFIGURATION of Grace. *Image.*
[18] We aH, with open face beholding as in a glass
the glory of the Lord, are changed into the same
image from glory to glory, *even* as by the Spirit
of the Lord.—2 Cor., ch. 3.

8881. —— in Prayer. *Jesus* [28] Took Peter
and John and James, and went up into a mountain to pray. [29] And as he prayed, the fashion
of his countenance was altered, and his raiment
was white *and* glistering.—Luke, ch. 9.

8882. TRANSLATION, Prepared for. *Enoch.*
[22] Enoch walked with God after he begat Methuselah three hundred years.. [24] And Enoch walked
with God : and he *was* not ; for God took him.
—Gen., ch. 5.

8883. TRAVELLERS for Canaan. *Passover.*
[11] Thus shall ye eat it ; *with* your loins girded,
your shoes on your feet, and your staff in your
hand ; and ye shall eat it in haste : it *is* the
Lord's passover.—Ex., ch. 12.

See other illustrations under :

JOURNEY.

Arrested. Edom said, Thou shalt not pass by me　4727
Christians. Get thee out of thy country..kindred　4728
Preparation. Elijah did eat..went in the strength　4729
Sad. Abraham rose up early..took Isaac　　　　4730
to Zion. A highway shall be there..no lion　　　4731

SHIPWRECK.

Perils by. Thrice I suffered shipwreck [Paul]　7839
Saved in. Some on boards, and some on broken　7840

8884. TREASURE, The Cross a. *To Moses.*
[26] Esteeming the reproach of Christ greater
riches than the treasures in Egypt : for he had
respect unto the recompense of the reward.
[27] By faith he forsook Egypt.—Heb., ch. 11.

8885. —— Discovery of. *Parable.* [44] The
kingdom of heaven is like unto treasure hid in
a field ; the which when a man hath found, he
hideth, and for joy thereof goeth and selleth all
that he hath, and buyeth that field.—Mat., ch.
13.

8886. TREASURES forsaken. *Jacob.* [19] Take
you wagons out of the land of Egypt for your
little ones, and for your wives, and bring your
father, and come, [20] Also regard not your stuff ;
for the good of all the land of Egypt *is* yours.
—Gen., ch. 45.

8887. —— in Heaven. *Young Ruler.* [21] One
thing thou lackest : go thy way, sell whatsoever
thou hast, and give to the poor, and thou shalt
have treasure in heaven..and follow me. [22] And
he was sad.—Mark, ch. 10.

8888. —— insecure. *Jesus said,* [19] Lay not
up for yourselves treasures upon earth, where
moth and rust doth corrupt, and where thieves
break through and steal.—Mark, ch. 6.

8889. —— restored. *Temple.* [11] All the vessels
of gold and of silver *were* five thousand and four
hundred. All *these* did Sheshbazzar bring up
with *them of* the captivity that were brought up
from Babylon unto Jerusalem.—Ezra, ch. 1.

8890. —— secure. *In Heaven.* [20] But lay up
for yourselves treasures in heaven, where neither
moth nor rust doth corrupt, and where thieves
do not break through nor steal : [21] For where
your treasure is, there will your heart be also.
—Mat., ch. 6.

8891. TREASURY watched. *By Jesus.*
[41] Jesus sat over against the treasury, and be-

held how the people cast money into the treasury.—MARK, ch. 12.

8892. TREASURER, A dishonest. *Judas.* [5] Why was not this ointment sold for three hundred pence, and given to the poor? [6] This he said, not that he cared for the poor ; but because he was a thief, and had the bag.—JOHN, ch. 12.

See WEALTH *and references.*

8893. TREACHERY, Artful. *Gibeonites.* [4] They did work wilily..as if they had been ambassadors, and took old sacks upon their asses, and wine bottles, old, and rent, and bound up ; [5] And old shoes and clouted upon their feet, and old garments upon them ; and all the bread of their provision was dry *and* mouldy. [6] And they went to Joshua.—JOSH., ch. 9.

8894. —— Bloody. *Joab.* [27] When Abner was returned to Hebron, Joab took him aside in the gate to speak with him quietly, and smote him there under the fifth *rib*, that he died, for the blood of Asahel his brother.—2 SAM.,ch. 3.

8895. —— Disgraceful. *David.* [15] He wrote in the letter, saying, Set ye Uriah in the forefront of the hottest battle, and retire ye from him, that he may be smitten, and die.—2 SAM., ch. 11. [To Joab.]

8896. —— Gain by. *Gibeonites.* [15] Made a league with them, to let them live : and the princes of the congregation sware unto them. [16]..three days after they had made a league with them..they heard that they *were* their neighbours.—JOSH., ch. 9.

8897. —— Hypocritical. *Pharisees.* [53] Scribes and the Pharisees began to urge *him* vehemently, and to provoke him to speak of many things : [54] Laying wait for him, and seeking to catch something out of his mouth, that they might accuse him.—LUKE, ch. 11.

8898. —— in Politics. *Babylonians.* [3] This Daniel was preferred above the presidents and princes, because an excellent spirit *was* in him ; and the king thought to set him over the whole realm.. [5] Then said these men, We shall not find any occasion against this Daniel, except.. concerning the law of his God.—DAN., ch. 6.

8899. —— Property by. *Ziba.* [3] Behold, he abideth at Jerusalem : for he said, To-day shall the house of Israel restore me the kingdom of my father. [4] Then said the king to Ziba, Behold, thine *are* all that *pertained* unto Mephibosheth.—2 SAM., ch. 16. [Mephibosheth was loyal to David.]

8900. —— punished. *Servitude.* [22] Wherefore have ye beguiled us, saying, We *are* very far from you ; when ye dwell among us ? [23] Now therefore ye *are* cursed, and there shall none of you be freed from being bondmen, and hewers of wood and drawers of water for the house of my God.—JOSH., ch. 9.

8901. —— suspected. *Jeremiah.* [12] Jeremiah went forth out of Jerusalem..to separate himself.. [13] And when he was in the gate of Benjamin, a captain of the ward *was* there..and he took Jeremiah the prophet, saying, Thou fallest away to the Chaldeans.—JER., ch. 37.

See other illustrations under :

SPIES.
Accusation. By the life of Pharaoh, surely ye are s. 8266
Church. Came in privily to spy out our liberty   8267

Disguised. Spies which should feign themselves   8268
Entertained. Joshua sent two men to spy out..J. 8269
Intimidated. We were in our own sight as grassh. 8270
Political. Absalom sent spies throughout all the   8271
Suspected. Hath not David sent..to spy it out   8272
    "   Hanun shaved off one half their b.   8273
Twelve. Moses sent them to spy out..Canaan   8274
Watchful. These men assembled and found Daniel 8275

TRAITORS.
Conspiring. Ahithophel is among the conspirators 8871
Defeated. Ahithophel saw his counsel not followed 8872
Repenting. Judas brought..30 pieces of silver   8873
Remorse. Judas..cast down the 30 pieces..hanged 8874
Suspected. Which..is for the king of Israel?   8875

See DECEPTION *and references.*

8902. TREASON, A justifiable. *Against Athaliah.* [12] He brought forth Jehoash the king's son, and put the crown upon him, and *gave him* the testimony ; and they made him king, and anointed him : and they clapped their hands, and said, God save the king.. [14]..all the people of the land rejoiced, and blew with trumpets : and Athaliah rent her clothes, and cried, Treason, Treason !—2 KINGS, ch. 11.

8903. —— Spiritual. *Korah.* [3] They gathered..against Moses and against Aaron, and said.. *Ye take* too much upon you, seeing all the congregation *are* holy, every one of them, and the Lord *is* among them : wherefore then lift ye up yourselves above the congregation of the Lord ?—NUM., ch. 16.

8904. —— Punished. [32] The earth opened her mouth..and their houses, and all the men that *appertained* unto Korah.. [33]..and all that *appertained* to them, went down alive into the pit, and the earth closed upon them. —NUM., ch. 16.

See TREACHERY *and references.*

8905. TREE of Life. *In Heaven.* [7] The Spirit saith unto the churches ; To him that overcometh will I give to eat of the tree of life, which is in the midst of the paradise of God. —REV., ch. 2.

8906. —— of Life debarred. *In Eden.* [22] Behold, the man is become as one of us, to know good and evil : and now, lest he..take also of the tree of life, and eat, and live for ever : [23] Therefore the Lord God sent him forth from the garden of Eden.—GEN., ch. 3.

8907. —— An aspiring. *Bramble.* [15] The bramble said unto the trees, If in truth ye anoint me king over you, *then* come *and* put your trust in my shadow ; and if not, let fire come out of the bramble, and devour the cedars of Lebanon. —JUDGES, ch. 9.

8908. —— The barren. *Cut it down.* [6] A certain man had a fig tree planted in his vineyard ; and he came and sought fruit thereon, and found none.—LUKE, ch. 13.

8909. —— A prohibited. *Tree of Knowledge.* [3] But of the fruit of the tree which *is* in the midst of the garden, God hath said, Ye shall not eat of it, neither shall ye touch it, lest ye die.—GEN., ch. 3.

8910. TREES, Humility of. *Parable.* [8] Trees went forth *on a time* to anoint a king over them ; and they said unto the olive tree, Reign thou over us. [9] But the olive tree said..Should I leave my fatness, wherewith by me they honour

God and man, and go to be promoted over the trees?—JUDGES, ch. 9.

8911. —— *Fig.* ¹⁰ The trees said to the fig tree, Come thou, *and* reign over us. ¹¹ But the fig tree said.. Should I forsake my sweetness, and my good fruit, and go to be promoted over the trees?—JUDGES, ch. 9.

8912. —— *Vine.* ¹² Said the trees unto the vine, Come thou, *and* reign over us. ¹³ And the vine said.. Should I leave my wine, which cheereth God and man, and go to be promoted over the trees?—JUDGES, ch. 9.

8913. —— *Bramble.* ¹⁴ Then said all the trees unto the bramble, Come thou, *and* reign over us.—JUDGES, ch. 9. [See No. 8907.]

8914. TRIAL forms Character. *Slaves made Freemen.* ³⁰ Israel saw the Egyptians dead upon the sea shore. ³¹ And Israel saw that great work which the Lord did upon the Egyptians : and the people feared the Lord, and believed the Lord, and his servant Moses.—EX., ch. 14.

8915. —— *Red Sea.* ²¹ Strong east wind all that night.. made the sea dry *land*, and the waters were divided. ²² And the children of Israel went into the midst of the sea upon the dry *ground;* and the waters *were* a wall unto them on their right hand, and on their left.—EX., ch. 14.

8916. —— **of Faith.** *Heaviness.* ⁶ Ye greatly rejoice, though now for a season, if need be, ye are in heaviness through manifold temptations : ⁷ That the trial of your faith, being much more precious than of gold that perisheth, though it be tried with fire, might be found unto praise and honour and glory at the appearing of Jesus Christ.—1 PETER, ch. 1.

8917. —— **Impenitence under.** *"Wild Bull."* ²⁰ Thy sons have fainted, they lie at the head of all the streets, as a wild bull in a net : they are full of the fury of the Lord, the rebuke of thy God.—ISA., ch. 51.

8918. —— **Life a.** *In Eden.* ¹⁶ God commanded the man, saying, Of every tree of the garden thou mayest freely eat : ¹⁷ But of the tree of the knowledge of good and evil, thou shalt not eat of it.. shalt surely die.—GEN., ch. 2.

8919. —— **A mock.** *Jesus.* ⁵⁵ The chief priests and all the council sought for witness against Jesus to put him to death ; and found none. ⁵⁶ For many bare false witness against him, but their witness agreed not together.—MARK, ch. 14.

8920. —— **proportioned.** *Exodus.* ¹⁷ When Pharaoh had let the people go.. God led them not *through* the way of the land of the Philistines, although that *was* near ; for God said, Lest peradventure the people repent when they see war, and they return to Egypt.—EX., ch. 13.

8921. —— **Stubbornness in.** *Ahaz.* ²² In the time of his distress did he trespass yet more against the Lord : this *is that* king Ahaz. ²³ For he sacrificed unto the gods of Damascus, which smote him : and he said, Because the gods of the kings of Syria help them, *therefore* will I sacrifice to them, that they may help me. But they were the ruin of him, and of all Israel.—2 CHRON., ch. 28.

8922. —— **A severe.** *Abraham's.* ² Take now thy son, thine only *son* Isaac, whom thou lovest, and get thee into the land of Moriah ; and offer him there for a burnt offering upon one of the mountains which I will tell thee off. —GEN., ch. 22.

8923. TRIALS in Business. *Jacob.* ⁴⁰ *Thus* I was ; in the day the drought consumed me, and the frost by night ; and my sleep departed from mine eyes.—GEN., ch. 31.

8924. —— **Backsliding amid.** *Israelites.* ¹⁸ Ye have wept in the ears of the Lord, saying, Who shall give us flesh to eat? for *it was* well with us in Egypt : therefore the Lord will give you flesh, and ye shall eat.—NUM., ch. 11.

8925. —— **a Blessing.** *Persecution.* ¹¹ Blessed are ye, when *men* shall revile you, and persecute *you*, and shall say all manner of evil against you falsely, for my sake. ¹² Rejoice, and be exceeding glad : for great *is* your reward in heaven.—MAT., ch. 5.

8926. —— **Comfort in.** *Ziklag burned.* ⁶ David was greatly distressed ; for the people spake of stoning him, because the soul of all the people was grieved, every man for his sons and for his daughters : but David encouraged himself in the Lord his God.—1 SAM., ch. 30.

8927. —— **Confidence in.** *Paul.* ³⁸ I am persuaded, that neither death, nor life, nor angels, nor principalities, nor powers, nor things present, nor things to come, ³⁹ Nor height, nor depth, nor any other creature, shall be able to separate us from the love of God, which is in Christ Jesus our Lord.—ROM., ch. 8.

8928. —— **winnow the Church.** *"No Root."* ¹⁶ Sown on stony ground ; who, when they have heard the word, immediately receive it with gladness ; ¹⁷ And have no root in themselves, and so endure but for a time : afterward, when affliction or persecution ariseth for the word's sake, immediately they are offended.—MARK, ch. 4.

8929. —— **after Deliverance.** *Marah.* ²² Moses brought Israel from the Red sea.. and they went three days in the wilderness, and found no water. ²³ And when they came to Marah, they could not drink of the waters of Marah, for they *were* bitter.—EX., ch. 15.

8930. —— **Darkness of.** *Providence.* ⁶ Know now that God hath overthrown me, and hath compassed me with his net. ⁷ Behold, I cry out of wrong, but I am not heard : I cry aloud, but *there is* no judgment. ⁸ He hath fenced up my way that I cannot pass, and he hath set darkness in my paths.—JOB, ch. 19.

8931. —— **Encouragement in.** *"Glory."* ¹⁷ Our light affliction, which is but for a moment, worketh for us a far more exceeding *and* eternal weight of glory ; ¹⁸ While we look not at the things which are seen, but at the things which are not seen.—2 COR., ch. 4.

8932. —— **Hope amid.** *Job.* ²⁵ I know *that* my Redeemer liveth, and *that* he shall stand at the latter *day* upon the earth : ²⁶ And *though* after my skin *worms* destroy this *body*, yet in my flesh shall I see God : ²⁷ Whom I shall see for myself, and mine eyes shall behold, and not another ; *though* my reins be consumed within me. —JOB, ch. 19.

8933. —— *David.* ⁵ Why art thou cast down, O my soul ? and *why* art thou disquieted in me? hope thou in God: for I shall yet praise him *for* the help of his countenance.—Ps. 42.

8934. —— —— *Apostles.* [8] *We are* troubled on every side, yet not distressed; *we are* perplexed, but not in despair; [9] Persecuted, but not forsaken; cast down, but not destroyed; [10] Always bearing about in the body the dying of the Lord Jesus.—2 Cor., ch. 4.

8935. —— Joy in. *Persecution.* [34] Ye had compassion on me in my bonds, and took joyfully the spoiling of your goods, knowing in yourselves that ye have in heaven a better and an enduring substance.—Heb., ch. 10.

8936. —— multiplied. *Job.* [18] Young children despised me; I arose, and they spake against me. [19] All my inward friends abhorred me: and they whom I loved are turned against me. [20] My bone cleaveth to my skin and to my flesh, and I am escaped with the skin of my teeth.—Job, ch. 19.

8937. —— Overburdening. *Moses.* [11] Thou layest the burden of all this people upon me? [12] . . have I begotten them, that thou shouldest say unto me, Carry them in thy bosom, as a nursing father beareth the sucking child, unto the land.—Num., ch. 11. [They murmured for flesh.]

8938. —— Rest from. *Elim.* [27] They came to Elim, where *were* twelve wells of water, and threescore and ten palm trees: and they encamped there by the waters.—Ex., ch. 15.

8939. —— Severe. *Apostles.* [11] We both hunger, and thirst, and are naked, and are buffeted, and have no certain dwellingplace; [12] And labour, working with our own hands: being reviled, we bless; being persecuted, we suffer it: [13] Being defamed, we entreat: we are made as the filth of the world.—1 Cor., ch. 4.

8940. —— —— *Paul.* [23] Are they ministers of Christ? . . I *am* more; in labours more abundant, in stripes above measure, in prisons more frequent, in deaths oft. [24] Of the Jews five times received I forty *stripes* save one. [25] Thrice was I beaten with rods, once was I stoned, thrice I suffered shipwreck, a night and a day I have been in the deep.—2 Cor., ch. 11.

8941. —— —— *P a u l.* [26] *In* journeyings often, *in* perils of waters, *in* perils of robbers, *in* perils by *mine own* countrymen, *in* perils by the heathen, *in* perils in the city, *in* perils in the wilderness, *in* perils in the sea, *in* perils among false brethren.—2 Cor., ch. 11.

8942. —— —— *Paul.* [27] In weariness and painfulness, in watchings often, in hunger and thirst, in fastings often, in cold and nakedness. [28] Beside those things that are without, that which cometh upon me daily, the care of all the churches.—2 Cor., ch. 11.

8943. —— Use of. *Canaanites.* [1] These *are* the nations which the Lord left, to prove Israel by them . . [3] *Namely,* five lords of the Philistines, and all the Canaanites, and the Sidonians, and the Hivites that dwelt in mount Lebanon.—Judges, ch. 3.

8944. —— —— *" More Fruit."* [1] I am the true vine, and my Father is the husbandman. [2] Every branch in me that beareth not fruit he taketh away: and every *branch* that beareth fruit, he purgeth it, that it may bring forth more fruit.—John, ch. 15.

8945. —— Victory over. *P a u l.* [35] Who shall separate us from the love of Christ? *shall* tribulation, or distress, or persecution, or famine, or nakedness, or peril, or sword? . . [37] Nay, in all these things we are more than conquerors through him that loved us.—Rom., ch. 8.

8946. —— understood. *"Partakers . . Glory."* [12] Beloved, think it not strange concerning the fiery trial which is to try you, as though some strange thing happened unto you: [13] But rejoice, inasmuch as ye are partakers of Christ's sufferings; that, when his glory shall be revealed, ye may be glad also with exceeding joy.—1 Peter, ch. 4.

See other illustrations under:

EXPERIMENT.

Dietetic. Ten days . . give us pulse to eat	2817
Faith's. Walked on the water to go to Jesus	2818

TEST.

Benevolence. One thing thou lackest . . go sell . . give	8726
Character. Ye shall not eat of it [tree] lest ye die	8727
Diet. Give us pulse to eat, and water to drink	8728
Exact. It was at the same hour . . Jesus said . . son	8729
Lord's. Man's rod whom I shall choose, shall b.	8730
Needful. Girded his sword . . I have not proved their	8731
Obedience. That saith, I know him, and keepeth	8732
Password. Say now, Shibboleth . . said Sibboleth	8733
Prayer. Call ye upon the names of your gods	8734
Question. Certain lawyer . . tempted him, saying	8735
Severe. Take now . . thine only son . . burnt offering	8736
Trials. To know whether they would hearken	8737
" That they which are approved . . made m.	8738

SUFFERINGS.

Apostolic. [Paul] Five times . . stripes . . thrice	8452
Chosen. Moses . . choosing rather to suffer . . than	8453
Recompensed. Moses . . had respect unto the r.	8454
Sacred. Remove this cup . . not my will [Jesus]	8455

VENTURE.

Believers. Went into the midst of the sea . . waters	9185
Shot. Drew a bow at a venture, and smote the	9186

See **ADVERSITIES, AFFLICTIONS, SUFFERING, TEMPTATIONS, TROUBLE.**

8947. TRIBULATION at the Judgment. *Sixth Seal.* [12] There was a great earthquake; and the sun became black as sackcloth of hair, and the moon became as blood; [13] And the stars of heaven fell . . [14] And the heaven departed as a scroll when it is rolled together; and every mountain and island were moved out of their places.—Rev., ch. 6. [See No. 4785.]

8948. —— Joy in. *Paul.* [4] I am filled with comfort, I am exceeding joyful in all our tribulation. [5] For, when we were come into Macedonia, our flesh had no rest, but we were troubled on every side; without *were* fightings, within *were* fears.—2 Cor., ch. 7.

8949. —— recompensed. *" White Robes."* [13] What are these which are arrayed in white robes? and whence came they? [14] And I said . . Sir, thou knowest. And he said to me, These are they which came out of great tribulation, and have washed their robes, and made them white in the blood of the Lamb.—Rev., ch. 7.

See other illustrations under:

CALAMITY.

Destructive. Wall fell upon 27,000 men that were	995
of God. Earth opened her mouth, and swallowed	996
Hardened. I have smitten you with blasting	1001
Indiscriminating. The L. maketh the earth	1002
Misjudged. Tower in Siloam fell, think . . they	1003

Predicted. Shall not be left one stone upon a. 997
Waiting. Jonah sat..see what would become 999

CRUELTY.
Captives. Joab put them under saws..harrows 1864
" Judah cast [10,000 men of Seir] from the 1858
Maternal. Athaliah..destroyed all the seed royal 1857

MASSACRE.
Intended. Letters were sent by post..to destroy 5249
Infants. Herod..slew all the children..in Bethlehem 5250
Treacherous. Jehu said, Proclaim an assembly for 5251

Forsaken in. Cry unto the gods which ye have chosen 6
See GRIEF and references.

8950. TRIBUTE from Enemies. *To Jotham.*
⁵ He fought..the Ammonites..And the children of Ammon gave him the same year a hundred talents of silver, and ten thousand measures of wheat, and ten thousand of barley..both the second year, and the third.—2 CHRON., ch. 27.

8951. —— levied. *"Fifty Shekels."* ²⁰ Menahem exacted the money of Israel, *even* of all the mighty men of wealth, of each man fifty shekels of silver, to give to the king of Assyria. —2 KINGS, ch. 15.

8952. —— in Sheep. *Mesha.* ⁴ Mesha king of Moab was a sheepmaster, and rendered unto the king of Israel a hundred thousand lambs, and a hundred thousand rams, with the wool. ⁵..when Ahab was dead..the king of Moab rebelled.—2 KINGS, ch. 3.

8953. —— in Silver. *Israelites.* ¹⁹ Pul the king of Assyria came against the land : and Menahem gave Pul a thousand talents of silver, that his hand might be with him to confirm the kingdom in his hand.—2 KINGS, ch. 15. [About $1,811,000.]

8954. —— A useless. *Ahaz'.* ²¹ Ahaz took away a portion *out* of the house of the Lord, and *out* of the house of the king, and of the princes, and gave *it* unto the king of Assyria : but he helped him not.—2 CHRON., ch. 28.
See TAX and references.

8955. TRICK, A diplomatic. *Gibeonites.* ⁷ Peradventure ye dwell among us ; and how shall we make a league with you? ⁸ And they said unto Joshua.. ⁹..From a very far country thy servants are come.—JOSH., ch. 9. [With mouldy bread and ragged shoes.]

8956. —— The Hypocrites'. *Is Tribute lawful?* ²⁰ Watched *him*, and sent forth spies, which should feign themselves just men, that they might take hold of his words, that so they might deliver him unto..the governor. ²¹ And they asked him, saying, Master, we know that thou sayest and teachest rightly, neither acceptest thou the person *of any*, but teachest the way of God truly.—LUKE, ch. 20.

8957. —— of Legerdemain. *Magicians.* ¹¹ The magicians of Egypt, they also did in like manner with their enchantments. ¹² For they cast down every man his rod, and they became serpents.—EX., ch. 7.

8958. —— A Politician's. *Babylonians.* ⁷ Whosoever shall ask a petition of any god or man for thirty days, save of thee, O king, he shall be cast into the den of lions. ⁸ Now, O king, establish the decree, and sign the writing, that it be not changed, according to the law of the Medes and Persians, which altereth not.— DAN., ch. 6.

See other illustrations under :
IMPOSTOR.
Called. Others said, Nay..he deceiveth the people 4352
Punished. Elymas the sorcerer..thou shalt be b. 4353
Treated as. Herod..arrayed him in a gorgeous r. 4354

IMPOSTORS.
Exposed. Seven sons of Sceva..fled out..wounded 4355
Punished. Hewers of wood and drawers of water 4356

STRATAGEM.
Battle. Joshua saw that the ambush had taken the 8366
Success. Joab's field..set it on fire [by Absalom] 8367
Subtile. Joseph's coat..dipped in the blood 8424

Disclosed. Joab put all these words in the mouth of 95
See DECEPTION and references.

8959. TRIFLES, Blinded by. *Pharisees.* ²⁴ Ye blind guides, which strain at a gnat, and swallow a camel. ²⁵ Woe unto you, scribes and Pharisees, hypocrites ! for ye make clean the outside of the cup and of the platter, but within they are full of extortion and excess.—MAT., ch. 23.

8960. —— Comparative. *Samson.* ² In the morning, when it is day, we shall kill him. ³ And Samson..arose at midnight, and took the doors of the gate of the city, and the two posts, and went away with them, bar and all.—JUDGES, ch. 16.

8961. —— magnified. *Tithes.* ²³ Woe unto you, scribes and Pharisees, hypocrites ! for ye pay tithe of mint, and anise, and cummin, and have omitted the weightier *matters* of the law, judgment, mercy, and faith.—MAT., ch. 23.

8962. —— —— Washing. ⁵ The Pharisees and scribes asked him, Why walk not thy disciples according to the tradition of the elders, but eat bread with unwashen hands?—MARK, ch. 7.

8963. —— observed. *"Washed."* ³⁷ A certain Pharisee besought him to dine with him : and he went in, and sat down to meat. ³⁸..he marvelled that he had not first washed before dinner.—LUKE, ch. 11.

8964. —— Theological. *Avoid.* ⁹ Avoid foolish questions, and genealogies, and contentions, and strivings about the law ; for they are unprofitable and vain.—TITUS, ch. 3.

Also see :
Little. There be four things..little..wise 5051

8965. TRINITY revealed, The. *Baptism.* ¹⁶ Lo, the heavens were opened unto him, and he saw the Spirit of God descending like a dove, and lighting upon him : ¹⁷ And lo a voice from heaven, saying, This is my beloved Son, in whom I am well pleased.—MAT., ch. 3.

8966. TRIUMPH of Christ. *Complete.* ⁴⁴ Whosoever shall fall on this stone shall be broken : but on whomsoever it shall fall, it will grind him to powder.—MAT., ch. 21.

8967. —— A glorious. *Paul.* ⁷ I have fought a good fight, I have finished *my* course, I have kept the faith : ⁸ Henceforth there is laid up for me a crown of righteousness.—2 TIM., ch. 4.

8968. —— Spiritual. *Stephen.* ⁵⁹ They stoned Stephen, calling upon *God*, and saying, Lord Jesus, receive my spirit. ⁶⁰ And he kneeled down and cried with a loud voice, Lord, lay not this sin to their charge. And when he had said this, he fell asleep.—ACTS, ch. 7.

8969. TROUBLE, Awakened by. *Idolaters.* [27] Saying to a stock, Thou *art* my father ; and to a stone, Thou hast brought me forth : for they have turned *their* back unto me, and not *their* face : but in the time of their trouble they will say, Arise, and save us.—JER., ch. 2.

8970. —— from Abundance. *Parable.* [16] The ground of a certain rich man brought forth plentifully : [17] And he thought within himself, saying, What shall I do, because I have no room where to bestow my fruits ?—LUKE, ch. 12.

8971. —— Borrowing. *By Red Sea.* [12] *Is* not this the word that we did tell thee in Egypt, saying, Let us alone, that we may serve the Egyptians ? For *it had been* better for us to serve the Egyptians, than that we should die in the wilderness.—Ex., ch. 14.

8972. —— —— *Forbidden.* [34] Take therefore no thought for the morrow : for the morrow shall take thought for the things of itself. Sufficient unto the day *is* the evil thereof.—MAT., ch. 6.

8973. —— Business. *Borrower.* [5] As one was felling a beam, the axe head fell into the water : and he cried, and said, Alas, Master ! for it was borrowed.—2 KINGS, ch. 6.

8974. —— Comfort in. *David.* [2] I poured out my complaint before him ; I shewed before him my trouble. [3] When my spirit was overwhelmed within me, then thou knewest my path. —Ps. 142.

8975. —— Despairing in. *Moses.* [13] Whence should I have flesh to give unto all this people ? for they weep unto me, saying, Give us flesh, that we may eat. [14] I am not able to bear all this people alone, because *it is* too heavy for me. [15] And if thou deal thus with me, kill me, I pray thee, out of hand.—NUM., ch. 11.

8976. —— Domestic. *Martha.* [40] Lord..my sister hath left me to serve alone ? bid her therefore that she help me. [41] And Jesus answered.. Martha, Martha, thou art careful and troubled about many things,—LUKE, ch. 10.

8977. —— delayed. *Wicked.* [17] Until I went into the sanctuary of God ; *then* understood I their end. [18] Surely thou didst set them in slippery places : thou castedst them down into destruction.—Ps. 73.

8978. —— A Dreamer's. *King.* [1] Nebuchadnezzar dreamed dreams, wherewith his spirit was troubled, and his sleep brake from him.— DAN., ch. 2.

8979. —— explained. *Moses said,* [3] He humbled thee, and suffered thee to hunger, and fed thee with manna, which thou knewest not, neither did thy fathers know ; that he might make thee know that man doth not live by bread only, but by every *word* that proceedeth out of the mouth of the Lord.—DEUT., ch. 8.

8980. —— Family. *Hannah by Peninnah.* [6] Because the Lord had shut up her womb. [7] And *as* he did so year by year, when she went up to the house of the Lord, so she provoked her ; therefore she wept, and did not eat.—1 SAM., ch. 1.

8981. —— Forsaking God in. *Ahaz.* [22] In the time of his distress did he trespass yet more against the Lord : this *is that* king Ahaz. [23] For he sacrificed unto the gods of Damascus, which smote him : and he said, Because the gods of the kings of Syria help them, *therefore* will I sacrifice to them, that they may help me. But they were the ruin of him, and of all Israel.— 2 CHRON., ch. 28.

8982. —— Helpless in. *Sinners.* [13] Ye have forsaken me, and served other gods : wherefore I will deliver you no more. [14] Go and cry unto the gods which ye have chosen ; let them deliver you in the time of your tribulation.— JUDGES, ch. 10.

8983. —— An increasing. *In Egypt.* [18] There shall no straw be given you, yet shall ye deliver the tale of bricks. [19] And the officers of the children of Israel did see *that* they *were* in evil *case*, after it was said, Ye shall not minish *aught*..of your daily task.—Ex., ch. 5.

8984. —— —— *Jacob.* [36] Me have ye bereaved *of my children :* Joseph *is* not, and Simeon *is* not, and ye will take Benjamin *away :* all these things are against me.—GEN., ch. 42.

8985. —— for Others. *Parable.* [20] Thou fool, this night thy soul shall be required of thee : then whose shall those things be, which thou hast provided ?—LUKE, ch. 12.

8986. —— Overwhelmed with. *Eli.* [17] And the messenger answered and said, Israel is fled before the Philistines, and there hath been also a great slaughter among the people, and thy two sons also, Hophni and Phinehas, are dead, and the ark of God is taken. [18] And it came to pass, when he made mention of the ark of God, that he fell from off the seat backward by the side of the gate, and his neck brake, and he died.—1 SAM., ch. 4.

8987. —— Prayer in. *David's.* [9] Have mercy upon me, O Lord, for I am in trouble : mine eye is consumed with grief, *yea*, my soul and my belly. [10] For my life is spent with grief, and my years with sighing.—Ps. 31.

8988. —— Penitence in. *Israelites.* [15] We have sinned : do thou unto us whatsoever seemeth good unto thee ; deliver us only, we pray thee, this day. [16] And they put away the strange gods from among them, and served the Lord : and his soul was grieved for the misery of Israel. —JUDGES, ch. 10.

8989. —— —— *Moses said,* [30] When thou art in tribulation, and all these things are come upon thee, *even* in the latter days, if thou turn to the Lord thy God, and shalt be obedient unto his voice ; [31] (For the Lord thy God *is* a merciful God ;) he will not forsake thee, neither destroy thee.—DEUT., ch. 4.

8990. —— Perplexing. *Jews.* [15] The king and Haman sat down to drink ; but the city Shushan was perplexed.—ESTHER, ch. 3.

8991. —— Patience with. *Waited.* [1] I waited patiently for the Lord ; and he inclined unto me, and heard my cry. [2] He brought me up also out of a horrible pit, out of the miry clay, and set my feet upon a rock, *and* established my goings.—Ps. 40.

8992. —— **Refuge in.** *God.* [1] God *is* our refuge and strength, a very present help in trouble. [2] Therefore will not we fear, though the earth be removed, and though the mountains be carried into the midst of the sea.—Ps. 46.

8993. —— **removed.** *Joy.* [22] I said in my haste, I am cut off from before thine eyes : nevertheless thou heardest the voice of my supplications when I cried unto thee. [23] O love the Lord, all ye his saints : *for* the Lord preserveth the faithful.—Ps. 31.

8994. —— **Royal.** *David.* [Abner assassinated.] [39] I *am* this day weak, though anointed king ; and these men the sons of Zeruiah *be* too hard for me.—2 Sam., ch. 3.

8995. —— **relieved.** *In Sanctuary.* [See Nos. 8977 and 8999.]

8996. —— **Retributive.** *Joseph's Brethren.* [21] We *are* verily guilty concerning our brother, in that we saw the anguish of his soul, when he besought us, and we would not hear ; therefore is this distress come upon us.—Gen., ch. 42.

8997. —— **seen.** *God.* [34] I have seen, I have seen the affliction of my people which is in Egypt, and I have heard their groaning, and am come down to deliver them. And now come, I will send thee into Egypt.—Acts, ch. 7.

8998. —— —— *Jesus.* [48] He saw them toiling in rowing ; for the wind was contrary unto them : and about the fourth watch of the night he cometh unto them, walking upon the sea.—Mark, ch. 6.

8999. —— **Sanctuary in.** *Church.* [3] For a long season Israel *hath been* without the true God, and without a teaching priest, and without law. [4] But when they in their trouble did turn unto the Lord God of Israel, and sought him, he was found of them.—2 Chron., ch. 15.

9000. —— **Shelter from.** *God.* [4] Thou hast been a strength to the poor, a strength to the needy in his distress, a refuge from the storm, a shadow from the heat, when the blast of the terrible ones *is* as a storm *against* the wall. —Isa., ch. 25.

9001. —— **Times of.** *Public.* [5] In those times *there was no* peace to him that went out, nor to him that came in, but great vexations *were* upon all the inhabitants of the countries.— 2 Chron., ch. 15.

9002. —— **Unendurable.** *Rebekah.* [46] Rebekah said to Isaac, I am weary of my life because of the daughters of Heth : if Jacob take a wife of the daughters of Heth, such as these *which are* of the daughters of the land, what good shall my life do me?—Gen., ch. 27.

9003. —— —— *Comparison.* [3] I was envious at the foolish, *when* I saw the prosperity of the wicked. [4] For *there are* no bands in their death : but their strength *is* firm. [5] They *are* not in trouble *as other* men : neither are they plagued like *other* men.—Ps. 73. [Also see No. 8977.]

9004. —— **Years of.** *Eight.* [33] He found a certain man named Eneas, which had kept his bed eight years, and was sick of the palsy. [34] And Peter said unto him, Eneas, Jesus Christ maketh thee whole.—Acts, ch. 9.

9005. —— —— *Twelve.* [25] A certain woman, which had an issue of blood twelve years, [26] And

had suffered many things of many physicians, and had spent all that she had, and was nothing bettered, but rather grew worse. — Mark, ch. 5.

9006. —— —— *Thirty-eight.* [5] A certain man was there, which had an infirmity thirty and eight years.. [7] The impotent man answered him, Sir, I have no man, when the water is troubled, to put me into the pool : but while I am coming, another steppeth down before me. —John, ch. 5.

See other illustrations under :

AGITATION.

Deception. Who art thou ?..Esau..Isaac trembled	256
Diffuses. Disputed he in the synagogue..market	257
Deplored. [Israelites] Made..abhorred..slay us	258
General. [Philistines] Trembling in the host..field	259
Mount. Sinai..quaked greatly	260
Overcome. [At sepulchre] Keepers did shake	261
Physical. Belshazzar's thoughts troubled..knees	262
Terror. [Job's vision] Trembling..my bones	263

ANXIETY.

Burdensome. They weep..not able to bear all this	453
God's Cause. Eli sat..trembled for the ark of G.	454
Forbidden. Take no thought..eat..put on	455
Parental. Thy father and I..sought the sorrowing	456
Relief. When they deliver you up, take no thought	457
Sleepless. King passed the night fasting	458
Sickness. Come down ere my child die	459
Worldly. Martha, thou art careful about many t.	460

DISCOURAGEMENT.

Contrast. But as for me, my feet were almost	2346
Defeat. Would to God, we had been content..other	2347
Evil-doers. I am..weak, though anointed king	2348
Failure. Neither hast thou delivered thy people	2349
" We have toiled all the night and taken	2350
Mismanagement. Men of Ai smote 36 men	2351
Ministerial. Some fell on stony ground..thorns	2352
Needless. They that be with us are more..with	2353
Overcome. He answered her not a word	2359
Reproved. Yet I have left me 7000 in I.	2354
Trials. I am not able to bear all the people..too	2355
Unbelief. Been better to have served the Egyp'ns	2356
Unreasonable. Wherefore have ye brought us out	2357
Without. We faint not..though our outward man	2358

DESPONDENCY.

Bereavement. Joseph is, without doubt, rent in	2226
Complaint. Since I came to Pharaoh..done evil	2227
Constitutional. Let us go..die with him	2230
Continued. My heart is smitten and withered like	2228
Cure. David was greatly distressed..spake of	2229
Difficulties. People was much discouraged	2231
Hope. Why art thou cast down, O my soul ?	2232
Hasty. Sun beat..Jonah fainted..wished to die	2233
Ill-timed. Handful of meal..little oil..die	2234
Loneliness. I only am left, and they seek my life	2235
Memories. By the rivers of Babylon we wept	2236
Overcare. If thou deal thus with me, kill me	2237
Prayer. How long wilt thou forget me, O Lord ?	2239
Public. Moses heard the people weeping..door	2238
Peril. Esau cometh..400 men..Jacob afraid	2240
Singular. Lord, take away my life..not better	2242
Vows. L. made a reproach unto me..derision	2243
Without. Troubled on every side..not in despair	2244

Consolation. Considereth the poor..L..deliver him	695
False Confidence. Unfaithful man in him of t. like	1533

See **ADVERSITY** and references.
See **DISTRESS** and references.
See **GRIEF** and references.
See **AFFLICTIONS** and **SORROW.**

9007. TRUCE, A valuable. *Saul came.* [2] Nahash the Ammonite answered them, On this *condition* will I make *a covenant* with you, that I may thrust out all your right eyes, and lay it *for* a reproach upon all Israel. [3] And the elders of Jabesh said .. Give us seven days' respite.—1 SAM., ch. 11.

9008. TRUST, An active. *Hezekiah.* [6] He clave to the Lord, *and* departed not from following him, but kept his commandments.. [7] And the Lord was with him ; *and* he prospered whithersoever he went forth : and he rebelled against the king of Assyria, and served him not. —2 KINGS, ch. 18.

9009. —— A courageous. *David.* [45] To the Philistine, Thou comest to me with a sword, and with a spear, and with a shield : but I come to thee in the name of the Lord of hosts, the God of the armies of Israel, whom thou hast defied. —1 SAM., ch. 17.

9010. —— Experience strengthens. *David.* [37] The Lord that delivered me out of the paw of the lion, and out of the paw of the bear, he will deliver me out of the hand of this Philistine. And Saul said unto David, Go, and the Lord be with thee.—1 SAM., ch. 17.

9011. —— An Egotist's. *Pharisee.* I..I.. I..I..I. [See No. 9023.]

9012. —— A fearless. *Three Hebrews.* [16] Nebuchadnezzar, we *are* not careful to answer thee in this matter. [17] If it be *so*, our God whom we serve is able to deliver us from the burning fiery furnace, and he will deliver *us* out of thine hand, O king.—DAN., ch. 3.

9013. —— Death. [4] Yea, though I walk through the valley of the shadow of death, I will fear no evil : for thou *art* with me ; thy rod and thy staff they comfort me.—Ps. 23.

9014. —— David. [5] I called upon the Lord in distress : the Lord answered me, *and set me* in a large place. [6] The Lord *is* on my side ; I will not fear : what can man do unto me?—Ps. 118.

9015. —— A fixed. *Job.* [15] Though he slay me, yet will I trust in him.—JOB, ch. 13.

9016. —— A foolish. *Bramble.* [15] The bramble said unto the trees, If in truth ye anoint me king over you, *then* come *and* put your trust in my shadow ; and if not, let fire come out of the bramble, and devour the cedars of Lebanon.— JUDGES, ch. 9.

9017. —— honoured. *Reuben—Gad.* [23] They were helped against them, and the Hagarites were delivered into their hand, and all that *were* with them : for they cried to God in the battle, and he was entreated of them ; because they put their trust in him.—1 CHRON., ch. 5.

9018. —— An honoured. *Protector.* [See No. 9027.] [35] The angel of the Lord went out, and smote in the camp of the Assyrians a hundred fourscore and five thousand : and when they arose early in the morning, behold, they *were* all dead.—2 KINGS, ch. 19.

9019. A hindering. *In Riches.* [24] The disciples were astonished at his words. But Jesus ..saith unto them, Children, how hard is it for them that trust in riches to enter into the kingdom of God !—MARK, ch. 10.

9020. —— An ill-timed. *From Philistines.* [3] The elders of Israel said, Wherefore hath the Lord smitten us to day before the Philistines ? Let us fetch the ark of the covenant of the Lord out of Shiloh unto us, that.. it may save us out of the hand of our enemies.—1 SAM., ch. 4.

9021. —— in Providence. *Paul.* [5] Be content with such things.. as ye have : for he hath said, I will never leave thee, nor forsake thee. [6] So that we may boldly say, The Lord *is* my helper, and I will not fear what man shall do unto me.—HEB., ch. 13.

9022. —— in Self. *Goliath.* [41] The Philistine.. drew near unto David ; and the man that bare the shield *went* before him. [42] And when the Philistine looked about, and saw David, he disdained him : for he was *but* a youth.—1 SAM., ch. 17.

9023. —— —— Pharisee. [11] God, I thank thee, that I am not as other men *are*, extortioners, unjust, adulterers, or even as this publican. [12] I fast twice in the week, I give tithes of all that I possess.—LUKE, ch. 18.

9024. —— —— Peter. [37] Peter said unto him, Lord, why cannot I follow thee now ? I will lay down my life for thy sake.—JOHN, ch. 13.

9025. —— in Self, No. *Paul.* [9] We had the sentence of death in ourselves, that we should not trust in ourselves, but in God which raiseth the dead.—2 COR., ch. 1.

9026. —— A safe. *Believers.* [1] They that trust in the Lord *shall be* as mount Zion, *which* cannot be removed, *but* abideth for ever. [2] *As* the mountains *are* round about Jerusalem, so the Lord *is* round about his people from henceforth even for ever.—Ps. 125.

9027. —— Trial of. *Rabshakeh said,* [30] Neither let Hezekiah make you trust in the Lord, saying, The Lord will surely deliver us, and this city.. [33] Hath any of the gods of the nations delivered at all his land out of the hand of the king of Assyria?—2 KINGS, ch. 18.

9028. —— A treacherous. *In Egypt.* [1] Woe to them that go down to Egypt for help ; and stay on horses, and trust in chariots, because *they are* many ; and in horsemen, because they are very strong : but they look not unto the Holy One of Israel, neither seek the Lord !— ISA., ch. 31.

9029. —— An unfaltering. *Asa's.* [9] There came out against them Zerah the Ethiopian with a host of a thousand thousand, and three hundred chariots.. [11] And Asa cried.. Lord, *it is* nothing with thee to help, whether with many, or with them that have no power : help us, O Lord our God ; for we rest on thee, and in thy name we go against this multitude.—2 CHRON., ch. 14.

9030. —— unshaken. *In God.* [See No. 9027.] [36] But the people held their peace, and answered him not a word : for the king's commandment was, saying, Answer him not.—2 KINGS, ch. 18.

9031. —— An unwarranted. *Presumption.* [6] If thou be the Son of God, cast thyself down : for it is written, He shall give his angels charge concerning thee : and in *their* hands they shall bear thee up.—MAT., ch. 4.

9032. TRUTH agitated. *At Athens.* [16] While
Paul waited..at Athens, his spirit was stirred
in him, when he saw the city wholly given to
idolatry. [17] Therefore disputed he in the synagogue with the Jews, and with the devout persons, and in the market daily with them that
met with him.—ACTS, ch. 17.

9033. —— Blood with the. *At Sinai.* [19] When
Moses had spoken every precept..he took the
blood of calves and of goats, with water, and
scarlet wool, and hyssop, and sprinkled both the
book and all the people.—HEB., ch. 9.

9034. —— convicts. *Felix.* [25] As he reasoned of righteousness, temperance, and judgment to come, Felix trembled.—ACTS, ch. 24.

9035. —— Conspiracy against. *Ananias—
Sapphira.* [8] Tell me whether ye sold the land for
so much? And she said, Yea, for so much. [9] Then
Peter said..How is it that ye have agreed together to tempt the Spirit of the Lord?—ACTS,
ch. 5.

9036. —— Conflict with. *Powder.* [44] Whosoever shall fall on this stone shall be broken:
but on whomsoever it shall fall, it will grind
him to powder.—MAT., ch. 21.

9037. —— Various Effects of. *Athens.* [32] When
they heard of the resurrection of the dead, some
mocked: and others said, We will hear thee
again of this *matter*.. [34] Howbeit, certain..be-
lieved..Dionysius the Areopagite, and a woman
named Damaris, and others with them.—ACTS,
ch. 17.

9038. —— Freedom in. *Believers.* [31] Said
Jesus to those Jews which believed on him, If
ye continue in my word, *then* are ye my disciples
indeed; [32] And ye shall know the truth, and the
truth shall make you free.—JOHN, ch. 8.

9039. —— Inquiry for. *Pilate.* [37] Every
one that is of the truth, heareth my voice. [38] Pilate saith unto him, What is truth? And when
he had said this, he..saith unto them, I find
in him no fault at all.—JOHN, ch. 18.

9040. —— Power of. *Josiah.* [11] When the
king had heard the words of the book of the
law..he rent his clothes.—2 KINGS, ch. 22.

9041. —— ridiculed. *At Athens.* [See No.
9037.]

9042. —— resisted. *Saul.* [5] Who art thou,
Lord? And the Lord said, I am Jesus whom
thou persecutest: *it is* hard for thee to kick
against the pricks.—ACTS, ch. 9.

9043. —— False Standard of. *Jesus said,*
[7] In vain do they worship me, teaching *for* doctrines the commandments of men.—MARK, ch. 7.

9044. —— Stumbling at. *Jews.* [45] Because
I tell *you* the truth, ye believe me not. [46] Which
of you convinceth me of sin? And if I say the
truth, why do ye not believe me?—JOHN, ch. 8.

9045. —— —— Disciples. [54] Whoso eateth
my flesh, and drinketh my blood, hath eternal
life; and I will raise him up at the last day..
[66] From that *time* many of his disciples went
back, and walked no more with him.—JOHN,
ch. 6.

9046. —— The whole. *Eli.* [16] Eli called
Samuel.. [17] And he said, What *is* the thing that
the Lord hath said unto thee? I pray thee hide *it*
not from me: God do so to thee, and more also,
if thou hide *any* thing from me.—1 SAM., ch. 3.

9047. —— Warfare of the. *Spiritual.*
[34] Think not that I am come to send peace on
earth: I came not to send peace, but a sword..
[36] And a man's foes *shall be* they of his own household.—MAT., ch. 10.

9048. TYRANNY, Unendurable. *Rehoboam*
[14] Spake to them after the counsel of the young
men, saying, My father made your yoke heavy,
and I will add to your yoke: my father *also*
chastised you with whips, but I will chastise
you with scorpions.—1 KINGS, ch. 12.

9049. TUMULT, Fear of. *Pilate.* [24] When
Pilate saw that he could prevail nothing, but
that rather a tumult was made, he took water,
and washed *his* hands before the multitude, say-

ing, I am innocent of the blood of this just person.—MAT., ch. 27.

9050. —— Peace in a. *Stephen.* [57] They cried out with a loud voice, and stopped their ears, and ran upon him with one accord.. [59] And they stoned Stephen, calling upon *God*, and saying, Lord Jesus, receive my spirit. [60] And he kneeled down, and cried with a loud voice, Lord, lay not this sin to their charge. And when he had said this, he fell asleep.—ACTS, ch. 7.

See other illustrations under :

MOB.

Bigots. Two hours cried out, Great is Diana	5487
Disturbance. Lewd fellows of the baser sort	5488
Murderous. City was moved..people ran..took	5489
Tumultuous. Left beating Paul..some cried one	5490
Trial by. Cried..loud voice..ran upon Stephen	5491
Workmen. By this craft we have our wealth	5492

9051. UNBELIEF corrected. *"See."* [22] Shall the flocks and the herds be slain for them, to suffice them? or shall all the fish of the sea be gathered together for them, to suffice them? [23] And the Lord said unto Moses, Is the Lord's hand waxed short? thou shalt see now whether my word shall come to pass unto thee or not.— NUM., ch. 11.

9052. —— condemns. *Jesus said,* [18] He that believeth on him is not condemned : but he that believeth not is condemned already, because he hath not believed in the name of the only begotten Son of God.—JOHN, ch. 3.

9053. —— a Detriment. *Wilderness.* [See No. 8920.]

9054. —— Discouragement from. *W a i t .* [13] Moses said..Fear ye not, stand still, and see the salvation of the Lord, which he will shew to you to day : for the Egyptians whom ye have seen to day, ye shall see them again no more for ever.—EX., ch. 14.

9055. —— Divided by. *At Rome.* [23] There came many to him into *his* lodging ; to whom he expounded and testified the kingdom of God, persuading them concerning Jesus, both out of the law of Moses, and *out of* the prophets, from morning till evening. [24] And some believed.. some believed not.—ACTS, ch. 28.

9056. —— excludes. *Heaven.* [11] I sware in my wrath, They shall not enter into my rest. [12] Take heed, brethren, lest there be in any of you an evil heart of unbelief, in departing from the living God.—HEB., ch. 3.

9057. —— Failure from. *D e m o n - b o u n d .* [19] Then came the disciples to Jesus apart, and said, Why could not we cast him out? [20] And Jesus said unto them, Because of your unbelief. —MAT., ch. 17.

9058. —— angers God. *Spies reported.* [11] The Lord said unto Moses, How long will this people provoke me? and how long will it be ere they believe me, for all the signs which I have shewed among them ? [12] I will smite them with a pestilence, and disinherit them, and will make of thee a greater nation and mightier than they. —NUM., ch. 14.

9059. —— from Incredulity. *D i s c i p l e s .* [14] When she knew Peter's voice, she..ran in, and told how Peter stood before the gate. [15] And they said unto her, Thou art mad. But she constantly affirmed that it was even so. Then said they, It is his angel.—ACTS, ch. 12.

9060. —— an Insult. *"Liar."* [10] He that believeth on the Son of God hath the witness in himself : he that believeth not God, hath made him a liar, because he believeth not the record that God gave of his Son.—1 JOHN, ch. 5.

9061. —— Natural. *Israelites.* [1] Moses answered..But, behold, they will not believe me, nor hearken unto my voice : for they will say, The Lord hath not appeared unto thee.—EX., ch. 4.

9062. —— punished. *E g y p t i a n s .* [19] The hail shall come down upon them, and they shall die. [20] He that feared the word of the Lord among the servants of Pharaoh made his servants and his cattle flee into the houses : [21] And he that regarded not the word of the Lord left his..cattle in the field.—EX., ch. 9.

9063. —— —— *Of Leaders.* [11] Water came out abundantly, and the congregation drank.. [12] And the Lord spake unto Moses and Aaron, Because ye believed me not, to sanctify me in the eyes of the children of Israel, therefore ye shall not bring this congregation into the land. —NUM., ch. 20.

9064. —— —— *Partial.* [28] Thus saith the Lord, Because the Syrians have said, The Lord *is* God of the hills, but he *is* not God of the valleys, therefore will I deliver all this great multitude into thine hand, and ye shall know that I *am* the Lord.—1 KINGS, ch. 20.

9065. —— Prayer against. *"Help."* [23] If thou canst believe, all things *are* possible to him that believeth. [24] And straightway the father of the child cried out, and said with tears, Lord, I believe; help thou mine unbelief.—MARK, ch. 9.

9066. —— reproved. *By Birds.* [24] Consider the ravens : for they neither sow nor reap ; which neither have storehouse nor barn ; and God feedeth them : how much more are ye better than the fowls?—LUKE, ch. 12.

9067. —— —— *By F l o w e r s .* [27] Consider the lilies how they grow : they toil not, they spin not ; and yet..Solomon in all his glory was not arrayed like one of these. [28] If then God so clothe the grass, which is to day in the field, and to morrow is cast into the oven ; how much more *will he clothe* you, O ye of little faith ? —LUKE, ch. 12.

9068. —— —— *Resurrection.* [13] They went and told *it* unto the residue : neither believed they them. [14] Afterward he appeared unto the eleven as they sat at meat, and upbraided them with their unbelief and hardness of heart, because they believed not them which had seen him after he was risen.—MARK, ch. 16.

9069. —— Remarkable. *Brother's.* [4] If thou do these things, shew thyself to the world. [5] For neither did his brethren believe in him.—JOHN, ch. 3.

9070. —— removed. *Queen of Sheba.* [6] She said to the king, It was a true report that I heard in mine own land of thy acts and of thy wisdom. [7] Howbeit I believed not the words, until I came, and mine eyes had seen *it ;* and, behold, the half was not told me.—1 KINGS, ch. 10.

9071. —— Sin of. *Rephidim.* [3] The people thirsted there for water ; and the people murmured against Moses, and said, Wherefore *is* this *that* thou hast brought us up out of Egypt, to kill us and our children and our cattle with thirst ?—Ex., ch. 17.

9072. —— **Suggestion of.** *Rephidim.* [7] He called the name of the place Massah, and Meri-bah, because of the chiding of the children of Israel, and because they tempted the Lord, say-ing, Is the Lord among us or not ?—Ex., ch. 17.

9073. —— **Secret of.** *Ambition.* [44] How can ye believe, which receive honour one of another, and seek not the honour that *cometh* from God only ?—John, ch. 5.

9074. UNBELIEF unnecessary. *Loved Dark-ness.* [19] This is the condemnation, that light is come into the world, and men loved darkness rather than light, because their deeds were evil. —John, ch. 3.

9075. —— **Wilful.** *Pharisees.* [25] Who art thou ? And Jesus said unto them, Even *the same* that I said unto you from the beginning.. [45] And because I tell *you* the truth, ye believe me not. [46].. And if I say the truth, why do ye not believe me ?—John, ch. 8.

See other illustrations under :

DOUBT.

Adversity. They hearkened not..for anguish　2493
Disappointment. Told them..he was alive　　2494
Forbidden. How much more will he clothe you　2495
Hurtful. King said, They know that we be hungry　2496
Impossible. Fire of the L. fell..licked up the w.　2497
Obedience. Do his will, he shall know of the d.　2498
Struggling. Hast thou eyes..seest thou as man　2499
Strong. Except I put my finger in the print　　2500
Snare. People is great and taller than we　　2501
Trouble. Would G. it were morning..were　　2502

INCREDULITY.

Disciples'. Words seemed to them as idle tales　4394
　　"　　Neither believed they them　　4395
Prayer. Gathered together praying [for Peter]　4397
Removed. Thomas, reach hither..My Lord　　4398
Unbelievers. Jews did not believe he had been　4397

Atheism. The fool hath said..no God　　　570
Rationalism. Cain brought of the fruit..an offering　6868

9076. UNBELIEVERS, End of. *"Second Death."* [8] The fearful, and unbelieving, and the abominable, and murderers, and whoremongers, and sorcerers, and idolaters, and all liars, shall have their part in the lake which burneth with fire and brimstone : which is the second death. —Rev., ch. 21.

9077. —— **UNCERTAINTY of the Future.** *Parable.* [19] I will say to my soul, Soul, thou hast much goods laid up for many years ; take thine ease, eat, drink, *and* be merry. [20] But God said unto him, *Thou* fool, this night thy soul shall be required of thee : then whose shall those things be, which thou hast provided ?—Luke, ch. 12.

9078. —— —— *"Know not."* [13] Go to now, ye that say, To day or to morrow we will go in-to such a city, and continue there a year, and buy and sell, and get gain : [14] Whereas ye know not what *shall* be on the morrow.—James, ch. 4.

9079. —— —— *Recognized.* [14] For what *is* your life ? It is even a vapour, that appeareth for a little time, and then vanisheth away. [15] For that ye *ought* to say, If the Lord will, we shall live, and do this, or that.—James, ch. 4.

9080. —— **of Riches.** *Proverb.* [5] Wilt thou set thine eyes upon that which is not ? for *riches* certainly make themselves wings ; they fly away as an eagle toward heaven.—Prov., ch. 23.

See other illustrations under :

FUTURE.

God's Will. If the L. will, we shall live and do this　3494
Ignorance. If thou hadst known..hid from thine　3495
Piety. Let me first go and bid them farewell　　3496
Presuming. I will pull down my barns..ease, eat　3497
Uncertainty. Boast not..of to-morrow..knowest　3498

Hesitation. I will follow thee, but　　　3964
　　See **UNBELIEVERS** and references.

9081. UNCLE, A gracious. *Abraham.* [8] Abram said unto Lot, Let there be no strife, I pray thee..for we *be* brethren. [9] *Is* not the whole land before thee? separate thyself, I pray thee, from me : if *thou wilt take* the left hand, then I will go to the right.—Gen., ch. 13.

9082. —— —— *Laban.* [13] When Laban heard the tidings of Jacob his sister's son..he ran to meet him, and embraced him, and kissed him, and brought him to his house. And he told Laban all these things.—Gen., ch. 29.

9083. —— **A kind.** *Esther's.* [7] She had nei-ther father nor mother, and the maid *was* fair and beautiful ; whom Mordecai, when her father and mother were dead, took for his own daugh-ter.—Esther, ch. 2.

9084. —— **A respected.** *Mordecai.* [20] Esther had not *yet* shewed her kindred nor her people, as Mordecai had charged her : for Esther did the commandment of Mordecai, like as when she was brought up with him.—Esther, ch. 2.

9085. UNCONSCIOUS of Condition. *Coin.* [8] Either what woman having ten pieces of silver, if she lose one piece, doth not light a candle, and sweep the house, and seek diligently till she find it ?—Luke, ch. 15.

9086. —— **of Glory.** *"Shone."* [29] When he came down from the mount, that Moses wist not that the skin of his face shone while he talk-ed with him.—Ex., ch. 34.

9087. —— **of Sin.** *Formalists.* [8] Will a man rob God ? Yet ye have robbed me. But ye say, Wherein have we robbed thee ? In tithes and offerings. [9] *Ye are* cursed with a curse.—Mal., ch. 3.

9088. UNCONSCIOUSNESS, Spiritual. *Samson.* [20] She said, The Philistines *be* upon thee, Sam-son. And he awoke out of his sleep, and said, I will go out as at other times before, and shake myself. And he wist not that the Lord was de-parted from him.—Judges, ch. 16.

9089. UNFAITHFUL, Surprise of the. *Parabl[e]* [50] The lord of that servant shall come in a day when he looketh not for *him*, and in an hour that he is not aware of, [51] And shall cut him asunder, and appoint *him* his portion with the hypocrites : there shall be weeping and gnash-ing of teeth.—Mat., ch. 24.

9090. —— **Slander of the.** *"One Talent."* [20] Behold, *here is* thy pound, which I have kept laid up in a napkin : [21] For I feared thee, be-cause thou art an austere man : thou takest up that thou layedst not down, and reapest that thou didst not sow.—Luke, ch. 19.

9091. —— **disqualifies.** *Mark.* [37] Barnabas

determined to take with them John, whose surname was Mark. [38] But Paul thought not good to take him with them, who departed from them from Pamphylia, and went not with them to the work.—ACTS, ch. 15.

9092. —— Hinderance by. *Pharisees.* [52] Woe unto you, lawyers! for ye have taken away the key of knowledge : ye entered not in yourselves, and them that were entering in ye hindered.— LUKE, ch. 11.

9093. —— Trouble from the. *Proverb.* [19] Confidence in an unfaithful man in time of trouble *is like* a broken tooth, and a foot out of joint.— PROV., ch. 25.

See other illustrations under :

APOSTASY.
Angelic. Angels which kept not their first estate 461
Age. When Solomon was old..turned..other gods 462
Deception. Latter times..heed to seducing spirits 463
Enmity. Alexander..did me much evil 464
Hopeless. If we sin wilfully..no more sacrifice 465
Inconsiderate. Gave Esau pottage..despised his b. 466
Idolatrous. Ahab..served Baal, and worshipped 467
Prosperity. Jeshurun waxed fat, and kicked 468
Responsibility. Whoso shall offend..millstone 469
Shipwreck. Made shipwreck..Hymeneus..Alex. 470

DESERTION.
Ignorance. Drinketh my blood..disciples went b. 2207
Painful. At my first answer..all men forsook me 2208
Prevented. Soldiers cut the ropes..boat..let her 2209

DISOBEDIENCE.
Apostasy. Solomon loved many strange women 2392
Curses upon. [See Deut. 28 : 15–51.]
Dangerous. Because thou hast let go out of..hand 2394
Death. Nadab and Abihu..offered strange fires 2395
Fear. Joseph was afraid..he turned aside..Galilee 2396
Hinderance. Say nothing..Jesus could no more 2397
Noble. Queen Vashti refused to come 2398
Peril. People..scattered..I offered a burnt o. 2399
Penalties. [See Leviticus 26 : 15–38.]
Progressive. Did not destroy..mingled..served 2401
Rebellion. To obey is better..for rebellion is 2402
Results. They shall be as thorns in your sides 2403
Unprofitable. Babylon..until the land enjoyed 2405
Warning. The L. shall scatter you among the n. 2406

OMISSION.
Cursed. Curse ye, Meroz..came not up to the help 5875
Deception. If any man be a hearer..and not a doer 5876
Great. When saw we thee a hungered..not minister 5877
Inexcusable. These shall go..everlasting punish't 5878
Nobles. Put not their necks to the work of the L. 5879
Sin. Ye pay tithe of mint..omitted weightier 5880

REBELLION.
Abominable. Rebellion is as the sin of 6874
Ingrates. Absalom sent spies..say Absalom 6875
Ill-government. Thy father made our yoke 6876
Jealousy. Ye take too much upon you [Korah] 6877
Mental. Not enter..ye rebelled against my word 6878
Sinners. We will not have this man to reign 6879
" This is the heir, come, let us kill him 6880
Tongue. Every kind of beasts..been tamed 6881
Uncontested. Ye shall not fight..return every man 6882
Vain. Sheba blew a trumpet..we have no part 6883
Will. How oft would I..but ye would not 6884

TREASON.
Justifiable. Athaliah rent her clothes and cried 8902
Spiritual. Wherefore lift ye up yourselves above 8903
" The earth opened..Korah..went down 8904

TRAITOR.
Conspiring. Ahithophel is among the conspirators 8871
Defeated. Ahithophel saw his counsel not followed 8872
Repenting. Judas brought..20 pieces of silver 8873
Remorse. Judas..cast down the 30 pieces..hanged 8874
Suspected. Which..is for the king of Israel? 8875

WANDERING.
Corrected. Before I was afflicted, I went astray 9282
Invitation. Return unto me, and I will return 9280
Restoration. Lovest thou me?..Feed my sheep 9279
Search. Having a hundred sheep, if he lose one 9284
Unsatisfied. Dove found no rest for the..foot 9285
Wicked. I will be a swift witness against thee 9281

See BACKSLIDERS.

9094. UNFORTUNATES, An Army of. *David's.* [2] Every one *that was* in distress..in debt, and..discontented, gathered themselves unto him ; and he became a captain over them..about four hundred men.—1 SAM., ch. 22.

See ADVERSITY and references.
See MISFORTUNE.

9095. UNHAPPINESS in Old Age. *Jacob.* [36] And Jacob their father said..Me have ye bereaved *of my children:* Joseph is not, and Simeon is not, and ye will take Benjamin *away:* all these things are against me.—GEN., ch. 42.

9096. —— by Covetousness. *Ahab.* [4] Ahab came into his house heavy and displeased because..Naboth..had said, I will not give thee the inheritance of my fathers. And he laid him down upon his bed, and turned away his face, and would eat no bread.—1 KINGS, ch. 21. [In his ivory house.]

9097. —— Pride gives. *Haman.* [11] Haman told them of the glory of his riches, and the multitude of his children, and all *the things* wherein the king had promoted him.. [13] Yet all this availeth me nothing, so long as I see Mordecai the Jew sitting at the king's gate.—ESTHER, ch. 5.

9098. —— Royal. *Darius.* [18] The king went to his palace..and passed the night fasting : neither were instruments of music brought before him ; and his sleep went from him. [19] Then the king arose very early in the morning, and went in haste unto the den of lions.—DAN., ch. 6.

See ADVERSITY and references.

9099. UNION in Building. *From Captivity.* [3] Let him go up to Jerusalem..and build the house of the Lord.. [4] And whosoever remaineth in any place where he sojourneth, let the men of his place help him with silver, and with gold, and with goods.—EZRA, ch. 1.

9100. —— in Blessing. *Pentecost.* [3] And there appeared unto them cloven tongues like as of fire, and it sat upon each of them. [4] And they were all filled with the Holy Ghost, and began to speak with other tongues, as the Spirit gave them utterance.—ACTS, ch. 2.

9101. —— with Christ. *Branch.* [5] I am the vine, ye *are* the branches. He that abideth in me, and I in him, the same bringeth forth much fruit.—JOHN, ch. 15.

9102. —— Constant. *"Never."* [5] Be content with such things as ye have : for he hath said, I will never leave thee, nor forsake thee. [6] So that we may boldly say, The Lord *is* my helper, and I will not fear what man shall do unto me.—HEB., ch. 13.

9103. —— in Charity. *Famine.* [29] Then the disciples, every man according to his ability, determined to send relief unto the brethren which dwelt in Judea.—ACTS, ch. 11.

9104. —— Communistic. *Christian.* [44] All that believed were together, and had all things common ; [45] And sold their possessions and goods, and parted them to all *men*, as every man had need.—ACTS, ch. 2.

9105. —— in Communion. *Passover.* [3] They shall take to them every man a lamb according to the house of *their* fathers, a lamb for a house : [4] And if the household be too little for the lamb, let him and his neighbour next unto his house take *it* according to the number of the souls.— Ex., ch. 12.

9106. —— in Distress. *With David.* [2] Every one *that was* in distress. .in debt, and. .discontented, gathered themselves unto him ; and he became a captain over them. .about four hundred men.—1 SAM., ch. 22.

9107. —— Effect of. *"Ask."* [7] If ye abide in me, and my words abide in you, ye shall ask what ye will, and it shall be done unto you.— JOHN, ch. 15.

9108. —— Eternal. *Paul writes,* [38] I am persuaded, that neither death, nor life, nor angels, nor principalities, nor powers, nor things present, nor things to come, [39] Nor height, nor depth, nor any other creature, shall be able to separate us from the love of God, which is in Christ Jesus our Lord.—ROM., ch. 8.

9109. —— of Forces. *A h a b* [4] Said unto Jehoshaphat, Wilt thou go with me to battle to Ramoth-gilead? And Jehoshaphat said to the king of Israel, I *am* as thou *art*, my people as thy people, my horses as thy horses.—1 KINGS, ch. 22.

9110. —— of Friends. *Ruth—Naomi.* [16] Ruth said, Entreat me not to leave thee, *or* to return from following after thee : for whither thou goest, I will go ; and where thou lodgest, I will lodge : thy people *shall be* my people, and thy God my God : [17] Where thou diest, will I die, and there will I be buried : the Lord do so to me, and more also, *if aught* but death part thee and me.—RUTH, ch. 1.

9111. —— A forbidden. *Gibeonites.* [4] They did work wilily, and went and made as if they had been ambassadors, and took old sacks upon their asses, and wine bottles, old, and rent, and bound up. . [21] Let them live ; but let them be hewers of wood and drawers of water unto all the congregation.—JOSH., ch. 9. [A treaty was made.]

9112. —— important. *Reuben—Gad.* [6] Moses said unto the children of Gad and. .of Reuben, Shall your brethren go to war, and shall ye sit here ? [7] And wherefore discourage ye the heart of the children of Israel.—NUM., ch. 32.

9113. —— in Prayer. *Successful.* [12] Moses' hands *were* heavy. .and Aaron and Hur stayed up his hands, the one on the one side, and the other on the other side ; and his hands were steady until the going down of the sun. [13] And Joshua discomfited Amalek and his people with the edge of the sword.—Ex., ch. 17.

9114. —— Perpetual. *"End."* [19] Go ye therefore, and teach all nations, baptizing them

in the name of the Father, and of the Son, and of the Holy Ghost : [20] Teaching them to observe all things whatsoever I have commanded you : and, lo, I am with you alway, *even* unto the end of the world.—MAT., ch. 28.

9115. —— Revival brings. *"As one man."* [1] All the people gathered themselves together as one man into the street that *was* before the water gate ; and they spake unto Ezra the scribe to bring the book of the law of Moses.—NEH., ch. 8.

9116. —— rejected. *"Burned."* [6] If a man abide not in me, he is cast forth as a branch, and is withered ; and men gather them, and cast *them* into the fire, and they are burned.—JOHN, ch. 15.

9117. —— Strength in. *Against Allies.* [11] Joab said, If the Syrians be too strong for me, then thou shalt help me : but if the children of Ammon be too strong for thee, then I will come and help thee. [12] Be of good courage, and let us play the men for our people.—2 SAM., ch. 10.

9118. —— of Two. *Against Philistines.* [13] Jonathan climbed up upon his hands and upon his feet, and his armourbearer after him : and they fell before Jonathan ; and his armourbearer slew after him. [14] And that first slaughter. .was about twenty men.—1 SAM., ch. 14.

9119. —— Unhallowed. *Building.* [1] When the adversaries. .heard that the children of the captivity builded the temple. . [2] Then they came to Zerubbabel, and to the chief of the fathers, and said. .Let us build with you : for we seek your God, as ye *do*.—EZRA, ch. 4.

9120. —— in Worship. *Pentecost.* [1] When the day of Pentecost was fully come, they were all with one accord in one place.—ACTS, ch. 2.

9121. UNITY by Creation. *"One Blood."* [26] Hath made of one blood all nations of men for to dwell on all the face of the earth, and hath determined the times before appointed, and the bounds of their habitation.—ACTS, ch. 17.

9122. —— Delightful. *Fraternal.* [1] Behold, how good and how pleasant *it is* for brethren to dwell together in unity ! [2] *It is* like the precious ointment upon the head. . [3] As the dew of Hermon, *and as the dew* that descended upon the mountains of Zion.—Ps. 133.

9123. —— Dangerous. *Babel-builders.* [5] The Lord came down to see the city and the tower. . [6] And the Lord said, Behold, the people *is* one, and they have all one language. .and now nothing will be restrained from them, which they have imagined to do.—GEN., ch. 11.

9124. —— with Diversity. *"Many Members."* [20] Now *are they* many members, yet but one body. [17] If the whole body *were* an eye, where *were* the hearing ? If the whole *were* hearing, where *were* the smelling ?—1 COR., ch. 12.

9125. —— Dependence in. *"Need."* [21] The eye cannot say unto the hand, I have no need of thee : nor again the head to the feet, I have no need of you. [22] Nay, much more those members of the body, which seem to be more feeble, are necessary.—1 COR., ch. 12.

9126. —— impracticable. *Image.* [32] This image's head *was* of fine gold, his breast and his arms of silver, his belly and his thighs of brass, [33] His legs of iron, his feet part of iron and part of clay. ³⁴ Thou sawest till that a stone was cut out without hands, which smote the image upon his feet *that were* of iron and clay, and brake them to pieces.—DAN., ch. 2.

9127. —— from Occupation. *Aquila.* ³ Because he was of the same craft, he abode with them, and wrought : (for by their occupation they were tentmakers.)—ACTS, ch. 18.

9128. —— Prayer for. *Church.* ²⁰ Neither pray I for these alone, but for them also which shall believe on me through their word ; ²¹ That they all may be one ; as thou, Father, *art* in me, and ɪ in thee, that they also may be one in us : that the world may believe that thou hast sent me.—JOHN, ch. 17.

9129. —— Remarkable. *Christian.* ³² The multitude of them that believed were of one heart and of one soul : neither said any *of them* that aught of the things which he possessed was his own ; but they had all things common.—ACTS, ch. 4.

9130. —— by the Spirit. *"One Body."* ¹² As the body is one, and hath many members, and all the members of that one body, being many, are one body : so also *is* Christ. ¹³ For by one Spirit are we all baptized into one body.—1 COR., ch. 12.

9131. —— Suffering in. *Body.* ²⁶ Whether one member suffer, all the members suffer with it ; or one member be honoured, all the members rejoice with it. ²⁷ Now ye are the body of Christ, and members in particular.—1 COR., ch. 12.

See other illustrations under :

ALLIANCE.

COMMUNION.

CONSPIRACY.

COVENANT.

FELLOWSHIP.

FRIENDSHIP.

See LOVE.

9132. UNSELFISHNESS, Godly. *N a a m a n.* ¹⁵ Now therefore, I pray thee, take a blessing of thy servant. ¹⁶ But he said, As the Lord liveth, before whom I stand, I will receive none. And he urged him to take *it;* but he refused.—2 KINGS, ch. 5.

9133. —— in Giving. *Feast.* ¹³ When thou makest a feast, call the poor, the maimed, the lame, the blind : ¹⁴ And thou shalt be blessed ; for they cannot recompense thee.—LUKE, ch. 14.

9134. —— manifested. *Spoils.* ²³ I will not take from a thread even to a shoelatchet, and that I will not take any thing that *is* thine, lest thou shouldest say, I have made Abram rich.— GEN., ch. 14.

9135. —— Official. *Nehemiah.* ¹⁸ *That* which was prepared *for me* daily *was* one ox *and* six choice sheep ; also fowls were prepared for me, and once in ten days store of all sorts of wine : yet for all this required not I the bread of the governor, because the bondage was heavy upon this people.—NEH., ch. 5.

9136. —— —— *Prophecy.* ²⁷ There ran a young man..and said, Eldad and Medad do prophesy in the camp. ²⁸ And Joshua..said, My lord Moses, forbid them. ²⁹ And Moses said.. Enviest thou for my sake? would God that all the Lord's people were prophets, *and* that the Lord would put his Spirit upon them.—NUM., ch. 11.

9137. —— in Popularity. *Baptist.* ²⁹ He that

hath the bride is the bridegroom : but the friend of the bridegroom, which standeth and heareth him, rejoiceth greatly because of the bridegroom's voice : this my joy therefore is fulfilled. [30] He must increase, but I *must* decrease.—JOHN, ch. 3.

9138. —— **Pious.** "*All Men.*" [33] I please all *men* in all *things*, not seeking mine own profit, but the *profit* of many, that they may be saved. —1 COR., ch. 10.

9139. —— *Daniel.* [17] Daniel answered ..Let thy gifts be to thyself, and give thy rewards to another ; yet I will read the writing unto the king, and make known to him the interpretation.—DAN., ch. 5.

9140. —— **A Rival's.** *Jonathan.* [3] He loved him as his own soul. [4] And Jonathan stripped himself of the robe that *was* upon him, and gave it to David, and his garments, even to his sword, and to his bow, and to his girdle.—1 SAM., ch. 18.

9141. —— **rewarded.** *Solomon.* [11] God said.. Because thou hast asked this thing, and hast not asked for thyself long life ; neither hast asked riches for thyself, nor hast asked the life of thine enemies ; but hast asked for thyself understanding to discern judgment.. [13] ..I have also given thee that which thou hast not asked, both riches, and honour.—1 KINGS, ch. 3.

9142. —— **Wise.** *Solomon.* [9] Give therefore thy servant an understanding heart to judge thy people, that I may discern between good and bad : for who is able to judge this thy so great a people ? [10] And the speech pleased the Lord, that Solomon had asked this thing.—1 KINGS, ch. 3.

See other Illustrations under :

GENEROSITY.

Royal. [David's] 3000 talents of gold..70,000 silver 3514
Tabernacle Builders. People..much more than 3511

GIFT.

Better. Silver and gold..none, but such as I have 3521
Declined. Daniel answered, Let thy gifts be to 3535
" Esau said, I have enough, my brother 3536
Jesus. Wise men..gold, frankincense, and myrrh 3543
Thanksgiving. Purim..sending portions..gifts to 3546
Unspeakable. God so loved the world..gave..Son 3529
Unaccepted. David said to Ornan..nay..will buy 3530
Valuable. Only handful of meal..little oil 3531
Value of. Two mites..widow hath cast in more 3548

GIVERS.

Disposition. Whose heart stirred him up..willing 3551
Grateful. Certain women which had been healed 3552
Happy. People rejoiced, for they offered willingly 3553
Lovely. Not grudgingly..loveth a cheerful giver 3554
Royal. Did Araunah as a king, give unto the king 3555

LIBERALITY.

Benevolent. Much entreaty, that we would receive 4949
Commended. Thine heart shall not be grieved 4950
Denominational. He followeth not us ; and we f. 4952
Pagan. He hath built us a synagogue 4954
Rule. Poor widow hath cast in more than all 4955
Returned. Liberal soul shall be made fat 4956
Return. Give, and it shall be given unto you 4957
Royal. Every one a loaf..flesh..wine 4958
Ungrudging. Thine heart shall not be grieved 4960

SELF-DENIAL.

Abstinence. David would not drink thereof 7701
Bodily. I keep under my body lest..be a castaway 7702

Better. People complained..fire consumed them 7703
Costly. If thy right hand offend thee, cut it off 7704
Difficult. [Young ruler] went away grieved 7705
Decent. Put a knife to thy throat..given to a. 7706
Essential. Let him deny himself..take up his c. 7707
Marvellous. Get thee out of thy country..kindred 7708
" Moses refused to be called the son 7709
" Unto this present hour we both h. 7710
for Others. If meat make my brother to offend 7711
Patriotic. Twelve years..not eaten the bread 7712
Positive. If..hate not his father..own life 7713
Rewarded. Ye also shall sit upon 12 thrones 7714
" Shall receive 100 fold..eternal life 7715
Saved by. Because strait is the gate and narrow 7716
Sabbath. If thou turn from doing thine own w. 7717

See BENEVOLENCE.

9143. UNWORTHINESS conferred. *Jacob.* [10] I am not worthy of the least of all the mercies, and of all the truth, which thou hast shewed unto thy servant ; for with my staff I passed over this Jordan ; and now I am become two bands.—GEN., ch. 32.

9144. —— —— *Centurion.* [6] The centurion sent friends to him, saying unto him, Lord, trouble not thyself ; for I am not worthy that thou shouldest enter under my roof : [7] Wherefore neither thought I myself worthy to come unto thee : but say in a word, and my servant shall be healed.—LUKE, ch. 7.

See CONFESSION and HUMILITY.

9145. USEFULNESS, The better Choice. *The Undemonized.* [18] When he was come into the ship, he that had been possessed with the devil prayed him that he might be with him. [19] Howbeit Jesus suffered him not, but saith unto him, Go home to thy friends, and tell them how great things the Lord hath done for thee, and hath had compassion on thee.—MARK, ch. 5.

See SERVICE and references.

9146. USURY abolished. *Nehemiah.* [10] I pray you, let us leave off this usury. [11] Restore, I pray you, to them, even this day, their lands, their vineyards, their oliveyards, and their houses, also the hundredth *part* of the money, and of the corn, the wine, and the oil, that ye exact of them.—NEH., ch. 5.

9147. —— **condemned.** *Nehemiah.* [6] I was very angry when I heard their cry and these words. [7] Then I consulted with myself, and I rebuked the nobles, and the rulers, and said unto them, Ye exact usury, every one of his brother. And I set a great assembly against them.—NEH., ch. 5.

9148. —— **Law of.** *Jewish.* [19] Thou shalt not lend upon usury to thy brother ; usury of money, usury of victuals, usury of any thing that is lent upon usury : [20] Unto a stranger thou mayest lend upon usury.—DEUT., ch. 23.

9149. —— **Opportunity for.** *Dearth.* [3] Some.. said, We have mortgaged our lands, vineyards, and houses, that we might buy corn, because of the dearth. [4] There were also that said, We have borrowed money for the king's tribute, *and that upon* our lands and vineyards.—NEH., ch. 5.

See EXTORTION.

9150. UTENSILS desecrated. *Holy.* [7] Cyrus the king brought forth the vessels of the house of the Lord, which Nebuchadnezzar had brought forth out of Jerusalem, and had put them in the house of his gods.—EZRA, ch. 1.

9151. —— restored. *Holy.* [See above.]
[11] All *these* did Sheshbazzar bring up with *them of* the captivity that were brought up from Babylon unto Jerusalem.—EZRA, ch. 1.

9152. —— Valuable. *From Temple.* [9] Thirty chargers of gold, a thousand chargers of silver, nine and twenty knives, [10] Thirty basins of gold, silver basins of a second *sort*, four hundred and ten, *and* other vessels a thousand. [11] All the vessels of gold and of silver *were* five thousand and four hundred.—EZRA, ch. 1.

9153. UTTERANCE, Deficient in. *Moses.*
[10] O my Lord, I *am* not eloquent, neither heretofore, nor since thou hast spoken unto thy servant : but I *am* slow of speech, and of a slow tongue.—EX., ch. 4.

9154. —— Gift for. *Promise.* [11] And the Lord said unto him, Who hath made man's mouth? or who maketh the dumb, or deaf, or the seeing, or the blind? have not I the Lord? [12] Now therefore go, and I will be with thy mouth, and teach thee what thou shalt say.—EX., ch. 4.

9155. —— —— *Pentecost.* [3] There appeared unto them cloven tongues like as of fire, and it sat upon each of them. [4] And they were all filled with the Holy Ghost, and began to speak with other tongues, as the Spirit gave them utterance.—ACTS, ch. 2.

See SPEECH and references.

9156. VACATION for Rest. *Apostles.* [30] The apostles gathered..unto Jesus, and told him all things, both what they had done, and what they had taught. [31] And he said unto them, Come ye yourselves apart into a desert place, and rest a while : for there were many coming and going, and they had no leisure so much as to eat.—MARK, ch. 6.

9157. VALLEY, A defiled. *Topheth.* [10] He defiled Topheth, which *is* in the valley of the children of Hinnom, that no man might make his son or his daughter to pass through the fire to Molech.—2 KINGS, ch. 23.

9158. —— An unsightly. *" Bones."* [1] The Spirit of the Lord..set me down in the midst of the valley which *was* full of bones. [2]..behold, *there were* very many in the open valley ; and, lo, *they were* very dry.—EZEK., ch. 37.

9159. VALOUR, Characteristic. *Benaiah.* [22] He slew two lionlike men of Moab : also he went down and slew a lion in a pit in a snowy day. [23] And he slew an Egyptian, a man of *great* stature, five cubits high ; and in the Egyptian's hand *was* a spear like a weaver's beam ; and he went down to him with a staff, and plucked the spear out of the Egyptian's hand. and slew him with his own spear.—1 CHRON., ch. 11.

See COURAGE and reference.

9160. VANITY forbidden. *Disciples.* [8] Be not ye called Rabbi ; for one is your Master, *even* Christ ; and all ye are brethren.—MAT., ch. 23.

9161. —— punished. *Hezekiah.* [13] Hezekiah ..shewed them all the house of his precious things, the silver, and the gold, and the spices, and the precious ointment, and *all* the house of his armour, and all that was found in his treasures : there was nothing in his house, nor in all his dominion, that Hezekiah shewed them not. —2 KINGS, ch. 20. [All were captured.]

9162. —— —— *Haman.* [11] Then took Haman the apparel and the horse, and arrayed Mordecai, and brought him on horseback through the street of the city, and proclaimed before him, Thus shall it be done unto the man whom the king delighteth to honour.—ESTHER, ch. 6.

9163. —— Religious. *Pharisees.* [5] All their works they do for to be seen of men : they make broad their phylacteries, and enlarge the borders of their garments, [6] And love the uppermost rooms at feasts, and the chief seats in the synagogues, [7] And greetings in the markets, and to be called of men, Rabbi, Rabbi.—MAT., ch. 23.

See other illustrations under :

OSTENTATION.

Forbidden. Be not called Rabbi..are brethren	5933
" Do not sound a trumpet before thee	5934
Purpose. Absalom prepared him chariots..50 men	5935
Prayer. Scribes..for a shew make long prayers	5936
Religious. To be seen..make broad their p.	5937

PRESUMPTION.

Daring. Egyptians went..midst of the sea	6535
Failure. Presumed to go up..Amalekites smote	6536
Future. Know not what shall be..morrow	6537
Impatience. Because..people scattered..I offered	6538
Pride. Uzziah..heart lifted up..burn incense	6539
Penalty. Death, except..king hold out..sceptre	6540
Religious. Prophet that shall presume to speak	6541
Rebuke. Uzziah..leprosy..priests thrust him out	6542
Sin. Much sorer punishment..under foot..blood	6543
" Doeth aught presumptuously..cut off	6545
Success. Israel made as if..beaten..Ai..drawn	6544
Temptation. Setteth him on a pinnacle..cast	6546
Unholy. Ye take too much upon you [Korah]	6547

See PRIDE.

9164. VEGETATION, Beginning of. *Creation.*
[11] God said, Let the earth bring forth grass, the herb yielding seed, *and* the fruit tree yielding fruit after his kind, whose seed *is* in itself, upon the earth : and it was so.—GEN., ch. 1.

9165. —— Development of. *For Harvest.*
[28] For the earth bringeth forth fruit of herself ; first the blade, then the ear, after that the full corn in the ear. [29] But when the fruit is brought forth, immediately he putteth in the sickle, because the harvest is come.—MARK, ch. 4.

9166. —— Mystery of. *" How."* [26] So is the kingdom of God, as if a man should cast seed into the ground : [27] And should sleep, and rise night and day, and the seed should spring and grow up, he knoweth not how.—MARK, ch. 4.

See other illustrations under :

GROWTH.

Beautiful. Soul shall be as a well watered garden	3739
Continuous. Flourish like the palm tree..fruit in	3740
Christian. Your faith groweth exceedingly	3741
Divine. Jesus increased in wisdom and stature	3742
Esteem. Samuel grew..in favour with G. and man	3743
Fruit. Branch that beareth not he taketh away	3744
Grace. Like a tree planted by the rivers of water	3745
Imperceptible. First the blade, then the ear..corn	3746
Inward. Leaven..meal till the whole was leavened	3747
Outward. Becometh greater than all herbs	3748
Perfection. Path..shineth more and more perfect	3749
Stages. Blade..ear..full corn in the ear	3750
Strength. Clean hands shall be stronger and S.	3751
Spiritual. Child [J. B.]..grew and waxed strong	3752

HARVEST.

Abundant. Joseph gathered corn..without num. 3803
First Fruits. Bring a sheaf of the first fruits 3804
Great. The field is the world..reapers the angels 3805
Cleaning. [Boaz to Ruth] Glean not in another 3806
Prayer. That he will send forth labourers 3807
Promise. While earth remaineth, seed time and 3808
Poor Man's. Not make clean the corners..poor 3809
Sowing. Ploughman..open and break the clods 3810
Secret. He that soweth sparingly shall reap also 3811

See AGRICULTURE.

9167. VEGETARIANS, Apostate. "*L a s t Days.*" ¹ In the latter times some shall depart from the faith, giving heed to seducing spirits, and doctrines of devils.. ³ Forbidding to marry, *and commanding* to abstain from meats, which God hath created to be received with thanksgiving of them which believe and know the truth.—1 Tim., ch. 4.

9168. —— **The first.** *Adam.* ²⁹ Behold, I have given you every herb bearing seed, which *is* upon the face of all the earth, and every tree, in the which *is* the fruit of a tree yielding seed ; to you it shall be for meat.—Gen., ch. 1.

Also see :
Fondness. We remember in E. cucumbers..melons 480

9169. VENGEANCE averted. *By A b i g a i l.* ²⁵ Let not my lord, I pray thee, regard this man of Belial, *even* Nabal..Nabal *is* his name, and folly *is* with him : but I thine handmaid saw not the young men of my lord, whom thou dist send. —1 Sam., ch. 25.

9170. —— —— *Thanks for.* ³³ Blessed *be* thy advice, and blessed *be* thou, which hast kept me this day from coming to *shed* blood, and from avenging myself with mine own hand.—1 Sam., ch. 25.

9171. —— **for Blood.** *Cain.* ¹³ Cain said unto the Lord, My punishment *is* greater than I can bear. ¹⁴ Behold, thou hast driven me out this day from the face of the earth.. I shall be a fugitive and a vagabond in the earth ; and.. every one that findeth me shall slay me.—Gen., ch. 4.

9172. —— **A call for.** *Zachariah said,* ²⁰ Thus saith God, Why transgress ye the commandments of the Lord, that ye cannot prosper ? because ye have forsaken the Lord, he hath also forsaken you. ²¹ And they conspired against him, and stoned him with stones at the commandment of the king in the court of the house of the Lord.—2 Chron., ch. 24.

9173. —— **Divine.** *Calamity.* ³⁵ To me *belongeth* vengeance, and recompense ; their foot shall slide in *due* time : for the day of their calamity *is* at hand, and the things that shall come upon them make haste.—Deut., ch. 32.

9174. —— —— *Terrible.* ⁴¹ If I whet my glittering sword, and mine hand take hold on judgment ; I will render vengeance to mine enemies, and will reward them that hate me. ⁴² I will make mine arrows drunk with blood, and my sword shall devour flesh.—Deut., ch. 32.

9175. —— **declined.** *Saul.* ¹² The people said unto Samuel, Who *is* he that said, Shall Saul reign over us ? bring the men, that we may put them to death. ¹³ And Saul said, There shall not a man be put to death this day : for to day the Lord hath wrought salvation in Israel.—1 Sam., ch. 11.

9176. —— **Fear of.** *Joseph's Brethren.* ¹⁵ When Joseph's brethren saw that their father was dead, they said, Joseph will peradventure hate us, and will certainly requite us all the evil which we did unto him.—Gen., ch. 50.

9177. —— **with God.** *By Nehemiah.* ¹³ Therefore *was* he hired, that I should be afraid, and do so, and sin, and *that* they might have *matter* for an evil report, that they might reproach me. ¹⁴ My god, think thou upon Tobiah and Sanballat according to these their works.—Neh., ch. 6.

9178. —— **Inappropriate.** *Parable.* ³² His lord..said..O thou wicked servant, I forgave thee all that debt, because thou desiredst me : ³³ Shouldest not thou also have had compassion on thy fellow servant, even as I had pity on thee?—Mat., ch. 18.

9179. —— **Mistaken.** *On Samaritans.* ⁵³ They did not receive him, because his face was as though he would go to Jerusalem. ⁵⁴ And when ..James and John saw *this,* they said, Lord, wilt thou that we command fire to come down from heaven, and consume them, even as Elias did?—Luke, ch. 9.

9180. —— **Monstrous.** *Haman's.* ⁵ When Haman saw that Mordecai bowed not, nor did him reverence, then was Haman full of wrath. ⁶ And he thought scorn to lay hands on Mordecai alone..Haman sought to destroy all the Jews that *were* throughout the whole kingdom. —Esther, ch. 3.

9181. —— **Prayer for.** *Samson.* ²⁸ Samson.. O Lord God, remember me, I pray thee, and strengthen me, I pray thee, only this once, O God, that I may be at once avenged of the Philistines for my two eyes. ²⁹ And Samson took hold of the two middle pillars.—Judges, ch. 16.

9182. —— **prohibited.** *Parable.* ³⁴ His lord was wroth, and delivered him to the tormentors, till he should pay all that was due unto him. ³⁵ So likewise shall my heavenly Father do also unto you, if ye from your hearts forgive not every one his brother their trespasses.—Mat., ch. 18.

9183. —— **undesired.** *David.* ⁶ They came thither into the midst of the house, as *though* they would have fetched wheat ; and they smote him under the fifth *rib :* and Rechab and Baanah his brother escaped.. ⁸..said to the king, Behold the head of Ish-bosheth the son of Saul thine enemy, which sought thy life : and the Lord hath avenged my lord the king this day of Saul, and of his seed.—2 Sam., ch. 4.

9184. —— **for Vengeance.** *Murderers.* [See above.] ¹¹ How much more, when wicked men have slain a righteous person in his own house upon his bed ? shall I not therefore now require his blood of your hand, and take you away from the earth ? ¹² And David commanded his young men, and they slew them.—2 Sam., ch. 4.

See REVENGE and references.

9185. VENTURE of Believers. *Red Sea.* ²² The children of Israel went into the midst of the sea upon the dry *ground :* and the waters *were* a wall unto them on their right hand, and on their left.—Ex., ch. 14.

9186. —— **Shot at a.** *Ahab slain.* ³⁴ A *certain* man drew a bow at a venture, and smote the king of Israel between the joints of the harness : wherefore he said unto the driver of his chariot,

Turn thine hand, and carry me out of the host ; for I am wounded.—1 KINGS, ch. 22.

9187. VEXATION from Entreaty. *Samson's.* [16] When she pressed him daily with her words, and urged him, *so* that his soul was vexed unto death ; [17] That he told her all his heart.— JUDGES, ch. 16.

See TROUBLE and references.

9188. VICE, Mental. *"Works."* [20] Idolatry, witchcraft, hatred, variance, emulations, wrath, strife, seditions, heresies, [21] Envyings, murders, drunkenness, revellings, and such like.—GAL., ch. 5.

9189. VICES, Physical. *"Works."* [19] The works of the flesh are manifest, which are *these*, Adultery, fornication, uncleanness, lasciviousness.—GAL., ch. 5.

9190. —— Pleasures of. *Proverb.* [33] Thine eye shall behold strange women, and thine heart shall utter perverse things. [34] Yea, thou shalt be as he that lieth down in the midst of the sea, or as he that lieth upon the top of a mast.—PROV., ch. 23.

See CRIME and references.
See SIN and references.

9191. VICTORY in Death. *Samson.* [29] Samson took hold of the two middle pillars upon which the house stood .. [30] .. And he bowed himself with *all his* might ; and the house fell upon the lords, and upon all the people that *were* therein. So the dead which he slew at his death were more than *they* which he slew in his life.—JUDGES, ch. 16.

9192. —— of Faith. *"Shouted"..."Fell."* [20] When the people heard the sound of the trumpet, and the people shouted with a great shout..the wall fell down flat, so that the people went up into the city, every man straight before him, and they took the city.—JOSH., ch. 6.

9193. —— —— In Adversity. [17] Although the fig tree shall not blossom, neither *shall* fruit *be* in the vines ; the labour of the olive shall fail, and the fields shall yield no meat ; the flock shall be cut off from the fold, and *there shall be* no herd in the stalls : [18] Yet I will rejoice in the Lord, I will joy in the God of my salvation.— HAB., ch. 3.

9194. —— from God. *Moab—Ammon.* [Jahaziel] [15] Said, Hearken ye, all Judah, and ye inhabitants of Jerusalem, and thou king Jehoshaphat, Thus saith the Lord unto you, Be not afraid nor dismayed by reason of this great multitude ; for the battle *is* not yours, but God's.—2 CHRON., ch. 20.

9195. —— —— Gideon. [2] The Lord said unto Gideon, The people that *are* with thee *are* too many for thee to give the Midianites into their hands, lest Israel vaunt themselves against me, saying, Mine own hand hath saved me. [3] Now therefore go to, proclaim in the ears of the people, saying, Whosoever *is* fearful and afraid, let him return and depart early from mount Gilead. —JUDGES, ch. 7.

9196. —— Joy of. *Over Philistines.* [6] When David was returned from the slaughter of the Philistines..the women came out of all cities of Israel, singing and dancing, to meet king Saul, with tabrets, with joy, and with instruments of music. [7] And..answered one another as they played, and said, Saul hath slain his thou-

sands, and David his ten thousands.—1 SAM., ch. 18.

9197. —— at the Last. *Paul.* [7] I have fought a good fight, I have finished *my* course, I have kept the faith: [8] Henceforth there is laid up for me a crown of righteousness.—2 TIM., ch. 4.

9198. —— Mourning in. *David.* [1] King weepeth and mourneth for Absalom. [2] And the victory that day was *turned* into mourning unto all the people : for the people heard say that day how the king was grieved for his son.—2 SAM., ch. 19.

9199. —— Mistake in. *"Gods."* [23] The lords of the Philistines gathered them together for to offer a great sacrifice unto Dagon their god, and to rejoice : for they said, Our god hath delivered Samson our enemy into our hand. [24] And when the people saw him, they praised their god.—JUDGES, ch. 16.

9200. —— by Flank Movement. *Over Philistines.* [23] When David inquired of the Lord, he said, Thou shalt not go up ; *but* fetch a compass behind them, and come upon them over against the mulberry trees. [24] And let it be, when thou hearest the sound of a going in the tops of the mulberry trees, that then thou shalt bestir thyself.—2 SAM., ch. 5.

9201. —— Monument of. *Eben-ezer.* [11] The men of Israel..pursued the Philistines, and smote them.. [12] Then Samuel took a stone, and set *it* between Mizpeh and Shen, and called the name of it Eben-ezer, saying, Hitherto hath the Lord helped us.—1 SAM., ch. 7.

9202. —— necessary. *In Canaan.* [55] If ye will not drive out the inhabitants of the land from before you ; then..those which ye let remain of them *shall be* pricks in your eyes, and thorns in your sides, and shall vex you.—NUM., ch. 33.

9203. —— A perilous. *Samson.* [21] Philistines took him, and put out his eyes, and brought him down to Gaza, and bound him with fetters of brass ; and he did grind in the prison house. [22] Howbeit the hair of his head began to grow again after he was shaven.—JUDGES, ch. 16.

9204. —— Piety brings. *Burnt Offering.* [10] As Samuel was offering up the burnt offering, the Philistines drew near to battle against Israel : but the Lord thundered with a great thunder on that day upon the Philistines, and discomfited them ; and they were smitten before Israel.—1 SAM., ch. 7.

9205. —— Promise of. *Ammon.* [16] Thus saith the Lord, Make this valley full of ditches. [17] For ..Ye shall not see wind, neither shall ye see rain ; yet that valley shall be filled with water, that ye may drink, both ye, and your cattle, and your beasts. [18] And this is *but* a light thing in the sight of the Lord : he will deliver the Moabites also into your hand.—2 KINGS, ch. 3.

9206. —— Prayer for. *Against Ethiopians.* [11] Asa cried..Lord, *it is* nothing with thee to help, whether with many, or with them that have no power : help us, O Lord our God ; for we rest on thee, and in thy name we go against this multitude. O Lord, thou *art* our God : let not man prevail against thee.—2 CHRON., ch. 14.

9207. —— —— Against Philistines. [See No. 9200.]

9208. —— **Spoils of.** *"Three Days."* [25] When Jehoshaphat and his people came to take away the spoil of them, they found..both riches with the dead bodies, and precious jewels, which they stripped off for themselves, more than they could carry away : and they were three days in gathering of the spoil, it was so much. —2 CHRON., ch. 20.

9209. —— **by Song.** *"Destroyed Another."* [22] When they began to sing and to praise, the Lord set ambushments against the children of Ammon, Moab, and mount Seir, which were come against Judah ; and they were smitten. [23] For the children of Ammon and Moab stood up against the inhabitants of mount Seir, utterly to slay and destroy *them :* and when they had made an end of the inhabitants of Seir, every one helped to destroy another.—2 CHRON., ch. 20.

9210. —— **Soul's.** *Death.* [54] Death is swallowed up in victory. [55] O death, where *is* thy sting ? O grave, where *is* thy victory ? [56] The sting of death *is* sin ; and the strength of sin *is* the law. [57] But thanks *be* to God, which giveth us the victory through our Lord Jesus Christ.— 1 COR., ch. 15.

9211. —— **Spiritual.** *Stephen.* [60] And he kneeled down, and cried with a loud voice, Lord, lay not this sin to their charge. And when he had said this, he fell asleep.—ACTS, ch. 7.

9212. —— **Song of.** *In Heaven.* [2] Stand on the sea of glass, having the harps of God. [3] And they sing the song of Moses the servant of God, and the song of the Lamb, saying, Great and marvellous *are* thy works, Lord God Almighty ; just and true *are* thy ways, thou King of saints. —REV., ch. 15.

9213. —— **over Trials.** *Conqueror's.* [35] Who shall separate us from the love of Christ ? *shall* tribulation, or distress, or persecution, or famine, or nakedness, or peril, or sword ? [37] Nay, in all these things we are more than conquerors through him that loved us.—ROM., ch. 8.

9214. —— **by Waiting.** *"Stand still."* [16] To morrow go ye down against them.. [17] Ye shall not *need* to fight in this *battle :* set yourselves, stand ye *still,* and see the salvation of the Lord with you, O Judah and Jerusalem : fear not, nor be dismayed.—2 CHRON., ch. 20.

See other illustrations under :
CONQUEST.
Preparation. Sent them to spy out the land of C. 1548
Unfortunate. Philistines took the ark of God 1549
Welcome. Women came..singing and dancing 1550
TRIUMPH.
Christ. It will grind him to powder 8966
Glorious. I have fought a good fight 8967
Spiritual. They stoned Stephen..he fell asleep 8968

9215. VIEWS, Opposite. *Of God.* [20] It came between the camp of the Egyptians and the camp of Israel ; and it was a cloud and darkness *to them,* but it gave light by night *to these.* —EX., ch. 14.

See other illustrations under :
OPINION.
Control. Nevertheless the lords favour thee not 5890
Changed. He is a murderer..he was a god 5891
Preconceived. I thought he will..come..stand..call 5893
OPINIONS.
Concealed. No man spake openly of him for fear 5893
Divided. Some said, He is a good man..others d. 5894

Diverse. A pestilent fellow..have..conscience 5895
" This is the prophet..Christ..was a div. 5896
Opposite. Cloud..darkness to them..light to these 5897
Prejudiced. They..found no answer, and yet had 5898
Undecided. How long halt ye between two 5899

9216. VIGILANCE, Christian. *Watch.* [35] Watch ye therefore : for ye know not when the master of the house cometh, at even, or at midnight, or at the cockcrowing, or in the morning : [36] Lest coming suddenly he find you sleeping. [37] And what I say unto you I say unto all, Watch.—MARK, ch. 13.

9217. —— **necessary.** *Sardis.* [1] I know thy works, that thou hast a name that thou livest, and art dead. [2] Be watchful, and strengthen the things which remain, that are ready to die : for I have not found thy works perfect before God.—REV. ch. 3.

9218. —— **in Uncertainty.** *Sardis.* [3] If therefore thou shalt not watch, I will come on thee as a thief, and thou shalt not know what hour I will come upon thee.—REV., ch. 3.

9219. —— **Want of.** *Evil Servant.* [48] My lord delayeth his coming ; [49] And shall begin to smite *his* fellow servants, and to eat and drink with the drunken : [50] The lord..shall come in a day when he looketh not for *him..* [51] And shall cut him asunder, and appoint *him* his portion with the hypocrites.—MAT., ch. 24.

Also see :
Prayerful. Made our prayer, and set watch day a. 5261
See **WATCHFULNESS** and references.

9220. VIGOR in Age. *Moses.* [7] Moses *was* a hundred and twenty years old when he died : his eye was not dim, nor his natural force abated.—DEUT., ch. 34.

9221. —— —— *Caleb.* [At eighty-five years.] [11] I *am as* strong this day as *I was* in the day that Moses sent me : as my strength *was* then, even so *is* my strength now, for war, both to go out, and to come in.—JOSH., ch. 14.

9222. —— —— *Caleb.* [12] Now therefore give me this mountain..for thou heardest in that day how the Anakim *were* there, and *that* the cities *were* great *and* fenced : if so be the Lord *will* be with me, then I shall be able to drive them out.—JOSH., ch. 14.
See **STRENGTH.**

9223. VINDICTIVENESS rebuked. *Samaritans.* [12] And when the day began to wear away, then came the twelve, and said unto him, Send the multitude away, that they may go into the towns and country round about, and lodge, and get victuals : for we are here in a desert place. —LUKE, ch. 9.
See **REVENGE** and references.

9224. VIOLENCE, Righteous. *Jesus.* [15] When he had made a scourge of small cords, he drove them all out of the temple, and the sheep, and the oxen ; and poured out the changers' money, and overthrew the tables.—JOHN, ch. 2.

9225. VISION, A comforting. *Stephen.* [54] They gnashed on him with *their* teeth. [55] But he, being full of the Holy Ghost, looked up steadfastly into heaven, and saw the glory of God, and Jesus standing on the right hand of God.—ACTS, ch. 7.

9226. —— **of God.** *Isaiah's.* [1] I saw also the Lord sitting upon a throne, high and lifted up, and his train filled the temple. ² Above it stood the seraphim : each one had six wings ; with twain he covered his face, and with twain he covered his feet, and with twain he did fly.—Isa., ch. 5.

9227. —— —— *Effect of.* ⁵ Then said I, Woe *is* me ! for I am undone ; because I *am* a man of unclean lips, and I dwell in the midst of a people of unclean lips : for mine eyes have seen the King, the Lord of hosts.—Isa., ch. 5.

9228. —— Instructed by. *Peter.* ¹³ There came a voice to him, Rise, Peter ; kill, and eat. ¹⁴ But Peter said, Not so, Lord ; for I have never eaten any thing that is common or unclean. ¹⁵ And the voice *spake* unto him again the second time, What God hath cleansed, *that* call not thou common.—Acts, ch. 10.

9229. —— Prepared for a. *Cornelius.* ³⁰ Cornelius said, Four days ago I was fasting until this hour ; and at the ninth hour I prayed in my house, and, behold, a man stood before me in bright clothing, ³¹ And said, Cornelius, thy prayer is heard.—Acts, ch. 10.

9230. —— perfected. *"Clearly."* ²³ He asked him if he saw aught. ²⁴ And he looked up, and said, I see men as trees, walking. ²⁵ After that he put *his* hands again upon his eyes, and made him look up ; and he was restored, and saw every man clearly.—Mark, ch. 8.

9231. —— of a Spirit. *Job.* ¹³ In thoughts from the visions of the night, when deep sleep falleth on men, ¹⁴ Fear came upon me, and trembling, which made all my bones to shake. ¹⁵ Then a spirit passed before my face ; the hair of my flesh stood up.—Job, ch. 4.

9232. —— Transforming. *" Shone."* ²⁹ When Moses came down from mount Sinai, with the two tables of testimony in Moses' hand..Moses wist not that the skin of his face shone.—Ex., ch. 34.

9233. —— —— *Christian.* ¹⁸ We all, with open face beholding as in a glass the glory of the Lord, are changed into the same image from glory to glory, *even* as by the Spirit of the Lord. —2 Cor., ch. 3.

9234. —— A Trance. *Peter's.* ¹⁰ Fell into a trance, ¹¹ And saw heaven opened, and a certain vessel descending unto him, as it had been a great sheet knit at the four corners, and let down to the earth : ¹² Wherein were all manner of fourfooted beasts of the earth, and wild beasts, and creeping things, and fowls of the air.—Acts, ch. 10.

Also see :
of God. Moses..elders..saw the G. of I..under his f. 50

9235. VOICE, The Lord's. *"Still small."* ¹¹ After the wind an earthquake ; *but* the Lord was not in the earthquake : ¹² And after the earthquake a fire ; *but* the Lord *was* not in the fire : and after the fire a still small voice. ¹³ And it was *so,* when Elijah heard *it,* that he wrapped his face in his mantle, and went out, and stood in the entering in of the cave.—1 Kings, ch. 19.

9236. —— —— *Baptism.* ¹⁶ Jesus, when he was baptized..lo, the heavens were opened unto him, and he saw the Spirit of God descending like a dove, and lighting upon him : ¹⁷ And lo a voice from heaven, saying, This is my beloved Son, in whom I am well pleased.— Mat., ch. 3.

9237. —— —— *" Trumpet."* ¹⁶ There were thunders and lightnings, and a thick cloud upon the mount, and the voice of the trumpet exceeding loud ; so that all the people that *was* in the camp trembled.—Ex., ch. 19.

9238. —— —— *Transfiguration.* ³⁵ There came a voice out of the cloud, saying, This is my beloved Son : hear him. ³⁶ And when the voice was past, Jesus was found alone.—Luke, ch. 9.

9239. —— —— *Mistaken.* ²⁸ Father, glorify thy name. Then came there a voice from heaven, *saying,* I have both glorified *it,* and will glorify *it* again. ²⁹ The people..said that it thundered : others said, An angel spake to him. ³⁰ Jesus..said, This voice came not because of me, but for your sakes.—John, ch. 12.

9240. —— —— *Awakening.* ⁴ He fell to the earth, and heard a voice saying unto him, Saul, Saul, why persecutest thou me ? ⁵ And he said, Who art thou, Lord ? And the Lord said, I am Jesus.—Acts, ch. 9.

9241. —— Only a. *Baptist.* ³ This is he that was spoken of by the prophet Esaias, saying, the voice of one crying in the wilderness, Prepare ye the way of the Lord, make his paths straight.—Mat., ch. 3.

See SPEECH and references.

9242. VOLUNTEER, A brave. *David.* ³² David said to Saul, Let no man's heart fail because of him ; thy servant will go and fight with this Philistine.—1 Sam., ch. 17.

9243. —— An inconsiderate. *A Scribe.* ¹⁹ Master, I will follow thee whithersoever thou goest. ²⁰ And Jesus saith unto him, The foxes have holes, and the birds of the air *have* nests ; but the Son of man hath not where to lay *his* head.—Mat., ch. 8.

9244. VOLUNTEERS, Call for. *Building.* ³ Who *is there* among you of all his people ? his God be with him, and let him go up to Jerusalem, which *is* in Judah, and build the house of the Lord..in Jerusalem.—Ezra, ch. 1.

9245. —— in Giving. *Building.* ⁴ Whosoever remaineth in any place where he sojourneth, let the men of his place help him with silver, and with gold, and with goods, and with beasts, besides the freewill offering for the house of God that *is* in Jerusalem.—Ezra, ch. 1.

See other illustrations under :
WILLINGNESS.
Believe. L. I believe ; help my unbelief   9595
Giving. I brought a willing offering for the tab.   9596
Love. If thou wilt thou canst..I will be thou clean 9597
    "   This man receiveth sinners and eateth with 9598

See CHOICE and references.

9246. VOW in Despondency. *Jeremiah.* ⁸ Because the word of the Lord was made a reproach unto me, and a derision, daily. ⁹ Then I said, I will not make mention of him, nor speak any more in his name. But *his word* was in mine heart as a burning fire shut up in my bones, and I was weary with forbearing, and I could not stay.—Jer., ch. 20.

9247. —— An inconsiderate. *Saul's.* ²⁴ The men of Israel were distressed that day : for Saul had adjured the people, saying, Cursed *be* the man that eateth *any* food until evening, that I may be avenged on mine enemies. So none of the people tasted *any* food.—1 Sam., ch. 14. [While pursuing the Philistines.]

9248. —— **of Obedience.** *All the People.* [29] They clave to their brethren, their nobles, and entered into a curse, and into an oath, to walk in God's law..and to observe and do all the commandments of the Lord our Lord.— Neh., ch. 10.

9249. —— **Observance of.** *"Pay."* [4] When thou vowest a vow unto God, defer not to pay it ; for *he hath* no pleasure in fools : pay that which thou hast vowed. [5] Better *is it* that thou shouldest not vow, than that thou shouldest vow and not pay.—Eccl., ch. 5.

9250. —— **A rash.** *Jephthah's.* [30] Jephthah vowed..if thou shalt without fail deliver the children of Ammon into mine hands, [31] Then it shall be, that whatsoever cometh forth of the doors of my house to meet me, when I return in peace..shall surely be the Lord's, and I will offer it up for a burnt offering.—Judges, ch. 11. [See No. 9253.]

9251. —— **A Sailor's.** *In Storm.* [15] They took up Jonah, and cast him forth into the sea : and the sea ceased from her raging, [16] Then the men feared the Lord exceedingly, and offered a sacrifice unto the Lord, and made vows.—Jonah, ch. 1.

9252. —— **in Trouble.** *Hannah's.* [11] She vowed a vow, and said, O Lord of hosts, if thou wilt indeed look on the affliction of thine handmaid, and remember me..wilt give unto thine handmaid a man child ; then I will give him unto the Lord all the days of his life.—1 Sam., ch. 1.

9253. —— **Trouble from a.** *Jephthah.* [See No. 9250.] [34] Jephthah came to Mizpeh unto his house, and, behold, his daughter came out to meet him with timbrels and with dances : and she *was his* only child.. [35]..he rent his clothes, and said, Alas, my daughter ! thou hast brought me very low.—Judges, ch. 11.

9254. —— **A Teetotaler's.** *Nazarene.* [2] When he shall vow a vow.. [3] He shall separate *himself* from wine and strong drink, and shall drink no vinegar of wine, or vinegar of strong drink, neither shall he drink any liquor of grapes, nor eat moist grapes, or dried.—Num., ch. 6.

See other illustrations under :

9255. WAGES, Back. *Collected.* [21] When ye go, ye shall not go empty : [22] But every woman shall borrow of her neighbour, and of her that sojourneth in her house, jewels of silver, and jewels of gold, and raiment.—Ex., ch. 3.

9256. —— **changed.** *Jacob's.* [6] Ye know that with all my power I have served your father. [7] And your father hath deceived me, and changed my wages ten times ; but God suffered him not to hurt me.—Gen., ch. 29.

9257. —— **Daily.** *Law.* [13] Thou shalt not defraud thy neighbour, neither rob *him* : the wages of him that is hired shall not abide with thee all night until the morning.—Lev., ch. 19.

9258. —— —— *Needed.* [15] At his day thou shalt give *him* his hire, neither shall the sun go down upon it ; for he *is* poor, and setteth his heart upon it : lest he cry against thee unto the Lord, and it be sin unto thee.—Deut., ch. 24.

9259. —— **of Others.** *"They murmured."* [12] These last have wrought *but* one hour, and thou hast made them equal unto us, which have borne the burden and heat of the day.— Mat., ch. 20.

9260. —— **unimportant.** *Moses' Mother.* [9] Pharaoh's daughter said..Take this child away, and nurse it for me, and I will give *thee* thy wages. And the woman took the child, and nursed it.—Ex., ch. 2.

9261. —— **withheld.** *Sin.* [4] Behold, the hire of the labourers who have reaped down your fields, which is of you kept back by fraud, crieth : and the cries of them which have reaped are entered into the ears of the Lord of Sabaoth. —James, ch. 5.

Also see :

9262. WAITING for Calamity. *Nineveh.* [6] Jonah went out of the city, and sat on the east side of the city, and there made him a booth, and sat under it in the shadow, till he might see what would become of the city.—Jonah, ch. 4.

9263. —— **Eager.** *Soul.* [5] I wait for the Lord, my soul doth wait, and in his word do I hope. [6] My soul *waiteth* for the Lord more than they that watch for the morning.—Ps. 130.

9264. —— **in Faith.** *Abraham.* [From his seventy-fifth to his one hundredth year.] [5] Look now toward heaven, and all the stars, if thou be able to number them : and he said unto him. So shall thy seed be. [6] And he believed in the Lord ; and he counted it to him for righteousness.—Gen., ch. 15.

9265. —— **on God.** *Eagles.* [31] They that

wait upon the Lord shall renew *their* strength ; they shall mount up with wings as eagles ; they shall run, and not be weary ; *and* they shall walk, and not faint.—ISA., ch. 40.

9266. —— **A long.** *Bethesda.* ⁵ A certain man was there, which had an infirmity thirty and eight years. ⁶ When Jesus saw him lie, and knew that . . he saith unto him, Wilt thou be made whole ?—JOHN, ch. 5.

9267. —— **Patient.** *Noah.* [After a year was past.] ¹⁵ God spake unto Noah, saying, ¹⁶ Go forth of the ark.—GEN., ch. 8.

9268. —— **for Power.** *Pentecost.* ⁴ Commanded them that they should not depart from Jerusalem, but wait for the promise of the Father.—ACTS, ch. 1.

9269. —— **rewarded.** *Simeon.* ²⁵ Waiting for the consolation of Israel : and the Holy Ghost was upon him . . ²⁸ Then took he him up in his arms, and blessed God, and said, ²⁹ Lord, now lettest thou thy servant depart in peace, according to thy word : ³⁰ For mine eyes have seen thy salvation.—LUKE, ch. 2.

9270. —— **Vigilant.** *"Lamps burning."* ³⁵ Let your loins be girded about, and *your* lights burning : ³⁶ And ye yourselves like unto men that wait for their lord, when he will return from the wedding.—LUKE, ch. 12.

9271. —— **Weariness from.** *Absalom said,* ³² Wherefore am I come from Geshur? *it had been* good for me *to have been* there still : now therefore let me see the king's face ; and if there be *any* iniquity in me, let him kill me.— 2 SAM., ch. 14.

9272. —— **and Watching.** *Abraham.* ¹⁰ He took unto him all these, and divided them in the midst, and laid each piece one against another : but the birds divided he not. ¹¹ And when the fowls came down upon the carcasses, Abram drove them away.—GEN., ch. 15.

9273. —— **for Work.** *Eighty Years.* ²⁹ Then fled Moses at this saying, and was a stranger in the land of Midian, where he begat two sons. ³⁰ And when forty years were expired, there appeared to him in the wilderness of mount Sinai an angel of the Lord.—ACTS, ch. 7.

See DELAY *and references.*

9274. WALK consecrated. *"Feet."* ²⁴ He brought Aaron's sons, and Moses put of the blood upon the tip of their right ear, and upon the thumbs of their right hands, and upon the great toes of their right feet.—LEV., ch. 8.

9275. —— **A holy.** *Enoch.* ²² Enoch walked with God after he begat Methuselah three hundred years . . ²⁴ And Enoch walked with God : and he *was* not : for God took him.—GEN., ch. 5.

9276. —— **A perfect.** *Noah.* ⁹ Noah was a just man *and* perfect in his generations, *and* Noah walked with God.—GEN., ch. 6.

9277. —— **Saintly.** *Duty.* ⁸ He hath shewed thee, O man, what *is* good ; and what doth the Lord require of thee, but to do justly, and to love mercy, and to walk humbly with thy God?—MICAH, ch. 6.

See other illustrations under :

CONDUCT.

Disposition. Samaritan had compassion   1467
Observed. David behaved himself . . much set by   1468
Strange. Turned aside quickly . . calf and worship it 1469

FEET.

Consecrated. Moses put of the blood . . on the great 3200
Hallowing. Put off thy shoes . . the place . . is holy   3201

Runner. Asahel was as light of foot as a wild roe 7482
Travellers. Eat it with your loins girded, your s.   8883
See WANDERING.

9278. WANDERER compassionated. *At Corinth.* ⁶ Sufficient to such a man *is* this punishment, which *was inflicted* of many. ⁷ So that contrariwise ye *ought* rather to forgive *him*, and comfort *him*, lest perhaps such a one should be swallowed up with overmuch sorrow.—2 COR., ch. 2.

9279. —— **restored, A.** *Peter.* ¹⁷ Peter was grieved because he said unto him the third time, Lovest thou me? And he said unto him, Lord, thou knowest all things ; thou knowest that I love thee. Jesus saith unto him, Feed my sheep.—JOHN, ch. 21.

9280. WANDERERS, Invitation to. *"Return."* ⁷ Even from the days of your fathers ye are gone away from mine ordinances, and have not kept them. Return unto me, and I will return unto you, saith the Lord of hosts. But ye said, Wherein shall we return ?—MAL., ch. 3.

9281. —— **Search for the.** *Wilderness.* ⁴ What man of you, having a hundred sheep, if he lose one of them, doth not leave the ninety and nine in the wilderness, and go after that which is lost, until he find it ?—LUKE, ch. 15.

9282. —— **Wicked.** *Immoral.* ⁵ I will come near to you to judgment ; and I will be a swift witness against the sorcerers, and against the adulterers, and against false swearers, and against those that oppress the hireling in *his* wages, the widow, and the fatherless.—MAL., ch. 3.

9283. WANDERING corrected. *Afflictions.* ⁶⁷ Before I was afflicted I went astray : but now have I kept thy word.—Ps. 119.

9284. —— **Folly of.** *Sheep.* ¹⁷⁶ I have gone astray like a lost sheep : seek thy servant ; for I do not forget thy commandments.—Ps. 119.

9285. —— **Unsatisfied.** *Dove.* ⁹ The dove found no rest for the sole of her foot, and she returned unto him into the ark, for the waters *were* on the face of the whole earth.—GEN., ch. 8.

Also see :
Faith in. Micah consecrated the Levite . . his priest 1519
See BACKSLIDING *and references.*

9286. WANT made a Blessing. *Prodigal.* ¹⁶ He would fain have filled his belly with the husks that the swine did eat : and no man gave unto him. ¹⁷ And when he came to himself, he said, How many hired servants of my father's have bread enough and to spare, and I perish with hunger ! ¹⁸ I will arise and go to my father. —LUKE, ch. 15.

9287. —— **Contentment in.** *Paul.* ¹¹ Not that I speak in respect of want : for I have learned, in whatsoever state I am, *therewith* to be content. ¹² I know both how to be abased, and I know how to abound.—PHIL., ch. 4.

9288. —— **Degraded by.** *At Samaria.* ²⁹ So we boiled my son, and did eat him : and I said unto her on the next day, Give thy son, that we many eat him : and she hath hid her son.—2 KINGS, ch. 6.

9289. —— **Frivolity brings.** *Proverb.* ¹⁹ He

that tilleth his land shall have plenty of bread :
but he that followeth after vain *persons* shall
have poverty enough.—Prov., ch. 28.

9290. —— **near Luxury.** *Parable.* [19] There
was a certain rich man, which was clothed in
purple and fine linen, and fared sumptuously
every day : [20] And there was a certain beggar
named Lazarus, which was laid at his gate full
of sores.—Luke, ch. 16.

9291. —— **to Plenty, From.** *Four Lepers.*
[8] When these lepers came to the uttermost part
of the camp, they went into one tent, and did
eat and drink, and carried thence silver, and
gold, and raiment, and went and hid *it ;* and
came again, and entered into another tent, and
carried thence *also*, and went and hid *it.*—2
Kings, ch. 7.

9292. —— **Sin brings.** *Proverb.* [26] By means
of a whorish woman *a man is brought* to a piece
of bread : and the adulteress will hunt for the
precious life.—Prov., ch. 6.

9293. WANTING, Weighed and. *Belshazzar.*
[5] In the same hour came forth fingers of a man's
hand, and wrote over against the candlestick
upon the plaster of the wall of the king's palace..
[27] TEKEL ; Thou art weighed in the balances,
and art found wanting.—Dan., ch. 5.

9294. WANTS, The higher. *Jesus said,*
[22] Take no thought for your life, what ye shall
eat ; neither for the body, what ye shall put on.
[23] The life is more than meat, and the body *is*
more than raiment.—Luke, ch. 12.

9295. —— **provided for.** *Food.* [24] Consider
the ravens : for they neither sow nor reap ;
which neither have storehouse nor barn ; and
God feedeth them : how much more are ye better than the fowls?—Luke, ch. 12.

9296. —— —— *Clothing.* [27] Consider the
lilies how they grow : they toil not, they spin
not ; and..Solomon in all his glory was not arrayed like one of these. [28] If then God so clothe
the grass, which is to day in the field, and to
morrow is cast into the oven ; how much more
will he clothe you, O ye of little faith?—Luke,
ch. 12.

9297. —— **supplied.** *Christians.* [32] Neither
said any *of them* that aught of the things which
he possessed was his own, but they had all things
common. [34] Neither was there any among them
that lacked.—Acts, ch. 4.

See other illustrations under :

DESTITUTION.
Physical. In hunger and thirst..in cold and n.   2246
Pastoral. Jesus was moved .sheep not having a   2247
Religious. For a long season I..without the true G. 2248

FAMINE.
Charity. Disciples determined to send relief   3023
Care. Shall eat bread by weight..water by w.   3024
Dying. Eaten no bread..three days..sick   3025
Distress. Delicate woman..children..eat them   3026
Exiled. Sojourn wherever thou canst..seven yrs.   2027
Escape. Abram went down into Egypt..famine   3028
Emigration. Elimelech went to sojourn in..famine   3029
Inhumanity. Give thy son, that we may eat him   3030
Sin. I will break the staff of bread   3031
  " Ye have forsaken the..L. and followed B.   3032
Seven Years. No bread..land of Canaan fainted   3033
Spiritual. I will send a famine..words of the L.   3034
Water. To kill us and our children..cattle   3035

NEEDS.
Clothing. God made coats of skins and clothed t.   5692
The One. But one thing is needful   5693
Supply of. I will rain bread from heaven [manna]   5694
  " " Your father knoweth that ye have n.   5695

9298. WAR a lost Art. *Messiah.* [4] He shall
judge among the nations..and they shall beat
their swords into ploughshares, and their spears
into pruninghooks : nation shall not lift up
sword against nation, neither shall they learn
war any more.—Isa., ch. 2.

9299. —— **Art aids.** *Canaanites.* [19] Judah
could not drive out the inhabitants of the valley,
because they had chariots of iron.—Judges, ch. 1.

9300. —— **Civilized.** *Fruit Trees.* [20] Only
the trees which thou knowest that they *be* not
trees for meat, thou shalt destroy and cut them
down ; and thou shalt build bulwarks against
the city that maketh war with thee, until it be
subdued.—Deut., ch. 21.

9301. —— **Challenge of.** *By Jehu.* [2] As
soon as this letter cometh to you, seeing your
master's sons *are* with you, and *there are* with
you chariots and horses, a fenced city also, and
armour ; [3] Look even out the best and meetest
of your master's sons, and set *him* on his father's
throne, and fight for your master's house.—2
Kings, ch. 10.

9302. —— **Dishonoured by.** *David.* [8] Thou
hast shed blood abundantly, and hast made
great wars : thou shalt not build a house unto
my name, because thou hast shed much blood
upon the earth in my sight.—1 Chron., ch. 22.

9303. —— **Exempt from.** *Housebuilders.*
[5] What man *is there* that hath built a new house,
and hath not dedicated it? let him go and return to his house, lest he die in the battle, and
another man dedicate it.—Deut., ch. 20.

9304. —— —— *Cowards.* [8] The officers
shall speak further unto the people..What man
is there that is fearful and fainthearted? let him
go and return unto his house, lest his brethren's
heart faint as well as his heart.—Deut., ch. 20.

9305. —— —— *Betrothed.* [7] What man *is*
there that hath betrothed a wife, and hath not
taken her? let him go and return unto his
house, lest he die in the battle, and another man
take her.—Deut., ch. 20.

9306. —— **Equipment for.** *Spiritual.* [11] Put
on the whole armour of God, that ye may be
able to stand against the wiles of the devil.—
Eph., ch. 6. [See chapter.]

9307. —— **with the Flesh.** *Spiritual.* [23] I
see another law in my members, warring against
the law of my mind, and bringing me into captivity to the law of sin which is in my members.
—Rom., ch. 7.

9308. —— **from Insult.** *To Messengers.*
[4] Hanun took David's servants, and shaved off
the one half of their beards, and cut off their
garments in the middle, *even* to their buttocks,
and sent them away.. [7] And when David heard
of *it*, he sent Joab, and all the host of the
mighty men.—2 Sam., ch. 10.

9309. —— **Levied for.** *Twelve Thousand.*
[3] Moses spake..Arm some of yourselves unto
the war, and let them go against the Midianites,
and avenge the Lord of Midian. [4] Of every
tribe a thousand, throughout all the tribes of
Israel, shall ye send to the war.—Num., ch. 31.

9310. —— **Lord in the.** *At Jericho.* [13] There stood a man over against him with his sword drawn in his hand : and Joshua went unto him, and said. . *Art* thou for us, or for our adversaries ? [14] And he said, Nay ; but *as* captain of the host of the Lord am I now come.—Josh., ch. 5.

9311. —— **Merciless.** *Chaldees.* [17] Therefore he brought upon them the king of the Chaldees, who slew their young men with the sword in the house of their sanctuary, and had no compassion upon young man or maiden, old man, or him that stooped for age.—2 Chron., ch. 36.

9312. —— **necessary.** *Reproach.* [1] The men of Jabesh said unto Nahash, Make a covenant with us, and we will serve thee. [2] . .answered them, On this *condition* will I make *a covenant* with you, that I may thrust out all your right eyes, and lay it *for* a reproach upon all Israel.— 1 Sam., ch. 11.

9313. —— **Prayer in.** *"Helped."* [20] They were helped against them, and the Hagarites were delivered into their hand, and all that *were* with them : for they cried to God in the battle, and he was entreated of them ; because they put their trust in him.—1 Chron., ch. 5.

9314. —— **Ruin by.** *Of Moabites.* [25] They beat down the cities, and on every good piece of land cast every man his stone, and filled it ; and they stopped all the wells of water, and felled all the good trees.—2 Kings, ch. 3.

9315. —— **Readiness for.** *Jabin.* [2] The Lord sold them into the hand of Jabin king of Canaan. . the captain of whose host *was* Sisera. . [3] And the children of Israel cried unto the Lord : for he had nine hundred chariots of iron. —Judges, ch. 4.

9316. WARFARE of the Truth. *Variance.* [34] Think not that I am come to send peace on earth : I am come not to send peace, but a sword. [35] For I am come to set a man at variance against his father, and the daughter against her mother. —Mat., ch. 10.

See other illustrations under :

ARMOUR.

Defenceless. [Goliath] had a helmet of brass	494
Rejected. David girded his sword. . I cannot go w.	495
Without. Neither sword nor spear. . land of I.	496

ARMY.

Great. [Uzziah's army] 37,500 men	497
Impressed. When Saul saw any strong man, he t.	498
Strange. Every one. . in distress, debt, discontent	499
Standing. Saul chose 3000. . the rest. . his tent	500
Scattered. [Zedekiah's] Chaldees pursued. . army	501

BATTLE.

Ambuscade. Beware thou pass not such a place	334
Disarmed. No smith. . lest Hebrews make swords	643
Hailstones. L. cast great stones from heaven	645
Lord's. When thou seest chariots, be not afraid	646
" L. saveth not with sword and spear	647
Needless. Need not to fight. . stand still and see	644
Prayer. They cried to God in the battle	648

CAPTIVES.

Compassion. I have heard. . groaning. . bondage	1022
Kindness. Gave them to eat. . feeble upon asses	1024
Mercy. Shalt not smite. . set bread. . go	1025
Mourning. By the rivers of Babylon. . we wept	1026
Songless. How shall we sing. . strange land	1027
Return. Come to Zion with songs. . joy and g.	1028

Sin. Walked in the sins of. . until removed	1029
" L. strengthened. . Moab against I. . done evil	1030
Unexpected. David and his men. . wives. . captives	1031
Victorious. Found a jawbone. . slew 1000 men	1032

FIGHTING.

Forbidden. Ye shall not fight your brethren. . I.	3217
God. Mountain was full of chariots. . fire	3218
for Jesus. Drew his sword, and struck a servant	3219

HEROISM.

Christian. Bonds. . abide me. . none of these things	3959
Needless. Three mighty men brake through. . well	3961
Numbers. Shamgar slew 600 with an ox-goad	3962
Patriotic. Jael. . smote the nail into his. . temples	3957
" Woman cast a stone upon Abimelech	3958

INSUBORDINATION.

Intimidating. He could not answer Abner a word	4773
Soldier's. To translate the kingdom from. . Saul	4774

MIGHTY MEN.

Adino. Mighty men whom David had. . chief	5332
Abishai. Chief among the three. . against 300. . slew	5336
Benaiah. Slew the lion-like men of Moab	5337
Eliezer. Smote the Philistines. . hand clave to his	5333
Shammah. Stood in the midst. . slew the Philistines	5334
Three. Brake through the host of the Philistines	5335

SOLDIER.

Brave. Jonathan climbed up. . his armourbearer	8161
Christian. Endure hardness as a good soldier of	8162
Magnanimous. Men of David said. . enemy in thine	8163
Pious. Cornelius, a centurion. . prayed to G. always	8164
" Joshua. . departed not from the tabernacle	8165
Pride. Abimelech. . say not of me, A woman slew	8166
Volunteer. I thy servant will go and fight this P.	8167

SWORD.

Flaming. Drove out the man. . flaming sword w.	8531
Lord's. They cried, The sword of the L. and G.	8532
Memorial. Sword of Goliath. . wrapped in a cloth	8533
Ominous. David saw the angel. . a drawn sword	8534
" Man against Joshua with a drawn s.	8535
Punishment. Ye have feared the sword, I will b.	8536
Rejected. Put up. . sword in his place. . perish with	8537
of the Spirit. Take. . the sword of the S. . the word	8538
Outfit. Word. . is sharper than any two-edged s.	8539
Tongue. Whose teeth are spears. . tongue a sharp	8540
" There is that speaketh like the piercing	8541

WEAPONS.

Faith. David chose him five smooth stones	9443
Rejected. Saul armed David. . helmet. . coat of	9444

Benaiah. Plucked the spear out of the Egyptian's	1543
Captains. [See Abner, Abishai, and Joab—1 and 2 Sam.]	
Divine. L. is my rock. . fortress. . high tower	1535
Faith. He took his staff. . five smooth stones	9443
Shield. Above all, taking the shield of faith	8669
Useless. Peter. . smote the high priest's servant	918

See VICTORY and references.

9317. WARNING of Destruction. *"Calamity."* [24] Because I have called, and ye refused ; I have stretched out my hand, and no man regarded ; [25] But ye have set at nought all my counsel, and would none of my reproof : [26] I also will laugh at your calamity ; I will mock when your fear cometh.—Prov., ch. 1.

9318. —— **by Dream.** *Pilate's Wife.* [19] When he was set down on the judgment seat, his wife sent unto him, saying, Have thou nothing to do with that just man : for I have suffered many things this day in a dream because of him.— Mat., ch. 27.

9319. —— **of Danger.** *By Elisha.* [8] King of Syria warred against Israel, and took counsel with his servants, saying, In such and such a place *shall be* my camp. [9] And the man of God sent unto the king of Israel, saying, Beware that thou pass not such a place ; for thither the Syrians are come down.—2 KINGS, ch. 6.

9320. —— **despised.** *Sodomites.* [14] Lot went out, and spake unto his sons in law..Up, get you out of this place ; for the Lord will destroy this city. But he seemed as one that mocked unto his sons in law.—GEN., ch. 19.

9321. —— **of Disobedience.** *Moses.* [17] If thine heart turn away, so that thou wilt not hear, but shalt be drawn away, and worship other gods, and serve them ; [18] I denounce unto you this day, that ye shall surely perish. –DEUT., ch. 30.

9322. —— **doubted.** *Peter.* [33] Peter answered and said unto him, Though all *men* shall be offended because of thee, *yet* will I never be offended.—MAT., ch. 26.

9323. —— **by Example.** *Sodom.* [7] Sodom and Gomorrah and the cities about them, in like manner giving themselves over to fornication, and going after strange flesh, are set forth for an example, suffering the vengeance of eternal fire.—JUDE.

9324. —— —— *Lot's Wife.* [32] Remember Lot's wife.—LUKE, ch. 17.

9325. —— **from Experience.** *Paul.* [14] Alexander the coppersmith did me much evil : the Lord reward him according to his works : [15] Of whom be thou ware also ; for he hath greatly withstood our words.—2 TIM., ch. 4.

9326. —— **Faithful.** *Ephesians.* [31] Watch, and remember, that by the space of three years I ceased not to warn every one night and day with tears.—ACTS, ch. 20.

9327. —— **Heedless.** *Sword.* [4] Whosoever heareth the sound of the trumpet, and taketh not warning ; if the sword come, and take him away, his blood shall be upon his own head.—EZEK., ch. 33.

9328. —— **heeded.** *Noah.* [7] By faith Noah, being warned of God of things not seen as yet, moved with fear, prepared an ark to the saving of his house.—HEB., ch. 11.

9329. —— **from History.** *Israelites.* [6] These things were our examples, to the intent we should not lust after evil things, as they also lusted. [7] Neither be ye idolaters, as *were* some of them.—1 COR., ch. 10. [See chapter.]

9330. —— —— *Solomon.* [25] Ye shall not give your daughters unto their sons, nor take their daughters unto your sons, or for yourselves. [26] Did not Solomon king of Israel sin by these things ?—NEH., ch. 13.

9331. —— **ignored.** *Asahel.* [19] Asahel pursued after Abner ; and in going he turned not to the right hand nor to the left from following Abner.. [22] And Abner said again to Asahel, Turn thee aside from following me : wherefore should I smite thee to the ground ? how then should I hold up my face to Joab thy brother ? [23] Howbeit he refused to turn aside : wherefore Abner with the hinder end of the spear smote him under the fifth *rib*.—2 SAM., ch. 2.

9332. —— **Punishment a.** *Miriam.* [10] Miriam *became* leprous, *white* as snow : and Aaron looked upon Miriam, and, behold, *she was* leprous. —NUM., ch. 12. [Nearly forty years later Moses said,] [9] Remember what the Lord thy God did unto Miriam by the way.—DEUT., ch. 24.

9333. —— **Preserved by.** *Jesus.* [13] The angel of the Lord appeareth to Joseph in a dream, saying, Arise, and take the young child and his mother, and flee into Egypt..for Herod will seek the young child to destroy him.—MAT., ch. 2.

9334. —— **Personal.** *To Peter.* [34] Jesus said unto him, Verily, I say unto thee, That this night, before the cock crow, thou shalt deny me thrice. [35] Peter said unto him, Though I should die with thee, yet will not I deny thee. Likewise also said all the disciples.—MAT., ch. 26.

9335. —— **repeated.** *At Sinai.* [20] And the Lord called Moses *up* to the top of the mount.. [21] And the Lord said unto Moses, Go down, charge the people, lest they break through unto the Lord to gaze, and many of them perish.—EX., ch. 19.

9336. —— **Saved by.** *"Taketh."* [5] He heard the sound of the trumpet, and took not warning ; his blood shall be upon him. But he that taketh warning shall deliver his soul.—EZEK., ch. 33.

9337. —— **A solemn.** *Last Supper.* [31] All ye shall be offended because of me this night : for it is written, I will smite the Shepherd, and the sheep of the flock shall be scattered abroad.—MAT., ch. 26.

9338. —— **A sorrowful.** *Betrayal.* [21] As they did eat, he said, Verily I say unto you, that one of you shall betray me. [22] And they were exceeding sorrowful, and began every one of them to say unto him, Lord, is it I ?—MAT., ch. 26.

9339. —— **The Wicked a.** *"Sign."* [9] Dathan and Abiram.. [10]..the earth opened her mouth, and swallowed them up together with Korah, when that company died, what time the fire devoured two hundred and fifty men : and they became a sign.—NUM., ch. 26.

9340. WARNINGS, Additional. *From Heaven.* [27] I pray thee therefore, father, that thou wouldest send him to my father's house : [28] For I have five brethren ; that he may testify unto them, lest they also come into this place of torment.—LUKE, ch. 16.

See other illustrations under :

VIGILANCE.

Christian. Watch..Master..cometh		9216
Necessary. Not found thy works perfect		9217
Uncertainty. If..not watch..will come as a thief		9218

See ADMONITION and references.

9341. WASTE, Complaint of. *Disciples.* [4] Why was this waste of the ointment made ? [5] For it might have been sold for more than three hundred pence, and have been given to the poor. And they murmured against her.—MARK, ch. 14.

Also see :

by Economy. New wine..in old bottles..spilled		1555
Prodigality. Wasted his substance with riotous		6625
" Earneth wages..put in a bag..holes		2616

See ECONOMY.

9342. WATCHING, Affectionate. *Miriam.* [3] Put the child therein ; and she laid *it* in the flags by the river's brink. [4] And his sister stood afar off, to wit what would be done to him.—EX., ch. 2.

9343. —— **Constant.** *Lord cometh.* [42] Watch therefore ; for ye know not what hour your Lord doth come. [43] But know this, that if the good-man of the house had known in what watch the thief would come, he would have watched, and would not have suffered his house to be broken up.—MAT., ch. 24.

9344. —— **the Dead.** *Rizpah.* [10] Rizpah.. took sackcloth, and spread it for her upon the rock, from the beginning of harvest until water dropped upon them out of heaven, and suffered neither the birds of the air to rest on them by day, nor the beasts of the field by night.—2 SAM., ch. 21.

9345. —— **Failure in.** *Gethsemane.* [39] O my Father, if it be possible, let this cup pass from me : nevertheless, not as I will, but as thou *wilt.* [40] And he cometh unto the disciples, and findeth them asleep, and saith unto Peter, What, could ye not watch with me one hour ?—MAT., ch. 26.

9346. —— **Hinderances to.** *Cares.* [34] Take heed to yourselves, lest at any time your hearts be overcharged with surfeiting, and drunkenness, and cares of this life, and *so* that day come upon you unawares.—LUKE, ch. 21.

9347. —— **Malicious.** *Pharisees.* [1] He entered again into the synagogue ; and there was a man there which had a withered hand. [2] And they watched him, whether he would heal him on the sabbath day ; that they might accuse him. —MARK, ch. 3.

9348. —— **with Prayer.** *Abram's Sacrifice.* [11] And when the fowls came down upon the carcasses, Abram drove them away.—GEN., ch. 15.

9349. —— —— *Wall-builders.* [9] Nevertheless we made our prayer unto our God, and set a watch against them day and night, because of them.—NEH., ch. 4.

9350. —— —— *Anna.* [37] She *was* a widow of about fourscore and four years, which departed not from the temple, but served *God* with fastings and prayers night and day.—LUKE, ch. 2.

9351. —— —— *Jesus.* [12] In those days.. he went out into a mountain to pray, and continued all night in prayer to God.—LUKE, ch. 6.

9352. —— **Vigilant.** *Master.* [35] Watch ye therefore : for ye know not when the master of the house cometh, at even, or at midnight, or at the cockcrowing, or in the morning : [36] Lest coming suddenly he find you sleeping.—MARK, ch. 13.

9353. —— **and watched.** *Witnesses.* [1] Seeing we also are compassed about with so great a cloud of witnesses, let us lay aside every weight, and the sin which doth so easily beset *us,* and let us run with patience the race that is set before us.—HEB., ch. 12.

9354. —— **The World's.** *"Observed."* [20] Herod feared John, knowing that he was a just man and a holy, and observed him ; and when he heard him, he did many things, and heard him gladly.—MARK, ch. 6.

9355. WATCHFULNESS, Lack of. *Foolish Virgins.* [7] Then all those virgins arose, and trimmed their lamps. [8] And the foolish said unto the wise, Give us of your oil ; for our lamps are gone out.—MAT., ch. 25.

9356. —— **Necessary.** *Adversary.* [8] Be sober, be vigilant ; because your adversary the devil, as a roaring lion, walketh about, seeking whom he may devour : [9] Whom resist steadfast in the faith.—1 PETER, ch. 5.

9357. —— **Personal.** *"Own House."* [3] Let not the gates of Jerusalem be opened until the sun be hot ; and while they stand by, let them shut the doors, and bar *them:* and appoint watchers of the inhabitants of Jerusalem, every one in his watch, and every one *to be* over against his house—NEH., ch. 7.

9358. —— **rewarded.** *"Blessed."* [37] Blessed *are* those servants, whom the lord when he cometh shall find watching : verily I say unto you, that he shall gird himself, and make them to sit down to meat, and will come forth and serve them.—LUKE, ch. 12.

See other illustrations under :

FIDELITY.

Required. Oughtest to have put my money to the 3214
Tested. Yielded their bodies..might not..any god 3215
Want of. Take thy bill..quickly write fifty 3216

Guard. Flaming sword..tree of life 3754
Ludicrous. Found keepers standing before the d. 275
Omitted. Amasa took no heed to the sword..in 523

9359. WATCH - NIGHT Meeting. *At Troy.* [7] Paul preached unto them, ready to depart on the morrow ; and continued his speech until midnight.—ACTS, ch. 20.

9360. WATER, Bitter. *Marah.* [23] When they came to Marah, they could not drink of the waters of Marah, for they *were* bitter.. [25].. Lord shewed him a tree, *which* when he had cast into the waters, the waters were made sweet.—EX., ch. 15.

9361. —— **Choice.** *Beth-lehem.* [15] David longed, and said, Oh that one would give me drink of the water of the well of Beth-lehem, which *is* by the gate !—2 SAM., ch. 23.

9362. —— **Famine, A.** *"No Water."* [3] Their nobles have sent their little ones to the waters : they came to the pits, *and* found no water ; they returned with their vessels empty ; they were ashamed and confounded, and covered their heads.—JER., ch. 14.

9363. —— —— *Relieved.* [6] I will stand before thee there upon the rock in Horeb ; and thou shalt smite the rock, and there shall come water out of it, that the people may drink.— EX., ch. 17.

9364. —— —— *At Kadesh.* [10] Moses and Aaron gathered the congregation together before the rock, and he said unto them, Hear now, ye rebels ; must we fetch you water out of this rock ? [11] And Moses lifted up his hand, and with his rod he smote the rock twice : and the water came out abundantly.—NUM., ch. 20.

9365. —— **Gift of.** *Disciple.* [42] Whosoever shall give to drink unto one of these little ones a cup of cold *water* only in the name of a disciple, verily I say unto you, he shall in no wise lose his reward.—MAT., ch. 10.

9366. —— **of Humiliation.** *"Drink it."* [20] He took the calf which they had made, and burnt *it* in the fire, and ground *it* to powder, and strewed *it* upon the water, and made the children of Israel drink *of it.*—EX., ch. 32.

9367. —— **improved.** *At Jericho.* [21] He went forth unto the spring of the waters, and cast the salt in there, and said, Thus saith the Lord, I have healed these waters ; there shall not be from thence any more death or barren *land.*—2 Kings, ch. 2.

9368. —— **Living.** *At Jacob's Well.* [14] Whosoever drinketh of the water that I shall give him shall never thirst ; but the water that I shall give him shall be in him a well of water springing up into everlasting life.—John, ch. 4.

9369. —— **by Measure.** *Scarcity.* [16] Son of man, behold, I will break the staff of bread in Jerusalem : and they shall eat bread by weight, and with care ; and they shall drink water by measure, and with astonishment.—Ezek., ch. 4.

9370. —— **Perishing for.** *Ishmael.* [14] She departed, and wandered in the wilderness of Beer-sheba. [15] And the water was spent in the bottle, and she cast the child under one of the shrubs.—Gen., ch. 21.

9371. —— **Saved from.** *Moses.* [10] Pharaoh's daughter, and he became her son. And she called his name Moses : and she said, Because I drew him out of the water.—Ex., ch. 2.

9372. —— **Invisible Supplies of.** *Elisha said,* [16] Thus saith the Lord, Make this valley full of ditches. [17] For thus saith the Lord, Ye shall not see wind, neither shall ye see rain ; yet that valley shall be filled with water, that ye may drink, both ye, and your cattle, and your beasts. —2 Kings, ch. 3.

9373. —— **Spiritual.** *"Rivers."* [37] In the.. great *day* of the feast, Jesus stood and cried, saying, If any man thirst, let him come unto me, and drink. [38] He that believeth on me, as the Scripture hath said, out of his belly shall flow rivers of living water.—John, ch. 7.

9374. —— **Walls of.** *Red Sea.* [22] The children of Israel went into the midst of the sea upon the dry *ground :* and the waters *were* a wall unto them on their right hand, and on their left.—Ex., ch. 14.

9375. —— **made Wine.** *At Cana.* [9] When the ruler of the feast had tasted the water that was made wine, and knew not whence it was, (but the servants which drew the water knew,) the governor of the feast called the bridegroom, [10] And saith unto him, Every man at the beginning doth set forth good wine ; and when men have well drunk, then that which is worse : *but* thou hast kept the good wine until now.—John, ch. 2.

9376. —— **Walking on.** *Christ.* [49] When they saw him walking upon the sea, they supposed it had been a spirit, and cried out : [50] For they all saw him, and were troubled..saith unto them, Be of good cheer : it is I ; be not afraid. —Mark, ch. 6.

9377. —— —— **Peter.** [29] He said, Come.. Peter..walked on the water, to go to Jesus. [30] But when he saw the wind boisterous, he was afraid ; and beginning to sink, he cried, saying, Lord, save me.—Mat., ch. 14.

9378. WATER-CURE, A marvellous. *Bethesda.* [4] An angel went down at a certain season into the pool, and troubled the water : whosoever then first after the troubling of the water stepped in was made whole of whatsoever disease he had.—John, ch. 5.

9379. WATERS, Increase of. *Vision.* [4] Again he measured a thousand, and brought me through the waters ; the waters *were* to the knees. Again he measured a thousand, and brought me through ; the waters *were* to the loins. [5] Afterward he measured a thousand ; *and it was* a river that I could not pass over : for the waters were risen, waters to swim in, a river that could not be passed over.—Ezek., ch. 47.

9380. WATERING-PLACE, A religious. *Enon.* [23] John also was baptizing in Enon near to Salim, because there was much water there : and they came, and were baptized.—John, ch. 3.

See other illustrations under·
RIVER.
First. A river went out of Eden..four heads		7453
Life. Clear as crystal..out of the throne of G.		7454
"　There is a river..make glad the city of G.		7455
Salvation. Waters were to the ankles..knees..loins		7456

See RAIN.

9381. WAVERING, Religious. *"Looking back."* [61] Lord, I will follow thee ; but let me first go bid them farewell, which are at home at my house. [62] And Jesus said unto him, No man having put his hand to the plough, and looking back, is fit for the kingdom of God.—Luke, ch. 9.

See other illustrations under:
FICKLENESS.
Burdensome. Ye have wept..was well with us in	3211
Purpose. No root in themselves..are offended	3212
Superstitious. The gods are come..stoned Paul	3213

HESITATION.
Discipleship. I will follow thee, but	3964
Punished. Fire of the L. burnt..uttermost parts	3965

Sad. Pilate sought to release..delivered he him　　4662

9382. WAY of Deliverance. *Red Sea.* [21] The Lord caused the sea to go *back* by a strong east wind all that night, and made the sea dry *land,* and the waters were divided. [22] And the children of Israel went into the midst of the sea upon the dry *ground :* and the waters *were* a wall unto them on their right hand, and on their left.—Ex., ch. 14.

9383. —— **A hidden.** *The Lord's.* [20] It came between the camp of the Egyptians and the camp of Israel ; and it was a cloud and darkness *to them,* but it gave light by night *to these :* so that the one came not near the other all the night.—Ex., ch. 14.

9384. —— **The Lord's.** *Considerate.* [17] When Pharaoh had let the people go..God led them not *through* the way of the land of the Philistines, although that *was* near ; for God said, Lest peradventure the people repent when they see war, and they return to Egypt.—Ex., ch. 13.

9385. —— —— **Differs.** [10] Elisha sent a messenger unto him, saying, Go and wash in Jordan seven times, and thy flesh shall come again to thee, and thou shalt be clean. [11] But Naaman was wroth, and went away, and said, Behold, I thought, He will surely come out to me, and stand, and call on the name of the Lord his God, and strike his hand over the place, and recover the leper.—2 Kings, ch. 5.

9386. —— —— **No Other.** [12] *Are* not Abana and Pharpar, rivers of Damascus, better than all the waters of Israel ? may I not wash in them, and be clean? So he turned and went away in a rage.—2 KINGS, ch. 5.

9387. —— —— *Simple.* [13] His servants.. said, My father, *if* the prophet had bid thee *do some* great thing, wouldest thou not have done *it?* how much rather then, when he saith to thee, Wash, and be clean.—2 KINGS, ch. 5.

9388. —— —— *Sure.* [14] Then went he down, and dipped himself seven times in Jordan, according to the saying of the man of God : and his flesh came again like unto the flesh of a little child, and he was clean.—2 KINGS, ch. 5.

9389. —— Man's. *Abraham.* [18] Abraham said unto God, O that Ishmael might live before thee !—GEN., ch. 17.

9390. —— of Transgressors. *Alarm.* [24] In the morning watch the Lord looked..through the pillar of fire and of the cloud, and troubled the host ot the Egyptians, [25] And took off their chariot wheels, that they drave them heavily : so that the Egyptians said, Let us flee from the face of Israel ; for the Lord fighteth for them.—Ex., ch. 14.

See WANDERING.

9391. WEAK, Care for the. "*Offend.*" [6] Whoso shall offend one of these little ones which believe in me, it were better for him that a millstone were hanged about his neck, and *that* he were drowned in the depth of the sea.—MAT., ch. 18.

9392. —— —— *Stumble.* [9] But take heed lest by any means this liberty of yours become a stumblingblock to them that are weak.—1 COR., ch. 8.

9393. —— Help for the. *The Ammonite.* [Eyes to be put out. See No. 9312.] [3] The elders of Jabesh said unto him, Give us seven days' respite, that we may send messengers unto all the coasts of Israel : and then, if *there* be no man to save us, we will come out to thee. —1 SAM., ch. 11. [Saul delivered them.]

9394. WEAKNESS of Believers. "*Babes.*" [1] I, brethren, could not speak unto you as unto spiritual, but as unto carnal, *even* as unto babes in Christ. [2] I have fed you with milk, and not with meat : for hitherto ye were not able *to bear it*, neither yet now are ye able.—1 COR., ch. 3.

9395. —— —— *Israelites.* [17] When Pharaoh had let the people go..God led them not *through* the way of the land of the Philistines, although that *was* near ; for God said, Lest peradventure the people repent when they see war, and they return to Egypt.—Ex., ch. 12.

9396. —— Conscious. *David.* [39] I *am* this day weak, though anointed king ; and these men the sons of Zeruiah *be* too hard for me : the Lord shall reward the doer of evil according to his wickedness.—2 SAM., ch. 3.

9397. —— of the Flesh. *Moses' Hands.* [12] Moses' hands *were* heavy ; and they took a stone, and put *it* under him, and he sat thereon ; and Aaron and Hur stayed up his hands, the one on the one side, and the other on the other side ; and his hands were steady until the going down of the sun.—Ex., ch. 17.

9398. —— of Instruments. *Lice—Flies.* [16] Say unto Aaron, Stretch out thy rod, and smite the dust of the land, that it may become lice throughout all the land of Egypt. [17] And they

did so ; for Aaron stretched out his hand with his rod, and smote the dust of the earth, and it became lice in man, and in beast ; all the dust of the land became lice.—Ex., ch. 8.

9399. —— Moral. *Peter.* [12] Before that certain came from James, he did eat with the Gentiles : but when they were come, he withdrew and separated himself, fearing them which were of the circumcision.—GAL., ch. 2.

9400. —— Personal. "*Do nothing.*" [5] I am the vine, ye *are* the branches. He that abideth in me, and I in him, the same bringeth forth much fruit ; for without me ye can do nothing. —JOHN, ch. 15.

9401. —— remembered. *Paul.* [3] I was with you in weakness, and in fear, and in much trembling.—1 COR., ch. 2.

9402. —— Submission from. *Ahab.* [2] Thus saith Ben-hadad, [3] Thy silver and thy gold *is* mine ; thy wives also and thy children, *even* the goodliest *are* mine. [4] And the king of Israel answered and said, My lord, O king, according to thy saying, I *am* thine, and all that I have.— 1 KINGS, ch. 20.

9403. —— Spiritless. *Fear.* [1] When all the kings of the Amorites, which *were* on the side of Jordan westward, and all the kings of the Canaanites, which *were* by the sea, heard that the Lord had dried up the waters of Jordan from before the children of Israel, until we were passed over..their heart melted, neither was there spirit in them any more.—JOSH., ch. 5.

9404. —— —— *Discouragement.* [5] The men of Ai smote of them about thirty and six men : for they chased them..and smote them in the going down : wherefore the hearts of the people melted, and became as water.—JOSH., ch. 7.

See other illustrations under:

Care. Brethren, comfort the feeble—1 Thess. 5 : 14.

Destroyed. Amalekites smote all..feeble—Deut. 25 : 18
Death. Abner dead, Ish-bosheth's..feeble—2 Sam. 4 : 1
Despised. What do these feeble Jews?   7429
Disqualifies. Any blemish let him not approach the 813
Exempt. Not one feeble person among their tribes 6723
Fear. Angel rolled back the stone..as dead men   261
One. One thing thou lackest..sell..give..cross   4876
"   When my master goeth..Rimmon to worship 3083
Overlooked. Jehu..thou hast done well..in part   4351
Tendency. People..set on mischief   8719
Weariness. Thou layest the burden of all..on me 9448
Without. Absalom..from the sole..without blemish 814

9405. WEALTH a Blessing. *To Laban.* [Abraham's servant said,] 35 The Lord hath blessed my master greatly, and he is become great : and he hath given him flocks, and herds, and silver, and gold, and menservants, and maidservants, and camels, and asses.—GEN., ch. 24.

9406. —— Contentment with. *A b r a m.* 22 Abram said to the king of Sodom, I have lifted up mine hand unto the Lord.. 23 That I will not *take* from a thread even to a shoelatchet, and that I will not take any thing that *is* thine, lest thou shouldest say, I have made Abram rich.— GEN., ch. 14.

9407. —— by Commerce. *Solomon.* 22 For the king had at sea a navy..once in three years came the navy of Tharshish, bringing gold, and silver, ivory, and apes, and peacocks. 23 So king Solomon exceeded all the kings of the earth for riches and for wisdom.—1 KINGS, ch. 10.

9408. —— at the Cross. *Joseph.* 57 When the even was come, there came a rich man of Arimathea, named Joseph, who also himself was Jesus' disciple : 58 He went to Pilate, and begged the body of Jesus.—MAT., ch. 27.

9409. —— in Cattle. *Reuben—Gad.* 1 The children of Reuben and the children of Gad had a very great multitude of cattle.—NUM., ch. 32.

9410. —— Covetous of. *Rich Fool.* 15 Beware of covetousness : for a man's life consisteth not in the abundance of the things which he possesseth. 16 And he spake a parable unto them, saying, The ground of a certain rich man brought forth plentifully.—LUKE, ch. 12.

9411. —— makes Difficulties. *"Grieved."* [See No. 9416.]

9412. —— Distribution of. *To Poor.* [See No. 9416.]

9413. —— Dispersion of. *By War.* 5 Then said Isaiah to Hezekiah, Hear the word of the Lord of hosts : 6 Behold, the days come, that all that *is* in thine house, and *that* which thy fathers have laid up in store until this day, shall be carried to Babylon : nothing shall be left, saith the Lord.—ISA., ch. 39.

9414. —— Danger of. *"Beware."* 12 Lest *when* thou hast eaten and art full, and hast built goodly houses, and dwelt *therein ;* 13 And *when* thy herds and thy flocks multiply, and thy silver and thy gold is multiplied, and all that thou hast is multiplied ; 14 Then thine heart be lifted up, and thou forget the Lord thy God, which brought thee out of the land of Egypt.— DEUT., ch. 8.

9415. —— Display of. *A h a s u e r u s.* 3 He made a feast.. 4 He shewed the riches of his glorious kingdom and the honour of his excel-

lent majesty many days, *even* a hundred and fourscore days.—ESTHER, ch. 1.

9416. —— Bondage to. *Young Ruler.* 21 Jesus beholding him loved him, and said..One thing thou lackest : go thy way, sell whatsoever thou hast, and give to the poor, and thou shalt have treasure in heaven : and come, take up the cross, and follow me. 22..went away grieved : for he had great possessions.—MARK, ch. 10.

9417. —— enough. *Esau.* 8 What *meanest* thou by all this drove which I met? And he said, *These are* to find grace in the sight of my lord. 9 And Esau said, I have enough, my brother ; keep that thou hast unto thyself.—GEN., ch. 33.

9418. —— separates Friends. *Abram—Lot.* 11 Lot chose him all the plain of Jordan ; and Lot journeyed east : and they separated themselves the one from the other. 12 Abram dwelt in the land of Canaan, and Lot dwelt in the cities of the plain, and pitched *his* tent toward Sodom. —GEN., ch. 13.

9419. —— —— *Jacob—Esau.* 6 Went into the country from the face of his brother Jacob. 7 For their riches were more than that they might dwell together : and the land..could not bear them because of their cattle.—GEN., ch. 36.

9420. —— Greatness in. *B o a z.* 1 Naomi had a kinsman of her husband's, a mighty man of wealth, of the family of Elimelech ; and his name *was* BOAZ.—RUTH, ch. 2.

9421. —— from God. *"He..giveth."* 17 Thou say in thine heart, My power and the might of *mine* hand hath gotten me this wealth. 18 But thou shalt remember the Lord thy God : for *it is* he that giveth thee power to get wealth.—DEUT., ch. 8.

9422. —— Inherited. *I s a a c.* 13 The man waxed great, and went forward, and grew until he became very great : 14 For he had possession of flocks, and possession of herds, and great store of servants : and the Philistines envied him.—GEN., ch. 26.

9423. —— Ill-gotten. *Proverb.* 6 The getting of treasures by a lying tongue *is* a vanity tossed to and fro of them that seek death. 7 The robbery of the wicked shall destroy them ; because they refuse to do judgment.—PROV., ch. 21.

9424. —— —— *For the Poor.* 8 He that by usury and unjust gain increaseth his substance, he shall gather it for him that will pity the poor.—PROV., ch. 18.

9425. —— lost. *Job.* 3 His substance also was seven thousand sheep, and three thousand camels, and five hundred yoke of oxen, and five hundred she asses, and a very great household ; so that this man was the greatest of all the men of the east.—JOB, ch. 1.

9426. —— Loss of. *Friends lost.* 13 He hath put my brethren far from me, and mine acquaintance are verily estranged from me. 14 My kinsfolk have failed, and my familiar friends have forgotten me.—JOB, ch. 19.

9427. —— Overflow of. *L o t.* 5 Lot also, which went with Abram, had flocks, and herds, and tents. 6 And the land was not able to bear them, that they might dwell together : for their substance was great, so that they could not dwell together.—GEN., ch. 13.

9428. —— **Obstructions of.** *"Cares."* [18] These are they which are sown among thorns : such as hear the word, [19] And the cares of this world, and the deceitfulness of riches, and the lusts of other things entering in, choke the word, and it becometh unfruitful.—MARK, ch. 4.

9429. —— **with Piety.** *Abram.* [2] Abram was very rich in cattle, in silver, and in gold.. [4] Unto the place of the altar, which he had made there at the first : and there Abram called on the name of the Lord.—GEN., ch. 13.

9430. —— **Perishable.** *" Flower of Grass."* [11] The sun is no sooner risen with a burning heat, but it withereth the grass, and the flower thereof falleth, and the grace of the fashion of it perisheth : so also shall the rich man fade away in his ways.—JAMES, ch. 1

9431. —— **A Prophet's.** *Elisha.* [19] Elisha.. was ploughing with twelve yoke of oxen before him, and he with the twelfth : and Elijah passed by him, and cast his mantle upon him.. [21] And he returned back from him, and took a yoke of oxen, and slew them, and boiled their flesh with the instruments of the oxen, and gave unto the people, and they did eat.—1 KINGS, ch. 19.

9432. —— **Pride in.** *" Lifted up."* [See Nos. 9414, 9421.]

9433. —— **and Poverty.** *Indifferent.* [9] Let the brother of low degree rejoice in that he is exalted : [10] But the rich, in that he is made low : because as the flower of the grass he shall pass away.—JAMES, ch. 1.

9434. —— **Poverty in.** *Proverb.* [7] There is that maketh himself rich, yet hath nothing : there is that maketh himself poor, yet hath great riches.—PROV., ch. 13.

9435. —— **Perplexities of.** *What ?* [17] And he thought within himself, saying, What shall I do, because I have no room where to bestow my fruits ?—LUKE, ch. 12.

9436. —— **regained.** *Job.* [12] The Lord blessed the latter end of Job more than his beginning : for he had fourteen thousand sheep, and six thousand camels, and a thousand yoke of oxen, and a thousand she asses.—JOB, ch. 42.

9437. —— **Sudden.** *Four Lepers.* [8] And when these lepers came to the uttermost part of the camp, they went into one tent, and did eat and drink, and carried thence silver, and gold, and raiment, and went and hid it; and came again, and entered into another tent, and carried thence also, and went and hid it.—2 KINGS, ch. 7.

9438. —— —— *Proverb.* [21] An inheritance may be gotten hastily at the beginning ; but the end thereof shall not be blessed.—PROV., ch. 20.

9439. —— **Selfish Use of.** *Rich Fool.* [18] And he said, This will I do : I will pull down my barns, and build greater ; and there will I bestow all my fruits and my goods. [19] And I will say to my soul, Soul, thou hast much goods laid up for many years ; take thine ease, eat, drink, and be merry.—LUKE, ch. 12.

9440. —— **Uncertain Use of.** *" Whose ?"* [20] But God said unto him, Thou fool, this night thy soul shall be required of thee : then whose shall those things be, which thou hast provided ? —LUKE, ch. 12.

9441. —— **unenjoyed.** *Nabal.* [2] There was a man in Maon, whose possessions were in Carmel ; and the man was very great, and he had three thousand sheep, and a thousand goats.. [3] ..but the man was churlish and evil in his doings ; and he was of the house of Caleb.—1 SAM., ch. 25.

9442. —— **of the Wicked.** *Transient.* [22] A good man leaveth an inheritance to his children's children : and the wealth of the sinner is laid up for the just.—PROV., ch. 13.

Also see :

Miscellaneous. Jacob had much cattle,maidservants 994

See MONEY, RICHES, and references.

9443. WEAPONS of Faith. *Simple.* [40] He took his staff in his hand, and chose him five smooth stones out of the brook, and put them in a shepherd's bag which he had, even in a scrip ; and his sling was in his hand : and he drew near to the Philistine.—1 SAM., ch. 17.

9444. —— **rejected.** *Saul's Armour.* [38] Saul armed David with his armour, and he put a helmet of brass upon his head : also he armed him with a coat of mail. [39] And David girded his sword upon his armour, and he assayed to go ; for he had not proved it. And David said unto Saul, I cannot go with these, for I have not proved them.—1 SAM., ch. 17.

See other illustrations under :

ARMOUR.

Defenceless. Goliath had a helmet of brass	494
Rejected. David girded his sword..I cannot	495
Without. Neither sword nor spear	496

SWORD.

Flaming. East of..Eden..flaming sword	8531
Lord's. Sword of the L..Gideon	8532
Memorial. Sword of Goliath..wrapped	8533
Ominous. D. saw..angel..drawn sword	8534
" Joshua..stood a man..sword drawn	8535
for Punishment. Feared the s., I will bring the s.	8536
Rejected. Said J., Put up again thy sword	8537
Spirit. Take the s...is word of God	8538
" Word of G. is sharper than any twoedged	8539
Sharpest. Whose..tongue a sharp s.	8540
" Speaketh like the piercing of a sword	8541

SWORDS.

Fallen. Of Benjamin..25,000 men	8542
Necessary. Beat your ploughshares into swords	8543
Transformed. Beat their s. into ploughshares	8544

9445. WEARINESS from Exhaustion. *Two Hundred.* [10] David pursued, he and four hundred men : for two hundred abode behind, which were so faint that they could not go over the brook Besor.—1 SAM., ch. 30.

9446. —— **of Formality.** *" Contemptible."* [12] Ye have profaned it, in that ye say, The table of the Lord is polluted ; and the fruit thereof, even his meat, is contemptible. [13] Ye said also, Behold, what a weariness is it ! and ye have snuffed at it, saith the Lord of hosts ; and ye brought that which was torn, and the lame, and the sick.—MAL., ch. 1.

9447. —— **of the Flesh.** *Gethsemane.* [42] He went away again the second time, and prayed, saying, O my Father, if this cup may not pass away from me, except I drink it, thy will be done. [43] And he came and found them asleep again : for their eyes were heavy.—MAT., ch. 26.

9448. —— **Impatience from.** *Moses.* [11] Moses said unto the Lord, Wherefore hast thou afflicted thy servant? and wherefore have I not found favour in thy sight, that thou layest the burden of all this people upon me?—Num., ch. 11.

9449. —— of Jesus. *At Sychar.* ⁶ Jacob's well was there. Jesus therefore, being wearied with *his* journey, sat thus on the well : *and* it was about the sixth hour.—John, ch. 4.

9450. —— Support in. *Moses.* [See No. 9397.]

9451. —— from Work. *Apostles.* ³¹ Come ye yourselves apart into a desert place, and rest a while : for there were many coming and going, and they had no leisure so much as to eat. —Mark, ch. 6.

Also see :
Affliction. Wearisome nights are appointed unto me 213
See WEAKNESS and references.

9452. WEATHER, Discernment of. *Signs.* ² When it is evening, ye say, It will be fair weather : for the sky is red. ³ And in the morning, It will be foul weather to day : for the sky is red and lowering. O ye hypocrites, ye can discern the face of the sky ; but can ye not *discern* the signs of the times ?—Mat., ch. 16.

See other illustrations under :
WHIRLWIND.
Destructive. Smote..the house..fell upon the y m. 9492
Glorious. Elijah went up by a whirlwind into h.　9493
See STORM and references.

9453. WEEPING, An affecting. *Esther.* ³ Esther spake yet again before the king, and fell down at his feet, and besought him with tears to put away the mischief of Haman the Agagite, and his device that he had devised against the Jews.—Esther, ch. 8.

9454. —— —— *Absalom's Rebellion.* ²³ All the country wept with a loud voice, and all the people passed over : the king also himself passed over the brook Kidron..toward the way of the wilderness.—2 Sam., ch. 15.

9455. —— All. *For Lazarus.* ³³ When Jesus therefore saw her weeping, and the Jews also weeping which came with her, he groaned in the spirit, and was troubled..³⁵ Jesus wept.— John, ch. 11.

9456. —— Appropriate. *Peter.* ⁷⁴ Immediately the cock crew. ⁷⁵ And Peter remembered the word of Jesus, which said unto him, Before the cock crow, thou shalt deny me thrice, And he went out, and wept bitterly.—Mat., ch. 26.

9457. —— Babe, A. *Moses.* ⁵ And the daughter of Pharaoh came down to wash *herself* at the river ; and her maidens walked along by the river's side : and when she saw the ark among the flags, she sent her maid to fetch it. ⁶ And when she had opened *it*, she saw the child : and, behold, the babe wept. And she had compassion on him, and said, This *is one* of the Hebrews' children.—Ex., ch. 2.

9458. —— in Bereavement. *Jacob.* ³³ Joseph is without doubt rent in pieces. ³⁴ And Jacob rent his clothes, and put sackcloth upon his loins, and mourned for his son many days.. ³⁵..and he said, For I will go down into the grave unto my son mourning. Thus his father wept for him.—Gen., ch. 37.

9459. —— of Captives. *Babylon.* ¹ By the rivers of Babylon, there we sat down, yea, we wept, when we remembered Zion. ² We hanged

our harps upon the willows in the midst thereof.— Ps. 137.

9460. —— for the Dying. *Hagar.* ¹⁵ The water was spent in the bottle, and she cast the child under one of the shrubs. ¹⁶ And she went, and sat her down over against *him* a good way off, as it were a bowshot : for she said, Let me not see the death of the child. And she..lifted up her voice, and wept.— Gen., ch. 21.

9461. —— excessive. *Soldiers.* ³ Ziklag..the city..*was* burned with fire ; and their wives, and their sons, and their daughters, were taken captives. ⁴ Then, David and the people that *were* with him lifted up their voice and wept, until they had no more power to weep.—1 Sam., ch. 30.

9462. —— for Flesh. *Wilderness.* ⁴ The mixed multitude that *was* among them fell a lusting : and the children of Israel also wept again, and said, Who shall give us flesh to eat ? —Num., ch. 11.

9463. —— Fruitless. *Reprobates.* ¹² Not having a wedding garment ? And he was speechless. ¹³ Then said the king to the servants, Bind him hand and foot, and take him away, and cast *him* into outer darkness ; there shall be weeping and gnashing of teeth.—Mat., ch. 22.

9464. —— Fictitious. *Ishmael.* ⁶ Ishmael.. went forth from Mizpah to meet them, weeping all along as he went : and..as he met them, he said unto them, Come to Gedaliah.. ⁷ And it was *so*, when they came into the midst of the city, that Ishmael the son of Nethaniah slew them.—Jer, ch. 41.

9465. —— A great. *Spies discouraged.* ³³ There we saw the giants, the sons of Anak.. and we were in our own sight as grasshoppers, and so we were in their sight.. ¹ And all the congregation lifted up their voice, and cried ; and the people wept that night.—Num., chs. 13 and 14.

9466. —— in Humiliation. *Absalom's Rebellion.* ³⁰ David went up by the ascent of *mount* Olivet, and wept as he went up, and had his head covered, and he went barefoot : and all the people that *was* with him covered every man his head, and they went up, weeping as they went up.—2 Sam., ch. 15.

9467. —— at the Judgment. *Jesus said,* ²⁸ There shall be weeping and gnashing of teeth, when ye shall see Abraham, and Isaac, and Jacob, and all the prophets, in the kingdom of God, and you *yourselves* thrust out.—Luke, ch. 13.

9468. —— for Joy. *Joseph.* ² He wept aloud : and the Egyptians and the house of Pharaoh heard. ³ And Joseph said unto his brethren, I am Joseph ; doth my father yet live ? —Gen., ch. 45.

9469. —— and Mourning. *Apostles.* ¹⁰ She went and told them that had been with him, as they mourned and wept. ¹¹ And they, when they had heard that he was alive, and had been seen of her, believed not.—Mark, ch. 16.

9470. —— Needless. *Mary.* ¹¹ Mary stood without at the sepulchre weeping : and as she wept, she stooped down, *and looked* into the sepulchre, ¹² And seeth two angels in white sitting, the one at the head, and the other at

the feet, where the body of Jesus had lain.—
JOHN, ch. 11.

9471. —— **Overwhelmed by.** *Paul.* [12] When
we heard these things, both we, and they of
that place, besought him not to go up to Jerusalem. [13] Then Paul answered, What mean ye
to weep and to break mine heart? for I am
ready not to be bound only, but also to die at
Jerusalem for the name of the Lord Jesus.—
ACTS, ch. 21.

9472. —— **for a Purpose.** *Samson's Wife.*
[17] And she wept before him the seven days,
while their feast lasted : and it came to pass on
the seventh day, that he told her, because she
lay sore upon him : and she told the riddle to
the children of her people.—JUDGES, ch. 14.

9473. —— **Patriotic.** *Jesus.* [41] He beheld
the city, and wept over it, [42] Saying, if thou
hadst known, even thou, at least in this thy
day, the things *which belong* unto thy peace !
but now they are hid from thine eyes.—LUKE,
ch. 19.

9474. —— **Pious.** *Rebuilding.* [12] Many of the
priests and Levites and chief of the fathers, *who
were* ancient men, that had seen the first house,
when the foundation of this house was laid before their eyes, wept with a loud voice ; and
many shouted aloud for joy.—EZRA, ch. 3.

9475. —— **Penitential.** *Hearers.* [9] This day
is holy unto the Lord your God ; mourn not,
nor weep. For all the people wept, when they
heard the words of the law.—NEH., ch. 8.

9476. —— —— *Woman* [38] Stood at his
feet behind *him* weeping, and began to wash his
feet with tears, and did wipe *them* with the hairs
of her head, and kissed his feet, and anointed
them with the ointment.—LUKE, ch. 7.

9477. —— —— *Israelites.* [3] I will not drive
them out from before you ; but they shall be *as
thorns* in your sides, and their gods shall be a
snare unto you. [4] . .when the Angel of the
Lord spake these words. .the people lifted up
their voice, and wept.—JUDGES, ch. 2.

9478. —— —— *Superficial.* [16] When David
had made an end of speaking these words unto
Saul. .Saul said, *Is* this thy voice, my son
David? And Saul lifted up his voice, and wept,
[17] And he said to David, Thou *art* more righteous
than I.—1 SAM., ch. 24.

9479. —— —— *Genuine.* [1] When Ezra had
prayed, and. .confessed, weeping and casting
himself down before the house of God, there
assembled unto him out of Israel a very great
congregation of men and women and children :
for the people wept very sore.—EZRA, ch. 10.

9480. —— **in Reconciliation.** *Jacob—Esau.*
[4] Esau ran to meet him, and embraced him, and
fell on his neck, and kissed him : and they wept.
—GEN., ch. 33.

9481. —— **at Separation.** *David* [41] Fell on
his face to the ground, and bowed himself three
times : and they kissed one another, and wept
one with another, until David exceeded. [42] And
Jonathan said to David, Go in peace.—1 SAM.,
ch. 20.

9482. —— —— *At Miletus.* [37] They all wept
sore, and fell on Paul's neck, and kissed him,
[38] Sorrowing most of all for the words which he
spake, that they should see his face no more.

And they accompanied him unto the ship.—
ACTS, ch. 20.

9483. —— —— *From Naomi.* [9] Then she
kissed them ; and they lifted up their voice, and
wept. [10] And they said unto her, Surely we will
return with thee unto thy people.—RUTH, ch. 1.

9484. —— **in Sickness.** *Hezekiah.* [1] In those
days was Hezekiah sick unto death. And the
prophet Isaiah. .said unto him, Thus saith the
Lord, Set thine house in order ; for thou shalt
die, and not live. [2] Then he turned his face to
the wall, and prayed unto the Lord. .[3] . .And
Hezekiah wept sore.—2 KINGS, ch. 20.

9485. —— **Useless.** *David.* [22] While the child
was yet alive, I fasted and wept : for I said,
Who can tell *whether* God will be gracious to
me, that the child may live? [23] But now he is
dead, wherefore should I fast? can I bring him
back again? I shall go to him, but he shall not
return to me.—2 SAM., ch. 12.

9486. —— **for the Wicked.** *By Elisha.*
[12] Hazael said, Why weepeth my lord? And he
answered, Because I know the evil that thou
wilt do unto the children of Israel : their strong
holds wilt thou set on fire, and their young men
wilt thou slay with the sword, and wilt dash
their children, and rip up their women with
child. [13] And Hazael said, But what, *is* thy
servant a dog, that he should do this great
thing?—2 KINGS, ch. 8.

See GRIEF and references.

9487. WEDDING, Heaven a. *Lamb.* [9] He
saith unto me, Write, Blessed *are* they which are
called unto the marriage supper of the Lamb.
—REV., ch. 19.

See MARRIAGE.

9488. WELCOME envied. *Saul.* [See below.]
[8] Saul was very wroth. .and he said, They have
ascribed unto David ten thousands, and to me
they have ascribed *but* thousands : and *what* can
he have more but the kingdom? [9] And Saul
eyed David.—1 SAM., ch. 18.

9489. —— **A Hero's.** *David.* [6] And it came
to pass as they came, when David was returned
from the slaughter of the Philistine, that the
women came out of all cities of Israel, singing and dancing, to meet king Saul, with tabrets, with joy, and with instruments of music.
[7] And the women answered one another as they
played, and said, Saul hath slain his thousands,
and David his ten thousands.—1 SAM., ch. 18.

9490. —— **The heavenly.** *"Well done."*
[21] His lord said. .Well done, *thou* good and faithful servant : thou hast been faithful over a few
things, I will make thee ruler over many things :
enter thou into the joy of thy lord.—MAT., ch. 25.

9491. —— —— *Friends.* [9] Make to yourselves friends of the mammon of unrighteousness ; that, when ye fail, they may receive you
into everlasting habitations.—LUKE, ch. 16.

See other illustrations under:

HOSPITALITY.

Christian. Paul entered. .a certain man's house	4098
Dangerous. Come home. .and eat. .I may not	4099
Forbidden. Diotrephes. .forbiddeth them that w.	4100
Grateful. Mephibosheth shall eat at the king's t.	4101
Increase by. How shall I. .before 100 men?	4102
Joyful. Zaccheus. .haste. .received him joyfully	4103
Odious. Baser sort. :assaulted the house of Jason	4104

Preservation. Tarry all night, and wash your feet 4105
of Poor. Widow did according to the saying of E. 4106
Pagan. Barbarous people..received us every one 4107
Refused. Samaritans did not receive him 4108
Repaid. Shunammite..make a little chamber 4109
Reward. Abraham ran to meet them..feast 4110
Treacherous. Pharisee brought him to dine with 4111
Unjust. Rich man..took the poor man's lamb 4112
Urgent. Lot pressed them greatly..his house 4113
   " Urged him, therefore he lodged there 4114
   " They constrained him..sat at meat 4115
Woman's. Lydia..came into my house..constrain'd 4116
Willing. Ungirded his camels..set meat before him 4117
Wanting. Simon, thou gavest me no water to wash 4118

INVITATION.

Bountiful. Come unto me..eat the fat of the land 4649
Benevolence. Whosoever is of a willing heart 4650
Christian. Can any good come out of Nazareth? 4651
Divine. Ho, every one that thirsteth, come 4652
Gospel. Sent..servants to call..to the wedding 4653
Grace. Spirit and the bride say, Come 4654
Heavenward. Come..we will do thee good..L. 4655
Pressing. I stand at the door and knock..voice 4656
Solicited. Bid me come unto thee upon the water 4657

Boisterous. When the ark of G. came into the camp 1521

9492. WHIRLWIND, A destructive. *Job.*
19 There came a great wind from the wilderness,
and smote the four corners of the house, and it
fell upon the young men, and they are dead.—
Job, ch. 1.

9493. —— A glorious. *" Horses of Fire."*
11 *There appeared* a chariot of fire, and horses of
fire, and parted them both asunder ; and Elijah
went up by a whirlwind into heaven.—2 Kings,
ch. 2.

See STORM.

9494. WICKED, Arts of the. *Proverb.* 13 He
winketh with his eyes, he speaketh with his
feet, he teacheth with his fingers.—Prov., ch. 6.

9495. —— Angered by. *God.* [See No.
9536.]

9496. —— in Bondage. *Proverb.* 22 His
own iniquities shall take the wicked himself,
and he shall be holden with the cords of his
sin.—Prov., ch. 5.

9497. —— Criticisms of the. *" Troubleth."*
17 When Ahab saw Elijah..Ahab said unto him,
Art thou he that troubleth Israel? 18..I have
not troubled Israel ; but thou, and thy father's
house, in that ye have forsaken the commandments of the Lord, and thou hast followed Baalim.—1 Kings, ch. 18.

9498. —— commended, The. *Prudence.* 7 And
how much owest thou? And he said, A hundred
measures of wheat. And he said unto him,
Take thy bill, and write fourscore. 8 And the
lord commended the unjust steward, because he
had done wisely.—Luke, ch. 16.

9499. —— Defeat of the. *Haman said,* 9 Thus
shall it be done to the man whom the king delighteth to honour. 10 Then the king said to
Haman, Make haste, *and* take the apparel and
the horse, as thou hast said, and do even so to
Mordecai the Jew.—Esther, ch. 6.

9500. —— End of the. *" Fire."* 49 So shall
it be at the end of the world : the angels shall
come forth, and sever the wicked from among
the just, 50 And shall cast then into the furnace

of fire : there shall be wailing and gnashing of
teeth.—Mat., ch. 13.

9501. —— Fear of the. *Proverb.* 1 The
wicked flee when no man pursueth : but the
righteous are bold as a lion.—Prov., ch. 28.

9502. —— fear the Good. *Saul.* 12 Saul was
afraid of David, because the Lord was with him,
and was departed from Saul.—1 Sam., ch. 13.

9503. —— —— *Joseph's Brethren.* 15 When
Joseph's brethren saw that their father was
dead, they said, Joseph will peradventure hate
us, and will certainly requite us all the evil
which we did unto him.—Gen., ch. 50.

9504. —— Flattering the. *Proverb.* 24 He
that saith unto the wicked, Thou *art* righteous ;
him shall the people curse, nations shall abhor
him : 25 But to them that rebuke *him* shall be
delight, and a good blessing shall come upon
them.—Prov., ch. 24.

9505. —— Fears of the. *Presence of God.*
10 As the ark of God came to Ekron..the Ekron-
ites cried out, saying, They have brought about
the ark of the God of Israel to us, to slay us
and our people.—1 Sam., ch. 5.

9506. —— —— *Peter and John released.*
21 They entered into the temple early in the
morning, and taught.. 24 Now when the high
priest and the captain of the temple and the
chief priests heard these things, they doubted of
them whereunto this would grow.—Acts, ch. 5.

9507. —— —— *" Shaken Leaf."* 36 I will
send a faintness into their hearts in the lands
of their enemies ; and the sound of a shaken
leaf shall chase them ; and they shall flee, as
fleeing from a sword ; and they shall fall when
none pursueth.—Lev., ch. 26.

9508. —— Hiding of the. *" Cave."* 16 The
five kings are found hid in a cave at Makkedah.
18 And Joshua said, Roll great stones upon the
mouth of the cave, and set men by it for to keep
them.—Josh., ch. 10.

9509. —— honoured, The. *Jeroboam.* 31 He
made a house of high places, and made priests
of the lowest of the people, which were not of
the sons of Levi.—1 Kings, ch. 12.

9510. —— Justifying the. *" Abomination."*
15 He that justifieth the wicked, and he that
condemneth the just, even they both *are* abomination to the Lord.—Prov., ch. 17.

9511. —— Overthrow of the. *" Moment."*
17 I went into the sanctuary of God ; *then* understood I their end. 18 Surely thou didst set
them in slippery places : thou castedst them
down into destruction. 19 How are they *brought*
into desolation, as in a moment ! they are utterly consumed with terrors.—Ps. 73.

9512. —— —— *" His Light."* 5 Yea, the
light of the wicked shall be put out, and the
spark of his fire shall not shine. 6 The light
shall be dark in his tabernacle, and his candle
shall be put out with him.—Job, ch. 18.

9513. —— —— *" His Strength."* 12 His
strength shall be hungerbitten, and destruction
shall be ready at his side. 13 It shall devour the
strength of his skin : *even* the firstborn of death
shall devour his strength.—Job, ch. 18.

9514. —— —— *" His Remembrance."* 17 His
remembrance shall perish from the earth, and
he shall have no name in the street. 18 He shall

be driven from light into darkness, and chased out of the world.—Job, ch. 18.

9515. —— Offences of. *"Refused."* [24] Because I have called and ye refused ; I have stretched out my hand, and no man regarded ; [25] But ye have set at nought all my counsel, and would none of my reproof.—Prov., ch. 1.

9516. —— overwhelmed. *"Whirlwind."* [26] I also will laugh at your calamity : I will mock when your fear cometh ; [27] When your fear cometh as desolation, and your destruction cometh as a whirlwind.—Prov., ch. 1.

9517. —— Pleasures of the. *"Gall."* [12] Though wickedness be sweet in his mouth, *though* he hide it under his tongue ; [13] *Though* he spare it, and forsake it not, but keep it still within his mouth ; [14] *Yet* his meat in his bowels is turned, *it is* the gall of asps within him.—Job, ch. 20.

9518. —— punish the Wicked. *Eglon.* [12] Israel did evil again in the sight of the Lord : and the Lord strengthened Eglon the king of Moab against Israel, because they had done evil. —Judges, ch. 3.

9519. —— refused. *Prayers of.* [28] Then shall they call upon me, but I will not answer ; they shall seek me early, but they shall not find me ; [29] For that they hated knowledge, and did not choose the fear of the Lord.—Prov., ch. 1.

9520. —— Riches of the. *"Vomit."* [15] He hath swallowed down riches, and he shall vomit them up again : God shall cast them out of his belly. [16] He shall suck the poison of asps : the viper's tongue shall slay him.—Job, ch. 20.

9521. —— Retribution for. *Haman.* [9] Harbonah, one of the chamberlains, said before the king, Behold also the gallows fifty cubits high, which Haman had made for Mordecai, who had spoken good for the king, standeth in the house of Haman. Then the king said, Hang him thereon.—Esther, ch. 7.

9522. —— restless. *"Troubled Sea."* [20] The wicked *are* like the troubled sea, when it cannot rest, whose waters cast up mire and dirt. [21] *There is* no peace, saith my God, to the wicked.—Isa., ch. 57.

9523. —— Seduced by the. *Israelites.* [9] But they hearkened not : and Manasseh seduced them to do more evil than did the nations whom the Lord destroyed before the children of Israel.—2 Kings, ch. 21.

9524. —— Trouble from. *David.* [38] A great man fallen this day in Israel? [39] And I *am* this day weak, though anointed king ; and these men the sons of Zeruiah *be* too hard for me : the Lord shall reward the doer of evil according to his wickedness.—3 Sam., ch. 3.

9525. —— Torments of the. *"Sound."* [21] A dreadful sound *is* in his ears : in prosperity the destroyer shall come upon him. [22] He believeth not that he shall return out of darkness, and he is waited for of the sword.—Job, ch. 15.

9526. —— unenvied, The. *Proverb.* [19] Fret not thyself because of evil *men*, neither be thou envious at the wicked ; [20] For there shall be no reward to the evil *man ;* the candle of the wicked shall be put out.—Prov., ch. 24.

9527. —— The Wealthy. *"Woe?"* [1] Go to now, *ye* rich men, weep and howl for your miseries that shall come upon *you.*—James, ch. 5. [See chapter.]

9528. —— warned. *Ananias.* [5] Ananias hearing these words fell down, and gave up the ghost : and great fear came on all them that heard these things.—Acts, ch. 5.

9529. —— Witness against the. *God.* [5] I will come near to you to judgment ; and I will be a swift witness against the sorcerers, and against the adulterers, and against false swearers, and against those that oppress the hireling in *his* wages, the widow, and the fatherless.—Mal., ch. 3.

9530. —— Way of the. *"Avoid."* [14] Enter not into the path of the wicked, and go not in the way of evil *men.* [15] Avoid it, pass not by it, turn from it, and pass away.. [19] The way of the wicked *is* as darkness : they know not at what they stumble.—Prov., ch. 4.

9531. WICKEDNESS, Audacious. *Josiah.* [11] He took away the horses that the kings of Judah had given to the sun, at the entering in of the house of the Lord.—2 Kings, ch. 23.

9532. —— Climax of. *"Kill."* [37] But last of all he sent unto them his son, saying, They will reverence my son. [38] But when the husbandmen saw the son, they said among themselves, This is the heir ; come, let us kill him, and let us seize on his inheritance.—Mat., ch. 21.

9533. —— delusive. *"Spirits."* [See No. 9540.]

9534. —— Desperation in. *After nine Plagues.* [28] Pharaoh said..Get thee from me, take heed to thyself, see my face no more ; for in *that* day thou seest my face thou shalt die. [29] And Moses said, Thou hast spoken well, I will see thy face again no more.—Ex., ch. 10.

9535. —— Depravity in. *Good Josiah.* [7] And he brake down the houses of the sodomites, that *were* by the house of the Lord, where the women wove hangings for the grove.—2 Kings, ch. 23.

9536. —— Exceeding. *Ahab's.* [33] Ahab made a grove ; and Ahab did more to provoke the Lord God of Israel to anger than all the kings of Israel that were before him.—1 Kings, ch. 16.

9537. —— Flagrant. *Parable.* [34] When the time of the fruit drew near, he sent his servants ..that they might receive the fruits of it. [35] And the husbandmen took his servants, and beat one, and killed another, and stoned another.— —Mat., ch. 21.

9538. —— in the Heart. *"Treasure."* [35] A good man, out of the good treasure of the heart, bringeth forth good things : and an evil man, out of the evil treasure, bringeth forth evil things.—Mat., ch. 12.

9539. —— Natural. *Antediluvians.* [5] God saw that the wickedness of man *was* great in the earth, and *that* every imagination of the thoughts of his heart *was* only evil continually. [6] And it repented the Lord that he had made man on the earth, and it grieved him at his heart.—Gen., ch. 6.

9540. —— Paternal. *Manasseh.* [6] He made his son pass through the fire, and observed times, and used enchantments, and dealt with familiar spirits and wizards : he wrought much wickedness in the sight of the Lord, to provoke *him* to anger.—2 KINGS, ch. 21.

9541. —— **Royal.** *Manasseh.* [3] He reared up altars for Baal, and made a grove, as did Ahab king of Israel ; and worshipped all the host of heaven, and served them. [4] And he built altars in the house of the Lord.—2 KINGS, ch. 21.

See other illustrations under :

BLASPHEMY.

Accused of. We stone thee not, but for blasphemy 801
Evidence of. High priest rent his clothes..spoken 802
Forbidden. Thou shalt not take the name..vain 803
Greatest. Word against the Son of man..be forgiven 804
Heedless. As the L. liveth, I will..take something 805
Habit. Stephen ceaseth not to speak blasphemous 806
Murdered. He ought to die..made himself the Son 807
No. Why..speak blasphemies?..Who can forgive 808
Punishment. All that heard laid their hands..head 809
Strange. Peter began to curse and swear 810
Unpardonable. Blasphemy against the H. G..not 811

CRUELTY.

Ambition. Athaliah..destroyed all the seed royal 1857
Captives. Judah cast [10,000 men of Seir] from the 1858
Failure. More they afflicted them, grew 1859
Insulting. Purple..crown of thorns..Hail king 1860
Pride. Mordecai bowed not..H. was full of wrath 1861
Reward. Cruel troubleth his own flesh 1862
Savage. Slew the sons of Z..before his eyes 1863
War. Joab put them under saws..harrows 1864

DESECRATION.

Bribery. Ahaz took..out of the house of the L. 2204
Removed. I. cast forth all the household stuff 2205
Sacrilegious. That his concubines might drink 2206

GUILT.

Accumulated. Upon you..all the righteous blood 3766
Cowardice. Adam and his wife hid 3767
Degrees. One owed 500 pounds, the other 50 3768
Panic. Egyptians said, Let us flee 3769

INJUSTICE.

Indignation. Rich man..took the poor man's l. 4499
Official. Because this widow troubleth me, I will 4500
" No fault..I will chastise him and release 4501

PROFANATION.

Sanctuary. Those that sold oxen..first visit 6626
" Sold and bought..Last visit 6627

SACRILEGE.

Presumptuous. They brought the golden vessels 7544
Priestly. Men abhorred the offering of the L. 7545
Unintended. Uzzah put forth his hand .ark 7546

See CRIME and references.
See SIN and references.

9542. WIDOW, Dilemma of. *Prophet's.* [1] There cried a certain woman of the wives of the sons of the prophets unto Elisha, saying, Thy servant my husband is dead ; and thou knowest that thy servant did fear the Lord : and the creditor is come to take unto him my two sons to be bondmen.--2 KINGS, ch. 4.

9543. —— **Gifts of a.** *"Two Mites."* [43] This poor widow hath cast more in, than all they which have cast into the treasury : [44] For all *they* did cast in of their abundance ; but she of her want did cast in all that she had, *even* all her living.—MARK, ch. 12.

9544. —— **An impoverished.** *Naomi.* [21] I

went out full, and the Lord hath brought me home again empty : why *then* call ye me Naomi, seeing the Lord hath testified against me, and the Almighty hath afflicted me?—RUTH, ch. 1.

9545. —— **Importunate.** *Unjust Judge.* [4] Though I fear not God, nor regard man ; [5] Yet because this widow troubleth me, I will avenge her, lest by her continual coming she weary me. —LUKE, ch. 18.

9546. —— **A pious.** *Anna* [37] *Was* a widow of about fourscore and four years, which departed not from the temple, but served *God* with fastings and prayers night and day.—LUKE, ch. 2.

9547. —— **remembered.** *Zarephath.* [14] Thus saith the Lord God of Israel, The barrel of meal shall not waste, neither shall the cruse of oil fail, until the day *that* the Lord sendeth rain upon the earth.—1 KINGS, ch. 17.

9548. —— —— **Again.** [23] Elijah took the child, and brought him down out of the chamber into the house, and delivered him unto his mother : and Elijah said, See, thy son liveth.— —1 KINGS, ch. 17.

9549. —— **relieved.** *Oil.* [5] When the vessels were full..she said unto her son, Bring me yet a vessel. And he said unto her, There is not a vessel more. And the oil stayed. [7] Then she came and told the man of God. And he said, Go, sell the oil, and pay thy debt, and live.— 2 KINGS, ch. 4. [See No. 4049.]

9550. —— **Son of a.** *Hiram.* [14] He *was* a widow's son of the tribe of Naphtali, and his father *was* a man of Tyre, a worker in brass : and he was filled with wisdom, and understanding, and cunning to work all works in brass.—1 KINGS, ch. 7.

9551. —— **Seven times a.** *Sadducees said,* [27] And last of all the woman died also. [28] Therefore in the resurrection, whose wife shall she be of the seven? for they all had her.—MAT., ch. 22.

9552. WIDOWS, Care for. *Murmured.* [1] When the number of the disciples was multiplied, there arose a murmuring of the Grecians against the Hebrews, because their widows were neglected in the daily ministration.—ACTS, ch. 6.

9553. —— **Home of.** *Ruth—Orpah—Naomi.* [3] Elimelech Naomi's husband died ; and she was left, and her two sons.. [5] And Mahlon and Chilion died also both of them ; and the woman was left of her two sons and her husband.— RUTH, ch. 1.

9554. —— **Provision for.** *Deacons.* [3] Look ye out among you seven men of honest report, full of the Holy Ghost and wisdom, whom we may appoint over this business.—ACTS, ch. 6.

9555. —— **in the Resurrection.** *Sadducees said,* [28] Therefore in the resurrection, whose wife shall she be of the seven? for they all had her.. [30] For in the resurrection they neither marry, nor are given in marriage, but are as the angels of God in heaven.—MAT., ch. 22. [See No. 9551.]

9556. —— **Wronging.** *Embezzlement.* [14] Woe unto you, scribes and Pharisees, hypocrites ! for ye devour widows' houses, and for a pretence make long prayers : therefore ye shall receive the greater damnation.—MAT., ch. 23.

9557. WIFE, Adornment of a. *"Quiet Spirit."* [3] Whose adorning, let it not be that outward *adorning* of plaiting the hair and of wearing of gold, or of putting on of apparel, [4] But *let it be* the hidden man of the heart, in that which is not corruptible, *even the ornament* of a meek and quiet spirit, which is in the sight of God of great price.—1 PETER, ch. 3.

9558. —— —— *"Good Works."* [9] That women adorn themselves in modest apparel, with shamefacedness and sobriety; not with braided hair, or gold, or pearls, or costly array; [10] But, which becometh women professing godliness, with good works.—1 TIM., ch. 2.

9559. —— Prior Claims of. *Adam said,* [23] She shall be called Woman, because she was taken out of man. [24] Therefore shall a man leave his father and his mother, and shall cleave unto his wife.—Ex., ch. 2.

9560. —— A contentious. *Proverb.* [19] *It is* better to dwell in the wilderness, than with a contentious and an angry woman.—PROV., ch. 21.

9561. —— —— *"Rainy Day."* [15] A continual dropping in a very rainy day and a contentious woman are alike. [16] Whosoever hideth her hideth the wind, and the ointment of his right hand, *which* bewrayeth *itself.*—PROV., ch. 27.

9562. —— Bad Counsels of. *Haman's.* [14] Then said Zeresh his wife and all his friends unto him, Let a gallows be made of fifty cubits high, and to morrow speak thou unto the king that Mordecai may be hanged thereon.—ESTHER, ch. 5. [Was himself hung thereon.]

9563. —— —— *Job's.* [9] Then said his wife unto him, Dost thou still retain thine integrity? curse God, and die. [10] But he said unto her, Thou speakest as one of the foolish women speaketh.—JOB, ch. 2.

9564. —— Corrupting. *Ahab.* [31] As if it had been a light thing for him to walk in the sins of Jeroboam..he took to wife Jezebel the daughter of Ethbaal king of the Zidonians, and went and served Baal.—1 KINGS, ch. 16.

9565. —— A contemptuous. *Michal.* [16] Saw king David leaping and dancing before the Lord; and she despised him in her heart.—2 SAM., ch. 6.

9566. —— Device of. *Michal.* [13] Michal took an image, and laid *it* in the bed, and put a pillow of goats' *hair* for his bolster, and covered *it* with a cloth.. [16] And when the messengers were come in, behold, *there was* an image in the bed, with a pillow of goats' *hair* for his bolster. —1 SAM., ch. 19.

9567. —— A disgraceful. *"Rottenness."* [4] A virtuous woman *is* a crown to her husband: but she that maketh ashamed *is* as rottenness in his bones.—PROV., ch. 12.

9568. —— A dangerous. *Jehoram.* [18] He walked in the way of the kings of Israel, as did the house of Ahab; for the daughter of Ahab was his wife: and he did evil in the sight of the Lord.—2 KINGS, ch. 8. [She was Jezebel's daughter.]

9569. —— A disobedient. *Vashti.* [12] Queen Vashti refused to come at the king's commandment by *his* chamberlains: therefore was the king very wroth, and his anger burned in him. —ESTHER, ch. 1.

9570. —— A falsifying. *Michal.* [17] Saul said unto Michal, Why hast thou deceived me so, and sent away mine enemy, that he is escaped? And Michal answered Saul, He said unto me, Let me go; why should I kill thee?—1 SAM., ch. 19.

9571. —— for her Husband. *Against Laban.* [14] Rachel and Leah answered..*Is there* yet any portion or inheritance for us in our father's house? [15] Are we not counted of him strangers? for he hath sold us, and hath quite devoured also our money.—GEN., ch. 31.

9572. —— saves her Husband. *From her Father.* [11] Michal David's wife told him, saying, If thou save not thy life to night, to morrow thou shalt be slain. [12] So Michal let David down through a window: and he went, and fled, and escaped.—1 SAM., ch. 19.

9573. —— An intelligent. *Of Manoah.* [22] Manoah said unto his wife, We shall surely die, because we have seen God. [23] But his wife said..If the Lord were pleased to kill us, he would not have received a burnt offering and a meat offering at our hand.—JUDGES, ch. 13.

9574. —— from the Lord, A. *Proverb.* [14] House and riches *are* the inheritance of fathers: and a prudent wife *is* from the Lord.— PROV., ch. 19.

9575. —— A loving. *Michal.* [19] When Merab Saul's daughter should have been given to David..she was given unto Adriel the Meholathite to wife. [20] And Michal Saul's daughter loved David: and they told Saul, and the thing pleased him.—1 SAM., ch. 18.

9576. —— lost, A. *Michal.* [44] Saul had given Michal his daughter, David's wife, to Phalti the son of Laish, which *was* of Gallim.— 1 SAM., ch. 25.

9577. —— —— *Samson's.* [20] Samson's wife was *given* to his companion, whom he had used as his friend.—JUDGES, ch. 15.

9578. —— Purchase of. *Dinah.* [11] Shechem said unto her father and unto her brethren, Let me find grace in your eyes, and what ye shall say unto me I will give. [12] Ask me never so much dowry and gift, and I will give according as ye shall say unto me: but give the damsel to wife.—GEN., ch. 34.

9579. —— Prudence of. *Abigail.* [3] The name of the man *was* Nabal, and..his wife Abigail; and *she was* a woman of good understanding, and of a beautiful countenance: but the man *was* churlish and evil in his doings.—1 SAM., ch. 25. [See chapter.]

9580. —— Piety of. *Elisabeth.* [5] Zacharias. and her name *was* Elisabeth. [6] And they were both righteous before God, walking in all the commandments and ordinances of the Lord blameless.—LUKE, ch. 1.

9581. —— regained, A. *Michal.* [14] David sent messengers to Ishbosheth, Saul's son, saying, Deliver me my wife Michal, which I espoused to me for a hundred foreskins of the Philistines. [16] And her husband went with her along weeping behind her to Bahurim. Then said Abner unto him, Go, return. And he returned.—2 SAM., ch. 3.

9582. —— Submission of. *After the Fall.* [16] Unto the woman he said, I will greatly multiply thy sorrow and thy conception ; in sorrow thou shalt bring forth children ; and thy desire *shall be* to thy husband, and he shall rule over thee.—Gen., ch. 3.

9583. —— **A subduing.** *Samson's.* [16] Samson's wife wept before him, and said, Thou dost but hate me, and lovest me not : thou hast put forth a riddle unto the children of my people, and hast not told *it* me.—Judges, ch. 14.

9584. —— **A sarcastic.** *Michal.* [20] David returned to bless his household. And Michal the daughter of Saul came out to meet David, and said, How glorious was the king of Israel to day, who uncovered himself to day in the eyes of the handmaids of his servants, as one of the vain fellows shamelessly uncovereth himself !— 2 Sam., ch. 6.

9585. —— **Selecting.** *Jacob's.* [1] Thou shalt not take a wife of the daughters of Canaan. [2] Arise, go to Padan-aram, to the house of Bethuel thy mother's father ; and take thee a wife from thence of the daughters of Laban thy mother's brother.—Gen., ch. 28.

9586. —— **Serving for a.** *"Seven Years."* [20] Jacob served seven years for Rachel ; and they seemed unto him *but* a few days, for the love he had to her.—Gen., ch. 29.

9587. —— **a Treasure.** *Proverb.* [22] *Whoso* findeth a wife findeth a good *thing,* and obtaineth favour of the Lord.—Prov., ch. 18.

9588. —— **A treacherous.** *Delilah.* [4] He loved a woman in the valley of Sorek, whose name *was* Delilah. [5] The lords of the Philistines .. said unto her, Entice him, and see wherein his great strength *lieth,* and by what *means* we may prevail against him, that we may bind him to afflict him : and we will give thee every one of us eleven hundred *pieces* of silver.—Judges, ch. 16.

9589. —— **An unworthy.** *Canaanite.* [46] Rebekah said to Isaac, I am weary of my life because of the daughters of Heth : if Jacob take a wife of the daughters of Heth, such as these *which are* of the daughters of the land, what good shall my life do me ?—Gen., ch. 27.

9590. —— **won by Merit.** *In Battle.* [25] The men of Israel came, Have ye seen this man that is come up? surely to defy Israel is he come up : and it shall be, *that* the man who killeth him, the king will enrich him with great riches, and will give him his daughter.—1 Sam., ch. 17.

9591. —— **Wicked.** *Herodias.* [3] Herod had laid hold on John, and bound him, and put *him* in prison for Herodias' sake, his brother Philip's wife. [4] For John said unto him, It is not lawful for thee to have her.. [10] And he sent, and beheaded John in the prison.—Mat., ch. 13.

See **MARRIAGE, WIVES.**

9592. WILDERNESS, Temptation in the. *Jesus.* [1] Then was Jesus led up of the Spirit into the wilderness to be tempted of the devil. [2] And when he had fasted forty days and forty nights, he was afterward a hungered.—Mat., ch. 4.

9593. WILL, A rebellious. *"Would not."* [37] O Jerusalem, Jerusalem, *thou* that killest the prophets, and stonest them which are sent unto thee, how often would I have gathered thy children together, even as a hen gathereth her chickens under *her* wings, and ye would not !— Mat., ch. 23.

9594. —— —— *Jews in Egypt.* [16] *As for* the word that thou hast spoken unto us in the name of the Lord, we will not hearken unto thee. [17] But we will certainly do whatsoever thing goeth forth out of our own mouth, to burn incense unto the queen of heaven.—Jer., ch. 44.

See other illustrations under :

CHOICE.

Better. Mary hath chosen that good part	1222
Decisive. Me and my house, we will serve the L.	1223
Desperate. So will I go..if I perish, I perish	1224
Difficult. David said..I am in a great strait	1225
Dangerous. Lot chose..toward Sodom	1226
Fruitful. Rod of Aaron..budded..almonds	1227
Foolish. Hewed them out..broken cisterns	1228
Heart. L. looketh on the heart	1229
Life or Death. Fiery serpent..looketh on it..live	1230
Murderers. Release unto us Barabbas	1231
Neglected. O that thou hadst hearkened	1232
Pious. Moses..refused to be called the son	1233
of Piety. How much better..than to get gold	1234
Rebellious. We will certainly..burn incense	1235
Responsibility. Set before you..blessing and a c.	1236
Results. Therefore shalt thou serve..enemies	1237
Saints. I will take you..for a people	1238
Unexpected. Remaineth the youngest..feedeth	1239
Worldly. Went away sorrowful..great possessions	1240

DETERMINATION.

Evil. We will certainly..burn incense to the queen	2260
Fixed. In every city bonds..none..move me	2261
" As the L. liveth..I will not leave thee	2262
Resolute. Absalom said..set it on fire	2263
Wanting. I will let him go..Pilate gave sentence	2264

OBDURACY.

Defiant. Who is the L..let Israel go ?	5755
Final. Pharaoh made ready his chariot..people	5756
Foolish. Ahaz in..distress did trespass more and	5757
Jewish. Thy neck is an iron sinew..brow brass	5758
Spiritual. If the mighty works..been done in Tyre	5759
Self-destructive. I know G. hath determined to	5760
Truth. Divers were hardened..spake evil	5761

OBSTINACY.

Provoking. The L. said..it is a stiffnecked people	5825
Rebuked. I..withstand thee..thy way is perverse	5826
Rebellious. People refused the voice of the L.	5827

PERSISTENCE.

Necessary. Aaron and Hur stayed up his hands	6067
Prayer. Let me go, for the day breaketh..will not	6068
Rewarded. As thy soul liveth, I will not leave thee	6069
Unchangeable. They spake daily..Mordecai	6070
Undiscouraged. Many charged Bartimeus..hold his	6071
" Because of his importunity he will	6077

SELF-CONTROL.

Lack. He that hath no rule over his own spirit	7698
Masterly. Children of Belial said..He held his p.	7699
Resolute. Put a knife to thy throat..much appetite	7700

SELF-DENIAL.

Abstinence. David would not drink thereof	7701
Bodily. I keep under my body lest..be a castaway	7702
Better. People complained..fire consumed them	7703
Costly. If thy right hand offend thee..cut it off	7704
Difficult. Young ruler went away grieved..great	7705
Decent. Put a knife to thy throat..given to a.	7706
Essential. Let him deny himself..take up his cross	7707
Marvellous. Get thee out of thy country..kindred	7708
" Moses refused to be called the son	7709
" Unto this present hour we both	7710
for Others. If meat make my brother to offend	7711
Patriotic. Twelve years..not eaten the bread of	7712

9595. WILLINGNESS to believe. *"One born blind."* [36] Said, Who is he, Lord, that I might believe on him? [37] And Jesus said..thou hast both seen him, and it is he that talketh with thee. [38] And he said, Lord, I believe. And he worshipped him.—JOHN, ch. 9.

9596. —— in Benevolence. *For Tabernacle.* [29] The children of Israel brought a willing offering unto the Lord, every man and woman, whose heart made them willing to bring for all manner of work, which the Lord had commanded to be made by the hand of Moses.—Ex., ch. 35. [See chapter.]

9597. —— to Save. *Jesus.* [2] There came a leper and worshipped him, saying, Lord, if thou wilt thou canst make me clean. [3] And Jesus put forth *his* hand, and touched him, saying, I will; be thou clean. And immediately his leprosy was cleansed.—MAT., ch. 8.

9598. —— —— *"Receiveth."* [2] The Pharisees and scribes murmured, saying, This man receiveth sinners, and eateth with them.—LUKE, ch. 15.

See other illustrations under:

9599. WIND, Master of the. *Jesus.* [24] Then he arose, and rebuked the wind and the raging of the water: and they ceased, and there was a calm.—LUKE, ch. 8. •

9600. —— A powerful. *Red Sea.* [21] The Lord caused the sea to go *back* by a strong east wind all that night, and made the sea dry *land*, and the waters were divided. [22] And the children of Israel went into the midst of the sea upon the dry *ground*: and the waters *were* a wall unto them.—Ex., ch. 14.

9601. —— A provident. *Quails.* [31] There went forth a wind from the Lord, and brought quails from the sea, and let *them* fall by the camp.—NUM., ch. 11.

9602. —— A perilous. *Euroclydon.* [14] There arose against it a tempestuous wind, called Euroclydon. [15] And when the ship was caught, and could not bear up into the wind, we let *her* drive.—ACTS, ch. 27.

9603. —— —— *Gennesaret.* [23] As they sailed,

he fell asleep: and there came down a storm of wind on the lake; and they were filled *with water*, and were in jeopardy. [24] And they came to him, and awoke him, saying, Master, Master, we perish.—LUKE, ch. 8.

9604. —— A rending. *Sinai.* [11] The Lord passed by, and a great and strong wind rent the mountains, and brake in pieces the rocks before the Lord; *but* the Lord *was* not in the wind.— 1 KINGS, ch. 19.

See other illustrations under:

9605. WINE, Changed by. *Nabal.* [37] In the morning, when the wine was gone out of Nabal, and his wife had told him these things..his heart died within him, and he became *as* a stone. —1 SAM., ch. 25.

9606. —— Changed to. *Water.* [7] Jesus saith unto them, Fill the waterpots with water. And they filled them up to the brim. [8] And he saith ..Draw out now, and bear unto the governor of the feast. And they bare *it*.—JOHN, ch. 2.

9607. —— Dangers of. *"Drunken."* [20] Noah began *to be* a husbandman, and he planted a vineyard: [21] And he drank of the wine, and was drunken; and he was uncovered within his tent.—GEN., ch. 9.

9608. —— a Mocker. *Proverb.* [1] Wine *is* a mocker, strong drink *is* raging: and whosoever is deceived thereby is not wise.—PROV., ch. 20.

9609. —— Misled by. *"Stingeth."* [31] Look not thou upon the wine when it is red, when it giveth his colour in the cup, *when* it moveth itself aright. [32] At the last it biteth like a serpent, and stingeth like an adder.—PROV., ch. 23.

9610. —— Medicinal. *To Timothy.* [23] Drink no longer water, but use a little wine for thy stomach's sake and thine often infirmities.—1 TIM., ch. 5.

9611. —— brings Poverty. *Proverb.* [20] Be not among winebibbers; among riotous eaters of flesh: [21] For the drunkard and the glutton shall come to poverty: and drowsiness shall clothe *a* man with rags.—PROV., ch. 23.

9612. —— Sorrows of. *Proverb.* [29] Who hath woe? who hath sorrow? who hath contentions? who hath babbling? who hath wounds without cause? who hath redness of eyes? [30] They that tarry long at the wine; they that go to seek mixed wine.—PROV., ch. 23.

9613. —— Sacramental. *First.* [18] Melchizedek king of Salem brought forth bread and wine:— and he *was* the priest of the most high God.— GEN., ch. 14. [For Abram.]

See **INTEMPERANCE** and references.

9614. WISDOM, Attraction of. *Solomon.* [31] For he was wiser than all men: than Ethan the Ezrahite, and Heman, and Chalcol, and Darda, the sons of Mahol: and his fame was in all nations round about.—1 KINGS, ch. 4.

9615. —— with Age. *Elihu.* [6] The Buzite answered and said, I *am* young, and ye *are* very old; wherefore I was afraid, and durst not shew you mine opinion. [7] I said, Days should speak, and multitude of years should teach wisdom.— JOB, ch. 32.

9616. —— **Beginning of.** *Fear of the Lord.*
[9] Give *instruction* to a wise *man*, and he will be yet wiser : teach a just *man*, and he will increase in learning. [10] The fear of the Lord *is* the beginning of wisdom.—Prov., ch. 9.

9617. —— **Benefits of.** *Riches—Honour.*
[18] Riches and honour *are* with me : *yea*, durable riches and righteousness. [19] My fruit *is* better than gold, yea, than fine gold ; and my revenue than choice silver. [20] I lead in the way of righteousness.—Prov., ch. 8.

9618. —— **Choice of.** *Solomon.* [5] In Gibeon the Lord appeared to Solomon in a dream by night : and God said, Ask what I shall give thee.. [9] Give therefore thy servant an understanding heart to judge thy people, that I may discern between good and bad : for who is able to judge this thy so great a people ? [10] And the speech pleased the Lord.—1 Kings, ch. 3.

9619. —— —— *Commended.* [11] God said unto him, Because thou hast asked this thing, and hast not asked for thyself long life ; neither hast asked riches for thyself, nor hast asked the life of thy enemies ; but hast asked for thyself understanding to discern judgment.. [13] And I have also given thee that which thou hast not asked, both riches, and honour.—1 Kings, ch. 3.

9620. —— **Commended.** *Worldly.* [7] Take thy bill, and write fourscore. [8] And the lord commended the unjust steward, because he had done wisely.—Luke, ch. 16.

9621. —— **Creative.** *Divine.* [27] When he prepared the heavens, I *was* there : when he set a compass upon the face of the depth : [28] When he established the clouds above : when he strengthened the fountains of the deep : [29] When he gave to the sea his decree, that the waters should not pass his commandment : when he appointed the foundations of the earth.—Prov., ch. 8.

9622. —— **A Child's.** *Jesus.* [47] All that heard him were astonished at his understanding and answers.—Luke, ch. 2.

9623. —— **Early.** *Hebrews.* [17] These four children, God gave them knowledge and skill in all learning and wisdom : and Daniel had understanding in all visions and dreams.—Dan., ch. 1.

9624. —— **Earthly.** *Greeks.* [17] Christ sent me not to baptize, but to preach the gospel : not with wisdom of words, lest the cross of Christ should be made of none effect. [18] For the preaching of the cross is to them that perish, foolishness ; but unto us which are saved, it is the power of God.—1 Cor., ch. 1.

9625. —— —— *Not saved by.* [21] For after that in the wisdom of God the world by wisdom knew not God, it pleased God by the foolishness of preaching to save them that believe. [22] For the Jews require a sign, and the Greeks seek after wisdom.—1 Cor., ch. 1.

9626. —— **First.** *Principal Thing.* [7] Wisdom *is* the principal thing ; *therefore* get wisdom : and with all thy getting get understanding. [8] Exalt her, and she shall promote thee.—Prov., ch. 4.

9627. —— **Fame for.** *Solomon.* [34] There came of all people to hear the wisdom of Solomon, from all kings of the earth, which had heard of his wisdom.—1 Kings, ch. 4.

9628. —— **Greatness of.** *Solomon.* [29] God gave Solomon wisdom and understanding exceeding much, and largeness of heart, even as the sand that *is* on the sea shore. [30] And Solomon's wisdom excelled the wisdom of all the children of the east country, and all the wisdom of Egypt. [31] For he was wiser than all men.—1 Kings, ch. 4.

9629. —— **incomparable.** *"Rubies."* [11] Wisdom *is* better than rubies, and all the things that may be desired are not to be compared to it. [12] I wisdom dwell with prudence, and find out knowledge of witty inventions.—Prov., ch. 8.

9630. —— **Lack of.** *"On Sand."* [26] And every one that heareth these sayings of mine, and doeth them not, shall be likened unto a foolish man, which built his house upon the sand : [27] And the rain descended, and the floods came, and the winds blew, and beat upon that house ; and it fell : and great was the fall of it. —Mat., ch. 7.

9631. —— **in Oppression, No.** *In Egypt.* [10] Let us deal wisely with them ; lest they multiply.. join also unto our enemies, and fight against us, and *so* get them up out of the land.. [12] But the more they afflicted them, the more they multiplied and grew.—Ex., ch. 1.

9632. —— **vs. Poverty.** *Solomon said,* [16] Then said I, Wisdom *is* better than strength : nevertheless the poor man's wisdom *is* despised, and his words are not heard.—Eccl., ch. 9.

9633. —— **prayed for.** *Solomon.* [See No. 9618.]

9634. —— **Earnest Pursuit of.** *Proverb.* [3] If thou criest after knowledge, *and* liftest up thy voice for understanding ; [4] If thou seekest her as silver, and searchest for her as *for* hid treasures ; [5] Then shalt thou understand the fear of the Lord, and find the knowledge of God. [6] For the Lord giveth wisdom.—Prov., ch. 2.

9635. —— **Practical.** *David.* [19] *Is not* the hand of Joab with thee in all this ? And the woman answered.. *As* thy soul liveth, my lord the king, none can turn to the right hand or to the left from aught that my lord the king hath spoken : for thy servant Joab, he bade me.—2 Sam., ch. 14.

9636. —— —— *Solomon.* [25] The king said, Divide the living child in two, and give half to the one, and half to the other. [26] Then spake the woman whose the living child *was* unto the king, for her bowels yearned upon her son, and she said, O my lord, give her the living child, and in no wise slay it.—1 Kings, ch. 3.

9637. —— **of Piety.** *"On a Rock."* [24] Whosoever heareth these sayings of mine, and doeth them, I will liken him unto a wise man, which built his house upon a rock : [25] And the rain descended, and the floods came, and the winds blew, and beat upon that house ; and it fell not : for it was founded upon a rock.—Mat., ch. 7.

9638. —— **prized.** *Divine.* [34] Blessed *is* the man that heareth me, watching daily at my gates, waiting at the posts of my doors. [35] For whoso findeth me findeth life, and shall obtain favour of the Lord. [36] But he that sinneth against me wrongeth his own soul : all they that hate me love death.—Prov., ch. 8.

9639. —— **more than Strength.** *Parable.*
[14] There was a little city, and few men within it ; and there came a great king against it, and besieged it, and built great bulwarks against it. [15] Now there was found in it a poor wise man, and he by his wisdom delivered the city.—ECCL., ch. 9.

9640. —— **separates.** *Jews.* [28] The rest of the people, the priests, the Levites, the porters, the singers, the Nethinim, and all they that had separated themselves from the people of the lands unto the law of God, their wives, their sons, and their daughters, every one having knowledge, and having understanding ; [29] They clave to their brethren.—NEH., ch. 10.

9641. —— **True.** *Proverb.* [10] The fear of the Lord is the beginning of wisdom : and the knowledge of the holy is understanding. [11] For by me thy days shall be multiplied, and the years of thy life shall be increased.—PROV., ch. 9.

9642. —— **Tribute to.** *Queen of Sheba.* It was a true report that I heard in mine own land of thy acts and of thy wisdom. [7] Howbeit I believed not the words, until I came, and mine eyes had seen it ; and, behold, the half was not told me : thy wisdom and prosperity exceedeth the fame which I heard.—1 KINGS, ch. 10.

9643. —— **Varied.** *Solomon* [32] Spake three thousand proverbs : and his songs were a thousand and five. [33] And he spake of trees, from the cedar tree that is in Lebanon even unto the hyssop that springeth out of the wall : he spake also of beasts, and of fowl, and of creeping things, and of fishes.—1 KINGS, ch. 4.

9644. —— **Worldly.** *Vanity.* [15] As it happeneth to the fool, so it happeneth even to me ; and why was I then more wise ? Then I said in my heart, that this also is vanity, [16] For there is no remembrance of the wise more than of the fool for ever.—ECCL., ch. 2.

9645. —— **of the World.** *" On Wall."* [8] Then came in all the king's wise men : but they could not read the writing, nor make known to the king the interpretation thereof. [9] Then was king Belshazzar greatly troubled.—DAN., ch. 5.

See EDUCATION, INTELLIGENCE, *and references.*

9646. WISH, An inconsiderate. *David.*
[15] David longed, and said, Oh that one would give me drink of the water of the well of Bethlehem, which is by the gate ! [16] And the three mighty men brake through the host of the Philistines, and drew water.—2 SAM., ch. 23.

See other illustrations under :

DESIRE.

Chief. Lord, that I might receive my sight   2210
Longing. Give me drink of..well of Beth-lehem   2211
Sanctuary. My soul longeth..for the courts of the   2212

9647. WITCH, A famous. *At En-dor.* [7] Said Saul unto his servants, Seek me a woman that hath a familiar spirit, that I may go to her and inquire of her..Behold, there is a woman that hath a familiar spirit at En-dor.—1 SAM., ch. 28.

9648. —— **Work of a.** *" Bring up."* [See above.] [11] Said the woman, Whom shall I bring up unto thee? And he said, Bring me up Samuel. [12] And when the woman saw Samuel, she cried with a loud voice.—1 SAM., ch. 28.

9649. WITCHCRAFT abolished. *By Josiah.*
[24] The workers with familiar spirits, and the wizards, and the images, and the idols, and all the abominations that were spied in the land of Judah and in Jerusalem, did Josiah put away.—2 KINGS, ch. 23.

9650. —— **Famous for.** *Simon.* [9] Simon, which beforetime in the same city used sorcery, and bewitched the people of Samaria, giving out that himself was some great one : [10] To whom they all gave heed, from the least to the greatest, saying, This man is the great power of God.—ACTS, ch. 8.

See other illustrations under :

SORCERY.

Captivating. Simon bewitched the people..all   8202
Curious Arts. [Ephesians] used curious arts..burn   908
Imposition. Magicians..cast down..rod..serpent   5162
Renounced. Simon himself believed..was bap'd   8203
    "   [Ephesians] used curious arts   8204

Magic. Magicians..cast down..rod..serpent   5162

9651. WITNESS, Altar for. *Beyond Jordan.*
[11] And the children of Israel heard say, Behold, the children of Reuben and..of Gad and the half tribe of Manasseh have built an altar..in the borders of Jordan, at the passage of the children of Israel.. [24] ..done it for fear..In time to come your children might speak unto our children, saying, What have ye to do with the Lord God of Israel?—JOSH., ch. 22.

9652. —— **An ancient.** *Abel's.* [4] By faith Abel offered unto God a more excellent sacrifice than Cain, by which he obtained witness that he was righteous, God testifying of his gifts : and by it he being dead yet speaketh.—HEB., ch. 11.

9653. —— **of Approval.** *Enoch.* [5] By faith Enoch was translated that he should not see death ; and was not found, because God had translated him : for before his translation he had this testimony, that he pleased God.—HEB., ch. 11.

9654. —— **Christ a.** *Before Pilate.* [37] Art thou a king then? Jesus answered, Thou sayest that I am a king. To this end was I born, and for this cause came I into the world, that I should bear witness unto the truth.—JOHN, ch. 18.

9655. —— **An effective.** *The Council.* [14] Beholding the man which was healed standing with them, they could say nothing against it.—ACTS, ch. 4.

9656. —— **A false.** *Proverb.* [18] A man that beareth false witness against his neighbour is a maul, and a sword, and a sharp arrow.—PROV., ch. 25.

9657. —— **by Fire.** *To Abram.* [17] When the sun went down, and it was dark, behold a smoking furnace, and a burning lamp that passed between those pieces. [18] In that same day the Lord made a covenant with Abram.—GEN., ch. 15.

9658. —— **The Father's.** *Baptism.* [16] Jesus ..went up straightway out of the water : and lo, the heavens were opened unto him, and he saw the Spirit of God descending like a dove, and lighting upon him : [17] And lo, a voice from heaven, saying, This is my beloved Son, in whom I am well pleased.—MAT., ch. 3.

9659. —— **A faithful.** *Stephen* [56] Said, Behold, I see the heavens opened, and the Son of man standing on the right hand of God. [57] Then they cried out with a loud voice, and stopped their ears, and ran upon him with one accord. —Acts, ch. 7.

9660. —— **of the Spirit.** *Inward.* [16] The Spirit itself beareth witness with our spirit, that we are the children of God : [17] And if children, then heirs.—Rom., ch. 8.

9661. —— **Insufficient, One.** *Law.* [15] One witness shall not rise up against a man for any iniquity, or for any sin, in any sin that he sinneth : that the mouth of two witnesses, or at the mouth of three witnesses, shall the matter be established.—Deut., ch. 19.

9662. —— —— *Law.* [30] Whoso killeth any person, the murderer shall be put to death by the mouth of witnesses : but one witness shall not testify against any person *to cause him* to die. —Num., ch. 35.

9663. —— **An influential.** *Lazarus.* [10] The chief priests consulted that they might put Lazarus also to death ; [11] Because that by reason of him many of the Jews went away, and believed on Jesus.—John, ch. 12.

9664. —— —— *Eneas* [33] Was sick of the palsy. [34] And Peter said..Eneas, Jesus Christ maketh thee whole : arise, and make thy bed. And he arose immediately. [35] And all that dwelt at Lydda and Saron saw him, and turned to the Lord.—Acts, ch. 9.

9665. —— **for Jesus.** *"The undemonized."* [19] Go home to thy friends, and tell them how great things the Lord hath done for thee, and hath had compassion on thee. [20] And he departed, and began to publish in Decapolis how great things Jesus had done for him : and all *men* did marvel.—Mark, ch. 5.

9666. —— **A joint.** *"With our."* [See No. 9660.]

9667. —— **A little.** *Captive Maid.* [2] The Syrians..had brought away captive out of the land of Israel a little maid ; and she waited on Naaman's wife. [3] And she said unto her mistress, Would God that my lord *were* with the prophet that *is* in Samaria ! for he would recover him of his leprosy.—2 Kings, ch. 5.

9668. —— **Neglect of a.** *"To utter."* [1] If a soul sin, and hear the voice of swearing, and *is* a witness, whether he hath seen or known *of it ;* if he do not utter *it,* then he shall bear his iniquity.—Lev., ch. 5.

9669. —— **punished, False.** *Law.* [18] Be a false witness, and hath testified falsely against his brother ; [19] Then shall ye do unto him, as he had thought to have done unto his brother. —Deut., ch. 19.

9670. —— **Power for.** *Pentecost.* [8] Ye shall receive power, after that the Holy Ghost is come upon you : and ye shall be witnesses unto me both in Jerusalem, and in all Judea, and in Samaria, and unto the uttermost part of the earth.—Acts, ch. 1.

9671. —— **Stone for.** *Reminder.* [26] Joshua wrote these words in the book of the law of God, and took a great stone, and set it up there under an oak, that *was* by the sanctuary of the Lord. [27] And Joshua said unto all the people,

Behold, this stone shall be a witness unto us ; for it hath heard all the words of the Lord which he spake unto us.—Josh., ch. 24.

9672. —— **An unknown.** *Moses.* [12] He looked this way and that way, and when he saw that *there was* no man, he slew the Egyptian, and hid him in the sand. [13] And when he went out the second day, behold, two men of the Hebrews strove together.. [14] And he said, Who made thee a prince and a judge over us ? intendest thou to kill me, as thou killedst the Egyptian ? And Moses feared, and said, Surely this thing is known.—Ex., ch. 2.

9673. —— **Voluntary.** *To Samaritans.* [28] The woman then left her waterpot, and went her way into the city, and saith to the men, [29] Come, see a man, which told me all things that ever I did : is not this the Christ ? [30] They they.. came unto him.—John, ch. 4.

9674. WITNESSES, Bold. *Apostles.* [13] When they saw the boldness of Peter and John, and perceived that they were unlearned and ignorant men, they marvelled ; and they took knowledge of them, that they had been with Jesus.— Acts, ch. 4.

9675. —— **Deeds are.** *Of Christ.* [3] Art thou he that should come, or do we look for another ? [4] Jesus answered..Go and shew John again those things which ye do hear and see : [5] The blind receive their sight, and the lame walk, the lepers are cleansed, and the deaf hear, the dead are raised up, and the poor have the gospel preached to them.—Mat., ch. 11.

9676. —— **disagreeing.** *Ananias' Court.* [58] We heard him say, I will destroy this temple that is made with hands, and within three days I will build another made without hands. [59] But neither so did their witness agree together.— Mark, ch. 14.

9677. —— **discredited.** *Mary.* [10] She went and told them that had been with him, as they mourned and wept. [11] And they, when they had heard that he was alive, and had been seen of her, believed not.—Mark, ch. 16.

9678. —— —— *Two Disciples.* [12] He appeared in another form unto two of them, as they walked, and went into the country. [13] And they went and told *it* unto the residue : neither believed they them.—Mark, ch. 16.

9679. —— —— *Ten.* [25] The other disciples therefore said..We have seen the Lord. But he said unto them, Except I shall see in his hands the print of the nails, and put my finger in the print of the nails, and thrust my hand into his side, I will not believe.—John, ch. 20.

9680. —— **False.** *For Jezebel.* [13] Two men, children of Belial..witnessed against him, *even* against Naboth, in the presence of the people, saying, Naboth did blaspheme God and the king. Then they carried him forth out of the city, and stoned him with stones that he died.—1 Kings, ch. 21.

9681. —— —— *Against Stephen.* [11] They suborned men, which said, We have heard him speak blasphemous words against Moses, and *against* God. [12] And they stirred up the people, and the elders, and the scribes, and came upon *him,* and caught him, and brought *him* to the council. [13] And set up false witnesses.—Acts, ch. 6.

9682. —— —— *Soldiers.* [12] When they were assembled with the elders, and had taken counsel, they gave large money unto the soldiers, [13] Saying, Say ye, His disciples came by night, and stole him *away* while we slept.—Mat., ch. 27.

9683. —— Greater. *Deeds.* [36] I have greater witness than *that* of John : for the works which the Father hath given me to finish, the same works that I do, bear witness of me, that the Father hath sent me.—John, ch. 5.

9684. —— Irrepressible. *Apostles.* [40] When they had..beaten *them*, they commanded that they should not speak in the name of Jesus, and let them go.. [42] And daily in the temple, and in every house, they ceased not to teach and preach Jesus Christ.—Acts, ch. 5.

9685. —— Imposition by. *"His Head."* [14] Bring forth him that hath cursed without the camp ; and let all that heard *him* lay their hands upon his head, and let all the congregation stone him.—Lev., ch. 24.

9686. —— intimidated. *Believers.* [12] Some said, He is a good man : others said, Nay ; but he deceiveth the people. [13] Howbeit no man spake openly of him for fear of the Jews.—John, ch. 7.

9687. —— Joyful. *Shepherds.* [19] Mary kept all these things, and pondered *them* in her heart. [20] And the shepherds returned, glorifying and praising God for all the things that they had heard and seen, as it was told unto them.—Luke, ch. 2.

9688. —— Subornation of. *Against Naboth.* [9] She wrote in the letters, saying, Proclaim a fast, and set Naboth on high among the people : [10] And set two men, sons of Belial, before him, to bear witness against him, saying, Thou didst blaspheme God and the king. And *then* carry him out, and stone him.—1 Kings, ch. 21.

9689. —— in the Scriptures. *For Jesus.* [39] Search the Scriptures ; for in them ye think ye have eternal life : and they are they which testify of me. [40] And ye will not come to me, that ye might have life.—John, ch. 5.

9690. —— unnecessary. *Thomas.* [27] Thomas, Reach hither thy finger, and behold my hands ; and reach hither thy hand, and thrust *it* into my side ; and be not faithless, but believing. [28] And Thomas answered..My Lord and my God.—John, ch. 20.

Also see:

Confounded. He that is without sin..first stone   86
 See EVIDENCE and references.
 See TESTIMONY.

9691. WIVES, Duty of. *Christian.* Ye wives, be in subjection to your own husbands ; that, if any obey not the word, they also may without the word be won by the conversation of the wives : [2] While they behold your chaste conversation *coupled* with fear.—1 Peter, ch. 3.

9692. —— by Kidnapping. *Benjamites.* [21] If the daughters of Shiloh come out to dance in dances, then come ye out of the vineyards, and catch you every man his wife of the daughters of Shiloh, and go to the land of Benjamin.—Judges, ch. 21.

9693. —— Numerous. *Solomon's.* [3] He had seven hundred wives, princesses, and three hundred concubines : and his wives turned away his heart.—1 Kings, ch. 11.

9694. —— Pernicious. *Solomon's.* [4] When Solomon was old..his wives turned away his heart after other gods.—1 Kings, ch. 11.

See WIFE.

9695. WOMAN, Benevolence of. *"Two Mites."* [43] This poor widow hath cast more in, than all they which have cast into the treasury. [44] For all *they* did cast in of their abundance : but she of her want did cast in all that she had, *even* all her living.—Mark, ch. 12.

9696. —— —— *Dorcas.* [36] There was at Joppa a certain disciple named..Dorcas : this woman was full of good works and almsdeeds which she did.—Acts, ch. 9.

9697. —— A Companion. *Eve.* [20] Adam gave names to all cattle, and to the fowl of the air, and to every beast of the field ; but for Adam there was not found a help meet for him.—Gen., ch. 2. [Cattle were insufficient.]

9698. —— A courteous. *Rebekah.* [18] She said, Drink, my lord : and she hasted, and let down her pitcher upon her hand, and gave him drink. [19] And when she had done giving him drink, she said, I will draw *water* for thy camels also. —Gen., ch. 24.

9699. —— Conspiracy of. *Delilah.* [18] She sent and called for the lords of the Philistines, saying, Come up this once..the Philistines..brought money in their hand. [19] And she made him sleep upon her knees ; and she called for a man, and she caused him to shave off the seven locks of his head ; and she began to afflict him, and his strength went from him.—Judges, ch. 16.

9700. —— A cursed. *Queen Jezebel.* [33] Jehu said, Throw her down. So they threw her down : and *some* of her blood was sprinkled on the wall, and on the horses : and he trode her under foot. [34] And when he was come in, he did eat and drink, and said, Go, see now this cursed *woman*, and bury her : for she is a king's daughter. [35]..but they found no more of her than the skull, and the feet, and the palms of *her* hands.—2 Kings, ch. 9.

9701. —— A disgracing. *Adulteress.* [32] Whoso committeth adultery with a woman lacketh understanding : he *that* doeth it destroyeth his own soul. [33] A wound and dishonour shall he get ; and his reproach shall not be wiped away. —Prov., ch. 6.

9702. —— A cruel. *Herodias.* [24] She went forth, and said unto her mother, What shall I ask ? And she said, The head of John the Baptist.—Mark, ch. 6.

9703. —— a Crown. *Proverb.* [4] A virtuous woman *is* a crown to her husband : but she that maketh ashamed *is* as rottenness in his bones. —Prov., ch. 12.

9704. —— leavens the Church. *Jesus said,* [33] The kingdom of heaven is like unto leaven, which a woman took, and hid in three measures of meal, till the whole was leavened.—Mat., ch. 13.

9705. —— for Christ. *Pilate's Wife.* [19] When he was set down on the judgment seat, his wife sent unto him, saying, Have thou nothing to do with that just man : for I have suffered many things this day in a dream because of him.— Mat., ch. 27.

9706. —— **Converted.** *First in Europe.* [14] A certain woman named Lydia, a seller of purple.. which worshipped God, heard *us* : whose heart the Lord opened, that she attended unto the things which were spoken of Paul. [15] And when she was baptized, and her household, she besought *us*, saying, If ye have judged me to be faithful to the Lord, come into my house, and abide *there*. And she constrained us.—ACTS, ch. 16.

9707. —— **The chosen.** *Delilah.* [3] Then his father and his mother said unto him, *Is there* never a woman among the daughters of thy brethren, or among all my people, that thou goest to take a wife of the uncircumcised Philistines? And Samson said unto his father, Get her for me ; for she pleaseth me well.—JUDGES, ch. 14.

9708. —— **Dependence on.** *Deborah.* [7] Sisera the captain of Jabin's army, with his chariots and his multitude ; and I will deliver him into thine hand. [8] And Barak said unto her, If thou wilt go with me, then I will go : but if thou wilt not go with me, *then* I will not go.—JUDGES, ch. 4. [See No. 9736.]

9709. —— **Disgraced by a.** *Reputation.* [See No. 9731.] [54] Then he called hastily unto the young man his armourbearer..Draw thy sword, and slay me, that men say not of me, A woman slew him. And his young man thrust him through.—JUDGES, ch. 9.

9710. —— **A determined.** *Shunammite.* [29] He said to Gehazi, Gird up thy loins, and take my staff in thy hand, and go thy way..and lay my staff upon the face of the child. [20] And the mother of the child said, *As* the Lord liveth, and *as* thy soul liveth, I will not leave thee. And he arose, and followed her.—2 KINGS, ch. 4. [Her dead child was restored.]

9711. —— **Device of a.** *Messengers.* [18] Which had a well in his court ; whither they went down. [19] And the woman took and spread a covering over the well's mouth, and spread ground corn thereon ; and the thing was not known. [20] And when Absalom's servants came.. to the house, they said, Where *is* Ahimaaz and Jonathan? And the woman said..They be gone over the brook.—2 SAM., ch. 17.

9712. —— **Devotion of.** *A Sinner* [38] Stood at his feet behind *him* weeping, and began to wash his feet with tears, and did wipe *them* with the hairs of her head, and kissed his feet, and anointed *them* with the ointment.—LUKE, ch. 7.

9713. —— **An energetic.** *Shunammite.* [24] She saddled an ass, and said to her servant, Drive, and go forward ; slack not *thy* riding for me, except I bid thee. [25] So she..came unto the man of God to mount Carmel.—2 KINGS, ch. 4.

9714. —— **An indiscreet.** *Proverb.* [22] *As* a jewel of gold in a swine's snout, *so is* a fair woman which is without discretion.—PROV., ch. 11.

9715. —— **Government by.** *Deborah.* [2] The Lord sold them into the hand of Jabin king of Canaan..the captain of whose host *was* Sisera.. [3]..Israel cried unto the Lord : for he had nine hundred chariots of iron ; and twenty years he mightily oppressed the children of Israel. [4] And Deborah, a prophetess, the wife of Lapidoth, she judged Israel at that time.—JUDGES, ch. 4.

9716. —— **A helpful.** *Phebe.* [2] That ye receive her in the Lord, as becometh saints, and that ye assist her in whatsoever business she hath need of you : for she hath been a succourer of many, and of myself also.—ROM., ch. 16.

9717. —— **honoured.** *Messiahship announced.* [At Jacob's well,] [25] The woman saith unto him, I know that Messias cometh, which is called Christ : when he is come, he will tell us all things. [26] Jesus saith unto her, I that speak unto thee am *he*.—JOHN, ch. 4.

9718. —— **A discreet.** *Abigail.* [18] Abigail made haste, and took two hundred loaves, and two bottles of wine, and five sheep ready dressed, and five measures of parched *corn*, and a hundred clusters of raisins, and two hundred cakes of figs.. [25] Let not my lord, I pray thee, regard this man of Belial, *even* Nabal : for as his name *is*, so *is* he ; Nabal *is* his name, and folly *is* with him.—1 SAM., ch. 25.

9719. —— **Importunity of.** *Delilah.* [15] How canst thou say, I love thee, when thine heart *is* not with me? Thou hast mocked me these three times, and hast not told me wherein thy great strength *lieth.* [16]..when she pressed him daily with her words, and urged him, *so*..his soul was vexed unto death ; [17] That he told her all his heart, and said..There hath not come a razor upon mine head.—JUDGES, ch. 16.

9720. —— **An irrepressible.** *Proverb.* [15] A continual dropping in a very rainy day and a contentious woman are alike. [16] Whosoever hideth her hideth the wind.—PROV., ch. 27.

9721. —— **An infamous.** *Jezebel.* [25] There was none like unto Ahab, which did sell himself to work wickedness in the sight of the Lord, whom Jezebel his wife stirred up. [26] And he did very abominably in following idols, according to all *things* as did the Amorites.—1 KINGS, ch. 21.

9722. —— **An intimidating.** *"Maid."* [67] When she saw Peter warming himself, she looked upon him, and said, And thou also wast with Jesus of Nazareth. [68] But he denied, saying, I know not, neither understand I what thou sayest.—MARK, ch. 14.

9723. —— **Influence of.** *Denial.* [See above.]

9724. —— **Intemperance injures.** *Vashti.* [See No. 9726.]

9725. —— **Jesus disclosed to.** *First.* [16] Jesus saith unto her, Mary. She turned herself, and saith unto him, Rabboni ; which is to say, Master.—JOHN, ch. 20.

9726. —— **A modest.** *Vashti.* [10] On the seventh day, when the heart of the king was merry with wine, he commanded.. [11] To bring Vashti the queen before the king with the crown royal, to shew the people and the princes her beauty : for she *was* fair to look on. [12] But the queen Vashti refused to come.—ESTHER, ch. 2.

9727. —— **A model.** *Housekeeper.* [11] The heart of her husband doth safely trust in her, so that he shall have no need of spoil. [12] She will do him good and not evil all the days of her life. [13] She seeketh wool, and flax, and worketh willingly with her hands.—PROV., ch. 31.

9728. —— **Memorial of.** *Love.* [8] She hath done what she could : she is come aforehand to anoint my body to the burying. [9] . . Wheresoever this gospel shall be preached throughout the whole world, *this* also that she hath done shall be spoken of for a memorial of her.—MARK, ch. 14.

9729. —— **Origin of.** " *Rib.*" [21] The Lord God caused a deep sleep to fall upon Adam, and he slept ; and he took one of his ribs, and closed up the flesh instead thereof. [22] And the rib, which the Lord God had taken from man, made he a woman, and brought her unto the man.—GEN., ch. 2.

9730. —— **A patriotic.** *Jael.* [21] Jael Heber's wife took a nail of the tent, and took a hammer in her hand, and went softly unto him, and smote the nail into his temples, and fastened it into the ground : for he was fast asleep and weary. So he died.—JUDGES, ch. 4.

9731. —— —— *Siege of Thebez.* [52] Abimelech came unto the tower, and fought against it, and went hard unto the door of the tower to burn it with fire. [53] And a certain woman cast a piece of a millstone upon Abimelech's head, and *all-to* brake his skull.—JUDGES, ch. 9.

9732. —— **punished.** *For Modesty.* [See No. 9726.] [15] What shall we do unto the queen Vashti according to law, because she hath not performed the commandment of the king Ahasuerus by the chamberlains?—ESTHER, ch. 1. [She was rejected.]

9733. —— **a Peacemaker.** *At Abel.* [19] I *am one of them that are* peaceable *and* faithful in Israel : thou seekest to destroy a city and a mother in Israel. . [21] . . deliver him only, and I will depart from the city. . [22] Then the woman went unto all the people in her wisdom : and they cut off the head of Sheba. . and cast it out to Joab.—2 SAM., ch. 20.

9734. —— **A remarkable.** *Miriam.* [20] Miriam the prophetess, the sister of Aaron, took a timbrel in her hand ; and all the women went out after her with timbrels and with dances. [21] And Miriam answered them, Sing ye to the Lord, for he hath triumphed gloriously : the horse and the rider hath he thrown into the sea.—EX., ch. 15.

9735. —— **A revengeful.** *Herodias.* [18] John had said unto Herod, It is not lawful for thee to have thy brother's wife. [19] Therefore Herodias had a quarrel against him, and would have killed him ; but she could not.—MARK, ch. 6.

9736. —— **A sensible.** *Deborah.* [See No. 9708.] [9] And she said, I will surely go with thee : notwithstanding the journey that thou takest shall not be for thine honour ; for the Lord shall sell Sisera into the hand of a woman. —JUDGES, ch. 4.

9737. —— **A treacherous.** *Jael.* [18] Jael went out to meet Sisera, and said unto him, Turn in, my lord, turn in to me ; fear not. And when he had turned in unto her into the tent, she covered him with a mantle.—JUDGES, ch. 4.

9738. —— **Tears of a.** *Samson's Wife.* [17] She wept before him the seven days, while their feast lasted : and. . he told her, because she lay sore upon him : and she told the riddle to the children of her people.—JUDGES, ch. 14.

9739. —— **A terrifying.** *Jezebel.* [1] Ahab told Jezebel all that Elijah had done, and withal how he had slain all the prophets with the sword. [2] Then Jezebel sent a messenger unto Elijah, saying, So let the gods do *to me,* and more also, if I make not thy life as the life of one of them by to morrow about this time.—1 KINGS, ch. 19. [He fled to Sinai.]

9740. —— **a Teacher.** *To Apollos.* [25] Being fervent in the spirit, he spake and taught diligently the things of the Lord, knowing only the baptism of John. [26] And he began to speak boldly in the synagogue : whom when Aquila and Priscilla had heard, they took him unto *them,* and expounded unto him the way of God more perfectly.—ACTS, ch. 18.

9741. —— **a Witness.** *Samaritan.* [28] The woman then left her waterpot, and went her way into the city, and saith to the men, [29] Come, see a man, which told me all things that ever I did : is not this the Christ ? [30] Then they went out of the city, and came unto him.—JOHN, ch. 4.

9742. —— **A wicked.** *Delilah.* [See No. 9583.] [5] The lords of the Philistines. . said unto her, Entice him, and see wherein his great strength *lieth,* and by what *means* we may prevail against him, that we may bind him to afflict him : and we will give thee every one of us eleven hundred *pieces* of silver.—JUDGES, ch. 16.

9743. WOMEN, Amusements of. *Dancing.* [21] If the daughters of Shiloh came out to dance in dances, then come ye out of the vineyards, and catch you every man his wife of the daughters of Shiloh, and go to the land of Benjamin.— JUDGES, ch. 21.

9744. —— **Benevolence of.** *To Jesus.* [1] He went throughout every city and village, preach. ing. . and the twelve *were* with him, [2] And certain women, which had been healed of evil spirits and infirmities, Mary called Magdalene, out of whom went seven devils, [3] And Joanna the wife of Chuza Herod's steward, and Susanna, and many others, which ministered unto him of their substance.—LUKE, ch. 8.

9745. —— **Consecration of.** *Gifts.* [8] He made the laver *of* brass, and the foot of it *of* brass, of the lookingglasses of *the women* assembling, which assembled *at* the door of the tabernacle. —EX., ch. 38.

9746. —— **Contributions of.** *For Tabernacle.* [25] All the women that were wise hearted did spin with their hands, and brought that which they had spun, *both* of blue, and of purple, *and* of scarlet, and of fine linen. [26] And all the women whose hearts stirred them up in wisdom spun goats' *hair.*—EX., ch. 35.

9747. —— **in the Church.** *Prophesy.* [Peter at Pentecost quoted from Joel,] [18] On my servants and on my handmaidens, I will pour out in those days of my spirit ; and they shall prophesy.—ACTS, ch. 2.

9748. —— **destroyed.** *By War.* [22] When their fathers or their brethren come unto us to complain. . we will say. . Be favourable unto them for our sakes : because we reserved not to each man his wife in the war.—JUDGES, ch. 21.

9749. —— **first in Duty.** *Resurrection.* [2] Very early in the morning, the first *day* of the week, they came unto the sepulchre at the rising of the sun.—Mark, ch. 16.

9750. —— **Faithful.** *Crucifixion.* [55] Many women were there (beholding afar off) which followed Jesus from Galilee, ministering unto him : [56] Among which was Mary Magdalene, and Mary the mother of James and Joses, and the mother of Zebedee's children.—Mat., ch. 27.

9751. —— *Crucifixion.* [25] There stood by the cross of Jesus his mother, and his mother's sister, Mary the *wife* of Cleophas, and Mary Magdalene.—John, ch. 19.

9752. —— **First Gifts from.** *For Tabernacle.* [21] Every one whose heart stirred him up, and every one whom his spirit made willing..they brought the Lord's offering to the work of the tabernacle..and for all his service, and for the holy garments. [22]..both men and women.— Ex., ch. 35. [*Lit.* " The men over and above the women."]

9753. —— **Irreligious.** *Antediluvians.* [2] The sons of God saw the daughters of men that they *were* fair ; and they took them wives of all which they chose.. [5] And God saw that the wickedness of man *was* great in the earth.— Gen., ch. 6.

9754. —— **leading in Sin.** *In Egypt.* [19] When we burned incense to the queen of heaven, and poured out drink offerings unto her, did we make her cakes to worship her, and pour out drink offerings unto her, without our men.— Jer., ch. 44.

9755. —— **Messengers.** *For Christ.* [7] Tell his disciples and Peter that he goeth before you into Galilee : there shall ye see him, as he said unto you. [8] And they went out quickly, and fled from the sepulchre ; for they trembled and were amazed : neither said they any thing to any *man;* for they were afraid.—Mark, ch. 16.

9756. —— **Ornaments of.** *" Works."* [9] In like manner also, that women adorn themselves in modest apparel, with shamefacedness and sobriety ; not with braided hair, or gold, or pearls, or costly array ; [10] But (which becometh women professing godliness) with good works. —1 Tim., ch. 2. [See No. 9557.]

9757. —— **Power of.** *In the Church.* [50] The Jews stirred up the devout and honourable women, and the chief men of the city, and raised persecution against Paul and Barnabas, and expelled them out of their coasts.—Acts, ch. 13.

9758. —— **Ruined by.** *Solomon.* [1] King Solomon loved many strange women, together with the daughter of Pharaoh, women of the Moabites, Ammonites, Edomites, Zidonians, *and* Hittites.. [4]..when Solomon was old..his wives turned away his heart after other gods.— 1 Kings, ch. 11.

9759. —— **Sympathy of.** *At Calvary.* [27] There followed him a great company of people, and of women, which also bewailed and lamented him. —Luke, ch. 23.

9760. —— **Sermon to.** *At Philippi.* [13] On the sabbath we went out of the city by a river side, where prayer was wont to be made ; and we sat down, and spake unto the women which resorted *thither.*—Acts, ch. 16.

9761. —— **Silence of.** *Disorders.* [11] Let the

woman learn in silence with all subjection. [12] But I suffer not a woman to teach, nor to usurp authority over the man, but to be in silence.—1 Tim., ch. 2.

See other illustrations under :

DAUGHTER.
Portion of. Caleb said, What wouldest thou ? 1935
Unfortunate. Jephthah..daughter came to meet 1936

DAUGHTER IN LAW.
Faithful. Ruth said, Entreat me not to return 1937
Unwelcome. Were a grief of mind unto Isaac and 1938

MOTHER.
Ambitious. Grant these my two sons may..kingd. 5570
Anxious. Rebekah said, I am weary of my life 5571
Brutalized. We boiled my son..Give thy son 5572
Cruel. Athaliah the mother..slew the seed 5573
Careful. Made Samuel a little coat..every year 5574
Care for. Behold thy mother [Jesus to John] 5575
Distress. Let me not see the death of the child 5576
Ingenious. Took an ark of bulrushes and daubed 5577
in Israel. I am one of them that are peaceable 5578
Revengeful. What shall I ask?..The head of John 5579
Robbery of. 1100 shekels of silver..I took it..M. 5580
True. Give her the living child, in no wise slay it 5581
Wicked. Rebekah put the skins upon his hands 5582
"   Maachah his mother..made an idol 5583

MOTHER IN LAW.
Beloved. Ruth said, Entreat me not to leave thee 5584
Tender. L. deal kindly with you as ye have..N. 5585
Vexed. Esau's wives, were a grief..unto..Rebekah 5586

WIDOW.
Dilemma. Creditor is come..two sons..bondmen 9542
Gifts. Of her want did cast in more 9543
Impoverished. I went out full..come..empty 9544
Importunate. Widow troubleth me..I will avenge 9545
Pious. Served God..night and day 9546
Remembered. Meal shall not waste 9547
"   Elijah said, See thy son liveth 9548
Relieved. Sell the oil and pay the debt 9549
Son of. Hiram..worker in brass 9550
Seven times. They [seven] all had her 9551

WIDOWS.
Care of. Widows..daily ministration 9552
Home of. Naomi..Orpah..Ruth 9553
Provision. Look ye out seven men..this business 9554
Resurrection. Whose wife of the seven 9555
Wronging. Devour widows' houses..long prayers 9556
See WIFE and WIVES.

9762. WONDERS, Demand for. *A Nobleman* [47] Besought him that he would come down, and heal his son : for he was at the point of death. [48] Then said Jesus unto him, Except ye see signs and wonders, ye will not believe.—John, ch. 4.

See other illustrations under :

ASTONISHMENT.
Mystery. Nebuchadnezzar .was astonied 565
Sacred. Angel ascended in the flame of the altar 566
Speech. All amazed..how hear we our own l. 567

SURPRISE.
Appalling. Haman..do even so to Mordecai 8488
Astounding. Men ye put in prison are..in the t. 8489
Choice. The youngest..keepeth the sheep 8490
Conspirators. Guests..were afraid..went his way 8491
Conquest. All the host run and cried and fled 8492
Family. I have provided me a king..his sons 8493
Great. Mordecai..went out in royal apparel 8494
Needless. Did eat, drank..until the day..flood 8495
Providential. I am Joseph your brother..G. did 8496

from Rejection. [Eliab] Look out on his s. 8497
Speechless. Doth my father live?..could not a. 8498
Worldly. As it was in the days of Lot..they sold 8499
World's. As it was in the days of Noe, so..son of 8500
Judgment Day. When saw we thee in prison ? 8496
Prostrating. Paul fell..on the earth..sore afraid 8723
Divine. Moses said, I exceedingly fear and quake 8725

Miracle. Now I know there is no God but 5444

9763. WORD, Divine. *Jesus.* ¹ In the beginning was the Word, and the Word was with God, and the Word was God.—JOHN, ch. 1.

9764. —— **An important.** "*Shibboleth.*" ⁶ Say now Shibboleth ; and he said Sibboleth : for he could not frame to pronounce *it* right. Then they took him, and slew him at the passages of Jordan : and there fell at that time of the Ephraimites forty and two thousand.—JUDGES, ch. 12.

9765. —— **Only a.** *John—Andrew.* ³⁵ John stood, and two of his disciples ; ³⁶ And looking upon Jesus as he walked, he saith, Behold the Lamb of God ! ³⁷ And the two disciples heard him speak, and they followed Jesus.—JOHN,ch.1.

9766. —— **of God.** *Limited.* ¹⁸ Balaam answered..the servants of Balak, If Balak would give me his house full of silver and gold, I cannot go beyond the word of the Lord my God, to do less or more.—NUM., ch. 22.

9767. —— —— *Effective.* ¹⁰ As the rain cometh down, and the snow from heaven, and returneth not thither, but watereth the earth, and maketh it bring forth and bud, that it may give seed to the sower, and bread to the eater : ¹¹ So shall my word be that goeth forth out of my mouth.—ISA., ch. 55.

9768. —— —— *Hammer.* ²⁹ *Is* not my word like as a fire? saith the Lord ; and like a hammer *that* breaketh the rock in pieces?—JER., ch. 23.

9769. WORDS, Accountability for. *Judgment.* ³⁶ Every idle word that men shall speak, they shall give account thereof in the day of judgment. ³⁷ For by thy words thou shalt be justified, and by thy words thou shalt be condemned. —MAT., ch. 12.

9770. —— **Cheerful.** *Proverb.* ²⁵ Heaviness in the heart of man maketh it stoop : but a good word maketh it glad.—PROV., ch. 12.

9771. —— —— *Medicine.* ²² A merry heart doeth good *like* a medicine : but a broken spirit drieth the bones.—PROV., ch. 17.

9772. —— **Effect of.** *Water.* ⁴ The words of a man's mouth *are* as deep waters, *and* the wellspring of wisdom *as* a flowing brook.—PROV., ch. 18.

9773. —— **Kind.** *Honey.* ²⁴ Pleasant words *are as* an honeycomb, sweet to the soul, and health to the bones.—PROV., ch. 16.

9774. —— **Listening to.** *Brotherly.* ¹⁶ They that feared the Lord spake often one to another : and the Lord hearkened, and heard *it :* and a book of remembrance was written before for them that feared the Lord, and that thought upon his name. ¹⁷ And they shall be mine, saith the Lord of hosts, in that day when I make up my jewels.—MAL., ch. 3.

9775. —— **Overflowing.** *Heart.* ³⁴ O generation of vipers, how can ye, being evil, speak good

things ? for out of the abundance of the heart the mouth speaketh. ³⁵ A good man out of the good treasure of the heart bringeth forth good things : and an evil man out of the evil treasure bringeth forth evil things.—MAT., ch. 12.

9776. —— **proven.** *By Deeds.* ²⁷ They told him all the words of Joseph, which he had said unto them : and when he saw the wagons which Joseph had sent to carry him, the spirit of Jacob their father revived.—GEN., ch. 45.

9777. —— **Reliance on.** *Christ's.* ²⁷ Jesus spake unto them, saying, Be of good cheer ; it is I ; be not afraid. ²⁸ And Peter answered him and said, Lord, if it be thou, bid me come unto thee on the water.—MAT., ch. 14.

<small>See other illustrations under :</small>

Heart in. By thy words shalt thou be justified 5612
Treasured. His mother kept all these..in her heart 7602
Talking vs. Doing. He shall be a mouth..take this 8591
Word of God. Came almost the whole city to hear 1334
<small>*See* SPEECH and references.</small>

9778. WORK, Anointing for. *Aaron.* ¹² He poured of the anointing oil upon Aaron's head, and anointed him, to sanctify him.—LEV., ch. 8.

9779. —— **abandoned.** *Mark.* ³⁷ Barnabas determined to take with them John, whose surname was Mark. ³⁸ But Paul thought not good to take him with them, who departed from them from Pamphylia, and went not with them to the work.—ACTS, ch. 15.

9780. —— **distributed.** *System.* ²¹ Thou shalt provide out of all the people able men, such as fear God, men of truth, hating covetousness ; and place *such* over them, *to be* rulers of thousands, *and* rulers of hundreds, rulers of fifties, and rulers of tens : ²² And let them judge the people at all seasons : and it shall be *that* every great matter they shall bring unto thee. —EX., ch. 18.

9781. —— **Devotion to.** *Nehemiah.* ² Sanballat and Geshem sent unto me, saying, Come, let us meet together.. ³ And I sent messengers ..saying, I *am* doing a great work, so that I cannot come down : why should the work cease, whilst I leave it, and come down to you?—NEH., ch. 6.

9782. —— **Excessive.** *Moses.* ¹⁷ Moses' father in law said unto him, The thing that thou doest *is* not good. ¹⁸ Thou wilt surely wear away, both thou, and this people that *is* with thee : for this thing *is* too heavy for thee ; thou art not able to perform it thyself alone.—EX., ch. 18.

9783. —— —— *Epaphroditus.* ³⁰ Because for the work of Christ he was nigh unto death, not regarding his life, to supply your lack of service toward me.—PHIL., ch. 2.

9784. —— **Earnest.** "*Violence.*" ¹² From the days of John the Baptist until now the kingdom of heaven suffereth violence, and the violent take it by force.—MAT., ch. 11.

9785. —— —— *Wall-building.* ⁶ So built we the wall ; and all the wall was joined together unto the half thereof : for the people had a mind to work.—NEH., ch. 4.

9786. —— —— *In Peril.* ¹⁷ They which builded on the wall, and they that bare burdens, with those that laded, *every one* with one of his hands wrought in the work, and with the other *hand* held a weapon.—NEH., ch. 4.

9787. —— **Encouragement for.** *"With you."*
⁴ Now be strong, O Zerubbabel, saith the Lord ; and be strong, O Joshua, son of Josedech, the high priest ; and be strong, all ye people of the land, saith the Lord, and work : for I *am* with you, saith the Lord of hosts.—HAG., ch. 2.

9788. —— **for Each.** *"His Work."* ³⁴ For *the Son of man is* as a man taking a far journey, who left his house, and gave authority to his servants, and to every man his work, and commanded the porter to watch.—MARK, ch. 13.

9789. —— **Early at.** *Twelve Years old.* ⁴⁸ They were amazed : and his mother said. . Son, why hast thou thus dealt with us ? behold, thy father and I have sought thee sorrowing. ⁴⁹ And he said. .How is it that ye sought me ? wist ye not that I must be about my Father's business ?—LUKE, ch. 2.

9790. —— **Grace for.** *Paul.* ¹⁰ His grace which was *bestowed* upon me was not in vain ; but I laboured more abundantly than they all : yet not I, but the grace of God which was with me.—1 COR., ch. 15.

9791. —— **God in the.** *Wall finished.* ¹⁶ When all our enemies heard *thereof*, and all the heathen that *were* about us saw *these things*, they were much cast down in their own eyes : for they perceived that this work was wrought of our God.—NEH., ch.6.

9792. —— **Hindering.** *Wall-builders.* [Their enemies] ⁷ Heard that the walls of Jerusalem were made up, *and* that the breaches began to be stopped, then they were very wroth, ⁸ And conspired all of them together to come *and* to fight against Jerusalem, and to hinder it.—NEH., ch. 4.

9793. —— —— *Opposition.* ¹⁶ From that time forth. .the half of my servants wrought in the work, and the other half of them held both the spears, the shields, and the bows, and the habergeons.—NEH., ch. 4.

9794. —— **Immortal in.** *Moses.* ¹ The Lord spake unto Moses, saying, ² Avenge the children of Israel of the Midianites : afterward shalt thou be gathered unto thy people.—NUM., ch. 31.

9795. —— **Incompetent for.** *Naaman came.* ⁷ When the king of Israel had read the letter. . he rent his clothes, and said, *Am* I God, to kill and to make alive, that this man doth send un-to me to recover a man of his leprosy ?—2 KINGS, ch. 5.

9796. —— **Joy in.** *Jesus.* ³³ Said the disciples one to another, Hath any man brought him *aught* to eat ? ³⁴ Jesus saith unto them, My meat is to do the will of him that sent me, and to finish his work.—JOHN, ch. 4.

9797. —— **neglected.** *Nobles.* ⁵ Tekoites repaired ; but their nobles put not their necks to the work of their Lord.—NEH , ch. 3.

9798. —— —— *Thessalonians.* ¹¹ We hear that there are some which walk among you disorderly, working not at all, but are busybodies. ¹² Now them that are such we command and exhort by our Lord Jesus Christ, that with quietness they work, and eat their own bread.—2 THESS., ch. 3.

9799. —— **Offerings of.** *Tabernacle.* ²⁵ All the women that were wise hearted did spin

with their hands, and brought that which they had spun, *both* of blue, and of purple, *and* of scarlet, and of fine linen. ²⁶ And all the women whose heart stirred them up in wisdom spun goats' *hair.*—EX., ch. 35.

9800. —— **the better Privilege.** *Undemonized.* ¹⁸ When he was come into the ship, he that had been possessed with the devil prayed him that he might be with him. ¹⁹ Howbeit Jesus suffered him not, but saith unto him, Go home to thy friends, and tell them how great things the Lord hath done for thee.—MARK, ch. 5.

9801. —— **Preparation for.** *"Live Coal."* ⁷ He laid *it* upon my mouth, and said, Lo, this hath touched thy lips; and thine iniquity is taken away, and thy sin purged. ⁸ Also I heard the voice of the Lord, saying, Whom shall I send, and who will go for us ? Then said I, Here *am* I ; send me.—ISA., ch. 6.

9802. —— **with Prayer.** *Wall-builders.* ⁹ Nevertheless we made our prayer unto our God, and set a watch against them day and night, because of them.—NEH., ch. 4.

9803. —— **Rigorous.** *Pharaoh.* ⁷ Let them go and gather straw for themselves. ⁸ And the tale of the bricks, which they did make heretofore, ye shall lay upon them ; ye shall not diminish *aught* thereof.—EX., ch. 5.

9804. —— **rewarded.** *Courage.* ⁷ Be ye strong therefore, and let not your hands be weak: for your work shall be rewarded. ⁸ And when Asa heard. .the prophecy of Oded the prophet, he took courage, and put away the abominable idols out of all the land of Judah.—2 CHRON., ch. 15.

9805. —— **ridiculed.** *Wall-builders.* ¹⁹ When Sanballat the Horonite, and Tobiah the servant, the Ammonite, and Geshem the Arabian, heard *it*, they laughed us to scorn, and despised us, and said, What *is* this thing that ye do ? will ye rebel against the king ?—NEH., ch. 2.

9806. —— **slandered.** *Pentecost.* ¹³ Others mocking said, These men are full of new wine. —ACTS, ch. 2.

9807. —— **vs. Stealing.** *Unjust Steward.* ³ Then the steward said within himself, What shall I do ? for my lord taketh away from me the stewardship : I cannot dig ; to beg I am ashamed.—LUKE, ch. 16. [He cut down the bills.]

9808. —— **or Want.** *Paul.* ¹⁰ When we were with you, this we commanded you, that if any would not work, neither should he eat.— 2 THESS., ch. 3.

9809. WORKS adorned by. *Women.* ⁹ That women adorn themselves in modest apparel, with shamefacedness and sobriety ; not with braided hair, or gold, or pearls, or costly array ; ¹⁰ But (which becometh women professing godliness) with good works.—1 TIM., ch. 2. [See No. 9557.]

9810. —— **evince Character.** *Jesus.* ³⁷ If I do not the works of my Father, believe me not. ³⁸ But if I do, though ye believe not me, believe the works ; that ye may know, and believe, that the Father *is* in me, and I in him.—JOHN, ch. 10.

9811. —— **Evidence in.** *Ephraim.* ¹⁵ Joshua answered them, If thou *be* a great people, *then* get thee up to the wood *country*, and cut down for thyself there in the land of the Perizzites and of the giants, if mount Ephraim be too narrow for thee.—JOSH., ch. 17,

9812. —— —— *Jesus said,* ²² Tell John what things ye have seen and heard ; how that the blind see, the lame walk, the lepers are cleansed, the deaf hear, the dead are raised, to the poor the gospel is preached.—LUKE, ch. 7.

9813. —— with Faith. *Moses' Parents.* ²³ By faith Moses, when he was born, was hid three months of his parents, because they saw *he was* a proper child ; and they were not afraid of the king's commandment.—HEB., ch. 11.

9814. —— —— *David* ⁴⁰ Chose him five smooth stones out of the brook, and put them in a shepherd's bag which he had, even in a scrip ; and his sling *was* in his hand : and he drew near to the Philistine.—1 SAM., ch. 17.

9815. —— —— *Dead Faith.* ¹⁷ Even so faith, if it hath not works, is dead, being alone. ¹⁸ Yea, a man may say, Thou hast faith, and I have works : shew me thy faith without thy works, and I will shew thee my faith by my works.—JAMES, ch. 2.

9816. —— —— *Ten Lepers.* ¹⁴ When he saw *them,* he said unto them, Go shew yourselves unto the priests..as they went, they were cleansed.—LUKE, ch. 17.

9817. —— Fruit of. *"By their Fruits."* ¹⁶ Ye shall know them by their fruits. Do men gather grapes of thorns, or figs of thistles ? ¹⁷ Even so every good tree bringeth forth good fruit ; but a corrupt tree bringeth forth evil fruit.—MAT., ch. 7.

9818. —— of the Flesh. *Hurtful.* ¹⁹ The works of the flesh are manifest, which are *these,* Adultery, fornication, uncleanness, lasciviousness, ²⁰ Idolatry, witchcraft, hatred, variance, emulations, wrath, strife, seditions, heresies, ²¹ Envyings, murders, drunkenness, revellings, and such like.—GAL., ch. 5.

9819. —— perfect Faith. *Abraham.* ²¹ Was not Abraham our father justified by works, when he had offered Isaac his son upon the altar ? ²² Seest thou how faith wrought with his works, and by works was faith made perfect ?—JAMES, ch. 2.

9820. —— of God. *The Wonderful.* [See Ps. 104.]

9821. —— Influence of. *"Light shine."* ¹⁵ Neither do men light a candle, and put it under a bushel, but on a candlestick : and it giveth light unto all that are in the house. ¹⁶ Let your light so shine before men, that they may see your good works, and glorify your Father which is in heaven.—MAT., ch. 5.

9822. —— Important. *Necessary Uses.* ¹⁴ Let ours also learn to maintain good works for necessary uses, that they be not unfruitful.—TITUS, ch. 3.

9823. —— of Jesus. *Benevolent.* [See No. 9812.]

9824. —— needful. . *To Poor.* ¹⁵ If a brother or sister be naked, and destitute of daily food, ¹⁶ And one of you say unto them, Depart in peace, be *ye* warmed and filled : notwithstanding ye give them not those things which are needful to the body ; what *doth it* profit ?—JAMES, ch. 2.

9825. —— Ostentation in. *"Sound a Trumpet."* ² When thou doest *thine* alms, do not sound a trumpet before thee, as the hypocrites do in the synagogues and in the streets, that they may have glory of men. Verily I say unto you, They have their reward. ³ But..let not thy left hand know what thy right hand doeth.—MAT., ch. 6.

9826. —— required. *"Hewn down."* ¹⁹ Every tree that bringeth not forth good fruit is hewn down, and cast into the fire.—MAT., ch. 7.

9827. —— of Religion. *Benevolent.* ²⁷ Pure religion and undefiled before God and the Father is this, To visit the fatherless and widows in their affliction, *and* to keep himself unspotted from the world.—JAMES, ch. 1.

9828. —— of Supererogation. *None.* ¹⁰ When ye shall have done all those things which are commanded you, say, We are unprofitable servants : we have done that which was our duty to do.—LUKE, ch. 17.

9829. —— Testimony of. *Paul.* ¹² Having your conversation honest among the Gentiles : that, whereas they speak against you as evil-doers, they may by *your* good works, which they shall behold, glorify God in the day of visitation.. ¹⁵ For so is the will of God, that with well-doing ye may put to silence the ignorance of foolish men.—1 PETER, ch. 2.

9830. —— Unprofitable. *Foolish Questions.* ⁹ Avoid foolish questions, and genealogies, and contentions, and strivings about the law ; for they are unprofitable and vain.—TITUS, ch. 3.

9831. WORKER forsaken, A. *Paul.* ⁹ Do thy diligence to come shortly unto me : ¹⁰ For Demas hath forsaken me, having loved this present world.—2 TIM., ch. 4.

9832. —— The model. *Jesus.* ⁴ I must work the works of him that sent me, while it is day : the night cometh, when no man can work.—JOHN, ch. 9.

9833. —— —— *"Finished."* ⁴ I have glorified thee on the earth ; I have finished the work which thou gavest me to do. ⁵ And now, O Father, glorify thou me with thine own self.—JOHN, ch. 17.

9834. —— A retiring. *Paul.* ⁷ I have fought a good fight, I have finished *my* course, I have kept the faith : ⁸ Henceforth there is laid up for me a crown of righteousness, which the Lord, the righteous judge, shall give me at that day. —2 TIM., ch. 4.

9835. WORKERS accepted. *Of Righteousness.* ¹ Lord, who shall abide in thy tabernacle ? who shall dwell in thy holy hill ? ² He that walketh uprightly, and worketh righteousness, and speaketh the truth in his heart.—Ps. 15.

9836. —— Abilities of. *Talents.* ¹⁴ The kingdom of heaven *is* as a man travelling into a far country, *who* called his own servants, and delivered unto them his goods. ¹⁵ And unto one he gave five talents, to another two, and to another one ; to every man according to his several ability ; and straightway took his journey.—MAT., ch. 25.

9837. —— Benedictions on. *Christian.* ⁷ To them who by patient continuance in well doing seek for glory and honour and immortality, eternal life.. ¹⁰ But glory, honour, and peace, to every man that worketh good ; to the Jew first, and also to the Gentile.—ROM., ch. 2.

9838. —— benefited. *Doer.* ²³ I any be a hearer of the word, and not a doer, he is like unto a man beholding his natural face in a glass : [24] For he beholdeth himself, and goeth his way, and straightway forgetteth what manner of man he was.—JAMES, ch. 1.

Also see:
with God. When thou hearest the sound of a going 7889
Hardships. Get you straw..yet not aught..dimin. 896
Personal. Philip..go join thyself to his chariot 773
See INDUSTRY and references.
See SERVICE and WAGES.

9839. WORLD, Attractions of the. "*Egypt.*"
[3] Wherefore hath the Lord brought us unto this land, to fall by the sword, that our wives and our children should be a prey ? were it not better for us to return into Egypt ? [4] And they said one to another, Let us make a captain, and let us return into Egypt.—NUM., ch. 14.

9840. —— **Bondage to.** *Young Ruler.*
[21] Come, take up the cross, and follow me. [22] And he was sad at that saying, and went away grieved : for he had great possessions.—MARK, ch. 10.

9841. —— **Conformity to.** "*Like all the Nations.*" [19] The people refused to obey the voice of Samuel ; and they said, Nay ; but we will have a king over us ; [20] That we also may be like all the nations.—1 SAM., ch. 8.

9842. —— **Choice of.** *Demas.* [10] Demas hath forsaken me, having loved this present world. —2 TIM., ch. 4.

9843. —— **Dominion of the.** *Jesus.* [18] All power is given unto me in heaven and in earth. [19] Go ye therefore, and teach all nations.. [20]..and, lo, I am with you alway, *even* unto the end of the world.—MAT., ch. 28.

9844. —— **Fear of.** "*Spared the Best.*" [24] Saul said unto Samuel, I have sinned : for I have transgressed the commandment of the Lord, and thy words : because I feared the people, and obeyed their voice. [25] Now therefore, I pray thee, pardon my sin, and turn again with me, that I may worship the Lord.—1 SAM., ch. 15.

9845. —— **forbidden, Love of the.** *Christian.* [15] Love not the world, neither the things that *are* in the world. If any man love the world, the love of the Father is not in him.—1 JOHN, ch. 2.

9846. —— **Forsaking.** *Sodom.* [17] When they had brought them forth abroad..he said, Escape for thy life ; look not behind thee, neither stay thou in all the plain ; escape to the mountain, lest thou be consumed.—GEN., ch. 19.

9847. —— **Hatred of the.** *Disciples.* [18] If the world hate you, ye know that it hated me before *it hated* you. [19] If ye were of the world, the world would love his own ; but because ye are not of the world, but I have chosen you out of the world, therefore the world hateth you.— JOHN, ch. 15.

9848. —— **Offers of the.** *To Balaam.* [16] Thus saith Balak..Let nothing, I pray thee, hinder thee from coming unto me : [17] For I will promote thee unto very great honour, and I will do whatsoever thou sayest unto me : come therefore, I pray thee, curse me this people.—NUM., ch. 22.

9849. —— **Price of the.** *Soul.* [26] For what is a man profited, if he shall gain the whole world, and lose his own soul.—MAT., ch. 16.

9850. —— **Preservation in the.** *Jesus.* [15] I pray not that thou shouldest take them out of the world, but that thou shouldest keep them from the evil. [16] They are not of the world, even as I am not of the world.—JOHN, ch. 17.

9851. —— **Separation from the.** "*Come out.*" [17] Come out from among them, and be ye separate, saith the Lord, and touch not the unclean *thing ;* and I will receive you, [18] And will be a Father unto you, and ye shall be my sons and daughters, saith the Lord Almighty.—2 COR., ch. 6.

9852. —— **unsatisfying, The.** *Haman.* [11] Haman told them of the glory of his riches, and the multitude of his children, and all *the things* wherein the king had promoted him.. [13] Yet all this availeth me nothing, so long as I see Mordecai the Jew sitting at the king's gate. —ESTHER, ch. 5.

9853. WORLDLINESS, Ambition in. *Babel.* [4] Go to, let us build us a city, and a tower, whose top *may reach* unto heaven ; and let us make us a name, lest we be scattered abroad upon the face of the whole earth.—GEN., ch. 11.

9854. —— **Curse of.** "*Desert.*" [5] Thus saith the Lord ; Cursed *be* the man that trusteth in man, and maketh flesh his arm, and whose heart departeth from the Lord. [6] For he shall be like the heath in the desert, and shall not see when good cometh ; but shall inhabit the parched places in the wilderness, *in* a salt land and not inhabited.—JER., ch. 17.

9855. —— **Evidence of.** "*Carnally.*" [5] For they that are after the flesh do mind the things of the flesh ; but they that are after the Spirit, the things of the Spirit. [6] For to be carnally minded *is* death ; but to be spiritually minded *is* life and peace.—ROM., ch. 8.

9856. —— **Entangled by.** *Soldier.* [4] No man that warreth entangleth himself with the affairs of *this* life ; that he may please him who hath chosen him to be a soldier.—2 TIM., ch. 2.

9857. —— **Excuses for.** *Supper.* [See No. 9863.]

9858. —— **prevents Faith.** *Pride.* [44] How can ye believe, which receive honour one of another, and seek not the honour that *cometh* from God only ?—JOHN, ch. 5.

9859. —— **neutralizes Faith.** "*Praise of Men.*" [42] Among the chief rulers also many believed on him ; but because of the Pharisees they did not confess *him*, lest they should be put out of the synagogue. [43] For they loved the praise of men more than the praise of God. —JOHN, ch. 12.

9860. —— **forbidden.** *Anxiety.* [31] Take no thought, saying, What shall we eat? or, What shall we drink ? or, Wherewithal shall we be clothed ? [32] (For after all these things do the Gentiles seek :) for your heavenly Father knoweth that ye have need of all these things.—MAT., ch. 6.

9861. —— **Fruit of.** *Lot.* [His home in Sodom brought poverty and shame. See Nos. 9864, 9866.]

9862. —— **Hostility from.** *Enemy.* [4] Ye adulterers and adulteresses, know ye not that the friendship of the world is enmity with God ? whosoever therefore will be a friend of the world is the enemy of God.—JAMES, ch. 4.

9863. —— **Hinderances from.** *Supper.* [18] They all with one *consent* began to make excuse : The first said..I have bought a piece of ground, and I must needs go and see it : I pray thee have me excused. [19]..I have bought five yoke of oxen, and I go to prove them : I pray thee have me excused. [20]..I have married a wife, and therefore I cannot come.—LUKE, ch. 14.

9864. —— **punished.** *Lot's Wife.* [26] His wife looked back from behind him, and she became a pillar of salt.—GEN., ch. 19.

9865. —— **rebuked.** *Usury.* [See No. 1839.] [7] I rebuked the nobles, and the rulers, and said unto them, Ye exact usury, every one of his brother. And I set a great assembly against them. [8] And I said unto them, We, after our ability, have redeemed our brethren the Jews, which were sold unto the heathen ; and will ye even sell your brethren ?—NEH., ch. 5.

9866. —— **Temptation to.** *Lot.* [10] Lot lifted up his eyes, and beheld all the plain of Jordan, that it *was* well watered every where, before the Lord destroyed Sodom and Gomorrah, *even* as the garden of the Lord, like the land of Egypt, as thou comest unto Zoar. [11] Then Lot chose him all the plain of Jordan.—GEN., ch. 13.

9867. —— **in Worship.** *Damascus.* [10] Went to Damascus to meet Tiglath-pileser king of Assyria, and saw an altar that *was* at Damascus : and king Ahaz sent to Urijah the priest the fashion of the altar, and the pattern of it, according to all the workmanship thereof. [11] And Urijah the priest built an altar according to all that king Ahaz had sent.—2 KINGS, ch. 16.

9868. —— —— **Changes.** [17] King Ahaz cut off the borders of the bases, and removed the laver from off them ; and took down the sea from off the brazen oxen that *were* under it, and put it upon a pavement of stones. [18] And the covert for the sabbath that they had built in the house, and the king's entry without, turned he from the house of the Lord for the king of Assyria.—2 KINGS, ch. 16.

See other illustrations under :

AVARICE.

SELFISHNESS.

9869. WORSHIP, Abuses in. *Divisions.* [18] First of all, when ye come together in the church, I hear that there be divisions among you ; and I partly believe it.—1 COR., ch. 11.

9870. —— —— *Sacrament.* [21] In eating every one taketh before *other* his own supper : and one is hungry, and another is drunken. [22] What ! have ye not houses to eat and to drink in? or despise ye the church of God ?—1 COR., ch. 11.

9871. —— **bid for.** *Satan.* [8] The devil taketh him up into an exceeding high mountain, and sheweth him all the kingdoms of the world, and the glory of them ; [9] And saith..All these things will I give thee, if thou wilt fall down and worship me.—MAT., ch. 4.

9872. —— **Changes in.** *Altar.* [10] King Ahaz went to Damascus to meet Tiglath-pileser king of Assyria, and saw an altar that *was* at Damascus : and king Ahaz sent to Urijah the priest the fashion of the altar, and the pattern of it, according to all the workmanship thereof. —2 KINGS, ch. 16.

9873. —— **Custom of.** *Jesus.* [16] He came to Nazareth, where he had been brought up : and, as his custom was, he went into the synagogue on the sabbath day.—LUKE, ch. 4.

9874. —— —— *Paul.* [1] They came to Thessalonica, where was a synagogue of the Jews : [2] And Paul, as his manner was, went in unto them, and three sabbath days reasoned with them out of the Scriptures.—ACTS, ch. 17.

9875. —— **Care in.** *"Not rash."* [1] Keep thy foot when thou goest to the house of God, and be more ready to hear, than to give the sacrifice of fools : for they consider not that they do evil. [2] Be not rash with thy mouth, and let not thine heart be hasty to utter *any* thing before God : for God *is* in heaven, and thou upon earth : therefore let thy words be few.—ECCL., ch. 5.

9876. —— **Convenient.** *Jeroboam.* [28] The king took counsel, and made two calves *of* gold, and said unto them, It is too much for you to go up to Jerusalem : behold thy gods, O Israel, which brought thee up out of the land of Egypt. [29] And he set the one in Beth-el, and the other put he in Dan.—1 KINGS, ch. 12.

9877. —— **Compulsory.** *"Image."* [6] Whoso falleth not down and worshippeth shall the same hour be cast into the midst of a burning fiery furnace.—DAN., ch. 3.

9878. —— **Daily.** *Temple.* [38] This *is that* which thou shalt offer upon the altar ; two lambs of the first year day by day continually. [39] The one lamb thou shalt offer in the morning ; and the other lamb thou shalt offer at even.—EX., ch. 29.

9879. —— **Delight in.** *David.* [1] How amiable *are* thy tabernacles, O Lord of hosts ! [2] My soul longeth, yea, even fainteth for the courts of the Lord : my heart and my flesh crieth out for the living God.—Ps. 84.

9880. —— **Devoted to.** *Joshua.* [11] The Lord spake unto Moses face to face, as a man speaketh unto his friend. And he turned again into the camp ; but his servant Joshua, the son of Nun, a young man, departed not out of the tabernacle.—Ex., ch. 33.

9881. —— **Expense in.** *David.* [See No. 9912.]

9882. —— **Family.** *Passover.* [3] In the tenth *day* of this month they shall take to them every man a lamb, according to the house of *their* fathers, a lamb for an house.—Ex., ch. 12.

9883. —— **Fear in.** *Manoah.* [21] Then Manoah knew that he *was* an angel of the Lord. [22] And Manoah said unto his wife, We shall surely die, because we have seen God.—Judges, ch. 13.

9884. —— —— **Removed.** [23] His wife said unto him, If the Lord were pleased to kill us, he would not have received a burnt offering and a meat offering at our hands, neither would he have shewed us all these *things*, nor would as at this time have told us *such things* as these.—Judges, ch. 13.

9885. —— **in Grief.** *Job.* [19] It fell upon the young men, and they are dead ; and I only am escaped alone to tell thee. [20] Then Job arose, and rent his mantle, and shaved his head, and fell down upon the ground, and worshipped.—Job, ch. 1.

9886. —— **Grace for.** *Repentance.* [10] I will pour upon the house of David, and upon the inhabitants of Jerusalem, the spirit of grace and of supplications : and they shall look upon me whom they have pierced, and they shall mourn for him, as one mourneth for *his* only *son*, and shall be in bitterness for *him*, as one that is in bitterness for *his* firstborn.—Zech., ch. 12.

9887. —— **Gladness in.** *" Good."* [1] *It is* a good thing to give thanks unto the Lord, and to sing praises unto thy name, O Most High : [2] To shew forth thy lovingkindness in the morning, and thy faithfulness every night.—Ps. 92.

9888. —— **Heartless.** *" Weariness."* [See No. 9919.]

9889. —— **Hope in.** *" Wait."* [14] Wait on the Lord : be of good courage, and he shall strengthen thine heart : wait, I say, on the Lord.—Ps. 27.

9890. —— **in Ignorance.** *Athenians.* [22] Paul stood in the midst of Mars' hill, and said, Ye men of Athens, I perceive that in all things ye are too superstitious. [23] For as I passed by, and beheld your devotions, I found an altar with this inscription, TO THE UNKNOWN GOD. Whom therefore ye ignorantly worship, him declare I unto you.—Acts, ch. 17.

9891. —— **Intimidated in.** *Disciples.* [19] The same day at evening, being the first *day* of the week, when the doors were shut where the disciples were assembled for fear of the Jews, came Jesus and stood in the midst, and saith unto them, Peace *be* unto you.—John, ch. 20.

9892. —— **Inconvenient.** *Temple at Jerusalem.* [22] Thou shalt observe the feast of weeks, of the firstfruits of wheat harvest, and the feast of ingathering at the year's end. [23] Thrice in the

year shall all your men children appear before the Lord God.—Ex., ch. 34.

9893. —— **Lip.** *Hypocrites.* [7] Ye hypocrites, well did Esaias prophesy of you, saying, [8] This people draweth nigh unto me with their mouth, and honoureth me with *their* lips ; but their heart is far from me.—Mat., ch. 15.

9894. —— **Mistaken.** *" Repetitions."* [7] When ye pray, use not vain repetitions, as the heathen *do :* for they think that they shall be heard for their much speaking.—Mat., ch. 6.

9895. —— **Public.** *" Congregation."* [7] Moses took the tabernacle, and pitched it . . afar off from the camp, and called it the Tabernacle of the congregation . . every one which sought the Lord went out unto the tabernacle.—Ex., ch. 33.

9896. —— **Preparation for.** *Carmel.* [30] Elijah said unto all the people, Come near unto me. And all the people came near unto him. And he repaired the altar of the Lord that was broken down.—1 Kings, ch. 18.

9897. —— **prostituted.** *Hoshea.* [4] He removed the high places, and brake the images, and cut down the groves, and brake in pieces the brazen serpent that Moses had made : for unto those days the children of Israel did burn incense to it : and he called it Nehushtan.—2 Kings, ch. 18.

9898. —— **Preservation by.** *David.* [2] My steps had well nigh slipped. [3] For I was envious of the foolish, *when* I saw the prosperity of the wicked . . [16] When I thought to know this, it *was* too painful for me. [17] Until I went into the sanctuary of God ; *then* understood I their end.—Ps. 73.

9899. —— **a Pretence.** *Herod.* [8] He sent them to Bethlehem, and said, Go and search diligently for the young child ; and when ye have found *him*, bring me word again, that I may come and worship him also.—Mat., ch. 2.

9900. —— **prohibited.** *" Lions."* [7] All the presidents of the kingdom, the governors, and the princes, the counsellors, and the captains, have consulted together to establish a royal statute, and to make a firm decree, that whosoever shall ask a petition of any God or man for thirty days, save of thee, O king, he shall be cast into the den of lions.—Dan., ch. 6. [See No. 6095.]

9901. —— **Purpose in.** *" Needed."* [24] God that made the world and all things therein, seeing that he is Lord of heaven and earth, dwelleth not in temples made with hands ; [25] Neither is worshipped with men's hands, as though he needed any thing, seeing he giveth to all life, and breath, and all things.—Acts, ch. 17.

9902. —— **Presumption in.** *King Saul.* [11] Saul said, Because I saw that the people were scattered from me, and *that* thou camest not within the days appointed . . [12] Therefore said I, the Philistines will come . . and I have not made supplication unto the Lord : and I forced myself therefore, and offered a burnt offering. [He thereby lost his throne.]—1 Sam., ch. 13.

9903. —— **remembered.** *Captives.* [5] If I forget thee, O Jerusalem, let my right hand forget *her* cunning. [6] If I do not remember thee, let my tongue cleave to the roof of my mouth ; if I prefer not Jerusalem above my chief joy.—Ps. 137.

9904. —— Relief in. *Trouble.* ⁴ One *thing* have I desired of the Lord, that will I seek after ; that I may dwell in the house of the Lord all the days of my life, to behold the beauty of the Lord, and to inquire in his temple. ⁵ For in the time of trouble he shall hide me in his pavilion : in the secret of his tabernacle shall he hide me.—Ps. 27.

9905. —— Readiness in. *Hearty.* ⁷ Hear, O Lord, *when* I cry with my voice : have mercy also upon me, and answer me. ⁸ *When thou saidst,* Seek ye my face ; my heart said unto thee, Thy face, Lord, will I seek.—Ps. 27.

9906. —— Reconciliation before. *Jesus said,* ²³ If thou bring thy gift to the altar, and there rememberest that thy brother hath aught against thee : ²⁴ Leave there thy gift before the altar, and go thy way ; first be reconciled to thy brother, and then come and offer thy gift.— MAT., ch. 5.

9907. —— Remembrance of. *David.* ⁴ I had gone with the multitude, I went with them to the house of God, with the voice of joy and praise, with a multitude that kept holyday. ⁵ Why art thou cast down, O my soul, and *why* art thou disquieted in me ? hope thou in God : for I shall yet praise him *for* the help of his countenance.—Ps. 42.

9908. —— Social. *Sinai.* ⁹ Then went up Moses, and Aaron, Nadab, and Abihu, and seventy of the elders of Israel : ¹⁰ And they saw the God of Israel: and *there was* under his feet as it were a paved work of a sapphire-stone, and as it were the body of heaven.—Ex., ch. 19.

9909. —— —— *Beneficial.* ²⁴ Thomas, one of the twelve, called Didymus, was not with them when Jesus came. ²⁵ The other disciples therefore said unto him, We have seen the Lord.—JOHN, ch. 20.

9910. —— —— *Waiting for.* ²⁶ After eight days again his disciples were within, and Thomas with them . then came Jesus, the doors being shut, and stood in the midst, and said, Peace *be* unto you. ²⁷ Then saith he to Thomas, Reach hither thy finger.—JOHN, ch. 20.

9911. —— Strength from. *" Eagles."* ³¹ They that wait upon the Lord shall renew *their* strength ; they shall mount up with wings as eagles ; they shall run, and not be weary ; *and* they shall walk, and not faint.—ISA., ch. 40.

9912. —— Sacrifice in. *David.* ²⁴ King David said to Ornan, Nay ; but I will verily buy it for the full price : for I will not take *that* which *is* thine for the Lord, nor offer burnt offerings without cost.—1 CHRON., ch. 21.

9913. —— Safety in. *At Feasts.* ²⁴ I will cast out the nations before thee, and enlarge thy borders : neither shall any man desire thy land, when thou shalt go up to appear before the Lord thy God thrice in the year.—Ex., ch. 34.

9914. —— Universal. *Creation.* ¹ Praise ye the Lord. Praise ye the Lord from the heavens : praise him in the heights. ² Praise ye him, all his angels : praise ye him, all his hosts. ³ Praise him, sun and moon : praise him, all ye stars of light. ⁴ Praise him, ye heavens of heavens, and ye waters that *be* above the heavens.—Ps. 148.

9915. —— Unauthorized. *Pharisees.* ⁹ In

vain they do worship me, teaching *for* doctrines the commandments of men.—MAT., ch. 15.

9916. —— —— *" Strange Fire."* ¹ Nadab and Abihu, the sons of Aaron, took either of them his censer, and put fire therein, and put incense thereon, and offered strange fire before the Lord. . ² And there went out fire from the Lord, and devoured them.—LEV., ch. 10.

9917. —— Unintimidated. *Daniel.* ¹⁰ When Daniel knew that the writing was signed, he went into his house ; and, his windows being open in his chamber toward Jerusalem, he kneeled upon his knees three times a day, and prayed, and gave thanks before his God, as he did aforetime.—DAN., ch. 6.

9918. —— Vows in. *Pay.* ⁴ When thou vowest a vow unto God, defer not to pay it ; for *he hath* no pleasure in fools : pay that which thou hast vowed. ⁵ Better *is it* that thou shouldest not vow, than that thou shouldest vow and not pay.—ECCL., ch. 5.

9919. —— Weariness in. *" Sick."* ¹³ Ye said also, Behold, what a weariness *is it !* and ye have snuffed at it, saith the Lord of hosts ; and ye brought *that which was* torn, and the lame, and the sick ; thus ye brought an offering : should I accept this of your hand ?—MAL., ch. 1.

9920. WORSHIPPERS, Mixed. *" Some doubted."* ¹⁶ The eleven disciples went away into Galilee, into a mountain where Jesus had appointed them. ¹⁷ And when they saw him, they worshipped him : but some doubted.—MAT., ch. 28.

9921. —— True. *To Samaritan.* ²³ The hour cometh, and now is, when the true worshippers shall worship the Father in spirit and in truth ; for the Father seeketh such to worship him. ²⁴ God *is* a spirit : and they that worship him must worship *him* in spirit and in truth.—JOHN, ch. 4.

9922. —— —— *Jews.* ⁵ Ezra opened the book. .and when he opened it, all the people stood up : ⁶ And Ezra blessed the Lord, the great God. And all the people answered, Amen, Amen. with lifting up their hands : and they bowed their heads, and worshipped the Lord with *their* faces to the ground.—NEH., ch. 8.

See other illustrations under :

DEVOTION.

9923. WORTH, Estimated. *By Others.* [4] When they came to Jesus, they besought him instantly, saying, That he was worthy for whom he should do this : [5] For he loveth our nation, and he hath built us a synagogue.—Luke, ch. 7.

9924. —— Promotion by. *David.* [18] Behold, I have seen a son of Jesse the Beth-lehemite, *that is* cunning in playing, and a mighty valiant man, and a man of war, and prudent in matters, and a comely person, and the Lord *is* with him. —1 Sam., ch. 16.

9925. —— Without. *Centurion.* [6] When he was now not far from the house, the centurion sent friends·to him, saying unto him, Lord, trouble not thyself ; for I am not worthy that thou shouldest enter under my roof : [7] Wherefore neither thought I myself worthy to come unto thee : but say in a word, and my servant shall be healed.—Luke, ch. 7.

See other illustrations under :

MERIT.
Disclaimed. Why look ye..as though by our own 5375
Honoured. Daniel was preferred above all the p. 5376
Unappreciated. Sought to find occasion against D. 5377

SUPERIORITY.
Claimed. Though all shall be offended..not I. 8471
Manifested. Aaron's rod swallowed up their rods 8472
"   Rod of Aaron..yielded almonds 8473
Unclaimed. Simon..lovest thou me more than t. 8474

9926. WRITING, An alarming. *Belshazzar.* [5] The king saw the part of the hand that wrote. [6] Then the king's countenance was changed, and his thoughts troubled him, so that the joints of his loins were loosed, and his knees smote one against another. [7] The king cried aloud to bring in the astrologers.—Dan., ch. 5. [See No. 4602.]

9927. —— A perishable. *"On the Ground."* [7] When they continued asking him, he lifted up himself, and said unto them, He that is without sin among you, let him first cast a stone at her. [8] And again he stooped down, and wrote on the ground.—John, ch. 8.

9928. —— Tenderness in. *Paul.* [4] Out of much affliction and anguish of heart I wrote unto you with many tears ; not that ye should be grieved, but that ye might know the love which I have more abundantly unto you.—2 Cor., ch. 2.

See other illustrations under :

ENGRAVING.
Inspiration. Filled Bezaleel with the Spirit 2671
Lord's. Tables..the writing of God 2672
Law. Set up great stones..write upon them 2673

MESSAGE.
Rejected. Hezekiah..wrote letters..come to the h. 5379
Received. Divers..humbled themselves and came 5380

Effective. Epistle hath made you sorry..season 4943
Shameful. David wrote a letter to Joab..by Uriah 5382
Terrible. Letters were sent..destroy all Jews 5386

9929. YEAR changed, The. *Jewish.* [1] The Lord spake unto Moses and Aaron in the land of Egypt, saying, [2] This month *shall be* unto you the beginning of months : it *shall be* the first month of the year to you.—Ex., ch. 12.

9930. —— of Jubilee. *Fiftieth.* [10] Ye shall hallow the fiftieth year, and proclaim liberty throughout *all* the land unto all the inhabitants thereof : it shall be a jubilee unto you ; and ye shall return every man unto his possession, and ye shall return every man unto his family.— Lev., ch. 25.

9931. —— A rest. *Seven.* [3] Six years thou shalt sow thy field ; and six years thou shalt prune thy vineyard, and gather in the fruit thereof ; [4] But in the seventh year shall be a sabbath of rest unto the land, a sabbath for the Lord : thou shalt neither sow thy field, nor prune thy vineyard.—Lev., ch. 25.

9932. YEARS, Burden of. *Barzillai.* [35] I *am* this day fourscore years old : *and* can I discern between good and evil ? can thy servant taste what I eat or what I drink ? can I hear any more the voice of singing men and singing women ? wherefore then should thy servant be yet a burden unto my lord the king.—2 Sam., ch. 19.

See TIME and references.

9933. YOKE, The easy. *Christ's.* [29] Take my yoke upon you, and learn of me : for I am meek and lowly in heart ; and ye shall find rest unto your souls. [30] For my yoke *is* easy, and my burden is light.—Mat., ch. 11.

9934. YOKES, Emblem of. *Bondage.* [2] Thus saith the Lord to me ; Make thee bonds and yokes, and put them upon thy neck, [3] And send them to the king of Edom..of Moab..of the Ammonites..of Tyrus, and to the king of Zidon, by the hand of the messengers which come to Jerusalem unto Zedekiah king of Judah.—Jer., ch. 27.

See BONDAGE, WORK, and references.

9935. YOUNG admonished, The. *" Son."* [1] My son, if thou wilt receive my words, and hide my commandments with thee ; [2] So that thou incline thine ear unto wisdom, *and* apply thine heart to understanding.—Prov., ch. 2.

**9936. —— *" My Law."* ** [1] Hear, ye children, the instruction of a father, and attend to know understanding. [2] For I give you good doctrine, forsake ye not my law.—Prov., ch. 4.

See CHILD and CHILDREN.

9937. YOUNG MAN, An ambitious. *Absalom.* [4] Oh that I were made judge in the land, that every man which hath any suit or cause might come unto me, and I would do him justice !— 2 Sam., ch. 15.

9938. —— An artful. *Absalom.* [5] When any man came nigh *to him* to do him obeisance, he put forth his hand, and took him, and kissed him. [6] And on this manner did Absalom to all Israel that came to the king for judgment : so Absalom stole the hearts of the men of Israel.— 2 Sam., ch. 15.

9939. —— advised. *By old Men.* [6] King Rehoboam consulted with the old men, that stood before Solomon his father while he yet lived, and said, How do ye advise that I may answer this people ? [7] If thou wilt be a servant unto this people this day, and wilt serve them, and answer them, and speak good words to them, then they will be thy servants for ever. —1 Kings, ch. 12.

9940. —— for Business. *Joseph.* [46] Joseph *was* thirty years old when he stood before Pharaoh..And Joseph went out from the presence of Pharaoh, and went throughout all the land of Egypt.. [48] And he gathered up all the food of the seven years.—Gen., ch. 41.

9941. —— A depraved. *Absalom.* [See 2 Sam. 16 : 22.]

9942. —— debauched. *"Hot Coals."* ²⁷ Can a man take fire in his bosom, and his clothes not be burned? ²⁸ Can one go upon hot coals, and his feet not be burned? ²⁹ So he that goeth in to his neighbour's wife.—Prov., ch. 6.

9943. —— A fast. *Absalom.* ¹ After this.. Absalom prepared him chariots and horses, and fifty men to run before him.—2 Sam., ch. 15.

9944. —— A handsome. *Absalom.* ²⁵ In all Israel there was none to be so much praised as Absalom for his beauty : from the sole of his foot even to the crown of his head there was no blemish in him.—2 Sam., ch. 14.

9945. —— A heartless. *Absalom.* ¹ Ahithophel said.. Let me now choose out twelve thousand men, and I will arise and pursue after David this night : ² And I will come upon him while he *is* weary and weak handed, and will make him afraid : and all the people that *are* with him shall flee ; and I will smite the king only : ⁴ And the saying pleased Absalom well, and all the elders of Israel.—2 Sam., ch. 17.

9946. —— A helpless. *Absalom.* ⁹ Absalom met the servants of David. And Absalom rode upon a mule, and the mule went under the thick boughs of a great oak, and his head caught hold of the oak, and he was taken up between the heaven and the earth : and the mule that *was* under him went away.—2 Sam., ch. 18. [Joab slew him.]

9947. —— An intriguing. *Absalom.* ¹⁰ Absalom sent spies throughout all the tribes of Israel, saying, As soon as ye hear the sound of the trumpet, then ye shall say Absalom reigneth in Hebron.—2 Sam., ch. 15.

9948. —— An ill-advised. *Rehoboam.* ¹⁰ The young men that were grown up with him spake unto him, saying, Thus shalt thou speak unto this people that spake unto thee, saying, Thy father made our yoke heavy, but make thou *it* lighter unto us ; thus shalt thou say unto them, My little *finger* shall be thicker than my father's loins.—1 Kings, ch. 12. [Ten tribes seceded.]

9949. —— An imprudent. *Asahel.* ²¹ Abner said to him, Turn thee aside to thy right hand or to thy left, and lay thee hold on one of the young men, and take thee his armour. But Asahel would not turn aside from following him.. ²³.. wherefore Abner with the hinder end of the spear smote him under the fifth *rib.*—2 Sam., ch. 2. [Abner was a great captain.]

9950. —— Prayer for a. *"Eyes opened."* ¹⁵ His servant said unto him, Alas, my master ! how shall we do? ¹⁶ And he answered, Fear not : for they that *be* with us *are* more than they that *be* with them. ¹⁷ And Elisha prayed, and said, Lord, I pray thee, open his eyes, that he may see.. and he saw : and behold, the mountain *was* full of horses and chariots of fire round about Elisha.—2 Kings, ch. 6.

9951. —— protected. *Elisha.* [By pious friendship. See above.]

9952. —— Prodigal. *Parable.* ¹³ The younger son gathered all together, and took his journey into a far country, and there wasted his substance with riotous living.—Luke, ch. 15.

9953. —— A ruinous. *Rehoboam.* [See No. 9948.]

9954. —— A rich. *Ruler.* ²¹ Jesus beholding him loved him, and said unto him, One thing thou lackest : go thy way, sell whatsoever thou hast, and give to the poor, and thou shalt have treasure in heaven : and come, take up the cross, and follow me. ²² And he was sad at that saying, and went away grieved : for he had great possessions.—Mark, ch. 10.

9955. —— A reverential. *Elihu.* ⁶ Elihu.. the Buzite answered and said, I *am* young, and ye *are* very old ; wherefore I was afraid, and durst not shew you mine opinion. ⁷ I said, Days should speak, and multitude of years should teach wisdom.—Job, ch. 32.

9956. —— Young Ruler. ¹⁷ When he was gone forth into the way, there came one running, and kneeled to him, and asked him, Good Master, what shall I do that I may inherit eternal life?—Mark, ch. 10.

9957. YOUNG MEN against Christ. *Disciples.* ¹⁵ Then went the Pharisees, and took counsel how they might entangle him in *his* talk. ¹⁶ And they sent out unto him their disciples with the Herodians.. ¹⁷ Tell us therefore, What thinkest thou ? Is it lawful to give tribute unto Cesar or not ?—Mat., ch. 22.

9958. —— Hope in. *For the State.* ¹³ There came a prophet unto Ahab king of Israel, saying ..Hast thou seen all this great multitude ? behold, I will deliver it into thine hand this day.. ¹⁴ And Ahab said, By whom? And he said, Thus saith the Lord, Even by the young men of the princes of the provinces.—1 Kings, ch. 20.

9959. —— Heroic. *Soldiers.* ¹³ Jonathan climbed up upon his hands and upon his feet, and his armourbearer after him : and they fell before Jonathan ; and his armourbearer slew after him. ¹⁴ And that first slaughter.. was about twenty men.—1 Sam., ch. 14. [The long imposed yoke of the Philistines was broken.]

9960. —— Trustful. *Soldiers.* ⁶ Jonathan said to the young man that bare his armour, Come, and let us go over unto the garrison of these uncircumcised : it may be that the Lord will work for us : for *there is* no restraint to the Lord to save by many or by few. ⁷ And his armourbearer said.. Do all that *is* in thy heart : turn thee ; behold, I *am* with thee according to thy heart.—1 Sam., ch. 14.

9961. —— Victory by. *Over Syria.* ¹⁹ These young men of the princes of the provinces came out of the city, and the army which followed them. ²⁰ And they slew every one his man : and the Syrians fled.. and Ben-hadad the king of Syria escaped on a horse.—1 Kings, ch. 20.

9962. —— for War. *David.* ³³ Saul said to David, Thou art not able to go against this Philistine to fight with him : for thou *art but* a youth, and he a man of war from his youth.—1 Sam., ch. 17.

9963. YOUNG PEOPLE, Care for. *Peter.* ¹⁶ He saith to him again the second time, Simon, *son* of Jonas, lovest thou me? He saith unto him, Yea, Lord ; thou knowest that I love thee. He saith unto him, Feed my sheep.—John, ch. 20. [*Lit.*, Half-grown sheep.]

9964. YOUNGER chosen, The. *Ephraim.* ¹⁷ When Joseph saw that his father laid his right hand upon the head of Ephraim, it displeased him : and he held up his father's hand, to remove it from Ephraim's head unto Manasseh's head.—Gen., ch. 48.

9965. YOUTH, Dreams of. *Joseph.* [6] Hear, I pray you, this dream which I have dreamed : [7] For, behold, we *were* binding sheaves in the field, and, lo, my sheaf arose, and also stood upright : and, behold, your sheaves stood round about, and made obeisance to my sheaf.—Gen., ch. 37.

9966. —— **Gentleness of.** *Gideon said,* [20] Unto Jether his firstborn, Up, *and* slay them. But the youth drew not his sword : for he feared, because he *was* yet a youth. [21] . . And Gideon arose, and slew Zebah and Zalmunnah, and took away the ornaments that *were* on their camels' necks.—Judges, ch. 8.

9967. —— **Piety in.** *"Before."* [1] Remember now thy Creator in the days of thy youth, while the evil days come not, nor the years draw nigh, when thou shalt say, I have no pleasure in them.—Eccl., ch. 12.

9968. —— **A religious.** *David.* [17] O God, thou hast taught me from my youth : and hitherto have I declared thy wondrous works. [18] Now also when I am old and grayheaded, O God, forsake me not.—Ps. 71.

9969. —— —— *David.* [45] Then said David to the Philistine, Thou comest to me with a sword, and with a spear, and with a shield : but I come to thee in the name of the Lord of hosts, the God of the armies of Israel, whom thou hast defied.—1 Sam., ch. 17.

9970. —— **secured.** *By Obedience.* [20] My son, keep thy father's commandment, and forsake not the law of thy mother : [21] Bind them continually upon thine heart, *and* tie them about thy neck. [22] When thou goest, it shall lead thee ; when thou sleepest, it shall keep thee ; and *when* thou awakest, it shall talk with thee.—Prov., ch. 6.

9971. —— **A spotless.** *Young Ruler.* [19] Thou knowest the commandments, Do not commit adultery, Do not kill, Do not steal, Do not bear false witness, Defraud not, Honour thy father and mother. [20] And he answered and said unto him, Master, all these have I observed from my youth.—Mark, ch. 10.

9972. —— **Selected.** *Hebrews.* [4] Children in whom *was* no blemish, but well favoured, and skilful in all wisdom, and cunning in knowledge, and understanding science, and such as *had* ability in them to stand in the king's palace, and whom they might teach the learning and the tongue of the Chaldeans.—Dan., ch. 1.

9973. —— **Temptations of.** *"Entice."* [10] My son, if sinners entice thee, consent thou not. [11] If they say, Come with us, let us lay wait for blood, let us lurk privily for the innocent without cause.—Prov., ch. 1. [See chapter.]

Also see :

Reverential. When I went out . . young men . . hid t. 246
Remembrance of. O that I was as in the days of   1005
See CHILD and YOUNG.

9974. ZEAL in Old Age. *Caleb.* [11] I *am* this day fourscore and five years old. [12] Now therefore give me this mountain . . thou heardest in that day how the Anakim *were* there, and *that* the cities *were* great *and* fenced : if so be the Lord *will be* with me, then I shall be able to drive them out, as the Lord said.—Josh., ch. 14.

9975. —— **An affecting.** *"Outwent."* [32] They departed into a desert place by ship privately. [33] . . and many knew him, and ran afoot thither out of all cities, and outwent them, and came together unto him. [34] And Jesus, when he came out, saw much people, and was moved with compassion.—Mark, ch. 6.

9976. —— **An acknowledged.** *Epaphras.* [12] Epaphras . . a servant of Christ, saluteth you, always labouring fervently for you in prayers, that ye may stand perfect and complete in all the will of God. [13] For I bear him record, that he hath a great zeal for you, and them *that are* in Laodicea.—Col., ch. 4.

9977. —— **An affectionate.** *Women.* [1] When the sabbath was past, Mary Magdalene, and Mary the *mother* of James, and Salome, had bought sweet spices, that they might come and anoint him. [2] And very early in the morning, the first *day* of the week.—Mark, ch. 16.

9978. —— **A burning.** *Baptist's.* [35] He was a burning and a shining light.—John, ch. 5.

9979. —— **A belated.** *Egyptians.* [33] The Egyptians were urgent upon the people, that they might send them out of the land in haste ; for they said, We be all dead *men.*—Ex., ch. 12.

9980. —— **Contagious.** *Benevolence.* [2] I know the forwardness of your mind, for which I boast of you to them of Macedonia, that Achaia was ready a year ago ; and your zeal hath provoked very many.—2 Cor., ch. 9.

9981. —— **desirable.** *Paul.* [18] But *it is* good to be zealously affected always in *a* good *thing.*—Gal., ch. 4.

9982. —— **A discreditable.** *"For the Law."* [20] They glorified the Lord, and said unto him, Thou seest, brother, how many thousands of Jews there are which believe ; and they are all zealous of the law.—Acts, ch. 21.

9983. —— **An excelling.** *Levites.* [34] The priests were too few, so that they could not flay all the burnt offerings : wherefore their brethren the Levites did help them, till the work was ended, and until the *other* priests had sanctified themselves : for the Levites *were* more upright in heart to sanctify themselves than the priests.—2 Chron., ch. 29.

9984. —— **Energetic.** *Nehemiah.* [24] Their children spake half in the speech of Ashdod, and could not speak in the Jews' language, but according to the language of each people. [25] And I contended with them, and cursed them, and smote certain of them, and plucked off their hair, and made them swear by God.—Neh., ch. 13.

9985. —— **A false.** *Pharisees'.* [4] They say unto him, Master, this woman was taken in adultery . . [5] Now Moses in the law commanded us, that such should be stoned : but what sayest thou ? [6] This they said, tempting him, that they might have to accuse him.—John, ch. 8.

9986. —— **of Hearers.** *"Outwent."* [See No. 9975.]

9987. —— **removes Hunger.** *Jesus.* [31] His disciples prayed him, saying, Master, eat. [32] But he said . . I have meat to eat that ye know not of. [33] Therefore said the disciples one to another, Hath any man brought him *aught* to eat ? [34] Jesus saith . . My meat is to do the will of him that sent me, and to finish his work.—John, ch. 4.

9988. —— with Humility. *Apollos.* [Eloquent Apollos taught more perfectly by mechanics, Aquila and Priscilla. See No. 4544.]

9989. —— A holy. *Apostles.* ²⁵ Then came one and told them, saying, Behold, the men whom ye put in prison are standing in the temple, and teaching the people.—Acts, ch. 5.

9990. —— of Hypocrites. *Pharisees.* ¹³ Woe unto you scribes and Pharisees, hypocrites! for ye compass sea and land to make one proselyte; and when he is made, ye make him twofold more the child of hell than yourselves.—Mat., ch. 23.

9991. —— A hurtful. *Healed Leper.* ⁴⁴ See thou say nothing to any man. . ⁴⁵ But he went out, and began to publish *it* much, and to blaze abroad the matter, insomuch that Jesus could no more openly enter into the city, but was without in desert places : and they came to him from every quarter.—Mark, ch. 1.

9992. —— An imprudent. *Asahel.* ¹⁸ Asahel *was as* light of foot as a wild roe. ¹⁹ And Asahel pursued. .he turned not to the right hand nor to the left from following Abner. ²⁰ Then Abner looked behind him, and said, *Art* thou Asahel? And he answered, I *am*. ²¹ And Abner said. . Turn thee aside to thy right hand or to thy left, and lay thee hold on one of the young men, and take thee his armour. But Asahel would not turn aside from following of him.—2 Sam., ch. 2. [The veteran soldier killed him.]

9993. —— An infatuated. *Christ's Murderers.* ²⁴ When Pilate saw that he could prevail nothing, but *that* rather a tumult was made, he took water, and washed *his* hands before the multitude, saying, I am innocent of the blood of this just person : see ye *to it.* ²⁵ Then answered all the people, and said, His blood *be* on us, and on our children.—Mat., ch. 27.

9994. —— for Labour. *Paul's.* ¹⁰ And his grace which *was bestowed* upon me was not in vain ; but I laboured more abundantly than they all : yet not I, but the grace of God which was with me.—1 Cor., ch. 15.

9995. —— Lack of. *"Woe."* ¹ Woe to them *that are* at ease in Zion, and trust in the mountain of Samaria, *which are* named chief of the nations, to whom the house of Israel came. —Amos, ch. 6.

9996. —— —— *Laodiceans.* ¹⁵ I know thy works, that thou art neither cold nor hot : I would thou wert cold or hot. ¹⁶ So then because thou art lukewarm, and neither cold nor hot, I will spew thee out of my mouth.—Rev., ch. 3.

9997. —— Misunderstood. *Jesus.* ²⁰ The multitude cometh together again, so that they could not so much as eat bread. ²¹ And when his friends heard *of it*, they went out to lay hold on him : for they said, He is beside himself.— Mark, ch. 3.

9998. —— —— *Paul's.* ²⁴ Festus said with a loud voice, Paul, thou art beside thyself ; much learning doth make thee mad. ²⁵ But he said, I am not mad, most noble Festus ; but speak forth the words of truth and soberness.— Acts, ch. 26.

9999. —— for Morality. *Zaccheus.* ⁸ Zaccheus stood, and said. .Behold, Lord, the half of my goods I give to the poor ; and if I have taken any thing from any man by false accusation, I restore *him* fourfold.—Luke, ch. 19.

10000. —— Ministerial. *Paul's.* ³¹ Therefore watch, and remember, that by the space of three years I ceased not to warn every one night and day with tears.—Acts, ch. 20.

10001. —— Misdirected. *Peter's.* ²² Then Peter took him, and began to rebuke him, saying, Be it far from thee, Lord : this shall not be unto thee. ²³ But he turned, and said unto Peter, Get thee behind me, Satan : thou art an offence unto me.—Mat., ch. 16.

10002. —— A Martyr's. *Paul.* ¹³ What mean ye to weep and to break mine heart? for I am ready not to be bound only, but also to die at Jerusalem for the name of the Lord Jesus.— Acts, ch. 21.

10003. —— An overcoming. *"Roof."* ³ One sick of the palsy, which was borne of four. ⁴ And when they could not come nigh unto him for the press, they uncovered the roof where he was : and when they had broken *it* up, they let down the bed wherein the sick of the palsy lay. —Mark, ch. 2.

10004. —— Patriotic. *Wall-builders.* ¹⁷ They which builded on the wall, and they that bare burdens, with those that laded, *every one* with one of his hands wrought in the work, and with the other *hand* held a weapon.—Neh., ch. 4.

10005. —— A prosperous. *"All his Heart."* ²⁰ Thus did Hezekiah throughout all Judah, and wrought *that which was* good and right and truth before the Lord his God. ²¹ And in every work that he began in the service of the house of God, and in the law, and in the commandments, to seek his God, he did *it* with all his heart, and prospered.—2 Chron., ch. 31.

10006. —— in Prayer. *Epaphras.* [See No. 9976.]

10007. —— A Persecutor's. *Saul.* ¹¹ I punished them oft in every synagogue, and compelled *them* to blaspheme ; and being exceedingly mad against them, I persecuted *them* even unto strange cities.—Acts, ch. 26.

10008. —— Revival. *Offerings.* ³¹ And the congregation brought in sacrifices and thankofferings ; and as many as were of a free heart, burnt offerings. ³² And the number of the burnt offerings. .was threescore and ten bullocks, a hundred rams, *and* two hundred lambs : all these *were* for a burnt offering to the Lord. ³³ And the consecrated things *were* six hundred oxen and three thousand sheep.—2 Chron., ch. 29.

10009. —— A Reformer's. *Nehemiah.* ²⁸ *One* of the sons of Joiada, the son of Eliashib the high priest, *was* son in law to Sanballat the Horonite : therefore I chased him from me.— Neh., ch. 13.

10010. —— —— *Asa's.* ¹¹ Asa did *that which was* right in the eyes of the Lord. . ¹². .he took away the sodomites out of the land, and removed all the idols that his fathers had made. ¹³ And also Maachah his mother. .he removed from *being* queen, because she had made an idol in a grove ; and Asa destroyed her idol.— 1 Kings, ch. 15.

10011. —— —— *Josiah's.* ²⁰ He slew all the priests of the high places that *were* there upon the altars, and burned men's bones upon them, and returned to Jerusalem.—2 Kings, ch. 23.

10012. —— **for Reformation.** *Jesus* [14] Found in the temple those that sold oxen and sheep and doves, and the changers of money sitting: [15] And when he had made a scourge of small cords, he drove them all out of the temple, and the sheep, and the oxen; and poured out the changers' money, and overthrew the tables.—John, ch. 2.

10013. —— **rewarded.** *Priestly.* [12] Behold, I give unto him my covenant of peace: [13] And he shall have it, and his seed after him, *even* the covenant of an everlasting priesthood; because he was zealous for his God, and made an atonement for the children of Israel.—Num., ch. 25.

10014. —— —— *Zaccheus'.* [5] When Jesus came to the place, he looked up, and saw him, and said unto him, Zaccheus, make haste, and come down: for to day I must abide at thy house. [6] And he made haste, and came down, and received him joyfully.—Luke, ch. 19.

10015. —— **in Repentance.** *Corinthians.* [11] Behold this selfsame thing, that ye sorrowed after a godly sort, what carefulness it wrought in you, yea, *what* clearing of yourselves, yea, *what* indignation, yea, *what* fear, yea, *what* vehement desire, yea, *what* zeal, yea, *what* revenge.—2 Cor., ch. 7.

10016. —— **Sudden.** *Services.* [35] So the service of the house of the Lord was set in order. [36] And Hezekiah rejoiced, and all the people, that God had prepared the people: for the thing was *done* suddenly.—2 Chron., ch. 29.

10017. —— **Self-sacrificing.** *Nehemiah.* [23] So neither I, nor my brethren, nor my servants, nor the men of the guard which followed me, none of us put off our cloth*es, saving that* every one put them off for washing.—Neh., ch. 11.

10018. —— **Spiritual.** *"As the hart panteth."* [1] As the hart panteth after the water brooks, so panteth my soul after thee, O God. [2] My soul thirsteth for God, for the living God: when shall I come and appear before God? [3] My tears have been my meat day and night, while they continually say unto me, Where *is* thy God?—Ps. 42.

10019. —— **for the Sabbath.** *Nehemiah.* [20] The merchants and sellers of all kind of ware lodged without Jerusalem once or twice. [21] Then I testified against them..Why lodge ye about the wall? if ye do *so* again, I will lay hands on you..came they no *more* on the sabbath.—Neh., ch. 13.

10020. —— **in seeking.** *Zaccheus.* [3] He sought to see Jesus who he was; and could not for the press, because he was little of stature. [4] And he ran before, and climbed up into a sycamore tree to see him: for he was to pass that *way.*—Luke, ch. 19.

10021. —— **A sacrificing.** *Paul's.* [7] What things were gain to me, those I counted loss for Christ. [8] Yea doubtless, and I count all things *but* loss for the excellency of the knowledge of Christ Jesus my Lord: for whom I have suffered the loss of all things, and do count them *but* dung, that I may win Christ.—Phil., ch. 3.

10022. —— **to testify.** *"Left."* [28] The woman then left her waterpot, and went her way into the city, and saith to the men, [29] Come, see a man, which told me all things that ever I did: is not this the Christ? [30] Then they.. came unto him.—John, ch. 4.

10023. —— **A terrible.** *Against Idolaters.* [16] [Jehu] said, Come with me, and see my zeal for the Lord. So they made him ride in his chariot. [17] ..he came to Samaria, he slew all that remained unto Ahab in Samaria..according to the saying of the Lord, which he spake to Elijah.—2 Kings, ch. 10.

10024. —— **A united.** *Soldiers.* [6] Jonathan said to the young man that bare his armour, Come, and let us go over unto the garrison of these uncircumcised: it may be that the Lord will work for us: for *there is* no restraint to the Lord to save by many or by few. [7] And his armourbearer said unto him, Do all that *is* in thy heart: turn thee; behold, I *am* with thee according to thy heart.—1 Sam., ch. 14.

10025. —— **Unwavering.** *Paul's.* [23] In every city, saying that bonds and afflictions abide me. [24] But none of these things move me, neither count I my life dear unto myself, so that I might finish my course with joy, and the ministry, which I have received of the Lord Jesus, to testify the gospel of the grace of God. —Acts, ch. 20.

10026. —— **A working.** *Wall.* [21] So we laboured in the work: and half of them held the spears from the rising of the morning till the stars appeared.—Neh., ch. 4.

10027. —— **A Wicked.** *Priests.* [17] Then the high priest rose up, and all..the sect of the Sadducees, and. were filled with indignation, [18] And laid their hands on the apostles, and put them in the common prison.—Acts, ch. 5.

See other illustrations under:

EARNESTNESS.

Angelic. [Lot] While he lingered..laid hold	2568
Bold. Second time..Joab's field..set it on fire	2569
Checked. Running and kneeled..master what	2570
Chosen. Every one that lappeth of the water	2571
Hospitality. [Lot] pressed upon them greatly	2572
Important. Aaron ran..plague begun..incense	2573
Influence. Because of his importunity, he will	2574
Lack. [Joash] Should have smitten 5 or 6 times	2575
Rewarded. Whoso first after the troubling	2576
Safety. Look not behind..escape to the mount	2577
" [Bartimeus] cried the more a great deal	2578
Seeking. Uncovered the roof..broke it..down	2579

ENTHUSIASM.

Brief. With joy receiveth..not root	2679
Benevolence. They said, He is beside himself	2680
Contempt. Michal saw king David leaping	2681
Misunderstood. He is beside himself	2682
Public. Take him by force, to make him king	2683

EXCITEMENT.

Abstinence. Saul rose from the earth..neither did	2777
Creating. [Stephen's enemies] stirred up the	2778
Ecstasy. Peter said..it is good for us to be here	2779
Evildoers. They were instant with loud voices	2780
General. Multitude cometh..could not eat	2781
Needless. Israel..to go up to war against	2782
Public. City was moved..This is Jesus	2783
Trembling. [Jailer] came trembling..what must	2784
Wild. Some cried one thing, some another	2785

FANATICISM.

Accused. His friends said..He is beside himself	3036
Fickle. Would have done sacrifice..stoned Paul	3037

Genuine. Two hours cried out, Great is Diana   3038
Idolatry. They cried out, and cut themselves   3039

FORWARDNESS.

Brave. Lord, bid me come unto thee on the water 3394
Checked. Other disciple did outrun Peter   3395
Failure. When he saw the wind boisterous..afraid 3396
Hazardous. [Peter] drew his sword..smote off his 3397

———

Bigots. Chief priests..vehemently accused him   81
Insanity. Multitude came..could not eat..beside h. 92
of Love. His [aged] father saw him..ran   157
   "   Mary cometh..dark to the sepulchre..run. 185
for Vengeance. Cursed be the man that eateth..I   97

10028. ZOOLOGIST, The first. *Adam.* [19] Out of the ground the Lord God formed every beast of the field, and every fowl of the air ; and brought *them* unto Adam to see what he would call them : and whatsoever Adam called every living creature, that *was* the name thereof.— GEN., ch. 2.

10029. —— A famous. *Solomon.* [33] He spake also of beasts, and of fowl, and of creeping things, and of fishes. [34] And there came of all people to hear the wisdom of Solomon, from all kings of the earth, which had heard of his wisdom.—1 KINGS, ch. 4.

TEXTUAL INDEX.

EXPLANATION.—The left-hand column of numbers found under the various chapters represent the verses belonging to those chapters which are quoted in this volume. The numbers which follow each of these show the reader where he may find the verse in one or more places in this volume by turning to corresponding numbers.